AWARDS, HONORS & PRIZES

ISSN 0196-6316

AWARDS, HONORS & PRIZES

An International Directory of Awards and Their Donors Recognizing Achievement in Advertising, Architecture, Arts and Humanities, Business and Finance, Communications, Computers, Consumer Affairs, Ecology, Education, Engineering, Fashion, Films, Journalism, Law, Librarianship, Literature, Medicine, Music, Performing Arts, Photography, Public Affairs, Publishing, Radio and Television, Religion, Science, Social Science, Sports, Technology, and Transportation

VOLUME 2

INTERNATIONAL

33rd EDITION

VERNE THOMPSON
PROJECT EDITOR

GALE
CENGAGE Learning

Detroit • New York • San Francisco • New Haven, Conn • Waterville, Maine • London

Awards, Honors and Prizes, 33rd Edition

Volume 2: International

Project Editor: Verne Thompson

Editorial Support Services: Charles Beaumont

Composition and Electronic Prepress: Charlie Montney

Manufacturing: Rita Wimberley

Product Management: Michele LaMeau

For product information and technology assistance, contact us at
Gale Customer Support, 1-800-877-4253.
For permission to use material from this text or product,
submit all requests online at **www.cengage.com/permissions.**
Further permissions questions can be emailed to
permissionrequest@cengage.com

Gale, Cengage Learning
27500 Drake Rd.
Farmington Hills, MI 48331-3535

ISBN-13: 978-1-4144-6826-6 (Set)
ISBN-10: 1-4144-6826-1 (Set)
ISBN-13: 978-1-4144-6828-0 (Volume 1, Part 1)
ISBN-10: 1-4144-6828-8 (Volume 1, Part 1)
ISBN-13: 978-1-4144-6829-7 (Volume 1, Part 2)
ISBN-10: 1-4144-6829-6 (Volume 1, Part 2)
ISBN-13: 978-1-4144-6830-3 (Volume 2)
ISBN-10: 1-4144-6830-X (Volume 2)

ISSN 0196-6316

Printed in the United States of America
1 2 3 4 5   16 15 14 13 12

ED087

Contents

United States and Canadian awards are covered in Volume 1.

Contents

Indexes

Volume 2 of Awards, Honors & Prizes (AHP) is the single most comprehensive source of information on awards offered by organizations in more than 140 countries around the world. These awards recognize achievements in all fields of human endeavor, including:

- Advertising
- Agriculture
- Arts and Humanities
- Botany
- Business and Finance
- Communications
- Computers
- Conservation
- Ecology
- Education
- Engineering
- Environment
- Ethics
- Fashion
- Films
- Journalism
- Law
- Library Science
- Literature
- Management
- Medical Research
- Music
- Performing Arts
- Photography
- Public Affairs
- Publishing
- Radio and Television
- Religion
- Safety
- Science
- Social Science
- Sports
- Technology
- Transportation

Volume 2 provides contact information for more than 2,300 organizations and 7,100 awards.

Features of This Edition

Awards, Honors & Prizes, 33rd Edition continues to track trends in award giving, which in turn reflect the current values and priorities of society. This edition features listings for new awards under organizations in such fields as art, literature, education, and science, and covering such contemporary issues as the environment, religion, AIDS, national security, and international relations. AHP also lists e-mail addresses for nearly 5,700 organizations and website addresses for more than 6,000 organizations.

Two Volumes Organized by Location

Volume 1: Parts 1 & 2. Profiles of awards offered by organizations in the United States and Canada, plus the Subject, Organization, and Awards Indexes.

Volume 2. Profiles of awards offered by organizations in 140 countries all over the world, plus the Subject, Organization, and Awards Indexes.

Many Uses for AHP

Awards, Honors & Prizes can be used:

- by organizations, associations, and individuals to locate information on awards in a particular field of interest or that are mentioned in the media;
- by organizations and individuals to determine their eligibility for particular awards;
- by organizations to provide guidance in establishing a new award or expanding an existing program; and
- by employers in evaluating the significance of the awards listed on a job applicant's resume.

Available in Electronic Formats

Licensing. Awards, Honors & Prizes is available for licensing. The complete database is provided in a fielded format and is deliverable on such media as disk or CD-ROM. For more information, contact Gale's Business Development Group at 1-800-877-GALE, or visit us on our web site at http://gale.cengage.com/bizdev/.

Online. The Directory is available online through the Gale Directory Library. For more information, call 1-800-877-GALE.

The greatest of humankind's efforts have long provided occasion for great recognition and celebration. From the ancient Greek Olympics to the Lemelson-MIT Prize for Invention and Innovation, societies worldwide continue to acknowledge extraordinary accomplishment in all fields of human endeavor.

Awards, Honors & Prizes seeks to honor individuals and groups who foster intellectual growth, set records, stimulate creativity, demonstrate courage, and inspire and encourage humanitarian efforts and international understanding. The following is a representative sampling of established awards designed to confer such recognition.

Science and Technology

- The Lemelson-MIT Prize for Invention and Innovation seeks to raise the status and visibility of American inventors and innovators. The annual award carries a $500,000 award for U.S. citizens who have shown excellence in creativity, invention, and/or innovation in the fields of medicine and health care, energy and environment, telecommunications and computing, consumer products or industrial products.

- Excellence in the field of aerospace engineering is rewarded by a gold medal and $100,000 by the American Institute of Aeronautics and Astronautics' Walter J. and Angeline H. Crichlow Trust Prize.

- The Richard M. Oster Gold Heart Award, the American Heart Associations' highest honor, recognizes outstanding service to the national heart program. The annual awards includes a certificate and a gold plaque.

- The World Wildlife Fund offers the J. Paul Getty Award for Conservation Leadership, which recognizes an individual who has shown leadership in conservation in one of three annually rotating themes: political leadership, scientific leadership, and community leadership. The award is unique in that it not only recognizes today's leaders in conservation but also helps develop conservation leadership for tomorrow by establishing graduate fellowships in the name of the winner and J. Paul Getty. A monetary prize of $200,000 is awarded annually.

Education

- The Thomas J. Brennan Award, given by the Astronomical Society of the Pacific, recognizes high school astronomy teachers for excellence in teaching.

- Students in eighth, ninth and tenth grades are given monetary awards for excellence in analytical thinking and writing through the Anthem Essay Contest, which is sponsored by the Ayn Rand Institute.

- The International Reading Association aims to recognize talent in the field of children's literature with the Children's and Young Adult's Book Awards. The awards are presented annually for fiction and nonfiction in each of three categories: primary, intermediate, and young adult. Winners receive a monetary prize.

- The Promising Young Writers Program rewards outstanding eighth-grade writers who have been nominated by their schools. Awards and certificates are granted by the National Council of Teachers of English.

International Relations

- A monetary prize of 5,000,000 Japanese yen is awarded annually by the Victor Company of Japan to the person, company, or group that best demonstrates the importance of international contribution and cooperation.

- The Edouard Saouma Award includes a monetary prize of $25,000 for the national or regional institution that has managed a particularly efficient project funded by the Food and Agriculture Organization of the United Nations.

- UNESCO, an organization of the United Nations, offers the Felix Houphouet-Boigny Peace Prize to honor those who have made a contribution to promoting, seeking, safeguarding, or maintaining peace through education, science, and culture. A monetary prize of 150,000 Euros, a gold medal, and a certificate are awarded annually.

Journalism

- The Goldsmith Prize for Investigative Reporting honors journalists whose investigative reporting best promotes more effective and ethical conduct of government, public policy making, or political practice.

• Distinct journalistic coverage of the problems of the disadvantaged is rewarded annually by the Robert F. Kennedy Memorial's Journalism Awards. The awards are granted in such diverse categories as print, television, cartoon, radio, and photojournalism.

• The Leukemia and Lymphoma Society provides their own media awards to recognize American journalists who have educated the public through their coverage of advancements in cancer treatment through leukemia research.

Arts and Entertainment

• The Australia Council for the Arts honors indigenous artists who have made a great contribution to the recognition of aboriginal and Torres Strait Island art and culture in the wider community at both the national and international levels with its Red Ochre Award. This award, which includes a cash prize of $50,000, was established to mark the International Year for the World's Indigenous People.

• The Jack Poppele Broadcast Award, presented by the Radio Club of America, recognizes important and long-term contributions to the improvement of radio broadcasting.

• The National Academy of Television Arts and Sciences recognizes excellence in primetime television programs. Established in 1949, the Primetime Emmy Awards are now presented in more than 100 categories.

Sports

• The ESPY Awards, established by ESPN Inc., honor excellence in 34 categories of sports performance.

• Commitment to the Amateur Athletic Union is rewarded with the National Gold Pin Awards. Individuals considered for this honor must have given at least 35 years of continued service to the advancement of amateur sports.

• Winners of the championship game of the Canadian football league are presented with the Grey Cup. Established in 1909, the annual presentation of the cup inspires a festival for celebration.

News reports, by their very nature, frequently convey information that is less than welcome to world audiences. War, civil unrest, political upheaval, crime, health and environmental concerns, and other issues and events claim a majority of media attention. Perhaps that is why news of awards and their recipients, often featured prominently in print and broadcast media reporting, comes as a welcome change.

Humankind has long celebrated achievement of all kinds and in every field, from art and literature to science and technology. Individuals of all ages and from all walks of life are recognized when they transcend the boundaries of the ordinary to provide encouragement and inspiration by establishing new records, exploring new frontiers, demon-strating extraordinary courage, challenging the intellect, establishing new standards of excellence, creating beauty, or improving the quality of everyday life.

Awards, Honors & Prizes (AHP), now in its 33rd edition, continues to provide perspective on the variety, scale, significance, and number of awards given throughout the world to acknowledge distinguished achievement. Volume 1 of AHP is the single major source of descriptive information on awards bestowed in all subject areas by organizations, foundations, corporations, universities, and government bodies in the United States and Canada. Volume 2 covers international awards.

Content and Arrangement

Volume 2 of *Awards, Honors & Prizes* comprises descriptive listings for awards and their administering organizations, and three indexes.

Descriptive Listings are arranged alphabetically by administering organization; entries for the awards administered by each organization are listed alphabetically following organization entries.

Subject Index of Awards classifies awards by their principal areas of interest.

Organization Index provides an alphabetical listing of all organizations appearing in both volumes that administer or sponsor awards, including alternate and foreign organization names.

Award Index provides an alphabetical listing of all award names, including alternate, former, and popular names listed in both volumes.

Preparation of This Edition

The 33rd Edition of *Awards, Honors & Prizes* represents the revision and updating of the previous edition. Information was obtained via correspondence through electronic mail and the web sites of administering organizations, as well as mail correspondence.

Volume 1 Covers U.S. and Canadian Awards

Information on awards given by organizations located in the United States and Canada is available in Volume 1 of *AHP*. It provides descriptive information on more than 14,500 awards and more than 3,600 organizations, foundations, universities, corporations, and government bodies located in the United States and Canada.

Volume 2 Covers International Awards Scene

Information on awards given by organizations located in countries other than the U.S. and Canada is available in Volume 2 of *AHP*. It provides descriptive information on more than 7,100 awards and more than 2,300 national and international organizations, foundations, universities, corporations, research centers, libraries and government bodies located in more than 140 countries.

Acknowledgements

The editors are grateful to the large number of individuals in organizations throughout the world who generously responded to our requests for updated information. Without their cooperation, this book would not be possible.

Comments and Suggestions Welcome

If you are interested in additional information about *AHP*, are interested in information about other Gale business products, if your award is listed in *AHP* and you have a question pertaining to your profile, or if you would like to have your award listed, please contact **Verne Thompson, Content Project Editor,** *Awards, Honors and Prizes*

Gale, Cengage Learning

27500 Drake Rd.

Farmington Hills, MI 48331

Phone: (248)699-GALE

Toll-free: (800)347-GALE

Fax: (248)699-8075

URL: www.gale.com

Descriptive Listings

The descriptive listings are arranged alphabetically by administering organization; entries on the awards administered by each organization follow that organization's listing.

The organization and award entries shown below illustrate the kind of information that is or might be included in these entries. Each item of information is preceded by a number and is explained in the paragraph of the same number following the sample entry.

Sample Entry

▮1▮ 4266 ■
▮2▮ Canadian Parks/Recreation Association
▮3▮ (Association Canadienne des Loirsirs/Parc)
▮4▮ 333 River Rd.
   Vanier City, ON, Canada K1L 8H9
▮5▮ Phone: (613)748-5651
▮6▮ Toll-Free: 800-748-5600
▮7▮ Fax: (613)748-5652
▮8▮ E-mail: par@rec.assn.can
▮9▮ URL: http://www.can.park.rec
▮10▮ Formerly: (1980) Canadian Parks Association
▮11▮ 4267 ■ ▮12▮ Award of Merit ▮13▮ (Prix de Merite)
▮14▮ To give national recognition for meritorious achievements at the municipal, regional, or provincial levels that have made significant and distinct contributions to the furtherance of some aspect of local parks/recreation. Canadian individuals or organizations are eligible. The deadline for applications is February 15. ▮15▮ A wood plaque is ▮16▮ awarded annually. ▮17▮ Established in 1965. ▮18▮ Sponsored by the Canadian Park Service. ▮19▮ Formerly: (1982) Canadian Park Service Award.

Descriptions of Numbered Elements

▮1▮ **Organization Entry Number:** Entries for administering organizations are listed alphabetically, each followed by an alphabetical listing of its awards. All entries—organization and award—are numbered in a single sequence. These numbers are used as references in the indexes. Organization entry numbers are preceded by a horizontal rule across the column.

▮2▮ **Organization Name:** The name of the organization administering the awards that follow.

▮3▮ **Organization Name in Alternate Language(s):** The name of the organization is given in up to two additional languages, when provided by the organization.

▮4▮ **Mailing Address:** The organization's permanent mailing address for information on awards.

▮5▮ **Telephone Number:** The telephone number(s) for the administering organization.

▮6▮ **Toll-free Number:** The toll-free telephone number for the administering organization.

▮7▮ **Fax Number:** The facsimile number for the administering organization.

▮8▮ **E-mail:** When provided in source material, electronic mail numbers are listed.

▮9▮ **URL:** Whenever possible, the home page or URL for Internet access to organization sites is provided.

▮10▮ **Former Name of Organization:** The former name of the organization is provided if the name has changed, the organization merged, or the organization absorbed another organization. The year the name change occurred is also provided, when available.

▮11▮ **Award Entry Number:** Entries on awards are listed alphabetically following the entry for their administering organization. All entries—organization and award—are numbered in a single sequence. These numbers are used as references in the indexes.

▮12▮ **Award Name:** Name of the award, honor, or prize is listed in English whenever possible.

▮13▮ **Award Name in Alternate Language(s):** The award name is provided in up to two additional languages, when provided by the organization.

▮14▮ **Purpose of Award and Eligibility Criteria:** The description of the award indicates the purpose for which it is given, the criteria for eligibility, whether one can apply or must be nominated for the award, and the application or nomination deadline.

▮15▮ **Character:** Identifies the nature of the award, such as a medal, monetary award, certificate, inclusion in a hall of fame, or the presentation of a lecture.

▮16▮ **Frequency:** Information on the frequency of award

presentation and the occasion on which it is presented.

▮17▮ Year Established: The year the award was established and in whose honor or memory it is presented.

▮18▮ Sponsor: The sponsor or co-sponsor of an award, if it is an organization other than the administering organization.

▮19▮ Former Name: The former name of an award and the year of the name change, if provided.

Indexes

Subject Index of Awards

The Subject Index of Awards classifies all awards described in this volume by their principal areas of interest. The index contains more than 400 subject headings. Identically named awards are followed by an indented alphabetical list of the organizations administering an award by that name. Each award is indexed under all relevant headings. The index also contains numerous cross-references to direct users to related topics. Awards are listed alphabetically under each subject heading, and the number following an award name identifies that award's entry in the descriptive listings portion of this volume.

Organization Index

The alphabetical Organization Index provides access to all sponsoring and administering organizations listed in both volumes, as well as to organization acronyms and alternate language and former names. Index references include the volume in which the organization appears and book entry numbers in the descriptive listings section. In the case of sponsoring organizations, citations are to the specific awards they sponsor.

Award Index

The Award Index provides an alphabetical listing of all award names listed in both volumes, as well as alternate-language, former, and popular award names, such as the Oscars and Tonys. In the case of generic award names (e.g., Gold Medal, Achievement Award, Grand Prize), the award name is followed by an alphabetical listing of the organizations administering an award by that name. References to the volume in which the award may be found followed by the award's entry number in the descriptive listings section follow each award citation.

Albania

1 ▪ Albania Art Institute
Torre DRIN, Shoping Ctr.
Nr. 27, Rr A. Toptani
Tirana, Albania
E-mail: info@albaniaartinstitute.org
URL: http://www.albaniaartinstitute.org

2 ▪ Tirana International Film Festival
To recognize the world's best filmmakers and to promote Albanian cinema across the globe. Categories include fiction, documentaries, animation, and experimental films. Awards are presented in each. Held annually. Established in 2003.

3 ▪ Albanian Political Science Association
(Shoqata Shqiptare e Shkencave Politike)
Mirela Bogdani, Contact
PO Box 8199
Tirana, Albania
E-mail: alpsa@alpsa.org
URL: http://alpsa.org

4 ▪ Supplementary Research Grants
To support scholars and students who are conducting research in political science or related disciplines, and are receiving or will receive research funding from at least one source. Grants up to US$500 are awarded annually.

5 ▪ Travel Grants
To provide financial assistance to participants who present scholarly papers at professional conferences in political science and related disciplines. Grants up to US$500 are awarded annually.

6 ▪ Bank of Albania
Sheshi Skenderbej, No. 1
Tirana, Albania
Ph: 355 4 2222 152
Fax: 355 4 2223 558
E-mail: public@bankofalbania.org
URL: http://www.bankofalbania.org

7 ▪ Governor's Award
To honor the best diploma thesis on the topic of Albanian economics, macroeconomics, and finance. Open to Albanian students worldwide. Gold, silver, and bronze medals are awarded annually. Established in 2006.

8 ▪ United States Agency for International Development, Albania
c/o American Embassy
Rr. Elbasanit, Nr. 103
Tirana, Albania
Ph: 355 42 247 285

E-mail: tirana-webcontact@usaid.gov
URL: http://albania.usaid.gov

9 ▪ Authentic Albania Quality Mark Award Program
To support enterprises in Albania's tourism industry by establishing quality hotel standards and building opportunities for tourism business. Establishments are judged on such criteria as professionalism, safety, cleanliness, and comfort. Gold, silver, and bronze awards are presented annually. Established in 2011.

American Samoa

10 ▪ American Samoa Chamber of Commerce
PO Box 2446
Pago Pago, American Samoa 96799
Ph: 684 699 1881
Fax: 684 699 1197
E-mail: president@amsamoachamber.com
URL: http://amsamoachamber.com

11 ▪ Business Awards
To recognize companies and business people in American Samoa. Awards presented include the Business Person of the Year, New Business of the Year, Young Business Person of the Year, Support of Business Development Award, Community Business Support Award, and the Green Business Award. Awarded annually. Established in 2006.

Andorra

12 ▪ Concurs Internacional de Piano
C/Prat Gran n 9, 2n
Escaldes-Engordany, Andorra
Ph: 376 826501
Fax: 376 864075
E-mail: info@pianocompetitionandorra.com
URL: http://www.pianocompetitionandorra.com

13 ▪ Premi Principat d'Andorra International Piano Competition
To honor outstanding pianists. Open to pianists of all nationalities and places of residence who are between the ages of 18 and 32 years. A gold medal, trophy, and monetary prize of 10,000 Euros are awarded for first place, a silver medal and 5,000 Euros are awarded for second place, and a bronze medal and 2,000 Euros are awarded for third place. In addition, several special prizes may be awarded, including the Audience Prize. Held annually. Established in 1995.

Angola

14 ▪ Sonangol
Rua 1 Congresso do MPLA, n. 8-16
Caixa Postal 1316
Luanda, Angola
Ph: 244 2 334448
Fax: 244 2 391782
E-mail: secretariageral@sonangol.co.ao
URL: http://www.sonangol.co.ao

15 ▪ Sonangol Literature Prize - Grand Prize
To encourage and recognize the creativity of established authors from Angola, Cabo Verde, and Sao Tome and Principe. A cash prize of US$20,000 along with the cost of publication of 1,500 copies of the winning title are awarded biennially in odd-numbered years. Established in 1999.

16 ▪ Sonangol Literature Prize - Revelation Prize
To encourage and recognize the creativity of young Angolan authors who have yet to publish a work. A cash prize of US$5,000 along with the cost of publication of 1,500 copies of the winning title are awarded annually. Established in 1993.

Anguilla

17 ▪ Anguilla Hotel and Tourism Association
Coronation Ave.
PO Box 1020
The Valley, Anguilla
Ph: 264497-2944
Fax: 264497-3091
E-mail: ahta@anguillanet.com
URL: http://www.ahta.ai

18 ▪ Anguilla Tourism Awards
To recognize individuals for the promotion of Anguilla as a travel destination. The following awards are presented: Pioneer Awards, Ports Employees of the Year, Allied Member of the Year, Employee of the Year, and Supervisor of the Year. Awarded annually as part of the Tourism Gala, usually held during the last week of November.

Antigua-Barbuda

19 ▪ Antigua Charter Yacht Show
English Harbour, Antigua-Barbuda
Ph: 268460-1059
Fax: 268460-1784
E-mail: info@antiguayachtshow.com
URL: http://www.antigua-charter-yacht-meeting.com

Awards are arranged in alphabetical order below their administering organizations

20 ■ Charter Chef Competition
To recognize the most talented yacht charter chefs. Dishes must be prepared onboard each chef's yacht. Presented in three categories: chefs from yachts that are at least 150 feet long, yachts between 90 and 149 feet, and yachts 89 feet and shorter. Held annually. Established in 2000.

21 ■ Friends of the Antigua Public Library
Market St.
St. Johns, Antigua-Barbuda
Fax: 268723-7740
E-mail: info@foapl.org
URL: http://www.foapl.org

22 ■ Antigua Literary Award
To recognize and celebrate literary achievements in the Caribbean. Awarded annually at the Antigua & Barbuda Literary Festival, which was established in 2006 as the Caribbean International Literary Festival.

Argentina

23 ■ Academia Nacional de Agronomia y Veterinaria
Dr. Norberto Ras, Honorary Pres.
Avda. Alvear 1711, 2 piso
1014 Buenos Aires, Argentina
Ph: 54 11 48124168
Ph: 54 11 48154616
Fax: 54 11 48124168
E-mail: acadagrovet@anav.org.ar
URL: http://www.anav.org.ar

24 ■ Premio Jose Maria Bustillo
For recognition of an outstanding contribution in the field of agricultural economics. Awarded biennially in even-numbered years. Established in 1975 by Maria Luisa Devoto de Bustillo in memory of her husband, Jose Maria Bustillo.

25 ■ Premio Osvaldo Eckell
Awarded for outstanding scientific works in veterinary sciences. A medal is awarded biennially.

26 ■ Premio Fundacion Alfredo Manzullo
For recognition of persons who have contributed to the field of public health. Awarded biennially in odd-numbered years. Established by Fundacion Manzullo in 1975.

27 ■ Dr. Antonio Pires Prize
In recognition of superior research, education, and development in agronomy and veterinary sciences. Awarded biennially in odd-numbered years. Established in honor of Dr. Antonio Pires.

28 ■ Antonio J. Prego Prize
For recognition of soil and water conservation and reclamation. Awarded biennially in even-numbered years. Established in 1994.

29 ■ Premio Academia Nacional de Agronomia y Veterinaria
For recognition of individuals or institutions that have contributed to progress in agriculture. Awarded biennially in odd-numbered years. Established in 1969 by the Academy as its highest award.

30 ■ Premio al Desarrollo Agropecuario
For recognition of individuals or institutions who have contributed to national agriculture. Awarded biennially in even-numbered years. Established in 1977 by Massey Ferguson Argentina s.a. Formerly: (1998) Premio Massey Ferguson.

31 ■ Premio Bayer en Ciencias Veterinarias
For recognition of contributions to veterinary science. Awarded biennially in odd-numbered years. Established in 1976 by Bayer Argentina.

32 ■ Premio Bolsa de Cereales de Buenos Aires
For recognition of contributions to the production, industrialization, and commercialization of grains. Awarded biennially in odd-numbered years. Established in 1979 by Bolsa de Cereales de Buenos Aires on the occasion of the 125th anniversary of its founding.

33 ■ Premio Camara Arbitral de la Bolsa de Cereales de Buenos Aires
Awarded for improvements in the industrialization and commercialization of seeds. Awarded biennially in even-numbered years.

34 ■ Academia Nacional de la Historia de la Republica Argentina
Dr. Eduardo Martire, Pres.
Balcarce 139
C1064AAC Buenos Aires, Argentina
Ph: 54 4343 4416
Ph: 54 4331 4633
Fax: 54 4331 4416
E-mail: admite@an-historia.org.ar
URL: http://www.an-historia.org.ar

35 ■ Premio a Egresado
Developed by the Academia Nacional de Historia and given to the best in their specialty. Awarded annually.

36 ■ Premio Enrique Pena
For recognition of the best historical work on the discovery, conquest, and settlement of the Rio de Plata. University students are eligible. Certificates are awarded annually. Established in 1944 in memory of the scholar, Dr. Enrique Pena.

37 ■ Premio Academia Nacional de la Historia
For recognition of the best works concerning the history of Argentina from its beginning until 1950. Published or unpublished works are eligible. A monetary prize and a certificate are awarded annually for first, second, and third place winners. Established in 1964 in honor of the founding of Argentina.

38 ■ Argentine Academy of Letters (Academia Argentina de Letras)
Bosch Ines, Pres.
Sanchez de Bustamante 2663
1425 Buenos Aires, Argentina
Ph: 54 1 48023814
Fax: 54 1 48023814
E-mail: aaldespa@fibertel.com.ar
URL: http://www.aal.edu.ar

39 ■ Premio Academia Argentina de Letras
For poetry, narrative, or essay.

40 ■ Premio Academia Argentina de Letras e Egresados de la carrera de Letras de universidades estatales o privadas

41 ■ Argentine Marketing Association (Asociacion Argentina de Marketing)
Gustavo Dominguez, Pres.
Viamonte 723
C1053ABO Buenos Aires, Argentina
Ph: 54 11 43224888
E-mail: aam@aam-ar.com
URL: http://www.aam-ar.org.ar

42 ■ Mercurio Award (Premio Mercurio)
To recognize the best commercial strategies of the year. A trophy is awarded in several categories each year.

43 ■ Argentine Society of Geographical Studies (Sociedad Argentina de Estudios Geograficos)
Dr. Dario Cesar Sanchez, Pres.
Rodriguez Pena 158, 4 piso, Dep 7
1020 Buenos Aires, Argentina

Ph: 54 11 43712076
Ph: 54 11 43730588
Fax: 54 11 43712076
E-mail: informes@gaea.org.ar
URL: http://www.gaea.org.ar

44 ■ Premio Dr. Carlos A. Biedma
Annual award of recognition. Established in 1953.

45 ■ Premio Francisco P. Moreno Award
Annual award of recognition. Established in 1952.

46 ■ Premio Consagracion a la Geografia
Annual award of recognition for scholars. Established in 1984.

Armenia

47 ■ Armenian Medical Association
Parounak Zelveian MD, Pres.
PO Box 143
375010 Yerevan, Armenia
E-mail: info@armeda.am
URL: http://armeda.am

48 ■ Garegin Harutyunyan Scholarship
To support one senior medical student of the Yerevan State Medical University for one academic year. Scholarship is awarded to a bright individual with potential leader abilities, interest in research, and motivation in professional development. A scholarship of $30,000 is awarded monthly.

49 ■ Honorary Award
For individuals with outstanding work in public and scientific activity.

50 ■ Center for Regional Development/ Transparency International - Armenia
Varuzhan Hoktanyan, Exec. Dir.
Aygestan 9th St., House 6
0025 Yerevan, Armenia
Ph: 374 10 569910
Ph: 374 10 553069
Fax: 374 10 571399
E-mail: info@transparency.am
URL: http://www.transparency.am

51 ■ Outstanding Contribution to the Anti-Corruption Movement in Armenia
To recognize the representatives of the state institutions, business sector, NGOs, media, and international organizations, who have shown genuine commitment, consistency, and enthusiasm in the fight against corruption. Awarded annually. Established in 2003.

52 ■ Golden Apricot (Yerevan) International Film Festival
3 Moskovyan St.
0001 Yerevan, Armenia
Ph: 374 10 521047
Fax: 374 10 521042
E-mail: info@gaiff.am
URL: http://www.gaiff.am

53 ■ Golden Apricot (Yerevan) International Film Festival
To honor films that that fall within the theme of "Crossroads of Cultures and Civilizations" by representing the human experience through diverse ethnic groups, religions, and nations. Golden Apricot and Silver Apricot awards are presented in three categories: International Feature Films, International Documentary Films, and the Armenian Panorama. Held annually. Established in 2004.

54 ■ Hayastan All-Armenian Fund
Government Bldg. 3
0010 Yerevan, Armenia
Ph: 374 10 526474

Awards are arranged in alphabetical order below their administering organizations

Fax: 374 10 523795
E-mail: info@himnadram.org
URL: http://www.himnadram.org

55 ■ President of the Republic Genocide Prize

To honor an individual for valuable contributions to the recognition of the Armenian Genocide of 1915. Two prizes are awarded annually, one to a citizen of the Republic of Armenia and one to a citizen of other countries. Each recipient is presented with a diploma and monetary prize of US$10,000.

56 ■ President of the Republic Prize

To recognize individuals, typically citizens of the Republic of Armenia, for valuable creations and inventions in eight disciplines: natural sciences, technical science and information technology, physics, medical sciences, art, literature, humanities, and activities and projects promoting the development and dissemination of humanistic values. A diploma and monetary prize of US$5000 are awarded in each category annually. Supported by the Boghossian Foundation of France.

57 ■ President of the Republic Youth Prize

To recognize young people for valuable creations and inventions in literature and in fine arts and film. Candidates must be between 18 and 25 years old and must be citizens of Armenia. A diploma and monetary prize of US$2500 are awarded in each category annually. Supported by the Boghossian Foundation of France.

58 ■ President of the Republic Youth Prize in Classical Music

To recognize young performers in classical vocal art and instrumental performing art. Candidates must be between 18 and 27 years old and must be citizens of Armenia. A diploma and monetary prize of US$5000 are awarded in each category annually. Supported by the Boghossian Foundation of France.

Aruba

59 ■ Aruba International Film Festival
Paseo Herencia Mall
J.E. Irausquin Blvd. 382-A
Aruba, Aruba
Ph: 297 586 7450
E-mail: info@aiff.aw
URL: http://www.aiff.aw

60 ■ Aruba International Film Festival

To recognize the finest of studio and independent films from around the world, and to encourage local emerging filmmakers. Held annually. Established in 2010.

61 ■ Crescendo Foundation
Irenestraat 13
Oranjestad, Aruba
E-mail: info@arubapianofestival.com
URL: http://www.arubapianofestival.com

62 ■ Crescendo Piano Competition

To honor talented youthful pianists from Aruba. Open to amateur Aruban pianists between the ages of 8 and 18 years. The winner is awarded a full year of piano lessons with the teacher of his or her choice, and is invited by the Classical Music Board Bonaire to perform in a recital. Held annually as part of the International Aruba Piano Festival. Established in 2006.

Australia

63 ■ Accounting and Finance Association of Australia and New Zealand
Ms. Cheryl Umoh, Exec. Dir.
Level 1, 156 Bouverie St.
Carlton, Victoria 3053, Australia

Ph: 61 3 93495074
Fax: 61 3 93495076
E-mail: cherylu@afaanz.org
URL: http://www.afaanz.org

64 ■ AFAANZ Fellowship

To recognize a member who has made a significant contribution to the Association's activities over a sustained period of time. Candidates must have been members of AFAANZ for at least 10 years, and must have held a position on a board, special interest group, or performed other duties of importance to the Association. Lifetime membership is conferred annually if merited.

65 ■ Outstanding Contribution to Accounting and Finance Education Award

To recognize a member for contributions to education in the field of accounting and finance. Awarded when merited.

66 ■ Outstanding Contribution to Accounting and Finance Practice Award

To recognize a member for outstanding contributions to accounting and finance practice. Awarded annually if merited. Established in 1999.

67 ■ Advanced Manufacturing Australia
Angela Krepcik, CEO
Ste. 8, 322 Mountain Hwy.
Wantirna South, Victoria 3152, Australia
Ph: 61 3 97381133
Fax: 61 3 97381733
E-mail: info@amaus.com.au
URL: http://www.amaus.com.au

68 ■ Master Toolmaker Award

For excellence in the tool making industry.

69 ■ African Studies Association of Australasia and the Pacific
Dr. Fernanda Claudio, Pres.
Graduate Student Association
University of Melbourne
Graduate Centre
Melbourne, Victoria 3010, Australia
Ph: 61 3 83448323
E-mail: treasurer@afsaap.org.au
URL: http://www.afsaap.org.au

70 ■ Postgraduate Essay Prize

Awarded annually for the best postgraduate essay. The winner will be given assistance in publishing the essay in a refereed journal. A monetary award of $500 is presented.

71 ■ Allen & Unwin Pty. Ltd.
Paul Donovan, Managing Dir.
PO Box 8500
St. Leonards, New South Wales 1590, Australia
Ph: 61 2 8425 0100
Fax: 61 2 9906 2218
E-mail: frontdesk@allen-unwin.com.au
URL: http://www.allenandunwin.com

72 ■ The Australian/Vogel Literary Award

To encourage young Australian writers of unpublished fiction, history, or biography manuscripts. Australian residents under 35 years of age are eligible. Manuscripts with a maximum of 100,000 and a minimum of 30,000 words must be submitted by May 31. A monetary prize of A$20,000 is awarded annually. Established in 1979 by Niels Stevens of Vogel's Australia.

73 ■ Appita - Technical Association for the Australian and New Zealand Pulp and Paper Industry
Adele Elice-Invaso, Exec. Dir.
255 Drummond St., Ste. 47, Level 1
Carlton, Victoria 3053, Australia
Ph: 61 3 93472377
Fax: 61 3 93481206
E-mail: admin@appita.com.au
URL: http://www.appita.com

74 ■ L. R. Benjamin Medal

To encourage technical excellence, innovation, and achievement by honoring an individual who has contributed in an outstanding way to the technical progress of the pulp and paper industry in Australia and New Zealand. The contribution should have been largely personal, and could be in research, development, engineering, or management (provided the work managed was technical in nature). The nominee need not be a member of Appita. A mounted silver medallion is awarded annually.

75 ■ Art and Australia
11 Cecil St.
Paddington, New South Wales 2021, Australia
Ph: 61 2 9331 4455
Fax: 61 2 9331 4577
URL: http://www.artaustralia.com

76 ■ Contemporary Art Award

To promote the work of emerging artists. Eligible to Australian and New Zealand citizens or permanent residents who have been practicing professionally for less than five years. The winning artwork is displayed on the back cover of Art and Australia magazine. Two winners are chosen every six months. Sponsored by Credit Suisse Private Banking. Formerly: (2010) ANZ Private Bank and Australia Contemporary Award.

77 ■ Art Gallery of New South Wales
Edmund Capon, Dir.
Art Gallery Rd.
The Domain
Sydney, New South Wales 2000, Australia
Ph: 61 2 9225 1700
Fax: 61 2 9225 1701
E-mail: artmail@ag.nsw.gov.au
URL: http://www.artgallery.nsw.gov.au

78 ■ Archibald Prize

For recognition of a portrait painting of a distinguished person in art, letters, science, or politics. Applicants must have been a resident of Australia for 12 months prior to closing date. A monetary prize of A$50,000 is awarded annually. Established in 1921 by a bequest of J.F. Archibald, in trust of the Perpetual Trustee Company.

79 ■ Sir John Sulman Prize

For recognition of a subject/genre painting and/or murals/mural project executed during the preceding two years. Applicants must have been a resident in Australia for a period of five years prior to the closing date. A monetary prize of A$20,000 is awarded annually.

80 ■ The Wynne Prize

Awarded to the best landscape painting of Australian scenery in oils or watercolors or for the best example of figure sculpture by Australian artists completed during the preceding 12 months. A monetary prize of A$25,000 is awarded annually. First awarded in 1897.

81 ■ Art Gallery of Western Australia
Perth Cultural Centre
James St.
PO Box 8363
Perth, Western Australia 6849, Australia
Ph: 61 8 9492 6622
E-mail: admin@artgallery.wa.gov.au
URL: http://www.artgallery.wa.gov.au

82 ■ Tom Malone Prize

To promote the creation, appreciation, and enjoyment of glass made in Australia. A monetary prize of A$10,000 is awarded annually; in addition, the winning work then becomes part of the State Art Collection at the Art Gallery of Western Australia. Established in 2003.

83 ■ Western Australian Premier's Indigenous Art Awards

To celebrate the diversity and richness of indig-

Awards are arranged in alphabetical order below their administering organizations

enous art from across Australia. The following awards are presented: Western Australian Indigenous Art Award of A$50,000, Western Australian Artist Award of A$10,000, and the People's Choice Award of A$5000. Awarded annually. Established in 2008.

84 ■ Year 12 Perspectives People's Choice Award
To recognize the artist and art work receiving the most votes from the public at the Year 12 Perspectives, an exhibition that aims to honor the talent and creativity of the next generation of artists and to provide audiences a unique opportunity to see the world through the eyes of today's youth. Open to all Year 12 secondary school students who studied the Year 12 Visual Art Courses in Western Australia. Awarded annually.

85 ■ Asia-Pacific Professional Services Marketing Association
Sonia Adams, Pres.
Ste. 23, Chatswood Village
47-53 Neridah St.
Chatswood, New South Wales 2067, Australia
Ph: 61 2 94112599
Fax: 61 2 94112544
E-mail: info@apsma.com.au
URL: http://www.apsma.com.au

86 ■ Seldon Gill Scholarship
To support members by providing a significant career development opportunity to junior and mid-level marketers. An award package up to $8,500 is awarded annually.

87 ■ Hall of Fame
To recognize the contributions of those who have contributed to the profession of the marketing industry through their involvement in the APSMA. One or more individuals are inducted annually.

88 ■ Asia Pacific Screen Awards
Level 25, Waterfront Pl.
1 Eagle St.
PO Box 7990
Brisbane, Queensland 4001, Australia
Ph: 61 7 3222 1010
Fax: 61 7 3221 1684
E-mail: info@spscreenawards.com
URL: http://www.asiapacificscreenawards.com

89 ■ Asia Pacific Screen Awards
To honor filmmaking in the Asia-Pacific region that best reflects its culture, origins, and cinematic excellence; to promote outstanding films to a global audience in order to broaden the market appeal of such works; and to develop, through film, greater understanding of the region's various cultures. Open to feature films, animated feature films, children's feature films, and documentary feature films. Awarded annually. Established in 2007.

90 ■ Asian Studies Association of Australia
Purnendra Jain, Pres.
Adelaide University
Centre for Asian Studies
Adelaide, South Australia 5005, Australia
Ph: 61 8 83034688
Fax: 61 8 83034388
E-mail: purnendra.jain@adelaide.edu.au
URL: http://www.asaa.asn.au

91 ■ President's Prize
To recognize an outstanding doctoral thesis about Asia written at an Australian university. A monetary prize of $1,500 is awarded. Awarded annually. Established in 1997.

92 ■ Association for the Study of Australian Literature
Paul Genoni, Pres.
University of Sydney
Dept. of English
School of Letters, Arts and Media
John Woolley Bldg. A20
Sydney, New South Wales 2006, Australia
Ph: 61 2 93516853
Fax: 61 2 93512434
E-mail: bernadette.brennan@arts.usyd.edu.au
URL: http://asaliterature.com
Absorbed: (1982) Australian Literature Society.

93 ■ Australian Literature Society Gold Medal
For recognition of an outstanding literary work published in Australia during the previous calendar year between January 1 and December 31. Nominations are accepted. A monetary prize of $1,000 and a gold medal are awarded annually at the annual conference of the Association. Established in 1928. Formerly: (1982) Herbert Crouch Medal.

94 ■ Mary Gilmore Award
For recognition of the best first book of poetry published in Australia in the preceding two calendar years. Nominations are accepted, but not required. A monetary prize of A$1,000 is awarded biennially in even-numbered years. Established in 1985 in honor of Mary Gilmore, an Australian poet.

95 ■ A.D. Hope Prize
To recognize the best conference paper delivered by a postgraduate student. The winning paper receives publication in *JASAL* and a cash prize of A$500. Awarded annually.

96 ■ Magarey Medal
To recognize the female author of the best biographical writing on an Australian subject in the preceding two years. A medal and monetary prize of at least A$10,000 are awarded biennially in even-numbered years. Established by Adjunct Professor Susan Magarey. Co-sponsored by the Australian Historical Association.

97 ■ A.A. Phillips Prize
To recognize a work of outstanding achievement in the field of Australian literary scholarship. A monetary award of about $500 is presented on occasion. First awarded in 1986.

98 ■ Walter McRae Russell Award
For recognition of the best book of literary scholarship on an Australian subject published in the preceding two calendar years. Nominations are accepted, but not required. A monetary prize of A$1,000 is awarded biennially in odd-numbered years. Established in 1983 in honor of Walter McRae Russell, last president of the Australian Literature Society.

99 ■ Association of Australasian Diesel Specialists
Mr. Mike Hurley, Pres.
PO Box 576
Crows Nest, New South Wales 2065, Australia
Ph: 61 2 94318685
Fax: 61 3 94318677
E-mail: aads@apcaust.com.au
URL: http://www.aads.com.au

100 ■ Keith Jurgs Award
To a financial service member with significant contribution to the promotion and growth of the association.

101 ■ President's Shield
For the best exhibition stand.

102 ■ Association of Chartered Certified Accountants - Australia and New Zealand
Frances Dwyer, Contact
68 York St., Ste. 402
Sydney, New South Wales 2000, Australia
Ph: 61 2 82450222
Fax: 61 2 82450211
E-mail: info@au.accaglobal.com
URL: http://australia.accaglobal.com

103 ■ Australia and New Zealand Awards for Sustainability Reporting
To recognize organizations that report and disclose environmental, social, or full sustainability information within Australia; to raise awareness of corporate transparency issues and increase accountability for responsiveness to stakeholders; and to encourage the uptake of environmental, social, and sustainability reporting. Awarded annually.

104 ■ Association of Regulatory and Clinical Scientists Australia
Katrina Campion, Pres.
28 Clarke St., Ste. 802
Crows Nest, New South Wales 2065, Australia
Ph: 61 2 89050829
Fax: 61 2 89050830
E-mail: arcs@arcs.com.au
URL: http://www.arcs.com.au

105 ■ Life Membership Award
To recognize an individual for contributions to the organization and its goals. Awarded when merited.

106 ■ Osmond-Russell Scholarship
For a qualified applicant and member of ARCS. A scholarship up to $10,000 is awarded annually. Established in 1987.

107 ■ Asthma Foundation of New South Wales
Craig Knowles, Pres.
Level 3, 486 Pacific Hwy.
St. Leonards, New South Wales 2065, Australia
Ph: 61 2 99063233
Fax: 61 2 99064493
E-mail: ask@asthmansw.org.au
URL: http://www.asthmafoundation.org.au

108 ■ Asthma Research Hall of Fame
Individuals funded by the Asthma Foundation NSE are eligible for this award. Inductees are chosen from researchers who have published a large amount of material on asthma and allergies. Established in 2005.

109 ■ Asthma Research Postgraduate Scholarships
To support new and emerging asthma research talent, encouraging young researchers to devote their energies and considerable talents to asthma research. Several scholarships are awarded annually.

110 ■ Asthma Research Sustainability Grants
To assist new and emerging research work to continue to develop to a level where it can attract other, more significant funding. Grants of $50,000 are awarded annually.

111 ■ Astronomical Society of Australia
Dr. Kate Staveley-Smith, Pres.
University of Sydney
Sydney Institute for Astronomy
School of Physics
Sydney, New South Wales 6009, Australia
Ph: 61 2 93513184
Fax: 61 2 93517726
E-mail: john.obyrne@sydney.edu.au
URL: http://www.astronomy.org.au

112 ■ David Allen Prize
Recognizes a published article that portrays an astronomical theme in an exciting and educative way. A monetary prize of $5,000 is awarded triennially.

113 ■ The Bok Prize
To recognize the best third- or fourth-year undergraduate student essay or project. A bronze medal and cash prize of $500 is awarded annually.

Awards are arranged in alphabetical order below their administering organizations

114 ■ The Ellery Lectureship
Recognizes outstanding contributions in astronomy or related fields. Awarded biennially in odd-numbered years.

115 ■ Charlene Heisler Prize
To recognize the most outstanding PhD thesis in astronomy or a closely related topic. A certificate and cash prize of $500 is awarded annually. Established in 2000.

116 ■ Page Medal
Recognizes excellence in amateur astronomy. Awarded biennially in even-numbered years.

117 ■ Astronomical Society of New South Wales
Les Sara, Sec.
PO Box 193
Ettalong Beach, New South Wales 2257, Australia
Ph: 61 2 43442874
Fax: 61 2 96881161
E-mail: secretary@asnsw.com
URL: http://www.asnsw.com

118 ■ Crago Award
To encourage a student or other member who has shown special interest in amateur astronomy by undertaking an activity or organizing an event. Awarded annually, if merited. Established in 1997.

119 ■ Editor's Award
For excellence in quantity or quality of astronomy writing. Selected and presented by the Society's editor. Awarded annually. Established in 1981.

120 ■ Education Officer's Award
To recognize the outstanding junior member of the Society. Established in the 1950s as the Junior Award.

121 ■ Life Membership
This, one of the Society's highest honors, is presented to a member for sustained, selfless dedication to the Society. Awarded as merited. Established in 1963.

122 ■ McNiven Medal
To recognize an amateur astronomer for significant contributions to the Society or to the science of astronomy. Awarded annually when merited. Established in 1973.

123 ■ President's Award
For the best contribution to the Society in the previous year. Awarded annually at the discretion of the president. Established in 1998.

124 ■ Southern Cross Award
This is the second-highest award of the Society and can be regarded as a runner-up to the McNiven Medal. Presented to recognize an individual for contributions to astronomy or the Society. Awarded annually, if merited. Established in 2000.

125 ■ Aurealis Awards
PO Box 1394
Toowong, Queensland 4066, Australia
E-mail: coordinator@.aurealisawards.com
URL: http://www.aurealisawards.com

126 ■ Aurealis Awards
To recognize the achievements of Australian science fiction, fantasy, and horror writers. Open to authors, editors, and illustrators who are Australian citizens or permanent residents. Awarded annually in 14 categories. In addition, the Peter McNamara Convenors' Award for Excellence may be presented. Established in 1995.

127 ■ Australasian Association of Convenience Stores
Sheryle Moon, Exec. Dir.
PO Box 499
Melbourne, Victoria 3058, Australia

Ph: 61 3 00736227
Fax: 61 3 82560143
E-mail: marketing@aacs.org.au
URL: http://www.aacs.org.au

128 ■ Distributor of the Year
Award of recognition.

129 ■ Peter Jowett Industry Award
To recognize young members who can present insight, innovation, and a clear understanding of current and future challenges and trends facing convenience retailing in Australasia. Candidates must be between the ages of 21 and 36 years. Awarded annually.

130 ■ Australasian College of Tropical Medicine
Prof. David Porter, Pres.
PO Box 123
Red Hill, Queensland 4059, Australia
Ph: 61 7 38722246
Fax: 61 7 38564727
E-mail: actm@tropmed.org
URL: http://www.tropmed.org

131 ■ ACTM Medal for Outstanding Contributions to Tropical Medicine
For outstanding contributions to the field of tropical medicine through research, development, and/or teaching. Awarded annually.

132 ■ ACTM Medal for Outstanding Service to the College
Award or recognition.

133 ■ ACTM Medal for Students
Recognizes excellence in scholarship and research by students.

134 ■ Australasian Federation of Family History Organisations
Mr. Andrew Peake, Pres.
PO Box 3012
Weston Creek, Australian Capital Territory 2611, Australia
E-mail: secretary@affho.org
URL: http://www.affho.org

135 ■ Award for Meritorious Service to Family History
Recognizes contributions to Australasian genealogy. Awarded triennially. Established in 1990.

136 ■ Australasian Medical Writers Association
Dr. Justin Coleman, Pres.
PO Box 1261
Chatswood, New South Wales 2067, Australia
Ph: 61 2 48785424
E-mail: president@medicalwriters.org
URL: http://www.medicalwriters.org

137 ■ AMWA Awards
For members undertaking a project that is worthy of AMWA support.

138 ■ Australasian Performing Rights Association
Mr. Michael Perjanik, Chm.
16 Mountain St.
Ultimo, New South Wales 2007, Australia
Ph: 61 2 99357900
E-mail: apra@apra.com.au
URL: http://www.apra-amcos.com.au

139 ■ Music Awards
To honor Australian composers and songwriters who have achieved the highest performances of their work and excellence in their craft over the previous year. Awarded in the categories of: Songwriter of the Year, Breakthrough Award, Most Played Australian Work, Most Played Foreign Work, Most Played Australian Work Overseas, Blues and Roots Work of the Year, Country Work of the Year, Dance Work of the

Year, Jazz Work of the Year, and Urban Work of the Year. In addition, the Ted Albert Award for Outstanding Services to Australian Music is presented. Awarded annually. Established in 1982.

140 ■ Professional Development Awards
To encourage and honor music writers of Australia in the early stages of their careers. Candidates must be at least 18 years old, and must be Australian citizens or legal residents of Australia for at least two years. Awards are presented in six categories: Popular Contemporary, Country, Jazz, Classical, Film and Television, and Indigenous. Gifts and cash prizes totaling $16,000 are awarded annually in each category. Established in 2001 to mark the Association's 75th anniversary.

141 ■ Screen Music Awards
To honor Australian music composers for excellence and innovation in the genre of screen composition. Awarded in 13 categories, including compositions for documentaries, short films, mini-series, children's television, and feature film scores. Awarded annually. Established in 2002. Co-sponsored by the Australian Guild of Screen Composers (AGSC).

142 ■ Song of the Year
To recognize the best song of the year, as determined from member votes. Awarded annually. Established in 1991.

143 ■ Australasian Pig Science Association
Ms. Karen Moore, Sec.
Locked Bag 4
Bentley, Western Australia 6983, Australia
Ph: 61 8 93683636
Ph: 61 8 93602012
Fax: 61 8 94741295
E-mail: karen.moore@agric.wa.gov.au
URL: http://www.apsa.asn.au

144 ■ APSA Fellow
To recognize significant contributions to the Association. Established in 2007.

145 ■ APSA Medal
For the best presentation of a first APSA paper. Awarded annually. Sponsored by Becan Consulting Group.

146 ■ Batterham Award
To recognize achievements in pig research and development in Australia by a young scientist. Sponsored by Ridley Agriproducts Pty Ltd.

147 ■ Poster Award
For the best poster at the annual conference. Awarded annually. Sponsored by Ridley Agriproducts Pty Ltd.

148 ■ Australasian Political Studies Association
Prof. Katharine Gelber, Pres.
6 Sullivan Crescent
Wanniassa
Canberra, Australian Capital Territory 2903, Australia
E-mail: mhapel5@gmail.com
URL: http://www.auspsa.org.au

149 ■ Crisp Medal
For recognition of originality and intellectual contribution of a work in political science published during the preceding three years. Citizens or permanent residents of Australia or New Zealand are eligible for nomination. Individuals who have held a doctorate for 10 years or more or whose first appointment to a tenurable post at a tertiary institution was ten or more years ago are not eligible. A monetary prize of $1,000 (Australian) and a medal are awarded biennially in even-numbered years. Established in 1988 by the Association and the Commonwealth Bank of

Awards are arranged in alphabetical order below their administering organizations

Australia in memory of Leslie Finlay Crisp, Foundation Professor of Political Science at Canberra University College (later The Australian National University) and Chairman of the Board of the Commonwealth Bank of Australia from 1975 until his death in 1984.

150 ■ Women in Politics Prize
For recognition of the best essay on the topic of women and politics, broadly defined. Awarded biennially in odd-numbered years. Established in 1981.

151 ■ Australasian Quaternary Association
Dr. Peter Almond, Pres.
University of Queensland
School of Geography, Planning and Architecture
Brisbane, Queensland 4072, Australia
Ph: 61 7 33656418
E-mail: president@aqua.org.au
URL: http://www.aqua.org.au

152 ■ J.M. Bowler Prize
Awarded to the best PhD and honors student papers presented at the biennial conference. Open to AQUA members who are currently enrolled in a degree program in Australia, Fiji, New Zealand or Papua New Guinea. Monetary prizes of A$500 and A$250 are presented to the winning post-graduate and undergraduate papers, respectively. Awarded annually. Established in 1989.

153 ■ Lifetime Achievement Award
Awarded for the outstanding and distinguished careers of AQUA members. A certificate and lifetime membership to the association are awarded periodically.

154 ■ Postgraduate Travel Award
To support a student currently enrolled in a postgraduate degree in Australia, New Zealand, Papua New Guinea, or Fiji in the field of quaternary studies, to attend an international conference at which they will present results of their research. A grant of A$1,000 is awarded annually.

155 ■ Australasian Society for Traumatic Stress Studies
Douglas Brewer, Pres.
PO Box 6227
Adelaide, South Australia 5000, Australia
Ph: 61 8 82315626
E-mail: davidk@victimsa.org
URL: http://www.astss.org.au

156 ■ Media Award
To promote sensitive reporting and responsible and credible coverage of crime, family violence, natural disasters, accidents, war, and genocide, and to advance knowledge and understanding about the nature and consequences of highly stressful events. Open to journalists, photographers, and broadcasters based in Australasia. A monetary prize of $1,000 is awarded annually.

157 ■ Australasian Society for Ultrasound in Medicine
Annie Gibbins, CEO
PO Box 943
Crows Nest
Sydney, New South Wales 1585, Australia
Ph: 61 2 94382078
Fax: 61 2 94383686
E-mail: asum@asum.com.au
URL: http://www.asum.com.au

158 ■ Best Poster Award
To honor the best posters submitted at the annual scientific meeting of the Society. Awarded annually.

159 ■ Best Research Presentation Award
To honor the best research papers submitted at the annual scientific meeting of the Society. Awarded annually.

160 ■ Best Sonographer Research Presentation Award
To honor the best research papers submitted at the annual scientific meeting of the Society. Awarded annually.

161 ■ Anthony Tynan Award for Best Clinical Presentation
To honor the best papers submitted at the annual scientific meeting of the Society. Awarded annually.

162 ■ Australasian Society of Clinical Immunology and Allergy
Prof. Jo Douglass, Pres.
PO Box 450
Balgowlah, New South Wales 2093, Australia
Fax: 61 2 99079773
E-mail: education@allergy.org.au
URL: http://www.allergy.org.au

163 ■ Media Awards
For outstanding medical/health reporting on allergic diseases or other immune diseases by a journalist in Australia and New Zealand. Two awards of A$1,000 each are presented annually.

164 ■ Australia Council
Literature Board
Kathy Keele, CEO
PO Box 788
Operations Section
Strawberry Hills, New South Wales 2012, Australia
Ph: 61 2 92159000
Fax: 61 2 92159111
E-mail: mail@australiacouncil.gov.au
URL: http://www.australiacouncil.gov.au

165 ■ Writers' Emeritus Award
To acknowledge the achievements of eminent literary writers over the age of 65 who have made outstanding and lifelong contributions to Australian literature. Literary excellence, importance of previous work and financial situation of the writer are the selection criteria. Nominated writers must have produced a critically acclaimed body of work over a long creative life and be able to document that their maximum annual income is less than $40,000. A monetary prize of up to A$50,000 is awarded annually.

166 ■ Australia Council for the Arts
Kathy Keele, CEO
372 Elizabeth St.
Surry Hills, New South Wales 2010, Australia
Ph: 61 2 92159000
Fax: 61 2 92159111
E-mail: mail@australiacouncil.gov.au
URL: http://www.australiacouncil.gov.au

167 ■ Don Banks Music Award
To recognize the finest Australian composers and to provide them with the means whereby they may devote one year fully to composition. A monetary prize of A$60,000 is awarded annually. Established in 1984 in honor of Don Banks, an Australian composer and the first chairperson of the Music Board. Formerly: (1997) Don Banks Composer Fellowship.

168 ■ Australia Council for the Arts
Visual Arts/Craft Board
Kathy Keele, CEO
372 Elizabeth St.
Surry Hills, New South Wales 2010, Australia
Ph: 61 2 92159000
Fax: 61 2 92159111
E-mail: mail@australiacouncil.gov.au
URL: http://www.australiacouncil.gov.au

169 ■ Red Ochre Award
To honor indigenous artists who have made a great contribution to the recognition of Aboriginal and Torres Strait Island art and culture in the wider community at both the national and international level. A monetary award of $50,000 per year for up to three years is presented. Established in 1993.

170 ■ Australian Academy of Science
Dr. Sue Meek, Chief Exec.
GPO Box 783
Canberra, Australian Capital Territory 2601, Australia
Ph: 61 2 62019400
Ph: 61 2 62019450
Fax: 61 2 62019494
E-mail: eb@science.org.au
URL: http://www.science.org.au

171 ■ Academy Medal for Contributions to Science and Technology
To recognize non-research related contributions to science by a person outside the Fellowship. Generally awarded no more than once every three years.

172 ■ MacFarlane Burnet Medal and Lecture
Recognizes biological research of high standing. Awarded every two years in even-numbered years. Established in 1971 in honor of Dr. Joseph Bancroft.

173 ■ Fenner Medal
Recognizes biology research, except biomedical sciences. Scientists under the age of 40 who are normally residents of Australia are eligible. Research must have been conducted mainly in Australia. An honorarium of A$1000 and a medal are awarded annually. Established in 2000.

174 ■ Matthew Flinders Medal and Lecture
Recognizes high standing scientific research in the field of physical science. Only Academy Fellows are eligible. An honorarium of A$200, a medal, honorary recognition, and an invitation to present the Matthew Flinders Lecture are awarded biennially in odd-numbered years, alternating with the Burnet Lecture. Established in 1956.

175 ■ Ruth Stephens Gani Medal in Human Genetics
To recognize exceptional research in genetics. Researchers under 40 years of age (except in the case of serious career interruption) who reside and conduct research primarily in Australia are eligible. Awarded annually. Established in 2008. Honors the contributions to human cytogenetics by Ruth Stephens Gani.

176 ■ Gottschalk Medal
Recognizes outstanding research in the medical sciences. Scientists who are under 40 years of age and not Fellows of the Academy and who have completed most of the research in Australia are eligible. An honorarium of A$1,000 and a medal is awarded annually. Established in 1976 by Dr. A. Gottschalk.

177 ■ Anton Hales Medal in Earth Sciences
To recognize exceptional research in the Earth sciences. Researchers under 40 years of age (except in the case of serious career interruption) who reside and conduct research primarily in Australia are eligible. Awarded annually. Established in 2009. Honors the late Prof. Anton L. Hales FAA.

178 ■ Hannan Medal
To recognize a scientist for distinguished research carried out mainly in Australia in mathematical sciences. Work carried out during the entire career of the candidates will be considered, but special weight will be given to their recent research. The award is given biennially in odd-numbered years, rotating among the following three categories: statistical science, pure

---

Awards are arranged in alphabetical order below their administering organizations

mathematics, and applied and computational mathematics. Established in 1994 in honor of the late E.J. Hannan, Professor and Professor Emeritus of Statistics of the Australian National University.

179 ■ Dorothy Hill Award
Supports research in aquatic Earth sciences, including ocean drilling, marine and reef science, and taxonomy in marine systems. Female researchers under the age of 40 are eligible. Candidates are normally Australian residents who have conducted research mainly in Australia. A monetary prize of A$5,000 is awarded annually. Established in 2002 in honor of Professor Dorothy Hills.

180 ■ Jaeger Medal
Recognizes outstanding investigations into the solid earth or its oceans. Investigations carried out in Australia or having some connection with Australian earth science are eligible. A medal is awarded biennially in odd-numbered years. Established in 1991 to honor the late John Conrad Jaeger.

181 ■ Haddon Forrester King Medal
Recognizes original and sustained contributions to earth and related sciences of particular relevance to the discovery, evaluation, and exploitation of mineral deposits, including the hydrocarbons. Scientist residents of Australia and elsewhere are eligible. A medal is awarded biennially in even-numbered years. Established in 1993 in honor of the late Haddon Forrester King. Sponsored by Rio Tinto.

182 ■ R.J.W. Le Fevre Memorial Prize
Recognizes the achievements of young researchers in chemistry, particularly physical chemistry. Scientists not more than 40 years of age are eligible. A monetary prize of A$3,000 is awarded annually. Established in 1989 in memory of the late Professor R.J.W. Le Fevre.

183 ■ Thomas Ranken Lyle Medal
Recognizes outstanding research in mathematics or physics. The research must have been completed during the previous five years, largely in Australia. A bronze medal and honorary recognition are awarded biennially in odd-numbered years. Established in 1931 in honor of Sir Thomas Ranken Lyle, FRS.

184 ■ Mawson Medal and Lecture
Recognizes contributions to the field of Earth Science. Australian scientists are eligible. A bronze medal, and an invitation to deliver a lecture at the convention of the Geological Society of Australia are awarded biennially in even-numbered years. Established in 1979 in honor of Sir Douglas Mawson, FAA FRS.

185 ■ Moran Medal
To recognize a scientist for distinguished research carried out mainly in Australia, in one or more of the fields of applied probability, biometrics, mathematical genetics, psychometrics, and statistics. Candidates must be no more than 40 years of age, or have significant interruptions to a research career. A monetary award of A$1,000 and a medal are awarded biennially in odd-numbered years. Established in 1990 to honor the late Professor P.A.P. Moran.

186 ■ Pawsey Medal
Recognizes contributions to research in physics. Scientists under 40 years of age and citizens of Australia are eligible. The research must be carried out mainly in Australia. A monetary prize of A$1,000 and a medal are awarded annually. Established in 1965 in honor of Dr. Pawsey and his contributions to science in Australia.

187 ■ Selby Fellowship
To recognize distinguished overseas scientists and to enable them to undertake public lectures and visit scientific centers in Australia. Fellowship trips should be more than two weeks but less than three months in duration. Up to A$10,000 is available to cover airfare and assistance toward living expenses. Awarded annually. Established in 1961. Financed through the Selby Scientific Foundation.

188 ■ Ian Wark Medal and Lecture
To recognize a scientist for a contribution to the prosperity of Australia where such prosperity is attained through the advance of scientific knowledge or its application, or both. Also, to focus attention on applications of scientific discoveries that have benefited the community. A medal and lecture are awarded biennially in even-numbered years. Established in 1987 in memory of Sir Ian Wark, whose work was at the interface of science and industry.

189 ■ Frederick White Prize
Recognizes scientific research achievement in the fields of mathematics, physics, astronomy, chemistry, and terrestrial and planetary sciences. Australian scientists under the age of 40 are eligible. Research must have been conducted primarily in Australia. A monetary prize of A$3,000 is awarded biennially in even-numbered years. Established in 1981 by Sir Frederick White.

190 ■ Australian Academy of the Humanities
Prof. Joseph Lo Bianco, Pres.
GPO Box 93
Canberra, Australian Capital Territory 2601, Australia
Ph: 61 2 61259860
Fax: 61 2 62486287
E-mail: enquiries@humanities.org.au
URL: http://www.humanities.org.au

191 ■ Crawford Medal
To recognize the outstanding achievements of scholars in the humanities in Australia. Australian humanities scholars in the early career stages are eligible. In making the award, the Council of the Academy shall take into account the actual or potential contributions of the research to the enrichment of cultural life in Australia. The medal is awarded biennially in even-numbered years. Established in 1992.

192 ■ Australian Acoustical Society
Mr. Richard Booker, Gen. Sec.
PO Box 1843
Toowong, Queensland 4066, Australia
Ph: 61 7 31222605
Fax: 61 7 31222605
E-mail: generalsecretary@acoustics.asn.au
URL: http://www.acoustics.asn.au

193 ■ President's Prize
Recognizes the best paper presented at annual conference. Awarded annually.

194 ■ Australian-American Fulbright Commission
Hon. Kevin Rudd MP, Co-Chm.
6 Napier Close, Level 1
PO Box 9541
Deakin, Australian Capital Territory 2600, Australia
Ph: 61 2 62604460
Fax: 61 2 62604461
E-mail: fulbright@fulbright.com.au
URL: http://www.fulbright.com.au

195 ■ Fulbright Awards - American Program
To enable American scholars to undertake study or research in Australia. Open to any American citizen not residing in Australia. Several programs are offered: Fulbright Postgraduate Scholarships, Fulbright Senior Scholarships, Fulbright Australian National University Distinguished Chair in American Political Science, and U.S. Senior Specialist.

196 ■ Fulbright Awards - Australian Program
To enable Australian scholars, professionals, postdoctoral fellows, and postgraduates to undertake 8 to 12 months study or research in the United States. Open to all Australian citizens. The following programs are offered: Fulbright Postgraduate Scholarships, Fulbright Postdoctoral Scholarships, Fulbright Senior Scholarships, Fulbright Professional Scholarships, Fulbright New Century Scholar Program, and Fulbright Scholar in Residence.

197 ■ Australian and New Zealand Association for the Advancement of Science
Mike Murray, Chm.
PO Box 788
Northcote, Victoria 3070, Australia
Ph: 61 408373114
E-mail: chair@anzaas.org.au
URL: http://www.anzaas.org.au

198 ■ Joyce Allen Lecture
To encourage scientific discussion and sharing of knowledge. Awarded biennially in odd-numbered years. Established in 1995 in honor of Joyce Allen, retired school teacher and dedicated member of ANZAAS.

199 ■ ANZAAS Medal
To recognize an individual for outstanding achievements in science. Individuals who normally reside in Australia or New Zealand may be nominated. A medal is awarded annually at the annual ANZAAS Congress. Established in 1965.

200 ■ Giblin Lecture
To recognize an individual for contributions to economics, public administration, and government. Awarded annually. Established in 1958 in honor of Professor L.F. Giblin, an economist and statistician of great renown.

201 ■ Liversidge Lecture
To recognize a distinguished scientist. Awarded annually. Established in 1930 in honor of Professor Archibald Liversidge, secretary of the Association for 20 years.

202 ■ Mueller Medal
For recognition of important contributions to anthropological, botanical, geological or zoological science. Preference is given to work having special reference to Australasia. There is no restriction on eligibility for the award. A medal is awarded annually. Established in 1902.

203 ■ Australian and New Zealand Bone and Mineral Society
Prof. Rebecca S. Mason, Pres.
145 Macquarie St.
Sydney, New South Wales 2000, Australia
Ph: 61 2 92565405
Ph: 61 2 93512561
Fax: 61 2 92518174
E-mail: anzbms@racp.edu.au
URL: http://www.anzbms.org.au

204 ■ Amgen-ANZBMS Outstanding Abstract Award
To honor a member for high standard bone and mineral research. A monetary prize of A$1,000 is awarded annually to one or more recipients. Established in 2003.

205 ■ Kaye Ibbertson Award for Metabolic Bone Disease
Awarded for outstanding and prolific contributions, as well as research in the field of metabolic bone disease. A monetary award of $1,000 is presented annually. Established in 2005 in honor of Prof. Kaye Ibbertson and his contributions to the ANZBMS.

206 ■ Christine and T. Jack Martin Research Travel Grant
To facilitate travel to undertake bone and mineral

Awards are arranged in alphabetical order below their administering organizations

research in any aspect of basic or clinical science. Open to financial members of the Society, and preference is given to members who are in the training phase of their careers. Grants up to A$15,000 are awarded annually. Established in 2002.

207 ■ Roger Melick Young Investigator Award

To support young members of the society currently working toward a higher degree. A monetary award of A$1,000 is presented annually. Established in 1996 in honor of the contributions of Dr. Roger Aziz Melick to student education and the science of endocrinology.

208 ■ Christopher and Margie Nordin Young Investigator Poster Award

To recognize the author of the best presenting paper to be delivered at the annual meeting. A monetary award of A$1,000 is presented annually. Established in 1997 in honor of Prof. Chris Nordin and his contributions to the ANZBMS.

209 ■ Sol Posen Research Award

To recognize a member for the best paper published in the previous 18 months of the closing date of the award. A monetary award of $1,000 is presented annually. Established in 2006 in honor of Sol Posen, one of the pioneers in the field of bone and mineral endocrinology in Australia.

210 ■ Australian and New Zealand Industrial and Applied Mathematics ANZIAM

Andrew Bassom, Sec.
Department of Mathematics
Australian National University
Canberra, Australian Capital Territory 0200, Australia
Ph: 61 2 6125 8922
Fax: 61 2 6125 8923
E-mail: office@austms.org.au
URL: http://www.anziam.org.au

211 ■ ANZIAM Medal

To recognize outstanding service to the profession of applied mathematics in Australia, through research achievements and activities enhancing applied or industrial mathematics. Members of ANZIAM are eligible. Awarded biennially in even-numbered years. Established in 1995.

212 ■ T. M. Cherry Prize

For recognition of the best student paper presented at the annual conference of ANZIAM. Any postgraduate student whose higher degree thesis has not been submitted more than three calendar months before the commencement of the annual conference is eligible. A monetary prize is awarded annually at the conference. Established in 1969 and renamed in 1976 in memory of T. M. Cherry, one of Australia's leading applied mathematicians.

213 ■ J.H. Michell Medal

For outstanding new researchers in industrial and applied mathematics who are in the first ten years of their research careers. They must be members of ANZIAM, and a significant proportion of their research must have been carried out in Australia or New Zealand. Awarded annually. Established in 1999.

214 ■ Australian and New Zealand Obesity Society

Prof. Nuala Byrne, Pres.
University of Sydney
Medical Foundation Bldg. K25
Sydney, New South Wales 2006, Australia
E-mail: office@asso.org.au
URL: http://www.asso.org.au/home
Formerly: (2008) Australasian Society for the Study of Obesity.

215 ■ ASSO Student Award

For the best scientific paper.

216 ■ Young Investigator Award

To recognize and encourage the research careers of young or recently graduated scientists active in obesity-related research. The award is based on a consideration of the originality, ingenuity and productivity of the applicant over the past five years and an assessment of their potential for further contribution. Candidates must be aged 35 years or younger; should have obtained or are currently undertaking a higher degree or award; and are in the early stages of a research career (i.e., within five (5) years of obtaining their postgraduate degree). A monetary prize of $2,000 is awarded annually.

217 ■ Australian and New Zealand Society of Blood Transfusion

Dr. Erica Wood, Pres.
145 Macquarie St.
Sydney, New South Wales 2000, Australia
Ph: 61 2 92565456
Fax: 61 2 92520294
E-mail: anzsbt@anzsbt.org.au
URL: http://www.anzsbt.org.au

218 ■ Presidential Symposium Award

To recognize the best oral presentation at the annual scientific meeting by a Society member. A monetary prize of $500 is awarded annually.

219 ■ Peter Schiff Award

To recognize and foster significant contributions to transfusion medicine through efforts in one or more of the following areas: Research into the nature and roles of blood products; Education of the medical community and special interest groups in the field of transfusion medicine; and Encouragement and promotion of the importance of blood and plasma donation and their appropriate clinical use leading to better healthcare in Australia or New Zealand. A monetary prize of $5,000 is awarded annually.

220 ■ Australian and New Zealand Society of Respiratory Science

Dr. Debbie Burton, Pres.
Charles Sturt University
School of Biomedical Sciences
Leeds Parade
Orange, New South Wales 2800, Australia
Ph: 61 2 63605555
Fax: 61 2 63605590
E-mail: dburton@csu.edu.au
URL: http://www.anzsrs.org.au

221 ■ Bird Healthcare Young Investigator Award

To encourage a presentation by junior members of the Society, as well as those members of the Society who have had limited opportunity to participate in research during their career as respiratory scientists/technologists. A monetary prize of $2,500 is awarded annually. Sponsored by Bird Healthcare.

222 ■ Compumedics Poster Prize

To recognize the best poster presentation at the annual scientific meeting of the society. A monetary prize of $500 is awarded annually. Sponsored by Compumedics.

223 ■ Life Membership

To recognize a member who has contributed in a major way to the development, promotion, and operation of the Society. A trophy and lifetime membership are awarded when merited.

224 ■ Niche Medical Best Oral Presentation

To recognize the best oral presentation at the annual scientific meeting of the Society. A monetary prize of $2,500 is awarded annually. Sponsored by Niche Medical. Formerly: Techni-pro Best Oral Presentation.

225 ■ Australian and New Zealand Solar Energy Society

George Hardy, Admin.
PO Box 148

Frenchs Forest, New South Wales 1640, Australia
Ph: 61 2 94021638
Fax: 61 2 94021638
E-mail: anzses@optusnet.com.au
URL: http://www.anzses.org

226 ■ Wal Read Memorial Student Prize

To recognize the most outstanding papers submitted to the annual conference by tertiary students and recent graduates who are residents of Australia, New Zealand, New Caledonia, Papua New Guinea, Vanuatu, Solomon Islands, or Fiji. Awarded in two categories: 1. final-year undergraduates whose substantial work was in the previous year; and 2. post-graduate work. A total of A$6,000 is awarded annually.

227 ■ Australian Archaeological Association

Lynley Wallis, Pres.
Railway Estate
3 Queens Rd.
Townsville, Queensland 4810, Australia
Ph: 61 3 99058465
Fax: 61 3 99052948
E-mail: secretary@australianarchaeology.com
URL: http://www.australianarchaeologicalassociation.com.au

228 ■ Rhys Jones Medal

This, the highest honor of the Association, is given to recognize an individual for an outstanding and sustained contribution to the field. Awarded annually. Established in 2002.

229 ■ Life Membership

To recognize an individual for significant and sustained contribution to the objects and purposes of the Association. Awarded annually.

230 ■ John Mulvaney Book Award

To recognize the significant contribution of individual or co-authored publications to Australian archaeology, either as general knowledge or as specialist publications. To be considered, books must have been published in the previous three calendar years. Awarded annually. Established in 2004.

231 ■ Bruce Veitch Award for Excellence in Indigenous Engagement

To recognize an individual or group who has undertaken an archaeological or cultural heritage project that has produced a significant outcome for Indigenous interests. Awarded annually. Established in 2005.

232 ■ Australian Association for Cognitive and Behaviour Therapy

Heather Green, Natl. Pres.
PO Box 853
West Perth, Queensland 6872, Australia
Ph: 61 7 55529086
E-mail: h.green@griffith.edu.au
URL: http://www.aacbt.org

233 ■ Distinguished Career Award

For cognitive behavioral researchers and clinicians whose total career achievements have made an outstanding contribution to behavior research and therapy.

234 ■ Tracy Goodall Early Career Award

For outstanding early career contributions to cognitive behavior research or therapy. A travel grant of $2,000 is awarded annually.

235 ■ Australian Association of Consulting Archaeologists

David Mott, Contact
University of Sydney
Box 214, Holme Bldg.
Sydney, New South Wales 2006, Australia
Ph: 61 8 83409566
Fax: 61 8 83409577
E-mail: membershipsecretary@aacai.com.au

Awards are arranged in alphabetical order below their administering organizations

URL: http://www.aacai.com.au

236 ■ Laila Haglund Prize for Excellence in Consultancy

For outstanding contribution to consultancy profession in Australia. Awarded annually. Established in 2001.

237 ■ Australian Athletes with a Disability

Gillian Ting, Exec. Off.
PO Box 4083
Homebush, New South Wales 2140, Australia
Ph: 61 2 81169720
Fax: 61 2 87321633
E-mail: info@sports.org.au
URL: http://www.sports.org.au

238 ■ Sir Ludwig Guttman Award

To recognize an individual who makes a significant contribution to wheelchair sport in Australia. Awarded biennially in even-numbered years. Established in 1981.

239 ■ The Lord's Taverners Award

To recognize an individual who makes a significant contribution to Junior Wheelchair Sport in Australia. Awarded biennially in odd-numbered years. Established in 1995.

240 ■ Australian Automotive Aftermarket Association

195 Wellington Rd., Bldg. 3, Ste. 16
Clayton, Victoria 3168, Australia
Ph: 61 3 95453333
Fax: 61 3 95453355
E-mail: info@aaaa.com.au
URL: http://www.aaaa.com.au

241 ■ Awards to Industry

To recognize excellence in the Australian automotive aftermarket industry. Gold medals are presented for: Best Trade Catalogue; Best Retail Catalogue; Best Print Media Advertisement; Best Radio Commercial; and Best Website. Gold, silver, and bronze medals are presented for: Excellence in Marketing and Excellence in Manufacturing. Special awards include: Kim Aunger Young Achiever Award; Outstanding Service to Industry Award; and Hall of Fame. Awarded biennially in odd-numbered years.

242 ■ Trade Show Awards

To recognize excellence in the Australian automotive aftermarket industry. Award categories include: Best New Aftermarket Product; Best New Servicing Product; Best Shell Scheme; and Best Stand. Gold medals are awarded in all categories. Awarded biennially in odd-numbered years.

243 ■ Australian Ballooning Federation

PO Box 402
Emerald, Victoria 3782, Australia
Ph: 61 3 59686533
Fax: 61 3 59686599
E-mail: AusBallooningFed@bigpond.com
URL: http://www.abf.net.au

244 ■ Australian Ballooning Hall of Fame

To recognize eminent members. Awardees are inducted into the Hall of Fame and presented with a small memento. Awarded as merited.

245 ■ William Dean Award

For individuals or organizations who have made valuable contributions to ballooning in Australia. Named in honor of 19th century ballooning pioneer William Dean.

246 ■ Gedge Trophy

To recognize a member who has made a considerable contribution to the Federation over a sustained period of time.

247 ■ Life Members

To recognize exemplary service to the Federation over a sustained period of time. A free lifetime membership is awarded as merited.

248 ■ Australian Booksellers Association

Jon Page, Pres.
828 High St., Unit 9
Kew East, Victoria 3102, Australia
Ph: 61 3 9859 7322
Fax: 61 3 9859 7344
E-mail: mail@aba.org.au
URL: http://www.aba.org.au

249 ■ Nielsen BookData Booksellers' Choice Award

To the most popular Australian book read and sold by Australian booksellers during the previous year. Awarded annually. Established in 1994. Sponsored by Nielsen BookData.

250 ■ Australian Business Awards

GPO Box 365
Melbourne, Victoria 3001, Australia
Ph: 61 1300 790593
Fax: 61 1300 790594
E-mail: info@businessawards.com.au
URL: http://www.businessawards.com.au

251 ■ Australian Business Awards

To recognize outstanding success and innovation by Australian businesses and organizations. Awards are offered across all industry sectors, and to all companies whether public or private. Categories include: Enterprise, Innovation, Service Excellence, Marketing Excellence, Recommended Employer, E-Business, Project Management, Public Service, Community Contribution, and Environmental Sustainability. Awarded annually. Established in 2006.

252 ■ Australian Ceramic Society

Prof. Chris Berndt, Pres.
543-545 Burwood Rd.
Hawthorn, Victoria 3122, Australia
Ph: 61 3 92148706
Fax: 61 3 92145050
E-mail: cberndt@groupwise.swin.edu.au
URL: http://www.austceram.com

253 ■ Australasian Ceramic Society/ Ceramic Society of Japan Joint Ceramic Award

To enhance cooperation in the field of ceramics between Australia and Japan by allowing an exchange of distinguished ceramists for short-term study or research. The Australian recipient receives airfare and up to A$5,000 in living expenses. Awarded annually. Established in 1993.

254 ■ Australian Cinematographers Society

Mr. Ron Johanson, Federal Pres.
47 Herbert St.
Artarmon, New South Wales 2064, Australia
E-mail: info@cinematographer.org.au
URL: http://www.cinematographer.org.au/home

255 ■ Hall of Fame

To recognize individuals who have made a substantial contribution to the industry and the Society, as well as having left a legacy of fine work and having been responsible for training and influencing others. One or more individuals are inducted annually. Established in 1997.

256 ■ International Award for Cinematography

To recognize excellence by a feature film cinematographer working on the international stage. Open to individuals of any nationality; membership is not a requirement. A trophy is awarded annually. Established in 2006.

257 ■ Milli Award

To recognize the overall best entry in the National Awards for Cinematography. A trophy is awarded annually. Established in 1968. Named for the abbreviation of the word "millimetre."

258 ■ National Awards for Cinematography

To honor the best cinematographic submissions in Australia. Awards are presented in dozens of categories, including experimental, music clips, current affairs, wildlife and nature, local and regional commercials, and news directors. Direct entry is not permitted; entries winners of Gold awards in the individual state and territory awards are automatically entered for the National Awards. The Golden Tripod is awarded for first place in each category; the Award of Distinction is presented for the runner-up. All Golden Tripod winners are reevaluated to determine the winner of the Milli Award (see separate entry). Awarded annually.

259 ■ Ross Wood Memorial Award

To encourage and recognize young cinematographers who has made, or intends to make, a contribution to cinematography and/or to develop their career in the areas of research, education, experimentation, or technical, scientific, or aesthetic innovation. A plaque and monetary prize are awarded annually. Established in 1994.

260 ■ Australian College of Educators

Margaret Clark, CEO
PO Box 445
Mawson, Australian Capital Territory 2607, Australia
Ph: 61 2 62812306
Fax: 61 2 62812394
E-mail: ace@austcolled.com.au
URL: http://www.austcolled.com.au

261 ■ College Medal

For recognition of an outstanding contribution to education in Australia. Australian citizens or long-term residents of Australia may be nominated for the Award. Selection is made by a committee. A medal and framed citation are awarded annually at the College national conference. Established in 1981. Formerly: (2006) Australian College of Education Medal.

262 ■ Fellowship of the Australian College of Educators

For recognition of a distinctive contribution to the advancement of education. College members must be nominated for selection by a committee. A parchment is awarded annually at the College national conference. Established in 1959.

263 ■ Australian College of Rural and Remote Medicine

Dr. Jeffrey Ayton, Pres.
GPO Box 2507
Brisbane, Queensland 4001, Australia
Ph: 61 7 31058200
Fax: 61 7 31058299
E-mail: acrrm@acrrm.org.au
URL: http://www.acrrm.org.au

264 ■ Distinguished Service Awards

For fellows, members, or non-medical persons who have provided specific and significant contributions to rural and remote medicine. Awarded annually.

265 ■ John Flynn Placement Program Awards

To enable medical students to work closely with rural doctor mentors. A grant in the amount of $500 per week is awarded to approximately 150 students each year. Formerly: John Flynn Scholarship.

266 ■ Honorary Fellowship

For individuals who have provided significant contributions to the organization. Awarded annually.

Awards are arranged in alphabetical order below their administering organizations

267 ■ Honorary Membership
For distinguished or significant service to the organization. Awarded annually.

268 ■ Life Fellowship
For fellows who have rendered outstanding and meritorious service to the College. Awarded annually.

269 ■ Medical Rural Bonded Scholarship
For new medical students prepared to commit to at least six years of rural practice once they completed their basic medical and postgraduate training. Approximately 100 scholarships of more than $20,000 per year are awarded annually. Established in 2001.

270 ■ MedicarePlus Procedural Training Grants
For support to procedural rural doctors in upgrading their skills in anesthetics, obstetrics and surgery. Grants of up to $20,000 per doctor per financial year are awarded annually.

271 ■ Australian Council for Educational Leaders
Jenny Lewis, CEO
PO Box 1891
Penrith, New South Wales 2751, Australia
Ph: 61 2 47321211
Fax: 61 2 47321711
E-mail: admin@acel.org.au
URL: http://www.acel.org.au

272 ■ Gold Medal
Recognizes outstanding contributions to the study and practice of educational administration. Educators are eligible. Awarded biennially in even-numbered years.

273 ■ Nganakarrawa Award
Recognizes general excellence in educational administration and significant contributions to ACEA. Awarded biennially in odd-numbered years.

274 ■ Australian Council for International Development
Mr. Marc Purcell, Exec. Dir.
14 Napier Close
Deakin, Australian Capital Territory 2600, Australia
Ph: 61 2 62851816
Fax: 61 2 62851720
E-mail: main@acfid.asn.au
URL: http://www.acfid.asn.au

275 ■ Sir Ron Wilson Human Rights Award
To recognize an individual or organization for outstanding contributions to the advancement of human rights in the international development sector. A trophy is awarded annually.

276 ■ Australian Council of Women and Policing
Carlene York, Pres.
PO Box 1485
Woden, Australian Capital Territory 2606, Australia
Ph: 61 3 92475455
Ph: 61 417 231838
E-mail: inquiry@acwap.com.au
URL: http://www.acwap.com.au

277 ■ Excellence in Policing for Women Award
To recognize an individual, unit, or agency in Australia, New Zealand, or the Pacific Islands who has improved policing for women. Awarded annually.

278 ■ Excellence in Policing in the Asia Pacific Region Award
To acknowledge and reward the achievements of women and men who are contributing to making policing and law enforcement better for women in the Asia Pacific region. Awarded annually.

279 ■ Excellence in Research on Improving Policing For Women Award
To recognize an individual for outstanding research that supports the advancement of policing and how it can better respond to women. Open to researchers in Australia, New Zealand, and the Pacific Islands. Awarded annually.

280 ■ Audrey Fagan Memorial Award
To recognize outstanding women who have demonstrated exceptional qualities as a mentor, role model, and leader of men and women in policing and law enforcement. Awarded annually. Established in memory of Audrey Fagan, the Chief Police Officer of the Australian Capital Territory.

281 ■ Hellweg Bravery Award
To recognize a woman who demonstrates great commitment, courage and determination in improving the lives of people. Awarded annually.

282 ■ Bev Lawson Memorial Award
This, the Council's most prestigious award, is given to recognize the most outstanding woman who has been first in any policing or law enforcement activity or support service. Open to current or former employees (sworn or unsworn) of an Australian, New Zealand, or Pacific Islands policing, law enforcement, or justice agency. Awarded annually.

283 ■ Most Outstanding Female Administrator Award
To a woman For making a significant impact on the lives of many women within the police service. Awarded annually.

284 ■ Most Outstanding Female Investigator Award
For a young woman who has been outstanding in her work investigating violence against women. Awarded annually.

285 ■ Most Outstanding Female Leader Award
To recognize a female employee (sworn or unsworn) of an Australian, New Zealand, or Pacific Islands policing, law enforcement, or justice agency for excellent leadership. Awarded annually.

286 ■ Most Outstanding Female Practitioner Award
To recognize a woman who is practicing any aspect of policing, including general duties, community policing, forensic science, operational support, and investigations. Open to current or former employees (sworn or unsworn) of an Australian, New Zealand, or Pacific Islands policing, law enforcement, or justice agency. Awarded annually.

287 ■ Australian Council on Healthcare Standards
Prof. Peter Woodruff, Pres.
5 Macarthur St.
Ultimo
Sydney, New South Wales 2007, Australia
Ph: 61 2 92819955
Fax: 61 2 92119633
E-mail: achs@achs.org.au
URL: http://www.achs.org.au

288 ■ Gold Medal
For individuals with exemplary contributions to the improvement of health services in Australia. Awarded annually.

289 ■ Quality Improvement Awards
To encourage quality activities, programs, projects, and strategies that demonstrate outstanding achievements. Awarded annually.

290 ■ Australian Curriculum Studies Association
Ms. Katherine Schoo, Exec. Dir.
PO Box 331
Deakin West, Australian Capital Territory 2600, Australia

Ph: 61 2 62605660
Fax: 61 2 62605665
E-mail: acsa@acsa.edu.au
URL: http://www.acsa.edu.au/pages/index.asp

291 ■ Garth Boomer Award
To recognize significant contributions to promoting collaborative principles in a school. Teams of two or more educators are eligible. Awarded biennially in odd-numbered years. Established in honor of educator, Garth Boomer.

292 ■ Innovative Curriculum Award
To recognize a pre-service teacher for outstanding curriculum innovation. Awarded biennially in odd-numbered years.

293 ■ Australian Department of the Prime Minister and Cabinet
Awards and Culture Branch
POB 6500
Canberra, Australian Capital Territory 2600, Australia
Ph: 61 2 6271 5601
Fax: 61 2 6271 5662
URL: http://www.itsanhonour.gov.au
Formerly: (1995) Council for the Order of Australia.

294 ■ Afghanistan Medal
Recognizes service of Australian Defence Personnel in designated operations in the Afghanistan region since October 11, 2001. Established in 2004.

295 ■ Ambulance Service Medal
To recognize distinguished service by members of Australian full-time and volunteer ambulance services. Recommendations are made by the responsible Minster to the Governor-General for approval. A medal in silver and bronze tones is awarded when merited. Established in 1999.

296 ■ Anniversary of National Service 1951-1972 Medal
To commemorate the service of persons who gave service under the National Service Act 1951, as the act was in force from time to time between 1951 and 1972, or who gave other service in discharge of the obligations to serve under that Act. The award is made by the Governor-General or his/her delegate. Established in 2001.

297 ■ Australian Antarctic Medal
To recognize outstanding service in scientific research or exploration, or in support of such work, in connection with Australian Antarctic expeditions. Recommendations are made by the responsible Minister to the Governor-General for approval. Awards are normally announced annually on June 21, Midwinter's Day, which is a traditional day of celebration for Antarctic expedition members. Established in 1987.

298 ■ Australian Bravery Decorations
To recognize Australian citizens and others for acts of bravery in other than warlike situations. There are five grades of award that can be made to individuals. The Cross of Valour - for acts of the most conspicuous courage in circumstances of extreme peril. The Star of Courage - for acts of conspicuous courage in circumstance of great peril. The Bravery Medal - for acts of bravery in hazardous circumstances. The Commendation for Brave Conduct - for other acts of bravery which are considered worthy of recognition. The Group Bravery Citation - for collective acts of bravery. Each decoration may be awarded posthumously. Nominations can be made by members of the public and are considered by the Australian Bravery Decorations Council. Awarded as merited. Established in 1975.

299 ■ Australian Cadet Forces Service Medal
To recognize 15 years of efficient service by officers and instructors in the Australian Cadet

Awards are arranged in alphabetical order below their administering organizations

Force. A nickel-silver medal is awarded when merited; a clasp is awarded for each additional five years of qualifying service. Recommendations are made by the Chief of the Defence Force or his/her delegate to the Governor-General for approval. Established in 1999.

300 ■ Australian Defence Medal
To recognize current and former Australian Defence Force personnel who demonstrated commitment and contribution to the nation by serving for an initial enlistment period or four years service, whichever was the lesser. A cupro-nickel medal with a stylized version of the Commonwealth Coat of Arms, hung on a red ribbon with black edges, is awarded when merited. Established in 2006.

301 ■ Australian Fire Service Medal
To recognize distinguished service by members of Australian full-time and volunteer fire services. Recommendations are made by the responsible Minister to the Governor-General for approval. An annual quota exists for each fire service. Established in 1988.

302 ■ Australian Police Medal
To recognize distinguished service by members of Australian police forces. Recommendations are made by the responsible Minister to the Governor-General for approval. An annual quota exists for each police service. Established in 1986.

303 ■ Australian Service Medal
To recognize service in prescribed areas. The Australian Active Service Medal 1945-1975 and the Australian Active Service Medal are given to recognize service in a prescribed warlike operation (the latter recognizes service from 1975 onwards). The Australian Service Medal 1945-1975 and the Australian Service Medal are given to recognize service in a declared peacekeeping or non-warlike operation. Awards are made by the Governor-General on the recommendation of the Chief of the Defence Force or his/her delegate. The four medals were established between 1988 and 1997.

304 ■ Australian Sports Medal
To recognize individuals who have made a contribution to Australian sport as a current of former participant or through the provision of support service to Australian sport. Awards are made by the Governor-General's recommendation to the Prime Minister or a person authorized by the Prime Minister. Established in 1999.

305 ■ Centenary Medal
To commemorate 100 years of federation and to acknowledge the challenges of the new century by recognizing citizens and other people who made a contribution to Australian society or government. Awards are made by the Governor-General on the recommendation of the Prime Minister or a person authorized in writing by the Prime Minister to make a recommendation. Established in 2001.

306 ■ Champion Shots Medal
To honor winners in the annual target shooting contest with standard issue weapons conducted by each arm of the Defence Force. Three medals (one for each Service) are awarded annually. The award is made with a clasp to denote the year of the competition and any subsequent award to the same person is made in the form of another clasp. Awards are made by the Governor-General on the recommendation of the Chief of the Defence Force or his/her delegate. Established in 1988.

307 ■ Civilian Service Medal 1939-1945
To recognize the service of civilians who served in Australia during World War II in organizations that were subject to military-like arrangements and conditions of service, in arduous circum-

stances, in support of the war effort. A bronze medal portraying the Southern Cross and surrounded by Golden Wattle is awarded. Established in 1994.

308 ■ Conspicuous Service Decorations
To recognize outstanding or meritorious achievement or devotion to duty in nonwarlike situations by members of the Defence Force and certain others. The Conspicuous Service Cross is given for outstanding devotion to duty or outstanding achievement in the application of exceptional skills, judgment, or dedication in nonwarlike situations. The Conspicuous Service Medal is also given for meritorious achievement or devotion to duty in nonwarlike situations. Each decoration may be awarded posthumously. Awards are presented annually on Australia Day and the Queen's Birthday. The awards are made by the Governor-General on the recommendation of the Minister for Defence. Established in 1989.

309 ■ Cross of Valour
To recognize acts of conspicuous courage in circumstances of extreme peril. It is the highest decoration for Australian bravery, the others being the Star of Courage, Bravery Medal, and Commendation for Brave Conduct. A gold medal shaped like a cross is awarded when merited, only rarely. Established in 1975.

310 ■ Defence Long Service Medal
To recognize 15 years of efficient service by members of the Australian Defence Force. Recommendations are made by the Chief of the Defence Force or his/her delegate to the Governor-General for approval. Members of philanthropic organizations who are serving with the Australian Defence Force are eligible for nomination. A clasp is awarded for each additional five years of qualifying service. Established in 1998.

311 ■ Distinguished Service Decorations
To recognize members of the Defence Force and certain others for distinguished command and leadership in action or distinguished performance of duties in warlike operations. There are three levels of awards. The Distinguished Service Cross is given for distinguished command and leadership in action. The Distinguished Service Medal is given for distinguished leadership in action. The Commendation for Distinguished Service is given for distinguished performance of duties in warlike operations. Each decoration may be awarded posthumously. The awards are made by the Governor-General on the recommendation of the Minister for Defence. Established in 1991.

312 ■ Emergency Services Medal
To recognize distinguished service by members of emergency services across Australia, and people who are involved in emergency management, training, or education. Recommendations are made by the responsible Minister to the Governor-General for approval. Awarded annually. Established in 1999.

313 ■ Gallantry Decorations
To recognize members of the Defence Force and certain others who perform acts of gallantry in action. There are four levels of awards. The Victoria Cross for Australia is given for acts of valour or self-sacrifice. The Star of Gallantry is given for acts of great heroism or conspicuous gallantry in action in circumstances of great peril. The Medal for Gallantry is given for acts of gallantry in action in hazardous circumstances. The Commendation for Gallantry is given for other acts of gallantry that are considered worthy of recognition. Each decoration may be awarded posthumously. The awards are made by the Governor-General on the recommendation of the Minister for Defence. The Governor-General may

also delegate his power to make immediate awards to military commanders in the field. Established in 1991.

314 ■ Humanitarian Overseas Service Medal
To recognize emergency humanitarian service in hazardous conditions outside Australia. A medal is awarded when merited; clasps denote the area of prescribed service. Established in 1999.

315 ■ International Force East Timor Medal
To recognize service by members of the Australian Defence Force who served in East Timor during the International Force East Timor (INTERFET) campaign (Sept. 1999-April 2000). The medal may also be awarded to members of an allied country's INTERFET operation. Awards are made by the Governor-General on the recommendation of the Chief of the Defence Force or his/her delegate. Established in 2000.

316 ■ Iraq Medal
Recognizes service with the Australian Defence Force in specified operations in the Iraq region from March 18, 2003. Awarded by the Governor General on recommendation of the Chief of the Defense Force. Established in 2004.

317 ■ National Medal
This, Australia's most awarded civilian medal, is given to recognize long service in the Australian Defence Force, including part-time and volunteer service, members of the Australian Protective Service, correctional and emergency services, and volunteer search and rescue groups. Many, but not all, eligible groups are uniformed. Fifteen years of service is required to qualify. A circular bronze medal is awarded when merited; a clasp is awarded for each additional ten years of qualifying service. Established in 1975.

318 ■ Nursing Service Cross
To recognize outstanding performance of nursing duties in both operational and nonoperational situations by members of the Defence Force and certain others. The decoration may be awarded posthumously. Awards are made by the Governor-General on the recommendation of the Minister for Defence. Established in 1989.

319 ■ Order of Australia
For recognition of achievement and merit in service of Australia. The Order of Australia consists of a Civil/General Division and a Military Division. Each division has four levels: Companion of the Order; Officer of the Order; Member of the Order; and Medal of the Order. Australian citizens, including members of the Defence Force, are eligible to be appointed to the Order as members in the General Division. Persons other than Australian citizens are eligible to be appointed to the Order as honorary members in the General Division or may be appointed a member if it is desirable that the person be honored by Australia. The Medal of the Order in the General Division may be awarded to Australian citizens and other persons. Appointments are announced each year on Australia Day (January 26) and on the celebration of The Queen's Birthday in June. Established in 1975.

320 ■ Police Overseas Service Medal
To recognize service with international peacekeeping organizations by officers of Australian police forces. The award is made with a clasp to denote the area of prescribed service and any subsequent award to the same person is made in the form of a further clasp with the prescribed service appropriately inscribed. Awards are made by the Governor-General on the recommendation of the Chief Officer of an Australian police force. Established in 1991.

321 ■ Public Service Medal
To recognize outstanding service by members of

Awards are arranged in alphabetical order below their administering organizations

Australian public services and other government employees, including those in local government. Recommendations are made by the responsible Minister to the Governor-General for approval. An annual quota exists for each government public service. Established in 1989.

322 ■ Unit Citations
To recognize gallantry in action or outstanding service in warlike operations by units of the Defence Force and/or units of the defence forces of other countries. The Unit Citation for Gallantry is given for extraordinary gallantry in action and the Meritorious Unit Citation is given for sustained outstanding service in warlike operations. Each citation consists of a certificate of citation to the Unit signed by the Governor-General and insignia for each recipient. Insignia may be awarded posthumously. The award is made by the Governor-General on the recommendation of the Minister for Defence. Established in 1991.

323 ■ Vietnam Logistic and Support Medal
To recognize service in Vietnam between May 29, 1964 and January 27, 1973. Qualifying service includes: 28 days in ships or craft on inland waters or off the coast of Vietnam; one day or more on the posted strength of a unit or formation on land; one operational sortie over Vietnam or Vietnamese waters by aircrew on the posted strength of a unit; or official visits either continuous or aggregate of 30 days. Established in 1968. Formerly: (1995) Vietnam Medal.

324 ■ Vietnam Medal
To recognize members of the Australian Defence Forces and members of accredited philanthropic organizations serving in South Vietnam during the Vietnam War. A nickel-silver medal is awarded when merited. Established in 1968.

325 ■ Australian Dermatology Nurses Association
Margaret Whitton, Pres.
PO Box 3148
East Blaxland, New South Wales 2774, Australia
Ph: 61 2 47392673
Fax: 61 2 47399615
E-mail: adna@adna.org.au
URL: http://www.adna.org.au/public/default.aspx

326 ■ DermaTech Educational Award
To recognize an active ADNA member who has contributed to the ongoing dermatology nursing education of the patients, the community, or colleagues. Awarded annually.

327 ■ Ego Nurses Fellowship
To assist Australian dermatology nurses to build their international contacts. Candidates must be working full-time in dermatology for at least three years and intend to work in dermatology for the next three years. A fellowship of $3,000 is awarded annually.

328 ■ Galderma Research/Literature Award
To recognize quality research in dermatology nursing, to improve dermatology patients' care, and to recognize excellence in dermatology nursing literature written by an active ADNA member. Awarded annually.

329 ■ Stiefel Clinical Practice Award
To recognize an active ADNA member whose professional practice and achievements best exemplify the goals and objectives of ADNA. Awarded annually.

330 ■ Australian Drug Foundation
John Rogerson, CEO
PO Box 818
North Melbourne, Victoria 3051, Australia
Ph: 61 3 92788100
Fax: 61 3 93283008
E-mail: druginfo@adf.org.au
URL: http://www.adf.org.au

331 ■ National Drug and Alcohol Awards
Recognizes those who aim to prevent drug problems in Australia. Several awards are presented: Excellence in Prevention, Excellence in Treatment, Excellence in Research, Excellence in Services for Young People, Excellence in Law Enforcement, Excellence in Alcohol and Drug Media Reporting, Excellence in School Drug Education, Excellence in Creating Healthy Sporting Communities, and the Honour Roll. Awarded annually. Established in 2004.

332 ■ Prime Minister's Award for Excellence and Outstanding Contribution in Drug and Alcohol Endeavours
To recognize an individual as having made a significant commitment and contribution to reducing the impact and negative effects of drug and alcohol use. Awarded annually as part of the National Drug and Alcohol Awards (see separate entry). Endorsed by the Prime Minister of Australia.

333 ■ Australian Entomological Society
Dr. Alice Wells, Honorary Sec.
Australian Entomological Society
GPO Box 787
Canberra, Australian Capital Territory 2601, Australia
Ph: 61 2 62509444
Fax: 61 2 62509555
E-mail: alice.wells@environment.gov.au
URL: http://www.austentsoc.org.au/wordpress

334 ■ Phil Carne Prize
Recognizes individuals who have fostered high quality entomological research in young scientists. Open to any honors or post=graduate students enrolled part-time or full-time at an Australian University. Named for Dr. Phil Carne and his outstanding contributions to the society and the science of entomology. Formerly: AES Student Prize.

335 ■ The Mackerras Medal
To recognize a member of the Society under 50 years of age who has demonstrated excellence in entomology. Awarded biennially in even-numbered years. Established in 1984.

336 ■ Australian Federation of Graduate Women
Jane Baker, Pres.
PO Box 224
Enmore, New South Wales 2042, Australia
E-mail: afgwoz@bigpond.com
URL: http://www.afgw.org.au
Formerly: (1989) Australian Federation of University Women - South Australia.

337 ■ Thenie Baddams Bursary
To assist women with research towards a Master's by research or PhD degree at a recognized higher education institution in Australia. Applicants must have completed one year of postgraduate research. There is no restriction on age or field of study. A monetary award of up to A$6,000 is presented. Established in 1986 to honor Thenie Baddams, President of AFUW from 1982 to 1985. Administered by the South Australia branch of AFUW.

338 ■ Cathy Candler Bursary
To assist women or men of any nationality complete a master's or PhD degree by research at a recognized higher education institution in South Australia. Applicants must have completed one year of post-graduate research. There is no restriction on age or field of study. Students in full-time employment are not eligible and evidence of enrollment must be provided at time of application. One monetary award of A$5,000 is awarded annually. Administered by the South Australia branch of AFUW.

339 ■ Barbara Crase Bursary
To assist women or men of any nationally complete a master's or PhD degree by research at a recognized higher education institution in South Australia. Applicants must have completed one year of post-graduate research. There is no restriction on age or field of study. Students in full-time employment are not eligible and evidence of enrollment must be provided at time of application. One monetary award of A$5,000 is awarded annually. Administered by the South Australia branch of AFUW.

340 ■ Diamond Jubilee Bursary
To assist women or men of any nationality complete a master's or PhD degree by course work at a recognized higher education institution in South Australia. There is no restriction on age or field of study. Students in full-time employment are not eligible and evidence of enrollment must be provided at time of application. Applicants must have an honors degree or equivalent. One monetary award of A$4,000 is awarded annually. Administered by the South Australia branch of AFUW.

341 ■ Doreen McCarthy Bursary
To assist women or men of any nationality to complete a master's degree by course work at a recognized higher education institution in South Australia. Applicants must have completed one year of post-graduate research. There is no restriction on age or field of study. Applicants must have an honors degree or equivalent and have completed one year of study. A monetary award of A$5,000 is awarded annually. Administered by the South Australia branch of AFUW.

342 ■ Padnendadlu Undergraduate Bursary
To provide financial assistance to Aboriginal and/or Torres Strait Islander Australian women undergraduates at any of the South Australian universities. Applicants must be undertaking subjects for the final year of their Bachelor degree, or undertaking an Honors year. A monetary award of up to A$700 is presented annually. Administered by the South Australia branch of AFUW.

343 ■ Winifred E. Preedy Postgraduate Bursary
To assist women who are or have been students in the Faculty of Dentistry in The University of Adelaide at the time of application to further their studies at postgraduate level in Dentistry or a related field. Applicants must have completed one year of their postgraduate degree. A monetary award of A$4,000 is presented annually. Established in 1992 from the bequest of Winifred E. Preedy BDS (1901-1989), a devoted Life Member of AFUWSA Inc., who graduated in 1927, the second woman to graduate BDS in the University of Adelaide. Administered by the South Australia branch of AFUW.

344 ■ Georgina Sweet Fellowship
Assists women in carrying out some advanced study or research in Australia for a period of four to 12 months. Application deadline is July 31 in the year of the offer. A fellowship of A$6,000 is awarded biennially in odd-numbered years. Established in 1965 in honor of Dr. Georgina Sweet, a foundation member and an active member of the Victorian Branch of the Federation.

345 ■ Australian Federation of Modern Language Teachers Associations
Sherryl Saunders, Pres.
PO Box 758
Belconnen, Australian Capital Territory 2616, Australia
E-mail: president@afmlta.asn.au
URL: http://www.afmlta.asn.au

Awards are arranged in alphabetical order below their administering organizations

346 ■ Certificate of Merit
To recognize an individual for dedicated and effective contribution to the work of the Federation over an extended period of time. Awarded annually.

347 ■ Medal for Outstanding Service to Language Teaching
To recognize an individual who has contributed to the teaching of languages other than English in Australia over an extended period of time. Recipients are usually those who are members of the Federation, but occasionally award is presented to a non-member. Awarded annually.

348 ■ Australian Film Institute
Damian Trewhella, CEO
236 Dorcas St.
South Melbourne, Victoria 3205, Australia
Ph: 61 3 96961844
Fax: 61 3 96967972
E-mail: info@afi.org.au
URL: http://www.afi.org.au

349 ■ AACTA Awards
To recognize achievement in Australian film, television, documentary, and shorts production. Awarded annually. Established in 1958. Administered by the Australian Academy of Cinema and Television Arts (AACTA). Formerly: (2011) AFI Awards.

350 ■ Byron Kennedy Award
To recognize an individual working in any area of the Australian film or television industry, whose quality of work is marked by the pursuit of excellence. A monetary award of A$10,000 and a trophy are presented annually as part of the AACTA Awards (see separate entry). Established in 1984. Formerly: (2004) Byron Kennedy Memorial Prize.

351 ■ Raymond Longford Award
For recognition of an individual who has made a significant contribution to Australian filmmaking. A trophy is awarded annually as part of the AACTA Awards (see separate entry). Established in 1968.

352 ■ Australian Fleet Managers Association
431 St. Kilda Rd., Ste. 30
Melbourne, Victoria 3004, Australia
Ph: 61 3 98666056
Fax: 61 3 98661304
E-mail: info@afma.net.au
URL: http://www.afma.net.au

353 ■ Fleet Awards
To recognize excellence in fleet management in Australia. Awards include Fleet Manager of the Year, Fleet Safety Award, and Fleet Environment Award. The Fleet Manager Award is for an individual; the Fleet Safety and Environment Awards are for organizations. Awarded annually.

354 ■ Australian Geography Teachers Association
Rebecca Nicholas, Sec.
26 Wesley St.
Lutwyche, Queensland 4030, Australia
Ph: 61 4 00121311
E-mail: bec_nic@hotmail.com
URL: http://www.agta.asn.au

355 ■ AGTA Awards
To recognize producers of materials used in the teaching of geography. Awarded in 13 categories biennially in even-numbered years.

356 ■ Australian Government Department of Innovation, Industry, Science and Research Science Group
Science Connections Program
GPO Box 5322
Kingston, Australian Capital Territory 2601, Australia

Ph: 61 2 62702865
Fax: 61 2 62702808
E-mail: sgismanager@innovation.gov.au
URL: http://grants.innovation.gov.au

357 ■ Malcolm McIntosh Prize for Physical Scientist of the Year
To recognize outstanding early-career research that advances, or has the potential to advance, human welfare or benefit society. Eligible to individuals who have completed their PhDs in the last 10 years. A grant of $50,000 is awarded.

358 ■ Prime Minister's Prize for Science
This, the most prestigious award for science excellence in Australia, recognizes an outstanding specific achievement in any area of science that advances human welfare or benefits society. Eligible to individuals or groups for research in biological, chemical, physical, or technological sciences. A monetary prize of A$300,000, a gold medallion, and a lapel pin are awarded.

359 ■ Prime Ministers Prizes for Excellence in Science Teaching
To recognize outstanding contributions to science education in Australia. Two awards are presented: Prime Minister's Prize for Excellence in Science Teaching in Primary Schools; and Prime Minister's Prize for Excellence in Science Teaching in Secondary Schools. Each award consists of a A$50,000 grant, a silver medallion, and a lapel pin. Established in 2002.

360 ■ Science Minister's Prize for Life Scientist of the Year
To recognize outstanding early-career research that advances, or has the potential to advance, human welfare or benefit society. Eligible to individuals who have completed their PhDs in the last 10 years. A grant of $50,000 is awarded.

361 ■ Australian Hotels Association NSW
Scott Leach, Pres.
Level 15 Hudson House
131 Macquarie St.
Sydney, New South Wales 2000, Australia
Ph: 61 2 92816922
Fax: 61 2 92815722
E-mail: enquiries@ahansw.com.au
URL: http://www.ahansw.com.au

362 ■ Awards for Excellence
To honor excellence in New South Wales hotels across a variety of segments, including accommodation, dining, entertainment, marketing, community service, and talented employees. Presented in more than 30 categories, such as Best Traditional Hotel Bar, Best Retail Liquor Outlet, Best Steak Venue, Best Gaming Venue, and Chef of the Year. In addition, awards are presented for Overall Country Hotel of the Year, Overall City Hotel of the Year, and Hall of Fame. Awarded annually.

363 ■ Awards for Excellence - Accommodation Division
To honor hotels for achievement in a variety of categories, such as training, environmental initiatives, exceptional employees, and food venues. Awarded annually.

364 ■ Awards for Excellence - General Division
To honor the achievement of excellence by "pub-style" hotel members of the Association. Awarded in a variety of categories annually.

365 ■ Best Practices
For hotels that demonstrate success in environmentally sympathetic operation and innovative approach to increasing health and safety awareness.

366 ■ Outstanding Achievement in Patron Transport Safety
For hotels that demonstrate achievement in the safe transportation of patrons.

367 ■ Outstanding Community Service and Achievement Award
To recognize hotels for active participation and support of community groups and activities. Awarded annually as part of the Awards for Excellence.

368 ■ Australian Hotels Association South Australian Branch
Mr. Peter Hurley, Pres.
PO Box 3092
Adelaide, South Australia 5000, Australia
Ph: 61 8 82324525
Fax: 61 8 82324979
E-mail: acaretti@ahasa.asn.au
URL: http://www.ahasa.asn.au

369 ■ Hotel Industry Awards for Excellence
To recognize those AHAISA member hotels who are deemed outstanding. Awards are presented in 25 categories each year. Winners in each category vie for the National Awards for Excellence (see separate entry).

370 ■ National Awards for Excellence
For excellence in all aspects of hotels, including bar presentation and service, gaming, bottleshops, redevelopment, and live music. Awarded annually to one or more recipients.

371 ■ Australian Human Resource Institute
Peter Wilson, Natl. Pres.
Level 13, 565 Bourke St.
Melbourne, Victoria 3000, Australia
Ph: 61 3 99189200
Fax: 61 3 99189201
E-mail: reception@ahri.com.au
URL: http://www.ahri.com.au

372 ■ AHRI/The CEO Institute Business Leadership Awards
To recognize CEOs and managers for excellence in people management practices. Awards include: Lynda Gratton CEO of the Year and Lynda Gratton Manager of the Year. Awarded annually. Formerly: People Management Awards.

373 ■ HR Leadership Awards
To recognize individual human resources practitioners for exceptional HR practices that contribute to positive business outcomes. Awards include: Dave Ulrich HR Leader of the Year; Dave Ulrich HR Practitioner of the Year; and Dave Ulrich Rising Star of the Year. Awarded annually.

374 ■ HR Student of the Year
For the highest achievement by a student completing the AHRI Professional Diploma of HR. Awarded annually.

375 ■ Organisational Awards
Recognizes organizations for outstanding people initiatives and strategies. Awards include: Wayne Cascio Award for Organisational Development and Leadership; Sir Ken Robinson Award for Workforce Flexibility; Martin Seligman Award for Health and Wellbeing; John Boudreau Award for Human Capital Management; Rob Goffee Award for Talent Management; and the Fons Trompenaars Award for Innovation and Creativity. Awarded annually. Formerly: People Initiative Awards.

376 ■ Australian Institute of Agricultural Science and Technology
Claire Howe, Communications Mgr.
PO Box 130
Curtin, Australian Capital Territory 2605, Australia
Ph: 61 2 61638122
Fax: 61 2 61638133
E-mail: members@aiast.com.au
URL: http://www.aiast.com.au

Awards are arranged in alphabetical order below their administering organizations

377 ■ Australian Medal of Agricultural Science

To recognize an individual who has made outstanding, specific contributions to the advancement of agriculture and natural resource management. Candidates must be residents of Australia. Up to three medals are awarded annually. Established in 1941.

378 ■ Fellow of the Australian Institute of Agricultural Science and Technology FAI-AST

To recognize members who have served the Institute and the profession with eminence and dedication. Candidates must be at least 35 years of age, be a financial member of the Institute, and have been engaged in practicing as a professional in agriculture or natural resource management for at least 10 years since gaining qualifications acceptable for membership of the Institute. Awarded when merited.

379 ■ Young Professionals in Agriculture Award

To recognize young professionals for outstanding specific contributions to the advancement of agriculture in Australia. Candidates must be no older than 35 years of age, and must be members domiciled in Australia. A medal is awarded annually if merited.

380 ■ Australian Institute of Architects

David Parken, CEO
PO Box 3373
Manuka, Australian Capital Territory 2603, Australia
Ph: 61 2 61212000
Fax: 61 2 61212001
E-mail: national@architecture.com.au
URL: http://www.architecture.com.au

381 ■ Robin Boyd Award for Residential Architecture - Houses

Recognizes residential architecture, including new buildings and extensions (not including major projects, such as hotels). Awarded annually as part of the National Architecture Awards. Established in 1981.

382 ■ Sir Zelman Cowen Award for Public Architecture

Recognizes non-residential work, including commercial, institutional, and recreational-type projects. Awarded annually as part of the National Architecture Awards. Established in 1981.

383 ■ Walter Burley Griffin Award for Urban Design

Recognizes excellence in the field of the design of civil amenities. Awarded annually as part of the National Architecture Awards. Established in 1989.

384 ■ Lachlan Macquarie Award for Heritage

Recognizes conservation and restoration in both domestic and commercial architecture, where the work has led to the restoration or conservation of the building with "due consideration for its historic purpose." Awarded annually as part of the National Architecture Awards. Established in 1982.

385 ■ Frederick Romberg Award for Residential Architecture - Multiple Housing

Recognizes excellence in multiple-residence architecture. Awarded annually as part of the National Architecture Awards.

386 ■ Harry Seidler Award for Commercial Architecture

Recognizes outstanding commercial architecture. Awarded annually as part of the National Architecture Awards.

387 ■ Emil Sodersten Award for Interior Architecture

Recognizes interiors completed for commercial or other purposes, new building interiors, or interior refurbishment of existing buildings. Awarded annually as part of the National Architecture Awards.

388 ■ John Utzon Award for International Architecture

Recognizes the overseas work of RAIA member architects in many parts of the world. Awarded annually as part of the National Architecture Awards. Established in 1991.

389 ■ Australian Institute of Energy

Ms. Candice Pribil, Sec.
PO Box 193
Surrey Hills, Victoria 3127, Australia
Ph: 61 1800629945
Fax: 61 398980249
E-mail: aie@aie.org.au
URL: http://www.aie.org.au

390 ■ Australian Institute of Energy Medal

For recognition of achievement in the field of energy. Members only may be nominated. A medal is awarded when merited. Established in 1980.

391 ■ Australian Institute of Genealogical Studies

Thomas Fred Smith, Pres.
41 Railway Rd.
PO Box 339
Blackburn, Victoria 3130, Australia
Ph: 61 3 98773789
E-mail: info@aigs.org.au
URL: http://www.aigs.org.au

392 ■ Alexander Henderson Award

To recognize the best family history published in Australia, improve the quality of published family histories, and encourage people to write their family history. Any writer is eligible. A trophy is awarded annually. Established in 1974.

393 ■ Manuscript Award

To recognize a member for the best manuscript of a family history. A trophy and certificate are awarded annually.

394 ■ President's Award

To recognize a secondary school student for compiling the most outstanding family history. Students must be 20 years or younger, and must be attending a secondary college within the Australian education system at the time of researching and compiling the entry. A trophy and certificate are awarded annually.

395 ■ Australian Institute of Landscape Architects

Petra Weisner, Natl. Mgr.
GPO Box 1646
Canberra, Australian Capital Territory 2601, Australia
Ph: 61 2 62489970
Fax: 61 2 62497337
E-mail: admin@aila.org.au
URL: http://www.aila.org.au

396 ■ Australian Medal for Landscape Architecture

To recognize outstanding landscaping design. Awarded annually.

397 ■ Awards of Excellence in Landscape Architecture

To recognize outstanding landscaping design. Awarded annually to one or more recipients.

398 ■ National Landscape Architecture Awards

To recognize outstanding landscaping projects. Awards are presented in the following categories: design, land management, landscape planning, and research and communication. Awarded annually to one or more recipients in each category.

399 ■ Australian Institute of Nuclear Science and Engineering

Dr. Dennis Mather, Managing Dir.
Locked Bag 2001
Kirrawee, New South Wales 2232, Australia
Ph: 61 2 97173376
Fax: 61 2 97179268
E-mail: ainse@ainse.edu.au
URL: http://www.ainse.edu.au

400 ■ AINSE Awards

To assist researchers from member universities to gain access to ANSTO and other AINSE facilities. Financial support is awarded annually.

401 ■ Gold Medal

For excellence in research, based on publications over the last five years. Awarded annually.

402 ■ Post Graduate Research Awards

For postgraduate students whose research projects are associated with nuclear science or its applications. Awarded annually.

403 ■ Australian Institute of Packaging

Pierre Pienaar, Pres.
34 Lawson St.
Oxley
Brisbane, Queensland 4075, Australia
Ph: 61 7 32784490
Fax: 61 7 32784492
E-mail: info@aipack.com.au
URL: http://www.aipack.com.au

404 ■ Australian Institute of Packaging Fellow

To honor individuals who have made significant contributions to the packaging industry over many years and have considerable knowledge of various aspects of packaging technology.

405 ■ Harry Lovell Award

To recognize the Australasian student achieving the highest final exam/dissertation results of the year. Awarded annually.

406 ■ Australian Institute of Physics

Dr. Marc Duldig, Pres.
61 Danks St. W
Port Melbourne, Victoria 3207, Australia
Ph: 61 3 96469515
Fax: 61 3 96456322
E-mail: aip@aip.org.au
URL: http://www.aip.org.au

407 ■ Award for Outstanding Service to Physics in Australia

To recognize outstanding service to the profession of physics. Society members are eligible for nomination. Awarded annually. Established in 1996.

408 ■ Walter Boas Medal

For recognition of original research by an Australian in physics. Institute members who are also Australian citizens are eligible. Self-nominations and nominations from other members are accepted. A medal is awarded annually. Established in 1984.

409 ■ Bragg Gold Medal for Excellence in Physics

To recognize the student who is judged to have completed the most outstanding PhD in physics under the auspices of an Australian university and whose degree has been approved in the previous 13 months. Awarded annually. Established in 1992 to commemorate the work of W. L. and W. H. Bragg.

410 ■ Harrie Massey Medal and Prize

Recognizes an Australian physicist or a non-Australian physicist working or residing in

Awards are arranged in alphabetical order below their administering organizations

Australia for contributions to physics or its application. Applicants must be members of the Australian Institute of Physics or the Institute of Physics (England). A medal is awarded annually. Established in 1988 in honor of Sir Harrie Massey.

411 ■ Alan Walsh Medal for Service to Industry

Recognizes research and/or development leading to patents, processes, or inventions that influence an industrial process. Physicists who have resided in Australia for at least five years of the preceding seven years prior to application date are eligible. A trophy is awarded biennially in even-numbered years.

412 ■ Australian Institute of Professional Photography

Alice Bennett, Chair
PO Box 372
North Melbourne, Victoria 3051, Australia
Ph: 61 3 93290044
Ph: 61 3 62292559
Fax: 61 3 93299933
E-mail: enquiries99@aipp.com.au
URL: http://www.aipp.com.au

413 ■ Commercial Photographer of the Year

To recognize the best commercial photography in the Canon AIPP Professional Photography Awards Competition. Includes advertising, fashion, architectural, industrial and editorial or commissioned or non-commissioned work. A trophy and $2,500 in photography products are awarded annually.

414 ■ Highest Scoring Print of the Year Award

Awarded for the highest scoring print in the Canon AIPP Professional Photography Awards Competition. Open to all photographers. A trophy and $600 in photography products are awarded annually.

415 ■ Landscape Photographer of the Year

Awarded for the best photographs of the natural or human environment in the Canon AIPP Professional Photography Awards Competition. A trophy and $2,500 in photography products are awarded annually.

416 ■ Open Category Award

Awarded for the highest aggregate score of prints entered into any two or more categories in the Canon AIPP Professional Photography Awards Competition. Open to all photographers. A trophy and $2,750 in photography products are awarded annually.

417 ■ Portrait Photographer of the Year

To recognize the best portrait photography in the Canon AIPP Professional Photography Awards Competition. Includes environmental, contemporary, traditional, groups and glamour photographs. A trophy and $2,500 in photography products are awarded annually.

418 ■ Professional Photographer of the Year

To the most outstanding professional photographer member in the Canon AIPP Professional Photography Awards Competition. A trophy and $20,000 in photography products are awarded annually.

419 ■ Student Photographer of the Year

To recognize the highest aggregate score of three student prints in the Canon AIPP Professional Photography Awards Competition. Open to all tertiary, AIPP student members studying photography. A trophy and $1,000 in photography products are awarded annually.

420 ■ Australian Institute of Project Management

Mr. Ian Baxter, Gen. Mgr.
Level 9, 139 Macquarie St.
Sydney, New South Wales 2000, Australia
Ph: 61 2 82888700
Fax: 61 2 82888711
E-mail: info@aipm.com.au
URL: http://www.aipm.com.au/html/default.cfm

421 ■ Project Management Achievement Awards

To recognize excellence in all aspects of project management across Australia. Awards are presented in 11 categories within two classifications: management of projects and individual project management achievement. Winners are selected at the chapter level in each Australian state and territory, and then state and territory winners are judged at the national level. Awarded annually. Established in 1999.

422 ■ Australian Institute of Quantity Surveyors

Mr. Terry Aulich, CEO
27-29 Napier Close
Deakin West, Australian Capital Territory 2600, Australia
Ph: 61 2 62822222
Fax: 61 2 62852427
E-mail: contact@aiqs.com.au
URL: http://www.aiqs.com.au

423 ■ National President's Award

To recognize the top students in Quantity Surveying degree courses. Awarded annually.

424 ■ Australian Insurance Law Association

David McKenna, Pres.
PO Box 93
Box Hill, Victoria 3127, Australia
Ph: 61 3 98995382
Fax: 61 3 98906310
E-mail: national@aila.com.au
URL: http://www.aila.com.au

425 ■ Insurance Prize

For persons who have made substantial contributions to the insurance industry.

426 ■ Australian Interactive Media Industry Association

John Butterworth, CEO
Level 2, 295-301 Pitt St.
Sydney, New South Wales 2000, Australia
Ph: 61 2 92487900
Fax: 61 2 92487950
E-mail: info@aimia.com.au
URL: http://www.aimia.com.au

427 ■ AIMIA Annual Awards

To recognize Australia's leading digital content developers, content providers, and application developers. Awards are presented in 23 categories each year.

428 ■ Australian Library and Information Association

Sue Hutley, Exec. Dir.
PO Box 6335
Kingston, Australian Capital Territory 2604, Australia
Ph: 61 2 62158222
Fax: 61 2 62822249
E-mail: enquiry@alia.org.au
URL: http://www.alia.org.au
Formerly: (1988) Library Association of Australia.

429 ■ H. C. L. Anderson Award

To recognize an individual who has rendered outstanding service to librarianship or to the library profession in Australia, or to the theory or practice of librarianship. Any member of the Association or the Council of a Division may nominate persons for this award. A statuette is awarded annually. Established in 1973 to honor Henry Charles Lennox Anderson, principal librarian of the Free Public Library of New South Wales from 1893 to 1906.

430 ■ ARL-Blackwells Practicum Prize

To recognize the top student in a practicum undertaken at a university or research institution. A monetary award of A$100 is awarded annually. Administered by the Academic and Research Libraries (WA) group of ALIA. Sponsored by Blackwells Book Services.

431 ■ ARL-DA Books Prize

To recognize an essay or presentation with a research component, undertaken as part of course work at final year undergraduate or graduate diploma level at Edith Cowan University, Curtin University, and Perth Central Metropolitan College of TAFE. A $100 DA book voucher is presented to three recipients annually. Administered by the Academic and Research Libraries (WA) group of ALIA. Sponsored by DA Information Services.

432 ■ Aurora Scholarship

To support an ALIA member attending the Aurora Leadership Institute. A scholarship up to A$4,000 is awarded annually.

433 ■ Australian Library and Information Association Fellow

Recognizes distinguished contribution to the theory of practice of library and information science. Nominees must have at least eight years' standing as a professional member of the Association. Any professional member(s) of the Association; be at least 30 years of age; and be a personal member of the Association or the Council of a Division may nominate a professional member for this distinction. A certificate is awarded irregularly. Established in 1963.

434 ■ Redmond Barry Award

To recognize outstanding service to the promotion of a library or of libraries, to the Association, to the theory or practice of librarianship, or to an associated field such as bibliography. Individuals who are not eligible to be professional members of the Association and who are not employed in a library are eligible. Any member of the Association or the council of a Division may nominate persons for this award. A statuette is awarded annually. Established to honor Sir Redmond Barry.

435 ■ Ray Choate Scholarship

To support students who investigate a particular aspect of reference or information services that will lead to improved practice in the area. The research topic should relate to the objectives of the Association. A scholarship up to A$4,000 is awarded annually.

436 ■ Marjorie Cotton Award

To recognize an individual for outstanding contribution to library services for young people. A monetary award of A$200 is presented biennially in even-numbered years. Administered by the Children's and Youth Services (NSW) group of ALIA.

437 ■ Excellence Award

To recognize individuals or groups for excellence in any area, field, or aspect of practice in the library and information services sector. Awarded annually.

438 ■ Anne Harrison Award

To support a research project in health librarianship. A cash award of A$3,000 is presented biennially in odd-numbered years. Established in 1987. Administered by the Health Libraries Australia group of ALIA.

439 ■ Twila Ann Janssen Herr Research Award for Disability Services

To provide an early career LIS practitioner with the opportunity to research or undertake a project, which may include travel, in the area of library and information services for people with a disability. A monetary prize of A$5,000 is awarded biennially in even-numbered years.

Awards are arranged in alphabetical order below their administering organizations

440 ■ Library Technician of the Year

To recognize outstanding contributions to the advancement of library technicians and/or the National Library Technicians group of the ALIA. A trophy and a citation are awarded annually. Established in 1989. Administered by the Association's National Library Technicians group.

441 ■ Queensland Library Achiever of the Year Award

To recognize an individual working in a library or information center in Queensland who shows outstanding service to the library profession. A plaque and monetary prize of A$300 are awarded annually. Established in 1995. Administered by the ALIA Queensland group.

442 ■ Queensland Library Technician of the Year (Recent Graduate) Award

This award, for recent graduates in library and information sciences in Queensland, aims to promote the role and image of library technicians in the library and information industry and/or in the wider community, and to encourage library technicians to join and support ALIA. Awarded annually. Administered by the Queensland Library Technician Group of ALIA. Sponsored by Queensland Library Supplies Pty. Ltd.

443 ■ F. A. Sharr Medal

To recognize the graduate who has just completed his or her final year of a library and information degree or diploma, or is in the first year of employment and exhibits the most potential and is most likely to have a positive impact on his or her preferred stream of the library profession. Candidates must be a resident of Western Australia. Awarded annually. Established in 1976 in honor of Francis Aubie (Ali) Sharr, State Librarian in Western Australia from 1953 to 1976. Administered by the ALIAWest group of ALIA.

444 ■ South Australian Library Achiever of the Year Award

To recognize a library or information center professional working in South Australia who shows outstanding service to the library profession. A monetary award of A$550 and plaque are awarded annually. Established in 2006. Administered by the ALIA SA group. Sponsored by Ex Libris.

445 ■ Student Award

To recognize the highest achieving graduating student in all ALIA-recognized librarianship and library technician courses. A certificate, one-year membership, and a subscription to an Association journal. Awarded annually.

446 ■ Study Grant Awards

To support professional members to undertake projects that they would otherwise be unable to do because of the time and costs involved. Monetary awards of up to A$5,000 are presented annually. Established in 1984.

447 ■ Bess Thomas Award

To recognize individuals, school libraries, public library services, regional services, and cooperative networks for the development of innovative and significant library services for young people. A grant of A$500 is awarded biennially in even-numbered years. Administered by the Children's and Youth Services (NSW) group of ALIA.

448 ■ WA Library Technicians Group (WALT) Conference Grant

To enable a WA library technician student or recent graduate to attend a national library technicians' conference. Open to members and non-members of ALIA. A travel grant of up to A$1,000 is awarded biennially in odd-numbered years. Administered by the WA Library Technicians group of ALIA.

449 ■ WA Special Librarian of the Year Award

To recognize outstanding contribution to the library profession by a special librarian. Nominees must be members of the ALIA Special Libraries Section WA Group and have demonstrated a willingness to share professional expertise and to participate in formal and informal networking activities, good management practices, and successful promotion of the library. A trophy and cash prize of A$250 are awarded annually. Administered by the ALIAWest group.

450 ■ YBP/Lindsay and Croft Research Award for Collection Services

To increase an individual's professional knowledge and experience; to provide him or her with the opportunity to investigate and research a particular aspect of the development of collection services; and to encourage practice-related research or projects that will inform and advance practice in collection services and management. A monetary prize of A$4,000 is awarded biennially in even-numbered years. In addition, the recipient is required to prepare a comprehensive report for publication in the *Australian Library Journal*.

451 ■ Australian Mammal Society
Tony Friend, Pres.
WA Wildlife Research Centre
PO Box 51
Wanneroo, Western Australia 2351, Australia
Ph: 61 8 94055159
Fax: 61 8 93061641
E-mail: amssecretary@australianmammals.org.au
URL: http://www.australianmammals.org.au

452 ■ Adolph Bolliger Award

To recognize the best spoken presentation by a student. Awarded annually.

453 ■ A.G. Lyne Award

To recognize the best poster presentation by a student. Awarded annually.

454 ■ Ellis Troughton Memorial Award

For outstanding service to Australian mammalogy. Awarded annually.

455 ■ Australian Marine Sciences Association
Ms. Narelle Hall, Treas.
PO Box 8
Kilkivan, Queensland 4600, Australia
Ph: 61 7 54841179
Fax: 61 7 54841456
E-mail: treasurer@amsa.asn.au
URL: http://www.amsa.asn.au

456 ■ Allen International Student Travel Award

To provide financial support to an outstanding graduate student, in any field of marine science, to attend an international conference each year. A maximum of A$2,500 is awarded annually. Supported by a bequest from the estate of the late K. Radway Allen.

457 ■ Peter Holloway Oceanography Prize

To recognize the best student presentation related to oceanography. Awarded annually.

458 ■ Ron Kenny Prizes

Two prizes are presented: Ron Kenny Student Presentation Prize for the best oral presentation of research results and the Ron Kenny Student Poster Prize for the best poster display of research results. Prizes are named in honor of Ron Kenny, a professor and associate member of the association, until his death in 1987.

459 ■ Silver Jubilee Award

To recognize a scientist who has made an outstanding contribution to marine research in Australia. Awarded annually. Established in 1998 to commemorate the Association's silver jubilee year.

460 ■ Australian Market and Social Research Society
Elissa Molloy, Exec. Dir.
Level 1, 3 Queen St.
Glebe, New South Wales 2037, Australia
Ph: 61 2 95663100
Fax: 61 2 95715944
E-mail: amsrs@amsrs.com.au
URL: http://www.amsrs.com.au

461 ■ George Camakaris Best Paper by a Young Researcher Award

For the best paper submitted by a young researcher at the Annual Conference. Eligible to researchers who are 31 years old or younger, or who are in the first five years of their careers. A prize of A$1,500 in credit towards industry-related events or courses is awarded annually. Sponsored by Quantum.

462 ■ Tony Wheeler Best Conference Paper Award

For the best paper presented at the Annual Conference. A A$2,000 Best Paper Award and a $1,000 People's Choice Award are presented annually. Sponsored by Millward Brown.

463 ■ Australian Mathematical Society
Dr. A. Howe, Treas.
Australian National University
Dept. of Mathematics
Canberra, Australian Capital Territory 0200, Australia
Ph: 61 2 61258922
Fax: 61 2 61258923
E-mail: office@austms.org.au
URL: http://www.austms.org.au

464 ■ Australian Mathematical Society Medal

For recognition of distinguished research in the mathematical sciences. Members who have not reached the age of 40 at the beginning of the year in which the Council makes the award are eligible. A significant portion of the work should have been carried out in Australia. A medal is awarded annually. Established in 1981.

465 ■ Mahler Lectureship

To support a distinguished mathematician who preferably works in an area of mathematics associated with the work of Professor Mahler. It is usually expected that the Lecturer will speak at one of the main Society Conferences and visit as many universities as can be reasonably managed. Awarded biennially in odd-numbered years. Established in 1991.

466 ■ Bernhard H. Neumann Prize

For recognition of the best student speech at the annual meeting. Students (part-time or full-time) who are members of the Society are eligible. A monetary prize of A$600 and a certificate are awarded each year at the annual meeting. Established in 1985 in honor of Professor Bernhard H. Neumann.

467 ■ George Szekeres Medal

To recognize outstanding research achievement in a 15-year period for work done primarily in Australia. A medal is awarded biennially in even-numbered years. Established in 2001 in honor of Professor George Szekeres.

468 ■ Australian Military Medicine Association
Dr. Greg Mahoney, Pres.
113 Harrington St.
Hobart, Tasmania 7000, Australia
Ph: 61 3 62347844
Fax: 61 3 62345958
E-mail: leanne@leishman-associates.com.au
URL: http://www.amma.asn.au

469 ■ Weary Dunlop Award

To recognize the best original paper presented at the Annual Scientific Conference by a member. A certificate and monetary prize of $750 are presented annually. Established in 1993.

Awards are arranged in alphabetical order below their administering organizations

470 ■ Patron's Prize
To recognize the best health-related article published in a peer-reviewed journal by an AMMA member. A monetary prize of A$250 is awarded annually.

471 ■ Australian Music Centre
John Davis, CEO
PO Box N690
Grosvenor Place, New South Wales 1220, Australia
Ph: 61 2 92474677
Fax: 61 2 92412873
E-mail: info@australianmusiccentre.com.au
URL: http://www.australianmusiccentre.com.au

472 ■ Classical Music Awards
To recognize distinguished contributions to Australian classical music. Eleven awards are presented annually: 1. Instrumental Work of the Year; 2. Orchestral Work of the Year; 3. Vocal or Choral Work of the Year; 4. Best composition by an Australian composer; 5. Best performance of an Australian composition; 6. Outstanding contribution by an organization; 7. Outstanding contribution by an individual; 8. Outstanding contribution to Australian music in education; 9. Outstanding contribution to Australian music in a Regional Area; 10. Long-term contribution to the advancement of Australian music; and 11. Distinguished Services to Australian Music. In addition, State Awards are presented. Established in 1988.

473 ■ Paul Lowin Prizes
To recognize outstanding Australian music compositions. Eligible composers must be at least 18 years of age, and be Australian citizens or residents of Australia for at least the two previous years. The Orchestral Prize ($25,000) is for a work for modern chamber or symphony orchestra of at least 30 players and 15 independent lines. The Song Cycle Prize ($15,000) is awarded to a work suitable for chamber performance, using no more than 1-8 independent vocal lines, accompanied by up to 10 instrumental players. Awarded every two or three years. Established in 1990.

474 ■ Australian National University
Crawford School of Economics and Government | Australian-Japan Research Centre
J.G. Crawford Building, No. 132
Lennox Crossing Rd.
Canberra, Australian Capital Territory 0200, Australia
Ph: 61 2 6125 3780
Fax: 61 2 6125 8448
E-mail: ajrc@anu.edu.au
URL: http://www.crawford.anu.edu.au/research_units/ajrc/index.php

475 ■ J. G. Crawford Award
To recognize the author of a research paper making a substantial and original contribution to scholarship on Japan or on Australia-Japan relations. Younger and new scholars developing a specialization in the areas of study specified are encouraged to apply. To be eligible for consideration, the paper should address some aspect of the operation of the Japanese economy or economic policy, or Japan's international relations or relations with Australia, or the political environment affecting these affairs. The value of the award is determined each year by a judging panel and in recent years has been A$2,500. Papers published, written for publication, or unpublished, but written the year of the award are eligible for nomination. Where possible, the paper selected for the award will be published by the Australia-Japan Research Centre as part of its *Pacific Economic Papers* series. Awarded annually. Established 1987.

476 ■ Australian Neuroscience Society
Prof. Sarah Dunlop, Pres.
PO Box 2331

Kent Town, South Australia 5071, Australia
Ph: 61 8 83620038
Fax: 61 8 83620038
E-mail: ans@sallyjayconferences.com.au
URL: http://www.ans.org.au

477 ■ A.W. Campbell Award
For the best contribution by a member of the society over the first five post-doctoral years. Awarded annually. Established in 1987.

478 ■ Nina Kondelos Prize
To recognize a female neuroscientist for outstanding contribution to basic or clinical neuroscience research. A certificate and monetary prize of $500 are awarded annually. Established in 2007.

479 ■ Paxinos-Watson Prize
For the most significant refereed paper in the neurosciences. Awarded annually. Established in 1997.

480 ■ Sir Grafton Elliot Smith Award
For the best poster by a student member at the Annual Meeting. Awarded annually.

481 ■ Istvan Tork Prize
For the best oral presentation by a student member at the annual meeting. Awarded annually. Established in 1996.

482 ■ Australian Nuclear Association
Dr. John Harries, Sec.
PO Box 472
Engadine, New South Wales 2233, Australia
E-mail: ana.info@optusnet.com.au
URL: http://www.nuclearaustralia.org.au

483 ■ Australian Nuclear Association Annual Award
Recognizes major contributions in the nuclear field. Awarded annually.

484 ■ Australian Numismatic Society
Rod Sell, Contact
PO Box 366
Brookvale, New South Wales 2100, Australia
E-mail: rodsell@rodsell.com
URL: http://www.the-ans.com

485 ■ Bronze Medal
For recognition of noteworthy services to Australian Numismatic Society and numismatics research. Only members of the Society are eligible. Established in 1983.

486 ■ Gold Medal and Fellowship of the Society
For recognition of long and distinguished service to the Society and numismatics research. Only members of the Society are eligible. Established in 1968.

487 ■ Silver Medal and Associate Fellowship of the Society
For recognition of long and distinguished service to the Society and numismatics research. Only members of the Society are eligible. Established in 1968.

488 ■ Australian Office of the Privacy Commissioner
GPO Box 5218
Sydney, New South Wales 2001, Australia
Fax: 61 2 9284 9666
E-mail: privacy@privacy.gov.au
URL: http://www.privacy.gov.au

489 ■ Australian Privacy Awards
To encourage, recognize, and reward businesses, government agencies, and not-for-profit organizations that engage in good privacy practices. Candidates must have engaged in good privacy practices and/or promotion of privacy messages through overall work or one or more of their projects, initiatives, campaigns,

or systems. Awarded annually in four categories: Large Businesses, Small-Medium Businesses, Community and Non-Government Organizations (NGOs), and Government Agencies. Established in 2008.

490 ■ Australian Privacy Medal
To honor an individual who has exhibited an outstanding level of achievement in advancing privacy in Australia. Awarded annually. Established in 2008.

491 ■ Australian Packaging and Processing Machinery Association
Rob Lawrence, Chm.
PO Box 2076
Rose Bay North, New South Wales 2030, Australia
Ph: 61 2 93712769
Fax: 61 2 93712769
E-mail: appma@appma.com.au
URL: http://www.appma.asn.au
Formerly: (2010) Australian Packaging Machinery Association.

492 ■ Awards of Excellence
To recognize companies for outstanding contribution to the packaging and processing industry. Awarded in four categories: Customer Participation, Design, Imported Equipment, and Export Achievement. Awarded annually.

493 ■ Australian Petroleum Production and Exploration Association
Ms. Belinda Robinson, Chief Exec.
PO Box 2201
Canberra, Australian Capital Territory 2601, Australia
Ph: 61 2 62470960
Fax: 61 2 62470548
E-mail: appea@appea.com.au
URL: http://www.appea.com.au

494 ■ Environment Award
To recognize production and exploration companies for showing environmental concern. Awards are offered in two categories: Category A for production companies and Category B for exploration companies. Membership in the Association and a permit to operate in Australia are required for eligibility. Awarded annually.

495 ■ JN Pierce Award for Media Excellence
For excellence in journalism about the upstream petroleum industry. All forms of media are eligible, including print, radio, television, and online. Awarded annually. Established in 2004 in honor of leading Australian resource writer, John Pierce.

496 ■ Safety Awards
To recognize outstanding safety performance. Awards include: Safety Performance Award; Safety Innovation Award; Contractor Safety Innovation Award; and Drilling Safety Award. Awarded annually. Established in 1987.

497 ■ Reg Sprigg Medal
To recognize an individual for outstanding service to the Australian petroleum exploration and production industry. Awarded annually. Established in 1989 as the Gold Medal, and renamed in 1995 to honor the Association's founding chairman, Dr. Reginald Sprigg.

498 ■ Lewis G. Weeks Gold Medal
To recognize an individual for outstanding contributions to the art, practice, and/or science of petroleum exploration. Awarded annually. Established in 1982.

499 ■ Australian Physiological Society
Dr. Robyn Murphy, Natl. Sec.
LaTrobe University
Dept. of Zoology

Awards are arranged in alphabetical order below their administering organizations

Melbourne, Victoria 3086, Australia
Ph: 61 3 94792302
Fax: 61 4 17335390
E-mail: r.murphy@latrobe.edu.au
URL: http://aups.org.au

500 ■ A.K. McIntyre Prize
For significant contributions to Australian physiological science during pre-doctoral and early post-doctoral years. Nominees must be financial Ordinary Members of the Society, and must normally have completed their PhD or equivalent doctoral degree not more than five years prior to the time of their nomination. A medal and monetary prize of $1,000 are awarded periodically.

501 ■ PhD Publication Prize
To recognize the best original paper published by an AuPS member during the course of their PhD studies. A monetary award of $500 is awarded annually.

502 ■ PostDoc Publication Prize
To recognize a member for the best original paper published during his or her first four postdoctoral years. A monetary prize of $500 is awarded annually.

503 ■ Student Presentation Prizes
Awarded at each meeting for the best oral and poster presentations by graduate students in physiology and related sciences. Co-sponsored by SDR Clinical Technology and Blackwell Scientific Publications. AuPS student members are eligible for prizes. Established in 1990.

504 ■ Australian Psychological Society
Prof. Simon Crowe, Pres.
PO Box 38
Melbourne, Victoria 8009, Australia
Ph: 61 3 86623300
Fax: 61 3 96636177
E-mail: contactus@psychology.org.au
URL: http://www.psychology.org.au

505 ■ APS College Awards of Distinction
For individuals who made outstanding contributions to their specialist field. One award is presented annually per College.

506 ■ APS College of Forensic Psychologists (NSW Section) Annual Awards
For excellence in Forensic psychology. Awarded annually in three categories: research, practitioner, and open. Established in 2003.

507 ■ APS Prize
For academic excellence in an APS-accredited course. Awarded annually to one or more recipients.

508 ■ Award For Excellent PhD Thesis in Psychology
To honor an outstanding research in psychology by candidates who have completed a PhD at an Australian University within the last calendar year. A monetary prize of $1,000 is awarded annually.

509 ■ Children's Peace Literature Award
To honor one or more Australian authors of books for children that encourage the peaceful resolution of conflict. A monetary prize of $2,000 is awarded biennially in odd-numbered years.

510 ■ Elaine Dignan Award
To encourage research about women, women's studies in psychology, and professional work with women in any field. Awarded annually. Established in 1992. Administered by the Women in Psychology Interest Group.

511 ■ Distinguished Scientific Contribution Award
To honor a distinguished theoretical for empirical contributions to psychology by psychologists at mid- career stage or later. A plaque is awarded annually, if merited.

512 ■ Early Career Research Awards
For excellence in scientific achievement in psychology among psychologists who are at early stages in their research careers. Awarded annually to one or more recipients.

513 ■ Ethics Prize
To APS members and subscribers who have made a significant scholarly, research, pedagogical or professional contribution in the areas of professional or research ethics. A monetary prize of $500 is awarded.

514 ■ Alastair Heron Prize
To a member of the APS College of Clinical Psychologists For applied research of exceptional quality in the area of normal adult ageing or age-related dementias. A monetary prize of $400 is awarded even-numbered years.

515 ■ Australian Publishers' Association
Ms. Maree McCaskill, CEO
89 Jones St., Ste. 60
Ultimo, New South Wales 2007, Australia
Ph: 61 2 92819788
Fax: 61 2 92811073
E-mail: maree.mccaskill@publishers.asn.au
URL: http://www.publishers.asn.au

516 ■ Australian Awards for Excellence in Educational Publishing
To recognize publishers for contributions that improve the quality of Australian educational materials. Judged for clarity of writing, pedagogical implications, illustrations, special features and characteristics, quality of subject matter, and innovation and flair. One publisher is honored as the overall winner, with the Primary Publisher of the Year and Secondary Publisher of the Year also named. Awarded annually. Established in 1994 by the APA and Sydney University's Teaching Resources and Textbooks Research Unit.

517 ■ Australian Book Industry Awards
To honor and recognize authors, booksellers, and publishers. Awards are presented in 11 categories, including Australian Biography of the Year, Australian Illustrated Book of the Year, Australian Newcomer of the Year, and the overall Australian Book of the Year.

518 ■ Book Design Awards
For recognition of excellence in book design in Australia. Entries must be published and designed in Australia, but may be printed anywhere. Awards are presented in various categories annually. Established in 1953.

519 ■ Pixie O'Harris Award
To recognize distinguished and dedicated service to the development and reputation of Australian children's books. A certificate, glass plate, and monetary prize of A$500 are awarded annually. Established in 1994 in honor of Rhona Olive Harris, one of Australia's best-loved illustrators of children's books.

520 ■ Australian Science Teachers Association
Anna Davis, Pres.
PO Box 334
Deakin, Australian Capital Territory 2600, Australia
Ph: 61 2 62829377
Fax: 61 2 62829477
E-mail: asta@asta.edu.au
URL: http://www.asta.edu.au

521 ■ Australian Museum Eureka Prizes
For Australian primary and secondary schools and their teachers. Awards include: Macquarie University Eureka Schools Science Prize for Action Against Climate Change; University of Sydney Skeek Geeks Science Eureka Prize; University of Technology, Sydney Eureka Prize for Science Teaching; and Australian Museum Eureka Prizes People's Choice Award. More than A$30,000 worth of cash awards and prizes are awarded annually.

522 ■ BHP Billiton Science Awards
These, the most prestigious student science awards in Australia, recognize exceptional and practical science research projects by students. Winner(s) represents Australia at the International Science and Engineering Fair.

523 ■ Australian Singing Competition
Vivian Zeltzer, Coor.
67 Castlereagh St., Level 4
Sydney, New South Wales 2000, Australia
Ph: 61 2 9231 4293
Fax: 61 2 9221 8201
E-mail: asc@mostlyopera.org.au
URL: http://www.aussing.com.au

524 ■ Mathy Awards
This, the richest and most prestigious singing competition in Australia, is held to encourage professional careers and to recognize exceptional classical singing talent. Numerous scholarships and awards are presented annually, including the Marianne Mathy Scholarship of A$30,000 and the Guildhall School of Music and Drama Award. Awarded annually. Established in 1982.

525 ■ Opera Awards
To recognize outstanding opera singers in Australia. Candidates must be an Australian citizen or resident, and have sung at least two principal roles with a recognized professional opera company during the previous two years. A monetary prize of $25,000 is awarded annually.

526 ■ Australian Skeptics - NSW Branch
Eran Segev, Pres.
PO Box 20
Beecroft, New South Wales 2119, Australia
Ph: 61 2 80941894
Fax: 61 2 80884735
E-mail: nsw@skeptics.com.au
URL: http://www.skeptics.com.au

527 ■ Australian Skeptics Prize for Critical Thinking
To recognize research projects, education programs, or media stories that encourage critical thinking about popular beliefs that owe nothing to rational thought or scientific validity. Eligible entries must have been undertaken/published/broadcast in Australia by an Australian citizen or permanent resident within the previous five years. A monetary prize of $10,000 is awarded annually. At the judges' discretion, two additional prizes of $2,000 each may be presented to runners up. Established in 2006.

528 ■ Bent Spoon Award
To recognize an individual or organization that makes the most outrageous claim of a paranormal or pseudoscientific nature in the preceding year. The name of the annual recipient is added to a perpetual trophy. Established in 1982 and named in commemoration of one of the less useful, though widely acclaimed, alleged paranormal claims: the psychic ability to distort items of cutlery.

529 ■ Journalism Award

530 ■ Australian Society for Antimicrobials
Dr. Graeme Nimmo, Pres.
PO Box 8266
South Perth, Western Australia 6151, Australia
Ph: 61 8 92242446
Fax: 61 8 94508553
E-mail: info@asainc.net.au
URL: http://www.asainc.net.au

531 ■ ASA Travel Awards
To enable members to attend the annual scientific meeting, where they will present an oral or poster paper. Awarded annually to one or more recipients.

532 ■ Australian Society for Biophysics
Paul Smith, Sec.
Australian National University
College of Science

Awards are arranged in alphabetical order below their administering organizations

Department of Chemistry
Canberra, Australian Capital Territory 0200, Australia
Ph: 61 2 61252021
E-mail: paul.smith@anu.edu.au
URL: http://www.biophysics.org.au

533 ■ McAulay-Hope Prize for Original Biophysics
Recognizes originality and innovation in the field of biophysics. A medal and a monetary award of $1,000 are presented. Awarded when merited.

534 ■ Bob Robertson Award
To recognize outstanding contributions to the field of biophysics in Australia and New Zealand and to commemorate the contributions to the Society and to Australian science in general of Sir Rutherford (Bob) Robertson. A medal and monetary prize of $250 are awarded annually. Established in 2002.

535 ■ Young Biophysicist Award
To encourage members of the Society who were about to or had recently embarked on a career in biophysics. Eligible individuals should be PhD candidates, or be within five years following the award of a PhD or equivalent degree. A cash prize of $500 is awarded annually.

536 ■ Australian Society for Fish Biology
Jeremy Lyle, Pres.
Australian Antarctic Division
Channel Hwy.
Kingston, Tasmania 7050, Australia
E-mail: treasurer@asfb.org.au
URL: http://www.asfb.org.au

537 ■ John Lake Poster Award
To encourage and support high quality poster presentations by students at the annual conference. Awarded in two categories: Junior and Senior. A monetary prize of $600 is awarded in each category annually. Established in 1987 in memory of John Lake.

538 ■ Gilbert P. Whitley Memorial Student Award
To encourage and support high quality oral presentations by students at the annual conference. Awarded in two categories: Junior and Senior. A monetary prize of $600 is awarded in each category annually.

539 ■ Australian Society for Medical Research
Catherine West, Sr. Exec. Off.
145 Macquarie St.
Sydney, New South Wales 2000, Australia
Ph: 61 2 92565450
Ph: 61 2 92565451
Fax: 61 2 92520294
E-mail: asmr@alwaysonline.net.au
URL: http://www.asmr.org.au

540 ■ Research Awards
To support research by students and recent graduates. Two research grants are awarded annually, one to a postgraduate student member nearing completion of his or her studies and one to a recently graduated postdoctoral member. A grant of $5,000 is bestowed for a short period of research in a laboratory outside of Australia, and $2,000 is given for work in a distal laboratory within Australia.

541 ■ Australian Society for Microbiology
Prof. John Turnidge, Pres.
Ste. 23, 20 Commercial Rd.
Melbourne, Victoria 3004, Australia
Ph: 61 3 98678699
Fax: 61 3 98678722
E-mail: admin@theasm.com.au
URL: http://www.theasm.org.au

542 ■ BD ASM Student Travel Award
To allow one student from each ASM State

Branch to attend the Annual Scientific Meeting and give an oral presentation. Open to postgraduate student members. Travel and accommodation expenses are awarded.

543 ■ Distinguished Service Award
To recognize outstanding service or contributions to the Society by an individual or organization. Open to members. Up to 10 awards may be presented annually.

544 ■ Frank Fenner Award
To recognize distinguished contributions to microbiology research in Australia. Focused on scientists who are at the formative stages of their careers and have been engaged in research for 15 years or less. Recipient delivers a lecture at the Annual Scientific Meeting. A monetary prize of A$1,000, a bronze plaque, and travel expenses are awarded.

545 ■ Honorary Life Membership
For members who have provided distinguished service to the Society. A free lifetime membership in the Society is awarded.

546 ■ Teachers' Travel Award
To encourage tertiary level teachers of microbiology to attend the Annual Scientific Meeting. Nominees need to be members of the Society for the last twelve months and be teaching at least part-time. Up to A$1,000 in travel expenses are awarded.

547 ■ David White Excellence in Teaching Award
Recognizes excellence in microbiology teaching or innovative teaching methods in microbiology. Nominees must have been members for at least two years. Recipient is expected to present a paper or participate in a workshop at the Annual Scientific Meeting. A monetary prize of A$1,000, a bronze plaque, and free registration at the Annual Scientific Meeting are awarded.

548 ■ Australian Society for Music Education
Dr. Kay Hartwig, Pres.
PO Box 141
Mawson, Australian Capital Territory 2607, Australia
Fax: 61 8 81255749
E-mail: asme@asme.edu.au
URL: http://www.asme.edu.au

549 ■ Callaway Doctoral Award
To recognize the best doctoral thesis in the area of music education from an Australian University. Awarded biennially in odd-numbered years. Established in 2005.

550 ■ Fellowship of the Australian Society for Music Education
To honor a member for outstanding and distinctive contributions to the advancement of music education. Awarded when merited.

551 ■ Australian Society for Parasitology
Denise Doolan, Pres.
300 Herston Rd.
Herston
Brisbane, Queensland 4006, Australia
Ph: 61 7 33620382
Fax: 61 7 33620105
E-mail: denise.doolan@qimr.edu.au
URL: http://parasite.org.au

552 ■ Bancroft - Mackerras Medal for Excellence
For recognition of achievements in the science of parasitology. Members of the Society must be nominated by September 30 each year. A medal is awarded annually when merited at the annual general meeting of the Society. Established in 1982 in honor of the Bancroft and Mackerras families.

553 ■ John Frederick Adrian Sprent Prize
For recognition of an outstanding PhD thesis in

parasitology published during the preceding three years. Members of the Society may apply. A monetary prize and medal are awarded triennially. Established in 1987.

554 ■ Australian Society of Anaesthetists
Dr. Andrew Mulcahy, Pres.
PO Box 600
Edgecliff, New South Wales 2027, Australia
Ph: 61 2 93274022
Fax: 61 2 93277666
E-mail: asa@asa.org.au
URL: http://www.asa.org.au

555 ■ Anaesthesia and Intensive Care Best Paper Award
To recognize the author of an outstanding paper in the field of anaesthesia, intensive care, and pain medicine. Criteria include scientific content, originality, relevance, and presentation. A monetary prize of A$2,000 is awarded annually. Established in 1997.

556 ■ Best Poster Presentation Prize
To recognize the contribution by delegates through their posters at the National Scientific Congress. A monetary prize of A$500 is awarded annually.

557 ■ Jeanne Collison Prize
To recognize excellence in original research within Australia in the fields of anaesthesia and pain management during the previous two years. A monetary prize of A$5,000 is awarded biennially in even-numbered years. Established in 2007 in memory of Dr. Jeanne Collison, a member of ASA for 52 years.

558 ■ Nerida Dilworth Prize
To recognize a registrar in anaesthesia in Western Australia for significant contributions to the ASA or to the Australian and New Zealand College of Anaesthetists (ANZCA). A monetary prize of A$400 is awarded once or twice per year. Established in 1985.

559 ■ Kevin McCaul Prize
To recognize the best paper on any aspect of anesthesia, pain relief, physiology, or pharmacology with particular focus on the female reproductive system. Candidates must be registrars-in-training or junior specialists within two years of obtaining a higher qualification in anesthesia or obstetrics and gynecology. A monetary prize of A$2,000 is awarded annually.

560 ■ Smith/ASA Young Investigator Awards
To recognize young professionals working in the field of anesthesia, enabling them to attend the ASA National Scientific Congress to present papers. Three awards are presented annually.

561 ■ Gilbert Troup Prize
To recognize a member who presents the best free paper at the ASA National Scientific Congress. Eligible papers must be based on original research performed in Australia. A medal and cash prize of A$2,000 are awarded annually.

562 ■ Australian Society of Archivists
Jackie Bettington, Pres.
PO Box 638
Virginia, Queensland 4014, Australia
E-mail: office@archivists.org.au
URL: http://www.archivists.org.au

563 ■ Distinguished Achievement Award
Conferred on a member who has been mainly or solely responsible for an outstanding development or achievement in archives work. The Council accepts recommendations from the Awards Committee. Awarded when merited every year. Established 1993. Formerly: (2000) Laureateship of the Australian Society of Archivists.

Awards are arranged in alphabetical order below their administering organizations

564 ■ Fellowship of the Australian Society of Archivists
Conferred on a professional member of the Society who has given at least ten years of distinguished service to the profession, to the theory, teaching or practice of archives work, or to writing about archives. Established 1993.

565 ■ Honorary Member
Conferred by a two-thirds majority vote at a general meeting of the society, upon the recommendation of the council, in recognition of services to the society or to the profession. Honorary members are entitled to all rights and privileges of professional membership without payment or subscriptions. Established in 1975.

566 ■ Margaret Jennings Award
Recognizes an outstanding student in each accredited diploma course in archives administration. The award consists of a certificate, one year's membership in the society, and a monetary prize of A$100. Awarded annually to one or more recipients. Established in 1989.

567 ■ Mander Jones Awards
To honor writings about archives in Australia or by Australians. Awards are presented in the following categories: (1) publication making the greatest contribution to Archives of a related field in Australia written by or on a corporate body; (2) publication making the greatest contribution to archives or a related field in Australia written by a person in their own right; (3) best finding aid to an archival collection held by an Australian institution or about Australia produced by an organization deemed eligible for Category A Institutional Membership; (4) best article about archives or a related field written by an Australian in a journal not primarily intended for archivists or record managers; (5) best article about archives or a related field written by an Australian in an archives or records management journal; (6) best article about archives or a related field written by a student (not more than 5000 words) in an entry level archives or records management course in Australia; and (7) Best academic work on archives or recordkeeping produced by a student in any Australian university course. Awarded annually. Established in 1996 in honor of the late Phyllis Mander Jones.

568 ■ Sharman Award
To recognize the significant contribution over the years by Robert Charles "Bob" Sharman to the Australian Society of Archivists and the archival cause generally in Australia. The award is in the form of financial assistance for selected members of the ASA to attend the annual conference. Established in 2000.

569 ■ Australian Society of Exploration Geophysicists
Phil Harman, Pres.
PO Box 8463
Perth, Western Australia 6849, Australia
Ph: 61 8 94270838
Ph: 61 3 99097655
Fax: 61 8 94270839
E-mail: secretary@aseg.org.au
URL: http://www.aseg.org.au

570 ■ Early Achievement Award
Awarded for the best publication in Exploration Geophysics or a related journal be a ASEG member who is under 36 years of age. Established in 2007.

571 ■ Gold Medal
Awarded for exceptional contribution to the science of geophysics. Members are eligible for award.

572 ■ Honorary Membership
Awarded for distinguished contributions to the profession of exploration geophysics and service to ASEG over an extended period of time. Only those who have been members of the ASEG for 20 years or more are eligible.

573 ■ Lindsay Ingall Memorial Award
To honor an individual for the promotion of geophysics to the wider community. Awarded when merited. Established in 2000.

574 ■ Grahame Sands Award
Recognizes innovation in applied geophysics and the 'development of benefit to Australian exploration geophysics in the field of instrumentation, data acquisition, interpretation or theory'. Award winners do not have to be members of the ASEG. Established in 1986.

575 ■ Service Certificate
Awarded for distinguished service to the association by a member and contribution to state branch committees, Federal committees, publications or conferences. Established in 1998.

576 ■ Service Medal
Awarded for outstanding contributions by an ASEG member to the society over a period of many years. Established in 1998.

577 ■ Australian Society of Plant Scientists
Dr. Ros Gleadow, Pres.
GPO Box 1600
Canberra, Australian Capital Territory 2601, Australia
Ph: 61 2 62465280
Fax: 61 2 62465399
E-mail: president@asps.org.au
URL: http://www.asps.org.au

578 ■ ASPS-FPB Best Paper Award
Awarded for the best paper published in the journal, Functional Plant Biology, in each calendar year. Co-sponsored by Functional Plan Biology. Eligible candidates must be a member of the ASPS and no more than 10 years post-PhD. Awarded annually

579 ■ Peter Goldacre Award
To recognize meritorious original research by a young scientist. Candidates should be Australian citizens, permanent residents, or have carried out all the research for the Award in Australia, and must have done the research within 10 years of their PhD, or within 10 cumulative years of employment subsequent to the year in which their PhD thesis was submitted. A medal and monetary prize of $2,000 are awarded annually. Established in 1965.

580 ■ Teaching Award
To recognize excellence, innovation, and/or contributions to the teaching of plant science at the university level in Australia. Awarded annually. Established in 1997.

581 ■ Australian Society of Sugar Cane Technologists
Mr. Arthur Pinkney, Honorary Gen. Sec.
PO Box 5596
Mackay Mail Centre
Mackay, Queensland 4741, Australia
Ph: 61 7 49543956
Fax: 61 7 49543956
E-mail: assctadmin@ozemail.com.au
URL: http://www.assct.com.au/assct_main.php?page_id=0

582 ■ President's Medal
To recognize the best research paper and the best industry paper of the ASSCT conference. A medal is awarded annually in each category.

583 ■ Rod Rookwood Award for Agriculture/Engineering Design
To recognize the best paper of the ASSCT conference focusing on innovation and excellence in agricultural or factory design of sugar industry equipment. A plaque and monetary prize of $500 are awarded annually.

584 ■ Australian Speech Science and Technology Association
Dr. David Grayden, Sec.
GPO Box 143
Canberra, Australian Capital Territory 2601, Australia
E-mail: secretary@assta.org
URL: http://www.assta.org

585 ■ New Researcher Award
To recognize the best papers submitted for presentation at the SST Conference. Open to students enrolled in postgraduate study at an Australian or New Zealand university who are no more than two years beyond their highest degree. A grant of A$750 is awarded to up to six recipients annually.

586 ■ PhD of the Year
To the best PhD thesis of the year in the area of speech science and technology. A monetary prize of $1,000 is awarded annually.

587 ■ PhD Study Award
To students who have passed confirmation of their PhD. Applicants must have been enrolled in a full-time PhD course of study at an Australasian academic institution for no less than six months and no more than 18 months at the time of this application. A monetary prize of $500 is awarded to up to four recipients each year.

588 ■ Research Event Awards
Presented for three different classes of events: seminars centered on a specific theme, groundwork meetings for new or existing research collaborations, or workshops on new theories or approaches. Full members of the ASSTA who are also employed full-time in Australia or New Zealand are eligible. Monetary awards of A$2,000 to A$5,000 are presented annually.

589 ■ Australian Sports Commission
Brent Espeland, Dir.
Leverrier St.
PO Box 176
Belconnen, Australian Capital Territory 2616, Australia
Ph: 61 2 62141111
Fax: 61 2 62512680
URL: http://www.ausport.gov.au

590 ■ Media Awards
To recognize journalists, broadcasters, and photographers for their focus on analytical, insightful reporting and the presentation of sport and sporting issues, with the ultimate aim of fostering improved coverage of key issues within sport. Awarded in nine categories each year.

591 ■ Australian Steel Institute
Mr. Don McDonald, CEO
Level 13, 99 Mount St.
North Sydney, New South Wales 2060, Australia
Ph: 61 2 99316666
Ph: 61 2 99316610
Fax: 61 2 99316633
E-mail: enquiries@steel.org.au
URL: http://steel.org.au

592 ■ Steel Awards
For high standard of design and execution achievable with the versatility of steel, aesthetics and the industry's capabilities and excellence.

593 ■ Australian Subscription Television and Radio Association
Steve Bracks, Chm.
55 Pyrmont Bridge Rd.
Pyrmont, New South Wales 2009, Australia
Ph: 61 2 97762684
Fax: 61 2 97762683
E-mail: astra@astra.org.au

Awards are arranged in alphabetical order below their administering organizations

URL: http://astra.org.au

594 ■ ASTRA Awards
To recognize talent and contributions to subscription television platforms and channels. Awards are presented in more than 30 categories each year.

595 ■ Australian Teachers of Media
Roger Dunscombe, Chm.
PO Box 2211
St. Kilda, Victoria 3182, Australia
Ph: 61 3 95349986
Fax: 61 3 95372325
E-mail: atom@atomvic.org
URL: http://www.atomvic.org

596 ■ Australian Teachers of Media Awards
To recognize and celebrate excellence in Australian and New Zealand film, television, animation, and educational content. Presented in dozens of categories within the broad classifications of: 1) School Students - open to students 18 years of age an under, attending a primary or high school; 2) Tertiary/Higher Education Students - productions made as assignments at a higher education institution; 3) General - open to anyone; and 4) Educational/Vocational - productions of an educational nature. Awarded annually. Established in 1982.

597 ■ Australian Veterinary Association
Dr. Barry Smyth, Pres.
6 Herbert St., Unit 40
St. Leonards, New South Wales 2065, Australia
Ph: 61 2 94315000
Fax: 61 2 94379068
E-mail: members@ava.com.au
URL: http://www.ava.com.au

598 ■ Gilruth Prize
To recognize an individual for meritorious service to veterinary science in Australia. Awarded annually. Established in 1953 to honor Dr. J.A. Gilruth, Dean of the Faculty of Veterinary Science of the University of Melbourne, the first Chief of the Division of Animal Health of the CSIRO, and an outstanding veterinary authority.

599 ■ Kendall Oration and Medal
To recognize outstanding Australian veterinarians. A medal is awarded when merited at the annual conference of AVA. Established in 1930 by the five sons of Dr. W.T. Kendall to honor his memory. Dr. William Tyson Kendall migrated to Australia in 1880 and he made a unique contribution to veterinary science in Australia.

600 ■ Don Kerr Veterinary Student Award
Commemorates the work of the late Don Kerr, who died in November 1992 while serving as President of the Association. Conferred upon a final year veterinary student from one of the veterinary schools for academic achievement and exceptional commitment to cattle medicine. A one-year membership and monetary prize of A$50 is awarded annually.

601 ■ Kesteven Medal
To recognize Australian veterinarians for distinguished contributions to international veterinary science in the fields of technical and scientific assistance to developing countries. A medal is presented annually.

602 ■ Meritorious Service Award
To recognize service by members to the Association, regional divisions, branches, or special interest groups. The award may also be made to persons who are not eligible for membership in the Association but who have provided meritorious service to it. Established in 1978.

603 ■ Australian Water Association
Peter Robinson, Pres.
PO Box 222
St. Leonards, New South Wales 1590, Australia

Ph: 61 1300 361426
Ph: 61 2 94360055
Fax: 61 2 94360155
E-mail: info@awa.asn.au
URL: http://www.awa.asn.au

604 ■ Peter Hughes Award
Recognizes outstanding contributions to the water industry. Awarded biennially in odd-numbered years.

605 ■ Stockholm Junior Water Prize
Recognizes high school seniors for a water science project. Awarded periodically. Established in 1995.

606 ■ Undergraduate Water Prize
For a final-year student in an Australian university undertaking a thesis or project related to water. Awarded annually.

607 ■ Water Environment Merit Award
Recognizes corporate contributions to water and the environment. Awarded biennially.

608 ■ Australian Women Pilots' Association
Jennifer Graham, Pres.
PO Box 90
Cairns, Queensland 4870, Australia
E-mail: national.president@awpa.org.au
URL: http://www.awpa.org.au

609 ■ Sir Donald Anderson Trophy
Recognizes the most meritorious academic progress towards professional aviation qualifications. Three trophies and monetary prizes are awarded annually.

610 ■ Aviation Award (W.A. Branch)
To assist a female pilot of the Western Australia in getting her Private Pilot's License. Up to $1,000 is awarded annually.

611 ■ Mrs. Harry (Lores) Bonny Award
For outstanding flight achievement(s) by a female pilot. Achievement could be: a record breaking flight or valiant attempt; representing Australia at the World Championship level; or a significant and recognized flight in the spirit of Lores Bonney. Nominees must be female and residents of Australia.

612 ■ Charts and Documents Award
To assist student pilots. Award consists of the charts and documents required for a Private Pilot. Two awards are presented annually, one for a female and one for a male pilot.

613 ■ Gliding Award
Recognizes the most meritorious gliding fight of the previous year, or an outstanding contribution to the advancement of gliding. Awarded annually.

614 ■ Robinson Silver Wings Award
To assist with ab-initio training, PPL, CPL, Aerobatic or PIFR training for a female pilot over 45 years old. Nominees must be permanent residents of Australia. Up to A$1,000 is awarded annually.

615 ■ SA Branch Memorial Incentive Award
To assist with a commendable aviation endeavor. Eligible to residents of South Australia with at least two years membership and a current aviation medical. Award amount is variable.

616 ■ Freda Thompson and Claire Embling Aviation Award
To advance practical and/or theoretical aviation training. Nominees must be female and permanent residents of Australia, with at least 50 hours of powered aircraft experience. Up to A$1,000 is awarded.

617 ■ Nancy-Bird Walton Memorial Trophy
Recognizes noteworthy contributions to aviation by an Australasian woman.

618 ■ Nancy Wells Award
To assist with CASA study fees. Nominees must be members of the Association or the 99s. A $300 prize is awarded.

619 ■ Australian Wound Management Association
351 Park St.
South Melbourne, Victoria 3205, Australia
Ph: 61 39 6961210
Fax: 61 39 6961684
E-mail: awma@ozemail.com.au
URL: http://www.awma.com.au

620 ■ Aaxis Pacific New Investigator Award
Awarded for the best oral presented during the annual conference. Co-sponsored by Aaxis Pacific.

621 ■ AWMA Conference Awards
Awarded for excellence poster or oral presentations during the AWMA annual conference.

622 ■ Comfeel Literary Awards
To recognize outstanding authorship and contribution to the AWMA Journal of Wound Practice and Research. A certificate and monetary prize of $1,000 are presented to one recipient in each of three categories: Original research article, Literature review/clinic practice, and Case study. Established in 1994.

623 ■ Australian Writers' Guild
Jacqueline Woodman, Exec. Dir.
5 Blackfriars St.
Chippendale, New South Wales 2008, Australia
Ph: 61 2 93190339
Fax: 61 2 93190141
E-mail: admin@awg.com.au
URL: http://www.awg.com.au

624 ■ FOXTEL Fellowship for Excellence in Television Writing
Recognizes a writer for the contribution of television writing to the development of the Australian cultural landscape. A grant of $25,000 is awarded for the development of a new project for television. Awarded annually. Established in 2007. Co-sponsored by FOXTEL.

625 ■ B & T Magazine
Tower 2, 475 Victoria Ave.
Locked Bag 2999
Chatswood, New South Wales 2067, Australia
Ph: 61 2 9422 2999
Fax: 61 2 9422 2922
E-mail: customerservice@reedbusiness.com.au
URL: http://www.bandt.com.au

626 ■ B & T Awards
To recognize excellence in all areas of marketing, media, and communications in Australia. Awards are presented in 25 categories each year.

627 ■ Banksia Environmental Foundation
1/40 Albert Rd.
South Melbourne, Victoria 3205, Australia
Ph: 61 3 96844667
Fax: 61 3 96844699
URL: http://www.banksiafdn.com

628 ■ Environmental Awards
To recognize individuals, companies, and organizations in Australia for contributions to the environment. Awards include: Achieving a Sustainable Australia; Recognising and Rewarding Environmental Excellence; Promoting Best Practice Principles; and Contributing to Action-Learning and Education. Awarded annually.

629 ■ Birds Australia
Dr. Graeme Hamilton, CEO
60 Leicester St., Ste. 2-05
Carlton, Victoria 3053, Australia

Awards are arranged in alphabetical order below their administering organizations

Ph: 61 3 93470757
Fax: 61 3 93479323
E-mail: mail@birdsaustralia.com.au
URL: http://www.birdsaustralia.com.au

630 ■ Stuart Leslie Bird Research Award
To support post-graduate field work and travel to scientific conferences by promising students working on ornithology in Australian universities. A grant of A$15,000 is awarded annually. Established in 1997.

631 ■ Brisbane Writers Festival
Michael Campbell, Dir.
PO Box 3453
South Brisbane, Queensland 4101, Australia
Ph: 61 7 3255 0254
Fax: 61 7 3255 0362
E-mail: info@bwf.com.au
URL: http://www.brisbanewritersfestival.com.au
Formerly: Brisbane Warana Festival Ltd..

632 ■ Steele Rudd Award
To recognize the best collection of short stories. Australian collections published in the preceding twelve months must be submitted by the end of April each year. A monetary award of $15,000 is presented annually at the opening of the Brubane Writers Festival in Brisbane each September. Sponsored by the Queensland Government.

633 ■ Building Designers Association of Australia
Monty East, Chm.
PO Box 592
Hunter Region Mail Centre, New South Wales 2310, Australia
E-mail: montyeast@bdaa.com.au
URL: http://www.bdaa.com.au

634 ■ National Design Awards
To honor the best and most innovative building designs. Awarded annually in 17 categories. Established in 1995.

635 ■ Cardiac Society of Australia and New Zealand
Mrs. Lynne Portelli, CEO
145 Macquarie St.
Sydney, New South Wales 2000, Australia
Ph: 61 2 92565452
Fax: 61 2 92477916
E-mail: info@csanz.edu.au
URL: http://www.csanz.edu.au

636 ■ Affiliate Clinical Development Award
To further develop an individual through an increase in his or her clinical knowledge and expertise, an increased awareness of research and evidence-based practice, and enable the successful candidate to build on his or her professional network. Five awards of A$1,000 are presented annually.

637 ■ R. T. Hall Prize
To recognize an individual investigator or group of investigators for work that advances knowledge of the cardiovascular system and its diseases and is published in a scientific journal or journals during the three-year period preceding the closing date. The work must have originated in Australia or New Zealand but the investigators need not be members of The Society. A monetary prize of A$10,000 is awarded annually.

638 ■ Traveling Fellowships to the European Society of Cardiology
To support members of the Cardiac Society attending the European Society of Cardiology Congress. The fellowships are intended to provide an opportunity for investigators in the early stage of their research career. Awarded annually.

639 ■ Centre for Asia Pacific Aviation
88 Phillip St., Aurora Pl., Level 4
Sydney, New South Wales 2000, Australia
Ph: 61 2 92413200
Fax: 61 2 92413400
E-mail: info@centreforaviation.com
URL: http://www.centreforaviation.com

640 ■ Aviation Awards for Excellence
To recognize excellence in the Asia Pacific aviation industry. Award categories include: Airline of the Year; Airline Turnaround of the Year; Aviation Executive of the Year; Aviation Minister of the Year; Cargo Airline of the Year; International Airport of the Year; Legends Award; Low Cost Airline of the Year; Low Cost Airport of the Year; National Tourism Organisation of the Year; New Airline of the Year; New Airport of the Year; and Regional Airline of the Year. Awarded annually.

641 ■ Chartered Institute of Logistics and Transport in Australia
Hal Morris, CEO
PO Box 4594
Robina, Queensland 4230, Australia
Ph: 61 2 92677538
E-mail: hal.morris@cilta.com.au
URL: http://www.cilta.com.au

642 ■ Achiever of the Year
To foster and acknowledge outstanding performance by individuals within the logistics and transport industry. Awarded annually.

643 ■ Young Achiever of the Year
To recognize the achievements in the field of logistics and transport by individuals aged 30 or younger. Awarded annually.

644 ■ Children's Book Council of Australia
Marj Kirkland, Pres.
PO Box 3203
Norwood, South Australia 5067, Australia
Ph: 61 8 83322845
Fax: 61 8 83330394
URL: http://cbc.org.au/Default.aspx

645 ■ Book of the Year Award: Early Childhood
Recognizes outstanding books of fiction, drama, or poetry for children who are at the pre-reading or early reading stages. They may be picture books, picture story books, or blocks in which illustrations play a substantial part in the story telling or concept development. Awarded annually.

646 ■ Book of the Year Award: Older Readers
To recognize outstanding books that generally require mature reading ability to appreciate the topics, themes, and the scope of emotional involvement. Awarded annually.

647 ■ Book of the Year Award: Picture Books
To recognize outstanding books in which the author and illustrator achieve artistic and literary unity; or in wordless books, where the story, theme, or concept is unified solely through illustrations. Awarded annually.

648 ■ Book of the Year Award: Younger Readers
For recognition of books for readers who have developed independent reading skills but are still developing in literary awareness. Awarded to books of fiction, drama, or poetry. Awarded annually.

649 ■ Crichton Award for New Illustrators
To recognize and encourage new talent in the field of Australian children's book illustration. Awarded annually. Established in 1988. Administered by the Victorian branch of the CBCA.

650 ■ Lady Cutler Award
For recognition of distinguished service to children's literature in New South Wales. Service should be well beyond a professional association with children's literature. The contributions should be primarily in New South Wales, and sympathetic to the aims of the Council. A trophy, citation certificate, and gift are awarded annually at the Lady Cutler Dinner. Established in 1981 in honor of the late Lady Cutler, Patron of the Children's Book Council and wife of Sir Roden Cutler, former governor of New South Wales. Administered by the New South Wales branch.

651 ■ Eve Pownall Award for Information Books
To recognize outstanding nonfiction books that present well-authenticated data in combination with imaginative presentation and variation of style. Awarded annually.

652 ■ Cladan Cultural Exchange Institute of Australia
Ms. Claire Dan, Managing Dir.
PO Box 420
Double Bay, New South Wales 1360, Australia
Ph: 61 2 93262405
Fax: 61 2 93262604
E-mail: sipca@bigpond.com
URL: http://www.sipca.com.au

653 ■ Sydney International Piano Competition of Australia
To encourage the careers of young concert pianists, to promote professional development, and to provide performance opportunities. Open to artists of any nationality, between 17 and not more than 30 years of age. The following monetary prizes in Australian dollars are awarded: (1) First prize - The Council of the City of Sydney Prize - A$25,000; (2) Second prize - A$10,000; (3) Third prize, donated by Theme & Variations - A$6,000; (4) Fourth prize - A$4,000; (5) Fifth prize, donated by Hunt and Hunt - A$2,500; (6) Sixth prize - A$2,500. In addition, many special prizes are also awarded. Held every four years. Established in 1977.

654 ■ Commonwealth Scientific and Industrial Research Organisation
Dr. Megan Clark, Chief Exec.
Locked Bag 10
Clayton South, Victoria 3169, Australia
Ph: 61 3 95452176
Fax: 61 3 95452175
E-mail: enquiries@csiro.au
URL: http://www.csiro.au

655 ■ Chairman's Medal
For a scientist commitment and dedication to the service of science and the public good. Awarded annually.

656 ■ Medal for Business Excellence
For commercial contribution to the organization's success and outstanding individual performances. Awarded annually.

657 ■ Medal for Lifetime Achievement
For individuals with a record of sustained and meritorious achievement over a prolonged period of service.

658 ■ Communications Alliance
John Stanton, CEO
PO Box 444
Milsons Point, New South Wales 1565, Australia
Ph: 61 2 99599111
Fax: 61 2 99546136
E-mail: info@einsteinz.com.au
URL: http://www.commsalliance.com.au

Awards are arranged in alphabetical order below their administering organizations

659 ■ ACOMM Awards, the Communications Alliance and Communications Day Awards
To recognize excellence in the wider communications industry, rewarding and profiling companies that have excelled within the industry around the nation, regardless of size, location, and whether service providers, equipment vendors, or suppliers of professional services. Awarded annually.

660 ■ Concrete Institute of Australia
Graeme Burns, CEO
PO Box 1227
North Sydney, New South Wales 2138, Australia
Ph: 61 2 97362955
Fax: 61 2 97362639
E-mail: admin@concreteinstitute.com.au
URL: http://www.concreteinstitute.com.au

661 ■ Award for Environmentally Sustainable Use of Concrete
Recognizes significant advances in the environmental sustainability of concrete. Established in 2008.

662 ■ Kevin Cavanagh Medal
Recognizes an outstanding contribution to the quality of concrete construction in Australia. Established in 1991.

663 ■ Consult Australia
Jamie Shelton, Pres.
Level 6, 50 Clarence St.
Sydney, New South Wales 2000, Australia
Ph: 61 2 99224711
Fax: 61 2 99572484
E-mail: acea@acea.com.au
URL: http://www.consultaustralia.com.au
Formerly: (2010) Association of Consulting Engineers of Australia.

664 ■ Awards for Excellence
To recognize engineering and technical consultants who maintain high ethical and professional standards and work to ensure the status of the engineering profession. Held annually.

665 ■ Convoy For Kids
PO Box 85
Park Orchards, Victoria 3114, Australia
Ph: 61 409 940378
Fax: 61 3 98762383
E-mail: admin@convoyforkids.org
URL: http://www.convoyforkids.org

666 ■ Convoy For Kids Grant
For childhood asthma research.

667 ■ Distinguished Award of Honour for Service to Children's Charities
For long-term voluntary work connected with Convoy for Kids.

668 ■ Life Governor
For long-term exemplary service to Convoy for Kids.

669 ■ Most Outstanding Volunteer
For outstanding service to Convoy for Kids above and beyond what is expected of a volunteer.

670 ■ President's Choice Award
For outstanding service to Convoy for Kids.

671 ■ Youth Ambassador
For children with asthma or another disability or illness who are an inspiration to other children and adults.

672 ■ Cooperative Research Centre for Polymers
Dr. Ian Dagley, CEO
8 Redwood Dr.
Notting Hill, Victoria 3168, Australia
Ph: 61 3 9518 0400
Fax: 61 3 9543 2167
E-mail: polymers@crcp.com.au
URL: http://www.crcp.com.au

673 ■ CRC for Polymers Prize
To recognize a report based on project work in any field of polymer science or engineering. The competition is open to all students who have completed a research project as part of the requirement for a Bachelors or Honours degree in a relevant area of engineering, materials science, or chemistry during the year. Candidates must be members of the Royal Australian Chemical Institute or the New Zealand Institute of Chemistry. A monetary prize of $1,500 and travel expenses are awarded annually.

674 ■ Country Music Association of Australia
John Williamson, Pres.
PO Box 298
Tamworth, New South Wales 2340, Australia
Ph: 61 67661577
Fax: 61 67667314
E-mail: info@country.com.au
URL: http://www.country.com.au

675 ■ Australian Country Music Industry Achiever Awards
To recognize individuals, companies, and organizations that have made major contributions to the development and promotion of Australian country music over the preceding 12 month period. Awarded annually in a variety of categories. Established in 1995.

676 ■ Country Music Awards of Australia
To recognize and promote excellence in Australian country music songwriting, performance, and recording. Awarded annually in a variety of categories. Established in 1973.

677 ■ Crime Writers Association of Australia
PO Box 3162
East Prahran, Victoria, Australia
E-mail: contact@nedkellyawards.com
URL: http://www.nedkellyawards.com

678 ■ Ned Kelly Awards for Crime Writing
To promote and encourage crime writing by Australians. Awards are presented in the following categories: First Fiction, True Crime, Fiction, and Lifetime Achievement. In addition, the S. D. Harvey Short Story Award is presented. Awarded annually. Established in 1996.

679 ■ Cystic Fibrosis Australia
Mr. Terry Stewart, CEO
21 Manning Rd.
North Ryde, New South Wales 2113, Australia
Ph: 61 2 98785250
Fax: 61 2 98785058
E-mail: general@cysticfibrosisaustralia.org.au
URL: http://www.cysticfibrosis.org.au

680 ■ Allied Health Fellowship
For allied health professionals involved in the treatment or care for people with Cystic Fibrosis. A fellowship in the amount of $4,000 is awarded annually.

681 ■ Post Graduate PhD Studentship Grant
For PhD students in Australia conducting research on Cystic Fibrosis. A grant of $5,000 per year for three years is awarded annually to one or more recipients.

682 ■ Deaf Australia
Ms. Karen Lloyd, Exec. Off.
PO Box 1083
Stafford, Queensland 4053, Australia
Ph: 61 7 33578266
Ph: 61 7 33578277
Fax: 61 7 33578377
E-mail: info@deafau.org.au
URL: http://www.deafau.org.au
Formerly: (2009) Australian Association of the Deaf.

683 ■ Dorothy Shaw Deaf Australian of the Year Award
Recognizes a deaf person who has made an outstanding contribution to the Deaf Community. In addition, the Dorothy Shaw Deaf Youth of the Year is also honored. Awarded annually when merited.

684 ■ Delta Society Australia
Phillip Palangas, Chm.
Shop 2, 50 Carlton Crescent
Summer Hill
Sydney, New South Wales 2130, Australia
Ph: 61 2 97977922
Fax: 61 2 97995009
E-mail: hollee@deltasociety.com.au
URL: http://www.deltasocietyaustralia.com.au

685 ■ Leigh Anne Snow Award
To recognize a volunteer for outstanding services to the Delta Therapy Dogs Program. Awarded annually. Formerly: (2007) Julie Mandile Award.

686 ■ Dromkeen Collection Art Gallery
1012 Kilmore Rd.
Riddells Creek, Victoria 3431, Australia
Ph: 61 3 5428 6799
Fax: 61 3 5428 6830
E-mail: dromkeen@scholastic.com.au
URL: http://www.scholastic.com.au/common/dromkeen

687 ■ Dromkeen Librarian's Award
To recognize a teacher, teacher/librarian, or a children's librarian currently working within or outside the educational systems for the important role of introducing children to literature. The award is presented each December at the Dromkeen Literary Luncheon. Established in 1994.

688 ■ Dromkeen Medal
To recognize an individual for an outstanding contribution to children's literature in Australia. A bronze medal, designed by Robert Ingpen, is awarded annually in March. Established in 1982 in memory of Courtney Thomas Oldmeadow, the founder of Dromkeen.

689 ■ Eaglehawk Dahlia and Arts Festival
David Richards, Pres.
40 Napier St.
Eaglehawk, Victoria 3556, Australia
Ph: 61 5 4469098
Fax: 61 5 4469098
E-mail: aylenehugh@bigpond.com
URL: http://dahlia.bendigo.net.au

690 ■ Literary Competition
To recognize outstanding literature. Australian citizens are eligible for original, unpublished works on an Australian theme. The following awards are presented: 1. Rolf Boldrewood Award for a short story on any topic. First prize is $200 and a certificate; second prize is $50; 2. Allan Llewellyn Award for Bush verse with an Australian theme, written in rhyme and traditional metre. First prize is $100 and a certificate. 3. Apollo Prize for poetry. First prize is $200; second prize is $50. Awarded at the Eaglehawk Dahlia and Arts Festival each year.

691 ■ Ecological Society of Australia
Prof. Kris French, Pres.
PO Box 2187
Windsor, Queensland 4030, Australia
Ph: 61 7 31620901
Fax: 61 7 37354209
E-mail: president@ecolsoc.org.au
URL: http://www.ecolsoc.org.au

692 ■ Australian Ecology Research Award
Recognizes excellence in recent research involv-

Awards are arranged in alphabetical order below their administering organizations

ing Australian ecology. Supports an invited lecture at the annual conference. Eligible to researchers based in Australia, or for research focused on Australian ecosystems. Candidates should be at the height of their careers and should have produced research that advanced the science of ecology. Travel expenses, accommodations, and registration are reimbursed for the award recipient. Awarded annually. Established in 2008.

693 ■ Gold Medal
To recognize ecologists for substantial contributions to Australian ecology over the course of their career, or to a member for significant contributions to Society operations. Awarded as merited.

694 ■ Nature Conservancy Applied Conservation Award
To support postgraduate research in applied conservation science. A grant of A$6,000 is awarded annually.

695 ■ Economic Society of Australia
Jane Oldroyd, Admin.
PO Box 937
St. Ives, New South Wales 2075, Australia
Ph: 61 2 94400241
Fax: 61 2 94400241
E-mail: ecosoc@ecosoc.org.au
URL: http://www.ecosoc.org.au

696 ■ Distinguished Fellow Award
To recognize Australian economist's contribution to the development of economics. A citation is awarded annually. Established in 1985.

697 ■ Honorary Fellow Award
To honor a member for significant and substantial contribution to the Society. Awarded annually. Established in 2005.

698 ■ Young Economist Award
To recognize an Australian economist under the age of 40 who is deemed to have made a significant contribution to economic thought and knowledge. Candidates must have studied and worked in Australia for five out of the previous 10 years. A citation is awarded annually. Established in 2006.

699 ■ Edublog Awards
URL: http://edublogawards.com

700 ■ EduBlog Awards
To recognize the world's best education-related blogs. Eddies Awards are presented in 19 categories, including Best Individual Blog, Best Library/Librarian Blog, and Most Influential Post. Awarded annually. Established in 2004.

701 ■ Endocrine Society of Australia
Prof. Vicki Clifton, Pres.
145 Macquarie St.
Sydney, New South Wales 2000, Australia
Ph: 61 2 92565405
Fax: 61 2 92518174
E-mail: esa@racp.edu.au
URL: http://www.endocrinesociety.org.au

702 ■ Bryan Hudson Clinical Endocrinology Award
To recognize the best clinical research presentation at the annual scientific meeting by a member of the Society early in his or her career. Candidates must be younger than 45 years of age or are within 10 years of obtaining professional qualifications. A monetary award of $3,500 is awarded annually. Established in 2004.

703 ■ Novartis Junior Scientist Award
To recognize the best presentation at the Annual Scientific Meeting by an advanced trainee or a person enrolled for a higher education degree. Awarded annually. Established in 1976. Sponsored by Novartis AG.

704 ■ Servier Young Investigator Award
To recognize the best scientific paper published in the previous 12 months written by a member of the Society early in his or her career. A monetary award of A$1,000 is presented annually. Established in 1991. Sponsored by Servier Laboratories Australia.

705 ■ Engineers Australia
Society for Engineering in Agriculture
Thomas Banhazi, Chm.
Engineering House
11 National Circuit
Barton, Australian Capital Territory 2600, Australia
Ph: 61 2 62706588
Fax: 61 2 62732358
E-mail: memberservices@engineersaustralia.org.au
URL: http://www.engineersaustralia.org.au/society-engineering-agriculture

706 ■ Agricultural Engineering Award and Life Membership
Recognizes significant national contributions to the field. Only members are eligible. Awarded biennially in even-numbered years. Established in 1986.

707 ■ Exhibition and Event Association of Australasia
Ms. Joyce DiMascio, Gen. Mgr.
PO Box 952
Chatswood, New South Wales 2057, Australia
Ph: 61 2 94139520
Fax: 61 2 80881325
E-mail: info@eeaa.com.au
URL: http://www.eeaa.com.au

708 ■ Awards for Excellence
To recognize outstanding achievements in the Australian exhibition and events industry. Award categories include: Best Consumer Show; Best Trade Show; Best New Show; Best New Zealand Show; Best Australian Show; Best Custom Stand; Most Innovative Promotional Campaign; Best Green Initiative; Best Show Team; Best Supplier Team; and the Richard Geddes Young Achiever Award. Awarded annually.

709 ■ Farrer Memorial Trust
B.D. Buffier, Dir. Gen.
c/o New South Wales Dept. of Primary Industries, Agriculture
PO Box K220
Haymarket, New South Wales 1240, Australia
Ph: 61 2 6391 3100
Fax: 61 2 6391 3336
E-mail: nsw.agriculture@agric.nsw.gov.au
URL: http://www.dpi.nsw.gov.au/agriculture/field/field-crops/farrer-memorial-trust

710 ■ Farrer Memorial Medal
To provide encouragement and inspiration to those engaged in agricultural science and to recognize an individual who has rendered distinguished service in agricultural science in Australia in the fields of research, education, or administration. The recipient of the medal is invited to deliver an oration on a topical subject of his own choice. Awarded annually. Established in 1936 in memory of William James Farrer, plant breeder.

711 ■ Feline Control Council of Western Australia
Sandy Baraiolo, Pres.
PO Box 915
Cannington, Western Australia 6107, Australia
Ph: 61 8 94522885
Fax: 61 8 94522885
E-mail: office@felinecontrolcouncilofwesternaustralia.com.au
URL: http://www.felinecontrolcouncilofwesternaustralia.com.au

712 ■ Cat of the Year Awards
Awards are given for best entire cat, kitten, desexed, and domestic felines. Awarded annually.

713 ■ Fellowship of Australian Writers NSW
Trevar Langlands, Pres.
PO Box 488
NSW Writers Ctre., Rm. 36
Rozelle, New South Wales 2039, Australia
Ph: 61 2 98101307
Fax: 61 2 98101307
E-mail: president@fawnsw.org.au
URL: http://www.fawnsw.org.au

714 ■ Marjorie Barnard Short Story Award
To recognize the author of an outstanding short story (under 3,000 words). A monetary prize of A$500 is awarded biennially in odd-numbered years at the Annual Members' Lunch. Winning story will be published in Writers Voice and on the Fellowship's website.

715 ■ Mona Brand Award Short Story Competition
To recognize winners of a short story competition. First prize is A$200, second prize is A$100, and third prize is A$50.

716 ■ Hilarie Lindway Young Writers Short Story Competition for School Children
To recognize and encourage young writers in Australia. Awards are offered in grade-based sections: Section 1 - Years 10, 11, and 12, a A$200 prize; Section 2 - Years 7, 8, and 9, a A$180 prize; Section 3 - Years 5 and 6, a A$160 prize; and Section 4 - Year 4 and under, a A$60 prize. Held annually.

717 ■ Jean Stone Award for Poetry
To recognize an outstanding poem or group of poems up to 60 lines. Open to residents of Australia who are 18 years or older. A monetary prize of A$500 is awarded biennially in even-numbered years.

718 ■ Walter Stone Memorial Award
For recognition of a monograph, biography, or bibliography dealing with some aspect of Australian literature. A monetary prize of A$1,000 is awarded biennially at the Seminar in October. Established in 1984 in honor of Walter Stone, publisher, and president of City Regional FAW and NSW State Council FAW.

719 ■ Wooden Horse Award
To recognize a first professionally published work. Works are judged by a committee appointed by the State Council. A carved wooden horse is awarded annually.

720 ■ Field Naturalists Club of Victoria
John Harris, Pres.
Locked Bag 3
Post Office
Blackburn, Victoria 3130, Australia
Ph: 61 3 98779860
Fax: 61 3 98779860
E-mail: admin@fncv.org.au
URL: http://www.fncv.org.au

721 ■ Australian Natural History Medallion
For recognition of the most meritorious contribution to the understanding of Australian natural history. A person of any age may be nominated by May 1 of any year for a contribution made in the preceding ten year period. A medal is awarded annually. Established in 1940 by Mr. J.K. Moir.

722 ■ Film and Television Institute of Western Australia
Graeme Sward, CEO
92 Adelaide St.
PO Box 579

Awards are arranged in alphabetical order below their administering organizations

Fremantle, Western Australia 6959, Australia
Ph: 61 8 94316700
Fax: 61 8 93351283
E-mail: fti@fti.asn.au
URL: http://www.fti.asn.au

723 ■ West Australia Screen Awards

For recognition of excellence, innovation, and talent in film or video making. Awards are given in the Industry Section, for commercial theatrical releases or significant television transmission, the Early Career Section for students who have not achieved commercial credits, and the Open section. In addition, individuals are eligible for the Outstanding Contribution to Industry Award and the Young Filmmaker of the Year. Held annually. Established in 1996. Formerly: (1998) Western Australia Film and Video Festival.

724 ■ Flying Fifteen International

Rupert Leslie, Sec.
14 Gardiner St.
East Perth, Western Australia 6004, Australia
Ph: 61 8 92723280
URL: http://www.flying15.org/ffi

725 ■ Flying Fifteen European Championship Awards

To honor the winners of the European Championships. Trophies are awarded in three categories: Open, Silver, and Classic. Held biennially in even-numbered years. Established in 2004.

726 ■ Flying Fifteen World Championship Awards

For recognition of the winners of the Flying Fifteen World Championships. The International Flying Fifteen Class is a one design racing keelboat. Members of FFL affiliated associations are eligible. Trophies are awarded in three categories: Open, Silver, and Classic. Held biennially in odd-numbered years. Established in 1979.

727 ■ Foundation for Australian Literary Studies

Dr. Stephen Torre, Exec. Dir.
James Cook University
School of Arts and Social Sciences
Department of Humanities
Townsville, Queensland 4811, Australia
Ph: 61 7 40421052
Fax: 61 7 40421390
E-mail: fals@jcu.edu.au
URL: http://www.jcu.edu.au/sass/humanities/fals/index.htm
Formerly: Townsville Foundation for Australian Literary Studies.

728 ■ Colin Roderick Lectures

To foster the study of Australian literature in the University and the wider community. To date, more than 20 of these series of lectures have been delivered and published in the Foundation's monograph series, and they have made a significant contribution to the critical discussion of Australian literature. Awarded annually. Established in 1966.

729 ■ Colin Roderick Prizes for Australian Literature

For recognition of the best book published each year in Australia that deals with any aspect of Australian life. Publications entered may be in any field of Australian writing and may be in verse or prose. Publications considered must be published in Australia, even though they may be printed elsewhere, and deal with some aspect of Australian life. A publication or any number of publications may be entered by any author or publisher by February 28 of the year following the year of publication. A monetary prize of A$10,000 Australian is awarded at the annual dinner of the Foundation. Since 1980, the win-

ner has also received the H. T. Priestley Memorial Medal. Established in 1967. Formerly: (1995) Townsville Foundation for Australian Literary Studies Award; (2006) .

730 ■ Genetics Society of Australasia

Prof. Phil Batterham, Pres.
8 Ewart St.
Malvern
Melbourne, Victoria 3144, Australia
Ph: 61 3 95090323
Fax: 61 3 95098206
E-mail: gsa@genetics.org.au
URL: http://www.genetics.org.au

731 ■ D.G. Catcheside Prize

To recognize research that has led to the award of a doctoral degree by an Australasian university. A monetary prize of A$1,000 is awarded annually.

732 ■ Spencer Smith-White Travel Prize

To assist a postgraduate student member of GSA to attend an overseas conference. A grant of up to A$1,750 is awarded annually.

733 ■ Geological Society of Australia

Sue Fletcher, Exec. Dir.
104 Bathurst St., Ste. 61
Sydney, New South Wales 2000, Australia
Ph: 61 2 92902194
Fax: 61 2 92902198
E-mail: info@gsa.org.au
URL: http://www.gsa.org.au

734 ■ W.R. Browne Medal

To a person distinguished For contributions to the geological sciences. Awarded biennially in even-numbered years.

735 ■ S.W. Carey Medal

To a person distinguished in the field of tectonics. Awarded biennially in even-numbered years.

736 ■ David I. Groves Award

To honor the best paper published in the *Australian Journal of Earth Sciences* by a young author. Candidates must have had their first degree in any relevant science for less than six years. A medal is awarded annually. Established in 2005.

737 ■ Joe Harms Medal

For excellence in mineral exploration and contribution to the discovery of ore deposits. Awarded biennially in even-numbered years.

738 ■ F.L. Stillwell Award

For the best paper published in the *Australian Journal of Earth Sciences*. Awarded annually.

739 ■ Girls' Brigade Australia

Mrs. Leonie Watson, Natl. Admin.
PO Box 811
Toongabbie, New South Wales 2146, Australia
Ph: 61 2 96313553
E-mail: gbaust@bigpond.net.au
URL: http://www.girlsbrigadeaustralia.org

740 ■ Blue Service Award

To recognize girls who have consistently attended company meetings and who have a satisfactory attitude as displayed by conduct and attendance.

741 ■ Gold Service Award

To recognize girls who fulfill the requirements of the Blue Service Award and who regularly attend Sunday School or other voluntary Christian service.

742 ■ Gliding Federation of Australia

Level 1/34 Somerton Rd.
Somerton, Victoria 3062, Australia
Ph: 61 3 93037805
Fax: 61 3 93037960
URL: http://www.gfa.org.au

743 ■ Life Membership of the GFA

This, the Federation's highest honor, is given to recognize a member for years of endeavor, both on and off the field of gliding. Awarded annually if merited. Established in 1981.

744 ■ Haematology Society of Australia and New Zealand

Lexy Harris, Admin. Off.
145 Macquarie St.
Sydney, New South Wales 2000, Australia
Ph: 61 2 92565456
Fax: 61 2 92520294
E-mail: hsanz@hsanz.org.au
URL: http://www.hsanz.org.au

745 ■ Albert Baikie Award

To recognize the best presentation (either oral or poster) at the Annual Scientific Meeting by a new investigator who is a financial member of the Society. Investigators awarded their postgraduate qualification (MSc, FRACP, FRCPA or PhD) within the past five years are eligible. The Baikie Medal and monetary prize of $3,000 are awarded annually.

746 ■ New Investigator Scholarship

To enhance the scientific stature of Australian and New Zealand haematology by providing the opportunity for medical or science graduates who are undertaking advanced training in haematology to gain experience in acknowledged centers of excellence. Three scholarships with a value of A$50,000 are awarded annually.

747 ■ Human Factors and Ergonomics Society of Australia

Ms. Christine Aickin, Pres.
Hills Corporate Centre, Ste. 18
11-13 Brookhollow Ave.
Baulkham Hills, New South Wales 2153, Australia
Ph: 61 2 96809026
Fax: 61 2 96809027
E-mail: secretariat@ergonomics.org.au
URL: http://www.ergonomics.org.au

748 ■ David Ferguson Award

Awarded for the best postgraduate project or undergraduate thesis completed in the previous 18 months. All students enrolled in a relevant program of study at an Australian University are eligible.

749 ■ John Lane Award

Presented to an individual, group or organization for contribution the advancing the science of human factors and ergonomics in Australia. Awarded for work carried out in the previous five to ten years.

750 ■ Society Medal

Awarded for service to the society over the previous seven years. Awarded to a member of the society in good standing.

751 ■ Alan Welford Award

Awarded for the best paper on ergonomics and human factors published in a peer-reviewed journal during the previous calendar year. Presented to an individual or group of individuals, of which one is a member of the society.

752 ■ Institute of Australian Geographers

Prof. Iain Hay, Pres.
GPO Box 2100
Adelaide, South Australia 5063, Australia
E-mail: iain.hay@flinders.edu.au
URL: http://www.iag.org.au/home

753 ■ Fellowship of the Institute of Australian Geographers

For distinguished service to the institute. Awarded annually, if merited.

754 ■ Postgraduate Award

For work undertaken during own research For a

Awards are arranged in alphabetical order below their administering organizations

higher degree; the paper could be submitted during the period of enrollment but should not be submitted later than one year after the award of the degree. A monetary prize of $200 is awarded annually.

755 ■ Griffith Taylor Medal
For distinguished contributions to geography in Australia. Awarded biennially in even-numbered years. Established in 1989.

756 ■ Institute of Chartered Accountants in Australia
Graham Meyer, CEO
33 Erskine St.
Sydney, New South Wales 2000, Australia
Ph: 61 2 92901344
Fax: 61 2 92621512
E-mail: graham.meyer@charteredaccountants.com.au
URL: http://www.charteredaccountants.com.au

757 ■ Business Leader Awards
To recognize innovation, leadership, and strategic thinking in Australian business leaders. Awards include Business Leader of the Year and Most Outstanding Chartered Accountant in Business. Established in 1999.

758 ■ Leadership in Government Awards
To recognize innovation, leadership, and strategic thinking in Australian government leaders. Eligible to current employees of the Australian Public Service.

759 ■ Institute of Quarrying - Australia
David Cilento, Pres.
PO Box 156
Oatley, New South Wales 2223, Australia
Ph: 61 2 94840577
Fax: 61 2 94840766
E-mail: admin@quarry.com.au
URL: http://www.quarry.com.au

760 ■ Atlas Copco Award
To recognize the best technical paper presented at an Institute meeting, published in *Quarry Magazine*, or presented at an Institute or outside seminar or conference during the previous 12 months. A monetary prize of A$2,000 is awarded annually. Sponsored by Atlas Copco.

761 ■ Alex Northover Award
To recognize the best prepared portfolio of evidence submitted in support of the applicant seeking accreditation for either Certificate IV or Diploma against the Extractive Industries Training Package. A grant of A$2,500 is awarded annually. Sponsored by the Australian Institute of Quarrying Education Foundation.

762 ■ Ron Parrott Award
To recognize the best exhibit at the Trade Exhibition at the Institute's Annual Conference. Criteria include technical advancement, industry benefits, and visual appeal. Awarded annually.

763 ■ Service Award
To recognize an individual who has demonstrated outstanding service to the Institute and the quarrying industry. Awarded annually.

764 ■ Institution of Engineers Australia/Engineers Australia
Peter Taylor, Chief Exec.
11 National Circuit
Engineering House
Barton, Australian Capital Territory 2600, Australia
Ph: 61 2 62706555
Fax: 61 2 62731488
E-mail: memberservices@engineersaustralia.org.au
URL: http://www.engineersaustralia.org.au

765 ■ Agricultural Engineering Award
For recognition of a project, invention, design, or manufacturing process that represents a significant agricultural engineering achievement and that has been completed within the previous two years. Nominees must be SEAg members. A monetary award and a plaque are awarded biennially. Established in 1986. Administered by the Society for Engineering in Agriculture (SEAg).

766 ■ G.N. Alexander Medal
To honor the author of the best paper on hydrology and/or water resources published in an Association publication. It is usually awarded every 18 months at the Hydrology and Water Resources Symposium. The first award was given in 1988, with selection responsibility being with the National Committee on Water Engineering.

767 ■ Australian Engineering Excellence Awards
To reward achievement, promote better engineering, show the community how good engineering creates wealth and improves living standards, and encourage young people to join the profession. Given annually, entries comprise the winning entrants from the Divisional competitions over the previous two years. A special issue of *Engineers Australia* gives details of all the entries. An award is given in each of the following categories: building and civil design; engineering products; engineering project management; engineering reports, procedures, and systems; environmental engineering; manufacturing facilities; public works; research; resource development; and the Sir William Hudson Award for the overall winner.

768 ■ Australian Geomechanics Award - John Jaeger Memorial Award
To recognize and promote contributions of the highest order in the field of Australian geomechanics. Contributions may take the form of papers published in any publication of the Society, Institution, or Institute or presented at any meeting, conference, or symposium of one of these bodies. Papers may also be the design, construction, or supervision of any project in the field of geomechanics. The award is not restricted to members of the Australian Geomechanics Society. A bronze medallion is awarded every four years. Established in 1980 in memory of Professor John Conrad Jaeger, who was Professor of Geophysics and Geochemistry at the Australian National University from 1953 until his death in 1979. Co-sponsored by the Australasian Institute of Mining and Metallurgy.

769 ■ Award for Achievement in Engineering Enterprise
To recognize a corporate member of the Institution who, by personal endeavors, has significantly contributed to an enterprise built around the successful commercialization of innovative engineering endeavor. A memento is presented as a recognition of the award. Established in 1986. Presented by the Victoria Division.

770 ■ O. F. Blakey Memorial Prize
For recognition of the best prepared paper of approximately 20 minutes duration delivered on an engineering subject to a meeting of the Western Australian Division by a graduate (under 30 years old) or student member of that Division. In the event of there being more entries than can be conveniently heard in one evening, preselection is carried out. A significant proportion of the points are awarded for the standard of presentation of the paper. The prize consists of the O.F. Blakey Memorial Medal and a monetary award. Awarded annually. Established in 1955 in memory of Professor O.F. Blakey, the first Professor of Civil Engineering at the University of Western Australia, who was a Councillor of the Institution from 1936 to 1951, Chairman of the former Perth Division in 1936 and 1942, and President of the Institution in 1945.

771 ■ John A. Brodie Medal
For recognition of a paper in chemical engineering considered superior by the College of Chemical Engineers. The award is not limited to members of the Institution. A bronze medal is awarded annually. Established in 1963 in honor of J.A. Brodie, a leading industrial innovator. Administered by the Chemical College of the Institution.

772 ■ Frederick Brough Memorial Prize
For recognition of the best prepared paper of approximately 20 minutes duration delivered on any engineering subject by a graduate or student member of the Tasmania Division. A monetary prize and a medal are awarded annually. Established in 1949 in memory of Mr. Frederick Brough who was Honorary Secretary of the Tasmania Division from 1929 until his death in 1948. He was a member of the staff of the Hydro-Electric Commission from 1920 to 1947.

773 ■ R. W. Chapman Medal
For recognition of a paper on structural engineering considered the best by the College of Civil Engineers. Members of the Institution are eligible. A bronze medal is awarded annually. Established in 1935 in memory of Sir Robert Chapman, President of the Institution in 1922. Administered by the Structural College of the Institution.

774 ■ Chemeca Medal
This, the most prestigious award in the profession of chemical engineering in Australia, is given for achievement and distinction in the profession. This award is not limited to members of the three sponsoring associations. A medal is awarded annually at the Chemeca Conference. Administered by the Chemical College of the Institution. Co-sponsored by: Engineers Australia, Chemical College; the Institution of Chemical Engineers in Australia; and the Royal Australian Chemical Institute, Industrial Chemical Division.

775 ■ College of Electrical Engineers Student Prizes
To raise the profile of the Institution and the Electrical College in electrical engineering schools of tertiary institutions, thereby encouraging students to become members. The college provides funds on the basis of $400 per electrical engineering school, to divisional electrical branches for allocation as appropriate to local circumstances. Established in 1990.

776 ■ Arthur Corbett Medal
To honor the top student graduating in engineering from the Australian Defence Force Academy of the University of New South Wales. A medal and a cash prize are awarded annually. Between 1971 and 1985, the award was made for the best final year engineering student from the Royal Military College Duntroon. Part of the Engineers Australia Awards.

777 ■ J.M.C. Corlette Medal
To annually recognize a final year student who completes the Bachelor of Engineering degree with First Class Honors at the University of Newcastle. A medal and a cash prize are awarded annually. Established in 1961. Administered by the Newcastle Division as part of the Engineers Australia Awards.

778 ■ E. H. Davis Memorial Lecture
To recognize a person selected for a distinguished recent contribution to the theory and practice of geomechanics in Australia. Awarded biennially. The selected lecturer is presented with a framed certificate. Established in 1985 in honor of E.H. Davis, who achieved eminence in the field of geomechanics.

779 ■ Russell Dumas Medal
To recognize University of Western Australia engineering students. The award is made annually to the student completing the Bachelor of Engineering degree at the University who, in the

opinion of the Board of Examiners in Engineering, has given the best academic performance in the final year of the course. A medal and a cash prize are awarded annually. Established in 1970. Administered by the Western Australia Division as part of the Engineers Australia Awards.

780 ■ L.R. East Medal

To honor final-year engineering students at the University of Melbourne. Based on academic record and involvement in extra-curricular activities and special projects. A medal and a cash prize are awarded annually as part of the Engineers Australia Awards. Selection is made by a Faculty/Campus Chapter Panel. Established in 1977.

781 ■ ESSO Award

For recognition of significant ongoing contributions to chemical engineering through innovations or a series of related publications over a number of years. A monetary prize and a certificate are awarded annually at the Chemeca Conference. Established in 1990. Sponsored by ESSO.

782 ■ Excellence in Engineering Journalism Award

To encourage and enhance the reporting of engineering issues to the public. A single award is presented for the Engineering Journalist of the Year, with commendations for runners-up. A monetary award of $5,000 and a suitably inscribed medal is awarded to the winner; runners-up receive certificates. Established in 1990.

783 ■ Faldt Guthrie Medal

To recognize University College of Central Queensland engineering students. The award is based on a final year project and selection is made on appraisal by faculty staff. A medal and a cash prize of $200 are awarded annually as part of the Engineers Australia Awards. Established in 1973.

784 ■ Ian Henderson Award

Recognizes the winner of a presentation competition for young engineers in the Newcastle division. A monetary prize and a medal are awarded annually. Established in 1977 in memory of Mr. I.F.G. Henderson who was employed by BHP Company Ltd. for over 45 years, and who was closely associated with the Newcastle Division for many years until his death in 1975.

785 ■ K. Johinke Medal

To annually recognize a final year engineering student at the University of South Australia who is selected on the basis of personality and a high level of academic attainment. A medal and a cash prize of $200 are awarded annually as part of the Engineers Australia Awards. Established in 1077.

786 ■ Sir George Julius Medal

For recognition of a paper on mechanical engineering considered the best by the College of Mechanical Engineers. Members of the Institution are eligible. A bronze medal and a certificate are awarded annually. Established in 1955 in memory of George Julius, inventor of the automatic totalizator and President of the Institution in 1925. Administered by the Mechanical College of the Institution. Formerly: (1976) Mechanical Engineering Prize.

787 ■ Allen Knight Medal

To honor the engineering student at the University of Tasmania, who on the appraisal of the faculty staff, shows the highest degree of proficiency in the subject of engineering design in the final year of the course. A medal and a cash prize are awarded annually as part of the Engineers Australia Awards. Established in 1963.

788 ■ Ian Langlands Medal

To honor final-year engineering students at Monash University. The award is based on academic record and involvement in extra-curricular activities and special projects. A medal and a cash prize are awarded annually as part of the Engineers Australia Awards. Established in 1977.

789 ■ Digby Leach Medal

To recognize a final year student at Curtin University of Technology on the basis of interest in the Institution, academic record, and qualities of leadership. A medal and a cash prize are awarded annually. Established in 1968. Administered by the Western Australia Division as part of the Engineers Australia Awards.

790 ■ Local Government Engineering Medal

To recognize the local government engineering project/design judged to be the best of those completed in the last two years. The award consists of a bronze medal for the engineer, and a certificate for the council that approved the project/design. Awarded biennially. Established in 1989.

791 ■ John Madsen Medal

To recognize the best paper written by a current member on electrical engineering and published in the Australian Journal of Electrical and Electronic Engineering. A bronze medal is awarded annually. A bronze medal and a certificate are awarded annually. Established in 1927; renamed in 1976 to honor Sir John Madsen, one of Australia's great electrical engineers and foundation professor of Electrical Engineering at the University of Sydney. Administered by the Electrical College of the Institution.

792 ■ A. G. M. Michell Medal

For recognition of a significant contribution through technical innovation to the science or practice of mechanical engineering, or for notable and sustained leadership pertaining to mechanical engineering. A bronze medal and a certificate are awarded annually. Established in 1978 in honor of Anthony George Maldon Michell, Australia's outstanding mechanical engineer, and inventor of the tilting-pad thrust bearing and the viscometer. Administered by the Mechanical College of the Institution.

793 ■ John Monash Medal

For recognition of outstanding contributions made by individuals towards increasing the awareness, and conservation, of Australia's natural heritage. Members and non-members of the Institution are eligible. A bronze medal and a certificate are awarded annually. Established in 1976 in honor of Sir John Monash, Australia's greatest military commander and an outstanding engineer.

794 ■ W.H.R. Nimmo Medal

To recognize University of Queensland engineering students. The award is based on a final year project and selection is made on faculty appraisal. A medal and a cash prize are awarded annually as part of the Engineers Australia Awards. Established in 1976.

795 ■ Sir Arvi Parbo Medal

To annually recognize a final year engineering student at the University of Adelaide who is selected on the basis of personality and high level of academic attainment. A medal and a cash prize are awarded annually as part of the Engineers Australia Awards. Established in 1977.

796 ■ R. W. Parsons Memorial Prize

To recognize a graduate or student member of the South Australian Division for the best prepared paper of approximately 20 minutes duration delivered on an engineering subject. In the event of there being more entries than can be conveniently heard in one evening, pre-selection of the papers is carried out. A significant proportion of the points awarded are for the standard of presentation of the paper. A monetary prize and a medal are awarded annually. Established in 1962 in memory of Mr. R.W. Parsons, a former Principal of the South Australian School of Mines (1940-1960) and a former Director of the South Australian Institute of Technology (1960-1961). Parsons was a Councillor of the Institution from 1947 to 1961, Chairman of the former Adelaide Division in 1943 and President of the Institution in 1955.

797 ■ President's Prize

To recognize individuals or organizations that have made considerable contributions to engineering in Australia, to the Institution, to the profession, or to the community. A certificate is awarded annually at the discretion of the National President. Established in 1990.

798 ■ R.A. Priddle Medal

To honor, on the recommendation of the Dean of the Faculty of Engineering, the candidate working toward a Bachelor of Engineering degree at the University of Sydney who shows the greatest proficiency. A medal and a cash prize are awarded annually as part of the Engineers Australia Awards. Established in 1978.

799 ■ Professional Engineer of the Year

To recognize a corporate member of the Institution for competence and significant achievement in community affairs, a demonstrated understanding of the role and purpose of the engineering profession within society, proficiency in the use of communication and managerial skills in engineering projects, and/or effective communication with the mass media. National nominees may only come from the winners of state and territory awards made by the divisions. A certificate is awarded annually.

800 ■ Queensland Division Chemical Branch Award

To recognize a chemical engineering student at the University of Queensland. A monetary award of $100 is presented. Co-sponsored by the ANC of the Institution of Chemical Engineers.

801 ■ Railway Engineering Award

For recognition of an outstanding contribution to railway engineering in Australia. A monetary prize of $2,000 and a plaque are awarded annually. Established in 1984 by the Institution's National Committee on Railway Engineering.

802 ■ Peter Nicol Russell Memorial Medal

This, the most prestigious award of the Institution, is given for notable contributions to the science and practice of engineering in Australia. Fellows of the Institution are eligible. A certificate is awarded annually. Established in 1923 in memory of Peter Nicol Russell, a Sydney industrialist who made major donations to the cause of engineering education in Australia.

803 ■ W.E. Sansum Medal

To recognize aeronautical engineering students at the University of Canberra. Based on academic record and involvement in extra-curricular activities and special projects. Awarded annually. Established in 1988 after the late Air Commodore "Bill" Sansum, who was elected as a Fellow of the Institution in 1981, was Chairman of the Canberra Branch of the Royal Aeronautical Society in 1987-1988, and Chairman of the Canberra Division of the Institution in 1988.

804 ■ M. A. Sargent Medal

To recognize the outstanding Australian electrical engineer of the year. Selection of the recipient is based on: a highly significant contribution, through technical innovation to the science or practice of electrical engineering; long-standing eminence in science or practice of electrical engineering; exceptional and sustained management or leadership relating to electrical engineer-

Awards are arranged in alphabetical order below their administering organizations

ing; or a notable combination of the foregoing qualities. A bronze medal is awarded annually. Established in 1989. Administered by the Electrical College of the Institution.

805 ■ Norman Selfe Medal

To recognize the best final-year project of the Bachelor of Engineering (Maritime) at Australian Maritime College. A medal and a cash prize are awarded annually as part of the Engineers Australia Awards. The medal is named in honor of Norman Selfe, who was a great promoter of technical education.

806 ■ Kevin Stark Memorial Award

To encourage excellence in coastal and ocean engineering. Any author who has a paper published in a forthcoming Australasian Conference on Coastal and Ocean Engineering, sponsored biennially by the National Committee on Coastal and Ocean Engineering, is eligible. The award is in the form of an engraved bronze medal. Awarded to one or more recipients in odd-numbered years. Established in 1993.

807 ■ D. H. Trollope Medal

Recognizes an outstanding paper on theoretical or applied geomechanics. Papers must have been undertaken in Australia by an author under 35 years old and have been published in the last four years. A bronze medal is awarded biennially. Established in 1987.

808 ■ Shedden Uhde Medal and Prize

To recognize young members of the Institution of Chemical Engineers or the College of Chemical Engineers, their practical services to the profession, and the practice of chemical engineering in Australia. Candidates must be under 40 years of age. Achievements may be in technical, marketing, or management fields and nominations may be made either by individuals themselves or by others. The award is donated by Shedden Pacific and consists of a medal and a cash prize. Awarded annually at the Chemeca Conference.

809 ■ W. H. Warren Medal

For recognition of a paper on civil engineering considered the best by the College of Civil Engineers. Members of the Institution are eligible. A bronze medal is awarded annually. Established in 1929 in honor of W.H. Warren, the First President of the Institution and first professor of Engineering at the University of Sydney. Administered by the Civil College of the Institution.

810 ■ Weir Minerals Design and Build Competition

To recognize outstanding students in their first or second year of engineering study in the Asia Pacific region. All recognized engineering teaching institutions may submit a team for the national award after conducting in-house competitions to ascertain their representations. A separate design problem is set each year. Awarded annually. Administered by the National Committee on Engineering Design, a committee of Engineers Australia. Sponsored by Weir Minerals Australia Ltd. Formerly: (2009) Warman International Students Design Award Competition.

811 ■ Young Professional Engineer of the Year

To recognize young professional engineers for achievement in community affairs, for an understanding of the role and purpose of the engineering profession in society, for proficiency in the use of communication skills in engineering projects, and for effective communication with public media. Candidates must be practicing engineers under the age of 35. Awarded annually.

812 ■ International Association of School Librarianship

Dr. Diljit Singh, Pres.
PO Box 83
Zillmere, Queensland 4034, Australia
Fax: 61 7 3633 0570
E-mail: iasl@iasl-online.org
URL: http://www.iasl-online.org

813 ■ Books for Children

To provide books for children in developing countries. Sponsored by IASL members and supporters. Several US$1,000 awards may be presented each year. Formerly: UNESCO Project Books for Children Award.

814 ■ IASL/Softlink Excellence Award

For library specialists, educators or researchers who have made significant contributions to school librarianship. A monetary prize of US$1,000 is awarded annually. Sponsored by Softlink International.

815 ■ School Library Technology Innovation Award

For a school librarian or a school library team for school library programs or projects that utilize emerging technologies. A monetary prize of A$1,000 is awarded annually. Sponsored by KB Enterprises Pty. Ltd.

816 ■ International Association of Trichologists

David Salinger, Dir.
185 Elizabeth St., Ste. 919
Sydney, New South Wales 2000, Australia
Ph: 61 2 92671384
Fax: 61 8 82968450
E-mail: dsalinger@trichology.edu.au
URL: http://www.trichology.edu.au

817 ■ Ronald Salinger Award

For the best trichology student in North America, Australia and New Zealand.

818 ■ International Colour Association (Association Internationale de la Couleur)

Nick Harkness, Sec.-Treas.
Birdcage 3.1
65 Doody St.
Alexandria, New South Wales 2015, Australia
Ph: 61 2 97008110
Fax: 61 2 97008112
E-mail: nick@nhpl.com.au
URL: http://www.aic-colour.org

819 ■ Judd Award

For recognition of research in color in all aspects, and its application to science, art, and industry. A plaque is awarded biennially in odd-numbered years. Established in 1973 by Mrs. Judd in honor of Dr. Deane B. Judd, internationally acclaimed authority on color and one of the founders of the Association.

820 ■ International Cost Engineering Council

Dr. Peter Smith, Sec.-Treas.
PO Box 301
Deakin West, Australian Capital Territory 2600, Australia
Ph: 61 2 62822222
Fax: 61 2 62852427
E-mail: icec@icoste.org
URL: http://www.icoste.org

821 ■ Distinguished International Fellow Award

Recognizes outstanding service to profession. Awarded biennially in even-numbered years. Established in 2002.

822 ■ Jan Korevaar Outstanding Paper Award

Presented to the author of the outstanding paper of each biennial congress. Established in 1992.

823 ■ International Research Society for Children's Literature

Clare Bradford, Pres.
Deakin University
Arts Faculty
221 Burwood Hwy.
Burwood, Victoria 3125, Australia
Ph: 61 3 92446487
Ph: 61 3 95009295
Fax: 61 3 92446755
E-mail: clarex@deakin.edu.au
URL: http://www.irscl.com

824 ■ IRSCL Award

Recognizes distinguished research in the field of children's literature published in the two previous years. Recipient must be a member in good standing who is nominated by another member. Established in 1994.

825 ■ IRSCL Fellows

To recognize members who have made outstanding contributions to the Society and to research in children's literature. Established in 2001.

826 ■ International Society for Antiviral Research

Dr. Susan Cox, Dir.
576 Swan St.
Richmond, Victoria 3121, Australia
Ph: 613 9208 4066
Fax: 613 9208 4100
E-mail: susancox@westnet.com.au
URL: http://isar.phrm.cf.ac.uk

827 ■ Award for Outstanding Contributions to the Society

To recognize an individual who has made significant contributions consistently over many years (at least 10 years) that are considered to have been essential to the continuing success of the Society and its annual Conference. Awarded periodically. Established in 2004.

828 ■ Award of Excellence

To recognize individuals who have made truly outstanding contributions to the field of antiviral research. Awarded periodically.

829 ■ Conference Poster Awards

To recognize young investigators for their outstanding contributions to antiviral research. Awards are based on such criteria as scientific excellence, innovative research methodology, clarity and organization of presentation materials, and competence of the investigator in responding to the poster audience. Awarded in three categories: Graduate students, Postdoctoral individuals, and Young investigators. Awarded annually.

830 ■ Gertrude Elion Memorial Lecture Award

To recognize an outstanding scientist, not necessarily in the field of antiviral research, who has made considerable contributions to the scientific field directly or peripheral to it. Candidates should be senior scientists (basic or clinical) of international stature. A travel stipend of $7,500 is awarded annually. Established in 2000.

831 ■ William Prusoff Young Investigator Lecture Award

To recognize an outstanding young scientist (not older than 45 years of age) who has demonstrated dedication and excellence in the field of antiviral research (basic or clinical, synthetic or pharmacological) and future potential for contribution to the field and the society. The award is intended to encourage young investigators in the

Awards are arranged in alphabetical order below their administering organizations

field, and by definition should not be a fully developed scientist. A travel stipend is awarded annually. Established in 2001.

832 ■ International Society for Behavioral Ecology
Robert Magrath, Sec.
Australian National University
School of Botany and Zoology
Canberra, Australian Capital Territory 0200, Australia
Ph: 61 2 6125 3060
Fax: 61 2 6125 5573
E-mail: robert.magrath@anu.edu.au
URL: http://www.behavecol.com

833 ■ Frank A. Pitelka Award for Excellence in Research
To recognize the senior or sole author of a significant paper published in *Behavioral Ecology* during the previous two years. A monetary prize of US$150 is awarded biennially in even-numbered years. Established in 1996.

834 ■ International Society for Neurochemistry
(Societe Internationale de Neurochimie)
Philip M. Beart, Sec.
University of Melbourne
Florey Neuroscience Institutes
Parkville
Melbourne, Victoria 3010, Australia
Ph: 61 3 83441955
Fax: 61 3 93470466
E-mail: isn.secretary@florey.edu.au
URL: http://www.neurochemistry.org

835 ■ *JNC* Editors' Award
To recognize the contribution of an outstanding young scientist to an exceptional research paper published in the *Journal of Neurochemistry* (*JNC*). To qualify, authors must be 35 years or younger and no more than eight years beyond their PhD. Awarded biennially in odd-numbered years. Established in 2009.

836 ■ Young Scientist Award
To recognize individuals for outstanding contributions to neuroscience. Scientists who are less than 35 years of age may be nominated. A travel award is presented biennially in odd-numbered years. Established in 1989.

837 ■ International Society of Biomechanics
Ton van den Bogert, Pres.
PO Box 3156
Sydney, New South Wales 6009, Australia
Ph: 61 4 27092523
Fax: 61 8 97641643
E-mail: gwood@cygnus.uwa.edu.au
URL: http://isbweb.org

838 ■ *Clinical Biomechanics* Award
To honor the best article submitted for publication in *Clinical Biomechanics*. A certificate, monetary prize of US$1,250, and publication are awarded biennially in odd-numbered years. Established in 1989.

839 ■ Muybridge Award
This, the most prestigious award of the Society, is given to honor an individual for career achievements in biomechanics. Awarded biennially in odd-numbered years. Established in 1987 in honor of the first person to use cinematography for the study of human and animal movement.

840 ■ Promising Young Scientist Award
To recognize individuals who have performed superior biomechanics research early in their career. A certificate and monetary prize of US$5,000 are awarded in each category biennially in odd-numbered years. Established in 1997.

841 ■ Wartenweiler Memorial Lecture
To honor an individual for contributions to the

study of biomechanics. Awarded biennially in odd-numbered years. Established in 1987 in honor of the first president of the Society.

842 ■ Young Investigator Awards
To honor individuals for the best oral presentation and the best poster presentation. A certificate and monetary prize of US$750 are awarded in each category biennially in odd-numbered years. Established in 1983.

843 ■ International Society on Toxinology
Prof. Julian White, Sec.-Treas.
Women's & Children's Hospital
Toxinology Department
North Adelaide, South Australia 5006, Australia
Fax: 61 8 81618024
E-mail: julian.white@adelaide.edu.au
URL: http://www.toxinology.org

844 ■ Redi Award
For recognition of outstanding contributions to the knowledge of natural-occurring poisons and venoms. Individuals without regard to nationality may be nominated and voted upon by present and past officers of the Society and past awardees. A monetary award, a plaque, a leather bound illuminated manuscript noting the accomplishments of the awardee, and travel expenses are awarded every three years at the International Congress. Established in 1967 in honor of Francisco Redi, an Italian anatomist of the 17th century who showed it was venom, not spirits, that were transferred from snake to victim.

845 ■ Liquor Merchants Association of Australia
Mr. Ralph Dunning, Chm.
Locked Bag 4100
Chatswood, New South Wales 2067, Australia
Ph: 61 2 94151199
Fax: 61 2 94151080
E-mail: info@liquormerchants.org.au
URL: http://www.liquormerchants.org.au

846 ■ LMA Award
For best red wine at the Royal Easter Show in Sydney.

847 ■ Live Performance Australia
Evelyn Richardson, Chief Exec.
Level 1, 15-17 Queen St.
Melbourne, Victoria 3000, Australia
Ph: 61 3 96141111
Fax: 61 3 96141166
E-mail: info@liveperformance.com.au
URL: http://www.liveperformance.com.au

848 ■ Helpmann Awards
To recognize distinguished artistic achievement and excellence in the performing arts in Australia. Productions of theatre, musical theatre, opera, ballet or dance, contemporary and classical music, visual or physical theatre, comedy, special events, new works, and children's presentations are eligible. Awards are presented in more than 40 categories. In addition, the J.C. Williamson Award and the Brian Stacey Award may be presented. Awarded annually. Established in 2001 in honor of Sir Robert Helpmann.

849 ■ Master Builders Association - New South Wales
52 Parramatta Rd.
Forest Lodge, New South Wales 2037, Australia
Ph: 61 2 8586 3555
Fax: 61 2 9660 3700
E-mail: enquiries@mbansw.asn.au
URL: http://www.mbansw.asn.au

850 ■ Excellence in Construction Awards
To recognize the best in commercial building in New South Wales, Australia. Awarded annually in a variety of categories. Winners in each category become finalists in the National Excel-

lence in Building and Construction Awards, presented by the national Master Builders Australia organization (see separate entry).

851 ■ Excellence in Housing Awards
To recognize the best in residential building in New South Wales, Australia. Open to project home builders, contract builders, multi-unit developers, medium density housing builders, and builders specializing in alterations and additions. Awarded annually in a variety of categories. Winners in each category become finalists in the National Excellence in Building and Construction Awards, presented by the national Master Builders Australia organization (see separate entry).

852 ■ Master Builders Association - Newcastle
Level 1, 165 Lambton Rd.
Broadmeadow, New South Wales 2292, Australia
Ph: 61 2 4953 9400
Fax: 61 2 4953 9433
E-mail: enquiries@newcastle-mba.com.au
URL: http://www.newcastle-mba.com.au

853 ■ Excellence in Building Awards
To encourage, promote, and recognize best practice in building and to establish benchmark projects for others in the industry to emulate. Open to residential and commercial builders in the Hunter, Central Coast, Manning Great Lakes, and Oxley regions of New South Wales, Australia. Awarded annually in a variety of categories. Winners in each category become finalists in the National Excellence in Building and Construction Awards, presented by the national Master Builders Australia organization (see separate entry). Established in 1995.

854 ■ Master Builders Association of the ACT
Hayley Symons, Events Coord.
1 Iron Knob St.
Fyshwick, Australian Capital Territory 2609, Australia
Ph: 61 2 62472099
Fax: 61 2 62498374
E-mail: canberra@mba.org.au
URL: http://www.mba.org.au

855 ■ Excellence in Building Awards
Recognizes excellence in Australian construction. Categories include Civil, Commercial, Occupational Health and Safety, Housing, Subcontractor, Environmental, Training Awards, Landscaping, Kitchens and Bathrooms, and Overall. Sponsored by Boral.

856 ■ Master Builders Association - South Australia
47 South Terr.
Adelaide, South Australia 5000, Australia
Ph: 61 8 8211 7466
Fax: 61 8 8231 5240
E-mail: buildsa@mbasa.com.au
URL: http://www.mbasa.com.au

857 ■ Building Excellence Awards
To recognize the best in the building and construction industry in South Australia. Awarded annually in a variety of categories. Winners in each category become finalists in the National Excellence in Building and Construction Awards, presented by the national Master Builders Australia organization (see separate entry).

858 ■ Master Builders Association - Tasmania
34 Patrick St.
Hobart, Tasmania 7000, Australia
Ph: 61 3 6234 3810
Fax: 61 3 6234 3860
URL: http://www.mbatas.org.au

859 ■ Excellence in Housing and Construction Awards
To recognize the best in the building and con-

Awards are arranged in alphabetical order below their administering organizations

struction industry in Tasmania, Australia. Awarded annually in a variety of categories. Winners in each category become finalists in the National Excellence in Building and Construction Awards, presented by the national Master Builders Australia organization (see separate entry).

860 ■ Master Builders Association - Victoria
332 Albert St. E
Melbourne, Victoria 3002, Australia
Ph: 61 3 9411 4555
Fax: 61 3 9411 4591
E-mail: mbassist@mbav.com.au
URL: http://www.mbav.com.au

861 ■ Excellence in Construction Awards
To recognize outstanding craftsmanship and professional standards in the commercial/industrial sector of the building industry throughout Victoria, Australia. Awarded annually in a variety of categories. Winners in each category become finalists in the National Excellence in Building and Construction Awards, presented by the national Master Builders Australia organization (see separate entry).

862 ■ Excellence in Housing Awards
To recognize outstanding craftsmanship and professional standards in the residential sector of the building industry throughout Victoria, Australia. Awarded annually in a variety of categories. Winners in each category become finalists in the National Excellence in Building and Construction Awards, presented by the national Master Builders Australia organization (see separate entry).

863 ■ Master Builders Association - Western Australia
35-37 Havelock St.
West Perth, Western Australia 6005, Australia
Ph: 61 8 9476 9800
Fax: 61 8 9476 9801
E-mail: mba@mbawa.com
URL: http://www.mbawa.com

864 ■ Excellence in Construction Awards
To recognize the best commercial, industrial, and civil engineering builders in Western Australia for excellence and quality of workmanship. Awarded annually in a variety of categories. Winners in each category become finalists in the National Excellence in Building and Construction Awards, presented by the national Master Builders Australia organization (see separate entry). Established in 1989. Sponsored by Bankwest.

865 ■ Housing Excellence Awards
To recognize the best residential builders in Western Australia for excellence and quality of workmanship. Open to new construction, display homes, renovations, single detached, and group housing projects. Awarded annually in a variety of categories. Winners in each category become finalists in the National Excellence in Building and Construction Awards, presented by the national Master Builders Australia organization (see separate entry). Established in 1981. Sponsored by Bankwest.

866 ■ Master Builders Australia
Level 1, 16 Bentham St.
PO Box 7170
Yarralumla, Australian Capital Territory 2600, Australia
Ph: 61 2 6202 8888
Fax: 61 2 6202 8877
E-mail: enquiries@masterbuilders.com.au
URL: http://www.masterbuilders.com.au

867 ■ National Excellence in Building and Construction Awards
To recognize excellence in the building and construction industry in Australia. Awards are presented in more than 30 categories. Nomina-

tions are submitted through State and Territory Master Builders associations, which have their own awards processes. These winners become finalists for the national awards and are judged accordingly. Awarded annually.

868 ■ National Export Awards
To recognize the outstanding export performance of members and others in the Australian building and construction industry in the export market. Awarded annually.

869 ■ National Lifestyle Housing for Seniors Award
To recognize builders, designers, and architects who are developing innovative housing options for older Australians and setting the pace in creating healthy, safe, comfortable, adaptable, and "age friendly" housing. Presented in two categories: 1) Purpose-built owner occupied dwellings, and 2) Owner occupied dwelling that have been extended or modified. Awarded annually.

870 ■ Master Builders Northern Territory
11/396 Stuart Hwy.
Winnellie, Northern Territory 0820, Australia
Ph: 61 8 8922 9666
Fax: 61 8 8922 9600
E-mail: info@mbant.com.au
URL: http://www.mbant.com.au

871 ■ Excellence in Building and Construction Awards
To recognize excellence in building and construction from the smallest renovation to the largest commercial project in the Northern Territory, Australia. Awarded annually in a variety of categories. Winners in each category become finalists in the National Excellence in Building and Construction Awards, presented by the national Master Builders Australia organization (see separate entry).

872 ■ Melbourne International Film Festival
225 Bourke St., Level 5
GPO Box 4982
Melbourne, Victoria 3001, Australia
Ph: 61 3 8660 4888
Fax: 61 3 9654 2561
E-mail: miff@melbournefilmfestival.com.au
URL: http://www.melbournefilmfestival.com.au

873 ■ Shorts Awards
To give encouragement, recognition and reward to short film makers. Short films less than 60 minutes in length are eligible. The following prizes are awarded: the City of Melbourne Grand Prize for Best Short Film - A$10,000; Film Victoria Erwin Radio Prize for Best Australian Short Film - A$7,000; Transmission Films Award for Emerging Australian Filmmaker - A$5,000; Cinema Nova Award for Best Fiction - A$5,000; Holmesglen Award for Best Animation - A$5,000; Swinburne Award for Best Documentary - A$5,000; and Award for Best Experimental Film - A$5,000. Awarded annually. Established in 1962.

874 ■ Mental Health Association NSW
Ms. Elizabeth Priestley, CEO
80 William St., Level 5
East Sydney, New South Wales 2011, Australia
Ph: 61 2 93396000
Fax: 61 2 93396066
E-mail: mha@mentalhealth.asn.au
URL: http://www.mentalhealth.asn.au

875 ■ Mental Health Matters Awards
To recognize the high standard and ongoing commitment demonstrated by those involved in innovative and effective programs which address key mental health issues at a local, regional, or state-wide level. Further, the awards encourage individuals and organizations to continue to

strive for excellence in their daily work and to continue to enhance their skills and experience within the mental health field. Awarded annually in a variety of categories.

876 ■ Moran Arts Foundation
Renee Ward, Admin.
13-15 Bridge St.
Sydney, New South Wales 2000, Australia
Ph: 61 2 92476666
Fax: 61 2 82720022
E-mail: moranprizes@moran.com.au
URL: http://www.moranprizes.com.au

877 ■ Doug Moran National Portrait Prize
For recognition of portraits by and of Australian citizens or permanent residents. Finalists tour nationally in Australia. Winners receive $100,000, and the winning painting becomes part of Tweed River Regional Art Gallery's Portrait Collection. Awarded annually. Established in 1988. Formerly: (1995) Douglas J. Moran Portraiture Prize.

878 ■ Mortgage and Finance Association of Australia
Phil Naylor, CEO
PO Box 604
Neutral Bay, New South Wales 2089, Australia
Ph: 61 2 89051316
URL: http://www.mfaa.com.au

879 ■ Excellence Awards
Recognizes individuals and organizations for excellence in mortgage and finance. Awards are offered in four individual categories and 11 company categories. Presented annually.

880 ■ Museums Australia
Lee Scott, Natl. Office Mgr.
PO Box 266
Civic Square, Australian Capital Territory 2608, Australia
Ph: 61 2 62732437
Fax: 61 2 62732451
E-mail: ma@museumsaustralia.org.au
URL: http://www.museumsaustralia.org.au

881 ■ Multimedia and Publication Design Awards
To recognize excellence in design and multimedia. Awards are presented in 12 categories. Awarded annually.

882 ■ National Association of Testing Authorities, Australia
7 Leeds St.
Rhodes, New South Wales 2138, Australia
Ph: 61 2 9736 8222
Fax: 61 2 9743 5311
URL: http://www.nata.com.au

883 ■ Young Scientists of the Year Awards
To foster interest in science among school children and to encourage students to consider how science impacts peoples' lives. Students between the ages of 7 and 12 years may enter. A monetary prize of A$3,000 is awarded to the winning school in each of three student age groups (7 and 8 years old, 9 and 10 years old, and 11 and 12 years old). In addition, A$500 is awarded to each winning student group. Awarded annually. Established in 2007.

884 ■ National Australia Day Council
Old Parliament House
King George Terr.
Parkes, Australian Capital Territory 2600, Australia
Ph: 61 2 61200600
Fax: 61 2 62738777
E-mail: info@australiaday.gov.au
URL: http://www.australiaday.gov.au/experience

885 ■ Australian of the Year Awards
Recognizes the achievements of leading citizens

Awards are arranged in alphabetical order below their administering organizations

who are role models for all Australians. Four awards are presented: Australian of the Year, Senior Australian of the Year, Young Australian of the Year, and Australia's Local Hero. Awarded annually.

886 ■ National Electrical and Communications Association
James Tinslay, CEO
PO Box 1818
St. Leonards, New South Wales 1590, Australia
Ph: 61 2 94398523
Fax: 61 2 94398525
E-mail: necanat@neca.asn.au
URL: http://www.neca.asn.au

887 ■ Apprentice Awards
To recognize senior apprentices who have shown outstanding commitment to the electrical and communications industry, both by developing technical skills in academia. Awarded annually.

888 ■ Electrotechnology School Student Awards
Recognizes high school students who are skilled in the area of electrotechnology and have also shown enthusiasm in their commitment to their school learning environment. Presented in two categories: Innovation and Commitment to Industry. Monetary prizes ranging from A$250 to A$1,000 are awarded annually in each category.

889 ■ Excellence Awards
To recognize members for outstanding electrical and communications projects. Presented in 10 categories, including Domestic Residence, Occupational Health and Safety, and Voice/Data. Awarded annually.

890 ■ National Health and Medical Research Council
Prof. Warwick Anderson AM, CEO
GPO Box 1421
Canberra, Australian Capital Territory 2601, Australia
Ph: 61 2 62179000
Fax: 61 2 62179100
E-mail: nhmrc@nhmrc.gov.au
URL: http://www.nhmrc.gov.au

891 ■ Neil Hamilton Fairley Fellowships
To provide training in scientific research methods, including those of the social and behavioral sciences, which can be applied to any area of clinical or community medicine. Fellowships are not restricted to medical and dental graduates. In considering applications, the Council places emphasis on the applied value of the proposed research training, with preference given to persons who already have research experience and are seeking advanced study not available in Australia. To be eligible to apply, candidates must: hold appropriate qualifications; hold a doctorate; have demonstrated their interest in, and ability to pursue, a career in research and/or teaching in the specific fields of applied health science and be currently engaged in such activities in Australia; not have more than two years' postdoctoral experience since the most recent doctoral award at the time of the application; be Australian citizens or be graduates from overseas, with permanent Australian resident status, not under bond to any foreign government; provide a specific study plan within a clearly defined area; organize affiliation with an overseas investigator/institution to carry out the study; and have reasonable prospects of a responsible position in Australia, on completion of the fellowship. The fellowships are usually awarded for a period of four years; the first two years are spent overseas and the remainder in Australia. The fellowships are named after the late Sir Neil Hamilton Fairley, an Australian scientist whose research in areas of preventive and tropical medicine received international acclaim.

892 ■ C. J. Martin Overseas Biomedical Fellowship
To enable fellows to work overseas on specific research projects within the biomedical sciences under nominated advisers. These fellowships are offered to a limited number of young persons of outstanding ability who wish to make medical research a full time career. To be eligible to apply, candidates must: hold a doctorate in a medical, dental, or related field of research or have submitted a thesis for such by December of the year of application. No offer of award is made unless written confirmation of submission is received; be actively engaged in such research in Australia; not have more than two years' postdoctoral experience at the time of the application; and be Australian citizens or be graduates from overseas, with permanent Australian resident status, not under bond to any foreign government. Candidates enrolled for a doctorate at the time of applying for this fellowship are expected to complete the degree successfully before the award can be taken up. The deadline for applications is July 31. The fellowships are usually awarded for a period of four years; two years are spent overseas and the remainder in Australia. The fellowships are named after the late Sir Charles Martin, a British scientist who had a profound influence on medical research and teaching in Australia early this century. Formerly: (2006) C. J. Martin Fellowships.

893 ■ Medical and Dental Postgraduate Research Scholarships
To assist medical or dental graduates to gain full time research experience. All candidates must enroll for a higher degree. The scholarships are held within Australia. Those eligible to apply are: Australian citizens who are graduates registered to practice within Australia, with the proviso that Dental Postgraduate Research Scholarships may be awarded prior to graduation provided that evidence of high quality work is shown; and overseas graduates who hold a qualification that is registered for practice in Australia and who have permanent resident status and are currently residing in Australia. The deadline for applications is June 30. A stipend is awarded for consumables and conference travel. The usual maximum period of the award is three years.

894 ■ National Library of Australia
Jan Fullerton, Dir. Gen.
Parkes Pl.
Canberra, Australian Capital Territory 2600, Australia
Ph: 61 2 6262 1111
Fax: 61 2 6257 1703
E-mail: exec@nla.gov.au
URL: http://www.nla.gov.au

895 ■ Harold White Fellowship
To promote the library as a centre of scholarly activity and research; to encourage scholarly and literary use of the collections and the production of publications based on them; and to publicize the library's collections. Open to established scholars, writers and librarians of any nationality. Grant-in-aid and traveling expenses are awarded annually. Established in 1983 to honor Sir Harold White, former National Librarian.

896 ■ National Space Society of Australia
Kirby Ikin, Chm.
GPO Box 7048
Sydney, New South Wales 2001, Australia
Ph: 61 2 91504553
E-mail: nssa@nssa.com.au
URL: http://nssa.com.au

897 ■ Advocate of the Year
To recognize a member for dedication and proactive service to the Society. Awarded annually.

898 ■ Chapter of the Year
To recognize a Society Chapter for exceptional activities and development in the previous year. Awarded annually.

899 ■ Outstanding Service Award
For contributions and personal service to the Society.

900 ■ Project of the Year
To recognize the chapter that undertook the most important project of the year. Awarded annually.

901 ■ Space Pioneer Award
To recognize an individual from the Australian space industry for outstanding and sustained service to the domestic space community.

902 ■ Young Space Achiever Award
Recognizes a young member for outstanding achievements during the previous year. Awarded annually.

903 ■ NBTA Asia Pacific
Glenn Buckingham, Exec. Dir./CEO
PO Box 812
Rockdale, New South Wales 2216, Australia
Ph: 61 2 95851945
Fax: 61 2 95851946
E-mail: abta@abta.com.au
URL: http://www2.nbta.org/asiapacific
Formerly: (2007) Australasian Business Travel Association.

904 ■ Qantas/ABTA Excellence Awards
To practitioners who have achieved excellence and implemented innovative and successful solutions in the business travel industry.

905 ■ New South Wales Ministry for the Arts
Carol Mills, Dir. Gen.
Level 9, St. James Centre
111 Elizabeth St.
PO Box A226
Sydney, New South Wales 1235, Australia
Ph: 61 2 9228 5533
Fax: 61 2 9228 4722
E-mail: mail@arts.nsw.gov.au
URL: http://www.arts.nsw.gov.au

906 ■ New South Wales Premier's Literary Awards
To honor distinguished achievement by Australian writers in the following categories of writing: fiction, nonfiction, poetry, children's books, and play and scriptwriting. Writers must be residents of Australia. Works may be nominated by writers or publishers. More than a dozen monetary prizes are awarded, including: Christina Stead Prize for Fiction - A$40,000; UTS Glenda Adams Award for New Writing - A$5,000; Douglas Stewart Prize for Non-Fiction - A$40,000; Kenneth Slessor Prize for Poetry - A$30,000; Patricia Wrightson Prize for Children's Fiction - A$30,000; Ethel Turner Prize for Young People's Literature - A$30,000; Play Award - A$30,000; Script Writing Award - A$30,000; and Community Relations Commission Award - A$20,000. Awarded annually. Established in 1979.

907 ■ NSW Premier's Translation Prize
To recognize Australian translators who translate literary works into English from other languages. Works can include stage and radio plays, poetry, and works of fiction and non-fiction. A medallion and monetary prize of A$30,000 are awarded annually as part of the New South Wales Premier's Literary Awards (see separate entry).

908 ■ Premier's History Awards
Honors distinguished achievement in history by Australians. Six prizes are awarded. Each prize includes a monetary award of $15,000. Prizes include: Australian History Prize, the General History Prize, Community and Regional History Prize, the Young People's History Prize, the

Awards are arranged in alphabetical order below their administering organizations

Audio/Visual History Prize and the John and Patricia Ward History Prize. Established in 1997.

909 ■ Northern Territory Library
Jo McGill, Dir.
GPO Box 42
Darwin, Northern Territory 0801, Australia
Ph: 61 8 9220785
Fax: 61 8 9220760
E-mail: ntl.info@nt.gov.au
URL: http://www.ntl.nt.gov.au

910 ■ Northern Territory Literary Awards
To encourage Territorians to express their creative and essay writing talents while promoting literacy and literary excellence. The following awards are presented: Chief Minister's History Book, Charles Darwin University Essay Award, Charles Darwin University Bookshop Travel Short Story Award, Dymocks Aboriginal Torres Strait Islander Writers' Award, Dymocks Arafura Short Story Award, Dymocks Red Earth Poetry Award, Kath Manzie Youth Literary Award, Darwin Festival Script Award, and the Birch Carroll and Coyle Screenwriting Award. Over $5,000 in prize money is awarded annually. The winners of each category receive a cheque and a certificate.

911 ■ Nursery and Garden Industry Australia
Mr. Robert Prince, CEO
PO Box 907
Epping, New South Wales 1710, Australia
Ph: 61 2 98765200
Fax: 61 2 98766360
E-mail: info@ngia.com.au
URL: http://www.ngia.com.au/MainMenu

912 ■ Community Award
Recognizes industry businesses for outstanding commitment to local communities, outside of those related to day-to-day business operations. Awarded biennially in even-numbered years.

913 ■ Environmental Award
Recognizes an industry business for showing initiative in environmental management. Awarded biennially in even-numbered years.

914 ■ Garden Centre Awards
To recognize the best garden centers in Australia. Awards are presented in three categories: Best Small Garden Centre (turnover up to A$750,000); Best Medium Garden Centre (turnover between A$750,000 and A$2 million); and Best Large Garden Centre (turnover greater than A$2 million). Awarded biennially in even-numbered years.

915 ■ Production Nursery Awards
To recognize the best production nurseries in Australia. Awards are presented in three categories based on FTE (full-time equivalent) staff numbers: Best Small Production Nursery (5 or fewer FTE staff); Best Medium Production Nursery (Six to 15 FTE staff); and Best Large Production Nursery (more than 15 FTE staff). Also recognizes the Best Government Nursery and Best Propagation Nursery. Awarded biennially in even-numbered years.

916 ■ Supplier Award
Recognizes product and service suppliers for outstanding contributions and exemplary services. Awarded biennially in even-numbered years.

917 ■ Training Award
Recognizes industry businesses for outstanding approaches and commitment to staff training. Awarded biennially in even-numbered years.

918 ■ Organ Historical Trust of Australia
Dr. Kelvin Hastie, Sec.
PO Box 200
Camberwell, Victoria 3124, Australia

Ph: 61 2 95252638
E-mail: khas@bigpond.com
URL: http://www.ohta.org.au

919 ■ Christopher Dearnley Award
To recognize new recordings or the re-release of archival recordings made on Australian pipe organs, or Australian recordings involving a significant local pipe organ component. A monetary prize is awarded periodically.

920 ■ Charles Ivor Matthews Memorial Scholarship
To stimulate research into the history of organ-building in Australia. Awarded annually.

921 ■ Pacific Area Newspaper Publishers' Association
Mark Hollands, CEO
69-71 Edward St., Level 4
Pyrmont, New South Wales 2009, Australia
Ph: 61 2 83386300
Fax: 61 2 83386311
E-mail: mark.hollands@panpa.org.au
URL: http://panpa.org.au

922 ■ Hegarty Prize
To recognize management potential in young newspaper executives. Prize includes a round the-world trip to study various newspaper operations (value of up to A$8,000) and a plaque. Awarded annually. Established in 1987.

923 ■ Newspaper of the Year Award
To recognize excellent in pre-production and production of newspapers. It rewards high quality results in registration, dot gain, color density, blank density, cut off accuracy, fold, pin marks and tears, and ink set-off. Awards in six circulation categories are presented annually.

924 ■ Park Centre for Mental Health Treatment, Research and Education Queensland Centre for Mental Health Research
John McGrath, Dir.
Dawson House, Level 3
The Park
Wacol, Queensland 4076, Australia
Ph: 61 7 3271 8660
Fax: 61 7 3271 8698
E-mail: john_mcgrath@qcmhr.uq.edu.au
URL: http://www.qcsr.uq.edu.au
Formerly: (2007) Queensland Centre for Schizophrenia Research.

925 ■ Zaccari Fellowship

926 ■ Pharmaceutical Society of Australia
Liesel Wett, CEO
PO Box 42
Deakin West, Australian Capital Territory 2600, Australia
Ph: 61 2 62834777
Fax: 61 2 62852869
E-mail: psa.nat@psa.org.au
URL: http://www.psa.org.au

927 ■ Lifetime Achievement Award
Recognizes dedication to the promotion of professional excellence in the pharmacy profession over a long period of time. Awarded to current PSA members or a retired pharmacists who was a member of PSA for 25 or more years. A monetary grant of $8,000 is presented.

928 ■ Pharmacist of the Year
To recognize a pharmacist for a significant achievement in an area of excellence within the previous year. A gold medal and grant of $8,000 are awarded annually.

929 ■ Young Pharmacist of the Year
To recognize a pharmacist under the age of 35 for a significant achievement in an area of excellence within the previous year. A silver medal and grant of $8,000 are awarded annually.

930 ■ Powerhouse Museum
PO Box K346
Haymarket, New South Wales 1238, Australia

Ph: 61 2 9217 0111
URL: http://www.powerhousemuseum.com

931 ■ International Lace Award
To present a provocative challenge to conventional notions of lace, to inspire new design applications of lace, and to attract a diversity of ideas from many global cultures. Judging criteria are: visual impact, originality and creativity, innovation in design, materials or techniques, skill in execution, and a conceptual interpretation of place. A prize of A$20,000 is awarded to the overall winner. Five A$4,000 prizes are awarded to winners in the following categories: fashion and accessories, traditional techniques, built environment, digital multimedia, and student work. In addition, a People's Choice Prize is awarded.

932 ■ Property Council of Australia
Peter Verwer, CEO
11 Barrack St., Level 1
Sydney, New South Wales 2000, Australia
Ph: 61 2 90331900
Fax: 61 2 90331967
E-mail: info@propertyoz.com.au
URL: http://www.propertyoz.com.au

933 ■ Innovation and Excellence Awards
To recognize outstanding property development in Australia. Awarded annually in a variety of categories. Sponsored by Rider Levett Bucknall. Formerly: Rider Hunt Awards.

934 ■ Psychotherapists and Counsellors Association of Western Australia
Rosemary Watkins, Pres.
PO Box 691
Subiaco, Western Australia 6904, Australia
Ph: 61 8 93887761
E-mail: admin@pacawa.asn.au
URL: http://www.pacawa.iinet.net.au

935 ■ Achievement Award
To recognize an individual whose endeavors in the field have made a significant difference to the profession. Awarded annually. Established in 2005.

936 ■ Recognition Award
To recognize a retiring member of the Association's Management Committee for exceptional contributions to the Association. Candidates must have contributed more than five years of service to the Management Committee. Awarded as merited. Established in 2004.

937 ■ Student Award
For outstanding performance by a student in psychotherapy and counseling, as determined by the student's university. Awarded annually. Established in 2004.

938 ■ Public Relations Institute of Australia
Jon Bisset, CEO
94 Oxford St., Ste. 33
Darlinghurst, New South Wales 2010, Australia
Ph: 61 2 93313346
Fax: 61 2 93313559
E-mail: info@pria.com.au
URL: http://www.pria.com.au

939 ■ National Golden Target Awards
To recognize excellence, best practice, and professionalism in public relations in Australia. Recipients are selected from among the winners of the State Awards for Excellence. Awarded annually.

940 ■ State Awards for Excellence
To recognize excellence, best practice, and professionalism in public relations in each state or territory of Australia. Awarded in the following categories: public affairs, government-sponsored campaigns, internal communications, emergency/crisis communications, community

Awards are arranged in alphabetical order below their administering organizations

relations, investor relations, consumer marketing, business-to-business marketing, special event/observance, environmental, arts, prescription medicines, health organizations, corporate social responsibility, low cost/pro bono, issues management, and recovery communications. Awarded annually. The winners compete for the National Golden Target Awards.

941 ■ Queensland Master Builders Association
417-419 Wickham Terr.
Brisbane, Queensland 4000, Australia
Ph: 61 7 3225 6444
Fax: 61 7 3225 6545
E-mail: ask@masterbuilders.asn.au
URL: http://www.masterbuilders.asn.au

942 ■ Housing and Construction Awards
To promote and showcase excellence in Queensland's housing and construction industry. Awarded annually in more than 50 categories. Winners in each category become finalists in the National Excellence in Building and Construction Awards, presented by the national Master Builders Australia organization (see separate entry).

943 ■ Railway Technical Society of Australasia
Mr. Martin Baggott, Chm.
PO Box 6238
Kingston, Australian Capital Territory 2604, Australia
Ph: 61 2 62706569
Fax: 61 2 62732358
E-mail: admin@rtsa.com.au
URL: http://rtsa.com.au

944 ■ Contact Mechanics Award
Awarded to the author of an outstanding final year undergraduate project on a topic related to the 'contact conditions between the wheel and rail and the consequence of those conditions in terms of material behavior and damage models'. Awarded annually. A monetary prize of $2,000 is presented.

945 ■ Industry Award
To recognize an engineering achievement in the railway industry that is considered worthy of public recognition. A plaque is awarded biennially in even-numbered years.

946 ■ Student Thesis Award
To recognize the author of an outstanding final year project undertaken in Australia or New Zealand on a topic in railway engineering. The project may be in any engineering discipline provided that it is the subject of railway engineering. A plaque and monetary prize of $4,000 are awarded biennially in even-numbered years.

947 ■ Young Railway Engineers Award
To recognize young professional engineers, technologists, or associates in Australia or New Zealand. Awarded annually.

948 ■ Risk Management Institution of Australasia
Mr. Brian Roylett, Pres.
Level 8, 600 Bourke St.
Melbourne, Victoria 3000, Australia
Ph: 61 3 83411000
Fax: 61 3 93475575
E-mail: customerservice@rmia.org.au
URL: http://www.rmia.org.au

949 ■ Risk Manager of the Year
To recognize an individual for delivering excellence in the management of risk for their organization. Awarded annually.

950 ■ RMIT University
GPO Box 2476
Melbourne, Victoria 3001, Australia
Ph: 61 3 9925 2000

Fax: 61 3 9663 2764
URL: http://www.rmit.edu.au

951 ■ J. N. McNichol Prize
For recognition of achievement and to encourage professional development in the field of technology. Nominees must have exhibited outstanding academic achievement, leadership potential, initiative, and successful completion of an undergraduate course at the Royal Melbourne Institute of Technology. A monetary award of A$3,000, medal, and certificate are awarded annually. Established in 1976 by E. J. Reilly in memory of J. N. McNichol for his assistance and encouragement to students.

952 ■ Francis Ormond Medal
To recognize a member of the Institute's academic, teaching, or general staff who has served the Institute with distinction or has given meritorious service which has not been recognized by the Institute by any other honorary award. A medal is awarded annually. Established in 1983 in memory of Francis Ormond, founder of the Institute and president of the Council (1882-1889).

953 ■ Royal Australasian College of Dental Surgeons
W. Bischof, Pres.
37 York St., Level 13
Sydney, New South Wales 2000, Australia
Ph: 61 2 92626044
Fax: 61 2 92621974
E-mail: registrar@racds.org
URL: http://www.racds.org

954 ■ Academic Prize
To honor final year dental students who have demonstrated outstanding academic achievement. A monetary prize of A$500 is awarded annually.

955 ■ F. G. Christensen Memorial Prize
For recognition of a candidate who gains the highest marks in the College's Primary Examination. A dentist who is enrolled with the College, and has passed the Primary Examination is eligible. A monetary prize of A$500 and a bronze medallion are awarded annually on the recommendation of the examiners. Established in 1971 by the late Dr. F.G. Christensen.

956 ■ Honorary Fellowship
To honor an individual who has rendered long distinguished service to the College and the profession. Awarded when merited. Established in 1965.

957 ■ Meritorious Service Award
To honor an individual who has rendered long distinguished service to the College. Awarded when merited. Established in 1983.

958 ■ Presidential Commendation
To honor an individual who has made a contribution of great significance to the College in its continuing development and activities. Awarded at the discretion of the President. Established in 1998.

959 ■ Kenneth J. G. Sutherland Prize
For recognition of a candidate who gains the highest marks in General Dentistry by demonstrating eminence in the elective section of the College's General Stream Final Examination. To be eligible, candidates must be dentists enrolled in the College and eligible to take the Final Examination held in late January each year. A monetary prize of A$500 and the College Medal are awarded annually when merited at Scientific Meetings of the College. Established in 1987 by Emeritus Professor Kenneth J.G. Sutherland, AM.

960 ■ Young Lecturer Award
To recognize a young dental surgeon for talent

in the manner and demeanor of his or her lecture at the biennial Convocation, as well as the lecture's scientific and clinical content. Candidates need not be members of the College; however, they must have graduated within 10 years prior to the Convocation. A monetary prize of A$2,500 is biennially in even-numbered years. Established in 1998.

961 ■ Royal Australian and New Zealand College of Ophthalmologists
Richard Stawell, Pres.
94-98 Chalmers St.
Surry Hills, New South Wales 2010, Australia
Ph: 61 2 96901001
Fax: 61 2 96901321
E-mail: ranzco@ranzco.edu
URL: http://www.ranzco.edu

962 ■ College Medal
This, the highest honor of the College, is given to recognize Fellows for service to the College and/or furtherance of its aims that is distinguished, meritorious, and selfless. Awarded annually.

963 ■ Distinguished Service Award
To recognize an individual for distinguished or signal service or for outstanding contribution to the College or the profession of ophthalmology. Awarded annually.

964 ■ Meritorious Service Award
Awarded at the branch or federal level for meritorious service or performance of duty to the College, medicine, ophthalmology, education, research or the community that is notable and worthy or recognition. Awarded annually.

965 ■ Royal Australian Chemical Institute
Prof. David Wood, Pres.
1/21 Vale St.
North Melbourne, Victoria 3051, Australia
Ph: 61 3 93282033
Fax: 61 3 93282670
E-mail: member@raci.org.au
URL: http://www.raci.org.au

966 ■ Applied Research Medal
For recognition of a significant contribution towards the development of innovation in applied research, or in industrial fields. Members of the Institute are eligible. An honorarium of A$250 and a bronze medal are awarded annually. Each awarding of the medal is named for a distinguished chemist. Established in 1980.

967 ■ Biota Award for Medicinal Chemistry
To encourage the design and development by younger chemists of small molecules as potential therapeutic agents for medicinal chemistry. The Medal will be awarded to the chemist judged to be responsible for the best drug design and development paper published, patent taken out, or commercial-in-confidence report concerning small molecules as potential therapeutic agents. Only members of the RACI under the age of 35 are eligible. A monetary prize of A$5,000 Australian and a medal are awarded annually. The recipient shall deliver a lecture on the topic of the award at a RACI meeting or a division meeting.

968 ■ A.J. Birch Medal
To recognize a member for excellence in organic chemical research conducted in Australia. A medal is awarded annually. Administered by the Institute's Organic Chemistry Division.

969 ■ Bruno Breyer Medal
To recognize an individual for internationally recognized contributions in the field of electrochemistry. Awarded every four years. Established in honor of Bruno Breyer, a pioneer of AC polarography in Australia. Administered by the Institute's Electrochemistry Division.

Awards are arranged in alphabetical order below their administering organizations

970 ■ Burrows Award

To recognize an individual for outstanding contributions to inorganic chemistry. A citation, metal sculpture, and travel expenses are awarded annually, if merited. Established in 1975 in honor of George Burrows, pioneer in metal-tertiary arsine complexes. Administered by the Institute's Inorganic Chemistry Division.

971 ■ Centenary of Federation Teaching Awards in Chemistry

To recognize and reward outstanding excellence in the teaching of chemistry in Australia at both school and university levels. The Primary and Secondary Award is offered on the basis of one per state; the Tertiary Award is made nationally to an individual who is a financial member of the Institute. Each award consists of an inscribed certificate and monetary prize of A$500. Awarded annually.

972 ■ Citations for Contributions to Chemistry and the Chemical Profession

To honor individuals who make substantial contributions to chemistry and especially to the progress of the profession over a period of many years. To provide recognition of these contributions, the Institute has initiated a series of citations. The awarding of citations are based on contributions to research, development or application of chemistry; contributions to chemistry in other disciplines or technologies; contributions to chemical education; contributions to the promotion of chemistry; service to RACI. Up to three citations may be awarded in a calendar year.

973 ■ Cornforth Medal

To recognize an RACI member for the most outstanding Ph.D. thesis submitted in a branch of chemistry, chemical science, or chemical technology in the previous 13 months. A candidate's degree must have been approved by the governing body of an Australian University, although not necessarily conferred, in the previous 13 months. No candidate may be nominated more than once. Each Australian university may nominate one candidate through the Deputy Vice-Chancellor (Research) or person holding the equivalent office of the University. A bronze relief medal and cash prize are awarded annually.

974 ■ Distinguished Fellowship Award

For recognition of highly distinguished contributions to the profession in academia, government or industry and the Institute. Awarded to an individual on, or very close to, retirement from principal professional role. Restricted to Fellows of the Institute. Usually not more than three fellowships are awarded per year. Established in 1996.

975 ■ Green Chemistry Challenge Awards

To recognize and promote fundamental and innovative chemical methods that accomplish pollution prevention through source reduction, and to recognize contributions to education in green chemistry, which involves a reduction in or elimination of the use or generation of hazardous materials from a chemical process. Awards are presented in three categories: small business sector; academic or government institution; and education. Awarded annually.

976 ■ Leighton Memorial Medal

For recognition of eminent services to chemistry in its broadest sense. A medal is awarded annually in May. The medal is silver and has a particularly beautiful design showing a profile of Leighton on the obverse, and a design symbolizing the chemical industry on the reverse. Established in 1965 in honor of A.E. Leighton.

977 ■ Masson Memorial Scholarship Prize

To facilitate further study in the field of chemistry.

Open to financial candidates wishing to proceed to BSc Honours or the fourth year of a BSc Honours course or the first postgraduate year following 4-year courses such as BAppScience, BSc (Industrial Chemistry), BSc (Chemical Engineering) or BE (Chemical Engineering) or their equivalent, at their own or any other approved institution. A monetary prize of A$500 is awarded annually. Established as a memorial to the late Sir David Orme Masson, Founder of the Institute.

978 ■ Organic Lectureship

To recognize a recently appointed organic chemist by allowing him or her to travel around Australia to present the results of his or her research work. There is no age limit, but nominees must have been appointed to their first academic or industrial position within the previous five years. Travel and accommodation expenses up to A$3,000 are awarded. Administered by the Institute's Organic Chemistry Division.

979 ■ Organometallic Chemistry Award

To recognize a member for exceptional contributions to the development of organometallic chemistry. A medallion and monetary prize are awarded annually. The recipient may also be invited to lecture at branch and divisional conferences.

980 ■ Physical Chemistry Division Medal

To recognize an individual for outstanding contributions to the field of physical chemistry in Australia. A medal and invitation to lecture are awarded no more frequently than every two years.

981 ■ C. S. Piper Prize

To recognize a RACI member for the best published original research work carried out mainly in Australia in the fields of either soil chemistry or the mineral nutrition of plants. The successful candidate will deliver a lecture on the occasion of the presentation of the award and may be invited to lecture to other branches of the Institute. A medal, a monetary prize of $8,000, plus $2,000 travel expenses, if required, are awarded biennially in even-numbered years when merited.

982 ■ Rennie Memorial Medal

For recognition of published research. Members of the Institute who have less than 8 years of professional experience since completing their degree, have contributed towards the development of some branch of chemical science can apply. A medal is awarded annually. Established in 1931 in honor of E.H. Rennie.

983 ■ Alan Sargeson Inorganic Lectureship Award

To recognize an early career researcher for significant and innovative contributions to inorganic chemistry. Candidates must be Australian or New Zealand nationals within 10 years of their PhD. Awarded every 18 to 24 months. Established in 2006. Administered by the Institute's Inorganic Chemistry Division.

984 ■ H. G. Smith Memorial Award

To recognize the individual who has contributed the most to the development of some branch of chemical science. The contribution is judged by research work published or accepted for publication during the ten years immediately preceding the award. Most of the work should have been done in Australia while the candidate was an Institute member. An honorarium and a bronze medal are awarded annually. Established in 1929 in memory of H.G. Smith. Formerly: (2006) H. G. Smith Medal.

985 ■ R.H. Stokes Medal

To recognize an individual for distinguished research in the field of electrochemistry carried

out mainly in Australia. A medal is awarded when merited. Administered by the Institute's Electrochemistry Division.

986 ■ Don Stranks Awards

To recognize student members for outstanding performance in research within a PhD candidature. Two awards of A$300 each are awarded biennially in odd-numbered years. Established in 2000. Administered by the Institute's Inorganic Chemistry Division.

987 ■ Weickhardt Medal for Distinguished Contribution to Economic Advancement

To recognize a member for significant contributions toward the economic advancement of the Australian economy through work in chemistry. A medal is awarded annually. Established in honor of Leonard William Weickhardt, a fellow of the Institute.

988 ■ Royal College of Nursing - Australia

Debra Cerasa, CEO
PO Box 219
Deakin West, Australian Capital Territory 2600, Australia
Ph: 61 2 62833400
Fax: 61 2 62823565
E-mail: canberra@rcna.org.au
URL: http://www.rcna.org.au

989 ■ National Research Grants and Scholarships

To assist registered nurses to undertake both tertiary and/or postgraduate education, training, and/or research activities. Several scholarships and grants are awarded annually.

990 ■ Patricia Slater Award

To honor a Registered/Division 1 nurse who is a member of RCNA. A certificate and travel grant are awarded annually.

991 ■ Royal Federation of Aero Clubs of Australia

Ms. Marj Davis, Pres.
PO Box 72
Canberra, Australian Capital Territory 2612, Australia
Ph: 61 2 62539724
Fax: 61 2 62539281
E-mail: rfaca@ozemail.com.au
URL: http://www.rfaca.com.au

992 ■ Jack Fahey Memorial Award

Recognizes an individual who have made distinguished contributions to the Aero club movement or who have developed new concepts that aid to the viability of Aero clubs. Only members of the RFACA are eligible.

993 ■ Federation Award

To recognize club members and/or employees who, by virtue of their individual commitment over many years, make an outstanding contribution to their Club. Up to four recipients are honored each year. Established in 1962.

994 ■ Oswald Watt Gold Medal

To recognize the most notable contribution to aviation by an Australian or in Australia. Established in 1921.

995 ■ Royal Historical Society of Queensland

Carolyn Nolan, Pres.
PO Box 12057
Brisbane, Queensland 4003, Australia
Ph: 61 7 32214198
Fax: 61 7 32214698
E-mail: info@queenslandhistory.org.au
URL: http://queenslandhistory.org.au

996 ■ Fellowships

To recognize conspicuous scholarly service to the Society. Nominees must have been Society members for at least 10 years. Up to three awards may be made each year.

Awards are arranged in alphabetical order below their administering organizations

997 ■ Honourary Life Membership

For long or outstanding service to the Society. A lifetime membership to the Society is awarded as merited.

998 ■ John Douglas Kerr Medal of Distinction for History

To recognize an individual for excellence in historiography (historical research and writing) in the context of Queensland history in any of its themes and disciplines. Awarded annually. Established in 2005.

999 ■ MacGregor Medal

For conspicuous service to the society, other than that of a scholarly nature. Eligible to members of at least 10 years. Up to three medals may be awarded each year.

1000 ■ Royal Society of New South Wales

Mr. J.R. Hardie, Pres.
University of Sydney
Bldg. H47
Sydney, New South Wales 2006, Australia
Ph: 61 2 90365282
Fax: 61 2 90365309
E-mail: info@nsw.royalsoc.org.au
URL: http://nsw.royalsoc.org.au

1001 ■ Walter Burfitt Prize

To recognize the worker whose contributions published during the past six years are deemed of the highest scientific merit in pure or applied science. Only investigations described for the first time and carried out by the author resident in Australia or New Zealand are considered. The prize is awarded triennially when merited. Established in 1957 as a result of generous gifts by Dr. and Mrs. W. F. Burfitt.

1002 ■ Clarke Memorial Lectureship

To recognize an individual for advancement in geology. Awarded biennially in odd-numbered years. The lectures are published in the Society's Journal. Established in 1903.

1003 ■ Clarke Memorial Medal

For recognition of distinguished work in the natural sciences done in or on the Australian Commonwealth and its territories in one of the following three categories: geology, mineralogy, and natural history. A medal is awarded annually when merited. Established in 1878 in memory of Reverend William Branwhite Clarke, Vice-President of the Society, 1866-1878.

1004 ■ James Cook Medal

For recognition of outstanding contributions to science and human welfare in and for the Southern Hemisphere. A medal is awarded periodically. Established in 1947.

1005 ■ Edgeworth David Medal

To recognize Australian research workers under the age of 35 for work done mainly in Australia or its territories, or for contributions to the advancement of Australian science. A medal is awarded annually when merited. Established in 1948.

1006 ■ Liversidge Lectureship

To recognize an individual for outstanding research in chemistry. Awarded biennially in even-numbered years. The lectures are published in the Society's Journal. Established under the terms of a bequest by Prof. Archibald Liversidge.

1007 ■ Archibald D. Olle Prize

To recognize the member of the Society who has submitted the best paper during the year. A cash award of A$500 is presented periodically. Established in 1956. Established under the terms of a bequest by Mrs. A. D. Olle.

1008 ■ Poggendorff Lecture

To recognize an individual for accomplishment in the broad field of Agriculture. Held every 2 or 3 years. In honor of Walter Hans George Poggendorff.

1009 ■ Pollock Memorial Lecture

Awarded approximately every four years in memory of Prof. J.A. Pollock, Dse, FRS, Professor of Physics, University of Sydney (1899-1922). The Lectures are published in the Society's Journal. Established 1949. Sponsored by the Royal Society of N.S.W. and the University of Sydney.

1010 ■ Society's Medal

To recognize a member of the Society for meritorious contributions to the advancement of science, including administration and organization of scientific endeavor, and for recognition of services to the Society. A medal is awarded annually when merited. Established in 1882.

1011 ■ Royal Society of South Australia

J.T. Jennings PhD, Pres.
North Terr.
Adelaide, South Australia 5005, Australia
Ph: 61 8 82077590
Fax: 61 8 82077222
E-mail: roysocsa@gmail.com
URL: http://www.adelaide.edu.au/rssa
Formerly: (1880) Adelaide Philosophical Society.

1012 ■ H.G. Andrewartha Medal

Recognizes outstanding contributions to research by a scientist aged a maximum of 40 years in the year of the award. Candidates should demonstrate a clear connection with South Australia by research field or employment. Selection is based on published research within the fields covered by the activities of the Society. Awarded annually.

1013 ■ Postgraduate Student Prize

Students in the natural sciences throughout South Australia are invited to present their research at an Ordinary meeting of the Society. Six to eight students are selected to make presentations throughout the year on the basis of their submitted abstract. The student adjudged to have made the best presentation receives free membership of the Society for one year, a one year subscription to the Transactions of the Royal Society of South Australia, and a cash prize. Established in 2000.

1014 ■ Publication Medal

Recognizes the most outstanding paper published in the Transactions of the Royal Society of South Australia. Authors aged 40 or younger who are Fellows of the Society are eligible. Also encourages and rewards high quality scientific publication by younger scientists. Awarded as merited.

1015 ■ Verco Medal

For recognition of distinguished scientific work published by a member of the Society. The Council of the Society makes the award on the recommendation of the Society's awards committee, which considers members of the Society who have been nominated by fellow members. A medal is awarded annually when merited. Established in 1928 in honor of Sir Joseph Verco (1851-1933). Formerly: (2006) Sir Joseph Verco Medal.

1016 ■ Royal Society of Victoria

Prof. L. Selwood, Pres.
9 Victoria St.
Melbourne, Victoria 3000, Australia
Ph: 61 3 96635259
Fax: 61 3 96632301
E-mail: rsv@sciencevictoria.org.au
URL: http://www.sciencevictoria.org.au

1017 ■ Research Medal

For recognition of scientific research of outstanding merit in one of the following four categories: biological sciences (non-human)- agriculture, biochemistry, botany, forestry, physiology, zoology, and related (non-human) sciences; earth sciences - geology, geochemistry, geochronology, geophysics, planetary physics, meteorology, oceanography, physical geography, and related sciences; physical sciences - astronomy, chemistry, engineering, mathematics, physics, and related sciences; and human health or medical sciences (human)- genetics, immunology, human physiology, human anatomy, pathology, necrology, epidemiology, parasitology, nuclear medicine, and related human sciences. The work must have been carried out in or on Australia with preference given to work done in Victoria or about Victoria. A silver medal is awarded annually at the Medal Lecture. Established in 1959, the centenary year of the society.

1018 ■ Royal Society of Western Australia

P. O'Brien PhD, Pres.
Locked Bag 49
Welshpool, Western Australia 6986, Australia
E-mail: rswa@museum.wa.gov.au
URL: http://www.rswa.org.au

1019 ■ Medal of the Royal Society of Western Australia

To provide recognition for distinguished work in natural and agricultural science connected with Western Australia. There are no restrictions on eligibility. A sterling silver medallion and a cash award of $250 are awarded every four years. Established in 1924.

1020 ■ Royal Western Australian Historical Society

Dr. Lenore Layman, Pres.
Stirling House
49 Broadway
Nedlands, Western Australia 6009, Australia
Ph: 61 8 93863841
Fax: 61 8 93863309
E-mail: histwest@git.com.au
URL: http://histwest.org.au

1021 ■ Lee-Steere Western Australian History Prize

To recognize outstanding essays on the history of Western Australia. Entries may be on any aspect of Western Australian history, and should be no more than 5,000 words. A monetary prize of A$500 is awarded annually. Established with funds donated by Sir Ernest Lee-Steere.

1022 ■ A. E. Williams History Prize

To recognize the best paper submitted on any aspect of Western Australian history. Open to members of Historical Societies and secondary school students of years 10 to 12 in Western Australia. A monetary award of $400 is awarded every four years, alternating in even-numbered years with the Lee-Steere Western Australian History Prize. Established in 1990.

1023 ■ Royal Zoological Society of New South Wales

Dr. Peter Banks, Pres.
PO Box 20
Mosman, New South Wales 2088, Australia
Ph: 61 2 99697336
Fax: 61 2 99697336
E-mail: office@rzsnsw.org.au
URL: http://www.rzsnsw.org.au

1024 ■ Whitley Awards

For recognition of outstanding publications (printed or electronic) on Australasian fauna or the history of Australasian zoology during the preceding year. Awards are presented in more than a dozen categories, including children's stories, field guides, urban zoology, interactive resources, periodicals, and pocket guides. A silver medal is awarded to the author of the outstanding book; the publisher receives a certificate and citation. Certificates of com-

Awards are arranged in alphabetical order below their administering organizations

mendation are awarded to category winners. Established in 1978 to honor Gilbert Whitley (1903-1975), an Australian zoologist.

1025 ■ Rugby League International Federation
Level 5, 165 Phillip St.
Sydney, New South Wales 2000, Australia
URL: http://www.rlif.co.uk

1026 ■ International Coach of the Year
To recognize an outstanding rugby coach among the member nations of the Federation. Awarded annually. Established in 2008.

1027 ■ International Player of the Year
To recognize an outstanding rugby player among the member nations of the Federation. Awarded annually. Established in 2008.

1028 ■ International Referee of the Year
To recognize an outstanding rugby referee among the member nations of the Federation. Awarded annually. Established in 2004.

1029 ■ Rookie of the Year
To recognize an outstanding rookie rugby player among the member nations of the Federation. Awarded annually. Established in 2008.

1030 ■ Spirit of Rugby League Award
To honor an individual who demonstrates the spirit and sportsmanship of the sport of rugby. Awarded annually. Established in 2008.

1031 ■ Team of the Year
To recognize an outstanding rugby team among the member nations of the Federation. Awarded annually. Established in 2008.

1032 ■ Rugby Union Players' Association
Mr. Rod Kafer, CEO
25 Bligh St., Level 22
Sydney, New South Wales 2000, Australia
Ph: 61 2 92300477
Fax: 61 2 92300489
E-mail: info@rupa.com.au
URL: http://www.rupa.com.au

1033 ■ Newcomer of the Year
To recognize a first- or second-year player who has demonstrated excellence on and off the field. Awarded annually. Established in 2007.

1034 ■ Rugby Medal for Excellence
To recognize a player for outstanding performance on the field as well as outstanding leadership, behavior, charitable work, and rugby community service off the field. Awarded annually. Established in 2001.

1035 ■ St. Kilda Film Festival
Paul Harris, Festival Dir.
Private Bag No. 3
St. Kilda, Victoria 3182, Australia
Ph: 61 3 9209 6490
Fax: 61 3 9209 6790
E-mail: filmfest@portphillip.vic.gov.au
URL: http://www.stkildafilmfestival.com.au

1036 ■ St. Kilda Film Festival
To recognize the best Australian independent short films. More than one dozen monetary prizes are awarded, including the A$10,000 Best Short Film Award, sponsored by the City of Port Phillip. Held annually. Established in 1984.

1037 ■ Society of Automotive Engineers - Australasia
Mr. Patrick Ross, Pres.
70 Dorcas St., Level 2, Ste. B
Southbank, Victoria 3051, Australia
Ph: 61 3 96965190
Fax: 61 3 96965865
E-mail: enquiries@sae-a.com.au
URL: http://www.saea.com.au

1038 ■ Automotive Engineering Excellence Awards
Recognizes excellence in the Australian automotive engineering industry. Awards include: Gold, Silver, and Bronze Awards; Certificate of Commendation; and Young Engineer Award. Awarded annually.

1039 ■ Society of Hospital Pharmacists of Australia
Yvonne Allison, CEO
65 Oxford St., Ste. 3
PO Box 1774
Collingwood, Victoria 3066, Australia
Ph: 61 3 9486 0177
Fax: 61 3 9486 0311
E-mail: shpa@shpa.org.au
URL: http://www.shpa.org.au

1040 ■ Fred J. Boyd Award
To recognize an individual for outstanding contributions to hospital pharmacy in Australia. An invitation to present a lecture is awarded biennially in odd-numbered years. Established in 1978 in honor of the founding president of the Society.

1041 ■ Society of Women Writers - Victoria
Tricia Veale, Pres.
73 Church Rd.
Carrum, Victoria 3197, Australia
Ph: 61 3 97722389
E-mail: fjbartosy@tadaust.org.au
URL: http://home.vicnet.net.au/~swwvic

1042 ■ Alice Award
For recognition of a distinguished and long-term contribution to literature by an Australian woman. Selection is by nomination. A non-acquisitive statuette (The Alice) designed by Alan Ingham accompanied by a hand-lettered certificate are awarded in even-numbered years at the biennial conference. Established in 1978 by the Federal Council to commemorate fifty years of the Society (1925-1975) and the late Alice Booth, a former school teacher and member of the Society in New South Wales.

1043 ■ South Australia Arts and Industry Development
Alex Reid, Exec. Dir.
GPO Box 2308
Adelaide, South Australia 5001, Australia
Ph: 61 8 84635444
Fax: 61 8 84635420
E-mail: artssa@dpc.sa.gov.au
URL: http://www.arts.sa.gov.au/site/page.cfm

1044 ■ Festival Awards for Literature
To recognize distinguished Australian writing in children's literature, fiction, innovation, non-fiction, and poetry. Several awards are presented: the Premier's Award of A$10,000, the Children's Literature Award (A$15,000), Fiction Award (A$15,000), Innovation Award (A$10,000), John Bray Poetry Award (A$15,000), Non-Fiction Award (A$15,000), and Young Adult Fiction Award (A$15,000). Awarded biennially in even-numbered years during Writers' Week as part of the Adelaide Festival. Established in 1976.

1045 ■ Premier's Award
To recognize the most outstanding published work submitted to the Festival Awards for Literature. A monetary prize of A$10,000 is awarded biennially in even-numbered years during Writers' Week as part of the Adelaide Festival.

1046 ■ Special Olympics Australia
Gill Stapleton, CEO
PO Box 62
Concord, New South Wales 2138, Australia
Ph: 61 2 81169833
Fax: 61 2 87321629

E-mail: info@specialolympics.com.au
URL: http://www.specialolympics.com.au

1047 ■ Hall of Fame
To recognize a volunteer who has shown outstanding service to Special Olympics and its athletes. One or more individuals are inducted annually. Established in 2000.

1048 ■ Student Journalism Award
To recognize tertiary students for outstanding journalism about the Special Olympics. Awarded annually.

1049 ■ Speech Pathology Australia
Ms. Gail Mulcair, CEO
2nd Fl., 11-19 Bank Pl.
Melbourne, Victoria 3000, Australia
Ph: 61 3 96424899
Fax: 61 3 96424922
E-mail: office@speechpathologyaustralia.org.au
URL: http://www.speechpathologyaustralia.org.au

1050 ■ Community Contribution Award
Recognizes outside agencies who have made valuable contribution of the profession of speech pathology.

1051 ■ Life Membership
Highest honor bestowed by the association.

1052 ■ Recognition of Service Award
To honor members who have provided ongoing, valuable, and voluntary service to the Association at either a national or branch level. Awarded to up to three recipients annually.

1053 ■ Rookie of the Year
Awarded to a new graduate practicing member if the association in recognition of valuable service to the association at the branch or national level. Award is open to all association members who have completed less than one year of employment as a speech pathologist.

1054 ■ Student Awards
To recognize final-year speech pathology students who have distinguished themselves through outstanding academic achievements including research throughout their course, and/or excellent clinical achievements throughout the course. Each university determines the winner of their Student Award in the way that best suits their institution. Awarded annually.

1055 ■ Elinor Wray Award
Awarded for outstanding contributions to the field of speech pathology in research, student training, innovations in diagnostic, assessment or treatment procedures or in the promotion of speech pathology. Any person within the speech pathology profession is eligible. Named in honor of Elinor Wray, founder of the speech pathology profession in Australia. Established in 1981.

1056 ■ Sport Australia Hall of Fame Ltd.
Robert Lay, Gen. Mgr.
615 St. Kilda Rd.
PO Box 6873
Melbourne, Victoria 8008, Australia
Ph: 61 3 9510 2066
Fax: 61 3 9510 2110
E-mail: mail@sahof.org.au
URL: http://www.sahof.org.au

1057 ■ Sport Australia Hall of Fame
For recognition of outstanding achievement in Australian sport (Member), and in functions associated with Australian sporting achievement, such as sports administration, coaching, science, or media (Associate Member). Nominations may be submitted by anyone but must be endorsed by the relevant national sporting association or the Hall of Fame Selection Committee. A medal is awarded to Members; a certificate is awarded to Associate Members. Awarded annually. Estab-

Awards are arranged in alphabetical order below their administering organizations

lished in 1985 by Garry Jeffery Daly. In 1995, the program was placed under the management of the National Sport Australia Hall of Fame Trust.

1058 ■ Sport Management Association of Australia and New Zealand
Assoc. Prof. Paul Jonson, Pres.
La Trobe University
School of Management
Centre for Sport and Social Impact
Bundoora, Victoria 3086, Australia
Ph: 61 3 94791343
Fax: 61 3 94791010
E-mail: info@smaanz.org
URL: http://www.smaanz.org

1059 ■ Student Research Award
To support research-based honors, masters, and doctoral degree candidates who have completed or are completing their degree in sport management. Awarded annually.

1060 ■ State Library of New South Wales
Macquarie St.
Sydney, New South Wales 2000, Australia
Ph: 61 2 9273 1414
Fax: 61 2 9273 1255
E-mail: library@sl.nsw.gov.au
URL: http://www.sl.nsw.gov.au

1061 ■ C. H. Currey Memorial Fellowship
To encourage the writing of Australian history from the original sources. A monetary prize of A$20,000 is awarded annually. Established in 1975 in honor of Charles Herbert Currey, an Australian historian.

1062 ■ Nancy Keesing Fellowship
For research into any aspect of Australian life and culture using the resources of the state library of New South Wales, Australia. A monetary prize of A$12,000 is awarded annually. Established in 1994 in honor of Nancy Keesing, author and poet.

1063 ■ Nita B. Kibble Literary Award
To encourage Australian women writers, to advance Australian literature, and to benefit the community. A monetary prize of A$30,000 is awarded annually. Established by Nita May Dobbie in memory of her aunt, the first woman appointed a librarian in the State Library of New South Wales.

1064 ■ State Library of Victoria
328 Swanston St.
Melbourne, Victoria 3000, Australia
Ph: 61 3 8664 7000
Fax: 61 3 9639 4737
E-mail: pla@slv.vic.gov.au
URL: http://www.slv.vic.gov.au
Formerly: (1997) Australia Arts Victoria.

1065 ■ Prize for Science Writing
To recognize a popular science book aimed at non-specialist readers. Its goal is to encourage discussion and understanding of scientific ideas in the wider community, to nurture a culture of innovation in Victoria through support of scientific endeavor, and to encourage the writing of popular science books for non-specialist readers. Awarded biennially in odd-numbered years.

1066 ■ Prize for Young Adult Fiction
To recognize an outstanding published novel or collection of short stories written for a readership between the ages of 13 and 18. Awarded annually.

1067 ■ Grollo Ruzzene Foundation Prize for Writing about Italians in Australia
To encourage people from all backgrounds to write about the experience of Italians in Australia. Eligible works include migration studies, histo-

ries, travel narratives, published plays and screenplays, biographies, collections of poems, and novels for adults or children. Awarded annually.

1068 ■ Village Roadshow Prize for Screen Writing
To recognize an outstanding screenplay of a feature-length fiction film or the script of a television drama program. Awarded annually.

1069 ■ Stroke Society of Australasia
Prof. Richard Lindley, Pres.
PO Box 576
Crows Nest, New South Wales 1585, Australia
Ph: 61 2 94318660
Fax: 61 2 94318677
E-mail: ssa@apcaust.com.au
URL: http://www.strokesociety.com.au

1070 ■ New Investigators Awards
To recognize the most outstanding presentations by new investigators at each annual scientific meeting. Candidates must be members of Society and be undergoing or have completed an accredited post-graduate/undergraduate training program, or commenced full-time academic research, whichever is most recent, no more than five years before the closing date for abstracts. Awarded to two recipients annually.

1071 ■ Sweet Mother International
Julie Anne Nze-Bertram, Coor.
9 Northside Ct.
Evanston Gardens
Gawler, South Australia 5116, Australia
Ph: 61 407918735
E-mail: sweetmotherinternational@yahoo.com
URL: http://sweetmother0.tripod.com

1072 ■ Golden Mother Award
Honors the mothers of distinguished personalities who have contributed the social development. Awardees have included the mothers of political leaders, sports heroes, musical stars, and academic luminaries.

1073 ■ Sydney Cultural Council
St. Martins Tower, Level 12
31 Market St.
Sydney, New South Wales 2000, Australia
Ph: 61 2 9261 8366
Fax: 61 2 9261 8161
E-mail: info@sydneyeisteddfod.com.au
URL: http://www.sydneyeisteddfod.com.au
Formerly: (1975) City of Sydney Eisteddfod.

1074 ■ Allison/Henderson Sydney Eisteddfod Piano Scholarship
To encourage professional piano development. Contestants must be between 16 and 25 years of age. Both amateur and professional pianists, men and women (a) born in Australia or New Zealand; or (b) naturalized citizens of Australia who have been domiciled in Australia or New Zealand for at least six years may enter. Finalists will perform their own choice of one major work with a performance time of minimum 14 and maximum 22 minutes. A scholarship totaling A$12,000 is awarded to the winner, with A$500 going to each finalist. Awarded annually. Established in 1982. Formerly: John Allison City of Sydney Piano Scholarship; (1998) City of Sydney Piano Scholarship.

1075 ■ McDonald's Ballet Scholarship
To encourage professional development in ballet. Dancers who are amateur or professional, male or female, between 15 and 19 years of age are eligible. Dancers must be citizens or permanent residents of Australia of New Zealand or have lived in these countries for more than three years. Outright winner receives a $3,000 cash prize and a $15,000 scholarship; second place winner receives a $2,000 cash prize and a

$10,000 scholarship; six finalists each receive $1,000 cash prizes. Established in 1974. Formerly: Rothmans Foundation Ballet Scholarship; (1998) GIO Australia Ballet Scholarship.

1076 ■ McDonald's Operatic Aria
To encourage professional vocal development. Both amateur and professional singers, men and women (a) born in Australia or New Zealand; or (b) naturalized citizens of Australia who have been domiciled in Australia or New Zealand for at least six years are eligible. No previous winners are eligible. The age limit is 35 years of age on December 31. The following prizes are awarded: (1) Grand Prize - a monetary prize of A$5,000, a scholarship of $35,000, a travel grant, and a portfolio of professional studio photographs; (2) Second Prize - A$5,000; (3) six finalists - A$1,000 each; and (4) eight semifinalists A$500 each. Awarded annually. Established in 1933. Formerly: Sydney *Sun* Aria Contest.

1077 ■ Sydney Film Festival
Clare Stewart, Dir.
PO Box 96
Strawberry Hills, New South Wales 2012, Australia
Ph: 61 9690 5333
Fax: 61 2 9319 0055
E-mail: info@sff.org.au
URL: http://www.sff.org.au

1078 ■ CRC Multicultural Award
To recognize the best film produced in Australia during the preceding year among the Dendy Award finalists that reflects the cultural diversity of Australia. Maximum running time is 59 minutes. To qualify, the film must meet one of the following criteria: treat issues arising from the Australian immigration and settlement process; address general issues in one or more cross-cultural settings; or contain material or languages that celebrate the cultural and linguistic diversity of Australia. A monetary award of A$5,000 is awarded annually in one of the following categories: documentary, fiction, and general, for films concerned with exploring the formal possibilities of film as an end in itself or made as a personal response to some area of the filmmaker's experience while articulating that response is an end in itself. Established in 1992. Sponsored by Community Relations Commission (CRC) for a Multicultural New South Wales.

1079 ■ Dendy Awards for Australian Short Films
To recognize the best films made in Australia during the preceding year. Maximum running time is 59 minutes at 24 frames per second. Films produced by television stations or made for a television series are not eligible. The following prizes are awarded: Live Action Short Award (A$5,000), Yoram Gross Animation Award (A$4,000), CRC Award (A$5,000), and the Rouben Mamoulian Award (A$5,000). Presented during the opening night ceremony of the Sydney Film Festival. Awarded annually. Established in 1970. Formerly: (1988) Greater Union Awards; (1974) Benson and Hedges Awards.

1080 ■ FOXTEL Australian Documentary Prize
To recognize the best documentary film at the Sydney Film Festival. A monetary prize of A$10,000 is awarded annually. Established in 2009.

1081 ■ Symphony Services Australia
Kate Lidbetter, CEO
1 Oxford St., Level 5, Ste. 2
PO Box 1145
Darlinghurst, New South Wales 1300, Australia
Ph: 61 2 8622 9400

Awards are arranged in alphabetical order below their administering organizations

Fax: 61 2 8622 9422
E-mail: info@symphony.net.au
URL: http://www.symphony.net.au

1082 ■ Young Performers Awards

To encourage professional development of young solo musicians. Awards are presented in three categories: strings, keyboard, and instrumental. Individuals under 18 and 30 years of age who are citizens or permanent residents of Australia are eligible. A monetary prize of A$5,000 is presented to the best performer in each category. The overall winner is designated the Young Performer of the Year and receives a monetary award of a further A$20,000 and concert engagements with Symphony Australia orchestras. Awarded annually. Established in 1944. Formerly: (1986) ABC Young Performers' Competition; (1985) Instrumental and Vocal Competition; (1967) ABC Concerts and Vocal Competition.

1083 ■ Trust Co., Ltd.
John Atkin, Managing Dir.
Level 4, 35 Clarence St.
GPO Box 4270
Sydney, New South Wales 2001, Australia
Ph: 61 2 8295 8100
Fax: 61 2 8295 8659
E-mail: info@trust.com.au
URL: http://www.trust.com.au

1084 ■ Miles Franklin Literary Award

To encourage and assist the advancement of Australian literature and for recognition of a novel or play that portrays an aspect of Australian life. Novels must be first published during the year preceding the award. A monetary prize of $42,000 (Australian) is awarded annually. Established in 1954 in memory of Miles Franklin, an Australian author.

1085 ■ Portia Geach Memorial Award

For recognition of the best portraits painted from life of a man or woman distinguished in art, letters, or the sciences. Any female artist, resident in Australia during the preceding twelve months, who was born in Australia or was British born or has become a naturalized Australian and whose place of domicile is Australia is eligible. A monetary prize of $18,000 is awarded annually. Established in 1965 by a bequest of Miss Florence Kate Geach, who died in 1962, in memory of her sister, Portia Geach.

1086 ■ Turner Syndrome Association of Australia
Sean Kenny, Natl. Pres.
PO Box 3112
Warner, Queensland 4500, Australia
Ph: 61 7 32986635
Fax: 61 7 32986647
E-mail: info@turnersyndrome.org.au
URL: http://www.turnersyndrome.org.au

1087 ■ Mandy Award

Awarded to an individual who supported individuals with Turner syndrome. A trophy is awarded annually. Established in honor of Mandy Fisher, who was born with Turner Syndrome in 1981.

1088 ■ *TV Week*
35-51 Mitchell St.
McMahons Point, New South Wales 2060, Australia
Ph: 61 2 9464 3300
Fax: 61 2 9464 3375
URL: http://tvweek.ninemsn.com.au
Formerly: (1995) Southdown Press.

1089 ■ Logie Awards

To acknowledge and honor Australia's most popular television performers and programs, along with outstanding contributions in all areas - from news and public affairs, to light entertain-

ment and drama. The program or performance must have occurred during the calendar year for which the awards are presented. Awards are given in the following categories: Public Voted Awards - Most Popular Personality on Australian TV, Most Popular Actor and Actress on Australian TV, Most Popular Comedy Personality, Most Popular Sports Program, Most Popular Comedy Program, Most Popular Light Entertainment/Program, Most Popular Light Entertainment Personality, Most Popular Sports Event, Most Popular Series, Most Popular Children's Program, Most Popular Public Affairs Program, and Most Popular New Talent in Australia; Most Popular Lifestyle/Information Program Most Popular Series, Most Popular Sports Event, and Panel Voted Awards - Hall of Fame, Most Outstanding Actor and Actress, Most Outstanding Achievement in Public Affairs, Most Outstanding Documentary (Series or Program), Most Outstanding Achievement in News, Most Outstanding Achievement in Sports, Most Outstanding Achievement in Drama, and Most Outstanding Achievement in Comedy. Statuettes, including Silver TV Week Logie Awards for Australia's most popular actor and actresses, and a Gold TV Week Logie Award for Australian television's most popular personality are awarded annually. Established in 1958. The TV Week Logie Award is named after Scottish John Logie Baird, the inventor of television.

1090 ■ United Nations Association of Australia, Victorian Division
Level 3, 190 Queen St.
GPO Box 45
Melbourne, Victoria 3001, Australia
Ph: 61 3 96707878
Fax: 61 3 96709993
E-mail: info@unaavictoria.org.au
URL: http://www.unaavictoria.org.au

1091 ■ Founders' Award

To recognize individuals who have demonstrated a commitment to peace, conflict resolution, human rights, and social justice. Established in 2000.

1092 ■ International Peace Award

To recognize an outstanding individual for efforts in promoting peace and resolving conflict. Awarded annually.

1093 ■ Media Peace Awards

Recognizes humanitarian and social justice contributions by the media in Australia. Major award categories include: Best Print (News, Feature); Best Television (News, Current Affairs and Features); Best Radio; Best Photojournalism; and Best Online. Special categories include: Promotion of Aboriginal Reconciliation; Promotion of Multicultural Issues; Increasing Understanding and Awareness of Children's Rights and Issues; Promotion of Positive Images of the Older Person; and Increasing Awareness and Understanding of Women's Rights and Issues. Established in 1979.

1094 ■ World Environment Day Awards

To recognize individuals and organizations from all Australian sectors for contributions to protecting, managing, and restoring the environment. Awards include: Lincolne Scott Sustainability Leadership Award; Szencorp Green Building Award; Building Commission Award for Best Sustainable Residential Development; Meeting the Greenhouse Challenge Award; Business Awards; Local Government Awards; Excellence in Sustainable Water Management; Education/School Award; Excellence in Marine and Coastal

Management Award; Media Award; Community Award; and Individual Award. Presented annually on World Environment Day.

1095 ■ University of Melbourne Assessment Research Centre
Prof. Patrick Griffin PhD, Dir.
Melbourne Graduate School of Education
100 Leicester St., Level 8
Parkville, Victoria 3010, Australia
Ph: 61 3 9035 4425
Fax: 61 3 8344 8739
E-mail: p.griffin@unimelb.edu.au
URL: http://www.edfac.unimelb.edu.au/arc

1096 ■ National Assessment Awards

For excellence in assessment practice. Awarded annually. Established in 1997.

1097 ■ University of Melbourne Faculty of Arts
Prof. Mark Considine, Dean
Old Arts Bldg., Rm. 104
Melbourne, Victoria 3010, Australia
Ph: 61 3 8344 6395
Fax: 61 3 9347 0424
E-mail: arts-enquiries@arts.unimelb.edu.au
URL: http://www.arts.unimelb.edu.au

1098 ■ Penguin Manuscript Prize

To encourage postgraduate students who are enrolled in Creative Writing to submit an extended prose manuscript with the opportunity for professional development and possible publication. Entrants must be Australian citizens. Manuscripts must be at least 40,000 words in any prose genre (poetry and scripts excluded). A monetary prize of A$5,000 plus 25 hours of editorial manuscript development assistance by the Penguin Group are awarded annually.

1099 ■ Wesley Michel Wright Prize for Poetry

For recognition of a composition of original English verse or poetry by an Australian citizen. Poems with 50 to 500 lines are eligible. A monetary prize of approximately A$4,000 is awarded annually. Established in 1982 by Wesley Michel Wright.

1100 ■ University of Melbourne Faculty of Science
Liz Sonenberg, Dean
Old Geology Bldg., Ground Fl.
Melbourne, Victoria 3010, Australia
Ph: 61 3 8344 6404
Fax: 61 3 8344 5803
E-mail: science-queries@unimelb.edu.au
URL: http://www.science.unimelb.edu.au

1101 ■ Amgen Australia Prize in Biotechnology

To recognize a student for outstanding achievement in biotechnological research. A monetary prize of A$1,000 is awarded annually. Established in 1994. Sponsored by Amgen Australia.

1102 ■ AMOS Prize

To recognize a student for the best thesis on a meteorological or oceanographic topic. A monetary prize of A$100 is awarded annually. Established in 2003. Sponsored by the Australian Meteorological and Oceanographic Society (AMOS).

1103 ■ J.S. Anderson Prize

To recognize a chemistry major who displays the greatest potential for research. A monetary prize of A$1,300 is awarded periodically.

1104 ■ Maurice H. Belz Prizes in Statistics

To recognize outstanding second-year students of statistics. Book vouchers of approximately A$440 and A$220 are awarded annually to the first-place and second-place winner, respectively.

Awards are arranged in alphabetical order below their administering organizations

1105 ■ Dame Margaret Blackwood Prize
To recognize an outstanding second-year student of genetics. A monetary prize of approximately A$1,500 is awarded annually. Established in 1984.

1106 ■ Botany Prize
To recognize an outstanding Australian student enrolled in the Bachelor of Science program of botany. A monetary prize of A$1,000 is awarded annually.

1107 ■ Kaye Merlin Brutton Prize
To recognize an individual for research into cancer, diseases of the liver, ophthalmic diseases, and angina pectoris. Monetary prizes are awarded to one or more recipients when merited.

1108 ■ Chemistry Research Excellence Award
To recognize students entering a postgraduate course in the School of Chemistry. A monetary prize of $1,000 per year for up to three years is awarded periodically.

1109 ■ CISRA Prize in Physics
To recognize a PhD student for the best referred publication during the previous year. Candidates must be enrolled in or recently graduated from the PhD program in the School of Physics. A monetary prize of $2,000 is awarded annually. Sponsored by Canon Information Systems Research Australia Pty. Ltd. (CISRA).

1110 ■ F.H. Drummond Prize
To recognize an outstanding undergraduate student of zoology. A monetary prize of A$500 is awarded annually.

1111 ■ Dublin Prize
To recognize students and graduates for outstanding contributions in art, music, literature, and science. A monetary prize of $4,000 is awarded every five years. Established in 1892.

1112 ■ Dulux Australia Prize
To recognize an outstanding third-year student of organic or physical chemistry. A monetary prize of A$1,000 is awarded annually. Established in 1991.

1113 ■ Dwight Prize in Chemistry
To recognize an outstanding first-year student of chemistry. A monetary prize of A$700 is awarded annually.

1114 ■ Dwight Prize in Genetics
To recognize an outstanding third-year student of genetics. A monetary prize of A$700 is awarded annually.

1115 ■ Dwight Prize in Mathematical Statistics
To recognize an outstanding fourth-year student of statistics. A monetary prize of A$700 is awarded annually.

1116 ■ Dwight Prize in Physics
To recognize an outstanding first-year student of physics. A monetary prize of A$700 is awarded annually.

1117 ■ Exhibition Prize in First-Year Chemistry
To recognize an outstanding first-year student of chemistry. A monetary prize of A$100 is awarded annually.

1118 ■ Exhibition Prize in Second-Year Biochemistry
To recognize an outstanding second-year student of biochemistry. A monetary prize of $100 is awarded annually.

1119 ■ Exhibition Prize in Second-Year Geology
To recognize an outstanding second-year student of geology. A monetary prize of A$400 is awarded annually.

1120 ■ Exhibition Prize in Third-Year Botany
To recognize an outstanding third-year student of botany. A monetary prize of A$700 is awarded annually.

1121 ■ Exhibition Prize in Third-Year Geology
To recognize an outstanding third-year student of geology. A monetary prize of A$700 is awarded annually.

1122 ■ Exhibition Prize in Third-Year Physiology
To recognize an outstanding third-year student of physiology. A monetary prize of $500 is awarded annually.

1123 ■ John and Allan Gilmour Research Award
To recognize an individual for scientific research that benefits mankind. A monetary prize of A$6,000 is awarded biennially in even-numbered years.

1124 ■ Grimwade Prize
To promote the study of industrial chemistry. Candidates must be undergraduates or undergraduates at the University of Melbourne or graduates from other tertiary institutions whose degrees are recognized by the Faculty of Science. A monetary prize of A$6,500 is awarded annually.

1125 ■ J.H. Harvey Prize
To recognize the recipient of the Professor Kernot Scholarship in Earth Sciences. A small monetary prize is awarded annually. Established in 1984.

1126 ■ Stanley Harvey Prize
To recognize the recipient of the Professor Kernot Scholarship in Chemistry. A small monetary prize is awarded annually. Established in 1984.

1127 ■ T.W. Healy Award
To recognize a postgraduate student in the School of Chemistry who presented a paper at a conference. Candidates must be in at least the second year of the PhD program. A monetary prize of A$2,200 is awarded annually. Established in 2002.

1128 ■ Huntsman Australia for Research Excellence
To recognize an outstanding student enrolling in a postgraduate research degree in the School of Chemistry. A monetary prize of A$1,000 is awarded when merited. Sponsored by Huntsman Corporation Australia Pty. Ltd.

1129 ■ Huntsman Australia Prize in Chemistry
To recognize an outstanding second-year student of chemistry who is proceeding to a major in chemistry. A monetary prize of A$500 is awarded annually. Established in 2001. Sponsored by Huntsman Corporation Australia Pty. Ltd.

1130 ■ Klein Prize in Experimental Physics
To recognize a student for the most original project in experimental physics. Candidates must have completed the fourth-year Honours and be currently enrolled in the degree of MSc or PhD in the School of Physics. A monetary prize of A$700 is awarded annually.

1131 ■ Megan Klemm Postgraduate Research Award
To recognize a graduate student for academic achievement in botany. Candidates must be enrolled as full- or part-time graduate students in the School of Botany. A monetary prize of A$3,500 is awarded annually.

1132 ■ Bruce Knox Honours Prize
To recognize an outstanding fourth-year student of botany. A monetary prize of A$1,200 is awarded annually. Established in 1997.

1133 ■ Lavarack Prize for Developmental Biology
To recognize an outstanding student who has completed the third-year course of Developmental Neurobiology. A monetary prize of $250 is awarded annually. Supported by the Department of Anatomy and Cell Biology.

1134 ■ Jasper Loftus-Hills Award
To recognize individuals for achievements in zoological research. A monetary prize of A$3,000 is awarded to up to three recipients annually.

1135 ■ E. R. Love Prize
To recognize an outstanding undergraduate student of mathematics. A monetary prize of approximately A$120 is awarded annually. Established in 1977.

1136 ■ John Lovering Prize
To recognize an outstanding student of earth sciences. A monetary prize of A$1,000 is awarded annually. Established in 2003.

1137 ■ Norma McArthur Prize
To recognize an outstanding third-year student of statistics. A monetary prize of approximately A$300 is awarded annually. Established in 1983.

1138 ■ McGraw-Hill Biology Award
To recognize an outstanding student enrolled in the first-year course of Biology of Australian Flora and Fauna. A book voucher of $200 is awarded annually. Sponsored by McGraw-Hill Publishing Co.

1139 ■ Ethel McLennan Award
To recognize a graduate student for academic achievement in botany. Candidates must be enrolled as full- or part-time graduate students in the School of Botany. A monetary prize of A$1,000 is awarded annually. Established in 2002.

1140 ■ MUPHAS Prize for Academic Excellence in Mathematics
To recognize a student enrolled in the Melbourne University Program for High Achieving Students (MUPHAS) who has completed an approved, year-long subject sequence in mathematics. A book voucher of $120 is awarded annually.

1141 ■ Professor Nanson Prize
To recognize a graduate student for the best original memoir on some subject in pure and applied mathematics. Candidates must be graduates of not more than seven years standing from first enrollment. A monetary prize of A$250 is awarded annually.

1142 ■ Ramm Prize in Experimental Physics
To recognize a student for research in experimental physics. A monetary prize of A$2,000 is awarded annually. Established in 1998.

1143 ■ Monica Elizabeth Reum Memorial Prize
To recognize an outstanding PhD thesis on some topic of organic chemistry. A monograph with inscribed bookplate and monetary prize of approximately A$500 are awarded periodically. Established in 1998.

1144 ■ Ronald Riseborough Prize
To recognize a fourth-year student for a research report in applied chemistry. Candidates must be graduates of an Institute of Technology. A monetary prize of approximately A$250 is awarded annually. Established in 1959.

1145 ■ Kingsley Rowan Marine Botany Prize
To recognize an outstanding student enrolled in the Marine and Freshwater Botany course. A monetary prize of A$800 is awarded annually.

1146 ■ T.F. Ryan Prize for Anatomy
To recognize an outstanding student enrolled in second-year anatomy. A medal and monetary prize of A$300 are awarded annually.

Awards are arranged in alphabetical order below their administering organizations

1147 ■ G. A. M. Scott Research Award

To recognize a postgraduate student enrolled in the School of Botany who has contributed to research in bryophytes. A monetary prize of A$2,000 is awarded annually.

1148 ■ Roy and Iris Simmons Award

To recognize a student, either undergraduate or postgraduate, for achievements in microbiology. A monetary prize of A$3,000 is awarded annually.

1149 ■ Baldwin Spencer Prize

To recognize undergraduate students in zoology. Each year, a monetary prize of A$125 is awarded to one first-year biomedical student and one first-year science student.

1150 ■ Sunderland Award for Neuroscience

To recognize an outstanding student who has completed the third-year course of Neuroscience Systems and Higher Function. A monetary prize of $250 is awarded annually. Supported by the Department of Anatomy and Cell Biology.

1151 ■ William Sutherland Prize

To recognize an outstanding second-year student of physics. A book voucher of A$145 is awarded annually. Established in 1920.

1152 ■ David Syme Research Prize

For recognition of the best original research in biology, chemistry, geology, or physics during the previous two years. Preference is given to work of value to the industrial and commercial interests of Australia. A monetary prize of A$7,000 and a bronze medallion are awarded annually. Established in 1904 by David Syme.

1153 ■ Third-Year Science Prize in Pharmacology

To recognize an outstanding third-year student of pharmacology. A monetary prize of $200 is awarded annually.

1154 ■ UMEP Prize for Academic Excellence in Biology

To recognize an outstanding student who completed a year-long subject sequence in biology as part of the University of Melbourne Extension Program (UMEP). A book voucher of $120 is awarded annually.

1155 ■ E.M. and J.F. Ward Prize in Experimental Physics

To recognize a student enrolled in the third-year or final-year of a physics degree program. A medallion and monetary prize of A$600 are awarded annually. Established in honor of Edith Ward, who in 1896 was among the first 55 women to graduate from the University of Melbourne.

1156 ■ Rowden White Foundation Prize

To recognize the student with the highest third-year faculty honors score. Candidates must be enrolled in the Bachelor of Science program. A monetary prize of $1,500 is awarded annually.

1157 ■ Norman Thomas Mortimer Wilsmore Research Prize

To recognize a visiting research fellow who is distinguished in the field of chemistry. A monetary prize of A$12,000 is awarded periodically.

1158 ■ Professor Wilson Prize

To recognize a student for the best thesis on some subject in pure and applied mathematics. Candidates must be graduates of not more than seven years standing from first enrollment. A monetary prize of A$450 is awarded annually.

1159 ■ Wood-Jones Award for Topographic Anatomy

To recognize an outstanding student who has completed the courses in Functional and Applied Anatomy and Advanced Studies in Human Anatomy. A monetary prize of $250 is awarded annually. Supported by the Department of Anatomy and Cell Biology.

1160 ■ R.D. Wright Prize

To recognize an outstanding undergraduate physiology student pursuing a degree other than Bachelor of Medicine and Bachelor of Surgery. Three monetary prizes of $1,000 are awarded annually.

1161 ■ University of Melbourne Faculty of Veterinary Science

Melbourne, Victoria 3010, Australia
Ph: 61 3 8344 7357
Fax: 61 3 8344 7374
URL: http://www.vet.unimelb.edu.au

1162 ■ Australian Veterinary Association (Australia) Prize

To recognize an outstanding second-year student in veterinary pathology. A book voucher is awarded annually. Sponsored by the Australian Veterinary Association (Australia).

1163 ■ Australian Veterinary Association (Victoria) Prize

To recognize an outstanding final-year student in veterinary science. A statuette is awarded annually.

1164 ■ Jan Blackburn Prize

To recognize an outstanding student in the area of small animal emergency and critical care. A monetary prize of $100 is awarded annually.

1165 ■ Hills Prize in Small Animal Medicine

To recognize an outstanding final-year student enrolled in the Bachelor of Veterinary Science program. A monetary prize of $400 is awarded annually.

1166 ■ Intervet Prize in Animal Reproduction

To recognize an outstanding student in the animal reproduction components of the final two clinical years of the Bachelor of Veterinary Science program. A monetary prize of $500 is awarded annually. Sponsored by Intervet.

1167 ■ Lyppard/Provet Victoria Colin Basset Prize

To recognize an outstanding student in the final two clinical years of the Bachelor of Veterinary Science program pertinent to large animal rural veterinary practice. A monetary prize of $250 is awarded annually.

1168 ■ Pfizer Animal Health Prize

To recognize an outstanding second-year student in veterinary microbiology. A monetary prize of $250 is awarded annually. Sponsored by Pfizer Animal Health.

1169 ■ Sir A.E. Rowden White Prize

To recognize an outstanding final-year student in veterinary science. A monetary prize of $1,500 is awarded annually.

1170 ■ University of New South Wales Student Information and Systems Office

Sydney, New South Wales 2052, Australia
Ph: 61 2 9385 1000
Fax: 61 2 9385 1252
E-mail: sisinfo@unsw.edu.au
URL: http://www.unsw.edu.au

1171 ■ Silver Dirac Medal

For recognition of contributions to the advancement of theoretical physics. The individual selected to deliver the Dirac Lecture receives a silver medal. Awarded at least biennially. Established in 1979 by the University of New South Wales to commemorate the only visit to Australasia of Professor P.A.M. Dirac, 1975, organized by the University. Co-sponsored by the Australian Institute of Physics (NSW Branch).

1172 ■ Victorian Artists Society

Gregory R. Smith, Pres.
430 Albert St.
East Melbourne, Victoria 3002, Australia
Ph: 61 3 96621484
Fax: 61 3 96622343
E-mail: admin@victorianartistssociety.com.au
URL: http://www.victorianartistssociety.com.au

1173 ■ Artist of the Year

To honor an exhibiting artist in the Artist of the Year Award Exhibition held in November of each year. The recipient is selected by peer artists. Awarded annually. Established in 1973.

1174 ■ Gordon Moffatt Award

To recognize the youngest artist who gained a place at the annual Award Exhibition. Founded by former Society treasurer, Gordon Moffatt.

1175 ■ Walkley Foundation

245 Chalmers St.
Redfern, New South Wales 2016, Australia
Ph: 61 2 9330
Fax: 61 2 9330
E-mail: walkleys@walkleys.com
URL: http://www.walkleys.com

1176 ■ The Walkley Awards

For recognition of the best examples of Australian journalism. Awards are presented in more than 30 categories covering photography, print, radio, television, and online journalism. In addition to awards in each category are several special awards: the Gold Award for the top winner among all categories; the Journalistic Leadership Award for outstanding acts of courage and bravery in the practice of journalism; and the Nikon-Walkley Press Photographer Prizes. Awarded annually. Established in 1956 by Sir William Gaston Walkley, founder of Ampol Petroleum and one of the pioneers of oil exploration in Australia.

1177 ■ Warringah Council

Rik Hart, Gen. Mgr.
Civic Ctre.
725 Pittwater Rd.
Dee Why, New South Wales 2099, Australia
Ph: 61 2 99422111
Fax: 61 2 99714522
E-mail: council@warringah.nsw.gov.au
URL: http://www.warringah.nsw.gov.au/home/index.aspx
Awards discontinued.

1178 ■ Australia Day Awards

To honor individuals and organizations that epitomize the pursuit of excellence, commitment to a tolerant and diverse society, a fair go, and public service. The following awards are presented: Citizen of the Year Award, Young Citizen of the Year Award, and Community Event of the Year. Awarded annually.

1179 ■ Garden Awards

To honor the best gardens in a variety of gardens. Open to all residents, businesses, and schools who have a great garden they want to share with others in the area. Awarded annually.

1180 ■ Outstanding Community Service Awards

Given to residents or non-residents of Warringah who should be rewarded for their longstanding efforts in helping the community. Up to ten residents and one non-resident will be recognized and honored for their involvement in voluntary community service. Awarded annually.

1181 ■ Weed Society of Victoria

James O'Brien, Pres.
PO Box 987
Frankston, Victoria 3199, Australia
Ph: 61 3 95762949
Ph: 61 3 92964647
Fax: 61 3 92964720
E-mail: secwssv@surf.net.au
URL: http://www.wsvic.org.au

Awards are arranged in alphabetical order below their administering organizations

1182 ■ Honorary Membership
To honor people who have made a major contribution to the Society and to Weed Science. Awarded annually.

1183 ■ Weed Book Prize
Recognizes excellence in some part of course work. Students studying weed science subjects at the Melbourne University Institutes of Land and Food Resources are eligible. Awarded annually.

1184 ■ Welding Technology Institute of Australia
Chris Smallbone, Exec. Dir.
Unit 50, 8 Avenue of the Americas
Newington, New South Wales 2127, Australia
Ph: 61 2 97484443
Fax: 61 2 97482858
E-mail: info@wtia.com.au
URL: http://www.wtia.com.au

1185 ■ Florence Taylor Award
Recognizes an individual who has a made a notable contribution to education and training in welding, and to the development of welding skills in the Northern Territory. Awarded annually.

1186 ■ Young Tradesperson of the Year
Recognizes an up-and-coming young welder. Awarded annually.

1187 ■ Wildlife Preservation Society of Australia
Suzanne Medway JP, Pres.
PO Box 42
Brighton-Le-Sands, New South Wales 2216, Australia
Ph: 61 2 95561537
Fax: 61 2 95990000
E-mail: info@wpsa.org.au
URL: http://www.wpsa.org.au

1188 ■ Community Wildlife Conservation Award
To recognize organizations that make a significant contribution to the preservation of Australian wildlife. A crystal trophy and monetary award of $2,500 is awarded annually.

1189 ■ Serventy Conservation Medal
To recognize an individual for conservation work that has been done outside of his or her professional career. A medal and monetary award of $2,000 is awarded annually. Established in 1999 in honor of the Society's President of Honour, Dr. Vincent Serventy, his brother and international ornithologist, Dr. Dominic Serventy, and his older sister, Lucy Seventy, who was the Society's oldest Life Member.

1190 ■ Wine Industry Suppliers Australia
Carol Haslam, Exec. Off.
GPO Box 1117
Adelaide, South Australia 5001, Australia
Ph: 61 8 82312091
Ph: 61 8 83038700
Fax: 61 8 82312092
E-mail: carol@wisa.org.au
URL: http://www.wisa.org.au

1191 ■ Supplier of the Year Awards
To honor wine industry suppliers who have actively added to the success of the Australian wine industry. The following awards are presented: Supplier of the Year, Innovation Award, Environmental and Sustainability Award, Export Award, and Chairman's Award. Awarded annually. Formerly: (2007) WOW Awards.

1192 ■ World Federation of Occupational Therapists
(Federation Mondiale des Ergotherapeutes)
E. Sharon Brintnell, Pres.
PO Box 30
Forrestfield, Western Australia 6058, Australia

Fax: 61 8 94539746
E-mail: admin@wfot.org.au
URL: http://www.wfot.org

1193 ■ Thelma Cardwell Foundation Award for Education and Research
To provide opportunities for occupational therapists to extend their knowledge, gain specialized skills, and mature professionally through study and research.

Austria

1194 ■ Amt der Tiroler Landesregierung, Kulturabteilung
Dr. Christoph Mader, Contact
Sillgasse 8
A-6020 Innsbruck, Austria
Ph: 43 512 508
Fax: 43 512 5082185
E-mail: post@tirol.gv.at
URL: http://www.tirol.gv.at/themen/kultur

1195 ■ Emil Berlanda Preis
For recognition of a contribution to the promotion and interpretation of contemporary music. Selection is by nomination. A monetary prize of 5,000 Euros is awarded biennially. Established in 1982 by Magdalena Berlanda and the Kulturabteilung in memory of Emil Berlanda (1905-1960), one of Tyrol's most important composers in the first half of the twentieth century.

1196 ■ Jakob Stainer Preis
For recognition of a contribution to the promotion of early music. Individuals from Tyrol and South Tyrol who are active in the field of early music may be nominated. A monetary prize is awarded biennially. Established in 1983 in memory of Jakob Stainer (1617-1683), world-famous violin maker, who was born in Absam near Innsbruck.

1197 ■ Tiroler Landespreis fur Kunst
For recognition of achievement in the arts. Artists from the Tyrol and South Tyrol may be nominated. A monetary prize of 14,000 Euros is awarded annually. Established in 1984. Formerly: (1983) Wurdigungspreis des Landes Tirol fur Literatur, Musik etc..

1198 ■ Tiroler Landespreis fur Wissenschaft
For recognition of achievement in the fields of humanities or science. Candidates from the Tyrol and South Tyrol may be nominated. A monetary prize of 14,000 Euros is awarded annually. Established in 1984.

1199 ■ Austria Press Agency
Laimgrubengasse 10
A-1060 Vienna, Austria
Ph: 43 1 360 600
E-mail: apa@apa.at
URL: http://www.apa.at

1200 ■ Austrian Prize for Press Photography
To recognize an outstanding press photographer in Austria. Criteria include topic, creativity, theme, and technical and artistic quality of photographs. Awarded annually. Established in 2006. Sponsored by Canon Austria.

1201 ■ Writing for CEE Award
To recognize outstanding journalism from Central and Eastern Europe (CEE) and South Eastern Europe for work that contributes to overcoming border and prejudices and enhances cultural diversity. A monetary prize of 5,000 Euros is awarded annually. Established in 2004. Sponsored by Bank Austria.

1202 ■ Austrian Broadcasting Corporation
(Landesstudio Oberosterreich)
Bianca Petscher, Contact
ORF/Prix Ars Electronica

Hauptstr. 2
A-4040 Linz, Austria
Ph: 43 732 7272 79
Fax: 43 732 7272 674
E-mail: info@prixars.aec.at
URL: http://www.aec.at/en/prix/index.asp

1203 ■ Prix Ars Electronica - International Competition for Cyberarts
Open to artists, scientists, researchers, and developers. Three monetary prizes are awarded in each of the following categories: Digital Communities, Interactive Art, Digital Music and Sound Art, "The Next Idea," Computer Animation/Film/VFX, Hybrid Art, and U19 - Create Your World. Held annually. Established in 1979.

1204 ■ Austrian Computer Society
(Osterreichische Computer Gesellschaft)
Dr. Gerald Futschek, Pres.
Wollzeile 1-3
A-1010 Vienna, Austria
Ph: 43 1 51202350
Fax: 43 1 51202359
E-mail: ocg@ocg.at
URL: http://www.ocg.at

1205 ■ Roland Wagner Award
To recognize an individual for achievements in the field of utilizing computers to assist people with special needs. A monetary prize of 3,000 Euros is awarded biennially in even-numbered years. Established in 2001.

1206 ■ Heinz Zemanek Award
Recognizes an outstanding researcher in information and computer science. A monetary prize of 2,000 to 4,000 Euros is awarded biennially in even-numbered years.

1207 ■ Austrian Neuroscience Association
(Osterreichische Gesellschaft fuer Neurowissenschaften)
Heinrich Romer, Pres.
Karl-Franzens-Universitat Graz
Institut fur Zoologie
Universitatsplatz 2
A-8010 Graz, Austria
Ph: 43 316 3805596
Fax: 43 316 3809876
E-mail: heinrich.roemer@uni-graz.at
URL: http://www.univie.ac.at/ANA/php/index3.php

1208 ■ Otto Loewi Award
To a young scientist (below the age of 40) in Austria for exceptional scientific achievement in a topical field of interest in neuroscience. A monetary prize of 5,300 Euros is awarded biennially in odd-numbered years.

1209 ■ Austrian Physical Society
(Oesterreichische Psysikalische Gesellschaft)
Dr. Karl Riedling, Mgr.
Vienna University of Technology
Institute of Sensor and Actuator Systems
Gusshausstrasse 27/366
A-1040 Vienna, Austria
Ph: 43 1 5880136658
Fax: 43 1 5880136699
E-mail: office@oepg.at
URL: http://www.oepg.at

1210 ■ Viktor Hess Preis
For scientific excellence.

1211 ■ Physik-Preis
For scientific excellence. A monetary prize of 2,200 Euros is awarded annually.

Awards are arranged in alphabetical order below their administering organizations

1212 ■ Roman Ulrich Sexl Prize
For excellence in physics. A monetary prize of 1,500 Euros is awarded.

1213 ■ Austrian Society for Geriatrics and Gerontology
(Osterreichische Gesellschaft fur Geriatrie and Gerontologie)
Dr. Peter Pietschmann, Pres.
Wahringer Gurtel 18-20
1090 Vienna, Austria
Ph: 43 1 404005126
E-mail: peter.pietschmann@meduniwien.ac.at
URL: http://www.geriatrie-online.at

1214 ■ Walter Doberaller Stipendium
To an individual under 40 years of age.

1215 ■ Cardiovascular and Interventional Radiological Society of Europe
Mr. Daniel Waigl, Exec. Dir.
Neutorgasse 9/6
AT-1010 Vienna, Austria
Ph: 43 1 9042003
Fax: 43 1 904200330
E-mail: info@cirse.org
URL: http://www.cirse.org

1216 ■ Editor's Medal
To recognize an outstanding article published in *CardioVascular and Interventional Radiology (CVIR)* during the previous year. Awarded annually. Established in 1997.

1217 ■ Education Grants
To provide advanced training and education in interventional radiology for CIRSE members. A variety of grants are awarded annually.

1218 ■ Gold Medal
To honor an individual for outstanding achievements in interventional radiology. Awarded annually. Established in 1994.

1219 ■ Andreas Gruentzig Lecture
To honor an individual for outstanding contributions to the field of interventional radiology. Awarded annually. Established in 1994.

1220 ■ Research Grant
For research in cardiovascular and interventional radiology.

1221 ■ Josef Roesch Lecture
To recognize a physician for a significant contribution to the field of interventional radiology. Awarded annually. Established in 2003.

1222 ■ DAAAM International Vienna
Karlsplatz 13/311
A-1040 Vienna, Austria
E-mail: webmaster@daaam.com
URL: http://www.daaam.com

1223 ■ Authors Club Certificate
To recognize authors who publish and/or present papers at five, 10, or 15 DAAAM International Symposiums. Awarded annually.

1224 ■ Best Paper Awards
To recognize excellence in the contributions of younger researchers and scientists. In addition to the Best Paper Award, the following awards are presented: Award for Best Poster Presentation, Award for Best Oral Presentation, Award for Best Visual Presentation, and a Special Award. Awarded annually.

1225 ■ Best Photo Award
To honor an individual for the best photograph taken during the International Symposium/Conference. Awarded annually.

1226 ■ Medal of DAAAM International
To honor an individual or institution for excellence in the science, technology, and international scientific cooperation in the framework of DAAAM International Vienna. A medal is awarded annually.

1227 ■ ENERGY GLOBE Portal
Muhlbach 7
A-4801 Traunkirchen, Austria
Ph: 43 761720900
Fax: 43 7617 209090
E-mail: contact@energyglobe.info
URL: http://www.energyglobe.com

1228 ■ ENERGY GLOBE Awards
Recognizes projects that conserve and protect the natural environment. Over 800 projects from around the world compete annually for these awards which are offered in the categories of Earth, Fire, Air, and Youth. Awards are presented nationally in over 100 countries. The World ENERGY GLOBE Award for Sustainability is awarded internationally. Established in 1999.

1229 ■ European Association for Programming Languages and Systems
Jens Knoop, Gen. Sec.
Argentinierstrasse 8/4/E185.1
Institut fur Computersprachen
Fakultat fur Informatik
Technische Universitat Wien
A-1040 Vienna, Austria
Ph: 43 1 58801 18510
Fax: 43 1 58801 18598
E-mail: knoop@complang.tuwien.ac.at
URL: http://eapls.org

1230 ■ Best PhD Dissertation Award
To recognize the PhD who has made the most original and influential contribution to the field of programming languages and systems in Europe. Awarded annually. Established in 2010.

1231 ■ European Association of Nuclear Medicine
P. Bourguet, Pres.
Hollandstr. 14, Mezzanine
A-1020 Vienna, Austria
Ph: 43 1 2128030
Fax: 43 1 21280309
E-mail: office@eanm.org
URL: http://www.eanm.org

1232 ■ Marie Curie Training Grant
To cover the expenses of young members of the association to obtain short-term training in a recognized and competent European training centre, thereby promoting the exchange and expansion of knowledge among junior members who have demonstrated an interest and involvement in research experience in nuclear medicine or related fields. Candidates must be junior members aged 38 years and younger who have demonstrated an interest and involvement in research experience in Nuclear Medicine or related fields. Up to five grants in the amount of 1,000 Euros are awarded every year.

1233 ■ Eckert and Ziegler Abstract Award
Encourages abstract submissions by young investigators at the annual EANM Congress.

1234 ■ European Federation for Medicinal Chemistry
Dr. Gerhard Ecker, Pres.
University of Vienna
Althanstrasse 14
A-1090 Vienna, Austria
Ph: 43 1 427755110
Fax: 43 1 42779551
E-mail: info@efmc.info
URL: http://www.efmc.info

1235 ■ Nauta Award on Pharmacochemistry
For outstanding achievements in the field of Medicinal Chemistry by a scientist working in Europe or European scientist abroad. A monetary prize of 7,500 Euros, a diploma, and an invitation to present a lecture are awarded biennially in even-numbered years.

1236 ■ Prous Institute-Overton and Meyer Award on New Technologies in Drug Discovery
For a scientist, without restrictions regarding nationality, who has made a discovery, evaluation or use of new technologies. A monetary prize of 7,500 Euros, a diploma, and an invitation to present a lecture are awarded biennially in even-numbered years.

1237 ■ UCB-Ehrlich Award for Excellence in Medicinal Chemistry
For a scientist, without restrictions regarding nationality, who has made an outstanding research in the field of Medicinal Chemistry. A monetary prize of 7,500 Euros, a diploma, and an invitation to present a lecture are awarded biennially in even-numbered years.

1238 ■ European Money and Finance Forum
(Societe Universitaire Europeenne de Recherches Financieres)
Michael Bailey, Exec. Sec.
Otto Wagner-Platz 3
A-1090 Vienna, Austria
Ph: 43 1 404207206
Ph: 43 1 404207216
Fax: 43 1 404207298
E-mail: suerf@oenb.at
URL: http://www.suerf.org

1239 ■ Marjolin Prize
Recognizes the best paper for the colloquium. Persons under the age of 40 are eligible. Awarded periodically. Established in honor of Robert Marjolin, a distinguished European economist.

1240 ■ European Society of Radiology
Mr. Peter Baierl, Contact
Neutorgasse 9
1010 Vienna, Austria
Ph: 43 1 53340640
Fax: 43 1 5334064448
E-mail: communications@myesr.org
URL: http://www.myesr.org
Formerly: European Association of Radiology.

1241 ■ Boris Rajewsky Medal
For recognition of scientific or professional contributions to European radiology. A medal is awarded to one or more recipients annually. Established in 1972.

1242 ■ Federal Ministry of Economy, Family and Youth
Stubenring 1
A-1011 Vienna, Austria
Ph: 43 1 711000
Fax: 43 1 7137995
E-mail: service@bmwfj.gv.at
URL: http://www.bmwfj.gv.at
Formerly: Austria Ministry of Economics and Labour.

1243 ■ National Prize for Advertising
(Staatspreise fur Werbung)
For recognition of an ordering enterprise or advertising agency for an outstanding advertising campaign. Certificates are awarded. Established in 1972.

1244 ■ National Prize for Consulting
(Staatspreis fur Consulting)
For recognition of outstanding consulting. Applications are accepted. Trophies and certificates are awarded annually. Established in 1990.

1245 ■ National Prize for the Most Beautiful Book
(Staatspreis fur das Schonste Buch)
For recognition of the best designed books. Austrian publishing houses are eligible. Five

Awards are arranged in alphabetical order below their administering organizations

monetary prizes and honorary recognition are awarded annually. Established in 1953. Formerly: Most Beautiful Books of Austria (Staatspreis fur die Schonsten Bucher Osterreichs).

1246 ■ Filmfestival of Nations
Erich Reiss, Dir.
Gaumbergstrasse 82
A-4060 Linz, Austria
Ph: 43 732 666 2666
Fax: 43 732 666 2666
E-mail: eva-video@netway.at
URL: http://www.8ung.at/filmfestival

1247 ■ Ebensee Bear
To honor the top three films in the Festival. All non-commercial films and videos are qualified to participate without restriction of topic, and the film must not be over two years old. The duration must be no more than 30 minutes. A jury selects the winner and the jury has the right to ask the author to participate in the deliberations. Ebensee Bears in Gold, Silver, and Bronze are awarded annually.

1248 ■ International Competition for Film and Video
For recognition of non-commercial amateur films and videos. The following formats are eligible: super 8 and 16mm films, and all video systems (preferably VHS and S-VHS). Films must not run over 30 minutes. The following awards are presented: The Austrian Education and Art Minister's Prize; the Ebensee Bear in Gold, Silver, and Bronze; Special Awards for Best Experimental Film; the Best Youth Film (under 21 years); Special Award for Best Film of the Competition - an invitation for free participation in the Festival of Nations the next year; and Cups and Certificates. Awarded annually. Established in 1972 by Franz David.

1249 ■ International Association for Cereal Science and Technology
Dr. Roland E. Poms, Sec. Gen./CEO
Marxergasse 2
A-1030 Vienna, Austria
Ph: 43 1 70772020
Fax: 43 1 70772040
E-mail: office@icc.or.at
URL: http://www.icc.or.at

1250 ■ Clyde H. Bailey Medal
To honor an outstanding scientist in the field of cereal science. Individuals may be nominated. A medal is awarded when merited, usually at the Cereal and Bread Congresses. Established in 1970 in memory of Dr. Clyde H. Bailey, a past president of the Association and renowned cereal scientist.

1251 ■ Harald Perten Prize
For recognition of outstanding achievements in the furtherance of cereal science. A monetary prize of US$3,000 is awarded annually at ICC meetings. Established in 1989 by Ing. Harald Perten. Sponsored by the Harald Perten Foundation.

1252 ■ Friedrich Schweitzer Medal
To honor distinguished service in furthering the aims and ideals of the ICC. The Medal is normally awarded annually at ICC meetings. Established in 1989 in memory of one of the founders of the Association, Prof. Dr. Friedrich Schweitzer, who served as President and Secretary General, and was renowned as a cereal scientist worldwide.

1253 ■ International Association for Plant Taxonomy
(Association Internationale pour la Taxonomie Vegetale)
Alessandra Ricciuti Lamonea, Managing Sec.
University of Vienna
Institute of Botany

Rennweg 14
A-1030 Vienna, Austria
Ph: 43 1 427754098
Fax: 43 1 427754099
E-mail: office@iapt-taxon.org
URL: http://www.botanik.univie.ac.at/iapt/index_layer.php

1254 ■ Engler Gold Medal
To recognize lifelong achievements in systematic botany. A gold medal is awarded every six years at the International Botanical Congresses. Established in 1987 in honor of Adolf Engler.

1255 ■ Engler Silver Medal
To recognize an outstanding publication in monographic and/or floristic plant systematics. Awarded annually if merited. Established in 1990.

1256 ■ Stafleu Medal
To recognize excellence in a publication dealing with historical, bibliographic, or nomenclatural aspects of plant systematics.

1257 ■ Stebbins Medal
To recognize an outstanding publication in plant systematics and plant evolution during a particular year. Established in 2004.

1258 ■ International Association of Philatelic Experts
(Association Internationale des Experts en Philatelie)
Carl Aage Moller, Pres.
Herzog-Friedrich-Strasse 19
A-6020 Innsbruck, Austria
Ph: 43 512 583764
Fax: 43 512 580682
E-mail: klaus.schoepfer@chello.at
URL: http://www.aiep-experts.net/cms

1259 ■ Hunziker Medal
To recognize a significant literary contribution or research work concerned with forgeries or philatelic expertising, or for expertising activities. Awarded annually. Established in 1996.

1260 ■ International Conference of Labour and Social History
(Internationale Tagung der Historikerinnen der Arbeiter-und anderer sozialer Bewegungen)
Berthold Unfried, Pres.
Wipplinger Strasse 6-8
Altes Rathaus
A-1010 Vienna, Austria
Ph: 43 1 2289469
Fax: 43 1 2289469
E-mail: ith@doew.at
URL: http://www.ith.or.at/start

1261 ■ Rene Kuczynski Prize
For outstanding publications in the field of social history. Awarded annually. Established in 1977.

1262 ■ Kaethe Leichter Prize
For women's research. Awarded annually. Established in 1991.

1263 ■ Herbert Steiner Prize
For outstanding research works in German or English on resistance, persecution, exile, and labor history. Awarded annually to one or more recipients.

1264 ■ International Coronelli Society for the Study of Globes
(Internationale Coronelli-Gesellschaft fuer Globenkunde)
Ms. Heide Wohlschlager, Treas.
Dominikanerbastei 21/28
A-1010 Vienna, Austria
Fax: 43 1 5320824
E-mail: coronelli.schmidt@aon.at
URL: http://www.coronelli.org

1265 ■ Fiorini-Haardt Prize
To further research into globes, particularly

among younger enthusiasts, by honoring research on old globes (pre-1945) and their producers. Awarded triennially.

1266 ■ Prize for Encouragement of Globe Studies
To honor the author of scientific studies on globes or cartography dealing with globology in the widest sense. Papers may be written in German or English, but must not be older than two years. Eligible individuals must be younger than 35 years old. A monetary prize of 500 Euros is awarded annually. Established in 2006.

1267 ■ International Federation for Information Processing
(Federation Internationale pour le Traitement de l'Information)
Leon Strous, Pres.
Hofstrasse 3
A-2361 Laxenburg, Austria
Ph: 43 2236 73616
Fax: 43 2236 736169
E-mail: ifip@ifip.org
URL: http://www.ifip.org

1268 ■ Isaac L. Auerbach Award
To recognize individuals whose service in support of IFIP in its mission is deemed to be extraordinary by their peers. A medal and an honorarium are awarded biennially in even-numbered years.

1269 ■ Kristian Beckman Award
To honor an individual for an outstanding contribution to security and protection in information processing systems. Awarded when merited.

1270 ■ Namur Award
To honor an individual for an outstanding contribution to the creation of awareness of the social implications of information technology. Presented biennially in Namur, Belgium. Administered by the Working Group on Social Accountability.

1271 ■ Outstanding Service Award
In recognition of services rendered to IFIP by Technical Committee and Working Group members not normally eligible for the Silver Core Award. Awarded annually to one or more recipients. Established in 1988.

1272 ■ Manfred Paul Award
To recognize an outstanding researcher for a published paper in the area of software theory and practice. A plaque/certificate and monetary prize of 1024 Euros are awarded annually. Established in honor of the chairman of the TC2 Group from 1977 to 1986.

1273 ■ Brian Shackel Award
To recognize the most outstanding contribution in the form of a referred paper submitted to and delivered at the INTERACT Conference. A plaque and certificate are awarded biennially in odd-numbered years.

1274 ■ Silver Core Award
For recognition of services rendered to IFIP. Silver Core pins and certificates are given to numerous recipients every three years. Established in 1974.

1275 ■ International Federation of Automatic Control
Schlossplatz 12
A-2361 Laxenburg, Austria
Ph: 43 2236 71447
Fax: 43 2236 72859
E-mail: secretariat@ifac-control.org
URL: http://www.ifac-control.org

1276 ■ Automatica Prize Paper Award
To recognize the best papers published in the IFAC journal *Automatica*. Monetary prizes are awarded to the authors of three papers every three years. Established in 1979.

Awards are arranged in alphabetical order below their administering organizations

1277 ■ High Impact Paper Award

To recognize a paper published in any of the official IFAC journals on the broad areas of automatic control theory and application. Awarded to one or two recipients every three years. Established in 2008.

1278 ■ Industrial Achievement Award

To recognize an individual or team of individuals for a significant contribution to industrial applications of control. A certificate and monetary prize are awarded every three years. Established in 2000.

1279 ■ Nathaniel B. Nichols Medal

To recognize outstanding contributions by an individual to design methods, software tools and instrumentation, or to significant projects resulting in major applications and advancement of control education. A medal and monetary prize are awarded every three years. Established in 1996.

1280 ■ Giorgio Quazza Medal

To recognize a distinguished control engineer. A medal and monetary prize are awarded every three years. Established in 1981.

1281 ■ International Federation of Purchasing and Supply Management
Charles Holden, Dir. Gen.
Laurenzenvorstadt 90
CH-5001 Aarau, Austria
E-mail: sapawson@gmail.com
URL: http://www.ifpmm.org

1282 ■ Garner-Themoin Medal

To recognize an individual for an outstanding contribution to international purchasing and materials management. A medal and a plaque are presented annually. Established in 1976 to commemorate two outstanding personalities, Mr. Garner from the United Kingdom, and Mr. Themoin from France.

1283 ■ Maple Leaf Award

To increase the availability of written communication world wide. A technical paper is selected in the competition. A monetary prize, a plaque, and a diploma are presented annually. Established in 1977.

1284 ■ Hans Ovelgonne - Purchasing Research Award

To recognize individuals who made outstanding contributions to the development of purchasing, materials management, and logistics. Awarded annually to one or two recipients.

1285 ■ Lewis E. Spangler - Purchasing Professional Award

To recognize individuals who made outstanding contributions to materials management, logistics, and the purchasing profession, and who support education and training. Awarded annually to one or two recipients.

1286 ■ International Fritz Kreisler Competition
Susanne Nitsch, Sec.
Postfach 76
A-1030 Vienna, Austria
Ph: 43 2252 41003
Fax: 43 2252 21993
E-mail: fritz-kreisler@music.at
URL: http://www.fritz-kreisler.music.at

1287 ■ International Fritz Kreisler Competition Prizes

To provide recognition for the best violin and viola performance. Monetary awards ranging from 5,000 Euros to 15,000 Euros are given to the six finalists. The winners of the first three prizes perform the final round in the Great Hall of the Wiener Konzerthaus with the Vienna Symphonic Orchestra. A solo performance is provided for the first prize winner. In addition, six special prizes of 2,000 Euros are presented. Held every five years. Established in 1979 in memory of Fritz Kreisler, the Austrian violinist and composer.

1288 ■ International Institute for Applied Systems Analysis
(Institut International pour l'Analyse des Systemes Appliques)
Prof. Detlof von Winterfeldt, Dir.
Schlossplatz 1
A-2361 Laxenburg, Austria
Ph: 43 2236 8070
Fax: 43 2236 71313
E-mail: inf@iiasa.ac.at
URL: http://www.iiasa.ac.at

1289 ■ Distinguished Principal Founding Member

For recognition of exemplary dedication to the ideals of the charter and support for the objectives of the institute, as well as distinguished accomplishments in promoting the research of the institute. Established in 1987.

1290 ■ Honorary Scholar

For recognition of outstanding contributions made to the development of the Institute and to the advancement of its objectives. Honorary recognition is awarded when merited. Established in 1975.

1291 ■ Peccei Scholarship

To recognize outstanding contributions of participants of the Young Scientists Summer Program (YSSP). A monthly scholarship for three months and travel expenses are awarded annually. Established in 1984 to commemorate Aurelio Peccei's contributions towards understanding global problems and promoting research through multinational collaboration.

1292 ■ International Music and Media Centre
(Internationales Musik Medienzentrum)
Franz Patay, Sec. Gen.
Stiftgasse 29
A-1070 Vienna, Austria
Ph: 43 1 8890315
Fax: 43 1 889031577
E-mail: office@imz.at
URL: http://www.imz.at/imz

1293 ■ Dance Screen Awards

To stimulate and disseminate the production of audiovisual dance programs. Awards are given in the following categories: Live Performance Relay, Camera Re-work, Screen Choreography, and Documentary. The competition is open to dance films, dance videos, and television programs on dance and ballet completed during the previous year. Certificates are awarded to the top submission in each category, and a monetary prize of 15,000 EUR is awarded to the best submission overall. Awarded annually. Established in 1990.

1294 ■ Honorary Members

To recognize individuals who have served as profound inspiration and as examples of extraordinary quality to many people through their outstanding commitment, dedication, and work for the arts.

1295 ■ MIDEM Classical Awards

To honor classical music in all of its forms and to recognize outstanding achievements in the international classical music scene. Candidates may be from any country. Available awards include Best Recording of the Year, Best Vocal Recital, Best Choral Work, Best Solo Instrument, Best Opera, Best Contemporary Music, Best Reissue/Archival/Historical Recording, Best Concerto, Best Symphonic Work, Outstanding Young Artist, Artist of the Year, and Lifetime Achievement Award. Awarded annually. Established in 2005.

1296 ■ International Organization of Supreme Audit Institutions
(Organisation Internationale des Institutions Superieures de Control des Finances Publiques)
Monika Gonzalez-Koss, Sec. Gen.
Rechunungshof
Dampfschiffstrasse 2
A-1031 Vienna, Austria
Ph: 43 1 711718474
Ph: 43 1 711718073
Fax: 43 1 7180969
E-mail: intosai@rechnungshof.gv.at
URL: http://www.intosai.org

1297 ■ Jorg Kandutsch Preis

To recognize important achievements and contributions in the field of auditing by supreme audit institutions. Nominations may be made for achievements or contributions in the three calendar years preceding the year of INTOSAI's triennial Congress. A wall plaque is awarded triennially. Established in memory of Dr. Jorg Kandutsch, former Secretary General of INTOSAI.

1298 ■ Elmer B. Staats Award

To encourage excellence in the writing of articles for the *International Journal of Government Auditing*. Authors of articles published in the journal in the three calendar years preceding the year of the triennial Congress are eligible for nomination. A sterling silver medallion and a scroll suitable for framing are awarded triennially. Established in 1983 in memory of Dr. Elmer B. Staats, former comptroller general of the United States, and former chairman of the Journal's Board of Editors. Formerly: (2006) Elmer B. Staats International Journal Award.

1299 ■ International Press Institute
David Dadge, Dir.
Spiegelgasse 2
A-1010 Vienna, Austria
Ph: 43 1 5129011
Fax: 43 1 5129014
E-mail: ipi@freemedia.at
URL: http://www.freemedia.at

1300 ■ Free Media Pioneer Award

To honor organizations that have fought to ensure freer and more independent media in their country or region. Awarded annually. Established in 1996.

1301 ■ International Society for Engineering Education
(Internationale Gesellschaft fur Ingenieur-padagogik)
Dr. Norbert Kraker, Pres.
Muhlgasse 67
2500 Baden, Austria
Ph: 43 2252 88570113
Fax: 43 2252 88570180
E-mail: office@igip.org
URL: http://www.igip.org

1302 ■ IGIP Award
(IGIP-Preis)

To honor outstanding scientific or practical works in the field of engineering education. A monetary award is presented biennially. Established in 1986.

1303 ■ International Solid Waste Association
Greg Vogt, Managing Dir.
15 Auerspergstrasse, Top 41, 4th Fl.
1080 Vienna, Austria
Ph: 43 1 2536001
Fax: 43 1 253600199
E-mail: iswa@iswa.org

Awards are arranged in alphabetical order below their administering organizations

URL: http://www.iswa.org

1304 ■ Communication Award
To recognize waste communications campaigns that increase public awareness and promote sustainable waste management. Open to members and non-members. Awarded annually.

1305 ■ Publication Award
To recognize an exceptional article, book, or publication in the field of solid waste management. A cash prize of 2,500 Euros and a commemorative prize are awarded annually.

1306 ■ International Union of Forest Research Organizations
(Union Internationale des Instituts de Recherches Forestieres)
Dr. Peter Mayer, Exec. Dir.
Hauptstrasse 7
A-1140 Vienna, Austria
Ph: 43 1 87701510
Ph: 43 1 877015112
Fax: 43 1 877015150
E-mail: office@iufro.org
URL: http://www.iufro.org

1307 ■ Advisory Council Award
To recognize an individual or group for outstanding contributions to the forest science/policy interface in the field of forestry, including the forest industry. Awarded when merited by the Advisory Council of IUFRO.

1308 ■ Best Poster Award
To encourage public dissemination of high quality research and to recognize distinguished poster presentations by young scientists during the IUFRO World Congress. Open to any presenter under 35 years of age. A certificate is awarded annually in each of the eight IUFRO divisions.

1309 ■ Certificate of Appreciation
To express appreciation for a significant contribution to the organization or activities of IUFRO, including conducting scientific meetings, hosting excursions, and supporting a cooperative research program. A certificate is awarded when merited.

1310 ■ Distinguished Service Award
To recognize individuals whose work has substantially furthered the aims of IUFRO. A plaque made of wood from five continents is awarded to up to three individuals per year. Established in 1981.

1311 ■ Honorary Membership
This, the IUFRO's highest award, recognizes individuals who have rendered particularly important services to the Union. A certificate is awarded approximately once per year, although up to five individuals may be honored at any one time during the five-year period between congresses. Established in 1953.

1312 ■ Outstanding Doctoral Research Award
To recognize outstanding individual scientific achievements among young doctoral researchers and to encourage further work within the fields of research covered by IUFRO. Candidates should have completed their dissertations no longer than six years prior to nomination. A medallion, certificate, and travel expenses to the World Congress are awarded in each IUFRO division, if merited.

1313 ■ Scientific Achievement Award
Selection is based on research results published in scientific journals, proceedings of scientific meetings, appropriate patents, or in books, which clearly demonstrate the importance of the advancement of forestry, forestry research, and forest products. made by a member of the parent organization, by a leader of Divisions, Subject, or Project Groups, Working Parties, and by other officers and knowledgeable persons associated with the Union (but no self-nominations). Nominations and supporting documents are sent to the Chairperson of the IUFRO Honors and Awards Committee approximately 15 months before a IUFRO World Congress. Awards consisting of a cash honorarium, a medal, and a scroll are presented every five years at the Congress. Established in 1971.

1314 ■ Student Award for Excellence in Forest Sciences
To recognize outstanding individual achievements in forest science made by Master's degree students (or equivalent), and to encourage their further work within the fields of research covered by IUFRO. A certificate and travel expenses to the IUFRO World Congress are awarded annually in each of the eight IUFRO divisions.

1315 ■ World Congress Host Scientific Award
To recognize an outstanding scientist from the host country/countries of the IUFRO World Congress who has elevated the profile of forest science and research accomplishments. A scroll and cash honorarium are presented annually.

1316 ■ Schweighofer Privatstifung Beteiligungsverwaltung GmbH
Margareta Patzelt, Contact
Favoritenstr. 7/2
A-1040 Vienna, Austria
Ph: 43 1 585 686228
Fax: 43 1 585 686220
E-mail: patzelt@schweighofer-prize.org
URL: http://www.schweighofer-prize.org

1317 ■ Schweighofer Prize
To honor European individuals or groups for innovation in forestry, wood technology, wood products, and multinational cooperation and education in the field of wood and wood products. A monetary prize of 100,000 Euros is awarded; in addition, four Schweighofer Innovation Prizes of 50,000 Euros each is awarded. Presented biennially in odd-numbered years. Established in 2003.

1318 ■ University Mozarteum, Salzburg
Mirabellplatz 1
A-5020 Salzburg, Austria
Ph: 43 662 6198
Fax: 43 662 6198 3033
E-mail: presse@moz.ac.at
URL: http://www.moz.ac.at

1319 ■ International Mozart Competition
(Internationaler Mozart Wettbewerb)
For recognition of outstanding singers, composers, pianoforte, violinists, and pianists. Musicians of all nationalities are eligible. Held every three or four years. Established in 1975 in memory of Wolfgang Amadeus Mozart.

1320 ■ University of Music and Dramatic Arts in Graz
(Hochschule fur Musik und Darstellende Kunst, Graz)
Prof. Dr. Georg Schulz, Rector
Leonhardstr. 15
A-8010 Graz, Austria
Ph: 43 316 389 1310
Fax: 43 316 389 1101
E-mail: info@kug.ac.at
URL: http://www.kug.ac.at

1321 ■ Franz Schubert and Modern Music International Competition
For recognition of an outstanding performance in three categories: Voice and Piano Duo; Violin and Piano Duo; and String Quartet. Monetary prizes ranging from 4,500 Euros to 18,000 Euros are awarded for first, second, and third place in each category. In addition, an Audience Prize as well as prizes for best interpretations are awarded. Held triennially. Established in 1989.

1322 ■ Vienna University of Music and Performing Arts
(Hochschule fur Musik und Darstellende Kunst, Wien)
Elga Ponzer, Sec. Gen.
Anton-von-Webern-Platz 1
A-1030 Vienna, Austria
Ph: 43 71155
Fax: 43 71155 199
E-mail: ponzer@mdw.ac.at
URL: http://www3.mdw.ac.at

1323 ■ International Beethoven Piano Competition Vienna
(Internationaler Beethoven Klavierwettbewerb)
To encourage the professional development of young pianists. Musicians between 17 and 32 years of age are eligible. The following prizes are awarded: the Beethoven Prize (7,500 Euros) for first place, Yujiro Kojima Prize (6,000 Euros) for second place, and the Vendome Prize (4,500 Euros) for third place. Held every four years. Established in 1961.

1324 ■ International Hilde Zadek Vocal Competition
To honor the world's best young singers. Spans music from four centuries, with a focus on the Modernist music of Schoenberg to the present day. Open to individuals of any nationality who have not turned 30 years old. Co-sponsored by the Hildegard Zadek Foundation.

1325 ■ International Joseph Haydn Chamber Music Competition
To honor the world's best piano trios and string quartets. Open to individuals of any nationality who have not turned 35 years old. Monetary prizes are presented biennially in odd-numbered years.

1326 ■ International Karl Scheit Guitar Competition
To honor the world's best young guitar players. Open to individuals of any nationality who have not turned 30 years old. Held every four years.

1327 ■ City of Villach
(Stadt Villach)
Rathausplatz 1
A-9500 Villach, Austria
Ph: 43 4242 205 1888
Fax: 43 4242 205 1899
E-mail: service@villach.at
URL: http://www.villach.at

1328 ■ Kulturpreis der Stadt Villach
For recognition of cultural and scientific achievements reflecting the cultural life of the city of Villach. A monetary prize is awarded annually. Established in 1986 by the Magistrat Villach.

1329 ■ Paracelsusring der Stadt Villach
For recognition of scientific or artistic achievements in the spirit of Paracelsus. A golden ring is awarded normally every three years. Established in 1953 by the City of Villach in honor of Theophrastus Bombastus von Hohenheim, called Paracelsus; and of his father, Wilhelm Bombast von Hohenheim, who lived and worked in Villach for 32 years.

1330 ■ World Association for the History of Veterinary Medicine
Dr. Gerald E. Weissengruber, Treas.
University of Veterinary Medicine Vienna
Dept. of Anatomy
Veterinaerplatz 1
1210 Vienna, Austria
Ph: 43 1 250772506
Fax: 43 1 250772590
E-mail: gerald.weissengruber@vu-wien.ac.at

Awards are arranged in alphabetical order below their administering organizations

URL: http://www.wahvm.umn.edu

1331 ■ Cheiron Medal

To recognize individuals for contributions of special merit involving the advancement of the history of veterinary medicine. A medal and a certificate are awarded at meetings of the World Association; as a rule, not more than two medals are awarded annually. Established in 1989 to commemorate the 20th anniversary of the Association.

Azerbaijan

1332 ■ Azerbaijan Cartoonists Union
Bayram Hajizadeh, Pres.
Inshaatchilar ave. 30, flat 10
1065 Baku, Azerbaijan
Ph: 994 12 5104025
E-mail: info@azercartoon.com
URL: http://www.azercartoon.com

1333 ■ International Cartoon Contest

To recognize outstanding print cartoons. Open to all professional and amateur cartoonists. Gold, silver, and bronze medals are awarded for first, second, and third place recipients. Held annually. Established in 2008.

1334 ■ Azerbaijan National Science Foundation
Fuad Ismayilov, Dir.
10 Istiglaliyyet St.
AZ-1001 Baku, Azerbaijan
Ph: 994 12 4973511
Fax: 994 12 4971526
E-mail: office@ansf.az
URL: http://ansf.az

1335 ■ Academician H. Abdullayev Award

To honor authors of prominent scientific articles on physics, biophysics, high-technology, and other similar areas of science. Four awards are presented: two awards of 1,000 manat each to doctors of science and doctoral students; four awards of 300 manat to postgraduates; six awards of 100 manat to students and Olympiad winners; and one award of 1,000 manat for the best article dedicated to the life and activity of Hasan Mammad Bagir Abdullayev. Awarded annually. Established in 2003.

1336 ■ Caspian Business Alliance LLC
International Trade Ctr., 6th Fl.
95 H. Aliyev Ave.
AZ-1033 Baku, Azerbaijan
Ph: 994 12 447 2186
E-mail: pr@brendaward.az
URL: http://brandaward.az

1337 ■ Brand Award Azerbaijan

To honor the best brands in Azerbaijan. Awards are presented in dozens of categories, such as entertainment, food products, education, office furniture, business credit, and Internet service providers. Established in 2008.

1338 ■ Embassy of the United States in Azerbaijan
83 Azadlig Prospecti
AZ-1007 Baku, Azerbaijan
Ph: 994 12 4980 335
Fax: 994 12 4656 671
URL: http://azerbaijan.usembassy.gov

1339 ■ Hafiz Pashayev Award for the Promotion of U.S.-Azerbaijan Relations

To recognize an Azerbaijani citizen who has made an outstanding contribution to promoting stronger relations between the United States and Azerbaijan. Awarded annually. Established in 2008.

Bahamas

1340 ■ Bahamas Hotel Association
Wendy Wong, Exec. Admin.
SG Private Banking Bldg.
PO Box N-7799
Nassau, Bahamas
Ph: 242322-8381
Ph: 242322-8382
Fax: 242502-4220
E-mail: bha@bahamashotels.org
URL: http://www.bhahotels.com

1341 ■ Bahamas Hotel Awards/Cacique Awards

Recognizes excellence in the Caribbean hotel industry. Awards include: Hotelier of the Year, Manager of the Year, Chef of the Year, Employee of the Year, Supervisor of the Year, and Sales Executive of the Year. Awarded annually.

1342 ■ Bahamas International Film Festival
Bldg. 10, Ground Fl.
4th Terrace East and Collins Ave.
PO Box SP 64008
Nassau, Bahamas
Ph: 242325-5747
Fax: 242356-2991
URL: http://www.bintlfilmfest.com

1343 ■ Bahamas International Film Festival

To provide the local community and international festival audience with a diverse presentation of films from the Bahamas and around the world. Four awards are presented: the Spirit of Freedom Award for dramatic film, Spirit of Freedom Award for documentary, New Vision Award, and the Award for Best Short Film. Held annually. Established in 2004.

1344 ■ Bahamas Web Awards
PO Box N-105
Nassau, Bahamas
URL: http://www.bahamaswebawards.com

1345 ■ Bahamas Web Awards

To honor individuals and companies for Web sites or Web pages created for, or by, Bahamian entities. Criteria include content, visual design, functionality, innovation, and whether the site has achieved its objectives. Awards are presented in various categories. In addition, the Best of the Bahamas Award and People's Choice Award are presented. Awarded annually. Established in 2003.

1346 ■ Governor General's Youth Award
11 Patton St.
Palmdale
PO Box SS-19228
Nassau, Bahamas
Ph: 242326-1760
Fax: 242328-4420
E-mail: ggya@coralwave.com
URL: http://www.bahamasggya.org

1347 ■ Governor General's Youth Award

To foster success in Bahaman youth through activities that encourage personal discovery and growth, self-reliance, perseverance, responsibility, and service to the community. Gold, silver, and bronze awards are presented annually. Established in 1987 as part of the Duke of Edinburgh Award Program.

1348 ■ Marlin Awards
c/o Harris Communications
PO Box SP-63808
Nassau, Bahamas
Ph: 242676-6719
Fax: 242327-1249
URL: http://marlinawards.com

1349 ■ Marlin Awards

To recognize the best in Caribbean Gospel music. Awards are offered in more than 50 categories, including the prestigious Song and Album of the Year categories. Established in 1996.

Bahrain

1350 ■ College of Health Sciences
Salmaniya Medical Complex
Manama, Bahrain
Ph: 973 172 86663
E-mail: samin@health.gov.bh
URL: http://www.chs.edu.bh

1351 ■ His Excellency Mr. Jawad S. Al-Arrayed Prize

To honor the best student graduating from the Bachelor of Science nursing program. Awarded annually.

1352 ■ Rafida Bint Saad Al-Aslamiya Prize

To honor the best graduating student in general nursing. Awarded annually.

1353 ■ Abu Rayhan Al-Bayronni Prize

To honor the best graduating student in pharmacy. Awarded annually.

1354 ■ Abu Abdulla Moh'd Al-Edreesi Prize

To honor the best graduating student in health teacher development. Awarded annually.

1355 ■ Ali Bin Al-Farabi Prize

To honor the best graduating student in public health. Awarded annually.

1356 ■ Abo Yousif Yaqoub Al-Kindi Prize

To honor the best graduating student in sports and physiotherapy. Awarded annually.

1357 ■ Ibn Al-Nafees Prize

To honor the best graduating student in cardiac care nursing. Awarded annually.

1358 ■ Muhammad Bin Zakariya Al Razi Prize

To honor the best graduating student in medical laboratory studies. Awarded annually.

1359 ■ Ommaya Qurabi Al-Tajer Prize

To honor the best graduating student in emergency nursing. Awarded annually.

1360 ■ Abdul Qassim Al-Zahrawi Prize

To honor the best graduating student in dental hygiene. Awarded annually.

1361 ■ Fatima Al-Zayani Prize

To honor the best graduating student in midwifery. Awarded annually.

1362 ■ His Excellency Dr. Ali Fakhro Prize

To honor the best graduating student in medical equipment maintenance and repair. Awarded annually.

1363 ■ Her Highness Shaikha Hessa Prize

To honor the best graduating student in community health nursing. Awarded annually.

1364 ■ Ishaq bin Omran Prize

To honor the best graduating student in psychiatric nursing. Awarded annually.

1365 ■ Ibn Sina Prize

To honor the best graduating student in radiography. Awarded annually.

1366 ■ Al-Sahabi Zaid Bin Thabit Prize

To honor the best graduating student in medical secretarial work. Awarded annually.

Awards are arranged in alphabetical order below their administering organizations

Bangladesh

1367 ■ Bangladesh Chemical Society
Prof. Tofail Ahmad Chowdhury, Sec.
10/11 Eastern Plz.
Hatirpool
Dhaka 1205, Bangladesh
Ph: 880 2 8614683
Fax: 880 2 8615583
E-mail: bchemsoc@bangla.net
URL: http://www.chemhome-bcs.org

1368 ■ Gold Medal
For outstanding and sustained contributions to chemistry in Bangladesh.

1369 ■ Bangladesh University of Engineering and Technology
Department of Architecture
Dhaka 1000, Bangladesh
Ph: 880 966 5633
Fax: 880 2 861 3046
E-mail: dsw@buet.edu
URL: http://www.buet.ac.bd/arch

1370 ■ Berger Awards for Students of Architecture
To recognize the talent of architecture students enrolled Bangladesh University of Engineering and Technology. Three awards are presented annually: Best Portfolio Award, Promising Designer Award, and Best Design Award. Established in 2006.

1371 ■ DHL Worldwide Express, Bangladesh National Office
Molly Capital Ctr., 4th and 5th Fl.
Road 127, Holding, 76 Gulshan Ave.
Dhaka 1212, Bangladesh
Ph: 88 2 988 1703
URL: http://www.dhl.com.bd

1372 ■ Bangladesh Business Awards
To recognize exceptional business leaders in Bangladesh. The following awards may be presented: Business Person of the Year, Outstanding Woman in Business, Enterprise of the Year, Best Financial Institution of the Year, and Best Joint Venture Enterprise of the Year; in addition, a Special Achievement Award may be presented. Awarded annually. Established in 2000.

1373 ■ Holcim (Bangladesh) Ltd.
House No. 8, Rd. No. 14
Baridhara
Dhaka 1212, Bangladesh
Ph: 880 2988 1002
Fax: 880 2988 6394
URL: http://www.holcim.com.bd/bd

1374 ■ Holcim Green Built Bangladesh Contest
To encourage Bangladesh engineers, architects, planners, and students to focus on sustainability and strive to develop the green-built concept in Bangladesh. Awards are presented in two categories: Built Projects, for projects that are already constructed, under construction, or approved for construction; and Idea Projects, for conceptual visions, even those with a low potential for realization. Monetary prizes are awarded for first, second, and third place winners in each category. Awarded annually.

1375 ■ UNESCO Dhaka Office
Derek Elias, Off.-in-Charge
House 122, Rd. 1
Block F
Banani
Dhaka 1213, Bangladesh
Ph: 880 2 9862073
Ph: 880 2 9873210
Fax: 880 2 9871150

URL: http://www.unescodhaka.org

1376 ■ UNESCO Bangladesh Journalism Award
To recognize and encourage quality investigative journalism that contributes to establishing transparency and accountability by exposing corruption and vices in various spheres of public life. A monetary prize of Tk 50,000 is awarded annually. Established in 2007.

Barbados

1377 ■ Barbados Association of Medical Practitioners
Dr. Carlos A. Chase, Pres.
BAMP Complex
Spring Garden
St. Michael, Barbados
Ph: 246429-7569
Fax: 246435-2328
E-mail: info@bamp.org.bb
URL: http://www.bamp.org.bb

1378 ■ Practitioner's Award for Excellence
Recognizes contributions to health care/medical education in Barbados. Awarded annually.

1379 ■ Barbados Employers' Confederation
Mr. Tony Walcott, Exec. Dir.
PO Box 33B
St. Michael, Barbados
Ph: 246620-4753
Ph: 246620-4755
Fax: 246620-2907
URL: http://www.barbadosemployers.com/cms

1380 ■ Barbados Employers' Confederation Scholarship
To support a Barbadian to read for a degree majoring in Management that includes a course in Industrial Relations at the University of the West Indies, Cave Hill Campus. The scholarship covers a period of up to three years. It is valued at BDS$1,500 per year and is to be used in meeting the student's maintenance costs, books, fees, and incidental expenses. Established in 1964.

1381 ■ Barbados International Film Festival
PO Box 988
General Post Office
Bridgetown, Barbados
Ph: 246231-2388
E-mail: info@barbadosfilmfestival.com
URL: http://www.barbadosfilmfestival.com

1382 ■ Barbados International Film Festival
To recognize the best of independent world cinema in order to enrich the film culture in Latin America and the Caribbean. Awards are presented in three categories: features, documentaries, and shorts. In addition, Audience Awards and Jury Prizes are presented. Held annually.

1383 ■ Barbados National Trust
Wildey House
Wildey
St. Michael, Barbados
Ph: 246426-2421
Ph: 246436-9033
Fax: 246429-9055
E-mail: natrust@sunbeach.net
URL: http://trust.funbarbados.com

1384 ■ Barbados National Trust Member
To recognize buildings of historical and architectural interest. Established in 1961.

1385 ■ Caribbean Tourism Organization
Hugh Riley, Sec. Gen.
1 Financial Pl.
Collymore Rock
St. Michael, Barbados

Ph: 246427-5242
Fax: 246429-3065
E-mail: ctobar@caribsurf.com
URL: http://www.onecaribbean.org

1386 ■ Lifetime Achievement Award
To recognize an individual who over his or her lifetime has made a difference in the industry by their actions, contributions, and great accomplishments in the Caribbean region and beyond. Awarded annually.

1387 ■ Frank Collymore Hall
Central Bank of Barbados
Spry St.
Bridgetown, Barbados
Ph: 246436-9083
Fax: 246228-2703
E-mail: fchmail@centralbank.org.bb
URL: http://www.fch.org.bb

1388 ■ Frank Collymore Literary Awards
To recognize outstanding works of poetry, drama, prose fiction, and non-fiction. Monetary prizes are awarded in each category. In addition, the John Wickham Prize honors the best writer under the age of 21. Awarded annually.

1389 ■ Insurance Association of the Caribbean
Mr. Douglas Camacho, Pres.
Thomas Pierce Bldg.
Lower Collymore Rock
St. Michael, Barbados
Ph: 246427-5608
Ph: 246427-5609
Fax: 246427-7277
E-mail: info@iac-caribbean.com
URL: http://www.iac-caribbean.com

1390 ■ Caribbean Education Award
To provide financial assistance to professionals in the pursuit of continuing education. Applicants must be: Caribbean nationals; employed by an IAC Member Company view members; full-time employees in the Claims Division; and enrolled in insurance-related course(s) from a school, university, or professional organization. Grants totaling US$5,000 are presented each year. Sponsored by Crawford & Company.

1391 ■ Timeless Barbados Entertainment Inc.
Ph: 246256-4364
Fax: 246256-4364
E-mail: timelessbb@yahoo.com
URL: http://www.timelessbarbados.com

1392 ■ Barbados Music Awards
To recognize outstanding musicians in Barbados. Awards are presented in numerous categories, including best soul/R&B single, best raga single, best social commentary, best Christmas album, and Songwriter of the Year. In addition, People's Choice Awards, International Award of Merit, Cornerstone Awards, and Lifetime Achievement Awards may be presented. Awarded annually. Established in 2006.

Belarus

1393 ■ Council of Ministers of the Republic of Belarus
11 Sovetskaya St.
220010 Minsk, Belarus
Ph: 375 8 17 222 6046
Fax: 375 8 17 222 6665
E-mail: contact@government.by
URL: http://www.government.by

1394 ■ Quality Prize of the Government of the Republic of Belarus
To recognize Belarus companies and organizations for high quality products, works, or services; for competitive excellence; for efficient quality

Awards are arranged in alphabetical order below their administering organizations

management methods; for the successful implementation of international standards; and for satisfying the needs of customers. Awarded annually to recipients in several categories. Established in 1999.

1395 ■ National Academy of Sciences of Belarus
Anatoly M. Rusetsky, Chm.
66 Independence Ave.
220072 Minsk, Belarus
Ph: 375 172 841801
Fax: 375 172 842816
E-mail: nasb@presidium.bas-net.by
URL: http://nasb.gov.by

1396 ■ Best Scientific Work
To recognize exceptional scientific work. Awarded biennially in odd-numbered years.

1397 ■ Best Scientific Work of a Young Scientist
To recognize exceptional scientific work by a young scientist. Awarded biennially in odd-numbered years.

1398 ■ Best Student Scientific Work
To recognize exceptional scientific work by a student. Awarded biennially in odd-numbered years.

Belgium

1399 ■ Association of European Journalists
N. Peter Kramer, Sec. Gen.
145, Avenue Baron Albert d'Huart
B-1950 Kraainem, Belgium
Ph: 32 47 8291 985
E-mail: npkramer@skynet.be
URL: http://www.aej.org

1400 ■ European Journalism Prize
To recognize a European journalist for outstanding achievements. Awarded annually.

1401 ■ Association of European Operational Research Societies
Philippe Van Asbroeck, Permanent Sec.
EURO Office
Universite Libre de Bruxelles
Service de mathematiques de la gestion
Bld. du Triomphe CP210/01
B-1050 Brussels, Belgium
Fax: 32 2 6505970
E-mail: Office@euro-online.org
URL: http://www.euro-online.org

1402 ■ Distinguished Service Medal
For distinguished service to the Society or to operation research. A medal, a diploma, and free registration at all future EURO Conferences is awarded annually when merited.

1403 ■ Doctoral Dissertation Award
To recognize an exceptional doctoral dissertation in operations research. Three finalists receive travel expenses and free registration to the conference at which they are competing. Winner is awarded monetary prize of 1,000 Euros and a certificate annually when merited.

1404 ■ Excellence in Practice Award
To recognize the best paper describing a practical application of operations research. A monetary prize of 3,000 Euros (to be equally divided in the case of multiple authors) and a certificate are awarded annually when merited.

1405 ■ Gold Medal
To recognize a prominent individual or institution for an outstanding contribution to operational research science. Generally awarded for a body of work over a sustained period of time. Recipient receives a gold medal, a diploma, travel expenses to the awarding conference, and free registration at all future EURO Conferences.

1406 ■ Management Science Strategic Innovation Prize
To recognize outstanding innovative contributions to specific application of operations research as it pertains to management. For prize consideration, the work must be submitted as a paper. The winning paper is presented at the conference and published in EJOR. A monetary prize of at least 12,000 Euros is awarded annually.

1407 ■ Association of European Operational Research Societies within IFORS
Ir. Philippe Van Asbroeck, Sec.
Universite Libre de Brussels
Blvd. du Triomphe CP 210-01
1050 Brussels, Belgium
Fax: 32 2 6505970
E-mail: office@euro-online.org
URL: http://www.euro-online.org/display.php?page=welcome

1408 ■ EURO Doctoral Dissertation Award
To recognize an early stage scientist on the basis of a doctoral dissertation in any area of operational research. A certificate and monetary prize of 1,000 Euros are awarded biennially in odd-numbered years. Established in 2006.

1409 ■ Association of European Refrigeration Component Manufacturers
Mr. Jochen A. Winkler, Pres.
Ave. du Bourget 40
1130 Brussels, Belgium
Ph: 32 30 21479872
Fax: 32 30 21479871
E-mail: winkler@asercom.org
URL: http://www.asercom.org
Formerly: Association of European Refrigeration Compressor and Controls Manufacturer.

1410 ■ Energy Efficiency Award
For the most valuable energy saving concept or system in refrigeration/air conditioning. A monetary prize of 10,000 Euros is awarded biennially in even-numbered years.

1411 ■ Belgian Neurological Society (Belgische Vereniging voor Neurologie)
Paul Boon, Pres.
CHR Citadelle
Dept. of Neurology
Bd du 12 de Ligne 1
B-4000 Liege, Belgium
Ph: 32 4 2256451
Ph: 32 4 2223857
Fax: 32 4 2262939
E-mail: mgonce@cma.neurosc.be
URL: http://www.neuro.be

1412 ■ BNS Travel Grants
To enable members to participate at International Congresses. A grant of 600 Euros is bestowed to attend a congress within Europe, and a grant of 1,000 Euros is awarded for a congress outside of Europe.

1413 ■ Research Fellowship for Young Investigators
To support young investigators. A fellowship in the amount of 10,000 Euros is awarded annually.

1414 ■ Belgian Operations Research Society
Prof. Patrick De Causmaecker, Pres.
Dept. di Informatique
University Libre de Bruzelles, CP 210/1
Blvd. du Triumph
B-1050 Brussels, Belgium
Ph: 32 2 6503095
Fax: 32 2 6293690
E-mail: bernard.fortz@ulb.ac.be
URL: http://www.orbel.be

1415 ■ ORBEL Award
To honor the author of a scientifically oriented student's thesis (excluding PhD theses). A monetary prize of 1,000 Euros is awarded annually.

1416 ■ Brussels International Festival of Fantastic Film
Georges Delmote, Chair
Gravin van Vlaanderenstraat 8
Rue de la Comtesse de Flandre
B-1020 Brussels, Belgium
Ph: 32 2 201 1713
Fax: 32 2 201 1469
E-mail: info@bifff.org
URL: http://www.bifff.org

1417 ■ Brussels International Festival of Fantastic Film (Festival International du Film Fantastique, de Science-Fiction, et Thriller de Bruxelles)
For recognition of outstanding fantasy and science fiction films. The following prizes are awarded: Golden Raven Grand Prix, Silver Raven, 7th Orbit, Silver Melies, Pegase, and the Thriller Award. Held annually. Formerly: (2006) Brussels International Festival of Fantasy, Thriller, and Science-Fiction Films.

1418 ■ BTC, the Belgian Development Agency Trade for Development Centre (Semaine du commerce equitable)
Rue Haute 147 Hoogstraat
B-1000 Brussels, Belgium
Ph: 32 2 505 3700
Fax: 32 2 502 9862
URL: http://www.befair.be

1419 ■ Be Fair Award
To recognize a Belgian business that sells fair trade products and/or delivers fair trade services. A monetary prize of 5,000 Euros is awarded annually during Fair Trade Week.

1420 ■ Be Sustainable Award
To recognize a Belgian business that sells sustainable products and/or delivers sustainable services. A monetary prize of 5,000 Euros is awarded annually during Fair Trade Week.

1421 ■ Dialogic Agency
5 Col Vert St.
B-1170 Brussels, Belgium
Ph: 32 2 426 6466
Fax: 32 2 426 5378
E-mail: info@dialogic-agency.com
URL: http://www.dialogic-agency.com

1422 ■ European Football Supporters Award
To honor a football club or association that has demonstrated exemplary action by trying to instill a positive spirit around any football game anywhere in Europe. Criteria include: 1) Respect for others, regardless of nationality, race, culture, and religion; 2) Respect for the moral and physical integrity of all players, which excludes all forms of violence, including verbal abuse; 3) Compliance with the rules and acceptance of the referees' decisions; 4) Promotion of fair play and the life skills of athletes; 5) Appreciation of the size of the festive and friendly sport, brotherhood between fans, and communion in the same passion; 6) Training of younger generations within crowds by spreading the principles of sports ethics; and 7) Solidarity with minority groups, motivated by a shared passion for football. A monetary prize of 6,000 Euros is awarded annually. Established in 2005 by the Dialogic Agency and the City of Brussels, Belgium.

1423 ■ EUREKA
Mr. Robert Verbruggen, Contact
Rue Neerveld 107
B-1200 Brussels, Belgium

Awards are arranged in alphabetical order below their administering organizations

Ph: 32 2 7770950
Fax: 32 2 7707495
E-mail: info@eurekanetwork.org
URL: http://www.eurekanetwork.org
Formerly: Eureka Secretariat.

1424 ■ Lillehammer Award
To recognize a contribution made by a project to improving Europe's environment by developing sustainable solutions to the problems of waste and pollution. A monetary prize of 10,000 Euros is awarded annually. Established in 1994.

1425 ■ European Advertising Standards Alliance
(Alliance Europeenne pour l'Ethique en Publicite)
Dr. Oliver W. Gray, Dir. Gen.
Rue de la Pepiniere
Boomkwekerijstraat 10-10a
B-1000 Brussels, Belgium
Ph: 32 2 5137806
Fax: 32 2 5132861
E-mail: info@easa-alliance.org
URL: http://www.easa-alliance.org

1426 ■ Best Practice Award
To recognize a self-regulatory organization that has most effectively implemented an element of the EASA best practice model. Awarded annually.

1427 ■ European Association for Battery, Hybrid and Fuel Cell Electric Vehicles
(Association Europeenne des Vehicules Electriques Routiers)
Philippe Aussourd, Pres.
Bd. de la Plaine, 2
B-1050 Brussels, Belgium
Ph: 32 2 6292363
E-mail: info@avere.org
URL: http://www.avere.org

1428 ■ Best Electrical Vehicle
For electrical vehicle manufacturers.

1429 ■ FQE Prizes
For the best students in overall and specific subjects.

1430 ■ European Association for Chemical and Molecular Sciences
Avenue E. van Nieuwenhuyse 4
B-1160 Brussels, Belgium
Ph: 32 2 792 7540
URL: http://www.euchems.eu

1431 ■ EuCheMS Lecture
To recognize a prominent chemist from a European country for contributions to chemical and molecular science. Awarded annually.

1432 ■ European Sustainable Chemistry Award
To recognize individual scientists and teams for contributions to sustainable chemistry. A monetary prize of 10,000 Euros is awarded biennially in even-numbered years. Established in 2010.

1433 ■ European Association for Research in Industrial Economics
Ene Kannel, Exec. Sec.
c/o European Institute for Advanced Studies in Management
Place de Brouckere Plein 31
B-1000 Brussels, Belgium
Ph: 32 2 226 6660
Fax: 32 2 512 1929
E-mail: kannel@eiasm.be
URL: http://www.earie.org

1434 ■ Paul Geroski Best Article of the Year Prize
To recognize the best articles published in the *International Journal of Industrial Organization* during the previous year. A monetary prize of US$1,000 and a certificate are awarded to two recipients annually. Established in 2007.

1435 ■ Young Economists' Essay Awards
To recognize young economists for exceptionally innovative and high-quality papers. Candidates must be younger than 35 years and must have completed their PhD less than five years ago. Awarded annually to one or more recipients. Established in 2000.

1436 ■ European Association of Communications Agencies
152 Blvd. Brand Whitlock
B-1200 Brussels, Belgium
Ph: 32 2 740 0710
Fax: 32 2 740 0717
URL: http://www.eaca.be

1437 ■ Care Awards
To recognize excellence in social marketing as part of the Association's overall commitment to promote corporate social responsibility, and to highlight the advertising industry's specific contributions to society by honoring the most successful creative social marketing campaigns. Awarded in six categories: nonprofit organizations and non-governmental bodies; government bodies and related organizations; local and regional authorities; public and private sector businesses; corporate governance; and volunteering and people-to-people activities. Awarded annually.

1438 ■ Euro Effie Awards
To promote and recognize excellence in marketing communications that can prove effectiveness in at least two European countries. Presented in several categories, including consumer goods, automotive, retail, and product/service launch. Established in 1996, and based on the Effie Awards that were established in 1968 by the New York American Marketing Association.

1439 ■ European Association of Directory and Database Publishers
(Association Europeenne des Editeurs d'Annuaires et Bases de Donrees)
Mrs. Luisa Piazza, Pres.
127 Ave. Franklin Roosevelt
B-1050 Brussels, Belgium
Ph: 32 2 6463060
Fax: 32 2 6463637
E-mail: mailbox@eadp.org
URL: http://www.eadp.org

1440 ■ European Awards for Quality and Excellence in Directory Publishing
To recognize quality and excellence in directory publishing. Awards are presented in two categories: Business-to-Business and Business-to-Consumer. Awarded annually.

1441 ■ European Association of Hospital Pharmacists
Rue de Abbe Cuypers, 3
B-1040 Brussels, Belgium
Ph: 32 2 741 6822
Fax: 32 2 734 7910
URL: http://www.eahp.eu

1442 ■ Student Science Award
To recognize and honor the best scientific research manuscript authored by an undergraduate hospital pharmacy student. Awarded annually. Co-sponsored by the European Pharmaceutical Student Association.

1443 ■ European Cancer Organization
Michel Ballieu, CEO
Avenue E Mounier 83
B-1200 Brussels, Belgium
Ph: 32 2 7720201
Fax: 32 2 7750200
E-mail: michel.ballieu@ecco-org.eu
URL: http://www.ecco-org.eu

1444 ■ Clinical Research Award
For an outstanding international contribution to the integration of scientific research and clinical practice in oncology.

1445 ■ ECCO/EJC Young Investigator's Award
For recent and original work in cancer care, research, or treatment by a young scientist or doctor. A monetary prize of 4,000 Euros, free conference registration, accommodations for the week of the conference, and reimbursement of travel expenses are awarded.

1446 ■ ECCO/EJC Young Investigator's Poster Awards
For the best poster by a young basic scientist or clinical oncologist at the ECCO/ESMO conference. Three awards are presented.

1447 ■ ECCO-ESMO Educational Awards
To allow clinicians and nurses who are not involved in research to attend the ECCO-ESMO conference. Award includes free registration and up to four nights accommodation.

1448 ■ Pezcoller Foundation-ECCO Recognition for Contributions to Oncology
To recognize an individual for contributions and dedication to the improvement of cancer care, research, and treatment. A monetary prize of 25,000 Euros and a plaque are awarded biennially.

1449 ■ European Cell Death Organization
Boris Zhivotovsky, Pres.
VIB-University of Gent
Dept. for Molecular Biomedical Research
Technologiepark 927
B-9052 Gent, Belgium
Ph: 32 9 3313682
Fax: 32 9 3313511
E-mail: ecdo@dmbr.ugent.be
URL: http://www.ecdo.eu

1450 ■ Career Award
For outstanding scientist with exceptional record in the cell death field. Awarded annually.

1451 ■ European Ceramic Society
Dr. Hasan Mandal, Pres.
Ave. Gouverneur Cornez 4
B-7000 Mons, Belgium
Ph: 32 65403421
Fax: 32 65403458
E-mail: ecers@bcrc.be
URL: http://www.ecers.org

1452 ■ International Prize
To recognize a ceramist who has contributed to the advancement of contacts between the European and the international ceramic community. Awarded biennially.

1453 ■ Stuijts Award
To recognize a ceramist noted for outstanding contributions to ceramic science or technology. Awarded biennially.

1454 ■ European Chemical Industry Council
Giorgio Squinzi, Pres.
Ave. E Van Nieuwenhuyse, 4 Box 1
B-1160 Brussels, Belgium
Ph: 32 2 6767211
Fax: 32 2 6767300
E-mail: mail@cefic.be
URL: http://www.cefic.org

1455 ■ European Responsible Care Awards
To recognize companies that serve as outstanding examples of good practice in responsible care of the environment. The winner receives a two-day consultancy on a responsible care objective or related subject of his or her choice. Awarded annually. Established in 2005.

1456 ■ LRI Innovative Science Award
To recognize an individual for a novel interdisciplinary research project in toxicology. A monetary prize of 100,000 Euros is awarded annually. Sponsored by the Long-Range Research Initiative (LRI).

Awards are arranged in alphabetical order below their administering organizations

1457 ■ Solvents Stewardship Awards

To promote and share best practice in the use of solvents by recognizing companies that undertake innovative ways to minimize the impact of solvent use on the environment and on health, and to share this information so that other solvent users and handlers can implement similar improvements. A trophy is awarded annually. Established in 1999. Administered by the European Solvents Industry Group (ESIG), a joint activity of the Oxygenated Solvents Producers Association (OSPA) and the Hydrocarbon Solvents Producers Association (HSPA), two sector groups of the European Chemical Industry Council (Cefic).

1458 ■ European Commission
Rafaella Di Iorio, Contact
Ph: 32 2 2984897
Fax: 32 2 2993746
URL: http://www.europa.eu

1459 ■ DesCartes Prize for Collaborative, Transnational Research

To recognize transnational teams that have achieved outstanding scientific or technological results through collaborative research in any field of science, such as social sciences, humanities and economics. A monetary award of 1.36 million Euros is to be shared among the recipients of the research prize, with an additional 30,000 Euros awarded to each of the four finalist teams. Awarded annually. Established in 2000.

1460 ■ European Business Awards for the Environment

Recognizes companies that integrate sustainable development into their activities. Awards are presented in four categories: management, process, product and international cooperation. Judges place special weight on initiatives that show improvements in greenhouse gases and climate change, air quality, health and environment, biodiversity, coastal and marine areas, soil degradation, civil protection, and solid waste. Awarded biennially in even-numbered years. Established in 1990.

1461 ■ Prize for Science Communication

To recognize excellence in the dissemination of research and science issues to European culture. A monetary prize of 60,000 Euros is awarded to up to three recipients, with an additional 5,000 Euros awarded to up three finalists. Awarded annually. Established in 2004. Formerly: (2007) Science Communication Prize.

1462 ■ European Commission - DG Development
Gino Debo, Contact
SC-15 00/70
1040 Brussels, Belgium
Ph: 32 2 299 2143
Fax: 32 2 296 4926
E-mail: gino.debo@ec.europa.eu
URL: http://ec.europa.eu/development

1463 ■ Lorenzo Natali Journalism Prize

To recognize journalists writing on topics of human rights and democracy in the developing world. A total of 50,000 euros is awarded annually to outstanding works of print and online journalism in Africa, Europe, the Middle East, Asia, and Latin America/Caribbean. Formerly: Lorenzo Natali Prize for Journalists.

1464 ■ European Convention for Constructional Steelwork (Convention Europeenne de la Construction Metallique)
Mrs. Veronique Baes-Dehan, Sec. Gen.
32, Ave. des Ombrages, bte 20
B-1200 Brussels, Belgium
Ph: 32 2 7620429
Fax: 32 2 7620935

E-mail: eccs@steelconstruct.com
URL: http://www.steelconstruct.com

1465 ■ European Steel Design Awards

To honor outstanding designs in steel constructions emphasizing the advantages of steel in construction, production, economy, and architecture. Awarded in each of 19 European countries. Awarded biennially in odd-numbered years.

1466 ■ Charles Massonnet Award

To recognize a prominent scientist who has highly contributed to the advancement of scientific and technical support to constructional steelwork. Awarded annually. Established in 1998.

1467 ■ European Council for Agricultural Law (Comite Europeen de Droit Rural)
Dr. Marc Heyerick, Gen. Sec.
Deinse Horsweg 33
B-9031 Gent, Belgium
Ph: 32 9 2771857
Fax: 32 9 2771857
E-mail: vero.de.rooze@telenet.be
URL: http://www.cedr.org

1468 ■ CEDR Medals

To recognize individuals who have rendered significant service to the Organization and to the development of the field of agricultural law. Awarded biennially in odd-numbered years.

1469 ■ Prix d'Honneur

To recognize the author of works on topics related to agricultural law. Awarded biennially in odd-numbered years.

1470 ■ European Council of Spatial Planners (Conseil Europeen des Urbanistes)
Bruno Clerbaux, Sec. Gen.
Ave. d' Auderghem 63
B-1040 Brussels, Belgium
Ph: 32 2 2346503
Ph: 32 2 6396300
Fax: 32 2 2346501
E-mail: secretariat@ectp-ceu.eu
URL: http://www.ceu-ectp.eu

1471 ■ European Urban and Regional Planning Awards

To recognize planning strategies, schemes, or developments that make an outstanding contribution to the quality of life in urban and rural regions of Europe. Awarded biennially in even-numbered years.

1472 ■ European Disposables and Nonwovens Association
Mr. Pierre Wiertz, Gen. Mgr.
Ave. Herrmann Debroux, 46
B-1030 Brussels, Belgium
Ph: 32 2 7349310
Ph: 32 2 7401823
Fax: 32 2 7333518
E-mail: info@edana.org
URL: http://www.edana.org/Content/Default.asp?

1473 ■ Innovation Awards

To encourage and acknowledge innovation and new ideas in nonwovens, their raw material, and the machinery used in making or converting nonwoven fabrics. A diploma and statuette are awarded to one recipient in each of six categories. Presented at the triennial congress. Formerly: (1995) European Disposables and Nonwovens Association Awards.

1474 ■ European Emergency Number Association
Avenue Louise 262
B-1050 Brussels, Belgium
E-mail: info@eena.org
URL: http://www.eena.org

1475 ■ 112 Awards

To recognize and honor individuals and organizations particularly engaged in improving and promoting the European emergency number 112. Presented in several categories, including Citizen and Emergency Rescue, Emergency Call Center, Political Initiative, and National 112 System. Awarded annually. Established in 2007.

1476 ■ European Generic Medicines Association
Mr. Greg Perry, Dir. Gen.
Rue d'Arlon, 50
B-1000 Brussels, Belgium
Ph: 32 2 7368411
Fax: 32 2 7367438
E-mail: info@egagenerics.com
URL: http://www.egagenerics.com

1477 ■ EGA Generic Medicines Award

To honor exemplary efforts in research, publications, and public awareness in the field of generic medicines. Awarded annually. Established in 1997.

1478 ■ European Health Management Association
Jennifer Bremner, Dir.
Rue Belliard 15-17, 6th Fl.
1040 Brussels, Belgium
Ph: 32 2 5026525
Fax: 32 2 5031007
E-mail: info@ehma.org
URL: http://www.ehma.org
Formerly: (1987) European Association of Programmes in Health Services Studies.

1479 ■ Baxter Award for Healthcare Management in Europe

To recognize an outstanding publication and/or practical contribution to excellence in healthcare management in Europe. Contributions can be in any of the following fields: management development initiatives, health services research, or innovations in management practice. Books, articles, or papers submitted must have been published within the last two years. The deadline is January 31st. A monetary award of $5,000 is presented at the Annual Conference of the EHMA. Established in 1986, the award is sponsored by Baxter Healthcare.

1480 ■ Karolinska Medical Management Centre/EHMA Research Award

To recognize the best publication associated with a doctoral thesis related to health management. A monetary prize of 1,000 Euros is presented at the annual EHMA Conference. Funded by Karolinska MMC.

1481 ■ European Logistics Association
Kunstlaan 19 Avenue des Arts
B-1210 Brussels, Belgium
Ph: 32 2 230 0211
Fax: 32 2 230 8123
URL: http://www.elalog.org

1482 ■ European Award for Logistics Excellence

To recognize an individual or company that has demonstrated outstanding achievement in logistics and supply chain management. Awarded annually.

1483 ■ European Marketing Academy
Veronica Wong, Pres.
European Institute for Advanced Studies in Management
Pl. de Brouckere Plein, 31
B-1000 Brussels, Belgium
Ph: 32 2 2266660
Ph: 32 2 2266661
Fax: 32 2 5121929
E-mail: emac@eiasm.be
URL: http://www.emac-online.org/r/default. asp?ild=IHGMD

Awards are arranged in alphabetical order below their administering organizations

1484 ■ McKinsey Marketing Dissertation Award
Recognizes and encourages distinguished dissertations in the field of marketing. Awarded annually. Established in 2009. Sponsored by McKinsey and Co.

**1485 ■ European Nuclear Society
(Europaische Kernenergie-Gesellschaft)**
Prof. Vladimir Slugen, Pres.
Rue Belliard 65
B-1040 Brussels, Belgium
Ph: 32 2 5053050
Fax: 32 2 5023902
E-mail: info@euronuclear.org
URL: http://www.euronuclear.org

1486 ■ Jan Runermark Award
To recognize an individual who has given outstanding service to the benefit of the young generation. Awarded annually. Established in 1995. Administered by the ENS Young Generation Network.

1487 ■ European Society for Cognitive Psychology
Cristina Cacciari, Pres.-Elect
Bernard Hamelinckstraat, 3
Drongen
9031 Gent, Belgium
E-mail: marilou.vandierendonck@telenet.be
URL: http://escop.eu

1488 ■ Paul Bertelson Award
To honor scientists at a relatively early stage of their scientific career who have made an outstanding contribution to European Cognitive Psychology. Candidates should normally have completed their doctoral thesis no more than 8 years before nomination, and be under 35 years of age. However, the committee does not wish to discriminate against researchers who have, for example, taken maternity leave or made career switches. Awarded biennially in odd-numbered years. Established in 2001.

**1489 ■ European Society for Engineering Education
(Societe Europeenne pour la Formation des Ingenieurs)**
Mrs. Francoise Come, Sec. Gen.
119, rue de Stassart
B-1050 Brussels, Belgium
Ph: 32 2 5023609
Fax: 32 2 5029611
E-mail: info@sefi.be
URL: http://www.sefi.be

1490 ■ Leonardo da Vinci Medal
This, the highest award of recognition that can be bestowed by the Society, is given to honor living persons who have made an outstanding contribution of international significance to engineering education. A medal is awarded annually. Established in 1983.

1491 ■ European Society for Radiotherapy and Oncology
Alessandro Cortese, Exec. Dir.
Ave. E Mounierlaan 83
B-1200 Brussels, Belgium
Ph: 32 2 7759340
Fax: 32 2 7795494
E-mail: info@estro.org
URL: http://www.estro.org
Formerly: (2011) European Society for Therapeutic Radiology and Oncology.

1492 ■ Accuray Award
To recognize excellence in radiotherapy and radiation technology. In even-numbered years, a monetary prize of 7,500 Euros is awarded to a radiotherapy professional for research in the field of radiobiology, radiation physics, clinical radiotherapy, or radiation technology. In odd-numbered years, 2,500 Euros is awarded to a physicist or radiation technologist, and to a radiation clinician.

1493 ■ Breur Lecture and Gold Medal Award
This, the highest honor that can be conferred on a member, is given to recognize an individual for a significant contribution to European radiotherapy. A gold medal and invitation to lecture are awarded annually. Established in 1982 in honor of Klaas Breur, one of the founders of ESTRO.

1494 ■ Marie Curie Medal
To recognize a brachytherapist or physicist who has made a major contribution to the development of the brachytherapy specialty. A medal is awarded every fourth year. Established in 1996.

1495 ■ Jack Fowler Award
To recognize the best abstract in the field of radiation physics or radiation technology. Candidates should be ESTRO members younger than 36 years (40 years for women whose research was interrupted for pregnancy/maternity reasons). A monetary prize of 1,000 Euros is presented annually.

1496 ■ GEC-ESTRO Iridium Award
To recognize a brachytherapist or physicist who has made a major contribution to the development of the brachytherapy specialty. A medal is awarded annually. Established in 2004. Administered by the GEC-ESTRO Committee

1497 ■ Honorary Physicist Award
To recognize an individual who, although not a physicist, has made an outstanding contribution to the cause of physics in ESTRO, to raising the profile of physicists in the radiation oncology community, or to the development of the field of physics in clinical radiotherapy. Awarded biennially in odd-numbered years. Established in 1993.

1498 ■ Nucletron Brachytherapy Award
To recognize the most innovative abstract submitted for presentation at the Annual Brachytherapy Meeting GEC-ESTRO. A monetary prize of 1,700 Euros is presented annually. Established in 1990.

1499 ■ Regaud Lecture Award
To recognize an individual for contributing in the spirit of Claudius Regaud, who introduced the principles of fractionation in his clinical practice. Awarded biennially in even-numbered years. Established in 1988.

1500 ■ Emmanuel van der Schueren Award
To recognize an individual for outstanding contributions to therapeutic radiology and oncology. Awarded annually.

1501 ■ VARIAN-Juliana Denekamp Award
To recognize young radiobiologists and radiotherapists who have demonstrated excellence and passion for biologically driven cancer research relevant for radiation oncology, and who show promise to assume a scientific leadership role in the future. Candidates should be ESTRO members younger than 36 years (40 years for women whose research was interrupted for pregnancy/maternity reasons). A monetary prize of 2,500 Euros is presented annually. Established in 2005. Sponsored by VARIAN Medical Systems.

1502 ■ VARIAN Research Award
To recognize research in radiotherapy and radiation technology. In even-numbered years, a monetary prize of 7,500 Euros is awarded to a radiotherapy professional for research in the field of radiobiology, radiation physics, clinical radiotherapy, or radiation technology. In odd-numbered years, 2,500 Euros is awarded to a physicist or radiation technologist, a radiation clinician, and/or a biologist. Established in 1985. Sponsored by VARIAN Medical Systems.

1503 ■ European Society of Anaesthesiology
Paolo Pelosi, Pres.
24 rue des Comediens

B-1000 Brussels, Belgium
Ph: 32 2 7433290
Fax: 32 2 7433298
E-mail: info@euroanaesthesia.org
URL: http://www.euroanesthesia.org

1504 ■ Research Grants
To promote anaesthesia-related research in Europe, and to encourage anaesthesiologists to extend the frontiers of their practice or understanding. Awards are made to a sponsoring institution, not to individuals or to departments. Any qualified member of a sponsoring institution in one of the European countries that is represented on the ESA Council may apply. Two types of grants are awarded: Project grants, of up to 60,000 euro each, to support work of up to two years duration; and Research support grants, for amounts up to 15,000 euro, to assist work in progress or pilot studies. Established in 1987 by ICI Germany. Formerly: (1997) ZENECA Research Scholarship.

1505 ■ European Society of Intensive Care Medicine
Nelly Le Devic, Exec. Off.
Rue Belliard, 19
B-1040 Brussels, Belgium
Ph: 32 2 5590350
Fax: 32 2 5590379
E-mail: administration@esicm.org
URL: http://www.esicm.org

1506 ■ Young Investigator Award
To enable young doctors to work full-time in a different intensive care unit (ICU) or laboratory. Candidates must be members of the Society, be European doctors, and be under the age of 40. A monetary prize of 20,000 Euros is presented annually.

1507 ■ European Society of Neuroradiology
Prof. Guido Wilms, Sec. Gen.
UZ Gasthuisberg
Herestraat 49
3000 Leuven, Belgium
E-mail: guido.wilms@uz.kuleuven.ac.be
URL: http://www.esnr.org

1508 ■ Lucien Appel Prize
For young neuroradiologists under the age of 40 years. A monetary prize of 4,000 Euros is awarded annually.

1509 ■ Federation of European Aquaculture Producers
Mr. John Stephanis, Pres.
9, Rue de Paris
B-4020 Liege, Belgium
Ph: 32 4 3382995
Fax: 32 4 3379846
E-mail: secretariat@feap.info
URL: http://www.feap.info/feap

1510 ■ Award for Excellence in European Aquaculture
To recognize an individual who has made innovative contributions to the field of aquaculture in Europe. A statuette of Poseidon is awarded annually.

1511 ■ Federation of European Direct and Interactive Marketing
Mr. Dieter V. Weng, Chm.
Ave. Ariane 5, 4th Fl.
1200 Brussels, Belgium
Ph: 32 2 7794268
Fax: 32 2 7789922
E-mail: info@fedma.org
URL: http://www.fedma.org

**1512 ■ Best of Europe - International Direct Marketing Awards
(Concours International de Campagnes de Marketing Direct)**
For recognition of the best direct marketing

Awards are arranged in alphabetical order below their administering organizations

campaigns in Europe. Awards are given in the following categories: consumer products, consumer services, business-to-business products, business-to-business services, non-profit, and multinational campaigns. Gold, silver, and bronze prizes, special awards, and letters of distinction are awarded annually. Established in 1976.

1513 ∎ Federation of European Securities Exchanges
Judith Hardt, Sec. Gen.
Ave. de Cortenbergh 52
B-1000 Brussels, Belgium
Ph: 32 2 5510180
Ph: 32 2 5510188
Fax: 32 2 5124905
E-mail: info@fese.eu
URL: http://www.fese.be

1514 ∎ Josseph de la Vega Prize
For outstanding research on the securities markets in Europe. Awarded annually. Established in 2000.

1515 ∎ Flanders International Film Festival - Ghent
(Internationaal Filmfestival van Vlaanderen - Gent)
Jacques Dubrulle, Managing Dir.
Leeuwstraat, 40b
B-9000 Gent, Belgium
Ph: 32 9 242 8060
Fax: 32 9 221 9074
E-mail: info@filmfestival.be
URL: http://www.filmfestival.be
Formerly: International Flanders Film Festival - Ghent.

1516 ∎ Impact of Music on Film Competition
(Competitie de Impact van Muziek op Film)
For recognition of achievement in incorporating music into film. Non-musical fiction films are eligible. An international jury awards four prizes: Grand Prize of the Flemish Community for Best Film (20,000 Euros); George Delerue Prize for Best Music (10,000 Euros); SABAM Prize for the Best Scenario (10,000 Euros); and De Robert Wise Award for Best Director (5,000 Euros). Established in 1985.

1517 ∎ Fonds National de la Recherche Scientifique
M.J. Simoen, Sec. Gen.
Rue d'Egmont 5
B-1000 Brussels, Belgium
Ph: 32 2 504 9211
Fax: 32 2 504 9292
E-mail: secr.gen@frs-fnrs.be
URL: http://www.frs-fnrs.be

1518 ∎ Iwan Akerman Award
To recognize an individual for innovative research on compressors and expansion machines and related technical disciplines such as aero- and thermodynamics, electromechanical drive systems, power electronics and high-speed motors, advanced bearing and seal concepts, and new high-performance materials and surface coatings. Candidates may be from any country but must hold a university degree in sciences or applied sciences. A monetary prize of 25,000 Euros is awarded biennially in even-numbered years.

1519 ∎ Gagna A. and Ch. Van Heck Prize
To honor a scientist or medical doctor in recognition of a body of research work that has contributed to the treatment of a disease currently incurable. A monetary prize of 75,000 Euros is awarded triennially. Established in 2003.

1520 ∎ Van Gysel Prize for Biomedical Research in Europe
To honor a researcher for making an important contribution to the biomedical sciences. Candidates must be members of a country of the European Union and must be under the age of 55. A monetary prize of 100,000 Euros is awarded triennially. Established in 1990.

1521 ∎ InBev-Baillet Latour Health Prize
To recognize individuals working in the field of scientific research and its practical applications. The prize recognizes the scientific merit of the winner and should assist him or her in the pursuit of his or her work. A monetary prize of 150,000 Euros is awarded annually.

1522 ∎ International Spa Foundation Prize
To recognize a research or team of researcher for experimental work that demonstrates the critical role of optimal hydration during aging. A monetary prize of 40,000 Euros is awarded biennially in odd-numbered years.

1523 ∎ Prix Centre d'etudes Princesse Josephine-Charlotte
To encourage scientific research in the field of viral infections. A monetary prize of 12,500 Euros is awarded biennially in odd-numbered years.

1524 ∎ Umicore Scientific Award
To recognize an individual for an original contribution in fine particle technology/applications, sustainable technology for metal containing compounds, sustainable energy, catalysis, or economic or societal issues involving metal containing compounds. Candidates must have obtained a PhD from a university in the European economic area or Switzerland during the previous two years. A monetary prize of 10,000 Euros is awarded biennially in even-numbered years. Sponsored by Umicore SA.

1525 ∎ Oswald Vander Veken Prize
To recognize an individual for an original contribution or an improvement to the understanding of tumors of the locomotor apparatus: their causes, their prevention, their diagnosis, and their treatment. Candidates must be researchers living and working in a country of the European Union. A monetary prize of 25,000 Euros is awarded triennially.

1526 ∎ Francqui Foundation
(Fondation Francqui)
Pierre Van Moerbeke, Exec. Dir.
Rue Defacqz 1
B-1000 Brussels, Belgium
Ph: 32 2 539 3394
Fax: 32 2 537 2921
E-mail: francquifoundation@skynet.be
URL: http://www.francquifoundation.be

1527 ∎ Francqui Prize
(Prix Francqui)
To recognize a Belgian scholar who has contributed to the prestige of Belgium. Awards are given in alternate years in the following categories: exact sciences, human sciences, biology and medical sciences. Candidates under 50 years of age may be nominated by a former prize winner or two members of a Belgian Academy. A monetary prize of 150,000 Euros is awarded annually. In addition, a prize of 25,000 Euros may be awarded to support the scientific work of an individual or a team. Established in 1932.

1528 ∎ International Association of Public Transport
Rue Sainte-Marie 6
B-1080 Brussels, Belgium
Ph: 32 2 673 6100
Fax: 32 2 660 1072
E-mail: rat.hans@uitp.org
URL: http://www.uitp.org

1529 ∎ PTx2 Awards
Also known as the Public Transport Times Two Awards, these awards recognize the efforts and reward the ambition of agencies, individuals, and groups that support the UITP goal of doubling the public transport market share worldwide between the years 2009 and 2025. Open to national and regional governments, cities and local authorities, operators, investors, industry and service suppliers, academics and researchers, and associations and non-governmental organizations (NGOs). Awards are presented in several categories. Established in 2010.

1530 ∎ International Dairy Federation
(Federation Internationale de Laiterie)
Mr. Christian Robert, Dir. Gen.
Diamant Bldg.
Blvd. Auguste Reyers 80
1030 Brussels, Belgium
Ph: 32 2 7339888
Fax: 32 2 7330413
E-mail: info@fil-idf.org

1531 ∎ IDF Award
To recognize an individual for contributions to progress in dairying worldwide. A medallion is awarded annually.

1532 ∎ Marketing Awards
To recognize dairy companies for outstanding marketing activities in the areas of innovation, nutri-marketing, and marketing communication. Awarded annually.

1533 ∎ Elie Metchnikoff Prize
To recognize an individual for outstanding discoveries in the fields of microbiology, biotechnology, nutrition, and health with regard to fermented milk. Awarded periodically.

1534 ∎ International Federation of Landscape Architects
Avenue d'Auderghem, 63
B-1040 Brussels, Belgium
Ph: 32 2 230 3757
Fax: 32 2 230 3757
E-mail: admin@iflaonline.org
URL: http://www.iflaonline.org

1535 ∎ Sir Geoffrey Jellicoe Award
To recognize a living landscape architect whose lifetime achievements and contributions have had a unique and lasting impact on the welfare of society and the environment and on the promotion of the profession of landscape architecture. Awarded every four years. Established in 2004.

1536 ∎ Student Design Competition
To recognize superior environmental design achievements made by students enrolled in landscape architecture programs or other allied disciplines around the world. The following awards are presented: Han Prize for Student Landscape Architecture for first place, the Zvi Miller Prize for second place, and the Merit Award for third place. In addition, one or more Jury Awards may be presented. Held annually.

1537 ∎ International Life Saving Federation
Gemeenteplein 26
B-3010 Leuven, Belgium
Ph: 32 16 896060
Fax: 32 16 897070
E-mail: ils.hq@pandora.be
URL: http://www.ilsf.org

1538 ∎ Citation of Merit
To recognize an individual who has contributed to the furtherance of lifesaving and the goals of the Federation in a manner of enduring, global importance. Awarded to one or more individuals annually. Established in 1997.

1539 ∎ Lifesaving Hall of Fame
To commemorate and recognize members and teams who have achieved outstanding ac-

Awards are arranged in alphabetical order below their administering organizations

complishments and exceptional contributions to the development of international lifesaving. Up to eight nominees are inducted biennially in even-numbered years. Established in 2010.

1540 ■ Order of Lifesaving
To recognize an individual who has given extraordinary service to the Federation and/or its regions over a period of years in a voluntary capacity. Individuals are recognized in two orders: Grand Knight (voluntary service of at least 15 years and membership for at least 25 years) and Knight (voluntary service of at least 10 years and membership for at least 20 years). Awarded annually to one or more meriting individuals. Established in 1994.

1541 ■ President's Award
To recognize an individual whose actions have significantly contributed to the Federation or to its Aims and Objectives as defined in the Federation Constitution. No more than three awards are issued each year. First presented in 2003.

1542 ■ Rescue Medal
To recognize an individual without formal lifesaving training who has knowingly and selflessly intervened in an instance of extreme peril in the aquatic environment in an effort to save the life of another person. No more than one ILS Medal shall be issued each year, unless by unanimous decision of the Board of Directors.

1543 ■ Rescue Medal of Valour
To recognize a lifesaver or group of lifesavers who is a member of any ILS member federation in good standing who has knowingly and selflessly intervened in an instance of the most extreme peril in the aquatic environment in an effort to save the life of another person. No more than one Medal of Valour shall be issued each year, unless by unanimous decision of the Board of Directors. To be eligible, the lifesaver or group of lifesavers must first receive the highest award for valour, if any, by the lifesaver's national federation and the action must be documented and verified. First presented in 2006.

1544 ■ International Navigation Association - Belgium
(Association Internationale de Navigation)
Sabine Van de Veld, Gen. Sec.
Graaf de Ferraris Bldg., 11th Fl.
Blvd. du Roi Albert II, 20-Box 3
B-1000 Brussels, Belgium
Ph: 32 2 5537161
Ph: 32 2 5537157
Fax: 32 2 5537155
E-mail: info@pianc.org
URL: http://www.pianc.org

1545 ■ De Paepe-Willems Award
To encourage young engineers, research workers, and others to pursue studies in the fields of interest to the Association and to submit articles on these subjects suitable for publication in the *PIANC Bulletin*. A monetary award of 5,000 Euros, a five-year membership, and an invitation to present the paper at the Annual Meeting are awarded annually at the General Assembly. Established in 1984 in memory of Professor Gustave Willems, and expanded in 2002 to honor Robert De Paepe. Formerly: (2006) Gustave Willems Prize.

1546 ■ International Network for Cancer Treatment and Research
Dr. Ian Magrath, Pres.
Institut Pasteur
Rue England 642
B-1180 Brussels, Belgium
Ph: 32 2 3739323
Fax: 32 2 3739313
E-mail: edupont@inctr.be
URL: http://www.inctr.org

1547 ■ Paul P. Carbone Award
For outstanding contributions to oncology or cancer research by an individual from a resource-rich country. Awarded annually.

1548 ■ Nazli Gad-el-Mawla Award
For outstanding contributions to cancer control by an individual for a country with limited resources. Awarded annually.

1549 ■ International Nuclear Law Association (Association Internationale du Droit Nucleaire)
Mr. M. Patrick Reyners, Sec. Gen.
Sq. de Meeus 29
B-1000 Brussels, Belgium
Ph: 32 2 5475841
Fax: 32 2 5030440
E-mail: info@aidn-inla.be
URL: http://www.aidn-inla.be

1550 ■ INLA Prize
To recognize an individual for contributions in the field of nuclear law. Candidates must have a law diploma or an academic diploma of a discipline including a "law" component. A monetary prize up to 2,000 Euros is awarded to cover the participation expenses to the Nuclear Inter Jura Congress. Awarded biennially in odd-numbered years.

1551 ■ Allen Keast Research Award
Awarded to students studying ornithology in Australian universities.

1552 ■ International Society for Scientometrics and Informetrics
Wolfgang Glanzel, Sec.-Treas.
Centre for R & D Monitoring
Katholieke Universiteit Leuven
Faculty of Business and Economics
Waaistraat 6, PB 3536
B-3000 Leuven, Belgium
Ph: 32 16 325 713
Fax: 32 16 325 799
E-mail: wolfgang.glanzel@econ.kuleuven.be
URL: http://www.issi-society.info

1553 ■ Derek John de Solla Price Memorial Medal
Awarded by the journal *Scientometrics* to recognize a scientist for outstanding contributions to the field of quantitative studies of science. Presented biennially in odd-numbered years. Established in 1984.

1554 ■ International Society of Orthopaedic Surgery and Traumatology
(Societe Internationale de Chirurgie Orthopedique et de Traumatologie)
Maurice Hinsenkamp, Pres.-Elect
Rue Washington, 40-B.9
B-1050 Brussels, Belgium
Ph: 32 2 6486823
Fax: 32 2 6498601
E-mail: hq@sicot.org
URL: http://www.sicot.org

1555 ■ Lester Lowe Awards
To recognize trainees who are graduates in medicine and are studying orthopedics and/or traumatology. Candidates must be under the age of 35. A monetary prize of up to US$1,000 is awarded to one or two recipients annually.

1556 ■ Oral Presentation Awards
To recognize the authors of the best oral presentations. A monetary prize of 500 Euros is awarded to three recipients triennially at the World Congress.

1557 ■ Poster Awards
To recognize the authors of the best posters. A monetary prize of 500 Euros is awarded to three recipients triennially at the World Congress.

1558 ■ SICOT/SIROT Award
To recognize the author of original research in

orthopedics of traumatology. Candidates must be members under the age of 45 years. A monetary prize of US$2,000 is awarded triennially at the World Congress.

1559 ■ International Taste and Quality Institute
55 rue des Trois Ponts
B-1160 Brussels, Belgium
Ph: 32 2 372 3422
Fax: 32 2 372 3421
E-mail: info@itqi.com
URL: http://www.itqi.com

1560 ■ Crystal Taste Award
To honor products that have received three-star Superior Taste Awards (see separate entry) for three consecutive years. Awarded annually, as merited.

1561 ■ Superior Taste Award
To honor branded and processed foods and beverages from around the world. Products are evaluated by chefs and sommeliers based on their individual merits and don't compete against each other. Three stars are awarded for products judged to be exceptional, two stars for those judged as remarkable, and one star for those judged to be notable in taste. Awarded annually.

1562 ■ International Union of Radio Science
(Union Radio Scientifique Internationale)
Prof. Paul Lagasse, Sec. Gen.
Gent University
Sint-Pietersnieuwstraat 41
B-9000 Gent, Belgium
Ph: 32 9 2643320
Fax: 32 9 2644288
E-mail: info@ursi.org
URL: http://www.ursi.org

1563 ■ Appleton Prize
To recognize an individual for outstanding contributions to ionospheric physics. A monetary prize of £250 is awarded triennially. Established in 1969 in memory of Sir Edward Appleton, president of the Union from 1934 to 1952.

1564 ■ Booker Gold Medal
To recognize an individual for outstanding contributions to telecommunications or a related discipline of direct interest to the Organization. Awarded triennially. Established in memory of Professor Henry G. Booker.

1565 ■ John Howard Dellinger Gold Medal
For recognition of outstanding work in radio science, preferably in radio wave propagation. Work must have been carried out during the six-year period preceding the year of the URSI General Assembly at which the medal is presented. A medal is awarded triennially at the URSI General Assembly. Established in 1966 by the United States Member Committee of URSI in honor of Professor John Howard Dellinger, Honorary President of URSI.

1566 ■ Issac Koga Gold Medal
For recognition of outstanding work in radio science carried out by a young scientist. Candidates must be 35 years of age or younger and the work must have been carried out during the six-year period preceding the year of the URSI General Assembly at which the medal is presented. A medal is awarded triennially at the URSI General Assembly. Established in 1984 by the URSI Member Committee in Japan in honor of Professor Issac Koga, Honorary President of URSI.

1567 ■ Balthasar Van der Pol Gold Medal
For recognition of outstanding work in radio science. Work must have been carried out in the six-year period preceding the year of the General Assembly at which the Medal is awarded. A medal with an effigy of Professor Van der Pol is

Awards are arranged in alphabetical order below their administering organizations

awarded every three years and presented on the occasion of the General Assembly. Established in 1963 in memory of Professor Balthasar van der Pol, Honorary President of the Union, by his widow, Mrs. P. Le Corbeiller-Posthuma.

1568 ■ King Baudouin Foundation
(Fondation Bonderjnstichting)
Baron Tayart de Borms, Managing Dir.
rue Brederodestraat 21
B-1000 Brussels, Belgium
Ph: 32 2 5111840
Fax: 32 2 5115221
E-mail: info@kbs-frb.be
URL: http://www.kbs-frb.be/start.aspx?goto=/index. aspx

1569 ■ King Baudouin International Development Prize
To recognize persons or organizations, without regard to national origin, who have made a substantial contribution to the development of the Third World or towards the cooperation and good relations between industrialized and developing countries, and among their peoples. Particular importance is attached to activities having a multiplier effect and those which make it possible for the populations of the Third World to provide for themselves by their own development. Individuals or organizations may be nominated. A monetary prize of 150,000 Euros is awarded biennially in odd-numbered years. Established in 1978.

1570 ■ League of Families
(La Ligue des Familles)
Ave. E. de Beco 109
B-1050 Brussels, Belgium
Ph: 32 2 507 7211
Fax: 32 2 507 7200
E-mail: info@liguedesfamilles.be
URL: http://www.citoyenparent.be/Public/ligue

1571 ■ Prix Bernard Versele
To encourage reading among children and to promote books of high literary, artistic, and educational value, not necessarily those best known on the market. Books are pre-selected by specialists in literature from those written in French and published during the preceding year. About 50,000 children from 3 to 14 years of age vote for the best liked children's books. Awards are given for books for children in the following age categories: from 3 years, from 5 years, from 7 years, from 9 years, and from 11 years. Five monetary prizes are awarded annually in June. Established in 1979 in memory of Bernard Versele, a young psychologist, who dedicated his professional life to children.

1572 ■ MEDEA Awards
Leuvensesteenweg 132
B-3370 Roosbeek, Belgium
Ph: 32 16 284 042
Fax: 32 16 223 743
E-mail: secretariat@medea-awards.com
URL: http://www.medea-awards.com

1573 ■ MEDEA Awards
To encourage innovation and good practice in the use of media (audio, video, graphics, and animation) in education, and to promote excellence in the production and pedagogical design of media-rich learning resources. A statuette is awarded annually. Established in 2007.

1574 ■ Queen Elisabeth International Music Competition of Belgium
(Concours Musical International Reine Elisabeth de Belgique)
Count Jean-Pierre de Launoit, Chm.
20, rue aux Laines
B-1000 Brussels, Belgium
Ph: 32 2 213 4050
Fax: 32 2 514 3297

E-mail: info@qeimc.be
URL: http://www.cmireb.be

1575 ■ Queen Elisabeth International Music Competition of Belgium
To recognize musicians who have completed their training and who are ready to launch their international careers. Covers the musical disciplines of piano, voice, violin, and composition. The performance sessions take place every three years, and the competition for composers is held before each instrumental session. The winning works of the composer's competition become compulsory pieces during the piano and violin sessions. Established in 1937.

1576 ■ Royal Academy of Medicine of Belgium
(Academie Royale de Medecine de Belgique)
Mr. Augustin Ferrant, Sec.
Palais des Academies
rue Ducale 1
B-1000 Brussels, Belgium
Ph: 32 2 5502255
Fax: 32 2 5502265
E-mail: contact@armb.be
URL: http://www.armb.be

1577 ■ Prijs Albert Van Dyck
To recognize an investigator in basic or clinical science who has acquired special merit in the study of leukemia or another disease that is considered incurable or fatal. Unpublished manuscripts as well as published work written in Dutch, French, English, or German are considered. A monetary prize of 3,500 Euros is awarded every four years. Established in 1971.

1578 ■ Prijs Franz Van Goidsenhoven
For recognition of an original paper dealing with clinical medicine, particularly, internal medicine. Manuscripts must be written in Dutch, French, English, or German. A monetary prize of 2,500 Euros is awarded every four years. Established in 1955.

1579 ■ Royal Academy of Sciences, Humanities and Fine Arts of Belgium
Division of Arts
(Academie Royale des Sciences, des Lettres et des Beaux-Arts de Belgique)
Beatrice Denuit, Sec.
Paleis der Academies
rue Ducale 1
B-1000 Brussels, Belgium
Ph: 32 2 550 2212
Fax: 32 2 550 2205
E-mail: academieroyale@cfwb.be
URL: http://www.academieroyale.be

1580 ■ Prix Ernest Acker
For recognition of an architectural project presented to the Academy on a subject chosen by the Classe des Beaux-Arts. Young Belgian architects are eligible. A monetary prize is awarded triennially. Established in 1922.

1581 ■ Prix Jos Albert
To encourage the work of a Belgian painter of the representational trend. A monetary prize of 2,000 Euros is awarded annually. Established in 1981.

1582 ■ Prix Paul Artot
To recognize the painter of a fresco or oil painting. The theme of the painting must be expressed by human figures. Belgian artists under the age of 40 are eligible. A monetary prize of 3,000 Euros is awarded biennially in odd-numbered years. Established in 1958.

1583 ■ Prix Paul Bonduelle
To recognize the originator(s) of a great architectural project. The subject is decided by the Classe des Beaux-Arts. Belgian architects who are not members of the Academy are eligible. A monetary prize of 5,000 Euros is awarded triennially. Established in 1956.

1584 ■ Prix Gustave Camus
To recognize a Belgian painter who has already accomplished a notable work. A monetary prize of 2,750 Euros is awarded biennially in even-numbered years. Established in 1990.

1585 ■ Prix Pierre Carsoel
For recognition of the most technically and artistically successful work conceived and executed by an architect during the preceding five year period. Belgian architects are eligible. A monetary prize is awarded every five years. Established in 1940.

1586 ■ Prix Charles Caty
To recognize a painter who has studied regularly and successfully at the Academy of Fine Arts at Mons. A monetary prize of 1,250 Euros is awarded triennially. Established in 1953.

1587 ■ Prix Emma du Cayla-Martin
To recognize the work of a painter not yet awarded by the Academy. A monetary prize of 2,000 Euros is awarded biennially in odd-numbered years. Established in 1991.

1588 ■ Prix Arthur DeGreef
For recognition of the best musical composition for piano solo conceived in the true tradition of the instrument and not aiming at virtuosity. Belgian composers are eligible. A monetary prize of 1,250 is awarded biennially in odd-numbered years. Established in 1989.

1589 ■ Prix Louise Dehem
To recognize a painter who has been out of a fine arts school or an academy less than ten years and whose works, preferably human figures or still life, have been shown publicly and have revealed a truly artistic temperament. A monetary prize of 1,250 Euros is awarded biennially in even-numbered years. Established in 1926.

1590 ■ Prix Irene Fuerison
For recognition of the best unpublished musical composition in the following categories: chamber music, orchestral music, vocal music, and electronic music. Young Belgian musicians or foreign musicians less than 50 years of age who have been residents of Belgium for three years are eligible. Awards are given in alternate years for chamber music, orchestral music, vocal music, and electronic music. A monetary prize of 2,700 Euros is awarded biennially in even-numbered years. Established in 1933.

1591 ■ Prix Baron Horta
To recognize the designer of an architectural work that has already been built or studied as a project. The finished work must have been constructed in one of the Common Market countries, or the project must have been planned for construction in Common Market countries. Architects of any nationality are eligible. A monetary prize of 4,000 Euros is awarded every five years. Established in 1948.

1592 ■ Prix Rene Janssens
To recognize outstanding Belgian painters. Awards are given in alternate years to a painter who has excelled at portraits and a painter who has excelled at paintings of interiors. An individual's entire work is considered. A monetary prize of 1,250 Euros is awarded triennially. Established in 1943.

1593 ■ Prix Jacques Lavalleye-Coppens
For recognition of achievements in the fields of archaeology, art history, or restoration of monuments. Awards are given in alternate years to the Belgian author or authors or the foreign author for the best published or unpublished work on archaeology or art history of ancient Southern Netherlands and the ancient ecclesiastic principalities of Liege and Stavelot; and the author of the best work on restoration of monu-

Awards are arranged in alphabetical order below their administering organizations

ments or works of art erected or preserved in Belgium. A monetary prize of 2,000 Euros is awarded every four years. Established in 1976.

1594 ■ Prix Joseph-Edmond Marchal
To recognize the author of the best work, published or manuscript, on national antiquities or archaeology. A monetary prize is awarded every five years. Established in 1918.

1595 ■ Prix Constant Montald
For recognition of a large fresco or a mural in oils, leaded glass, or tapestry, portraying human figures. The work must be at least one meter high. A monetary prize of 1,200 Euros is awarded triennially. Established in 1944.

1596 ■ Prix Jules Raeymaekers
To encourage an artistic activity that uses color as its form of expression. A monetary prize of 5,000 Euros is awarded triennially. Established in 1981.

1597 ■ Prix Egide Rombaux
To recognize a sculptor for a work on a subject chosen by the Academy in decorative or monumental art. Belgian sculptors between 25 and 45 years of age are eligible. A sculpture is awarded triennially. Established in 1943.

1598 ■ Prix Emile Sacre
To recognize the painter of the most noteworthy work that was executed and publicly displayed during the preceding six year period. A monetary prize of 1,250 Euros is awarded every six years. Established in 1909.

1599 ■ Royal Academy of Sciences, Humanities and Fine Arts of Belgium
Division of Letters and Moral and Political Sciences
Serge Alexandre, Sec.
Palais des Academies
rue Ducale 1
B-1000 Brussels, Belgium
Ph: 32 2 550 2212
Fax: 32 2 550 2205
E-mail: academieroyale@cfwb.be
URL: http://www.academieroyale.be

1600 ■ Prix Franz Cumont
For recognition of a work on the ancient history of religion or science in the Mediterranean basin before Mohammed. Belgian or foreign authors are eligible. A monetary prize is awarded triennially. Established in 1937.

1601 ■ Prix Eugene Goblet d'Alviella Prize
For recognition of the best work of a strictly scientific and objective character on the history of religions. Belgian authors are eligible. A monetary prize is awarded every five years. Established in 1926.

1602 ■ Prix Joseph De Keyn
For recognition of works by Belgian authors on secular instruction and education. Awards are given in alternate years in the following categories: (1) works useful for primary schools; and (2) works on secondary instruction or education, including industrial art. A monetary prize is awarded biennially in even-numbered years. Established in 1880.

1603 ■ Prix Emile de Laveleye
To recognize a scholar whose total work has brought about important progress in political economy and social science, including finance, international and public law, and general or national politics. Living Belgian or foreign scholars are eligible. A monetary prize is awarded every six years. Established in 1895.

1604 ■ Prix Polydore De Paepe
For recognition of the best account of a spiritualist philosophy founded on pure reason or

experience. Preference is given to works which develop the principles stated by Paul Le Monyne in *De l'Idee de Dieu, sa transformation, ses consequences morales et sociales*. Belgian or foreign authors are eligible. A monetary prize is awarded every five years. Established in 1907.

1605 ■ Prix Baron de Saint-Genois
To recognize the author of the best historical or literary work written in Dutch. A monetary prize is awarded every five years. Established in 1867.

1606 ■ Prix Ernest Discailles
For recognition of the best work on the history of French literature or on contemporary history. Awards are given in alternate years in the following categories: (1) history of French literature; and (2) contemporary history. Belgians are eligible for the former, and foreigners who are studying or have studied at the University of Ghent are eligible for the latter. A monetary prize is awarded every five years. Established in 1907.

1607 ■ Prix Jules Duculot
For recognition of a manuscript or printed work on the history of philosophy. Belgians or foreigners with a degree from a Belgian university may submit works written in French. A monetary prize awarded every five years. Established in 1965.

1608 ■ Prix Joseph Gantrelle
For recognition of a work in classical philology. Belgian authors are eligible. A monetary prize is awarded every five years. Established in 1890.

1609 ■ Prix Joseph Houziaux
For recognition of a work in romance philology or in dialects of Belgo-Romance. All nationalities are eligible. A monetary prize is awarded triennially. Established in 1994.

1610 ■ Prix Tobie Jonckheere
For recognition of a manuscript or printed work on the science of education. A monetary prize is awarded every five years. Established in 1957.

1611 ■ Prix Eugene Lameere
For recognition of the best history textbook for Belgian primary and secondary schools and colleges of education, in which illustrations play an important part in making the text understandable. A monetary prize is awarded every five years. Established in 1902.

1612 ■ Prix Henri Lavachery
For recognition of a written work or filmed commentary on ethnology. Belgian authors may submit works written in French and published in the preceding five years. A monetary prize is awarded every five years. Established in 1961.

1613 ■ Prix Leon Leclere
For recognition of the best manuscript or printed work on national or general history. First works by a young historian are eligible. A monetary prize is awarded every five years. Established in 1928.

1614 ■ Prix de Psychologie
For recognition of the best doctoral thesis on scientific psychology, earned in a Belgian university by a Belgian citizen during the three preceding years. A monetary prize is awarded triennially. Established in 1961.

1615 ■ Prix Herman Schoolmeesters
For recognition of a manuscript or printed work useful in promoting small and medium-sized firms. A monetary prize is awarded every five years. Established in 1943.

1616 ■ Prix Baron de Stassart
To recognize a noted Belgian. The award is given in alternate years to: (1) historians; (2) writers; and (3) scientists and artists. A monetary prize is awarded every six years. Established in 1851.

1617 ■ Prix de Stassart
For recognition of an outstanding contribution to national history. A monetary prize is awarded every six years. Established in 1859.

1618 ■ Prix Suzanne Tassier
To recognize a woman who has obtained her doctorate at a Belgian university, and who has written an important scientific work in the fields of history, philology, law, or the social sciences. If no worthy work is found in these categories, a work on natural, medical, or mathematical sciences will be considered. A monetary prize is awarded every three years. Established in 1956.

1619 ■ Prix Victor Tourneur
To encourage numismatic and sigillographical studies, and to encourage the art of medal making. A monetary prize of 1,200 Euros is awarded alternately every five years by the Classe des Lettres and the Classe des Beaux Arts. Established in 1958.

1620 ■ Royal Academy of Sciences, Humanities and Fine Arts of Belgium
Division of Sciences
Francoise Thomas, Sec.
Palais des Academies
rue Ducale 1
B-1000 Brussels, Belgium
Ph: 32 2 550 2212
Fax: 32 2 550 2205
E-mail: academieroyale@cfwb.be
URL: http://www.academieroyale.be

1621 ■ Prix Henri Buttgenbach
For recognition of studies on mineralogy, petrography and paleontology that are based on materials gathered in Belgium. Belgian scientists are preferred. Dutch, French, or English scientists can be considered. A monetary prize is awarded triennially. Established in 1945.

1622 ■ Prix Eugene Catalan
To recognize a Belgian or French scholar who has made important progress in pure mathematics. Works must be submitted in French and must have been published during the five preceding years. A monetary prize is awarded every five years. Established in 1964.

1623 ■ Prix de Boelpaepe
For recognition of an important discovery likely to bring about progress in photography. The work can be on the properties of emulsions, and physico-chemical techniques used in photographic processes, or can be used for a new development in photography that may add to scientific progress. Belgian researchers are eligible. A monetary prize of 1,500 Euros is awarded biennially in even-numbered years. Established in 1926.

1624 ■ Prix Theophile de Donder
For recognition of the best original work on mathematical physics. Candidates under 40 years of age are eligible. A monetary prize is awarded triennially. Established in 1958.

1625 ■ Prix de la Fondation Jean-Marie Delwart
For recognition of the best works in the field of chemical communication between organisms (including human beings) or in the field of human ethology and cultural anthropology. A monetary prizes is awarded biennially in even-numbered years. Established in 1993.

1626 ■ Prix Francois Deruyts
To recognize one or more authors who have made progress in synthetic or analytic superior geometry. Belgian researchers are eligible. A monetary prize is awarded every four years. Established in 1902.

1627 ■ Prix Jacques Deruyts
For recognition of progress in mathematical analysis. Belgian researchers are eligible. A monetary prize is awarded every four years. Established in 1948.

Awards are arranged in alphabetical order below their administering organizations

1628 ■ Prix Dubois - Debauque

For recognition of the best works relating to the production of electrical currents by living organisms, and the nature of these currents. Belgian or foreign scientists are eligible. A monetary prize is awarded every four years. Established in 1950.

1629 ■ Fondation Octave Dupont

To recognize projects of fundamental scientific research in the fields of human an animal physiology and physiopathology. Reserved for Belgian French-speaking scientists. Administration of this biennial award rotates among four Belgian organizations, including the Royal Academy of Medicine of Belgium. Established in 1989.

1630 ■ Prix Leo Errera

To recognize the author or authors of the best original work on general biology. A monetary prize is awarded triennially. Established in 1906.

1631 ■ Prix Paul Fourmarier

To recognize a scholar who, during the preceding ten years, has made important discoveries or has brought about considerable progress in theoretical concepts in the geological sciences. Work in geology and its applications, petrography, relations with the creation and evaluation of mineral masses, physical geography, paleontology, or understanding of the general evolution of the earth is eligible. A monetary prize of 1,500 Euros is awarded every ten years. Established in 1937.

1632 ■ Prix Leon et Henri Fredericq

To recognize a scholar who has distinguished himself by original experimental research in physiology or any related science (biochemistry, biophysics, pharmacodynamics, molecular biology, etc.). Belgian and foreign scientists whose research is done in a Belgian laboratory are eligible. Individuals must be under 45 years of age. A monetary prize of 2,000 Euros is awarded biennially in odd-numbered years. Established in 1969.

1633 ■ Prix Theophile Gluge

For recognition of the best work on physiology. Belgian and foreign researchers are eligible. A monetary prize of 1,000 Euros is awarded biennially in even-numbered years. Established in 1902.

1634 ■ Prix Charles Lagrange

For recognition of the best mathematical or experimental work contributing to the progress of mathematical knowledge in the world. Belgian or foreign researchers are eligible. A monetary prize is awarded every four years. Established in 1901.

1635 ■ Prix Lamarck

For recognition of morphological works published in French or Flemish and dealing with a zoological group including humans. All of the author's work must have brought to light the greatest number of facts and new explanations on animal evolution or zoological phylogeny. A monetary prize is awarded every five years. Established in 1913.

1636 ■ Prix Emile Laurent

For recognition of outstanding work in the field of botany. Awards are given in alternate years for: (1) the best work on the flora or vegetation of Zaire (including works on the anatomy and physiology of plants from Zaire); and (2) the best work on botany including agriculture and horticulture. Belgian researchers are eligible. A monetary prize is awarded every four years. Established in 1907.

1637 ■ Prix Charles Lemaire

For recognition of the best published report on public works related preferably to experiences and practical works on engineering or theoretical research on the resistance of materials, the stability of buildings, or hydraulics. A monetary prize of 1,250 Euros is awarded biennially in even-numbered years. Established in 1891.

1638 ■ Prix Edmond de Selys Longchamps

For recognition of the best original work on present day Belgian fauna. If no entry on this subject is deemed worthy, works on Belgian fauna in the past or on the fauna of Zaire will be considered. Belgian and foreign researchers are eligible. A monetary prize of 1,500 Euros is awarded every five years. Established in 1901.

1639 ■ Prix Edouard Mailly

To recognize a scientist who has contributed to progress in astronomy or has helped spread interest in and knowledge of this science. Belgian or naturalized Belgian scientists are eligible. A monetary prize is awarded every four years. Established in 1892.

1640 ■ Fondation Max Poll

For recognition of the best work on zoology (systematic, comparative anatomy, zoo geography, or animal ecology). Reserved for researchers of Belgian French-speaking or Zairian universities. A monetary prize is awarded triennially. Established in 1991.

1641 ■ Prix de la Belgica

To recognize a scholar or a group of scholars who have successfully devoted themselves to scientific research inside the Antarctic Polar Circle. Scientists of all nationalities are eligible. Surplus funds of the foundation may be given to subsidize oceanographic work by Belgians. A gold medal is awarded every five years. Established in 1901.

1642 ■ Prix Joseph Schepkens

For recognition of work in the field of botany or agronomical research. Awards are given in alternate years for: (1) the best experimental work on the genetics of plants, particularly highly cultivated plants; (2) the best work on phytopathology and applied entomology; and (3) agronomical research. A monetary prize of 1,000 Euros is awarded annually. Established in 1922.

1643 ■ Prix Paul et Marie Stroobant

To recognize the Belgian or French scientist who has written the best theoretical or observational work on astronomy. A monetary prize of 1,000 Euros is awarded biennially in even-numbered years. Established in 1950.

1644 ■ Prix Frederic Swarts

To reward the best work, published or in manuscript form, in the field of pure or industrial chemistry. The work has to be written in French or in Flemish and must be the work of a Belgian citizen who holds an engineering degree from one of the Belgian universities of the Ecole des Mines de Mons, and who graduated in the preceding eight years. If the prize is not awarded for two consecutive periods, it may be awarded to a chemist with a doctorate. A monetary prize is awarded biennially in even-numbered years. Established in 1938.

1645 ■ Prix Pol et Christiane Swings

For recognition of outstanding research in the field of astrophysics. Scientists who are not older than 40 years of age are eligible. The prize is awarded in alternate years to a Belgian and to a foreigner. A monetary prize of 1,200 Euros is awarded every four years. Established in 1977.

1646 ■ Prix Pierre-Joseph et Edouard Van Beneden

To recognize the author or authors of the best original manuscript or published work on embryology or cytology during the preceding three-year period. Belgian or foreign researchers are eligible. A monetary prize of 1,400 Euros is awarded triennially. Established in 1913 by P. Nolf.

1647 ■ Prix Baron Van Ertborn

For recognition of the best published work on geology. Belgian authors who are not members of the Academy are eligible. A monetary prize is awarded biennially in odd-numbered years. Established in 1922.

1648 ■ Prix Georges Vanderlinden

For recognition of the best discovery or the most noteworthy work in the physical sciences, in particular, radio-electricity. The prize is given alternately for national and international works. For the national competition, the work should be written in French or Dutch. For the international competition, the work should be in English, German, or Italian. A monetary prize of 1,200 Euros is awarded every four years. Established in 1958.

1649 ■ Royal Academy of Sciences, Humanities and Fine Arts of Belgium
Division of Technology and Society
Paleis der Academies
rue Ducale 1
B-1000 Brussels, Belgium
Ph: 32 2 550 2213
Fax: 32 2 550 2205
E-mail: academieroyale@cfwb.be
URL: http://www.academieroyale.be

1650 ■ Prix Professeur Louis Baes

For recognition of the best discovery or the most noteworthy studies on elasticity, plasticity, resistance of materials, the stability of buildings and the calculation of machine parts, including theoretical and practical applications. Candidates must be from Common Market countries and papers must be in French. A monetary prize of 1,000 Euros is awarded biennially in odd-numbered years. Established in 1960.

1651 ■ Royal Carillon School Jef Denyn (Koninklijke Beiaardschool Jef Denyn)
Frederik de Merodestraat 63
B-2800 Mechelen, Belgium
Ph: 32 15 204792
Fax: 32 15 203176
E-mail: info@beiaardschool.be
URL: http://www.beiaardschool.be

1652 ■ International Carillon Competition - Queen Fabiola (Internationale Beiaardwedstrijd Koningin Fabiola)

For recognition of outstanding performance of original carillon compositions. Carillonneurs from all over the world may participate. All candidates must present nine original carillon compositions, including three baroque, three romantic, and three modern works. All compositions must be of a very high virtuosity level. The following prizes are awarded: first prize - a monetary prize of 3,000 Euros, a bronze bell in a frame, diploma, and a concert tour through Belgium; second prize - a monetary prize of 2,000 Euros plus a medal and diploma; third prize - a monetary prize of 1,500 Euros plus a medal and diploma; fourth prize - a monetary of 1,300 Euros plus a diploma; fifth prize - a monetary prize of 1,000 Euros plus a diploma; and sixth prize - a monetary prize of 1,000 Euros plus a diploma. Established in 1987 under the patronage of Her Majesty Queen Fabiola. Held every five years.

1653 ■ International Carillon Composition Contest

For recognition of a composition for a four octave carillon (c tot c''''), three pages minimum, lasting a maximum of eight minutes. The composer has free choice of a musical form in Category I. In Category II, the carillon compositions are based on an old folksong or use a folksong as a basic element. Compositions already published, performed, or sent in on the occasion of previous competitions are not allowed, and not more than one work by the same composer may obtain a prize. The following monetary prizes, each of

Awards are arranged in alphabetical order below their administering organizations

them with a diploma, may be awarded: Category I: first prize - Jef Denyn Prize of 1,500 Euros; second prize - Stad Mechelen Prize of 1,000 Euros; third prize - Carillon School Prize of 750 Euros; and Category II: first prize - Staf Nees Prize of 1,500 Euros; and second prize - Tower and Carillon Prize of 1,000 Euros. Awarded every five years. Established in 1952. Formerly: Internationale Kompositiewedstrijd voor Beiaard.

1654 ■ Royal Film Archive of Belgium (Cinematheque Royale)
Hotel van Cleves
Rue Ravenstein 3
B-1000 Brussels, Belgium
Ph: 32 2 551 1900
Fax: 32 2 551 1904
E-mail: info@cinematek.be
URL: http://www.cinematheque.be

1655 ■ Age d'Or Prize
To promote the creation and distribution of films that depart from all cinematographic conformities by the originality, the oddity of their substance, and form. Competing films must be longer than 60 minutes and completed in the preceding three years. The films must be presented in their original and uncut version. If not in English, French, or Dutch, the films must be subtitled in one of these languages. A monetary prize is awarded to the winning film chosen from one of five films awarded the Royal Film Archive of Belgium's Prizes for the Distribution of Quality Films in Belgium. This sum is given to the Belgian distributor, who may, within one year, present proof of genuine distribution in Belgium and of possession of a print of the film in its original version, subtitled in French and Dutch. Another monetary prize is divided into two parts and are awarded to the producer and director. Formerly: Prix de l'Age d'Or.

1656 ■ Prizes for the Distribution of Quality Films in Belgium (Premies voor de verspreiding van de betere film in Belgie)
To provide recognition for quality films of any country, longer than 60 minutes, whose innovative nature makes their release problematic; and to recognize the Belgian distributors who may, within one year of the award, present proof of distribution of these films in original and uncut versions with French and Dutch subtitles. Five monetary awards are awarded annually. In Addition, one film from among these 5 award winners is singled out by the jury for the Age d'or Prize.

1657 ■ SECO: Technical Control Bureau for Construction
Yves Pianet, CEO
rue d'Arlon 53
B-1040 Brussels, Belgium
Ph: 32 2 2382211
Ph: 32 2 2382250
Fax: 32 2 2382261
E-mail: mail@seco.be
URL: http://www.seco.be/Public
Formerly: Bureau of Security Control of Construction.

1658 ■ Gustave Magnel Prize
For recognition of scientific work in the area of safety control of construction that has practical application for the field. The research results must be written in French, Dutch, German, or English. The author must be attached to a university or a research institute of a member country of the European Union, and must be no older than 40 years of age. A monetary award of 10,000 Euro is awarded every four years. Established in 1964.

1659 ■ Verdeyen Prize for Soil Mechanics
For recognition of scientific research on soil mechanics, with practical application for control and safety of constructions. The work must be written in French, Dutch, German, or English. Research workers not older than 40 years of age are eligible. A monetary award of 7,500 Euro is awarded every four years. Established in 1974.

1660 ■ SIGNIS, World Catholic Association for Communication
Fr. Bernardo Suate, Dir.
310, rue Royale
1210 Brussels, Belgium
Ph: 32 2 7349708
Fax: 32 2 7347018
E-mail: sg@signis.net
URL: http://www.signis.net
Formed by merger of: Unda International Catholic Association for Radio and Television; OCIC, for Cinema and Audiovisual.

1661 ■ Ecumenical Prize
For recognition of films from any country that promotes human and spiritual values. A bronze medal is awarded at film festivals throughout the world, such as Cannes, Locarno, Montreal, Moscow, Berlin, and others. Established in 1974.

1662 ■ SIGNIS Award (Colombe Unda)
To recognize radio and television programs of high technical quality that convey a spiritual message at the International Television Festival of Monte Carlo. Applications are accepted. Awards are presented for fiction programs and current affairs. A trophy is awarded annually in February. Established in 1962. Formerly: (2002) Unda Dove.

1663 ■ Societe Royale Belge des Electriciens (Koninklijke Belgische Vereniging der Elektrotechnici)
Christian Pierlot, Gen. Pres.
VUB-IrW-ETEC
2 Blvd. de la Plaine
B-1050 Brussels, Belgium
Ph: 32 2 6292819
Ph: 32 2 6292804
Fax: 32 2 6293620
E-mail: srbe-kbve@vub.ac.be
URL: http://www.kbve-srbe.be

1664 ■ Prix de la SRBE
For individual doing original work in the field of electrical engineering.

1665 ■ Robert Sinave Prix
To honor outstanding work in electrical engineering.

1666 ■ Societe Royale de Chimie
Anne Choprix, Sec.
Universite Libre de Bruxelles
Ave. F.D. Roosevelt 50
CP 160/07
B-1050 Brussels, Belgium
Ph: 32 2 6505208
Fax: 32 2 6505184
E-mail: src@ulb.ac.be
URL: http://www.src.be
Formerly: (1986) Societe Chimique de Belgique.

1667 ■ Prix Triennal de la Societe Royale de Chimie
To honor a chemist whose work has received international recognition. Members of the Society of any nationality who are living permanently in Belgium or Belgian chemists living abroad are eligible. The candidate cannot be older than 40 years of age, and must have been a Society member for at least five years. A monetary prize of 2,500 Euros is awarded triennially. Established in 1969.

1668 ■ The University Foundation (Fondation Universitaire)
Eric de Keuleneer, Exec. Dir.
rue d'Egmont 11
B-1000 Brussels, Belgium
Ph: 32 2 545 0400
Fax: 32 2 513 6411
E-mail: fu.us@universityfoundation.be
URL: http://www.universitairestichting.be

1669 ■ Fernand Collin Prize for Law
To stimulate junior researchers at Belgian institutions in the area of law by recognizing a Dutch-language scholarly work on law. Candidates must be researchers at Belgian academic institutions. A monetary prize of 7,500 Euros is awarded biennially. Established in 1962.

1670 ■ World Veterinary Association (Welt-Tierarztegesellschaft)
Dr. Tjeerd Jorna, Pres.
1, Rue Defacqz
B-1000 Brussels, Belgium
Ph: 32 2 5337022
Fax: 32 2 5372828
E-mail: secretariat@worldvet.org
URL: http://www.worldvet.org

1671 ■ Gamgee Gold Medal
To individuals who have made outstanding contributions to veterinary science.

Belize

1672 ■ Belize Audubon Society
12 Fort St.
PO Box 1001
Belize City, Belize
Ph: 501 223 5004
Fax: 501 223 4985
E-mail: base@btl.net
URL: http://www.belizeaudubon.org

1673 ■ James A. Waight Award
To recognize an individual or organization for outstanding achievements in the protection and enhancement of Belize's environment. A trophy is presented annually. Established in 1987 in honor of the Society's first president.

1674 ■ Belize Chamber of Commerce and Industry
Withfield Tower, 2nd Fl.
4792 Coney Dr.
PO Box 291
Belize City, Belize
Ph: 501 223 5330
Fax: 501 223 5333
E-mail: bcci@belize.org
URL: http://www.belize.org

1675 ■ Expo Booth Awards
To recognize outstanding booth displays at the Expo Belize Marketplace, the largest consumer tradeshow in Belize. Plaques for first, second, and third place winners are awarded annually. Established in 1990.

1676 ■ Belize International Film Festival
c/o Bliss Centre
Southern Foreshore
Belize City, Belize
Ph: 501 227 2110
E-mail: belizefilmfestival@yahoo.com
URL: http://www.belizefilmfestival.com

1677 ■ Belize International Film Festival
To promote films from Belize and the neighboring regions of the Caribbean, Central America, and Southern Mexico. Awards are presented for best feature-length fiction, feature-length documentary, short fiction, and short documentary. In addition, special awards may be presented, among them the Green Award and an award for the best short script. Held annually. Established in 2006.

1678 ■ Belize Tourism Board
Mr. Michael Singh, CEO
64 Regent St.
Belize City, Belize

Awards are arranged in alphabetical order below their administering organizations

Ph: 501 227 2420
Fax: 501 227 2423
URL: http://www.belizetourism.org

1679 ■ National Tourism Awards
To recognize organizations and individuals who have committed to the development of tourism in Belize. The following awards are presented: Minister's Award, Lifetime Achievement Award, Hotel of the Year, Tour Operator of the Year, Corporate Organization of the Year, Tour Guide of the Year, Frontline Person of the Year, Environmental Organization of the Year, Education Award of the Year, Cultural Award of the Year, Receptive Service of the Year, Small Hotel of the Year, and Small Vendor of the Year. Awarded annually.

1680 ■ Taste of Belize Culinary Competition
To showcase the finest culinary and bartending talent in Belize. Designed for individual competitors in the following categories: Professional Chef, Young Professional and Apprentice Chef, Bartender, and Cake Decorating. Trophies are awarded annually. Established in 2002.

1681 ■ Government of Belize
Ministry of the Public Service, Governance Improvement, Elections and Boundaries and Sports
Sir Edney Cain Bldg., North Wing
Belmopan, Belize
Ph: 501 822 2204
Fax: 501 822 2206
URL: http://www.mps.gov.bz

1682 ■ Ministry/Department of the Year
To recognize the government ministry or department that has: 1) demonstrated the practice of good governance principles for two consecutive years; 2) developed new tools and implemented innovative solutions to improve access to, as well as delivery of, programs and services to Belizeans; and 3) forged partnerships with businesses, industries, educational institutions, and other governmental agencies. A plaque and certificate are awarded annually as part of the Belize Public Service Awards.

1683 ■ Public Officer of the Year
To recognize an individual who has demonstrated exceptional results toward the achievement of the Ministry's or Department's mission by developing an innovative and/or solution that contributed to improved efficiency and effectiveness, and who has consistently provided outstanding service to customers, both internal and external. A plaque, certificate, and monetary prize are awarded annually as part of the Belize Public Service Awards.

1684 ■ Twenty-Five Years Long Service Award
To honor an individual for 25 years of continuous service in Belize government. A plaque and certificate are awarded annually as part of the Belize Public Service Awards.

Bermuda

1685 ■ Bermuda Department of Community and Cultural Affairs
81 Court St.
PO Box HM 886
Hamilton, Bermuda
Ph: 441292-1681
Fax: 441292-2474
URL: http://www.communityandculture.bm

1686 ■ Brian Burland Prize for Fiction
To recognize an individual for a published novel or collection of short stories. Awarded annually.

1687 ■ Cecile N. Musson Prize for Poetry
To honor a significant selection of new work by a poet published in book form. Awarded annually.

1688 ■ Prize for Children and Young Adult Fiction
To recognize an individual for a published work of fiction or collection of short stories written for a readership between the ages of birth to 20 years old. Awarded annually.

1689 ■ Prize for Drama
To recognize an individual for a script written for theater or radio. Awarded annually.

1690 ■ Prize for Non-Fiction
To recognize an individual for a published work of non-fiction. Awarded annually.

1691 ■ The Bermuda Insurance Institute
Cedarpark Centre
48 Cedar Ave.
PO Box HM 2911
Hamilton HM LX, Bermuda
Ph: 441295-1596
Fax: 441295-3532
URL: http://www.bii.bm

1692 ■ Lifetime Achievement Award
To recognize an individual who has distinguished himself or herself in the insurance industry over the course of his or her career. Awarded annually as part of the Insurance Industry Awards. Established in 1999.

1693 ■ Re(insurance) Person of the Year
To recognize an individual from the executive ranks who has made a significant contribution to his or her organization, or the Bermuda insurance market as a whole, over the course of the previous year. Awarded annually as part of the Insurance Industry Awards. Established in 1999.

1694 ■ Young Re(insurance) Person of the Year
To recognize an individual under the age of 35 who, over the course of the previous year, has made a significant contribution to his or her organization, or the Bermuda insurance market as a whole, by promoting professionalism through education, conduct, or ethics. Awarded annually as part of the Insurance Industry Awards. Established in 1999.

1695 ■ Bermuda International Film Festival
PO Box HM 2963
Hamilton, Bermuda
Ph: 441293-3456
Fax: 441293-7769
E-mail: info@biff.bm
URL: http://www.biff.bm

1696 ■ Bermuda Children's Film Festival
To honor the best in children's films from around the world. Prizes are presented in two age groups. Held annually in October. Established in 2004.

1697 ■ Bermuda International Film Festival
To showcase and honor independent films from around the world. Awards are presented for best narrative feature film, best documentary, and audience choice. In addition, the Bermuda Shorts Award is also presented, and qualifies the winner to compete in the Short Film Category of the Oscars, the awards of the Academy of Motion Picture Arts and Sciences. Held annually. Established in 1997.

1698 ■ Bermuda Public Services Union
Edward G. Ball Jr., Gen. Sec.
PO Box HM 763
Hamilton HM CX, Bermuda
Ph: 441292-6985
Ph: 441292-6484
Fax: 441292-1149
E-mail: info@bpsu.bm
URL: http://www.bpsu.bm

1699 ■ Local and Overseas Education Awards
To provide financial support for post-secondary school education. Six scholarships of $3,000 each are awarded annually for overseas study, and six scholarships of $1,000 each are awarded annually for local study.

1700 ■ The Bermudian Publishing Co., Ltd.
PO Box HM 283
Hamilton HM AX, Bermuda
Ph: 441232-7041
Fax: 441232-7042
E-mail: info@thebermudian.com
URL: http://www.thebermudian.com

1701 ■ Best of Bermuda Awards
To celebrate all that is best on the island of Bermuda. Awards are presented in various categories among Food, Drink, and Entertainment; People and Places; Shopping and Services; and Clothing and Accessories. Winners are highlighted in the summer edition of *The Bermudian* magazine. Awarded annually. Established in 1989.

1702 ■ Interior Design Awards
To recognize Bermuda's outstanding interior designers, interior design firms, and architectural firms that practice interior design. Winners are highlighted in the fall edition of *The Bermudian* magazine. Awarded annually. Established in 2004.

1703 ■ Masterworks Foundation
PO Box HM 1929
Hamilton, Bermuda
Ph: 441236-2950
Fax: 441236-4402
E-mail: mworks@logic.bm
URL: http://www.bermudamasterworks.com

1704 ■ Charman Prize Competition
To recognize local artists. Open to artists who are residents of Bermuda. Judged on four categories of criteria: Design and Composition; Use of Material; Distinctive and Convincing Style; and Source of Inspiration. A $2,500 prize is awarded in each category, along with three $100 certificates in each category for honorable mentions. A grand prize of $10,000 is also offered for the artwork that best encompasses all four categories. Held annually. Established in 2008. Sponsored by John Charman, a local businessman and art collector.

1705 ■ Visitor Industry Partnership
PO Box 668
Flatts FL BX, Bermuda
Ph: 441734-8125
E-mail: info@vip.bm
URL: http://www.vip.bm

1706 ■ Excellence Awards
To honor individuals for outstanding promotion and development of hospitality and tourism in Bermuda. A monetary prize of $20,000 is awarded to the "Best of the Best" recipient. Awarded annually. Established in 2001.

1707 ■ Lifetime Achievement Award
To recognize an individual for a lifetime of achievement and contribution to the hospitality industry in Bermuda. Awarded annually.

Bhutan

1708 ■ Bhutan Department of Trade
Ministry of Economic Affairs
PO Box 141
Thimphu, Bhutan
URL: http://www.moea.gov.bt

1709 ■ Bhutan Seal of Excellence
To recognize Bhutanese handicrafts that uphold

Awards are arranged in alphabetical order below their administering organizations

rigorous standards of excellence, including the design, selection of materials, quality, pricing, and environmental responsibility of production. Each qualified product is awarded a certificate that can be used as a promotional tool. Awarded biennially in even-numbered years. Established in 2008.

1710 ■ Bhutan Seal of Quality
To establish a credible quality standard by recognizing high quality Bhutanese handicrafts. Each qualified product is awarded a certificate that can be used as a promotional tool. Awarded biennially in even-numbered years. Established in 2008.

1711 ■ Bhutan Ministry of Information and Communications
PO Box 278
Thimphu, Bhutan
Ph: 975 2 322144
Fax: 975 2 324860
URL: http://www.moic.gov.bt

1712 ■ Media Awards
To recognize and reward the best in Bhutanese media, including print, radio, and television. Awarded annually. Established in 2009.

1713 ■ Motion Pictures Association of Bhutan
BCCI Compound
Doeburn Lam
PO Box 1388
Chubachu
Thimphu, Bhutan
Ph: 975 331715
Fax: 975 331715
URL: http://www.bhutanesefilm.bt

1714 ■ Bhutan National Film Festival
To honor and promote filmmaking in Bhutan. Awards are presented in various categories each year. Established in 2002.

1715 ■ MPC Bhutan Entertainment
Karma Khangzang Complex, 4th Fl.
PO Box 748
Thimphu, Bhutan
Ph: 975 2 336378
Fax: 375 2 336379
E-mail: info@missbhutan.bt
URL: http://www.missbhutan.bt

1716 ■ Miss Bhutan
To support young Bhutanese women in the advancement of their careers, personal life, and humanitarian goals. The winning contestant receives the official Miss Bhutan Crown, a cash award of Nu. 100,000, and other prizes. She also represents Bhutan at international pageants, such as the Miss Earth pageant and the Miss Young International pageant. Awarded annually. Established in 2008.

1717 ■ Royal University of Bhutan
Sherubtse College
Kanglung, Bhutan
Ph: 975 4 535100
Fax: 375 4 535129
E-mail: director@sherubtse.edu.bt
URL: http://www.sherubtse.edu.bt

1718 ■ President's Award for Academic Excellence
To recognize students from any program who have secured the highest marks in their class. Awarded annually.

1719 ■ Principal's Medal
To honor the outgoing Social Service Unit Coordinator. Awarded annually.

1720 ■ Jigme Dorji Wangchuck Gold Medal
To recognize a graduating student who has

excelled in academic work and co-curricular activities, and whose contribution to the college is considered outstanding. Awarded annually.

Bolivia

1721 ■ Bienal Internacional del Cartel Bolivia
David Criado Angulo, Dir.
Edificio Italia II 12B
Av. Saavedra Esq. Villalobos - Miraflores
La Paz, Bolivia
Ph: 591 725 49734
E-mail: dcriado@grupocatalografica.com
URL: http://www.bicebebolivia.com

1722 ■ International Poster Show of Bolivia - Bienal Internacional del Cartel Bolivia
To recognize outstanding posters by design students, graphic designers, plastic artists, photographers, and graphic producers in general. Open to all individuals of any age and nationality. The following prizes are awarded in several categories: first place - US$3,000, a medal, and a diploma; second place - a medal and diploma; and third place - a medal and diploma.

1723 ■ Conservation International - Bolivia
Calle 13 de Calacoto, No. 8008
PO Box 13593
La Paz, Bolivia
Ph: 591 2 279 7700
Fax: 591 2 211 4228
E-mail: mmariaca@conservation.org
URL: http://www.conservation.org.bo

1724 ■ Biodiversity Reporting Award
To encourage the coverage of environmental and biodiversity issues. Awarded annually. Established in 1999.

Bosnia-Hercegovina

1725 ■ Gardens of the Righteous Worldwide (GARIWO) - Sarajevo
Ivana Gorana Kovacica 1
Sarajevo, Bosnia-Hercegovina
Ph: 38 7 33 259 455
Fax: 38 7 33 259 456
URL: http://www.gariwo.org

1726 ■ Dusko Kondor Civil Courage Award
To honor individuals who have demonstrated civil courage by risking their lives in standing up to negative authorities and acting according to their values. Awarded annually to one or more recipients. Established in 2008 in memory of Dusko Kondor, a human rights activist who was assassinated in his home in 2007.

1727 ■ Sarajevo Film Festival
Zelenih beretki 12
Sarajevo, Bosnia-Hercegovina
Ph: 38 7 33 221 516
Fax: 38 7 33 263 381
E-mail: info-sff@sff.ba
URL: http://www.sff.ba

1728 ■ Sarajevo Film Festival
To recognize films and filmmakers from southeast Europe. The Heart of Sarajevo Award is presented in three categories: Feature Film, Short Film, and Documentary. In addition, special and honorary awards may be presented. Held annually. Established in 1995.

Botswana

1729 ■ Botswana Institute of Bankers
Plot 767
GIB Bldg., 2nd Fl.
Gaborone, Botswana

Ph: 267 395 2493
Fax: 267 390 4307
E-mail: biob@info.bw
URL: http://www.biob.co.bw

1730 ■ Examination Prizes
To honor students for the highest marks in the Institute's examinations. Prizes are presented for specific subjects, as well as for overall performance. Awarded twice each year.

1731 ■ Student of the Year Award
To honor the student who completes the Certificate in Banking, the Intermediate Diploma, and either the Associate Diploma Stage 1 or 2 at any one sitting of the examinations. Awarded annually. Sponsored by the Bank of Botswana.

1732 ■ Botswana Ministry of Education Teaching Service Management Unit
Block 6, Government Enclave
Private Bag 00206
Gaborone, Botswana
Ph: 267 365 7300
Fax: 267 397 5315
E-mail: tsm.registry@gov.bw
URL: http://www.moe.gov.bw/tsm

1733 ■ Long and Distinguished Service Medal
To honor teachers who have completed 30 or more years of continuous and reputable service. Up to 10 awards may be presented annually as part of Botswana Teachers Day each June. Established in 1999.

1734 ■ Meritorious Service Medal
To honor teachers for exceptional service both in and out of the classroom. Up to 20 medals may be presented annually as part of Botswana Teachers Day each June. Established in 1999.

1735 ■ Mid-Career Medal
To honor teachers who have completed 15 or more years of continuous and reputable service. Up to 100 awards may be presented annually as part of Botswana Teachers Day each June. Established in 1999.

1736 ■ Silver Jubilee Medal
To honor teachers who have completed 25 or more years of continuous and reputable service. Up to 50 awards may be presented annually as part of Botswana Teachers Day each June. Established in 1999.

1737 ■ Botswana National Sports Council
Botswana Bureau of Standards Bldg.
Plot 55745
Airport Rd., Block 8
PO Box 1404
Gaborone, Botswana
Ph: 267 395 3449
Fax: 267 390 1607
URL: http://www.bnsc.co.bw

1738 ■ Sports Awards
To reward performance by athletes and sports-related individuals of Botswana. Awarded in nearly 20 categories, including Female and Male Sportsperson, Sports Code, Umpire/Referee, Print Media, and the Chairperson's Special Award. Awarded annually. Established in 1981.

1739 ■ Bessie Head Heritage Trust
PO Box 70401
Gaborone, Botswana
Ph: 267 395 2517
E-mail: bessiehead@gmail.com
URL: http://www.bessiehead.org

1740 ■ Bessie Head Literature Awards
To recognize the finest in English-language writing by residents and citizens of Botswana. Presented in four categories: Novel, Short Story, Poetry, and Children's Literature. Each year, the

Awards are arranged in alphabetical order below their administering organizations

categories of novel and short story are offered; the poetry and children's literature categories alternate annually. Monetary prizes are awarded for first, second, and third place in each category. Established in 2007 in memory of Botswana's most famous author. Sponsored by Pentagon Publishers.

Brazil

1741 ■ American Chamber of Commerce of Brazil (Rio de Janeiro, Brazil)
Henrique Rzezinski, Pres.
Praca Pio X, 15, Andar 5
Candelaria
Centro
20040-020 Rio de Janeiro, Rio de Janeiro, Brazil
Ph: 55 21 32139200
Fax: 55 21 32139201
E-mail: liliane@amchamrio.com
URL: http://www.amchamrio.com.br

1742 ■ FIGO/Ernst Schering Research Foundation Fellowship
For postgraduate research in human reproduction by junior obstetricians and gynecologists from developing nations for study at a center of excellence either at home or abroad. Airfare and living expenses are awarded.

1743 ■ American Chamber of Commerce of Brazil (Sao Paulo, Brazil)
(Camara Americana de Comercio de Sao Paulo)
Eduardo Wanick, Pres.
Rua da Paz, 1431
04713-001 Sao Paulo, Sao Paulo, Brazil
Ph: 55 11 33240194
Fax: 55 11 51803777
E-mail: ombudsman@amchambrasil.com.br
URL: http://www.amcham.com.br

1744 ■ ECO Award
To recognize an individual for social contribution. Awarded annually. Established in 1982.

1745 ■ Brazil Office of the President
Luis Inacio Lula da Silva, Pres.
Palacio do Planalto
Praca des Tres Poderes
70150-900 Brasilia, Federal District, Brazil
Ph: 55 61 3411 1596
E-mail: imprensa@planalto.gov.br
URL: http://www.presidencia.gov.br

1746 ■ Order of Rio Branco
For recognition of outstanding service to the Brazilian nation by a citizen or a foreigner. The order is conferred in five classes: Grand Cross, Grand Official, Knight Commander, Official, and Knight. Established in 1963.

1747 ■ Roquette Pinto Prize
To provide recognition for the best adaptation from a book to a film scenario by a Brazilian author.

1748 ■ Brazilian Academy of Letters
(Academia Brasileira de Letras)
Marcos Vinicios Vilaca, Pres.
Av. Presidente Wilson 203, Castelo
20030-021 Rio de Janeiro, Rio de Janeiro, Brazil
Ph: 55 21 39742500
E-mail: academia@academia.org.br
URL: http://www.academia.org.br

1749 ■ Afonso Arinos Prize
For recognition of the best work of fiction published or written during the two years preceding the year of award. A monetary prize is awarded annually.

1750 ■ Machado de Assis Prize
This, one of Brazil's highest literary awards, is given to recognize an outstanding Brazilian

writer for the sum of his work. A monetary prize of 200,000 Brazilian cruzeiros is awarded annually. Established in 1943.

1751 ■ Brazilian Book Chamber
(Camara Brasileira do Livro)
Karine Goncalves Pansa, Pres.
Rua Cristiano Viana, 91
05411-000 Sao Paulo, Sao Paulo, Brazil
Ph: 55 11 30691300
Fax: 55 11 30691300
E-mail: cbl@cbl.org.br
URL: http://www.cbl.org.br

1752 ■ Friend of the Book
(Amigo Del Libro)
To recognize individuals who stimulate the importance of reading books. Awarded annually.

1753 ■ Brazilian Chemical Society
Av. Prof. Lineu Prestes, 748
05508-900 Sao Paulo, Brazil
Ph: 55 11 30322299
Fax: 55 11 38145602
E-mail: sbqsp@iq.usp.br
URL: http://www.sbq.org.br

1754 ■ Simao Mathias Medal
To recognize contributions to the Society and to the development of chemistry in Brazil. Established in 1997.

1755 ■ Brazilian Metallurgy and Materials Association
(Associacao Brasileira de Metalurgia e Materiais)
Nelson Guedes de Alcantara, Pres.
Rua Antonio Comparato, 218
Campo Belo
04605-030 Sao Paulo, Sao Paulo, Brazil
Ph: 55 11 55344333
Fax: 55 11 55344330
E-mail: abm@abmbrasil.com.br
URL: http://www.abmbrasil.com.br

1756 ■ Gold Medal
Recognizes an individual providing outstanding service to the association. Awarded annually.

1757 ■ Silver Medal
Recognizes outstanding service to the association. Applicants must be association members. Awarded periodically.

1758 ■ Brazilian Society of Biochemistry and Molecular Biology
(Sociedade Brasileira de Bioquimica e Biologia Molecular)
Cynthia Sayuri Bando, Exec. Sec.
Av. Prof. Lineu Prestes
748 - bloco 3 superior - sala 0367 Butanta
CP 26077
05513-970 Sao Paulo, Sao Paulo, Brazil
Ph: 55 11 38155798
Fax: 55 11 38155798
E-mail: sbbq@iq.usp.br
URL: http://sbbq.iq.usp.br/v2

1759 ■ Prize in Life Sciences for a Young Scientist
For a student (undergraduate or graduate) in biochemistry or molecular biology. A monetary prize of $1,500, an invitation to present research, and plane tickets to an International Congress are awarded.

1760 ■ International Association for the Study of Clays
(Association Internationale pour l'Etude des Argiles)
Dr. Daisy Barbosa Alves SA, Sec. Gen.
Rua Horacio Macedo 950
Cidade Universitaria - Ilha do Fundao
21941-915 Rio de Janeiro, Rio de Janeiro, Brazil
Ph: 55 21 38656438
Fax: 55 21 38654562

E-mail: daisy@petrobras.com.br
URL: http://www.aipea.org

1761 ■ AIPEA Medals
To honor clay scientists in recognition of their contributions to clay science. A maximum of two medals are awarded quadrennially.

1762 ■ Bradley Award
To enable young clay scientists to attend the International Conference for the purpose of presenting his or her paper. A travel stipend of up to $1,000 is awarded annually.

1763 ■ International Confederation for Thermal Analysis and Calorimetry
Eder Cavalheiro, Sec.
Universidade de Sao Paulo
Instituto de Quimica de Sao Carlos
Av. do Trabalhador Sao-carlense, 400
13566-390 Sao Carlos, Sao Paulo, Brazil
Ph: 55 16 33738054
Fax: 55 16 33739987
E-mail: sec@ictac.org
URL: http://www.ictac.org
Formerly: (1993) International Confederation for Thermal Analysis.

1764 ■ Young Scientist Award
To encourage young scientists early in their careers to consider and utilize thermoanalytical methods. Scientists under 35 years of age are eligible. All necessary financial support to attend the ICTA Congress is awarded every four years. Established in 1985.

1765 ■ Latin American Thyroid Society
Ana Maria Masini-Repiso, Sec.
Departamento de Fisiologia e Biofisica
ICB-USP
05508-900 Sao Paulo, Sao Paulo, Brazil
Ph: 55 11 36098845
Ph: 55 11 36096389
Fax: 55 11 8187285
E-mail: amasini@mail.fcq.edu.ar
URL: http://www.lats.org/index.asp

1766 ■ Young Investigator Award
To honor young members for scientific achievements. Awarded to one or more recipients biennially in odd-numbered years.

1767 ■ Sao Paulo International Film Festival
(Mostra Internacional de Cinema Em Sao Paulo)
R. Antonio Carlos, 288
01309-010 Sao Paulo, Sao Paulo, Brazil
Ph: 55 11 3141 0413
Fax: 55 11 3266 7066
E-mail: info@mostra.org
URL: http://www.mostra.org

1768 ■ Sao Paulo International Film Festival
For recognition of the best films of the festival. Feature films or shorts not previously shown in Brazil must be submitted by August 13. The festival has two sections: the International Perspective and the New Filmmakers Competition for films by new directors. In the first week of the Festival, the public chooses ten films, and the jury chooses the final winners in the second week. The Bandeira Paulista, a flag of Sao Paulo stylized by the designer, Tomie Ohtake, is awarded annually. The Public Award and the Critic Award are also presented. Established in 1977 by Leon Cakoff.

1769 ■ Villa-Lobos Museum
(Museu Villa-Lobos)
Turibio Santos, Dir.
Rua Sorocaba, 200
22271-110 Botafogo, Rio de Janeiro, Brazil
Ph: 55 21 2266 1024
Fax: 55 21 2266 1024
E-mail: mvillalobos@museuvillalobos.org.br

Awards are arranged in alphabetical order below their administering organizations

URL: http://www.museuvillalobos.org.br

1770 ■ International Villa-Lobos Guitar Competition
(Concorso Internacional de Violao Villa-Lobos)

To recognize the best guitarist in the competition, and to encourage the development of Villa-Lobos works and Brazilian works in general. Guitarists of any age may submit entries and tapes by April 20. The following monetary prizes are awarded biennially: (1) First prize - $3,000 US; and (2) Second prize - $2,000 US. Established in 1971 by Museu Villa-Lobos in honor of Heitor Villa-Lobos.

1771 ■ International Villa-Lobos Piano Competition
(Concorso Internacional de Piano Villa-Lobos)

To recognize the best pianist in the competition, and to encourage the development of Villa-Lobos works and Brazilian works in general. Pianists of any age may submit entries and tapes by April 20. The following prizes are awarded: (1) first prize - 200,000,000 Brazilian cruzeiros; (2) second prize - 100,000,000 Brazilian cruzeiros; and (3) third prize - 50,000,000 Brazilian cruzeiros. Semi finalists may be awarded Distinctions. The winner also accepts the commitment to perform a pre-selected work by Villa-Lobos with orchestra. Held annually in November. Established in 1974 by Museu Villa-Lobos in honor of Heitor Villa-Lobos.

Brunei Darussalam

1772 ■ Authority for Info-Communications Technology Industry of Brunei Darussalam
Block B14, Spg. 32-5
Kg. Anggerek Desa
Jalan Berakas BB 3713, Brunei Darussalam
Ph: 673 232 3232
Fax: 673 238 1265
E-mail: hamdani.gani@aiti.gov.bn
URL: http://www.aiti.gov.bn

1773 ■ Brunei Info-Communications Technology Awards

To stimulate innovation and creativity in the Brunei Info-Communications Technology (ICT) industry among individuals and organizations, particularly small and medium enterprises (SMEs). Open to secondary schools, tertiary schools, and members of the ICT industry. Awards are presented in a variety of categories, such as Communication, e-Government, e-Health, Security, and Start-Up Companies. In addition, four special awards may be presented: the Patron's Award, Made in Brunei Product Award, Green ICT Award, and the Islamic Award. Winners may also be selected to represent Brunei Darussalam in the Asia Pacific ICT Alliance Awards. Presented annually. Established in 2004.

1774 ■ Brunei Darussalam Computer Society
(Persatuan Komputer Brunei Darussalam)
Helena Hj Mohd Mahathir, Sec.-Treas.
1st Fl., Unit 6, Bgn. Desa Delima
Spg. 44, Jln Muara
Bandar Seri Begawan BB 4513, Brunei Darussalam
Ph: 673 2334621
Ph: 673 2334997
Fax: 673 2334997
E-mail: pkbd@brunet.bn
URL: http://www.pkbd.org.bn/org/pkbd/index.html

1775 ■ Bursary Awards

Awarded to students who excel in the computer sciences.

1776 ■ Brunei Ministry of Communications
Jalan Menteri Besar
Besar BB 3910, Brunei Darussalam
Ph: 673 2383 838

Fax: 673 2380 398
E-mail: info@bicta.gov.bn
URL: http://www.bicta.gov.bn

1777 ■ Brunei Information-Communication Technology Awards BICTA

To stimulate innovation and creativity in the information-communication technology industry among individual and associations in Brunei, and to reduce the gap of the digital divide in the Asia Pacific region. Awards are presented each year in 16 categories.

1778 ■ Brunei Ministry of Industry and Primary Resources
Jalan Menteri Besar
Bandar Seri Begawan BB3910, Brunei Darussalam
Ph: 673 238 0599
Fax: 673 238 2474
URL: http://www.bruneimipr.gov.bn

1779 ■ National Awards for SMEs

To recognize small and medium enterprises (SMEs) for achievements in strengthening their role in Brunei's development. Awards are presented in four categories based on size and revenue. Awarded biennially.

1780 ■ Council of Women of Negara Brunei Darussalam
(Majlis Wanita Negara Brunei Darussalam)
12 Simpang 32-66-9
Jalan Stadium
Bolkiah
Bandar Seri Begawan 4313, Brunei Darussalam
Ph: 673 2 340524
Fax: 673 2 340525
URL: http://www.womencouncil.org.bn

1781 ■ Council of Women Award

To recognize the outstanding contributions of members who have elevated the vision and objectives of the Council and have distinguished themselves in volunteer work. Awarded biennially.

1782 ■ Mother of the Year Award

To honor an exemplary mother who has made extraordinary contributions to her family and community. Awarded biennially.

Bulgaria

1783 ■ Bulgarian Academy of Sciences Rostislaw Kaischew Institute of Physical Chemistry
(Institut po Fizikokhimiya)
Prof. Ivan Krastev, Dir.
Acad. G. Bonchev Str., Bl. 11
1113 Sofia, Bulgaria
Ph: 359 2 727 550
Fax: 359 2 971 2688
E-mail: krastev@ipchp.ipc.bas.bg
URL: http://www.ipc.bas.bg

1784 ■ Professor Rostislaw Kaischew Award

For young specialists in the field of physical chemistry.

1785 ■ Bulgarian Book Association
Silva Papazian, Exec. Sec.
64 Vitosha Blv., Fl. 2, Ap.4
BG-1463 Sofia, Bulgaria
Ph: 359 2 9581525
Fax: 359 2 9589211
E-mail: bba@otel.net
URL: http://www.abk.bg

1786 ■ Bronze Lion Award

To honor the best book issued in Bulgaria. Awarded annually.

1787 ■ Knight of the Book Award

To recognize special merit to the development of the book publishing industry in Bulgaria. Awarded annually.

1788 ■ Bulgarian National Television
(Bulgarska Natcionalna Televiziya)
International Relations Dept.
29 San Stefano Str.
BG-1504 Sofia, Bulgaria
Ph: 359 2 9461034
Fax: 359 2 9461034
E-mail: intr@bnt.bg
URL: http://www.bnt.bg
Formerly: (1995) Bulgarian Television and Radio.

1789 ■ Golden Chest International Television Festival
(Zlatnata Rakla)

To promote international television cooperation and a better knowledge of achievements in the field of television drama and to expand contacts between authors and producers from across the world. Productions must be on a contemporary theme and must be based on a literary work of national origin; plays written for television; TV-versions of theatre plays or television dramatizations. The programs may not offend the dignity of any country or nation, nor may they propagate violence, pornography, or religious fanaticism. The award is given in two categories: (1) Television drama for adults (running time of up to 100 minutes); and (2) Television drama for children and adolescents (70 minutes). The productions must have been released during the preceding year. Programs that have already won international awards and programs containing advertisements are not eligible. The following prizes are awarded: Category One - The Golden Chest Prize and the Special Prize of the Novotel Plovdiv. Category Two The Golden Chest Prize and the Special Prize of the Plovdiv Municipality. Other prizes may be awarded for special achievements in both categories: best actor, best actress; best child actor (awarded by the Union of Bulgarian Actors); best scriptwriter; best director; best director of photography; best set director (awarded by the Union of Bulgarian Filmmakers). The juries awarding the prizes shall be a seven-member international jury for Category One, and a five-member international jury for Category Two. Established in 1968 by Bulgarian Television.

1790 ■ Bulgarian Society of Ophthalmology
Dept. of Ophthalmology
67 - A, Bd., Stoletov
1233 Sofia, Bulgaria
Ph: 359 2 9268195
URL: http://www.mdsupport.org/resources/oph_societies.html████

1791 ■ Dalov's Award

For the best research done by a young ophthalmologist.

1792 ■ Boris Christoff International Competition for Young Opera Singers Foundation
Plamen Djouroff, Chm.
41, Tzar Boris III Blvd.
BG-1612 Sofia, Bulgaria
Ph: 359 2 9515 903
Fax: 359 2 9521 558
E-mail: borischristoff@abv.bg
URL: http://www.borischristoff.dir.bg

1793 ■ Boris Christoff International Competition for Young Opera Singers
(Concours International de Jeunes Chanteurs d'Opera)

For recognition of the achievements of young opera singers. Singers of all nationalities can take part in the Competition. Men may not be older than 35, and women not older than 33 years of age. The Competition takes place in

Awards are arranged in alphabetical order below their administering organizations

three stages; the third one involves singing a principal part in a regular performance of the Sofia National Opera. The Grand Prix of Sofia consists of a monetary prize of US$7,000, a gold medal, a gold ring, and a diploma. The following prizes are also awarded to both men and women: (1) First prize - US$5,000, a gold medal, and a diploma; (2) Second prize - US$3,000, a silver medal, and a diploma; and (3) Third prize US$2,000, a bronze medal, and a diploma. The winners are offered invitations for guest performances in Bulgaria and other countries of Europe. Awarded every four years. Established in 1961.

1794 ■ European Colloid and Interface Society
Prof. Peter Kralchevsky, Gen. Sec.
Sofia University
Department of Chemical Engineering
Faculty of Chemistry
James Bourchier Blvd., No. 1
BG-1164 Sofia, Bulgaria
Ph: 359 2 8161262
Ph: 359 2 9625310
Fax: 359 2 9625643
E-mail: pk@lcpe.uni-sofia.bg
URL: http://www.ecis-web.eu

1795 ■ Rhodia European Colloid and Interface Prize
To a European scientist who has published a work in an international journal for colloids and interfaces. Awarded annually.

1796 ■ International Academy of Architecture - Bulgaria
Prof. Georgi Stoilov, Pres.
35 Oborishte St.
BG-1504 Sofia, Bulgaria
Ph: 359 2 9446297
Ph: 359 2 9434950
Fax: 359 2 9434959
E-mail: 0882@mail.bol.bg
URL: http://www.iaa-ngo.org/home.php

1797 ■ IAA Gold Medal
For architectural achievements.

1798 ■ Transparency International - Bulgaria
Ognyan Minchev, Chm.
PO Box 72
Sofia, Bulgaria
Ph: 359 2 9867713
Ph: 359 2 9867920
Fax: 359 2 9867834
E-mail: mbox@transparency.bg
URL: http://www.transparency.bg

1799 ■ Integrity Awards
For individuals or organizations fighting corruption around the world.

1800 ■ Union of Scientists in Bulgaria
Prof. Damyan Damyanov, Pres.
39 Madrid Blvd., Fl. 2
BG-1505 Sofia, Bulgaria
Ph: 359 2 9430128
Ph: 359 2 9441157
Fax: 359 2 9441590
E-mail: science@usb-bg.org
URL: http://www.usb-bg.org

1801 ■ Honorary Sign
To recognize leading Bulgarian or foreign researchers who maintain beneficial contacts with units or members of the Union. Candidates must be nationally or internationally recognized. Awarded annually.

1802 ■ Scientific Achievement Competition
To recognize scientific achievements by members of the USB. Awards are presented in several categories each year, traditionally on the eve of November 1st, which is the Day of the Bulgarian Revival Leaders and the Bulgarian Scientist.

1803 ■ USB Certificate
To recognize an individual or organization for exceptional assistance or contribution to USB or its units. Candidates may be individuals; sections, branches, or other USB units; higher schools and research organizations; or business or trade juridical bodies. Awarded annually.

1804 ■ Varna International Ballet Competition (Concours International de Ballet, Varna)
6 Serdika St., 1st Fl.
BG-1000 Sofia, Bulgaria
Ph: 359 2 988 3377
Fax: 359 2 986 1901
E-mail: varna_ibc@mail.bol.bg
URL: http://www.varna-ibc.org

1805 ■ Varna International Ballet Competition (Concours International de Ballet, Varna)
For recognition of outstanding ballet dancers. Men and women dancers from all nationalities can take part in the Competition. Awards are presented in two independent classes: (1) Class A (Seniors) - for ballet dancers not older than 26 years of age; and (2) Class B (Juniors) - for boys and girls from 14 to 19 years of age. Competitors under 19 years of age who wish to compete in Class A - Seniors should receive special permission from the international jury. If the candidates decide to dance a pas de deux in one of the three stages of the competition, the ballet couples may be formed from one and the same class or from the two different classes. The candidates have to perform five pieces. The following prizes are awarded in Class A - Seniors: (1) Laureate of the International Ballet Competition and the Grand Prix of Varna - 20,000 leva, a gold medal and a diploma; (2) First Prizes (one for men and one for women) - 15,000 leva each, a gold medal, and a diploma; (3) two Second Prizes - 10,000 leva each, a silver medal, and a diploma; (4) Third Prize - 8,000 leva, a bronze medal, and a diploma; (5) Special Prize Nina Ricci - 12,000 leva, a commemorative medal and a diploma; and (6) Special Prize Repetto - 12,000 leva, a commemorative medal and a diploma. The following prizes are awarded in Class B - Juniors: (1) Excellent Performer of the International Ballet Competition and Special Distinction of the Youth Organization of Varna 10,000 leva, a diploma, concerts, and a medal; (2) First Class Awards (one for girls and one for boys) - 6,000 leva each, a diploma and a medal; (3) two Second Class Awards - 4,000 leva each, a diploma and a medal; and (4) two Third Class Awards - 2,000 leva each, a diploma and a medal. Special awards, token awards and distinctions are also awarded. Awarded biennially in even-numbered years. Established in 1964. Varna is one of four locations for the International Ballet Competition, the others being Moscow, Russia; Jackson, Mississippi, USA; and Helsinki, Finland.

Burkina Faso

1806 ■ Burkina Faso Ministry of Culture, Tourism and Communication
11 BP 852 CMS
Ouagadougou 11, Burkina Faso
Ph: 226 50 330963
Fax: 226 50 330964
E-mail: mctc@cenatrin.bf
URL: http://www.culture.gov.bf

1807 ■ National Prizes of Arts and Literature
To honor and promote talent in Burkina Faso. Prizes are presented in the following categories: Dramatic Art, Visual Art, Literature, Cooking, and Traditional Sport (wrestling and archery). Monetary prizes are awarded in each category and subcategory. Awarded biennially in even-

numbered years as part of the National Culture Week of Burkina Faso, or La Semaine Nationale de la Culture. Established in 1983.

Cambodia

1808 ■ Cambodian Ministry of Foreign Affairs and International Cooperation
No. 3, Samdech Hun Sen St.
Sangkat Tonle Bassac
Khan Chamcar Mon
Phnom Penh, Cambodia
Ph: 855 23 214 441
Fax: 855 23 216 144
E-mail: mfaicinfo@online.com.kh
URL: http://www.mfaic.gov.kh

1809 ■ Royal Order of Sahametrei
To honor a non-Cambodian for dedication and service to the Royal Government and the people of Cambodia. Awarded when merited.

1810 ■ Cambodian National Volleyball League (Disabled)
Christopher Minko, Sec. Gen.
Phnom Penh, Cambodia
E-mail: cminko@standupcambodia.net
URL: http://www.standupcambodia.net

1811 ■ Cambodian National Disability Awards
To recognize and celebrate outstanding contributions by corporations and institutions to raising awareness and positive action in support of issues of disability in Cambodia. Presented in four categories: Corporate Social Responsibility, Employer, Education, and Media. Awarded annually. Established in 2008.

Cameroon

1812 ■ EduArt Inc.
PO Box 90, Buea
Southwest Province, Cameroon
E-mail: eduartinc@yahoo.com
URL: http://www.eduartinc.org

1813 ■ EduArt Awards for Literature
To recognize outstanding literary works written by citizens of Cameroon. Awards are presented in three categories: fiction, drama, and poetry. Awarded annually.

Cayman Islands

1814 ■ Cayman Islands Society of Human Resource Professionals
PO Box 904 GT
Grand Cayman, Cayman Islands
Ph: 345949-1345
E-mail: info@cishrp.ky
URL: http://www.cishrp.ky

1815 ■ Top Employer Award
To recognize Cayman's leading organizations that attract and retain employees, contribute to the community through employee participation programs, and create an environment that exemplifies respect, fairness, and pride. Awarded annually. Established in 2009.

1816 ■ Cayman Islands Tourism Association
Largatos Bldg., 2nd Fl.
73 Lawrence Blvd.
PO Box 31086
Grand Cayman, Cayman Islands
Ph: 345949-8522
Fax: 345949-8522
E-mail: info@cita.ky
URL: http://www.cita.ky

Awards are arranged in alphabetical order below their administering organizations

1817 ■ Stingray Tourism Awards
To recognize individuals who have excelled in Cayman's tourism operations and have made great contributions to the interests and well-being of the Islands' hospitality industry and Association affairs during the year. Awarded annually in a variety of categories. Established in 2004.

1818 ■ Cayman National Cultural Foundation
F. J. Harquail Cultural Centre
17 Harquail Dr.
PO Box 30201
Grand Cayman, Cayman Islands
Ph: 345949-5477
Fax: 345949-4519
E-mail: admincncf@candw.ky
URL: http://www.artscayman.org

1819 ■ National Arts and Culture Awards
To recognize individuals who have attained a level of merit in their artistic discipline; contribute to the arts, culture, and heritage of the Cayman Islands; and support the work of the Cayman National Cultural Foundation. The Heritage Cross is awarded in gold, silver, and bronze for a minimum of 20, 10, and five years, respectively, of consistent and active engagement to Caymanian cultural heritage. The Star for Creativity in the Arts is awarded for artistic endeavor, achievement, and excellence. In addition, the Volunteer of the Year, Sponsor of the Year, and the Chairman's Award may be presented. Awarded annually. Established in 1994.

1820 ■ The Office of His Excellency the Governor of the Cayman Islands
c/o Governor's Awards
10 Market St., Ste. 710
Grand Cayman, Cayman Islands
URL: http://www.governorsaward.ky

1821 ■ Governor's Award for Design and Construction Excellence in the Cayman Islands
To encourage, foster, and maintain innovation, sustainability, and excellence in the Cayman Islands construction industry. Criteria include design excellence, creativity and innovation, sustainability and environmental, value, buildability, and cultural response. Awarded annually by the Governor. Sponsored by the Cayman Society of Architects, Surveyors and Engineers (CASE) and the Cayman Contractors Association (CCA).

Chile

1822 ■ Chile Ministry of Education Library
Sergio Bitar, Min.
Direccion de Bibliotecas
Archivos y Museos
Ave. Libertador Bernardo O'Higgins No. 651
Santiago 1371, Chile
Ph: 56 2 3904 000
Fax: 56 2 6381975
E-mail: bndir@oris.renib.d
URL: http://www.mineduc.cl/biblio

1823 ■ Premio Nacional de Artes Musicales
To recognize an individual for outstanding contributions in music. Awarded annually.

1824 ■ Premio Nacional de Ciencias Aplicadas
To recognize an individual for outstanding contributions in applied science. Awarded annually.

1825 ■ Premio Nacional de Ciencias Naturales
To recognize an individual for outstanding contributions in natural science. Awarded annually.

1826 ■ Premio Nacional de Historia
To recognize an individual for outstanding contributions in history. Awarded annually.

1827 ■ Premio Nacional de Literatura
To recognize a Chilean author of distinction in any of the literary fields of the novel, poetry, theater, essay, and literary criticism. Chilean writers must be nominated by an accredited academic institution and three or more people associated with the prize. A monetary prize and a certificate are awarded biennially in even-numbered years. Established in 1942 by Por Ley de la Republica.

1828 ■ Premio Nacional de Periodismo
To recognize a Chilean journalist distinguished by his or her method of communication or expression and for significant support of written or audiovisual journalism. A monetary prize is awarded biennially in odd-numbered years.

1829 ■ Engineers' Association of Chile (Colegio de Ingenieros de Chile A.G)
Fernando Aguero Garces, Pres.
Avenida Santa Maria 0508
Providencia
Santiago, Chile
Ph: 56 2 5701900
Fax: 56 2 5701903
E-mail: soporte@ingenieros.cl
URL: http://www.ingenieros.cl

1830 ■ Premio Nacional
Recognizes contributions to the engineering field. Awarded annually.

Colombia

1831 ■ Colombia Ministry of National Defence
Carrera 54 N 26
Bogota, Colombia
Ph: 57 1 2884184
E-mail: usuarios@mindefensa.gov.co
URL: http://www.mindefensa.gov.co

1832 ■ Medalla Militar Francisco Jose de Caldas
To recognize officials of the military forces who obtained the title of Military Professor, and alumni of the Escuela Superior de Guerra. Gold, silver, and bronze medals and a diploma are awarded annually.

1833 ■ Medalla Militar Soldado Juan Bautista Solarte Obando
To recognize the best soldier or sailor in each contingent of the Armed Forces who has distinguished himself by his excellent conduct, military qualities, ability to learn, and comradeship. A silver medal and a diploma are awarded annually.

1834 ■ Medalla Servicios Distinguidos a la Aviacion Naval
To recognize members of the Armed Forces for outstanding service.

1835 ■ Medalla Servicios Distinguidos la Fuerza de Superficie
To recognize members of the Armed Forces for outstanding service.

1836 ■ Orden del Merito Militar Antonio Narino
This, the highest award for military virtues, is conferred on the military and civilian personnel of the Colombian Military Forces. Awards are given in the following classes: (1) Great Cross; (2) Great Official; (3) Commander; (4) Official; (5) Knight; and (6) Companion. A medal and a diploma are awarded annually.

1837 ■ Orden del Merito Naval Almirante Padilla
For recognition of members of the Navy for outstanding services to the nation. Awards are given in the following classes: (1) Great Cross; (2) Great Official; (3) Official; and (4) Companion. A cross and a diploma are awarded annually.

1838 ■ Orden del Merito Sanitario Jose Fernandez Madrid
For recognition of personnel of the Health Section of the Armed Forces for extraordinary services in their profession. Awards are given in the following classes: (1) Grand Cross; (2) Grand Officer; (3) Office; (4) Knight; (5) Member; and (6) Commander. A medal and a diploma are awarded annually.

1839 ■ Servicios Distinguidos a la Fuerza Submarina
To recognize members of the Armed Forces for outstanding service.

1840 ■ Colombia Ministry of Transportation
Avenida el Dorado
Bogota, Colombia
Ph: 57 1 3240800
Fax: 57 1 2215767
E-mail: mintrans@mintransporte.gov.co
URL: http://www.mintransporte.gov.co

1841 ■ Orden al Merito Julio Garavito
To recognize the merits of certified Colombian engineers who have rendered distinguished service to the nation. The following orders may be awarded: (1) Gran Cruz con Placa de Oro - the Great Cross with the Plaque of Gold. This may be awarded only to former Colombian presidents; (2) Gran Cruz the Great Cross is presented to those who have held the offices of the Minister of Dispatch, President of the Society of Colombian Engineers, Rector of the University, and Manager of the Department of Public Decentralization; (3) Gran Oficial - the Plaque of the Great Official is presented to those who have held the offices of Secretary General, Director of the Ministry, president of some society of engineers, of an academic group, or a national servant such as a congressional representative, or those who have merited the title of Professor Emeritus or won some of the prizes conferred by the Colombian Society of Engineers; (4) Cruz de Plata - the silver cross is presented to official organizations or jurists who have distinguished themselves in service to the country; (5) Cruz de Comendador - the Cross of Commendation is presented to those who have served as chief of a branch of the Ministry or the equivalent, a noted public servant or jurist, university professor of engineering, or persons of equivalent status; (6) Cruz Oficial - the Official Cross is presented to those who have served as chiefs of a Division of the Ministry, or its equivalent, members of professional councils of engineering and architecture, or held other public office; and (7) Cruz de Caballero - the Knight's Cross is presented to those who are judged by the Order's council to be deserving of the honor through professional service. Awarded annually. Established in 1963 by the President of the Republic.

1842 ■ Alejandro Angel Escobar Foundation (Fundacion Alejandro Angel Escobar)
Camila Botero, Dir.
Calle 26, No. 4A-45, Piso 10
Bogota, Colombia
Ph: 57 1 281 8711
Fax: 57 1 243 3104
E-mail: info@faae.org.co
URL: http://faae.org.co

1843 ■ Science Prizes
To recognize Colombian citizens for scientific accomplishments in three categories: 1. Exact, Physical, and Natural Sciences; 2. Social Sciences and Humanities; and 3. Environment and Development. A monetary prize, silver medal,

Awards are arranged in alphabetical order below their administering organizations

and diploma are awarded annually in each category. Established in 1954 by Dr. Angel Escobar in his will.

1844 ■ Latin American and Caribbean Economic Association (Asociacion de Economia de America Latina y el Caribe)
Carolina G. Prada, Asst. Mgr.
Calle 78, No. 9-91
Bogota, Colombia
Ph: 57 1 3259777
Fax: 57 1 3259770
E-mail: lacea@fedesarollo.org.co
URL: http://www.lacea.org

1845 ■ Carlos Diaz-Alejandro Prize
To recognize an individual who has made a significant contribution or a body of contributions to the economic analysis of issues relevant to Latin America. A monetary prize of US$1,500 is awarded biennially in even-numbered years.

1846 ■ National Federation of Coffee Growers of Colombia (Federacion Nacional de Cafeteros de Columbia)
Juan Valdez, Contact
Oficina Central
Calle 73, No. 8-13
Bogota, Colombia
Ph: 57 1 3136600
E-mail: juan.valdez@juanvaldez.com
URL: http://www.cafedecolombia.com

1847 ■ Manuel Mejia Award
To support individuals and institutions that have significantly contributed to the global coffee business. Awarded annually. Established in 1960.

1848 ■ Pan-American Association of Educational Credit Institutions (Asociacion Panamericana de Instituciones de Credito Educativo)
Jorge Tellez Fuentes, Exec. Dir.
Calle 57, No. 8B-05, Local 46
Bogota, Colombia
Ph: 57 1 2126054
Ph: 57 1 2123926
Fax: 57 1 2124318
E-mail: apice@apice.org.co
URL: http://www.apice.org.co

1849 ■ International Order of Educational Credit
For promotion of student loan.

1850 ■ Medal of Honor of the Great Promoters of Education

1851 ■ Solidarity of Educational Credit Order
For outstanding development in financing of education and student loans.

1852 ■ Universidad del Valle
Calle 13 No. 100-00
Cali, Colombia
Ph: 57 2 321 2100
Fax: 57 2 339 8520
URL: http://www.univalle.edu.co

1853 ■ Gran Cruz de la Universidad del Valle
For recognition of outstanding services to the University by those serving on the staff, or for outstanding investigations and intellectual contributions by members of the University community. Faculty members who have been retired for over a year, who have been residents of the state of Valle for more than fifteen years, and who hold no public office are eligible. A cross is awarded annually. Established in 1954.

Cook Islands

1854 ■ Cook Islands Tourism Awards
Chris McGeown, Contact
c/o Edgewater Resort and Spa
PO Box 121, Avarua
Rarotonga, Cook Islands
Ph: 682 254 35
Fax: 682 254 75
E-mail: chris.mcgeown@edgewater.co.ck
URL: http://www.cookislandstourismawards.co.ck

1855 ■ Cook Islands Tourism Awards
To recognize excellence and innovation within the tourism and hospitality industry of the Cook Islands. Presented in several categories, including accommodations, tourism attractions, festival and event organizers, and tourism industry support. Awarded biennially in odd-numbered years. Sponsored by Air New Zealand.

Costa Rica

1856 ■ Costa Rica Ministry of Culture, Youth and Sport
Guido Saenz, Min.
Apartado 10227
San Jose 1000, Costa Rica
Ph: 506 331471
Fax: 506 337066
E-mail: mincjd@costarricense.cr
URL: http://www.mcjdcr.go.cr

1857 ■ Aquileo J. Echeverria Prize (Los Premios Nacionales Aquileo J. Echeverria)
To recognize Costa Rican citizens for excellence in the fields of literature (novel, short story, poetry, essay, scientific literature); history; theatre; music; and fine arts. Monetary prizes of 250,000 colones divided amongst the selected works, the total sum of awards not exceeding 8,000,000 Costa Rican colones, and a certificate are awarded annually. Established in 1962.

1858 ■ Joaquin Garcia Monge Prize (El Premio Nacional Joaquin Garcia Monge)
To recognize a foreign or Costa Rican journalist for promoting and disseminating literary, scientific and artistic works of Costa Ricans, or for pointing out cultural values of Costa Rica. Monetary prize of 818,800 colones and honorary recognition are awarded annually.

1859 ■ Los Premios Nacionales Interpretacion en Musica, Teatro, Danza
For recognition of achievement in the theatre. The following awards are presented: (1) Premio Olga Zuniza - best young actress; (2) Premio Eugenio Arias - best young actor; (3) best actress; (4) best actor; (5) best supporting actress; (6) best supporting actor; (7) best director; (8) best scenario; and (9) best theatrical group. Monetary prizes of 250,000 Costa Rican colones and a plaque are awarded annually. Established in 1972.

1860 ■ Premio Nacional de Periodismo Pio Viquez
To recognize a journalist for outstanding contributions. Monetary prizes of 250,000 Costa Rican colones are awarded annually. Established in 1972.

Croatia

1861 ■ Croatian Cartoonist Association
Savska 100
10000 Zagreb, Croatia
Ph: 385 1 4923 673
Fax: 385 1 6687 695

E-mail: hrvdrukar@gmail.com
URL: http://www.hdk.hr

1862 ■ International Cartoon Exhibition Zagreb
Recognizes outstanding print cartoons. Open to all professional and amateur cartoonists, regardless of nationality.

1863 ■ Croatian Library Association
Marijana Misetic, Pres.
National and University Library
Hrvatske bratske zajednice 4
CT-10000 Zagreb, Croatia
Ph: 385 1 615 9320
Fax: 385 1 615 9320
E-mail: hkd@nsk.hr
URL: http://www.hkdrustvo.hr

1864 ■ Kukuljevic's Charter (Kukuljeviceva povelja)
For recognition of achievement in librarianship to prominent librarians with many years of experience (age 50 and older). Society membership is necessary for consideration. A charter is awarded at the CLA convention irregularly. Established in 1968 in honor of Croatia's meritorious bibliophile and bibliographer Ivan Kukuljevic Sakcinski (1816-1889).

1865 ■ Eva Verona Award
Recognizes achievement in librarianship to young librarians (age 35 or younger). Society membership is necessary for consideration. A charter is awarded at the CLA convention every two years. The award has been named by the professor Eva Verona, PhD (1905-1996), who was Croatia's eminent librarian and scientist in the field of cataloging. Established in 1998.

1866 ■ Croatian National Theatre Split (Hrvatsko narodno kazaliste Split)
Trg Gaje Bulata 1
Porinova 4
CT-21000 Split, Croatia
Ph: 385 21 344
Fax: 385 21 361 260
E-mail: hnk-split@hnk-split.hr
URL: http://www.hnk-split.hr

1867 ■ Split Summer Festival (Splitsko ljeto)
To recognize achievement in opera, drama and ballet programs of the festival. Bronze sculptures by Vasko Lipovac are awarded annually in July or August. Established in 1984 by the journal *Danas*, in memory of Marko Marulic, the first writer on Croatian language. Sponsored by the Split newspaper, *Slobodna Dalmacija*.

1868 ■ Croatian Pharmaceutical Society (Hrvatsko Farmaceutsko Drustvo)
Maja Jaksevac-Miksa, Contact
Masarykova 2
HR-10000 Zagreb, Croatia
Ph: 385 1 4872849
Fax: 385 1 4872853
E-mail: hfd-fg-ap@zg.t-com.hr
URL: http://www.hfd-fg.hr

1869 ■ Julije Domac Medal (Medalja Julije Domac)
For recognition of a contribution to the development of pharmaceutical science and the profession. Members of the Society are eligible. A medal is awarded annually when merited. Established in 1955 in memory of Julije Domac, professor of The Pharmaceutical Faculty in Zagreb, Institute for Pharmacognosy (1886 to 1924).

1870 ■ International Animated Film Association (Association Internationale du Film d'Animation)
Nelson Shin, Pres.
Hrvatskog proljeca 36
CT-10040 Zagreb, Croatia

Awards are arranged in alphabetical order below their administering organizations

Ph: 385 1 2991395
Fax: 385 1 2991395
E-mail: secretary@asifa.net
URL: http://asifa.net

1871 ■ Special Award

To recognize a film or person or entity for the best contribution to international understanding through the art of animation. Nomination may be made to the ASIFA Board. Established in 1985.

1872 ■ International Association of Theatre for Children and Young People (Association Internationale du Theatre pour l'Enfance et la Jeunesse)
Dr. Wolfgang Schneider, Pres.
Petra Preradovica 44/II
HR-10 000 Zagreb, Croatia
Ph: 385 1 4667034
Ph: 385 1 4667225
Fax: 385 1 4667225
E-mail: sec.gen@assitej-international.org
URL: http://www.assitej-international.org/english/home.aspx

1873 ■ Honorary President Award

To recognize an artist or company who has achieved noteworthy excellence in theatre for children and young people. Awarded triennially.

1874 ■ Republic of Croatia Ministry of Science, Education and Sports (Ministarstvo Znanosti, Obrazovanja i Sporta, Republike Hrvatske)
Stanislava Rogic, Sec. Gen.
Donje Svetice 38
CT-10000 Zagreb, Croatia
Ph: 385 1 4569 000
Fax: 385 1 4594 301
E-mail: office@mzos.hr
URL: http://public.mzos.hr

1875 ■ Annual Award for Junior Researchers

To recognize prominent work of young researchers, publishing a prominent article in a journal with an international review or in a journal of corresponding excellence, or for publishing a book. Up to six awards are presented annually.

1876 ■ Annual Award for Popularization and Promotion of Science

To recognize contribution in spreading scientific knowledge through popular presentation of valuable professional and scientific knowledge and other forms of presentation in the following fields: natural sciences; biomedical sciences; technical sciences; biotechnical sciences; social sciences; and the humanities. A monetary award equal to 7,000 Croatian kuna is awarded; up to three awards shall be awarded annually for all fields.

1877 ■ Annual Science Award

To recognize important scientific achievement, scientific innovation, and application of results obtained by scientific-research activities in the following fields: natural sciences, biomedical sciences, technical sciences, biotechnical sciences, social sciences and humanities. A Monetary award equal to 10,000 Croation kuno is awarded. Up to three awards can be awarded annually for each scientific field.

1878 ■ Franjo Bucar National Sports Award

To recognize individuals for exceptional achievement in the field of sports and for outstanding contribution to its development in the Republic of Croatia. Available to professional and public workers in the field of sports, sportsmen, persons engaged in sports activities, and other individuals who contributed to the development of sports. Each year, up to 12 silver-plated medals may be presented; in addition, the National Lifetime Achievement Award, a gold-plated medal, may be presented to one or two individuals. Established in 1991.

1879 ■ Ivan Filipovic Award

To recognize research work in the field of education and teaching, the promotion of pedagogical theory and practice, and the development of educational systems in general. A monetary prize of 5,000 dinars is awarded annually. An additional prize of 20,000 dinars is given annually for life-long contributions to teaching. Awarded annually. Established in 1964.

1880 ■ Lifetime Achievement Award for Science

To recognize an individual for long-term contributions to science. Up to six awards are presented annually.

1881 ■ Minister's Certificate of Merit

To honor educational institutions, educators, teachers, and professors for achievement in work results, community reputation, and success of their students in further education and competitions in knowledge, skills, and competencies. Awarded annually. Established in 2000.

1882 ■ National Award for Technical Culture Faust Vrancic

To recognize individuals, associations, and other organizations for outstanding achievement in technical culture. Each year, up to 10 awards are presented to individuals, and up to five are presented to technical culture associations, companies, and other legal entities. Established in 1992.

1883 ■ Luka Ritz Award

To honor students who promote tolerance and violence-free schools, to encourage young people to adopt an active approach to fighting violence, and to make children, parents, and teachers more aware of the need for violence prevention. A statuette and scholarship in the amount of HrK 1,000 per month are awarded annually. Established in 2008 in memory of Luka Ritz, a high-school pupil who was beaten to death by a group of youths.

1884 ■ State Awards for Top-Level Sporting Achievements

To recognize athletes, sports teams, coaches, and active expert sports workers for sporting achievements of particular value and importance. Monetary prizes are awarded annually.

1885 ■ Faust Vrancic Lifetime Achievement Award

To honor individuals for their longstanding contribution and work in the development of technical culture, for extraordinary results of lasting value in the enhancement and development of scientific and technical literacy, and for development of technology and technical innovation in the Republic of Croatia and abroad. Awarded annually.

1886 ■ Zagreb World Festival of Animated Films - ANIMAFEST Zagreb (Svjetski Festival Animiranih Filmova, Zagreb)
Darko Krec, Pres.
Nova ves 18/3
CT-10000 Zagreb, Croatia
Ph: 385 1 390 7074
Fax: 385 1 4666 443
E-mail: info@animafest.hr
URL: http://www.animafest.hr

1887 ■ Audience Award

To recognize the audience's favorite feature film of the Animation Festival. Awarded annually.

1888 ■ Golden Zagreb Prize

Encourages creativity and innovation in artistic achievement. A cash award of 3,000 Euros and a statue are presented.

1889 ■ Grand Prize (Svjetski Festival Animiranih Filmova)

Awarded to the best short film of the festival. A

monetary prize and statue are awarded. Winner also becomes honorary President at the next festival. Established in 1972.

Cuba

1890 ■ Academy of Sciences of Cuba
Alejandro Caballero Rivero, Contact
Industria y San Jose, Capitolio Nacional
Habana Vieja
Havana 12400, Cuba
Ph: 53 7 862 6545
Fax: 53 7 867 0599
E-mail: alejandro@academiaciencias.cu
URL: http://www.academiaciencias.cu

1891 ■ Scientific Book Award

To promote science development in Cuba and to encourage scientific researchers to publish their works for a Cuban audience. Awarded annually. Established in 2003.

1892 ■ Festival Internacional del Nuevo Cine Latinoamericano
Calle 2, No. 411, entre 17 y 19
Vedado
Havana 10400, Cuba
E-mail: festival@festival.icaic.cu
URL: http://www.habanafilmfestival.com

1893 ■ International Festival of the New Latin American Cinema

To promote and honor those works whose significance and artistic values contribute to enrich and reaffirm the Latin American and Caribbean cultural identity. Coral Awards are presented in a variety of categories. Awarded annually. Established in 1979.

Cyprus

1894 ■ Cyprus Dance Association
14 Democratias Ave.
PO Box 70640
Ayios Dometios 2370, Cyprus
Ph: 357 2278 0876
Fax: 357 2278 0874
E-mail: cyprusdanceassociation@cytanet.com.cy
URL: http://www.cydanceassociation.org

1895 ■ Pancyprian Ballet Competition

To discover talented Cypriot dancers and promote them in Cyprus and abroad, as well as to bridge relationships between Cyprus and the international scenery of dancing. Participants, who must be permanent residents of Cyprus, compete in two classifications: Children's Group (11-14 years old) and Adolescents' Group (15-20 years old). Scholarships and monetary prizes are awarded to the first, second, and third place dancers in each category. Held annually. Established in 2006.

1896 ■ Cyprus Employers and Industrialists Federation (Omospondia Ergodoton ke Biomichanon Kyprou)
Ms. Michael Pilikos, Dir. Gen.
30 Grivas Dhigenis Ave.
PO Box 21657
Nicosia CY-1511, Cyprus
Ph: 357 22 665102
Fax: 357 22 669459
E-mail: info@oeb.org.cy
URL: http://www.oeb.org.cy

1897 ■ Cyprus Innovation Awards

To recognize the innovation and continuous improvement of competitiveness of Cyprus companies. Awards are presented in four categories: Primary Sector (agriculture, fishing, and mining businesses); Manufacturing Sector (all industrial businesses); Services Sector (compa-

Awards are arranged in alphabetical order below their administering organizations

nies of the tertiary sector); and Public Sector (public services, local authorities, and governmental organizations). Awarded annually. Established in 2006.

1898 ■ Cyprus Professional Engineers Association
(Syndesmos Epistimonon Michanikon Kyprou)
Pavlos Demetriou, Sec. Gen.
PO Box 28772
Nicosia 2082, Cyprus
Ph: 357 2 314556
Fax: 357 2 492032
E-mail: sem.kyprou@cytanet.com.cy
URL: http://www.feani.org/webfeani

1899 ■ CPEA Educational Award
For students.

1900 ■ Cyprus Sport Organization
Nikous Kartakoullis, Pres.
PO Box 24804
Nicosia 1304, Cyprus
Ph: 357 22 897000
Fax: 357 22 358222
E-mail: info@sport-koa.org.cy
URL: http://www.cyprussports.org

1901 ■ Best Athlete
To sport champions.

1902 ■ Best Team
To sport champions.

Czech Republic

1903 ■ Association of Czech Insurance Brokers
(Asociace ceskych pojistovacich makleru)
Zdenka Indruchova, Exec. Dir.
nam. W Churchilla 2
CZ-130-00 Prague, Czech Republic
Ph: 42 2 34462166
Fax: 42 2 34462167
E-mail: info@acpm.cz
URL: http://www.acpm.cz

1904 ■ Insurance Company of the Year
For insurance companies.

1905 ■ Charta 77 Foundation
Jan Kacer, Mgr.
Melantrichova 5
CS-110 00 Prague 1, Czech Republic
Ph: 42 224 214 452
Fax: 42 224 213 647
E-mail: nadace77@bariery.cz
URL: http://www.bariery.cz

1906 ■ Dr. Frantisek Kriegel Prize
(Cena Frantisek Kriegel)
For recognition of contributions to the human and civil rights movement and civil courage in the Czech Republic and the Slovak Republic. Individuals who promote human rights and civic freedom are considered. A monetary award of 100,000 Czech crowns and a diploma are awarded annually. Established in 1987 in memory of Frantisek Kriegel (1908-1978), a promoter of Prague spring and the only leader who refused to sign the acceptance of Soviet rule in August 1968.

1907 ■ Jaroslav Seifert Prize
(Cena Jaroslava Seiferta)
For recognition of the best work in Czech and Slovak literature. A monetary award of 250,000 Czech crowns and a diploma made by one of the well known Czechoslovak artists are awarded. Established in 1986 in memory of Jaroslav Seifert, Nobel Prize Winner (1984) and Czech poet.

1908 ■ Tom Stoppard Prize
To recognize authors of Czech origin for a major,

predominantly essayist, work that serves as a source of inspiration in terms of its philosophical contribution. Awarded annually. Established in 1983 in honor of the English dramatist of Czech origin.

1909 ■ Josef Vavrousek Prize
To recognize an individual for contributions toward protecting the environment or implementing the concept of sustainable development. Awarded annually. Established in 1996.

1910 ■ Czech Chemical Society
(Ceska Spolecnost Chemicka)
Prof. Jitka Ulrichova, Pres.
Novotneho Lavka 5
CZ-116 68 Prague 1, Czech Republic
Ph: 42 2 21082383
Fax: 42 2 22220184
E-mail: csch@csch.cz
URL: http://www.csch.cz

1911 ■ Alfred Bader Prize
To recognize young Czech organic and bio-organic/bio-inorganic chemists for scientific achievement. Awarded to two individuals annually. Established in 1994.

1912 ■ Hanus Medal
This, the highest award bestowed by the Society, recognizes high scientific achievements in chemistry. Awarded to one or more recipients annually.

1913 ■ Heyrovsky-Ilkovic-Nernst Lecture
To initiate or improve the interaction between research institutions in the Czech and Slovak republics as well as with Germany. Awarded annually. Established in 2002.

1914 ■ Milos Hudlicky Prize
To honor the best paper printing in one of the European journals in which CCS is a partner or owner. Awarded annually. Established in 2001.

1915 ■ Karel Preis Prize
To recognize the best article published the *Chemicke Listy* journal. Awarded annually. Established in 1995.

1916 ■ Czech Publishers Association
(Unie Vydavatelu)
Peter Mark, Pres.
Na Porici 30
CZ-110 00 Prague, Czech Republic
Ph: 42 2 21733427
Ph: 42 2 21733527
E-mail: unie@unievydavatelu.cz
URL: http://www.unievydavatelu.cz

1917 ■ Best Magazine of the Year
To recognize the best magazine. Awarded annually.

1918 ■ Zlaty Stocek Golden Printing Block
For the best advertisement published in the Czech periodical press.

1919 ■ Czech Radiological Society
(Ceska Radiologicka Spolecnost)
Prof. Jiri Ferda PhD, Scientific Sec.
University Hospital
Clinic of Diagnostic Radiology
Alej Svobody 80
CZ-306 40 Plzen 100, Czech Republic
Ph: 42 377103436
Fax: 42 377103438
E-mail: ferda@fnplzen.cz
URL: http://www.crs.cz

1920 ■ Sigmund's Prize
For publication with scientific value.

1921 ■ European Association of Archaeologists
Sylvie Kvetinova, Admin.
Institute of Archaeology
Letenska 4

118 01 Prague, Czech Republic
Ph: 42 257014411
Fax: 42 257014411
E-mail: eaa@arup.cas.cz
URL: http://www.e-a-a.org

1922 ■ European Archaeological Heritage Prize
To recognize an individual, institution, or a local or regional government for an outstanding contribution to the protection and presentation of European archaeological heritage. A work of art, diploma, and a monetary prize are awarded annually. Established in 1999.

1923 ■ Student Award
To recognize the best paper presented at the EAA conference by a student or archaeologist working on a dissertation. Awarded annually. Established in 2002.

1924 ■ Festa Musicale
Slovenska 5
PO Box 55
CZ-771 11 Olomouc, Czech Republic
Ph: 42 587 420 334
Fax: 42 587 420 334
E-mail: info@festamusicale.com
URL: http://www.festamusicale.cz

1925 ■ Mundi Cantant - International Choir Festival
For recognition of achievement in the singing competition, Iuventus Mundi Cantat. Members of choirs of all categories, including pre-school children's choir; children's choirs; selected choirs; boys' choirs; youth choirs; women choirs; men's choirs; and others are eligible. Winners are awarded by jury according to their gained points. Gold, silver, and bronze medals are awarded biennially at the Festival "Holidays of Songs." Established in 1987 by the Ministry of Culture.

1926 ■ Musica Religiosa - International Choir Festival of Sacred and Clerical Music
To recognize excellence in religious choral performance. Open to amateur choirs. Awards are presented in the following categories: Children's Choirs, Boys' Choirs, Youth Choirs, Adult Choirs, Chamber Choirs, Polyphony, and Gregorian Chant. Held annually. Established in 2003.

1927 ■ Prague Spring International Music Festival
(Mezinarodni hudebni festival Prazske jaro)
Ing. Roman Belor, Dir.
Hellichova 18
CZ-118 00 Prague 1, Czech Republic
Ph: 42 257 312547
Fax: 42 257 313725
E-mail: info@festival.cz
URL: http://www.festival.cz

1928 ■ Prague Spring International Music Competition
(Mezinarodni hudebni soutez Prazske jaro)
For recognition of an outstanding performance in the field of music by young talent. Open to musicians of all nationalities who are under the age of 30. Categories change annually, and there may be more than one category within any given competition. Monetary awards are given in the amounts of 200,000 Czech Koruna for first place; 100,000 Czech Koruna for second; and 50,000 Czech Koruna for third place. Held annually. Established in 1948. Sponsored by the Ministry of Culture.

1929 ■ Radio Prague
(Cesky Rozhlas, Praga)
Vinohradska 12
CZ-120 99 Prague 2, Czech Republic
Ph: 42 221 552 933

Awards are arranged in alphabetical order below their administering organizations

Fax: 42 221 552 903
E-mail: cr@radio.cz
URL: http://www.radio.cz

1930 ■ Concertino Prague International Radio Competition for Young Musicians (Mezinarodni Rozhlasova Soutez Mladych Hudebniku Concertino Praha)
To recognize young talented musicians and enable them to compare their skills on an international scale, to acquaint the broad radio audiences with their performances, and to assist in establishing contacts among the youngest artistic generation. The competition is open to soloists in the categories of piano, violin, and violoncello. Musicians no older than 16 years of age are eligible. Candidates take part in the competition through tape recordings sent in by radio organizations associated in the European Broadcasting Union. Each radio organization can enter one participant in each competition category. In case one of the three instruments is not represented, the second competitor may be admitted for one of the remaining categories. The selection of soloists whose performances have to be judged is made by the participating radio organization itself. In each competition category, the jury awards first and second prizes. On consideration, the jury may award an honorary diploma to runners-up whose score comes close to those of the first and second prize winners. The winners, first, and second prize laureates are invited by the organizer to perform at public concerts in Prague and at the South Bohemia Concertino Praga Festival to defend their victory. The concerts are offered to members of the broadcasting unions for live or delayed broadcasts. Expenses for the winners' stay in Prague and at the South Bohemian Concertino Praga Festival, and travel to and from the Festival are paid by Czech Radio. Awarded annually. Established in 1966.

1931 ■ Society for Geology Applied to Mineral Deposits (Societe de Geologie Appliquee aux Gites Mineraux)
Dr. Jan Pasava, Exec. Sec.
Czech Geological Survey
Klarov 131/3
CZ-118 21 Prague 1, Czech Republic
Ph: 42 2 51085506
Fax: 42 2 51818748
E-mail: secretary@e-sga.org
URL: http://www.e-sga.org

1932 ■ Best Paper Award
To recognize the best paper published in the Society's journal, *Mineralium Deposita*, during the previous two years. Awarded biennially in odd-numbered years. Established in 1999.

1933 ■ Best Student Oral and Poster Presentation Award
To recognize students for outstanding quality and scientific merit of posters and oral presentations delivered at the Biennial Meeting. A certificate and monetary prize of US$300 are awarded for best poster and oral presentation. Awarded biennially in odd-numbered years.

1934 ■ SGA-Barrick Young Scientist Award
To recognize a young scientist who contributes to the understanding of mineral deposits. Candidates must be younger than 37 year old on January 1 of the year in which the award is given. Awarded biennially in odd-numbered years. Established in 2003. Sponsored by Barrick Gold Corp.

1935 ■ SGA-Newmont Gold Medal
To recognize an individual for outstanding career performance that has forwarded the work of the mineral deposit sector through research, mine geology, and exploration. Awarded biennially in odd-numbered years. Established in 2006. Sponsored by Newmont Mining Corp.

1936 ■ Society of Czech Architects (Obec Architektu)
Ing. Arch. Jan Melichar, Pres.
Revolucni 23
CZ-110 00 Prague, Czech Republic
Ph: 42 257 535025
Ph: 42 732 554698
Fax: 42 257 535033
E-mail: obecarch@architekt.cz
URL: http://www.architekt.cz
Formerly: (1990) Union of Czech Architects.

1937 ■ Grand Prix in Architecture (Cena Obce Architektu za Realizaci Roku)
For recognition of contemporary national architecture in the fields of new buildings, reconstructions, interior design, town planning, landscape architecture, and garden design. The competition is open to projects designed by Czech or foreign architects and created in the territory of the Czech Republic. Held annually. Established in 1993.

Denmark

1938 ■ Danish Academy of Technical Sciences (Akademiet for de Tekniske Videnskaber)
Prof. Klaus Bock, Pres.
266 Lundtoftevej
DK-2800 Lyngby, Denmark
Ph: 45 45881311
Ph: 45 45960822
Fax: 45 45881351
E-mail: lsr@atv.dk
URL: http://www.atv.dk/index.php

1939 ■ Knud Lind Larsen Prize
Recognizes a young Danish chemistry researcher who is outstanding in the field and shows potential for future growth. Awarded biennially in even-numbered years.

1940 ■ Danish Association of the Specialist Press (Dansk Fagpresse)
Henrik Thogersen, Contact
Pressens Hus
Skindergade 7
DK-1159 Copenhagen K, Denmark
Ph: 45 33974000
E-mail: specialmedierne@specialmedierne.dk
URL: http://www.specialmedierne.dk

1941 ■ Anders-Bording Prisen
To recognize a freelance journalist. Awarded annually.

1942 ■ Danish DX Group
Allis Andersen, Treas.
Kagsaavej 34
DK-2730 Herlev, Denmark
Ph: 45 4485 2530
E-mail: oz1acb@qrz.dk
URL: http://www.ddxg.dk

1943 ■ Copenhagen Award
To recognize any amateur radio operator, worldwide, who has made contact with stations in the area of Copenhagen, Denmark. A certificate is awarded when merited. Established in 1967.

1944 ■ Cross Country award
To recognize Scandinavian amateur radio operators who have made contact with at least 10 counties in Denmark; extra points are given for contact made with Greenland. A certificate is awarded when merited.

1945 ■ Danish Island Award
To recognize any amateur radio operator or short wave listener, worldwide, who has made contact with or heard the Danish islands after January 1, 1997. A certificate is awarded when merited.

1946 ■ Danish Lighthouse Award
To recognize any amateur radio operator, worldwide, who has made contact with Danish lighthouses.

1947 ■ Danish Underground Radio Award
To recognize any amateur radio operator, worldwide, who has made contact with station OZ5MAY. A certificate is awarded when merited.

1948 ■ Field Day Award
To recognize a member for making contact with a minimum of 15 Danish Club stations at the Annual Field Day. A certificate is awarded when merited.

1949 ■ Greenland Award
To recognize amateur radio operators either for 2xCW or Phone contact with a minimum of five different amateurs from a minimum of three different locations. A certificate is awarded when merited.

1950 ■ OZ Locator Award
To recognize any amateur radio operator, worldwide, who has made contact with stations in at least 10 locator-squares after January 1, 1985. A certificate is awarded when merited.

1951 ■ OZ Prefix Award
To recognize any amateur radio operator, worldwide, who has made contact with a certain number of stations prefixed with OZ. A certificate is awarded when merited.

1952 ■ Danish Huntington Association (Lansforeningen mod Huntingtons Chorea)
Sven Asger Sorensen PhD, Exec. Pres.
Bystaevneparken 25, 701
2700 Copenhagen, Denmark
Ph: 45 9 8575323
E-mail: lhc@lhc.dk
URL: http://www.lhc.dk

1953 ■ Danish Huntington Association (Lansforeningen mod Huntingtons Chorea)
Dr. Bettina Thoby, Exec. Pres.
Bystaevneparken 23, 701
2700 Bronshoj, Denmark
Ph: 45 9 8575323
E-mail: kontor@lhc.dk
URL: http://www.lhc.dk

1954 ■ Awards for Editorial Excellence
To recognize editorial excellence in both traditional and new media, and to encourage editorial vitality throughout the region. Awarded annually in various categories. Established in 1999.

1955 ■ Landsforeningen mod Huntingtons Choreas Forskningsfond
For research.

1956 ■ Danish Library Association (Danmarks Biblioteksforening)
Winnie Vitzansky, Dir.
Farvergade 27D, 2 sal
DK-1463 Copenhagen V, Denmark
Ph: 45 33250935
Fax: 45 33257900
E-mail: webmaster@dbf.dk
URL: http://www.dbf.dk

1957 ■ R. Lysholt Hansens Bibliotekspris
To recognize special achievement in library or cultural work. Nominations must be submitted. A monetary award is presented annually when merited. Established in 1983 to honor R. Lysholt Hansen.

Awards are arranged in alphabetical order below their administering organizations

1958 ■ Edvard Pedersens Biblioteks-fonds Forfatterpris
To recognize outstanding authors. A monetary award of 25,000 Koruna is presented annually. Established in 1986 to honor Edvard Pedersen.

1959 ■ Danish Union of Journalists (Dansk Journalistforbund)
Fred Jacobsen, VP
Gl. Strand 46
DK-1202 Copenhagen K, Denmark
Ph: 45 33428000
Fax: 45 33428030
E-mail: dj@journalistforbundet.dk
URL: http://journalistforbundet.dk

1960 ■ Cavling Prize
For outstanding journalism. Awarded annually.

1961 ■ Carsten Nielsen Prize
Award of recognition. A monetary prize of 20,000 kroner is awarded annually.

1962 ■ Danish Writers Association (Dansk Forfatterforening)
Strandgade 6
DK-1401 Copenhagen K, Denmark
Ph: 45 32955100
E-mail: df@danskforfatterforening.dk
URL: http://www.danskforfatterforening.dk

1963 ■ Dansk Oversaetterforbunds Aere-spris
For recognition of an outstanding translation of foreign literature into Danish. A monetary prize of 30,000 Danish kroner and a diploma are awarded annually. Established in 1954. Sponsored by Denmark - Ministry of Cultural Affairs.

1964 ■ Holberg Medal
To provide recognition for outstanding contributions to Danish literature. A monetary prize of 30,000 Danish kroner and a medal are awarded annually.

1965 ■ European Association for Lexicography
Lars Trap-Jensen, Sec.-Treas.
Society for Danish Language and Literature
Christians Brygge 1
1219 Copenhagen, Denmark
Ph: 45 33 130360
E-mail: ltj@dsl.dk
URL: http://www.euralex.org

1966 ■ Laurence Urdang Award
To support unpaid lexicographical work of any type, including study. A monetary grant ranging from £250 to £1,500 is awarded annually. Established in 1990. Formerly: Verbatim Award.

1967 ■ Geological Society of Denmark (Dansk Geologisk Forening)
Lars Nielsen, Chm.
Geological Museum
Oster Voldgade 5
DK-1350 Copenhagen, Denmark
Ph: 45 35322354
E-mail: dgfemail@gmail.com
URL: http://2dgf.dk/dgf_uk

1968 ■ Danish Geology Prize
To recognize an individual or group for the publication of one or more articles or maps that have provided an exceptional contribution to the understanding of the geology of Denmark or Greenland. Articles and maps must have been published within the last five years. Nominees must have been employed at a Danish or Greenland institution or company. A monetary prize of 25,000 Danish Krone is awarded annually. Established in 1993.

1969 ■ Steno Medal
To recognize outstanding contributions to geology. A gold medal is awarded every four or

five years. Established in 1969 in honor of Niels Nicolaus Steno (1638-1686), a pioneer in the fields of crystallography and stratigraphy.

1970 ■ Gyldendal
Klareboderne 3
DK-1001 Copenhagen K, Denmark
Ph: 45 33 755555
Fax: 45 33 755556
E-mail: gyldendal@gyldendal.dk
URL: http://www.gyldendal.dk

1971 ■ Soren Gyldendal Prisen
To recognize authors of fiction or of scientific or educational work. A writer in the middle of his or her creative process is eligible. A monetary prize of 150,000 Danish kroner is awarded annually. Established in 1958 in memory of Soren Gyldendal, founder of Gyldendal, in connection with his birthday, April 12 (1742).

1972 ■ Medicon Valley Alliance
Arne Jacobsens Alle 15, 2
DK-2300 Orestad City, Denmark
Ph: 45 70 201503
E-mail: mva@mva.org
URL: http://www.mva.org

1973 ■ Elite Research Prize
To recognize outstanding researchers under 45 years of age in the fields of science, social science, and the humanities. Five recipients are awarded a personal honorary prize of 200,000 DDK, plus a monetary award of 800,000 DDK for further research.

1974 ■ Carl Nielsen International Music Competitions (Internationale Carl Nielsen Musik Konkurrencer)
Marianne Granvig, Sec. Gen.
Odense Symphony Orchestra
Claus Bergs Gade 9
DK-5000 Odense C, Denmark
Ph: 45 6612 0057
Fax: 45 6591 0047
E-mail: carlnielsencompetition@odensesymfoni.dk
URL: http://cncomp.odensesymfoni.dk

1975 ■ Carl Nielsen International Music Competitions (De Internationale Carl Nielsen Musik Konkurrencer)
To recognize musicians of outstanding talent under 30 years of age and of all nationalities. Four separate competitions are held on an annually rotating basis - for violin, clarinet, flute, and organ. Monetary prizes totaling approximately DKK350,000 and concert engagements are awarded. Held annually. Established in 1980 to honor the Danish composer Carl Nielsen.

1976 ■ Nordic Council (Nordiska Radet)
Jan Erik Enestam, Sec. Gen.
Ved Stranden 18
DK-1061 Copenhagen K, Denmark
Ph: 45 33960400
Fax: 45 33111870
E-mail: nordisk-rad@norden.org
URL: http://www.norden.org/sv

1977 ■ Film Prize
To recognize outstanding film manuscript writers, directors, and producers from Nordic countries for the creation of an artistically original film that is rooted in Nordic cultural circles, in which the various elements of the film unite to form a harmonious work. A monetary prize of DKK 350,000 is awarded annually.

1978 ■ Literature Prize (Litteraturpris)
To increase the interest in the literature of the Nordic countries. Works by living authors from Nordic countries (Denmark, Finland, Greenland,

Iceland, Norway, and Sweden), which have been produced during the preceding two years are eligible. The literary work may be in one of the languages of the Nordic region, including Faeroese, Greenlandic, and Sami. A monetary prize of 350,000 Danish kroner is presented annually at the time of the Nordic Council's session. Established in 1962 by the Nordic governments.

1979 ■ Music Prize (Musikpris)
To recognize a living Nordic composer for a recent musical work and in alternate years a living Nordic performer. The selection is made by NOMUS - Nordic Music Committee, which is an expert committee consisting of two members from each Nordic country. Candidates for the prize are nominated by the delegates of the respective countries. A monetary prize of 350,000 Danish kroner is awarded annually. Established in 1965.

1980 ■ Nature and Environment Prize
To recognize individuals and organizations from Nordic countries for achievements in environmental conservation. A monetary prize of DKK 350,000 is awarded annually. Established in 1995.

1981 ■ Novo Nordisk Foundation
Birgitte Nauntofte, Exec. Dir.
Tuborg Havnevej 19
DK-2900 Hellerup, Denmark
Ph: 45 3527 6600
Fax: 45 3527 6601
E-mail: nnfond@novo.dk
URL: http://www.novonordiskfonden.dk

1982 ■ H. C. Jacobaeus Lectures
The lectures should be held in Scandinavian university cities or other European cities with association to medical research. The subject of the lectures should be within the field of physiology or endocrinology. A monetary award of 50,000 Danish kroner is presented in connection with the lecture. Awarded annually. Established in 1939.

1983 ■ Marie and August Krogh Prize
For recognition of outstanding research in medical sciences. Any Danish doctor is eligible. A monetary award of 100,000 Danish kroner is awarded annually. Established in 1969. Formerly: (2009) August Krogh Prize.

1984 ■ Novo Nordisk Foundation Lecture
For recognition of outstanding scientific work within the field of diabetes research and/or treatment. A monetary award of 50,000 Danish kroner is presented annually to an active outstanding Nordic scientist. The lecture is given in connection with the annual meeting of the Scandinavian Society for the Study of Diabetes (SSSD). Established in 1995.

1985 ■ Novo Nordisk Prize
To recognize a considerable contribution, particularly a Danish contribution, in the field of medical science. A monetary personal award of 250,000 Danish kroner and an award of 750,000 Danish kroner to be used for research are presented annually to a scientist working in a Danish university or institution. Established in 1963.

1986 ■ Odense International Film Festival
Birgitte Weinberger, Dir.
Farvergarden 7
DK-5000 Odense C, Denmark
Ph: 45 66 512821
E-mail: filmfestival@odense.dk
URL: http://www.filmfestival.dk

1987 ■ Odense Film Festival
For recognition of outstanding films in the following categories: Fairy tale films, including live or animated films of 45 minutes maximum running

Awards are arranged in alphabetical order below their administering organizations

time and experimental/imaginative films. Approximately 11 awards are presented, including the Grand Prize, Award for Best Danish Documentary, and Award for Best Danish Short Fiction. Awarded annually. Established in 1975.

1988 ■ Odense International Organ Competition and Festival
Kultursekretariatet
Norregade 36-38
DK-5100 Odense C, Denmark
Ph: 45 5194 1816
E-mail: jr@organcompetition.dk
URL: http://www.organcompetition.dk

1989 ■ Carl Nielsen International Organ Competition
For recognition of young organists of all nationalities. Held as one of the four Carl Nielsen International Music Competitions. The following prizes are awarded: first prize - 40,000 Danish kroner; second prize - 15,000 Danish kroner; third prize - 10,000 Danish kroner; and fourth prize - 5,000 Danish kroner. Organ pipes with inscription are also awarded. Special prize for the best performance of the Danish piece - 5,000 Danish kroner. Held every four years. Established in 1986 under the patronage of His Royal Highness, Prince Henrik of Denmark. Formerly: (2009) Odense International Organ Competition.

1990 ■ Royal Danish Geographical Society
(Kongelige Danske Geografiske Selskab)
Prof. Ole Mertz, Sec. Gen.
Oester Voldgade 10
DK-1350 Copenhagen K, Denmark
Ph: 45 35322500
E-mail: rdgs@geo.ku.dk
URL: http://www.rdgs.dk

1991 ■ Galathea Medal
(Galathea Medaillen)
For recognition of geographical investigations and research outside the Arctic areas. Geographers of any nation are eligible. A medal is awarded when merited. Established in 1916.

1992 ■ Leonie Sonnings Music Foundation
(Leonie Sonnings Musikfond)
Torsten Hoffmeyer, Sec.
Philip Heymans Alle 7
DK-2900 Hellerup K, Denmark
Ph: 45 33 344231
Fax: 45 33 344232
E-mail: bl@horten.dk
URL: http://www.sonningmusik.dk

1993 ■ Leonie Sonning Music Prize
(Leonie Sonnings Musikpris)
For recognition of outstanding achievement in music. Composers, conductors, musicians, and singers are eligible for consideration. A monetary award of 300,000 Danish kroner and a diploma are awarded annually. Established in 1959 by Mrs. Leonie Sonning.

1994 ■ University of Copenhagen
(Kobenhavns Universitet)
Norregade 10
PO Box 2177
DK-1017 Copenhagen K, Denmark
Ph: 45 3532 2626
Fax: 45 3532 2628
E-mail: ku@ku.dk
URL: http://www.ku.dk

1995 ■ Sonning Prize
To recognize a man or woman who has made an outstanding contribution toward the advancement of European civilization. Recommendations for candidates are invited from European universities. A monetary prize of 1 million Danish kroner is awarded biennially on April 19, Mr. Sonning's birthday, biennially in even-numbered years. Established in 1949 in memory of C.J. Sonning, a writer and editor; first given as a special award to Winston Churchill in 1950.

Dominica

1996 ■ Discover Dominica Authority
Financial Centre, 1st Fl.
Roseau, Dominica
Ph: 767448-2045
Fax: 767448-5840
E-mail: tourism@dominica.dm
URL: http://www.dominica.dm

1997 ■ Tourism Recognition Awards
To recognize individuals in the tourism industry who have demonstrated commitment to the development of their sub-sector and tourism as a whole. Awards are presented in the categories of accommodation, community tourism, employee, responsible tourism, and tour operator. In addition, awards are presented for Tourism Vendor of the Year, Tour Guide of the Year, and Tourism Taxi Service Provider of the Year. Awarded annually.

1998 ■ Government of the Commonwealth of Dominica
Information and Communication Technology Unit
General Post Office Bldg., 2nd Fl.
Dame Mary Eugenia Charles Blvd.
Roseau, Dominica
Ph: 767266-5241
Fax: 767448-0005
URL: http://www.dominica.gov.dm

1999 ■ Dominica Award of Honour
To honor an individual for outstanding contributions. Awarded annually to one or more individuals.

2000 ■ Long Service Medal
To honor an individual for long-term contributions. Awarded annually to one or more individuals.

2001 ■ Meritorious Service Award
To honor an individual for meritorious service. Awarded annually to one or more individuals.

2002 ■ Services Medal of Honour
To honor an individual for outstanding contributions. Awarded annually to one or more individuals.

2003 ■ Sisserou Award of Honour
To honor an individual for meritorious service. Awarded annually to one or more individuals.

Dominican Republic

2004 ■ Global Foundation for Democracy and Development
C/Capitan Eugenio de Marchena, No. 26
La Esperilla, Dominican Republic
Ph: 809685-9966
URL: http://www.drglobalfilmfestival.org

2005 ■ Dominican Short Film Competition
To promote the short film industry in the Dominican Republic, and to increase the visibility of local production in the national and international film community. To qualify, films must not be longer than 15 minutes in length, the director of the film must be of Dominican nationality, and the films must utilize a minimum of 70 percent Dominican actors. Awards are presented in the categories of fiction, animation, documentaries, and fantasy films. Awarded annually. Established in 2009.

Egypt

2006 ■ Anna Lindh Foundation
PO Box 732 El Mansheia
Alexandria, Egypt
Ph: 20 3 4820 342

Fax: 20 3 4820 471
E-mail: info@euromedalex.org
URL: http://www.euromedalex.org

2007 ■ Euro-Med Award for Dialogue between Cultures
To recognize the achievements of individuals and organizations that have been at the forefront of promoting dialogue in the Euro-Mediterranean region. Candidates must bear nationality of one of the 43 member countries of the Euro-Med Partnership or of its observer countries (Libya and Sudan). Awarded annually. Established in 2006.

2008 ■ Arab Fertilizer Association
Dr. Shafik Ashkar, Sec. Gen.
PO Box 8109
Nasr City
Cairo 11371, Egypt
Ph: 20 2 24172347
Ph: 20 2 24172349
Fax: 20 2 24173721
E-mail: info@afa.com.eg
URL: http://www.afa.com.eg

2009 ■ AFA Annual Award
To honor and encourage researchers for contributions to the progress of research activity in the fertilizer industry. Awarded annually.

2010 ■ Arab Institute of Navigation
Dr. Refaat Rashad, Pres.
Sebaei Bldg.
Cross Road of Sebaei St. and 45th St.
Miami
Alexandria, Egypt
Ph: 20 3 5509824
Ph: 20 3 5509686
Fax: 20 3 5509686
E-mail: ain@aast.edu
URL: http://www.ainegypt.org

2011 ■ Navigation Distinction
For graduates of naval college and faculty of maritime transport with top mark in navigation.

2012 ■ Egypt Web Academy
61 Mostafa El Nahas St.
Nasr City, Egypt
Ph: 20 22 2275 5425
Fax: 20 22 2287 0311
E-mail: info@egyptwebacademy.org
URL: http://www.egyptwebacademy.org

2013 ■ Egypt Web Awards
To discover creativity and innovation in Web design and development, and to give Egyptian Web designers the opportunity to market their talent and obtain notice by regional players. Web sites are judged on four criteria: design and innovation, programming and technology, content and copywriting, and interactivity. Presented in 13 categories, from Arts/Advertising to Trade/Retail. Winners represent Egypt in the Pan Arab Web Awards (see separate entry). Awarded annually. Established in 2008.

2014 ■ Egyptian Computer Society
Dr. Ahmed E. Sarhan, Contact
PO Box 9009
Nasr City
Cairo, Egypt
Ph: 20 2 2608182
Fax: 20 2 2603880
E-mail: ecomps@ritsec3.com.eg
URL: http://www.ifip.or.at/members/egypt.htm

2015 ■ Sarhan's Award
For those making strides in computer science.

2016 ■ Egyptian Nuclear Physics Association
Dr. Mohammad Nassef H. Comsan, Pres.
3 Ahmed El Zomor St.
Nasr City
Cairo 11787, Egypt

Awards are arranged in alphabetical order below their administering organizations

Ph: 20 2 24021018
Fax: 20 2 22876031
E-mail: comsanmn@hotmail.com
URL: http://www.physicsegypt.org/Enpa.html

2017 ■ Award in Environmental Physics
For original and outstanding research presented at the corresponding conference.

2018 ■ Award in Nuclear and Particle Physics
For original and outstanding research presented at the corresponding conference.

2019 ■ Egyptian Ophthalmological Society
Prof. Dr. Gamal Abdelatif Radwan, Pres.
42 Kasr El-Einy St.
Cairo, Egypt
Ph: 20 2 7923941
Ph: 20 2 7923942
Fax: 20 2 7941538
E-mail: eos@eyegypt.com
URL: http://www.eos1902.com

2020 ■ Mohamed el Aswad Prize
To recognize the best paper published in the *Bulletin of the Ophthalmological Society of Egypt* on the topic of refractive surgery. Eligible papers must be written by active members under 40 years of age.

2021 ■ Adham Ayoub Prize
To recognize the best paper published in the *Bulletin of the Ophthalmological Society of Egypt* on the topic of cataract surgery. Eligible papers must be written by active members under 40 years of age.

2022 ■ Salwa Eid Prize
To recognize the best paper published in the *Bulletin of the Ophthalmological Society of Egypt* on the topic of corneal blindness. Eligible papers must be written by active members under 40 years of age.

2023 ■ Yehia El-Gammal Prize
To recognize the best paper published in the *Bulletin of the Ophthalmological Society of Egypt* on the topic of ophthalmic microsurgery or pathology. Eligible papers must be written by active members under 40 years of age.

2024 ■ Amin El-Maghrabi Prize
To recognize an outstanding paper published in the *Bulletin of the Ophthalmological Society of Egypt*. Eligible papers must be written by active members under 40 years of age.

2025 ■ Ahmed Abdel-Reheim Fahmy Prize
To recognize the best paper published in the *Bulletin of the Ophthalmological Society of Egypt* on the topic of ophthalmic surgery. Eligible papers must be written by active members under 40 years of age.

2026 ■ Kamel Sabri Kamel Prize
To recognize the best paper published in the *Bulletin of the Ophthalmological Society of Egypt* on the topic of ophthalmic diagnostics. Eligible papers must be written by active members under 40 years of age.

2027 ■ Sabri Kamel Prize
To recognize the best paper published in the *Bulletin of the Ophthalmological Society of Egypt* on the topic of cataract management. Eligible papers must be written by active members under 40 years of age.

2028 ■ M. Abdel Moneim Labib Prize
To recognize the best paper published in the *Bulletin of the Ophthalmological Society of Egypt* on the topic of glaucoma. Eligible papers must be written by active members under 40 years of age.

2029 ■ Ibrahim Ahmed Mohamed Prize
To recognize the best work in the field of ophthalmia (inflammation of the eye). Candidates must be active members of the Society under the age of 40 years.

2030 ■ Ophthalmological Gold Medal
For recognition of major services and activities in the Society and ophthalmology. Members of the Society who are over 50 years of age are considered for services and activities other than scientific activities. A gold medal is awarded when merited. Established in 1943.

2031 ■ Wedad Saeed Prize
To recognize the best paper published in the *Bulletin of the Ophthalmological Society of Egypt* on the topic of eye squint. Eligible papers must be written by active members under 40 years of age.

2032 ■ Mohamed Sobhi Prize
To honor the best article published in the *Bulletin of the Ophthalmological Society of Egypt* written by an active member under 40 years of age.

Estonia

**2033 ■ Association of Construction Material Producers of Estonia
(Eesti Ehitusmaterjalide Tootjate Liit)**
Viktor Valkianen, Managing Dir.
Kiriku 6
EE-10130 Tallinn, Estonia
Ph: 372 64 81918
Fax: 372 64 89062
E-mail: eetl@hot.ee
URL: http://www.eetl.ee

2034 ■ Estonian Concrete Construction of the Year
For individual member. Awarded annually.

**2035 ■ Association of Estonian Broadcasters
(Eesti Ringhaalingute Liit)**
Mr. Urmas Loit, Managing Dir.
Ulemiste tee 3A
EE11415 Tallinn, Estonia
Ph: 372 6333235
Fax: 372 6333235
E-mail: erl@online.ee
URL: http://www.ringhliit.ee/eng/general.html

2036 ■ Golden Microphone
To honor a broadcast journalist for professionalism, creativity, and achievement within national broadcasting culture.

**2037 ■ Estonian Academy of Sciences
(Eesti Teaduste Akadeemia)**
Mr. Richard Villems, Pres.
Kohtu 6
EE-10130 Tallinn, Estonia
Ph: 372 6 442129
Fax: 372 6 451805
E-mail: akadeemia@akadeemia.ee
URL: http://www.akadeemia.ee/et

2038 ■ Nikolai Alumae Medal
To recognize excellence in research in engineering and informatics. Awarded every four years.

2039 ■ Paul Ariste Medal
To recognize excellence in research in the humanities and social sciences. Awarded every four years.

2040 ■ Karl Ernst von Baer Medal
To recognize excellence in research in biology. Awarded every four years.

2041 ■ Letter of Appreciation
To recognize long-term service to the Academy. Members and nonmembers are eligible. Awarded when merited.

2042 ■ Medal of the Estonian Academy of Sciences
To recognize individuals for outstanding services in development of Estonian science or in helping its development, as well as for services in performance of tasks of the Academy. Awarded periodically.

2043 ■ Wilhelm Ostwald Medal
To recognize contributions in chemistry and related fields. Awarded annually.

2044 ■ Prize for Popularisation of Estonian Science
To acknowledge the merits of science popularization and to recognize efforts in presenting science and research in a manner that is understandable to a wider public. Awarded annually. Co-sponsored by the Archimedes Foundation and the Finland Ministry of Education and Research.

2045 ■ Karl Schlossmann Medal
To recognize excellence in research in natural sciences. Awarded every four years.

2046 ■ Bernhard Schmidt Prize
To recognize young scientists and engineers for excellent results in applied sciences and innovation. Awarded biennially.

2047 ■ Student Research Prize
To recognize students for outstanding results in scientific work and to stimulate independent research of talented and capable students. A monetary award is given annually.

**2048 ■ Estonian Association for Personnel Development
(Eesti Personalitoo Arendamise Uhing)**
Piret Puss, Managing Dir.
Joe 5
10151 Tallinn, Estonia
Ph: 372 6 116411
Ph: 372 6 116410
Fax: 372 6 116410
E-mail: pare@pare.ee
URL: http://www.pare.ee

2049 ■ Best HR Projects in Estonia
To promote the importance of the work with human capital in society by honoring human resources projects that contributes efficiently to businesses. Awarded annually. Established in 2000.

2050 ■ Best Potential in HR Management
To recognize students who have the potential to succeed in the field of Human Resource Management.

**2051 ■ Estonian Education Personnel Union
(Eesti Haridustootajate Liit)**
Sven Rondik, Pres.
Gonsiori St. 21
10147 Tallinn, Estonia
Ph: 372 6419803
Fax: 372 6419802
E-mail: ehl@ehl.org.ee
URL: http://www.ehl.org.ee

2052 ■ Teacher of the Year Award
Recognizes effective work on the professional level and activeness on the social level. Awarded annually.

**2053 ■ Union of Estonian Psychologists
(Eesti Psuhholoogide Liit)**
Tiia Tulviste, Pres.
Psuhholoogia Osakond
Tartu Ulikool
Tiigi 78
EE-50410 Tartu, Estonia
Ph: 372 7 375902
Fax: 372 7 375900
E-mail: helves@tlu.ee
URL: http://www.epl.org.ee

2054 ■ Past President's Award
For the best BSC and MSC thesis in psychology.

Falkland Islands

2055 ■ Falkland Islands Tourist Board
Jetty Visitor Centre
PO Box 618
Stanley, Falkland Islands

Awards are arranged in alphabetical order below their administering organizations

Ph: 500 22215
Fax: 500 27020
E-mail: info@falklandislands.com
URL: http://www.falklandislands.com

2056 ■ Falklands Exposed!

To honor the best photographs taken on the Falkland Islands. Open to amateur, professional, and young photographers. Categories include Wildlife, Landscapes, Heritage, Island Life, Active/Outdoors, and a Face from the Place (Falkland residents). Awarded biennially in even-numbered years.

Fiji

2057 ■ Bula Fiji Tourism Exchange
590 Ratu Mara Rd.
Nabua
PO Box 17506
Suva, Fiji
Ph: 679 338 0683
Fax: 679 998 0758
E-mail: bfte@connect.com.fj
URL: http://www.bfte.com.fj

2058 ■ Air Pacific Tabua Marketing Awards

To acknowledge the talent, creativity, and resourcefulness of marketing efforts by those who promote Fiji and South Pacific tourism around the world. Awards are presented in 13 categories. In addition, the Chairman's Award may be presented. Awarded annually.

2059 ■ Fiji Audio Visual Commission
Civic House, Ground Fl.
Victoria Parade
GPO Box 18080
Suva, Fiji
Ph: 679 330 6662
Fax: 679 331 4662
E-mail: info@fijiaudiovisual.org.fj
URL: http://www.fijiaudiovisual.com

2060 ■ TFL Kula Film Awards

To stimulate the interest of young people in the creative arts and thereby encourage them to consider the career opportunities in the audio-visual industry. Participation is open to secondary and tertiary school students in Fiji. Awards are presented for best film, best actor, best actress, best director, and most popular film. Held annually. Sponsored by TFL.

2061 ■ Fiji Chess Federation
Jashint Maharaj, Gen. Sec.
PO Box 14117
Suva, Fiji
Ph: 679 9279 547
E-mail: info@fijichess.com
URL: http://www.fijichess.com

2062 ■ Fiji Chess Championships

To recognize Fiji's best chess players. Championships include the Brijlal Open Chess Championship, Kundan Singh Open Chess Championship, Grand Prix, J.R. White National Championship, Fiji Day Open Chess Championship, Carlton Brewery Chess Championship, Rajnesh Parmeshwar Memorial Open, and the Oceania Zonal Chess Championship. Each is held annually.

2063 ■ Fiji Islands Trade and Investment Bureau
Civic Tower, 6th Fl.
Victoria Parade
PO Box 2303
Government Buildings
Suva, Fiji
Ph: 679 331 5988
Fax: 679 330 1783
E-mail: info@ftib.org.fj

URL: http://www.ftib.org.fj

2064 ■ Prime Minister's Exporter of the Year Award

To honor Fiji's exporters for their achievements and contributions to the economy. In addition to the Exporter of the Year Award, prizes are presented in 16 other sponsored categories. Awarded annually. Established in 1993.

2065 ■ Save the Children Fiji
PO Box 2249
Government Bldg.
Suva, Fiji
Ph: 679 331 3178
Fax: 679 330 2214
E-mail: info@savethechildren.org
URL: http://www.savethechildren.org.fj/index.html

2066 ■ National Photographic Competition

To recognize the best in photographs of children to draw awareness to the food, clothing, and educational needs of the 18,000 displaced children in Fiji. Open to amateur, professional, and young photographers. A plaque is awarded to the winner in each of eight categories. Held annually. Established in 2007.

Finland

2067 ■ Design Forum Finland
Mikko Kalhama, Managing Dir.
Erottajankatu 7
FIN-00130 Helsinki, Finland
Ph: 358 9 6220810
Ph: 358 9 62208112
Fax: 358 9 62208181
E-mail: info@designforum.fi
URL: http://www.designforum.fi

2068 ■ Estlander Prize

For organizations promoting design in significant ways. A monetary prize of 5,000 Euros is awarded biennially in even-numbered years. Established in 2000.

2069 ■ Fennia Prize

For companies that excel in design. A grand prize of 20,000 Euro and two Fennia prizes of 7,500 Euros each are awarded biennially in odd-numbered years.

2070 ■ Kaj Franck Design Prize

For a distinguished designer or team. The Kaj Franck Medal and monetary prize of 10,000 Euro is awarded annually. Established in 1992.

2071 ■ Young Designer of the Year Prize

For a promising young designer. A monetary prize of 5,000 Euro is awarded annually. Established in 2000.

2072 ■ European Society for the Study of English
Prof. Fernando Galvan, Chm.
University of Joensuu
PO Box 111
FIN-80101 Joensuu, Finland
Ph: 358 13 2514320
Fax: 358 13 2514211
E-mail: john.stotesbury@joensuu.fi
URL: http://www.ESSEnglish.org

2073 ■ Book Awards

To recognize excellence in scholarly works in the field of English studies. Prizes are awarded for a book in each of the following categories: English language and linguistics; Literatures in the English Language; and Cultural Studies in English. Monetary prizes of 1,500 Euros are awarded biennially in even-numbered years.

2074 ■ Finnish Amateur Radio League (Suomen Radioamatööriliitto ry)
Raimo Lehto, Chair/Pres.
PO Box 44
FIN-00441 Helsinki, Finland

Ph: 358 9 5625973
Ph: 358 9 5625974
Fax: 358 9 5623987
E-mail: hq@sral.fi
URL: http://www.sral.fi

2075 ■ The Lakes of Finland Award

To recognize the achievement of operating 25 Finnish radio stations that are located within 100 meters of a lake. Open to amateur radio operators, radio clubs, and short wave listeners in Finland.

2076 ■ OH Awards

To recognize amateur radio operators, radio clubs, and short wave listeners who work stations situated in Finland. Awards are presented in various categories depending on the accomplishments of the individuals and clubs. Awarded when merited.

2077 ■ The OH County Award

To recognize the achievement of operating in OH counties. Open to amateur radio operators, radio clubs, and short wave listeners in Finland.

2078 ■ The OHA Plaques

To recognize the achievement of operating OHA-1000, OHA-2500, and OHA-5000 stations. Open to amateur radio operators, radio clubs and short wave listeners in Finland.

2079 ■ OHA-VHF Award

For workers in VHF, UHF and SHF bands. Open to amateur radio operators, radio clubs and short wave listeners in Finland.

2080 ■ Finnish Association of Designers Ornamo (Teollisuustaiteen Liitto Ornamo)
Tapani Hyvonen, Pres.
Unioninkatu 26
FIN-00130 Helsinki, Finland
Ph: 358 9 6877740
Fax: 358 9 68777468
E-mail: info@ornamo.fi
URL: http://www.ornamo.fi

2081 ■ Glass Designer of the Year

To honor an outstanding Finnish glass designer. Awarded annually.

2082 ■ Graphic Designer of the Year

To honor an outstanding Finnish graphic designer. Awarded annually.

2083 ■ Interior Designer of the Year

To honor an outstanding Finnish interior designer. Awarded annually.

2084 ■ Ornamo Globe

To honor an outstanding Finnish design firm. Awarded annually. Established in 1961.

2085 ■ Finnish Association of Graduate Engineers (Tekniikan Akateemisten Liito Tek)
Mr. Heikki Kauppi, Exec. Dir.
Ratavartijankatu 2
FIN-00520 Helsinki, Finland
Ph: 358 9 229121
Fax: 358 9 22912911
E-mail: jasenrekisteri@tek.fi
URL: http://www.tek.fi

2086 ■ Finnish Engineering Award

To recognize notable engineering or architectural work that has remarkably advanced technical competence in Finland. Basic evaluation criteria are distinctiveness of the work, creative contribution, and practical application of the idea or the theory. A certificate of honor and a monetary prize of 17,000 Euros is awarded annually. Established in 1981.

2087 ■ Finnish Book Publishers Association (Suomen Kustannusyhdistys)
Mr. Sakari Laiho, Dir.
PO Box 177
Lonnrotinkatu 11A

Awards are arranged in alphabetical order below their administering organizations

FIN-00121 Helsinki, Finland
Ph: 358 9 22877250
Ph: 358 9 22877258
Fax: 358 9 6121226
E-mail: sakari.laiho@kustantajat.fi
URL: http://www.kustantajat.fi/en

2088 ■ Finlandia Junior Prize for Literature
To recognize the best Finnish book for children and young people. A monetary prize of 26,000 Euros is awarded annually. Established in 2000.

2089 ■ Finlandia Prize for Literature
To recognize the best novel written by a Finnish citizen. A monetary prize of 26,000 Euros is awarded annually. Established in 1984.

2090 ■ Alvar Renqvist Prize
To recognize a publishing editor for distinguished work for the benefit of Finnish books and literature, whether in the field of domestic or translated literature, book for children and young people, non-fiction, textbooks, or electronic publishing. A monetary prize of 3000 Euros is awarded annually. Established in 1998.

2091 ■ Tieto-Finlandia Prize for Non-Fiction
To recognize the year's best Finnish non-fiction book or textbook. A monetary prize of 26,000 Euros is awarded. Established in 1989.

2092 ■ Finnish Paper Engineers' Association
(Finska Pappesingeniorsforeningen)
Mikko Jokio, Chm.
PO Box 118
00171 Helsinki, Finland
Ph: 358 9 1326688
Ph: 358 2 4626450
E-mail: info@papereng.fi
URL: http://www.papereng.fi

2093 ■ Andritz Oy Award
To recognize an individual for outstanding academic work dealing with fibre processes. Established in 1999.

2094 ■ Johan Gullichsen Prize
To recognize the most outstanding presentation at the Johan Gullichsen Colloquium. A monetary prize of 2000 Euros is presented biennially.

2095 ■ C.J. Jansson Prize
To recognize the best publication or most valuable original research published in Finland by a member in the field of wood pulp, chemical pulp, or paper. Awarded annually at the General Meeting.

2096 ■ Lampen Medal
For outstanding technical and scientific work contributed to the Association. Established in 1967.

2097 ■ Metso Paper Mechanical Pulping Award
To recognize students and researchers for exceptional academic studies in the field of mechanical pulping recycled fiber and stock preparation technology and their practical applications. A monetary prize of 2000 Euros is presented annually. Established in 1989.

2098 ■ Plaquette of Merit
For outstanding contributions done in the association's field. Established in 1978.

2099 ■ Stenback Plaquette
To recognize a member for outstanding work done in the association's field. Established in 1967.

2100 ■ Finnish Society of Chemical Engineers
Kemiallisteknillinen Yhdistys
Urho Kekkosen katu 8 c 31
FIN-00100 Helsinki, Finland
Ph: 358 50 351 8303

Fax: 358 9 454 20440
E-mail: kty@kty.fi
URL: http://www.kty.fi

2101 ■ Post-graduate Research Prize
To encourage study in chemical engineering. Awarded biennially.

2102 ■ Finnish Society of Sciences and Letters
(Societas Scientiarum Fennica)
Prof. Carl G. Gahmberg, Sec.
Regeringsgatan 2 B
FIN-00170 Helsinki, Finland
Ph: 358 9 633005
Fax: 358 9 661065
E-mail: societas@scientiarum.fi
URL: http://www.scientiarum.fi

2103 ■ Professor Magnus Ehrnrooth Prize
To recognize outstanding contributions to the fields of chemistry, mathematics, and physics (categories alternate each year). A monetary award of 12,000 Euro is presented annually.

2104 ■ Professor Theodor Homen Prize
To recognize outstanding research contributions in the fields of physics and Finnish history (category alternates each year the award is presented). Members of the Society may submit nominations. A monetary award of 15,000 Euro is presented triennially.

2105 ■ Medal of the Society
To recognize an individual for outstanding efforts on behalf of the Society. A medal, either in bronze or silver, is awarded.

2106 ■ E. J. Nystrom Prize
(Professor E. J. Nystroms Prize)
To recognize outstanding scientific contributions. Members of the Society may submit nominations. A monetary award of 20,000 Euro is presented annually. Established in 1962 to honor Professor E. J. Nystrom, former president of the Society, who died in 1960.

2107 ■ Upper Secondary School Teachers Prizes
Recognizes excellent teaching in schools. Two monetary awards of 5,000 Euro are presented annually, one for teachers of science and the other for teachers of the humanities or social science. Established in 1998.

2108 ■ Foundation for the Promotion of Finnish Music
(Luovan Saveltaiteen Edistamissaatio)
Ms. Jutta Jaakkola, Sec.
Lauttasaarentie 1
FIN-00200 Helsinki, Finland
Ph: 358 9 68101252
Fax: 358 9 6820770
E-mail: luses@luses.fi
URL: http://www.luses.fi/fimic/luses.nsf/webpages/hakuajat?opendocument

2109 ■ Music Grants
(Apuraha tai Palkinto)
For recognition of teachers of music, representatives of the science of music, composers, performers of music, and persons who have in other ways meritoriously promoted music in Finland. Only Finnish citizens are eligible. Grants are available in the following categories: production of recordings; marketing of recordings; concerts; travel; publication, marketing, and export of sheet music, training events, and research in musical culture; working; and commission. Monetary awards are presented every year on the birthday of Jean Sibelius, the famous Finnish composer. Established in 1955 by the Finnish Parliament which donated the basic capital

for the establishment of the Foundation on the occasion of the 90th birthday of Professor Jean Sibelius, who died in 1957.

2110 ■ GRAFIA - Association of Professional Graphic Designers in Finland
Marita Sandelin, Exec. Dir.
Uudenmaankatu 11 B 9
SF-00120 Helsinki, Finland
Ph: 358 9 601942
Ph: 358 9 601941
E-mail: grafia@grafia.fi
URL: http://www.grafia.fi

2111 ■ The Best of Finnish Graphic Design and Advertising Competition
To recognize creative designers working in graphic design, illustration, layout and book jacket and package design. The following awards are presented: Golden Award, Silver Award, Platinum Award, and Junior Award. Held annually.

2112 ■ Albert Gebhard Medal
To recognize an individual or group that has promoted the development and appreciation of drawing and graphic design in Finland, as well as performed a notable act that has promoted the cultural agenda of the Association and its members. Primarily awarded to Finnish individuals and groups, but can also be awarded to foreign individuals or groups. A diploma and bronze medal designed by Olof Eriksson are awarded annually. Established in 1963.

2113 ■ Honorary Member
To honor individuals who have, over the course of decades, broadened the Finnish world view and increased the societal appreciation of creative visual communication and graphic professionalism. Awarded when merited.

2114 ■ Rudolf Koivu Prize
To recognize a Finnish citizen for outstanding illustration of books for children or youths. Open to all illustrations regardless of production or technique. A monetary prize of 10,000 Euros is awarded biennially in odd-numbered years. Established in 1949.

2115 ■ International Accordionists Confederation
(Confederation Internationale des Accordeonistes)
Kyrosselankatu 3
FIN-39500 Ikaalinen, Finland
Ph: 358 3 4400221
Fax: 358 3 4589071
E-mail: hanuritalo@harmonikkainstituutti.net
URL: http://www.accordions.com/cia

2116 ■ Merit Awards
To recognize individuals who advance and promote accordion music around the world. Awarded annually to one or more recipients. Established in 1963.

2117 ■ International Federation of the Phonographic Industry - Finland
(Musiikkituottajat)
Lauri Rechardt, Contact
Yrjonkatu 3B
FIN-00120 Helsinki, Finland
Ph: 358 9 68034050
Fax: 358 9 68034055
E-mail: ifpi@ifpi.fi
URL: http://www.ifpi.fi

2118 ■ Emma Awards
To recognize the best artists in the Finnish music industry. Awarded in more than a dozen categories, including best song, best hip-hop album, best female soloist, and best producer. Awarded annually. Established in 1983.

Awards are arranged in alphabetical order below their administering organizations

2119 ■ Muuvi Awards
To honor outstanding music videos of Finnish origin. Gold, silver, and bronze statuettes are awarded annually. Established in 1991.

2120 ■ Oulu International Children's and Youth Film Festival
Eszter Vuojala, Dir.
Hallituskatu 7
FIN-90100 Oulu, Finland
Ph: 358 8 881 1293
Fax: 358 8 881 1290
E-mail: eszter.vuojala@oufilmcenter.fi
URL: http://www.oulunelokuvakeskus.fi

2121 ■ Kaleva Award
To recognize the director of the best film at the festival. A monetary award of 3,000 Euros is awarded annually. Established in 1992 by *Kaleva Newspaper*. Formerly: Star Boy Award.

2122 ■ Little Bear Award
To award a Finnish script-writer, director, or producer who contributed with distinction to children's film making in Finland. May also be given to recognize lifetime achievement in the field. Established in 2004 by POEM - Northern Film and Media Foundation.

2123 ■ Rural Youth Europe
Amanda Hajnal, Sec. Gen.
Karjalankatu 2A
FIN-00520 Helsinki, Finland
Ph: 358 45 2345629
E-mail: office@ruralyoutheurope.com
URL: http://www.ruralyoutheurope.com

2124 ■ Rural Youth Europe Awards
To further the work of 4H Clubs and related rural and farming organizations by recognizing young people living in rural areas. Presented annually.

2125 ■ Sibelius Academy
Anna Krohn, Sec.
PO Box 86
FIN-00251 Helsinki, Finland
Ph: 358 20 7539 645
Fax: 358 20 7539 600
E-mail: anna.krohn@siba.fi
URL: http://www.siba.fi/sibeliuscompetition

2126 ■ International Jean Sibelius Violin Competition
To recognize the best violinists of the Competition. Violinists of any nationality born in 1975 or later are eligible. Monetary prizes totaling 47,000 Euro are awarded every five years. In addition, the Finnish Broadcasting Company awards 2,000 Euro for the best performance of the Sibelius Violin Concerto; the Sibelius family awards 1,000 Euro to second-round finalists; and the city of Jarvenpaa grants a special prize of 1,500 Euro. Established in 1965 to commemorate one hundred years after the birth of Jean Sibelius by the Sibelius Society of Finland.

2127 ■ Tampere Film Festival (Tampereen elokuvajuhlat)
Jukka-Pekka Laakso, Dir.
Tullikamarinaukio 2
PO Box 305
FIN-33101 Tampere, Finland
Ph: 358 3 223 5681
Fax: 358 3 223 0121
E-mail: office@tamperefilmfestival.fi
URL: http://www.tamperefilmfestival.fi
Formerly: (1980) Society for Film Art in Tampere.

2128 ■ Tampere International Short Film Festival (Tampereen Kansainvaliset lyhytelokuva-juhlat Grand Prix)
For recognition of short films in a national and international competition of a high standard that have a human theme and seek new forms of cinematic expression. Films produced during the two years preceding the festival are eligible in the following categories: animated films, documentary films, and fiction films. An international jury awards the following prizes for the film directors: Grand Prix - a monetary award of 5000 Euros and a "Kiss" statuette; Category Prizes three monetary prizes of 1500 Euros each and a "Kiss" Statuette; The Special Prize of the Jury - a monetary prize of 1500 Euros and a "Kiss" statuette; and Diplomas of Merit. Held annually in March. Established in 1970.

2129 ■ Union of Finnish Writers (Suomen Kirjailijaliitto)
Varis Tuula-Liina, Chm.
Runeberginkatu 32 C 28
FIN-00100 Helsinki, Finland
Ph: 358 9 445392
Ph: 358 9 449752
Fax: 358 9 492278
E-mail: info@suomenkirjailijaliitto.fi
URL: http://www.suomenkirjailijaliitto.fi/index_eng.asp

2130 ■ Tirlittan Prize
To recognize outstanding literature for children's and adolescents. Awarded annually.

2131 ■ Union's Award for Merit
To recognize a writer for professional achievement. Awarded annually.

2132 ■ Ursa Astronomical Association (Tahtitieteellinen yhdistys Ursa)
Matti Suhonen, Contact
Raatimiehenkatu 3 A 2
FIN-00140 Helsinki, Finland
Ph: 358 9 6840400
Fax: 358 9 68404040
E-mail: ursa@ursa.fi
URL: http://www.ursa.fi

2133 ■ Stella Arcti Award
For advanced amateur astronomers. Awarded annually to up to three recipients. Established in 1988.

France

2134 ■ Academie des Beaux-Arts
Yves Millecamps, Pres.
Institut de France
23, Quai de Conti
F-75270 Paris Cedex 06, France
Ph: 33 1 44414320
E-mail: contact@academie-des-beaux-arts.fr
URL: http://www.academie-des-beaux-arts.fr

2135 ■ Prix Charles Abella
To provide financial assistance to a student of architecture. Candidates must be age 35 or younger. A monetary prize of 25,000 Euros is awarded annually. Established in 1975.

2136 ■ Prix Antoine-Nicolas Bailly
For recognition of an architectural work or a publication on architecture. For two consecutive times, the prize is awarded to a French architect; then on the third time, to a French author. A monetary prize is awarded periodically, when the funds permit it.

2137 ■ Prix Claude Berthault
To recognize painters, sculptors, or architects who have created a beautiful work of art or decoration in the best French spirit. Artists born in France are eligible. A monetary prize is awarded annually. Awarded by the Fondation de Madame Claude Berthault.

2138 ■ Prix Georges Bizet
For recognition of a music composer. Awarded periodically.

2139 ■ Prix Catenacci
For recognition of outstanding architectural contributions in the categories of interior or exterior ornamentation of a building, garden, or public square and publication of deluxe illustrated books. Two equal monetary prizes are awarded periodically, when the funds permit it.

2140 ■ Prix Alphonse Cellier
To recognize a painter who is a student of l'Ecole des Beaux-Arts and is less than 30 years of age. Awarded annually.

2141 ■ Prix Chaudesaigues
To recognize a young architect. French architects who are under 32 years of age may submit sketches on the assigned subject. The 12 candidates who have the best sketches are invited to present a project based on their sketch. A monetary prize is awarded periodically, when the funds permit it.

2142 ■ Grand Prix d'Architecture
To recognize architects or architectural students under 35 years of age for outstanding work. The competition consists of three phases: candidates submit a draft on the subject proposed by the Academy, 20 candidates who have the most interesting drafts submit a sketch, and 10 candidates who have the best sketches submit an architectural project. Three annual prizes are awarded: Grand Prize/Charles Abella Prize - 20,000 Euros; Second Prize/Andre Arfvidson Prize - 9,000 Euros; and Third Prize/Paul Arfvidson Priz - 4,000 Euros. Established in 1975.

2143 ■ Prix Achille Leclere
For recognition of the best architectural project on a specific subject assigned by the Academy. Architects under 31 years of age are eligible. Collaboration in the execution of the projects is not permitted. The prize may not be awarded to the same person more than once. A monetary prize is awarded periodically, when the funds permit it.

2144 ■ Prix Hector Lefuel
For recognition of a painting, sculpture, work of architecture, or musical composition. Awards are given in alternate years in the categories of painting, sculpture, architecture, and musical composition. A monetary prize is awarded periodically, when the funds permit it.

2145 ■ Prix du Baron de Joest
For recognition of a discovery or work in the field of art history that is most useful to the public good. A monetary prize is awarded periodically, when the funds permit it.

2146 ■ Prix Rouyer
For recognition of a survey of French architecture. A monetary prize is awarded periodically, when the funds permit it.

2147 ■ Prix Ruhlmann
To recognize a student architect for the best project in interior design. A monetary prize is awarded periodically, when the funds permit it.

2148 ■ Prix Thorlet
To encourage scholarly works on the history of art, in particular on painting. A monetary prize is awarded periodically, when the funds permit it.

2149 ■ Prix de Dessin Pierre David Weill
For recognition of excellence in drawing competitions. Artists must be under 30 years of age and, if foreigners, must have lived at least one year in France. All drawing techniques are allowed with the exception of water color, gouache and pastel. A monetary prize of 6,100 Euros is awarded for first place, 2,285 Euros for second place, and 1,525 Euros for third place.

Awards are arranged in alphabetical order below their administering organizations

Awarded annually. At least the 50 best entries are publicly exhibited. Established in 1971. Sponsored by the Pierre David - Weill Foundation.

2150 ■ Academie des Inscriptions et Belles-Lettres
M. Jean Lectant, Sec.
Institut de France
23, quai de Conti
F-75006 Paris, France
Ph: 33 1 44414310
Fax: 33 1 44414311
E-mail: j.leclant.aibl@dial.oleane.com
URL: http://www.aibl.fr

2151 ■ Prix Honore Chavee
To encourage work in linguistics and, in particular, research on Romance languages. A monetary prize is awarded biennially in odd-numbered years.

2152 ■ Prix Charles Clermont-Ganneau
For recognition of a work or collection of studies on the epigraphy of Semitic people (from Syria, Phoenicia, Palestine, Cyprus, Carthage and other Punic colonies) or on the ancient history of these regions (studies on Syrian history may only go up to the Crusades). A monetary prize is awarded every five years. Established by the Duke of Loubat.

2153 ■ Prix de Chenier
To recognize the author of the best method for teaching Greek or for the work that seems the most useful for studying Greek language and literature. A monetary prize is awarded every five years.

2154 ■ Prix Delalande-Guerineau
For recognition of work on the Orient published during the two years preceding the award. A monetary prize is awarded biennially in even-numbered years.

2155 ■ Prix Edmond Drouin
For recognition of a manuscript or published work on Oriental numismatics. Authors are eligible without regard to nationality. A monetary prize is awarded every four years.

2156 ■ Prix Duchalais
For recognition of the best work on the numismatics of the Middle Ages appearing in the preceding two years. A monetary prize is awarded biennially in even-numbered years.

2157 ■ Prix Raoul Duseigneur
For recognition of work on Spanish art and archaeology from the beginning of history to the end of the 16th century, or on the artistic, archaeological treasures of these epochs in the public or private Spanish collections. A monetary prize is awarded triennially. Established by the Marquise Arconati-Visconti.

2158 ■ Prix Estrade-Delcros
For recognition of a work re-examining the arrangement of studies by the Academy. The award is not to be divided. A monetary prize is awarded every five years.

2159 ■ Prix de la Fons-Melicocq
For recognition of the best work on the history and the antiquities of Picardy and Ile-de-France (except Paris). A monetary prize is awarded every three years.

2160 ■ Prix Louis Fould
For recognition of the best work on the history of drawing up to the end of the 16th century. A monetary prize is awarded biennially in even-numbered years.

2161 ■ Prix Roman et Tania Ghirshman
For recognition of the best publication on pre-Islamic Iran. Works may be written on the history of civilization, the history of religion or art, numismatics, or the epigraphy or philology of Elamit, old-Persian, Armenian, Greek or Pahlavi writings. French or foreign authors are eligible. A monetary prize is awarded annually.

2162 ■ Prix Stanislas Julien
For recognition of the best work related to China. A monetary prize is awarded annually.

2163 ■ Prix Emile Le Senne
To encourage historical, archaeological, artistic or iconographic studies on Paris and the Seine department. A monetary prize is awarded biennially in odd-numbered years.

2164 ■ Prix Gaston Maspero
For recognition of a work or collection of works on Ancient Egypt. A monetary prize is awarded every five years. Established by the Duke of Loubat.

2165 ■ Prix Gustave Mendel
For recognition of a detailed scientific catalogue, written in French, of part or of a whole collection of Ancient Greek monuments or objects. If no such catalogue is submitted, a scientific work on Greek archaeology is considered. A monetary prize is awarded annually. Established by Louis Gaillet-Billotteau.

2166 ■ Prix de La Grange
For recognition of the publication of a previously unpublished poem of an early poet of France. If no unpublished work is submitted, the prize may go to the best work on a published poem of the early poets. A monetary prize is awarded annually.

2167 ■ Prix du Baron de Joest
To recognize an individual who has made a discovery or written a book best serving the public interest during the preceding year. A monetary prize is awarded annually and is given alternately by one of the five Academies of the Institut.

2168 ■ Prix du Duc de Loubat
For recognition of the best work on the history, geography, and archaeology of the New World. A monetary prize is awarded triennially.

2169 ■ Prix Gabriel-Auguste Prost
To recognize the author of the best historical work on Metz or neighboring areas. A monetary prize is awarded annually.

2170 ■ Prix Gustave Schlumberger
For recognition of studies in the following categories: (1) Byzantine History; (2) Byzantine Archeology; and (3) the history and archaeology of the Latin Orient. A monetary prize is awarded alternately in the three categories. Awarded annually.

2171 ■ Prix Toutain-Blanchet
For recognition of work either on the history of Ancient Gaul, before the advent of Clovis (485 A.D.), or on the history of Northern Africa before the end of the Byzantine domination (715 A.D.). A monetary prize is awarded triennially.

2172 ■ Prix Volney
For recognition of a work of comparative philology. Awarded annually.

2173 ■ Academie des Sciences
Jean Dercourt, Sec.
Institut de France
23, quai de Conti
F-75006 Paris, France
Ph: 33 1 44414367
Fax: 33 1 44414363
E-mail: disc@academie-sciences.fr
URL: http://www.academie-sciences.fr

2174 ■ Prix Anatole et Suzanne Abragam
For recognition of a researcher under 40 years of age in the field of physics. A monetary prize of 1,500 Euros is awarded biennially in even-numbered years. Established in 1987.

2175 ■ Prix Alcan
To recognize young researchers with doctorates, whose work has contributed to progress in the aluminum industry or, more broadly, the field of metallurgy. The selection is made by a commission composed of members of the Academy or members of CADAS. One of the Institute's Grand Prizes. A monetary prize of 15,000 Euros is awarded annually. Established in 1986.

2176 ■ Prix Ampere d'Electricite de France
To recognize one or several French scientists for remarkable research work in the field of mathematics or physics, fundamental or applied. One of the Institute's Grand Prizes. A monetary prize of 30,500 Euros is awarded annually. Established in 1974 by Electricite de France in memory of the scientist, Ampere, whose 200th birthday was celebrated in 1975.

2177 ■ Prix Louis Armand
For recognition of a young researcher (30 years of age or younger) for an outstanding work in the field of applied mathematics, mechanical engineering, physics, chemistry, biology, or earth science. A monetary prize of 1,500 Euros is awarded biennially in odd-numbered years. Established in 1987 by the Association des Amis de Louis Armand.

2178 ■ Prix Louis-Daniel Beauperthuy
For recognition of work in epidemiology that contributes to the amelioration of the human condition. A monetary prize of 3,000 Euros is awarded biennially in even-numbered years. Established in 1982.

2179 ■ Prix de Madame Claude Berthault
For recognition of a scientific work that increases the influence of the French nation. French citizens are eligible. A monetary prize of 1,500 Euros is awarded annually. Established in 1921.

2180 ■ Medaille Berthelot
To recognize a scientist who has received a prize for chemistry during the preceding year. Awarded annually. Established in 1902.

2181 ■ Prix Paul Bertrand, G. Deflandre, M. Deflandre-Rigaud, and Jean Cuvillier
For recognition of outstanding work in paleobotany or stratigraphic geology dedicated to coal-bearing formations. Awards are given in alternate years in the two categories. If there are no candidates in these disciplines, the award goes to a work of anatomy or descriptive botany. A monetary prize of 3,000 Euros is awarded every four years. Established in 1960.

2182 ■ Prix Paul Betrand, Georges Deflandre et Marthe Deflandre-Rigaud, Jean Cuvillier
For recognition of a work in micro-paleontology, concerning in particular: evolution, phylogenesis, ontogenesis, ecology, paleobiology, or morphology. Scientists without regard to nationality or age are eligible. A monetary prize of 3,000 Euros is awarded triennially. Established in 1960.

2183 ■ Prix Binoux, Henri de Parville, Jean-Jaques Berger, Remlinger
For recognition of outstanding work in geography, navigation, or the history or philosophy of science. Awards are given in alternate years. A monetary prize of 1,500 Euros is awarded every four years. Established in 1889.

2184 ■ Prix Edmond Brun
For recognition of work in the mechanics of fluids, thermics, or astronautics. A monetary prize of 3,000 Euros is awarded annually. Established in 1980.

Awards are arranged in alphabetical order below their administering organizations

2185 ■ Prix Lazare Carnot
To recognize excellent research works. One of the Institute's Grand Prizes. A monetary award of 30,500 Euros is given biennially in odd-numbered years. Established in 1992.

2186 ■ Prix Elie Cartan
To recognize a mathematician who has introduced new ideas or solved a difficult problem. Individuals over 45 years of age of any nationality are eligible. A monetary prize of 3,000 Euros is awarded triennially. Established in 1980.

2187 ■ Prix L. La Caze, A. Policart-Lacassagne
For recognition of outstanding work in the field of physics, chemistry, or physiology. All nationalities are eligible. A monetary prize of 1,500 Euros is awarded quadrennially. Awarded alternately by the Commission for physics, chemistry, and physiology. Established in 1865 (La Caze) and 1958 (Policort-Lacassagne).

2188 ■ Prix Auguste Chevalier
To recognize the author of one or more works relating to plants (systems, biology, and geography) of tropical and subtropical French-speaking countries, in particular to plants from West Africa. A monetary prize of 1,500 Euros is awarded every four years. Established in 1955.

2189 ■ Prix Clavel-Lespiau
For recognition of work in organic chemistry. A monetary prize of 3,000 Euros is awarded every four years. Established in 1979.

2190 ■ Prix du Commisariat a l'Energie Atomique
To recognize one or several Frenchmen for an important scientific or technical discovery in the following fields: physics, mechanics, astronomy, and their applications; and chemistry, biology, human biology, and medical sciences, as well as their applications. The Academie awards an equal number of prizes in each of the two fields. One of the Institute's Grand Prizes. A monetary prize of 30,500 Euros is awarded annually. Established in 1977 by the Commissioner of Atomic Energy.

2191 ■ Prix Adrien Constantin de Magny
To recognize a craftsman or scientist whose practical works are considered remarkable by the Academie. Individuals are not required to have a diploma to be eligible. A monetary prize of 7,600 Euros is awarded biennially in odd-numbered years. Established in 1963 by the Fondation Rheims.

2192 ■ Prix Jean Dagnan-Bouveret
To encourage medical studies. A monetary prize of 1,500 Euros is awarded biennially in odd-numbered years. Established in 1924.

2193 ■ Prix Dandrimont-Benicourt
For recognition of research in the field of cancer. A monetary prize of 3,000 Euros is awarded annually. Established in 1993 by the Fondation de l'Institute de France.

2194 ■ Prix Ernest Dechelle
For recognition of the work of a French scientist in the physical sciences. A monetary prize of 1,500 Euros is awarded every four years. Established in 1943.

2195 ■ Prix Deslandres
For recognition of the best work in spectral analysis and its applications. French or foreign scientists are eligible. A monetary prize of 7,600 Euros is awarded biennially in even-numbered years. Established in 1946.

2196 ■ Prix Pierre Desnuelle
To recognize works by biological chemists. A monetary award of 1,500 Euros is given every four years. Established in 1991.

2197 ■ Prix Charles Dhere
For recognition of work in biochemistry. A monetary prize of 2,300 Euros is awarded annually. Established in 1955.

2198 ■ Prix Paul Doistau - Emile Blutet de l'Information Scientifique
Recognizes a work in information science. A monetary prize of 3,000 Euros is awarded biennially in even-numbered years. Established in 1995.

2199 ■ Prix Rene Dujarric de la Riviere
For recognition of work in biology with application to rural economics and veterinary medicine. A monetary prize of 3,800 Euros is awarded quadrennially. Established in 1970.

2200 ■ Prix Leon-Alexandre Etancelin
To encourage or recognize discoveries valuable to humanity, primarily in the fight against cancer and other incurable diseases. French citizens or research work done by a French institute or laboratory are eligible. A monetary award of 7,500 Euros is awarded biennially in odd-numbered years. Established in 1945.

2201 ■ Prix Fonde par l'Etat
For recognition of outstanding works in mathematics and physics and their applications; or for works in the chemical, natural, biological, and medical sciences and their applications. Each year, the prize is awarded on alternating topics: mathematics, physics, chemistry, and biology. A monetary prize is awarded every four years. Established in 1795.

2202 ■ Prix Foulon
For recognition of outstanding work in the fields of botany, rural economics, zoology, and neuroscience. A monetary prize of 7,500 Euros is given annually. Established in 1940.

2203 ■ Prix France Telecom
To award one or more researchers or engineers for research work in telecommunications. One of the Institute's Grand Prizes. A monetary award of 30,500 Euros is given annually. Established in 1992.

2204 ■ Prix Gaz de France
For recognition of French researchers or researchers from the European Community in the fields of engineering, chemistry, materials, energy, or first matter that contributes to an increase in knowledge of interest to the gas industry. A monetary prize is awarded annually. Established in 1987.

2205 ■ Prix Jean-Marie Le Goff, Lemonon, Houry, Laveran
To encourage research in biological chemistry, in particular the study of red blood cells in diabetics and the physiological and therapeutic properties of cobalt and its derivatives. A monetary prize of 3,000 Euros is awarded annually. Established in 1942.

2206 ■ Prix Grammaticakis-Neuman
For recognition of the best work in organic chemistry concerning photochemistry or spectrochemistry, experimental chemistry, mathematical applications in biology, or the philosophy of science. Awards are given alternately in the categories of organic chemistry, mathematical applications in biology (preferably human physiology), and the philosophy of science (preferably the pragmatic approach). A monetary prize is awarded annually. In addition, in the area of organic chemistry concerning photochemistry or spectrochemistry, a monetary prize of 3,000 Euros is awarded annually. Established in 1982.

2207 ■ Prix Philippe A. Guye
For recognition of work in the field of physical chemistry. A monetary prize of 7,500 Euros is awarded biennially in even-numbered years. Established in 1941.

2208 ■ Prix Max-Fernand Jayle
For recognition of original research in the biochemistry or the physiology of sexual hormones, in particular, research on the function of reproduction of mammals, primates, and humans. French citizens who are at least 45 years of age are eligible. The prize is not be divided. A monetary prize of 3,000 Euros is awarded every four years. Established in 1981.

2209 ■ Prix Jecker, Cahours, Paul Marguerite de la Charlonie, Houzeau, and J. B. Dumas
For recognition of original research in chemistry, agriculture, and physics. Awards are given in alternate years in the following categories: chemistry, agriculture, and physics. A monetary prize of 1,500 Euros is awarded every four years. Established between 1851 and 1943.

2210 ■ Prix Alexandre Joannides
For recognition of scientific, medical, or other research useful to the public good. The prize is awarded alternately by the division of chemistry and natural sciences and the division of mathematics and physics. A monetary prize of 7,500 Euros is awarded annually. Established in 1958.

2211 ■ Prix Emile Jungfleisch
To recognize a Frenchman for important work or discoveries in organic chemistry. One of the Institute's Grand Prizes. A monetary prize of 150,000 Euros is awarded biennially in odd-numbered years. Established in 1923.

2212 ■ Prix du Docteur et de Madame Henri Labbe
For recognition of scientific work in biochemistry and nutrition. A monetary prize of 1,500 Euros is awarded biennially in even-numbered years. Established in 1948.

2213 ■ Prix Andre Lallemand
For recognition of outstanding work in the different fields of astronomy. Preference is given to works that have application in some other field. Individuals or teams are eligible. A monetary prize of 7,600 Euros is awarded biennially in odd-numbered years. Established in 1990.

2214 ■ Prix Lamb
For recognition of the best studies on the national defense of France. A monetary prize of 7,600 Euros is awarded biennially in odd-numbered years. Established in 1938.

2215 ■ Prix Leconte
For recognition of discoveries and of new applications in mathematics, physics, chemistry, natural history, and medical science. A monetary prize of 2,500 Euros is awarded every four years. Established in 1886.

2216 ■ Prix de l'Institut Francais du Petrole
To recognize a French or foreign researcher or research team for a scientific work that contributes to progress in understanding techniques directly or indirectly of interest to the hydrocarbon industry. Techniques concerning action that satisfies the needs of humanity for energy and its products and materials while respecting the environment are eligible. One of the Institute's Grand Prizes. A monetary prize of 20,000 Euros is awarded annually. Established in 1990 and awarded for the first time in 1994.

2217 ■ Prix Richard Lounsbery
For recognition of research in medicine and biology. Scientists under 40 years of age are eligible. A monetary prize of $50,000 is awarded annually. The prize is awarded alternately by the National Academy of Sciences in Washington, D.C., U.S.A., and by the Academie des Sciences in Paris. Established in 1978 and first awarded in 1979 in Washington.

2218 ■ Prix Leon Lutaud
For recognition of work that makes progress in a

Awards are arranged in alphabetical order below their administering organizations

discipline of geology. A monetary prize of 7,500 Euros is awarded biennially in even-numbered years. Established in 1982 on the occasion of the election of Jean Aubouin to l'Academie des Sciences. Sponsored by Comite National Francais de Geologie.

2219 ■ Prix des Sciences de la Mer de l'Ifremer

To recognize research works in physical oceanography, marine ecology, chemistry, and biology. A monetary award is given biennially in odd-numbered years. Established in 1992.

2220 ■ Prix et medaille Georges Millot

To recognize the author of a work in the field of geochemistry in one of the many areas of earth science, including geology, sedimentology, oceanology, pedology, metallurgy, and ecology. A medal and a monetary award of 1,500 Euros are awarded triennially. Established in 1979.

2221 ■ Prix Octave Mirbeau et Valentine Allorge

To honor authors of works on cryptograms. A monetary award of 1,500 Euros is given every four years. Established in 1990.

2222 ■ Prix Michel Monpetit

To recognize a French researcher or engineer in the field of computer sciences or automation. The judges are guided by such factors as the originality of basic ideas and the serious nature of the work, the confirmation of the results obtained, and the possibility of its practical application in the French computer sciences and automation industries. A monetary prize of 4,500 Euros is awarded annually. Established in 1977 by the Institut National de Recherche en Informatique et en Automatique and le Club de la Peri-Informatique.

2223 ■ Prix Montyon de Physiologie

For recognition of the most useful work on experimental physiology. A monetary prize of 1,500 Euros is awarded every four years. Established in 1818.

2224 ■ Prix Victor Noury, Thorlet, Henri Becquerel, Jules and Augusta Lazare

For recognition of outstanding scientific research in cellular and molecular biology. A monetary prize of 1,500 Euros is awarded every four years. Established in 1950.

2225 ■ Prix Henri de Parville, Artur du Fay, Alexandre Givry

For recognition of outstanding work in the fields of mechanics or physics. Awards are given in alternate years in the two categories. A monetary prize of 1,500 Euros is awarded every four years. Established in 1891.

2226 ■ Prix Blaise Pascal du GAMNI-SMAI

To recognize one or several researchers for a remarkable work done in France using the applied numerical methods of the Science of Engineering. A monetary prize of 1,500 Euros is awarded annually. Established in 1984 by le Groupement pour l'Avancement des Methodes Numerique de l'Ingenieur (GAMNI) and the Societe de Mathematiques appliques et Industrielles (SMAI).

2227 ■ Prix Paul Pascal

For recognition of research work in physical chemistry, particularly in magnetochemistry and its eventual extensions. Young or middle-aged researchers are eligible. A monetary prize of 1,500 Euros is awarded annually. Established in 1972.

2228 ■ Prix Petit d'Ormoy, Carriere, Thebault

For recognition of contributions to mathematics. A monetary prize of 1,500 Euros is awarded every four years. Established in 1875 (d'Ormay), 1932 (Carriere), and 1943 (Thebault).

2229 ■ Prix Ivan Peyches

For recognition of work that studies the condition and usefulness of solar energy or similar applied science fields. A monetary prize of 7,600 Euros is awarded biennially in odd-numbered years. Established in 1978.

2230 ■ Prix Plumey

To recognize an individual who perfects steam engines or other devices that contribute to the progress of navigation. A monetary prize of 1,500 Euros is awarded biennially in odd-numbered years. Established in 1859.

2231 ■ Prix Gustave Ribaud

For recognition of work in the area of thermal exchanges or high frequency. Awards alternate between the fields of applied physics and theoretical physics. A monetary prize of 1,500 Euros is awarded every four years. Established in 1965.

2232 ■ Prix L. E. Rivot

To recognize the four students who graduate from l'Ecole polytechnique in first and second place in the department of mines and the department of bridges and highways. Monetary prizes for first place and second place are awarded annually. The prize is to be used to buy science books, and for travel expenses for study. Established in 1890.

2233 ■ Prix Gaston Rousseau

To provide recognition for scientific research leading toward an improvement in human welfare, and especially toward the cure of diseases, such as cancer. A scientist or a team of scientists working in the same field (without respect to nationality) are eligible. A monetary prize of 3,000 Euros is awarded every biennially in even-numbered years. Established in 1970 and first awarded in 1978.

2234 ■ Prix Gustave Roussy

For recognition and encouragement of cancer research. A monetary prize of 3,000 Euros is awarded every four years. Established in 1967.

2235 ■ Prix Charles-Louis de Saulses de Freycinet

To aid scientists whose resources are insufficient to permit them to pursue their scientific research, or to encourage research or work in mathematics. A monetary prize of 1,500 Euros is awarded biennially in odd-numbered years. Established in 1925.

2236 ■ Prix Servant

For recognition of outstanding works in mathematics and physics. A monetary prize of 7,500 Euros is awarded annually. Established in 1952.

2237 ■ Prix Gabrielle Sand et Marie Guido Triossi

To recognize a scientist for an invention for the good of mankind. Awards are given in alternate years in the categories of mathematics, physics, and chemistry and natural sciences. A monetary prize is awarded every four years. Established in 1908 (Sand) and 1939 (Triossi).

2238 ■ Prix Leon Velluz

For recognition of a discovery in chemistry or organic biochemistry leading to human therapy. One of the Institute's Grand Prizes. The prize is not to be divided, but may be awarded to a team for a discovery. A monetary prize of 25,000 Euros is awarded biennially in odd-numbered years. Established in 1986.

2239 ■ Prix Alfred Verdaguer

For recognition of a remarkable work in art, literature, or science. A monetary prize of 3,000 Euros is awarded every four years. Established in 1948 by a large bequest of Alfred Verdaguer.

2240 ■ Prix Aniuta Winter-Klein

To recognize young researchers whose work contributes to the knowledge or application of the physical chemistry of the solid noncrystalline vitreous state. Individuals of any nationality and residence are eligible. The winner gives one or two lectures in memory of Aniuta Winter Klein. A monetary prize if 7,500 Euros is awarded biennially in even-numbered years. Established in 1982.

2241 ■ Academie des Sciences Morales et Politiques

Michel Albert, Sec.
Institut de France
23, quai de Conti
F-75006 Paris, France
Ph: 33 1 44414326
Fax: 33 1 44414327
E-mail: secretaireperpetuel@asmp.fr
URL: http://www.asmp.fr

2242 ■ Prix Gustave Chaix d'Est Ange

For recognition of a work of documentary history about the Chartists movement. A medal is awarded annually.

2243 ■ Prix Odilon Barrot

For recognition of the best work on juries, both criminal and civil and for recognition of the most practical and liberal work on decentralization of government. A medal is awarded triennially.

2244 ■ Prix Claude Berthault

For recognition of an artistic or scientific work that increases the reputation of the French nation. Families of farmers or sailors of the coast of the Marche on the ocean, with preference given to veterans of World War I are eligible. A monetary prize of 3,000 francs is awarded annually. Established in 1921.

2245 ■ Prix Bigot de Morogues

For recognition of the best work on poverty in France and remedies for that poverty. A medal is awarded every ten years.

2246 ■ Bourse Marcelle Blum

To provide the opportunity for studies in female psychology. A grant of 1,500 Euros is awarded annually.

2247 ■ Prix Bordin

For recognition of papers on subjects touching the public interest, the good of humanity, the progress of science, and national honor. Awards are given in alternate years by the following sections of the academy: philosophy, morals, legislation, political economy, and history. A medal is awarded biennially in odd-numbered years.

2248 ■ Prix Carlier

For recognition of the best treatise on new methods to improve moral and material conditions of the largest social class in Paris. A medal is awarded annually.

2249 ■ Prix Rene Cassin

For recognition of a legal work of value or to recognize the author of an action or work of civic merit. A monetary prize of 750 Euros is awarded biennially in odd-numbered years.

2250 ■ Prix Corbay

For recognition of a useful contribution in the fields of science, art, law, agriculture, industry, or business. A medal is awarded annually.

2251 ■ Prix Victor Cousin

To recognize the author of a treatise on the history of ancient philosophy. A medal is awarded triennially.

2252 ■ Prix Crouzet

For recognition of the best treatise on philosophical or religious questions exclusively from the point of view of natural religion without any diversion into the area of the supernatural. A medal is awarded every five years.

2253 ■ Prix Dagnan-Bouveret

To encourage the study of psychology and for

Awards are arranged in alphabetical order below their administering organizations

recognition of a work in psychology. A medal is awarded annually. Established by the parents of M. Dagnan-Bouveret, who died for France.

2254 ■ Prix Felix de Beaujour
To recognize the author of the best treatise that contributes to the solution of the plight of the poor in different countries, particularly France. A medal is awarded every five years.

2255 ■ Prix Lucien de Reinach
For recognition of a work on the overseas territories written in French during the preceding two years. A medal is awarded biennially in odd-numbered years.

2256 ■ Prix Victor Delbos
For recognition of publications that promote spiritual life and religious philosophy in the past and future. A medal is awarded biennially in even-numbered years.

2257 ■ Prix Demolombe
To recognize an author whose works are within the scope of the academie. Awards are given in alternate years in the following categories: philosophy, morality, law, political economy, and history and geography. Monetary awards are presented by one of the five sections of the academie. A medal is awarded every four years.

2258 ■ Prix Le Dissez de Penanrun
For recognition of works published during the preceding six years on a topic proposed by one of the six sections of the academie. A medal is awarded annually.

2259 ■ Prix Paul Vigne d'Octon
To recognize the author, preferably a physician, who has demonstrated through his writings his professional behavior and life, an authentic and tangible devotion to the cause of progress of human relationships or of relationships between groups of human beings. A monetary prize of 800 Euros is awarded biennially in even-numbered years.

2260 ■ Prix Drouyn de Lhuys
For recognition of a published or unpublished work on history. A medal is awarded annually.

2261 ■ Prix Joseph du Teil
For recognition of a work on diplomatic history. A medal is awarded annually.

2262 ■ Prix Dulac
For recognition of acts of courage or devotion. Members of the police or military are eligible. A medal is awarded annually.

2263 ■ Prix Charles Dupin
For recognition of the best treatise or work on statistics or political economics. A medal is awarded biennially in even-numbered years.

2264 ■ Prix Lucien Dupont
To recognize an individual who by some action has contributed to the elimination of legal and administrative procedures and formalities that complicate the life of a citizen. A monetary prize of 5,000 Euros is awarded annually.

2265 ■ Prix Joseph Dutens
For recognition of the best book or treatise related to political economics, or its history and applications. A medal is awarded every five years.

2266 ■ Prix Leon Faucher
For recognition of a treatise on a question of political economics or on the life of a famous economist. A medal is awarded triennially.

2267 ■ Prix Le Fevre-Deumier de Ports
For recognition of a remarkable work on mythology, philosophy, or comparative religion. A medal is awarded every ten years.

2268 ■ Prix Jean Finot
For recognition of a work with profoundly humanitarian social tendencies. A medal is awarded biennially in odd-numbered years.

2269 ■ Prix Marcel Flach
For recognition of a work on the history of Alsace after 1648. A medal is awarded biennially in odd-numbered years. Established by Madame Jacques Flach at the bequest of her husband, a member of the academie.

2270 ■ Prix Edmond Freville
For recognition of the best original work, book, or article that discusses the organization, function, or work of the ministries of defense, Army or Navy. The work may deal with topics such as central administration, commanding, officers, troops, and different services. Works written in French and published in the preceding two years are considered. A monetary prize of 3,000 Euros is awarded annually.

2271 ■ Prix Gallet
To recognize the Catholic person or group having contributed the most to the improvement of French law and organization as it relates to the Catholic point of view. French citizens are eligible. A medal is awarded annually.

2272 ■ Prix Gegner
To recognize a philosopher-writer whose works contribute to the progress of positive science. A medal is awarded annually.

2273 ■ Prix Emile Girardeau
For recognition of a work or treatise on the subject of economics or sociology. A monetary prize of 5,500 Euros is awarded annually.

2274 ■ Prix Joseph Hamel
For recognition of a work on commercial financial law. A monetary prize of 600 Euros is awarded biennially in even-numbered years.

2275 ■ Prix Jules et Louis Jeanbernat et Bathelemy de Ferrari Doria
For recognition of a work of literature, art, or science by a young French author. A medal is awarded every five years.

2276 ■ Prix de Joest
For recognition of a discovery or written work that is most useful for the public good. A medal is awarded every five years.

2277 ■ Prix Koenigswarter
For recognition of the best book on the history of law published during the preceding five years. A monetary prize is awarded every five years.

2278 ■ Prix Charles Lambert
To recognize the author of the best published study or manuscript on the future of spiritualism. A monetary prize is awarded triennially.

2279 ■ Prix Docteur Rene-Joseph Laufer
For recognition of the best work on social prophylaxis. A monetary prize of 1,500 Euros is awarded biennially in even-numbered years.

2280 ■ Prix Jules Lefort
To recognize the author or authors of working manuscripts on private and social insurance for the common classes, and on mutuality and future planning among the common social classes. A medal is awarded every ten years. Established by M. and Mme. Lefort in memory of their son, Jules Lefort.

2281 ■ Prix Ernest Lemonon
For recognition of a work concerning contemporary foreign politics or contemporary French or foreign economics and social questions. A medal is awarded annually.

2282 ■ Prix Paul Leroy-Beaulieu
To recognize and encourage effective publicity in favor of increasing the French birth rate and defending the rights and interests of large and average families. A medal is awarded triennially.

2283 ■ Prix Louis Liard
For recognition of a work on education, philoso-

phy, or the history of philosophy, using rational or experimental methods and marked by precision results. A medal is awarded triennially.

2284 ■ Prix Limantour
For recognition of the best work on law, history, or political economy. Prizes are awarded in alternate years in the following categories: law by the Legislative Section, history by the History Section, and political economics by the Political Economics Section. Work published in the past three years is eligible. A medal is awarded biennially in odd-numbered years.

2285 ■ Prix Charles Lyon-Caen
To recognize the author of a work on philosophy, moral sciences, law, political economics, or history. Prizes are awarded in alternate years in the following categories: philosophy, moral sciences, law, political economics, and history. A medal is awarded triennially. Established by friends and associates of M. Charles-Lyon Caen on the occasion of the 40th anniversary of his election to the academy.

2286 ■ Prix Maisondieu
To recognize the author or founder of a work that contributes to the improvement of the conditions of the working classes. A medal is awarded biennially in even-numbered years.

2287 ■ Prix Malouet
To recognize a secondary school teacher in France with at least four children of whose professional merits and devotion to family deserve public recognition. A medal is awarded annually.

2288 ■ Prix Zerilli Marimo
To recognize an outstanding liberal economist. A monetary prize of 13,500 Euros is awarded annually. Established in 1984.

2289 ■ Prix Georges Mauguin
For recognition of a scholarly work on Napoleon Bonaparte or his era. A monetary prize of 1,000 Euros is awarded biennially in odd-numbered years.

2290 ■ Prix Gabriel Monod
For recognition of a published work on the sources of the national history of France, or on any subjects favored by Gabriel Monod. A medal is awarded triennially.

2291 ■ Prix Fondation du General Muteau
To recognize individuals or institutions who have contributed to the glory of France by their heroism, actions, or writings. A monetary prize of 400 Euros is given every four years.

2292 ■ Prix Ugo Papi - Gaston Leduc
For recognition of an outstanding work on economy. A monetary prize of 7,500 Euros is awarded every three years. Established in 1985.

2293 ■ Prix Paul-Michel Perret
For recognition of a book on history. Books published during the preceding three years are eligible. A medal is awarded annually. Established by Madame Dupont de Latuillerie in memory of her son.

2294 ■ Prix Rossi
For recognition of the best treatise on a question of social and political economics. A medal is awarded annually.

2295 ■ Prix Joseph Saillet
For recognition of the best work on a subject of rationalist moral philosophy or scientific morality, independent of any religious ideas. Published or unpublished works written in French may be submitted. All nationalities are eligible. A medal is awarded annually.

2296 ■ Prix Saintour
For recognition of works of philosophy, morality,

law, political economy, or history and geography. Monetary awards are given in alternate years by one of the six sections of the academie. A medal is awarded biennially in even-numbered years.

2297 ■ Prix Eugene Salvan
For recognition of an act of courage or self-sacrifice. A medal is awarded annually.

2298 ■ Prix Stassart
For recognition of the best oration of a moralist or for recognition of a work on a question of morality. A medal is awarded every six years.

2299 ■ Prix Tanesse
To recognize an individual who contributed the most to improving the condition of women during the preceding three years. A medal is awarded triennially.

2300 ■ Prix Henri Texier I
To recognize the author of a treatise on individual freedom and in support of actions directed toward the defense of individual liberty. A monetary prize of 1,000 Euros is awarded annually.

2301 ■ Prix Henri Texier II
For recognition of a work to preserve the beauty of France. A monetary prize of 2,000 Euros is awarded annually.

2302 ■ Prix Ernest Thorel
For recognition of the best work designed to educate the people. Pamphlets or books of current reading, other than textbooks are considered. A medal is awarded biennially in even-numbered years.

2303 ■ Prix Maurice Travers
For recognition of works relative to international public or private law, or comparative law; or for works on diplomatic history. Prizes are awarded in alternate years in international public or private law or comparative law and diplomatic history. A medal is awarded biennially in odd-numbered years.

2304 ■ Prix Blaise des Vosges
For recognition of the best treatise, manuscript, or book published in French having as its object the moral and material improvement of industrial and agricultural workers through instruction, unionization, or any other means. Individuals are eligible without regard to nationality. A medal is awarded triennially.

2305 ■ Prix Wolowski
For recognition of a work of law or political economy published during the preceding eight years. Awards are given in alternate years in law and political economy. A medal is awarded every four years.

2306 ■ Amaury Sport Organisation
253 Quai de la Bataille de Stalingrad
92137 Issy-les-Moulineaux, France
Ph: 33 1 41331400
E-mail: asotv@aso.fr
URL: http://www.aso.fr

2307 ■ Tour de France
This, the world's most prestigious bicycle endurance race, is open to the world's top men's professional cycling teams. The Tour is a 22-day cycling race that covers approximately 3,500 kilometers during the month of July. Monetary prizes in excess of 3 million Euros are awarded. Held annually in July. Established in 1903.

2308 ■ Amiens International Film Festival (Festival International du Film d'Amiens)
Jean-Pierre Bergeon, Festival Dir.
c/o MCA
Place Leon Gontier
F-80000 Amiens, France
Ph: 33 3 2271 3570
Fax: 33 3 2292 5304

E-mail: contact@filmfestamiens.org
URL: http://www.filmfestamiens.org

2309 ■ Amiens International Film Festival (Festival International du Film d'Amiens)
For recognition of the best quality film produced during the previous year. A Golden Unicorn trophy is awarded for the Best Fiction Feature Film, the Best Short Film, and the Best Actor and Actress. Awarded annually. Established in 1980.

2310 ■ Association Aeronautique et Astronautique de France
Michel Scheller, Pres.
6 rue Galilee
F-75116 Paris, France
Ph: 33 1 56641230
Fax: 33 1 56641231
E-mail: secr.exec@aaaf.asso.fr
URL: http://www.aaafasso.fr

2311 ■ Grand Prix
To recognize a person who has gained distinction through his or her works or services rendered to aeronautics or astronautics. Citizens of France or other countries are eligible. A medal and a diploma are awarded annually. Established in 1973.

2312 ■ Prix d'Aeronautique
To recognize an individual who has gained distinction through his or her work in the field of aeronautics. French citizens are eligible. A medal and a diploma are awarded annually. Established in 1974.

2313 ■ Prix d'Astronautique
To recognize an individual for outstanding work in the field of astronautics. A medal and a diploma are awarded annually. Established in 1974.

2314 ■ Prix des Jeunes
To recognize an individual who has distinguished himself through scientific work, originality of writings, or an enterprising spirit. Individuals under 30 years of age are eligible. A monetary prize and a diploma are awarded annually. Established in 1973.

2315 ■ Association of Chemists of the Textile Industry (Association des Chimistes de l'Industrie Textile)
Georges Merand, Sec.
37-39 rue de Neuilly
F-92110 Clichy, France
Ph: 33 1 47563170
Ph: 33 1 47563176
Fax: 33 1 47302709
E-mail: contact@acit.asso.fr
URL: http://www.acit.asso.fr

2316 ■ A.C.I.T. Award
For original scientific and technical work.

2317 ■ Avenir Award
For research in textile chemistry.

2318 ■ Ernest Sack Award
For original scientific and technical work.

2319 ■ Association of European Schools of Planning
Anna Geppert, Sec. Gen.
Universite de Reims
Institut d'Amenagement du Territoire et d'Environment de l'U
57 bis, rue Pierre Taittinger
F-51096 Reims, France
E-mail: secretariat@aesopsg.eu
URL: http://www.aesop-planning.com

2320 ■ Best Congress Paper Prize
To recognize the best paper presented at the Congress. Awarded annually. Established in 2005.

2321 ■ Best Published Paper Prize
To recognize the best paper published in a European planning journal. Papers must be on spatial planning. Established in 1995.

2322 ■ Excellence in Teaching Prize
To encourage planning schools to implement new pedagogy, theories, and/or technologies. Member schools are eligible. Awarded annually. Established in 2002.

2323 ■ Association of Schools of Public Health in the European Region (Association des Ecoles de Sante Publique de la Regional Europeenne)
Antoine Flahault, Pres.
9-11, rue Benoit Malon
F-92150 Suresnes, France
E-mail: office@aspher.org
URL: http://www.aspher.org

2324 ■ Andrija Stampar Medal
To recognize a distinguished person for excellence in the field of public health. Awarded annually.

2325 ■ Automobile Club de l'Ouest
Remy Brouard, CEO
Circuit des 24 heures
F-72019 Le Mans, France
Ph: 33 2 4340 2424
Fax: 33 2 4340 2415
E-mail: tickets@lemans.org
URL: http://www.lemans.org

2326 ■ Le Mans 24-hour Grand Prix d'Endurance
To recognize the winning team in a 24 hour endurance race on the famous Sarthe track located 3 miles south of Le Mans, France. The track, which is part raceway and part roadway, is 13.535 km (8.5 miles) long. The race is held annually in June. Established in 1923.

2327 ■ Bioelectrochemical Society
Prof. Ana Maria Oliveria Brett, Pres.
UMR 5089
CNRS-IPBS
205 Rte. de Narbonne
F-31077 Toulouse Cedex, France
E-mail: justin.teissie@ipbs.fr
URL: http://www.bes-online.usf.edu

2328 ■ Luigi Galvani Prize
To recognize young scientists who have documented an outstanding contribution to biochemistry or bioenergetics. Eligible candidates must have achieved a PhD and must be younger than 45 years of age. A monetary prize of 1,000 Euros, a citation, and an invitation to present a lecture are awarded biennially in odd-numbered years.

2329 ■ Giulio Milazzo Prize
To honor a member of the Society who has demonstrated excellence in science and contributed to the expansion of the field of bioelectrochemistry. A monetary prize of 2,000 Euros is awarded biennially in odd-numbered years. Established in honor of the founder and first president of the Society.

2330 ■ Cafe des Deux Magots
6 Place Saint Germain des Pres
F-75006 Paris, France
Ph: 33 145 485525
Fax: 33 145 493139
E-mail: cafe.lesdeuxmagots@free.fr
URL: http://www.lesdeuxmagots.com

2331 ■ Deux Magots Literary Prize (Prix des Deux-Magots)
For recognition of an avant-garde book by a young writer. The selection is made by a jury of 13 judges, as was the first prize in 1933. A monetary prize of 7700 Euro is awarded annu-

Awards are arranged in alphabetical order below their administering organizations

ally in January at the Cafe des Deux Magots, named after *The Two Magots of China,*, a successful play in 1813. Established in 1933 by Henri Philippon with writers, painters, and sculptors who frequented the cafe and each provide monetary contributions for the prize.

2332 ■ COGEDIM
Jean-Claude Borda, Pres.
8, avenue Delcasse
F-75008 Paris Cedex 16, France
Ph: 33 1 5626 2400
E-mail: contact-internet@cogedim.fr
URL: http://www.cogedim.fr

2333 ■ Prix COGEDIM
To recognize young architects who have not had a contract for a major real estate development during the preceding year. The first prize is the development of apartments in Paris. Awarded annually.

2334 ■ Committee on Space Research (Comite pour la Recherche Spatiale)
Dr. J.L. Fellous, Exec. Dir.
2 Pl. Maurice Quentin
75039 Paris Cedex 01, France
Ph: 33 1 44767510
Fax: 33 1 44767437
E-mail: cospar@cosparhq.cnes.fr
URL: http://cosparhq.cnes.fr

2335 ■ COSPAR Space Science Award
To honor a scientist who has made outstanding contributions to space science. All scientists working in fields covered by COSPAR are eligible. Awarded biennially in even-numbered years at the COSPAR Scientific Assembly. Established in 1984.

2336 ■ Distinguished Service Medal
To recognize extraordinary services rendered to COSPAR over many years. Awarded when merited. Established in 1992.

2337 ■ International Cooperation Medal
Given for significant contributions, by an individual or a group, to the promotion of international scientific cooperation. Awarded biennially in even-numbered years. Established in 1984.

2338 ■ Jeoujang Jaw Award
To recognize scientists who have made distinguished pioneering contributions to promoting space science research, establishing new space science research branches, and founding new exploration programs. Awarded biennially in even-numbered years jointly with the Chinese Academy of Sciences. Established in 2008.

2339 ■ Massey Award
In recognition of outstanding contributions to the development of space research, interpreted in the widest sense, in which a leadership role is of particular importance. Awarded biennially in even-numbered years. Established in 1990 in honor of Sir Harrie Massey. Awarded jointly with the Royal Society of London.

2340 ■ William Nordberg Medal
To honor distinguished contributions to the application of space science in a field covered by COSPAR. Awarded biennially in even-numbered years. Established in 1988.

2341 ■ Vikram Sarabhai Medal
To recognize exceptional contributions to space research in developing countries. Awarded biennially in even-numbered years jointly with the Indian Space Research Organization. Established in 1990.

2342 ■ Zeldovich Medals
To acknowledge excellence and achievements of young scientists. One medal is awarded for each COSPAR Scientific Commission. Awarded biennially in even-numbered years. Established in 1990. Awarded jointly with the Russian Academy of Sciences.

2343 ■ Cooperation Centre for Scientific Research Relative to Tobacco (Centre de Cooperation pour les Recherches Scientifiques Relatives au Tabac)
Pierre-Marie Guitton, Sec. Gen.
11 rue du Quatre Septembre
F-75002 Paris, France
Ph: 33 1 58625870
Fax: 33 1 58625879
E-mail: fjacob@coresta.org
URL: http://www.coresta.org

2344 ■ CORESTA Prize (Prix CORESTA)
For recognition of achievement in tobacco science or technology. A monetary prize of about Euro 10,000, a diploma, and travel are presented biennially in even-numbered years at a Congress. Established in 1978. Formerly: (1978) Philip Morris International Prize.

2345 ■ Council of Europe (Conseil de l'Europe)
Thorbjorn Jagland, Sec. Gen.
Ave. de l'Europe
F-67075 Strasbourg Cedex, France
Ph: 33 3 88412029
Ph: 33 3 88412000
Fax: 33 3 88412754
E-mail: visites@coe.int
URL: http://www.coe.int

2346 ■ Crystal Scales of Justice Prize
To discover and highlight innovative and efficient practices used in European courts for court organization or for the conduct of civil proceedings, and deserving to be drawn to the attention of policy-makers and the judicial community so as to improve the operation of the public system of justice. Awarded annually by COE's European Commission for the Efficiency of Justice. Established in 2005. Co-administered by the European Commission.

2347 ■ Europe Prize
Awarded to a local or regional municipality for active promotion of the European ideal through such activities as twinnings, European events, and exchange visits. The winning authority is chosen by the Parliamentary Assembly, and receives a trophy (retained for one year), a bronze medal, and a diploma. A cash prize of 7,600 Euros is awarded to the winning municipality, to be spent on a study visit in Europe by some of its young citizens. Awarded annually. Established in 1955.

2348 ■ European Diploma
To reward local and regional authorities for their active promotion of the European ideal, via twinnings, European events, exchange visits, etc. Awarded by the Parliamentary Assembly as the first step toward the Europe Prize. A diploma is awarded annually to approximately 30 authorities.

2349 ■ European Diploma of Protected Areas
The Committee of Ministers awards this diploma on the advice of the Committee for the Activities of the Council of Europe in the field of Biological and Landscape Diversity. Awarded to natural parks, reserves, or sights of international importance which meet certain criteria for safeguarding the natural heritage, and takes their scientific, cultural, and recreational value into account. Established in 1965.

2350 ■ European Drug Prevention Prize
To encourage active youth participation in drug prevention in all communities in Europe by recognizing innovation in projects that are currently in operation in one or more members states of the Council of Europe. Eligible projects must involve young people under the age of 25 years. The jury is composed of seven young people from member states. A monetary sum of 5,000 Euros is awarded to three winning projects. Awarded biennially in even-numbered years. Administered by the COE's Pompidou Group.

2351 ■ Flag of Honour
To reward local and regional authorities for their active promotion of the European ideal, via twinnings, European events, exchange visits, etc. Awarded by the Parliamentary Assembly as the second step toward the Europe Prize. An embroidered flag is awarded annually to 20 to 25 authorities.

2352 ■ Museum Prize
To honor a museum judged to have made an original contribution to the preservation of the European heritage. The prize consists of a bronze statuette donated by the Spanish Artist Joan Miro and a monetary award of 5,000 Euros. The winning museum is selected by the Parliamentary Assembly's Committee on Culture, Science and Education. Awarded annually. Established in 1977.

2353 ■ North-South Prize
To recognize individuals for: the defense and promotion of human rights and pluralistic democracy; the development of intercultural dialogue; raising of public awareness of the issues of global interdependence and solidarity; or reinforcement of the North-South partnership. A statuette is awarded annually to two recipients, one from the north and one from the south. Administered by the COE's European Centre for Global Interdependence and Solidarity, more commonly known as the North-South Centre. Established in 1995.

2354 ■ Plaque of Honour
To reward local and regional authorities for their active promotion of the European ideal, via twinnings, European events, exchange visits, etc. Awarded by the Parliamentary Assembly as the third step toward the Europe Prize. An plaque is awarded annually to eight to 10 authorities.

2355 ■ Prix Europa
To promote the creativity and diversity of European television, radio, and Internet products. Producers, broadcasting organizations, and associations of broadcasting organizations are eligible. Categories include Internet, Radio Drama, Radio Documentary, TV Fiction, TV Documentary, TV Multicultural Programs, and TV Current Affairs. Awarded annually.

2356 ■ Young Active Citizens Award
To promote active participation of young people in society by recognizing the value and practice of co-management between young people and public authorities at the local, regional, and national levels. Open to youth organizations involving individuals between the ages of 16 and 30. A diploma and monetary prize of 1,000 Euros is awarded to five recipients annually. Established in 2002.

2357 ■ Danone Institute
Rte. Departementale 128
F-91757 Palaiseau, France
Ph: 33 1 69 357634
URL: http://www.danoneinstitute.org

2358 ■ Danone International Prize for Nutrition
To recognize a single researcher or research team who discovered or developed a novel concept of nutrition that advanced human nutrition science, either basic or applied. A monetary prize of 120,000 Euros is to be split between the recipient and his or her not-for-profit primary

Awards are arranged in alphabetical order below their administering organizations

research institution. Awarded biennially in odd-numbered years. Established in 1997. Sponsored by Groupe Danone.

2359 ∎ European Association for Geochemistry
Bernard Bourdon, Pres.
Gopel-Bureau 566
1, rue Jussieu
F 75238 Paris Cedex 5, France
E-mail: gopel@ipgp.fr
URL: http://www.eag.eu.com

2360 ∎ Paul W. Gast Lecture Series
For outstanding contributions to geochemistry by a scientist under 45 years of age. The recipient presents a lecture at the EAG/GS Goldschmidt Conference.

2361 ∎ Houtermans Medal
For exceptional contributions to geochemistry by a scientist no more than 35 years of age. Awarded annually. Named in honor of physicist Friedrich Georg Houtermans.

2362 ∎ Science Innovation Award
To recognize significant and innovative breakthroughs in geochemistry. Eligible to scientists between 35 and 55 years of age. Subject area varies by year. A medal and certificate are awarded annually.

2363 ∎ Urey Medal
For outstanding contributions to geochemistry over a career. Awarded annually without regard to nationality. Named in honor of Nobel Award winning physical chemist Harold Clayton Urey.

2364 ∎ European Environmental Mutagen Society
Dr. Robert A. Baan, Treas.
Unit of Carcinogen Identification and Evaluation
Intl. Agency for Research on Cancer
150 cours Albert Thomas
F-69008 Lyon, France
Ph: 33 4 72738659
Fax: 33 4 72738319
E-mail: baan@iarc.fr
URL: http://www.eems-eu.org

2365 ∎ Frits Sobels Award
For recognition of an excellent scientific contribution in the field of environmental mutagenesis. The EEMS Awards Committee makes the selection. A monetary prize of 3,000 Euros is awarded and travel expenses are awarded annually. Established in 1986. Formerly: (1997) EEMS Award.

2366 ∎ Young Scientist of the Year
To recognize an outstanding scientist who is no more than 35 years old. A certificate, travel expenses, and monetary prize of £1,000 are awarded annually. Established in 1981.

2367 ∎ European Geosciences Union
Donald Bruce Dingwell, Pres.
5, rue Rene Descartes
67084 Strasbourg, France
Ph: 33 3 88450191
Fax: 33 3 88603887
E-mail: president@egu.eu
URL: http://www.egu.eu

2368 ∎ Julius Bartels Medal
To recognize scientists for their outstanding achievements in solar-terrestrial sciences. Awarded annually by the Division on Solar-Terrestrial Sciences. Established in 1996 in honor of the scientific achievements of Julius Bartels.

2369 ∎ Sir David Robert Bates Medal
To recognize scientists for their exceptional contributions to planetary and solar system sciences. Awarded when merited. Established in 1992 in recognition of the Scientific and editorial achievements of Sir David Robert Bates. Administered by the Division on Planetary and Solar System Sciences.

2370 ∎ Vilhelm Bjerknes Medal
To recognize distinguished research in atmospheric science. Awarded annually by the Division on Atmospheric Sciences. Established in 1995 in recognition of the scientific achievements of Vilhelm Bjerknes.

2371 ∎ Jean Dominique Cassini Medal and Honorary Membership
This, one of the three equally-ranked most prestigious awards bestowed by the Union, is reserved for scientists who have achieved exceptional international standing in geophysics, defined in its widest sense. Awarded annually if merited. Established in 1973.

2372 ∎ Beno Gutenberg Medal
To recognize individuals for their outstanding contributions to seismology. Awarded annually by the Division on Seismology. Established in 1996 in honor of the scientific achievements of Beno Gutenberg.

2373 ∎ Arthur Holmes Medal and Honorary Membership
This, one of the three equally-ranked most prestigious awards bestowed by the Union, is given to recognize a scientist who has achieved exceptional international standing in Solid Earth Geosciences through merit and scientific achievements. The recipients may be citizens of any country in the world. The medal may be jointly awarded to two scientists or more, whether they have worked together or not in the case of simultaneous and identical or complementary discoveries. The medal, bearing a likeness of Arthur Holmes and the recipient's name, both engraved, is awarded annually either for a specific major discovery or for the achievement of a life-time career.

2374 ∎ Milutin Milankovic Medal
To recognize scientists for their outstanding achievements in long-term climatic changes and modeling. Awarded annually by the Division on Climate: Past, Present & Future. Established in 1993 by the Section on Oceans and Atmosphere in recognition of the scientific and editorial achievements of Milutin Milankovic.

2375 ∎ Fridtjof Nansen Medal
To recognize distinguished research in oceanography. Awarded annually by the Division on Ocean Sciences. Established in 1996 in honor of the scientific achievements of Fridtjof Nansen.

2376 ∎ Louis Neel Medal
To recognize scientists for outstanding achievements in the fertilization of the Earth Sciences by the transfer and application of fundamental theory and/or experimental techniques of solid state physics, as defined in its broadest sense. Awarded annually by the Division on Magnetism, Palaeomagnetism and Rock Physics. Established in 1993 in recognition of the scientific achievements of Louis Eugene Felix Neel, who shared the 1970 Nobel Prize of Physics for his fundamental research and discoveries concerning antiferromagnetism.

2377 ∎ Arne Richter Award for Outstanding Young Scientists
To recognize scientific achievements in any field made by a young scientist. Candidates must be aged 35 years or younger, and must have received their PhD within the previous five years. Awarded annually to one or more recipients. Formerly: (2011) Outstanding Young Scientist Award.

2378 ∎ Runcorn-Florensky Medal
To recognize a scientist for exceptional contributions to planetology, defined in its widest sense. Awarded annually if merited by the Division on Planetary and Solar System Sciences. Honors the scientific achievements of Keith Runcorn and Cyril Florensky. Formerly: Keith Runcorn Travel Award.

2379 ∎ Sergey Soloviev Medal
To recognize scientists for their exceptional contributions to natural hazards and their research into improving our knowledge of basic principles, as well as for the assessment and proper mitigation of hazards in view of environmental protection and the integrity of human life and socio-economic systems. Awarded annually by the Division on Natural Hazards. Established in 1996 in honor of Sergey Soloviev.

2380 ∎ Alfred Wegener Medal and Honorary Membership
This, one of the three equally-ranked most prestigious awards bestowed by the Union, is given to recognize a scientist who has achieved exceptional international standing in atmospheric, hydrological, or ocean sciences. The recipients may be citizens of any country in the world. The medal may be jointly awarded to two scientists or more, whether they have worked together or not in the case of simultaneous and identical or complementary discoveries. Awarded annually. The medal, bearing a likeness of Alfred Wegener and the recipient's name, both engraved, is awarded annually either for a specific major discovery or for the achievement of a life-time career.

2381 ∎ Young Scientists Travel Awards
To enable European scientists or young scientists working in Europe to attend the scientific conferences of the Society by providing a financial contribution to the cost of travel and free registration. Candidates must be age 35 years or younger, and must be undergraduate or postgraduate students or have received their highest degree qualification within the last seven years. Established in 1977.

2382 ∎ European Materials Research Society
Prof. Paul Siffert, Gen. Sec.
23 Rue du Loess
BP 20
F-67037 Strasbourg Cedex 02, France
Ph: 33 3 88106372
Ph: 33 3 88106543
Fax: 33 3 88106293
E-mail: emrs@emrs-strasbourg.com
URL: http://www.emrs-strasbourg.com

2383 ∎ Graduate Student Award
For participation at the E-MRS Meeting as an author or co-author of a symposium paper, which shows significant and timely research results.

2384 ∎ European Membrane Society
Lidetta Giorno, Pres.
Universite Paul Sabatier
Laboratoire de Genie Chimique
118, Rte. de Narbonne
F-31062 Toulouse Cedex, France
Fax: 33 561 558199
E-mail: ems@chimie.ups-tlse.fr
URL: http://81.255.167.59/~iodeco/ems/site/home/index.php

2385 ∎ EMS Award
To recognize a researcher under 35 years for the best published journal paper on the topic of membrane science and engineering. Awarded annually.

2386 ∎ European Physical Society
Mr. David Lee, Gen. Sec.
6 rue des Freres Lumiere
F-68200 Mulhouse Cedex, France
Ph: 33 3 89329440

Awards are arranged in alphabetical order below their administering organizations

Fax: 33 3 89329449
E-mail: d.lee@eps.org
URL: http://www.eps.org

2387 ■ Accelerator Prize
To recognize an individual in the early part of his/her career having made a recent, original contribution to the accelerator field, as well as to recognize an individual for outstanding work in the accelerator field with no age limit. A cash prize and diploma are awarded to a recipient in each category biennially. Awarded by the Accelerators Division.

2388 ■ Hannes Alfven Prize
To recognize one or more individuals for outstanding contributions to plasma physics in experimental, theoretical, or technological areas. A medal, diploma, and cash prize are awarded annually. Administered by the Plasma Physics division of the Society.

2389 ■ Europhysics Prize
For recognition of outstanding achievement in physics of condensed matter. Nominations are submitted to the EPS Secretariat for the Selection Committee. A monetary prize and a certificate are awarded annually at the Conference. Established in 1975.

2390 ■ Experimental Physics Control Systems Prize
To recognize one or more individuals aged 35 or younger for outstanding contributions to the field of experimental physics control systems in experimental, theoretical, or technological areas. A diploma and cash prize are awarded biennially. Administered by the Experimental Physics Control Systems division of the Society.

2391 ■ Gribov Medal
To recognize a physicist aged 35 or younger for outstanding work performed in the field of theoretical particle physics and/or field theory. A medal and diploma are awarded biennially. Established in honor of Vladimir Naumovich Gribov.

2392 ■ High Energy and Particle Physics Prize
For recognition of important contributions to theoretical or experimental particle physics. Awarded to one or more individuals in the area of physics of condensed matter, specifically work leading to advances in the fields of electronic, electrical and materials engineering. Nominations are invited. A monetary prize, medal, and certificate are awarded biennially in odd-numbered years. Established in 1989 by the EPS High Energy and Particle Physics (HEPP) Division.

2393 ■ Medal for Public Understanding of Physics
To recognize an individual who has contributed greatly to the understanding of physics by the non-scientific public. A diploma and cash prize are awarded every three years.

2394 ■ Lise Meitner Prize
To recognize one or more individuals for outstanding contributions in nuclear science and related technologies. A diploma and cash prize are awarded biennially. Administered by the Nuclear Physics division of the Society. Sponsored by Eurisys Measures.

2395 ■ Outreach Prize
To recognize one or more individuals for outstanding outreach achievement in connection to high energy physics and/or particle astrophysics. A diploma and cash prize are awarded annually. Administered by the High Energy and Particle Physics division of the Society.

2396 ■ Cecil F. Powell Memorial Medal
To recognize an individual for the purpose of delivering a lecture on the subject of physics and society. A medal is awarded triennially.

2397 ■ Quantum Electronics Prize
To honor outstanding contributions to quantum electronics and optics. Awards are presented in two categories: fundamental aspects and applied aspects. A medal and monetary prize of 5000 Euros are awarded annually in each category.

2398 ■ Gero Thomas Prize
To recognize an individual for valuable contributions to the Society. Awarded every three years.

2399 ■ Young Particle Physicist Prize
To recognize a physicist aged 35 or younger for outstanding work performed in the fields of high energy physics and/or particle astrophysics. A diploma and cash prize are awarded biennially. Administered by the High Energy and Particle Physics division of the Society.

2400 ■ European Psychiatric Association (L'Association Europeenne de Psychiatrie)
Caroline Martin, Contact
15, Ave. de la Liberte
F-67000 Strasbourg, France
Ph: 33 3 88239930
Fax: 33 3 88352973
E-mail: hq@europsy.net
URL: http://www.europsy.net

2401 ■ European Bristol-Myers Squibb Prevention Award in Psychiatry
To recognize distinguished research in the field of prevention of psychiatric disorders, including psychosis, depression, anxiety, and dementia. A monetary prize of 20,000 Euros is awarded annually. Established in 2007.

2402 ■ Research Prizes
To recognize early career psychiatrists working in Europe who have published outstanding scientific papers during the previous year. Candidates must be younger than 40 years. Presented in four categories: 1) Clinical psychopathology and refinement of psychiatric diagnostic categories; 2) Biological correlates and treatments of mental disorders; 3) Psychiatric epidemiology, social psychiatry, and psychotherapeutic interventions in mental disorders; and 4) Child and adolescent psychiatry. A monetary prize of 2,500 Euros is awarded annually in each category.

2403 ■ European Research Consortium for Informatics and Mathematics
Mr. Keith Jeffrey, Pres.
2004, Rte. des Lucioles
BP 93
F-06902 Sophia Antipolis, France
Ph: 33 4 92385010
Fax: 33 4 92387822
E-mail: contact@ercim.org
URL: http://www.ercim.org

2404 ■ Cor Baayen Award
To recognize the most promising young researcher in computer science and applied mathematics. Nominees must have carried out their work in one of the "ERCIM countries": Austria, Belgium, Czech Republic, Denmark, Finland, France, Germany, Greece, Hungary, Ireland, Italy, Luxembourg, Norway, Poland, Portugal, Spain, Sweden, Switzerland, the Netherlands, and the United Kingdom. A certificate and monetary prize of 5,000 Euros are awarded annually. Established in 1995 to honor ERCIM's first president.

2405 ■ European Society for Clinical Virology
Prof. Dr. Bruno Lina, Pres.
Institut de Microbiologie
Laboratoire de Virologie Est
Centre de Biologie et de Pathologie Est
61 Blvd. Pinel
F-69677 Lyon, France

Ph: 33 4 72129657
Ph: 33 4 72129500
Fax: 33 4 72129500
E-mail: lina@univ-lyon1.fr
URL: http://www.escv.org

2406 ■ Abbott Diagnostic Award
For original contributions in the field of viral diagnosis. Eligible to members with less than 10 active years in virology after receiving a PhD or MD. Nominees must have authored one or more papers on viral diagnosis that have been published in a refereed journal in the previous two years. Awarded annually. Sponsored by Abbott Diagnostics.

2407 ■ Gardner Lectureship
To provide for a lecture by an eminent virologist, preferably with a focus on diagnostic or clinical virology. Awarded annually. Established in 1995 with a bequest by the late Prof. Philip Gardner.

2408 ■ Heine-Medin Award
To recognize scientific work that promotes understanding of viral diseases. Awarded annually to a promising young scientist who presents a paper at the Annual Meeting. Honors German orthopedic surgeon Jacob Von Heine and Swedish pediatrician Oscar Medin, both who made important contributions to recognizing poliomyelitis as a disease.

2409 ■ European Society for Surgery of Shoulder and Elbow (Societe Europeenne pour la Chirurgie de L'Epaule et du Coude)
Sylvie Noel, Sec.
50-52, Ave. Chanoine Cartellier
F-69230 St. Genis Laval, France
Ph: 33 1 472395301
Fax: 33 1 472395302
E-mail: secec@wanadoo.fr
URL: http://www.secec.org

2410 ■ Didier Patte Prize
For a piece of European scientific research of outstanding merit pertaining to the shoulder or the elbow. The author should be under the age of 45 years. A monetary prize of 3,000 Euros is awarded biennially in odd-numbered years. Established in 1992.

2411 ■ Ian Wolboumers Award
For physicians.

2412 ■ Federation Internationale de l'Art Photographique
Emile Wanderscheid, Pres.
37, rue du Chanzy
75011 Paris, France
Ph: 33 1 43723724
Fax: 33 1 43723728
E-mail: fiap@fiap.net
URL: http://www.fiap.net

2413 ■ World Cup
For recognition of outstanding photography in monochrome prints and color prints. Eligible to photography clubs; membership is not required. Prizes include: Clubs World Cup - for the best club; Gold Medal - for club coming in second; Silver Medal - for club coming in third; Bronze Medal - for club coming in fourth; and six Honourable Mentions for fifth through tenth place. Held annually. Established in 2006.

2414 ■ Festival du Film Court de Villeurbanne
Laurence Hughes, Managing Dir.
117 Cours Emile Zola
F-69100 Villeurbanne, France
Ph: 33 4 7893 4265
Fax: 33 4 7243 0962
E-mail: lezola@wanadoo.fr
URL: http://www.lezola.com

2415 ■ Festival du Film Court de Villeurbanne
To recognize the best French-spoken short film

Awards are arranged in alphabetical order below their administering organizations

made during the preceding year. The following prizes are awarded: Grand Prix de la Ville de Villeurbanne, Prix de Gnseil Regional, Prix Fuji, Prix Pyral, Prix du Public, and Prix TPS. Awarded annually. Established in 1980. Sponsored by the City of Villeurbanne, Region Rhone-Alpes Geonseil General du Rhone, France - Ministry of Culture and Communication, Centre National de la Cinematographie, and Groupement Regional d'Action Cinematographique.

2416 ■ Festival International de Musique de Besancon et de Franche-Comte
Square Saint-Amour
3 bis, rue leonel de Moustier
F-25000 Besancon, France
Ph: 33 8125 0585
Fax: 33 8181 5215
E-mail: contact@festival-besancon.com
URL: http://www.festival-besancon.com

2417 ■ Besancon International Competition for Young Conductors (Concours International de Jeunes Chefs d'Orchestre Besancon)
To recognize the aptitudes of young artists for conducting, rather than to check their technical knowledge. Individuals who are less than 35 years of age are eligible. A monetary prize and opportunities to conduct various orchestras are awarded annually. Established in 1951.

2418 ■ Besancon International Competition of Music Composition (Concours International de Composition Musicale)
To recognize an outstanding music composition for an orchestra. The contest is open to composers of any nationality who are under 40 years of age. Recipients are awarded Prize of the Festival of Besancon and a monetary prize. The piece that wins first place is played at the final session of the Young Conductors Contest of the Music Festival of Besancon the following year. Awarded annually. Established in 1988.

2419 ■ Festival International du Film de Vol Libre
Marie-Claude Previtali, Press Off.
Office du tourisme
102 route des 3 villages
F-38660 St. Hilaire du Touvet, France
Ph: 33 4 7608 3399
Fax: 33 4 7697 2056
E-mail: info@coupe-icare.org
URL: http://www.coupe-icare.org

2420 ■ International Free Flight Film Festival (Festival International du Film de Vol Libre)
For the promotion of all forms films dealing with air, wind, and flight. Film topics can include, but are not limited to: aerial sports, hot-air balloons, human-powered aircraft, sail planes, bungee jumping, base jumping, kites, boomerangs, motorized gliders, aerial acrobatics, and birds or related species. The following prizes are awarded: Grand Prix du Festival, Prix du Public, Prix de la Critique, Mention Special du Jury, Mention Reportage, Prize for the Best Film Script, Prize for the Best Artistic Film, Prize for the Best Documentary or News Film, and Prize for the Best Advertising Film. Trophies are awarded annually in September. Established in 1983.

2421 ■ Foundation for Medical Research
54, rue de Varenne
F-75335 Paris, France
Ph: 33 1 44 397575
Fax: 33 1 44 397586
URL: http://www.frm.org

2422 ■ Jean-Paul Binet Prize
To recognize an individual for outstanding cardiovascular or xenografts research. Awarded annually.

2423 ■ Grand Prize
To honor an individual for outstanding contributions to medical knowledge. Awarded annually.

2424 ■ Adrienne and Frederick Herbert Prize
To recognize an individual for outstanding research in leukemia, Alzheimer's disease, or childhood diseases. Awarded annually.

2425 ■ Rose Lamarca Prize
To recognize an individual for outstanding clinical research. Awarded annually.

2426 ■ Ana and John Paneboeuf Prize
To recognize an individual for outstanding research in leukemia. Awarded biennially in odd-numbered years.

2427 ■ Jacques Piraud Prize
To recognize an individual for outstanding research in the field of infections. Awarded annually.

2428 ■ Line Renaud Prize
To recognize an individual for outstanding research in virology, particularly AIDS. Awarded annually.

2429 ■ Lucien Tartois Prize
To recognize an individual for outstanding research in the fields of immunology, oncology, and virology. Awarded annually.

2430 ■ France Ministry of Defense
14, rue Saint Dominique
F-75700 Paris, France
Ph: 33 1 42193011
URL: http://www.defense.gouv.fr

2431 ■ Croix de Guerre
To recognize fighting units for feats of arms and acts of devotion. Civilians, men or women, towns, various institutions, in combat areas, and foreigners mentioned in Army orders as having rendered distinguished services in the front line are eligible. The holders of the Croix de Guerre do not constitute an order and have no degrees of rank; the number of clasps attached to the ribbon being the only token of special distinction. The medal, Florentine bronze, 35 millimeters in diameter, consists of a cross with four branches supported on two crossed swords. On the obverse, there is an effigy of the Republic wearing a Phrygian (Liberty) cap, a wreath of laurel, and the inscription "Republicque Francaise." On the reverse, there is the date. Established in 1915; confirmed in 1921 for Theaters of Overseas Operations and again in September 1939.

2432 ■ Medaille Militaire
To reward acts of bravery and distinguished military service by noncommissioned officers and soldiers. The award is by decree of the President of the Republic. Established in 1852.

2433 ■ Prix Science et Defense
For recognition of outstanding research work or studies which advance the science and technology in fields pertaining to national defense. A monetary prize is awarded annually. Established in 1983.

2434 ■ French Academy of Sciences (Academie des Sciences - Institut de France)
Alain Carpentier, Pres.
23 quai de Conti
F-75006 Paris, France
Ph: 33 1 44414366
Fax: 33 1 44414363
E-mail: alain.carpentier@academie-sciences.fr
URL: http://www.academie-sciences.fr

2435 ■ Grande Medaille
To recognize a French or foreign scholar who has contributed to the development of science. Awarded annually. Established in 1997.

2436 ■ French Chemical Society (Societe Francaise de Chimie)
Olivier Homolle, Pres.
28, rue Saint-Dominique
F-75007 Paris, France
Ph: 33 1 40467162
Fax: 33 1 40467163
E-mail: secretariat@societechimiquedefrance.fr
URL: http://www.societechimiquedefrance.fr

2437 ■ Grand Prix de Chimie Industrielle
To recognize an industrial researcher for an important contribution in the field of industrial chemistry. A monetary prize is awarded when merited. Established in 1988. Co-sponsored by the Societe de Chimie Industrielle. Formerly: Grand Prix de la Societe de Chimie.

2438 ■ Prix Le Bel
For recognition of research contributions in the field of stereo chemistry or on a subject of particular interest to Le Bel. A monetary prize is awarded annually. Established in 1942 in memory of Le Bel, a benefactor of the Society.

2439 ■ Prix Pierre Sue
For recognition in the field of chemistry. A prize is awarded annually. Established in 1964 in memory of Pierre Sue, Secretary General of the Society from 1962 to 1967.

2440 ■ French Diabetes Association (Association Francaise des Diabetiques)
88, rue de la Roquette
F-75544 Paris Cedex 11, France
Ph: 33 1 40092425
Fax: 33 1 40092030
E-mail: afd@afd.asso.fr
URL: http://www.afd.asso.fr

2441 ■ Prix Madame Gay
For a diabetic student or mother.

2442 ■ French League for Animal Rights Foundation (Fondation Ligue Francaise des Droits de l'Animal)
39, rue Claude Bernard
F-75005 Paris, France
Ph: 33 1 4707 9899
Fax: 33 1 4707 9998
E-mail: contact@fondation-droits-animal.org
URL: http://www.fondation-droits-animal.org

2443 ■ Prix de Biologie Alfred Kastler
To encourage research and experimental methods that are not traumatic for animals. French-speaking researchers in the fields of biology, medicine, pharmacy, and veterinary research are eligible. A monetary prize of 25,000 francs is awarded annually. Established in 1985 in memory of Professor Alfred Kastler, French winner of the 1966 Nobel Prize of Physics and president of the League from 1979 to 1984. Formerly: Prix Alfred Kastler.

2444 ■ French Ministry of Culture and Communication
Paul Rechter, Department Chief
Departement de l'information et de la communication
3, rue de Valois
F-75033 Paris Cedex 01, France
Ph: 33 1 4015 8120
Fax: 33 1 4015 8172
E-mail: point-culture@culture.gouv.fr
URL: http://www.culture.gouv.fr

2445 ■ Order of the Academic Palms (Palmes Academiques)
To reward distinguished service in public

Awards are arranged in alphabetical order below their administering organizations

education. The Order consists of the grades of Chevalier, Officer, and Commander. Nominees should have rendered at least 15 years of service in public education to be nominated for the grade of Chevalier and at least five years for the grades of Officer and Commander. Awarded semiannually. The Order was established on October 4, 1955, to replace the honorary distinctions of the Academic Palms, which had been founded in 1808.

2446 ■ French National Center for Scientific Research
(Centre national de la recherche scientifique)
Campus Gerard-Megie
3, Rue Michel-Ange
F-75794 Paris, France
Ph: 33 1 4496 4000
Fax: 33 1 4496 5390
URL: http://www.cnrs.fr

2447 ■ Bronze Medal
To recognize young researchers for their first work, usually a thesis, which shows promise and encourages them to continue their work. Research fields cover all disciplines. A bronze medal is awarded annually to approximately 40 researchers. Established in 1954.

2448 ■ Gold Medal
To recognize an internationally renowned scientist who has made an outstanding contribution to the advancement and worldwide impact of French research. Research fields cover all disciplines. A gold medal is awarded annually. Established in 1954.

2449 ■ Silver Medal
To recognize researchers in mid-career whose works are nationally and internationally renowned for their originality, quality, and importance. Research fields cover all disciplines. A silver medal is awarded annually to approximately 15 scientists. Established in 1954.

2450 ■ French Society for Metallurgy and Materials
(Societe Francaise de Metallurgie et de Materiaux)
Bruno Dubost, Chm.
250 rue Saint Jacques
F-75005 Paris, France
Ph: 33 1 46330800
Fax: 33 1 46330880
E-mail: sfmm@wanadoo.fr
URL: http://www.sf2m.asso.fr

2451 ■ Grande Medaille
For prominent accomplishment in the field of metallurgy or materials. Awarded annually. Established in 1949.

2452 ■ Medaille Jean Rist
To recognize young metallurgy or materials science specialists for their scientific or applied accomplishments in the field of materials. Awarded annually to four recipients. Established in 1949.

2453 ■ Geological Society of France
(Societe Geologique de France)
Christian Ravenne, Pres.
77, rue Claude-Bernard
F-75005 Paris, France
Ph: 33 1 43317735
Fax: 33 1 45357910
E-mail: accueil@sgfr.org
URL: http://sgfr.free.fr/index_gb.html

2454 ■ Prix Leon Bertrand
To recognize a geologist for work in the field of applied geology. Members of the Society are eligible. Awarded every four years. Established in 1949 by Leon Bertrand.

2455 ■ Prix Fontannes
To recognize the French author of the best strati-graphic work published during the last five years. A medal is awarded every four years. Established in 1888 by a bequest of F. Fontannes.

2456 ■ Prix Raymond et Madeleine Furon
For recognition in the field of endogenous geology. A medal is awarded every four years. Established in 1977 by Raymond Furon.

2457 ■ Prix Gosselet
For recognition of a work of applied geology in water management, the environment, or civil engineering. A medal is awarded every four years. Established in 1910 by Jules Gosselet.

2458 ■ Prix Prestwich
To encourage new research and to recognize one or several geologists, preferably by men or women from a country other than France, who have displayed a zeal for the progress of the science of geology. A medal is awarded every four years. Established in 1902 by a bequest of Sir J. Prestwich.

2459 ■ Prix Fondation Pierre Pruvost
For recognition in the field of structural geology. A medal is awarded every four years. Established in 1960 by Pierre Pruvost.

2460 ■ Prix van Straelen
To recognize the best paper in the field of either Earth surface or inner-Earth geology, with the topics alternating each year. A monetary prize of 2,287 Euros is awarded annually. Established in 1993 in memory of Professor Victor Van Straelen.

2461 ■ Prix Wegmann
For recognition of a work concerning the history of geology. Awarded periodically. Established in 1984 by a bequest of E. Wegmann.

2462 ■ Guilde Europeenne du Raid
Olivier Allard, Managing Dir.
11, rue de Vaugirard
F-75006 Paris, France
Ph: 33 1 4326 9752
Fax: 33 1 4634 7545
E-mail: infos@la-guilde.org
URL: http://www.la-guilde.org

2463 ■ International Adventure Film Festival
(Les Ecrans De L'Aventure)
For recognition of documentary 16mm films or videos about any kind of adventure, such as mountain expeditions, arctic travels, sailing races around the world, ballooning, underwater diving, speleology, outstanding sport performances, and any dramatic events that are milestones in adventurism. Within this framework, the festival attempts to bring together the best of recently produced or non released films from all parts of the world. Among the prizes awarded are: Toison d'Or for the best adventure documentary film; Jury's Special Prize; Jean-Marc Boivin Prize for the genuineness and ethical dimension of the adventure; Adventurer of the Year; Peter Bird's Trophy for perseverance and tenacity in an adventure; Alain Bombard Prize for adventure with a teaching value; Dijon Young Jury's Prize; and Young Director Prize. Held annually. Established in 1977. Sponsored by Dijon - Bourgogne. Formerly: Festival International du Film d'Aventure de la Plagne.

2464 ■ Human Rights Institute of the Bar of Bordeaux
(Institut des Droits de l'Homme du Barreau de Bordeaux)
Maison de l'Avocat
18-20 Rue du Marechal-Joffre
F-33000 Bordeaux, France
Ph: 33 556 442076
Fax: 33 656 791433
E-mail: idhbb@idhbb.org
URL: http://www.idhbb.org

2465 ■ Ludovic-Trarieux International Human Rights Prize
Awarded to a lawyer, regardless of nationality or Bar, who has encountered personal suffering through the defense of human rights, the supremacy of law, or the struggle against racism, and intolerance of any form. A monetary prize is awarded annually. Co-sponsored by the European Bar Human Rights Institute.

2466 ■ Institut de Biologie Physico-Chimique
Francis-Andre Wollman, Dir.
13, rue Pierre et Marie Curie
F-75005 Paris, France
Ph: 33 1 58415000
Fax: 33 1 58415020
E-mail: webmaster@ibpc.fr
URL: http://www.ibpc.fr

2467 ■ Nine Choucroun Prize
To recognize a young researcher for work in the field of physical-chemical biology. Researchers under 30 years of age are eligible. A monetary prize of 5,000 Euros is awarded biennially in even-numbered years. Established in 1980.

2468 ■ Pierre Gilles de Gennes Prize
To recognize a young researcher for outstanding achievement. Candidates must have received his or her doctorate in the previous two years. A monetary prize of 8,000 Euros is awarded biennially in odd-numbered years.

2469 ■ Institut de France
23, quai Conti
F-75006 Paris, France
Ph: 33 1 4441 4441
Fax: 33 1 4441 4341
E-mail: fondations@institut-de-france.fr
URL: http://www.institut-de-france.fr

2470 ■ Prix Jeanne Burdy
To recognize a painter. Awarded biennially on the recommendation of the Academie des Beaux-Arts by the Institut. Established in 1983.

2471 ■ Prix Hercule Catenacci
To encourage the publication of beautifully illustrated books of poetry, literature, history, archaeology, or music. Each of three Academies awards this prize annually.

2472 ■ Prix Jules et Louis Jeanbernat et Barthelemy de Ferrari Doria
To recognize a young French author for a book of literature, science, or art. The prize is awarded periodically by each of the five Academies. Established by Emmanuel Jeanbernat in memory of her two sons who died for France.

2473 ■ Prix Osiris
For recognition of a discovery or outstanding work in the field of science, literature, art, industry, or generally any field that affects the public. Awarded every three years by a special commission whose members are from each of the five Academies.

2474 ■ International Academy for Production Engineering
(College International pour la Recherche en Productique)
Prof. Didier Dumur, Sec. Gen./Treas.
9, rue Mayran
F-75009 Paris, France
Ph: 33 1 45262180
Fax: 33 1 45269215
URL: http://www.cirp.net
Formerly: International Institution for Production Engineering Research.

2475 ■ General Pierre Nicolau Award
For scientific and industrial contributions to a specific area within the field of production engineering. Awarded annually. Established in 2001.

Awards are arranged in alphabetical order below their administering organizations

2476 ■ F. W. Taylor Medal

To recognize younger research workers of outstanding merit who author original scientific research papers on topics falling within the fields of CIRP. Candidates for the award must have personally presented their research at a Paper Session during the two years preceding their nomination. Recipients are not to be over 35 years of age in the year of the presentation of their paper. A medal is awarded annually. Established in 1958.

2477 ■ International Academy of Comparative Law
28 rue Saint-Guillaume
F-75007 Paris, France
Ph: 33 1 44398629
Fax: 33 1 44398628
E-mail: secretariat@iuscomparatum.org
URL: http://www.iuscomparatum.org

2478 ■ Canada Prize

To recognize an original, critical work comparing common law and civil law systems. Work may be in French or English, and should be of high scientific quality and suitable for publication in monograph form. A monetary prize of C$10,000 is awarded every four years. Established in 1994.

2479 ■ International Agency for Research on Cancer
(Centre International de Recherche sur le Cancer)
Dr. Christopher Wild, Dir.
150, Cours Albert Thomas
F-69372 Lyon Cedex 08, France
Ph: 33 4 72738485
Fax: 33 4 72738575
URL: http://www.iarc.fr

2480 ■ Cancer Research Training Fellowship

To support junior scientists from low- or medium-resource countries who are committed to pursuing a career in cancer research. Candidates must have a Master's degree in an appropriate subject (medicine, epidemiology, biostatistics, genetics, or laboratory research) and wish to study for a PhD degree in the field of epidemiology or biostatistics in a research Group at IARC in Lyon. Awarded to several recipients annually.

2481 ■ Visiting Scientist Award for Senior Scientists

To support a qualified and experienced investigator with recent publications in international peer-reviewed scientific journals who wishes to spend from six to twelve months at the IARC working on a collaborative project in a research area related to the Agency's programs: epidemiology, biostatistics, environmental chemical carcinogenesis, cancer etiology and prevention, infection and cancer, molecular cell biology, molecular genetics, molecular pathology, and mechanisms of carcinogenesis. A grant up to US$80,000 is awarded annually.

2482 ■ International Association for Suicide Prevention
Dr. Lanny Berman, Pres.
La Barade
F-32330 Gondrin, France
Ph: 33 5 62291142
E-mail: iasp1960@aol.com
URL: http://www.iasp.info

2483 ■ De Leo Fund Award

To recognize outstanding research on suicidal behaviors in developing countries. Eligibility criteria include: born in a developing country; carried research out in a developing country; be a young or mid-career researcher (no more than 20 years from degree); and demonstrate competence in the field through international publications. Established to honor the memory of Nicola and Vittorio, beloved children of past IASP president Prof. Diego De Luna.

2484 ■ Farberow Award

To recognize an individual for significant contributions to the field of suicide survivors. Awarded biennially in odd-numbered years. Established in 1997. Honors Prof. Norman Farberow, a founding member and driving force behind the Association.

2485 ■ Ringel Service Award

For distinguished service in the field of suicidology. Awarded biennially in odd-numbered years. Established in 1995. Named in honor of Erwin Ringel, founding president of the Association.

2486 ■ Stengel Research Award

Recognizes outstanding research in the field of suicidology. Nominees must be active researchers with at least 10 years of scientific activity in the field who have authored or co-authored an international book. Awarded biennially in odd-numbered years. Established in 1977. Honors Prof. Erwin Stengel, on of the Association's founders.

2487 ■ International Association of Cancer Registries
Dr. David Forman, Exec. Sec.
150, cours Albert Thomas
69372 Lyon Cedex 08, France
Ph: 33 4 72738417
Fax: 33 4 72738575
E-mail: iacr@iarc.fr
URL: http://www.iacr.com.fr

2488 ■ Honorary Member

For recognition of achievement in the field of cancer registration. Nominations must be made by a member or members of the Association. A certificate is awarded annually at scientific meetings of the Association. Established in 1980.

2489 ■ International Association of Gerontology and Geriatrics
Prof. Bruno Vellas MD, Pres.
Faculte de Medecine
Institut du Vieillissement
37 Allees Jules Guesde
31000 Toulouse, France
Ph: 33 5 61145639
Fax: 33 5 61145640
E-mail: contact@iagg.info
URL: http://www.iagg.info

2490 ■ Ewald W. Busse Research Awards

To promote international research in gerontology. Awards shall be selected on an international basis. Two awards are given biennially, one recognizing a researcher from the social/behavioral sciences and the other from the biomedical sciences. Awards of US$4,000 plus $3,000 for travel expenses to the conference are supported from an endowment made by Gerontology International in honor of Ewald W. Busse M.D., past president of the Association and founding director of the Duke Aging Center. Established in 1987.

2491 ■ Hall of Great Names

To honor individuals who have made a significant difference in the study of aging. Awarded when merited.

2492 ■ Presidential Award

To recognize individuals who have contributed to the enhancement and dignity of the International Association of Gerontology through specific tasks, such as acting as former officers. The awards are presented to those devoted to enhancing the Association's international recognition, promoting research in the aging field, and

preserving the historical background of the Association. The President of the Association is responsible for the nomination. Established in 1993.

2493 ■ International Association of Hydrological Sciences
(Association Internationale des Sciences Hydrologiques)
Dr. Pierre Hubert, Sec. Gen.
Universite Pierre and Marie Curie
Case 105, 4 Pl. Jussieu
F-75252 Paris Cedex 05, France
Ph: 33 1 44272373
Fax: 33 1 44275125
E-mail: pjy.hubert@free.fr
URL: http://iahs.info

2494 ■ International Hydrology Prize

To recognize an individual who has made an outstanding contribution to hydrology such as confers on the candidate universal recognition of his international stature. The contribution should have an identifiable international dimension extending beyond both the country of normal work and the specific field of interest of the candidate. The contribution may have been made through scientific work, as evidenced by the publication in international journals of scientific literature of a high standard, and/or through practical work, as evidenced by reports of the projects concerned. Preference should be given to candidates who have contributed through both scientific and practical work. The Prize may be awarded to hydrologists of long international standing or to those who, while having gained such standing only recently, exhibit the qualities of international leadership in the science and practice of hydrology. An active involvement in the work of IAHS and other international organizations in the field of hydrology should be counted as an advantage. A silver medal is presented annually. Established in 1981. Sponsored by UNESCO and World Meteorological Organization.

2495 ■ Tison Award

To promote excellence in research by young hydrologists. Outstanding papers published by IAHS in a period of two years previous to the deadline for nominations are eligible. Candidates for the award must be under 41 years of age at the time their paper was published. A monetary prize of US$1,000 and a citation are awarded annually during either an IUGG/IAHS General Assembly or an IAHS Scientific Assembly.

2496 ■ International Association of Survey Statisticians
(Association Internationale des Statisticiens d'Enquetes)
Evelyne Coutant, Sec.
3 rue de la Cite
F-33500 Libourne, France
Ph: 33 5 57555607
Fax: 33 5 57555620
E-mail: evelyne.coutant@insee.fr
URL: http://isi.cbs.nl/iass/index.htm

2497 ■ Cochran-Hansen Prize

For a young statistician from a developing or transition country. Books and journals valued at 500 Euros are awarded biennially in odd-numbered years. Established in 1999.

2498 ■ International Astronautical Federation
(Federation Internationale d'Astronautique)
Mr. Philippe Willekens, Exec. Dir.
94 bis, Ave. de Suffren
75015 Paris, France
Ph: 33 1 45674260
Fax: 33 1 42732120
E-mail: secretariat.iaf@iafastro.org
URL: http://www.iafastro.com/index.html?title=Main_Page

Awards are arranged in alphabetical order below their administering organizations

2499 ■ Allan D. Emil Memorial Award
For recognition of an outstanding contribution in space science, space technology, space medicine, or space law which involved the participation of more than one nation and/or which furthered the possibility of greater international cooperation in astronautics. An IAF member society may make nominations. A monetary award of $1,000 US and a diploma are awarded annually during the IAF Congress. Established in 1977 in memory of Allan D. Emil.

2500 ■ Frank J. Malina Astronautics Medal
To recognize an educator who has demonstrated excellence in taking the fullest advantage of the resources available to promote the study of astronautics and related space sciences. Awarded annually.

2501 ■ Luigi G. Napolitano Award
To recognize a young scientist, below 30 years of age, who has contributed significantly to the advancement of the aerospace science. The individual must have presented a paper at the IAF Congress on this contribution. Awarded annually by the IAF Education Committee.

2502 ■ Student Awards
To recognize the best papers submitted by undergraduate and graduate students at the IAF Congress. Awarded annually.

2503 ■ International Automobile Federation
(Federation Internationale de l'Automobile)
Jean Todt, Pres.
8, Pl. de la Concorde
75008 Paris, France
Ph: 33 1 43124455
Fax: 33 1 43124466
E-mail: admin@fiacommunications.com
URL: http://www.fia.com/en-GB/Pages/HomePage.aspx

2504 ■ Championships, Cups, and Trophies
Championships recognize the winners of the following races: the European Rally Championship, the African Continent Rally Challenge, the Middle East Rally Championship, the Asia Pacific Rally Championship, the Asia-Pacific Touring Car, the GT Championship, the European Championships for Autocross and Rallycross Drivers, the European Hill Climb Championship and Challenge, the European Challenge for Historic Touring Cars, and the European Drag Racing Championship. The following cups and trophies are also awarded: the FIA World Cup for Cross Country Rallies, the FIA Marathon Trophy, the Touring Car World Cup, the European 1600 Cup for Autocross, the European Truck Racing Cup, the Electro Solar Cup, the FIA Intercontinental Formula 3 Cup, the European Trophy for Historic Sports Car, the Cup for Historic Grand Touring Cars, the Cup for Thoroughbred Grand Prix Cars, the Lurani Trophy for Formula Junior Class, the European Historic Rally Trophy, the Inter Nations Cup for Rallycross, Lurani Trophy for Formula Junior Cars, Trophy for Historic Regularity Rallies, and the European Drag Racing Championship.

2505 ■ Formula One World Champion
To recognize the winning driver of the Series of Formula One races. A prize is also given to the manufacturers. Established in 1950.

2506 ■ World Rally Champion
To recognize the winning driver of the World Rally and the manufacturer of the winning automobile.

2507 ■ International Competition of the City of Paris
(Concours Internationaux de la Ville de Paris)
5 Passage River
F-75011 Paris, France
Ph: 33 1 4033 4535

Fax: 33 1 4033 4538
E-mail: info@civp.com
URL: http://www.civp.com

2508 ■ Lily Laskine Harp Competition
To recognize outstanding harp performances. Open to individuals of any age from any country. Held every three years. Established in 1993.

2509 ■ International Consultative Research Group on Rapeseed
(Groupe Consultatif International de Recherche sur le Colza)
Dr. Petr Baranyk, Pres.
12 Ave. George
V-75008 Paris, France
Ph: 33 1 56895705
Fax: 33 1 56895704
E-mail: lot@cetiom.fr
URL: http://www.gcirc.cetiom.fr

2510 ■ International Rapeseed Award
This award, also known as the Eminent Scientist Award, recognizes scientific achievement in the framework of rapeseed research. A plaque is awarded quadrennially. Established in 1983.

2511 ■ International Council on Large Electric Systems
(Conseil International des Grands Reseaux Electriques)
Francois Meslier, Sec. Gen.
21 rue d'Artois
75 008 Paris, France
Ph: 33 1 53891290
Ph: 33 1 53891291
Fax: 33 1 53891299
E-mail: francois.meslier@cigre.org
URL: http://www.cigre.org

2512 ■ Distinguished Member
For distinguished members.

2513 ■ Honorary Member
For honorary members.

2514 ■ Technical Committee Award

2515 ■ International Council on Monuments and Sites
(Conseil International des Monuments et des Sites)
Gustavo Araoz, Pres.
49-51 rue de la Fed.
75015 Paris, France
Ph: 33 1 45676770
Fax: 33 1 45660622
E-mail: secretariat@icomos.org
URL: http://www.icomos.org

2516 ■ Gazzola Prize
(Prix Gazzola)
To recognize a person or group of persons whose life's work has furthered the aims and objectives of ICOMOS, and the defense of conservation and restoration of historic monuments and sites. Members of ICOMOS may be nominated. A monetary prize of US $10,000, a commemorative medal, and a diploma are awarded triennially on the occasion of the General Assembly of ICOMOS. Established in 1979 in honor of Piero Gazzola, one of the founders of ICOMOS and its first President.

2517 ■ Honorary Membership
To recognize individuals who have rendered distinguished service in the field of conservation, restoration, and enhancement of historical monuments, sites, and groups of buildings. Awarded triennially to one or more recipients. Established in 1975.

2518 ■ International Federation of Adapted Physical Activity
Claire Boursier, Pres.
58-60 avenue des landes
F-92150 Suresnes, France

Ph: 33 14097 4175
E-mail: claire.boursier@inshea.fr
URL: http://www.ifapa.biz

2519 ■ Elly D. Friedmann Award for Outstanding APA Contributions
To recognize an individual for long-standing leadership as well as outstanding academic and professional achievements in the field of adapted physical activity (APA). Awarded annually. Established in 1991.

2520 ■ Young Professional Award in Adapted Physical Activity
To encourage, recognize, and support young professionals interested in physical activity for people of all abilities. Candidates must be younger than 40 years of age. Each year, one award is presented by IFAPA and a second award by the local organizing committee of the Symposium. Awarded annually. Established in 1991.

2521 ■ International Federation of Classification Societies
Patrice Bertrand, Sec.
Universite Paris-Dauphine
Place du Marechal de Lattre de Tassigny
F-75775 Paris, France
E-mail: patrice.bertrand@ceremade.dauphine.fr
URL: http://www.classification-society.org

2522 ■ Chikio Hayashi Awards
To recognize young researchers with a promising track record in classification, data analysis, or related areas. Candidates must be under the age of 35 years. Up to five monetary prizes of $1,000 each are presented biennially in odd-numbered years.

2523 ■ International Fertilizer Industry Association
Luc Maene, Dir. Gen.
28 rue Marbeuf
F-75008 Paris, France
Ph: 33 1 53930500
Fax: 33 1 53930545
URL: http://www.fertilizer.org

2524 ■ International Crop Nutrition Award
To recognize an individual for research that has led to a significant and practical advance in the efficiency of fertilizer. Eligible to researchers from both the public and private sectors. Award alternates yearly between research relating to fertilizer use in industrialized and developing countries. Awarded annually.

2525 ■ Safety, Health, Environment Award
To recognize individual production sites for contributions and/or innovations that enhance safety, health, and environmental performance. Eligible only to members.

2526 ■ International Finn Association
Corinne McKenzie, Exec. Dir.
39 Rue du Portal d'Amont
F-66370 Pezilla-la-Riviere, France
Ph: 33 468 926046
Fax: 33 468 926046
E-mail: corinne.mckenzie@orange.fr
URL: http://www.finnclass.org

2527 ■ World Championship
To recognize an individual for achievement in sailing. The Finn Gold Cup is awarded annually in July. Established in 1956 by Tony Mitchell.

2528 ■ International Institute of Refrigeration
(Institut International du Froid)
Prof. E. Joachim Paul, Pres.
177 Blvd. Malesherbes
F-75017 Paris, France
Ph: 33 1 42273235

Awards are arranged in alphabetical order below their administering organizations

Fax: 33 1 47631798
E-mail: iif-iir@iifiir.org
URL: http://www.iifiir.org

2529 ■ Clarence Birdseye Young Researcher Award

To recognize a young researcher for outstanding work in the field of food science and engineering. Candidates must be 35 years of age or younger. A medal, certificate, and monetary prize of 800 Euros are awarded every four years. Established in 2001.

2530 ■ Sadi Carnot Young Researcher Award

To recognize a young researcher for outstanding work in the field of thermodynamics. Candidates must be 35 years of age or younger. A medal, certificate, and monetary prize of 800 Euros are awarded every four years. Established in 2001.

2531 ■ Alexis Carrel Young Researcher Award

To recognize a young researcher for outstanding work in the field of cryobiology or cryomedicine. Candidates must be 35 years of age or younger. A medal, certificate, and monetary prize of 800 Euros are awarded every four years. Established in 2001.

2532 ■ Willis H. Carrier Young Researcher Award

To recognize a young researcher for outstanding work in the field of air conditioning and heat pumps. Candidates must be 35 years of age or younger. A medal, certificate, and monetary prize of 800 Euros are awarded every four years. Established in 2001.

2533 ■ James Harrison Young Researcher Award

To recognize a young researcher for outstanding work in the field of refrigerated storage and transport. Candidates must be 35 years of age or younger. A medal, certificate, and monetary prize of 800 Euros are awarded every four years. Established in 2001.

2534 ■ James Joule Young Researcher Award

To recognize a young researcher for outstanding work in the field of systems and equipment for refrigeration. Candidates must be 35 years of age or younger. A medal, certificate, and monetary prize of 800 Euros are awarded every four years. Established in 2001.

2535 ■ Peter Kapitza Young Researcher Award

To recognize a young researcher for outstanding work in the field of cryophysics. Candidates must be 35 years of age or younger. A medal, certificate, and monetary prize of 800 Euros are awarded every four years. Established in 2001.

2536 ■ Gustav Lorentzen Medal

To honor an individual for outstanding and original achievements in academic or industrial research, innovation or development, in all fields of refrigeration, thus promoting creativity and renewal in the fields of competence of the IIR. Candidates are not limited to individuals from IIR member countries, however, active officers of the IIR are not eligible. Nomination shall be supported by a sponsor who is a member of an IIR commission. Winner will receive a medal, certificate, 8,000 Euros (minus travel expenses, accommodation costs and registration fees for the Congress, which the winner must attend, and at which winner may make a short speech). Awarded every four years. Established in 1997 to honor the memory of Prof. Gustav Lorentzen, Honorary President of the IIR.

2537 ■ Science and Technology Medal

To recognize an individual who, over an extended period of time, in science and/or technology in one of the fields of competence of the Institute. A medal, certificate, and monetary prize of 1,600 Euros are awarded every four years. Established in 2001.

2538 ■ Carl von Linde Young Researcher Award

To recognize a young researcher for outstanding work in the field of cryogenic engineering. Candidates must be 35 years of age or younger. A medal, certificate, and monetary prize of 800 Euros are awarded every four years. Established in 2001.

2539 ■ International Institute of Space Law
Tanja Masson-Zwaan, Pres.
94bis, Ave. de Suffren
75015 Paris, France
Ph: 33 1 45674260
Fax: 33 1 42732120
E-mail: cmj@advancingspace.com
URL: http://www.iislweb.org

2540 ■ Diederiks-Verschoor Award

To recognize the best paper accepted for presentation at the Institute's Colloquium by an author not older than 40 years and who has not published more than five papers in the Proceedings of IISL Colloquia. A monetary prize of 500 Euros is awarded annually. Established in 2001 in honor of Prof. Dr. Ph. Diederiks-Verschoor.

2541 ■ Manfred Lachs Trophy

To recognize the winner of the world finals of the Manfred Lachs Space Law Moot Court competition. Awarded annually. Established in 1992.

2542 ■ International Institute of Welding
(Institut International de la Soudure)
Mireille Aubert, Admin./Finance Asst.
90 rue des Vanesses
F-93420 Villepinte Cedex, France
Ph: 33 1 49903679
E-mail: m.aubert@iiwelding.org
URL: http://www.iiwelding.org

2543 ■ Yoshiaki Arata Award

Recognizes a person who has realized outstanding achievements in fundamental researches in welding science and technology and its allied areas and which has been recognized as a great contribution to the progress of welding engineering and related fields. A monetary prize of $5,000 is awarded annually.

2544 ■ Edstrom Medal

Recognizes persons who have made an exceptional and distinguished contribution which furthers, in a significant manner, the aims and objectives of the IIW. The contribution may be related to any aspect of IIW business and can come from individuals either actively engaged in the IIW or those who are not usually associated with IIW affairs. A medal is awarded as merited. Sponsored by the Swedish delegation.

2545 ■ Henry Granjon Prize

To recognize authors of papers devoted to research into welding technology or a related subject, ultimately to stimulate interest in welding and allied processes among young people. Papers (thesis, research reports, state-of-the-art surveys) must be single authored, based on recent work carried out in a University, other appropriate Institutions, or in Industry. The work must fall within four categories of technology related to joining, surfacing, or cutting: 1) Joining and fabrication technology; 2) Materials behavior and weldability; 3) Design and structural integrity; and 4) Human related subjects. A plaque is awarded annually in each category. Established in 1991 to honor Henri Granjon of Institut de Soudure, Paris.

2546 ■ Guerrera Prize

Recognizes one engineer or technician espe-

cially responsible for the Fabrication of an outstanding welded construction of particular interest. Judged from the point of view of design, or materials or fabrication methods. A gold medal and a diploma are awarded every three years. Established in 2000. Sponsored by the Italian Institute of Welding.

2547 ■ Andre Leroy Prize

Recognizes education in the field of welding. Awarded to large circulation multi media document, including video and computer programs, intended for use in education and training in any aspect of welding and allied processes, including brazing, hot spraying, thermal cutting, at any level, including engineers, technicians, and welders. A medal is awarded in even years. Established in 1980 in honor of Andre Leroy.

2548 ■ Evgenij Paton Prize

Recognizes an individual who has made a significant contribution to science and technology through their life time dedication. Work must be in the areas of applied research and development in the field of advanced technologies, materials and equipment for welding and allied processes. A medal, diploma, and a visit of E.O Pateon Electric Welding Institute in Kiev Ukraine are awarded every even year.

2549 ■ Arthur Smith Award

Given to an individual who has given dedicated service to the IIW which enabled the objective of the Institute to be significantly advanced. Recipients are individuals who have contributed to the activities of the Institute for a significant number of years, particularly in the work of Commissions. A silver plate is awarded annually.

2550 ■ Sossenheimer Software Innovation Award

To recognize the winner of a competition for modeling and simulation software documents covering any aspect of joining and allied processes which contribute to the improvement of quality/safety of joining, cutting, or surfacing operations. A monetary prize of 2,000 Euros and a medal is awarded. Prize-winning software is presented during the Annual Assembly Week. Established in 2001. Sponsored by the German Delegation.

2551 ■ Thomas Medal

Recognizes an individual who has been involved in IIW/ISO international standards activities. Requires the presentation of a lecture that illustrates the incorporation of global studies in the standardization of welding technology. A medal is awarded annually. Established in 1998.

2552 ■ International Meat Secretariat
Mr. Laurence Wrixon, Sec. Gen.
6 rue de la Victoire
F-75009 Paris, France
Ph: 33 1 45266897
Fax: 33 1 45266898
E-mail: info@meat-ims.org
URL: http://www.meat-ims.org/en/index.php

2553 ■ Prize for Meat and Technology

To recognize scientific and technological excellence in red meat research. Eligible to individuals or groups. Individual, or lead scientist if a group, must be 40 years old or younger. A monetary prize of $5,000 is awarded annually.

2554 ■ International Music Council
(Conseil International de la Musique)
Frans de Ruiter, Pres.
1, rue Miollis
75732 Paris Cedex 15, France
Ph: 33 1 45684850
Fax: 33 1 45684866
E-mail: imc@unesco.org
URL: http://www.imc-cim.org

Awards are arranged in alphabetical order below their administering organizations

2555 ■ International Music Award

Recognizes international excellence in music. Awards are organized in collaboration with the Haydn Festival at the Esterhazy Palace in Eisenstadt, Austria and the International Music Centre in Vienna, Austria. This award replaces, and continues, the former IMC/UNESCO International Music Prize.

2556 ■ International Professional Hairdressing Magazines Association
(Association Internationale Presse Professionelle Coiffure)
5, rue Boudreau
F-75009 Paris, France
E-mail: info@aipp.net
URL: http://www.aipp.net

2557 ■ Grand Trophy Award

To recognize outstanding achievement by professional hairdressers in the photography and presentation of their work. Open to hairdressers from around the world. Awards are presented in five categories: Avant-Garde Fashion Collection, Commercial Collection, Best Photograph, Men's Collection, and Best Video. The overall winner receives the Grand Trophy. Awarded annually. Established in 1997.

2558 ■ International Radiation Protection Association
Mr. Jacques Lochard, Exec. Off.
28 rue de la Redoute
F-92260 Fontenay-aux-Roses, France
Ph: 33 1 55521920
Fax: 33 1 55521921
E-mail: irpa.exof@irpa.net
URL: http://www.irpa.net

2559 ■ Rolf M. Sievert Award

For recognition of contributions to radiological protection. A monetary prize and a certificate are awarded at the International IRPA Congress, which is held every three or four years. Established in 1973 in honor of Rolf Sievert.

2560 ■ International Real Estate Federation - France
(Federation Internationale des Professions Immobilieres)
Alexander Romanenko, Pres.
17 rue Dumont d'Urville
F-75116 Paris, France
Ph: 33 1 73795830
Fax: 33 1 73795833
E-mail: info@fiabci.org
URL: http://www.fiabci.com

2561 ■ Prix d'Excellence

Given to those outstanding real estate developments which show excellence in all aspects of their creation from initial design through construction, financials, marketing, community benefit and environmental impact. Awards are made each year in a maximum of seven categories (residential, retail, office-industrial, public sector, rural, specialized, leisure), and are presented at the annual FIABCI World Congress in May annually.

2562 ■ International Social Science Council
(Conseil International des Sciences Sociales)
Dr. Heide Hackmann, Exec. Dir.
UNESCO House
1 rue Miollis
F-75732 Paris Cedex 15, France
Ph: 33 1 45684860
Fax: 33 1 45667603
E-mail: issc@worldsocialscience.org
URL: http://www.worldsocialscience.org

2563 ■ Mattei Dogan Prize

To recognize an individual for outstanding contributions to interdisciplinary excellence within the social sciences. A monetary prize of US $5,000 is awarded when merited.

2564 ■ Stein Rokkan Prize in Comparative Social Science Research

For recognition of a contribution in comparative social science research in either manuscript or book form; and to encourage younger scholars. Submissions cab be either an unpublished manuscript of book length or a printed book or collected works published within the past two years. Candidates must be under 40 years of age at the time of the award presentation. The laureate receives a diploma and a cash prize of 5,000 Euros. Awarded biennially in even-numbered years jointly by the International Social Science Council and the Conjunto Universitario Candido Mendes of Brazil. Established in 1980.

2565 ■ International Speech Communication Association
Isabel Trancoso, Pres.
4 Rue des Fauvettes - Lous Tourils
F-66390 Baixas, France
E-mail: secretariat@isca-speech.org
URL: http://www.isca-speech.org

2566 ■ Best Paper Published in the Speech Communication Journal

To recognize the best paper published in the *Speech Communication Journal*. Awarded annually.

2567 ■ Best Student Paper Award

To recognize the best student paper on speech communications. Awarded annually.

2568 ■ Medal for Scientific Achievement

To recognize scientific achievement in speech communication. Awarded annually at the Eurospeech Conference.

2569 ■ Special Service Medal

To acknowledge those scientists instrumental in promoting the Association. Awarded as merited.

2570 ■ International Sunflower Association
Mr. Carlos Feoli, Pres.
12 Ave. George V
75008 Paris, France
Ph: 33 56 895705
Fax: 33 56 895704
E-mail: lot@cetiom.fr
URL: http://www.isa.cetiom.fr

2571 ■ V. S. Pustovoit Award

To recognize outstanding contributions in theoretical or applied research in any field dealing with sunflowers (for example, but not limited to: genetics, breeding, physiology, chemistry, phytopathology, crop science, entomology, weed science, oil technology, etc.) that have stimulated the development of the sunflower crop and enriched the literature. A plaque will normally be awarded every four years, to coincide with the International Sunflower Conference. Established in 1979.

2572 ■ International Union Against Tuberculosis and Lung Disease
(Union Internationale Contre la Tuberculose et les Maladies Respiratoires)
Dr. S.B. Squire, Pres.
68 Blvd. St. Michel
F-75006 Paris, France
Ph: 33 1 44320360
Fax: 33 1 43299087
E-mail: union@iuatld.org
URL: http://www.theunion.org

2573 ■ Princess Chichibu Memorial TB Global Award

To a person who has shown great achievements in anti-tuberculosis activities. A monetary prize of $10,000 is awarded annually.

2574 ■ Honorary Member

To recognize an individual who has distinguished himself or herself in active participation in the Union's activities and fulfillment of its goals. Awarded when merited.

2575 ■ Scientific Prize

To recognize a young researcher (under 45 years of age) for his or her work on tuberculosis or non-tuberculosis lung disease published in the previous two years. A monetary prize of US$2,000 is awarded annually.

2576 ■ Stop TB Partnership/Kochon Prize

To recognize an individual, institution, or organization for a great achievement in combating tuberculosis, contribution toward the formulation and implementation of a system or policy for anti-tuberculosis, or contribution to education and training for the prevention of tuberculosis. A medal and monetary prize of at least US$65,000 are awarded annually. Established in 2006. Sponsored by the Kochon Foundation and the Stop TB Partnership.

2577 ■ Karel Styblo Public Health Prize

To recognize a health worker for his or her contribution to tuberculosis control or non-tuberculosis lung disease. A monetary prize of US$2,000 is awarded annually.

2578 ■ The Union Medal

To members who have made outstanding contributions to the control of tuberculosis or non-tuberculosis lung disease. Awarded annually.

2579 ■ International Union for Electricity Applications
(Union Internationale pour les applications d l'electricite)
5, rue Chante-Coq
F-92808 Puteaux Cedex, France
Ph: 33 1 41265648
Fax: 33 1 41265649
E-mail: uie@uie.org
URL: http://www.uie.org

2580 ■ UIE Electroheat Prize for Young Engineers

For outstanding young engineers.

2581 ■ International Union for the Scientific Study of Population
(Union Internationale pour l'Etude Scientifique de la Population)
Peter McDonald, Pres.
3-5 rue Nicolas
F-75980 Paris Cedex 20, France
Ph: 33 1 56062173
Fax: 33 1 56062204
E-mail: iussp@iussp.org
URL: http://www.iussp.org

2582 ■ IUSSP Laureates

To honor a member who gave an outstanding contribution to the advancement of the population sciences and rendered distinguished service. Awarded annually. Established in 1991.

2583 ■ International Union of Architects
(Union Internationale des Architectes)
Louise Cox, Pres.
Tour Maine Montparnasse - B.P. 158
33 Ave. du Maine
75755 Paris, France
Ph: 33 1 45243688
Fax: 33 1 45240278
E-mail: uia@uia-architectes.org
URL: http://www.uia-architectes.org

2584 ■ Sir Patrick Abercrombie Prize

For recognition of outstanding work in the field of town planning or territorial development. Awarded triennially at the Congress of the Union. Established in 1961 in memory of Sir Patrick Abercrombie, first president of the UIA.

2585 ■ Gold Medal for Outstanding Architectural Achievement

This, the highest individual award of the UIA, is bestowed upon an architect or group of architects for outstanding contributions to architecture and

---

Awards are arranged in alphabetical order below their administering organizations

design excellence over an extended period of time. A jury of international renown selects the Gold Medalist from nominations submitted by UIA National Sections. A gold medal is awarded triennially. Established in 1984.

2586 ■ Sir Robert Matthew Prize
For recognition of an outstanding improvement in the quality of human settlements. Awarded triennially at the Congress of the Union. Established in 1978 in memory of Sir Robert Matthew, a past president of the UIA.

2587 ■ Auguste Perret Prize
For recognition of a project which is particularly remarkable for applied technology in architecture. Awarded triennially at the Congress of the Union. Established in 1961 in memory of Auguste Perret, a past honorary president of the UIA.

2588 ■ Jean Tschumi Prize
For recognition of architectural criticism or architectural education. Awarded triennially at the Congress of the Union. Established in 1967 in memory of John Tschumi, a past president of the UIA.

2589 ■ International Union of Laboratories and Experts in Construction Materials, Systems and Structures
(Reunion Internationale des Laboratoires et Experts des Materiaux, Systemes de Constructions et Ouvrages)
Dr. Peter Richner, Pres.
157 rue des Blains
F-92220 Bagneux, France
Ph: 33 1 45361020
Fax: 33 1 45366320
E-mail: sg@rilem.org
URL: http://www.rilem.net

2590 ■ Robert L'Hermite Medal
To recognize an author of less than 40 years who has made a written contribution of outstanding quality in the scientific journal *Materials and Structures*. Awarded annually. Established in 1975.

2591 ■ NCC Partners
25, Cours d'Estienne d'Orves
F-13001 Marseille, France
Ph: 33 491 315217
Fax: 33 491 143199
URL: http://www.imgawards.com

2592 ■ International Mobile Gaming Awards
To recognize the most innovative and creative mobile games in the world. Presented in six categories: Excellence in Design, Excellence in Game Play, Best Casual Game, Best Real World Game, Most Innovative Game, and Best Sports Game. Awarded annually. Established in 2004.

2593 ■ Observ'ER
(Observatoire des Energies Renouvelables)
146 rue de L 'Universite
F-75007 Paris, France
Ph: 33 1 44180080
Fax: 33 1 44180036
E-mail: observ.er@energies-renouvelables.org
URL: http://observ-er.org/accueil_observ-er.asp

2594 ■ Habitat Solaire, Habitat d'aujourd'hui
For recognition of individuals who have constructed or occupied buildings created successfully by solar architecture principles. Awards are given for individual houses, apartment housing and all types of professional buildings. Co-sponsored by Observ'ER, Ademe, the French Ministry of Environment, the Camif Group and Electricite de France. Held annually. Formerly: (1998) Maisons solaire, maisons, d'aujourd'hui.

2595 ■ Prix Theophraste Renaudot
Tour Eve
3610 La Defense
F-92800 Puteaux, France

E-mail: celine-albin.faivre@club-internet.fr
URL: http://prixrenaudot.free.fr

2596 ■ Prix Theophraste Renaudot
To provide recognition for a novelist showing talent and originality. Novels published during the preceding year are considered by a jury of 10 members. A luncheon in the winner's honor and honorary recognition are awarded annually at the Restaurant Drouan at the same time as the Prix Goncourt. Established in 1925.

2597 ■ Rencontres Internationales de la Photographie
Francois Barre, Pres.
10 rond point des Arenes
F-13200 Arles, France
Ph: 33 9096 7606
Fax: 33 9049 9439
E-mail: info@rencontres-arles.com
URL: http://www.rencontres-arles.com

2598 ■ Contemporary Book Award
To recognize the author of the best contemporary photography book of the year. The prize aims to promote the quality of photography publishing and to encourage production. A monetary prize of 8,000 Euros is awarded annually. Established in 1974.

2599 ■ Discovery Award
To recognize a photographer or artist making use of photography whose work has been recently discovered, or deserves to be discovered, in the international level. A monetary prize of 25,000 Euros is awarded annually.

2600 ■ Historical Book Award
To recognize the best documented book on photography. Entries may be either thematic or monographic. A monetary prize of 8,000 Euros is awarded annually. Established in 2007.

2601 ■ Sauve Qui Peut le Court Metrage
Jean-Claude Saurel, Pres.
6 place Michel-de-L'Hospital
F-63058 Clermont-Ferrand Cedex 1, France
Ph: 33 473 916573
Fax: 33 473 921193
E-mail: info@clermont-filmfest.com
URL: http://www.clermont-filmfest.com

2602 ■ Clermont-Ferrand International Short Film Festival
(Festival International du Court Metrage de Clermont-Ferrand)
To recognize short films in the international competition. The following prizes are awarded: Grand Prize; Audience Prize, Special Jury Prize, Best Soundtrack Creation, Best Animation Film, Canal+ Award, Youth Jury Prize, Press Prize, and Special Mentions of the Jury. Held annually. Established in 1988.

2603 ■ Clermont-Ferrand National Short Film Festival
(Festival National du Court Metrage de Clermont-Ferrand)
To recognize short films in the national competition. The following prizes are awarded: Grand Prize; Audience Prize, Special Jury Prize, Best First Film, Best Actor and Actress, Best Soundtrack Creation, Best Animation Film, Canal+ Award, Procirep's Award for Best Producer, FNAC Award, Youth Jury Prize, Press Prize, and Special Mentions of the Jury. Held annually. Established in 1978.

2604 ■ Societe Astronomique de France
Philippe Morel, Chm.
3, rue Beethoven
F-75016 Paris, France
Ph: 33 1 42241374
Fax: 33 1 42307547
E-mail: ste.astro.france@wanadoo.fr
URL: http://www2.saf-lastronomie.com

2605 ■ Medaille des Soixantenaire et Fondation Manley-Bendall
To recognize individuals who have been members of the Society for sixty years. A bronze medal is awarded annually. Established in 1957.

2606 ■ Prix Georges Bidault de l'Isle
To encourage young people who show a special talent for astronomy or meteorology. Individuals are chosen from participants at courses and conferences, collaboration at the Observatory, or through communications in the bulletin during the preceding year. A bronze medal is awarded annually. Established in 1925.

2607 ■ Plaquette du Centenaire de Camille Flammarion
For recognition of long and continuous service to the Society. A silver plaque is awarded annually. Established in 1956.

2608 ■ Prix Gabrielle et Camille Flammarion
For recognition of an important discovery and marked progress in astronomy or in a sister science, to aid an independent researcher, or to assist a young researcher to begin work in astronomy. A silver medal is awarded annually. Established in 1930.

2609 ■ Prix Edmond Girard
To encourage a beginning vocation in astronomy or scientific exploration of the sky above the Observatoire de Juvisy. A medal is awarded annually. Established in 1974.

2610 ■ Prix Marius Jacquemetton
For recognition of a work or research by a member of the Society, a student, or a young astronomer. A silver medal is awarded annually.

2611 ■ Prix Jules Janssen
This, the highest award of the Society, is given for recognition of outstanding work in the field of astronomy. The award is given alternately to a professional French astronomer and a foreign one. A medal is awarded annually. Established in 1897.

2612 ■ Prix Dorothea Klumpke - Isaac Roberts
To encourage the study of the wide and diffuse nebulae of William Herschel, the obscure objects of Barnard, or the cosmic clouds of R.P. Hagen. A silver medal is awarded biennially in even-numbered years. Established in 1931.

2613 ■ Medaille des Anciens Presidents
For recognition of past presidents of the Society when they leave office. A silver medal is awarded every three years.

2614 ■ Prix Marcel Moye
To encourage a young member of the Society for his or her observations. Individuals must be 25 years of age or less. A silver medal is awarded annually. Established in 1946.

2615 ■ Prix des Dames
To recognize women for service to the Society. A silver medal is awarded annually. Established in 1897 by three women.

2616 ■ Prix Henri Rey
For recognition of an important work in astronomy. A silver medal is awarded annually. Established in 1926.

2617 ■ Prix Julien Saget
To recognize an amateur for his or her remarkable astronomic photography. A bronze medal is awarded annually. Established in 1969.

2618 ■ Prix Viennet-Damien
For recognition of a beautiful piece of optics or

Awards are arranged in alphabetical order below their administering organizations

for some work in this branch of astronomy. A silver medal is awarded in odd-numbered years when merited, alternating with the Prix Dorothea Klumpke-Isaac Roberts.

2619 ■ Societe de Chimie Therapeutique
Herve Galons, Sec. Gen.
5 rue Jean-Baptiste Clement
F-92296 Chatenay-Malabry Cedex, France
Ph: 33 1 46835684
E-mail: sct@sct.asso.fr
URL: http://www.sct-asso.fr

2620 ■ Lecon Paul Ehrlich
To enable a well-known scientist to deliver a lecture on new trends in medicinal chemistry. A monetary prize of 3,500 Euros is awarded annually. Established in 1989 in honor of Paul Ehrlich, a great scientist in medicinal chemistry.

2621 ■ Prix Charles Mentzer
To recognize a researcher or a team of researchers for work in the field of therapeutic chemistry. Members of the Society may submit nominations. A monetary prize of 3,500 Euros is awarded biennially in even-numbered years. Established in 1971 in honor of Charles Mentzer, a researcher in therapeutic chemistry.

2622 ■ Prix d'Encouragement a la Recherche en Chimie Therapeutique
To provide encouragement for a young researcher in therapeutic chemistry to create new medicines. Candidates must be aged 36 years or younger. A monetary prize of 3050 Euros is awarded annually. Established in 1984.

2623 ■ Societe de Pathologie Exotique
Ambroise Thomas, Pres.
28, rue du Docteur-Roux
F-75724 Paris, France
Ph: 33 1 45668869
Ph: 33 1 45688222
Fax: 33 1 45664485
E-mail: socpatex@pasteur.fr
URL: http://www.pathexo.fr

**2624 ■ Gold Medal
(Medaille d'Or)**
For recognition of exceptional merit in the field of exotic pathology. A medal is awarded periodically at the convention of the Society. Established in 1908.

**2625 ■ Research Grant
(Bourse de la SPE)**
To encourage a young researcher in the field of pathology. A monetary prize of is awarded every two years. Established in 1997.

2626 ■ Societe des Auteurs, Compositeurs et Editeurs de Musique
Jean-Luc Vialla, Exec. Dir.
225, av. Charles de Gaulle
F-92528 Neuilly-sur-Seine, France
Ph: 33 1 47154715
E-mail: drim@sacem.fr
URL: http://www.sacem.fr

2627 ■ Grand Prix de la Chanson Francaise
For recognition of the best French songwriter. A monetary prize and a medal are awarded annually in December. Established in 1982.

2628 ■ Grand Prix de la Musique Symphonique
For recognition in the field of symphonic music. A monetary prize and a medal are awarded annually in December. Established in 1982.

2629 ■ Grand Prix de l'Edition Musicale
To recognize a French music publisher. A medal is awarded annually in December. Established in 1984.

2630 ■ Grand Prix de l'Humour
For recognition in the field of comedy. A monetary prize and a medal are awarded annually in December. Established in 1983.

2631 ■ Grand Prix des Poetes
For recognition in the field of poetry. A monetary prize and a medal are awarded annually in December. Established in 1982. Formerly: Grand Prix de la Poesie.

2632 ■ Grand Prix du Jazz
To recognize an outstanding jazz composer. A monetary prize and a medal are awarded annually in December. Established in 1982.

**2633 ■ Society of Dramatic Authors and Composers
(Societe des Auteurs et Compositeurs Dramatiques)**
Pascal Rogard, Dir. Gen.
9 Rue Ballu
F-75009 Paris Cedex 09, France
Ph: 33 1 40234455
E-mail: international@sacd.fr
URL: http://www.sacd.fr

2634 ■ Grand Prix
To recognize the most outstanding playwright or a composer on the basis of his entire dramatic work. A monetary prize is awarded annually.

2635 ■ Henri Jeanson Prize
To honor an author whose humor and dramatic power perpetuate the memory of one of the most famous authors and dialogue writers of French cinema. Awarded annually. Established in 2004.

2636 ■ Prix Nouveau Talent
To recognize new talent in theatre, music, cinema, television, radio, and dance. Monetary prizes are awarded annually in each category.

2637 ■ Maurice Yvain Prize
To recognize an outstanding composer of light music and operetta. Awarded annually. Established in 1976.

**2638 ■ UNESCO
Intergovernmental Oceanographic Commission
(Commission Oceanographique Intergouvernementale)**
Javier Valladares, Chm.
1 rue Miollis
F-75015 Paris Cedex 15, France
Ph: 33 1 45683984
Fax: 33 1 45685810
E-mail: ioc.secretariat@unesco.org
URL: http://ioc-unesco.org

2639 ■ Innovative Coastal Research Grants
For innovative research projects finding solutions to local problems.

2640 ■ Travel Grants
To a marine student/professional from a developing country to participate in a scientific/technical conference, workshop or meeting with a clearly defined ocean oriented nature.

2641 ■ Union des Annonceurs
Loic Armand, Pres.
53, Ave. Victor Hugo
F-75116 Paris, France
Ph: 33 1 45007910
Fax: 33 1 45005579
E-mail: infos@uda.fr
URL: http://www.uda.fr

2642 ■ Phenix UDA
For recognition of the actions of the most highly skilled sponsors of enterprises for their undertakings, and to promote new techniques of communication and new talents among those who daily witness the increasing integration of enterprises into the life of the city. Awards are given in the following categories: culture, heritage, humanitarian causes, audiovisual programs, adventure, sport, education, and environment. A

trophy is awarded annually in each category as well as honorable mention and Special Jury Prizes.

**2643 ■ Union of International Fairs
(Union des Foires Internationales)**
Mr. Paul Woodward, Managing Dir.
35 bis, rue Jouffroy d'Abbans
F-75017 Paris, France
Ph: 33 1 42679912
Fax: 33 1 42271929
E-mail: info@ufi.org
URL: http://www.ufinet.org

2644 ■ ICT Award
To recognize the best exhibition industry initiatives related to information and communication technologies (ICT). Awarded annually. Established in 2008.

2645 ■ Marketing Award
To honor the best marketing initiatives undertaken by exhibition professionals. Open to members and non-members. Awarded annually. Established in 2001.

2646 ■ Operations Award
To recognize the best exhibition industry initiatives connected to operations issues, and to honor those in the industry who have successfully implemented creative and results-oriented initiatives. Awarded annually.

**2647 ■ United Nations Educational, Scientific and Cultural Organization
(Organisation des Nations Unies pour l'Education, la Science et la Culture)**
Irina Bokova, Dir. Gen.
7, pl. de Fontenoy
F-75352 Paris, France
Ph: 33 1 45681000
E-mail: bpi@unesco.org
URL: http://www.unesco.org/new/en/unesco

2648 ■ Bilbao Prize for the Promotion of a Culture of Human Rights
To recognize the efforts of institutions, organizations, and individuals that have made a particularly important and effective contribution to the promotion of a culture of human rights at regional and international levels. A monetary prize of US$20,000 and a trophy are awarded biennially in even-numbered years. Established in 1978 on the occasion of the 30th anniversary of the Universal Declaration of Human Rights. Formerly: UNESCO Prize for Human Rights Education.

2649 ■ Carlos J. Finlay Prize
To promote research and development in microbiology by rewarding a person or group of persons for an outstanding contribution in that field. Member states of UNESCO make the nominations. A monetary prize of $5,000 and a silver medal are awarded biennially in odd-numbered years coinciding with the year of UNESCO's General Conference. Established in 1980 in memory of Carlos J. Finlay, a Cuban scientist whose discoveries led to the conquest of yellow fever.

2650 ■ Felix Houphouet-Boigny Peace Prize
To honor individuals, bodies, or institutions that have made a significant contribution to promoting, seeking, safeguarding, or maintaining peace through education, science, and culture. Nominations may be made by Member States and nongovernmental organizations as well as other specified groups. A monetary prize of 150,000 Euros, a gold medal, and a certificate are awarded annually. Established in 1989.

2651 ■ Javed Husain Prize for Young Scientists
For recognition of outstanding pure or applied research carried out by young scientists. Eligible

Awards are arranged in alphabetical order below their administering organizations

applicants include individuals who, in the opinion of the jury, have done the most to advance the progress of scientific research as judged by the quality of their publications and/or patents; or individuals whose age does not exceed 35 years at the time of announcement of the Prize. Research specifically aimed at the development of weapons or other military devices shall not be considered for the Prize. A monetary prize representing half the biennial interest earned from the Fund, a medal, and a certificate are awarded biennially in odd-numbered years. Established in 1987 by a donation made by Dr. Javed Husain, an Indian physicist who has held university professional posts in Saudi Arabia and the United States.

2652 ■ The International Jose Marti Prize
In recognition of an activity of outstanding merit in accordance with the ideals and spirit of Jose Marti (Struggle for Liberty) contributing to unity and integration of countries in Latin America/Caribbean; and the preservation of identities. A monetary prize of $5,000 is awarded biennially in odd-numbered years to coincide with the meeting of the General Conference. Established in 1995 in honor of the centenary of the death of Jose Marti.

2653 ■ International Simon Bolivar Prize
For recognition of activity of outstanding merit that, in accordance with the ideals of Simon Bolivar, has contributed to the freedom, independence, and dignity of peoples and to the strengthening of solidarity among nations; and has fostered their development or facilitated the establishment of a new international economic, social, and cultural order. Such activity may take the form of intellectual or artistic creation, a social achievement, or the mobilization of public opinion. A monetary prize of US$25,000 is awarded every four years. Established in 1978. Sponsored by the Government of Venezuela.

2654 ■ Kalinga Prize for the Popularization of Science
For recognition of outstanding interpretation of science to the general public. Persons actively involved in the promotion of public understanding of science and technology are eligible. National Commissions for UNESCO make the nominations. A monetary prize of US$20,000, a medal, and a plaque are awarded biennially in odd-numbered years. Established in 1952 by Mr. B. Patnaik, an Indian industrialist. The prize is named after the ancient Indian emperor who in the second century BC renounced war and devoted his power to the development of science, culture, and education.

2655 ■ Sultan Qaboos Prize for Environmental Preservation
For recognition of outstanding contributions by individuals, groups of individuals, institutes, or organizations in the management or preservation of the environment, consistent with the policies, aims, and objectives of UNESCO, and in relation to the organization's programs in this field (i.e., environmental and natural resources research, environmental education and training, creation of environmental awareness through the preparation of environmental information materials, and activities aimed at establishing and managing protected areas such as Biosphere Reserves and Natural World Heritage Sites). A monetary prize of US$30,000 is awarded biennially in odd-numbered years. Established in 1989.

2656 ■ UNESCO Award for Distinguished Services to Physical Education and Sport
For recognition of distinguished services to physical education and sport in accordance with the principles of the International Charter of Physical Education and Sport adopted by the General Conference of UNESCO at its twentieth

session. The award is given in two different categories: to an institution or body that has made an outstanding contribution to the development of physical education and sport for all; and to a person who, by his or her active participation, has made a significant contribution to the development of physical education and sport for all. Candidates are selected by the Member States of UNESCO. A diploma of honor and medal are awarded biennially. Established in 1985.

2657 ■ UNESCO Award of Excellence for Handicrafts
To encourage and sustain the production of handicrafts using traditional skills. Established in 2001. Formerly: (2005) UNESCO Crafts Prize.

2658 ■ UNESCO Prize for Peace Education
For recognition of a particularly outstanding example of activity designed to alert public opinion and mobilize the conscience of mankind in the cause of peace. The following criteria are considered: the mobilization of the consciences in the cause of peace; the implementation, at international or regional level, of programs of activity designed to strengthen peace education by enlisting the support of public opinion; the launching of important activities contributing to the strengthening of peace; education action to promote human rights and international understanding; the promotion of public awareness of the problems of peace through the media and other effective channels; and any other activity recognized as essential to the construction of the defenses of peace in the minds of men. Member states of UNESCO, intergovernmental organizations, non-governmental organizations granted consultative status with UNESCO, and persons whom the Director-General deems qualified in the field of peace may nominate an individual, a group of individuals, or an organization considered to merit the distinction of this Prize by virtue of their activities. A monetary prize is awarded biennially in even-numbered years. Established in 1981 by the Japan Shipbuilding Industry Foundation.

2659 ■ UNESCO Science Prize
To recognize a person or group of persons for an outstanding contribution, through the application of science and technology, to the development of a developing member state or region, especially in the fields of scientific and technological research and education, or in the fields of engineering and industrial development. Nomination is by governments of UNESCO member states and non-governmental organizations having consultative status with UNESCO. A monetary prize of $15,000, a medal, and a plaque are awarded biennially in odd-numbered years. Established in 1968.

2660 ■ Vieilles Maisons Francaises
Philippe Toussaint, Pres.
93, rue de l'Universite
F-75007 Paris, France
Ph: 33 1 4062 6171
Fax: 33 1 4551 1226
E-mail: revue@vmf.net
URL: http://www.vmf.net

2661 ■ Concours Annuel de Sauvegarde
For recognition of outstanding contributions to the safeguarding of old French houses. A monetary prize of 15,000 Euros is awarded annually. Established in 1966.

2662 ■ World Association of Newspapers
(Association Mondiale des Journaux)
Mr. Gavin O'Reilly, Pres.
7 Rue Geoffroy St. Hilaire
F-75005 Paris, France
Ph: 33 1 47428500

Ph: 33 1 47428539
Fax: 33 1 47424948
E-mail: contact_us@wan.asso.fr
URL: http://www.wan-press.org/index.php3

2663 ■ Golden Pen of Freedom Award
Presented to individuals, groups, or institutions working for freedom of the press. Awarded annually. Established in 1961.

2664 ■ World Federation of Engineering Organisations
(Federation Mondiale des Organisations d'Ingenieurs)
Maria J. Prieto Laffargue, Pres.
Maison de l'UNESCO
1, Rue Miollis
F-75015 Paris, France
Ph: 33 1 45684846
Ph: 33 1 45684847
Fax: 33 1 45684865
E-mail: executivedirector@wfeo.net
URL: http://www.wfeo.org

2665 ■ Medal of Excellence in Engineering Education
To recognize an teacher for contributions to engineering education. Awarded biennially in odd-numbered years.

2666 ■ Hassib Sabbagh Award for Engineering Construction Excellence
To recognize an engineer or team of engineers for a successfully completed project demonstrating the role of engineering in sustainable development. A medal, certificate, and cash prize of US$10,000 are awarded biennially in odd-numbered years. Established in 2002.

2667 ■ World Organisation for Animal Health
(Organisation Mondiale de la Sante Animale)
Dr. Bernard Vallat, Dir. Gen.
12, rue de Prony
F-75017 Paris, France
Ph: 33 1 44151888
Fax: 33 1 42670987
E-mail: oie@oie.int
URL: http://www.oie.int/en

2668 ■ Gold Medal
For outstanding services to international veterinary science.

2669 ■ Meritorious Medal
For special services to veterinary science.

2670 ■ Young Writer's Award Association
(Association Prix du Jeune Ecrivain)
18 rue de Louge
BP 40055
F-31602 Muret, France
Ph: 33 561 561315
Fax: 33 561 510292
E-mail: pje@pjef.net
URL: http://www.pjef.net

2671 ■ Prix du Jeune Ecrivain
For recognition of outstanding writing by a young French writer between 15 and 25 years of age. Unpublished works of prose, such as short stories, drama, or fiction are eligible. Publication of the work is awarded annually in May and edited by Le Mercure de France. Established in 1985. Co-sponsored by Fondation BNP Paribas.

2672 ■ Prix du Jeune Ecrivain Francophone
For recognition of outstanding writing by a young, French-speaking writer between 15 and 27 years of age who lives outside France. Unpublished works such as short stories, drama, or fiction are eligible. Publication of the work is awarded annually in May. Established in 1985.

Gambia

2673 ■ The President's International Award
PO Box 2659
Serra Kunda, Gambia

Awards are arranged in alphabetical order below their administering organizations

Ph: 220 449 6541
URL: http://www.thegambiaintaward.org

2674 ■ The President's International Award

To encourage the development of Gambian youth, and to foster in them an attitude of service to others. Open to young people between the ages of 14 and 25 years. Gold, silver, and bronze awards are presented in the areas of skills training, service, physical recreation, adventurous journey, and residential projects. Awarded annually.

Georgia

2675 ■ Administration of the President of the Republic of Georgia
Maia Shiukashvili, Secretariat
1 M. Abdushelishvili St.
0103 Tbilisi, Georgia
Ph: 995 32 282736
E-mail: info@president.gov.ge
URL: http://www.president.gov.ge

2676 ■ David Agmashenebeli Order

To honor regular citizens, military personnel, and clerical personnel for an immense contribution to Georgia, for fighting toward the independence of Georgia and its revival, and for significantly contributing to the social consolidation and democracy development of the nation. A medal is awarded when merited. Established in 1992.

2677 ■ Golden Fleece Order

To honor individuals with foreign citizenship, and those holding no citizenship, who have significantly contributed to Georgian governmental development, national security interests, sovereignty and protection of territorial unity, formation of democratic and free society, formation of useful bilateral relationship with foreign countries and international organizations, protection of rights of Georgian citizens living abroad, popularization of the Georgian culture, and development of Georgian science and art. A medal is awarded when merited. Established in 1992.

2678 ■ Honor Medal

To honor Georgian citizens who actively participated in the revival of Georgia and devoted themselves to noble deeds. A medal is awarded when merited. Established in 1992.

2679 ■ Military Courage Medal

To honor military and police personnel for protection of the Georgian motherland while displaying bravery and courage when carrying out military duties. A medal is awarded when merited. Established in 1992.

2680 ■ Military Honor Medal

To honor Georgian military personnel and citizens who actively participated in the protection of their motherland and its territorial unity. A medal is awarded when merited. Established in 1992.

2681 ■ National Hero Award

This, the most honorable governmental title in Georgia, is awarded to a Georgian citizen for distinct, heroic actions. A medal is awarded when merited. Established in 1992.

2682 ■ Order of Honor

To honor Georgian citizens who took part in the building process of an independent Georgian government by devoting themselves, displaying heroism, and actively participating in approving and sustaining the following: governing, defense, law and order, farming, health protection, achievement in the fields of science, education, culture, literature, art, and sports. A medal is awarded when merited. Established in 1992.

2683 ■ St. George's Victory Order

To honor a Georgian citizen who has significantly contributed to victorious battles involving the Republic of Georgia. A medal is awarded when merited. Established in 1992.

2684 ■ Vakhtang Gorgasal's Order

To honor Georgian military personnel who displayed courage and heroism in the fight for protection of their motherland and its territorial unification, while skillfully leading them, protecting their military division, and creating and carrying out military operations. There are three ranks of the order: the I Rank Order is awarded to individuals who outstandingly contributed to their nation and motherland, and devoted and sacrificed their lives; II Rank Order is awarded to military and police personnel who successfully carried out orders given out by military leaders; and III Rank Order is awarded to individuals who displayed maximum battling preparedness when fulfilling their duties at a workplace. Medals are awarded when merited. Established in 1992.

2685 ■ Style Magazine
33 Pekini str.
Tbilisi, Georgia
Ph: 995 32 372634
E-mail: nino@style-magazine.com.ge
URL: http://www.style-magazine.com.ge

2686 ■ Architectural Awards

To stimulate architects and interior designers, promote their works, and increase popularity of construction and architecture in the Republic of Georgia. Open to architects and designers from any country. Awards are presented in approximately 10 categories, including single-family houses, public construction, residential interior design, and student projects. Awarded annually. Established in 2006.

2687 ■ Tbilisi International Film Festival
164, David Agmashenebeli av.
0112 Tbilisi, Georgia
Ph: 995 32 356760
E-mail: office@tbilisifilmfestival.ge
URL: http://www.tbilisifilmfestival.ge

2688 ■ Tbilisi International Film Festival

To recognize Georgian films and promote the development of the Georgian film industry. Four prizes are awarded: the Golden Prometheus for best film, the Silver Prometheus for best director, the FIPRESCI Prize for the film critics' international federation choice, and the Parajanov Prize for the most outstanding poetic vision. Held annually. Established in 2000.

Germany

2689 ■ Academy of Visual Arts
Leipzig College of Graphic Arts and Book Design
(Hochschule fur Grafik und Buchkunst Leipzig)
Waechterstrasse 11
D-04107 Leipzig, Germany
Ph: 49 341 21350
Fax: 49 341 2135166
E-mail: hgb@hgb-leipzig.de
URL: http://www.hgb-leipzig.de

2690 ■ Walter Tiemann Award

To recognize the design achievements of typographers and illustrators. One to three different titles published within the preceding two years may be submitted. A small sculpture and monetary prizes are awarded biennially in even-numbered years. Established in 1992 in honor of Walter Tiemann, a teacher and the rector from 1920 to 1945 at the former Leipzig Academie for Graphic Arts and Book Production, now College of Graphic Arts and Book Design, Leipzig.

2691 ■ American Chamber of Commerce in Germany (Frankfurt, Germany)
Dr. Dierk Muller, Gen. Mgr.
Borsenplatz 7-11

D-60313 Frankfurt, Germany
Ph: 49 69 92910420
Ph: 49 69 9291040
Fax: 49 69 92910411
E-mail: dmueller@amcham.de
URL: http://www.amcham.de

2692 ■ AmCham Transatlantic Partnership Award

For significant contributions to the German-American relationship. Candidates must be from Germany or the United States, living in either the United States or Germany; have notable achievements in business, politics, science, arts, or culture; and whose accomplishments receive wide public attention. Awarded annually.

2693 ■ Anna-Monika Foundation (Anna-Monika-Stiftung)
Michael Bommers, Managing Dir.
Kieshecker Weg 240
D-40468 Dusseldorf, Germany
Ph: 49 211 43718713
Fax: 49 211 43718723
E-mail: m.bommers@gospax.com
URL: http://www.anna-monika-stiftung.com

2694 ■ Anna-Monika Foundation Prize Competition

For academic research into psychiatry. Exact subject varies by year. A prize of 25,000 Euros is awarded annually.

2695 ■ Association for Aerosol Research (Gesellschaft fur Aerosolforschung e.V.)
Dr. Gerhard Kasper, Pres.
Postfach 3640
D-76021 Karlsruhe, Germany
Ph: 49 721 60824800
Fax: 49 721 60824857
E-mail: treasurer@gaef.de
URL: http://www.gaef.de

2696 ■ Fissan-Pui-TSI International Collaboration Award

For international collaboration in aerosol science and technology between researchers residing on at least two different continents. Awarded to individuals or teams; award may be shared. Established in 2006 by a donation from TSI Incorporated.

2697 ■ Fuchs Memorial Award

For exceptionally meritorious research contributions to aerosol science and technology. Awarded every four years. Named in honor of Prof. Nikolai Albertovich Fuchs.

2698 ■ International Aerosol Fellow Award

Recognizes contributions to aerosol science through education, research, service, and technical development. A certificate and a citation are awarded biennially to one or two recipients.

2699 ■ Junge Memorial Award

To recognize an individual for outstanding research contributions to aerosol science and technology. Preference is given to senior scientists for a career of accomplishments. Award consists of a certificate, a citation, free registration for the awarding conference, and the awards dinner. Awarded as merited. Honors Prof. Christian Junge for his contributions to atmospheric research.

2700 ■ Smoluchowski Award

To recognize significant contributions to aerosol science. Scientists under 40 years of age who have achieved and published new results in aerosol science in the previous three years are

---

Awards are arranged in alphabetical order below their administering organizations

eligible. A monetary award of 2,000 Euros and a certificate are awarded annually. Named in honor of physicist Marian Smoluchowski.

2701 ■ Association of Chemical Pulp and Paper Chemists and Engineers (Verein der Zellstoff-und Papier-Chemiker und-Ingenieure)
Dr. Wilhelm Busse, Exec. Dir.
Emilstrasse 21
D-64293 Darmstadt, Germany
Ph: 49 6151 33264
Fax: 49 6151 311076
E-mail: zellcheming@zellcheming.de
URL: http://www.zellcheming.com/startseite/start_e.php

2702 ■ Georg Jayme Denkmunze
For recognition of outstanding technical and scientific achievements which promote research and development of the pulp chemistry. Scientists without regard to nationality are eligible. A medal showing the bust of Georg Jayme, and on the reverse, the emblem of the association and the inscription "in recognition of outstanding service" is awarded periodically. Established in 1989.

2703 ■ Bavarian Academy of Fine Arts (Bayerische Akademie der Schonen Kunste)
Katja Schaefer MA, Gen. Sec.
Max Joseph-Platz 3
D-80539 Munich, Germany
Ph: 49 89 2900770
Fax: 49 89 29007723
E-mail: info@badsk.de
URL: http://www.badsk.de

2704 ■ Friedrich Baur Prize
To honor artists and arts institutions in four categories: visual arts, literature, music, and performing arts. Awarded annually. Established in 1990.

2705 ■ Gerda and Gunter Bialas Award
To honor outstanding composers. A monetary prize is awarded biennially in even-numbered years. Established in 1998.

2706 ■ Horst Bienek Preis fur Lyrik
To recognize outstanding poetry. A monetary award is presented annually. Established in 1991 to honor Horst Bienek. Sponsored by the Horst Bienek Stiftung.

2707 ■ Grosser Literaturpreis der Bayerischen Akademie der Schonen Kunste
To recognize an author for his or her literary work. A monetary prize is awarded annually. Established in 1950. Formerly: (1986) Literaturpreis der Bayerische Akademie der Schonen Kunste.

2708 ■ Thomas Mann Prize
To recognize accomplishment in literature. Awarded annually. Established in 1950. Formerly: Grober Literaturpreis Wilhelm-Hausentein-Ehrung.

2709 ■ Bavarian Academy of Sciences and Humanities (Bayerische Akademie der Wissenschaften)
Bianca Marzocca, Gen. Sec.
Alfons-Goppel-Str. 11
D-80539 Munich, Germany
Ph: 49 89 230310
Fax: 49 89 23031100
E-mail: info@badw.de
URL: http://www.badw.de

2710 ■ Bavarian Academy of Science Prize
For recognition of an outstanding achievement in science. A monetary prize is awarded irregularly when merited. Established in 1956 by the Foundation for the Advancement of Science in Bavaria.

2711 ■ Bene merenti Medals
For recognition of outstanding work for the Academy. Gold, silver, and bronze medals are awarded irregularly; the gold is seldom awarded, while the silver is awarded most years. Established in 1759.

2712 ■ Silver Medal of Special Merit
To recognize members, employees, and former employees who have demonstrated exceptional loyalty to the Academy's principles. Established in 2003.

2713 ■ Arnold Sommerfeld Prize
For recognition of outstanding achievement in science. A monetary prize is awarded annually. Established 1993.

2714 ■ Max Weber Award
For recognition of outstanding achievement in humanities. A monetary prize is awarded annually. Established 1993.

2715 ■ Berlin International Film Festival (Internationale Filmfestspiele Berlin)
Dieter Kosslick, Dir.
Potsdamer Str. 5
D-10785 Berlin, Germany
Ph: 49 30 259 20 0
Fax: 49 30 259 20 299
E-mail: info@berlinale.de
URL: http://www.berlinale.de

2716 ■ Amnesty International Film Prize
To recognize a film that draws the attention of audiences to the theme of human rights. Documentaries are given special attention for this award. A monetary prize of 5,000 Euros is presented annually.

2717 ■ Alfred Bauer Prize
To recognize a film at the festival which takes the art of film in a new direction. Awarded by the International Jury. Awarded annually.

2718 ■ Berlin International Film Festival (Internationale Filmfestspiele Berlin)
To recognize the best feature and short films which are not only of interest to selected and expert audiences, but also films of quality that reach a wide public. The competition is limited to feature films and short films (less than 15 minutes) produced during the year preceding the Festival, not having been released outside their countries of origin, and not having participated in another competition or film festival. Priority is given to films not yet released. Held annually in February. Established in 1951.

2719 ■ Berlin Today Award
To recognize a short film that has something to do with Berlin and was developed by an international team. Awarded annually.

2720 ■ Berlinale Camera
To recognize a film personality or an institution to whom the film festival feels especially attached. This award is given as an expression of thanks. Established in 1986.

2721 ■ Caligari Film Prize
To recognize a film presented at the festival. A monetary award of 4,000 Euros is presented annually. Sponsored by the *German Federal Association of Communal Film Work* and *filmdienst* magazine.

2722 ■ Crystal Bear Awards
To recognize films that depict or are produced for children. Awarded annually.

2723 ■ DAAD Scholarship
To enable a filmmaker to spend three months of study in Berlin within the framework of the Artists-in-Berlin program. Awarded annually by the International Short Film Jury. Sponsored by the German Academic Exchange Service (DAAD).

2724 ■ Femina Film Prize
To recognize an outstanding artistic contribution by a female in a German-language feature film. The award covers the areas of set design, camera work, costumes, music, or editing. A monetary prize of 3,000 Euros is awarded annually.

2725 ■ Golden Bear Awards
To recognize the best film in the festival. Awarded annually by the International Jury.

2726 ■ Honorary Golden Bear
To recognize a particularly outstanding career in the film industry. A golden bear sculpture is presented annually.

2727 ■ NETPAC Prize
The Network for the Promotion of Asian Cinema (NETPAC) presents this award to recognize and promote Asian film at the festival. Awarded annually.

2728 ■ Panorama Audience Award
To recognize the audience's favorite film through a vote of the audience. Awarded annually. Established in 1999.

2729 ■ Peace Film Prize
To recognize a film that encourages peace. A monetary prize of 5,000 Euros is presented annually.

2730 ■ Manfred Salzgeber Prize
To recognize a film that broadens the boundaries of cinema today. Only films that have not yet been distributed in more than one European country are eligible. Awarded annually. Established in honor of Manfred Salzgeber, the former director.

2731 ■ Score Competition
To recognize young, outstanding sound designers and composers. An international jury judges a two-minute film clip with sound recordings. The winner receives a trip to Los Angeles. Formerly: Volkswagen Score Competition.

2732 ■ Silver Bear Awards
To recognize achievement in films at the festival. Awarded as the Jury Grand Prize, and for best director, best actress, best actor, best script, and outstanding artistic contribution in the categories of camera, editing, score, costumes, and set design. Awarded annually by the International Jury.

2733 ■ Teddy Awards
To recognize films that have gay and lesbian content. A monetary award is presented. A monetary prize of 3,000 Euros is presented to a feature film, a short film, and a documentary each year.

2734 ■ Bertelsmann Stiftung
Ines Koring, Proj. Dir.
Carl-Bertelsmann-Strasse 256
D-33311 Gutersloh, Germany
Ph: 49 5241 810
Fax: 49 5241 816 81396
E-mail: info@bertelsmann-stiftung.de
URL: http://www.bertelsmann-stiftung.de

2735 ■ Neue Stimmen International Singing Competition (Neue Stimmen Internationaler Gesangswettbewerb)
For recognition of young opera singers. Female singers who are 30 years of age or younger, and male singers who are 32 years of age or younger may submit applications. The following monetary awards are presented: first prize: 15,000 Euro; second prize: 10,000 Euro; third prize: 8000 Euro; 4th, 5th, and 6th prize: 4000 Euro each. Plus: Audience Prize, CD/DVD recording Neue Stimmen, radio and television broadcast, possible participation in one of the master classes

Awards are arranged in alphabetical order below their administering organizations

Neue Stimmen. Held biennially in odd-numbered years. Established in 1987.

2736 ■ Berthold Leibinger Stiftung GmbH
Johann-Maus-Strasse 2
D-71254 Ditzingen, Germany
Ph: 49 7156 303 35201
Fax: 49 7156 303 35205
URL: http://www.leibinger-stiftung.de

2737 ■ Berthold Leibinger Innovation Prize
To honor scientists and developers who make advancements in the field of laser technology. Monetary prizes of 30,000 Euros, 20,000 Euros, and 10,000 Euros are awarded for first, second, and third place, respectively. Awarded biennially in even-numbered years. Established in 2000.

2738 ■ Braun GmbH
Bernard Wild, Chm.
Frankfurter Strasse 145
D-61476 Kronberg, Germany
Ph: 49 6173 300
Fax: 49 6173 302875
E-mail: info@braunprize.com
URL: http://www.braunprize.com

2739 ■ Braun Prize
To recognize the creativity of young designers and the richness of their ideas. The total prize money gifted through the competition is 36,000 Euros, with the overall winner receiving 12,000 Euros and a six-month paid internship within the Braun design department. The remaining money is then bestowed to the other finalists (5,000 Euros each) with the rest being distributed in the form of special recognition awards at the discretion of the jury. Awarded biennially in odd-numbered years. Established in 1967.

2740 ■ Braunschweig City Cultural Office (Stadt Braunschweig-Kulturamt)
Platz der Deutschen Einheit, 1
38100 Braunschweig, Germany
Ph: 49 531 470 1
Fax: 49 531 151 12
E-mail: stadt@braunscheig.de
URL: http://www.braunschweig.de

2741 ■ Braunschweig Research Prize
To recognize outstanding international research in the fields of technology, life sciences, and cultural sciences. A monetary prize of 30,000 Euros is awarded biennially in odd-numbered years.

2742 ■ Friedrich-Gerstaecker-Preis
To recognize living authors of young peoples' books which convey adventures in the wide world with captivating style, as did world traveler/author Friedrich Gerstaecker, a citizen of Braunschweig. The book, written in German, must have been published within the preceding three years. A monetary prize of 6,500 Euros is awarded biennially in odd-numbered years. Established in 1947.

2743 ■ Gauss Medal
To honor a scientist for outstanding lifetime achievement. A medal is awarded annually. Established in memory of one of Brunswick's most prominent citizens and scientists, Carl Friedrich Gauss.

2744 ■ Technology Transfer Prize
To recognize individuals and groups working in either academic fields or research and development facilities for outstanding work in transferring research and development findings and applying them to economic situations. A monetary prize of 10,000 Euros is awarded annually.

2745 ■ City of Buxtehude (Stadt Buxtehude)
Helmar Putz, Contact
Breite Strasse 2
D-21614 Buxtehude, Germany
Ph: 49 4161 5010
Fax: 49 4161 501318
E-mail: stadtverwaltung@stadt.buxtenude.de
URL: http://www.stadt.buxtehude.de
Formerly: (1981) Buchhandlung Ziemann & Ziemann, Buxtehude.

2746 ■ Buxtehuder Bulle
For recognition of the best book of the year for young people. Books written in German, and published during the preceding year are considered. A monetary of 5,000 Euros and a plaque are awarded annually. Established in 1971 by Winfried Ziemann in honor of Ferdinand, the peace-loving bull in a famous children's story.

2747 ■ Chopin Society in the Federal Republic of Germany (Chopin-Gesellschaft in der Bundesrepublik Deutschland)
John F.-Kennedy-Haus
Kasinostrasse 3
D-64293 Darmstadt, Germany
Ph: 49 6151 25957
Fax: 49 6151 25957
E-mail: i.hoerl@chopin-gesellschaft.de
URL: http://www.chopin-gesellschaft.de

2748 ■ International Chopin Piano Competition, Darmstadt
To promote outstanding Chopin interpretation. The competition is open to all pianists who are not older than 30 years of age. Monetary prizes ranging from 10,000 Euros to 1,000 Euros are awarded triennially. Established in 1983.

2749 ■ Christian European Visual Media Association (Christliche Europaische Arbeitsgemeinschaft fur Visuelle Medien)
Liliana Oliveri, Chm.
ERF TV
D-35573 Wetzlar, Germany
Ph: 49 6441 957266
Fax: 49 6441 957130
E-mail: info@cevma.net
URL: http://www.cevma.net

2750 ■ CEVMA Awards
To encourage and recognize excellence in films and videos that reflect Christian values. Awards are offered for content and production. Awarded biennially at the CEVMA Film Festival. Established in 1982.

2751 ■ City of Nuremberg Office of Human Rights
Rathausplatz 2
D-90403 Nuremberg, Germany
Ph: 49 911 231 5029
Fax: 49 911 231 3040
E-mail: menschenrechte@stadt.nuernberg.de
URL: http://www.menschenrechte.nuernberg.de

2752 ■ Nuremberg Award for Company Culture without Discrimination
To honor local companies that are committed to the protection of the dignity and rights of all of their staff, and are committed to the support of the city of Nuremberg in its activities against racism and discrimination, beyond the scope stipulated by legal norms. Awarded biennially in even-numbered years. Established in 2010.

2753 ■ Nuremberg International Human Rights Award
To honor individuals or groups who have committed themselves to human rights, to contribute to the protection of endangered human rights defenders, and to encourage others to commit themselves to human rights. A monetary prize of 15,000 Euros is presented biennially in odd-numbered years. First awarded on September 17, 1995, almost 60 years after the publication of the National Socialist racial laws and 50 years after the end of WWII. It is intended to symbolize

that no signals are to radiate from Nuremberg except those of peace, reconciliation, and respect for human rights.

2754 ■ Confederation of European Baseball (Confederation Europeenne de Baseball)
Samuel Pelter, Sec. Gen.
Otto-Fleck-Schneise 12
D-60528 Frankfurt, Germany
Ph: 49 69 6700284
Fax: 49 69 67724212
E-mail: office@baseballeurope.com
URL: http://www.baseballeurope.com

2755 ■ European Baseball Championships (Campionato Europeo Baseball)
For recognition of the national team that wins the European Championship. Awarded annually. Established in 1954. In addition, a Cup of Cups, the CEB-Cup, Junior European Baseball Champion, European Cadets, and European Juvenile Championships are awarded.

2756 ■ European Baseball Cup
Awarded annually to the National Club Champions. Established in 1963.

2757 ■ Deutsche Gesellschaft fur Parasitologie
Prof. Dr. Brigitte Frank, Mgr.
Universitat Hohenheim
FG Parasitologie
D-70599 Stuttgart, Germany
Ph: 49 711 4592277
Fax: 49 711 4592276
E-mail: brifrank@uni-hohenheim.de
URL: http://www.dgparasitologie.de

2758 ■ Rudolph Leuckart Medal
To recognize individuals who have gained special merit by the furtherance of parasitology. Awarded annually to one or more recipients. Established in 1974.

2759 ■ Gerhard Piekarski Prize
To recognize the author of a doctoral thesis and resulting publications in the field of parasitology, preferably on parasitic protozoa. Publications must not be older than 30 months at the time of submission. Candidates must give an oral presentation of their thesis during the biannual General Meeting of the Society. Awarded annually.

2760 ■ Karl Asmund Rudolphi Medal (Carl-Asmund-Rudolphi-Medaille)
For recognition of outstanding scientific achievement in the area of parasitological research and its application. Scientists not older than 38 years who are involved in the field of biology and medical science are eligible. A monetary prize of 500 Euros is awarded annually. Established in 1986 in memory of Carl Asmund Rudolphi (1771-1832), a scientist in the area of parasitological research and its application.

2761 ■ Deutsche Meteorologische Gesellschaft
Marion Schnee, Sec.
Carl-Heinrich-Becker-Weg 6-10
Freie Universitat Berlin
D-12165 Berlin, Germany
Ph: 49 30 79708324
Fax: 49 30 7919002
E-mail: sekretariat@dmg-ev.de
URL: http://www.dmg-ev.de

2762 ■ Albert Defant Medaille
For recognition of outstanding scientific achievement in physical oceanography. Awarded triennially. Established in 1984 in honor of Albert Defant.

2763 ■ Forderpreis
To recognize young meteorologists for outstand-

Awards are arranged in alphabetical order below their administering organizations

ing achievement in the field. Works that are completed by individuals under 35 years of age and that have been published are considered. There may be no more than three years between publication and awarding of the prize. A monetary prize is awarded annually. Established in 1966. Formerly: Deutsche Meteorologische Gesellschaft e.V. Jugendpreis.

2764 ■ Honorary Membership
To honor members of the meteorological society for special service to meteorology or to the organization. A certificate is awarded when merited. Established in 1966.

2765 ■ Alfred Wegener Medaille
To recognize persons for exemplary service and contributions to meteorological science. A medal is awarded triennially. Established in 1966 in honor of Alfred Wegener.

2766 ■ Deutsche Mineralogische Gesellschaft
Dr. Ralf Milke, Contact
Institut fur Geologische Wissenschaften
Freie Universitat Berlin
Malteserstrasse 74-100
12249 Berlin, Germany
Ph: 49 30 83870864
E-mail: milke@zedat.fu-berlin.de
URL: http://www.dmg-home.de

2767 ■ Georg Agricola Medaille
For recognition of outstanding contributions in the field of applied (industrial) mineralogy. Individuals must be nominated. A bronze medal is awarded when merited at the convention. Established in 1974 in honor of Georg Argricola.

2768 ■ Viktor Moritz Goldschmidt Preis
For recognition of important scientific contributions of younger scientists. Members of the Society, generally younger than 38 years of age, must be nominated. A monetary prize is awarded at the convention. Established in 1957 in honor of Victor Moritz Goldschmidt.

2769 ■ Paul Ramdohr Prize
Award of recognition. A monetary prize of 1,000 Euros is awarded annually.

2770 ■ Abraham Gottlob Werner Medaille
For recognition of outstanding scientific contributions to mineralogy. Individuals must be nominated. Gold and silver medals are awarded annually at the convention. Established in 1950 in honor of Abraham Gottlob Werner.

2771 ■ Deutsche Physikalische Gesellschaft
Anne Friedrich, Contact
Hauptstrasse 5
D-53604 Bad Honnef, Germany
Ph: 49 2224 92320
Ph: 49 2224 923210
Fax: 49 2224 923250
E-mail: dpg@dpg-physik.de
URL: http://www.dpg-physik.de/index.html

2772 ■ Max Born Prize
For recognition of outstanding scientific contributions to physics. Awards are given in alternate years to German and British physicists by the combined British Institute of Physics and the Deutsche Physikalische Gesellschaft. A monetary prize of 3,000 Euros, a silver medal bearing the likeness of Mr. Born (designed by his daughter, Mrs. Margaret Pryce) on one side and a formula on the other, and a certificate are awarded annually. Established in 1973.

2773 ■ Otto-Hahn-Preis fur Chemie und Physik
To recognize German individuals who have performed a unique service to the development of chemistry, physics, or applied research. A monetary prize of 50,000 Euros, a gold medal bearing the likeness of Mr. Hahn on one side,

and a certificate are awarded by the Deutscher Zentralausschuss fur Chemie and the Deutsche Physikalishe Gesellschaft when merited. Established in 1955.

2774 ■ Gustav Hertz Prize
To recognize a recently completed, outstanding publication by a younger physicist. A prize is awarded in both experimental and theoretical physics when merited. A monetary prize of 7,500 Euros and a certificate are awarded annually. Established in 1942. Formerly: Preis der Deutschen Physikalische Gesellschaft.

2775 ■ Gentner Kastler Prize
To recognize alternately French and German physicists for outstanding contributions to physics. A monetary prize of 3,000 Euros, a silver medal bearing the likeness of Mr. Gentner and Mr. Kastler on one side, and a certificate are awarded annually by the Societe Francaise de Physique and the Deutsche Physikalische Gesellschaft. Established in 1985.

2776 ■ Medaille fur Naturwissenschaftliche Publizistik
For recognition of journalistic achievement contributing to the expansion of natural scientific physical thought in the German-speaking realm. A silver medal and a certificate are awarded when merited. Established in 1984.

2777 ■ Max Planck Medaille
For recognition of outstanding theoretical work in quantum theory. A gold medal bearing the likeness of Mr. Planck on one side and a certificate are awarded annually. Established in 1929.

2778 ■ Robert Wichard Pohl Prize
For recognition of outstanding achievements in physics, especially radiation and other disciplines of science and technology and the dissemination of scientific knowledge through the teaching of physics. A monetary prize of 5,000 Euros and a certificate are awarded annually when merited. Established in 1979.

2779 ■ Walter-Schottky-Preis fur Festkorperforschung
For recognition of outstanding publications and research in solid state physics by a younger scientist. A monetary prize of 15,000 Euros and a certificate are awarded annually. Established in 1972. Sponsored by Siemens AG.

2780 ■ Deutsches Forum fur Figurentheater und Puppenspielkunst e.V.
Annette Dabs, Managing Dir.
Hattinger Str. 467
D-44795 Bochum 1, Germany
Ph: 49 234 47720
Fax: 49 234 47735
E-mail: info@fidena.de
URL: http://www.dfp.fidena.de

2781 ■ Fritz Wortelmann Preis of the City of Bochum for Amateur Puppetry (Fritz Wortelmann-Preis der Stadt Bochum fur das Amateur-Figurentheater)
To recognize the best groups of amateur puppeteers. Monetary prizes are awarded biennially in November. Established in 1959.

2782 ■ City of Dortmund (Stadt Dortmund)
Friedensplatz 3
D-44122 Dortmund, Germany
Ph: 49 231 50 29731
Fax: 49 231 50 22497
E-mail: redaktion@dortmund.de
URL: http://www.dortmund.de

2783 ■ Literature preis der Stadt Dortmund - Nelly-Sachs-Preis
For recognition of personal achievement that has promoted the cultural relationship between

people by stressing the ideals of tolerance and reconciliation. A monetary prize is awarded biennially. Established in 1961.

2784 ■ Ecological Society of Germany, Austria, and Switzerland (Gesellschaft fur Oekologie)
Prof. Dr. Volkmar Wolters, Pres.
Technische Universitat Berlin
Institute of Ecology
Rothenburgstr. 12
D-12165 Berlin, Germany
Ph: 49 30 31471396
Fax: 49 30 31471355
E-mail: info@gfoe.org
URL: http://www.gfoe.org

2785 ■ Horst-Wiehe Award
To recognize an individual for outstanding work in ecology. Awarded biennially in odd-numbered years.

2786 ■ Thesis Awards
To recognize outstanding PhD and Master's/Diploma theses in ecology. A monetary prize of 1,500 Euros is awarded for the winning PhD thesis and 1,000 Euros is awarded for the winning Master's/Diploma thesis. Established in 2007.

2787 ■ Electric Power Society Association of German Electrical Engineers
VDE Headquarters
Stresemannallee 15
D-60596 Frankfurt, Germany
Ph: 49 69 63080
Fax: 49 69 6312925
E-mail: service@vde.com
URL: http://www.vde.com/de/Seiten/Homepage.aspx

2788 ■ Herbert-Kind-Preis
For recognition of outstanding academic achievement. Students of electrical power engineering may be nominated. A monetary prize of 8,000 Euros and a certificate of award are presented annually. Established in 1982 in memory of Dr. Herbert Kind.

2789 ■ VDE/ETG Award
For recognition of excellence in scientific publications in the field of electric power. Members of the Society under the age of 40 are eligible. A monetary prize of 3,000 Euros and a certificate are awarded several times a year. Established in 1975. Formerly: (2006) Literaturpreis der ETG.

2790 ■ Eppendorf AG
Barkhausenweg 1
D-22339 Hamburg, Germany
Ph: 49 4053 8010
Fax: 49 4053 801556
E-mail: webmaster@eppendorf.com
URL: http://www.eppendorf.com

2791 ■ Eppendorf Award for Young European Investigators
To honor young scientists for outstanding achievements in the field of biomedical research based on methods of molecular biology. A monetary prize of 15,000 Euros is awarded annually. Established in 1995. Presented in partnership with the scientific journal *Nature*.

2792 ■ International Eppendorf and *Science* Prize for Neurobiology
To recognize a young scientist for outstanding neurobiological research based on methods of molecular and cell biology conducted by him or her during the previous three years. Candidates must be aged 35 years or younger. A monetary prize of 25,000 Euros is awarded annually. Established in 2002. Presented in partnership with the scientific journal *Science*.

2793 ■ European Academy of Facial Plastic Surgery
Prof. Pietro Palma, Pres.
Nibelungenstr. 87
D-23562 Lubeck, Germany

Awards are arranged in alphabetical order below their administering organizations

Fax: 49 451 5824 9981
E-mail: info@eafps.org
URL: http://www.eafps.org

2794 ■ Joseph Prize
For the writer of outstanding original paper in reconstructive surgery.

2795 ■ European Aluminum Foil Association
Francois Coeffic, Pres.
Am Bonneshof 5
40474 Dusseldorf, Germany
Ph: 49 211 4796150
Fax: 49 211 4796408
E-mail: enquiries@alufoil.org
URL: http://www.alufoil.org/front_content.php

2796 ■ Alufoil Trophy
Recognizes technical innovation and excellence in aluminum foil packaging. Trophies are awarded annually.

2797 ■ European Association for the Study of Diabetes
Dr. Viktor Joergens, Exec. Dir.
Rheindorfer Weg 3
D-40591 Dusseldorf, Germany
Ph: 49 221 7584690
Fax: 49 221 75846929
E-mail: secretariat@easd.org
URL: http://www.easd.org

2798 ■ Claude Bernard Lecture
To recognize an individual's innovative leadership and outstanding contributions to the advancement of knowledge in the field of diabetes mellitus and related diseases. Members may submit nominations by April 15. Travel expenses to the annual meeting of EASD and the Claude Bernard Medal are awarded annually. Established in 1969 by the Paul Neumann Laboratory, in Paris, France.

2799 ■ Eli Lilly/EASD Research Fellowship in Diabetes and Metabolism
To encourage research in the field of diabetes and metabolism and to promote excellence in medical education in Europe. Applications may be made by European members of the EASD under the age of 38 who hold an M.D. degree or European equivalent. The deadline is February 15. Two fellowships of 50,000 Euros each are awarded annually. Established in 1991. Administered by the European Foundation for the Study of Diabetes.

2800 ■ Minkowski Prize
For recognition of outstanding publications that increase knowledge concerning diabetes mellitus. Research must be carried out in Europe by a person normally a resident in Europe, who is under the age of 45. A monetary prize of 20,000 Euros, a certificate, and travel expenses to the annual meeting of EASD are awarded annually. Established in 1966 by Farbwerke Hoechst AG.

2801 ■ Castelli Pedroli Prize
For recognition of work concerned with the histopathology, pathogenesis, prevention, and treatment of the complications of diabetes mellitus. Works published in internationally recognized scientific journals during the previous five-year period are considered. Members of the Association who are residents in Europe may be nominated by members only by February 15. A monetary prize of 8,000 Euros is awarded each year at the annual meeting. In addition, the winner is named the Golgi Lecturer and presents a lecture. Established in 1986 by the family of the late Maria Carla Castelli Pedroli in honor of Camillo Golgi.

2802 ■ Albert Renold Prize Lecture
To recognize an individual for outstanding achievements in research on the islets of Langerhans. Candidates may be of any age from any country. A monetary prize of 20,000 Euros plus travel expenses is awarded annually. In addition, the recipient is invited to deliver a lecture at the Annual Meeting. Established in 2007.

2803 ■ Albert Renold Travel Fellowship
To encourage young European investigators to visit another laboratory or laboratories to gain experience in new techniques and methodology, to receive postdoctoral training or to carry out collaborative research. Members under 40 years of age may apply. One Fellowship valued at up to 7,000 Euros is awarded annually. Established in memory of Professor Albert Ernst Renold (1923-1988), the founding Secretary of the European Association for the Study of Diabetes. Administered by the European Foundation for the Study of Diabetes.

2804 ■ European Association of Event Centers (Europaischer Verband der Veranstaltungs-Centren)
Ms. Martina Fritz, Contact
Ludwigstrasse 3
D-61348 Bad Homburg, Germany
Ph: 49 6172 2796900
Ph: 49 6172 2796906
Fax: 49 6172 2796909
E-mail: info@evvc.org
URL: http://www.evvc.org

2805 ■ Best Center Award
To honor the best centers of the year. Awarded in three categories each year.

2806 ■ European Association of Organic Geochemists
Dr. L. Schwark, Awards Contact
Ludewig-Meyn-Str. 10
Institute of Geosciences
Christian-Albrechts-University of Kiel
D-24118 Kiel, Germany
Ph: 49 431 880 2850
Fax: 49 431 880 4376
E-mail: ls@gpi.uni-kiel.de
URL: http://www.eaog.org

2807 ■ Pieter Schenck Award
To recognize a young scientist who has made a major contribution in any specific area of organic geochemistry or a related field. Candidates are typically younger than 35 years of age. Awarded biennially in odd-numbered years. Established in 1993.

2808 ■ European Association of Personality Psychology
Dr. Jens Asendorpf, Pres.
Rudower Chaussee 18
Institute of Psychology
Humboldt University Berlin
D-12489 Berlin, Germany
E-mail: president@eapp.org
URL: http://www.eapp.org

2809 ■ Distinguished Personality Psychologist Award
To promote personality psychology in Europe and to increase the visibility of outstanding European personality psychologists, both to the scientific community and the general public. Awarded biennially in even-numbered years. Established in 2006.

2810 ■ European Association of Psychological Assessment
Karl Schweizer, Pres.
Mertonstrasse 17
Institute of Psychology
Goethe University
D-60054 Frankfurt am Main, Germany
E-mail: president@eapa-homepage.org
URL: http://www.eapa-homepage.org

2811 ■ Award for Distinguished Scientific or Professional Contributions to Psychological Assessment
To recognize a European psychologist who has made a distinguished contribution to psychological assessment as a science or as a profession in the last five years. A monetary prize of 2,000 Euros is awarded biennially in odd-numbered years. Established in 1994.

2812 ■ European Association of Social Psychology
Sibylle Classen, Exec. Off.
PO Box 420143
D-48068 Munster, Germany
E-mail: sibylle@easp.eu
URL: http://www.easp.eu

2813 ■ Jos Jaspers Awards
To recognize young scholars who have made an outstanding research contribution to social psychology. Candidates must be under the age of 30 years and must have obtained their PhD within the previous three years. Awarded to three recipients every three years at the General Meeting. Established in 1990.

2814 ■ Kurt Lewin Awards
To recognize mid-career members for outstanding scientific contributions to social psychology. Awarded to three recipients every three years at the General Meeting. Established in 2005.

2815 ■ Henri Tajfel Award
To recognize a member for a distinguished lifetime achievement in social psychology. A medal and invitation to lecture are presented every three years at the General Meeting. Established in 1982.

2816 ■ European Coordinating Committee for Artificial Intelligence
Gerhard Brewka, Chm.
Leipzig University
Informatics Institute
Augustusplatz 10-11
04109 Leipzig, Germany
Ph: 49 341 9732235
Fax: 49 341 9732299
E-mail: brewka@informatik.uni-leipzig.de
URL: http://www.eccai.org

2817 ■ Artificial Intelligence Dissertation Award
To recognize and encourage scientific and technological advances in the field of artificial intelligence. A monetary prize of 1,500 Euros is awarded annually. Established in 1998.

2818 ■ ECCAI Travel Awards
To support students, young researchers, and faculty who are members of an ECCAI affiliated society participating in ECAI or ACAI. Monetary prizes of 400 Euros each are to be used to reimburse travel and registration fees. Awarded annually.

2819 ■ European Federation for the Science and Technology of Lipids
Dr. Frank Amoneit, Managing Dir.
Varrentrappstr. 40-42
60486 Frankfurt, Germany
Ph: 49 69 7917345
Fax: 49 69 7917564
E-mail: amoneit@eurofedlipid.org
URL: http://www.eurofedlipid.org

2820 ■ European Lipid Awards
Recognizes distinguished individuals in the field of lipid science and technology. Three awards

Awards are arranged in alphabetical order below their administering organizations

are offered: European Lipid Science Award; European Lipid Technology Award; and European Young Lipid Scientist Award. Presented annually.

2821 ■ European Federation of Chemical Engineering
(Europaische Foderation fur Chemie-Ingenieur-Wesen)
Dr. Willi Meier, Gen. Sec.
Theodor-Heuss-Allee 25
D-60486 Frankfurt, Germany
Ph: 49 69 7564143
Ph: 49 69 7564209
Fax: 49 69 7564201
E-mail: honndorf@dechema.de
URL: http://www.efce.info

2822 ■ EFCE Excellence Awards
To recognize PhD theses or publications of young researchers published in preceding years that demonstrate the most outstanding contribution to research and/or practice in the scientific fields of the EFCE Working Parties. The following awards are presented: Excellence Award in Recognition of an Outstanding PhD Thesis on CAPE; Excellence Award in Crystallization; Excellence Award in Process Intensification; Excellence Award in Process Safety; and Excellence Award in Thermodynamics and Transport Properties. Awarded annually.

2823 ■ European Federation of Corrosion
(Federation Europeenne de la Corrosion)
Prof. Philippe Marcus, Pres.
Theodor-Heuss-Allee 25
D-60486 Frankfurt, Germany
Ph: 49 69 7564209
Ph: 49 69 7564143
Fax: 49 69 7564299
E-mail: meier@dechema.de
URL: http://www.efcweb.org

2824 ■ Cavallaro Medal
For recognition of outstanding achievement in basic research in the field of corrosion and corrosion protection. Awarded biennially in even-numbered years. Established in 1965 by the Universite de Ferrara in memory of Professor Leo Cavallaro, founder of the Center for the Study of Corrosion.

2825 ■ European Corrosion Medal
For recognition of achievements by a scientist, or group of scientists in the application of corrosion science in the chemical, petroleum, and nuclear industries. The recipients must be of a nationality(ies) corresponding to one, or more, of the member Societies of the EFC and the work must be conducted within a European country. Proposals for recipients may be submitted mainly by the EFC member Societies; selection is by a Jury. A bronze medal, diploma, and cash prize of 1000 Euros are awarded biennially in odd-numbered years. Established in 1985 by DECHEMA.

2826 ■ Marti I. Franques Medal
For recognition of outstanding contributions to the advancement of science and technology of corrosion through international cooperation with the EFC, transfer of knowledge, and education. Established by the Sociedad Espanola de Quimica Industrial and awarded for the first time in 1993.

2827 ■ Kurt Schwabe Prize
To recognize a young scientist for his or her scientific and technical contribution to the field of corrosion on the basis of publication. Candidates

must be aged 35 years or younger. A monetary prize of 300 Euros is awarded triennially. Established in 2000. Supported by the Kurt Schwabe Foundation.

2828 ■ European Federation of the Associations of Dietitians
(Federation Europeenne des Associations de Dieteticiens)
Judith Liddell, Sec.-Treas.
Ziegeleiweg 4
D-46446 Emmerich am Rhein, Germany
Ph: 49 2822 68367
E-mail: secretariat@efad.org
URL: http://www.efad.org/everyone

2829 ■ European Student Dietitian of the Year
To promote the work of dietitians and to stimulate students to develop their professional skills in dietetic research. A statuette is awarded annually.

2830 ■ European Film Academy
Mr. Pascal Edelmann, Hd. of Press and PR
Kurfurstendamm 225
D-10719 Berlin, Germany
Ph: 49 30 8871670
Fax: 49 30 88716777
E-mail: efa@europeanfilmacademy.org
URL: http://www.europeanfilmacademy.org

2831 ■ European Film Awards
To honor the greatest achievements in European cinema. Awards are presented in 15 categories: European Film; European Director; European Actress; European Actor; European Screenwriter; Carlo Di Palma European Cinematographer Award; European Composer; European Discovery; European Film Academy Prix d'Excellence; Lifetime Achievement; European Achievement in World Cinema; Critics Award - Prix Fipresci; Prix Arte for Documentary; Prix Uip for Short Film; and the People's Choice Award For Best European Film. Awarded annually.

2832 ■ European Landscape Contractors Association
(Union Europeenne des Entrepeneurs du Paysage)
Emmanuel Mony, Pres.
Alexander-von-Humboldt-Strasse 4
D-53604 Bad Honnef, Germany
Ph: 49 2224 770720
Fax: 49 2224 770777
E-mail: contact@elca.info
URL: http://www.elca.info

2833 ■ Trend Award
For landscaping projects (public or private) with pioneering trends in building greenery as well as gardens and innovative system solutions which were possibly jointly planned and realized by the client, architect and landscaping company. Awarded annually to one or more recipients.

2834 ■ European Life Scientist Organization
Dr. Kai Simons, Pres.
Pfotenhauerstr. 108
01307 Dresden, Germany
E-mail: simons@mpi-cbg.de
URL: http://www.elso.org

2835 ■ Early Career Award
To recognize a woman or a man who has made a very significant contribution to the molecular life sciences during their early career as an independent scientist in Europe. Candidates normally have obtained his or her PhD less than 10 years ago, but exceptional circumstances can be taken into account. A monetary prize of 1,000 Euros is awarded annually.

2836 ■ European Meteorological Society
Martina Junge, Exec. Sec.
c/o Freie Universitat Berlin
Carl-Heinrich-Becker-Weg 6-10

D-12165 Berlin, Germany
Ph: 49 30 79708328
Fax: 49 30 7919002
E-mail: ems-sec@met.fu-berlin.de
URL: http://www.emetsoc.org

2837 ■ Broadcast Meteorologist Award
To recognize lifetime achievements in broadcast meteorology. Candidates must be European broadcast meteorologists with long professional careers. Awarded annually. Established in 2007.

2838 ■ Outreach and Communication Award
To recognize projects that explore innovative and effective ways to communicate the sciences of climatology, meteorology, and related fields to the general public. Individuals and project teams are eligible. A trophy is awarded annually. Established in 2008.

2839 ■ Silver Medal
For distinguished contributions to meteorology in Europe. Awarded annually.

2840 ■ TV Weather Forecast Trophy Award
To recognize an outstanding meteorology video clip. Eligible to European broadcast meteorologists. Awarded annually.

2841 ■ Young Scientist Award
To recognize excellence in young meteorology scientists. Eligible to scientists under 35 years old who work and/or study in Europe, and who have written a high quality publication in a reviewed scientific journal, or an outstanding PhD thesis. Travel expenses to the Annual Meeting are awarded annually, as well as a monetary prize of 1,000 Euros.

2842 ■ European Molecular Biology Organization
Prof. Maria Leptin, Dir.
Meyerhofstrasse 1
D-69117 Heidelberg, Germany
Ph: 49 6221 88910
Fax: 49 6221 8891200
E-mail: embo@embo.org
URL: http://www.embo.org

2843 ■ EMBO Medal
For recognition of contributions in Western Europe to the development of molecular biology. European citizens under the age of 40 are eligible. A monetary prize of 10,000 Euros and a medal are awarded annually. Established in 1986.

2844 ■ European Optical Society
Klaus Nowitzki, Exec. Dir.
Hollerithallee 8
D-30419 Hannover, Germany
Ph: 49 511 2788115
Fax: 49 511 2788119
E-mail: info@myeos.org
URL: http://www.myeos.org

2845 ■ EOS Prize
To recognize an outstanding paper in optics.

2846 ■ European Parking Association
Gerhard Trost-Heutmekers, Sec.
Richartzstrasse 10
D-50667 Cologne, Germany
Ph: 49 221 2571018
Fax: 49 221 2571019
E-mail: epa@europeanparking.eu
URL: http://www.europeanparking.eu

2847 ■ European Parking Award
For excellence in parking structures. Categories include New Parking Structures, Renovated Structures, Innovative Scheme in any Aspect of Parking, and On Street Parking Projects. Awarded biennially in odd-numbered years.

Awards are arranged in alphabetical order below their administering organizations

2848 ■ European Standard Parking Award
To recognize car parks that have met certain standards for safety and customer friendliness. Standards include: lighting and reflective services; vehicular entry and exit; parking areas; pedestrian routes; lifts and stairwells; security; maintenance; and more.

2849 ■ European Rotogravure Association
James Siever, Sec. Gen.
Swakopmunder Strasse 3
D-81827 Munich, Germany
Ph: 49 89 4395051
Fax: 49 89 4394107
E-mail: info@era.eu.org
URL: http://www.era.eu.org

2850 ■ Packaging Gravure Awards
To recognize gravure quality in packaging printing. Competition is open to members and non-members from around the world. Award categories include: flexible packaging (subdivided into substrate types); shrinkwrap sleeves; labels; cartonboard; specialty, security and intelligent printing; and innovation (for technical developments and new fields of application). Special awards include a newcomers' prize and best use of a PDF-based workflow prize.

2851 ■ European Society for Microcirculation
Prof. Dr. Axel R. Pries, Gen. Sec.
Charite-Universitatsmedizin Berlin
Campus Benjamin Franklin
Institut fur Physiologie
Arnimallee 22
14195 Berlin, Germany
Ph: 49 30 450528501
Ph: 49 30 450528502
Fax: 49 30 450528910
E-mail: esmmail@charite.de
URL: http://www.esmicrocirculation.eu

2852 ■ Lars-Erik Gelin Conference Travel Award
Together with the submission of an abstract for an international conference of the ESM, young scientists may apply for a travel grant which will cover the registration fee and support their travel costs. Prizes are awarded on the basis of the quality of the submitted abstracts. A grant of 500 Euros are awarded to one or more recipients biennially in even-numbered years.

2853 ■ Honorary Membership
To award researchers who have been active in microcirculatory research for a long time (they may be retired from their professional duties). Honorary membership may be awarded upon suggestion by national societies or individual members.

2854 ■ Malpighi Medal
Recognizes scientific achievements of a long scientific career. A medal is awarded annually.

2855 ■ Van Leeuwenhoek Distinctive Travel Award
To allow researchers entering the area of microcirculatory and vascular biology research to visit research laboratories in order to learn new techniques and discuss topics, methods and perspectives with established researchers. A monetary prize of 2,500 Euros is awarded biennially in even-numbered years.

2856 ■ European Society of Gastrointestinal Endoscopy
Horst Neuhaus, Pres.
HG Editorial and Management Services
Mauerkircher Str. 29
81679 Munich, Germany
Ph: 49 89 907793600
Fax: 49 89 907793620
E-mail: secretariat@esge.com
URL: http://www.esge.com

2857 ■ European Postgraduate Grants
To support fully trained East- and Central-European endoscopists who wish to undertake further training in highly specialized endoscopic techniques at an officially recognized ESGE training centre. Applicants must below the age of 40 and must have a high proficiency in English, French, or German. Awarded annually.

2858 ■ European Society of Ophthalmic Plastic and Reconstructive Surgery
Prof. Dr. C. Hintschich, Sec.
Ludwig-Maximilians-University Munich
Dept. of Ophthalmology
Mathildenstr. 8
80336 Munich, Germany
Ph: 49 89 51603811
Ph: 49 89 51603001
Fax: 49 89 51605160
E-mail: christoph.hintschich@med.uni-muenchen.de
URL: http://www.esoprs.com

2859 ■ Junior Award
Recognizes the best research in ophthalmology by a young scientist. Based on papers submitted and read at the Annual Meeting. Author must be under 35 years of age. A monetary prize of 3,000 Euros to further the education of the recipient is awarded annually.

2860 ■ European Thyroid Association (Association Europeenne Thyroide)
Peter Laurberg, Pres.
EndoScience Endokrinologie Service GmbH
Hopfenartenweg 19
90518 Nuremberg, Germany
Ph: 49 6136 762197
Fax: 49 6136 761953
E-mail: euro-thyroid-assoc@endoscience.de
URL: http://www.eurothyroid.com

2861 ■ Brahm's Young Investigators Award
To recognize young investigators for outstanding accomplishments in thyroid research. Awarded annually.

2862 ■ Genzyme Prize
To recognize a member of the Association for a major contribution to thyroid research. Awarded biennially in even-numbered years. Formerly: Henning Prize.

2863 ■ Harington-De Visscher Prize
To recognize a European scientist, not older than 42 years, for outstanding contributions to thyroid research. Awarded biennially in even-numbered years.

2864 ■ Max Pierre Koenig/Organon/ Nourypharma Poster Prize
To recognize the authors of the best poster presentation at the annual meeting. Awarded annually if merited. Established in 1989.

2865 ■ Lissitzky Career Award
To recognize a scientist for outstanding contributions over a lifetime to thyroid research. Individuals should preferably work in Europe. Awarded biennially in odd-numbered years. Established in 1997.

2866 ■ Merck-Serono Award
To recognize research into thyroid conditions. Recipient gives a lecture at the annual meeting. Awarded annually. Established in 1992.

2867 ■ Merck-Serono Prize
To recognize outstanding thyroid research. Recipients are invited to present a lecture detailing their findings. Awarded annually. Sponsored by Merck-Serono. Formerly: Merck KGaA Prize.

2868 ■ European Tube Manufacturers Association
Mr. Gregor Spengler, Sec. Gen.
Am Bonneshof 5
Haus der Metalle, 2nd Fl.

D-40474 Dusseldorf, Germany
Ph: 49 211 4796144
Fax: 49 211 479625141
E-mail: info@etma-online.org
URL: http://www.etma-online.org

2869 ■ Tubes of the Year
Recognizes excellence in tube manufacturing and design. Awards are offered in three tube categories: plastic, laminate, and metal. Also presents and award for a prototype category, which is open to any type of tubing. Awarded annually.

2870 ■ European Water Association
Dr. Jean Philippe Torterotot, Pres.
Theodor-Heuss-Allee 17
D-53773 Hennef, Germany
Ph: 49 22 42872189
Fax: 49 22 42872135
E-mail: info@ewa-online.eu
URL: http://www.EWA-online.eu

2871 ■ William Dunbar Medal
To recognize applied technology development in the field of waste water treatment and water protection. A gold medal, certificate, and monetary prize of 5,000 Euros are awarded triennially. Established in 1973.

2872 ■ EUROSOLAR - The European Association for Renewable Energy
Irm Pontenagel, Managing Dir.
Kaiser-Friedrich Str. 11
D-53113 Bonn, Germany
Ph: 49 228 362373
Ph: 49 228 362373
Fax: 49 228 361279
E-mail: info@eurosolar.org
URL: http://www.eurosolar.org

2873 ■ European Solar Prizes
Recognizes individuals, associations, communities, municipal enterprises, and towns for contributions to renewable energy. Multiple prizes are awarded throughout Europe. Established in 1994.

2874 ■ Federal Association of the Gem, Stone and Diamond Industry (Bundesverband der Edelstein- und Diamantindustrie)
Paul Otto Caesar, Chm.
Hauptstrasse 161
D-55714 Idar-Oberstein, Germany
Ph: 49 6781 944240
Fax: 49 6781 944266
E-mail: info@bv-edelsteine-diamanten.de
URL: http://www.bv-edelsteine-diamanten.de

2875 ■ German Award for Jewelry and Precious Stones
To recognize innovative and positive developments in gemstone and jewelry design. Awarded annually.

2876 ■ Federal Chamber of Architects, Germany (Bundesarchitektenkammer)
Sigurd Trommer, Pres.
Askanischer Platz 4
10963 Berlin, Germany
Ph: 49 30 2639440
Fax: 49 30 26394490
E-mail: info@bak.de
URL: http://www.bak.de/site/163/default.aspx

2877 ■ Taut-Prize
For the four best students of architecture in Germany.

2878 ■ Federal Union of German Associations of Pharmacists (Bundesvereinigung Deutscher Apothekerverbande)
Heinz-Gunter Wolf, Pres.
Jagerstrasse, 49/50
D-10117 Berlin, Germany

Awards are arranged in alphabetical order below their administering organizations

Ph: 49 30 400040
Fax: 49 30 40004598
E-mail: pressestelle@abda.aponet.de
URL: http://www.abda.de

2879 ■ Ehrennadel der Deutschen Apotheker
To recognize an outstanding German pharmacist. A lapel pin and a certificate are awarded at infrequent intervals. Established in 1975.

2880 ■ Hans Meyer Medaille
For recognition of service to the German pharmaceutical profession and pharmaceutical medicine. A silver medal and a certificate are awarded annually. Established in 1971 by the executive councils of the Professional Association of German Pharmacists, and the Federal Chamber of Pharmacists.

2881 ■ Federation of European Neuroscience Societies
Meino Gibson, Contact
Max Delbruck Center for Molecular Medicine
Robert-Rossle Str. 10
D-13092 Berlin, Germany
Ph: 49 3 94063133
Ph: 49 3 94063133
Fax: 49 3 94062813
E-mail: meino.gibson@fens.org
URL: http://fens.mdc-berlin.de

2882 ■ Boehringer Ingelheim FENS Research Award
For outstanding and innovative scientific contributions to neuroscience. Eligible to scientists under 40 years of age who are working in a European institute or are of European origin. A monetary award of 25,000 Euros is presented. Sponsored by Boehringer Ingelheim.

2883 ■ EJN Award
To recognize outstanding scientific work in neuroscience. Eligible to European scientists working in Europe or abroad. Recipient is required to give a lecture at the FENS Forum. A monetary prize of £10,000 is awarded biennially in even-numbered years. Recipient is also invited to write a minireview for publication in the *European Journal of Neuroscience* (EJN). Sponsored by Wiley-Blackwell.

2884 ■ EJN Young Investigator Award
To recognize a young investigator for outstanding scientific work in neuroscience. Candidates should be under 40 years of age and working at a European institute or of European origin. A monetary prize of £7,000 is awarded biennially in even-numbered years. Co-sponsored by the *European Journal of Neuroscience* (EJN) and Wiley-Blackwell.

2885 ■ Foerderkreis Deutscher Schriftsteller in Baden-Wuerttemberg
Meike Gerhardt, Managing Dir.
Postfach 80 03 24
D-70503 Stuttgart, Germany
E-mail: info@schriftsteller-in-bawue.de
URL: http://www.schriftsteller-in-bawue.de

2886 ■ Thaddaeus Troll Preis
For recognition of German writers in the field of literature. Baden-Wuerttemberg authors are eligible. An endowment of 10,000 Euros and a certificate are awarded annually. Established in 1981 in memory of Thaddaeus-Troll who was dedicated to promoting young literary talent.

2887 ■ Foundation of Lower Saxony (Stiftung Niedersachsen)
Dr. Joachim Werren, Sec. Gen.
Sophienstrasse 2
Kunstlerhaus
D-30159 Hannover, Germany
Ph: 49 511 990540
Fax: 49 511 9905499

E-mail: info@stnds.de
URL: http://www.stnds.de/en/meta/homepage/index. html

2888 ■ Hanover International Violin Competition (Internationaler Violin-Wettbewerb Hannover)
To encourage professional development of young violinists and to recognize their achievements. The competition is open to violinists of all nationalities between 16 and 28 years of age. The following prizes are presented: first place - 50,000 Euros; second place - 30,000 Euros; third place - 20,000 Euros. Fourth, fifth, and sixth-place finalists receive 8,000 Euros, and 7th through 12th place semi-finalists receive a scholarship valued at 1,000 Euros. In addition, a Music Critics' Prize of 5,000 Euros and an Audience Prize of 5,000 Euros are awarded. Held triennially. Established in 1991 and dedicated to Joseph Joachim.

2889 ■ Franz Moll Foundation
Ganghoferstr. 52
D-80339 Munich, Germany
Ph: 49 89 2865 9714
Fax: 49 89 2865 9715
E-mail: info@nuclear-free.com
URL: http://www.nuclear-free.com

2890 ■ Nuclear-Free Future Award
To recognize individuals or organizations worldwide who are actively engaged in the struggle for a post-nuclear society. Awarded in three categories: Solutions, Education, and Resistance. A monetary prize of US$10,000 is awarded annually in each category. Established in 1999.

2891 ■ Fraunhofer-Gesellschaft zur Forderung der Angewandten Forschung
Prof. Dr. Hans-Jorg Bullinger, Pres.
PO Box 20 07 33
80007 Munich, Germany
Ph: 49 89 12050
Fax: 49 89 12057531
E-mail: info@zv.fraunhofer.de
URL: http://www.fraunhofer.de

2892 ■ Hugo Geiger Prize
To recognize outstanding, application-oriented theses or dissertations in the life sciences field. A monetary prize of 5,000 Euros is awarded for first place, 3,000 Euros for second place, and 2,000 for third place. Sponsored by the Bavarian Ministry of Economic Affairs, Infrastructure, Transport and Technology.

2893 ■ Technology Prize for Human-Centered Technology
To recognize members of staff whose research and development work has made a significant contribution to the quality of life, enabling people to remain fit and active in their daily lives through an advanced age. A monetary prize of 10,000 Euros is awarded biennially.

2894 ■ Joseph von Fraunhofer Prize
To recognize outstanding scientific achievements by Fraunhofer researchers in solving application-related problems. Three monetary prizes of 20,000 Euros are awarded annually.

2895 ■ German Academy of Language and Poetry (Deustche Akademie fur Sprache und Dichtung)
Dr. Bernd Busch, Gen. Sec.
Gluckert-Haus
Alexandraweg 23
D-64287 Darmstadt, Germany
Ph: 49 6151 40920
Fax: 49 6151 409299
E-mail: sekretariat@deutscheakademie.de
URL: http://www.deutscheakademie.de

2896 ■ Georg Buchner Preis
To recognize writers and poets whose works further the cultural heritage of Germany. A monetary prize of 40,000 Euros is awarded annually. Established in 1923 for the arts and literature, and changed to a literature prize in 1951.

2897 ■ Sigmund Freud Preis
For recognition of a scientific work which constitutes an effective piece of prose. A monetary of 12,500 Euros is awarded annually. Established in 1964.

2898 ■ Friedrich-Gundolf-Preis fur die Vermittlung deutscher Kultur im Ausland
To recognize persons who have rendered outstanding service to the promulgation of German culture on foreign soil. A monetary prize of 12,500 Euros is awarded annually. Established in 1964.

2899 ■ Johann Heinrich Merck Preis
For recognition of works of literary criticism and essays. A monetary prize of 12,500 Euros is awarded annually. Established in 1964.

2900 ■ Johann-Heinrich-Voss-Preis fur Uebersetzung
For recognition of excellence in translation of a life's work and also individual works of poetry, drama, or essays. A monetary prize of 15,000 Euros is awarded annually. Established in 1958.

2901 ■ German Adult Education Association (Deutscher Volkshochschul-Verband)
Dr. Roland Schwartz, Dir.
Obere Wilhelmstrasse 32
D-53225 Bonn, Germany
Ph: 49 228 975690
Fax: 49 228 9756955
E-mail: info@dvv-international.de
URL: http://www.dvv-international.de/index. php?article_id=1&clang=1

2902 ■ Adolf Grimme Preis
Recognizes outstanding educational television programs. Awarded annually.

2903 ■ German Agricultural Society (Deutsche Landwirtschafts-Gesellschaft)
Carl-Albrecht Bartmer, Pres.
Eschborner Landstrasse 122
D-60489 Frankfurt, Germany
Ph: 49 69 247880
Fax: 49 69 247881100
E-mail: info@dlg.org
URL: http://www.dlg.org

2904 ■ International DLG Prize (Internationaler DLG-Preis)
For recognition of exceptional professional and honorary achievement in agriculture and its related industry and to provide further and supplementary training. Individuals who are 18 to 36 years of age may be nominated. The following grants for training are awarded: (1) Junior-Prize, for individuals 18-24 years of age - 2,500 Euros; (2) Supplemental Training Prize, for individuals 24-36 years of age - 4,000 Euros. Established in 1986 by Deutsche Landwirtschafts-Gesellschaft on the occasion of its 100-year anniversary.

2905 ■ German Association for Physiotherapy (Deutscher Verband fur Physiotherapie)
Heinz Christian Esser, Managing Dir.
Postfach 210280
D-50528 Cologne, Germany
Ph: 49 221 9810270
Fax: 49 221 98102725
E-mail: info@zvk.org
URL: http://www.zvk.org

Awards are arranged in alphabetical order below their administering organizations

2906 ■ Scientific Award
For scientific research.

2907 ■ German Association for Water, Wastewater and Waste
Theodor-Heuss-Allee 17
D-53773 Hennef, Germany
Ph: 49 2242 872333
Fax: 49 2242 872100
E-mail: mitgliederbetreuung@dwa.de
URL: http://www.dwa.de/portale/dwahome/dwahome.nsf/home?readform

2908 ■ Ernst-Kuntze Prize
For a practitioner's thesis in the field of wastewater. A monetary prize of 5,000 Euros is awarded annually.

2909 ■ German Association of Market and Social Researchers
(Berufsverband Deutscher Markt- und Sozialforscher)
Wolfgang Dittrich, CEO
Friedrichstrasse 187
D-13187 Berlin, Germany
Ph: 49 30 49907420
Fax: 49 30 49907421
E-mail: info@bvm.org
URL: http://www.bvm.org

2910 ■ Lifetime Award
To honor an individual for lifelong commitment to the marketing research industry and its image. Awarded annually.

2911 ■ Research Personality of the Year
To honor an individual who has provided outstanding services to the market research sector. Awarded annually.

2912 ■ Study of the Year Award
To recognize an outstanding market research study, which should be exciting, introduce innovative methodology, and prove relevant to the company concerned and its success. Awarded annually.

2913 ■ Tool of the Year Award
To recognize a market research instrument that is innovative in its field of research and represents a significant advantage in comparison to other approaches. Awarded annually.

2914 ■ Young Researcher Award
To recognize an outstanding dissertation, diploma paper, or thesis on the topic of market research. Awarded annually.

2915 ■ German Atomic Forum
(Deutsches Atomforum)
Dr. Dieter H. Marx, Sec. Gen.
Robert-Koch-Platz 4
D-10115 Berlin, Germany
Ph: 49 30 498555
Fax: 49 30 498555
E-mail: info@kernenergie.de
URL: http://www.atomforum.de/kernenergie

2916 ■ Karl-Winnacker-Preis
For outstanding journalistic work on nuclear energy.

2917 ■ German Bunsen Society for Physical Chemistry
(Deutsche Bunsen-Gesellschaft fur Physikalische Chemie)
Dr. Andreas Foerster, Sec. Gen.
Theodor-Heuss Allee 25
D-60486 Frankfurt, Germany
Ph: 49 69 7564621
Fax: 49 69 7564622
E-mail: woehler@bunsen.de
URL: http://www.bunsen.de

2918 ■ Paul Bunge Prize
The Hans R. Jenemann Foundation honors work in the area of scientific historic instruments, jointly with Gesellschaft Deutscher Chemiker. Established in 1992. Awarded annually.

2919 ■ Theodor Foerster Memorial Lecture
For recognition of outstanding work in the area of photochemistry. A lecture and travel expenses are awarded. Established to honor Theodor Foerster. Awarded jointly with the Gesellschaft Deutscher Chemiker.

2920 ■ Wilhelm Jost Memorial Lecture
Established by H. Roeck, jointly with and under administration of the Akademie der Wissenschaften, Goettingen. Annual proposal of a lecturer by the Bunsen-Gesellschaft. Honors the famous physicochemist W. Jost and lectures are given in the university cities of Jost's work.

2921 ■ Nernst-Haber-Bodenstein-Preis
For recognition of achievement in physical chemistry. Scientists who are less than 40 years of age are eligible. A monetary award is presented annually. Established in 1953 by German industry.

2922 ■ German Chemical Society
(Gesellschaft Deutscher Chemiker)
Prof. Wolfram Koch, Exec. Dir.
Postfach 90 04 40
D-60444 Frankfurt am Main, Germany
Ph: 49 69 79170
Fax: 49 69 7917232
E-mail: gdch@gdch.de
URL: http://www.gdch.de

2923 ■ Adolf-von-Baeyer-Denkmunze
For recognition of the best published work of the preceding year in the area of organic chemistry, especially on experimental dye or pharmaceutical chemistry, or for contributions to the German chemical industry through the discovery of organic preparations, important dyes or pharmaceutical preparations, perfumes or other products. German chemists are eligible. A monetary prize and a gold medal are awarded biennially in odd-numbered years. Established in 1910 by Carl Duisberg.

2924 ■ August-Wilhelm-von-Hofmann-Denkmunze
To honor non-German chemists and German scientists who are not chemists but who have made special contributions to chemistry. A gold medal is awarded when merited. Established in 1902.

2925 ■ Gmelin Beilstein Denkmunze
For special recognition of contributions to chemical literature or the history of chemistry, hence also the goals of the German Chemical Society. German and non-German chemists are eligible. A monetary award and a silver medal are awarded every few years. Established in 1954 by Hoechst AG.

2926 ■ Carl Duisberg Gedachtnispreis
For recognition of research in chemistry. Younger scientists qualified as university lecturers are eligible. A monetary award is given annually. Established in 1935.

2927 ■ Carl Duisberg Plakette
For recognition of special contributions to the advancement of chemistry and the goals of the society. A gold plaque is awarded when merited. Established in 1953 by Bavarian AG.

2928 ■ Emil Fischer Medaille
For recognition of the best work in the field of organic chemistry. German chemists are eligible. A monetary award and a gold medal are awarded biennially in even-numbered years when merited. Established in 1912.

2929 ■ Fresenius-Preis
For recognition of special contributions to the scientific development of analytical chemistry. A monetary award and a gold medal are awarded biennially in odd-numbered years. Established in 1961.

2930 ■ Wilhelm Klemm Preis
For recognition of outstanding work in the field of inorganic chemistry. German and non-German scientists are eligible. A monetary award and a gold medal are awarded biennially in odd-numbered years. Established in 1984 by Degussa AG.

2931 ■ Joseph Konig Gedenkmunze
For recognition of special contributions to the scientific development of food chemistry and for the advancement and recognition of food chemistry. German and non-German scientists are eligible. A monetary award and a bronze medal are awarded every few years. Established in 1934.

2932 ■ Liebig-Denkmunze
For recognition of outstanding achievements by German chemists. A monetary award and a silver medal are given biennially in even-numbered years. Established in 1903.

2933 ■ Horst Pracejus Preis
For eminent contributions to the advancement of research in chirality. A monetary award is given biennially in odd-numbered years. Established in 1999.

2934 ■ Preis der Gesellschaft Deutcher Chemiker fur Schriftsteller
For recognition of outstanding publications that inform the public about problems of chemistry and their solutions. Journalists and authors are eligible. A monetary award is presented annually if merited. Established in 1980. Formerly: Preis der Gesellschaft Deutscher Chemiker fur Journalistin und Schrif tsteller.

2935 ■ Arfvedson Schlenk Preis
To honor outstanding scientific and technical achievements in the field of lithium chemistry. A monetary award is awarded biennially in odd-numbered years. Established in 1997.

2936 ■ Hermann Staudinger Preis
For recognition of contributions in the field of macromolecular chemistry. German and foreign scientists are eligible. A monetary award and a gold medal are awarded every three years. Established in 1970 by BASF AG.

2937 ■ Alfred Stock Gedachtnispreis
For recognition of an outstanding independent scientific experimental investigation in the field of inorganic chemistry. A monetary award and a gold medal are awarded biennially in even-numbered years. Established in 1950.

2938 ■ Friedrich Wohler Preis fur Ressourcenschonende Prozesse
For recognition of achievements in chemistry, chemical technology, and similar fields which improve the use of materials and reduce waste, solvents, energy, or hazards. A monetary award is presented every two or three years. Established in 1997.

2939 ■ German Dental Association
(BundeszahnArztekammer-BZAK)
Andreas Kunzler, Contact
Chausseestrasse 13
D-10115 Berlin, Germany
Ph: 49 30 400050
Ph: 49 30 40005113
Fax: 49 30 40005200
E-mail: info@bzaek.de
URL: http://www.bzaek.de

2940 ■ Goldene Nadel Award
For outstanding service to the profession.

2941 ■ German Design Council
(Rat fur Formgebung)
Prof. Dr. Peter Pfeiffer, Pres.
Dependance/Messegelande

Awards are arranged in alphabetical order below their administering organizations

Ludwig-Erhard-Anlage 1
D-60327 Frankfurt am Main, Germany
Ph: 49 69 7474860
Fax: 49 69 74748619
E-mail: info@german-design-council.de
URL: http://www.german-design-council.de

2942 ■ Design Award of the Federal Republic of Germany (Designpreis der Bundesrepublik Deutschland)
To recognize the best in German product and communication design. Entries are judged on creative and technical innovation, design strategy, utility, human benefits, and sustainability. To be considered, products must be nominated by the Ministers or Senators for Economics and Culture of the German Lander and the Federal Minister of Economics and Employment. Awarded biennially. Established in 1969 by the German Ministry for Economics and Technology. Formerly: (1990) Bundespreis Gute Form.

2943 ■ German Geological Society (Deutschen Gesellschaft fur Geowissenshaften)
Dr. Stefan Wohnlich, Chm.
Stilleweg 2
D-30655 Hannover, Germany
Ph: 49 511 6433567
Ph: 49 511 8980561
Fax: 49 511 6433667
E-mail: dgg@bgr.de
URL: http://www.dgg.de

2944 ■ Herman Credner Preis
For a geologist or geoscientist. A monetary prize is awarded annually.

2945 ■ Teichmueller Stipendium
For geologist or geoscientist. A monetary prize is awarded annually.

2946 ■ German Geophysical Society
Birger G. Luehr, Contact
GeoForschungsZentrum Potsdam
Telegrafenberg
D-14473 Potsdam, Germany
Ph: 49 331 2881206
Fax: 49 331 2881204
E-mail: ase@gfz-potsdam.de
URL: http://www.dgg-online.de

2947 ■ Gunter Bock Prize
To recognize a young geophysicist for an outstanding scientific publication in the field. Established in 2006.

2948 ■ Walter Kertz Medal
To recognize outstanding interdisciplinary achievements in promoting geophysics. Established in 2000.

2949 ■ Ernst von Rebeur Paschwitz Medal
To recognize outstanding scientific achievements in geophysics. Established in 2004.

2950 ■ Emil Wiechert Medal
For outstanding work in geophysics. Established in 1955.

2951 ■ Karl Zoeppritz Prize
For young researchers in geophysics. Established in 2003.

2952 ■ German Informatics Society (Gesellschaft fuer Informatik)
Dr. Peter Federer, CEO
Ahrstrasse 45
D-53175 Bonn, Germany
Ph: 49 228 302145
Fax: 49 228 302167
E-mail: gs@gi-ev.de
URL: http://www.gi.de

2953 ■ Award for Teachers
To honor outstanding teachers of informatics. Open to teachers of any age pupil in any type of school. Awarded annually.

2954 ■ Dissertation Prize
To recognize outstanding works covering all kinds of topics in informatics, including advances in technology, new applications, or the interrelation with the general society. Awarded annually. Established in 1994.

2955 ■ Innovation Prize
To recognize inventions or innovations covering typical problem areas in informatics. Awarded annually. Established in 2005.

2956 ■ Konrad-Zuse-Medaille
Recognizes an outstanding contributor to computer science. Awarded annually if merited. Established in 1987.

2957 ■ German Interior Architects Association (Bund Deutscher Innenarchitekten)
Prof. Rudolf Schricker, Pres.
Konigswinterer Str. 675
D-53227 Bonn, Germany
Ph: 49 228 9082940
Fax: 49 228 90829420
E-mail: info@bdia.de
URL: http://www.bdia.de

2958 ■ Deutscher Innenarchitektur Preis
To recognize outstanding interior architects. Awarded to up to three recipients.

2959 ■ Forderpreis
To recognize students of interior architecture. Awarded to up to three recipients.

2960 ■ German Language Society (Geselleschaft fur deutsche Sprache)
Dr. Karin M. Eichoff-Cyrus, Contact
Spiegelgasse 13
D-65183 Wiesbaden, Germany
Ph: 49 611 999550
Fax: 49 611 9995530
E-mail: sekr@gfds.de
URL: http://www.gfds.de

2961 ■ Medienpreis fur Sprachkultur
For the promotion of media communications, journalism, radio, and television, and for recognition of outstanding endeavors in promoting the German language. A certificate and monetary prize of 5,000 Euros are awarded biennially in even-numbered years. Established in 1985.

2962 ■ Alexander Rhomberg Preis
For the encouragement of young journalists, and for the cultivation and promotion of the German language. A monetary prize of 5,000 Euros is awarded biennially in even-numbered years. Established in 1994 as an extension of the Medienpreis fur Sprachkultur.

2963 ■ German Medical Association (Bundersarztekammer)
Prof. Joerg-Dietrich Hoppe, Pres.
Herbert-Lewin-Platz 1
D-10623 Berlin, Germany
Ph: 49 30 4004560
Fax: 49 30 400456388
E-mail: info@baek.de
URL: http://www.baek.de

2964 ■ Ernst-von-Bergmann-Plakette
For recognition of outstanding contributions in the field of CME. Individuals of all lands are eligible. A medal and certificate are awarded annually. Established in 1962.

2965 ■ Paracelsus Medaille
This, the highest honor of the Assembly, is given for recognition of outstanding medical achievement, contributions to the medical profession, and notable advances in the science of medicine. Doctors are eligible. A medal and a certificate are awarded annually. Established in 1952.

2966 ■ German National Mathematical Society (Deutsche Mathematiker Vereinigung)
Ms. Roswitha Jahnke, Sec.
Mohrenstrasse 39

D-10117 Berlin, Germany
Ph: 49 30 20372306
Fax: 49 30 20372307
E-mail: dmv@wias-berlin.de
URL: http://www.dmv.mathematik.de

2967 ■ Carl Friedrich Gauss Prize
To honor scientists whose mathematical research has had an impact outside mathematics, whether in technology, business, or everyday life. A medal and monetary prize are awarded every four years. Established in 2006 in honor of the mathematician Carl Friedrich Gauss. Co-sponsored by the International Mathematical Union.

2968 ■ German Neuroscience Society (Neurowissenschaftliche Gesellschaft e.V.)
Dr. Sigrun Korsching, Pres.
Max Delbruck Center for Moleculare Medizin
Robert Roessle Str. 10
D-13122 Berlin, Germany
Ph: 49 30 94063133
Fax: 49 30 94063819
E-mail: gibson@mdc-berlin.de
URL: http://nwg.glia.mdc-berlin.de/de

2969 ■ Schilling Research Award
To recognize a researcher under the age of 35 for outstanding contributions in the field of brain research. A monetary prize of 20,000 Euros is awarded biennially in odd-numbered years.

2970 ■ German Ophthalmological Society (Deutsche Ophthalmologische Gesellschaft)
Dr. Philip Gass, Managing Dir.
Platenstr. 1
D-80336 Munich, Germany
Ph: 49 89 550576815
E-mail: geschaeftsfuehrer@dog.org
URL: http://www.dog.org

2971 ■ AMD Award
For innovative developments and therapies for age-related macular degeneration. Sponsored by Novartis Pharma GmbH.

2972 ■ Glaucoma Research Award
To recognize excellence in glaucoma research. Work must have been published in a scientific magazine. Awarded annually. Sponsored by Alcon Pharma GmbH.

2973 ■ Leonard Klein Award
Recognizes innovation in the development and application of microsurgical instruments or microsurgical operating techniques in ophthalmic surgery. Eligible to individuals or research teams. A monetary prize of 15,000 Euros for continued research in ophthalmology is awarded.

2974 ■ Research Award for Innovative Work in Anterior-Segment Surgery
For innovative research in the field of anterior-segment surgery. Awarded biennially. Sponsored by Pharmacia GmbH.

2975 ■ Research Promotion for Innovative Work in Treating Glaucoma With Medication
For innovative research on treating glaucoma with medication. Work must have been published in a scientific magazine. Awarded annually. Sponsored by Pharmacia GmbH.

2976 ■ Retinitis Pigmentosa Research Award for Prevention of Blindness
For research into retinitis pigmentosa. Awarded annually. Co-sponsored by Pro Retina Deutschland e.V. and RP-Association Switzerland.

2977 ■ German Organization of Endocrinology (Deutsche Gesellschaft fur Endokrinologie)
Prof. Dr. Andreas Pfeiffer, Pres.
Mozartstrasse 23
93128 Regenstauf, Germany

Awards are arranged in alphabetical order below their administering organizations

Ph: 49 9402 9481112
Fax: 49 9402 9481119
E-mail: dge@endokrinologie.net
URL: http://www.endokrinologie.net

2978 ■ Von-Recklinghausen-Preis
For recognition of outstanding work in the field of clinical and experimental research on osteopathy and ca-metabolism. Scientists residing in Europe who are 40 years of age are eligible. A monetary prize of 5,000 Euros is awarded annually. Established in 1987 by Henning/Merrell Dow, Berlin.

2979 ■ German Ornithologists' Society
Dr. Franz Bairlein, Pres.
Institut fur Vogelforschung
Vogelwarte Helgoland
An der Vogelwarte 21
D-26386 Wilhelmshaven, Germany
Ph: 49 176 78114479
Fax: 49 4421 968955
E-mail: geschaeftsstelle@do-g.de
URL: http://www.do-g.de

2980 ■ Foerderpreis der Werner-Sunkel-Stiftung
To support work on bird migration and bird banding. Members of the German Ornithological Society (DOG) may be nominated. A monetary prize of 2,600 Euro is awarded biennially. Established in 1985 by Mrs. Sunkel in honor of Werner Sunkel.

2981 ■ Ornithologen-Preis
For recognition of important accomplishments in ornithological research. Selection is by nomination. A monetary prize of 5,000 Euro, a medal, and a diploma are awarded annually or biennially. Established in 1985 by Klaus Schmidt-Koenig.

2982 ■ Preis der Horst Wiehe-Stiftung
For recognition of a scientific contribution to bird ecology. A monetary prize of 26,000 Euro and a diploma are awarded biannually. Established in 1993.

2983 ■ Erwin-Stresemann-Foerderung
For recognition of an important ornithological research or publication. The author must be a member of DOG, may be of any nationality and under 40 years of age. A monetary prize of 5,000 Euro, a medal, and a diploma are awarded biennially in odd-numbered years. Established in 1969.

2984 ■ German Phytomedical Society
(Deutsche Phytomedizinische Gesellschaft e.V.)
Prof. Andreas Von Tiedemann, Chm.
Messeweg 11/12
D-38104 Braunschweig, Germany
Ph: 49 531 2993213
Fax: 49 531 2993019
E-mail: geschaeftsstelle@dpg.phytomedizin.org
URL: http://www.phytomedizin.org

2985 ■ Otto Appel Medal
To honor extraordinary scientific and organistic work in plant pathology. A medal is awarded biennially in even-numbered years. Established in 1959 in memory of Otto Appel, past master in plant pathology in Germany.

2986 ■ Anton de Bary Medal
To promote international research in phytopathology. A medal is awarded annually. Established in 1989 in memory of Anton de Bary (who died in 1888), mycologist and one of the founders of plant pathology.

2987 ■ Julius Kuhn Prize
To promote research in phytopathology. Scientists who are under 40 years of age are eligible. A monetary prize of 2,000 Euros is awarded biennially in even-numbered years. Established in 1978 in memory of Julius Kuhn (1825-1910), founder of the German plant pathology.

2988 ■ German Publishers and Booksellers Association
(Boersenverein des Deutschen Buchhandels e.V.)
Dr. Joachim Treeck, Contact
Grosser Hirschgraben 17 - 21
D-60311 Frankfurt am Main, Germany
Ph: 49 69 13060
Fax: 49 69 1306201
E-mail: info@boev.de
URL: http://www.boersenverein.de/de/portal/index.html
Formerly: German Booksellers Association.

2989 ■ Peace Prize of the German Book Trade
(Friedenpreis des Deutschen Buchhandels)
To recognize people of any nationality or religion who have made noteworthy contributions to literature, science, and art in the service of peace. A monetary prize of 25,000 Euros is awarded annually during the Frankfurt Book Fair. Established in 1950 by a group of publishers.

2990 ■ German Research Foundation
(Deutsche Forschungsgemeinschaft)
Prof. Dr. Matthias Kleiner, Pres.
Kennedyallee 40
D-53175 Bonn, Germany
Ph: 49 228 8851
Fax: 49 228 8852777
E-mail: postmaster@dfg.de
URL: http://www.dfg.de

2991 ■ Copernicus Award
To recognize young researchers in Germany and Poland for outstanding achievements in German-Polish scientific cooperation, in particular for young researchers. A monetary prize of 50,000 Euros is divided between two recipients (one from Germany and one from Poland) every two years. Co-administered by the Foundation for Polish Science.

2992 ■ Gottfried Wilhelm Leibniz Prize
To improve the working conditions of outstanding scientists and academics, expand their research opportunities, relieve them of administrative tasks, and help them employ particularly qualified young researchers. Up to 10 prizes are awarded annually, with a maximum of 2.5 million Euros per award. Established in 1985.

2993 ■ Heinz Maier-Leibnitz Prize
For young scientists who excel in research work. A monetary prize of 10,000 Euros is awarded annually. Established in 1977.

2994 ■ Albert Maucher Prize in Geoscience
To recognize young researchers for outstanding research finding and original approaches they have produced by using DFG funds. Candidates must be 35 years or younger. Awarded biennially in odd-numbered years.

2995 ■ Eugen and Ilse Seibold Prize
To promote science, research, and understanding between Germany and Japan by recognizing an individual for exceptional contribution toward advancing understanding between these two countries. A monetary prize of 10,000 Euro is awarded to two recipients (one from Germany and one from Japan) biennially in odd-numbered years.

2996 ■ German Society for Biochemistry and Molecular Biology
(Gesellschaft fur Biochemie und Molekularbiologie e.V.)
Tino Apel, Contact
Morfelder Landstr. 125
D-60598 Frankfurt, Germany
Ph: 49 69 6605670
Fax: 49 69 66056722
E-mail: info@gbm-online.de
URL: http://www.gbm-online.de/v2

2997 ■ Otto Warburg Medaille
For recognition in the field of biochemistry. Individuals must be nominated. A medal and document are awarded annually. Established in 1963.

2998 ■ German Society for Fat Science
(Deutsche Gesellschaft fur Fettwissenschaft e.V.)
Dr. Frank Amoneit, CEO
Varrentrappstr. 40-42
60486 Frankfurt, Germany
Ph: 49 69 7917529
Ph: 49 69 7917533
Fax: 49 69 7917564
E-mail: info@dgfett.de
URL: http://www.dgfett.de

2999 ■ Honorary Membership
To honor an individual for outstanding contributions to fats science and the Society. Awarded when merited. Established in 1939.

3000 ■ Kaufmann Memorial Lecture
For outstanding research in the fat science field. The honoree presents a lecture at the convention. Awarded biennially in odd-numbered years. Established in 1974 in memory of H. P. Kaufmann, the society's founder.

3001 ■ H. P. Kaufmann Prize
For recognition of outstanding work in the field of fat and fat product chemistry and technology. Included are studies of fatty acids and their derivatives, as well as related materials and their uses. Members of related sciences are eligible, particularly chemists, biologists, medical and pharmaceutical scientists, and engineers under age 35. A monetary prize, a plaque, and a certificate are awarded to one or two recipients. Established in 1972 in memory of the society's founder and president, H. P. Kaufmann.

3002 ■ Wilhelm Normann Medal
To recognize an individual for excellence in the study of fats and fats technology or for achievements in the promotion of fat science and the work of the Society. Awarded annually. Established in 1940.

3003 ■ Student Award
To honor outstanding student research papers in the area of fats science and technology. Open to students of all schools up to the 13th grade. A monetary prize is awarded annually. Established in 2007.

3004 ■ German Society for Mining, Metallurgy, Resource and Environmental Technology
(Gesellschaft fur Bergbau, Metallurgie, Rohstoff-und Umwelttechnik e.V.)
Dr. Hans Jacobi, Pres.
Paul-Ernst-Strasse 10
38678 Clausthal-Zellerfeld, Germany
Ph: 49 5323 93790
Fax: 49 5323 937937
E-mail: stiftung@gdmb.de
URL: http://gdmb.de
Formerly: German Society of Metallurgical and Mining Engineers.

3005 ■ Gratitude Medal
To recognize an individual for special technical-scientific and social acts of merit that have been exceptionally helpful in supporting the Society or the constitutional aims of the Society. Awarded when merited.

3006 ■ Dr. Paul Grunfeld Commemorative Award
To recognize young engineers and scientists in

Awards are arranged in alphabetical order below their administering organizations

the field of special metals in Europe. Individuals from Europe who are under 35 years of age may be nominated by the GDMB Committee for Special Metals. A monetary prize and a plaque are awarded biennially at the general assembly of GDMB. Established in 1986 by Ernst Grunfeld, London (Metallurgy) in memory of his father, Paul Grunfeld.

3007 ■ Reden Badge
To recognize students of metallurgy and mining at German technical universities who have passed their examinations with honors. A brass plaque is awarded. Established in 1935.

3008 ■ German Society for Non-Destructive Testing
(Deutschen Gesellschaft fur Zerstorungsfreie Prufung)
Mr. Matthias Purschke, CEO
Max-Planck-Strasse, 6
D-12489 Berlin, Germany
Ph: 49 30 67807
Fax: 49 30 67807
E-mail: mail@dgzfp.de
URL: http://www.dgzfp.de

3009 ■ Berthold-Preis
For recognition of achievement in non-destructive testing and of the promotion of this field. Individuals under 40 years of age may submit an application. A monetary prize of 4,000 Euros is awarded annually at the convention. Established in 1973 in honor of Professor Dr. Rudolf Berthold, founder of the Society.

3010 ■ Schiebold-Gedenkmunze
For recognition of achievement in non-destructive testing. Students of universities and institutes of technology up to 30 years of age having finished a scholarly paper or thesis may submit an application. A commemorative medal together with a monetary prize of 4000 Euros is awarded annually at the convention. Established in 1996 in honor of Professor Dr. Ernst Schiebold, a pioneer of non-destructive testing.

3011 ■ German Society of Glass Technology
(Deutsche Glastechnische Gesellschaft)
Dr. Ulrich Roger, Managing Dir.
Siemensstrasse 45
D-63071 Offenbach, Germany
Ph: 49 69 9758610
Fax: 49 69 97586199
E-mail: info@hvg-dgg.de
URL: http://www.hvg-dgg.de

3012 ■ Adolf-Dietzel-Industriepreis der DGG
For recognition of valuable work in the committees of the Society and to provide an incentive for younger glass workers. A monetary prize of 1,500 Euros and a glass box are awarded every two to three years. Established in 1952. Formerly: (1995) Industriepreis fur technisch-wissenschaftliche Arbeiten.

3013 ■ Goldener Gehlhoff-Ring
To recognize people who have contributed significantly to the development of the Society and those who have tried to improve deficiencies in glass manufacturing, science, and technology. A gold ring is awarded when merited. Established in 1950 in honor of the German physicist Georg Gehlhoff.

3014 ■ German Society of Human Genetics
(Deutsche Gesellschaft fur Humangenetik)
Christine Scholz, Exec. Managing Dir.
Inselkammerstr. 5
82008 Munich, Germany
Ph: 49 89 61456959
Fax: 49 89 55027856
E-mail: organisation@gfhev.de
URL: http://www.gfhev.de

3015 ■ Medal of Honor
To recognize an individual for significant contributions to the field of human genetics. A medal is awarded annually. Established in 2003.

3016 ■ German Society of Nutrition
(Deutsche Gesellschaft fur Ernahrung e. V.)
Dr. Helmut Oberritter, CEO
Godesberger Allee 18
D-53175 Bonn, Germany
Ph: 49 228 3776600
Fax: 49 228 3776800
E-mail: webmaster@dge.de
URL: http://www.dge.de

3017 ■ Journalist Prize
(Journalistenpreis of the DGE)
For recognition of journalists, reporters, and authors of press, radio, and television for contributions in the field of nutrition. The jury consists of members of the German Nutrition Society, sciences, consumer societies, nutrition industry, and the German Nutrition Foundation. Monetary prizes of 2,000 Euros are awarded in five categories: daily newspapers, journals, radio, television, and Internet. Awarded annually. Established in 1989.

3018 ■ Hans Adolf Krebs Prize
To encourage young scientists in the field of nutrition and food sciences. A monetary prize of 5,000 Euros is awarded every four years. Sponsored by the Stiftung zur Forderung der DGE (German Nutrition Foundation) since 1981.

3019 ■ Max Rubner Prize
For recognition and promotion of research that contributes to the development of preventive and practical dietetics for physicians. A monetary prize is awarded every four years. Sponsored by the German Nutrition Foundation since 1988.

3020 ■ German Society of Pediatrics and Adolescent Medicine
(Deutsche Gesellschaft fur Kinder- und Jugendmedizin)
Sabine Kuhne, Asst. Sec.
Chausseestr. 128/129
D-10115 Berlin, Germany
Ph: 49 30 3087779
Fax: 49 30 3087779
E-mail: info@dgkj.de
URL: http://www.dgkj.de

3021 ■ Adalbert Czerny Preis
To stimulate research in pediatrics. Pediatricians from German speaking countries are eligible. A monetary prize of 10,000 Euro and a medal are awarded annually. Established in 1961.

3022 ■ Otto Heubner Preis
For recognition of scientific achievements of the members of the German Pediatric Association. A gold medal is awarded every five years. Established before the First World War and renewed in 1953.

3023 ■ German Society of Plastic and Reconstructive Surgery
(Deutsche Gesellschaft fur Plastische und Wiederherstellungschirurgie e.V.)
Prof. Dr. Doris Henne-Bruns, Pres.
Elise-Averdieck-Str. 17
27356 Rotenburg, Germany
Ph: 49 4261 772127
Ph: 49 4261 772126
Fax: 49 4261 772128
E-mail: info@dgpw.de
URL: http://www.dgpw.de/home

3024 ■ Hans von Seemen Preis
To encourage professional development in the field of plastic and reconstructive surgery. Work published during the preceding two years and submitted to the Society is eligible. A monetary prize of 1,500 Euros and a diploma are awarded biennially. Established in 1984 in honor of Hans von Seemen, founder of the Society.

3025 ■ German Society of School Music Educators
(Verband Deutscher Schulmusiker)
Dorothee Pflugfelder, Sec.
Bundesgeschaftsstelle
Weihergarten 5
D-55116 Mainz, Germany
Ph: 49 6131 234049
Fax: 49 6131 234006
E-mail: vds@vds-musik.de
URL: http://www.vds-musik.de

3026 ■ Leo Kestenberg Medal
For outstanding contributions in promoting music education. Awarded biennially in even-numbered years.

3027 ■ VDS-Media Award
To recognize innovative music education software and media. Awarded biennially.

3028 ■ Gesellschaft Deutscher Naturforscher und Arzte
Prof. Dr. Fred R. Heiker, Gen. Sec.
Hauptstrasse 5
D-53604 Bad Honnef, Germany
Ph: 49 2224 980713
Fax: 49 2224 980789
E-mail: info@gdnae.de
URL: http://www.gdnae.de

3029 ■ Lorenz Oken Medaille
For recognition of the writing and/or editing of publications for the promotion of the general understanding, general knowledge, and the image of the natural sciences and medicine, and for contributions that promote the image of the organization. Selection is by nomination. A gold medal and a document are awarded biennially. Established in 1983 in memory of Lorenz Oken, who founded the Association by initiating the first meeting of German natural scientists and physicians in Leipzig in 1822.

3030 ■ Goethe Institute
(Goethe Institut)
Dr. Hans-Georg Knopp, Sec. Gen.
Dachauer Str. 122
D-80637 Munich, Germany
Ph: 49 89 159 210
Fax: 49 89 159 21450
E-mail: info@goethe.de
URL: http://www.goethe.de

3031 ■ Goethe Medaille
To recognize of outstanding services in the promotion of international cultural exchange, especially in the field of promoting the German language in foreign countries. Special literary, scientific, pedalogical, or organizational achievement that promotes interaction between the cultures of Germany and the host country is considered. Individuals of any nationality are eligible, but Germans only as an exception. Every year, a maximum of five medals and certificates are awarded at the official presentation taking place on March 22, the anniversary of the death of Goethe. Established in 1954.

3032 ■ Gutenberg Society: International Association for Past and Present History of the Art of Printing
(Gutenberg-Gesellschaft: Internationale Vereinigung fuer Geschichte und Gegenwart der Druckkunst)
Jens Beutel, Pres.
Liebfrauenplatz 5
D-55116 Mainz, Germany
Ph: 49 6131 226420
Ph: 49 6131 233530
Fax: 49 6131 233530
E-mail: info@gutenberg-gesellschaft.de
URL: http://www.gutenberg-gesellschaft.de

Awards are arranged in alphabetical order below their administering organizations

**3033 ■ Gutenberg Award
(Gutenberg-Preis)**
To recognize exceptional achievements relating to in artistic, technical, and scholarly fields. Individuals in the fields of typeface design, typography, printing, and printing technology and scholars in bibliographic studies from all over the world may be nominated. A monetary award of 10,000 Euros and a diploma are presented biennially in even-numbered years. Established in 1968 by the Gutenberg Society and the City of Mainz on the Rhine in memory of Johannes Gutenberg, master printer and inventor of moveable type in Mainz, 500 years after his death in 1468 A.D.

3034 ■ IFRA
Dr. Horst Pirker, VP
Washingtonplatz 1
D-64287 Darmstadt, Germany
Ph: 49 6151 7336
Fax: 49 6151 733800
E-mail: info@ifra.com
URL: http://www.ifra.net

3035 ■ International Newspaper Color Quality Club Awards
Recognizes excellence in color print quality. Awarded biennially in even-numbered years.

3036 ■ Information Technology Society
Prof. Dr. Ingo Wolff, Chm.
Stresemannallee 15
D-60596 Frankfurt, Germany
Ph: 49 69 6308 360
Fax: 49 69 6312 925
E-mail: itg@vde.com
URL: http://www.vde.com/en/Technical%20Societies/
Pages/ITG.aspx

3037 ■ Forderpreis der ITG
For recognition of excellent scientific dissertations in the field of telecommunication. Members of the Society under 30 years of age are eligible. A monetary prize and a certificate of award are presented up to three times per year. Established in 1993.

**3038 ■ Karl Kupfmuller Prize
(Karl-Kupfmuller-Preis)**
For recognition of outstanding significant technical or scientific achievements or contributions in the field of telecommunications engineering. Individuals may be nominated. A monetary prize and a certificate of award are presented every four years. Established in 1984 in memory of Karl Kuepfmueller, Professor of Engineering.

**3039 ■ International Academy of Cytology
(L'Academie Internationale De Cytologie)**
Fernando Schmitt MD, Sec.-Treas.
PO Box 1347
D-79013 Freiburg, Germany
Ph: 49 761 2923801
Fax: 49 761 2923802
E-mail: centraloffice@cytology-iac.org
URL: http://www.cytology-iac.org

3040 ■ Maurice Goldblatt Cytology Award
To recognize an individual(s) for outstanding contributions to the advancement of cytologic science and research in applied cellular studies. A medal is awarded annually at the International Congress of Cytology where the honoree delivers the Goldblatt Lecture of the Congress. Established in 1960 to honor Maurice Goldblatt, the Chairman of the Board of the Cancer Research Foundation of the University of Chicago, for his dedication to career research.

3041 ■ International Cytotechnologist of the Year Award
To recognize outstanding achievement and contribution by persons who have distinguished themselves as cytotechnologists. Technologists, educators, researchers and administrators are

eligible. Nominations are accepted from members (MIAC, PMIC or CMIAC) or fellows (FIAC or CFIAC) of IAC. A medal, a diploma and an honorarium are awarded annually. Awardees also present a special lecture during the meeting at which they are honored. Established in 1975 through a gift from the Tutorials of Cytology, Chicago, Illinois.

3042 ■ Kazumasa Masubuchi Lifetime Achievement Award
To recognize an individual for outstanding and long-term contributions to clinical cytology. Awarded triennially. Established in 1995.

3043 ■ James W. Reagan Lecture Award
To recognize an individual for extraordinary contributions to clinical cytology. Awarded triennially. Established in 1995.

3044 ■ George L. Wied Lifetime Achievement Award
To recognize an individual for outstanding and long-term contributions to cytologic research. Awarded triennially. Established in 1995.

**3045 ■ International Association for Sports and Leisure Facilities
(Internationale Vereinigung Sport- und Freizeiteinrichtungen)**
Siegfried Hoymann, Sec. Gen.
Eupener Str. 70
D-50933 Cologne, Germany
Ph: 49 221 1680230
Fax: 49 221 16802323
E-mail: iaks@iaks.info
URL: http://www.iaks.info

3046 ■ IOC/IAKS Award
Recognizes exemplary architecture of sports and leisure facilities already in operation. Medals in gold, silver and bronze are awarded biennially in odd-numbered years. Established in 1987. Co-sponsored by the International Olympic Committee (IOC).

**3047 ■ International Association of Geodesy
(Association Internationale de Geodesie)**
Michael G. Sideris, Pres.
Alfons-Goppel-Str. 11
D-80539 Munich, Germany
Ph: 49 89 230311107
Fax: 49 89 230311240
E-mail: iag@dgfi.badw.de
URL: http://www.iag-aig.org

3048 ■ Best Paper Award for Young Scientists
To recognize the best article published in the *Journal of Geodesy* that was written by a scientist aged 35 years or younger. Awarded annually.

3049 ■ Guy Bomford Prize
For recognition of outstanding individual contributions to geodetic studies. Individuals under 40 years of age are eligible. A monetary prize of $2,000 is awarded every four years at the General Assembly. Established in 1975 in honor of Brigadier Guy Bomford, formerly President of the International Association of Geodesy and Chairman of the British National Committee.

3050 ■ Levallois Medal
To recognize an individual for distinguished contribution to the Association and/or to the science of geodesy in general. Awarded every four years. Established in 1979 in honor of Jean-Jacques Levallois.

3051 ■ Young Authors' Award
To recognize the best paper written by a scientist aged 35 years or younger. A certificate and monetary prize of US$500 are awarded triennially.

3052 ■ International Association of Political Consultants
Nancy Tood Tyner, Treas.
Uerdingerstrasse 449
D-47800 Krefeld, Germany

Ph: 49 2151 590276
Fax: 49 2151 501014
E-mail: info@rapiddonor.com
URL: http://www.iapc.org

3053 ■ International Democracy Award
To recognize an individual or organization for courageously fostering, promoting, and sustaining the democratic process anywhere in the world. The Democracy medal, a bronze medal with a burnished rendering of the Acropolis etched in relief, and a certificate are awarded annually. Established in 1982.

3054 ■ International Bankers Forum
Dr. Nader Maleki, Pres.
Wiesenau 1
D-60323 Frankfurt am Main, Germany
Ph: 49 69 97176180
Ph: 49 69 27172349
Fax: 49 69 97176355
E-mail: center@ibf-ev.org
URL: http://www.ibf-ev.org

3055 ■ European Banker of the Year
For European bankers.

**3056 ■ International Council of Christians and Jews
(Internationalen Rat der Christen und Juden)**
Dr. Deborah Weissman, Pres.
PO Box 1129
D-64629 Heppenheim, Germany
Ph: 49 6252 6896810
Fax: 49 6252 68331
E-mail: info@iccj.org
URL: http://www.jcrelations.net

3057 ■ International Sternberg Award
For recognition of sustained intellectual contribution to the furtherance of inter-religious understanding, particularly, but not exclusively, in the field of Jewish-Christian relations. One or more individuals, institutions, or organizations may be recognized for achievements of international significance with impact beyond the recipient's own country. A monetary prize awarded annually when merited. Established in 1985 by Sir Sigmund Sternberg, K.C.S.G., J.P.

**3058 ■ International Council of Environmental Law
(Conseil International du Droit de l'Environnement)**
Dr. Wolfgang E. Burhenne, Exec. Governor
Godesberger Allee 108-112
D-53175 Bonn, Germany
Ph: 49 228 2692240
Fax: 49 228 2692251
E-mail: icel@intlawpol.org
URL: http://www.i-c-e-l.org

3059 ■ Elizabeth Haub Prize for Environmental Diplomacy
For recognition of practical accomplishments in the field of environmental diplomacy. Awarded annually. Established in 1998 by the ICEL and Pace University, New York.

3060 ■ Elizabeth Haub Prize for Environmental Law
For recognition of practical accomplishments in the field of environmental law. No restrictions exist as to membership or citizenship. A jury composed of representatives of ICEL and of the Universite Libre de Bruxelles makes the selection. A monetary prize to be used for specified purposes associated with environmental law and a gold medal are awarded annually. Established in 1974 by the ICEL and the Universite Libre de Bruxelles in honor of Elizabeth Haub.

**3061 ■ International Council of Sport Science and Physical Education
(Conseil International pour l'Education Physique et la Science du Sport)**
Mr. Detlef Dumon, Exec. Dir.
Hanns-Braun-Strasse Friesenhaus II
14053 Berlin, Germany

Awards are arranged in alphabetical order below their administering organizations

Ph: 49 30 36418850
Fax: 49 30 8056386
E-mail: icsspe@icsspe.org
URL: http://www.icsspe.org
Formerly: (1983) International Council of Sport and Physical Education.

3062 ■ Philip Noel Baker Research Award

To recognize an individual for both scientific work and personal contribution to the Council's activities. A diploma is awarded annually. Established in 1969 to honor Lord Philip Noel Baker, first president of ICSSPE and Laureat of the Nobel Prize for Peace.

3063 ■ Sport Science Award of the IOC President

To recognize outstanding scientific achievements in the field of sport and physical education. A US$5,000 grant is awarded in alternative years in two areas: biomedical sciences and social/human sciences. Accomplishments in the following areas are considered which: (1) study the development of the Olympic movement and world sport and their impact upon peace and international understanding; (2) substantially contribute to the knowledge of sport and physical education in general and in their various branches; (3) study the implications of life-long participation in sport on personality development and health; or (4) contribute to the further development of sport science and its disciplines.

3064 ■ International Ecology Institute
Prof. Otto Kinne, Dir./Pres.
Nordbunte 23
D-21385 Oldendorf, Germany
Ph: 49 4132 7127
Fax: 49 4132 8883
E-mail: ir@int-res.com
URL: http://www.int-res.com/ecology-institute

3065 ■ ECI Prize

To recognize ecologists for outstanding scientific achievements who are able and willing to provide a critical synthesis and evaluation of their field of expertise, addressing an audience beyond narrow professional borderlines. In an annually rotating pattern, awards are presented in the fields of marine, terrestrial, and limnetic ecology. All ecologists engaged in scientific research are eligible. A 6,000 Euros stipend is awarded annually. In addition, the winner of the prize is requested to author a 200 to 300 printed-page book, to be published by ECI in the series *Excellence in Ecology* and to be made available worldwide at cost price. The Prize is considered unique for two reasons: it was established and is financed by research ecologists, and the prize gives and takes, by both honoring the recipient and requiring him or her to serve science. Established in 1984 by Prof. Otto Kinne. Formerly: Ecology Institute Prize.

3066 ■ IRPE Prize

To recognize a young ecologist under the age of 40 who has conducted and published uniquely independent, original, and/or challenging research efforts representing an important scientific breakthrough. A 3,000 Euros stipend is awarded when merited. Formerly: International Recognition of Professional Excellence Prize.

3067 ■ International Federation of Film Critics
Schleissheimer Str. 83
D-80797 Munich, Germany
Ph: 49 89 182303
Fax: 49 89 184766
E-mail: info@fipresci.org
URL: http://www.fipresci.org

3068 ■ FIPRESCI Prize

To recognize outstanding films at more than 20 international film festivals or at film festivals of

particular importance. A diploma is awarded annually. Established in 2000.

3069 ■ International Film Festival Mannheim-Heidelberg
(Internationale Filmwoche Mannheim)
Dr. Michael Koetz, Dir.
Collini-Center, Galerie
D-68161 Mannheim, Germany
Ph: 49 621 102943
Fax: 49 621 291564
E-mail: ifmh@iffmh.de
URL: http://www.mannheim-filmfestival.com

3070 ■ International Film Festival Mannheim/Heidelberg
(Internationale Filmwoche Mannheim)

To recognize outstanding films. This small but well-known film festival is one of the oldest in the Federal Republic of Germany. Since 1994, its venues have been in the cities of Mannheim and Heidelberg. Films must be German premiers unawarded in other European Festivals such as Cannes (all sections), Berlin (all sections), Locarno (competition), and Venice (competition). New features form the backbone of the competitive festival, which prides itself on making artistic discoveries and supporting independent filmmaking. Awards are presented in the following categories: Best Feature Film, for films at least 70 minutes in length; Rainer Werner Fassbinder Prize, for the best unconventionally narrated feature film at least 60 minutes in length; Special Award of the Jury; Audience Prize; International Film Critics' Prize; Ecumenic Film Prize; and Special Mentions. Held annually. Established in 1959. Formerly: Mannheim International Filmweek.

3071 ■ International Institute of Public Finance
(Institut International de Finances Publiques)
Barbara Hebele, Admin. Mgr.
PO Box 860446
81631 Munich, Germany
Ph: 49 89 92241281
Fax: 49 89 9077952281
E-mail: hebele@iipf.org
URL: http://www.iipf.net

3072 ■ Best Paper Award

Recognizes the best paper presented at annual conference. Awarded annually.

3073 ■ Peggy and Richard Musgrave Prize

To honor and encourage younger scholars whose work meets the high standards of scientific quality, creativity, and relevance. Candidates must be younger than 40 years of age. Awarded annually. Established in 2003.

3074 ■ Young Economists Award

To encourage younger scholars to present papers at the IIPF annual congress by honoring those that demonstrate exceptional scientific quality, creativity, and relevance. Candidates must be younger than 40 years of age. Awarded annually to up to three recipients. Established in 2008.

3075 ■ International Joseph A. Schumpeter Society
Prof. Dr. Horst Hanusch, Sec. Gen.
University of Augsburg
Chair of Economics V
Universitatsstr. 16
D-86135 Augsburg, Germany
Ph: 49 821 5984179
Fax: 49 821 5984229
E-mail: horst.hanusch@wiwi.uni-augsburg.de
URL: http://www.iss-evec.de

3076 ■ Schumpeter Prize
(Schumpeter-Preis)

For recognition of a recent scholarly contribution

in economics on a designated topic related to Schumpeter's work. Applications are accepted. A monetary prize of 10,000 Euro is awarded biennially in even-numbered years. Established in 1986 in honor of Joseph Alois Schumpeter. Sponsored by *Wirtschaftswoche*, a German economic weekly.

3077 ■ International Society for Aerosols in Medicine
(Societas Internationalis Aerosolibus in Medicina)
William D. Bennett, Pres.
Wohraer Str. 37
D-35285 Gemunden, Germany
Ph: 49 6453 648180
Fax: 49 6453 6481822
E-mail: office@isam.org
URL: http://www.isam.org

3078 ■ Career Achievement Award

To recognize a senior investigator whose body of work demonstrates a lifetime of outstanding achievement in aerosol science. Awarded biennially in odd-numbered years. Established in 1987.

3079 ■ Juraj Ferin Award

To recognize an individual for outstanding contributions to the Society. Awarded biennially in odd-numbered years.

3080 ■ Student Research Award

To honor a student who has demonstrated outstanding independent research in the field of aerosols. Candidates must be full-time students enrolled in an MD, PhD, or Masters program. The first-place winner receives a cash prize and an invitation to publish part of his or her work in the *Journal of Aerosol Medicine*. Awarded biennially in odd-numbered years. Established in 2001.

3081 ■ Young Investigator Award

To recognize a member for significant contributions to the field of aerosols in medicine. Candidates must be no older than 40 years. Awarded biennially in odd-numbered years. Established in 1993.

3082 ■ International Society for Extremophiles
Dr. Ralf Grote, Sec. Gen.
Kasernenstr. 12
Institute of Technical Microbiology
Hamburg University of Technology
D-21073 Hamburg, Germany
Ph: 49 40 42878 3336
Fax: 49 40 42878 2582
E-mail: grote@tuhh.de
URL: http://extremophiles.org

3083 ■ Lifetime Achievement Award

To recognize an individual for outstanding contributions to the field of research on extremophiles. Awarded annually.

3084 ■ International Society for Oncodevelopmental Biology and Medicine
Dr. Petra Stieber, Pres.
Institut fur Klinische Chemie
Klinikum Grosshadern
Marchionini Strasse 15
D-81377 Munich, Germany
Ph: 49 89 70953115
Fax: 49 89 70956298
E-mail: petra.stieber@med.uni-muenchen.de
URL: http://isobm.org

3085 ■ Abbott Award

For anyone in the scientific or medical community who made an outstanding contribution in the field of basic or clinical oncology. Awarded annually. Established in 1990.

3086 ■ International Society for Pediatric and Adolescent Diabetes
Ragnar Hanas MD, Exec. Sec.
Kurfurstendamm 71
10709 Berlin, Germany
Ph: 49 30 24603210
Fax: 49 30 24603200
E-mail: secretariat@ispad.org
URL: http://www.ispad.org

3087 ■ Prize for Achievement
This, the Society's highest honor, is given to an individual who has made outstanding contributions in the areas of science, education, or advocacy that have had a major impact on childhood and adolescent diabetes. Awarded annually.

3088 ■ Young Investigator Award
To honor an outstanding young investigator. Awarded annually.

3089 ■ International Society of Arachnology
Nikolaj Scharff, Pres.
Museum f. Naturkunde
Humboldt Univ. zu Berlin
Invalidenstrasse 43
D-10115 Berlin, Germany
Ph: 49 30 20938516
Fax: 49 30 20938528
E-mail: dunlop@arachnology.org
URL: http://www.arachnology.org

3090 ■ Pierre Bonnet Award
To honor an individual for outstanding services to the arachnological community. Established in 2007.

3091 ■ Paulo Marcello Brignoli Award
To honor an individual for a single piece or body of exceptional research in the field of arachnology. Established in 2007.

3092 ■ Honorary Member
To honor senior colleagues who have made important contributions to the Society or the field of arachnology over the years. Awarded when merited.

3093 ■ Eugene Simon Award
To honor an individual for lifetime achievement in the field of arachnology. Established in 2007.

3094 ■ International Society on Oxygen Transport to Tissue
Dr. Oliver Thews, Sec.
Institute of Physiology
University of Halle
Magdeburger Str. 6
D-06097 Halle, Germany
Ph: 49 345 557 4048
Fax: 49 345 557 4019
E-mail: oliver.thews@medizin.uni-halle
URL: http://isott.org

3095 ■ Britton Chance Award
To recognize an outstanding young investigator in the field of oxygen transport to tissue. Candidates must not have passed his or her 30th birthday. Awarded annually. Established in 2004.

3096 ■ Melvin H. Knisely Award
To recognize outstanding young investigators in the field of oxygen transport to tissue. Candidates must have a PhD, MD, or equivalent degree, and must not have passed his or her 36th birthday. Awarded annually. Established in 1983.

3097 ■ Dietrich W. Lubbers Award
To recognize an outstanding young investigator in the field of oxygen transport to tissue. Candi-

dates must not have passed his or her 30th birthday. Awarded annually. Established in 1994.

3098 ■ International Solar Energy Society
Ms. Christine Hornstein, Exec. Dir.
Villa Tannheim
Wiesentalstrasse 50
D-79115 Freiburg, Germany
Ph: 49 761 459060
Fax: 49 761 4590699
E-mail: hq@ises.org
URL: http://www.ises.org

3099 ■ Advancing Solar Energy Policy Award
To recognize an individual for significant contributions to the advancement of solar energy policy. Awarded biennially in odd-numbered years. Established in 2011.

3100 ■ Karl W. Boer Solar Energy Medal of Merit
To recognize an individual for significant pioneering contributions to the promotion of solar energy as an alternate source of energy through research, development, or economic enterprise, or to recognize an extraordinarily valuable and enduring contribution to the field of solar energy in other ways. A bronze medal and monetary prize of US$40,000 are awarded biennially in odd-numbered years. Established in 1993.

3101 ■ Farrington Daniels Award
For recognition of outstanding contributions to science, technology, or engineering of solar energy applications leading toward ameliorating the conditions of humanity, and for furthering this cause through the International Solar Energy Society. Members may be nominated by October 31 in even-numbered years. A certificate is presented biennially at the International Congress. The recipient of the award is invited to deliver an address on a topic of his or her choice in the field of solar energy application at the international meeting at which the award is conferred. Established in 1974 in memory of Professor Emeritus Farrington Daniels of the University of Wisconsin.

3102 ■ Christopher A. Weeks Achievement through Action Award
To recognize an individual, group, or corporation for an important contribution to the harnessing of solar energy for practical use, or for a new concept, development, or product for the same purpose. A monetary prize is awarded biennially in odd-numbered years. Established in 1983.

3103 ■ International Youth Library (Internationale Jugendbibliothek)
Dr. Christiane Raabe, Dir.
Schloss Blutenburg
D-81247 Munich, Germany
Ph: 49 89 8912110
Ph: 49 89 121142
Fax: 49 89 8117553
E-mail: info@ijb.de
URL: http://www.ijb.de

3104 ■ White Ravens
To promote high quality children's books of international interest. About 250 children's books, by authors and illustrators from all over the world, are given recognition. Children's books submitted by publishers during the year prior to the award are considered. White Ravens books are listed in the annual international selected bibliography and exhibited during the Children's Book Fair in Bologna, Italy, and thereafter upon request in libraries and other institutions. Awarded annually. Established in 1984.

3105 ■ Internationale Muenchner Filmwochen GmbH
Andreas Strohl, Festival Dir.
Sonnenstrasse 21
D-80331 Munich, Germany

Ph: 49 89 3819040
Fax: 49 89 38190426
E-mail: info@filmfest-muenchen.de
URL: http://www.filmfest-muenchen.de

3106 ■ Munich International Festival of Film Schools (Internationales Festival der Filmhochschulen Munchen)
To encourage the professional development of young filmmakers. Films by film students can only be entered by the respective film schools. Awards and prize money totaling approximately 100,000 Euros are awarded. Held annually. Established in 1981.

3107 ■ Kiel Institute for the World Economy (Institut fur Weltwirtschaft)
Prof. Dennis J. Snower PhD, Pres.
Hindenburgufer 66
D-24105 Kiel, Germany
Ph: 49 431 8814 1
Fax: 49 431 8585 3
E-mail: dennis.snower@ifw-kiel.de
URL: http://www.ifw-kiel.de

3108 ■ Excellence Award in Global Economic Affairs
To recognize young researchers in the area of global economic affairs. Winners receive intellectual, financial, and administrative support to pursue focused programs of research in designated areas. Awarded to four recipients annually. Established in 2007.

3109 ■ Global Economy Prize
To recognize an economist, a politician, and a businessperson who have made an outstanding contribution to establishing a just and protective society based on individual initiative and responsibility. Awarded annually in each category. Established in 2005.

3110 ■ Bernhard Harms Medal
To recognize individuals who have contributed to the Institute's research on the world economy in the tradition of Bernhard Harms. Awarded periodically. Established in 1980.

3111 ■ Bernhard Harms Prize
For recognition of special research achievements in the field of international economics. Professors who have distinguished themselves through extraordinary achievement in the field of international economics or individuals in the business world who have made significant contributions to the improvement of world economic relations are eligible. Individuals are nominated by a nomination committee. A monetary award of 25,000 Euros and a medal are presented biennially at Kieler Woche. Established in 1964 in memory of Bernhard Harms, professor of economics and the founder of the Kiel Institute of World Economics. Sponsored by Gesellschaft zur Forderung des Instituts fur Weltwirtschaft. In addition, the Bernhard Harms Medal, established in 1980, is awarded at irregular intervals.

3112 ■ Konrad Adenauer Foundation - Germany (Konrad Adenauer Stiftung)
Dr. Hans-Gert Poettering, Chm.
Rathausallee 12
D-53757 St. Augustin, Germany
Ph: 49 2241 2460
Ph: 49 30 269963222
Fax: 49 2241 246591
E-mail: zentrale@kas.de
URL: http://www.kas.de/wf/en/

3113 ■ Literaturpreis
For outstanding literary works. A monetary prize is given annually. Established in 1993.

Awards are arranged in alphabetical order below their administering organizations

3114 ■ Lokaljournalistenpreis
Annual monetary award for local journalism.

3115 ■ Landscape Association of Westfalen-Lippe
(Landschaftsverband Westfalen-Lippe)
Wolfgang Kirsch, Dir.
Freiher-vom-Stein-Platz 1
D-48147 Munster, Germany
Ph: 49 2 51 59101
Fax: 49 2 51 5913300
E-mail: lwl@lwl.org
URL: http://www.lwl.org/LWL
Formerly: (1953) Provinzialverband Westfalen.

3116 ■ Annette von Droste Hulshoff Preis
For recognition of special achievement in poetry written in either high or low German. Every third time it can be awarded for creative musical achievement. Recipients must be natives or residents of the Westfalian Lippe region of Germany. A monetary prize and a certificate are awarded biennially. Established in 1946 by the Provinzialverband Westfalen in memory of the German and Westfalian poetess, Annette von Droste-Hulshoff (1797-1848). Formerly: Westfaelischer Literaturpreis.

3117 ■ Konrad von Soest Preis
For recognition of special achievement in the field of fine and graphic arts. Recipients must be natives or residents of the Westfalian - Lippe region of Germany. A monetary prize and a certificate are awarded biennially. Established in 1952 by the Provinzialverband Westfalen in memory of the great Westfalian medieval artist, Konrad von Soest (about 1400). Formerly: Westfaelischer Kurstpreis.

3118 ■ Leopoldina, the German Academy of Sciences
(Deutsche Akademie der Naturforscher Leopoldina)
Prof. Dr. Jorg Hacker, Pres.
Emil-Abderhalden-Str. 37
Postfach 110543
D-06019 Halle, Germany
Ph: 49 345 472390
Fax: 49 345 4723919
E-mail: leopoldina@leopoldina.org
URL: http://www.leopoldina-halle.de/cms

3119 ■ Carus Medal
To recognize younger natural scientists or physicians who have distinguished themselves with pioneering research achievements. A monetary prize of 5,000 Euros is awarded biennially. Established in honor of the 13th Academy President, Carl Gustav Carus (1789-1869).

3120 ■ Cothenius Medal
To recognize an individual for outstanding scientific lifework. A gold medal is awarded biennially. Established in 1954 in honor of Christian Andreas von Cothenius (1708-1789).

3121 ■ Early Career Award
To recognize scientists for outstanding performance in one of the research fields of the Leopoldina. A monetary prize of 30,000 Euros is awarded annually. First awarded in 2010.

3122 ■ Medal of Merit
To recognize an individual for major contributions to the benefit of the Academy. Awarded periodically.

3123 ■ Mendel Medal
To recognize an individual for special contributions to general biology (molecular biology and genetics). Awarded biennially. Established in 1965 honor of Gregor Mendel (1822-1884).

3124 ■ Prize for Junior Scientists
To recognize men or women who have made a distinguished achievement in natural sciences, medical science, or the history of science and who are under the age of 30. A monetary prize of 2,000 Euros is awarded biennially in odd-numbered years. Established in 1993.

3125 ■ Schleiden Medal
To recognize an individual for significant achievements in the field of cell research. Awarded biennially. Established in 1955 in honor of Matthias Jacob Schleiden (1804-1881).

3126 ■ Thieme Award for Medicine
To recognize junior scientists who have made a major contribution in the fields of etiology, pathogenesis, therapy, or the prevention of human diseases. A monetary prize of 15,000 Euros is awarded annually. Established in 2007.

3127 ■ Georg Uschmann Award for the History of Science
To recognize junior scientists who have written an outstanding doctoral thesis. A monetary prize of 2,000 Euros is awarded annually. Established in 2001.

3128 ■ Carl Friedrich von Weizsacker Prize
To recognize scientists or teams of researchers for their scientific contribution to socially critical questions. A monetary prize of 50,000 Euros is awarded annually. Established in 2009.

3129 ■ City of Mannheim
(Stadt Mannheim)
Rathaus E 5
D-68159 Mannheim 1, Germany
Ph: 49 621 2930
Fax: 49 621 293 9532
E-mail: masta@mannheim.de
URL: http://www.mannheim.de

3130 ■ Konrad Duden Preis
For recognition of an outstanding contribution to the German language. The prize is non-competitive. A monetary is awarded biennially. Established in 1960 in memory of Konrad Duden (1829-1911), a linguist and authority on German orthography. Co-sponsored by the Bibliographic Institute of Mannheim.

3131 ■ Max-Eyth Society for Agricultural Engineering of the VDI
(Max-Eyth-Gesselschaft Agrartechnik im VDI)
Dr. Andreas Herrmann, CEO
PO Box 10 11 39
D-40002 Dusseldorf, Germany
Ph: 49 211 6214266
Ph: 49 211 6214372
Fax: 49 211 6214177
E-mail: meg@vdi.de
URL: http://www.vdi.de/6470.0.html

3132 ■ Max Eyth Commemorative Medal
(Max-Eyth-Gedenkmunze)
To recognize an individual for outstanding contributions that are an integral part of the historical development of agricultural engineering. A bronze medal is awarded. Established in 1950.

3133 ■ Max Planck Society for the Advancement of Science
Max Planck Institute for Molecular Biomedicine
(Max-Planck-Institut fur Molekulare Biomedizin)
Dr. Ralf H. Adams, Mng. Dir.
Rontgenstrasse 20
D-48149 Munster, Germany
Ph: 49 251 703650
Fax: 49 251 70365 499
E-mail: ralf.adams@mpi-muenster.mpg.de
URL: http://www.mpi-muenster.mpg.de

3134 ■ Werner-Risau Prize
To recognize outstanding studies in endothelial cell biology by a young scientist (within the first five years after obtaining a PhD or MD). A diploma and monetary prize of 4,000 Euros is awarded annually.

3135 ■ Munich Department of Arts and Culture
(Munchen Kulturreferat)
Burgstr. 4
D-80331 Munich, Germany
Ph: 49 89 233 96939
E-mail: kulturreferat@muenchen.de
URL: http://www.muenchen.de/Rathaus/kult/37585/index.html

3136 ■ Kultureller Ehrenpreis
To recognize a person of international prominence for their cultural or scientific achievements. A monetary prize of $10,000 is awarded annually. Established in 1958.

3137 ■ LiteraVision Preis
To recognize an outstanding television program or movie covering books or writers. German-speaking individuals and programs are eligible. Two monetary awards of 5,000 Euros are presented annually. Established in 1991.

3138 ■ Promotional Prizes
To honor outstanding contributions to German culture in various fields of the arts. Monetary prizes are awarded annually in film, art, music, and dance.

3139 ■ Scholarships of the City of Munich
To honor outstanding contributions to German culture in the fields of literature, fine arts, music, theater, and dance. A number of scholarships of various amounts are awarded annually. Established in 1991.

3140 ■ Geschwister Scholl Preis
To honor a book that presents intellectually important insights on civic freedom, morality, and aesthetics. A monetary prize of 10,000 Euros is awarded annually. Established in 1980. Co-sponsored with the Bavarian Publishers and Booksellers Association.

3141 ■ Music School of Ettlingen
(Musikschule der Stadt Ettlingen)
Pforzheimer Strasse 25
D-76275 Ettlingen, Germany
Ph: 49 7243 101312
Fax: 49 7243 101436
E-mail: musikschule@ettlingen.de
URL: http://www.musikschule-ettlingen.de

3142 ■ Ettlingen International Competition for Young Pianists
(Internationaler Wettbewerb fur Junge Pianisten Ettlingen)
To recognize outstanding young pianists. Pianists of all nationalities are eligible. Awards are given in two categories: those up to 15 years of age and those up to 20 years of age. A monetary award is given to the first place winner in the younger age group, and the older age group. Special prizes are also given. Awarded biennially. Established in 1988.

3143 ■ National Association of Financial Services
(Bundesverband Finanzdienstleistungen)
Rechtsanwalt Norman Wirth, Managing Dir.
Ackerstr. 3
10115 Berlin, Germany
Ph: 49 30 20454403
Fax: 49 30 20634759
E-mail: office@afw-verband.de
URL: http://www.afw-verband.de

3144 ■ Best Journalist of the Year
For journalists.

3145 ■ Paleontological Society - Germany
Dr. Bettina Reichenbacher, Pres.
Dept. fur Geo- und Umweltwissenschaften
Ludwig-Maximilians-Universitat Munchen

Awards are arranged in alphabetical order below their administering organizations

Richard-Wagner-Str. 10
D-80333 Munich, Germany
Ph: 49 89 21806603
E-mail: b.reichenbacher@lrz.uni-muenchen.de
URL: http://www.palaeo.de/palges

3146 ■ Friedrich von Alberti Prize
To honor an individual for outstanding work in palaeontology. Awarded annually. Established in 1998.

3147 ■ Tilly Edinger Prize
To honor an individual for outstanding work in palaeontology. Awarded annually. Established in 2004.

3148 ■ Karl Alfred von Zittel Medaille
For recognition of exceptional merits in paleontology by amateurs. A certificate and a medal are awarded annually at the convention of the Society. Established in 1984 in honor of Professor Dr. Karl Alfred von Zittel (1839-1904) of Munich, a famous palaeontologist and author of an internationally known handbook.

3149 ■ Pascher + Heinz GmbH
Sigmund-Riefler Bogen 2
D-81829 Munich, Germany
Ph: 49 89 944 1960
Fax: 49 89 944 19629
URL: http://www.pascher-heinz.com

3150 ■ ispo BrandNew Awards
To honor innovation and creativity in the sporting goods industry by entrepreneurs and young companies. Awards are presented in seven categories: summer hardware, winter hardware, accessories, hardware accessories, sportswear, personal design, and style. The winner in each category receives a fully equipped complimentary booth at the BrandNew Village. In addition, an award is presented to the overall winner. The BrandNew Competition is held each year at ispo, the world's largest trade fair of the sporting goods industry. Awarded annually.

3151 ■ Physical Society of Berlin
c/o Paul Drude Institute for Solid State Electronics
Hausvogteiplatz 5-7
D-10117 Berlin, Germany
Ph: 49 30 20377 318
Fax: 49 30 20377 301
URL: http://www.pgzb.tu-berlin.de

3152 ■ Karl Scheel Prize
For recognition of published works in the field of physics. Young physicists in Berlin are eligible. A monetary prize of 5,000 Euros, a bronze plaque, and a certificate are awarded annually. Established in 1958.

3153 ■ Prix Jeunesse Foundation
Kirsten Schneid, Coor.
c/o Bayerischer Rundfunk
Rundfunkplatz 1
D-80335 Munich, Germany
Ph: 49 89 5900 2058
Fax: 49 89 5900 3053
E-mail: info@prixjeunesse.de
URL: http://www.prixjeunesse.de

3154 ■ International Munich Festival and Competition for Children's and Youth Television
To stimulate production of more and better children's and youth programs, to develop internationally applicable standards for such programs, to awaken and deepen understanding among young people of all nations, and to intensify international program exchange. Television programs for children and young people, including fiction (animation, drama, story-telling, light entertainment) and nonfiction (documentary, magazines, mixed forms, natural history, etc.) are considered in the following categories: up to

7 years of age, 7 to 12 years of age, and 12 to 15 years of age. Telecasters authorized under national and international law to operate broadcasting services may enter programs and send experts to the contest. All programs must have been produced and broadcast within the two years preceding the contest. Six prizes are awarded biennially. A trophy and a "kinetic object" created out of stainless steel and acrylic are awarded in each category. Held biennially in even-numbered years. Established in 1964.

3155 ■ Robert Schumann Society Zwickau e.V.
Stadtverwaltung Zwickau
Cultural Office
Kolpingstr. 8
D-08058 Zwickau, Germany
Ph: 49 375 834130
Fax: 49 375 834141
E-mail: kulturbuero@zwickau.de
URL: http://www.schumannzwickau.de

3156 ■ International Robert Schumann and Piano and Song Competition
For recognition of the best performances of Schumann's piano works and songs (lieder). The following prizes are awarded: first place - a monetary prize and a gold medal; second place - a monetary prize and a silver medal; third place - a monetary prize and a bronze medal; and a special monetary prize. Held annually.

3157 ■ International Robert Schumann Choral Competition
For recognition of the best music performance of Schumann's work and contemporary compositions. Amateur male, female, and mixed choirs are eligible. Held every four years. Established in 1992.

3158 ■ Society for Chemical Engineering and Biotechnology (Gesellschaft fur Chemische Technik und Biotechnologie)
Dr. Hans Jurgen Wernicke, Chm.
Theodor-Heuss-Allee 25
D-60486 Frankfurt, Germany
Ph: 49 69 75640
Fax: 49 69 7564201
E-mail: info@dechema.de
URL: http://www.dechema.de

3159 ■ ACHEMA Plaque in Titanium (ACHEMA-Plakette in Titan)
For recognition of outstanding service to DECHEMA, in particular to the ACHEMA Exhibition-Congresses, and to the DECHEMA's non-profit scientific activities. The plaque is awarded triennially. The ACHEMA Plaque was founded by DECHEMA in 1970 to commemorate the 50th Jubilee of the ACHEMA Exhibition-Congress and was first awarded during the ACHEMA of 1973.

3160 ■ ACHEMA Television Prize
To recognize the author of an exceptional German TV documentary on some aspect of chemical engineering, biotechnology, or environmental protection. Awarded triennially.

3161 ■ Jochen Block Prize
For research and development by young scientists (maximum of 35 years of age) in the field of catalysis. The prize consisting of a certificate and a monetary award is awarded in irregular intervals. Established in 1996. Sponsored by DECHEMA Subject Group Catalysis.

3162 ■ DECHEMA Award of the Max Buchner Research Foundation (DECHEMA Preis der Max Buchner Forschungsstiftung)
For recognition of an outstanding and already published research and development work in the field of chemical apparatus, and its fundamentals in technical chemistry, the materials sciences,

measurement and control technology, process engineering, and biotechnology on chemical apparatus or plant development. Preference is given to the works of younger scientists of demonstrated merit from whom further development and application in chemical engineering can be expected. A monetary prize, a gold medal, and a certificate are awarded annually. Established in 1950.

3163 ■ DECHEMA Honorary Membership (DECHEMA Ehrenmitgliedschaft)
This, the highest award of DECHEMA, is given for recognition of outstanding supporters of chemical equipment manufacture, chemical engineering, and biotechnology or to the society itself. Awarded when merited.

3164 ■ DECHEMA Medal (DECHEMA-Medaille)
For recognition of outstanding achievement in the field of chemical apparatus technology. The DECHEMA Medal is traditionally awarded triennially during ACHEMA International Meeting on Chemical Engineering and Biotechnology to one outstanding scientist each in the fields of engineering, chemistry, and biotechnology. Established in 1951.

3165 ■ Hellmuth Fischer Medal
To recognize primarily younger scientists whose works have advanced the science of electrochemistry, corrosion, or corrosion protection or works that have led to its exemplary application in industrial practice. A medal is given triennially. Established in 1988.

3166 ■ Willy Hager Medal
To recognize a scientist for an outstanding theoretical and practical contribution to water and waste water treatment. Awarded triennially. Administered jointly with the Water Chemistry Division of the German Chemical Society.

3167 ■ Willy Hager Prize
To recognize a young university scientist for outstanding work in the field of water and waste water treatment. Awarded annually. Administered jointly with the Water Chemistry Division of the German Chemical Society.

3168 ■ Hochschullehrer-Nachwuchs Prize
To recognize exceptional lectures presented at the Meeting for Up-and-Coming Teachers in Higher Education.

3169 ■ Alwin Mittasch Medal
For recognition of scientific works that broaden the fundamentals of catalysis, or their exemplary application in industry. The work must have been conducted in a European country. A medal is awarded triennially. Established in 1988. Co-sponsored by the BASF AG.

3170 ■ Polytechnic Award
For the best thesis in technical chemistry or biotechnology at a polytechnics or comprehensive university. A monetary prize of 500 Euros is awarded.

3171 ■ Otto Roelen Medal
For essential innovations in homogeneous catalysis, like introduction of a new process to industrial application, investigations of kinetics and mechanisms or improving the knowledge base of homogeneous catalysis. The work must have been conducted in a European country by a young scientist. The prize consists of a medal and cash and is awarded biannually. Established in 1997. Sponsored by Celanese AG.

3172 ■ Student Awards
To recognize outstanding students in technical chemistry, chemical process engineering, and biotechnology. Eligible to students who complete their studies in a particularly short period of time

Awards are arranged in alphabetical order below their administering organizations

while still achieving excellent results. Award consists of a two-year membership in the Society, invitation to an award winners colloquium, and travel expenses to attend two conferences. Established in 1993.

3173 ■ Society for Medicinal Plant Research (Gesellschaft fur Arzneipflanzenforschung)
Dr. Birgit Benedek, Sec.
Society of Medicinal Plant and Natural Product Research
Uttenreuther Strasse 1
D-91077 Neunkirchen am Brand, Germany
Ph: 49 9134 707247
Fax: 49 3212 1216038
E-mail: ga-secretary@ga-online.org
URL: http://www.ga-online.org
Formerly: German Society for Medicinal Plant Research.

3174 ■ Bionorica Phytoneering Award
To recognize outstanding research in the field of development and application of phytopharmaceutical products. Awarded annually. Established in 2009.

3175 ■ Dr. Willmar Schwabe Award
To motivate young scientists to resolve phytotherapeutical and phytopharmaceutical problems in an interdisciplinary approach, in order to support the evidence-based use of natural products. Awarded annually. Established in 1961.

3176 ■ Egon Stahl Award (Egon Stahl Preis)
To honor and encourage younger scientists in the field of pharmacognosy (pharmaceutical biology) and analytical phytochemistry. A monetary award of 3,000 Euros and a silver medal are presented to scientists not older than 40 years of age, and a monetary prize of 2,000 Euros and a bronze medal are presented to scientists not older than 30 years of age. Awarded annually. Established in 1955 to honor Egon Stahl, founder of the Prize, on his 60th birthday.

3177 ■ Egon Stahl Award in Gold
This, the highest scientific honor of the Society, acknowledges a research scientist for a lifetime of scientific work in pharmaceutical biology. Awarded triennially. Established in 1999.

3178 ■ Society for Spinal Research (Gesellschaft fur Wirbelsaulenforschung)
Prof. Dr. H. Sturz, Contact
Orthopadische Klinik
Justus Liebig University
Paul Meimberg Str. 3
35392 Giessen, Germany
Ph: 49 4721 49746
Fax: 49 641 9942 909
E-mail: Dr.Peter-Edelmann@t-online.de
URL: http://gwsf.de

3179 ■ Georg Schmorl Preis
To recognize physicians for outstanding publications in the field of spinal column research. A monetary prize of at least 1000 Euro is awarded biennially. Established in 1963 to honor pathologist Georg Schmorl.

3180 ■ Society of German Cooks (Verband der Koche Deutschlands)
Robert Oppeneder, Acting Pres.
Steinlestrasse 32
D-60596 Frankfurt, Germany
Ph: 49 69 6300060
Fax: 49 69 63000610
E-mail: koeche@vkd.com
URL: http://www.vkd.com

3181 ■ Culinary Olympics
To recognize outstanding culinary ability. The competition is built around research and development and the establishment of food trends for the future. Medals are awarded. The Culinary Olympics are held every four years. Winners of the other international regional competitions participate: Culinary World Cup (Luxembourg), Salon Culinaire Mondial (Basel, Switzerland), Food & Hotel Asia Competition (Singapore), Culinary Arts Salon (USA), Hotelympia (London), Chef Ireland (Ireland), and Culinary Masters (Canada). Established in 1900.

3182 ■ Stadt Pforzheim, Kulturamt
Marktplatz 1
D-75175 Pforzheim, Germany
Ph: 49 7231 390
Fax: 49 7231 392303
E-mail: poststelle@stadt-pforzheim.de
URL: http://www.pforzheim.de/leben-in-pforzheim/kultur-bildung.html

3183 ■ Reuchlinpreis der Stadt Pforzheim
For recognition of a work in the humanities that represents an advancement. Works in German are nominated by the Heidelberg Academy of Sciences and the Lord Mayor of Pforzheim. A monetary award is awarded biennially when merited. Established in 1955. Sponsored by the City Council of Pforzheim.

3184 ■ Stiftung Internationaler Karlspreis zu Aachen
Bernd Vincken, Managing Dir.
Theaterstr. 67
D-52062 Aachen, Germany
Ph: 49 241 401 7770
Fax: 49 241 401 7771
E-mail: info@karlspreis.de
URL: http://www.karlspreis.de

3185 ■ International Charlemagne Prize of Aachen (Internationaler Karlspreis zu Aachen)
For recognition of the most notable achievement in encouraging international understanding and cooperation in the European sphere through political, economic, and literary endeavors. Individuals without respect to nationality, religion, or race who further the idea of the creation of the United States of Europe are eligible. A monetary prize an illuminated document, and a medallion, one side of which is embossed with the ancient Aachen City seal dating from the 12th century, and the reverse side, which contains an inscription concerning the winner of the prize, are awarded annually. Established in 1949 by a number of public-minded Aachen citizens. Formerly: (1988) Internationalen Karlpreis der Stadt Aachen.

3186 ■ Stress and Anxiety Research Society
Prof. Dr. Sonja Rohrmann, Sec.-Treas.
Dorfstr. 6-8
D-40667 Meerbusch, Germany
Fax: 49 69 79823363
E-mail: rohrmann@psych.uni-frankfurt.de
URL: http://www.star-society.org

3187 ■ Early Career Award
To recognize early career achievements in stress research. Eligible to members under 40 years of age. A plaque is awarded annually. Established in 1999.

3188 ■ Lifetime Career Award
To recognize a member for sustained and distinguished contributions in the fields of stress, coping, emotions, and health. Nominees must be over 50 years of age and/or at least 20 years past the granting of their doctoral degree. A plaque is awarded annually. Established in 1998.

3189 ■ Student Development Award
For the best paper on stress, anxiety, and coping in theory, practice, or research in a student paper competition. Eligible to graduate students; work must be unpublished. Winner receives a year membership, free registration at the award-ing conference, a plaque, and a monetary prize of 100 Euros. Paper will be reviewed for publication in the Society's journal, Anxiety, Stress and Coping. Awarded annually. Established in 2006.

3190 ■ Stuttgart City Council (Landeshauptstadt Stuttgart)
Kulturamt
Marktplatz M1
D-70173 Stuttgart, Germany
Ph: 49 711 2160
Fax: 49 711 216 4773
E-mail: post@stuttgart.de
URL: http://www.stuttgart.de

3191 ■ Hegel-Preis der Landeshauptstadt Stuttgart
For recognition of an outstanding contribution to the advancement of human sciences. A monetary prize of 12,000 Euro and a certificate are awarded triennially. Established in 1967.

3192 ■ Otto Hirsch Medaille
To recognize exceptional merits in the field of Christian-Jewish cooperation and understanding. A certificate and medal are awarded annually. Established in 1985.

3193 ■ Hans-Molfenter-Preis der Landeshauptstadt Stuttgart/Galerie
For recognition of artistic achievement in fine arts in the Baden-Wurttemberg region. A monetary prize of 12,000 Euro is awarded triennially. Established in 1983 in memory of the Stuttgart artist, Hans Molfenter (1884-1979).

3194 ■ Umweltpreis der Landeshauptstadt Stuttgart
For recognition of outstanding contributions to the retention of the natural environment of Stuttgart or the improvement of environmental conditions. Candidates must be residents, employees in, or businessmen of the city. Monetary prizes and certificates are awarded biennially. Established in 1985.

3195 ■ Stuttgart International Festival of Animated Film (Internationales Trickfilm Festival Stuttgart)
Ulrich Wegenast, Artistic Managing Dir.
Schlosstr. 84
D-70176 Stuttgart, Germany
Ph: 49 711 92546 0
Fax: 49 711 92546 150
E-mail: kontakt@festival-gmbh.de
URL: http://www.itfs.de

3196 ■ Stuttgart International Festival of Animated Film (Internationales Trickfilm Festival Stuttgart)
For recognition of outstanding animated short films produced in the previous 12 months. The following prizes are awarded: the Grand Prix (15,000 Euros), SWR Audience Award (6,000 Euros), International Promotion Award (10,000), Award for Best Student Film (2,500 Euros), Award for Best Animated Children's Film (4,000 Euros), Award for Best Animated Feature Film (2,500 Euros), and the Award for Best Animated TV series (2,500 Euros). Held annually. Established in 1990.

3197 ■ Taxpayers Association of Europe (Bund der Steuerzahler Europa)
Rolf von Hohenhau, Pres.
Nymphenburger Strasse 118
D-80636 Munich, Germany
Ph: 49 89 12600820
Fax: 49 89 12600827
E-mail: info@taxpayers-europe.org
URL: http://www.taxpayers-europe.org

3198 ■ Taxpayers Award
To honor an individual who defends the rights of taxpayers by fighting to achieve relief in high

Awards are arranged in alphabetical order below their administering organizations

taxes, undue bureaucracy, and avoidance of new taxes. A bronze sculpture is awarded annually.

3199 ■ Alfred Toepfer Stiftung F.V.S.
Sibylle Benecke, Sec.
Georgsplatz 10
D-20099 Hamburg, Germany
Ph: 49 40 334020
Fax: 49 40 335860
E-mail: mail@toepfer-fvs.de
URL: http://www.toepfer-fvs.de

3200 ■ Hamburg Max Brauer Prize
To recognize personalities and institutions in the Free Hanseatic City of Hamburg who have rendered outstanding services to the cultural, scientific, or intellectual life of the city. A monetary prize of 15,000 Euros is awarded annually. First awarded in 1993.

3201 ■ Hansischer Goethe Prize
To provide recognition for overriding humanitarian achievements in Europe. A monetary prize of 25,000 Euros is awarded biennially in Hamburg.

3202 ■ Herder Prizes
To provide recognition for outstanding work by individuals from Albania, Belarus, Bosniekercegovine, Bulgaria, Croatia, the Czech Republic, Estonia, Greece, Hungary, Latvia, Lithuania, Poland, Romania, Slovakia, Slovenia, Ukraine, and the remains of Yugoslavia, who have contributed to the preservation and renewal of the European cultural heritage. Seven monetary prizes are awarded annually through the University of Vienna, Austria. Established in 1964.

3203 ■ Alexander Petrowitsch Karpinskij Prize
To recognize outstanding accomplishments in the field of science, ecology, and protection of the environment and the nature in the C.I.S. A monetary prize is awarded annually. Established in 1985.

3204 ■ Montaigne Prize
To recognize eminent Europeans from Romance-language speaking countries who further European humanitarian values in the sphere of literature, the arts, or the humanities. A monetary prize of 20,000 Euros is awarded annually through the University of Tubingen. Established in 1968.

3205 ■ Wilhelm Leopold Pfeil Prize
To provide recognition for exemplary forestry practice in Europe. A monetary prize of 2,000 Euros is awarded annually. Established in 1963.

3206 ■ Alexander Sergejewitsch Puschkin Prize
To recognize extraordinary works in modern Russian literature. A monetary prize of 15,000 Euros is awarded annually in cooperation with the Russian PEN Club in Moscow. Established in 1989.

3207 ■ Fritz Schumacher Prize
To provide recognition for outstanding work in the preservation of monuments, architecture, urban areas, and the management of land areas. Established in 1949. A monetary prize is awarded annually since 1960 through the Technical University of Hanover, from 1950 until 1955 through the University of Hamburg.

3208 ■ Shakespeare Prize
To recognize individuals in Great Britain who have rendered distinguished services in the field of literature, the humanities, and the visual arts. A monetary prize of $20,000 is awarded annually, along with an $11,040 scholarship to study at a German academy or university. Established in 1937 and re-established in 1967.

3209 ■ Henrik Steffens Prize
To recognize cultural achievements in the Scandinavian countries. A monetary prize of 20,000 euros is awarded annually in Kiel or Lubeck through the Christian Albrechts University, Kiel. Established in 1935-36 and re-established in 1965.

3210 ■ Heinrich Tessenow Gold Medal
To recognize achievements in the field of handicraft and industrial design. Awarded annually. Co-sponsored with the Heinrich-Tessenow-Gesellschaft in Dresden-Hellerau.

3211 ■ Justus Von Liebig Prize
To provide recognition for outstanding achievements in practical agriculture in Europe or in scientific or technical work in the field. A monetary prize of $15,000 is awarded biennially through the Agricultural Faculty of the University of Kiel. Established in 1949.

3212 ■ Freiherr Von Stein Prize
To recognize exemplary or innovative contributions to the common good achieved by individuals, groups, or institutions in the new German Lander, notably through the solution of economic, social, and cultural problems resulting from the reunification of Germany. A monetary prize of 25,000 Euros is awarded annually through the Humboldt University, Berlin. Established in 1954.

3213 ■ Underground Transportation Research Association (Studiengesellschaft fur Unterirdische Verkehrsanlagen)
Dr. Roland Leucker, Exec. Dir.
Mathias-Brueggen-Strasse 41
D-50827 Cologne, Germany
Ph: 49 221 597950
Ph: 49 221 5979510
Fax: 49 221 5979550
E-mail: info@stuva.de
URL: http://www.stuva.de

3214 ■ STUVA Prize
Recognizes innovations in the field of underground construction. Awarded biennially in odd-numbered years.

3215 ■ Universitat Karlsruhe (Technische Hochschule)
Prof. Dr. Horst Hippler, Pres.
Kaiserstrasse 12
D-76131 Karlsruhe, Germany
Ph: 49 721 6080
Fax: 49 721 6084290
E-mail: rektor@verwaltung.uni-karlsruhe.de
URL: http://www.uni-karlsruhe.de

3216 ■ Heinrich Hertz Preis
For recognition of an outstanding scientific and technological achievement in the field of energy technology. Contributions may be of a technological or technical economic character, or relate to work in experimental or theoretical physics. They should have led to important new findings and developments or be conducive to new developments. A monetary prize of 10,000 Euros and a medal are awarded. Established in 1975 to commemorate the 150th anniversary of the University of Karlsruhe.

3217 ■ Verein Deutscher Textilveredlungsfachleute e.V
Kurt Van Wersch, Pres.
Postfach 1449
D-69172 Leimen, Germany
Ph: 49 6224 73197
Ph: 49 6224 829623
Fax: 49 6224 829624
E-mail: mail@vdtf.de
URL: http://www.vdtf.de

3218 ■ Gerhard Dierkes Prize
To recognize an individual for outstanding accomplishments. A monetary prize of DM 1,000 is awarded periodically. Established in 1994.

3219 ■ Egon - Elod Award
To recognize the best publication of the last three years. A monetary prize of DM 1,000 is awarded annually. Established in 1978.

3220 ■ Max Kehren Medal
To recognize an individual for outstanding achievements in the fields of textile chemicals, textile technology, textile machinery and equipment, and fiber chemistry. Awarded annually.

3221 ■ Medal of Honor
To recognize an individual for outstanding achievements in fields that relate directly or indirectly to the textile finishing industry. Awarded annually.

3222 ■ Otto N. Witt Medal
To recognize an individual for outstanding and innovative achievements in the fields of dye, fiber, and textile chemicals. Awarded annually.

3223 ■ Verein Fur Socialpolitik
Prof. Lars-Hendrik Roller, Chm.
Wilhelm-Epstein-Str. 14
D-60431 Frankfurt, Germany
Ph: 49 69 56807610
Fax: 49 69 56807615
E-mail: office@socialpolitik.org
URL: http://www.socialpolitik.org/vfs.php?mode=start

3224 ■ Gossen Award
To promote the internationalization of German economic sciences. Candidates must be economists from German language areas who are under 45 years of age. A monetary prize of 10,000 Euros is awarded annually.

3225 ■ Reinhard Selten Award
To recognize a student for an excellent paper presented at the annual meeting. Author must be under 32 years of age. A monetary award of 3,000 Euros is awarded annually.

3226 ■ Gustav Stolper Award
For an influential economist who has contributed to the understanding of economic problems in the real world. Open to members. A monetary prize of 5,000 Euros is awarded annually,

3227 ■ Alexander von Humboldt-Stiftung Foundation
Helmut Schwarz, Pres.
Jean-Paul-Strasse 12
D-53173 Bonn, Germany
Ph: 49 228 8330
Fax: 49 228 833199
E-mail: info@avh.de
URL: http://www.humboldt-foundation.de

3228 ■ Humboldt Research Fellowships
To enable highly qualified foreign scholars holding doctorate degrees to carry out a research project in the Federal Republic of Germany. Individuals under the age of 40 from any discipline may submit applications at any time during the year. Scholars from all nations are eligible. Application requirements include: an examination equivalent to the doctorate degree (Ph.D., C.Sc., or equivalent); high academic qualifications; academic publications; a detailed research plan; command of the German language (humanities scholars); and at least command of the English language for science scholars (including medicine and engineering). Up to 600 fellowships for six to 18 months are awarded annually. Family allowance, travel expenses, grants for language classes and monthly monetary prizes are awarded.

3229 ■ JSPS Research Fellowship for Postdoctoral Researchers
To enable post-doctoral researchers from Germany to carry out a research project at a selected national research institution in Japan. Up to 20 fellowships are granted annually. Sponsored by the Japan Society for the Promotion of Science (JSPS).

Awards are arranged in alphabetical order below their administering organizations

3230 ■ Feodor Lynen Research Fellowships

To enable German scholars, not over age 38, to conduct research abroad in cooperation with a former Humboldt Fellow or Awardee. Open to all disciplines. Application requirements include a doctorate degree, high academic qualifications, a detailed research proposal approved by the host, and a good knowledge of English or the respective country's language. Fellowships are for a period of one to four years. A monthly stipend, travel expenses, and assistance upon return are awarded. Up to 150 fellowships are given annually.

3231 ■ Max Planck Research Award

To recognize outstanding achievements of internationally renowned foreign and German scientists of any academic discipline and to promote intensive cooperation between foreign and German scientists. German or foreign scholars (generally full/associate professors) of any age may be nominated by eminent German scholars (in special cases more than one German and/or foreign scholar may be nominated). On an annually-alternating basis, the call for nominations addresses areas within the natural and engineering sciences, the life sciences, and the humanities. Two research awards are granted every year, one to a researcher working in Germany and one to a researcher working abroad. Each award is endowed with 750,000 Euros and may be used over a period of three to five years to fund research chosen by the award winner. Co-sponsored by the Max Planck Society.

3232 ■ Alexander von Humboldt Award for Scientific Cooperation

To encourage scientific cooperation between Germany and other countries. World-renowned researchers of any age specially engaged in bilateral scientific cooperation in any discipline are eligible. Nominations of foreign scholars are directed by German researchers to the Alexander von Humboldt Foundation, which is entrusted with the selection and administration. The selection of the German scholars is coordinated by partner organizations in other countries. Agreements with counterparts exist in Australia, Belgium, Brazil, Canada, Chile, China, Finland, France, Hungary, India, Israel, Japan, Korea, Netherlands, New Zealand, Poland, South Africa, Spain, Sweden, and Taiwan. The award consists of a prize and invitation for a period of several months to do research work in the partner's country.

3233 ■ Philipp Franz von Siebold Award for Japanese Research

To recognize a Japanese scholar who has played an important part in promoting understanding between Japan and the Federal Republic of Germany. Awardees spend a lengthy research period in Germany and receive a monetary prize. A grant of 50,000 Euros is awarded annually. Established in 1978.

3234 ■ Ernst von Siemens Music Foundation (Ernst Von Siemens-Musikstiftung)
Michael Rossnagl, Contact
Wittelsbacherplatz 2
D-80333 Munich, Germany
Ph: 49 89 636 33202
Fax: 49 89 636 33285
E-mail: rossnagl@evs-musikstiftung.ch
URL: http://www.evs-musikstiftung.ch

3235 ■ Ernst von Siemens Music Prize (Ernst von Siemens-Musikpreis)

For recognition of an outstanding achievement in music. Famous composers or performers from anywhere in the world are eligible. A monetary prize of 200,000 Euro is awarded annually. Established 1972. In addition, each year around 2.3 million Euro is awarded for specified purposes to music institutions, ensembles and individuals, in Germany and abroad, who have made a special contribution to contemporary music.

3236 ■ Wissenschaftsstadt Darmstadt (Stadt Darmstadt)
c/o Magistrat, Hauptamt
Postfach 11 07 80
Luisenplatz 5
W-64283 Darmstadt, Germany
Ph: 49 6151 131
Fax: 49 6151 13 3777
E-mail: info@darmstadt.de
URL: http://www.darmstadt.de

3237 ■ Ricarda-Huch-Preis

For recognition of outstanding literary works that support German culture and freedom. A monetary prize is awarded triennially. Established in 1978 in memory of the uprising June 17, 1953 and the poetess Ricarda Huch who stood up against the Nazi oppression and for cultural freedom.

3238 ■ Kunstpreis der Stadt Darmstadt

To recognize outstanding artists of the city. Individuals, under 50 years of age, who enter the art exhibition and who have not previously won prizes, are eligible. A monetary prize, a certificate, and travel costs are awarded annually. The prize may be divided. Established in 1955.

3239 ■ Literarischer Marz

For recognition of the most outstanding young lyric authors of the biennial lyric festival, "The Last Week in March." German speaking lyricists, under 35 years of age, who have won no previous prizes are eligible. Awarded biennially. Established in 1978.

3240 ■ Johann-Heinrich-Merck Ehrung

To recognize individuals for contributions in various fields such as science, art, economics, and architecture. Awarded several times annually. Established in 1955.

3241 ■ World Veterinary Poultry Association (Asociacion Mundial Veterinaria de Avicola)
Dr. Ursula Heffels-Redmann, Sec.-Treas.
Clinic for Birds, Reptiles, Amphibian and Fish
Justus Liebig University Giessen
Frankfurter Str. 91-93
D-35392 Giessen, Germany
E-mail: ursula.heffels-redmann@vetmed.uni-giessen.de
URL: http://www.wvpa.net

3242 ■ Houghton Lecture Award

To recognize innovative contributions to any branch of research concerned with poultry diseases. Nominees must be under 45 years of age at the time of the relevant congress. The travel expenses to the WVPA Congress will be met, and a memento will be awarded. In addition, the registration fee will be waived and a contribution made to the cost of the recipient's accommodations and subsistence. Awarded in odd-numbered years at the WVPA Congress. Established in 1993.

3243 ■ Bart Rispens Award

For recognition of achievements in the field of avian diseases. The authors of the best papers published in *Avian Pathology* during the preceding two calendar years are eligible. A monetary award, medallion, and a certificate are awarded biennially. Established in 1975 in honor of Dr. Bart Rispens.

3244 ■ Writers Ink eV
Sabine Meier, Chair
Alte Poststr. 39
D-38239 Salzgitter, Germany
E-mail: sabine.meier@writers-ink.de

URL: http://www.writers-ink.de

3245 ■ Daniil Pashkoff Prize

To recognize outstanding creative writing in English by a non-native speaker of the language. Open to any writer around the world whose mother tongue is not English. Prizes are awarded in two categories (poetry and prose fiction) within two age groups (older than 21 years and 21 years and younger). Presented biennially in even-numbered years. Established in 2000 in memory of the first Russian student to study English at the Technical University of Branschweig.

3246 ■ Wurzburg International Film Weekend (Internationales Filmwochenende Wurzburg)
Friedenstr. 19
D-97072 Wurzburg, Germany
Ph: 49 931 15077
Fax: 49 931 15078
E-mail: info@filmwochenende-wuerzburg.de
URL: http://uploader.wuerzburg.de/ifw

3247 ■ Audience Prizes

To recognize and honor the best films as chosen by the audience. Only films by invited directors are eligible for the award. Monetary prizes are awarded for the Best Film, Best Children's Film, and Best Short Film. Presented annually at the festival. Established in 1989.

3248 ■ Best Children's Film Prize

To honor the best children's film at the Festival. A monetary prize of several thousand Euros is awarded annually.

3249 ■ Best Short Film Prize

To honor the best short film at the Festival. A monetary prize of several thousand Euros is awarded annually.

Ghana

3250 ■ Ghana Base Music
c/o Lyon Media Ltd.
PO Box 5676
Accra, Ghana
URL: http://www.ghanabase.com

3251 ■ Ghana Music Awards

To foster the development of the Ghanaian music industry and honor those in the industry who have excelled in the five main music genres of Ghana: gospel, hip-life, highlife, reggae, and traditional. Trophies and cash prizes are awarded annually in 19 categories. Established in 2000.

3252 ■ Ghana Ministry of Communications
PO Box M38
Accra, Ghana
Ph: 233 21 666465
Fax: 233 21 667114
E-mail: info@moc.gov.gh
URL: http://www.moc.gov.gh

3253 ■ Ghana ICT Awards

To promote awareness of the role of information and communications technology (ICT) in public services, to motivate stakeholders in effective utilization of ICT for citizen's services, to ensure that ICT professionals are provided a benchmark for recognizing and validating outstanding contribution, and to transform and promote Ghana into an information- and knowledge-driven nation. Awarded annually in 13 categories, including ISP of the Year, Hardware Company of the Year, and Internet Cafe of the Year. Established in 2007. Sponsored by the Ghana Internet Service Providers Association and the Ghana Association of Software and IT Services Companies.

3254 ■ Ghana Property Awards
Property Express Bldg.
No. 64 Palace St.
North Kaneshie Swalake Junction

Awards are arranged in alphabetical order below their administering organizations

North Kaneshie
Accra, Ghana
E-mail: info@ghanapropertyawards.com
URL: http://www.ghanapropertyawards.com

3255 ■ Ghana Property Awards

To recognize and reward excellence in the Ghanaian real estate and allied sectors, and to encourage innovative real estate solutions within the industry. Presented in several commercial categories, such as interior design, retail development, and property finance, as well as three residential builder of the year categories. In addition, special awards may be presented for public service development, recreational facility, property marketing, and personality of the year. Awarded annually. Established in 2007.

3256 ■ The Head of State Award Scheme - Ghana

Teachers Hall Complex
PO Box 13539
Accra, Ghana
Ph: 233 21 7010 231
E-mail: hosa_gh@yahoo.com
URL: http://hosa.wetpaint.com

3257 ■ Head of State Awards - Ghana

To provide Ghanaian youth with a sense of responsibility, instilling and abiding in them developmental skills that are beneficial to themselves and the community. Open to individuals aged 14 to 25 years. Covers service projects, adventurous journey, skills, and physical recreation. Gold, silver, and bronze awards are presented annually. Established in 1967 as part of the Duke of Edinburgh Award Program.

Gibraltar

3258 ■ Gibraltar Festival for Young Musicians

PO Box 1358
Gibraltar, Gibraltar
E-mail: info@gibfym.com
URL: http://www.gibfym.com

3259 ■ Gibraltar Festival for Young Musicians

To promote and encourage music performance among the children in Gibraltar. Open to young musicians aged 18 or under, as well as amateur adult musicians. Medals and trophies are awarded in a variety of classes. Held annually. Established in 2005.

3260 ■ Gibraltar Song Festival

John Jones, Sec.
14/2 S Barrack Ramp
Gibraltar, Gibraltar
E-mail: secretary@gibraltarsongfestival.com
URL: http://www.gibraltarsongfestival.com

3261 ■ Gibraltar Song Festival

To promote local and international talent and to raise proceeds for charities in Gibraltar. Composers are awarded the following prizes: £3,000 for first place, £1,000 for second place, and £500 for third place; singers are awarded trophies. Held annually. Established in 1965.

3262 ■ Gibtelecom International Chess Festival

c/o Caleta Hotel
PO Box 73
Gibraltar, Gibraltar
Ph: 350 76501
Fax: 350 71050
URL: http://www.gibraltarchesscongress.com

3263 ■ Gibtelecom International Chess Festival

To recognize the best chess players in Gibraltar. Monetary prizes up to £12,000 are awarded annually. Established in 2003. Sponsored by Gibtelecom.

3264 ■ Health Promotion Group Gibraltar

17 Johnstone's Passage
Gibraltar, Gibraltar
Ph: 350 72266
Fax: 350 43864
URL: http://www.health.gov.gi

3265 ■ Good Health Award

To recognize catering establishments for helping to reduce the high incidence of coronary hearth disease in Gibraltar by promoting healthy food and a healthy eating environment. Open to workplace catering establishments, school and hospital canteens, sandwich bars, social clubs, pubs, hotels and restaurants, and take-away outlets. Gold, Silver, and Bronze awards are awarded annually.

Greece

3266 ■ Athenaeum International Cultural Center

Louli Psychouli, Pres.
3, Adrianou St.
GR-105 55 Athens, Greece
Ph: 30 210 321 1987
Fax: 30 210 321 1196
E-mail: contact@athenaeum.com.gr
URL: http://www.athenaeum.com.gr

3267 ■ Maria Callas Grand Prix for Opera

To recognize outstanding singers. Male singers between 18 and 32 years of age and female singers between 18 and 30 years of age are eligible. The following awards are presented in both male and female categories: Grand Prize - the Maria Callas Gold Medal, a cash prize of 9,000 Euros, and a diploma; Second Prize - a silver medal, a cash prize of 5,000 Euros, and a diploma; Third Prize - a silver medal, a cash prize of 3,000 Euros, and a diploma. Held biennially in odd-numbered years. Established in 1975. Formerly: (1994) Maria Callas International Opera, Oratorio-Lied Competition.

3268 ■ Maria Callas Grand Prix for Piano

To recognize outstanding young pianists of any nationality. Open to individuals 19 to 33 years of age. A gold medal and monetary prize of 12,000 Euros is presented to the grand prize recipient. Second and third place prizes consist of silver medals and cash prizes of 6,000 Euros and 3,000 Euros, respectively. Awarded biennially in even-numbered years.

3269 ■ Biopolitics International Organization

Dr. Agni Vlavianos-Arvanitis, Founder/Pres.
10 Tim Vassou
115 21 Athens, Greece
Ph: 30 21 6432419
Fax: 30 21 6434093
E-mail: bios@otenet.gr
URL: http://www.biopolitics.gr

3270 ■ Bios Prizes

Awarded to those who have contributed to the evaluation or priorities in society and the development of new models and thinking for the future, in terms of environmental protection.

3271 ■ Circle of the Greek Children's Book

Loty Petrovits, Pres.
Bouboulinas 28
GR-106 82 Athens, Greece
Ph: 30 210 8222 296
Fax: 30 210 8222 296
E-mail: kyklos@greekibby.gr

URL: http://www.greekibby.gr

3272 ■ Book Prizes

To recognize the writers and illustrators of the best Greek children's book of the previous year. Greek citizens must submit books published in the previous calendar year by December 31. Monetary prizes are awarded in four categories: authors of books for younger children, authors of books for intermediate readers, authors of books for older children and young adults, and illustrators. Presented annually on April 2, the International Children's Book Day. Established in 1988.

3273 ■ Penelope Delta Award

To recognize a distinguished writer of Greek children's books for the entire body of his or her work. Greek citizens must be nominated. A diploma is awarded annually. Established in 1988 in memory of Penelope Delta (1874-1941), a famous Greek writer for children.

3274 ■ European Association for Signal and Image Processing

Marc Moonen, Pres.
PO Box 74251
161 10 Kaisariani, Greece
URL: http://www.eurasip.org
Formerly: (1998) European Association for Signal Processing.

3275 ■ Paper Awards

To recognize the authors of outstanding papers on signal processing. Awards are presented in the following categories: signal processing, image communication, speech communication, *EURASIP Journal on Advances in Signal Processing*, and *EURASIP Journal on Wireless Communications and Networking*. Awarded biennially.

3276 ■ Athanasios Papoulis Award

To honor scientists whose work has had a major impact in various aspects on signal processing education. Awarded periodically when merited.

3277 ■ European Association for Theoretical Computer Science

Dr. Ioannis Chatzigiannakis, Sec.
University of Patras Campus
Research Academic Computer Technology Institute
1 N Kazantzaki St.
26504 Rio, Greece
E-mail: secretary@eatcs.org
URL: http://www.eatcs.org

3278 ■ Godel Prize

For outstanding papers in the area of theoretical computer science. A monetary prize of US$5,000 is awarded annually to one or more recipients. Established in honor of Kurt Godel.

3279 ■ European Association of Developmental Psychology

Prof. Frosso Motti-Stefanidi, Sec.
School of Philosophy, Div. 505
Department of Psychology
University of Athens
157 84 Athens, Greece
Ph: 30 210 7277 525
E-mail: frmotti@psych.uoa.gr
URL: http://www.esdp.info

3280 ■ George Butterworth Young Scientist Award

To recognize an outstanding PhD dissertation in developmental psychology. To qualify, the dissertation must be written in English and must have been successfully defended at a university in any European country during the previous two years. A monetary prize of 500 Euros is awarded biennially in odd-numbered years. Established in 2007.

Awards are arranged in alphabetical order below their administering organizations

3281 ■ William Thierry Preyer Award for Excellence in Research on Human Development

To honor a European psychologist (or group of European psychologists) who is recognized internationally for an original and substantial contribution to a better understanding of human development and its contexts, as demonstrated by first-rate publications in scholarly journals, based on empirical research into the antecedents, processes, and outcomes of human development-in-context. Awarded biennially in odd-numbered years. Established in 2007.

3282 ■ European Design Awards
Sokratous 157
Athens, Greece
Ph: 30 210 959 3033
Fax: 30 210 952 3607
E-mail: info@ed-awards.com
URL: http://www.ed-awards.com

3283 ■ European Design Awards

To celebrate European design with all its regional distinctive elements as well as its common grounds; to facilitate European designers to meet, benchmark, be inspired, and build networks; to promote and raise standards for communication design throughout Europe, and to properly honor and award people who invest their passion in design. Trophies are presented in 30 categories, divided into seven groups. In addition, two overall prizes are presented: the Jury's Prize and Agency of the Year. Awarded annually. Established in 2007.

3284 ■ Federation of European Societies of Plant Biology
Prof. Heinz Rennenberg, Pres.
PO Box 2208
71409 Heraklion, Greece
Ph: 30 81 394072
Ph: 30 81 394073
Fax: 30 81 394408
E-mail: heinz.rennenberg@ctp.uni-freiburg.de
URL: http://www.fespb.org

3285 ■ Awards to Young European Scientists

For recognition of outstanding scientific work in recent years. Plant biologists who are under 35 years of age may be nominated by each of the national societies that constitute the federation. A diploma, plenary lecture, and travel and participation expenses, and a cash prize are awarded biennially. Established in 1986. Sponsored by Academic Press and Jouan, France.

3286 ■ Foundation for Research and Technology - Hellas
PO Box 1385
Heraklion
GR-711 10 Crete, Greece
Ph: 30 2810 391500
Fax: 30 2810 391555
E-mail: central@admin.forth.gr
URL: http://www.forth.gr

3287 ■ Stratis V. Sotirchos Memorial Lectureship

To recognize an engineer-scientist who has produced original and fundamentally important results in some research and development field within the broader context of chemical engineering. Candidates must be younger than 40 years of age. An invitation to lecture is awarded biennially.

3288 ■ Vasilis Xanthopoulos Award

To recognize an individual for excellence in academic teaching. Candidates may be members of the educational and research staff of Greek universities, specialized scientists, or members of research centers with university teaching work. A monetary prize of 3,000 Euro is

awarded annually. Established in 1991 in memory of the University of Crete professor who was assassinated in 1990 while fulfilling teaching duties.

3289 ■ Greek Alzheimer's Association
Mr. Nina Kotras, Exec.Dir.
Charisio Old People's Home
Terma Dimitriou Charisi
A. Toumba
Thessaloniki
GR-54352 Hellas, Greece
Ph: 30 2310 925802
Ph: 30 2310 909000
Fax: 30 2310 925802
E-mail: info@alzheimer-hellas.gr
URL: http://www.alzheimer-hellas.gr

3290 ■ Conference Award

To recognize the best research initiative of the previous two years. A monetary prize of 30,000 Euros is awarded biennially in odd-numbered years.

3291 ■ International Society for the Psychological Treatments for the Schizophrenias and Other Psychoses
Paktolou 7-9
165 61 Athens, Greece
Ph: 30 210 961 8012
E-mail: isps@isps.org
URL: http://www.isps.org

3292 ■ Barbro Sandin Award

To recognize a female leader in psychological treatment of schizophrenias and other psychoses. A US$250 cash prize, plaque, and US$1,200 travel award are presented biennially in even-numbered years. Established in 2008.

3293 ■ Near East South Asia Council of Overseas Schools
David Chojnacki, Exec. Dir.
Gravias 6
Aghia Paraskevi
GR-153 42 Athens, Greece
Ph: 30 210 600 9821
Fax: 30 210 600 9928
E-mail: nesa@nesacenter.org
URL: http://www.nesacenter.org

3294 ■ Finis Engleman Award

To recognize an individual for outstanding dedication and service to schools in the NESA region. Awarded annually. Established in 1981 in honor of one of the founders of the Council.

3295 ■ Alexander S. Onassis Public Benefit Foundation
Anthony S. Papadimitriou, Pres.
Athens Office
56 Amalias Ave.
GR-105 58 Athens, Greece
Ph: 30 210 3713 000
Fax: 30 210 3713 013
E-mail: pubrel@onassis.gr
URL: http://www.onassis.gr

3296 ■ Onassis Award for Culture (Letters, Arts and Humanities)

A monetary award of $250,000, a gold, silver, and bronze medal, and a scroll are awarded in Athens, Greece. Established in 1979 by the Board of Directors of the Foundation according to the will of Aristotle Onassis. Formerly: Onassis Prize for Man and Culture - Olympia.

3297 ■ Onassis Award for International Understanding and Social Achievement

To recognize individuals for their cultural, professional, and social contributions to international understanding. Nominees must actively participate in their relevant activities and must not be in the course of retirement. Nominations are accepted from individuals as well as institutions. A monetary prize of $250,000 is awarded when merited. Established in 1979.

3298 ■ Onassis Award for the Environment

To recognize individuals or organizations for a notable contribution in the field of the protection of the natural environment. Nominations and applications to the International Committee for the Onassis Prizes are accepted from individuals and organizations. A monetary prize of $250,000, a silver medal, and a scroll are awarded when merited in Athens, Greece. Established in 1988. Formerly: Onassis Prize for Man and His Environment - Delphi.

3299 ■ Onassis International Prize in Finance

To recognize an academic of international stature for lifetime achievement in the sector of finance. A monetary prize of $200,000 is awarded triennially. Established in 2007. Co-sponsored by the Corporation of the City of London and the Cass Business School of the City University of London.

3300 ■ Onassis International Prize in Law

To recognize distinguished personalities who have contributed to improving understanding between states and cultures and to the protection of human rights. A monetary prize of 250,000 Euros is awarded biennially, alternating years with the Prize in the Humanities. Established in 2008.

3301 ■ Onassis International Prize in Shipping

To recognize an academic of international stature for lifetime achievement in the sector of shipping. A monetary prize of $200,000 is awarded triennially. Established in 2007. Co-sponsored by the Corporation of the City of London and the Cass Business School of the City University of London.

3302 ■ Onassis International Prize in the Humanities

To recognize individuals who have concentrated their studies on Greek culture and the promotion of Greek cultural heritage in the fields of archaeology, history, and literature. A monetary prize of 250,000 Euros is awarded biennially, alternating years with the Prize in Law. Established in 2008.

3303 ■ Onassis International Prize in Trade

To recognize an academic of international stature for lifetime achievement in the sector of trade. A monetary prize of $200,000 is awarded triennially. Established in 2007. Co-sponsored by the Corporation of the City of London and the Cass Business School of the City University of London.

3304 ■ Onassis Prize in Shipping, Trade and Finance

To recognize lifetime achievement by an academic of international stature. Awarded in the sectors of shipping, trade, and finance on a rotating basis. A monetary prize of US$200,000 is awarded every three years. Established in 2007.

3305 ■ Radio Amateur Association of Greece
Darkadakis Manos, Chm.
PO Box 3564
GR-10210 Athens, Greece
Ph: 30 5226516
Fax: 30 5226505
E-mail: raag-hq@raag.org
URL: http://www.raag.org

3306 ■ Alexander the Great Award

For listeners or radio amateurs who have confirmed contacts with countries that were crossed by Alexander the Great.

3307 ■ Ancient Greek Cities Award

For radio amateur listeners who had contacts with stations near ancient Greek cities.

3308 ■ Athenian Award

For working and confirming 25 different stations located in greater Athens.

Awards are arranged in alphabetical order below their administering organizations

3309 ■ Athens Summer Olympic Games Award
For listeners or radio amateurs who had contacts with different Greek stations in a given period of time.

3310 ■ Greek Islands Award
For confirming and working ten contacts with at the very least three different groups of Greek islands.

3311 ■ RAAG Award
For those who worked and confirmed contacts with at least seven Greek stations from the nine SV call areas.

3312 ■ Thessaloniki International Film Festival
(Centre du Cinema Grec)
Dimitris Eipides, Dir.
9 Alexandras Ave.
GR-114 73 Athens, Greece
Ph: 30 210 8706 000
Fax: 30 210 6448 143
E-mail: info@filmfestival.gr
URL: http://www.filmfestival.gr

3313 ■ Thessaloniki Film Festival
To encourage the production of films and to recognize short and feature length documentary films. The Ministry of Culture awards the Golden Alexander to the outstanding film overall, and awards three monetary prizes for the best film in each category. The awards are given to the directors and producers. In addition, a prize is given for: (1) Best first feature film; (2) Best Screenplay; (3) Best Actor; (4) Best Supporting Actor; (5) Best Actress; (6) Best Supporting Actress; (7) Best Music; (8) Best Sound; (9) Best Makeup; (10) Best Costumes; (11) Best Technical Contribution; and (12) Best Editing. The Jury of the Festival presents honorary awards in the following categories: (1) Grand Prize for the best feature film; (2) Grand Prize for the best documentary; (3) Best Director; (4) Best Director for a first feature film; (5) Best Photography; (6) Best Actress; (7) Best Actor; (8) Best Screenplay; and (9) prizes for music, costumes, editing, decoration, sound, makeup, special effects and supporting roles. In addition, the Human Values Award of 15,000 Euros, the Woman and Equal Opportunities Award, and the Thrace Award are presented. Held annually. Established in 1959 by the International Fair of Thessaloniki.

3314 ■ World Chess Federation
(Federation Internationale des Echecs)
Kirsan Ilyumzhinov, Pres.
9 Singrou Ave.
11743 Athens, Greece
Ph: 30 210 9212047
Fax: 30 210 9212859
E-mail: office@fide.com
URL: http://www.fide.com

3315 ■ Chess World Champions
For recognition of the winner of the Individual World Championship. Champions have been recognized since 1886.

3316 ■ FIDE Master
For recognition of achievement in the game of chess. The title FIDE Master is awarded for any of the following: a rating of at least 2300 based on the completion of at least 24 related games (the national federation is responsible for the payment of the fee established in the financial regulations); first place in the IBCA World Junior Championship with a rating of 2205; first place in the World Championships, Continental Championships, or the Arab Championships in specific age groups (in the event of a tie in either the Continental or Arab Championships, each of the tied players shall be awarded the title of FIDE Master - subject to a maximum of three players); a score of 50 percent or better on the Zonal Tournament of at least nine games; and runners-up of the IBCA World Championship with a rating of 2205. A title, a medal, and a diploma are awarded annually. Established in 1946.

3317 ■ Gold Diploma of Honor
To recognize an exceptional contribution to international chess over a period of years. A plaque is awarded annually by the FIDE Congress. Established in 1980.

3318 ■ Grandmaster
For recognition of achievement in the game of chess. The title Grandmaster is given for any of the following: two or more Grandmaster results in events covering at least 24 games and a rating of at least 2500 in the current FIDE Rating List, or within seven years of the first title result; qualification for the Candidates Competition for the World Championship; one Grandmaster result in a FIDE Internzonal tournament; first place in the Women's World Championship or World Junior Championship; first place in the Continental Junior Championship or the Women's Candidates Tournament is equivalent to one nine-game Grandmaster result; a tie for first place in the World Junior Championship (equivalent to one nine-game Grandmaster result); and one 13-game Grandmaster result in the Olympiad, which leads to the award of a full title. A title, a medal, and a diploma are awarded annually. Established in 1946.

3319 ■ International Arbiter
To recognize individuals knowledgeable of the Laws of Chess and Federation Regulations for chess competitions. The title of International Arbiter is awarded for all of the following: knowledge of the laws of chess and Federation Regulations; knowledge of at least one official Federation language; objectivity; and experience as chief or deputy arbiter in at least four Federation rated events, such as the following: the final of the National Individual Adult Championship (not more than two), all official Federation tournaments and matches, international title tournaments and matches, and international chess festivals with at least 100 contestants. Awarded annually.

3320 ■ International Master
For recognition of achievement in the game of chess. The title International Master is given for any of the following: two or more International Master results in events covering at least 24 games, and a rating of at least 2400 in the current FIDE Rating List, or within seven years of the first title result; first place in one of the following events: Women's Candidates Tournament, Zonal Tournament, Continental Individual Championship, Continental Individual Junior Championship, Arab Individual and Junior Championships, Centroamerican-Caribbean Junior Championship, World Under-18 Championship, International Braille Chess Association World (IBCA) Championship (champion is given a rating of 2205), and International Committee of Silent Chess World Championship (in the event of a tie for first place in any of the above listed events, each of the tied players shall be awarded the title - subject to a maximum of three players); the top three medalist in the World Junior Championship; qualification for the Interzonal Tournament of the World Championship cycle; one International Master result in the cycle of the Individual World Championship, of at least 13 games; a score of 66 2/3 percent or better in a Zonal Tournament of at least nine games; first place in the World Under-16 Championship and the Continental Under-18 and Under-16 Championships (equivalent to one nine-game International Master result); and one 13-game International Master result in the Olympiad, which leads to the award of the full title. A title, a medal, and a diploma are awarded annually. Established in 1946.

3321 ■ Woman FIDE Master
To recognize the achievements of a female in the game of chess. The title of Woman FIDE Master is given for any of the following: a rating of at least 2100 after the completion of at least 24 games (the national federation is responsible for the payment of the fee established by the financial regulations); first place in any of the following events: World Girls' Championships in specific age groups, Continental Women's Championship, Arab Women's Championship, Continental Girls Championship in specific age groups, and IBCA Women's World Championship with a rating of at least 2005 (in the event of a tie for first place in any of the above events, each of the tied players will receive the title of WFM - subject to a maximum of three players); and a score of 50 percent or better in a Woman's Zonal tournament of at least nine games. A title, a medal, and a diploma are awarded annually.

3322 ■ Woman Grandmaster
To recognize the achievement of a female in the game of chess. The title of Woman Grandmaster is given for any of the following: two or more Woman Grandmaster results in events covering at least 24 games and a rating of at least 2300 in the FIDE Rating List, or within seven years of the first title result; qualification for the Candidates Competition for the Women's World Championship; one Woman Grandmaster result in the cycle of the Individual Women's World Championship, of at least 13 games; first place in the World Girls Championship (equivalent to one nine-game Woman Grandmaster result); first place in the Continental Girls Championship (equivalent to one nine-game WGM result); and one 13-game Woman Grandmaster result in the Olympiad, which leads to a full title. A title, a medal, and diploma are awarded annually.

3323 ■ Woman International Master
To recognize the achievement of a female in the game of chess. The title of Woman International Master is given for any of the following: two or more WIM results in events covering at least 24 games and a rating of at least 2200 in the FIDE Rating List, within seven years of the first title result; qualification for the Interzonal Tournament for the Women's World Championship; first place in any of the following events: Continental Women's Championship, Arab Women's Championship, World Girls Under-18 Championship, Continental Girls Under-20 Championship. In the event of a tie in any of the above events, each of the tied players will be awarded the title of WIM (subject to a maximum of three players); top three medalists in the World Girl Under-20 Championship; one WIM result in the cycle of the Individual Women's World Championship, of not less than 13 games; a score of 66 2/3 percent or better in a Women's World Championship Zonal Tournament of at least 9 games; first place in the World Girls Under-16 Championship and the Continental Girls Under-18 and Under-16 Championships is equivalent to one 9-game WIM result; or one 13-game WIM result in the Olympiad will result in the award of a full title. A title, medal, and diploma are awarded annually.

Greenland

3324 ■ Greenland Bureau of Minerals and Petroleum
Imaneq 29
PO Box 930
Nuuk, Greenland
Ph: 299 34 6800
Fax: 299 32 4302
E-mail: bmp@nanoq.gl
URL: http://www.bmp.gl

Awards are arranged in alphabetical order below their administering organizations

3325 ■ Greenland Prospector and Developer of the Year
To recognize an individual or company who has executed an extraordinary effort in the geological exploration of Greenland. Awarded annually.

Grenada

3326 ■ Grenada Triathlon Association
Clare Morrall, Pres.
PO Box 170
St. George's, Grenada
Fax: 473440-4137
URL: http://www.grenadatriathlon.com

3327 ■ Triathlon Awards
To honor the athletes who performed the best at the Annual Triathlon, an event featuring Olympic-distance swimming, bicycling, and running. Trophies and cash prizes are given for the first, second, and third place winners in various age groups and well for the top men and women overall. Held annually in May. Established in 1998.

Guatemala

**3328 ■ American Chamber of Commerce of Guatemala
(Camara de Comercio Guatemalteco-Americana)**
Carolina Castellanos, Exec. Dir.
5 Av. 5-55, Zona 14 Edif. WBC Torre 1
Nivel 5 Europlaza
01014 Guatemala City, Guatemala
Ph: 502 2 4170800
Fax: 502 2 4170777
E-mail: recepcion@amchamguate.com
URL: http://www.amchamguate.com

3329 ■ AmCham Annual Awards
To recognize a person who makes efforts in promoting trade and investment. Awarded annually.

Guyana

3330 ■ Guyana Business Coalition on HIV/AIDS
Lot 108 Orange Walk
Dorothy Bailey Compound
Bourda
Georgetown, Guyana
Ph: 592 225 0972
E-mail: info@guybizcoalition.org
URL: http://www.guybizcoalition.org

3331 ■ Awards for Business Excellence
To recognize valuable contributions made by the private sector in the fight against HIV and AIDS in Guyana during the year. Awards are presented in five categories: workplace programs, peer educators, core competency, community investment, and advocacy and individual leadership. Awarded annually.

3332 ■ Guyana Central Arya Samaj
Central Vaidik Mandir
78-79 Prem Niranjan Pl.
Prashad Nagar
Georgetown, Guyana
Ph: 592 227 2210
E-mail: secretary@aryasamaj.org.gy
URL: http://www.aryasamaj.org.gy

3333 ■ National Arya Samaj Award
To honor an Arya Samajist for outstanding lifelong service to the ideals and vision of the Arya Samaj in Guyana. Awarded annually. Established in 2000.

3334 ■ Office of the President of the Cooperative Republic of Guyana
New Garden St.
Georgetown, Guyana
Ph: 592 225 13308
E-mail: opmed@op.gov.gy
URL: http://opnew.op.gov.gy

3335 ■ Cacique's Crown of Honour
To honor a citizen or organization for service to Guyana. Awarded when merited.

3336 ■ Cacique's Crown of Valour
To honor an individual for acts of bravery. Awarded when merited.

3337 ■ Golden Arrow of Achievement
To honor a citizen or organization for service to Guyana. Awarded when merited.

3338 ■ Golden Arrow of Courage
To honor an individual for acts of bravery. Awarded when merited.

3339 ■ Medal of Service
To honor a citizen or organization for service to Guyana. Awarded when merited.

3340 ■ Order of Excellence of Guyana
This, the highest national award in Guyana, is awarded to honor an individual for achievements of national or international significance. Shall be held by no more than 25 living citizens at any given time. Awarded when merited.

3341 ■ Order of Roraima of Guyana
To honor a citizen of Guyana for outstanding service to the nation. Shall be held by no more than 35 living citizens at any given time. Awarded when merited.

**3342 ■ University of Guyana
Faculty of Agriculture and Forestry**
Dillon Husbands, Mgr.
PO Box 10-1110
Georgetown, Guyana
Ph: 592 222 5402
Fax: 592 222 2490
E-mail: dillonhusbands2002@yahoo.com
URL: http://www.uog.edu.gy/faculties/faf

3343 ■ Naseer Ahmad Shield
To honor the best graduating student in the field of soil science. Awarded annually.

3344 ■ Barama Company Award
To honor the best graduating student in the Diploma of Forestry Programme. Awarded annually.

3345 ■ Dwarka (Agriculture) Award
To honor the best graduating student in the Diploma of Forestry Programme. Awarded annually.

3346 ■ Bernard Gonsalves Memorial Award
To honor the best full-time student (other than the holder of a full scholarship in the Bachelor of Science in Agriculture Programme) who has completed the third year of the program. Awarded annually.

3347 ■ Guyana National Cooperative Bank Award
To honor the best first-year student. Awarded annually.

3348 ■ Guyana Sugar Corporation Award for Soil Science
To honor the best graduating student in the field of soil science. Awarded annually.

3349 ■ Oscar Sydney James Shield and Trophy
To honor the best graduating student in the field of animal husbandry. Awarded annually.

3350 ■ Gavin B. Kennard Award
To honor the best overall student in the Faculty of Agriculture. Awarded annually.

3351 ■ Ministry of Agriculture Award
To honor the best third-year student. Awarded annually.

3352 ■ Ministry of Agriculture Award for Soil Science
To honor the best third-year student in the field of soil science. Awarded annually.

3353 ■ National Bank of Industry and Commerce Award
To honor the best graduating student in the field of agricultural economics and agricultural extension. Awarded annually.

3354 ■ Winston J. Phillips Award
To honor the second-best overall student in the Faculty of Agriculture. Awarded annually.

3355 ■ Ptolemy A. Reid Award for Animal Science
To honor the best graduating student in the field of animal science. Awarded annually.

3356 ■ Ptolemy A. Reid Award for Crop Science
To honor the best graduating student in the field of crop science. Awarded annually.

3357 ■ University of Guyana Awards
To honor outstanding first-year, second-year, and third-year students. Awarded annually.

3358 ■ University of Guyana Guild of Graduates Ontario Award
To honor an outstanding student entering the second, third, or fourth year at the undergraduate level. Awarded annually.

Hungary

**3359 ■ Association of Hungarian Geophysicists
(Magyar Geofizikusok Egyesulete)**
Fo utca 68
H-1027 Budapest, Hungary
Ph: 36 1 2019815
E-mail: mageof@elgi.hu
URL: http://www.mageof.hu/index.htm

**3360 ■ Laszlo Egyed Medal
(Egyed Laszlo emlekerem)**
For recognition of outstanding professional performance in the field of geophysics, in honor of Hungarian geophysicist Lazlo Egyed. The award may be awarded for an outstanding performance in any special area of geophysics; for achievements in the teaching of geophysics; for writing and editing special geophysics papers; and for lifetime service in the profession. Established in 1985, the award is given biennially.

3361 ■ Lorand Eotvos Medal
For recognition of achievements in research, in both theoretical and practical geophysics, during the past six years. Hungarian geophysicists who are regular members of the association are eligible. A medal with the figure of R. Eotvos on one side is awarded triennially. Established in 1957.

3362 ■ Honorary Membership
For recognition of outstanding achievements in geophysics and related sciences, or in attainment of the association's purposes. Both Hungarian and foreign citizens are eligible. Honorary memberships are awarded triennially. Established in 1954.

Awards are arranged in alphabetical order below their administering organizations

3363 ■ Janos Renner Medal
For recognition of outstanding performance within and on behalf of the Association. The medal may be awarded for significant social activities; for merits shown in organizing and developing Association activities; and for research in scientific history. In honor of Janos Renner, a renowned Hungarian geophysicist. Awarded annually. Established in 1985.

3364 ■ Association of Hungarian Inventors
(Magyar Feltalalok Egyesuletenek)
Mr. Andras Vedres PhD, Sec. Gen.
PO Box 426
H-1519 Budapest, Hungary
Ph: 36 1 2203040
Fax: 36 1 2203040
E-mail: genius@inventor.hu
URL: http://www.inventor.hu

3365 ■ Genius Prize
To recognize exceptional inventions. Criteria include inventiveness, potential, and quality of display and presentation. Awarded biennially in even-numbered years at the Genius International Fair of Inventions. Established in 1998.

3366 ■ Association of Hungarian Librarians
(Magyar Konyvtarosok Egyesulete)
Dr. Agnes Hajdu Barat, VP
Budavari Palota, F Bldg.
H-1827 Budapest, Hungary
Ph: 36 1 3118634
Fax: 36 1 3118634
E-mail: mke@oszk.hu
URL: http://mke.info.hu

3367 ■ A Magyar Konyvtarosok Egyesuleteert Emlekerem
For association officials who showed professional merit.

3368 ■ Association of Hungarian Medical Societies
(Magyar Orvostudomanyi Tarsasagok es Egyesuletek Szovetsege)
Dr. Tibor Ertl, Pres.
1443 Budapest, Pf. 145
H-1051 Budapest, Hungary
Ph: 36 1 3324556
Ph: 36 1 3116687
Fax: 36 1 3837918
E-mail: office@motesz.hu
URL: http://www.motesz.hu

3369 ■ MOTESZ Award
For outstanding work promoting the activity of Federation.

3370 ■ Food and Agriculture Organization of the United Nations - Regional Office for Europe
(Organizacion de la Naciones Unidas para La Agricultura y la Alimentacion)
Ludmilla Vorobej, Sec.
Benczur utca 34
H-1068 Budapest, Hungary
Ph: 36 1 4612000
Fax: 36 1 3517029
E-mail: fao-seur@fao.org
URL: http://www.fao.org/world/regional/reu

3371 ■ A. H. Boerma Award
To recognize journalists who have helped to focus public attention on important aspects of the world food problem and have stimulated interest in and support for measures leading to their solutions. An article, articles, and productions in television and radio may be submitted by nationals of any member country of FAO. A monetary prize of $10,000 US and a scroll describing the recipient's achievements are awarded biennially in even-numbered years. Established in 1975 in honor of Mr. Addeke H. Boerma, Director-General of FAO from 1968 to 1975.

3372 ■ Edouard Saouma Award
To recognize a national or regional institution that managed a particularly efficient project funded under FAO's Technical Cooperation Programme. A medal, scroll, and cash prize of US$25,000 is awarded biennially in odd-numbered years. Established in 1993 to honor Mr. Edouard Saouma, who served as Director General of FAO from 1976 to 1993.

3373 ■ B. R. Sen Award
To recognize FAO field officers who have made outstanding contributions to the advancement of the country or countries to which he/she was assigned. Candidates must have served in the year for which the Award is granted and must have at least two years' continuous service in the field. All FAO field officers are eligible. The Award consists of a medal bearing the recipient's name, a scroll describing achievements, a cash prize of US $5,000 and round-trip airfare to FAO headquarters in Rome for the recipient and spouse. Awarded annually. Established in 1968.

3374 ■ Hungarian Academy of Sciences Veterinary Medical Research Institute
Prof. Tibor Magyar DVM, Dir.
PO Box 18
H-1581 Budapest, Hungary
Ph: 36 1 2522455
Fax: 36 1 2521069
E-mail: tibor.magyar@vmri.hu
URL: http://www.vmri.hu

3375 ■ Aujeszky Medal
For experts working with Aujeszky disease.

3376 ■ Csontos Medal
For excellence in veterinary science.

3377 ■ Hungarian Anatomical Society
Prof. Dr. Gyula Lazar, Contact
University Medical School
Dept. of Anatomy
Szigeti ut 12
Pecs, Hungary
Ph: 36 72 324122
Fax: 36 72 326244
E-mail: lazargy@apacs.pote.hu
URL: http://www.efem.eu/council.php

3378 ■ Lenhosseks Prize
To young morphologists who have been successful in publishing outstanding articles in the field of anatomy, histology and embryology.

3379 ■ Hungarian Chemical Society
(Verein Ungarischer Chemiker)
Dr. Simonne Sarkadi Livia, Pres.
Fo utca 68
H-1027 Budapest, Hungary
Ph: 36 1 2016883
Fax: 36 1 2018056
E-mail: mail@mke.org.hu
URL: http://www.mke.org.hu

3380 ■ Rudolf Fabinyi Medal
To recognize a non-member for contributions that increase the reputation of the Society. A bronze medal and diploma are awarded annually. Established in 2007.

3381 ■ Ignac Pfeifer Award
To recognize a member who has provided at least 20 years of dedication to the chemical industry. A bronze medal and monetary prize are awarded every one or two years. Established in 1968.

3382 ■ Miklos Preisich Award
To recognize a member for a sustained contribution to the Society and the chemical industry. A diploma and monetary prize are awarded every one or two years. Established in 1994.

3383 ■ Karoly Than Award
For service to the organization.

3384 ■ Vince Wartha Memorial Plaquettes
To recognize a member for outstanding achievements to chemical engineering. A bronze medal and monetary prize are awarded every one or two years. Established in 1955.

3385 ■ Hungarian Dermatological Society
(Magyar Dermatologiai Tarsulat)
Dr. Norbert Wikonkal, Sec. Gen.
Semmelweis University Budapest
Dept. of Dermatology
Faculty of Medicine
Maria Str. 41
H-1085 Budapest, Hungary
Ph: 36 1 2660465
Fax: 36 1 2676974
E-mail: office@derma.hu
URL: http://www.derma.hu

3386 ■ Mor Kaposi Medal
To recognize an individual for outstanding work in the field of dermato-venereology. Awarded annually.

3387 ■ Hungarian Publishers and Booksellers Association
Mr. Peter Laszlo Zentai, Dir.
Pf. 130
H-1367 Budapest, Hungary
Ph: 36 1 3432540
Ph: 36 1 3432538
Fax: 36 1 3432541
E-mail: mkke@mkke.hu
URL: http://www.mkke.hu

3388 ■ Book of the Year
For recognition of the best published book of the year in all categories of literature. Held annually. Co-sponsored by Artisjus, Hungarian Organization for Defence of Copyright.

3389 ■ International Association for Hungarian Studies
(Association Internationale des Etudes Hongroises)
Istvan Monok, Gen. Sec.
Terez krt. 13. II/205-207
H-1067 Budapest, Hungary
Ph: 36 1 3214407
Fax: 36 1 3214407
E-mail: admin@nmtt.hu
URL: http://www.iahs.eu

3390 ■ John Lotz Commemorative Medal
(Lotz Janos Emlekerem)
To recognize scholars living outside of Hungary for an outstanding contribution to the teaching of Hungarian Studies in the fields of Hungarian language, literature, and ethnography. A special award committee makes the nomination. A medal is awarded every five years on the occasion of the general meetings of IAHS. Established in 1981 in memory of John Lotz (1913-1973), a Hungarian philologist, linguist, and educator.

3391 ■ Endre Szirmai Prize
To recognize scholarly excellence in the field of Hungarian studies. Individuals from any country are eligible. Criteria are the discovery of any hitherto unknown or unfound relic or source of Hungarian cultural or historical interest, or a published scholarly work in Hungarian studies written in an international language of scholarship (English, French, German, Italian, Russian, or Spanish). Awarded triennially. Established in 1987.

3392 ■ International Fair Play Committee
Istvanmezei ut 1-3
H-1146 Budapest, Hungary
Ph: 36 1 460 6957
Fax: 36 1 460 6956
E-mail: cifp@fairplayinternational.org
URL: http://www.fairplayinternational.org

Awards are arranged in alphabetical order below their administering organizations

3393 ■ Jean Borotra World Fair Play Trophy

To recognize a person for his/her remarkable general attitude shown throughout his/her sport career, for an outstanding and constant spirit of fair play, and for observing the unwritten rule of sport not to take advantage of an opponent's bad luck. Awarded annually as part of the Fair Play Prizes. Established in 1965.

3394 ■ Pierre de Coubertin World Fair Play Trophy

To recognize an athlete or a team for a gesture of fair play that cost, or could have cost, his/her victory, or could have downgraded his or her sport performance. Awarded annually as part of the Fair Play Prizes. Established in 1965.

3395 ■ Willi Daume World Fair Play Trophy

To recognize a person or organization for an activity aimed at promoting fair play by organizing national or local campaigns, giving lectures, writing articles in the press, or making comments on the radio or television. Awarded annually as part of the Fair Play Prizes. Established in 1965.

3396 ■ Fair Play Prizes

To recognize individuals and teams for the promotion of fair play in sports. Awarded in three categories: 1) to an athlete or a team for a gesture of fair play; 2) to a person for a general attitude of fair play showed during his/her career; and 3) to a person or an organization for promoting fair play. Letter of Congratulations, Diplomas of Honour, and trophies (see separate entries) are awarded in each category annually. Established in 1965.

3397 ■ International Federation of Inventors' Associations
PO Box 319
1591 Budapest, Hungary
Ph: 36 1 422 0936
Fax: 36 20 945 8078
E-mail: ifia@inventor.hu
URL: http://www.invention-ifia.ch

3398 ■ Arpad Bogsch Memory Medal

To recognize individuals for invention and innovation. A medal is presented to one or more recipients per year.

3399 ■ International Order of Merit of the Inventors

To recognize inventors and their supporters for exceptionally meritorious conduct in the performance of outstanding invention activity, services, and achievements. Issued in four degrees: Knight, Officer, Commander, and Grand Master. Established in 2008.

3400 ■ International Judo Federation
(Federation Internationale de Judo)
Mr. Marius Vizer, Pres.
Jozsef Attila Str. 1
1051 Budapest, Hungary
Ph: 36 1 302 7270
Fax: 36 1 3027271
E-mail: president@ijf.org
URL: http://www.ijf.org

3401 ■ International Judo Federation Awards

To promote the spread and development of the spirit and techniques of judo by sponsoring world championships. Awards include the Gold Award, Silver Award, and Bronze Award. Awarded annually when merited.

3402 ■ Judo Hall of Fame

To honor the achievements of those judokas, referees, coaches, and contributors who have given outstanding contributions, leadership, and abilities to the development and diffusion of the sport of judo on a worldwide level. To qualify for consideration, athletes must have been retired for at least three years, referees must have been retired for at least five years, and coaches must have coached for 25 years or have been retired for at least five years; contributors are eligible after having retired from their capacity in the sport.

3403 ■ International Measurement Confederation
(Internationale Messtechnische Konfoderation)
Ms. Karolina Havrilla, Sec.
PO Box 457
H-1371 Budapest V, Hungary
Ph: 36 1 3531562
Fax: 36 1 3531562
E-mail: imeko@t-online.hu
URL: http://www.imeko.org

3404 ■ Distinguished Service Award

To recognize an individual for outstanding service to the Confederation. Candidates must have been active for many years as well-known specialists in the field of measurement. Awarded triennially to several recipients.

3405 ■ Gyorgy Striker Junior Paper Award

To recognize a junior author under the age of 35 who presents a paper reflecting a deep understanding of the scope of a World Congress. A diploma and $1,000 is awarded at the Closing Session of the World Congress. Established in 1992.

3406 ■ International Society for Inventory Research
Kiraly u. 12
H-1061 Budapest, Hungary
Ph: 36 1 267 8740
Fax: 36 1 267 8740
E-mail: isir@isir.hu
URL: http://isir.hu

3407 ■ Fellow of ISIR

To recognize members who have significantly advanced the goals of the Organization through their general contributions to knowledge, the formation of professionals, the promotion of international cooperation, and/or exemplary practice. Awarded biennially in even-numbered years. Established in 1996.

3408 ■ Service Award

To recognize an individual who has performed invaluable service to the Organization over a number of years both in official roles and in providing help whenever needed. Awarded biennially in even-numbered years. Established in 1996.

3409 ■ International Weightlifting Federation
Dr. Tamas Ajan, Pres.
Istvanmezei ut 1-3
H-1146 Budapest, Hungary
Ph: 36 1 3530530
Ph: 36 1 3318153
Fax: 36 1 3530199
E-mail: iwf@iwfnet.net
URL: http://www.iwf.net

3410 ■ Award of Merit

To recognize individuals for outstanding service to the development of the sport of weightlifting. Proposals to confer the award must be submitted by the national or continental federations or executive board members.

3411 ■ Weightlifting Hall of Fame

To honor the sport's most prominent representatives. Candidates may be athletes, coaches, officials, journalists, or sponsors. To qualify, athletes must have been retired for at least five years, coaches must have worked for weightlifting for at least 25 years, officials must have at least 25 years of service in weightlifting, and other individuals must have significantly assisted the weightlifting sport. As many as 10 individuals may be inducted annually. Established in 1992.

3412 ■ John Von Neumann Computer Society - Hungary
(Neumann Janos Szamitogep-tudomanyi Tarsasag)
Prof. Gabor Peceli, Pres.
Bathori u. 16
H-1054 Budapest, Hungary
Ph: 36 1 4722730
Ph: 36 1 4722710
Fax: 36 1 4722739
E-mail: titkarsag@njszt.hu
URL: http://www.njszt.hu/neumann/neumann.main.page

3413 ■ Kalmar Prize

To recognize outstanding experts in practical applications of computer sciences. Established in 1976 in honor of Laszlo Kalmar, the late Professor at the Science University of Szeged.

3414 ■ John Kemeny Prize

To recognize young scholars (under 30 years of age) for professional works and publications. Awarded annually. Established in 2000 in honor of one of the developers of the BASIC computer language.

3415 ■ Neumann Medal

To recognize individuals who have rendered outstanding services in or for the Society or have otherwise gained distinction in the dissemination of computer culture. Awarded annually. Established in 1976 in honor of the founder of the Society.

3416 ■ Neumann Plaquette and Certificate

To recognize illustrious computer specialists from abroad who contribute to the development and foreign recognition of Hungarian computer science. Awarded annually.

3417 ■ Tarjan Prize

To recognize individuals for contributions to basic and further education in informatics.

Iceland

3418 ■ Evangelical Lutheran Church of Iceland
Laugavegur 31
IS-150 Reykjavik, Iceland
Ph: 354 535 1500
Fax: 354 551 3284
E-mail: kirkjan@kirkjan.is
URL: http://www.kirkjan.is

3419 ■ Church of Iceland Film Award

To recognize an outstanding film that deals with existential, ethical, or religious questions. Awarded annually as part of the Reykjavik International Film Festival.

3420 ■ Iceland Music Export
Borgartun 35
105 Reykjavik, Iceland
Ph: 354 571 5660
E-mail: info@icelandmusic.is
URL: http://www.icelandmusic.is

3421 ■ Icelandic Music Awards

To encourage and reward Icelandic musicians and to further the local and international reputation of Icelandic music. Awarded annually in a variety of categories. Established in 1993.

3422 ■ Icelandic Centre for Research
(Rannsoknarrad Islands)
Hallgrimur Jonasson, Gen. Dir.
Laugavegur 13
IS-101 Reykjavik, Iceland

Awards are arranged in alphabetical order below their administering organizations

Ph: 354 5155800
Fax: 354 5529814
E-mail: rannis@rannis.is
URL: http://www.rannis.is/forsida

3423 ■ Research Grant
For scientific, technological quality and socio economic relevance.

3424 ■ Icelandic Film and Television Academy
Hverfisgata 54
101 Reykjavik, Iceland
URL: http://www.icelandicfilmcentre.is

3425 ■ Edda Awards for Icelandic Film and Television
To recognize the best in Icelandic film and television productions. Open to features, documentaries, shorts, television shows, and music videos. Awarded annually in a variety of categories. Established in 1999.

3426 ■ Icelandic Publishers' Association
(Felag Islenskra Bokautgefenda)
Kristjan B. Jonasson, Contact
Baronsstig 5
IS-101 Reykjavik, Iceland
Ph: 354 5118020
Ph: 354 4313271
Fax: 354 5115020
E-mail: baekur@simnet.is
URL: http://www.bokautgafa.is

3427 ■ Icelandic Literature Prize
To recognize the best books published in Iceland during the year. Awarded annually in two categories: fiction and nonfiction. Established in 1989.

3428 ■ Icelandic Radio Amateurs
(Islenskir Radioamatorar)
Jonas Bjarnason, Chm.
PO Box 1058
IS-121 Reykjavik, Iceland
E-mail: formadur@ira.is
URL: http://www.ira.is/homepage.action

3429 ■ The Iceland Award
For being able to contact or hear Icelandic amateur radio stations within one year. Awarded when merited.

3430 ■ Iceland on Six Meters Award
For being able to contact or hear Icelandic amateur radio stations on six meters. Awarded when merited.

3431 ■ Icelandic JOTA Award
For contacting Icelandic JOTA amateur radio stations. Awarded when merited.

3432 ■ Icelandic Radio Amateurs Award
For radio amateurs outside Iceland. Awarded when merited.

3433 ■ IRA Zone 40 Award
For being able to contact with each of the countries specified by the club. Awarded when merited.

3434 ■ Worked All Nordic Countries Award
For licensed radio amateurs. Awarded when merited.

3435 ■ Office of the President of Iceland
Soleyjargotu 1
IS-101 Reykjavik, Iceland
Ph: 354 540 4400
Fax: 354 562 4802
E-mail: president@president.is
URL: http://www.forseti.is

3436 ■ Medal of Icelandic Red Cross
To honor individuals for humanitarian deeds. A medal is awarded when merited. Established in 1949.

3437 ■ Medallion of the Republic of Iceland
To honor individuals who endangered their lives or health to save Icelanders from mortal danger. A medal is awarded when merited. Established in 1950.

3438 ■ Order of the Falcon
To honor Icelanders and non-nationals for achievements in the interest of Iceland or in the international arena. The Order has the following classes: Grand Cross, Commander with a Star, Commander, and Knight. A medal is awarded when merited. Established in 1921.

India

3439 ■ Aeronautical Society of India
Dr. Vijay Kumar Sarswat, Chm.
PO. Kanchanabagh
Hyderabad 500058, Andhra Pradesh, India
Ph: 91 40 24341207
E-mail: info@aesi-hyd.com
URL: http://www.aesi-hyd.com

3440 ■ Excellence in Aerospace Education Award
To recognize an outstanding contribution in the field of aerospace education. Individuals actively engaged in the teaching profession in the aeronautical field are eligible. A monetary award of 20,000 rupees is presented annually at the annual meeting. Established in 1991.

3441 ■ Dr. V. M. Ghatage Award
For recognition of an outstanding contribution in the field of design, development, manufacture, operation, training, maintenance and allied areas in aviation and space. Scientific and technical institutions are invited to make recommendations to an Awards Committee, upon whose recommendation the Council makes the final decision. A monetary prize of 20,000 rupees is awarded annually. Established in 1984 in honor of Dr. V.M. Ghatage, on the occasion of his 75th birthday, by his students and colleagues.

3442 ■ Indigenisation of Aeronautical Equipment Award
Recognizes outstanding achievements in indigenisdion of aeronautical equipment, including ground handling equipment. A monetary prize of 20,000 rupees is awarded annually. Established in 1994 by S.I.A.T.L.

3443 ■ Swarna Jayanti Award
For outstanding contribution by a young achiever in the field of aviation, aeronautics, or aerospace. Candidates must be members below the age of 40 years. A monetary prize of 50,000 rupees is awarded annually. Established in 1999 on the golden jubilee of the society.

3444 ■ National Aeronautical Prize
For recognition of an outstanding fundamental and applied work in aeronautical science and technology. A monetary prize of 100,000 rupees is awarded annually. Established in 1988 by the Aeronautics Research & Development Board, Ministry of Defence of the Government of India, New Delhi.

3445 ■ Production Technology Award
To encourage and recognize outstanding contributions by technicians in the making of aero products. A monetary prize of 20,000 rupees is awarded annually. Established in 1993.

3446 ■ Dr. Biren Roy Space Science and/or Design Award
To encourage Indian space scientists and to recognize an outstanding contribution in space science. The Awards Committee selects the nominees and makes recommendations to the Council for a final decision. A monetary prize of 20,000 rupees is awarded annually. Established in 1985 by Dr. Biren Roy (Charitable) Trust, Roy Mansions, Behala, Calcutta - 34, well known for its grants for medical relief and scientific progress.

3447 ■ Dr. Biren Roy Trust Award
For recognition of an outstanding contribution in the field of design, development, manufacture, operation, training, maintenance and allied areas in aviation and space. Scientific and technical institutions are invited to make recommendations to an Awards Committee, upon whose recommendation the Council makes the final decision. A monetary prize of 20,000 rupees is awarded annually. Established in 1983 by Dr. Biren Roy (Charitable) Trust, Calcutta.

3448 ■ All India Management Association
Mr. Gautam Thapar, Pres.
Mgt. House
14 Institutional Area
Lodhi Rd.
New Delhi 110 003, Delhi, India
Ph: 91 11 24617354
Ph: 91 11 24645100
Fax: 91 11 24626689
E-mail: dg@aima-ind.org
URL: http://www.aima-ind.org

3449 ■ Creativity and Innovation Award for Small Enterprises
To recognize small enterprises for creativity and innovation. Awarded annually. Established in 2003.

3450 ■ JRD Tata Corporate Leadership Award
To recognize corporate leaders for contributions to the Society and the nation at large. Awarded annually. Established in 1995.

3451 ■ Lifetime Achievement Award for Management
To recognize managers who are acknowledged leaders in his or her own organization, who have left footprints in the management profession, management thought, and culture, and whose organization operates in India. Candidates are generally about 75 years old. Awarded annually. Established in 1999.

3452 ■ Public Service Excellence Award
To recognize individuals who have awareness and commitment to nationally important issues. Awarded annually. Established in 1998.

3453 ■ Bharatiya Jnanpith
18 Institutional Area
PO Box 3113
Lodhi Rd.
New Delhi 110 003, Delhi, India
Ph: 91 2462 6467
Fax: 91 2465 4197
E-mail: jnanpith@satyam.net.in
URL: http://jnanpith.net

3454 ■ Jnanpith Award
To recognize the best creative literary writing by any Indian citizen. Awarded annually. Established in 1965.

3455 ■ Moortidevi Award
To recognize an individual for a contemplative or creative literary work that expresses, underlines, and illuminates human values rooted in the broad vision of Indian philosophy and cultural heritage. Awarded annually.

3456 ■ Bombay Natural History Society
Dr. Ashok S. Kothari, Honorary Sec.
Hornbill House
Shaheed Bhagat Singh Rd.
Mumbai 400 001, Maharashtra, India
Ph: 91 22 22821811
Fax: 91 22 22837615

Awards are arranged in alphabetical order below their administering organizations

E-mail: bnhs@bom4.vsnl.net.in
URL: http://www.bnhs.org

3457 ■ Salim Ali International Award
For outstanding contribution in the field of nature conservation.

3458 ■ Children's Film Society, India
Nandita Das, Chair
Films Division Complex
24, Dr. G. Deshmukh Marg
Mumbai 400 026, Maharashtra, India
Ph: 91 22 23521120
Ph: 91 22 23516136
Fax: 91 22 23522610
E-mail: cfsi@cfsindia.org
URL: http://www.cfsindia.org

3459 ■ International Children's Film Festival of India
For recognition of outstanding films for children. The objects of the festival are to promote and encourage the Children's Film Movement, to foster a closer relationship among the international fraternity of children's film makers and organizations and to afford them an opportunity to exchange their films, and to exhibit the best of the children's films from different countries of the world with a view to promote international understanding and brotherhood among the children of the world. There are three sections at the festival: competitive, information Asian Panorama, and market. The following awards are presented: Golden Elephant Award for the Best Live-Action Feature Length Film - 100,000 rupees; Silver Elephant Award for the Best Short Film - 50,000 rupees; Silver Elephant Award for the Second Best Live-Action Feature-Length Film 50,000 rupees; Silver Elephant Award for the Best Animation Film - 50,000 rupees; Silver Elephant Award for the Best Puppet Film; Silver Elephant Award for the Best Director - 50,000 rupees; Silver Elephant Award for the Best Child Artist; Silver Elephant Award for the Best Cinematographer; Silver Elephant Award for the Special Jury Prize - 50,000 rupees; and Golden Plaque Award for the Most Popular Children's Film determined by a jury of 15 children. Held biennially in odd-numbered years. Established in 1979.

3460 ■ CLFMA of India
Commander S. Jaikumar, Exec. Dir.
111, Mittal Chamber, 11th Fl.
Nariman Pt.
Mumbai 400 021, Maharashtra, India
Ph: 91 22 22026103
Fax: 91 22 22880128
E-mail: clafma@bom4.vsnl.net.in
URL: http://www.clfmaofindia.org

3461 ■ CLFMA Award
For original research on applied animal nutrition for commercial exploitation by the compound feed industry. Awarded triennially.

3462 ■ Clothing Manufacturers Association of India
Mr. Rahul Mehta, Pres.
902 Mahalaxmi Chambers
22, Bhulabhai Desai Rd.
Mumbai 400 026, Maharashtra, India
Ph: 91 22 23538245
Ph: 91 22 23538986
Fax: 91 22 23515908
E-mail: cmai@vsnl.com
URL: http://www.cmai.in

3463 ■ APEX Awards
To recognize excellence in apparel manufacturing, marketing, and supply chain management,

as well as to honor significant contributions to the industry from allied industries. Awards are presented annually in 30 categories.

3464 ■ Confederation of Indian Textile Industry
D.K. Nair, Sec. Gen.
6th Fl., Narain Manzil
23 Barakhamba Rd.
New Delhi 110 001, Delhi, India
Ph: 91 11 23325012
Ph: 91 11 23325013
Fax: 91 11 41519602
E-mail: mail@citiindia.com
URL: http://www.citiindia.com

3465 ■ Birla Awards
To recognize textile companies for excellence. A monetary prize of Rs. 2 lakh is awarded annually.

3466 ■ Consulting Engineers Association of India
Mr. P.K. Datta, Exec. Dir.
OCF Plot No. 2, Pocket 9, Sector B
Vasant Kunj
New Delhi 110070, Delhi, India
Ph: 91 11 26524644
Ph: 91 11 26139658
Fax: 91 11 26139658
E-mail: ceai.ceai@gmail.com
URL: http://www.ceaindia.org

3467 ■ Major General Harkirat Singh Memorial Award
For student securing highest marks in civil engineering final year at Indian Institute of Technology, Delhi.

3468 ■ Cotton Textiles Export Promotion Council
Mr. Rajagopal Siddhartha, Exec. Dir.
Engineering Ctre., 5th Fl.
9 Mathew Rd.
Mumbai 400004, Maharashtra, India
Ph: 91 22 23632910
Ph: 91 22 23632912
Fax: 91 22 23632914
E-mail: info@texprocil.org
URL: http://www.texprocil.org

3469 ■ Export Awards
To Indian exporters for excellence in export performance in cotton yarn, fabrics, and made-ups. Gold, silver, and bronze awards are presented in various categories each year.

3470 ■ Council of Scientific and Industrial Research, India
Institute of Himalayan Bioresource Technology
Paramvir Singh Ahuja PhD, Dir.
PO Box 6
Palampur 176 061, Himachal Pradesh, India
Ph: 91 1894 230411
Fax: 91 1894 230433
E-mail: psahuja@ihbt.res.in
URL: http://www.ihbt.res.in

3471 ■ CSIR Case Award
For the promotion of science at the college level.

3472 ■ Technology Adoption Award

3473 ■ Delhi Management Association
Mr. S. Varadarajan, Pres.
India Habitat Centre
Core 6A, 1st Fl.
Lodhi Rd.
New Delhi 110 003, Delhi, India
Ph: 91 11 24649552
Fax: 91 11 24649553
E-mail: dmadelhi@sify.com
URL: http://www.dmadelhi.org

3474 ■ Erehwon Award for Innovative HR Initiatives
To recognize companies for innovative HR practices that result in improved business performance. Established in 2003. Co-sponsored by Erehwon Consulting.

3475 ■ NTPC Book Award
To recognize excellence in books on management. First prize is Rs.15,000, second prize is Rs.10,000, and third prize is Rs.5,000. Awarded annually.

3476 ■ Shiram Award
For original contributions to management topics. Established in 1969.

3477 ■ ELCINA Electronic Industries Association of India
Mr. Robert John, Pres.
Elcina House
422 Okhla Industrial Estate
New Delhi 110 020, Delhi, India
Ph: 91 11 26928053
Ph: 91 11 26924597
Fax: 91 11 26923440
E-mail: elcina@vsnl.com
URL: http://www.elcina.com

3478 ■ ELCINA/Dun & Bradstreet Awards for Excellence in Electronics Hardware
To recognize the achievements of electronics and information technology manufacturing companies in India. Awards are presented in the following categories: Exports; Research and Development; Quality; Indigenous Development of Capital Goods; Environment Management; and Business Excellence. In addition, the Electronics Man of the Year may be presented to honor outstanding individual contributions to the overall development of electronics in India. Awarded annually. Sponsored by Dun & Bradstreet.

3479 ■ Engineering Export Promotion Council
Mr. Rantideb Maitra, Exec. Dir.
1st Fl., International Trade Facilitation Centre
1/1, Wood St.
Calcutta 700016, West Bengal, India
Ph: 91 33 22890651
Ph: 91 33 22890652
Fax: 91 33 22890654
E-mail: eepcho@eepcindia.net
URL: http://www.eepcindia.org

3480 ■ Outstanding Export Performance
For outstanding company members.

3481 ■ Fertiliser Association of India
S. Nand, Dir.
10 Shaheed Jit Singh Marg
New Delhi 110 067, Delhi, India
Ph: 91 11 26567144
Fax: 91 11 26960052
E-mail: general@faidelhi.org
URL: http://www.faidelhi.org

3482 ■ Award for Production, Promotion, and Marketing of Biofertilizer
To encourage and recognize quality production, promotion, and marketing of biofertilizer. A plaque and monetary prize of 15,000 rupees are awarded annually. Co-sponsored by National Fertilisers Ltd.

3483 ■ IMPHOS-FAI Award on the Role of Phosphorus on Yield and Quality of Crops
To encourage and recognize outstanding fundamental or applied research work done on phosphorus. A gold medal and monetary prize of 25,000 rupees are awarded annually. Co-sponsored by the World Phosphate Institute of Casablanca, Morocco.

3484 ■ IPI-FAI Award for Outstanding Doctoral Research in the Field of Balanced and Integrated Fertilizer Use with Emphasis on Potassium
To honor and encourage high quality fundamental or applied research amongst doctoral students in India in the field of balanced and integrated fertilizer usage. A gold medal, citation, and monetary prize of 25,000 rupees are awarded biennially in odd-numbered years. Co-sponsored by the International Potash Institute (IPI).

Awards are arranged in alphabetical order below their administering organizations

3485 ■ IPNI-FAI Award for Best Research on Management and Balanced Use of Inputs in Achieving Maximum Yield
To encourage and recognize outstanding fundamental or applied research work done on management and balanced use of inputs. A gold medal, citation, and monetary prize of 25,000 rupees are awarded biennially. Co-sponsored by the International Plant Nutrition Institute (IPNI).

3486 ■ Gem and Jewelry Export Promotion Council
Shri Rajiv Jain, Chm.
391-A, Diamond Plz.
5th Fl., Dr. Dadasaheb Bhadkamkar Marg
Mumbai 400 004, Maharashtra, India
Ph: 91 22 43541800
Fax: 91 22 23808752
E-mail: ho@gjepcindia.com
URL: http://www.gjepc.org

3487 ■ Costume and Fashion Jewelry Award
To recognize exceptional jewelry. Awarded annually.

3488 ■ Cut and Polished Colored Gemstones Award
To recognize exceptional jewelry. Awarded annually.

3489 ■ Cut and Polished Diamonds Award
To recognize exceptional jewelry. Awarded annually.

3490 ■ Cut and Polished Synthetic Stones Award
To recognize exceptional jewelry. Awarded annually.

3491 ■ Pearls Award
Award of recognition.

3492 ■ Plain Gold Jewelry Award
To recognize exceptional jewelry. Awarded annually.

3493 ■ Plain Precious Metal Jewelry Award
To recognize exceptional jewelry. Awarded annually.

3494 ■ Sales to Foreign Tourists Award
To recognize outstanding sales of jewelry. Awarded annually.

3495 ■ Silver Jewelry Award
To recognize exceptional jewelry. Awarded annually.

3496 ■ Studded Gold Jewelry Award
To recognize exceptional jewelry. Awarded annually.

3497 ■ Studded Precious Metal Jewelry Award
To recognize exceptional jewelry. Awarded annually.

3498 ■ India Office of the Prime Minister
South Block
Raisina Hill
New Delhi 110 011, Delhi, India
Ph: 91 11 2301 2312
Fax: 91 11 2301 9545
URL: http://pmindia.nic.in

3499 ■ Padma Vibhushan
For recognition of exceptional and distinguished service in any field, including service rendered by Government servants. Any person without distinction of race, occupation, position or sex is eligible for the award which may be awarded posthumously. The names of the persons, upon whom the decoration is conferred, is published in the Gazette of India and a register of all recipients is maintained under the direction of the President. A decoration of toned bronze with embossing in white gold is awarded annually by the President.

3500 ■ Param Vir Chakra
This, the highest decoration for valor, is given for the most conspicuous bravery of some daring or pre-eminent act of valor or self-sacrifice in the presence of the enemy, whether on land, at sea or in the air. Members of the military are eligible.

3501 ■ Param Vishisht Seva Medal
To recognize personnel of all three Services for distinguished service of the most exceptional order.

3502 ■ Shaurya Chakra
For recognition of an act of gallantry. Members of the military are eligible.

3503 ■ Vir Chakra
This, the third in the order of valor awards, is given for acts of gallantry in the presence of the enemy, whether on land, at sea or in the air. Members of the military are eligible.

3504 ■ Vishisht Seva Medal
To recognize personnel of all three Services for recognition of distinguished service.

3505 ■ Indian Adult Education Association
K.C. Choudhary, Pres.
17-B Indraprastha Estate
New Delhi 110 002, Delhi, India
Ph: 91 11 23379282
Ph: 91 11 23379306
Fax: 91 11 23378206
E-mail: iaeaindia@yahoo.com
URL: http://www.iaea-india.org

3506 ■ Nehru Literacy Award
For recognition of an outstanding contribution to the promotion of literacy and adult education in India. Individuals or institutions are eligible. A monetary award of 21,000 rupees, a plaque, a citation, and a shawl are awarded annually. Established in 1968.

3507 ■ Tagore Literacy Award
To recognize individuals or institutions for outstanding contribution toward the promotion and development of literacy among women. A plaque, shawl, citation, and monetary prize of 21,000 rupees are awarded annually. Established in 1987.

3508 ■ Indian Association for the Cultivation of Science
Prof. Debashis Mukherjee, Chm.
2A and 2B Raja S C Mullick Rd.
Calcutta 700 032, West Bengal, India
Ph: 91 33 24734971
Ph: 91 33 24735374
Fax: 91 33 24732805
E-mail: root@iacs.res.in
URL: http://www.iacs.res.in

3509 ■ Shanti Swarup Bhatnagar Award
For outstanding scientists in different branches of science.

3510 ■ Indian Association of Cardiovascular Thoracic Anaesthesiologists
Dr. Sandeep Chauhan, Pres.
All India Institute of Medical Sciences
CN Center, Rm. 8, 7th Fl.
Ansari Nagar
New Delhi 110029, Delhi, India
Ph: 91 11 9971698138
E-mail: mahesh_iacta@rediffmail.com
URL: http://www.iacta.in

3511 ■ Late Brig PN Bhatt Memorial Oration
To honor a cardiothoracic anaesthesiologist in India. A gold medal and invitation to deliver a lecture are awarded annually.

3512 ■ Dr. Janak H. Mehta Award
To honor the best paper presented by a junior member (aged under 35 years) at the Annual Conference. A monetary prize of 5,000 rupees is awarded annually.

3513 ■ Indian Chemical Society
Sir P.C. Ray, Pres.
92 Acharya Prafulla Chandra Rd.
Calcutta 700 009, West Bengal, India
Ph: 91 33 23503478
Ph: 91 33 23609497
Fax: 91 33 23503478
E-mail: indi3478@dataone.in
URL: http://indianchemsoc.org/index.htm

3514 ■ Professor B.N. Ghoah Memorial Award
Awarded annually.

3515 ■ Professor Priyadaranjan Ray Memorial Award
Awarded annually.

3516 ■ Dr. Ghanshyam Srivastava Memorial Award
Awarded annually.

3517 ■ Indian Council for Cultural Relations
Dr. Karan Singh, Pres.
Azad Bhavan
Indraprastha Estate
New Delhi 110002, Delhi, India
Ph: 91 11 23379309
Ph: 91 11 23379314
Fax: 91 11 23378639
E-mail: president@iccrindia.net
URL: http://www.iccrindia.net

3518 ■ Jawaharlal Nehru Award for International Understanding
To recognize a person who has contributed to the promotion of international understanding, goodwill, and friendship among peoples of the world. Individuals may be nominated regardless of nationality, race, creed, or sex. Work achieved within the five years preceding nomination is considered. A monetary prize of about rupees 15 lakhs and a citation are awarded annually. Established in 1965 by the Government of India as a tribute to the memory of Jawaharlal Nehru, independent India's first Prime Minister and his life long dedication to the cause of world peace and international understanding. Sponsored by the Government of India.

3519 ■ Indian Council of Agricultural Research
Dr. S. Ayyappan, Dir. Gen.
Krishi Bhavan, Dr. Rajendra Prasad Rd.
New Delhi 110 114, Delhi, India
Ph: 91 11 23386711
Ph: 91 11 23382629
Fax: 91 11 23384773
E-mail: dg.icar@nic.in
URL: http://www.icar.org.in

3520 ■ Fakhruddin Ali Ahmed Award for Tribal Areas
To recognize accomplishments in agriculture research in tribal areas. A monetary award of 50,000 rupees is presented biennially. Established in 1977.

3521 ■ Hari Om Ashram Trust Award
To recognize published original research in crop science, horticulture, animal management, and resource management. Four monetary prizes of 40,000 rupees each are awarded biennially. Established in 1972.

3522 ■ Award for Outstanding Multidisciplinary Team Research in Agriculture and Allied Sciences
To recognize outstanding interdisciplinary team research in agriculture and allied sciences to promote the culture of interdisciplinary team ef-

Awards are arranged in alphabetical order below their administering organizations

fort in the solution of inherently interdisciplinary problem. Nine awards of Rupees 1 lakh each are presented to a team of scientists (normally restricted to eight members) every in two years.

3523 ■ Punjab Rao Deshmukh Woman Agricultural Scientist Award
To recognize women scientists working at an Institution under the ICAR system. Two monetary awards of 50,000 rupees are annually. Established in 1995.

3524 ■ Rafi Ahmed Kidwai Award
To recognize research and work in agriculture, animal husbandry, and allied sciences. Nine awards of rupees 3 lakh each are awarded every one or two years. Established in 1956.

3525 ■ Jagjivan Ram Kisan Puruskar
To recognize outstanding contributions and distinguished farming attributes of individual farmers in the area. A monetary prize of rupees 1 lakh is awarded annually.

3526 ■ Choudhary Devi Lal Outstanding All-India Coordinated Research Project Award
To recognize excellence in performing an all-India coordinated research project. A monetary prize of rupees 1 lakh is awarded annually.

3527 ■ Vasantrao Naik Award
To recognize a work published by a scientist that suggests reforming water conservation and dry-land farming. A monetary prize of rupees 1 lakh is awarded annually. Established in 1994.

3528 ■ National Krishi Vigyan Kendra Award
To recognize outstanding institutional performance by Krishi Vigyan Kendras that have run for a minimum period of five years. Three monetary awards are presented annually.

3529 ■ Jawaharlal Nehru Award
To recognize young scientists for excellence in postgraduate agricultural research. A gold medal and monetary prize of 20,000 rupees are awarded annually to 18 recipients.

3530 ■ Sardar Patel Outstanding ICAR Institution Award
To recognize the best performance in agricultural research, extension, and education. Three awards of rupees 5 lakh each is awarded annually to two ICAR institutes and one state agricultural university.

3531 ■ Dr. Rajendra Prasad Puruskar
To provide recognition to the Indian writer/author for the best book in the Hindi language on the topic of agriculture and allied sciences. Eight awards of 50,000 rupees each are presented biennially.

3532 ■ N. G. Ranga Farmer Award For Diversified Agriculture
To recognize contributions in diversified agriculture activities. A monetary prize of rupees 1 lakh is awarded annually. Established in 2001.

3533 ■ Swamy Sahajanand Saraswati Extension Scientist/Worker Award
To recognize outstanding extension scientists or workers for their innovative research in developing extension education programs, adopting extension methodologies, and creating impact on the farming community, especially to the downtrodden. Four awards of 25,000 rupees, along with a citation and a plaque, are presented biennially. Established in 1995.

3534 ■ Lal Bahadur Shastri Young Scientist Award
To recognize outstanding research efforts in selected areas of agriculture and allied sciences. A monetary prize of 25,000 rupees is awarded biennially.

3535 ■ Chaudhary Charan Singh Award for Excellence in Journalism in Agricultural Research and Development
To recognize an individual for a significant contribution in writing, analyzing, or reporting for the promotion of Indian agriculture. A monetary prize of Rupees 1 lakh is awarded annually. Established in 2000.

3536 ■ Bharat Ratna Dr. C Subramaniam Outstanding Teacher Award
To recognize excellent teachers in the field of agriculture. Eight awards of 50,000 rupees each are awarded biennially. Established in 1994.

3537 ■ Indian Council of Medical Research
Dr. Vishwa Mohan Katoch, Dir. Gen.
V. Ramalingaswami Bhawan
Ansari Nagar
New Delhi 110029, Delhi, India
Ph: 91 11 26588895
Ph: 91 11 26588980
Fax: 91 11 26588713
E-mail: icmrhqds@sansad.nic.in
URL: http://www.icmr.nic.in

3538 ■ Professor B. K. Aikat Oration Award
To recognize an eminent scientist for outstanding work carried out in the field of tropical diseases. The criteria for award of the prize are the significance and value of the addition to existing knowledge contributed by a worker in the field of tropical diseases in which he has been actively engaged over a number of years and has shown sustained activity in research. A certificate and monetary prize of 20,000 rupees is awarded biennially in even-numbered years. Established in 1984.

3539 ■ Dr. B. R. Ambedkar Centenary Award for Excellence in Biomedical Research
To recognize excellence in any field of biomedical research, as evidenced by scientific publications in internationally recognized journals, and contribution to advancement of knowledge and/or improvements in medical practices and health programs. Eligible categories of nominees include: members of the ICNR governing body; vice-chancellors of universities; principles, deans, or directors of recognized medical colleges; directors and deans of university-level institutions; secretaries of science and health departments; directors of major R and D organizations; chairman of the Atomic Energy Commission; directors of ICMR labs; and members of the ICMR Scientific Advisory Board. A certificate and monetary prize of 100,000 rupees is awarded biennially in odd-numbered years. Established in 1991-1992 as part of the Dr. Ambedkar Birth Centenary Celebrations.

3540 ■ BGRC Silver Jubilee Oration Award
To recognize an eminent scientist for outstanding work carried out in the field of haematology and immunohaematology. The criteria for award of the prize are the significance and value of the addition to existing knowledge contributed by a worker in this specialty in which he has been actively engaged over a number of years and has shown sustained activity in research. A certificate and monetary prize of 20,000 rupees is awarded biennially in even-numbered years. Established in 1982 by the Institute of Immunohaematology, formerly the Blood Group Reference Center (BGRC).

3541 ■ Basanti Devi Amir Chand Prize
For recognition of work of outstanding merit in any subject in the field of biomedical science, including clinical research. Senior research workers of more than 10 years are eligible. The criteria for award of the prize are the significance and value of the addition to existing knowledge

contributed by a worker in a particular field in which he has been actively engaged over a number of years and has shown sustained activity in research. A certificate and monetary prize of 50,000 rupees is awarded annually. Established in 1953.

3542 ■ Shakuntala Amir Chand Prizes
For recognition of the best published research on any subject in the field of biomedical sciences, including clinical research, by an individual under 40 years of age. Clinical research covers research into the mechanism and causation of diseases and its prevention and cure, and includes work on patients in hospitals, field studies in epidemiology and social medicine, and observations in general practice. Both medical and non-medical graduates are eligible. Prizes awarded to Indian nationals for work done in any institution in India. Work started in India but completed abroad will not be acceptable. Papers published both in Indian and foreign journals in the previous two years are considered for the award. Four monetary prizes of 10,000 rupees each are awarded annually. Established in 1953.

3543 ■ Dr. Dharamvir Datta Memorial Oration Award
To recognize a scientist (medical or non-medical) below 40 years of age for work carried out in the last five years in India in the field of liver diseases. The criteria include significance and value of addition to existing knowledge contributed by a worker in this specialty, with special reference to application of findings to clinical hepatology. A certificate and monetary prize of 10,000 rupees is awarded biennially in even-numbered years.

3544 ■ Dr. H. B. Dingley Memorial Award
To recognize individuals for outstanding contribution to research in the field of pediatrics by Indian scientists below the age of 40 years. The work to be assessed would be research work carried out in India and published in scientific journals during the three years preceding the year for which the award is to be given. A certificate and monetary prize of 10,000 rupees is awarded annually. Established in 1988.

3545 ■ Smt. Swaran Kanta Dingley Oration Award
To recognize an eminent scientist for outstanding contribution in the field of reproductive biology. The work should highlight the underlying mechanisms and/or prevention of the various diseases related to reproductive science. A certificate of honor and monetary prize of 20,000 rupees is awarded biennially in odd-numbered years. Established in 1984.

3546 ■ Chaturvedi Ghanshyam Das Jaigopal Memorial Award
To recognize an eminent scientist for outstanding work carried out in the field of immunology. The criteria for award of the prize are the significance and value of the addition to existing knowledge contributed by a worker on a subject in which he has been actively engaged over a number of years and has shown sustained activity in research. A certificate, gold medal, and monetary prize of 20,000 rupees are awarded biennially in odd-numbered years. Established in 1985.

3547 ■ Dr. M. O. T. Iyengar Memorial Award
To recognize an eminent scientist for an outstanding contribution in the fields of malaria, filariasis, plague or medical entomology. The criteria for award of the prize are the significance and value of the addition to existing knowledge contributed by a worker in any of the fields of malaria, filariasis, plague or medical entomology in which he has been actively engaged over a number of years and has shown sustained activ-

Awards are arranged in alphabetical order below their administering organizations

ity in research. A certificate and monetary prize of 20,000 rupees are awarded biennially in odd-numbered years. Established in 1983.

3548 ■ Dr. C. G. S. Iyer Oration Award
To recognize a scientist under the age of 40 for an outstanding contribution in the field of leprosy. The criterion for award of the prize is the significance and value of the addition to existing knowledge contributed by a worker in this specialty in which he/she has been actively engaged over a number of years and has shown sustained activity in research. A certificate and monetary prize of 10,000 rupees are awarded biennially in even-numbered years.

3549 ■ Chaturvedi Kalawati Jaghmohan Das Memorial Award
For recognition of research in the field of cardio-vascular diseases. Eminent scientists, preferably medical persons, are eligible. The criteria include the significance and value of addition to existing knowledge contributed by a worker in cardiovascular diseases in which he or she has been actively engaged over a number of years and has shown sustained activity in research. A certificate, gold medal, and monetary prize of 20,000 rupees are awarded biennially in odd-numbered years. Established in 1975.

3550 ■ JALMA Trust Fund Oration Award
For recognition of outstanding work carried out in the field of leprosy. The criterion for award of the prize is the significance and value of addition to existing knowledge contributed by a worker on any aspect of leprosy in which he or she has been actively engaged over a number of years and has shown sustained activity in research. A monetary prize of 20,000 rupees, a gold medal, and a certificate are awarded annually. Established with funds donated by the Japan Leprosy Mission for Asia (JALMA).

3551 ■ Lala Ram Chand Kandhari Award
To recognize an eminent scientist for new outstanding research in the fields of dermatology and sexually transmitted diseases. The criteria for the award are the significance and value of the addition to existing knowledge contributed by the worker on a subject in which he has been actively engaged over a number of years and has shown sustained activity in research. A certificate and monetary prize of 20,000 rupees are awarded biennially in even-numbered years.

3552 ■ Kshanika Oration Award
To recognize an eminent Indian woman scientist for outstanding work carried out in any branch of biomedical science, contributing to the alleviation of human suffering. The criteria for award of this prize are the significance and value of the addition to existing knowledge contributed by her in any field of biomedical sciences in which she has been actively engaged over a number of years and has shown sustained activity in research. A monetary prize of 20,000 rupees and a certificate are awarded annually. Established in 1977.

3553 ■ Amrut Mody Unichem Prize
Awarded to a scientist for the research carried out in the field of gastroenterology, cardiology, neurology, maternal and child health, or chest diseases. Based on contributions made by a worker to the existing knowledge in a subject area in which he/she has been actively engaged. A certificate and monetary prize of 20,000 rupees is awarded annually. Established in 1985 by Unichem Laboratories.

3554 ■ Prof. Surindar Mohan Marwah Award
To recognize an Indian scientist for significant contribution to the field of geriatrics, through sustained research in India on the problems of the aged as evidenced by research papers in science publications. The subject matter could be biomedical or psychosocial research on problems of the aged, both basic and applied. A certificate and monetary prize of 20,000 rupees are awarded biennially in even-numbered years. Established in 1993.

3555 ■ Novartis Oration Award for Research in the Field of Cancer
For recognition of an outstanding contribution toward the control, prevention, and cure of cancer that is recognized nationally and internationally. A certificate, gold medal, and monetary prize of 20,000 rupees are awarded biennially in even-numbered years. Established in 1970. Formerly: (2006) Sandoz Oration Award for Research in Cancer.

3556 ■ Dr. V. N. Patwardhan Prize
For recognition of outstanding work carried out in India on fundamental, clinical or field studies in nutritional sciences. Eminent scientists, not older than 40 years of age, are eligible. The criteria for the award of the prize are the contribution of a worker to nutritional sciences in which he or she has been actively engaged over a number of years and has shown sustained activity in research. A certificate and monetary prize of 10,000 rupees are awarded biennially in even-numbered years. Established in 1973.

3557 ■ Drs. Kunti and Om Prakash Oration Award
To recognize a scientist for excellence achieved in the field of Biomedical Sciences. The research conducted should have a major impact on healthcare and the research should have been conducted in India. A monetary award of 100,000 rupees, a certificate, and gold medal are awarded biennially in even-numbered years. Established in 2005.

3558 ■ Dr. D. N. Prasad Memorial Oration Award
To recognize an Indian scientist for significant contribution to research in the field of pharmacology, carried out in India, as evidenced by research papers and innovations. The criteria for the award will be the significance and value of addition to existing knowledge in research in pharmacology. A gold medal, certificate, and monetary prize of 20,000 rupees are awarded biennially in odd-numbered years. Established in 1991.

3559 ■ Prize for Biomedical Research Conducted in Underdeveloped Areas
To recognize an eminent scientist for outstanding contributions in any field of biomedical sciences. The criteria for award of the prize are the significance and value of biomedical research carried out by a worker based in underdeveloped parts of the country, or for work carried out in under-developed parts of the country over a period of five years preceding the year for which the award is to be given. A certificate and monetary prize of 20,000 rupees are awarded annually. Established in 1983.

3560 ■ Prize for Biomedical Research for Scientists Belonging to Underprivileged Communities
To recognize an eminent scientist for outstanding contributions in any field of the biomedical sciences. The criterion for award of the prize is the significance and value of addition to existing knowledge contributed by a worker in the particular field in which he has been actively engaged over a number of years and has shown sustained activity in research. Scientists belonging to under privileged communities are eligible. A certificate and monetary prize of 20,000 rupees is awarded annually. Established in 1983.

3561 ■ Dr. P. N. Raju Oration Award
For recognition of outstanding work of national importance in the field of medicine or public health. Eminent scientists, preferably medical specialists, are eligible. A certificate and monetary prize of 20,000 rupees are awarded biennially in even-numbered years. Established in 1965.

3562 ■ Dr. T. Ramachandra Rao Award
To recognize a young scientist under the age of 40 for an outstanding contribution in the field of medical entomology. The criterion for award of the prize is the significance and value of the addition to existing knowledge contributed by a worker in this specialty in which he/she has been actively engaged over a number of years and has shown sustained activity in research. A certificate and monetary prize of 10,000 rupees are awarded biennially in even-numbered years. Established in 1985.

3563 ■ Tilak Venkoba Rao Award
To recognize a young yet eminent scientist for research in the field of psychological medicine and reproductive physiology. Awards are given in alternate years in the following categories: psychological medicine and reproductive physiology. Candidates must be younger than 40 years. A certificate and monetary prize of 10,000 rupees are awarded annually. Established in 1982.

3564 ■ Dr. Y. S. Narayana Rao Oration Award
For recognition of outstanding work in the field of microbiology. The criteria for the award of the prize are the significance and value of the addition to existing knowledge contributed by a worker in the field of microbiology in which he has been actively engaged over a number of years and has shown sustained activity in research. A certificate and monetary prize of 20,000 rupees are awarded biennially in even-numbered years. Established in 1972.

3565 ■ Dr. Vidya Sagar Award
To recognize an eminent scientist for outstanding contributions made in the field of mental health. The criteria for award of the prize are the significance and value of the addition to existing knowledge contributed by a worker in the field of mental health in which he has been actively engaged over a number of years and has shown sustained activity in research. A certificate and monetary prize of 20,000 rupees are awarded biennially in even-numbered years. Established in 1985.

3566 ■ Smt. Kamal Satbir Award
To recognize individuals under the age of 40 for outstanding contribution to research on non-tuberculosis chest diseases, especially respiratory allergy and chronic obstructive lung diseases, pertaining to mechanism and causation of diseases, their prevention and/or management. The work to be assessed would be the research carried out in India and published in scientific journals during the three years preceding the year for which the award is to be given. A certificate and monetary prize of 10,000 rupees are awarded annually. Established in 1987.

3567 ■ M. N. Sen Oration Award
For recognition of outstanding work in medical practice (clinical, laboratory or therapeutic). Eminent scientists are eligible. The criterion for award of the prize is the significance and value of addition to existing knowledge contributed by a worker to the practice of medicine in which he or she has been actively engaged over a number of years and has shown sustained activity in research. A certificate and monetary prize of 20,000 rupees are awarded biennially in even-numbered years. Established in 1977.

3568 ■ Dr. M. K. Seshadri Prize
To recognize an eminent scientist or institution

Awards are arranged in alphabetical order below their administering organizations

whose original work has led to useful inventions in, or otherwise significantly contributed to, the practice of community medicine. A gold medal, certificate, and monetary prize of 20,000 rupees are awarded biennially in even-numbered years. Established in 1977.

3569 ■ Maj. Gen. Saheb Singh Sokhey Award
To recognize a scientist below the age of 40 years for his or her outstanding contribution to the field of communicable diseases. The facets of work to be considered could be basic or applied research that adds to the knowledge on the mechanism and causation of communicable diseases, their prevention and/or their management. The work to be assessed would be the research carried out in India and published in scientific journals, during the three years preceding the year for which the award is to be given. A certificate of honor and monetary prize of 10,000 rupees are awarded annually. Established in 1988.

3570 ■ Dr. J. B. Srivastav Oration Award
To recognize an eminent scientist for outstanding work in virology. The criterion for award of the prize is the significance and value of addition to existing knowledge contributed by a worker in virology in which he or she has been actively engaged over a number of years and has shown sustained activity in research. A certificate and monetary prize of 20,000 rupees are awarded biennially in odd-numbered years. Established in 1978.

3571 ■ Prof. B. C. Srivastava Foundation Award
To recognize a scientist under 40 years of age for work in the field of community medicine in medical colleges/recognized institutions. The criterion for the award is the significance of research contributions to the practice of community medicine by a worker. A certificate and monetary prize of 10,000 rupees are awarded biennially in even-numbered years. Established in 1987.

3572 ■ Dr. Prem Nath Wahi Award
To recognize an eminent scientist for outstanding contribution in the field of basic and/or clinical cytology, and/or preventive oncology. The criterion for the award is the significance and value of addition to existing knowledge contributed by a worker on the subject in which he or she has been actively engaged over a number of years and has shown sustained activity in research. A certificate and monetary prize of 100,000 rupees are awarded biennially in odd-numbered years. Established in 1990.

3573 ■ Indian Dairy Association
Dr. N.R. Bhasin, Chm.
Ida House
Sector IV, R.K. Puram
New Delhi 110 022, Delhi, India
Ph: 91 11 26170781
Ph: 91 11 26165355
Fax: 91 11 26174719
E-mail: ida@nde.vsnl.net.in
URL: http://www.indairyasso.org

3574 ■ Best Paper Award
To encourage the dissemination of scientific information. Papers published in the IDA-periodicals, such as *Indian Dairyman* and *Indian Journal of Dairy Science*, are considered. A monetary award and a certificate are presented annually during the Dairy Industry Conference. Established in 1991.

3575 ■ Dr. Kurien Award
To recognize the achievement of dedicated individuals and institutions and to provide impetus for further progress in every field associated with Indian dairying. A monetary prize of 100,000 rupees and a citation are awarded biennially at the time of the Dairy Industry Conference. The first Dr. Kurien Award was given in 1991.

3576 ■ Patrons and Fellows
For recognition of outstanding achievements in the field of dairy science and the dairy industry. Nomination is required. A plaque and citation are awarded from time to time to Patrons and Fellows at the general body meeting or any other important function. Established in 1978.

3577 ■ Indian Drug Manufacturers' Association
N.R. Munjal, Pres.
102-B Poonam Chambers
Dr. A.B. Rd.
Worli
Mumbai 400 018, Maharashtra, India
Ph: 91 22 24974308
Ph: 91 22 24944624
Fax: 91 22 24950723
E-mail: idma1@idmaindia.com
URL: http://www.idma-assn.org

3578 ■ G.P. Nair Awards
For all First Rank B.Pharm. students in Indian universities. Awarded annually. Established in 1970.

3579 ■ Indian Footwear Components Manufacturers Association
Mr. S.K. Verma, Deputy Dir.
FDDI Complex, A-10/A, Sector-24
Noida 201301, Uttar Pradesh, India
Ph: 91 120 4225763
Fax: 91 120 2411572
E-mail: ifcoma@airtelmail.in
URL: http://ifcoma.org/index.asp

3580 ■ Excellence Awards
To honor individuals for outstanding performance or contribution to the industry. Awarded annually to one or more recipients.

3581 ■ Indian Institute of Architects
Vinay M. Parelkar, Pres.
Prospect Chambers Annex
Dr. D.N. Rd., Ft.
Mumbai 400 001, Maharashtra, India
Ph: 91 22 22046972
Ph: 91 22 22884805
Fax: 91 22 22832516
E-mail: iia@vsnl.com
URL: http://www.iia-india.org

3582 ■ Madhav Achwal Gold Medal
For a teacher, professor, lecturer or administrator who has made a lasting and dedicated contribution of architectural education and community service. Awarded annually.

3583 ■ Dharmasthala Manjunatheswara Award
For works that are carried out in rural or semi-urban areas For a building or project of any size which reflects outstanding qualities in architecture. Awarded annually.

3584 ■ Baburao Mhatre Gold Medal
To a distinguished architect or man of science who has produced works which promote or facilitate the knowledge of architecture or the various branches of science connected therewith. Awarded annually.

3585 ■ Snowcem Award
For creative excellence and/or unique contribution in the field of architecture. Awarded annually.

3586 ■ Surfa-Coats-Piloo Mody Awards
To student for the best project work during his or her 4th year. Awarded annually.

3587 ■ Indian Institute of Metals
Dipankar Banerjee, Pres.
Metal House, Plot 13/4
Block AQ, Sector V
Salt Lake City
Calcutta 700091, West Bengal, India
Ph: 91 33 23675004
Ph: 91 33 23677089
Fax: 91 33 23675335
E-mail: iiomcal@dataone.in
URL: http://www.iim-india.net

3588 ■ Vidya Bharathi Prize
To recognize the student who secures the highest marks on the final B. Tech. B.E. in Metallurgy examination. Awarded annually. Established in 1978.

3589 ■ Binani Gold Medal
To recognize the contributions made in the non-ferrous group through their reference work and published in the Transactions of the Institute. A gold medal is awarded annually. Established in 1959 by the House of Binanis.

3590 ■ G. D. Birla Memorial Gold Medal
To recognize a distinguished research worker for continuing and outstanding research work in the field of materials sciences and technology. A gold medal is awarded annually. Established in memory of the industrialist, G. D. Birla.

3591 ■ Dr. A. K. Bose Medal
To recognize the best Mechanical Engineering Thesis. Awarded annually. Established in 1972 in honor of the late Dr. A. K. Bose.

3592 ■ Bralco Gold Medal
To recognize a member for contributions made to the development of the non-ferrous metal industry. A medal is awarded triennially. Established in 1972 by Bralco Metal Industries, Bombay.

3593 ■ Essar Gold Medal
To recognize outstanding contributions to metallurgical industries in general and in the field of secondary steel making, particularly electrometallurgy. Awarded annually. Established in 1996 by Essar Steel Ltd.

3594 ■ Sir Padamji Ginwala Gold Medal
To recognize a candidate securing the highest marks in the Associate Membership Examination (Part-I) of the Institute. A gold medal is awarded annually. Established in 1963 in memory of Sir Padamji Ginwala, Ex-President of IIM.

3595 ■ Hindustan Zinc Gold Medal
To recognize distinguished personalities for significant contributions to non-ferrous metallurgical industries and to advance the art and science relating to non-ferrous metallurgical industries. A gold medal is awarded annually. Established in 1991 to commemorate the silver jubilee of Hindustan Zinc Ltd.

3596 ■ Honorary Member
To recognize distinguished service to the metallurgical profession and to the IIM.

3597 ■ O. P. Jindal Gold Medal
To recognize outstanding contributions to the development of ferrous metals and alloys. A gold medal is awarded annually. Established in 1996 to commemorate the golden jubilee of IIM by the Jindal Group of Industries.

3598 ■ Lifetime Achievement Award
To recognize an outstanding metallurgical engineer, material scientist, researcher, or academic for lifetime achievements in the field of metallurgy. Indian citizens over 70 years of age who carried out most of their work in India are eligible. A scroll, a citation, and a monetary prize of Rs. 2,00,000 is awarded.

3599 ■ MECON Award
To recognize outstanding contributions by an individual under the age of 50 years in the development of process engineering and equipment. A scroll of honor and monetary prize

Awards are arranged in alphabetical order below their administering organizations

of 10,000 rupees is awarded annually at the National Metallurgists Day Celebration. Established in 1984 by Metallurgical and Engineering Consultants (India) Limited (MECON).

3600 ■ Metallurgist of the Year Award
To recognize outstanding contributions to the science and technology of metals. Generally two awards are given for ferrous metallurgy, and one each for non-ferrous, metal sciences, and environment (energy conservation and waste management). Candidates must be 55 years of age or younger. Five awards of 75,000 rupees are awarded annually.

3601 ■ National Metallurgist of the Year
To recognize outstanding original contributions to one or more of the following fields in metallurgy in the last 20 years: Leadership; HRD and Entrepreneurial Development; Cost Control and Reduction; Industrial Productivity; Resources and Capacity Utilization; Material and Process Review; Product Quality Improvement; Energy and Waste Management; Environment; and Research and Development. Indian citizens 70 years old or younger who carried out most of their work in India are eligible. A scroll of honor, a citation, and a monetary prize of Rs. 1.50,000 are awarded annually.

3602 ■ Platinum Medal
To recognize an eminent metallurgist for outstanding lifetime contributions to the metallurgical profession and to create an incentive by the recognition of such a contribution. A platinum medal is awarded as merited.

3603 ■ Quality Awards
To give recognition to the Ferrous and Non-Ferrous divisions of the IIM for the quality, highest product development, profit making, and environmental performances during the previous year. Awards are offered in the categories of: Integrated Steel Plants; Secondary Steel and Alloy Steel Plants; and DR Plants, Pig Iron Plants, and Major Rolling Units. Awarded annually.

3604 ■ Rolling Trophy
To recognize chapters for overall performance and for enrolling the maximum number of new members. Awards are offered for large, medium, and small chapters. Established in 1982.

3605 ■ Sail Gold Medal
To recognize the best paper published in the Transactions of the Institute during the preceding year. A medal is awarded annually. Established in 1933 by Steel Authority of India, Ltd. Formerly: Kamani Gold Medal.

3606 ■ N.B. Sen Medal and Prize
For the student who earns the highest marks in aggregate of Part II AMIIM Examination in two consecutive attempts. A bronze medal and textbooks worth RS. 700 are awarded annually when merited. Honors Nalin Behari Sen.

3607 ■ SMS-DEMAG Excellence Award
To recognize an outstanding executive from the industrial sector for contributions to the iron, steel, or non-ferrous industry in India. Eligible to Indian citizens. A medal is awarded annually when merited. Established in 2002 by SMS Demag Pvt. Ltd.

3608 ■ Steel Eighties Award
For recognition of a significant R and D contributions to steel making and metallurgy. A monetary prize of 21,000 rupees is awarded annually.

3609 ■ Tata Gold Medal
To recognize a distinguished personality actively connected with the metallurgical industry. A medal is awarded annually. Established in 1980 in honor of Mr. J. R. D. Tata.

3610 ■ Young Metallurgist of the Year Award
To recognize contributions to the science and

technology of metals by a young metallurgist. Generally one award each is given for ferrous, non-ferrous, and metal sciences. Candidates must be no older than 35 years. Three awards of 31,000 rupees each are awarded annually.

3611 ■ Indian Merchants' Chamber
Shri Arvind Pradhan, Dir. Gen.
IMC Bldg., IMC Marg
Churchgate
Mumbai 400 020, Maharashtra, India
Ph: 91 22 2046633
Fax: 91 22 2048508
E-mail: imc@imcnet.org
URL: http://www.imcnet.org

3612 ■ Community Welfare Award
For outstanding contribution by an individual, firm, association, social welfare organization, relief organization, or voluntary organization. Awarded annually.

3613 ■ Contribution by Business Community Award
For outstanding contribution by a businessman or executive. Awarded annually.

3614 ■ Environment, Agriculture, and Rural Development Award
For outstanding contribution in the field of control of air and water pollution, rural development, and agriculture. Awarded annually.

3615 ■ Industry and Technology Award
For any original research, discovery, invention scientific and technical. Awarded annually.

3616 ■ Platinum Jubilee Award
For outstanding contribution towards alleviation of human suffering or any other socially desirable cause. Awarded annually.

3617 ■ Promotion of Savings, Consumer Protection, and Export Performance Award
For outstanding contribution towards promotion savings, consumer protection, and enhancing export performance. Awarded annually.

3618 ■ Indian National Science Academy
Dr. Krishan Lal, Pres.
Bahadur Shah Zafar Marg
New Delhi 110 002, Delhi, India
Ph: 91 11 23221931
Ph: 91 11 23221950
Fax: 91 11 23235648
E-mail: insa@giasdl01.vsnl.net.in
URL: http://www.insa.ac.in/html/home.asp

3619 ■ Dr. Nitya Anand Endowment Lecture
To recognize a scientist who has done outstanding work in any area of biomedical research including new drug development. The award is based on work done in India during the previous 10 years. Nominations for consideration for the award are invited from the Fellowship. The lecture is delivered in any institution involved in work in this area but not in the award winner's own institution. The lecturer is paid 25,000 rupees including funds for journeys performed to deliver the lecture. Awarded biennially in odd-numbered years. Established in 1986 to celebrate the 60th birthday of Dr. Nitya Anand, an eminent chemist and a Fellow of the Academy.

3620 ■ Aryabhata Medal
For recognition of achievement in any branch of science. A copper medal (gold plated) is awarded biennially in even-numbered years. Established in 1977.

3621 ■ Prof. Rango Krishna Asundi Memorial Lecture
To recognize persons who have made outstanding contributions in the field of spectroscopy. The lecturer is paid an honorarium of 25,000 rupees

and travel expenses for journeys performed to deliver the lecture. Awarded every four years. Established in 1983 to commemorate Professor Asundi, a Fellow of the Academy, distinguished for research in spectroscopy.

3622 ■ Vainu Bappu Memorial Award
To recognize an astronomer/astrophysicist of international recognition. A monetary award of 25,000 rupees and a bronze medal are awarded triennially. Established in 1985 from an endowment by Mrs. Sunanna Bappu, mother of the late Dr. M.K.V. Bappu, an eminent astronomer and Fellow of the Academy.

3623 ■ Professor Sadhan Basu Memorial Lecture
To recognize a scientist who has made outstanding contributions in the field of chemical science. An honorarium of 25,000 rupees and travel expenses for journeys performed to deliver the lecture are awarded. Awarded triennially. Established in 1993.

3624 ■ Homi Jehangir Bhabha Medal
For recognition of work in the field of experimental physics. A copper medal (silver plated) is awarded triennially. Established in 1978.

3625 ■ Professor K.P. Bhargava Memorial Medal
To recognize eminent scientist who has done outstanding work in the area of Basic Medical Sciences. Applicants must be under the age of 50. A monetary prize of 25,000 rupees, a bronze medal, and a citation are awarded triennially. Established in 1992 to commemorate the memory of the late Professor K.P Bhargava, an eminent Pharmacologist and distinguished Fellow of the Academy.

3626 ■ Shanti Swarup Bhatnagar Medal
For recognition of an outstanding contribution to any branch of science. A copper medal (gold plated) is awarded biennially in odd-numbered years. Established in 1959.

3627 ■ Professor Krishna Sahai Bilgrami Memorial Medal
To recognize a scientist who has made outstanding contributions in the field of plant sciences including agriculture and forestry. A monetary prize of 25,000 rupees and a bronze medal are awarded triennially. Established in 1998.

3628 ■ Jagadis Chandra Bose Medal
For recognition of contributions to biochemistry, biophysics, molecular biology, and related fields. A copper medal (silver plated) is awarded triennially. Established in 1977.

3629 ■ Satyendranath Bose Medal
For recognition of achievement in the field of theoretical physics. A copper medal (silver plated) is awarded triennially. Established in 1977.

3630 ■ Anil Kumar Bose Memorial Award
For recognition of the best research paper published in a reputable journal by a recipient of the INSA Medal for Young Scientists on work done in India within five years from the date of receipt of the INSA Young Scientist Medal. Candidates must be below the age of 40 years as of December 31 preceding the year of the award. A bronze medal, a monetary prize of 1,000 rupees, and a certificate are awarded in two categories: physical sciences and biological sciences. Established in 1987.

3631 ■ Dr. Guru Prajad Chatterjee Memorial Lecture
For recognition of outstanding contributions in engineering sciences. The lecture is to be given once every five years. The lecturer is paid an honorarium of 25,000 and travel expenses for journeys made to deliver the lecture. Established in 1979 to commemorate Dr. Guru Prasad Chatterjee, an eminent metallurgist and Fellow of the Academy.

Awards are arranged in alphabetical order below their administering organizations

3632 ■ Bashambar Nath Chopra Lecture

For recognition of a distinctive contribution in any branch of biological sciences. The lecturer is paid an honorarium of 25,000 rupees besides expenses for the journey to deliver the award lecture. Awarded triennially. Established in 1968.

3633 ■ Shri Dhanwantari Prize

To recognize an eminent scientist who has done outstanding work in the field of medical sciences in its widest sense including research in drugs and methodology of Ayurveda. This includes research in medical as well as chemical, physical and biological sciences aimed at the amelioration of human suffering. Its scope shall also include any outstanding discovery in drugs, mode of treatment, or inventions considered as a landmark in medical sciences in its widest sense. A monetary prize of 25,000 rupees and a bronze medal are awarded. Established in 1969 by an endowment of 18,500 rupees by Shri A.K. Asundi in memory of his youngest daughter, Shrimati Akkadevi.

3634 ■ Indira Gandhi Prize for Popularization of Science

To encourage and recognize popularization of science in any Indian language including English. The nominee must have had a distinguished career as a writer, editor, journalist, lecturer, radio or television program director, science photographer or as an illustrator, which has enabled him/her to interpret science (including medicine), research and technology to the public. He/she should have knowledge of the role of science, technology and research in the enrichment of cultural heritage and in the solution of problems of humanity. The prize is open to any Indian national residing in the country. A monetary prize of 10,000 rupees and a bronze medal are awarded biennially in even-numbered years. Established in 1986.

3635 ■ Golden Jubilee Commemoration Medal for Biological Sciences

For recognition in the field of biological sciences. A copper medal (silver plated) is awarded triennially. Established in 1986. Formerly: Golden Jubilee Commemoration Medal for Animal Sciences.

3636 ■ Golden Jubilee Commemoration Medal for Chemical Sciences

For recognition in the field of chemical sciences. A copper medal (silver plated) is awarded triennially. Established in 1986.

3637 ■ Sunder Lal Hora Medal

To recognize a scientist who has distinguished himself in plant and animal sciences. A copper medal (silver plated) is awarded triennially. Established in 1960.

3638 ■ Chandrakala Hora Memorial Medal

To recognize an eminent scientist who has done outstanding work in the development of fisheries, aquatic biology, and related areas in India during the five years preceding the year of award. A bronze medal and monetary prize of 25,000 rupees are awarded every five years. Established in 1945 from an endowment by Dr. and Mrs. S.L. Hora in memory of their daughter.

3639 ■ Daulat Singh Kothari Memorial Lecture Award

To recognize a scientist who has made an outstanding contribution to any branch of science. A lectureship and an honorarium of 25,000 rupees are awarded triennially. Established in 1993 from the General Funds of the Academy in the memory of the late Professor Daulat Singh Kothari, an esteemed Fellow and a past President of the Academy. The first award was made in 1996.

3640 ■ Kariamanikkam Srinivasa Krishnan Memorial Lecture

To recognize a scientist who has made an outstanding contribution to any branch of science. Awarded triennially. Established in 1965 in memory of Professor Kariamanikkam Srinivasa Krishnan, a Fellow of the Academy.

3641 ■ Prof. L. S. S. Kumar Memorial Award

To recognize a recipient of INSA Medal for Young Scientists in the disciplines of Plant Sciences, Animal Sciences and Agriculture by rotation. In case of more than one person being recommended by the Sectional Committee for the award of the INSA Medal for Young Scientists, the person who is first in order of merit in the list is given the award. A monetary award of 1,000 rupees is awarded annually. Established in 1986.

3642 ■ Prasanta Chandra Mahalanobis Medal

For recognition of an outstanding contribution to mathematics. A copper medal (silver plated) is awarded triennially. Established in 1978.

3643 ■ Prof. Panchanan Maheshwari Memorial Lecture

To recognize persons who have made outstanding contributions in any area of plant sciences. The lecturer is paid an honorarium of 25,000 rupees as well as travel expenses to deliver the lecture. Awarded every four years. Established in 1984 by the colleagues and friends of the late Professor Panchanan Maheshwari, a distinguished botanist and a Fellow of the Academy.

3644 ■ Medal for Young Scientists

For recognition of outstanding work in the field of science and technology. Any citizen of India below the age of 35 is eligible for nomination. Bronze medals and cash prizes of 25,000 rupees are awarded annually to a maximum of 30 recipients. In addition, in exceptional cases, the recipient may be considered for start-up research support with seed money. Established in 1974.

3645 ■ Sisir Kumar Mitra Memorial Lecture

For recognition of a distinguished contribution to any branch of the sciences. Established in 1963 in memory of Professor Sisir Kumar Mitra, a foundation fellow and past president of the Academy.

3646 ■ Professor K. Naha Memorial Medal

To recognize an eminent scientist who has done outstanding work in the area of Earth Sciences. A monetary prize of 25,000 rupees and a bronze medal are awarded triennially. Established in 1996 from an endowment by the family members of Professor Naha to commemorate the memory of late Professor K. Naha, an eminent geologist of our country.

3647 ■ Professor Vishnu Vasudeva Narlikar Memorial Lecture

To recognize a scientist who has made outstanding contributions in the field of Applied Mathematics, including Gravitational Theory. The lecturer is paid an honorarium of 25,000 rupees plus travel expenses for journeys performed to deliver the lecture. Awarded triennially. Established in 1992.

3648 ■ Professor Shambu Nath De Memorial Lecture

To recognize a scientist who has made outstanding contributions in biochemistry and biophysics. The lecturer is paid an honorarium of 25,000 rupees plus travel expenses for journeys performed to deliver the lecture. Awarded triennially. Established in 1992.

3649 ■ Professor Vishwa Nath Memorial Lecture

To recognize outstanding contributions to biochemistry and biophysics. An honorarium of 25,000 rupees and travel expenses for journeys performed to deliver the lecture are awarded. Awarded triennially. Established in 1992.

3650 ■ Jawaharlal Nehru Birth Centenary Lectures

To recognize Indian scientists in the fields of biological sciences and physical sciences. Every three years, an invitation to lecture and an honorarium of 25,000 rupees are awarded to two recipients, one in each category. Established in 1989.

3651 ■ Jawaharlal Nehru Birth Centenary Medal

For recognition of international cooperation in science and technology. Scientists of all nations are eligible. A bronze medal, citation and travel expenses are awarded annually. Established in 1989.

3652 ■ Professor Brahm Prakash Memorial Medal

To recognize an eminent scientist who has done outstanding work in any area of Engineering and Technology. A monetary prize of 25,000 rupees and a bronze medal are awarded triennially. Established in 1987 from an endowment by Mrs. R. Brahm Prakash and friends of late Dr. Brahm Prakash, an eminent Fellow of the Academy.

3653 ■ Prof. M. R. N. Prasad Memorial Lecture

To recognize an individual who has made an outstanding contribution in the field of animal physiology in its widest sense. The lecture is to be given once in three years. An honorarium of 25,000 rupees and travel expenses are awarded triennially. Established in 1989.

3654 ■ Prize for Materials Science

For recognition of outstanding contributions in materials science. Any citizen of India is eligible for consideration for the prize for outstanding work done in India. A monetary prize of 25,000 rupees is awarded biennially in odd-numbered years. Established in 1986.

3655 ■ Prof. G. N. Ramachandran 60th Birthday Commemoration Medal

To recognize an individual who has made outstanding contributions in the field of molecular biology, biophysics and crystallography. The lecture is to be given once in three years. The lecturer is awarded a bronze medal, and a monetary prize of 25,000 rupees. Established in 1989.

3656 ■ Chandrasekhara Venkata Raman Medal

For recognition of contributions to the promotion of science. Scholars who have done outstanding work in any branch of science are eligible. A copper medal (silver plated) is awarded biennially in odd-numbered years. Established in 1979.

3657 ■ Kalpathi Ramakrishna Ramanathan Medal

For recognition in the field of atmospheric sciences and meteorology. A cooper medal (silver plated) is awarded triennially. Established in 1987.

3658 ■ Srinivasa Ramanujan Medal

For recognition of outstanding work in the field of mathematics or a related subject. A copper medal (silver plated) is awarded triennially. Established in 1962.

3659 ■ Prof. K. Rangadhama Rao Memorial Lecture

To recognize a person who has done exemplary work in the field of spectroscopy. A lectureship and an honorarium of 25,000 rupees are awarded every four years, alternating with the Professor Rk Asundi Memorial Lecture. Established in 1979 in memory of Dr. K. Rangadhama Rao, an eminent physicist and a distinguished Fellow of the academy.

3660 ■ Dr. Biren Roy Memorial Lecture

To recognize a scientist who has made outstand-

Awards are arranged in alphabetical order below their administering organizations

ing contributions to physics. An honorarium of 25,000 rupees and travel expenses for journeys performed to deliver the lecture are awarded. Awarded triennially. Established in 1993.

3661 ■ Meghnad Saha Medal
For recognition of a distinguished contribution to science. A copper medal (gold plated) is awarded biennially in even-numbered years. Established in 1958.

3662 ■ Professor Shyam Bahadur Saksena Memorial Medal
To recognize an eminent scientist who had done outstanding work in any branch of Botany. A monetary prize of 25,000 rupees and a bronze medal are awarded triennially. Established in 1989 from an endowment of 50,000 rupees by Mrs. Sarla Saksena to commemorate the memory of late Professor Shyam Bahadur Saksena, a distinguished botanist and Fellow of the Academy.

3663 ■ Professor T. R. Seshadri Seventieth Birthday Commemoration Medal
For recognition of meritorious work in any branch of chemistry and chemical technology. Eminent chemists of Indian nationality are eligible. A monetary prize of 25,000 rupees and a bronze medal are awarded triennially. Established in 1971 by an endowment of 10,000 rupees by the students of Professor T. R. Seshadri, an eminent organic chemist and a Fellow of the Academy.

3664 ■ Dr. Jagdish Shankar Memorial Lecture
Recognizes a scientist under the age of 50 who has made outstanding contributions in the field of Chemical Sciences. A monetary prize of 25,000 rupees is awarded triennially. Established in 1992 in memory of Dr. Jagdish Shankar, a distinguished scientist in nuclear and radiation chemistry.

3665 ■ Silver Jubilee Commemoration Medal
For recognition of an outstanding contribution to the agricultural sciences and applied sciences. A copper medal (silver plated) is awarded triennially. Established in 1970.

3666 ■ Dr. Yellapragada SubbaRow Memorial Lecture
To recognize a scientist who has made outstanding contributions in the field of biomedical science. An honorarium of 25,000 rupees and travel expenses for journeys performed to deliver the lecture are awarded triennially. Established in 1995.

3667 ■ Professor S. Swaminathan 60th Birthday Commemoration Lecture
To recognize scientist who has made outstanding contributions in the field of Chemical Sciences. The lecturer is paid an honorarium of 25,000 rupees plus travel expenses for journeys performed to deliver the lecture. Awarded biennially in even-numbered years. Established in 1990.

3668 ■ Professor Har Swarup Memorial Lecture
For recognition of outstanding contributions in the field of zoology. The lecture is to be given once in five years. The lecturer is paid an honorarium of 25,000 as well as travel expenses for journeys performed to deliver the lecture. Established in 1981 by Dr. (Mrs.) Savitri Swarup to commemorate Professor Har Swarup, a Fellow of the Academy distinguished for his researches on endocrinology, physiology and developmental biology.

3669 ■ Prof. Bal Dattatraya Tilak Lecture
To recognize persons who have made outstanding contributions to rural economy and life through innovative and effective application of

science and technology. The lecturer is paid an honorarium 25,000 rupees and travel expenses for journeys performed to deliver the lecture. Awarded annually. Established in 1982 to commemorate Professor B.D. Tilak, a Fellow of the Academy, distinguished for research in the field of dyestuffs chemistry and organic chemical technology.

3670 ■ Dr. T.S. Tirumurti Memorial Lecture
To recognize outstanding contributions in the field of medical sciences. The lecturer is paid an honorarium 25,000 rupees as well as travel expenses for journeys performed to deliver the lecture. Awarded biennially in odd-numbered years. Established in 1985 by Mrs. Janaki Ramachandran, daughter of the late Dr. T.S. Tirumurti, who made notable contributions to pathology and medicine and was a Foundation Fellow of the Academy.

3671 ■ Vishwakarma Medal
To recognize eminent scientists who have done outstanding work or whose discovery or invention has led to the start of a new industry in India or to a significant improvement of an existing process resulting in a cheaper or better product. A monetary prize of 25,000 rupees and a bronze medal are awarded triennially. Established in 1976 from an endowment by Dr. P.B. Sarkar, FNA.

3672 ■ Darashaw Nosherwanji Wadia Medal
To recognize an individual who has done outstanding work in the field of earth sciences (geology, geophysics, geography). A copper medal (silver plated) is awarded triennially. Established in 1977.

3673 ■ Syed Husain Zaheer Medal
To recognize an individual who has made outstanding contributions in the field of engineering and technology. A copper medal (silver plated) is awarded triennially. Established in 1980.

3674 ■ Indian Pharmaceutical Association
Mr. S.D. Joag, Hon. Gen. Sec.
Kalina
Santa Cruz
Mumbai 400 098, Maharashtra, India
Ph: 91 22 26671072
Fax: 91 22 26670744
E-mail: ipacentre@ipapharma.org
URL: http://www.ipapharma.org

3675 ■ Best Paper Awards
To recognize the best papers published by Indian scientists. Awarded annually in five categories.

3676 ■ Eminent Pharmacist Award
To recognize a pharmacist of Indian origin for outstanding contributions toward the advancement of the pharmaceutical profession. A monetary prize of 15,000 rupees is awarded annually.

3677 ■ Prof. M.L. Khorana Memorial Award
To honor the student scoring the highest marks in the final year B. Pharm. examinations among all colleges and universities in India. A medal and cash prize of 1,500 rupees are awarded annually. Established in 1999.

3678 ■ Lifetime Achievement Award
To recognize senior pharmacists for longtime contributions to the field of pharmacy. A monetary prize of 5,000 rupees is awarded annually to one or more recipients. Established in 2003.

3679 ■ Prof. M.L. Schroff Award
To honor the student scoring the highest marks in the final year B. Pharm. examinations among

all colleges and universities in India. A medal and cash prize of 1,000 rupees are awarded annually. Established in 1999.

3680 ■ Indian Physics Association
Dr. S. Kailas, Pres.
PRIP Shed, Rm. No. 4
Bhabha Atomic Research Centre
Trombay
Mumbai 400 085, Maharashtra, India
Ph: 91 22 25505138
E-mail: ipa.india@gmail.com
URL: http://www.ipa1970.org.in

3681 ■ Award for Best Thesis Presentation in Solid State Physics
To recognize the author of an outstanding thesis on the topic of solid state physics. Candidates must be Indian students who have either submitted their thesis or have been awarded their PhD within the previous calendar year. A citation and monetary prize of 1,000 rupees are awarded annually.

3682 ■ Prof. C.V.K. Baba Award for Best Thesis Presentation in Nuclear Physics
To recognize the author of an outstanding thesis on the topic of nuclear physics. Candidates must be Indian students who have either submitted their thesis or have been awarded their PhD within the previous calendar year. A citation and monetary prize of 3,000 rupees are awarded annually.

3683 ■ C.L. Bhat Memorial Award for Indian Astronomy Olympiad
To honor the best student at the Indian Astronomy Olympiad Camp. A certificate and monetary prize of 1,000 rupees are awarded in the junior and senior levels each year. Established in 2004.

3684 ■ R. D. Birla Award
To recognize an Indian citizen for achievement in the field of physics. A citation, gold medal, and monetary prize of 50,000 rupees are awarded annually. Established in 1980.

3685 ■ Buti Foundation Award
To recognize a scientist for outstanding contributions in the area of theoretical physics, astrophysics, or biophysics. A citation, gold medal, and cash prize of 25,000 rupees are awarded annually. Established in 2006.

3686 ■ Murli M. Chugani Memorial Award for Excellence in Applied Physics
To recognize a scientist who has made outstanding contributions in the area of applied physics. Candidates must be Indian citizens working in India. A citation, gold medal, and monetary prize of 100,000 rupees are awarded annually. Established in 1998.

3687 ■ Physics Olympiad Awards
To recognize outstanding performance at the International Physics Olympiad Camp. Awards are presented in two categories: 1) Best solution to a challenging problem, and 2) Best performance in the experimental program. In each category, a certificate and 3,000 rupees in cash and books is awarded. Awarded annually.

3688 ■ N. S. Satyamurthy Award for Young Scientists
To recognize a young individual for outstanding contributions to the growth of physics in India by way of research, applications, or other activities. Candidates must be below the age of 35 years. A citation and monetary prize of 20,000 rupees are awarded annually. Established in 1992.

3689 ■ S. N. Seshadri Memorial Instrumentation Award
To recognize a young scientist for innovation and/or excellence in indigenous instrumentation development in the physical sciences. Candi-

Awards are arranged in alphabetical order below their administering organizations

dates must be below the age of 40 years. A citation and cash prize of 20,000 rupees are awarded annually. Established in 1986.

3690 ■ Indian Phytopathological Society
Dr. S.C. Chatterjee, Sec.
Indian Agricultural Research Inst.
Div. of Plant Pathology
New Delhi 110 012, Delhi, India
Ph: 91 11 25848418
Ph: 91 11 25843474
Fax: 91 11 25843113
E-mail: ipsdis@indiatimes.com
URL: http://www.ipsdis.org

3691 ■ Best Research Paper
For the best paper by a member published in Indian Phytopathology. A certificate is awarded annually.

3692 ■ Prof. S.N. Dasgupta Memorial Lecture
For an exceptional plant pathologist. Recipient delivers a lecture to the Society. Established in 1994.

3693 ■ Fellow of Indian Phytopathological Society
For eminent plant pathologists. Nominees must have been continuous members of the Society for a minimum of 10 years.

3694 ■ Jeersannidhi Award Lecture
For an exceptional plant pathologist. Recipient delivers a lecture to the Society. Established in 1994.

3695 ■ K.C. Mehta and Manoranjan Mitra Award
To recognize a review article in Indian Phytopathology.

3696 ■ K.P.V. Menon Best Poster Paper Award
To encourage participation at the Annual Meeting and National Symposium. A medal and a certificate are awarded annually for the best paper presented during the poster session.

3697 ■ A.P. Misra Lifetime Achievement Award
To recognize an eminent plant pathologist. Established in 2000.

3698 ■ Mundkur Memorial Lecture Award
For an eminent plant pathologist. Recipient delivers a lecture to the Society. Established in 1963.

3699 ■ Prof. M.J. Narasimhan Academic Merit Award Contest
To encourage young scientists in plant pathology. A cash award and a certificate are awarded annually.

3700 ■ Prof. M.K. Patel Memorial Young Scientist Award
Recognizes a young scientist for professional contributions to plant pathology. Open to Society members under 40 years of age. Awarded annually.

3701 ■ Prof. M.S. Pavgi Award Lecture
For an eminent plant pathologist. Recipient delivers a lecture to the Society. Established in 1990.

3702 ■ Travel Sponsorships for Young Scientists
To aid graduate students in attending the Annual Meeting. Eligible to members who are PhD students under 30 years of age. Travel expenses, waiving of the registration fee, and certificates are awarded to four students annually.

3703 ■ Indian Plumbing Association
Mr. Kamal Harpalani, Exec. Sec.
E-117, L.G.F.
Greater Kailash - 3
Masjid Moth

New Delhi 110 048, Delhi, India
Ph: 91 11 29220063
Fax: 91 11 29220063
E-mail: hq@indianplumbing.org
URL: http://www.indianplumbing.org

3704 ■ Flow Guard Plumbing Personality Award
To the most productive member of the association.

3705 ■ IPA Jaquar Felicitations
To 5 eminent plumbing professionals.

3706 ■ Indian Science Congress Association
Prof. Geetha Bali, Gen. Pres.
14 Dr. Biresh Guha St.
Calcutta 700017, West Bengal, India
Ph: 91 33 22474530
Ph: 91 33 22815323
Fax: 91 33 22402551
E-mail: iscacal@vsnl.net
URL: http://www.sciencecongress.nic.in

3707 ■ Prof. Hira Lal Chakravarty Awards
To recognize talented young scientists doing significant research in the field of botany within the country. Candidates must be under 40 years of age on December 31 of the preceding year for the Award and must have a Ph.D. degree in any branch of botany, either pure or applied. The awards are given for original, independent, published work carried out in India within three years prior to the award. A monetary prize of 4,000 rupees and a certificate are awarded annually during the Inaugural Function of the Congress. Established in 1984.

3708 ■ G. P. Chatterjee Memorial Award
To recognize a distinguished scientist for his/her outstanding original contribution related to some aspect of Science and Man. The awardee may deliver a lecture at the annual session of the Indian Science Congress Association on the subject of his/her specialization. A monetary prize of 10,000 rupees is awarded annually. Established in 1981.

3709 ■ Dr. B. C. Deb Memorial Award for Popularisation of Science
To recognize an Indian national who has sustained interest for popularizing science. The candidate must have a degree in science/technology, be under 45 years old, and should have ten years experience in publishing articles/monographs/books for popularizing science. A monetary prize of 5,000 rupees and a plaque is awarded annually. The recipient also delivers a lecture on the topic of his/her contributions during the Science Congress. Established in 1994-95.

3710 ■ Dr. B. C. Deb Memorial Award for Soil/Physical Chemistry
To recognize outstanding contributions in any branch of Soil/Physical Chemistry. Candidates must have published research papers either independently or as a research guide and the research work must have been carried out in India. Candidate also must have a PhD in any branch of Soil/Physical Chemistry and be under 45 years old. A monetary prize of 5,000 rupees and a plaque are awarded annually. The recipient also delivers a lecture on the topic of his/her contributions during the Science Congress. Established in 1994-95.

3711 ■ Raj Kristo Dutt Memorial Award
The awardee may deliver a lecture on the topic of his/her specialization during the Science Congress. A monetary prize of 10,000 rupees and a plaque is awarded annually. Established in 1991.

3712 ■ Excellence in Science and Technology
To recognize a distinguished and respected

scientist for outstanding contributions to science and technology. A monetary prize of Rs 2.00 lakh is awarded annually. Award is presented by the Prime Minister of India at the Inaugural Function of the Annual Session.

3713 ■ Dr. Gouri Ganguly Memorial Award for Young Scientists in Animal Science
To recognize an outstanding young scientist. Individuals must be 35 years old or younger. A monetary prize of 5,000 rupees and a plaque are awarded annually. Established in 2002.

3714 ■ B. C. Guha Memorial Lecture
The topic of the lecture should have some relevance to the science of nutrition and is to be delivered during the annual session of the Indian Science Congress Association. A monetary prize of 3,000 rupees and a plaque is awarded annually. Established in 1965.

3715 ■ Infosys Foundation - ISCA Travel Award
For deserving students to attend the Annual Session. Travel expenses and plaques are awarded to five students annually.

3716 ■ Prof. S. S. Katiyar Commemoration Lecture
To recognize original contributions in the areas related to biological or chemical sciences. A monetary prize of 20,000 rupees and a plaque is awarded annually. Established in 2003.

3717 ■ Prof. R. C. Mehrotra Commemorative Lecture
To recognize an individual for outstanding contributions in the chemical sciences field. A monetary prize of 10,000 rupees is awarded biennially. Established in 1998.

3718 ■ Asutosh Mookerjee Memorial Award
To honor a distinguished scientist of the country. Nominations must be received by July 31. A gold medal is awarded annually. Established in 1988 in memory of Sir Asutosh Mookerjee, the first General President of Association and a great educationist of the country.

3719 ■ Prof. Sushil Kumar Mukherjee Commemorative Lecture
To recognize a distinguished scientist in any branch of agricultural science. Awarded annually. Established in 1999.

3720 ■ Jawaharlal Nehru Birth Centenary Award
Two awards are given annually by the Association. Nominations must be submitted by July 31. Plaques are awarded annually. Each recipient will be asked to speak, one on Science and Nation Building in the Indian Context and the other on Outstanding Contributions in Science. Established in 1989 to commemorate the birth centenary of the late Indian Prime Minister, Pandit Jawaharlal Nehru.

3721 ■ C. V. Raman Birth Centenary Award
To honor a distinguished scientist of the country. Nominations must be received by July 31. A gold medal is awarded annually. Each awardee may be requested to deliver a lecture at the headquarters of a Regional Chapter of ISCA or ISCA Headquarters. Established in 1989.

3722 ■ Srinivasa Ramanujan Birth Centenary Award
To honor a distinguished scientist of the country. Nominations must be submitted by July 31. A gold medal is awarded annually. Each awardee may be requested to deliver a lecture at the headquarters of a Regional Chapter of ISCA or ISCA headquarters. The award was established in 1989 to commemorate the birth of the Indian mathematician Srinivasa Rmamnujan.

Awards are arranged in alphabetical order below their administering organizations

3723 ■ Prof R. C. Saha Memorial Lecture
To recognize a scientist with accomplishments in chemistry. Individual should not be over 45 years old. A plaque and monetary prize of 5,000 rupees is awarded annually. Established in 1995.

3724 ■ Birbal Sahni Birth Centenary Award
To recognize outstanding contributions to the Association. A gold medal is awarded biennially. Established in 1993.

3725 ■ Prof. Anima Sen Memorial Lecture
To recognize an outstanding scientist in any branch of psychology and educational science. A monetary prize of 5,000 rupees is awarded biennially. Established in 2000.

3726 ■ Professor R. C. Shah Memorial Lecture
To recognize an individual who publishes outstanding research papers in any field of organic, pharmaceutical and biological chemistry either independently or under supervisors in India. Candidates should be under 45 years old. A monetary prize of 5,000 rupees and a plaque are awarded annually. The recipient will deliver a lecture on the topic of his/her contributions in the section of Chemistry during the Science Congress. Nominations must be submitted by July 31. Established in 1989.

3727 ■ Professor Umakant Sinha Memorial Award
To recognize an individual's original independent published work in a discipline of Plant Sciences related to Biochemistry, Biophysics Molecular biology or Molecular Genetics applied to plant sciences. The award is given annually and candidates must be under 40 years old. The recipient has to deliver a lecture on his/her specialization during the Science Congress. A monetary prize of 4,000 rupees and a certificate are awarded annually. Established in 1991.

3728 ■ Pran Vohra Award
To recognize an individual for contributions in Agricultural Science. Candidates must be under 35 years of age on December 31 of the preceding year of the award and have a PhD degree in agricultural sciences from any university or institution in India. A monetary prize of 10,000 rupees and a certificate are awarded annually. The awardee is required to deliver a lecture on the topic of his/her specialization. Established in 1989.

3729 ■ Young Scientists' Awards
To encourage young scientists. Candidates must be under 30 years of age and members of the Association. The papers submitted for consideration must not be submitted for any other awards and the work must have been carried out in India. A monetary prize of 25,000 rupees and a Certificate of Merit are awarded annually to 14 recipients, one for each Section of the Association. Established in 1981.

3730 ■ Indian Silk Export Promotion Council
Subhash Mittal, Chm.
62 Mittal Chambers, Nariman Point
Mumbai 400 021, Maharashtra, India
Ph: 91 22 22025866
Ph: 91 22 22027662
Fax: 91 22 22874606
E-mail: isepc@bom2.vsnl.net.in
URL: http://www.silkepc.org

3731 ■ Outstanding Export Performance Awards
To honor members who have shown outstanding performance in exporting. Awards are presented in five categories: fabrics, garments, made-ups, carpets, and sarees. In addition, an overall winner is recognized. Awarded annually.

3732 ■ Indian Society for Medical Statistics
Babu L. Verma, Pres.
Department of Social and Preventive Medicine

MLB Medical College and Hospital Institute of Medical Sciences
Jhansi 284128, Uttar Pradesh, India
E-mail: contact@isms-india.org
URL: http://www.isms-india.org

3733 ■ Smt. Suraj Kali Jain Award
To recognize the best paper on any area related to medical statistics, published by a young scientist in a scientific journal during three preceding years from the year of the annual conference. Candidates must be younger than 40 years of age. A gold medal and scroll of honor are awarded annually.

3734 ■ Prof. B.G. Prasad Award
To recognize the best published paper in a scientific journal during the last two calendar years, on any topic related to biostatistics applied to epidemiology. A gold medal and scroll of honor are awarded annually. Established in 1985.

3735 ■ Indian Society of Advertisers
Bharat Patel, Chm.
Army and Navy Bldg., 3rd Fl.
148, Mahatma Gandhi Rd.
Mumbai 400001, Maharashtra, India
Ph: 91 22 22856045
Ph: 91 22 22843583
Fax: 91 22 22042116
E-mail: isa.ed@vsnl.net
URL: http://www.isanet.org.in

3736 ■ The ISA Gold Medal
For significant contributions to Indian advertising.

3737 ■ Indian Society of Agricultural Economics
Dr. C.L. Dadhich, Honorary Sec.-Treas.
Krishi Vikas Sadan, 1st Fl.
Veer Savarkar Marg
Dadar W
Mumbai 400 028, Maharashtra, India
Ph: 91 22 28493723
Fax: 91 22 28493724
E-mail: isae@bom7.vsnl.net.in
URL: http://www.isaeindia.org

3738 ■ Dr. D.K. Desai Prize Award
Recognizes the best articles published in the *Indian Journal of Agricultural Economics*. A monetary prize of 5,000 rupees is awarded annually.

3739 ■ Dr. S.R. Sen Prize
To honor a book on agricultural economics and rural development published by an Indian author below the age of 45 years on the date of publication of the book. Awarded biennially.

3740 ■ Indian Society of Nephrology
Dr. Vivekanand Jha, Sec.
Postgraduate Institute of Medical Education and Research
Dept. of Nephrology
Chandigarh 160 012, Punjab, India
Ph: 91 172 2756733
Fax: 91 172 2744401
E-mail: vjha@pginephro.org
URL: http://www.isn-india.com

3741 ■ Janseen-Cilag Award for Excellence in Nephrology
To honor members younger than age 40 for published research from India in the field of chronic renal failure. Established in 1999.

3742 ■ Indian Textile Accessories and Machinery Manufacturers' Association
Shri J.H. Shah, Pres.
Bhogilal Hargovindas Bldg., 2nd Fl.
18/20 Kaikhushru Dubash Marg
Mumbai 400 001, Maharashtra, India
Ph: 91 22 22844350
Ph: 91 22 22844401
Fax: 91 22 22874060

E-mail: itamma@mtnl.net.in
URL: http://www.itamma.org

3743 ■ Export Promotion and Research and Development
For excellence in the member's field of activities.

3744 ■ India's National Academy of Letters
Rabindra Bhavan
35 Ferozeshah Rd.
New Delhi 110 001, Delhi, India
Ph: 91 11 338 6626
Fax: 91 11 338 2428
E-mail: secy@sahitya-akademi.org
URL: http://www.sahitya-akademi.org

3745 ■ Bhasha Samman Awards
To recognize writers/scholars for significant contributions to the languages not formally recognized by the Academy. A plaque and monetary prize of 50,000 rupees are awarded annually.

3746 ■ Sahitya Akademi Awards
To recognize outstanding writers for books of high literary merit written in each of the 24 languages of India that are recognized by the Academy. Indian nationals only are eligible. A monetary prize of 50,000 rupees and an inscribed copper plaque are awarded annually by the President of the Sahitya Akademi.

3747 ■ Sahitya Akademi Fellowship
This, the highest literary honor in India, is conferred on persons of undisputed eminence in literature. The highest standard of Fellowship is ensured by limiting the number of living Fellows to 21 at any one time. An inscribed copper plaque is presented to the Fellows, along with a shawl by the President of the Akademi.

3748 ■ Sahitya Akademi Translation Prize
To encourage translation activity in India. This award is given for the best translated creative and critical works in the 24 languages recognized by the Academy. Both the translator and the original author should be Indian nationals. A monetary prize of 20,000 rupees and an inscribed copper plaque are presented annually by the President of the Sahitya Akademi. Established in 1989.

3749 ■ Indo-French Chamber of Commerce and Industry
Mr. Jacques Michel, Pres.
French Bank Bldg.
62 Homji St.
Mumbai 400 001, Maharashtra, India
Ph: 91 22 22618180
Ph: 91 22 22064660
Fax: 91 22 22621969
E-mail: contact@ifcci.org.in
URL: http://www.ifcci.org.in

3750 ■ Europe Impresa Award
For members who have given exceptional service to the institute.

3751 ■ Institution of Electronics and Telecommunication Engineers
Lt. Gen. Ashok Agarwal, Pres.
2 Institutional Area
Lodhi Rd.
New Delhi 110 003, Delhi, India
Ph: 91 11 24631810
Ph: 91 11 43538800
Fax: 91 11 24649429
URL: http://www.iete.org

3752 ■ Prof. S.V.C. Aiya Memorial Award
To honor a person for providing guidance in electronics and telecommunication research work during the past five years. A citation and monetary prize of 2,000 rupees are awarded annually.

Awards are arranged in alphabetical order below their administering organizations

3753 ■ Bimal Bose Award

To honor a person For original outstanding contributions in the field of power electronics. A monetary prize of 10,000 rupees is awarded annually.

3754 ■ Flt. Lt. Tanmaya Singh Dandass Memorial Award

To honor a person or group of persons For outstanding contributions in the field of avionics, covering education, research, design, development and production. A medal and citation are awarded annually.

3755 ■ Prof. S.N. Mitra Memorial Award

To honor a person for outstanding contributions and leadership role in radio broadcast science and technology during the last ten years. A citation and monetary prize of 2,000 rupees are awarded annually.

3756 ■ Prof. K. Sreenivasan Memorial Award

For outstanding performance in teaching electronics and telecommunication engineering during the past five years. A citation and monetary prize of 2,000 rupees are awarded annually.

3757 ■ Hari Ramji Toshniwal Gold Medal

To honor a person for outstanding innovative ideas having practical application in industry. A medal and citation are awarded annually.

3758 ■ Lal C. Verman Award

To honor a person for outstanding contributions in the areas of standardization, quality control and precision measurements, during the last ten years. A medal and citation are awarded annually.

3759 ■ Ram Lal Wadhwa Gold Medal

To honor a professional for outstanding contributions in the field of electronics and telecommunications engineering during the last ten years. A medal and citation are awarded annually.

3760 ■ International Commission on Irrigation and Drainage (Commission Internationale des Irrigations et du Drainage)

Mr. Mukuteswara Gopalakrishnan, Sec. Gen.
48 Nyaya Marg
Chanakyapuri
New Delhi 110 021, Delhi, India
Ph: 91 11 26115679
Ph: 91 11 26116837
Fax: 91 11 26115962
E-mail: icid@icid.org
URL: http://www.icid.org

3761 ■ Best Paper Award

For an outstanding paper contributed to Irrigation and Drainage, the journal of the ICID. Awarded annually. Established in 2006.

3762 ■ Best Performing National Committee Award

To recognize the best performing National Committee. A shield and citation are awarded triennially. Established in 2002.

3763 ■ Best Performing Workbody Award

To recognize exceptional performance by a workbody in contributing to the mission of the Commission. Awarded triennially. Established in 2003.

3764 ■ WatSave Awards

Recognizes outstanding contributions to water conservation in agriculture. Open to individuals and teams. Awards include the WatSave Technology Award, the WatSave Innovative Water Management Award, and the WatSave Young

Professional Award. Each award consists of a $2,000 cash prize and a certificate. Awarded annually. Established in 1998.

3765 ■ International Commission on Physics Education

Dr. Pratibha Jolly, Chm.
Miranda House
Univ. of Delhi
New Delhi 110007, Delhi, India
Fax: 91 11 27667437
E-mail: pjolly@vsnl.com
URL: http://web.phys.ksu.edu/ICPE

3766 ■ ICPE Medal

Recognizes outstanding contribution to physics education. A medal is awarded annually. Established in 1979.

3767 ■ International Federation of Pigment Cell Societies

Prasad Kumarasinghe, Sec.
c/o Asian Society for Pigment Cell Research
PO Box 1510
Department of Dermatology
Postgraduate Institute of Medical Education and Research
Chandigarh 160012, India
Ph: 91 172 274 2211
E-mail: ifpcs@ifpcs.org
URL: http://www.ifpcs.org

3768 ■ Thomas B. Fitzpatrick Medal

To recognize the best article published in the journal Pigment Cell & Melanoma Research during the previous three years. A medal is awarded triennially at the International Pigment Cell Conference.

3769 ■ Myron Gordon Award

To recognize one or more scientists for distinguished and outstanding contributions to the pigment cell field. A plaque is awarded triennially at the International Pigment Cell Conference. Established in 1961.

3770 ■ Seiji Memorial Lectureship

To recognize an eminent scientist for distinguished and long-standing contributions to the pigment cell field. A plaque is awarded triennially at the International Pigment Cell Conference. Established in 1983 in memory of Makoto Sieji.

3771 ■ National Association for the Blind, India

11/12 Khan Abdul Gaffar Khan Rd.
Worli Seaface
Mumbai 400 025, Maharashtra, India
Ph: 91 22 4988134
Fax: 91 22 4932539
E-mail: nabin@bom3.vsnl.net.in
URL: http://www.nabindia.com

3772 ■ Alpaiwala Award

For promoting blind welfare.

3773 ■ Optical Society of India

Dr. K. Bhattacharya, Gen. Sec.
92, Acharya Prafulla Chandra Rd.
Calcutta 700 009, West Bengal, India
Ph: 91 33 23522411
Fax: 91 33 23522411
E-mail: osiindia@rediffmail.com
URL: http://www.osiindia.org

3774 ■ Satgur Prasad-Prag Parmeshwari Devi Memorial Award

To recognize the best presentation of a research paper at the Symposium of the OSI. Candidates must be under 30 years of age.

3775 ■ Optical Society of India Award

To recognize a scientist of Indian origin having made significant contribution in the field of optics and optoelectronics. Candidates must have been

members of the OSI for at least last three consecutive years and must have a membership for at least ten years in total.

3776 ■ Harbans Singh Memorial Award

Recognizes the article published in the Journal of Optics. Scientists under 30 years of age are eligible. Awarded periodically.

3777 ■ Protein Foods and Nutrition Development Association of India

Dr. G.M. Tewari, Chm.
Mahalaxmi Chambers
22 Bhulabhai Desai Rd.
Mumbai 400 026, Maharashtra, India
Ph: 91 22 23538858
Ph: 91 22 23538998
Fax: 91 22 23538998
E-mail: pfndai@pfndai.org
URL: http://www.pfndai.org

3778 ■ Toppers in Food Technology

To first rankers at university.

3779 ■ Society of Biological Chemists, India

Dr. V. Nagaraja, Pres.
Indian Institute of Science
Bangalore 560 012, Karnataka, India
Ph: 91 80 23601412
Fax: 91 80 23601412
E-mail: sbci@satyam.net.in
URL: http://www.iisc.ernet.in/sbci

3780 ■ A.N. Bhaduri Memorial Lecture Award

To honor an individual for outstanding contributions to biological chemistry and allied sciences, preferably related to parasitic infections. Candidates must be younger than 50 years of age, and must hold permanent positions in universities, publicly funded institutes, or national laboratories. A citation and monetary prize of Rs. 10,000 are awarded triennially. Established in 2006.

3781 ■ Prof. I.S. Bhatia Award

To recognize an individual for long-term achievements in original research in plant biochemistry, molecular biology, and allied sciences. A citation and monetary prize of Rs. 10,000 are awarded triennially. Established in 2000.

3782 ■ D.P. Burma Memorial Lecture Award in Biological Sciences

To honor an eminent scientist for outstanding lifetime contributions in the field of biological sciences. A citation and monetary prize of Rs. 20,000 are awarded triennially. Established in 2007.

3783 ■ A. Krishnamurthy Award

For the best paper published in an Indian journal. A citation and monetary prize of 2,000 rupees are awarded annually. Established in 1976.

3784 ■ C.R. Krishnamurti Lecture Award

For the best work done in the field of biochemistry and allied sciences in India. A citation and monetary prize of 10,000 rupees are awarded triennially. Established in 1995.

3785 ■ Prof. P.A. Kurup Endowment Award

To recognize an individual for contributions to biomedical research. Candidates must be younger than 60 years of age. A citation and monetary prize of Rs. 10,000 are awarded triennially. Established in 1991.

3786 ■ P.B. Rama Rao Memorial Award

For the best work done in the field of biochemistry and allied sciences in India. A citation and monetary prize of 10,000 rupees are awarded triennially. Established in 1973.

3787 ■ P.S. Sarma Memorial Award

For the best work done in the field of biochemis-

Awards are arranged in alphabetical order below their administering organizations

try and allied sciences in India. A citation and monetary prize of 10,000 rupees are awarded triennially. Established in 1973.

3788 ■ Prof. M. Shadakshara Swamy Endowment Lecture Award
For eminent teachers in biological chemistry and allied sciences at the postgraduate level in Indian universities, deemed universities and institutions of higher learning for their contributions in teaching and research. A citation and monetary prize of 10,000 rupees are awarded triennially. Established in 1982.

3789 ■ M. Sreenivasaya Memorial Award
For the best work done in the field of biochemistry and allied sciences in India. A citation and monetary prize of 10,000 rupees are awarded triennially. Established in 1972.

3790 ■ Solvent Extractors' Association of India
Dr. B.V. Mehta, Exec. Dir./CEO
142, Jolly Maker Chambers No. 2, 14th Fl.
225 Nariman Point
Mumbai 400 021, Maharashtra, India
Ph: 91 22 22021475
Ph: 91 22 22822979
Fax: 91 22 22021692
E-mail: solvent@mtnl.net.in
URL: http://www.seaofindia.com

3791 ■ SEA Awards
To recognize the most successful processor of oil meal and most successful exporter of oilseed or oilcake.

3792 ■ Sports Goods Export Promotion Council
Mr. Anil Mukim, Chm.
1-E/6 Swami Ram Tirth Nagar
New Delhi 110055, Delhi, India
Ph: 91 11 23525695
Ph: 91 11 23516183
Fax: 91 11 23632147
E-mail: mail@sgepc.in
URL: http://www.sportsgoodsindia.org

3793 ■ Export Awards
To recognize the top Indian sports exporters. Categories include: Highest Export Awards; Outstanding Export Awards; Export Excellence Awards; and Indian Brand Promotion Awards. Awarded annually.

3794 ■ Sugar Technologists' Association of India
V.K. Goel, Pres.
21 Community Centre, East of Kailash
New Delhi 110 065, Delhi, India
Ph: 91 11 6237196
Ph: 91 11 6482351
Fax: 91 11 6216217
E-mail: staidel@nda.vsnl.net.in
URL: http://members.tripod.com/~staicurrentscene

3795 ■ Noel Deerr Gold Medal
To recognize the distinguished work done by members in the fields of agriculture, engineering, and manufacturing. Awarded annually by the Sugarcane Agriculture Section and the Equipment Design and Maintenance Engineering Section.

3796 ■ Sugar Industry Cup
For the distinguished work done by members in the fields of agriculture, engineering and manufacturing.

3797 ■ Sulabh International Social Service Organisation
Dr. Bindeshwar Pathak, Founder
Sulabh Gram
Mahavir Enclave
Palam Dabri Rd.
New Delhi 110 045, Delhi, India

Ph: 91 11 25032617
Ph: 91 11 25031518
Fax: 91 11 25034014
E-mail: sulabhinfo1@gmail.com
URL: http://www.sulabhinternational.org

3798 ■ Global Sanitation Award
To recognize an organization for its critical role in the promotion of hygiene, environmental sanitation, and social justice. A gold medal and monetary prize are awarded annually. Established in 2002.

3799 ■ Synthetic and Rayon Textiles Export Promotion Council
E. L. Paulo, Dir./Sec.
Resham Bhavan
78 Veer Nariman Rd.
Churchgate
Mumbai 400 020, Maharashtra, India
Ph: 91 22 22048797
Ph: 91 22 22048690
Fax: 91 22 22048358
E-mail: srtepc@vsnl.com
URL: http://www.srtepc.org

3800 ■ Export Awards
To recognize exporters of synthetic and rayon textile items for outstanding export performance during the year. Trophies are awarded in 12 categories each year.

3801 ■ Tibetan Youth Congress
Tsewang Rigzin, Pres.
PO Box Mcleod Ganj
Dharamsala 176 219, Himachal Pradesh, India
Ph: 91 1892 221554
Ph: 91 1892 221239
Fax: 91 1892 221849
E-mail: tyc@vsnl.com
URL: http://www.tibetanyouthcongress.org

3802 ■ Culture and Literature Award
Recognizes outstanding contribution to the field of Tibetan literature and culture. Applicants must be Tibetan citizens. Awarded triennially.

3803 ■ Social Service Award
Triennial award of recognition.

3804 ■ Urological Society of India
S.V. Kotwal, Pres.
Christian Medical Colorado and Hospital
Ludhiana 141008, Punjab, India
Ph: 91 161 5026999
Fax: 91 161 5010909
E-mail: kjmammen@gmail.com
URL: http://usi.org.in

3805 ■ Member Travel Fellowship
For an individual who has been a full member for a minimum of three years and who is less that 45 years of age. A certificate and cash prize of 4,000 rupees are awarded annually.

3806 ■ Dr. G.M. Phadke Oration
To recognize the outstanding achievements of a non-member. A monetary prize of 2,000 rupees and an invitation to lecture are awarded annually.

3807 ■ Late G.M. Phadke Travelling Award
For a senior postgraduate student. Two fellowships of 3,000 rupees are awarded annually.

3808 ■ President's Gold Medal
For a member's outstanding contribution to the progress of urology in India. A certificate and medal are awarded annually.

3809 ■ Dr. R. Sitharman Memorial Essay Competition
For the best essay written by a member of the society. A monetary prize of 10,000 rupees and an invitation to lecture are awarded annually.

3810 ■ Teacher Travel Fellowship Award
For a teacher in urology. A cash prize of 4,000 rupees is awarded annually.

3811 ■ World Association for Small and Medium Enterprises
Mr. Sunil D. Sharma ED, Exec. Dir.
Plot No. 4, Institutional Area, Sector 16A
Noida 201301, Uttar Pradesh, India
Ph: 91 120 2515241
Ph: 91 120 4216284
Fax: 91 120 2515243
E-mail: feedback@wasmeinfo.org
URL: http://www.wasmeinfo.org

3812 ■ Legion of Honor Award
For recognition of outstanding achievement in the field of small and medium enterprises. Individuals who have at least 15 years of uninterrupted service to the small and medium enterprises sector in any part of the world either at national, regional, or global level irrespective of age, religion, or citizenship are eligible. A gold medal and a citation are awarded biennially. Established in 1980.

3813 ■ Special Honour Award
To recognize institutions and individuals for their outstanding contribution in promoting small businesses in economics or at regional or international level for a minimum period of 10 years. Awarded when merited.

Indonesia

3814 ■ Australian Embassy in Indonesia
Jalan HR Rasuna Said Kav C 15-16
12940 Jakarta, Indonesia
Ph: 62 21 2550 5555
Fax: 62 21 2550 5467
E-mail: public-affairs-jakt@dfat.gov.au
URL: http://www.indonesia.embassy.gov.au

3815 ■ Australian Alumni Awards
To recognize the contributions to Indonesia made by Indonesians who have studies at Australian schools, universities, and technical colleges. Awards may be presented in the following categories: entrepreneurship, sustainable and economic development, research and innovation, business leadership, culture and arts, creativity and design, and journalism and media. Awarded annually. Established in 2008.

3816 ■ Elizabeth O'Neill Journalism Award
To honor print, radio, television, and Internet journalists who foster a better understanding of Australian-Indonesian relations. Awarded annually to two individuals, one Australian and one Indonesian. Established in 2007.

3817 ■ Gadjah Mada University Center for Population and Policy Studies (Pusat Studi Kependudukan Dan Kebijakan)
Prof. Muhadjir Darwin, Dir.
Bulaksumur G-7
55281 Yogyakarta, Indonesia
Ph: 62 2 7456 3079
Fax: 62 2 7458 2230
E-mail: cpps-gmu@cpps.or.id
URL: http://www.cpps.or.id

3818 ■ Masri Singarimbun Research Awards
To enhance the opportunities of junior researchers in Indonesia and to develop networking among advanced researchers concerned with reproductive health issues.

3819 ■ Indonesia Travel and Tourism Awards Foundation
Ruko Permata 7E
Jl. Curug Raya Kalimalang Jatiwaringin
Jakarta, Indonesia

Awards are arranged in alphabetical order below their administering organizations

Ph: 62 21 709 0887
Fax: 62 21 8690 5677
URL: http://www.indonesiatraveltourismawards.org

3820 ■ Indonesia Travel and Tourism Awards

To recognize, reward, and celebrate excellence across all sectors of the Indonesia travel and tourism industry. Presented in many categories within the classifications of 1) Hotels, 2) Resorts, Suites, and Villas, 3) Destination and Tourism Boards, 4) Tourist Attractions and Travel Agents, 5) On-Ground Transportation, and 6) Special Tourism. In addition, the Indonesia Tourism Personality of the Year and the Indonesia Tourism Lifetime Contribution Award may be presented. Awarded annually.

3821 ■ Society of Indonesian Films
JI. Sutan Syahrir IC, Blok 3-4
10350 Jakarta, Indonesia
Ph: 62 21 319251
Fax: 62 21 31925360
E-mail: info@jiffest.org
URL: http://www.jiffest.org

3822 ■ Jakarta International Film Festival

To foster the local film industry, to showcase the growth and development of contemporary Indonesian cinema, and to strengthen the network between filmmakers and film professionals in southeast Asia. The Indonesian Feature Film Competition honors the Best Indonesian Film and the Best Indonesian Director. In the Script Development Competition, awards are presented for Best Documentary Film Script, Best Short Film Script, and Best Feature Film Script. Held annually. Established in 1999.

Iran

3823 ■ Children's Book Council of Iran
(Shoraye Ketabe Koodak)
PO Box 13145-133
Tehran, Iran
Ph: 98 21 66408074
Ph: 98 21 66492721
Fax: 98 21 66408074
E-mail: info@cbc.ir
URL: http://www.cbc.ir

3824 ■ CBCI Award
(Jayezeye Shoraye Ketabe Koudak)
For recognition of a contribution in the field of children's literature in Iran. Iranian writers, illustrators, and translators are eligible. A plaque or diploma is awarded annually at the Founding Day Celebration. Established in 1971 by A. Yamini Sharif.

3825 ■ Diploma of Appreciation
To recognize members and non-members for exceptional efforts in support of the Council's aims and objectives. Awarded annually.

3826 ■ Special Commendation
To recognize authors for outstanding works of children's fiction, translation, illustration, poetry, and non-fiction. It may also be awarded to a publisher for a significant contribution to children's literature. A diploma is awarded annually.

3827 ■ Iranian Research Organization for Science and Technology
No. 71 Sh. Mousavi St.
Enghelab Ave.
PO Box 15819-3538
Tehran 15819, Iran
Ph: 98 21 8882 8051
Fax: 98 21 8883 8341
E-mail: admin@irost.org
URL: http://www.irost.org

3828 ■ Kharazmi International Award
To recognize the efforts made by researchers, innovators, and inventors worldwide, and to show appreciation for their invaluable achievements and contributions to various fields of science and technology. Eligible fields are human sciences, engineering, basic sciences, agriculture, biotechnology, and emerging technologies (nanotechnology). A certificate, trophy, and monetary prize of US$7,000 are awarded annually. Established in 1982 in memory of Mohammad Bin Moussa Kharazmi, an Iranian mathematician and astronomer.

Ireland

3829 ■ Association of Chartered Certified Accountants - Ireland
Liz Hughes, Hd.
9 Leeson Park
Dublin 6, Dublin, Ireland
Ph: 353 1 4988900
Ph: 353 1 4988906
Fax: 353 1 4963615
E-mail: info@ie.accaglobal.com
URL: http://ireland.accaglobal.com

3830 ■ ACCA Ireland Sustainability Reporting Awards
To recognize organizations that report and disclose environmental, social, or full sustainability information; to raise awareness of corporate accountability and transparency issues; and to encourage the uptake of environmental, social, sustainability reporting. Awarded annually. Established in 2001.

3831 ■ Children's Books Ireland
Mags Walsh, Dir.
17 N Great Georges St., 1st Fl.
Dublin 1, Dublin, Ireland
Ph: 353 1 8727475
Fax: 353 1 8727476
E-mail: info@childrensbooksireland.com
URL: http://www.childrensbooksireland.com

3832 ■ Bisto Book of the Year Award
To honor authors and illustrators of children's books who were born in or are residents of Ireland. The winner is awarded a trophy and monetary prize of 10,000 Euros, and three Honours Awards recipients share a prize fund of 6,000 Euros. Awarded annually. Established in 1991. Sponsored by Premier Foods Ireland (Bisto).

3833 ■ Eilis Dillon Award
To recognize an outstanding author or illustrator of children's books in Ireland. A trophy and monetary prize of 3,000 Euros are awarded annually.

3834 ■ Front Line
Mary Lawlor, Dir.
81 Main St.
Blackrock
Dublin, Dublin, Ireland
Ph: 353 1 2123750
Fax: 353 1 2121001
E-mail: info@frontlinedefenders.org
URL: http://www.frontlinedefenders.org

3835 ■ Front Line Award for Human Rights Defenders at Risk
Recognizes outstanding individuals who put their lives at risk on a daily basis to defend the lives of others. A monetary donation of 10,000 Irish pounds is donated to the work of the human rights defender; in addition, the recipient is also awarded a monetary prize of 5,000 Irish pounds. Awarded annually. Established in 2004.

3836 ■ Small Grants Program
Grants are given to human rights organizations all over the world for the specific purpose of strengthening the protection of human rights defenders at risk. Established in 2007.

3837 ■ Genealogical Society of Ireland
(Cumann Geinealais na heireann)
Mr. Michael Merrigan MA, Gen. Sec.
11 Desmond Ave.
Dun Laoghaire, Dublin, Ireland
E-mail: eolas@familyhistory.ie
URL: http://www.familyhistory.ie

3838 ■ GSI Medallion
Award of recognition.

3839 ■ Guild of Agricultural Journalists of Ireland
Damien O'Reilly, Chm.
Irish Food Publishers Media
Irish Farm Centre
Bluebell
Dublin 12, Dublin, Ireland
E-mail: colmcronin@live.com
URL: http://www.agriguild.ie

3840 ■ Agricultural Journalism Awards
For outstanding journalistic work in the fields of agriculture, food, and rural affairs. Awards are presented in seven categories: National Print, Local Print, National Broadcasting, Local Broadcasting, Technical Journalism, Targeted Communications, and Photography. In addition, the Bull Bronze Trophy is awarded for the best overall entry. Awarded biennially in even-numbered years.

3841 ■ Institute for Numerical Computation and Analysis
Diarmuid Herlihy, Sec.
7-9 Dame Ct.
Dublin 2, Dublin, Ireland
E-mail: info@incaireland.org
URL: http://www.incaireland.org

3842 ■ Victor W. Graham Perpetual Trophy
To recognize a school teacher in Ireland for achievement in applied mathematics. Awarded annually.

3843 ■ Institute of Advertising Practitioners in Ireland
Brian Swords, Pres.
8 Upper Fitzwilliam St.
Dublin 2, Dublin, Ireland
Ph: 353 1 6765991
Fax: 353 1 6614589
E-mail: info@iapi.com
URL: http://www.iapi.ie

3844 ■ Advertising Effectiveness Awards
To honor the most effective advertising campaigns that appeared in both Irish and international markets. Presented in a variety of categories, including packaged and frozen food packaging, electrical consumer goods, and automotive. Awarded biennially in even-numbered years. Established in 1996.

3845 ■ Institute of Chemistry of Ireland
(Instiiuid Ceimice Na hEireann)
Dr. James P. Ryan, Honorary Sec.
PO Box 9322
Cardiff Ln.
Dublin 2, Dublin, Ireland
E-mail: info@instituteofchemistry.org
URL: http://www.chemistryireland.org

3846 ■ Johnny Dwyer Memorial Award
To recognize the best presentations in four categories: oral presentations in physical chemistry, inorganic chemistry, organic chemistry, and analytical chemistry. Winners receive one year free graduate membership to the Institute. Awarded annually.

Awards are arranged in alphabetical order below their administering organizations

3847 ■ Boyle Higgins Gold Medal and Lecture Award
To recognize outstanding and internationally acclaimed contributions to the advancement of chemistry by a chemist of any nationality working in Ireland or by an Irish chemist working overseas. Open to research in pure chemistry, applied and industrial chemistry, and chemical education. Awarded annually.

3848 ■ ICI Annual Award for Chemistry
To recognize major contributions by individuals to the field of chemistry. The recipient presents a keynote lecture in several Irish locations each year. Awarded annually. Established in 2005.

3849 ■ Institute of Designers in Ireland
Rachael Murtagh, Exec. Off.
The Digital Hub, Roe Ln.
Thomas St.
Dublin 8, Dublin, Ireland
Ph: 353 1 4893650
Ph: 353 1 2084150
Fax: 353 1 4885801
E-mail: info@idi-design.ie
URL: http://www.idi-design.ie

3850 ■ Graduate Designer Awards
To recognize innovative and creative students graduating from recognized design courses throughout the country. Awards are presented in several categories. In addition, a Grand Prix recipient is selected. Awarded annually.

3851 ■ IDI Design Awards
To celebrate the excellent standard of design achieved by designers on the island of Ireland. Companies, design consultancies, architects, advertising agencies, direct marketing agencies, printers, and client companies from outside the island of Ireland are eligible, provided that the client's headquarters are on the island. Awards are presented in the following categories: Commercial Interior and Exhibition Design; TV/Theater/Film Design; Visual Communications; Fashion and Textile Design; Multimedia Design; Product Design; Design for All; and Design Sustainability. The Grand Prix award for the designer of the year is selected from all the category winners. Awarded annually.

3852 ■ International Academy of Broadcasting
George T. Waters, Pres.
PO Box 9502
Dublin 18, Dublin, Ireland
Fax: 3531 2899412
E-mail: seminar@iab.ch
URL: http://www.iab.ch

3853 ■ Radharc Awards
To recognize the producers of documentaries of outstanding quality that address national or international topics of social justice, morality, or faith. There is no requirement that the documentary be of any specific religious adherence, but it should portray positive human values and should imply a challenge to the moral conscience. Two categories of award are presented: 1. Full-length Documentaries - that had been broadcast on island of Ireland; and 2. Short Documentaries - that must have been produced by an Irish production team or by a team based in Ireland. A bronze statuette is awarded in each category. Awarded biennially in even-numbered years.

3854 ■ International Bureau for Epilepsy
Mr. Mike Glynn, Pres.
11 Priory Hall
Stillorgan
Dublin 18, Dublin, Ireland
Ph: 353 1 2108850
Fax: 353 1 2108450
E-mail: ibedublin@eircom.net
URL: http://www.ibe-epilepsy.org

3855 ■ Ambassador for Epilepsy Award
To honor individuals for extraordinary actions in the field of epilepsy. A maximum of 12 awards are presented biennially at the International Epilepsy Congress. Established in 1961. Cosponsored by the International League Against Epilepsy.

3856 ■ Award for Social Accomplishment
For those who have performed outstanding activities aimed at the social benefit of people with epilepsy. A glass trophy, certificate, and monetary prize of $5,000 are awarded annually.

3857 ■ International Federation of Surgical Colleges
Prof. S.W.A. Gunn, Sec. Gen.
123 St. Stephen's Green
Dublin 2, Dublin, Ireland
Ph: 353 1 4022707
Fax: 353 1 4022230
E-mail: ifsc@rcsi.ie
URL: http://www.ifsc-net.org

3858 ■ Sandoz Garcia Prize
For best scientific paper published in Folia Phoniatrica et Logopaedica between congresses.

3859 ■ IFSC Travel Grants
For promising surgeons in developing countries.

3860 ■ MBC/IFSC Scholarship
For young surgeons, with special attention to those from developing countries.

3861 ■ International Society of Biomechanics in Sports
Dr. Drew Anderson, Sec. Gen.
University of Limerick
Department of Physical Education and Sports Science
Limerick, Limerick, Ireland
Ph: 353 61 202809
Fax: 353 61 202814
E-mail: drew.harrison@ul.ie
URL: http://www.csuchico.edu/isbs/index.htm

3862 ■ Geoffrey Dyson Lecture
This, the Society's most prestigious award, is given to recognize sport scientists who, throughout their professional careers, bridge the gap between biomechanics research and practice in sport. Awarded annually. Established in 1987.

3863 ■ Fellow Award
To honor individuals who have made outstanding contributions in biomechanics related to sports over a period of years. Awarded when merited. Established in 1989.

3864 ■ Hans Gros New Investigator Award
To recognize and encourage new researchers to become productive members of the Society by expanding the knowledgebase of sports biomechanics through study and dissemination of information. Candidates must have completed their terminal degree within the previous two years. Awarded annually to one or more recipients. Established in 1990.

3865 ■ Life Membership Award
To honor members who have made outstanding contributions to the Society. Awarded when merited. Established in 1989.

3866 ■ Irish Astronomical Association
Mr. Daniel Collins, Sec.
5 Fairhill Rd.
Carnmoney
County Antrim
Newtownabbey BT36 6LY, Ireland
E-mail: iaa@irishastro.com
URL: http://irishastro.org.uk

3867 ■ Aidan P. Fitzgerald Memorial Medal
Award of recognition for outstanding service to the association. Awarded periodically.

3868 ■ Irish Exporters Association
John Whelan, Chief Exec.
28 Merrion Sq.
Dublin 2, Dublin, Ireland
Ph: 353 1 6612182
Fax: 353 1 6612315
E-mail: iea@irishexporters.ie
URL: http://www.irishexporters.ie

3869 ■ Export Industry Awards
To recognize achievements of small and large export companies. The following awards are presented: Emerging Exporter of the Year, Multinational Exporter of the Year, Life Sciences Exporter of the Year, Services Exporter of the Year, Manufacturing Exporter of the Year, Software Exporter of the Year, Seafood Exporter of the Year, Food and Drink Exporter of the Year, Innovation Export of the Year, First Flight Export of the Year, Short Sea Shipping Company of the Year, and Logistics Company of the Year. Awarded annually.

3870 ■ Irish Franchise Association
Tom Shanahan, Exec. Dir.
Kandoy House
2 Fairview Strand
Dublin 3, Dublin, Ireland
Ph: 353 1 8134555
Fax: 353 1 8134575
E-mail: info@irishfranchiseassociation.com
URL: http://www.irishfranchiseassociation.com

3871 ■ Best Emerging Franchise Award
To honor a franchisor who has established a new Irish franchise system during the past five years that is considered to have good potential for development. Awarded annually.

3872 ■ Franchise of the Year
To recognize and Irish business with outstanding achievement in the franchise industry. Awarded annually.

3873 ■ Franchise Person of the Year
To recognize an individual who has made a valuable contribution toward raising the profile of franchising in Ireland. Awarded annually.

3874 ■ Franchisee of the Year
To recognize franchisees with a single or multiple outlet of any established franchise system in North and/or South Ireland. Awards are presented annually in two categories: Retail and Service. Awarded annually.

3875 ■ Irish Georgian Society
Desmond Fitzgerald, Pres.
74 Merrion Sq.
Dublin 2, Dublin, Ireland
Ph: 353 1 6767053
Fax: 353 1 6620290
E-mail: info@igs.ie
URL: http://www.igs.ie

3876 ■ Conservation Grants
To support the restoration and conservation of historic buildings, interiors, monuments, and gardens in Ireland. A variety of grants are awarded throughout the year.

3877 ■ Irish Haemophilia Society
Brian O'Mahony, Chief Exec.
1st Fl., Cathedral Ct.
New St.
Dublin 8, Dublin, Ireland
Ph: 353 1 6579900
Fax: 353 1 6579901
E-mail: info@haemophilia.ie
URL: http://www.haemophilia.ie

Awards are arranged in alphabetical order below their administering organizations

3878 ■ Maureen Downey Memorial Grant
To provide financial support to a person with haemophilia or related bleeding disorder to attend a
post-second-level education course. Awarded
annually. Established in the late 1980s.

3879 ■ Honorary Life Member
To honor a member for 1) exceptional service to
the Society, or 2) maintaining 30 years of
continuous membership. Awarded annually.

3880 ■ Bill O'Sullivan Fundraiser Award
To recognize an individual for fundraising efforts.
Awarded annually.

3881 ■ Irish Hospitality Institute
Natasha Kinsella, Chief Exec.
8 Herbert Ln.
Dublin 2, Dublin, Ireland
Ph: 353 1 6624790
Fax: 353 1 6624789
E-mail: info@ihi.ie
URL: http://www.ihi.ie

3882 ■ Catering Manager of the Year
To recognize the professionalism and excellence
of managers in the Irish catering industry. Open
to senior managers at the general, deputy, or
departmental levels in an individual or group role
in any sector of the catering industry in Ireland.
Candidates must have had at least five years of
experience in a management position at any
level. Awarded annually. Sponsored by Unilever
Foodsolutions.

3883 ■ Hotel Manager of the Year
Recognizes individuals who have demonstrated
an exceptional ability to manage and deliver
excellent service quality and strong leadership.
Eligible candidates must have at least five years
management in experience and be age 30 years
or older. Awarded annually.

**3884 ■ Young Hospitality Manager of the
Year**
Recognizes excellence by young managers in
the hospitality and tourism industry. Eligible
candidates must have at least two years of
experience in a management position and be 30
years or younger on the final date for nomination.
Awarded annually.

**3885 ■ Irish Institute of Purchasing and
Materials Management
(An Foras um Cheannacht agus Bainistocht
Abhar)**
Des Crowther, CEO
17 Lower Mount St.
Dublin 2, Dublin, Ireland
Ph: 353 1 6449660
Fax: 353 1 6449661
E-mail: iipmm@iipmm.ie
URL: http://www.iipmm.ie

3886 ■ Lambert Memorial Award
For the best overall student.

**3887 ■ Irish Institute of Training and Develop-
ment
(Foras Oiliuna agus Forbartha Eireann)**
John Gorman, Pres.
Millennium Business Park
4 Sycamore House
Naas, Kildare, Ireland
Ph: 353 45 881166
Fax: 353 45 881192
E-mail: info@iitd.com
URL: http://www.iitd.com

3888 ■ National Training Awards
To recognize organizations with outstanding
training and development practices. Presented
in several categories annually.

**3889 ■ Irish Playwrights and Screenwriters
Guild**
Joe O'Byrne, Chm.
Art House
Curved St.

Temple Bar
Dublin 2, Dublin, Ireland
Ph: 353 1 6709970
E-mail: info@script.ie
URL: http://script.ie

3890 ■ ZeBBie Awards
To recognize the best scripts written by Irish
playwrights and screenwriters during the previous year. Awarded in four categories: television,
radio, theater, and film. In addition, the Honorary
Services to Writers Award may be presented.
Awarded annually. Established in 2007 and
named in honor of O.Z. "Zebby" Whitehead.

3891 ■ Irish Security Industry Association
Mr. Barry Brady, Exec. Dir.
42-44, Northumberland Rd.
Dublin 4, Dublin, Ireland
Ph: 353 1 4847206
E-mail: info@isia.ie
URL: http://www.isia.ie

3892 ■ ISIA Awards
Annual awards of recognition for police and com-
munity groups. The following awards are pre-
sented: Community Person of the Year, National
Courage Award, Security Officer of the Year,
Student of the Year, and the Premier Award.

3893 ■ Irish Society of Human Genetics
Collette Hand, Pres.
Dublin City University
School of Biotechnology
Dublin 9, Dublin, Ireland
Ph: 353 1 7008499
Fax: 353 1 7005284
E-mail: anne.parle-mcdermott@dcu.ie
URL: http://irishsocietyofhumangenetics.blogspot.
com

3894 ■ Young Investigator Awards
To recognize the best oral presentation at the
Annual Conference. Candidates must be clinicians in training, graduate students, or young
postdoctoral fellows presenting work done during their PhD projects. Awarded annually.

**3895 ■ Irish United Nations Veterans Associa-
tion**
Michael Butler, Chm.
Arbour House
Mt. Temple Rd.
Dublin 7, Dublin, Ireland
Ph: 353 1 6791262
URL: http://www.iunva.com

3896 ■ Service Medal
Award of recognition for two years of service to
the association.

3897 ■ Irish Youth Foundation
Liam O'Dwyer, Chief Exec.
56 Fitzwilliam Sq., 2nd Fl.
Dublin 2, Dublin, Ireland
Ph: 353 1 6766535
Fax: 353 1 6769893
E-mail: info@iyf.ie
URL: http://www.iyf.ie/intro.html

3898 ■ Irish Youth Foundation Award
Award of recognition for nongovernmental organizations working with disadvantaged young
people. Presented three times per year.

3899 ■ National Irish Safety Organisation
Pauric Corrigan, Pres.
A11 Calmount Park
Calmount Ave.
Ballymount
Dublin 12, Dublin, Ireland
Ph: 353 1 4659760
Fax: 353 1 4659765
E-mail: info@niso.ie
URL: http://www.niso.ie

**3900 ■ NISO Safety Representative of the
Year Award**
To an individual who contributed to the advance-
ment of health and safety in the workplace.

**3901 ■ Pitch and Putt Union of Ireland
(Aontas Teilgin Agus Amais na h'Eireann)**
Michael Murphy, Honorary Sec./Office Admin.
Sport HQ
13 Joyce Way
Park W
Dublin 12, Dublin, Ireland
Ph: 353 1 6251110
Fax: 353 1 6251111
E-mail: office@ppui.ie
URL: http://www.ppui.ie

3902 ■ Club Development Award
Given to clubs for improvement of facilities
and/or purchase of equipment. Awarded
annually. Established in 1998.

3903 ■ Psychological Society of Ireland
Mary Morrissey, Pres.
Grantham House, 2nd Fl.
Grantham St.
Dublin 2, Dublin, Ireland
Ph: 353 1 4720105
Fax: 353 1 4244051
E-mail: info@psihq.ie
URL: http://www.psihq.ie

3904 ■ Special Award
For outstanding contribution to the discipline of
psychology, or to work in the society.

3905 ■ Young Psychologist of the Year
To an outstanding student.

3906 ■ Royal Academy of Medicine in Ireland
John J. O'Connor, Gen. Sec.-Treas./Asst. Ed.
Frederick House, 4th Fl.
19 S Frederick St.
Dublin 2, Dublin, Ireland
Ph: 353 1 6334820
Fax: 353 1 6334918
E-mail: secretary@rami.ie
URL: http://www.rami.ie

3907 ■ Donal Burke Memorial Lecture
An invitation lecture organized by the Section of
General Practice of the Royal Academy of
Medicine in Ireland. A monetary award and a
silver medal are awarded annually. The first
lecture was given in 1984.

3908 ■ Conway Review Lecture
To encourage research in the biological sciences.
Workers in the biological sciences who are
nominated by two Fellows of the Academy are
eligible. A monetary award and a silver medal
are awarded annually. Established in 1977 by
the Biological Sciences Section of the Academy
in memory of Edward J. Conway, FRS.

3909 ■ Graves Lecture
To encourage clinical research in Ireland. Doctors under 40 years of age who are nominated
by two Fellows of the Academy and whose
research has been carried out wholly or partly in
Ireland are eligible. A monetary award and a
silver medal are awarded annually. Established
in 1960 by the Royal Academy of Medicine and
the Medical Research Council of Ireland in
memory of Robert Graves.

3910 ■ Saint Luke's Lecture
To encourage research in the field of oncology.
Doctors who are nominated by two Fellows of
the Academy and whose research has been carried out wholly or partly in Ireland are eligible. A
monetary award and a silver medal are awarded
annually. Established in 1975 by The Royal
Academy of Medicine and Saint Luke's Hospital.

3911 ■ Silver Medal
Awarded to the recipients of the Graves Lecture

Awards are arranged in alphabetical order below their administering organizations

(of clinical interest embodying original research) and the St. Luke's Lecture (in the field of oncology). Awarded annually.

3912 ■ Royal College of Physicians of Ireland
Dr. John Donohoe, Pres.
Frederick House
19 S Frederick St.
Dublin 2, Dublin, Ireland
Ph: 353 1 8639700
Fax: 353 1 6724707
E-mail: college@rcpi.ie
URL: http://www.rcpi.ie/pages/home.aspx

3913 ■ Reuben Harvey Memorial Prize
To recognize the student who has achieved the highest aggregate marks in the final examination in Medicine, Surgery and Obstetrics from each of the Dublin Medical Colleges/Universities: the Royal College of Surgeons in Ireland; Trinity College, Dublin; and University College, Dublin. Awarded annually. Established in 1885 in honor of Rueben Joshua Harvey, a pioneer in practical physiological teaching in Dublin.

3914 ■ Royal Dublin Society
Michael Duffy, Chief Exec.
Anglesea Rd.
Ballsbridge
Dublin 4, Dublin, Ireland
Ph: 353 1 6680866
Fax: 353 1 6604014
E-mail: info@rds.ie
URL: http://www.rds.ie

3915 ■ Allotment Awards
To recognize the hard work, dedication, and attention to detail that is being undertaken by those involved in allotment gardening, and to promote an area that encourages people to become more aware of rural issues. Presented in the categories of Experienced Individual Gardeners, Novice Individual Gardeners, and Groups (local authorities, allotment societies, community gardening groups, etc.). Medals, certificates, and monetary prizes totaling 3,000 Euros are awarded in each category. Awarded annually.

3916 ■ Boyle Medal for Scientific Excellence
To honor an individual for scientific research of exceptional merit carried out in Ireland. A medal and cash prize of 20,000 Euros are awarded biennially in odd-numbered years, alternating between a scientist based in Ireland and an Irish scientist based abroad. Established in 1899 in honor of Robert Boyle. Co-sponsored by the *Irish Times*.

3917 ■ Champion of Champions Awards
To encourage innovation and improvement in the Irish cattle breeding sector. Candidates are nominated by their cattle breed societies to compete to become a Champion of Champions. The winner in each breed is awarded a silver medal, a trophy, and a monetary prize of 1,000 Euros. Awarded annually. Established in 2006.

3918 ■ Dublin Horse Show
For recognition of outstanding exhibits, horses, and riders entered in horse show competitions. Awards are presented in the categories of international jumping, national jumping, showing classes, Samsung Super League, and Hunt Chase. Held annually. Established in 1868.

3919 ■ Gold Medal Award for Industry
To recognize an individual who has made an exceptional impact on industry and commerce. Candidates must have shown considerable professional and leadership skills, and have an outstanding track record in business achievement that has contributed to employment and economic development in Ireland. Awarded annually. Established in 1992.

3920 ■ Horticulture Student of the Year Award
To recognize final-year horticulture students in Ireland for their career to date, knowledge of horticulture, and future career plans. A silver medal, trophy, and monetary prize of 2,500 Euros are presented annually to the winner, with a certificate and monetary prize of 1,000 Euros presented to the runner-up.

3921 ■ McWilliams Young Science Writers' Competition
To encourage scientific investigation and foster literary skills by Irish youth between the ages of 12 and 19 years. Prizes are awarded in three aged-based categories: 12-13 years, 14-16 years, and 17-19 years; in addition, an overall winner is selected. Held annually.

3922 ■ National Crafts Competition
To promote Irish craft and design. Open to professional and amateur craft workers living in Ireland and Irish designer based abroad. More than 40 prizes totaling 28,000 Euros are awarded in 20 categories. In addition to dozens of sponsored awards, the RDS presents the following prizes: Award of Excellence (7,000 Euros); Reserve Prize (3,500 Euros); New Entrants Prize (1,500 Euros); Graduate Prize (1,500 Euros); and the William Smith O'Brien Perpetual Challenge Cup. Held annually. Established in 1968. Sponsored by the Crafts Council of Ireland.

3923 ■ RDS-Forest Service Irish Forestry Awards
To recognize and reward farmers who are employing the basic principles of sustainable forestry management on their properties including: sound commercial management; environmental protection; bio-diversity and social amenity. Awarded in two categories: Farm Forestry and Bio-Diverse Forestry/Woodlands. A silver medal, trophy, and monetary prize of 2,000 Euros are awarded in each category annually. Established in 1987. Supported by the Forest Service of the Department of Agriculture, Fisheries, and Food.

3924 ■ Student Art Awards
To recognize excellence and best practice in the work of students who are registered in full- and part-time award bearing art classes in Ireland. Monetary prizes totaling more than 18,000 Euros are awarded. Nearly one dozen prizes are awarded, including the Taylor Art Award, which has been awarded since 1860. Awarded annually.

3925 ■ Young Sheep Farmer Award
To promote sheep farming as a viable career for young Irish farmers. Candidates must be under 35 years of age, and must be either full- or part-time sheep farmers or students aspiring to become a sheep farmer. A silver medal and international travel bursary of 3,000 Euros is awarded annually. Established in 2010.

3926 ■ Royal Horticultural Society of Ireland
Cabinteely House
The Park
Cabinteely
Dublin 18, Dublin, Ireland
Ph: 353 1 2353912
Fax: 353 1 2353912
E-mail: info@rhsi.ie
URL: http://www.rhsi.ie

3927 ■ Banksian Medal
Annual award of recognition for contribution to horticulture in Ireland. Instituted in 1920 in commemoration of Sir Joseph Banks, one of the founders of the Society.

3928 ■ Royal Irish Academy (Acadamh Rioga na hEireann)
Patrick Buckley, Exec. Sec.
19 Dawson St.
Dublin 2, Dublin, Ireland

Ph: 353 1 6762570
Fax: 353 1 6762346
E-mail: p.buckley@ria.ie
URL: http://www.ria.ie

3929 ■ Gold Medal
To recognize Ireland's foremost thinkers in the humanities, social sciences, physical and mathematical sciences, life sciences, engineering sciences, the environment, and geosciences. Two medals are awarded annually, one in the sciences and one in the humanities. Each of the science medals are presented once over a four-year cycle, while the humanities and social sciences are awarded on alternate years. Established in 2005.

3930 ■ Eoin O'Mahony Bursary
To assist Irish scholars undertaking overseas research on historical subjects of Irish interest. Preference will be given to projects concerning family history, in particular those which are associated with the "wild geese". Special consideration will be given to those who have been active in local learned societies. A grant of 1,500 Euros is awarded annually. Established in 1978 by friends of the late Eoin O'Mahony, Barrister-at-Law, Knight of Malta, and genealogist who died in 1970.

3931 ■ Scouting Ireland CSI
Michael Devins, Natl. Sec.
Larch Hill
Dublin 16, Dublin, Ireland
Ph: 353 1 4956300
Fax: 353 1 4956301
E-mail: questions@scouts.ie
URL: http://www.scouts.ie

3932 ■ Service Awards
To recognize adults for service in any recognized Scout or Guide association. A gold award is presented for 25 years of service; silver awards for 15 and 20 years of service; and bronze awards for 5 and 10 years of service. Awarded when merited.

3933 ■ Ulster Bank Ireland Ltd.
Ulster Bank Group Centre
George's Quay
Dublin 2, Ireland
Ph: 353 1 608 4000
URL: http://www.ulsterbank.ie

3934 ■ Business Achievers Awards
To recognize the achievement of entrepreneurs in Ireland. One winner is selected in each of eight categories in the four regions of Leinster, Ulster, Munster, and Connaught; from these 32 candidates, one national winner is declared in each category; finally, a single All-Island Overall Business Achiever is selected. Awarded annually. Established in 2008.

Israel

3935 ■ Arthur Rubinstein International Music Society
Mr. J. Bistritzky, Artistic Dir.
12 Huberman St.
64075 Tel Aviv, Israel
Ph: 972 3 6856684
Ph: 972 3 6856628
Fax: 972 3 6854924
E-mail: competition@arims.org.il
URL: http://www.arims.org.il/main.htm

3936 ■ Arthur Rubinstein International Piano Master Competition
To foster young pianists with outstanding musicianship and a talent for persuasive, versatile rendering and creative interpretation of works, ranging from the pre-classical to the contemporary. The competition also aims to

Awards are arranged in alphabetical order below their administering organizations

establish a world forum for fostering talented and aspiring young interpreters and promoting their future artistic careers. The International Jury's task is to select pianists with more than average concert standard, who have attained a mature intellectual and emotional response to music. Open to pianists of all nationalities between 18 and 32 years of age. The Screening Committee prefers candidates who have either won top prizes at other important international competitions or who have been recommended specifically by world renowned artists. Approximately 15 prizes are presented, including: (1) The Arthur Rubinstein Award for first place - US$25,000 and a gold medal; (2) Sara and Moshe Mayer Prize for second place - US$15,000 and a silver medal; (3) Majorie and the late Arnold Ziff Prize for third place - US$10,000 and a bronze medal; and (4) US$3,000 each fourth, fifth, and sixth prizes. The Competition's Secretariat undertakes to help promote the artistic careers of the prize winners by recommending them for engagements with leading orchestras, concert managements and recording companies. Held triennially by the President of the State of Israel at the Laureates Gala Concert in Tel Aviv. Established in 1973.

3937 ■ Association for Civil Rights in Israel
(Haagudah Lezechuyot Haezrach Beyisrael)
Mr. Sammi Michael, Pres.
PO Box 34510
IL-91000 Jerusalem, Israel
Ph: 972 2 6521218
Fax: 972 2 6521219
E-mail: mail@acri.org.il
URL: http://www.acri.org.il

3938 ■ Emil Grunzweig Human Rights Award
To recognize an individual or NGO that has made a unique contribution to the advancement of human rights in Israel. Awarded annually.

3939 ■ Book Publishers' Association of Israel
Mordechai Bernstein Fund
29 Carlebach St.
PO Box 20123
61201 Tel Aviv, Israel
Ph: 972 3 5614 121
Fax: 972 3 5611 996
E-mail: hamol@tbpai.co.il
URL: http://www.tbpai.co.il

3940 ■ Golden Book Certificate
To recognize books that have sold 20,000 copies. A scroll is presented to the author and publisher annually.

3941 ■ Platinum Book Certificate
To recognize books that have sold 40,000 copies. A scroll is presented to the author and publisher annually.

3942 ■ Dan David Prize Organization
Ms. Smadar Fisher, Dir.
Eitan Berglas Blgd. No. 199
Tel Aviv University
PO Box 39040
Ramat Aviv
69978 Tel Aviv, Israel
Ph: 972 3 6406615
Fax: 972 3 6406613
E-mail: fisher@post.tau.ac.il
URL: http://www.dandavidprize.org

3943 ■ Dan David Prize
Awards three prizes of $1 million each for outstanding cultural, social, scientific or technological impact on our world. Awarded annually. Each year three time dimensions - past, present and future - are chosen.

3944 ■ Federation of European Biochemical Societies
Prof. Israel Pecht, Sec. Gen.
The Weizmann Institute of Science
Department of Immunology

PO Box 26
76100 Rehovot, Israel
Ph: 972 8 9344019
Fax: 972 8 9465264
E-mail: febs@weizmann.ac.il
URL: http://www.febs.org

3945 ■ Anniversary Prizes of the Society for Biochemistry and Molecular Biology
To recognize outstanding achievements in biochemistry, molecular biology, or related fields. Generally awarded to scientists less than 40 years of age who presented an invited lecture at one of the Society's meetings. Two monetary prizes of 2,000 Euros and diplomas are awarded. Co-sponsored by Boehringer Mannheim GmbH and Eppendorf Geratebau Netheler and Hinz GmbH.

3946 ■ Theodor Bucher Lecture and Medal
For outstanding achievements in biochemistry, molecular biology, or related fields. Recipient should be active in European research and is expected to present a plenary lecture at the Congress. Travel expenses and a silver medal are awarded.

3947 ■ Datta Lectureship and Medal
For outstanding achievements in biochemistry, molecular biology, or related fields. Awarded to one of the plenary lecturers. A medal and travel expenses are awarded. Sponsored by Elsevier Science Publishers.

3948 ■ FEBS/EMBO Women in Science Award
To highlight the major contributions made by female scientists in the life sciences. Eligible to female scientists from member countries who have made outstanding contribution to their field in the last five years. Recipient presents a plenary lecture at the Congress. A monetary prize of 10,000 Euros is awarded. Established in 2007. Co-sponsored by the European Molecular Biology Organisation (EMBO).

3949 ■ FEBS Journal Prize for Young Scientists
For the best paper in the *FEBS Journal* by a graduate student or young post-doctoral researcher (no more than three years post-doctoral) published in the previous calendar year. Recipient must be the first author of the paper. A monetary prize of 10,000 Euros is awarded annually.

3950 ■ FEBS Letters Young Scientist Award
For the author of the most outstanding research letter published in *FEBS Letters* during the previous calendar year. Author must be 40 years or younger at the time of manuscript acceptance. A monetary prize of 10,000 Euros is awarded. Established in 2003.

3951 ■ Sir Hans Krebs Lecture and Medal
To recognize outstanding achievements in biochemistry, molecular biology, or related fields. Recipient should be active in European research and is expected to present a plenary lecture at the Congress. A silver medal and travel expenses are awarded. Endowed by the Lord Rank Centre for Research.

3952 ■ Hebrew University of Jerusalem
Center for Research on the History and Culture of Polish Jews
(Ha-Merkar Le-Heker Yehudey Polin)
Prof. Israel Bartal, Dir.
Rabin Bldg. 2303
Mount Scopus
91905 Jerusalem, Israel
Ph: 972 2 588 1767
Fax: 972 2 588 1767
E-mail: bartalisr@yahoo.com

URL: http://jewish.huji.ac.il/Research/polin/index.htm

3953 ■ Solomon Prize
For a Master's or Doctoral thesis on Polish Jewry.

3954 ■ International Harp Contest in Israel
(Concours International de Harpe en Israel)
34, Techeskel St.
62595 Tel Aviv, Israel
Ph: 972 3 6041 808
Fax: 972 3 6041 688
E-mail: harzimco@netvision.net.il
URL: http://harpcontest-israel.org.il

3955 ■ International Harp Contest in Israel
(Concours International de Harpe en Israel)
To encourage and recognize excellence in playing the harp. Harpists of all nationalities under 35 years of age are eligible. The following prizes are awarded: first prize - Lyon and Healy Concert Grand Harp; second prize, (the Rosalind G. Weindling Prize) - US$6,000; a third prize of US$4,000 (in memory of Rachel Graetz); the Aharon Zvi and Mara Propes Prize of US$2,500 for an Israeli work; and the Mario Falcao Prize of US$1,500 for the best performance of the free choice, contemporary piece, in Stage II. Held every three years. Established in 1959 by Aharon Zvi Propes and the Israel Festival.

3956 ■ Israel Chemical Society
(Hachevrah Hayisraelit Lechimia)
Prof. Shlomo Margel, Pres.
Bar-Ilan University
Dept. of Chemistry
IL-52900 Ramat Gan, Israel
Ph: 972 3 5318861
Ph: 972 8 9343829
Fax: 972 3 5351250
E-mail: shlomo.margel@mail.biu.ac.il
URL: http://www.weizmann.ac.il/ICS

3957 ■ Israel Chemical Society Medal
To recognize an individual for outstanding contributions to the development and establishment of chemistry in Israel. Awarded annually. Established in 2002.

3958 ■ Outstanding Young Scientist Prize
To recognize young researchers for outstanding contributions to chemistry. Awarded to one or two recipients annually. Established in 1987.

3959 ■ Prize for Excellence
To recognize individuals for outstanding contributions to chemistry. Awarded to one or two recipients annually. Established in 1999.

3960 ■ Israel Democracy Institute
Prof. Arye Carmon, Pres.
4 Pinsker St.
91046 Jerusalem, Israel
Ph: 972 2 5300888
Fax: 972 2 5300837
E-mail: info@idi.org.il
URL: http://www.idi.org.il/Pages/Home_Page.aspx

3961 ■ Democracy Award
To recognize a figure of international stature in recognition of his or her significant contribution to strengthening democracy. Awarded annually.

3962 ■ Israel Geological Society
Ezra Zilberman, Pres.
PO Box 1239
IL-91000 Jerusalem, Israel
E-mail: gsi@igs.org.il
URL: http://www.igs.org.il

3963 ■ Professor Raphael Freund Award
To recognize a member for an excellent publication on the topic of earth sciences. Awarded annually.

Awards are arranged in alphabetical order below their administering organizations

3964 ■ Dr. Peretz Grader Award
For original work in earth sciences. Candidates must be below age 36. Awarded annually.

3965 ■ IGS Medal
To recognize a member for outstanding contribution to public awareness of the earth sciences. Awarded annually.

3966 ■ Israel Physical Society
Prof. Avishai Dekel, Pres.
Racah Institute of Physics
The Hebrew University of Jerusalem
IL-91904 Jerusalem, Israel
Ph: 972 2 6585512
Fax: 972 2 5611519
E-mail: dekel@phys.huji.ac.il
URL: http://www.israelphysicalsociety.org

3967 ■ IPS Prize
To honor students for outstanding research. Awarded annually to one or more recipients.

3968 ■ Israel Society for Biochemistry and Molecular Biology
Prof. Michael Eisenbach, Pres.
PO Box 9095
IL-52190 Ramat Efal, Israel
Ph: 972 3 6355038
Fax: 972 3 5351103
E-mail: isbmb1@gmail.com
URL: http://www.tau.ac.il/lifesci/isbmb

**3969 ■ Hestrin Prize
(Pras Hestrin)**
For recognition of achievement in the field of biochemistry. Israeli citizens under 44 years of age may be nominated. A monetary prize of 12,000 NIS and a plaque are awarded annually. Established in 1964 in memory of Professor Shlomo Hestrin.

3970 ■ Teva Prize
To recognize outstanding PhD students in the fields of biochemistry and molecular biology. A monetary prize of 9,500 NIS is awarded to two students biennially in odd-numbered years. Established in 2003.

**3971 ■ Israel Translators Association
(Agudat Hametargmim Beyisrael)**
Pascale Amozig-Bukszpan, Chair
PO Box 16133
IL-61161 Tel Aviv, Israel
E-mail: chair@ita.org.il
URL: http://www.ita.org.il

3972 ■ Prize to Outstanding Student of Translation
To recognize a student for extraordinary accomplishments and promise as a translator. Awarded annually.

3973 ■ Israel Vacuum Society
Alon Hoffman, Pres.
Technion Israel Institute of Technology
Faculty of Chemistry
32000 Haifa, Israel
Ph: 972 54 5580727
Fax: 972 4 8241602
URL: http://science.co.il/ivs

3974 ■ Edwards Vacuum Ltd. Israel Research Excellence Prize
To honor an Israeli scientist performing outstanding internationally acclaimed research in the fields that are fostered and encouraged by the IVS. Formerly: Rafael Research Excellence Award.

3975 ■ Odem Technical Excellence Award
For technical excellence and outstanding

achievement in the field of vacuum science and technology including all fields of endeavor of the Society in Israel. Formerly: Elop Technical Excellence Award.

3976 ■ Israeli Association of Grid Technologies
Mr. Avner Algom, CEO
PO Box 4058
46140 Herzliya, Israel
Ph: 972 54 4276528
Fax: 972 9 9564410
E-mail: info@grid.org.il
URL: http://www.grid.org.il

3977 ■ IGT Award
To create awareness about grid technologies; to help ISVs working on grid solutions to get market recognition; to help enterprises understand the value and relevance of grid technologies to its business; and to motivate grid research and development. Awarded annually.

3978 ■ Israeli Society for Bioinformatics and Computational Biology
Prof. Ron Unger, Pres.
Technion - Israel Institute of Technology
Faculty of Biology
32000 Haifa, Israel
Ph: 972 4 8293958
Ph: 972 4 8294258
Fax: 972 4 8225153
E-mail: yaelmg@tx.technion.ac.il
URL: http://www.weizmann.ac.il/ISBCB

3979 ■ Distinguished Service Award
To recognize an individual for outstanding contribution to bioinformatics. Awarded biennially in even-numbered years.

3980 ■ Israeli Society of Gene and Cell Therapy
Prof. Eithan Galun MD, Pres.
PO Box 12000
91120 Jerusalem, Israel
Ph: 972 2 6778589
Ph: 972 2 6777762
Fax: 972 2 6430982
E-mail: gtx@hadassah.org.il
URL: http://www.isgt.org.il

3981 ■ Award for Excellent Oral Presentation
To recognize the best oral presentation by a researcher during the annual conference. A monetary prize of 1,500 NIS is awarded annually.

3982 ■ Award for Excellent Poster Presentation
To recognize the best paper submitted to a panel. A monetary prize of 750 NIS is awarded annually to two recipients.

3983 ■ Mordechai Bernstein Literary Prizes Association
Amnon Ben-Shumel, Managing Dir.
29 Carlebach St.
PO Box 20123
61201 Tel Aviv, Israel
Ph: 972 3 5614121
Fax: 972 3 5611996
E-mail: hamol@tbpai.co.il
URL: http://www.tbpai.co.il

**3984 ■ Award for Literary Criticism
(Pras l'Bikoret Sifrutit)**
To recognize an outstanding newspaper book review of an original Hebrew novel, play, poetry, or short story in the daily Hebrew press. A monetary prize of 10,000 NS is awarded biennially. Established in 1979 to honor Mordechai Bernstein, an Israeli author.

**3985 ■ Award for Original Hebrew Novel
(Pras l'Roman Ivri Mekori)**
To encourage authors under the age of 50 who

write Hebrew novels. A monetary award of 50,000 NS is presented biennially. Established in 1977 to honor Mordechai Bernstein, an Israeli author.

**3986 ■ Award for Original Hebrew Poetry
(Pras l'Sefer Shira Ivri Mekori)**
To encourage Hebrew poets under the age of 50. A monetary award of 25,000 NS is presented biennially. Established in 1981 to honor Mordechai Bernstein, an Israeli author.

3987 ■ First Novel Award
Recognizes the first novel written in Hebrew by an immigrant new to Israel. A monetary award of 20,000 NS is presented biennially. Established in 1999 in honor of Mordechai Bernstein, an Israeli author.

3988 ■ First Poetry Book Award
Recognizes a first poetry book in Hebrew by an immigrant new to Israel. A monetary award of 20,000 NS is presented biennially. Established in 1999 in honor of Mordechai Bernstein, an Israeli author.

3989 ■ Hebrew Play Award
Recognizes an outstanding Hebrew play. A monetary award of 10,000 NS is presented biennially. Established in 1999 in honor of Mordechai Bernstein, an Israeli author.

3990 ■ Tel Aviv Museum of Art
Prof. Mordechai Omer, Contact
27 Shaul Hamelech Blvd.
64329 Tel Aviv, Israel
Ph: 972 3 607 7000
Fax: 972 3 695 8099
E-mail: daria@tamuseum.com
URL: http://www.tamuseum.com

3991 ■ Dr. Haim Gamzu Prize
For recognition in the field of the arts. Awarded annually. Established in 1984.

3992 ■ Nathan Gottesdiener Prize
To recognize an Israeli artist. Awarded annually.

3993 ■ Eugene Kolb Prize
For recognition of a work of Israeli graphic art. Awarded annually. Established in 1983.

3994 ■ Mendel and Eva Pundik Prize
To provide for the acquisition of Israeli art. Awarded annually. Established in 1984.

3995 ■ U.S.-Israel Binational Science Foundation
Dr. Yair Rotstein, Exec. Dir.
PO Box 45086
IL-91450 Jerusalem, Israel
Ph: 972 2 5828239
Fax: 972 2 5828306
E-mail: bsf@bsf.org.il
URL: http://www.bsf.org.il/BSFPublic/Default.aspx

3996 ■ Prof. E. D. Bergmann Memorial Award
To encourage and assist young scientists. Any U.S. or Israeli BSF grantee under 35 years of age, who received his or her doctoral degree within the previous five years, is eligible. A grant of US$5,000 is awarded annually. Established in 1977 in memory of Ernst D. Bergmann.

3997 ■ Prof. Henry Neufeld Memorial Award
To encourage young scientists in the health sciences. The BSF grantee proposing the most outstanding and original project in health science is selected by a committee. A grant of US$10,000 is awarded annually. Established in 1987 in memory of Professor Henry Neufeld.

3998 ■ Prof. Amnon Pazy Memorial Award
To recognize the most outstanding and original

Awards are arranged in alphabetical order below their administering organizations

new project in the mathematical sciences (mathematics and computer science). A monetary prize of US$10,000 is awarded annually. Established in 2007.

3999 ■ Wolf Foundation
(Keren Wolf)
Yaron E. Gruder, Dir. Gen.
39 Hamaapilim St.
PO Box 398
46103 Herzlia Bet, Israel
Ph: 972 9 955 7120
Fax: 972 9 954 1253
E-mail: wolffund@netvision.net.il
URL: http://www.wolffund.org.il

4000 ■ Krill Prizes for Excellence in Scientific Research
To recognize faculty members at universities in Israel for excellence in exact sciences, life sciences, medicine, agriculture, and engineering. Six prizes of $10,000 each are awarded annually. Established in 2005.

4001 ■ The Wolf Prizes
To recognize outstanding scientists and artists irrespective of nationality, race, color, religion, sex, or political views, for achievements in the interest of humankind and friendly relations among peoples. Individuals may be nominated by universities, academies of science, and former recipients by August 31. The recipients are selected by international prize committees. The Prize in each area consists of a diploma and $100,000 (US) equally divided among co-recipients. Awards are given in the fields of agriculture, physics, chemistry, medicine, and mathematics. There may be a sixth prize for the arts (music, painting, sculpture, architecture), or one of the five science prizes may be awarded for art rather than science. Official presentation of the prizes takes place at the Knesset (Israel's Parliament) and the winners are presented their awards by the President of the State in a special ceremony. The Wolf Foundation was established in 1978 by the Israeli chemist, Dr. Ricardo Wolf.

4002 ■ Yad Vashem, The Holocaust Martyrs' and Heroes' Remembrance Authority
Mr. Avner Shalev, Chm.
PO Box 3477
IL-91034 Jerusalem, Israel
Ph: 972 2 6443400
Ph: 972 2 6443453
Fax: 972 2 6443443
E-mail: general.information@yadvashem.org.il
URL: http://www.yadvashem.org

4003 ■ Bergson Award
Awarded for a term paper on the Holocaust.

4004 ■ Brandt Award
Award for children's Holocaust literature.

4005 ■ Buchman Award
Award for literature/research on the Holocaust.

4006 ■ Najmann Award
Award for excellence in the field of Holocaust education.

4007 ■ Uveeler Award
Award for outstanding papers.

Italy

4008 ■ Abdus Salam International Centre for Theoretical Physics
Ms. Anne Gatti, Asst. Dir.
Strada Costiera 11
I-34151 Trieste, Italy
Ph: 39 402240111
Fax: 39 40224163
E-mail: sci_info@ictp.it
URL: http://www.ictp.it

4009 ■ Dirac Medal
For recognition of significant contributions to theoretical physics and mathematics. Selection is by nomination. The Dirac Medals are not awarded to Nobel laureates or Wolf Foundation Prize winners. A monetary prize of US$5,000 is awarded annually. The winners are announced on August 8, Dirac's birthday. Established in 1985 in honor of Paul Adrien Maurice Dirac (United Kingdom), Nobel Laureate for physics.

4010 ■ ICO-ICTP Gallieno Denardo Award
To recognize a researcher under 40 years of age from a developing country who has made significant contributions to the field of optics. A certificate, cash prize of $1,000, and an invitation to attend and deliver a lecture at the next conference on optics are awarded annually. Co-sponsored by the International Commission for Optics (ICO). Formerly: (2008) ICO-ICTP Prize.

4011 ■ ICTP Prize
To recognize an outstanding and original contribution made by a scientist from and working and living in a developing country in a particular field of physics and mathematics. Individuals under 40 years of age are eligible. A monetary award of 3,000 Euros, a sculpture, and a certificate are awarded annually. Established in 1982.

4012 ■ Prizes for Leadership in Islamic Thought and Applied Sciences
To recognize exploration of links between Islamic thought and applied science (e.g., medicine, agriculture, engineering, and technology). Individuals must hold a doctorate degree and be younger than 45 years old. Two awards of $20,000 are presented annually.

4013 ■ Ramanujan Prize for Young Mathematicians from Developing Countries
Awarded to a researcher less than 45 years old from a developing country, who has conducted outstanding research in mathematics in a developing country. A monetary prize of $15,000 is awarded annually. Established in 2005.

4014 ■ Abdus Salam Prize for Leadership in Islamic Thought and the Physical Sciences
To recognize an individual for exploration of links between physical science and Islamic thought. Candidates must hold a doctorate degree and be younger than 45 years old. An award of $20,000 is presented annually.

4015 ■ Ahmed Zewail Prize for Leadership in Islamic Thought and Biological Science
To recognize exploration of links between biology and Islamic thought. Individuals must hold a doctorate degree and be younger than 45 years old. An award of $20,000 is presented annually.

4016 ■ Ahmed Zewail Prize for Leadership in Islamic Thought and Chemical Science
To recognize exploration of links between chemical sciences and Islamic thought. Individuals must hold a doctorate degree and be younger than 45 years old. An award of $20,000 is presented annually.

4017 ■ Accademia delle Scienze di Torino
Dr. Chiara Mancinelli, Chancellor
Via Maria Vittoria 3
I-10123 Turin, Italy
Ph: 39 11 5620047
Fax: 39 11 532619
E-mail: iniziative@accademia.csi.it
URL: http://www.accademiadellescienze.it

4018 ■ Premio Herlitzka
For recognition of outstanding work in physiology during the preceding ten academic years. Proposals are admitted only upon invitation by the Academy. A monetary prize is awarded every four years. Established in 1986.

4019 ■ Premio Internazionale Panetti-Ferrari
(Professor Modesto Panetti International Prize with Gold Medal)
To honor a scientist who has particularly distinguished himself or herself in work in applied mechanics during the ten years preceding the prize. Scientists who are not national or foreign members of the Academy are eligible to be proposed by national and foreign members of the Classe di Scienze Fisiche, Matematiche e Naturali of the Accademia delle Scienze di Torino as well as presidents of scientific Italian and foreign academies. Proposals are admitted only upon invitation by the Academy. A monetary award and a gold medal are awarded biennially in odd-numbered years. Established in 1998 by the merger of two awards honoring Professors Modesto Panetti and Carlo Ferrari.

4020 ■ Accademia Nazionale dei Lincei
Prof. Lamberto Maffei, Pres.
Palazzo Corsini
Via della Lungara 10
I-00165 Rome, Italy
Ph: 39 6 680271
Fax: 39 6 6893616
E-mail: segreteria@lincei.it
URL: http://www.lincei.it

4021 ■ Dr. Joseph Borgia Prize
To recognize an individual for an outstanding contribution to chemistry. A monetary prize of 10,000 Euros is awarded annually.

4022 ■ Antonio Feltrinelli Prizes
To honor distinguished scholars in the various fields of science and the arts. Open to individuals of any nationality. Conferred annually on a rotating basis among: Humanities; Physical, mathematical, and natural sciences; Literature; Arts; and Medicine. In addition, an award may be presented for an exceptional enterprise of high moral and humanitarian value. Awarded annually.

4023 ■ Lincei Prize for Astronomy
To recognize an individual for an outstanding contribution to astronomy. A monetary prize of 10,000 Euros is awarded annually.

4024 ■ National Institute of Insurance International Prizes
(Premio Internazionali dell' Instituto Nazionale delle Assicurazioni)
To recognize a person of renown in the insurance field. A monetary prize of 25,000 Euros is awarded annually on a rotating basis in four categories: law; economics, finance, and statistics; mathematics and technique; and in a different area from the other three. (If none is available, then one of the three categories is used.) The emphasis is upon private insurance. Established in 1962.

4025 ■ Prof. Luigi Tartufari Prizes
To honor distinguished scholars in the four scientific disciplines of mathematics, physics, geology, and biology. Open to individuals of any nationality. A monetary prize of 25,000 Euros is awarded annually in each category.

4026 ■ Association of Italian Clinical Dermatologists
Dr. Agostino Crupi, Pres.
Via Nicolo Dell'Arca 7
70121 Bari, Italy
Ph: 39 080 5240633
Fax: 39 080 5240633
E-mail: direttivo@aida.it
URL: http://web.ilds.org/cms

4027 ■ Best Free Communication
For innovative therapy or clinical management.

Awards are arranged in alphabetical order below their administering organizations

4028 ■ **Best Poster of the Year**
For unusual clinical case.

4029 ■ **Associazione Culturale Antonio Pedrotti**
Lucio Chiricozzi, Pres.
Centro S. Chiara-via S. Croce 67
I-38100 Trento, Italy
Ph: 39 461 231223
Fax: 39 461 1820531
E-mail: pedrotticompetition@fastwebnet.it
URL: http://www.concorsopedrotti.it

4030 ■ **Antonio Pedrotti International Competition for Orchestra Conductors (Concurso Internazionale per Direttori d'Orchestra Antonio Pedrotti)**
To encourage professional activity of young orchestra conductors. Applicants must be between 18 and 35 years of age. First place winner is awarded 10,000 Euros and the opportunity to perform in several orchestras. Second and third place winners receive 5,000 Euros and 3,000 Euros, respectively. Held biennially in even-numbered years. Established in 1989 by Andrea Mascagni.

4031 ■ **Associazione Internazionale Guido Dorso**
Antonio Pisanti, Sec. Gen.
Corso Umberto I, 22
I-80138 Naples, Italy
Ph: 39 81 5527 744
Fax: 39 81 5527 744
E-mail: info@assodorso.it
URL: http://www.assodorso.it
Formerly: (1990) Centro Studi Nuovo Mezzogiorno.

4032 ■ **International Guido Dorso Prize**
For recognition of achievement in, or contribution to, political, economic, managerial, scientific, cultural, educational, and publishing activities, specifically focused on southern Italy's growth. Applications must be submitted for the "ordinaria" section, and for the other sections nomination is necessary. Monetary prizes and trophies are awarded annually in the autumn. Established in 1970 by Dott. Nicola Squitieri in honor of Guido Dorso.

4033 ■ **Associazione per il Disegno Industriale**
Yara Cutolo, Sec. Gen.
Via Bramante 29
I-20154 Milan, Italy
Ph: 39 2331 0241
Fax: 39 23310 0878
E-mail: info@adi-design.org
URL: http://www.adi-design.org

4034 ■ **Gold Compass Prize (Premio Compasso d'oro)**
For recognition in the field of Italian industrial design. Awarded triennially. Established in 1954.

4035 ■ **Bagutta Restaurant**
Via Bagutta 14
I-20121 Milan, Italy
Ph: 39 2 76000 902
Fax: 39 2 799613
E-mail: segreteria@bagutta.it
URL: http://www.bagutta.it

4036 ■ **Bagutta Prize**
This, one of Italy's oldest and most prestigious literary awards, is given for recognition of the best book of the year in several categories. Established and young distinguished authors of many literary forms, including the novel, poetry, and journalism are eligible. Submissions are not accepted. A monetary award and honorary recognition are awarded annually at Bagutta, a small restaurant at Via Baguttain, Milan. Established in 1927.

4037 ■ **Bergamo Film Meeting**
Via Pignola 123
I-24121 Bergamo, Italy
Ph: 39 035 363087

Fax: 39 035 341255
E-mail: info@bergamofilmmeeting.it
URL: http://www.bergamofilmmeeting.it

4038 ■ **Rosa Camuna**
To recognize and honor films of high quality and art for sale and distribution in Italy. Participating films are included by invitation of the organizers. Films must not have been previously released in Italy nor have been shown in any other Italian film festival. Three plaques are awarded annually in March at the end of the Bergamo Film Meeting Festival - a gold, silver, and bronze Rosa Camuna, the symbol of Regione Lombardia. Established in 1983. Sponsored by Regione Lombardia.

4039 ■ **Campiello Foundation (Fondazione Il Campiello)**
Andrea Riello, Pres.
Vio Torino, 151 C
I-30172 Mestre-Venice, Italy
Ph: 39 41 2517 511
Fax: 39 41 2517 576
E-mail: info@premiocampiello.org
URL: http://www.premiocampiello.org

4040 ■ **Campiello Prize (Premio Campiello)**
To provide recognition for the best Italian prose works of the year. Books of fiction by Italian citizens published during the preceding 12 months are considered. Five monetary prizes and plaques are awarded with additional money for the super prize winner. A monetary prize is awarded annually for the super prize. Established in 1963 by Mario Valeri Manera, Associazioni Industriali del Veneto.

4041 ■ **Cinema Giovani - Torino Film Festival (Festival Internazionale Cinema Giovani)**
Lorenzo Ventavoli, Pres.
Via Montevello, 15
I-10124 Turin, Italy
Ph: 39 11 813 8811
Fax: 39 11 813 8890
E-mail: info@torinofilmfest.org
URL: http://www.torinofilmfest.org

4042 ■ **Turin International Film Festival (Festival Internazionale Cinema Giovani)**
For recognition of outstanding films submitted to the Festival. Prizes are awarded in two competitions: International Feature Films Competition and International Short Films Competition. Two special jury awards are also given. Held annually.

4043 ■ **Club Tenco**
Via Matteotti, 226
C.P. 1
I-18038 San Remo, Italy
Ph: 39 184 505011
Fax: 39 184 577289
E-mail: info@clubtenco.org
URL: http://www.clubtenco.org

4044 ■ **Premio Tenco**
For recognition of musical artists who have always worked in the musical world with cultural, poetic and social aims. Musical performers may be nominated. A trophy is awarded annually in October. Established in 1974 in honor of Luigi Tenco. Sponsored by the San Remo Municipality.

4045 ■ **Concorso Pianistico Internazionale Alessandro Casagrande**
Via I Maggio, 65
I-05100 Terni, Italy
Ph: 39 744 549713
Fax: 39 744 449877
E-mail: fondazionecasagrande@gmail.com
URL: http://www.concorsocasagrande.org

4046 ■ **Alessandro Casagrande International Piano Competition (Concorso Pianistico Internazionale Alessandro Casagrande)**
To recognize and encourage young pianists.

Pianists of any nationality under 30 years of age are eligible. Concert engagements and monetary awards are presented. Awarded biennially in even-numbered years. Established in 1966 by the Municipality of Terni.

4047 ■ **Courmayeur Noir in Festival**
Simonetta Pacifico, Receptionist
Via Panaro, 17
I-00199 Rome, Italy
Ph: 39 6 8603 111
Fax: 39 6 8621 3298
E-mail: noir@noirfest.com
URL: http://www.noirfest.com
Formerly: Noir International Festival.

4048 ■ **International Mystery Festival**
To recognize and promote outstanding film achievement in various mystery genres (crime story, suspense, thriller, horror, fantasy, spy story, etc.) in Italy and throughout the world. The following prizes are awarded: Black Lyon for best film; Napapijri Award for best leading actress/actor; Optical Special Citation Award at jury's discretion; Audience Award for audience favorite; and Mystery Award for best short film. Trophies are awarded annually. Established by Mr. Giorgio Gosetti in 1991.

4049 ■ **Cultural Association "Rodolfo Lipizer" (Associazione Culturale "Rodolfo Lipizer")**
Prof. Lorenzo Qualli, Pres.
Via don Giovanni Bosco 91
I-34170 Gorizia, Italy
Ph: 39 481 547863
Fax: 39 481 536710
E-mail: lipizer@lipizer.it
URL: http://www.lipizer.it

4050 ■ **International Violin Competition - Rodolfo Lipizer Prize (Concorso Internazionale di Violino - Premio Rodolfo Lipizer)**
To promote Rodolfo Lipizer's work and help the debut of young concert artists. Cash awards and concert engagements are awarded annually. First prize is 10,000 lira (indivisible), with diploma and silver medal offered by the President of the Italian Republic. Second prize is 6,000 lira and a diploma. Third prize is 4,000 lira and a diploma. Fourth prize is 2,500 lira and a diploma. Fifth prize is 2,000 lira and a diploma. Sixth prize is 1,500 lira and a diploma. Established in 1982 by Professor Lorenzo Qualli, an ex-pupil of Rodolfo Lipizer.

4051 ■ **Ente David di Donatello**
Gian Luigi Rondi, Pres.
Via di Villa Patrizi 10
I-00161 Rome, Italy
Ph: 39 6 4402766
Fax: 39 6 8411746
E-mail: segreteria@daviddidonatello.it
URL: http://www.daviddidonatello.it

4052 ■ **David Film Awards (Premi David di Donatello per la Cinematografia Internazionale)**
For recognition of outstanding Italian films; and to stimulate, with the collaboration of authors, critics, technicians, and personalities of industry, culture, and the arts, an adequate form of competition in the sphere of cinematographic production. The Premi David di Donatello are awarded for Italian films and for foreign films. A reproduction of the famous David statue by Donatello is awarded annually in a variety of categories. Established in 1954/55 under the sponsorship of the President of the Italian Republic.

4053 ■ **European Association for Animal Production (Federation Europeenne de Zootechnie)**
Andrea Rosati, Sec. Gen.
Via G. Tomassetti 3, 1/A
00161 Rome, Italy

Awards are arranged in alphabetical order below their administering organizations

4054 ■ Distinguished Service Award
To recognize outstanding contributions in the service of European and Mediterranean animal production and science. Individuals retired from active service may be nominated. A silver medal and diploma are awarded a maximum of three times in one year when merited. Established in 1989.

4055 ■ A. M. Leroy Fellowship
To recognize an individual for significant contributions to research or development in the animal sector in Europe and the Mediterranean Basin. By nomination only. A silver plaque and diploma are awarded annually when merited. Established in 1989 by E.A.A.P. to honor Prof. A. M. Leroy.

4056 ■ Romert Politiek Award
To recognize the best poster presented at the Annual Meeting. Awarded annually.

4057 ■ Young Scientist Awards
For recognition of the best scientific/technical paper in the field of animal production presented at the annual meeting of each one of the seven commissions of the organization. Individuals under 30 years of age are chosen by the Commission Boards. Scientific/technical papers are considered. Between 12 and 20 trophies and diplomas are awarded annually. Established in 1983. Formerly: (1995) EAAP Annual Meeting Awards.

4058 ■ European Association of Environmental and Resource Economists
Ms. Monica Eberle, Sec. Gen.
Fondazione Eni Enrico Mattei
I-30124 Venice, Italy
Ph: 39 41 2700438
Fax: 39 41 2700412
E-mail: eaere@eaere.org
URL: http://www.eaere.org

4059 ■ European Lifetime Achievement Award in Environmental Economics
To recognize outstanding and sustained contributions to environmental economics, generally by a retired or retiring practitioner. Awarded as merited.

4060 ■ European Practitioner Achievement Award in Applying Environmental Economic
To recognize practical applications of environmental economics. Awarded annually if merited.

4061 ■ Erik Kempe Award in Environmental and Resource Economics
Recognizes the best paper in the field of environmental and resource economics. Eligible papers must have been published in refereed journals by an author affiliated with a European research institute. The prize is awarded biennially in odd-numbered years, with the prize being conveyed at the first conference and the winner(s) presenting a lecture and leading seminars at the second conference. A monetary prize of 100,00 SEK is awarded.

4062 ■ European Association of Veterinary Anatomists
(Societas Europaea Anatomorum Veterinariorum)
Dr. Francesco Abbate, Sec. Gen.
Faculty of Veterinay Science
Polo Universitario Annunziata
98168 Messina, Italy
Ph: 39 90 3503598
Fax: 39 90 3503935
E-mail: abbatef@unime.it
URL: http://www.eava.eu/modules/info/index.php?id=7:17

Ph: 39 6 44202639
Fax: 39 6 86329263
E-mail: eaap@eaap.org
URL: http://www.eaap.org

4063 ■ Berlin Poster Prize
For an individual with the best poster presentation at the EAVA congress. Awarded biennially in even-numbered years.

4064 ■ Simic-Grau Award
For a young veterinary anatomist with the best paper presentation at the EAVA congress. Awarded biennially in even-numbered years.

4065 ■ European Bridge League
Yves Aubry, Pres.
Via Ciro Menotti 11/C
I-20129 Milan, Italy
Ph: 39 2 7384450
Fax: 39 2 5609996
E-mail: ebl@federbridge.it
URL: http://www.eurobridge.org

4066 ■ European Bridge Champion
To recognize the country whose bridge team wins the European Bridge Championships. The Championships are held biennially in odd-numbered years. Medals are awarded. Established in 1940.

4067 ■ European Committee for the Advancement of Thermal Sciences and Heat Transfer
Prof. Hans Muller-Steinhagen, Pres.
University of Pisa
Department of Energetics
Via Diotisalvi 2
56126 Pisa, Italy
Ph: 39 50 2217107
Fax: 39 50 2217150
E-mail: p.dimarco@ing.unipi.it
URL: http://termserv.casaccia.enea.it/eurotherm

4068 ■ EUROTHERM Young Scientist Prizes and Awards
For research work in the field of thermal sciences. Awarded to three recipients every four years.

4069 ■ European Economic Association
Christopher Pissarides, Pres.
Universita Cattolica
Instituto di Economia dell'Impresa e del Lavoro
Via P. Necci, 5
20123 Milan, Italy
Ph: 39 2 72343050
Fax: 39 2 72343051
E-mail: eea@unicatt.it
URL: http://www.eeassoc.org

4070 ■ Yrjo Jahnsson Award
To recognize a young European economist who has made a contribution in theoretical and applied research. Candidates must be aged 45 years or younger. Awarded annually.

4071 ■ Hicks Tinbergen Medal
To recognize an outstanding article published in the *Journal of the European Economic Association*. Awarded annually.

4072 ■ European Hotel Managers Association
Peter Bierwirth, Pres.
Hotel Quirinale
Via Nazionale 7
I-00184 Rome, Italy
Ph: 39 6 4818888
Fax: 39 6 47880826
E-mail: secretariat.ehma@ehma.com
URL: http://www.ehma.com

4073 ■ Hotel Manager of the Year
To recognize managers of European hotels. Awarded annually. Established in 1999.

4074 ■ European Society of Biomechanics
Dr. Gabriele Dubini, Sec. Gen.
Politecnico di Milano
Piazza Leonardo da Vinci, 32
20133 Milan, Italy

Ph: 39 2 23994254
Fax: 39 2 23994286
E-mail: gabriele.dubini@polimi.it
URL: http://www.esbiomech.org

4075 ■ Clinical Biomechanics Award
Recognizes biomechanics research of exceptional clinical relevance. A monetary prize of 1,000 Euros is awarded biennially in even-numbered years.

4076 ■ S. M. Perren Research Award
To recognize the first author of the best scientific paper. An honorarium of 10,000 Swiss francs and an invitation to present a lecture are awarded biennially in even-numbered years. Established in 2002. Formerly: (2002) ESB Research Award.

4077 ■ Poster Award
To stimulate the quality of the poster presentations on biomechanics. Winning posters are selected based on clarity of presentation and scientific quality. A monetary prize of 300 Euros and a certificate are awarded at each biannual congress of the ESB.

4078 ■ Student Award
Recognizes biomechanics research of research students. A monetary award of 1,000 Euros for first place and 250 Euros for runner-up are awarded biennially in even-numbered years. Established in 1998.

4079 ■ Festival dei Popoli - International Review of Social Documentary Film
(Festival dei Popoli - Internazionale del Film di Documentazione Sociale)
Giorgio Bonsanti, Pres.
Borgo Pinti 82 rosso
I-50121 Florence, Italy
Ph: 39 55 244778
Fax: 39 55 241364
E-mail: festivaldeipopoli@festivaldeipopoli.191.it
URL: http://www.festivaldeipopoli.org

4080 ■ Festival dei Popoli
For recognition of outstanding social documentary films dealing with social anthropological, political, and historical topics, as well as art, music, and cinema. Films must be completed in the previous year. The following awards are presented: Best Documentary, Best Research, and Best Anthropological Film. Awarded annually. Established in 1959. Formerly: (1987) Marzocco d'Ora.

4081 ■ Focolare Movement - Italy
(Movimento dei Focolari)
Maria Voce, Pres.
Via di Frascati, 306
I-00040 Rocca di Papa, Italy
Ph: 39 6 947989
Fax: 39 6 9497460
E-mail: sif@focolare.org
URL: http://www.focolare.org

4082 ■ Luminosa Award for Unity
Recognizes outstanding contributions to the cause of unity among religion, ethnic groups, and related organizations. Awarded annually. Established in 1998.

4083 ■ Hot Bird TV Awards
Corso Palladio 114
36100 Vicenza, Italy
Ph: 39 444 543133
Fax: 39 444543466
URL: http://www.hotbirdtvawards.com

4084 ■ Hot Bird TV Awards
To recognize excellence and innovation in thematic satellite television. Presented in the following categories: Children's, Cinema, Culture/ Education, Documentaries, Fiction, HDTV, Lif-

Awards are arranged in alphabetical order below their administering organizations

estyle, Music, National Window, News, and Sports. Awarded annually. Established in 1998.

4085 ■ International Balzan Prize Foundation (Fondazione Internazionale Balzan)
Bruno Bottai, Chm.
Piazzetta Umberto Giordano 4
I-20122 Milan, Italy
Ph: 39 2 7600 2212
Fax: 39 2 7600 9457
E-mail: balzan@balzan.it
URL: http://www.balzan.org

4086 ■ Balzan Prizes (Premio Balzan)
These, Italy's most prestigious academic awards, are given to promote the most deserving humanitarian and cultural works throughout the world, regardless of nationality, race, or religion. Four prizes are awarded: two in literature, moral sciences, and the arts, and two in the physical, mathematical, and natural sciences and medicine. At intervals of not less than three years, the Foundation also awards a prize for Humanity, Peace, and Brotherhood among Peoples. Awarded annually. Established in 1961 by Eugenio Balzan.

4087 ■ International Centre for the Study of the Preservation and Restoration of Cultural Property (Centre international d'etudes pour la conservation et la restauration des biens culturels)
Dr. Mounir Bouchenaki, Dir. Gen.
Via di San Michele 13
I-00153 Rome, Italy
Ph: 39 6 585 531
Fax: 39 6 585 53349
E-mail: iccrom@iccrom.org
URL: http://www.iccrom.org

4088 ■ ICCROM Award
For recognition of a person with exceptional talent in the field of preservation, protection, and restoration of cultural property who has contributed in an exceptional way to the development of ICCROM. The ICCROM Council makes nominations. A bronze sculpture by Peter Rockwell and a citation are awarded biennially at the General Assembly in November. Established in 1979.

4089 ■ Media Save Art Award
An international press competition for articles dealing with the preservation of cultural heritage. The competition is held every two years and is open to journalists worldwide. The award and cash prizes are presented at the ICCROM General Assembly.

4090 ■ International Committee for Animal Recording (Comite International pour le Controle des Performances en Elevage)
Mr. Andrea Rosati, Sec. Gen.
Via Tomasetti 3-1/A
00161 Rome, Italy
Ph: 39 6 44202639
Fax: 39 6 44266798
E-mail: icar@icar.org
URL: http://www.icar.org

4091 ■ Distinguished Certificate Award
To recognize volunteer service to the Committee. Awarded to outstanding members of Sub-Committees and Working Groups upon completion of their terms in office. Awarded annually. Established in 2009.

4092 ■ Distinguished Service Award
For outgoing chairmen of the Committee's Working Groups, Task Forces, and Sub-Committees. Awarded annually. Established in 2006.

4093 ■ President Award
Recognizes an industry professional for outstanding expertise in research. Awarded annually. Established in 2006.

4094 ■ International Federation of Beekeepers' Associations (Federation Internationale des Associations Apicoles)
Mr. Riccardo Jannoni-Sebastianini, Sec. Gen.
Corso Vittorio Emanuele 101
I-00186 Rome, Italy
Ph: 39 6 6852286
Fax: 39 6 6852287
E-mail: apimondia@mclink.it
URL: http://www.apimondia.org

4095 ■ International Federation of Beekeepers' Associations Medals
To recognize national beekeepers associations, and to encourage the dissemination of information regarding new techniques, the results of scientific research, and economic developments in beekeeping. The Federation sponsors competitions, conducts symposia, and bestows awards on occasion of the biennial International Apicultural Congress in odd-numbered years.

4096 ■ International Federation of Clinical Chemistry and Laboratory Medicine (Federation Internationale de Chimie Clinique)
Graham Beastall, Pres.
Via Carlo Farini 81
I-20159 Milan, Italy
Ph: 39 2 66809912
Fax: 39 2 60781846
E-mail: ifcc@ifcc.org
URL: http://www.ifcc.org

4097 ■ Abbott Award for Significant Contributions to Molecular Diagnostics
To recognize an individual for unique contributions to the application of molecular biology in clinical chemistry and laboratory medicine. Awarded annually. Established in 2002. Sponsored by Abbott Diagnostics.

4098 ■ Award for Distinguished Contributions in Education
Recognizes an individual for outstanding contributions to developing and establishing educational materials for clinical chemistry and laboratory medicine. Awarded triennially. Established in 1999. Sponsored by Beckman Coulter.

4099 ■ Distinguished Award for Laboratory Medicine and Patient Care
To recognize an individual for contributions to Laboratory medicine, especially its application to improving patient care and impacting clinical medicine. Sponsored by Ortho Diagnostics. Awarded triennially. Established in 2008.

4100 ■ Distinguished Clinical Chemist Award
Recognizes an individual for outstanding contributions to clinical chemistry and laboratory medicine or the application of chemistry to the understanding/solution of medical problems. Awarded triennially. Established in 1969. Sponsored by Bayer Diagnostics.

4101 ■ Henry Wishinsky Award for Distinguished International Service
To recognize an individual for unique contributions to the promotion and understanding of clinical chemistry and laboratory medicine on an international level. Awarded triennially. Established in 1981 in honor of distinguished international scientist, Henry Wishinsky. Sponsored by Bayer Diagnostics.

4102 ■ International Federation of Sports Medicine (Federation Internationale de Medecine du Sport)
Prof. Fabio Pigozzi MD, Pres.
University of Rome "Foro Italico"
Department of Health Sciences

Piazza Lauro de Bosis, 15
00135 Rome, Italy
Ph: 39 6 36733569
Ph: 39 6 36733597
Fax: 39 6 36733351
E-mail: fabio.pigozzi@uniroma4.it
URL: http://www.fims.org

4103 ■ Bronze Medal
To recognize individuals who have contributed to the work of the Federation in the past. Awarded when merited. Established in 1978.

4104 ■ Citation of Honor
To recognize an individual who has made outstanding contributions to sports medicine in one or more of the following categories: research; scholarly activity and publication; medical care of athletes; regional and/or national leadership; and service to the Federation. Awarded when merited. Established in 1993.

4105 ■ Gold Medal
To recognize outstanding contributions to sports medicine over a period of years in leadership, education, research and practice. Nominations may be made by the Executive Committee to the Council of Delegates. A gold medal is presented biennially when the Council of Delegates meets. Established in 1932.

4106 ■ International Society for Applied Phycology
Roberto de Philippis, Sec.-Treas.
Piazzale delle Cascine 24
Dipartimento di Biotecnologie Agrarie
Universita degli Studi di Firenze
I-50144 Florence, Italy
Ph: 39 055 3288 284
Fax: 39 055 3288 272
E-mail: roberto.dephilippis@unifi.it
URL: http://www.appliedphycologysoc.org

4107 ■ Honorary Membership
To recognize a scientist for continuous and outstanding contributions to the field of applied phycology. Awarded annually, if merited. Established in 2002.

4108 ■ International Society of Hypnosis
Via Tagliamento, 25
I-00198 Rome, Italy
Ph: 39 06 854 8205
Fax: 39 06 854 8205
E-mail: contact@ish-hypnosis.org
URL: http://www.ish-hypnosis.org

4109 ■ Benjamin Franklin Gold Medal
To recognize a member for a distinguished life career in promoting hypnosis worldwide, both clinically and experimentally. A gold medal is awarded triennially. Established in 1976.

4110 ■ Jay Haley Early Career Award for Innovative Contributions
To recognize an individual early in his or her career whose writing, teaching, leadership, and clinical/scientific work have shown substantive advances in the understanding and practice of hypnosis. Awarded annually, if merited. Established in 2009.

4111 ■ Ernest R. Hilgard Award for Scientific Excellence
To recognize an individual whose lifetime of published experimental work substantially advances the understanding of the process of hypnosis and the ability to predict the outcome of its applications. Awarded annually, if merited. Established in 1997.

4112 ■ Pierre Janet Award for Clinical Excellence
To recognize an individual whose lifetime of published clinical experience substantially advances the understanding of the uses of hypnosis in obtaining effective results in clinical practice. Awarded annually, if merited. Established in 1997.

Awards are arranged in alphabetical order below their administering organizations

4113 ■ Kay F. Thompson Award for Clinical Excellence in Dentistry
To recognize an individual whose lifetime of demonstrated clinical experience substantially advances the understanding of the uses of hypnosis in obtaining effective results in dental practice. Awarded annually, if merited. Established in 2009.

4114 ■ Istituto Nazionale di Studi Romani
Prof. Paolo Sommella, Pres.
Piazza dei Cavalieri di Malta 2
I-00153 Rome, Italy
Ph: 39 6 5743 442
Fax: 39 6 5743 447
E-mail: studiromani@studiromani.it
URL: http://www.studiromani.it

4115 ■ Certamen Capitolinum
To provide recognition for the best works on the Latin language and literature. Teachers, scholars, and students are eligible. The competition is held annually. Established in 1950.

4116 ■ Istituto Paolo VI: International Centre for Study and Documentation
(Istituto Paolo VI: Centro Internazionale di Studi e Documentazione)
Dr. Giuseppe Camadini, Pres.
Via Guglielmo Marconi, 15
I-25062 Brescia, Italy
Ph: 39 30 3756468
Ph: 39 30 2807336
Fax: 39 30 46597
E-mail: info@istitutopaolovi.it
URL: http://www.istitutopaolovi.it/index.asp

4117 ■ International Paul VI Prize
Presented for contributions to religious research. Awarded periodically.

4118 ■ Italian Association for Metallurgy
(Associazione Italiana di Metallurgia)
Piazzale R. Morandi 2
I-20121 Milan, Italy
Ph: 39 2 76021132
Ph: 39 2 76397770
Fax: 39 2 76020551
E-mail: aim@aimnet.it
URL: http://www.metallurgia-italiana.net

4119 ■ Aldo Dacco Award
To recognize the best paper dealing with the various techniques used in ferrous and nonferrous foundries.

4120 ■ Felice de Carli Award
To recognize outstanding students in metallurgy. New graduates in the last year of study are eligible.

4121 ■ Gold Medal
(Medaglia d'Oro)
To recognize outstanding contributions to the field of metallurgy.

4122 ■ Italian Association for Metallurgy Awards
To recognize individuals for contributions to materials science and technology that promote progress in traditional and advanced metallurgy. Awards are given biennially.

4123 ■ Eugenio Lubatti Award
To recognize the best paper dealing with electrothermic processes.

4124 ■ Italian Chemical Society
(Societa Chimica Italiana)
Prof. Vincenzo Barone, Pres.
Viale Liegi 48c
I-00198 Rome, Italy
Ph: 39 6 8549691
Ph: 39 6 8553968
Fax: 39 6 8548734
E-mail: soc.chim.it@agora.it

URL: http://www.soc.chim.it

4125 ■ Medaglia Stanislao Cannizzaro
For recognition in the field of chemistry. A medal is awarded at the National Congress of the Societa Chimica Italiana. Awarded triennially. Established in 1956.

4126 ■ Medaglia d'oro Domenico Marotta
Recognizes distinguished persons for their achievements in the field of chemistry and in promoting chemistry. A medal is awarded triennially at the Society's national congress. Established in 1962.

4127 ■ Medaglia d'oro Giulio Natta
Recognizes distinguished researchers for their achievements in the field of chemistry. A medal is awarded triennially at the Society's national congress. Established in 1991.

4128 ■ Medaglia Emanuele Paterno
For recognition of outstanding achievement in chemistry. A medal is awarded in occasion of a national congress of the Societa Chimica Italiana. Awarded triennially. Established in 1923.

4129 ■ Italian Geological Society
(Societa Geologica Italiana)
Prof. Carlo Doglioni, Pres.
Piazzale Aldo Moro 5
I-00185 Rome, Italy
Ph: 39 6 4959390
Fax: 39 6 49914154
E-mail: info@socgeol.it
URL: http://www.socgeol.it

4130 ■ Premio Giorgio Dal Piaz
For recognition in the field of geology. Awarded biennially.

4131 ■ Italian Institute of Packaging
(Istituto Italiano Imballaggio)
Ms. Alessandra Alessi, PR and Communication Mgr.
via Cosimo del Fante 10
I-20122 Milan, Italy
Ph: 39 2 58319624
Fax: 39 2 58319677
E-mail: istituto@istitutoimballaggio.it
URL: http://www.istitutoimballaggio.it

4132 ■ Oscar dell'imballaggio Award
To recognize the best packaging produced or used in Italy. Presented in several categories, including food and pet food, communication products, chemicals and household products, liquid food and drink, and pharmaceuticals, cosmetics, and personal care. Awarded annually.

4133 ■ T.I.L.L. Photonics Technology Award
For young researchers under 35 years of age.

4134 ■ Italian Mathematical Union
(Unione Matematica Italiana)
Franco Brezzi, Pres.
Piazza Porta San Donato, 5
40126 Bologna, Italy
Ph: 39 51 243190
Fax: 39 51 4214169
E-mail: umi@dm.unibo.it
URL: http://umi.dm.unibo.it

4135 ■ Premio Giuseppe Bartolozzi
For recognition of achievement in the field of mathematics. Italian citizens under 33 years of age must apply or be nominated. A monetary prize of 1,500 Euros is awarded biennially in odd-numbered years. Established in 1969 in honor of the Giuseppe Bartolozzi family.

4136 ■ Premio Renato Caccioppoli
For recognition of achievement in the field of mathematics. Italian citizens under 38 years of age must apply or be nominated. A monetary prize of 10,000 Euros is awarded every four years. Established in 1960 in honor of Renato Caccioppoli's brother.

4137 ■ Premio Franco Tricerri
For recognition of achievement in the field of differential geometry. A monetary prize of 1,000 Euros is awarded biennially in odd-numbered years. Established in 1995.

4138 ■ Italian PEN Club
(PEN Club Italiano)
Lucio Lami, Pres.
Via Daverio 7
I-20122 Milan, Italy
Ph: 39 2 3357350966
Fax: 39 2 363350654
E-mail: segreteria@penclub.it
URL: http://www.penclub.it
Formerly: PEN Club Italiano.

4139 ■ Italian PEN Prize
To recognize the poem, novel, or essay voted by Italian PEN members as most outstanding. A monetary prize is awarded in the medieval village of Campiano (Parma) in September. Established in 1991.

4140 ■ Italian Society of Pharmacology
(Societa Italiana di Farmacologia)
Carlo Riccardi, Pres.
Viale Abruzzi 32
I-20131 Milan, Italy
Ph: 39 2 29520311
Fax: 39 2 29520179
E-mail: sifcese@comm2000.it
URL: http://www.sifweb.org
Formerly: Italian Pharmacological Society.

4141 ■ Farmindustria Awards for Pharmacological Research
(Premi SIF Farmindustria)
To recognize young society members (maximum of 35 years old) for research in pharmacology. Awarded to one or more recipients annually. Established in 2002.

4142 ■ North American Academy of Liturgy
Dr. Donald LaSalle, Sec.
Curia Generalizia dei Monfortani
Viale dei Monfortani, 65
00135 Rome, Italy
E-mail: donlasalle@fastmail.fm
URL: http://www.naal-liturgy.org

4143 ■ Berakah Award
To recognize distinguished contributions by members to the study and the renewal of the liturgy. Nominations from the membership are accepted. A framed parchment with a text indicating the awardee's contribution to the liturgy is presented annually. Established in 1976. The name of the award, "Berakah," is the Hebrew word for blessing, or a prayer of blessing.

4144 ■ Diekmann Award
To recognize an individual who have made a contribution to the liturgical life of the world. Recipients are typically not members of the Academy. Awarded periodically. Established in 2003 in memory of Benedictine Father Godfrey Diekmann of Saint John's Abbey in Collegeville Minnesota.

4145 ■ Organization for the Phyto-Taxonomic Investigation of the Mediterranean Area
(Organisation pour l'Etude Phyto-Taxonomique de la Region Mediterraneenne)
Werner Greuter, Sec.
via Lincoln, 2/A
90123 Palermo, Italy
Ph: 39 91 23891209
Fax: 39 91 6238203
E-mail: secr@optima-bot.org
URL: http://www.optima-bot.org

4146 ■ OPTIMA Gold Medal
For recognition of an outstanding contribution to the phytotaxonomy of the Mediterranean area.

Awards are arranged in alphabetical order below their administering organizations

Individuals must not be members of the OPTIMA Prize Commission to be eligible for the award. A medal is awarded triennially, at the OPTIMA meetings. Established in 1977.

4147 ■ OPTIMA Silver Medal
For recognition of the authors of the best papers or books on the phytotaxonomy of the Mediterranean area, published in the three years preceding the award. Individuals must not be current members of the OPTIMA Prize Commission or the OPTIMA International Board to be eligible for the award. Medals are awarded triennially at the OPTIMA meetings. Established in 1977.

4148 ■ Pezcoller Foundation
(Fondazione Pezcoller)
Marco Clerici, Sci. Dir.
Via Dordi 8
I-38100 Trento, Italy
Ph: 39 461 980250
Fax: 39 461 980350
E-mail: pezcoller@pezcoller.it
URL: http://www.pezcoller.it

4149 ■ AACR-Pezcoller International Award for Cancer Research
Recognizes a scientist: who has made a major scientific discovery in basic cancer research or who has made significant contributions to translational cancer research; who continues to be active in cancer research and has a record of recent, noteworthy publications; and whose ongoing work holds promise for continued substantive contributions to progress in the field of cancer who has made a major scientific discovery in the field of cancer. A grant of 75,000 Euros is awarded annually. Established in 1997. Co-sponsored by the American Association for Cancer Research (AACR).

4150 ■ Concorso Internazionale di Chitarra Classica Michele Pittaluga Premio Citta' di Alessandria
Piazza Garibaldi 16
I-15100 Alessandria, Italy
Ph: 39 131 235507
Fax: 39 131 251207
E-mail: concorso@pittaluga.org
URL: http://www.pittaluga.org

4151 ■ Michele Pittaluga International Classical Guitar Competition - City of Alessandria Award
(Concorso Internazionale di Chitarra Classica Michele Pittaluga Premio Citta' di Alessandria)
For recognition of outstanding performance on the classical guitar. Soloists of any nationality under 30 years of age are eligible. First place receives 13,000 Euros, a concert tour in Italy and other countries, and a silver plaque. Second prize is 4,500 Euros and a silver plaque. Third prize is 2,500 Euros and a silver plaque. Held annually in September. Established in 1968.

4152 ■ Sondrio Festival, the International Festival of Documentary Films on Parks
(Comune di Sondrio Mostra Internazionale dei Documentari sui Parchi)
Via Perego 1
I-23100 Sondrio, Italy
Ph: 39 342 526260
Fax: 39 342 526437
E-mail: info@sondriofestival.it
URL: http://www.sondriofestival.it

4153 ■ Sondrio International Documentary Film Festival on Parks
(Mostra Internazionale die Documentari Sui Parchi)
To recognize the makers of documentary films on national parks, national reserves, and other protected areas. Films should focus on the ethnographic, naturalistic, and management aspects of parks. Prizes include: First prize/Town

of Sondrio Award - 5,000 Euros; Stelvio National Park Award - 3,000 Euros; and Lombardy Region Special Award - 3,000 Euros. Other special prizes may also be awarded.

4154 ■ Strega Alberti Benevento SpA
Piazza Vittoria Colonna, 8
I-82100 Benevento, Italy
Ph: 39 824 54292
Fax: 39 824 21007
E-mail: info@strega.it
URL: http://www.strega.it

4155 ■ Strega Prize
To recognize an Italian novel published during the preceding year. The winner is selected by a grand jury of approximately 400 persons. A monetary prize is awarded annually at the Villa Giulia, one of the most fascinating buildings of the Rome Renaissance. Established in 1947 by the Strega liquor producer, Guido Alberti, and the Italian writers, Goffredo and Maria Bellonci.

4156 ■ Teatro Municipale Valli
(Fondazione I Teatri)
Piazza Martiri del 7 Luglio, no. 7
I-42100 Reggio Emilia, Italy
Ph: 39 522 458811
Fax: 39 522 458922
E-mail: uffstampa@iteatri.re.it
URL: http://www.iteatri.re.it

4157 ■ Premio Paolo Borciani - International String Quartet Competition (Concorso Internazionale per Quartetto d'Archi)
To recognize outstanding string quartets of any nationality. Individual members must be 35 years of age or younger; the total age of the ensemble must not exceed 120 years. First place receives the Premio Paolo Borciani, 20,000 Euros, and contracts for international tours; finalists receive 6,000 Euros. Additionally, a Special Prize of 2,500 Euros and the Public's Prize of 1,000 Euros are presented. Held annually. Established in 1987.

4158 ■ TWAS, The Academy of Sciences for the Developing World
Prof. Romain Murenzi, Exec. Dir.
Strada Costierra 11
I-34151 Trieste, Italy
Ph: 39 40 2240327
Fax: 39 40 224559
E-mail: info@twas.org
URL: http://www.twas.org

4159 ■ Ernesto Illy Trieste Science Prize
To recognize scientists from developing countries who have made outstanding contributions to sustainability science. Awarded annually, the prize rotates among various fields of science, such as climate change, renewable energies, materials science, and human health. A medal and monetary prize of US$100,000 are awarded annually. Established in 2005.

4160 ■ Medal Lecturers
To recognize members for their achievements in their fields of scientific research. A plaque and invitation to present a lecture are awarded annually to three recipients. Established in 1996.

4161 ■ C.N.R. Rao Prize for Scientific Research
To honor a distinguished scientist from the developing world, especially from the world's scientifically and technologically lagging countries. A monetary prize of US$5,000 is awarded every three years. Established in honor of the Academy's Founding Fellow and former president.

4162 ■ Abdus Salam Medal for Science and Technology
To recognize highly distinguished personalities

who have served the cause of science in the Third World. Awarded annually, if merited. Established in 1995 in honor of the Academy's founder and first president.

4163 ■ TWAS-AAS-Microsoft Award for Young Scientists
To recognize young scientists in Africa whose research in computer sciences promises to have a positive impact in the developing world. Each year, three winners are selected from different countries on the African continent. Each recipient is awarded a cash prize of 7,000 Euros, contributed by Microsoft Corp. Co-sponsored by the African Academy of Sciences (AAS).

4164 ■ TWAS Prizes
To honor individual scientists who have been working and living in a developing country for at least 10 years. Presented in the following eight fields of science: agricultural sciences, biology, chemistry, earth sciences, engineering sciences, mathematics, medical sciences, and physics. A monetary prize of US$15,000 is awarded to one recipient in each branch of science annually. Established in 1985.

4165 ■ UNESCO Regional Bureau for Science and Culture in Europe
Mr. Engelbert Ruoss, Dir.
Palazzo Zorzi
Castello 4930
30122 Venice, Italy
Ph: 39 41 2601511
Fax: 39 41 5289995
E-mail: veniceoffice@unesco.org
URL: http://www.unesco.org/venice

4166 ■ BICI-UNESCO (ROSTE)
For PhD students and young researchers mainly from Eastern European countries to participate in BICI scientific educational meetings.

4167 ■ SMI-UNESCO (ROSTE)
For students attending graduate courses in Mathematics at the Scuola Normale Superiore Cortona and at the University of Perugia Italy.

4168 ■ Villa I Tatti
Harvard University Center for Italian Renaissance Studies
Joseph Connors, Dir.
Via di Vincigliata 26
I-50135 Florence, Italy
Ph: 39 55 603251
Fax: 39 55 603383
E-mail: info@itatti.it
URL: http://www.itatti.it

4169 ■ I Tatti Fellowships
To provide fellowships for post-doctoral scholars doing advanced research in any aspect of the Italian Renaissance. These are normally reserved for scholars in the early stages of their career. Candidates of any nationality are eligible to apply by October 15. Each Fellow is offered a place to study, use of the Biblioteca and Fototeca Berenson, lunches on weekdays, various other privileges of membership in the I Tatti community, and an opportunity to meet scholars from various countries working in related fields. Awarded annually.

4170 ■ Mellon Research Fellowship
To support Czech, Hungarian, Polish, Slovak, Bulgarian, Romanian, Estonian, Latvian, and Lithuanian post-doctoral scholars. The fellowship carries an award of $5,000 per month plus a one-time supplement toward transportation expenses. Awarded annually.

4171 ■ Craig Hugh Smyth Visiting Fellowship
To support students engaged in some aspect of Italian Renaissance studies who hold demanding positions that permit little time for research.

Awards are arranged in alphabetical order below their administering organizations

Fellowships are awarded in two categories: Museum and Library Professionals, and Mothers. Up to three fellowships for residence at Villa I Tatti for periods up to three months are offered each year.

Jamaica

4172 ■ Institute of Jamaica
African-Caribbean Institute of Jamaica/
Jamaica Memory Bank
Bernard Jankee, Dir.
12 Ocean Blvd.
Kingston, Jamaica
Ph: 876922-4793
Fax: 876924-9361
E-mail: acij@cwjamaica.com
URL: http://www.instituteofjamaica.org.jm/ACIJ/acij.aspx

4173 ■ Musgrave Medals
This, Jamaica's highest cultural honor, is awarded for recognition of achievement in the fields of art, science, and literature. Gold, silver, and bronze medals are awarded to one or more recipients annually. Established in 1889 in memory of Sir Anthony Musgrave, former Governor of Jamaica who founded the Institute of Jamaica in 1879.

4174 ■ Jamaica Exporters Association
Jean Smith, Gen. Mgr.
1 Winchester Rd.
Kingston 10, Jamaica
Ph: 876968-5812
Ph: 876960-4908
Fax: 876960-9869
E-mail: jea@exportja.org
URL: http://www.exportjamaica.org

4175 ■ Champion Exporter
To recognize a Jamaican company excelling at exporting. Awarded annually.

4176 ■ Champion Manufacturer
To recognize a Jamaican manufacturer for successful export sales. Awarded annually.

4177 ■ Jamaica Hotel and Tourist Association
Wayne Cummings, Pres.
2 Ardenne Rd.
Kingston 10, Jamaica
Ph: 876926-3635
Ph: 876920-3482
Fax: 876929-1054
E-mail: info@jhta.org
URL: http://www.jhta.org

4178 ■ Hotel Worker of the Year
To honor a Jamaican hotel worker for performance during the previous calendar year, as well as his or her overall service record both in the tourist industry and in his/her local community. Awarded annually.

4179 ■ Hotelier of the Year
To honor a Jamaican hotelier for demonstrated achievements in hotel operations in the previous year, as well as achievements in community affairs. Candidates may be owners/operators; hotel general managers/managing directors; and owners of hotels. Awarded annually.

4180 ■ Abe Issa Award for Excellence
To honor individuals, groups, and entities who have contributed significantly to the tourism industry by promoting the reputation and image of Jamaica as a tourist destination. Awarded annually.

4181 ■ Local Transportation Company of the Year
For the best provider of local transportation services. Part of the Allied Member Services Awards. Awarded annually.

4182 ■ Jamaica Manufacturers' Association
Mr. Omar Azan, Pres.
85a Duke St.
Kingston, Jamaica
Ph: 876922-8880
Ph: 876922-8869
Fax: 876922-9205
E-mail: jma@cwjamaica.com
URL: http://www.jma.com.jm

4183 ■ Best Environmental Management Program Award
To recognize a Jamaican manufacturing company for environmental awareness and reduction of environmental impact in the manufacturing process. Awarded annually.

4184 ■ Breakthrough Product of the Year
To recognize a new Jamaican product based on number of products manufactured and number of products sold. Awarded annually.

4185 ■ Champion Exporter Award
To recognize a Jamaican manufacturing company for outstanding achievements in export. Awarded annually.

4186 ■ Ray Hadeed Award for Best Small and Medium-Sized Enterprise
To recognize the most outstanding Jamaican manufacturing company with 50 or fewer employees. Awarded annually.

4187 ■ Manufacturer of the Year
To recognize the Jamaican manufacturing company for outstanding achievements during the year. Awarded annually.

4188 ■ Ministry of Industry, Investment and Commerce Award for Competitiveness
To recognize a Jamaican manufacturing company for success in innovation and competition. Awarded annually.

4189 ■ New Manufacturer of the Year
To recognize the most outstanding Jamaican company that has been in existence for less than six years. Awarded annually.

4190 ■ Product Group Award
To recognize a Jamaican manufacturing company for value of production and capital over the previous three years. Awarded annually.

4191 ■ Skills and Productivity Award
To recognize a Jamaican manufacturing company for achievements in productivity and the nurturing of skills of employees. Awarded annually.

4192 ■ Jamaica Teachers' Association
Michael Stewart, Pres.
97 Church St.
Kingston, Jamaica
Ph: 876922-1385
Ph: 876922-1386
Fax: 876922-3257
URL: http://www.jamaicateachers.org.jm

4193 ■ Golden Torch Award
To recognize Jamaican teachers in the public and private educational systems with 35 years or more of service. Awarded annually.

4194 ■ Ben Hawthorne Award
To recognize members who have given a minimum of 20 years distinguished service to education in Jamaica, to the Association, and to the community. Awarded annually to one male and one female.

4195 ■ Edith-Dalton James Award
To recognize members with at least 25 years of service to education in Jamaica and who have been members of the JTA for a minimum of 20 years. Awarded annually.

4196 ■ Roll of Honour Award
This, the most prestigious award given by the Association, recognizes outstanding service to the Association, to education, and to the national and international communities. Awarded annually.

4197 ■ R.C. Tavares Award
To recognize members who are younger than 40 years old and have been teachers for at least 10 years. Awarded annually.

4198 ■ Private Sector Organisation of Jamaica
Mr. Joseph Matalon, Pres.
39 Hope Rd.
Kingston 10, Jamaica
Ph: 876927-6957
Ph: 876978-6795
Fax: 876927-5137
E-mail: psojinfo@psoj.org
URL: http://www.psoj.org

4199 ■ Job Creation Awards
To recognize companies that contribute to the economy of Jamaica through the creation of sustainable jobs. The Job Creation Award recognizes companies or entrepreneurs who have made new investments within the last 12 months and have created at least 25 new employment opportunities. The Small Business Award recognizes companies that have created at least five jobs in the last year. The Award for Companies in Operation for Over 40 Years honors companies that have created jobs over a sustained period. Awarded annually. Established in 2002. Sponsored by Cable and Wireless (Jamaica) Ltd. and National Commercial Bank of Jamaica Ltd.

4200 ■ Private Sector Hall of Fame
Recognizes outstanding contribution to the development of private sectors as well as the nation. Awarded annually. Established in 1992.

4201 ■ Recording Industry Association of Jamaica
Frankie Campbell, Acting Chm.
16a Worthington Terr.
Kingston 5, Jamaica
Ph: 876906-0953
Fax: 876929-9688
E-mail: info@riajamaica.com
URL: http://www.riaa.com

4202 ■ Reggae Academy Awards
To recognize outstanding contributions to reggae music. Awards are presented in various categories, including best song, best solo vocal performance, best album, best instrumental recording, and best dancehall vocal. In addition, the Reggae Trailblazer Award, Reggae Legend Award, and Reggae Icon Award may be presented. Awarded annually.

4203 ■ World Federation of Consuls
3 Brompton Rd.
Kingston KGN5, Jamaica
Ph: 876946-1005
Fax: 876927-6978
E-mail: secretariat@ficacworld.org
URL: http://www.ficacworld.org

4204 ■ Gold Star and Citation
To honor distinguished world leaders. Awarded only when merited.

Japan

4205 ■ The Asahi Glass Foundation
Hiromichi Seya, Chm.
Science Plaza, 2nd Fl.
5-3, Yonbancho

Awards are arranged in alphabetical order below their administering organizations

Chiyoda-ku
Tokyo 102-0081, Japan
Ph: 81 3 5275 0620
Fax: 81 3 5275 0871
E-mail: post@af-info.or.jp
URL: http://www.af-info.or.jp

4206 ■ Blue Planet Prize
To recognize outstanding environmental contributions by individuals or institutions of any nationality. The award is offered to spur research and activity in global environmental issues. The deadline each year for nomination is October 15. Two monetary awards of ¥50 million each are presented annually. Established in 1992.

4207 ■ Comprehensive Research Grant
To support research in environmentally related projects that will produce comprehensive results. Grants in the range of ¥10 to ¥12 million are awarded annually.

4208 ■ Human and Social Sciences Research Grant
To support research in human and social science that suggests solutions to the serious issues confronting society as it undergoes rapid change. Multiple awards are presented annually.

4209 ■ Natural Science Grants
To recognize and encourage original research in the field of natural science, including chemistry, materials, bioscience, physics, electronics, information, machinery, metallurgy, architecture, and urban engineering. Multiple awards presented annually.

4210 ■ Overseas Research Grant
To support research on topics of specific regional interest. Awarded annually.

4211 ■ Asian-Oceanian Computing Industry Organization
Dr. Wong Say Ho, Sec. Gen.
9th Fl., Nittobo Bldg.
2-8-1 Yaesu, Chuo-ku
Tokyo 104-0028, Japan
Ph: 81 3 62140035
Fax: 81 3 62141123
E-mail: lucas@asocio.org
URL: http://www.asocio.org

4212 ■ ASOCIO IT Award
To honor the contributions made by leading industry or government personalities of Asian/Oceanic countries for their leadership in developing the information technology industry in their economies. Awarded annually. Established in 1995.

4213 ■ Asian Productivity Organization
Ryuichiro Yamazaki, Sec. Gen.
Hirakawa-cho Dai-ichi Seimei Bldg., 2nd Fl.
1-2-10 Hirakawa-cho, Chiyoda-ku
Tokyo 102-0093, Japan
Ph: 81 3 52263920
Fax: 81 3 52263950
E-mail: apo@apo-tokyo.org
URL: http://www.apo-tokyo.org

4214 ■ APO National Awards
To recognize outstanding contributions to the cause of productivity promotion. Established in 1985. Formerly: (1986) APO Special National Award.

4215 ■ APO Regional Awards
To recognize outstanding contributions to the cause of productivity promotion. Established in 1978. Formerly: (1986) APO Award.

4216 ■ Chemical Society of Japan
Prof. Yasuhiro Iwasawa, Pres.
5 Kanda-Surugadai 1-Chome
Chiyoda-ku
Tokyo 101-8307, Japan

Ph: 81 3 32926169
Fax: 81 3 32926317
E-mail: member@chemistry.or.jp
URL: http://www.csj.jp

4217 ■ Award for Chemistry Education
For recognition of a distinguished contribution in the field of chemistry education. Society members are eligible. A plaque and a certificate is presented annually to up to three recipients. Established in 1976.

4218 ■ Award for Technical Achievements
To recognize an individual for a contribution to the improvement/development of devices/instruments/plants for chemistry and the chemical industry. A plaque and a certificate are presented annually to one or more recipients.

4219 ■ Award for Technical Development
For recognition of a distinguished contribution to technological development in the chemical industry. Industries in Japan are eligible. A plaque and a certificate are awarded annually to up to five recipients. Established in 1951.

4220 ■ Award for Young Chemists
To recognize chemists under 35 years of age who have made distinguished contributions in the field of pure and applied chemistry. Society members are eligible. A plaque and a certificate are awarded annually to up to 10 recipients.

4221 ■ Award for Young Chemists in Technical Development
To recognize chemists under 40 years of age who have made distinguished contributions in the field of chemical industry. Society members are eligible. A plaque and a certificate are awarded to one or more recipients annually. Established in 1995.

4222 ■ Award of Merit for Chemistry Education
To recognize teachers who have made a distinguished contribution to chemistry education in specific areas. Society members and members of the Division of Chemical Education are eligible. A plaque and a certificate are presented annually to up to five recipients.

4223 ■ Chemical Society of Japan Award
For recognition of a distinguished contribution in the field of pure and applied chemistry. Society members are eligible. A plaque and certificate is awarded annually to up to six recipients. Established in 1948.

4224 ■ Institute of Electronics, Information and Communication Engineers
Hiroshi Yasuda, Pres.
Kikai-Shinko-Kaikan Bldg.
5-8, Shibakoen 3 chome
Minato-ku
Tokyo 105-0011, Japan
Ph: 81 3 34336691
Ph: 81 3 34336692
Fax: 81 3 34336659
E-mail: member@ieice.org
URL: http://www.ieice.org

4225 ■ Achievement Award
To recognize individuals for fundamental research involving new inventions, theories, experiments, and methods, or for the development or improvement of new devices or methods related to electronic engineering or communications. A certificate, medal, and monetary prize of ¥30,000 are awarded annually.

4226 ■ Best Paper Award
To outstanding authors of papers published in *IEICE Transactions*. A monetary prize of ¥100,000 is awarded annually.

4227 ■ Distinguished Achievement and Contributions Award
For outstanding contribution to the study of electronic engineering. A certificate and medal are awarded annually.

4228 ■ Inose Award
To the author of the most outstanding paper. A certificate, medal, and monetary prize are awarded annually.

4229 ■ Young Researchers' Award
Awarded to promising upcoming scientists and engineers. Candidates must be younger than 33 years old. A monetary prize of ¥50,000 is awarded annually.

4230 ■ International Association for Pattern Recognition
Ms. Linda J. O'Gorman, Sec.-Treas.
Shizuoka University
Dept. of Computer Science
Faculty of Information
3-5-1 Johoku
Hamamatsu 432-8011, Japan
Fax: 81 53 4781499
E-mail: abe@cs.inf.shizuoka.ac.jp
URL: http://www.iapr.org

4231 ■ J.K. Aggarwal Prize
To recognize a young scientist for a substantial contribution to a field that is relevant to the IAPR community and whose research work has had a major impact on the field. Candidates must be under 40 years old. A certificate and monetary prize are awarded biennially in even-numbered years. Established in 2006.

4232 ■ Certificate of Appreciation
To recognize individuals for outstanding contributions to the IAPR. Awarded to one or more recipients biennially in even-numbered years. Established in 1998.

4233 ■ Outstanding Achievement Award
To recognize individuals who have made outstanding contributions to the field of document analysis and recognition in one or more of the following areas: research, training of students, research/industry interaction, and service to the profession. A certificate is awarded biennially in odd-numbered years at the International Conference on Document Analysis and Recognition. Established in 1997.

4234 ■ Young Scientist Award
To recognize individuals who have made outstanding contributions to the field of document analysis and recognition in one or more of the following areas: research, training of students, research/industry interaction, and service to the profession. Candidates must be under 40 years old. A certificate is awarded biennially in odd-numbered years at the International Conference on Document Analysis and Recognition. Established in 1997.

4235 ■ P. Zamperoni Award
To recognize a student for the best paper, based on contribution to the field of pattern recognition, technical soundness, and presentation. Established in honor of Peter Zamperoni, an outstanding educator in pattern recognition. Awarded biennially in even-numbered years. Established in 1996.

4236 ■ International Association of Traffic and Safety Sciences
(Kokusai Kotsu Anzen Gakkai)
Yasuhei Oguchi, Chm.
6-20-2-chome, Yaesu
Chuo-ku
Tokyo 104-0028, Japan
Ph: 81 3 32737884
Fax: 81 3 32727054
E-mail: mail@iatss.or.jp
URL: http://www.iatss.or.jp

4237 ■ Achievement Award
To recognize an individual or organization for an

Awards are arranged in alphabetical order below their administering organizations

outstanding achievement during the previous three years in the development of an ideal mobile society. A plaque is awarded annually. Established in 1974.

4238 ■ International Commission of Agricultural Engineering (Commission Internationale du Genie Rural)

Prof. Toshinori Kimura, Sec. Gen.
Hokkaido University
Research Faculty of Agriculture
Research Group of Bioproduction Engineering
N-9, W-9, Kita-ku, Hokkaido
Sapporo 060-8589, Japan
Ph: 81 11 7063885
Fax: 81 11 7064147
E-mail: cigr_gs2010@bpe.agr.hokudai.ac.jp
URL: http://www.cigr.org

4239 ■ Armand Blanc Prize

To recognize the best paper presented at CIGR Congresses by a young student or agricultural engineer. Citizens of CIGR member countries who are not more than 30 years of age may submit papers on a topic dealing with the Congresses' program. A medal and expenses are awarded every five years on the occasion of each CIGR Congress. Established in 1964 to honor Armand Blanc, Honorary General Director of Agricultural Engineering and Hydraulics, founder-member and former President of CIGR.

4240 ■ E-Journal Prize

To recognize authors who have contributed outstanding papers to the Commission's electronic journals published since the preceding World Congress. Awarded biennially in even-numbered years. First awarded in 2000.

4241 ■ Merit Award

To recognize members who have achieved remarkable works for the Commission. Awarded biennially in even-numbered years. First awarded in 1998.

4242 ■ International Society of Developmental Biologists

Claudio Stern, Pres.
RIKEN Center for Developmental Biology
2-2-3 Minatojima Minamimachi
Chuo-ku
Kobe 650-0047, Japan
Ph: 81 78 3060111
Fax: 81 78 3060101
E-mail: sipp@cdb.riken.jp
URL: http://www.developmental-biology.org

4243 ■ Ross G. Harrison Prize

To recognize scientists whose contributions have significantly advanced the field of developmental biology. Awarded once every four years at a ceremony at the ISDB Congress. Established in 1981.

4244 ■ Medical Student Prize

To honor a report submitted by an undergraduate student on subject related to sexually transmitted diseases, genitourinary medicine, or HIV infection. A monetary prize of £200 is awarded annually.

4245 ■ International Society of Paddy and Water Environment Engineering

c/o Japanese Society of Irrigation, Drainage & Reclamation Eng.
Nogyo-doboku Kaikan
5-34-4 Shinbashi
Minato-ku
Tokyo 105-0004, Japan
Ph: 81 3 3436 3418
Fax: 81 3 3435 8494
E-mail: suido@jsidre.or.jp
URL: http://pawees.net

4246 ■ International Award

To recognize an individual for exceptional and valuable achievements to the advancement of paddy and water environment engineering. Awarded annually to several recipients. Established in 2003.

4247 ■ Paper Award

To recognize the author of an original article of extraordinary significance published during the previous year. Awarded annually to several recipients. Established in 2004.

4248 ■ Reviewer Award

To recognize paper reviewers for excellent reviews that enhance the standard of paddy and water environments. Awarded annually to one or more recipients. Established in 2004.

4249 ■ Iron and Steel Institute of Japan

Akira Kojima, Exec. Dir.
2nd Fl., Niikura Bldg.
2 Kanda-Tsukasacho 2-chome
Chiyoda-ku
Tokyo 101-0048, Japan
Ph: 81 3 52097011
Fax: 81 3 32571110
E-mail: admion@isij.or.jp
URL: http://www.isij.or.jp

4250 ■ Asada Medal

For recognition of an important contribution to interdisciplinary fields of iron and steel. One award is presented annually.

4251 ■ Hattori Prize

For recognition of contributions to the steel industry. Awarded annually.

4252 ■ Honorary Member

To recognize individuals who have contributed to the steel industry of Japan and have honorable fame in the industry. Honorary members are nominated by the council. Awarded annually.

4253 ■ Meritorious Prize for Scientific Achievement

To recognize excellent achievements in scientific and technological research on iron and steel. Three awards are presented each year.

4254 ■ Mishima Medal

For recognition of important inventions and research in the field of cast steel, magnets, heat treatment and metal forming as well as the commercialization of these fields. Three awards are presented annually.

4255 ■ Nishiyama Medal

For recognition of contributions to the steel industry. One award is presented annually.

4256 ■ Satomi Prize

For recognition of important research in metal surface treatment. Open only to ISIJ members and associated researchers. One award is presented annually.

4257 ■ Tawara Gold Medal

To recognize a member, regardless of nationality, who has rendered outstanding contributions to the development of science and technology, and has an internationally established fame. A certificate of merit and a gold medal are awarded.

4258 ■ G. Watanabe Medal

For recognition of contributions to the steel industry. One award is presented annually.

4259 ■ Japan Advertising Agencies Association

Toshiharu Kanesaka, Exec. Dir.
Dentsu Ginza Bldg.
4-17 Ginza, 7-chome
Chuo-Ku
Tokyo 104-0061, Japan
Ph: 81 3 55680876
Fax: 81 3 55680889

E-mail: info@jaaa.ne.jp
URL: http://www.jaaa.ne.jp

4260 ■ Yoshida Hideo Memorial Award

Recognizes a person who contributed to the improvement and development in the advertising industry. Awarded annually. Established in 1964.

4261 ■ Japan Art Association

Mr. Hieda Hisashi, Chm.
1-2 Ueno-park Taito-ku
Tokyo 110-0007, Japan
Ph: 81 3 58326464
Fax: 81 3 58326465
URL: http://www.praemiumimperiale.org/eg/jaahome/home.html

4262 ■ Praemium Imperiale

To honor artistic values and contributions of surpassing importance in the arts beyond the boundaries of nations and races. These international awards are given to anyone in the world in the following areas: sculpture, painting, music, architecture, and theatre and film. Recipients are selected on the basis of recommendations of an appointed panel of advisors. A monetary prize of ¥15 million and a medal are awarded in each category annually. Established in 1988 in memory of His Imperial Highness Prince Takamatsu. The prize reflects Japan's growing global commitment to support of the arts, and is a reminder that a nation's cultural heritage is as precious as its economic accomplishments could ever be.

4263 ■ Japan Association of Adult Orthodontics

Motohiko Sato, Pres.
Shibuya Kurosutawa, 21st Fl.
2-15-1 Shibuya Shibuya-ku
Tokyo 150-0002, Japan
Ph: 81 3 34992222
Fax: 81 3 34992221
E-mail: info@jaao.jp
URL: http://www.jaao.jp

4264 ■ Beautiful E-line Award

To Japanese female who is active and with good tooth alignment, acceptable occlusion, attractive profile, physically and mentally healthy and well-balanced body proportion.

4265 ■ Japan Construction Mechanization Association (Nihon Kensetsu Kikai-ka Kyokai)

Seizo Tsuji, Chm.
ShibaKoen 3-5-8
Minato-ku
Tokyo 105-0011, Japan
Ph: 81 3 34331501
Fax: 81 3 34320289
E-mail: info@jcmanet.or.jp
URL: http://www.jcmanet.or.jp

4266 ■ Chairman's Award

To recognize an individual for outstanding achievements in research, technical development, and practical applications in construction mechanization for Japanese projects. Established in 1988.

4267 ■ Japan Industrial Design Promotion Organization

Kazunori Iizuka, Pres.
Midtown Tower, 5th Fl.
9-7-1, Akasaka
Minato-ku
Tokyo 107-6205, Japan
Ph: 81 3 67433772
Fax: 81 3 67433775
E-mail: f-press@g-mark.org
URL: http://www.jidpo.or.jp

4268 ■ Good Design Award

Recognizes outstanding examples of industrial

Awards are arranged in alphabetical order below their administering organizations

design. The award focuses on industrial products but includes products in a wide variety of fields such as architecture, the environment, communication, and even experimental design in state-of-the-art technical fields and business models that have design at their core. Awarded annually. Established in 1957.

**4269 ■ Japan Newspaper Publishers and Editors Association
(Nihon Shinbun Kyokai)**
Nippon Press Center Bldg.
2-2-1 Uchisaiwai-cho
Chiyoda-ku
Tokyo 100-8543, Japan
E-mail: editor@pressnet.or.jp
URL: http://www.pressnet.or.jp

**4270 ■ Nihon Shinbun Kyokai Awards
(Shinbum Kyokai Sho)**
For recognition of distinguished contributions towards promoting the credibility and authority of newspapers, news agencies, and broadcasting organizations in the eyes of the general public. Members of the Association are eligible. Certificates and medals are given in the following categories: editorial field, management and business field, and technical field. Awarded annually. Established in 1957.

4271 ■ Japan Office of the Prime Minister
Cabinet Public Relations Office
1-6-1 Nagata-cho
Chiyoda-ku
Tokyo 100-8968, Japan
Ph: 81 3 3581 2361
URL: http://www.kantei.go.jp

4272 ■ Order of the Sacred Treasure
To recognize men and women of Japanese or foreign origin who have rendered distinguished services to Japan. This Order is divided into eight classes. A badge and a star are awarded. The design of the Order features the sacred mirror of the Grand Shrine of Ise, surrounded by profuse shafts of light. Established in 1888 by Emperor Meiji.

**4273 ■ Japan Society for the Promotion of Science
(Nihon Gakujutsu Shinko-kai)**
Motoyuki Ono, Pres.
Sumitomo-Ichibancho FS Bldg.
6 Ichibancho
Chiyoda-ku
Tokyo 102-8471, Japan
Ph: 81 3 32631722
Fax: 81 3 32212470
URL: http://www.jsps.go.jp

**4274 ■ International Prize for Biology
(Kokusai Seibutsugaku-sho)**
To recognize an individual for an outstanding contribution to the advancement of research in fundamental biology. The specialty within the field of biology for which the Prize is awarded is decided upon annually. There are no restrictions on the nationality of the recipient. Nominations must be submitted by relevant organizations and authoritative individuals by May 7. A monetary award of ¥10 million, a medal, and an Imperial gift are awarded annually in Tokyo in the autumn. The Prize is normally made to one individual. In the event of a Prize being shared by two or more individuals, each receives a medal and an equal share of the monetary prize. Established in 1985 to celebrate the sixty-year reign of His Majesty the Emperor Showa of Japan and to commemorate the Emperor's longtime devotion to research in biology.

4275 ■ JSPS Prize
To recognize and support young researchers in the fields of the humanities, social sciences, and natural sciences. Candidates must be younger

than 45 years, have obtained a doctorate degree, and be Japanese citizens. Prize money in the amount of 1.1 million yen is awarded annually to approximately 20 recipients. Established in 2004.

**4276 ■ Japan Society of Mechanical Engineers
(Nihon Kikai Gakkai)**
Yochiro Matsumoto, Pres.
Shinanomachi-Rengakan Bldg.
Shinanomachi 35, Shinjuku-ku
Tokyo 160-0016, Japan
Ph: 81 3 53603500
Fax: 81 3 53603508
E-mail: admin@jsme.or.jp
URL: http://www.jsme.or.jp

4277 ■ Education Award
To recognize excellence in the teaching of mechanical engineering. Awarded annually to one or more recipients. Established in 2001.

4278 ■ Excellent Product Award
To recognize outstanding new uses of mechanical engineering. Awarded annually to one or more recipients. Established in 2005.

4279 ■ Medal for Distinguished Engineers
To recognize outstanding Japanese engineers. Awarded annually to one or more recipients.

4280 ■ Medal for New Technology
To recognize individuals and companies for technological innovation. Awarded annually to one or more recipients.

4281 ■ Medal for Outstanding Paper
For recognition of outstanding technical papers and for recognition of achievement in developing new techniques in the field of mechanical engineering. Members are eligible. A medal and certificate of merit are awarded annually at the Plenary Meeting. Established in 1958.

4282 ■ Young Engineers Award
To recognize outstanding young Japanese engineers. Awarded annually to one or more recipients.

4283 ■ Japanese Biochemical Society
Kiyoshi Kita, Pres.
25-16 Hongo 5-chome
Bunkyo-ku
Tokyo 113-0033, Japan
Ph: 81 3 38151913
Fax: 81 3 38151934
E-mail: jb-jbs@jbsoc.or.jp
URL: http://www.jbsoc.or.jp

4284 ■ *JB* Award
To recognize an outstanding article published in the *Journal of Biochemistry*. Awarded annually. Established in 1993.

4285 ■ Young Investigator Awards
To encourage the professional development of young biochemists. Members who are under 40 years of age are eligible. A monetary prize of ¥100,000 and a plaque are awarded annually to one or more recipients in October. Established in 1955 by Professor Soda Tokuro.

4286 ■ Japanese Peptide Society
Prof. Saburo Aimoto, Pres.
4-1-2 Ine
Minoh 562-8686, Japan
Ph: 81 72 7294125
Fax: 81 72 7294165
E-mail: jps@senri-inter.jp
URL: http://www.peptide-soc.jp

4287 ■ Akabori Memorial Award
For contributions to the field of peptides. Recipient will present a lecture at the Society's Symposium. Established in 2000 to honor Dr. Shiro Akabori.

4288 ■ Award for Young Investigator
To recognize a young investigator in the field of peptides. Membership is required. Awarded annually.

4289 ■ JPS Award
For contributions to the Society. Membership is required. Awarded biennially.

4290 ■ Japanese Society of Applied Entomology and Zoology
Dr. Akira Kawai, Pres.
2-28-10 Nakazato
Kita-ku
Tokyo 114-0015, Japan
Ph: 81 3 59800281
Fax: 81 3 59800282
E-mail: aez_sg@naro.affrc.go.jp
URL: http://odokon.org

4291 ■ Society Fellowship Award
For a member who displays remarkable achievement in applied entomology/zoology. Two awards are presented annually.

4292 ■ Young Scientist Award
For a young member (under 40 years old) who displays potential in applied entomology/zoology. One or two awards are presented annually.

4293 ■ Japanese Society of Hypertension
Kazuyuki Shimada, Pres.
3-28-8, Hongo
Bunkyo-ku
Tokyo 113-0033, Japan
Ph: 81 3 68019786
Fax: 81 3 68019787
E-mail: office@jpnsh.org
URL: http://www.jpnsh.org

4294 ■ Novartis Award for Hypertension Research
To honor individuals for outstanding contributions to hypertension research. Awarded annually.

4295 ■ Young Investigators Award
For distinguished researcher under 40 years old.

4296 ■ Min-On Concert Association
Hiroyasu Kobayashi, Pres.
Min-On Culture Ctr.
8 Shinano-machi
Shinjuku-ku
Tokyo 160-8588, Japan
Ph: 81 3 5362 3400
Fax: 81 3 5365 3401
E-mail: publicrelations@min-on.or.jp
URL: http://www.min-on.org

**4297 ■ Tokyo International Music Competition
(Internationaler Musikwettbewerb Tokyo)**
For recognition of outstanding work in the field of music. Open to individuals of any nationality who are between the ages of 18 and 33. The following awards are presented: (1) first place - a monetary award of ¥2 million, a certificate, and medal; (2) second place - ¥1 million, a certificate, and a medal; and (3) third place - ¥500,000, a certificate, and a medal. Held annually. Established in 1966.

4298 ■ Mita Society for Library and Information Science
Kimio Hosono, Chm.
Keio University
2-15-45 Mita
Minato-ku
Tokyo 108-8345, Japan
Ph: 81 3 34534511
Ph: 81 3 34533147
E-mail: mslis@slis.keio.ac.jp
URL: http://wwwsoc.nii.ac.jp/mslis

**4299 ■ Mita Society for Library and Information Science Prize
(Mita Toshokan Joho Gakkai-Sho)**
For recognition of achievement in the field of

Awards are arranged in alphabetical order below their administering organizations

library and information science. Papers published in the *Library and Information Science* are eligible for consideration. A monetary prize is awarded annually at the Society convention. Established in 1977.

4300 ■ National Federation of UNESCO Associations in Japan
(Nihon UNESCO Kyokai Renmei)
Masatake Matsuda, Pres.
Asahi Seimei Ebisu Bldg., 12th Fl.
1-3-1 Ebisu
Shibuya-ku
Tokyo 150-0013, Japan
Ph: 81 3 54241121
Fax: 81 3 54241126
E-mail: nfuaj@unesco.or.jp
URL: http://www.unesco.jp/en

4301 ■ Mitsubishi Asian Children's Enikki Festa
To honor illustrated diaries produced by children ages six to 12 years old, and to promote the teaching of reading and writing for young people throughout the nations of Asia. The following prizes are awarded to one or more recipients from each of 22 nations: Grand Prix, Mitsubishi Public Affairs Committee Award, National Federation of UNESCO Associations in Japan Award, and the Excellence Award. Held triennially. Established in 1990 to mark the United Nations' International Literacy Year. Formerly: (2006) Festival of Asian Children's Art.

4302 ■ UNESCO Japan Fair Play Award

4303 ■ Youth Awards for International Understanding Activities

4304 ■ Niwano Peace Foundation
(Niwano Heiwa Zaidan)
Kinjiro Niwano, Chm.
Shamvilla Catherina, 5th Fl.
1-16-9, Shinjuku
Shinjuku-ku
Tokyo 160-0022, Japan
Ph: 81 3 32264371
Fax: 81 3 32261835
E-mail: info@npf.or.jp
URL: http://www.npf.or.jp

4305 ■ Niwano Peace Prize
To recognize an individual or organization that is making a significant contribution to world peace through promoting inter-religious cooperation. The Foundation solicits nominations from people of recognized intellectual stature around the world. A prize of ¥20 million, a medal, and a certificate are awarded annually. Established in 1983.

4306 ■ Oita Sports Association for the Disabled
Katsusada Hirose, Pres.
3-1-1, Ohte-machi
Oita 870-8501, Japan
E-mail: kurumaisu-marathon@pref.oita.lg.jp
URL: http://www.wheelchair-marathon.com

4307 ■ Oita International Wheelchair Marathon
To encourage people with physical disabilities in Japan and other countries and territories for further social participation, and to deepen citizens' understanding toward persons with disabilities through wheelchair racing. Disabled persons over 16 years of age using a wheelchair may apply by August 31. Trophies are awarded to the top 10 runners, cups to the male and female winners of the total marathon, medals to the top runners of the four classes, and certifi-

cates are awarded to all who complete the course. Awarded annually. Established in 1981 by Hiramatsu Morihiko, Oita Prefectual Governor.

4308 ■ Pharmaceutical Society of Japan
(Nippon Yakugakkai)
Hiromichi Kimura, Chm.
12-15, Shibuya 2-Chome, Shibuya-ku
Tokyo 150-0002, Japan
Fax: 81 3 34981835
E-mail: doi@pharm.or.jp
URL: http://www.pharm.or.jp/index_e.html

4309 ■ Award for Divisional Scientific Contributions
(Nihon Yakugakkai Gakujutsukokensho)
To recognize a contribution to a divisional field of the pharmaceutical sciences. Society members are eligible. A monetary prize and a medal are awarded annually in five divisional fields: chemistry (two awards), physical chemistry, biology, public health, and pharmaceutics. Established in 1994.

4310 ■ Award for Divisional Scientific Promotions
To recognize mid-career researchers in the six divisional fields of pharmaceutical sciences: chemistry (two awards), physical chemistry, biology, public health, and pharmaceutics. Candidates must be no older than 50 years. Awarded annually.

4311 ■ Award for Drug Research and Development
(Nihon Yakugakkai Gijutsusho)
For recognition of achievement in the field of research and development of a new drug (including intermediates of a new drug, diagnostic reagent, etc.). Society members and non-members are eligible. A monetary prize and a medal are awarded annually to one or two recipients. Established in 1987.

4312 ■ Award for Young Scientists
(Nihon Yakugakkai Shoreisho)
To encourage young researchers in all fields of pharmaceutical sciences. Society members aged 38 years or younger are eligible. A monetary prize and a medal are awarded annually to up to eight recipients. Established in 1955.

4313 ■ PSJ Award
(Nihon Yakugakkai sho)
For recognition of achievement in the field of pharmaceutical sciences. Society members are eligible. A monetary prize and a medal are awarded annually to up to four recipients. Established in 1921.

4314 ■ Phytopathological Society of Japan
Tomonori Shiraishi, Pres.
Shokubo Bldg.
1-43-11 Komagome
Toshima-Ku
Tokyo 170-8484, Japan
Ph: 81 3 39436021
Fax: 81 3 39436086
E-mail: byori@juno.ocn.ne.jp
URL: http://www.ppsj.org

4315 ■ Fellow of the Phytopathological Society of Japan
For recognition of achievement in phytopathology, or for contributions to the Society. A monetary award of ¥100,000, a certificate, and a watch are awarded annually. Established in 1953.

4316 ■ Young Scientist Award
To encourage professional development in the field of phytopathology. A monetary award of ¥50,000, a certificate, and a medal are awarded annually. Established in 1953.

4317 ■ Recording Industry Association of Japan
Naoki Kitagawa, Chm./CEO
11 Fl., Kita-Aoyama Yoshikawa Bldg.
2-12-16 Kita-Aoyama

Minato-ku
Tokyo 107-0061, Japan
Ph: 81 3 64060510
Fax: 81 3 64060520
URL: http://www.riaj.or.jp/e

4318 ■ Japan Gold Disk Awards
To honor the artists and their works that had made great contributions in the development of the music recording industry. Awards are given annually in various categories, including Artist of the Year, Single of the Year, Album of the Year, and Traditional Japanese Music Album of the Year. Established in 1987.

4319 ■ Science and Technology Foundation of Japan
Masao Ito, Pres.
Akasaka Twin Tower E, 13th Fl.
2-17-22 Akasaka
Minato-ku
Tokyo 107-0052, Japan
Ph: 81 3 55450551
Fax: 81 3 55450554
E-mail: info@japanprize.jp
URL: http://www.japanprize.jp
Formerly: (1983) Japan Prize Preparatory Foundation.

4320 ■ Japan Prize
This, the most prestigious and honored scientific prize in Japan, is given to recognize scientists and technologists from all parts of the world. It is awarded to persons recognized as having served the cause of peace and prosperity for mankind through original and outstanding achievements in science and technology which have advanced the frontiers of knowledge in these fields. No distinctions are made as to nationality, occupation, race or sex, but only living persons may be named Japan Prize Laureates. Award categories change annually. Two laureates are selected each year. A monetary award of ¥50 million, a medal and a certificate are awarded in April during Japan Prize Week. Established in 1982; first presented in 1985.

4321 ■ Seismological Society of Japan
(Zisin Gakkai)
6-26-12, Hongo, Bunkyo-ku
Tokyo RS Bldg.
Tokyo 113-0033, Japan
Ph: 81 3 58039570
Fax: 81 3 58039577
E-mail: zisin-koho@tokyo.email.ne.jp
URL: http://wwwsoc.nii.ac.jp/ssj

4322 ■ Academic Prize
For an excellent thesis.

4323 ■ Society for Biotechnology, Japan
Shinji Iijima, Pres.
Osaka University
Faculty of Engineering
2-1 Yamadaoka, Suita
Osaka 565-0871, Japan
Ph: 81 6 68762731
Fax: 81 6 68792034
E-mail: info@sbj.or.jp
URL: http://www.sbj.or.jp

4324 ■ Eda Award
To recognize members for contributing to the progress of theory or technology regarding brewing. Awarded annually.

4325 ■ Excellent Paper Award
For several papers published in the *Journal of Bioscience and Bioengineering* that have prominently contributed to the progress of biotechnology. Awarded annually.

4326 ■ Saito Award
To honor young researchers for contributing to the progress of basic studies in the field of biotechnology. Awarded annually.

Awards are arranged in alphabetical order below their administering organizations

4327 ■ Society Award
To honor members for outstanding contributions in the field of biotechnology. Awarded annually.

4328 ■ Technical Award
To members for outstanding contributions to industrial research and development in the field of biotechnology. Awarded annually.

4329 ■ Terui Award
To honor young researchers for contributing to progress in the field of biochemical engineering. Awarded annually.

4330 ■ Young Asian Biotechnologist Prize
To honor young scientists in Asia, other than Japan, who have achieved outstanding accomplishments in the field of biotechnology. Awarded annually.

4331 ■ Suntory Foundation
Suntory Annex 9F
2-1-5, Doujima
Kita-Ku
Osaka 530-8204, Japan
Ph: 81 6 6342 6221
Fax: 81 6 6342 6220
E-mail: sfnd@suntory-foundation.or.jp
URL: http://www.suntory.co.jp/sfnd

4332 ■ Suntory Prize for Community Cultural Activities
To recognize individuals and organizations for outstanding contributions to the cultural life of their communities. Wide-ranging activities intended for the creation or furtherance of local cultures are eligible for this prize, such as arts, literature, publication, succession of traditions, beautification of environment, and even food, shelter, and clothing, as well as international exchange and community activities. Awarded annually. Established in 1979.

4333 ■ Suntory Prize for Social Sciences and Humanities
To recognize pioneering achievements by rising critics and researchers in the following four fields: political science and economics, literary and art criticism, life and society, and history and civilization. The work must have been published in Japanese during the preceding year. Awarded annually. Established in 1979.

4334 ■ Tokyo International Film Festival
Tatsumi Yoda, Chm.
Tsukiji Yasuda Bldg., 5F
2-15-14 Tsukiji
Chuo-ku
Tokyo 104-0045, Japan
Ph: 81 3 3524 1081
Fax: 81 3 3524 1087
E-mail: info@tiff-jp.net
URL: http://www.tiff-jp.net

4335 ■ Tokyo International Film Festival
To promote cultural exchange, friendship, mutual understanding, and cooperation among the nations of the world through films, as well as to raise the motion picture arts and sciences and develop the international film industry. The Festival consists of the following competitive sections: (1) The International Competition; and (2) Young Cinema. Films produced in 35mm or 70mm during the 18 months preceding the Festival that have not won an award at other competitive events may be entered by June 10 in the International Competition. The following prizes are awarded: (1) Tokyo Grand Prix - a statuette sculpted by the late Sebo Kitamura; (2) Special Jury Prize; (3) Best Director; (4) Best Actress; (5) Best Actor; (6) Best Artistic Contribution; and (7) Best Screenplay. Each winner receives a trophy and a diploma. The Young Cinema Festival section is designed to encourage the development of world cinema arts by providing promising young international filmmakers, upon whose cinematic talents the film industries of tomorrow depend, with venues for interchange and competition. Film directors satisfying either one of the following categories are eligible: (a) under 35 years of age and directed no more than five commercially exploited films; or (b) made debut as a film director with this entry film. The international jury of Young Cinema will then judge the winners to receive two awards from those four film candidates: (1) Sakura Gold - for one film, with the prize money of ¥20 million to the director; and (2) Sakura Silver - for one film, with the prize money of ¥10 million to the director. The festival is held biennially in even-numbered years. Established in 1985.

4336 ■ Union of Japanese Scientists and Engineers
Hiromasa Yonekura, Chm.
1-2-1, Koenji-Minami
Suginami-ku
Tokyo 166-0003, Japan
Ph: 81 3 53789812
Fax: 81 3 53781220
E-mail: juse@juse.or.jp
URL: http://www.juse.or.jp

4337 ■ Deming Prizes (Demingu Sho)
This, the most prestigious industrial award in Japan, is given to recognize companies that demonstrate their commitment to quality control. Three awards are presented: the Deming Prize for Individuals, the Deming Application Prize, and the Quality Control Award for Operations Business Units. Monetary prizes are awarded annually. Established in 1951 to recognize Dr. W. Edwards Deming, an American statistician and proponent of quality control techniques.

4338 ■ Japan Quality Medal
To further develop the world of quality control. Awarded annually. Created to commemorate the first International Conference on Quality Control (ICQC), held in October 1969 in Tokyo, and to maintain an up-grade the spirit of the conference long into the future.

4339 ■ Nikkei QC Literature Prize
To recognize outstanding literature on the study of total quality management (TQM) or statistical methods used for TQM. A certificate and monetary prize are awarded annually. Established in 1954. Funded by Nippon Keizai Shimbun.

4340 ■ Waseda University (Waseda Daigaku)
Office of International Exchange
1-104, Totsuka-machi
Shinjuku-ku
Tokyo 169-8050, Japan
Ph: 81 3 3203 4141
Fax: 81 3 3202 8638
E-mail: intl-ac@list.waseda.jp
URL: http://www.waseda.jp

4341 ■ Award for Distinguished Services to Art (Geijyutsu Korosha)
To honor alumni who have made a distinguished contribution to the promotion of art. Individuals must be over 70 to be eligible. A gold medal and honorable mention are awarded when merited. Established in 1982.

4342 ■ Award for Distinguished Services to Sports
To honor alumni over 70 years of age who have made a distinguished contribution to the promotion of sports. Awarded annually. Established in 1982.

4343 ■ Honorary Doctorate
To honor individuals who have achieved distinction in academia, culture, and other fields. Awarded annually to one or more recipients. Established in 1957.

4344 ■ Okuma Academic Commemorative Prize (Okuma Gakujutsu Kinensho)
To recognize faculty members whose research achievements have been recognized as distinguished, and who have greatly contributed to the progress in the field of study. A monetary award of ¥1 million and honorable mention are presented annually. Established in 1958 in memory of Marquis Shigenobu Okuma, founder of the University.

4345 ■ Okuma Academic Encouragement Prize (Okuma Gakujutsu Shoreisho)
To recognize faculty members who have obtained outstanding research results. A monetary award of ¥500,000 plus honorable mention are presented annually. Established in 1958 in memory of Marquis Shigenobu Okuma, founder of the University.

4346 ■ Azusa Ono Memorial Awards for Academic Studies
To recognize students whose dissertations, graduation theses, or seminar reports have been recognized as outstanding in quality. Awarded annually during graduation ceremonies. Established in 1959 in honor of Azusa Ono, co-founder of Waseda University.

4347 ■ Azusa Ono Memorial Awards for Art
To recognize students whose art productions have been recognized as outstanding in quality. Awarded annually during graduation ceremonies. Established in 1959 in honor of Azusa Ono, co-founder of Waseda University.

4348 ■ Azusa Ono Memorial Awards for Sports
To recognize students who have established a world record or the equivalent in various athletic events. Awarded annually during graduation ceremonies. Established in 1959 in honor of Azusa Ono, co-founder of Waseda University.

4349 ■ World Association of Societies of Pathology and Laboratory Medicine
Prof. Masami Murakami, Exec. Dir.
WASPaLM Administrative Office
2F UI Bldg., 2-2 Kanda Ogawa-machi
Chiyoda-ku
Tokyo 101-0052, Japan
Ph: 81 3 32950353
Fax: 81 3 32950352
E-mail: info@waspalm.org
URL: http://www.waspalm.org

4350 ■ Gold-Headed Cane
For recognition of a special contribution to the World Association. The former president of the World Association is ordinarily nominated for this award by the Awards Committee. A gold headed cane and a certificate are awarded when merited at the convention. Established in 1969.

4351 ■ Gordon Signy Foreign Fellowship
To foster cooperation between members, sponsor congresses and conventions, and improve standards in anatomic and clinical pathology by furthering the training of a pathologist from a developing country. Awarded when merited.

4352 ■ World Society for Stereotactic and Functional Neurosurgery - Canada
Takaomi Taira MD, Pres.
Tokyo Women's Medical University
Dept. of Neurosurgery
8-1 Kawada-cho, Shinjuku-ku
Tokyo 162-8666, Japan
Ph: 81 3 33538111
Fax: 81 3 52697599
E-mail: ttaira@nij.twmu.ac.jp
URL: http://www.wssfn.org

4353 ■ Spiegel-Wycis Award
To recognize senior neurosurgeons who,

Awards are arranged in alphabetical order below their administering organizations

throughout their career, have contributed to the advancement of the field of stereotactic and functional neurosurgery. Awarded to one or two scientists every four years. Established in 1977.

Jordan

4354 ■ Amman Filmmakers Cooperative
Zahran St.
PO Box 454
Amman, Jordan
Ph: 962 776 400434
E-mail: jordanianfilms@gmail.com
URL: http://www.jordanfilmfestival.com

4355 ■ Jordan Short Film Festival
To promote intercultural understanding and to advance the cause of independent filmmaking. Open to films from around the world that are no longer than 30 minutes in length. A monetary prize of US$1,000 each is awarded to the best Arab film and the best international film. Held annually. Established in 2005.

4356 ■ Islamic Academy of Sciences
Abdul Salam Majali, Pres.
PO Box 830036
Amman, Jordan
Ph: 962 6 5522104
Ph: 962 6 5523385
Fax: 962 6 5511803
E-mail: secretariat@ias-worldwide.org
URL: http://www.ias-worldwide.org

4357 ■ Ibrahim Memorial Award
To honor an individual for outstanding research in medical field.

4358 ■ Jordan Hotel Association
Jawadat Shasha'a St., Bldg. 9
PO Box 9905
Amman, Jordan
Ph: 962 6 567 7777
Fax: 962 6 567 1692
E-mail: jha@johotels.org
URL: http://www.johotels.org

4359 ■ Tourism Distinction Award
To encourage agencies that have promoted tourism and attracted visitors to the Kingdom of Jordan's wealth of diverse historical, cultural, religious, and natural attractions. Awarded annually. Established in 2009.

4360 ■ MediaScope Ltd.
PO Box 3645
Amman, Jordan
Ph: 962 6 5538 369
Fax: 962 6 5514 943
E-mail: info@mediascope.com.jo
URL: http://www.mediascope.com.jo

4361 ■ Jordan Advertising Awards
To honor the standard of creative excellence in advertising and marketing communications originating in Jordan. Open to all Jordan-based advertising agencies, design houses, production houses, and below-the-line (BTL)/direct marketing companies. Presented in dozens of subcategories within the larger categories of press, outdoor, below-the-line (BTL), Internet, ambient media, radio, and television. Gold, silver, and bronze award are presented annually. Established in 2000.

4362 ■ Jordan Web Awards
To foster the spirit of innovation and creativity among Web designers in Jordan, to raise the standards of Web design and Web sites, to advocate the growth and development of local talent, to promote intellectual property awareness, and to encourage all industries to showcase their Web sites and become more involved in the digital economy. Web sites are judged on

five criteria: concept/creativity, technical/ease of use/navigation, content/structure, visual design solution/aesthetics, and interactivity. Presented in dozens of categories, including airlines, culture, fashion and art, industrial, and sports. Winners represent Jordan in the Pan Arab Web Awards (see separate entry). Awarded annually. Established in 2006.

4363 ■ Abdul Hameed Shoman Foundation
PO Box 940255
Amman, Jordan
Ph: 962 6 4633 627
Fax: 962 6 4633 565
E-mail: ahsf@shoman.org.jo
URL: http://www.shoman.org

4364 ■ Abdul Hameed Shoman Award for Children's Literature
To recognize an individual for contributions toward enhancing the literature for children in order to achieve ongoing innovation and improvement and to promote interest in reading among Arab children. Awarded annually in the following categories: story, poetry, novel, and literary criticism.

4365 ■ Abdul Hameed Shoman Award for Teachers of Science
To recognize science teachers in Jordan's schools for the scientific subjects taught at the elementary and secondary school levels. Awarded biennially. Established in 1982.

4366 ■ Abdul Hameed Shoman Award for Translation
To honor and reward Arab translators for their contributions toward bringing to the readership the books published in scientific, technical, social, and humanities fields. Eligible works are translated into the Arabic language or from the Arabic language to other languages. Open to all Arab translators or to those of Arab descent throughout the world. Awarded annually.

4367 ■ Abdul Hameed Shoman Award for Young Arab Researchers
To promote Arab scientific research and provide incentives to upcoming generations of young Arab scientists. Each year, six scientific fields are selected. Candidates must be Arab citizens or of Arab ancestry, be no more than 45 years of age, and should be working in an Arab country. Awarded annually. Established in 1982.

4368 ■ Abdul Majeed Shoman International Award for Jerusalem
To honor individuals for their lifelong intellectual, academic, literary, or artistic contributions that exhibit originality and excellence, and that genuinely enhance and further the knowledge of Jerusalem in terms of its history, geography, demography, and culture. Granted every two years in one of the following fields on Jerusalem: historical research, research in modern life of the city, creative literary works, and creative artistic works. Established in 1999.

Kenya

4369 ■ African Academy of Sciences
Prof. Shem Arungu-Olende Prof., Sec. Gen.
PO Box 14798
Nairobi, Kenya
Ph: 254 2 884401
Ph: 254 2 884405
Fax: 254 2 884406
E-mail: aas@aasciences.org
URL: http://www.aasciences.org

4370 ■ AAS Prize in Agricultural Biosciences
To recognize an individual for outstanding contributions in the field of agricultural bioscience. Awarded when merited. Established in 1990.

4371 ■ Olusegun Obasanjo Prize in Technological Innovation
To recognize an individual or institution that has developed exemplary technological innovation. Open to all African Scientists and technologies. A gold medal and monetary prize of US$5,000 are awarded annually.

4372 ■ Thomas R. Odhiambo Prize in Basic and Applied Sciences
To recognize a young outstanding and promising researcher (under age 40) in the basic sciences, engineering, and technology. Awarded annually. Established in 1996. Co-sponsored by ICIPE and the Academy of Sciences for the Developing World (TWAS).

4373 ■ African Association for Public Administration and Management
Mr. Tlohang Sekhamane, Pres.
PO Box 48677
Nairobi, Kenya
Ph: 254 20 2730555
Ph: 254 20 2730505
Fax: 254 20 2731153
E-mail: aapam@aapam.org
URL: http://www.aapam.org

4374 ■ Award for Best Student Essay/Report
To recognize student scholarship in African public administration; to encourage good writing and analytical skills, which are essential to a successful leadership career in the public service; and to attract top students into careers in the public service. A cash prize of US$300 is awarded to up to three recipients annually. Established in 2005.

4375 ■ Award for Excellence in the Teaching of Public Administration in Africa
To recognize outstanding accomplishment that is worthy of emulation and to encourage and recognize exceptional talent of effective and creative teaching of public administration and management in Africa. A bronze statuette is awarded annually. Established in 2005.

4376 ■ Award for Innovative Management
To recognize an individual for organizational achievement in the public sector through the introduction of new ideas and new operational and management methods. Awarded annually. Established in 2005.

4377 ■ Award for Outstanding Contribution to Knowledge in Public Administration and Management
To recognize the finest article published in the *African Journal of Public Administration and Management*. A glass trophy is awarded annually. Established in 2005.

4378 ■ Gold Medal Award
This, the Association's highest award bestowed on an individual, is presented to a person who has shown distinctive leadership in advancing public administration and management in Africa. Awarded when merited. Established in 2005.

4379 ■ International Centre of Insect Physiology and Ecology
Prof. Christian Borgemeister, Dir. Gen./CEO
PO Box 30772-00100
Nairobi, Kenya
Ph: 254 20 8632000
Fax: 254 20 8632001
E-mail: icipe@icipe.org
URL: http://www.icipe.org

Awards are arranged in alphabetical order below their administering organizations

4380 ■ Outstanding Researcher

Recognizes an outstanding researcher. Selection is based on originality, impact, and contribution to ICIPE's goals. Awarded periodically.

4381 ■ Kenya Association of Hotelkeepers and Caterers
Jaideep S. Vohra, Chm.
PO Box 9977
Nairobi, Kenya
Ph: 254 2 604419
Ph: 254 2 602538
Fax: 254 2 602539
E-mail: info@kahc.co.ke
URL: http://www.kahc.co.ke

4382 ■ Tom Tyrell Trophy and Award

For the best student in hotel management at the national tourism training college.

4383 ■ Kenya Institute of Management
Mr. David Muturi, Exec. Dir./CEO
PO Box 43706
Nairobi, Kenya
Ph: 254 20 2445600
Ph: 254 20 2445555
E-mail: kim@kim.ac.ke
URL: http://www.kim.ac.ke

4384 ■ Company of the Year Awards

To identify and publicly recognize companies that demonstrate excellence and integrity in their management practices. Companies are grouped in the following sectors: Service; Manufacturing; Small and Medium Enterprises; and Parastatals. Awarded annually. Established in 2000.

4385 ■ Kenya National Academy of Sciences
Ministry of Research, Science and Technology
Prof. Joseph O. Malo, Chm.
PO Box 39450
Nairobi, Kenya
Ph: 254 20 311714
E-mail: knas@iconnect.co.ke
URL: http://www.nationalacademies.org/nairobi/org/kenya.html

4386 ■ Honorary Fellow

To recognize an individual for an outstanding contribution to science and technology. Conferred at the discretion of the Governing Council of the Academy.

4387 ■ Kenyan Publishers Association
Mr. Lawrence Njagi, Chm.
PO Box 42767
Nairobi, Kenya
Ph: 254 20 3752344
Fax: 254 20 3754076
E-mail: info@kenyapublishers.org
URL: http://www.kenyapublishers.org

4388 ■ Jomo Kenyatta Prize for Literature

Recognizes the best newly published books. Awarded in five categories: Adult English, Adult Kiswahili, English Youth, Kiswahili Youth, and English Children's. A monetary prize is given biennially.

4389 ■ Kenyan Section of the International Commission of Jurists
George Kegoro, Exec. Dir.
PO Box 59743
Nairobi, Kenya
Ph: 254 20 3875980
Ph: 254 20 3875981
Fax: 254 20 3875982
E-mail: info@icj-kenya.org
URL: http://www.icj-kenya.org

4390 ■ Jurist of the Year Award

To recognize an outstanding jurist who has consistently, fearlessly, and impartially promoted the rule of law and human rights in Kenya during the year. Awarded annually. Established in 1993.

4391 ■ SEED Initiative
Helen Marquard, Exec. Dir.
United Nations Environment Programme
Division of Communications and Public Information
PO Box 30552
Nairobi, Kenya
URL: http://www.seedinit.org

4392 ■ SEED Awards for Entrepreneurship in Sustainable Development

To support and encourage locally-led entrepreneurial partnerships in developing countries. Award winners receive $5,000 worth of business and partnership support services. Awarded annually.

4393 ■ SEED Gold Awards

To support and encourage locally-led entrepreneurial partnerships in developing countries. Selected from the winners of the SEED Awards. Recipients receive an additional $35,000 worth of business support services, $25,000 of which is managed directly by the winner. Awarded annually.

4394 ■ UN-Habitat
PO Box 30030, GPO
Nairobi, Kenya
Ph: 254 20 762 1234
Fax: 254 20 762 4266
E-mail: infohabitat@unhabitat.org
URL: http://www.unhabitat.org

4395 ■ Habitat Business Award

To recognize and publicize outstanding achievements contributing to sustainable urbanization through corporate responsible practices. For-profit commercial enterprises and businesses are eligible. A trophy and certificate are awarded in five categories: Affordable housing solutions; Sustainable water, sanitation waste management, and urban infrastructure solutions; Clean urban energy solutions, mitigation and adaptation to climate change; Innovative information and communications technology solutions for the urban development and management; and Conflict-related and natural and disaster mitigation and post-disaster reconstruction. Awarded annually. Established in 2008.

4396 ■ Lecture Award

To recognize and encourage outstanding and sustained contribution to research, thinking, and practice in the human settlements field, either urban or rural. A plaque and monetary prize of US$1,000 is awarded annually; in addition, the recipient is invited to present a lecture at the World Urban Forum.

4397 ■ Scroll of Honour Award

To recognize an individual for contributions toward improving the lives of the poor through better housing policies and urban development. Awarded annually.

4398 ■ Shaikh Khalifa Bin Salman Al Khalifa Habitat Award

To promote the ideals and principles of good governance and equity in housing and urban development policies and practice. A monetary prize of US$100,000 is awarded biennially in even-numbered years at the World Urban Forum. Established in 2008.

4399 ■ United Nations Environment Programme
Division of Communication and Public Information
(Programme des Nations Unies pour l'Environnement)
PO Box 30552
Nairobi, Kenya
Ph: 254 20 762 1234
Fax: 254 20 762 4489
E-mail: unepinfo@unep.org
URL: http://www.unep.org/dcpi

4400 ■ Champions of the Earth

To recognize outstanding environmental leaders around the world. Awarded in four categories: policy leadership, science and innovation, entrepreneurial vision, and inspiration and action. A crystal trophy and monetary prize of US$40,000 are awarded in each category annually. Established in 2004.

4401 ■ The Green Awards

Recognizes outstanding work that conveys the importance of sustainable development and ethical best practices in promoting waste awareness, renewable energy, and resource efficiency. Awarded annually in 13 categories, such as Green Leadership, Green Investment, Cradle-to-Cradle Initiatives, and Green Game Changer. Established in 2006.

4402 ■ The Green Star Awards

Recognizes those who have make outstanding efforts to prevent and respond to environmental disasters all over the world. Awarded biennially in odd-numbered years. Awards are given jointly by the United Nations Environment Programme, the UN Office for the Coordination of Humanitarian Affairs and the Green Cross International.

4403 ■ Ozone Awards

Recognizes outstanding achievements in areas related to protecting the Earth's ozone layer by highlighting scientific contributions in understanding ozone depletion. Introduced in 1995. Awarded periodically.

4404 ■ SEED Awards

Recognizes innovation in local, environmentally responsible and sustainable entrepreneurship. Award winners are announced annually at the United Nations Commission for Sustainable Development in New York.

4405 ■ University of Nairobi
PO Box 30197
Nairobi, Kenya
Ph: 254 2 318262
Fax: 254 2 318262
URL: http://www.uonbi.ac.ke

4406 ■ African Development and Economic Consultants Prize

To honor the best final-year student in the School of Economics. A monetary prize of KShs. 3000 is awarded annually.

4407 ■ African Urban Quarterly Prize

To honor the best final-year student with the highest marks in Geography, Faculty of Arts. A monetary prize of KShs. 5000 is awarded annually.

4408 ■ Asian Commercial Community Academic Awards

To recognize the best accounting students in the Faculty of Business. Monetary prize totaling KShs. 20,000 are awarded annually.

4409 ■ Yusuf Dawood Award

To honor the best final-year student in the Department of Literature, Faculty of Arts. A badge, certificate, gift of books, and monetary prize of KShs. 5000 is awarded annually

4410 ■ Rahima Dawood Prize

To recognize the best overall final-year student in the Department of Surgery, School of Medicine. A badge and monetary prize of KShs. 5000 are awarded annually.

4411 ■ Dr. A.C.L. De'Souza Memorial Prize

To recognize the best first-year student in the Faculties of Arts, Science, and School of Business. A monetary prize of KShs. 1000 is awarded annually.

Awards are arranged in alphabetical order below their administering organizations

4412 ■ Dr. Eddah Gachukia Science Prize
To honor the best final-year female student from the departments of Agriculture, Civil, Electrical and Electronics, and Mechanical Engineering. A cup and monetary prize of KShs. 5000 are awarded annually.

4413 ■ Kaplan and Stratton Prize
To recognize the best overall final-year student in the School of Law. A monetary prize of KShs. 12,500 is awarded annually.

4414 ■ Kenya National Chamber of Commerce and Industry Prize
To recognize the best final-year student in the School of Business. A monetary prize of KShs. 1000 is awarded annually.

4415 ■ N.H.O. Mahondo Award
To honor the best student in Constitutional Law, School of Law. A monetary prize of KShs. 5000 is awarded annually.

4416 ■ Mutiso Menezes International Prize
To honor the best fourth- and fifth-year students in the Department of Agriculture. A monetary prize of KShs. 1500 is awarded annually.

4417 ■ Gandhi Smarak Nidhi Trustee Fund Gold Prize
To recognize the best overall student at the University of Nairobi. A gold medal is awarded annually. In addition, monetary prizes of KShs. 7500 are given to the best final-year student in each Faculty/Institute/School.

4418 ■ Norbrook Award
To honor the best final-year student in the course of medicine, Faculty of Veterinary Medicine. A trophy and monetary prize of KShs. 5000 are awarded annually.

4419 ■ Dr. Marjorie Oludhe Award
To honor the best Master of Arts student in the Department of Literature, Faculty of Arts. A cup and monetary prize of KShs. 5000 are awarded annually.

4420 ■ Daramola Oluyemisi Memorial Prize
To honor the best final-year female pharmacy student who has shown consistent academic performance and leadership skills in the professional years. A floating trophy, silver cup, and monetary prize of KShs. 5000 are awarded annually.

4421 ■ Elida Ponds Prize
To honor the best student in each of the four departments in the School of Dental Sciences. A monetary prize of KShs. 10,000 is awarded annually.

4422 ■ Professor Arthur T. Porters Prize
To honor the best final-year student in the College of Humanities and Social Sciences. A monetary prize of KShs. 3000 is awarded annually.

4423 ■ Sakarben Sheth Prize
To recognize the best overall second-year student in the School of Law. A monetary prize of KShs. 5000 is awarded annually.

4424 ■ Paul Musili Wambua Award
To honor the best student in Civil Procedure, School of Law. A certificate and monetary prize of KShs. 2500 are awarded annually.

4425 ■ Professor L.R. Whittaker's Annual Prize
To honor the best final-year postgraduate student in the Department of Diagnostic Radiology, School of Medicine. A book is awarded annually.

Kuwait

4426 ■ Islamic Organization for Medical Sciences
Dr. Abdul Rahman Al-Awadi, Pres.
PO Box 31280
Sulaibekhat 90803, Kuwait
Ph: 965 4834984
Fax: 965 4837854
E-mail: ioms@islamset.org
URL: http://www.islamset.org/ioms/main.html

4427 ■ KFAS Awards in Islamic Medical Sciences
For original and academically significant contribution in the field of Islamic medical sciences.

4428 ■ Organization of Arab Petroleum Exporting Countries (Organization de Paises Arabes Exportadores de Petroleo)
Abbas Ali Naqi, Sec. Gen.
PO Box 20501
Safat 13066, Kuwait
Ph: 965 4959000
Fax: 965 4959755
E-mail: oapec@oapecorg.org
URL: http://www.oapecorg.org

4429 ■ Award for Scientific Research
To promote and encourage scientific research by recognizing the outstanding research paper on a specified topic. Papers may be submitted by May 31 of even-numbered years. A monetary award of 7,000 Kuwaiti dinars for first place and 5,000 Kuwaiti dinars for second place are presented biennially in even-numbered years. Established in 1985.

4430 ■ Regional Organization for the Protection of the Marine Environment
Dr. Abdul Rahman Al-Awadi, Exec. Sec.
PO Box 26388
Safat 13124, Kuwait
Ph: 965 25312140
Fax: 965 25324172
E-mail: ropme@qualitynet.net
URL: http://www.ropme.com

4431 ■ Environmental Prize
To honor individuals who have contributed outstanding work or had achievements in the field of marine environment. A monetary prize of US$20,000 is awarded triennially. Established in 1984.

Latvia

4432 ■ Latvian Academy of Sciences (Latvijas Zinatnu Akademija)
Prof. Juris Ekmanis, Pres.
Akademijas laukums 1
LV-1050 Riga, Latvia
Ph: 371 7225361
Ph: 371 7211405
Fax: 371 7821153
E-mail: lza@lza.lv
URL: http://www.lza.lv

4433 ■ Karlis Balodis Prize
To recognize an individual for contributions in Latvian economy. Awarded when merited.

4434 ■ Fricis Brivzemnieks Prize
To recognize an individual for contributions in Latvian folklore studies and ethnography. Awarded when merited.

4435 ■ Fridrihs Canders Prize
To recognize an individual for contributions in physics, mathematics, or engineering sciences. Awarded when merited.

4436 ■ Janis Endzelins Prize
To recognize an individual for contributions in Latvian linguistics or Baltology. Awarded when merited.

4437 ■ Grand Medal
To honor scientists of Latvia and foreign countries for their outstanding creative contributions to the academy.

4438 ■ Paulis Lejins Prize
To recognize an individual for contributions in agricultural sciences. Awarded when merited. Co-sponsored by the Latvian Academy of Agriculture and Forestry.

4439 ■ Vilis Pludonis Prize
To recognize an individual for contributions in literary criticism. Awarded when merited.

4440 ■ Heinrichs Skuja Prize
To recognize an individual for contributions in biological sciences. Awarded when merited.

4441 ■ Pauls Stradins Prize
To recognize an individual for contributions in practical medicine, the science of medicine, or the history of medicine. Awarded when merited. Co-sponsored by the Pauls Stradins Museum of the History of Medicine.

4442 ■ Student Awards
To recognize outstanding scientific work by students of Latvian institutions of higher education. Nine awards are granted annually, three each in chemical and biological sciences; physical, mathematics, and engineering sciences; and humanities and social sciences.

4443 ■ Arveds Svabe Prize
To recognize an individual for contributions in the history of Latvia. Awarded when merited.

4444 ■ Gustavs Vanags Prize
To recognize an individual for contributions in chemical sciences. Awarded when merited.

4445 ■ Latvian Art Directors Club
13 Janvara Str., 33
LV-1050 Riga, Latvia
Ph: 371 34 7228218
Fax: 371 34 7503616
E-mail: info@adclub.lv
URL: http://www.adclub.lv

4446 ■ ADwards
To recognize creative excellence in advertisement. Awarded annually. Established in 2006.

Lebanon

4447 ■ Delegation of the European Union to the Republic of Lebanon
490 Harbour Dr. Bldg.
Charles Helou Ave., Saifi
PO Box 11-4008 Riad el Solh
Beirut, Lebanon
Ph: 961 1 569 400
Fax: 961 1 569 415
E-mail: delegation-lebanon@ec.europa.eu
URL: http://ec.europa.eu/delegations/lebanon/about_us/contacs/index_en.htm

4448 ■ Prix Marguerite Delahautemaison
To recognize an individual for outstanding contributions to laboratory research. French laboratory researchers are eligible. The award is presented in alternate years in the following categories: nephrology research and cancer research. A monetary award of 9,000 Euros is presented annually. Established in 1977.

4449 ■ Prix Raymond Rosen
For recognition of outstanding research in cancer. Well-known French researchers are eligible. A monetary prize of 30,000 Euros is awarded annually.

4450 ■ Pan Arab Web Awards Academy
PO Box 45-71 Hazmieh
Beirut, Lebanon
Ph: 961 1 392 822

Awards are arranged in alphabetical order below their administering organizations

Fax: 961 1 392 822
E-mail: president@panarabwebawards.org
URL: http://www.panarabwebawards.org

4451 ■ Bahrain Web Awards
To foster the spirit of innovation and creativity among Web designers in Bahrain, to raise the standards of Web design and Web sites, to advocate the growth and development of local talent, to promote intellectual property awareness, and to encourage all industries to showcase their Web sites and become more involved in the digital economy. Web sites are judged on five criteria: concept/creativity, technical/ease of use/navigation, content/structure, visual design solution/aesthetics, and interactivity. Presented in dozens of categories, including airlines, culture, fashion and art, industrial, and sports. Winners represent Bahrain in the Pan Arab Web Awards (see separate entry). Awarded annually. Established in 2006.

4452 ■ Lebanon Web Awards
To foster the spirit of innovation and creativity among Web designers in Lebanon, to raise the standards of Web design and Web sites, to advocate the growth and development of local talent, to promote intellectual property awareness, and to encourage all industries to showcase their Web sites and become more involved in the digital economy. Web sites are judged on five criteria: concept/creativity, technical/ease of use/navigation, content/structure, visual design solution/aesthetics, and interactivity. Presented in dozens of categories, including airlines, culture, fashion and art, industrial, and sports. Winners represent Lebanon in the Pan Arab Web Awards (see separate entry). Awarded annually. Established in 2003.

4453 ■ Pan Arab Web Awards
To foster the spirit of innovation and creativity among Web designers, to raise the standards of Web design and Web sites, to advocate the growth and development of local talent, to promote intellectual property awareness, and to encourage all industries to showcase their Web sites and become more involved in the digital economy. To be eligible to compete in the Pan Arab Web Awards, individuals must first qualify in the national Web Awards competition of the following countries: Bahrain, Egypt, Jordan, Lebanon, Oman, Kuwait, Saudi Arabia, Syria, United Arab Emirates, Qatar, and Yemen (see separate entries). Web sites are judged on five criteria: concept/creativity, technical/ease of use/ navigation, content/structure, visual design solution/aesthetics, and interactivity. Presented in dozens of categories, including airlines, culture, fashion and art, industrial, and sports. Awarded annually. Established in 2004.

4454 ■ Radio Amateurs of Lebanon
Hani Raad, Pres.
PO Box 11-8888
Beirut, Lebanon
Ph: 961 70970922
Fax: 961 1798479
E-mail: ral@ral.org.lb
URL: http://www.ral.org.lb

4455 ■ Worked Oscar Delta Award
To recognize any amateur radio operator, worldwide, who confirms contact with a minimum of five different Oscar Delta (OD) land stations in Lebanon. A certificate is awarded when merited.

4456 ■ Syria Web Awards
PO Box 45-71 Hazmieh
Beirut, Lebanon
Ph: 961 1 385 293
E-mail: president@syriawebawards.org
URL: http://www.syriawebawards.org

4457 ■ Syria Web Awards
To foster the spirit of innovation and creativity among Web designers in Syria, to raise the standards of Web design and Web sites, to advocate the growth and development of local talent, to promote intellectual property awareness, and to encourage all industries to showcase their Web sites and become more involved in the digital economy. Web sites are judged on five criteria: concept/creativity, technical/ease of use/navigation, content/structure, visual design solution/aesthetics, and interactivity. Presented in dozens of categories, including advertising and production, culture, fashion and clothing, industrial, and sports. Winners represent Syria in the Pan Arab Web Awards (see separate entry). Awarded annually.

4458 ■ UAE Web Awards
PO Box 45-71 Hazmieh
Beirut, Lebanon
Ph: 961 1 385 293
E-mail: president@uaewebawards.org
URL: http://www.uaewebawards.org

4459 ■ UAE Web Awards
To foster the spirit of innovation and creativity among Web designers in the United Arab Emirates, to raise the standards of Web design and Web sites, to advocate the growth and development of local talent, to promote intellectual property awareness, and to encourage all industries to showcase their Web sites and become more involved in the digital economy. Web sites are judged on five criteria: concept/creativity, technical/ease of use/navigation, content/ structure, visual design solution/aesthetics, and interactivity. Presented in dozens of categories, including advertising and production, culture, fashion and clothing, industrial, and sports. Winners represent the United Arab Emirates in the Pan Arab Web Awards (see separate entry). Awarded annually.

Lesotho

4460 ■ National University of Lesotho
Faculty of Education
Roma 180, Lesotho
Ph: 266 2221 3679
Fax: 266 2234 0000
URL: http://www.nul.ls/faculties/education

4461 ■ Moletsane and Sets'abi Award
To honor the student with the best performance in Year IV Adult Education. Awarded annually.

4462 ■ Paragon Lesotho Award
To honor the student with the best performance in the Faculty of Education. Awarded annually.

4463 ■ Sesotho Academy Award
To honor the student with the best performance in Year IV Curriculum Studies in Sesotho. Awarded annually.

4464 ■ South African High Commission Award
To honor the student with the best performance in Education Foundations. Awarded annually.

4465 ■ National University of Lesotho
Faculty of Law
Roma 180, Lesotho
Ph: 266 2221 3679
Fax: 266 2234 0000
URL: http://www.nul.ls/faculties/law

4466 ■ African Regional Intellectual Property Organisation Prize
To honor the student with the best dissertation in the Law of Intellectual Property. Awarded annually.

4467 ■ Juta Prize
To honor the best student in the LLB program who attains a minimum mean of 70 percent. Awarded annually.

4468 ■ Mokhele Kabi Memorial Prize
To honor the student with the best average mark in Mercantile Law I and Mercantile Law II. Awarded annually.

4469 ■ Lesotho National Insurance Corporation Prize
To honor the best fourth-year student in the Bachelor of Arts Law program who attains a minimum mean of 70 percent. Awarded annually.

4470 ■ Maile Mosisili Memorial Award
To honor the best student in Constitutional Law who attains a minimum mean of 70 percent. Awarded annually.

Libyan Arab Jamahiriya

4471 ■ African Organization of Supreme Audit Institutions
(Organizacion de Entidades Fiscalizadoras Superiors de Africa)
Prof. Ali Al-Hesnawi, Sec. Gen.
PO Box 2879
Tripoli, Libyan Arab Jamahiriya
Ph: 218 21 4448171
Ph: 218 21 4440630
Fax: 218 21 4440630
E-mail: afrosai@libyansai.ly.org
URL: http://www.intosai.org/en/portal/regional_ working_groups/afrosai

4472 ■ AFROSAI Prize
For commitment to AFROSAI.

Liechtenstein

4473 ■ Liechtenstein Football Association
(Liechtenstein Fussballverband)
Landstrasse 149
Schaan, Liechtenstein
Ph: 423 237 4747
Fax: 423 237 4748
E-mail: info@lf.li
URL: http://www.lfv.li

4474 ■ Liechtenstein Football Cup
To recognize the champion football (soccer) team in Liechtenstein. The winner of the championship represents Liechtenstein in the Europa League, organized by the Union of European Football Associations (UEFA). Awarded annually. Established in 1946.

4475 ■ University of Liechtenstein
Graduate School
Furst-Franz-Josef-Strasse
9490 Vaduz, Liechtenstein
Ph: 423 265 1241
Fax: 423 265 1112
E-mail: master.bfm@uni.li
URL: http://www.uni.li/graduateschool

4476 ■ Banking Award Liechtenstein
To recognize a student for outstanding academic achievement in the field of banking and finance while completing a Bachelor's or Master's thesis. Graduates from all Bachelor's and Master's programs in Banking and Financial Management at the University of Liechtenstein whose thesis was rated at least 5.0 points are eligible. A monetary prize of 5,000 Swiss francs is awarded annually. Sponsored by the Liechtenstein Bankers Association.

Lithuania

4477 ■ American Chamber of Commerce in Lithuania
Zivile Sabaliauskaite, Acting Exec. Dir.
Lukiskiu str. 5, Rm. 204
LT-01108 Vilnius, Lithuania

Awards are arranged in alphabetical order below their administering organizations

Ph: 370 5 2611181
E-mail: acc@iti.lt
URL: http://www.amcham.lt

4478 ■ Best Business Plan
To a university student with the best business plan.

4479 ■ Lithuanian Association of Literary Translators
(Lietuvos literaturos verteju sajunga)
Ms. Jurgita Mikutyte, Chair
Sv. Ignoto g. 5-264
LT-01120 Vilnius, Lithuania
Ph: 370 698 18116
Ph: 370 682 42977
E-mail: info@llvs.lt
URL: http://www.llvs.lt

4480 ■ Best Translated Book of the Year
To recognize the best contemporary books of world literature published for the first time in Lithuanian during the previous year. Open to adult fiction novels, playwriting, poetry, and literary essays first published abroad no earlier than 30 years ago. The Association invites the public to read the nominated books and vote for their favorite. Winners are announced on April 23rd, World Book and Copyright Day.

4481 ■ Companion Prize
To recognize a person or organization for special merits in regards to literary translation and the profession of translation. A diploma and honorary gift are awarded annually.

4482 ■ St. Jerome Award
To recognize a translator of literature for the most professional and skillful translations into Lithuanian. Awarded annually. Established in 2005.

4483 ■ Dominykas Urbas Prize
To recognize a young translator for the best first or second translation into Lithuanian of a book-length literary work. Candidates must not be older than 35 years. Awarded annually on April 28th, the birthday of the outstanding translator, editor, and linguist, Dominykas Urbas.

4484 ■ President of the Republic of Lithuania
Valdas Adamkus, Pres.
Simono Daukanto sq. 3
LT-2008 Vilnius, Lithuania
Ph: 370 5 266 4154
Fax: 370 5 266 4145
E-mail: adamkus@president.lt
URL: http://adamkus.president.lt

4485 ■ Independence Medal
To honor an individual for distinction in the cause of restoration and consolidation of the Independent State of Lithuania during the period from 1990 to 2000. A medal is awarded when merited. Established in 1928.

4486 ■ Life Saving Cross
To honor a Lithuanian citizen or a foreign national who, despite danger to him or her, performed acts of bravery in saving the life of other people. May be awarded for saving human life within the territory of Lithuania and for saving the life of Lithuanian citizens in foreign countries. A medal is awarded when merited.

4487 ■ Medal of Darius and Girenas
To honor an individual for contributions to aviation in Lithuania. A medal is awarded when merited. Established in 1933 to commemorate the flight across the Atlantic by pilots Steponas Darius and Stasys Girenas.

4488 ■ Medal of January 13
To honor a Lithuanian citizen or a foreign national for outstanding performance in defending the freedom and independence of Lithuania during the months of January through September 1991.

A medal is awarded when merited. Established to commemorate the tragic events that took place in Vilnius on January 13, 1991.

4489 ■ Medal of the Founding Volunteers of the Lithuanian Army
To honor an individual for contributions to the establishment of the Armed Forces of Lithuania and to the strengthening of the national defense system of the country. A medal is awarded when merited. Established in 1928.

4490 ■ Medal of the Order of the Lithuanian Grand Duke Gediminas
To honor a Lithuanian citizen or a foreign national for distinguished services to Lithuania. Medals are conferred in three classes. Awarded when merited. Established in 1930.

4491 ■ Order of the Cross of Vytis (the Knight)
To honor an individual for acts of bravery performed in defending the freedom and independence of the Republic of Lithuania. Medals are conferred in five classes. Awarded when merited. Established in 1991.

4492 ■ Order of the Lithuanian Grand Duke Gediminas
To honor a Lithuanian citizen or a foreign national for outstanding performance in civil and public duties. Medals are conferred in five classes. Awarded when merited. Established in 1930.

4493 ■ Order of Vytautas the Great
To honor a Lithuanian citizen or a foreign national for distinguished services to the State of Lithuania and for contributions to the Lithuanian nation or to the welfare of mankind. A medal is awarded when merited. Established in 1930 to commemorate the 500th anniversary of the death of the Lithuanian Grand Duke Vytautas the Great.

4494 ■ United Nations Development Programme
Lithuania Office
Lyra Jakuleviciene, Mgr.
Gostauto 40A, 10th Fl.
Central PO Box 62
LT-01112 Vilnius, Lithuania
Ph: 370 5 2107 400
Fax: 370 5 2107 401
E-mail: lyra.jakuleviciene@undp.org
URL: http://www.undp.lt

4495 ■ National Responsible Business Award
To recognize companies for successful implementation of Corporate Social Responsibility (CSR) principles in business practices. Awarded annually. Established in 2008.

Luxembourg

4496 ■ Jeune Chambre Economique du Grand-Duche de Luxembourg
Federation Mondiale de Jeunes Leaders et Entrepreneurs
7 rue Alcide de Gasperi
L-2981 Luxembourg, Luxembourg
E-mail: info@jcluxembourg.com
URL: http://www.jcluxembourg.com

4497 ■ Creative Young Entrepreneur Luxembourg Award
To honor outstanding young entrepreneurs in Luxembourg. Candidates must be between the ages of 18 and 40, and must be owner/managers who are primarily responsible for the performance of a privately held business or activity. Awarded annually.

4498 ■ Luxembourg Society for Contemporary Music
BP 828
L-2018 Luxembourg, Luxembourg
Ph: 352 22 5821

Fax: 352 22 5823
E-mail: info@lgnm.lu
URL: http://www.lgnm.lu

4499 ■ International Composition Prize
To recognize composers from around the world for outstanding concert pieces written for the ensemble Luxembourg Sinfonietta. Monetary prizes of 3,000 Euros, 2,000 Euros, and 1,000 Euros are awarded annually for first, second, and third place, respectively. Established in 2002.

4500 ■ Vatel-Club Luxembourg
Armand Steinmetz, Pres.
BP. 271
L-9003 Ettelbruck, Luxembourg
Ph: 352 802453
Fax: 352 809897
E-mail: president@vatel.lu
URL: http://www.vatel-club.lu

4501 ■ Culinary World Cup
To recognize outstanding culinary ability. The competition is built around research and development and establishing food trends for the future. Medals are awarded at the EXPOGAST trade show held quadrennially in Luxembourg. Established in 1980.

Macao

4502 ■ Environment Council of Macao
Ala. Dr. Carlos D'Assumpcao, No. 393 a 437
Edif. Dynasty Plz, 10 andar
Macau, Macao
Ph: 853 2872 5134
Fax: 853 2872 5129
E-mail: ca@ambiente.gov.mo
URL: http://www.ambiente.gov.mo

4503 ■ Macao Green Hotel Award
To honor hotels that have committed to environmental management. Criteria include green leadership and innovation, green program performance, and partner synergy. Awarded annually to one or more recipients in two categories. Established in 2007.

4504 ■ Macao Polytechnic Institute
(Instituto Politecnico de Macau)
Rua de Luis Gonzaga Gomes
Macau, Macao
Ph: 853 2857 8722
Fax: 853 2830 8801
E-mail: dge@ipm.edu.mo
URL: http://www.ipm.edu.mo

4505 ■ Degree Program Distinguished Teacher Award
To commend and reward teachers for distinguished performance, to promote the quality of teaching, to upgrade professional teaching standards, and to enhance the development of the MPI. Candidates must be full-time degree program teachers who have taught at the MPI for three full academic years or longer. Awarded in each of the MPI degree programs: Business, Public Administration, and Health Sciences. A trophy and monetary prize are awarded triennially.

4506 ■ English-Speaking Competition
To encourage people from all walks of life to learn English, to promote English-language teaching, and to enhance English proficiency through Macao. Participants must be citizens of Macao whose mother tongue is not English. Monetary prizes are presented for first, second, and third place winners in six categories: Open, College, Senior High School, Junior High School, Upper Primary School, and Lower Primary School. Winners may be selected to represent Macao at China's national competition. Held annually.

Awards are arranged in alphabetical order below their administering organizations

4507 ■ Teaching Excellence Award
To promote high quality and standards of teaching, to commend and reward full-time teachers for excellent performance, and to encourage enthusiasm in teaching. Candidates must have taught at the MPI for three full academic years or longer. Awarded in each of the MPI schools: Arts, Public Administration, Business, Physical Education and Sports, Language and Translation, and Health Sciences. A certificate and monetary prize are awarded triennially.

Macedonia

4508 ■ Office of the President of the Republic of Macedonia
Natasha Savova, Sec. Gen.
Vila Vodno
Aco Karamanov bb
MK-1000 Skopje, Macedonia
Ph: 389 2 311 1568
Fax: 389 2 311 2643
URL: http://www.president.gov.mk

4509 ■ Decoration for Service to the Country
To honor an individual for contributions to the development and enhancement of the Macedonian spirit and nationality. Awarded when merited. Established in 2002.

4510 ■ Decoration of the Republic of Macedonia
This, the highest national award in Macedonia, is awarded to honor an individual for achievements of national or international significance. Awarded when merited. Established in 2002.

4511 ■ Medal for Service to the Country
To honor an individual for contributions to the development and enhancement of the Macedonian spirit and nationality. Awarded when merited. Established in 2002.

4512 ■ Medal of Honour
To honor an individual for courageous acts. Awarded when merited. Established in 2002.

4513 ■ War Service Decoration
To honor an individual for military service benefiting Macedonia. Awarded when merited. Established in 2002.

Malawi

4514 ■ National Research Council of Malawi
PO Box 30745
Lilongwe 3, Malawi
Ph: 265 1 771550
Ph: 265 1 774869
Fax: 265 1 772431
E-mail: nrcm@sdnp.org.mw
URL: http://www.sdnp.org.mw/nrcm/

4515 ■ Malawi Award for Scientific and Technological Achievement
To recognize individuals and institutions for outstanding scientific performance as well as the social significance of their achievements in support of the poverty alleviation program. Awarded annually.

Malaysia

4516 ■ Asia-Pacific Association of Forestry Research Institutions
Dr. Sim Heok-choh, Exec. Dir.
Kepong
52109 Selangor, Malaysia
Ph: 60 3 62722516
Fax: 60 3 62773249
E-mail: secretariat@apafri.org

URL: http://www.apafri.org

4517 ■ Dr. Y.S. Rao Forestry Research Award
To recognize a young researcher who has made outstanding contributions in forestry research and development. A plaque is awarded triennially. Established in 2000.

4518 ■ Asia-Pacific Broadcasting Union
Javad Mottaghi, Sec. Gen.
PO Box 12287
50772 Kuala Lumpur, Malaysia
Ph: 60 3 22823592
Ph: 60 3 22822480
Fax: 60 3 22825292
E-mail: info@abu.org.my
URL: http://www.abu.org.my

4519 ■ ABU Prizes for Radio and Television Programs
For recognition of the high standard of a production in the field of radio and television programs. Prizes are awarded in the following categories for radio: Drama, Infotainment; News & Documentary; Children and Youth; and External Broadcasts; and in the following categories for television: Drama; Entertainment; Children and Youth; News & Documentary; and Sports. Awarded annually. Established in 1964.

4520 ■ Dennis Anthony Memorial Award
To honor the best news coverage of the year by a member of Asiavision, the daily news exchange among member stations of the Asia-Pacific Broadcasting Union (ABU). A trophy is awarded annually. Sponsored by CNN, which selects the winner. Established in honor of a former ABU Senior Officer who died in 1996.

4521 ■ Asiavision Annual Awards
To honor members for important contributions to the news exchange. A monetary prize of US$700 is awarded annually to one or more recipients.

4522 ■ Asiavision Award for Contributions to ASEAN Television News
To recognize outstanding contributions to ASEAN Television News, a weekly news exchange among the 10 national broadcasters of the Association of Southeast Asian Nations (ASEAN). Awarded annually.

4523 ■ Engineering Excellence Awards
To encourage technical writing in broadcast engineering. ABU members are eligible. Two awards are presented: Broadcast Engineering Excellence Award and the Engineering Industry Excellence Award. Awarded annually. Established in 1973.

4524 ■ Asian Football Confederation
Mohamed bin Hammam, Pres.
AFC House Jalan 1/155B
Bukit Jalil
57000 Kuala Lumpur, Malaysia
Ph: 60 3 89943388
Fax: 60 3 89942689
URL: http://www.the-afc.com

4525 ■ AFC Annual Awards
To recognize outstanding performance. The following awards are presented at an annual ceremony: Diamond of Asia; Association of the Year (men and women); Fair Play Association of the Year (men and women); Referee of the Year (men and women); Assistant Referee of the Year (men and women); Match Commissioner of the Year (men and women); Coach of the Year (men); Club of the Year (men); National Team of the Year (men and women); Youth Player of the Year (men and women); and Player of the Year.

4526 ■ Association of Chartered Certified Accountants - Malaysia
Jennifer Lopez, Country Hd.
27th Fl., Sunway Tower
86 Jalan Ampang

50450 Kuala Lumpur, Malaysia
Ph: 60 3 27135051
Fax: 60 3 27135052
E-mail: info@my.accaglobal.com
URL: http://malaysia.accaglobal.com

4527 ■ ACCA Malaysia Sustainability Reporting Awards
To recognize organizations that report and disclose environmental, social, and full sustainability information; to encourage the uptake of such reporting; and to raise awareness of corporate transparency issues. Awarded annually. Formerly: ACCA Malaysia Environmental and Social Reporting Awards.

4528 ■ Badminton World Federation
Dr. Kang Young Joong, Pres.
Batu 3 1/2 Jalan Cheras
56000 Kuala Lumpur, Malaysia
Ph: 60 3 92837155
Ph: 60 3 92836155
Fax: 60 3 92847155
E-mail: bwf@bwfbadminton.org
URL: http://www.bwfbadminton.org
Formerly: (2007) International Badminton Federation.

4529 ■ Certificate of Commendation
To be awarded, where appropriate, to commercial undertakings and other external organizations that have rendered significant services to the game. Nominations to be made by Member Associations. Service shall have been for a period of at least three years and will have made a significant contribution to the nominating organization. Awarded annually to multiple recipients.

4530 ■ Eddy Choong Most Promising Player of the Year Award
To honor an individual based on performance in the Super Series events and such major tournaments as the World Championship, the Sudirman Cup, and the Thomas/Uber Cup. Awarded annually.

4531 ■ Distinguished Service Award
For recognition of major support in the development of badminton. Nominations must be made by resolution of a standing committee of the Council. Awarded annually to 75 recipients.

4532 ■ Hall of Fame
To honor players and administrators who have enhanced their sport through exceptional achievements. Nominees must be members of the badminton fraternity who have retired from the sport of badminton for a period of five years or more. Only in special circumstances will the Administration Committee consider a recommendation to Council of a nominee who is still involved in badminton.

4533 ■ Lifetime Achievement Award
To honor an individual who has made a significant and lifetime contribution toward the advancement and promotion of badminton worldwide. Awarded annually.

4534 ■ Meritorious Service Award
For recognition of long and meritorious service to badminton. Long service means at least fifteen years. Nominations should preferably be received from the nominee's National Organization but the Council may dispense with the requirement. A certificate and a lapel badge are awarded when merited. Established in 1985.

4535 ■ Player of the Year Awards
To recognize the best male and female badminton players, based on performance in the Super Series events and major BWF tournaments (the World Championships, the Sudirman Cup, and the Thomas/Uber Cup). Awarded annually.

Awards are arranged in alphabetical order below their administering organizations

4536 ■ Herbert Scheele Trophy
To recognize an individual for outstanding and exceptional services to badminton. Awarded annually.

4537 ■ Dermatological Society of Malaysia (Persatuan Dermatologi Malaysia)
Dr. Mardziah Alias, Pres.
Damansara Specialist Hospital
119, Jalan SS20/10 Damansara Utama
47400 Petaling Jaya, Malaysia
Fax: 60 3 77222617
E-mail: info@dermatology.org.my
URL: http://www.dermatology.org.my

4538 ■ Honorary Membership
To honor distinguished individuals who have rendered notable service to the Society or to the advancement of dermatology in Malaysia.

4539 ■ Research Grant
For research.

4540 ■ Enterprise Asia
Jaya One Commercial Hub, 33-5-3A
Block C, Jaya One, 72A
Jalan Universiti
46200 Petaling Jaya, Malaysia
Ph: 60 3 7955 3325
Fax: 60 3 7955 3326
E-mail: info@enterpriseasia.org
URL: http://www.enterpriseasia.org

4541 ■ Asia Pacific Entrepreneurship Awards
To recognize business leadership for outstanding entrepreneurship, and to enhance the awareness of the importance of entrepreneurship amongst the general public and, in turn, stimulate the growth of local and regional brands and enterprises. Open to individuals in Australia, Brunei, Cambodia, China, Hong Kong, India, Indonesia, Japan, Korea, Malaysia, Singapore, Thailand, and Vietnam. Awarded annually.

4542 ■ Asia Responsible Entrepreneurship Awards
To recognize and honor Asian businesses for championing sustainable and responsible entrepreneurship in the following categories: Green Leadership, Community Engagement, Investment in People, and Responsible Business Leadership. Awarded annually.

4543 ■ Malaysian Association of Professional Secretaries and Administrators
Melissa Ong, Pres.
15 Lorong Tempinis Kiri Satu
Lucky Garden, Bangsar
59100 Kuala Lumpur, Malaysia
Ph: 60 3 22828308
Fax: 60 3 22825884
E-mail: officeadministration@mapsa-malaysia.com
URL: http://www.mapsa-malaysia.com

4544 ■ Boss of the Year Award
To honor the boss who has demonstrated the most ideal and professional relationship with his or her assistant/secretary at the workplace. Awarded annually. Established in 1976.

4545 ■ Member of the Year Award
To recognize a secretary/administrative professional for commitment and dedication to the profession; involvement in MAPSA activities; contribution towards the progress and promotion of the profession; inclination to undertake work beyond her/his call of duty; and contribution to the local community. Awarded annually.

4546 ■ Malaysian Institute of Certified Public Accountants
Dato Ahmad Johan Mohammad Raslan, Pres.
15, Jalan Medan Tuanku
50300 Kuala Lumpur, Malaysia
Ph: 60 3 26989622

Fax: 60 3 26989403
E-mail: micpa@micpa.com.my
URL: http://www.micpa.com.my

4547 ■ Excellence Award for Best Accounting Graduate
For the best accounting graduate from each of the local universities that offer the Bachelor of Accountancy Programme. A certificate, pewter trophy, and cash prize of RM500 are awarded annually. Established in 1992.

4548 ■ Excellence Award for Most Outstanding CPA Student
For a CPA student who has achieved excellence in the MIPCA examinations. A certificate, pewter trophy, and cash prize of RM500 are awarded annually. Established in 1994.

4549 ■ Gold Medals
To recognize the students who have passed the MICPA examination with high distinction. A certificate and medal are awarded annually to one or more recipients.

4550 ■ National Chamber of Commerce and Industry of Malaysia (Dewan Perniagaan dan Perindustrian Kebangsaan Malaysia)
Mr. Wong Kum Sin, Exec. Dir.
Level 3, W Wing
Menara Matrade, Jalan Khidmat Usaha, Off Jalan Duta
50480 Kuala Lumpur, Malaysia
Ph: 60 3 62049811
Fax: 60 3 62049711
E-mail: enquiry@nccim.org.my
URL: http://www.nccim.org.my/t1/index.php

4551 ■ Efficiency Service Awards for the Public Sector
For deserving and outstanding government ministries or agencies.

4552 ■ Pacific Association of Quantity Surveyors
Ms. Katherine Thiang, Sec.
The Institute of Surveyors Malaysia
3rd Fl., Bangunan Jurukur
64-66 Jalan 52/4
Petaling Jaya
46200 Selangor, Malaysia
Ph: 60 3 79551773
Fax: 60 3 79550253
E-mail: secretariat@ism.org.my
URL: http://www.paqs.net

4553 ■ Service Award
To recognize outstanding service to international Quantity Surveying and cost engineering that exceeds the expectations of the individual's local PAQS member Institution. Awarded to one or more recipients annually. Established in 2002.

Maldives

4554 ■ Maldives Breakout Festival
Lot No. 1/55, 1st Fl.
Boduthakurufaanu Magu
Male, Maldives
Ph: 960 330 3023
Fax: 960 330 3024
E-mail: info@maldivesbreakoutfestival.com
URL: http://maldivesbreakoutfestival.com

4555 ■ Maldives Breakout Festival
To recognize up-and-coming musical bands from the Maldives, and to provide opportunities on an international scale. Finalists from three regional competitions vie at the Maldives Breakout Festival, where one winning band is awarded the opportunity to perform for U.K. music executives. Held annually. Established in 2008.

Malta

4556 ■ Computer Society of Malta
Dr. Brian Warrington, Chm.
Kordin Business Incubation Centre
Kordin Industrial Centre
Paola PLA 08, Malta
Ph: 356 2398 0131
E-mail: info@csm.org.mt
URL: http://www.csm.org.mt

4557 ■ e-Business Solution Award
To recognize projects, products, or business solutions making use of Internet technology. Awarded annually.

4558 ■ Information Society Award
To honor an individual or organization for the promotion of digital literacy or the encouragement of a greater use of technology in everyday life.

4559 ■ IT Company Award
To recognize growth and revenue for suppliers of information technology products and services. Candidates may be suppliers of computer hardware, networking, software products, software development services, and Web technology, as well as training and educational services. Awarded annually.

4560 ■ IT Education Award
To recognize excellence in the use of information technology solutions in the educational or training sector. Awarded annually.

4561 ■ IT Product Award
To recognize achievement in the development of new products or enhancement of existing products in the field of information and communications technology. Awarded annually.

4562 ■ IT Project Award
To recognize end-user projects that have exploited information technology to achieve benefits in efficiency, effectiveness, service delivery or quality, and cost reduction. Awarded annually.

4563 ■ Micro-Enterprise Award
To recognize a company or public body outside of the information technology field that demonstrates the best use of information technology throughout its organization to meet objectives, achieve greater competitiveness, or improve public services. To qualify, organizations must have fewer than 50 employees. Awarded annually.

4564 ■ R & D Award
To recognize creative effort and achievement in the acquisition or application of knowledge, or the development of cutting-edge techniques in the field of information and communications technology. Awarded annually.

4565 ■ Institute of Maltese Journalists (Institut Tal-Gurnalisti Maltin)
Mr. Joe A. Vella, Gen. Sec.
280/3, Republic St.
3rd Fl., Rm. 120
Valletta VLT 1112, Malta
Ph: 356 21316958
Ph: 356 99450746
E-mail: joeavella@onvol.net
URL: http://www.maltapressclub.org.mt

4566 ■ Malta Journalism Awards
To recognize excellence by Maltese journalists. Awards are presented in 12 categories. The first-place winner each category receives a certificate, trophy, and monetary prize of 350 Euros. In addition, the Gold Award is presented. Awarded annually.

4567 ■ Malta Amateur Radio League
PO Box 575
Valletta CMR 01, Malta
Ph: 356 21423608

Awards are arranged in alphabetical order below their administering organizations

Fax: 356 21423608
E-mail: email@m.a.r.l.
URL: http://www.9h1mrl.org/

4568 ■ All Malta Award
To recognize any amateur radio operator who accrues at least five points, awarded for contact with 9H stations. Diplomas are awarded when merited.

4569 ■ Diploma Mediterranean Award
To recognize any amateur radio operator who confirms contact with at least 15 of the 30 Mediterranean countries. Diplomas are awarded when merited.

4570 ■ Office of the Prime Minister of Malta
Transcontinental House
Zachary St.
Valletta 1210, Malta
Ph: 356 22 001 852
Fax: 356 22 001 851
E-mail: customercare.opm@gov.mt
URL: http://www.opm.gov.mt

4571 ■ Malta Self-Government Re-introduction Seventy-Fifth Anniversary Medal
To recognize persons living on the 7th of June, 1996 who at any time since the 1st of November, 1921, was, or is, a Member of the Senate, Legislative Assembly or House of Representatives.

4572 ■ Medal for Bravery (Midalja ghall-Qlubija)
To recognize a Maltese citizen for exceptional bravery. A medal is awarded by the President of the Republic of Malta, on the written advice of the Prime Minister, when merited and may be awarded posthumously. Established in 1975 by the Government of Malta.

4573 ■ Medal for Service to the Republic (Midalja ghall-Qadi tar-Repubblika)
To recognize distinguished service to Malta. Maltese citizens are eligible, and citizens of other countries are eligible on an honorary basis. A medal is awarded by the President of the Republic of Malta when merited (on the written advice of the Prime Minister). No more than 10 awards may be made in one year, and the total number of recipients may not exceed 100. Established in 1975 by the Government of Malta.

4574 ■ National Order of Merit
To recognize Maltese citizens who distinguish themselves in different fields of endeavor. Maltese citizens may be appointed members of the Order and honorary memberships may be conferred on foreign nationals who have distinguished themselves by their service in the promotion and fostering of international relations or who have earned the respect and gratitude of the people of the Maltese Islands. There are four grades of the Order: Companion of Honor, Companion, Officer, and Member. Established in 1990 by the Government of Malta as a consolidation of the Gieh ir-Repubblika Act, 1975.

4575 ■ Xirka Gieh ir-Repubblika
Induction to this honor society recognizes distinguished persons who have demonstrated merit in the service of Malta or of humanity. Maltese citizens may be appointed members of the Society and others may be appointed honorary members by the President of the Republic of Malta on the written advice of the Prime Minister. The total membership is limited to 20 persons. New appointments are made only when a vacancy occurs. Established in 1975.

Mauritius

4576 ■ National Productivity and Competitiveness Council
Level 4, Alexander House
Cybercity
Ebene City, Mauritius
Ph: 230 467 7700
Fax: 230 467 3838
E-mail: natpro@intnet.mu
URL: http://www.npccmauritius.com

4577 ■ Innovators Mauritius Award
To encourage innovation on a specific theme. Awarded biennially in even-numbered years. Established in 2004.

Mexico

4578 ■ Centre for Latin American Monetary Studies (Centro de Estudios Monetarios Latinoamericanos)
Javier Guzman Calafell, Dir. Gen.
Durango No. 54
Col. Roma
06700 Mexico City, Federal District, Mexico
Ph: 52 55 50616640
Ph: 52 55 50616641
Fax: 52 55 50616695
E-mail: direccion@cemla.org
URL: http://www.cemla.org

4579 ■ Rodrigo Gomez Prize
Recognizes outstanding contributions in the areas of economic, jury, finance, and monetary studies. Awarded annually. Established in 1970.

4580 ■ Chemical Organization of Mexico (Sociedad Quimica de Mexico)
Eusebio Juaristi Cosio, Pres.
Barranca del Muerto No. 26
Col. Credito Constructor, Delegacion Benito Juarez
CP 03940 Mexico City, Federal District, Mexico
Ph: 52 55 56626837
Ph: 52 55 56626823
Fax: 52 55 56626823
E-mail: soquimex@prodigy.net.mx
URL: http://www.sqm.org.mx

4581 ■ Andres Manuel del Rio National Prize in Chemistry (Premio Nacional de Quimica Andres Manuel del Rio)
To recognize chemistry professionals who have contributed extraordinarily towards raising the quality and the prestige of the chemistry profession in Mexico. Awards are made in two categories: academic and industrial. Members of the Society must make nominations by June 30. Medals and diplomas are awarded annually to one or more recipients. Established in 1964 in memory of Andres Manuel del Rio (1764-1849), the discoverer of the element Vanadium, atomic number 23, in 1801.

4582 ■ Consejo Nacional de Ciencia y Tecnologia
Juan Carlos Romero Hicks, Dir. Gen.
Av. Insurgentes Sur 1582
Col. Credito Constructor
Del. Benito Juarez
03940 Mexico City, Federal District, Mexico
Ph: 52 55 53227700
E-mail: contacto@conacyt.mx
URL: http://www.conacyt.mx

4583 ■ Premio Nacional de Ciencia y Tecnologia de Alimentos
To recognize outstanding work and stimulate research in the field of nutrition. Awards are given in the following categories: (1) Premio Na-

cional al Merito; (2) Professional; and (3) Student. Awarded annually.

4584 ■ Fundacion Miguel Aleman
Miguel Aleman Velazco, Pres.
Ruben Dario 187
Colonia Chapultepec Morales
11570 Mexico City, Federal District, Mexico
Ph: 52 9 1260700
Fax: 52 9 1260762
E-mail: fundacionmiguelaleman@frna.org.mx
URL: http://www.miguelaleman.org.mx

4585 ■ Premio Miguel Aleman Valdes
To recognize and stimulate young researchers and to promote research in the knowledge, prevention, and control of the principal maladies affecting the country's health. Mexican citizens under 40 year of age who are registered researchers in the biological, biomedical, and technological sciences are eligible. A monetary prize of 25,000 Mexican pesos and the support of the project are awarded annually. Established in 1985.

4586 ■ Inter-American Society of Cardiology (Sociedad Interamericana de Cardiologia)
Dr. Wistremundo Dones, Pres.
Juan Badiano No. 1
Edificio Galas P.B.
14080 Mexico City, Federal District, Mexico
Ph: 52 55 55135177
Fax: 52 55 55135177
URL: http://www.soinca.org

4587 ■ Professor Ignacio Chavez Young Investigator Award (Premio Joven Investigador Profesor Ignacio Chavez)
To recognize the best cardiological work presented at the Interamerican Congress of Cardiology. The Congress is held every two years in a city of the continent (America).

4588 ■ Mexican Academy of Dermatology (Academia Mexicana de Dermatologia)
Dr. Laura Juarez Navarrete, Pres.
Filadelfia No. 119 PH
Colonia Napoles
03810 Mexico City, Federal District, Mexico
Ph: 52 56 822545
Ph: 52 55 435354
Fax: 52 56 828963
URL: http://www.amd.org.mx

4589 ■ Dr. Antonio Gonzalez Ochoa Award
For best resident paper in clinical or basic research.

4590 ■ Mexican Academy of Sciences (Academia Mexicana de Ciencias)
Dr. Arturo Menchaca Rocha, Pres.
Calle Cypresses s/n
Km 23.5 de la carretera federal Mexico-Cuernavaca
San Andres Totoltepec
14400 Tlalpan, Federal District, Mexico
Ph: 52 5 8494905
Fax: 52 5 58495112
E-mail: academia@amc.unam.mx
URL: http://www.amc.unam.mx
Formerly: (1997) Academy of Scientific Research; Academia de la Investigacion Cientifica.

4591 ■ Scientific Research Prizes (Premios de Investigacion Cientifica)
For recognition of contributions to scientific research in the following areas: (1) natural sciences; (2) social sciences; (3) exact sciences; (4) technological innovation; and (5) humanities. Scientists and researchers working permanently in Mexico and under 40 years of age are eligible. The awards are given for a complete career rather than for a single publication or research

Awards are arranged in alphabetical order below their administering organizations

paper. A monetary prize in Mexican pesos and a diploma are awarded annually for each field. The monetary prize changes every year. Established in 1961.

4592 ■ Weizmann Prizes
(Premios Weizmann de la Academia Mexicana de Ciencias)
For recognition of the best doctoral thesis in the field of: (1) natural sciences and (2) exact sciences. Originality and scientific importance are considered. Individuals under 35 years of age are eligible for thesis research done in Mexico and the degree must be conferred by a Mexican institution. A monetary prize in Mexican pesos and a diploma is awarded for each thesis annually. Established in 1986. Formerly: (1997) Weizmann Prizes of the Academy of Scientific Research (Premios Weizmann de la Academia de la Investigacion Cientifica).

4593 ■ National Chamber of the Restaurant and Seasoned Food Industry
(Camara Nacional de la Industria de Restaurantes y Alimentos Condimentados)
Mr. Braulio Cardenas Cantu, Natl. Pres.
Aniceto Ortega 1009
Colonia del Valle
03100 Mexico City, Federal District, Mexico
Ph: 52 55 56040478
Fax: 52 55 56044086
E-mail: orientaciongeneral@canirac.org.mx
URL: http://canirac.org.mx

4594 ■ Annual Restaurant Merit Award
To recognize Mexican cuisine, innovative features, chains, fast-foods, Mexican traditions, foreign cuisine, regional cuisine, banquets and catering. Awarded annually.

4595 ■ United Nations High Commissioner for Refugees - Regional Office Mexico
Presidente Masaryk No. 29, Piso 6
11570 Polanco, Federal District, Mexico
Ph: 52 55 52639864
E-mail: mexme@unhcr.org
URL: http://www.unhcr.ch

4596 ■ Nansen Refugee Award
To recognize individual or organizations that have distinguished themselves in work on behalf of refugees. A medal and monetary prize of $100,000 is awarded annually. Established in 1954. Formerly: (2006) Nansen Medal.

4597 ■ World Boxing Council
(Consejo Mundial de Boxeo)
Jose Sulaiman, Pres.
Cuzco 872
Colonia Lindavista
07300 Mexico City, Federal District, Mexico
Ph: 52 55 51195276
Fax: 52 55 51195293
E-mail: contact@wbcboxing.com
URL: http://www.wbcboxing.com/indexEng.php

4598 ■ Hall of Fame
To recognize individuals who have made extraordinary contributions to the sport of boxing.

4599 ■ World Boxing Council Awards
To recognize the winners of world boxing title fights. Champions are declared in approximately 17 divisions, from Heavyweight to Strawweight.

4600 ■ World Cultural Council
(Consejo Cultural Mundial)
Ms. Lilian Hernandez, Sec. Gen.
Apartado Postal 10-1083
CP 11002 Mexico City, Federal District, Mexico
Ph: 52 55 55892907
Fax: 52 55 55898857
E-mail: info@consejoculturalmundial.org
URL: http://www.consejoculturalmundial.org

4601 ■ Leonardo da Vinci World Award of Arts
To recognize artists, avant guardists, or art authorities whose works constitute a significant contribution to the artistic legacy of the world. A monetary prize of US$10,000, a medal, and a diploma are awarded biennially in odd-numbered years. Established in 1989.

4602 ■ Albert Einstein World Award of Science
To recognize individuals for scientific and technological achievements that have brought progress to science and benefit to humankind. Candidates must be nominated. A monetary prize of US$10,000, a medal, and a diploma are awarded annually. Established in 1984.

4603 ■ Jose Vasconcelos World Award of Education
To recognize an educator, an authority in the field of teaching, or a legislator of education policies who has had a significant influence on the advancement of human culture. Candidates must be nominated. A monetary prize of US$10,000, a medal, and a diploma are awarded biennially in even-numbered years. Established in 1985.

Moldova

4604 ■ American Chamber of Commerce in Moldova
John Maxemchuk, Pres.
202, Stefan cel Mare St.
MD-2004 Chisinau, Moldova
Ph: 373 22 211 781
Fax: 373 22 211 782
E-mail: info@amcham.md
URL: http://www.amcham.md

4605 ■ Corporate Social Responsibility Awards
To raise public awareness to corporate social responsibility and to showcase companies that have made notable contributions to further corporate citizenship in Moldova. Four awards are presented: General Award, SME Award for small and medium enterprises, Partnership Award, and the Philanthropy Award. Awarded annually. Established in 2008.

Monaco

4606 ■ Monaco Charity Film Festival Association
31-B, ave. Princess Grace, 1st Fl.
MC-98000 Monaco, Monaco
E-mail: info@monacofilmfestival.org
URL: http://www.monacofilmfestival.org

4607 ■ Monaco Charity Film Festival
To encourage and assist independent and emerging filmmakers to promote their films and obtain financing, and to raise money to benefit poor children around the world. A jury selects the best film, best director, best scriptwriter, and best actors from among the films screened during the weeklong festival. Held annually. Established in 2006.

4608 ■ Peace and Sport
Immeuble les Mandariniers
42 ter, Boulevard du Jardin Exotique
98000 Monaco, Monaco
Ph: 377 9797 7800
Fax: 377 9797 1891
E-mail: contact@peace-sport.org
URL: http://www.peace-sport.org

4609 ■ Best Corporate Social Responsibility Initiative of the Year
To recognize an international corporation that has particularly shown its citizenship by using sport as a tool for peace education. Awarded annually. Established in 2008.

4610 ■ Best Project for Peace from an International Sports Federation
To recognize excellence from an International Federation that has put its sport at the service of social action, while also contributing to the national development of the sport. Awarded annually. Established in 2008.

4611 ■ Champion for Peace of the Year
To recognize an international athlete who has made the greatest contribution throughout the year to promoting and using sport for the cause of sustainable peace. Awarded annually. Established in 2008.

4612 ■ Non-Governmental Organization for Peace of the Year
To recognize a non-governmental organization that has demonstrated real expertise in using sport as a tool for peace education and has delivered an impact on the people with whom it works. Awarded annually. Established in 2008.

4613 ■ Peace and Sport Image of the Year
To honor a photograph of fraternity in sport that has succeeded in integrating sport into the global agenda for peace. Awarded annually. Established in 2008.

4614 ■ Special Jury Prize
To recognize creative initiatives (such as films, books, exhibitions, art, etc.) that have highlighted the positive role that sport can play for sustainable peace. Awarded annually. Established in 2008.

4615 ■ Sports Event for Peace of the Year
To recognize an event demonstrating an ability to effectively promote a message of peace through sport, which also contributes to implement sustainable peace within the communities involved. Awarded annually. Established in 2008.

Morocco

4616 ■ American Chamber of Commerce in Morocco
Kamal Kassis, Pres.
67, Blvd. Massira Al Khadra, 3rd Fl., Apt. 6
Casablanca 20100, Morocco
Ph: 212 2 522250736
Ph: 212 2 522250737
Fax: 212 2 522250730
E-mail: amcham@amcham-morocco.com
URL: http://www.amcham-morocco.com

4617 ■ Corporate Citizenship Award
To recognize organizations for outstanding corporate citizenship activities. Awards are presented in three categories based on size of organization. Awarded annually.

4618 ■ Moroccan-American Trade and Investment Award
To recognize organizations for outstanding contributions to Moroccan trade in the form of merchandise or services. Awarded annually. Co-sponsored by Groupe OCP.

Namibia

4619 ■ Hospitality Association of Namibia
Box 86078
Windhoek, Namibia
Ph: 264 61 222 904
Fax: 264 61 222 904
URL: http://www.hannamibia.com

4620 ■ Award of Excellence
To honor accommodation establishments in Namibia for hard work, dedication, and eagerness to demonstrate the quality of their products

Awards are arranged in alphabetical order below their administering organizations

and services. Recipients are determined by survey of guests. Gold, silver, and bronze certificates are awarded annually to multiple recipients.

4621 ■ Eco Award Namibia
To serve as a mark of distinction for accommodation establishments that are planned and managed according to eco-friendly principles. Based on seven criteria: water and waste water management, waste management including recycling practices, energy management, approach towards the ecology, sustainable construction and landscaping practices, staff welfare and development programs, and involvement in and social responsibility towards local communities. Winning establishments are awarded the Desert Flower emblem, which not only symbolizes roots, earth, water, leaves, and the sun of Namibia, but also the human being. Awarded annually.

4622 ■ Eco Media Awards Namibia
To recognize, encourage, and honor published work and broadcasts for outstanding achievements that contribute to the advancement of environmental reporting in the media landscape of Namibia, and also to encourage the promotion of environmental awareness in all areas of Namibian society and trade. Open to all local and national media houses, private, and public radio and TV broadcasters and news agencies stationed in Namibia, all Namibian publications, and editors, journalists, reporters, writers for news agencies, stringers, freelance journalists, and broadcasters. Awarded annually. Sponsored by Namibia Breweries Ltd.

4623 ■ Personality of the Year
To honor a dynamic, dedicated, and determined member for his or her unselfish input to the development of the tourism and hospitality industry in Namibia. Awarded annually.

4624 ■ Media Institute of Southern Africa - Namibia
Kaitira Kandjii, Regional Dir.
Private Bag 13386
Windhoek, Namibia
Ph: 264 61 232975
Fax: 264 61 248016
URL: http://www.misa.org

4625 ■ John Manyarara Investigative Journalism Awards
To recognize excellence in investigative journalism in any form of media in the Southern African Development Community. Awarded for an article or series of articles that demonstrate investigative journalism skills and presentation of facts. Two awards are presented: John Manyarara Investigative Journalist of the Year, which carries a monetary prize of 4000 Euros, and the John Manyarara Upcoming Investigative Journalist of the Year, which carries a cash prize of 2000 Euros plus a scholarship of 6000 Euros. Awarded annually. Supported by the Netherlands Institute of Southern Africa and the Forum for African Investigate Reporters.

4626 ■ Press Freedom Award
To recognize an individual for efforts in support of journalistic freedom in the southern Africa region, including Angola, Botswana, Lesotho, Malawi, Mozambique, Namibia, South Africa, Swaziland, Tanzania, Zambia, and Zimbabwe. Open to all forms of media. A monetary prize of US$2500 is awarded annually.

4627 ■ Namibia Nature Foundation
Julian Fennessy, Dir.
76-78 Frans Indongo St.
PO Box 245
Windhoek, Namibia
Ph: 264 61 248345
Fax: 264 61 248344
E-mail: sw@nnf.org.na

URL: http://www.nnf.org.na

4628 ■ Environment Award
To honor individuals and organizations for achievements in the environmental field. Awarded annually.

4629 ■ Go-Green Journalism Award
To honor an outstanding environmental journalism in Namibia. Awarded annually.

Nepal

4630 ■ Nepal Academy of Science and Technology
Prof. Dr. Prakash Chandra Adhikari, Sec.
PO Box 3323
Kathmandu, Nepal
Ph: 977 1 547715
Ph: 977 1 547717
Fax: 977 1 547713
E-mail: info@nast.org.np
URL: http://www.nast.org.np
Formerly: (2007) Royal Nepal Academy of Science and Technology.

4631 ■ M.D. Basnyat Technology Award
To recognize an outstanding scientist in technology. Awarded biennially.

4632 ■ Bhubaneswor Low Cost Technology Award
To recognize an outstanding scientist in the field of low-cost technology. Awarded biennially.

4633 ■ J.B. Nakarmi Metalwork Award
To recognize an outstanding scientist in metalwork. Awarded biennially.

4634 ■ Nature Conservation Award
To recognize individuals and institutions for contributions in nature conservation under any genre of science and technology. Awarded biennially. Established in 2005.

4635 ■ S & T Promotion Award
To recognize Nepali individuals and institutions for the promotion of science and technology (S & T) and for creating public awareness on the importance of science and technology. One or two awards are presented annually.

4636 ■ Science and Technology Award
To honor Nepali researchers for remarkable contributions in the field of science and technology. Awarded biennially. Established in 1986.

4637 ■ Young Scientist Award
To recognize young Nepali scientists for outstanding endeavor and dedication in their field of expertise. Candidates must be younger than 40 years of age. Awarded annually to up to five individuals.

4638 ■ Nepal Vista
URL: http://www.nepalvista.com

4639 ■ New Nepali Website Award
To recognize the best new Web sites based on site design and maintenance. Sites must have content relevant to the Nepal region. Awarded annually to one or more recipients.

4640 ■ Site of the Year
To recognize the most outstanding Nepali Website of the year. Awarded annually. In addition, Site of the Month awards are conferred throughout the year.

4641 ■ Tourism Award
To honor Webmasters and people involved in the tourism industry who have designed outstanding Websites. Awarded annually to one or more recipients.

4642 ■ Trekking Agencies' Association of Nepal
Mr. Sitaram Sapkota, Pres.
PO Box 3612

Ganesthan, Maligaun
Kathmandu, Nepal
Ph: 977 1 4440920
Ph: 977 1 4427473
Fax: 977 1 4419245
E-mail: taan@wlink.com.np
URL: http://www.taan.org.np

4643 ■ Sagarmatha Award
To recognize climbers of Mount Everest (Sagarmatha). A monetary prize of Nrs. 50,000 is awarded annually as part of International Everest Day. Established in 2008.

4644 ■ Tenzing-Hillary Award
To recognize Nepali journalists and photographers. A monetary prize of Rs. 25,000 is awarded.

Netherlands

4645 ■ Association of Dutch Designers (Beroepsorganisatie Nederlandse Ontwerpers)
Mr. Rob Huisman, Dir.
Postbus 20698
NL-1001 NR Amsterdam, Netherlands
Ph: 31 20 6244748
Fax: 31 20 6278585
E-mail: bno@bno.nl
URL: http://www.bno.nl

4646 ■ Dutch Design Awards
For the most characteristic, trendsetting, fashionable, functional, admirable, innovative, smart, astounding, provocative, impressive, creative, or just plain design. Awarded annually.

4647 ■ Piet Zwart Prize
For an individual excelling in one or more fields that Piet Zwart covered with his work, including graphic design, industrial design, interior design, and photography.

4648 ■ Chancery of Netherlands Orders (Kanselarij der Nederlandse Orden)
Nassaulaan 18
PO Box 30436
NL-2500 GK The Hague, Netherlands
Ph: 31 70 375 1200
Fax: 31 70 365 2923
E-mail: infor@kanselaeij.nl
URL: http://www.lintjes.nl

4649 ■ Military William Order
To recognize Netherlanders or foreigners for conspicuous gallantry in the presence of the enemy. Awarded in four classes. Dutch citizens have to start as Knights 4th class, but can be promoted for further acts of bravery to Knight 3rd Class, Knight 2nd Class and Knight Commander. Such promotions are relatively rare. Established in 1815.

4650 ■ Order of Orange-Nassau (Orde van Oranje-Nassau)
To recognize Dutch citizens or foreigners who have made themselves particularly deserving towards the Dutch people and the State, or towards society. This Order has six classes: Grand Cross; Grand Officer; Commander; Officer; Knight; and Member. Awarded in two divisions: with swords, for military recipients; and a general division for others. Established in 1892.

4651 ■ Order of the Golden Ark
To recognize outstanding service to the conservation of wildlife and the natural environment. Established in 1972 by H.R.H. Prince Bernhard of the Netherlands, founder-President of the World Wildlife Fund. (The Order of the Golden Ark is a private award of H.R.H. Prince Bernhard of the Netherlands and does not belong to the Netherlands' Orders of Knighthood).

4652 ■ Order of the Netherlands Lion
To recognize Netherlanders who have displayed

Awards are arranged in alphabetical order below their administering organizations

tested patriotism, unusual dedication and loyalty in the carrying out of their civil duties, or extraordinary skill and performance in the sciences and arts. This Order, in exceptional cases, is given to foreigners, and consists of three classes: Grand Cross; Commander; and Knight. Established in 1815.

4653 ■ Collective Promotion for the Dutch Book
(Stichting Collectieve Propaganda van het Nederlandse Boek)
Postbus 10576
NL-1001 EN Amsterdam, Netherlands
Ph: 31 20 626 4971
Fax: 31 20 623 1696
E-mail: info@cpnb.nl
URL: http://www.cpnb.nl

4654 ■ Prijs van de Jonge Jury
Dutch children between the ages of 12 and 15 elect the best Dutch book for children. Books must have been published during the previous year in the Netherlands. Established in 1998.

4655 ■ Prijs van de Nederlandse Kinderjury
To recognize the best children books that were published during the preceding year in two age categories (6 to 9 years and 9 to 12 years). The prize is awarded by Dutch children ages six to twelve. Two diplomas are awarded annually. Established in 1988.

4656 ■ Conamus
(Stichting Conamus)
PO Box 929
NL-1200 AX Hilversum, Netherlands
Ph: 31 35 621 8748
Fax: 31 35 621 2750
E-mail: info@bumacultuur.nl
URL: http://www.conamus.nl

4657 ■ Export Award
To recognize Dutch performers based on the figures of records-sales abroad. These figures are obtained from records companies, music publishers, and personal or business managers of qualifying artists. A trophy is awarded annually. Formerly: Conamus Export Prize.

4658 ■ Golden Harp
This, the highest award in light music in Holland, recognizes individuals who have contributed to national light music in exceptional ways. A trophy is awarded annually to three or four recipients. Established in 1962.

4659 ■ Pop Award
To recognize the Dutch artist who made the biggest contribution to Dutch pop music in the previous year. Awarded annually.

4660 ■ Silver Harp
To encourage young Dutch artists in the field of entertainment who are expected to develop into credits to their trade. A trophy is awarded annually to three or four recipients.

4661 ■ Dutch Society for Biomaterials and Tissue Engineering
(Nederlandse vereniging voor Biomaterialen en Tissue Engineering)
Dr. Jenneke Klein-Nulend, Chm.
ACTA - Vrije Universiteit
Dept. of Oral Cell Biology
Van der Boechorststraat 7
1081 BT Amsterdam, Netherlands
Ph: 31 20 4448660
Fax: 31 20 4448683
E-mail: j.kleinnulend@vumc.nl
URL: http://www.nbte.nl

4662 ■ Pauline van Wachem Award
To recognize the best thesis in biomaterials science or tissue engineering in the Netherlands. Awarded biennially in odd-numbered years.

4663 ■ Edison Foundation
(Edison Stichting)
Albertus Perkstraat 36
NL-1217 NT Hilversum, Netherlands
Ph: 31 35 625 4411
Fax: 31 35 625 4410
E-mail: info@nvpi.nl
URL: http://www.edisons.nl

4664 ■ Edison Classical Music Award
To recognize classical (sound carrier) productions for artistic value. Awarded in the following categories: chamber music, vocal, concerts, instrumental solo series, opera, contemporary music, baroque, Middle Ages and Renaissance, orchestra music, choir music, special historical recordings, and DVDs. Statues are awarded annually. Established in 1960.

4665 ■ Edison Jazz/World Music Awards
To recognize the best artists in jazz and world music. Presented in the following categories: National Jazz, International Jazz, Jazz Vocal, and World Music. In addition, the Jazz Lifetime Achievement Award may be presented. Statuettes are awarded annually. Established in 2007.

4666 ■ Edison Popular Music Awards
To recognize outstanding pop music artists and groups. Statuettes are awarded in a variety of categories each year. Established in 1960. Formerly: Edison Populair - Awards for Popular Music.

4667 ■ ESOMAR: World Association of Opinion and Marketing Research Professionals
Dieter Korczak, Pres.
Eurocenter 2, 11th Fl.
Barbara Strozzilaan 384
1083 HN Amsterdam, Netherlands
Ph: 31 20 6642141
Ph: 31 20 5897800
Fax: 31 20 6642922
E-mail: customerservice@esomar.org
URL: http://www.esomar.org

4668 ■ Excellence Award for Best Paper
To recognize the highest quality paper presented at an ESOMAR event. Papers are judged on their success in demonstrating a concrete contribution to the decision-making process while sustaining the ESOMAR best practices. A monetary prize of 4,000 Euros is awarded annually. Established in 1978.

4669 ■ John and Mary Goodyear Award
To recognize the best international research paper presented at ESOMAR events. Original, unpublished papers dealing with international research or being of strong relevance to international research; presented at the ESOMAR Congress, ESOMAR Conferences and other major conferences, seminars, symposia, and other events, which ESOMAR will hold alone or in cooperation with other organizations in a given calendar year. The award carries a prize of 3500 Euro, and is awarded annually. Established in 1999.

4670 ■ Young Researcher of the Year Award
To recognize individuals for outstanding original research projects. Research, which must be no older than 6 months, should contribute to societal excellence and best practice in research. A trophy is awarded annually. Established in 2009.

4671 ■ Europa Nostra Pan European Federation for Heritage
(Federation pan-europeenne du patrimoine)
Mrs. Sneska Quaedvlieg-Mihailovic, Sec. Gen.
Lange Voorhout 35
NL-2514 EC The Hague, Netherlands

Ph: 31 70 3024050
Fax: 31 70 3617865
E-mail: info@europanostra.org
URL: http://www.europanostra.org

4672 ■ European Union Prize for Cultural Heritage/Europa Nostra Awards
To promote high standards of conservation practice, to stimulate the exchange of knowledge and experience throughout Europe, and to encourage further efforts through the power of example. Monetary prizes are awarded in the following categories: Conservation of architectural heritage, cultural landscapes, collections of works of art, and archaeological sites; Outstanding study in the field of cultural heritage; and Dedicated service to heritage conservation by individuals or groups. Awarded annually. Established in 2002.

4673 ■ European Association of Geoscientists and Engineers
John Underhill, Pres.
PO Box 59
3990 DB Houten, Netherlands
Ph: 31 88 9955055
Fax: 31 30 6343524
E-mail: eage@eage.org
URL: http://www.eage.org

4674 ■ Nigel Anstey Award
To recognize a member who has made a contribution of distinctly valuable and tangible bearing on one or more of the disciplines in the Association. A medal and a certificate are awarded annually. Established in 2003.

4675 ■ Guido Bonarelli Award
To recognize the best oral presentation at the EAGE Annual Conference in the calendar year preceding the Award. A certificate is awarded annually. Established in 1989.

4676 ■ Louis Cagniard Award
To recognize the best poster presentation at the EAGE Annual Conference in the calendar year preceding the Award. A certificate is awarded annually. Established in 1997.

4677 ■ Lorand Eotvos Award
To recognize the author(s) of the best paper published in *Geophysical Prospecting* (or in *First Break* in a related topic) in the calendar year preceding the award. The paper should be of high scientific standard and should represent a significant contribution or an outstanding tutorial in one or more of the disciplines in the Association. A certificate and specially bound copy of the issue in which the paper appears are awarded annually. Established in 1988.

4678 ■ Desiderius Erasmus Award
To recognize a member for outstanding and lasting achievements in the field of resource exploration and development. A medal and a certificate are awarded annually. Established in 1999.

4679 ■ Norman Falcon Award
To recognize the author(s) of the best paper published in *Petroleum Geoscience* (or in *First Break* in a related topic) in the calendar year preceding the award. The paper should be of high scientific standard and should represent a significant contribution to one or more of the disciplines in the Association. A certificate and specially bound copy of the issue in which the paper appears are awarded annually. Established in 1999.

4680 ■ Life Membership Award
To honor a member who has rendered major and exceptionally valuable services to the Association. In special cases, Life Membership may also be conferred upon ex-members of the Association. A certificate and a lifelong EAGE membership are awarded when merited. First presented in 2005.

Awards are arranged in alphabetical order below their administering organizations

4681 ■ Ludger Mintrop Award
To recognize the author(s) of the best paper published in *Near Surface Geophysics* (or in *First Break* in a related topic) in the calendar year preceding the award. The paper should be of high scientific standard and should represent a significant contribution to one or more of the disciplines in the Association. A certificate and specially bound copy of the issue in which the paper appears are awarded annually. Established in 1997.

4682 ■ Conrad Schlumberger Award
Recognizes outstanding contribution over a period of time to the scientific and technical advancement of geophysics or other service to the geophysical community. A certificate and medal are awarded annually.

4683 ■ Arie van Weelden Award
Recognizes an individual under age 30 for significant contributions to one or more of the disciplines of the Association. A medal and monetary prize are awarded annually.

4684 ■ Alfred Wegener Award
To recognize a member who has made an outstanding contribution over a period of time to the scientific and technical advancement of one or more of the disciplines in the Association, particularly petroleum geoscience and engineering. A medal and a certificate are awarded annually. Established in 1998.

4685 ■ European Association of Plastic Surgeons
University Medical Center Utrecht
Department of Plastic Surgery
PO Box 85500
NL-3508 GA Utrecht, Netherlands
Ph: 31 88 7556 897
Fax: 31 30 2516 097
E-mail: euraps@umcutrecht.nl
URL: http://www.euraps.org

4686 ■ Hans Anderl Award
To promote excellence in the field of plastic surgery in Europe by recognizing an individual for outstanding and pioneer achievements in the field of plastic-reconstructive and aesthetic surgery. A monetary prize of 4,000 Euros is awarded annually. Established in 2005.

4687 ■ European Association of Tax Law Professors
Joke Straver, Contact
c/o International Bureau of Fiscal Documentation
H.J.E. Henckebachweg 210
NL-1096 AS Amsterdam, Netherlands
E-mail: j.straver@ibfd.org
URL: http://www.eatlp.org

4688 ■ European Academic Tax Thesis Award
To recognize an outstanding doctoral or post-doctoral thesis on issues of comparative, European, and/or international tax law. Authors must be no older than 35 years of age, and the thesis must be accepted by a European university. Awarded annually. Co-administered by the European Commission's Directorate General Taxation and Customs Union.

4689 ■ European Association of Urology
PO Box 30016
NL-6803 AA Arnhem, Netherlands
Ph: 31 26 389 0680
Fax: 31 26 389 0674
URL: http://www.uroweb.org

4690 ■ Frans Debruyne Lifetime Achievement Award
To recognize an individual for a long-standing and important contribution to the activities and development of the Association. Awarded annually. Established in 2006.

4691 ■ Willy Gregoir Medal
To recognize an individual for a significant contribution to the development of the urological specialty in Europe. Awarded annually. Established in 1988.

4692 ■ Hans Marberger Award
To recognize an outstanding European paper published on the topic of minimally invasive surgery in urology. Awarded annually. Established in 2004.

4693 ■ Crystal Matula Award
To recognize a young, promising European urological academician. Awarded annually. Established in 1996.

4694 ■ European Biophysical Societies' Association
Prof. J. Antoinette Killian, Sec.
Utrecht University
Chemical Biology and Organic Chemistry
Hugo R. Kruyt Bldg., Rm. W 804
Kruytgebouw, Padualaan 8
NL-3584 CH Utrecht, Netherlands
Ph: 31 30 2533442
Fax: 31 30 2533969
E-mail: j.a.killian@uu.nl
URL: http://www.ebsa.org

4695 ■ EBSA Prize and Lecture
To recognize a promising young scientist in biophysics. Candidates should be under 40 years of age (barring special circumstances) and working in a member country. Recipient is expected to give a lecture at the Congress. A monetary prize of 2,000 Euros is awarded.

4696 ■ European Federation of Food Science and Technology
Prof. Dr. Dietrich Knorr, Pres.
Bornse Weilanden 9
PO Box 17
NL-6708 WG Wageningen, Netherlands
Ph: 31 317 480297
E-mail: info@effost.org
URL: http://www.effost.org

4697 ■ Alexander Gottlieb Baumgarten Award
Recognizes outstanding young scientists. Awarded biennially in even-numbered years. Established in 2002.

4698 ■ Gustav Theodor Fechner Award
Recognizes scientific contribution to the field of empirical/experimental aesthetics. Awarded biennially in even-numbered years. Established in 1996.

4699 ■ Sir Francis Galton Award
For scientific contribution to the field of empirical aesthetics. Awarded biennially in even-numbered years. Established in 1996.

4700 ■ European Hematology Association
Koninginnegracht 12b
NL-2514 AA The Hague, Netherlands
Ph: 31 70 3020 099
E-mail: info@ehaweb.org
URL: http://www.ehaweb.org

4701 ■ Jean Bernard Lifetime Achievement Award
To honor outstanding physicians and scientists for their lifetime contributions to the advancement of hematology. Awarded annually. Established in 2008.

4702 ■ Jose Carreras Award
To recognize an established and active investigator who has made a large contribution to hematology. Awarded annually. Established in 1999 in collaboration with the Jose Carreras Foundation.

4703 ■ European Institute of Public Administration
(Institut Europeen d'Administration Publique)
Prof. Marga Prohl MD, Dir. Gen.
PO Box 1229

NL-6201 BE Maastricht, Netherlands
Ph: 31 43 3296296
Ph: 31 43 3296202
Fax: 31 43 3296296
E-mail: info@eipa.eu
URL: http://www.eipa.nl

4704 ■ Alexis de Tocqueville Prize
To recognize one or more persons, or a group of people, whose work and commitment have made a considerable contribution to improving public administration in Europe. Awarded biennially in odd-numbered years. Established in 1987.

4705 ■ European Organization for Caries Research
(Organisme Europeen de Recherche sur la Carie)
Dr. Monique van der Veen, Sec. Gen.
Dept. of Preventive Dentistry, ACTA
Gustav Mahlerlaan 3004
NL-1081 LA Amsterdam, Netherlands
Ph: 31 20 5980437
E-mail: m.vd.veen@acta.nl
URL: http://www.orca-caries-research.org

4706 ■ Young Investigator's Award
To encourage research by scientists aged 35 or under. A certificate and payment of the registration fee for a future ORCA Congress are awarded annually. Established in 2007.

4707 ■ Zsolnay Prize
For recognition of merit in any aspect of caries research. The field of scientific investigation from which a recipient is selected should be as broad as possible. A porcelain prize is awarded annually. Established in 1964.

4708 ■ European Public Health Association
Ms. Dineke Zeegers Paget PhD, Exec. Dir.
PO Box 1568
NL-3500 BN Utrecht, Netherlands
Ph: 31 30 2729709
Fax: 31 30 2729729
E-mail: office@eupha.org
URL: http://www.eupha.org

4709 ■ Best Abstract Award
To honor the highest scoring abstract submitted to the conference. Awarded annually.

4710 ■ European Society for Hyperthermic Oncology
Mrs. S. van der Sluis, Contact
Erasmus MC
Department of Radiation Oncology
Hyperthermia Unit
PO Box 5201
NL-3008 AE Rotterdam, Netherlands
E-mail: s.vandersluis@erasmusmc.nl
URL: http://www.esho.info

4711 ■ ESHO-BSD Award
To recognize an individual for exceptional contributions to hyperthermic oncology. Awarded annually.

4712 ■ FLEUROSELECT
Nils Klemm, Pres.
Parallel Blvd., 214d
NL-2202 HT Noordwijk, Netherlands
Ph: 31 71 3649101
Fax: 31 71 3649102
E-mail: info@fleuroselect.com
URL: http://www.fleuroselect.com
Formerly: European Organization for Testing New Flower Seeds.

4713 ■ Gold Medal
To recognize good performance and the presentation of the best new flower seeds of exceptional quality. Society members are eligible. A medal is awarded annually at the convention. Established in 1970.

Awards are arranged in alphabetical order below their administering organizations

4714 ■ Industry Award

To recognize the breeder of an outstanding plant in terms of point of sale performance, commercial potential, and overall appeal. Awarded annually. Established in 2009.

4715 ■ Quality Award

To recognize novelties and new varieties of flower seeds that are found to be improvements in comparison to an existing assortment. Winning varieties may carry the Fleuroselect Quality Mark logo. Awarded annually.

4716 ■ International Apparel Federation
PO Box 428
NL-3700 AK Zeist, Netherlands
Ph: 31 30 2320908
Fax: 31 30 2320
E-mail: nep@iafnet.com
URL: http://www.iafnet.com

4717 ■ International Designer Awards

To recognize and encourage innovative, original, and creative emerging fashion designers. Each member association is invited to nominate one designer from its country who has been in the business for at least three years. Participants are free to use any fabric/material that they choose, and no design restrictions apply. First prize is awarded for the most creative design; second prize for the most commercial design; and third prize for the best method of working with fabric. Awarded annually.

4718 ■ Student Award

To recognize and encourage outstanding final-year students enrolled at IAF Education Institutions. Selected candidates are invited to participate in a six-month internship at companies sponsoring the awards. Awarded annually.

4719 ■ International Association for the Evaluation of Educational Achievement
(Association Internationale pour l'Evaluation du Rendement Scolaire)
Dr. Hans Wagemaker, Exec. Dir.
Herengracht 487
NL-1017 BT Amsterdam, Netherlands
Ph: 31 20 6253625
Fax: 31 20 4207136
E-mail: department@iea.nl
URL: http://www.iea.nl

4720 ■ Bruce H. Choppin Memorial Award

For recognition of achievement in empirical research using data from studies conducted by the Association. The competition is open to persons from any nation who have completed a master's or doctoral thesis within the preceding three years that used data collected in connection with any IEA study, and that used statistical methods to analyze the data. Applications are accepted by March 31 of each year. A certificate and monetary prize of 500 Euros are awarded annually. Established in 1983 in honor of Bruce H. Choppin.

4721 ■ Dick Wolf Memorial Award

To recognize the author of a published paper in the field of educational research. A certificate and monetary prize of 500 Euros is awarded annually.

4722 ■ International Association for Vegetation Science
Wes Beekhuizenweg 3
NL-6871 VJ Renkum, Netherlands
E-mail: admin@iavs.org
URL: http://www.iavs.org

4723 ■ Editor's Award

To recognize outstanding papers in *Applied*

Vegetation Science and the *Journal of Vegetation Science*. Awarded annually for each magazine. Established in 2001.

4724 ■ International Association of Dredging Companies
Mr. Rene Kolman, Sec. Gen.
PO Box 80521
NL-2508 GM The Hague, Netherlands
Ph: 31 70 3523334
Fax: 31 70 3512654
E-mail: info@iadc-dredging.com
URL: http://www.iadc-dredging.com

4725 ■ IADC Award

To stimulate the promotion of new ideas and to encourage the younger men or women working in the dredging industry and related fields by honoring the best paper presented at conferences. A monetary prize of 1,000 Euros is awarded annually.

4726 ■ International Association of Logopedics and Phoniatrics
Mara Behlau PhD, Pres.
Tilweg 1
NL-9971 CW Ulrum, Netherlands
Fax: 31 595 401661
E-mail: office@ialp.info
URL: http://ialp.info

4727 ■ Student Award

To recognize a student for excellence in research. Awarded annually.

4728 ■ International Association of Sedimentologists
(Association Internationale de Sedimentologistes)
Poppe de Boer, Pres.
Utrecht University
PO Box 80021
TA 3508 Utrecht, Netherlands
E-mail: pdeboer@geo.uu.nl
URL: http://www.sedimentologists.org

4729 ■ Honorary Membership

Awarded to members who have given outstanding service to the association. Awarded periodically when merited. Established in 1975.

4730 ■ International Association of Sedimentologists Grants

To promote the study of sedimentology and the interchange of research, particularly where international cooperation is desirable.

4731 ■ Sorby Medal

This, the highest honor of the IAS, is given to recognize scientists of eminent distinction in sedimentology. Awarded every four years. Established in 1978.

4732 ■ International Bird Strike Committee
Dr. Luit Buurma, Honorary Vice Chm.
PO Box 20703
NL-2500 ES The Hague, Netherlands
Ph: 31 70 3396346
Fax: 31 70 3396347
E-mail: luitbuurma@worldmail.nl
URL: http://www.int-birdstrike.org

4733 ■ Mike Kuhring Award

Recognizes individuals for achievements toward improved flight safety concerning the bird problems of aviation. Awarded biennially in even-numbered years. Established in 1979.

4734 ■ International Confederation of Midwives
(Confederation Internationale des Sages-Femmes)
Frances Day-Strik, Pres.
Laan van Meerdervoort 70
NL-2517 AN The Hague, Netherlands
Ph: 31 70 3060520

Fax: 31 70 3555651
E-mail: info@internationalmidwives.org
URL: http://www.internationalmidwives.org

4735 ■ Marie Goubran Award

To assist in the furthering of midwifery education and practice in countries with special needs and limited funding opportunities, through the provision of grants, scholarships, and awards to midwives who have demonstrated the potential to act as change agents in their region or country. Awarded every three years to one or more recipients. Established in 1993.

4736 ■ International Federation of Agricultural Journalists
Connie Siemes, Exec. Sec.
PO Box 205
6920 AE Duiven, Netherlands
Ph: 31 573 451975
Fax: 31 613 398465
E-mail: secretary@ifaj.org
URL: http://www.ifaj.org

4737 ■ IFAJ-Alltech Young Leaders in Agricultural Journalism Award

To contribute to the global advancement of agricultural journalism and communication by supporting Congress participation by young members with leadership potential. Eligible to members under 35 years of age who are nominated by their guild. Awards of $1,000 are presented to 10 recipients annually.

4738 ■ Star Prize for Agricultural Photography

To recognize the winners of a photo contest for the best agricultural photograph of the previous year. Awards are presented in three categories, with the winner of each category awarded a diploma and a cash prize of 250 Euros. An overall winner is chosen from the category winners and awarded a trophy, a golden pin, and a cash prize of 500 Euros.

4739 ■ Star Prize for Print

To recognize the best agricultural writing of the previous year. Journalists in member countries are eligible. First prize is a trophy, a gold pin, a certificate and a 1,000 Euro cash prize. Second prize is a gold pin, a certificate, and a 500 Euro cash prize. Awarded annually.

4740 ■ International Federation of Library Associations and Institutions
Ms. Jennefer Nicholson, Sec. Gen.
PO Box 95312
NL-2509 CH The Hague, Netherlands
Ph: 31 70 3140884
Fax: 31 70 3834827
E-mail: ifla@ifla.org
URL: http://www.ifla.org

4741 ■ Honorary Fellow

To honor an individual for long and distinguished service to the Association. Awarded only four or five times each decade.

4742 ■ Honorary President

For recognition of outstanding service. Awarded when merited.

4743 ■ IFLA Medal

For recognition of outstanding service in the field of librarianship. There are no age, society, or citizenship restrictions. A medal and scroll are awarded to one or two recipients in odd-numbered years at the conference. IFLA's Council may also confer the title of Honorary Fellow of IFLA. Established in the 1930s.

4744 ■ Dr. Shawky Salem Conference Grant

To enable one expert in library science, who is a national of an Arabic country, to attend an IFLA Conference. A grant is awarded annually. Established in 1992.

Awards are arranged in alphabetical order below their administering organizations

4745 ■ Guust van Wesemael Literary Prize
To aid a public or school library in a developing country to perform activities in the field of literacy: collection development, promotion, training, policy development, or otherwise. A monetary prize of 3,000 Euro is awarded biennially in odd-numbered years. Established in 1991.

4746 ■ Margaret Wijnstroom Fund
To support IFLA's Regional Offices, to involve librarians from developing world in the work of IFLA's professional groups, and to support projects in the developing world. A grant is awarded periodically.

4747 ■ International Institute for Geo-Information Science and Earth Observation
Prof. Dr. Martien Molenaar, Contact
PO Box 217
NL-7500 Enschede, Netherlands
Ph: 31 53 4874444
Ph: 31 53 4874229
Fax: 31 53 4874400
E-mail: info@itc.nl
URL: http://www.itc.nl

4748 ■ Klaas Jan Beek Award
To recognize the best MSc thesis. A certificate, monetary prize of 1,000 Euros, and roundtrip travel from the home country of the winner to the Netherlands is awarded annually.

4749 ■ Research Award
To recognize the best ISI publication by a PhD candidate. A certificate and monetary prize of 1,000 Euros is awarded annually.

4750 ■ International Korfball Federation
Ms. Kate Mazak, Contact
PO Box 417
NL-3700 AK Zeist, Netherlands
Ph: 31 34 3499655
Fax: 31 34 3499650
E-mail: office@ikf.org
URL: http://www.korfball.org

4751 ■ Badge of Honour
For recognition of a contribution to a field of activity over a period of time. Individuals may apply. A badge of honor is awarded at the annual general meeting. Established in 1946.

4752 ■ Honorary Member
For recognition of a contribution to a field of activity over a period of time (more than 12 years). Three Pin of Merit for recognition of a contribution to a field of activity over a period of time (more than 6 years). Awarded at the annual general meeting. Established in 1995.

4753 ■ International Pharmaceutical Federation
(Federation Internationale Pharmaceutique)
A.J.M. Hoek, Gen. Sec./CEO
PO Box 84200
NL-2508 AE The Hague, Netherlands
Ph: 31 70 3021970
Fax: 31 70 3021999
E-mail: fip@fip.org
URL: http://www.fip.org/www

4754 ■ Andre Bedat Award
To recognize a pharmacist, or a person eligible to be licensed as a pharmacist, who is an outstanding practitioner and has made significant contributions to pharmacy at the international level. A winner is determined by the Board of Pharmaceutical Practice. An engraved steel plaque and the recipient's travel expenses are awarded at an FIP Congress. Awarded biennially in even-numbered years. Established in 1986 to honor Andre Bedat, president of FIP from 1978 to 1986.

4755 ■ Bio-Tech Award
To recognize an individual who has significantly contributed to the rapidly developing field of biotechnology. Awarded biennially in odd-numbered years. Established in 1999.

4756 ■ Distinguished Practice Award
To recognize an individual or group who has made an outstanding contribution to pharmaceutical practice. Awarded biennially in odd-numbered years. Established in 1994.

4757 ■ Distinguished Science Award
To recognize an individual or group who has made an outstanding contribution to pharmaceutical sciences. Awarded biennially in even-numbered years. Established in 1994.

4758 ■ Distinguished Service Award
To recognize officers and employees of the Federation who have rendered exceptional and distinguished service. Awarded when merited. Established in 2005.

4759 ■ FIP Fellowships
To permit the recipient to perform research and/or be trained outside his/her own home country. The subject of research or training must be in line with the objectives of the Foundation. Anyone employed in either the practice of pharmacy or the pharmaceutical sciences may apply. Selection is based on: originality/ novelty and creativity; relevance to the Foundation's objectives and current priorities; conciseness and clarity of presentation; application's qualifications and background; demonstration that the project is innovative and needed; the international character of the project; appropriateness of the project design to the stated goals; methods of evaluation, including both the monitoring of project developments and the achievement of project goals; specificity and practicality of the project schedule; specificity and practicality of the budget; and documentation of the institutional commitments (funds, materials, facilities, and/or personnel provided).

4760 ■ Honorary Member
To honor individuals who have rendered significant services to the Federation. Awarded periodically, when merited.

4761 ■ Host-Madsen Medal
To recognize pharmacists who have particularly distinguished themselves by their work in the field of pharmaceutical sciences and to encourage pharmacists in scientific research. Scientists from any country are eligible. Nominations may be submitted by members of the Federation and the Board of Pharmaceutical Sciences makes the selection. A gold medal is awarded biennially in odd-numbered years. Established in 1955, and awarded for the first time to Dr. Host-Madsen to honor his services to the Federation.

4762 ■ Lifetime Achievement in the Pharmaceutical Practice Award
To recognize an individual who has, over many years, contributed to the development of the practice of pharmacy. Awarded biennially in odd-numbered years. Established in 1994.

4763 ■ Lifetime Achievement in the Pharmaceutical Science Award
To recognize an individual who has, over many years, contributed to the development of the pharmaceutical sciences. Awarded biennially in even-numbered years. Established in 1994.

4764 ■ International Project Management Association
Mr. Roberto Mori, Pres.
PO Box 1167
NL-3860 BD Nijkerk, Netherlands
Ph: 31 33 2473430
Fax: 31 33 2460470
E-mail: info@ipma.ch
URL: http://www.ipma.ch/Pages/default.aspx

4765 ■ International Project Management Awards
To recognize the most successful project teams in the world. The award identifies examples of excellent project management and acknowledges innovative projects. It supports professional project management in achieving high performance in projects and motivates project teams to identify and optimize the use of their strengths. Awarded to several recipients each year.

4766 ■ International School Psychology Association
Dr. Helen Bakker, Pres.
Spangenhof 29
1083 JJ Amsterdam, Netherlands
E-mail: bakkerhe@planet.nl
URL: http://www.ispaweb.org

4767 ■ Distinguished Services Award
To honor members for distinguished contributions to the association. Awarded to one or more recipients annually. Established in 1998.

4768 ■ International Society for Contemporary Music
c/o Muziek Centrum Nederland
Rokin 111
NL-1012 KN Amsterdam, Netherlands
Ph: 31 20 344 6060
E-mail: info@iscm.org
URL: http://www.iscm.org

4769 ■ Young Composer Award
To recognize an outstanding young composer whose work is featured in the annual ISCM World New Music Days Festival. Candidates must be under the age of 35 years. Awarded annually. Established in 2002.

4770 ■ International Society for Microbial Ecology - Netherlands
Sarash de Wilde, Mgr.
PO Box 50
NL-6708 PB Wageningen, Netherlands
Ph: 31 317 473467
Fax: 31 317 210138
E-mail: office@isme-microbes.org
URL: http://www.isme-microbes.org

4771 ■ Jim Tiedje Award
To honor an individual for outstanding lifetime contributions to microbial ecology. Awarded biennially in even-numbered years.

4772 ■ David C. White Award
To stimulate innovating thinking and to honor a student for the most innovative poster presentation. Awarded biennially in even-numbered years. Established in 2008.

4773 ■ Young Investigator Award
To recognize a young scientist who has made a significant contribution to microbial ecology. Awarded biennially in even-numbered years.

4774 ■ International Society of Blood Transfusion
(Societe Internationale de Transfusion Sanguine)
Geoff Daniels, Sec. Gen.
Jan van Goyenkade 11
NL 1075 HP Amsterdam, Netherlands
E-mail: centraloffice@isbtweb.org
URL: http://www.isbtweb.org

4775 ■ International Women in Transfusion Award
To honor a woman for lifetime achievements in transfusion medicine and science. A monetary prize of 1,000 Euro as well as an invitation and travel expenses to lecture at an annual meeting are awarded annually. Established in 2005.

4776 ■ ISBT Award
To recognize an individual or organization for

Awards are arranged in alphabetical order below their administering organizations

outstanding contribution to the education of blood transfusion or transfusion medicine science. Awarded annually to one or more recipients.

4777 ■ Jean Julliard Prize

For recognition of recently completed scientific work on blood transfusion and related subjects. In general, the prize is awarded to one individual; in special cases, the prize may be shared by more than one scientist. Scientists under 40 years of age may submit manuscripts. A monetary prize of $5,000 and a certificate are awarded biennially in even-numbered years. Established in 1964 in memory of Jean Julliard, the first secretary general of the Society.

4778 ■ Presidential Award

To recognize a senior individual for eminent contributions to transfusion medicine or a related field through basic or applied research, the practice of transfusion therapy, or significant educational and/or service contributions to the field. A medal, certificate, and monetary prize are awarded biennially in even-numbered years. Established in 2000.

4779 ■ International Society of City and Regional Planners

3rd Fl., Rm. 318/320
Laan van Meerdervoort 70
PO Box 983
NL-2501 CZ The Hague, Netherlands
Ph: 31 70 346 2654
Fax: 31 70 361 7909
E-mail: isocarp@isocarp.org
URL: http://www.isocarp.org

4780 ■ Gerd Albers Award

To recognize members for outstanding publications that further the aims of the Society. Eligible publications include books, chapters, journal articles, and published project reports. A monetary prize of 400 Euros is awarded annually. Established in 1999.

4781 ■ Awards for Excellence

To recognize a city, region, or institution for exceptionally innovative urban and regional initiatives. Criteria include content, process, and innovation. Awarded annually. First awarded in 2005.

4782 ■ Sam van Embden Award for Members' Initiatives

To honor and support members and their initiatives. A monetary prize of 1,000 Euros is awarded annually.

4783 ■ International Society of Olympic Historians

Anthony Th. Bijkerk, Sec. Gen.
Vogelrijd 16
NL-8428 HJ Fochteloo, Netherlands
Ph: 31 516 588520
Fax: 31 516 588260
E-mail: tony.bijkerk@planet.nl
URL: http://www.isoh.org/pages/index.html

4784 ■ Article Award

To recognize the best article on the subject of the Olympic movement or Olympic history published during the previous year. A monetary prize of US$250 is awarded annually. Established in 2003.

4785 ■ *Journal of Olympic History* Award

To recognize the best article published in the *Journal of Olympic History* during the previous year. A monetary prize of US$250 is awarded annually. Established in 2003.

4786 ■ Lifetime Contribution Award

To honor an Olympic historian for contributions over a lifetime. Awarded annually. Established in 2003.

4787 ■ Monograph Award

To recognize the best monograph on the subject of the Olympic movement or Olympic history published during the previous year. A monetary prize of US$500 is awarded annually. Established in 2003.

4788 ■ International Statistical Institute (Institut International de Statistique)

Ms. Ada van Krimpen, Sec.-Treas.
PO Box 24070
2490 AB The Hague, Netherlands
Ph: 31 70 3375737
Fax: 31 70 3860025
E-mail: isi@cbs.nl
URL: http://isi-web.org

4789 ■ Jan Tinbergen Awards for Young Statisticians from Developing Countries

To encourage the professional development of statisticians by honoring the authors of papers on any topic within the broad field of statistics. Individuals under the age of 32 who are residents of developing countries are eligible. A monetary prize of 2,269 Euros and travel expenses to present the winning paper are awarded biennially. Established in 1981. Formerly: (1995) Competition for Young Statisticians from Developing Countries.

4790 ■ International Union of Microbiological Societies (Union Internationale des Societes de Microbiologie)

Robert A. Samson, Sec. Gen.
PO Box 85167
3508 AD Utrecht, Netherlands
Ph: 31 30 2122600
Fax: 31 30 2512097
E-mail: r.samson@cbs.knaw.nl
URL: http://www.iums.org

4791 ■ Arima Award for Applied Microbiology

To recognize an individual for contributions to applied microbiology. A monetary award of US$1,000, a plaque, and travel expenses to present a lecture are awarded every three years at the International Congress. Established in 1989 to honor Professor Kli Arima, former president of IUMS.

4792 ■ Stuart Mudd Award for Studies in Basic Microbiology

To recognize an individual for contributions to basic microbiology. A monetary award of US$1,000,, a plaque, and travel expenses to present a lecture are awarded every three years at the International Congress. The recipient also becomes a Fellow in the World Academy of Art and Science. Established in 1978 to honor Professor Stuart Mudd.

4793 ■ Van Niel International Prize for Studies in Bacterial Systematics

To recognize an individual for contributions to bacterial systematics. A monetary award of approximately $2,000 is presented every three years at the International Congress. Established in 1986 by Dr. Vic Skerman to honor Professor Van Niel. The International Committee of Systematic Bacteriology plays an advisory role in the award program.

4794 ■ International World Games Association

Co Koren, Sec. Gen.
Office of the IWGA Secretary General
Slot Aldeborglaan 33
NL-6432 JM Hoensbroek, Netherlands
Ph: 31 45 5631089
Fax: 31 45 5631079
E-mail: sec@worldgames-iwga.org
URL: http://www.worldgames-iwga.org

4795 ■ The World Games

To recognize the world's best athletes in more

than 30 diverse sports. Open to athletes who are members of the 32 International Sports Federations that make up the International World Games Association. Held every four years over a period of 11 days. Established in 1981.

4796 ■ Netherlands Physical Society (Nederlandse Natuurkundige Vereniging)

Anja Al, Sec.
PO Box 41882
1009 DB Amsterdam, Netherlands
Ph: 31 20 5922211
Ph: 31 20 5922212
Fax: 31 20 5925155
E-mail: bureau@nnv.nl
URL: http://www.nnv.nl

4797 ■ Physica Prize

To an outstanding physicist.

4798 ■ Netherlands Psychiatric Association (Nederlandse Vereniging voor Psychiatrie)

PO Box 20062
NL-3502 LB Utrecht, Netherlands
Ph: 31 30 2823303
Fax: 31 30 2888400
E-mail: info@nvvp.net
URL: http://www.nvvp.net/nvvppublic/default.ashx?ShowPoll=0

4799 ■ Ramaermedaille

To recognize a citizen of the Netherlands who has produced the most meritorious contribution to psychiatric science, in particular to clinical psychiatry. A specially appointed committee makes the selection. A medal is awarded biennially. Established in 1918 by the Nederlandse Vereniging voor Psychiatrie en Neurologie in honor of Dr. J. N. Ramaer, founder of the Netherlands Psychiatric Association.

4800 ■ Netherlands Society for English Studies

Dr. Roger Eaton, Sec.-Treas.
University of Amsterdam
Dept. of English
Spuistraat 210
NL-1012 VT Amsterdam, Netherlands
E-mail: roger.eaton@hum.uva.nl
URL: http://nses.let.uu.nl

4801 ■ Graduation Prize

To recognize the graduate in English studies who produced the finest dissertation or final project. Awarded biennially.

4802 ■ NSES Award

To recognize an individual for journalistic contribution to English studies. Awarded biennially.

4803 ■ Permanent Court of Arbitration (Cour permanente d'arbitrage)

Mr. Christiaan M.J. Kroner, Sec. Gen.
Peace Palace
Carnegieplein 2
NL-2517 KJ The Hague, Netherlands
Ph: 31 70 3024165
Fax: 31 70 3024167
E-mail: bureau@pca-cpa.org
URL: http://www.pca-cpa.org

4804 ■ Financial Assistance Fund for Settlement of International Disputes

Awarded to developing countries in need of financial assistance for resolution of disputes under PCA auspices. Established in 1994.

4805 ■ Poetry International Foundation (Stichting Poetry International)

Bas Kwakman, Exec. Dir.
Eendrachtsplein 4
NL-3012 LA Rotterdam, Netherlands
Ph: 31 10 282 2777
Fax: 31 10 444 4305
E-mail: info@poetry.nl
URL: http://www.poetry.nl

Awards are arranged in alphabetical order below their administering organizations

4806 ■ C. Buddingh' Prize
To recognize the best debut collection of Dutch-language poetry. A monetary prize of 1,200 is presented along with the opportunity for the winner and nominees to present their work at the Poetry International Festival. Established in 1988.

4807 ■ Poetry Day Prizes
For the three best poems of the past year. Prizes are awarded annually on Poetry Day. Monetary prizes of 2,500 are presented, consisting partly of book tokens.

4808 ■ Poetry International Festival
To recognize outstanding poets. Alongside the nightly international series of readings, the festival offers a variety of related activities: poetry and music projects, exhibitions, and a series of lectures on famous poets. The C. Buddingh Prize for New Dutch Poetry is presented. The Festival is held annually. Established in 1970.

4809 ■ Rijksakademie van Beeldende Kunsten
Martijntje van Schooten, Prize Coor.
Sarphatistraat 470
NL-1018 GW Amsterdam, Netherlands
Ph: 31 20 527 0300
Fax: 31 20 527 0301
E-mail: info@rijksakademie.nl
URL: http://www.rijksakademie.nl

4810 ■ Prix de Rome - Architecture
To recognize and encourage architects under 35 years of age. Individuals of Dutch nationality or those who have lived and worked in Holland for a minimum of two years are eligible. The winner receives a monetary prize of 45,000 Euros and the runner-up receives 20,000 Euros; in addition, two prizes of 10,000 Euros each are awarded. Awarded every four years. Established in 1870 by King William III of the Netherlands.

4811 ■ Prix de Rome - Visual Arts
This, the largest prize for young artists in the Netherlands, is presented to recognize and encourage artists under 35 years of age. Individuals of Dutch nationality or those who have lived and worked in Holland for a minimum of two years are eligible. The winner receives a monetary prize of 45,000 Euros and the runner-up receives 20,000 Euros; in addition, two prizes of 10,000 Euros each are awarded. Awarded biennially in odd-numbered years. Established in 1870 by King William III of the Netherlands.

4812 ■ Royal Dutch Geographical Society (Koninklijk Nederlands Aardrijkskundig Genootschap)
Henk Ottens, Chm.
PO Box 80123
NL-3508 TC Utrecht, Netherlands
Ph: 31 30 2361202
Fax: 31 30 2631290
E-mail: info@knag.nl
URL: http://www.knag.nl

4813 ■ Glazen Globe (Glass Globe)
To recognize authors of youth literature for contributions to the understanding of the world in which children live. Books that help children understand other cultures are considered. A specially designed globe of glass is awarded biennially in odd-numbered years. Established in 1987.

4814 ■ Royal Netherlands Academy of Arts and Sciences (Koninklijke Nederlandse Akademie van Wetenschappen)
Prof. Robbert Dijkgraaf, Pres.
PO Box 19121
NL-1000 GC Amsterdam, Netherlands

Ph: 31 20 5510700
Fax: 31 20 6204941
E-mail: knaw@bureau.knaw.nl
URL: http://www.knaw.nl

4815 ■ Academy Medal
To recognize an individual who has made a particular contribution in the Netherlands to the flourishing of the sciences in a broad sense. Awarded annually on an alternating basis between the Science Division and the Humanities and Social Sciences Division. Established in 1983.

4816 ■ Buys Ballot Medal
To recognize a scientist for outstanding contributions to the field of meteorology. A silver medal is awarded every 10 years. Established in 1888.

4817 ■ M. W. Beijerinck Virology Prize
To recognize a scientist for outstanding international achievement in virology, including the biochemical and biophysical aspects. A gold medal and cash prize of 34,000 Euros are awarded triennially. Established in 1965.

4818 ■ De la Court Prize
For conspicuous achievements by non-salaried researchers in the fields of humanities and social sciences. A silver medal and cash prize of 6,800 Euros are awarded triennially. Established in 1985.

4819 ■ Dow Energy Dissertation Prizes
To recognize researchers who have recently completed their doctoral research in a subject that has or could promote sustainable development in the process industry. Awarded to two recipients biennially in odd-numbered years. Established in 1998. Sponsored by Dow Chemical Co. in Terneuzen, Netherlands.

4820 ■ Dow Energy Prize
To recognize an individual in the Netherlands who have made a particular contribution to sustainable development in the process industry. Open to researchers, engineers, and technicians working at a university and/or industry in the Netherlands. A monetary prize of 25,000 Euros is awarded to one or two recipients biennially in odd-numbered years. Established in 1985. Sponsored by Dow Chemical Co. in Terneuzen, Netherlands.

4821 ■ Dr. A.H. Heineken Prize for Art
For recognition of promising and established artists working in the Netherlands. A monetary prize of 50,000 Euros is awarded biennially in even-numbered years. Financed by the Alfred Heineken Fondsen Foundation. Established in 1988. Formerly: (1995) Amsterdam Prize for Art.

4822 ■ Dr. H.P. Heineken Prize for Biochemistry and Biophysics
For recognition of exceptional discoveries in the fields of biochemistry and biophysics, including microbiology and the physiology of seed germination. A monetary prize of US$150,000 and a crystal trophy are awarded biennially in even-numbered years. Established in 1963 by Heineken N.V. in memory of Dr. H.P. Heineken, past president of Heineken Brewery. Sponsored by the Dr. H.P. Heineken Foundation.

4823 ■ Dr. A.H. Heineken Prize for Cognitive Science
To recognize outstanding scientific achievements in the field of cognitive research. A trophy and monetary prize of US$150,000 is awarded biennially in even-numbered years. Established in 2005. Financed by the Dr. H.P. Heineken Foundation and the Alfred Heineken Fondsen Foundation.

4824 ■ Dr. A.H. Heineken Prize for Environmental Sciences
To recognize scientists or institutions for signifi-

cant contributions to a better relation between man and his natural environment in one of the following fields: the natural sciences, engineering sciences, or the social sciences. A monetary prize of US$150,000 is awarded biennially in even-numbered years. Financed by the Alfred Heineken Fondsen Foundation. Established in 1990. Formerly: (1995) Amsterdam Prize for the Environment.

4825 ■ Dr. A.H. Heineken Prize for History
For recognition of work in the field of European history from antiquity to the present day. Preference is given to work which makes a significant contribution to an understanding of Europe generally. A monetary prize of US$150,000 is awarded biennially in even-numbered years. Established in 1990. Financed by the Alfred Heineken Fondsen Foundation. Formerly: (1995) Amsterdam Prize for History.

4826 ■ Dr. A.H. Heineken Prize for Medicine
For recognition of outstanding scientific research in the field of medicine. A monetary prize of US$150,000 is awarded biennially in even-numbered years. Financed by the Alfred Heineken Fondsen Foundation. Established in 1989. Formerly: (1995) Amsterdam Prize for Medicine.

4827 ■ Heineken Young Scientists Awards
To recognize young scientists whose outstanding scientific or scholarly work sets an example for other young researchers. Candidates must work for Dutch research organizations and have received their doctoral degrees no more than five years previously. A monetary prize of 10,000 Euros is awarded to five recipients biennially in even-numbered years. Established in 2010.

4828 ■ Holleman Prize, Dutch Foundation for Chemistry
To recognize a Dutch researcher for a project completed during the previous five years in the field of scientific and technical chemistry. Awarded every five years. Established in 1952 by Professor Dr. A.F. Holleman.

4829 ■ Gilles Holst Medal
For recognition of outstanding contributions to applied chemistry and applied physics by Dutch scientists. A gold medal is awarded every four years. Established in 1939.

4830 ■ Christiaan Huygens Science Award
To recognize a researcher who, in a recently defended dissertation, has made an important contribution to science in an innovative way. Open to the fields of study of information and communication technology, physics, space studies, economics, and actuarial studies and econometrics. Candidates must have defended their dissertation in the previous four years. Awarded annually. Established in 1998.

4831 ■ Leeuwenhoek Medal
To recognize a scientist for outstanding work in the field of microbiology. A gold medal is awarded every ten years. Established in 1877 in memory of the Dutch microbiologist, Antonie van Leeuwenhoek (1632-1723).

4832 ■ Lorentz Medal
To recognize a scientist for contributions to the field of physics. A gold medal is awarded every four years. Established in 1926 in memory of Professor H.A. Lorentz (1853-1928).

4833 ■ Dr. Hendrik Muller Prize for Behavioural and Social Sciences
To recognize researchers for exceptional achievements in the field of behavioral and social sciences. Open to Dutch researchers as well as researchers who work in the Netherlands. A monetary prize of 25,000 Euros is awarded biennially in odd-numbered years. Established in 1990.

Awards are arranged in alphabetical order below their administering organizations

4834 ■ Theodore Roosevelt American History Awards

To recognize the best thesis on American history defended at Dutch universities. First place winner receives a trip to the United States; second place winner receives a diploma and a cash sum of 250 Euros; third place winner receives a monetary award of 125 Euros. Awarded annually. Established in 1987.

4835 ■ Bakhuys Roozeboom Medal

To recognize a scientist for outstanding contributions to the field of chemistry, particularly phase theory. A gold medal is awarded every four years. Established in 1911 in memory of Professor H.W. Bakhuys Roozeboom (1854-1907).

4836 ■ Van Walree Prize

To recognize the best journalistic achievement in the field of medico-scientific research. A monetary prize of 12,000 Euros is awarded biennially in odd-numbered years. Established in 1987.

4837 ■ Society of Netherlands Literature (De Maatschappij der Nederlandse Letterkunde)

Ernestine Van Der Wall, Pres.
PO Box 9501
NL-2300 RA Leiden, Netherlands
Ph: 31 715144962
E-mail: mnl@library.leidenuniv.nl
URL: http://www.
maatschappijdernederlandseletterkunde.nl

4838 ■ Henriette de Beaufort-prijs

To recognize the author of a biographical work. A monetary prize is awarded every three years, alternately, to a Dutch and a Flemish author. Established in 1986.

4839 ■ Dr. Wijnaendts Francken-prijs

For recognition of a literary work in the following categories: essays in literary criticism, and cultural history. A monetary prize is awarded in each of the two categories alternately. The prize is awarded triennially. The work must have been published during the preceding six years. Established in 1935.

4840 ■ Frans Kellendonk-prijs

To recognize an author, preferably 40 years of age or younger, of literary works (prose, essay, theater, or poetry) reflecting intellectual independency and an original view on social or existential questions. A monetary prize of 5,000 Euros is awarded every three years. Established in 1993.

4841 ■ Kruyskamp-prijs

To recognize an author in the field of lexicography, lexicology, or edition and annotation of old Dutch texts. A monetary prize is awarded triennially. Established in 1992.

4842 ■ WMC Foundation (Stichting Wereld Muziek Concours Kerkrade)

Oranjestraat 2a
PO Box 133
NL-6460 AC Kerkrade, Netherlands
Ph: 31 45 545 5000
Fax: 31 45 535 3111
E-mail: info@wmc.nl
URL: http://www.wmc.nl

4843 ■ World Music Contest, Kerkrade (Wereld Muziek Concours Kerkrade)

For recognition of outstanding amateur bands and orchestras. Participants may enter one or more of the following competitions: concert competitions - participation in the concert competition is open to the following amateur orchestral categories: symphonic windbands, including harmony-orchestras of the French and Dutch variety as well as American style symphonic windbands; brassbands of the continental type, also known as fanfare orchestras; and brassbands of the English type; counter competition

for the drumband - sector - participation is open to the drum-ensembles of various compositions, such as percussion ensembles, mallet ensembles and fife piccolo bands marching competitions participation in the marching competitions is open to all bands of the above mentioned categories and drumbands of various compositions, such as drum and bugle bands, pipebands, etc.; concert competition for the Drumband-Sector - participation is open to drum-ensembles of various compositions, such as percussion ensembles, mallet ensembles and fife and piccolo bands; show competitions - participation in the show competitions is open to bands and orchestras with or without majorettes and/or showgirls; and marching parade is open to marching bands and orchestras with a minimum of 24 musicians; the marching parade has only one division. A first prize with distinction, first prize, second prize, and third prize are awarded every four years in each competition.

4844 ■ World Association of Research Professionals

Dieter Korczak, Pres.
Barbara Strozzilaan 384
Eurocenter 2, 11th Fl.
NL-1083 HN Amsterdam, Netherlands
Ph: 31 20 6642141
Ph: 31 20 5897800
Fax: 31 20 6642922
E-mail: customerservice@esomar.org
URL: http://www.esomar.org

4845 ■ Fernanda Monti Award

To recognize the best paper in any field presented at the Congress. A monetary award of 2,500 Euros is given annually.

4846 ■ World Ploughing Organization (Organisation Mondiale de Labourage)

Hans Spieker, Gen. Sec.
Grolweg 2
NL-6964 BL Hall, Netherlands
Ph: 31 313 619634
Fax: 31 313 619735
E-mail: hans.spieker@worldploughing.org
URL: http://www.worldploughing.org

4847 ■ World Ploughing Championship Awards (Weltmeister im Pflugen)

To encourage improved skills of ploughing the land, and to recognize the highest standards of soil tillage. Individuals qualify through local, regional, and national matches to enter the world championship. The following prizes are awarded for conventional plowing: Golden Plough Trophy for the champion; Silver Rose Bowl for the runner-up; Friendship Trophy for the third place winner and Golden Furrows Challenge Trophy for reversible champion. Awarded annually. Established in 1952.

4848 ■ World Press Photo

Jacob Obrechtstraat 26
NL-1071 KM Amsterdam, Netherlands
Ph: 31 20 676 6096
Fax: 31 20 676 4471
E-mail: office@worldpressphoto.org
URL: http://www.worldpressphoto.org

4849 ■ World Press Photo Contest

For recognition of the best press photographs of the preceding year. Awards are presented in 10 categories: Spot News; General News; People in the News; Sports Action; Sports Features; Contemporary Issues; Daily Life; Portraits; Arts and Entertainment; and Nature. First, second, and third prizes are awarded in each category. In addition, the photographer of the best single image and the photographer of the best story/portfolio in each category is awarded the Golden Eye Award of 1,500 Euros. The World Press Photo of the Year Award of 10,000 Euros is

presented to the best entry overall. Held annually. Established in 1955.

4850 ■ Worldwide Association of Self-Adhesive Labels and Related Products (Federation Internationale des fabricants et transformateurs d'Adhesifs et Thermocollants sur papiers et autres supports)

Mr. Jules Lejeune, Managing Dir.
PO Box 85612
NL-2508 CH The Hague, Netherlands
Ph: 31 70 3123910
Fax: 31 70 3636348
E-mail: info@finat.com
URL: http://www.finat.com
Formerly: (2003) International Federation of Manufacturers and Converters of Pressure-Sensitive and Heatseals on Paper and Other Base Materials.

4851 ■ World Label Association Awards

For recognition of research to improve the quality and utilization of pressure-sensitive and heat-seal materials. In order to be eligible, entries must have won their local label awards competition first; each association then selects entries for the world competition. Awarded annually in 27 categories. Sponsored by the World Label Association.

Netherlands Antilles

4852 ■ St. Maarten Hospitality and Trade Association

WJA Nisbeth Rd., No. 33a
PO Box 486
Philipsburg, Netherlands Antilles
Ph: 599 542 0108
Fax: 599 542 0107
E-mail: info@shta.com
URL: http://www.shta.com

4853 ■ Crystal Pineapple Awards

To recognize individuals for outstanding performance in or contribution to the St. Maarten tourism industry. Awarded annually. Established in 2006.

New Zealand

4854 ■ American Psychological Association Society for the Psychology of Aesthetics, Creativity and the Arts (Division 10)

Lisa F. Smith, Pres.
University of Otago
College of Education
PO Box 56
Dunedin, New Zealand
Ph: 64 3 479 9014
E-mail: lisa.smith@otago.ac.nz
URL: http://www.apa.org/divisions/div10

4855 ■ Arnheim Award

To recognize an individual for outstanding achievement in psychology and the arts. An invitation to lecture is presented annually. Established in 1990 in honor of Rudolph Arnheim, who served as Division president three times.

4856 ■ Frank X. Barron Award

To recognize a student for superior contributions to the psychology of aesthetics, creativity, and the arts. Awarded annually. Established in 2006 in honor of notable creativity researcher, Frank X. Barron.

4857 ■ Berlyne Award

To recognize an individual for outstanding research by a junior scholar. Candidates must have received a PhD in the past 10 years. A monetary prize of $500 and an invitation to lecture are awarded annually. Established in 1992 in honor of Daniel E. Berlyne, who served as Division president.

Awards are arranged in alphabetical order below their administering organizations

4858 ■ Farnsworth Award
To recognize an individual for outstanding service to the Division. Awarded periodically. Established in 2000 in honor of Paul Farnsworth, the first Division president.

4859 ■ Association of Consulting Engineers of New Zealand
Mr. Kieran Shaw, CEO
PO Box 10247
Wellington 6143, New Zealand
Ph: 64 4 4721202
Fax: 64 4 4733814
E-mail: service@acenz.org.nz
URL: http://www.acenz.org.nz

4860 ■ Awards of Excellence
Made to projects of ACENZ members that show excellence in consulting engineering. The award is given annually at the conference in August and is for ACENZ members only. The awards are made at the Gold, Silver, and Merit levels to recognize innovation, excellence in technique, excellence in business relationships, community benefit, environmental sensitivity, and fair methods. The award is a framed certificate presented to the consultant firm and the client who commissioned the project. A magazine is published highlighting all entries.

4861 ■ Fourth-Year Student Award
Recognizes excellence in report writing based on the report on a work experience project. Students entering their fourth year at universities offering four-year engineering degrees are eligible. One student from each University is awarded a framed certificate and monetary prize annually.

4862 ■ President's Award
Made to an individual within the membership who has provided outstanding support to the association. May be, but is not required to be, awarded at the annual conference in August, and the winner is selected by the President and given a plaque.

4863 ■ Association of Social Anthropologists of Aoteaora/New Zealand
Dr. Chrystal Jaye, Treas.
University of Otago
Department of General Practice
PO Box 913
Dunedin 9054, New Zealand
URL: http://asaanz.rsnz.org

4864 ■ Peter Wilson Memorial Award
To honor the best paper presented at the annual conference.

4865 ■ Australasian Society for Biomaterials and Tissue Engineering
Dr. Tim Woodfield, Sec.
PO Box 4345
Christchurch 8140, New Zealand
Ph: 64 3 3641086
Fax: 64 3 3640909
E-mail: tim.woodfield@otago.ac.nz
URL: http://www.biomaterials.org.au
Formerly: (2008) Australasian Society for Biomaterials.

4866 ■ Conference Travel Grants
To provide financial assistance to postgraduate research students and early career researchers who wish to attend the Annual ASBTE Conference. Up to 10 grants of $500 each are awarded annually.

4867 ■ Lab Travel Grants
To provide financial assistance to postgraduate researchers and early career researchers for travel to laboratories. One or more grants up to a total of $5,000 is awarded for international travel, and two grants of $1,000 each for local travel is awarded. Presented annually.

4868 ■ Booksellers New Zealand
Lincoln Gould, CEO
PO Box 25033
Wellington, New Zealand
Ph: 64 4 4721908
Fax: 64 4 4721912
E-mail: info@booksellers.co.nz
URL: http://www.booksellers.co.nz

4869 ■ Maori Language Award
To recognize an outstanding New Zealand book written in the Te Reo language. Awarded as part of the New Zealand Post Book Awards (see separate entry). A monetary prize of NZ$10,000 is awarded annually.

4870 ■ New Zealand Post Book Awards
Recognizes outstanding adult books published in New Zealand. Awards are made in four categories: Fiction, Poetry, Illustrated Non-Fiction, and General Non-Fiction. The winner in each category receives a prize of NZ$10,000; the overall winner, the Book of the Year, is awarded NZ$15,000. The following awards are also presented: Reader's Choice Award (NZ$5,000), Maori Language Award (see separate entry), and three Best First Book Awards (NZ$2,500 each). Awarded annually. Established in 1996. Sponsored by the New Zealand Post. Formerly: (2010) Montana New Zealand Book Awards.

4871 ■ New Zealand Post Children's Book Awards
To honor excellence in children's literature, recognizing the best books for children and teenagers published in New Zealand. Awards are made in four categories: Young Adult Fiction, Junior Fiction, Non-Fiction, and Picture Book. A monetary prize of NZ$7,500 is awarded in each category (in the Picture Book category, the author and illustrator share equally in the prize). Two additional types of awards may be presented: Best First Book Award (NZ$2,000) and Honour Awards (NZ$500). Awarded annually. Established in 1997. Sponsored by the New Zealand Post.

4872 ■ Canterbury Historical Association
Judy Robertson, School Admin.
University of Canterbury
School of Humanities
Private Bag 4800
Christchurch 1, New Zealand
Ph: 64 3 3642104
Fax: 64 3 3642003
E-mail: judy.robertson@canterbury.ac.nz
URL: http://www.hist.canterbury.ac.nz

4873 ■ J. M. Sherrard Award
To encourage scholarly research and publication in the field of New Zealand regional and local history. Amateur and professional historians are eligible. All history titles included in the National Bibliography for the preceding two years are considered. A monetary award of approximately NZ$1,000 is awarded biennially as one major award, and may be divided equally among as many as four winners. Established in 1972 in honor of J. M. Sherrard.

4874 ■ Christian Booksellers Association of New Zealand
Mr. Rosalie McGeorge, Sec.
85 Guyton St.
Wanganui 4500, New Zealand
Ph: 64 6 3458220
E-mail: info@cba.net.nz
URL: http://www.cba.net.nz

4875 ■ Christian Album of the Year
To recognize the Christian album considered to have the greatest impact on the listener during the previous 12 months. Awarded annually.

4876 ■ Christian Book of the Year
To recognize the Christian book considered to have the most impact on readers during the previous 12 months. Awarded annually.

4877 ■ New Zealand Christian Book of the Year
To recognize the Christian publication published in New Zealand, or written by a resident in New Zealand at the time of publication. Awarded annually.

4878 ■ Young Persons Book of the Year
To recognize the publication targeted at young people which has had the greatest impact on the reader during the previous 12 months. Awarded annually.

4879 ■ Communication Agencies Association of New Zealand
Rick Osborne, CEO
PO Box 105 052
Auckland, New Zealand
Ph: 64 9 3030435
Fax: 64 9 3030460
E-mail: office@caanz.co.nz
URL: http://www.caanz.co.nz

4880 ■ AXIS Awards
To recognize creative excellence in advertising in New Zealand. Awards are awarded in a variety of categories each year.

4881 ■ EFFIE Awards - New Zealand
To honor creative achievement in meeting and exceeding advertising objectives. Awarded in various categories each year. The EFFIE award program, established in 1968 by the New York American Marketing Association in 1968, is held in more than 25 countries on five continents. Formerly: CANS Award.

4882 ■ Media Awards
To recognize excellence in strategy and implementation of advertising campaigns. Awards are awarded in a variety of categories each year.

4883 ■ Designers Institute of New Zealand
Sean McGarry, Pres.
PO Box 109423
Newmarket
Auckland 1149, New Zealand
Ph: 64 9 5291713
Fax: 64 9 5291714
E-mail: designer@dinz.org.nz
URL: http://www.dinz.org.nz
Formerly: New Zealand Society of Designers.

4884 ■ BeST Design Awards
To recognize professional designers, students, and organizations in New Zealand and to strengthen the design profession by promoting high standards in the design field, including graphic, product, and interior design. Several awards are presented annually, including Best of Discipline, Best of Category, Student Award, Outstanding Achievement Award, and the John Britten Award. Established as the National Graphic Design Awards in 1976.

4885 ■ Design Ambassador Awards
To promote design excellence for recently graduated and emerging designers and to build connections between the design communities in Britain and New Zealand. The following awards are presented: Dyson Product Design Ambassador Award, Deutz Fashion Design Ambassador Award, and the PANPRINT Graphics and New Media Design Ambassador Award. Awarded annually.

4886 ■ Design in Business Awards
To establish design as a key driver of business performance and to honor New Zealand companies that have strategically used design to drive innovation and business growth. Entries are

Awards are arranged in alphabetical order below their administering organizations

specific design projects or design strategies (not specific products) that have generated measurable results for an organization, such as an increase in sales, revenue, profitability, brand value, market share, internal economic improvements, or improvements in staff morale and productivity. Awarded annually. Established in 1997.

4887 ■ Entomological Society of New Zealand
Pauline Syrett, Sec.
Lincoln University
PO Box 84
Canterbury 7647, New Zealand
Ph: 64 3 3840163
E-mail: secretary@ento.org.nz
URL: http://www.ento.org.nz

4888 ■ 21st Anniversary Research Grants
To encourage entomological research by groups, clubs, or individuals whether or not they are members of the society. Grants are to be used mainly to encourage "amateurs." Grants ranging between $2,000 and $3,000 are awarded annually. Established in 1972.

4889 ■ Clare Butcher Awards
To honor exhibits in school sciences fairs within Christchurch, Dunedin, Hawkes Bay, and Auckland, New Zealand. Book token prizes are awarded annually. Established in 1993.

4890 ■ K.J. Fox Memorial Awards
To provide financial assistance to enable "amateur" (non-funded) members of the Society to attend the annual conference. Awarded annually. Established in 1988.

4891 ■ Bruce Given Awards
To honor excellent papers and posters presented by students at the annual conference. A monetary prize of $75 is awarded for the best paper and $50 for best poster or photo. Awarded annually. Established in 1998.

4892 ■ Health Research Council of New Zealand
Dr. Robin Olds, Chief Exec.
PO Box 5541
Wellesley St.
Auckland 1141, New Zealand
Ph: 64 9 3035200
Ph: 64 9 3035204
Fax: 64 9 3779988
E-mail: info@hrc.govt.nz
URL: http://www.hrc.govt.nz

4893 ■ Liley Medal for Health Research
For outstanding contribution to health and medical sciences. A medal is awarded annually.

4894 ■ MacDiarmid Young Scientist of the Year
For best communication of research, including techniques and outcomes. The winner receives a monetary prize of $10,000; the runner-up and five category winners each receive $5,000. Awarded annually.

4895 ■ Historical Branch Advisory Committee
Historical Branch
Department of Internal Affairs
PO Box 805
Wellington 6140, New Zealand
Ph: 64 4 4957200
Fax: 64 4 4957212
E-mail: info@dia.govt.nz
URL: http://www.dia.govt.nz

4896 ■ Awards in History
To encourage and support research into, and the writing of, the history of New Zealand. Applications from researchers and writers of projects relating to New Zealand history are eligible. Assistance is not normally available for projects that are eligible for university research

funds, nor for university theses. Grants totaling $80,000 to $90,000 are awarded annually in December. Established in 1989. Funded by the New Zealand History Research Trust Fund.

4897 ■ Awards in Oral History
To provide financial help for projects using oral resources relating to the history of New Zealand/ Aoetearoa and New Zealand's close connections with the Pacific. Awards are made to individuals, groups, communities, and institutions. Available to those normally resident in New Zealand. Grants are awarded annually. Established in 1990 by the Australian people to commemorate New Zealand's sesquicentennial. Funded by the Australian Sesquicentennial Gift Trust for Awards in Oral History.

4898 ■ Institute of Chartered Accountants of New Zealand
Dinu Harry, Pres.
PO Box 11342
Wellington 6142, New Zealand
Ph: 64 4 4747840
Fax: 64 4 4736303
E-mail: customer@nzica.com
URL: http://www.nzica.com//AM/Template.cfm?Section=Home1

4899 ■ Annual Report Awards
To recognize and celebrate best practice in annual reporting by New Zealand organizations. Open to any New Zealand organization that produces an annual report, from small community groups to multinational corporations. Annual reports are judged on how clearly they communicate the objectives, highlights, performance, management, and personnel of the organization. Judges consider the size, complexity, and sophistication of each entry, as well as the resources the organization has available. Presented in four categories: Corporate organizations, Public sector organizations, Not-for-profit organizations, and Best Sustainability Reporting. Awarded annually.

4900 ■ Best Public Sector CFO of the Year
To recognize a chief financial officer (CFO) for effective financial management leadership and added value to his or her public sector employer. Awarded annually.

4901 ■ Crombie Lockwood Chartered Accountant of the Year
To recognize the top professional accountant in New Zealand. Criteria include contributions to the accounting profession, community involvement, and specialist expertise. Award consists of a $7,000 travel package, a telecom credit of $2,000, and $3,000 worth of leadership training. Awarded annually. Sponsored by Crombie Lockwood. Formerly: Hays Chartered Accountant of the Year.

4902 ■ Outstanding Service to the Profession Award
To recognize a member who has demonstrated outstanding service to the accounting profession throughout his or her career. Awarded annually.

4903 ■ Westpac Outstanding New Member of the Year
To recognize a new member of the Institute for effective leadership and outstanding contribution to the success of his or her employer, clients, and the accounting profession. There is no age limit, but the winner should likely have achieved success within approximately five years of becoming a full member of the Institute. Awarded annually.

4904 ■ Institution of Professional Engineers New Zealand
Andrew Cleland, Chief Exec.
PO Box 12241
Wellington, New Zealand

Ph: 64 4 4739444
Fax: 64 4 4748933
E-mail: ipenz@ipenz.org.nz
URL: http://www.ipenz.org.nz/ipenz

4905 ■ Angus Award
To recognize engineering excellence in water, waste, and amenities, specifically, the design, construction and operation of reliable supply of services to communities and/or their distribution networks in respect of any of water supply, water storage, waste water, flood works, and community amenities (swimming pools, beaches, marinas, and solid waste), but excluding transportation, communications and energy services. A trophy and a certificate are awarded biennially in odd-numbered years. Presented as part of the Supreme Technical Awards for Engineering Achievers. Formerly: Infrastructure, Utilities, and Transport.

4906 ■ John Cranko Award
To recognize engineering excellence in mechanical and manufacturing-based engineering, specifically, the design, development or operation of improved or new products, processes, or services using mechanical engineering, mechatronics, or that which arises in the manufacturing sector. A trophy and a certificate are awarded biennially in even-numbered years. Presented as part of the Supreme Technical Awards for Engineering Achievers.

4907 ■ Freyssinet Award
To recognize engineering excellence in buildings and construction, specifically, the design and construction of buildings, including fire engineering, building services, geotechnical, structural, and earthquake engineering. A trophy and certificate are awarded biennially in odd-numbered years. Presented as part of the Supreme Technical Awards for Engineering Achievers.

4908 ■ Fulton-Downer Gold Medal
Recognizes outstanding achievement in the public service aspects of the engineering profession. Members and group are eligible. A gold medal is awarded annually. Established in 1989. Formerly: (2005) President's Award.

4909 ■ Furkert Award
To recognize engineering excellence in sustainability and clean technologies. A trophy and certificate are awarded biennially in even-numbered years. Presented as part of the Supreme Technical Awards for Engineering Achievers.

4910 ■ Hume Prize
To recognize the best paper presented by a member at a meeting during the year. A monetary award is presented annually. Administered by the Auckland Branch of IPENZ.

4911 ■ MacLean Citation
To recognize persons who have rendered exceptional and distinguished service to the profession. A citation is awarded when merited. Established in 1954 in memory of Francis William MacLean, a former President of the Institution, who displayed exceptional devotion to the profession of engineering and to his fellow engineers.

4912 ■ Arthur Mead Environmental Award
To recognize an Auckland branch member for outstanding work in engineering that shows consideration for the environment. A plaque is presented annually. Administered by the Auckland Branch of IPENZ.

4913 ■ Ray Meyer Medal for Excellence in Student Design
To recognize and foster the steel design abilities of undergraduate engineers. Open to all fields of IPENZ-accredited engineering. In judging the

Awards are arranged in alphabetical order below their administering organizations

award, consideration will be given to the project design, the business case, and the presentation and communication of ideas. A medal and certificate is presented. Finalists' reasonable travel and entry expenses will also be met to enable them to attend the IPENZ Awards Dinner during the IPENZ annual Convention. Awarded annually. Established in 1999. Sponsored by GHD.

4914 ■ G. T. Murray Memorial Award
To recognize the best paper presented by a student or graduate member. Two monetary prizes are awarded annually. Administered by the Auckland Branch of IPENZ.

4915 ■ Evan Parry Award
To recognize engineering excellence in energy systems, specifically, the design, development, implementation, or operation of improved or new products or services for generation, transmission, reticulation, or use of gas, electricity, including motor, and engine technology. A trophy and certificate are awarded biennially in odd-numbered years. Presented as part of the Supreme Technical Awards for Engineering Achievers.

4916 ■ Rabone Award
To recognize engineering excellence in ICEET (Information, Communication, Electrical, and Electronic Technology), specifically, the design, development, or operation of improved or new communications, hardware and/or software, embedded systems, broadcasting, telecoms, electrical, or electronic products and controls. A trophy and certificate are awarded biennially in even-numbered years. Presented as part of the Supreme Technical Awards for Engineering Achievers.

4917 ■ Skellerup Award
To recognize engineering excellence in food, bioprocess, and chemical technologies, specifically, the development of improved or new bioprocess technology involving chemical processes, biological processes, food processing, storage, and specialized transport and materials handling. A trophy and certificate are awarded biennially in odd-numbered years. Presented as part of the Supreme Technical Awards for Engineering Achievers.

4918 ■ Technician of the Year Award
To recognize an excellent student in his or her final year of the NZCE course at a participating institution. A monetary prize is awarded annually. Administered by the Auckland Branch of IPENZ.

4919 ■ Templin Scroll Competition
To recognize the best written and best presented paper by a student. A monetary award and a scroll are presented annually. Established in 1941 by J.R. Templin. Administered by the Canterbury Branch of IPENZ.

4920 ■ Transpower Neighborhood Engineers Award
To encourage a greater awareness of the engineering profession and foster innovative thinking in engineering and technology. Primary, intermediate, and secondary schools in New Zealand are eligible. Established in 2001. Sponsored by Transpower.

4921 ■ Turner Award for Professional Commitment
To recognize a corporate member of the Institution for his continuing contribution to the profession of engineering, to the activities of the Institution, and to society. The recipient should be over the age of 40 years. The following attributes are sought in nominees for this award: upholding the image of the profession, publicizing engineering achievement and promoting the interests of the profession and industry, emphasis of the Institution's code of ethics and the profession's exper-

tise and experience, encouragement to young people to enter the profession and young engineers to take an active role in Institution affairs, participation in community affairs, assistance with career counseling and recruitment to the Institution, and dissemination of technical and welfare information within the profession. A certificate and trophy are presented annually at the Institution's annual conference. Established in 1981 by R.J. McCarten.

4922 ■ International Council of Associations for Science Education
(Federacion Internacional de Asociaciones de Profesores de Ciencias)
Ms. Beverley Cooper, Sec.
University of Waikato
Faculty of Education
Private Bag 3106
Hamilton 3104, New Zealand
Ph: 64 7 8384382
E-mail: bcooper@waikato.ac.nz
URL: http://www.icaseonline.net

4923 ■ Distinguished Service Award
To recognize science educators for outstanding contributions to international science education over a sustained period of time.

4924 ■ International Viola Society
Michael Vidulich, Pres.
PO Box 47-126
Ponsonby
Auckland 1144, New Zealand
E-mail: vervid@xtra.co.nz
URL: http://www.internationalviolasociety.org

4925 ■ Golden Viola Clef
To honor servants of the viola who are without peer for exceptionally distinguished and unique contributions to the instrument. Awarded rarely.

4926 ■ Honorary Membership
To honor individuals for careers that exponentially furthered the purposes of the Society. Awarded when merited.

4927 ■ Silver Viola Clef
To honor an individual for an outstanding contribution to the viola and/or the Society. Awarded annually if merited.

4928 ■ Library and Information Association of New Zealand Aotearoa
Alli Smith, Exec. Dir.
PO Box 12212
Wellington 6144, New Zealand
Ph: 64 4 4735834
Fax: 64 4 4991480
E-mail: admin@lianza.org.nz
URL: http://www.lianza.org.nz
Formerly: (1995) New Zealand Library Association.

4929 ■ 3M Award for Innovation in Libraries
To recognize a librarian, information specialist, or team for innovation and the use of entrepreneurial skills in business. 3M products valued at $4,000 are awarded for first place, $1,000 for second place, and $500 for third place. Awarded annually. Established in 1996. Sponsored by 3M New Zealand Ltd.

4930 ■ Edith Jessie Carnell Travelling Scholarship
To enhance the knowledge and development of the profession in New Zealand, the aims of the Association, and to further the continuing professional development of the successful applicant. The grant is awarded for the purpose of assisting an individual to travel outside New Zealand for research, a study visit, or attending a conference. Awarded biennially in even-numbered years. Established in 1998.

4931 ■ Russell Clark Award
For recognition of the most distinguished illustra-

tions in a children's book with or without text. The illustrator must be a citizen of New Zealand, and the book must have been published during the preceding year. A monetary award of $1,000 and a bronze medal are presented annually as part of the Children's Book Awards. Established in 1975 in memory of Russell Clark (1905-1966), a New Zealand illustrator, artist and sculptor.

4932 ■ Ada Fache Fund
To support a member in his or her professional development. A grant of approximately NZ$600 is awarded annually. Established in honor of Ada Fache, who worked as an assistant in the Dunedin Public Library.

4933 ■ Mary Fleming Prize
To recognize the best student enrolled in LIBR 526 at Victoria University. a book voucher of NZ$200 is awarded annually. Established in 1964 in honor of Mary Smith Fleming.

4934 ■ Esther Glen Award
To recognize the author of the most distinguished contribution to literature for children. Authors of books published during the preceding year who are citizens or residents of New Zealand are eligible. A monetary award of NZ$1,000 and a bronze medal are awarded annually as part of the Children's Book Awards. Established in 1944 in memory of Esther Glen (1881-1940), a New Zealand journalist and editor active in promoting children's literature.

4935 ■ John Harris Award
To recognize an outstanding published work that represents a contribution to New Zealand librarianship. A diploma and monetary prize are awarded annually. Established in 1961.

4936 ■ Elsie Locke Award
To recognize a distinguished contribution to nonfiction for young people. Citizens or residents of New Zealand are eligible. A monetary award of NZ$1,000 and a medal are presented annually as part of the Children's Book Awards. Established in 1986.

4937 ■ Paul Szentirmay Special Librarianship Scholarship
To enhance the knowledge and development of library and information services, particularly in the area of special needs, in New Zealand. Awarded triennially.

4938 ■ Te Kura Pounamu Award
To recognize a distinguished contribution written in Te Reo Maori to the literature for children or young people. A greenstone pendant and monetary prize of NZ$1,000 are awarded annually as part of the Children's Book Awards. Established in 1995.

4939 ■ David Wylie Prize
To recognize the authors of works dealing with library and information issues. Two book vouchers of NZ$200 are awarded annually. Established in 1986.

4940 ■ YBP Award for Collection Services
To recognize the contributions made by library staff in the years of collection development, collection management, acquisitions, and cataloging. A citation and grant of $2,000 are presented annually. Established in 2001. Sponsored by YBP.

4941 ■ Logistics and Transport New Zealand
Marilyn Henderson, Admin. Mgr.
PO Box 1281
Shortland St.
Auckland, New Zealand
Ph: 64 9 3684970
Fax: 64 9 3684971
E-mail: info@cilt.co.nz
URL: http://www.cilt.co.nz/MainMenu

Awards are arranged in alphabetical order below their administering organizations

4942 ■ Award for Most Meritorious Presentation
To honor the most meritorious New Zealand presentation to a supply chain management/logistics or transport forum during the year. A trophy and plaque are awarded annually.

4943 ■ Award for Supply Chain Innovation
To honor notable innovation in systems and technology in the New Zealand supply chain sector. Criteria include economic benefits and originality. A plaque and certificate are awarded annually.

4944 ■ Ministry of Transport Award for Best Student Research
For the best undergraduate student research project/paper at the 300 academic level in a tertiary institution in New Zealand. A plaque and monetary award of $1,000 is given annually.

4945 ■ Norman Spencer Memorial Award
For personal achievements, and service to the institute, the profession, and the community in the field of transport, including expertise, experience and other criteria. A trophy is awarded annually.

4946 ■ Meteorological Society of New Zealand
Jim Renwick, Contact
PO Box 6523
Te Aro
Wellington, New Zealand
E-mail: info@metsoc.rsnz.org
URL: http://metsoc.rsnz.org

4947 ■ Edward Kidson Medal
To encourage advancement in the science of meteorology (including climatology) and its applications. Awarded biennially.

4948 ■ New Zealand Academy of Fine Arts
Ian Hamlin, Pres.
1 Queens Wharf
Wellington, New Zealand
Ph: 64 4 4998807
Fax: 64 4 4992612
E-mail: info@nzafa.com
URL: http://www.nzafa.com

4949 ■ Governor-General Art Award
To recognize New Zealand artists for outstanding service to the Academy and the arts over a sustained period of time. A bronze sculpture and a lifetime membership are awarded annually when merited. Established in 1983.

4950 ■ New Zealand Accordion Association
John Statham, Pres.
4 O'Neills Ave.
Takapuna
Auckland 0622, New Zealand
Ph: 64 9 4898316
E-mail: nzaasecretary@yahoo.com
URL: http://www.accordion.co.nz

4951 ■ Coupe Mondiale International Competition for Accordionists
To encourage excellence in accordion playing by individuals and ensembles. Open to accordionists from all nationalities. Categories include: Coupe Mondiale; Junior Coupe Mondiale; International Competition for Piano Accordion; International Competition for Virtuoso Entertainment Music; Junior International Competition for Virtuoso Entertainment Music; International Competition for Ensemble Music; and Coupe Mondiale Digital Accordion Competition. First, second, and third prizes are offered in most categories, with prizes ranging from 250 to 1,800 Euros. The first prize for the International Competition for Virtuoso Entertainment Music is a monetary award (NZ$5,000).

4952 ■ International Accordion Competition
To recognize excellence in accordion music. Established in 2008.

4953 ■ New Zealand Association of Scientists
Prof. Neil Curtis, Pres.
PO Box 1874
Wellington, New Zealand
Ph: 64 4 3895096
E-mail: david.lillis@rsnz.org
URL: http://nzas.rsnz.org

4954 ■ Sir Ernest Marsden Medal for Outstanding Service to Science
For recognition of a meritorious contribution to the cause and/or the development of science. Any person who has made an outstanding contribution to science is eligible. An engraved medal is awarded annually. Established in 1973.

4955 ■ Research Medal
To honor a young scientist aged under 40 for outstanding research work, principally undertaken in New Zealand during the three preceding years. Awarded annually. Established in 1990.

4956 ■ Science Communicator Award
To honor a practicing scientist for excellence in communicating to the general public in any area of science and technology. An engraved medal is awarded annually. Established in 1951.

4957 ■ Shorland Medal
To honor the significance and originality of a personal, lifetime contribution to basic or applied research in New Zealand. Awarded annually.

4958 ■ New Zealand Committee for the Scientific Investigation of Claims of the Paranormal
Vicky Hyde, Chair
PO Box 30-501
Lower Hutt 5040, New Zealand
Fax: 64 3 3845138
E-mail: chair@skeptics.org.nz
URL: http://skeptics.org.nz

4959 ■ Bent Spoon Award
To recognize the New Zealand organization that has shown the most egregious gullibility or lack of critical thinking in the public coverage of, or commentary on, a science-related issue. Awarded annually. Established in 1992.

4960 ■ Bravo Awards
To recognize media professionals and those with a high public profile who have provided food for thought, critical analysis, and important information on topics of relevance to the scientific investigation of the paranormal. Awarded annually to one or more recipients. Established in 1995.

4961 ■ New Zealand Dental Therapists' Association
Ngaire Mune, Exec. Off.
PO Box 24557
Auckland 1345, New Zealand
E-mail: nzdta@nzdta.co.nz
URL: http://www.nzdta.co.nz

4962 ■ New Zealand Dental Therapist Student Award
To 2nd year students demonstrating leadership attitude.

4963 ■ New Zealand Freshwater Sciences Society
Dr. Brian Sorrell, Sec.-Treas.
NIWA
PO Box 8602
Riccarton
Christchurch, New Zealand
E-mail: b.sorrell@niwa.co.nz

4964 ■ Guest Lecturer Award
For overseas limnologists whose visits benefit the New Zealand's limnological research. A grant up to $2,000 is awarded annually.

4965 ■ Travel Award
To enable outstanding young scientists to attend overseas conferences, seminars, or workshops, or to visit institutions to learn techniques, develop expertise, use equipment, collections, or library facilities not available in New Zealand. Preference is given to candidates less than 35 years of age, or who graduated in the previous 10-year period. A grant up to $2,000 is awarded annually.

4966 ■ New Zealand Geographical Society
Prof. Tony Binns, Pres.
University of Auckland
Private Bag 92019
Auckland, New Zealand
Ph: 64 9 3737599
Fax: 64 9 3737434
E-mail: nzgs@auckland.ac.nz
URL: http://www.nzgs.co.nz

4967 ■ Distinguished Geographer Medal
For significant contribution to geography by a New Zealander. Awarded biennially.

4968 ■ New Zealand Geotechnical Society
Philip Robins, Chm.
PO Box 12-241
Wellington, New Zealand
Ph: 64 4 4739444
Fax: 64 4 4748933
E-mail: ann.williams@beca.com
URL: http://www.nzgs.org

4969 ■ Geomechanics Award
To honor the author with the best paper published during the preceding three years. A certificate and monetary prize are awarded triennially.

4970 ■ Student Award
To honor outstanding students in the field of rock mechanics, soil mechanics, and engineering geology. Two awards of $500 each are awarded.

4971 ■ New Zealand Guild of Agricultural Journalists and Communicators
Sue Miller, Sec.
PO Box 54-234
Mana
Wellington 5026, New Zealand
Ph: 64 4 2331842
E-mail: secretary@guildag.co.nz
URL: http://www.guildag.co.nz

4972 ■ Bank of New Zealand Farm Business Writing Award
To recognize high quality writing about farm business, a topic that encompasses management and leadership practices relating to farming including - but not limited to - planning, leading people, and financial management, as differentiated from technical management (e.g., stock and pasture management). A monetary prize of $1,000 is awarded annually. Sponsored by the Bank of New Zealand.

4973 ■ Bank of New Zealand Rongo Award
To recognize excellence in agricultural journalism, both broadcast and written. A trophy and monetary prize of $2,000 are awarded for first place and $500 is awarded for second place. Awarded annually. Sponsored by the Bank of New Zealand.

4974 ■ New Zealand Institute of Physics
Dr. Ben Ruck, Pres.
PO Box 31310
Lower Hutt 5040, New Zealand
Ph: 64 4 9313220

Awards are arranged in alphabetical order below their administering organizations

E-mail: secretary@nzip.org.nz
URL: http://nzip.org.nz

4975 ■ High School Physics Prize
To honor any school with a corporate NZIP staff member.

4976 ■ New Zealand Mathematical Society
Dr. Alex James, Sec.
University of Canterbury
Private Bag 4800
Christchurch 8140, New Zealand
E-mail: a.james@math.canterbury.ac.nz
URL: http://nzmathsoc.org.nz

4977 ■ Aitken Prize
To recognize the best contributed talk by a student at the NZ Mathematics Colloquium. Candidates must be enrolled (or have been enrolled) for a degree in mathematics at a university or other tertiary institution in New Zealand. A certificate and check for NZ$250 are awarded annually to one or two recipients. Established in 1995.

4978 ■ NZMS Research Award
To foster mathematical research in New Zealand and to recognize excellence in research carried out by New Zealand mathematicians. Awarded annually. Established in 1990.

4979 ■ New Zealand Olympic Committee
Kereyn Smith, Sec. Gen.
PO Box 643
Wellington 6140, New Zealand
Ph: 64 4 3850070
Fax: 64 4 3850090
E-mail: office@olympic.org.nz
URL: http://www.olympic.org.nz/Front.aspx?ID=3783

4980 ■ Robert Swan Aitchison Memorial Trophy
To recognize the best New Zealand archer participating in the Games of the Olympiad. A trophy is awarded every four years, on Olympic Day in the first year of each Olympiad. Established in 1996.

4981 ■ Sir Lance Cross Memorial Cup
To recognize a member of the media for significant contributions to the Olympic or Commonwealth Games. Awarded biennially in odd-numbered years. Established in 1993.

4982 ■ Leonard A. Cuff Medal
To honor an individual for contributions to Olympism in New Zealand. A medal and diploma are awarded every four years, on Olympic Day in the first year of each Olympiad. Established in 2000.

4983 ■ IOC Annual Trophy
To honor an individual or organization for distinguished achievement in the teaching of Olympism. Awarded annually. Established in 1985.

4984 ■ Kodak Media Photography Award
To honor the best photograph of an Olympic or Commonwealth Games sport taken during the previous year. A diploma is awarded biennially in odd-numbered years, on Olympic Day in a non-Games year. Established in 1995 by Kodak New Zealand Ltd.

4985 ■ Lonsdale Cup
To recognize the competing New Zealand who made the most outstanding contribution to Olympic and Commonwealth sport during the year. Awarded annually. Established in 1911.

4986 ■ New Zealand Olympic Order
To recognize an individual or organization for outstanding service to the Olympic Movement. A pin and diploma are awarded annually. Established in 1991.

4987 ■ New Zealand Psychological Society
Frank O'Connor, Pres.
PO Box 4092
Wellington 6140, New Zealand

Ph: 64 4 4734884
Fax: 64 4 4734889
E-mail: office@psychology.org.nz
URL: http://www.psychology.org.nz/cms_display.php

4988 ■ C.J. Adcock Award
To honor the most valuable contribution in any of the areas like philosophy of science, psychological theory, personality, cybernetics, cognition, perception, linguistics, and the use of multivariate statistical techniques. Awarded triennially.

4989 ■ Best Student Conference Paper Prizes
To recognize student members who present the best paper at the society's annual conference. Awarded annually

4990 ■ G.V. Goddard Early Career Award
To recognize early career achievement and excellence in research and the scholarship in basic psychological science. Candidates must be no longer than seven years past the completion of his or her highest post-graduate degree in psychology. A monetary prize of NZ$500 is awarded biennially.

4991 ■ Hunter Award
To recognize and encourage excellence in scholarship, research, and professional achievement in psychology. A monetary prize of $1,000 is awarded triennially. Established in 1972 in memory of Sir Thomas Hunter.

4992 ■ Jamieson Award
To recognize an individual for significant contributions to industrial/organizational psychology in New Zealand. A monetary prize of $1,000 is awarded every four years. Established in 2006 in honor of Bruce Jamieson.

4993 ■ The President's Maori Scholarship
To provide financial support for post-graduate students that are of the Maori ethnicity and are involved in the Maori community. A scholarship in the amount of NZ$2,000 is awarded annually.

4994 ■ Public Interest Award
To recognize an individual for valuable contributions to psychology in the service of the public interest.

4995 ■ New Zealand Recreation Association
Steve Gibling, Chief Exec.
PO Box 11132
Wellington 6142, New Zealand
Ph: 64 4 8015598
Ph: 64 4 8019364
Fax: 64 4 8015599
E-mail: info@nzrecreation.org.nz
URL: http://www.nzrecreation.org.nz

4996 ■ Ian Galloway Memorial Cup
To recognize an individual for outstanding personal contribution to the parks management industry. A memorial cup and plaque are awarded annually.

4997 ■ Mark Mitchell Memorial Trophy
To recognize an individual for outstanding personal contribution to the recreation industry. A memorial cup and plaque are awarded annually.

4998 ■ National Pool Lifeguard Award
To recognize and reward employees who have made outstanding contributions to the delivery and development of aquatic services in New Zealand. Awarded annually. Established in 2007.

4999 ■ Outstanding Awards
To recognize excellence, innovation, and effectiveness in New Zealand recreational facilities. Awards are presented in six categories: project, park, pool, facility, event, and community recreation program. Awarded annually.

5000 ■ Outstanding Contribution Award
To recognize an individual for outstanding service to the New Zealand parks and open space industry. Awarded annually.

5001 ■ Outstanding Research, Planning, and Policy Award
To recognize an individual for applied work in research, policy development, or planning in the general recreation/leisure industry in New Zealand. Awarded annually.

5002 ■ Paul Stuart Memorial Award
To recognize an individual for outstanding personal contribution to the facility management industry. A memorial award and plaque are awarded annually. Established in 1995.

5003 ■ Young Amenity Horticulturist of the Year
To honor young horticulturists employed in the wider horticulture industry. Candidates must be under the age of 30 years. Awarded annually.

5004 ■ New Zealand Society for Earthquake Engineering
Win Clark, Exec. Off.
PO Box 2193
Wellington 6140, New Zealand
Ph: 64 4 5653650
Fax: 64 4 5653650
E-mail: exec@nzsee.org.nz
URL: http://nzsee.org.nz

5005 ■ Otto Glogau Award
For the author(s) presenting the best paper during the three preceding years. Any paper published in the Society's Bulletin, or published elsewhere by a member of the society, is eligible. A monetary prize to purchase books and a certificate are awarded annually. Established in 1978.

5006 ■ Ivan Skinner Award
To promote research which reduces the impact of earthquakes on New Zealand communities. Co-sponsored by the Earthquake Commission.

5007 ■ New Zealand Society for Music Therapy
Daphne Rickson, Pres.
New Zealand School of Music
PO Box 2332
Wellington 6143, New Zealand
Ph: 64 4 8015799
E-mail: daphne.rickson@nzsm.ac.nz
URL: http://www.musictherapy.org.nz

5008 ■ Mary Lindgren Award
To provide financial assistance for the study, research, and projects that promote the advancement of music therapy in New Zealand. Awarded annually.

5009 ■ New Zealand Society of Authors
Maggie Tarver, Exec. Dir./CEO
PO Box 7701
Wellesley St.
Auckland 1141, New Zealand
Ph: 64 9 3794801
Fax: 64 9 3794801
E-mail: office@nzauthors.org.nz
URL: http://www.authors.org.nz
Formerly: (1995) PEN New Zealand, Inc..

5010 ■ Hubert Church Best First Book Award for Fiction
To recognize a New Zealand author for his or her first fiction book. Awarded annually.

5011 ■ Jessie Mackay Best First Book Award for Poetry
To recognize a New Zealand author for his or her first poetry book. Awarded annually.

5012 ■ E.H. McCormick Best First Book Award for Non-Fiction
To recognize a New Zealand author for his or her first non-fiction book. Awarded annually.

Awards are arranged in alphabetical order below their administering organizations

5013 ■ Mid-Career Writers Award
To recognize the oeuvre of published work by a mid-career writer (defined as being one who has published a minimum of three books and a maximum of six). Open to writers of fiction, poetry, short fiction collections, drama, and literary non-fiction. A monetary prize of NZ$3,500 is awarded annually.

5014 ■ NZSA/Pindar Publishing Prize
To create a publishing opportunity for a New Zealand writer. Open to unpublished manuscripts in fiction, non-fiction, short fiction, and poetry. The winning title is professionally edited, designed, printed, and distributed. Awarded biennially in even-numbered years. Established in 2009. Supported by Creative New Zealand. Sponsored by Pindar NZ.

5015 ■ Lilian Ida Smith Award
To assist Society of Authors members 35 years of age or older to embark on or further a literary career. An award of NZ$3,000 is made to assist a writer in the completion of a specific writing project. Projects may be nonfiction, fiction, poetry, or drama for children or adults. Recipients must be NZSA (PEN NZ Inc.) members. Awarded biennially in odd-numbered years. Established in 1986 from a bequest made by Lillian Ida Smith, a music teacher who had an interest in the arts.

5016 ■ New Zealand Society of Plant Biologists
Dr. Mike Clearwater, Pres.
University of Waikato
Dept. of Biological Sciences
Private Bag 3105
Hamilton 3240, New Zealand
Ph: 64 7 8384613
E-mail: president@plantbiology.science.org.nz
URL: http://plantbiology.science.org.nz
Formerly: (2007) New Zealand Society of Plant Physiologists.

5017 ■ Roger Slack Award in Plant Biology
To honor a member for an outstanding contribution to the study of plant biology. Awarded annually. Established in 2001. Formerly: (2007) Outstanding Plant Physiologist Award.

5018 ■ Student Travel Grants
To provide financial assistance to student members who are presenting material at any international conference. Two awards of $250 or more are presented annually. Established in 1997.

5019 ■ New Zealand Statistical Association
Jennifer Brown, Pres.
PO Box 1731
Wellington, New Zealand
Ph: 64 3 3642987
Ph: 64 3 3748769
Fax: 64 3 3642587
E-mail: j.brown@math.canterbury.ac.nz
URL: http://www.stats.org.nz

5020 ■ Campbell Award
To promote statistics within New Zealand and to recognize an individual's contribution to the promotion and development of statistics. A plaque and certificate are awarded annually, if merited.

5021 ■ Visiting Lecturer
To provide financial assistance for a distinguished overseas statistician to tour New Zealand universities. Typically the recipient, known as the NZSA Visiting Lecturer, spends two to three days at each of the six main university centers, and gives at least two lectures at each place: one for a general audience, and one more closely tied to his or her own particular research interests. Awarded when merited.

5022 ■ New Zealand Trade and Enterprise
Jon Mayson, Chm.
Symonds St.
PO Box 8680

Auckland 1150, New Zealand
Ph: 64 9 3549000
Fax: 64 9 3549001
URL: http://www.nzte.govt.nz/Pages/default.aspx

5023 ■ Agritechnology, Life Sciences and Biotechnology Exporter of the Year
To recognize the top New Zealand exporters. Awarded annually. Established in 1965.

5024 ■ New Zealand Veterinary Association
Julie Hood, CEO
PO Box 11-212
Wellington 6142, New Zealand
Ph: 64 4 4710484
Fax: 64 4 4710494
E-mail: nzva@vets.org.nz
URL: http://www.nzva.org.nz

5025 ■ Honorary Life Membership
To honor individuals for service to the profession.

5026 ■ NZVA Clinical Studies Award
To professional associations under veterinary science.

5027 ■ Outstanding Service Award
For outstanding work within the profession.

5028 ■ Packaging Council of New Zealand
Paul Curtis, Exec. Dir.
PO Box 58899
Manukau City, New Zealand
Ph: 64 9 271 4044
Fax: 64 9 271 4041
E-mail: pac.nz@packaging.org.nz
URL: http://www.packaging.org.nz

5029 ■ Environmental Packaging Awards
To recognize environmental standards, best practices, and initiatives achieved in New Zealand by packaging manufacturers, brand owners, retailers, recycling operators, young designers, and users of packaging. Awards are presented in 10 categories; in addition, the Supreme Awards is presented. Awarded biennially in odd-numbered years. Established in 1999.

5030 ■ Physiological Society of New Zealand
Dr. Kirk L. Hamilton, Sec.
University of Otago
Otago School of Medical Sciences
Dept. of Physiology
Private Bag 913
Otago, New Zealand
Ph: 64 3 4797252
Fax: 64 3 4797323
E-mail: kirk.hamilton@stonebow.otago.ac.nz
URL: http://www.physoc.org.nz/index.html

5031 ■ Mary Bullivant Student Prize
Recognizes the best student presentation at the annual conference. A certificate and monetary award of $100 is presented annually.

5032 ■ John Hubbard Memorial Prize
Recognizes excellence in studies toward a PhD degree. Awarded annually. Established in 1997.

5033 ■ Playmarket
Andrew Caisley, Pres.
Level 2, 16 Cambridge Terr.
PO Box 9767, Te Aro
Wellington, New Zealand
Ph: 64 4 382 8462
Fax: 64 4 382 8461
E-mail: info@playmarket.org.nz
URL: http://www.playmarket.org.nz

5034 ■ Bruce Mason Playwrighting Award
To recognize the work on an outstanding emerging New Zealand playwright. The recipient will receive a $10,000 full-length commission and an annual playreading. Awarded annually. Established in 1983 to honor Bruce Mason, one of

New Zealand's finest playwrights and theater critics. Formerly: *The Dominion Sunday Times* Bruce Mason Playwrights Award.

5035 ■ Restaurant Association of New Zealand
Mike Egan, Pres.
PO Box 8287
Symonds St.
Auckland 1, New Zealand
Ph: 64 9 6388403
Fax: 64 9 6384209
E-mail: info@restaurantnz.co.nz
URL: http://www.restaurantnz.co.nz

5036 ■ Continuing Education Grant
To encourage continuing education for hospitality professionals who are currently employed in a New Zealand hospitality/foodservice workplace. A grant of $12,000 is awarded annually.

5037 ■ Hall of Fame Award
To recognize individuals who have made a significant contribution and have given exceptional service to the foodservice and hospitality industry in New Zealand. A greenstone sculpture based on the Maori myth "The Great Bird of Ruakapanga" is awarded annually. Established in 1992.

5038 ■ Innovator Award
To honor an individual or company for innovation within the restaurant industry and for achievement at the highest level. Awarded annually. Established in 1999.

5039 ■ Merit Scholarships for Hospitality Students
To assist individuals who are pursuing further training through tertiary hospitality training or a Modern Apprenticeship program. Four scholarships of $3,500 are awarded annually.

5040 ■ Merit Scholarships for Secondary School Students
To assist secondary school students planning to work toward national recognized hospitality qualification. Three scholarships of $3,500 are awarded annually.

5041 ■ Tutor Work Study Grant
To assist individuals who wish to gain knowledge and insight into today's work environment. A grant of $5,000 is awarded annually.

5042 ■ Royal Astronomical Society of New Zealand
Rory O'Keeffe, Sec.
PO Box 3181
Wellington, New Zealand
E-mail: secretary@rasnz.org.nz
URL: http://www.rasnz.org.nz

5043 ■ Murray Geddes Memorial Prize
For contributions to astronomy in New Zealand. Candidates must be New Zealand residents but need not be members of the Society. Awarded annually. Established in 1945.

5044 ■ Kingdon-Tomlinson Grants
To support projects or ventures that promote the progress of astronomy in New Zealand.

5045 ■ Royal New Zealand Aero Club
Wayne Matheson, Pres.
PO Box 1191
Blenheim, New Zealand
E-mail: dave@flyingnz.co.nz
URL: http://www.flyingnz.co.nz

5046 ■ Aero Engine Services Trophy
For recognition of achievement in basic aerobatics by student pilot or trainee. Competitors must perform five aerobatic maneuvers: Loop, Barrel Roll, Roll off the Top, Slow Roll, and Stall Turn. A trophy is awarded annually. Established in 1969.

Awards are arranged in alphabetical order below their administering organizations

5047 ■ Airways Corporation Trophy

For recognition of achievement in general flying by student pilots/trainees. Competitors must perform three in-flight maneuvers from a list of five options. A cup is awarded annually. Established in 1991 by Airways Corporation of New Zealand Ltd.

5048 ■ Airwork Cup

For recognition of achievement in lowflying. Competitors must perform maneuvers at a height under 500 feet. A cup is awarded annually. Presented in 1987 by Airwork Ltd.

5049 ■ D.M. Allan Memorial Cup

For recognition of achievement in intermediate aerobatics for New Zealand professional club pilots. Entrants in the competition are eligible. A cup is awarded annually. Established in 1949 in honor of D.M. Allan.

5050 ■ Jean Batten Memorial Trophy

For recognition of achievement in takeoff, circuit, preflight inspection, and landing. Open to student pilots/trainees. A monetary grant and trophy are awarded annually. Established in 1989 in honor of Jean Batten.

5051 ■ Bledisloe Aviation Trophy

For recognition of achievement in navigation for pilots who have gone solo in the preceding year. Open to PPL and student pilots/trainees who have flown no more than 150 hours. A trophy is awarded annually. Established in 1934. Presented by the Governor-General of N.Z. & Lady Bledisloe.

5052 ■ Civil Aviation Authority (CAA) Trophy

For recognition of achievement in aircraft pre-flight inspections. All RNZAC National Championship competing pilots are eligible. A trophy is awarded annually. Presented by the Civil Aviation Authority since 1985.

5053 ■ Cory-Wright Cup

For recognition of achievement in aerobatics for club-trained pilots. A cup is awarded annually. Established in 1931 in memory of Cyril W. Cory-Wright.

5054 ■ Gloucester Challenge Trophy

For recognition of achievement in "air safari" navigation. A trophy is awarded annually. Established in 1950 to commemorate the visit of the Duke of Gloucester 1934-35.

5055 ■ W. A. Morrison Trophy

For recognition of achievement in three aircraft flying in formation. Private or commercial pilot license holders in affiliated clubs are eligible. A trophy is awarded annually. Presented by WA Morrison 1981.

5056 ■ New Zealand Herald Challenge Trophy

For recognition of achievement in navigation. Open to PPL/RPL with more than 150 hours of total flight time. A trophy is awarded annually. Established in 1947. Presented by Wilson & Houghton Ltd.

5057 ■ Newman Cup

For recognition of achievement in takeoff, circuit, and landing by female pilots. A cup is awarded annually. Established in 1935. Presented by Mrs. T. Newman.

5058 ■ North Shore Trophy

For recognition of achievement for the most points amassed by a club at the RNZAC Annual National Championships. Clubs with pilots competing at the National Championships are eligible. A trophy is awarded annually. Presented by the North Shore Aero Club since 1988.

5059 ■ Rotorua Trophy

For recognition of achievement in a mock bomb-ing competition. Student or private pilot license holders who are Club members are eligible. A trophy is awarded annually. Established in 1981 by the Rotorua Aero Club.

5060 ■ Sir Francis Boys Cup

For recognition of achievement in takeoff, circuit, and spot landings. Competitors must be PPL or student pilot/trainees. A cup is awarded annually. Established in 1931. Presented by Sir Francis Boys K.B.E. First President of New Zealand Aero Club.

5061 ■ G. M. Spence Trophy

For recognition of achievement in forced landings without power. A trophy is awarded annually. Established in 1935 by G.M. Spence.

5062 ■ Waitemata Aero Club Cup

For recognition of achievement in CIVA Sportsman aerobatics. A trophy is awarded annually. Established in 1993.

5063 ■ Wanganui Trophy

For recognition of achievement in a low-flying competition. The competition is open to pilots of affiliated clubs who hold a commercial pilot's license and who are not in full-time employment as pilots. A trophy is awarded annually. Established in 1989. Presented by the Wanganui Aero Club.

5064 ■ Ivon Warmington Trophy

For recognition of achievement in life raft dropping from a plane. Club pilots who hold private pilot licenses are eligible. A trophy is awarded annually. Presented in 1975 by Mr. I. Warmington D.F.C.

5065 ■ Wigram Cup

For recognition of achievement in landing, instrument flying, and non-instrument circuit flying by nonprofessional pilots. A cup is awarded annually. Established in 1931. Presented by Sir Henry Wigram.

5066 ■ Wigram Cup (Sub-Competition) - Instrument Flying

For recognition of achievement in flying using a limited panel of flight instruments. A cup is awarded annually. Established in 1955. originally for aerobotics changed to Instrument Flying in 1963 Presented by M.N. McLaren.

5067 ■ Wigram Cup (Sub-Competition) - Junior Landing

For recognition of achievement in powered approach and landing. A cup is awarded annually. Established in 1956. Presented by J.R. Franklin.

5068 ■ Wigram Cup (Sub-Competition) - Non-instrument Circuits

For recognition of achievement in flying two circuits without the assistance of flight instruments. A cup is awarded annually. Established in 1956 originally for bombing-changed to Non-instrument Circuits in 1981.

5069 ■ Wigram Cup (Sub-Competition) - Senior Landing

For recognition of achievement in short landing. A cup is awarded annually. Established in 1956.

5070 ■ Royal Society of New Zealand
Dr. Di McCarthy, Chief Exec.
PO Box 598
Wellington 6011, New Zealand
Ph: 64 4 4727421
Fax: 64 4 4731841
E-mail: di.mccarthy@royalsociety.org.nz
URL: http://www.royalsociety.org.nz

5071 ■ Leonard Cockayne Memorial Lecture

For encouragement of botanical research in New Zealand. An invitation to deliver a lecture is awarded triennially. Established in 1964 to commemorate the life and work of the late Leonard Cockayne.

5072 ■ E. R. Cooper Memorial Medal and Prize

For the encouragement of scientific research in the fields of physics or engineering. The award consists of a medal and prize - a book or books, suitably inscribed - and is made every two years to the persons who, in the opinion of the Selection Committee, published the best single account of original research in physics or engineering. Preference is given to contributions to the development of New Zealand natural resources. Awarded biennially in even-numbered years. Established in 1958 by the Dominion Physical Laboratory in memory of E. R. Cooper.

5073 ■ Charles Fleming Award for Environmental Achievement

To recognize individuals, groups, or organizations who have achieved distinction in the protection, maintenance, management, improvement, or understanding of the environment. Nominations may be made by New Zealand citizens. A monetary grant, a plaque, and an expense paid lecture tour are awarded triennially.

5074 ■ Hamilton Memorial Prize

For the encouragement of beginners in scientific research in New Zealand or in the islands of the South Pacific. Works published within seven years preceding the last day of January prior to the annual meeting where the award is made are eligible. Such publications must include the first investigation published by the candidate. A certificate and monetary prize of NZ$1,000 are awarded annually.

5075 ■ Hector Memorial Medal and Prize

To recognize advancement and achievement, on a rotating basis, in the following scientific areas: chemical sciences, physical sciences, and mathematical and information sciences. Investigators working within New Zealand are considered for the award. A bronze medal is awarded annually. Established in 1910 by the Hector Memorial Fund of the New Zealand Institute in memory of Sir James Hector, second President of the New Zealand Institute.

5076 ■ Hutton Memorial Medal and Prize

To recognize advancement and achievement, on a rotating basis, in the following scientific areas: earth sciences, plant sciences, and animal sciences. Researchers who have received the greater part of their education in New Zealand or who have resided in New Zealand for not less than ten years are eligible for the award. A bronze medal is awarded annually. Established in 1909 by the New Zealand Institute in memory of Professor Sir Frederick Wollaston Hutton, F.R.S., its first President.

5077 ■ New Zealand Science and Technology Medals

To recognize individuals who have made exceptional contributions to New Zealand society and culture through activities in the fields of science and technology. A medal is awarded for each of the following types of achievement: (1) for eminent research by a person or a group in any field of science or technology that is recognized internationally and that has contributed to public awareness of the field concerned; (2) for conspicuous, continuing contributions to science and technology over an extended period; and (3) for outstanding specific contributions to the advancement of science and technology, including an excellent piece of research, an outstanding inventions or technological innovation, or exceptional service to a society or institution. Bronze medals and up to 10 silver medals are awarded annually.

5078 ■ New Zealand Science, Mathematics and Technology Teacher Fellowship

To enable outstanding teachers to further understand the role of science, mathematics, social

Awards are arranged in alphabetical order below their administering organizations

science, and technology in New Zealand's economy and society, and to provide them with new experiences outside the classroom that can enable them to become more effective science teachers. Primary, intermediate, or secondary school teachers of science, mathematics, and technology are eligible. Awarded annually.

5079 ■ T. K. Sidey Medal and Prize
For the promotion and encouragement of scientific research in the study of light visible and invisible, and other solar radiations in relation to human welfare, or, at the discretion of the Society, of research on radiations of any kind. A medal is awarded triennially. Established in 1933 by the transfer to the New Zealand Institute of £500 collected to commemorate the passing of the Summer-Time Act (1927) through the instrumentality of Sir Thomas A. Sidey.

5080 ■ Thomson Medal
For recognition of outstanding contributions to the organization, administration, or application of science. A medal and monetary prize of NZ$15,000 are awarded annually. Established in 1985 to commemorate the contributions made to science by George Malcolm Thomson (1848-1933) and his son, James Allan Thomson (1881-1928).

5081 ■ Tourism Industry Association New Zealand
Tim Cossar, Chief Exec.
PO Box 1697
Wellington, New Zealand
Ph: 64 4 4990104
Fax: 64 4 4990827
E-mail: info@tianz.org.nz
URL: http://www.tianz.org.nz

5082 ■ New Zealand Tourism Awards
To encourage and recognize excellence in tourism and tourist products in New Zealand; to improve and enhance the quality of the New Zealand tourism experience offered; and to encourage significant initiatives taken by individuals and/or organizations to develop tourism and tourist products in New Zealand. Open to any individual, company or organization. Awards are judged in a variety of categories; in addition, several special awards are presented. Held annually. Established in 1955.

5083 ■ University of Otago
PO Box 56
Dunedin, New Zealand
Ph: 64 3 479 1100
Fax: 64 3 479 8692
E-mail: university@otago.ac.nz
URL: http://www.otago.ac.nz

5084 ■ Professor Erkin Bairam Memorial Prize
To recognize an outstanding paper written by a third-year student in economics. Awarded annually. Established in 2003. Administered by the University's Department of Economics.

5085 ■ Jessie Kinder Prize
To recognize an outstanding student completing the degree of Bachelor of Consumer and Applied Sciences. A scholarship is awarded annually. Established in 1948 in honor of Jessie Kinder, who completed a diploma in Home Science in 1936.

5086 ■ Water New Zealand
Murray Gibb, Chief Exec.
PO Box 1316
Wellington 6140, New Zealand
Ph: 64 4 4728925
Ph: 64 4 4950896
Fax: 64 4 4728926
E-mail: murray.gibb@waternz.org.nz
URL: http://www.waternz.org.nz

Formerly: (2009) New Zealand Water and Wastes Association.

5087 ■ Exhibitors Awards
To honor the best expo stands at the Annual Conference. The winner receives a certificate and voucher for a free stand at the Annual Conference Expo. Awarded annually.

5088 ■ Ronald Hicks Memorial Award
To recognize a paper that presents significant solutions to sewage treatment or water pollution problems in New Zealand. A certificate and cash prize are awarded annually.

5089 ■ Hynds Paper of the Year Award
To recognize the best technical and presented paper at the NZWWA Annual Conference. Awarded annually. Sponsored by the Hynds Group.

5090 ■ Orica Chemnet Operations Award
To recognize a member for efforts made in solving an operating difficulty or problem at a water or wastewater treatment plant. Awarded annually.

5091 ■ Poster of the Year Award
To honor the best poster presentation at the Annual Conference. Awarded annually.

5092 ■ Women's Studies Association
Mary Mowbray, Contact
PO Box 5382
Wellington, New Zealand
E-mail: marytrevor.mowbray@paradise.net.nz
URL: http://www.wsanz.org.nz

5093 ■ Rosemary Seymour Award
For a research or archive project that meets aims of the organization. Two awards of $500 are available each year - one for which only Maori women may apply; the other is open to all women. Established in 1985.

Nigeria

5094 ■ Benin National Congress
No. 1, Ogbelaka St.
Benin, Nigeria
Ph: 234 522 54558
E-mail: beninnationalcongress@yahoo.com
URL: http://www.benincongress.org

5095 ■ Benin National Merit Award
To recognize the contributions of individuals to the growth and development of the Benin community and humanity as a whole. Awarded annually. Established in 2005.

5096 ■ Nigeria LNG Ltd.
C & C Towers
Plot 1684 Sanusi Fafunwa St.
Victoria Island
PMB 12774 (Marina)
Lagos, Lagos, Nigeria
Ph: 234 1 262 4190
Fax: 234 1 261 6976
E-mail: info@nlng.com
URL: http://www.nlng.com

5097 ■ Nigeria Prize for Literature
To recognize the author of the best book published in Nigeria during the previous four years. Rotates among four literary genres each year: prose fiction, poetry, drama, and children's literature. A monetary prize of $50,000 is awarded annually. Established in 2004.

5098 ■ Nigeria Prize for Science
To create awareness, stimulate competition, and recognize excellence in science and technology

in Nigeria. Open to all scientists who are residents and working in Nigeria. A monetary prize of $50,000 is awarded annually. Established in 2004.

5099 ■ Nigerian Library Association
Sanusi Dantata House
PMB 1
Abuja, Nigeria
Ph: 234 805 536 5245
E-mail: info@nla-ng.org
URL: http://www.nla-ng.org

5100 ■ Best State Public Library Services Award
To recognize a state-level public library for exceptional accomplishments and programs, including physical achievements, level of computerization, Internet connectivity, budget allocation, readership promotion campaign, innovation, publications, and support for NLA. Awarded annually.

5101 ■ Science Teachers Association of Nigeria
Dr. Prince Okorie, Pres.
The STAN Pl.
PMB 777
Abuja, Nigeria
Ph: 234 708 2743110
Fax: 234 708 2743110
E-mail: stan@stanonline.org
URL: http://www.stanonline.org

5102 ■ Branches of the Year
To recognize the best five branches of STAN. Awarded annually.

5103 ■ Distinguished and Sustained Service to Science Education Award
To recognize an individual for outstanding science education. Awarded annually.

5104 ■ President's Award
To recognize the science teacher of the year. Awarded annually.

5105 ■ West African College of Surgeons (College Ouest Africain des Chirurgiens)
Dr. Clement C. Nwawolo, Sec. Gen.
West African Health Committee Bldg.
6 Taylor Dr., Edmond Crescent
Private Mail Bag 1067
Yaba
Lagos, Nigeria
Ph: 234 1 7616563
Ph: 234 1 8980038
E-mail: info@wacs-coac.org
URL: http://www.wacs-coac.org

5106 ■ Patron/Matrons Award
For contributions to the development of community and support to the organization.

5107 ■ Women's Health and Economic Development Association
Mrs. Fidela Etim Ebuk, Natl. Coor.
No. 3B, Ekpo Obot St.
PO Box 2665
Uyo, Nigeria
Fax: 234 85 204344
URL: http://www.kabissa.org/civiorg/387

5108 ■ Best Paper Award
For recognition of the best paper presented at scientific meeting. Grants and scholarships are also awarded.

Northern Mariana Islands

5109 ■ Northern Mariana Islands Council for the Humanities
Scott Russell, Exec. Dir.
PO Box 506437
Saipan, Northern Mariana Islands MP 96950

Awards are arranged in alphabetical order below their administering organizations

Ph: 670 2354785
Fax: 670 2354786
URL: http://www.nmihumanities.org

5110 ■ Governor's Award for Lifetime Achievement in the Humanities
This, the Council's most prestigious award, is given to recognize individuals for significant contributions in one or more fields of humanities over the course of multiple decades (typically three or more). Awarded when merited.

5111 ■ Governor's Award for Outstanding Humanities Teacher
To recognize individuals for significant contributions to humanities instruction. Candidates may be classroom teachers (Kindergarten through college) or individuals involved in humanities instruction outside of the formal classroom setting. Awarded annually.

5112 ■ Governor's Award for Preservation of CNMI History
To recognize individuals for significant contributions to preserving history relating to the Commonwealth of the Northern Mariana Islands. Awarded annually.

5113 ■ Governor's Award for Preservation of Traditional Cultural Practices
To recognize individuals for significant contributions to the preservation of traditional cultural practices relating to such topics as language, subsistence, medicine, law, kinship, religion, construction, and transportation. Awarded annually.

5114 ■ Governor's Award for Research and Publication in the Humanities
To recognize individuals for original scholarly research in one or more of the humanities fields that resulted in a manuscript or in the publication of a book or article. Research and publications must relate directly to the Northern Mariana Islands or to the greater Pacific region. Awarded annually.

5115 ■ Sengebau Poetry Competition
To encourage student poets and to foster poetry as a literary form in the Commonwealth of the Northern Mariana Islands. Trophies are awarded in two categories: Junior Division (7th and 8th grades) and Senior Division (9th through 12th grades). Held annually. Established in 2004.

Norway

5116 ■ Association for Promotion of Skiing
Kongevei 5
N-0787 Oslo, Norway
Ph: 47 2 22923200
Fax: 47 2 22923250
E-mail: post@skiforeningen.no
URL: http://www.skiforeningen.no

5117 ■ Holmenkoll Medal (Holmenkollmedaljen)
To recognize outstanding skiers and to promote the sport of skiing. Individuals who have been active in skiing in Holmenkollen for at least one year are eligible. Awarded to one or more recipients annually. Established in 1895.

5118 ■ Holmenkollen Ski Festival
To recognize outstanding skiers at the annual Ski Festival. The following events are held: Combined, Jump, Men's 50 Km, Men's 18 Km, Men's 15 Km, Women's 30, Women's 20 Km, Women's 10 Km, Women's 5 Km, Women's Relay and Men's Relay. The Trophy of Holmenkollen (Holmenkollpokal) is awarded annually. Established in 1892.

5119 ■ Bergen International Festival (Festspillene I Bergen)
Per Boye Hansen, Festival Dir.
Vagsallmenningen 1
PO Box 183

Sentrum
N-5804 Bergen, Norway
Ph: 47 55 210630
Fax: 47 55 210640
E-mail: festspillene@fib.no
URL: http://www.fib.no

5120 ■ Robert Levins Festspillfond
To encourage and promote a higher level of quality among younger, Norwegian pianists. Norwegian citizens are eligible. A monetary prize of 15,000 Norwegian kroner is awarded annually during the Festival in May/June. Established in 1985 in honor of Robert Levin.

5121 ■ Operasangerinnen Fanny Elstas Fond
To encourage, promote and improve Norwegian vocal music, both composition and singing. Stipends, scholarships, and invitations to master classes are awarded annually during the Festival in May/June. Established in 1979 in honor of Fanny Elsta.

5122 ■ Sigbjorn Bernhoft Osas Festspillfond
For recognition of outstanding achievements within the field of Norwegian folk-music. A monetary prize is awarded annually during the Festival in May/June. Established in 1986 in honor of Sigbjorn Bernhoft Osa.

5123 ■ European Association for Computer Science Logic
Marc Bezem, Contact
Instututt for Informatikk
Universitetet i Bergen
PO Box 7803
N-5020 Bergen, Norway
Ph: 47 555 84177
Fax: 47 555 84199
E-mail: bezem@ii.uib.no
URL: http://www.eacsl.org

5124 ■ Ackermann Award
To recognize an outstanding dissertation on logic in computer science. Awarded annually.

5125 ■ Ludvig Holberg Memorial Fund
University of Bergen
PO Box 7800
N-5020 Bergen, Norway
Ph: 47 55 586992
E-mail: info@holbergprisen.no
URL: http://www.holbergprisen.no

5126 ■ Holberg International Memorial Prize
To recognize a scholar for outstanding contributions to research in the arts and humanities, social science, law, or theology, either within one of these fields or through interdisciplinary work. A monetary prize of 4.5 million Norwegian krone is awarded annually. Established in 2003.

5127 ■ Nils Klim Prize
To recognize a young Nordic researcher for outstanding contributions to research in the arts and humanities, social science, law, or theology, either within one of these fields or through interdisciplinary work. Candidates must be under the age of 35. A monetary prize of 250,000 Norwegian krone is awarded annually. Established in 2003.

5128 ■ Ibsen Awards
Skien Municipality, Culture Department
PO Box 4
N-3701 Skien, Norway
Ph: 47 3558 1000
E-mail: post@ibsenawards.com
URL: http://www.ibsenawards.com

5129 ■ International Ibsen Award
To honor an individual, organization, or institution within the arts and culture sector for excep-

tional achievements defined within the spirit of Henrik Ibsen's work. A monetary prize of 2.5 million Norwegian kroner is awarded annually. Established by the Norwegian Parliament in 2007.

5130 ■ Norwegian Ibsen Award
To honor contemporary Norwegian dramatists and to advance drama in Norway. A monetary prize of 150,000 Norwegian kroner is awarded annually. Established in 1986.

5131 ■ International Council for Open and Distance Education
(Conseil International de l'Enseignement a Distance)
Carl Holmberg, Sec. Gen.
Lilleakerveien 23
N-0283 Oslo, Norway
Ph: 47 22 062630
Fax: 47 22 062631
E-mail: icde@icde.org
URL: http://www.icde.org

5132 ■ Prize of Excellence
To recognize for excellence and dedication to distance education. Awarded annually in three categories: individual, institutional, and lifelong contributions to the field.

5133 ■ Norway Ministry of Foreign Affairs
Bjorn T. Grydeland, Sec. Gen.
7 juni plassen
Victoria Terrasse
PO Box 8114 Dep.
N-0032 Oslo, Norway
Ph: 47 23 950000
Fax: 47 23 950099
E-mail: post@mfa.no
URL: http://www.regjeringen.no/en/dep/ud.html?id=833

5134 ■ Royal Norwegian Order of Merit
To recognize foreign nationals and Norwegian nationals living permanently abroad for outstanding service to Norway. It may also be given to foreign civil servants in Norway for diplomatic/consular service, as well as to Norway's honorary consuls. The Order has five classes: Grand Cross, Commander with Stars, Commander, Officer and Knight. The insignia of Officer of the Royal Norwegian Order of Merit ("Ridder I" in Norwegian) consists of a gold cross. The insignia of Knight ("Ridder" in Norwegian) are silver. Established in 1985.

5135 ■ Royal Norwegian Order of St. Olav
To recognize Norwegian citizens for outstanding service to their native country and humanity. A decoration and a diploma are awarded when merited in the following classes: Grand Cross with Collar; Grand Cross; Commander with Star; Commander; Knight First Class; and Knight. Awarded when merited. Established in 1847 by King Oscar I.

5136 ■ St. Olav Medal
To recognize individuals who have promoted knowledge of Norway abroad or have strengthened the cultural ties between Norwegian emigrants and their home country. The medal is silver. Awarded when merited. Established in 1939 by H.M. King Haakon VII.

5137 ■ Norwegian Academy of Science and Letters
(Det Norske Videnskaps-Akademi)
Prof. Oyvind Osterud, Pres.
Drammensveien 78
N-0271 Oslo 2, Norway
Ph: 47 22121090
Fax: 47 22121099
E-mail: dnva@online.no
URL: http://www.dnva.no

Awards are arranged in alphabetical order below their administering organizations

5138 ■ Abel Prize
To recognize an individual for outstanding scientific work in the field of mathematics. A monetary prize of 6 million Norwegian kroner is awarded annually. Established in 2003.

5139 ■ Kavli Prize in Astrophysics
To recognize an individual for outstanding achievement in advancing knowledge and understanding in the origin, evolution, and properties of the universe. A scroll, medal, and monetary prize of US$1 million are awarded biennially in even-numbered years. Established in 2008.

5140 ■ Kavli Prize in Nanoscience
To recognize an individual for outstanding achievement in the science and application of the unique physical, chemical, and biological properties of the atomic, molecular, macromolecular, and cellular structures and systems that are manifest in the nanometer scale. A scroll, medal, and monetary prize of US$1 million are awarded biennially in even-numbered years. Established in 2008.

5141 ■ Kavli Prize in Neuroscience
To recognize an individual for outstanding achievement in advancing knowledge and understanding of the brain and nervous system. A scroll, medal, and monetary prize of US$1 million are awarded biennially in even-numbered years. Established in 2008.

**5142 ■ Norwegian International Film Festival
(Norske Filmfestivalen)**
Gunnar Johan Lovvik, Festival Dir.
PO Box 145
N-5501 Haugesund, Norway
Ph: 47 52 743370
Fax: 47 52 743371
E-mail: info@filmfestivalen.no
URL: http://www.filmweb.no/filmfestivalen

**5143 ■ Amanda Award for
Cinematographic Merit
(Amanda Film - OG Fjernsynspris)**
For recognition of outstanding achievement in the preceding season's (July-July) national film and television production. Norwegian film productions may be submitted to the appointed "Amanda" jury/juries. Awards are given in the following categories: Best Norwegian Feature, Best Nordic Feature, Best Documentary, Best Artistic Short Film, Best Actor, Best Actress, Best Professional Achievement, Best Foreign Feature, Best TV-drama, Gullklapperen (Honorary Award to Filmmakers), and Amanda-Komiteens Aerespris (Special Honorary Award). A bronze statuette awarded annually. Established in 1985.

**5144 ■ Norwegian International Film
Festival**
To honor films of artistic merit and interest to a Norwegian and Scandinavian audience. The following awards are presented: Film Critics Award, Ray of Sunshine Award, Audience Award, Andreas Award, and the Golden Ribbon. Held annually.

**5145 ■ Norwegian Press Association
(Norsk Presseforbund)**
Per Edgar Kokkvold, Gen. Sec.
Radhusgatan 17
Postboks 46 Sentrum
N-0101 Oslo, Norway
Ph: 47 22 405040
Fax: 47 22 405055
E-mail: pfu@presse.no
URL: http://presse.no

**5146 ■ Grand Journalism Prize
(Den Store Journalistprisen)**
For recognition of outstanding efforts in journalism by Norwegian citizens. A monetary prize of 100,000 kroner and a plaque are awarded annually when merited. Established in 1991. Spon-

sored by the Norwegian Union of Journalists, the Editors Association, the Norwegian Newspaper Publishers Association, and the Norwegian Broadcasting Corporation.

**5147 ■ The Norwegian Short Film Festival
(Stiftelsen Kortfilmfestivalen)**
Torunn Nyen, Dir.
Filmens Hus
Dronningensgt. 16
N-0152 Oslo, Norway
Ph: 47 22 474646
Fax: 47 22 474690
E-mail: short@shortfilm.no
URL: http://www.kortfilmfestivalen.no

5148 ■ Audience Award
To recognize the best film in the competition, as selected by the audience. A video distribution deal is awarded annually.

5149 ■ The Documentary Award
To recognize the best film in the documentary film competition. A monetary prize of 50,000 Norwegian kroner is awarded annually. Sponsored by the Norwegian Broadcasting Corp.

5150 ■ Film Critics Award
To recognize the best Norwegian film in the short film competition. A jury selected by the Norwegian Film Critics Association presents an award annually.

5151 ■ Filmpolitiets Short Film Award
To recognize the best short film in the online competition. A monetary prize of 10,000 Norwegian kroner is awarded annually in cooperation with the Norwegian Broadcasting Corp.

5152 ■ The Golden Chair
This is a special jury prize of the Festival. There are no conditions; the jury may award the prize to whomever it finds suitable. The Golden Chair trophy, made of blue glass, and a monetary prize of 50,000 Norwegian kroner are awarded annually.

5153 ■ Grand Prix Grimstad
To recognize the best film in the international short film competition. A monetary prize of 2,500 Euros is awarded annually. Sponsored by Nordisk Film.

5154 ■ Hour Glass
To recognize the best script for a short or midlength fiction film in the Norwegian short film competition. A jury selected by the Norwegian Playwrights' Association presents a monetary prize of 10,000 Norwegian kroner annually.

5155 ■ Norwegian Film Workers Association Technical Award
To recognize the individual who represents the best technical achievement among the Norwegian films in the competition. A monetary prize of 10,000 Norwegian kroner is awarded annually.

**5156 ■ Norwegian Short Film Festival
Prize
(Stiftelsen Kortfilmfestivalen)**
To recognize the best short film of the Festival. The film director must be a Norwegian citizen. Monetary prizes are awarded annually. Established in 1983.

5157 ■ Prix UIP Grimstad
To recognize the best European short film in the international competition. A monetary prize of 2,000 Euros is awarded annually. Additionally, the winner is automatically nominated for the European Film Academy Short Film Award. Sponsored by United International Pictures (UIP).

5158 ■ Terje Vigen Award
This is a special jury prize of the Festival. There are no conditions; the jury may award the prize to whomever it finds suitable. A statuette in

bronze of Terje Vigen, a person from one of Henrik Ibsen's poems, is awarded annually. Established in 1988 by the Grimstad City Council.

**5159 ■ Norwegian Society for Immunology
(Norsk Selskap for Immunologi)**
Fridtjof Lund-Johansen PhD, Pres.
Norwegian Radium Hospital
Montebello
N-0310 Oslo, Norway
E-mail: elsmar@rr-research.no
URL: http://www.norwegianimmunology.org

5160 ■ NSI Research Award
To honor the first author of an outstanding original scientific paper in the field of immunology. Awarded biennially in even-numbered years.

**5161 ■ Norwegian Society of Financial
Analysts
(Norske Finansanalytikeres Forening)**
Ms. Guri Angell-Hansen, Managing Dir.
PO Box 1276 VIKA
N-0111 Oslo, Norway
Ph: 47 22 129210
Ph: 47 22 129218
Fax: 47 22 129211
E-mail: nff@finansanalytiker.no
URL: http://www.finansanalytiker.no

5162 ■ Stockman Award
To recognize those companies listed on the Oslo stock Exchange that provide the best investor relations efforts to the capital market. Two awards are presented annually, one in the Open Class and the other for smaller and mid-sized companies.

**5163 ■ Women's International Shipping and
Trading Association Norway**
Marita Scott, Pres.
I.M. Skaugen ASA
Karenlyst Alle 8b
0212 Oslo, Norway
Ph: 47 23 120300
Fax: 47 55 120401
URL: http://www.wista.no

5164 ■ WISTA Personality of the Year
To recognize an individual who has made contributions to the maritime industry. Awarded annually.

5165 ■ Yara Foundation
Ingegerd Rafn, Sec. Gen.
Bygdoy Alle 2
N-0202 Oslo, Norway
Ph: 47 91 840620
Fax: 47 24 157224
E-mail: ingegerd.rafn@yara.com
URL: http://www.yara.com

**5166 ■ Yara Prize for an African Green
Revolution**
To support and direct attention to efforts made to fight poverty and hunger in Africa and to recognize measures that increase food production and value creation in any field related to African agriculture. A glass trophy, diploma, and monetary prize of US$100,000 are awarded annually. Established in 2005.

Oman

5167 ■ Oman Economic Review
c/o United Press & Publishing LLC
PO Box 3305
Ruwi 112, Oman
Ph: 968 2470 0896
Fax: 968 2470 7939
E-mail: editor@oeronline.com
URL: http://www.oeronline.com

Awards are arranged in alphabetical order below their administering organizations

5168 ■ Oman Green Awards
To honor outstanding environmental vision, endeavors, and achievements of corporations and individuals. Presented in nine categories: Innovation, Campaign, Habitat, Champion, Research, Landscape, Footprint, Guardian, and Education. Awarded annually.

5169 ■ Omani Economic Association
Mohamed Abdullah Hamed Alharthy, Chm.
PO Box 1211
Muscat 131, Oman
Fax: 968 24 664491
E-mail: info@oea-oman.org
URL: http://www.oea-oman.org

5170 ■ Association Award for Economic Research
To encourage economic research to support the process of development in Oman. Entries should focus on new, applied economic research and should include a proposal for future development in Oman. Open to Omanis and researchers from other nationalities. Monetary prizes ranging from 1,000 to 3,000 Oman rials are awarded in the general category, and from 200 to 500 Oman rials in the student category. Awarded annually.

5171 ■ Royal Oman Police
Muscat, Oman
Ph: 968 2456 9944
Fax: 968 2456 2708
URL: http://www.rop.gov.om

5172 ■ Medal for Courage
To honor members of the police department for an outstanding act of bravery. A medal is awarded when merited. Established in 1975.

5173 ■ Medal for Efficiency
To honor members of the police department for outstanding service. A medal is awarded when merited. Established in 1975.

5174 ■ Medal for Long Service and Good Conduct
To honor members of the police department for outstanding service. A medal is awarded when merited. Established in 1975.

5175 ■ Sultan Qaboos Police Medal
To honor members of the police department for outstanding service. A medal is awarded when merited. Established in 1975 as the Medal for Excellent Service; renamed in 1980.

5176 ■ SJS Group (Oman)
PO Box 2058
Ruwi 112, Oman
Ph: 968 2478 9680
Fax: 968 2475 1019
E-mail: spotlight@sjsoman.com
URL: http://www.sjsoman.com

5177 ■ Kuwait Web Awards
To foster the spirit of innovation and creativity among Web designers in Kuwait, to raise the standards of Web design and Web sites, to advocate the growth and development of local talent, to promote intellectual property awareness, and to encourage all industries to showcase their Web sites and become more involved in the digital economy. Web sites are judged on five criteria: concept/creativity, technical/ease of use/navigation, content/structure, visual design solution/aesthetics, and interactivity. Presented in dozens of categories, including art and design, education, real estate, and sports. Winners represent Kuwait in the Pan Arab Web Awards (see separate entry). Awarded annually.

5178 ■ Oman Web Awards
To foster the spirit of innovation and creativity among Web designers in Oman, to raise the standards of Web design and Web sites, to advocate the growth and development of local talent, to promote intellectual property awareness, and to encourage all industries to showcase their Web sites and become more involved in the digital economy. Web sites are judged on five criteria: concept/creativity, technical/ease of use/navigation, content/structure, visual design solution/aesthetics, and interactivity. Presented in dozens of categories, including art and culture, education, real estate, and sports. Winners represent Oman in the Pan Arab Web Awards (see separate entry). Awarded annually. Established in 2005.

5179 ■ Qatar Web Awards
To foster the spirit of innovation and creativity among Web designers in Qatar, to raise the standards of Web design and Web sites, to advocate the growth and development of local talent, to promote intellectual property awareness, and to encourage all industries to showcase their Web sites and become more involved in the digital economy. Web sites are judged on five criteria: concept/creativity, technical/ease of use/navigation, content/structure, visual design solution/aesthetics, and interactivity. Presented in dozens of categories, including advertising and production, culture, fashion and art, industrial, and sports. Winners represent Qatar in the Pan Arab Web Awards (see separate entry). Awarded annually. Established in 2009.

Pakistan

5180 ■ Association of Chartered Certified Accountants - Pakistan
Afra Sajjad, Contact
61-C, Main Gulberg
Main Blvd.
Lahore 54660, Pakistan
Ph: 92 42 111222275
Fax: 92 42 5759346
E-mail: afra.sajjad@pk.accaglobal.com
URL: http://pakistan.accaglobal.com

5181 ■ ACCA-WWF Pakistan Environmental Reporting Awards
To recognize organizations that disclose information about the environmental and social impacts of their activity, to raise awareness of corporate transparency issues, and to encourage the uptake of environmental and sustainability reporting. Awarded annually. Established in 2004. Co-sponsored by WWF Pakistan.

5182 ■ Institution of Engineers - Pakistan
Engr. Ayaz Mirza, Sec.
Karachi Centre
IEP Bldg., 4th Fl.
177/2, Liaquat Barracks
Karachi 75530, Pakistan
Ph: 92 21 32780233
Ph: 92 21 32781492
Fax: 92 21 32783442
E-mail: info@iepkc.org
URL: http://www.iepkc.org

5183 ■ Honorary Fellowship
To honor an individual of distinction for services rendered to the Institution or whose association is deemed to be of benefit to the Institution. Awarded when merited.

5184 ■ Iqbal Academy Pakistan
Academy Block, 6th Fl.
Aiwan-e-Iqbal Complex
Egerton Rd.
Lahore, Pakistan
Ph: 92 42 6314510
Fax: 92 42 6314496
E-mail: info@iap.gov.pk
URL: http://www.allamaiqbal.com

5185 ■ International Iqbal Award
For promotion and recognition of original research work of high caliber to a foreign national in the field of Iqbal studies. A monetary prize of US$5,000 and a medal are awarded triennially. Established in 1977 by the President of Pakistan in honor of Dr. Sir Allama Mohammad Iqbal. Sponsored by the Pakistan Ministry of Education.

5186 ■ National Iqbal Award
To honor the best books on Allama Iqbal published in Urdu and English. Each recipient for Urdu- and English-language books is given a gold medal and cash prize of 50,000 rupees. In addition, six awards are presented for the best books in regional languages of Pakistan, namely Punjabi, Sindhi, Pashto, Baluchi, Brahvi, and Siriaki; each of these awards carries a cash prize of 30,000 rupees. Awarded triennially.

5187 ■ Pakistan Academy of Sciences
Prof. Ishfaq Ahmad, Pres.
3-Constitution Ave., Sector G-5/2
Islamabad 44000, Pakistan
Ph: 92 51 9204657
Fax: 92 51 9225159
E-mail: pasisb@yahoo.com
URL: http://www.paspk.org

5188 ■ Dr. M.N. Azam Prize
To recognize a Pakistani scientist for contributions in the field of computer software. A certificate and monetary prize of 15,000 rupees are awarded annually.

5189 ■ Comstech Prize in Computer Sciences/Information Technology
To recognize a Pakistani scientist for contributions in the field of computer sciences and information technology. A certificate and monetary prize of 15,000 rupees are awarded annually.

5190 ■ Distinguished Scientist of the Year
To recognize a Pakistani scientist for a contribution to the progress of scientific research of benefit and relevance to Pakistan. A gold medal, certificate, and monetary prize of 300,000 rupees are presented annually.

5191 ■ Gold Medal
To recognize Pakistani scientists for original research contributions. Awards are presented in 15 categories: agriculture, biochemistry, biology, botany, chemistry, computer software, computer information technology, earth sciences, engineering and technology, mathematics, medical sciences, molecular biology, pharmaceutical sciences, physics, and zoology. A gold medal, certificate, and monetary prize of 15,000 rupees are presented annually.

5192 ■ Gold Medals
To recognize achievements in scientific and technological research in various disciplines of science, and in engineering and technology for those who have developed patents and processes of far-reaching national importance. Medals are given in 15 categories: Agriculture, Biochemistry, Biology, Botany, Chemistry, Computer Science (Software), Computer Science (Information Technology), Earth Sciences, Engineering & Technology, Mathematics, Medical Sciences, Molecular Biology, Pharmaceutical Sciences, Physics, and Zoology. Pakistani scientists must be nominated by a Fellow of the Academy or rector/head of a university or scientific organization, within the time period specified. A gold medal and monetary prize of 15,000 rupees is awarded annually at an investiture ceremony. Established in 1967.

5193 ■ Dr. Atta Ur Rahman Prize in Chemistry
To recognize a Pakistani scientist for contributions in the field of chemistry. A gold medal, certificate, and monetary prize of 20,000 rupees are awarded annually.

Awards are arranged in alphabetical order below their administering organizations

5194 ■ Dr. M. Raziuddin Siddiqi Prize for Scientists Under 40
To recognize a Pakistani scientist below the age of 40 for contributions in science. Awards are presented on a rotating basis in the fields of chemistry, mathematics, and physics. A gold medal, certificate, and monetary prize of 15,000 rupees are awarded annually.

5195 ■ TWAS Prize for Young Scientists in the South
To recognize a Pakistani scientist below the age of 40 for contributions in science. Awards are presented on a rotating basis in the fields of biology, chemistry, mathematics, and physics. A certificate and monetary prize of $2,000 are awarded annually. Sponsored by the Third World Academy of Sciences (TWAS).

5196 ■ Pakistan Advertising Association
Mukthar Ahmed Azmi, Chm.
232, Hotel Metropole, Club Rd.
Karachi 75520, Pakistan
Ph: 92 21 5671567
Fax: 92 21 5671571
E-mail: paa@cyberaccess.com.pk
URL: http://www.pakistanadvertising.com/Associations/association.asp?id=12

5197 ■ Excellence Awards
To recognize excellence in advertising. Awards are presented in various categories each year.

5198 ■ Pakistan Society of Cardiovascular and Thoracic Surgeons
Prof. Jawad Sajid Khan, Pres.
Punjab Institute of Cardiology
Conference Rm., 2nd Fl.
(Gaus-ul-Azam) Jail Rd.
Lahore, Pakistan
Ph: 92 42 9203206
Fax: 92 42 9203207
E-mail: info@pakscts.org
URL: http://www.pakscts.org

5199 ■ Research Grant
To provide financial support to residents/trainees in Pakistan for research projects. Awarded annually.

5200 ■ University of Karachi Marine Reference Collection and Resource Center
Dr. Quddusi B. Kazmi, Dir.
University Rd.
Karachi 75270, Pakistan
Ph: 92 21 924 3680
Fax: 92 21 924 3680
E-mail: mrrcc@uok.edu.pk
URL: http://www.uok.edu.pk/research_institutes/mrrcc/index.php

5201 ■ NM Tirmizi Gold Medal
For marine science.

5202 ■ World Association of Detectives
Rashid Ali Malik, Chm.
One Anjum Plaza
Karachi 75400, Pakistan
Ph: 92 21 111002000
Fax: 92 21 4549554
E-mail: main@security2000.com
URL: http://www.wad.net

5203 ■ Investigator of the Year
To recognize an individual who has demonstrated outstanding professional service in the calendar year. Awarded annually.

5204 ■ Hal Lipset "Truth in Action" Award
To recognize a non-member for distinguished service and contribution to the profession of private investigation, private security, or law enforcement. Awarded annually.

5205 ■ Security Professional of the Year
To recognize individuals who have demonstrated outstanding professional service in the calendar year. Awarded annually.

5206 ■ Norman J. Sloan Memorial Award
This, the Association's highest honor, is awarded to a member who has contributed an exceptional amount of his or her time, energy, and effort to the betterment of the investigative or security professions. Awarded annually.

Panama

5207 ■ Florida State University, Panama
Edificio 227
Ciudad del Saber
Panama City, Panama
Ph: 507 317 0367
Fax: 507 317 0366
E-mail: fsupanama-awards@fsu.edu
URL: http://panama.fsu.edu

5208 ■ Distinguished Former Student Award
To recognize a former student of Florida State University Panama whose contributions have enhanced society on a significant level. Candidates must be students who completed their last class at least seven years ago. Awarded annually.

5209 ■ Promising Former Student Award
To recognize a recent graduate of Florida State University Panama for significant achievement and contribution to society. Candidates must be students who completed their last class no more than seven years ago. Awarded annually.

Papua New Guinea

5210 ■ Office of the Prime Minister of Papua New Guinea
Morauta House, 3rd Fl.
PO Box 639
Waigani, Papua New Guinea
Ph: 675 327 6525
Fax: 675 323 3943
E-mail: pmsmedia@pm.gov.pg
URL: http://www.pm.gov.pg

5211 ■ Companion of the Star of Melanesia
To honor an individual for distinguished service of a high degree in any field to Papua New Guinea and the Asia Pacific region, particularly the Melanesian nations, or to humanity, considered to be inspirational and significant at the national level, and sustained over a period of no less than 15 years. A medal is awarded when merited.

5212 ■ Cross of Valour
To honor an individual for selfless acts of extreme courage taken at the very great risk of one's life. Awarded to one or more recipients annually.

5213 ■ Grand Companion of Logohu
To honor a citizen of Papua New Guinea and other individuals for eminent achievement and merit of the highest degree in service sustained over a period of no less than 20 years. Excluding the Governor-General and honorary appointments, this award is limited to 50 living persons. A medal is awarded when merited.

5214 ■ Medals of the Orders
To honor an individual for meritorious service in the State Services or the community over a minimum period of three years. Awarded when merited.

5215 ■ Member of Logohu
To honor an individual for commendable service in a particular area of endeavor, or a combination of areas of service to the national or a local community for a period of at least seven years. A medal is awarded when merited.

5216 ■ National Logohu Medal
To honor individuals who have rendered exemplary service in their careers or professional or industry group or to the community generally over a period of at least five years. A medal is awarded when merited.

5217 ■ Officer of Logohu
To honor an individual for distinguished service to the nation or a local community sustained over a minimum period of 10 years. A medal is awarded when merited.

People's Republic of China

5218 ■ Association of Asia Pacific Physical Societies
Jie Zhang, Pres.
PO Box 603
Beijing 100080, People's Republic of China
E-mail: aapps@aapps.org
URL: http://www.aapps.org

5219 ■ Chen Ning Yang Award
To encourage young physicists in the Asia/Pacific region and to introduce excellent activities in the region. Awarded annually. Established in 1997.

5220 ■ Association of Chartered Certified Accountants - Hong Kong
Brendan Murtagh, Pres.
World Wide House, 19th Fl., Rm. 1901
19 Des Voeux Rd.
Central
Hong Kong, People's Republic of China
Ph: 852 25244988
Fax: 852 28684909
E-mail: info@hk.accaglobal.com
URL: http://hongkong.accaglobal.com

5221 ■ ACCA Hong Kong Awards for Sustainability Reporting
To recognize organizations that report and disclose environmental, social, or full sustainability information; to raise awareness of corporate transparency issues; and to encourage the uptake of environmental and sustainability reporting. Awarded annually.

5222 ■ Capital Corporation Image Institution
No.2, Wan Hong Xi Jie
Chaoyang District
Beijing 100015, People's Republic of China
Ph: 86 10 84567727
Fax: 85 10 64355550
E-mail: logo@ccii.com.cn
URL: http://www.ccii.com.cn

5223 ■ Logo Awards
To recognize the best logos. Awards include: Trademark/Logo Award; Visual Images Series Award; Spark Creation Award; Corporation Image Management Award; and Promoting Award. Awarded biennially in even-numbered years. Established in 1998.

5224 ■ Chartered Institute of Management Accountants - Hong Kong Division
Mr. Harold Baird, Pres.
Tower One, 20th Fl., Ste. 2005
Times Square
1 Matheson St.
Causeway Bay
Hong Kong, People's Republic of China
Ph: 852 25112003
Fax: 852 25074701

Awards are arranged in alphabetical order below their administering organizations

E-mail: hongkong@cimaglobal.com
URL: http://www.cimaglobal.com

5225 ■ Management Accounting Award
Recognizes exceptional CIMA publications and recommended readings for CIMA exams. Awarded annually.

5226 ■ China Foundry Association
Zhang Shufan, Exec. VP
3rd Fl., A-32 Zizhuyuan Rd.
Haidian District
Beijing 100044, People's Republic of China
Ph: 86 10 68418899
Fax: 86 10 68458356
E-mail: cfa@foundry-china.com
URL: http://www.foundry-china.com

5227 ■ Fine Craftsmanship Award for Young Foundrymen
To young foundrymen.

5228 ■ Outstanding Contributions Award
To foundries.

5229 ■ China Toy Association
Xiaoguang Shi, Pres.
101 Fu Xing Men Nei St.
Beijing 100031, People's Republic of China
Ph: 86 10 66038881
Ph: 86 10 66038225
Fax: 86 10 66033964
E-mail: cta@toy-cta.org
URL: http://www.toy-cta.org

5230 ■ Toy Star Award
To encourage innovative design of toys. Awarded to numerous recipients each year. Established in 2002.

5231 ■ Chinese American Librarians Association
Haipeng Li, Exec. Dir.
Hong Kong Baptist University
Kowloon Tong
Hong Kong, People's Republic of China
Ph: 852 34117368
E-mail: haipeng4cala@gmail.com
URL: http://www.cala-web.org

5232 ■ Distinguished Service Award
To recognize individuals who have consistently demonstrated outstanding leadership and achievement in library and information services at the national and/or international level. A plaque and recognition are awarded annually at the annual meeting held in June or July.

5233 ■ Chinese Anti-Cancer Association
Xishan Hao, Council Chm.
Tianjin New Technology Industrial Park Zone
Lanyuan Rd., 10 Fl., Bldg. A
Tianjin 300384, People's Republic of China
Ph: 86 22 23359958
Fax: 86 22 23526512
E-mail: commun@caca.sina.net
URL: http://www.caca.org.cn

5234 ■ CACA Award to Qualified Current Published Papers
To persons younger and older than 55 years of age who have current contributions.

5235 ■ Scientific Awards
To improve the national health by promoting the research of oncology in China by rewarding those oncology workers who made outstanding contribution to the progress of Chinese medical research and technology on oncology in order to give full play to initiative and creativity of Chinese scientists and medical workers. Each year, five first prizes, 10 second prizes, and 15 third prizes are awarded. Established in 2009.

5236 ■ Chinese Chemical Society
No. 2 Beiyijie St.
Zhong Guan Cun
Beijing 100080, People's Republic of China
Ph: 86 10 62564020
Ph: 86 10 62568157
Fax: 86 10 62568157
E-mail: qiuxb@iccas.ac.cn
URL: http://www.ccs.ac.cn/indexen.asp

5237 ■ Graduate Education Award
To an advisor of graduate students in polymer and coordination chemistry.

5238 ■ Graduate Student Award
To graduate students of polymer and inorganic chemistry.

5239 ■ Composers and Authors Society of Hong Kong
Prof. Chan Wing Wah JP, Chm.
18/F, Universal Trade Centre
3 Arbuthnot Rd.
Central
Hong Kong, People's Republic of China
Ph: 852 28463268
Fax: 852 28463261
E-mail: general@cash.org.hk
URL: http://www.cash.org.hk

5240 ■ Golden Sail Most Performed Works Award
To recognize the musical works that performed the most frequently during the year. Awards are given in the following categories: Cantonese Pop Work, Mandarin Pop Work, English (Foreign) Pop Work, Original Local Serious Work, Chinese Operatic Work, Highest Number of New Works Performed, and Highest Number of Active Works Performed. Awarded at the Annual Dinner Party.

5241 ■ Golden Sail Music Awards
To recognize outstanding musical works as well as vocal performances of musical works first commercially released or performed in Hong Kong within a specified period of the past year. Criteria include artistic, creative, and technical achievements of each piece of work or recorded performance. Awarded annually. Established in 2001.

5242 ■ Hall of Fame Award
Recognizes achievements and contribution to local music scenes. Awarded annually.

5243 ■ Federation of Hong Kong Industries
Mr. Roy Chung, Chm.
Hankow Centre, 4th Fl.
31/F, Billion Pl.
8 Cheung Yue St., Cheung Sha Wan, Kowloon
Hong Kong, People's Republic of China
Ph: 852 27323188
Fax: 852 27213494
E-mail: fhki@fhki.org.hk
URL: http://www.industryhk.org

5244 ■ Hong Kong Awards for Industries - Consumer Product Design
To promote and recognize the importance of product design in Hong Kong, and to encourage local entrepreneurs to improve the design, research, and development of their products. Eligible entries are consumer products or consumer-related products that are designed wholly or in part by Hong Kong designers and that have been on the market for two years or less. Criteria include external design, innovation, technological advancement and application, quality, usefulness, marketability, and safety. Awarded annually.

5245 ■ Industrialist of the Year
To honor an outstanding industrialist who has made significant contributions to industry and the Hong Kong community. Awarded annually. Established in 2002.

5246 ■ Young Industrialist Awards of Hong Kong
To recognize outstanding industrialists for their achievements and commitment to manufacturing

industry and to encourage them to further contribute their expertise to the territory's economic development. Industrialists who have resided in Hong Kong for more than seven years and are between the ages of 21 and 45 are eligible for nomination. A trophy is awarded annually.

5247 ■ Feng Zikai Chinese Children's Picture Book Award Committee
30/F, Wyndham Pl.
40-44 Wyndham St., Central
Hong Kong, People's Republic of China
Ph: 852 3167 4169
Fax: 852 2877 0434
E-mail: enquiries@fengzikaibookaward.org
URL: http://www.fengzikaibookaward.org

5248 ■ Feng Zikai Chinese Children's Picture Book Award
To promote the importance of original quality children's picture books and to recognize the contributions of writers, illustrators, and publishers of children's picture books. The following awards are presented: one Best Children's Picture Book Award of US$20,000; one Judging Panel's Recommended Illustration Award of US$10,000; one Judging Panel's Recommended Writing Award of US$10,000; and 10 Outstanding Children's Picture Book Award of US$1,000 each. Awarded annually. Established in 2008 in honor of Mr. Feng Zikai, a Chinese artist who was concerned with the welfare of children.

5249 ■ Geographical Society of China
No. A 11, Datun Rd.
Beijing 100101, People's Republic of China
Ph: 86 10 64870663
Fax: 86 10 64889598
E-mail: gsc@igsnrr.ac.cn
URL: http://www.gsc.org.cn

5250 ■ National Award for Middle School Teacher
For middle school teachers.

5251 ■ National Award of Science and Technology for Young Geographer
To honor young geographers. Awarded annually to 10 recipients.

5252 ■ Hong Kong Arts Centre
8/F, 2 Harbour Rd.
Wanchai
Hong Kong, People's Republic of China
Ph: 852 2824 5329
Fax: 852 2519 2032
E-mail: ifva@hkac.org.hk
URL: http://www.hkac.org.hk

5253 ■ Hong Kong Independent Short Film and Video Awards
To promote quality non-commercial short films and encourage creature independent production in Hong Kong. Films must be directed by Hong Kong residents with Hong Kong identity cards and must be no longer than 60 minutes in length. Awards are presented in five categories: Open, Youth, Animation, Interactive Media, and the Asian New Force. Held annually in the spring. Established in 1992.

5254 ■ Hong Kong Digital Entertainment Association
Mr. Gariel Pang, Chm.
Hong Kong Polytechnic University
School of Design
Hunghom
Kowloon
Hong Kong, People's Republic of China
Ph: 852 27664344
Fax: 852 23338812
E-mail: info@hkdea.org
URL: http://www.hkdea.org

Awards are arranged in alphabetical order below their administering organizations

5255 ■ Digital Animation - Feature Film Award
For best digital animation for a video or film featuring computer animation of not less than 25 minutes for mass media.

5256 ■ Digital Animation - Short Film Award
For best digital animation for a video or film featuring computer animation of not more than 25 minutes for mass media.

5257 ■ Digital Entertainment Software Award
For best digital entertainment software for computer terminals and TV sets.

5258 ■ Student Award
For best productions of digital entertainment software and video or film featuring computer animation.

5259 ■ Hong Kong Film Awards Association
Michelle Tsang, Admin.Mgr.
Rm 304 Ashley Centre
25 Ashley Rd.
Tsimshatsui
Hong Kong, People's Republic of China
Ph: 852 2367 7892
Fax: 852 2723 9597
E-mail: hkfaa@hkfaa.com
URL: http://www.hkfaa.com
Formerly: (1994) Hong Kong International Film Festival.

5260 ■ Hong Kong Film Awards
To promote Hong Kong films in Hong Kong and abroad, to recognize local film professionals, to encourage professional development, and to promote film culture. Awards are given in the following categories: Best Film, Best Director, Best Actor, Best Actress, Best Supporting Actor, Best Supporting Actress, Best New Performer, Best Screenplay, Best Cinematography, Best Film Editing, Best Art Direction, Best Costume and Makeup Design, Best Action Choreography, Best Original Film Score, and Best Original Film Song. All films with a general release in the preceding year are considered. Trophies are awarded annually at the award ceremony. Established in 1982. Formerly: Hong Kong International Film Festival.

5261 ■ Hong Kong Institute of Landscape Architects
Mr. Leslie Chen, Pres.
PO Box 20561
Hennessy Rd. Post Office
Wanchai
Hong Kong, People's Republic of China
Ph: 852 28962833
Fax: 852 28963938
E-mail: secretary@hkila.com
URL: http://www.hkila.com/index2.htm

5262 ■ Design Awards
To promote excellence in landscape planning, design, and research, and to recognize outstanding achievements by landscape architects and students. Awards are presented in five categories: landscape planning/research study; conceptual landscape project, landscape design project, environmental design project, and student landscape design project. Gold, silver, and merit awards are presented annually.

5263 ■ Hong Kong Jewelry Manufacturers Association
Mr. Sunny Chan, Chm.
Unit G, 2nd Fl.
Kaiser Estate, Phase 2
51 Man Yue St.
Hunghom, Kowloon
Hong Kong, People's Republic of China
Ph: 852 27663002
Fax: 852 23623647

E-mail: enquiry@jewelry.org.hk
URL: http://www.jewelry.org.hk

5264 ■ Outstanding Achievement Award - Hong Kong Jewelry Industry
For jewelry founders.

5265 ■ Hong Kong Management Association
Dr. Elizabeth S.C. Shing JP, Dir. Gen.
W Haking Management Development Center
Fairmont House, 14th Fl.
8 Cotton Tree Dr.
Central
Hong Kong, People's Republic of China
Ph: 852 27663303
Fax: 852 28684387
E-mail: hkma@hkma.org.hk
URL: http://www.hkma.org.hk/front.asp

5266 ■ Award for Excellence in Training and Development
To recognize individuals and companies for achievements in training and development. Gold, silver, and bronze prizes are awarded to the top training programs. Individuals receive the Distinguished Trainer Award and the Outstanding New Trainer Award. Awarded annually. Established in 1990.

5267 ■ Award for Marketing Excellence
To recognize organizations and marketers who have, though outstanding marketing programs, broken barriers and raised the standard of the marketing profession in Hong Kong. Gold, silver, and bronze prizes are awarded to the top marketing campaigns. Individuals receive the Distinguished Marketing Leadership Award, Outstanding Marketing Professional Award, and the CIM Marketer of the Year Award (sponsored by the Chartered Institute of Marketing). Awarded annually.

5268 ■ Best Annual Reports Awards
To encourage the publication of annual reports and accounts that are accurate, informative, and well-presented to shareholders, employees, and others who may have an interest in the activities of the organization in question. Awarded annually.

5269 ■ Distinguished Salesperson Award
To recognize successful salespersons for their achievements, to help improve the quality of salesmanship, and to promote the image of selling and marketing as a prestigious profession. Awarded annually.

5270 ■ Hong Kong Management Game Competition
To challenge teams of business executives to outwit each other in the making of management decisions. The winning team receives a trip to Malaysia, a trophy, and a cash prize of HK$28,000. The first runner-up receives HK$14,000, and the second runner-up receives HK$8,000. Held annually.

5271 ■ Quality Award
To recognize organizations that have achieved outstanding standards of quality and have made a lasting commitment to the process of quality management. Awarded annually.

5272 ■ Hong Kong Medical Association
Dr. Yvonne Leung, Chief Exec.
Duke of Windsor Social Service Bldg., 5th Fl.
15 Hennessy Rd.
Hong Kong, People's Republic of China
Ph: 852 25278285
Fax: 852 28650943
E-mail: hkma@hkma.org
URL: http://www.hkma.org

5273 ■ T.M. Gregory Memorial Scholarship Fund

5274 ■ Hong Kong Political Science Association
Baohui Zhang, Pres.
University of Hong Kong

Dept. of Politics and Public Administration
Pokfulam Rd.
Hong Kong, People's Republic of China
URL: http://www.hkpsa.org

5275 ■ Best Dissertation Award
For the dissertation or thesis that has made an original contribution political science. Awarded annually.

5276 ■ Hong Kong Productivity Council
Mr. Clement Chen Cheng-jen, Chm.
HKPC Bldg.
78 Tat Chee Ave.
Kowloon
Hong Kong, People's Republic of China
Ph: 852 27885678
Fax: 852 27885900
E-mail: gzo@gzo-hkpc.org
URL: http://www.hkpc.org/html/eng/common/index.jsp

5277 ■ Hong Kong Awards for Industries
To recognize outstanding achievements of Hong Kong enterprises in their move toward higher technology and higher value-added activities. Awards are presented in seven categories: Consumer product design, Machinery and equipment design, Customer service, Environmental performance, Innovation and creativity, Productivity and Quality, and Technological Achievement. Awarded annually. Established in 2005.

5278 ■ Hong Kong Society of Nephrology
Dr. Leung Chi Bon, Chm.
Alice Ho Miu Ling Nethersole Hospital
Department of Medicine
11 Chuen On Rd.
Tai Po, NT
Hong Kong, People's Republic of China
E-mail: office@hksn.org
URL: http://hksn.org

5279 ■ Hong Kong Nephrology Research Grants
To promote research culture among members, and to support local research projects in nephrology, which can be clinical, basic scientific, psychosocial, nursing or related to health economics. Grants are awarded in three categories: clinical research, basic science research, and nursing research. Grants ranging from HK$20,000 to HK$60,000 are awarded annually.

5280 ■ ICCHK Scholarships
For business related studies at the undergraduate level at the HK University of Science and Technology.

5281 ■ Young Nephrology Investigator Scholarship
To encourage young members of the Society to conduct studies and present their research in the international meetings, and to provide financial support for young nephrologists and nurses to attend international nephrology meetings for educational purposes. Ten scholarships up to HK$15,000 are awarded annually.

5282 ■ Indian Chamber of Commerce Hong Kong
M. Arunachalam, Chm.
Hoseinee House, 2nd Fl.
69 Wyndham St.
Central
Hong Kong, People's Republic of China
Ph: 852 25233877
Ph: 852 25250138
Fax: 852 28450300
E-mail: indcham@icchk.org.hk
URL: http://www.icchk.org.hk

Awards are arranged in alphabetical order below their administering organizations

5283 ■ Hong Kong Medical Association Prize
To medical students or interns.

5284 ■ International Association for Cross-Cultural Psychology
Kwok Leung, Pres.
City University of Hong Kong
Hong Kong, People's Republic of China
E-mail: mkkleung@cityu.edu.hk
URL: http://www.iaccp.org

5285 ■ Harry and Pola Triandis Doctoral Thesis Award
For outstanding dissertations in any area of culture and psychology. A monetary prize of US$500 is awarded biennially in even-numbered years. Established in 2000.

5286 ■ Witkin-Okonji Memorial Fund Award
To defray travel expenses to IACCP Congresses. Awards are presented on the basis of need and contribution to the Congress. Named in honor of Michael Okonji and Hy Witkin.

5287 ■ International Association of Schools of Social Work (Association Internationale des Ecoles de Travail Social)
Prof. Angelina Yuen PhD, Pres.
Hong Kong Polytechnic University
Dept. of Applied Social Sciences
Hong Kong, People's Republic of China
Ph: 852 27665718
Fax: 852 27736546
E-mail: angie.yuen@inet.polyu.edu.hk
URL: http://www.iassw-aiets.org

5288 ■ Katherine Kendall Award
To acknowledge significant contributions to the development of social work education at the international level. Awarded biennially in even-numbered years. Established in 1992.

5289 ■ International Federation of the Phonographic Industry - Hong Kong
Unit A, Tower A, Billion Centre, 18 Fl., No. 1
Wang Kwong Rd.
Kowloon Bay
Hong Kong, People's Republic of China
Ph: 852 28614318
Fax: 852 28666859
E-mail: enquiry@ifpihk.org
URL: http://www.ifpihk.org/www_1/index01e.php

5290 ■ Gold Disc Award
Awarded when merited to a pop music recording selling 25,000 copies in Hong Kong and/or 10,000 copies internationally. Additional awards are also awarded in the classical, extended play, and multi-unit set categories.

5291 ■ Platinum Disc Award
Awarded when merited to a pop music recording selling 50,000 copies in Hong Kong and/or 20,000 copies internationally. Additional awards are also awarded in the classical, extended play, and multi-unit set categories.

5292 ■ International Society for Photogrammetry and Remote Sensing
Mr. Chen Jun, Sec. Gen.
National Geomatics Center of China
28 Lianhuachixi Rd.
Haidian District
Beijing 100830, People's Republic of China
Ph: 86 10 63881102
Ph: 86 10 63881101
Fax: 86 10 63881905
E-mail: chenjun@nsdi.gov.cn
URL: http://www.isprs.org

5293 ■ Best Poster Paper Awards
To recognize the best poster presentations during the Society's Congress. A certificate and gift are awarded to two recipients.

5294 ■ Brock Gold Medal Award
For recognition of an outstanding contribution to the evolution of photogrammetric theory, instrumentation, or practice. Nomination by two member societies to which the nominee does not belong is required. A gold medal is awarded every four years at the Quadrennial Congress. Established in 1952 by the American Society for Photogrammetry and Remote Sensing in honor of Dr. G.C. Brock.

5295 ■ Gino Cassinis Award
Awarded to a person who has significantly enhanced the mathematical and statistical foundations of the photogrammetry, remote sensing or spatial information sciences in the four years preceding the congress. A certificate and monetary prize of 2,500 Swiss francs is awarded annually. Established in 2000.

5296 ■ The CATCON Prizes
Awarded at the Computer Assisted Teaching Contest, which is held to promote the development and dissemination of outstanding, user-friendly software packages. A gold award (1,000 Swiss francs), silver award (700 Swiss francs), and bronze award (500 Swiss francs) are awarded annually. Established in 1996.

5297 ■ Eduard Dolezal Award
To assist individuals or representatives of institutions from developing or reform countries to participate in the ISPRS Congress. Awarded annually. Established in 1996.

5298 ■ Samuel Gamble Award
For recognition of personal contributions to the administration of the Society or to the organization of activities of the Society's Commissions. Individuals irrespective of nationality are eligible. A certificate is awarded to up to three individuals every four years at the Quadrennial Congress. Established in 1985 in honor of Dr. Sam G. Gamble. Sponsored by the Canadian Institute of Surveying and Mapping.

5299 ■ U.V. Helava Award
Awarded to the author(s) of the most outstanding paper published exclusively in the ISPRS international Journal of Photogrammetry. A plaque and monetary prize of 10,000 Swiss francs is awarded annually. Established in 2000.

5300 ■ Honorary Member
To recognize distinguished services to the ISPRS and its aims. There may be no more than 10 living Honorary Members at any given time. A maximum of two Honorary Members may be elected at any Congress. Established in 1926.

5301 ■ Karl Kraus Medal
To honor the author of an outstanding textbook in the scientific fields of photogrammetry, remote sensing, and spatial information sciences. A medal and certificate are awarded annually. Established in 2009.

5302 ■ President's Honorary Citation
Awarded to a chairperson, co-chairperson or member of a working group of each ISPRS Technical Commission. A certificate is awarded annually. Established in 1988.

5303 ■ Prizes for Best Papers by Young Authors
Awarded to authors who are less than 35 years old and are the sole author of a high quality paper presented to the congress. A certificate and grant of 2,500 Swiss francs is awarded annually.

5304 ■ Willem Schermerhorn Award
To recognize a Working Group member(s) who, through commitment, has achieved successful scientific meetings at a very high level during the four year Congress period. Established in 1988. Sponsored by the Netherlands Society of Photogrammetry.

5305 ■ Schwidefsky Medal
To recognize individuals who have made significant contributions to photogrammetry and remote sensing, either through the medium of publication as author or editor, or in another form. A medal is awarded to one or two recipients every four years. Established in 1986 in memory of Prof. Dr. rer. techn. Dr.-Ing. E.h. Kurt Schwidefsky, honorary member of the Society. Sponsored by the Deutsche Gesselschaft fur Photogrammetrie und Fernerkundung.

5306 ■ Otto von Gruber Award
For recognition of a significant paper on photogrammetry or an allied subject, written in the four year period preceding the Congress. A monetary award and a gold medal are awarded every four years at the Quadrennial Congress. Established in 1964 by the ITC-Foundation (International Institute for Aerial Survey Sciences, the Netherlands) in honor of Otto von Gruber.

5307 ■ Sherman Wu Young Authors Award
To recognize the best paper by an author under 35 years of age. Established by Sherman Wu, a scientist well-known for his efforts in mapping Mars.

5308 ■ Wang Zhizhuo Award
Awarded to a person who has made significant achievement or innovation in the spatial information sciences. A medal and monetary prize of 2,500 Swiss francs is awarded every four years. Established in 2008.

5309 ■ International Society of Heterocyclic Chemistry
Prof. Dawei Ma, Pres.-Elect
Shanghai Institute of Organic Chemistry
Dept. of Chemistry
345 Lingling Rd.
Shanghai 200032, People's Republic of China
E-mail: madw@mail.sioc.ac.cn
URL: http://web.me.com/tpettus/ISHC/Welcome.html

5310 ■ Katritzky Junior Award in Heterocyclic Chemistry
To honor outstanding individuals in the field of heterocyclic chemistry. A monetary prize of US$3,000 is awarded biennially in odd-numbered years. Established in honor of Alan Katritzky.

5311 ■ Senior Award in Heterocyclic Chemistry
To honor outstanding individuals in the field of heterocyclic chemistry. Candidates may be any scientist whose research has directly or indirectly had a significant impact on heterocyclic chemistry. A monetary prize of US$5,000 is awarded biennially in odd-numbered years. Established in 1979.

5312 ■ Life Underwriters Association of Hong Kong
Ms. Angela Cheng, Asst. Dir.
Unit A-D, 23rd Fl.
Seabright Plz.
9-23 Shell St.
North Point
Hong Kong, People's Republic of China
Ph: 852 25702256
Fax: 852 25701525
E-mail: info@luahk.org
URL: http://www.luahk.org/www/main.asp

5313 ■ Distinguished Agent Award
To honor an outstanding life insurance agent in Hong Kong. Awarded annually.

5314 ■ Distinguished Manager Award
To honor an outstanding life insurance manager in Hong Kong. Awarded annually.

5315 ■ Toys Manufacturers' Association of Hong Kong
Mr. Samson Chan, Pres.
Metroplaza, Tower 2, Rm. 1302
223 Hing Fong Rd.

Awards are arranged in alphabetical order below their administering organizations

Kwai Chung
New Territories
Hong Kong, People's Republic of China
Ph: 852 24221209
Fax: 852 31880982
E-mail: info@tmhk.net
URL: http://www.tmhk.net

5316 ■ Toy Design Competition
To recognize local design talents, to encourage creativity as well as quality and competence in the toy design profession, and to stimulate and promote public interests in toy design in Hong Kong. Held annually. Established in 1999 by the Association and the Hong Kong Polytechnic University.

Peru

5317 ■ Peruvian Association for Conservation of Nature
(Asociacion Peruana para la Conservacion de la Naturaleza)
Cecilia Rosa F. Yockteng, Pres.
Parque Jose de Acosta 187
Magdalena del Mar
Lima 17, Peru
Ph: 51 1 2645804
Fax: 51 1 2673027
URL: http://www.apeco.org.pe

5318 ■ Global 500
Recognizes exemplary efforts of NGOs in the areas of conservation of natural resources. Awarded annually. Established in 1987.

5319 ■ Regional Centre for Seismology for South America
(Centro Regional de Sismologia para America del Sur)
Daniel Huaco Oviedo PhD, Exec. Dir.
Apartado 14-0363
Lima, Peru
Ph: 51 1 2256283
Fax: 51 1 2245144
E-mail: dhuaco@ceresis.org
URL: http://www.ceresis.org/portal/index.php

5320 ■ CERESIS Award
(Premio Ceresis)
For recognition of exceptional contributions to the advancement of seismology and related fields, relevant to South America. Selection is by nomination and unanimous approval of the member states. A plaque and a diploma are awarded biennially. Established in 1979.

Philippines

5321 ■ Asian Association of Social Psychology
Dr. Allan B.I. Bernardo, Sec. Gen.
De La Salle University
College of Education
Yuchengco Hall, Rm. 601
2401 Taft Ave.
Manila 1004, Philippines
E-mail: bernardoa@dlsu.edu.ph
URL: http://www.asiansocialpsych.org

5322 ■ Park Jung-heun Young Scholar Award
To provide financial travel assistance for young Asian psychologists to attend the Biennial Conference of AASP.

5323 ■ Misumi Award
To recognize the author of the article in the *Asian Journal of Social Psychology* of which contribution to the development of social psychology in Asia is most prominent. A monetary prize of $1,000 is awarded annually.

5324 ■ Association of Development Financing Institutions in Asia and the Pacific
Octavio B. Peralta, Sec. Gen.
2nd Fl., Skyland Plz.

Sen. Gil Puyat Ave.
Makati City 1200, Philippines
Ph: 63 2 8161672
Ph: 63 2 8430932
Fax: 63 2 8176498
E-mail: inquiries@adfiap.org
URL: http://www.adfiap.org

5325 ■ Distinguished Person Award
To honor an individual who has, in his or her chosen career, excelled and made a mark in the country or internationally, and who has made outstanding accomplishments in the field of development in general, and in the development banking profession in particular. Awarded annually.

5326 ■ Honorary Member
For recognition of achievement or contribution to the advancement of the development banking profession in the Asia-Pacific region. Individuals may be nominated if they have gained recognition in the field on development banking because of any of the following services: they have created, developed, and actualized an innovative concept, system, or technology that has been responsible for the improvement of development financing in the region; they have been the leading figure in the founding, development, and the operation of a pioneering institution that provides either development, financing or support, and assistance to other development financing institutions; or they have been recognized by peers and the leaders of their country for outstanding contributions to the field of development financing. A life-time membership in the Association is awarded when merited. Established in 1983.

5327 ■ Outstanding CEO Award
To recognize a practicing chief executive officer whose singular talent, leadership, vision, and achievement render him or her distinctive. Criteria include the stature of the individual, the positive effect that the person's leadership has had on his or her institution, and the impact his or her decisions have had on the development banking profession, in particular, and on the development of the country, in general. Awarded annually.

5328 ■ Outstanding Development Project Award
To recognize and honor member-banks that have undertaken and/or assisted projects that have created a development impact in their respective countries. Awards are presented in nine categories. Awarded annually.

5329 ■ International Federation of Asian and Western Pacific Contractors' Associations
Conrad Wong, Pres.
Padilla Bldg., 3rd Fl.
Ortigas Ctr.
F. Ortigas, Jr. Rd.
Pasig City 1605, Philippines
Ph: 63 2 6312782
Ph: 63 2 6312789
Fax: 63 2 6312773
E-mail: ifawpca@ifawpca.org
URL: http://www.ifawpca.org

5330 ■ Builders' Awards
To promote the development of operational and technical advancement in the field of construction, and to encourage the involvement of the construction industry in national welfare. Association members are eligible. A gold or silver medal is awarded in two classifications, Building Construction and Civil Engineering Construction, at the Association's convention. Established in 1964.

5331 ■ IFAWPCA-CHOI Construction Fieldman Award
To encourage the development of construction

field management systems, procedures, construction methods, and techniques; and to promote the cause of man-made power training. Candidates may be nominated. A monetary award or a citation is presented annually at the convention. Established in 1982 by Mr. Choi Chong-Whan, Past President of IFAWPCA, and President of Samwhan Corporation of Korea.

5332 ■ International Society for Southeast Asian Agricultural Sciences
University of the Philippines Los Banos
Dept. of Agricultural Economics
Laguna 4031, Philippines
Ph: 63 49 536 5816
Fax: 63 49 536 5816
E-mail: secretariat_phil@issaas.org
URL: http://www.issaas.org

5333 ■ Matsuda Award
To recognize an outstanding individual or group for distinguished contribution over a period of time toward the advancement of agricultural sciences and agricultural development in Southeast Asia.

5334 ■ Dr. Priscilla C. Sanchez Awards
To recognize individuals for excellence in leadership and research in agriculture and scientific communities in Southeast Asia. Awarded in three categories: Leadership Excellence, Excellence in Research, and Scientific Cooperation. Awarded biennially in odd-numbered years. Established in 2007.

5335 ■ Scientific Award
To recognize a member who has made a significant contribution to the advancement of Southeast Asian agricultural sciences.

5336 ■ Ramon Magsaysay Award Foundation
Ground Floor, Ramon Magsaysay Center
1680 Roxas Blvd.
PO Box 3350
Manila, Philippines
Ph: 63 2 521 3166
Fax: 63 2 521 8105
E-mail: rmaf@rmaf.org.ph
URL: http://www.rmaf.org.ph

5337 ■ Ramon Magsaysay Award
Awarded to individuals and organizations in Asia whose civic contributions and leadership exemplify the greatness of spirit, integrity, and devotion to freedom of Ramon Magsaysay, former president of the Philippines who died tragically in an airplane crash. Often regarded as the Nobel Prizes of Asia, these awards are presented in six categories: Government service; Public service; Community leadership; Journalism, literature, and creative communication arts; Peace and international understanding; and Emergent leadership. Awarded annually. Established in 1957.

5338 ■ National Commission for Culture and the Arts
(Pambansang Komisyon para sa Kultura at mga Sining)
Malou Jacob, Exec. Dir.
633 NCCA Bldg.
General Luna St.
Intramuros
Manila 1002, Philippines
Ph: 63 2 5272192
Ph: 63 2 5272202
Fax: 63 2 5272194
E-mail: info@ncca.gov.ph
URL: http://www.ncca.gov.ph

5339 ■ Dangal ng Haraya (Achievement Award)
To recognize living Filipino artists, cultural workers, historians, artistic or cultural groups, historical societies, institutions, foundations, and

Awards are arranged in alphabetical order below their administering organizations

councils for outstanding achievements in their particular fields that have made an impact and significant contribution to Philippine culture and arts. Awarded annually.

5340 ■ Gawad Alab ng Haraya (Alab ng Haraya Awards)
To honor outstanding achievements in the performing arts, cultural conservation, arts management, library and information services program, theater production, cultural journalism and documentation, and other fields in the Philippines. Awarded annually.

5341 ■ National Living Treasures Awards (Gawad Manlilikha Ng Bayan (GAMABA))
To recognize the vital role of the traditional Filipino artist in preserving and developing their indigenous artistic heritage, and to honor artists for their technical skills and outstanding creativity. Awards are presented in the categories that include, but are not limited to: folk architecture, maritime transport, weaving carving, performing arts, literature, graphic and plastic arts, ornament, textile or fiber art, pottery, and other artistic expressions of traditional culture. A gold medallion, initial grant of 100,000 pesos, and lifetime monthly stipend of 10,000 pesos are awarded annually. Established in 1992.

5342 ■ Order of National Artists of the Philippines (Orden ng Gawad Pambansang Alagad ng Sining)
To recognize Filipino individuals who have made significant contributions to the development of Philippine arts; namely, Music, Dance, Theater, Visual Arts, Literature, Film and Broadcast Arts, and Architecture and Allied Arts. The order is jointly administered by the NCCA and the Cultural Center of the Philippines (CCP), and conferred by the President of the Philippines upon recommendation by both institutions. Recipient is awarded the rank and title of National Artist; the National Artist medallion and citation; and a cash award of 100,000 pesos (for living artists) or 75,000 pesos (for posthumous artists, payable to their heirs).

5343 ■ National Research Council of the Philippines (Pambansang Sanggunian sa Pananaliksik ng Pilipinas)
Dr. Cecilia P. Reyes, Exec. Dir.
Department of Science and Technology
General Santos Ave.
Bicutan
Taguig 1631, Philippines
Ph: 63 2 8376143
Ph: 63 2 8376142
Fax: 63 2 8390275
E-mail: nrcpinfo@yahoo.com
URL: http://www.nrcp.dost.gov.ph

5344 ■ Achievement Awards
Recognizes exemplary achievement in the sciences. Awards are presented in the categories of mathematics, medicine, pharmaceuticals, biology, agriculture/forestry, social sciences, engineering/industrial research, physics, chemistry, humanities, and Earth and space sciences. Awarded annually.

5345 ■ Nutrition Foundation of the Philippines
Rodolfo F. Florentino PhD, Chm./Pres.
107 E. Rodriguez Sr. Blvd.
Quezon City 1102, Philippines
Ph: 63 2 7121474
Ph: 63 2 7113980
Fax: 63 2 7121474
E-mail: nfp_ngo@hotmail.com
URL: http://www.iuns.org/adhering-bodies/report/philippines.htm

5346 ■ Dr. Juan Salcedo Jr. Memorial Lecture
For Filipinos excelling in the fields of nutrition and dietetics, public health, and biochemistry.

5347 ■ Operating Room Nurses Association of the Philippines
Romeo E. Santarina, Pres.
Unit 915, Le Gran Condominium
Eisenhower St.
Greenhills, San Juan
Manila, Philippines
URL: http://www.ornap.org

5348 ■ Consuelo Gomez-Arabit Award for Excellence in Perioperative Nursing
To recognize outstanding operating room nurses in the Philippines. Awarded annually. Established in 1990 in honor of the founding president of the Association.

5349 ■ Carlos Palanca Foundation
1 World Square Bldg.
10 Upper McKinley Rd.
McKinley Town Ctr.
Fort Bonifacio
Taguig City 1634, Philippines
Ph: 63 2 856 0808
Fax: 63 2 856 5005
E-mail: cpawards@palancaawards.com.ph
URL: http://www.palancaawards.com.ph

5350 ■ Memorial Awards for Literature
For recognition of outstanding literature in English, Filipino, and Regional languages (Hiligaynon, Iluko, Cebuano). Awards are presented in nine categories: short stories, short stories for children, poetry, essays, one-act plays, full-length plays, teleplays, and screenplays. Cash prize, certificate and medallion are awarded annually.

5351 ■ Palanca Hall of Fame
To recognize those individuals who have won at least five first prizes in the Memorial Awards for Literature. Individuals are inducted when merited. Established in 1995.

5352 ■ Philippine Association of the Record Industry
Cely Cruz, Office Mgr.
Greenhills Mansion, Ste. 207
37 Annapolis St., Greenhills
San Juan
Manila, Philippines
Ph: 63 2 7250770
Ph: 63 2 7258754
Fax: 63 2 7250786
E-mail: writeus@pari.com.ph
URL: http://www.pari.com.ph

5353 ■ AWIT Awards
To recognize Filipino performing artists and others involved in Filipino recorded music. Awards are given in dozens of subcategories within the broader divisions of Performance, Creativity, Technical Achievement, Album Packaging, and Music Videos. Awarded annually.

5354 ■ Philippine Society of Anesthesiologists
Maria Minerva P. Calimag MD, Pres.
PMA Bldg., Rm. 102
North Ave.
Diliman
Quezon City 1100, Philippines
Ph: 63 2 4558263
Ph: 63 2 4558264
Fax: 63 2 9295852
URL: http://www.psa-ph.org

5355 ■ Quintin J. Gomez Award
To an individual or an institution that has made outstanding contribution(s) to the science and practice of anesthesiology.

5356 ■ Philippines Department of Science and Technology National Academy of Science and Technology
Dr. Estrella F. Alabastro, Sec.
DOST Complex
2/F Philippine Science Heritage Center
Bicutan, Taguig
Manila 1631, Philippines
Ph: 63 2 838 7739
Fax: 63 2 837 3170
E-mail: secretariat@nast.ph
URL: http://www.dost.gov.ph

5357 ■ Julian A. Banzon Medal for Applied Research
To recognize an individual or group for outstanding contributions through applied research in agriculture, industry and engineering, or health and social science. A medal and monetary prize of PhP 150,000 are awarded annually.

5358 ■ Hugh Greenwood Environmental Science Award
To recognize outstanding scientific and technological research works that contribute to environmental protection and conservation. Candidates must be Filipino citizens affiliated with a scientific society, research institution or firm, college or university, non-governmental organization, or environmental organization. A monetary prize of US$1,000 is awarded annually. Administered by the National Academy of Science and Technology.

5359 ■ Magsaysay Future Engineers/Technologists Award
To recognize outstanding research results in engineering and technology at the collegiate level and to encourage young Filipino students to pursue a career in science. Open to Bachelor of Science students enrolled in an engineering program or related fields; areas of study include biotechnology, machinery, engineering products, engineering sources, and product development. Monetary prizes of PhP 50,000, PhP 30,000, and PhP 20,000 are awarded for first, second, and third place, respectively. Awarded annually.

5360 ■ NAST-LELEDFI Award for Outstanding Research in Tropical Medicine
To recognize outstanding achievements in the research of tropical medicine, particularly the prevention and containment of the spread of tropical disease, the nature of the problem, and solutions to minimize or eradicate such diseases. Awarded annually. Established in 1976. Administered by the National Academy of Science and Technology. Co-sponsored by the LEL Educational Development Foundation Inc. (LELEDFI).

5361 ■ Outstanding Book and/or Monograph Awards
To recognize outstanding books and/or monographs published in the Philippines or elsewhere by Filipino authors during the previous five years. Eligible works are written on the topics of agriculture sciences; biological sciences; chemical, mathematical, and physical sciences; engineering sciences and technology; health sciences; and social sciences. A plaque is awarded annually. Administered by the National Academy of Science and Technology.

5362 ■ Outstanding Scientific Paper Award
To recognize outstanding papers published in Philippine scientific or technical journals within the previous five years. Eligible papers are written on the topics of agriculture sciences; biological sciences; chemical, mathematical, and physi-

Awards are arranged in alphabetical order below their administering organizations

cal sciences; engineering sciences and technology; health sciences; and social sciences. A plaque is awarded annually. Administered by the National Academy of Science and Technology.

5363 ■ Outstanding Young Scientist Award
To recognize Filipino scientists under the age of 41 for significant contributions to science and technology. A total of 10 awards are presented in the following divisions: agriculture sciences; biological sciences; chemical, mathematical, and physical sciences; engineering sciences and technology; health sciences; and social sciences. A trophy and monetary prize is awarded to each recipient annually. Administered by the National Academy of Science and Technology.

5364 ■ Philippine Mathematical Olympiad
To recognize secondary students with mathematical talents. Certificates of achievement, monetary prizes, trophies, medals, and plaques are awarded annually. Established in 1984. Jointly sponsored by the Philippines' Department of Science and Technology-Science Education Institute, Department of Education, Culture, and Sports, the Mathematical Society of the Philippines, and the PCI Bank Group.

5365 ■ Philippine Physics Olympiad
To recognize Philippine secondary school students with talent in physics and to stimulate the improvement of physics education. Certificates of merit, monetary prizes, trophies, medals, and plaques are given biennially. Established in 1992. Sponsored jointly by the Philippines' Department of Science and the Science and Technology-Science Education Institute, the Department of Education, Culture, and Sports, and the Samahang Pisika ng Pilipinas.

5366 ■ Pro Scientia Transformatrix Award
To recognize corporate institutions or foundations operating within the Philippines for notable practical success directly due to pioneering and novel science/technology, leading to measurable increases in the global competitiveness of the Philippines. Awarded annually. Administered by the National Academy of Science and Technology.

5367 ■ Eduardo A. Quisumbing Medal for Basic Research
To recognize an individual or group for outstanding contributions through basic research in mathematics, physical science, or life science. A medal and monetary prize of PhP 150,000 are awarded annually.

5368 ■ TWAS Prize for Young Scientist in the Philippines
To recognize an outstanding Filipino scientist under the age of 40 years. Focus shifts between chemistry, mathematics, and physics on an annually rotating basis. A plaque and monetary prize of US$2,000 are awarded annually. Administered by the National Academy of Science and Technology. Co-sponsored by the Third World Academy of Sciences (TWAS).

5369 ■ Dioscoro L. Umali Medal for Outstanding Science Administrator
To recognize science and technology or research and development administrators who have made significant contributions to science and technology through effective management and implementation of plans and programs. Open to administrators in the academe, private sector, or government. A medal and monetary prize of PhP 150,000 are awarded annually.

5370 ■ Gregorio Y. Zara Medal for Outstanding Technology Commercialization
To recognize the efforts of technology genera-

tors and developers whose technologies have been commercialized. A medal and monetary prize of PhP 150,000 are awarded annually.

5371 ■ University of the Philippines Alumni Association
Ang Bahay ng Alumni, Rm. 211
Magsaysay Ave.
University of the Philippines, Diliman Campus
Quezon City, Philippines
Ph: 63 920 6871
Fax: 63 920 6875
E-mail: up.alum.assn@pacific.net.ph
URL: http://www.upalumni.ph

5372 ■ Community Service Award
To recognize alumni for outstanding accomplishments and notable service in a particular community in the Philippines. Awards may be presented for each of the following levels: National, Luzon, Visayas, and Mindanao. Awarded annually.

5373 ■ Distinguished Alumnus/Alumna Award
To recognize alumni who have attained national or international prestige for programs and projects that have brought honor and distinction to the University and the nation. Awarded annually.

5374 ■ Lifetime Distinguished Achievement Award
To recognize alumni for illustrious and meritorious service and contributions to their field of expertise. Awarded annually.

5375 ■ Outstanding Alumni Chapter Award
To recognize Association chapters for meritorious and exceptional activities, projects, and other accomplishments. Two awards may be presented annually, one to a local chapter and one to a foreign-based chapter.

5376 ■ Outstanding Graduate Award
To recognize graduates of the current school year. Candidates must be of good moral character, have potential for leadership and service to the University and the nation, and have achieved excellent academic performance and participation. Two awards may be presented annually, one for a male graduate and one for a female graduate.

5377 ■ Outstanding Professional Award
To recognize alumni who have excelled in the respective fields of their professions. Awards are given in 26 categories, from agriculture to veterinary medicine. Awarded annually.

5378 ■ Service Award
To recognize alumni for meritorious service to the Association directly or through a special project of the Association. Awarded annually.

5379 ■ Special Recognition Award
To recognize an individual or group of alumni that, through special outstanding efforts or achievements during the past year, gave honor and prestige to a profession, the University, the community, and the nation. Awarded annually.

Poland

5380 ■ Central Institute for Labor Protection National Research Institute
Prof. Danuta Koradecka PhD, Dir.
Czerniakowska Str. 16
00-701 Warsaw, Poland
Ph: 48 22 623 3698
Fax: 48 22 623 3693
E-mail: dakor@ciop.pl
URL: http://www.ciop.pl

5381 ■ PRO LABORE SECURO Statuette
Recognizes extraordinary public service in aid of the protection of man in the working environment. Awarded annually.

5382 ■ European Association for Sociology of Sport
Prof. Andrzej Pawlucki, Sec. Gen.
University School of Physical Education in Wroclaw
51-617 Warsaw, Poland
Ph: 48 71 347 3169
E-mail: asp48@wp.pl
URL: http://www.eass-sportsociology.eu

5383 ■ Young Researcher's Awards
To facilitate the integration of outstanding graduate students and young researchers into the European community of sociology of sport scholars. Candidates must be students who are registered for Master's or doctoral level graduate work, and must be younger than 35 years of age who was awarded a PhD not earlier than five years previously. Awarded annually.

5384 ■ European Sports Press Union (Union Europeenne de la Presse Sportive)
Jerzy Jakobsche, Pres.
Ul. Bracka 6/8
00-502 Warsaw, Poland
Ph: 48 22 6216584
Fax: 48 22 6213875
E-mail: j.jakobsche@pap.com.pl
URL: http://www.uepsmedia.com

5385 ■ European Sportsman and Sportswoman of the Year (Sportive et Sportif Europeen de l'Annee)
To honor the best male and female European athlete of the year. A trophy is awarded annually. Established in 1983.

5386 ■ Frederick Chopin Society (Towarzystwo imienia Fryderyka Chopina)
Antoni Grudzinski, Gen. Dir.
43 Tamka St.
PL-00-355 Warsaw, Poland
Ph: 48 22 8266549
Ph: 48 22 8283873
Fax: 48 22 8279589
E-mail: info@chopin.pl
URL: http://www.chopin.pl

5387 ■ Grand Prix du Disque Frederic Chopin
To recognize an outstanding recording of a work by Chopin. Awards are presented in three categories: 1. Contemporary recordings; 2. Historical recordings; and 3. Remasterings of historical mechanical recordings/pianola recordings. Held every five years. Established in 1985.

5388 ■ International Frederic Chopin Piano Competition
To recognize outstanding pianists of work by Chopin. Pianists of all nationalities between 17 and 30 years of age may apply. The following prizes are awarded: first prize - 30,000 Euros and a gold medal; second prize - 25,000 Euros and a silver medal; third prize - 20,000 Euros and a bronze medal; fourth prize - 15,000 Euros; fifth prize - 10,000 Euros; and sixth prize - 7,000 Euros. In addition, each finalist receives 4,000 Euros, and five special prizes of 3,000 Euros may be awarded. Held every five years. Established in 1927 by Professor Jerzy Zurawlew in memory of Frederic Chopin.

5389 ■ Ministry of Justice, Poland Institute of Forensic Research
Aleksander Glazek, Dir.
ul. Westerplatte 9
31-033 Krakow, Poland
Ph: 48 12 422 8755

Awards are arranged in alphabetical order below their administering organizations

Fax: 48 12 422 3850
E-mail: ies@ies.krakow.pl
URL: http://www.ies.krakow.pl

5390 ■ Robel Award
To recognize the best Master's, Bachelor's, or diploma thesis in the field of forensic sciences.

5391 ■ Polish Chemical Society
(Polskie Towarzystwo Chemiczne)
Dr. Pawel Kafarski, Pres.
ul. Freta 16
PL-00-227 Warsaw, Poland
Ph: 48 22 831304
Fax: 48 22 831304
E-mail: zgptchem@chemix.ch.pw.edu.pl
URL: http://www.ptchem.lodz.pl

5392 ■ Jan Harabaszewski Medal
For recognition of outstanding contributions to the field of chemistry education. Nominees for the awards are named by the Presidium of General Council of the Society or by Division of Educational Chemistry. A medal is awarded annually. Established in 1989 in honor of Jan Harabaszewski, a Polish scientist.

5393 ■ Honorary Membership
To recognize distinguished chemists, regardless of their nationality and affiliation, for outstanding scientific achievements and contributions to the development of the Society and chemistry in Poland. Nominees for the awards are named by the Presidium of General Council of the Society or by its regional councils and are determined by the General Assembly.

5394 ■ Wiktor Kemula Medal
To recognize an individual for achievements in analytical chemistry. Awarded annually. Established in 1998.

5395 ■ Stanislaw Kostanecki Medal
For recognition of contributions to the fields of physical and inorganic chemistry. Nominees for the awards are named by the Presidium of General Council of the Society or by its regional councils. Awarded annually if merited. Established in 1978.

5396 ■ Ignacy Moscicki Medal
To recognize an individual for achievements in chemical technology. Awarded annually. Established in 2000.

5397 ■ Maria Sklodowska-Curie Medal
In recognition of outstanding foreign chemists who have made significant contributions to science and/or technology and have strong ties with Polish chemical institutions, particularly academic. Awarded annually by the General Assembly of the Society. Established in 1996. Formerly: Polish Chemical Society Medal.

5398 ■ Jedrzej Sniadecki Medal
This, the Society's highest distinction, is given in recognition of prominent achievements in chemistry. Nominees for the awards are named by the Presidium of General Council of the Society or by its regional councils. Awarded annually if merited. Established in 1965.

5399 ■ Jan Zawidzki Medal
For recognition of outstanding contributions to the fields of physical and inorganic chemistry. Nominees for the awards are named by the Presidium of General Council of the Society or by its regional councils. Awarded annually. Established in 1979.

5400 ■ Polish Composers Union
(Zwiazek Kompozytorow Polskich)
Jerzy Kornowicz, Pres.
Rynek Starego Miasta 27
PL-00-272 Warsaw, Poland
Ph: 48 22 8311741
Fax: 48 22 8874052

E-mail: zkp@zkp.org.pl
URL: http://www.zkp.org.pl

5401 ■ Tadeusz Baird Memorial Competition for Young Composers
(Konkurs Mlodych Kompozytorow im. Tadeusza Bairda)
For recognition of outstanding young composers. Polish citizens who are 35 years of age or younger are eligible. First prize of the Tadeusz Baird Award, accompanied by $2,500, is awarded annually; also awarded are two honorable mentions. Established in 1958 by the Board of the Polish Composers Union and renamed in 1990 in honor of Tadeusz Baird.

5402 ■ PCU Award
(Nagroda Zwiazku Kompozytorow Polskich)
To honor Polish composers, performers, musicologists, music teachers, and music life organizers for eminent achievements. A monetary award and a diploma are presented annually in January. Established in 1949 by the Polish Composers Union to commemorate the liberation of Warsaw on January 17, 1945.

5403 ■ Polish Physical Society
(Polskie Towarzystwo Fizyczne)
Prof. Wieslaw A. Kaminski, Pres.
ul. Hoza 69
PL-00-681 Warsaw, Poland
Ph: 48 22 6212668
Fax: 48 22 6212668
E-mail: ptf@fuw.edu.pl
URL: http://ptf.fuw.edu.pl

5404 ■ Award for Promotion of Physics
For the promotion of physics and of the public understanding of physics. A monetary prize and certificate are awarded.

5405 ■ Grzegorz Bialkowski Prize
For outstanding teacher of physics. A monetary prize and certificate are awarded.

5406 ■ Honorary Membership
Given by the general ensemble of the Society when merited.

5407 ■ Nagroda Naukowa Scientific Prize
For outstanding achievements in physics. A monetary prize and certificate are awarded.

5408 ■ Arkadiiusz Piekara Prize
For outstanding master's thesis for physics. A monetary prize and certificate are awarded.

5409 ■ Marian Smoluchowski Medal
(Medal Mariana Smoluchowskiego)
For recognition of a splendid contribution to science and to international scientific cooperation in physics. Scientists may be nominated. A medal and a special diploma in Polish and Latin are awarded annually when merited. Established in 1967 in memory of Marian Smoluchowski, a Polish physicist famous for his achievements in the kinetic theory of matter.

5410 ■ Smoluchowski-Warburg Prize
For outstanding contributions to pure or applied physics. Awarded to Polish and German physicists alternately every two years. A monetary prize of 1,000 Euros, a silver medal, and a certificate are awarded.

5411 ■ Special Prize
For special services for physics and Polish Physical Society. A monetary prize and certificate are awarded annually if merited. Established in 1982.

5412 ■ Polish Society of Veterinary Science
(Polskie Towarzystwo Nauk Weterynaryjnych)
Prof. Andrew Koncicki, Pres.
ul.Nowoursynowska 159c
02-776 Warsaw, Poland
Ph: 48 22 5931606

Fax: 48 22 5931606
E-mail: ptnw@sggw.pl
URL: http://www.ptnw.pl

5413 ■ Science Award
To young scientists.

5414 ■ Warsaw Philharmonic
(Filharmonia Narodowa w Warszawie)
Antoni Wit, General and Artistic Dir.
c/o National Orchestra and Choir of Poland
ul. Jasna 5
PL-00-950 Warsaw, Poland
Ph: 48 22 55 17 111
Fax: 48 22 55 17 200
E-mail: sekretariat@filharmonia.pl
URL: http://www.filharmonia.pl

5415 ■ Witold Lutoslawski International Composers Competition
(Miedzynarodowy Konkurs Kompozytorski im-Witolda Lutoslawskiego)
To recognize outstanding compositions. Compositions may be submitted in the following categories: symphony orchestra; choir and symphony orchestra; solo voice or voices and symphony orchestra; solo instrument or instruments and symphony orchestra; and choir, solo voice or voices and symphony orchestra. Composers of all ages and nationalities may submit scores by December 31. Pieces not performed in public and not rewarded at any other competition are eligible. Three monetary prizes ranging from $1,000 to $3,000 and performance of the winning pieces are awarded biennially. Established in 1988.

Portugal

5416 ■ Cinema Novo Fantasporto
Rua Anibal Cunha 84, sala 1.6
P-4050-046 Porto, Portugal
Ph: 351 2220 58819
Fax: 351 2220 58823
E-mail: info@fantasporto.com
URL: http://www.fantasporto.com

5417 ■ Best Actor
Awarded to the best actor in a film at the awards show. Awarded annually.

5418 ■ Best Actress
Awarded to the best actress in a film at the awards show. Awarded annually.

5419 ■ Best Direction
Awarded to the best director of a film at the awards show. Awarded annually.

5420 ■ Best Fantasy Short
Awarded to the best short fantasy film at the awards show. Awarded annually.

5421 ■ Best Film Award
Awarded to the best overall film at the awards show. Awarded annually.

5422 ■ Best Screenplay
Awarded to the best screenplay for a film at the awards show. Awarded annually.

5423 ■ Best Special Effects
Awarded to the best special effects in a film at the awards show. Awarded annually.

5424 ■ Oporto International Film Festival - Fantasporto
(Festival Internacional de Cinema do Porto - Fantasporto)
To promote imaginary films on an international level that seek new forms and methods of filmmaking, and in which the creative powers of the imagination have a treatment of quality. The Festival has eight sections, the first three of which are competitive: 1. Official Section - Competition for Fantasy Films; 2. Directors'

Awards are arranged in alphabetical order below their administering organizations

Week - Competition for Feature Films; 3. Orient Express Official Section for Asiatic Feature Films; 4. Panorama and Premiere Films of the World; 5. Love Connection; 6. Anima-te (Animation Features); 7. Porto in Shorts; and 8. Retrospectives. Trophies and certificates are awarded in the competitive sections. Held annually in February. Established in 1980 by the magazine, *Cinema Novo*.

5425 ■ Special Prize of the Jury
To recognize a film that is the favorite of the jury at the festival. Awarded annually.

5426 ■ European Imaging and Sound Association
Patricia Barbosa, Contact
R.D. Joao V, 6-R/C Esq.
1250-090 Lisbon, Portugal
Ph: 351 21 319 0654
Fax: 351 21 319 0659
E-mail: patricia.barbosa@eisa.eu
URL: http://www.eisa.eu

5427 ■ Audio and Home Theater Awards
To recognize outstanding new audio and home theater products in Europe. To qualify, products must have been for sale to the general public in at least 10 European countries. Recipients are selected by panels representing more than 50 prominent industry magazines from up to 19 European countries. Awarded in several categories each year. Established in 1992.

5428 ■ Mobile Devices Awards
To recognize outstanding new mobile products in Europe. To qualify, products must have been for sale to the general public in at least 10 European countries. Recipients are selected by panels representing more than 50 prominent industry magazines from up to 19 European countries. Awarded in several categories, including tablets, desktop speakers, headphones, social media phones, mobile phones, and camera phones. Awarded annually. Established in 2005.

5429 ■ International Commission on Mathematical Instruction
Jaime Carvalho e Silva, Sec. Gen.
Departamento de Matematica
Apartado 3008
EC Universidade
3001-454 Coimbra, Portugal
Ph: 351 239 791199
Fax: 351 239 793069
E-mail: jaimecs@mat.uc.pt
URL: http://www.mathunion.org

5430 ■ Hans Freudenthal Award
To recognize an individual for a major cumulative program of research in mathematics education. A medal is awarded biennially in odd-numbered years. Established in 2003.

5431 ■ Felix Klein Award
To recognize an individual for a lifetime of achievement in mathematics education. A medal is awarded biennially in odd-numbered years. Established in 2003.

5432 ■ International Society for Rock Mechanics
(Societe Internationale de Mecanique des Roches)
Prof. John A. Hudson, Pres.
Avenida Brasil, 101
1700-066 Lisbon, Portugal
Ph: 351 21 8443419
Fax: 351 21 8443021
E-mail: secretariat.isrm@lnec.pt
URL: http://www.isrm.net

5433 ■ Muller Award
To recognize an individual for a contribution in

the field of rock mechanics. A medal and travel expenses are awarded every four years at the ISRM Congress. Established in 1989 to honor Prof. Leopold Muller.

5434 ■ Manuel Rocha Medal
For recognition of an outstanding doctoral thesis in the field of rock mechanics that is accepted during the two years preceding the conferment. A monetary prize, a bronze medal, and travel expenses to receive the award are presented annually. Established in 1981 in honor of Manuel Rocha, past president of the Society and Portuguese scientist.

Qatar

5435 ■ Oryx Advertising Co. WLL
PO Box 3272
Doha, Qatar
Ph: 974 4467 2139
Fax: 974 4455 0982
E-mail: info@omsqatar.com
URL: http://www.omsqatar.com

5436 ■ *Qatar Today* Green Awards
To recognize and honor organizations for outstanding environmental vision, endeavors, and achievements. Presented in several categories, including Green Innovation, Green Retailer, Environment Leadership, and Best Public Awareness Campaign. Awarded annually. Established in 2008. Sponsored by *Qatar Today* magazine.

5437 ■ *Qatar Today* Restaurant Awards
To recognize the best restaurants in Qatar, as selected by readers of *Qatar Today* magazine. Categories include Most Authentic Arabic Food and the Restaurant with the Best Ambience. Awarded annually. Sponsored by *Qatar Today* magazine.

Republic of Korea

5438 ■ Asia-Pacific Satellite Communications Council
Inho Seo, Dir.
Ste. T-1602, Poonglim Iwantplus
255-1 Seohyun-dong, Bundang-gu
Kyungin-do
Seongnam 463-862, Republic of Korea
Ph: 82 31 7836244
Ph: 82 31 7836246
Fax: 82 31 7836249
E-mail: info@apscc.or.kr
URL: http://www.apscc.or.kr

5439 ■ Lifetime Achievement Award
For organizations and individuals who have made significant contributions to the advancement of the satellite and space related industries.

5440 ■ Satellite Executive of the Year
To honor individuals who have made significant contributions to the advancement of the satellite and space related industries.

5441 ■ The International Association of Forensic Toxicologists
Ms. Hee-Sun Chung, Sec.
c/o National Institute of Scientific Investigation
331-1 Shinwol-dong
Yangcheon-ku
Seoul, Republic of Korea
E-mail: info@tiaft.org
URL: http://www.tiaft.org

5442 ■ Achievement Award
To recognize a young member for outstanding achievements in forensic toxicology through his or her scientific activities and outputs. Candidates must be younger than 46 years of age. Awarded annually. Established in 2000.

5443 ■ Alan Curry Award
This, the Association's most prestigious award, is presented to a member who has a long history of distinguished contributions to the field of forensic toxicology and to the Association. Awarded annually. Established in 1993.

5444 ■ International Radiation Commission
Byung-Ju Sohn, Sec.
School of Earth and Environmental Sciences
Seoul National University
Gwanak-ro 577, Gwanak-gu
Seoul 151-747, Republic of Korea
Ph: 82 2 880 7783
Fax: 82 2 872 8156
E-mail: sohn@snu.ac.kr
URL: http://www.irc-iamas.org

5445 ■ Gold Medal
To honor a senior scientist who has made contributions of lasting significance to the field of radiation research. Awarded every four years at the International Radiation Symposium.

5446 ■ Young Scientist Award
To recognize a young scientist who has made recent noteworthy contributions to radiation studies and is regarded as having great potential to become a leading radiation scientist in the future. Candidates should be under 40 years of age and within 10 years of having received the PhD degree. A monetary prize of $1,000 is awarded every four years at the International Radiation Symposium.

5447 ■ Korean Chemical Society
Choon Ho Do, Contact
34-1, 5-ga, Anam-dong
Seongbuk-gu
Seoul 136-075, Republic of Korea
Ph: 82 2 9532095
Fax: 82 2 9532093
E-mail: webmaster@kcsnet.or.kr
URL: http://new.kcsnet.or.kr

5448 ■ Academic Excellence Prize
To chemists who have performed excellent research in chemical technology. Awarded annually.

5449 ■ Analytical Chemistry Division Award for Excellent Research
To recognize an individual for outstanding research results in analytical chemistry within the past three years. Awarded annually.

5450 ■ Award for Advancement of Industry
To chemists who have made contribution in the advancement and development of the Korean chemical technology. Awarded annually.

5451 ■ Award for Advancement of Science
To chemists who have published excellent research in the journals of KCS. Awarded annually.

5452 ■ Award for Chemical Education
To teachers who have made distinguished achievement in the advancement of chemical education. Awarded biennially.

5453 ■ Award for Excellent Chemistry Teachers
To recognize secondary school teachers for outstanding performance in teaching chemistry. Awarded annually.

5454 ■ Award for Excellent Research Paper
To chemists who have published the paper most frequently cited in the journals of KCS. Awarded annually.

5455 ■ Chemistry Award for Young Physical Chemists
To recognize young researchers for outstanding

Awards are arranged in alphabetical order below their administering organizations

research contributions to physical chemistry. Candidates must be less than 45 years of age. Awarded annually by the Physical Chemistry Division.

5456 ■ Excellent Poster Presentation Prize
To recognize students for outstanding poster presentations at the annual meeting of the KCS. Awarded annually.

5457 ■ Inorganic Chemistry Division Award for Excellent Research
To recognize an individual for outstanding research results in organic chemistry within the past three years. Awarded annually.

5458 ■ Ipjae Award in Physical Chemistry
To honor a member for outstanding contributions to the development of the physical chemistry industry in Korea, or for outstanding research results in the physical chemistry field. Awarded annually by the Physical Chemistry Division.

5459 ■ Macromolecular Chemistry Division Award for Advancement of Science
To recognize an individual for distinguished contributions to polymer chemistry. Awarded annually.

5460 ■ Material Chemistry Division Award for Excellent Research
To recognize young researchers for outstanding research contributions to material chemistry. Candidates must be less than 45 years of age. Awarded annually.

5461 ■ Merit Award
Awarded for distinguished achievement in the advancement and development of KCS. Awarded triennially.

5462 ■ Organic Chemistry Division Award for Excellent Research
To recognize an individual for distinguished contributions to organic chemistry. Awarded annually.

5463 ■ Taikyue Ree Academic Award
To recognize an individual for distinguished contributions to the chemical industry. Awarded annually by the Taikyue Ree Commemoration Foundation.

5464 ■ Korean Society for Biochemistry and Molecular Biology
Korea Science and Technology Ctr. 801
635-4 Yeoksam-dong
Kangnam
Seoul, Republic of Korea
Ph: 82 2 565 1621
Fax: 82 2 508 7578
E-mail: ksbmb@biochem.or.kr
URL: http://www.biochem.or.kr

5465 ■ Dongchun Lecture
To support a lecture by a member who has recently published an exceptional paper in the Journal of Biochemistry and Molecular Biology. Established to honor Prof. Moon-Hi Han.

5466 ■ Moosa Lecture
To support a lecture by a distinguished scholar in biochemistry or molecular biology. Established in honor of Prof. Keun-Bai Lee.

5467 ■ Korean Society of Pharmacology
Ho Seok Jeong, Pres.
208 Hyunil Tower Officetel
Seongsan-dong
Mapo-gu
Seoul 121-250, Republic of Korea
Ph: 82 2 3260370
Fax: 82 2 3260371
E-mail: head@kosphar.org
URL: http://www.kosphar.org

5468 ■ Chung-Wae Award
For exemplary scientific papers.

5469 ■ Korean Society of Soil Science and Fertilizer
Kwang Yong Jung, Pres.
No. 249 Seodun-dong
Gwonseon-ku
Gyeonggi-Do
Suwon 441-709, Republic of Korea
Ph: 82 31 2957335
Ph: 82 31 2900100
Fax: 82 31 2957335
E-mail: ksssf249@hanmail.net
URL: http://www.ksssf.or.kr

5470 ■ Academy Prize
For members who made outstanding contributions to soil research.

5471 ■ Music Association of Korea
Yong-Jin Kim, Hon. Pres.
1-117 Tong-Sung Dong, Chong-Ro Ku
Seoul 110-765, Republic of Korea
Ph: 82 2 7448060
Ph: 82 2 7448061
Fax: 82 2 7412378
URL: http://www.mak.or.kr/english/e-index.htm

5472 ■ Korean Composition Awards
To encourage and contribute to professional development in the field of Korean music. Applicants must be Korean. Works composed and performed within five years, including the year the award is given, that are more than 10 minutes duration may be submitted by late September. The following awards are presented: (1) The Most Outstanding Award 3,000,000 won for one, plus a concert; (2) The Outstanding Award - 2,000,000 won, plus a concert engagement, for six in the categories of Korean Classical Music and Western Music. Awarded annually from 1977 to 1982, and biennially since 1982.

5473 ■ Seoul International Music Festival Awards
To recognize top musicians performing at the Festival. Held biennially in odd-numbered years. Established in 1993.

5474 ■ Student Competition for Overseas Music Study Award
To recognize outstanding student musicians. Awarded annually. Established in 1982.

5475 ■ National Academy of Sciences of the Republic of Korea
Kim Sang-joo, Pres.
59 gil 37, Banpodaero
Seocho-gu
Seoul 137-044, Republic of Korea
Ph: 82 2 34005250
Fax: 82 2 5373183
E-mail: academy@mest.go.kr
URL: http://nas.go.kr

5476 ■ National Academy of Sciences Award
To recognize a citizen for contributions to the academic development through his or her outstanding academic works. A monetary prize is given annually.

Republic of South Africa

5477 ■ Actuarial Society of South Africa
Wim Els, Exec. Dir.
PO Box 4464
Cape Town 8000, Republic of South Africa
Ph: 27 21 5095242
Ph: 27 21 5097697
Fax: 27 21 5090160
E-mail: wim@actuarialsociety.org.za
URL: http://www.actuarialsociety.org.za

5478 ■ Murray Medal
To recognize a member for outstanding service. Awarded annually.

5479 ■ President's Award
To recognize an individual for excellent service to the profession. A monetary prize is awarded annually. Established in 1992.

5480 ■ The Swiss Re Award
To recognize a meritorious paper that broadens or deepens actuaries' understanding of risks that can in some manner be managed, or the process of management of such risks. A monetary prize is awarded annually if merited. Established in 1998.

5481 ■ Aero Club of South Africa
Jeff Earle, Chm.
PO Box 18018
Germiston 1401, Republic of South Africa
Ph: 27 11 0821100
Fax: 27 86 6353755
E-mail: info@aeroclub.org.za
URL: http://www.aeroclub.org.za

5482 ■ James Gilliland Trophy
For the most meritorious feat of the year. Awarded annually.

5483 ■ Gold Wings
For significant contribution to sport aviation in South Africa.

5484 ■ Dennis Jankelow Trophy
For airmanship.

5485 ■ Lewis Lang Trophy
For pilot of the year.

5486 ■ SA Eagle Trophy
To recognize an individual for the most meritorious achievement at an international event. Awarded periodically.

5487 ■ Africa Investor
93 Protea Rd.
Chislehurston
Sandton
Gauteng 2146, Republic of South Africa
Ph: 27 11 783 2431
Fax: 27 11 783 2430
URL: http://www.africainvestor.com

5488 ■ Financial Reporting Awards
To recognize analysts, investor relations professionals, and the financial media for outstanding coverage at the company and sectoral level. Presented in three categories: Best Financial Reporting Company, Best Financial News Reporting, and Best Analyst. Awarded annually at the Analysts Forum.

5489 ■ Africagrowth Institute
Canal Edge 2
Tyger Waterfront
Carl Cronje Dr.
Bellville 7535, Republic of South Africa
Ph: 27 21 914 6778
Fax: 27 21 946 1652
E-mail: info@africagrowth.com
URL: http://www.africagrowth.com

5490 ■ SMME Awards
To support and showcase Africa's finest entrepreneurial achievements in the small, medium, and micro enterprise sector. Awards are presented in the following categories: industrial, trade, services, best new business, and most innovative. In addition, the Young Enterprise Award and African Union SMME of the Year may be presented. Awarded annually. Established in 2007.

5491 ■ African National Congress
54 Sauer St.
PO Box 61884
Marshalltown

Awards are arranged in alphabetical order below their administering organizations

Johannesburg 2001, Republic of South Africa
Ph: 27 86 376 1000
Fax: 27 86 633 1402
URL: http://www.anc.org.za

5492 ■ Anton Lembede Award
To recognize the best performing youth league ANC branch. Awarded annually. Established in 2000.

5493 ■ Z.K. Matthews Award
To recognize the best performing group of ANC councilors. Awarded annually. Established in 2000.

5494 ■ Charlotte Maxeke Award
To recognize the best performing women's league ANC branch. Awarded annually. Established in 2000.

5495 ■ Sol Plaatje Award
To recognize the best performing ANC branch. Awarded annually. Established in 2000.

5496 ■ Agricultural Economics Association of South Africa
Mr. Ronald Ramabulana, Pres.
Private Bag x935
Pretoria 0001, Republic of South Africa
Ph: 27 12 3411115
E-mail: ronald@namc.co.za
URL: http://www.aeasa.org.za

5497 ■ Award for Best Final Year Student in Agricultural Economics
For student who has achieved an average mark of at least 70% in Agricultural Economics throughout the years of study. Awarded annually.

5498 ■ Best Contributed Paper Award
To honor a member for the best paper submitted to the Contributed Paper Session of the annual conference. A monetary prize of 3,000 rand is awarded for first place, 2,000 rand for second place, and 1,000 rand for third place. Awarded annually.

5499 ■ Best Master's Thesis Award
To honor a member for the best thesis in the field of agricultural economics. A monetary prize of 4,000 rand is presented for first place, and 1,500 is awarded for second place. Awarded annually.

5500 ■ Leopard Award
To honor a member for an outstanding contribution in the field of agricultural economics. A certificate is awarded annually.

5501 ■ American Chamber of Commerce in South Africa
Mrs. Carol O'Brien, Exec. Dir.
PO Box 1132
Houghton
Johannesburg 2041, Republic of South Africa
Ph: 27 11 7880265
Fax: 27 11 8801632
E-mail: admin@amcham.co.za
URL: http://www.amcham.co.za

5502 ■ Star of the Community Award
To a member of society in the corporate social responsibility field.

5503 ■ Stars of Africa Award
For excellence in corporate social responsibility projects. Awarded annually.

5504 ■ Animal Feed Manufacturers Association
Dr. De Wet Boshoff, Exec. Dir.
PO Box 8144
Centurion 0046, Republic of South Africa
Ph: 27 12 6639097
Ph: 27 12 6639361
Fax: 27 12 6639612
E-mail: admin@afm.co.za

URL: http://www.afma.co.za

5505 ■ Koos van der Merwe Prize
For best final year student in animal nutrition. One scholarship is awarded annually.

5506 ■ Barney van Niekerk/AFMA Technical Person of the Year
Recognizes technical contributions within the industry. A trophy and monetary prize are awarded annually.

5507 ■ Association of South African Quantity Surveyors
Egon Wortmann, Exec. Dir.
PO Box 3527
Halfway House 1685, Republic of South Africa
Ph: 27 11 3154140
Fax: 27 11 3153785
E-mail: associations@asaqs.co.za
URL: http://www.asaqs.co.za

5508 ■ Gold Medal of Honour
This, the Association's highest honor, is given for outstanding service to the building industry in general and to quantity surveying in particular. Members are eligible. A gold medal and a citation are awarded when merited. Established in 1977.

5509 ■ Astronomical Society of Southern Africa
Ian Glass, Pres.
PO Box 9
Observatory 7935, Republic of South Africa
E-mail: membership@assa.saao.ac.za
URL: http://assa.saao.ac.za

5510 ■ Director's Award Certificate
To recognize individuals who report observations considered worthy of an honorable distinction.

5511 ■ General Observer's Certificate
To recognize individuals who report observations of at least three observing sessions.

5512 ■ Gill Medal
For recognition of services to astronomy. Preference is given to work done in Southern Africa. Society members and non-members are eligible. Not more than one award is made in any year. Established in 1955, the medal commemorates Sir David Gill, HM Astronomer at the Cape.

5513 ■ Long Service Award
To recognize members for long and outstanding service to the Society. To recognize members for long and outstanding service to the Society.

5514 ■ McIntyre Award
For recognition of significant contributions to astronomy in the form of: (1) a work to be published or which has been published in book form; or (2) a journal of recognized standing within the previous five years. Living persons of any nationality are eligible. The award derived from the interest on the bequest made to the Society by the late Donald G. McIntyre, is awarded irregularly.

5515 ■ President's Award Certificate
To recognize individuals who report multiple, exceptional observations. To recognize individuals who report multiple, exceptional observations.

5516 ■ Botanical Society of South Africa (Botaniese Vereniging van Suid-Afrika)
Dr. John Rourke, Pres.
Private Bag X 10
Claremont 7735, Republic of South Africa
Ph: 27 21 7972090
Fax: 27 21 7972376
E-mail: info@botanicalsociety.org.za
URL: http://www.botanicalsociety.org.za

5517 ■ Bolus Medal
To recognize an amateur botanist who has made

a significant contribution to our knowledge of flora through publications in recognized scientific literature. Awarded annually.

5518 ■ Certificate of Merit
To recognize a member of the Society for valuable contributions made to the promotion of the flora of Southern Africa. Awarded annually.

5519 ■ Dudley D'Ewe Medal
To recognize any person who effectively promotes the flora of Southern Africa and its conservation through the media. Awarded annually.

5520 ■ Flora Conservation Medal
To recognize any person who has contributed considerably towards the preservation and conservation of the flora of Southern Africa. Awarded annually.

5521 ■ Denys Heesom Medal
To recognize any person or organization that has made a significant contribution to the eradication of alien vegetation in Southern Africa. Awarded annually.

5522 ■ Honorary Life Membership
To honor any member of the Society who has rendered exceptional services to the Society or one of its branches. Awarded annually.

5523 ■ Cythna Letty Medal
To recognize any person who has made a significant contribution to the promotion of South African flora through the medium of published botanical illustrations. Awarded annually.

5524 ■ Marloth Medal
To recognize any amateur or professional botanist who has produced scientific literature of a popular nature to stimulate public interest. Awarded annually.

5525 ■ Schelpe Award
To recognize the best article in *Veld and Flora* in any given year covering any aspect of horticulture. Awarded annually.

5526 ■ Percy Sergeant Medal
To recognize person who effectively promotes the flora of Southern Africa and its conservation through the medium of photography. Awarded annually.

5527 ■ Cape Town Regional Chamber of Commerce and Industry
Michael Bagraim, Pres.
19 Louis Gradner St.
Cape Town 8001, Republic of South Africa
Ph: 27 21 4024300
Ph: 27 21 4222860
Fax: 27 21 4024302
E-mail: info@capechamber.co.za
URL: http://www.capetownchamber.com

5528 ■ Western Cape Exporter of the Year
To recognize Western Cape exporters in the manufacturing and non-manufacturing sectors. Awarded annually.

5529 ■ Youth Webstar Competition
For students to design a website in either brochure or database driven category.

5530 ■ Concrete Society of Southern Africa
John Sheath, CEO
PO Box 75364
Lynnwood Ridge 0040, Republic of South Africa
Ph: 27 12 3485305
Ph: 27 12 3481319
Fax: 27 12 3486944
E-mail: admin@concretesociety.co.za
URL: http://www.concretesociety.co.za

5531 ■ Chairman's Award
To recognize the greatest contribution made to the achievement of excellence in the use or ap-

Awards are arranged in alphabetical order below their administering organizations

plication of concrete made by a hands-on operative. Awarded annually by the Inland Branch. Established 1996.

5532 ■ Concrete Achiever of the Year
For recognition of the person doing the most to promote the use of concrete and the standards of excellence in its use. Awarded annually. Established in 1982.

5533 ■ Fulton Award
To recognize professionals, contractors, and owners for their outstanding achievements and determination to challenge new frontiers. Awarded in various categories biennially in odd-numbered years.

5534 ■ Consulting Engineers South Africa
Zulch Lotter, CEO
PO Box 68482
Bryanston
Johannesburg 2021, Republic of South Africa
Ph: 27 11 4632022
Fax: 27 11 4637383
E-mail: general@cesa.co.za
URL: http://www.saace.co.za
Formerly: (2008) South African Association of Consulting Engineers.

5535 ■ CESA/Glenrand M.I.B. Engineering Excellence Awards
To recognize outstanding achievement of member firms. Awarded in three categories based on project size. The following awards may also be presented: Business Excellence Award, Young Company of the Year, International Business Developer of the Year, Mentoring Company of the Year, Young Engineer of the Year, Mentor of the Year, Visionary Client of the Year, and Publisher of the Year. Certificates are awarded annually.

5536 ■ Dorper Sheep Breeders' Society of South Africa
(Dorpers Skaaptelersgenootskap van Suid-Afrika)
Attie Westraad, Dir.
2 van Reenen St.
Middelburg 5900, Republic of South Africa
Ph: 27 49 8422241
Fax: 27 49 8423589
E-mail: dorperinfo@adsactive.com
URL: http://www.dorpersa.co.za

5537 ■ Honorary Certificate
Recognizes outstanding contributions to Dorper breed of sheep. Awarded annually.

5538 ■ English Academy of Southern Africa
Prof. Stanley Ridge, Pres.
PO Box 124
Wits 2050, Republic of South Africa
Ph: 27 11 7179339
Fax: 27 11 7179339
E-mail: englishacademy@societies.wits.ac.za
URL: http://www.englishacademy.co.za

5539 ■ Academy Gold Medal
To recognize an individual who has conspicuously served the cause of English over a number of years, or performed signal service in the cause of English. A medal is awarded annually. Established in 1989.

5540 ■ Percy FitzPatrick Award for Youth Literature
Recognizes achievement by Southern African writers publishing in Southern Africa in the field of books directed toward children between the ages of 10 and 14 years. Awarded biennially in even-numbered years. Established in 1970. Sponsored by *Media Tenor South Africa*. Formerly: (2006) Percy FitzPatrick Prize.

5541 ■ Sol Plaatje Award for Translation
To recognize an outstanding translation of a prose passage or poetry into English from any of the other 11 official languages in the South African Republic. Awarded biennially in odd-numbered years. Established in 2007.

5542 ■ Thomas Pringle Award
For recognition of work written in English and published in newspapers and periodicals in Southern Africa. Material published in the following categories is considered: reviews of books, plays, films, and television in newspapers or periodicals; literary articles or substantial book reviews; articles on language, the teaching of English, and educational topics in academic, teachers', and other journals, and in newspapers; short stories and one act plays in periodicals; and poetry in periodicals (a single poem could be sufficient for an award). The first category is considered annually for an award. The other four categories are considered in alternate years over a two-year period. Monetary prizes and an illuminated certificate are awarded. A maximum of three awards is made annually. Established in 1962.

5543 ■ Olive Schreiner Prize
To recognize the first major work in English by a new South African writer. Awards are given in one of three categories: poetry, drama, and prose (rotating in the order given). South Africans and Namibians are eligible for work published in South Africa. A monetary prize of 5000 rand and an illuminated certificate are awarded annually. Established in 1961 by the South African Academy for Sciences and Arts.

5544 ■ Federated Hospitality Association of Southern Africa
PO Box 71517
Bryanston 2021, Republic of South Africa
Ph: 27 861 333628
Fax: 27 867 347000
E-mail: fedhasa@fedhasa.co.za
URL: http://www.fedhasa.co.za

5545 ■ Imvelo Awards for Responsible Tourism
To recognize tourism and hospitality businesses that make a real, measurable, and sustained contribution to responsible tourism in South Africa. Awarded in several categories, including Best Social Investment Program, Best Overall Environmental Management System, and the Chairman's Award. Presented annually. Established in 2002, the word "Imvelo" means "nature" in South Africa's Nguni languages.

5546 ■ Fertilizer Society of South Africa
(Die Misstofvereniging van Suid-Afrika)
Gert van der Linde, Dir.
PO Box 75510
Lynnwood Ridge 0040, Republic of South Africa
Ph: 27 12 3491450
Fax: 27 12 3491463
E-mail: general@fssa.org.za
URL: http://www.fssa.org.za
Awards discontinued.

5547 ■ Gold Medal Award
(MVSA Goue Medalje)
For recognition of contributions to agriculture in South Africa over a long period of time. The deadline for nomination is August. A medal is awarded annually at the general meeting of the Society. Established in 1968.

5548 ■ Silver Medal Award
(MVSA Silwer Medalje vir Navorsing)
For recognition of contributions to crop production and soil fertility research over a long period of time. The nomination deadline falls in August. A medal is awarded annually at the general meeting of the Society. Established in 1968.

5549 ■ Free Market Foundation
Leon M. Louw, Exec. Dir.
PO Box 785121
Sandton 2146, Republic of South Africa
Ph: 27 11 8840270
Fax: 27 11 8845672
E-mail: fmf@mweb.co.za
URL: http://www.freemarketfoundation.com

5550 ■ Free Market Award
To honor individuals who have made an outstanding contribution to the cause of economic freedom in South Africa. Selection is by nomination. A certificate and Kruger Rand are awarded annually. Established in 1980.

5551 ■ Genealogical Society of South Africa
Andre Heydenrych, Treas.
Postnet X2600, Ste. 143
Houghton 2041, Republic of South Africa
E-mail: aheydenr@mweb.co.za
URL: http://gensa.info.www19.jnb2.host-h.net

5552 ■ Genealogist of the Year
To recognize an individual for significant contributions in advancing, promoting, or furthering the science of genealogy within the borders of South Africa. Awarded annually.

5553 ■ Geological Society of South Africa
Dr. Craig Smith, Exec. Mgr.
PO Box 61809
Marshalltown 2107, Republic of South Africa
Ph: 27 11 4923370
Fax: 27 11 4923371
E-mail: info@gssa.org.za
URL: http://www.gssa.org.za

5554 ■ Corstorphine Medal
To provide recognition for the best student thesis embodying the results of original research on geological subjects. Students of any university in Southern Africa are eligible. A bronze medal is awarded annually when merited. Established in 1925 to honor Geo. S. Corstorphine, Honorary Editor of the *Transactions of the Geological Society of South Africa* (1903-1905 and 1910-1915).

5555 ■ Des Pretorius Memorial Award
To recognize work in economic geology in Africa. A monetary award and a certificate are awarded annually. Established in 1998 in memory of Prof. Des Pretorius.

5556 ■ Draper Memorial Medal
For recognition of a past record of research with particular reference to the advancement of South African geology. Members of the Society for at least five years are eligible. A bronze medal showing a bust of Dr. David Draper, the first Honorary Secretary of the Society, is awarded annually. Established in 1932.

5557 ■ John Handley Award
To recognize the best thesis at a South African university in the year preceding the award. A certificate and monetary award are presented annually.

5558 ■ Haughton Award
To recognize an outstanding thesis at a South African university in the year preceding the award. A monetary award and a certificate are awarded annually.

5559 ■ Honorary Member
To recognize outstanding contributions to the field of geology. Awarded when merited, the recipient receives a certificate.

5560 ■ Honours Award
To recognize a member or group of members of the Society who has made a particularly meritorious contribution to the Geological Society of South Africa or the Geological Fraternity of South Africa. A shield on which the recipient's name is inscribed is awarded when merited. Established in 1978.

5561 ■ Jubilee Medal
For recognition of a paper of particular merit

Awards are arranged in alphabetical order below their administering organizations

published by the Society in any year. Members of the Society are eligible. A gold medal weighing one ounce is awarded annually. Established in 1945 on the 50th anniversary of the founding of the Society.

5562 ■ Grassland Society of Southern Africa
Ms. Freyni Du Toit, Admin.
PO Box 41
Hilton 3245, Republic of South Africa
Ph: 27 49 8424335
Ph: 27 83 2567202
Fax: 27 86 6227576
E-mail: admin@grassland.org.za
URL: http://www.gssa.co.za

5563 ■ Award for Best Ecological Project
To recognize young scientists (under 35 years old) for an outstanding project pertaining to an ecological issue, such as rangelands, pastures, rehabilitation, alien and invasive species, game surveys, and animal production. At the regional level, the prize consists of a certificate for each member of the winning team. At the national level, a certificate and medal is awarded. Presented annually.

5564 ■ Institute for Landscape Architecture in South Africa
Ms. Cynthia Badenhorst, Client Mgr.
PO Box 868
Ferndale 2160, Republic of South Africa
Ph: 27 11 7891384
Fax: 27 11 7892116
E-mail: ilasa@vdw.co.za
URL: http://www.ilasa.co.za
Formerly: (2009) Institute of Landscape Architects of South Africa.

5565 ■ Merit Award
Recognizes outstanding landscape architecture projects, studies, and research. Awarded in various categories biennially in odd-numbered years.

5566 ■ Institute of Quarrying - Southern Africa
Gert Coffee, Chm.
PO Box 6068
Cresta 2052, Republic of South Africa
Ph: 27 11 7916655
Fax: 27 11 7917655
E-mail: iqsa@global.co.za
URL: http://www.iqsa.co.za

5567 ■ Chairman's Award
For best M level student.

5568 ■ Nordberg Shield
For best N level student.

5569 ■ International Council for the Control of Iodine Deficiency Disorders
Dr. Pieter Jooste, Sec.
Nutritional Intervention Research Unit
South African Medical Research Council
Tygerberg, Republic of South Africa
Ph: 27 21 938 0370
E-mail: secretary@iccidd.org
URL: http://www.iccidd.org

5570 ■ John T. Dunn Award
To honor individuals who have rendered exceptional service to the Organization. Awarded when merited. Established in 2007.

5571 ■ *Mail and Guardian*
PO Box 91667
Auckland Pk.
Johannesburg 2006, Republic of South Africa
Ph: 27 11 250 7300
Fax: 27 11 250 7503
URL: http://mg.co.za

5572 ■ Greening the Future Awards
To honor and celebrate the achievements by companies and organizations that are playing a

role in ensuring a sustained and healthy planet for all people. Awarded annually during World Environmental Week in June.

5573 ■ National Research Foundation
Dr. Albert S. van Jaarsveld, Pres./CEO
PO Box 2600
Pretoria 0001, Republic of South Africa
Ph: 27 12 4814000
Fax: 27 12 3491179
E-mail: info@nrf.ac.za
URL: http://www.nrf.ac.za

5574 ■ Lifetime Achievement Award
To recognize a South African individual for extraordinary contributions to the development of science in and for South Africa. Awarded when merited. Established in 2004.

5575 ■ President's Awards
To recognize South African scientists for their achievements as indicated through the Foundation's rating system. Awarded in two categories: P-rating (for young researchers) and A-rating (for internationally recognized researchers). Awarded annually.

5576 ■ Transforming the Science Cohort Award
To encourage black scientists to engage in world-class research and to promote the notion of transforming the science cohort to be more representative of the South African demographic make-up. Established in 2007.

5577 ■ National Wool Growers' Association of South Africa (Nasionale Wolkwekersvereeniging van Suid-Afrika)
Adele Rhode, Sec.
Posbus 34291
Port Elizabeth 6055, Republic of South Africa
Ph: 27 41 3655030
Fax: 27 41 3655035
E-mail: nwga@nwga.co.za
URL: http://www.nwga.co.za

5578 ■ Golden Ram Award (Goueram-Toekenning)
To recognize members of the Association who have delivered exceptional service to the wool industry. The Central Executive may nominate presidents of the Association, or persons who have delivered exceptional service to the industry. A medal and certificate are awarded when merited at the Congress. Established about 1964.

5579 ■ Nematological Society of Southern Africa (Nematologiese Vereniging van Suidelike Afrika)
Prof. Driekie Fourie, Pres.
North-West University
Private Bag X6001
Potchefstroom 2520, Republic of South Africa
Ph: 27 82 5641848
Fax: 27 18 2947146
E-mail: driekie.fouriehd@nwu.ac.za
URL: http://www.sanematodes.com

5580 ■ George Martin Memorial Scholarship
To promote nematology in Southern Africa, preferably by assisting the successful candidate to attend a recognized course in nematology. Applicants must be serious about pursuing a career in nematology and about furthering the science of nematology, and must be from countries of Southern Africa (South Africa, Botswana, Lesotho, Swaziland, Mozambique, Malawi, Zimbabwe, and Namibia). A scholarship in the amount of 4,000 rand is awarded annually. In addition, the recipient is expected to give a paper at the next NSSA symposium and/or report in the Society's newsletter.

5581 ■ Rhone-Poulenc Award
For the advancement of nematology.

5582 ■ Van Der Linde Award
For best paper.

5583 ■ Wirsam Scientific Award
For best poster.

5584 ■ Occupational Therapy Association of South Africa
Lana van Niekerk, Pres.
PO Box 11695
Hatfield 0028, Republic of South Africa
Ph: 27 12 3625457
Fax: 27 86 6515438
E-mail: otoffice@otasa.org.za
URL: http://www.otasa.org.za

5585 ■ Vona and Marie du Toit Foundation Student Prize
To recognize the best undergraduate research project in the year, thereby encouraging newly qualified occupational therapists to contribute to the body of knowledge of occupational therapy profession by studying the effect and outcomes of their occupational therapy interventions. Awarded annually. Sponsored by the Vona and Marie du Toit Foundation.

5586 ■ Vona du Toit Memorial Award and Lecture
To honor an occupational therapist who excels in the profession. A certificate and monetary prize are awarded annually. Established in 1976 in memory of Vona du Toit, who was a pioneer in the development of the occupational therapy profession.

5587 ■ Life Esidimeni Award
To recognize an individual for exceptional research in psychiatry and mental health. A certificate and monetary prize are awarded annually.

5588 ■ Albie Sachs Award
To recognize a practitioner working in the field of occupational therapy who has made a significant contribution in the lives of people with disabilities. A trophy and monetary prize are awarded annually.

5589 ■ Parasitological Society of Southern Africa (Parasitologiese Vereniging van Suidelike Afrika)
Prof. Banie L. Penzhorn, Pres.
University of Pretoria
Faculty of Veterinary Science
Dept. of Veterinary Tropical Diseases
Private Bag X04
Pretoria 0110, Republic of South Africa
Ph: 27 12 5298253
Fax: 27 12 5298312
E-mail: banie.penzhorn@up.ac.za
URL: http://www.parsa.ac.za

5590 ■ Elsdon Dew Medal
Award of recognition for distinguished service in Parasitology in Africa. Awarded every one or two years.

5591 ■ W.O. Neitz Junior Medal/Senior Medal
Recognizes the best postgraduate (MSc and PhD) thesis in parasitology. Awarded annually in each category.

5592 ■ Pharmaceutical Society of South Africa
Sybil Seoka, Pres.
PO Box 26039
Arcadia 0007, Republic of South Africa
Ph: 27 12 6537351
Fax: 27 12 6537355
E-mail: sseoka@lantic.net
URL: http://www.pssa.org.za

Awards are arranged in alphabetical order below their administering organizations

5593 ■ Fellowship of the Pharmacy Society of South Africa
To an individual making an outstanding achievement in pharmacy or in related field.

5594 ■ Professional Hunters' Association of South Africa
Adri Kitshoff, CEO
PO Box 10264
Centurion 0046, Republic of South Africa
Ph: 27 12 6672048
Fax: 27 12 6672049
URL: http://www.phasa.co.za

5595 ■ Nature Conservation Officer of the Year
For outstanding officer.

5596 ■ Coenraad Vermaak Award
For person with outstanding service to PHASA.

5597 ■ Wildlife Utilisation Award
For person who made an outstanding contribution to wildlife.

5598 ■ Project Management South Africa
Danie de Waal, Pres.
PO Box 1714
Halfway House
Johannesburg 1685, Republic of South Africa
Ph: 27 11 2578003
Fax: 27 11 6622961
E-mail: admin@projectmanagement.org.za
URL: http://www.pmisa.co.za

5599 ■ Project Management Excellence Award
To honor a team that excels in project management performance. Awarded annually.

5600 ■ Public Relations Institute of Southern Africa
Ronel Rensburg, Pres.
PO Box 2825
Pinegowrie 2123, Republic of South Africa
Ph: 27 11 3261262
Fax: 27 11 3261259
E-mail: info@prisa.co.za
URL: http://www.prisa.co.za

5601 ■ Gold Medal
To honor a South African citizen who, through his or her profession, raises the profile of the nation by using outstanding public relations techniques to place South Africa on the global map. Awarded when merited. Established in 1968.

5602 ■ Long Service Award
To recognize volunteers who serve on the regional committees, board, council, and other committees in the Institute for a period of at least five consecutive years. A certificate is awarded when merited.

5603 ■ President's Award
To recognize a member for exceptional service and contribution to the Institute. A certificate is awarded annually, if merited, to one or more recipients. Established in 1986.

5604 ■ Prism Awards
To recognize public relations and communication professionals who have successfully incorporated strategy, creativity, and professionalism into public relations and communication programs and strategies that showcase a successful public relations campaign. Awards are presented in 20 categories each year.

5605 ■ Royal Society of South Africa
Prof. Donald Cowan, Pres.
University of Cape Town
4.17 PD Hahn Bldg.
Rhodes Gift
Cape Town 7700, Republic of South Africa
Ph: 27 21 6502543
E-mail: royalsociety@uct.ac.za
URL: http://www.royalsocietysa.org.za

5606 ■ John F. W. Herschel Medal
To recognize persons or teams who have made outstanding contributions in a wide range of fields, especially those of a multidisciplinary scientific nature that have been completed in South Africa or that are relevant to South Africa. A medal is awarded annually when merited. Established in 1984 in honor of John F. W. Herschel, a scientist and a renowned polymath.

5607 ■ S. Meiring Naude Medal
To recognize persons or teams who have made outstanding contributions to science, especially those of a multidisciplinary scientific nature that have been completed in South Africa or that are relevant to South Africa. Scientists under 35 years of age who are residents or who are visiting South Africa are eligible. A medal is awarded annually when merited. Established in 1984 in honor of Stefan Meiring Naude, a renowned South African scientist, discoverer of the N15 isotope, and past president of the Society.

5608 ■ Rural Doctors Association of Southern Africa
Karl le Roux, Chm.
PO Box 19063
Tygerberg 7505, Republic of South Africa
Ph: 27 21 9389108
Fax: 27 21 9314220
E-mail: karlleroux@gmail.com
URL: http://www.rudasa.org.za

5609 ■ Pierre Jaques Rural Doctor of the Year Award
To recognize an outstanding rural doctor in South Africa. Awarded annually. Established in 2002.

5610 ■ Sanlam Life Insurance Ltd.
PO Box 1
Sanlamhof 7532, Republic of South Africa
Ph: 27 21 947 9111
URL: http://www.sanlam.co.za

5611 ■ Financial Journalism Awards
To recognize excellence in financial journalism in South Africa. Open to journalists in South Africa who are in the full-time employment of any media group or who are mainly dependent on freelance journalism for their livelihood. Categories include economy and industry, markets and companies, personal finance, broadcast media, development economics, and members of the Foreign Correspondents' Association. A monetary prize of R15,000 is awarded to the winner in each category; in addition, the overall winner receives an additional R25,000. Awarded annually. Established in 1974.

5612 ■ Society of Medical Laboratory Technologists of South Africa (Vereniging van Geneeskundige Laboratorium Tegnoloe van Suid-Afrika)
Mr. Donald J. Alexander, Admin. Mgr.
PO Box 6014
Roggebaai 8012, Republic of South Africa
Ph: 27 21 4194857
Fax: 27 21 4212566
E-mail: smltsa@iafrica.com
URL: http://www.smltsa.org.za

5613 ■ Abbott Award for Innovative Research and Development in Virology
To recognize innovative research and development in virology. A monetary prize of R2,000 is awarded biennially, in addition to a commemorative plaque. Sponsored by Abbott Laboratories S.A. (PTY) LTD, Diagnostic Division.

5614 ■ Bactlab Systems Gold Award for the Best Paper
To recognize the person who made significant contributions to the academic improvement of posters presented in either of the following categories: microbiology, serology, or flow-cytometry. Preference will be given to original work. The recipient should be a member in good standing of the SMLTSA and must have been qualified for a period of at least 3 years. A check for R500, a floating trophy, and a miniature are awarded biennially in odd-numbered years at the SMLTSA National Congress. Sponsored by Bactlab Systems (Pty.) Ltd.

5615 ■ Bactlab Systems Premier Award for Best Paper
To recognize the person who has contributed most to improving the standard of academic papers in the category of microbiology. Preference will be given to authors or co-authors who have completed their papers with minimal outside help. The recipient should be a member of the SMLTSA in good standing and should have been qualified for a period of at least 5 years. A floating trophy, miniature, and certificate are awarded biennially in odd-numbered years at the SMLTSA National Congress. Sponsored by Bactlab Systems (Pty.) Ltd.

5616 ■ Bayer Diagnostics Academic Achievement Award
To recognize the author or co-author of a paper published in any recognized journal or presentation at Congress in the fields of haematology, immunology clinical chemistry, or laboratory computers. Candidates must show why the award should be made to them, how the award will be used, and what benefit will be gained from it. A monetary prize of 5,000 rand is awarded biannually toward study or as a travel grant to further professional career. Presented at the National Congress of the SMLTSA. Sponsored by Bayer SA.

5617 ■ Bayer/Sakura Histology Achievement Award
To recognize achievement in the field of histology. A trip to the U.K. to attend the Bayer Histology in Focus Meeting is awarded annually. Sponsored by Bayer SA and Sakura Europe. Formerly: (1995) Bayer-Mills Histology Award; (1995) Ames Histology Award.

5618 ■ Dade Behring Award
To sponsor the attendance of a student of immunology to attend a course on presentation skills. A monetary prize of 500 rand is awarded to the winning student, with an additional 250 rand to his or her branch. Awarded biennially in odd-numbered years at the SMLTSA National Congress. Sponsored by Dade Behring SA (Pty.) Ltd.

5619 ■ Joseph Award
To recognize the author or authors of the highest standard paper published in *Medical Technology: SA Journal*. A monetary prize of R800 is awarded biennially at the SMLTSA National Congress.

5620 ■ Labotec-Shandon Award for Achievement in the Field of Cytology
To recognize achievement in the field of cytology, service to the profession, original research, and/or publication of outstanding papers. A monetary prize of 1,000 rand is awarded biennially in odd-numbered years at SMLTSA National Congress. Formerly: (1995) Premier Technology Shandon Award.

5621 ■ Merck Award
To recognize the most successful candidate in the categories of cytopathology or microbiology. A monetary prize of 1,000 rand is awarded biennially at the National Congress of the SMLTSA. Sponsored by Merck.

5622 ■ Roche Award
To recognize a member of the Society who has contributed most significantly toward the aims of

Awards are arranged in alphabetical order below their administering organizations

medical technology. Travel expenses and a stipend of DM1,000 is awarded biennially at the National Congress of the SMLTSA. Sponsored by Roche Diagnostics. Formerly: (2006) Boehringer Mannheim S.A. Award.

5623 ■ Technologist of the Year
Award to the technologist of the year. A monetary prize of R1,000 and a plaque are awarded biennially at a National Congress. Administered by the SA Scientific Group.

5624 ■ Thistle Student Award
To recognize the academic achievement of students at the relevant Technikon. Recipient must be a pre-diplomat and must have been a member of the Society for a period of not less than one year. A trophy, which remains the property of the relevant Branch, a miniature, and R100 is awarded annually. Formerly: (1995) Wellcome Diagnostics Student Award.

5625 ■ South African Academy for Science and Arts
(Die Suid-Afrikaanse Akademie vir Wetenskap en Kuns)
Prof. Nellie Engelbrecht, Contact
Private Bag XII
Arcadia 0007, Republic of South Africa
Ph: 27 12 3285082
Fax: 27 12 3285091
E-mail: akademie@akademie.co.za
URL: http://akademie.org.za/tuisblad

5626 ■ Dominee Pieter Drimmelen Medal
To recognize the work of an individual in the following fields: translation of the Bible, theological textbooks in Afrikaans for use by university students, published books of sermons, religious teaching, and the writing, translation, composition, and improvement of Afrikaans psalms and hymns. Awarded annually.

5627 ■ Frans du Toit Medal for Business Leadership
To recognize an individual for creative contributions to South African business, sustained contribution over a long period to the areas in which Frans du Toit was engaged, and leadership and the impetus for further development of those areas that he inspired. A gold medal is awarded annually.

5628 ■ FARMOVS Prize for Pharmacology and Medicine Development
To recognize outstanding contributions to a branch of pharmacology and medicine development. Awarded annually.

5629 ■ Havenga Prize
For recognition of original research in the natural sciences and/or the field of technology. The prize is awarded alternately in three main fields: (1) Biological sciences; (2) Human natural sciences, and (3) Mathematical, chemical, and physical sciences. A gold medal is awarded annually.

5630 ■ Hertzog Prize for Literature
For recognition of the best literary work written in Afrikaans during the three years preceding the award. The prize rotates in the following categories: poetry, drama, and prose. A monetary prize of 17,000 rand is awarded annually.

5631 ■ Louis Hiemstra Prize for Nonfiction
To recognize works of nonfiction. Works must be in Afrikaans. Awarded every three years.

5632 ■ Tienie Holloway Medal
To recognize writers who have written the best work in Afrikaans for children, primarily under eight years of age. A gold medal is awarded every three years.

5633 ■ C. J. Langenhoven Prize
For recognition of outstanding scientific and/or creative work, including lexicography in Afrikaans. Awarded every three years.

5634 ■ Eugene Marais Prize
For recognition of an first or second work in belles lettres written in the Afrikaans language. A monetary prize of 10,000 rand is awarded annually.

5635 ■ Medal of Honour for Afrikaans Radio Feature Programme
To honor excellence in Afrikaans radio feature programs and in Afrikaans radio plays. Works broadcast by all broadcasting networks in the two previous calendar years will be considered. Awarded each year, alternately for Afrikaans radio plays and Afrikaans radio feature programs.

5636 ■ Medal of Honour for the Promotion of History
To recognize the promotion of History. Candidate must play a dynamic role in the promoting of history by the publication of quality books/articles, by initiating research projects that lead to publications, by participating in History societies, or by contributing to the development of the teaching of History. Awarded annually.

5637 ■ Gustav Preller Prize
To provide recognition for works of literary science and criticism in Afrikaans. A monetary prize is awarded every three years.

5638 ■ Scheepers Prize for Youth Literature
To provide recognition for the advancement of Afrikaans literature for young people. Works must be of literary and educational value to the young reader and aimed at the older child. A monetary prize is awarded every three years, since 1974. Established in 1956.

5639 ■ Senior Captain Scott Commemoration Medal
To recognize a biologist in southern Africa who has attained outstanding achievements in his or her field of work. Awarded annually.

5640 ■ Junior Captain Scott Commemorative Medal
To recognize the best dissertation submitted at a South African university for an M.Sc. degree. Awarded alternately in the animal and plant sciences.

5641 ■ Stals Prize for the Humanities
To recognize an outstanding publication or a series of outstanding publications preferably, but not exclusively, in Afrikaans. The prize is awarded in 14 fields that rotate every three years. Awarded annually.

5642 ■ Elizabeth C. Steijn Medal
To recognize exceptional teaching and educating in any subject, both inside and outside the classroom. The recipient must be an Afrikaans-speaking teacher. Awarded every three years.

5643 ■ M. T. Steyn Prize for Natural Science and Technical Achievement
For recognition of leadership at the highest level in the fields of natural sciences and technology. The prize may be awarded only once to a candidate, as it is regarded as a seal of excellence on his or her career. A gold medal is awarded annually. Established in 1964.

5644 ■ Totius Prize for Theology and Study of the Original Languages of the Bible
For recognition of publications in Afrikaans in the field of Christian theology and the original languages of the Bible. Awarded biennially.

5645 ■ Toon Van Den Heever Prize for Jurisprudence
To provide recognition for original legal works in Afrikaans or full-length articles of outstanding quality in Afrikaans that have appeared in accredited law journals. Awarded every three years.

5646 ■ N. P. van Wyk Louw Medal
To recognize an individual for a creative contribu-

tion to the development, organization, and sustained extension of a branch/branches of the human sciences. The contribution must be fundamental and important to the promotion of the human sciences and to their successful application in the national interest. A medal is awarded annually. Established in 1991 in honor of N. P. van Wyk Louw, Afrikaans poet, dramatist, essayist, and man of letters (1906-1970).

5647 ■ Markus Viljoen Medal for Journalism
To provide recognition for work of long duration and high standard in Afrikaans journalism. A gold medal is awarded every three years.

5648 ■ Christo Wiese Medal for an Emerging Entrepreneur
To recognize the special qualities of entrepreneurship, vision, and perseverance in a private entrepreneur. Candidates must be South African citizens 40 years old or younger and be a business professional who has overcome obstacles in order to achieve success. The award can be presented only once to any particular person.

5649 ■ South African Association for Food Science and Technology
Owen Frisby, Exec. Sec.
PO Box 1935
Durban 4000, Republic of South Africa
Ph: 27 31 3688000
Fax: 27 31 3686623
E-mail: info@saafost.org.za
URL: http://www.saafost.org.za

5650 ■ Academic Achievement Award
To recognize the most deserving student for a completed first degree or completed four semesters for a diploma in Food Science/Technology at qualifying South African tertiary institutions. A certificate and monetary prize of R1,000 is awarded annually to one or more recipients. Established in 1979.

5651 ■ Dreosti Award
To recognize young individuals for the best oral paper presented at the Biennial Congress. Candidates must be under the age of 35. A monetary prize of R1,000 is awarded biennially in odd-numbered years. Established in 1983.

5652 ■ Ginsburg Award
To recognize young individuals for the best poster presented at the Biennial Congress. Candidates must be under the age of 35. A monetary prize of R1,000 is awarded biennially in odd-numbered years. Established in 1995.

5653 ■ Koeppen Memorial Scholarship
For students who have registered for masters or doctorate degrees in the Department of Food Science. A scholarship in the amount of R25,000 is awarded annually. Established in 1980.

5654 ■ Aubrey Parsons Study Grant
To provide financial assistance to qualified researchers in the final year of undergraduate/diplomate study. Candidates must be non-working, non-sponsored citizens of South Africa with a record of academic distinction. Grants valued at R20,000 are awarded annually.

5655 ■ South African Association for Learning and Educational Difficulties
Sally Mayhew, Contact
PO Box 55023
Northlands
Johannesburg 2116, Republic of South Africa
Ph: 27 11 6485779
Fax: 27 11 6485779
E-mail: membership@saaled.org.za
URL: http://www.saaled.org.za

5656 ■ SAALED Bursary
To encourage students to engage in further study in the field of disadvantaged/learning-disabled

Awards are arranged in alphabetical order below their administering organizations

children. Full- and part-time students applying for a course at Tertiary institutions are eligible; preference is given to Association members. A monetary prize of 4,000 rand is awarded annually. Established in 1986.

5657 ■ South African Association of Botanists
Mr. Myke Scott, Sec.
PO Box 3268
Matieland 7602, Republic of South Africa
Ph: 27 21 8813167
Fax: 27 21 5457933
E-mail: forsaab@telkomsa.net
URL: http://www.sabotany.com

5658 ■ Certificate for Young Botanists
To honor a young individual for outstanding contributions to the field of botany. Awarded annually. Established in 1982.

5659 ■ Certificate of Merit
To honor an individual for outstanding contributions to the field of botany. Awarded when merited. Established in 1977.

5660 ■ Gold Medal for Botany
For recognition of outstanding botanical research. The premier award for Botany in South Africa. A gold medal is awarded annually when merited. Established in 1972.

5661 ■ Honorary Member
To honor an individual for outstanding contributions to the field of botany. Awarded when merited.

5662 ■ Junior Medal for Botany
For recognition of an outstanding thesis on a botanical subject resulting in a doctorate degree at a Southern African University. A bronze medal is awarded annually. Established in 1977.

5663 ■ Senior Medal for Botany
For recognition of outstanding research and/or other contributions to advancement of botany in South Africa. A silver medal is awarded annually. Established in 1977.

5664 ■ South African Association of Competitive Intelligence Professionals
Mr. Steve Whitehead, Pres.
PO Box 16063
Pretoria 0140, Republic of South Africa
Ph: 27 12 6643157
Fax: 27 12 6643180
E-mail: info@saacip.co.za
URL: http://www.saacip.co.za

5665 ■ Meritorious Award
For pioneering work and effort to promote competitive intelligence.

5666 ■ Johan Pretorius Academic Award
For contributions to the indigenous body of knowledge of competitive intelligence.

5667 ■ South African Association of Women Graduates
Ms. Margaret Edwards, Pres.
Postnet 329
Private Bag X18
Rondebosch 7701, Republic of South Africa
Ph: 27 11 8834847
Ph: 27 11 4443161
Fax: 27 11 8834847
E-mail: medwards@netactive.co.za
URL: http://ifuw.org/southafrica

5668 ■ Fellowship International Award
To a foreign student enrolled in a South African university. Awarded triennially.

5669 ■ Mary Agard Pocock Award
For postgraduate study in botany and related studies. Awarded annually.

5670 ■ Hansi Pollak Scholarship
For postgraduate research directed toward bettering social conditions in South Africa. The recipient is required to spend at least two years in South Africa after completion of the degree to implement the results of his or her research. Awarded annually.

5671 ■ Isie Smuts Award
For postgraduate study in any field. Awarded annually.

5672 ■ Bertha Stoneman Award
To honor a postgraduate for botany and related studies, including environmental studies. Awarded annually.

5673 ■ South African Chemical Institute (Suid-Afrikaanse Chemiese Instituut)
Prof. Ivan Green, Pres.
PO Box 407
Wits 2050, Republic of South Africa
Ph: 27 11 7176741
Fax: 27 11 7176779
E-mail: saci.chem@wits.ac.za
URL: http://www.saci.co.za

5674 ■ Chemical Education Medal
To recognize a person who has made an outstanding contribution to chemical education, as judged by works published within the previous five years. Published works may be in any form and may be related to any level or education context. The deadline for applications and nominations is March 31. A medal struck in silver bearing the Institute's crest and name on the obverse is awarded.

5675 ■ Gold Medal
To recognize an individual whose scientific contributions in the field of chemistry or chemical technology are adjudged to be of outstanding merit. A member of the South African Chemical Institute may nominate individuals. A gold medal and monetary prize of 5,000 rand are awarded annually when merited. Established in 1967.

5676 ■ Industrial Chemistry Medal
To recognize an individual who has conducted novel research or enhanced existing chemical research in a particular field in an industrial laboratory that is judged to be of outstanding merit, taking into account the benefits to the individual's company and the chemical community at large. The deadline for nominations and applications is March 31. A medal struck in silver bearing the Institute's crest and name on the obverse is awarded.

5677 ■ Merck Medal
To recognize the senior author of a research paper that has been published in the *South African Journal of Chemistry* and is considered to have made the most significant contribution to scientific knowledge in that field of chemistry. Each year, the award is considered for papers in one of the following four fields of chemistry: analytical, organic, physical, and inorganic, in the defined sequence. A gold medal is awarded annually when merited. Established in 1961. Sponsored by Merck & Co. Formerly: (2006) AECI Medal.

5678 ■ James Moir Medal
To recognize the best BSc Honours student in chemistry at each University, and the best BTech student in chemistry at each Technikon, or University or Institute of Technology. To be eligible for the award the student must have achieved a minimum final pass mark of 75 percent. One medal shall be available for award annually for each University, Technikon, and University or Institute of Technology in the Republic of South Africa.

5679 ■ Raikes Medal
To recognize an individual whose original chemi-

cal research shows outstanding promise, as adjudged by publication in reputable journals. The research must have been performed in South Africa. Individuals under the age of 40 on March 31 during the year of the award may be nominated by a member of the South African Chemical Institute, or may apply. A gold medal is awarded annually when merited. Established in 1960 in honor of Humphrey Raikes, a former professor of Chemistry at the University of the Witwatersrand.

5680 ■ Sasol Post-Graduate Medal
To recognize students who are engaged in research towards the M.Sc. or PhD degree in Chemistry, or the Master's Diploma of a Technikon, and who are considered to be young, innovative chemists. A maximum of five silver medals are available to be awarded annually, and the award is accompanied by a cash prize of 2,000 rand. Established in 1984. Sponsored by Sasol Ltd.

5681 ■ Hendrik Van Eck Medal
To recognize a member of the Institute who has made exceptional contributions in the business or industrial sectors and/or to the community as a whole in South Africa. Members of the South African Chemical Institute may be nominated by a member of the SACI. A gold medal is awarded annually when merited. Established in 1983 in honor of Hendrik van Eck, a major South African industrialist.

5682 ■ South African Council of Shopping Centres
Greg Azzopardi, Pres.
PO Box 784937
Sandton 2146, Republic of South Africa
Ph: 27 11 8848940
Fax: 27 11 8848941
E-mail: ayesha@sacsc.org.za
URL: http://www.shoppingcouncil.co.za

5683 ■ Footprint Marketing Awards
To recognize outstanding and highly effective retail marketing initiatives. Gold, silver, and bronze awards are presented in various categories each year. Established in 2008.

5684 ■ South African Department of Science and Technology
Private Bag X894
Pretoria 0001, Republic of South Africa
Ph: 27 12 843 6300
URL: http://www.dst.gov.za

5685 ■ Best Emerging Young Woman Scientist Award
To recognize a young female scientist for outstanding scientific contribution to the advancement of science and building of the knowledge base within the fields of natural sciences or engineering. Candidates must hold a PhD and have less than five years of post-doctoral experience in either natural sciences or engineering. A monetary prize of 50,000 rand is awarded annually.

5686 ■ Distinguished Scientist Award for Contribution to the Improvement of the Quality of Life of Women
To recognize a scientist (male or female) for outstanding scientific contribution to improvement in the quality of life for women. Candidates must hold a PhD and have at least five years of post-doctoral experience. A monetary prize of 50,000 rand is awarded annually.

5687 ■ Distinguished Woman Scientist Award
To recognize a female scientist for outstanding scientific contribution to the advancement of science and building of the knowledge base within the fields of natural sciences or engineering. Candidates must hold a PhD and have at least

Awards are arranged in alphabetical order below their administering organizations

five years of post-doctoral experience in either natural sciences or engineering. A monetary prize of 50,000 rand is awarded annually.

5688 ■ South African Geophysical Association
Ms. Charlene Skipp, Admin.
PostNet, Ste. 417
Private Bag X19
Gardenview 2047, Republic of South Africa
Ph: 27 83 7807209
Ph: 27 12 3826279
Fax: 27 86 6605640
E-mail: admin@sagaonline.co.za
URL: http://www.sagaonline.co.za

5689 ■ Best Paper Award
To honor an outstanding research paper. Awarded biennially in odd-numbered years. Established in 2001. Formerly: SAGA-FUGRO Best Paper Award.

5690 ■ Krahman Medal
To honor deserving members. Awarded periodically. Established in 1988.

5691 ■ South African Institute of Architects
Mrs. Su Linning, Exec. Off.
Private Bag X10063
Randburg 2125, Republic of South Africa
Ph: 27 11 7821315
Fax: 27 11 7828771
E-mail: admin@saia.org.za
URL: http://www.saia.org.za

5692 ■ Architectural Critics and Writers Award
For recognition of a distinguished contribution to architectural criticism and/or writing. Established in 1977.

5693 ■ Award for Excellence
For outstanding contributions to the field of architecture. Awarded to one or more recipients biennially in even-numbered years.

5694 ■ Award of Merit
To recognize good design or a significant contribution in the field of architecture. Awarded to one or more recipients biennially in even-numbered years.

5695 ■ Gold Medal for Architecture
For recognition of an outstanding contribution to architecture through practice and design. Members of the Institute are eligible. A silver gilt medal is awarded when merited. Established in 1958.

5696 ■ Medal of Distinction
For recognition of services to the profession of architecture. Members of the Institute are eligible. A medal is awarded when merited. Established in 1981.

5697 ■ Patron of Architecture Award
For recognition of achievement in architecture and allied fields. An individual, government, department, or other organization is eligible. Awarded when merited. Established in 1981.

5698 ■ South African National Council for the Blind
Jill Wagner, CEO
514 White St.
Bailey's Muckleneuk
Pretoria 0181, Republic of South Africa
Ph: 27 12 4523811
Fax: 27 12 3461177
E-mail: admin@sancb.org.za
URL: http://www.sancb.org.za

5699 ■ R. W. Bowen Medal
For recognition of lifelong meritorious service to the visually disabled people of South Africa. South Africans from all walks of life may be nominated. A medal and citation are awarded

biennially. Established in 1962 in memory of R. W. Bowen, a blinded veteran of the 1914-1918 War, and first chairman of the South African National Council for the Blind.

5700 ■ South African National Defence Force
c/o Department of Defense Information Centre
Private Bag X161
Pretoria 0001, Republic of South Africa
Ph: 27 12 355 6321
Fax: 27 12 355 6398
E-mail: info@mil.za
URL: http://www.dod.mil.za

5701 ■ General Service Medal
To recognize members of the SA Defence Force who have rendered service as part of military operations within the borders of the Republic of South Africa for the prevention or suppression of terrorism or internal disorder or who have served for the preservation of life, health or property, or maintenance of essential services, including the maintenance of law and order or the prevention of crime in co-operation with the South Africa Police. A silver medal displaying a pentagon and wreath, worn from an orange, white, and blue ribbon is bestowed. Established January 1983.

5702 ■ Military Merit Medal
To recognize members of the SA Defence Force who have distinguished themselves by the rendering of services of a high order. A medal worn from a blue and red striped ribbon is bestowed. A bar is presented for successive awards. Formerly: C SADF Commendation Medal; Chief of the South African Defense Force Commendation Medal.

5703 ■ Unitas Medal
A round bronze medal depicting a seven-pointed star with a Greek lower-case alpha in the center worn from a light blue, green, and white ribbon is bestowed. Established in 1994 to commemorate the new constitutional dispensation introduced in South Africa.

5704 ■ South African Orthopaedic Association
(Suid-Afrikaanse Ortopediese Vereniging)
Mrs. Leana Fourie, CEO
PO Box 12918
Brandhof 9324, Republic of South Africa
Ph: 27 51 4303280
Fax: 27 51 4303284
E-mail: info@saoa.org.za
URL: http://www.saoa.org.za

5705 ■ GT du Toit Registrar Prize
To honor the best registrar paper presented at the Annual Congress.

5706 ■ President's Medal
To recognize a member for an outstanding essay on a subject of Orthopaedic interest. Awarded by the President biennially in odd-numbered years.

5707 ■ Research Grant
For research carried out in South Africa.

5708 ■ Travel Grant
To provide financial support for members to travel.

5709 ■ South African Society for Basic and Clinical Pharmacology
Prof. Vanessa Steenkamp, Sec. Gen.
North-West University
Faculty of Natural Sciences
Internal Box 60
Potchefstroom 2520, Republic of South Africa
Ph: 27 18 2992304
Ph: 27 12 3192547
Fax: 27 18 2992447
E-mail: office@sapharmacol.co.za
URL: http://www.sapharmacol.co.za

Formerly: (2007) South African Pharmacology Society.

5710 ■ Young Scientist Award
To foster and promote research in pharmacology among young scientists by honoring the best podium presentation at the Congress. A monetary prize of 10,000 rand and 4,000 rand is awarded for first and second place, respectively.

5711 ■ South African Society for Enology and Viticulture
(Suid Afrikaanse Wingerd en Wynkundevereniging)
Mrs. Melinda van der Ryst, Admin. Mgr.
PO Box 2092
Dennesig 7601, Republic of South Africa
Ph: 27 21 8896311
Ph: 27 21 8896312
Fax: 27 21 8896335
E-mail: sasev@sasev.org
URL: http://www.sasev.org

5712 ■ Journal Prize
For the best article in the annual journal. A cash prize is awarded annually.

5713 ■ Medal of Merit
To a person who made an exceptional contribution over many years to the industry. Awarded annually.

5714 ■ Paper and Poster Prizes
To recognize the best paper and poster presented at the Annual Congress. Student prizes are also awarded. Awarded annually.

5715 ■ SASEV Award
To the most outstanding scientific contribution published in the journal or the most outstanding innovation in the industry. A cash prize is awarded annually.

5716 ■ Student Prize
For the top students in Viticulture and Enology at the University of Stellenboch and Cellar Technology at the Elsenburg College. Awarded annually.

5717 ■ Table Grape Award
To the most outstanding scientific contribution published in journal or the most outstanding innovation in table and raisin grape industry. A cash prize is awarded annually.

5718 ■ South African Society for Professional Engineers
W. Stewart, CEO/VP
PO Box 78433
Sandton 2146, Republic of South Africa
Ph: 27 11 8075990
Fax: 27 11 5076821
E-mail: spe@professionalengineers.co.za
URL: http://www.professionalengineers.co.za

5719 ■ Engineer of the Year
For distinguished contributions to engineering profession. Awarded annually.

5720 ■ South African Society of Occupational Health Nursing Practitioners
Ms. Linda Stokes, Contact
215 Leeuwpoort St.
Boksburg 1470, Republic of South Africa
Ph: 27 11 8923174
Fax: 27 11 8925355
E-mail: sasohnoffice@mweb.co.za
URL: http://www.sasohn.org.za

5721 ■ Mike Baker Bursary Award
To provide financial support to students in the field of occupational health. A maximum of R10,000 is awarded annually.

Awards are arranged in alphabetical order below their administering organizations

5722 ■ Occupational Health Practitioner of the Year
For outstanding contribution to the practice of occupational health in South Africa. Awarded annually.

5723 ■ South African Statistical Association (Suid-Afrikaanse Statistiese Vereniging)
Ms. Marie F. Smith MSC, Sec.
PO Box 3341
Matieland
Stellenbosch 7602, Republic of South Africa
Ph: 27 12 9970653
Ph: 27 83 3062753
Fax: 27 12 9970653
E-mail: marie.smith@stats4science.com
URL: http://www.sastat.org.za

5724 ■ Herbert Sichel Medal
For excellent published articles. Awarded annually. Established in 1997.

5725 ■ South African Sugar Technologists' Association
Ms. Danile Macdonald, Admin.
Private Bag X 02
Mount Edgecombe 4300, Republic of South Africa
Ph: 27 31 5087543
Fax: 27 31 5087420
E-mail: sasta@sugar.org.za
URL: http://www.sasta.co.za

5726 ■ Gold Medal
For recognition of outstanding contributions to technology in the South African sugar industry. Members of the Association are eligible. A gold medal is awarded periodically at the annual general meeting. Established in 1968.

5727 ■ South African Translators' Institute (Suid-Afrikaanse Vertalersinstituut)
Ms. Marion Boers, Exec. Dir.
PO Box 1710
Rivonia
Johannesburg 2128, Republic of South Africa
Ph: 27 11 8032681
Fax: 27 11 8032681
E-mail: office@translators.org.za
URL: http://translators.org.za

5728 ■ Johan Kruger Prize
For service to the institute or to the profession.

5729 ■ Prizes for Outstanding Translation
To recognize excellence in published translations and dictionaries in South Africa's official languages. Presented in five categories: literary translation, non-fiction translation, translation of children's literature, service translation, and translation of dictionaries. A monetary prize of R10,000 is awarded in each category annually. Established in 2000.

5730 ■ South African Veterinary Association
Dr. Colin Cameron, CEO
PO Box 25033
Monument Park
Pretoria 0152, Republic of South Africa
Ph: 27 12 3461150
Fax: 27 12 3462929
E-mail: elize@sava.co.za
URL: http://www.sava.co.za

5731 ■ Boswell Award
To recognize members for selfless and eminent service rendered to the profession through the SAVA. The award may be bestowed upon more than one person in a particular year.

5732 ■ Gold Medal
Awarded to any person resident in South Africa, or a veterinarian who is not resident in South Africa but who is a member of the SAVA, in

recognition of outstanding scientific achievement and advancement of veterinary science. The medal will only be awarded once to a particular person.

5733 ■ Southern Africa Association for the Advancement of Science (Suider-Afrika Genootskap vir die Bevordering van die Wetenskap)
Mrs. Shirley A. Korsman, Sec.
PO Box 366
Irene 0062, Republic of South Africa
Ph: 27 12 6672544
Fax: 27 12 6672544
E-mail: s2a3@global.co.za
URL: http://s2a3.up.ac.za

5734 ■ British Association Medal
Recognizes exceptional scientific achievement, international participation and publications. Applicants must be under 40 years if age. A silver medal is awarded annually.

5735 ■ Bronze Medal
To recognize the student at each South African university who has submitted the best Master's dissertation in one of the branches of science, either natural or human sciences. Awarded annually.

5736 ■ Certificate of Merit
To recognize persons who have contributed to the advancement of science in South Africa. Awarded when merited.

5737 ■ South Africa Medal
Recognizes exceptional scientific achievement, international participation and publications. A gold medal is awarded annually.

5738 ■ Southern Africa Institute for Management Services
Mr. Eddie Morrison, Sec.-Treas.
PO Box 693
Pretoria 0001, Republic of South Africa
Ph: 27 12 4979183
Fax: 27 12 5587183
E-mail: saimas@global.co.za
URL: http://www.saimas.org.za

5739 ■ President's Award for Excellence
For involvement with SAIMAS and the management profession.

5740 ■ Southern African Society for Plant Pathology
Prof. Teresa Coutinho, Pres.
University of Pretoria
Forestry and Agricultural Biotechnology Institute
Private Bag X28
Pretoria 0002, Republic of South Africa
Ph: 27 12 4203934
Fax: 27 12 4203960
E-mail: teresa.coutinho@up.ac.za
URL: http://www.saspp.co.za
Formerly: South African Society for Plant Pathology and Microbiology; South African Society for Plant Pathology.

5741 ■ Applied Plant Pathology Award
For an outstanding recent contribution to applied plant pathology. Membership is not required. A certificate is awarded annually. Established in 2002.

5742 ■ E.M. Doidge Memorial Lecture
Invites a leading South African scientist to present the keynote address at the systematics session of the Society's Congress. Established in 2003.

5743 ■ Fellow of the Society
For recognition of service to the Society and to teaching and/or research in plant pathology. Individuals who have ten years of uninterrupted membership may be nominated by the members and elected by the Council. A certificate is awarded when merited. Established in 1984.

5744 ■ Honorary Member
For recognition of an outstanding contribution to plant pathology or the Society. Election is by ballot at the annual general meeting. A certificate is awarded when merited. Established in 1963.

5745 ■ Inqaba Molecular Biology Prize
To recognize the best student paper in molecular biology presented at the Biennial Congress. A book prize worth R500 is awarded biennially. Established in 2007.

5746 ■ John and Petakin Mildenhall Award
To recognize an outstanding young researcher in plant pathology. Open to young South African applied and basic researchers who have been Society members for at least two years. Preference is given to graduate students. A cash prize and a certificate are awarded biennially.

5747 ■ Pannar Seed Floating Trophy
For the best student paper presented at the Annual Congress. A monetary prize of R1,000 and a trophy are awarded annually. Established in 1996.

5748 ■ Christiaan Hendrik Persoon Medal
For recognition of an outstanding achievement in the field of plant pathology. Nominations are accepted. A medal is awarded triennially when merited. Established in 1979.

5749 ■ Publicity Award
To recognize a member for recent contributions to general public awareness of plant pathology and related issues. A certificate is presented annually. Established in 2002.

5750 ■ J.E. Vanderplank Award
To recognize an outstanding young plant pathologist. Members who received their doctorate degrees in the ten years immediately preceding the award are eligible. A plaque is awarded annually.

5751 ■ J.E. Vanderplank Lecture
Invites a leading South African scientist to present the opening keynote address at the Society's Congress. Established in 1999.

5752 ■ Southern African Society of Human Genetics
Dr. Zane Lombard, Sec.-Treas.
University of the Witwatersrand
National Health Laboratory Service
Division of Human Genetics
PO Box 1038
Johannesburg 2000, Republic of South Africa
Ph: 27 11 4899344
Fax: 27 11 4899226
E-mail: zane.lombard@nhls.ac.za
URL: http://www.sashg.org

5753 ■ Student Bursaries
For students.

5754 ■ Tourism Business Council of South Africa
PO Box 11655
Centurion 0046, Republic of South Africa
Ph: 27 12 654 7525
Fax: 27 12 654 7394
URL: http://www.tbcsa.travel

5755 ■ Tourism Business Leadership Award
To recognize and reward an individual who has made an extraordinary contribution to lifting the profile of the tourism industry in South Africa through promoting growth, investment, innovation, and excellence across all tourism sectors. Awarded annually during the Hotel Investment Conference Africa (HICA).

5756 ■ VinPro
PO Box 1411
Suider Paarl 7624, Republic of South Africa
Ph: 27 21 807 3322

Awards are arranged in alphabetical order below their administering organizations

Fax: 27 21 863 3079
E-mail: info@vinpro.co.za
URL: http://www.vinpro.co.za

5757 ■ Veritas Awards

To recognize the outstanding wines of South Africa. Double gold, gold, silver, and bronze awards are presented for wine in each of 15 varieties. Awarded annually.

5758 ■ Water Institute of Southern Africa
Dr. Kevin Pietersen, Pres.
PO Box 6011
Halfway House 1685, Republic of South Africa
Ph: 27 11 8053537
Fax: 27 11 3151258
E-mail: wisa@wisa.org.za
URL: http://www.wisa.org.za/Home/Home.htm

5759 ■ Aqua Vita Est Award

To recognize individuals and groups for their material contributions to WISA. A monetary prize of 750 rand is awarded annually to one or more recipients.

5760 ■ Burke Award

To recognize organizations for outstanding safety programs and safety records. Awarded when merited.

5761 ■ Dr. G. G. Cillie Floating Trophy

To recognize the high level research in anaerobic and sludge processes and technologies by a university student. A floating trophy and a cash prize of 3,000 rand are awarded biennially in even-numbered years. Established in 1989 to honor the research contributions on water treatment by Dr. G. G. Cillie.

5762 ■ Foundation for Water Research (UK) Award

To recognize the best paper dealing with water by a young South African writer. Awarded biennially in even-numbered years.

5763 ■ Potable Water Award

To recognize a South African water purification institution for competence and initiative. Awarded biennially in even-numbered years.

5764 ■ Umgeni Award

To encourage excellence in the fields of water science and engineering by recognizing a paper that makes a noteworthy contribution to water science and engineering. Members are eligible for papers published through WISA. A monetary award of 1,000 rand is awarded annually. Established in 1988 to mark the inauguration of the Water Institute of Southern Africa. Sponsored by Umgeni Water.

5765 ■ Piet Vosloo Award

To recognize an innovative project in the water field that represents a notable technical achievement. Awarded biennially in even-numbered years.

5766 ■ Wilson Award (Wilson - Toekenning)

To recognize the combined competence and initiative of the owner and works manager of a Waste Water Treatment Works, having a total design capacity of up to 25,000 kl/day average DWF. The criteria that are considered include treatment and operating efficiency, maintenance and servicing, laboratory control, housekeeping, safety, and administration. A certificate is awarded biennially in even-numbered years at the Conference. Established in 1976 to honor Dr. Harold Wilson (1887-1974), a founding member and first Chairman of the South African Branch of the Institute of Water Pollution Control in 1937. Administered by the Nutrient Management Division of WISA.

5767 ■ World Luxury Hotel Awards
PO Box 4
Stellenbosch
Western Cape 7599, Republic of South Africa

Ph: 27 21 888 5547
Fax: 27 21 886 8881
E-mail: enquiries@luxuryhotelawards.com
URL: http://www.luxuryhotelawards.com

5768 ■ World Luxury Hotel Awards

To recognize and celebrate the facilities and service provided by luxury hotels around the world. Presented in a variety of categories, including Business Hotels, City Hotels, Airport Hotels, Casino Resorts, Family Hotel, Golf Resort, and Private Island Resort. Awarded annually. Established in 2007.

5769 ■ Zoological Society of Southern Africa (Dierkundige Vereniging van Suidelike Afrika)
Prof. Colleen T. Downs, Treas.
University of KwaZulu-Natal
School of Biological, Conservation Sciences
Private bag X01
Scottsville 3209, Republic of South Africa
Ph: 27 33 2605104
Ph: 27 33 2605127
Fax: 27 33 2605105
E-mail: downs@ukzn.ac.za
URL: http://www.zssa.co.za

5770 ■ Award to the Most Outstanding Third Year Student in Zoology

Awarded each year to the best third-year and honors students in zoology at each of the universities in southern Africa. Each student also receives free membership for one year. Awards are based on the recommendation of department heads. Awarded annually. Formerly: Certificate of Merit.

5771 ■ Gold Medal

To recognize a zoologist of exceptional merit in the field of zoology in southern Africa. A medal is awarded annually if merited. Established in 1970.

5772 ■ Lawrence Memorial Grant

To recognize and support research on the litter fauna of the forest floor. Candidates are typically in the midst of the beginning of their research careers. Awarded annually if fund are available from the Lawrence Estate Bequest. Established in honor of Reginald Frederick Lawrence.

5773 ■ Stevenson - Hamilton Award

To recognize an amateur zoologist for exceptional contributions to zoology in southern Africa. Individuals may be nominated by members of the Society before May of each year. A medal is awarded annually if merited. Established in 1988.

5774 ■ Student Prize

To honor the best paper presented by a student at the annual scientific meeting. Any full-time student registered at any South African university is eligible. A citation and cash prize of R300 are awarded annually.

Russia

5775 ■ All Russia Association of the Blind (Vserossiiskoe Obschestvo Slepykn)
Alexandr Y. Neumyvakin, Pres.
Novaya Ploschad, 14
109012 Moscow, Russia
Ph: 7 495 6286513
Ph: 7 495 6281374
Fax: 7 495 6237600
E-mail: info@vos.org.ru
URL: http://www.vos.org.ru

5776 ■ Certificate of Good Work

To honor an individual for contribution to the association.

5777 ■ Excellent Member of VOS

For an outstanding individual who has made remarkable contributions to the association.

5778 ■ Honorary Member of VOS

For an individual's contribution to the association.

5779 ■ Gerontological Society of the Russian Academy of Sciences
Dr. Vladimir N. Anisimov, Pres.
68, Leningradskaya St., Pesochny-2
197758 St. Petersburg, Russia
Ph: 7 812 5968607
Ph: 7 812 2351832
Fax: 7 812 2351832
E-mail: aging@mail.ru
URL: http://www.iagg.com.br/webforms/iaggMembers.aspx

5780 ■ Junior Research Award in Gerontology

For researchers under age 35.

5781 ■ Russian Academy of Sciences
Yuri S. Osipov, Pres.
Leninskii ave. 14
GSP 1
119991 Moscow, Russia
Ph: 7 495 9380309
Fax: 7 495 9381844
E-mail: info-kadr@pran.ru
URL: http://www.ras.ru

5782 ■ A.A. Andronov Prize

To recognize an individual for outstanding contributions to classical mechanics and control theory. Awarded to one or more recipients triennially. Established in 1994. Administered by the Academy's Division of Machine Engineering, Mechanics, and Control Processes.

5783 ■ P.P. Anosov Prize

To recognize an individual for the best scientific results in metallurgy, metal science, and heat treatment of metals and alloys. Awarded triennially. Established in 1993. Administered by the Academy's Division of Physico-Chemistry and Technology of Inorganic Materials.

5784 ■ A.D. Arkhangelskii Prize

To recognize an individual for the best research works in regional geology. Awarded triennially. Established in 1996. Administered by the Academy's Division of Geology, Geophysics, Geochemistry, and Mining Sciences.

5785 ■ L.A. Artsimovich Prize

To recognize an individual for the best results in experimental physics. Awarded triennially. Established in 1995. Administered by the Academy's Division of General Physics and Astronomy.

5786 ■ A.N. Bakh Prize

To recognize an individual for the best results in biochemistry. Awarded triennially. Established in 1996. Administered by the Academy's Division of Physico-Chemical Biology.

5787 ■ A.A. Balandin Prize

To recognize an individual for outstanding contributions to catalysis. Awarded to one or more recipients triennially. Established in 1995. Administered by the Academy's Division of General and Technical Chemistry.

5788 ■ I.P. Bardin Prize

To recognize an individual for the best work in metallurgy. Awarded triennially. Established in 1995. Administered by the Academy's Division of Physico-Chemistry and Technology of Inorganic Materials.

5789 ■ A.A. Belopol'skii

To recognize an individual for outstanding contributions to astrophysics. Awarded to one or more recipients triennially. Established in 1993. Administered by the Academy's Division of General Physics and Astronomy.

5790 ■ A.N. Belozerskii Prize

To recognize an individual for the best results in

molecular biology. Awarded triennially. Established in 1995. Administered by the Academy's Division of Physico-Chemical Biology.

5791 ■ N.N. Bogoliubov Gold Medal
To recognize a Russian or foreign scientist for outstanding achievements in mathematics, theoretical physics, or mechanics. Awarded every five years. Administered by the Academy's Division of Mathematics. Established in 1999.

5792 ■ F.A. Bredikhin Prize
To recognize an individual for the best results in astronomy. Awarded triennially. Established in 1995. Administered by the Academy's Division of General Physics and Astronomy.

5793 ■ A.M. Butlerov Prize
To recognize an individual for the best results in organic chemistry. Awarded triennially. Established in 1994. Administered by the Academy's Division of General and Technical Chemistry.

5794 ■ A.V. Chayanov Prize
To recognize an individual for the best works in agrarian economics. Awarded when merited. Established in 1996. Administered by the Academy's Division of Economics.

5795 ■ P.A. Cherenkov Prize
To recognize an individual for outstanding achievements in experimental high energy physics. Awarded biennially in even-numbered years. Established in 1999. Administered by the Academy's Division of Nuclear Physics.

5796 ■ L.A. Chugaev Prize
To recognize an individual for the best results in the chemistry of complex compounds. Awarded triennially. Established in 1994. Administered by the Academy's Division of Physico-Chemistry and Technology of Inorganic Materials.

5797 ■ A.Y. Fersman Prize
To recognize an individual for the best research work in mineralogy and geochemistry. Awarded triennially. Established in 1994. Administered by the Academy's Division of Geology, Geophysics, Geochemistry, and Mining Sciences.

5798 ■ E.S. Fiodorov Prize
To recognize an individual for the best results in crystallography. Awarded to one or more recipients triennially. Established in 1994. Administered by the Academy's Division of General Physics and Astronomy.

5799 ■ V.A. Fok Prize
To recognize an individual for the best results in theoretical and mathematical physics. Awarded triennially. Established in 1995. Administered by the Academy's Division of General Physics and Astronomy.

5800 ■ A.M. Fridman Prize
To recognize an individual for the best results in cosmology and gravitation. Awarded to one or more recipients triennially. Established in 1996. Administered by the Academy's Division of Nuclear Physics.

5801 ■ B.B. Golitsyn Prize
To recognize an individual for the best research work in geophysics. Awarded triennially. Established in 1994. Administered by the Academy's Division of Geology, Geophysics, Geochemistry, and Mining Sciences.

5802 ■ L.V. Grebenschikov Prize
To recognize an individual for the best results in chemistry, physical chemistry, and technology of glass. Awarded triennially. Established in 1994. Administered by the Academy's Division of Physico-Chemistry and Technology of Inorganic Materials.

5803 ■ A.A. Grigorev Prize
To recognize an individual for outstanding

contributions to physical geography. Awarded to one or more recipients biennially in odd-numbered years. Established in 1994. Administered by the Academy's Division of Oceanology, Atmosphere Physics, and Geography.

5804 ■ I.M. Gubkin Prize
To recognize an individual for the best research works in oil and gas geology. Awarded triennially. Established in 1995. Administered by the Academy's Division of Geology, Geophysics, Geochemistry, and Mining Sciences.

5805 ■ A.F. Ioffe Prize
To recognize an individual for the best results in physics. Awarded triennially. Established in 1993. Administered by the Academy's Division of General Physics and Astronomy.

5806 ■ V.N. Itat'ev Prize
To recognize an individual for the best results in technical chemistry. Awarded triennially. Established in 1994. Administered by the Academy's Division of General and Technical Chemistry.

5807 ■ L.V. Kantorovich Prize
To recognize an individual for the best works in economical mathematical models and techniques. Awarded triennially. Established in 1996. Administered by the Academy's Division of Economics.

5808 ■ N.I. Kareev Prize
To recognize an individual for substantial contributions in the research of problems of general history. Awarded triennially. Established in 1994. Administered by the Academy's Division of History.

5809 ■ V.A. Kargin Prize
To recognize an individual for the best results in high-molecular compounds. Awarded triennially. Established in 1996. Administered by the Academy's Division of General and Technical Chemistry.

5810 ■ V.G. Khlopin Prize
To recognize an individual for the best results in radiochemistry. Awarded triennially. Established in 1995. Administered by the Academy's Division of General and Technical Chemistry.

5811 ■ V.O. Klyuchevskii Prize
To recognize an individual for a substantial contribution in Russian history and Slavic studies. Awarded biennially in even-numbered years. Established in 1994. Administered by the Academy's Division of History.

5812 ■ A.N. Kolmogorov Prize
To recognize an individual for outstanding accomplishments in mathematics. Awarded triennially. Established in 1994. Administered by the Academy's Division of Mathematics.

5813 ■ N.K. Kol'tsov Prize
To recognize an individual for the best works in molecular genetics. Awarded triennially. Established in 1994. Administered by the Academy's Division of Physico-Chemical Biology.

5814 ■ V.L. Komarov Prize
To recognize an individual for the best works in botany, systematics, botanical geography, paleobotany, and the anatomy and morphology of plants. Awarded triennially. Established in 1996. Administered by the Academy's Division of General Biology.

5815 ■ N.D. Kondrat'ev Prize
To recognize an individual for the best works in general economical theory. Awarded triennially. Established in 1995. Administered by the Academy's Division of Economics.

5816 ■ A.F. Koni Prize
To recognize an individual for the best scientific

works in law. Awarded triennially. Administered by the Academy's Division of Philosophy, Sociology, Psychology, and Law.

5817 ■ D.S. Korzhinskii Prize
To recognize an individual for the best research work in physico-chemical petrology and mineralogy. Awarded triennially. Established in 1995. Administered by the Academy's Division of Geology, Geophysics, Geochemistry, and Mining Sciences.

5818 ■ S.V. Kovalevskaya Prize
To recognize an individual for outstanding accomplishments in mathematics. Awarded triennially. Established in 1997. Administered by the Academy's Division of Mathematics.

5819 ■ A.O. Kovalevskii Prize
To recognize an individual for the best works in development biology or general, comparative, and experimental embryology of invertebrates and vertebrates. Awarded triennially. Established in 1994. Administered by the Academy's Division of General Biology.

5820 ■ M.M. Kovalevskii Prize
To recognize an individual for the best scientific works in sociology. Awarded triennially. Established in 1995. Administered by the Academy's Division of Philosophy, Sociology, Psychology, and Law.

5821 ■ A.N. Krylov Prize
To recognize an individual for the best results in the use of computers in solving problems of mechanics and mathematical physics. Awarded triennially. Established in 1995. Administered by the Academy's Division of Informatics, Computer Technologies, and Automation.

5822 ■ G.M. Krzhizhanovskii Prize
To recognize an individual for the best research work in complex problems of energetics. Awarded triennially. Established in 1993. Administered by the Academy's Division of Physical and Technical Problems of Energetics.

5823 ■ M.A. Lavrent'ev Prize
To recognize an individual for outstanding accomplishments in mathematics and mechanics. Awarded triennially. Established in 1994. Administered by the Academy's Division of Mathematics.

5824 ■ S.A. Lebedev Prize
To recognize an individual for the best results in computer system development. Awarded every four years. Established in 1994. Administered by the Academy's Division of Informatics, Computer Technologies, and Automation.

5825 ■ S.V. Lebedev Prize
To recognize an individual for the best results in the chemistry and technology of synthetic rubber and other synthetic polymers. Awarded triennially. Established in 1995. Administered by the Academy's Division of General and Technical Chemistry.

5826 ■ N.I. Lobachevskii Prize
To recognize an individual for outstanding accomplishments in geometry. Awarded every four years. Established in 1996. Administered by the Academy's Division of Mathematics.

5827 ■ M.V. Lomonosov Great Gold Medal
For recognition of outstanding works in the natural, physical, and social sciences. Two gold medals with the profile of the Russian scientist, M.V. Lomonosov, are awarded annually: one to a Soviet scientist and one to a foreign scholar. First awarded in 1959.

5828 ■ A.M. Lyapunov Prize
To recognize an individual for outstanding ac-

Awards are arranged in alphabetical order below their administering organizations

complishments in mathematics and mechanics. Awarded triennially. Established in 1995. Administered by the Academy's Division of Mathematics.

5829 ■ S.O. Makarov Prize
To recognize an individual for the best research works, discoveries, and inventions in oceanology. Awarded when merited. Established in 1996. Administered by the Academy's Division of Oceanology, Atmospheric Physics, and Geography.

5830 ■ A.I. Maltsev Prize
To recognize an individual for outstanding accomplishments in mathematics. Awarded triennially. Established in 1994. Administered by the Academy's Division of Mathematics.

5831 ■ L.I. Mandel'shtam Prize
To recognize an individual for outstanding accomplishments in physics. Awarded triennially. Established in 1994. Administered by the Academy's Division of General Physics and Astronomy.

5832 ■ A.A. Markov Prize
To recognize an individual for outstanding contributions to mathematics. Awarded triennially. Established in 1997. Administered by the Academy's Division of Mathematics.

5833 ■ F.F. Martens Prize
To recognize an individual for the best scientific works in international law and international relations. Awarded triennially. Established in 1995. Administered by the Academy's Division of Philosophy, Sociology, Psychology, and Law along with the Division of International Relations Studies.

5834 ■ I.I. Mechnikov Prize
To recognize an individual for the best scientific works in immunology and in comparative and experimental pathology, as well as substantial scientific achievements in biology and biomedicine. Awarded triennially. Established in 1996. Administered by the Academy's Division of General Biology.

5835 ■ N.V. Mel'nikov Prize
To recognize an individual for the best research works in complex mining. Awarded triennially. Established in 1995. Administered by the Academy's Division of Geology, Geophysics, Geochemistry, and Mining Sciences.

5836 ■ N.N. Miklukho-Maklai Prize
To recognize an individual for substantial contributions to the research of ethnology and anthropology problems. Awarded triennially. Established in 1993. Administered by the Academy's Division of History.

5837 ■ V.S. Nemchinov Prize
To recognize an individual for the best works in economical mathematical models and techniques. Awarded triennially. Established in 1993. Administered by the Academy's Division of Economics.

5838 ■ A.N. Nesmeyanov Prize
To recognize an individual for the best results in hetero-organic compounds. Awarded triennially. Established in 1994. Administered by the Academy's Division of General and Technical Chemistry.

5839 ■ V.A. Obruchev Prize
To recognize an individual for the best research works in the geology of Asia. Awarded triennially. Established in 1996. Administered by the Academy's Division of Geology, Geophysics, Geochemistry, and Mining Sciences.

5840 ■ S.F. Ol'denburg Prize
To recognize an individual for the best works in Orientalistics. Awarded triennially. Established in 1994. Administered by the Academy's Division of History.

5841 ■ L.A. Orbeli Prize
To recognize an individual for the best works in evolutionary physiology. Awarded triennially. Established in 1995. Administered by the Academy's Division of Physiology.

5842 ■ Y.A. Ovchinnikov Prize
To recognize an individual for the best works in physico-chemical biology and biotechnology. Awarded triennially. Established in 1994. Administered by the Academy's Division of Physico-Chemical Biology.

5843 ■ E.N. Pavlovskii Prize
To recognize an individual for the best works in zoology and parasitology. Awarded triennially. Established in 1996. Administered by the Academy's Division of General Biology.

5844 ■ B.N. Petrov Prize
To recognize an individual for the best results in automatic control theory and systems. Awarded triennially. Established in 1995. Administered by the Academy's Division of Machine Engineering, Mechanics, and Control Processes Problems.

5845 ■ I.G. Petrovskii Prize
To recognize an individual for outstanding accomplishments in mathematics. Awarded every six years. Established in 1995. Administered by the Academy's Division of Mathematics.

5846 ■ G.V. Plekhanov Prize
To recognize an individual for the best scientific works in philosophy. Awarded triennially. Established in 1994. Administered by the Academy's Division of Philosophy, Sociology, Psychology, and Law.

5847 ■ D.N. Pryanishnikov Prize
To recognize an individual for the best works in plant nutrition and use of fertilizers. Awarded triennially. Established in 1996. Administered by the Academy's Division of Physico-Chemical Biology.

5848 ■ A.A. Raspletin Prize
To recognize an individual for the best achievements in creating radioengineering automatic control systems. Awarded triennially. Established in 1994. Administered by the Academy's Division of Informatics, Computer Technologies, and Automation.

5849 ■ P.A. Rebinder Prize
To recognize an individual for the best results in colloid chemistry and the chemistry of surface phenomena. Awarded triennially. Established in 1995. Administered by the Academy's Division of General and Technical Chemistry.

5850 ■ D.S. Rozhdestvenskii Prize
To recognize an individual for the best results in optics. Awarded triennially. Established in 1995. Administered by the Academy's Division of General Physics and Astronomy.

5851 ■ S.L. Rubinshtein Prize
To recognize an individual for the best scientific results in psychology. Awarded triennially. Established in 1996. Administered by the Academy's Division of Philosophy, Sociology, Psychology, and Law.

5852 ■ F.P. Savarenskii Prize
To recognize an individual for the best work in the study of waters of the dry land. Awarded triennially. Established in 1995. Administered by the Academy's Division of Oceanology, Atmospheric Physics, and Geography.

5853 ■ A.N. Severtsov Prize
To recognize an individual for the best results in developmental morphology. Awarded triennially. Established in 1993. Administered by the Academy's Division of General Biology.

5854 ■ A.A. Shakhmatov Prize
To recognize an individual for the best works in

source science, textology, and linguistics. Awarded triennially. Established in 1994. Administered by the Academy's Division of Literature and Language.

5855 ■ N.S. Shatskii Prize
To recognize an individual for the best research works in tectonics. Awarded triennially. Established in 1994. Administered by the Academy's Division of Geology, Geophysics, Geochemistry, and Mining Sciences.

5856 ■ M.M. Shemyakin Prize
To recognize an individual for the best works in bioorganic chemistry. Awarded triennially. Established in 1995. Administered by the Academy's Division of Physico-Chemical Biology.

5857 ■ I.I. Shmal'gauzen Prize
To recognize an individual for the best works in developmental morphology. Awarded triennially. Established in 1995. Administered by the Academy's Division of General Biology.

5858 ■ O.Y. Shmidt Prize
To recognize an individual for the best works in the exploration of the Arctic. Awarded triennially. Established in 1995. Administered by the Academy's Division of Oceanology, Atmospheric Physics, and Geography, as well as the Division of Geology, Geophysics, Geochemistry, and Mining Sciences.

5859 ■ K.I. Skryabin Prize
To recognize an individual for the best research in helminthology and parasitology. Awarded triennially. Established in 1996. Administered by the Academy's Division of General Biology.

5860 ■ S.S. Smirnov Prize
To recognize an individual for the best research works in mineral deposits and metallogeny. Awarded triennially. Established in 1994. Administered by the Academy's Division of Geology, Geophysics, Geochemistry, and Mining Sciences.

5861 ■ L.A. Spendiarov International Geological Prize
For recognition of advanced scientific research, and to strengthen international cooperation in the field of geosciences. Citizens of the country which is the organizer of the International Geological Congress at which the prize is awarded are eligible. A monetary prize and a diploma are awarded every four years. Established in 1897 by A. Spendiarov, in memory of his son, Leonid A. Spendiarov, who perished during a geological excursion at the 7th IGC in St. Petersburg.

5862 ■ A.G. Stoletov Prize
To recognize an individual for the best results in physics. Awarded to one or more recipients triennially. Established in 1996. Administered by the Academy's Division of Physical and Technical Problems of Energetics.

5863 ■ V.N. Sukachev Prize
To recognize an individual for the best works in ecology. Awarded triennially. Established in 1995. Administered by the Academy's Division of General Biology.

5864 ■ I.Y. Tamm Prize
To recognize an individual for the best results in theoretical physics, elementary particles, and field theory. Awarded triennially. Established in 1995. Administered by the Academy's Division of Nuclear Physics.

5865 ■ Y.V. Tarle Prize
To recognize an individual for the best research works in world history and modern development of international relations. Awarded triennially. Established in 1994. Administered by the Academy's Division of International Relations Studies and the Division of History.

Awards are arranged in alphabetical order below their administering organizations

5866 ■ K.A. Timiryazev Prize
To recognize an individual for the best work in the physiology of plants. Awarded triennially. Established in 1995. Administered by the Academy's Division of Physico-Chemical Biology.

5867 ■ F.A. Tsander Prize
To recognize an individual for the best theoretical results in missile and space science. Awarded triennially. Established in 1996. Administered by the Academy's Division of Machine Engineering, Mechanics, and Control Processes Problems.

5868 ■ K.E. Tsiolkovskii Prize
To recognize an individual for the best results in interplanetary communications and use of outer space. Awarded triennially. Established in 1996. Administered by the Academy's Division of Machine Engineering, Mechanics, and Control Processes Problems.

5869 ■ A.N. Tupolev Prize
To recognize an individual for the best results in aviation science and aerotechnics. Awarded triennially. Established in 1994. Administered by the Academy's Division of Machine Engineering, Mechanics, and Control Processes Problems.

5870 ■ A.A. Ukhtomskii Prize
To recognize an individual for the best works in neurophysiology and physiology of labor activity. Awarded triennially. Established in 1994. Administered by the Academy's Division of Physiology.

5871 ■ E.S. Varga Prize
To recognize an individual for the best research work in world economy. Awarded triennially. Established in 1994. Administered by the Academy's Division of International Relations Studies.

5872 ■ V.I. Veksler Prize
To recognize an individual for the best results in the physics of accelerators. Awarded triennially. Established in 1994. Administered by the Academy's Division of Nuclear Physics.

5873 ■ A.N. Veselovskii Prize
To recognize an individual for the best works in the theory of literature, comparative literary science, and folkloristics. Awarded biennially in odd-numbered years. Established in 1996. Administered by the Academy's Division of Literature and Language.

5874 ■ A.P. Vinogradov Prize
To recognize an individual for the best research work in geochemistry, biogeochemistry, and cosmochemistry. Awarded triennially. Established in 1996. Administered by the Academy's Division of Geology, Geophysics, Geochemistry, and Mining Sciences.

5875 ■ I.M. Vinogradov Prize
To recognize an individual for outstanding accomplishments in mathematics. Awarded triennially. Established in 1995. Administered by the Academy's Division of Mathematics.

5876 ■ S.N. Vinogradskii Prize
To recognize an individual for the best works in general microbiology. Awarded triennially. Established in 1994. Administered by the Academy's Division of Physico-Chemical Biology.

5877 ■ P.N. Yablochkov Prize
To recognize an individual for the best results in electrical physics and electrical engineering. Awarded biennially in even-numbered years. Established in 1994. Administered by the Academy's Division of Physical and Technical Problems of Energetics.

5878 ■ I.Y. Zabelin Prize
To recognize an individual for substantial contributions in the research of problems of archaeology. Awarded triennially. Established in 1994. Administered by the Academy's Division of History.

5879 ■ N.D. Zelinskii Prize
To recognize an individual for the best works in organic chemistry and petrochemistry. Awarded triennially. Established in 1996. Administered by the Academy's Division of General and Technical Chemistry.

5880 ■ Russian Academy of Sciences Section of Social Science
Leninskii ave. 14
GSP 1
119991 Moscow, Russia
Ph: 7 95 938 0309
Fax: 7 95 938 1844
E-mail: info@pran.ru
URL: http://www.ras.ru

5881 ■ Alexander Sergeovich Pushkin Prize
To recognize Soviet scientists for outstanding work in the Russian language and literature. A monetary prize of 2,000 rubles is awarded triennially. Established in 1969. Administered by the Division of Literature and Language.

5882 ■ Russian Council of Shopping Centers
Oleg Voytsekhovskiy, Managing Dir.
PO Box 48
125315 Moscow, Russia
Ph: 7 495 7999000
E-mail: voytsekhovsky@rcsc.ru
URL: http://www.icsc.org/about/affiliates_russia.php

5883 ■ Shopping Center Awards
To recognize the best performance in the shopping center industry. Awards are presented in four categories: small shopping centers, medium shopping centers, large shopping centers, and superregional shopping centers. In addition, outstanding consultants and individuals are recognized. Awarded annually.

5884 ■ World Trade Center Moscow
Mr. Valery M. Serov, Dir. Gen.
Krasnopresnenskaya nab., 12
123610 Moscow, Russia
Ph: 7 495 2581212
Ph: 7 495 2538252
Fax: 7 495 2531041
E-mail: sb@wtc.msk.ru
URL: http://www.wtcmoscow.ru

5885 ■ Order of Hospitality
For distinction in work.

Rwanda

5886 ■ Imbuto Foundation
Kigali, Rwanda
Ph: 250 5906 2082
E-mail: info@www.imbutofoundation.org
URL: http://www.imbutofoundation.org

5887 ■ Celebrating Young Rwandan Achievers Award CYRWA
To recognize outstanding young Rwandans who strive toward the highest levels of personal and professional accomplishment, who excel in their chosen field, devote time and energy to their community in a meaningful way, and forge paths of leadership for all Rwandan youth to follow. Candidates must be aged between 18 and 35 years, and of Rwandan nationality, living in Rwanda or abroad. Awarded annually.

5888 ■ Rwanda Development Board
Blvd. de l'Umuganda
Gishushu, Nyarutarama Rd.
PO Box 6239
Kigali, Rwanda
Fax: 250 252 580388
E-mail: info@rdb.rw
URL: http://www.rdb.rw

5889 ■ Business Excellence Awards
To recognize the achievement of businesses, individuals, and small and medium enterprises (SMEs) that have made an outstanding contribution to Rwanda's economic growth. Presented in a variety of sector categories as well as special categories. In addition, special awards are presented for Investor of the Year, Exporter of the Year, and SME of the Year. Awarded annually.

St. Lucia

5890 ■ Government of St. Lucia
Greaham Louisy Administrative Bldg.
Waterfront
Castries, St. Lucia
Ph: 758468-2116
Fax: 758453-1614
E-mail: info@dis.gov.lc
URL: http://www.stlucia.gov.lc

5891 ■ Grand Cross of the Order of Saint Lucia
To honor the individual appointed to the office of Governor-General of St. Lucia. A gold medal is awarded when merited.

5892 ■ Les Pitons Medal of the Order of Saint Lucia
To honor an individual who has performed long and meritorious service to St. Lucia tending to promote loyal public service, national welfare, or inculcate and strengthen community spirit. A bronze, silver, or gold medal is awarded when merited.

5893 ■ Medal of Honour of the Order of Saint Lucia
To honor an individual who has rendered eminent service of national importance to St. Lucia or who has performed an outstanding brave or humane act to a national of St. Lucia or other country. A silver or gold medal is awarded when merited.

5894 ■ Medal of Merit of the Order of Saint Lucia
To honor an individual who has performed long and meritorious service to St. Lucia in the fields of arts, sciences, literature, or other such fields. A silver or gold medal is awarded when merited.

5895 ■ National Service Cross of the Order of Saint Lucia
To honor an officer who has rendered loyal and devoted service beneficial to Saint Lucia. Candidates may be officers of the Royal Saint Lucia Police Force not below the rank of Assistant Superintendent, an Officer of the Fire Service not below the rank of Deputy Fire Chief, or an Officer of the Prison Service not below the rank of Deputy Chief Prisons Officer. A medal is awarded when merited.

5896 ■ National Service Medal of the Order of Saint Lucia
To honor an individual for outstanding and meritorious service to members of the Royal Saint Lucia Police Force, the Saint Lucia Fire Service, the Saint Lucia Prison Service, and Commissioned officers of a Cadet Corps. A medal is awarded to up to four individuals annually.

5897 ■ St. Lucia Cross
To honor an individual who has rendered distinguished and outstanding service of national importance to St. Lucia. A gold medal is awarded when merited. The number of recipients is limited to 25 at any given time.

5898 ■ St. Lucia Music Awards
Vide Boutielle
PO Box 1058
Castries, St. Lucia

Awards are arranged in alphabetical order below their administering organizations

Ph: 758452-6299
Fax: 758452-7571
URL: http://www.stluciamusicawards.org

5899 ■ St. Lucia Music Awards
To foster the development of the national musical industry by recognizing the works of writers, performers, and producers, and to encourage the continued quest for excellence by St. Lucians involved in the industry. Awards are presented in 22 categories. Held annually in February.

Saudi Arabia

5900 ■ Islamic Development Bank
Dr. Ahmad Mohamed Ali, Pres.
PO Box 5925
Jeddah 21432, Saudi Arabia
Ph: 966 2 6361400
Fax: 966 2 6366871
E-mail: idbarchives@isdb.org
URL: http://www.isdb.org

5901 ■ Prize for Science and Technology
To recognize the critical role that science and technology plays in socio-economic development, and to encourage the development and implementation of relevant projects and programs in IDB member countries. A trophy, certificate, and monetary prize of US$100,000 is awarded to three institutions annually.

5902 ■ Prizes in Islamic Economics and Islamic Banking
To recognize, reward, and encourage creative efforts of outstanding merit in the fields of Islamic economics and Islamic banking. Such efforts may take the form of research, teaching, training, mobilization of intellectual and scientific capabilities that would contribute to the promotion of Islamic values in economics and banking, or any other related activity. Individuals, universities, academic, financial, and Islamic institutions throughout the world may nominate whoever they deem eligible. One prize is awarded annually, alternating between Islamic economics and Islamic banking. A monetary award of 30,000 Islamic dinars and a citation are awarded for each. Established in 1986.

5903 ■ King Fahd University of Petroleum and Minerals
Center for Environment and Water
Dr. Alaadin A. Bukhari, Dir.
PO Box 5040
Dhahran 31261, Saudi Arabia
Ph: 966 3 860 3232
Fax: 966 3 860 3220
E-mail: cew@kfupm.edu.sa
URL: http://www.kfupm.edu.sa/ri/cew

5904 ■ Best Technical and/or Administrative Services Award

5905 ■ Distinguished Applied Research Manager
To an employee on his or her outstanding performance in project management.

5906 ■ Distinguished Applied Research Team
To a research team on successful completion of a project with great significance.

5907 ■ Distinguished Applied Researcher
Given to an employee on his or her outstanding performance in research.

5908 ■ Organization of Islamic Capitals and Cities
(Organisation des Capitales et des Villes Islamiques)
PO Box 13621
Jeddah 21414, Saudi Arabia
Ph: 966 2 69821414

Fax: 966 2 6981053
E-mail: secrtriat@oicc.org
URL: http://www.oicc.org
Formerly: (1984) Islamic Capitals Organization.

5909 ■ Organization of Islamic Capitals and Cities Awards
To recognize outstanding achievements in the domains of writing, accomplishments, translation, and projects in the fields of architecture, urban planning, environment, services, organization, and municipal legislation. They aim at encouraging municipalities and local authorities and individuals to contribute effectively to the achievement of sustainable urban development and the preservation of the heritage and the identity of Islamic cities. Prizes are awarded every three years.

Serbia

5910 ■ Chamber of Commerce and Economy of Serbia
Slobodan Milosavljevic, Pres.
Resavska 13-15
Y-11000 Belgrade, Serbia
Ph: 381 11 3300900
Fax: 381 11 3230949
E-mail: pks@pks.co.yu
URL: http://www.pks.co.yu

5911 ■ Award of the Serbian Chamber of Commerce
To honor an outstanding individual contribution in the development and improvement of the economy of the Republic of Serbia. A plaque and monetary prize are awarded annually.

5912 ■ International Board on Books for Young People - Serbian National Section
Ms. Vuk Vukicevic, Liaison Off.
Dimitrija Tucovica 41
11000 Belgrade, Serbia
Ph: 381 11 4121359
Fax: 381 11 4121359
E-mail: sekretar@izdavaci.rs
URL: http://www.ibbyserbia.org

5913 ■ Dusko Radovic Prize
To honor the best children's book written in a given year by a Serbian author.

5914 ■ International Institute for the Science of Sintering
Ms. Maria V. Nikolic, Assoc. Ed.
PO Box 315
Knez-Mihailova 35/IV
YU-11001 Belgrade, Serbia
Ph: 38 11 2637367
Ph: 38 11 2637239
Fax: 38 11 2637239
E-mail: scisint@sanu.ac.rs
URL: http://www.iiss.sanu.ac.rs

5915 ■ Frenkel Prize
For extraordinary contribution to the science of sintering.

5916 ■ Kuczynski Prize
For the paper that is considered to be a particular contribution to the sintering theory.

5917 ■ Samsonov Prize
For the best paper published in the journal, *Science of Sintering*.

Singapore

5918 ■ Asia-Pacific Council of American Chambers of Commerce
Walter Blocker, CEO/Chm.
Pacific Architects & Engineers
1 Scotts Rd., No. 19-01

Singapore 228208, Singapore
Ph: 65 7373600
Fax: 65 7373476
URL: http://www.apcac.org

5919 ■ APCAC Award
To recognize an individual or organization that has made an outstanding contribution to furthering U.S. business interests in the Asia-Pacific region. Awarded annually.

5920 ■ Asian and Pacific Federation of Clinical Biochemistry
Joseph B. Lopez, Pres.
150 Cecil St., No. 10-06
Singapore 069543, Singapore
Ph: 65 62239118
Fax: 65 62239131
E-mail: consulting@solidtract.com.sg
URL: http://www.apfcb.org

5921 ■ BD AFCB Distinguished Service Award
For outstanding contribution to APFCB for the advancement of clinical biochemistry in the Asia-Pacific region.

5922 ■ The Asian Banker
10 Hoe Chiang Rd.
No. 14-06 Keppel Tower
Singapore 089315, Singapore
Ph: 65 6236 6500
Fax: 65 6236 6530
E-mail: adm@theasianbanker.com
URL: http://www.theasianbanker.com

5923 ■ Best Retail Bank by Country Awards
To recognize the best retail bank in each country in Central Asia, the Gulf Region, and Asia Pacific. Awarded annually as part of the Excellence in Retail Financial Services International Awards.

5924 ■ Best Retail Bank in Asia Pacific
Recognizes the retail bank deemed to be the best in the Asia Pacific region. Awarded annually as part of the Excellence in Retail Financial Services International Awards. Established in 2004.

5925 ■ Best Retail Bank in Central Asia
Recognizes the retail bank deemed to be the best in Central Asia. Awarded annually as part of the Excellence in Retail Financial Services International Awards. Established in 2007.

5926 ■ Best Retail Bank in the Gulf States
Recognizes the retail bank deemed to be the best in the Gulf region. Awarded annually as part of the Excellence in Retail Financial Services International Awards. Established in 2007.

5927 ■ Most Admired Bank
Recognizes the best bank outside of the Asia Pacific, Central Asia, and Gulf regions. Winner is determined by a vote of the Asian retail community. Awarded annually as part of the Excellence in Retail Financial Services International Awards. Established in 2007.

5928 ■ Products and Processes Awards
Recognizes excellence in a product or process released during the previous year by a single player in the Asia Pacific, Central Asia, and Gulf region. Awarded in more than 20 categories, including Payment Products, Automobile Lending, Microfinance, and Credit Collection. Awarded annually as part of the Excellence in Retail Financial Services International Awards.

5929 ■ Special Banking Awards
To recognize excellence in key strategic areas to the financial services industry. Presented in several categories, including Best Customer Relationship Management, Best Brand Building

Awards are arranged in alphabetical order below their administering organizations

Initiative, and Best Business Model. Awarded annually as part of the Excellence in Retail Financial Services International Awards.

5930 ■ Association of Accredited Advertising Agents Singapore
Ms. Chua Bee Hong, Contact
Marsh & McLennan Centre
18 Cross St., No. 07-05
Singapore 069545, Singapore
Ph: 65 68360600
Fax: 65 68360700
E-mail: info@4as.org.sg
URL: http://www.4as.org.sg

5931 ■ Creative Circle Awards
To honor the best in creative communications in four disciplines: advertising, design, direct marketing/promotional, and interactive. Awarded annually. Established in 1980.

5932 ■ Crowbar Awards
To honor emerging talent in creative communications and design. Awards are presented in six categories: advertising, design, interactive, photography, film, and the Crowbar Challenge. Awarded annually. Established in 2001.

5933 ■ Association of Chartered Certified Accountants - Singapore
Ho Yew Mun, Pres.
435 Orchard Rd.
No. 15-04/05, Wisma Atria
Singapore 238877, Singapore
Ph: 65 67348110
Fax: 65 67342248
E-mail: info@sg.accaglobal.com
URL: http://singapore.accaglobal.com

5934 ■ ACCA Singapore Awards for Sustainability Reporting
To recognize organizations that report and disclose environmental, social, and full sustainability information; to encourage the uptake of such reporting; and to raise awareness of corporate transparency issues. Awarded annually. Established in 2003. Formerly: Singapore Environmental and Social Reporting Awards.

5935 ■ Dermatological Society of Singapore
Dr. Chan Yuin Chew, Pres.
Bukit Timah Post Office
PO Box 310
Singapore 915811, Singapore
Ph: 65 91294583
E-mail: info@dermatology.org.sg
URL: http://www.dermatology.org.sg

5936 ■ Book Prize
To recognize the final-year medical student with the highest score on the dermatology examination. Awarded annually. Established in 1974.

5937 ■ V.S. Rajan Gold Medal
To recognize the final year medical student with outstanding results in the dermatology examination conducted by the National University of Singapore. The student with the second-highest score is awarded the Book Prize. Awarded annually.

5938 ■ V.S. Rajan Memorial Fund
To provide financial support to members of the medical and allied professions to conduct research in the field of dermatology. Established in 1983.

5939 ■ Franchising and Licensing Association Singapore
Dr. T. Chandroo, Chm./CEO
32 Maxwell Rd., No. 02-14
Singapore 069115, Singapore
Ph: 65 63330292
Fax: 65 63330962

E-mail: enquiry@flasingapore.org
URL: http://www.flasingapore.org

5940 ■ Franchisor of the Year
To recognize and reward the most thriving franchising business in Singapore. A trophy is awarded annually.

5941 ■ Promising Franchisor of the Year
To recognize a new franchisor who shows the most promise to succeed and make an indelible mark on the franchising scene in Singapore. A trophy is awarded annually.

5942 ■ Freedom to Create Prize
UOB Plaza 1, Level 46
80 Raffles Pl.
Singapore 048624, Singapore
Ph: 65 6210 5560
E-mail: info@freedomtocreateprize.com
URL: http://www.freedomtocreateprize.com

5943 ■ Freedom to Create Prize
To celebrate the courage and creativity of artists around the world who use their talents to build the foundations for open societies and inspire the human spirit. Open to artists in all creative fields. Awards are presented in three categories: the Main Prize of US$75,000, the Youth Prize of US$25,000, and the Imprisoned Artist Prize of US$25,000. Awarded annually. Established in 2008.

5944 ■ Global Scholars and Leaders Council
Office of Admissions and Financial Aid
10 Anson Rd.
No. 10-15 International Plz.
Singapore 079903, Singapore
E-mail: admissions@global-leaders.org
URL: http://www.global-leaders.org

5945 ■ Founders' Award
To recognize school chapter founders, presidents, and vice-presidents for extraordinary excellence in leadership. Awarded when merited.

5946 ■ Global Youth Excellence Awards, an International Award Scheme
To inspire and challenge students around the world to achieve their full scholastic and leadership potentials. Open to all young people between the age of 14 and 30 years. To participate, students must first obtain the Global Scholar's Record Book. They must then complete four Sections, demonstrating Character, Leadership, Scholarship, and Service (the additional Section of Allegiance/Citizenship is required for platinum level). Awards are presented in four levels: Bronze (eligible for students over 14 years old), Silver (for students over 15), Gold (for students over 16), and Platinum (for students over 17). Awarded twice each year to all qualifying students.

5947 ■ International Federation of Interior Architects/Designers (Federation Internationale des Architectes d'Interieur)
Shashi Caan, Pres.
317 Outram Rd.
No. 02-57 Concorde Shopping Ctre.
Singapore 169075, Singapore
Ph: 65 63386974
Fax: 65 63386730
E-mail: info@ifiworld.org
URL: http://www.ifiworld.org

5948 ■ Design Excellence Awards
To recognize the best examples of interior design excellence from around the world. Categories include residential, corporate, retail, leisure and hospitality, healthcare, public design, and sustainable design. Awarded biennially in odd-numbered years. Established in 1985.

5949 ■ Design for All Award
To promote the work of interior architects and

designers in the field of socially responsible and sustainable design. Awarded biennially in odd-numbered years. Established in 2003.

5950 ■ International Water Association, Singapore National Committee
Tang Kin Fei, Pres.
80 Toh Guan Rd. E
Training Block, 3rd Fl.
Singapore 608575, Singapore
Ph: 65 65150812
Fax: 65 65150813
E-mail: enquiry@swa.org.sg
URL: http://www.swa.org.sg

5951 ■ Honorary Member
Recognizes outstanding contribution in the field of environmental engineering. Awarded periodically to one or more recipients.

5952 ■ National Book Development Council of Singapore
Ms. Serene Wee, Chair
50 Geylang E Ave. 1
Singapore 389777, Singapore
Ph: 65 68488290
Fax: 65 67429466
E-mail: info@bookcouncil.sg
URL: http://www.bookcouncil.sg

5953 ■ Book Awards
To encourage and develop Singapore literary talent and to give recognition to excellence in writing. Awards are presented in five categories (fiction, non-fiction, poetry, children and young people, and drama) in each of the four official languages (Chinese, English, Malay, and Tamil). Awarded biennially in even-numbered years. Established in 1972.

5954 ■ Singapore Literature Prize
To provide incentives and public support for creative writing in Singapore, and to promote Singapore literary talent through recognition to outstanding published works by Singapore authors in any of the four official languages (Chinese, English, Malay, and Tamil). Open to Singapore citizens and permanent residents of Singapore who are at least 18 years old. A monetary prize of $10,000 is awarded in each of the four categories. In the event there is no winner, a Merit Prize of $5,000 or a Commendation prize of $1,000 is awarded. Awarded biennially in even-numbered years. Established in 1991.

5955 ■ National University of Singapore
21 Lower Kent Ridge Rd.
Singapore 119077, Singapore
Ph: 65 6516 6666
URL: http://www.nus.edu.sg

5956 ■ Emeritus Professor
To recognize an individual for distinguished scholarship and outstanding service to the University. The title of Emeritus Professor is conferred when merited.

5957 ■ Outstanding Service Award
To recognize a member of the University community for sustained meritorious service rendered to the department, faculty, university, national and/or international communities, as well as to governmental and non-governmental organizations. Awarded annually.

5958 ■ Special Commendation
To honor an individual or group of people for exceptional achievements. Awarded when merited.

5959 ■ National University of Singapore Centre for Development of Teaching and Learning
10 Kent Ridge Crescent
Singapore 119260, Singapore
Ph: 65 6516 2071

Awards are arranged in alphabetical order below their administering organizations

Fax: 65 6777 0342
E-mail: cdtsec@nus.edu.sg
URL: http://www.cdtl.nus.edu.sg

5960 ■ Annual Teaching Excellence Award
To recognize faculty members who have displayed a high level of commitment to their teaching. Awarded annually to one or more recipients. Individuals who win this award three times are placed on the Honour Roll.

5961 ■ Outstanding Educator Award
To recognize faculty members who have excelled in engaging and inspiring students in their discovery of knowledge. A monetary prize and teaching grant are awarded annually to one or more recipients.

5962 ■ National University of Singapore Division of Research and Technology
University Hall, UHL-05-02J
21 Lower Kent Ridge Rd.
Singapore 119077, Singapore
Ph: 65 6516 6666
Fax: 65 6775 6467
E-mail: dprmyn@nus.edu.sg
URL: http://www.nus.edu.sg/dpr

5963 ■ Outstanding Researcher Award
To recognize researchers for research excellence over a period of time and for having achieved significant breakthroughs or outstanding accomplishments in his or her field. Each year, a cash prize of S$3,000 and a research grant of S$15,000 are awarded. Established in 1997.

5964 ■ Young Researcher Award
To honor researchers below 40 years of age based on their potential impact in their respective areas of research. Each year, a cash prize of S$2000 and a research grant of S$10,000 are awarded. Established in 1997.

5965 ■ Securities Investors Association - Singapore
Mr. David Gerald, Pres.
7 Maxwell Rd. No. 05-03
MND Bldg. Annex B
Singapore 088902, Singapore
Ph: 65 62272683
Fax: 65 62206614
E-mail: admin@sias.org.sg
URL: http://www.sias.org.sg

5966 ■ Best Financial Journalist of the Year
To honor a journalist who makes an impact on improving the investing environment of investors. Awarded annually.

5967 ■ Model Shareholder of the Year Award
To shareholder who serves as a good role model for investors.

5968 ■ Most Transparent Company Award
To encourage public listed companies to be more transparent so as to help investors make informed decisions on their investments. Candidates are judged on timeliness, sustainability, clarity of news release, degree of media access, and availability of segmental information and communication channels. Awarded annually. Established in 2000.

5969 ■ Singapore Corporate Governance Award
To honor companies who strive to embrace the Code of Corporate Governance, which contains the best corporate governance practices and serves as a model and benchmark for Singapore companies. Awarded annually. Established in 2003.

5970 ■ Singapore Association of Administrative Professionals
Josephine Kwan, Honorary Sec.
20 Maxwell Rd.
No. 08-06 Maxwell House
Singapore 069113, Singapore
Ph: 65 63237523
Fax: 65 63237591
E-mail: admin@saap.org.sg
URL: http://www.saap.org.sg

5971 ■ Administrative Professionals Award
For contributions to organizational performance, productivity and community development. Formerly: Professional Secretary Award.

5972 ■ Singapore Exhibition Services Pte. Ltd.
Stephen Tan, CEO
Pacific Tech Centre
No. 1 Jalan Kilang Timor, No. 09-02
Singapore 159303, Singapore
Ph: 65 6233 6638
Fax: 65 6233 6633
E-mail: events@sesallworld.com
URL: http://www.sesallworld.com

5973 ■ FHA Culinary Challenge
To recognize outstanding culinary ability. The following competition components are featured: National Team Challenge, Gourmet Team Challenge, Dream Team Challenge, and Individual Challenge. Held biennially in even-numbered years. Formerly: (2006) FHA International Salon Culinaire.

5974 ■ Singapore Industrial Automation Association
Dr. Tan Guan Hong, Pres.
1010 Dover Rd., No. 03-17
Singapore 139658, Singapore
Ph: 65 67491822
Fax: 65 68413986
E-mail: secretariat@siaa.org
URL: http://www.siaa.org

5975 ■ Asia Pacific Industrial Technologies Awards
To recognize outstanding performance by companies in the electronics and security, industrial automation and process control, energy and power systems, chemicals materials and food industries, as well as new and emerging technologies across these industries. Awarded annually. Established in 2006.

5976 ■ Singapore Infocomm Technology Federation
Tan Yen Yen, Chair
SITF House
55/55A Neil Rd.
Singapore 088892, Singapore
Ph: 65 63259700
Ph: 65 63259710
Fax: 65 63254993
E-mail: info@sitf.org.sg
URL: http://www.sitf.org.sg

5977 ■ Infocomm Singapore Awards
To recognize and encourage local infocomm technologies to grow beyond the shores of Singapore. Presented in 16 categories. Awarded biennially in even-numbered years.

5978 ■ Singapore Institute of Food Science and Technology
Mrs. Ser-Low Wai Ming, Pres.
93 Toa Payoh Central, No. 05-01
Toa Payoh Community Bldg.
Singapore 319194, Singapore
Ph: 65 6 7721120
Ph: 65 6 5501523
Fax: 65 6 2524533
E-mail: admin@sifst.org.sg
URL: http://www.sifst.org.sg

5979 ■ Best Product Award
To honor the best food product in Singapore. Open to local food companies as well as overseas establishments that are either owned by Singaporeans or Singapore companies. Awarded annually.

5980 ■ Healthier Choice Award
To honor the best health food product in Singapore. Open to local food companies as well as overseas establishments that are either owned by Singaporeans or Singapore companies. Awarded annually.

5981 ■ Innovation Awards
To honor the most original and creativity of a food product in Singapore. Open to local food companies as well as overseas establishments that are either owned by Singaporeans or Singapore companies. Awarded annually.

5982 ■ Singapore National Olympic Council
Mr. Chris Chan, Sec. Gen.
230 National Stadium Blvd.
Singapore 397799, Singapore
Ph: 65 6 3459273
Fax: 65 6 3459274
E-mail: admin@snoc.org.sg
URL: http://www.snoc.org.sg

5983 ■ Singapore Sports Awards
To recognize the achievements of sportsmen and sportswomen locally, regionally, and internationally. Awards include: Sportsman of the Year, Sportswoman of the Year, Sportsboy of the Year, Sportsgirl of the Year, Team of the Year, Junior Team of the Year, Coach of the Year, Meritorious Award, and a Special Award. Awarded annually. Established in 1967.

5984 ■ Singapore Psychological Society
Col. Bernard Lim PhD, Pres.
93 Toa Payo Central, No. 05-01
Toa Payoh Central Community Bldg.
Singapore 319194, Singapore
E-mail: enquiries@singaporepsychologicalsociety.org
URL: http://singaporepsychologicalsociety.org

5985 ■ Award for Outstanding Contribution to Psychology in Singapore
To honor psychologists working in Singapore for outstanding achievements in the field of psychology. Awarded annually. Established in 2003.

5986 ■ Singapore Retailers Association
Jannie Chan, Pres.
371 Beach Rd., No. 02-04/05
Singapore 199597, Singapore
Ph: 65 62952622
Fax: 65 62952722
E-mail: info@sra.org.sg
URL: http://www.retail.org.sg

5987 ■ Retail Industry Awards
To recognize retailers for the impact they have made on the retail landscape in Singapore. The following awards are presented: Best New Entrant of the Year, Best Retail Concept of the Year, Best Retail Event of the Year, Retail Manager of the Year, and Young Retail Executive of the Year. Trophies are awarded annually. In addition, the winners of the Retail Manager of the Year and Young Retail Executive of the Year receive a S$4,000 educational reward. Awarded annually. Established in 2000.

5988 ■ Tan Kah Kee Foundation
Level 1, 43 Bukit Pasoh Rd.
Singapore 089856, Singapore
E-mail: tkkf@tkkfoundation.org.sg

Awards are arranged in alphabetical order below their administering organizations

URL: http://www.tkk.wspc.com.sg

5989 ■ Young Inventors' Award
To stimulate creativity among young Singaporeans and to promote scientific and technological research in Singapore. Categories include Junior, Student, Senior, Open, and Defense Science. Awarded annually. Established in 1987.

5990 ■ Ten Alps Communications Asia
Fiona Lawson-Baker, Contact
Ubi Ave. 1
No. 06-06 Starhub Green (North Wing)
Singapore 408942, Singapore
Ph: 65 6521 9777
Fax: 65 6521 9788
E-mail: fionalb@tenalpsasia.com
URL: http://www.tenalpsasia.com

5991 ■ Asian Television Awards
To showcase and reward the best in television programming from throughout the Asia Pacific region. Awarded annually in more than 30 categories. Established in 1996.

5992 ■ World Organization of Family Doctors
Dr. Alfred W.T. Loh, CEO
7500-A Beach Rd., No. 12
303 The Plz.
Singapore 199591, Singapore
Ph: 65 62242886
Fax: 65 63242029
E-mail: admin@wonca.com.sg
URL: http://www.globalfamilydoctor.com

5993 ■ WONCA Foundation Award
To foster and maintain high standards of care in general practice/family medicine by enabling physicians to travel to appropriate countries to instruct in general practice/family medicine, and appropriate physicians from developing countries to spend time in areas where they may develop special skills and knowledge in general practice/family medicine. Awarded triennially at the world conference. Established by a donation from the Royal College of General Practitioners.

Slovakia

5994 ■ Bibiana, International House of Art for Children
Peter Cacko, Dir.
Panska ul. 41
815 39 Bratislava, Slovakia
Ph: 421 2 5443 4986
Fax: 421 2 5443 4986
E-mail: bibiana@bibiana.sk
URL: http://www.bibiana.sk

5995 ■ Biennial of Animation Bratislava
Also known as the International Festival of Animated Films for Children, this program recognizes outstanding animated films for children. Several prizes are awarded, including the Viktor Kubal Prize for the best film; Albin Brunovsky Honorary Medal to authors of animated films for their outstanding contributions to animated film production; and the Prix Klingsor, which is presented as a life achievement award. Held biennially in even-numbered years.

5996 ■ The Most Beautiful and the Best Children's Books in Slovakia
To recognize Slovak publishing companies for the most artistically valuable books produced for children and youth. A plaque is awarded each spring, summer, autumn, and winter. Established in 1990.

5997 ■ International Commission on Glass
Peter Simurka, Exec. Sec.
c/o Slovak Glass Society
Nabrezna 5
911 01 Trencin, Slovakia

E-mail: psimurka@stonline.sk
URL: http://www.icg.group.shef.ac.uk

5998 ■ Gottardi Prize
To recognize young individuals with outstanding achievements in the field of glass research and development, teaching, writing, management, or commerce. Awarded annually. Established in 1987 in memory of Prof. V. Gottardi.

5999 ■ President's Award
To recognize outstanding lifetime contributions to the international glass community in areas such as scientific discoveries, engineering developments, artistic accomplishments leadership, and communications. Awarded triennially. Established in 1995.

6000 ■ Turner Award
To recognize an individual who has made a noteworthy contribution to the ICG Technical Committees. Awarded annually. Established in 2002.

6001 ■ Woldemar A. Weyl International Glass Science Award
To recognize an outstanding young scientist working in glass research. Awarded triennially. Established in 1976.

6002 ■ Office of the President of the Slovak Republic
Hodzovo nam. 1
PO Box 128
810 00 Bratislava, Slovakia
E-mail: informacie@prezident.sk
URL: http://www.prezident.sk

6003 ■ Medal for Bravery
To honor an individual for acts of bravery. Awarded when merited.

6004 ■ Order of the White Double Cross
To honor citizens of other countries for extraordinary service to the Slovak Republic. A medal is awarded in three classes when merited.

6005 ■ Pribina Cross
To honor citizens of the Slovak Republic for outstanding economic, social, or cultural service to the nation. A medal is awarded in three classes when merited.

6006 ■ M.R. Stefanik Cross
To honor individuals for outstanding service to the Slovak Republic. A medal is awarded in three classes when merited.

6007 ■ L'Udovit Stur Order
To honor individuals for outstanding service to the Slovak Republic. A medal is awarded in three classes when merited.

Slovenia

6008 ■ International Centre of Graphic Arts (Mednarodni Graficni Likovni Center)
Lili Sturm, Contact
Pod turnom 3
SLO-1000 Ljubljana, Slovenia
Ph: 386 1 2413800
Fax: 386 1 2413821
E-mail: lili.sturm@mglc-lj.si
URL: http://www.mglc-lj.si

6009 ■ International Biennial of Graphic Art (Biennale Internationale de Gravure)
For recognition of achievement in the field of graphic art. Both black-and-white and color reproductive printmaking techniques (monotype excluded) are taken into consideration, regardless of style and technical execution. Medals are awarded for the Grand Prix and for second and third prizes. The Grand Prix d'Honneur (Grand Prize of Honor) is given to artists who prove their

constant high level during the years of participating. Held biennially in odd-numbered years. Established in 1955.

6010 ■ Slovenia Ministry of Higher Education, Science and Technology
Metrology Institute of the Republic of Slovenia
Tkalaka ulica 15
SI-3000 Celje, Slovenia
Ph: 386 3 428 0750
Fax: 386 3 428 0760
E-mail: gp.mirs@gov.si
URL: http://www.mirs.gov.si

6011 ■ National Quality Award
To recognize the quality of business excellence as a result of the development of knowledge and innovation. A certificate and statuette are awarded annually.

6012 ■ Slovenian Business Excellence Prize
To recognize achievements in the field of quality of products and services. A certificate and statuette are awarded annually.

6013 ■ Tourism and Hospitality Chamber of Slovenia
Ms. Majda Dekleva, Contact
Society and Industry of Slovenia
Dimiceva 13
SI-1504 Ljubljana, Slovenia
Ph: 386 1 5898225
Ph: 386 1 5898000
Fax: 386 1 5898224
URL: http://www.gzs.si/slo

6014 ■ Achievement Award
To recognize individuals for exemplary business and entrepreneurial achievements. Awarded annually to approximately six recipients. Established in 1969.

6015 ■ Union of Associations of Slovene Librarians
(Zveza Bibliotekarskih Drustev Slovenije)
Melita Ambrozic PhD, Pres.
Turjaska 1
SI-1000 Ljubljana, Slovenia
Ph: 386 1 2001207
Fax: 386 1 4257293
E-mail: zbds2010@gmail.com
URL: http://www.zbds-zveza.si

6016 ■ Copova Diploma
For recognition of an outstanding contribution in the field of libraries. Members of the Association are eligible. A plaque and a diploma are awarded annually. Established in 1967 in honor of Matija Cop (1797-1835), Slovenian librarian.

6017 ■ Pavle Kalan Fund Award
To recognize the best written text in the field of library information systems. A biennial award and grant established in 1974 in honor of Pavle Kalan (1900-1974), Slovenian librarian.

6018 ■ Stepinsnki Fund Award
Award that encourages the development and professional work in the field of mobile librarianship. Awarded to main libraries for a specific professional achievement. Established in honor of the first Slovene librarian, Lovro Stepisnik (1834-1912).

Spain

6019 ■ Barcelona Graduate School of Economics
Ramon Trias Fargas, 25-27
08005 Barcelona, Spain
Ph: 34 93 542 1222
Fax: 34 93 542 1223
E-mail: info@barcelonagse.eu

Awards are arranged in alphabetical order below their administering organizations

URL: http://www.barcelonagse.eu

6020 ■ Calvo-Armengol International Prize

To recognize a young economist or social scientist for his or her contributions to the understanding of social structure and its implications for economic interactions. Open to individuals 40 years of age or younger. A monetary prize of 30,000 Euros is awarded biennially in even-numbered years. Established in 2009 in memory of Toni Calvo-Armengol, affiliated professor at the Barcelona Graduate School of Economics.

6021 ■ Editorial Planeta SA
Diagonal, 662-664
E-08034 Barcelona, Spain
Ph: 34 93 2285 800
Fax: 34 93 2177 140
URL: http://www.editorial.planeta.es

6022 ■ Azorin Prize
To recognize a novel written in Spanish. Awarded annually. Established in 1994.

6023 ■ Premi de les Lletres Catalanes Ramon Llull
To recognize an author of any nationality for an outstanding novel of at least 200 pages, written in Catalonian Spanish, and to promote the production of novels in Catalonian Spanish. A monetary prize is awarded annually. Established in 1968, and re-established in 1980.

6024 ■ Premio de Novela Fernando Lara
Annual award of recognition. Established by the Jose Manuel Lara Foundation and Editorial Planeta in 1996. Named in honor of the youngest son of Jose Manuel Lara Hernandez.

6025 ■ Premio Planeta de Novela
For recognition of the best unpublished novel. Writers of Spanish speaking countries who write in Castillian Spanish are eligible. The prize must be awarded each year. Established in 1952 by Jose Manuel Lara Hernandez, director of Editorial Planeta.

6026 ■ European Society of Rheology
Prof. Crispulo Gallegos, Pres.
Universidad de Huelva
Campus del Carmen
Facultad de Ciencias Experimentales
21071 Huelva, Spain
Ph: 34 959219987
Fax: 34 959219983
E-mail: cgallego@uhu.es
URL: http://www.rheology-esr.org

6027 ■ Weissenberg Award
To honor rheologists with outstanding and long-term achievements in rheology. A bronze statuette is awarded annually.

6028 ■ European Software Institute
Mr. Manu Prego, Managing Dir.
Parque Tecnologico de Zamudio, No. 204
Zamudio
E-48170 Bizkaia, Spain
Ph: 34 94 4209519
Fax: 34 94 4209420
E-mail: info@esi.es
URL: http://www.esi.es

6029 ■ Awards for Software Excellence
To recognize efforts made by companies in software process improvement and with a visible commitment to continuous improvement. A glass trophy is awarded in four categories: International; European; SME; and Cluster Approach Project.

6030 ■ European Survey Research Association
Wiebke Weber, Contact
Passeig de Circumval lacio 8
Edifici Franca, Despatx 70.380

Universitat Pompeu Fabra
E-08003 Barcelona, Spain
E-mail: esra@sqp.nl
URL: http://surveymethodology.eu

6031 ■ Early-Career Researcher Award
To recognize excellence in scholarly research by new researchers in the field of survey research, including research on: 1) theoretical issues in survey methodology; 2) the use of statistical techniques in the design, adjustment, or analysis of survey data; and 3) empirical applications of survey methodology. Candidates must have completed their PhD within the previous five years. A monetary prize of 600 Euros is awarded biennially in odd-numbered years. Established in 2010.

6032 ■ Federacion Empresarial de la Industria Quimica Espanola
Fernando Iturrieta, Pres.
Hermosilla 31
E-28001 Madrid, Spain
Ph: 34 91 4317964
Fax: 34 91 5763381
E-mail: info@feique.org
URL: http://www.feique.org

6033 ■ Science Education Award
For a member granted by a jury.

6034 ■ Film Festival of Huesca (Certamen Internacional de Films Cortos, Ciudad de Huesca)
Domingo Malo Arilla, Pres.
Avda. Parque 1, no. 2
E-22002 Huesca, Spain
Ph: 34 974 212582
Fax: 34 974 210065
E-mail: info@huesca-filmfestival.com
URL: http://www.huesca-filmfestival.com

6035 ■ Huesca International Short Film Contest (Certamen International de Films Cortos, Ciudad de Huesca)
To promote the diffusion of short films in Spain. Any Spanish foreign short film accepted by the Selection Committee can take part in the Contest. Although there are no restrictions in the choice of theme, those that deal exclusively with tourism or publicity cannot be presented. The following prizes are awarded annually: Danzante Award - 10,000 Euros; Special Prize of the Jury - 3,000 Euros; Youth Jury Award - 5,000 Euros; and the Francisco Garcia de Paso Award.

6036 ■ International Association for Engineering Geology and the Environment (Association Internationale de Geologie de l'Ingenieur)
Prof. Carlos Delgado, Pres.
Escuela Universitaria de Ingenieria
Tecnica de Obras Publicas
Calle Alfonso XII, no 3 y 5
28014 Madrid, Spain
Ph: 34 91 3367757
Fax: 34 91 3367961
E-mail: carlos.delgado@upm.es
URL: http://www.iaeg.info

6037 ■ Hans Cloos Medal
To recognize an individual for outstanding contributions to engineering geology in his or her written papers or to the development of engineering geology and/or the Association in his or her field. Awarded biennially in even-numbered years. Established in 1977.

6038 ■ International Association for Shell and Spatial Structures (Association Internationale pour les Voiles Minces en Beton)
Marta Sanchez de Juan, Sec.
Laboratorio Central de Estructuras y Materiales
C/Alfonso XII, 3
28014 Madrid, Spain

Ph: 34 91 3357409
Fax: 34 91 3357422
E-mail: iass@cedex.es
URL: http://www.iass-structures.org

6039 ■ Eduardo Torroja Medal
To recognize outstanding and distinguished contributions to the development of the field of shell and spatial structures, and/or for exceptional service to the association. Awarded periodically. Established in honor of the founder of the Association.

6040 ■ International Association of Hydraulic Engineering and Research
Prof. Roger Falconer, Pres.
Paseo Bajo Virgen del Puerto, 3
28005 Madrid, Spain
Ph: 34 91 3357986
Ph: 34 91 3357908
Fax: 34 91 3357935
E-mail: iahr@iahr.org
URL: http://www.iahr.net/site/index.html

6041 ■ Honorary Member
For recognition of individuals who have made outstanding contributions to hydraulic research. Awarded biennially in odd-numbered years during IAHR Biennial Congresses.

6042 ■ Arthur Thomas Ippen Award
To recognize a member of IAHR who has developed an outstanding record of accomplishment as demonstrated by research, publications, and/or conception and design of significant engineering hydraulic works; and who holds great promise for a continuing level of productivity in the field of basic hydraulic research and/or applied hydraulic engineering. Preference is given to members under 45 years of age. An honorarium of $1,500 is awarded biennially in odd-numbered years. The recipient delivers the Arthur Thomas Ippen Lecture. Established in 1977 to honor Professor Ippen, IAHR President (1959-1963), IAHR Honorary Member (1963-1974), and for many decades an inspirational leader in fluids research, hydraulic engineering, and international cooperation and understanding.

6043 ■ John F. Kennedy Student Paper Competition
To recognize outstanding student papers. Selection is based on written and oral presentations. A monetary award and a plaque are awarded at the Congress closing ceremony. Additional monetary awards and certificates are presented to runners-up. Awarded biennially in odd-numbered years. Established in 1992 in memory of Professor John F. Kennedy, IAHR President (1979-1983) and honorary member (1989-1991), remembered particularly for his efforts to foster younger-member membership and participation.

6044 ■ Lecturer Award
To provide an institute of research or higher learning with an IAHR lecturer. The lecturer is appointed by the Secretary-General. The award consists of a maximum of US$2,500 travel allowance, an honorarium of US$2,500, and a certificate. Awarded annually. Established in 1985.

6045 ■ Harold Jan Schoemaker Award
To recognize the most outstanding paper that was published in the IAHR *Journal of Hydraulic Research* during the preceding two-year period. IAHR members may submit candidates for nomination by December 15. A bronze medal and a certificate are awarded biennially in odd-numbered years. Established in 1980 in memory of Prof. Schoemaker, Secretary (1960-1979) who guided the *Journal of Hydraulic Research* in its formative years.

6046 ■ M. Selim Yalin Lifetime Achievement Award
To honor a member whose experimental, theo-

Awards are arranged in alphabetical order below their administering organizations

retical, or numerical research has resulted in significant and enduring contributions to the understanding of the physics of phenomena and/or processes in hydraulic science and engineering, and who demonstrated outstanding skills in graduate teaching and supervision. A certificate and monetary prize are presented biennially in odd-numbered years. Established in 2006.

6047 ■ International Association of Volcanology and Chemistry of the Earth's Interior (Association Internationale de Volcanologie et de Chimie de l'Interieur de la Terre)
Ray Cas, Pres.
Rambla Principal, 19
Vilanova i la Geltru
08800 Barcelona, Spain
Ph: 34 938934020
Fax: 34 938934208
E-mail: ageyer@ija.csic.es
URL: http://www.iavcei.org

6048 ■ Honorary Membership
To honor individuals who have made outstanding contributions to the volcanological community, and in particular to the Association. Three individuals are recognized every four years at the General Assembly. Established in 2003.

6049 ■ Krafft Medal
To recognize outstanding contributions to volcanology through service to the scientific community or to communities threatened by volcanic activity. Awarded every four years. Established in honor of Katia and Maurice Krafft, who were killed while photographing a pyroclastic flow on Mount Unzen, Japan, in 1991.

6050 ■ Thorarinsson Medal
For recognition of excellence in volcanological research. A medal and $2,000 US for travel expenses is awarded every four years at the IAVCEI General Assembly. Established in 1987 in honor of Professor Sigurdur Thorarinsson of Reykjavik University.

6051 ■ Wager Medal
For recognition of outstanding contributions to the study of volcanic rocks. Scientists under 40 years of age on December 31 of the year preceding the award are eligible. A monetary prize of $2,000 US to attend the IAVCEI General Assembly, where the award is presented, is awarded every four years. Established in 1975 by the Volcanology Subcommittee of the Royal Society (London) to commemorate the work of the late Professor L. R. Wager. Formerly: (1994) Wager Prize.

6052 ■ George Walker Awards
To recognize the achievements of two outstanding recent graduates in the fields of research encompassed by IAVCEI. A monetary prize and a certificate are awarded every four years. Established in 2004.

6053 ■ International Commission for Optics (Commission Internationale d'Optique)
Mrs. Rosario de Cecilio, Admin. Sec.
Universida Complutense de Madrid
Departamento de Optica
Facultad de Fisicas
E-28040 Madrid, Spain
Ph: 34 91 3944555
Fax: 34 91 3944683
E-mail: rcecilio@fis.ucm.es
URL: http://www.ico-optics.org

6054 ■ ICO/ICTP Gallieno Denardo Award
To recognize young researchers from developing countries (as defined by the United Nations) who conduct their research in a developing country. Candidates, who must be younger than 40 years, must be active in research in optics

and must have contributed to the promotion of research activities in optics in their own or another developing country. A diploma and monetary prize of US$1,000 are awarded annually. Established in 2000. Co-sponsored by the Abdus Salam International Centre for Theoretical Physics (ICTP).

6055 ■ Galileo Galilei Award
For recognition of outstanding contributions to the field of optics that are achieved under comparatively unfavorable circumstances. The Galileo Galilei Medal, funding of registration and approved local expenses at the next ICO General meeting, and special attention and appropriate measures of ICO to support the future activities of the award winner are presented annually. Established in 1994.

6056 ■ International Commission for Optics Prize
To recognize an individual for outstanding achievement in the field of optics. Individuals under 40 years of age are eligible. A monetary award of US$2,000, travel bursary of US$1,000, and a medal are presented annually. Established in 1982.

6057 ■ IUPAP Young Scientist Prize in Optics
To recognize a young scientist who has made noteworthy contributions to applied optics and photonics. The qualify, the candidate must have conducted such research no more than eight years after receiving his or her PhD degree. A medal, citation, and monetary prize of 1,000 Euros are awarded annually. Established in 2005 by the International Union of Pure and Applied Physics (IUPAP); adopted by the ICO in 2008.

6058 ■ International Committee for Coal and Organic Petrology
Dr. Petra David, Pres.
Instituto Nacional del Carbon, CSIC
Apartado 73
33080 Oviedo, Spain
Ph: 34 98 5119090
Fax: 34 98 5297662
E-mail: petra.david@wintershall.com
URL: http://www.iccop.org

6059 ■ Organic Petrology Award
Recognizes outstanding contributions by coal and organic petrologists at the mid-career level. Nominees must be under 50 years of age. Medals and certificates are awarded as biennially in even-numbered years. Established in 2004.

6060 ■ Thiessen Medal
This, the highest award offered by the Committee, recognizes outstanding contributions and lifetime achievements in coal and organic petrology. Nominations are called for every two years, and medals are awarded as merited. Established in 1956.

6061 ■ International Corrosion Council
Dr. Daniel dela Fuente, Sec.-Treas.
University of Erlangen-Nuremberg
Dept. of Materials Engineering, Degradation and Durability
Centro Nacional de Investigaciones Metalurgicas
Avenida Gregorio del Amo, 8
28040 Madrid, Spain
Ph: 34 91 5538900
Fax: 34 91 5347425
E-mail: delafuente@cenim.csic.es
URL: http://www.icc-net.org

6062 ■ Marcel Pourbaix Award for Promotion of International Cooperation
To recognize corrosion scientists and engineers for outstanding contributions to international cooperation, to the exclusion of personal and commercial interests. A certificate is awarded.

6063 ■ Young Researcher Travel Award
To enable a young researcher to present a paper

at the International Corrosion Congress. Preference is given to candidates from developing countries. Researcher must be under 35 years of age to be eligible. Up to 1,000 Euros is awarded annually for travel to the Congress.

6064 ■ International Federation of Women's Travel Organizations
Faye Alexander, Chair
Avda. Palma d'Mallorca 15
Edificio Espana 1
29620 Torremolinos, Spain
Ph: 34 95 2057060
Fax: 34 95 2058418
E-mail: ifwto@ifwto.org
URL: http://www.ifwto.org

6065 ■ Benger-Sullivan Award
For individuals who make significant contributions to the advancement of travel and tourism.

6066 ■ SPIRIT Award
Award of recognition.

6067 ■ International Society for Transgenic Technologies
Centro Nacional de Biotecnologia
Campus de Cantoblanco
C/Darwin 3
28049 Madrid, Spain
Ph: 34 9158 54844
Fax: 34 9158 54506
E-mail: istt@transtechsociety.org
URL: http://www.transtechsociety.org

6068 ■ ISTT Prize
To recognize a scientist for outstanding contributions to the field of transgenic technologies. A silver model of a mouse blastocyst is awarded annually. Established in 2001.

6069 ■ Young Investigator Award
To recognize outstanding achievements by a young scientist who will keep the field of transgenic technologies vibrant with new ideas. Candidates must have received his or her advanced professional degree within the past 10 years. A travel stipend of up to 1,500 Euros is awarded annually.

6070 ■ International Society of Bioethics (Sociedad Internacional de Bioetica)
Marcelo Palacios, Pres.
Plaza del Humedal 3
Asturias
33205 Gijon, Spain
Ph: 34 98 5348185
Ph: 34 98 5354666
Fax: 34 98 5353437
E-mail: bioetica@sibi.org
URL: http://www.sibi.org

6071 ■ SIBI Prize
To honor the person, group, or entity that has brought forward the most relevant work, publication, or teaching in the field of bioethics, or contributed the most to build the language of bioethics. Awarded biennially in odd-numbered years to one or more recipients.

6072 ■ International Society on Multiple Criteria Decision Making
Francisco Ruiz, Sec.
Department of Applied Mathematics
Campus de Teatinos
University of Malaga
E-29071 Malaga, Spain
E-mail: secretary@mcdmsociety.org
URL: http://www.mcdmsociety.org

6073 ■ Georg Cantor Award
To recognize a scholar who, over a distinguished career, has personified the spirit of independent inquiry, and whose many innovative ideas and achievements are decidedly reflected in the

Awards are arranged in alphabetical order below their administering organizations

theory, methodology, and current practice of multiple criteria decision making (MCDM). Awarded biennially in odd-numbered years. Established in 1992.

6074 ■ Edgeworth-Pareto Award

To recognize a researcher who, over a distinguished career, has established a record of creativity to the extent that the field of multiple criteria decision making (MCDM) would not exist in its current form without the far-reaching contributions from this distinguished scholar. Awarded biennially in odd-numbered years. Established in 1992.

6075 ■ Gold Medal

To recognize a scholar who, over a distinguished career, has devoted much of his or her talent, time, and energy to advancing the field of multiple criteria decision making (MCDM), and who has markedly contributed to the theory, methodology, and practice of MCDM. Awarded biennially in odd-numbered years. Established in 1992.

6076 ■ International Sociological Association (Association Internationale de Sociologie)
Izabela Barlinska PhD, Exec. Sec.
University Complutense
Faculty of Political Sciences and Sociology
E-28223 Madrid, Spain
Ph: 34 91 3527650
Fax: 34 91 3524945
E-mail: isa@isa-sociology.org
URL: http://www.isa-sociology.org

6077 ■ Best Student Paper in Sociological Theory Award

To recognize the best paper in sociological theory authored by one or more graduate students. A citation and travel expenses up to $750 are awarded every four years. Administered by the ISA's Research Committee 16.

6078 ■ Frederick H. Buttel International Award for Distinguished Scholarship in Environmental Sociology

To recognize outstanding contributions by scholars to the study of environment-society relations. A certificate or plaque is awarded every four years. Established in 2005. Administered by the ISA's Research Committee on Environment and Society (RC24).

6079 ■ Distinguished Contribution to Sociological Theory Award

To recognize a living thinker who has made a significant contribution to sociological theory over the last two decades. A certificate and invitation to deliver a presentation are awarded every four years. Administered by the ISA's Research Committee 16.

6080 ■ Essay Competition on Women in Society

To recognize outstanding papers on the changing position of women throughout the world, with an emphasis on the analysis of social movements. Essays should provide an analysis of the effects of women's movements in bringing about change in the cultural, religious, ethnic, and national political sphere of women's lives, with particular concern for the issues of violence, sexuality, and reproductive rights as matters of social justice. Held every four years. Established in 2001. Administered by the ISA's Research Committee on Women in Society (RC32).

6081 ■ Adam Podgorecki Prize

To recognize an individual for outstanding achievements in socio-legal research, either in the form of distinguished and outstanding lifetime achievements or in the form of outstanding scholarship of a socio-legal researcher at an earlier stage of his or her career. Awarded annually. Established in 2004. Administered by the Research Committee on Sociology of Law (RC12)

6082 ■ Worldwide Competition for Junior Sociologists

To recognize young scholars engaged in social research. Individuals under 35 years of age who hold a Master's degree (or an equivalent graduate diploma) in sociology or in a related discipline may submit essays focusing on socially relevant issues. Essays may be written in one of the following languages: English, French, Spanish (the three languages of the ISA) as well as Arabic, Chinese, German, Italian, Japanese, Portuguese, and Russian. A Merit Award certificate, a four-year membership in the ISA, and an invitation to attend the World Congress, of Sociology are awarded every four years. Established in 1987.

6083 ■ Young Leisure Scholar Award

To recognize the young scholar who contributes the best paper in the field of leisure studies. Candidates must be age 40 years or younger. A certificate and monetary prize of US$100 are awarded annually. Established in 2009. Administered by the Research Committee on Sociology of Leisure (RC14).

6084 ■ Prince of Asturias Foundation (Fundacion Principe de Asturias)
D. Matias Inciarte, Pres.
General Yague, 2
Principado de Asturias
E-33004 Oviedo, Spain
Ph: 34 985 258755
Fax: 34 985 242104
E-mail: info@fpa.es
URL: http://www.fpa.org

6085 ■ Prince of Asturias Award for Communications and Humanities (Premios Principe de Asturias)

To recognize an individual, institution, or group whose work or research constitutes a significant contribution to universal culture in these fields. Awarded annually. Established in 1981.

6086 ■ Prince of Asturias Award for Concord

To recognize an individual, group, or institution whose work has made an exemplary and outstanding contribution: to mutual understanding and peaceful coexistence amongst men; to the struggle against injustice, poverty, disease, or ignorance; to defense of freedom; or whose work has widened the horizons of knowledge or has been outstanding in protecting and preserving humankind's heritage. Awarded annually. Established in 1986.

6087 ■ Prince of Asturias Award for International Cooperation

To recognize an individual, group, or institution whose work has contributed to the mutual understanding, progress, and brotherhood among nations in an exemplary and significant way. Awarded annually. Established in 1981.

6088 ■ Prince of Asturias Award for Sports

To recognize an individual, group, or institution whose lives and works are not only examples to others, but who have also reached new heights in humankind's quest to surpass itself, and whose efforts have contributed to the advancement, nurturing, promotion, or dissemination of sport. Awarded annually. Established in 1987.

6089 ■ Prince of Asturias Award for the Arts

To recognize an individual, group, or institution for significant contributions to the arts, including architecture, cinematography, dance, music, painting, and sculpture. Awarded annually. Established in 1981.

6090 ■ Prince of Asturias for Technical and Scientific Research

To recognize an individual, group, or institution for discoveries or research that represent a significant contribution to science and technology, includes the fields of biology, chemistry, earth and space sciences, mathematics, medicine, and physics. Awarded annually. Established in 1981.

6091 ■ Fernando Rielo Foundation
Jorge Juan 82, no. 1, 6
E-28009 Madrid, Spain
Ph: 34 915 754091
Fax: 34 915 780772
E-mail: fundacion@rielo.com
URL: http://www.rielo.com

6092 ■ World Mystical Poetry Prize

For recognition of outstanding mystical poetry (poetry expressing humanity's spiritual values in their profound religious significance). Any previously unpublished poem or group of poems with a total length of 600 to 1300 lines and written or translated into Spanish is eligible. The deadline is October 15. A monetary prize of 7,000 Euros and publication of the entry are awarded annually. Established in 1981 by Fernando Rielo, Spanish philosopher and poet.

6093 ■ San Sebastian International Film Festival
Mikel Olaciregui, Dir.
Plaza Okendo, 1
PO Box 397
E-20080 San Sebastian, Spain
Ph: 34 943 481212
Fax: 34 943 481218
E-mail: ssiff@sansebastianfestival.com
URL: http://www.sansebastianfestival.com

6094 ■ San Sebastian International Film Festival Awards

To recognize superb international films in an official competitive section, an unofficial section, and a variety of retrospectives. Many awards are presented each year, including the Donostia Award, which honors a great film personality. Held annually. Established in 1953.

6095 ■ Skal, the International Association of Travel and Tourism Professionals
Avda. Palma de Mallorca, N 15-1
Edificio Espana
E-29620 Torremolinos, Spain
Ph: 34 95 238 9111
Fax: 34 95 237 0013
E-mail: skal@akal.org
URL: http://www.skal.org

6096 ■ Sustainable Development in Tourism Awards

To highlight and acknowledge the best sustainable practices in tourism and travel around the world. Open to companies from the public and private sectors, as well as non-governmental organizations (NGOs). Presented in eight categories: tour operators/travel agents, urban accommodation, rural accommodation, transportation, general countryside, cities/villages, educational programs/media, and global corporate establishments. Awarded annually. Established in 2002.

6097 ■ Sociedad Espanola para el Estudio de la Obesidad
Xavier Formiguera Sala, Pres.
Paseo de la Bonanova, 47
E-08017 Madrid, Spain
Ph: 34 91 5360814
E-mail: contacto@seedo.es
URL: http://www.seedo.es

6098 ■ Wassermann Prize

For outstanding senior research in obesity.

Awards are arranged in alphabetical order below their administering organizations

6099 ■ Young Investigator

**6100 ■ Spanish ALS Association
(Association Espanola de Esclerosis Lateral
Amiotrofica)**
Adriana Guevara de Bonis, Pres.
C/. Emilia, 51
E-28029 Madrid, Spain
Ph: 34 91 3113530
E-mail: adela@adelaweb.com
URL: http://www.adelaweb.com

6101 ■ Ayuda a la Investigacion
For biomed research.

**6102 ■ Spanish Royal Society of Physics
(Real Sociedad Espanola de Fisica)**
Ms. Maria del Rosario Heras Celemin, Pres.
Universidad Complutense de Madrid
Facultades de Ciencias Fisicas
E-28040 Madrid, Spain
Ph: 34 91 3944359
Ph: 34 91 3944350
Fax: 34 91 3944162
E-mail: rsef@fis.ucm.es
URL: http://www.rsef.org

**6103 ■ Award for the Teaching of Phys-
ics**
To recognize outstanding teachers of physics.
Awarded annually in two categories: university
education and secondary education.

6104 ■ Premio a Investigadores Noveles
Recognizes scientific merit and publications. A
monetary prize is given annually to one or more
recipients.

**6105 ■ Spanish Society of Anatomy
(Sociedad Anatomica Espanola)**
Prof. Fermin Viejo Tirado, Sec.
Universidad Complutense
Facultad de Medicina
Departamento de Anatomia y Embriologia Hu-
mana I
28040 Madrid, Spain
Ph: 34 1 913941374
Fax: 34 1 913941374
E-mail: fviejo@med.ucm.es
URL: http://www.sociedadanatomica.es

6106 ■ Premio Enrique Martinez Moreno
To the best article published in the European
Journal of Anatomy.

**6107 ■ Torello Mountain Film Festival
Foundation**
Joan Salarich, Dir.
Anselm Clave 5, 3er 2a
PO Box 19
E-08570 Torello, Spain
Ph: 34 93 8504321
Fax: 34 93 8504321
E-mail: info@torellomountainfilm.com
URL: http://www.torellomountainfilm.com
Formerly: Torello Excursionist Center; Torello
International Festival of Mountain and Adventure
Films.

6108 ■ Unnim Mountain Film Festival
An international film contest of mountain cinema.
Films related to mountains and ecology, such as
alpinism, climbing, excursions, expeditions,
mountain sports, skiing, speleology, and protection of nature, flora, and fauna are considered.
The following prizes are awarded: Grand Prix
Vila de Torello - Gold Edelweiss and a monetary
prize to the best film; Silver Edelweiss and a
monetary prize to the best mountaineering film;
Silver Edelweiss and a monetary prize to the
best mountain environment film; Silver Edelweiss
and a monetary prize to the best film of mountain
sports; Silver Edelweiss and a monetary prize
for the jury prize; Medal Federacion Espanola
de Montanismo and a monetary prize for the best
film by a Spanish director; and Silver Edelweiss

and a monetary prize for best script. Awarded
annually. Established in 1983. Formerly: (2010)
Torello International Festival of Mountain and
Adventure Films.

6109 ■ Tusquets Editores S.A.
Cesare Cantu, 8
E-08023 Barcelona, Spain
Ph: 34 93 253 0400
Fax: 34 93 417 6703
E-mail: general@tusquets-editores.es
URL: http://www.tusquets-editores.es

**6110 ■ Premio Comillas de Biografia, Au-
tobiografia y Memorias**
To promote unpublished biographies, memoirs,
and autobiographies written in Spanish
language. A monetary award and a trophy are
presented annually when merited. Established in
1988.

**6111 ■ Vertical Smile La Sonrisa Vertical
(Premio La Sonrisa Vertical)**
To promote the knowledge of great erotic authors
and revitalize this marginal genre of Castilian
literature. Works must be written in Spanish to
be considered. A monetary award and an art
object are awarded annually in January. Established in 1978 in honor of Lopez Barbadillo, the
first to publish a collection of erotic narratives.

**6112 ■ Francisco Vinas International Singing
Competition
(Concurs Internacional de Cant Francesc Vi-
nas)**
Manuel Garcia Gascons, Org. Sec.
Bruc 125
E-08037 Barcelona, Spain
Ph: 34 934578646
Fax: 34 934574364
E-mail: info@francisco-vinas.com
URL: http://www.francisco-vinas.com

**6113 ■ Francisco Vinas International
Singing Contest
(Concurs Internacional de Cant Francesc
Vinas)**
To encourage talented young singers all over
the world. Female singers between 18 and 32
years of age, and male singers between 20 and
35 years of age are eligible. A monetary prize of
15,000 Euro and a gold plated silver medal are
awarded to the grand prize winners in the male
and female categories. Other official, special,
and extraordinary prizes including scholarships
are awarded. The competition is held annually,
usually in January. Established in 1963 by Dr.
Jacinto Vilardell in memory of Francisco Vinas, a
well-known Catalan opera tenor.

Sri Lanka

**6114 ■ Association of Chartered Certified Ac-
countants - Sri Lanka**
Mrs. Nilusha Ranasinghe, Contact
No. 424 R A De Mel Mawatha
Colombo 3, Sri Lanka
Ph: 94 11 2301920
Ph: 94 11 2301923
Fax: 94 11 7667780
E-mail: info@lk.accaglobal.com
URL: http://www.accaglobal.com/contacts/offices/
srilanka

**6115 ■ ACCA Sri Lanka Awards for Sus-
tainability Reporting**
To promote good corporate citizenship and
encourage companies to be more open and ac-
countable for the social, environmental, and
economic impact of their activities. Awarded
annually. Established in 2004.

**6116 ■ British Computer Society - Sri Lanka
Section**
Dr. Gihan Wikramanayake, Chm.
51, Sir Marcus Fernando Mawatha
Colombo 7, Sri Lanka

Ph: 94 11 2665 262
Fax: 94 11 4713 821
URL: http://www.bcssrilanka.org

**6117 ■ National Best Quality Software
Awards**
To recognize outstanding achievements of
individuals and organizations in Sri Lanka that
have contributed to the development of information computer technology; to create a window to
gain international recognition for locally developed information computer technology products;
and to improve standards and the quality of local
information computer technology products and
services to be able to compete in the international market place. Gold, silver, and bronze
awards are presented in 16 categories. Awarded
annually. Established in 1997.

**6118 ■ Chartered Institute of Management Ac-
countants - Sri Lanka**
Radley Stephen, Communications Mgr.
356 Elvitigala Mawatha
Colombo 5, Sri Lanka
Ph: 94 11 250 3880
Fax: 94 11 250 3881
E-mail: colombo@cimaglobal.com
URL: http://www.cimaglobal.com

**6119 ■ Global Compact Sri Lanka
Network/CIMA Sustainability Awards**
To recognize companies that demonstrate best
practice in sustainability in Sri Lanka and a
genuine commitment to triple bottom line management by upholding the United Nations Global
Compact ten principles. The practices should
demonstrate that the company has a sincere
ongoing commitment to any of the four areas of
the Global Compact: human rights, labor, environment, or anti-corruption. Awarded annually.
Established in 2007. Co-sponsored by Global
Compact Sri Lanka Network.

6120 ■ The Gratiaen Trust
c/o Marga Institute
941/1 Jayanthi Mawatha
Kotte Rd.
Colombo 7, Sri Lanka
Ph: 94 777 335 301
E-mail: malawana@wow.lk
URL: http://www.gratiaen.com

**6121 ■ H.A.I. Goonetileke Prize for
Translation**
To recognize the best translation into English of
a work originally written in the Sinhala and Tamil
languages of Sri Lanka. A monetary prize of Sri
Lankan rupees 200,000 is awarded annually.

6122 ■ The Gratiaen Prize
To recognize the best work of literary writing in
English by a resident Sri Lankan. Eligible works
are fiction, poetry, drama, or literary memoir
either published during the previous year or still
in manuscript format. A monetary prize of Sri
Lankan rupees 200,000 is awarded annually.
Established in 1992 by Michael Ondaatje, author
of The English Patient.

6123 ■ Institution of Engineers - Sri Lanka
Engr. Arundathi Wimalasuriya, Exec. Sec.
120/15 Wijerama Mawatha
Colombo 7, Sri Lanka
Ph: 94 11 2698426
Fax: 94 11 2699202
E-mail: es@iesl.lk
URL: http://www.iesl.lk

**6124 ■ Ceylon Development Engineering
Award**
To recognize the author(s) of the best article in
the quarterly journal, Engineer, published each
year. Expertise in the relevant field is necessary
for consideration. A monetary prize of 3,000 Sri
Lanka rupees is awarded annually at the
convention. Established in 1980. Sponsored by
the Ceylon Development Engineering Company,
Ltd.

Awards are arranged in alphabetical order below their administering organizations

6125 ■ Junior Inventor of the Year

To encourage originality and inventiveness of technical minded and talented students. Sri Lankan students between 12 and 20 years of age must be nominated. Monetary prizes, medals, and certificates are awarded annually. Established in 1988. Co-sponsored by Lanka Electricity Company (Private) Ltd.

6126 ■ Professor E. O. E. Pereira Award

To recognize the author(s) of the best paper in the field of engineering at the annual convention of the Institution. Members of the Institution may submit papers by June 30 every year. Books or publications valued at 1,000 Sri Lanka rupees are awarded annually at the convention. Established in 1973 in honor of Professor E.O.E. Pereira, first Dean, Faculty of Engineering and first Engineer Vice Chancellor of the Peradeniya Campus of the University of Ceylon.

6127 ■ Sri Lanka Association for the Advancement of Science
Dr. Lalini C. Rajapaksa, Gen. Pres.
120/10 Vidya Wijerma Rd.
Colombo 7, Sri Lanka
Ph: 94 1 688740
Fax: 94 1 691681
E-mail: hqslaas@gmail.com
URL: http://www.slaas.org

6128 ■ Environmental Award

To recognize significant contributions in sustainable management of the environment. Students, individuals, organizations, and institutions in both the public and private sector are eligible. Awarded annually.

6129 ■ General Research Committee Award

Recognizes the best total research contribution by a Sri Lankan scientist. Awarded annually.

6130 ■ Manamperi (Engineering) Award

To recognize the best undergraduate engineering research project carried out at a Faculty of Engineering in a Sri Lankan university. Awarded annually.

6131 ■ Physical Science Award

To recognize undergraduate students or recent graduates who have completed research projects (individual) in the field of Physics, Computer Science, Mathematics, or Statistics as a partial requirement for BSc degree in a Sri Lankan university during the previous year. Awarded annually.

6132 ■ Sri Lanka Standards Institution
Mr. Kanchana Ratwatte, Chm.
17 Victoria Pl.
Elvitigala Mawatha
Colombo 8, Sri Lanka
Ph: 94 11 267 1567
Ph: 94 11 267 1573
Fax: 94 11 267 1579
E-mail: slsi@slsi.slt.lk
URL: http://www.slsi.lk

6133 ■ Sri Lanka National Quality Awards

To honor Sri Lankan businesses that have demonstrated clear, proven strategies for success. Awards are presented in four categories: large companies; medium-sized companies; small companies; and manufacturing/service/education/health organizations. Awarded annually.

Sweden

6134 ■ Dataspelsbranschen, the Swedish Games Industry
Box 3139
SE-103 62 Stockholm, Sweden
URL: http://www.dataspelbranschen.se

6135 ■ Swedish Video Game Awards

To recognize and highlight development, creativity, and innovation in video games released in Sweden during the previous year. Presented in several categories, including Game of the Year and Swedish Game of the Year. Awarded annually. Established in 2000.

6136 ■ European Atherosclerosis Society
Prof. John Chapman, Pres.
Kronhusgatan 11
SE-411 05 Goteborg, Sweden
Ph: 46 31 7242795
Fax: 46 31 7242701
E-mail: office@eas-society.org
URL: http://www.eas-society.org

6137 ■ Anitschkow Prize

To recognize an individual for outstanding research in the field of atherosclerosis and linked metabolic disturbances. A medal and monetary prize of 10,000 Euros are awarded annually.

6138 ■ Prizes for Young Scientists in Atherosclerosis Research

To recognize young scientists that contribute to the advancement of knowledge in the field of atherosclerosis and linked metabolic disturbances. Awards are presented in two categories: clinical and basic research. A monetary prize of 2,000 Euros is presented in each category annually.

6139 ■ European Federation for Pharmaceutical Sciences
Hans H. Linden MSc, Exec. Dir.
Veddesta Business Center
SE-175 72 Stockholm, Sweden
Ph: 46 8 50582040
Fax: 46 8 4113217
E-mail: secretariat@eufeps.org
URL: http://www.eufeps.org

6140 ■ Best Paper Award

Recognizes the best paper published in the European Journal of Pharmaceutical Sciences in the preceding year. A monetary prize and a certificate are presented annually. Established in 2001. Sponsored by Elsevier.

6141 ■ New Safe Medicines Faster Award

To recognize an individual scientist or team of scientists for outstanding contributions to new methodology or technology that have made the drug development process more efficient. The innovation must have happened in the preceding 10 years. The winner(s) receive a monetary prize, certificate, and travel expenses. Awarded annually. Established in 2002. Sponsored by Sanofi-Aventis.

6142 ■ Giorgio Segre Prize

For investigators who show distinction in the fields of pharmacokinetics (PK) and pharmacodynamics (PD). Generally eligible to investigators who are 40 years of age or younger. A monetary prize, certificate, and travel expenses are awarded biennially in even-numbered years. Established in 1998.

6143 ■ Young Investigator's Award

Recognizes a young investigator for distinction in communicating research achievements. Awarded biennially in even-numbered years.

6144 ■ European Histamine Research Society
Prof. Anita Sydbom PhD, Pres.
PO Box 287
SE-171 77 Stockholm, Sweden
Ph: 46 730 412599
Fax: 46 8 300619
E-mail: anita.sydbom@ki.se
URL: http://www.ehrs.org.uk

6145 ■ Student Travel Bursaries

To students attending the annual meeting of the society.

6146 ■ Young Investigator Awards

For pre-doctoral students, MD and post-doctoral trainees with no more than 3 years post-doctoral research training.

6147 ■ Federation of International Bandy
Boris Skrynnik, Pres.
PO Box 91
SE826 23 Soderhamn, Sweden
Ph: 46 70 3232698
Fax: 46 27 018014
E-mail: bo.nyman@sensusinvest.se
URL: http://www.internationalbandy.com

6148 ■ Competitions and Tournaments

To promote the game of Bandy, a sport related to ice hockey, but played on a larger ice rink, with 11 players on a team, using a plastic ball and curved sticks and no play behind goals. The Federation sponsors the Senior World Championship and a Junior Boys Championship for boys between 17 and 19 years of age. Held biennially. Established in 1957.

6149 ■ Gold Medal

For recognition of contributions to the sport of bandy, a predecessor of the modern sport of ice hockey.

6150 ■ International Council of the Aeronautical Sciences
Anders Gustafsson, Exec. Sec.
Swedish Defence Research Agency
SE-164 90 Stockholm, Sweden
Ph: 46 8 55503151
Fax: 46 8 55503397
E-mail: secr.exec@icas.org
URL: http://www.icas.org

6151 ■ Daniel and Florence Guggenheim Memorial Lecture Award

To recognize and honor a scientist or engineer of eminence who in a long and productive career has made a significant contribution to progress in aeronautics. Awarded annually.

6152 ■ International Research Group on Wood Protection
(Groupe International de Recherches sur la Preservation du Bois)
Mr. Joran Jermer, Sec. Gen.
IRG Secretariat
Box 5609
SE-11486 Stockholm, Sweden
Ph: 46 8 101453
Fax: 46 8 108081
E-mail: irg@sp.se
URL: http://irg-wp.com

6153 ■ Ron Cockcroft Award

To promote international wood preservation research through the Research Group by assisting selected individuals to attend IRG congresses. The award is intended to be particularly available to postgraduate students and active young scientists and also non-members who otherwise cannot attend an IRG meeting. Applications must be submitted by December 15. Travel assistance is awarded annually prior to each congress. Established in 1988 in memory of Ron Cockcroft, secretary-general of the IRG.

6154 ■ IRG Travel Award

Contributes to the realization of the scientific objectives of the IRG. Missions shall strengthen the networks by allowing scientists to go to a laboratory in another country or in some instances within their own country, to learn a new technique or to make measurements using instruments and/or methods not available in their own laboratory. The applicant will normally be a scientist or student establishing himself/herself in the field of wood preservation, or in a field related directly to wood preservation interests. The host institution can be public or private, but

Awards are arranged in alphabetical order below their administering organizations

most have a member of IRG on staff, or be a sponsor member of the IRG.

6155 ■ National Association of Swedish Architects
Box 9225
S-102 73 Stockholm, Sweden
Ph: 46 8 50557700
E-mail: kansli@arkitekt.se
URL: http://www.arkitekt.se/s20287

6156 ■ Ralph Erskine Award
To recognize an individual, group, or organization for innovation in architecture and urban design with regard to social, ecological, and aesthetic aspects. A monetary prize up to US$10,000 is awarded annually. Established in 1988.

6157 ■ Kasper Salin Prize
(Kasper Salinpriset)
For recognition of the best Swedish architecture. Any building completed during the preceding year is eligible for consideration. A plaque is awarded annually. Established in 1961 by the Kasper Salin Foundation in memory of Kasper Salin, a city planning architect of Stockholm, Sweden (1898-1919).

6158 ■ Nordic Association for Hydrology
(Nordisk Hydrologisk Forening)
Hans Stjarnskog, Treas.
Sveriges Meteorologiska och Hydrologiska Institut
S-601 76 Norrkoping, Sweden
Ph: 46 11 4958267
Fax: 46 11 4958573
E-mail: hans.stjarnskog@smhi.se
URL: http://www.nhf-hydrology.org

6159 ■ Great Prizes
For the best scientific article in *Nordic Hydrology*. Awarded annually.

6160 ■ Olof Palme Memorial Fund for International Understanding and Common Security
PO Box 836
S-101 36 Stockholm, Sweden
Ph: 46 8 677 5790
Fax: 46 8 677 5771
E-mail: palmefonden@palmecenter.se
URL: http://www.palmefonden.se

6161 ■ Olof Palme Memorial Fund Scholarships
To encourage the study of peace and disarmament and for work against racism and hostility to foreigners. Scholarships are awarded twice a year. Established in 1986.

6162 ■ Olof Palme Prize
For recognition of an outstanding achievement in the areas of peace, disarmament, international understanding and common security. The Board of the Fund makes the selection. A monetary prize of $75,000 and diploma are awarded annually. Established in 1987 in honor of Olof Palme, former Prime Minister of Sweden.

6163 ■ Polar Music Prize Committee
PO Box 55777
SE-114 83 Stockholm, Sweden
Ph: 46 8 629 5300
E-mail: info@polarmusicprize.org
URL: http://www.polarmusicprize.org

6164 ■ Polar Music Prize
To recognize individuals, groups, and institutions for exceptional achievements in music. Without any restrictions of nationality, the prize is presented "for significant achievements in music and/or musical activity, or for achievements which are found to be of great potential importance for music or musical activity, and it shall be referable to all fields within or closely con-

nected with music." A monetary prize of 1 million Swedish kroner is awarded annually to one or more recipients. Established in 1989 by the late Stig "Stikkan" Anderson, publisher, lyricist, and manager of the band Abba.

6165 ■ Right Livelihood Award Foundation
PO Box 15072
S-104 65 Stockholm, Sweden
Ph: 46 8 702 0340
Fax: 46 8 702 0338
E-mail: info@rightlivelihood.org
URL: http://www.rightlivelihood.org

6166 ■ Right Livelihood Award
To honor and support those working on exemplary and practical solutions to the real problems in the world today, thereby forming an essential contribution to making life more whole and healing our planet. The awards have become known as the Alternative Nobel Prize. Selection is by a jury that accepts nominations (no self-nomination). Monetary prizes totaling 200,000 Euros are shared by three recipients for use in ongoing successful wok. In addition, an Honorary Award may be presented to an individual or group whose work the Jury wishes to recognize but who is not in need of monetary support. Awarded annually in Stockholm, Sweden. Established in 1980 by Jakob von Uexkull, a Swedish-German writer, philatelic expert, Chairman of the Foundation, and former member of the European Parliament.

6167 ■ Royal Physiographical Society of Lund
(Kungliga Fysiografiska Sallskapet)
Prof. Rolf Elofsson, Perpetual Sec.
Stortorget 6
S-222 23 Lund, Sweden
Ph: 46 132528
Ph: 46 304153
Fax: 46 131944
E-mail: kansli@fysiografen.se
URL: http://www.fysiografen.se

6168 ■ Sven Berggrens pris
For meritorious service to Swedish science, trade, and industry. Awarded annually. Established in 1995.

6169 ■ Rolf Dahlgrens Pris
For meritorious work on the systematics and evolution of the flowering plants. International prize, awarded triennially. Established in 1990.

6170 ■ Fabian Gyllenbergs pris
For recognition of the best thesis in the field of chemistry in the last three years at the University of Lund. Awarded triennially, the award carries a cash prize of 60,000 kroner. Established in 1972.

6171 ■ Assar Haddings pris
For recognition in the field of geology. A monetary prize of 260,000 kroner is awarded triennially. Established in 1959.

6172 ■ Bengt Jonssons pris
For recognition of meritorious work in the field of botany by young scientists at the University of Lund. A monetary prize of 70,000 kroner is awarded every five years. Established in 1940.

6173 ■ Thunberg Medal
(Thunbergmedaljen)
For recognition in the field of physiology. Scandinavian scientists are eligible. A medal is awarded biennially. Established in 1954.

6174 ■ Wilhelm Westrups Prize
For recognition in the field of applied science, especially benefiting the economy of the Swedish province of Skane (Scania). Awarded every five years. Established in 1923.

6175 ■ Royal Swedish Academy of Engineering Sciences
Bjorn O. Nilsson, Pres.
PO Box 5073
S-102 42 Stockholm, Sweden

Ph: 46 8 7912900
Fax: 46 8 6115623
E-mail: info@iva.se
URL: http://www.iva.se

6176 ■ Brinell Medal
For research and publication in mining, metallurgy, and processing of iron and steel. A gold medal is awarded intermittently. Established as an international prize in 1954.

6177 ■ Emblem of Appreciation
To recognize: 1) members of the Executive Committee of the Academy for valuable contributions to the Academy; 2) individuals who have made lasting and successful contributions as leaders within one of the Academy's committees; and 3) other individuals within or outside the Academy to whom the Academy owes a particular debt of gratitude. Awarded annually. Established in 1974.

6178 ■ Gold Medal
To recognize 1) considerable achievement within one of the Academy's fields, and 2) considerable contributions to the application and development of knowledge and engineering, as well as for considerable administrative and organizational work to support research and development within the Academy's fields. Three Gold Medals are awarded each year - two of them for the first purpose and one for the second.

6179 ■ Great Gold Medal
This, the highest award of the academy, is given to recognize outstanding scientific and technological achievements within the academy's sphere of activity. Another medal, the Gold Medal, is given for meritorious contributions in the academy's sphere of activity. Awarded annually. Established in 1921.

6180 ■ Honorary Member's Emblem
This, the Academy's foremost mark of distinction, is awarded to an individual who has assisted the Academy significantly in achieving its goal. Awarded annually. Established in 1989.

6181 ■ Royal Swedish Academy of Sciences
(Kungl. Vetenskapsakademien)
Per Hedenqvist, Exec. Dir.
PO Box 50005
S-104 05 Stockholm, Sweden
Ph: 46 8 6739500
Ph: 46 8 6739595
Fax: 46 8 155670
E-mail: info@kva.se
URL: http://www.kva.se

6182 ■ Gregori Aminoff Prize
For recognition of an outstanding documented, individual contribution in the field of crystallography, including areas concerned with the dynamics of the formation and dissolution of crystal structures. Awarded to up to three individuals annually. Established in 1979.

6183 ■ Crafoord Prize
For recognition of excellence in mathematics, astronomy, biosciences (particularly ecology), geosciences, and polyarthritis. A monetary prize of approximately $500,000 and a gold medal are awarded annually. Established in 1980 by Anna-Greta and Holger Crafoord, chairman of the medical supply firm Gambro AB, to help the areas of science not covered by the Nobel prizes.

6184 ■ Nobel Prizes
To honor international achievements in physics, chemistry, and economics. A medal and cash prize are awarded annually in each category. The prize-giving ceremony takes place on December 10, the anniversary of the death of Alfred Nobel, the benefactor of the prizes. Established in 1901. The prizes are described in detail under the Nobel Foundation (see separate entry).

Awards are arranged in alphabetical order below their administering organizations

6185 ■ Rolf Schock Prizes

To recognize individuals in the fields of logic and philosophy, mathematics, visual arts, and music. Monetary prizes are awarded in each category. Awarded triennially. The awards in logic/philosophy and mathematics are awarded by the Royal Swedish Academy of Sciences, and those in the visual arts and music are awarded by the Royal Academy of Fine Arts and the Royal Swedish Academy of Music, respectively.

6186 ■ Soderstromska medaljen i guld

To recognize a Swedish citizen or resident of Sweden for outstanding work in economic science or law. Awarded every other year.

6187 ■ Sture Centerwalls Pris

To recognize conservationists who best promote the protection of animal life in Sweden. Awarded annually.

6188 ■ Wahlbergska Minnesmedaljen I guld

For recognition of accomplishment in the natural sciences. Open to Swedish or foreign citizens. Awarded every fifth year.

6189 ■ Stockholm International Water Institute
Drottninggatan 33
SE-111 51 Stockholm, Sweden
Ph: 46 8 522 13960
Fax: 46 8 522 13961
E-mail: siwi@siwi.org
URL: http://www.siwi.org

6190 ■ Stockholm Water Prize

To honor an individual, institution, or organization whose work contributes broadly to the conservation and protection of water resources and to improved health of the planet's inhabitants and ecosystems. Open to candidates from around the world and across a broad range of water-related activities, professions, and scientific disciplines. A crystal sculpture and monetary prize of US$150,000 are awarded annually. Established in 1991. H.M. King Carl XVI Gustaf of Sweden is the Patron of the prize.

6191 ■ Swedish Baltic Sea Water Award

To recognize an individual, company, organization, or public authority for innovation, commitment, and new methods that protect the Baltic Sea water environment. A crystal sculpture and monetary prize of 250,000 SEK are awarded annually. Established in 1999.

6192 ■ Swedish Academy
(Svenska Akademien)
Peter Englund, Sec.
PO Box 2118
S-103 13 Stockholm, Sweden
Ph: 46 8 55512500
Fax: 46 8 55512549
E-mail: sekretariat@svenskaakademien.se
URL: http://www.svenskaakademien.se/web/hem.aspx

6193 ■ Carl Akermarks Stipendium

For recognition of outstanding achievements in Swedish theatre. Up to five monetary prizes of 50,000 Swedish kronor are awarded annually. Established in 1984 by Carl Akermarks.

6194 ■ Ida Backmans Stipendium

For recognition of a work of Swedish literature or journalism that represents an idealistic view of the world. A monetary prize of 80,000 Swedish kronor is awarded biennially in even-numbered years. Established in 1953 by Ida Backmans in memory of the Swedish writers, Gustaf Froding (1860-1911) and Selma Lagerlof (1858-1940).

6195 ■ Bellmanpriset

To recognize a truly outstanding Swedish poet. A monetary prize of 250,000 Swedish kronor is awarded annually. Established in 1920 by the Swedish painter, Anders Zorn.

6196 ■ Beskowska resestipendiet

For recognition of a literary work by a Swedish writer. A monetary prize of 70,000 Swedish kronor for travel expenses is awarded biennially in even-numbered years. Established in 1873 by Bernhard von Beskow.

6197 ■ Birger Scholdstroms pris

For recognition of a work on the history of literature, or for a biography written by a Swedish author. A monetary prize of 65,000 Swedish kronor is awarded biennially in even-numbered years. Established in 1960.

6198 ■ Blomska stipendiet

For recognition of scientific work on the Swedish language. A monetary prize of 40,000 Swedish kronor is awarded annually. Established in 1945 by Edward and Eva Blom.

6199 ■ Doblougska priset

For recognition of outstanding literary works by Norwegian and Swedish writers. Two monetary prizes of 150,000 Swedish kronor each are awarded annually in each category. Established in 1951.

6200 ■ Gun och Olof Engqvists stipendium

For recognition of a work of Swedish literature, or to recognize a journalist who writes about Swedish culture. A monetary prize of 160,000 Swedish kronor is awarded annually. Established in 1975 by Gun and Olof Engqvist.

6201 ■ Lydia och Herman Erikssons stipendium

For recognition of poetry or prose by a Swedish author. A monetary prize of 100,000 Swedish kronor is awarded biennially in odd-numbered years. Established in 1976.

6202 ■ Karin Gierows pris

To recognize Swedish journalists who promote knowledge by means of writing. A monetary prize of 80,000 Swedish kronor is awarded annually. Established in 1976 by Karl Ragnar Gierow.

6203 ■ Grand Prize
(Stora priset)

For recognition of an outstanding contribution to Swedish culture. A gold medal is awarded when merited. During the 20th century, 20 persons received the medal. Established in 1786 by King Gustavus III of Sweden.

6204 ■ Axel Hirschs pris

For recognition of biographical or historical work by Swedish writers or scientists. Monetary prizes totaling 120,000 Swedish kronor are awarded annually. Established in 1967.

6205 ■ Kallebergerstipendiet

For recognition of a work of prose or poetry. A monetary prize of 50,000 Swedish kronor is awarded annually. Established in 1977 by Gosta Ronnstrom and Tekla Hansson.

6206 ■ Kellgrenpriset

For recognition of important achievements in any of the fields of the Academy. A monetary prize of 200,000 Swedish kronor is awarded annually. Established in 1979 by Karl Ragnar Gierow.

6207 ■ Ilona Kohrtz' stipendium

For recognition of a work of prose or poetry in Swedish. A monetary prize of 35,000 Swedish kronor per year is awarded biennially in odd-numbered years. Established in 1962.

6208 ■ Kungliga priset

For recognition of a contribution to Swedish culture or for a literary or artistic work. A monetary prize of 60,000 Swedish kronor is awarded annually. Established in 1835 by King Karl XIV Johan of Sweden.

6209 ■ Nordiska Priset

For recognition of important achievements in any of the fields of interest of the Academy. Citizens of any of the Scandinavian countries are eligible. A monetary prize of 350,000 Swedish kronor is awarded annually. Established in 1986 by the Academy in connection with its 200th anniversary.

6210 ■ Oversattarpris

For recognition of the best translations of foreign literature into the Swedish language. Translations in other humanistic disciplines are also eligible. A monetary prize of 40,000 Swedish kronor is awarded annually. Established in 1953.

6211 ■ Margit Pahlsons pris

For recognition of works on linguistics or Swedish language cultivation. A monetary prize of 100,000 Swedish kronor is awarded annually. Established in 1981 by Ms. Margit Pahlson.

6212 ■ Schuckska priset

For recognition of a work on the history of Swedish literature. A monetary prize of 100,000 Swedish kronor is awarded annually. Established in 1946.

6213 ■ Signe Ekblad-Eldhs pris

To recognize an eminent Swedish writer. A monetary prize of 125,000 Swedish kronor is awarded annually. Established in 1960.

6214 ■ Stiftelsen Natur och Kulturs oversattarpris

For recognition of good translations of foreign literature into Swedish or of Swedish literature into foreign languages. Two monetary prizes of 40,000 Swedish kronor are awarded annually. Established in 1985 by the Natur och Kultur Foundation.

6215 ■ Svenska Akademiens pris for introduktion av svensk kultur utomlands

To recognize important contributions to the introduction of Swedish culture abroad. Two monetary prizes of 40,000 Swedish kronor each are awarded annually. Established in 1992.

6216 ■ Svensklararpris

To recognize teachers for stimulating young people's interest in the Swedish language and literature. Three monetary prizes of 25,000 Swedish kronor each are awarded annually. Established in 1987 by the Crafoord Foundation.

6217 ■ Teaterpriset

To recognize actors, actresses, producers, and playwrights who have made outstanding achievements in the Swedish theater. A monetary prize of 75,000 Swedish kronor is awarded annually. Established in 1963.

6218 ■ Stipendium ur Lena Vendelfelts minnesfond

For recognition of a literary work, particularly poetry. A monetary prize of 60,000 Swedish kronor is awarded annually. Established in 1981 by Mr. and Mrs. Erik Vendelfelt.

6219 ■ Zibetska priset

For recognition of a work on the history or culture of the period of King Gustavus III, or for a literary work with special regard to this period. A monetary prize of 70,000 Swedish kronor is awarded biennially in odd-numbered years. Established in 1809 in memory of King Gustavus III.

6220 ■ Swedish Academy of Pharmaceutical Sciences
PO Box 1136
S-111 81 Stockholm, Sweden
Ph: 46 8 7235000
Fax: 46 8 205511
E-mail: apotekarsocieteten@swepharm.se
URL: http://www.swepharm.se

6221 ■ Scheele Prize

For recognition of outstanding scientific contribu-

Awards are arranged in alphabetical order below their administering organizations

tions in the field of pharmaceutical sciences. A monetary prize of 200,000 Swedish kronor and a medal are awarded and the winner presents the Scheele Memorial Lecture. Awarded annually in October/November in connection with the annual congress. Established in 1961 in memory of C. W. Scheele (1742-1786).

6222 ■ Swedish Arts Council
(Kulturradet)
PO Box 27215
Borgvagen 1-5
SE-102 53 Stockholm, Sweden
Ph: 46 8 51926400
Fax: 46 8 51926499
E-mail: artscouncil@artscouncil.se
URL: http://www.alma.se

6223 ■ Astrid Lindgren Memorial Award
To promote children's and youth literature around the world. Authors, illustrators, story-tellers, and individuals or organizations that make valuable contributions to the promotion of reading are eligible. A monetary prize of 5 million Swedish crowns is awarded annually. Established by the Swedish government in 2002 in honor of Astrid Lindgren, the Swedish author of such literary characters as Pippi Longstocking.

6224 ■ Swedish Entrepreneurship Forum
Jarntorgsgatan 3
SE-703 61 Orebro, Sweden
Ph: 46 19 333700
Fax: 46 19 333701
E-mail: info@entreprenorskapsforum.se
URL: http://entreprenorskapsforum.se
Formerly: Swedish Foundation for Small Business Research.

6225 ■ Global Award for Entrepreneur-
ship Research
To recognize a scholar who has produced scientific work of outstanding quality and importance, thereby giving a significant contribution to theory-building concerning entrepreneurship and small business development, the role and importance of new firm formation, and the role of small and medium-sized enterprises (SMEs) in economic development. The "The Hand of God" statuette and a monetary sum of 100,000 Euros is awarded annually. Established in 1996. Co-sponsored by the Swedish Agency for Economic and Regional Growth and the Research Institute of Industrial Economics (IFN). Formerly: FSF-NUTEK Award.

6226 ■ Global Student Entrepreneur
Award
To recognize an outstanding student entrepreneur. Candidates must be: 1) an undergraduate student at a recognized university or college; 2) the owner, founder, or controlling shareholder of his or her company, and principally responsible for its operation; and 3) the company must be a for-profit business that has been in operation for at least the past six consecutive months. Awarded annually.

6227 ■ Young Researcher Award
To recognize a promising young researcher in the field of entrepreneurship. A monetary prize of 50,000 Swedish Krona is awarded annually. Established in 2003. Co-sponsored by the Swedish Agency for Economic and Regional Growth.

6228 ■ Swedish Fellowship of Reconciliation
(Kristna Fredsrorelsen)
Elisabeth Lundgren, Gen. Sec.
Ekumeniska Centret
Starrbacksgatan 11
S-172 99 Sundbyberg, Sweden
Ph: 46 8 4536840
E-mail: kristna.freds@krf.se
URL: http://www.krf.se

6229 ■ Nonviolence Award
(Ickevaldspris)
To recognize an individual or group that works for the goal of non-violence. Awarded annually.

6230 ■ Swedish Film Institute
(Svenska Filminstitutet)
Hakan Tidlund, Chm.
PO Box 27126
S-102 52 Stockholm, Sweden
Ph: 46 8 6651100
Fax: 46 8 6611820
E-mail: registrator@sfi.se
URL: http://www.sfi.se
Awards discontinued.

6231 ■ Audience Award
To recognize the Swedish film that Swedish cinemagoers vote for as their favorite over the previous year. Awarded annually during the Guldbagge ceremony. Established in 2006.

6232 ■ Golden Bug Award
(Guldbagge Award)
For recognition of meritorious contributions to Swedish film. Awards are given approximately 12 categories, including Best Picture, Best Director, Best Actor/Actress, Best Screenplay, Best Foreign Language Film, and Best Documentary. In addition, the Lifetime Achievement Award and up to three Special Achievement Awards may be presented. Awarded annually. Established in 1963.

6233 ■ Gullspira Award
To honor an individual who has made a special contribution to children's films. Awarded annually. Established in 2006.

6234 ■ Swedish Library Association
(Svensk Biblioteksforening)
Niclas Lindberg, Sec. Gen.
Box 70380
107 24 Stockholm, Sweden
Ph: 46 8 54513230
Fax: 46 8 54513231
E-mail: info@biblioteksforeningen.org
URL: http://www.biblioteksforeningen.org

6235 ■ Aniara Prize
(Aniara Priset)
For recognition of the best book written in Swedish by a Swedish author. A monetary prize of 50,000 kroner is awarded annually. Established in 1974 in honor of Swedish author, Harry Martinsson, and his book *Aniara*.

6236 ■ Elsa Beskow Plaque
(Elsa Beskow Plaketten)
To recognize the illustrator of the best children's book published during the preceding year. A monetary prize of 25,000 kroner is awarded annually. Established in 1958 in honor of Elsa Beskow, well-known children's book designer.

6237 ■ Nils Holgersson Plaque
(Nils Holgersson Plaketten)
To recognize the author of the best book for youth published during the preceding year. A plaque of glass and a 25,000 kroner scholarship are awarded annually. Established in 1950 in honor of Swedish author, Selma Lagerlof.

6238 ■ Swedish National Association of the Deaf
(Sveriges Dovas Riksforbund)
Box 4194
S-102 64 Stockholm, Sweden
Ph: 46 8 4421460
Fax: 46 8 4421499
E-mail: sdr@sdr.org
URL: http://www.sdrf.se/sdr

6239 ■ Kruth Award
For great contributions to the deaf community.

6240 ■ Swedish Society of Aeronautics and Astronautics
(FlygTekniska Foreningen)
Anna Rathsman, Contact
Box 4207
S-171 04 Solna, Sweden
Ph: 46 8 6276262
E-mail: anna.rathsman@ssc.se
URL: http://www.flygtekniskaforeningen.org

6241 ■ Thulin Medal
(Thulinmedaljen)
For recognition of outstanding achievement in the field of aeronautics. The following awards are presented: a gold medal for achievement of the highest merit; a silver medal for an independent work, thesis, or design to aeronautical development; and a bronze medal for the furtherance of the goals of the Society. Awarded annually (the bronze medal may be given more often). Established in 1944 by Tord Angstrom.

6242 ■ Swedish Society of Crafts and Design
(Svensk Form)
Ewa Kumlin, Mgr.
Box 204
SE-101 24 Stockholm, Sweden
Ph: 46 8 4633130
Ph: 46 8 4633138
E-mail: info@svenskform.se
URL: http://www.svenskform.se

6243 ■ Excellent Swedish Design Prize
(Utmarkt Svensk Form)
For recognition of outstanding Swedish design products during the preceding year. Products should be well designed and of high quality with regard to function, materials, and manufacture. The jury also takes resources and environmental factors into account. The products should be produced in quantity and available on the market. Products may be entered by application or nomination. Swedish manufacturers and designers are eligible. Plaques are awarded annually. Established in 1983. Formerly: Excellence in Swedish Design Prize.

6244 ■ Uppsala International Short Film Festival
Niclas Gillberg, Festival Dir.
PO Box 1746
S-751 47 Uppsala, Sweden
Ph: 46 18 120025
Fax: 46 18 121350
E-mail: info@shortfilmfestival.com
URL: http://www.shortfilmfestival.com

6245 ■ Uppsala International Short Film Festival
To recognize outstanding films and to encourage professional development. The following awards are presented: Uppsala Grand Prix, Special Prize of the Jury, Honorary Mentions, and Audience Award. Held annually. Established in 1982. In addition, prizes are awarded in two other competitions: the Children's Film Festival and the National Short Film Festival.

6246 ■ Volvo Environment Prize Foundation
Ms. Annelie Karlsson, Contact
Chalmers University of Technology
1650 VHK
SE-412 96 Goteborg, Sweden
Ph: 46 31 7724961
Fax: 46 31 7724958
E-mail: info@environment-prize.com
URL: http://www.environment-prize.com

6247 ■ Volvo Environment Prize
To promote research and development across the environmental spectrum by acknowledging individuals who have made an outstanding

Awards are arranged in alphabetical order below their administering organizations

contribution to understanding or protecting the environment through scientific, socio-economic, or technological innovation or discovery of global or regional importance. A diploma, glass sculpture, and monetary prize of 1.5 million Swedish krona are awarded annually. Established in 1988.

6248 ■ Marcus Wallenberg Foundation
SE-791 80 Falun, Sweden
Ph: 46 1046 71214
Fax: 46 23 711581
E-mail: info@mwp.org
URL: http://www.mwp.org

6249 ■ Marcus Wallenberg Prize
To recognize, encourage, and stimulate ground-breaking scientific achievements that contribute significantly to broadening knowledge and technical development within the fields of importance to forestry and forest industries. Awarded annually. Established in 1981.

Switzerland

6250 ■ Aga Khan Trust for Culture
Aga Khan Development Network
1-3 Ave. de la Paix
PO Box 2049
CH-1211 Geneva, Switzerland
Ph: 41 22 909 7200
Fax: 41 22 909 7292
E-mail: information@aiglemont.org
URL: http://www.akdn.org/aktc.asp

6251 ■ Aga Khan Award for Architecture
For recognition of architectural excellence; to nurture a heightened awareness of Islamic culture within the architectural profession, related disciplines, and society; and to encourage buildings for tomorrow's needs. In its selection process, the independent master jury considers the context in which architecture is practiced, and the social, economic, technical, and environmental factors to which the project responds. Particular consideration is given to those projects that use available resources and initiatives appropriately and creatively, that meet both the functional and cultural needs of their users, and that have the potential to stimulate related development elsewhere. Projects that have been completed within the past twelve years and that have been in use for at least one year may be nominated. The projects must be located in the Islamic world or intended for use primarily by Muslims. Monetary prizes totaling US$500,000, trophies, and certificates are awarded to those contributors including architects, construction professionals, craftsmen, and clients who are considered most responsible for the success of a project. Awarded triennially. Established in 1977 by His Highness the Aga Khan, chairman of the Award Steering Committee.

6252 ■ American Citizens Abroad
Marylouise Serrato, Exec. Dir.
5, Rue Liotard
CH-1202 Geneva, Switzerland
Ph: 41 22 3400233
Fax: 41 22 3400233
E-mail: info.aca@gmail.com
URL: http://www.americansabroad.org

6253 ■ Eugene Abrams Award
To honor an American citizen residing abroad who, through voluntary work, has made an exceptional contribution to his or her community. The purpose of the award is to acknowledge publicly meritorious voluntary work performed by Americans abroad in fields such as education, health care, care of children or the elderly, among many others as well as original initiatives taken for the benefit of a community or group of people abroad. Awarded annually.

6254 ■ Thomas Jefferson Award
To recognize outstanding service to American citizens overseas by a US State Department employee. Awarded annually. Established in 1994 to commemorate the 250th anniversary of the birth of Thomas Jefferson, America's first Secretary of State, who himself lived outside the new republic for many years in order to promote its interests.

6255 ■ Association of National Olympic Committees
(Association des Comites Nationaux Olympiques)
Mario Vazquez Rana, Pres.
Rue du Grand-Chene 6
1003 Lausanne, Switzerland
Ph: 41 21 3215260
Fax: 41 21 3215261
E-mail: info@acnolympic.org
URL: http://www.acnolympic.org/acno/index.php

6256 ■ Merit Awards
Recognizes merits in support of ANOC and it members. A plaque and laurel chains are presented to laureates. Awarded to one or more recipients annually. Established in 1983.

6257 ■ Clara Haskil Association
Patrick Peikert, Dir.
31, rue du Conseil
Case postale 234
CH-1800 Vevey, Switzerland
Ph: 41 21 922 6704
Fax: 41 21 922 6734
E-mail: info@clara-haskil.ch
URL: http://www.regart.ch/clara-haskil

6258 ■ Clara Haskil Competition
(Concours Clara Haskil)
To recognize and help a young pianist whose approach to piano interpretation is "of the same spirit that constantly inspired Clara Haskil and that she illustrated so perfectly." Male and female pianists from any country who are 27 years of age or younger are eligible to apply by July 1. A monetary prize of 20,000 Swiss francs, a broadcasted public concert (together with the other finalists), a concert engagement during the Festival, and concerts at other music centers in Europe are awarded to the winner. In addition, an Audience Prize of 3,000 Swiss francs is awarded. Held biennially in odd-numbered years. Established in 1963 by the Clara Haskil Association and the Lucerne Festival in memory of Clara Haskil, a Romanian pianist famous for her interpretive skills. From 1973 through 1984 the Competition was organized by the Montreux-Vevey Music Festival. Since 1985, the Competition has been organized independently.

6259 ■ Debiopharm Group
Chemin Messidor 5-7
Case postale 5911
CH-1002 Lausanne, Switzerland
Ph: 41 21 3210111
Fax: 41 21 3210169
URL: http://www.debiopharm.com

6260 ■ Debiopharm Life Sciences Award, Switzerland
To motivate young, innovative European researchers in the life sciences field. Recognizes a young investigator (under 45 years of age) for contributions in biology and immunology. A prize of 50,000 Swiss francs is awarded, one fifth of which is a personal award and the remainder to support the recipient's research. In addition, two Junior Awards of 25,000 Swiss francs each are awarded to young researchers under the age of 33 and working at a Swiss institution.

6261 ■ Prix Debiopharm/Valais pour les Sciences de la Vie
To recognize inventors of marketable innovative

products, technologies, or services in the life sciences sector. Students, scientists, and small to medium-sized companies in the canton of Valais are eligible. A monetary prize of 20,000 CHF is awarded.

6262 ■ European Association for Computer Graphics
Roberto Scopigno, Chm.
Ave. de Frontenex 32
CH-1207 Geneva, Switzerland
E-mail: secretary@eg.org
URL: http://www.eg.org

6263 ■ Distinguished Career Award
To recognize a professional in computer graphics who has made outstanding technical contributions to the field and has shaped computer graphics in Europe, e.g., by building an internationally leading group, by creating a school of young researchers, by establishing the field in a certain country, or by advancing the field within a certain research organization. A statue is awarded biennially in even-numbered years. Established in 2004.

6264 ■ John Lansdown Prize for Interactive Digital Art
To recognize an individual for creative use of the digital medium for interactive art in any form. A monetary prize of 750 Euros is awarded to the winner, with 250 Euros awarded to the runner-up. Awarded annually.

6265 ■ Medical Prize
To recognize researchers and developers who demonstrate that a particular benefit has resulted from the use of computer graphics technology in a medical application. The top three entries receive a monetary prize of 500 Euros, 300 Euros, and 200 Euros, respectively. Awarded biennially in odd-numbered years at the Eurographics conference.

6266 ■ Outstanding Technical Contributions Award
To recognize an individual for an outstanding technical achievement in computer graphics. A statuette is awarded annually. Established in 2004.

6267 ■ Young Researcher Award
To recognize individuals in the early part of their career who have already made a notable contribution to computer graphics in Europe and who show promise for future achievements. A statuette is awarded annually to two recipients. Established in 2004.

6268 ■ European Athletic Association
(Association Europeenne d'Athletisme)
Christian Milz, Dir. Gen.
Ave. Louis-Ruchonnet 18
CH-1003 Lausanne, Switzerland
Ph: 41 21 3134356
Ph: 41 21 3134358
Fax: 41 21 3134351
E-mail: anti-doping@european-athletics.org
URL: http://www.european-athletics.org

6269 ■ Waterford Crystal European Athlete of the Year Award
Recognizes outstanding athletic performances. Winners are selected through voting on an on-line poll on the European Athletics Web site. Presented to one male and one female athlete annually.

6270 ■ European Broadcasting Union
(Union Europeenne de Radio-Television)
Jean-Paul Philippot, Pres.
L'Ancienne-Rte. 17A
CH-1218 Grand-Saconnex, Switzerland
Ph: 41 22 7172111
Fax: 41 22 7474000
E-mail: ebu@ebu.ch

Awards are arranged in alphabetical order below their administering organizations

URL: http://www.ebu.ch

6271 ■ EBU Award
To honor outstanding contributions on the part of an individual or institution supporting or defending public service broadcasting. A glass sculpture is awarded when merited. Established in 1996.

6272 ■ Eurovision Dance Contest
To recognize the best dancers in Europe. National representatives are selected by their respective national public broadcasters, who are active members of the European Broadcasting Union. Held annually. Established in 2007.

6273 ■ Eurovision for Young Dancers
To encourage the rising generation of performers of dance. This competition will include all genres of modern dance. Contestants must be between the ages of 15 and 20. First prize is 5,000 Euros. Held biennially in odd-numbered years.

6274 ■ Eurovision Song Contest
To encourage the creation of original songs. National representatives are selected by their respective national public broadcasters, who are active members of the European Broadcasting Union. Held annually. Established in 1956.

6275 ■ Geneva-Europe Prizes
To assist in discovering new talents and to stimulate the growth of audiovisual culture in Europe. Two awards are presented: European Grand Prize for TV Scenarios (10,000 Swiss francs is awarded annually for the best European television drama script) and the European Bursaries for TV Film Writing (10,000 Swiss francs is awarded biennially to assist potential television writers develop a script for a television drama).

6276 ■ Junior Eurovision Song Contest
To encourage the rising generation of performers of classical music. Contestants must be aged 19 or under. Held annually. Established in 2003.

6277 ■ Prix Ex Aequo - International Children's and Youth Radio Drama Festival
To promote the creation of works in the field of children's and youth radio drama; to stimulate the international exchange of radio drama productions, text and artists; and to stimulate the exchange of theoretical and technical expertise at an international level. The festival is open to all Active and Associate EBU Members organizations. Organizations may submit programs in radio drama aimed at children and young people. Programs should have been first produced and broadcasted since the previous festival. Each organization may submit two programs for each category that do not exceed 90 minutes. The festival will be held biennially in Bratislava, Slovakia. There are two categories for the contest; radio fairy tales/radio plays for children and radio plays for youth. In each category, an award will be given to an organization for the best fairy tale or children's radio play and for the best youth radio play. In each category an award will be given to an individual creator for the exceptional artistic execution of a fairy tale or children's radio play and for the exceptional artistic execution of a youth radio play.

6278 ■ European League Against Rheumatism
(Ligue Europeenne Contre le Rhumatisme)
Prof. Maxime Dougados, Pres.
Seestrasse 240
CH-8802 Kilchberg, Switzerland
Ph: 41 44 7163030
Ph: 41 44 7163032
Fax: 41 44 7163039
E-mail: eular@eular.org

URL: http://www.eular.org

6279 ■ EULAR Stene Prize
Awarded for the best essay on a pre-determined topic. Prize includes the cost of travel to the Annual EULAR Congress. Awarded every other year.

6280 ■ European Photochemistry Association
Prof. Dr. Eric Vauthey, Pres.
University of Geneva
30 quai Ernest-Ansermet
CH-1211 Geneva 4, Switzerland
Ph: 41 22 3796537
Ph: 41 44 8235453
Fax: 41 22 3796518
E-mail: eric.vauthey@chiphy.unige.ch
URL: http://www.photochemistry.eu

6281 ■ Prize for PhD Thesis in Photochemistry
To recognize an exceptional PhD thesis in photochemistry. A monetary prize of 1,000 Euros, a free one-year membership, and travel expenses to the Symposium are awarded.

6282 ■ European Rare-Earth Actinide Society
Prof. Jean-Claude G. Bunzli, Sec.-Treas.
Swiss Federal Institute of Technology
Inst. of Chemical Sciences and Engineering
Laboratory of Lanthanide Supramolecular Chemistry
CH-1015 Lausanne, Switzerland
Ph: 41 21 6939821
Fax: 41 21 6939825
E-mail: jean-claude.bunzli@epfl.ch
URL: http://ereswww.epfl.ch

6283 ■ LeCoq de Boisbaudran Award
For outstanding and long-lasting contribution to the science and/or technology of the f-elements. Candidates may be of any nationality and may be located in an academic, governmental or industrial institution, or elsewhere. Awarded every three years.

6284 ■ Junior Award
For an innovative contribution to the science and/or technology of the f-elements. Candidates should be under the age of 35 and may be of any nationality and may be located in an academic, governmental or industrial institution, or elsewhere. A monetary prize of 1,000 Euros is awarded every three years.

6285 ■ European Rhinologic Society
J.S. Lacroix, Pres.
Clinic of ORL Hopital Cantonal
Rue Micheli-du-Crest 24
CH-1211 Geneva, Switzerland
E-mail: silvain.lacroix@hcuge.ch
URL: http://www.europeanrhinologicsociety.org

6286 ■ Research Prizes
To stimulate and recognize young scientists in rhinologic research. Two awards are presented: one for original basic research and the other for original clinical research. Candidates must be members below the age of 40. A monetary prize of 1,500 Euros is presented in each category at the biennial Congress. Established in 1986.

6287 ■ European Society for Dermatological Research
Prof. V. Piguet, Pres.
7 Rue Cingria
1205 Geneva, Switzerland
Ph: 41 22 3214890
Fax: 41 22 3214892
E-mail: office@esdr.org
URL: http://www.esdr.org

6288 ■ ESDR Travel Grants
To assist young researchers to attend the Society's Annual Meeting.

6289 ■ Honorary Membership
To honor individuals who have contributed greatly to dermatological research worldwide. Awarded to one or more individuals annually.

6290 ■ European Society of Clinical Microbiology and Infectious Diseases
Ms. Judith Zimmermann, Admin./Finance Mgr.
PO Box 214
CH-4010 Basel, Switzerland
Ph: 41 61 5080153
Fax: 41 61 5080151
E-mail: info@escmid.org
URL: http://www.escmid.org

6291 ■ Award for Advances in Clinical Microbiology
To outstanding young scientists from Central and Eastern Europe.

6292 ■ Award for Excellence in Clinical Microbiology and Infectious Diseases
To recognize and reward an outstanding senior scientist for a lifetime contribution in the areas of science, education, or professional affairs in clinical microbiology and/or infectious diseases. A monetary prize of 10,000 Euros is awarded annually.

6293 ■ Young Investigator Awards for Research in Clinical Microbiology and Infectious Diseases
To recognize excellence in scientific research and to stimulate further research of the highest scientific level. Candidates should be aged 40 or younger. A monetary prize of 7,500 Euros is awarded to two recipients each year.

6294 ■ Federation Aeronautique Internationale
Dr. John Grubbstrom, Pres.
Ave. Mon Repos 24
CH-1005 Lausanne, Switzerland
Ph: 41 21 3451070
Fax: 41 21 3451077
E-mail: sec@fai.org
URL: http://www.fai.org

6295 ■ Aeromodelling Gold Medal
To recognize aeromodellers of an FAI member for outstanding merit in organization activities. Recipients must have: fulfilled at least twice the function of Competition Director or a similar function at World or European Championships; or fulfilled at least three times the function of an FAI jury member at World or European Championships; or fulfilled at least five times the function of a judge or a similar function at World or Continental Championships; or served at least three years as a delegate to the FAI Aeromodelling Commission, or served another function therein; or shown outstanding merits in developing aeromodelling by organizational activities. Awarded annually. Established in 1987.

6296 ■ Air Sport Medal
To recognize individuals or groups for outstanding services in connection with air sport activities. Any number of medals may be awarded at any time for work in FAI Commissions and Committees; organizing World and Continental championships; training and education of new pilots, parachutists, or aeromodellers; or promoting aviation in general and especially with young people. Awarded annually to several recipients. Established in 1991, the 100th anniversary of Lilienthal's first flights.

6297 ■ Antonov Aeromodelling Diploma
To recognize technical innovations in aeromodelling. Each year an active member of the FAI may submit the name of one candidate by November 15. The Antonov Diploma can be granted more than once to the same person for different technical innovations made in different years. A diploma donated by the National Aeroclub of Russia is awarded annually. Established in 1987.

Awards are arranged in alphabetical order below their administering organizations

6298 ■ Leon Biancotto Aerobatics Diploma

To recognize individuals or organizations that have contributed significantly to the sport of aerobatics. Awarded annually if merited. Established in 1993. Honors renowned aerobatics pilot Leon Biancotto.

6299 ■ Louis Bleriot Medal

To recognize the holders of the highest records for speed, altitude, and distance in a straight line attained in the previous year by light aircraft. Three medals are awarded annually (unless the records of the preceding year have not been broken). Established in 1936 in memory of Louis Bleriot, an aviation pioneer and vice president of FAI.

6300 ■ Bronze Medal

To recognize individuals who have rendered eminent services to the FAI in administrative work, in commissions or committees, or in organizations of international sporting competitions. The award is decided by the Council by a simple majority vote. A medal is awarded annually upon proposal by the Secretary General of FAI. Established in 1962.

6301 ■ Colibri Diploma

To recognize outstanding contributions to the development of microlight aircraft by action, work, achievements, initiative, or devotion. Each active member of the FAI may submit the name of a candidate. Only one Diploma may be awarded annually. Established in 1983.

6302 ■ Leonardo da Vinci Parachuting Diploma

To recognize a male or female parachutist. Eligible candidates include those who have: obtained at least three times consecutively the title of National Parachuting Champion; or obtained at least once the title of World Absolute Parachuting Champion and at least twice the title of Combined Champion at an international parachuting competition; or successfully fulfilled the function of Chief Judge at least twice at an international competition and at least once at a World Parachuting Championship; or fulfilled at least three times consecutively the function of International Judge at a World Parachuting Championship; or established at least three World Parachuting records; fulfilled at least twice the function of Competition Director at an International Parachuting Contest and at least once at a World Parachuting Championship; or been or nominated Honorary President of the FAI Parachuting Commission; or been for at least 10 consecutive years, and still are a national delegate to the FAI Parachuting Commission. A diploma may be awarded annually. Established in 1970.

6303 ■ De La Vaulx Medal

To recognize the holders of absolute world records achieved during the previous year. A medal or several medals may be awarded annually. Established in 1933 in memory of Comte de La Vaulx, a founder-member and President of FAI.

6304 ■ Diploma for Outstanding Airmanship

For recognition of a pilot or flight crew on an aircraft in sub-orbital flight for a feat of outstanding airmanship having occurred during one of the previous two years and that resulted in the saving of life, or that was carried out with that objective. Eligible nominees include pilots, flight crew, or any person being temporarily in charge of an aircraft in the air. A pilot or crew engaged in a routine search and rescue mission is not eligible. A diploma may be awarded annually. Established in 1985.

6305 ■ Santos Dumont Gold Airship Medal

To recognize Alberto Santos-Dumont for his contributions to the development and the sport of flying airships. A medal may be awarded on recommendation of the Ballooning Commission to reward: the best sporting performance in the previous Montgolfier year in airships; and a major contribution to the development of the sport of airship flying in general. Each year an FAI member may submit the name of one candidate. A medal is awarded annually when merited. Established in 1994.

6306 ■ Frank Ehling Diploma

To recognize an individual or an organization for exceptional accomplishment in the promotion of aviation through the use of flying models. One diploma awarded annually.

6307 ■ Yuri A. Gagarin Gold Medal

To recognize the astronaut who, in the previous year, has accomplished the highest achievement in the conquest of space. An active member may submit one candidate of the same nationality. The medal may be awarded posthumously. A gold medal may be awarded annually. Established in 1968 in memory of Astronaut Yuri A. Gagarin, who performed the first human space flight in 1961 and who lost his life in an aircraft accident while carrying out a training flight.

6308 ■ Pirat Gehriger Diploma

To recognize outstanding service to international gliding. One or two diplomas are awarded annually.

6309 ■ Sabiha Gokcen Medal

To recognize outstanding female pilots. Awarded annually. Established in 2002.

6310 ■ Gold Air Medal

This medal, one of FAI's two highest awards, is given for recognition of outstanding contributions to the development of aeronautics through activities, work, achievements, initiative, or devotion to the cause of aviation. Active members may submit one candidate who is of the same nationality. The medal may be awarded posthumously. A gold medal is awarded annually. Established in 1924.

6311 ■ Gold Parachuting Medal

For recognition of an outstanding accomplishment in parachuting. Contributions in the realm of sport, safety, or, at the option of the Commission, an invention are considered. Each year, an active member of the FAI may submit the name of one candidate who is not a member of the FAI Parachute Commission. A medal may be awarded annually. Established in 1968.

6312 ■ Gold Rotorcraft Medal

To reward a particularly remarkable achievement in rotorcraft, including the use of a sporting vehicle or eminent services to the development of rotorcraft over an extended period of time. A medal is awarded annually if merited. Established in 1993.

6313 ■ Gold Space Medal

This medal, one of FAI's two highest awards, is awarded to individuals who have contributed greatly to the development of astronautics by their activities, work, achievements, initiative, or devotion to the cause of space. An active member may submit one candidate of the same nationality. The medal may be awarded posthumously. A gold medal is awarded annually. Established in 1963.

6314 ■ Hang Gliding Diploma

To recognize an individual who has made an outstanding contribution to the development of hang gliding by initiative, work, or leadership in flight achievements. Nominations are accepted by the FAI Hang Gliding Commission. A diploma may be awarded annually. Established in 1979.

6315 ■ Honorary Group Diploma

To recognize a group of people who has made notable contributions to the progress of aeronautics or astronautics during the previous year or years. Each year, an active member of the FAI may submit the names of two candidates, one for aeronautics and one for astronautics. Established in 1965.

6316 ■ V. M. Komarov Diploma

To recognize astronauts and members of multiseater crews for outstanding achievements in the exploration of outer space during the previous year. Each year, an active member of the FAI may submit the name of two astronauts (multi-spaceship crews) from his country. A diploma or diplomas may be awarded annually to up to three crews. Established in 1970 in memory of V. M. Komarov, the cosmonaut who participated in the World Space record flight of Voskhod 1 in 1964 and who lost his life while on duty on a cosmic flight.

6317 ■ Korolev Diploma

To recognize technicians or engineers who, having worked in orbit or on a celestial body in building structures and/or equipment or in a non-planned restoration or repair of a broken device to make possible the continuation of a mission, have shown human work in space. One diploma is awarded each year. Established in 1988.

6318 ■ Lilienthal Gliding Medal

For recognition of a particularly remarkable performance in gliding or for eminent services to gliding over a long period of time. A glider pilot who has broken an international record during the past year, made a pioneer flight during the past year, or has given eminent services to gliding over a long period of time and is still an active glider pilot is eligible. Each year, an active member of the FAI may submit the name of one candidate. A medal may be awarded annually. Established in 1938.

6319 ■ Charles Lindbergh General Aviation Diploma

For recognition of a significant contribution for more than 10 years to the progress and success of general aviation in either its sporting or transportation manifestations or in the work of international bodies; or to recognize technical breakthroughs in the field of General Aviation as an incentive toward general progress and for the purpose of stimulating research and development of new concepts and equipment contributing to operational efficiency and flight safety. One diploma is awarded annually. Established in 1983.

6320 ■ Pepe Lopes Hang Gliding Medal

To recognize outstanding contributions to sportsmanship or international understanding in the sport of hang gliding. Awarded annually when merited. Established in 1993 in memory of Pedro Paulo ("Pepe") Lopes, World Hang Gliding Champion in 1981.

6321 ■ Pelagia Majewska Gliding Medal

To recognize a female glider pilot for a particularly remarkable performance in gliding during the past year, or eminent services to gliding over a long period of time. Each year any FAI member may submit the name of one candidate to be considered and acted upon by the FAI Gliding Commission and the Council. A medal is awarded annually. Established in 1989 following a proposal by the Aero Club of Poland in memory of Madame Pelagia Majewska, eminent Polish glider pilot who was awarded the Lilienthal Medal in 1960, holds 17 world gliding records, and lost her life in an air accident in 1988.

6322 ■ Montgolfier Ballooning Diploma

To recognize each of the following: the best sporting performance in the previous Montgolfier year of a gas balloonist; the best sporting performance in the previous Montgolfier year of

Awards are arranged in alphabetical order below their administering organizations

a hot air balloonist; and a major contribution to the development of the sport of ballooning in general. Sporting performances, including; records for distance, altitude, duration, and precision of landing: number of ascents; hours of flying; or any other performance that might be judged by the FAI Ballooning Commission to be most meritorious may be submitted for consideration. Up to three diplomas may be awarded annually if merited. Established in 1960.

6323 ■ Nile Gold Medal
For recognition of distinguished work in the field of aerospace education, particularly during the preceding year. A person, group of persons, or organization is eligible. Each active member of the FAI may propose one candidate each year. A gold medal donated by the Aero Club of Egypt is presented annually. Established in 1972.

6324 ■ Odyssey Diploma
To recognize a person or a group of persons whose actions, achievements, or works on earth, in space, or on a celestial body have safeguarded or may safeguard human life in space. Each year, an FAI member may submit the name of one candidate. Awarded annually. Established in 1988.

6325 ■ Past Presidents Diploma
To recognize eminent services rendered to the FAI by a past president. Established in 1973.

6326 ■ Alphonse Penaud Aeromodelling Diploma
To recognize an aeromodeller of FAI members who have: obtained at least three times consecutively the title of National Champion or at least once obtained the title of World Champion; or established at least three world records; or been at least twice Competition Director or a similar function at world and/or continental championships; or been at least three times an FAI jury member at world and/or continental championships; or been at least three times an FAI judge at world and/or continental championships; or been at least for three years Delegate of their NAC to CIAM; or shown outstanding merits in developing aeromodelling as a sport, technique, or organization. A diploma is awarded annually. Established in 1979 and amended in 1980.

6327 ■ Phoenix Group Diploma
To recognize a group for the best reconstruction or restoration of an old aircraft. Established in 1990.

6328 ■ Silver Medal
To recognize an outstanding leader in the Federation or an aeronautical organization in a member country. A silver medal is awarded annually.

6329 ■ Paul Tissandier Diploma
For recognition of distinguished service to the cause of aviation in general and sporting aviation in particular. Each active member of the FAI may submit the name of a candidate. A diploma is awarded annually. Established in 1952 in memory of Paul Tissandier, Secretary General of FAI from 1919 to 1945.

6330 ■ Andrei Tupolev Aeromodelling Diploma
For recognition of an outstanding record performance in aeromodelling. Each year an active member of the FAI may submit the name of one candidate. A diploma donated by the NAC of Russia is awarded annually. Established in 1989.

6331 ■ Andrei Tupolev Aeromodelling Medal
To recognize aeromodellers who, in the same year, win the World and National Aeromodelling Championships in the same class of models. A medal donated by the NAC of Russia is awarded each year when merited. Established in 1989.

6332 ■ Faust Vrancic Medal
To recognize outstanding achievement in parachuting. Awarded annually when merited.

6333 ■ Ann Welch Diploma
To recognize the pilot or crew of a Mircolight who made the most meritorious flight while setting a world record during the year. Awarded annually. Established in 2006. Honors former FAI Vice President and Editor Ann Welch.

6334 ■ Young Artists Contest
To make the children of FAI-member countries more familiar with aeronautics and astronautics. Winners are chosen from three age classes: 6-9, 10-13, and 14-17. Gold, silver, and bronze FAI medals and a diploma are awarded to three winners in each age class at the Annual General Conference. Established in 1986. Sponsored by the FAI Aerospace Education Committee (CIEA) with the help of national and regional aero clubs.

6335 ■ Fondation Louis-Jeantet
Prof. Jean-Louis Carpentier, Chm.
PO Box 270
1211 Geneva, Switzerland
Ph: 41 22 7043636
Fax: 41 22 7043637
E-mail: info@jeantet.ch
URL: http://www.jeantet.ch

6336 ■ Louis-Jeantet Prize for Medicine (Prix Louis-Jeantet de medecine)
To enable researchers to continue biomedical research projects, either fundamental or clinical, of a very high level. Individuals or groups must be proposed by scientists, doctors, or institutions who are familiar with the work of the candidates. To be eligible, researchers must be working in a European country that is a member of the Council of Europe. The deadline for entry is February 15. Monetary awards amounting to a maximum of 2 million Swiss francs are awarded annually. Established in 1986.

6337 ■ Informa plc
Informa Sports Group
Gubelstr. 11
CH-6300 Zug, Switzerland
Ph: 41 41 444 1344
E-mail: info@informasportsgroup.com
URL: http://www.iirme.com

6338 ■ International Sports Event Management Awards
To recognize excellence in the global sports event management industry. Presented in 11 categories, included Brand Presentation, Event Services, and Sports City. Awarded annually. Established in 2007.

6339 ■ Institute of International Law (Institut de Droit International)
Mrs. Isabelle Gerardi, Contact
132, rue de Lausanne
CH-1211 Geneva 21, Switzerland
Ph: 41 22 9085720
Fax: 41 22 9086277
E-mail: isabelle.gerardi@gmail.com
URL: http://www.idi-iil.org

6340 ■ James Brown Scott Prizes
For recognition of contributions to international law in theory and practice. Thirteen prizes are designed to reward the authors of the best dissertations devoted to a specific topic of public international law. These prizes bear the following names: Prix Andres Bello, Prix Carlos Calvo, Prix Grotius, Prix Francis Lieber, Prix Frederic de Martens, Prix Mancini, Prix Samuel Pufendorf, Prix Louis Renault, Prix G. Rolin-Jaequemyns, Prix Emer de Vattel, Prix Vitoria, Prix John Westlake, and Prix Henri Wheaton. The prizes are offered for competition in rotation so that one prize may, where appropriate, be awarded every four years. The prize awarded in

1950 bore the name of Grotius. Thereafter, the order of rotation was in the alphabetical order of the names. The competition is open to any person, except members and former members, associates and former associates of the institute. Dissertations must be submitted by December 31 of the preceding year. The topic and the amount suggested for the Prize are printed each year in the *Annuaire de l'Institut de Droit international*. This information can be obtained through the Secretariat of the Institute. The prizes were established in 1931 by James Brown Scott in memory of his mother and his sister, Jeannette Scott.

6341 ■ International AIDS Society - Switzerland
Julio S.G. Montaner, Pres.
PO Box 28
CH-1216 Geneva, Switzerland
Ph: 41 22 7 100800
Fax: 41 22 7 100 899
E-mail: info@iasociety.org
URL: http://www.iasociety.org

6342 ■ ANRS/IAS Prize
To recognize young researchers who demonstrate excellence in the area of research programs related to the scale-up of prevention and treatment services in resource-limited settings. A monetary prize of US$3000 is awarded to one or more recipients annually. Co-sponsored by the Agence Nationale de Recherches sur le SIDA (ANRS).

6343 ■ IAS/ANRS Young Investigator Award
To encourage young researchers and to recognize excellence in their HIV/AIDS research. Awarded in six tracks: Track A: Basic Sciences; Track B: Clinical Sciences; Track C: Biomedical Prevention; Track D: Operations Research; Track E: Economics, Operations Research, Care and Health Systems; and Track F: Policy, Law, Human Rights and Political Science. A monetary prize of US$2,000 is awarded in each category. Co-sponsored by the Agence Nationale de Recherche sur le SIDA (ANRS).

6344 ■ Women, Girls and HIV Investigator's Prize
To recognize a young female investigator from a resource-limited setting whose abstract demonstrates excellence in research and/or practice that addresses women, girls, and gender issues related to HIV/AIDS. A monetary prize of US$2,000 is awarded annually. Established in 2006. Co-sponsored by the International Center for Research on Women and the International Community of Women Living with HIV/AIDS.

6345 ■ International Air Transport Association - Switzerland
PO Box 416
1215 Geneva, Switzerland
Ph: 41 22 7702525
E-mail: info.ch@iata.org
URL: http://www.iata.org/about/offices.htm

6346 ■ Eagle Awards
To recognize airports and air navigation service providers for providing exemplary service and value to airline customers. Air navigation service providers and airports handling a minimum of 5 million passengers annually are eligible. Awarded annually. Established in 1998.

6347 ■ International Association for Bridge and Structural Engineering (Internationale Vereinigung fur Bruckenbau und Hochbau)
Mr. Ueli Brunner, Exec. Dir.
ETH Honggerberg HIL E21.3
Wolfgang-Pauli-Strasse 15
CH-8093 Zurich, Switzerland
Ph: 41 44 6332647

Awards are arranged in alphabetical order below their administering organizations

Ph: 41 44 6332648
Fax: 41 44 6331241
E-mail: secretariat@iabse.org
URL: http://www.iabse.org

6348 ■ Honorary Membership
To honor the dedicated service of long-standing members. Awarded annually to one or more recipients. Established in 1949.

6349 ■ IABSE Prize
To honor an individual early in his or her career for an outstanding achievement in the field of structural engineering. Members 40 years of age or younger are eligible. A medal and a certificate are awarded annually at the conference. Established in 1983.

6350 ■ International Award of Merit in Structural Engineering
For recognition of outstanding contributions in the field of construction engineering, with special reference to their usefulness to society. Contributions may include the following aspects: planning, design, and construction; materials and equipment; and education, research, government, and management. Structural engineers who are members or non-members of the Association are eligible. A medal and a certificate are awarded annually at the conference. Established in 1975.

6351 ■ Outstanding Paper Award
To recognize an outstanding article published in *Structural Engineering International*. Awarded annually. Established in 1993.

6352 ■ Outstanding Structure Award
Recognizes not necessarily the largest, longest, highest, but clearly the most remarkable, innovative, creative, or otherwise stimulating structures. Awarded periodically. Established in 1998.

6353 ■ International Association for the Study of Insurance Economics
(Association International pour l'Etude de l'Economie de l'Assurance)
Dr. Nikolaus von Bomhard, Chm.
53 Rte. de Malagnou
CH-1208 Geneva, Switzerland
Ph: 41 22 7076600
Fax: 41 22 7367536
E-mail: secretariat@genevaassociation.org
URL: http://www.genevaassociation.org

6354 ■ Ernst Meyer Prize
(Prix Ernst Meyer)
To recognize university research work that makes a significant and original contribution to the study of risk and insurance economics. Students or researchers may apply for the award mainly by the presentation of a Ph.D. thesis. A monetary prize of 5,000 Swiss francs is awarded annually. Established in 1974 by the Geneva Association. The award honors Ernst Meyer, former Managing Director of the Allianz and founding father of the Geneva Association.

6355 ■ International Association of Paediatric Dentistry
Joseph Chan, Sec. Gen.
Tour de Cointrin
Ave. Louis Casai 84
Case Postale 3
Cointrin-Geneve
1216 Geneva, Switzerland
Ph: 41 22 5608150
Fax: 41 22 5608140
E-mail: iapd@fdiworldental.org
URL: http://www.iapdworld.org

6356 ■ Jens Andreasen Award
To recognize the best trauma poster displayed in each IAPD Congress. A monetary award of £400 is presented biennially in odd-numbered years.

6357 ■ Bright Smiles, Bright Futures Award
To recognize a community education program

and stimulate the development of innovative programs worldwide, and to facilitate information sharing and transfer in children's dentistry. Awarded at the biennial congress held in odd-numbered years.

6358 ■ Dr. Sam Harris Travel Bursaries
To support individuals who wish to attend IAPD International Congresses. Persons who have not received a bursary previously and those from less wealthy nations will be given preference. A travel grant of US$1,000 is awarded biennially in odd-numbered years.

6359 ■ Bengt Magnusson Memorial Prize
Recognizes the best essay in the field of child dental health by a young pediatric dentist. Supporting members are eligible. Awarded biennially in odd-numbered years.

6360 ■ Morita Prize
To recognize the best poster, on any clinical field, presented in each IAPD Congress. A monetary award is presented biennially in odd-numbered years. Sponsored by the Morita Corporation.

6361 ■ International Board on Books for Young People
(Union Internationale pour les livres de jeunesse)
Ms. Elizabeth Page, Exec. Dir.
Nonnenweg 12
Postfach
CH-4003 Basel, Switzerland
Ph: 41 61 2722917
Fax: 41 61 2722757
E-mail: ibby@ibby.org
URL: http://www.ibby.org
Formerly: (1989) International Board on Books for Young People (IBBY) - Canadian Section.

6362 ■ Hans Christian Andersen Awards
To recognize a living author and illustrator whose complete works have made a lasting contribution to children's literature. Recipients are selected by an international jury of children's literature specialists. A gold medal and diploma are presented biennially in even-numbered years. The Hans Christian Andersen Medal for Writing was established in 1956, and the Hans Christian Andersen Medal for Illustration was established in 1966.

6363 ■ Claude Aubry Award
(Prix Claude Aubry)
For recognition of achievement in the field of Canadian children's literature. Canadian citizens who have made lasting and significant contributions to the development and/or promotion of Canadian children's literature are eligible for the award. A monetary award of $1,000 is presented biennially. Established in 1981 in honor of Claude Aubry, a Canadian author and librarian. Administered by IBBY Canada.

6364 ■ Honour List
To recognize outstanding, recently published books from IBBY member countries. Books are judged to be representative of the best in children's literature from the country of origin, and are suitable for publication throughout the world, providing insight into the diverse cultural, political, and social setting in which children live and grow. Awards are given to numerous recipients in three categories: writers, illustrators, and translators. Awarded biennially in even-numbered years.

6365 ■ IBBY-Asahi Reading Promotion Award
To recognize groups or institutions for outstanding and lasting contributions to reading promotion programs for children and young people. A diploma and monetary prize of US$10,000 are presented to up to two groups biennially, in even-numbered years. Established in 1986. Sponsored by the Asahi Shimbun newspaper company.

6366 ■ Elizabeth Mrazik-Cleaver Canadian Picture Book Award
(Prix Elizabeth Mrazik Cleaver pour le Meilleur Livre d'Images Canadien)
For recognition of excellence in the area of the Canadian picture books and to give some financial support to Canadian illustrators of children's books. Living Canadian citizens who are illustrators of picture books published in Canada in English or French during the previous calendar year are eligible. A monetary award of C$1,000 and a certificate are awarded annually. Established in 1986 by Elizabeth Cleaver, an internationally known illustrator of Canadian picture books, who died in 1985, and left in her will the original fund of C$10,000 for the establishment of the award. Administered by IBBY Canada.

6367 ■ Frances E. Russell Award
(Prix Frances E. Russell)
To encourage research in Canadian children's literature. Applicants must be Canadian citizens or landed immigrants and must submit applications by September 30. A grant of C$1,000 is awarded annually. Established in 1982 by Marjorie Russell in memory of Frances E. Russell. Administered by IBBY Canada.

6368 ■ International Committee of the Red Cross - Switzerland
(Comite International de la Croix-Rouge)
Yves Daccord, Dir. Gen.
19, Ave. de la Paix
CH-1202 Geneva, Switzerland
Ph: 41 22 7346001
Fax: 41 22 7332057
E-mail: press.gva@icrc.org
URL: http://www.icrc.org

6369 ■ Florence Nightingale Medal
(Medaille Florence Nightingale)
To recognize qualified male or female nurses and voluntary nursing aides who are active members or regular helpers of a National Red Cross or Red Crescent Society, or of an affiliated medical or nursing institution, for having distinguished themselves in time of peace or war, by exceptional courage and devotion to wounded, sick, or disabled persons or to civilian victims of a conflict or disaster and by exemplary services or creative and pioneering spirits in the areas of public health or nursing education. The medal may be awarded posthumously if the prospective recipient has fallen on active service. The award is presented by the International Committee of the Red Cross (ICRC) on proposals made to it by National Red Cross and Red Crescent Societies. The deadline is March 12 of odd numbered years. A medal and a diploma are awarded biennially. The medal is silver-gilt with a portrait of Florence Nightingale and the words "Ad memoriam Florence Nightingale 1820-1910" inscribed on the obverse, and "Pro vera misericordia et cara humanitate perennis decor universalis" on the reverse. The name of the holder and the date of the award are engraved in the center. The medal is attached by a red and white ribbon to a laurel crown surrounding a red cross. No more than 50 medals are issued at any one distribution. Established in 1912 by contributions from National Societies of the Red Cross in memory of the distinguished services of Florence Nightingale for the improvement of the care of the wounded and sick.

6370 ■ Paul Reuter Prize
To recognize a work aimed at improving knowledge or understanding of international humanitarian law. The work must either be unpublished or have been published since the closing date

Awards are arranged in alphabetical order below their administering organizations

for submissions for the previous award. A monetary prize of 5,000 Swiss francs is awarded triennially. Established in 1983.

6371 ■ International Council of Nurses (Conseil International des Infirmieres)
Rosemary Bryan, Pres.
3, Pl. Jean Marteau
CH-1201 Geneva, Switzerland
Ph: 41 22 9080100
Fax: 41 22 9080101
E-mail: icn@icn.ch
URL: http://www.icn.ch

6372 ■ Christiane Reimann Prize
To recognize registered nurses (first level) who have made a significant impact on the nursing profession internationally, or through the nursing profession for the benefit of humanity. A cash prize and a hand-painted porcelain statue of a nurse are awarded every four years to one or more nurses. Established in 1985.

6373 ■ International Electrotechnical Commission (Commission Electrotechnique Internationale)
Mr. Jacques Regis, Pres.
3, rue de Varembe
PO Box 131
CH-1211 Geneva 20, Switzerland
Ph: 41 22 9190211
Fax: 41 22 9190300
E-mail: info@iec.ch
URL: http://www.iec.ch

6374 ■ Lord Kelvin Award
To honor individuals who have contributed in an exceptional, dedicated way to the technical work of the IEC in the field of electrotechnology standardization and related activities, for a significant period of at least five years. Awarded annually. Established in 1995 in honor of the IEC's first president, the Rt. Hon. Lord Kelvin.

6375 ■ International Equestrian Federation (Federation Equestre Internationale)
Avenue du Rumine 37
CH-1005 Lausanne, Switzerland
Ph: 41 21 310 4747
Fax: 41 21 310 4760
URL: http://www.fei.org

6376 ■ Best Athlete Award
To recognize a rider, driver, or vaulter who, over the past year, has shown exceptional sportsmanship and equestrian prowess and has taken the sport to a new level. Open to individuals around the world. Awarded annually as part of the FEI Awards. Established in 2009.

6377 ■ International Federation of Consulting Engineers (Federation Internationale des Ingenieurs Conseils)
Gregs Thomopulos, Pres.
World Trade Center II
Geneva Airport
29 Rte. de Pre-Bois, Cointrin
CH-1215 Geneva 15, Switzerland
Ph: 41 22 7994900
Fax: 41 22 7994901
E-mail: fidic@fidic.org
URL: http://www.fidic.org

6378 ■ Louis Prangey Award
Recognizes significant contribution to the consulting industry. Awarded annually.

6379 ■ International Federation of Social Workers
PO Box 6875
Schwartzorstr. 22
CH-3001 Bern, Switzerland
Ph: 41 22 548 3625

Fax: 41 31 380 8301
URL: http://www.ifsw.org

6380 ■ Andrew Mouravieff-Apostol Medal
To recognize an individual or organization that has stimulated the further development of international social work and over time made an outstanding contribution to the social work profession on an international level, transcended national borders, and reflected social work values. Awarded biennially in even-numbered years.

6381 ■ International Federation of Sound Hunters (Federation Internationale des Chassuers de Sons)
Helmut Weber, Sec. Gen.
Riedernrain 264
CH-3027 Bern, Switzerland
Ph: 41 31 9916240
Fax: 41 31 9503135
E-mail: h.weber@soundhunters.com
URL: http://www.soundhunters.com

6382 ■ Jean Thevenot Medal (Medaille Jean Thevenot)
To recognize the entry with the best sound in the RPS International Audio-Visual Festival. A monetary prize, medal, trophy, and equipment are awarded annually. The contest is held in even-numbered years at the Royal Agricultural College in Cirencester, England. Established in 1984 in honor of Jean Thevenot, founder of FICS.

6383 ■ International Federation of Standards Users
Mr. Ross Wraight, Pres.
1, ch. de la Voie-Creuse
Casa Postale 56
CH-1211 Geneva 20, Switzerland
Ph: 41 22 7490335
Fax: 41 22 7333430
E-mail: zaech@iso.org
URL: http://www.ifan.org/ifanportal/livelink/fetch/2000/2035/36282/394607/index.html

6384 ■ Georges Garel Award
Presented to individuals for their outstanding services to the international community of standards users. Awarded periodically. Established 1979.

6385 ■ International Federation of University Women - Switzerland (Federation Internationale des Femmes Diplomees des Universites)
Leigh Bradford Ratteree, Sec. Gen.
10 rue du Lac
CH-1207 Geneva, Switzerland
Ph: 41 22 7312380
Fax: 41 22 7380440
E-mail: info@ifuw.org
URL: http://www.ifuw.org/index.shtml

6386 ■ Fellowship Competition
To encourage advanced scholarship by enabling university women to undertake original research in some country other than that in which they have received their education or habitually reside. A fellowship is not awarded for the first year of a PhD program. The following fellowships and grants are awarded biennially: British Federation Crosby Hall Fellowship (£2,500); CFUW A. Vibert Douglas International Fellowship (C$12,000); Ida Smedley Maclean Fellowship (10,000 Swiss francs); Marjorie Shaw International Fellowship (£3,500); Ruth Bowden International Fellowship (8,000 Swiss francs); Australian Universities Grant (5,000 Swiss francs); Dorothy Leet Grant (6,000 Swiss francs); Daphne Purves Grant (3,000 Swiss francs); Winifred Cullis Grant (6,000 Swiss francs).

6387 ■ Recognition Award
To honor individuals for outstanding contribu-

tions to the Federation and industry. A monetary prize of 1,000 Swiss francs is awarded to one or more recipients biennially.

6388 ■ International Handball Federation (Federation Internationale de Handball)
Dr. Hassan Moustafa, Pres.
Peter Merian-Strasse 23
CH-4002 Basel, Switzerland
Ph: 41 61 2289040
Fax: 41 61 2289055
E-mail: ihf.office@ihf.info
URL: http://www.ihf.info/Home/tabid/40/Default.aspx

6389 ■ Hans Baumann Trophy
To recognize the member association of the IHF that has most successfully contributed to the development and propagation of handball in their country or in the whole world. A trophy is awarded biennially in odd-numbered years at the ordinary IHF Congress. Established in memory of Hans Baumann, second president of the International Handball Federation.

6390 ■ Handball Player of the Year
To recognize an individual for outstanding handball performance and overall contributions to the sport. Awarded to a man and a woman annually.

6391 ■ International Hockey Federation
Rue du Valentin 61
CH-1004 Lausanne, Switzerland
Ph: 41 21 641 0606
Fax: 41 21 641 0607
E-mail: info@fih.ch
URL: http://www.fih.ch

6392 ■ Diploma of Merit
To honor individuals, whether members or ex-members of the FIH. For shorter period of distinguished service or lesser service than that required for those receiving the Order of Merit, extended by a continuation of the individual's devotion to field hockey (for past members of FIH). No more than six awards may be given during each two-year period. Established in 1994.

6393 ■ Pablo Negre Trophy
To recognize the National Association that has, by its activities, initiatives ,and sportsmanship, served best the course of field hockey and made it more popular during the previous two years. Awarded annually. Established in 1973 by the family of Paplo Negre, who rendered exceptional services to hockey.

6394 ■ Order of Merit
To honor individuals, whether members of FIH or not. In the case of FIH members, for distinguished service over a period of at least ten years, or for exceptional achievement or contribution that is important in the international field. In the case of those who are not members of the FIH, constructive and positive activity over a period of at least 15 years, or unique personal achievement or contribution that has benefited international hockey. No more than four awards may be given during each two-year period. Established in 1974.

6395 ■ Player of the Year Awards
To recognize outstanding field hockey players from around the world. Presented in four categories: Men, Women, Young Men, and Young Women. Awarded annually. Established in 1997.

6396 ■ President's Award
To recognize individuals who are not members of the FIH for long and valuable services to hockey, whether direct or indirect, or services

Awards are arranged in alphabetical order below their administering organizations

that have had an indisputable beneficial effect for field hockey at international level. No more than 10 awards during a two-year period. Established in 1994.

6397 ■ International Hotel and Restaurant Association
Dr. Ghassan Aidi, Pres.
42 Ave. General Guisan
1009 Lausanne, Switzerland
Ph: 41 21 7114283
Fax: 41 21 7114285
E-mail: info@ih-ra.com
URL: http://www.ih-ra.com

6398 ■ Environmental Award
To recognize a hotel that has made outstanding efforts to protect the environment. Awarded annually. Established in 1990. Sponsored by American Express Ltd.

6399 ■ International Ice Hockey Federation
Rene Fasel, Pres.
Brandschenkestr. 50
Postfach
CH-8027 Zurich, Switzerland
Ph: 41 44 5622200
Fax: 41 44 5622229
E-mail: office@iihf.com
URL: http://www.iihf.com

6400 ■ International Ice Hockey Federation Championships
To encourage the playing of ice hockey by organizing regular international competitions and championships. Championships include the World Championships, World Women's Championships, World U20 Championships, World U18 Championships, and World Women's U18 Championships.

6401 ■ International Institute for Promotion and Prestige
(Institut International de Promotion et de Prestige)
Jean-Marie Lavie, Science and Technological Programme Dir.
1, rue de Varembe
CH-1202 Geneva, Switzerland
Ph: 41 22 7338614
Fax: 41 22 7342538
E-mail: info@iipp.org
URL: http://www.iipp.org

6402 ■ International Humanitarian Medal
To honor and encourage individuals, companies, and groups whose endeavors lead to the improvement of human life. Awarded annually.

6403 ■ International Promotion Prize
To recognize rapidly growing companies for success in foreign markets. Awarded annually.

6404 ■ International Trophy
To honor companies and institutions for outstanding international prestige and reputation in their particular fields. Awarded annually.

6405 ■ Merit Prize for Development
To encourage private individuals, institutions, communities, and companies who contribute to the development of an activity field in the economic, industrial, craft industry, or cultural and social sectors. Awarded annually.

6406 ■ International Motorcycling Federation
(Federation Internationale de Motocyclisme)
Guy Maitre, CEO
11, Rte. de Suisse
CH-1295 Mies, Switzerland
Ph: 41 22 9509500
Fax: 41 22 9509501
E-mail: info@fim-live.com
URL: http://www.fim-live.com/en

6407 ■ Environment Award
To reward a significant contribution to environ-

mental protection, such as prevention of oil and fuel leakage, litter, and inordinate sound levels. A trophy and monetary prize of $5,000 are awarded when merited. Established in 1995.

6408 ■ Fair Play Trophy
(Trophee du Fairplay FIM)
For recognition of fair play in the world of motorcycling. Awarded when merited. Established in 1983.

6409 ■ Gold Medal
For recognition of outstanding accomplishments in the sport of motorcycling. Awarded when merited. Established in 1963.

6410 ■ Motorcycling Merit Diploma
For recognition of contributions to the sport of motorcycling. Gold, silver, and bronze medals are awarded when merited. Established in 1983.

6411 ■ World Motorcycle Championships
To encourage and draw up regulations for the sport of motorcycling in all of its disciplines by controlling worldwide through its members the application of rules, standards, and, in particular, its codes. The FIM is the sole international authority empowered to control international motorcycling activities organized under its jurisdiction throughout the world. The official titles of World Championships, Intercontinental Championships, Continental Championships, and FIM Prize Events, in all disciplines of the motorcycle sport belong to the FIM. Motorcycle World Championship events held each year determine: Road Racing World Champions, World Champions Motocross and Supercross, Trial World Champions, Enduro World Champions, and World Track Racing Champions.

6412 ■ International Olympic Committee
(Comite International Olympique)
Jacques Rogge, Pres.
Chateau de Vidy
Case postale 356
CH-1001 Lausanne, Switzerland
Ph: 41 21 6216111
Fax: 41 21 6216216
URL: http://www.olympic.org/ioc

6413 ■ Olympiart
To recognize an artist who has distinguished him/herself through the creation of works of outstanding aesthetic qualities in the field of the visual and plastic arts, architecture, literature, or music, and for his/her interest in youth, peace, and sport. Established in 1992.

6414 ■ Olympic Cup
(Coupe Olympique)
For recognition of an institution or association with a general reputation for merit and integrity that has been active and efficient in the service of sport and has contributed substantially to the development of the Olympic Movement. The Cup remains at the Chateau de Vidy, and a reproduction is awarded annually. Established by the Baron de Coubertin in 1906.

6415 ■ Olympic Medals and Diplomas
(Medailles et Diplomes Olympique)
To recognize winners of individual and team events at the summer and winter Olympics. The following awards are given: first prize - a silvergilt medal and a diploma; second prize - a silver medal and a diploma; and third prize - a bronze medal and a diploma. The medals must bear the name of the sport concerned and be fastened to a detachable chain or ribbon to be hung around the neck of the athlete. Diplomas, not medals, are also awarded for the fourth, fifth, sixth, seventh and eighth places, if any. All participants in a tie for first, second and third places are entitled to receive a medal and a diploma. The names of all winners are inscribed upon the walls of the main stadium where the Olympic Games have taken place. Awarded every four years. Established in 1896.

6416 ■ Olympic Order
To recognize an individual who has illustrated the Olympic ideal through his action, has achieved remarkable merit in the sporting world, or has rendered outstanding services to the Olympic cause, either through his own personal achievement or his contribution to the development of sport. Nominations are proposed by the Olympic Order's Council and decided upon by the Executive Board. Active members of the IOC may not be admitted as such into the Olympic Order. From 1974 through 1984, the award was presented in three Orders: gold, silver and bronze. Since 1984, there has been no distinction between the silver and bronze Order. The insignia of the Olympic Order and the diploma are conferred upon the recipient by the President, by a member of the IOC nominated by him, or, failing that, by someone approved by the President. Awarded annually. Established in 1974.

6417 ■ International Organisation for the Elimination of All Forms of Racial Discrimination
(Organisation Internationale pour l'Elimination de Toutes les Formes de Discrimination Raciale)
Abdalla Sharafeddin, Pres.
5, Rte. Des Morillons
Case Postale 2100
CH-1211 Geneva 2, Switzerland
Ph: 41 22 7886233
Fax: 41 22 7886245
E-mail: info@eaford.org
URL: http://www.eaford.org

6418 ■ Fellowship Award
For students preparing doctoral dissertations on racism.

6419 ■ International Award for the Promotion of Human Understanding
To recognize outstanding books in English, French, Arabic, Spanish, and Portuguese are made by EAFORD in accordance with its purposes, which include the "confirmation of the moral and human values of equality, brotherhood and justice without discrimination by reason of race, color, descent or national or ethnic origin." A monetary prize of $5,000 is awarded.

6420 ■ International Philatelic Federation
(Federation Internationale de Philatelie)
Andree Trommer-Schiltz, Sec. Gen.
Biberlinstrasse 6
CH-8032 Zurich, Switzerland
Ph: 41 44 3122827
E-mail: ats@f-i-p.ch
URL: http://www.f-i-p.ch

6421 ■ Medal for Research
For research in a special philatelic field.

6422 ■ Medal for Service
For outstanding service to the federation or organized philately for more than 10 years.

6423 ■ International Road Transport Union
(Union Internationale des Transports Routiers)
Martin Marmy, Sec. Gen.
3 Rue de Varembe
CH-1211 Geneva 20, Switzerland
Ph: 41 22 9182700
Fax: 41 22 9182741
E-mail: iru@iru.org
URL: http://www.iru.org

6424 ■ Grand Prix d'Honneur
To recognize an act of outstanding bravery by a professional road transport driver of a bus, coach, or truck accomplished in the course of professional duties. Candidates may be nominated by IRU member associations (in the United

Awards are arranged in alphabetical order below their administering organizations

States, the America Trucking Association-ATA). A monetary prize, a diploma, and a gold button badge are awarded biennially at the IRU Congress. Established in 1967.

6425 ▪ International Service for Human Rights - Switzerland
Isabelle Scherer, Dir.
PO Box 16
CH-1211 Geneva, Switzerland
Ph: 41 22 9197100
Fax: 41 22 9197125
E-mail: information@ishr.ch
URL: http://www.ishr.ch

6426 ▪ Human Rights Award
Recognizes exceptional contributions to the work of the UN Commission on Human Rights. Diplomats and UN experts are eligible. Awarded annually if merited.

6427 ▪ International Ski Federation
(Federation Internationale de Ski)
Gian Franco Kasper, Pres.
Marc Hodler House
Blochstrasse 2
CH-3653 Oberhofen, Switzerland
Ph: 41 33 2446161
Fax: 41 33 2446171
E-mail: mail@fisski.ch
URL: http://www.fis-ski.com

6428 ▪ Alpine Skiing World Cup Champions
To recognize the men's and women's overall champion in the ski racing competition. In addition, the following awards are presented: Alpine World Cup Medals - to recognize men and women in five categories: slalom, giant slalom, downhill, combined, and super G; The Nations Cup - to recognize the country whose skiers accumulate the most points in the competition; World Cup Jumping Leaders - established in 1981; Nordic World Cup Leaders - established in 1974; Nordic Combined World Cup Leaders established in 1984; and Skier of the Year - established in 1975. Awarded annually. Established in 1967.

6429 ▪ International Society for Cerebral Blood Flow and Metabolism
c/o Kenes International
1-3, rue de Chantepoulet
PO Box 1726
CH-1211 Geneva, Switzerland
Ph: 41 22 906 9155
Fax: 41 22 732 2607
E-mail: info@iscbfm.org
URL: http://www.iscbfm.org

6430 ▪ Niels Lassen Award
To recognize an outstanding scientific contribution made by a young scientist. Candidates must be members of the Society, younger than 36 years of age, and the primary author of an abstract submitted for presentation at the Brain Meeting. A certificate, cash prize of $1,500, and travel bursary are awarded biennially in odd-numbered years. Established in 1999.

6431 ▪ Lifetime Achievement Award
To recognize an individual for exceptional contributions to the Society. Awarded biennially in odd-numbered years. Established in 1997.

6432 ▪ International Society for Neuroimaging in Psychiatry
Dr. Thomas Dierks, Contact
University Hospital of Psychiatry
Dept. of Psychiatric Neurophysiology
Bolligenstr. 111
CH-3000 Bern, Switzerland
Ph: 41 31 930 9716
Fax: 41 31 930 9961
URL: http://isnip.org

6433 ▪ Membership Awards
To support and promote the research of young scientists in the field of neuroimaging in psychiatry. One-year free membership in the Society is awarded to 10 individuals annually. Established in 2011.

6434 ▪ Young Scientist Award
To recognize the best paper published in *Psychiatry Research: Neuroimaging* during the previous year. Candidates are authors not older than 35 years and are involved in research and/or clinical projects related to neuroimaging in psychiatry. A monetary prize of 1,000 Euros is awarded annually. Established in 2011.

6435 ▪ International Society of Electrochemistry
M. Orazem, Pres.
Rue de Sebeillon 9b
CH-1004 Lausanne, Switzerland
Fax: 41 21 6483975
E-mail: info@ise-online.org
URL: http://www.ise-online.org

6436 ▪ Brian Conway Prize for Physical Electrochemistry
To recognize an individual for achievements in physical electrochemistry during recent years. Awarded biennially in even-numbered years.

6437 ▪ Oronzio and Niccolo De Nora Foundation Prize of ISE on Electrochemical Technology and Engineering
Recognizes recent application-oriented achievements in the field of electrochemical technology and engineering. Applicants must be under the age of 35 on January 1 of the year of the award. Awarded annually.

6438 ▪ Oronzio and Niccolo De Nora Foundation Young Author Prize
Recognizes published work in the areas of corrosion, electrodeposition or surface treatment. Applicants must be electrochemists under the age of 30. Awarded annually.

6439 ▪ Electrochimica Acta Gold Medal
To recognize contributions in the field of electrochemistry. Work must have been completed in the past two years. A certificate and medal are awarded biennially in even-numbered years.

6440 ▪ Electrochimica Acta Travel Award for Young Electrochemists
To recognize young electrochemists for outstanding contributions. Individuals must be ISE members who have obtained their PhD not earlier than six years before application. Awarded annually.

6441 ▪ Hans-Jurgen Engell Prize
Recognizes work in the field of corrosion, electrodeposition, or surface treatment. Applicants must be young electrochemists. Awarded annually.

6442 ▪ Frumkin Memorial Medal
Recognizes outstanding contributions of a living individual over his/her life in the field of fundamental electrochemistry. Awarded biennially in odd-numbered years.

6443 ▪ Alexander Kuznetsov Prize for Theoretical Electrochemistry
To recognize an individual who has made a groundbreaking contribution to the theory of electrochemical phenomena, including theory of charge transfer at interfaces and conductive media, structure and dynamics of electrified interfaces at molecular level, and related phenomena. A bronze medal, certificate, and monetary prize of 1,000 Euros are awarded biennially in even-numbered years.

6444 ▪ Katsumi Niki Prize for Bioelectrochemistry
To recognize an individual for outstanding contribution to the field of bioelectrochemistry. Awarded biennially in odd-numbered years.

6445 ▪ Prix Jacques Tacussel
Recognizes contributions to an electrochemical technique. Awarded biennially in odd-numbered years.

6446 ▪ Tajima Prize
Recognizes the work of young electrochemists. Applicants must be under the age of 40. Winners are selected based on published work. Awarded annually if merited.

6447 ▪ International Society of Paediatric Oncology
(Societe Internationale d'Oncologie Pediatrique)
Dr. Gabriele Calaminus, Pres.
1-3 Rue de Chantepoulet
PO Box 1726
1211 CH Geneva, Switzerland
Ph: 41 22 9069169
Fax: 41 22 9069140
E-mail: irah@kenes.com
URL: http://www.siop.nl

6448 ▪ Schweisguth Prize
For recognition of the best clinical or basic science contribution presented in the format of a full manuscript related to the field of pediatric oncology. The manuscript must describe work performed by a trainee while they were still in their training period and must be submitted within one year of completion of their training period. Criteria for awarding the prize include originality, completeness, scientific accuracy, and contribution to science. An all-expenses paid trip to the annual conference and presentation/publication of the winning article are awarded each year at the annual conference. Established in 1985 in honor of Dr. Odile Schweisguth, founding member and first president of the Society.

6449 ▪ SIOP Awards
To stimulate the research and development of pediatric oncology by rewarding the quality of either an oral or poster presentation during annual SIOP meetings. The two highest scoring abstracts in the fields of basic science and clinical science are presented orally during the congress. A jury selected by the Scientific Committee will judge which abstracts are worthy of the first prize. The main authors of the winning abstracts are awarded a certificate and 1,000 Euro. Awarded annually. Established in 1991. Formerly: (1998) Nycomed Prize.

6450 ▪ International Society of Surgery
(Societe Internationale de Chirurgie)
Prof. Jean-Claude Givel, Sec. Gen.
Seltisbergerstrasse 16
CH-4419 Lupsingen, Switzerland
Ph: 41 61 8159666
Fax: 41 61 8114775
E-mail: surgery@iss-sic.ch
URL: http://www.iss-sic.ch

6451 ▪ Robert Danis Prize
To recognize the surgeon/author of the most important and personal work in connection with surgical treatment of fractures (orthopaedic treatment excluded). Surgeon nationals of one of the countries represented at the ISS/SIC are eligible. Work can be in connection with technics, clinics, or experimentation. Awarded every two to four years. Established in 1947.

6452 ▪ Rene Leriche Prize
For recognition of the most valuable work on the surgery of arteries, veins, or the heart which has appeared in the previous few years. Awarded every two to four years. Established in 1947.

6453 ▪ Prize of the Societe Internationale de Chirurgie
To recognize the surgeon who has a published work that has made the most notable and useful contribution to surgical science. The prize win-

Awards are arranged in alphabetical order below their administering organizations

ner need not necessarily be a member of the Society. Awarded every two to four years. Established in 1953.

6454 ■ International Sport Press Association (Association Internationale de la Presse Sportive)
Gianni Merlo, Pres.
Maison du Sport International
Ave. de Rhodanie 54
1007 Lausanne, Switzerland
Ph: 41 21 6013980
Fax: 41 21 6017923
E-mail: info@aipsmedia.com
URL: http://www.aipsmedia.com

6455 ■ AIPS Awards
For recognition of worldwide achievement in sports. Awards are given in the following categories: Best Male Athlete, Best Female Athlete, Best Sports Team, and Best Press Facilities. Trophies are awarded annually during the AIPS Congress. Established in 1977.

6456 ■ International Union Against Cancer (Union Internationale Contre le Cancer)
Dr. Eduardo Cazap, Pres.
62 Rte. de Frontenex
CH-1207 Geneva, Switzerland
Ph: 41 22 8091811
Fax: 41 22 8091810
E-mail: membership@uicc.org
URL: http://www.uicc.org

6457 ■ American Cancer Society International Fellowships for Beginning Investigators
To assist investigators, clinicians, epidemiologists, and public health professionals in the early stages of their academic careers from low-, lower-middle-, and upper-middle-income countries. Candidates generally have a minimum of two and a maximum of 10 years post-doctoral experience. Six to eight fellowships of US$45,000 each are awarded annually. Sponsored by the American Cancer Society. Formerly: American Cancer Society Eleanor Roosevelt International Cancer Fellowships.

6458 ■ Asia-Pacific Cancer Society Training Grants (APCASOT)
To assist the work of voluntary cancer societies in the Asian-Pacific region by providing their English-speaking staff and accredited volunteers with non-medical training opportunities in: prevention & early detection education programs; non-medical patient services; advocacy; fundraising; behavioral research; media relations; organization & managerial skills; and surveillance of cancer statistics at established cancer societies in Australia and others in the region. Grants cover a duration of one to two weeks, and training at two societies is encouraged. Three to five fellowships with an average value of US $1,800 are awarded each year. Applications must be submitted by September 15. Funded by the William Rudder Memorial Fund.

6459 ■ Award for Outstanding Government Official
To recognize an elected or appointed government official whose support for national cancer control efforts has significantly raised health standards for his or her country. Awarded annually.

6460 ■ Award for Outstanding UICC Member Organization
To recognize a UICC member cancer organization that has demonstrated excellence in cancer control in and beyond its borders. Awarded annually.

6461 ■ Award for Outstanding Volunteer
To recognize an individual who has demonstrated excellence in fighting cancer in or beyond his/her discipline and who has strong links to UICC. Awarded annually.

6462 ■ Yamagiwa-Yoshida Memorial International Cancer Study Grants
To enable cancer investigators from any country who are actively engaged in cancer research to undertake joint research/study abroad or to establish bilateral research projects, including advanced training in experimental methods and special techniques. The applications deadline is January 15 and July 1. On average, 15 grants with a value for 3 months of $10,000 are made annually. Selections take place twice a year, in spring and autumn. Sponsored by the Japan National Committee for UICC and the Toray Industries Inc., and Kyowa Hakko Kogyo Co. Ltd. in Tokyo.

6463 ■ International Waterski and Wakeboard Federation
Postbox 564
CH-6314 Unteraegeri, Switzerland
E-mail: iww@iwwfed.com
URL: http://www.iwsf.com

6464 ■ Athlete of the Year
To recognize outstanding male and female waterskiers around the world. Awarded annually.

6465 ■ Hall of Fame
To recognize water skiing and officials for outstanding contributions to the international sport of water skiing. For a skier to be eligible, he or she must have competed in at least two World Championships and must have been retired from Open competition for at least two additional World Championships. Officials are selected primarily based on significant contributions to water skiing at the international level over a period of at least 15 years. A maximum of five individuals are inducted biennially in odd-numbered years. Established in 1989.

6466 ■ Order of Merit
To recognize individuals who have made meaningful contributions to the sport of water skiing that do not fall within the guidelines for the Hall of Fame. Awarded biennially in odd-numbered years, if merited.

6467 ■ Localization Industry Standards Association
Mr. Michael Anobile, Managing Dir.
Domaine en Prael
CH-1323 Romainmotier-Envy, Switzerland
Ph: 41 24 4532310
Fax: 41 24 4532312
E-mail: lisa@lisa.org
URL: http://www.lisa.org

6468 ■ Business Leader of the Year
For outstanding corporate leader.

6469 ■ Nestle SA
Creating Shared Value Section
CH-1800 Vevey, Switzerland
Ph: 41 21 924 2111
URL: http://www.nestle.com/csv

6470 ■ Nestle Prize in Creating Shared Value
To recognize an individual, business, or nongovernmental organization for developing an outstanding innovation that has high promise of improving rural development, nutrition, access to clean water, or having a significant impact on water management. A monetary prize of 500,000 Swiss francs is awarded biennially in even-numbered years. Established in 2009.

6471 ■ Prix de Lausanne
Patricia Leroy, Sec. Gen.
Palais de Beaulieu
Av. Bergieres 6
CH-1004 Lausanne, Switzerland
Ph: 41 21 643 2405
Fax: 41 21 643 2409
E-mail: info@prixdelausanne.org

URL: http://www.prixdelausanne.org

6472 ■ Prix de Lausanne
To help promising young dancers between 15 and 18 years of age to embark on a professional career. Up to nine scholarships for a year's study in a world renowned school of dance or ballet company are awarded. Winners choose the school or the company they wish to attend from a list furnished by the competition. Established in 1973 by Philippe Braunschweig.

6473 ■ Pro Carton, the Association of European Cartonboard and Carton Manufacturers
Roland Rex, Pres.
c/o AC Fiduciaire SA
Todistrasse 47
PO Box 1507
CH-8027 Zurich, Switzerland
Ph: 41 43 676 4244 637
E-mail: rex@procarton.com
URL: http://www.procarton.com

6474 ■ Design Award
To recognize creative, but as yet unrealized, design ideas in carton packaging. Awarded biennially in even-numbered years. Established in 2004.

6475 ■ Pro Carton/ECMA Awards
To recognize outstanding packaging produced predominantly from cartonboard or cartonboard laminated to microflute. To qualify, all entries must have been produced and sold in the previous three years. Presented in a variety of categories, including beverages, beauty and cosmetics, confectionery, and pharmaceutical. Awarded annually. Established in 1997.

6476 ■ Rolex Awards for Enterprise
PO Box 1311
CH-1211 Geneva 26, Switzerland
Ph: 41 22 302 2200
Fax: 41 22 302 2585
E-mail: secretariat@rolexawards.com
URL: http://www.rolexawards.com

6477 ■ Rolex Awards for Enterprise
To encourage outstanding personal enterprise and to provide financial support for the implementation of projects. These should break new ground in one of five major sectors of human endeavor: Cultural Heritage, Environment, Exploration and Discovery, Science and Medicine, and Technology and Innovation. Projects must expand knowledge of our world, improve the quality of life on the planet, or contribute to the betterment of humankind. Each recipient is awarded a solid gold Rolex chronometer and a monetary prize of US$100,000. Awarded biennially in even-numbered years. Established in 1976 by Montres Rolex SA on the occasion of the 50th anniversary of the invention of the Rolex Oyster, the world's first waterproof wrist watch.

6478 ■ Rose d'Or AG (Societe Suisse de Radiodiffusion et Television et la Ville de Montreux)
Dina Baenninger, Mgr.
Sempacherstr. 3
CH-6003 Lucerne 8, Switzerland
Ph: 41 41 242 0905
Fax: 41 41 242 0906
E-mail: info@rosedor.com
URL: http://www.rosedor.com
Formerly: Swiss Broadcasting Corporation and the City of Montreux.

6479 ■ Rose d'Or Festival
Recognizes the best of the year in new entertainment and television programming. Awards are offered for Arts Documentary, Comedy, Drama,

Awards are arranged in alphabetical order below their administering organizations

Entertainment, Game Show, Multi-Platform, Performing Arts, Pitch Pilot, Reality, and Sitcom. Held annually. Established in 1961.

6480 ■ Swiss Academy of Medical Sciences (Schweizerische Akademie der Medizinischen Wissenschaften)
Dr. Hermann Amstad, Sec. Gen.
Petersplatz 13
CH-4051 Basel, Switzerland
Ph: 41 61 2699030
Fax: 41 61 2699039
E-mail: mail@samw.ch
URL: http://www.samw.ch/de/Aktuell/News.html

6481 ■ Robert Bing Prize
To encourage younger scientists, up to 45 years of age, who have done outstanding work that has helped in the recognition, treatment and cure of neurological diseases. A monetary prize and a certificate are awarded biennially in even-numbered years. Established in 1956 by Professor Robert Bing.

6482 ■ Theodore Ott Prize (Prix Theodore Ott)
To encourage established, internationally recognized scientists and medical researchers who have performed outstanding scientific work in basic neurology research. Nominations or personal applications are accepted. A monetary prize of 50,000 Swiss francs is awarded approximately every five years. Established in 1992.

6483 ■ Swiss Association for Theatre Studies (Schweizerische Gesellschaft fur Theaterkultur)
Susann Moser-Ehinger, Contact
Lothringerstrasse 55
CH-4056 Basel, Switzerland
Ph: 41 61 3211060
Fax: 41 61 3211075
E-mail: redaktion@theater.ch
URL: http://www.theater.ch

6484 ■ Hans Reinhart Ring
To recognize an artist for an outstanding theatrical performance. Swiss stage artists or foreign artists performing in Switzerland are eligible. A gold ring is awarded annually. Established in 1957 in memory of the ring's founder, Winterthur poet, Hans Reinhart.

6485 ■ Swiss Chemical Society (Schweizerische Chemische Gesellschaft)
David Spichiger, Exec. Dir.
Schwarztorstrasse 9
CH-3007 Bern, Switzerland
Ph: 41 31 3104090
Fax: 41 31 3104029
E-mail: info@scg.ch
URL: http://www.swiss-chem-soc.ch
Formerly: Swiss Association of Chemists.

6486 ■ Balmer Prize
To recognize a teacher working in Switzerland at the high school level for innovation in chemistry teaching. A medal and monetary prize is awarded annually to the teacher and his or her school's chemistry department.

6487 ■ Grammaticakis-Neumann Prize
To recognize a young scientist (under 40 years old) who carries out an excellent research program in photochemistry, photophysics, or molecular photobiology. A monetary prize of 5,000 Swiss francs is awarded annually.

6488 ■ Dr. Max Luthi Award (Prix Dr. Max-Luthi)
To recognize the author of a work of exceptional quality in the Department of Chemistry in a technical Swiss school. A bronze medal and monetary prize of 1,000 Swiss francs are awarded annually.

6489 ■ Paracelsus Prize
For recognition of outstanding research in the field of chemistry. A gold medal and cash prize of 20,000 Swiss francs are awarded biennially in even-numbered years. Established in 1938.

6490 ■ Sandmeyer Prize (Prix Sandmeyer)
To recognize a researcher or a group of researchers for outstanding work in the chemical industry field or studies. The work must take place in Switzerland, or in a foreign country by a group of researchers with participation of Swiss citizens. A monetary prize of 10,000 Swiss francs is awarded to an individual; a prize of 20,000 Swiss francs is awarded to groups. Awarded annually.

6491 ■ Werner Prize
To recognize a young scientist who has obtained very good research results in the field of chemistry. Candidates should be younger than 40 years old. A bronze medal and monetary prize of 10,000 Swiss francs are awarded annually. Established in 1915 in honor of Professor Werner.

6492 ■ Swiss Electrotechnical Association (Schweizerischer Elektrotechnischer Verein)
Willy R. Gehrer, Chm.
Luppmenstrasse 1
CH-8320 Fehraltorf, Switzerland
Ph: 41 1 9561111
Fax: 41 1 9561122
E-mail: info@electrosuisse.ch
URL: http://www.electrosuisse.ch

6493 ■ ETG Innovation Award
To recognize an individual for innovative work in the field of electrical engineering. A monetary prize of 10,000 Swiss francs is awarded annually. Administered by the Power Engineering Society (ETG) of the Association.

6494 ■ Swiss Federal Institute of Technology Zurich (Eidgenossische Technische Hochschule Zurich)
Raemistr. 101
CH-8092 Zurich, Switzerland
Ph: 41 1 632 1111
Fax: 41 1 632 1010
URL: http://www.ethz.ch

6495 ■ Georg A. Fischer Prize
For recognition of outstanding student scientific works. In particular, diploma theses or doctoral dissertations in mechanical engineering are considered. Awarded to one or more candidates annually on ETH-Day (Dies Academicus) and Promotion-Day. Established in 1970 by Mrs. Katja Fischer in honor of Mr. Georg A. Fischer, a mechanical engineer at ETH.

6496 ■ Heinrich Hatt-Bucher Prize
For recognition of outstanding student scientific work in the final diploma in the field of architecture and civil engineering. Monetary prizes of 5,000, 4,000, and 3,000 Swiss francs, respectively, are awarded annually at ETH-Day (Dies-Academicus). Established in 1986 by Heinrich Ernst Hatt-Bucher.

6497 ■ Hilti-Preis
For recognition of a scientifically outstanding diploma or Ph.D. thesis in applied research. A prize of 5,000 Swiss francs is awarded annually on the ETH-Day (Dies Academicus) or at a Promotion Ceremony. Established in 1989 by Hilti AG, Schaan, FL.

6498 ■ Otto Jaag-Gewasserschutz-Preis
For recognition of outstanding student scientific works, particularly for diploma theses or doctoral dissertations in protection of water. A monetary prize of 1,000 Swiss francs is awarded annually on ETH-Day (Dies Academicus). Established in 1980 in honor of Professor Dr. Otto Jaag.

6499 ■ Fritz Kutter-Preis
For recognition of an outstanding diploma or Ph.D. thesis in computer science, with a significant contribution in information processing or a valuable implementation of know-how, at a Swiss University or Swiss Federal Institute of Technology. A monetary prize of 10,000 francs is awarded. Established in 1975.

6500 ■ Latsis-Preis
For recognition of outstanding scientific work. Candidates who are 40 years of age and younger are eligible. The candidates are evaluated by the Research Committee of the ETH Zurich. A monetary prize of 25,000 Swiss francs is awarded annually. Established in 1984 by Fondation Latsis Internationale in honor of Dr. John Latsis. Sponsored by Forschungskommission ETH Zurich.

6501 ■ Ruzicka Prize (Ruzicka-Preis)
For recognition of an outstanding work in the field of chemistry. Work that has already been published and completed in Switzerland or by a Swiss national abroad under 40 years of age is eligible. A monetary prize, medal, document, and colloquium are awarded. Established in 1957 by Schweizerische Chemische Industrie in memory of Dr. Leopold Ruzicka, winner of the Nobel Prize for Chemistry, 1945.

6502 ■ Willi Studer Preis
To recognize the best diploma in the year of every department of Swiss Federal Institute of Technology. Awarded annually.

6503 ■ Swiss International Festival of Mountain and Environment Films (Festival International du Film Alpin et de l'Environment de Montagne, Les Diablerets, Suisse)
Charles Pascal Ghiringhelli, Pres.
CP 3
CH-1865 Les Diablerets, Switzerland
Ph: 41 24 492 2040
Fax: 41 24 492 2348
E-mail: info@fifad.ch
URL: http://www.fifad.ch

6504 ■ Les Diablerets Film Festival
To encourage and develop the production of films which will stimulate, both in Switzerland and abroad, an interest in the Alps and in the people who live and work in the mountains. An "Alpine Film" is to be understood as any film or video tape with action situated in the mountains, and a "Mountain Environment Film" as any production focusing attention on, or portraying, a place or region which deserves to be preserved or which is already protected. The Festival is open to all filmmakers, professional, free-lance, or amateurs. Films must be submitted in 16mm or 35mm formats, with optical magnetic or double band (sepmag) sound. Established in 1975.

6505 ■ Swiss Music Edition (Schweizer Musikedition)
Postfach 7851
CH-6000 Lucerne 7, Switzerland
Ph: 41 41 210 6070
Fax: 41 41 210 6070
E-mail: mail@musicedition.ch
URL: http://www.musicedition.ch

6506 ■ Swiss Music Edition (Schweizer Musikedition)
To recognize the publication of compositions of contemporary music. Swiss citizens or other citizens living in Switzerland are eligible.

6507 ■ Swiss Physiological Society
Prof. Francois Verrey, Pres.
University of Zurich
Winterthurerstr. 190

Awards are arranged in alphabetical order below their administering organizations

CH-8057 Zurich, Switzerland
Ph: 41 44 6355044
Ph: 41 44 6355046
Fax: 41 44 6356814
E-mail: verrey@access.uzh.ch
URL: http://www.swissphysio.org

6508 ■ Asher-Hess Prize
To honor the best presentations (oral) by doctoral students and post-doctoral fellows. Awarded annually.

6509 ■ Swiss Society for Infectious Diseases (Schweizerische Gesellschaft fur Infektiologie)
Prof. Dr. Ursula Fluckiger, Pres.
University Hospital Basel
Petersgraben 4
CH-4031 Basel, Switzerland
Ph: 41 61 2653851
Fax: 41 61 265 38 54
E-mail: info@sginf.ch
URL: http://www.sginf.ch
Formerly: Swiss Society for Infectious Diseases, Division for Infectiology and Hospital Epidemiology.

6510 ■ Boehringer Ingelheim Grant
For outstanding research paper in the field of clinical infectious epidemiology. A grant of 20,000 Swiss francs is awarded annually.

6511 ■ Bristol-Myers Squibb AG Grant
To a young investigator in an experimental research project in the field of HIV. A grant of 20,000 Swiss francs is awarded annually.

6512 ■ Swiss Society for Microbiology
Irene Muller, Sec.
Sonnenrain 10
3150 Schwarzenburg, Switzerland
Ph: 41 31 7312505
Fax: 41 31 7312594
E-mail: irene.mueller@pop.agri.ch
URL: http://www.swissmicrobiology.ch

6513 ■ Encouragement Award
To honor young investigators in the field of microbiology for achievements that are outstanding in terms of their originality and particular scientific value. A monetary prize of 5,000 Swiss francs is awarded annually. Established in 1996.

6514 ■ United Nations Office of the High Commissioner for Human Rights
Palais des Nations
CH-1211 Geneva, Switzerland
Ph: 41 22 9179220
E-mail: infodesk@ohchr.org
URL: http://www.ohchr.org/EN/Pages/WelcomePage.aspx

6515 ■ United Nations Prize in the Field of Human Rights (Prix pour les Droits de l'Homme)
To recognize individuals and organizations who have made outstanding contributions to the promotion of the protection of human rights and fundamental freedoms. Nominations obtained from member states of the United Nations, specialized agencies, international non-governmental organizations, in consultative status with the Economic and Social Council, are presented to the selection committee composed of the President of the United Nations General Assembly, the President of the Economic and Social Council, the Chairman of the Commission on Human Rights, the Chairman of the Sub-Commission on Prevention of Discrimination and Protection of Minorities, and the Chairman of the Commission on the Status of Women. A citation on a plaque is awarded at intervals of not less than every five years. Established in 1966. Formerly: Human Rights Prize.

6516 ■ Universal Postal Union (Union Postale Universelle)
Edouard Dayan, Dir. Gen.
Case Postale 13

CH-3000 Bern 15, Switzerland
Ph: 41 31 3503111
Fax: 41 31 3503110
E-mail: info@upu.int
URL: http://www.upu.int

6517 ■ International Letter-Writing Competition for Young People
To develop young people's facility in composition and the subtlety of their thought and to contribute to the strengthening of international friendship which is one of the essential missions of the Universal Postal Union. Individuals who are 15 years of age and under may participate in the Competition organized at the national level by Postal Administrations belonging to the UPU. Letters may be submitted until April 30 each year. Gold-plated, silver and bronze medals, diplomas, and postage stamp albums are awarded annually. A jury of UNESCO, which chooses the winning letters, also awards three bronze medals. Ceremonies are organized by the winning Postal Administrations and prizes are presented to the winners on October 9, the anniversary of the founding of the UPU. Established in 1971.

6518 ■ University of Basel (Universitat Basel)
Petersplatz 1
CH-4003 Basel, Switzerland
Ph: 41 61 267 3111
Fax: 41 61 267 3013
E-mail: kommunikation@unibas.ch
URL: http://www.unibas.ch

6519 ■ Amerbach Prize
For recognition of the best essay written by a young scholar. Students or alumni of the various departments of the University are eligible. A monetary award of 5,000 Swiss francs and a medal are awarded annually on the occasion of the Dies Academicus. Established in 1962.

6520 ■ Credit Suisse Award for Best Teaching
To promote the quality of academic teaching and training, and to strengthen Switzerland as a place of knowledge and research. Awarded annually. Endowed by Credit Suisse AB.

6521 ■ Faculty of Business and Economics Prize
To honor an individual for outstanding achievements in the study of business and economics. Awarded annually to one or two recipients. Endowed by Coop Schweiz.

6522 ■ Faculty of Humanities Prize
To honor an individual for outstanding achievements in the study of humanities. Awarded annually to one or two recipients. Endowed by Migros Cooperative Basel.

6523 ■ Faculty of Law Prize
To honor an individual for outstanding achievements in legal studies. Awarded annually to one or two recipients. Endowed by Bank Sarasin and Cie.

6524 ■ Faculty of Medicine Prize
To honor an individual for outstanding achievements in medical studies. Awarded annually to one or two recipients. Endowed by Roche Research Foundation.

6525 ■ Faculty of Psychology Prize
To honor an individual for outstanding achievements in psychological studies. Awarded annually to one or two recipients.

6526 ■ Faculty of Science Prize
To honor an individual for outstanding achievements in scientific studies. Awarded annually to one or two recipients. Endowed by Migros Cooperative Basel.

6527 ■ Faculty of Theology Prize
To honor an individual for outstanding achievements in theological studies. Awarded annually to one or two recipients.

6528 ■ Emilie Louise Frey Award for the Promotion of Talented Female Scholars
To promote young female researchers and to encourage young women to pursue research careers by recognizing either an outstanding dissertation or Master's thesis written by a female researcher. Rotates annually among faculties/departments. Awarded annually. Established in 2008 in honor of the first female student to receive a PhD at the University of Basel, the physician Emilie Louise Frey (1869-1937).

6529 ■ Schwizerhuesli Young Researchers Award
To recognize the best Master's dissertation in science, as selected by the Schwizerhuesli Student Fraternity. Awarded annually on the occasion of the Dies Academicus. Established in 2009.

6530 ■ Irma Tschudi Steiner Award
To recognize the best doctoral dissertation in the pharmaceutical sciences submitted by a female candidate. Awarded biennially in odd-numbered years.

6531 ■ Visions du Reel International Documentary Film Festival
Jean Schmutz, Pres.
18 rue Juste-Olivier
CH-1260 Nyon, Switzerland
Ph: 41 22 365 4455
Fax: 41 22 365 4450
E-mail: docnyon@visionsdureel.ch
URL: http://www.visionsdureel.ch

6532 ■ Visions du Reel International Documentary Film Festival
To recognize documentary films on an international perspective. Works are classified into the International Competition, New Perceptions (beginning, self-taught, and student filmmaker), and the Showcase of Swiss Film Industry (best of recent Swiss productions). Monetary prizes accompany Visions du Reel prizes. Held annually.

6533 ■ World Conservation Union
Julia Marton-Lefevre, Dir. Gen.
Rue Mauverney 28
CH-1196 Gland, Switzerland
Ph: 41 22 999 0000
Fax: 41 22 999 0002
E-mail: webmaster@iucn.org
URL: http://www.iucn.org

6534 ■ Honorary Membership
To recognize individuals for outstanding service in the field of conservation of nature and natural resources. Awarded when merited.

6535 ■ IUCN - Reuters - COMplus Media Awards
To help raise global awareness of environmental and sustainable development issues by encouraging high standards in environmental reporting worldwide. A certificate and cash prize of US$500 are awarded to each of six regional winners, with one overall recipient awarded a cash prize of US$5,000 and a travel stipend to attend the awards ceremony. Awarded biennially in even-numbered years. Established in 1998. Co-sponsored by the Thomson Reuters Foundation and COMplus.

6536 ■ Kenton R. Miller Award for Innovation in Protected Areas Management
To recognize individuals for innovation in communications, planning and management, finance and economics, assessment, monitoring, and evaluation, learning and capacity building, or governance. A stipend of US$5,000 is awarded annually.

6537 ■ Fred M. Packard Award
To recognize individuals or groups for outstanding service to protected areas. A certificate and

Awards are arranged in alphabetical order below their administering organizations

medal are presented annually at the World Conservation Congress; in some cases, a monetary award is also presented. Established in 1979 and now given in honor of Fred M. Packard, who initiated the award. Formerly: (1982) Valor Award.

6538 ■ John C. Phillips Memorial Medal
For recognition of distinguished service in international conservation. A sterling silver medal is awarded triennially at ordinary sessions of the IUCN General Assembly. Established in 1963 by Friends of John C. Phillips and the American Committee for International Wild Life Protection in memory of John C. Phillips, distinguished United States naturalist, explorer, author and conservationist.

6539 ■ Sir Peter Scott Medal for Conservation Merit
To recognize highly significant achievement in conservation in however small a field. Accomplishments to be recognized may involve one or more specific events, or they may reflect sustained activity over a period of time. The recipient may be one or more individuals, an organization or an institution.

6540 ■ Tree of Learning Award
To recognize individuals who have contributed to environmental protection through education and communications. The prize is awarded every three years at the IUCN members' assembly of the World Conservation Congress. Awarded to one or more recipients.

6541 ■ Young Conservationist Award
To recognize young conservationists for outstanding contributions to the management of protected areas. Candidates must be under the age of 35. Awarded annually.

6542 ■ World Federation of Neurosurgical Societies
Mrs. Janette A. Joseph, Dir.
5 Rue Du Marche
1260 Nyon, Switzerland
Ph: 41 22 362 4303
Fax: 41 22 362 4352
E-mail: janjoseph@wfns.ch
URL: http://www.wfns.org

6543 ■ Gold Medal of Honor
For excellence in neurosurgery. A monetary award is given quadrennially.

6544 ■ Scoville Award
For excellence in neurosurgery. A monetary award is given quadrennially.

6545 ■ Young Neurosurgeons Award
To recognize young neurosurgeons for original, unpublished work related to basic science or clinical work in neurosurgery. Candidates must be within 10 years of having obtained his or her neurosurgical qualification. A monetary award of US$1,500 is awarded to five recipients every four years at the World Congress.

6546 ■ World Health Organization (Organisation Mondiale de la Sante)
Dr. Margaret Chan, Dir. Gen.
20, Ave. Appia
CH-1211 Geneva 27, Switzerland
Ph: 41 22 7912111
Ph: 41 22 7912222
Fax: 41 22 7913111
E-mail: info@who.int
URL: http://www.who.int

6547 ■ Leon Bernard Foundation Prize
For recognition of outstanding service in the field of social medicine. No condition is made as to age, sex, profession, or nationality. Only nominations put forward by national health administrations of WHO Member States and by former recipients of the awards are acceptable. A

monetary prize of 2,500 Swiss francs and a bronze medal are awarded biennially in odd-numbered years. Established in 1948.

6548 ■ Darling Foundation Prize
For recognition of outstanding work in the control of malaria. Only nominations put forward by national health administrations of WHO Member States and by former recipients of the award are acceptable. A monetary prize of 2,500 Swiss francs and a bronze medal are awarded periodically. Established in 1948 in memory of Dr. Samuel Taylor Darling, a noted malaria researcher.

6549 ■ Ihsan Dogramaci Family Health Foundation Prize
For recognition of outstanding services in the field of family health. Only nominations put forward by national health administrations of WHO member states and by former recipients of the award are acceptable. A monetary prize of US$20,000 and a bronze medal are awarded biennially in odd-numbered years. Established in 1980. Formerly: (1996) Child Health Foundation Prize.

6550 ■ Down Syndrome Research Prize in the Eastern Mediterranean Prize
To honor one or more persons considered to have made an outstanding contribution in the field of research related to Down syndrome. A bronze medal and a monetary prize of US$2,000 are awarded biennially. Established in 1999.

6551 ■ Dr. Lee Jong-Wook Memorial Prize for Public Health
Awarded to one or more persons, institutions, governmental or non-governmental organizations who have made extraordinary contributions into one or more of the following areas: prevention, treatment and control of HIV/AIDS; control of communicable diseases; or control of tropical diseases. Awarded annually. A monetary prize of up to $85,000 is presented. Awarded annually during a special assembly at the World Health Assembly. Established in 2008.

6552 ■ Jacques Parisot Foundation Fellowship
To support research in social medicine or public health. The regional offices of the WHO are invited in turn to submit candidatures. A fellowship of US$5,000 and a bronze medal are awarded biennially in even-numbered years. Established in 1969.

6553 ■ Dr. Comlan A. A. Quenum Prize for Public Health
To honor an individual considered to have made the most significant contribution to improving health in the geographical area of Africa. A bronze medal and monetary prize of US$2,000 are awarded biennially. Established in 1987.

6554 ■ Sasakawa Health Prize
To recognize an individual, institution, or non-governmental organization for outstanding innovative work in health development. Only nominations put forward by national health administrations of WHO Member States and by former recipients of the award are acceptable. A monetary prize of US$100,000 and a crystal statuette are awarded annually. Established in 1984 upon the initiative of Mr. Ryoichi Sasakawa of Japan, a great supporter of WHO, and President of the Sasakawa Memorial Health Foundation.

6555 ■ Dr. A. T. Shousha Foundation Prize
To recognize an individual for a significant contribution to improving health in the Eastern Mediterranean. A bronze medal and monetary prize of 2,500 Swiss francs is awarded annually. Established in 1966.

6556 ■ State of Kuwait Prize for Research in Health Promotion
Awarded to one or more persons, institutions or

nongovernmental organizations that have made an extraordinary contribution to research in health promotion. A certificate, plaque and a monetary award of up to $40,000 are awarded annually at a special assembly during the World Health Assembly. Established in 2004.

6557 ■ United Arab Emirates Health Foundation Prize
To honor one or more persons, institutions, or nongovernmental organizations that have made an outstanding contribution to health development. A certificate, plaque, and monetary prize up to US$40,000 are awarded annually. Established in 1995.

6558 ■ World Meteorological Organization (Organisation Meteorologique Mondiale)
Dr. David Grimes, Pres.
7bis, ave. de la Paix
CH-1211 Geneva 2, Switzerland
Ph: 41 22 7308111
Fax: 41 22 7308181
E-mail: wmo@wmo.int
URL: http://www.wmo.int/pages/index_en.html

6559 ■ Norbert Gerbier-Mumm International Award
To encourage and reward an original scientific paper on the influence of meteorology in a particular field of the physical, natural, or human sciences, or on the influence of one of these sciences on meteorology. The award aims at stimulating interest in such research in support of WMO programs. Only papers published during the 18-month period immediately preceding the year when the award is made are eligible for consideration. A medal bearing the likeness of Mr. Norbert Gerbier and 7,600 Euro are awarded annually.

6560 ■ International Meteorological Organization Prize
For recognition of outstanding work in the field of meteorology or in any related field. A monetary prize of SFr 10,000, a gold medal, and a parchment scroll with a citation are given annually. Established in 1956.

6561 ■ Research Award for Young Scientists
To encourage young scientists, preferably in developing countries, who are working in the fields of meteorology and hydrology. Individuals who are under 35 years of age may be nominated by Permanent Representatives of Member States with WMO. A monetary award of $1,000 and a citation are awarded annually.

6562 ■ Prof. Dr. Vilho Vaisala Award
To encourage and stimulate interest in important research programs in the field of instruments and methods of observation in support of WMO programs. Scientists may submit papers through the Permanent Representatives of Member States with WMO. A monetary prize of $5,000, a medal, and a diploma are awarded biennially in even-numbered years. Established in 1986 in honor of Dr. Vilho Vaisala, founder of the Vaisala Oy. In addition, the New Prof. Dr. Vilho Vaisala Award, created in 2004, awards $10,000 biennially to recognize work in developing countries and countries with economies in translation.

6563 ■ World Organization of the Scout Movement
Mr. Luc Panissod, Sec. Gen.
Rue du Pre-Jerome 5
PO Box 91
CH-1211 Geneva, Switzerland
Ph: 41 22 7051010
Fax: 41 22 7051020
E-mail: worldbureau@scout.org
URL: http://www.scout.org

6564 ■ Bronze Wolf (Loup de Bronze)
To recognize an individual for outstanding

Awards are arranged in alphabetical order below their administering organizations

services of the most exceptional character to the world scout movement. A bronze medal in the form of an wolf is awarded triennially at the World Scout Conferences. Established in 1935 by Robert Baden-Powell, founder of the Scout movement.

6565 ■ Scouts of the World Award
To contribute to the enrichment of young people in two areas: community service and international cooperation. Candidates must demonstrate awareness of world issues through the Scouts of the World Discovery program and acquire the necessary experience and skills to become a citizen of the world through a voluntary service. Open to scouts in the Senior Sections (15-26 age range). Awarded when merited by the scout's provincial/national headquarters. Established in 2000.

6566 ■ Worlddidac Foundation
Paul Perjes, Contact
Bollwerk 21
PO Box 8866
CH-3001 Bern, Switzerland
Ph: 41 31 311 7682
Fax: 41 31 312 1744
E-mail: info@worlddidac.org
URL: http://www.worlddidac.org

6567 ■ Worlddidac Award
To promote the quality improvement and the creativity of the international educational materials industry. The products entered are divided into the following product groups: school supplies, vocational and scientific equipment, visual and audiovisual media, furniture/equipment, printed and published products, informatics and multimedia technologies. There is a further classification into entry groups based on the educational level of the respective products: preschools, elementary schools, secondary/senior schools, universities, institutes of technology, professional training and further education, and special education. Products newly released in the past two years are eligible. Gold, silver, bronze award certificates are presented biennially at the International Exhibition for Educational Materials and Professional Training WORLDDIDAC in Basel, Switzerland. Established in 1984.

6568 ■ WWF International
Yolanda Kakabadse, Pres.
Av. du Mont-Blanc
CH-1196 Gland, Switzerland
Ph: 41 22 3649111
Fax: 41 22 3648836
URL: http://wwf.panda.org
Formerly: World Wildlife Fund.

6569 ■ Award for Conservation Merit
To recognize grassroots conservation work that has significantly contributed to local conservation and conservation achievement over a long period. Individuals, groups, and institutions or associations are eligible. Awarded annually.

6570 ■ Duke of Edinburgh Conservation Medal
To recognize individuals for outstanding achievements in conservation. Awarded annually.

6571 ■ Gold Panda Award
This, WWF's highest award, is given for highly meritorious and strictly personal services to the conservation of wildlife and natural resources. Nominations are made, screened, and judged through an internal consultative process. A gold medal is awarded annually. Established in 1970.

6572 ■ Roll of Honour
A posthumous honor for people having rendered outstanding services to the cause of conservation, not only to WWF. Awarded when merited. Established in 1973.

6573 ■ Y's Men International
Takao Nishimura, Sec. Gen.
9 Ave. Ste-Clotilde

CH-1205 Geneva, Switzerland
Ph: 41 22 8091530
Fax: 41 22 8091539
E-mail: ihq@ysmen.org
URL: http://www.ysmen.org

6574 ■ Harry M. Ballantyne Award
This, the highest honor of the Y's Men International, is given to recognize especially deserving friends of Y's Men International who over a long period of time have rendered service of special value and helpfulness to the Y's Men's movement. A medal, a trophy, and a framed diploma are awarded annually. Established in 1957 by Harry M. Ballantyne.

6575 ■ Elmer Crowe Memorial Award
To recognize an outstanding district governor. A bronze wall plaque is awarded annually.

Taiwan

6576 ■ Architectural Institute of the Republic of China
Prof. Chiang Che-Ming, Pres.
13F-3, 51, Keelung Rd., Sec. 1
Taipei 110, Taiwan
Ph: 886 2 27350338
Fax: 886 2 27396917
E-mail: chiairoc@ms21.hinet.net
URL: http://www.airoc.org.tw

6577 ■ Architecture Award
For elementary through high school scientific works related to architecture.

6578 ■ Institute Fellowship Award
For achievement in architectural research or planning and design.

6579 ■ Master Thesis Award
For a master's thesis on architecture.

6580 ■ Research Paper Award
For a paper appearing in the Journal of Architecture.

6581 ■ Center for Chinese Studies
Karl Min Ku, Dir.
20 Chungshan South Rd.
Taipei 10001, Taiwan
Ph: 886 2 23147321
Fax: 886 2 23712126
E-mail: ccswww@msg.ncl.edu.tw
URL: http://ccs.ncl.edu.tw/ccs/ccs.asp
Formerly: (1987) Resource and Information Center for Chinese Studies.

6582 ■ Research Grant Program to Assist Foreign Scholars in Chinese Studies
To enhance scholarly communication in the field of Chinese studies and encourage foreign scholars of Chinese studies to carry out research work in the Republic of China. PhD candidates, assistant professors, associate professors, professors, and researchers at institutes are eligible to apply. The content of the research, to be undertaken in Taiwan, should be within the field of Chinese studies. Research grants for 3 to 12 months are awarded annually. The amount of each grant is determined by the candidate's rank at the time of application. Established in 1988 by the R.O.C. Center for Chinese Studies.

6583 ■ International Ergonomics Association
Andrew S. Imada PhD, Pres.
National Tsing Hua University
Dept. of Industrial Engineering and Engineering Management
101, Sec. 2, Guang Fu Rd.
Hsinchu 30013, Taiwan
Ph: 886 3 5742649
Fax: 886 3 5726153
E-mail: mywangeric@gmail.com
URL: http://www.iea.cc

6584 ■ Distinguished Service Award
For an outstanding contribution to the promotion, development, and advancement of IEA. Awarded triennially.

6585 ■ Ergonomics Development Award
For a contribution that advances the existing ergonomics sub-specialty or opens up a new area of ergonomics research or application. Awarded triennially.

6586 ■ Liberty Mutual Prize in Occupational Safety and Ergonomics
For outstanding original research leading to the reduction or mitigation of work related injuries and/or advancement of theory, understanding, and development of occupational safety research. A cash prize of US$10,000 is awarded.

6587 ■ Outstanding Educators Award
For an outstanding contribution in the area of ergonomics education. Awarded triennially.

6588 ■ President's Award
For an outstanding contribution to ergonomics. Awarded triennially.

6589 ■ K.U. Smith Student Paper Award
For a deserving student responsible for an application or contribution to ergonomics. A cash prize of US$3,000 is awarded triennially.

6590 ■ National Science Council of Taiwan
Lou- Chuang Lee, Minister
No. 106 Hoping E Rd., Sect. 2
Taipei 10622, Taiwan
Ph: 886 2 27377992
Ph: 886 2 27377501
Fax: 886 2 27377566
E-mail: nsc@nsc.gov.tw
URL: http://web1.nsc.gov.tw

6591 ■ Tsungming Tu Award
To recognize a foreign scientist of international renown for outstanding discoveries or achievements in his or her chosen academic research field. Awarded annually. Established in 2006 in honor of Dr. Tsungming Tu, a legendary figure in Taiwan's medical field.

6592 ■ Taipei Golden Horse Film Festival
7 F, No. 196, Jhonghua Rd.
Taipei 10850, Taiwan
Ph: 886 2 2370 0456
Fax: 886 2 2370 0366
E-mail: info@goldenhorse.org.tw
URL: http://www.goldenhorse.org.tw
Formerly: Taipei International Film Exhibition.

6593 ■ Golden Horse Awards
To encourage film production in Taiwan and Hong Kong. The Festival is comprised of three major events each year: Golden Horse Awards - a prestigious competition designed to promote the production of Chinese-language cinema; International Film Exhibition - a non-competitive annual showcase of a wide range of the most outstanding films from around the world to enhance the public's appreciation of cinematic art and to foster understanding among diverse cultures; and Chinese Film Exhibition - a showcase of Chinese films retrospectively on different topics, recent products and overseas Chinese film production. Awards are given in the following categories: Best Picture, Best Short Film, Best Documentary as well as Best Animation. Individual Awards are given for Best Director, Best Leading Actor/Actress, Best Supporting Actor/Actress, Best New Performer, Best Original Screenplay, Best Screenplay Adaptation, Best Cinematography, Best Visual Effects, Best Art Direction, Best Make Up & Costume Design, Best Action Choreography, Best Original Film Score, Best Original Film Song, Best Editing, and Best Sound Effects. Special awards include Taiwanese Film of the Year and Taiwanese Film-

Awards are arranged in alphabetical order below their administering organizations

maker of the Year. A non-competition award is given to the Audience Choice Award. Held annually. Established in 1980.

6594 ■ Taiwan Ministry of Economic Affairs Small and Medium Enterprise Administration
3rd Fl., No. 95, Sec. 2
Roosevelt Rd.
Taipei 10646, Taiwan
Ph: 886 2 2368 6858
Fax: 886 2 2367 1134
URL: http://www.moeasmea.gov.tw

6595 ■ Business Start-Up Award
To discover start-up enterprises with potential in Taiwan, and to develop Taiwan as the start-up and innovation base for the Asia Pacific area.

6596 ■ Golden Book Award
To encourage publishers to introduce series of outstanding books beneficial to management level. Awarded annually to several recipients. Established in 1996.

6597 ■ National Outstanding Small and Medium Enterprise Award
To encourage and demonstrate successful examples of small and medium enterprises in Taiwan. Awarded annually. Established in 1992.

6598 ■ Rising Star Award
To recognize small and medium enterprises that display excellence in global trading. Awarded annually to several recipients. Established in 1998.

6599 ■ Small and Medium Enterprise Innovation Research Award
To recognize and encourage small and medium enterprises nationwide to engage in innovation and in research and development. Awarded annually to several recipients. Established in 1993.

6600 ■ Taiwan Pediatric Association
Mei-Hwei Chang, Pres.
10 Fl.-1, No. 69, Hang-Chow S Rd.
Sect. 1
Taipei 100, Taiwan
Ph: 886 2 23516446
Fax: 886 2 23516448
E-mail: tpa98@www.pediatr.org.tw
URL: http://www.pediatr.org.tw

6601 ■ E. Mead Johnson Award for Research in Pediatrics
To recognize clinical and laboratory research achievements in pediatrics. Two awards are presented annually, consisting of a plaque, $15,000 honorarium, and travel expenses to present review at the Society's annual meeting.

Thailand

6602 ■ Ensign Media (Bangkok) Co., Ltd.
55 Bio House Bldg., 5th Fl.
Soi Prompong
Klongton Nua, Wattana
Bangkok 10110, Thailand
Ph: 66 2 662 5195
Fax: 66 2 662 5198
E-mail: bangkok@ensign-media.com
URL: http://www.ensign-media.com

6603 ■ South East Asia Property Awards
To recognize the high quality of the real estate industry throughout Southeast Asia. Covers the countries of Indonesia, Malaysia, Singapore, Thailand, and Vietnam. Presented in dozens of categories within the classifications of 1) Developers; 2) Real Estate Agencies; 3) Development; 4) Architecture/Interior Design; 5) Marketing; and 6) Publisher's Choice. Awarded annually. Established in 2011.

6604 ■ Thailand Property Awards
To promote, reward, and showcase the best in Thailand's real estate industry. Presented in dozens of categories within the classifications of 1) Developers; 2) Real Estate Services; 3) Development; 4) Architecture/Interior Design; and 5) Publisher's Choice. Awarded annually. Established in 2006.

6605 ■ Southeast Asian Ministers of Education Organization
Dr. Ahamad bin Sipon, Dir.
Mom Luang Pin Malakul Centenery Bldg., 4th Fl.
920 Sukhumvit Rd.
Klongtoey, Prakanong
Bangkok 10110, Thailand
Ph: 66 2 3910144
Fax: 66 2 3812587
E-mail: secretariat@seameo.org
URL: http://www.seameo.org

6606 ■ SEAMEO-Australia Press Award
To recognize outstanding coverage of education issues by print journalists in Southeast Asia. Open to print journalists of SEAMEO Member Countries, namely, Brunei Darussalam, Cambodia, Indonesia, Lao PDR, Malaysia, Myanmar, the Philippines, Singapore, Thailand, Timor-Leste, and Vietnam. Candidates must be working in print media, including online newspapers and online magazines that publish recognized articles that subscribe to the ideals of professional journalism. Awarded annually. Established in 2000. Supported by the Australian government.

6607 ■ Service Award
To recognize staff members who have demonstrated exceptionally high levels of achievement in such areas as work performance, innovation and creativity, professionalism, and commitment that contribute to the success of the Organization's mission and goals. Awarded annually to a recipient in each SEAMEO unit.

6608 ■ Thai Chamber of Commerce
Mr. Prapatchot Thanavorasart, Exec. Dir.
150 Rajbopit Rd.
Pranakhon District
Bangkok 10200, Thailand
Ph: 66 2 6221860
Ph: 66 2 6221876
Fax: 66 2 2253372
E-mail: tcc@thaiechamber.com
URL: http://www2.thaiechamber.com

6609 ■ Management Award
To effective leaders of provincial chambers.

6610 ■ United Nations Economic and Social Commission for Asia and the Pacific
Noeleen Heyzer, Exec. Sec.
The United Nations Bldg.
Rajadamnern Nok Ave.
Bangkok 10200, Thailand
Ph: 66 2 2881234
Fax: 66 2 2881000
E-mail: unescap@unescap.org
URL: http://www.unescap.org

6611 ■ HRD Award
Recognizes social development in Asia and Pacific. Awarded annually.

Trinidad and Tobago

6612 ■ ANSA McAL Foundation
TATIL Bldg., 9th Fl.
11 Maraval Rd.
PO Box 600
Port of Spain, Trinidad and Tobago
Ph: 868625-3670
Fax: 868622-3491
E-mail: anscafe@ansamcal.com
URL: http://www.ansamcal.com

6613 ■ Anthony N. Sabga Caribbean Awards for Excellence
To recognize significant Caribbean achievement and to encourage and support the pursuit of excellence by Caribbean individuals for the benefit of the region. Open to candidates from any country in the Caribbean Community (CARICOM). Presented in three categories: Arts and Letters, Science and Technology, and Public and Civic Contributions. A gold medal and monetary prize of TT$500,000 is awarded annually in each category. Established in 2005.

6614 ■ Government of the Republic of Trinidad and Tobago
Office of the Prime Minister
Whitehall
29 Maraval Rd.
Port of Spain, Trinidad and Tobago
Ph: 868622-1625
URL: http://www.opm.gov.tt

6615 ■ Chaconia Medal
To honor an individual for long and meritorious service to Trinidad and Tobago that promotes the national welfare or strengthens the community spirit. Awarded annually when merited.

6616 ■ Hummingbird Medal
To honor an individual for loyal and devoted service beneficial to Trinidad and Tobago in any field of human endeavor or for gallantry or other humane action. Awarded annually when merited.

6617 ■ Medal of Merit
To honor an individual for outstanding and meritorious service in the Public Service, the Defense and Protective Services, or with Statutory Bodies performing national functions. Awarded annually when merited.

6618 ■ Prime Minister's Awards for Innovation and Invention
To acknowledge and reward individuals who demonstrate innovative thinking, particularly in the arena of science and technology. Individuals aged nine to 17 are eligible for the Junior Division; individuals 18 and older are eligible for the Senior Division. Awards are presented in two categories within each division: 1. Innovation and Invention and 2. Design Challenge. Awarded biennially in even-numbered years. Established in 2000.

6619 ■ Trinity Cross
To honor an individual for distinguished and outstanding service to Trinidad and Tobago. Awarded annually when merited.

6620 ■ Information and Communications Technology Society of Trinidad and Tobago
Fenwick Reid, Pres.
PO Box 5045
Port of Spain, Trinidad and Tobago
Ph: 868675-9204
Fax: 868675-9204
E-mail: secretartiat@icts.org.tt
URL: http://www.icts.org.tt

6621 ■ Excellence Awards
To recognize and reward outstanding performance by information and communications technology projects and individuals. Held annually.

6622 ■ National Carnival Bands Association of Trinidad and Tobago
1 Picton St.
Newtown
Port of Spain, Trinidad and Tobago
Ph: 868628-3143
Ph: 868628-8650
Fax: 868622-1978
E-mail: info@ncbatt.com
URL: http://www.ncbatt.com

Awards are arranged in alphabetical order below their administering organizations

6623 ■ Junior Carnival Awards
To promote the traditional Carnival (Mas) and to recognize bandleaders, designers, craftsmen, costume builders, masqueraders, and other involved in Carnival activity. Awards are presented in several categories. Held annually.

6624 ■ Senior Carnival Awards
To promote the traditional Carnival (Mas) and to recognize bandleaders, designers, craftsmen, costume builders, masqueraders, and other involved in Carnival activity. Awards are presented in several categories, including the naming of the King and Queen. Held annually.

6625 ■ National Institute for Higher Education, Research, Science and Technology
43-45 Woodford St.
Newtown
Port of Spain, Trinidad and Tobago
Ph: 868622-7880
Fax: 868622-1589
E-mail: innovation@niherst.gov.tt
URL: http://www.niherst.gov.tt

6626 ■ Awards in Science and Technology
To reward and recognize individuals for outstanding contributions made to the field of science and technology, including science education. A plaque or trophy is awarded annually. Established in 2005.

6627 ■ Frank Rampersad Scientific and Technological Award
To recognize an outstanding postgraduate student engaged in food, agriculture, or environmental research. A plaque and monetary prize of TT$20,000 are awarded every four years. Established in 2000.

6628 ■ Trinidad and Tobago Football Federation
Oliver Camps, Pres.
43 Dundonald St.
PO Box 400
Port of Spain, Trinidad and Tobago
Ph: 868623-7312
Fax: 868623-8109
E-mail: ttff1908@yahoo.com
URL: http://ttffonline.com

6629 ■ Football Awards
To recognize the best male and female athletes, coaches, and officials. Awards include Footballer of the Year, Player of the Year, Team of the Year, Super League Awards, Fair Play Award, Most Valuable Player, Referee of the Year, Administrator of the Year, and Coach of the Year. Awarded annually.

Turkey

6630 ■ International Centre for Heat and Mass Transfer
Graham de Vahl Davis, Pres.
Middle East Technical University
Mechanical Engineering Dept.
TR-06531 Ankara, Turkey
Ph: 90 312 2105213
Ph: 90 312 2105214
Fax: 90 312 2101429
E-mail: ichmt@ichmt.org
URL: http://www.ichmt.org

6631 ■ Fellowship Awards
For recognition of a contribution to a field of heat and mass transfer science and for enhancement of the progress in scientific and technological cooperation connected to the ICHMT activities. Awarded to no more than two individuals each year. Established in 1975.

6632 ■ Hartnett-Irvine Award
To recognize an individual for the best paper on heat or mass transfer presented at an ICHMT conference, symposium, or seminar. A medal and certificate are awarded annually. Established in 2007 in honor of James P. Hartnett and Thomas F. Irvine, founders of ICHMT.

6633 ■ Luikov Medal
For recognition of an outstanding contribution to the heat and mass transfer science and art. Nominations are accepted by January. A medal is awarded biennially in even-numbered years. Established in 1975 in honor of A.V. Luikov.

6634 ■ Scientific and Technical Research Council of Turkey
(Turkiye Bilimsel ve Teknolojik Arastirma Kurumu)
Prof. Dr. Nuket Yetis, Pres.
Tunus No. 80
Kavaklidere
TR-06100 Ankara, Turkey
Ph: 90 312 4685300
E-mail: aysegul.gungor@tubitak.gov.tr
URL: http://www.tubitak.gov.tr

6635 ■ Junior Science Award
(Tesvik Odulu)
To recognize and encourage the potential for future outstanding scientific contributions. Living Turkish scientists under 40 years of age are eligible. A monetary prize in Turkish liras, a silver plaque, and a certificate are awarded annually. Established in 1968.

6636 ■ Science Award
(Bilim Odulu)
For recognition of contributions to scientific research at the international level, or to the development of the country. Living Turkish scientists are eligible. A monetary prize in Turkish liras, a golden plaque, and a certificate are awarded annually. Established in 1965.

6637 ■ Scientific Service Award
To recognize an individual who has significantly served science, either by training high-level scientists, by contributing to the institutionalization of a branch of science, or by contributing to the establishment of a scientific institution.

6638 ■ Technology Award
To encourage innovation and technology development by recognizing companies for their comprehensive technological development activities.

6639 ■ Tubitak-TWAS Science Award
To recognize a scientist who has made a significant contribution to the advancement of science in general. Co-sponsored by the Third World Academy of Sciences (TWAS).

6640 ■ Turkish Society of Cardiology
(Turk Kardiyoloji Dernegi)
Mr. Ahmet Unver, Exec. Off.
Darulaceze Cd. Fulya Sk.
Eksioglu Is Merkezi, No. 9/1
Okmeydani
34384 Istanbul, Turkey
Ph: 90 212 2211730
Ph: 90 212 2211738
Fax: 90 212 2211754
E-mail: tsc@tkd.org.tr
URL: http://www.tkd.org.tr

6641 ■ Young Investigator Award
To recognize a young scientist in cardiology. Awarded annually. Established in 1993.

Turks and Caicos Islands

6642 ■ Turks & Caicos Conch Festival
Providenciales, Turks and Caicos Islands
Ph: 649331-6832
URL: http://www.conchfestival.com

6643 ■ Turks and Caicos Conch Festival
To recognize the best dishes made with conch. Open to restaurants on Turks & Caicos Islands. Awards are presented in several categories, such as conch chowder and conch salad, with an overall winner declared the Grand Champion. Held annually in November. Established in 2004.

6644 ■ Turks & Caicos Islands Tourist Board
Stubbs Diamond Plz.
Providenciales, Turks and Caicos Islands
Ph: 649946-4970
Fax: 649941-5494
E-mail: info@turksandcaicostourism.com
URL: http://www.turksandcaicostourism.com

6645 ■ Kite Flying Competition
To recognize locally-made kites from Providenciales and North Caicos. Presented in the following categories: Smallest Kite, Largest Kite, Most Artistic Kite, National Pride Kite, and Best Traditional Kite. Held annually. Established in 1993.

6646 ■ Underwater Photo Competition
To recognize the best photographs taken in the territorial waters of the Turks & Caicos Islands during the competition period. Cash prizes of $3,000, $2,000, and $1,000 are awarded to first, second, and third place winners, respectively. In addition, winning photographs are published by the government of the Turks & Caicos Islands as a set of commemorative postage stamps. Held annually. Established in 2005.

6647 ■ Turks & Caicos Society for the Prevention of Cruelty to Animals
Susie Turn Plz.
Leeward Hwy.
Providenciales, Turks and Caicos Islands
Ph: 649941-8846
E-mail: tcspca@tciway.tc
URL: http://tcspca.tc

6648 ■ Festival of the Wagging Tails Dog Show
To recognize outstanding dogs on Turks & Caicos Islands. Awards are presented in the following categories: Best Trick, Most Original Potcake, Looks Most Like Owner, Best at Obstacle Course, Cutest Tail, and Best Looking Male and Female. An overall winner is declared the Best in Show. Held annually. Established in 2005.

Uganda

6649 ■ Amakula Kampala Cultural Foundation
Plot 266, Kivebulaya Rd., Mengo
PO Box 10020
Kampala, Uganda
Ph: 256 41 427 3532
URL: http://www.amkula.com

6650 ■ Golden Impala Eastern Africa Short Film Award
To recognize the most outstanding short film and video production in the Amakula Kampala International Film Festival. Open to productions no longer than 30 minutes made by directors from Uganda, Tanzania, Kenya, Rwanda, Burundi, Zambia, Malawi, Mozambique, Congo, Sudan, Ethiopia, Somalia, Djibouti, and Eritrea. Awarded annually.

6651 ■ Young Achievers Awards
Plot 33A Bukoto Crescent
PO Box 12632
Kampala, Uganda
Ph: 256 752 845460
E-mail: mail@youngachievers.ug
URL: http://www.youngachievers.ug

6652 ■ Young Achievers Awards
To recognize and appreciate outstanding contri-

Awards are arranged in alphabetical order below their administering organizations

butions by young individuals or groups in the areas of business, leadership, and development; to promote a spirit of entrepreneurship, innovation, and excellence; and to support ideas of creating new employment opportunities outside the traditional job market. Open to Ugandan citizens aged between 18 and 35 years. Awards are presented in 11 categories: Construction Skills, Hospitality Skills, Agriculture Skills, Business and Trade, Journalism, Social Entrepreneurs, Corporate and Professional, Art/Fashion/Design, Music and Entertainment, Sports, and Information Communication Technology Solutions. In addition, the following special awards are presented: Young Achiever of the Year, Heroes/Heroines Award, and Lifetime Achievement Award. Presented annually. Established in 2009.

Ukraine

6653 ■ Office of the President of Ukraine
c/o Public Reception Office
12 Shovkovychna St.
Kiev, Ukraine
Ph: 380 44 226 2077
URL: http://www.president.gov.ua

6654 ■ Medal for Irreproachable Service
To honor an individual for exceptional service to Ukraine. Awarded when merited.

6655 ■ Medal for Military Service to Ukraine
To honor an individual for outstanding military service to Ukraine. Awarded when merited.

United Arab Emirates

6656 ■ Abu Dhabi Authority for Culture and Heritage
Zayed 1st str, Al-Khalidya
PO Box 2380
Abu Dhabi, United Arab Emirates
Ph: 971 2 657 6171
Fax: 971 2 441 8418
E-mail: info@adach.ae
URL: http://www.adach.ae

6657 ■ Emirates Film Competition
To recognize and support the film industry in the Emirates. Open to UAE national writers, directors, and/or producers who have completed a short, feature, or documentary film. Awards are presented in various categories. Held annually. Established in 2001.

6658 ■ Sheikh Zayed Book Award
To recognize an outstanding Arab writer, intellectual, publisher, or young talent for writings and translations of humanities that have enriched Arab cultural, literary, and social life. A monetary prize of AED 7 million is awarded annually. Established in memory of Sheikh Zayed Bin Sultan Al Nahyan.

6659 ■ American Business Council of Dubai and the Northern Emirates
John Podgore, Pres.
PO Box 37068
Dubai, United Arab Emirates
Ph: 971 4 3407566
Fax: 971 4 3407565
E-mail: director@abcdubai.com
URL: http://www.abcdubai.com

6660 ■ American Business Award
To honor a UAE national for an outstanding contribution to the development of relations between the United Arab Emirates and the United States of America. Awarded annually.

6661 ■ *Arabian Business* Magazine
ITP Publishing Group Ltd.
Al Hilal Bldg.
Garhoud Rd.

PO Box 500024
Dubai, United Arab Emirates
Ph: 971 4 210 8000
Fax: 971 4 210 8080
E-mail: info@itp.com
URL: http://www.arabianbusiness.com

6662 ■ Arabian Business Achievement Awards
To honor Arab individuals and corporations for business achievement. Presented in a variety of categories, including technology, logistics, investment banking, healthcare, industrial, and residential development. In addition, the Businessman of the Year may be presented. Trophies are awarded annually. Established in 2000.

6663 ■ Emirates Environmental Group
Villa No. JMR 68, Jumeirah 1
PO Box 7013
Dubai, United Arab Emirates
Ph: 971 4 344 8622
Fax: 971 4 344 8677
E-mail: eeg@emirates.net.ae
URL: http://www.eeg-uae.org

6664 ■ Arabia Corporate Social Responsibility Awards
To recognize and honor organizations in the Arab region that demonstrate outstanding leadership and commitment to corporate sustainability, and to promote corporate social responsibility as an essential element of a successful business model in the Arab region. Presented in three categories: small companies (up to 99 employees), medium companies (100 to 499 employees), and large companies (500 and more companies). Awarded annually. Established in 2008.

6665 ■ Sheikh Hamdan Bin Rashid Award for Medical Sciences
PO Box 22252
Dubai, United Arab Emirates
Ph: 971 4 398 6777
Fax: 971 4 398 0
E-mail: shhaward@emirates.net.ae
URL: http://www.hmaward.org.ae

6666 ■ Grand Hamdan International Award
To honor individuals whose contributions to health care delivery have left an indelible mark by their quality, originality, and impact. Universities, research centers, science institutions, and physicians and scientists are eligible to nominate individuals. Open to candidates from any country. A monetary prize of AED 250,000 is awarded annually.

6667 ■ Hamdan Award for an Outstanding Clinical Department in the Public Sector in the UAE
To recognize an outstanding clinical department in the public sector that has provided exemplary medical services and care to the people of the United Arab Emirates. A certificate, trophy, and monetary prize of AED 700,000 are awarded annually.

6668 ■ Hamdan Award for Medical Research Excellence
To recognize medical researchers for innovative methods and research that resulted in novel discoveries and inventions. Open to candidates from any country. A certificate, trophy, and monetary prize of AED 300,000 are awarded to three individuals annually.

6669 ■ Hamdan Award for Original Research Paper Published in SHAMS
To encourage individuals working both inside and outside the UAE to undertake medical research and to publish the results in *SHAMS, the Journal of Medical Sciences.* Two awards of AED 25,000 are presented, one for research conducted within the UAE and the other for research conducted outside the UAE. Awarded biennially.

6670 ■ Hamdan Award for the Best Medical College/Institute or Centre in the Arab World
To recognize a prominent medical institution in Arab countries in order to provide an incentive for the development of excellence in research and education in Arab countries so that they can conform to international standards. Two recipients are each awarded AED 500,000 annually.

6671 ■ Hamdan Award for Volunteers in Humanitarian Medical Services
To recognize institutions and individuals who provide important voluntary services and who significantly contribute to alleviating the suffering of a large number of human beings subjected to exceptional circumstances such as catastrophes, epidemics, famine, war, and natural calamities. Open to candidates from any country. Four awards are presented annually: two institutions each receive AED 100,000, and two individuals each receive AED 50,000.

6672 ■ Zayed International Prize for the Environment
PO Box 28399
Dubai, United Arab Emirates
Ph: 971 4 332 6666
Fax: 971 4 332 6777
E-mail: zayedprz@emirates.net.ae
URL: http://www.zayedprize.org.ae

6673 ■ Zayed International Prize for the Environment
To recognize and promote pioneering contributions in the field of environment and sustainable development. Open to individuals, organizations, and partnerships or projects. Monetary prizes are awarded in three categories: 1. Global leadership in environment and sustainable development (US$500,000); 2. Scientific/technological achievements in environment (US$300,000); and 3. Environmental action leading to positive change in society (US$200,000). Awarded biennially in odd-numbered years. Established in 1999.

United Kingdom

6674 ■ Academi - Welsh National Literature Promotion Agency and Society for Authors
3rd Fl., Mount Stuart House
Mount Stuart Sq.
Cardiff CF10 5FQ, United Kingdom
Ph: 44 29 2047 2266
Fax: 44 29 2047 2930
E-mail: post@academi.org
URL: http://www.academi.org

6675 ■ Lingo Newydd Short Story Competition
To promote short story writing in the Welsh language. A monetary prize of £50 is awarded for first place. Held annually. Sponsored by *Lingo* magazine.

6676 ■ Wales Book of the Year Awards
To recognize works of exceptional merit by Welsh authors (by birth or residence) that have been published during the previous calendar year. Works may be written in Welsh or English. Two prizes of £10,000 are awarded to the first place winners. Awarded annually. Established in 1992. Funded by the Arts Council of Wales and supported by the Welsh Books Council. Formerly: Welsh Arts Council Prizes.

6677 ■ Acuity
Ian Rough, Chm.
5 St. Vincent St.
Edinburgh EH3 6SW, United Kingdom
Ph: 44 131 2204542
E-mail: info@sco-online.org
URL: http://www.sco-online.org/index.html

Awards are arranged in alphabetical order below their administering organizations

Formerly: (2010) Scottish Committee of Optometrists.

6678 ■ SCO Prizes
For the best ophthalmic and the best dispensing student at Glasgow Caledonian University. Awarded annually in each category.

6679 ■ Aerosol Society
Mrs. Virginia Foot, Pres.
PO Box 34
Portishead
Bristol BS20 7FE, United Kingdom
Ph: 44 1275 849019
Fax: 44 1275 844877
E-mail: admin@aerosol-soc.org.uk
URL: http://www.aerosol-soc.org.uk

6680 ■ C.N. Davies Award
To a new graduate undertaking a course of study leading to a Doctorate at UK or Irish university. Awarded annually.

6681 ■ Whytlaw-Gray Studentship
To a new graduate undertaking a course of study leading to a Doctorate at UK or Irish university. Awarded annually.

6682 ■ African Studies Association of the United Kingdom
Ms. Gemma Haxby, Sec.
36 Gordon Sq.
London WC1H 0PD, United Kingdom
Ph: 44 20 30738335
Fax: 44 20 30738340
E-mail: secretary@asauk.net
URL: http://www.asauk.net

6683 ■ Distinguished Africanist Award
To honor individuals who have made exceptional contributions to the field of African studies in the United Kingdom. Awarded annually to one or more recipients. Established in 2001.

6684 ■ Audrey Richards Prize
Recognizes the best doctoral thesis in African studies that has been successfully examined in a United Kingdom institute of higher education during the previous two years. Awarded biennially in even-numbered years.

6685 ■ Agricultural Economics Society
Sophia Davidova, Pres.
Holtwood
Red Lion St.
Cropredy
Banbury OX17 1PD, United Kingdom
Ph: 44 1295 750182
Fax: 44 1295 750182
E-mail: aes@cingnet.org.uk
URL: http://www.aes.ac.uk

6686 ■ Outstanding Young Researcher Award
To recognize the outstanding achievements of a researcher under 40 years of age. Awarded annually.

6687 ■ Prize Essay Competition
To honor the best essay submitted by young recent graduates of agricultural economics. Authors must be within six years of graduation or, in the case on non-graduates, be under 30 years old. A monetary prize of £1,000 and publication of the winning essay in the *Journal of Agricultural Economics* are awarded annually. Established in 1963.

6688 ■ Air League
Andrew Brookes, Dir.
Broadway House
Tothill St.
London SW1H 9NS, United Kingdom
Ph: 44 20 72228463
E-mail: exec@airleague.co.uk
URL: http://www.airleague.co.uk

6689 ■ Challenge Trophy
Awarded through annual competition among the Voluntary Gliding Schools of the (RAF) Air Cadets organization. A silver Challenge Cup is awarded annually. Established in 1921 by Major General Sir Sefton Brancker KCB AFC and Philip Foster Esq.

6690 ■ Founders' Medal
For recognition of the most meritorious achievement in the field of British aviation during the year. British nationals and, exceptionally, foreign nationals are eligible. A medal is awarded annually when merited. Established in 1960 by a gift of the late Stephen Marples to commemorate the Founders of the Air League in 1909.

6691 ■ Framed Scrolls
To honor individuals for meritorious achievements in aviation. Awarded when merited.

6692 ■ Gold Medal
For outstanding service to the causes of the Air League. Awarded when merited. Established in 1998 by the Royal Force Historical Society.

6693 ■ Marshall of Cambridge Medal
To honor a young member for exceptional support of the Air League Educational Trust. Awarded annually if merited. Established in 2002.

6694 ■ Jeffrey Quill Medal
For an outstanding contribution to the development of air-mindedness in Britain's youth. Awarded annually. Established in 1997 in memory of the late Jeffrey Quill.

6695 ■ Scott-Farnie Medal
To recognize work in the field of air education. Awarded annually. Established in 1969 in memory of G. R. Scott-Farnie.

6696 ■ Amateur Entomologists' Society
Mr. Dafydd Lewis, Sec.
PO Box 8774
London SW7 5ZG, United Kingdom
URL: http://www.amentsoc.org

6697 ■ Ansorge Bequest
To recognize the best entomological exhibit by a junior member at the Annual Exhibition and Trade Fair. Awarded annually. Established in 1977.

6698 ■ Bradford Award
To recognize the best entomological exhibit at the Annual Exhibition and Trade Fair by an adult member of the Society. Awarded annually. Established in 2005.

6699 ■ Cribb Award
To recognize a U.K. resident for outstanding contributions to insect conservation. Awarded annually.

6700 ■ Gardiner Award
To recognize the best article submitted by a young member to the *Bug Club Magazine*. Awarded annually.

6701 ■ Hammond Award
To honor a member for the best article published in *The Bulletin*. A certificate and monetary prize of £100 are awarded annually.

6702 ■ Amateur Swimming Association
John Crowther, Chm.
SportPark
3 Oakwood Dr.
Leicestershire
Loughborough LE11 3QF, United Kingdom
Ph: 44 1509 618700
E-mail: customerservices@swimming.org
URL: http://www.swimming.org/asa

6703 ■ Henry Benjamin National Memorial Trophy
For recognition of the club with the most points

in the following National Championships and the National Winter Championships for Men, viz: 50, 100, 200, 400, 1,500 metres Freestyle; Long Distance; 100 and 200 metres Backstroke, Breaststroke and Butterfly; and 200 and 400 metres Individual Medley, Club Medley Team, and Club Freestyle Team. The total number of points obtained by the clubs either through their team or individual entries are added together on completion of the championships and the club obtaining the highest aggregate is declared the winner.

6704 ■ Mary Black Award
Recognizes a person who is a member of an affiliated club and who has given outstanding service to synchronized swimming during the year. Given by the Synchronized Swimming Committee.

6705 ■ G. Melville Clark National Memorial Trophy
For recognition of the club with the highest points in the Diving Championships. The competition for the G. Melville Clark National Memorial Trophy is open to all men's clubs or men's sections of clubs affiliated to the ASA. The competitions are confined to the following championships: All ASA Summer and Winter Diving Championships and the two principal District Diving Championships other than plain diving, which are declared by each District Association no later than June 1 in each year. The trophy is awarded annually.

6706 ■ Dawdon Trophy
For recognition of the winning club of the ASA Age Group Diving Competitions. The total number of points obtained by each club is added together on December 31 each year, and the club obtaining the highest total is declared the winner. The winning club is entitled to hold the trophy. Awarded annually.

6707 ■ Harold Fern Award
To recognize the most outstanding contribution to swimming on the national or international level through education or instructional achievement, for architectural design of swimming facilities, for writing or development of original material, or for competitive performance. Clubs, individuals, or associations (amateur and professional) may be nominated by District Associations. A monetary award of £50 and a framed certificate are presented each year in February at the annual council meeting. Established in 1961 in honor of Harold E. Fern C.B.E. J.P., Secretary to the ASA from 1921 to 1969.

6708 ■ Harold Fern National Trophy
For recognition of the club with the most points in the National Championships and the National Winter Championships for Women 50, 100, 200, 400, 800 metres Freestyle; Long Distance; 100 and 200 metres Backstroke, Breaststroke and Butterfly; and 200 and 400 metres Individual Medley, Club Medley Team, and Club Freestyle Team. The total number of points obtained by the clubs either through their team or individual entries, are added together on completion of the Championships, and the club obtaining the highest aggregate is declared the winner. The winning club is entitled to hold the Harold Fern National Trophy. Awarded annually.

6709 ■ George Hearn Trophy
To recognize the senior level diver who is a member of a club affiliated with the ASA whose performance is adjudged by the ASA Diving Committee to be the best for the year. Awarded annually. Established to honor George Hearn, Present of the ASA in 1908.

6710 ■ Alan Hime Memorial Trophies
To recognize the male and the female swimmers who are members of a club affiliated to the ASA

Awards are arranged in alphabetical order below their administering organizations

and whose performance is adjudged by the ASA Swimming Committee to be the best at the ASA National Winter Championships. A memento is awarded to each annually.

6711 ■ Holland Trophy
For the senior synchronized swimmer with the highest total of routine scores in the solo duet and team events at the National Championships. Awarded annually.

6712 ■ Alan Lawrence Trophy
To honor a junior female and male swimmer whose performance is judged to be the best at the National Youth Championship. Awarded annually to two recipients. Established in 1999.

6713 ■ Shacklock Trophy
For the junior swimmer with the highest total of routine scores in the solo, duet, and team events at the National Championships. Awarded annually.

6714 ■ Norma Thomas National Memorial Trophy
To recognize a junior diver who is a member of a club affiliated to the ASA and whose performance is adjudged by the ASA Diving Committee to be the best for the year. Awarded annually. Established in 1985.

6715 ■ Alfred H. Turner Award
For recognition of outstanding contributions to swimming on the national or international level, through educational or instructional achievement, for architectural design of swimming facilities, for writing or development of original material, or for competitive performance. This award is given to a female if the Harold Fern trophy is given to a male, and vice versa. A monetary award of £50 and a framed certificate are awarded each year at the annual council meeting held in February. Established in 1982 to honor Alfred H. Turner, O.B.E., A.I.B., the Honorary Treasurer from 1968 to 1985, and the President in 1982.

6716 ■ Belle White National Memorial Trophy
For recognition of the club with the highest points in the Diving Championships. All women's clubs or women's sections of clubs affiliated to the ASA are eligible. The competitions are confined to the following championships: All ASA summer and winter Championships and the two principal District Diving Championships other than plain diving, which are declared by each District Association not later than June 1 in each year. A trophy is awarded annually.

6717 ■ Gemma Yates Trophy
Recognizes endeavor. Applicants must be members of an affiliated club who have overcome anything which has made it difficult for them, yet still gives 100% to the sport of synchronized swimming. Awarded annually.

6718 ■ T.M. Yeaden Memorial Trophy
To honor the swimmer whose performance is adjudged by the ASA Board to be the best for that year. Awarded annually. Established in 1970.

6719 ■ T. M. Yeadon Memorial Trophy
To recognize the swimmer whose performance is the best for the year as judged by the Amateur Swimming Association Committee. A trophy is presented annually. Established in 1970 in memory of T. M. Yeadon, an ASA officer and President in 1924.

6720 ■ The Ammies, the African Music Awards
76 Druridge Dr.
Newcastle upon Tyne NE5 3JS, United Kingdom
E-mail: info@ammies.com
URL: http://www.ammies.com

6721 ■ The Ammies, African Music Awards
To publicize and showcase African music to the largely untapped non-African population in Europe, Asia, and America, and to maintain a strong presence of African music on the international state and position it in the mainstream of the music industry. Awards are presented in 18 categories, including the African Most Popular Song of the Year. Awarded annually.

6722 ■ Anti-Slavery International
Aidan McQuade, Dir.
Thomas Clarkson House
The Stableyard
Broomgrove Rd.
London SW9 9TL, United Kingdom
Ph: 44 20 75018920
Fax: 44 20 77384110
E-mail: info@antislavery.org
URL: http://www.antislavery.org/english/default.aspx

6723 ■ Anti-Slavery Award
To recognize an individual or organization performing outstanding work in the fight against contemporary slavery. Applicants must have worked for a number of years on an issue related to slavery, be involved in direct intervention, be involved in an on-going campaign, and see a need for international pressure to enhance his or her work. Awarded annually. Established in 1991.

6724 ■ Applied Vision Association
Prof. Tom Troscianko, Sec.
University of Bristol
Dept. of Experimental Psychology
12 A Priory Rd.
Bristol BS8 1TU, United Kingdom
Ph: 44 117 9288565
Fax: 44 117 9288588
E-mail: tom.troscianko@bristol.ac.uk
URL: http://www.theava.net

6725 ■ Vision Scientist Memorial Fund
To the most productive junior vision scientists.

6726 ■ Von Karman Award for International Cooperation in Aeronautics
For exceptional achievement in international cooperation in the field of aeronautics.

6727 ■ Arboricultural Association
Nick Eden, Dir.
Ullenwood Ct.
Cheltenham GL53 9QS, United Kingdom
Ph: 44 1242 522152
Fax: 44 1242 577766
E-mail: admin@trees.org.uk
URL: http://www.trees.org.uk

6728 ■ Arboricultural Association Award
To recognize an individual for services to arboriculture. Awarded annually.

6729 ■ Architectural Association
Brett Steele, Dir.
36 Bedford Sq.
London WC1B 3ES, United Kingdom
Ph: 44 20 78874000
Fax: 44 20 74140782
E-mail: membership@aaschool.ac.uk
URL: http://www.aaschool.ac.uk

6730 ■ Anthony Pott Memorial Award
To assist studies or the publication of studies related to the field of architecture. Architects and students of architecture and related subjects may apply. Candidates wishing to use the award for research rather than the publication of studies will, in their application, either have to demonstrate some pre-knowledge of the proposed field of study or satisfy the Award Committee that they are sufficiently competent to undertake new work. Projects are to be related to the subject of architecture and design, taken in its widest sense. A monetary award of £2,000 is presented biennially. Established in memory of Anthony Pott who was a student at the Architectural Association, a distinguished member of the staff of the Building Research Station, and Chief Architect of the Ministry of Education.

6731 ■ Michael Ventris Memorial Award
To promote the study of architecture and the study of Mycenaean civilization. It is intended that the award should support a specific project rather than a continuing program of study. Architects or students of not less than RIBA Intermediate status or other comparable level of achievement from all countries may apply. A monetary award of to £2,000 is awarded annually for each field of study. Established in 1957 in memory of Michael Ventris, in appreciation of his work in the fields of architecture and Mycenaean civilization.

6732 ■ Bernard Webb Studentship
For the encouragement of the study of architecture. Students of post graduate standing, 32 years of age and under, who are citizens of the British Commonwealth and have been members of the Architectural Association for not less than two years may apply. A stipend of £1,500 and travel expenses are awarded biennially for a three-month architecture study visit, based on the British School at Rome.

6733 ■ Arts and Business
Colin Tweedy, Chief Exec.
Nutmeg House
60 Gainsford St.
Butler's Wharf
London SE1 2NY, United Kingdom
Ph: 44 20 73788143
Fax: 44 20 74077527
E-mail: contactus@artsandbusiness.org.uk
URL: http://artsandbusiness.org.uk

6734 ■ Arts and Business Awards
To recognize and encourage imaginative and effective support of the arts by commercial organizations. The Awards are open to all companies sponsoring arts events, projects, or organizations in the United Kingdom, and all companies sponsoring British arts events overseas. Nominations should be submitted on the nomination form and the major part of the sponsorship should have taken place in the 12 months prior to the closing date. Awarded in a variety of categories annually in November.

6735 ■ BP/A & B Sustained Partnership Award
To recognize an established, ongoing partnership that continues to set standards in creative arts-business collaborations. Awarded to up to five recipients annually. Sponsored by BP plc.

6736 ■ Business Volunteer of the Year Award
To recognize a volunteer business professional who has added outstanding benefit to an arts organization through transferal of skills, knowledge, inspiration, and strategic direction. Awarded annually.

6737 ■ Classic FM/A & B International Award
To recognize a global-level partnership that builds brand reputation and audience for both the arts organization and business across international borders through an event or marketing project. Awarded to up to five recipients annually. Sponsored by the British Council. Formerly: British Council/AandB International Award.

6738 ■ Community and Young People Award
To recognize a partnership that has harnessed the power of the arts to engage young people and that delivers regeneration or specific community engagement with the arts. Awarded annually. Sponsored by Jaguar Land Rover.

Awards are arranged in alphabetical order below their administering organizations

6739 ■ Garrett Award
To recognize an individual for outstanding achievement in a professional capacity in the encouragement of the business support for the arts. Awarded annually. Established in honor of the Arts and Business's founding deputy chairman, Tony Garrett.

6740 ■ Goodman Award
To recognize an individual for outstanding achievement in a voluntary capacity in the encouragement of the business support for the arts. Awarded annually. Established in honor of the Arts and Business's founding chairman, Lord Goodman.

6741 ■ Prudential/A & B People Development Award
To recognize a partnership that embeds culture as a core element of employee development. The winning business demonstrates significant business improvement through skills enhancement and innovation building. Awarded annually. Sponsored by Prudential.

6742 ■ Telegraph Media Group/A & B Cultural Branding Award
To recognize a partnership that reinforces the branding and marketing activity of a business through the use of culture. The winning business demonstrates an integral connection with culture that has increased brand equity and therefore business performance. Awarded annually. Sponsored by the Telegraph Media Group.

6743 ■ Arts Council of England
Alan Davey, Chief Exec.
14 Great Peter St.
London SW1P 3NQ, United Kingdom
Ph: 44 845 3006200
Ph: 44 20 79736564
Fax: 44 161 9344426
E-mail: enquiries@artscouncil.org.uk
URL: http://www.artscouncil.org.uk

6744 ■ Chrisi Bailey Award
To recognize children under the age of 10 for achievements in exploring photography, digital art, animation, and video as creative visual media and forms of communication rather than as documentaries or records of events. Monetary prizes of £1,000 and £500 are awarded for first and second place, respectively. Awarded annually.

6745 ■ David Cohen British Literature Prize
To honor an individual for a lifetime of literary achievement. A monetary prize of £30,000 plus an additional £10,000 to fund new work is awarded annually.

6746 ■ Raymond Williams Community Publishing Prize
To commend an outstanding creative and imaginative work which reflects the values of ordinary people and their lives, and is submitted by nonprofit-making publishers producing books in mutual and cooperative ways. Monetary prizes of £3,000 and £2,000 are awarded for first and second place, respectively. Awarded annually.

6747 ■ Peter Wolff Theatre Trust Award
For recognition of the best original play of the year. The award is intended to help further the careers and enhance the reputations of younger British playwrights, and to draw public attention to the importance of writers in contemporary theater. The following criteria are considered in judging a play: writing of special quality, relevance and importance to contemporary life, and potential value to the British theater. The judges shall not have regard to whether or not the play has received a production, or is likely to receive a production or publication. To be considered, British playwrights must, over the previous two

years, have had either an offer of an award under the Arts Council Theatre Writing Schemes, a commission from one of those theater companies in receipt of annual subsidy from either the Arts Council or a Regional Arts Board, or a premiere production by a theater company in receipt of annual subsidy from either the Arts Council or a Regional Arts Board. No writer who has previously won the award may reapply, and no play that has previously been submitted for the award is eligible. A monetary prize of £6,000 is awarded annually. Established in 1965 in memory of John Whiting for his contribution to post-war British theater. Formerly: (2007) John Whiting Award.

6748 ■ Arts Council of Northern Ireland (Airts Cooncil o Norlin Airlann)
Roisin McDonough, Chief Exec.
MacNeice House
77 Malone Rd.
Belfast BT9 6AQ, United Kingdom
Ph: 44 28 90385200
Fax: 44 28 90661715
E-mail: info@artscouncil-ni.org
URL: http://www.artscouncil-ni.org

6749 ■ Arts Council of Northern Ireland Funding and Awards
To provide support for creative and performing artists active in the fields of drama and dance, music and jazz, literature, traditional arts, community arts, and visual arts. Artists who are residents in Northern Ireland for at least one year, contribute regularly to the artistic activity of the community, and who were previous award holders are eligible.

6750 ■ Arvon Foundation
Free Word
60 Farringdon Rd.
London EC1R 36A, United Kingdom
Ph: 44 20 7324 2554
E-mail: london@arvonfoundation.org
URL: http://www.arvonfoundation.org

6751 ■ International Poetry Competition
For recognition of outstanding poetry submitted by individuals from Great Britain and abroad. Each entry must be written in English. The following prizes are awarded biennially: (1) First prize - £5,000; (2) Second prize - £2,500; (3) Third prize - £1,000 and (4) Fourth prizes of £500. Established in 1980. Sponsored by Duncan Lawrie Limited. Deadline is May 31.

6752 ■ Ashden Awards for Sustainable Energy
Allington House
150 Victoria St.
London SW1E 5AE, United Kingdom
Ph: 44 20 7410 0330
E-mail: info@ashdenawards.org
URL: http://www.ashdenawards.org

6753 ■ Ashden Awards for Sustainable Energy
To encourage the greater use of local sustainable energy solutions to address climate change, alleviate poverty, and improve quality of life. Open to projects in the United Kingdom and the developing world. Awarded to multiple recipients annually. Established in 2001.

6754 ■ Association for Clinical Biochemistry
Dr. Michael Thomas, Pres.
130-132 Tooley St.
London SE1 2TU, United Kingdom
Ph: 44 20 74038001
Fax: 44 20 74038006
E-mail: admin@acb.org.uk
URL: http://www.acb.org.uk

6755 ■ Foundation Award
To recognize a member of the Association,

normally a resident in the British Isles, who is acknowledged as having made an outstanding contribution to clinical biochemistry. The subject matter of the Foundation Award Lecture should reflect the interests of the award recipient, and should be of a scientific nature, reflecting the state of the art in one area of clinical biochemistry. Nominations for the award may be made by any three members of the Association. The award, which is presented by the President or Chairman of the Association, comprises a suitable memento and an honorarium. Prior to the presentation, the recipient delivers the ACB Foundation Award Lecture. Awarded annually. Established in 1990 by the ACB Foundation.

6756 ■ President's Shield
To honor an individual for outstanding contribution to the Association. Awarded annually at the discretion of the Association's president. Established in 1990.

6757 ■ Professors' Prize
To recognize general achievements within the field of clinical biochemistry. Clinical biochemists, or those in related fields such as molecular biology or clinical medicine, who are under 40 years of age are eligible. A diploma and an honorarium are awarded when merited. Established in 1994.

6758 ■ Siemens Award Lecture
To honor a medical scientist whose work has been of major importance to clinical biochemistry, in practice, research, or in education, leading to improved international co-operation between workers in the specialty, particularly those within Europe. Nominated persons are typically practicing clinical biochemists from outside the United Kingdom. A monetary prize is awarded annually. Established in 1981. Sponsored by Siemens Healthcare Diagnostics. Formerly: Dade Behring Award.

6759 ■ Siemens Medal
To recognize a junior member of the Association who has presented the best scientific paper at a national meeting. Members of the Association under 35 years of age are eligible to participate in the competition. A monetary award of £1,000 and a silver medal are awarded annually. Established in 1971. Sponsored by Siemens Medical Solutions Diagnostics Ltd. Formerly: Bayer Award.

6760 ■ Thermo Electron Clinical Chemistry and Automation Systems Award
To honor a medical scientist whose work has been of major importance to clinical biochemistry. Medical students whose work in practice, research, or education has led to improved international cooperation particularly in Europe may be nominated. A monetary award for travel to present the lecture is awarded annually. Established in 1981.

6761 ■ Association for Consultancy and Engineering
Nelson Ogunshakin OBE, Chief Exec.
Alliance House
12 Caxton St.
London SW1H 0QL, United Kingdom
Ph: 44 20 72226557
Ph: 44 20 72271881
Fax: 44 20 79909202
E-mail: consult@acenet.co.uk
URL: http://www.acenet.co.uk

6762 ■ ACE Engineering Excellence Awards
To recognize the most innovative and original projects from across the consultancy and engineering sector in the United Kingdom. Awards are presented in eight categories: transport; sustainability; water; low carbon technology; prop-

Awards are arranged in alphabetical order below their administering organizations

erty; research, studies, and consulting; small projects; and large projects. In addition, the Engineering Ambassador Award is presented. Awarded annually.

6763 ■ NCE/ACE Young Consultant of the Year Award
To recognize excellence and talent in the field of consultancy and engineering by individuals under the age of 35. A trophy and monetary prize of £1,000 are awarded annually. Sponsored by Hays Consulting Engineering.

6764 ■ Association for Heritage Interpretation
Ruth Taylor, Chair
54 Balmoral Rd.
Kent ME7 4PG, United Kingdom
Ph: 44 5602 747737
E-mail: mail@ahi.org.uk
URL: http://www.ahi.org.uk

6765 ■ Interpret Britain and Ireland Awards
To recognize outstanding practice in interpretation throughout Britain and Ireland. Awarded annually to one or more recipients.

6766 ■ Association for Industrial Archaeology
Marilyn Palmer, Honorary Pres.
Ironbridge Institute
Ironbridge Gorge Museum
Coalbrookdale
Telford TF8 7DX, United Kingdom
Ph: 44 174 656280
E-mail: aia-enquiries@contacts.bham.ac.uk
URL: http://www.industrial-archaeology.org

6767 ■ British Archaeological Awards
To advance public education in the study and practice of archaeology in all its aspects in the United Kingdom, and in particular by the granting of awards for excellence and/or initiative. The awards are committed to recognizing significant contributions to knowledge and the importance of research, professional standards and excellence, involvement of local communities in the study of archaeology, effective dissemination and presentation of archaeological knowledge, and innovation and originality of approach. Awards are presented in 14 categories within: Best Archaeological Project, Best Independent or Amateur Archaeological Project, Best Archaeological Book, Best Scholarly Archaeological Book, Best Archaeological TV/Radio Programme, Best Archaeological Discovery, Best Archaeological Innovation, Best ICT Project, Lifetime Achievement, and Young Archaeologist of the Year. Awarded annually. Established in 1976. Formerly: Ironbridge Award.

6768 ■ Dorothea Award for Conservation
To support and encourage voluntary conservation work on sites and artifacts of industrial, agricultural, and domestic importance. A plaque and monetary award of £500 are presented annually. Established in 1984.

6769 ■ Fieldwork and Recording Awards
To recognize exemplary fieldwork and archaeological recording practices in industrial archaeology. Two awards are presented annually: 1) individuals and groups paid for their work, and 2) research undertaken on a voluntary basis. Additionally, a Student Award is presented. Awarded annually. Formerly: (2007) Fieldwork Award.

6770 ■ Peter Neaverson Awards
To recognize outstanding scholarship in industrial archaeology. Any work published in English in the last two years is eligible. Works may be published anywhere in the world and include articles, books, papers, and published theses. Awarded annually. Honors British industrial archaeologist Peter Neaverson.

6771 ■ Publications Award
To encourage high standards in local society publications sympathetic to the aims of industrial archaeology, but excluding those solely concerned with transport history. A local society is defined as being based on a town, county, district or region in England, Wales, Scotland, and Ireland, but excluding societies with a nationwide remit. Three categories exist: newsletters; journals produced on a regular basis; and occasional publications. All entries must have been published in the 18 months prior to the year of the competition. A monetary award of £200 is awarded to the winner of each category annually.

6772 ■ Recording and Fieldwork Awards
To recognize an industrial archeological project involving a substantial element of site recording in the field, together with supporting research. Open to all amateur and professional individuals and groups. Three awards are presented: the main award of £500 for the best piece of fieldwork submitted that year, a student award of £200 for the best entry by a student, and the initiative award of £300 for innovative projects. Awarded annually.

6773 ■ Association for Literary and Linguistic Computing
(Association de Litterature et de Linguistique Computationnelles)
Mr. Paul Spence, Honorary Treas.
King's College London
Centre for Computing in the Humanities
Strand
London WC2R 2LS, United Kingdom
Ph: 44 20 78365454
Fax: 44 20 78482980
E-mail: paul.spence@kcl.ac.uk
URL: http://www.allc.org

6774 ■ Roberto Busa Award
To honor outstanding lifetime achievement in the application of information and communications technologies to humanistic research. A monetary prize of £1,500 is awarded triennially. Established in 1998.

6775 ■ Student Prize
To stimulate students who have a significant contribution to make in the field of humanities computing, and to promote the involvement of outstanding young scholars in the application of computing in humanistic research. A monetary prize of £500 is awarded annually.

6776 ■ Association for Project Management
Dr. Martin Barnes, Pres.
Ibis House, Regent Park
Summerleys Rd.
Buckinghamshire
Princes Risborough HP27 9LE, United Kingdom
Ph: 44 845 4581944
E-mail: info@apm.org.uk
URL: http://www.apm.org.uk

6777 ■ Sir Monty Finniston Award
For an individual or organization who has made an outstanding contribution to the development of project management as a vehicle for effective change. Awarded annually.

6778 ■ Programme of the Year
To the organization that has achieved a common objective through effective management of a portfolio of projects. Awarded annually.

6779 ■ Project Manager of the Year
To the project manager who provides the most effective demonstration of project management. Awarded annually.

6780 ■ Project of the Year
To the company with the project delivered within the UK whose outcomes and results exceeded or aligned most closely to its objectives, completed or successfully commissioned during the last year. Awarded annually.

6781 ■ Brian Willis Award
To the student under the age of 30 who has achieved the highest mark of all candidates in the past year's APMP examination. Awarded annually.

6782 ■ Association for Radiation Research
Dr. Kaye J. Williams, Chm.
University of Manchester
School of Pharmacy and Pharmaceutical Sciences
Oxford Rd.
Manchester M13 9PL, United Kingdom
Ph: 44 116 2752428
Fax: 44 116 2752396
E-mail: kaye.williams@manchester.ac.uk
URL: http://www.le.ac.uk/cm/arr/home.html

6783 ■ Weiss Medal
For distinguished contributions to radiation science. Awarded biennially in odd-numbered years. Established in 1972 in memory of Professor J. Weiss, professor of radiation chemistry at the University of Newcastle-on-Tyne.

6784 ■ Association for the Study of Obesity
Dr. Susan Jebb, Chair
Eversheds House
70 Great Bridgewater St.
Manchester M1 5ES, United Kingdom
Ph: 44 1304 367788
E-mail: catherine.stone@aso.org.uk
URL: http://www.aso.org.uk

6785 ■ Best Practice Award
To a member either as an individual or representative of a group working in the field of obesity. Awarded annually.

6786 ■ Student Researcher Award
To individuals of any age but who are registered for a higher degree. A monetary prize of £200 is awarded annually.

6787 ■ Young Achiever Award
To a member who has made a significant contribution to scientific or clinical knowledge. A monetary prize of £300 is awarded annually.

6788 ■ Association for Veterinary Teaching and Research Work
Dr. Adrian Philbey, Sec.
PO Box 3
Penicuik EH26 0RZ, United Kingdom
Ph: 44 131 4454508
Fax: 44 131 5353103
E-mail: enquiries@avtrw.co.uk
URL: http://www.avtrw.co.uk

6789 ■ President's Prize
To a young scientist with the best first paper.

6790 ■ Undergraduate and Postgraduate Bursaries
For an applicant with merit on a presented case for consideration.

6791 ■ Association in Scotland to Research into Astronautics
Mr. Duncan A. Lunan MA, Sec.
Flat 65, Dalriada House
Anderston
Glasgow G2 7PE, United Kingdom
Ph: 44 141 2217658
E-mail: duncanlunan@talktalk.net

6792 ■ Oscar Schwiglhofer Trophy
To recognize the winning team in the International Rocketry Weekend Aquajet (water rocket) Contest. Awarded annually. Established in 1984.

6793 ■ Association of British Climatologists
104 Oxford Rd.
Reading RG1 7LL, United Kingdom
Ph: 44 118 9568500

Awards are arranged in alphabetical order below their administering organizations

Fax: 44 118 9568571
E-mail: chiefexec@tarmets.org
URL: http://www.rmets.org/activities/groups/SIG/detail.php?ID=6

6794 ■ Frisby-Green Dissertation Prize

For undergraduates in H.E. in U.K. for meteorology/climatology dissertation.

6795 ■ Association of British Philatelic Societies

Alan Godfrey, Membership Sec.
Gerard Rd.
Warwickshire
Alcester B49 6QC, United Kingdom
E-mail: membership@abps.org.uk
URL: http://www.abps.org.uk

6796 ■ Award of Merit

To honor an individual for voluntary efforts in philately on a local and/or regional level. A certificate is awarded annually to no more than 15 recipients.

6797 ■ Congress Medal

Awarded for outstanding service to British philately at a national level. The candidate must be a member of an organization affiliated to the Association of British Philatelic Societies (ABPS) and there is only one recipient each year, with presentation being made at the annual Philatelic Congress of Great Britain.

6798 ■ The Roll of Distinguished Philatelist

Established in 1921, the signing of the Roll has been regarded for many years as one of the world's pre-eminent philatelic honors. Candidates can be nominated by existing Signatories to the Roll, National Federations accredited to the Federation Internationale de Philatelie (FIP), regional UK Federations and a number of UK specified societies, should be philatelists who have been performed services to philately, either by research work made available to others or in some public or other capacity.

6799 ■ Association of British Travel Agents

Daniele Broccoli, Contact
30 Park St.
London SE1 9EQ, United Kingdom
Ph: 44 20 31170500
Ph: 44 20 31170503
Fax: 44 20 31170581
E-mail: abta@abta.co.uk
URL: http://www.abta.com/home

6800 ■ Gold Training Award

Recognizes exceptional levels of training. Only members are eligible. Awarded periodically.

6801 ■ Association of Building Engineers

Colin Bell, Pres.
Lutyens House
Billing Brook Rd.
Weston Favell
Northamptonshire
Northampton NN3 8NW, United Kingdom
Ph: 44 845 1261058
Fax: 44 1604 784220
E-mail: building.engineers@abe.org.uk
URL: http://www.abe.org.uk

6802 ■ Fire Safety Award

For significant contributions to fire safety, fire protection, or fire engineering. Awarded annually. Established in 1994.

6803 ■ Outstanding Service Award

To recognize a member's contribution to the advancement of the aims and the objectives of the Association. Awarded annually. Formerly: Lutyens Award.

6804 ■ Peter Stone Award

For personal service and valuable contribution to the advancement of building engineering. An engraved silver salver is awarded annually. Established in 1982.

6805 ■ Association of Chartered Certified Accountants - United Kingdom

Branden Murtagh, Chief Exec.
29 Lincoln's Inn Fields
London WC2A 3EE, United Kingdom
Ph: 44 20 70595000
Fax: 44 20 70595050
E-mail: info@accaglobal.com
URL: http://www.uk.accaglobal.com
Formerly: (1974) Association of Certified Accountants.

6806 ■ ACCA U.K. Awards for Sustainability Reporting

To recognize companies that report and disclose environmental, social, and full sustainability information, and to raise awareness of corporate transparency issues. Awarded annually. Established in 1991.

6807 ■ Association of Chief Estate Surveyors and Property Managers in Local Government

Tim Foster, Sec.
23 Athol Rd.
Cheshire
Bramhall SK7 1BR, United Kingdom
Ph: 44 161 4399589
Fax: 44 161 4407383
E-mail: secretary@aces.org.uk
URL: http://www.aces.org.uk

6808 ■ ACES Award for Excellence in Property Management

For good practice and innovation.

6809 ■ Association of Chief Police Officers of England, Wales and Northern Ireland

Sir Hugh Orde OBE, Pres.
10 Victoria St., 1st Fl.
London SW1H 0NN, United Kingdom
Ph: 44 20 70848950
Fax: 44 20 70848951
E-mail: info@acpo.pnn.police.uk
URL: http://www.acpo.police.uk

6810 ■ Police Public Bravery Awards

For recognition of an act of bravery in support of law and order performed by a member of the public anywhere in England or Wales outside the area controlled by the Metropolitan Police and City of London Police. Individuals may be nominated. Gold and silver medals are awarded annually. Established in 1965. Formerly: Provincial Police Award.

6811 ■ Association of Commonwealth Universities

Prof. John Wood CBE, Sec. Gen.
Woburn House
20-24 Tavistock Sq.
London WC1H 9HF, United Kingdom
Ph: 44 20 73806700
Fax: 44 20 73872655
E-mail: info@acu.ac.uk
URL: http://www.acu.ac.uk

6812 ■ Canada Memorial Foundation Scholarships

To facilitate postgraduate study by U.K. students leading to a university degree in Canada. Candidates must be individuals of high academic promise and leadership potential who will play a full part in the life of the Canadian community which they visit and who will return to contribute fully to UK society. Additionally, they must hold, or expect to attain, a minimum of an upper second class degree. Awards are available for one year of taught study only at any university or other appropriate institution in Canada subject to

the approval of the Canada Memorial Foundation. Awards are not offered for study at doctoral level. Awarded annually.

6813 ■ Commonwealth Scholarship and Fellowship Plan

Encourages students to study in a Commonwealth country other than their own. Applicants must be Commonwealth postgraduate students. Awarded annually.

6814 ■ Commonwealth Shared Scholarship Scheme

For study in the United Kingdom. Applicants must be students from developing Commonwealth countries with a fluency in English. Awarded annually.

6815 ■ Marshall Scholarships

Encourages U.S. graduate students to study in the United Kingdom. Awarded annually.

6816 ■ PR, Marketing and Communications Awards

To encourage and reward good practice among higher education institutions. Open to all member universities. Awarded in four categories: student publications, corporate publications, Web sites, and outreach and community relations. Awarded annually. Established in 2005.

6817 ■ Association of Community Rail Partnerships

Neil Buxton, Gen. Mgr.
Rail and River Centre
Canal Side, Civic Hall
15a New St.
Slaithwaite
Huddersfield HD7 5AB, United Kingdom
Ph: 44 1484 847790
Fax: 44 1484 847877
E-mail: office@acorp.uk.com
URL: http://www.acorp.uk.com

6818 ■ Community Rail Awards

To honor outstanding delivery of the community rail strategy. Awarded annually in a variety of categories. Established in 2005.

6819 ■ Association of Cricket Statisticians and Historians

Andrew Hignell, Sec.
Archives Department
Glamorgan Cricket
Sophia Gardens
Cardiff CF11 9XR, United Kingdom
Ph: 44 2920 419383
E-mail: secretary@acscricket.com
URL: http://acscricket.com

6820 ■ Les Hatton Second Eleven Player of the Season

To recognize an outstanding cricket player in the English First-Class Second Eleven competitions. Awarded annually. Established in 2001.

6821 ■ Statistician of the Year

To recognize cricket historians and/or statisticians. Awarded annually. Established in 1987.

6822 ■ Association of Event Organisers

Austen Hawkins, CEO
119 High St.
Hertfordshire
Berkhamsted HP4 2DJ, United Kingdom
Ph: 44 1442 285810
Fax: 44 1442 875551
E-mail: info@aeo.org.uk
URL: http://www.aeo.org.uk

6823 ■ Excellence Awards

To recognize organizers, venues and contractors operating in trade, consumer exhibition, and events industry. Awarded annually in a variety of categories.

6824 ■ Association of Industrial Laser Users

Dr. Mike Green, Exec. Sec.
Oxford House
100 Ock St.

Awards are arranged in alphabetical order below their administering organizations

Oxfordshire
Abingdon OX14 5DH, United Kingdom
Ph: 44 1235 539595
Fax: 44 1235 550499
E-mail: m.sharp@ljmu.ac.uk
URL: http://www.ailu.org.uk

6825 ■ AILU Award

To recognize a pioneering individual in the United Kingdom for significant contribution to laser materials processing and that preferably has wider benefit for the industrial laser user community. Awarded annually.

6826 ■ Association of Interior Specialists
Martin Romaine, Pres.
Olton Bridge
245 Warwick Rd.
Solihull B92 7AH, United Kingdom
Ph: 44 121 7070077
Fax: 44 121 7061949
E-mail: info@ais-interiors.org.uk
URL: http://ais-interiors.org.uk
Formerly: (1998) Partitioning and Interiors Association; Partitioning Industry Association.

6827 ■ Contractors' Awards

To promote and encourage high levels of craftsmanship in six categories: interior fit-outs, ceilings, partitioning, drywall construction, specialist joinery, and operable walls. Certificates are presented to the winner in each category. In addition, the Judge's Award may be presented. Awarded annually.

6828 ■ Association of Learned and Professional Society Publishers
Audrey McCulloch, Exec. Dir.
1-3 Ship St.
Shoreham-by-Sea
West Sussex BN43 5DH, United Kingdom
Ph: 44 1442 828928
E-mail: audrey.mcculloch@alpsp.org
URL: http://www.alpsp.org

6829 ■ Award for Best New Journal

To recognize an outstanding peer-reviewed journal launched in the previous one to three years. Criteria include the main aspects of the journal, such as its launch, market research, editorial strategy, marketing, and commercial success. Awarded annually.

6830 ■ Award for Publishing Innovation

To recognize a truly innovative approach to any aspect of publication. Applications are judged on their originality and innovative qualities, together with their utility, benefit to their community, and long-term prospects. Awarded annually.

6831 ■ Association of Mining Analysts
Tony Mahalski, Chm.
Bankside plc.
1 Frederick's Pl.
London EC2R 8AE, United Kingdom
Ph: 44 20 88782308
Fax: 44 20 83921220
E-mail: info@ama.org.uk
URL: http://www.ama.org.uk

6832 ■ Mining Analyst of the Year

For the greatest contribution to the mining industry in the form of research output.

6833 ■ Association of National Park Authorities
Kathryn Cook, Coor.
126 Bute St.
Cardiff Bay
Cardiff CF10 5LE, United Kingdom
Ph: 44 29 20499966
E-mail: info@anpa.gov.uk
URL: http://www.nationalparks.gov.uk

6834 ■ National Conservation Award

For contributions to national parks purposes. A trophy is awarded biennially.

6835 ■ Association of Paediatric Anaesthetists of Great Britain and Ireland
Dr. R. Bingham, Treas.
21 Portland Pl.
London W1B 1PY, United Kingdom
Ph: 44 20 76318887
Fax: 44 20 76314352
E-mail: apagbiadministration@aagbi.org
URL: http://www.apagbi.org.uk

6836 ■ Paediatric Anaesthesia Research Fund Grant

To support projects that serve scientific development in basic or clinical research in the field of pediatric anesthesia. A maximum of £10,000 is available per year.

6837 ■ Travel Grants

To enable members to travel to overseas meetings with direct relevance to the practice of pediatric anesthesia. Grants are limited to the amount of £500 for speakers and presenters, and £ for other delegates.

6838 ■ Association of Photographers
Kingsley Marten, Managing Dir.
81 Leonard St.
London EC2A 4QS, United Kingdom
Ph: 44 20 77396669
Fax: 44 20 77398707
E-mail: general@aophoto.co.uk
URL: http://home.the-aop.org
Formerly: Association of Fashion Advertising and Editorial Photographers.

6839 ■ Assistants Awards

To recognize the potential of photographic assistants who will be the future's professional advertising, editorial, and creative photographers. Open to all Assistants Members who enter individual images or portfolios into four categories. Awarded annually. Established in 1990. Formerly: Fuji/Association of Photographers Assistants' Awards.

6840 ■ Photographers Awards

To recognize talent within the professional advertising, fashion, and editorial fields of photography. Awards are presented in 18 categories. Gold and silver trophies and Merit certificates are awarded annually. Established in 1983. Formerly: (1990) AFAEP Awards.

6841 ■ Students Awards

To encourage the development of students training to succeed in fashion, advertising, and editorial photography and to creatively and technically satisfy briefs devised and judged by major photographers and art directors in fashion, advertising, and editorial photography. A monetary award and a certificate are awarded annually. Established in 1981. Formerly: (1990) AFAEP/Kodak Student Competition.

6842 ■ Association of Professional Landscapers
Alison Smith, Admin.
Horticulture House
19 High St.
Theale
Berkshire
Reading RG7 5AH, United Kingdom
Ph: 44 118 9303132
Fax: 44 118 9323453
E-mail: apl@the-hta.org.uk
URL: http://www.landscaper.org.uk

6843 ■ APL Awards

To recognize and promote the best in landscap-

ing undertaken by APL members. Categories range from smaller projects to garden maintenance to contract of over £100,000. Awarded annually.

6844 ■ Association of Sign Language Interpreters
Sarah Haynes, Chm.
Fortuna House
S Fifth St.
Milton Keynes MK9 2EU, United Kingdom
Ph: 44 871 4740522
Fax: 44 1908 325259
E-mail: chair@asli.org.uk
URL: http://www.asli.org.uk/default.aspx

6845 ■ Ben Steiner Award

To recognize an individual for outstanding, positive, and consistent contributions and achievements over a number of years toward the development of sign language interpreting. Awarded triennially.

6846 ■ Association of Social Anthropologists of the UK and the Commonwealth
Rohan Jackson, Admin.
50 Fitzroy St.
London W1T 5BT, United Kingdom
E-mail: admin@theasa.org
URL: http://www.theasa.org

6847 ■ Harold Blakemore Prize

To recognize the best essay by a postgraduate student. Awarded annually.

6848 ■ Association of Surgeons of Great Britain and Ireland
Prof. John MacFie, Pres.
35-43 Lincoln's Inn Fields
London WC2A 3PE, United Kingdom
Ph: 44 20 79730300
Fax: 44 20 74309235
E-mail: admin@asgbi.org.uk
URL: http://www.asgbi.org.uk

6849 ■ Moynihan Prize

For the author of the best short paper on new work that is read at the Annual Meeting. A medal and monetary prize of £1,000 are awarded annually. Established in 1951.

6850 ■ Overseas Surgical Fellowship

To sponsor surgeons wishing to work in a developing country, primarily in the least developed countries, on a short-term basis for the purpose of providing training and support for overseas medical schools in the development of their postgraduate training programs and, thereby, establishing links with these centers. At least five fellowships of £2,000 each are awarded annually.

6851 ■ Association of the British Pharmaceutical Industry
Martin Anderson, Dir. of Commercial Affairs
7th Fl., Southside
105 Victoria St.
London SW1E 6QT, United Kingdom
Ph: 44 870 8904333
Fax: 44 20 77471414
E-mail: manderson@abpi.org.uk
URL: http://www.abpi.org.uk

6852 ■ Pharmacy Award

For innovative pharmacy practice that brings benefits to patients. Awarded annually to one winner from each of the following regions: England, Scotland, Wales, and Northern Ireland.

6853 ■ Association of Veterinary Anaesthetists
Ms. Karen Walsh, Sec.
Highlands Rd.
Shirley
West Midlands

Awards are arranged in alphabetical order below their administering organizations

Solihull B90 4NH, United Kingdom
Ph: 44 121 7127070
Fax: 44 121 7127077
E-mail: secretary@ava.eu.com
URL: http://www.ava.eu.com

6854 ■ Educational Trust Awards
To provide financial assistance to trainee veterinary anaesthetists for purposes relevant to their training. Awarded twice each year to one or more individuals.

6855 ■ Langley Award
To recognize the best paper in the journal *Veterinary Anaesthesia and Analgesia*. A monetary prize of £250 is awarded annually. Established in 1985.

6856 ■ Association of Zimbabwe Journalists in the United Kingdom
83 Glendale Dr.
Surrey
Burpham GU4 7JA, United Kingdom
E-mail: feedback@zimbabwejournalists.com
URL: http://www.zimbabwejournalists.com

6857 ■ Mark Chavhunduka Award
To recognize a Zimbabwe journalist for outstanding contributions. Established in honor of the Zimbabwe journalist who was arrested and tortured for his reporting.

6858 ■ Automobile Association Ltd.
Hotel Services Section
Fanum House, 14th Fl.
Basing View
Basingstoke RG21 4EA, United Kingdom
Ph: 44 1256 494974
Fax: 44 1256 491647
E-mail: hotelservicescustomersupport@theaa.com
URL: http://www.theaa.com

6859 ■ B & B Awards
To recognize excellent services provided by bed and breakfast (B & B) establishments in the United Kingdom. Awarded in six categories: London B & B of the Year; Friendliest Landlady of the Year; Funkiest B & B of the Year; and Guest Accommodation of the Year in England, Scotland, and Wales. Awarded annually.

6860 ■ Campsite of the Year
To recognize the most outstanding campsites in England, Scotland, and Wales. Awarded annually.

6861 ■ Hospitality Awards
To recognize the success of establishments and individuals in the hospitality industry in the United Kingdom. Awarded in a variety of categories, including hotel groups, restaurants, wine, pubs, and chefs. Awarded annually.

6862 ■ Housekeeper of the Year
To recognize and reward the most diligent and outstanding housekeepers in Britain and Northern Ireland. Awarded annually.

6863 ■ BackCare, The Charity for Healthier Backs
Sean McDougall, Acting Chief Exec.
16 Elmtree Rd.
Middlesex
Teddington TW11 8ST, United Kingdom
Ph: 44 20 89775474
Ph: 44 20 86148186
Fax: 44 20 89435318
E-mail: info@backcare.org.uk
URL: http://www.backcare.org.uk
Formerly: (2004) National Back Pain Association.

6864 ■ BackCare Medal
To recognize the best research paper presented at the annual meeting of the Society for Back Pain Research. Awarded annually.

6865 ■ National Back Pain Association Medal
For recognition of the most outstanding scientific research paper on the subject of back pain published during the year in one or more scientific journals in the English language. The paper must have come to the attention of the awarding committee of the Society for Back Pain Research. A monetary prize of £200, a medal, and a certificate are awarded annually. Established in 1978. Formerly: (1990) Back Pain Association Medal.

6866 ■ Badminton England
Geoff Rofe, Pres.
Natl. Badminton Ctre.
Bradwell Rd.
Milton Keynes MK8 9LA, United Kingdom
Ph: 44 1908 268400
Fax: 44 1908 268412
E-mail: info@badmintonengland.co.uk
URL: http://www.badmintonengland.co.uk/homepage.asp

6867 ■ English Badminton Award
To recognize long-standing exceptional service to badminton in England. An EBA badge and a certificate are presented to the recipient(s) annually. Established in 1993.

6868 ■ Herbert Scheele Medal
To recognize outstanding contributions to the development and administration of the sport of badminton. Consideration is given to a member of the Association or its other national governing bodies. A silver medal is presented as merited at All-England Championships. Established in 1981. The award commemorates Herbert Scheele, a one-time secretary of the Association and of the International Badminton Federation.

6869 ■ Yonex National Badminton Awards
To honor members who volunteer their time as coaches, officials, administrators, committee members, and other roles. Awards are presented in two categories: Volunteer of the Year and Young Volunteer of the Year. All-expense paid trips to the semi-finals and finals of the Yonex All England Championships are awarded annually.

6870 ■ BCA Productions
Power Road Studios, G.09
114 Power Rd.
London W4 5PY, United Kingdom
Ph: 44 20 89876400
E-mail: va@ucgtv.com
URL: http://www.britishcomedyawards.com

6871 ■ British Comedy Awards
Recognizes the best of the year in British comedy. Annual awards are presented in more than a dozen categories, including Best Comedy Panel Show, Best Male and Female TV Comics, Best Comedy Performance in Film, and Lifetime Achievement Award. Established in 1990.

6872 ■ Beatson Institute for Cancer Research
Prof. Karen H. Vousden, Dir.
Garscube Estate
Switchback Rd.
Bearsden
Glasgow G61 1BD, United Kingdom
Ph: 44 141 330 3953
Fax: 44 141 942 6521
E-mail: beatson@gla.ac.uk
URL: http://www.beatson.gla.ac.uk

6873 ■ John Paul Career Award
Recognizes the most promising student at the Beatson Institute. Candidates prepare a progress report of their work, present a lecture to staff and other students, and are interviewed by a selection committee. Awarded annually.

6874 ■ Belgian Luxembourg Chamber of Commerce in Great Britain
Mr. Michel Vanhoonacker, Chm.
Westwood House
Annie Med Ln.

South Cave HU15 2HG, United Kingdom
Ph: 44 207 1274292
Fax: 44 870 4292148
E-mail: info@blcc.co.uk
URL: http://www.blcc.co.uk

6875 ■ Golden Bridge Export Award
To honor the most successful Belgian or Luxembourg company exporting to the United Kingdom, in both the service and manufacturing sector. Awarded annually.

6876 ■ Bibliographical Society - United Kingdom
Ms. Margaret Ford, Honorary Sec.
University of London
Institute of English Studies
Senate House
Malet St.
London WC1E 7HU, United Kingdom
E-mail: secretary@bibsoc.org.uk
URL: http://www.bibsoc.org.uk

6877 ■ Medal for Services to Bibliography
For recognition of achievement in the field of bibliographical studies. Individuals are elected. A gold medal is awarded biennially in odd-numbered years. Established in 1929. Formerly: Silver-gilt Medal for Bibliography.

6878 ■ Biochemical Society - England
Chris Kirk, Chief Exec.
3rd Fl., Eagle House
16 Procter St.
London WC1V 6NX, United Kingdom
Ph: 44 20 72804131
Ph: 44 20 76852400
Fax: 44 20 72804170
E-mail: genadmin@biochemistry.org
URL: http://www.biochemistry.org

6879 ■ Centenary Award
Awarded to a biochemist of distinction from any part of the world. Recipient presents the Sir Frederick Gowland Hopkins Memorial Lecture. A monetary award of £3,000 and medal are awarded annually. Established in 2010.

6880 ■ Early Career Research Awards
To recognize exceptional impact by early career scientists. Eligible to scientists who received the PhD in the preceding five years. Honorariums of £1,000 and medals are awarded annually to one or more recipients. Established in 2009.

6881 ■ Life Sciences Bursaries
To support biochemical students who are interested in life-science research. Grants are awarded annually.

6882 ■ Sir Philip Randle Lecture
To recognize a scientist for contributions to the understanding of mammalian metabolism. The recipient presents a lecture at an appropriate meeting. A monetary prize of £2,000 and a certificate are awarded biennially in odd-numbered years. Established in 2011.

6883 ■ Scientific Outreach Grants
To support schools and young bioscientists who conduct outreach programs that communicate the excitement of bioscience to young scientists. Grants in the amount of £1,000 are awarded annually.

6884 ■ The Black and White Spider Awards
8 Shepherd Market, Ste. 639
Mayfair
London W1J 7JY, United Kingdom
Ph: 44 207 239490
E-mail: info@thespiderawards.com
URL: http://www.thespiderawards.com

6885 ■ Black and White Spider Awards
To honor excellence in professional and amateur

Awards are arranged in alphabetical order below their administering organizations

black and white photography from around the world. Awarded annually in more than one dozen categories; additionally, one entry is named the Photographer of the Year. Established in 2004.

6886 ■ BMJ Group
BMA House
Tavistock Sq.
London WC1H 9JR, United Kingdom
Ph: 44 20 7387 4410
Fax: 44 20 7387 6400
URL: http://group.bmj.com

6887 ■ BMJ Awards
To recognize individuals, organizations, and initiatives that have demonstrated outstanding and measurable contributions to health care in the United Kingdom. Eleven awards are presented, including Research Paper of the Year, Corporate Social Responsibility Award, Health Communicator of the Year, Junior Doctor of the Year, Best Quality Improvement, and the Award for Lifetime Achievement. Awarded annually. Established in 2009.

6888 ■ Boardman Tasker Charitable Trust
Maggie Body, Sec.
Pound House
Llangennith
West Glamorgan
Swansea SA3 1JQ, United Kingdom
Ph: 44 1792 386215
Fax: 44 1792 386215
E-mail: margaretbody@lineone.net
URL: http://www.boardmantasker.com

6889 ■ Prize for Mountain Literature
For recognition of an original literary work. The central theme must be concerned with the mountain environment. Fiction, nonfiction, drama, or poetry written (whether initially or in translation) in the English language may be nominated by publishers only. Books must have been published or distributed in the United Kingdom for the first time between November 1 of the preceding year and October 31 of the year the prize is awarded. A monetary award of £3,000 is awarded annually. Established in 1983 in memory of Peter Boardman and Joe Tasker, authors of mountain literature who disappeared on Mt. Everest in 1982.

6890 ■ Bookseller Information Group
Endeavour House
189 Shaftesbury Ave.
London WC2H 8TJ, United Kingdom
Ph: 44 20 7420 6006
Fax: 44 20 7420 6103
E-mail: info@booksellersubs.com
URL: http://www.thebookseller.com

6891 ■ Award for Expanding the Retail Market
Part of the Retail Awards. Awarded annually.

6892 ■ Bookseller Industry Awards
To recognize excellence among booksellers in the United Kingdom. Presented in a variety of categories. Awarded annually.

6893 ■ Children's Bookseller of the Year
To recognize an outstanding retailer of children's books in the United Kingdom. Awarded annually as part of the Bookseller Industry Awards (see separate entry).

6894 ■ Children's Independent of the Year
To recognize an outstanding independent retailer of children's books in the United Kingdom. Awarded annually as part of the Bookseller Industry Awards (see separate entry).

6895 ■ Green Initiative Award
Recognizes bookseller excellence in the United Kingdom. Part of the Retail Awards. Awarded annually.

6896 ■ Independent Bookseller of the Year
To recognize an outstanding independent book store in the United Kingdom. Awarded annually as part of the Bookseller Industry Awards (see separate entry).

6897 ■ Manager of the Year
To recognize an outstanding manager of a book store in the United Kingdom. Awarded annually as part of the Bookseller Industry Awards (see separate entry).

6898 ■ Booksellers Association of the United Kingdom and Ireland
Jane Streeter, Pres.
Minster House
272 Vauxhall Bridge Rd.
London SW1V 1BA, United Kingdom
Ph: 44 20 78020802
Fax: 44 20 78020803
E-mail: mail@booksellers.org.uk
URL: http://www.booksellers.org.uk

6899 ■ Costa Book Awards
To celebrate the best contemporary British writing. Books are considered in five categories: novel, first novel, biography/autobiography, poetry, and children's book. Authors who have been living in Great Britain or Ireland for three or more years are eligible. Selection is made from books first published in the United Kingdom or Ireland within the previous year. Works must be submitted by publishers only. The following monetary awards are presented: £5,000 each for the winner in each category, and an additional £30,000 to the overall winner, Costa Book of the Year, chosen from the five category winners. Awarded annually in January. Established in 1971. Sponsored by Costa Coffee. Formerly: (2006) Whitebread Literary Awards.

6900 ■ BBC Samuel Johnson Prize for Non-Fiction
To reward the best of non-fiction in English by writers of any nationality. Open to authors of all non-fiction books in the areas of current affairs, history, politics, science, sport, travel, biography, autobiography, and the arts. The winning author receives £20,000. Awarded annually. Formerly: (1996) AT&T Nonfiction Award.

6901 ■ Booktrust
Viv Bird, CEO
Book House
45 East Hill
London SW18 2QZ, United Kingdom
Ph: 44 20 8516 2977
Fax: 44 20 8516 2978
E-mail: query@booktrust.org.uk
URL: http://www.booktrust.org.uk
Formerly: (1986) National Book League (England).

6902 ■ BBC National Short Story Award
To recognize the best short stories in the United Kingdom. Open to all British nationals and U.K. residents aged 18 years or older. Stories must contain no more than 8,000 words. The following monetary prizes are awarded: £15,000 for the winner, £3,000 for the runner-up, and £500 for three shortlisted stories. Awarded annually. Established in 2006. Co-sponsored by the British Broadcasting Corp. (BBC).

6903 ■ Blue Peter Book Awards
To recognize U.K. authors and illustrators of books that guide children toward high quality literature, thereby encouraging them to read and establish a love of reading for life. Awarded in three categories: Favorite Story, Most Fun Story with Pictures, and Best Book with Facts. One overall winner is selected as the Blue Peter Book of the Year. Awarded annually. Established in 2000.

6904 ■ Roald Dahl Funny Prize
To reward authors and artists who write and il-

lustrate books for children with the use of humor. Open to stories, poetry, and fiction in two categories: children aged six and under, and children aged seven to 14. A monetary prize of £2,500 is awarded annually in each category. Established in 2008.

6905 ■ Early Years Awards
To the best books for children under the age of five. Awards are granted in three categories: best book for babies under one year old; best book for pre-school children, up to five years of age; and award for the best new illustrator. A monetary prize of £2,000 is awarded in each category. Formerly: Sainsbury's Baby Book Award.

6906 ■ Independent Foreign Fiction Prize
To honor a great work of fiction by a living author that has been translated into English from any other language, and published in the United Kingdom. A monetary prize of £10,000 is shared equally between the author and the translator. Awarded annually. Established in 1990.

6907 ■ Orange Award for New Writers
For the best work of fiction by an emerging female author. All first works of fiction are eligible, including short story collections and novellas. Judging is based on originality, accessibility, and promise. Awarded annually. Established in 2005.

6908 ■ Orange Prize for Fiction
For the best full-length novel by a woman. Eligible entries must be written in English. The novel must be published for the first time in the United Kingdom. All genres are accepted. A monetary prize of £30,000 and a limited edition bronze figurine known as a "Bessie" are awarded annually. Established in 1996.

6909 ■ John Llewellyn Rhys Prize
For recognition of a memorable literary work of fiction, nonfiction, or poetry written in English and published in the UK during the current year. British or Commonwealth writers who are under 35 years of age at the time of publication are eligible. A monetary prize of £5,000 is awarded annually. Established in 1941 by the widow of John Llewellyn Rhys, an airman killed while on active duty. Formerly: (1989) John Llewellyn Rhys Memorial Prize.

6910 ■ Teenage Prize
For an outstanding book in the category of contemporary teenage fiction. Prize is open to works of fiction, including novels, short story collections, and graphic novels. A trophy and monetary prize of £2,500 are awarded annually.

6911 ■ Kim Scott Walwyn Prize
Honors professional achievements of women in publishing. A monetary prize of £1,000 is awarded annually. Established in 2005 in honor of Kim Scott Walwyn, a publishing director at Oxford University Press.

6912 ■ Brazilian Chamber of Commerce in Great Britain
Mr. Jaime Gornsztejn, Chm.
32 Green St.
London W1K 7AT, United Kingdom
Ph: 44 20 73999281
Fax: 44 20 74990186
E-mail: brazilianchamber@brazilianchamber.org.uk
URL: http://brazilianchamber.org.uk

6913 ■ Personality of the Year Awards
To honor two outstanding individuals, one from the United Kingdom and one from Brazil, whose companies have significantly contributed to furthering trade and investment between the two countries. Awarded annually.

6914 ■ Brick Development Association
Simon Hay, CEO
The Building Ctre.
26 Store St.

Awards are arranged in alphabetical order below their administering organizations

London WC1E 7BT, United Kingdom
Ph: 44 20 73237030
Fax: 44 20 75803795
E-mail: brick@brick.org.uk
URL: http://www.brick.org.uk

6915 ■ Brick Awards
To recognize and reward excellence in use of brick. Awards are presented in 15 categories covering different aspects of design and construction. Trophies are awarded annually in each category.

6916 ■ Bridport Arts Centre
Polly Gifford, Dir.
South St.
Dorset
Bridport DT6 3NR, United Kingdom
Ph: 44 1308 427183
E-mail: info@bridport-arts.com
URL: http://www.bridport-arts.com

6917 ■ Bridport Prize
To encourage people to write. Awards are given for poetry and short stories. Entries should be written in English, of the length specified in the current conditions of entry. A monetary first prize of £5,000, a second prize of £1,000, and a third prize of £500 are awarded in each category annually. Established in 1980. Formerly: Creative Writing Competition.

6918 ■ British Academy
Dr. Robin Jackson, Chief Exec./Sec.
10-11 Carlton House Terr.
London SW1Y 5AH, United Kingdom
Ph: 44 20 79695200
Ph: 44 20 79695257
Fax: 44 20 79695300
E-mail: chiefexec@britac.ac.uk
URL: http://www.britac.ac.uk

6919 ■ Derek Allen Prize
To recognize outstanding contributions to musicology, numismatics, or Celtic Studies. Awarded annually. Established in 1976 to commemorate Derek Fortrose Allen, former secretary of the Academy.

6920 ■ British Academy Fellow
To recognize scholars for outstanding distinctions in most branches of the humanities. Up to 35 scholars under the age of 70, and up to three scholars over the age of 70, are selected annually. Formerly: (2009) Ordinary Fellow.

6921 ■ Burkitt Medal for Biblical Studies
To recognize outstanding contributions to Biblical studies. A bronze medal is awarded annually. Established in 1925.

6922 ■ Grahame Clark Medal
To recognize outstanding contributions to the study of prehistoric archaeology. Awarded biennially in even-numbered years. Established in 1992.

6923 ■ John Coles Medal for Landscape Archaeology
To recognize distinguished achievements, by any scholar based in Britain and Ireland, in landscape archaeology in any part of the world and in any period. Awarded annually. Established in 2007.

6924 ■ Rose Mary Crawshay Prize for English Literature
To recognize a woman of any nationality who, in the judgment of the Council of the British Academy, has written or published within three years next preceding the year of the award an historical or critical work of sufficient value on any subject connected with English Literature, preference being given to a work regarding one of the poets Byron, Shelley, and Keats. Presented to two recipients annually. Established in 1888.

6925 ■ Sir Israel Gollancz Prize
To recognize published work of sufficient value on subjects connected with Anglo-Saxon, Early English Language and Literature, English Philology, or the History of English Language; or for original investigations connected with the history of English Literature or the works of English writers. Awarded biennially in odd-numbered years. Established in 1995.

6926 ■ Kenyon Medal for Classical Studies
To recognize an individual for contributions to classical literature or archaeology. Awarded biennially in odd-numbered years. Established to honor Sir Frederic Kenyon, former President and secretary of the Academy.

6927 ■ President's Medal
To honor an individual or organization for signal service to the cause of the humanities and social sciences. Up to five medals are awarded annually. Established in 2009.

6928 ■ Research Grants
To provide research funding to postdoctoral level scholars in all subjects within the remit of humanities and social studies. Grants of various amounts are awarded annually.

6929 ■ Serena Medal for Italian Studies
To recognize an individual for services toward the furtherance of the study of Italian history, literature, art, or economics. Awarded annually. First awarded in 1920.

6930 ■ Wiley Prize in Psychology
To honor excellence in research in psychology. Alternatively rewards lifetime achievement by an outstanding international scholar and promising early career work by a U.K.-based psychologist. A monetary prize of £5,000 is awarded annually. Established in 2009. Sponsored by Wiley-Blackwell.

6931 ■ British Academy of Film and Television Arts
Tim Corrie, Chm.
195 Piccadilly
London W1J 9LN, United Kingdom
Ph: 44 20 77340022
Fax: 44 20 77341792
E-mail: info@bafta.org
URL: http://www.bafta.org
Formerly: (1976) Society of Film and Television Arts.

6932 ■ British Academy Television Awards
For recognition of outstanding television programs in the areas of performance, and craft and production. The voting lists are compiled from suggestions received from academy members throughout the year. The nominations for the Production, Direction, and Craft Awards are determined by vote. Juries decide the winner in each category. The Best Television Performance Awards are decided by membership vote. Awards are given in more than two dozen categories, including Single Drama, Drama Series, Comedy Program, and Leading Actor and Actress. Trophies are awarded annually. Awards related to the Academy go back as far as 1947.

6933 ■ Orange British Academy Film Awards
For recognition of outstanding films in the areas of performance, and craft and production. The voting lists are compiled from suggestions received from academy members throughout the year. The nominations for the Production, Direction, and Craft Awards are determined by vote. Juries decide the winner in each category. The Best Film and Performance Awards are decided by membership vote. Awards are given in more than two dozen categories, including Original Screenplay, Leading Actress and Actor, Cinematography, Production Design, and Academy Fellowship. Trophies are awarded annually.

6934 ■ British Air Line Pilots Association
Capt. Mark Searle, Chm.
BALPA House
5 Heathrow Blvd.
278 Bath Rd.
West Drayton UB7 0DQ, United Kingdom
Ph: 44 20 84764000
Ph: 44 20 84764099
Fax: 44 20 84764077
E-mail: balpa@balpa.org
URL: http://www.balpa.org

6935 ■ BALPA Award
For services to aviation/piloting profession.

6936 ■ British and Irish Association of Law Librarians
Elaine Bird, Sec.
58 Carey St.
Edinburgh WC2A 2JD, United Kingdom
E-mail: admin@biall.org.uk
URL: http://www.biall.org.uk

6937 ■ Wallace Breem Memorial Award
To recognize particularly good contributions to law librarianship, or to provide financial assistance for special research or other projects at doctorate level or above. Awarded biennially in even-numbered years. Established in 1990.

6938 ■ Legal Journals Award
To honor the publishing profession for quality products and outstanding contributions in the field of legal serial titles. A certificate is awarded annually. Established in 2001.

6939 ■ British Animation Awards Ltd.
219 Archway Rd.
London N6 5BN, United Kingdom
Ph: 44 7897 467376
E-mail: info@britishanimationawards.com
URL: http://www.britishanimationawards.com

6940 ■ British Animation Awards
To recognize outstanding United Kingdom animation, including student work, commercials, children's entertainment, short and experimental art films, music videos, and new technologies. Awarded biennially in even-numbered years. Established in 2006.

6941 ■ British Association for Applied Linguistics
Jeanie Taylor, Admin.
PO Box 6688
London SE15 3WB, United Kingdom
Ph: 44 207 6390090
Ph: 44 845 4568208
Fax: 44 207 6356014
E-mail: admin@baal.org.uk
URL: http://www.baal.org.uk

6942 ■ Book Prize
For recognition of an outstanding book in applied linguistics. Books published during the preceding calendar year are eligible. Books must be nominated by their publisher. Awarded annually. Established in 1984.

6943 ■ Postgraduate Scholarship
Assists in furthering education in applied linguistics. Applicants must be postgraduate students. Two scholarships are awarded annually.

6944 ■ British Association for Biological Anthropology and Osteoarchaeology
Holger Schutkowski, Chm.
Durham University
Department of Archaeology
South Rd.
Durham DH1 3LE, United Kingdom

Awards are arranged in alphabetical order below their administering organizations

URL: http://www.babao.org.uk

6945 ■ Jane Moore Prize
To recognize the most outstanding student presentation. Awarded annually.

6946 ■ Small Research Project Grants
To support research in biological anthropology and osteoarchaeology. Two grants are awarded: one for research in the contract sector (£1,500) and the other for research in the academic sector (£1,000). Awarded annually.

6947 ■ British Association for Cancer Research
Prof. Sir Bruce Ponder, Pres.
St. James's University Hospital
Clinical Sciences Bldg.
Beckett St.
Leeds LS9 7TF, United Kingdom
Ph: 44 113 2065611
Fax: 44 113 2429886
E-mail: bacr@leeds.ac.uk
URL: http://www.bacr.org.uk

6948 ■ AstraZeneca Young Scientist Frank Rose Award
To recognize and reward the achievements of a young scientist in any field of cancer research. Candidates should be age 35 or younger. A monetary prize of £1,000 and an invitation to present an oral paper are awarded annually.

6949 ■ BACR Travel/Exchange Fellowships
To enable members to visit institutions other than their own for the purposes of lecture tours, courses, or to carry out collaborative work. Open to all members but with preference given to individuals of 40 years of age or under, or with less than five years of post-doctoral experience. Visits may be abroad or within the United Kingdom. Fellowships up to £2,000 are awarded, and may be used for travel and/or living expenses.

6950 ■ Hamilton-Fairley Young Investigator Award
To recognize and encourage the talents of junior cancer researchers. Candidates must be clinically or scientifically qualified individuals who are not more than five years post PhD/MD. A monetary prize of £300 is awarded annually.

6951 ■ Translational Research Award
To recognize and reward the achievements of an individual whose work has made significant contributions to translational (laboratory-to-clinic) cancer research. Candidates must be 35 years of age or younger. A monetary prize of £1,000 is awarded annually.

6952 ■ British Association for Immediate Care
Richard Steyn, Chm.
Turret House, Turret Ln.
Suffolk
Ipswich IP4 1DL, United Kingdom
Ph: 44 1473 218407
Fax: 44 1473 280585
E-mail: admin@basics.org.uk
URL: http://www.basics.org.uk

6953 ■ BASICS Award
To recognize members and other individuals who have provided valuable service to the Association. Awarded annually. Established in 1986.

6954 ■ Asmund S. Laerdal Award
To an individual who has made an outstanding contribution to the field of immediate care. Awarded annually. Established in 1984.

6955 ■ British Association for Sexual Health and HIV
Dr. Keith Radcliffe, Pres.
1 Wimpole St.
London W1G 0AE, United Kingdom

Ph: 44 20 72902968
Ph: 44 20 72903904
Fax: 44 20 72902989
E-mail: bashh@rsm.ac.uk
URL: http://www.bashh.org

6956 ■ BASHH Undergraduate Prize
To recognize a report submitted by an undergraduate student on a subject related to sexually transmitted diseases, genitourinary medicine, or HIV infection. A monetary prize of £200 is awarded annually.

6957 ■ British Association of Aviation Consultants
John Wheeler, Chm.
16 Connaught Pl.
London W2 2ES, United Kingdom
E-mail: committee@baac.org.uk
URL: http://www.baac.org.uk

6958 ■ Sir Peter Masefield Gold Medal
To recognize an individual for prolonged and outstanding service to aviation. A medal is awarded annually. Established in 1987.

6959 ■ British Association of Dermatologists
Ms. Marilyn Benham, CEO
4 Fitzroy Sq.
London W1T 5HQ, United Kingdom
Ph: 44 20 73830266
Fax: 44 20 73885263
E-mail: admin@bad.org.uk
URL: http://www.bad.org.uk

6960 ■ British Association of Dermatologists Fellowships
To recognize undergraduates for outstanding contributions to dermatology. Awards include the Essay Prize, Elective Prize, Medical Student Project Grant, and the Intercalated Degree Grant. Awarded annually.

6961 ■ Intercalated Degree Grant
To recognize and support an undergraduate medical student with an intercalated degree which includes a project that is relevant to dermatology or skin biology. A monetary prize of £5,000 is awarded annually.

6962 ■ Postgraduate Awards
To recognize outstanding work completed by postgraduate members.

6963 ■ Undergraduate Award
To recognize a medical school student for outstanding academic achievement.

6964 ■ Undergraduate Dermatology Elective/Project Grants
To recognize undergraduate medical students at United Kingdom universities who will be undertaking an election in an overseas dermatology department. Nine monetary awards of £500 each are presented annually.

6965 ■ Undergraduate Essay Prize
To recognize a paper on a topic related to dermatology. Essays should be 2500 words long. A monetary award of £500 is presented for the winning essay, and three runners-up receive £250 each. Awarded annually.

6966 ■ British Association of Landscape Industries
Paul Cowell, Chm.
Landscape House
Stoneleigh Park
Warwickshire
Coventry CV8 2LG, United Kingdom
Ph: 44 24 76690333
Fax: 44 24 76690077
E-mail: contact@bali.org.uk
URL: http://www.bali.org.uk

6967 ■ National Landscape Awards
To draw attention to the landscape industry's

participation in creating an improved environment, and for recognition of the best contributions by BALI Members made to this aim. Landscape construction must have been undertaken by a BALI Member and completed within two years of the entry date to be eligible. Plaques are awarded annually at BALI's National Landscape Awards Luncheon. There is a Grand Award, for the overall winner. Established in 1976.

6968 ■ British Association of Otorhinolaryngologists - Head and Neck Surgeons
Nechama Lewis, Admin. Mgr.
35-43 Lincoln's Inn Fields
London WC2A 3PE, United Kingdom
Ph: 44 20 74048373
Ph: 44 20 76111731
Fax: 44 20 74044200
E-mail: admin@entuk.org
URL: http://www.entuk.org

6969 ■ Undergraduate Essay Prize
For the best essay by clinical medical student on a topic determined annually. A monetary prize of £500 is awarded annually.

6970 ■ British Association of Sport and Exercise Sciences
Dr. Claire Hitchings, Exec. Off.
Leeds Metropolitan University
Carnegie Faculty of Sport and Education
Fairfax Hall
Headingley Campus, Beckett Park
Leeds LS6 3QS, United Kingdom
Ph: 44 113 8126162
Fax: 44 113 8126162
E-mail: jbairstow@bases.org.uk
URL: http://www.bases.org.uk

6971 ■ BASES Annual Conference Awards
To recognize excellence in sport and exercise sciences and to reward members who have made outstanding achievements. Two types of awards are presented: Scientific Communications Oral Presentations Awards and Scientific Communications Poster Presentation Awards. Awarded annually.

6972 ■ Early Career Researcher Awards
To recognize excellence in early career members researching within the field sport and/or exercise sciences. A monetary award of £500 is awarded annually.

6973 ■ Undergraduate Dissertation of the Year Award
To recognize the best undergraduate dissertation in the area of sport and/or exercise sciences. A monetary prize of £200 is awarded annually to two recipients.

6974 ■ British Astronomical Association
Dr. David Boyd, Pres.
Burlington House
Piccadilly
London W1J 0DU, United Kingdom
Ph: 44 20 77344145
Fax: 44 20 74394629
E-mail: office@britastro.org
URL: http://www.britastro.org/baa

6975 ■ Lydia Brown Award for Meritorious Service
For recognition of prolonged and valuable service to the BAA in an honorary capacity. Members of the BAA are eligible. A monetary prize and a silver-gilt medal are usually awarded biennially. Established in 1972.

6976 ■ Walter Goodacre Medal
For recognition of prolonged and outstanding contribution to the progress of astronomy. Members of the BAA are eligible. A monetary prize and a silver gilt medal are awarded biennially in even-numbered years. Established in 1930.

Awards are arranged in alphabetical order below their administering organizations

6977 ■ Merlin Medal

For recognition of an outstanding discovery and contribution to astronomy. Members of the BAA are eligible. A monetary prize and a silver medal are awarded annually. Established in 1961.

6978 ■ Steavenson Memorial Award

For recognition of diligence and excellence as an astronomical observer. Members of the BAA are eligible. A book chosen by the recipient is awarded annually. Established in 1975.

6979 ■ British Broadcasting Corp.
Broadcasting House
Portland Pl.
London W1A 1AA, United Kingdom
Ph: 44 20 7580 4468
Fax: 44 20 7637 1630
URL: http://www.bbc.co.uk

6980 ■ Cardiff Singer of the World Competition

To recognize outstanding singers at the beginning of their professional careers. Open to individual from around the world who are at least 18 years old and no older than 32. In the main competition, singers are required to demonstrate their prowess in the disciplines of opera or concert music. In the Song Prize competition, which is open to all competitors but not compulsory, each singer performs this or her own choice of Lieder or art song. Three prizes are awarded: BBC Cardiff Singer of the Year (£15,000), BBC Cardiff Singer of the World Song Prize (£5,000), and Dame Joan Sutherland Audience Prize (£2,000). Held biennially in odd-numbered years. Established in 1983.

6981 ■ Food and Farming Awards

To promote and acknowledge outstanding food and food service in the United Kingdom. Awards are granted in a number of categories, including Best Takeaway, Farmer of the Year, and Best Local Food Retailer. Awarded annually.

6982 ■ Mastermind Award

To recognize the winner of a television program quiz. The winner is determined through 12 first-round heats, four quarter-finals, and the grand final. A Caithness (engraved) Glass Trophy is awarded annually. Established in 1972.

6983 ■ British Canoe Union
Albert Woods, Pres.
18 Market Pl.
Bingham
Nottingham NG13 8AP, United Kingdom
Ph: 44 845 3709500
Ph: 44 300 0119500
Fax: 44 845 3709501
E-mail: info@bcu.org.uk
URL: http://www.bcu.org.uk

6984 ■ Lifeguard Awards

To recognize individuals on everything from basic canoe rescue skills to advanced lifeguarding and first aid. Awards are presented in various levels when merited.

6985 ■ British Cartographic Society
Mr. Peter Jolly, Pres.
1 Kensington Gore
London SW9 2AR, United Kingdom
Ph: 44 115 9328684
Fax: 44 115 9328684
E-mail: admin@cartography.org.uk
URL: http://www.cartography.org.uk

6986 ■ Avenza Award for Electronic Mapping

To recognize an outstanding map available in electronic format. A trophy and certificate are awarded annually. Supported by Avenza.

6987 ■ John C. Bartholomew Award

For recognition of originality and excellence in the field of thematic (non-topographic, 1:100,000 and smaller) cartography with emphasis on effective communication of the intended theme or themes. A certificate and a trophy are awarded annually at the September symposium. Established in 1980. Sponsored by Collins Bartholomew.

6988 ■ British Cartographic Society Award

For recognition of the most outstanding entry among the winning entries for the Stanfords Award, Avenza Award, John C. Bartholomew Award, and the Ordnance Survey MasterMap Award (see separate entries). A silver medal and a trophy are awarded annually. Established in 1978.

6989 ■ Henry Johns Award

For recognition of the most outstanding article published in *The Cartographic Journal*. A monetary prize and certificate are awarded annually at the September symposium. Established in 1975. Formerly: Survey and General Instrument Company Award; (1996) Ryser SGI.

6990 ■ National Geographic Society New Mapmaker Award

To recognize people who have demonstrated outstanding achievement in Cartography for two years or more, including college students and new employees in commercial firms or government. The award includes a prize and certificate. The BCS will also pay for one year's membership. Established in 1993. Sponsored by National Geographic Society.

6991 ■ Ordnance Survey MasterMap Award

To encourage innovation and stimulating map products derived from, and composed mainly of, Ordnance Survey MasterMap data. A trophy and certificate are awarded annually.

6992 ■ Society Medal

To honor an individual who has made a distinguished contribution to cartography. Awarded biennially in even-numbered years. Established in 1984.

6993 ■ UKHO Junior Mapmaker Award

To encourage the creative representation, by children, of their environment in graphic form. Awarded in four categories: Atlas (7-9 years), Mercator (9-11 years), Ortelius (11-14 years), and Ptolemy (14-16 years). A certificate and monetary prize of £50 are awarded in each category biennially in even-numbered years. Established in 2008. Sponsored by the United Kingdom Hydrographic Office (UKHO).

6994 ■ British Cave Research Association
David Checkley, Chm.
The Old Methodist Chapel
Great Hucklow
Derbyshire
Buxton SK17 8RG, United Kingdom
Ph: 44 1298 873810
Ph: 44 161 4394387
Fax: 44 1298 873801
E-mail: bcra-enquiries@bcra.org.uk
URL: http://www.bcra.org.uk

6995 ■ Arthur Butcher Award

For contributions to cave surveying. A monetary prize of £100 is awarded annually. First awarded in 1988.

6996 ■ Cave Radio and Electronics Group Award

For achievements in the field of caving electronics. Awarded annually. Established in 2001.

6997 ■ Cave Science and Technology Research Initiative Awards CSTRI

For approved research in cave or karst related subjects. Approximately £5,000 in grants is awarded annually.

6998 ■ Alex Pitcher Award

To support young cavers going on their first expedition. One or two monetary prizes of £100 are awarded annually.

6999 ■ E.K. Tratman Award

For the best piece of caving literature. A monetary prize of £50 is awarded annually. First awarded in 1979.

7000 ■ British Christmas Tree Growers Association
13 Wolrige Rd.
Edinburgh EH16 6HX, United Kingdom
Ph: 44 131 6641100
Fax: 44 131 6642669
E-mail: rogermhay@btinternet.com
URL: http://www.christmastree.org.uk

7001 ■ Christmas Tree Competition

To recognize the best growers of Christmas trees and wreaths. Awards are presented in the following categories: container-grown tree, pine tree, spruce tree, fir tree, undecorated wreath, and decorated wreath. Held annually.

7002 ■ British Computer Society
David Clarke, Chief Exec.
North Star House
1st Fl., Block D
N Star Ave.
Swindon SN2 1FA, United Kingdom
Ph: 44 1793 417417
Ph: 44 1793 417424
Fax: 44 1793 417444
E-mail: bcshq@hq.bcs.org.uk
URL: http://www.bcs.org

7003 ■ APM Group IT Trainer of the Year

To recognize an individual for outstanding training for customers, businesses, and other IT professionals. Awarded annually. Sponsored by APM Group.

7004 ■ BT Flagship Award for Innovation

To recognize particularly innovative projects. Awarded annually. Sponsored by BT.

7005 ■ Business Analyst of Year

To recognize an individual for outstanding achievement in identifying system requirements and the demonstration of workable solutions that make a positive impact. Awarded annually as part of the UK IT Industry Awards program.

7006 ■ Business-to-Business Project Award

To recognize outstanding projects that improve business efficiency within and between businesses. Awarded annually. Sponsored by IBM.

7007 ■ Commercial Organisation of the Year

To recognize commercial companies for project development in information technology. Awarded annually.

7008 ■ Consumer Goods and Services Organisation of the Year

To recognize organizations like airlines and hotels for project development in information technology.

7009 ■ Entertainment and Media Project Award

To recognize outstanding projects dealing with media, music, and image applications. Projects can be for specialists or general users.

7010 ■ Financial Sector Organisation of the Year

To recognize a financial sector organization for outstanding project development in information technology. Awarded annually.

7011 ■ GCS Women in IT Award

To recognize organizations that can demonstrate

Awards are arranged in alphabetical order below their administering organizations

how they enhance opportunities for women in the field of information technology. Awarded annually. Sponsored by GCS.

7012 ■ Green Organisation of the Year
To recognize organizations that strive to help the environment. Awarded annually.

7013 ■ Intel IT Leader of the Year
To recognize an individual for covering the role of CIO or IT/IS Director. Awarded annually. Sponsored by Intel Corp.

7014 ■ IT Consultancy of the Year
To recognize consultancies in the technology and information management industry for project development in information technology. Awarded annually.

7015 ■ Lovelace Lecture and Medal
To recognize individuals for outstanding contributions in the advancement of information systems. Awarded annually. Established in 1998.

7016 ■ Mobile Technology Project Award
To recognize outstanding projects in mobile solutions, wireless technology, PDAs, and notebooks. Awarded annually. Supported by CMA.

7017 ■ Roger Needham Award and Lecture
To recognize distinguished research contributions in computer science by a UK-based researcher within 10 years of his or her PhD. A monetary prize £1,000 and an invitation to present a lecture are awarded annually.

7018 ■ Project Manager of the Year
To recognize an individual for outstanding management on a project or program. Awarded annually.

7019 ■ Public Sector Organisation of the Year
To recognize local governments, councils, and government departments for outstanding achievement in the field. Awarded annually.

7020 ■ Ricoh Information Security and Data Management Project Award
To recognize outstanding projects in data protection, disaster recovery, and data management. Awarded annually. Sponsored by Ricoh.

7021 ■ Service Manager of the Year
To recognize an individual for outstanding service and management in an outsourced or in-house delivery function. Awarded annually. Sponsored by itSMF.

7022 ■ SME Supplier Organisation of the Year
To recognize supplier of hardware and software for development in information technology. Open to small and medium-sized enterprises. Awarded annually.

7023 ■ Social Contribution Project Award
To recognize outstanding projects that benefit the general society and especially disadvantaged individuals. Awarded annually.

7024 ■ Systems Developer of the Year
To recognize an individual for outstanding efforts in business, functional, and technological development. Awarded annually.

7025 ■ Web-based Technology Project Award
To recognize outstanding projects in Web-based applications or services available to the public. Awarded annually.

7026 ■ Wilkes Award
To recognize the most outstanding paper in *The Computer Journal*. Authors under 30 years of age are eligible. A monetary prize of £500 and a medal are awarded annually.

7027 ■ Young IT Practitioner of the Year
To recognize a qualified specialist who shows outstanding potential. Individual must be 30 years or younger. Awarded annually as part of the UK IT Industry Awards program.

7028 ■ British Contact Lens Association
Vivien Freeman, Sec. Gen.
7/8 Market Pl.
London W1W 8AG, United Kingdom
Ph: 44 20 75806661
Fax: 44 20 75806669
E-mail: vfreeman@bcla.org.uk
URL: http://www.bcla.org.uk

7029 ■ Da Vinci Award
To honor a work or an idea from any member of the contact lens industry who is not an established contact lens researcher. A monetary prize of £1,000 is awarded annually.

7030 ■ Dallos Award
For a research project that is likely to further the scientific community's understanding of a topic related to contact lenses or the anterior eye. A grant of £5,000 is awarded annually.

7031 ■ British Council for Offices
Gerald Kaye, Pres.
78-79 Leadenhall St.
London EC3A 3DH, United Kingdom
Ph: 44 20 72830125
Fax: 44 20 76261553
E-mail: mail@bco.org.uk
URL: http://www.bco.org.uk

7032 ■ BCO Awards
To recognize top quality design and functionality in office space. Categories include corporate workplace, commercial workplace, fit-out of workplace, refurbished/recycled workplace, project up to 2,000 square meters, and innovation. Buildings are submitted by region: Scotland; the north of England, North Wales, and Northern Ireland; the Midlands and East Anglia; London and the South East; and the South West of England and South Wales. Awarded annually. Established in 1992.

7033 ■ British Culinary Federation
Jayne Mottram, Admin.
PO Box 10532
Alcester B50 4ZY, United Kingdom
Ph: 44 1789 491218
E-mail: secretary@britishculinaryfederation.co.uk
URL: http://www.britishculinaryfederation.co.uk

7034 ■ Salon Culinaire International de Londres
To recognize outstanding culinary ability of chefs in the United Kingdom and around the world. More than 80 competition classes are held. Gold awards, silver awards, bronze awards, and certificates of merit are presented in each class. Held annually. Formerly: Hotelympia Competition.

7035 ■ Student Challenge Cook and Serve Competition
To recognize the best teams of culinary students. Contestants must be full-time students at any college or university. Each team, consisting of two chefs and one waiter, must prepare, cook, and serve a meal in 90 minutes using a pre-defined set of ingredients. The Team of the Year receives £500 in catering equipment. Held annually.

7036 ■ Young Chef of the Year Award
To recognize the best young chef. Contestants are required to create a three-course meal within two hours. The winner receives the David Bache Trophy, monetary prize of £300, and trip to Luxembourg. Awarded annually. Established in 1997.

7037 ■ British Dam Society
Mr. Martin Airey, Chm.
1 Great George St.

Westminster
London SW1P 3AA, United Kingdom
Ph: 44 20 76652234
Fax: 44 20 77991325
E-mail: bds@ice.org.uk
URL: http://www.britishdams.org

7038 ■ BDS Prize
For papers on research, design, construction, or supervision of dams. Candidates should be under the age of 35 years. A monetary prize of £300 is awarded. Established in 1984.

7039 ■ British Deaf Association
Mr. Terry Riley, Chm.
18 Leather Ln., 3rd Fl.
Holborn
London EC1N 7SU, United Kingdom
Ph: 44 207 4050090
E-mail: bda@bda.org.uk
URL: http://bda.org.uk

7040 ■ Medal of Honour
For recognition of services to the British deaf community. Individuals who are British or foreign, deaf or hearing, members or nonmembers may be nominated. A medal is awarded at the Congress or occasionally at a conference. Established in 1959.

7041 ■ British Design and Art Direction
9 Graphite Sq.
Vauxhall Walk
London SE11 5EE, United Kingdom
Ph: 44 20 78401111
Fax: 44 20 78400840
E-mail: contact@dandad.org
URL: http://www.dandad.org

7042 ■ Design and Art Direction Awards
Recognizes creative excellence in the categories of Broadcast, Print and Editorial, Digital and Wireless, 3D Design, Direct, Branding, Integrated, and Ambient. Awarded annually.

7043 ■ British Ecological Society
Dr. Hazel J. Norman, Exec. Dir.
12 Roger St.
London WC1N 2JU, United Kingdom
Ph: 44 207 6852500
Fax: 44 207 6852501
E-mail: info@britishecologicalsociety.org
URL: http://www.britishecologicalsociety.org

7044 ■ Best Poster Prizes
To recognize the best poster by a research student at the Symposium and Annual General Meeting. Any full-time post-graduate student is eligible to enter as is anyone whose research training was completed within the past six months. Awarded annually.

7045 ■ Ecological Engagement Award
To recognize an exceptional contribution to facilitating the use and understanding of ecology. A certificate and monetary prize of £1,000 are awarded annually.

7046 ■ Founders' Prize
To recognize an outstanding ecologist, in his or her early career, who is making a significant contribution toward the science of ecology. Candidates are typically younger than 40 years of age. The award is normally biennial, in tandem with the President's Medal. A monetary prize of £500 and a certificate are awarded. The recipient will be invited to give a forty-minute paper at the BES Winter Meeting. Established in 1997.

7047 ■ Anne Keymer Prize
To recognize the best oral presentation by a postgraduate student at the Annual Meetings. Those eligible to enter must present a paper at the BES Annual Meeting and should normally be a current graduate student, or one who has recently graduated and is presenting work that

Awards are arranged in alphabetical order below their administering organizations

was completed when they were still a student. An honorarium of £250 is presented to the winner, with two runners-up each receiving £100. Awarded annually. Named in the memory of Anne Keymer, one of the first winners of the previously-unnamed prize in 1981.

7048 ■ Marsh Award for Ecology
To recognize outstanding achievements and contributions to the science of ecology. Open to distinguished ecologists from around the world. An honorarium of £1,000 and a certificate are awarded annually.

7049 ■ President's Medal
To recognize individuals in mid-career for exceptional achievement in ecology. Awarded biennially when merited. Established in 1987.

7050 ■ Small Ecological Project Grants
To promote all aspects of ecological research and ecological survey. A maximum grant of £2,500 is awarded twice per year.

7051 ■ British Fashion Council
Somerset House, South Wing
Strand
London WC2R 1LA, United Kingdom
Ph: 44 20 7759 1999
E-mail: info@britishfashioncouncil.com
URL: http://www.britishfashioncouncil.com

7052 ■ British Fashion Awards
To celebrate the contributions of British designers, creatives, and models to the international fashion scene. Presented in the following categories: Accessory Design, Menswear Design, Models, and Designer Brand. In addition, the following awards are presented: Outstanding Achievement in Fashion Design, Designer of the Year, Isabella Blow Award for Fashion Creator, Swarovski Emerging Talent Award for Accessories, Swarovski Emerging Talent Award for Ready to Wear, Outstanding Contribution to British Fashion, and the London 25 Award. Held annually. Established in 1989.

7053 ■ British Fertility Society
Mr. Peter Brinsden, Pres.
22 Apex Ct.
Bradley Stoke
Bristol BS32 4JT, United Kingdom
Ph: 44 1454 642217
Fax: 44 1454 642222
E-mail: bfs@bioscientifica.com
URL: http://www.fertility.org.uk

7054 ■ H.S. Jacobs President's Lecture
To honor an individual who has made an outstanding contribution to the field of reproductive medicine and command an international reputation. The recipient delivers a lecture at the Annual BFS meeting. A medal is awarded annually.

7055 ■ Patrick Steptoe Memorial Lecture
To honor an individual who has made an outstanding contribution to the field of reproductive medicine and command an international reputation. The recipient delivers a lecture at the Annual BFS meeting. A medal is awarded annually. Sponsored by Organon Laboratories.

7056 ■ British Film Institute
Greg Dyke, Chm.
21 Stephen St.
London W1T 1LN, United Kingdom
Ph: 44 20 72551444
E-mail: greg.dyke@bfi.org.uk
URL: http://www.bfi.org.uk

7057 ■ British Film Institute Fellowships
To provide recognition for outstanding contribution to film or television culture in the United Kingdom. Established in 1983.

7058 ■ Sutherland Trophy
Awarded to the most original and imaginative film screened at the BFI London Film Festival. Awarded annually. First presented in 1958 on behalf of the BFI by the Duke of Sutherland.

7059 ■ British Florist Association
PO Box 674
Wigan
Lancashire WN1 9LL, United Kingdom
Ph: 44 844 800 7299
E-mail: info@britishfloristassociation.org
URL: http://www.britishfloristassociation.org

7060 ■ FleurEx - Chrysal Competition
To recognize the talented floral designers in the United Kingdom. Monetary prizes are presented to first, second, and third place winners. Held at FleurEx, an annual trade show for professional florists. Sponsored by Chrysal International.

7061 ■ FleurEx - Smithers-Oasis Competition
To recognize the talented floral designers in the United Kingdom. The Smithers-Oasis Trophy is presented to the first place winner. Held at FleurEx, an annual trade show for professional florists. Sponsored by Smithers-Oasis U.K. Ltd.

7062 ■ FleurEx - Student Competition
To recognize a high standard of design and technical skill in student floral designers in the United Kingdom. Competitors must have less than three years of experience. The Sylvia Bird Cup and monetary prize of £50 is presented to the first place winner. Held at FleurEx, an annual trade show for professional florists.

7063 ■ Florist of the Year Competition
To recognize the most talented floral designer in the United Kingdom. Candidates must be aged 25 years or older. The winner represents Great Britain in the Europa Cup, the most coveted floristry competition in Europe, which is held every four years. Held annually.

7064 ■ Honorary Membership
To honor members for extensive contributions to the floristry industry in the United Kingdom. Awarded as merited at the sole discretion of the Association president.

7065 ■ British Geotechnical Association
Ms. Shelagh Fleming, Admin.
1 Great George St.
London SW1P 3AA, United Kingdom
Ph: 44 20 76652316
Fax: 44 20 77991325
E-mail: bga@britishgeotech.org.uk
URL: http://www.britishgeotech.org.uk

7066 ■ Cooling Prize
To honor the best presentation on a geotechnical topic. A glass decanter is awarded annually. Established in 1971.

7067 ■ Rankine Lecture
To honor an individual for outstanding contributions to geotechnics. An invitation to present a lecture is awarded annually, in even-numbered years to a U.K. recipient and in odd-numbered years to a scientist from outside the United Kingdom. Established in 1961 in honor of W.J.M. Rankine, one of the first engineers in the United Kingdom to make a significant contribution to soil mechanics.

7068 ■ British Grassland Society
Mr. John Downes, Pres.
Unit 32 C
StoneLeigh Deer Park
Stareton
Warwickshire
Kenilworth CV8 2LY, United Kingdom
Ph: 44 2476 696600
E-mail: office@britishgrassland.com

URL: http://www.britishgrassland.com

7069 ■ British Grassland Society Award
To acknowledge those who have made an outstanding contribution to the understanding or application of grassland and forage crop husbandry and technology. A member of the Society may be nominated by any one member supported by two others. A trophy is awarded annually at the Winter Meeting in December. Established in 1979.

7070 ■ British Guild of Travel Writers
Robert Ellison, Sec.
335 Lordship Rd.
London N4 2TN, United Kingdom
Ph: 44 20 81448713
E-mail: secretariat@bgtw.org
URL: http://www.bgtw.org

7071 ■ Best Overseas Tourism Project Award
To recognize the best new overseas tourism project, which not only has a tourist potential but is of benefit to the local community and environment. Qualifying projects must be younger than two years old. Awarded annually.

7072 ■ Best U.K. Tourism Project Award
To recognize the best new tourism project in the United Kingdom, which not only has a tourist potential but is of benefit to the local community and environment. Qualifying projects must be younger than two years old. Awarded annually.

7073 ■ Globe Award
To recognize the best major, new tourism project worldwide, which combines responsible tourism development with local economic, environmental, and community benefits. Qualifying projects must be younger than two years old and must have projected visitor number of more than 250,000 per year. Awarded annually. Established in 2001.

7074 ■ Anne Gregg/Ed Lacy Memorial Award for Travel Broadcasting
To recognize outstanding travel broadcasting by members of the Guild. Awarded annually.

7075 ■ Lifetime Achievement Award
To honor an individual for long-term contributions to the travel industry. Awarded annually.

7076 ■ Members' Writing Awards
To recognize outstanding writing by members of the Guild. Awards are presented in a variety of categories, including Best Short Destination Feature, Best Trade/Business Feature, Best Online Travel Writer, and Best Travel Book. In addition, the Travel Writer of the Year Award, sponsored by Saga Holidays, may be presented. Awarded annually.

7077 ■ Photographer of the Year Award
To recognize outstanding photography by members of the Guild. Awarded annually.

7078 ■ Silver Otter Award
For tourism projects abroad which benefit the local community and environment. A trophy is awarded annually.

7079 ■ British Health Care Association
Rosa Mcalindon, Contact
PO Box 6752
Elgin IV30 9BN, United Kingdom
Ph: 44 1343 544841
E-mail: info@bhca.org.uk
URL: http://www.bhca.org.uk

7080 ■ BHCA Awards
For caring individuals who work in or alongside the National Health Service.

7081 ■ British HIV Association
Dr. Ian G. Williams, Chm.
1 Mountview Ct.
310 Friern Barnet Ln.

Awards are arranged in alphabetical order below their administering organizations

London N20 0LD, United Kingdom
Ph: 44 20 83695380
Fax: 44 20 84469194
URL: http://www.bhiva.org

7082 ■ Research Award

To recognize research projects that help improve the clinical care and management of individuals in the UK who are living with HIV. A monetary award of up to £30,000 is available to be distributed among successful applicants, with a maximum award of £10,000 per application. Awarded annually. Established in 2006.

7083 ■ British Infection Society

Dr. Jane Stockley, Pres.
Hartley Taylor Ltd.
Henderson House
New Rd.
Bucks
Princes Risborough HP27 0JN, United Kingdom
Ph: 44 1844 275650
Ph: 44 7578 599902
Fax: 44 1494 274407
E-mail: secretariat@britishinfection.org
URL: http://www.britishinfection.org/drupal

7084 ■ Barnett Christie Lectureship

To recognize an individual for excellence in original research. Candidates must be: based in Ireland or the United Kingdom; be clinically-qualified trainees in infection or infection-related specialties; be post-doctoral scientists within four years of a PhD; and not in a tenured academic or top grade scientist position. The recipient is invited to give a lecture at the annual meeting of the Federation of Infection Societies, Edinburgh. Awarded annually. Established in 1991.

7085 ■ *Journal of Infection* Young Investigator's Prize

To recognize outstanding articles published in the *Journal of Infection*. Open to all trainees in infection or infection-related disciplines who are the first authors on an accepted paper. A journal subscription and monetary prize of £3,000 are awarded annually.

7086 ■ British Institute Interior Design

Katherine Elworthy, Exec. Mgr.
Units 109-111 The Chambers
Chelsea Harbour
London SW10 0XF, United Kingdom
Ph: 44 20 73490800
Fax: 44 20 73490500
E-mail: info@biid.org.uk
URL: http://www.biid.org.uk
Formerly: (2009) British Interior Design Association.

7087 ■ BIDA Charitable Trust Bursary Award

For those intending to advance knowledge and skills upon which interior designers and decorators depend.

7088 ■ BIDA Foundation BA Award

For 3-year BA interior design honor student.

7089 ■ Emergent Designer Award

To showcase the creativity, resourcefulness, and practical skills of emerging interior design practitioners. Open to recently qualified and practicing interior designers with no more than four years of working experience. Awarded annually.

7090 ■ Graduate Product Award

To support emerging talent in contemporary furniture design and to celebrate excellence in product design. Candidates must be students in their final year of study or must have graduated

in the last 12 months. A monetary prize of £2,500 is awarded annually. In addition, Muralto ZA, the award's sponsor, will produce the winning design.

7091 ■ British Institute of Non-Destructive Testing

Matt Gallagher, Chief Exec.
Newton Bldg.
St. George's Ave.
Northampton NN2 6JB, United Kingdom
Ph: 44 1604 893811
Fax: 44 1604 893861
E-mail: info@bindt.org
URL: http://www.bindt.org

7092 ■ John Grimwade Medal

To recognize the best paper written in *Insight, the Journal of the British Institute of Non-Destructive Testing*. Works by any member of the Institute are automatically eligible for consideration. A medal is presented at the Annual British Conference on NDT. Established in 1981 in memory of John G. Grimwade, an Honorary Fellow of the Institute.

7093 ■ Ron Halmshaw Award

In recognition of the best paper published in *Insight* on any aspect of industrial radiography or radiology, contributed by a member of the Institute of any grade in the preceding year. A certificate and monetary prize of £300 are awarded annually at the Institute's Conference. Established in 1994 by Dr. Ron Halmshaw, MBE.

7094 ■ Hugh MacColl Award

For recognition of practical innovation in non-destructive testing condition monitoring. A certificate is awarded and £300 is held in credit for the recipient to spend in improving his technical education. Awarded annually at the Institute's Conference. Established in 1988 in memory of Hugh MacColl, a founder member of the NDT Society of Great Britain and a pioneer of NDT education.

7095 ■ Nemet Award

To recognize examples of effective use of NDT, especially those that might encourage small firms to apply NDT methods for the first time. A certificate is awarded to the company operating the successful scheme, and a monetary prize of £500 to the person or persons nominated by the company as responsible for the innovation. Awarded annually at the Institute's Conference. Established in 1989 by Dr. A. Nemet.

7096 ■ Roy Sharpe Prize

To recognize a significant contribution through research and development in any branch of NDT to the benefit of industry or society. A certificate plus a monetary prize of £300 are presented annually at the Institute's Conference. Established in 1989 in honor of Roy Sharpe.

7097 ■ British Insurance Law Association

Mr. Stephen Lewis, Chm.
47 Bury St.
Suffolk
Stowmarket IP14 1HD, United Kingdom
Ph: 44 7776 115795
Fax: 44 1449 770941
E-mail: secretariat@bila.org.uk
URL: http://www.bila.org.uk

7098 ■ Book Prize

To recognize the author of a published work with the most notable contribution to literature in the field of law as it affects the insurance industry. A monetary prize of £1,000 is awarded annually.

7099 ■ British Interactive Media Association

Justin Cooke, CEO
The Lightwell
12-16 Laystall St.
London EC1R 4PF, United Kingdom

Ph: 44 20 78436797
E-mail: info@bima.co.uk
URL: http://www.bima.co.uk

7100 ■ BIMA Awards

To honor an individual who has showed creative excellence in interactive design. Awards are presented in nine categories: business-to-business; business-to-consumer; Web sites; games; integrated campaigns; social media; film and animation; students; and talent. Awarded annually. Established in 1984.

7101 ■ British Interior Textiles Association

5 Portland Pl.
London W1B 1PW, United Kingdom
Ph: 44 20 76367788
Ph: 44 20 78439460
Fax: 44 20 76367515
E-mail: enquiries@interiortextiles.com
URL: http://www.interiortextiles.co.uk

7102 ■ Emerging Talent Award

To promote the new talent of graduates from colleges and universities in the United Kingdom. Open to any final year undergraduate and those who have graduated in the recent past. A monetary prize of £1,000 is awarded annually.

7103 ■ British Lichen Society

Dr. Stephen Ward, Pres.
Natural History Museum
Department of Botany
Cromwell Rd.
London SW7 5BD, United Kingdom
E-mail: c.ellis@rbge.org.uk
URL: http://www.thebls.org.uk

7104 ■ British Lichen Society Awards

To recognize professional, academic, and amateur lichenologists involved in research. Awards are bestowed annually at the convention in January.

7105 ■ British Long Distance Swimming Association

Mrs. Beverly Thomas, Pres.
1 Cairns Rd.
Murton Seaham
Durham SR7 9TD, United Kingdom
Ph: 44 1915 264215
Ph: 44 1925 730652
E-mail: membership_bldsa@yahoo.co.uk
URL: http://www.bldsa.org.uk

7106 ■ Hans Belay Trophy

To recognize the swim of the year. Awarded annually.

7107 ■ Breaststroke Trophy

To recognize a breaststroke endurance swim. Awarded annually.

7108 ■ James Brennan Memorial Trophy

For outstanding service rendered to the Association. Awarded annually.

7109 ■ Elise Brook Trophy

To recognize a junior swimmer during his or her last year as a junior. Awarded annually.

7110 ■ Tom Butcher Trophy

To recognize a junior swimmer of the year. Awarded annually.

7111 ■ Avril and Allan Mitchell Trophy

To recognize a veteran swimmer of the year. Awarded annually.

7112 ■ Harry Moffat Memorial Trophy

To recognize services to the Pilot Lifesaver scheme. Awarded annually.

7113 ■ Fred Slater Trophy

To recognize the most outstanding swimmer of the year. Awarded annually.

7114 ■ British Machine Vision Association and Society for Pattern Recognition

Dr. Andrew Fitzgibbon, Chm.
95 Queen St.
Sheffield S1 1WG, United Kingdom

Awards are arranged in alphabetical order below their administering organizations

Ph: 44 114 2720306
Fax: 44 114 2726158
E-mail: chair@bmva.org
URL: http://www.iapr.org

7115 ■ Distinguished Fellow Award
To honor a researcher who has contributed significantly to the field of research and the reputation of the British machine vision community. Awarded annually. Established in 2000.

7116 ■ Sullivan Thesis Prize
To recognize the best doctoral thesis submitted to a U.K. university in the field of computer or natural vision. A monetary prize of £300 is awarded annually. Established in 1998 in honor of Professor Geoff Sullivan.

7117 ■ British Medical Association
Dr. Hamish Meldrum, Chm.
Tavistock Sq.
London WC1H 9JP, United Kingdom
Ph: 44 20 73874499
Ph: 44 20 73836254
E-mail: bmanews@bma.org.uk
URL: http://www.bma.org.uk

7118 ■ Vera Down Grant
To assist research into neurological disorders. Candidates must be registered medical practitioners. A grant of £55,000 is awarded annually.

7119 ■ Gold Medal for Distinguished Merit
To recognize individuals who have conspicuously raised the character of the medical profession by scientific work, by extra-ordinary professional services, or by special services rendered to the British Medical Association. A gold medal is awarded when merited. Established in 1877.

7120 ■ T. P. Gunton Grant
To assist research into public health education with special regard to the early diagnosis and treatment of cancer. Both medical and non-medical researchers are eligible. A grant of £35,000 is awarded annually.

7121 ■ Nathaniel Bishop Harman Award
For recognition of research in regard to the outcome of treatment in hospital practice. Candidates must be registered medical practitioners on the staff of a hospital in Great Britain or Northern Ireland and not members of the staff of a recognized undergraduate or post-graduate medical school. A monetary prize of £2,125 is awarded biennially in even-numbered years.

7122 ■ Charles Oliver Hawthorne Award
For recognition of observation, research and record keeping in general practice. Candidates must be members of the Association and engaged in general practice. A monetary prize of £2,350 is awarded biennially.

7123 ■ Doris Hillier Grant
To assist research into rheumatism and arthritis. Candidates must be registered medical practitioners. A grant of £50,000 is awarded annually.

7124 ■ Insole and Clegg Grant
To assist research into the mental health of adults or children in difficult economic environments. Candidates must be registered medical practitioners in the United Kingdom. A grant of £35,000 is awarded annually.

7125 ■ T. V. James Fellowship
For recognition of and to assist research into the nature, causation, prevention or treatment of bronchial asthma. Members of the Association are eligible. A monetary prize of £15,600 is awarded annually.

7126 ■ H. C. Roscoe Research Grant
To promote research into the elimination of the common cold and/or diseases of the human respiratory system. Candidates must be members of the Association or non-medical scientists working in association with a member. A monetary prize of £50,000 is awarded annually.

7127 ■ Helen Tomkinson Award
For recognition of cancer research. Candidates must be members of the Association. A monetary prize of £11,250 is awarded annually.

7128 ■ Edith Walsh Grant
To provide financial assistance to support research into cardiovascular disease. Candidates must be members of the Association. A grant of £44,000 is awarded annually.

7129 ■ Elizabeth Wherry Award
For recognition of research into kidney disease. Candidates must be registered medical practitioners. A monetary prize of £7,250 is awarded annually.

7130 ■ British Mexican Society
Richard Maudslay, Chm.
PO Box 251
Morpeth NE61 9DH, United Kingdom
Ph: 44 870 9220679
E-mail: enquiries@britishmexicansociety.org.uk
URL: http://www.britishmexicansociety.org.uk

7131 ■ Postgraduate Prize
For recognition of the best PhD thesis on a topic relating to Mexico. The prize is open to students of any nationality and in any academic discipline. The thesis must be produced at a British university (or other institute of higher education). A monetary prize of £500 is awarded annually. Established in 1984.

7132 ■ British Microcirculation Society
Dr. Lopa Leach, Hon. Sec.
University of Bristol
Faculty of Medicine and Oral and Dental Science
Lower Maudlin St.
Bristol BS1 2LY, United Kingdom
Ph: 44 115 8230175
E-mail: lopa.leach@nottingham.ac.uk
URL: http://www.microcirculation.org.uk

7133 ■ Laboratory Visit Grant
To provide financial assistance to an eligible student or junior postdoctoral worker to visit a laboratory for the purpose of learning new techniques or other worthwhile scientific purposes related to microvascular research. A maximum of £600 per year is awarded.

7134 ■ Microcirculation Conference Grant
To provide financial assistance to two eligible student members to attend the European Society for Microcirculation Conferences or the International Microcirculation Conferences. A maximum of £500 per year is awarded per student.

7135 ■ Student Assistance Scheme
To promote student interest in and attendance at Society meetings by providing financial assistance. A maximum of £250 per year is awarded annually.

7136 ■ British Music Society
John McCabe, Pres.
7 Tudor Gardens
Upminster RM14 3DE, United Kingdom
Ph: 44 1708 224795
E-mail: sct.bms1943@amserve.com
URL: http://www.britishmusicsociety.com

7137 ■ British Music Society Awards
To encourage the performance of neglected British music (especially by dead composers 1850-1950) through a contest for young performers. Students of a British music college may be nominated by the college. A certificate and recital are awarded biennially at the Society's annual general meeting. Established in 1988.

7138 ■ British Mycological Society
Dr. Lynne Boddy, Pres.
City View House
5 Union St.
Manchester M12 4JD, United Kingdom
Ph: 44 161 2777638
Ph: 44 161 2777639
Fax: 44 161 2777634
E-mail: admin@britmycolsoc.info
URL: http://www.britmycolsoc.org.uk

7139 ■ Berkeley Award
For outstanding original scientific contribution to mycology. Candidates must be 35 years of age or younger. Awarded annually. Established in memory of Rev. M.J. Berkeley (1803-1889).

7140 ■ Howard Eggins Award
To a young scientist who presents the most outstanding paper in the annual meeting. Awarded annually.

7141 ■ Microscopy Award
For the best paper presented by a postgraduate student on an aspect of mycology at a meeting of the society. Awarded annually.

7142 ■ Undergraduate Student Bursaries
For research in any branch of mycology. Stipends in the amount of £150 per week are awarded annually.

7143 ■ British Numismatic Society
Dr. Robin J. Eaglen, Pres.
Woburn Sq.
London WC1H 0AB, United Kingdom
E-mail: secretary@britnumsoc.org
URL: http://www.fitzmuseum.cam.ac.uk/dept/coins/britnumsoc

7144 ■ Blunt Prize
To recognize an individual for a significant recent contribution to the study of numismatics. Preferable candidates are under 35 years of age, and need not be members of the Society. Awarded triennially. Established in 1986. Named in honor of the contributions made by Christopher Evelyn Blunt.

7145 ■ North Book Prize
To recognize the best book on British numismatics. A monetary prize of £500 is awarded biennially in even-numbered years. Established in 2006 with a donation by Jeffrey North.

7146 ■ Jeffrey North Medal for Service
To recognize members of the Society for exceptional service to the Society or to British numismatics. Inscribed medals are awarded when merited. Established in 2008.

7147 ■ John Sanford Saltus Gold Medal
To recognize individuals for scholarly contributions to British numismatics. Members and non-members are eligible. A gold medal is awarded triennially. Established in 1910 by John Sanford Saltus.

7148 ■ British Occupational Hygiene Society
Alex Bianchi, Pres.
5/6 Melbourne Business Ct.
Millennium Way
Pride Park
Derby DE24 8LZ, United Kingdom
Ph: 44 1332 298101
Ph: 44 1332 250701
Fax: 44 1332 298099
E-mail: admin@bohs.org
URL: http://www.bohs.org/standardTemplate.aspx

7149 ■ Bedford Award
To individuals for outstanding contributions to

Awards are arranged in alphabetical order below their administering organizations

the discipline of occupational hygiene, either in the general field or in work for the society. A medal is awarded annually. Established in 1978.

7150 ■ Thomas Bedford Memorial Prize
To the author or authors of the most outstanding paper published in the annals of occupational hygiene during the relevant period. A monetary prize of £500 is awarded to one or more recipients every two years.

7151 ■ David Hickish Award
For candidates who have achieved the diploma of professional competence in occupational hygiene. A monetary prize of £250 is awarded annually.

7152 ■ Working for a Healthier Workplace - The Peter Isaac Award
For individual members, or any other POOSH Professional Organizations in Occupational Safety and Health. A trophy, certificate, and monetary prize of £1,000 are awarded annually.

7153 ■ Ted King Award
For candidates who have achieved the certificate of operational competence in occupational hygiene. A monetary prize of £250 is awarded annually.

7154 ■ British Origami Society
Mick Guy, Chm.
2A The Chestnuts
Countesthorpe
Leicester LE8 5TL, United Kingdom
URL: http://www.britishorigami.info

7155 ■ Sidney French Medal
Recognizes outstanding contribution to origami and the society. Awarded annually to one or more recipients.

7156 ■ British Ornithologists' Union
Dr. Alistair Dawson, Pres.
PO Box 417
Peterborough PE7 3FX, United Kingdom
Ph: 44 733 844820
Fax: 44 733 844820
E-mail: bou@bou.org.uk
URL: http://bou-online.blogspot.com

7157 ■ Godman-Salvin Medal
To any person as an honor for excellent ornithological work. Awarded periodically when merited. Established in 1922.

7158 ■ Ibis Award
To recognize the outstanding achievement of younger ornithologists. Awarded annually if merited. Established in 2003.

7159 ■ Alfred Newton Lecture
To honor an internationally renowned figure in ornithology. An invitation to lecture is awarded when merited. Established in 1994.

7160 ■ Union Medal
To recognize any member in recognition of outstanding services to ornithology and to the organization. Awarded periodically when merited. Established in 1912.

7161 ■ British Orthodontic Society
Nigel Harradine, Chm.
12 Bridewell Pl.
London EC4V 6AP, United Kingdom
Ph: 44 20 73538680
Fax: 44 20 73538682
E-mail: ann.wright@bos.org.uk
URL: http://www.bos.org.uk

7162 ■ Maurice Berman Prize
To recognize outstanding achievement in clinical presentation of a treated case. A monetary prize of £800 is awarded annually.

7163 ■ Chapman Prize Essay
To encourage professional development in the field of orthodontics. Any member or international member of the society is eligible. An article which must contain original material on an orthodontic or allied subject, not more than 8000 words must be submitted. A monetary prize of £1,200 is awarded annually.

7164 ■ Houston Research Scholarship
Allows research scholars to pursue an academic or clinically based research project which promotes the specialty of orthodontics. This should not be part of an Msc project undertaken during the 3 year orthodontic specialty training program. Any member of the British Orthodontic Society is eligible. Sponsored by British Orthodontic Society.

7165 ■ Journal of Orthodontics Scientific Paper of the Year
To recognize the best article published in the Journal of Orthodontics during the year. A monetary prize of £750 is awarded annually.

7166 ■ Northcroft Lectureship
Application is by invitation only. For recognition of a contribution to orthodontics on an international basis. International reputation and original work are considered. A certificate is awarded annually when merited. Established in 1947 in honor of George Northcroft.

7167 ■ Research and Audit Poster Prizes
Encourages research or audit in a clinically related project of value to the orthodontic specialty. This should into be part of an MSC project undertaken in the three year training program. The orthodontist named in the application should be a Society member, but coauthors could be scientists or clinicians who are not members of the Society. Various grants are awarded annually.

7168 ■ Gunter Russell Prize
Recognizes the best poster demonstrations at the British Orthodontic Conference. Any member of the Society is eligible. A medal and monetary prize of £800 is awarded for first place; second and third place recipients are awarded £400 and £300, respectively. Awarded annually.

7169 ■ Laurence Usiskin Student Elective Prize
To recognize the best protocol for an elective study. A monetary prize of £1,000 is awarded annually.

7170 ■ British Phonographic Industry
Tony Wadsworth, Chm.
Riverside Bldg., County Hall
Westminster Bridge Rd.
London SE1 7JA, United Kingdom
Ph: 44 20 78031300
Ph: 44 20 78031326
Fax: 44 20 78031310
E-mail: general@bpi.co.uk
URL: http://www.bpi.co.uk

7171 ■ BRIT Awards
To honor the best of British and international music talent. Twelve categories of awards are voted for by an Academy of approximately 1,000 people. Seven categories are open to British nominees (Male artist, Female artist, Breakthrough Act, Single, Group, Critics' Choice, and the MasterCard British Album of the Year) and five are open to international nominees (Male artist, Female artist, The categories are as follows: Best British Single, Best British Group, Best British Female Solo Artist, Best British Male Solo Artist, Best British Breakthrough Act, Breakthrough Act, Album, and Group). Awarded annually. Established in 1977.

7172 ■ Certified Awards
To measure the performance of music singles, records, and CDs based on sales to the trade each week. Certification levels for Singles are: Silver - 200,000 units; Gold - 400,000 units; and Platinum - 600,000 units. Certification levels for Albums are: Silver - 60,000 units; Gold - 100,000 units; and Platinum - 300,000 units. Certification for music CDs are: Gold - 25,000 units; and Platinum - 50,000 units. Established in 1973.

7173 ■ British Printing Industries Federation
Kathy Woodward, Chief Exec.
Farringdon Point
29-35 Farringdon Rd.
London EC1M 3JF, United Kingdom
Ph: 44 20 79158300
Ph: 44 20 79158309
Fax: 44 20 74057784
E-mail: info@britishprint.com
URL: http://www.britishprint.com

7174 ■ British Book Design and Production Awards
To promote and acknowledge the excellence of the British book design and production industry. Awards are presented in the following categories: Limited edition and fine binding; Digitally printed books; Exhibition catalogs; Photographic books and art/architecture monographs; Trade illustrated; Literature; Primary education; Secondary education; Tertiary education; Scholarly and reference; Children's trade; and Brand or series identity. In addition, the following awards are presented: Book of the Year, Environmental Award, Best Jacket/Cover Design, Best Student Book of the Year, and Best British Book. Awarded annually.

7175 ■ Excellence Awards
To recognize U.K.-based firms and their employees for achievement in the printing industry. Awarded in various categories each year.

7176 ■ National Calendar Awards
To recognize outstanding printed calendars, to extend the use of printed business calendars, and to encourage high standards in their design and production. Awards are given in the following categories: Business, Retail, Student, Cause-Related, and Blank. Additionally, Special Awards and Awards of Excellence are awarded. A trophy is awarded to the publisher of the winning entry in each of the categories. Awarded annually in January. Established in 1968 by the London College of Printing, BPIF, and the British Advertising Calendar Association. Formerly: (2009) National Business Calendar Awards.

7177 ■ National Training Awards
To encourage, recognize and promote excellence in training and development throughout the printing, packaging, and graphic communications industry in the UK. Four monetary awards are presented annually: Employer's Award, Individual Award, Apprentice of the Year, and Digital Apprentice of the Year.

7178 ■ UK Company of the Year
To recognize all round business excellence in the printing, packaging, and graphic communications industry. A trophy is presented annually.

7179 ■ British Psychological Society
Sue Gardner, Pres.
St. Andrews House
48 Princess Rd. E
Leicester LE1 7DR, United Kingdom
Ph: 44 116 2549568
Fax: 44 116 2771314
E-mail: enquiries@bps.org.uk
URL: http://www.bps.org.uk

7180 ■ Award for Distinguished Contributions to Professional Psychology
To recognize a psychologist who has made an outstanding contribution to professional practice. Open to any current practitioner of psychology in any area of professional applied psychology, and not restricted to members of the Society. A

Awards are arranged in alphabetical order below their administering organizations

certificate and life membership are awarded annually. Administered by the Professional Practice Board of the Society.

7181 ■ Book Award
To recognize the authors of recently published books that have made significant contributions to the advancement of psychology in one or more ways and are likely to achieve a noteworthy place in the literature of psychology. Candidates must be residents of the United Kingdom and must not have published their book prior to three years before the date of the award. A monetary award of £500 and a certificate are presented at the annual conference each year. Administered by the Society's Research Board.

7182 ■ May Davidson Award
To honor a clinical psychologist for an outstanding contribution to the development of clinical psychology within the first 10 years of work. An invitation to present a lecture is awarded annually. Established in 1985. Administered by the Society's Division of Clinical Psychology.

7183 ■ Distinguished Contribution to the Field of Sport and Exercise Psychology Award
To honor a member of the Division of Sport and Exercise Psychology for a significant contribution to the field of sport and exercise psychology in any relevant area. Awarded biennially in even-numbered years. Established in 2008. Administered by the Society's Division of Sport and Exercise Psychology.

7184 ■ Margaret Donaldson Early Career Prize
To honor an individual for an outstanding contribution within the field of developmental psychology. Candidates are eligible within 10 years of their PhD. A monetary prize of £300 plus up to £200 in travel expenses are awarded annually. Administered by the Society's Developmental Psychology Section.

7185 ■ Excellence in Psychology Education Award
To recognize inspiring and dedicated teachers of psychology. Covers teachers from all areas of training and education, including pre-degree teaching, teaching at first and higher degree levels, training of professional applied psychologists, the teaching of psychology to other professions, and adult and continuing education. A certificate and life membership are awarded annually. Administered by the Psychology Education Board of the Society.

7186 ■ Honorary Fellow
To recognize an individual for an entire career in the field of psychology.

7187 ■ Honorary Life Member
To recognize the major contribution individuals make to the development of the Society. The award consists of a commemorative certificate, free life membership of the Society, and free registration at a Society Conference each year. On occasions the award may be made to non-psychologists who have similarly made outstanding services to psychology through their involvement with the activities of the Society.

7188 ■ William Inman Prize
To recognize the author of an outstanding published article on the effects of psychological factors upon physical conditions. Preference is given to psychodynamic or psychotherapeutics factors and to conditions of the eye. Papers must have been published within the past five years. A monetary prize of £2,000 is awarded annually. Administered by the Research Board of the Society.

7189 ■ Lifetime Achievement Award - Academics and Researchers
To honor an individual for distinctive and exem-

plary contributions to psychological knowledge. Candidates need not be members of the Society, but they must be residents of the United Kingdom. A certificate, life membership, and monetary prize of £1,000 are awarded when merited. Administered by the Research Board of the Society.

7190 ■ Lifetime Achievement Award - Professional Psychology
To honor an individual for unusually significant and sustained contributions in a career as a practitioner of applied psychology. Candidates need not be members of the Society nor must they be residents of the United Kingdom. A certificate and life membership are awarded when merited. Established in 2006. Administered by the Professional Practice Board of the Society.

7191 ■ Neil O'Connor Award
To recognize published research on cognitive abnormalities that appear during development and persist throughout life. A monetary prize of £300 plus up to £200 in travel expenses are awarded annually. Administered by the Society's Developmental Psychology Section.

7192 ■ Outstanding Doctoral Research Award
To recognize superb research in the field of psychology. Nominees must have had their work reported in one or more articles which have appeared in refereed journals, and must be directly derived from research for a doctoral degree in psychology. A certificate and monetary prize of £500 are awarded annually. Established in 1997. Administered by the Society's Research Board.

7193 ■ Practitioner of the Year Award
To identify, reward, and publicize excellence in the practical application of occupational psychology, with a clear focus on client benefits. Awards are presented in four categories: Organizational change, Assessment, Development, and Health and Wellbeing. In addition, and overall Practitioner of the Year is recognized. Awarded annually. Established in 2006. Administered by the Society's Division of Occupational Psychology.

7194 ■ Presidents' Award
For recognition of achievement in the field of scientific research that contributes to psychological knowledge. This mid-career award is intended as a timely acknowledgement of the achievements of those currently engaged in research of outstanding quality. Awarded annually. Established in 1981. Administered by the Society's Research Board.

7195 ■ M.B. Shapiro Award
To honor a psychologist in the latter part of his or her career for professional eminence. An invitation to present a lecture is awarded annually. Established in 1984. Administered by the Society's Division of Clinical Psychology.

7196 ■ Spearman Medal
For recognition of published work of outstanding merit in psychology. Individuals with more than 10 years of full time employment or further study in psychology (or their part-time equivalent) and who reside in the United Kingdom may be nominated. A medal is awarded annually. Established in 1965. Administered by the Society's Research Board.

7197 ■ H.T.A. Whiting Undergraduate Dissertation Prize
To honor an outstanding dissertation on any aspect of sport and exercise psychology. Entries must have been submitted as a final-year undergraduate project and any institution of higher education in the United Kingdom. A monetary

prize of £50 is awarded annually. Established in 1999. Administered by the Society's Division of Sport and Exercise Psychology.

7198 ■ British Science Fiction Association
Peter Wilkinson, Membership Sec.
Flat 4, Stratton Lodge
79 Bulwer Rd.
Barnet EN5 5EU, United Kingdom
E-mail: bsfamembership@yahoo.co.uk
URL: http://www.bsfa.co.uk

7199 ■ BSFA Awards
Recognizes the science fiction or fantasy novel, short fiction, artwork, and non-fiction considered the best of the year. Awarded annually. Established in 1969.

7200 ■ British Security Industry Association
James Kelly, Chief Exec.
Kirkham House
John Comyn Dr.
Worcester WR3 7NS, United Kingdom
Ph: 44 845 3893889
Fax: 44 845 3890761
E-mail: c.brooks@bsia.co.uk
URL: http://www.bsia.co.uk

7201 ■ BSIA/IFSEC Security Industry Awards
To promote the highest standards of excellence in the field of security by recognizing not only the best new products developed in the last year, but also excellence in the fields of exporting, project innovation, and people within the industry. Trophies are awarded annually in several categories.

7202 ■ Security Officer Awards
To recognize security officers who demonstrate dedication, loyalty, teamwork, customer service skills, use of technology, and bravery on a daily basis. Presented at a regional and national level each year.

7203 ■ British Show Pony Society
124 Green End Rd.
Sawtry
Huntingdon PE28 5XS, United Kingdom
Ph: 44 1487 831376
Fax: 44 1487 832779
E-mail: info@bsps.com
URL: http://www.britishshowponysociety.co.uk

7204 ■ British Show Pony Society Rosettes
To recognize a mare or gelding as the best pony of the year. Rosettes are awarded at all affiliated shows to the Champion and Reserve Show Pony, Working Hunter Pony, Show Hunter Pony, and Intermediate, Mini and Heritage Champions and Reserves.

7205 ■ Show Hunter Ponies Awards
To recognize the best ponies of the year in the following areas: (1) Novice Show Hunter Pony; and (2) Open Show Hunter Pony. A mare or gelding, four years of age or over, that has not won a first prize of £5.00 prior to October 1, and that is registered with the Society is eligible for novice classes. Awards are presented at shows of the Society, and are awarded by a panel of judges.

7206 ■ Show Ponies Awards
To provide recognition for the best show ponies of the year. The following general awards are given: (1) British show pony cups and trophies - to recognize members of the Society with ponies registered with the Society. A cup or trophy is presented annually, to be held for one year, and returned to the Society. Show ponies that are registered with the Society are eligible in the following categories: (1) Novice Show Pony - to a pony four years of age or older; (2) Three year old pony; and (3) Open Show Pony - to a pony four years of age or older. Ponies must not have

Awards are arranged in alphabetical order below their administering organizations

won a first prize of £5.00 or over prior to October 1 to be eligible for novice classes. Cups and trophies are presented at shows of the Society, and are awarded by a panel of judges.

7207 ■ Working Hunter Ponies Awards
To recognize the best ponies of the year in the following areas: (1) Novice Working Hunter Pony; and (2) Open Working Hunter Pony. A mare or gelding four years of age or over, that has not won a first prize of £5.00 or over prior to October 1, and that is registered with the Society is eligible for novice classes. Awards are presented at shows of the Society, and are awarded by a panel of judges.

7208 ■ British Small Animal Veterinary Association
Grant Petrie, Pres.
Woodrow House
1 Telford Way
Waterwells Business Park
Quedgeley
Gloucester GL2 2AB, United Kingdom
Ph: 44 1452 726700
Fax: 44 1452 726701
E-mail: administration@bsava.com
URL: http://www.bsava.com

7209 ■ Amoroso Award
For recognition of outstanding contributions to small animal studies by a non-clinical member of University staff. A textbook and monetary award are presented annually.

7210 ■ Blaine Award
For recognition of outstanding contributions to the advancement of small animal medicine or surgery. Veterinarians and non-veterinarians are eligible for nomination. A plaque and a monetary award are presented annually.

7211 ■ Bourgelat Award
For recognition of outstanding contributions to the field of small animal practice. An engraved decanter and a scroll are awarded annually.

7212 ■ Dunkin Award
For recognition of the most valuable article published in the *Journal of Small Animal Practice* by a small animal practitioner during the 12 months ending on October 31. An engraved decanter and a scroll are awarded annually.

7213 ■ Melton Award
For recognition of meritorious contributions by veterinary surgeons to small animal practice. Veterinary surgeons in general practice are eligible. A scroll and monetary awarded are presented annually. Established in 1981.

7214 ■ Petsavers Award
For recognition of the best clinical research article published in the JSAP during the 12 months ending on October 31. Awarded annually.

7215 ■ Simon Award
For recognition of outstanding contributions in the field of veterinary surgery. Members of the Association are eligible. A statuette is awarded annually.

7216 ■ J.A. Wight Memorial Award
For recognition of outstanding contributions to the welfare of companion animals. Veterinarians on the RCVS register are eligible. A monetary prize is awarded annually.

7217 ■ Woodrow Award
For recognition of outstanding contributions to the field of small animal veterinary medicine. Members of the Association are eligible. A scroll is awarded annually.

7218 ■ British Society for Antimicrobial Chemotherapy
Tracey Guise, Exec. Off.
Griffin House
53 Regent Pl.

Birmingham B1 3NJ, United Kingdom
Ph: 44 121 2361988
Ph: 44 121 2621830
Fax: 44 121 2129822
E-mail: enquiries@bsac.org.uk
URL: http://www.bsac.org.uk

7219 ■ Garrod Medal
For recognition of achievement in the field of antimicrobial chemotherapy. Nominations are made by the Council of the Society. A medal and an invitation to present the Garrod Memorial Lecture are awarded annually. Established in 1982 in honor of L.P. Garrod, whose writing and influence on the field was important to the development of the discipline.

7220 ■ Sir Richard Sykes Prize
To recognize a young investigator for the best contribution published in the *Journal of Antimicrobial Chemotherapy* during the preceding year. To qualify, authors must be members of the Society under 35 years of age. A monetary prize of £500 is awarded annually.

7221 ■ British Society for Clinical Neurophysiology
Prof. Peter Heath, Pres.
Frenchay Hospital
Clinical Neurophysiology Department
Bristol BS16 1LE, United Kingdom
E-mail: nick.kane@nbt.nhs.uk
URL: http://www.clinicalneurophysiology.org.uk

7222 ■ Gray Matter Medal
For distinguished service to a relevant science.

7223 ■ British Society for Geomorphology
Dr. David Robinson, Honorary Treas.
Royal Geographical Society
1 Kensington Gore
London SW7 2AR, United Kingdom
E-mail: d.a.robinson@sussex.ac.uk
URL: http://www.geomorphology.org.uk

7224 ■ Dick Chorley Award for Postgraduate Research
Awarded annually for the most significant original published contribution to geomorphology by a current or recently graduated student. Created in the memory of Dick Chorley.

7225 ■ David Linton Award
For an outstanding geomorphologist who made a leading contribution to the society. Awarded annually. Established in 1981.

7226 ■ Marjorie Sweeting Dissertation Prize
To honor the best undergraduate geomorphological dissertation at an UK university. Awarded annually to one or more recipients.

7227 ■ Gordon Warwick Award
For excellence in geomorphological research as recorded in a named publication or set of publications. Candidates must be younger than 35 years of age or have commenced work on their doctorate not more than 15 years previously. Awarded annually. Established in 1986.

7228 ■ Wiley Award
Awarded to the best paper published in the BSG's journal, *Earth Surface Processes and Landforms*. Awarded annually.

7229 ■ British Society for Middle Eastern Studies
Prof. James Dickins, Exec. Dir.
University of Durham
Institute for Middle Eastern and Islamic Studies
Elvet Hill Rd.
Durham DH1 3TU, United Kingdom
Ph: 44 191 3345179
Fax: 44 191 3345661
E-mail: a.l.haysey@dur.ac.uk

URL: http://www.brismes.ac.uk

7230 ■ Book Prize
To honor the best scholarly work in English on the subject of the Middle East that was published in its first edition in the United Kingdom. Qualifying topics include language and literature, Islamic studies, Islamic art and archaeology, and sociology, anthropology, history, politics, geography, economics, and international relations. A total monetary prize of £10,000 is awarded to one or more recipients.

7231 ■ British Society for Neuroendocrinology
Prof. Alison Douglas, Chm.
University of Nottingham Medical School
School of Biomedical Sciences
Queen's Medical Centre
Nottingham NG7 2UH, United Kingdom
Ph: 44 115 8230164
Fax: 44 115 8230142
E-mail: fran.ebling@nottingham.ac.uk
URL: http://www.neuroendo.org.uk

7232 ■ Research Visit Grant
To enable postgraduate students to visit research laboratories in the United Kingdom or abroad in order to learn a new technique. A grant up to £1,000 is awarded twice each year.

7233 ■ Student Travel Award
To provide financial assistance to enable student members to attend the annual BSN meetings in the United Kingdom. Grants up to £150 are awarded annually.

7234 ■ British Society for Plant Pathology
Prof. George Salmond, Pres.
Marlborough House
Basingstoke Rd.
Spencers Wood
Reading RG7 1AG, United Kingdom
Ph: 44 1603 880313
Fax: 44 1603 208493
E-mail: secretary@bspp.org.uk
URL: http://www.bspp.org.uk

7235 ■ P.H. Gregory Prize
To honor the best presentation of an oral paper at the Presidential Meeting. Awarded annually.

7236 ■ British Society for Research on Ageing
Matthew Hardman, Sec.
University of Manchester
Faculty of Life Sciences
AV Hill Bldg.
Manchester M13 9PT, United Kingdom
E-mail: secretary@bsra.org.uk
URL: http://www.bsra.org.uk

7237 ■ Lord Cohen Medal
To recognize an individual who has made a considerable contribution to ageing research, either through original discoveries or in the promotion of the subject of gerontology in its broadest aspects. The recipient is invited to give a lecture to the Society. Awarded periodically.

7238 ■ British Society for Rheumatology
Sue Murray-Johnson, Deputy Chief Exec.
Bride House
18-20 Bride Ln.
London EC4Y 8EE, United Kingdom
Ph: 44 20 78420900
Fax: 44 20 78420901
E-mail: bsr@rheumatology.org.uk
URL: http://www.rheumatology.org.uk
Formed by merger of: (1983) Heberden Society; British Association of Rheumatology and Rehabilitation.

7239 ■ Garrod Prize
To recognize young scientists (under age 35) working in the United Kingdom in a rheumatol-

Awards are arranged in alphabetical order below their administering organizations

ogy department or performing work closely related to the discipline. A monetary prize of £1,000 and an invitation to give a presentation of the work during the Society's annual meeting are awarded annually.

7240 ■ Innovation Awards
To honor examples of innovation and excellence within rheumatology medicine that has benefited the treatment and care of rheumatology patients. Awarded in two categories: Innovation in Practice (improvements in patient care) and Innovation in Development (a pioneering new strategy or concept). A cash prize of £250 is awarded to the winner in each category, with an additional £250 to be donated to the charity of each recipient's choice. Awarded annually.

7241 ■ Michael Mason Prize
For recognition of excellence in clinical or scientific research in the field of rheumatology. Members of the Society are eligible. A monetary prize of £1000 and a medal are awarded annually at the annual general meeting. Established in 1986.

7242 ■ Osteoporosis Award
To acknowledge outstanding work in the diagnosis and treatment of osteoporosis. A monetary prize of £500 is awarded annually. Established in 2007.

7243 ■ Young Investigator Award
To encourage the work of young investigative rheumatologists. Entries should include an imaginative hypothesis with results that could advance knowledge within the field. A monetary prize of £500 is awarded annually. Established in 2000.

7244 ■ British Society of Animal Science
Prof. Ian Givens, Pres.
PO Box 3
Penicuik EH26 0RZ, United Kingdom
Ph: 44 131 4454508
Fax: 44 131 5353103
E-mail: bsas@sac.ac.uk
URL: http://www.bsas.org.uk
Formerly: (1995) British Society of Animal Production.

7245 ■ Murray Black Award
To support young members of the society in the early years of their careers. A scholarship ranging from £500 to £1,500 is awarded annually for use in travel or research.

7246 ■ Sir Kenneth Blaxter Scholarship
To support young members of the society in the early years of their animal-science careers. A scholarship of approximately £1,500 is awarded annually for use in the United Kingdom or overseas.

7247 ■ BSAS/Biosciences KTN Vacation Scholarships
To encourage undergraduates into research in the field of farm animal genetics and genomics. Scholarships are available for a minimum of six and a maximum of eight weeks' work and carry a stipend of £200 per week. Awarded annually. Sponsored by Biosciences Knowledge Transfer Network (KTN). Formerly: Genesis-Faraday/BSAS Vacation Scholarships.

7248 ■ Sir John Hammond Memorial Prize
To recognize an individual who works or has worked in research, teaching, advising, farming, or affiliated professions, and has made a significant contribution to the development of animal production based on the application of knowledge of animal physiology. A monetary award and a certificate are presented at the annual meeting of the Society. Established in 1968.

7249 ■ President's Prize
To recognize members of the society for outstanding papers presented at the annual conference. Awarded in two categories: theater paper and poster paper. A monetary prize of £150 is awarded annually in each category.

7250 ■ Alan Robertson Fund
To support research and education in the application of genetics to livestock production. A monetary prize of approximately £1,400 is awarded annually. Established in honor of Professor Alan Robertson, a past president of the Society.

7251 ■ RSPCA Award for Innovative Developments in Animal Welfare
To recognize original developments in the promotion of animal welfare. To recognize original developments in the promotion of animal welfare. A trophy and monetary prize of £100 are awarded annually. Co-sponsored by the Royal Society for the Prevention of Cruelty to Animals (RSPCA).

7252 ■ Summer Placement Scheme
To support students' work experience in environments that match their areas of study. A monetary prize of £500 is presented annually. Established in 1995.

7253 ■ British Society of Hearing Aid Audiologists
Roger Lewin, Pres.
Remo House, 6th Fl.
310-312 Regent St.
London W1B 3BS, United Kingdom
E-mail: secretary@bshaa.com
URL: http://www.bshaa.com

7254 ■ Cunningham-Beatie Award
For outstanding merit.

7255 ■ British Society of Magazine Editors
Gill Branston, Admin.
137 Hale Ln.
Edgware
Middlesex HA8 9QP, United Kingdom
Ph: 44 20 89064664
E-mail: admin@bsme.com
URL: http://www.bsme.com

7256 ■ Awards for Editorial and Publishing Excellence
To recognize outstanding achievement through editorial and publishing excellence over the last year. The following awards are presented: Business Magazine Website of the Year, Consumer Magazine Website of the Year, The Mark Boxer Award, Editors' Editor of the Year, Art Director of the Year, Launch of the Year, Campaign of the Year, Innovation/Brandbuilding Initiative of the Year, and Fiona Macpherson New Editor of the Year. Awarded annually. Established in 1979.

7257 ■ Editors of the Year Awards
To honor those who have shown outstanding editing skills during the year. Any editor of a British magazine that is published at least four times per year is eligible. Awards are presented annually in the following weekly and non-weekly categories: business and professional magazines, customer magazines, entertainment and celebrity magazines, lifestyle magazines, men's magazines, newspaper magazines, special interest and current affairs magazines, women's magazines, and youth magazines. Awarded annually.

7258 ■ Fiona Macpherson New Editor of the Year Award
To recognize the most promising new editor. Awarded annually.

7259 ■ British Society of Periodontology
Helen Clough, Admin. Mgr.
PO Box 228
Selby
Bubwith YO8 1EY, United Kingdom
Ph: 44 844 3351915
Fax: 44 844 3351915
URL: http://www.bsperio.org.uk

7260 ■ Frank Ashley Undergraduate Prize
To encourage dental undergraduates to carry out projects related to periodontology. Open to students in United Kingdom dental schools. Two monetary prize of £500 are awarded annually.

7261 ■ Clinical Fellowship Awards
To enhance clinical training, the aim being to facilitate applications for training places and reduce the risk of dropouts for those U.K./European Union citizens in GDC recognized courses. Up for four awards of up to £4,000 each are awarded annually. Formerly: Marsh Midda Fellowship.

7262 ■ Sir Wilfred Fish Research Prize
To encourage researchers in the early states of their career. A monetary prize of £1,000 is awarded annually. Established in 1970.

7263 ■ Research Grants
To support research projects by full or associate members of the BSP. Grants up to £5,000 are awarded annually.

7264 ■ British Society of Rheology
Dr. Oliver Guy Harlen, Pres.
University of Wales
Institute of Mathematical and Physical Sciences
Ceredigion
Aberystwyth SY23 3BZ, United Kingdom
Ph: 44 1970 622775
Fax: 44 1970 622826
E-mail: dmb@aber.ac.uk
URL: http://www.bsr.org.uk

7265 ■ Scott Blair Biorheology Scholarship
The award is similar to the BSR Scott Blair Scholarship, but the recipient must work in the field of biorheology. Awarded occasionally. Established in 1989 to commemorate the work of the late Dr. G.W. Scott Blair, who was the first print editor of Biorheology Journal.

7266 ■ British Society of Rheology Annual Award
To recognize a significant or promising contribution and/or services to the advancement of rheology in any of its many aspects. Individuals, groups, or institutions are eligible. A certificate or monetary prize appropriate to the nature and significance of the contribution is awarded annually. Established in 1978.

7267 ■ Gold Medal
To recognize distinguished work in the theory and application of rheology. Individual scientists are eligible. A gold medal is awarded when merited. Established in 1966.

7268 ■ Vernon Harrison Annual Doctoral Prize
To recognize the postgraduate member who has made the most original and significant contribution to any branch of rheological research (experimental, computational, or theoretical) leading to the award of a PhD degree in a given academic year. A certificate and monetary prize of £500 are awarded annually. Established in 2003.

7269 ■ British Society of Scientific Glassblowers
Mr. William Fludgate, Chm.
Glendale, Sinclair St.
Caithness
Thurso KW14 7AQ, United Kingdom
Ph: 44 1847 802121
Ph: 44 1847 895637
Fax: 44 1847 802971
E-mail: ian.pearson@dounreay.com

Awards are arranged in alphabetical order below their administering organizations

URL: http://www.bssg.co.uk

7270 ■ Norman Collins Memorial Award

To provide an opportunity for experienced scientific glassblowers to demonstrate their outstanding skills in scientific glassware. All members of the society are eligible. Winners of the A.D. Wood Cup are automatically considered. A trophy to be held for one year is awarded annually at the symposium. Established in 1980 in memory of Norman Collins.

7271 ■ David Flack Memorial Award

To provide an opportunity for scientific glassblowers to express their artistic talent in the medium of glass. Members of the society are eligible. A trophy to be held for one year and a pewter tankard for the winner to keep are awarded annually at the symposium. Established in 1972 in memory of David Flack, by his parents.

7272 ■ Lucy Oldfield Cup

For recognition of contributions to the society journal. A trophy and certificates of achievement are awarded annually. Established in 1982 by Dr. Lucy Oldfield.

7273 ■ Thames Valley Award

To recognize a member who has contributed most to the society. A trophy to be held for one year is awarded annually at the annual symposium. Established in 1970 by members of the Thames Valley Section of the society.

7274 ■ TSL Trophy

To encourage excellence in scientific vitreous silica glassworking. All members of the society are eligible. A trophy to be held for one year and a pewter tankard for the winner to keep are awarded annually at the symposium. Established in 1969 by Thermal Syndicate, Ltd. (TSL).

7275 ■ A. D. Wood Cup

To encourage excellence in scientific borosilicate glassworking. Members of the society who have less than three years experience are eligible. A cup to be held for one year, a replica, and a £50 prize are awarded annually at the symposium. Established in 1966 by Mr. A.D. Wood of A.D. Wood Ltd.

7276 ■ British Thematic Association
John Hayward, Pres.
9 Oaklands Park
Herts
Bishop's Stortford CM23 2BY, United Kingdom
URL: http://www.brit-thematic-assoc.com

7277 ■ BTA Trophy

For the best exhibit as judged by National Thematic rules. A trophy is awarded annually.

7278 ■ British Toy and Hobby Association
Roland Earl, Dir. Gen./Sec.
80 Camberwell Rd.
London SE5 OEG, United Kingdom
Ph: 44 207 7017271
Fax: 44 207 7082437
E-mail: queries@btha.co.uk
URL: http://www.btha.co.uk

7279 ■ Toy Industry Awards

To recognize the best in toy design and retailing in the United Kingdom. Awarded in two general categories: Retailer of the Year Awards (includes awards for various regions within the U.K.) and Supplier of the Year Awards (includes Toy of the Year, Creative Toy of the Year, and Boys' and Girls' Ranges of the Year). Awarded annually.

7280 ■ British Transplantation Society
Mr. Keith Rigg, Pres.
Chester House
68 Chestergate
Cheshire
Macclesfield SK11 6DY, United Kingdom

Ph: 44 1625 664547
Fax: 44 1625 664510
E-mail: secretariat@bts.org.uk
URL: http://www.bts.org.uk

7281 ■ Astellas and Novartis Research Fellowships

For individuals in training who are interested in transplantation. A grant up to £60,000 is awarded annually to two recipients.

7282 ■ BTS/Morris Travelling Fellowship

For trainees in the field of transplantation. A grant up to £5,000 is awarded annually.

7283 ■ Roy Calne Award

To honor a member for the most outstanding contribution published in a peer review journal as a single paper. A certificate and monetary prize of £500 are awarded annually.

7284 ■ St. John Ambulance Air Wing Travelling Fellowship

To honor workers in all aspects of transplantation for the benefit of transplant patients. Awards of up to £10,000 are awarded annually.

7285 ■ Wyeth Fellowship

To trainees in the field of transplantation. An award up to £5,000 is awarded annually.

7286 ■ British Trust for Ornithology
Dr. Andy Clements, Dir.
The Nunnery
Norfolk
Thetford IP24 2PU, United Kingdom
Ph: 44 1842 750050
Fax: 44 1842 750030
E-mail: info@bto.org
URL: http://www.bto.org

7287 ■ Jubilee Medal

For recognition of services to the trust that are not scientific. Members of the trust are eligible. A medal is awarded annually. Established in 1983 to commemorate 50 years of the BTO.

7288 ■ Bernard Tucker Medal

For recognition of scientific services. Members of the trust are eligible. A medal is awarded annually. Established in 1954 in honor of Bernard Tucker.

7289 ■ British Universities Film and Video Council
Luis Carrasqueiro, Chief Exec.
77 Wells St.
London W1T 3QJ, United Kingdom
Ph: 44 20 73931500
Ph: 44 20 73931505
Fax: 44 20 73931555
E-mail: ask@bufvc.ac.uk
URL: http://bufvc.ac.uk
Formed by merger of: (2005) British Universities Film and Video Council; Society for Screen-Based Learning.

7290 ■ Channel 4 Archaeological Film Awards

To recognize cinematic achievements in the field of archaeology. Awards are presented in two categories: broadcast programs (including radio and television) and ICT projects (CD-ROMs, websites or integrated multimedia packages). Entries may deal with any aspect of archaeology, including industrial archaeology, and may have been made for broadcast, educational, promotional or site-specific purposes. To be eligible, they must be British-produced and have been made or broadcast during the previous two years. Winners in each of the three categories will be awarded a cash prize of £750. Held biennially in even-numbered years. Part of the British Archaeological Awards.

7291 ■ Learning on Screen Awards

To celebrate and reward excellence in the use of

moving image, sound, and related media in learning, teaching, and research. Presented in six categories: General Education Broadcast, General Education Non-Broadcast, General Education Multimedia, Course and Curriculum-Related Content, Undergraduate Student Production, and Post-Graduate Student Production. In addition, the Premier Award and the Special Jury Award are presented. Awarded annually.

7292 ■ British Veterinary Association
Harvey Locke, Pres.-Elect
7 Mansfield St.
London W1G 9NQ, United Kingdom
Ph: 44 20 76366541
Fax: 44 20 79086349
E-mail: bvahq@bva.co.uk
URL: http://www.bva.co.uk

7293 ■ Trevor Blackburn Award

To honor a member for contributions to animal health and welfare in a developing country. Awarded annually. Established in 2006.

7294 ■ Chiron Award

To recognize outstanding contributions to veterinary science and the veterinary profession. Awarded annually. Established in 1992.

7295 ■ Dalrymple-Champneys Cup and Medal

To recognize a member for outstanding work and merit in the advancement of veterinary science. Awarded annually. Established in 1934.

7296 ■ William Hunting Award

To recognize the best practitioner-based paper to be published in the previous year. Awarded annually. Established in 1997.

7297 ■ Overseas Travel Grants

To support undergraduate students attending veterinary school in the United Kingdom. Individuals should be undertaking a project that includes a strong element of agricultural development. Grants of up to £500 are awarded annually to one or more recipients. Established in 1983.

7298 ■ Harry Steele-Bodger Memorial Travel Scholarship

To assist a visit by an individual to a veterinary or agricultural school or research institute. Open to graduates of the veterinary schools in the United Kingdom and Ireland who have been qualified for no more than three years. A scholarship in the amount of £1,000 is awarded annually. Established in 1953 in memory of Henry W. Steele-Bodger, president of the Association from 1939 to 1941.

7299 ■ British Wildlife Photography Awards
PO Box 1481
Kingston upon Thames KT1 9Qp, United Kingdom
URL: http://www.bwpawards.org

7300 ■ British Wildlife Photography Awards

To recognize outstanding wildlife photography. Competition is open to photographers of all nationalities who are working in the United Kingdom. Awards include: British wildlife Photographer Award - £5,000; Young British Wildlife Photographer Award (12 to 18 years) - £500; Young British Wildlife Photographer Award (up to 11 years) - £300; Schools, Youth and Community Group Award - £1,000; and seven individual category awards of £1,000 each.

7301 ■ British Women Pilots' Association
Caroline Gough-Cooper, Chair
Brooklands Museum
Brooklands Rd.
Weybridge KT13 0QN, United Kingdom
E-mail: info@bwpa.co.uk

Awards are arranged in alphabetical order below their administering organizations

URL: http://www.bwpa.co.uk

7302 ■ Faith Bennet Navigation Trophy
To recognize a navigation exercise of special interest or one that stretches the pilot's experience and limits. Awarded annually when merited.

7303 ■ Brabazon Cup
Recognizes a particularly outstanding performance in aviation. Awarded annually when merited.

7304 ■ Jack Brackenbury Photography Trophy
For the best photograph submitted for the Association's archives, newsletter, or website. Awarded annually when merited.

7305 ■ Chairwoman's Challenge
To recognize the winner of an annual flying challenge. Awarded annually when merited.

7306 ■ Naomy Christy Award
To recognize personal achievement in aviation. Awarded annually when merited.

7307 ■ Hilda Hewlet Trophy
To recognize a younger member who has shown initiative and commitment in gaining her pilot's license. Awarded annually when merited.

7308 ■ O.P. Jones Cup
To recognize a noteworthy performance in gliding or hang-gliding. Awarded annually when merited.

7309 ■ Jean Lennox Bird Pendant
For service to aviation over a sustained period of time. Awarded annually when merited.

7310 ■ Jackie Moggridge Trophy
To recognize a female pilot for achieving excellent qualifications in her chosen career. Awarded annually when merited.

7311 ■ Muriel Sells Trophy
To support the Association by attending events or working to further the Association's goals. Awarded annually when merited.

7312 ■ Business Archives Council
Ms. Karen Sampson, Hon. Sec.
Lloyds TSB Group Archives
48 Chiswell St., 2nd Fl.
London EC1Y 4XX, United Kingdom
Ph: 44 20 78605762
URL: http://www.businessarchivescouncil.org.uk

7313 ■ Wadsworth Prize for Business History
For recognition of an outstanding contribution to British business history in any one calendar year. Books or articles on British business history published during the year are eligible. A monetary prize is awarded annually. Established in 1978 upon the retirement from the Council of Professor J. E. Wadsworth after 50 years continuous association.

7314 ■ Calouste Gulbenkian Foundation
United Kingdom Branch
50 Hoxton Sq.
London N1 6PB, United Kingdom
Ph: 44 20 7012 1400
Fax: 44 20 7739 1961
E-mail: info@gulbenkian.org.uk
URL: http://www.gulbenkian.org.uk

7315 ■ Calouste Gulbenkian Foundation Grants
To encourage and to provide support for programs in the arts, education, social welfare, and Anglo-Portuguese cultural relations. Grant applications for projects (not individuals) in the United Kingdom and the Republic of Ireland whose principal beneficiaries are people in these countries are accepted. Preference is given to original new developments, not yet a part of the regular running costs of an organization; to developments which are either strategic, such as practical initiatives directed to helping tackle the underlying causes of problems, or seminal, because they seem likely to influence policy and practice elsewhere; or to projects which are of more than local significance. The majority of grants are for less than £15,000. Awarded annually.

7316 ■ Camanachd Association (Cumunn na Camanachd)
Mr. Archie Robertson, Pres.
Alton House
4 Ballifeary Rd.
Inverness IV3 5PJ, United Kingdom
Ph: 44 1463 715931
Fax: 44 1463 226551
E-mail: admin@shinty.com
URL: http://www.shinty.com

7317 ■ Club of the Year
To recognize the year's most successful shinty team. Awarded annually.

7318 ■ Coach of the Year
To recognize the year's most successful shinty coach. Awarded annually.

7319 ■ Donella Crawford Award for Youth and Schools
To honor a student for outstanding contributions in school shinty. Awarded annually.

7320 ■ Marine Harvest Centenary Award for Outstanding Services to Shinty
To honor an older individual for contributions to the sport of shinty. Awarded triennially.

7321 ■ Player of the Year
To recognize the year's most outstanding player of shinty, a team-based sport that involves hitting a ball with a curved, wooden stick. Awarded annually.

7322 ■ Referee of the Year
To recognize the year's best referee of shinty. Awarded annually.

7323 ■ Under 14 Player of the Year
To recognize the year's most outstanding young player of shinty. Candidates must be younger than 14 years of age. Awarded annually.

7324 ■ Under 17 Player of the Year
To recognize the year's most outstanding young player of shinty. Candidates must be younger than 17 years of age. Awarded annually.

7325 ■ Under 21 Player of the Year
To recognize the year's most outstanding young player of shinty. Candidates must be younger than 21 years of age. Awarded annually.

7326 ■ Volunteer of the Year
To recognize an individual for volunteer contributions to the game of shinty. Awarded annually.

7327 ■ Campaign for the Protection of Rural Wales (Ymgyrch Diogelu Cymru Wledig)
Dr. Jean Rosenfeld, Chm.
Ty Gwyn
31 High St.
Welshpool SY21 7YD, United Kingdom
Ph: 44 1938 552525
Ph: 44 1938 556212
Fax: 44 1938 871552
E-mail: info@cprwmail.org.uk
URL: http://www.cprw.org.uk
Formerly: Council for the Protection of Rural Wales.

7328 ■ Rural Wales Award
To recognize work by individuals and organizations that is consciously intended to enhance the appearance or amenities of the Welsh countryside. Local branches of the organization make the awards. Framed certificates and a wooden plaque are awarded annually. Established in 1983. Sponsored by the Post Office Ltd.

7329 ■ Candlestar
8 Hammersmith Broadway
London W6 7AL, United Kingdom
Ph: 44 20 8741 6025
Fax: 44 20 8563 9700
E-mail: info@candlestar.co.uk
URL: http://www.candlestar.co.uk

7330 ■ Magic of Persia Contemporary Art Prize
To recognize the talent of emerging Iranian artists. Open to painting, photography, sculpture, and new media. Awarded annually. Established in 2009.

7331 ■ Prix Pictet
To honor the use of photography to communicate crucial messages of sustainability to a global audience. A monetary prize of 100,000 Swiss francs is awarded annually. Established in 2008. Supported by Pictet & Cie.

7332 ■ Care Forum Wales
Sue Thomas, Contact
PO Box 2195
Wrexham LL13 7WL, United Kingdom
Ph: 44 1978 755400
E-mail: enquiries@careforumwales.co.uk
URL: http://www.careforumwales.co.uk

7333 ■ Wales Cares Awards
To recognize providers of health and social care services for adults and children in Wales. The following awards are presented: Excellence in Catering Award, Newcomer to Care Award, Craig Thomas Lifetime Achievement in Care Award, Excellence in Training Award, Promoting Fulfilled Lives Award, Outstanding Service Award, Registered Manager Award, Nurse of the Year Award, Excellence in Dementia Care Award, Care Practitioner Award, Excellence in Palliative Care Award, Spirit of Care Award, and the Peter Clarke Award for Excellence in Children's Care. Trophies are awarded annually.

7334 ■ Celtic Media Festival
Jude MacLaverty, Festival Producer
249 W George St.
Glasgow G2 4QE, United Kingdom
Ph: 44 141 302 1737
Fax: 44 141 302 1738
E-mail: info@celticmediafestival.co.uk
URL: http://www.celticmediafestival.co.uk
Formerly: (1988) Association for Film and Television in the Celtic Countries.

7335 ■ Celtic Media Festival
For recognition of achievement by outstanding filmmakers and to encourage younger filmmakers. Individuals who reside or work in Celtic countries may apply. Awards are presented in 19 categories each year. Formerly: International Festival of Film and Television in the Celtic Countries.

7336 ■ Central Chancery of the Orders of Knighthood
Honours and Appointments
Ground Fl.
Admiralty Arch
London SW1A 2WH, United Kingdom
Ph: 44 20 7276 2777
Fax: 44 20 7276 2766
E-mail: honours@cabinet-office.x.gsi.gov.uk
URL: http://www.honours.gov.uk

7337 ■ Air Force Cross
To recognize all ranks of the Royal Air Force for outstanding services in flying operations not against the enemy. It can also be awarded to

Awards are arranged in alphabetical order below their administering organizations

equivalent ranks of the Royal Navy and the Army for similar services. Established in 1918. Administered by the Ministry of Defense.

7338 ■ British Empire Medal
To recognize men and women who do not qualify for the higher awards in the order of the British Empire. The British Empire Medal ceased being awarded in the United Kingdom in 1992, but is still awarded by some Commonwealth Countries.

7339 ■ Distinguished Flying Cross
To recognize non-commissioned ranks of the Royal Air Force for bravery in air operations against the enemy. It can also be awarded to equivalent ranks of the Royal Navy and the Army for similar services. Established in 1918. Administered by the Ministry of Defense.

7340 ■ Distinguished Service Order
To honor leadership in action displayed by officers of the armed forces of the Crown. It can be awarded to officers of the Merchant Navy. It is now the only gallantry award which cannot be given posthumously. Established in 1886.

7341 ■ George Cross
To honor great heroism or conspicuous courage and equivalent to the rank of the Victoria Cross. It was intended primarily for civilians but is not limited to them; in practice more servicemen and women have received it than civilians. Established in 1940.

7342 ■ George Medal
For recognition of an act of bravery that has not been sufficiently outstanding to merit the Cross. It can be awarded to foreigners. Established in 1940.

7343 ■ Military Cross
To recognize all ranks for gallant and distinguished services in the presence of the enemy on land. Established in 1914. Administered by the Ministry of Defense.

7344 ■ Most Honourable Order of the Bath
For recognition of conspicuous services to the Crown. This Order is open to both sexes. The Great Master and First or Principal Knight Grand Cross is the Prince of Wales. There are two divisions, military and civil. Ranks in the order, and their customary abbreviations, are: (1) Knight or Dame Grand Cross: G.C.B.; (2) Knight or Dame Commander: K.C.B. or D.C.B.; and (3) Companion: C.B. Established as a separate order in 1725 but with medieval origins.

7345 ■ Order of Merit
For recognition of eminent services rendered in the armed services, or towards the advancement of art, literature and science. It is open to both sexes. The Order is limited to 24 members, plus foreign honorary members. The insignia is awarded in either a military or a civil form. Established in 1902.

7346 ■ Order of St. Michael and St. George
For recognition of service overseas or in connection with foreign or Commonwealth affairs. The Grand Master is the Duke of Kent. Ranks in the Order, and their customary abbreviations, are: (1) Knight or Dame Grand Cross G.C.M.G.; (2) Knight or Dame Commander - K.C.M.G. or D.C.M.G.; and (3) Companion - C.M.G. Founded in 1818.

7347 ■ Order of the British Empire
To recognize civilians or service personnel for public services or other distinctions. The Grand Master is the Duke of Edinburgh. There are two divisions, military and civil. Ranks in the Order, which is open to both sexes, and the customary abbreviations, are: (1) Knight or Dame Grand Cross - G.B.E.; (2) Knight or Dame Commander - K.B.E. or D.B.E.; (3) Commander - C.B.E.; (4) Officer - O.B.E.; and (5) Member - M.B.E. Founded in 1917.

7348 ■ Queen's Fire Service Medal
For recognition posthumously. There is also the Queen's Fire Service Medal for Distinguished Service. Instituted in 1954.

7349 ■ Queen's Gallantry Medal
To recognize acts of exemplary bravery. The medal is intended primarily for civilians but may be awarded to military personnel for actions for which purely military honors are not granted. Established in 1974.

7350 ■ Queen's Police Medal for Distinguished Service
For recognition posthumously. There is also The Queen's Police Medal for Distinguished Service. Established in 1954.

7351 ■ Royal Red Cross
To recognize exceptional services by nurses rendered in any of the fighting services. There is also a second class of award known as "Associate." Established in 1883.

7352 ■ Royal Victorian Order
To reward services to the Royal Family. The Grand Master is Queen Elizabeth The Queen Mother. Ranks in the Order, which is open to both sexes, and the customary abbreviations, are: (1) Knight or Dame Grand Cross - G.C.V.O.; (2) Knight or Dame Commander - K.C.V.O. or D.C.V.O.; (3) Commander - C.V.O.; (4) Lieutenant L. D. V.; and (5) Member 5th Class M.V.O. Established in 1896 by Queen Victoria.

7353 ▪ Victoria Cross
This, the most esteemed of all British gallantry medals, is given to honor outstanding valor in the presence of the enemy. Normally intended for servicemen but it may be conferred on civilians serving under military command. A tax-free annuity of £1,300 a year is payable to holders of the Cross. Established in 1856.

7354 ■ Challenger Society for Marine Science
Jennifer Jones, Exec. Sec.
National Oceanography Centre
Waterfront Campus, Rm. 346/10
Southampton SO14 3ZH, United Kingdom
E-mail: jxj@noc.soton.ac.uk
URL: http://www.challenger-society.org.uk/the_society
Formerly: (1988) Challenger Society.

7355 ■ Cath Allen Prize
To encourage good poster presentations at the biennial UK Oceanography meeting. A monetary prize and a certificate are awarded biennially at the UK Oceanography meeting. Established in 1988 in honor of Dr. Catherine M. Allen. Formerly: (1991) Poster Prize.

7356 ■ Challenger Medal
This, the premier award of the Society, is given to honor a distinguished U.K. marine scientist or other individual who has made a single or sustained contribution to the development of marine science. Awarded biennially in even-numbered years.

7357 ■ Norman Heaps Prize
To encourage good presentations by young oceanographers. Individuals who are 35 years of age or younger are considered. A monetary prize and a certificate are awarded at the biennial UK Oceanography meeting. Established in 1988 in honor of Dr. Norman S. Heaps. Formerly: World Development Awards for Business.

7358 ■ Chartered Institute of Architectural Technologists
Mr. Adam Endacott, Public Relations Dir.
397 City Rd.
London EC1V 1NH, United Kingdom
Ph: 44 20 72782206
Fax: 44 20 78373194

E-mail: info@ciat.org.uk
URL: http://www.ciat.org.uk
Formerly: (1994) British Institute of Architectural Technicians.

7359 ■ Gold Award
To honor members who have demonstrated an outstanding service or commitment to the Institute, the construction industry, or the region. A gold medal is awarded annually to one or more recipients. Established in 1999.

7360 ■ Alan King Prize
To recognize individuals for achievement of technical excellence in construction in projects valued at £500,000 or less. A certificate, a plaque for permanent attachment to the project, and monetary prize of £1,500 are awarded for first place. Awarded annually. Established in 2005.

7361 ■ Open Award for Technical Excellence in Architectural Technology
To recognize achievement of technical excellence in construction by illustrating the composition of ideas put into practice and presented in a working format. First prize of £1,500 is awarded annually; second and third place winners receive £750 and £550, respectively. Established in 1994.

7362 ■ Student Award for Technical Excellence
To recognize students who demonstrate their achievement of technical excellence in architectural technology by illustrating the composition of ideas put into practice. Entries can be taken from any university/college assignment or a project from place of employment. A certificate, a trophy, and monetary prize of £750 are awarded for first place. Awarded annually. Established in 1983. Formerly: National Student Award.

7363 ■ Chartered Institute of Building
Chris Blythe, Chief Exec.
Englemere
Kings Ride
Berkshire
Ascot SL5 7TB, United Kingdom
Ph: 44 1344 630700
Fax: 44 1344 630777
E-mail: reception@ciob.org.uk
URL: http://www.ciob.org.uk/home

7364 ■ Building Manager of the Year Awards
To recognize outstanding performance in the management of building projects. Nominations are accepted for projects carried out in the United Kingdom. Awards and medals are bestowed annually. Established in 1979 in honor of Queen Elizabeth II's Silver Jubilee.

7365 ■ Construction Manager of the Year Awards
To recognize individuals for management achievement. Open to site-based project managers with overall responsibility for the delivery of any U.K. construction project. Gold and silver medals are presented in 11 categories. Awarded annually. Established in 1983.

7366 ■ Faculty of Architecture and Surveying Innovation Award
To recognize an individual for innovative practice in the areas of architecture or surveying. Awarded annually.

7367 ■ Innovation Competition
To encourage the sharing of innovative ideas and practices that can provide real benefits to members and other practitioners operating within the construction industry. A medal and monetary prize of £600 is awarded to the first-place winner, and a medal and £300 to second-place recipient. Held annually.

7368 ■ International Construction Project Management Association Award
To recognize projects that focus on practical in-

Awards are arranged in alphabetical order below their administering organizations

novation in the field of construction project management. A medal and monetary prize of 1,000 Euros is awarded to the first-place winner, and a medal and 500 Euros to second-place recipient. Awarded annually. Established in 2007.

7369 ∎ Masters Dissertation Award
To recognize dissertation research undertaken at the Master's degree level. A medal and monetary prize of £750 is awarded to the first-place winner, and a medal and £500 to second-place recipient. Awarded annually.

7370 ∎ Pera Prize
To recognize an individual for an innovative concept that is capable of being patented. Candidates must be based in the United Kingdom or Europe. A monetary prize of 55,000 Euros in business consultancy is awarded annually. Sponsored by Pera, an international network of technology development and industry support centers.

7371 ∎ Site Management Awards
To engage candidates who have completed the Certificate state of education and are currently progressing through the Diploma. Gold, silver, and bronze medals are awarded annually. Established in 2006.

7372 ∎ Student Challenge
To encourage students to enhance construction skills and knowledge by finding solutions to a topical industry problem. Held annually. First place winners receive a monetary prize of £200.

7373 ∎ Undergraduate Dissertation Award
To recognize outstanding dissertation research from students who are enrolled in degree programs accredited by the CIOB. A medal and monetary prize of £750 is awarded to the first-place winner, and a medal and £500 to second-place recipient. Awarded annually.

7374 ∎ Chartered Institute of Journalists
Dominic Cooper, Gen. Sec.
2 Dock Offices
Surrey Quays Rd.
London SE16 2XU, United Kingdom
Ph: 44 20 72521187
Fax: 44 20 72322302
E-mail: memberservices@cioj.co.uk
URL: http://cioj.co.uk
Formerly: Institute of Journalists.

7375 ∎ Gold Medal
For recognition of outstanding service to journalism and the fundamental freedom of the press. Journalists and others of any nationality are eligible. A gold medal with the Institute emblem on the reverse and the name of the recipient, wreathed on the obverse, is awarded when merited. Established in 1963.

7376 ∎ Chartered Institute of Library and Information Professionals
Brian Hall, Pres.
7 Ridgmount St.
London WC1E 7AE, United Kingdom
Ph: 44 20 72550500
Ph: 44 20 72550505
Fax: 44 20 72550501
E-mail: info@cilip.org.uk
URL: http://www.cilip.org.uk/pages/default.aspx
Formerly: (2004) Institute of Information Scientists; Library Association.

7377 ∎ Carnegie Medal
To an outstanding book for children and young people. All book categories are eligible. Book must have received its first publication in the United Kingdom. Judging is based on plot, characterization and style. The winner receives a golden medal and £500 for the purchase of books to donate to a library of their choice. Established in 1936 for Andrew Carnegie, an industrialist who set up over 2,800 libraries during his lifetime.

7378 ∎ Kate Greenaway Medal
For outstanding illustration in a book for children. All book categories are eligible. Book must have received its first publication in the United Kingdom. Judging is based on artistic style, format, synergy of illustration and text, and the visual experience. The winner receives a golden medal and £500 for the purchase of books to donate to a library of their choice. Established in 1955 for Kate Greenaway, a nineteenth-century artist known for her children's illustrations.

7379 ∎ Chartered Institute of Logistics and Transport
Prof. Alan Waller, Pres.
Earlstrees Ct.
Earlstrees Rd.
Northants
Corby NN17 4AX, United Kingdom
Ph: 44 1536 740100
Fax: 44 1536 740101
E-mail: enquiry@ciltuk.org.uk
URL: http://www.cilt-international.com/web/pages/home

7380 ∎ Excellence in Information Management Award
To honor outstanding development in information technology or management that gives organizational, supply chain, and/or other business benefits. Awarded annually.

7381 ∎ Excellence in Materials Handling Equipment and Technology Award
To honor outstanding achievement in the use of materials handling equipment and technology at any stage throughout the supply chain, including raw materials, manufacturing, distribution, and retail operations. Awarded annually.

7382 ∎ Excellence in Passenger Transport Award
To honor outstanding achievement in the transport of passenger by road, rail, water, and air. Awarded annually.

7383 ∎ Excellence in Transport Policy and Planning Award
To honor outstanding achievement in transport planning. Awarded annually.

7384 ∎ Sir Robert Lawrence Award
To honor an individual or organization for achievement in logistics and transport. Awarded annually.

7385 ∎ Logistics Best Practice Award
To honor outstanding development that benefits logistics and supply chains in any mode or combination of modes. Awarded annually.

7386 ∎ Logistics Dissertation of the Year
To recognize BSc, MSc/MBA, and PhD students for outstanding dissertations. A monetary prize of £500 is awarded annually.

7387 ∎ Chartered Institution of Building Services Engineers - England
Stephen Matthews, Chief Exec./Sec.
222 Balham High Rd.
London SW12 9BS, United Kingdom
Ph: 44 20 86755211
Ph: 44 20 87723638
Fax: 44 20 86755449
E-mail: smatthews@cibse.org
URL: http://www.cibse.org

7388 ∎ Barker Silver Medal
For recognition of papers contributing substantially to heating, ventilating, and air conditioning associated with the built environment. Papers that describe the author's experience in the application of engineering/scientific knowledge may be submitted. A silver medal is awarded annually when merited. Established in 1958 in honor of Mr. A. H. Barker.

7389 ∎ Carter Bronze Medal
For recognition of the best paper presented to the Institution on the application and development of heating, ventilating, and air conditioning. A bronze medal and a certificate are awarded annually when merited. Established in 1977.

7390 ∎ Dufton Silver Medal
For recognition of a paper that advances the science of building services through original research that leads to new development. A silver medal is awarded annually when merited. Established in 1958 in honor of Mr. A. F. Dufton.

7391 ∎ Leon Gaster Memorial Award
For recognition of the best paper presented to the Institution dealing with the research or theory of lighting and/or vision. A bronze medal and a certificate are awarded annually. Established in 1931 in honor of Mr. Leon Gaster.

7392 ∎ Honorary Fellows of CIBSE
To recognize outstanding service to CIBSE. Awarded annually to one or more recipients.

7393 ∎ Napier Shaw Bronze Medal
For recognition of the best paper presented to the institution dealing with the research or theory of heating, ventilating, and air conditioning. A bronze medal and a certificate are awarded annually when merited. Established before 1948.

7394 ∎ Walsh - Weston Memorial Award
For recognition of the best paper presented to the Institution dealing with the development of light sources or lighting application. A bronze medal and a certificate are awarded annually. Established in 1963 in memory of Dr. J. W. T. Walsh and Mr. H. C. Weston.

7395 ∎ Chartered Institution of Civil Engineering Surveyors
Mr. Jason Smith, Pres.
Dominion House, Sibson Rd.
Cheshire
Sale M33 7PP, United Kingdom
Ph: 44 161 9723100
Fax: 44 161 9723118
E-mail: president@cices.org
URL: http://www.cices.org

7396 ∎ Richard Carter Prize
To recognize a geospatial engineer who is judged to have made an outstanding contribution to the civil engineering surveying industry, either individually or through team leadership. Designed to encourage applicants from all backgrounds and is not restricted solely to members of ICES. A medal, certificate, and monetary prize of £500 are awarded biennially in even-numbered years.

7397 ∎ Chartered Institution of Water and Environmental Management
Nick Reeves, Exec. Dir.
15 John St.
London WC1N 2EB, United Kingdom
Ph: 44 20 78313110
Fax: 44 20 74054967
E-mail: admin@ciwem.org
URL: http://www.ciwem.org

7398 ∎ Certificate and Diploma in Environmental Management
For candidates who achieved overall highest marks in certain modules. A certificate and monetary prize of £500 are awarded annually.

7399 ∎ Living Wetlands Award
To recognize multi-functional projects that demonstrate the sustainable use of wetland habitats. The Mance Memorial Trophy and a monetary prize of £1,500 are awarded annually. Established in 2002.

7400 ∎ President's Award
To recognize a member for exceptional service to the work of the institution. A badge and certificate are awarded annually.

Awards are arranged in alphabetical order below their administering organizations

7401 ■ World of Difference Award
To recognize innovation in sustainable water technology. A trophy and monetary prize of £1,000 are awarded annually.

7402 ■ Young Members' Award
To recognize outstanding contribution to environmental understanding made by a young member (under age 35). A trophy and monetary prize of £1,000 are awarded annually.

7403 ■ Chartered Insurance Institute
Chris Hanks, Pres.
42-48 High Rd.
S Woodford
London E18 2JP, United Kingdom
Ph: 44 20 89898464
Fax: 44 20 85303052
E-mail: customer.serv@cii.co.uk
URL: http://www.cii.co.uk/cii.aspx

7404 ■ AIRMIC Prize
To recognize members for outstanding accomplishments in the risk-management field. A monetary prize of £100 is awarded.

7405 ■ Stanley Brown Prize
To recognize members for outstanding accomplishments in the liability insurance field. A monetary prize of £100 is awarded.

7406 ■ The Chubb Insurance Company of Europe Prize
To recognize a CII member employed by an insurance broker or a reinsurer. A monetary prize of £300 along with a ten-day work experience placement with Chubb Loss Control Services is provided.

7407 ■ H. J. Greening Prize
To recognize members for outstanding achievements in the life assurance field. A monetary prize of £100 is awarded.

7408 ■ Healthcare Award: Advanced Level
To recognize outstanding accomplishments in the private medical-insurance field. A monetary prize of £100 is awarded.

7409 ■ International Underwriting Association Marine Prize
To recognize and support members for outstanding accomplishments in the field. A monetary prize of £250 is awarded.

7410 ■ Layborn Prize
To recognize outstanding accomplishments in unit J06, concerning investment principles, markets, and environments. A monetary award of 100 Euros is presented.

7411 ■ London Business Interruption Association Prize
To recognize members for outstanding accomplishments in the principles of property insurance. A monetary prize of £250 is awarded.

7412 ■ Boleslaw Monic Prize
To recognize members for outstanding accomplishments in the field and principles of reinsurance. A monetary prize of £100 is awarded.

7413 ■ Morgan Owen Medal
To recognize a notable essay or work of research by an individual in the field of insurance. A monetary award of £2,000 and a medal are awarded annually . Established in 1933 by a bequest of O. Morgan Owen, FCII, president of the Institute in 1911.

7414 ■ John Poel Prize
To recognize BIBA members for outstanding work. A monetary prize of £250 is awarded.

7415 ■ Burton Rowe Prize
To recognize outstanding accomplishments in the insurance brokering field by U.K. citizens. A monetary prize of £80 is awarded.

7416 ■ Rutter Gold Medal and Prize
To recognize the individual with the highest score on completing the qualifying examination for fellowship of the Chartered Insurance Institute. Members of the Institute are eligible. A monetary award of £1,000 and a medal are presented annually . Established in 1914 by Sir Frederick Pascoe Rutter, FCII, President of the Institute from 1910-1911.

7417 ■ Chartered Society of Designers
Christopher Ramsden, Pres.
1 Cedar Ct.
Bermondsey St.
Royal Oak Yard
London SE1 3GA, United Kingdom
Ph: 44 20 73578088
Fax: 44 20 74079878
E-mail: info@csd.org.uk
URL: http://www.csd.org.uk

7418 ■ Honorary Fellow
To recognize distinguished persons outside the design profession who have been of material assistance to design or to the Society.

7419 ■ Minerva Medal
To recognize an individual for a lifetime achievement in the field of design. A sterling silver medal bearing the profile of Minerva, Roman goddess of wisdom, is awarded at the annual Minerva Dinner event. Formerly: (1987) SIAD Medal.

7420 ■ Minerva Service Award
To recognize members of the Society for outstanding contributions that have helped with the success of the Society. Established in 2005.

7421 ■ Prince Philip Prize
To recognize a British designer or design team leader for outstanding work that has affected the public perception of design. Awarded annually. Established in 1959 by HRH The Duke of Edinburgh.

7422 ■ Student Medals
To recognize a second-year design student in any full-time design course around the world. Candidates present a project for judging by a panel of CSD and design industry professionals. A winner is selected in each of seven design disciplines: Exhibition, Fashion, Graphic, Interactive Media, Interior, Product, and Textile. Awarded annually.

7423 ■ Chromatographic Society
Jordanhill Campus
76 S Brae Dr.
Glasgow G13 1PP, United Kingdom
Ph: 44 141 4341500
Fax: 44 141 4341519
E-mail: chromsoc@meetingmakers.co.uk
URL: http://www.chromsoc.com

7424 ■ Jubilee Medal
To recognize a young scientist for contributions to chromatography. Awarded annually. Established in 1982 to commemorate the Society's Silver Jubilee.

7425 ■ Martin Medal
To recognize a scientist who has made outstanding contributions to the advancement of separation science. Awarded annually to one or more recipients. Established in 1978 in honor of Professor A.J.P. Martin.

7426 ■ Circus Maniacs
Unit 62, Basepoint Business Centre
Oakfield Close
Tewkesbury Business Park
Tewkesbury
Gloucestershire GL20 8SD, United Kingdom
Ph: 44 1684 854412
Fax: 44 1684 854445
E-mail: info@circusmaniacs.com

URL: http://www.circusmaniacs.com

7427 ■ Circus Maniacs Awards
To recognize and encourage the circus skills of students aged seven years and older. Awarded in four categories: Acrobatics, Juggling and Manipulation, Equilbristics, and Trapeze and Aerial Acrobatics. Certificates are awarded when merited.

7428 ■ Unicycling Awards
To recognize and encourage the skills of unicycling students. Fifty levels are acknowledged within five groups: Beginners, Elementary, Intermediate, Advanced, and Super-Professional. Awarded when merited.

7429 ■ City and Guilds of London Institute
Michael Howell, Chm.
1 Giltspur St.
London EC1A 9DD, United Kingdom
Ph: 44 84 475430000
Fax: 44 20 72942400
E-mail: enquiry@city-and-guilds.co.uk
URL: http://www.cityandguilds.com/int-home.html

7430 ■ The Associateship of the City and Guilds of London Institute
Conferred exclusively on the engineering graduates of the City and Guilds College, Imperial College of Science, Technology and Medicine, London University. It denotes the ability to demonstrate, to the level equivalent to that of a degree of Bachelor of Science (Engineering), Bachelor of Engineering, or Master of Engineering, the understanding and application of the principles of a branch of Engineering or of Computing Science approved by the Institute. Established in 1887.

7431 ■ Fellowship of the City and Guilds of London Institute
The Fellowship is the highest distinction that can be given by the Institute. It signifies the ability to manage people, information, and operations in complex professional or technical situations and to formulate and implement strategies at the highest levels of responsibility. This achievement is to be demonstrated over a number of years in demanding appointments. The Fellowship may be conferred *Honoris Causa* (HonFCGI) on individuals whose professional achievement and advancement have been of outstanding significance over a period of years and/or who have made an outstanding contribution to the Institute's affairs. It was, until 1990, exclusive to former students of the City and Guilds College. Since 1990, applicants for the Fellowship may come from any profession or industry. Fellows of the Institute may be of any nationality and either sex. There is no restriction on the number of Fellowships which may be conferred annually. Established in 1892.

7432 ■ Graduateship of the City and Guilds of London Institute
To recognize achievements in industry, commerce, and the public services. The Graduateship denotes the ability to understand and apply the principles of a technical subject or professional activity. This ability is to be demonstrated in an employment-based context through the design, development, improvement, or critical assessment of an artifact, process, system, or service. Established in 1990.

7433 ■ Medals for Excellence
To recognize the candidates who have demonstrated outstanding ability in their particular subjects. Three types of medals are awarded: Bronze - to candidates gaining a City and Guilds qualification at Level 1 or 2; Silver - to candidates gaining a City and Guilds qualification at Level 3 or 4; and Gold - to candidates gaining a City and Guilds qualification at National Vocational Qualification (NVQ) Level 5 or gaining Graduateship

Awards are arranged in alphabetical order below their administering organizations

(GCGI), Associateship (ACGI), or Membership (MCGI) of the Institute. Medals are awarded to recognize excellence and a determined commitment to a high quality of work. To support an application, examples of work may be submitted which show: highly developed skills, outstanding knowledge of a subject directly related to the City and Guilds assessment undertaken, innovation and originality, enterprise, and versatility and adaptability. Also of relevance to an application would be examples that show a candidate has: made a significant contribution to his or her place of work, made a significant contribution to a special project, and overcome significant hardship or disability. Nominations will be accepted from any center in the UK and EC that is registered with City and Guilds. Medals will also be awarded to overseas candidates. Awarded annually.

7434 ■ Membership of the City and Guilds of London Institute
To recognize achievement in industry, commerce, and the public services. The Membership denotes the ability to exercise personal, professional responsibility for the design, development, or improvement of an artifact, process, system, or service. The emphasis is on individual competence and application of knowledge. The level of competence required is that which could be expected of a holder of a master's degree, with subsequent years of supervisory management or advanced technical experience, similar to that required for full membership of a major professional body. A diploma is awarded that specifies the subject area of the award. Holders are entitled to use the letters MCGI after their names and to wear the approved gown, hood, and mortar board. Established 1990.

7435 ■ City of London Corp.
Guildhall
PO Box 270
London EC2P 2EJ, United Kingdom
Ph: 44 20 7606 3030
E-mail: pro@cityoflondon.gov.uk
URL: http://www.cityoflondon.gov.uk

7436 ■ Clean City Awards
To raise the profile of effective waste management by recognizing and rewarding good practice and encouraging the wider adoption of the principles of "Reduce, Reuse and Recycle." Awarded annually in a variety of categories. Established in 1994.

7437 ■ Lord Mayor's Dragon Awards
To recognize the contribution made by London companies towards the social and economic regeneration of their local communities. A dragon statuette is awarded annually. Established in 1987.

7438 ■ Sustainable City Awards
To recognize and reward U.K. organizations and to promote outstanding achievements and innovation across all aspects of sustainability. Open to all sizes of organizations, from small charities to multinational corporations. Winners become eligible for the European Business Awards. Awarded annually. Established in 2001.

7439 ■ Clan Hunter Association
Madam Pauline Hunter, Clan Chief
Hunterston Castle
West Kilbride KA23 9QG, United Kingdom
E-mail: clanchief@clanhunter.com
URL: http://hunterclan.co.uk/html/home.htm

7440 ■ Order of the Royal Huntsman
For outstanding personal contributions to the Association. A plaque is awarded annually. Established in 1988.

7441 ■ Clinical Genetics Society
Ms. Dina Kotecha, Exec. Off.
Clinical Genetics Unit
Birmingham Women's Hospital

Edgbaston
Birmingham B15 2TG, United Kingdom
Ph: 44 121 6272634
Fax: 44 121 6236971
E-mail: cgs@bshg.org.uk
URL: http://www.bshg.org.uk

7442 ■ Carter Medal
To recognize an individual who has made an outstanding contribution to clinical genetics. A medal and an invitation to present a lecture is awarded annually. Established in 1984.

7443 ■ CNN MultiChoice African Journalist Awards
Kevin Talbot, Contact
CNN
PO Box 2537
London W1A 3HT, United Kingdom
Ph: 44 20 7693 0846
Fax: 44 20 7693 0847
E-mail: cnnafrica.competition@turner.com
URL: http://www.cnn.com/WORLD/africa/africanawards

7444 ■ CNN MultiChoice African Journalist Awards
To reinforce the importance of the journalist's role in Africa's development and to recognize journalistic talent across all disciplines. Open to African professional journalists (including freelancers) working on the continent for African-owned or -headquartered media organizations that produce a print publication or broadcast through an electronic medium (TV, radio, or Internet) primarily targeted to and received by an African audience. Awards are presented in 16 categories and include the Free Press Africa Award, Henry J. Kaiser Family Foundation Award, and the Mohamed Amin Photographic Award. In addition, the CNN MultiChoice African Journalist of the Year is named. Awarded annually. Established in 1995.

7445 ■ College of Piping
Robert Wallace, Contact
16-24 Otago St.
Glasgow G12 8JH, United Kingdom
Ph: 44 141 3343587
Fax: 44 141 3376068
E-mail: college@college-of-piping.co.uk
URL: http://www.college-of-piping.co.uk

7446 ■ Balvenie Medal
For recognition of services to piping. A silver medal, struck in Edinburgh, which carries a likeness of William Grant, the founder of The Glenfiddich Distillery, on the face is awarded annually. Established in 1985.

7447 ■ Glenfiddich Trophy
For recognition of outstanding piping. There are two panels of three judges for each of the two sections of the championships: 1. Piobaireachd, with each piper submitting six tunes in advance from which the judges will select one; and 2. March, Strathspey, and Reel, with the judges selecting three tunes from those submitted. The following prizes are awarded: first overall prize - one year's retention of the Glenfiddich Trophy, £600, and an inscribed sgian dhu; second prize - £300; and third prize - £150. Additional prizes are also awarded annually. Established in 1974.

7448 ■ Commonwealth Association of Architects
Mubasshar Hussain, Pres.
PO Box 508
London HA8 9XZ, United Kingdom
Ph: 44 20 89510550
Fax: 44 20 89510550
E-mail: info@comarchitect.org
URL: http://comarchitect.org

7449 ■ International Student Design Competition
To encourage innovation, creativity, and inter-

disciplinary work in design by architecture students. Each competition focuses on a specific design challenge. Open to all students who are studying in a Commonwealth country. Held every three years. First place winners receive a monetary prize of £1,200.

7450 ■ Robert Matthew Award
For recognition of specific buildings which, in the opinion of member institutes, show a significant response to the cultural, physical, and climatic context of the country. A scroll is awarded every three or four years at the CAA General Assembly. Established in 1965 in honor of Sir Robert Matthew, founder and first President of the Association. Formerly: (1983) CAA National Awards.

7451 ■ Commonwealth Association of Science, Technology and Mathematics Educators
Dr. Bridget Egan, Chair
University of Winchester
Faculty of Education
Winchester SO22 4NR, United Kingdom
E-mail: bridget.egan@winchester.ac.uk
Formerly: (1982) Commonwealth Association of Science and Mathematics Educators.

7452 ■ Alexander Prize
To recognize a woman or group of women for significant contributions to encouraging the scientific, technological, or mathematical education of girls or women in a situation of scarce resources. A monetary prize of £350 is awarded annually. Supported by the ASE, the UK Association for Science Education.

7453 ■ CASTME Awards
To encourage teaching of the social significance of science, technology and mathematics around the world. The scope of the awards is interpreted broadly, and social aspects include the relevance of science, technology and mathematics curricula to local needs and conditions and to the impact of technology, industry and agriculture on the local community. Teachers and officials (advisors, inspectors, etc.) working in primary, secondary and tertiary education in Commonwealth countries are eligible to enter. Individuals or syndicates may enter. The following awards are presented: Gold Prize (£500), Silver Prize (£400), Bronze Prize (£300), and the Alexander Prize (£350). Awarded annually. Established in 1974. Sponsored by the Commonwealth Foundation. Formerly: (1982) CASME Award.

7454 ■ Commonwealth Broadcasting Association
Sally-Ann Wilson, Sec. Gen.
17 Fleet St.
London EC4Y 1AA, United Kingdom
Ph: 44 20 75835550
Fax: 44 20 75835549
E-mail: sally-ann@cba.org.uk
URL: http://www.cba.org.uk

7455 ■ Elizabeth R. Award for Exceptional Contribution to Public Service Broadcasting
To honor an individual who has made an exceptional contribution to public service broadcasting. Awarded annually as part of the CBA Broadcasting Awards.

7456 ■ Rolls-Royce Award for Exceptional News Feature
For a news feature on radio or television that pushes out the boundary of media freedom. Awarded annually as part of the CBA Broadcasting Awards. Sponsored by Rolls-Royce.

7457 ■ Commonwealth Forestry Association
Jim Ball, Pres.
The Crib
Dinchope

Awards are arranged in alphabetical order below their administering organizations

Shropshire
Craven Arms SY7 9JJ, United Kingdom
Ph: 44 1588 672868
Fax: 44 870 0116645
E-mail: cfa@cfa-international.org
URL: http://www.cfa-international.org

7458 ■ Tom Gill Memorial Award
To encourage literary achievement in forestry related subjects. Essays may be submitted. A monetary award and a medal with Tom Gill's head and CFA logo are presented annually at each Commonwealth Forestry Conference. Bequeathed in 1972 by Tom Gill through his will.

7459 ■ Queen's Award for Forestry
To recognize an individual for mid-career forestry achievement with the potential to benefit and communicate to others in the land-based disciplines. Members of the Commonwealth between 30 and 55 years of age are eligible. A travel fellowship worth £2,000 approximately and a scroll signed by Her Majesty are awarded every 2 years. Established in 1987 by Her Majesty Queen Elizabeth.

7460 ■ Regional Awards
To recognize the professional excellence of foresters working at a national and regional level. Open to citizens of all nationalities, whether members or non-members. Awarded in five regions: Europe, Africa, South Asia, Southeast Asia and Pacific, and the Americas and the Caribbean. Awarded annually.

7461 ■ Young Forester Award
To support the professional development of foresters below 35 years of age through short-term work placement in a country other than their own. Designated placement as well as a bursary of between £1,000 and £1,500 are awarded annually.

7462 ■ Young Scientist Publication Award
To promote the careers of young forest scientists and managers through publication in the *International Forestry Review*. Candidates must be under 30 years of age, and must not have been published in any peer-reviewed international technical journal. A complimentary membership in CFA is awarded annually to up to four recipients.

7463 ■ Commonwealth Foundation
Dr. Danny Sriskandarajah, Interim Dir.
Marlborough House
Pall Mall
London SW1Y 5HY, United Kingdom
Ph: 44 20 79303783
Fax: 44 20 78398157
E-mail: geninfo@commonwealth.int
URL: http://www.commonwealthfoundation.com

7464 ■ Commonwealth Short Story Competition
To recognize short stories suitable for radio. The original short stories must be in English, be no more than 4 to 5 minutes in duration, and must be previously unpublished. Commonwealth citizens are eligible. Winning stories will be read by high quality actors, recorded in the BBC World Service Studios London and broadcast throughout the Commonwealth on national broadcasting stations. First prize also consists of £2,000; four regional winners receive £500. Awarded annually. Administered by Commonwealth Broadcasting Association.

7465 ■ Commonwealth Writers' Prize
To reward and encourage writing in all parts of the Commonwealth. A major prize of £10,000 for the best entry and an award of £5,000 for the best newly published book are awarded annually

for works of fiction. These are selected from eight regional winners, who each receive prizes of £1,000. Established in 1987.

7466 ■ Commonwealth Games Federation (Federation des Jeux du Commonwealth)
Michael Fennell, Pres.
2nd Fl., 138 Piccadilly
London W1J 7NR, United Kingdom
Ph: 44 20 74918801
Fax: 44 20 74097803
E-mail: info@thecgf.com
URL: http://www.thecgf.com

7467 ■ Commonwealth Games
To recognize athletic achievement among countries in the Commonwealth. Also known as the "Friendly Games," the event includes a minimum of 10 core sports and up to seven additional sports. Held every four years. Established in 1930 as the British Empire Games.

7468 ■ Commonwealth Partnership for Technology Management
Dr. Mihaela Y. Smith PJN, CEO
63 Catherine Pl.
London SW1E 6DY, United Kingdom
Ph: 44 20 77982500
Fax: 44 20 77982525
E-mail: smart.partnership@cptm.org
URL: http://www.cptm.org

7469 ■ Companions Awards
To honor distinguished professionals.

7470 ■ Commonwealth Pharmacists Association
Ivan Kotze, Pres.
1 Lambeth High St.
London SE1 7JN, United Kingdom
Ph: 44 20 75722216
Fax: 44 20 75722504
E-mail: admin@commonwealthpharmacy.org
URL: http://www.commonwealthpharmacy.org
Formerly: (2007) Commonwealth Pharmaceutical Association.

7471 ■ Albert Howells Award
Recognizes outstanding contributions to pharmacy at the commonwealth level. Applicants must be pharmacists. Awarded annually to one or more recipients.

7472 ■ Conservation Foundation
David Shreeve MA, Dir./Co-Founder
1 Kensington Gore
London SW7 2AR, United Kingdom
Ph: 44 20 75913111
Fax: 44 20 75913110
E-mail: info@conservationfoundation.co.uk
URL: http://www.conservationfoundation.co.uk

7473 ■ London's Green Corners Awards
To identify beautiful, unusual, unexpected, inspirational, and witty gardening projects in London. Awarded in 11 categories, including Edible Green Corners, No Man's Land, and Sacred Spaces. One winner from each category is chosen monthly, with overall winners selected annually.

7474 ■ Young Scientists for Rainforests
To enable young scientists to develop their ethno-medical research work. Grants of approximately £1,000 are available. Awarded throughout each year. Established in 1985.

7475 ■ Conservation Leadership Programme
Robyn Dalzen, Exec. Mgr.
c/o Birdlife International
Welbrook Center
Girton Rd.
Cambridge CB3 0NA, United Kingdom
Ph: 44 1223 277318
Fax: 44 1223 277200

E-mail: clp@birdlife.org
URL: http://conservation.bp.com

7476 ■ Conservation Follow-up Awards
To enable a team or individual to address a conservation issue raised by a previous project. Teams or individuals are eligible. Up to five $25,000 awards are available annually.

7477 ■ Conservation Leadership Award
To enable a longer-term project by a team that has had successful conservation projects in the past. Two $50,000 awards are granted annually.

7478 ■ Future Conservationist Awards
To recognize leadership potential in biodiversity conservation. Young conservation teams are eligible. Up to 20 awards of $12,500 are presented annually.

7479 ■ Kate Stokes Award
Recognizes a previous winner of the Follow-Up or Leadership Awards. An additional $5,000 is awarded annually.

7480 ■ Council for British Archaeology
Dr. Mike Heyworth MBE, Dir.
St. Mary's House
66 Bootham
York YO30 7BZ, United Kingdom
Ph: 44 1904 671417
Fax: 44 1904 671384
URL: http://www.britarch.ac.uk

7481 ■ Best Archaeological Book Award
To honor a publication that increases understanding of the past and introduces it to new audiences. Awarded biennially in even-numbered years.

7482 ■ Best Archaeological Project Award
To recognize the best archaeological project undertaken by a professional team or mixed professional/voluntary partnership demonstrating a commitment to recognized professional standards and ethics. Awarded biennially in even-numbered years. Formerly: ICI Award.

7483 ■ Grants for Publication
Grants are made available for publications which contribute substantially to research on problems of national or special regional significance. No grant will be made for the publication of records or of publications based exclusively on records, or for the publication of excavation reports where the excavation has been financed by government agencies. Awards are made three times a year by the CBA Publications Committee.

7484 ■ Keith Muckelroy Award
For published work on British maritime archaeology which best reflects the pioneering ideas and scholarly aspirations of the late Keith Muckelroy.

7485 ■ Young Archeologist of the Year Award
To recognize outstanding young archeologists. Awards are presented in two age categories: 8-12 and 13-16. Awarded biennially in even-numbered years. Sponsored by the Young Archeologists' Club.

7486 ■ Creative Scotland
Mr. Andrew Dixon, Chief Exec.
Waverley Gate
2-4 Waterloo Pl.
Edinburgh EH1 3EG, United Kingdom
Ph: 44 330 3332000
Fax: 44 131 5230001
E-mail: enquiries@creativescotland.com
URL: http://www.creativescotland.com
Formed by merger of: (2010) Scottish Arts Council; Scottish Screen.

7487 ■ Administrative Grant
To artistic organizations and projects.

Awards are arranged in alphabetical order below their administering organizations

7488 ■ Research Grant

7489 ■ Daiwa Anglo-Japanese Foundation
Prof. Marie Conte-Helm, Gen. Dir.
Daiwa Foundation Japan House
13/14 Cornwall Terr.
London NW1 4QP, United Kingdom
Ph: 44 20 74864348
Fax: 44 20 74862914
E-mail: office@dajf.org.uk
URL: http://www.dajf.org.uk

7490 ■ Daiwa Adrian Prizes
To recognize outstanding scientific collaboration between British and Japanese research teams in the field of pure science or applied science. Monetary prizes totaling £15,000 are awarded triennially. Established in 1992. Named in honor of Lord Adrian, an eminent scientist and founding trustee of the Foundation.

7491 ■ Daiwa Foundation Awards
To support relationships between institutions and organizations in a number of fields. Monetary awards ranging from £7,000 to £15,000 are presented to British and Japanese partners that work together. Awarded twice each year.

7492 ■ Daiwa Foundation Small Project Grants
To support individuals, societies, associations, or other bodies in the U.K. or Japan that promote integration between the two countries. Monetary awards ranging from £3,000 to £7,000 are presented to two or three projects annually.

7493 ■ Daiwa Scholarships
To enable outstanding young UK graduates of any discipline to acquire a lasting knowledge of Japanese life and culture and of spoken and written Japanese. Individuals must be citizens of the United Kingdom. Application deadline is December. Nineteen-month scholarships, including grants, tuition fees, and travel expenses, are awarded annually. One-year scholarships may be awarded to candidates with an excellent grasp of spoken and written Japanese. Awarded annually to numerous recipients. Established in 1991.

7494 ■ The Royal Society-Daiwa Anglo-Japanese Foundation Joint Project Grants
To support collaborative projects between British and Japanese researchers in the field of science. A relationship between both parties should already be established. A monetary award up to £6,000 is presented annually.

7495 ■ Data Publishers Association
Jerry Gosney, Exec. Dir.
Queens House
28 Kingsway
London WC2B 6JR, United Kingdom
Ph: 44 20 74050836
Fax: 44 20 74044167
E-mail: info@dpa.org.uk
URL: http://www.dpa.org.uk

7496 ■ Advertising Sales Team of the Year
To recognize the teams that have made a significant impact on the business. Awarded annually.

7497 ■ Best Marketing of the Year
To recognize subscription and marketing campaigns. Awarded annually.

7498 ■ Directory of the Year - Business
To recognize consistently high-quality directory, either in print or online. Awarded annually.

7499 ■ Directory of the Year - Consumer
To recognize consistently high-quality directory, either in print or online. Awarded annually.

7500 ■ New Product of the Year
To recognize an outstanding new directory, database, or search engine. Awarded annually.

7501 ■ Online Directory of the Year - Business
To recognize outstanding Web sites, CDs, search engines, or other online products. Awarded annually.

7502 ■ Online Directory of the Year - Consumer
To recognize outstanding Web sites, CDs, search engines, or other online products. Awarded annually.

7503 ■ Printer of the Year
To recognize a printer with a proven track record of excelling in his or her field. Awarded annually.

7504 ■ Publisher of the Year
To honor the most successful publisher of the year. Awarded annually.

7505 ■ Subscription Sales Team of the Year
To recognize the teams that have made a significant impact on the business. Awarded annually.

7506 ■ Supplier of the Year
To recognize a supplier with a proven track record of excelling in their field. Awarded annually.

7507 ■ Delphinium Society
Mrs. Shirley E. Bassett, Membership Sec.
Summerfield
Church Rd.
Biddestone
Chippenham SN14 7DP, United Kingdom
E-mail: david.bassett@care4free.net
URL: http://www.backyardgardener.com/delp

7508 ■ Delphinium Society Awards
To encourage the culture of delphiniums and the production of new and improved varieties by sponsoring competitions. Cups, medals, and certificates of merit are awarded.

7509 ■ Design Business Association
Deborah Dawton, Chief Exec.
35-39 Old St.
London EC1V 9HX, United Kingdom
Ph: 44 20 72519229
Fax: 44 20 72519221
E-mail: deborah.dawton@dba.org.uk
URL: http://www.dba.org.uk

7510 ■ Design Effectiveness Awards
To recognize design projects, either re-designs or new products, that demonstrate the effectiveness of design in significant situations for a client or a company. Awards are presented in 14 categories each year.

7511 ■ Design Council
David Kester, CEO
34 Bow St.
London WC2E 7DL, United Kingdom
Ph: 44 20 74205200
Fax: 44 20 74205300
E-mail: info@designcouncil.org.uk
URL: http://www.designcouncil.org.uk

7512 ■ British Design Awards
To promote the importance of good design by identifying and publicizing outstanding examples of British design within the areas of medical equipment, automotive, computer software, consumer and contract goods, and engineering products and components. Products that have been in production and service for some time and were designed by a British designer working in the U.K. or abroad, or by a designer resident in the U.K. are eligible. Certificates are awarded

and publicity and the use of the British Design Award logo are also provided. Established in 1957. Formerly: Design Council Awards.

7513 ■ Prince Philip Prize for the Designer of the Year
To recognize the designer who has made the greatest contribution to design. A certificate is presented to the winner at a ceremony at Buckingham Palace by Prince Philip. Awarded annually. Established in 1958. Formerly: Duke of Edinburgh's Designer's Prize.

7514 ■ Digital and Screen Printing Association
Mr. John Keith, Bus. Mgr.
Innovation Way
South Yorkshire
Barnsley S75 1JL, United Kingdom
Ph: 44 1226 321202
Fax: 44 1226 294797
E-mail: info@prismuk.org
URL: http://www.prismuk.org

7515 ■ DSPA Awards for Printing
For an individual who demonstrates excellence in printing through the use of the latest digital technologies.

7516 ■ Direct Marketing Association
David Metcalfe, Chm.
DMA House
70 Margaret St.
London W1W 8SS, United Kingdom
Ph: 44 207 2913300
Fax: 44 207 3234426
E-mail: info@dma.org.uk
URL: http://www.dma.org.uk
Formerly: (2004) British Direct Marketing Association.

7517 ■ DMA Awards
To recognize outstanding work in direct marketing in the United Kingdom. Presented in 35 categories among the broader classifications of Business Sectors, Digital, Craft, Other Channels, and Special Awards. A trophy is presented to the winner in each of the categories. A Grand Prix award is presented to the overall winner for the most outstanding work selected from the winner of each category. Awarded annually. Established in 1980. Formerly: BDMA/Post Office Direct Marketing Awards; (2004) DMA/Royal Mail Direct Marketing Awards.

7518 ■ Direct Selling Association - United Kingdom
Joanne Stevens, Treas.
30 Billing Rd.
Northampton
London NN1 5DQ, United Kingdom
Ph: 44 1604 625700
E-mail: info@dsa.org.uk
URL: http://www.dsa.org.uk

7519 ■ Excellence Award
To recognize a company for outstanding success in direct selling. Awarded annually.

7520 ■ Dorset Natural History and Archaeological Society
Dorset County Museum
High West St.
Dorchester DT1 1XA, United Kingdom
Ph: 44 1305 262735
E-mail: enquiries@dorsetcountymuseum.co.uk
URL: http://80.68.95.48/~dcmresearch/index.html
Formed by merger of: (1928) Dorset Natural History; Antiquarian Field Club.

7521 ■ Cecil Memorial Trust Competition
To encourage essays on Dorset chemistry or electricity as applied to healing and medicine, farm or garden cultivation, and motor power and machinery. Open to individuals aged between 16

Awards are arranged in alphabetical order below their administering organizations

and 30 who were either born in Dorset or has lived there for at least a year. A monetary prize of £250 is awarded annually.

7522 ■ Mansel-Pleydell Trust Essay Competition
To encourage essays on Dorset archaeology, geology, local, and natural history containing original research and material hitherto unpublished. Papers must be submitted by persons living in Dorset or having past or present connections with the county. A monetary prize of £1,000, along with publication in the *Proceedings of the Dorset Natural History and Archaeology Society*, is awarded to long essays (approximately 10,000 words). Shorter essays (approximately 2,000 words) on any subject related to Dorset generally compete for a monetary prize of £250. Held annually. Established in 1905 in honor of John Clavell Mansel-Pleydell, a founder of the Dorset Natural History and Antiquarian Field Club.

7523 ■ Dracula Society
Bernard Davies, Pres.
PO Box 30848
London W12 0GY, United Kingdom
E-mail: info@thedraculasociety.org.uk
URL: http://www.thedraculasociety.org.uk

7524 ■ Children of the Night Award
To the best piece of literature publishing in the Gothic (including horror and supernatural) genre for the previous year. Open to novels, short stories, and biography. Awarded annually.

7525 ■ Hamilton Deane Award
For recognition of the most significant contribution to the gothic genre in the performing arts. Any performance or technical contribution to a production in a given year is eligible. The winner is voted upon by the members of the Society. A framed scroll is awarded annually. Established in 1974 in memory of Hamilton Deane, the dramatizer of "Dracula." Formerly: (1977) Actor of the Year Award.

7526 ■ Edinburgh Festival Fringe
Tim Hawkins, Gen. Mgr.
180 High St.
Edinburgh EH1 1QS, United Kingdom
Ph: 44 131 226 0026
Fax: 44 131 226 0016
E-mail: admin@edfringe.com
URL: http://www.edfringe.com

7527 ■ Amused Moose Laugh Off Awards
To recognize the best comics in the United Kingdom and Ireland. Qualifying comics progress through heats, quarterfinals, and semi-finals, with the top eight comics vying at the Fringe festival. Awarded annually. Sponsored by the Amused Moose Comedy Club.

7528 ■ The Arches Brick Award
To recognize the Fringe performance that deserves to be staged at the Glasgow Theatre. Open to all performance and disciplines, including dance, physical theater, and text-based work. The winning performance receives a monetary prize of £1,000 toward performance expenses. Awarded annually. Established in 2007.

7529 ■ Evening News Awards
To recognize outstanding work by local companies during the Fringe festival. Two awards are presented: Best Musical Award and Best Play Award. Awarded annually. Sponsored by the *Evening News* newspaper. Established in 2008.

7530 ■ Fringe First Awards
To recognize the best new writing among the theater, dance and physical theater, musical and opera, and children's shows sections of the Fringe festival. Presented weekly during the Fringe to any number of recipients.

7531 ■ Fringe Review Outstanding Theatre Awards
To honor theater or theater-related productions that are deemed to be outstanding. Up to three productions are selected to receive a certificate and engraved teapot award. Presented annually. Sponsored by the *Fringe Review*.

7532 ■ Funny Women Awards
To recognize the best new female comedy acts at the Fringe festival. Open to any act that performs at least five minutes of comedy, including stand-up, funny songs and poetry, impressions, ventriloquism, and sketch and character acts. Awarded annually.

7533 ■ Holden Street Theatre Award
To recognize the Fringe performance that deserves to be staged at Holden Street Theatres in Adelaide, Australia. Criteria include artistic merit, production value, touring possibilities, venue compatibility, marketing viability, and the Holden Street Theater's core audience. The winning production receives an all-expense paid premiere in Adelaide, Australia. Awarded annually.

7534 ■ Mervyn Stutter's Spirit of the Fringe Awards
To honor the talent, hard work, and pluck demanded of performers from all genres at the Fringe festival. Up to six awards are presented annually. Established in 1992.

7535 ■ The MTM:UK Musical Theatre Matters Awards
To champion the next generation of musical theater producers, writers, and shows, recognizing the companies creating new and exciting musical theater work, and the individuals behind it. To qualify, the production must be playing during the second and third week of the Fringe festival. Awarded annually. Established in 2007.

7536 ■ The Stage Awards for Acting Excellence
To recognize acting excellence at the Edinburgh Festival Fringe. Companies/performers listed in the Theatre section of the Fringe program are considered. Presented in four categories: Best Actor, Best Actress, Best Ensemble, and Best Solo Show. Winners are determined by a review team from *The Stage* newspaper. Awarded annually. Established in 1995.

7537 ■ Carol Tambor Best of Edinburgh Award
To recognize the best new play of the Fringe festival. All productions given 4 or 5 stars by *The Scotsman* reviewers are eligible. The winning production receives an all-expense paid premiere in New York City, including publicity and theater expenses. Awarded annually. Established in 2004.

7538 ■ ThreeWeeks Editors' Awards
To honor the top 10 happenings at the Fringe, from people, plays, and productions to companies, venues, and even whole festivals. Judged and selected by the editors of the *ThreeWeeks* festival newspaper. Awarded annually.

7539 ■ Jack Tinker Spirit of the Fringe Award
To recognize people, production, or performances for outstanding talent, dedication, and creativity at the Fringe festival. Awarded annually.

7540 ■ Zebra Awards
To celebrate achievement in designing posters for the Fringe festival. Posters are judged on the degree to which they are eye-catching, informative, and marketable. Monetary prizes are awarded annually.

7541 ■ Edinburgh Geological Society
Mrs. Christine L. Thompson, Membership Sec.
85 Grange Loan
Edinburgh EH9 2ED, United Kingdom

Ph: 44 131 6675429
E-mail: membership@edinburghgeolsoc.org
URL: http://www.edinburghgeolsoc.org

7542 ■ Clough Medal
To recognize a geologist whose original work has increased the knowledge of the geology of Scotland and/or north England, and has significantly advanced the knowledge of any aspect of geology. A medal is awarded annually. Established in 1935.

7543 ■ Clough Memorial Award
To recognize a geologist of British nationality and up to 35 years old whose research on some aspect of the geology of Scotland or the north of England is considered as having outstanding merit. Awarded biennially in odd-numbered years. Established in 1962.

7544 ■ Edinburgh International Film Festival
Ginnie Atkinson, Managing Dir.
Filmhouse
88 Lothian Rd.
Edinburgh EH3 9BZ, United Kingdom
Ph: 44 131 228 4051
Fax: 44 131 229 5501
E-mail: info@edfilmfest.org.uk
URL: http://www.edfilmfest.org.uk

7545 ■ Edinburgh International Film Festival
For recognition of outstanding films screened at the Festival. The following prizes are awarded: Michael Powell Award - for the best new British feature; McLaren Award - for best new British animation; Standard Life Audience Award - audience vote; Guardian New Director's Award recognizing innovation; Kodak U.K. Film Council Award - for best British short film; European Film Academy Short Film Award/Priz UIP - for the best new filmmaker; and Saltire Society Award - for best short documentary. Held annually. Established in 1947.

7546 ■ Emap Ltd.
Greater London House
Hampstead Rd.
London NW1 7EJ, United Kingdom
Ph: 44 20 7728 4692
URL: http://www.emap.com

7547 ■ BETT Awards
To recognize extraordinary digital products intended for the education marketplace. Open to products that have already been launched in the open marketplace that can be purchased as an individual item or are freely available without charge. Awarded annually in 12 categories.

7548 ■ Energy Institute
Louise Kingham, Chief Exec.
61 New Cavendish St.
London W1G 7AR, United Kingdom
Ph: 44 20 74677100
Fax: 44 20 72551472
E-mail: info@energyinst.org
URL: http://www.energyinst.org

7549 ■ Melchett Medal
For outstanding work involving the scientific preparation or use of energy, the results of which have recently been made available to the community. Awarded annually. Established in 1930.

7550 ■ Thring Award
For outstanding project which demonstrates the likelihood of significant energy savings from recommendations. A monetary prize of £100 is awarded annually.

7551 ■ Engineers' Company
Mr. John H. Robinson, Master
Wax Chandlers Hall
6 Gresham St.

Awards are arranged in alphabetical order below their administering organizations

London EC2V 7AD, United Kingdom
Ph: 44 20 77264830
Fax: 44 20 77264820
E-mail: clerk@engineerscompany.org.uk
URL: http://www.engineerscompany.org.uk

7552 ■ Baroness Platt of Writtle Award
To individuals pursuing final year studies in the Engineering Council's Incorporated Engineer Grade. A medal and monetary prize of £1,000 are awarded annually.

7553 ■ Engineering Heritage Award
To honor an individual for a significant contribution to the understanding and development of engineering through the interpretation of historical sites or processes. Awarded periodically.

7554 ■ Fiona and Nicholas Hawley Award
To honor a young engineer for the application of proven technology to positively improve the environment. Candidates must be residents of the United Kingdom under 30 years of age. A medal and monetary prize of £5,000 are awarded annually.

7555 ■ Mercia Prize
To encourage postgraduate study in medical engineering. Candidates must be under 30 years old. A medal and monetary prize of £500 are awarded.

7556 ■ Service Awards
To recognize undergraduates, postgraduates, and engineering training students and staff for service to the industry and the Company. Awarded in a variety of categories.

7557 ■ Cadzow Smith Award
To encourage business enterprise in young engineers by recognizing excellence on an accredited undergraduate engineering course. A medal and monetary prize of £2,000 are awarded annually.

7558 ■ Stephenson Award
To honor an individual for excellence in inspiring young people into engineering with particular reference to mechanical engineering. A medal and monetary prize of £500 are awarded annually. Established in 1997.

7559 ■ Water Engineering Award
To honor an individual for postgraduate research in water engineering. A medal is awarded annually.

7560 ■ English Centre of International PEN
Dr. Lisa Appignanesi, Pres.
60 Farringdon Rd.
London EC1R 3GA, United Kingdom
Ph: 44 20 73242535
E-mail: enquiries@englishpen.org
URL: http://www.englishpen.org

7561 ■ J. R. Ackerley Prize for Autobiography
For recognition of outstanding literary achievement. Trustees of the J.R. Ackerley Trust consider submissions are not required autobiographies published during the previous calendar year. A monetary prize of £2,000 is awarded annually at the PEN International Writers' Day. Established in 1982 to honor Joe Randolph Ackerley by his sister Nancy.

7562 ■ Golden PEN Award
To recognize the writers whose work has given both pleasure to readers and inspiration to their fellow writers. An engraved golden pen and £1,000 in charitable donations is awarded when merited.

7563 ■ Hessell-Tiltman Prize
To recognize a historical work of high literary merit covering any period until the end of the second world war. A monetary prize of £3,000 is awarded annually. Established in 2002 through a bequest by Marjorie Hessell-Tiltman.

7564 ■ Entertainment and Leisure Software Publishers Association
Michael Rawlinson, Dir. Gen.
167 Wardour St.
London W1F 8WL, United Kingdom
Ph: 44 20 75340580
Fax: 44 20 75340581
E-mail: info@elspa.com
URL: http://www.elspa.com

7565 ■ Volume Sales Achievement Awards
Recognizes retail sales of published software titles achieving 100,000 (Silver), 200,000 (Gold), 300,000 (Platinum), 600,000 (Double Platinum), and 1 million (Diamond) units within 12 months of release.

7566 ■ Environmental Association for Universities and Colleges
University of Gloucestershire
The Park, Cheltenham
Gloucestershire GL50 2RH, United Kingdom
Ph: 44 1242 714321
E-mail: info@eauc.org.uk
URL: http://www.eauc.org.uk

7567 ■ Green Gown Awards
To recognize exceptional environmental and sustainability initiatives being undertaken by universities and the learning and skills sector across the United Kingdom. Awarded annually in 12 categories. Established in 2004.

7568 ■ Environmental Transport Association
Andrew Davis, Dir.
68 High St.
Surrey
Weybridge KT13 8RS, United Kingdom
Ph: 44 845 3891010
Fax: 44 845 3891015
E-mail: eta@eta.co.uk
URL: http://www.eta.co.uk

7569 ■ Green Car Awards
To recognize the most environmentally sound cars based on their power, emissions, fuel efficiency, and the amount of noise they make. Awarded in a variety of categories, including small family car, city car, off-road car, and luxury car. One overall winner is named the Green Car of the Year. Awarded annually. Formerly: Green Apple Awards.

7570 ■ Erin Arts Centre
Raymond Leppard, Pres.
Victoria Square
Port Erin IM9 6LD, United Kingdom
Ph: 44 1624 835858
Fax: 44 1624 836658
E-mail: information@erinartscentre.com
URL: http://www.erinartscentre.com
Formerly: Mananan Festival Trust.

7571 ■ Lionel Tertis International Viola Festival and Competition (Internationaler Wettbewerb und Seminar fur Bratsche)
To recognize outstanding viola players. Individuals of any nationality not over 30 years of age are eligible. The following prizes are awarded: first place - Ruth Fernoy Memorial Prize (£3,000); second place - Artur Rubinstein Memorial Prize (£2,000); and third place - Lilian Tertis Award (£1,500). In addition, several special awards may be presented. Held triennially. Established in 1980.

7572 ■ Estuarine and Coastal Sciences Association
Dr. Mark Fitsimons, Sec.
University of Plymouth
Biogeochemistry Research Centre
Plymouth
Devon PL4 8AA, United Kingdom
E-mail: jwilson@tcd.ie
URL: http://www.ecsa-news.org

7573 ■ Subsistence Award
For student member.

7574 ■ Travel Award
For student member.

7575 ■ Eurobest Advertising Festival
Greater London House
Hampstead Rd.
London NW1 7EJ, United Kingdom
Ph: 44 20 7728 4034
Fax: 44 20 7728 4044
URL: http://www.eurobest.com

7576 ■ EuroBest Awards
For recognition of advertising excellence for campaigns presented in Europe across a range of media categories: Print, TV/Cinema, Outdoor, Radio, Interactive, Direct, and Integrated. Trophies are awarded annually at the awards ceremony in December. Established in 1988.

7577 ■ European Association for Cancer Research
Richard Marais, Sec. Gen.
University of Nottingham
School of Pharmacy
Nottingham NG7 2RD, United Kingdom
Ph: 44 115 9515116
Fax: 44 115 9515115
E-mail: eacr@nottingham.ac.uk
URL: http://www.eacr.org

7578 ■ Anthony Dipple Carcinogenesis Award
Recognizes outstanding contributions to research in the field of carcinogenesis. Awarded biennially in even-numbered years. Sponsored by Oxford University Press.

7579 ■ Faustus Poster Awards
Recognizes the best poster as selected by the EACR Committee for Reviewing Posters.

7580 ■ Travel Fellowships
To enable cancer researchers, preferably under 35 years of age, to undertake further research in another location. Researchers must be sponsored by members of the Association. Fellowships of up to 2,500 Euros are awarded annually.

7581 ■ Young Cancer Researcher Award
To recognize a young cancer researcher (under the age of 40) from European countries to give a presentation at an EACR meeting. A monetary prize of 2,000 Euro plus expenses (travel, accommodation and congress fees) is awarded annually.

7582 ■ Young Cancer Researcher Award Lecture
Assists young scientists to attend conferences in order to present papers. Young scientists showing active participation by submission of abstracts for poster or oral presentation at the meeting are eligible. A monetary prize of 2,000 Euro plus travel expenses to present the paper are awarded biennially in even-numbered years.

7583 ■ European Association for Chinese Studies
Prof. Roel Sterckx, Sec.
University of Cambridge
Department of East Asian Studies
Sidgwick Ave.
Cambridge CB3 9DA, United Kingdom
E-mail: rs10009@cam.ac.uk
URL: http://www.soas.ac.uk/eacs

7584 ■ Young Scholar Award
To encourage research in Chinese studies among young scholars, especially, but not

Awards are arranged in alphabetical order below their administering organizations

exclusively, scholars studying and working at European institutions. Candidates must be 35 years of age or younger, and their rank of academic employment should be below that of Associate Professor or Senior Lecturer or the equivalent ranks in other systems. Awarded biennially in even-numbered years. Established in 2004.

7585 ■ European Association for Computer Assisted Language Learning
Mrs. Toni Patton, Sec.
University of Ulster
School of Languages, Literatures and Cultures
Coleraine BT52 1SA, United Kingdom
E-mail: t.patton@ulster.ac.uk
URL: http://www.eurocall-languages.org

7586 ■ EUROCALL Research Award
Recognizes an outstanding original article on computer-assisted and technology-enhanced language learning. Awarded annually.

7587 ■ European Association for Cranio-Maxillofacial Surgery
Mrs. Jill McFarland, Sec. Gen.
PO Box 85
Midhurst GU29 9WS, United Kingdom
Ph: 44 1730 810951
Fax: 44 1730 812042
E-mail: secretariat@eacmfs.org
URL: http://www.eurofaces.com

7588 ■ Educational Grants
To support trainee members in attending a rolling program of education. A monetary grant of 150 Euros is awarded annually.

7589 ■ Leibinger Prize
To support trainee members who wish to spend a period of targeted education and training within Europe away from their host programs. Two monetary prizes, of 5,000 Euros and 2,500 Euros, are awarded biennially.

7590 ■ Mondeal Prize
To recognize members who presented or published a meritorious paper in the period leading to the biennial congress. A monetary prize of 5,000 Euros is awarded biennially in even-numbered years.

7591 ■ Hugo Obwegeser Travelling Scholarship
To encourage trainee members who wish to travel to other countries to enhance their education and training.

7592 ■ European Association for Palliative Care
Sheila Payne, Pres.
Lancaster University
Institute for Health Research
Lancaster LA1 4YT, United Kingdom
Ph: 44 152 459 3701
E-mail: s.a.payne@lancaster.ac.uk
URL: http://www.eapcnet.eu

7593 ■ Young Investigator Award
To recognize a young researcher for outstanding contributions to palliative care in Europe. Awarded biennially in odd-numbered years.

7594 ■ European Association for the Study of Obesity
113-119 High St.
Hampton Hill
Middlesex TW12 1NJ, United Kingdom
Ph: 44 20 8783 2256
Fax: 44 20 8979 6700
E-mail: enquiries@easo.org
URL: http://www.easo.org

7595 ■ Friedrich Wassermann Award for Lifetime Achievement
To recognize a European researcher for out-

standing and sustained scientific contributions to the advancement of knowledge in the field of obesity. Candidates must be senior scientists who have carried out the majority of their work in Europe. Awarded biennially in odd-numbered years.

7596 ■ Young Investigators United Best Thesis Award
To recognize younger scientists and their contribution to the obesity field. Candidates must be nearly completing or have completed their PhD thesis, and must have carried out the majority of their work in Europe. A certificate and monetary prize of 1,000 Euros are awarded biennially in odd-numbered years.

7597 ■ European Consortium for Political Research
Clare Dekker, Admin. Dir.
University of Essex
Wivenhoe Park
Colchester CO4 3SQ, United Kingdom
Ph: 44 1206 872501
Fax: 44 1206 872500
E-mail: ecpr@essex.ac.uk
URL: http://www.ecprnet.eu

7598 ■ Jean Blondel PhD Prize
To honor the best thesis in politics. Awarded annually. Established in 2003.

7599 ■ Mattei Dogan Foundation Prize in European Political Sociology
To recognize a scholar who has produced a major contribution to the advancement of political sociology by an ensemble of outstanding scientific publications and constructive professional achievements. A monetary prize of US$3000 is awarded biennially in odd-numbered years.

7600 ■ Lifetime Achievement Award
To recognize a scholar who has made an outstanding contribution to European political science. Awarded biennially in odd-numbered years. Established in 2005.

7601 ■ Stein Rokkan Prize in Comparative Social Science Research
For social science research. Awarded biennially in even-numbered years. Established in 1981.

7602 ■ Standing Group Grants
To support activities by existing standing groups, or to provide the funds to establish a new standing group. Up to £500 per year is awarded. In addition, Standing Group Summer School Grants up to £4,000 per year are also available.

7603 ■ Wildenmann Prize
To recognize a young colleague for an outstanding paper at the workshop. Candidates must be within five years of receiving his or her PhD. Awarded annually. Established in 1997.

7604 ■ European Council for Cardiovascular Research
Michael Mulvany, Pres.
Hampton Medical Conferences Ltd.
113-119 High St.
Hampton Hill
Middlesex
London TW12 1NJ, United Kingdom
Ph: 44 20 89798300
Fax: 44 20 89796700
E-mail: eccr@hamptonmedical.com
URL: http://www.eccr.org

7605 ■ ECCR Scholarships
To persons under 40 years of age.

7606 ■ European Council of International Schools
Jean Vahey, Exec. Dir.
21B Lavant St.
Hampshire

Petersfield GU32 3EL, United Kingdom
Ph: 44 1730 268244
Fax: 44 1730 267914
E-mail: ecis@ecis.org
URL: http://www.ecis.org

7607 ■ Adult Award for Promotion of International Education
To recognize an adult for exemplary contributions to the promotion of international education. A plaque may be awarded annually by each ECIS member institution.

7608 ■ Student Award for International Understanding
To recognize students who are good representatives of their countries, display a positive attitude towards the life and culture of others, have the ability to converse in at least two languages, are contributing forces in the life of the school, and have an ability to bring different people together in a sense of community, thus furthering the cause of international understanding. Nominees are selected by the student's school faculty. Awarded annually to a student in each participating member school.

7609 ■ European Dystonia Federation
Alistair Newton, Exec. Dir.
2 Muttoes Ct.
St. Andrews KY16 9AY, United Kingdom
Ph: 44 77 36625450
Fax: 44 1334 474662
E-mail: sec@dystonia-europe.org
URL: http://www.dystonia-europe.org

7610 ■ David Marsden Award
To honor the best research paper on dystonia by a scientist under age 40. A monetary prize of 2,500 Euros is presented biennially in odd-numbered years. Established in 2003.

7611 ■ European Federation of Societies for Ultrasound in Medicine and Biology
Lynne Rudd, Gen. Sec.
36 Portland Pl.
London W1B 1LS, United Kingdom
Ph: 44 20 70997140
Fax: 44 20 74367934
E-mail: lynnerudd@efsumb.org
URL: http://www.efsumb.org/intro/home.asp

7612 ■ Young Investigators Award
To recognize and encourage new work in the fields of clinical and/or basic research. Members under 35 years of age are eligible. A monetary prize is awarded annually for first and second place recipients at the Federation Congress. Established in 1990.

7613 ■ European Federation of the Contact Lens Industry
Steve Wheeler, Exec. Dir.
108 Stortford Hall Park
Bishops Stortford
Herts
Chelmsford CM23 5AN, United Kingdom
Ph: 44 1279 659235
E-mail: steve@efclin.com
URL: http://www.efclin.com

7614 ■ EFCLIN Award
To recognize individuals who have contributed to the contact lens industry in an outstanding way. Awarded annually. Established in 1996.

7615 ■ Laureate Award
This, the Federation's most prestigious award, is given to honor an individual who has given an outstanding and long-term contribution to the Federation. Awarded periodically. Established in 1998.

Awards are arranged in alphabetical order below their administering organizations

7616 ■ Technology Award
To recognize individuals who have contributed to the contact lens industry with innovative technological developments. Awarded annually. Established in 1996.

7617 ■ European General Galvanizers Association
(Association Europeene des Galvanisateurs)
Mrs. Frances Holmes, Sec.
Maybrook House
Godstone Rd.
Caterham CR3 6RE, United Kingdom
Ph: 44 188 3331277
Fax: 44 188 3331287
E-mail: mail@egga.com
URL: http://www.egga.com

7618 ■ Bablik Medal
For individuals nominated by members.

7619 ■ European Orthodontic Society
David Suarez Quintanilla, Pres.
49 Hallam St., Flat 20
London W1W 6JN, United Kingdom
Ph: 44 20 76370367
Fax: 44 20 73230410
E-mail: eoslondon@aol.com
URL: http://www.eoseurope.org

7620 ■ Distinguished Teacher Award
To honor a well-known speaker and teacher in the orthodontic field. The recipient is invited to undertake four one-day lectures in different areas of Europe. Awarded annually.

7621 ■ Ernest Sheldon Friel Memorial Lecture
For recognition of work in the field of orthodontics. The award is associated with a named lecture known specifically as the Friel Memorial Lecture, which is presented at an annual congress and published in the Society's journal. A monetary prize of £2,500 is payable upon publication of the lecture in the *European Journal of Orthodontics*. Established in 1973 by the family of the late Professor Ernest Sheldon Friel to commemorate his services to orthodontics and to the European Orthodontic Society, of which he was a president and honorary member.

7622 ■ Grants to Eastern Europeans
Provides academic colleagues from Eastern European countries the chance to visit educational facilities in the West for a period of up to one month. Full-time university postgraduate teachers are eligible. A monetary sum of £2,000 is awarded annually.

7623 ■ W. J. B. Houston Research Awards
To recognize outstanding presentations at the annual congress. Awards are presented for the best research paper and the best poster presenting the results of original research on a topic of orthodontic interest. Papers and posters must be presented in English by a member under the age of 35. A scroll and monetary award of £1,000 is presented in each category. Established in 1993 in memory of W. J. B. Houston, honorary editor and past president and secretary of the Society.

7624 ■ W. J. B. Houston Scholarship Award
To recognize the research worker who has submitted the best prospective research proposal to the Society. A monetary award of no more than £60,000 is awarded every three years. Established in 1993 in memory of W.J.B. Houston, honorary editor and past president and secretary of the Society.

7625 ■ Poster Award
To recognize an outstanding poster presented by a non-member at the meeting on any topic. Three awards of £500 are awarded annually.

7626 ■ Research Grants
Provides funding for research grants. Grants ranging from £5,000 to £15,000 are awarded each year.

7627 ■ Beni Solow Award
To recognize an outstanding article published in the *European Journal of Orthodontics*. A monetary prize of £2,500 and a certificate are awarded annually.

7628 ■ European Process Safety Centre
Christian Jochum, Dir.
165-189 Railway Terrace
Rugby CV21 3HQ, United Kingdom
Ph: 44 1 788 534409
Fax: 44 1 788 560833
E-mail: epsc@icheme.org
URL: http://www.epsc.org

7629 ■ EPSC Award
Recognizes outstanding achievement in advancing the theory or practice of process safety in Europe. Awarded annually. Established in 1998.

7630 ■ European Society for Organ Transplantation
Mr. J.L.R. Forsythe, Sec.
Royal Infirmary of Edinburgh
Little France Crescent
Transplant Unit, Rm. S3316
Edinburgh EH16 5SA, United Kingdom
Ph: 44 131 2421715
Ph: 44 131 2421739
Fax: 44 131 2421739
E-mail: secretariat@esot.org
URL: http://www.esot.org

7631 ■ Best Abstract Presentation Award
To honor the best clinical/research abstract and presentation. Awarded annually.

7632 ■ Best Poster Award
To recognize the three best poster presentations at the ESOT Congress. A monetary prize of 1,000 Euros is awarded to each recipient biennially in odd-numbered years.

7633 ■ Biotest Best Oral Presentation Award
To honor the three best clinical and three best basic science oral presentations. A monetary prize of 2,500 Euros is awarded to six recipients annually. Sponsored by Biotest.

7634 ■ Euroliver Foundation Award
To recognize young transplant clinicians or coordinators for contributions to the expansion of the donor pool or the quality of life after transplantation. Candidates must be under 40 years of age. A monetary prize of 1,000 Euros is awarded to three recipients biennially in odd-numbered years. Funded by the Euroliver Foundation.

7635 ■ Young Investigator Award
To recognize young clinicians or scientists for outstanding abstracts submitted for the ESOT Congress. Candidates must be under 25 years of age. A monetary prize of 1,500 Euros is awarded to 10 recipients biennially in odd-numbered years.

7636 ■ European Society for Paediatric Endocrinology
Dr. Franco Chiarelli, Sec. Gen.
BioScientifica
Euro House
22 Apex Ct.
Woodlands
Bristol BS32 4JT, United Kingdom
Ph: 44 1454 642246
Fax: 44 1454 642222
E-mail: espe@eurospe.org
URL: http://www.eurospe.org

7637 ■ Henning Andersen Prizes
For the most highly rated clinical and experimental abstracts. Awarded annually. Established in 1985.

7638 ■ Hormone Research Prize
For best original paper published in *Hormone Research*. Awarded annually. Established in 2004.

7639 ■ Outstanding Clinician Award
To recognize an individual for an outstanding clinical contribution. Awarded annually. Established in 2001.

7640 ■ Andrea Prader Prize
To recognize an individual for lifetime achievement in teaching and research. Awarded annually.

7641 ■ Research Award
To recognize an individual for outstanding research achievement in the field of endocrine science. Awarded annually. Established in 1995.

7642 ■ Young Investigator Award
To recognize a young European pediatrician for his/her scientific publications. Candidates must be no older than 40 years. Awarded annually. Established in 1992.

7643 ■ European Society of Paediatric Radiology
Dr. Catherine M. Owens, Gen. Sec.
Great Ormond Street Hospital for Children
Department of Imaging
London WC1N 3JH, United Kingdom
E-mail: president@espr.org
URL: http://www.espr.org

7644 ■ Gold Medal
To recognize an individual for long service to paediatric radiology and for dedication to the Society. Established in 2007.

7645 ■ Jacques Lefebvre Award
To encourage professional development in the field of pediatric radiology. Members of the Society under 34 years of age may submit papers. A monetary prize is awarded annually at the Congress. Established in 1976 in memory of Dr. Lefebvre.

7646 ■ Poster Award
To recognize the best poster presented at a meeting of the Society. Awarded annually. Established in 1994.

7647 ■ President Award
To recognize an individual for contributions to paediatric radiology. Awarded annually, if merited. Established in 2004.

7648 ■ Young Researcher Award
To recognize a young scientist for outstanding research in the field of paediatric radiology. Awarded annually. Established in 2003.

7649 ■ European Sponsorship Association
Claremont House, Ste. 1
22-24 Claremont Rd.
Burbiton
Surrey KT6 4QU, United Kingdom
Ph: 44 20 8390 3311
Fax: 44 20 8390 0055
E-mail: enquiries@sponsorship.org
URL: http://www.sponsorship.org

7650 ■ European Sponsorship Awards
To recognize sponsorship projects for excellence in Europe. Categories include business-to-business, business-to-community, business-to-consumer, business-to-employee, and multinational campaigns. In addition, the Rights Holder Awards may be presented for the best sponsorship partnership. All applicants must be

Awards are arranged in alphabetical order below their administering organizations

based in Europe, and all projects must reflect activity based within at least one European market. Awarded annually. Established in 2007.

7651 ■ European Study Group on Lysosomal Diseases
Prof. Volkmar Gieselmann, Chm.
Pediatric Storage Disorders Lab, Box P040
Center Cellular Basis of Behaviour, Department Neurosciences
Institute of Psychiatry, King's College London
125 Coldharbour Ln.
London SE5 9NU, United Kingdom
Ph: 44 20 78480281
E-mail: j.cooper@iop.kcl.ac.uk
URL: http://www.esgld.org

7652 ■ Travel Grants/Scholarships
To promote the exchange of techniques and personnel among member laboratories by providing travel expenses within Europe for young scientists. Up to three grants are awarded per year.

7653 ■ European Surfing Federation
Karen Walton, Sec. Gen.
16 Beacon Estate
Penzance TR20 8QR, United Kingdom
Ph: 44 7773 332054
E-mail: karen@eurosurfing.org
URL: http://www.eurosurfing.org

7654 ■ European Surfing Championships - Open Champion
To recognize the winners of the annual European surfing championships. A trophy is awarded annually. Established in 1965.

7655 ■ Experimental Psychology Society
Dr. Helen Cassaday, Honorary Sec.
University of Nottingham
Dept. of Psychology
University Park
Nottingham NG7 2RD, United Kingdom
E-mail: michelle.dorman@nottingham.ac.uk
URL: http://www.eps.ac.uk

7656 ■ Sir Frederic Bartlett Lecture
For recognition of contributions to experimental psychology or cognate subjects. An honorarium, expenses for travel, and the opportunity to present a lecture are awarded annually. Established in 1966 in honor of Sir Frederic Bartlett, a British psychologist.

7657 ■ Experimental Psychology Society Prize
For recognition of distinguished work in experimental psychology or a cognate discipline by an individual in an early stage of his or her career. An honorarium and the opportunity to present a lecture are awarded annually. Established in 1993.

7658 ■ Grants for Postgraduate and Postdoctoral Workshops
To support workshops that are designed to bring together postgraduate students and postdoctoral researchers who are working on similar topics. The maximum grant for a one-day meeting is £1,200 and for a two-day workshop is £2,500. Awarded annually.

7659 ■ Grants for Study Visits
To support postgraduate students' research in experimental psychology. Grants of no more than £1,200 are awarded annually.

7660 ■ Grindley Grants for Conference Attendance
To support individuals attending academic conferences relevant to the applicant's work. Grants up to £500 are awarded annually.

7661 ■ Mid-Career Award
To recognize an experimental psychologist who is actively researching and has shown a distin-

guished research record over a substantial period. Candidates typically gained their PhD during the previous 15 to 25 years. A monetary prize and invitation to lecture are awarded annually. Established in 2002.

7662 ■ Undergraduate Research Bursaries
To support undergraduate students in the summer vacation immediately prior to their final year. Five monetary awards of £2,000 are presented annually.

7663 ■ FAB Awards
Riverbank House
1 Putney Bridge Approach
London SW6 3JD, United Kingdom
Ph: 44 20 7751 0354
Fax: 44 20 7751 0352
E-mail: info@fabawards.com
URL: http://www.fabawards.tv

7664 ■ FAB Awards, the International Food and Beverage Creative Excellence Awards
To recognize outstanding creative marketing work in the food and beverage industry. Awarded in various categories within the groups of: Retailers, Health Foods, Dairy Products, Baking and Sweet Foods, Savory Foods, Alcoholic Drinks, Non-Alcoholic Drinks, Confectionery and Snacks, Pet Foods, and Sponsorships. In addition, the FABulous Client of the Year is presented to a client who has made an unusually significant contribution to the development of outstanding creative work. Awarded annually. Established in 1999.

7665 ■ Faculty of Astrological Studies
Carole Taylor, Pres.
BM Box 7470
London WC1N 3XX, United Kingdom
Ph: 44 7000 790143
Fax: 44 7000 790143
E-mail: info@astrology.org.uk
URL: http://www.astrology.org.uk

7666 ■ Academic Awards
For academic excellence in exams. Awards are given annually.

7667 ■ Falklands Conservation
1 Princes Ave.
London N3 2DA, United Kingdom
E-mail: info@conservation.org.fk
URL: http://www.falklandsconservation.com

7668 ■ Falklands Conservation Wildlife Photo Competition
To recognize photography on the Falkland Islands. Open to residents, visitors, and military personnel. Awarded in three categories for adults: Wildlife and Environment, Attention to Detail, and Behaviour of Animals; a Junior category is open to photographers under the age of 18. Awarded annually. Established in 2009.

7669 ■ Federation of Children's Book Groups
Adam Lancaster, Chm.
2 Bridge Wood View
Horsforth
West Yorkshire
Leeds LS18 5PE, United Kingdom
Ph: 44 113 2588910
E-mail: info@fcbg.org.uk
URL: http://www.fcbg.org.uk

7670 ■ Red House Children's Book Award
To recognize the achievement of authors and illustrators who give children so much pleasure, and to foster an interest in children's books among children and parents. Works of fiction suitable for children that were published for the first time in the United Kingdom in the previous year are eligible for consideration. Entries are

judged entirely by children. The overall winner is presented with a silver and oak prize valued at over £7,000 and a presentation book filled with letters, pictures, reviews, and comments from the children who are the judges. Awards are also presented in three categories: Books for Younger Children, Books for Younger Readers, and Books for Older Readers. The "Pick of the Year" booklist is produced annually in the spring. Established in 1980. Sponsored by Red House Books.

7671 ■ Federation of Commercial Audiovisual Libraries International
79 College Rd.
Harrow HA1 1BD, United Kingdom
Ph: 44 20 3178 3535
Fax: 44 20 3178 3533
E-mail: info@focalint.org
URL: http://www.focalint.org

7672 ■ FOCAL International Awards
To honor outstanding use of footage archive images in the creative media. Awards are presented in approximately one dozen categories, such as footage in a factual production, sports footage, and footage in a cinema production. In addition, several special awards are presented, including Footage Library of the Year, Footage Librarian of the Year, and the Jane Mercer Footage Researcher of the Year. Awarded annually.

7673 ■ Federation of Family History Societies
Philippa McCray, Admin.
PO Box 8857
Lutterworth LE17 9BJ, United Kingdom
Ph: 44 1455 203133
E-mail: admin@ffhs.org.uk
URL: http://www.ffhs.org.uk

7674 ■ Best Website Award
To honor the member society that publishes and maintains the best web site. A monetary prize of £100 is awarded annually. Established in 2001.

7675 ■ Elizabeth Simpson Award
To recognize the member society that publishes the journal making the best contribution to family history. A monetary prize of £100 is awarded annually. Established in 1979.

7676 ■ Federation of Muslim Organisations, Leicestershire
99 Melbourne Rd.
Leicester LE2 0GW, United Kingdom
Ph: 44 116 262 2111
E-mail: info@fmo.org.uk
URL: http://www.fmo.org.uk

7677 ■ Youth and Community Awards
To highlight and acknowledge the effort of young Muslims and those working in the community in various fields of endeavor across the United Kingdom. Awarded in six categories: community, creativity, education, humanity, literature, and sports.

7678 ■ Federation of Plastering and Drywall Contractors
Gavin Colclough, Pres.
4th Fl., 61 Cheapside
London EC2V 6AX, United Kingdom
Ph: 44 20 76349480
Ph: 44 20 76349481
Fax: 44 20 72483685
E-mail: donna.rickaby@fpdc.org
URL: http://www.fpdc.org
Formerly: (1995) National Federation of Plastering Contractors.

7679 ■ Plaisterers' Trophy
To recognize the highest standards of skill and excellence in plastering, drylining, and associated trades in the United Kingdom. Presented in six categories: Fibrous and GRG, Plastering,

Awards are arranged in alphabetical order below their administering organizations

Screeding, Drylining, Steel Framed Systems, and Technical Ceilings. A trophy is awarded annually to the winner in each category. Organized in association with Royal Institute of British Architects and Worshipful Company of Plasterers, and sponsored by British Gypsom.

7680 ■ FeRFA Resin Flooring Association
Helen McGachie, CEO
16 Edward Rd.
Surrey
Farnham GU9 8NP, United Kingdom
Ph: 44 1252 714250
E-mail: lisa@ferfa.org.uk
URL: http://www.ferfa.org.uk/html

7681 ■ Contractor of the Year
For all-round performance, quality and variety of technique. Awarded annually.

7682 ■ Manufacturer of the Year
For innovation, new products and quality of service offered to customers. Awarded annually.

7683 ■ Project of the Year
To recognize projects based on innovation, aesthetics, size, duration, difficult conditions, challenges, and overall approach. Awarded annually.

7684 ■ Trainer of the Year
To recognize a member company's continuing commitment to training, development of staff, and training achievement. Awarded annually.

7685 ■ Filtration Society
Prof. Richard Wakeman, Sec.
19 Clyst Valley Rd.
Winslade Park
Clyst St. Mary
Exeter EX5 1DD, United Kingdom
Ph: 44 1392 874398
Ph: 44 7849 69060
Fax: 44 1392 874398
E-mail: richard.wakeman@lineone.net
URL: http://www.filtsoc.org

7686 ■ Gold Medal
To recognize the most meritorious original paper on filtration and separation technology. A medal and a certificate are awarded biennially. Established in 1966.

7687 ■ H. K. Suttle Award
To encourage and recognize the achievements of younger workers in the field of filtration and separation technology. Authors under 35 years of age may submit papers in English. A monetary prize of £500 and a certificate are awarded biennially. Established in 1971 in honor of the Founder-Chairman of the Society, Harold K. Suttle.

7688 ■ Fingerprint Society
Karen Stow, Pres.
Derbyshire Constabulary
Scientific Support Unit
Butterley Hall
Derbyshire
Ripley DE5 3RS, United Kingdom
E-mail: karen.stow.9864@derbyshire.pnn.police.uk
URL: http://www.fpsociety.org.uk
Formerly: (1976) National Society of Fingerprint Officers.

7689 ■ Aziz ul Haque and Hem Chandra Bose prize
To recognize innovative projects in the area of forensic identification with high potential to make an impact in the field. Awarded in three categories: undergraduate student project, postgraduate student project, and practitioner project. Awarded annually. Established in honor of Aziz ul Haque and Hem Chandra Bose, two Indian officers recruited by Sir Edward Henry to utilize anthropometry in the advancement of the science.

7690 ■ Henry Medal
To recognize individuals or organizations that have made an outstanding contribution for the good of the profession of fingerprint analysis. Awarded periodically. Established in 2001.

7691 ■ Lewis Minshall Award
For recognition of outstanding contributions to the science of fingerprints, identification, or research, world-wide. Members or non-members of the Society are eligible. A trophy is presented annually when merited at the general meeting. Established in 1980 by the widow of Detective Superintendent Lewis Minshall, Queen's Police Medal, in memory of her husband, the first president of the Fingerprint Society.

7692 ■ Fire Protection Association - England
Jonathan O'Neill, Managing Dir.
London Rd.
Moreton-in-Marsh GL56 0RH, United Kingdom
Ph: 44 1608 812500
Ph: 44 1608 812524
Fax: 44 1608 812501
E-mail: fpa@thefpa.co.uk
URL: http://www.thefpa.co.uk

7693 ■ Fire Excellence Awards
To recognize and celebrate excellence in fire safety engineering, product design and innovation, and fire and rescue practice. Awarded in a variety of categories each year.

7694 ■ Fleet News
Bauer Media Ltd.
21 Holborn Viaduct
London EC1A 2DY, United Kingdom
Ph: 44 1733 468123
URL: http://www.fleetnews.co.uk

7695 ■ Fleet News Awards
To recognize outstanding contributions to the fleet industry in the United Kingdom. Awards are presented in the categories of Fleet, Manufacturers, Suppliers, and Headline. Awarded annually.

7696 ■ Folklore Society
Mr. Robert McDowall, Pres.
Woburn Sq.
London WC1H 0AB, United Kingdom
Ph: 44 20 78628564
E-mail: enquiries@folklore-society.com
URL: http://www.folklore-society.com

7697 ■ Katharine Briggs Folklore Award
To encourage a high standard of publication and scholarship in folklore. Books published for the first time in English in the United Kingdom and Ireland between June 1 and May 31 are eligible. Included are scholarly revised editions of previously published texts, but excluded are reprints or folktales retold for children. A monetary prize of £200 and an engraved goblet are awarded annually. Established in 1982 in honor of Dr. Katharine Briggs, a distinguished English folktale and literary scholar, and a past president of the Society.

7698 ■ Coote Lake Medal for Folklore Research
For recognition of research in the field of folklore studies and for service to the Folklore Society. Individuals must be nominated by a committee of the Society. A medal is awarded when merited. Established in 1941 by Mrs. H. A. Lake-Barnett, a treasurer and secretary of the Folklore Society, in memory of Harold Coote Lake, the founder's brother and a treasurer and secretary of the Folklore Society.

7699 ■ Foreign Press Association in London
Mr. Christopher Wyld, Dir.
25 Northumberland Ave.
London WC2N 5AP, United Kingdom
Ph: 44 20 79300445

E-mail: christopherwyld@fpalondon.org
URL: http://www.fpalondon.org

7700 ■ Media Awards
To recognize the best foreign or domestic articles, photographs, and radio and television stories in the British media. U.K. journalists are eligible. Awarded in 11 categories annually.

7701 ■ Forensic Science Society
Ann Priston, Pres.
Clarke House
18A Mt. Parade
N Yorkshire
Harrogate HG1 1BX, United Kingdom
Ph: 44 1423 506068
Fax: 44 1423 566391
E-mail: info@forensic-science-society.org.uk
URL: http://www.forensic-science-society.org.uk

7702 ■ P.W. Allen Award
To recognize the most meritorious paper published in *Science and Justice* during the year. Awarded annually. Established in 1996.

7703 ■ J.B. Firth Essay Prize
To recognize an outstanding essay written by a student member on the topic of forensic science and/or forensic medicine. Open to students worldwide who are in the penultimate or final year of their studies at a recognized institute of higher education. A monetary prize of £200 and a set of text books are awarded annually.

7704 ■ Student Prizes
To recognize the achievement of the most meritorious students in forensic science programs. Awarded in two categories: undergraduate programs and post-graduate MSc degree programs. Awarded annually.

7705 ■ Fork Lift Truck Association
David Ellison, Chief Exec.
Manor Farm Bldg.
Lasham
Alton GU34 5SL, United Kingdom
Ph: 44 1256 381441
Fax: 44 1256 381735
E-mail: mail@fork-truck.org.uk
URL: http://www.fork-truck.org.uk

7706 ■ Awards for Excellence
To recognize individuals in the materials handling industry in the United Kingdom. Awarded in 11 categories encompassing innovation, environment, ergonomics, and safety. Awarded annually.

7707 ■ Franco-British Society
Mrs. Kate Brayn, Exec. Sec.
3 Dovedale Studios
465 Battersea Park Rd.
London SW11 4LR, United Kingdom
Ph: 44 20 79243511
E-mail: francobritish@googlemail.com
URL: http://www.francobritishsociety.org.uk

7708 ■ Franco-British Landscape Gardening Award
To draw attention to an outstanding horticultural achievement each year, either in Britain or France, thus encouraging and developing further contacts between the two countries in the areas of garden history and landscape design. Established in 1988.

7709 ■ Enid McLeod Literary Prize
To recognize the author of the work of literature that has contributed the most to Franco-British understanding. A monetary prize of £500 is awarded annually. Established in 1983.

7710 ■ Vlado Perlemuter Piano Scholarship
To select from auditions the British piano student, between 17 and 25 years old, whose career would benefit most from an international sum-

Awards are arranged in alphabetical order below their administering organizations

mer school course Academie Internationale de Musique Ravel in France. The annual winner of the scholarship receives fare, tuition, travel, and expenses to study at the Academie Internationale de Musique Maurice Ravel, St. Jean-de-Luz, near Biarritz. Established in 1983 in honor of the distinguished pianist, Vlado Perlemuter, pupil of Ravel.

7711 ■ Freshwater Biological Association
Dr. Michael Dobson, Dir.
The Ferry Landing
Far Sawrey
Ambleside
Cumbria LA22 0LP, United Kingdom
Ph: 44 15394 42468
Fax: 44 15394 46914
E-mail: info@fba.org.uk
URL: http://www.fba.org.uk

7712 ■ Hugh Cary Gilson Memorial Award
To assist a member with a piece of original freshwater research, either biological or limnological. A monetary prize of £4,000 is awarded annually.

7713 ■ GARDENEX: Federation of Garden and Leisure Manufacturers
Amanda Sizer Barrett MBE, Dir. Gen.
The White House
High St.
Kent
Brasted TN16 1JE, United Kingdom
Ph: 44 1959 565995
Fax: 44 1959 565885
E-mail: info@gardenex.com
URL: http://www.gardenex.com/index.html

7714 ■ Roy Hay Memorial Award
Recognizes services rendered to British gardening industry. Awarded annually.

7715 ■ Gen Foundation
Dr. Takashige Shimizu, Founder
45 Old Bond Rd.
London W1S 4DN, United Kingdom
Ph: 44 20 74955564
Fax: 44 20 74999590
E-mail: info@genfoundation.org.uk
URL: http://www.genfoundation.org.uk

7716 ■ Gen Foundation Awards
To support research and study of the natural sciences and the arts. Special attention is given to studies in biology, chemistry, botany, language, music, and arts. Candidates must hold a Bachelor's degree or the equivalent. Grants of £3,000 are offered periodically. Established in 1999.

7717 ■ Geological Society of London
Edmund Nickless, Exec. Sec.
Burlington House
Piccadilly
London W1J 0BG, United Kingdom
Ph: 44 20 74349944
Fax: 44 20 74398975
E-mail: enquiries@geolsoc.org.uk
URL: http://www.geolsoc.org.uk

7718 ■ Aberconway Medal
For recognition of distinguished contributions to the advancement of the profession and practice of geology. Individuals under 45 years of age may be nominated. A medal is awarded biennially in odd-numbered years. Established in 1980 by Lord Aberconway of Bodnant.

7719 ■ Major John Sacheverell A'Deane Coke Medal
To recognize scientists for their contributions to geology, and for recognition of significant service to geology, for example through administrative, organizational, or promotional activities resulting in benefits to the community. Also the field may

be extended to include scientists whose training and interests are outside the main fields of geology but whose contributions are of great significance to our science. A medal is awarded annually.

7720 ■ Bigsby Medal
To recognize an individual under 45 years of age for imminent services in any department of geology. A medal is awarded annually. Established in 1877.

7721 ■ Distinguished Service Award
To recognize an individual who has made a significant contribution to geoscience and the geoscience community by virtue of his or her professional, administrative, organizational, or promotional activities. Awarded annually. Established in 1998.

7722 ■ Major Edward D'Ewes Fitzgerald Coke Medal
To recognize scientists for their contributions to geology, and for recognition of significant service to geology through administrative, organizational, or promotional activities resulting in benefits to the community. Also the field may be extended to include scientists whose training and interests are outside the main fields of geology but whose contributions are of great significance to our science. A medal is awarded annually.

7723 ■ Sue Tyler Friedman Medal
To recognize an individual for distinguished contributions to the recording of the history of geology. Awarded annually. Established in 1987 by a gift from a Northeastern Science Foundation of Troy, New York.

7724 ■ Honorary Fellowships
To honor individuals around the world for their achievements, not only in science, but in acting as ambassadors for geological science and promoting its aims to the wider public. Awarded annually. Established in 1807.

7725 ■ Lyell Medal
To recognize an individual who has made a significant contribution to the science by means of a substantial body of research. Workers in both pure and applied aspects of the geological sciences are eligible. A medal is awarded annually. Established in 1876.

7726 ■ Murchison Medal
To recognize authors of memoirs or persons actually employed in any enquiries bearing upon the science of geology. A monetary prize and a medal are awarded annually. Established in 1873 through the will of Sir Roderick Impey Murchison (1792-1871).

7727 ■ President's Awards
To recognize geologists who are under the age of 30 and who made a notable early contribution to the science. Awarded annually to one or more recipients. Established in 1980 by Professor Perce Allen.

7728 ■ Prestwich Medal
To recognize scientists who have undertaken special research bearing on stratigraphical or physical geology. A medal is awarded triennially. Established in 1903 under the will of Sir Joseph Prestwich (1812-96).

7729 ■ William Smith Medal
For recognition of excellence in contributions to applied and economic aspects of the science. Candidates must have initiated significant contributions, which will normally take the form of published papers. A medal is awarded annually. Established in 1977.

7730 ■ Wollaston Medal
This, the highest award of the Society, is normally given to geologists who have had a significant influence by means of a substantial body of

excellent research in either or both pure and applied aspects of the science. A medal is awarded annually. Established in 1831.

7731 ■ R. H. Worth Prize
For recognition of meritorious geological research carried out by amateur geologists, or for the encouragement of geological research by amateurs.

7732 ■ Gibraltar Amateur Radio Society
Jorma Saloranta, Contact
PO Box 292
Gibraltar, United Kingdom
E-mail: jorma.saloranta@kolumbus.fi
URL: http://www.gibradio.net

7733 ■ ZB2 Award
To recognize any amateur radio operator who has worked or heard any six stations. Awarded when merited.

7734 ■ ZB2BU Award
To recognize any amateur radio operator who has worked or heard the club station on three bands in any mode. Awarded when merited.

7735 ■ Gibraltar Tourist Board
179 Strand
London WC2R 1EL, United Kingdom
URL: http://www.gibraltar.gov.uk

7736 ■ Ed Lacy Award
To recognize staff writers and freelance journalists for a published feature or broadcast on Gibraltar. A crystal trophy and monetary prize of £500 are awarded annually. Established in 1998 in memory of the popular travel writer and broadcaster Ed Lacy.

7737 ■ Girls' Brigade International Council
Mrs. Ruth Chikasa, Pres.
Challenge House
29 Canal St.
Glasgow G4 0AD, United Kingdom
Ph: 44 141 3329696
URL: http://www.gbic.org

7738 ■ International Award
Award of recognition. Members of brigade over the age of 18 are eligible. Awarded annually. Established in 1968.

7739 ■ Queen's Award
To encourage girls and young women to a personal commitment to Jesus Christ, and to inspire them to greater endeavor in service within the general community and the worldwide concept of the Brigade. Members of the Brigade in countries holding the Queen of England as head of state are eligible. Awarded annually.

7740 ■ Glasgow Natural History Society
Mary Child, Sec.
University of Glasgow
Graham Kerr Bldg.
Glasgow G12 8QQ, United Kingdom
Ph: 44 141 3391343
E-mail: info@glasgownaturalhistory.org.uk
URL: http://www.glasgownaturalhistory.org.uk

7741 ■ Professor Blodwen Lloyd Binns Prize
To recognize papers submitted for publication in the *Glasgow Naturalist*. Awarded annually.

7742 ■ Global Lung Cancer Coalition
Emma Gunby, Contact
134 Douglas St.
Glasgow G2 4HF, United Kingdom
Fax: 44 141 3314530
E-mail: glcc@roycastle.org
URL: http://www.lungcancercoalition.org

7743 ■ Lung Cancer Journalism Awards
To recognize excellence in lung cancer reporting.

Awards are arranged in alphabetical order below their administering organizations

Awards are presented in three categories: medical articles, consumer articles, and broadcast reports. A research grant of £2,000 is awarded annually in each category. Established in 2006.

7744 ■ Good Safari Guide
Miranda Travel Group
PO Box 135
Wantage OX12 9WX, United Kingdom
Ph: 44 1865 989280
Fax: 44 1865 989281
URL: http://www.goodsafariguide.com

7745 ■ Safari Awards
To recognize excellence among the best safari lodges, operators, and related services in Africa. Presented in more than 20 categories, including Best Safari Property, Best Safari Spa, Best Tourism Board in Africa, Best Air Charter in Africa, and Best Wildlife Organization. Awarded annually. Established in 2008.

7746 ■ Green Organisation
Roger Wolens, Contact
The Mill House
Mill Ln.
Earls Barton
Northampton NN6 0NR, United Kingdom
Ph: 44 1604 810507
E-mail: rogerwolens@btconnect.com
URL: http://www.thegreenorganisation.info

7747 ■ Green Apple Awards
To recognize, reward, and promote eco-friendly practice around the world. Trophies are awarded annually in three categories: 1. Best Practice; 2. Retail and Wholesale; and 3. the Built Environment and Architectural Heritage.

7748 ■ Greeting Card Association
Sharon Little, Gen. Mgr.
United House
North Rd.
London N7 9DP, United Kingdom
Ph: 44 20 76190396
E-mail: gca@max-publishing.co.uk
URL: http://greetingcardassociation.org.uk/home

7749 ■ Henries Awards
To recognize the best of the greeting card industry in the United Kingdom. Awards are presented in 15 product categories. In addition, three special awards may be presented: Most Promising Young Designer or Artist; Best Service to the Independent Retailer; and the Honorary Achievement Award. Awarded annually. Established in 1996 in honor of Sir Henry Cole, who produced the first commercial Christmas cards over 150 years ago.

7750 ■ Guild of Agricultural Journalists
Adrian Bell, Chm.
62 Percy St.
Shrewsbury SY1 2QG, United Kingdom
Ph: 44 1743 344986
E-mail: lizsnaith@btopenworld.com
URL: http://www.gaj.org.uk

7751 ■ Netherthorpe Communicator of the Year
To recognize a guild member who has made an outstanding and sustained contribution to the dissemination of knowledge and understanding about agriculture. A trophy and a certificate are bestowed annually. Established in 1977. The award honors the late Lord Netherthorpe.

7752 ■ Guild of Air Pilots and Air Navigators
Mr. Paul Tacon BA, Clerk
Cobham House
9 Warwick Ct.
Gray's Inn
London WC1R 5DJ, United Kingdom
Ph: 44 20 74044032
Fax: 44 20 74044035

E-mail: gapan@gapan.org
URL: http://www.gapan.org

7753 ■ Cumberbatch Trophy
To recognize an individual, a team, group, or organization for an outstanding contribution to air safety, whether by the development of techniques contributing to safer flight, by improvements in ground equipment and services, or by improvements in aircraft and component design. Awarded annually.

7754 ■ Hugh Gordon-Burge Memorial Award
To recognize a member or members of a crew whose outstanding behavior and action contributed to the saving of their aircraft or passengers. Awarded annually.

7755 ■ Guild Award of Honour
To honor an individual who has made an outstanding lifetime contribution to aviation. Awarded periodically. Established in 1999.

7756 ■ Sir James Martin Award
To recognize an individual, a group, team, or organization that has made an outstanding, original, and practical contribution leading to the safer operation of aircraft or the survival of aircrew or passengers. Awarded annually.

7757 ■ Prince Philip Helicopter Rescue Award
To recognize an individual member of a helicopter crew, a complete crew, or the crews of multiple helicopters for an act of outstanding courage or devotion to duty in the course of land or sea search and rescue operations. Awarded annually.

7758 ■ Guild of Air Traffic Control Officers
Mr. Steve Brindley, Pres./CEO
4 St. Mary's Rd.
Nottinghamshire
Bingham NG13 8DW, United Kingdom
Ph: 44 1949 876405
Fax: 44 1949 876405
E-mail: caf@gatco.org
URL: http://www.gatco.org

7759 ■ Hunt Trophy
For services to air traffic control.

7760 ■ Guild of Fine Food Retailers
Linda Farrand, Contact
Station Rd.
Somerset
Wincanton BA9 9FE, United Kingdom
Ph: 44 1963 824464
Fax: 44 1963 824651
E-mail: info@finefoodworld.co.uk
URL: http://www.finefoodworld.co.uk

7761 ■ Great Taste Awards
To honor the best specialty food and drink manufactured in the United Kingdom. Awards are presented in several categories annually.

7762 ■ World Cheese Awards
To honor the world's most delicious cheeses. Awards are presented in more than 60 categories annually.

7763 ■ Guild of Food Writers
Mr. Jonathan Woods, Admin.
255 Kent House Rd.
Kent
Beckenham BR3 1JQ, United Kingdom
Ph: 44 20 86590422
E-mail: guild@gfw.co.uk
URL: http://www.gfw.co.uk

7764 ■ Guild of Food Writers Award
Recognizes excellence in food writing. The following awards are presented: Food Book of the Year, Cookery Book of the Year, Michael Smith Award for Work on British Food, Derek Cooper

Award for Campaigning and Investigative Food Writing, Miriam Polunin Award for Work on Healthy Eating, Jeremy Round Award for the Best First Book, Evelyn Rose Award for Cookery Journalist of the Year, Restaurant Reviewer of the Year, Food Journalist of the Year, New Media Award, Food Broadcast Award, and the Lifetime Achievement Award. Awarded annually.

7765 ■ Guild of International Professional Toastmasters
Ivor Spencer MBE, Pres./Founder
12 Little Bornes
London SE21 8SE, United Kingdom
Ph: 44 20 86705585
Fax: 44 20 86700055
E-mail: ivor@ivorspencer.com
URL: http://www.ivorspencer.com

7766 ■ Ivor Spencer Best After Dinner Speaker of the Year
To recognize the best after dinner speaker of the year. Selection is by members of the Guild. A trophy is awarded annually. Established in 1967 by Ivor Spencer. Formerly: (1997) Guild of Professional Toastmasters Best After Dinner Speaker of the Year.

7767 ■ Guild of Motoring Writers
Patricia Lodge, Gen. Sec.
40 Baring Rd.
Bournemouth BH6 4DT, United Kingdom
Ph: 44 1202 422424
E-mail: generalsec@gomw.co.uk
URL: http://www.gomw.co.uk/home/welcome

7768 ■ Driver of the Year Award
To recognize a driver for his skill, courage and endurance. Awarded annually.

7769 ■ Sir William Lyons Award
To encourage young writers in automotive journalism, and to foster interest in the motoring industry. British citizens resident in the United Kingdom between 17 and 23 years of age may submit essays. A monetary award of £2,000 is presented annually. Established in 1966.

7770 ■ Pemberton Trophy
To recognize a Guild member for achievements in furthering the cause of motoring.

7771 ■ Guild of Television Cameramen
Graeme McAlpine, Chm.
Briar Cottage
Holyhead Rd.
Gwynedd LL61 5YX, United Kingdom
Ph: 44 300 1114123
E-mail: administration@gtc.org.uk
URL: http://www.gtc.org.uk

7772 ■ Awards for Excellence
To recognize examples of outstanding camerawork. Awards are presented in the following categories: Entertainment, Drama, Extreme Conditions, Factual, Multi-Camera, and Natural History. Awarded annually. Awarded annually.

7773 ■ Mike Baldock Award
To recognize an individual who has rendered valuable service to the Guild. Awarded annually. Established in memory of Mike Baldock, a Thames TV cameraman who died in 1979.

7774 ■ Fellowship of the Guild of Television Cameramen
To honor a member who, in the opinion of the majority of the Council, has made a significant contribution to television camerawork or has assisted the Guild to function. Lifetime membership is awarded annually.

7775 ■ Honorary Membership
To honor a non-member who, in the opinion of the majority of the Council, has made a signifi-

Awards are arranged in alphabetical order below their administering organizations

cant contribution to television camerawork or has assisted the Guild to function. Lifetime membership is awarded annually.

7776 ■ Seal of Approval
To recognize a manufacturer for a piece of equipment that has significantly aided cameramen in the advancement of their craft. Awarded annually.

7777 ■ Television Cameraman's Award
To recognize an individual who has furthered the cause of the Guild by fostering and improving the art and craft of the professional television cameraman over many years. Awarded annually.

7778 ■ Guildhall School of Music and Drama
Silk St.
Barbican
London EC2Y 8DT, United Kingdom
Ph: 44 20 7628 2571
Fax: 44 20 7256 9438
E-mail: info@gsmd.ac.uk
URL: http://www.gsmd.ac.uk

7779 ■ Gold Medal
This, the School's premier prize, is presented to singers and instrumentalists. Awarded annually, alternating between singing and instruments. Established in 1915.

7780 ■ Haemophilia Society
Christopher James, Chief Exec.
1st Fl., Petersham House
57a Hatton Garden
London EC1N 8JG, United Kingdom
Ph: 44 207 8311020
Fax: 44 207 4054824
E-mail: info@haemophilia.org.uk
URL: http://www.haemophilia.org.uk

7781 ■ Haemophilia Award
To recognize an individual for contributions to the well-being of people with bleeding disorders in the United Kingdom. Awarded annually.

7782 ■ Macfarlane Award
To recognize an individual for medical achievements in haemophilia. Awarded annually.

7783 ■ Philip Morris Art Award
To recognize an individual with haemophilia or a related bleeding disorder who are studying music or another art form. A monetary prize of approximately £400 is awarded annually. Established in memory of the Honorary Treasurer of the Society in its early days.

7784 ■ Sports Award
To honor a young person, under 18 years old, with haemophilia or another bleeding disorder who works hard at any sport. The prize for the junior and senior award winners is £100 of sports vouchers, and two runners up each receive £50 of sports vouchers. Awarded annually.

7785 ■ Hairdressers Journal International
Quadrant House
The Quadrant
Sutton
Surrey SM2 5AS, United Kingdom
Ph: 44 20 8652 8852
URL: http://www.hji.co.uk

7786 ■ British Hairdressing Awards
To inspire creativity and recognize excellence in hairdressing in the United Kingdom. Awards are presented in nine regional categories as well as the following: British Hairdresser of the Year, Afro Hairdresser of the Year, Artistic Team of the Year, Avant Garde Hairdresser of the Year, Men's Hairdresser of the Year, Newcomer of the Year, and the Schwarzkopf Professional British Colour Technician of the Year. Awarded annually. Established in 1985.

7787 ■ Healthcare People Management Association
Kelvin Cheatle, Pres.
Gothic House
3 The Green

Richmond TW9 1PL, United Kingdom
Ph: 44 20 83344530
Fax: 44 20 83344531
E-mail: admin@hpma.org.uk
URL: http://www.hpma.org.uk

7788 ■ Excellence in HRM Awards
To recognize the best human resource managers. Awarded annually in a variety of categories.

7789 ■ William Hill plc
Greenside House
50 Station Rd.
Wood Green
London N22 7TP, United Kingdom
Ph: 44 208 918 3600
Fax: 44 208 918 3775
E-mail: customerhelp@williamhill.co.uk
URL: http://www.williamhillplc.co.uk

7790 ■ William Hill Sports Book of the Year
To honor the best sports book of the year in the United Kingdom. Books published in the United Kingdom during the previous calendar year are eligible. A monetary prize of £22,000, a free £2,000 bet, and a leather bound book are awarded annually. Established in 1989.

7791 ■ Hire Association Europe
Kevin McGuinness, Pres.
2450 Regents Ct.
Birmingham Business Park
Solihull B37 7YE, United Kingdom
Ph: 44 121 3804600
Fax: 44 121 3334109
E-mail: mail@hae.org.uk
URL: http://www.hae.org.uk/pages/index.cfm

7792 ■ Hire Awards of Excellence
To recognize members who have made outstanding contributions to the hire and rental industry. Awarded in a variety of categories each year.

7793 ■ Historical Association
Prof. Anne Curry, Pres.
59a Kennington Park Rd.
London SE11 4JH, United Kingdom
Ph: 44 20 77353901
Fax: 44 20 75824989
E-mail: enquiry@history.org.uk
URL: http://www.history.org.uk

7794 ■ Norton Medlicott Medal
For recognition of an outstanding major contribution to the field of history. Nominations may be submitted. A medal is awarded annually. Established in 1984 in honor of Professor W. Norton Medlicott, past president of the Association.

7795 ■ Historical Metallurgy Society
Mr. David Cranstone, Honorary Gen. Sec.
267 Kells Ln.
Gateshead NE9 5HU, United Kingdom
Ph: 44 191 4821037
E-mail: hon-sec@hist-met.org
URL: http://hist-met.org

7796 ■ Historical Metallurgy Society Grants
To encourage the preservation and study of all aspects of metallurgical history, including the extraction of ores and minerals, the melting and working of metals, and the preservation of archaeological and historical sites and objects. Grants for research, excavations, and travel to conferences are awarded.

7797 ■ HR Society
Ms. Lara Roberts, Sec.
The Old Stables
Redenham Park Farm
Redenham

Hampshire SP11 9AQ, United Kingdom
Ph: 44 1264 774004
Fax: 44 1264 774009
E-mail: lararoberts@hrsociety.co.uk
URL: http://www.hrsociety.co.uk

7798 ■ Student Best Essay Award
For best essay.

7799 ■ Humane Slaughter Association
Dr. James K. Kirkwood, Chief Exec./Scientific Dir.
The Old School
Brewhouse Hill
Wheathampstead AL4 8AN, United Kingdom
Ph: 44 1582 831919
Fax: 44 1582 831414
E-mail: info@hsa.org.uk
URL: http://www.hsa.org.uk

7800 ■ Humane Slaughter Association Award
To recognize individuals and organizations whose work has resulted in significant advances in the humane slaughter of farmed livestock, including cattle, sheep, pigs, other mammals, poultry, and fish. Open to individuals and organizations worldwide. A plaque and monetary prize of £1,000 are awarded annually.

7801 ■ Poultry Catching Award
To recognize the poultry plant or independent catching team that has made the greatest improvement to animal welfare in one of the following ways: catching training program, catching protocol, or innovative equipment/system to improve catching of one or more poultry species. A plaque and monetary prize of £1,000 are awarded annually. Established in 2005.

7802 ■ Dorothy Sidley Memorial Award
To encourage young people in the UK to take an interest in the Association's specialist area of food animal welfare, thereby improving welfare conditions for food animals and birds in livestock markets, during transit or in slaughterhouses. Students in agricultural, veterinary, or meat sciences, and trainees in the livestock and meat industries are eligible. A monetary award of £2,000 is presented annually. Established in 1986 in memory of Dorothy Sidley MBE, who was General Secretary of the Association for 48 years.

7803 ■ Hunterian Society
Betty Smallwood, Gen. Admin.
11 Chandos St.
Lettsom House
London W19 9EB, United Kingdom
Ph: 44 20 74367363
E-mail: info@hunteriansociety.org.uk
URL: http://www.hunteriansociety.org.uk

7804 ■ Hunterian Medal
To stimulate an original contribution in essay form on a medical scientific topic chosen by the Society. Registered Medical Practitioners in Great Britain are eligible. A gold medal is awarded annually. Established in 1984 in honor of John Hunter.

7805 ■ Mo Ibrahim Foundation
35 Portman Sq., 3rd Fl. N
London W1H 6LR, United Kingdom
Ph: 44 20 7535 5063
URL: http://www.moibrahimfoundation.org

7806 ■ Mo Ibrahim Prize for Achievement in African Leadership
To recognize excellence in African leadership. Awarded to a democratically elected former African Executive Head of State or Government who has served his or her term in office within the limits set by the country's constitution and has left office in the last three years. The Ibra-

Awards are arranged in alphabetical order below their administering organizations

him Prize consists of US$5 million over 10 years and US$200,000 annually for life thereafter. Awarded annually. Established in 2007.

7807 ■ IC Events
7 Coldbath Sq.
London EC1R 4LQ, United Kingdom
Ph: 44 20 7841 3218
Fax: 44 20 7841 3211
URL: http://www.ic-events.net

7808 ■ African Banker Awards
To recognize excellence in banking and finance in Africa, and to reward the people and financial institutions that are making a difference on the continent. Presented in more than a dozen categories each year. Established in 2008.

7809 ■ African Business Awards
To recognize individuals and organizations that are making a significant contribution to Africa's business climate and economic development. Presented in approximately 12 categories each year. Established in 2008.

7810 ■ ICHCA International Limited
John Strang, Intl. Chm.
Ste. 2, 85 Western Rd.
Essex
Romford RM1 3LS, United Kingdom
Ph: 44 1708 735295
Fax: 44 1708 735225
E-mail: info@ichca.com
URL: http://www.ichcainternational.co.uk

7811 ■ ICHCA Australia Award
For contribution to industry development.

7812 ■ ICHCA Finland Award
For contribution to industry development.

7813 ■ Infection Prevention Society
Mrs. Lynne Duncan, Contact
Drumcross Hall
Bathgate EH48 4JT, United Kingdom
Ph: 44 1506 811077
E-mail: lynne@fitwise.co.uk
URL: http://www.ips.uk.net
Formerly: (2007) Infection Control Nurses' Association.

7814 ■ J and J Award
For further education.

7815 ■ Informa plc
30-32 Mortimer St.
London W1W 7RE, United Kingdom
Ph: 44 20 7017 5000
URL: http://www.informa.com

7816 ■ AfricaCom Awards
To reward and recognize the success of the African communications market. Open to any operator, vendor, or regulator that offers solutions or products anywhere in Africa. Awarded annually. Established in 2008.

7817 ■ Institute of Acoustics
Kevin Macan-Lind, Chief Exec.
77A St. Peter's St.
Hertfordshire
St. Albans AL1 3BN, United Kingdom
Ph: 44 1727 848195
Fax: 44 1727 850553
E-mail: ioa@ioa.org.uk
URL: http://www.ioa.org.uk

7818 ■ Rayleigh Medal
For recognition of outstanding contributions to acoustics by a United Kingdom and a foreign acoustician, alternately. A medal and a citation are awarded annually. Established in 1975 by the British Acoustical Society in memory of John William Strutt, Third Baron Rayleigh, a physicist and physician who won a Nobel Prize for physics in 1904.

7819 ■ Stephens Lecture
To honor distinguished acousticians. The lecture is held annually at the spring conference and is intended to be an important occasion at an IOA Meeting, marked by the presentation of a scroll to the lecturer. Established in 1984 in honor of Dr. Ray Stephens, a graduate of Imperial College, London where he subsequently created his Acoustics Research group, and also the first President of the Institute of Acoustics, which he was instrumental in creating. The Stephens Lecture was set up in honor of his 80th birthday.

7820 ■ Tyndall Medal
For recognition of achievement and service in the field of acoustics. Citizens of the United Kingdom, preferably under the age of 40, are eligible. A medal and a citation are awarded biennially in even-numbered years. Established in 1975 by the British Acoustical Society in memory of John Tyndall (1820-1893), an experimental physicist and one of the world's most brilliant scientific lecturers.

7821 ■ A. B. Wood Medal and Prize
For recognition of distinguished contributions in the application of acoustics, with preference given to candidates whose work is associated with the sea. The prize is awarded alternately to a person domiciled in the United Kingdom, and in the United States or Canada. The Acoustical Society of America selects recipients from the United States or Canada. Individuals, preferably under 35 years of age in the year of the award, are considered. A silver-gilt medal, a parchment scroll, and a monetary prize are awarded annually.

7822 ■ Institute of Actuaries - United Kingdom
Derek Cribb, Acting Chief Exec.
Staple Inn Hall
High Holborn
London WC1V 7QJ, United Kingdom
Ph: 44 207 6322100
Fax: 44 207 6322111
E-mail: institute@actuaries.org.uk
URL: http://www.actuaries.org.uk

7823 ■ Finlaison Medal
For recognition of services to the actuarial profession in furthering one or more of the various objectives set out in the Royal Charter. Awarded when merited. Established in 1966. Named after John Finlaison (1783-1860), the first president of the Institute of Actuaries. Formerly: (1985) Silver Medal.

7824 ■ Gold Medal
For recognition of work of pre-eminent importance either in originality, content, or consequence in the actuarial field. Awarded when merited. Established in 1919.

7825 ■ Institute of Administrative Management
Jenny Hewell, Chief Exec.
6 Graphite Sq.
Vauxhall Walk
London SE11 5EE, United Kingdom
Ph: 44 20 70912600
Fax: 44 20 70917340
E-mail: info@instam.org
URL: http://www.instam.org

7826 ■ Educational Awards
To recognize professional managers and to promote and develop the science of administrative management. The Institute's educational programs can lead to the award of certificate, diploma, advanced diploma, and BA (Hons) degree in Administrative Management. The fol-

lowing awards are presented: Michael Guthrie Prize, A. J. Shawcross Prize, Sir Joseph Burn Prize, and the Leonard W. Green Prize.

7827 ■ Institute of Cast Metals Engineers
Dr. Pam Murrell, Operations Dir.
47 Birmingham Rd.
West Bromwich B70 6PY, United Kingdom
Ph: 44 121 6016979
Fax: 44 121 6016981
E-mail: info@icme.org.uk
URL: http://www.icme.org.uk

7828 ■ British Foundry Medal and Prize
To recognize the best technical paper published in the *Foundry Trade Journal* during the previous year. Awarded annually.

7829 ■ E.J. Fox Medal
To recognize an individual who has made a significant contribution to the development of the foundry industry through an invention or a piece of research. Awarded annually.

7830 ■ M.M. Hallett Award
Awarded every three years to an individual, group, or an organization who has made outstanding contributions to the foundry industry by the creation of new ideas or inventions. Awarded triennially.

7831 ■ ICME Diploma
To recognize the best technical paper published in the *Foundry Trade Journal* during the previous year. Awarded annually.

7832 ■ Meritorious Services Medal
To honor a longstanding member who has made a significant contribution to the Institute or the industry as a whole.

7833 ■ Oliver Stubbs Medal
For recognition of achievement in the development of the cast metals industry and for imparting knowledge to fellow members of the Institute. Institute members are eligible. A medal is awarded annually. Established in 1922 by Oliver Stubbs, past president of the Institute.

7834 ■ Institute of Chartered Accountants of Scotland
Iain McLaren, Pres.
CA House
21 Haymarket Yards
Edinburgh EH12 5BH, United Kingdom
Ph: 44 131 3470100
Fax: 44 131 3470105
E-mail: enquiries@icas.org.uk
URL: http://www.icas.org.uk

7835 ■ David Bogie Prize
To recognize an outstanding performance in the Assurance and Business Systems section of the Test of Professional Skills (TPS) exam. Awarded four times per year.

7836 ■ J. C. Burleigh Prize
To award the candidate whose performance in the November Exam Diet of the Test of Professional Expertise is the most meritorious. Awarded annually.

7837 ■ Canadian Institute of Chartered Accountants Prize
To reward the winner of the Institute's Gold Medal. A monetary award is presented annually. Established 1967.

7838 ■ Walid Chorbachi Prizes
To recognize the candidates who placed first and second in the May Exam Diet of the Test of Professional Expertise. Awarded annually.

7839 ■ James M. Cowie Prize
To award the candidate at the November Exam Diet of the Test of Professional Expertise who is judged to be second in merit. Awarded annually.

Awards are arranged in alphabetical order below their administering organizations

7840 ■ Gold Medal
To encourage the professional development of the Institute's students. The award is given to the candidate whose performance, over all parts of the Institute's professional examinations, is judged to be most meritorious. A gold medal is awarded twice each year, at the May and November Exam Diets. Established in 1961.

7841 ■ Guthrie Prize
To award the candidate in the Test of Professional Expertise who is fourth in order of merit in the May Exam Diet. Awarded annually. Honors Isabel Guthrie, the first female member of the institute.

7842 ■ John Mann Prize
To recognize an outstanding performance in the Taxation section of the Test of Professional Skills (TPS) exam. Awarded four times per year.

7843 ■ Robert McArthur Prize
To award the candidate at the May Exam Diet of the Test of Professional Expertise who is judged to be third in order of merit. Awarded annually.

7844 ■ Sir William McLintock Prize
To recognize an outstanding performance in the Assurance and Business Systems section of the Test of Professional Skills (TPS) exam. Awarded in two parts four times per year.

7845 ■ Forbes Murphy Prize
To recognize an outstanding performance in the Financial Reporting section of the Test of Professional Skills (TPS) exam. Awarded in two parts four times per year.

7846 ■ Primrose Scott Prize
To recognize the TOPP's candidate at the November and May Exam Diets of the Test of Professional Expertise whose performance is judged to be most meritorious. Formerly: Lady Members Group Prize.

7847 ■ John Munn Ross Prize
To recognize an outstanding performance in the Taxation section of the Test of Professional Skills (TPS) exam. Awarded in two parts four times per year.

7848 ■ Helen Sommerville Prize
To recognize the candidate whose performance in the November Exam Diet of the Test of Professional Expertise is fifth in order of merit. Awarded annually.

7849 ■ Albert J. Watson Prize
To recognize the candidate whose performance in the Test of Professional Skills (TPS) was second in order of merit. Awarded four times per year.

7850 ■ C. J. Weir Prize
To recognize the candidate whose performance in the November Exam Diet of the Test of Professional Expertise is fourth in order of merit. Awarded annually.

7851 ■ Ronald Williamson Prize
To recognize the candidate whose performance in the Test of Professional Skills (TPS) was the most meritorious. Awarded four times per year.

7852 ■ Institute of Clerks of Works and Construction Inspectorate of Great Britain
Mr. Vaughan Jones, Gen. Sec.
Equinox
28 Commerce Rd.
Lynch Wood
Peterborough PE2 6LR, United Kingdom
Ph: 44 1733 405160
Fax: 44 1733 405161
E-mail: info@icwci.org
URL: http://www.icwci.org

7853 ■ Building on Quality Awards
For outstanding skills and abilities of clerks of works within the construction process. Awarded in three categories: 1. New Build Works, 2. Civil Engineering, and 3. Refurbishment and Maintenance. Awarded biennially in odd-numbered years.

7854 ■ Institute of Domestic Heating and Environmental Engineers
Chris Laughton, Chm.
New Forest Enterprise Centre, Unit 35A
Chapel Ln.
Totton
Southampton SO40 9LA, United Kingdom
Ph: 44 2380 668900
Fax: 44 2380 660888
E-mail: admin@idhee.org.uk
URL: http://www.idhee.org.uk

7855 ■ Advanced Diploma
For an understanding of the design and installation of energy efficient central heating and domestic air conditioning systems.

7856 ■ Associate Member Diploma
For an understanding of the design and installation of energy efficient central heating systems.

7857 ■ Certificate in Energy Efficiency For Domestic Central Heating
Award of recognition.

7858 ■ Technician Diploma
For an understanding of the installation of energy efficient central heating systems.

7859 ■ Institute of Ergonomics and Human Factors
Mr. David O'Neill, Chief Exec.
Elms Ct.
Elms Grove
Loughborough LE11 1RG, United Kingdom
Ph: 44 1509 234904
Fax: 44 1509 235666
E-mail: iehf@ergonomics.org.uk
URL: http://www.ergonomics.org.uk
Formerly: (2009) Ergonomics Society - England.

7860 ■ Ulf Aberg Post Graduate Award
To recognize the best postgraduate student project in ergonomics. The postgraduate project should be in an area of ergonomics; however, the postgraduate course need not be one recognized by the Society. Winners receive a monetary award of £100. In addition, a certificate and expenses to attend the Annual Dinner are awarded. Established in 1977. Formerly: (1985) Student Award - Postgraduate Division.

7861 ■ Sir Frederic Bartlett Medal
To honor an individual(s) who has made significant contributions to original research, the development of methodology, or application of knowledge within the field of ergonomics. Entries may be submitted by October 31. A medal, a certificate, and expenses to attend the Annual Dinner are awarded annually when merited. Established in 1971.

7862 ■ Paul Branton Meritorious Service Award
Awarded for altruistic service to the society over many years. A medal and certificate are awarded annually. Established in 1984.

7863 ■ Otto Edholm Award
To honor an individual or individuals who have made significant contributions to basic or applied research in ergonomics. Entries may be submitted by October 31. A certificate and expenses to attend the Annual Dinner are awarded. The award was established to honor Otto Edholm, who was born in 1909 and studied Medicine at St George's Hospital, London.

7864 ■ William Floyd Award
Awarded to individuals, institutions or groups who have made innovative or outstanding contributions to ergonomics. A certificate and medal are awarded annually. Established in 1985.

7865 ■ Richard Clive Holman Memorial Prize
Awarded to a writer of an outstanding essay on information technology linked to ergonomics. A certificate and monetary prize of £300 is awarded annually.

7866 ■ Hywel Murrell Award
To recognize the best undergraduate student project in ergonomics. The undergraduate project should be in an area of ergonomics; however, the undergraduate course need not be one recognized by the Society. Entries may be submitted by the student's supervisor or head of department by July 31. Winners receive a monetary award of £100. In addition, a certificate and expenses to attend the Annual Dinner are awarded. Established in 1977. Formerly: (1984) Student Award - Undergraduate Division.

7867 ■ President's Medal
Awarded to institutions or organizational groups whose work has made a significant contribution to original research, development of methods or application of knowledge within the field of ergonomics. A medal and certificate are awarded annually. Established in 1983

7868 ■ Student Prize
Awarded to the writer of an essay whose title is set each year by the society. A certificate and monetary prize of £1,000 is awarded annually. Established in 1992.

7869 ■ Institute of Financial Accountants
Eric Anstee, Chm.
Burford House
44 London Rd.
Sevenoaks TN13 1AS, United Kingdom
Ph: 44 1732 458080
Fax: 44 1732 455848
E-mail: mail@ifa.org.uk
URL: http://www.ifa.org.uk
Formerly: (1987) Institute of Administrative Accountants.

7870 ■ Institute of Financial Accountants Awards
To recognize individuals for: (1) excellence of achievement in the examinations for the awards of Associate and Fellow of the Institute; (2) outstanding contributions to the theory of accountancy; and (3) high levels of performance in the practice of the profession. Examination prizes are awarded twice a year in June and December. Formerly: Institute of Administrative Accountants Awards.

7871 ■ Institute of Financial Services - England
Bruce Carnegie-Brown, Pres.
100 Cannon St., 6th Fl.
London EC4N 6EU, United Kingdom
Ph: 44 20 74447111
Fax: 44 20 74447115
E-mail: customerservices@ifslearning.com
URL: http://www.ifslearning.com

7872 ■ Financial Innovation Awards
To recognize financial services organizations that have demonstrated excellence in one of the 22 award categories. Awarded annually.

7873 ■ Institute of Heraldic and Genealogical Studies
Cecil Humphery-Smith, Principal
79-82 Northgate
Canterbury CT1 1BA, United Kingdom
Ph: 44 1227 768664
Fax: 44 1227 765617
E-mail: admin@ihgs.ac.uk
URL: http://www.ihgs.ac.uk/index.html

Awards are arranged in alphabetical order below their administering organizations

7874 ■ Julian Bickersteth Memorial Medal

To honor individuals who have made significant contributions to family history studies. The Trustees of the Institute may nominate individuals. A gold medal is awarded annually when merited at the annual luncheon. Established in 1962 by Cecil R.J. Humphery-Smith.

7875 ■ Certificates, Diplomas, and Licentiates in Genealogy and Heraldry

To recognize achievement in genealogical study. Awarded when merited.

7876 ■ Institute of Internal Communication

Kathie Jones, Chief Exec.
Oak House, Ste. GA2
Woodlands Business Park
Linford Wood
Milton Keynes MK14 6EY, United Kingdom
Ph: 44 1908 313755
Ph: 44 1908 313711
Fax: 44 1908 313661
E-mail: enquiries@ioic.org.uk
URL: http://www.ioic.org.uk
Formerly: (1996) British Association of Industrial Editors.

7877 ■ Communicator of the Year

To recognize outstanding internal and external communication strategies that engage, enthuse, inspire, inform, or excite an organization's people or its clients. Awarded annually. In addition, the Internal Communicator of the Year is awarded to the communicator who is deemed to have made the biggest contribution to internal communications. Established in 1976.

7878 ■ Communicators in Business Awards

For recognition of achievement in corporate communication journalism. Internal and external magazines, newspapers, newsletters, and other publications published during the preceding year are eligible. All entries must be printed in English, but house journals from across the world are welcome. Awards are given in various categories, including Internal Newspapers; External publications; Financial Publications; Audio Visual; and News Photography Trophies and certificates are awarded annually at the spring convention. Established in 1954. Formerly: (1982) BACB National House Journal Competition; (1996) BAIE Editing for Industry Awards; BAIE Editing for Industry Awards.

7879 ■ Institute of Leadership and Management

Peter Cheese, Chm.
Stowe House
Netherstowe
Staffordshire
Lichfield WS13 6TJ, United Kingdom
Ph: 44 1543 266886
Ph: 44 1543 266867
Fax: 44 1543 266893
E-mail: customer@i-l-m.com
URL: http://www.i-l-m.com

7880 ■ Awards for Excellence

To recognize and reward forward-thinking individuals who have achieved outstanding results through leadership and management development. Two awards are presented annually: the Learner of the Year and the Achiever of the Year.

7881 ■ Keith Thurley Award

To recognize the best project at certificate level. Awarded when merited.

7882 ■ Institute of Legal Cashiers and Administrators

Dawn Chapman, Chm.
Marlowe House, 2nd Fl.
109 Station Rd.
Sidcup
Kent DA15 7ET, United Kingdom
Ph: 44 20 83022867
Fax: 44 20 83027481
E-mail: info@ilca.org.uk
URL: http://www.ilca.org.uk

7883 ■ Wilfred Owen Awards

Recognizes individuals for the highest examination marks at the Diploma, Associate, and Fellowship level. Medals are awarded annually.

7884 ■ Institute of Management

David Howard, Pres.
2 Savoy Ct., 3rd Fl.
Strand
London WC2R OEZ, United Kingdom
Ph: 44 20 74970580
Fax: 44 20 74970463
E-mail: enquiries@managers.org.uk
URL: http://www.managers.org.uk

7885 ■ John Ellis Award

To honor the best candidate to complete the Institute's Diploma in Management. Awarded annually.

7886 ■ Sir Henry Flides Award

To honor the best candidate to complete the Institute's Executive Diploma in Management. Awarded annually.

7887 ■ Gold Medal

This, the Institute's highest honor, is given to recognize an individual who exemplifies the highest standards in managing people and leading organizations. Awarded annually. Established in 1980.

7888 ■ Petrie Memorial Award

To honor the best candidate to complete the Institute's Executive Diploma in Strategic Management. Awarded annually.

7889 ■ Institute of Marine Engineering, Science and Technology

Prof. C.G. Hodge, Chm.
80 Coleman St.
London EC2R 5BJ, United Kingdom
Ph: 44 20 73822600
Fax: 44 20 73822670
E-mail: info@imarest.org
URL: http://www.imarest.org
Formerly: (2004) Institute of Marine Engineers.

7890 ■ Denny Medal

To recognize the best paper(s) published in the *Journal of Marine Engineering and Technology* or the *Journal of Operational Oceanography*. A silver gilt medal is awarded to up to three recipients annually. Established in 1893 in honor of Peter Denny.

7891 ■ Duke of Edinburgh's Award

To recognize an individual or group for current examples of best practice in research, development, design, manufacture, production, or construction of an engineering product or process that contributes to the protection or enhancement of the marine environment. A certificate and engraved memento are awarded every three years upon approval by the Duke of Edinburgh.

7892 ■ Stanley Gray Award - Branch Certificate

Awarded by each Branch for the best presentation made as part of their programs within the technical year. Certificates are awarded annually.

7893 ■ Stanley Gray Silver Medal

To enable post-graduate students to undertake research in approved maritime subjects. Applicants must have obtained an approved engineering degree or the DTp Extra First Class Certificate of Competency and be members of the Institute. The deadline for applications is July 31. A monetary award of £2,000 per year (for a maximum of three years) is presented annually.

7894 ■ Donald Maxwell Award

For recognition of the best paper presented to, or published by, the Institute by a member or nonmember of any nationality on the research and/or development of some aspect of marine equipment and its market potential. Joint authors are also eligible. Papers are to be assessed by the IMarE Technical Papers and Conferences Committee, whose recommendations are passed to the Donald Maxwell Fund Trustees for approval. A monetary prize of £1,000 is awarded annually.

7895 ■ President's Award

To recognize an individual or group for distinction in a maritime technology subject through outstanding achievement, the writing and presentation of a significant technical paper, or the writing of a technical book during the past 10 years. Open to members and non-members of any nationality. A certificate and monetary prize up to £10,000 is awarded when merited, roughly every five years.

7896 ■ Institute of Measurement and Control

Bill Bardo, Pres.
87 Gower St.
London WC1E 6AF, United Kingdom
Ph: 44 20 73874949
Fax: 44 20 73888431
URL: http://www.instmc.org.uk

7897 ■ Honeywell Prize

To recognize the best article for publication in *Measurement and Control*, the institute journal. The criteria for the assessment of these articles are as follows: general interest to the institute's members, importance of the subject to the institute, and lucidity and originality. A monetary award of £100 is awarded annually.

7898 ■ Institute of Physics

Prof. Jocelyn Bell-Bernell, Pres.
76 Portland Pl.
London W1B 1NT, United Kingdom
Ph: 44 20 74704800
Fax: 44 20 74704848
E-mail: physics@iop.org
URL: http://www.iop.org

7899 ■ Appleton Medal and Prize

For distinguished research in environmental, earth, or atmospheric physics. A monetary prize of £1,000, a silver medal, and a certificate are awarded biennially in even-numbered years. Established in 1939. Formerly: (2008) Charles Chree Medal and Prize.

7900 ■ Max Born Medal and Prize

In recognition of outstanding contributions to physics. A monetary prize of 3,000 Euros, a silver medal, and a certificate are awarded annually in even-numbered years to a physicist based in Germany, and in odd-numbered years to a physicist based in Ireland or the United Kingdom. Established in 1972. Co-administered by the German Physical Society.

7901 ■ Bragg Medal and Prize

For distinguished contributions to the teaching of physics. A monetary prize of £1,000, a bronze medal, and a certificate are awarded annually. Established in 1965 in honor of Sir Lawrence Bragg, teacher and popularizer of physics.

7902 ■ Business and Innovation Medal

For outstanding contributions to the organization or application of physics in an industrial or commercial setting. A medal, a certificate, and a monetary prize of £1,000 are awarded.

7903 ■ Chadwick Medal and Prize

Recognizes distinguished research in particle

Awards are arranged in alphabetical order below their administering organizations

physics. A medal, a certificate, and a monetary prize of £1,000 are awarded biennially in odd-numbered years. Established in 2008.

7904 ■ Dirac Medal
For outstanding contributions to theoretical (including mathematical and computational) physics. A monetary prize of £1,000, a silver medal, and a certificate are awarded annually. Established in 1985 in memory of Paul A. M. Dirac, an Honorary Fellow of The Institute of Physics.

7905 ■ Faraday Medal
To recognize a physicist of international reputation for contributions to experimental physics. A monetary prize of £1,000, a silver gilt medal, and a certificate are awarded annually. Established in 1914. Formerly: (2008) Guthrie Medal and Prize.

7906 ■ Franklin Medal and Prize
For distinguished research in physics as applied to the life sciences. A medal, a certificate, and a monetary prize of £1,000 is awarded biennially in even-numbered years. Established in 2008.

7907 ■ Gabor Medal and Prize
To recognize an individual or team for distinguished work in the application of physics in an industrial, commercial, or business context, including work that has enhanced the economic or social well-being of the United Kingdom or Ireland. A monetary prize of £1,000, a bronze medal, and a certificate are awarded biennially in even-numbered years. Established in 1923. Formerly: (2008) Duddell Medal and Prize.

7908 ■ Glazebrook Medal
In recognition of outstanding leadership contributions in the organization, utilization, or application of physics. A monetary prize of £1,000, a silver gilt medal, and a certificate are awarded annually. Established in 1965 by the Institute of Physics and the Physical Society in honor of Sir Richard Glazebrook, the first director of the National Physical Laboratory.

7909 ■ Holweck Medal and Prize
For distinguished work in any aspect of physics that is ongoing or has been carried out within the 10 years preceding this award. Awarded annually - in odd-numbered years to a physicist based in France, and in even-numbered years to a physicist based in Ireland or the United Kingdom. A gold medal and monetary prize of 3,000 Euros are presented. Established in 1945. Co-administered by the Societe Francaise de Physique (French Physical Society).

7910 ■ Hoyle Medal and Prize
For distinguished research in astrophysics, gravitational physics, or cosmology. A medal, a certificate, and a monetary prize of £1,000 is awarded biennially in even-numbered years. Established in 2008.

7911 ■ Joule Medal and Prize
For distinguished research in applied physics. A medal, a certificate, and a monetary prize of £1,000 is awarded biennially in odd-numbered years. Established in 2008.

7912 ■ Harrie Massey Medal
Recognizes contributions to physics or the applications of physics. A medal and a certificate are awarded biennially in even-numbered years. Awarded jointly by the Institute and the Australian Institute of Physics. Established in 1988.

7913 ■ Maxwell Medal and Prize
To recognize a young physicist for outstanding contributions to theoretical physics, mathematical physics, or computational physics. Open to physicists who are in the first 12 years of their research career. A monetary prize of £1,000, a bronze medal, and a certificate are awarded annually. Established in 1961.

7914 ■ Moseley Medal and Prize
In recognition of distinguished research in experimental physics. Candidates should be in the early port of their careers. A monetary prize of £1,000, a silver medal, and a certificate are awarded annually. Established in 1944. Formerly: (2008) Boy's Medal and Prize.

7915 ■ Mott Medal and Prize
Recognizes distinguished research in condensed matter or materials physics. A silver medal, a certificate, and a monetary prize of £1,000 is awarded biennially in odd-numbered years. Established in 1997.

7916 ■ Isaac Newton Medal
Recognizes a physicist for outstanding contributions to the field of physics. A medal, a certificate, and a monetary prize of £1,000 are awarded annually. Recipient may be invited to give a lecture.

7917 ■ Occhialini Medal and Prize
For distinguished work in physics during the preceding 10 years. Award is presented to physicists in Italy in even-numbered years and physicists in the U.K. or Ireland in odd-numbered years. A silver medal and a monetary prize of £3,000 are awarded annually. Established in 2007.

7918 ■ Paterson Medal and Prize
To recognize a young physicist for distinguished research in applied physics. Candidates must be in the first 12 years of their research career. A monetary prize of £1,000, a bronze medal, and a certificate are awarded annually. Established in 1981 in honor of Sir Clifford Paterson, founder of GEC Research Laboratories and a past president of the Institute.

7919 ■ Payne-Gaposchkin Medal and Prize
Recognizes distinguished research in plasma, solar, or space physics. A medal, a certificate, and a monetary prize of £1,000 is awarded biennially in odd-numbered years. Established in 2008.

7920 ■ President's Medal
To recognize individuals for meritorious service to the Institute or to physics in general. One or two awards are made per presidency. Established in 1997.

7921 ■ Rayleigh Medal and Prize
For distinguished research in theoretical, mathematical, or computational physics. A medal, a certificate, and a monetary prize of £1,000 is awarded biennially in odd-numbered years. Established in 2008.

7922 ■ Rutherford Medal and Prize
To recognize an individual or team for contributions to nuclear physics or nuclear technology. A monetary prize of £1,000, a bronze medal, and a certificate are awarded biennially in even-numbered years. Established in 1939 in memory of Lord Rutherford of Nelson. Formerly: Rutherford Memorial Lecture.

7923 ■ Simon Memorial Prize
In recognition of distinguished work in experimental or theoretical low-temperature physics. A monetary prize of £300, a bronze plaque, and a certificate are awarded approximately every three years. Administered by the Low Temperature Group of the Physical Society. Established in 1958 in memory of Sir Francis Simon.

7924 ■ Tabor Medal and Prize
Recognizes distinguished research in surface or nanoscale physics. A medal, a certificate, and a monetary prize of £1,000 is awarded biennially in odd-numbered years. Established in 2008.

7925 ■ Thomson Medal and Prize
For distinguished research in atomic or molecular

physics. A medal, a certificate, and a monetary prize of £1,000 is awarded biennially in even-numbered years. Established in 2008.

7926 ■ Thomas Young Medal and Prize
To honor an individual or team in recognition of work in optics, including work related to physics outside the visible region. A monetary prize of £1,000, a bronze medal, and a certificate are awarded biennially in odd-numbered years. Established in 1907 as the Thomas Young Oration by the Optical Society, taken over by the Physical Society of London in 1932, and changed to its present state in 1961 by the amalgamated Institute of Physics and Physical Society. Formerly: Thomas Young Oration.

7927 ■ Institute of Physics and Engineering in Medicine
Dr. Chris J. Gibson, Pres.
Fairmount House
230 Tadcaster Rd.
York YO24 1ES, United Kingdom
Ph: 44 1904 610821
Fax: 44 1904 612279
E-mail: office@ipem.ac.uk
URL: http://www.ipem.ac.uk

7928 ■ Founders' Prize
To recognize an individual for distinction in the practice of physics or engineering in relation to medicine. Awarded annually.

7929 ■ IPEM/AAPM Travel Award
To provide financial assistance to a member for IPEM-related travel in the U.S. or Canada. Awarded annually. Supported by the American Association of Physicists in Medicine (AAPM).

7930 ■ Manufacturers' Award
To recognize a member for significant contributions to the technology associated with medical physics or clinical engineering. Awarded annually.

7931 ■ Institute of Practitioners in Advertising
Hamish Pringle, Dir. Gen.
44 Belgrave Sq.
London SW1X 8QS, United Kingdom
Ph: 44 20 7235 7020
Fax: 44 20 7245 9904
E-mail: web@ipa.co.uk
URL: http://www.ipa.co.uk

7932 ■ Effectiveness Awards
to provide a data bank of case history material to demonstrate the contribution that advertising can make to successful marketing. The main objectives are to improve understanding of the crucial role advertising plays in marketing; to provide documented analyses of advertising effectiveness and to encourage use of methods of evaluation; and to generate objective case studies about how advertising works, which could then be used in connection with marketing training. In odd-numbered years, the contest is limited to agencies with marketing budgets up to £2.5 million and a maximum word count of 3,000; in even-numbered years, it is open to agencies worldwide and has a maximum word count of 4,000. Winning cases are awarded between one and five stars. The overall winner is presented with the Grand Prize. The winning case studies and a selection from the commended papers are published in a book, *Advertising Works*. Presented annually. Established in 1980.

7933 ■ Institute of Quarrying - England
Martin Isles, Pres.
7 Regent St.
Nottingham NG1 5BS, United Kingdom
Ph: 44 115 9453880
Fax: 44 115 9484035
E-mail: mail@quarrying.org
URL: http://www.quarrying.org

Awards are arranged in alphabetical order below their administering organizations

7934 ■ Ruston Bucyrus Award

To recognize the author(s) of papers presented at Institute seminars, conferences, courses, or symposia. A monetary prize of £200 is awarded annually to one or two recipients. Established in 1963.

7935 ■ Caernarfon Award

To recognize the best paper given at an Institute conference, seminar, or meeting that is adjudged to have contributed the most to the advancement of some aspect of the industry, including technical, environmental, and strategic. A monetary prize of £1,000 is awarded annually. Established in 1989 and named in honor of the town where the first Institute meeting took place in 1917.

7936 ■ Citation Award

To honor a long-serving member who is held in particularly high regard because of a long period of outstanding service to the Institute. Awarded annually to one or more recipients. Established in 1979.

7937 ■ Honorary Fellowship

To recognize an individual for distinguished service, either to the Institute or to the quarrying industry, at the highest levels. Awarded annually.

7938 ■ Marston Award

To recognize the best paper presented to a branch meeting by a U.K. member of any grade employed within the quarrying industry. A monetary prize of £200 is awarded annually. Established in 1974. Endowed by C.E. Marston, former president of the Institute.

7939 ■ McPherson Memorial Lecture

To recognize the author of an outstanding technical paper. A monetary prize of £1,000 and an invitation to lecture are awarded triennially. Established in 1974 in honor of Simon McPherson, one of the founders of the Institute.

7940 ■ Institute of Refrigeration
Dr. Andy Pearson, Pres.
Kelvin House, 76 Mill Ln.
Surrey
Carshalton SM5 2JR, United Kingdom
Ph: 44 20 86477033
Fax: 44 20 87730165
E-mail: ior@ior.org.uk
URL: http://www.ior.org.uk

7941 ■ J and E Hall Gold Medal

To recognize an individual for a significant practical contribution to the development of refrigeration and air conditioning technology. The recipient is awarded a cash prize of £5,000, a silver medal, and the retention of the Gold medal for a full year. Awarded annually. Established in 1977. Sponsored by J & E Hall.

7942 ■ Ted Perry Award

To honor a young individual for research of a practical nature related to the field of refrigeration. An engraved tankard and monetary prize of £500 is awarded annually. Established in 1991.

7943 ■ Service Engineer Lifetime Achievement Award

To recognize a service engineer for outstanding individual achievement and exceptional contribution to the industry the United Kingdom. Candidates must have at least 25 years of experience in the industry. A trophy/certificate and monetary prize of £400 is awarded annually.

7944 ■ Institute of Scientific and Technical Communicators
Mr. Paul Ballard, Pres.
Airport House
Purley Way
Croydon CR0 0XZ, United Kingdom

Ph: 44 20 82534506
Fax: 44 20 82534510
E-mail: istc@istc.org.uk
URL: http://www.istc.org.uk

7945 ■ Mike Austin Award

To recognize an individual for a considerable contribution to the Institute over a period of time. Awarded periodically.

7946 ■ Horace Hockley Award

To recognize an individual for work done in the scientific and technical communication industry over a period of time. Awarded annually.

7947 ■ UK Technical Communication Awards

To recognize individuals or teams for clear, concise, and effective information products. Awarded annually.

7948 ■ Institute of Trichologists
Mrs. Marilyn Sherlock, Chair
24 Langroyd Rd.
London SW17 7PL, United Kingdom
Ph: 44 845 6044657
Fax: 44 1722 741380
E-mail: admin@trichologists.org.uk
URL: http://www.trichologists.org.uk

7949 ■ MacDonald Award

For the best student in levels 2 and 3 institute examinations.

7950 ■ Institution of Agricultural Engineers
Mr. Christopher R. Whetnall, Chief Exec./Sec.
The Bullock Bldg.
University Way
Cranfield
Bedford MK43 0GH, United Kingdom
Ph: 44 1234 750876
Fax: 44 1234 751319
E-mail: secretary@iagre.org
URL: http://www.iagre.org

7951 ■ Award for Contribution to the Land Based Sector

To recognize a member for a sustained contribution to the land-based sector throughout his or her career. Established in 2005.

7952 ■ Award of Merit

For a person who has rendered services to the institution. Awarded when merited.

7953 ■ Douglas Bomford Paper Award

To recognize the author of a paper that was published in full in the Institution's journal *Landwards*. Awarded annually.

7954 ■ Michael Dwyer Memorial Prize

For mid-career engineer who has made outstanding progress in the agricultural engineering industry. Awarded annually.

7955 ■ Honorary Fellowship

For a person who has rendered services to the institution. Awarded when merited.

7956 ■ Johnson New Holland Trophy Award

For innovation by students of Agricultural Engineering or related subjects. Awarded annually.

7957 ■ Institution of Chemical Engineers
Desmond King, Pres.
Davis Bldg.
Railway Terr.
Rugby CV21 3HQ, United Kingdom
Ph: 44 1788 578214
Fax: 44 1788 560833
E-mail: onlineassistance@icheme.org
URL: http://www.icheme.org

7958 ■ Brennan Medal

To recognize the best book published by the

institution each year. Awarded annually. Established in 1988 to honor Basil Brennan, the Institution's first General Secretary.

7959 ■ Council Medal

To recognize a member or non-member who has given exceptional service on a special project. Awarded annually. Established in 1967.

7960 ■ George E. Davis Medal

For recognition of a contribution in the field of chemical engineering. Awarded not more than every three years. Established in 1965 in honor of George E. Davis, the father of the discipline.

7961 ■ Donald Medal

To recognize an individual for outstanding services to biochemical engineering. Awarded annually. Established in 1988 to honor Prof. Donald, a long-serving Honorary Secretary and former Ramsay Professor at University College London, where biochemical engineering was first established in the United Kingdom.

7962 ■ Ned Franklin Medal

To recognize an individual for outstanding service in the fields of occupational health, safety, loss prevention, and care for the environment. Awarded annually. Established to honor Ned Franklin, a past president of the institution and a major personality in the development of the nuclear power industry.

7963 ■ Arnold Greene Medal

For recognition of the most meritorious contribution to the progress of the institution. Awarded annually. Established in 1928 in honor of F. A. Greene, a founder member and honorable treasurer for 33 years. Formerly: (1964) Osborne Reynolds Medal.

7964 ■ Hanson Medal

For recognition of the best article contributed to the institution's monthly publication, *The Chemical Engineer*. A medal is awarded annually. Established in 1987.

7965 ■ John William Hinchley Medal

To recognize the fourth-year undergraduate student at Imperial College London with the best performance in the final examinations in chemical engineering. Awarded annually. Established in 1988 to honor John William Hinchley, the driving force behind the founding of the institution in 1922.

7966 ■ Hutchison Medal

To recognize the author of the best paper that is either philosophical in nature or deals with practical matters. Awarded annually. Established in 1991 to honor Sir Kenneth Hutchison, former president (1959-1960) of the institution.

7967 ■ MacNab Medal

For recognition of the best answer to the institution's Design Project in any year. Awarded annually. Established in 1935 to honor William MacNab, former president of the Institution.

7968 ■ Moulton Medal

For recognition of the best paper published of a mature nature by the institution during the year. Awarded annually. Established in 1929.

7969 ■ Junior Moulton Medal

For recognition of the best paper published by the institution during the year. Papers written by members under 30 years of age are considered. Awarded annually. Established in 1929.

7970 ■ Institution of Civil Engineers
Peter Hansford, Pres.
One Great George St.
Westminster
London SW1P 3AA, United Kingdom
Ph: 44 20 72227722
Ph: 44 20 76652227

Awards are arranged in alphabetical order below their administering organizations

E-mail: secretariat@ice.org.uk
URL: http://www.ice.org.uk/homepage/index.asp

7971 ■ Associate and Technicians Award
To recognize the best paper submitted by an associate or technician member of the ICE. Established in 1970.

7972 ■ Baker Medal
To recognize outstanding service or promotion of the engineering practice. Established in 1934 in honor of Sir Benjamin Baker.

7973 ■ Best Civil Engineering Student Award
To recognize students for advances in science, engineering, and technology (SET). A monetary prize of £250 is awarded annually.

7974 ■ Brunel Medal
To recognize an individual, team, or organization for excellence in civil engineering. Awarded annually. Established in 1981.

7975 ■ Karen Burt Award
To recognize a newly chartered female engineer for outstanding commitment to the promotion of the profession. Awarded annually.

7976 ■ Robert Alfred Carr Prize
To recognize the author of the best paper on dock, railway, and gas engineering subjects published by the Institution during the past year. A monetary prize of £50 and a certificate are awarded annually. Established in 1963 by Robert Alfred Carr (1864-1942) in memory of his father Robert Carr and his brother Harold Oswald Carr, both members of the Institution.

7977 ■ Civil Engineering Manager of the Year Award
To recognize the chartered civil engineer who has shown, in a given year, the finest management qualities on a construction project. The award, which comprises a medal and £500, can be made to a manager of a huge scheme, someone responsible for a substantial element of such a scheme, or an engineer in charge of a modest site.

7978 ■ Civil Engineering Students Papers Competition
For recognition of a paper on engineering design, research, or practice. Undergraduates of universities and polytechnics in the United Kingdom may be nominated by the heads of the engineering colleges. A monetary prize of £150 and a medal are awarded annually. All authors presenting papers in the final and not awarded the medal receive a monetary prize of £100 and a certificate. Established in 1946. Formerly: (1987) Institution Medal and Premium (London Universities) Competition; (1997) Institution Medal and Premium (Universities) Competition.

7979 ■ Coopers Hill War Memorial Prize
For recognition of a paper by a corporate member published by the Institution. The award is made irrespective of the age of the author and of any other award made for the same paper. A monetary prize, medal, and certificate are awarded annually. Established in 1921 by the Coopers Hill Society in memory of its members and relatives of its members who fell in the First World War.

7980 ■ Crampton Prize
For recognition of the best paper on practical geotechnical engineering. A monetary prize and a certificate are awarded annually. Established in 1890 following a bequest by Thomas Russell Crampton (1816-1888).

7981 ■ Bill Curtin Medal
To recognize the best paper presented to the Institution on innovative design in civil engineering. A medal is awarded annually.

Established in 1992 by Curtins Consulting Engineers to commemorate W. G. Curtin's contribution to engineering.

7982 ■ James Alfred Ewing Medal
For recognition of contributions to the science of engineering in the field of research. Members or nonmembers of the Institution are eligible. Recommendations are made by the Institute of Civil Engineers, the Institute of Mechanical Engineers, the Royal Institution of Naval Architects, and the Institution of Electrical Engineers. A gold medal with a bronze replica is awarded annually jointly with the Royal Society. Established in 1936 in memory of Sir Alfred Ewing (1855-1935), Honorary Member.

7983 ■ Geotechnical Research Medal
To recognize the author(s) of the best contribution in the field of research in geotechnical engineering published by the Institution in the previous year. A medal is awarded annually. Established in 1989 following a bequest by the late A. W. Bishop.

7984 ■ Gold Medal
To recognize an individual for valuable contributions to civil engineering over many years. This may cover contributions in one or more areas, such as, design, research, development, investigation, construction, management (including project management), education, and training. Eligible candidates are those who are in the course of, or have just completed, their active careers. Awarded annually. Established in 1993.

7985 ■ Graduates and Students Papers Competition
For recognition of a paper on engineering design, research, or practice that has been presented at a local association meeting. Nominations may be submitted by the committees of the local associations. Associate members, graduates, and students may be nominated. A monetary prize and a medal are awarded annually. All authors presenting papers at the final and not awarded the medal receive a monetary prize and a certificate. Established in 1951. Formerly: (1997) Institution Medal and Premium (Local Association) Competition.

7986 ■ Halcrow Prize
To recognize the author of the best paper published by the Institution on Maritime Engineering. A monetary prize is awarded annually. Established in 1960 by a bequest of Sir William Halcrow, president of the Institution in 1946-1947.

7987 ■ Edmund Hambly Medal
To recognize outstanding creative design in an engineering project that makes a substantial contribution to sustainable development.

7988 ■ James Hill Prize
To recognize a paper published in Municipal Engineer on the topic of municipal engineering. A monetary award of £100 and certificate are presented annually.

7989 ■ David Hislop Award
To recognize the best paper published in ICE Proceedings. A certificate and monetary prize of £100 are awarded annually. Founded in 1975 in honor of David Atholl Hislop.

7990 ■ Howard Medal
To recognize the author of a paper about the uses and properties of iron or steel, or associated process development. Candidates must be corporate member, graduate member, or student member of ICE. Awarded annually. Established in 1872.

7991 ■ T. K. Hsieh Award
To recognize the author(s) of the best paper published by the institution in the field of structural and soil vibration caused by mechanical plant, winds, waves, or seismic effects. A monetary prize of £100 is awarded annually. Established in 1979 in memory of Dr. Tso Kung Hsieh.

7992 ■ Renee Redfern Hunt Memorial Prize
For recognition of the best essays written in the spring, autumn, and overseas sessions of the professional examination for corporate membership of the Institution. A monetary prize of £100 and a certificate are awarded. Established in 1982 in memory of Miss Renee Redfern Hunt, MBE.

7993 ■ International Medal
To recognize a civil engineer for outstanding contributions to civil engineering in the United Kingdom. Awarded annually. Established in 2000.

7994 ■ Rees Jeffreys Award
To recognize the author of the best paper on highway engineering published in Municipal Engineer or Transport. A monetary prize of £200 is awarded annually.

7995 ■ James Prescott Joule Medal
For recognition of the best paper presented on an engineering subject, preferably one dealing with the transformation of energy. Associate members under 27 years of age or students of the Institution may submit papers. A medal is awarded triennially.

7996 ■ John Henry Garrood King Medal
To recognize the best paper published by an ICE member about tunnels, soil mechanics, or bridges. Awarded annually. Established in 2000.

7997 ■ Lindapter Award
To recognize the author of the best paper submitted to the Institution's Medal and Premium (Local Associations and Universities) Competitions. Students pursuing a course of study approved by the Institution are eligible. A monetary prize of £200 is awarded. The winner's name and that of the university/college is recorded on a trophy and displayed by that university/college for the following eight months. Sponsored by Lindapter International Ltd.

7998 ■ Manby Prize
To recognize an outstanding paper published by the Institution. A monetary prize of £100 and a certificate is presented annually. Established in 1857 by Charles Manby.

7999 ■ Overseas Prize
For recognition of the best papers received during the year on a subject connected with works carried out outside the British Isles. Corporate members of the Institution are eligible. Two monetary prizes and certificates are awarded annually.

8000 ■ Frederick Palmer Prize
For recognition of a paper published by the Institution. Preference is given to papers of merit dealing with the economic and financial aspects of civil engineering. A monetary prize and a certificate are awarded annually. Established in 1960 by a bequest made by John Palmer to mark the centenary of the birth of his father, Sir Frederick Palmer (1862-1934), president of the Institution in 1926-1927.

8001 ■ Parkman Medal
For recognition of the best paper published by the Institution in the previous year on the practical aspects of the control or management of the design and/or construction of a specific scheme. A medal is awarded annually. Established in 1988 by the Parkman Group to commemorate their centenary.

8002 ■ Paterson Prize
To recognize a Welsh resident for the best writ-

Awards are arranged in alphabetical order below their administering organizations

ten assignment or test produced during each of the U.K. Spring and Autumn Review sessions. A monetary award of £100 and certificate are presented. Established in honor of Colonel Paterson. Administered by the ICE Wales branch.

8003 ■ QUEST Travel Award
To recognize and support a member of ICE who wishes to study abroad. The course of study should last no more than 12 months. A travel grant up to £1,500 is awarded by the Queen's Jubilee Scholarship Trust (QUEST).

8004 ■ QUEST Undergraduate Scholarship
To recognize and support undergraduate scholars. Individuals must be enrolled in an ICE accredited civil engineering course. Financial support up to £3,000 per year is awarded by the Queen's Jubilee Scholarship Trust (QUEST).

8005 ■ Reed and Mallik Medal
To recognize the author of the best paper on urban design published in the previous year. A monetary prize and a medal are awarded annually. Established in 1983 following a donation by the Rush & Tompkins Group plc to commemorate the achievements of their civil engineering contracting subsidiary Reed and Mallik Ltd.

8006 ■ Region Merit Awards
Each Region of the ICE has an annual Award for excellence in a construction project within its area completed in the previous calendar year. The Award seeks to recognize and publicize works of merit - principally for innovation, engineering excellence, or physical achievement and contributions towards sustainability. Presented by the President of ICE at the relevant Region's Annual Dinner.

8007 ■ James Rennie Medal
To recognize the best Chartered Professional Review candidate of the year. A medal, certificate, and monetary prize of £500 are awarded annually.

8008 ■ Safety in Construction Medal
To recognize the author of a paper published by the Institution in the previous year that discusses a project or feature within a project that best describes the measures taken to safeguard the health and safety of the construction team, the user, and the public. A medal is awarded annually. Established in 1992 by John Derrington, president of the Institution in 1984-1985, to foster actively improved health and safety in construction works.

8009 ■ Telford Medal
This, the highest award of the Institution for a paper, is given to recognize a paper or series of papers presented to the Institution, irrespective of any previous recognition. Up to four medals and monetary prizes are awarded annually when merited. Established in 1835 by a bequest made to the Institution by Thomas Telford (1757-1834), first president of the Institution.

8010 ■ Trevithick Prize
For recognition of a paper presented to the Institution. A monetary prize and a certificate are awarded annually. Established in 1890 in memory of Richard Trevithick (1771-1833) and augmented in 1932 by a gift from Mrs. H. K. Trevithick.

8011 ■ Warren Medal
To recognize a member for outstanding service to his or her region. To recognize a member for outstanding service to his or her region.

8012 ■ Garth Watson Medal
To recognize dedicated and valuable service to the Institution related to any field of its activities or for a contribution to a specific Institution project by a member or a member of staff. Awarded annually. Established in 1993 in honor of Garth Watson, a respected past secretary of the Institution.

8013 ■ James Watt Medal
For recognition of papers on mechanical engineering subjects. A medal is awarded annually. Established in 1858 to honor James Watt, Scottish mechanical engineer and inventor.

8014 ■ Webb Prize
For recognition of papers on railway engineering and transportation in general. Two monetary prizes and certificates are awarded annually. Established in 1908 by a bequest of Francis William Webb (1838-1906), vice president.

8015 ■ Zienkiewicz Medal and Prize
To recognize a postgraduate researcher under the age of 40 for an outstanding paper. A monetary award of £1,000 and a silver medal are presented biennially.

8016 ■ Institution of Diagnostic Engineers
Mr. Bill Parker, CEO
16 Thistlewood Rd.
Wakefield WF1 3HH, United Kingdom
Ph: 44 192 4821000
Fax: 44 192 4821200
E-mail: admin@diagnosticengineers.org
URL: http://www.diagnosticengineers.org

8017 ■ Collacott Prize
To encourage members to submit information of diagnostic interest and of value to increasing a member's store of knowledge and events that can or may occur, and of techniques of deduction. Entries should be brief and factual, preferably illustrated by line sketches. A monetary prize is awarded annually. Established in 1985.

8018 ■ Institution of Engineering and Technology
Nigel Fine, Chief Exec./Sec.
Michael Faraday House
Herts
Stevenage SG1 2AY, United Kingdom
Ph: 44 1438 313311
Fax: 44 1438 765526
E-mail: postmaster@theiet.org
URL: http://www.theiet.org
Formerly: (2006) Institution of Electrical Engineers; Institution of Incorporated Engineers.

8019 ■ Achievement Medals
For recognition of achievement in the following categories: electronics; information technology; communications; control; power; transport; manufacturing; and any field within the scope of the IET. Awarded annually.

8020 ■ Blumlein-Brown-Willans Premium
For recognition of papers on the science and art of television or pulse and wideband techniques. Papers published in IEE publications are eligible. A monetary prize of £150 and a certificate are awarded annually in October. Established in 1954.

8021 ■ Faraday Medal
This, the most prestigious of the achievement medals, recognizes notable scientific or industrial achievement in electrical engineering, or for conspicuous service rendered to the advancement of electrical science. There are no restrictions as regards nationality, country of residence, or membership in the institution. A bronze medal and vellum certificate are awarded annually in March.

8022 ■ Mary George Memorial Prize for Apprentices
To recognize an outstanding young female engineering apprentice who has made exceptional contributions in the work place. Women currently employed in U.K. engineering apprenticeships are eligible. A monetary award of £750, an engraved trophy, and a certificate are awarded.

8023 ■ Dennis Hill Award
To recognize exceptional work in the field of health care technologies. Students in MSc programs in the field of health care technologies and related subjects are eligible. A monetary prize of £150, a year's membership in the Institute, and a certificate are awarded annually.

8024 ■ IERE Benefactors Premium
For recognition of a paper on the application of broadcast and communication technology, including papers on applications for educational purposes. A monetary prize of £150 is awarded annually in October.

8025 ■ William James Award
Recognizes outstanding work with research and development in the field of biomedical engineering. All PhD students in biomedical engineering are eligible. A monetary prize of £200, a plaque, and a certificate are awarded.

8026 ■ J. A. Lodge Award for Medical Engineering
Recognizes an electronic or electrical engineer, in the early stage of his/her career, who has shown promise through a significant innovation in the field of research and development in medical engineering. A monetary prize of £250, a certificate, and a one-year membership are awarded annually.

8027 ■ Sir Eric Mensforth International Manufacturing Gold Medal
To recognize outstanding contributions to the advancement of manufacturing engineering technology or manufacturing management. A gold medal is awarded annually in October.

8028 ■ Mountbatten Medal
Recognizes individuals for outstanding contributions to electronics and information technology over a sustained period of time. Awarded annually.

8029 ■ Viscount Nuffield Medal
To recognize a member of the Institution for meritorious contribution to the progress of the manufacturing profession. A medal is awarded annually in October.

8030 ■ A. H. Reeves Premium
To recognize the best paper published in any Institution publication on digital coding. A monetary prize of £150 and a certificate are presented annually. Established in honor of Alec Harley Reeves for his work on PCM at the laboratories of STC (1902-1971).

8031 ■ Sir Henry Royce Award
To recognize a younger member who shows excellence in his or her work in industry or for the profession. A monetary prize of £250, a medal, and a certificate are awarded annually in October.

8032 ■ Mike Sargeant Career Achievement Award
To recognize young professionals who have made significant progress in their careers over a period of time. A cash prize of £500 and a certificate are awarded.

8033 ■ J. Langham Thompson Premium
To recognize a paper published in the *Electronics & Communication Engineering Journal*. A monetary prize of £150 and a certificate are awarded annually. Established in 1962.

8034 ■ J. J. Thomson Medal
For recognition of outstanding work by a person

Awards are arranged in alphabetical order below their administering organizations

or group of persons in electronics theory, practice, development, or manufacture. There are no restrictions regarding nationality, country of residence, or membership of the Institution. A bronze medal is awarded annually.

8035 ■ Young Woman Engineer of the Year
To recognize the best young female engineer in the United Kingdom. Candidates must be under the age of 30. Recipient serves as an ambassador for women in engineering. A monetary prize of £1,000 is awarded at a national prize-giving ceremony with media coverage. Awarded annually. Established in 1978.

8036 ■ Institution of Engineering Designers
Mrs. Libby Brodhurst, Sec./Chief Exec.
Courtleigh
Westbury Leigh
Wiltshire
Westbury BA13 3TA, United Kingdom
Ph: 44 1373 822801
Fax: 44 1373 858085
E-mail: libby@ied.org.uk
URL: http://www.ied.org.uk

8037 ■ Founders Award
To recognize an individual for distinguished services to the Institution. Awarded annually. Established in 1986.

8038 ■ Gerald Frewer Memorial Trophy
For outstanding contributions in the field of engineering design, design management, education and training, or design philosophy. Awarded annually.

8039 ■ Institution of Gas Engineers and Managers
Jeremy Bending, Pres.
IGEM House
High St.
Derbyshire
Kegworth DE74 2DA, United Kingdom
Fax: 44 1509 678198
E-mail: general@igem.org.uk
URL: http://www.igem.org.uk

8040 ■ Birmingham Medal
To encourage the extension of the uses of coal gas. It is bestowed for originality in connection with the manufacture and application of gas, such qualification to be interpreted in its widest possible sense. Members may submit names of individuals who are members of the Institution or any of its affiliated organizations for the consideration of the Council. A medal is awarded biennially when merited. Established in 1881.

8041 ■ Bronze Medal
For recognition of a paper accepted for presentation to and read at a General Meeting of a Gas Association in the calendar year preceding the year of the award. A Presidential Address is not eligible for the award and the author of a paper must be a member of the Gas Association before which the paper is read. A bronze medal is awarded annually. Established in 1905.

8042 ■ Gold Medal
For recognition of a paper on any subject, accepted for presentation to and read at a General Meeting of the Institution in the calendar year preceding the year of the award. Individuals who are members of the Institution or any of its affiliated organizations are eligible. A gold medal is awarded annually. Established in 1912.

8043 ■ H. E. Jones London Medal
For recognition of a paper accepted for presentation to and read at a General Meeting of the Institution in the calendar year preceding the year of the award. The paper must deal with the principles involved in the construction of works or plants for the manufacture or distribution of

gas and/or the points of good management of a gas undertaking considered in relation to the management of labor, the facilitating and popularizing the use of gas for general purposes, or improvement in carbonizing and purifying processes, or in the development of residuals. Individuals who are members of the Institution or any of its affiliated organizations are eligible. A medal is awarded annually. Established in 1905.

8044 ■ James Ransom Memorial Medals
For recognition of the best paper presented by an Associate member (Technician Engineer Grade) of the Institution, who is registered with the Engineering Council as an Incorporated Engineer. The Medal will be awarded annually by the Council for a paper presented to any meeting of the Institution, its Sections, any affiliated body, or any other relevant meeting. To be presented in the calendar year preceding the award. Established in 1979 to honor James Ransom for his work in the field of education and training in the gas industry.

8045 ■ Silver Medal
For recognition of a paper accepted for presentation to and read at a General Meeting of a District Section of the Institution or of an Affiliated District Association in the calendar year preceding the year of the award. A Chairman's or a Presidential Address is not eligible for the award and the author of a paper must be a member in any class of the Institution. A silver medal is awarded annually. Established in 1905.

8046 ■ Sugg Heritage Award
For recognition of a paper judged to contribute most to the understanding of the history, traditions or aspirations and achievements of the gas industry (as defined by By-Law 1 of the Institution of Gas Engineers) as to a particular activity or period of either engineering, scientific or social import. Individuals who are members of the Institution or any of its affiliated organizations are eligible. The paper is to be selected by a Panel comprising the Chairman and two members or nominees of the Panel for the History of the Industry from those accepted for presentation to a General Meeting of a District Section or Gas Association of Great Britain or a paper accepted for presentation to a General Meeting of the Institution in the calendar year preceding the award. A trophy is presented at the Institution Annual General Meeting. Established in 1981.

8047 ■ Institution of Mechanical Engineers
Prof. R.A. Smith, Chm.
1 Birdcage Walk
Westminster
London SW1H 9JJ, United Kingdom
Ph: 44 20 72227899
Fax: 44 20 72224557
E-mail: enquiries@imeche.org
URL: http://www.imeche.org

8048 ■ Contribution to Special Needs Award
To recognize members who have worked to benefit those with special needs. Members are eligible. A monetary prize of £1,000 is awarded.

8049 ■ Student Awards
To recognize student achievement by mechanical engineering students at IMechE accredited schools. Awards include the Frederic Barnes Waldron Best Student Award and the Best Student Certificate.

8050 ■ Institution of Occupational Safety and Health
Rob Strange, Chief Exec.
The Grange
Highfield Dr.
Leicestershire
Wigston LE18 1NN, United Kingdom
Ph: 44 116 2573100

Fax: 44 116 2573101
E-mail: reception@iosh.co.uk
URL: http://www.iosh.co.uk

8051 ■ Lifetime Achievement Award
Recognizes individuals who have furthered the status of occupational health and safety practice. Awarded annually.

8052 ■ Practical Project Award
To recognize a project or device that has practical applications in improving occupational safety and health in the United Kingdom. Awarded annually.

8053 ■ Technician Safety Practitioner Scholarship
To recognize an individual for achievements in occupational safety and health in the United Kingdom. Awarded annually.

8054 ■ Institution of Railway Signal Engineers
Mr. Colin Porter, Chief Exec./Sec.
4th Fl., 1 Birdcage Walk
Westminster
London SW1H 9JJ, United Kingdom
Ph: 44 20 78081180
Ph: 44 20 78081190
Fax: 44 20 78081196
E-mail: hq@irse.org
URL: http://www.irse.org

8055 ■ Dell Award
For achievement of a high standard of skill in the science and application of railway signaling. A plaque and monetary prize of £300 are awarded annually. Established at the bequest of the late Robert Dell, a former president of the Institution.

8056 ■ Wing Award for Safety
To recognize an individual who is innovative, promotes awareness, and has made an outstanding contribution to the vital business of lineside safety. A certificate and monetary prize of £500 are awarded annually. Established in 1994 in honor of Peter Wing.

8057 ■ Institution of Structural Engineers
Mr. Martin Powell, Chief Exec.
11 Upper Belgrave St.
London SW1X 8BH, United Kingdom
Ph: 44 20 72354535
Fax: 44 20 72354294
URL: http://www.istructe.org/Pages/Default.aspx

8058 ■ Gold Medal
This, the highest individual award, is for recognition of outstanding personal contributions to the advancement of structural engineering. Individuals from anywhere in the world are eligible. A gold medal is awarded when merited. Established in 1922.

8059 ■ Kenneth Severn Award
To recognize a young author for an original paper of value to the structural engineering profession. Candidates must be 28 years of age or younger. A monetary prize of £500 is awarded to the winner, and the winning paper is published in The Structural Engineer. Awarded annually. Established in 2006.

8060 ■ Structural Awards
For recognition of structural engineering excellence, as expressed in a physical form in an existing building or structure. Organizations from anywhere in the world are eligible. An appropriate award and a plaque are awarded when merited. Established in 1968.

8061 ■ International Alliance of ALS/MND Associations
Gudjon Sigurdsson, Chm.
PO Box 246
Northampton NN1 2PR, United Kingdom
Ph: 44 1604 700653

Awards are arranged in alphabetical order below their administering organizations

Fax: 44 1604 624726
E-mail: alliance@alsmndalliance.org
URL: http://www.alsmndalliance.org

8062 ■ Humanitarian Award
To recognize and encourage individuals and/or groups from a non-scientific background whose work makes, or has made, a contribution of international significance for people affected by ALS/MND. Awarded annually. Established in 2000.

8063 ■ Forbes Norris Award
To encourage management of and research into the disease to the benefit of people living with ALS/MND. Awarded annually. Established in 1994.

8064 ■ International Aluminium Institute (Institut International d'Aluminium)
Ron Knapp, Sec. Gen.
New Zealand House, 8th Fl.
Haymarket
London SW1Y 4TE, United Kingdom
Ph: 44 207 9300528
Fax: 44 207 3210183
E-mail: iai@world-aluminium.org
URL: http://www.world-aluminium.org

8065 ■ Honorary Member
To recognize a person who has made a significant contribution to the work of the Institute, the furtherance of the objects of the Institute, or the furtherance of the interests of aluminum producers. Individuals may be recommended by the Board of Directors. Honorary membership and its rights are awarded when merited. Established in 1976.

8066 ■ International Association for Religious Freedom
Jeffrey Teagle, Treas.
Essex Hall
1-6 Essex St.
London WC2R 3HY, United Kingdom
E-mail: hq@iarf.net
URL: http://www.iarf.net

8067 ■ Albert Schweitzer Award
For recognition of distinguished service in promoting human rights and in serving the poor. Members of the Association may nominate individuals who have exhibited exemplary commitment in this regard. A plaque is awarded every four years, at each IARF World Congress. Established in 1975 in memory of Albert Schweitzer.

8068 ■ International Association for the Scientific Study of Intellectual Disabilities
Glynis Murphy, Pres.
University of Kent
Tizard Centre
Kent
Canterbury CT2 7LZ, United Kingdom
Ph: 44 1227 823960
Fax: 44 1227 763674
E-mail: g.h.murphy@kent.ac.uk
URL: http://www.iassid.org
Formerly: International Association for the Scientific Study of Mental Deficiency.

8069 ■ Distinguished Achievement Award - Research
To honor formulations and investigations that have contributed significantly to the sciences related to intellectual disabilities for either a major single contribution or a sustained and important contribution over a lifetime. Awarded every four years at the Congress.

8070 ■ Distinguished Achievement Award - Scientific Literature
To recognize an outstanding publication, published since the last Congress, that contributes substantially to the literature in the field of intellectual disabilities. Awarded every four years at the Congress.

8071 ■ Distinguished Achievement Award - Service
To recognize contributions to the improvement of services to persons with intellectual disability that result in substantive contributions to prevention or amelioration. Awarded every four years at the Congress.

8072 ■ Distinguished Service Citation
To recognize outstanding or exemplary service to the Association by a person who has served as an officer, councilor, member of a committee, or otherwise, who actively participated in the affairs and activities of the Association. Awarded every four years at the Congress.

8073 ■ International Association for the Study of Obesity
Charles Darwin House
12 Roger St.
London WC1N 2JU, United Kingdom
Ph: 44 20 7685 2580
Fax: 44 20 7685 2581
E-mail: enquiries@iaso.org
URL: http://www.iaso.org

8074 ■ Andre Mayer Award for Young Investigators
To recognize outstanding research in the field of obesity by an investigator under the age of 40. Awarded every four years. Established in 1983.

8075 ■ New Investigator Award
To recognize the most outstanding new international investigator in the field of obesity research. Awarded every four years. Established in 2002.

8076 ■ Population Science and Public Health Award
To recognize an individual for outstanding contribution to the field of epidemiology and public health issues relating to obesity. Awarded every four years. Established in 2006.

8077 ■ Wertheimer Award
To recognize an individual for outstanding contributions to basic investigations in obesity. Awarded every four years. Established in 1986.

8078 ■ Willendorf Award
To recognize an individual for outstanding contributions to clinical research in obesity. Awarded every four years. Established in 1980.

8079 ■ International Association of Book-Keepers
Mr. Fabian Hamilton, Pres.
40 Churchill Sq., Ste. 30
Kings Hill
Kent
West Malling ME19 4YU, United Kingdom
Ph: 44 1732 897750
Fax: 44 1732 897751
E-mail: mail@iab.org.uk
URL: http://www.iab.org.uk

8080 ■ Business Enterprise Awards
To encourage and support best practice across the small business sector by rewarding the efforts of individual and companies whose work might otherwise be overlooked. Awards are presented in three categories: 1. FE Sector: Top College of the Year, Lecturer of the Year, Outstanding Student of the Year; 2. Business Sector: Business Entrepreneur of the Year, Bookkeeper of the Year, Business of the Year, and Payroll Professional of the Year; and 3. Not for Profit Sector: Social Entrepreneur of the Year and Armed Forces Award. Awarded annually.

8081 ■ International Association of Broadcasting Manufacturers
Peter White, Dir. Gen.
PO Box 2264
Berkshire
Reading RG31 6WA, United Kingdom

Ph: 44 118 9418620
Fax: 44 118 9418630
E-mail: info@theiabm.org
URL: http://www.theiabm.org

8082 ■ Peter Wayne Award
To recognize the company that produced the best designed, most innovative product displayed at the annual exhibit of the International Broadcasting Convention. Awarded annually. Established in 1990.

8083 ■ International Association of Music Libraries, Archives and Documentation Centres - United Kingdom and Ireland
Mr. Geoff Thomason, Gen. Sec.
Royal Northern College of Music Library
124 Oxford Rd.
Manchester M13 9RD, United Kingdom
Ph: 44 161 9075245
Fax: 44 161 2737611
E-mail: general_secretary@iaml-uk-irl.org
URL: http://www.iaml.info/organization/national_branches/uk_and_ireland

8084 ■ E.T. Bryant Memorial Prize
To recognize a student of Library and Information Science, or a librarian in his or her first five years in music librarianship, for a significant contribution to the literature of music librarianship. Candidates must be resident in the U.K. or Republic of Ireland during the year of entry. A monetary prize of £200 is awarded annually. Established in 1994. Co-sponsored by the Music Libraries Trust.

8085 ■ Excellence Award for Music Libraries
To highlight and celebrate activity in music libraries showing sustained good work and good practice that has the potential to be adopted and adapted by others. Open to all music libraries in the United Kingdom and Ireland regardless of their sector, size, or type. Awarded biennially in even-numbered years. Established in 2009.

8086 ■ C. B. Oldman Prize
For recognition of the best work of music bibliography, librarianship, or reference. Individuals living in the United Kingdom are eligible. A monetary prize of £200 is awarded annually at the IAML (UK) annual study weekend. Established in 1988.

8087 ■ International Association of Women Police
Jane Townsley, Pres.
British Transport Police
25 Camden Rd.
London NW1 9LN, United Kingdom
Ph: 44 7900 578615
E-mail: janetownsley.iawp@blueyonder.co.uk
URL: http://www.iawp.org

8088 ■ International Recognition and Scholarship Award
To recognize the accomplishments of an officer from outside North America. The candidate must have the qualifications required for active membership in IAWP, and must be able to communicate in English or to provide an interpreter. The recipient attends the annual conference, where she is expected to give a short presentation on the role of women officers in her country. Travel expenses are awarded annually.

8089 ■ International Awards for Liveable Communities
Globe House
Crispin Close
Reading RG4 7JS, United Kingdom
Ph: 44 118 9461680
E-mail: info@livcomawards.com
URL: http://www.livcomawards.com

8090 ■ LivCom Awards
Recognizes individuals and communities for Best

Awards are arranged in alphabetical order below their administering organizations

Practices in managing the local environment. Awards include: Whole City Award; Project Award; Bursary Award; and Personal Award. Established in 1997.

8091 ■ International Bar Association (Association Internationale du Barreau)
Akira Kawamura, Pres.
1 Stephen St., 10th Fl.
London W1T 1AT, United Kingdom
Ph: 44 20 76916868
Fax: 44 20 76916544
E-mail: member@int-bar.org
URL: http://www.ibanet.org

8092 ■ Human Rights Award
To recognize personal endeavor in the field of law that makes an outstanding contribution to the promotion, protection, and advancement of human rights and the rule of law. Awarded biennially in even-numbered years. Established in 1995.

8093 ■ Rule of Law Award
To recognize an individual who has made significant and lasting contributions to upholding the rule of law worldwide. Awarded annually.

8094 ■ Bernard Simons Memorial Award
To recognize personal endeavors in the practice of criminal law that make a substantial contribution to the promotion, protection, and the advancement of human rights. Awarded biennially in even-numbered years. Established in 1995. Administered by the Association's Human Rights Institute.

8095 ■ William Reece Smith Jr. Outstanding Young Lawyer of the Year Award
To recognize a promising young lawyer. Candidates must be 35 years of age or younger, and must demonstrate professional excellence as well as a reputation for legal ethics and professional responsibility. A monetary prize of US$5,000 is awarded annually. Established in 2008.

8096 ■ International Behavioural and Neural Genetics Society
Cathy Fernandes, Treas.
Institute of Psychiatry
Psychological Medicine and Psychiatry, PO 82
De Crespigny Park
London SE5 8AF, United Kingdom
Ph: 44 207 8480662
E-mail: cathy.fernandes@iop.kcl.ac.uk
URL: http://www.ibangs.org

8097 ■ Distinguished Scientist Award
To honor members for achievements in the field of research. Awarded annually.

8098 ■ Young Scientist Award
To honor young members for achievements in the field of research. Candidates must have fewer than seven years of post-first faculty or faculty-equivalent appointment. Awarded annually.

8099 ■ International Byron Society
Acushla
Halam Rd.
Southwell
Nottinghamshire NG25 0AD, United Kingdom
Ph: 44 1636 813818
E-mail: whitelady@white-lady.co.uk
URL: http://www.internationalbyronsociety.org

8100 ■ Elma Dangerfield Award
To identify and reward scholarship for publication of new and original work related to the life, works, and times of the 6th Lord George Gordon Noel Byron the Poet. Awarded annually.

8101 ■ International Cartographic Association (Association Cartographique Internationale)
David Fairbairn, Sec. Gen./Treas.
Newcastle University
School of Civil Engineering and Geosciences

Newcastle upon Tyne NE1 7RU, United Kingdom
Ph: 44 191 2226353
Fax: 44 191 2228691
E-mail: dave.fairbairn@newcastle.ac.uk
URL: http://icaci.org

8102 ■ Honorary Fellowship
To recognize individuals who have contributed to ICA affairs. Presented quadrennially.

8103 ■ Carl Mannerfelt Gold Medal
To recognize cartographers of outstanding merit who have made significant contributions of an original nature to the field of cartography. Awarded when merited.

8104 ■ International Committee on Seafarers' Welfare
Cygnet House
12-14 Sydenham Rd.
Croydon CR0 2EE, United Kingdom
Ph: 44 300 012 4279
Fax: 44 300 012 4280
URL: http://www.seafarerswelfare.org

8105 ■ Port of the Year
To recognize the port that has done the most for the provision of and access to high quality welfare services and facilities for seafarers. Awarded annually. Established in 2010.

8106 ■ Seafarer Centre of the Year
To recognize the seafarer center that has done the most to provide high quality welfare services and facilities for visiting seafarers. Awarded annually. Established in 2010.

8107 ■ Shipping Company of the Year
To recognize the shipping company that has made the biggest difference to seafarers' welfare onboard their vessels and in port. Awarded annually. Established in 2010.

8108 ■ Welfare Personality of the Year
To recognize an individual for an outstanding contribution to seafarers' welfare. Awarded annually. Established in 2010.

8109 ■ International Egg Commission (Commission Internationale des Oeufs)
Julian Madeley, Dir. Gen.
89 Charterhouse St., 2nd Fl.
London EC1M 6HR, United Kingdom
Ph: 44 20 74903493
Fax: 44 20 74903495
URL: http://www.internationalegg.com

8110 ■ Golden Egg Award
For recognition of outstanding efforts in the fields of promotion and marketing of eggs. The IEC nominates a country which then selects an award winner. A trophy is presented annually. Established in 1970. Formerly: (1991) International Egg Marketing Award.

8111 ■ International Exhibition Logistics Associates
Alan Hunter, Exec. Dir.
119 High St.
Hertfordshire
Berkhamsted HP4 1DJ, United Kingdom
Ph: 44 845 0714395
Fax: 44 1442 869090
E-mail: adminiela@iela.org
URL: http://www.iela.org

8112 ■ International Exhibition Logistics Associates Awards
To recognize outstanding contributions in the field of exhibition organization. Awarded annually at the Congress.

8113 ■ International Federation for Theatre Research (Federation Internationale pour la Recherche Theatrale)
Prof. David Whitton, Sec. Gen.
Lancaster University
Lancaster LA1 4YN, United Kingdom

E-mail: d.whitton@lancaster.ac.uk
URL: http://www.firt-iftr.org

8114 ■ New Scholar's Prize
To recognize the best essay by a new scholar under the age of 35. The essay must not exceed 4,000 words and may be written in English or French. Airfare, fees, and accommodation for the Conference, and one year's membership in the organization are awarded annually.

8115 ■ International Federation of Air Line Pilots Associations (Federation Internationale des Associations de Pilotes de Ligne)
Capt. Don Wykoff, Pres.
Interpilot House
Gogmore Ln.
Surrey
Chertsey KT16 9AP, United Kingdom
Ph: 44 1932 571711
Fax: 44 1932 570920
E-mail: ifalpa@ifalpa.org
URL: http://www.ifalpa.org

8116 ■ Polaris Award
For recognition of acts of heroism and/or exceptional airmanship in civil aviation. Selection is by nomination. A medal is awarded annually at the Conference. Established in 1983.

8117 ■ Clarence N. Sayen Award
To honor a person whose personal contribution towards the achievement of the Federation's aims and objectives has been outstanding. Awarded annually. Established in 1965.

8118 ■ Scroll of Merit
For recognition of the sustained efforts of individuals who have served IFALPA with loyalty, honor, and distinction. Awarded to one or more recipients annually. Established in 1969.

8119 ■ International Federation of Airworthiness (Federation Internationale de Navigabilite Aerospatiale)
Mr. John W. Saull, Exec. Dir.
14 Railway Approach
West Sussex
East Grinstead RH19 1BP, United Kingdom
Ph: 44 1342 301788
Fax: 44 1342 317808
E-mail: sec@ifairworthy.org
URL: http://www.ifairworthy.com
Formerly: IFA International Aviation Scholarship.

8120 ■ International Federation of Airworthiness Scholarship
Each year, a candidate is selected from within IFA's membership to receive training in an airworthiness related discipline. A scholarship up to £3,000 is awarded annually.

8121 ■ Whittle Safety Award
A selection board reviews entrants, from within the aerospace community, each year for this award, and it honors the work of Sir Frank Whittle. The winner receives a medal and a citation. Traditionally, this award is presented at the annual IASS Global Safety Conference. Established in 1998.

8122 ■ International Federation of Gynecology and Obstetrics
FIGO House, Ste. 3
Waterloo Ct.
10 Theed St.
London SE1 8ST, United Kingdom
Ph: 44 20 7928 1166
Fax: 44 20 7928 7099
URL: http://www.figo.org

8123 ■ Awards in Recognition of Women Obstetricians/Gynecologists
To recognize female women gynecologists and obstetricians who, in their daily practice or in

Awards are arranged in alphabetical order below their administering organizations

their research laboratories, have contributed significantly to the improvement of health care for women. Presented predominantly to female practitioners from low- and middle-income countries/territories. Awarded biennially in even-numbered years. Established in 1997.

8124 ■ International Federation of Hydrographic Societies
Ms. Helen Atkinson, Operations and Publications Mgr.
PO Box 103
Plymouth PL4 7YP, United Kingdom
Ph: 44 1752 223512
Fax: 44 1752 223512
E-mail: helen@hydrographicsociety.org
URL: http://www.hydrographicsociety.org

8125 ■ Best First Paper Prize
For the best paper published in the *Hydrographic Journal* by an author or authors who have not previously been published in the journal. A monetary prize of £200 is awarded annually.

8126 ■ Best Paper Prize
For the best paper published in the *Hydrographic Journal*. A monetary prize of £200 is awarded annually.

8127 ■ Educational Fund Bursaries
For students of hydrography and related disciplines or those at the outset of their career. A financial award of £2,000 per year is awarded annually.

8128 ■ International Federation of Societies of Cosmetic Chemists
Mr. Alberto Martin, Pres.
Langham House E, Ste. 6
Mill St.
Beds
Luton LU1 2NA, United Kingdom
Ph: 44 1582 726661
Fax: 44 1582 405217
E-mail: enquiries@ifscc.org
URL: http://www.ifscc.org

8129 ■ Congress Awards
For recognition of the most meritorious paper presented at an IFSCC Congress. Papers that are original and that have important scientific content and relevance to the cosmetic and toiletry industry may be submitted nine months before a Congress meets. The IFSCC Award includes a monetary prize of 7,500 Swiss francs. Also awarded is an Honorable Mention prize of 2,000 Swiss francs, plus illuminated scrolls commending the achievement. Awarded biennially in even-numbered years. Established in 1970.

8130 ■ Poster Award
For recognition of the most meritorious poster presented at an IFSCC Congress. Posters that are original and that have important scientific content and relevance to the cosmetic and toiletry industry may be submitted nine months before a Congress meets. A monetary prize of 1,000 Swiss francs and a scroll are awarded biennially in even-numbered years.

8131 ■ International Gaming Awards
Park Plaza, Ste. 105
Point South
Hayes Way
Cannock WS12 2DB, United Kingdom
Ph: 44 1543 578689
URL: http://www.gaming-awards.com

8132 ■ International Gaming Awards
To reward excellence in all areas of the gaming industry. Prizes are awarded in nearly 20 categories, such as Bingo Operator Award, Casino Interior Design Award, Eco-Friendly Company Award, and Slot Manager Award. Awarded annually. Established in 2008.

8133 ■ International Glaciological Society
D. MacAyeal, Pres.
Scott Polar Research Institute
Lensfield Rd.
Cambridge CB2 1ER, United Kingdom
Ph: 44 1223 355974
Fax: 44 1223 354931
E-mail: igsoc@igsoc.org
URL: http://www.igsoc.org

8134 ■ Honorary Membership
For recognition of eminent contributions to the objects of the Society, namely to stimulate interest in and encourage research into all aspects of snow and ice in all countries, and to facilitate and increase the flow of glaciological ideas and information. Membership shall not exceed 12 in number. Established in 1962.

8135 ■ Richardson Medal
To recognize an individual for outstanding service to glaciology and to the Society. Awarded periodically. Established in 1993.

8136 ■ Seligman Crystal
For recognition of unique contributions to snow and ice studies that enrich the subject significantly. A hexagonal 5 1/2 inch column of crystal glass that is engraved with an ice crystal on a sloping top surface is awarded when merited. Established in 1963.

8137 ■ International Harm Reduction Association
Rick Lines, Exec. Dir.
Unit 701-The Chandlery
50 Westminster Bridge Rd.
London 3051, United Kingdom
Ph: 44 20 79537412
Fax: 44 20 79537404
E-mail: info@ihra.net
URL: http://www.ihra.net

8138 ■ Film Festival Award
To recognize the best film or documentary at the International Drugs and Harm Reduction Film Festival. Awarded annually.

8139 ■ International Rolleston Award
To recognize an individual who has made an outstanding contribution to reducing harm for psychoactive substances at an international level. Awarded annually. Established in 1992 in honor of Sir Humphrey Rolleston.

8140 ■ Carol and Travis Jenkins Award
To recognize a current or former drug user who has made an outstanding contribution to reducing drug related harm. Awarded annually. Established in 2005.

8141 ■ National Rolleston Award
To recognize an individual or organization for their outstanding contributions to reducing harm from psychoactive substances at the national level in the country that is hosting the harm reduction conference. Awarded annually. Established in 1992 in honor of Sir Humphrey Rolleston.

8142 ■ International Hologram Manufacturers Association
Ian M. Lancaster, Gen. Sec.
4 Windmill Business Village
Sunbury-on-Thames TW16 7DY, United Kingdom
Ph: 44 1932 785680
Fax: 44 1932 780790
E-mail: info@ihma.org
URL: http://www.ihma.org

8143 ■ Excellence in Holography Awards
To recognize outstanding holographic projects of the year. Awards are presented in the following categories: Security/Authentication; Packaging; Promotion/Illustration; Industrial; New Holographic Product; New Holographic Technique; and the Brian Monaghan Award for Business Innovation. Awarded annually.

8144 ■ International Map Collectors' Society
Sue Booty, Membership Sec.
Rogues Roost
Poudsgate
Devon
Newton Abbot TQ13 7PS, United Kingdom
Fax: 44 13 64631042
E-mail: financialsecretariat@imcos.org
URL: http://www.harvey27.demon.co.uk/imcos

8145 ■ International Map Collectors' Society Awards
To promote map collecting and the study of cartography and its history. Various awards are presented annually.

8146 ■ Helen Wallis Award
To recognize the cartographic contribution of greatest merit and widest interest to map collectors worldwide. A salver, certificate, and monetary prize of £300 are awarded annually. Established in 1983. Formerly: (2006) Tooley Award.

8147 ■ International Menopause Society
Ms. Lee Tomkins, Exec. Dir.
PO Box 98
Cornwall
Camborne TR14 4BQ, United Kingdom
Ph: 44 1209 711054
Fax: 44 1209 610530
E-mail: leetomkinsims@btinternet.com
URL: http://www.Imsociety.org

8148 ■ Henry Burger Prize
To recognize the investigator who is judged as having published the most significant contribution(s) to the field of menopause in basic science or clinical studies in the two-year period immediately following the preceding World Congress. Awarded triennially. Sponsored by Wyeth Pharmaceuticals.

8149 ■ Thomas Clarkson Prize
To recognize the best communication on menopause and cardiovascular health. Awarded triennially at the World Congress. Sponsored by Bayer Schering Pharma AG.

8150 ■ Robert B. Greenblatt Prizes
To recognize junior investigators who present the best papers in the field of menopause. Awarded in two categories: basic science and clinical work. Awarded triennially.

8151 ■ Hermann Schneider Prize
To recognize the best communication on menopause and breast health. Awarded triennially at the World Congress. Sponsored by Bayer Schering Pharma AG.

8152 ■ International Organ Festival at St. Albans
Dr. Peter Hurford, Founder/Pres.
PO Box 80
St. Albans AL3 4HR, United Kingdom
Ph: 44 1727 844765
Fax: 44 1727 868941
E-mail: info@organfestival.com
URL: http://www.organfestival.com
Formerly: International Organ Festival Society.

8153 ■ Improvisation Competition
For recognition of outstanding organ improvisation. Individuals under the age of 33 may compete. A monetary prize of £6,000 and recital engagements at such venues as Ste Clotilde (Paris) and St. Albans Cathedral are presented to the winner. Held biennially in odd-numbered years. Established in 1973 by Madame Tournemire in honor of Charles Tournemire.

8154 ■ Interpretation Competition
For recognition of the outstanding organ performance during the St. Albans International Organ Festival interpretation competition. Individuals under the age of 33 may compete. A monetary prize of £6,000 and recital engagements at various venues are awarded for first prize; £2,500

Awards are arranged in alphabetical order below their administering organizations

and recital engagements for second prize; and £500 and recital engagements for the winner of an audience prize. Also presents the John Mc-Cabe Prize of £500 for the best performance of the commissioned work. Held annually.

8155 ■ Douglas May Award
For recognition of the best performance of any competition piece in the quarterfinal and semi-final rounds of the Interpretation Competition or the Improvisation Competition. A monetary prize of £800 is awarded to a competitor who is not the recipient of any other prize. The festival and competitions are held in July of odd-numbered years. Established in 1963 by Dr. Peter Hurford.

8156 ■ International Organization for Medical Physics
Fairmount House
230 Tadcaster Rd.
York YO24 1ES, United Kingdom
URL: http://www.iomp.org

8157 ■ Harold Johns Medal
To honor scientists who have distinguished themselves through excellence in teaching and contributions to international education. Awarded triennially at the IOMP World Congresses.

8158 ■ Marie Sklodowska-Curie Award
To honor scientists who have distinguished themselves by their contributions in 1) education and training of medical physicists, medical students, medical residents, and allied health personnel; and/or 2) advancement of medical physics knowledge based upon independent original research and/or development; and/or 3) advancement of the medical physics profession in the IOMP adhering national and international organizations. Awarded triennially at the IOMP World Congresses.

8159 ■ Young Scientist Award in Medical Physics
To recognize a young scientist for original and/or applied work of outstanding scientific quality in medical physics. Preference is given to young medical physicists from developing countries. Candidates should have a maximum of eight years of research experience following the attainment of a PhD. A medal and cash prize of $1,000 are awarded annually.

8160 ■ International Planned Parenthood Federation
4 Newhams Row
London SE1 3UZ, United Kingdom
Ph: 44 20 7939 8200
Fax: 44 20 7939 8300
E-mail: info@ippf.org
URL: http://www.ippf.org

8161 ■ Individual Volunteer Award for Contributions to Sexual and Reproductive Health and Rights
To recognize a volunteer who has contributed significantly to the promotion, realization, and defense of sexual and reproductive health and rights around the world. Awarded annually. Established in 2008.

8162 ■ International Award for Contributions to Sexual and Reproductive Health and Rights
To recognize an individual who has contributed significantly to the promotion, realization, and defense of sexual and reproductive health and rights around the world. Awarded annually. Established in 2008.

8163 ■ Member Association Award for Contributions to Sexual and Reproductive Health and Rights
To recognize a member association who has contributed significantly to the promotion, realization, and defense of sexual and reproductive health and rights around the world. Awarded annually. Established in 2008.

8164 ■ Staff Award for Contributions to Sexual and Reproductive Health and Rights
To recognize a staff member who has contributed significantly to the promotion, realization, and defense of sexual and reproductive health and rights around the world. Awarded annually. Established in 2008.

8165 ■ Youth Award for Contributions to Sexual and Reproductive Health and Rights
To recognize a young person who has contributed significantly to the promotion, realization, and defense of sexual and reproductive health and rights around the world. Awarded annually. Established in 2008.

8166 ■ International Police Association
Mr. Georgios Karsaropoulos, International Sec. Gen.
Intl. Administration Ctre.
1 Fox Rd.
West Bridgford
Nottingham NG2 6AJ, United Kingdom
Ph: 44 115 9455985
Fax: 44 115 9822578
E-mail: isg@ipa-iac.org
URL: http://www.ipa-iac.org

8167 ■ World Police Prize
In recognition of exceptional service rendered (by an individual or group) to the police or the IPA. Nominees may or may not be members of the police or the IPA. A monetary prize of 10,000 Swiss francs, a certificate, and a statuette are awarded annually. Established in 1994.

8168 ■ International Psychoanalytical Association
(Association Psychanalytique Internationale)
Charles M.T. Hanly, Pres.
Broomhills
Woodside Ln.
London N12 8UD, United Kingdom
Ph: 44 20 84468324
Fax: 44 20 84454729
E-mail: ipa@ipa.org.uk
URL: http://www.ipa.org.uk

8169 ■ Elise M. Hayman Award
For the most cogent, relevant and commendable work on the Holocaust and genocide, current or historical. A prize of US$4,000 is awarded annually. Established in 1989.

8170 ■ Hayman Prize for Published Work Pertaining to Traumatized Children and Adults
To the author or authors of the best paper about Holocaust effects published in a book or in a recognized psychoanalytic or other scientific journal. A prize of US$4,000 is awarded annually. Established in 1997.

8171 ■ Psychoanalytic Training Today Award
For the best submitted paper on the study and development of psychoanalytic training models. A certificate is awarded annually. Established in 2002.

8172 ■ Cesare Sacerdoti Award
For the best individual paper submitted by a relatively young author who is presenting a paper at an international congress for the first time. A prize of £500 is awarded annually. Established in 1987.

8173 ■ International Public Relations Association
Elizabeth Ananto, Pres.
12 Dunley Hill Ct.
Ranmore Common
Surrey
Dorking RH5 6SX, United Kingdom

Ph: 44 1483 280130
Fax: 44 1483 280131
E-mail: info@ipra.org
URL: http://www.ipra.org

8174 ■ Golden World Awards for Excellence
To recognize and to acclaim excellent public relations programs carried out at least partially during the preceding two-year period. Business enterprises, associations, private institutions, and government bodies anywhere in the world may submit entries. Public relations firms and consultancies can enter on behalf of clients and share honors with them. The public relations program can be of any kind and be local, regional, national, or international in scope. Awards are presented in 30 categories. Awarded annually.

8175 ■ President's Award
To recognize contributions to a better world understanding. A trophy is awarded annually. Established in 1977.

8176 ■ International Sailing Federation
Ariadne House
Town Quay
Southampton
Hampshire SO14 2AQ, United Kingdom
Ph: 44 2380 635111
Fax: 44 2380 635789
URL: http://www.sailing.org

8177 ■ Beppe Croce Trophy
This, the Federation's most prestigious award, is presented to an individual who has made an outstanding voluntary contribution to the sport of sailing. Awarded annually. Established in 1988.

8178 ■ Long Service Medal
To recognize an individual for services to the Federation. Awarded annually. Established in 1990.

8179 ■ Rolex World Sailor of the Year Award
To recognize the highest achievers from all disciplines of the sport of sailing, from windsurfers and dinghy sailors to offshore specialists. A trophy is awarded annually to one man and one woman. Established in 1994.

8180 ■ Sailing Hall of Fame
To honor individuals who have made a significant impact on the sport of sailing during his or her life. One or more individuals are inducted annually. Established in 2007.

8181 ■ International Sheep Dog Society
Norman Lorton, Chief Exec.
Clifton House
4a Goldington Rd.
Bedford MK40 3NF, United Kingdom
Ph: 44 1234 352672
Fax: 44 1234 348214
E-mail: office@isds.org.uk
URL: http://www.isds.org.uk

8182 ■ Supreme Champion
For recognition of the achievements of the outstanding handler of a working border collie. Individuals must be members of the Society to be eligible. A monetary prize of £500 and numerous trophies are awarded annually. Established in 1930.

8183 ■ Young Handler Award
To recognize an outstanding young handler of sheep dogs. Presented annually.

8184 ■ International Society for Cutaneous Lymphomas
Sean Whittaker, Sec.-Treas.
St. Johns Institute of Dermatology
9th Fl., Tower Wing

Awards are arranged in alphabetical order below their administering organizations

Great Maze Pond
King's College London
London SE1 9RT, United Kingdom
Ph: 44 20 7188 6412
Fax: 44 20 7188 8050
E-mail: sean.whittaker@kcl.ac.uk
URL: http://www.cutaneouslymphoma.org

8185 ■ Herschel Zackheim Lectureship

To recognize an individual who has contributed to research in lymphoma-related biology. Awarded annually. Established in 2006.

8186 ■ International Society for Professional Innovation Management
PO Box 18
Worsley
Manchester M28 1XP, United Kingdom
Ph: 44 161 408 0409
E-mail: membership@ispim.org
URL: http://www.ispim.org

8187 ■ Best Student Paper Award

To recognize an outstanding Conference/ Symposium paper written by a student. Awarded annually. Established in 2005.

8188 ■ Knut Holt Award

To recognize an outstanding Conference/ Symposium paper. Awarded annually. Established in 2003.

8189 ■ ISPIM-Wiley Innovation Management Dissertation Award

To recognize PhD researchers who have demonstrated insight, theories, and tools to shape the future of innovation management thinking and action. The winner receives a monetary prize of 1,500 Euros, and two runners-up receive 500 Euros each. Awarded annually. Established in 2011. Sponsored by John Wiley & Sons.

8190 ■ Scientific Panel Award

To recognize a member of the Scientific Panel for useful and extensive contribution to the Panel during the year. Awarded annually. Established in 2010.

8191 ■ International Society for Reef Studies
Rupert Ormond, Sec.
c/o Marine Conservation International
5/6 Lang Rigg
South Queensferry
Edinburgh EH30 9WN, United Kingdom
E-mail: rupert.ormond.mci@gmail.com
URL: http://www.coralreefs.org

8192 ■ Darwin Medal

To honor a senior member who is recognized worldwide for major contributions to reef studies throughout his or her career. A medal is awarded every four years. Established in 1988.

8193 ■ International Society for Soil Mechanics and Geotechnical Engineering (Societe Internationale de Mecanique des Sols et de la Geotechnique)
Prof. R.N. Taylor, Sec. Gen.
City University
Northampton Sq.
London EC1V 0HB, United Kingdom
Ph: 44 20 70408154
Fax: 44 20 70408832
E-mail: secretariat@issmge.org
URL: http://www.issmge.org/web/page.aspx

8194 ■ Kevin Nash Gold Medal

For recognition of outstanding contributions to practice, research, and teaching in the field of geotechnical engineering. Members of the Society are eligible. A medal is awarded every four years. Established in 1985 in honor of Kevin Nash, former secretary general of the Society.

8195 ■ International Society for Trenchless Technology
Dr. Samuel Ariaratnam, Chm.
15 Belgrave Sq.
London SW1X 8PS, United Kingdom

E-mail: info@istt.com
URL: http://www.istt.com

8196 ■ International No-Dig Award

Recognizes the most notable contribution to trenchless technology during the year. Awarded annually at the International No-Dig Conference and Exhibition. Prizes are awarded in four categories: Best Product, Best Project, Best Academic Project or Research, and Best Student. Best Student prize receives £500 plus travel costs; others receive trophy, certificate, and publicity within the industry. Established in 1986.

8197 ■ International Society of Chemotherapy (Societe Internationale de Chimiotherapie)
Fiona MacKenzie, Exec. Dir.
Medical Microbiology
Aberdeen Royal Infirmary
Aberdeen AB25 2ZN, United Kingdom
Ph: 44 1224 552127
Ph: 44 1224 554954
Fax: 44 1224 550632
E-mail: isc@ischemo.org
URL: http://www.ischemo.org

8198 ■ Tom Bergan Memorial Award

To recognize young scientists for contributions to the science of chemotherapy in countries with limited resources. Two awards of $250 each are awarded biennially in odd-numbered years. Established in honor of a former president of the ISC.

8199 ■ Masaaki Ohkoshi Award

To recognize the best clinical study on the subject of urinary tract infections. A monetary prize of $1,500 is awarded biennially in odd-numbered years. Established in 1995.

8200 ■ Hamao Umezawa Memorial Award

For recognition of outstanding research and life's work in chemotherapy. Nominations are accepted a half year before the award is given. A monetary prize, a medal, and a document are presented biennially in odd-numbered years at the International Congress of Chemotherapy. Established in 1979 in honor of Professor Dr. Hamao Umezawa as the highest award of the Society.

8201 ■ John David Williams Memorial Award

To recognize young scientists from countries with limited resources for contributions to the science of chemotherapy. Two awards of $250 each are awarded biennially in odd-numbered years. Established in 2007 in honor of a former president of the ISC.

8202 ■ International Society of Gynecological Pathologists
Wilson Glenn McCluggage, Sec.
Royal Group of Hospitals Trust
Department of Pathology
Grosvenor Rd.
Belfast BT12 6BL, United Kingdom
Fax: 44 28 90 233643
URL: http://www.isgyp.com

8203 ■ Platform Presentation Award

To recognize an outstanding gynecologic pathology platform presentation at the annual United States and Canadian Academy of Pathology meeting. A monetary prize of $500 is awarded annually. Established in 2011.

8204 ■ Robert E. Scully Young Investigator Award

To recognize the best article published in the International Journal of Gynecological Pathology.

Authors must be members who are no older than 40 years of age. A plaque and monetary prize of $1,000 are awarded annually. Established in 1998.

8205 ■ International Society of Hypertension - United Kingdom
AM Heagerty, Pres.
113-119 High St.
Hampton Hill TW12 1NJ, United Kingdom
Ph: 44 20 8979 8300
Fax: 44 20 8979 6700
E-mail: secretariat@ish-world.com
URL: http://www.ish-world.com/default.aspx?Home

8206 ■ AstraZeneca Award

To honor a distinguished investigator responsible for outstanding work related to clinical pharmacology and therapy of arterial hypertension. A certificate is awarded biennially in even-numbered years. Established in 1979. Supported by AstraZeneca AB.

8207 ■ Boehringer Ingelheim Developing World Award

To recognize a researcher in the developing world who has done outstanding work in the region. A certificate is awarded biennially in even-numbered years. Established in 2002. Sponsored by Boehringer Ingelheim GmbH.

8208 ■ Distinguished Member Award

To honor members who have given outstanding service to the Society and have made unusually distinguished contributions to experimental and clinical research in hypertension. A plaque is awarded biennially in even-numbered years. Established in 2002.

8209 ■ Austin Doyle Award

To recognize a graduate for the best original presentation relevant to clinical medicine at the Biennial Scientific Meeting. Candidates must be within five years of post-graduate qualification. A certificate is awarded biennially in even-numbered years. Established in 1994.

8210 ■ Honorary Member Award

To recognize individuals who have not been regular members of the Society but have made extraordinary contributions to the Society in providing long and continuous support of research or of the other activities of the Society. Awarded when merited.

8211 ■ Stevo Julius Award

To recognize a person or persons demonstrating exceptional and continuous commitment to the dissemination of information, knowledge, and skills in the field of hypertension to: (a) general public; (b) medical community; (c) specialists in the hypertension field; and (d) to investigators involved in hypertension research. A certificate is awarded biennially in even-numbered years. Established in 2000.

8212 ■ Pfizer Award

To honor two investigators for research projects in the study of basic mechanisms by which blood pressure and lipids interact in the development of cardiovascular disease. A certificate is awarded biennially in even-numbered years. Established in 1990. Sponsored by Pfizer Inc.

8213 ■ Robert Tigerstedt Award

To recognize an individual, group, or institution for distinguished work relating to aetiology, epidemiology, pathology, or treatment of high blood pressure. A certificate is awarded biennially in even-numbered years. Established in 1974.

8214 ■ Franz Volhard Award and Lectureship

To honor an individual who has initiated in a field of hypertension, or in a related discipline, a concept that remains of current interest. A

Awards are arranged in alphabetical order below their administering organizations

diploma and invitation to lecture are awarded biennially in even-numbered years. Established in 1974.

8215 ■ International Society of Neuropathology
(Societe Internationale de Neuropathologie)
Dr. David Hilton, Sec. Gen.
Dept. of Cellular and Anatomical Pathology
Derriford Hospital
Plymouth PL6 8DH, United Kingdom
Ph: 44 175 2763599
Fax: 44 175 2763590
E-mail: davidhilton@nhs.net
URL: http://www.intsocneuropathol.com

8216 ■ Franz Nissl Young Investigator Award
For young neuroscientists (under 35 years of age) for an outstanding research contribution to neuropathology. Covers reasonable expenses for travel, accommodation, and registration for international congresses of neuropathology.

8217 ■ International Society of Psychiatric Genetics
Nick Craddock, Pres.
Wellcome Bldg. for Biomedical Research in Wales
Academic Ave.
Psychological Medicine Dept.
School of Medicine, Cardiff University
Cardiff CF14 4XN, United Kingdom
URL: http://www.ispg.net

8218 ■ Lifetime Achievement Award
To recognize a scientist who has made a major contribution to the advancement of the field of psychiatric genetics. A golden DNA helix is awarded annually at the World Congress of Psychiatric Genetics. Established in 1993.

8219 ■ Theodore Reich Young Investigator Award
To recognize young scientists for published work on psychiatric genetics that is of exceptional merit. Candidates must be 40 years old or younger. Awarded annually. Established in 2004.

8220 ■ International Society of Typographic Designers
Freda Sack, Pres.
PO Box 7002
Somerset
London W1A 2TY, United Kingdom
E-mail: mail@istd.org.uk
URL: http://www.istd.org.uk

8221 ■ International TypoGraphic Awards
To honor typographic excellence across a broad range of design disciplines. In 16 categories, three levels of awards are presented: a Certificate of Excellence, for all finalists; the Premier Award, for each outstanding submission; and the International TypoGraphic Award, for outstanding achievement. Awarded biennially in even-numbered years.

8222 ■ International Society of Ultrasound in Obstetrics and Gynecology
Ann Tabor, Pres.
Unit 4
Blythe Mews
Blythe Rd.
London W14 OHW, United Kingdom
Ph: 44 20 74719955
Fax: 44 20 74719959
E-mail: info@isuog.org
URL: http://www.isuog.org

8223 ■ Ian Donald Gold Medal
To honor an individual who has made an outstanding scientific contribution to the field of ultrasound in obstetrics and gynecology. Awarded annually.

8224 ■ Honorary Fellowship
To honor individuals who have shown outstanding commitment to the development of the society. Awarded when merited.

8225 ■ International Society on General Relativity and Gravitation
Prof. Malcolm A.H. MacCallum, Pres.
Queen Mary, University of London
School of Mathematical Sciences
Mile End Rd.
London E1 4NS, United Kingdom
Ph: 44 20 78825445
Fax: 44 20 89819587
E-mail: m.a.h.maccallum@qmul.ac.uk
URL: http://grg.maths.qmul.ac.uk/grgsoc

8226 ■ Hartle Awards
To recognize the best student presentations at the triennial conferences. A monetary prize and free three-year membership are awarded to one or more recipients triennially.

8227 ■ Xanthopoulos Prize
To recognize a scientist below the age of 40 who has made outstanding (preferably theoretical) contributions to the area of gravitational physics. A monetary prize of approximately US$10,000 is awarded triennially. Established in honor of Basilis C. Xanthopoulos. Funded by the Foundation for Research and Technology, Hellas.

8228 ■ International Spinal Cord Society
Marianne Bint, Exec. Admin.
Stoke Mandeville Hospital
National Spinal Injuries Centre
Aylesbury HP21 8AL, United Kingdom
Ph: 44 1296 315866
Fax: 44 1296 315870
E-mail: admin@iscos.org.uk
URL: http://www.iscos.org.uk

8229 ■ Hans Frankel Scholarship
To members.

8230 ■ Society Medal
To recognize an individual who has made an outstanding contribution to the prevention or treatment of spinal cord injury or to research related to spinal cord injury. Awarded annually. Established in 1975.

8231 ■ Spinal Cord Prize
To encourage younger members of the Society to submit well presented papers on original work for publication in *Spinal Cord* and for submission at the Annual Scientific Meeting. Authors must be younger than 39 years. A silver medal and monetary prize of £500 are awarded biennially in odd-numbered years.

8232 ■ International Tennis Federation
(Federation Internationale de Tennis)
Francesco Ricci Bitti, Pres.
Bank Ln.
Roehampton
London SW15 5XZ, United Kingdom
Ph: 44 20 88786464
Fax: 44 20 88787799
E-mail: ipin@itftennis.com
URL: http://www.itftennis.com

8233 ■ Award for Services to the Game
For recognition of long service or special service to tennis, or to recognize individuals working closely with the ITF. Individuals may be nominated at any time. A plaque is awarded to one or more recipients each year. Established in 1979.

8234 ■ Davis Cup Award of Excellence
To honor a living player, doubles team, or captain who made a significant contribution to the Davis Cup from the country or the region in which the Final is played. Awarded annually. Established in 2001.

8235 ■ Grand Slams of Tennis
To recognize the male or female tennis player or doubles team that wins all the following championships in a calendar year: Wimbledon, the Australian Open, the United States Open, and the Roland Garros. Awarded when merited. The first Grand Slam Champion was Don Budge, recognized in 1938.

8236 ■ Tennis World Champions
To recognize the outstanding male and female, singles and doubles, tennis players of the year. Named annually.

8237 ■ International Thermoelectric Society
David Rowe, Sec.
Cardiff University
School of Engineering
Cardiff, United Kingdom
Ph: 44 1433 203 460
E-mail: rowedm1@cardiff.ac.uk
URL: http://www.its.org

8238 ■ Best Paper Awards
To recognize the best scientific and application paper awards. A monetary prize of US$500 is awarded in each of the two categories.

8239 ■ Goldsmid Award
To recognize a graduate student for excellence in research in thermoelectrics. A certificate and monetary prize are awarded annually. Established in 1999.

8240 ■ Outstanding Achievement Award
To recognize the outstanding achievements of a senior scientist for his or her contributions to the field of thermoelectricity. A trophy and monetary prize of $2,000 are awarded annually. Established in 2011.

8241 ■ Young Investigator Award
To recognize a young investigator who has exhibited a record of excellent original work and significant results in the field of thermoelectrics or thermoelectric materials. Candidates must hold a researcher/engineer position in academia, industry, government laboratories, or scientific institutes. A certificate and monetary prize of US$2,000 are awarded annually.

8242 ■ International Tube Association
Mr. Phillip G. Knight, Exec. Sec.
46 Holly Walk
Warwickshire
Leamington Spa CV32 4HY, United Kingdom
Ph: 44 1926 834681
Fax: 44 1926 314755
E-mail: info@itatube.org
URL: http://www.itatube.org

8243 ■ Papers Award
For recognition of technical quality of papers that further tube technology and are presented at the Association's International Conference. The Hugh Sansome President's Trophy is awarded annually. Established in 1982.

8244 ■ International Union of Air Pollution Prevention and Environmental Protection Associations
Hanlie Liebenberg Enslin, Pres.
Oakwood House
11 Wingle Tye Rd.
Burgess Hill RH15 9HR, United Kingdom
Ph: 44 1444 236848
Fax: 44 1444 236848
E-mail: iuappa@btinternet.com
URL: http://www.iuappa.org

8245 ■ Christopher E. Barthel, Jr. Award
For recognition of outstanding service to the cause of clean air throughout the world over many years. Contributions of a civic, administrative, legislative, or judicial nature are considered. Nomination is by a member or contributing as-

Awards are arranged in alphabetical order below their administering organizations

sociate without further restriction. An illuminated parchment is awarded triennially at the World Clean Air Congress. Established in 1980 in honor of Christopher E. Barthel, Jr., a founding member of IUAPPA.

8246 ■ World Clean Air Congress Award
To recognize an individual (or group of individuals) who has made a contribution of outstanding significance internationally to the progress of science or technology pertaining to air pollution. An illuminated parchment is awarded triennially at the World Clean Air and Environmental Protection Congress. Established in 1989.

8247 ■ International Union of Crystallography (Union Internationale de Cristallographie)
Prof. Sine Larsen, Pres.
2 Abbey Sq.
Chester CH1 2HU, United Kingdom
Ph: 44 1244 345431
Fax: 44 1244 344843
E-mail: execsec@iucr.org
URL: http://www.iucr.org

8248 ■ Ewald Prize
For recognition of outstanding contributions to the science of crystallography. Selection is by nomination. A monetary award of US$30,000, a medal, and a certificate are awarded triennially at the International Congresses of Crystallography. Established in 1986 in honor of Professor Paul Peter Ewald, who made significant contributions to the foundations of crystallography and to the founding of the IUC.

8249 ■ International Visual Communications Association
Marco Forgione, CEO
1st Fl., 23 Golden Sq.
London W1F 9JP, United Kingdom
Ph: 44 20 72871002
Fax: 44 20 72872651
E-mail: info@ivca.org
URL: http://www.ivca.org
Formed by merger of: International Television Association.

8250 ■ International Visual Communications Association Awards
For recognition of effective and excellent business communications in film, video, multimedia and live events. Awarded in 33 categories within the broader groups of: (1) Film; (2) Digital; (3) Production Arts and Crafts; and (4) Special Awards. Gold, Silver, and Bronze Awards are presented to the best entries in each category. The Grand Prix Award is selected by a jury from all the category Gold Award winners, and is awarded to the most outstanding work submitted. Awarded annually. Established in 1968 by the British Industrial and Scientific Association.

8251 ■ International Water Association
Mr. Paul Reiter, Exec. Dir.
Alliance House
12 Caxton St.
London SW1H 0QS, United Kingdom
Ph: 44 20 76545500
Fax: 44 20 76545555
E-mail: water@iwahq.org
URL: http://www.iwahq.org/1nb/home.html

8252 ■ Honorary Membership
Recognizes individuals who make outstanding contribution to IWA and water pollution research and control. A medal is awarded biennially.

8253 ■ Imhoff - Koch Award for Outstanding Contribution to Water Management and Science
Recognizes the individual making contribution of international impact relating to facilities involved in water quality control. A medal is awarded biennially at the World Congress. Named in honor of Dr. Karl Imhoff and Dr. Pierre Koch.

8254 ■ Samuel H. Jenkins Outstanding Service Award
Recognizes meritorious contribution and service to IWA. Awarded biennially at the World Congress.

8255 ■ Publishing Award
Recognizes the best paper by an IWA member at biennial conference. Awarded periodically.

8256 ■ International Wine and Food Society (London, United Kingdom)
Judy Tayler-Smith, Chm.
4 St. James's Sq.
London SW1Y 4JU, United Kingdom
E-mail: judyts@iwfs.co.uk
URL: http://www.iwfs.org

8257 ■ Andre Simon Medal
To recognize individuals for contributions to gastronomy. Society members are eligible. Gold and silver medals are awarded at the discretion of the Council; bronze medals are awarded by area committees. Established in 1960 to honor Andre Louis Simon, CBE, the first president and founder of the Society.

8258 ■ InterNICHE
Nick Jukes, Coor.
42 S Knighton Rd.
Leicester LE2 3LP, United Kingdom
Ph: 44 116 2109652
Fax: 44 116 2109652
E-mail: coordinator@interniche.org
URL: http://www.interniche.org

8259 ■ Humane Education Award
To support ethical and effective life science education and training. A grant of 20,000 Euros is awarded annually.

8260 ■ Investor Relations Society
Michael Mitchell, Gen. Mgr.
3 Bedford St.
Bedford House
London WC2E 9HD, United Kingdom
Ph: 44 20 73791763
Fax: 44 20 72401320
E-mail: enquiries@irs.org.uk
URL: http://www.ir-soc.org.uk

8261 ■ Investor Relations Best Practice Awards
For companies that lead the way in the practice of investor communications. Awarded annually in various categories.

8262 ■ Irish Hang Gliding and Paragliding Association
Graham Tobin, Sec.
39 Garden Village Court
Kilpedder, United Kingdom
URL: http://www.ihpa.ie

8263 ■ Hang Gliding Cross Country Championship Trophy
For the hang gliding pilot who clocks up the most distance in the XC League during the preceding year. Best five flights are used. Awarded annually.

8264 ■ Hang Gliding Cross Country Trophy
For the hang gliding pilot who made the longest XC during the preceding year. Awarded annually.

8265 ■ Shane O'Reilly Memorial Hang Gliding Competitions Trophy
For the hang gliding pilot who clocks up the highest number of points in the IHPA Competitions League during the preceding year. Awarded annually.

8266 ■ Paragliding Cross Country Competitions Trophy
For the winner of the IHPA Paragliding Competitions League. At least five tasks need to be run to qualify. Awarded annually.

8267 ■ Paragliding Cross Country League Millennium Falcon Trophy
For the paragliding pilot who clocks the most distance in the XC League during the preceding year. Best five flights are used. Awarded annually.

8268 ■ Trevor Wilde Award
To recognize a member for outstanding contributions to hang gliding during the preceding year. The Pilots Trophy is awarded annually.

8269 ■ Japan Society - United Kingdom
Heidi Potter, Chief Exec.
Swire House
59 Buckingham Gate
London SW1E 6AJ, United Kingdom
Ph: 44 20 7828 6330
Fax: 44 20 7828 6331
E-mail: info@japansociety.org.uk
URL: http://www.japansociety.org.uk

8270 ■ Japan Society Small Grants
To recognize an individual for significant work in the field of U.K.-Japanese relations. A certificate and inscribed glass bowl are presented annually. Established in 1994.

8271 ■ Jowett Car Club
Ms. Mary Young, Contact
15 Second Ave.
Essex CM1 4ET, United Kingdom
URL: http://jowett.org

8272 ■ Horace Grimley Award
For recognition of outstanding service to the marque and the Club. Members are eligible. A monetary prize is awarded annually at the general meeting. Established in 1985 to honor Horace Grimley, a relative of the founders of Jowett Cars Ltd. who worked for the company for 33 years and was responsible for engineering development.

8273 ■ King's School
The Precincts
Canterbury CT1 2ES, United Kingdom
Ph: 44 1227 595501
Fax: 44 1227 595595
E-mail: info@kings-school.co.uk
URL: http://www.kings-school.co.uk

8274 ■ Calvin and Rose G. Hoffman Prize for Distinguished Publication on Christopher Marlowe
For recognition of the unpublished essay that most informatively examines and discusses in depth the life and works of Christopher Marlowe and the authorship of the plays and poems now commonly attributed to William Shakespeare. The deadline for entry is September 1. A monetary prize of not less than £6,500 is awarded annually. Established in 1988 by a bequest of Calvin Hoffman in memory of Calvin and Rose G. Hoffman.

8275 ■ Laboratory Animal Science Association
David Smith, Pres.
PO Box 524
Hull HU9 9HE, United Kingdom
Ph: 44 8456 711956
Fax: 44 8456 711957
E-mail: info@lasa.co.uk
URL: http://www.lasa.co.uk

8276 ■ LASA Award
To honor an individual, group, or organization of any nationality for contributions to laboratory animal science, including the welfare of laboratory animals. A medal is awarded annually.

8277 ■ Ladies' Golf Union
Shona Malcolm, Pres.
The Scores
Fife

Awards are arranged in alphabetical order below their administering organizations

St. Andrews KY16 9AT, United Kingdom
Ph: 44 1334 475811
Fax: 44 1334 472818
URL: http://www.lgu.org

8278 ■ Ladies' British Open Amateur Championship
To recognize the winner of the annual amateur golf championship. A Challenge Cup is awarded. Established in 1893.

8279 ■ Ricoh Women's British Open Championship
To recognize the winners of the annual golf championship. Trophies and monetary prizes are awarded annually. Established in 1976. Sponsored by Ricoh Co., Ltd. Formerly: (2007) Weetabix Women's British Open Championship.

8280 ■ Landscape Research Group
Prof. Dr. Eckart Lange, Hd.
The University of Sheffield
Department of Landscape
Arts Tower, 3rd Fl.
Western Bank
Sheffield S10 2TN, United Kingdom
Ph: 44 114 2220605
E-mail: e.lange@sheffield.ac.uk
URL: http://lrg.ethz.ch/lrg_main.html

8281 ■ Dissertation Prize
To honor undergraduate and postgraduate students for outstanding dissertations. Awarded annually. Established in 2001.

8282 ■ Law Society
Linda Lee, Pres.
113 Chancery Ln.
London WC2A 1PL, United Kingdom
Ph: 44 20 72421222
Fax: 44 20 78310344
E-mail: contact@lawsociety.org.uk
URL: http://www.lawsociety.org.uk/home.law

8283 ■ Award for Excellence in Equality and Diversity
To honor a law firm or team for excellence in the promotion of equality and diversity in the solicitors' profession. Awarded annually.

8284 ■ Award for Excellence in Exporting Legal Services
To honor a law firm that can show that it has broken new ground in the export of legal services. Entries should demonstrate the strategic nature of the firm's exporting objectives; the active development of new export markets (either geographical or sectoral) that have turned into results impacting on the firm's revenue; and the coherent integration of this export activity into wider business development plans. Awarded annually.

8285 ■ Award for Excellence in Marketing and Business Development
To recognize the most innovative, creative, and inspiring business development campaign executed by a law firm or in-house legal department. Awarded annually.

8286 ■ Award for Excellence in Pioneering Legal Services
To honor innovative teams across the legal services sector who can demonstrate cutting edge business practices and client service. Awarded annually.

8287 ■ Award for Excellence in Social Responsibility
To honor a law firm or team for original ideas and significant outcomes in social responsibility and community engagement, from small-scale community involvement to large-scale pro bono projects. Awarded annually.

8288 ■ Barrister of the Year Award
To honor an outstanding barrister. Awarded annually.

8289 ■ CLS Award for Excellence in Client Service
To honor a law firm or team for excellence in client care and innovative approaches to maintaining and developing client-focuses services. Awarded annually. Sponsored by Conveyancing Liability Solutions Ltd. (CLS).

8290 ■ Junior Lawyer of the Year Award
To honor an outstanding member of the Society's Junior Lawyers Division. Awarded annually.

8291 ■ Junior Lawyers Division Pro Bono Awards
To recognize and celebrate the value work of students, trainees, and junior solicitors in providing free legal services to help the most disadvantaged members of the community. Open to LPC students, trainee solicitors, and solicitors with up to five years of experience. Awards are presented in five categories. In addition, discretionary cash prizes of up to £1000 may be awarded to support the pro bono projects of the winners.

8292 ■ Legal Executive of the Year Award
To honor an outstanding legal executive. Awarded annually.

8293 ■ Lexcel Award for Excellence in Practice Standards
To honor excellence in practice management and service delivery from practices that have successfully implemented the Lexcel standards. Open to Lexcel-accredited practices only. Awarded annually. Sponsored by Lloyds TSB.

8294 ■ Solicitor of the Year Award
To honor an outstanding solicitor. Awarded annually.

8295 ■ Graham Turnbull Essay Competition
To recognize law students, trainee solicitors, and young lawyers in or from England and Wales. Monetary prizes of £500 and £250 are awarded to first- and second-place winners, respectively. Held annually. Established in honor of the English solicitor who was killed in 1997 while working as a United Nations rights monitor in Rwanda.

8296 ■ Wig & Pen Prize
To honor a junior solicitor practicing within London or Westminster, England. Awarded annually as part of the Junior Lawyers Division Pro Bono Awards. Sponsored by the City of London and the City of Westminster.

8297 ■ Lawn Tennis Association
Roger Draper, CEO
The National Tennis Centre
100 Priority Ln.
Roehampton
London SW15 5JQ, United Kingdom
Ph: 44 20 84877000
Fax: 44 20 84877301
E-mail: info@lta.org.uk
URL: http://www.lta.org.uk

8298 ■ Lawn Tennis Association National Awards
For recognition of performance, standards, and achievements in the field of lawn tennis. Awards are given in the following categories: Player of the Year; Junior Player of the Year; Disabled Player of the Year; Coach of the Year; Club of the Year; School of the Year; Local Authority of the Year; Volunteer of the Year; Official of the Year; and Marsh Team of the Year. Engraved cups or plates are presented to the winners annually at the LTA Awards Dinner. Established in 1982.

8299 ■ Lead Contractors Association
Dave Martin, Chm.
Centurion House
36 London Rd.

East Grinstead RH19 1AB, United Kingdom
Ph: 44 1342 317888
Fax: 44 1342 303200
E-mail: info@lca.gb.com
URL: http://www.leadcontractorsassociation.com

8300 ■ Murdoch Award
To honor the best technical design and installation of leadwork in the United Kingdom. Awarded annually. Established in 1996 in honor of Richard Murdoch.

8301 ■ LEPRA Health in Action
Ms. Nicolette Dawson, Communications Off.
28 Middleborough
Colchester CO1 1TG, United Kingdom
Ph: 44 1206 216700
Fax: 44 1206 762151
E-mail: lepra@leprahealthinaction.org
URL: http://www.leprahealthinaction.org
Formerly: (2008) LEPRA - England.

8302 ■ Medical Student Elective Grant
To encourage medical students who wish to undertake a leprosy assignment overseas during their elective period. Eligible placements must enable the student to make a worthwhile contribution and must fit into the life and work of the overseas institute he or she will be attached to. Awarded annually.

8303 ■ Liberal International (Internationale Liberale)
Mr. Hans van Baalen, Pres.
1 Whitehall Pl.
London SW1A 2HD, United Kingdom
Ph: 44 20 78395905
Fax: 44 20 79252685
E-mail: all@liberal-international.org
URL: http://www.liberal-international.org

8304 ■ Prize for Freedom
To recognize an individual for outstanding contributions to human rights and political freedoms. Selection is by nomination. A plaque is awarded annually. Established in 1985.

8305 ■ Libertarian Alliance
Dr. Tim Evans, Pres.
2 Lansdowne Row, Ste. 35
London W1J 6HL, United Kingdom
Ph: 44 20 7956472199
E-mail: tim@libertarian.co.uk
URL: http://www.libertarian.co.uk
Formerly: (1979) Radical Libertarian Alliance.

8306 ■ Liberty Awards
To recognize individuals for contributions to the cause of liberty and freedom. A framed certificate is awarded when merited.

8307 ■ Library and Information Research Group
Christine Irving, Honorary Sec.
7 Ridgmount St.
London WC1E 7AE, United Kingdom
Ph: 44 20 72550500
Fax: 44 20 72550501
E-mail: info@cilip.org.uk
URL: http://www.cilip.org.uk/specialinterestgroups/bysubject/research

8308 ■ LIRG Research Award
To encourage research and innovation in library and information science. Particular attention will be paid to proposals intended to improve the accessibility, retrievability, and usefulness of information. An award of up to £1,000 is awarded annually to fund research.

8309 ■ Student Prize
To promote a greater awareness among students of the importance of research and to facilitate the dissemination of the results of outstanding projects. To qualify, projects must be a final-year

Awards are arranged in alphabetical order below their administering organizations

undergraduate project or a post-graduate dissertation. A monetary prize of £300 is awarded annually.

8310 ■ Lighting Association
Jonathan Lucas, Pres.
Stafford Park 7
Shropshire
Telford TF3 3BQ, United Kingdom
Ph: 44 1952 290905
Fax: 44 1952 290906
E-mail: enquiries@lightingassociation.com
URL: http://www.lightingassociation.com
Formerly: Decorative Lighting Association.

8311 ■ Student Lighting Design Awards
To recognize student designers at the start of their careers in the lighting industry. Students of design at educational institutions in the United Kingdom and Europe are eligible. Monetary prizes totaling £5,000 are awarded annually. Established in 1985.

8312 ■ Linnean Society of London
Ms. Victoria Smith, Mgr.
Burlington House
Piccadilly
London W1J 0BF, United Kingdom
Ph: 44 20 74344479
Fax: 44 20 72879364
E-mail: info@linnean.org
URL: http://www.linnean.org

8313 ■ Bicentenary Medal
To recognize achievements of a biologist under the age of 40. Any biologist who is not at the time a member of the Council is eligible. A silver medal is awarded annually. Established in 1978 to commemorate the two-hundredth anniversary of the death of Linneaus.

8314 ■ H. H. Bloomer Award
To recognize an amateur naturalist who has made an important contribution to biological knowledge. The award may be given to any person not at the time a member of the Council. Presented alternately to a botanist and a zoologist. A silver medal is awarded annually. Established in 1963 from a legacy by the late Harry Howard Bloomer.

8315 ■ Linnean Medal
To recognize a botanist and/or a zoologist for service to science. Any biologist, who is not at the time a member of the Council, is eligible. A medal is awarded at the Anniversary Meeting. Established in 1888 in connection with the Centenary of the Society.

8316 ■ Irene Manton Prize
To recognize the best thesis in botany examined for a doctorate of philosophy during the year beginning in September and ending in August. It is open to candidates whose research has been carried out while registered at any institution in the United Kingdom. Theses on the full range of plant sciences are eligible. A piece of sculpture or other work of fine art is awarded, to which the Society has added £1,000. Awarded annually. Established in 1990.

8317 ■ Jill Smythies Award
To recognize published illustrations, such as drawings or paintings, in aid of plant identification, with the emphasis on botanical accuracy and the accurate portrayal of diagnostic characteristics. Illustrations of cultivars of garden origin are not eligible. Individuals who are not at the time members of the Council are eligible. A silver medal and a purse are awarded, usually annually. Established in 1986 by Mr. B.E. Smythies, FLS, in honor of his wife, the late Florence Mary Smythies ("Jill"), whose career as a botanical artist was cut short by an accident to her right hand.

8318 ■ Lloyd's List
Informa UK Ltd.
Telephone House
69-77 Paul St.
London EC2A 4LQ, United Kingdom
Ph: 44 20 70175531
Fax: 44 20 70174975
E-mail: info@lloydslist.com
URL: http://www.lloydslist.com

8319 ■ Asia Awards
Recognizes excellence in the shipping Industry in Asia. Awards are presented to firms and individuals. Award categories include: Shipbuilding, Ship Repair Yard, Ship of the Year, Container Terminal Operator of the Year, Classification Society, Ship Manager of the Year, Training and Crewing, Logistics, Safety, Environmental Protection, Tanker Owner, Financier of the Year, Asian Container Shipping Line of the Year, Dry Bulk Owner/Operator, Innovation, Ship Broker, Shipping Lawyer of the Year, Best Marine Insurance Provider, Newsmaker of the Year, and Lifetime Achievement. Awarded annually.

8320 ■ Global Awards
Recognizes excellence in the shipping industry. Awards are presented to firms and individuals. Award categories include: Clean Seas, Training, Shipmaster of the Year, Ship of the Year, Shipping Financier of the Year, Shipping Lawyer of the Year, Amver-Assisted Rescue at Sea, Port Operator of the Year, Innovation, Marine Insurance, Protection and Indemnity, Safety at Sea, Cruise and Ferry, Classification Society, Ship Agency, Ship Broker, Ship Repair and Conversion, Shipbuilding and Construction, Personality of the Year, Newsmaker of the Year, and Lifetime Achievement. Awarded annually.

8321 ■ Greek Shipping Awards
Recognizes excellence in the shipping industry in Greece. Awards are presented to firms and individuals. Award categories include: Dry Cargo Company of the Year, Tanker Company of the Year, Passenger Line of the Year, Shipbroker of the Year, Shipping Financier of the Year, Technical Innovation, International Personality of the Year, Ship of the Year, Achievement in Safety or Environmental Protection, Seafarer of the Year, Newsmaker of the Year, Personality of the Year, Lloyd's List/Propeller Club Lifetime Achievement, and Piraeus International Centre Award. Non-Greek companies are eligible provided they have been demonstrably active in the Greek shipping industry. Awarded annually.

8322 ■ Italian Shipping Awards
Recognizes excellence in the shipping industry in Italy. Awards are presented to firms and individuals. Award categories include: Dry Cargo Operator of the Year, Tanker Company of the Year, Passenger/Ro-Ro Operator of the Year, Maritime Services, Ship Agent of the Year, Shipping Financier of the Year, Marine Broker of the Year, Achievement in Safety or Environmental Protection, Training and Education, Port or Terminal of the Year, Yacht Builder of the Year, New Generation Award, Shipping Newsmaker of the Year, Personality of the Year, and the Cristoforo Colombo Award (special achievement). Awarded annually.

8323 ■ Middle East and Indian Subcontinent Awards
Recognizes excellence in the shipping industry in the Middle East and the Indian Subcontinent. Awards are presented to firms and individuals. Award categories include: Shipowner/Operator, Clean Seas and Environment, Shipbuilding and Repair, Innovation, Safety at Sea, Maritime Training, Port Authority/Terminal Operator, Ship of the Year, Maritime Services, Classification Society, Freight/Transport/Logistics, Energy, Infrastructure, Personality of the Year, Newsmaker of the Year, and Lifetime Achievement. Awarded annually.

8324 ■ Turkish Shipping Awards
Recognizes excellence in the Turkish shipping industry. Awards are presented to firms and individuals. Award categories include: Dry Cargo Company of the Year, Tanker Company of the Year, Ship of the Year, Shipyard of the Year, Yacht Building Company of the Year, Shipping Financier of the Year, Port or Terminal of the Year, Training and Education, Maritime Service, Achievement in Safety or Environmental Protection, New Generation Award, Personality of the Year, and Lifetime Achievement. Awarded annually.

8325 ■ London Chamber of Commerce and Industry
Stella Fernandes, Pres.
33 Queen St.
London EC4R 1AP, United Kingdom
Ph: 44 20 72484444
Ph: 44 20 72031881
Fax: 44 20 74890391
E-mail: lc@londonchamber.co.uk
URL: http://www.londonchamber.co.uk

8326 ■ Entrepreneur of the Year
To honor an individual who had led the growth of his/her business. Awarded annually.

8327 ■ London Mathematical Society
A.J. Macintyre, Pres.
De Morgan House
57-58 Russell Sq.
London WC1B 4HS, United Kingdom
Ph: 44 20 76373686
Fax: 44 20 73233655
E-mail: lms@lms.ac.uk
URL: http://www.lms.ac.uk

8328 ■ Berwick Prize
For recognition of a definite piece of mathematical research published by the Society in any of its publications during the preceding eight years. Members who have fewer than 15 years of involvement in mathematics at the postdoctoral level are eligible. A monetary prize and a certificate are awarded biennially in odd-numbered years. Established in 1946 by Mrs. Berwick in memory of Professor William Edward Hodgson Berwick, ScD, member of the Society (1914-1944), Council (1925-1929), and Vice President (1929).

8329 ■ Senior Berwick Prize
For recognition of a definite piece of mathematical research published by the Society in any of its publications during the preceding eight years. Members of the Society are eligible. A monetary prize and a certificate are awarded biennially in even-numbered years. Established in 1946 by Mrs. Berwick in memory of Professor William Edward Hodgson Berwick, ScD, member of the Society (1914-1944), Council (1925-1929), and Vice President (1929).

8330 ■ De Morgan Medal
This, the Society's highest honor, is given for recognition of an individual's contributions to mathematics. Mathematicians who are normally resident in the United Kingdom are eligible. A gold medal is awarded triennially. Established in 1884 in memory of Professor A. De Morgan, first President of the Society.

8331 ■ Naylor Prize and Lectureship
For recognition of contributions to applied mathematics and/or the applications of mathematics. Mathematicians who are normally resident in the United Kingdom in the year of the award are eligible. A monetary prize, a certificate, and an invitation to present a lecture are awarded biennially in odd-numbered years. Established in 1976 in memory of Vernon Dalrymple Naylor, by his sons.

8332 ■ Polya Prize
For recognition of outstanding creativity in, imaginative exposition of, or distinguished

Awards are arranged in alphabetical order below their administering organizations

contribution to mathematics within the United Kingdom. A monetary prize and a certificate are awarded annually. Established in 1986 by a donation from Mrs. Polya in memory of Professor G. Polya, member of the London Mathematical Society (1925-1985), and Honorary Member (1956-1985).

8333 ■ Whitehead Prize
For recognition of work in and influence on mathematics, including applied mathematics, mathematical physics, and mathematical aspects of computer science. Members who have fewer than 15 years of involvement in mathematics at the postdoctoral level are eligible. A monetary prize and a certificate are awarded to up to four recipients annually. Established in 1973 by Professor Whitehead's friends and a donation from Mrs. Whitehead in memory of Professor J.H.C. Whitehead, LMS President (1953-55).

8334 ■ Senior Whitehead Prize
For recognition of work in, influence on, and service to mathematics, as well as lecturing abilities. Mathematicians who are normally resident in the United Kingdom on January 1 of the year of the award are eligible. A monetary prize and a certificate are awarded biennially in odd-numbered years. Established in 1973 by Professor Whitehead's friends and a donation from Mrs. Whitehead in memory of Professor J.H.C. Whitehead, LMS President (1953-55).

8335 ■ Macmillan Education Ltd.
Between Towns Rd.
Oxford OX4 3PP, United Kingdom
Ph: 44 1865 405700
Fax: 44 1865 405701
E-mail: elt@macmillan.com
URL: http://www.macmillaneducation.com

8336 ■ Macmillan Writer's Prize for Africa
To promote and celebrate story writing from across the African continent. Open to those aged 16 or over who are nationals or naturalized citizens of any of the countries that make up the continent of Africa, and to those who were born as citizens in those countries. Awards are presented in three categories: Junior - a prize of US$5,000 for an unpublished story geared to children between the ages of 8 and 12 years; Senior - a prize of US$5,000 for an unpublished story geared to children between the ages 13 and 17; and New Children's Writer - a prize of US$3,000 for the most promising writer in either the Junior or Senior category who has never had a book published. Awarded biennially in even-numbered years. First awarded in 2002.

8337 ■ Making Music
Robin Osterley, Chief Exec.
2-4 Great Eastern St.
London EC2A 3NW, United Kingdom
Ph: 44 20 74228280
Fax: 44 20 74228299
E-mail: info@makingmusic.org.uk
URL: http://www.makingmusic.org.uk
Formerly: (2001) National Federation of Music Societies.

8338 ■ Philip and Dorothy Green Award for Young Concert Artists
To assist young solo performers in obtaining concert engagements at the beginning of their professional careers. Professional musicians under the age of 28 (32 for singers) who hold European Community passports and are normally residents of Great Britain are eligible. The award, consisting of concert engagements with music clubs and societies, is presented to a performer in several categories, such as piano, violin, tenor, harp, and saxophone; categories vary by year. Finalists are awarded engagements. Held annually. Established in 1961.

8339 ■ Sir Charles Grove Prizes
Recognizes outstanding contribution to British music life. Individuals and groups are eligible. Nominations must be made by society members. Awarded annually. Established in 1990.

8340 ■ Malacological Society of London
Mark Davies, Pres.
Kingston University
School of Life Sciences
Penrhyn Rd.
Kingston upon Thames
London KT1 2EE, United Kingdom
E-mail: webmanager@malacsoc.org.uk
URL: http://www.malacsoc.org.uk/index.html

8341 ■ Malacological Society of London Annual Award
To recognize exceptionally promising initial contributions to the study of molluscs. A monetary prize of £500 is awarded annually.

8342 ■ Sir Charles Maurice Yonge Award
To honor researchers for excellent achievements in the study of Bivalvia. Awarded annually.

8343 ■ Manufacturing Technologies Association
Bob Hunt, Pres.
62 Bayswater Rd.
London W2 3PS, United Kingdom
Ph: 44 20 72986400
Ph: 44 20 72986408
Fax: 44 20 72986430
E-mail: info@mta.org.uk
URL: http://www.mta.org.uk/home

8344 ■ TDI Awards
To promote the work of manufacturing technologies and engineering students and to celebrate the creativity and innovation taking place inside the curriculum. Open to all schools and colleges in the United Kingdom. Criteria are innovation; manufacturing and engineering; use of technology; production; presentation; research & development; and reflective practice. Awarded in three categories: Group A: 11-14 years; Group B: 15-16 years; and Group C: 17-19 years. Awarded annually.

8345 ■ Marine Biological Association of the United Kingdom
Geoffrey Holland, Pres.
The Laboratory
Citadel Hill
Devon
Plymouth PL1 2PB, United Kingdom
Ph: 44 1752 633207
Fax: 44 1752 633102
E-mail: sec@mba.ac.uk
URL: http://www.mba.ac.uk

8346 ■ Ray Lankester Investigatorship
To advance knowledge on marine animals and plants, and to further the development of marine biology. An honorarium of £1,500 per month for a maximum of five months is awarded, and winners may use laboratory facilities at MBA Plymouth. Awarded to one or two recipients annually. Established in 1911 by Dr. G.P. Bidder in honor of Sir Ray Lankester, president of the MBA.

8347 ■ Mensa International
Saint John's House
Saint John's Sq.
Wolverhampton WV2 4AH, United Kingdom
Ph: 44 1902 772771
Fax: 44 1902 392500
URL: http://www.mensa.org

8348 ■ Mensa International Competitions
To recognize individuals from 100 countries whose intelligence, as measured by standardized tests, is within the top 2 percent of the general population, and to promote social contact among intelligent people. Competitions are sponsored periodically and awards are given.

8349 ■ Mind - National Association for Mental Health
Paul Farmer, Chief Exec.
15-19 Broadway
London E15 4BQ, United Kingdom
Ph: 44 20 85192122
Fax: 44 20 85221725
E-mail: contact@mind.org.uk
URL: http://www.mind.org.uk

8350 ■ Book of the Year Award
For recognition of the book that makes the greatest contribution to public understanding of the experience, nature, cause, treatment, or consequences of mental health problems. Books published in the United Kingdom are eligible. A monetary prize of £1,500 is awarded annually. Established in 1981 in honor of Allen Lane.

8351 ■ Champion of the Year
To recognize an individual who has made an outstanding contribution to mental health in the United Kingdom over the past year. Worthy contributions include campaigning, speaking out against stigma, or improving the lives of people with mental distress. Candidates are nominated and voted for by the public. Awarded annually.

8352 ■ Journalist of the Year
To recognize excellence in reporting on mental health issues in the United Kingdom. Open to print journalists who have raised awareness and promoted understanding of mental distress. Awarded annually.

8353 ■ Mental Health Media Awards
To celebrate the best portrayal of mental distress and the reporting of mental health in broadcast media in the United Kingdom. Awarded in a variety of categories, including Factual Radio, Radio Drama, and Television Documentary. Awarded annually.

8354 ■ Student Journalist of the Year
To encourage outstanding reporting on mental health issues among young journalists in the United Kingdom. Awarded annually.

8355 ■ Mineralogical Society
Kevin B. Murphy, Exec. Dir.
12 Baylis Mews
Amyand Park Rd.
Middlesex
Twickenham TW1 3HQ, United Kingdom
Ph: 44 20 88916600
Fax: 44 20 88916599
E-mail: info@minersoc.org
URL: http://www.minersoc.org

8356 ■ Collins Medal
To recognize a scientist who, during a long and active career, has made an outstanding contribution to pure or applied aspects of mineral sciences and associated studies. Awarded annually. Established in 2008 in honor of Joseph Henry Collins (1841-1916), a founding member of the Society.

8357 ■ Max Hey Medal
To recognize existing and ongoing research of excellence carried out by young workers within the fields of either Mineralogy, Crystallography, Petrology or Geochemistry. Candidates must normally be under 35 years of age, except where there has been a career break, in which case the committee chair may agree to accept nominations from older candidates. Awarded annually. Established in 1993.

8358 ■ Schlumberger Medal
To recognize scientific excellence in mineralogy and its applications; mineralogy being broadly

Awards are arranged in alphabetical order below their administering organizations

defined and reflecting the diverse and worldwide interests and membership of the Society with its various specialist groups. A medal is awarded annually. Established in 1990. Sponsored by Schlumberger Cambridge Research.

8359 ■ Minerals Engineering Society
Andrew W. Howells, Natl. Sec.-Treas.
2 Ryton Close
Blyth
Nottinghamshire
Worksop S81 8DN, United Kingdom
Ph: 44 1909 591787
Ph: 44 1909 591940
Fax: 44 1909 591940
E-mail: secretary@mineralsengineering.org
URL: http://www.mineralsengineering.org
Formerly: Coal Preparation Society.

8360 ■ Lessing Medal
This, the Society's highest honor, is given for recognition of persons whose contributions to the field of mineral processing engineering have made them eminent in this sphere. Nominations are made in council, but may be initiated by a section committee or any group of ten members. Awarded from time to time in memory of Rudolph Lessing who, in the 1920s and 30s, was a determined advocate of the economic benefits to be obtained from coal cleaning and a pioneer in the introduction and establishment of coal preparation techniques.

8361 ■ Papers and Publications Committee Prizes
To recognize the authors of the best practical and theoretical papers given at National and Group meetings and submitted for publication in the Society's official journal, *Mine, Quarry & Recycling.* A prize is presented in each category at the annual meeting.

8362 ■ Travel Award
To subsidize an individual visit or attendance at a relevant conference or some other activity related to minerals engineering. Open to any person who is training or engaged in minerals engineering. A monetary award of £350 is awarded as merited.

8363 ■ Ministry of Defence
MOD Medal Office
Bldg. 250
RAF Innsworth
Gloucester GL3 1HW, United Kingdom
Ph: 44 141 2243600
URL: http://www.mod.uk

8364 ■ Iraq Medal
To honor an individual for 30 consecutive days of service on Op Telic in Iraq. Established in 2003.

8365 ■ MND Scotland
Craig Stockton, Chief Exec.
76 Firhill Rd.
Glasgow G20 7BA, United Kingdom
Ph: 44 141 9451077
Fax: 44 141 9452578
E-mail: info@mndscotland.org.uk
URL: http://www.mndscotland.org.uk
Formerly: (2009) Scottish Motor Neurone Disease Association.

8366 ■ John Macleod Memorial Award
To honor an individual for exceptional contributions to Scotland's motor neurone disease community. Awarded annually.

8367 ■ Mobile Data Association
Mike Short, Honorary Pres.
PO Box 9347
Sleaford NG34 4DA, United Kingdom
Ph: 44 870 2255632
E-mail: mda@themda.org

URL: http://www.themda.org

8368 ■ Best Consumer Mobile Data Application Award
To honor those U.K. companies and individuals who have made an outstanding contribution to the uptake and success of mobile data for consumers in the previous year. A glass trophy is awarded annually.

8369 ■ Best Corporate Mobile Data Application Award
To honor those U.K. companies and individuals who have made an outstanding contribution to the uptake and success of mobile data for the corporate world in the previous year. A glass trophy is awarded annually.

8370 ■ Multiple Sclerosis International Federation
Peer Baneke, CEO
3rd Fl., Skyline House
200 Union St.
London SE1 0LX, United Kingdom
Ph: 44 20 76201911
Fax: 44 20 76201922
E-mail: info@msif.org
URL: http://www.msif.org/language_choice.html

8371 ■ Jean-Martin Charcot Award
For recognition of lifetime achievement in pioneering research in multiple sclerosis. Nominations are accepted. A monetary grant of £1,500, travel expenses up to £6,000, and a plaque are presented biennially in odd-numbered years at the Multiple Sclerosis World Conference. Established in 1969 in honor of Professor Jean-Martin Charcot.

8372 ■ Jacqueline du Pre Fellowship
To support research in MS for young researchers by enabling them to undertake short visits to other MS research centers to either learn or jointly carry out research. The award is generally, but not exclusively, available for young and talented researchers from emerging countries. The two-year Fellowship includes an annual grant to cover travel and living costs, plus an additional contribution of up to £5,000 per year to the host research center. Established in 1999.

8373 ■ Evelyn Nicholson Award for International Caregiver
For recognition of a caregiver for a person with multiple sclerosis. Individuals must be recommended by national MS Society and reviewed by an awards committee. A monetary prize of £500 is awarded annually. Established in 1994.

8374 ■ James D. Wolfensohn Award
For recognition of an outstanding person with multiple sclerosis for his or her valuable contribution to fight MS. Individuals must be recommended by national MS Societies and reviewed by an awards committee. A monetary prize and a plaque are awarded annually with applicable travel and accommodation expenses. Presented biennially in odd-numbered years. Established in 1984.

8375 ■ Music Industries Association - England
Mr. Paul McManus CIPD, Chief Exec.
Ivy Cottage Offices
Finch's Yard
Eastwick Rd.
Great Bookham
Surrey KT23 4BA, United Kingdom
Ph: 44 1372 750600
Fax: 44 1372 750515
E-mail: enquiries@mia.org.uk
URL: http://www.mia.org.uk

8376 ■ Music Awards
To recognize innovation, commercial success, and value for money. Awards cover the whole

industry including contemporary and classical instruments, music publishing, and outstanding individuals within the music industry. Awarded annually.

8377 ■ Music Producers Guild
Mr. Steve Levine, Chm.
The Stables
Manor Farm
Chavenage
Tetbury GL8 8XW, United Kingdom
Ph: 44 20 32397606
Ph: 44 77 98621891
Fax: 44 79 76654643
E-mail: sue@whitenoisepr.co.uk
URL: http://www.mpg.org.uk/home

8378 ■ MPG Awards
To recognize producers and professionals in the U.K. recording industry. Awards are presented in a variety of categories, including Producer of the Year, Recording Engineer of the Year, U.K. Single of the Year, and Best Recording Studio. Established in 2009.

8379 ■ Producers Guild Fellowship Award
Nomination by other members.

8380 ■ Musicians Benevolent Fund
7-11 Britannia St.
London WC1X 9JS, United Kingdom
Ph: 44 20 7239 9100
Fax: 44 20 7713 8942
URL: http://www.helpmusicians.org.uk

8381 ■ Postgraduate Performance Awards
To assist outstandingly talented instrumentalists and singers with full-time study costs or toward the costs of buying a musical instrument. Awards range from £1,000 to £5,000, and include several named awards and scholarships. Awarded annually.

8382 ■ National Association of Hospital Fire Officers
David Cox, Treas.
University Hospital of Wales
Cardiff and Vales NHS Trust
Health Park
Cardiff CF14 4XW, United Kingdom
Ph: 44 29 20744646
Fax: 44 29 20744789
URL: http://www.nahfo.org

8383 ■ Merit Award
Recognizes significant contribution to healthcare fire safety. Personnel outside of the association are eligible. Awarded annually.

8384 ■ National Association of Licensed Paralegals
Amanda Hamilton, Contact
3.08 Canterbury Ct.
1-3 Brixton Rd.
London SW9 6DE, United Kingdom
Ph: 44 20 31760900
E-mail: info@nationalparalegals.co.uk
URL: http://www.nationalparalegals.com

8385 ■ Bronze Medal
To recognize the student obtaining the third-highest marks for the examinations to obtain the Higher Certificate in Paralegal Studies. Awarded annually.

8386 ■ Gold Medal
To recognize the student obtaining the highest marks for the examinations to obtain the Higher Certificate in Paralegal Studies. Awarded annually.

Awards are arranged in alphabetical order below their administering organizations

8387 ■ Silver Medal
To recognize the student obtaining the second-highest marks for the examinations to obtain the Higher Certificate in Paralegal Studies. Awarded annually.

8388 ■ National Association of Shopfitters
Richard Easton, Pres.
NAS House
411 Limpsfield Rd.
Warlingham CR6 9HA, United Kingdom
Ph: 44 1883 624961
Fax: 44 1883 626841
E-mail: enquiries@shopfitters.org
URL: http://www.shopfitters.org

8389 ■ Design Partnership Award
To recognize excellence in interior design and shopfitting contracting with emphasis on the special partnership between designer/architect and contractor that shopfitting demands. The competition is open to architects and designers practicing in the United Kingdom. The design project should be one for which the contract works have been completed and carried out in the United Kingdom by a member of the Association. The judges take into consideration the following: suitability of the design for the location and purpose of the project, choice of materials with particular reference to the needs of both design and cost effectiveness laid down in the design brief, creativity and originality in interpreting the design brief and to overcome problems inherent in the site or premises, and special design features of functional or decorative relevance. The entry judged the Best of Competition receives the overall Design Partnership Award. Awarded annually.

8390 ■ National Eisteddfod of Wales
(Eisteddfod Genedlaethol Frenhinol Cymr)
40 Parc Ty Glas
Llanishen
Cardiff CF14 5DU, United Kingdom
Ph: 44 29 2076 3777
Fax: 44 29 2076 3737
E-mail: gwyb@eisteddfod.org.uk
URL: http://www.eisteddfod.org.uk

8391 ■ Gorsedd of Bards Membership
(Aelod o Orsedd Beirdd Ynys Prydain)
In recognition of service to Wales, its language and culture, and also to honor Welshmen prominent in other fields of endeavor. Familiarity with the Welsh language, the oldest living language in Europe, is required. Membership in the Gorsedd of Bards - an association whose members consist of poets, writers, musicians, artists, and individuals who have made a distinguished contribution to the Welsh nation, language, and culture - entitles the holders to take part in the colorful ceremonial at the Royal National Eisteddfod. Bestowed annually during the first week of August. Established in 1772 by Iolo Morgannwg. Sponsored by the Gorsedd Board.

8392 ■ W. Towyn Roberts Vocal Scholarship
(Ysgoloriaeth W. Towyn Roberts)
To promote solo singing in Wales and to enable the most promising competitor in a special competition to follow a course of vocal instruction in a recognized school or college of music. The scholarship is open to those born in Wales or of Welsh parents, any person who has resided or worked in Wales for the three years prior to the date of the Eisteddfod, or any person able to speak or write the Welsh language. Competitors are expected to prepare a contrasting program of songs from different periods to be sung in Welsh. The program must include one song by a contemporary Welsh composer. A scholarship of £3,000 is awarded for the first place winner; £2,000 for second place winner; £1,000 for third place; and £500 for fourth place. Awarded annu-

ally during the first week of August. Established in 1982 by W. Towyn Roberts in memory of Violet Jones, Nantclwyd, the founder's wife.

8393 ■ National Music Council of The United Kingdom
Dame Cleo Laine, Pres.
British Music House
26 Berners St.
London W1T 3LR, United Kingdom
Ph: 44 170 7662662
Fax: 44 170 7662662
E-mail: info@nationalmusiccouncil.org.uk
URL: http://www.nationalmusiccouncil.org.uk

8394 ■ Local Education Authority Music Awards
To recognize local education authorities that have demonstrated imaginative, inclusive, and high quality music provision during the year. Awarded biennially.

8395 ■ National Operatic and Dramatic Association
Tony Gibbs, Chief Exec.
NODA House
58-60 Lincoln Rd.
Peterborough PE1 2RZ, United Kingdom
Ph: 44 1733 865790
Fax: 44 1733 319506
E-mail: info@noda.org.uk
URL: http://www.noda.org.uk

8396 ■ Long Service Awards
To recognize 25 years of service by individuals who are involved in amateur stage performances. Every five years thereafter, recipients become eligible for an additional Silver Bar to the medal, culminating after 50 years service with the Gold Bar, and after 60 years with the most prestigious award of all, the Diamond Bar. Awarded as merited.

8397 ■ National Piers Society
Neville C. Taylor, Membership Sec.
128 Gloucester Terr.
Flat 1
London W2 6HP, United Kingdom
Ph: 44 20 75865154
E-mail: nationalpierssociety@googlemail.com
URL: http://www.piers.co.uk

8398 ■ Peter Mason Award
Recognizes engineering excellence in pier restoration. Awarded triennially.

8399 ■ Photographic Competition
To honor the best photographs of piers in the United Kingdom. Monetary prizes are awarded for first, second, and third place winners. Awarded annually. Established in 2010.

8400 ■ Pier of the Year Award
Annual award of recognition. Voted on by membership ballot. Established in 1996.

8401 ■ National Portrait Gallery
Sandy Nairne, Dir.
St. Martins Pl.
London WC2H 0HE, United Kingdom
Ph: 44 171 306 0055
Fax: 44 171 306 0056
E-mail: snairne@npg.org.uk
URL: http://www.npg.org.uk

8402 ■ BP Portrait Award
To honor outstanding portrait painters. Open to painters from around the world who are older than 18 years of age. The first-place winner receives a monetary award of £25,000 and a commission for painting by the National Portrait Gallery. Awarded annually in June. Established in 1980. Sponsored by BP plc. Formerly: (1990) John Player Portrait Award; (1983) Imperial Tobacco Portrait Award.

8403 ■ BP Young Artist Award
To encourage young painters to specialize in portraiture, to foster new talent, and to help sustain Britain's long tradition of portraiture. Open to painters from around the world between the ages of 18 and 30 years. The first-place winner receives a monetary award of £5,000. Awarded annually. Established in 1980. Sponsored by BP plc.

8404 ■ Taylor Wessing Photographic Portrait Prize
To honor outstanding works of contemporary portrait photography. Open to photographers aged 18 years and over. Awarded annually. Sponsored by Taylor Wessing LLP.

8405 ■ National Register of Warranted Builders
Richard Diment, Dir. Gen.
Gordon Fisher House
14-15 Great James St.
London WC1N 3DP, United Kingdom
Ph: 44 20 72427583
Fax: 44 20 74040296
URL: http://www.fmb.org.uk

8406 ■ Master Builder of the Year Awards
To recognize excellent building skills and business performance in the United Kingdom. Awards are presented in nine categories. In addition, the following awards are presented: Master Builder of the Year (£20,000), Client of Master Builder of the Year (£3,000), Apprentice of the Year (£1,000), and Investor in Workforce Training (£500).

8407 ■ National Rifle Association of the United Kingdom
Glynn Alger, Sec. Gen.
Bisley
Surrey
Brookwood GU24 0PB, United Kingdom
Ph: 44 1483 797777
Fax: 44 1483 797285
E-mail: secgen@nra.org.uk
URL: http://www.nra.org.uk

8408 ■ Queen's Prize
To recognize an individual who has achieved the highest aggregate score in a course of rifle fire over distances of 300, 500, 600, 900, and 1,000 yards. A monetary prize of £250, a gold medal, and a badge are awarded annually on the fourth Saturday in July. Established in 1860 by H.M. Queen Victoria. The award was given as the King's Prize from 1901 through 1951. Formerly: (1951) King's Prize.

8409 ■ National Small-Bore Rifle Association
Allan Boosey, Chm.
Lord Roberts Ctre.
Bisley Camp
Brookwood
Woking GU24 0NP, United Kingdom
Ph: 44 1483 485505
Ph: 44 1483 485570
Fax: 44 1483 476392
E-mail: info@nsra.co.uk
URL: http://www.nsra.co.uk

8410 ■ Distinguished Service Award
To recognize secretaries' long service to affiliated clubs and organizations. Awarded when merited. Established in 1937.

8411 ■ National Sporting Club
Oak Cottage
County Oak Way
Crawley RH11 7ST, United Kingdom
Ph: 44 845 619 7070
Fax: 44 845 619 7171
E-mail: info@thenationalsportingclub.co.uk
URL: http://www.thenationalsportingclub.co.uk

Awards are arranged in alphabetical order below their administering organizations

8412 ■ British Sport Books Awards
To recognize the best U.K. books on sports. Awarded in the following categories: Best Autobiography, Best Biography, Best New Writer, Best Publicity Campaign, Best Illustrated Title, Best Racing Book, Best Football Book, Best Rugby Book, Best Cricket Book, and Best Sports Book Retailer.

8413 ■ National Vegetable Society
Mr. David Thornton, Sec.
14 Dronley Rd.
Birkhill
Dundee DD2 5QD, United Kingdom
Ph: 44 1382 580394
Ph: 44 1924 271869
E-mail: neil_hope@hotmail.com
URL: http://www.nvsuk.org.uk/index.php

8414 ■ Ron Fletcher Award
To recognize a group of members or a branch/district association that has made a considerable impact on the public by advancing the aims and objectives of the Society. Awarded annually.

8415 ■ Gold Medal
To recognize a member who has devoted a minimum of 15 years of service to the Society, Branch, or District Association.

8416 ■ Martin Robinson Award
To recognize the work done by a member of the Society or an affiliated society (branch, district association, or other affiliated society) over many years in the field of vegetable cultivation. Awarded annually.

8417 ■ Silver Medal
To recognize a member who has devoted a minimum of 12 years of service to the Society, Branch, or District Association.

8418 ■ Networking Culture Ltd.
Derby House
3 Market Pl.
Brackley NN13 7AB, United Kingdom
Ph: 44 704 404 7497
E-mail: admin@citywomen.co.uk
URL: http://www.citywomen.co.uk

8419 ■ Women in the City Achievement Awards
To recognize professional women who go above and beyond their professional and/or technical competencies by demonstrating ability to lead, develop people, build and nurture networks, and promote women's progress within their sector and the wider business world. Awards are presented in seven categories: accountancy services, alternative investment, financial services, insurance services, legal services, management consultancy, and property and facilities management. In addition, one woman is named the Woman of Achievement. Awarded annually. Established in 2007.

8420 ■ *New Statesman*
Jason Cowley, Ed.
John Carpenter House, 7th Fl.
7 Carmelite St.
Blackfriars EC4Y 0BS, United Kingdom
Ph: 44 20 7936 6400
Fax: 44 20 7936 6501
E-mail: info@newstatesman.co.uk
URL: http://www.newstatesman.co.uk

8421 ■ Edge Upstarts Awards
Recognizes social entrepreneurs who launch ideas or projects to challenge social exclusion in their communities. Awards are presented in five categories annually. Established in 2001. Sponsored by the Edge Foundation. Formerly: Upstarts Awards.

8422 ■ Nuclear Institute
Mr. Edmund Morgan-Warren, Exec. Sec.
Allan House
1 Penerley Rd.

London SE6 2LQ, United Kingdom
Ph: 44 20 86958220
Fax: 44 20 86958229
E-mail: admin@nuclearinst.com
URL: http://www.nuclearinst.com/ibis/Nuclear%20Institute/Home

8423 ■ Conference Awards
A limited number of awards are considered on the merit of the application. Applicants must be no more than 35 years old. Additional consideration will be given to those who intend to present their paper at the event. There are usually a maximum of four awards available per each major conference.

8424 ■ International Conference Award
Enables a young person to attend and thereby make a contribution and benefit from an international conference on a topic related to the science, engineering, safety, or economics of nuclear energy. Applicants must be no more than 30 years old and a member of the Society. Conference fees and living expenses are awarded annually. Established in 1998.

8425 ■ Oil and Colour Chemists' Association
Chris Pacey-Day, Gen. Sec.
3 Eden Ct., 1st Fl.
Eden Way
Leighton Buzzard LU7 4FY, United Kingdom
Ph: 44 1525 372530
Fax: 44 1525 372600
E-mail: membership@occa.org.uk
URL: http://www.occa.org.uk/home.lasso

8426 ■ Ellinger-Gardonyi Medal
To recognize the best paper presented at the Association's conferences and symposia. Both members and non-members are eligible. The silver medal is awarded annually. Established in 1989 in memory of Dr. Marianne Ellinger.

8427 ■ Jordan Award
To recognize the best paper published or submitted for publication in the Association's journal *Surface Coatings International*. Members under the age of 35 are eligible. A monetary award of £200 and a silver medal are awarded annually. Established in 1970.

8428 ■ Stern Award
To recognize the best paper, monograph, review, or special publication published by the Association during the year. Authors of any age are eligible, and need not be members of the Association. Awarded annually. Established in 1995 in memory of Dr. H.J. Stern, the Association's longest serving member and long-time member of the Publications Committee.

8429 ■ Oil Firing Technical Association for the Petroleum Industry
Foxwood House
Dobbs Ln.
Kesgrave
Ipswich IP5 2QQ, United Kingdom
Ph: 44 845 6585080
Fax: 44 845 6585181
E-mail: enquiries@oftec.org
URL: http://www.oftec.co.uk

8430 ■ Awards for Excellence
To recognize oil heating technicians, companies, distributors, and training centers for skill, hard work, and dedication to the oil industry. Gold, silver, and bronze awards are awarded in the following categories: Service and Commissioning Technician of the Year, Oil Distributor of the Year, Oil Boiler Installer of the Year, Oil Tank Installer of the Year, Trainee of the Year, Marketing Campaign of the Year, Training Centre of the Year, Oil Cooker/Stove Installer of the Year, and Green Initiative of the Year. Awarded annually.

8431 ■ Operational Research Society of the United Kingdom
Gavin Blackett, Sec./Gen. Mgr.
Seymour House

12 Edward St.
Birmingham B1 2RX, United Kingdom
Ph: 44 121 2339300
Fax: 44 121 2330321
E-mail: email@theorsociety.com
URL: http://www.theorsociety.com

8432 ■ Beale Medal
Recognizes sustained contributions to practice or theory of operational research. Awarded annually.

8433 ■ Goodeve Medal
Recognizes the most outstanding contribution to the philosophy, theory, or practice of operational research that was published in the *Journal of the OR Society*, the *European Journal of Information Systems*, or *OR Insight*. Awarded annually.

8434 ■ President's Medal
Annual award for the best account of OR practice given at the Society's annual conference.

8435 ■ Oppenheim-John Downes Memorial Trust
50 Broadway
London SW1H 0BL, United Kingdom
Ph: 44 20 7727 7000
Fax: 44 20 7222 3480
E-mail: emmatucker@bdb-law.co.uk
URL: http://www.oppenheimdownestrust.org

8436 ■ Oppenheim-John Downes Memorial Trust Awards
To enable deserving artists of any kind to pursue their vocation. Artists unable to pursue their vocation by reason of their poverty are eligible to apply. The following qualifications are mandatory: Individuals must be over 30 years of age and natural born British subjects born within Great Britain, Northern Ireland, The Channel Islands, or The Isle of Man; their parents must be British subjects born within the British Isles and neither parent may be of colonial or overseas origin after 1900 (Section 34 of the Race Relations Acts applies). Monetary awards of £1,000 are presented annually in December. Established in 1969 by Mrs. G.E. Downes in honor of her father, E. Phillips Oppenheim and his grandson, John Downes.

8437 ■ Ornithological Society of the Middle East, the Caucasus and Central Asia
Mr. Ian Harrison, Sec.
Bedfordshire
Sandy SG19 2DL, United Kingdom
E-mail: secretary@osme.org
URL: http://www.osme.org

8438 ■ Conservation Research Grants
For research projects involving nationals from the Middle East. Grants up to £500 are awarded three times per year.

8439 ■ Oxford Preservation Trust
10 Turn Again Ln.
St. Ebbes
Oxford OX1 1QL, United Kingdom
Ph: 44 1865 242918
Fax: 44 1865 251022
E-mail: info@oxfordpreservation.org.uk
URL: http://www.oxfordpreservation.org.uk

8440 ■ Oxford Preservation Trust Awards
To recognize projects that make a significant contribution to the conservation and improvement of the built or natural environment of Oxford and its green setting. To be eligible, projects must be within the public domain and must have been completed within three years of entry. Nominations are welcome from owners, architects, and public and voluntary organizations. Entries are judged in five categories: landscape and environmental enhancement; building conservation; new buildings; small projects; and

Awards are arranged in alphabetical order below their administering organizations

community projects. Plaques and certificates are awarded annually. Established in 1977. Formerly: (2010) Environmental Awards.

8441 ■ Packt Publishing Ltd.
32 Lincoln Rd.
Birmingham B27 6PA, United Kingdom
Ph: 44 121 683 1170
Fax: 44 121 535 7039
E-mail: contact@packtpub.com
URL: http://www.packtpub.com

8442 ■ Open Source Awards
To encourage, support, recognize, and reward a wide range of open source projects, including content management systems (CMS). Awards are presented in the following categories: Open Source CMS, Hall of Fame CMS, Most Promising Open Source Project, Open Source E-Commerce Applications, Open Source JavaScript Libraries, and Open Source Graphics Software. Monetary prizes of $2,500, $1,000, and $500 are awarded in each category. Awarded annually. Established in 2006.

8443 ■ Palaeontological Association
Dr. Tim J. Palmer, Exec. Off.
University of Wales-Aberstywyth
Institute of Geography and Earth Sciences
Ceredigion
Aberystwyth SY23 3DB, United Kingdom
E-mail: palass@palass.org
URL: http://www.palass.org

8444 ■ Mary Anning Award
For a non-professional who has made a remarkable contribution to palaeontology. A scroll and monetary prize are awarded annually.

8445 ■ Hodson Award
To recognize a palaeontologist who is under the age of 35 and who has made a notable early contribution to the science. A monetary prize of £1,000 is awarded annually. Established in 2001.

8446 ■ Lapworth Medal
To recognize a palaeontologist who has made a significant contribution to the science by means of a substantial body of research. Awarded annually. Established in 2000.

8447 ■ President's Medal
A mid-career award awarded to a palaeontologist in recognition of outstanding contributions in his/her earlier career, coupled with an expectation that he or she is not too old to contribute significantly to the subject in further years. Awarded annually. Established in 2008.

8448 ■ Paper Industry Technical Association
Barry Read, Contact
5 Frecheville Ct.
Bury BL9 0UF, United Kingdom
Ph: 44 161 7645858
Fax: 44 161 7645353
E-mail: info@pita.co.uk
URL: http://www.pita.co.uk

8449 ■ Julius Grant Essay Prize
To recognize an exceptional essay on paper technology. A monetary prize of £1,000 is awarded when merited.

8450 ■ Parker Harris Partnership
15 Church St.
Esher KT10 8QS, United Kingdom
Ph: 44 1372 462190
Fax: 44 1372 460032
E-mail: info@parkerharris.co.uk
URL: http://www.parkerharris.co.uk

8451 ■ Daiwa Foundation Art Prize
To offer a solo exhibition in Japan to a British artist. Open to artists working in any medium, including painting, photography, print, drawing, sculpture, ceramics, installation, and moving image. The winning artist is offered the opportunity to stage a solo show at Scai the Bathhouse in Tokyo, Japan. Awarded annually. Established in 2008.

8452 ■ EAC Over 60s Art Award
To recognize and encourage the artistic talents of older people. Open to all artists over 60 years of age. Awarded annually.

8453 ■ International Print Biennale
To recognize the best in new British and international printmaking. Open to British and International artists. Works in any medium are eligible. Formerly: (2011) Northern Print Biennale.

8454 ■ Jerwood Drawing Prize
To recognize excellence in drawing by established and emerging artists. Open to all artists who live in the U.K. Awarded annually.

8455 ■ Jerwood Sculpture Prize
To provide support and encouragement to emerging talent within the medium of outdoor sculpture to artists who are within 15 years of graduation from a recognized School of Art in the United Kingdom. A commissioning prize of £25,000 is awarded annually; in addition, the commissioned work joins the Jerwood Foundation's Sculpture collection at Ragley. Established in 2001.

8456 ■ Lynn Painter-Stainers Prize
To encourage representational painting and promote draughtsmanship. Open to all U.K. artists. Monetary prizes and medals are awarded annually. Established in 2005.

8457 ■ Sunday Times Watercolour Competition
To encourage the use of watercolor and water-based media painting among both amateur and professional artists in the United Kingdom. The following prizes are awarded: first place (£10,000); second place (£6,000); Vintage Classics Prize for Cover Art (£500); and the Smith & Williamson Cityscape Prize (£1,500). Held annually. Formerly: Singer Friedlander/Sunday Times Watercolour Competition.

8458 ■ Pathological Society of Great Britain and Ireland
Prof. Andrew H. Wyllie, Pres.
2 Carlton House Terr.
London SW1Y 5AF, United Kingdom
Ph: 44 20 79761260
Fax: 44 20 79302981
E-mail: admin@pathsoc.org
URL: http://www.pathsoc.org

8459 ■ Doniach Lectureship and Award
For a senior member of the society with substantial contribution to cellular pathology. Awarded annually. Established in 2003 in honor of Professor Israel Doniach.

8460 ■ Goudie Lectureship and Medal
For an active scientist with outstanding contributions to pathological science. Candidates shall normally be aged 40 years or more. Awarded annually.

8461 ■ Pensions Management Institute
Vince Linnane BA, Chief Exec.
4/10 Artillery Ln.
London E1 7LS, United Kingdom
Ph: 44 20 72471452
Fax: 44 20 73750603
E-mail: membership@pensions-pmi.org.uk
URL: http://www.pensions-pmi.org.uk

8462 ■ Covenant Assessment Provider of the Year
To honor achievements in innovation, client service, and commitment to improving pension provision in the United Kingdom. Awarded annually. Administered by the Institute's Accounting Specialist Industry Group.

8463 ■ Diploma in International Employee Benefits
Annual award of recognition. Individuals who have passed 2 exams are eligible.

8464 ■ Pension Scheme Accountant of the Year
To honor achievements in innovation, client service, and commitment to improving pension provision in the United Kingdom. Awarded annually. Administered by the Institute's Accounting Specialist Industry Group.

8465 ■ Pensions Management Institute Associateship
Annual award of recognition. Individuals who have passed 9 exams and have relevant experience are eligible.

8466 ■ Performing Right Society
Ellis Rich, Chm.
Copyright House
29-33 Berners St.
London W1T 3AB, United Kingdom
Ph: 44 20 75805544
Ph: 44 845 3039300
Fax: 44 20 73064455
E-mail: customerservice@prsformusic.com
URL: http://www.prsformusic.com

8467 ■ Leslie Boosey Award
To recognize an individual - not primarily a composer, conductor or soloist - who has made an outstanding contribution to the furtherance of contemporary music and, in particular, British music. A bronze trophy specially commissioned from the distinguished sculptress Dame Elisabeth Frink is held for two years by the recipient, who also receives a medallion to keep. Awarded biennially in odd-numbered years. Established in 1980 to honor Leslie Boosey, President of Honour who died in 1979 at the age of 92.

8468 ■ *Personnel Today*
Quadrant House, 3rd Fl.
The Quadrant
Sutton
Surrey SM2 5AS, United Kingdom
Ph: 44 20 8652 8026
Fax: 44 20 8652 8839
E-mail: alma.watson@rbi.co.uk
URL: http://www.personneltoday.com

8469 ■ *Personnel Today* Awards
To recognize and reward human resources teams that are making an impact with their people policies while delivering bottom-line benefits. Awarded annually in 13 categories.

8470 ■ Pharmaceutical and Healthcare Sciences Society
Mr. James Drinkwater, Chm.
6a Kingsdown Orchard
Wiltshire
Swindon SN2 7RR, United Kingdom
Ph: 44 1793 824254
Ph: 44 1264 835818
Fax: 44 1793 832551
E-mail: info@phss.co.uk
URL: http://www.phss.co.uk

8471 ■ George Sykes Memorial Award
To encourage the furtherance of knowledge in the field of parenteral science. Awarded annually.

8472 ■ Photo Imaging Council
Pam Hyde, Sec.
Airport House
Purley Way
Surrey
Croydon CR0 0XZ, United Kingdom
Ph: 44 208 2534507
Fax: 44 208 2534510
E-mail: pic@admin.co.uk
URL: http://www.pic.uk.net

Awards are arranged in alphabetical order below their administering organizations

8473 ■ PIC Award
To recognize student photographers in the United Kingdom. Awarded annually to one or more recipients. Established in 1992.
*

8474 ■ Phytochemical Society of Europe
Dr. Angela Stafford, Gen. Sec.
University of London
School of Pharmacy
Centre for Pharmacognosy and Phytotherapy
29-39 Brunswick Sq.
London WC1N 1AX, United Kingdom
Ph: 44 20 77535845
Ph: 44 14 33620281
Fax: 44 20 77535909
E-mail: amstafford@hotmail.co.uk
URL: http://www.phytochemicalsociety.org

8475 ■ Phytochemical Society of Europe Medal
To recognize individuals who have made an outstanding contribution to the Society or to the furtherance of plant science in general. The medal, which is struck in silver, shows an oak tree, representing plant science superimposed on a map of Europe. Awarded periodically. Established in 1986.

8476 ■ Plain English Campaign
Tony Maher, Gen. Mgr.
New Mills
PO Box 3
High Peak SK22 4QP, United Kingdom
Ph: 44 1663 744409
Fax: 44 1663 747038
E-mail: info@plainenglish.co.uk
URL: http://www.plainenglish.co.uk

8477 ■ Foot in Mouth Award
To recognize particularly baffling quotes by public figures. Awarded annually. Established in 1993.

8478 ■ Golden Bull Award
To recognize the best examples of gobbledygook, or tripe, during the preceding year. Awarded annually. Established in 1991.

8479 ■ Inside Write Awards
To recognize internal government documents for their clear use of English. Awarded annually to one or more recipients. Established in 1980.

8480 ■ Media Awards
To recognize media (television, radio, newspapers) that exhibited the best use of Plain English. Nominations are made on a regional and national level. Awarded annually. Established in 1991.

8481 ■ Osborne Memorial Award
For an individual or organization that made a major contribution to the Plain English cause. Awarded annually. Established in 2005 in memory of Geoffrey Osborne, a supporter of the Plain English campaign.

8482 ■ Plain English Awards
To promote the use of plain English and clear layout in forms, leaflets, and consumer agreements, and to recognize the best in official writing. Categories include: written documents, internal documents, and online documents. Trophies are presented to one or more recipients in each category annually. Established in 1980.

8483 ■ Web Award
To recognize the clearest website of the year. Awarded annually. Established in 2000.

8484 ■ Play Therapy International
Prof. Monika Jephcott, Pres.
The Coach House
Belmont Rd.
East Sussex
Uckfield TN22 1BP, United Kingdom
Ph: 44 1825 761143
Fax: 44 1825 769913

E-mail: ptukorg@aol.com
URL: http://www.playtherapy.org

8485 ■ Play Therapy International Award
To recognize an individual for an outstanding effort in advancing play therapy as a profession. A plaque is awarded annually.

8486 ■ Playwrights' Studio, Scotland
350 Sauchiehall St.
Glasgow G2 3JD, United Kingdom
Ph: 44 141 332 4403
Fax: 44 141 332 3208
E-mail: info@playwrightsstudio.co.uk
URL: http://www.playwrightsstudio.co.uk

8487 ■ Meyer-Whitworth Award
To encourage the careers of playwrights from the United Kingdom who are not yet established. Plays must be in English and have been produced professionally in the United Kingdom for the first time between August 1 and July 31 of the preceding year. Directors of professional theater companies may nominate plays. A monetary prize of £10,000 is awarded annually.

8488 ■ Poetry Society
Laura Bamford, Acting Chair
22 Betterton St.
London WC2H 9BX, United Kingdom
Ph: 44 20 74209880
Fax: 44 20 72404818
E-mail: info@poetrysociety.org.uk
URL: http://www.poetrysociety.org.uk

8489 ■ National Poetry Competition
For recognition of an outstanding unpublished poem. Individuals over 17 years of age who live anywhere are eligible. Entries must be submitted by October 31. Monetary prizes of £5,000 (for 1st place), £2,000 (2nd), £1,000 (3rd), and seven special commendations of £100 each are awarded annually. Established in 1978.

8490 ■ Corneliu M. Popescu Prize for European Poetry Translation
For recognition of a book of poems in translation of poetry from any European language into English. Eligible works are collections of poetry published within the previous 24 months that feature poetry translated from a European language into English. A monetary prize of £1,500 is awarded biennially in odd-numbered years. Established in 1983 by Mihail Popescu of Romania in memory of his son, a young poet and translator who died in the 1977 Romanian earthquake at the age of 17.

8491 ■ Police Federation of England and Wales
Paul McKeever, Chm.
Federation House
Highbury Dr.
Surrey
Leatherhead KT22 7UY, United Kingdom
Ph: 44 1372 352000
E-mail: gensec@polfed.org
URL: http://www.polfed.org

8492 ■ Police Bravery Award
Recognizes police officers who put themselves at risk of death or serious harm while performing their duties. Awarded annually to numerous recipients at the regional level, with one overall winner declared nationally.

8493 ■ Political Studies Association
Prof. Charlie Jeffery, Chm.
University of Newcastle
Dept. of Politics
Newcastle upon Tyne NE1 7RU, United Kingdom
Ph: 44 191 2228021
Fax: 44 191 2223499
E-mail: psa@ncl.ac.uk
URL: http://www.psa.ac.uk

8494 ■ W. J. M. MacKenzie Book Prize
For recognition of publications in political science. Nominations by publishers are accepted. A monetary prize of £100 and a plaque are awarded annually. Established in 1987 in honor of W.J.M. MacKenzie.

8495 ■ Politzer Society - International Society for Otological Surgery
Dr. O. Nuri Ozgirgin, Pres.
106 Harley St.
London W1G7JE, United Kingdom
Ph: 44 20 79350646
E-mail: eardoctor@afoc.org.uk
URL: http://www.politzersociety.org

8496 ■ Politzer Prize
To recognize the best clinical and science papers by scientists aged 40 years or younger. Two awards of 1,000 Euros are presented biennially.

8497 ■ Pony Club
Judy Edwards, Chief Exec.
Stoneleigh Park
Warwickshire
Kenilworth CV8 2RW, United Kingdom
Ph: 44 2476 698300
Ph: 44 2476 698304
Fax: 44 2476 696919
E-mail: enquiries@pcuk.org
URL: http://www.pcuk.org

8498 ■ Cubitt Award
To recognize individuals for long, devoted, and distinguished service in a voluntary capacity to the Club. Individuals who have served over 15 years, and preferably over 20 years, are eligible. A certificate and a badge are awarded annually at Council meetings. Established in 1988 to honor Colonel C. G. Cubitt, past chairman and president of the Club.

8499 ■ Prehistoric Society
Dr. Alison Sheridan, Pres.
University College London
Institute of Archaeology
31-34 Gordon Sq.
London WC1H 0PY, United Kingdom
E-mail: prehistoric@ucl.ac.uk
URL: http://www.prehistoricsociety.org
Formerly: (1935) Prehistoric Society of East Anglia.

8500 ■ R. M. Baguley Award
For recognition of an archaeological publication. Papers published in the proceedings of the Society are considered. A trophy, donated by R.M. Baguley, is awarded annually. Established in 1979.

8501 ■ Bob Smith Research Award
To fund research in the field of prehistory. Members must submit applications to the Society's research fund. A monetary award of £100 to £ 1,000 is presented annually in February. Established in 1987 by Dr. G.J. Wainwright in memory of Dr. Bob Smith.

8502 ■ Premenstrual Society
Dr. M.G. Brush, Chm.
PO Box 429
Addlestone KT15 1DZ, United Kingdom
Ph: 44 1932 872560
URL: http://www.patient.co.uk/showdoc/26739112

8503 ■ PMS Grants
For professionals in the field.

8504 ■ Producers and Composers of Applied Music
Jonathan Goldstein, Chm.
Birchwood Hall
Storridge
Worcestershire
Malvern WR13 5EZ, United Kingdom
Ph: 44 20 85638589

Awards are arranged in alphabetical order below their administering organizations

Ph: 44 20 89600111
E-mail: info@pcam.co.uk
URL: http://www.pcam.co.uk

8505 ■ PCAM Music Award
For best original music in a commercial.

8506 ■ Professional Golfers' Association - England
Sandy Jones, Chief Exec.
Centenary House
The De Vere Belfry
West Midlands
Sutton Coldfield B76 9PT, United Kingdom
Ph: 44 1675 470333
Fax: 44 1675 477888
E-mail: simmon.higginbottom@pga.org.uk
URL: http://www.pga.info

8507 ■ Whitcombe Cox Trophy
To recognize the PGA Trainee of the Year who is considered by the examiners to be the best overall candidate in the final examinations. A trophy and a monetary award of £3,500 are awarded annually. The award was introduced in 1974 and the trophy was commissioned in 1991.

8508 ■ PGA Assistants' Championship
To recognize the winning PGA of America Assistant Professional from all 41 PGA of America sections, plus Australia, Canada, Great Britain, and New Zealand. The winner receives £5,000, plus an invitation to participate in the Australian PGA Futures Championship and the BMW PGA Championship at Wentworth. Held annually. Established in 1930.

8509 ■ PGA Professional Championship
To recognize the best players at the annual PGA Club Professional Championship. Features a total purse of more than £78,000 that is awarded in Section, Regional, and National championships. Held annually. Established in 1973.

8510 ■ PGA Seniors Championship
To honor the best legendary golfer over the age of 50. Over £300,000 is prize money is presented. Held annually. Established in 1957.

8511 ■ Ryle Memorial Medal
Awarded to recognize the winner of the British Open Golf Championship. Candidates must be members of the PGA. Awarded annually. Established in 1901.

8512 ■ Braid Taylor Memorial Medal
To recognize the member of the PGA who finishes highest in the British Open Golf Championship. Candidates must have been born in the United Kingdom or Republic of Ireland, or at least one of their parents must have been. Awarded annually. Established in 1966.

8513 ■ Harry Vardon Trophy
To recognize the winner of the European Tour Order of Merit. Awarded annually. Established in 1939 to honor Harry Vardon, an internationally famous British golfer.

8514 ■ Professional Publishers Association
Mr. Barry McIlheney, CEO
Queens House
28 Kingsway
London WC2B 6JR, United Kingdom
Ph: 44 20 74044166
Fax: 44 20 74044167
E-mail: barry.mcilheney@ppa.co.uk
URL: http://www.ppa.co.uk
Formerly: (2010) Periodical Publishers Association.

8515 ■ Marcus Morris Award
For an individual who has made a significant

and longstanding contribution to the magazine publishing business. A trophy, citation, and honorarium of £1,000 are awarded annually. Established in 1990.

8516 ■ Public Relations Consultants Association
David Gallagher, Chm.
Willow House
17-23 Willow Pl., 1st Fl.
London SW1P 1JH, United Kingdom
Ph: 44 20 72336026
Fax: 44 20 78284797
E-mail: communications@prca.org.uk
URL: http://www.prca.org.uk

8517 ■ PRCA Awards
To celebrate the best in public relation consultancy in the United Kingdom. Open to all PR consultancies, all in-house communications or PR teams, and all freelance PR professionals working for in-house or consultancy clients. Presented in 26 categories. Certificates are awarded annually. Established in 1987. Formerly: Awards for Outstanding Consultancy Practice.

8518 ■ Publicity Club of London
Sue Ash, Chm.
Sheraton House
15-19 Great Chapel St.
London W1F 8FN, United Kingdom
Ph: 44 20 77345666
Fax: 44 20 77349666
E-mail: sue@ashcommunications.com
URL: http://www.thepcl.co.uk

8519 ■ FE Cook Cup and Keliher
For leading students in the annual communication advertising and marketing education foundation examinations.

8520 ■ Publishers Publicity Circle
Jessica Axe, Chair
65 Airedale Ave.
London W4 2NN, United Kingdom
Ph: 44 20 89941881
Ph: 44 20 74057422
E-mail: ppc-@lineone.net
URL: http://www.publisherspublicitycircle.co.uk

8521 ■ PPC Annual Awards
To recognize the best publicity campaigns from book publishing houses and freelance public relations agencies. Awards are presented in nine categories: Hardback Non-Fiction, Hardback Non-Fiction (Celebrity), Hardback Fiction, Paperback (2nd edition either fiction or non-fiction), Paperback Original Fiction, Paperback Original Non-Fiction, Children's Book, Generic Campaign, and Newcomer (3 years publicity experience or less). Awarded annually.

8522 ■ PPC Quarterly Awards
To recognize the best publicity campaigns from book publishing houses and freelance public relations agencies. Awards are presented in nine categories: Hardback Non-Fiction, Hardback Non-Fiction (Celebrity), Hardback Fiction, Paperback (2nd edition either fiction or non-fiction), Paperback Original Fiction, Paperback Original Non-Fiction, Children's Book, Generic Campaign, and Newcomer (3 years publicity experience or less). Awarded four times per year.

8523 ■ Quaternary Research Association
Prof. Dan Charman, Pres.
University of Exeter
Department of Geography
Exeter EX4 4RJ, United Kingdom
E-mail: d.j.charman@exeter.ac.uk
URL: http://www.qra.org.uk

8524 ■ Bill Bishop Award
For full or part-time M.Phil/PhD students. A grant of £800 is awarded annually.

8525 ■ New Research Workers' Awards
For new or young researchers registered for a postgraduate degree. Grants are typically for the amount of up to £400.

8526 ■ Postgraduate QRA Meetings Award
To enable postgraduate members to attend QRA meetings. A total of 15 travel stipends are awarded annually.

8527 ■ Quaternary Conference Fund Awards
To assist members of the QRA, particularly postgraduate students, with limited alternative sources of funding in attending QRA conferences and field meetings.

8528 ■ Quaternary Research Fund Awards
To foster research by members of the QRA. Grants ranging from £50 to £600 are awarded annually.

8529 ■ Queen's English Society
Dr. Bernard Lamb, Pres.
1 Oban Gardens
Woodley
Reading RG5 3RG, United Kingdom
E-mail: enquiries@queens-english-society.com
URL: http://www.queens-english-society.com

8530 ■ Arthur and Marjorie Goodchild Prize for Excellent English
For excellence in writing in the English language. A monetary award is given annually.

8531 ■ Racegoers Club
John Phillips, Club Exec.
Winkfield Rd.
Ascot SL5 7HX, United Kingdom
Ph: 44 1344 625912
E-mail: racegoersclub@rcarcl.co.uk
URL: http://www.racegoersclub.co.uk/Pages/Home.aspx

8532 ■ Racehorse of the Year Award
For recognition of the outstanding racehorse of the year. The award originated as a publicity idea designed to stimulate public interest in horseracing. Any horse that has raced on a British racecourse during the year is eligible. A panel of journalists selects the winner. A twelve-inch bronze statuette sculpted by Jean Walwyn and entitled "The Winner" is awarded annually. Established in 1965 by the Racecourse Association which invited The Racegoers Club to take over the award in 1978.

8533 ■ Ramsay Memorial Fellowships Trust
Gary Hawes, Exec. Sec.
University College London
Academic Services Department
2 Taviton St.
London WC1E 6BT, United Kingdom
Ph: 44 20 7679 8592
Fax: 44 20 7679 8595
E-mail: g.hawes@ucl.ac.uk
URL: http://www.ucl.ac.uk/ramsay-trust

8534 ■ Ramsay Memorial Fellowships for Postdoctoral Chemical Research
To enable the holder to devote himself or herself full-time to postdoctoral research in chemistry. Individuals preferably born within the British Commonwealth who graduated with honors in chemistry from a commonwealth university may apply by November 15. One or more Fellowships, tenable for two years in the United Kingdom, are awarded annually. Established in 1920 in memory of Sir William Ramsay, KCB FRS (1852-1916).

8535 ■ Regional Studies Association
Sally Hardy, Chief Exec.
PO Box 2058
Seaford BN25 4QU, United Kingdom

Awards are arranged in alphabetical order below their administering organizations

Ph: 44 1323 899698
Fax: 44 1323 899798
E-mail: info@rsa-ls.ac.uk
URL: http://www.regional-studies-assoc.ac.uk

8536 ■ Bill Ogden Memorial Prize
To recognize students for the best research paper. Publication and a monetary prize are awarded annually.

8537 ■ Remote Sensing and Photogrammetry Society
Dr. Samantha Lavender, Chair
University of Nottingham
School of Geography
University Park
Nottingham NG7 2RD, United Kingdom
Ph: 44 115 9515435
Fax: 44 115 9515249
E-mail: rspsoc@rspsoc.org
URL: http://www.rspsoc.org

8538 ■ Len Curtis Award
For recognition of distinguished technical articles published in the *International Journal of Remote Sensing* during the previous year. Certificate and books valued at £200 are awarded annually. Formerly: (1991) Eurosense Award.

8539 ■ Poster Paper Prize
For recognition of the best poster papers presented at the Society's annual conference. The first place winner receives the Main Award (£100) and the runner-up receives the Merit Award (£25). Awarded annually.

8540 ■ Remote Sensing and Photogrammetry Society Award
This, the highest award of the Society, is given for recognition of an outstanding contribution in the field of remote sensing. A gold medal and honorary lifetime membership in the Society are awarded periodically. Formerly: (2004) Remote Sensing Society Medal.

8541 ■ Student Awards
For recognition of the best Doctoral and Masters theses on the subject of remote sensing and/or photogrammetry. Certificates and monetary awards of £500 (Doctoral) and £250 (Masters) are awarded annually.

8542 ■ Taylor and Francis Best Letter Award
For recognition of the best letter published in the *International Journal of Remote Sensing* during the previous year. A certificate and prizes valued at £100 are awarded annually.

8543 ■ E. H. Thompson Award
For recognition of the best paper published in the *Photogrammetric Record* during the previous two years. A certificate and monetary award of £100 is awarded when merited. Formerly: (2004) Remote Sensing Society President's Prize.

8544 ■ Renal Association
Dr. Charlie Tompson, Pres.
Durford Mill
Hampshire
Petersfield GU31 5AZ, United Kingdom
Ph: 44 870 4584155
Fax: 44 870 4429940
E-mail: renal@mci-group.com
URL: http://www.renal.org/pages

8545 ■ Raine Award
To recognize a junior investigator who has made a significant contribution to renal research. Candidates are typically aged 35 years or younger. A monetary prize of £300 is awarded annually. Established in 1996.

8546 ■ Research and Development Society
Mr. Richard Sykes, Pres.
18 Grantchester Rd.
Cambridge CB3 9ED, United Kingdom

Ph: 44 1223 356728
Fax: 44 1223 560032
E-mail: rdsociety@royalsociety.org
URL: http://www.rdsoc.org

8547 ■ Duncan Davies Medal
For an individual who has made an outstanding contribution toward making the United Kingdom the best-performing research and development environment in the world. Awarded annually.

8548 ■ Romantic Novelists' Association
Katie Fforde, Pres.
North End Cottage
Kingston Winslow
Swindon SN6 8NG, United Kingdom
Ph: 44 1793 710252
E-mail: ncornick@madasafish.com
URL: http://www.rna-uk.org

8549 ■ Joan Hessayon New Writers' Award
To recognize new romance writers for an unpublished full-length novel. Probationary members of the RNA are eligible. A silver salver to be held for one year and a monetary award are presented annually in April. Established in 1962. Formerly: (1995) Nevva Muskett Award.

8550 ■ Love Story of the Year
To honor outstanding category romance stories, which are shorter romances with a strong emphasis on the central relationship. A cash prize and Rose Bowl are awarded annually. Established in 2003.

8551 ■ Romantic Novel of the Year (RoNA) Awards
To recognize the best romantic novels published in English in the United Kingdom during the year. Presented in five categories: Contemporary, Epic, Historical, Comedy, and Young Adult. The winner of each category is eligible to receive the overall Romantic Novel of the Year Award. Monetary prizes and trophies are presented annually. Established in 1960. Formerly: Foster-Grant Reading Glasses Romantic Novel of the Year; (1988) Boots Romantic Novel of the Year; (1998) Romantic Novel of the Year.

8552 ■ ROSL Arts
Anna Maciuk, Admin. Asst.
Over-Seas House
Park Pl.
St. James's St.
London SW1A 1LR, United Kingdom
Ph: 44 20 7408 0214
Fax: 44 20 7499 6738
E-mail: culture@rosl.org.uk
URL: http://www.roslarts.co.uk

8553 ■ Award for Keyboard
To recognize an outstanding keyboardist at the Annual Music Competition. A monetary prize of £5,000 is awarded annually. Formerly: Coutts and Co. Award for Keyboard.

8554 ■ Award for Strings
To recognize an outstanding string player at the Annual Music Competition. A monetary prize of £5,000 is awarded annually.

8555 ■ Irene Brown Memorial Prize
To recognize a New Zealand musician at the Annual Music Competition. A monetary prize of £1,000 is awarded annually. Formerly: Irene Brown Memorial Prize.

8556 ■ Phillip Cranshaw Memorial Prize
To recognize an outstanding musician from outside the United Kingdom at the Annual Music Competition. A monetary prize of £1,000 is awarded annually.

8557 ■ Pamela Faulkner Award for Singers
To recognize an outstanding singer at the Annual Music Competition. A monetary prize of £5,000 is awarded annually.

8558 ■ Gold Medal and First Prize
To recognize the most extraordinary musician at the Annual Music Competition. A monetary prize of £10,000 is awarded annually.

8559 ■ Len Lickorish Memorial Prize
To recognize a string player of promise at the Annual Music Competition. A monetary prize of £1,000 is awarded annually.

8560 ■ McCallum Prize
To recognize a pianist of promise at the Annual Music Competition. A monetary prize of £1,000 is awarded annually.

8561 ■ Mitchell Award
To recognize a New Zealand musician at the Annual Music Competition. A monetary prize of £1,000 is awarded annually.

8562 ■ New Zealand Society Prize
To recognize a New Zealand musician at the Annual Music Competition. A monetary prize of £1,000 is awarded annually.

8563 ■ Audrey Strange Memorial Prize
To recognize a singer of promise at the Annual Music Competition. A monetary prize of £1,000 is awarded annually.

8564 ■ Sussex Prize
To recognize an outstanding woodwind player at the Annual Music Competition. A monetary prize of £1,000 is awarded annually.

8565 ■ Lorna Viol Memorial Prize
To recognize the most outstanding competitor from outside the United Kingdom at the Annual Music Competition. A monetary prize of £1,500 is awarded annually.

8566 ■ Rough and Smooth Collie Training Association
Mrs. Jean Tuck, Sec.
1 Leigh Ln.
Bramshall
Staffordshire
Uttoxeter ST14 5DN, United Kingdom
Ph: 44 1889 568090
Fax: 44 1889 568090
E-mail: jean@rscta.co.uk
URL: http://www.rscta.co.uk

8567 ■ Achievement Awards
Recognizes members achieving the highest number of club points with a rough or smooth collie in agility, breed league, obedience, and versatility. Awarded annually.

8568 ■ Royal Academy of Arts
Sir Nicholas Grimshaw, Pres.
Burlington House
Piccadilly
London W1J 0BD, United Kingdom
Ph: 44 20 73005737
Ph: 44 20 73008000
Fax: 44 20 73008032
E-mail: library@royalacademy.org.uk
URL: http://www.royalacademy.org.uk

8569 ■ Jack Goldhill Award for Sculpture
For recognition of outstanding sculpture in each year's Summer Exhibition (see separate entry). A monetary award of £10,000 is presented annually. Established by the Jack and Grete Goldhill Charitable Trust.

8570 ■ Summer Exhibition Awards
For recognition of different categories of work exhibited in the Royal Academy's annual Summer Exhibition: an open competition of works featuring painting, sculpture, architecture and engraving, print-making and draftsmanship. A total of £65,000 is awarded in prizes. Held annually. Established in 1769.

8571 ■ Charles Wollaston Award
For recognition of the most distinguished exhibit

Awards are arranged in alphabetical order below their administering organizations

in the Summer Exhibition (see separate entry). A monetary award of £25,000 is awarded annually. Established in 1977 by Charles Wollaston, Esquire.

8572 ■ Royal Academy of Dance
Luke Rittner, Chief Exec.
36 Battersea Sq.
London SW11 3RA, United Kingdom
Ph: 44 20 73268000
E-mail: info@rad.org.uk
URL: http://www.rad.org.uk

8573 ■ Associate of the Royal Academy of Dance
To recognize full members over the age of 18 years who have passed the Advanced Examination or the Advanced Teaching Examination. Awarded annually by the Executive Committee.

8574 ■ Fellow of the Royal Academy of Dance
To recognize members for outstanding service to the Academy over a long period of time. Awarded annually.

8575 ■ Honorary Fellow of the Royal Academy of Dance
To recognize non-Academy members for outstanding service over a long period of time. Awarded annually.

8576 ■ President's Award
To honor an individual from anywhere throughout the world who has given dedicated service to the Academy. Established in 1992.

8577 ■ Queen Elizabeth II Coronation Award
To recognize an individual who has made a significant contribution to the art of ballet. A plaque is awarded annually. Established in 1954 by Dame Adeline Genee, founding President of the Royal Academy of Dancing in honor of Her Majesty, Queen Elizabeth II, who succeeded her grandmother, Queen Mary, as Patron of the Academy.

8578 ■ Royal Academy of Engineering
Philip Greenish, Chief Exec.
3 Carlton House Terr.
London SW1Y 5DG, United Kingdom
Ph: 44 20 77660600
Fax: 44 20 79301549
E-mail: kim.turner@raeng.org.uk
URL: http://www.raeng.org.uk
Formerly: Fellowship of Engineering.

8579 ■ Innovation in Education Prize
To recognize the work of a visiting professor, particularly one who has made the most significant contribution to the field of engineering education. A trophy and monetary prize of £10,000 are awarded annually. In addition, prizes of £1,000 are awarded to runners up. Established in 2006.

8580 ■ International Medal
To recognize a resident outside the European Union for his or her outstanding and sustained personal achievement in the broad field of engineering, including commercial or academic leadership. Awarded periodically. Established in 2006.

8581 ■ MacRobert Award
For recognition of an outstanding contribution by way of innovation in engineering or the physical technologies, or in the application of the physical sciences which is or will be for the benefit of the community. A gold medal is awarded to the winner, and each nominee receives a bronze medal. In addition, a cash prize of £50,000 is split among the winning team members. Awarded annually. Established in 1968 by the MacRobert Trusts.

8582 ■ President's Medal
Recognizes contributions to the Academy's aims and work. Organizations and individuals not eligible for membership in the academy are eligible. Awarded not more than once a year. Established in 1987.

8583 ■ Prince Philip Medal
Recognizes contribution to engineering as a whole through practice, management, or education. Engineers of any nationality are eligible. A solid gold medal is awarded biennially in even-numbered years. Established in 1989.

8584 ■ Rooke Medal for the Public Promotion of Engineering
To recognize an individual, small team, or organization that has contributed to the Academy's aims and work through initiative in promoting engineering to the public. An antiqued silver medal is awarded annually. Established in 2002.

8585 ■ Silver Medal
To recognize an individual for outstanding contributions to British engineering. Candidates must have fewer than 22 years of full-time employment as an engineer in the United Kingdom. Awarded annually to up to four recipients. Established in 1994.

8586 ■ Sustained Achievement Award
To honor an engineer, normally a resident of the United Kingdom, whose achievements have had a profound impact upon his or her engineering disciplines. Applies particularly to those engineers who have not been recognized earlier in their careers for such reasons as latency in the impact of their work or late disclosure due to national or commercial secrecy. A medal is awarded annually. Established in 2005.

8587 ■ Sir Frank Whittle Medal
To recognize an engineer, normally resident in the United Kingdom, for outstanding and sustained achievement that has contributed to the well-being of the nation. Awarded annually. Established in 1999.

8588 ■ Royal Aero Club
David Phipps, Gen. Sec.
31, St. Andrew's Rd.
Leicester LE2 8RE, United Kingdom
Ph: 44 116 2440182
Fax: 44 116 2440645
E-mail: secretary@royalaeroclub.org
URL: http://www.royalaeroclub.org

8589 ■ Breguet Trophy
For achievement in the field of rotary winged flight, including jet-lift and VTOL. Awarded jointly with Aero Club de France.

8590 ■ Britannia Trophy
Recognizes the British aviator who accomplishes the most meritorious performance in aviation during the preceding year. Awarded annually.

8591 ■ Certificate of Appreciation
To recognize sponsorship and support of Club activities or member organizations through the provision of facilities. Established in 1997.

8592 ■ Certificate of Merit
To recognize service to the Club, sporting aviation, or aviation in general.

8593 ■ Companion of the RAeC
To recognize significant contributions to the Club. Established in 1996.

8594 ■ Cowburn and Kay - Old and Bold Trophy
To recognize an older person for their devotion to, contributions, and/or achievements in aviation. Eligible to people who are 65 years of age or older and who have ceased flying in the previous year. Established in 1997.

8595 ■ Gold, Silver, and Bronze Medals
For outstanding achievement in aviation during the preceding year, or over a number of years. Awarded annually.

8596 ■ Nexus Sport Aviation Journalist of the Year Trophy
To recognize a journalist, producer, or author for an outstanding media item on sporting and/or recreational aviation during the previous year. Awarded annually. Established in 1997.

8597 ■ Norton-Griffiths Challenge Trophy
To recognize aviators for adventurous endeavors that go well beyond traditional aviation sporting events. Established in 2008.

8598 ■ President's Rolex Trophy
To recognize a young person for outstanding achievement, performance, or work in any aspect of aerospace activity. Eligible to young people between 14 and 21 years of age. Awarded annually. Established in 1988.

8599 ■ Prince of Wales Cup
Recognizes a team or group for the most meritorious event, feat, or performance during the previous year. Awarded annually. Established in 1976.

8600 ■ Royal Aero Club Diploma
To recognize outstanding service to the Club, sporting aviation, or aviation in general. Established in 1984.

8601 ■ Ann Welch Memorial Award
To recognize major contributions to flying instruction to the benefit of the BGA, BMAA, or BHPA. Established in 2005.

8602 ■ Royal Aeronautical Society - United Kingdom
Graham Roe, Chief Exec.
4 Hamilton Pl.
London W1J 7BQ, United Kingdom
Ph: 44 20 76704300
E-mail: raes@aerosociety.com
URL: http://www.raes.org.uk

8603 ■ Aircraft Maintenance Engineers Turnbuckle Award
To recognize long and valued service in the field of aircraft maintenance. Awarded annually when merited. Established in 1998. Formerly: Silvered Turnbuckle Award.

8604 ■ John Britten Prize
To recognize the best paper on light aviation or lighter-than-air aviation published by the Society. Awarded annually.

8605 ■ Flight Simulation Silver Medal
To recognize an individual for significant long-term contributions, in an international context, in the field of flight simulation. A medal is awarded annually. Established in 1991.

8606 ■ Hafner VTOL Prize
To recognize the best paper published by the Society on VTOL Technology by an individual under 30 years old. Awarded annually.

8607 ■ Sir Robert Hardingham Presidential Sword
To recognize a member for outstanding services to the Society over a period of time. Awarded at the discretion of the president of the Society.

8608 ■ Heritage Awards
Recognizes significant contributions to aeronautics within the United Kingdom. Plaques are erected to commemorate people, places, and things that have had an exceptional positive impact. Established in 2008.

8609 ■ Hodgson Prize
For recognition of the best paper on general

subjects, such as policy, law, operations, management, education, and history, published by the Society. Awarded annually.

8610 ■ Honorary Companionship
For recognition of important service to the profession of aerospace by someone outside the industry. Awarded when merited to not more than three individuals. Established in 1950.

8611 ■ Honorary Fellowship
This, the greatest distinction of the Society, is given for long and distinguished contributions to aerospace. Awarded when merited. Established in 1920.

8612 ■ Herbert Le Sueur Young Persons Award
To assist a student or graduate member where studies or experience will be enhanced by attending the European Rotorcraft Forum or similar event. Awarded annually. Established in 1999.

8613 ■ Alan Marsh Medal
For recognition of outstanding helicopter pilotage achievement in the field of helicopter research. British pilots are eligible. A medal is awarded annually. Established by the Helicopter Association of Great Britain in 1955 to commemorate the work of Henry Alan Marsh, the outstanding test pilot who was killed in 1950 while flying the Cierva Air Horse, at that time the largest helicopter to be built in the United Kingdom.

8614 ■ Geoffrey Pardoe Space Award
To recognize a significant contribution to space. Awarded annually. Established in 1999.

8615 ■ President's Award
To recognize individuals who displayed outstanding skill and professionalism in aeronautics and aviation, especially in adverse circumstances. Awarded at the discretion of the Society's president.

8616 ■ R38 Memorial Prize
To recognize a paper or work on airships. Awarded annually.

8617 ■ Frank Radcliffe Travelling Fellowship in Reliability and Quality Assurance
To enable a lecturer to give a presentation at all universities and in the United Kingdom with aeronautical engineering courses. Awarded annually.

8618 ■ RAeS Bronze Medal
For recognition of a work leading to an advance in aerospace. A bronze medal is awarded annually to individuals and teams. Established in 1908.

8619 ■ RAeS Gold Medal
To recognize an individual for work of an outstanding nature in aerospace. A gold medal is awarded annually to individuals and teams. Established in 1909.

8620 ■ RAeS Silver Medal
To recognize work contributing to major advances in aerospace. A silver medal is awarded annually to individuals and teams. Established in 1909.

8621 ■ N.E. Rowe Award
To recognize the best lecture presented before any branch of the Society by young members. Awards are presented in two age-based groups: the under age 25 group and the 25 to 30 age group. Awarded annually.

8622 ■ Ackroyd Stuart Prize
For recognition of the best paper on propulsion published by the Society. Awarded annually.

8623 ■ George Taylor (of Australia) Prize
For recognition of the best paper on design,

construction, production, and fabrication (including structures and materials) published by the Society. Awarded annually.

8624 ■ Wakefield Gold Medal
For recognition of contributions towards safety in aerospace. A gold medal is awarded irregularly. Established in 1926 by Castrol Limited in memory of the company's founder, Viscount Wakefield of Hythe. Sponsored by Kidde-Grininer.

8625 ■ Young Persons' Achievement Award
To recognize an individual or team for exceptional achievement or contribution in aerospace. Awarded annually.

8626 ■ Royal Agricultural Society of England
Mike Tomlinson, Pres.
Stoneleigh Park
Coventry CV8 2LZ, United Kingdom
Ph: 44 24 76696969
Fax: 44 24 76696900
E-mail: info@rase.org.uk
URL: http://www.rase.org.uk

8627 ■ Bledisloe Gold Medal for Landowners
To recognize a landowner for distinguished achievement in the successful land management and development of an agricultural estate in England. A gold medal, certificate, and honorary membership are awarded annually. Established in 1957 by the First Viscount Bledisloe.

8628 ■ Sir Roland Burke Perpetual Challenge Machinery Trophy
To recognize a British manufacturer of agricultural implements or machines which has made an outstanding impact on farming generally or on a particular branch of agriculture or horticulture. A trophy is awarded annually at the Royal Show. Established in 1970. Formerly: (1981) Burke Perpetual Challenge Trophy.

8629 ■ "Eqvalan Duo" Equine Thesis of the Year Award
To recognize academic achievement in the equestrian field. A trophy, certificate, monetary prize of £500, and five-year membership are awarded annually. Sponsored by Merial.

8630 ■ Excellence in Practical Farming and Business Award
To reward farmers and farm managers setting a lead for others as practical farmers willing to impart their knowledge to others. Up to three awards may be made annually. A slate plaque and life membership in the society are awarded to the winners at the Scientific Awards Ceremony in London in February. Established in 1999.

8631 ■ Honorary Fellow
To recognize individuals for outstanding contributions to the agricultural industry. Awarded when merited.

8632 ■ Long Service Award
To recognize approved and continuous land-based services of more than 40 years. A medal and certificate are awarded annually to all qualified individuals.

8633 ■ National Agricultural Award
For recognition of outstanding contributions to the advancement of agriculture in the United Kingdom. A trophy, medal, and honorary membership are awarded annually at an award ceremony in London in October. Established in 1964. Sponsorship of the award and lecture was assumed by the society in 1999.

8634 ■ Research Medal
For recognition of outstanding research work carried out in the United Kingdom that has proved or is likely to be of benefit to agriculture. Workers actually engaged in active research are

eligible. A monetary award of 300 guineas and a medal are awarded annually at the Scientific Awards. Established in 1954; absorbed the Bledisloe Veterinary Award in 2003.

8635 ■ Talbot-Ponsonby Prize for Agricultural Valuation
Established in 1957, the award is given to the first placed candidate in the entrance examinations to the Central Association of Agricultural Valuers. A bronze medal is awarded, usually annually, at the Royal Show.

8636 ■ Technology Award
To recognize individuals who, working in a commercial environment, have applied scientific advance into technology through the development of a product or process, which are likely to lead to cost effective improvements for farmers in any aspect of practical agriculture. A monetary prize of 300 guineas and a medal are awarded annually. Established in 1985.

8637 ■ Royal and Ancient Golf Club of St. Andrews
Colin M. Brown, Contact
St. Andrews
Fife KY16 9JD, United Kingdom
Ph: 44 1334 460000
Fax: 44 1334 460001
URL: http://www.randa.org

8638 ■ Open Championship
To recognize the winner of the annual golf tournament. Amateur and professional golfers are eligible. The competition is held in three stages: Regional Qualifying Competitions, Final Qualifying Competitions, and Open Championship. A maximum of 156 competitors participate in the Open Championship. The winner is designated Champion Golfer of the Year, and receives the Championship Trophy, also known as the Claret Jug, to retain for one year along with the Championship Gold Medal. The first amateur in the Championship, unless he or she is the winner, receives a Silver Medal, provided that 72 holes have been completed. Other amateurs who complete 72 holes receive a Bronze Medal. Prize money is awarded only to professional golfers. The Champion Golfer of the Year receives £750,000 for first place. In addition, the Professional Golfers Association awards various trophies at the competition. Established in 1860 by the Prestwick Golf Club, Ayrshire, Scotland; the Championship has been organized by the Royal and Ancient Gold Club of St. Andrews since 1920.

8639 ■ Royal Anthropological Institute of Great Britain and Ireland
Dr. David Shankland, Dir.
50 Fitzroy St.
London W1T 5BT, United Kingdom
Ph: 44 20 73870455
Fax: 44 20 73888817
E-mail: admin@therai.org.uk
URL: http://www.therai.org.uk

8640 ■ Curl Essay Prize
For recognition of the best essay not exceeding 10,000 words relating to the results or analysis of anthropological work. A monetary prize of £1,100 is awarded annually. Established in 1951.

8641 ■ J. B. Donne Essay Prize on the Anthropology of Art
To recognize an essay on any aspect of the anthropology of art, including the visual and performing arts. The essay must be unpublished, 10,000 words or less, and available for publication by the institute. Essays must be submitted by October 31. A monetary prize of £700 is awarded biennially in odd-numbered years. Established in 1987.

8642 ■ Amaury Talbot Prize for African Anthropology
For recognition of the most valuable work of

anthropological research published during the preceding calendar year. Preference is given to first works relating to Nigeria, and then to any other part of West Africa or West Africa in general, although works relating to other regions of Africa may also be considered. A monetary prize of £500 is awarded annually. Established in 1961.

8643 ■ Wellcome Medal for Anthropology as Applied to Medical Problems
To encourage the development of medical anthropology through recognition of an outstanding published work. Nominations or applications are accepted. Candidates in the early part of their careers are considered more favorably. A bronze medal and £600 are awarded biennially in even-numbered years. Established in 1931 by Sir Henry Wellcome. Sponsored by the Wellcome Trust.

8644 ■ Royal Archaeological Institute
Ms. Sharon Gerber-Parfitt, Admin.
Burlington House
Piccadilly
London W1J 0BE, United Kingdom
E-mail: admin@royalarchinst.org
URL: http://www.royalarchinst.org

8645 ■ Tony Clark Memorial Fund
To support the scientific elements of archaeological projects in the United Kingdom. A grant of £500 is awarded annually.

8646 ■ RAI Research Grants
To support archaeological research in the United Kingdom. Grants ranging from £700 to £5,000 are awarded annually.

8647 ■ Royal Asiatic Society of Great Britain and Ireland
Alison Ohta, Dir.
14 Stephenson Way
London NW1 2HD, United Kingdom
Ph: 44 20 73884539
Fax: 44 20 73919429
E-mail: info@royalasiaticsociety.org
URL: http://www.royalasiaticsociety.org/site

8648 ■ Professor Mary Boyce Prize
To recognize outstanding scholarly articles relating to the study of religion in Asia. A monetary prize of £250 is awarded annually.

8649 ■ Sir Richard Burton Medal
To encourage Asian studies through travel. A medal is presented at intervals of at least three years. Established in 1923 in memory of Sir Richard Burton, the explorer.

8650 ■ New Barwis-Holliday Award
To recognize new research in anthropology, art, history, literature, or religion in Japan, China, Korea, or the eastern regions of the former Soviet Union. A monetary prize of £250 is awarded annually. Established in 1981.

8651 ■ Royal Asiatic Society Award
To recognize outstanding research that is considered to have contributed the most to the advancement of Asian studies. The research must be published either in books or articles, in English or as Asian texts with editorial matter in English. An award is presented every three years.

8652 ■ Denis Sinor Medal
To recognize outstanding scholarship in the field of Inner Asian studies. Awarded when merited. Established in 1993.

8653 ■ Sir George Staunton Prize
To recognize young scholars working in the fields of history, archaeology, literature, language,

religion, archeology, or art of Asia. Submission should be close to 6,000 words in length. A monetary prize of £250 is awarded annually.

8654 ■ Royal Astronomical Society
Prof. R.L. Davies, Pres.
Burlington House
Piccadilly
London W1J 0BQ, United Kingdom
Ph: 44 20 77343307
Ph: 44 20 77344582
Fax: 44 20 74940166
E-mail: webmaster@ras.org.uk
URL: http://www.ras.org.uk

8655 ■ Award for Service to Astronomy and Geophysics
To recognize an individual for outstanding or exceptional work that has aided and advanced the sciences of astronomy, geophysics, or solar system sciences. A suitable gift is awarded irregularly.

8656 ■ Chapman Medal
For recognition of specific investigations of outstanding merit in the fields of solar-terrestrial physics, including geomagnetism and aeronomy. A medal is awarded annually. Established in 1973 to honor Professor Sidney Chapman.

8657 ■ George Darwin Lecture
To recognize outstanding achievement in astronomy, cosmology, or astroparticle physics. Awarded annually.

8658 ■ Eddington Medal
To recognize specific investigations of outstanding merit in the field of theoretical astrophysics. A medal is awarded annually. Established in 1953 in honor of Sir Arthur Stanley Eddington.

8659 ■ Fowler Prizes
To recognize individuals who have made particularly noteworthy contributions to the astronomical and geophysical sciences in the early stages of their careers. Two prizes are awarded annually.

8660 ■ Gold Medal
To recognize outstanding achievement in geophysics, solar physics, solar-terrestrial physics, or planetary sciences. Awarded annually.

8661 ■ Group Achievement Award
To recognize outstanding achievement by a large group or branch of astronomy or geophysics where it is not appropriate to present one of the other awards of the Society. Awarded when merited.

8662 ■ Herschel Medal
To recognize investigations of outstanding merit in observational astrophysics. A medal is awarded annually. Established in 1974 to honor Sir William Herschel.

8663 ■ Jackson-Gwilt Medal
For recognition of the invention, improvement, or development of astronomical instrumentation or techniques; for achievement in observational astronomy; or for achievement in research into the history of astronomy. A monetary award and a bronze medal are presented annually. Established in 1897 to honor Mrs. Hannah Jackson-Gwilt.

8664 ■ Harold Jeffreys Lecture
To recognize outstanding achievement in geophysics, solar physics, solar-terrestrial physics, or planetary sciences. Awarded annually.

8665 ■ Michael Penston Astronomy Prize
To recognize the best thesis in the astronomy and astrophysics fields. Open to students of all nationalities who are registered at universities in the United Kingdom. A monetary prize of £1,000 is awarded annually.

8666 ■ Price Medal
To recognize specific work in the fields of solid-earth geophysics, oceanography, or planetary sciences. Awarded annually. Established in 1993 to honor Professor Albert Thomas Price.

8667 ■ Keith Runcorn Prize
To recognize the best theses in the solar-system sciences and geophysics fields. Award is open to students of all nationalities and is not restricted to society members. A cash prize of £1,000 is awarded annually. Sponsored by Wiley-Blackwell. Formerly: RAS-Blackwell Prize.

8668 ■ Gerald Whitrow Lecture
To recognize outstanding achievement in cosmology. Awarded biennially. To recognize outstanding achievement in cosmology. Awarded biennially.

8669 ■ Royal British Society of Sculptors
Anne Rawcliffe-King, Dir.
108 Old Brompton Rd.
London SW7 3RA, United Kingdom
Ph: 44 20 73738615
E-mail: info@rbs.org.uk
URL: http://www.rbs.org.uk

8670 ■ Bursary Awards
Recognizes promise and dedication in the art form of sculpture. Ten awards are presented annually.

8671 ■ Royal College of General Practitioners
Dr. Iona Heath, Pres.
1 Bow Churchyard
London EC4M 9DQ, United Kingdom
Ph: 44 20 31887400
Fax: 44 20 31887401
E-mail: info@rcgp.org.uk
URL: http://www.rcgp.org.uk

8672 ■ Adolescent Health Care Award in memory of Dr. Kathy Phipps
To recognize an individual general practitioner or practice that has demonstrated a significant innovation or improvement in the standard of care provided for young people in the previous two years. A plaque and monetary prize of £2,500 are awarded annually. Established in 2009.

8673 ■ Disability Care Award
To recognize an individual or team for innovative/significant developments in the organization. A monetary prize of £5,000 is awarded annually.

8674 ■ Foundation Council Award
To recognize an individual for special meritorious work in connection with the College. A silver gavel is awarded annually.

8675 ■ Paul Freeling Award
To members of fellows of the RCGP in good standing. A monetary prize of £1,000 is awarded annually. Established in 2004.

8676 ■ John Fry Award
To recognize a member or Fellow who has promoted the discipline of general practice through research and publishing as a practicing general practitioner. A silver medal is awarded annually.

8677 ■ GP Registrar Awards
For original and innovative projects undertaken during the course of vocational training in UK. Monetary prizes ranging from £400 to £1,000 are awarded annually.

8678 ■ Honorary Fellowship
This, the most distinguished honor of the College, is awarded for outstanding work toward the objectives of the College. Open to doctors and non-doctors from the United Kingdom and overseas. Awarded to one or more recipients annually.

Awards are arranged in alphabetical order below their administering organizations

8679 ■ John Horder Award
To recognize exceptional contributions of members of staff who have given a considerable amount of service to the College. Awarded annually.

8680 ■ John Hunt Lectureship
To honor an individual who is not medically qualified as a general practitioner/family doctor. A medal is awarded triennially.

8681 ■ James Mackenzie Lectureship
To honor an individual in the field of clinical medicine. A medal is awarded triennially.

8682 ■ National GP of the Year Award
To honor a general practitioner (GP) for excellence in general practice. Candidates are nominated by patients. Awarded annually. Established in 2010.

8683 ■ Patient Participation Award
To any member of the practice team, patient group, or patient of a practice. Awarded annually. Established in 1996.

8684 ■ William Pickles Lectureship
To honor an individual in the field of medicine as it relates to education. A medal is awarded triennially.

8685 ■ President's Medal
To honor a Fellow for dedication in promoting the aims and objectives of the College. Candidates are individuals that would otherwise not receive recognition for that contribution. Awarded annually.

8686 ■ RGCP/SAPC Elective Prize
For the best proposal by a medical student for an elective project. A monetary prize of £500 is awarded annually.

8687 ■ Rose Prize
To recognize original work in the history of general practice in the British Isles. Non-professional historians are eligible.

8688 ■ Royal College of Obstetricians and Gynaecologists - United Kingdom
Dr. Anthony Falconer, Pres.
27 Sussex Pl.
Regent's Park
London NW1 4RG, United Kingdom
Ph: 44 20 77726200
Ph: 44 20 77726228
Fax: 44 20 77230575
E-mail: examsadmin@rcog.org.uk
URL: http://www.rcog.org.uk

8689 ■ AGC/GVS Fellowship
To enable the recipient to visit, make contact with and gain knowledge from a specific centre offering new techniques or methods of clinical management within the specialty of obstetrics and gynaecology. Open to specialist registrars in the British Isles and, in the USA, to junior fellows or those in residency programs in obstetrics and gynaecology. A maximum of £1,000 will be awarded for traveling expenses. Established in 1990 by the American Gynecological Club (AGC) and the Gynaecological Visiting Society of Great Britain and Ireland (GVS). Formerly: USA/British Isles Visiting Fellowship.

8690 ■ Bernhard Baron Travelling Scholarship
To provide funds for short-term travel to expand the applicant's experience in areas where he or she already has experience. Fellows and members of the college may apply. Funds for travel up to £6,000 are awarded annually. Established in 1953.

8691 ■ William Blair-Bell Memorial Lectureship in Obstetrics and Gynaecology
To honor members by inviting them to present lectures on either obstetrics or gynaecology, or closely related subjects. Preference is given to lectures based on original work, particularly in regard to the morphology, physiology, and pathology of the female reproductive organs, but this need not be considered an absolute condition of the appointment, particularly if the alternative be a problem connected with malignant neoplastic disease. An honorarium of £500 is awarded to no more than two recipients each year.

8692 ■ Eden Travelling Fellowship in Obstetrics and Gynaecology
To enable the holder to visit, for a specified period of time, another department(s) of obstetrics and gynaecology or of closely related disciplines where the applicant may gain additional knowledge and experience in the pursuit of a specific research project in which he or she is currently engaged. Open to medical graduates of not less than two years' standing of any approved university. A maximum of £5,000 is awarded annually. Endowed by Dr. Thomas Watts Eden.

8693 ■ Edgar Gentilli Prize
For recognition of original work on the cause, nature, recognition, and treatment of any form of cancer of the female genital tract. All medical practitioners are eligible. A monetary prize of £750 and book tokens of a valuing up to £250 are awarded annually. Established in 1960 by the late Mr. and Mrs. Gilbert Edgar.

8694 ■ Green-Armytage and Spackman Travelling Scholarship
To enable scholarship holders to visit centers where similar work to their own is being conducted on some particular aspect of obstetrical or gynaecological practice. Fellows and members of the college may apply. Funds for travel up to £4,000 are awarded annually. Established in 1969 in honor of Mr. V. B. Green-Armytage and Colonel W. C. Spackman.

8695 ■ John Lawson Prize
Recognizes the best article on a topic of obstetrics or gynaecology derived from work carried out in Africa between the tropics of Capricorn and Cancer. The record of the work can be submitted by way of an original manuscript. If joint authorship is involved, the candidate must identify his or her involvement in the publication. A monetary prize of £100 is awarded annually.

8696 ■ Malcolm Black Travel Fellowship
To enable a college member or fellow to travel, either to the British Isles or from the British Isles abroad, for a period of time to attend postgraduate training courses or to visit centers of research or particular expertise within the specialty of obstetrics and gynaecology. Travel and subsistence costs up to £1,000 are awarded biennially. Established in 1987 by Mrs. Mattie Black in memory of her husband, Malcolm Duncan Black, a member of the college in 1935 who was elevated to the fellowship in 1947.

8697 ■ Harold Malkin Prize
For recognition of the best original work of an individual while holding a registrar or senior registrar post in a hospital in the United Kingdom or the Republic of Ireland. Members or candidates for membership in the RCOG are eligible. A first place monetary prize of £250 and a second place prize of £150 are awarded annually. Established in 1971 by the late Harold Malkin.

8698 ■ Royal College of Physicians and Surgeons of Glasgow
Ian Anderson, Pres.
232-242 St. Vincent St.
Glasgow G2 5RJ, United Kingdom
Ph: 44 141 2216072
Ph: 44 141 2273219
Fax: 44 141 2211804
E-mail: president@rcpsg.ac.uk
URL: http://www.rcpsg.ac.uk/Pages/RCPSG_Welcome.aspx

8699 ■ Rod Cawson Prize Lecture
To recognize and encourage excellence in the science and practice of Oral pathology. Eligible to any person involved in the practice of oral pathology, including researchers, scientists, and clinicians. A monetary prize of £1,000 is awarded biennially and the recipient is invited to present a lecture at the Biennial Congress.

8700 ■ Davies Foundation Travelling Fellowship
For fellows and members who wish to take a sabbatical to travel and conduct research in cancer, palliative care, or a related field. Two awards of £10,000 are given for travel and expenses. Sponsored by the William and Elizabeth Davies Foundation.

8701 ■ T. C. White Grant
To encourage Fellows and Members in Dental Surgery of the College to further their education and experience by visits to centers abroad. Up to three grants of £2,000 are awarded annually.

8702 ■ T. C. White Prize Lecture
To recognize a dental graduate of not more than 12 years standing. An invitation to deliver a lecture on a subject related to the original work done by the prize winner is awarded annually. The value of the award is £1,000. Established in 1984.

8703 ■ Royal College of Psychiatrists
Prof. Sue Bailey, Pres.
17 Belgrave Sq.
London SW1X 8PG, United Kingdom
Ph: 44 20 72352351
Fax: 44 20 72451231
E-mail: rcpsych@rcpsych.ac.uk
URL: http://www.rcpsych.ac.uk

8704 ■ Thomas Bakewell Prize
To recognize an exceptional essay by medical students in the West Midlands. A monetary prize of £200 is awarded annually. Presented by the West Midlands Division.

8705 ■ Douglas Bennett Prize
Recognizes an exceptional psychiatry paper. Psychiatrists in training, including staff and associate specialists or those within two years of consultant appointment, are eligible. A monetary prize of at least £200 is awarded annually. Administered by the Faculty of Rehabilitation and Social Psychiatry.

8706 ■ Professor Joan Bicknell Essay Prize
To recognize the best essay written by a medical student about his or her contact with a person with learning disability during the course of studies. The award aims to raise the awareness of issues of disability in medical training and to encourage students to pursue further study and professional training in this area. Clinical medical students in Ireland and the United Kingdom are eligible. A monetary prize of £250 is awarded annually. Supported by the Faculty of the Psychiatry of Learning Disability.

8707 ■ Burden Research Prize
To recognize outstanding research work that has either been published, accepted for publication, or presented as a paper to the learning society during the three year period ending December 31. Applicants must be registered medical practitioners, the greater part of whose time is spent working in the field of learning disabilities in the United Kingdom or the Republic of Ireland. The prize consists of an award of £1,000. Awarded triennially. Established in 1969.

Awards are arranged in alphabetical order below their administering organizations

8708 ■ Child and Adolescent Faculty Poster Prize for SHOs/STs

To recognize senior house officers (SHOs) and specialty trainees (STs) 1-3 for the best poster on a topic relevant to child and adolescent mental health. Only individuals not currently working in the field of child and adolescent psychiatry are eligible. A monetary prize of £300 is awarded annually. Supported by the Faculty of Child and Adolescent Psychiatry.

8709 ■ Child and Adolescent Faculty Specialist Registrar Poster Prize

To recognize specialist registrars (SpRs) for the best poster on a topic relevant to child and adolescent mental health. A monetary prize of £300 is awarded annually. Supported by the Faculty of Child and Adolescent Psychiatry.

8710 ■ Clinical Audit Prize, West Midlands Division

To recognize an exceptional clinical audit by a junior doctor. Psychiatric trainees below specialist registrar and non consultant level are eligible. A trophy is awarded annually. Presented by the West Midlands Division.

8711 ■ Natalie Cobbing Travelling Fellowship

To further the training of specialists in the psychiatry of learning disability by enabling them to extend their experience with travel to appropriate centers overseas. All applicants must possess the MRCPsych and, must be working in the United Kingdom or Republic of Ireland. A fellowship of £3,000 is awarded biennially in even-numbered years.

8712 ■ Margaret Davenport Prize

To recognize the best presentation made by a trainee or newly appointed consultant at the Residential Meeting of the Child and Adolescent Psychiatry Faculty. A monetary prize of £100 is awarded annually in memory of Dr. Margaret Davenport.

8713 ■ Philip Davis Prize

For recognition of an essay, between 4,000 and 6,000 words, on a broadly-based clinical topic relating to the care of the elderly mentally ill. Only members or inceptors of the college below the rank of consultant psychiatrist or the equivalent are eligible. A monetary prize of £300 is awarded annually. Established in 1991 in honor of the late Dr. Philip R. H. Davis.

8714 ■ Eastern Division Research Prize

For the best research project conducted by any doctor of non-consultant grade working within the Eastern Division. A monetary prize of £500 is awarded annually.

8715 ■ Forensic Faculty Poster Prizes for SpRs and STs 1 - 3

To recognize specialist registrars (SpRs) and specialty trainees (STs) 1 - 3 for the best poster on a topic relevant to forensic psychiatry. A monetary prize of £300 is awarded annually. Supported by the Faculty of Forensic Psychiatry.

8716 ■ Forensic Faculty Senior House Officer Poster Prize

To recognize senior house officers (SHOs) for the best poster on a topic relevant to forensic psychiatry. A monetary prize of £300 is awarded annually. Supported by the Faculty of Forensic Psychiatry.

8717 ■ Dr. Thomas Freeman Psychotherapy Award

To recognize an exceptional paper or long case relevant to psychotherapy. Trainees working in Northern Ireland and anyone within two years of taking up a career post in Northern Ireland are eligible. A monetary prize of £150 and a medal are awarded biennially. Honors Dr. Thomas Freeman's contributions to psychiatry and psychotherapy. Presented by the Northern Ireland Division.

8718 ■ Gaskell Medal and Prize

To recognize individuals who have been qualified medical officers in one or more mental hospitals or clinics in psychiatry in the United Kingdom or elsewhere in the British Commonwealth for at least two years, and have passed the MRCPsych examination or equivalent examination within the last four years. The top 20 candidates in the MRCPsych examinations are invited to take the Gaskell Prize examination. A medal is awarded annually. Established in 1886 in honor of Samuel Gaskell, Medical Superintendent of the County Asylum, Lancaster.

8719 ■ John Hamilton Traveling Fellowship

To encourage psychiatrists working in the field of forensic psychiatry to broaden their knowledge and experience through travel to recognized forensic centers. Proposals to visit forensic services which are developing in order to support, advise and teach will be considered. Candidates may wish to pursue a research topic or a comparative study. A fellowship of £2,000 is awarded biennially in odd-numbered years.

8720 ■ Inter-Schools World Mental Health Day Public Speaking Competition

Recognizes the winners of a speaking competition for school children. Each team of two children speaks for up to four minutes on a mental illness issue. Teams are drawn from interested schools in Northern Ireland. Prizes are awarded annually. Presented by the Northern Ireland Division.

8721 ■ Irish College of Psychiatrists Faculty of Addictions Essay Competition

Recognizes the winner of an essay contest. Essay may be on any topic relevant to psychiatry. Trainees in psychiatry who are working in Ireland are eligible. A monetary prize of £500 is awarded annually.

8722 ■ Ferdinande Johanna Kanjilal Traveling Fellowship

To further the experience of senior trainees in psychiatry from countries overseas who wish to study in the United Kingdom or the Republic of Ireland for a short period. Applicants must submit an account of their previous psychiatric experience and their training needs, and describe the way in which they consider that the use of the Fellowship might benefit the psychiatric services in their home countries. A fellowship of £2,000 is awarded to cover the expenses, either wholly or in part, of such trainees who wish to come to the United Kingdom or the Republic of Ireland, for a short period of further study, research or clinical training. Awarded biennially in even-numbered years. Named in memory of Ferdinande Johanna, wife of Dr. C. Kanijilal.

8723 ■ Laughlin Prize

To recognize the candidate who obtains the highest marks and the best recommendation from the examiners in the MRCPsych Examinations. A monetary prize of £250 is awarded twice a year after the spring and autumn examinations. Established in 1979.

8724 ■ Morris Markowe Public Education Prize

For recognition of an article on a psychiatric topic of approximately 1,000 words, suitable for publication in a regional newspaper, lay journal, the paramedical press, or a general practitioners' magazine, or an article published in the last year (between May and May) of approximately 1,000 words in the above types of publications, or an article commissioned for publication in a regional newspaper, lay journal, paramedical press, or general practitioner's magazine by the Public Education Committee. Entries should be submitted by May 1 of each year. A monetary prize of £1,000 is awarded annually. Established in 1989 in memory of Dr. Morris Markowe, Honorary Fel-

low and Registrar of the Royal College of Psychiatrists from 1972-78.

8725 ■ Medical Student Essay Prize in Addictions Psychiatry

To recognize fourth- and fifth-year medical students for essays on the topic of addictions psychiatry. Students in Ireland and the United Kingdom are eligible. A monetary prize of £200 is awarded annually. Supported by the Faculty of Addictions Psychiatry.

8726 ■ Medical Student Essay Prize in Child and Adolescent Mental Health

To recognize medical students in their third through fifth year for essays on the topic of child and adolescent mental health. Students in Ireland and the United Kingdom are eligible. A monetary prize of £500 is awarded annually. Established in 2001. Supported by the Faculty of Child and Adolescent Psychiatry.

8727 ■ Medical Student Essay Prize in Forensic Psychiatry

To recognize medical students for an essay on the topic of forensic psychiatry. A monetary prize of £300 is awarded annually. Supported by the Faculty of Forensic Psychiatry.

8728 ■ Medical Student Essay Prize in General and Community Psychiatry

To recognize medical students for an essay on the topic of adult general and community psychiatry. Clinical medical students in Ireland and the United Kingdom are eligible. A monetary prize of £500 is awarded annually. Supported by the Faculty of General and Community Psychiatry.

8729 ■ Medical Student Essay Prize in Liaison Psychiatry

To recognize medical students for an essay on the topic of psychiatry among other medical disciplines. Clinical medical students in Ireland and the United Kingdom are eligible. A monetary prize of £500 is awarded annually. Supported by the Faculty of Liaison Psychiatry.

8730 ■ Spike Milligan Trophy and Prize

To recognize the winners of the Irish Intervarsity Public Speaking Competition. Student teams from each Medical School are eligible to participate. A monetary prize of £2,500 and a trophy are awarded to the two students on the winning team; additional prizes are awarded to the runners up. Awarded annually. Honors Spike Milligan and his work in destigmatizing mental illness.

8731 ■ Mohsen Naguib Memorial Prize

To recognize the best short scientific paper presented by a trainee. Trainees or new consultants presenting work undertaken during the training period are eligible, as are colleagues in Europe. A monetary prize of £250 is presented annually. Formally established in 1998.

8732 ■ Brian Oliver Prize

Recognition for research in the psychiatry of learning disabilities. Applicants may be trainees or consultants in psychiatry within three years of their first consultant appointment. Submissions may take the form of an original piece of work or a literature review and may be presented in the form of an essay or dissertation. A monetary prize of £500 is awarded annually. Established in 1991 in memory of the late Dr. Brian Oliver, who was Honorary Secretary of the Mental Handicap Psychiatry Specialist Advisory Committee.

8733 ■ Oral and Poster Presentation Prize

To recognize the best poster and oral presentation in the area of adult general and community psychiatry. Psychiatrists in training grades and consultants in their first year of practice are

Awards are arranged in alphabetical order below their administering organizations

eligible. A monetary prize of £250 is awarded annually. Supported by the Faculty of General and Community Psychiatry.

8734 ■ Oral and Poster Prize in the Psychiatry of Learning Disability
To recognize the best poster and oral presentation in the area of the psychiatry of learning disability. Psychiatrists in training grades and consultants in their first year of practice are eligible. A monetary prize of £200 is awarded annually. Supported by the Faculty of the Psychiatry of Learning Disability.

8735 ■ Gillian Page Prize
To recognize an original piece of work in the field of adolescent psychiatry. The work may take the form of a research project, a review, or a study of some clinical innovation. Candidates must be Members or Inceptors of the College below the rank of consultant psychiatrist or equivalent. A monetary prize of £500 is awarded biennially in odd-numbered years. Established in 1986.

8736 ■ Felix Post Prize
To promote research-oriented thinking among clinical teams. Non-consultant grade career psychiatrists in non-academic units are invited to submit an essay on how an innovative task contributed to management of older patients suffering from functional illness. A monetary prize of £500 is awarded annually. Established in 2004. Honors the contributions of Dr. Felix Post to old age psychiatry. Administered by the Faculty of Old Age.

8737 ■ Poster Prize for Trainees in Addictions Psychiatry
To recognize the psychiatric trainee who presents the best poster at the Annual Meeting of the Faculty of Addictions Psychiatry. A monetary prize of £300 is awarded annually.

8738 ■ Psychotherapy Prize
To recognize a paper relevant to psychotherapy, including psychodynamic, systemic, cognitive-behavioral, or other area as practiced in the field of psychiatry. Open to all eligible College Members from any discipline. A monetary prize of £500 is awarded biennially in even-numbered years. Administered by the Faculty of Psychotherapy of the RCP.

8739 ■ Research Presentation Prize, West Midlands Division
To recognize the best presentation of a piece of psychiatry research. Trainee and consultant psychiatrists in their first year of employment in the West Midlands are eligible. A trophy is awarded annually. Presented by the West Midlands Division.

8740 ■ Research Prize and Bronze Medal
For recognition of research. Members or inceptors of the College below the rank of consultant psychiatrist or equivalent at the time the research is submitted to the Royal College are eligible. Research involving collaboration between workers, whether psychiatrists or in other disciplines, may be submitted, but the prize may be shared between no more than two eligible psychiatrists. The research should be presented in the form of an essay or dissertation with accompanying tables or figures. Entries may be submitted to the Dean by April 30 of each year. A monetary prize of £5,000, a bronze medal, and registration fees and travel expenses are awarded annually. Established in 1882.

8741 ■ Scottish Division Research Prize
To recognize an exceptional psychiatry paper published in a peer-reviewed journal during the preceding year. Psychiatrists working in Scotland who are under 40 years of age or within five years of their first consultant appointment are eligible. A monetary prize of £500 is awarded at the Scottish Division Meeting.

8742 ■ Alec Shapiro Prize
To recognize the best verbal presentation and the best poster presentation in the field of learning disabilities. Applicants must submit an account of their previous experience in the area of learning disabilities and published or unpublished work that they feel would be an appropriate recipient of the prize by August 31. All applicants must possess the MRCPsych, be working in the UK or the Republic of Ireland, and be of SHO or Specialist Registrar status. Two prizes of £100 are awarded annually. Named in honor Dr. Alexander Shapiro, one of the great figures in the tradition of learning disabilities.

8743 ■ SIGP Prize for Best Published Paper on Psychopharmacology
To recognize an exceptional paper on Psychopharmacology published in the preceding 12 months. Clinical Psychopharmacology papers published in the British Journal of Psychiatry, the Psychiatric Bulletin, or Advances in Psychiatric Treatment are eligible. A monetary prize for the author to attend the College Annual Meeting is awarded annually. Presented by the Special Interest Group for Psychopharmacology.

8744 ■ South West Division Innovation Prize
To recognize innovation or leadership in modern psychiatric practice. Consultants, Associate Specialists, and Staff Grade doctors who have worked in the South West Division for at least six months and are Fellows or Members of the College are eligible. A monetary prize of £500 is awarded annually. Presented by the South West Division.

8745 ■ South West Division Poster Prize
Recognizes the winner of a poster competition. Specialist Registrars are eligible to submit a poster and abstract on a project that is near completion or an audit. First prize is a monetary award of £250 and second prize is a monetary award of £100. Awarded biennially.

8746 ■ South West Division Trainees Prize
To recognize the best essay submitted and presented at the Spring Biannual Meeting. Pre-Membership Psychiatric Trainees or trainee members of the Royal College of Psychiatrists who have worked in the division for the last six months are eligible. A monetary prize of £250 is awarded annually. Presented by the South West Division.

8747 ■ Spirituality and Psychiatry Prize
To recognize an exceptional study, research, review, or essay on spirituality and psychiatry. All members and affiliates of the College are eligible. A monetary prize of £250 is awarded annually. Presented by the Spirituality and Psychiatry Special Interest Group.

8748 ■ Standish-Barry Prize
To recognize the best results by an Irish Graduate in the MCRPsych Membership Examinations. A monetary prize of £200 is awarded annually. Established in 1998 as a result of a bequest made by Dr. Standish-Barry.

8749 ■ Trainee Prize - Northern and Yorkshire Division
To recognize the most outstanding oral and poster presentation by psychiatry trainees. Eligible to Trainee Psychiatrists in the Northern and Yorkshire Divisions. A monetary prize of £200 and a certificate of merit are awarded for the best oral presentation; a certificate of merit is awarded for the best poster. Awarded annually. Presented by the Northern and Yorkshire Division.

8750 ■ Trent Division Research Presentation Prize
For the best presentation of a piece of psychiatry research. Trainee psychiatrists in the Trent Region are eligible. A monetary prize of £200 and a certificate are awarded annually. Presented by the Trent Division.

8751 ■ Women in Psychiatry Special Interest Group Prize
For an original presentation on a mental health issue for women. Psychiatry trainees in a recognized unit in the UK or Ireland who are non-career grade or within three years of appointment as a consultant are eligible. A monetary prize of £250 is awarded annually. Presented by the Women in Psychiatry Special Interest Group.

8752 ■ Woodford-Williams Prize
To recognize research in the prevention of dementia. Research involving collaboration may be submitted, but the award may be shared by no more than two eligible applicants. Submissions of recently published essays or dissertations should be between 10,000 and 30,000 words. A monetary award of £300 is presented every three years. Established in 1984 to honor Dr. Eluned Woodford-Williams, CBE, a pioneer of British geriatrics and former Director of the Health Advisory Service.

8753 ■ Royal College of Radiologists - United Kingdom
Andrew Hall, Chief Exec.
38 Portland Pl.
London W1B 1JQ, United Kingdom
Ph: 44 20 76364432
Fax: 44 20 73233100
E-mail: enquiries@rcr.ac.uk
URL: http://www.rcr.ac.uk

8754 ■ George and Vera Ansell Poster Prize
To recognize the best clinical radiology proffered poster presented at an annual meeting in the category of original scientific presentation. Awarded annually.

8755 ■ Ellis Barnett Prize
To recognize the most outstanding paper with an ultrasound content published in Clinical Radiology in a given year. A medal is awarded annually to one or more recipients. Established in 1987.

8756 ■ Frank Doyle Medal
To recognize outstanding candidates in the First FRCR Examination. A medal is awarded annually. Established in 1984.

8757 ■ Editor's Medal
To recognize the first author of the best paper published in Clinical Radiology in a given year. A medal is awarded annually to one or more recipients. Established in 1990.

8758 ■ Robert and Elma Kemp Harper Prize
To recognize the best paper on gastrointestinal radiology published in Clinical Radiology in a given year. Awarded annually to one or more recipients. Established in 1997.

8759 ■ Ella Preiskel Prize
To recognize the most outstanding paper on paediatric radiology published in Clinical Radiology in a given year. A medal is awarded annually to one or more recipients. Established in 1989 in the memory of Dr. Ella Preiskel.

8760 ■ Royal College of Veterinary Surgeons
Dr. Jerry Davies, Pres.
Belgravia House
62-64 Horseferry Rd.
London SW1P 2AF, United Kingdom
Ph: 44 20 72222001
Ph: 44 20 72020727
Fax: 44 20 72222004
E-mail: admin@rcvs.org.uk
URL: http://www.rcvs.org.uk

Awards are arranged in alphabetical order below their administering organizations

8761 ■ Alison Alston Canine Award
To enable the holder to undertake studies related to the dog and is open to any Fellow or Member of the Royal College of Veterinary Surgeons who can show evidence of postgraduate experience in an appropriate field of veterinary science.

8762 ■ Robert Daubney Research Fellowship in Virology and Helminthology
To enable the holder to undertake a period of research in the fields of virology and helminthology. The Fellowship is open to any Fellow or member who shows evidence of postgraduate experience in an appropriate field of veterinary science. The fellowship is tenable for a maximum of three years. A grant between £10,000 and £20,000 is awarded annually.

8763 ■ Royal Economic Society
R. Blundell, Pres.
University of St. Andrews
School of Economics and Finance
Fife
St. Andrews KY16 9AL, United Kingdom
Ph: 44 1334 462479
Fax: 44 1334 462444
E-mail: royaleconsoc@st-andrews.ac.uk
URL: http://www.res.org.uk

8764 ■ Conference Grants
To provide financial assistance to members who are presenting a paper or acting as a principal discussant at a conference. Application deadlines are January 31, May 31, and September 30. Grants of up to £500 are awarded three times a year.

8765 ■ Junior Fellowship Awards
To enable students to attend universities in the United Kingdom for a period of one year. Students who have completed at least two years of work toward a doctoral thesis are eligible. Six fellowships valued at £8,000 (£11,000 in London) are awarded annually.

8766 ■ Royal Economic Society Prize
To recognize the best article published in *The Economic Journal*. Members of the Society may make submissions. A monetary prize of £3,000 is awarded annually. Established in 1990.

8767 ■ Royal Entomological Society
Prof. Stuart Reynolds, Pres.
The Mansion House
Chriswell Green Ln.
St. Albans AL2 3NS, United Kingdom
Ph: 44 1727 899387
Fax: 44 1727 894797
E-mail: info@royensoc.co.uk
URL: http://www.royensoc.co.uk

8768 ■ Agricultural and Forest Entomology Journal Award
To recognize the best paper published in *Agricultural and Forest Entomology* during the previous two years. A certificate and monetary prize of £600 are awarded biennially in even-numbered years.

8769 ■ Ecological Entomology Journal Award
To recognize the best paper published in *Ecological Entomology* during the previous two years. A certificate and monetary prize of £600 are awarded biennially in even-numbered years.

8770 ■ L. J. Goodman Award for Insect Biology
To recognize an individual for advancing the education of the public in the knowledge, understanding, and appreciation of all aspects of insect physiology, thereby promoting the control and conservation of insect species. A monetary prize of £1,000 is awarded annually. Established in honor of L. G. Goodman.

8771 ■ Insect Conservation and Diversity Journal Award
To recognize the best paper published in *Insect Conservation and Diversity* during the previous two years. A certificate and monetary prize of £600 are awarded biennially in even-numbered years.

8772 ■ Insect Molecular Biology Journal Award
To recognize the best paper published in *Insect Molecular Biology* during the previous two years. A certificate and monetary prize of £600 are awarded biennially in even-numbered years.

8773 ■ Marsh Award for Insect Conservation
To recognize individuals for lifetime achievement or for an exceptional contribution to the field of insect conservation. A certificate and monetary award of £1,000 are presented annually.

8774 ■ Medical and Veterinary Entomology Journal Award
To recognize the best paper published in *Medical and Veterinary Entomology* during the previous two years. A certificate and monetary prize of £600 are awarded biennially in odd-numbered years.

8775 ■ Physiological Entomology Journal Award
To recognize the best paper published in *Physiological Entomology* during the previous two years. A certificate and monetary prize of £600 are awarded biennially in odd-numbered years.

8776 ■ Student Award
To recognize students for articles about any entomological topic that would be of interest to the general public. Individuals may be undergraduates or postgraduates and may be full- or part-time students. A monetary prize of £350 is awarded for first place, £250 for runner-up, and £150 for third place. In addition, the top three articles are published in *Antenna*.

8777 ■ Systematic Entomology Journal Award
To recognize the best paper published in *Systematic Entomology* during the previous two years. A certificate and monetary prize of £600 are awarded biennially in odd-numbered years.

8778 ■ Alfred Russel Wallace Award
To recognize postgraduate students for outstanding work. A monetary award of £800, certificate, and one-year membership are presented annually.

8779 ■ J.O. Westwood Medal for Excellence in Insect Taxonomy
To recognize exceptional comprehensive taxonomic work on a group of insects or related arthropods. Scientists of all nationalities are eligible provided they meet the criteria. Award consists of a silver gilt medal and travel expenses to the International Congress of Entomology. Awarded biennially in even-numbered years. Established in 2008. Cosponsored by the Natural History Museum, London.

8780 ■ Wigglesworth Lecture and Medal Award
For recognition of outstanding contributions to the field of entomology at the international level. Society members make the selection. A silver medal is awarded every four years. Established in 1980 in honor of Professor Sir Vincent Wigglesworth FRS, the first recipient.

8781 ■ Royal Forestry Society
Dr. John Jackson, Chief Exec.
102 High St.
Hertfordshire
Tring HP23 4AF, United Kingdom
Ph: 44 1442 822028
Fax: 44 1442 890395
E-mail: rfshq@rfs.org.uk

URL: http://www.rfs.org.uk

8782 ■ Randle Travel Fund
To provide financial assistance to individual members of the RFS for subsistence and travel costs when taking part in: 1. RFS Overseas Study Tours organized by its Head Office; 2. tours those run by local divisions and approved by Head Office; or 3. for individual trips abroad specifically designed to enhance their forestry knowledge. Travel grants in the range of £200 to £500 are awarded annually.

8783 ■ Yorkshire Bursary
To provide financial assistance for a younger person to carry out a forestry related project at home or abroad. A grant of £600 is awarded annually. Administered jointly by the Yorkshire Division of the RFS and the Yorkshire Agricultural Society.

8784 ■ Royal Geographical Society with the Institute of British Geographers
Michael Palin CBE, Pres.
1 Kensington Gore
London SW7 2AR, United Kingdom
Ph: 44 20 75913000
Ph: 44 20 75913004
Fax: 44 20 75913001
E-mail: membership@rgs.org
URL: http://www.rgs.org/HomePage.htm
Formerly: (1997) Royal Geographic Society.

8785 ■ Back Award
To recognize individuals for applied or scientific geographical studies that make an outstanding contribution to the development of national or international public policy. Awarded annually when merited. Established in 1882 by Admiral Sir George Back.

8786 ■ Ralph Brown Expedition Award
For leaders of research expeditions associated with the study of rivers, wetlands, coral reefs or the shallow marine environment. Applicants may be of any nationality but must be over 25. The project can be located anywhere in the world, and must be of potential advantage to the host country. Close involvement of host country institutions is essential and strong preference will be given to teams involving host country nationals. The period of research should be at least six weeks. A grant of £12,500 is awarded annually. Established in 1996.

8787 ■ Busk Medal
To recognize an individual for fieldwork abroad in geography or in a geographical aspect of an allied science. The Medal is granted irrespective of age or nationality. Individuals cannot apply for this medal. A silver medal is awarded annually. Established in 1974.

8788 ■ Monica Cole Research Grant
To recognize a female physical geographer undertaking original field research overseas. A monetary prize of £1,000 is awarded annually. Given in memory of eminent physical geography researcher Prof. Monica Cole.

8789 ■ Geographical Award
To recognize an individual or company that has provided outstanding non-commercial support for individuals or groups learning through scientific expeditions. Awarded annually. Established in 1988. Cosponsored by the Institute of British Geographers.

8790 ■ Gilchrist Fieldwork Award
To recognize small teams of qualified academics and researchers who affect important and valuable research within short and limited periods of time. It should be original and challenging research to be carried out overseas, preferably of potential applied benefit to the host country or region. It may be multi-disciplinary or devoted to a single scientific objective. Applicants should be

Awards are arranged in alphabetical order below their administering organizations

British, undertaking a field session of over six weeks. A monetary prize of £15,000 is awarded biennially in even-numbered years. Established in 1990.

8791 ■ Gill Memorial Award
For encouragement of geographical research in young researchers who have shown great potential. Awarded annually. Established in 1886 by the gift of Miss Gill.

8792 ■ Gold Medals
To encourage and promote geographical science and discovery. Individuals cannot apply for this medal. One gold Founder's Medal and gold Patron's Medal is awarded annually. Established in the 1830s by H. M. King William IV at the foundation of the Society.

8793 ■ Honorary Membership
To acknowledge persons who have rendered particularly important services to the Union. A certificate is awarded annually.

8794 ■ Cherry Kearton Medal and Award
To recognize an explorer concerned with the study or practice of natural history, with a preference for those with an interest in nature photography, art, or cinematography. A monetary award and a bronze medal are awarded annually. Established in 1967 by a bequest of Mrs. Cherry Kearton to honor her late husband, Cherry Kearton.

8795 ■ Murchison Award
To recognize an individual for a publication that contributes the most to geographical science. Monetary awards for individuals to do fieldwork or for authors of memoirs are presented annually. Established in 1882 by a bequest of Sir Roderick Murchison.

8796 ■ Ness Award
To recognize explorers who have successfully popularized geography and the wider understanding of our world and its environments. Awarded annually. Established in 1953 by Mrs. Patrick Ness.

8797 ■ Cuthbert Peek Award
To recognize individuals who advance geographical knowledge of human impact on the environment through the application of contemporary methods, including those of earth observation and mapping. Awarded annually. The award may be given to the same explorer for more than one year. Established in 1883.

8798 ■ Neville Shulman Challenge Award
To further the understanding and exploration of the planet while promoting personal development through the intellectual or physical challenges involved in undertaking the research and/or expeditions. Applicants must be U.K. nationals and over the age of 25. The project can be desk or field based and be carried out in the United Kingdom or overseas. Applicants are required to demonstrate what new knowledge the project contributes to our understanding and exploration of the planet; why this is; and in what ways the project is intellectually or physically challenging. A grant of £10,000 is awarded annually.

8799 ■ Victoria Medal
To recognize an individual for conspicuous merit in scientific research in geography. Individuals cannot apply for this medal. Awarded annually. Established in 1902 to honor Queen Victoria.

8800 ■ Royal Historical Society - United Kingdom
Sue Carr, Exec. Sec.
University College London
Gower St.
London WC1E 6BT, United Kingdom
Ph: 44 20 73877532
Fax: 44 20 73877532
E-mail: s.carr@ucl.ac.uk
URL: http://www.royalhistoricalsociety.org

8801 ■ Alexander Prize
To recognize an individual for an essay on any historical subject. Candidates must be doctoral student in History at a U.K. institution, or be within two years of having completed a doctorate in History at a U.K. institution. A monetary award of £250 and publication of the paper in the Society's *Transactions* are awarded annually. Established in 1897 by L.C. Alexander.

8802 ■ David Berry Prize
To recognize an individual for an essay on any subject dealing with Scottish history. The essay must be an unpublished work of original research and should be between 6,000 and 10,000 words. A monetary prize of £250 is awarded annually. Established in 1929 by David Anderson Berry in memory of his father, the Reverend David Berry.

8803 ■ Frampton and Beazley Prizes
To recognize the best performance in the History A-level examinations of each of the examining boards in the United Kingdom. A monetary award of £100 is presented annually.

8804 ■ German History Society Essay Prize
To recognize an outstanding essay dealing with any aspect of German history, including German-speaking people in any part of the world. A monetary award of £500 is presented annually. Awarded in conjunction with the German History Society.

8805 ■ Gladstone History Book Prize
To recognize an author who has written a book on any non-British historical subject. It must be the author's first solely written book, and be an original and scholarly work of historical research. A monetary award of £1,000 is presented annually.

8806 ■ *History Scotland* Prize
To recognize outstanding dissertation work done by undergraduate students on any aspect of Scottish history. A monetary prize of £250 is awarded annually. In addition, the dissertation may be published in *History Scotland* magazine.

8807 ■ *History Today* Prize
Recognizes a paper based on original historical research. Third-year undergraduates enrolled in a higher education institution in the United Kingdom are eligible. A monetary prize of £250 and publication in *History Today* are awarded annually.

8808 ■ Whitfield Book Prize
To provide recognition for the best work within a field of British history. It must be the author's first solely written history book, and be an original and scholarly work of historical research. A monetary prize of £1,000 is awarded annually. Established in 1976 out of the bequest of the late Professor Archibald Stenton Whitfield.

8809 ■ Royal Horticultural Society
Elizabeth Banks, Pres.
80 Vincent Sq.
London SW1P 2PE, United Kingdom
Ph: 44 845 2605000
Ph: 44 845 0621111
E-mail: info@rhs.org.uk
URL: http://www.rhs.org.uk

8810 ■ Associateship of Honour
To recognize an individual for service to the field of horticulture over the course of a long period. Individuals of British nationality employed in the field of horticulture are eligible. Awarded as merited to one or more recipients. The number of Associates of Honour may not exceed 100 at any given time. Established in 1930.

8811 ■ Peter Barr Memorial Cup
To recognize an individual for excellence in connection with daffodils. Awarded annually by the Daffodil and Tulip Committee. Established in 1912 by the Trustees of the Peter Barr Memorial Fund.

8812 ■ Bowles Cup
For recognition of daffodils shown by amateurs. Three stems of each of fifteen cultivars of daffodils representing not fewer than four Divisions may be shown by an amateur. Awarded annually at the Daffodil Show. Established in 1949 by the late J.L. Richardson.

8813 ■ Britain in Bloom Awards
To recognize U.K. cities, towns, and villages for improvements in overall appearance through the planting of trees, shrubs, and flowers, thereby increasing local pride in the environment and attracting more business and tourism. Gold, Silver-Gilt, Silver, and Bronze awards are presented in 12 categories based on size of locale. In addition, one locale is named the Champion of Champions. Each year, two finalists are invited to represent the United Kingdom in Entente Florale Europe, the European horticultural campaign, alongside communities from 11 other European countries. Awarded annually.

8814 ■ Reginald Cory Memorial Cup
To encourage the production of new hardy hybrids of garden origin. A cup is awarded annually at the London Flower Show. Established in 1962. Formerly: Cory Cup.

8815 ■ Devonshire Trophy
For recognition of the best exhibit of twelve daffodil cultivars representing at least three Divisions, one stem of each. Awarded annually at the Daffodil Competition. Established in 1958 by Mary, Duchess of Devonshire in memory of the 10th Duke of Devonshire, a keen daffodil grower.

8816 ■ E. H. Trophy
For recognition of the best exhibit of cut flowers shown to the Society during the year. Awarded annually by the Herbaceous Plant Committee. Established in 1961 by the late W.J.M. Hawkey in memory of his grandmother, mother and wife, Mrs. Elizabeth, Mrs. Ellen and Mrs. Emma Hawkey.

8817 ■ Engleheart Cup
For recognition of the best exhibit of one stem daffodils of each twelve cultivars raised by the exhibitor. Awarded annually at the Daffodil Show in April. Established in 1913.

8818 ■ Farrer Trophy
For recognition of the best exhibit of plants suitable for the rock garden or alpine house staged during the year at one of the Society's Shows. Awarded annually by the Rock Garden and Alpine Club Committee. Established in 1959 in memory of Reginald Farrer (1880-1920), the plant collector and authority on alpine plants.

8819 ■ Gordon-Lennox Trophy
For recognition of the best exhibit of vegetables staged during the year at one of the Society's Shows. Awarded annually. Established in 1913 by the late Lady Algernon Gordon-Lennox.

8820 ■ Holford Medal
For recognition of the best exhibit of plants and/or flowers (fruit and vegetables excluded) shown by an amateur or group of amateurs at one of the Society's Shows. Awarded annually. Established in 1928 in memory of the late Sir George Holford.

8821 ■ Honorary Fellowship
To recognize significant contributions to the Society. Awarded when merited.

8822 ■ Lawrence Medal
For recognition of the best exhibit shown to the

Awards are arranged in alphabetical order below their administering organizations

Society during the year. Awarded annually at the London Flower Show. No exhibitor may receive this medal more than once in three years. Established in 1906 to celebrate Sir Trevor Lawrence's twenty-one years' tenure of office as President of the Society.

8823 ■ Loder Rhododendron Cup
For recognition of the best exhibit of one truss of a Rhododendron hybrid. Awarded annually at the Rhododendron Show. Established by the late Gerald Loder (Lord Wakehurst) and transferred to the Society in 1946.

8824 ■ George Moore Medal
To recognize the exhibitor of the new hybrid *Paphiopedilum, Selenipedium, Phragmipedium,* or an intergeneric hybrid between these genera that shows the greatest improvement on those of the same or similar parentage and that was submitted to the Society during the year. Awarded annually at the London Flower Show. Established in 1926 by the late G.F. Moore.

8825 ■ Richardson Trophy
For recognition of the best exhibit of twelve cultivars of daffodils, representing not fewer than three Divisions, to be selected from Division 1 to 4, one stem of each, shown by an amateur at the Daffodil Show. Awarded annually. Established in 1976.

8826 ■ Mrs. F. E. Rivis Prize
To encourage excellence in cultivation and to recognize the gardener or other employee responsible for the cultivation of the exhibit for which the Williams Memorial Medal is awarded. Awarded annually at the London Flower Show. Established in 1960 by Miss A.K. Hincks in commemoration of her sister, Mrs. F.E. Rivis.

8827 ■ Rothschild Challenge Cup
For recognition of the best exhibit in which rhododendrons predominate, shown to the Society during the year. Awarded annually at the London Flower Show by the Rhodendron and Camellia Committee. Established by the late Lionel de Rothschild and transferred to the Society in 1946.

8828 ■ Veitch Memorial Medal
For recognition of contributions to the advancement of the science and practice of horticulture, and for special exhibits. Medals and prizes are awarded to one or more recipients annually. Established in 1870 in memory of James Veitch of Chelsea.

8829 ■ Victoria Medal of Honour in Horticulture
To recognize an individual as deserving of a special honor at the hands of the Society for contributions in the field of horticulture. Horticulturists who are residents of the United Kingdom are eligible. Awarded to one or more recipients each year. In total, no more than 63 individuals can hold the title at any given time, symbolic of the 63 year reign of Her Majesty Queen Victoria. Established in 1897.

8830 ■ A. J. Waley Medal
To recognize a working gardener who has helped the cultivation of rhododendrons. Awarded annually. Established in 1937 by the late Alfred J. Waley.

8831 ■ Westonbirt Orchid Medal
For recognition in the field of orchid cultivation in the following categories: to the exhibitor of the best cultivar of an orchid species or of a hybrid grex that has been shown to the Society for the first time and received an award during the year or which, having received an award during the previous five years, has had the award raised during the year; for the most meritorious group of orchids staged in the Society's Halls during the year; for the most finely grown specimen

orchid shown to the Society during the year; or for any scientific, literary, or any other outstanding personal achievement in connection with orchids. Awarded annually at the London Flower Show. Established in 1960 by Mr. H.G. Alexander, in commemoration of the collection of orchids made at Westonbirt.

8832 ■ Wigan Cup
For recognition of the best exhibit shown to the Society during the year by a local authority. Awarded annually at the London Flower Show. Established in 1911.

8833 ■ Williams Memorial Medal
For recognition of a group of plants and/or cut blooms of one genus (fruit and vegetables excepted) that show excellence in cultivation, staged at one of the Society's Shows during the year. No exhibitor may win this award more than once in a three-year period. Awarded annually at the London Flower Shop. Established in 1896 by the Trustees of the Williams Memorial Fund in commemoration of B.S. Williams.

8834 ■ Guy Wilson Memorial Vase
For recognition of the best exhibit of six cultivars of white daffodils representing any or all of Divisions 1 to 3, three stems of each, at the Daffodil Show. Awarded annually. Established in 1982.

8835 ■ Royal Humane Society
Mr. Richard Titley, Chm./Treas.
50/51 Temple Chambers
3/7 Temple Ave.
London EC4Y 2942, United Kingdom
Ph: 44 20 79362942
Fax: 44 20 79362942
E-mail: info@royalhumanesociety.org.uk
URL: http://www.royalhumanesociety.org.uk

8836 ■ Bronze Medal
To recognize individuals who put their own lives at great risk to save someone else. Awarded throughout the year as merited. Established in 1837.

8837 ■ Certificate of Commendation
To recognize individuals under 18 years old who have helped in a potentially life-threatening situation, but have not necessarily put themselves at risk. A certificate is awarded throughout the year as merited.

8838 ■ In Memoriam Testimonial
To recognize someone who has lost his or her life in the attempt to save someone else. When possible, the Testimonial is presented to the next-of-kin. Awarded throughout the year as merited.

8839 ■ Resuscitation Certificate
To recognize individuals for successful resuscitation of someone through mouth-to-mouth resuscitation or heart-and-lung massage. Awarded throughout the year as merited.

8840 ■ Silver Medal
To recognize individuals who have put themselves in extreme danger, have carried out a difficult rescue, have returned to dangerous situations, or have performed similar actions. Awarded throughout the year as merited. Established in 1775.

8841 ■ Stanhope Medal
This, the Society's most prestigious award, also known as the Gold Medal, is given to honor an existing medal winner nominated by the following humane societies: Royal Humane Society, Royal Humane Society of Australasia, Royal Humane Society of New Zealand, Royal Humane Society New South Wales, Royal Canadian Humane Association, and the Liverpool Shipwreck and Humane Society. Awarded annually. First awarded in 1873.

8842 ■ Testimonial on Parchment
To recognize individuals for putting themselves in harm's way to save, or attempt to save someone else. This award is often presented to someone who has swum to the rescue of someone else. Awarded throughout the year as merited.

8843 ■ Testimonial on Vellum
To recognize individuals for putting themselves in harm's way to save, or attempt to save, someone else. Awarded throughout the year as merited.

8844 ■ Royal Incorporation of Architects in Scotland
Sholto Humphries, Pres.
15 Rutland Sq.
Edinburgh EH1 2BE, United Kingdom
Ph: 44 131 2297545
Fax: 44 131 2282188
E-mail: info@rias.org.uk
URL: http://www.rias.org.uk/content

8845 ■ Sir Rowand Anderson Silver Medal
To recognize the best portfolio by a fifth-year Scottish student. Portfolios must be submitted to the Secretary of the RIAS by October 31. Candidates, who must be within a year of passing Part II, would normally be sponsored by a school of architecture. A silver medal, a certificate, and monetary prize of £1,200 are awarded annually. Established in 1966.

8846 ■ Sir John Burnet Memorial Award
To test students' skill in architectural design and ability to communicate their proposals in response to a client's brief through drawings, prepared within a predetermined time limit. Competitors must be student members of the RIAS who have passed the Part I examination or equivalent and who have not passed the RIBA Part III examination or equivalent. Arrangements are made by each school to hold the *en loge,* normally in February. A monetary prize of £150 and a certificate are awarded annually.

8847 ■ Andrew Doolan Best Building in Scotland Award
To honor the best building in Scotland. All types of architectural projects in Scotland are eligible, including new-build, regeneration, restoration, extensions, and interiors. Awarded annually. Established in 2002, and named in honor of the RIAS founder.

8848 ■ Sir Robert Lorimer Memorial Award
For recognition of the best set of freelance sketches by students. Applications must be submitted by January 31 of each year. Competitors must be associate members or student members who are under the age of 29 years. The sketches should be analytical and illustrate in graphic form any architectural subject either existing or projected, and can be in any medium. A book voucher of £125 and a certificate are awarded annually. Established in 1933.

8849 ■ Thomas Ross Award
To provide for the production of a thesis or report resulting from research or study of: ancient Scottish buildings or monuments, or matters pertaining particularly to Scotland and to Scottish architecture and/or environment. Candidates must be members of the RIAS, be otherwise of graduate status, or submit other evidence of their qualifications as may satisfy the requirements of RIAS. An outline of the proposed subject of study must be submitted by January 31. A monetary prize of £600, with the possibility of additional help towards publication, and a certificate are awarded biennially. At the outset of the study, the nominee for the award is paid the sum of £300 which must be repaid if an acceptable

Awards are arranged in alphabetical order below their administering organizations

study is not submitted within a two-year period. The final bound report must be presented for consideration by the first day in March two years following. If acceptable, the balance of £300 is paid. Awarded annually. Established in 1966.

8850 ■ Scottish Student Awards for Architecture
To recognize the achievement of individual students and their schools of architecture, and to serve as a mark of the continuing high standards of Scottish architectural education. Awarded in five categories annually. Established in 2003. Co-sponsored by Access to Architecture at the Lighthouse.

8851 ■ Royal Institute of British Architects
Harry Rich, Chief Exec.
66 Portland Pl.
London W1B 1AD, United Kingdom
Ph: 44 20 75805533
Fax: 44 20 72551541
E-mail: info@inst.riba.org
URL: http://www.architecture.com

8852 ■ Client of the Year Award
Recognizes the key role that a good client plays in the creation of fine architecture. Clients are nominated by members. A plaque is awarded annually.

8853 ■ Housing Design Awards
To recognize incomplete projects or completed schemes that reflect the highest standards in housing design. Developments may consist of private or public sector new buildings, conversions, or renovation schemes in England, provided they are of four or more dwellings. Schemes including non-residential uses may be entered provided housing constitutes a major element. Criteria include: relationship to surroundings and neighborhood; response to site constraints and opportunities; layout, grouping, and landscaping; planning of roads and footpaths; handling of garages and car parking; attention to safety, security, and accessibility; external appearance and internal planning; sustainability in construction; and finishes, detailing, and workmanship. Awarded annually to multiple recipients in the two categories of incomplete and completed projects. Awarded annually. Established in 1981.

8854 ■ Royal Gold Medal
This, the architectural world's most prestigious individual award, is given to recognize an architect, or group of architects, for work of high merit; or to recognize another distinguished person or group whose work has promoted either directly or indirectly the advancement of architecture. The award is approved by Her Majesty, the Queen, on the recommendation of RIBA. A gold medal is awarded annually. Established in 1848.

8855 ■ Royal Institute of British Architects Awards
For recognition of an outstanding building or group of buildings in the European Union completed up to two years and three months preceding the award. The architect responsible for the project must be a member of the RIBA, RIAS, or RSUA. For the purposes of these awards, the country is divided into 13 regions, and awards are given in each region at the discretion of the jury. Plaques are presented to the award winning buildings. Diplomas are given to the architect or firm of architects, the owner of the building, and the building contractor. Award-winning buildings receive a plaque. Awarded annually. Established in 1966.

8856 ■ Royal Institute of Navigation (Association Internationale des Instituts de Navigation)
David Barnes OBE, Pres.
1 Kensington Gore
London SW7 2AT, United Kingdom
Ph: 44 20 75913130
Fax: 44 20 75913131
E-mail: info@rin.org.uk
URL: http://www.rin.org.uk
Formerly: (1972) Institute of Navigation.

8857 ■ Honorary Fellow
To recognize distinguished persons in the field of navigation. The Council of the Institute makes the selection.

8858 ■ Royal Institute of Navigation Fellowship
To recognize individuals who fall into one of the following categories: those who achieve distinction as professional navigators; those who contribute to navigation by invention, research, literature, or in other ways, or who achieve distinction in the field of training; or those who perform exceptional feats of navigation. Awarded annually.

8859 ■ Royal Institution of Great Britain
Chris Rofe, CEO
21 Albemarle St.
London W1S 4BS, United Kingdom
Ph: 44 20 74092992
Ph: 44 20 76702991
Fax: 44 20 76702920
E-mail: ri@ri.ac.uk
URL: http://www.rigb.org

8860 ■ Henry Dale Prize
To a scientist of any discipline who has performed outstanding work on a biological topic.

8861 ■ Science Graduate of the Year
To young researchers in British and Irish universities.

8862 ■ Royal Institution of Naval Architects
Mr. Trevor Blakeley, Chief Exec.
10 Upper Belgrave St.
London SW1X 8BQ, United Kingdom
Ph: 44 20 72354622
Fax: 44 20 72595912
E-mail: hq@rina.org.uk
URL: http://www.rina.org.uk

8863 ■ Samuel Baxter Prize
For recognition of the best paper published by the Institution on the subject of safety by a member under the age of 30. The Council considers nominations after October 31. A monetary prize of up to £100 is awarded annually.

8864 ■ Calder Prize
For recognition of the best paper published by the Institution on the subject of small or high-speed craft by a member under the age of 30 The essay may also be considered for publication in *The Naval Architect*. Submissions are accepted until September 1. A monetary prize of £100 is awarded annually.

8865 ■ William Froude Medal
To recognize a person of any nationality who, in the judgment of the Council of the Institution, has made some conspicuous contribution to naval architecture and/or shipbuilding and whose outstanding services and personal achievements in this direction merit special consideration. Nominations may be made by November. A gold medal is awarded when merited. Established in 1955.

8866 ■ Froude Research Scholarship in Naval Architecture
To enable Graduate Members of the Institution who have been offered a post-graduate place at a university in the United Kingdom to carry out research into hydrodynamics or other problems related to maritime technology. British subjects and citizens of EEC countries under the age of 30 who are members of the Institution may

submit applications. A scholarship in the amount of £700 per year is awarded annually as funds permit. Established in 1948.

8867 ■ Small Craft Group Medal
To recognize individuals for significant contributions to the development of small craft. Awarded annually.

8868 ■ Wakenham Prize
For recognition of the best paper written by a Junior Member of the Institution and accepted for publication. Individuals under the age of 30 are eligible. Books, instruments, and computer hardware or software to the value of £100 are awarded annually.

8869 ■ Sir William White Scholarship
To enable British and EEC graduate students of naval architecture or marine engineering under the age of 30, who have at some time been employed in shipbuilding or marine engineering, and who have passed with merit through an approved course of study in a university or college, to carry out research work into problems connected with the design and construction of ships and their machinery, or to follow a post-graduate advanced course of study relevant to ship technology. A scholarship of £700 per annum plus fees is awarded and is tenable for two years subject to a satisfactory report at the end of the first year. Presented annually. Established in 1915 in memory of Sir William H. White, K.C.B., LL.D. (1845-1913), who was a distinguished Director of Naval Construction and an Honorary Vice-President of The Institution of Naval Architects.

8870 ■ Royal Meteorological Society
Paul Hardaker, Chief Exec.
104 Oxford Rd.
Reading RG1 7LL, United Kingdom
Ph: 44 118 9568500
Fax: 44 118 9568571
E-mail: chiefexec@rmets.org
URL: http://www.rmets.org

8871 ■ Gordon Manley Weather Prize
To recognize an outstanding contribution to the Society journal *Weather* through a paper or other outstanding service in the preceding five years that has furthered the public understanding of meteorology and oceanography. Awarded annually.

8872 ■ Mason Gold Medal
To recognize an individual for outstanding contributions to the understanding of the fundamental processes that determine the variability and predictability of weather and climate. A gold medal is awarded biennially in even-numbered years. First awarded in 2006 to Paul Mason.

8873 ■ Symons Memorial Medal
For recognition of distinguished work in the field of meteorology. Meteorologists of any nationality are eligible. An inscribed silver gilt medal is awarded biennially in odd-numbered years. Established in 1901 in memory of George J. Symons, F.R.S.

8874 ■ Royal Musical Association
Dr. Jeffrey Dean, Exec. Off.
4 Chandos Rd.
Chorlton-cum-Hardy
Manchester M21 0ST, United Kingdom
Fax: 44 161 8617543
E-mail: jeffrey.dean@stingrayoffice.com
URL: http://www.rma.ac.uk

8875 ■ Dent Medal
For recognition of an outstanding contribution and important original research in the field of musicology. Musicologists of any country are eligible. Candidates, who are normally under 40 years of age, are nominated by the Directorium

Awards are arranged in alphabetical order below their administering organizations

of the International Musicological Society and the Council of the Royal Musical Association. A bronze medal is awarded annually. Established in 1961.

8876 ■ Jerome Roche Prize
To recognize a distinguished article by a scholar in the early stages of his or her career. Articles may be considered from journals, edited volumes, or books of conference proceedings. Awarded annually. Established in 2001.

8877 ■ Royal National Rose Society
Rod Petty SM, Pres.
Chiswell Green Ln.
Hertfordshire
St. Albans AL2 3NR, United Kingdom
Ph: 44 1727 850461
Fax: 44 1727 850360
E-mail: mail@rnrs.org.uk
URL: http://www.rnrs.org

8878 ■ Dean Hole Medal
Recognizes an individual who has given services to the society and the rose. Awarded annually.

8879 ■ Royal Philatelic Society
Brian Trotter, Pres.
41 Devonshire Pl.
London W1G 6JY, United Kingdom
Ph: 44 20 74861044
Fax: 44 20 74860803
E-mail: secretary@rpsl.org.uk
URL: http://www.rpslcatalogue.org.uk/home.asp

8880 ■ Crawford Medal
For recognition of the most valuable and original contribution to the study and knowledge of philately published in book form during the two years preceding the award. The award is open to worldwide competition. A silver gilt medal is awarded annually. Established in 1920 in honor of the 26th Earl of Crawford KT, president of the society (1910-1913).

8881 ■ Tapling Medal
For recognition of the best paper that is written by a fellow or member and published in the society's journal The London Philatelist during the two years preceding the date of the award. A silver medal is awarded annually. Established in 1920 in honor of Thomas Keay Tapling MP, Vice President of the society (1881-1891).

8882 ■ Tilleard Medal
For recognition of the best large display of any aspect of philately given by one or two Fellows or Members of the Society during the previous two years. A silver medal is awarded annually. Established in 1920 in honor of John Alexander Tilleard M.V.O., Honorary Secretary of the society, (1894-1913).

8883 ■ Royal Philharmonic Society
John Gilhooly, Chm.
10 Stratford Pl.
London W1C 1BA, United Kingdom
Ph: 44 207 4918110
Fax: 44 207 4937463
E-mail: admin@royalphilharmonicsociety.org.uk
URL: http://www.royalphilharmonicsociety.org.uk

8884 ■ Emily Anderson Prize for Violin
To recognize outstanding violinists of any nationality under the age of 21. A monetary prize of £2,500 is awarded annually. Established in 1969 at the bequest of Emily Anderson, editor and translator of the letters of Mozart and Beethoven.

8885 ■ Sir John Barbirolli Memorial Scholarship
To offer financial assistance to purchase better instruments for worthy students. Priority is given to students entering into full-time study of music at Conservatoire level. Awarded annually.

8886 ■ Leslie Boosey Award
Awarded biennially in association with the Performing Right Society, the award honors an individual who has made an outstanding contribution to the furtherance of contemporary music in Britain. It is not given to those who are primarily practitioners, but rather to those who work 'back stage', including programmers, publishers, broadcasters, administrators, educationalists, and representatives from the recording industry. The recipient receives a bronze eagle commissioned from Elizabeth Frink.

8887 ■ Gold Medal
This, the Society's highest honor, is given to recognize outstanding musicianship over a period of years. A gold medal is awarded when merited. Established in 1870 to commemorate the centenary of Beethoven's birth.

8888 ■ Honorary Member
Honorary membership in the RPS is given in recognition of service to music. Awarded annually. First awarded in 1826.

8889 ■ Julius Isserlis Scholarship
To enable music students (between the ages of 15 and 25) in selected performing categories and of any nationality, but domiciled in the United Kingdom, to study outside the British Isles for two years. The scholarship is awarded by competition and candidate will be expected to prepare a recital program of 45 minutes in duration as well as give an outline of their proposed course of study abroad and two references. A scholarship of £30,000 (£15,000 per year for two years) is awarded biennially in odd-numbered years.

8890 ■ Music Awards
For recognition of outstanding achievement in brass music, judged by experts and by the public to be the best of their kind in the United Kingdom in the preceding calendar year. Awards are given in 13 categories: Audience Development, Chamber Music and Song, Chamber-Scale Composition, Concert Series and Festivals, Conductor, Creative Communication, Education, Ensemble, Instrumentalist, Large-Scale Composition, Opera and Music Theatre, Singer, and Young Artists. Winners receive a silver trophy. Awarded annually. Established in 1989. Formerly: RPS Charles Heidseick Award.

8891 ■ Royal Philosophical Society of Glasgow
Prof. Roddy Macsween, Pres.
160 Bothwell St.
Glasgow G2 7EL, United Kingdom
Ph: 44 141 5643841
Ph: 44 141 9464358
E-mail: info@royalphil.org
URL: http://www.royalphil.org

8892 ■ Graham Medal
Recognizes distinction in research in a chemical discipline. The recipient is invited to present the Graham Lecture. Awarded annually.

8893 ■ Kelvin Medal
Recognizes distinction in fields associated with Lord Kelvin, former Society President. Awarded annually.

8894 ■ Royal Photographic Society of Great Britain
Mr. Stuart Blake, Dir. Gen.
Fenton House
122 Wells Rd.
Bath BA2 3AH, United Kingdom
Ph: 44 1225 325733
E-mail: reception@rps.org
URL: http://www.rps.org

8895 ■ Centenary Medal
To recognize sustained and significant contribu-

tions to the art of photography. A gold medal (plus Honorary Fellowship) of the Society are awarded annually. Established in 1993.

8896 ■ Davies Medal
To recognize an individual for a significant contribution in the field of digital imaging science. Awarded annually. Established in 1998.

8897 ■ Terence Donovan Award
To recognize an individual for a major achievement by a British photographer in the field of commercial, advertising, or editorial work. Awarded annually.

8898 ■ Fenton Medal
To recognize an individual for outstanding contributions to the work of the Society. Both members and non-members of the Society are eligible for nomination. Awarded annually to one or more recipients. Established in 1980 to honor Roger Fenton, a Society founder who, for several years after its foundation, filled the post of Honorary Secretary.

8899 ■ Colin Ford Award
To recognize an individual who has contributed in a major way to the unique partnership between the Society and the Museum. Awarded annually. Established in 2003.

8900 ■ Honorary Fellowship
To recognize distinguished individuals having, from their position or attainments, an intimate connection with the science or fine art of photography. Both members and non-members of the Society are eligible for nomination. Awarded to up to eight recipients each year.

8901 ■ Hood Medal
To recognize an individual for meritorious performance in some branch of photography, with particular emphasis on any exhibit that revealed the most outstanding advance in photography for public service. Established in 1933 by Harold Hood.

8902 ■ J. Dudley Johnston Award
To recognize a major achievement in the field of photographic criticism or the history of photography. Awarded annually. Established in honor of the Society's former president.

8903 ■ Lumiere Award
To recognize an individual for a major achievement in British cinematography, video, or animation. Awarded annually. Established in 1999.

8904 ■ Member's Award
To recognize members who have rendered distinguished service to the Society or to photography for a number of years. Honorary life membership is awarded annually. Established in 2005.

8905 ■ Vic Odden Award
To recognize an individual for a notable achievement in the art of photography by a British photographer aged 35 years or younger. Awarded annually.

8906 ■ Progress Medal
This, the Society's premier award, recognizes an individual for any invention, research, publication, or other contribution that has resulted in an important advance in the scientific or technological development of photography or imaging in its widest sense. Both members and non-members of the Society are eligible for nominations. A silver medal is awarded annually. Established in 1878.

8907 ■ Royal Colleges Medal
To recognize an individual for outstanding contributions to photography in the service of medicine and surgery. Established in collabora-

Awards are arranged in alphabetical order below their administering organizations

tion with the Royal College of Physicians of London, the Royal College of Surgeons of England, and the Royal College of Obstetricians and Gynaecologists.

8908 ■ Saxby Award
To recognize an individual for achievement in the field of three-dimensional imaging. Awarded annually. Established in 1998.

8909 ■ Selwyn Award
To recognize individuals who have conducted research leading to the solution of one or more technical problems connected with imaging in general, or photography in particular. Scientists under the age of 35 are eligible. Established in 1994 in memory of E.W.H. Selwyn. Sponsored by The Imaging Science and Technology Group of The Society.

8910 ■ Royal School of Church Music
Lindsay Gray, Dir.
19 The Close
Salisbury
Wiltshire SP1 2EB, United Kingdom
Ph: 44 1722 424848
Fax: 44 1722 424849
E-mail: enquiries@rscm.com
URL: http://www.rscm.com

8911 ■ Harold Smart Competition
To recognize composers for works tailored to the technical resources of choirs with limited ability. A monetary award of £100 and possible publication of the winning composition are awarded annually. Established in 1988 to honor Dr. Harold Smart.

8912 ■ Royal Scottish Academy
Bill Scott, Pres.
The Mound
Edinburgh EH2 2EL, United Kingdom
Ph: 44 131 2256671
Ph: 44 131 6246277
Fax: 44 131 2206016
E-mail: info@royalscottishacademy.org
URL: http://www.royalscottishacademy.org

8913 ■ Annual Exhibition
To present a comprehensive cross section of contemporary art in Scotland. Features painting, sculpture, film making, photography, printmaking, architecture, and installation. The main body of the exhibition is by RSA Academicians and selected submissions from leading and emerging artists from across the country. The following major awards are presented: RSA Medal for Architecture - for recognition of outstanding work, preferably a drawing, and to encourage younger architects; RSA Guthrie Award - for the best work by a young artist (under 33 years of age who has passed the usual years of training in painting, sculpture or architecture); and RSA Benno Schotz Prize - for promising work by a young sculptor domiciled in Scotland. Held annually. Established in 1826.

8914 ■ Royal Scottish Geographical Society
Mike Robinson, Chief Exec.
Lord John Murray House
15-19 N Port
Perth PH1 5LU, United Kingdom
Ph: 44 1738 455050
E-mail: enquiries@rsgs.org
URL: http://www.rsgs.org

8915 ■ John Bartholomew Essay Competition
To recognize outstanding geography essays written by primary and secondary schools students throughout the former Strathclyde region of Scotland. Presentations may take one of three forms: written or typed essay of approximately 1,500 words; a PowerPoint presentation of up to 20 slides; and a video presentation lasting up to

10 minutes. Prizes are presented to the winning school and the winning pupil(s) in three age categories. Held annually.

8916 ■ Bartholomew Globe
For outstanding lifetime contributions to cartography in Scotland. Awarded periodically.

8917 ■ Coppock Research Medal
For recognition of outstanding contributions in the field of geographical enquiry and the development of geography as a discipline. Individuals of any nationality are eligible. A silver gilt medal is awarded annually. Established in 1931. Formerly: (2009) Centenary Medal.

8918 ■ Honorary Fellowship
To recognize an individual for distinguished contributions to the Society or to geography and public life in Scotland. Applications and nominations are not accepted. A certificate of Fellowship is awarded to one or more recipients each year. Established in 1888.

8919 ■ Livingstone Medal
For recognition of outstanding public service in which geography has played an important part, either by exploration, by administration, or in other areas where its principles have been applied to the benefit of the human race. Individuals of any nationality are eligible. No nominations or applications are accepted. A gold medal is awarded periodically. Established in 1901 by Mrs. A. Livingstone Bruce to honor David Livingstone.

8920 ■ Mungo Park Medal
In recognition of outstanding contributions to geographical knowledge through exploration and/or research, and/or work of a practical nature of benefit to humanity in potentially hazardous physical and/or social environments. Individuals of any nationality are eligible. A silver medal is awarded annually. Established in 1930.

8921 ■ Newbigin Prize
To recognize the author of the most meritorious learned article published in the *Scottish Geographical Journal* during the previous year, as judged by the Publication Committee of the Society. A monetary award of £100 is presented each year. Established in 1938 in memory of Marion Newbigin, Editor of the *Scottish Geographical Magazine*.

8922 ■ President's Medal
To recognize the achievement of a research geographer at a mid-career stage. Awarded annually. Established in 1989.

8923 ■ Professional Associateship
To recognize professional geographers, as well as to enhance the professional status of geography, to create a forum for professional geographers, and to increase the influence of geography in relation to Scottish affairs. Individuals who have academic training as geographers, plus at least three years of relevant employment experience are eligible. Recipients are selected based on recommendations of the validating committee of the Society. Awarded when merited.

8924 ■ Scottish Geographical Medal
To recognize work of conspicuous merit within the science of geography. Research, whether in the field or otherwise, or any other contribution or cumulative service to the advancement of science is considered. Individuals of any nationality are eligible. A gold medal is awarded annually. Established in 1890. Formerly: (1933) Gold Medal.

8925 ■ Joy Tivy Education Medal
To recognize an outstanding contribution to geographical education. Established in 2008.

8926 ■ University Medal
To recognize the best graduating honours geog-

raphy student in each of the Scottish universities, being intended to provide essential support to young researchers, and to encourage excellence in the field of geographical research in Scotland. Awarded annually. Established in 1993.

8927 ■ Royal Society
Sir Paul Nurse, Pres.
6-9 Carlton House Terr.
London SW1Y 5AG, United Kingdom
Ph: 44 20 74512500
Fax: 44 20 79302170
E-mail: info@royalsoc.ac.uk
URL: http://royalsociety.org

8928 ■ Armourers and Brasiers' Company Award
To recognize individuals for excellence in materials science and materials technology. A monetary prize of £2,000 and a silver medal are awarded biennially in even-numbered years. Established in 1984 by agreement with the Worshipful Company of Armourers & Brasiers'.

8929 ■ Buchanan Medal
To recognize individuals for distinguished original research in the broad area of medical sciences. A silver gilt medal and monetary prize of £1,000 are awarded biennially in even-numbered years. Established in 1897.

8930 ■ Copley Medal
This, the premier award of the Society, is presented for outstanding achievements in research in any branch of science. Each year, the award alternates between the physical sciences and the biological sciences. A silver gilt medal and monetary prize of £5,000 are awarded annually. Established in 1731.

8931 ■ Darwin Medal
To recognize individuals for work of acknowledged distinction in the broad area of biology in which Charles Darwin worked, notably in evolution, population biology, organismal biology, and biological diversity. A silver medal and monetary prize of £1,000 are awarded biennially in even-numbered years. Established in 1890.

8932 ■ Davy Medal
To recognize an individual for an outstandingly important recent discovery in any branch of chemistry. A bronze medal and monetary prize of £1,000 are awarded annually. Established in 1877.

8933 ■ Michael Faraday Prize
To recognize individuals for excellence in communicating science to audiences in the United Kingdom. Scientists and engineers in the U.K. are eligible. A monetary award of £2,500, a silver gilt medal, and an invitation to present a lecture at the Society's annual meeting are awarded each year. Established in 1986.

8934 ■ Rosalind Franklin Award
To recognize an individual for an outstanding contribution to any area of natural science, engineering, or technology (SET). Nominees are required to propose a project that they will undertake to raise the profile of women in SET in their organization or subject area. Recipient is expected to give a lecture as part of the university's lecture series. A grant of £30,000 and a silver gilt medal are awarded annually. Established in 2003.

8935 ■ Gabor Medal
To recognize an individual for outstanding interdisciplinary work between life sciences and other disciplines. A silver gilt medal and monetary prize of £1,000 are awarded annually. Established in 1989 in memory of Dennis Gabor, F.R. S., by his brother, Andre Gabor.

8936 ■ GlaxoSmithKline Prize and Lecture
In recognition of original contributions to medi-

Awards are arranged in alphabetical order below their administering organizations

cine and veterinary sciences published within ten years from the date of the award. A monetary prize of £2,500, a gold medal, and an invitation to present a lecture are awarded biennially in even-numbered years. Established in 1979 by a donation from the Wellcome Foundation Sponsored by GlaxoSmithKline plc. Formerly: (2002) Wellcome Prize.

8937 ■ Dorothy Hodgkin Fellowship
To provide financial support to exceptional scientists in the United Kingdom at an early state of their career who require a flexible working pattern due to personal circumstances such as parenting or caring responsibilities or health issues. Female candidates are encouraged. Covers all areas of the life and physical sciences, including engineering, but excluding clinical medicine. Provides funding to cover salary costs, estate costs, and indirect expenses for a maximum of four years. Research expenses (up to £13,000 for the first year and up to £11,000 annually thereafter) are provided. Awarded annually to approximately 10 recipients.

8938 ■ Hughes Medal
To recognize an original discovery in the physical sciences, particularly electricity and magnetism or their applications. A silver gilt medal and monetary prize of £1,000 are awarded annually. Established in 1902.

8939 ■ King Charles II Medal
To recognize foreign Heads of State for outstanding contributions to advancing scientific research in their country. Awarded only in exceptional circumstances. A silver-gilt medal is presented, generally on the occasion of State Visits. Established in 1997.

8940 ■ Kohn Award
To reward practicing scientists or science communicators in their engagement with society in matters of science and its societal dimension. A monetary prize of £2,500, a grant of £7,500 for science communication activities, and a silver gilt medal are awarded annually. Supported by the Kohn Foundation.

8941 ■ Leverhulme Medal
To recognize an outstandingly significant contribution in the field of pure or applied chemistry or engineering, including chemical engineering. A gold medal and monetary prize of £2,000 are awarded triennially. Established in 1960 on the tercentenary of the Society. Sponsored by the Leverhulme Trust Fund.

8942 ■ Mullard Award
To recognize a young individual for an outstanding academic record in any area of natural science, engineering, or technology, and whose work is currently making or has the potential to make a contribution to national prosperity in the United Kingdom. Eligible candidates should be in early to mid-career stages. A monetary award of £2,000, a travel grant of £2,000, and a silver gilt medal are awarded biennially in odd-numbered years. Established in 1967.

8943 ■ Royal Medals
These medals, also known as the Queen's Medals, are given to recognize important contributions to natural and applied sciences. Three medals are presented annually: two for contributions to the advancement of natural knowledge and the other for distinguished contributions in the applied sciences. Silver medals and a monetary prize of £5,000 are awarded annually by the Sovereign upon the recommendation of the Council of the Royal Society.

8944 ■ Royal Society and Academie des sciences Microsoft Award
To recognize and support scientists working in Europe for significant contributions to the advancement of science through computational methods. Research scientists and engineers of any nationality who have resided in Europe for at least 12 months prior to the award are eligible. A trophy and an award of 250,000 Euros for research (7,500 of which constitutes prize money) is awarded.

8945 ■ Royal Society Pfizer Award
To recognize and support a young scientist based in Africa for innovative contributions to the biological sciences. A grant of £60,000 for a research project, and a monetary prize of £5,000 for the recipient are awarded annually. Sponsored by Pfizer Ltd.

8946 ■ Royal Society Winton Prizes for Science Books
To recognize the very best in popular science writing for adults and children. Two prizes are awarded annually: the General Prize, for a book intended for general readership, and the Junior Prize, for a book written for children under the age of 14. A monetary prize of £10,000 is awarded to the winner in each category, with an award of £1,000 for each of six finalists. Awarded annually. Established in 1988. Formerly: (2011) Royal Society Prizes for Science Books.

8947 ■ Rumford Medal
To recognize an outstandingly important recent discovery in the field of thermal or optical properties of matter made by a scientist working in Europe. A silver gilt medal and monetary prize of £1,000 are awarded biennially in even-numbered years. Established in 1800.

8948 ■ Sylvester Medal
To encourage mathematical research by an early- to mid-career scientist. A bronze medal and monetary prize of £1,000 are awarded biennially in even-numbered years. Established in 1901 in honor of James Joseph Sylvester.

8949 ■ Royal Society for Public Health
Prof. Richard Parish, Chief Exec.
John Snow House
59 Mansell St.
London E1 8AN, United Kingdom
Ph: 44 20 72657300
Fax: 44 20 72657301
E-mail: rsph@rsph.org
URL: http://www.rsph.org.uk
Formerly: (2004) Royal Society of Health.

8950 ■ Lord Cohen Gold Medal
For recognition of outstanding work in the field of health. A gold medal is awarded triennially.

8951 ■ Donaldson Gold Medal
To recognize an outstanding worker in any of the professions and disciplines identified with health. Awarded triennially.

8952 ■ Honorary Fellows Award
To recognize any person actively engaged and distinguished in the promotion of health. Awarded annually.

8953 ■ Ian Macmillan Prize
To recognize the individual who attains the highest marks in the RSPH exams. Awarded annually.

8954 ■ Benjamin Ward Richardson Gold Medal
To recognize outstanding innovative work in the field of food hygiene. Awarded triennially.

8955 ■ Vice Presidents Emiriti Award
To recognize Society members' meritorious service to the Society. Awarded annually.

8956 ■ Royal Society for the Encouragement of Arts, Manufactures, and Commerce
Matthew Taylor, Chief Exec.
8 John Adam St.
London WC2N 6EZ, United Kingdom
Ph: 44 20 79305115
Ph: 44 20 74516883
Fax: 44 20 78385805
E-mail: general@rsa.org.uk
URL: http://www.thersa.org

8957 ■ Albert Medal
To recognize individuals who contribute to social innovation. A gold medal is awarded annually. Established 1864 in memory of Prince Albert (1819-61), a former President of the Society.

8958 ■ Benjamin Franklin Medal
To recognize a global 'big thinker' who has shifted public debate in an innovative way and contributed to furthering public discourse on human progress. Awarded annually. Established in 1956.

8959 ■ Royal Designer for Industry Award
To encourage a high standard of industrial design and enhance the status of designers. It is awarded to individuals who have achieved sustained excellence in aesthetic and efficient design for industry. Such work can range from fashion to engineering, theatre to product design, graphics to environmental design. Only 200 designers may hold the distinction Royal Designer for Industry at any time. In addition, the Society confers on a limited number of distinguished international industrial designers the award of Honorary Royal Designer for Industry (HonRDI). Established in 1936.

8960 ■ Royal Society for the Prevention of Accidents
Jo Bullock, Contact
RoSPA House
28 Calthorpe Rd.
Edgbaston
Birmingham B15 1RP, United Kingdom
Ph: 44 121 2482000
Ph: 44 121 2482233
Fax: 44 121 2482001
E-mail: help@rospa.com
URL: http://www.rospa.com

8961 ■ MORR Trophy
For the best performance by a MORR (Managing Occupational Road Risk) Award winner. Awarded annually.

8962 ■ Sector Awards
To recognize the most outstanding performance in health and safety by a company or organization within a particular industry sector. Entrants must demonstrate four years of consistently excellent or continuously improving health and safety performance with a high standard of safety policy and commitment. An engraved trophy is awarded annually in each of several categories. Established in 1993.

8963 ■ Workforce Involvement in Safety and Health Trophy
To recognize the Sector Award nominee who demonstrates the best employee involvement in their organization's health and safety management performance. Awarded annually. Sponsored by Springfields Fuels Ltd.

8964 ■ Royal Society for the Prevention of Cruelty to Animals
Wilberforce Way
Southwater, Horsham
West Sussex RH13 9RS, United Kingdom
Ph: 44 300 1234 555
Fax: 44 303 1230 284
URL: http://www.rspca.org.uk

8965 ■ Community Animal Welfare Footprints Achiever Awards
To reward and promote good practice in animal welfare by local authorities and housing providers in England and Wales. Covers four areas of

Awards are arranged in alphabetical order below their administering organizations

work (footprints) that impact on animal welfare: stray dog services, housing, contingency planning, and animal welfare principles. Gold, silver, and bronze prizes are presented. In addition, the Innovator in Animal Welfare Award may be presented. Awarded annually. Established in 2008.

8966 ■ Good Business Awards
To promote animal welfare as a facet of ethical business policy in the United Kingdom by honoring companies in the fashion and food industries that have demonstrated innovation and excellence in advancing animal welfare. Awarded annually. Established in 2005.

8967 ■ Young Photographer Awards
To encourage young people's interest in photography and show their appreciation and understanding of the animals around them. Open to United Kingdom youth under age 19. In addition to an overall winner, awards are presented in the following categories: Under 12 Years, from 12 to 18 Years, Pet Personalities, and the Olympus Portfolio. Awarded annually. Established in 1991.

8968 ■ Royal Society of British Artists
James Horton, Pres.
17 Carlton House Terr.
London SW1Y 5BD, United Kingdom
Ph: 44 20 79306844
Fax: 44 20 78397830
E-mail: info@mallgalleries.com
URL: http://www.royalsocietyofbritishartists.org.uk

8969 ■ De Laszlo Medal
For recognition of the best painting or sculpture at the Society's Annual Exhibition. A medal is awarded annually. Established in 1910.

8970 ■ St. Cuthbert's Mill Award for Works on Paper
To recognize the best work on paper at the Society's Annual Exhibition. Awarded annually.

8971 ■ Royal Society of Chemistry
Prof. David Phillips PhD, Pres.
Burlington House
Piccadilly
London W1J 0BA, United Kingdom
Ph: 44 20 74378656
Fax: 44 20 74378883
URL: http://www.rsc.org
Formerly: Chemical Society.

8972 ■ Applied Catalysis Award
To recognize an individual for creativity and excellence in novel approaches or uses of catalysis in industry. A medal, a certificate, and a monetary award of £2,000 are awarded biennially in even-numbered years. Established in 2008.

8973 ■ Applied Inorganic Chemistry Award
For outstanding contributions to the development of applications in any branch of organic chemistry. A medal, a certificate, and a monetary award of £2,000 are awarded biennially in odd-numbered years. Established in 2008.

8974 ■ Award for Service
To honor an individual for outstanding non-academic service to the Society. Awarded annually to one or more recipients. Established in 1981.

8975 ■ Bader Award
To recognize an individual for outstanding achievement in organic chemistry. Open to U.K. and Irish academics only. A medal, certificate, and monetary prize of £2,000 are awarded annually. Established in 1989 by an endowment from Dr. Alfred Bader.

8976 ■ Barrer Award
To recognize the most meritorious recent pure or applied work in the field of porous inorganic materials. Open to U.K. and international scientists; membership is not required. A medal, certificate, and monetary prize of £500 are awarded triennially. Established in 1983.

8977 ■ Sir Derek Barton Gold Medal
To recognize work in any area of organic chemistry. Nominees must have had work published after 60 years of age. A medal, a certificate, and a monetary award of £2,000 are awarded biennially in even-numbered years. Established in 2001 to commemorate the life and work of Sir Derek Barton.

8978 ■ Beilby Medal and Prize
To recognize scientists or engineers for original work of exceptional significance in the fields of chemical engineering, applied materials science, energy efficiency, or a related topic. Preference is given to candidates under the age of 40. A medal, certificate, and monetary prize of £1,000 are awarded annually. Established in 1924 in memory of Sir George Beilby, and co-administered by the Society of Chemical Industry and the Institute of Materials.

8979 ■ Ronald Belcher Award
To encourage graduate students to make a positive contribution to, and to take an active interest in, the profession of analytical chemistry. Open to graduate students of British and Irish universities. Recipient is required to give a presentation of his/her work at the Analytical Research Forum Meeting. A certificate and monetary prize of £500 are awarded annually. Established in 1983 in memory of Professor Ronald Belcher. Formerly: Ronald Belcher Memorial Lectureship.

8980 ■ Bioinorganic Chemistry Award
To recognize outstanding research in any area of bioinorganic chemistry. Nominees must be in mid-career, and no older than 55 years. A medal, a certificate, and a monetary award of £2,000 are awarded biennially in odd-numbered years. Established in 2008.

8981 ■ Bioorganic Chemistry Award
To recognize excellence in any area of bioorganic chemistry. A medal, a certificate, and a monetary award of £2,000 are awarded biennially in even-numbered years. Established in 2008.

8982 ■ Joseph Black Award
To recognize a young scientist in any field related to the practice and teaching of analytical science. Nominees must be in mid-career, and no older than 40 years. A medal, a certificate, and a monetary award of £2,000 are awarded annually. Established in 2008.

8983 ■ Bourke Award
To enable distinguished scientists from overseas to lecture in the United Kingdom in the field of physical chemistry or chemical physics. An honorarium of £2,000, a silver medal, and a certificate are awarded annually. Established in 1954 in memory of Lieutenant Colonel Bourke, a benefactor of the Society. Formerly: Bourke Lectureship.

8984 ■ Robert Boyle Prize for Analytical Science
To honor an scientist who has made outstanding contributions to analytical science, A medal, certificate, and monetary prize of £5,000 are awarded biennially in even-numbered years. Established in 1981. Formerly: Robert Boyle Medal.

8985 ■ S. F. Boys - A Rahman Award
To recognize an individual for outstanding innovative research in the area of computational chemistry, including both quantum chemistry and molecular simulations. Open to individuals of any age and nationality. Membership in the Society is not a requirement. A monetary award of £2,000, a certificate, and a silver medal are presented biennially in odd-numbered years. Established through funds derived from the 1987 International Conference on the Impact of Supercomputers on Chemistry. Formerly: S. F. Boys - A Rahman Lectureship.

8986 ■ Malcolm Campbell Memorial Prize
To recognize an individual or team at a United Kingdom academic or industry organization that has made significant contributions to biological chemistry. A medal, a certificate, and a monetary award of £2,000 are awarded biennially in odd-numbered years.

8987 ■ Capps Green Zomaya Award
To recognize exceptional work in medicinal or computational medicinal chemistry. U.K. and international scientists 40 years of age or younger are eligible. A monetary award of £1,000 and a certificate are awarded biennially in even-numbered years. Established in 2002 to honor the memory of chemists Nigel Capps, Richard Green, and Alex Zomaya.

8988 ■ Catalysis in Organic Chemistry Award
For the discovery or development of a catalytic process that has applications in organic chemistry. A medal, a certificate, and a monetary award of £2,000 are awarded biennially in even-numbered years. Established in 2008.

8989 ■ Centenary Prizes
To promote the interchange of chemists between Britain and overseas countries. Any scientist normally working outside of the United Kingdom is eligible. Three awards of a medal, a certificate, a monetary prize of £5,000, and the opportunity to visit a number of scientific centers in the British Isles are presented annually. Established in 1949 by the British Chemical Industry to commemorate the centenary of the Chemical Society. Formerly: Centenary Lectureships.

8990 ■ Joseph Chatt Award
To recognize an individual who has made a contribution to interdisciplinary work in the areas which fall between inorganic chemistry and biochemistry. There are no age or nationality restrictions. A medal, certificate, and monetary prize of £2,000 are awarded biennially in even-numbered years. Established in 1995. Formerly: Joseph Chatt Lectureship.

8991 ■ Chemical Dynamics Award
For outstanding innovative research on the dynamics of molecules. A medal, a certificate, and a monetary award of £2,000 are awarded annually.

8992 ■ Chemistry of Transition Metals Award
To recognize outstanding research in any area of the chemistry of d-and f-block elements. Nominees must be in their early careers, and no older than 40 years. A medal, a certificate, and a monetary award of £2,000 are awarded biennially in even-numbered years.

8993 ■ Chemistry World Entrepreneur of the Year
To recognize an individual for the commercialization of chemistry research. U.K. residents are eligible. A trophy, a certificate, and a monetary award of £4,000 are awarded annually. Recipient is also be featured in the magazine Chemistry World.

8994 ■ Corday-Morgan Prize
To recognize meritorious contributions to experimental chemistry. British chemists under 40 years of age are eligible. Up to three awards, each consisting of a monetary prize of £5,000, a certificate, and a silver medal, are presented annually for work in different branches of chemistry. Established in 1949.

Awards are arranged in alphabetical order below their administering organizations

8995 ■ Rita and John Cornforth Award
To recognize and support scientists working as part of collaborative research teams in chemistry and the life sciences. A medal, a certificate, and a monetary award of £2,000 are awarded annually. Established in 2008.

8996 ■ Corrosion Science Award
For research leading to new concepts in corrosion science and technology. U.K. and Commonwealth-based scientists are eligible. Medals, certificates, and monetary prizes of £500 are awarded biennially in even-numbered years. Sponsored by Chemetall Ltd.

8997 ■ Creativity in Industry Prize
To recognize an individual for outstanding achievement in the chemical sciences industry. A memento, a certificate, and a monetary prize of £5,000 are awarded biennially in odd-numbered years. Established in 2008.

8998 ■ Dalton Young Researchers Award
To recognize achievements by young research chemists. Nominees should be under 27 years of age. A medal, a certificate, and a monetary prize of £1,000 are awarded annually.

8999 ■ Peter Day Award
For outstanding contributions to, and advancement of, materials chemistry. Award alternates between broad areas of soft matter and broad areas of extended solids. Mid-career members who are 55 years of age or younger are eligible. A medal, a certificate, and a monetary award of £2,000 are awarded annually. Established in 2008.

9000 ■ de Gennes Prize
For exceptional work in the field of materials chemistry. A medal, a certificate, and a monetary award of £5,000 are awarded biennially in odd-numbered years. Established in 2008.

9001 ■ Distinguished Service Award
To recognize exceptional and sustained service to the Society's Analytical Division. Open to members who have served the division for at least ten years. A certificate and a monetary award of £1,000 are awarded annually.

9002 ■ Education Award
To recognize exceptional contributions to education in the chemical sciences. A medal, a certificate, and a monetary award of £2,000 are awarded annually. Established in 2008.

9003 ■ Environment Prize
To recognize outstanding contributions to chemical sciences in the areas of environment, sustainability, and energy. A medal, a certificate, and a monetary award of £5,000 are awarded biennially in odd-numbered years. Established in 2008.

9004 ■ Environment, Sustainability and Energy Forum Early Career Award
Recognizes young scientists for exceptional contributions to the chemical sciences in the areas of environment, sustainability, and energy. Nominees must be in their early careers and no older than 40 years. A medal, a certificate, and a monetary award of £2,000 are awarded biennially in odd-numbered years. Established in 2008.

9005 ■ Faraday Lectureship Prize
To recognize a physical/theoretical chemist. A bronze medal, a certificate, a monetary prize of £5,000, and an invitation to present the Faraday Lecture are awarded biennially in even-numbered years. Established in 1867 in memory of Michael Faraday, a Fellow of the Society from 1842 to 1867.

9006 ■ Flavours and Fragrances Award
For research leading to new flavours or fragrances. Open to U.K. and Commonwealth-based scientists who are no older than 55 years.

A medal, a certificate, and a monetary prize of £500 are awarded biennially in odd-numbered years. Established in 2002. Sponsored by AkzoNobel.

9007 ■ Frankland Award
For recognition of meritorious contributions to pure and applied research in the field of organo-metallic chemistry or coordination chemistry. Candidates must be in their mid-career. A medal, certificate, and monetary prize of £2,000 are presented biennially in even-numbered years. Established in 1982. Formerly: Sir Edward Frankland Prize Lectureship.

9008 ■ Sir Edward Frankland Fellowship
For the encouragement of research in organo-metallic chemistry or co-ordination chemistry of transition metals. A monetary prize of £2,000, a medal, and a certificate are awarded biennially in odd-numbered years. Established in 1984.

9009 ■ Geochemistry Award
For studies on the chemical composition of the earth. Nominees should be mid-career and no older than 55 years. A medal, a certificate, and a monetary prize of £500 are awarded biennially in odd-numbered years. Established in 2002. Sponsored by BP Exploration.

9010 ■ Gibson-Fawcett Award
Recognizes original and independent contributions to materials chemistry. Nominees should be in their early careers and no older than 40 years. A medal, a certificate, and a monetary award of £2,000 are awarded biennially in even-numbered years. Established in 2008.

9011 ■ John B. Goodenough Award
Recognizes exceptional and sustained contributions to the field of materials chemistry. A medal, a certificate, and a monetary award of £2,000 are awarded biennially in odd-numbered years. Established in 2008. Honors the chemistry work of John Bannister Goodenough.

9012 ■ Green Chemistry Award
Recognizes the design, development, or implementation of novel chemical processes or products. A medal, a certificate, and a monetary award of £2,000 are awarded biennially in even-numbered years. Established in 2001.

9013 ■ Harrison-Meldola Memorial Prize
To recognize the most meritorious and promising original investigations in chemistry and published results of those investigations. Candidates should be 32 years of age or younger, and should be working in the United Kingdom. A medal, certificate, and monetary prize of £5,000 are awarded annually to up to three recipients. Established in 1922 in memory of Colonel Edward Frank Harrison and Raphael Meldola. Formerly: (2008) Edward Harrison Memorial Prize; Medola Medal and Prize.

9014 ■ Haworth Memorial Lectureship
To recognize an eminent chemist in the area of carbohydrate chemistry. The lecture deals with the advances in any subject of carbohydrate chemistry including contributions that further the better understanding of other branches of chemical science. A monetary prize of £500, a silver medal, and a lectureship are awarded annually. Established in 1969 in memory of Sir Norman Haworth, a President of the Society. Administered by the RSC Carbohydrate Group.

9015 ■ Norman Heatley Award
To recognize and encourage inter- and multi-disciplinary research between chemistry and the life sciences. A medal, a certificate, and a monetary award of £2,000 are awarded annually. Established in 2008.

9016 ■ Higher Education Teaching Award
To recognize outstanding teaching skills, includ-

ing the development of innovative materials or methods. A medal, a certificate, and a monetary award of £2,000 are awarded annually.

9017 ■ Homogeneous Catalysis Award
To recognize outstanding homogeneous catalysis. A medal, a certificate, and a monetary award of £2,000 are awarded biennially in odd-numbered years. Established in 2001.

9018 ■ Inorganic Mechanisms Award
To recognize studies leading to a better understanding of reaction mechanisms in any branch of inorganic chemistry. A medal, a certificate, and a monetary award of £2,000 are awarded biennially in odd-numbered years. Established in 2008.

9019 ■ Inspiration and Industry Awards
To recognize an individual in industry for the outreach, promotion, or teaching of chemical sciences. Open to U.K. residents. A memento, a certificate, and a monetary award of £2,000 are awarded annually. Established in 2008.

9020 ■ Interdisciplinary Prizes
To draw attention to the importance of interdisciplinary studies, particularly those of public interest, involving chemistry and one or more other sciences, and to the Society's interest in the willingness to encourage such work that reaches across traditional boundaries; and to enable work that involves chemists working with scientists from different disciplines to be appropriately rewarded and publicized. A medal, certificate, and monetary prize of £5,000 are awarded to up to two recipients annually. Established in 1986.

9021 ■ John Jeyes Award
To recognize the individual who has made the most meritorious contributions to the general theme of "Chemistry in Relation to the Environment." A monetary prize of £2,000, a medal, and a certificate are awarded biennially in even-numbered years. Established in 1976 by the Jeyes Group in memory of John Jeyes. Formerly: John Jeyes Lectureship.

9022 ■ Khorana Prize
Recognizes outstanding achievement in the interface of chemistry and life sciences. A medal, a certificate, and a monetary award of £5,000 are awarded biennially in even-numbered years. Established in 2008.

9023 ■ Jeremy Knowles Award
To recognize and encourage inter- and multi-disciplinary research between chemistry and the life sciences. A medal, a certificate, and a monetary award of £2,000 are awarded annually. Established in 2008.

9024 ■ Stephanie L. Kwolek Award
To recognize exceptional contributions to materials chemistry by a scientist working outside the United Kingdom. A medal, a certificate, and a monetary award of £2,000 are awarded biennially in even-numbered years. Established in 2008.

9025 ■ Liversidge Award
For outstanding contributions to physical chemistry. A medal, a certificate, and a monetary award of £2,000 are awarded biennially in even-numbered years. Established in 1928.

9026 ■ Longstaff Prize
To recognize a member of the Society who has done the most to promote the science of chemistry by research. A monetary prize of £5,000, a medal, and a certificate are awarded triennially. Established in 1881 in memory of Dr. George Dixon Longstaff, an original member and benefactor of the Society. Formerly: Longstaff Medal.

9027 ■ Lord Lewis Prize
For distinctive and distinguished chemical or scientific achievements along with contributions

Awards are arranged in alphabetical order below their administering organizations

to the development of science policy. A medal, a certificate, and a monetary award of £5,000 are awarded biennially in even-numbered years. Established in 2008. Honors the contributions of Lord Lewis to chemistry and the advancement of science policy.

9028 ■ Main Group Chemistry Award
Recognizes outstanding research in any area of the chemistry of the s and p block elements. A medal, a certificate, and a monetary award of £2,000 are awarded biennially in even-numbered years. Established in 1970.

9029 ■ Marlow Award
To recognize an individual for physical chemistry or chemical physics. Candidates must be aged 35 or younger. A medal, certificate, and monetary prize of £2,000 are awarded annually. Established in 1957. Formerly: Marlow Medal and Prize.

9030 ■ Material for Industry - Derek Birchall Award
To recognize an individual for creativity and excellence in the application of materials chemistry in industry. A medal, a certificate, and a monetary award of £2,000 are awarded biennially in odd-numbered years. Established in 2008.

9031 ■ Merck Award
For contributions to any area of chemistry by a researcher under 45 years of age. A medal, a certificate, and a monetary award of £2,000 are awarded annually. Established in 2009.

9032 ■ Ludwig Mond Award
To recognize accomplishments in the general area of inorganic chemistry. A medal, certificate, and monetary prize of £2,000 are awarded annually. Established in 1981 through an endowment from Imperial Chemical Industries. Formerly: Ludwig Mond Lectureship.

9033 ■ Nyholm Prize for Education
To recognize an individual for outstanding accomplishments in education relating to the chemical sciences. A medal, certificate, and monetary prize of £5,000 are awarded biennially in odd-numbered years. Established in 1973 in memory of Sir Ronald Nyholm, a President of the Society. Formerly: Sir Ronald Nyholm Lectureship.

9034 ■ Organic Industry Chemistry Award
Recognizes an individual or team for an application of organic chemistry in an industrial context. A medal, a certificate, and a monetary award of £2,000 are awarded biennially in odd-numbered years. Established in 2008.

9035 ■ Organic Stereochemistry Award
For studies of stereochemistry related to structure, reactivity, or synthesis. A medal, a certificate, and a monetary award of £2,000 are awarded biennially in odd-numbered years. Established in 2008.

9036 ■ Organometallic Chemistry Award
To recognize any aspect of the organic chemistry of the main group and transition metals. A medal, a certificate, and a monetary award of £2,000 are awarded biennially in odd-numbered years.

9037 ■ Pedler Award
To recognize contributions to any area of organic chemistry by a researcher under the age of 55. A monetary prize of £2,000, a silver medal, and a certificate are awarded annually. Established in 1927 in memory of Sir Alexander Pedler, a benefactor of the Society. Sponsored by Pfizer Ltd. Formerly: Pedler Lectureship.

9038 ■ Perkin Prize for Organic Chemistry
To recognize sustained achievement and originality in any area of organic chemistry. A medal,

a certificate, and a monetary award of £5,000 are awarded biennially in odd-numbered years. Established in 2008. Sponsored by AstraZeneca.

9039 ■ Physical Organic Chemistry Award
For achievement regarding the relationship between structure and molecular behaviors in chemistry. A medal, a certificate, and a monetary award of £2,000 are awarded biennially in odd-numbered years. Established in 2008.

9040 ■ Process Technology Award
Recognizes novel approaches to chemical process technology in industry that lead to superior process economics and sustainability. A medal, a certificate, and a monetary award of £2,000 are awarded biennially in odd-numbered years.

9041 ■ Theophilus Redwood Award
To recognize a leading analytical scientist. A medal, certificate, and monetary prize of £2,000 are awarded annually. Established in 1972 to commemorate the 1874 formation of the Society of Public Analysts (now the Analytical Division of the Royal Society of Chemistry). Formerly: Theophilus Redwood Lectureship.

9042 ■ Charles Rees Award
To recognize excellence in the field of heterocyclic chemistry. A medal, a certificate, and a monetary award of £2,000 are awarded biennially in even-numbered years. Established in 2008. Honors Charles Wayne Rees CBE, FRE who dedicated his career to heterocyclic chemistry.

9043 ■ Robert Robinson Award
To recognize contributions to any area of organic chemistry by a researcher over the age of 55. A monetary prize of £2,000, a silver medal, and a certificate are awarded annually. Established in 1962 in honor of Sir Robert Robinson on his seventieth birthday. Formerly: Robert Robinson Lectureship.

9044 ■ Schools Education Award
To recognize a teacher or other education professional for significant contributions to the teaching of chemical sciences. A medal, a certificate, and a monetary award of £2,000 are awarded annually.

9045 ■ Society for Analytical Chemistry Silver Medal
To encourage young scientists working in any field covering the practices and teaching of the analytical sciences. Scientists under the age of 35 are eligible. A monetary prize of £500 and a silver medal are awarded annually. Established in 1973.

9046 ■ Soft Matter and Biophysical Chemistry Award
Recognizes outstanding and innovative research in condensed matter and/or the application of physical-chemical techniques in biological problems. A medal, a certificate, and a monetary award of £2,000 are awarded annually. Established in 2008.

9047 ■ George and Christine Sosnovsky Award in Cancer Therapy
To recognize outstanding achievement in the prevention, control, and cure of cancers using chemotherapy, including gene and immunotherapy. A medal, a certificate, and a monetary award of £2,000 are awarded biennially in even-numbered years. Honors George and Christine Sosnovsky for their contributions to chemical sciences.

9048 ■ Spiers Memorial Award
To recognize an exceptional contributor to one of the year's four Faraday Discussions, which are international discussion meetings that focus on rapidly developing areas of physical

chemistry. An honorarium of £2,000, a silver medal, and a lectureship are awarded annually. Established in 1928 by the Faraday Society in memory of F. S. Spiers, the first Secretary of the Society.

9049 ■ Sir George Stokes Award
Recognizes outstanding and sustained contributions to analytical science by an individual in a complimentary field. A medal, a certificate, and a monetary award of £2,000 are awarded biennially in odd-numbered years. Sponsored by the Analytical Chemistry Trust Fund.

9050 ■ Supramolecular Chemistry Award
To recognize research leading to the design of functionally useful supramolecular species. A medal, a certificate, and a monetary award of £2,000 are awarded biennially in even-numbered years. Established in 2001.

9051 ■ Surfaces and Interfaces Award
For outstanding and innovative research on the behaviour of chemical systems at surfaces or interfaces. A medal, a certificate, and a monetary award of £2,000 are awarded annually. Established in 2008.

9052 ■ Sustainable Energy Award
For chemical science contributions to sustainable energy. A medal, a certificate, and a monetary award of £2,000 are awarded biennially in odd-numbered years. Established in 2008.

9053 ■ Sustainable Water Award
To recognize chemical science contributions to sustainable water. A medal, a certificate, and a monetary award of £2,000 are awarded biennially in even-numbered years. Established in 2008.

9054 ■ Synthetic Organic Chemistry Award
To recognize the development of new methods or strategies useful in the construction of organic molecules. A medal, a certificate, and a monetary award of £2,000 are awarded biennially in odd-numbered years.

9055 ■ Teamwork in Innovation Award
To recognize and encourage innovation and creativity in chemistry through teamwork in industry. Teams in industry and academia in the United Kingdom are eligible. A memento, a certificate, and a monetary prize of £4,000 is awarded annually.

9056 ■ Tilden Prizes
To recognize individuals for advances in chemistry. A medal, certificate, and monetary award of £5,000 are awarded to three recipients annually. Established in 1939 in memory of Sir William Agustus Tilden, a President of the Society. Formerly: Tilden Lectureships.

9057 ■ Toxicology Award
To recognize chemical science contributions to occupational and environmental toxicology. A medal, a certificate, and a monetary award of £2,000 are awarded biennially in odd-numbered years. Established in 2008.

9058 ■ Young Industrialist of the Year Award
To recognize an individual for significant contributions to the industry early in their career. Nominees should be no older than 36 years. A memento, a certificate, and a monetary award of £2,000 are awarded annually. Established in 2008.

9059 ■ Royal Society of Edinburgh
Dr. William Duncan, Chief Exec.
22-26 George St.
Edinburgh EH2 2PQ, United Kingdom
Ph: 44 131 2405000
Ph: 44 131 2405009

Awards are arranged in alphabetical order below their administering organizations

Fax: 44 131 2405024
URL: http://www.royalsoced.org.uk

9060 ■ David Anderson-Berry Medal
For recognition of recent work on the effects of X-rays and other forms of radiation on living tissues. Published work will be taken into consideration if submitted to the Society with the application. A medal is awarded every five years. Established in 1930.

9061 ■ BP Prize Lectureship in the Humanities
To recognize an individual working in a Scottish institution of higher education. Awards are given in alternate years in the following categories: languages, literature, and the arts; archaeological and historical studies; social studies; and philosophy, theology, and law. A monetary prize of £500 plus a lecture to be held at the society is awarded biennially. Established in 1990 by British Petroleum (BP).

9062 ■ W. S. Bruce Medal
For recognition of some notable contribution to the natural sciences, such as zoology, botany, geology, meteorology, oceanography, and geography. The contributions must be in the nature of new knowledge and be the outcome of a personal visit to polar regions on the part of the recipient. The recipient should preferably be at the outset of his or her career as an investigator. A medal is awarded every five years. Established in 1923 to commemorate the work of Dr. W. S. Bruce as an explorer and scientific investigator in polar regions.

9063 ■ Bruce-Preller Prize Lectureship
To recognize an outstanding scientist. The subject is to be, in sequence, in earth sciences, engineering sciences, medical sciences, and biological sciences. An honorarium is awarded biennially in odd-numbered years. Established in 1929 by the bequest of the late Dr. Charles Du Riche Preller.

9064 ■ Alexander Ninian Bruce Prize
For recognition of meritorious research in medical or veterinary physiology. Individuals under 40 years of age and working in a Scottish institution are eligible. A monetary prize of £250 is awarded every five years. Established in 1991.

9065 ■ Caledonian Research Foundation Prize Lectureship in Biomedical Sciences and Arts and Letters
To recognize an individual who has an international reputation in the fields of biological sciences and arts and letters subjects. A monetary prize of £1500 plus a lecture to be given by the winner at various locations throughout Scotland is awarded, alternating annually between Biomedical Sciences and Arts & Letters subjects. Established in 1990 and sponsored by Caledonian Research Foundation.

9066 ■ Henry Dryerre Prize Lectureship
To recognize a distinguished scholar in the field of medical research. A monetary prize of £500 plus a lecture to be held at the Society is awarded quadrennially. Established in 1991 in honor of Professor Henry Dryerre.

9067 ■ Henry Duncan Prize Lectureship
For recognition of a work of a scholar of any nationality for work of international reputation in Scottish studies. A monetary prize of £500 plus a lecture to be held at the Society is awarded triennially. Established in 1990 by Trustees Savings Bank (TSB) Scotland in memory of the Reverend Henry Duncan who founded the first TSB.

9068 ■ Keith Medal
For recognition of a paper on a scientific subject presented to the Royal Society of Edinburgh. Preference is given to a paper containing a

discovery. The medal is awarded alternately in quadrennial periods, provided papers worthy of recommendation have been communicated to the society for publications in: Proceedings A (Mathematics) or Transactions (Earth Sciences). Established in 1827.

9069 ■ MakDougall-Brisbane Prize
For promotion of research in science, either an individual engaged in scientific pursuit, a paper written on a scientific subject, or a discovery in science. Preference is given to a person working in Scotland. Awarded in odd-numbered years in the following successive subjects: physical sciences, engineering sciences, and biological sciences. Established in 1855.

9070 ■ Neill Medal
For recognition of a work or publication by some Scottish naturalist, on some branch of natural history completed or published within five years of the time of award. A medal is awarded triennially. Established in 1859 by a bequest from the late Dr. Patrick Neill.

9071 ■ Royal Medal
To honor individuals who have achieved distinction and are of international repute in any of the following categories: life science; physical and engineering sciences; humanities and social sciences; and business and commerce. Only Fellows of the Society can make nominations. Candidates need not be Fellows and should, preferably, have a Scottish connection irrespective of place of domicile. Awarded annually to one or more recipients. Established in 2000 by Her Majesty the Queen.

9072 ■ James Scott Prize Lectureship
To provide for a lecture on the fundamental concepts of natural philosophy. Awarded quadrennially. Established in 1918 by the Trustees of the James Scott Bequest.

9073 ■ Gunning Victoria Jubilee Prize Lectureship
In recognition of original work in physics, chemistry, or pure or applied mathematics. A monetary prize of £500 for a lecture is awarded quadrennially to scientists resident in or connected with Scotland. Established in 1887 by Dr. R. H. Gunning.

9074 ■ Royal Society of Literature
Maggie Fergusson, Sec.
Somerset House
Strand
London WC2R 1LA, United Kingdom
Ph: 44 20 78454676
Fax: 44 20 78454679
E-mail: info@rslit.org
URL: http://www.rslit.org

9075 ■ Benson Medal
To recognize a lifetime of outstanding works of poetry, fiction, history, or belles-lettres. A silver medal is awarded periodically when merited. Established in 1916 by Dr. A. C. Benson.

9076 ■ Ondaatje Prize
For recognition of a distinguished work of fiction, non-fiction, or poetry that evokes the spirit of a place. Full-length works written by British or Irish citizens and published in the United Kingdom are eligible. A monetary prize of £10,000 is awarded annually. Established in 1966. Formerly: (2003) Winifred Holtby Memorial Prize.

9077 ■ V.S. Pritchett Memorial Prize
Recognizes an outstanding published short story. A monetary prize of £1,000 is given annually. Established in 1999.

9078 ■ Royal Society of Medicine
Ms. Janice Liverseidge, Dir.
1 Wimpole St.
London W1G 0AE, United Kingdom

Ph: 44 207 2902900
Ph: 44 207 2902991
Fax: 44 207 2902989
E-mail: membership@rsm.ac.uk
URL: http://www.rsm.ac.uk

9079 ■ Anaesthesia Essay Prize - Students
Open to all medical students currently enrolled in recognized teaching institutions in the United Kingdom. The essay may contain information original research, audit, or a case report. Winner receives a monetary award of £400 and a certificate, and may be invited to present his or her work at the Section's meeting.

9080 ■ Barbara Ansell Prize
To recognize an individual for an outstanding presentation in rheumatology and rehabilitation. Candidates may be rheumatology specialist registrars and research fellows. Two monetary prizes are awarded annually, £200 for first place and £100 for second place. Administered by the Rheumatology and Rehabilitation Section of the Society.

9081 ■ John Arderne Medal
To recognize a recipient selected by the Council of the Section of Coloproctology for the quality of presentation and the content of a paper delivered at a meeting of the Section. The recipient must be a person who has not yet reached consultant status; exceptionally, the award may be made to a person who is not medically qualified. The successful candidate need not be a Fellow of the Royal Society of Medicine. The award consists of a medal struck in silver-gilt and an honorarium. The medal and prize are presented annually to the recipient by the President of the Section at the annual dinner.

9082 ■ Dame Josephine Barnes Award
To recognize the author of an original essay. Medical students are eligible. A monetary prize of £100 is awarded annually. Administered by the Obstetrics and Gynaecology Section of the Society.

9083 ■ Black and Minority Health Section Essay Prize
To recognize an outstanding essay written by a trainee who is currently practicing medicine in the United Kingdom or Ireland. A monetary prize of £250 is awarded annually.

9084 ■ Eric Bywaters Prize
To recognize an individual for the best 10-minute presentation of his or her work in progress in the field of rheumatology and rehabilitation. A monetary prize of £200 is awarded annually. Administered by the Rheumatology and Rehabilitation Section of the Society.

9085 ■ Cardiology Section President's Medal
To recognize original research for specialist registrars in cardiology. A monetary prize of £1,000 and a medal are awarded annually for first place. A monetary prize of £500 is presented for second place.

9086 ■ Colyer Prize
For recognition of the best original work in dental science completed during the previous five years by a dental surgeon educated at any duly recognized dental school in Great Britain or Northern Ireland, and who has not been qualified to practice more than 10 years at the date of the award. Applications from candidates, together with a general account of their projects, must be submitted to the Prize Committee not later than March 31 preceding the date of the award. A monetary prize of £100 is awarded.

9087 ■ A. C. Comfort Prize
For recognition of a 5,000-word essay on some aspects of clinical research in geriatric medicine,

Awards are arranged in alphabetical order below their administering organizations

written by a practitioner of not more than five years' standing from qualification, or by a student or intern approaching the medical degree. A monetary prize of £300 and the cost of publishing the award-winning paper are presented biennially. Established by Dr. Alex Comfort in 1981 as a memorial to his late father, A. C. Comfort. Administered by the Geriatrics and Gerontology Section.

9088 ■ Tim David Prize
To recognize the best paper presented by a paediatric trainee. A monetary prize of £150 is awarded annually to the first-place winner; a second-place prize of £100 is also presented. Administered by the Paediatrics and Child Health Section of the Society.

9089 ■ Alan Edwards Prize
To advance the study of clinical medical science. Individuals who have not yet gained consultant status are eligible for the case presentation in each session adjudged most likely to advance the study of clinical medical science. A £100 book token is awarded annually. Established in 1979 in memory of Alan Edwards. Administered by the Clinical Section.

9090 ■ Ellison-Cliffe Medal and Lecture
To provide for a lecture by a medically qualified person of eminence in his or her field at the Society's House on a subject connected with the contribution of fundamental science to advances in medicine. Invitations to the Lecture are not restricted to members of the Society and special care is taken to invite scientists working in areas that could become related to medicine. A medal and expenses for the lecturer are awarded annually. Established by Percy Cliffe and his wife, Carice Ellison.

9091 ■ Alan Emery Prize
To recognize an individual for a published research article in medical genetics. Eligible articles must have been published in a peer-reviewed journal during the previous two years. A monetary prize of £500 for current members or £300 plus a one-year membership for non-members is awarded annually. Administered by the Medical Genetics Section of the Society.

9092 ■ Finzi Prize
To recognize a trainee for the best 10-minute presentation of his or her work in progress in the field of radiology. Monetary prizes are awarded annually: £600 for first place, £300 for second place, and £150 for third place. Administered by the Radiology Section of the Society.

9093 ■ Geriatrics and Gerontology Section Trainees' Prize
To recognize the best short papers in geriatrics, gerontology, or a related field. Winners receive an engraved decanter, and are invited to make a poster presentation at the meeting. Awarded annually.

9094 ■ Malcolm Harrington Prize
To recognize an occupational physician in training for the presentation that best describes work that is most likely to advance the study of occupational medicine in its broadest sense. A monetary prize of £250 is awarded annually. Administered by the Occupational Medicine Section of the Society.

9095 ■ Brigadier Haywood Prize
To recognize the medical student for a case presentation that is most likely to advance the study of clinical medical science. A book token valued at £100 is awarded annually. Administered by the Clinical Section of the Society.

9096 ■ Gordon Holmes Prize
To recognize outstanding research by trainees in neuroscience, including nerology, neurosurgery, neurophysiology, neuroradiology, and neuropathology. A monetary prize of £300 is awarded annually. Administered by the Clinical Neurosciences Section of the Society.

9097 ■ Jephcott Lecture
To provide for lectures in the field of medicine. An honorarium is awarded annually. Established in 1959.

9098 ■ Sylvia Lawler Prize
To recognize the best scientific paper and best clinical paper presented at a meeting of the Oncology Section of the Society. A monetary prize of £500 is awarded annually in each category.

9099 ■ Ian MacKay Essay Prize
To recognize a trainee for an outstanding essay. A monetary prize of £1,000 is awarded annually. Administered by the Laryngology and Rhinology Section of the Society.

9100 ■ MIA Prize
To recognize a surgery registrar for a laboratory-based research paper. A monetary prize of £250 is awarded annually. Administered by the Surgery Section of the Society.

9101 ■ Oswald Morton Essay Prize
To recognize the author of the best essay on a topic in pharmaceutical medicine. Fellows, young fellows, associate members, and students are eligible. A monetary prize of £200 is awarded annually by the Pharmaceutical Medicine and Research Section.

9102 ■ Nuffield Lecture
To provide for a lecture to be delivered from time to time as decided upon by the Council of the Society (but not more than once in any calendar year) on October 10, or on the nearest suitable day in honor of Lord Nuffield and to advance the science and art of medicine. Lecturers are appointed by t he Council of the Society on the recommendation of a Committee consisting of the President of the Society for the time being, all living past presidents of the Society willing to serve, and, during the lifetime of Lord Nuffield, three other members nominated by him. A gold medal and an honorarium of 100 guineas are awarded every three to four years. Established in 1959 by Lord Nuffield.

9103 ■ Odontology Section President's Prize
To recognize the best research paper and best clinical paper presented at a meeting of the Odontology Section of the Society. A monetary prize of £100 is awarded annually in each category.

9104 ■ Palliative Care Section MSc/MA Research Prize
To recognize students for outstanding oral presentations. Candidates must be students wither currently studying, or within 18 months of completion, of MSc or MA in palliative medicine or an allied discipline. A monetary prize of £250 is awarded for first place, £100 for second place, and £50 for third place. Awarded annually.

9105 ■ Pathology Section President's Prize
To recognize junior pathologists and young scientists in the field of pathology. A monetary prize of £500 is awarded for first place and a prize of £250 for second place. Awarded annually.

9106 ■ Psychiatry Section Mental Health Foundation Research Prize
To recognize the author of the most outstanding published paper reporting original research conducted during the previous year. Candidates may be psychiatrists and psychologists practicing in the United Kingdom or the Republic of Eire and in training at any grade. Monetary prizes of £750 and £100 are awarded annually.

9107 ■ Herbert Reiss Trainees Prize
To recognize the best presentations of short papers and posters at a meeting of the Obstetrics and Gynaecology Section of the Society. Monetary prizes up to £150 are awarded annually.

9108 ■ Norah Schuster Essay Prize
To recognize the best essay submission by pre-clinical, clinical medical, and dental students. A book token valued at £100 is awarded annually. Administered by the History of Medicine Section of the Society.

9109 ■ Adrian Tanner Prize
To recognize a surgical trainee for an outstanding clinical case report. A monetary prize of £250 is awarded annually. Administered by the Surgery Section of the Society.

9110 ■ Hugh Wallace's Registrars' Prize
To recognize a dermatologist of registrar or senior registrar grade (or of equivalent academic status) considered to have made the most outstanding contribution at Section Meetings during the session preceding the year of award. A Selection Committee is established annually to submit a recommendation to the Council of the Society. Two monetary prizes of £150 are awarded annually. Established in honor of Hugh Wallace, a former president of the Section. Administered by the Dermatology Section.

9111 ■ Royal Society of Miniature Painters, Sculptors and Gravers
Patricia Houchell, Exec. Sec.
119 Dunstans Rd.
London SE22 0HD, United Kingdom
Ph: 44 208 6939536
E-mail: tattyhouchell@googlemail.com
URL: http://www.royal-miniature-society.org.uk

9112 ■ Gold Memorial Bowl
Recognizes the best piece of miniature work in any medium. Awarded annually.

9113 ■ Royal Society of Tropical Medicine and Hygiene
Hazel Dockrell, Pres.
303-306 High Holborn
London WC1V 7JZ, United Kingdom
Ph: 44 20 74052628
Fax: 44 20 72424487
E-mail: info@rstmh.org
URL: http://www.rstmh.org

9114 ■ Chalmers Memorial Medal
For recognition of research of outstanding merit contributing to knowledge of tropical medicine or tropical hygiene. Only individuals 46 years of age or under on the 1st of June of the year of the award are eligible. A silver-gilt medal is awarded annually. Established in 1923 in memory of Dr. Albert John Chalmers, who was known for his work in tropical medicine.

9115 ■ Sir Rickard Christophers Medal
For recognition of work in tropical medicine and hygiene in its broadest sense, with particular consideration given to practical and field applications. A bronze medal is awarded triennially. Established in 1979 in memory of Sir Rickard Christophers, for a lifetime spent in the relentless and inspired pursuit of knowledge.

9116 ■ George Macdonald Medal
For recognition of outstanding research leading to improvement of health in tropical countries. The London School Council and the Council of the Society propose the names of the candidates. A medal is awarded triennially. Established in 1968 in memory of Dr. George Macdonald, Professor of Tropical Hygiene at the London School of Hygiene and Tropical Medicine, and Director of the Ross Institute. Cosponsored by the London School of Hygiene and Tropical Medicine.

9117 ■ Donald Mackay Medal
For recognition of outstanding work in tropical

Awards are arranged in alphabetical order below their administering organizations

health, especially relating to improvements in the health of rural or urban workers in the tropics. There are no restrictions as to the nationality or sex of the candidates. Preference will be given to suitable medically qualified candidates, but those in other disciplines are eligible. The Medal is awarded annually - in odd-numbered years by the Royal Society of Tropical Medicine and Hygiene, and in even-numbered years by the American Society of Tropical Medicine and Hygiene. Established in 1990 in memory of Dr. Donald Mackay, who was Deputy Director of the Ross Institute at the London School of Hygiene and Tropical Medicine, who died in 1981 after many years of outstanding work in tropical occupational health, especially on the tea plantations of South Asia.

9118 ■ Manson Medal
This, the Society's highest mark of distinction, is given for contribution to any branch of tropical medicine or tropical hygiene. A bronze medal is awarded triennially. Established in 1922 in memory of Sir Patrick Manson, first president of the Society.

9119 ■ Medical Student Elective Prize
To recognize a medical student for an account of work carried out during an elective period in a tropical or developing country. The work, which may be the product of a student of any nationality, must contribute to the knowledge or understanding of tropical diseases. A monetary prize of £500 is awarded annually.

9120 ■ Research Grant
Awarded to physicists/mathematicians who have obtained their PhD not before four years.

9121 ■ Section Grant
Awarded to physicist or mathematician from a developing country who wishes to organize an international or regional conference in one of the areas of study of the ICTP.

9122 ■ Undergraduate Project Prize
To recognize an undergraduate student for an account of work carried out of relevance to tropical or developing countries. The work, which may be laboratory-based and not necessarily carried out in a tropical or developing country, should contribute to the knowledge of human or veterinary health or hygiene in the tropics. A monetary prize of £500 is awarded annually.

9123 ■ Royal Society of Wildlife Trusts
The Kiln Waterside
Mather Rd.
Nottinghamshire
Newark NG24 1WT, United Kingdom
Ph: 44 16 36677711
Fax: 44 16 36670001
E-mail: enquiry@wildlifetrusts.org
URL: http://www.rswt.org/welcome.php
Formerly: (2004) Royal Society for Nature Conservation.

9124 ■ Christopher Cadbury Medal
For recognition of services to the advancement of nature conservation in the British Islands. A silver medal is awarded annually. Established in 1990 in honor of the late Christopher Cadbury, former president of the Royal Society for Nature Conservation, who retired in 1988.

9125 ■ Charles Rothschild and Miriam Rothschild Medal
To recognize outstanding achievements in the conservation, management, promotion, or study of the natural environment.

9126 ■ Royal Television Society
Simon Albury, Chief Exec.
Kildare House, 5th Fl.
3 Dorset Rise
London EC4Y 8EN, United Kingdom

Ph: 44 207 8222810
Fax: 44 207 8222811
E-mail: info@rts.org.uk
URL: http://www.rts.org.uk

9127 ■ Craft and Design Awards
To recognize excellence in regional or network broadcast television in England. Awards are given in the following categories: Graphic Design; Make-up Design; Costume Design; Production Design; Visual Effects; Lighting, Photography and Camera; Sound; Tape and Film Editing; and Music. Additional awards that may be presented at the discretion of the Jury include the Design and Craft Innovation Award, Judges' Award, and Lifetime Achievement Award. Awards are presented annually.

9128 ■ Educational Television Awards
To recognize programs that constitute an outstanding contribution to the educational use of the broadcasting television medium. Awards are given in the following categories: Schools; Adult Education; Educational Impact in Primetime; and Innovation in Education. In addition, the Judge's Award and Lifetime Achievement Award may be presented. Awarded annually.

9129 ■ Programme Awards
For recognition of the best television programs during the previous year. Awards are given annually in numerous subcategories within the classifications of: Drama, Entertainment and Comedy, Performance, Presenter, Factual, Children's, and Nations and Regions. In addition, the Digital Channel Programme Award, International Award, Judges' Award, and Lifetime Achievement Award may be presented. Awarded annually.

9130 ■ Student Television Awards
To recognize undergraduate and graduate student programming that shows outstanding visual and aural creativity, a mastery of craft skills, innovation, and initiative. Open to students attending educational institutions offering approved BTEC, degree, and postgraduate courses in design, media, and media-related studies, and to film and television associations at these institutions. Awards are given in the following categories: Animation, Factual, Drama, and Entertainment/Factual Entertainment. Winners are presented with an award at a national ceremony each year.

9131 ■ Television Journalism Awards
To recognize creativity and excellence in news and current affairs television programs. Awards are given in numerous subcategories within the classifications of: News, Current Affairs, and Nations and Regions. In addition, the following awards may be presented: Scoop of the Year, Innovative News Award, Specialist Journalist Award, Young Journalist of the Year, Television Journalist of the Year, Camera Operator of the Year, Presenter of the Year, Judges' Award, and Lifetime Achievement Award. Awarded annually. Established in 1978.

9132 ■ Television Sports Awards
To recognize sports news items covered by United Kingdom broadcasting organizations or agencies. Entries must be up to 15 minutes and networked. Awards are presented in the following categories: Sports Coverage, Regional Sports, Sports Presenter or Commentator, and Judges' Award. Awarded annually.

9133 ■ Royal Town Planning Institute
Richard Summers BA, Pres.
41 Botolph Ln.
London EC3R 8DL, United Kingdom
Ph: 44 207 9299494
Fax: 44 207 9299490
E-mail: online@rtpi.org.uk
URL: http://www.rtpi.org.uk

9134 ■ George Pepler International Award
To enable individuals of any country to visit Britain for a short time to study an aspect of town and country planning or a related subject. Individuals under 30 years of age are eligible. A monetary prize of £1,500 is awarded biennially in even-numbered years. Established in 1963 by Lady Pepler in memory of Sir George Pepler, one of the Founders of the Town Planning Institute.

9135 ■ Young Planner of the Year Award
Recognizes outstanding young planners who made contributions to planning and to the profession in general. Institute members under the age of 35 are eligible. Awarded annually.

9136 ■ Royal United Services Institute for Defence and Security Studies
Sir Paul Lever, VP
Whitehall
London SW1A 2ET, United Kingdom
Ph: 44 20 77472600
E-mail: membership@rusi.org
URL: http://www.rusi.org

9137 ■ Chesney Gold Medal
This, the highest honor bestowed by the Institute, is given to recognize the originator of distinguished or authoritative work or works that have added to knowledge or achieved advances in the defense and international security fields to the benefit of the U.K. and/or the Western Alliance. A gold medal is awarded when merited. Established in 1900 in memory of General Sir George Chesney, military author, reformer, and engineer.

9138 ■ Duke of Westminster Medal for Military Literature
To recognize the best book in the English language, regardless of nationality, gender, or age of the author, that represents a notable and original contribution to the study of international or national security and defense. A medal and monetary prize of £1,000 are awarded annually. Created with the support of His Grace, the Duke of Westminster.

9139 ■ Trench Gascoigne Prize
To encourage original writing on contemporary issues of defense and international security, ideally with an emphasis on the military sciences. Open to authors of any nationality, and entries are particularly welcome from members of the Armed Forces. One or more awards totaling up to £1,000 are awarded annually. Established in 1897 by Colonel F. C. Trench Gascoigne.

9140 ■ Salters' Institute
Mrs. Audrey Strong, Institute Mgr.
Salters' Hall
4 Fore St.
London EC2Y 5DE, United Kingdom
Ph: 44 20 76285962
Fax: 44 20 76383679
E-mail: institute@salters.co.uk
URL: http://www.salters.co.uk/institute

9141 ■ City and Guilds Prizes
To recognize top students at each level of the Process Plant Operation Scheme. A monetary prize of £1,000 is awarded annually.

9142 ■ National Awards for Science Technicians
To recognize science technicians on a national level. Science technicians in schools and colleges who have more than five total years of experience are eligible. Awarded to several recipient each year. Established in 2002. Co-sponsored by the Association of Education, the Institute of Biology, the Royal Society, and the Royal Society of Chemistry.

9143 ■ Salters Advanced Chemistry Prize
To recognize individuals who have achieved the

Awards are arranged in alphabetical order below their administering organizations

highest grades in the Salters' Advanced Chemistry exams. Monetary prizes are awarded to the top four or five candidates. Awarded annually. Established in 1988. Formerly: A-Level Chemistry Prizes.

9144 ■ Salters' Graduate Prizes
In recognition of academic merit in chemistry or chemical engineering at British universities and of potential to occupy a leading position in the United Kingdom chemical industry. Final year undergraduates, who must be nominated by the head of the department and who expect to graduate with honors in chemistry or chemical engineering and have the intention of taking a post in a United Kingdom chemical industry, may apply by late January each year. Monetary awards of £1,000 and certificates are awarded to up to 10 recipients each year. Established in 1979.

9145 ■ Salters Horners Advanced Physics Prize
For the candidates who achieve the highest marks on the Salters-Nuffield Physics exams. Prizes are awarded annually. Established in 1996.

9146 ■ Salters-Nuffield Advanced Biology Awards
For the candidates who achieve the highest marks on the Salters-Nuffield Biology exams. Prizes are awarded annually. Established in 2006.

9147 ■ Saltire Society
Magnus Linklater, Pres.
9 Fountain Close
22 High St.
Edinburgh EH1 1TF, United Kingdom
Ph: 44 131 5561836
Fax: 44 131 5571675
E-mail: saltire@saltiresociety.org.uk
URL: http://www.saltiresociety.org.uk

9148 ■ Arts and Crafts in Architecture Award
For recognition of works of art and craft that are designed to enhance and enrich buildings. Eligible works include sculpture, painting, tilework, ceramics, mosaic, tapestry, textile hangings, glass, plaster, metalwork, and enamel. Work must be located in Scotland and be an intrinsic part of a building or group of buildings. Awarded biennially in odd-numbered years. Established in 1971.

9149 ■ Civil Engineering Awards
To encourage the highest standards in the design and construction of civil engineering projects completed in the previous two years in Scotland. Projects may be entered in the following categories: Project, Design, Construction, Structural, Conservation, Environmental Sustainable Construction, and Small Community Project. A plaque is awarded annually to the winner in each category. Established in 1981. Co-sponsored by the Scottish Association of the Institution of Civil Engineers.

9150 ■ Grierson Documentary Film Award
To assist young filmmakers in developing their careers. Candidates are first- and second-time short documentary filmmakers, either working in or from Scotland. A monetary prize of £1,000 is awarded annually. Established in 1999.

9151 ■ Housing Design Awards
For recognition of housing design in Scotland. Entries may be submitted by owners, builders, public or semi-public bodies, and individuals who have commissioned works in Scotland, or by the architects employed by them. Awarded annually. Established in 1937.

9152 ■ Scots and Gaelic Song Competition
To encourage the singing of Scottish songs by children by honoring school and junior choirs who are the winners of first and second places at their local music competition festivals. Trophies are awarded annually in two classes. Established in 1975.

9153 ■ Scottish Book of the Year Awards
For recognition of the Scottish Book of the Year and the Scottish First Book of the Year. The competition is open to any author of Scottish descent or living in Scotland, or for a book by anyone which deals with the work or life of a Scot or with a Scottish problem, event or situation. In 1988, the Award was extended to include the first published work by a new author. Entries are submitted to the Society by literary editors of leading newspapers, magazines, and periodicals. A monetary prize of £5,000 is awarded for the Book of the Year, and £1,500 for the First Book of the Year. Awarded annually. Established in 1982. Formerly: Saltire Society Scottish Literary Awards.

9154 ■ Scottish History Book of the Year Award
For recognition of a published work of Scottish historical research, including intellectual history and the history of science. A monetary prize of £1,500 is awarded annually. Established in 1965 in memory of Agnes Mure MacKenzie. Formerly: (1998) Agnes Mure MacKenzie Award.

9155 ■ Scottish Research Book Award
To recognize books that represent a significant body of research, offer new insight or dimension to the subject, and add knowledge and understanding of Scotland and the Scots. A monetary prize of £1,500 is awarded annually. Established in 1998. Co-administered by the National Library of Scotland.

9156 ■ Scottish Science Award
To recognize individuals making a major contribution to science, whose merit has not been previously recognized by public honors or by election to one of the senior learned societies, and who are able to communicate their scientific results to the wider public. Candidates must be between the ages of 30 and 50 years, and must have lived and worked continuously in Scotland for not less than five years or is of Scottish descent. Presented within five branches of science in rotation annually: medicine and veterinary medicine, physical science and mathematics, biological sciences, earth sciences, and cell and molecular biology. A medallion, a certificate, and a monetary prize are awarded annually. Established in 1989. Sponsored by Scottish & Newcastle plc. Formerly: (1995) Saltire Society and The Royal Bank of Scotland - Scottish Science Award.

9157 ■ TES Scotland/Saltire Educational Publications Award
Encourages the best examples of published work that enhances the curriculum for Scottish schools. The work must be relevant to Scottish school children, ages 3-18. Established in 1993. Awarded jointly with the Times Educational Supplement Scotland (TES Scotland).

9158 ■ Science Fiction Foundation
Roger Robinson, Contact
75 Rosslyn Ave.
Harold Wood
Essex
Romford RM3 0RG, United Kingdom
E-mail: chair@sf-foundation.org
URL: http://www.sf-foundation.org

9159 ■ Arthur C. Clarke Award
To recognize the best science fiction novel first published in the United Kingdom. Awarded annually. Established in 1987. Supported by the British Science Fiction Association and SF Crowsnest.

9160 ■ Scottish Ecological Design Association
Robin Baker, Chm.
35/1 Granton Crescent
Edinburgh EH5 1BN, United Kingdom
E-mail: info@seda.uk.net
URL: http://www.seda.uk.net

9161 ■ Design Competition
To recognize an individual for a design proposal of a structure to be utilized at the annual festival. A grant up to £2,000 is awarded annually.

9162 ■ Krystyna Johnson Student Travel Award
To further the study and development of ecological design by encouraging students to explore the latest developments in this and other countries. Open to matriculated students at any design-related courses at the University of Strathclyde. A grant up to £1,500 is awarded annually.

9163 ■ Scottish Engineering
Dr. Peter T. Hughes OBE, Chief Exec.
105 W George St.
Glasgow G2 1QL, United Kingdom
Ph: 44 141 2213181
Fax: 44 141 2041202
E-mail: consult@scottishengineering.org.uk
URL: http://www.scottishengineering.org.uk

9164 ■ Scottish Engineering Award
To recognize the Scottish manufacturing organization that, in the past year, has significantly contributed to the progress of the industry and enhanced its image at home and abroad. Awarded annually.

9165 ■ Scottish Engineering/Hammermen Award
To recognize an engineer or manger who has shown outstanding quality in the application of knowledge or innovation to his or her employer's business such as to result in a significant contribution to that business. A monetary prize of £1,000 is awarded annually. Co-sponsored by the Incorporation of Hammermen of Glasgow.

9166 ■ Scottish Federation of Meat Traders Association
8-10 Needless Rd.
Perth PH2 0JW, United Kingdom
Ph: 44 1738 637472
Fax: 44 1738 441059
E-mail: enquiries@sfmta.co.uk
URL: http://www.sfmta.co.uk

9167 ■ Meat to Go Awards
To recognize the best meat products. Diamond, gold, and silver awards are presented in three categories: ready to cook, ready to eat, and ready to heat. Awarded annually. Established in 1994. Formerly: Make It With Meat Awards.

9168 ■ Scottish International Piano Competition
Ian Mills, Admin.
100 Renfrew St.
Glasgow G2 3DB, United Kingdom
Ph: 44 141 270 8322
Fax: 44 141 332 8901
E-mail: sipc@rsamd.ac.uk
URL: http://www.
scottishinternationalpianocompetition.com

9169 ■ Scottish International Piano Competition
For recognition of achievement in the piano competition. Applications are accepted from individuals up to 30 years of age of any

Awards are arranged in alphabetical order below their administering organizations

nationality. The following monetary prizes are awarded: first prize - £10,000; second prize -£7,500; third prize - £5,000; and £1,000 for each semi-finalist. In addition, a £500 prize for the best performance of the commissioned work, and a £500 prize for the best performance in the chamber music section of the final. Held triennially. Established in 1986 in memory of Frederic Lamond (1868-1948).

9170 ■ Scottish Joint Industry Board for the Electrical Contracting Industry
Fiona Harper, Sec.
The Walled Garden
Bush Estate
Midlothian EH26 0SB, United Kingdom
Ph: 44 131 4459216
Fax: 44 131 4455548
E-mail: employment.affairs@sjib.org.uk
URL: http://www.sjib.org.uk

9171 ■ Apprentice of the Year
For skill and personality.

9172 ■ Scottish Photographic Federation
Neil Smith, Gen. Sec.
34 Braemer Crescent
Carluke ML8 4BH, United Kingdom
Ph: 44 1555 750737
E-mail: libby.neilsmith@btinternet.com
URL: http://www.scottish-photographic-federation.org

9173 ■ Scottish Salon of Photography
For recognition of outstanding photography from artists around the world. The Federation presents Gold Medals in four categories: Best Contemporary Slide, Best Traditional Slide, Best Monochrome Print, and Best Color Print. It also presents four gold medals to Scottish residents in four categories: Best General Slide, Best Natural History Slide, Best Monochrome Print, and Best Color Print. The Federation Internationale de l'art Photographique (FIAP) awards Gold Medals in four categories: Best Landscape Slide, Best Natural History Slide, Best Monochrome Landscape Print, and Best Color Landscape Print. In addition, the Dumfries Octocentenary Trophy is awarded to the best entry from a Scottish Club. Held annually. Established in 1910.

9174 ■ Seatrade Communications Ltd.
Seatrade House
42 N Station Rd.
Colchester CO1 1RB, United Kingdom
Ph: 44 1206 545121
Fax: 44 1206 545190
E-mail: mail@seatrade-global.com
URL: http://www.seatrade-global.com

9175 ■ Seatrade Asia Awards
To honor business excellence, best practices, and innovation across various sectors of the Asian maritime industry. Awards are presented in approximately 20 categories, including Safety, Port Authority, Repair Yard, Technical Innovation, and Shipbuilding. Awarded annually. Established in 2008.

9176 ■ Seatrade Awards
To honor individuals and organization that have demonstrated innovative solutions for safe, efficient, and environmentally friendly shipping. Awards are presented for: Protection of the Marine and Atmospheric Environment, Innovation in Ship Operations, Investment in People, Lifetime Achievement, Personality of the Year, Young Person in Shipping, and Global Performer. Awarded annually. Established in 1988.

9177 ■ Seatrade China Awards
To honor business excellence, best practices, and innovation across various sectors of the China maritime industry. Awards are presented in nearly 20 categories, including Ship of the Year, Corporate Responsibility, Offshore Yard, Tanker Operator, Ship Manager, Port of the Year, and Lifetime Achievement. Awarded annually.

9178 ■ Seatrade Insider Cruise Awards
To recognize companies and individuals for excellence in the cruise tourism industry. Seven categories of awards are presented: Ports, Destinations, Onboard Suppliers, Environmental Initiatives, Marketing Initiatives, Innovative Shore Excursions, and Mediterranean Cruise Personality. A trophy is awarded annually in each category. Established in 2007.

9179 ■ Seatrade Middle East and Indian Subcontinent Awards
To honor business excellence, best practices, and innovation across various sectors of the Middle Eastern and Indian Subcontinent maritime industry. Awards are presented in more than 20 categories, including Corporate Responsibility, Safety and Quality, Environmental Protection, Port Authority, Marine Insurance, and Ship Manager. Awarded annually.

9180 ■ Sir Henry Royce Memorial Foundation
Lt. Col. Eric B. Barrass OBE, Pres.
The Hunt House
Northamptonshire
Paulerspury NN12 7NA, United Kingdom
Ph: 44 1327 811048
Fax: 44 1327 811797
E-mail: philiphall@rrec.org.uk
URL: http://www.henryroyce.org.uk

9181 ■ Sir Henry Royce Foundation Trophy
To recognize an individual for a significant contribution to the Foundation's goals and objectives. The perpetual trophy is awarded annually. Established in 1997.

9182 ■ Skytrax Research
29 Harley St.
London W1G 9QR, United Kingdom
Ph: 44 2070 162197
Fax: 44 8700 512321
E-mail: miller@airlinequality.com
URL: http://www.skytraxresearch.com

9183 ■ World Airline Awards - Passenger's Choice Awards
To recognize the world's best airlines, as determined by their customers. A survey measures nearly 40 aspects of passenger satisfaction in product and service, including airline Web site, boarding procedures, baggage delivery, cabin seat comfort, in-flight entertainment, friendliness of staff, clarity of public address announcements, and consistency of service across different flights. Awards are presented across a variety of categories, cabin sizes, and regions, with an overall Airline of the Year selected. Awarded annually. Established in 2001.

9184 ■ World Airport Awards
To recognize the world's best airports, as determined by their customers. A survey measures nearly 40 aspects of passenger satisfaction in product and service, including airport accessibility, availability of luggage trolleys, clarity of public address system, terminal signage, prices in bars and restaurants, and smoking policy and lounges. Awards are presented across a variety of categories and regions, with an overall Airport of the Year selected. In addition, awards are presented for Most Improved Airport, Best Low-Cost Airport, and Staff Service Excellence. Awarded annually. Established in 1999.

9185 ■ Social Research Association
Barbara Doig, Chair
24-32 Stephenson Way
London NW1 2HX, United Kingdom
Ph: 44 20 73882391
Ph: 44 20 73882401
E-mail: admin@the-sra.org.uk
URL: http://www.the-sra.org.uk

9186 ■ Mark Abrams Prize
To honor a piece of work that best links survey research, social policy, and social theory. Awarded annually. Established in 1986.

9187 ■ Society for Applied Microbiology
Philip Wheat, CEO
Bedford Heights
Brickhill Dr.
Bedford MK41 7PH, United Kingdom
Ph: 44 1234 326661
Fax: 44 1234 326678
E-mail: pfwheat@sfam.org.uk
URL: http://www.sfam.org.uk

9188 ■ Communications Award
To recognize individuals who have communicated their work in specific or applied microbiology in general to the general public. The nature of the communication can be local, national, or international, and could be factual or fictional works, such as fiction books, factual books, popular science books, newspaper or magazine articles, film, television (series or documentary), lectures or lecture series, classroom demonstrations, and works of art or exhibitions. A monetary prize of £1,000 is awarded annually.

9189 ■ W. H. Pierce Memorial Prize
To recognize a young microbiologist for a substantial contribution to bacteriology, such as publication in the *Journal of Applied Bacteriology* or a presentation at the Symposium held at the summer conference of the Society. Members of the Society who are under 40 years of age are eligible for nomination by other members. A monetary award of £3,000 and a scroll are awarded annually. Established in 1984 by Oxoid Ltd. in honor of W. H. (Bill) Pierce, former chief bacteriologist.

9190 ■ Summer Conference Student Prizes
To recognize the students delivering the best oral presentation and displaying the best poster. Awarded annually to two individuals.

9191 ■ Don Whitley Travel Scholarship
To enable microbiologists to attend scientific meetings. Application by letter to Society office. Awarded annually.

9192 ■ Society for Environmental Exploration
Ms. Eibleis Fanning, Managing Dir.
50-52 Rivington St.
London EC2A 3QP, United Kingdom
Ph: 44 20 76132422
Fax: 44 20 76132992
E-mail: info@frontier.ac.uk
URL: http://www.frontier.ac.uk

9193 ■ BTEC Advanced Certificate in Expedition Management
Award of recognition for gaining the knowledge and skills needed to manage and organize expeditions.

9194 ■ BTEC Advanced Certificate in Tropical Habitat Conservation
Award of recognition for gaining knowledge of management and issues relating to the conservation of tropical habitats.

9195 ■ Society for Experimental Biology (Societe de Biologie Experimentale)
Paul Hutchinson, CEO
Charles Darwin House
12 Roger St.
London WC1N 2JU, United Kingdom
Ph: 44 207 6852600
Fax: 44 207 6852601
E-mail: c.trimmer@sebiology.org
URL: http://www.sebiology.org

9196 ■ Irene Manton Award
Recognizes the best postgraduate cell, plant, and animal biology posters by a PhD student or a PhD in their first post doctoral year. Awarded annually.

Awards are arranged in alphabetical order below their administering organizations

9197 ■ President's Medal
Recognizes research in new areas of science that have great success. Individuals under the age of 35 are eligible. Awarded annually.

9198 ■ Society for Medicines Research
Dr. Phillip Cowley, Chm.
840 Melton Rd.
Thurmaston
Leicester LE4 8BN, United Kingdom
Ph: 44 116 2691048
Fax: 44 116 2640141
E-mail: secretariat@smr.org.uk
URL: http://www.smr.org.uk
Formerly: Society for Drug Research.

9199 ■ Award for Drug Discovery
To recognize researchers in academic institutions and the pharmaceutical industry as well as other concerned individuals. Awarded biennially in odd-numbered years.

9200 ■ Society for Medieval Archaeology
Dr. Dawn Hadley, Honorary Sec.
Maney Publishing
Ste. 1C, Joseph's Well
Hanover Walk
Leeds LS3 1AB, United Kingdom
Ph: 44 113 2497481
Fax: 44 113 2486983
E-mail: d.m.hadley@sheffield.ac.uk
URL: http://www.medievalarchaeology.co.uk

9201 ■ John Hurst Award
To recognize the author of an undergraduate dissertation that makes the most original contribution to medieval archaeology. A monetary prize of £100, a three-year membership, and the possibility of publication in *Medieval Archaeology* are awarded annually.

9202 ■ Martyn Jope Award
To recognize the best novel interpretation, application, or presentation of new findings. A monetary award of £200 is presented annually. Established in 2007.

9203 ■ Medieval Archaeology Research Grant
To encourage research in medieval archaeology. A cash award of up to £2,000 to be used for research is presented annually. Established in 1990.

9204 ■ Sudreys Award
To encourage research in the field of Viking studies. Awardees receive up to £500 for travel-related research. Awarded annually. Established in 1992.

9205 ■ Society for Research into Higher Education
Helen Perkins, Dir.
44 Bedford Row
London WC1R 4LL, United Kingdom
Ph: 44 20 74472525
Fax: 44 20 74472526
E-mail: srheoffice@srhe.ac.uk
URL: http://www.srhe.ac.uk

9206 ■ Society for Research into Higher Education Awards
To recognize individuals involved in higher education research and to conduct educational programs. The Society bestows awards at its annual conference.

9207 ■ Society for Research into Hydrocephalus and Spina Bifida
Mr. Roger Strachan, Honorable Treas.
The James Cook University Hospital
Dept. of Neurosurgery
Marton Rd.
Cleveland
Middlesborough TS4 3BW, United Kingdom
Fax: 44 1642 282770

E-mail: srhsb@asbah.org
URL: http://www.srhsb.org

9208 ■ Casey Holter Memorial Prize
For recognition of an essay reporting original work bearing on the pathogenesis or treatment of hydrocephalus or spina bifida. Any professional worker in a field concerned with hydrocephalus and/or spina bifida may submit an essay in a form suitable for publication. Essays should include personal observations and experiences collected by the candidate in the course of his work and must not have been previously published. A monetary prize of £250 is awarded triennially. Established in 1966 by Mr. J. W. Holter in memory of his son.

9209 ■ Society for the Advancement of Anaesthesia in Dentistry
Nigel Robb, Pres.
21 Portland Pl.
London W1B 1PY, United Kingdom
Ph: 44 20 76318893
E-mail: saad@aagbi.org
URL: http://www.saad.org.uk

9210 ■ Drummond-Jackson Essay Prize
To recognize an outstanding essay on the topic of anaesthesia in dentistry. Open to graduates and undergraduates of dentistry and medicine from anywhere in the world. A monetary prize of £1,000 is awarded triennially.

9211 ■ Student and Nurse Essay Prizes
To honor the best essays written by dental students and by dental nurses. The dental student essay should not exceed 3,000 words and the dental nurse essay should not exceed 2,500 words. A monetary prize of £300 is awarded in each category.

9212 ■ Society for the History of Alchemy and Chemistry
John Perkins, Honorary Treas.
19 Nethercote Rd.
Tackley
Oxford OX5 3AW, United Kingdom
E-mail: shacperkins@googlemail.com

9213 ■ Partington Prize
To recognize an original and unpublished essay on any aspect of the history of alchemy or chemistry by a young scholar. It is open to anyone with a scholarly interest in the history of alchemy or chemistry who has not reached 35 years of age, or if older, has completed a doctoral thesis in the history of science within the previous three years. A monetary prize of £500 and a certificate are awarded triennially. Established in 1975 in memory of Professor J. R. Partington.

9214 ■ Society for the History of Natural History
Mrs. Lynda Brooks, Honorary Sec.
Cromwell Rd.
London SW7 5BD, United Kingdom
E-mail: info@shnh.org.uk
URL: http://www.shnh.org.uk

9215 ■ Founders' Medal
For contribution to the study of the history or bibliography of natural history. Awarded annually to one or more recipients.

9216 ■ Honorary Membership
For persons who have performed signal services to the Society. The number of honorary members is limited to ten.

9217 ■ John Thackray Medal
For contribution to the history of natural history realized in the preceding 12 months. Awarded annually. Established in 2000.

9218 ■ Alwyne Wheeler Bursary
For original contribution to the study of the history of natural history by a person under the age of 30. Awarded annually.

9219 ■ Society for the Study of Addiction to Alcohol and Other Drugs
Dr. Gillian Tober, Pres.
Leeds Addiction Unit
19 Springfield Mt.
Leeds LS2 9NG, United Kingdom
Ph: 44 113 2952787
Ph: 44 113 2951335
Fax: 44 113 2952787
E-mail: membership@addiction-ssa.org
URL: http://www.addiction-ssa.org

9220 ■ SSA Bursaries
To provide financial assistance to individuals who have been offered a place on a University validated program in specialist addiction studies, and who have a demonstrable commitment to working in the addictions field. Bursaries of up to £750 are awarded.

9221 ■ SSA Traveling Scholarship
To support any younger member of the Society to travel to international meetings, laboratories, and/or clinics to further their training. A scholarship in the amount of £2,500 is awarded twice a year, in March and October.

9222 ■ Society for the Study of Human Biology
Paula Griffiths, Sec.
Loughborough University
Department of Human Sciences
Leicestershire
Loughborough LE11 3TU, United Kingdom
Ph: 44 1509 228486
Ph: 44 1509 228812
E-mail: p.griffiths@lboro.ac.uk
URL: http://www.sshb.org

9223 ■ Postgraduate Student Travel Prize
To support the presentation of student research at academic and professional conferences. Two awards of £500 each are awarded annually.

9224 ■ Society for Theatre Research
Timothy West, Pres.
The National Theatre Archive
83-101 The Cut
London SE1 8LL, United Kingdom
E-mail: contact@str.org.uk
URL: http://www.str.org.uk

9225 ■ William Poel Memorial Festival
To encourage good stage speech, especially in sixteenth/seventeenth century drama. Entry is restricted to nominees from invited professional theatre schools in Great Britain. The festival currently takes place annually at the Royal National Theatre, normally in May. A small prize may be awarded at the Society's discretion. Established in 1952 by Dame Edith Evans in memory of William Poel (1852-1934), an innovative theatre director.

9226 ■ Research Awards
To provide for research on the history and practice of the British theatre. Private scholars, theatre professionals, academic staff, and students, unrestricted as to status or nationality, may apply for grants. Monetary awards range from £100 to £2,000. The following grants are awarded: The Anthony Denning Award, Kathleen Barker Award, Stephen Joseph Award, John Ramsden Awards, as well as other, unnamed grants. Frequency of the grants vary.

9227 ■ Society of Academic and Research Surgery
Prof. A. Bradley, Pres.
Royal College of Surgeons of England
35-43 Lincoln's Inn Fields

Awards are arranged in alphabetical order below their administering organizations

London WC2A 3PE, United Kingdom
Ph: 44 20 78696640
Fax: 44 20 78696644
E-mail: sking@rcseng.ac.uk
URL: http://www.surgicalresearch.org.uk

9228 ■ Patey Prize

To recognize the best paper presented at annual meeting.

9229 ■ President's Poster Prize

To recognize the best poster presented at the Society's annual meeting. Awarded annually. Established in 2004.

9230 ■ Society of Antiquaries of Scotland
Dr. Simon Gilmour MA, Dir.
National Museums Scotland
Chambers St.
Edinburgh EH1 1JF, United Kingdom
Ph: 44 131 2474133
Ph: 44 131 2474115
Fax: 44 131 2474163
E-mail: info@socantscot.org
URL: http://www.socantscot.org

9231 ■ Chalmers-Jervize Prize

To recognize the best essay relating to the archaeology or history of Scotland before the year 1100 AD. A monetary prize of £500 is awarded biennially.

9232 ■ Gunning Jubilee Gift

To enable experts to visit museums, collections, or materials of archaeological science at home or abroad for the purposes of Scottish-related special investigation and research. Open to non-Fellows. A monetary prize is awarded annually. Established in 1887 by Dr. Gunning.

9233 ■ Dorothy Marshall Medal

To recognize an individual for an outstanding contribution, in a voluntary capacity, to Scottish archaeological or related work. Awarded triennially.

9234 ■ Research Grants

To finance archaeological and historical research relating to Scotland. Awarded annually.

9235 ■ RBK Stevenson Award

To recognize the author of the article published in the *Proceedings* on a topic that best reflects the scholarship and high standards of R.B.K. Stevenson, who was for many years the Keeper of the National Museum of Antiquities of Scotland. A monetary prize of £50 is awarded annually.

9236 ■ Young Fellows Bursaries

To enable young Fellows of the Society to read papers on Scottish themes at conferences of international standing within Britain or abroad. Candidates must be under 25 years of age. Individual bursaries up to £300 are awarded annually.

9237 ■ Society of Architectural Historians of Great Britain
Mr. David McKinstry MA, Membership Sec.
6 Fitzroy Sq.
London W1T 5DX, United Kingdom
E-mail: membership@sahgb.org.uk
URL: http://www.sahgb.org.uk

9238 ■ Conference Bursaries

To provide financial assistance to bona fide students covering expenses involved in attending the Annual Conference. Awarded annually to two recipients.

9239 ■ Essay Medal

To encourage young or new architectural historians by honoring the author of the best essay. A medal and monetary prize of £200 are awarded annually. Established in 1982.

9240 ■ Alice Davis Hitchcock Medallion

To honor the author of the best architectural history book published in the past four years by a British author or by a foreign author on a British architectural historical subject. Awarded annually. Established in 1959.

9241 ■ Dorothy Stroud Bursary

To support research in architectural history for publication. A grant up to £500 is awarded twice each year.

9242 ■ Society of Army Historical Research
Guy Sayle, Membership Sec.
The Cavalry and Guards Club
127 Piccadilly
London W1J 7PX, United Kingdom
Ph: 44 7901951007
Fax: 44 2076299546
E-mail: guysayle@hotmail.com
URL: http://www.sahr.co.uk

9243 ■ Templer Medal

For recognition of the book making the most notable contribution to the history of the British Army or its predecessors and of the land forces of The Empire and Commonwealth. The award committee makes the selection from books published during the preceding calendar year that have been nominated. The medal and a cash prize of £5,000 are awarded at the annual general meeting. Established in 1982 in memory of Field Marshal Sir Gerald Templer KG, President of the Society.

9244 ■ Society of Authors - England
Emma Boniwell, Membership Sec.
84 Drayton Gardens
London SW10 9SB, United Kingdom
Ph: 44 20 73736642
Fax: 44 20 73735768
E-mail: info@societyofauthors.org
URL: http://www.societyofauthors.org

9245 ■ K. Blundell Grants

To assist young published authors working on their next book. British authors under 40 years of age whose work is for a British Publisher. The project must aim to increase social awareness, and can be fiction or non-fiction. Please note: the Trust does not cover self-published authors as grants cannot be awarded to help towards the costs of publication. A monetary prize of £1,000 to £4,000 is awarded annually. Established in 1987 by Kathleen Blundell.

9246 ■ Cholmondeley Award for Poets

To recognize and encourage poets of any age, sex, or nationality. The complete work of the poet is considered, rather than a specific book of poetry. Submissions are not accepted. Monetary prizes totaling £8,000 are awarded annually. Established in 1966 by the Marchioness of Cholmondeley.

9247 ■ Encore Award

To reward the best second novel of the year. The winner receives a monetary prize of £10,000. Awarded biennially in odd-numbered years. Established in 1990.

9248 ■ John Florio Prize

For recognition of the best translation from Italian into English of an Italian work of literary merit and general interest written in the last 100 years. Works published in the United Kingdom by a British publisher during the award year and the preceding year are eligible. A monetary prize of £3,000 is awarded biennially in even-numbered years. Established in 1963 under the auspices of the Italian Institute of Culture for the United Kingdom, the British Italian Society, and the Society of Authors.

9249 ■ Eric Gregory Awards

To encourage young poets. Candidates who are British subjects by birth, residents of the United Kingdom, and under 30 years of age may submit a published or unpublished volume of belles-lettres, drama poems, or poetry. Monetary awards totaling over £24,000 are awarded annually. Established by the late Eric Gregory.

9250 ■ Calouste Gulbenkian Prize

To recognize the best translation from Portuguese into English. The translation must have been first published in the United Kingdom in the award year and two preceding years. A monetary prize of £3,000 is awarded every four years.

9251 ■ Imison Award

To encourage new talent and high standards in writing for radio. Awarded for the best original radio drama script by a writer new to radio. A monetary prize of £1,500 is awarded annually. Established in 1994. Formerly: Richard Imison Memorial Award.

9252 ■ Premio Valle Inclan

To recognize published translations into English from Spanish. The original may be from any period or country, provided it is in the Spanish language. The translation must have been first published in the United Kingdom during the award year. A monetary prize of £2,000 is awarded annually.

9253 ■ Somerset Maugham Awards

To recognize a promising British author for a published work in the field of poetry, fiction, criticism, biography, history, philosophy, belles-lettres, or travel. Authors must be under 35 years of age. The award is designed to encourage writers to travel and acquaint themselves with the customs of other countries, and to extend the basis and influence of British literature. Monetary awards of £12,000 are awarded annually. Established in 1946 by the late Somerset Maugham.

9254 ■ McKitterick Prize

To recognize the best first novel published by an author over the age of 40. Published and unpublished novels are eligible. A monetary prize of £4,000 is awarded annually. Established in 1990.

9255 ■ Medical Book Awards

To recognize an author(s) or editor(s) of medical books published in Britain and to encourage authors who work in the United Kingdom to write for medical students, medical professionals, or the general public. The following awards are presented: Richard Asher Prize (£1,200), New Authored Book (£1,200), New Edited Book (£1,800), New Non-Clinical Medical Book (£600), New Edition Authored Book (£600), New Edition Edited Book (£600), the Minty Prize of the Medico-Legal Society (£1,000), New Medical or Healthcare Book for the General Reader (£600), and the RSM Literary Prize (£1,200). Awarded annually. Established in 1983. Sponsored by the Royal Society of Medicine. Formerly: (1985) Abbott Prize; Glaxo Prize for Medical Writing; Medical Book Prize.

9256 ■ Scott Moncrieff Prize

For recognition of the best translation from French to English of a French work of literary merit and general interest written in the last 100 years. Works published in the United Kingdom by a British publisher during the award year may be submitted by the publisher. A monetary prize of £2,000 is awarded annually. Established in 1964.

9257 ■ Bernard Shaw Prize

To recognize the best translation from Swedish into English. The translation must have been first published in the United Kingdom during the award year and the two preceding years. A monetary prize of £2,000 is awarded triennially. Established in 1991.

9258 ■ Tom-Gallon Trust Award

To recognize authors of short stories. Published

and unpublished works are eligible. A monetary prize of £1,000 is awarded biennially in odd-numbered years. Established in 1946. Formerly: Tom-Gallon Award.

9259 ■ Betty Trask Prize and Awards

To recognize authors under the age of 35 for a first novel, published or unpublished, of a romantic or traditional nature. British/Commonwealth citizens are eligible. Monetary awards totaling £20,000, which must be used for travel abroad, are presented annually. Established in 1983 by Margaret Elizabeth Trask, an author of romantic novels.

9260 ■ Travelling Scholarships

To enable British writers to travel abroad. Monetary awards of varying amounts are presented annually. Established in 1944.

9261 ■ Vondel Translation Prize

To recognize translations of Dutch and Flemish works of literature into English. The translation must have been first published in the United Kingdom or the United States in the award year or the preceding year. A monetary prize of £2,000 is awarded biennially in odd-numbered years. Established in 1995.

9262 ■ Society of Biology

Dr. Mark Downs, CEO
Charles Darwin House
12 Roger St.
London WC1N 2JU, United Kingdom
Ph: 44 20 76852550
E-mail: info@societyofbiology.org
URL: http://www.societyofbiology.org
Formed by merger of: (2009) Biosciences Federation; Institute of Biology.

9263 ■ Science Communication Award

To recognize bioscience researchers from U.K. universities and institutes who have made an outstanding and consistent contribution to communicating science. A monetary prize is awarded in two categories: new researchers (£750) and established researchers (£1,500). Awarded annually.

9264 ■ Society of Border Leicester Sheep Breeders

Ian J.R. Sutherland, Sec.
Rock Midstead
Northumberland
Alnwick NE66 2TH, United Kingdom
Ph: 44 7891 245870
Fax: 44 1665 579326
E-mail: info@borderleicesters.co.uk
URL: http://www.borderleicesters.co.uk

9265 ■ Best in Breed Award

Recognize members whose sheep win championships.

9266 ■ Society of Chemical Industry

Joanne Lyall, Exec. Dir.
14-15 Belgrave Sq.
London SW1X 8PS, United Kingdom
Ph: 44 20 75981500
Ph: 44 20 75981579
Fax: 44 20 75981545
E-mail: secretariat@soci.org
URL: http://www.soci.org

9267 ■ Henry E. Armstrong Memorial Lecture

To recognize an individual for contributions to process engineering. A scroll is awarded when merited by SCI's Process Engineering Group. Established in 1943 in memory of Professor H.E. Armstrong (1848-1937), regarded as one of the fathers of chemical engineering; it was his life's work to teach chemistry as part of an education in engineering.

9268 ■ Award for Science Communication

Recognizes outstanding contributions to the public understanding of chemistry or related sciences. Part of the Society's Peoples Awards. Awarded biennially. Established in 2006.

9269 ■ Award for Science Education

To recognize outstanding contributions to the field of scientific education. Part of the Society's Peoples Awards. Awarded biennially. Established in 2006.

9270 ■ Award for the Environment

Recognizes an individual or team for contributions to environmental understanding, protection, or performance as the result of the creation and application of science or technology in any chemistry-related field, including chemical engineering. Formerly: Environment Medal.

9271 ■ Baekeland Lecture

To recognize an individual for contributions to the science of polymeric materials. A scroll is awarded every four years by SCI's Materials Chemistry Group. Established in 1943 to commemorate the work of Dr. Leo H. Baekeland (1863-1944) of the USA on synthetic resins.

9272 ■ Hans R. Bolliger Memorial Lecture

To recognize an individual for contributions to a chemical aspect of health and safety. A certificate is awarded by SCI's Health and Safety Group. Established in 1977.

9273 ■ Canada International Award

To recognize an individual for outstanding service to the Canadian chemical industry in the international sphere. Awarded biennially by the SCI's Canada regional group. Established in 1976. Formerly: Canadian International Medal Lecture.

9274 ■ Canada Medal

For recognition of outstanding service to chemical industry in Canada. A medal is awarded biennially by the SCI's Canada regional group. Established in 1939.

9275 ■ Castner Medal and Lecture

To recognize an individual for contributions to applied electrochemistry in a subject related to chemical research. Awarded biennially by SCI's Electrochemical Technology Group. Established in 1946 to honor Hamilton Young Castner (1858-1899), a pioneer in the field of industrial electrochemistry.

9276 ■ Wesley Cocker Award

To recognize the best paper or patent on a topic of relevance to the industrial chemistry field. PhD and BSc students in Ireland who are Society's members are eligible. A monetary prize of 500 Euros, a certificate, and a year's membership in the Society are awarded annually. Established in 2008. Honors the late Professor Cocker's long service to the Society and chemistry in Ireland.

9277 ■ Carl Hanson Medal

To recognize an individual for achievements in solvent extraction science and technology. A bronze medal is awarded triennially by the Separation Science and Technology Group. Established in 1986 in memory of Carl Hanson, renowned for his work on all aspects of solvent extraction. Awarded jointly with DECHEMA.

9278 ■ Roland Harper Lecture

To recognize an individual for advanced work in consumer and/or sensory science. A scroll is awarded as merited by SCI's Food Group. Established in 1993 to commemorate Dr. Roland Harper (1916-92), an international figure in the growth and application of sensory sciences.

9279 ■ Hilditch Memorial Lecture

To recognize an individual for exceptional contributions to education as it relates to oil and fats or applied chemistry. A scroll is awarded every two or three years by SCI's Lipid Group. Estab-

lished in 1967 in memory of Professor T.P. Hilditch (1886-1965), the first holder of the Campbell Brown Chair of Industrial Chemistry in the University of Liverpool, who made outstanding contributions to the knowledge of oils and fats.

9280 ■ Robert Horne Memorial Lecture

A lecture on non-ferrous metals or a related subject is delivered at intervals in Bristol or in South Wales. Awarded triennially. Established in 1943 in memory of Viscount Horne, the first Chairman of the Imperial Smelting Corporation. Administered by the Bristol and the South Wales Sections of the Society.

9281 ■ Hurter Memorial Lecture

A lecture delivered at intervals on applied chemistry. Awarded periodically by the Society's Liverpool and North West Group. Established in 1898 as a memorial to Dr. Ferdinand Hurter (1844-1898), an authority on the Leblanc system for soda production.

9282 ■ Lampitt Medal

For recognition of outstanding service to the society through the groups and sections. No more than two medals and certificates are awarded annually. Established in 1958 to commemorate Dr. Leslie H. Lampitt, who played a major role in the society's affairs for 37 years.

9283 ■ LeSueur Memorial Award

Recognizes technical excellence in a university, research, or industrial setting in Canada. A medal and an invitation to address the Canada Group Meeting are awarded biennially. Administered by the Society's Canada Group. Established in 1955 to honor Ernest A. LeSueur, who made many outstanding contributions to early industrial chemistry in Canada, including the first successful commercial electrolytic cell for the manufacture of chlorine and caustic soda.

9284 ■ Leverhulme Lecture

To promote research and education in connection with the chemical industry. Awarded every two or three years by the Society's Liverpool and North West Group. Established in 1943 by the Leverhulme Trust in memory of the first Viscount Leverhulme (1851-1925), the founder of Port Sunlight.

9285 ■ Ivan Levinstein Memorial Lecture

To recognize an individual for excellence in chemical research and knowledge. An invitation to present a lecture is awarded triennially by the Society's Liverpool and North West Group. Established in 1946 in memory of Ivan Levinstein (1845-1916), a pioneer in the manufacture of synthetic dyestuffs.

9286 ■ Julia Levy Award

To recognize an individual or team for a successful commercial innovation in the field of biomedical science and engineering in Canada. Awarded irregularly. Established in 2004. Sponsored by the Canada International Group Committee. Honors Dr. Julia Levy one of the founders of QLT Inc.

9287 ■ Julius Lewkowitsch Memorial Lecture

To recognize an individual for contributions to the science of oils and fats and their products. Awarded biennially by SCI's Lipids Group. Established in 1980 to commemorate the work of Julius Lewkowitsch in the oils and fats field.

9288 ■ Lipids Group International Lecture

To recognize an individual for contributions to the field of lipids. Awarded biennially by Society'S Lipids Group. Established in 1964. Formerly: Oil and Fats Group International Lecture.

9289 ■ Lister Memorial Lecture

A lecture on chemistry and medical science.

Awards are arranged in alphabetical order below their administering organizations

Lecture is later published. Awarded periodically by the Society'S Scotland Group. Endowed in 1944 to commemorate the first Baron Lister (1827-1912), the pioneer of antiseptic surgery.

9290 ■ Mond Health and Safety Award
For significant achievement in health and safety, in either the work place or in any aspect of general public or consumer safety. Covers achievements in food, pharmaceuticals, construction materials, environmental protection, and petrochemicals. Awarded biennially. Established in 1999. Honors Ludwig Mond the principal founder of the Society.

9291 ■ Gordon E. Moore Medal
To recognize an industrial scientist for a significant innovation early in their career. Industrial scientists who are under 45 years of age and U.S. citizens or residents are eligible. A medal is awarded annually. Established in 2004. Honors Gordon E. Moore, one of the founders of Intel Corp. and author of Moore's Law.

9292 ■ Kalev Pugi Award
To recognize an individual or team for exceptional achievements in research and development in the chemical industry field. A medal is awarded irregularly. Established in 2002. Presented by the Canada International Group Awards Committee. Honors Kalev Pugi's contributions to nylon intermediate manufacturing and continuous polymerization of nylon.

9293 ■ Purvis Memorial Award
To recognize an individual for dedication and service to the Canadian chemical industry. A plaque is awarded periodically by the Society'S Canada Group. Established in 1947 to commemorate Rt. Hon. Arthur B. Purvis (1890-1941).

9294 ■ Sir Eric Rideal Lecture
To honor an individual for a significant and sustained contribution to the field of colloid science in the United Kingdom. Each year, one individual is awarded a scroll and an invitation to deliver a lecture at the Annual General of the Colloid and Surface Science Group. Established in 1970 to commemorate Sir Eric Rideal, President of the Society from 1944 to 1946.

9295 ■ Richard Seligman Lecture
To recognize an individual for contributions any aspect of engineering or processing in the food or beverage industries in order to advance the education of the public in such matters. Awarded no less than every three years. Established in 1974 in memory of Dr. Richard Seligman, founder of the company who had been a member of the society for over 50 years. Administered by SCI's Food Group.

9296 ■ Separation Science Lecture
A lecture on a branch of separation science and technology. A scroll is awarded periodically by the Separation Science and Technology Group. Established in 1995.

9297 ■ Society Award
To recognize an outstanding and internationally-useful innovation that has benefited consumers or society in general. Individuals and teams are eligible. Awarded biennially. Established in 2007.

9298 ■ Society of Cosmetic Scientists
Mrs. Gem Bektas, Sec. Gen.
Langham House East
Mill St., Ste. 6
Bedsfordshire
Luton LU1 2NA, United Kingdom
Ph: 44 1582 726661
Fax: 44 1582 405217
E-mail: ifscc.scs@btconnect.com
URL: http://www.scs.org.uk

9299 ■ Publications Prize
To the author of the best original scientific paper published in the *International Journal of Cosmetic Science*. A monetary prize of £500 is awarded annually.

9300 ■ Society of Dyers and Colourists - England
Susie Hargreaves, CEO
Perkin House
82 Grattan Rd.
PO Box 244
Bradford BD1 2JB, United Kingdom
Ph: 44 1274 725138
Fax: 44 1274 392888
E-mail: info@sdc.org.uk
URL: http://www.sdc.org.uk

9301 ■ Centenary Medal
To recognize an author of a paper published by the Society in the area of educational, management, or review. Awarded annually. Established in 1984.

9302 ■ LSDC Licentiateship
A diploma is awarded when merited to members who have passed the prescribed Society examinations (or possess an equivalent qualification) and who have provided evidence of having satisfactory experience in color science or color technology.

9303 ■ Medal of the Society of Dyers and Colourists
For recognition of exceptional services to the Society or in the interests of the tinctorial and allied industries. Gold, Silver, Bronze, and Centenary Medals are awarded annually. Established in 1908.

9304 ■ Perkin Medal
For recognition of exceptional services in the interests of the tinctorial and allied industries. A gold medal is awarded when merited. Established in 1908 in memory of Sir William Henry Perkin, the founder of the coal-tar dye industry, and President of the Society in 1907.

9305 ■ Turner - Scholefield Award
To recognize an Associate under the age of 33 who has made notable and meritorious contributions to the science or technology of coloring matters or their application, or has demonstrated the ability to apply his or her knowledge and skills in an appropriate field of color science or technology. Awarded annually or when merited. Established in 1970 under the will of the late Mr. H. A. Turner in memory of Fred Scholefield.

9306 ■ Worshipful Company of Dyers Research Medal
To recognize the authors of papers embodying the results of scientific research or technical investigation connected with the tinctorial arts published in the *Journal* of the Society. A gold or silver medal is awarded annually. Established in 1908.

9307 ■ Society of Floristry
Lucy Todman, Sec.
Wilcot Chapel
Kinton
Shropshire SY4 1AZ, United Kingdom
Ph: 44 870 2410432
E-mail: info@societyoffloristry.org
URL: http://www.societyoffloristry.org

9308 ■ Higher Diploma in Floristry
To recognize an individual for success in the Level 4 examination. Formerly: (2006) Intermediate Certificate in Floristry.

9309 ■ Master Diploma in Professional Floristry
To recognize an individual for success in the Level 5 examination. Formerly: (2006) National Diploma of the Society of Floristry.

9310 ■ Society of Food Hygiene and Technology
Simon Houghton-Dodd, Chm.
The Granary
Middleton House Farm
Tamworth Rd.
Staffs
Middleton B78 2BD, United Kingdom
Ph: 44 1827 872500
Fax: 44 1827 875800
E-mail: admin@sofht.co.uk
URL: http://www.sofht.co.uk

9311 ■ SOFHT Awards
To recognize and celebrate the excellence within the food industry and its associated industries. Six awards are presented: Best New Product, Company of the Year, Best Trainer, Best Training Company, Best Auditor or Technologist, and the SOFHT Award for the Most Significant Contribution. Awarded annually.

9312 ■ SOFHT Fellowship
For members who have given exceptional service to the Society.

9313 ■ Society of Glass Technology
Kevin Green, Contact
9 Churchill Way
Chapeltown
Sheffield S35 2PY, United Kingdom
Ph: 44 114 2634455
Fax: 44 114 2634411
E-mail: info@sgt.org
URL: http://www.sgt.org

9314 ■ Oldfield Award
To recognize the best research projects conducted by undergraduates or taught Masters students. Open to students worldwide. Research topics should be any experimental or theoretical investigation related to amorphous solids, glasses, glass-ceramics, sol-gel materials or ormocers, glass history and archaeology, or glass commerce and design. Monetary prizes are awarded for first (£500), second (£350), and third (£150) place. Awarded annually. Established in 2003 in honor of Lucy Oldfield.

9315 ■ Paul Award
To recognize the best student paper presentation at the New Researchers Forum. A monetary prize of £250 is awarded annually. Established in 2007 in honor of Amalendu Paul.

9316 ■ SGT Fellowship
To recognize members who have met certain criteria for achievements, education, and service.

9317 ■ SGT Travel Grant
For student travel to university/work experience.

9318 ■ Society of Indexers (Societe des Indexateurs)
Mr. Paul Machen, Office Mgr.
Woodbourn Business Centre
10 Jessell St.
Sheffield S9 3HY, United Kingdom
Ph: 44 114 2449561
E-mail: info@indexers.org.uk
URL: http://www.indexers.org.uk

9319 ■ Carey Award
For recognition of services to indexing. Individuals are nominated by the Council of the Society. A framed parchment is awarded when merited. Established in 1977 in honor of Gordon V. Carey, the first President of the Society.

9320 ■ Wheatley Medal
For recognition of an outstanding index first

Awards are arranged in alphabetical order below their administering organizations

published in the United Kingdom during the preceding three years. Printed indexes to any type of publication must be submitted provided that the whole work (including the index), or the index alone, has originated in the United Kingdom. A medal and monetary prize of £500 is awarded annually. Established in 1962 in honor of Henry B. Wheatley, sometimes referred to as "the father of British indexing."

9321 ■ Society of Leather Technologists and Chemists
Mrs. Pat Potter, Membership Sec.
8 Copper Leaf Close
Moulton
Northampton NN3 7HS, United Kingdom
Ph: 44 1604 892059
Fax: 44 1604 711183
E-mail: office@sltc.org
URL: http://www.sltc.org

9322 ■ Procter Memorial Prize
For outstanding contributions to the journal of SLTC.

9323 ■ Society of London Theatre
Richard Pulford, Chief Exec.
32 Rose St.
London WC2E 9ET, United Kingdom
Ph: 44 20 75576700
Fax: 44 20 75576799
E-mail: enquiries@solttma.co.uk
URL: http://www.solt.co.uk
Formerly: (1996) Society of West End Theatre.

9324 ■ Laurence Olivier Awards
To recognize distinguished artistic achievement in the West End Theatre. Awards are given in 24 categories, including Best Actor, Best Actress, Best Revival, Best New Musical, Outstanding Achievement in Opera, and Best Entertainment. Held annually. Established in 1976. Sponsored by MasterCard. Formerly: (1996) Society of West End Theatre.

9325 ■ Society of Ornamental Turners
Michael R. Windsor, Treas.
9 Rhodes Ave.
London N22 4UR, United Kingdom
Ph: 44 208 8883688
E-mail: webmaster@the-sot.com
URL: http://the-sot.com

9326 ■ Cattell Cup
To encourage the design and making of suitable apparatus for ornamental turning. Society members are eligible. A silver cup is awarded annually. Established in 1989 by Mr. S.N. Cattell.

9327 ■ Haythornthwaite Cup
For recognition of high practical and artistic skills in the art of both plain and ornamental turning. Members of the Society for fewer than five years are eligible. A cup is awarded annually.

9328 ■ Howe Cup
For recognition of high practical and artistic skills in the art of hand turning. Members of the Society are eligible. A cup is awarded annually.

9329 ■ President's Cup
To recognize the member who has consistently provided interesting displays at meetings during the year. Society members are eligible. A silver cup is awarded annually. Established in 1989.

9330 ■ Tweddle Medal
For recognition of high practical and artistic skills in the art of ornamental turning. Members of the Society are eligible. A medal is awarded annually.

9331 ■ Society of Procurement Officers in Local Government
Peter Howarth, CEO/Managing Dir.
113-117 London Rd.
Leicestershire

Leicester LE2 0RG, United Kingdom
Ph: 44 141 4311839
E-mail: k.may@espo.org
URL: http://www.sopo.org

9332 ■ Awards for Outstanding Achievement in Procurement
To recognize the variety of approaches to procurement made by local authorities. Trophies are awarded in four categories: County Council, Single-Tier (Unitary) Authority, Non-Unitary District/Borough Council, and Other (e.g., Police, Fire, Consortia). Awarded annually. Established in 2002.

9333 ■ Society of Professional Engineers
Dr. Hugh Wynne, Pres.
Lutyens House
Billing Brook Rd.
Weston Favell
Northampton NN3 8NW, United Kingdom
Ph: 44 1604 415729
E-mail: spe@abe.org.uk
URL: http://www.professionalengineers-uk.org

9334 ■ Gardner Award
Demonstrating high level of practical engineering achievement.

9335 ■ Society of Teachers of Speech and Drama
Mrs. Felicity Amor, Chair
73 Berry Hill Rd.
Nottinghamshire
Mansfield NG18 4RU, United Kingdom
E-mail: stsd@stsd.org.uk
URL: http://www.stsd.org.uk

9336 ■ John Holgate Memorial Award
To provide financial assistance to individuals training to become teachers. Awarded annually to one or more recipients.

9337 ■ Society of Technical Analysts
Deborah Owen, Chair
Dean House
Vernham Dean SP11 0JZ, United Kingdom
Ph: 44 20 71250038
Fax: 44 20 79002585
E-mail: info@sta-uk.org
URL: http://sta-uk.org

9338 ■ PMRS Awards
To top students.

9339 ■ Bronwen Wood Memorial Prize
To recognize the student on the Diploma Course who has the best paper. Awarded annually. Established in 2006.

9340 ■ Society of Wildlife Artists
Harriet Mead, Pres.
Federation of British Artists
17 Carlton House Terr.
London SW1Y 5BD, United Kingdom
Ph: 44 207 9306844
URL: http://www.swla.co.uk

9341 ■ Artists for Nature Foundation Award
Presented at the Society's annual exhibition.

9342 ■ RSPB Fine Art Award
To honor artwork depicting wildlife subjects that is shown at the annual exhibition of the Society, which takes place each autumn at the Mall Galleries. Awarded annually.

9343 ■ Society of Women Artists
Barbara Penketh Simpson, Pres.
1 Knapp Cottages
Wyke
Dorset
Gillingham SP8 4NQ, United Kingdom
Ph: 44 1747 825718
Fax: 44 1747 826835

E-mail: pamhendersons@dsl.pipex.com
URL: http://www.society-women-artists.org.uk

9344 ■ HRH Princess Michael of Kent Award
Annual award of recognition for the artist with the best watercolor painting.

9345 ■ President & Vice President's Choice Award
Award of recognition for a painting.

9346 ■ Barbara Tate Award
Annual award of recognition for the artist with best oil painting.

9347 ■ Winsor & Newton Choice Award
Annual award of recognition for a painting.

9348 ■ Soil Association
Helen Browning, Dir.
South Plz.
Marlborough St.
Bristol BS1 3NX, United Kingdom
Ph: 44 117 3145000
Fax: 44 117 3145001
E-mail: memb@soilassociation.org
URL: http://www.soilassociation.org

9349 ■ Natural and Organic Products Awards
To recognize innovation, quality, and commitment within the organic and natural health and beauty industry in Europe. Awards are presented in various categories, such as Best Organic Retailer, Best Organic Bodycare Product, and Best New Non-Food Product. Awarded annually at the Natural and Organic Products Europe trade show. Sponsored by *Natural Products* magazine.

9350 ■ Organic Food Awards
To recognize, celebrate, and promote the best organic foods on the market. Open to any product registered as organize under European Union regulation 834/07 and certified by a recognized organize certification body within the European Union. Awarded in 12 categories, such as baked goods, dairy, and wine and spirits. Held biennially in even-numbered years.

9351 ■ Specialty Coffee Association of Europe
Nils Erichsen, Pres.
Oak Lodge Farm
Leighams Rd.
Bicknacre
Essex
Chelmsford CM3 4HF, United Kingdom
Ph: 44 1245 426060
Fax: 44 1245 426080
E-mail: secretary@scae.com
URL: http://scae.com

9352 ■ Hidden Treasure Award
To honor an unrecognized coffee enthusiast who has done more than his/her fair share of promoting quality coffee. He or she must have a direct contact with coffee, but at any stage of production, e.g. as a grower, shipper, roaster, cafe owner, or barista. Awarded annually.

9353 ■ Lifetime Achievement Award
To honor an institution or person who has furthered the interests of the industry by promoting the concept of quality coffee in a statesman-like manner. Awarded annually.

9354 ■ Passionate Communicator Award
To honor an individual who has made a concerted effort to communicate to others the wonderful pleasure that coffee can bring to us. All communication tools that appeal to our five senses can be used: the spoken, written or printed word, the arts such as photography and painting, or even through music and drama.

Awards are arranged in alphabetical order below their administering organizations

9355 ■ Young Entrepreneur Award
To honor an enthusiastic member of the coffee industry, preferably under 35 years old, who shows great drive both to persevere in his/her field and to be successful in the business. Awarded annually.

9356 ■ *The Spectator*
22 Old Queen St.
London SW1H 9HP, United Kingdom
Ph: 44 20 7961 0200
Fax: 44 20 7242 0603
E-mail: spectator@solodigital.co.uk
URL: http://www.spectator.co.uk

9357 ■ Threadneedle/Spectator Parliamentarian of the Year Awards
For recognition of parliamentary contributions. The following awards are presented: Politician of the Year, Parliamentarian of the Year, Newcomer of the Year, Inquisitor of the Year, Peer of the Year, Speech of the Year, Resignation of the Year, Minister to Watch, Campaigner of the Year, Readers' Representative, Survivor of the Year, and Backbencher of the Year. Awarded annually.

9358 ■ Sports Journalists' Association of Great Britain
Barry Newcombe, Chm.
Unit 92, Capital Business Ctre.
22 Carlton Rd.
Surrey
South Croydon CR2 0BS, United Kingdom
Ph: 44 20 89162234
Fax: 44 20 89162235
E-mail: barrynewcombe@gmail.com
URL: http://www.sportsjournalists.co.uk

9359 ■ J.L. Manning Award
To recognize an individual for services to sport off the field of play. Awarded annually. Established in 1974.

9360 ■ Bill McGowran Award
To recognize a disabled sport personality. Awarded annually. Established in 1963

9361 ■ Sports Feature Writer Award
To recognize the author of an outstanding sports feature story. Awarded annually.

9362 ■ Sports Personalities of the Year (Men, Women, Team)
To recognize reigning world champions. Awarded annually.

9363 ■ Sports Photographer of the Year
To recognize an outstanding sports photographer. Awarded annually.

9364 ■ Sports Writer of the Year
To recognize a sports journalist, staff member, or freelance contributor to UK national newspaper. Awarded annually.

9365 ■ Tea Council
William Gorman, Exec. Chm.
Crown House, 4th Fl.
1 Crown Sq., Ste. 10
Woking GU2 6HR, United Kingdom
Ph: 44 20 73717787
Ph: 44 1483 750559
Fax: 44 20 73717958
E-mail: info@teacouncil.co.uk
URL: http://www.tea.co.uk

9366 ■ Top Tea Places of the Year
Recognizes tearooms and hotels across Britain for outstanding quality and consistent high standards in tea service. Criteria include variety and excellence of teas offered, service, decor, ambience, and presentation. Awarded annually to several recipients.

9367 ■ Television and Radio Industries Club
George Stone, Dir.
Hill Farm
Margaretting Rd.

Essex
Galleywood CM2 8TS, United Kingdom
Ph: 44 1245 290480
Fax: 44 1245 265963
E-mail: info@tric.org.uk
URL: http://www.tric.org.uk
Formerly: (1981) Radio Industries Club.

9368 ■ TRIC Awards
For recognition of the best in contributions in radio and television in the previous twelve months. Awards are given in 16 categories: Satellite/Digital TV Personality, Radio/Digital Radio Personality, TV Personality, Sports Presenter, Newscaster/Reporter, TV Weather Presenter, New TV Talent, TV Arts/Documentary Program, Satellite/Digital Program, Radio/Digital Program, TV Comedy Program, TV Drama Program, TV Daytime Program, TV Entertainment Program, TV Soap of the Year, and the TRIC Special Award. Monetary prizes, trophies and certificates are awarded annually. Established in 1969.

9369 ■ Tenovus Scotland
Mr. Iain McFadzean, Gen. Sec.
234 St. Vincent St.
Glasgow G2 5RJ, United Kingdom
Ph: 44 1292 443387
Ph: 44 141 2216268
E-mail: gen.sec@talk21.com
URL: http://www.tenovus-scotland.org.uk

9370 ■ Lady Illingworth Award
Rewards a major contribution made towards improving the quality of life for the elderly. Individuals or teams that have been actively engaged in research and/or in the development of a piece of medical/dental equipment, which has resulted in the improved welfare of the elderly, the quality of life for the elderly; elderly, for the purpose of this Award is 65 years of age and over, are eligible. Work must have been carried out within the British Isles. A monetary awarded is given every five years.

9371 ■ Textile Institute
Prof. Andreas Weber, Pres.
St. James's Buildings, 1st Fl.
79 Oxford St.
Manchester M1 6FQ, United Kingdom
Ph: 44 161 2371188
Fax: 44 161 2361991
E-mail: tiihq@textileinst.org.uk
URL: http://www.texi.org

9372 ■ Carothers Medal
To recognize creativity in the production or use of fibres. Awarded annually. Established in 1992 in memory of Wallace H. Carothers, who discovered nylon (polyamide).

9373 ■ Companion Membership
Awarded to institute members (over 40 years of age) who are considered to have substantially advanced the general interests of the textile industry. Awarded annually. Established in 1956 and limited to 50 living members worldwide.

9374 ■ Development Award
To recognize individuals, groups, or organizations for outstanding achievements in enhancing international textile interests through commerce or marketing or economic development. Awarded annually. Established in 1990.

9375 ■ Holden Medal
In recognition of an outstanding contribution to education for, or to the technology of, the apparel sector. Awarded annually. Established in 1981.

9376 ■ Honorary Fellow
This, the highest honor within the Institute, is given for recognition of creativity and the advancement of knowledge achieved by an indi-

vidual as a result of ingenuity and application over many years. It covers all occupational areas of the Institute's work, including science, technology, marketing and management. Awarded annually. Established in 1928.

9377 ■ Honorary Life Member
This, the highest award granted for service to the Institute, is given to recognize exceptional and sustained service to the Institute in the furtherance of its Charter objectives and to the textile industry in general. Awarded annually. Established in 1979.

9378 ■ Institute Medal
For recognition of distinguished services to the textile industry in general, and to the Institute. Awarded annually. Established in 1921.

9379 ■ Institute Medal for Design
To recognize professional designers or groups of designers who have devoted themselves to, and made significant contributions in the field of textile design or design management or both. Aesthetic appeal and commercial success are both taken into account. Awarded annually. Established in 1971.

9380 ■ Jubilee Award
For recognition of successful research and invention by teams or groups of researchers working within any appropriate organization. Awarded annually. Established in 1960 to commemorate the Institute's Golden Jubilee Year.

9381 ■ Lemkin Medal
For recognition of exceptional service to the Institute in the areas of clothing and footwear. Awarded annually. Established in 1960.

9382 ■ Service Medal
In recognition of valuable services rendered to the Institute. Awarded annually. Established in 1940.

9383 ■ S. G. Smith Memorial Medal
To recognize individuals for contributions to the furtherance of scientific knowledge concerned with the physical and structural properties of fibers, whether such work has been published or not. Awarded annually. Established in 1964.

9384 ■ Warner Memorial Medal
To recognize outstanding work in textile science and technology, the results of which have been published, and particularly for work published in the *Journal of the Textile Institute*. Awarded annually. Established in 1930.

9385 ■ Weaver's Company Medal and Prize
To recognize outstanding contributions to the weaving sector of the United Kingdom textile industry. Awarded annually. Established in 1979 by Worshipful Company Of Weavers', the oldest of the Livery Companies of the City of London.

9386 ■ Theatre Centre
Shoreditch Town Hall
380 Old St.
London EC1V 9LT, United Kingdom
Ph: 44 20 7729 3066
Fax: 44 20 7739 9741
E-mail: admin@theatre-centre.co.uk
URL: http://www.theatre-centre.co.uk

9387 ■ Brian Way Award
To honor playwrights who write plays for young people. Submitted plays must be at least 45 minutes long and must have been produced professionally during the previous year. A monetary prize of £6,000 is awarded annually. Established in 2001.

9388 ■ Thomson Reuters Foundation
Monique Villa, CEO
30 S Colonnade
London E14 5EP, United Kingdom

Awards are arranged in alphabetical order below their administering organizations

Ph: 44 20 75427015
URL: http://www.trust.org
Formerly: Reuters Foundation.

9389 ■ Oxford University Fellowship
The fellowship offers outstanding journalists the opportunity to spend three months studying at Oxford University to study subjects of their choice. The fellowship is open to writers and broadcasters from the United States, including specialists in economic, environmental, medical and scientific subjects. Applicants must be citizens of the United States; full-time journalists or regular contributors to newspapers, news agencies, magazines, radio or television; established journalists with a minimum five years' professional experience and a clear commitment to a career in journalism. Fellowship covers travel expenses, tuition and monthly living expenses. Applications are due by October 31. Established in 1996.

9390 ■ Stanford Fellowship
To provide individuals an opportunity to research and create prototype technology solutions that will benefit the under-served communities in developing countries. As part of the Digital Vision Program, the fellowship supports social entrepreneurs who seek to leverage technology-based solutions in the interest of humanitarian, educational, and sustainable development goals. The nine-month fellowship is based at the Stanford Center for the Study of Language and Information on the campus of Stanford University. The Reuter Foundation pays the costs of the return fare between the Fellow's home and the University, tuition fees, and living expenses. Each Fellowship is tenable for one, two, or three academic terms. Certificates are awarded at the completion of the fellowship. Established in 1982.

9391 ■ Time Out Group Ltd.
Cathy Runciman, Mng. Dir.
Universal House
251 Tottenham Court Rd.
London W1T 7AB, United Kingdom
Ph: 44 20 7813 3000
Fax: 44 20 7813 3438
E-mail: cathyrunciman@timeout.com
URL: http://www.timeout.com

9392 ■ Eating and Drinking Awards
For recognition of outstanding area restaurants. Winners and runners-up are named in the following categories: Best New Coffee Bar, Best New Cafe, Best New Bar, Best New Gastropub, Best New Cheap Eats, Best New Restaurant, Best New Local Restaurant, Best Spanish Food and Drink, and Best New Design. Awarded annually.

9393 ■ Live Awards
For recognition of achievement in the London theatre, dance, and comedy scene. Awards are given in the categories of nightlife, music, theatre, classical music, comedy, and dance. Plaques are awarded annually. Established in 1986. Formerly: *Time Out*/01 - for London Awards.

9394 ■ Tourism Society
Gregory Yeoman, Exec. Dir.
Trinity Ct.
34 West St.
Surrey
Sutton SM1 1SH, United Kingdom
Ph: 44 20 86614636
Fax: 44 20 86614637
E-mail: admin@tourismsociety.org
URL: http://www.tourismsociety.org

9395 ■ Tourism Society Award
For exceptional contributions to the development of tourism in the United Kingdom. Awarded annually. Established in 1997.

9396 ■ Triangle Management Services Ltd.
4 The Courtyard
Furlong Rd.
Bourne End
Bucks SL8 5AU, United Kingdom
Ph: 44 1628 642910
URL: http://www.triangle.eu.com

9397 ■ World Mail Awards
To recognize and encourage postal services for best practice within the mail industry worldwide. Awarded in the categories: Corporate Social Responsibility, Customer Service, e-Commerce, Growth, Industry Leadership, Innovation, People Management, Retail Project, Security, and Technology. Presented annually. Established in 2000.

9398 ■ UBM Aviation
The OAG Bldg.
Church St.
Dunstable LU5 4HB, United Kingdom
Ph: 44 1582 600111
Fax: 44 1582 695230
URL: http://www.ubmaviationnews.com

9399 ■ Aircraft Technology Engineering and Maintenance Awards
To recognize excellence in aircraft technology engineering and maintenance. Awarded in a variety of categories, including Best Airframe MRO Provider, Best OEM for Aftermarket Support, and Editors Award for Technology and Innovation. Awarded annually.

9400 ■ UK Association of Online Publishers
Tim Faircliff, Chm.
55/56 Lincolns Inn Fields
Holborn
London WC2A 3LJ, United Kingdom
Ph: 44 20 74044166
Fax: 44 20 74044167
E-mail: info@ukaop.org.uk
URL: http://www.ukaop.org.uk

9401 ■ Online Publishing Awards
For excellence in digital publishing. Awarded in a variety of categories each year.

9402 ■ UK Fashion Exports
Paul Alger, Exec. Dir.
5 Portland Pl.
London W1B 1PW, United Kingdom
Ph: 44 20 76365577
Ph: 44 20 76367788
Fax: 44 20 76367515
URL: http://www.5portlandplace.org.uk

9403 ■ UK Fashion Export Awards
To recognize companies, irrespective of size, who have demonstrated export excellence. Awards are presented in eight categories: Menswear; Men's Accessories; Women's wear; Women's Accessories; Children's wear; Ethical Fashion; Lingerie/Beach Fashion; and New Exporter. The Exporter of the Year Award and the Export Personality of the Year Award are also presented. Awarded annually.

9404 ■ U.K. Irrigation Association
Mr. Melvyn Kay, Exec. Sec.
Moorland House
10 Hayway
Northants
Rushden NN10 6AG, United Kingdom
Ph: 44 1427 717627
Fax: 44 1427 717624
E-mail: m.kay@ukia.org
URL: http://79.170.40.182/iukdirectory/com/iuk

9405 ■ Jack Wright Memorial Travel Grants
To support young people wishing to travel overseas to study aspects of water management in agriculture, including irrigation. One or more scholarships, with a maximum value of up to £1,750, are awarded every year.

9406 ■ Ulster Teachers' Union
Avril Hall-Callaghan, Gen. Sec.
94 Malone Rd.
Belfast BT9 5HP, United Kingdom
Ph: 44 28 90662216
Fax: 44 28 90683296
E-mail: office@utu.edu
URL: http://www.utu.edu

9407 ■ Honorary Member
Recognizes special services to Northern Ireland education. An honorary membership is awarded periodically.

9408 ■ Honorary Vice President
Recognizes special services to Northern Ireland education. Awarded periodically.

9409 ■ United Business Media Ltd.
Ludgate House
245 Blackfriars Rd.
London SE1 9UY, United Kingdom
Ph: 44 20 7921 5000
E-mail: simon.thorpe@ubm.com
URL: http://www.ubm.com

9410 ■ National Customer Service Awards
To celebrate the effort and impact of excellent customer service on the customer and the business in the United Kingdom. Open to any customer service professional in the United Kingdom. Awards are presented in a variety of categories for individuals and teams. In addition, the following awards may be presented: Best Use of Technology in Customer Service, Field Service Award, and the SOCAP Award for Innovation in Customer Service. Awarded annually. Established in 2006.

9411 ■ United Kingdom Department for Business, Innovation and Skills
1 Victoria St.
London SW1H 0ET, United Kingdom
Ph: 44 20 7215 5000
Fax: 44 20 7215 0105
URL: http://www.bis.gov.uk
Formed by merger of: (2009) Department for Business, Enterprise and Regulatory Reform; Department for Innovation, Universities and Skills.

9412 ■ SPUR: Support for Products Under Research
To provide help with the development of new products and processes which involve a significant technological advance. Established businesses in Great Britain with up to 250 employees and either an annual turnover not exceeding ECU 20 million or a balance sheet total not exceeding ECU 10 million are eligible. Projects must cost a minimum of £50,000 and be 6 to 36 months duration. The grant is normally 30 percent of the project costs up to a maximum grant of ECU 200,000, but SMART winners may receive a higher percentage grant rate. In addition, for a small number of exceptional projects which have a strategic significance for an industry sector and high R&D costs, there is the possibility of receiving a grant of up to £450,000 under a separate element of the scheme SPUR Plus.

9413 ■ United Kingdom eInformation Group
Ms. Christine Baker, Contact
Piglet Cottage
Redmire
Leyburn DL8 4EH, United Kingdom

Awards are arranged in alphabetical order below their administering organizations

Ph: 44 1969 625751
Fax: 44 1969 625751
E-mail: cabaker@ukeig.org.uk
URL: http://www.ukeig.org.uk

9414 ■ Jason Farradane Award
To an individual or a group of people for outstanding work in the information field. Awarded annually.

9415 ■ Tony Kent Strix Award
To individuals or groups for an outstanding contribution to the field of information retrieval. Awarded annually.

9416 ■ Research Award
For small research project in the broad area of electronic information. A monetary prize of £1,000 is awarded annually.

9417 ■ Student Bursary
To a student studying information management in the UK. A monetary prize of £2,500 is awarded annually.

9418 ■ United Kingdom Warehousing Association
Roger Williams, CEO
Walter House
418-422 Strand
London WC2R 0PT, United Kingdom
Ph: 44 20 78365522
Fax: 44 20 74389379
E-mail: dg@ukwa.org.uk
URL: http://www.ukwa.org.uk

9419 ■ Journalist of the Year
To recognize an journalist who has made the most qualitative and consistent contribution to the materials handling trade publications sector during the year. Awarded annually.

9420 ■ Training Award
To recognize an individual and/or organization for significant personal and/or team achievement at any level of warehouse related training. Awarded annually.

9421 ■ Warehouse Person of the Year
To honor an individual who demonstrated a significant and improved performance in carrying out his primary task during the year. Awarded annually.

9422 ■ Universities Federation for Animal Welfare
The Old School
Brewhouse Hill
Wheathampstead AL4 8AN, United Kingdom
Ph: 44 1582 831818
Fax: 44 1582 831414
E-mail: ufaw@ufaw.org.uk
URL: http://www.ufaw.org.uk

9423 ■ Small Project and Travel Awards
To support the benefit of animal welfare, particularly the welfare of farm, companion, laboratory, and captive wild animals as well as free-living wild animals whose welfare is compromised by humans. Applications may be made for the purchase of equipment, for the organization of (and, sometimes, to support attendance at) educational meetings, lectures and courses, and for publication, translation, or transmission of information on animal welfare and for other small projects in support of UFAW's objectives. Monetary grants of up to £3,500 are awarded annually.

9424 ■ Wild Animal Welfare Award
To recognize innovations that are relevant to improving the welfare of captive wild animals, or that alleviates or prevents anthropogenic (human-induced) harm to animals in the wild. Two awards of £1,000 are presented annually. Established in 1986. Formerly: (2006) Zoo Animal Welfare Award.

9425 ■ University of Edinburgh Department of English Literature
David Hume Tower
George Sq.
Edinburgh EH8 9JX, United Kingdom
Ph: 44 131 650 3620
Fax: 44 131 650 6898
E-mail: english.literature@ed.ac.uk
URL: http://www.englit.ed.ac.uk

9426 ■ James Tait Black Memorial Prizes
For recognition of the best biography or work of that nature, and the best work of fiction, published during the calendar year. Works of fiction and biographies written in English, originating with a British publisher, and first published in Britain in the 12-month period prior to the submission date are eligible. Two monetary prizes of £10,000 each are awarded annually. Established in 1918 in memory of James Tait Black, a partner in the publishing house of A.C. Black Ltd.

9427 ■ University of Oxford Faculty of Music
Dr. Susan Wollenberg, Chair
St. Aldates
Oxford OX1 1DB, United Kingdom
Ph: 44 1865 276125
Fax: 44 1865 276127
E-mail: chairman@music.ox.ac.uk
URL: http://www.music.ox.ac.uk

9428 ■ Donald Tovey Memorial Prize
To provide assistance for research in the philosophy, history, or understanding of music. Men or women without regard to nationality, age, or membership of a university are eligible. A monetary prize is awarded as funds allow.

9429 ■ Viking Society for Northern Research
Christopher Abram, Hon. Asst. Sec.
University College London
Gower St.
London WC1E 6BT, United Kingdom
E-mail: vsnr@ucl.ac.uk
URL: http://www.vsnr.org

9430 ■ Margaret Orme Prize
To recognize an undergraduate or new graduate student of universities and colleges in the U.K. and Eire (other than Oxford and the University College London) for distinguished contributions to the fields of study appropriate to the Society's interests. Recipient receives a five-year membership in the Society and a monetary prize of £50. Awarded annually.

9431 ■ Voice of the Listener and Viewer
Sue Washbrook, Membership Sec.
PO Box 401
Kent
Gravesend DA12 9FY, United Kingdom
Ph: 44 1474 338716
Ph: 44 1474 338711
Fax: 44 1474 325440
E-mail: info@vlv.org.uk
URL: http://www.vlv.org.uk

9432 ■ Awards for Excellence in Broadcasting
Recognizes the best radio and television program and personalities of the year. Awarded in various categories annually. Formerly: (2004) National Awards.

9433 ■ Wales Craft Council
Philomena Hearn, Chair
London House
The Square
Corwen LL21 0DE, United Kingdom
Ph: 44 1938 555313
Ph: 44 1490 412911
Fax: 44 1938 556237
E-mail: info@walescraftcouncil.co.uk
URL: http://www.walescraftcouncil.co.uk

9434 ■ Best Stand Award
To recognize the best exhibition stand in the Wales Spring Fair. Awarded annually.

9435 ■ *Wanderlust* Magazine
PO Box 1832
Windsor
Berkshire SL4 1YT, United Kingdom
Ph: 44 1753 620426
Fax: 44 1753 620474
E-mail: info@wanderlust.co.uk
URL: http://www.wanderlust.co.uk

9436 ■ Paul Morrison Guide Awards
To recognize the best tour guides in the world. Monetary prizes are awarded to the top three recipients. Awarded annually. Established in 2006.

9437 ■ Travel Photo of the Year Competition
To recognize the best amateur travel photographs. Awards are presented in four amateur categories (People, Wildlife, Landscape, and Travel Icons) and one comprehensive Portfolio category for professional photographers. Awarded annually. Winning photographs may be published in *Wanderlust* magazine.

9438 ■ Wanderlust Travel Awards
To recognize the best the world has to offer in travel, as voted upon by readers of *Wanderlust* magazine. Awarded in several categories, including Best Country, Best Low-Cost Airline, Best Travel Writer, Best Guidebook Series, Best TV Program, and Best Tour Operator. Awarded annually.

9439 ■ Welsh Amateur Music Federation (Ffederasiwn Cerddoriaeth Amatur Cymru)
Keith Griffin, Dir.
Wales Millenium Ctr.
Bute Pl.
Cardiff CF10 5AL, United Kingdom
Ph: 44 29 20635640
Fax: 44 29 20635641
E-mail: enquiries@tycerdd.org

9440 ■ W.S. Gwynn Williams Award
To amateur music promoting societies. Awarded annually.

9441 ■ Welsh Books Council (Cyngor Llyfrau Cymru)
Elwyn Jones, Dir.
Castell Brychan, Ceredigion
Aberystwyth SY23 2JB, United Kingdom
Ph: 44 1970 624151
Fax: 44 1970 625385
E-mail: castellbrychan@wbc.org.uk
URL: http://www.wbc.org.uk
Formerly: (1990) Welsh National Centre for Children's Literature.

9442 ■ Mary Vaughan Jones Award
For recognition of outstanding services to the field of children's literature in Wales over a period of time. A silver trophy is awarded triennially in November. Established in 1985 in memory of Mary Vaughan Jones, one of the main benefactors of children's literature in Wales for a period of over 30 years.

9443 ■ Tir na n-Og Awards (Gwobrau Tir na n-Og)
To raise the standard of children's and young people's books and to encourage the buying and reading of good books. Three awards of £1,000

Awards are arranged in alphabetical order below their administering organizations

each are presented annually: (1) Best English-language book, fiction or non-fiction, with an authentic Welsh background; (2) Best original Welsh-language book aimed at the primary sector; and (3) Best original Welsh-language book aimed at the secondary sector. Established in 1976. Co-sponsored by the Chartered Institute of Library and Information Professionals.

9444 ■ Wetnose Animal Aid
Newgate Lodge
Kirby Cane
Newgate NR35 2PP, United Kingdom
Ph: 44 1508 518 650
URL: http://www.wetnoseanimalaid.com

9445 ■ Wetnose Awards
To recognize the valuable and tireless work of small, independent rescue centers that help animals in the United Kingdom and overseas. Awards are presented in the following categories: Dog Rescue, Cat Rescue, Small Animal Rescue (rodent), Fibrevore Rescue (rabbit, guinea pig, chinchilla), Greyhound Rescue, Horse/Donkey Rescue, and Best Rescue Story. In addition, one overall winner is awarded a £500 cash prize and is named the Best U.K. Rescue Center. Awarded annually. Established in 2010.

9446 ■ Whitley Fund for Nature
33 Drayson Mews
London W8 4LY, United Kingdom
Ph: 44 20 7368 6568
E-mail: info@whitleyaward.org
URL: http://www.whitleyaward.org

9447 ■ Whitley Award
To recognize exceptional contributions to nature conservation. Up to nine Whitley Awards, and one Gold Award are presented. The Whitley Awards offer a £30,000 prize. The winners of these awards are automatically entered into consideration for the Gold Award of £60,000 over two years.

9448 ■ Wiener Library Institute of Contemporary History
Ben Barkow, Dir. Gen.
4 Devonshire St.
London W1W 5BH, United Kingdom
Ph: 44 20 7636 7247
Fax: 44 20 7636 6428
E-mail: info@wienerlibrary.co.uk
URL: http://www.wienerlibrary.co.uk

9449 ■ Fraenkel Prize in Contemporary History
To recognize outstanding work in the field of twentieth-century history. Eligible works must be finished but unpublished written in English, French, or German that cover one of the tradi-tional fields of interest to the Wiener Library, such as political history of Central and Eastern Europe; Jewish history; the two world wars; anti-Semitism; and the ideologies and movements of political extremism and totalitarianism. The deadline is May 15. Two distinct awards are made: US $6,000, open to all entrants (length not less than 50,000 words and not more than 150,000 words); and US $4,000, open to entrants who have yet to publish a major work (length not less than 25,000 words and not more than 100,000 words). The Wiener Library may invite the winner of the award to give a public lecture in London. The Wiener Library will have the op-tion to publish part of the award-winning work in the *Journal of Contemporary History*. Awarded annually in late summer. Established in 1989 by Ernst Fraenkel, chairman of the Institute.

9450 ■ Wolfson Foundation
8 Queen Anne St.
London W1G 9LD, United Kingdom
Ph: 44 20 7323 5730
Fax: 44 20 7323 3241

URL: http://www.wolfson.org.uk

9451 ■ Wolfson History Prizes
To promote and encourage standards of excel-lence in the writing of history for the general public. Books published in the United Kingdom during the year are eligible. Two prizes are awarded annually, with an occasional special prize given for an individual's distinguished contribution to the writing of history. Established in 1972.

9452 ■ Women in Banking and Finance
Sylvana Caloni, Pres.
PO Box 122
West Wickham BR4 9WW, United Kingdom
Ph: 44 20 87776902
Fax: 44 20 87777064
E-mail: christine.lawrence@wibf.org.uk
URL: http://www.wibf.org.uk

9453 ■ Awards for Achievement
For individuals who have demonstrated leader-ship, professionalism, or community service in the banking and finance industry. Awards are presented in three categories: achievement, outstanding contribution, and lifetime achievement. Awarded annually.

9454 ■ Women in Publishing
Claire Pimm, Treas.
4 Barnard Hill
London N10 2HB, United Kingdom
E-mail: info@womeninpublishing.org.uk
URL: http://www.womeninpublishing.org.uk

9455 ■ New Venture Award
Recognizes a pioneering woman or group of women who have embarked on a venture whose aim is to highlight the work and lives of under-represented groups of society. An engraved silver letter opener or pen is awarded annually. Established in 1987.

9456 ■ Pandora Award
Recognizes the promotion of positive images of women in publishing, bookselling and related trades. Individuals or organizations are eligible. A writing box which is passed on from winner to winner is awarded annually. Established in 1981.

9457 ■ Women's Engineering Society
Dawn Fitt, Sec.
Michael Faraday House
Six Hills Way
Hertfordshire
Stevenage SG1 2AY, United Kingdom
Ph: 44 1438 765506
E-mail: info@wes.org.uk
URL: http://www.wes.org.uk

9458 ■ Karen Burt Memorial Award
To encourage women to aim for Chartered Engineer and corporate status by honoring a newly Chartered female engineer. Awarded periodically. Established in 1998.

9459 ■ Lady Finniston Award
To enable women, who otherwise might be prevented from doing so on grounds of hard-ship, to take up places on and begin recognized engineering degree or HND courses in British universities and colleges. Monetary awards rang-ing between £500 and £1,000 are awarded annually. Established in 1991.

9460 ■ Scott Trust Technology Bursaries
To assist students who face financial difficulty in attaining the necessary qualifications needed to pursue a career in software development for the Web. Two monetary awards are given annually.

9461 ■ World Association of Christian Radio Amateurs and Listeners
(Association Mondiale des Radio-Amateurs et des Radioclubs Chretiens)
Steve Nicholls, Pres.
51, Alma Rd.
S Devon

Brixham TQ5 8QR, United Kingdom
Ph: 44 1803 854504
E-mail: g3xnx@wacral.org
URL: http://www.wacral.org

9462 ■ Countries Awards
To recognize individuals achieving contact over the air with stations operated by WACRAL members in different countries. Gold, silver, and bronze awards are presented for contact with 18, 12, and 8 countries, respectively. Awarded when merited.

9463 ■ Graded Awards
For recognition of individuals achieving contact over the air with WACRAL members. Proof of contact is required. Awards are presented in the following grades, in ascending order: Basic, Bronze, Silver, Gold, Emerald, and Diamond. Awarded when merited.

9464 ■ Heavenly Pilot Award
To recognize individuals achieving contact with five stations operated by WACRAL members who are full-time ministers, pastors, officers in the Church Army, or officers in the Salvation Army. Awarded when merited.

9465 ■ Special Event Station Awards
To recognize individuals achieving contact with six special event stations operated by WACRAL members. Awarded when merited.

9466 ■ World Association of Girl Guides and Girl Scouts
(Asociacion Mundial de las Guias Scouts)
Mary Mc Phail, Chief Exec.
World Bureau, Olave Centre
12c Lyndhurst Rd.
London NW3 5PQ, United Kingdom
Ph: 44 20 77941181
Fax: 44 20 74313764
E-mail: wagggs@wagggsworld.org
URL: http://www.wagggsworld.org/en/home

9467 ■ FAO-WAGGGS Nutrition Medal
To recognize a Girl Guide/Girl Scout group for relevant work to eradicated hunger and malnutri-tion in the world. Awarded periodically. Estab-lished in 1995.

9468 ■ Olave Award
To recognize a Girl Guide/Girl Scout group or unit for outstanding community service work. Awarded periodically.

9469 ■ WAGGGS Medal
To honor individuals for remarkable service at both national and global levels. Awarded annually.

9470 ■ Women of Outstanding Achieve-ment
To honor women who stand out as models in their professional and volunteer work who have achieved much in the promotion of women's rights and to advance the status of women. Awarded to one woman from each region every three years.

9471 ■ World Confederation for Physical Therapy
(Confederation Mondiale pour la Therapie Physique)
Marilyn Moffat, Pres.
Victoria Charity Centre
11 Belgrade Rd.
London SW1V 1RB, United Kingdom
Ph: 44 20 79316465
Fax: 44 20 79316494
E-mail: info@wcpt.org
URL: http://www.wcpt.org

9472 ■ Mildred Elson Award
To honor an individual for significant contribu-tions to the development of physical therapy on an international basis through his or her efforts,

Awards are arranged in alphabetical order below their administering organizations

dedication, and leadership. A plaque is awarded every four years at the International Congress. Established in 1987 by the American Physical Therapy Association in honor of Mildred Elson, first president of the Confederation.

9473 ■ Humanitarian Service Award
To recognize individual physical therapists who have improved people's lives through their exceptional care, compassion, dedication, and personal commitment at a national or international level. Awarded annually.

9474 ■ International Service Award
To recognize individuals who have made a great contribution toward physical therapy internationally or within their region. Recipients are determined based on the international scope and impact of their contribution in one or more of the following areas: practice, education, research, and administration and policy development. Awarded annually to one or more recipients.

9475 ■ Leadership in Rehabilitation Award
To recognize an individual or group/organization who has made a great contribution to international rehabilitation and/or global health. Awarded annually.

9476 ■ Recognition of Service Award
To recognize individuals who have contributed to WCPT as chairs of regions and subgroups and through membership committees. Awarded annually.

9477 ■ World Curling Federation
Kate Caithness, Pres.
74 Tay St.
Perth 8NP, United Kingdom
Ph: 44 1738 451630
Fax: 44 1738 451641
E-mail: info@worldcurling.org
URL: http://www.worldcurling.org

9478 ■ Frances Brodie Award
To honor the female curler who, by deed and action in the course of her performance, best exemplifies the traditional curling values of skill, honesty, fair play, friendship, and sportsmanship. Awarded annually at the conclusion of the World Women's Curling Championship. Established in 1989 in honor of Frances Brodie, the driving force behind the group that established the first World Ladies Curling Championship in 1979.

9479 ■ Collie Campbell Memorial Award
To honor the player selected by his fellow competitors in the World Curling Championship for the Air Canada Silver Broom who best exemplifies the traditional curling values of gentlemanly skill, fair play, and sportsmanship. Awarded annually. Established in 1979 in memory of the president of the International Curling Federation (1969-1978).

9480 ■ WJCC Sportsmanship Award
To honor junior competitors that best exemplify the traditional curling values of skill, honesty, fair play, friendship, and sportsmanship. Awarded annually to one male and one female at the conclusion of the World Junior Curling Championships (WJCC). Established in 1975.

9481 ■ World Curling Freytag Award
To honor curlers for world-championship-level playing ability, sportsmanship, character, and the achievement of extraordinary distinction, and to honor builders, those individuals who display distinguished service and major contributions to the development and advancement of international curling. Awarded annually. Established in memory of Elmer Freytag, an American founder of the International Curling Federation (now WCF).

9482 ■ WWhCC Sportsmanship Award
To honor wheelchair-bound competitors that best exemplify the traditional curling values of skill, honesty, fair play, friendship, and sportsmanship. Awarded annually at the conclusion of the World Wheelchair Curling Championships (WWhCC). Established in 2002.

9483 ■ *World Fishing* Magazine
Mercator Media Ltd.
The Old Mill
Lower Quay
Fareham
Hampshire PO16 0RA, United Kingdom
Ph: 44 1329 825335
Fax: 44 1329 825330
E-mail: editor@worldfishing.net
URL: http://www.worldfishing.net

9484 ■ Icelandic Fisheries Awards
To recognize excellence within the Icelandic and international fishing industries. Presented in more than a dozen categories, including Outstanding Icelandic Skipper, Outstanding Icelandic Fleet, Outstanding Icelandic Processor, and Best New Product. Awarded triennially as part of the Icelandic Fisheries Exhibition. Established in 1999.

9485 ■ World Organisation of Systems and Cybernetics
(Organisation Mondiale pour la Systemique et la Cybernetique)
Dr. Alex Andrew, Dir. Gen.
95 Finch Rd., Earley
Reading RG6 7JX, United Kingdom
Ph: 44 118 9269328
E-mail: alexandrew@tiscali.co.uk
URL: http://cybsoc.org/wosc

9486 ■ Honorary Fellowship
To honor eminent scientists in the fields of cybernetics, systems, computers, and related disciplines.

9487 ■ Norbert Wiener Memorial Gold Medal
For achievement in the field of cybernetics or systems. Awarded periodically. Established in 1978.

9488 ■ World Petroleum Council
(Congres Mondiaux du Petrole)
Randy Gossen, Pres.
1 Duchess St., 4th Fl., Ste. 1
London W1W 6AN, United Kingdom
Ph: 44 20 76374958
Fax: 44 20 76374965
E-mail: info@world-petroleum.org
URL: http://www.world-petroleum.org

9489 ■ Dewhurst Lecture and Award
To recognize an individual for scientific and technological excellence in the petroleum industry. The recipient is invited to present a lecture at the World Petroleum Congress. Awarded triennially. Established in 1991.

9490 ■ Excellence Awards
To distinguish companies, institutions, or any public or private organization engaged in the oil and gas industry for promoting or operating with high excellence standards in two categories: Technological Development and Social Responsibility. Presented triennially.

9491 ■ World Ship Trust - United Kingdom
Hon. Lord Greenway, Chm.
Iconoclast, Nine Elms Pier
Tideway Walk
London SW8 5PZ, United Kingdom
Ph: 44 20 76271550
Fax: 44 20 70001251
E-mail: info@worldshiptrust.org
URL: http://www.worldshiptrust.org

9492 ■ International Maritime Heritage Award
To recognize and encourage especially meritori-

ous ship preservation achievements on a worldwide basis. A medal is awarded at the discretion of the Trustees when merited. Established in 1980.

9493 ■ World Travel Awards
12-16 Laystall St.
London EC1R 4PF, United Kingdom
Ph: 44 20 7925 0000
Fax: 44 20 7925 2552
E-mail: awards@worldtravelawards.com
URL: http://www.worldtravelawards.com

9494 ■ World Travel Awards
To acknowledge, reward, and celebrate the achievements to be found in all sectors of the global travel industry. Awards are given in dozens of countries (as well as some states/provinces in Canada and the United States) around the world. Categories include airlines, airports, car rental, conference centers, family resorts, golf resorts, hotels, safaris, spa resorts, tourist boards, and travel agencies. Awarded annually. Established in 1994.

9495 ■ World's Poultry Science Association
Dr. Kelvin J. McCracken, Asst. Sec.-Treas.
2 Edengrove Park E
Ballynahinch BT24 8DP, United Kingdom
E-mail: wpsa@hotmail.co.uk
URL: http://www.wpsa-uk.com

9496 ■ International Poultry Hall of Fame
To recognize individuals who have contributed to the worldwide poultry industry above and beyond the call of duty. Open to individuals from any country. One or more individuals are inducted annually. Established in 1984.

9497 ■ Macdougall Medal
To recognize individuals for outstanding services to the Association. Any member of the WPSA is eligible. A gold medal is awarded intermittently by a decision of the Council of WPSA. Established in 1962 in memory of Major I. Macdougall.

9498 ■ Worshipful Company of Scientific Instrument Makers
Neville Watson, Clerk
Glaziers Hall
9 Montague Close
London SE1 9DD, United Kingdom
Ph: 44 20 74074832
Fax: 44 20 74071565
E-mail: theclerk@wcsim.co.uk
URL: http://www.wcsim.co.uk

9499 ■ Achievement Awards
Annual awards of recognition. Awards are given in the forms of scholarships, bursaries, achievement.

9500 ■ Yachting Journalists' Association
Rachel Nuding, Membership Sec.
36 Church Ln.
Hants
Lymington SO41 3RB, United Kingdom
Ph: 44 1590 673894
E-mail: secretary@yja.co.uk
URL: http://www.yja.co.uk
Formerly: Guild of Yachting Writers.

9501 ■ Yachtsman of the Year Award
For recognition of achievement in the field of boating by a British citizen during the previous year. Nominations may be made by anyone, but are shortlisted by members belonging to the Association. The entire Association votes for the final winner. The trophy, a silver navigation buoy on a sea of crystal, is awarded annually, as well as a keepsake replica for the winner. Established in 1955 by Sir Max Aitken.

9502 ■ Young Sailor of the Year Award
To recognize endeavor and achievement by

Awards are arranged in alphabetical order below their administering organizations

young sailors. Open to young sailors who are under 18 years of age before December 31 of the award year and who have a British passport or are immediately eligible to receive a British passport. Nominations may be submitted by members of each of the Royal Yachting Association's 13 regions which submit one candidate each, the regional winner. The entire association votes for the final winner. A trophy, held for one year by the recipient, and cash prizes are awarded for the final three competitors. Cash prizes are held in trust by the RYA for the winners to use for approved sailing-related expenses. Awarded annually. Established in 1993.

9503 ■ Young Composer of Dyfed (Cyfansoddwr Ifanc Dyfed)
Cathy Morris, Admin.
Llys Melus
75 Roath Court Rd.
Cardiff CF24 3SF, United Kingdom
E-mail: morris.c@ntlbusiness.com
URL: http://www.ycod.org.uk

9504 ■ Young Composer of Dyfed
To recognize musical composition talent in young artists. Awards are offered in three categories: Group A - under 16 years old; Group B - 16 to 18 years old; and Group C - 19 to 22 years old. Each group winner receives a prize: Group A - £100; Group B - £150; and Group C - £200. Also presents the Young Composer of Dyfed Award (£250) and the Greenhalgh Prize and Trophy (£100) for audience favorite.

9505 ■ Young Concert Artists Trust
Alasdair Tait, Chief Exec.
23 Garrick St.
London WC2E 9BN, United Kingdom
Ph: 44 20 7379 8477
Fax: 44 20 7379 8467
E-mail: info@ycat.co.uk
URL: http://www.ycat.co.uk

9506 ■ Young Concert Artists Trust Award
To recognize outstanding young musicians (instrumentalists and singers), and to promote their careers until they are established with a recognized commercial agent. Auditions are open to all instruments, but the categories vary each year. The applicants must be under 29 years for instrumentalists; under 31 for singers; and be British citizens or resident in the United Kingdom. The deadline for applications is in early February. Management services and promotion of career are awarded annually. Established in 1984 by W. H. Smith and Son, the founding sponsor. Supported by numerous trusts and foundations.

9507 ■ Zoological Society of London
Prof. Patrick Bateson FRS, Pres.
Regent's Park
Outer Circle
London NW1 4RY, United Kingdom
Ph: 44 20 77223333
Ph: 44 20 74496228
E-mail: membership@zsl.org
URL: http://www.zsl.org

9508 ■ Frink Medal for British Zoologists
To recognize professional zoologists who have made substantial and original contributions to the advancement of zoology. British citizens who are residents of the United Kingdom and whose work is based there may be nominated. A bronze medal designed by Elisabeth Frink is awarded annually when merited. Established in 1973.

9509 ■ Thomas Henry Huxley Award
To recognize postgraduate research students for original work in zoology. Postgraduate students attending a university in Great Britain or Northern Ireland who were awarded the Doctor of Philosophy degree during the preceding year may be nominated. A bronze medal and a sum of money are awarded annually when merited; a certificate may be awarded as an honorable mention. Established in 1961.

9510 ■ Marsh Award for Conservation Biology
To recognize contributions of fundamental science and its application to the conservation of animal species and habitats. A certificate and a sum of money are awarded annually when merited. Established in 1992.

9511 ■ Prince Philip Award
To recognize students for an account of practical work involving some aspect of animal biology. Pupils of schools in Great Britain, Northern Ireland, the Channel Isles, and the Isle of Man who are under 19 years of age are eligible. A bronze medal and a certificate are awarded annually when merited. The winner's school will also receive an award of money to be used in promoting the teaching of animal biology. Prizes of books or a certificate may also be awarded as honorable mentions. Awarded annually. Established in 1961.

9512 ■ Stamford Raffles Award
To recognize amateur zoologists who have made distinguished contributions to zoology or to recognize professional zoologists who have made contributions outside the scope of their professional activities and principal specialization. Nominations are accepted. A bronze sculpture by Anita Mandl is awarded annually when merited. Established in 1961.

9513 ■ Scientific Medal
For recognition of distinguished work in zoology. Men and women under 40 years of age may be nominated. Up to three silver medals may be awarded each year. Established in 1938.

9514 ■ Silver Medal
To recognize persons who have contributed to the understanding and appreciation of zoology. Selection is based on such activities as public education in natural history and wildlife conservation. A silver medal is awarded periodically when merited. Nominations are requested annually. Established in 1837 and first awarded in 1847.

United Republic of Tanzania

9515 ■ Publishers Association of Tanzania
Abdullah Saiwaad, Dir.
PO Box 76440
Dar es Salaam, United Republic of Tanzania
Ph: 255 22 2183643
E-mail: khalaf@mcmillanaidan.com
URL: http://www.ipa-uie.org/ipa/members.html

9516 ■ Best Book Awards
For a book assessed by the panel to have the best content and design.

9517 ■ Tanzania Commission for Science and Technology
COSTECH Bldg.
Ali Hassan Mwinyi Rd.
PO Box 4302
Dar es Salaam, United Republic of Tanzania
Ph: 255 22 700 745
Fax: 255 22 775 313
E-mail: info@costech.or.tz
URL: http://www.costech.or.tz

9518 ■ National Award for Environmental Management
To recognize a Tanzanian scientist for contributions to environmentally sound technologies, pollution control, hazardous waste reduction, food, agriculture, natural resources, and wildlife. Awarded annually.

9519 ■ National Award for Research in Science and Technology
To recognize and support high caliber scientific research or technology development work carried out by a Tanzanian scientist or technologist has made significant and outstanding contributions to the advancement of science and technology. Awarded annually.

9520 ■ School Science Award
To generate a scientific culture at the grassroots level by recognizing schools that have best registered an improvement in the utilization of science and technology through innovation and/or adaptation in the year under consideration. May be presented at a science fair organized at regional and national level. Awarded annually.

9521 ■ Tanzania Award for Scientific and Technological Achievements
To promote research and development across the environmental spectrum by acknowledging Tanzanian individuals or institutions that have made significant and outstanding contributions in the management of the environment, including environment protection, conservation through scientific, socio-economic or technological innovation, or discovery. The following awards are presented annually: Gold TASTA Award of Tshs 5 million; Silver TASTA Award of Tshs 3 million; and Bronze TASTA Award of Tshs 1 million. Established in 1982.

9522 ■ Tanzania Industrial Research and Development Organization (Shirika la Utafiti na Maendeleo va Viwanda, Tanzania)
Dr. A.P. Nanyaro, Dir. Gen.
PO Box 23235
Dar es Salaam, United Republic of Tanzania
Ph: 255 22 2666034
Ph: 255 22 2668822
Fax: 255 22 2666034
E-mail: info@tirdo.org
URL: http://www.tirdo.org

9523 ■ Research Award
For technical personnel.

9524 ■ Tanzania Tourist Board
IPS Bldg.
PO Box 2485
Dar es Salaam, United Republic of Tanzania
Ph: 255 22 2111 244
Fax: 255 22 2116 420
E-mail: safari@ud.co.tz
URL: http://tanzaniatouristboard.com

9525 ■ Tanzania Tourism Awards
To honor travel professionals and media who have worked to promote Tanzania from the world tourism market. Awarded to one or more recipients annually. Established in 2001.

9526 ■ Zanzibar International Film Festival
PO Box 3032
Zanzibar, United Republic of Tanzania
Ph: 255 777 411499
Fax: 255 777 419955
E-mail: ziff@ziff.or.tz
URL: http://www.ziff.or.tz

9527 ■ Air Tanzania Award for the Best East African Film
To honor the best film in the Festival from the East African region. Awarded annually. Established in 1997.

9528 ■ Best Short/Animation Film
To honor the best short film in the Festival that reflects mastery of the short film structure and aesthetics. Awarded annually. Established in 1997.

Awards are arranged in alphabetical order below their administering organizations

9529 ■ Chairman's Award
To honor a film that reveals an acute reflection on contemporary issues in a balanced manner in these times of polarized perspectives. Awarded annually. Established in 1997.

9530 ■ East Africa Award
To honor the best film in the Festival by an East African filmmaker that demonstrates the greatest commercial aptitude and potential marketability. Awarded annually. Established in 1997.

9531 ■ East African Talent Award
To honor the film that best showcases talent from the East African region. Awarded annually. Established in 1997.

9532 ■ Fipresci Jury Prize
To honor a feature film from the Dhow countries that combines cultural astuteness and commercial potential. Awarded annually. Established in 1997.

9533 ■ Sembene Ousmane Prize
To honor a film that takes a particular look at topics of development cooperation. Awarded annually. Established in 1997.

9534 ■ Signis Jury Award
To honor a film that is deemed to exemplify universal and spiritual values that enhance human dignity, justice, and tolerance. Awarded annually. Established in 1997.

9535 ■ UNICEF Award
To honor the film that best encapsulates issues of children and women. Awarded annually. Established in 1997.

9536 ■ Verona Jury Award
To honor a film deemed the best African feature film in the Festival. Awarded annually. Established in 1997.

Uruguay

9537 ■ International Council for Adult Education
(Conseil International d'Education des Adultes)
Paul Belanger, Pres.
Avenida 18 de julio 2095 apto. 301
11200 Montevideo, Uruguay
Ph: 598 2 4097982
Fax: 598 2 4097982
E-mail: secretariat@icae.org.uy
URL: http://www.icae2.org

9538 ■ Dame Nita Barrow Award
To recognize and support regional or national adult education organizations who have made a significant contribution towards the empowerment of women in the adult education movement. All ICAE member organizations are eligible to apply. The organization must demonstrate that women's active participation has increased in leadership and decision-making roles and planning and policy advisory positions. The organization must also show that it has promoted the discussion of gender issues and their participating social movements, and included gender issues in all aspects of the organization and on agenda and programs. A monetary award of $2,000 (Canadian) is granted annually. Established in 1990 to honor Nita Barrow for her longtime service as President of the ICAE, her commitment to the international adult education movement, and her firm support of women's full and equal participation in organizational and global issues.

9539 ■ Nabila Breir Award
For recognition of women's organizations engaged in innovative educational programming or projects for Palestinian women. The objectives of the award are: to support women's educational programs aimed at enhancing the socio-economic development of Palestinian communities, and the quality of life and self-sufficiency of women in particular; to provide opportunities for Palestinian women grassroots educators to exchange educational experiences with women educators from other regions; and to provide opportunities for participation in ICAE's regional and international workshops, seminars, and conferences for Palestinian women educators. A monetary prize of $2,000 (Canadian) is awarded annually. Established in 1987 in memory of Nabila Breir, an active member of ICAE women's program who was murdered in Beirut at the age of 42.

9540 ■ J. Roby Kidd Award
To recognize an individual or individuals who have made a particularly significant contribution to adult education at the local or national level. In particular, the aim of the award is to recognize and encourage innovative contributions of women and men, practitioners of whatever age, who could be considered as recent practitioners in adult education and thus carry out Roby Kidd's interest in attracting new people with new ideas. Individuals of any nationality, religion, race, sex, or age are eligible. A monetary award of $2,000 (Canadian) is granted annually. Established in memory or Roby Kidd, a pioneer in the field of adult education and founding Secretary-General of the ICAE.

Uzbekistan

9541 ■ Uzbekistan Teachers of English Association
Saida Nuriddinova, Award Coor.
48, Navoi St.
Tashkent, Uzbekistan
Ph: 998 71 252 7752
Fax: 998 71 252 7752
E-mail: uzteainfo@rambler.ru
URL: http://uztea.uz

9542 ■ Teaching English Excellence Award
To improve the practice of English teaching in Uzbekistan and to recognize outstanding English teachers. Each of the 14 branches of the Association organizes a regional competition, and the winners compete for the national award. Awarded annually.

Vanuatu

9543 ■ Vanuatu Tourism Office
Pilioko House, 1st Fl.
PO Box 209
Port Vila, Vanuatu
Ph: 678 775 8381
E-mail: reynolds@vanuatu.com.vu
URL: http://vanuatu.travel

9544 ■ Vanuatu Tourism Awards
To recognize tourism operators and associated entities for their contribution to Vanuatu tourism. Award in nearly 20 categories, including Best Resort, Best Tour Guide, Best Adventure/Eco Tour, and Best Specialist Tourism Business. Awarded annually. Established in 2005.

Vatican City

9545 ■ The Vatican
Papal Secretariat of State
I-00120 Vatican City, Vatican City
Ph: 39 06 6982
URL: http://www.vatican.va

9546 ■ Benemerenti Medal
To recognize a well deserving person for exceptional accomplishment and service. Men and women are eligible. Medals of gold, silver or bronze, bearing the likeness of the reigning Pope on one side and a laurel crown and the letter B on the other, are conferred by the Pope.

9547 ■ Order of Pius
For recognition of outstanding service to the Church and society. Four classes of knighthood may be awarded: (1) the Class of the Grand Collar; (2) Knights of the Grand Cross; (3) Knights of the Second Class; and (4) Commander and Knights of the Third Class. Christian or non-Christian heads of state are eligible. Membership is determined by the Pope. Pontifical Orders of Knighthood are awarded. Founded in 1847, and restricted to heads of state in 1966 by Paul VI.

9548 ■ Order of St. Gregory the Great
To recognize people who are distinguished for personal character and reputation, and for notable accomplishment. This secular honor of merit has civic and military divisions. Membership is determined by the Pope. Pontifical Orders of Knighthood are awarded. Established in 1831.

9549 ■ Order of St. Sylvester
For recognition of outstanding service to the Church. A secular honor of merit, formerly a part of the Order of the Golden Spur, is now awarded separately with three possible degrees: (1) Knights of the Grand Cross; (2) Knight Commanders, with or without emblem; and (3) Knights. Membership is determined by the Pope. Pontifical Orders of Knighthood are awarded. Established in 1841 by Gregory XVI and redefined in 1905 by Pius X.

9550 ■ Order of the Golden Spur (Golden Militia)
To recognize Christian heads of state. This secular honor of merit is one of the oldest knighthoods. The award was restricted in 1966 by Paul VI to Christian heads of state. Membership is determined by the Pope. Pontifical Orders of Knighthood are awarded. Established in 1841 by Gregory XVI as the Order of St. Sylvester. In 1905, Pius X restored the Order of the Golden Spur, separating it from the Order of Sylvester.

9551 ■ Pro Ecclesia et Pontifice Medal
For recognition of outstanding service to the Church and the papacy. Men and women are eligible. A gold medal with the likeness of Leo XIII is awarded. Established in 1888.

9552 ■ Supreme Order of Christ (Militia of Our Lord Jesus Christ)
For recognition of a Christian head of state. A secular honor of merit, originally meant to continue the suppressed Order of Templars in Portugal during the 14th and 15th centuries, this Order is now restricted to Christian heads of state. Membership in this highest and most exclusive Pontifical Order of Knighthood is determined by the Pope. Founded in 1319, and restricted to heads of state in 1966 by Paul VI.

Venezuela

9553 ■ Academy of Physical, Mathematical and Natural Sciences
(Academia de Ciencias Fisicas, Matematicas y Naturales)
Benjamin Scharifker, Pres.
Palacio de las Academias
Bolsa a San Francisco
Apartado Postal No. 1421
Caracas 1010-A, Venezuela
Ph: 58 212 4822954
Ph: 58 212 4827513
Fax: 58 212 4846611
E-mail: info@acfiman.org.ve
URL: http://www.acfiman.org

Awards are arranged in alphabetical order below their administering organizations

9554 ■ Juan Alberto Olivares' Foundation Award

To recognize Venezuelan or foreign scientists whose careers have been mostly developed in the country, whose achievements in their areas are both original and outstanding, and have resulted of importance, significance and projection; as well as resulted in a better understanding of sciences or universal welfare. Awarded annually.

9555 ■ Arnoldo Gabaldon Award

For Venezuelan scientists not older than 40 years of age. Awarded in the fields of biology, physics, chemistry, and mathematics, which alternate annually. A diploma and monetary prize of US$1,000 is awarded.

9556 ■ Radio Club Venezolano
Alfredo Medina, Pres.
Apartado Postal 2285
Caracas 1010-A, Venezuela
Ph: 58 212 7814878
Ph: 58 212 7935404
E-mail: presidencia@radioclubvenezolano.org
URL: http://www.radioclubvenezolano.org

9557 ■ Venezuelan Islands Award

To recognize any amateur radio operator, worldwide, who confirms contact with each of the Venezuelan islands after January 1, 1980. A certificate is awarded when merited.

Vietnam

9558 ■ Vietnam Standards Center
8 Hoang Quoc Viet
Cau Giay
Hanoi, Vietnam
Ph: 84 4 791 2619
Fax: 84 4 836 1771
E-mail: tttt@tcvn.gov.vn
URL: http://www.tcvn.gov.vn

9559 ■ Vietnam Quality Award

To encourage production business and service organizations in Vietnam to improve the quality of their activities for higher competitiveness in domestic and overseas markets. Several Vietnam Quality Awards (VQAs) are presented each year. In addition, the Vietnam Quality Gold Prize is awarded to up to six outstanding VQA recipients. Established in 1995.

9560 ■ VietNamNet
VietNamNet Tower
No. 4 Lang Ha St.
Dong Da District
Hanoi, Vietnam
Ph: 84 4 7722 729
Fax: 84 4 7722 733
E-mail: evnn@vietnamnet.vn
URL: http://www.vietnamnet.vn

9561 ■ Best of Vietnam Awards

To recognize the best products and services provided by Vietnamese companies in 50 different business fields. Open to all enterprises, domestic-owned or foreign-invested, that have been operating in Vietnam for at least three years and have a minimum capital of 3 billion Vietnamese dollars. Entries are judged on quality, price, trademark, post-sales service, technology, and impact on market. Awarded annually. Established in 2007.

Western Samoa

9562 ■ Samoa Association of Sport and National Olympic Committee
PO Box 1301
Apia, Western Samoa
Ph: 685 25033

Fax: 685 26701
E-mail: asip@sasnoc.ws
URL: http://www.sportingpulse.com/assoc_page.cgi?c=2-3855-0-0-0

9563 ■ Sports Awards

To recognize the achievements of athletes, officials, coaches, and administrators of sports in Western Samoa. Awards are presented in nine categories, including Overall Sportsperson of the Year, Athlete with a Disability of the Year, and Team of the Year. In addition, individuals may be inducted into the Hall of Fame for long-term contributions to sport in Samoa. Awarded annually.

Yemen

9564 ■ E-Commerce Yemen Co., Ltd.
26 Mujahed St.
Sana'a, Yemen
Ph: 967 1 514794
Fax: 967 1 514796
E-mail: info@ecommerce-ye.com
URL: http://www.ecommerce-ye.com

9565 ■ Yemen Web Awards

To foster the spirit of innovation and creativity among Web designers in Yemen, to raise the standards of Web design and Web sites, to advocate the growth and development of local talent, to promote intellectual property awareness, and to encourage all industries to showcase their Web sites and become more involved in the digital economy. Web sites are judged on five criteria: concept/creativity, technical/ease of use/navigation, content/structure, visual design solution/aesthetics, and interactivity. Presented in dozens of categories. Winners represent Yemen in the Pan Arab Web Awards (see separate entry). Awarded annually. Established in 2009.

9566 ■ Yemen Explorers
PO Box 23091
Sana'a, Yemen
Ph: 967 1 404838
Fax: 967 1 404837
E-mail: yescom@yemen.net.ye
URL: http://www.yemen-explorers.com

9567 ■ Yemen Panther Award

To honor Web sites that promote Yemen and Arabia. Criteria include context, creativity, design, and interactive features. Awarded when merited.

Zambia

9568 ■ National Arts Council of Zambia
Mulungushi International Conference Centre Annex
PO Box 50812
Lusaka, Zambia
Ph: 260 211 220639
Fax: 260 211 220638
E-mail: nacz@coppernet.zm
URL: http://www.nationalartscouncil.org.zm

9569 ■ Ngoma Awards

To honor deserving artists whose works and exploits merit recognition, and to encourage artistic excellence on both amateur and professional levels in Zambia. Trophies and monetary prizes of K1.5 million are awarded in 25 categories each year. Established in 1997. Named for the word that means "drum" in many Zambian tribes and dialects.

Zimbabwe

9570 ■ Boy Scouts Association of Zimbabwe
Mr. Nelson Sakala, Chief Commissioner
PO Box 669
Harare, Zimbabwe

Ph: 263 4 746644
Ph: 263 4 746830
E-mail: nsaks@yahoo.co.uk
URL: http://www.angelfire.com/sc/matabeles/zimbabwe

9571 ■ Golden Lion

For services of "Most Exceptional Character" and "Unrestricted Gift of the Chief Scout."

9572 ■ Silver Eagle

For special distinguished service to the scout movement.

9573 ■ Environment Africa
Ms. Charlene Hewat, CEO
76 Queen Rd.
Greendale
Harare, Zimbabwe
Ph: 263 77 4168260
E-mail: info@environmentafrica.org
URL: http://www.environmentafrica.org

9574 ■ Environmental Reporter Award

For reporting that covers topical and important issues in ways that highlight the diversity of the environment and the importance of mankind's impact on the environment. Quarterly winners receive an engraved trophy, a cash prize, and a travel stipend; one annual winner receives a floating trophy and a large cash sum. Established in 1996.

9575 ■ Reporter of the Year

For journalists.

9576 ■ Zimbabwe Institute of Engineers
Engr. Martin Manuhwa, Pres.
Conquenar House
256 Samora Machel Ave.
Harare, Zimbabwe
Ph: 263 4 746821
Fax: 263 4 746652
E-mail: zie@zarnet.ac.zw
URL: http://www.zie.org.zw

9577 ■ Engineering Achievement Award

To provide public recognition of noteworthy engineering achievements in Zimbabwe with the two-fold aim of challenging and encouraging engineers to strive for professional excellence, and drawing public attention to the contribution the engineering profession makes to the quality of life. Nominees do not have to be members of this Institution but the submission must be by a member of the Zimbabwe Institution of Engineers. Nominations for achievements in every branch of engineering and in such fields as research, invention, construction or design, amongst others may be submitted by March 31. A certificate and an inscribed plaque are awarded.

9578 ■ P. H. Haviland Award

To recognize an individual who has made an outstanding contribution in the field of water engineering, irrigation, or the prevention of water pollution and allied fields. Such contribution may be either in engineering or in administration and may arise from outstanding work in a person's field of employment. The award consists of a plaque, framed in wood, and a check in the value of $100.

9579 ■ SKF Award

For recognition of a service to engineering, noteworthy achievements, or unpaid social or public service. Members of any grade of the Institution are eligible for nomination. A monetary prize of $500 is awarded annually. Established in 1982 in honor of Wingquist. Formerly: (1996) Wingquist Award.

9580 ■ K. G. Stevens Award

To encourage the presentation of papers of outstanding merit. Corporate members of the

Awards are arranged in alphabetical order below their administering organizations

Institution and Editorial Committee may make nominations. A monetary prize of $200 and a bookplate are awarded annually. Established in 1981 in honor of K.G. Stevens. Sponsored by K.G. Stevens Trust.

Awards are arranged in alphabetical order below their administering organizations

The Subject Index of Awards classifies all awards described in this volume by their principal areas of interest. The index contains some 400 subject headings, and each award is indexed under all relevant headings. The index also contains see and see also references. Awards are arranged alphabetically under each subject heading. Identically named awards are followed by an indented alphabetical list of the organizations administering an award by that name. The numbers following award and organization names are book entry numbers, not page numbers.

Companion of the RAeC [8593]
Cory-Wright Cup [5053]
Cowburn and Kay - Old and Bold Trophy [8594]
De La Vaulx Medal [6303]
Diploma for Outstanding Airmanship [6304]
Eagle Awards [6346]
Frank Ehling Diploma [6306]
Excellence in Aerospace Education Award [3440]
Federation Award [993]
Flight Simulation Silver Medal [8605]
Founders' Medal [6690]
Framed Scrolls [6691]
Pirat Gehriger Diploma [6308]
Dr. V. M. Ghatage Award [3441]
James Gilliland Trophy [5482]
Gliding Award [613]
Gloucester Challenge Trophy [5054]
Sabiha Gokcen Medal [6309]
Gold Air Medal [6310]
Gold Medal [6692]
Gold, Silver, and Bronze Medals [8595]
Gold Wings [5483]
Grand Prix [2311]
Guild Award of Honour [7755]
Hafner VTOL Prize [8606]
Sir Robert Hardingham Presidential Sword [8607]
Heritage Awards [8608]
Hilda Hewlet Trophy [7307]
Hodgson Prize [8609]
Honorary Group Diploma [6315]
Indigenisation of Aeronautical Equipment
     Award [3442]
Dennis Jankelow Trophy [5484]
Swarna Jayanti Award [3443]
O.P. Jones Cup [7308]
Lewis Lang Trophy [5485]
Herbert Le Sueur Young Persons Award [8612]
Jean Lennox Bird Pendant [7309]
Charles Lindbergh General Aviation Diploma [6319]
Marshall of Cambridge Medal [6693]
Sir Peter Masefield Gold Medal [6958]
Medal of Darius and Girenas [4487]
Jackie Moggridge Trophy [7310]
National Aeronautical Prize [3444]
New Zealand Herald Challenge Trophy [5056]
Nexus Sport Aviation Journalist of the Year Tro-
     phy [8596]
North Shore Trophy [5058]
Norton-Griffiths Challenge Trophy [8597]
Alphonse Penaud Aeromodelling Diploma [6326]
Phoenix Group Diploma [6327]
Polaris Award [8116]
President's Award [8615]
President's Rolex Trophy [8598]
Prince of Wales Cup [8599]
Prix d'Aeronautique [2312]
Prix des Jeunes [2314]
Production Technology Award [3445]
Jeffrey Quill Medal [6694]
R38 Memorial Prize [8616]
RAeS Bronze Medal [8618]
Robinson Silver Wings Award [614]
N.E. Rowe Award [8621]
Dr. Biren Roy Memorial Lecture [3660]
Dr. Biren Roy Trust Award [3447]
Royal Aero Club Diploma [8600]
SA Branch Memorial Incentive Award [615]
SA Eagle Trophy [5486]
Clarence N. Sayen Award [8117]
Scott-Farnie Medal [6695]
Scroll of Merit [8118]
Muriel Sells Trophy [7311]
Silver Medal [6328]
Ackroyd Stuart Prize [8622]
Freda Thompson and Claire Embling Aviation
     Award [616]
Thulin Medal [6241]
Paul Tissandier Diploma [6329]
A.N. Tupolev Prize [5869]
Von Karman Award for International Cooperation in
     Aeronautics [6726]
Faust Vrancic Medal [6332]
Nancy-Bird Walton Memorial Trophy [617]
Oswald Watt Gold Medal [994]
Ann Welch Diploma [6333]
Ann Welch Memorial Award [8601]

Nancy Wells Award [618]
Young Artists Contest [6334]
Young Persons' Achievement Award [8625]

Aerospace

Advocate of the Year [897]
Aeromodelling Gold Medal [6295]
Air Sport Medal [6296]
Antonov Aeromodelling Diploma [6297]
Prix Edmond Brun [2184]
Chapter of the Year [898]
COSPAR Space Science Award [2335]
Distinguished Service Medal [2336]
Allan D. Emil Memorial Award [2499]
Jack Fahey Memorial Award [992]
Yuri A. Gagarin Gold Medal [6307]
Dr. V. M. Ghatage Award [3441]
Gold Space Medal [6313]
Hugh Gordon-Burge Memorial Award [7754]
Grand Prix [2311]
Honorary Companionship [8610]
Honorary Fellowship [8611]
Honorary Group Diploma [6315]
Christiaan Huygens Science Award [4830]
Indigenisation of Aeronautical Equipment
     Award [3442]
International Cooperation Medal [2337]
Swarna Jayanti Award [3443]
Kavli Prize in Astrophysics [5139]
V. M. Komarov Diploma [6316]
Korolev Diploma [6317]
Mike Kuhring Award [4733]
Frank J. Malina Astronautics Medal [2500]
Massey Award [2339]
Luigi G. Napolitano Award [2501]
Nile Gold Medal [6323]
William Nordberg Medal [2340]
Odyssey Diploma [6324]
Outstanding Service Award [899]
Geoffrey Pardoe Space Award [8614]
Prix d'Astronautique [2313]
Production Technology Award [3445]
Project of the Year [900]
RAeS Gold Medal [8619]
RAeS Silver Medal [8620]
Dr. Biren Roy Space Science and/or Design
     Award [3446]
Dr. Biren Roy Trust Award [3447]
Vikram Sarabhai Medal [2341]
Space Pioneer Award [901]
Student Awards [2502]
F.A. Tsander Prize [5867]
K.E. Tsiolkovskii Prize [5868]
Andrei Tupolev Aeromodelling Diploma [6330]
Andrei Tupolev Aeromodelling Medal [6331]
Wakefield Gold Medal [8624]
Young Artists Contest [6334]
Young Space Achiever Award [902]
Zeldovich Medals [2342]

African art *see also* *African studies*

Ngoma Awards [9569]

African studies *see also* *African art*

Distinguished Africanist Award [6683]
Postgraduate Essay Prize [70]
Audrey Richards Prize [6684]
Amaury Talbot Prize for African Anthropology [8642]

Aging *see also* *Geriatrics; Gerontology*

Hall of Great Names [2491]
McKitterick Prize [9254]

Agricultural economics

Award for Best Final Year Student in Agricultural
     Economics [5497]
Best Contributed Paper Award [5498]
Best Master's Thesis Award [5499]
Premio Jose Maria Bustillo [24]
A.V. Chayanov Prize [5794]
Prix Rene Dujarric de la Riviere [2199]
Excellence in Practical Farming and Business
     Award [8630]
Prix Foulon [2202]
Leopard Award [5500]

National Bank of Industry and Commerce
     Award [3353]
Outstanding Young Researcher Award [6686]
Prize Essay Competition [6687]
Talbot-Ponsonby Prize for Agricultural Valua-
     tion [8635]

Agricultural education

Naseer Ahmad Shield [3343]
Barama Company Award [3344]
Dwarka (Agriculture) Award [3345]
Excellence in Practical Farming and Business
     Award [8630]
Bernard Gonsalves Memorial Award [3346]
Guyana National Cooperative Bank Award [3347]
Guyana Sugar Corporation Award for Soil Sci-
     ence [3348]
Oscar Sydney James Shield and Trophy [3349]
Gavin B. Kennard Award [3350]
Mutiso Menezes International Prize [4416]
Ministry of Agriculture Award [3351]
Ministry of Agriculture Award for Soil Science [3352]
National Bank of Industry and Commerce
     Award [3353]
Winston J. Phillips Award [3354]
Ptolemy A. Reid Award for Animal Science [3355]
Ptolemy A. Reid Award for Crop Science [3356]
Swamy Sahajanand Saraswati Extension Scientist/
     Worker Award [3533]
University of Guyana Awards [3357]
University of Guyana Guild of Graduates Ontario
     Award [3358]

Agricultural engineering

Agricultural Engineering Award [765]
Agricultural Engineering Award and Life Member-
     ship [706]
Armand Blanc Prize [4239]
Sir Roland Burke Perpetual Challenge Machinery
     Trophy [8628]
International Crop Nutrition Award [2524]
Merit Award [4241]
Safety, Health, Environment Award [2525]
Technology Award [8636]
D. H. Trollope Medal [807]

Agriculture *see also* *Agricultural economics;*
Agricultural education; Agricultural engineering;
Agronomy; Animal husbandry; Dairy industry;
Forestry; Irrigation; Poultry science; Rural
economics

AAS Prize in Agricultural Biosciences [4370]
AFA Annual Award [2009]
Agricultural Journalism Awards [3840]
Fakhruddin Ali Ahmed Award for Tribal Areas [3520]
Allotment Awards [3915]
Hari Om Ashram Trust Award [3521]
Australian Medal of Agricultural Science [377]
Award for Outstanding Multidisciplinary Team
     Research in Agriculture and Allied Sciences [3522]
Julian A. Banzon Medal for Applied Research [5357]
Bledisloe Gold Medal for Landowners [8627]
British Grassland Society Award [7069]
CEDR Medals [1468]
Champion of Champions Awards [3917]
Prix Corbay [2250]
Noel Deerr Gold Medal [3795]
Dr. D.K. Desai Prize Award [3738]
Punjab Rao Deshmukh Woman Agricultural Scientist
     Award [3523]
Environment, Agriculture, and Rural Development
     Award [3614]
"Eqvalan Duo" Equine Thesis of the Year
     Award [8629]
Excellence in Practical Farming and Business
     Award [8630]
Farrer Memorial Medal [710]
Fellow of the Australian Institute of Agricultural Sci-
     ence and Technology FAIAST [378]
Ron Fletcher Award [8414]
Gold Medal Award [5547]
Gold Medals [5192]
Honorary Fellow [8631]
Humane Slaughter Association Award [7800]
IFAJ-Alltech Young Leaders in Agricultural Journal-
     ism Award [4737]

Archery

Architectural criticism

Architecture see also Architectural criticism; Construction; Historic preservation; Housing; Landscape architecture; Monument restoration; Park planning; Planning

Archival science see Library and information services

Art see also African art; Art education; Art history; Design; Exhibiting; Photography; specific disciplines, e.g. Ceramics

Charles Wollaston Award [8571]
Year 12 Perspectives People's Choice Award [84]

Art education

Dr. A.C.L. De'Souza Memorial Prize [4411]
Faculty of Humanities Prize [6522]
Philip Morris Art Award [7783]
Azusa Ono Memorial Awards for Art [4347]
Student Art Awards [3924]

Art history

Prix Louis Fould [2160]
Prix Roman et Tania Ghirshman [2161]
Prix du Baron de Joest [2145]
Prix Thorlet [2148]

Arts and humanities see also Antiquity;
Archaeology; Ethics; Humanities research;
Museums; Philosophy; Philosophy of science;
Religion

Academy Medal [4815]
Albert Medal [8957]
Arnheim Award [4855]
Arts and Business Awards [6734]
Balzan Prizes [4086]
Frank X. Barron Award [4856]
Alexander Gottlieb Baumgarten Award [4697]
Berlyne Award [4857]
BP Prize Lectureship in the Humanities [9061]
Crawford Medal [191]
Daiwa Foundation Art Prize [8451]
Dangal ng Haraya (Achievement Award) [5339]
De la Court Prize [4818]
EAC Over 60s Art Award [8452]
Faculty of Humanities Prize [6522]
Farnsworth Award [4858]
Gustav Theodor Fechner Award [4698]
Fellowship Competition [6386]
Antonio Feltrinelli Prizes [4022]
Benjamin Franklin Medal [8958]
Sir Francis Galton Award [4699]
Gawad Alab ng Haraya (Alab ng Haraya Awards)-
  [5340]
Gen Foundation Awards [7716]
Gold Medal
  Guildhall School of Music and Drama [7779]
  Royal Irish Academy [3929]
Governor's Award for Lifetime Achievement in the
  Humanities [5110]
Governor's Award for Outstanding Humanities
  Teacher [5111]
Governor's Award for Preservation of Traditional
  Cultural Practices [5113]
Holberg International Memorial Prize [5126]
Honorary Members [1294]
International Ibsen Award [5129]
International Print Biennale [8453]
JSPS Prize [4275]
Nils Klim Prize [5127]
Medal of Merit of the Order of Saint Lucia [5894]
Medal of the Society [2105]
Montaigne Prize [3204]
National Arts and Culture Awards [1819]
National Prizes of Arts and Literature [1807]
Onassis International Prize in the Humanities [3302]
Lynn Painter-Stainers Prize [8456]
President of the Republic Prize [56]
President's Medal [6927]
Prince of Asturias Award for Communications and
  Humanities [6085]
Prince of Asturias Award for the Arts [6089]
Research Grants [6928]
Royal Medal [9071]
Anthony N. Sabga Caribbean Awards for Excel-
  lence [6613]
Shakespeare Prize [3208]
Silver Medal of Special Merit [2712]
Stals Prize for the Humanities [5641]
Tiroler Landespreis fur Wissenschaft [1198]
Max Weber Award [2714]

Asian American culture

Distinguished Service Award [5232]

Asian studies see also Japanese culture

Dennis Anthony Memorial Award [4520]
APO National Awards [4214]
APO Regional Awards [4215]
Professor Mary Boyce Prize [8648]
Sir Richard Burton Medal [8649]
Prix Delalande-Guerineau [2154]
International Iqbal Award [5185]
Prix Stanislas Julien [2162]
National Iqbal Award [5186]
New Barwis-Holliday Award [8650]
President's Prize [91]
Research Grant Program to Assist Foreign Scholars
  in Chinese Studies [6582]
Royal Asiatic Society Award [8651]
Denis Sinor Medal [8652]
Sir George Staunton Prize [8653]
Student Competition for Overseas Music Study
  Award [5474]
Young Scholar Award [7584]

Astronautics see Aerospace

Astrology

Academic Awards [7666]
Advocate of the Year [897]
Chapter of the Year [898]
Outstanding Service Award [899]
Project of the Year [900]
Space Pioneer Award [901]
Young Space Achiever Award [902]

Astronomy

David Allen Prize [112]
Stella Arcti Award [2133]
Award for Service to Astronomy and Geophys-
  ics [8655]
Vainu Bappu Memorial Award [3622]
Sir David Robert Bates Medal [2369]
A.A. Belopol'skii [5789]
Medaille des Soixantenaire et Fondation Manley-
  Bendall [2605]
C.L. Bhat Memorial Award for Indian Astronomy
  Olympiad [3683]
Prix Georges Bidault de l'Isle [2606]
The Bok Prize [113]
F.A. Bredikhin Prize [5792]
Lydia Brown Award for Meritorious Service [6975]
Prix du Commisariat a l'Energie Atomique [2190]
Crafoord Prize [6183]
Crago Award [118]
George Darwin Lecture [8657]
Prix Ernest Dechelle [2194]
Director's Award Certificate [5510]
Eddington Medal [8658]
Editor's Award [119]
Education Officer's Award [120]
The Ellery Lectureship [114]
Aidan P. Fitzgerald Memorial Medal [3867]
Plaquette du Centenaire de Camille Flam-
  marion [2607]
Prix Gabrielle et Camille Flammarion [2608]
Fowler Prizes [8659]
Murray Geddes Memorial Prize [5043]
General Observer's Certificate [5511]
Gill Medal [5512]
Prix Edmond Girard [2609]
Gold Medal [8660]
Walter Goodacre Medal [6976]
Group Achievement Award [8661]
Charlene Heisler Prize [115]
Herschel Medal [8662]
Christiaan Huygens Science Award [4830]
Jackson-Gwilt Medal [8663]
Prix Marius Jacquemetton [2610]
Prix Jules Janssen [2611]
Jeoujang Jaw Award [2338]
Harold Jeffreys Lecture [8664]
Kavli Prize in Astrophysics [5139]
Kingdon-Tomlinson Grants [5044]
Prix Dorothea Klumpke - Isaac Roberts [2612]
Prix Andre Lallemand [2213]
Life Membership [121]
Lincei Prize for Astronomy [4023]
Long Service Award [5513]

Prix Edouard Mailly [1639]
Frank J. Malina Astronautics Medal [2500]
McIntyre Award [5514]
McNiven Medal [122]
Medaille des Anciens Presidents [2613]
Merlin Medal [6977]
Prix Marcel Moye [2614]
Luigi G. Napolitano Award [2501]
Page Medal [116]
Michael Penston Astronomy Prize [8665]
President's Award [123]
President's Award Certificate [5515]
Prix des Dames [2615]
Research Medal [1017]
Prix Henri Rey [2616]
Keith Runcorn Prize [8667]
Prix Julien Saget [2617]
Southern Cross Award [124]
Steavenson Memorial Award [6978]
Prix Paul et Marie Stroobant [1643]
Student Awards [2502]
Prix Pol et Christiane Swings [1645]
Prix Viennet-Damien [2618]
Frederick White Prize [189]
Gerald Whitrow Lecture [8668]

Athletics see Physical education; Sports; Track
  and field

Atmospheric science see Meteorology

Atomic energy see also Nuclear engineering

Nuclear-Free Future Award [2890]
Jan Runermark Award [1486]

Audiology see Speech and hearing

Audiovisuals

Dance Screen Awards [1293]
FOCAL International Awards [7672]
Learning on Screen Awards [7291]
Phenix UDA [2642]
Worlddidac Award [6567]

Auto racing

Championships, Cups, and Trophies [2504]
Driver of the Year Award [7768]
Formula One World Champion [2505]
Le Mans 24-hour Grand Prix d'Endurance [2326]
World Rally Champion [2506]

Automobile industry

Awards for Excellence [7706]
Awards to Industry [241]
Trade Show Awards [242]

Automobiles

FQE Prizes [1429]
Horace Grimley Award [8272]
Sir William Lyons Award [7769]
Pemberton Trophy [7770]
Sir Henry Royce Foundation Trophy [9181]

Automotive engineering

Automotive Engineering Excellence Awards [1038]
FQE Prizes [1429]

Aviation see Aeronautics and aviation

Aviation safety

Cumberbatch Trophy [7753]
Hunt Trophy [7759]
International Federation of Airworthiness Scholar-
  ship [8120]
Sir James Martin Award [7756]
Prince Philip Helicopter Rescue Award [7757]
Whittle Safety Award [8121]

Aviculture see Ornithology

Bacteriology see Microbiology

Badminton

Certificate of Commendation [4529]
Distinguished Service Award [4531]
English Badminton Award [6867]
Lifetime Achievement Award [4533]
Meritorious Service Award [4534]
Player of the Year Awards [4535]
Herbert Scheele Medal [6868]
Herbert Scheele Trophy [4536]
Yonex National Badminton Awards [6869]

Ballet

Associate of the Royal Academy of Dance [8573]
Eurovision for Young Dancers [6273]
Fellow of the Royal Academy of Dance [8574]
Honorary Fellow of the Royal Academy of Dance [8575]
McDonald's Ballet Scholarship [1075]
Pancyprian Ballet Competition [1895]
President's Award [8576]
Queen Elizabeth II Coronation Award [8577]
Varna International Ballet Competition [1805]

Banking

African Banker Awards [7808]
Awards for Achievement [9453]
Banking Award Liechtenstein [4476]
Best Retail Bank by Country Awards [5923]
Best Retail Bank in Asia Pacific [5924]
Best Retail Bank in Central Asia [5925]
Best Retail Bank in the Gulf States [5926]
Distinguished Person Award [5325]
European Banker of the Year [3055]
Examination Prizes [1730]
Honorary Member [5326]
Most Admired Bank [5927]
Outstanding CEO Award [5327]
Outstanding Development Project Award [5328]
Prizes in Islamic Economics and Islamic Banking [5902]
Products and Processes Awards [5928]
Special Banking Awards [5929]
Student of the Year Award [1731]

Baseball

European Baseball Championships [2755]
European Baseball Cup [2756]

Beauty contests

Miss Bhutan [1716]

Bibliography

Redmond Barry Award [434]
Medal for Services to Bibliography [6877]
C. B. Oldman Prize [8086]
Walter Stone Memorial Award [718]

Bicycling

Tour de France [2307]
Triathlon Awards [3327]
Unicycling Awards [7428]

Biochemistry

Anniversary Prizes of the Society for Biochemistry and Molecular Biology [3945]
Henry E. Armstrong Memorial Lecture [9267]
A.N. Bakh Prize [5786]
BD AFCB Distinguished Service Award [5921]
A.N. Bhaduri Memorial Lecture Award [3780]
Prof. I.S. Bhatia Award [3781]
Jagadis Chandra Bose Medal [3628]
Theodor Bucher Lecture and Medal [3946]
Caledonian Research Foundation Prize Lectureship in Biomedical Sciences and Arts and Letters [9065]
Centenary Award [6879]
Nine Choucroun Prize [2467]
Conference Travel Grants [4866]
Datta Lectureship and Medal [3947]
Dr. B. C. Deb Memorial Award for Soil/Physical Chemistry [3710]
Prix Charles Dhere [2197]
Dongchun Lecture [5465]
Early Career Research Awards [6880]

Exhibition Prize in Second-Year Biochemistry [1118]
FEBS/EMBO Women in Science Award [3948]
FEBS Journal Prize for Young Scientists [3949]
FEBS Letters Young Scientist Award [3950]
Foundation Award [6755]
Prix Leon et Henri Fredericq [1632]
Luigi Galvani Prize [2328]
Prix Jean-Marie Le Goff, Lemonon, Houry, Laveran [2205]
Dr. H.P. Heineken Prize for Biochemistry and Biophysics [4822]
Hestrin Prize [3969]
Honorary Membership [2999]
Prix Max-Fernand Jayle [2208]
JB Award [4284]
Sir Hans Krebs Lecture and Medal [3951]
Prof. P.A. Kurup Endowment Award [3785]
Lab Travel Grants [4867]
Prix du Docteur et de Madame Henri Labbe [2212]
Giulio Milazzo Prize [2329]
Moosa Lecture [5466]
Wilhelm Normann Medal [3002]
Y.A. Ovchinnikov Prize [5842]
President's Shield [6756]
Prize in Life Sciences for a Young Scientist [1759]
Professors' Prize [6757]
D.N. Pryanishnikov Prize [5847]
Sir Philip Randlo Lecture [6882]
Research Medal [1017]
Science Communication Award [9263]
Professor R. C. Shah Memorial Lecture [3726]
M.M. Shemyakin Prize [5856]
Siemens Award Lecture [6758]
Siemens Medal [6759]
Professor Umakant Sinha Memorial Award [3727]
Student Award [3003]
Teva Prize [3970]
Thermo Electron Clinical Chemistry and Automation Systems Award [6760]
Prix Leon Velluz [2238]
A.P. Vinogradov Prize [5874]
Otto Warburg Medaille [2997]
Frederick White Prize [189]
Young Investigator Awards [4285]

Biography

J. R. Ackerley Prize for Autobiography [7561]
Benson Medal [9075]
Birger Scholdstroms pris [6197]
James Tait Black Memorial Prizes [9426]
Costa Book Awards [6899]
Dr. Wijnaendts Francken-prijs [4839]
Axel Hirschs pris [6204]
Somerset Maugham Awards [9253]
Premio Comillas de Biografia, Autobiografia y Memorias [6110]
Walter Stone Memorial Award [718]
Strega Prize [4155]
Wales Book of the Year Awards [6676]

Biology see also Anatomy; Biochemistry; Biophysics; Biomedical engineering; Biotechnology; Botany; Genetics; Marine biology; Microbiology; Mycology; Nature; Ornithology; Physiology; Zoology

Prix Louis Armand [2177]
Award for Divisional Scientific Promotions [4310]
Awards for Excellence [362]
Karl Ernst von Baer Medal [2040]
Bancroft - Mackerras Medal for Excellence [552]
A.N. Belozerskii Prize [5790]
Prix Paul Betrand, Georges Deflandre et Marthe Deflandre-Rigaud, Jean Cuvillier [2182]
Bicentenary Medal [8313]
Jagadis Chandra Bose Medal [3628]
Anil Kumar Bose Memorial Award [3630]
Bruce-Preller Prize Lectureship [9063]
D.P. Burma Memorial Lecture Award in Biological Sciences [3782]
Caledonian Research Foundation Prize Lectureship in Biomedical Sciences and Arts and Letters [9065]
Alexis Carrel Young Researcher Award [2531]
Bashambar Nath Chopra Lecture [3632]
Prix du Commisariat a l'Energie Atomique [2190]
Conference Travel Grants [4866]
Conway Review Lecture [3908]

Craoford Prize [6183]
Henry Dale Prize [8860]
Darwin Medal [8931]
Distinguished Service Award [3979]
Dongchun Lecture [5465]
Prix Dubois - Debauque [1628]
EMBO Medal [2843]
Eppendorf Award for Young European Investigators [2791]
Prix Leo Errera [1630]
Fenner Medal [173]
Thomas B. Fitzpatrick Medal [3768]
Prix Fonde par l'Etat [2201]
Gabor Medal [8935]
Gen Foundation Awards [7716]
Pierre Gilles de Gennes Prize [2468]
Hugh Cary Gilson Memorial Award [7712]
Gold Medals [5192]
Golden Jubilee Commemoration Medal for Biological Sciences [3635]
Myron Gordon Award [3769]
Gottschalk Medal [176]
Prix Grammaticakis-Neuman [2206]
Van Gysel Prize for Biomedical Research in Europe [1520]
Hall of Fame Award [5037]
Ross G. Harrison Prize [4243]
Hector Memorial Medal and Prize [5075]
Honorary Membership [2999]
International Eppendorf and Science Prize for Neurobiology [2792]
International Prize for Biology [4274]
International Women in Transfusion Award [4775]
ISBT Award [4776]
Prix de Biologie Alfred Kastler [2443]
Kavli Prize in Nanoscience [5140]
Keith Medal [9068]
A.O. Kovalevskii Prize [5819]
Kshanika Oration Award [3552]
Lab Travel Grants [4867]
John Lake Poster Award [537]
Prix Lamarck [1635]
Louis-Jeantet Prize for Medicine [6336]
Prix Richard Lounsbery [2217]
MakDougall-Brisbane Prize [9069]
Irene Manton Award [9196]
George Martin Memorial Scholarship [5580]
Kazumasa Masubuchi Lifetime Achievement Award [3042]
McGraw-Hill Biology Award [1138]
I.I. Mechnikov Prize [5834]
Medal of the Society [2105]
Mendel Medal [3123]
Prix des Sciences de la Mer de l'Ifremer [2219]
Moosa Lecture [5466]
Professor Vishwa Nath Memorial Lecture [3649]
National Awards for Science Technicians [9142]
Wilhelm Normann Medal [3002]
Outstanding Book and/or Monograph Awards [5361]
Outstanding Scientific Paper Award [5362]
Outstanding Young Scientist Award [5363]
Postgraduate Student Travel Prize [9223]
Presidential Award [4778]
President's Medal [9197]
Prince of Asturias for Technical and Scientific Research [6090]
Prize in Life Sciences for a Young Scientist [1759]
D.N. Pryanishnikov Prize [5847]
Prof. G. N. Ramachandran 60th Birthday Commemoration Medal [3655]
James W. Reagan Lecture Award [3043]
Rhone-Poulenc Award [5581]
Karl Asmund Rudolphi Medal [2760]
Salters-Nuffield Advanced Biology Awards [9146]
Schleiden Medal [3125]
Science Graduate of the Year [8861]
Scientific Research Prizes [4591]
Senior Captain Scott Commemoration Medal [5639]
Scottish Science Award [9156]
Seiji Memorial Lectureship [3770]
A.N. Severtsov Prize [5853]
I.I. Shmal'gauzen Prize [5857]
SIBI Prize [6071]
K.I. Skryabin Prize [5859]
Heinrichs Skuja Prize [4440]
Frits Sobels Award [2365]

John Frederick Adrian Sprent Prize [553]
Egon Stahl Award [3176]
Egon Stahl Award in Gold [3177]
Student Award [3003]
David Syme Research Prize [1152]
Prof. Luigi Tartufari Prizes [4025]
Teva Prize [3970]
TWAS Prize for Young Scientists in the South [5195]
UMEP Prize for Academic Excellence in Biology [1154]
Prix Pierre-Joseph et Edouard Van Beneden [1646]
Van Der Linde Award [5582]
Werner-Risau Prize [3134]
Gilbert P. Whitley Memorial Student Award [538]
Don Whitley Travel Scholarship [9191]
George L. Wied Lifetime Achievement Award [3044]
Wirsam Scientific Award [5583]
Young Investigators Award [7612]
Herschel Zackheim Lectureship [8185]
Ahmed Zewail Prize for Leadership in Islamic Thought and Biological Science [4015]

Biomedical engineering

Clinical Biomechanics Award [838]
Eppendorf Award for Young European Investigators [2791]
Van Gysel Prize for Biomedical Research in Europe [1520]
William James Award [8025]
C. J. Martin Overseas Biomedical Fellowship [892]
Muybridge Award [839]
Promising Young Scientist Award [840]
Wartenweiler Memorial Lecture [841]
Young Investigator Awards [842]

Biophysics

Jagadis Chandra Bose Medal [3628]
EBSA Prize and Lecture [4695]
Prix Leon et Henri Fredericq [1632]
Dr. H.P. Heineken Prize for Biochemistry and Biophysics [4822]
McAulay-Hope Prize for Original Biophysics [533]
Giulio Milazzo Prize [2329]
Y.A. Ovchinnikov Prize [5842]
Prof. G. N. Ramachandran 60th Birthday Commemoration Medal [3655]
Bob Robertson Award [534]
Professor Umakant Sinha Memorial Award [3727]
Young Biophysicist Award [535]

Biotechnology

ACHEMA Television Prize [3160]
Amgen Australia Prize in Biotechnology [1101]
Henry E. Armstrong Memorial Lecture [9267]
Bio-Tech Award [4755]
DECHEMA Award of the Max Buchner Research Foundation [3162]
DECHEMA Honorary Membership [3163]
DECHEMA Medal [3164]
Eda Award [4324]
Excellent Paper Award [4325]
Hochschullehrer-Nachwuchs Prize [3168]
Y.A. Ovchinnikov Prize [5842]
Polytechnic Award [3170]
Poster Award [4077]
Saito Award [4326]
Society Award [4327]
Student Awards [3172]
Technical Award [4328]
Terui Award [4329]
Young Asian Biotechnologist Prize [4330]

Blindness

Alpaiwala Award [3772]
R. W. Bowen Medal [5699]
Certificate of Good Work [5776]
Excellent Member of VOS [5777]
Honorary Member of VOS [5778]
Ben Steiner Award [6845]

Boating

Beppe Croce Trophy [8177]
Flying Fifteen European Championship Awards [725]
Flying Fifteen World Championship Awards [726]

Lifeguard Awards [6984]
Long Service Medal [8178]
Peter Mason Award [8398]
Pier of the Year Award [8400]
Port of the Year [8105]
Rolex World Sailor of the Year Award [8179]
Sailing Hall of Fame [8180]
Seafarer Centre of the Year [8106]
Shipping Company of the Year [8107]
Welfare Personality of the Year [8108]
World Championship [2527]
Yachtsman of the Year Award [9501]
Young Sailor of the Year Award [9502]

Book and newspaper design

Book Design Awards [518]
British Book Design and Production Awards [7174]
Friend of the Book [1752]
Walter Tiemann Award [2690]

Book collecting

Christian Album of the Year [4875]
Christian Book of the Year [4876]
New Zealand Christian Book of the Year [4877]
Young Persons Book of the Year [4878]

Book illustration *see Illustration*

Books *see Publishing*

Botany

Otto Appel Medal [2985]
ASPS-FPB Best Paper Award [578]
Awards to Young European Scientists [3285]
Prix Paul Bertrand, G. Deflandre, M. Deflandre-Rigaud, and Jean Cuvillier [2181]
Prof. I.S. Bhatia Award [3781]
H. H. Bloomer Award [8314]
Bolus Medal [5517]
Botany Prize [1106]
British Lichen Society Awards [7104]
W. S. Bruce Medal [9062]
Certificate for Young Botanists [5658]
Certificate of Merit
   Botanical Society of South Africa [5518]
   South African Association of Botanists [5659]
Prof. Hira Lal Chakravarty Awards [3707]
Prix Auguste Chevalier [2188]
Clarke Memorial Medal [1003]
Leonard Cockayne Memorial Lecture [5071]
Community Award [912]
Anton de Bary Medal [2986]
Dudley D'Ewe Medal [5519]
Editor's Award [4723]
Engler Gold Medal [1254]
Engler Silver Medal [1255]
Environmental Award [913]
Exhibition Prize in Third-Year Botany [1120]
Fellow of the Phytopathological Society of Japan [4315]
Fellow of the Society [5743]
Flora Conservation Medal [5520]
Prix Foulon [2202]
Garden Centre Awards [914]
Gen Foundation Awards [7716]
Gold Medal for Botany [5660]
Peter Goldacre Award [579]
Hector Memorial Medal and Prize [5075]
Denys Heesom Medal [5521]
Dr. H.P. Heineken Prize for Biochemistry and Biophysics [4822]
Dean Hole Medal [8878]
Honorary Life Membership [5522]
Honorary Member
   South African Association of Botanists [5661]
   Southern African Society for Plant Pathology [5744]
Sunder Lal Hora Medal [3637]
Hutton Memorial Medal and Prize [5076]
Bengt Jonssons pris [6172]
Junior Medal for Botany [5662]
Megan Klemm Postgraduate Research Award [1131]
Bruce Knox Honours Prize [1132]
V.L. Komarov Prize [5814]
Julius Kuhn Prize [2987]

Prof. L. S. S. Kumar Memorial Award [3641]
Prix Emile Laurent [1636]
Cythna Letty Medal [5523]
Linnean Medal [8315]
Prix Edmond de Selys Longchamps [1638]
Prof. Panchanan Maheshwari Memorial Lecture [3643]
Irene Manton Prize [8316]
Marloth Medal [5524]
Ethel McLennan Award [1139]
Mueller Medal [202]
OPTIMA Gold Medal [4146]
OPTIMA Silver Medal [4147]
Christiaan Hendrik Persoon Medal [5748]
Production Nursery Awards [915]
D.N. Pryanishnikov Prize [5847]
Research Medal [1017]
Kingsley Rowan Marine Botany Prize [1145]
Professor Shyam Bahadur Saksena Memorial Medal [3662]
Schelpe Award [5525]
Prix Joseph Schepkens [1642]
Junior Captain Scott Commemorative Medal [5640]
G. A. M. Scott Research Award [1147]
Senior Medal for Botany [5663]
Percy Sergeant Medal [5526]
Professor Umakant Sinha Memorial Award [3727]
Jill Smythies Award [8317]
Stafleu Medal [1256]
Egon Stahl Award [3176]
Stebbins Medal [1257]
Supplier Award [916]
Teaching Award [580]
K.A. Timiryazev Prize [5866]
Training Award [917]
Whitley Awards [1024]
Young Scientist Award [4316]

Boxing

Hall of Fame [4598]
World Boxing Council Awards [4599]

Bravery *see Heroism*

Bridge

European Bridge Champion [4066]

Broadcast journalism

Asiavision Award for Contributions to ASEAN Television News [4522]
Stanford Fellowship [9390]
Television Journalism Awards [9131]

Broadcasting *see also Broadcast journalism; Media; Radio; Sports broadcasting; Television; Video*

Awards for Excellence in Broadcasting [9432]
EBU Award [6271]
Elizabeth R. Award for Exceptional Contribution to Public Service Broadcasting [7455]
Engineering Excellence Awards [4523]
Golden Microphone [2036]
Anne Gregg/Ed Lacy Memorial Award for Travel Broadcasting [7074]
IERE Benefactors Premium [8024]
Medal of Honour for Afrikaans Radio Feature Programme [5635]
Mental Health Media Awards [8353]
Nihon Shinbun Kyokai Awards [4270]
Radharc Awards [3853]
Rolls-Royce Award for Exceptional News Feature [7456]
Peter Wayne Award [8082]

Brotherhood

Balzan Prizes [4086]
Jawaharlal Nehru Award for International Understanding [3518]

Burglar and fire alarms *see Security*

Business *see also* *Accounting; Advertising; Business education; Business history; Business journalism; Conventions; Economics; Management; Manufacturing; Marketing*

ACCA Hong Kong Awards for Sustainability Reporting [5221]
ACCA Ireland Sustainability Reporting Awards [3830]
ACCA Malaysia Sustainability Reporting Awards [4527]
ACCA Sri Lanka Awards for Sustainability Reporting [6115]
ACCA-WWF Pakistan Environmental Reporting Awards [5181]
Administrative Professionals Award [5971]
African Business Awards [7809]
Albert Medal [8957]
AmCham Transatlantic Partnership Award [2692]
American Business Award [6660]
APEX Awards [3463]
Arabia Corporate Social Responsibility Awards [6664]
Arabian Business Achievement Awards [6662]
Asia Pacific Entrepreneurship Awards [4541]
Asia Responsible Entrepreneurship Awards [4542]
Australia and New Zealand Awards for Sustainability Reporting [103]
Australian Business Awards [251]
Australian Institute of Packaging Fellow [404]
Award of the Serbian Chamber of Commerce [5911]
Awards of Excellence [492]
Bangladesh Business Awards [1372]
Barbados Employers' Confederation Scholarship [1380]
BCO Awards [7032]
Be Fair Award [1419]
Be Sustainable Award [1420]
Best Business Plan [4478]
Best Center Award [2805]
Best Corporate Mobile Data Application Award [8369]
Best Emerging Franchise Award [3871]
Best Financial Journalist of the Year [5966]
Best of Vietnam Awards [9561]
Best Stand Award [9434]
Boss of the Year Award [4544]
Business Achievers Awards [3934]
Business Awards [11]
Business Leader of the Year [6468]
Business Start-Up Award [6595]
Business Volunteer of the Year Award [6736]
Champion Exporter [4175]
Classic FM/A & B International Award [6737]
CLFMA Award [3461]
Community Welfare Award [3612]
Contribution by Business Community Award [3613]
Prix Corbay [2250]
Creative Young Entrepreneur Luxembourg Award [4497]
Josseph de la Vega Prize [1514]
Design in Business Awards [4886]
Distinguished Agent Award [5313]
Distinguished Manager Award [5314]
Frans du Toit Medal for Business Leadership [5627]
ECO Award [1744]
Efficiency Service Awards for the Public Sector [4551]
Entrepreneur of the Year [8326]
Environment, Agriculture, and Rural Development Award [3614]
Europe Impresa Award [3750]
European Business Awards for the Environment [1460]
Excellence Award [7519]
Excellence Awards [6823]
Export Industry Awards [3869]
Max Eyth Commemorative Medal [3132]
Financial Assistance Fund for Settlement of International Disputes [4804]
Flow Guard Plumbing Personality Award [3704]
Footprint Marketing Awards [5683]
Franchise of the Year [3872]
Franchise Person of the Year [3873]
Franchisee of the Year [3874]
Franchisor of the Year [5940]
Benjamin Franklin Medal [8958]
Garrett Award [6739]
Global Award for Entrepreneurship Research [6225]

Global Student Entrepreneur Award [6226]
Gold Medal Award for Industry [3919]
Golden Bridge Export Award [6875]
Goodman Award [6740]
Graduateship of the City and Guilds of London Institute [7432]
Higher Diploma in Floristry [9308]
Hire Awards of Excellence [7792]
Hong Kong Medical Association Prize [5283]
HRD Award [6611]
ICHCA Australia Award [7811]
ICHCA Finland Award [7812]
Industry and Technology Award [3615]
Investor Relations Best Practice Awards [8261]
IPA Jaquar Felicitations [3705]
Abe Issa Award for Excellence [4180]
Journalist of the Year [9419]
Local Transportation Company of the Year [4181]
Logo Awards [5223]
Harry Lovell Award [405]
Management Award [6609]
Master Diploma in Professional Floristry [9309]
Medals for Excellence [7433]
Member of the Year Award [4545]
Membership of the City and Guilds of London Institute [7434]
Meritorious Award [5665]
Model Shareholder of the Year Award [5967]
Most Transparent Company Award [5968]
Murray Medal [5478]
National Awards for SMEs [1779]
National Outstanding Small and Medium Enterprise Award [6597]
National Quality Award [6011]
Onassis International Prize in Trade [3303]
Order of Hospitality [5885]
Outstanding Export Performance Awards [3731]
Personality of the Year Awards [6913]
Platinum Jubilee Award [3616]
President's Award [5479]
Johan Pretorius Academic Award [5666]
Promising Franchisor of the Year [5941]
Promotion of Savings, Consumer Protection, and Export Performance Award [3617]
Prudential/A & B People Development Award [6741]
Qantas/ABTA Excellence Awards [904]
Retail Industry Awards [5987]
Royal Medal [9071]
Prix Herman Schoolmeesters [1615]
Shopping Center Awards [5883]
Singapore Corporate Governance Award [5969]
Slovenian Business Excellence Prize [6012]
Small and Medium Enterprise Innovation Research Award [6599]
SMME Awards [5490]
Special Honour Award [3813]
Sri Lanka National Quality Awards [6133]
Star of the Community Award [5502]
Stars of Africa Award [5503]
Student Best Essay Award [7798]
The Swiss Re Award [5480]
Telegraph Media Group/A & B Cultural Branding Award [6742]
Training Award [9420]
Vietnam Quality Award [9559]
Warehouse Person of the Year [9421]
Western Cape Exporter of the Year [5528]
Christo Wiese Medal for an Emerging Entrepreneur [5648]
WISTA Personality of the Year [5164]
Women in the City Achievement Awards [8419]
Young Industrialist Awards of Hong Kong [5246]
Young Researcher Award [6227]
Youth Webstar Competition [5529]

Business administration *see* *Management*

Business education

Asian Commercial Community Academic Awards [4408]
Award for Excellence in the Teaching of Public Administration in Africa [4375]
Dr. A.C.L. De'Souza Memorial Prize [4411]
Faculty of Business and Economics Prize [6521]
Kenya National Chamber of Commerce and Industry Prize [4414]

Business history

Wadsworth Prize for Business History [7313]

Business journalism

Awards for Editorial and Publishing Excellence [7256]
Communicators in Business Awards [7878]
Sir William Lyons Award [7769]

Calligraphy *see* *Graphic arts*

Camping *see* *Recreation*

Canadian literature

Claude Aubry Award [6363]
Elizabeth Mrazik-Cleaver Canadian Picture Book Award [6366]
Frances E. Russell Award [6367]

Cancer *see also* *Radiology*

Abbott Award [3085]
American Cancer Society International Fellowships for Beginning Investigators [6457]
Asia-Pacific Cancer Society Training Grants (APCA-SOT) [6458]
AstraZeneca Young Scientist Frank Rose Award [6948]
Award for Outstanding Government Official [6459]
Award for Outstanding UICC Member Organization [6460]
Award for Outstanding Volunteer [6461]
BACR Travel/Exchange Fellowships [6949]
Tom Bergan Memorial Award [8198]
CACA Award to Qualified Current Published Papers [5234]
Cancer Research Training Fellowship [2480]
Paul P. Carbone Award [1547]
Clinical Research Award [1444]
Prix Dandrimont-Benicourt [2193]
Prix Marguerite Delahautemaison [4448]
Anthony Dipple Carcinogenesis Award [7578]
ECCO/EJC Young Investigator's Award [1445]
ECCO/EJC Young Investigator's Poster Awards [1446]
ECCO-ESMO Educational Awards [1447]
ESHO-BSD Award [4711]
Prix Leon-Alexandre Etancelin [2200]
Faustus Poster Awards [7579]
Nazli Gad-el-Mawla Award [1548]
Garrod Medal [7219]
Edgar Gentilli Prize [8693]
T. P. Gunton Grant [7120]
Hamilton-Fairley Young Investigator Award [6950]
Adrienne and Frederick Herbert Prize [2424]
Honorary Member [2488]
Sylvia Lawler Prize [9098]
Novartis Oration Award for Research in the Field of Cancer [3555]
Ana and John Paneboeuf Prize [2426]
John Paul Career Award [6873]
Pezcoller Foundation-ECCO Recognition for Contributions to Oncology [1448]
Prix Raymond Rosen [4449]
Prix Gustave Roussy [2234]
Saint Luke's Lecture [3910]
Schweisguth Prize [6448]
Scientific Awards [5235]
SIOP Awards [6449]
Sir Richard Sykes Prize [7220]
Lucien Tartois Prize [2429]
Helen Tomkinson Award [7127]
Translational Research Award [6951]
Travel Fellowships [7580]
Hamao Umezawa Memorial Award [8200]
Visiting Scientist Award for Senior Scientists [2481]
John David Williams Memorial Award [8201]
Yamagiwa-Yoshida Memorial International Cancer Study Grants [6462]
Young Cancer Researcher Award Lecture [7582]

Canoeing *see* *Boating*

Cardiology

Affiliate Clinical Development Award [636]
Ibn Al-Nafees Prize [1357]

Jean-Paul Binet Prize [2422]
Cardiology Section President's Medal [9085]
Professor Ignacio Chavez Young Investigator Award [4587]
Thomas Clarkson Prize [8149]
Education Grants [1217]
R. T. Hall Prize [637]
Amrut Mody Unichem Prize [3553]
Research Grant [1220]
Traveling Fellowships to the European Society of Cardiology [638]
Edith Walsh Grant [7128]
Young Investigator Award [6641]

Career achievement see Academic achievement; Professional and personal achievement

Cars see Automobiles

Cartography see also Geography

Avenza Award for Electronic Mapping [6986]
John C. Bartholomew Award [6987]
Bartholomew Globe [8916]
British Cartographic Society Award [6988]
Honorary Fellowship [8102]
International Map Collectors' Society Awards [8145]
Henry Johns Award [6989]
Carl Mannerfelt Gold Medal [8103]
National Geographic Society New Mapmaker Award [6990]
Ordnance Survey MasterMap Award [6991]
Prize for Encouragement of Globe Studies [1266]
Society Medal [6992]
UKHO Junior Mapmaker Award [6993]
Helen Wallis Award [8146]

Cartoons see also Animated films; Drawing; Humor

Biennial of Animation Bratislava [5995]
International Cartoon Contest [1333]
International Cartoon Exhibition Zagreb [1862]
The Walkley Awards [1176]

Catholic literature

Diekmann Award [4144]
Prix Gallet [2271]

Cats see Animal care and training

Ceramic engineering

Adolf-Dietzel-Industriepreis der DGG [3012]
Goldener Gehlhoff-Ring [3013]

Ceramics see also Glass

Australasian Ceramic Society/Ceramic Society of Japan Joint Ceramic Award [253]
Governor-General Art Award [4949]
International Prize [1452]
National Crafts Competition [3922]
Stuijts Award [1453]

Charity activities see Philanthropy; Volunteerism

Chemical engineering

ACHEMA Television Prize [3160]
Henry E. Armstrong Memorial Lecture [9267]
Jochen Block Prize [3161]
Brennan Medal [7958]
John A. Brodie Medal [771]
DECHEMA Award of the Max Buchner Research Foundation [3162]
Chemeca Medal [774]
Council Medal [7959]
George E. Davis Medal [7960]
DECHEMA Honorary Membership [3163]
DECHEMA Medal [3164]
Donald Medal [7961]
EFCE Excellence Awards [2822]
ESSO Award [781]
Ned Franklin Medal [7962]
Gold Medal [7686]
Arnold Greene Medal [7963]
Willy Hager Prize [3167]

Hanson Medal [7964]
John William Hinchley Medal [7965]
Hutchison Medal [7966]
Leverhulme Medal [8941]
MacNab Medal [7967]
Moulton Medal [7968]
Junior Moulton Medal [7969]
Post-graduate Research Prize [2101]
Queensland Division Chemical Branch Award [800]
Otto Roelen Medal [3171]
Salters' Graduate Prizes [9144]
Skellerup Award [4917]
H. K. Suttle Award [7687]
Shedden Uhde Medal and Prize [808]

Chemical industry

AFA Annual Award [2009]
Award for Science Communication [9268]
Award for Science Education [9269]
Award for Technical Development [4219]
Award for Young Chemists in Technical Development [4221]
Baekeland Lecture [9271]
Hans R. Bolliger Memorial Lecture [9272]
Canada Medal [9274]
Career Achievement Award [3078]
Cavallaro Medal [2824]
Wesley Cocker Award [9276]
European Corrosion Medal [2825]
Rudolf Fabinyi Medal [3380]
Juraj Ferin Award [3079]
Hellmuth Fischer Medal [3165]
Marti I. Franques Medal [2826]
Professor B.N. Ghoah Memorial Award [3514]
Roland Harper Lecture [9278]
Leverhulme Lecture [9284]
Ivan Levinstein Memorial Lecture [9285]
Julia Levy Award [9286]
Alwin Mittasch Medal [3169]
James Moir Medal [5678]
Mond Health and Safety Award [9290]
Gordon E. Moore Medal [9291]
Miklos Preisich Award [3382]
Kalev Pugi Award [9292]
Purvis Memorial Award [9293]
Professor Priyadaranjan Ray Memorial Award [3515]
Sir Eric Rideal Lecture [9294]
Andres Manuel del Rio National Prize in Chemistry [4581]
Separation Science Lecture [9296]
Society Award [9297]
Solvents Stewardship Awards [1457]
Dr. Ghanshyam Srivastava Memorial Award [3516]
Student Research Award [3080]
Hendrik Van Eck Medal [5681]
Friedrich Wohler Preis fur Ressourcenschonende Prozesse [2938]
Young Investigator Award [3081]

Chemistry see also Biochemistry; Chemical engineering; Chemical industry; Color technology; Fiber science; Geochemistry; Industrial chemistry

Abbott Award for Significant Contributions to Molecular Diagnostics [4097]
Academic Excellence Prize [5448]
ACHEMA Plaque in Titanium [3159]
A.C.I.T. Award [2316]
Adolf-von-Baeyer-Denkmunze [2923]
Gregori Aminoff Prize [6182]
Analytical Chemistry Division Award for Excellent Research [5449]
J.S. Anderson Prize [1103]
Applied Catalysis Award [8972]
Applied Inorganic Chemistry Award [8973]
Applied Research Medal [966]
Prix Louis Armand [2177]
Henry E. Armstrong Memorial Lecture [9267]
August-Wilhelm-von-Hofmann-Denkmunze [2924]
Avenir Award [2317]
Award for Advancement of Industry [5450]
Award for Advancement of Science [5451]
Award for Chemical Education [5452]
Award for Chemistry Education [4217]
Award for Distinguished Contributions in Education [4098]

Award for Divisional Scientific Promotions [4310]
Award for Excellent Chemistry Teachers [5453]
Award for Excellent Research Paper [5454]
Award for Service [8974]
Award for Technical Achievements [4218]
Award for Young Chemists [4220]
Award of Merit for Chemistry Education [4222]
Bader Award [8975]
Alfred Bader Prize [1911]
A.A. Balandin Prize [5787]
Balmer Prize [6486]
Barrer Award [8976]
Sir Derek Barton Gold Medal [8977]
Beilby Medal and Prize [8978]
Gmelin Beilstein Denkmunze [2925]
Ronald Belcher Award [8979]
Medaille Berthelot [2180]
Bioinorganic Chemistry Award [8980]
Bioorganic Chemistry Award [8981]
Biota Award for Medicinal Chemistry [967]
A.J. Birch Medal [968]
Joseph Black Award [8982]
Dr. Joseph Borgia Prize [4021]
Bourke Award [8983]
Robert Boyle Prize for Analytical Science [8984]
S. F. Boys - A Rahman Award [8985]
Bruno Breyer Medal [969]
Paul Bunge Prize [2918]
Burrows Award [970]
A.M. Butlerov Prize [5793]
Malcolm Campbell Memorial Prize [8986]
Canada International Award [9273]
Medaglia Stanislao Cannizzaro [1125]
Capps Green Zomaya Award [8987]
Castner Medal and Lecture [9275]
Catalysis in Organic Chemistry Award [8988]
Prix L. La Caze, A. Policart-Lacassagne [2187]
Cecil Memorial Trust Competition [7521]
Centenary of Federation Teaching Awards in Chemistry [971]
Centenary Prizes [8989]
Joseph Chatt Award [8990]
Chemical Dynamics Award [8991]
Chemical Education Medal [5674]
Chemical Society of Japan Award [4223]
Chemistry Award for Young Physical Chemists [5455]
Chemistry of Transition Metals Award [8992]
Chemistry Research Excellence Award [1108]
Chemistry World Entrepreneur of the Year [8993]
L.A. Chugaev Prize [5796]
Citations for Contributions to Chemistry and the Chemical Profession [972]
City and Guilds Prizes [9141]
Prix Clavel-Lespiau [2189]
Prix du Commisariat a l'Energie Atomique [2190]
Congress Awards [8129]
Brian Conway Prize for Physical Electrochemistry [6436]
Corday-Morgan Prize [8994]
Rita and John Cornforth Award [8995]
Cornforth Medal [973]
Corrosion Science Award [8996]
Creativity in Industry Prize [8997]
Dalton Young Researchers Award [8998]
Davy Medal [8932]
Peter Day Award [8999]
Prix de Boelpaepe [1623]
de Gennes Prize [9000]
Oronzio and Niccolo De Nora Foundation Prize of ISE on Electrochemical Technology and Engineering [6437]
Oronzio and Niccolo De Nora Foundation Young Author Prize [6438]
DECHEMA Honorary Membership [3163]
DECHEMA Medal [3164]
Prix Pierre Desnuelle [2196]
Distinguished Award for Laboratory Medicine and Patient Care [4099]
Distinguished Clinical Chemist Award [4100]
Distinguished Fellowship Award [974]
Distinguished Service Award [9001]
Carl Duisberg Gedachtnispreis [2926]
Carl Duisberg Plakette [2927]
Dulux Australia Prize [1112]
Dwight Prize in Chemistry [1113]
Johnny Dwyer Memorial Award [3846]

Education Award [9002]
Lecon Paul Ehrlich [2620]
Electrochimica Acta Gold Medal [6439]
Ellinger-Gardonyi Medal [8426]
Hans-Jurgen Engell Prize [6441]
Environment Prize [9003]
Environment, Sustainability and Energy Forum Early
    Career Award [9004]
EuCheMS Lecture [1431]
European Sustainable Chemistry Award [1432]
Ewald Prize [8248]
Excellent Poster Presentation Prize [5456]
Exhibition Prize in First-Year Chemistry [1117]
Faraday Lectureship Prize [9005]
Emil Fischer Medaille [2928]
Hellmuth Fischer Medal [3165]
Flavours and Fragrances Award [9006]
Theodor Foerster Memorial Lecture [2919]
Prix Fonde par l'Etat [2201]
Francqui Prize [1527]
Frankland Award [9007]
Sir Edward Frankland Fellowship [9008]
Fresenius-Preis [2929]
Frumkin Memorial Medal [6442]
Prix Gaz de France [2204]
Gen Foundation Awards [7716]
Geochemistry Award [9009]
Gibson-Fawcett Award [9010]
Pierre Gilles de Gennes Prize [2468]
Gold Medal
    Bangladesh Chemical Society [1368]
    South African Chemical Institute [5675]
Golden Jubilee Commemoration Medal for Chemical
    Sciences [3636]
John B. Goodenough Award [9011]
Graduate Education Award [5237]
Graduate Student Award [5238]
Prix Grammaticakis-Neuman [2206]
Grammaticakis-Neumann Prize [6487]
L.V. Grebenschikov Prize [5802]
Green Chemistry Award [9012]
Green Chemistry Challenge Awards [975]
Grimwade Prize [1124]
Prix Philippe A. Guye [2207]
Fabian Gyllenbergs pris [6170]
Willy Hager Medal [3166]
Otto-Hahn-Preis fur Chemie und Physik [2773]
Carl Hanson Medal [9277]
Hanus Medal [1912]
Jan Harabaszewski Medal [5392]
Harrison-Meldola Memorial Prize [9013]
Stanley Harvey Prize [1126]
Haworth Memorial Lectureship [9014]
T.W. Healy Award [1127]
Norman Heatley Award [9015]
Hector Memorial Medal and Prize [5075]
Heyrovsky-Ilkovic-Nernst Lecture [1913]
Boyle Higgins Gold Medal and Lecture Award [3847]
Higher Education Teaching Award [9016]
Hilditch Memorial Lecture [9279]
Holleman Prize, Dutch Foundation for Chemis-
    try [4828]
Gilles Holst Medal [4829]
Homogeneous Catalysis Award [9017]
Honorary Membership
    International Glaciological Society [8134]
    Polish Chemical Society [5393]
Robert Horne Memorial Lecture [9280]
Milos Hudlicky Prize [1914]
Huntsman Australia for Research Excellence [1128]
Huntsman Australia Prize in Chemistry [1129]
Hurter Memorial Lecture [9281]
ICI Annual Award for Chemistry [3848]
Industrial Chemistry Medal [5676]
Inorganic Chemistry Division Award for Excellent Re-
    search [5457]
Inorganic Mechanisms Award [9018]
Inspiration and Industry Awards [9019]
Interdisciplinary Prizes [9020]
Ipjae Award in Physical Chemistry [5458]
Israel Chemical Society Medal [3957]
V.N. Itat'ev Prize [5806]
Prix Jecker, Cahours, Paul Marguerite de la Charlo-
    nie, Houzeau, and J. B. Dumas [2209]
John Jeyes Award [9021]
JNC Editors' Award [835]

Jordan Award [8427]
Wilhelm Jost Memorial Lecture [2920]
Jubilee Medal [7424]
Prix Emile Jungfleisch [2211]
Professor Rostislaw Kaischew Award [1784]
V.A. Kargin Prize [5809]
Katritzky Junior Award in Heterocyclic Chemis-
    try [5310]
Kaufmann Memorial Lecture [3000]
H. P. Kaufmann Prize [3001]
Kavli Prize in Nanoscience [5140]
Wiktor Kemula Medal [5394]
V.G. Khlopin Prize [5810]
Khorana Prize [9022]
Wilhelm Klemm Preis [2930]
Jeremy Knowles Award [9023]
Joseph Konig Gedenkmunze [2931]
Stanislaw Kostanecki Medal [5395]
A. Krishnamurthy Award [3783]
C.R. Krishnamurti Lecture Award [3784]
Alexander Kuznetsov Prize for Theoretical Electro-
    chemistry [6443]
Stephanie L. Kwolek Award [9024]
Prix Le Bel [2438]
S.V. Lebedev Prize [5825]
Prix Leconte [2215]
Leighton Memorial Medal [976]
LeSueur Memorial Award [9283]
Leverhulme Medal [8941]
Julius Lewkowitsch Memorial Lecture [9287]
Liebig-Denkmunze [2932]
Prix de l'Institut Francais du Petrole [2216]
Lipids Group International Lecture [9288]
Liversidge Award [9025]
Liversidge Lectureship [1006]
Longstaff Prize [9026]
Lord Lewis Prize [9027]
Dr. Max Luthi Award [6488]
Macromolecular Chemistry Division Award for
    Advancement of Science [5459]
Main Group Chemistry Award [9028]
Marlow Award [9029]
Medaglia d'oro Domenico Marotta [4126]
Material Chemistry Division Award for Excellent Re-
    search [5460]
Material for Industry - Derek Birchall Award [9030]
Simao Mathias Medal [1754]
Prix des Sciences de la Mer de l'Ifremer [2219]
Merck Award [9031]
Merck Medal [5677]
Merit Award [5461]
Ludwig Mond Award [9032]
Ignacy Moscicki Medal [5396]
Prof. Sushil Kumar Mukherjee Commemorative Lec-
    ture [3719]
Medaglia d'oro Giulio Natta [4127]
Nauta Award on Pharmacochemistry [1235]
Nernst-Haber-Bodenstein-Preis [2921]
A.N. Nesmeyanov Prize [5838]
Nobel Prizes [6184]
Nyholm Prize for Education [9033]
Organic Chemistry Division Award for Excellent Re-
    search [5462]
Organic Industry Chemistry Award [9034]
Organic Lectureship [978]
Organic Stereochemistry Award [9035]
Organometallic Chemistry Award
    Royal Australian Chemical Institute [979]
    Royal Society of Chemistry [9036]
Wilhelm Ostwald Medal [2043]
Outstanding Book and/or Monograph Awards [5361]
Outstanding Scientific Paper Award [5362]
Outstanding Young Scientist Award [5363]
Outstanding Young Scientist Prize [3958]
Paracelsus Prize [6489]
Partington Prize [9213]
Prix Paul Pascal [2227]
Medaglia Emanuele Paterno [4128]
Pedler Award [9037]
Perkin Prize for Organic Chemistry [9038]
Ignac Pfeifer Award [3381]
Physical Chemistry Division Medal [980]
Physical Organic Chemistry Award [9039]
Phytochemical Society of Europe Medal [8475]
C. S. Piper Prize [981]
Polytechnic Award [3170]

Poster Award [8130]
Horst Pracejus Preis [2933]
Preis der Gesellschaft Deutcher Chemiker fur Schrift-
    steller [2934]
Karel Preis Prize [1915]
Prince of Asturias for Technical and Scientific Re-
    search [6090]
Prix Triennal de la Societe Royale de Chimie [1667]
Prize for Excellence [3959]
Prize for PhD Thesis in Photochemistry [6281]
Process Technology Award [9040]
Procter Memorial Prize [9322]
Prous Institute-Overton and Meyer Award on New
    Technologies in Drug Discovery [1236]
Dr. Atta Ur Rahman Prize in Chemistry [5193]
Raikes Medal [5679]
Ramsay Memorial Fellowships for Postdoctoral
    Chemical Research [8534]
P.B. Rama Rao Memorial Award [3786]
P.A. Rebinder Prize [5849]
Theophilus Redwood Award [9041]
Taikyue Ree Academic Award [5463]
Charles Rees Award [9042]
Rennie Memorial Medal [982]
Research Medal [1017]
Monica Elizabeth Reum Memorial Prize [1143]
Richardson Medal [8135]
Sir Eric Rideal Lecture [9294]
Ronald Riseborough Prize [1144]
Robert Robinson Award [9043]
Bakhuys Roozeboom Medal [4835]
Ruzicka Prize [6501]
Ernest Sack Award [2318]
Prof R. C. Saha Memorial Lecture [3723]
Salters Advanced Chemistry Prize [9143]
Salters' Graduate Prizes [9144]
Sandmeyer Prize [6490]
Alan Sargeson Inorganic Lectureship Award [983]
P.S. Sarma Memorial Award [3787]
Sasol Post-Graduate Medal [5680]
Arfvedson Schlenk Preis [2935]
Schools Education Award [9044]
Science Education Award [6033]
Scientific Research Prizes [4591]
Seligman Crystal [8136]
Senior Award in Heterocyclic Chemistry [5311]
Professor T. R. Seshadri Seventieth Birthday Com-
    memoration Medal [3663]
Prof. M. Shadakshara Swamy Endowment Lecture
    Award [3788]
Professor R. C. Shah Memorial Lecture [3726]
Dr. Jagdish Shankar Memorial Lecture [3664]
M.M. Shemyakin Prize [5856]
Dr. M. Raziuddin Siddiqi Prize for Scientists Under
    40 [5194]
Maria Sklodowska-Curie Medal [5397]
H. G. Smith Memorial Award [984]
Jedrzej Sniadecki Medal [5398]
Society for Analytical Chemistry Silver Medal [9045]
Soft Matter and Biophysical Chemistry Award [9046]
George and Christine Sosnovsky Award in Cancer
    Therapy [9047]
Spiers Memorial Award [9048]
M. Sreenivasaya Memorial Award [3789]
Hermann Staudinger Preis [2936]
Stern Award [8428]
Alfred Stock Gedachtnispreis [2937]
Sir George Stokes Award [9049]
R.H. Stokes Medal [985]
Don Stranks Awards [986]
Student Awards [3172]
Prix Pierre Sue [2439]
Supramolecular Chemistry Award [9050]
Surfaces and Interfaces Award [9051]
Sustainable Energy Award [9052]
Sustainable Water Award [9053]
Prix Frederic Swarts [1644]
David Syme Research Prize [1152]
Synthetic Organic Chemistry Award [9054]
Prix Jacques Tacussel [6445]
Tajima Prize [6446]
Teamwork in Innovation Award [9055]
Karoly Than Award [3383]
Tilden Prizes [9056]
Toxicology Award [9057]
Prix Gabrielle Sand et Marie Guido Triossi [2237]

TWAS Prize for Young Scientist in the Philippines [5368]
TWAS Prize for Young Scientists in the South [5195]
UCB-Ehrlich Award for Excellence in Medicinal Chemistry [1237]
Gustavs Vanags Prize [4444]
Prix Leon Velluz [2238]
Gunning Victoria Jubilee Prize Lectureship [9073]
A.P. Vinogradov Prize [5874]
Vince Wartha Memorial Plaquettes [3384]
Weickhardt Medal for Distinguished Contribution to Economic Advancement [987]
Werner Prize [6491]
Norman Thomas Mortimer Wilsmore Research Prize [1157]
Prix Aniuta Winter-Klein [2240]
Henry Wishinsky Award for Distinguished International Service [4101]
The Wolf Prizes [4001]
Young Industrialist of the Year Award [9058]
Young Scientist Award
    International Confederation for Thermal Analysis and Calorimetry [1764]
    International Society for Neurochemistry [836]
Jan Zawidzki Medal [5399]
N.D. Zelinskii Prize [5879]

Chess

Chess World Champions [3315]
FIDE Master [3316]
Fiji Chess Championships [2062]
Gibtelecom International Chess Festival [3263]
Gold Diploma of Honor [3317]
Grandmaster [3318]
International Arbiter [3319]
International Master [3320]
Woman FIDE Master [3321]
Woman Grandmaster [3322]
Woman International Master [3323]

Child welfare   *see also* Youth work

National Photographic Competition [2066]

Children and youth

Books for Children [813]
Carnegie Medal [7377]
Child and Adolescent Faculty Poster Prize for SHOs/STs [8708]
Child and Adolescent Faculty Specialist Registrar Poster Prize [8709]
Ihsan Dogramaci Family Health Foundation Prize [6549]
Early Years Awards [6905]
FAO-WAGGGS Nutrition Medal [9467]
Kate Greenaway Medal [7378]
Gullspira Award [6233]
International Award [7738]
International Munich Festival and Competition for Children's and Youth Television [3154]
Medical Student Essay Prize In Child and Adolescent Mental Health [8726]
Olave Award [9468]
Prix Ex Aequo - International Children's and Youth Radio Drama Festival [6277]
Queen's Award [7739]
Service Awards [3932]
Women of Outstanding Achievement [9470]

Children's literature

Hans Christian Andersen Awards [6362]
Claude Aubry Award [6363]
Australian Awards for Excellence in Educational Publishing [516]
Australian Book Industry Awards [517]
BBC National Short Story Award [6902]
Elsa Beskow Plaque [6236]
Bisto Book of the Year Award [3832]
Blue Peter Book Awards [6903]
Book Awards [5953]
Book of the Year Award: Early Childhood [645]
Book of the Year Award: Older Readers [646]
Book of the Year Award: Picture Books [647]
Book of the Year Award: Younger Readers [648]
Book Prizes [3272]
Buxtehuder Bulle [2746]

CBCI Award [3824]
Russell Clark Award [4931]
Costa Book Awards [6899]
Crichton Award for New Illustrators [649]
Lady Cutler Award [650]
Roald Dahl Funny Prize [6904]
Penelope Delta Award [3273]
Eilis Dillon Award [3833]
Diploma of Appreciation [3825]
Dromkeen Librarian's Award [687]
Dromkeen Medal [688]
Festival Awards for Literature [1044]
Finlandia Junior Prize for Literature [2088]
Percy FitzPatrick Award for Youth Literature [5540]
Friedrich-Gerstaecker-Preis [2742]
Glazen Globe [4813]
Esther Glen Award [4934]
Nils Holgersson Plaque [6237]
Tienie Holloway Medal [5632]
Honour List [6364]
IBBY-Asahi Reading Promotion Award [6365]
IRSCL Award [824]
IRSCL Fellows [825]
Mary Vaughan Jones Award [9442]
Rudolf Koivu Prize [2114]
Astrid Lindgren Memorial Award [6223]
Literary Competition [690]
Elsie Locke Award [4936]
Macmillan Writer's Prize for Africa [8336]
Memorial Awards for Literature [5350]
The Most Beautiful and the Best Children's Books in Slovakia [5996]
Elizabeth Mrazik-Cleaver Canadian Picture Book Award [6366]
New South Wales Premier's Literary Awards [906]
New Zealand Post Children's Book Awards [4871]
Pixie O'Harris Award [519]
Eve Pownall Award for Information Books [651]
Premier's Award [1045]
Prize for Children and Young Adult Fiction [1688]
Dusko Radovic Prize [5913]
Red House Children's Book Award [7670]
Frances E. Russell Award [6367]
Scheepers Prize for Youth Literature [5638]
Abdul Hameed Shoman Award for Children's Literature [4364]
Special Commendation [3826]
Tir na n-Og Awards [9443]
Prijs van de Jonge Jury [4654]
Prijs van de Nederlandse Kinderjury [4655]
Prix Bernard Versele [1571]
White Ravens [3104]
Feng Zikai Chinese Children's Picture Book Award [5248]

Choral music

Mundi Cantant - International Choir Festival [1925]
Musica Religiosa - International Choir Festival of Sacred and Clerical Music [1926]
Scots and Gaelic Song Competition [9152]
Harold Smart Competition [8911]

Choreography

Dance Screen Awards [1293]
Live Awards [9393]
Laurence Olivier Awards [9324]

Christianity   *see also* Catholic literature

Dominee Pieter Drimmelen Medal [5626]
Otto Hirsch Medaille [3192]
Order of Pius [9547]
Order of St. Sylvester [9549]
Order of the Golden Spur (Golden Militia) [9550]
Pro Ecclesia et Pontifice Medal [9551]
SIGNIS Award [1662]
Supreme Order of Christ (Militia of Our Lord Jesus Christ) [9552]
Totius Prize for Theology and Study of the Original Languages of the Bible [5644]

Cinema   *see* Films

Citizenship and patriotism

David Agmashenebeli Order [2676]
Australia Day Awards [1178]

Benin National Merit Award [5095]
Cacique's Crown of Honour [3335]
Chaconia Medal [6615]
Companion of the Star of Melanesia [5211]
Corporate Citizenship Award [4617]
Decoration for Service to the Country [4509]
Decoration of the Republic of Macedonia [4510]
Distinguished Alumnus/Alumna Award [5373]
Dominica Award of Honour [1999]
European Diploma [2348]
Flag of Honour [2351]
Golden Arrow of Achievement [3337]
Golden Fleece Order [2677]
Grand Companion of Logohu [5213]
Grand Cross of the Order of Saint Lucia [5891]
Head of State Awards - Ghana [3257]
Honor Medal [2678]
Hummingbird Medal [6616]
Independence Medal [4485]
Les Pitons Medal of the Order of Saint Lucia [5892]
Long Service Medal [2000]
Medal for Bravery [6003]
Medal for Irreproachable Service [6654]
Medal for Service to the Country [4511]
Medal of Honour of the Order of Saint Lucia [5893]
Medal of January 13 [4488]
Medal of Merit [6617]
Medal of Merit of the Order of Saint Lucia [5894]
Medal of Service [3339]
Medal of the Order of the Lithuanian Grand Duke Gediminas [4490]
Medals of the Orders [5214]
Member of Logohu [5215]
Meritorious Service Award [2001]
Military Honor Medal [2680]
Prix Fondation du General Muteau [2291]
National Arya Samaj Award [3333]
National Hero Award [2681]
National Logohu Medal [5216]
National Service Cross of the Order of Saint Lucia [5895]
National Service Medal of the Order of Saint Lucia [5896]
Officer of Logohu [5217]
Order of Excellence of Guyana [3340]
Order of Honor [2682]
Order of Orange-Nassau [4650]
Order of Rio Branco [1746]
Order of Roraima of Guyana [3341]
Order of the Cross of Vytis (the Knight) [4491]
Order of the Falcon [3438]
Order of the Lithuanian Grand Duke Gediminas [4492]
Order of the Netherlands Lion [4652]
Order of the White Double Cross [6004]
Order of Vytautas the Great [4493]
Plaque of Honour [2354]
Pribina Cross [6005]
Royal Norwegian Order of St. Olav [5135]
Royal Order of Sahametrei [1809]
St. George's Victory Order [2683]
St. Lucia Cross [5897]
St. Olav Medal [5136]
Services Medal of Honour [2002]
Sisserou Award of Honour [2003]
M.R. Stefanik Cross [6006]
Trinity Cross [6619]
L'Udovit Stur Order [6007]
Vakhtang Gorgasal's Order [2684]
Yemen Panther Award [9567]

City management

Britain in Bloom Awards [8813]
Young Planner of the Year Award [9135]

City planning   *see also* Park planning; Planning

Sir Patrick Abercrombie Prize [2584]
Gerd Albers Award [4780]
Awards for Excellence [4781]
Sam van Embden Award for Members' Initiatives [4782]
European Parking Award [2847]
European Standard Parking Award [2848]
European Urban and Regional Planning Awards [1471]

The Royal Society-Daiwa Anglo-Japanese Foundation Joint Project Grants [7494]
Scholarships of the City of Munich [3139]
Geschwister Scholl Preis [3140]
Svenska Akademiens pris for introduktion av svensk kultur utomlands [6215]
Telegraph Media Group/A & B Cultural Branding Award [6742]
Jose Vasconcelos World Award of Education [4603]

Cycling *see* Bicycling

Dairy industry

IDF Award [1531]
Dr. Kurien Award [3575]
Marketing Awards [1532]
Elie Metchnikoff Prize [1533]
Patrons and Fellows [3576]

Dance *see also* Ballet; Choreography

The Arches Brick Award [7528]
Arts Council of Northern Ireland Funding and Awards [6749]
Dance Screen Awards [1293]
Eurovision Dance Contest [6272]
Grand Prix [2634]
Live Awards [9393]
Laurence Olivier Awards [9324]
Prix de Lausanne [6472]
Prix Nouveau Talent [2636]
Promotional Prizes [3138]
Scholarships of the City of Munich [3139]
Split Summer Festival [1867]

Data base management *see* Information management

Data processing *see* Computer science

Deafness *see also* Speech and hearing

Cunningham-Beatie Award [7254]
Medal of Honour [7040]
Dorothy Shaw Deaf Australian of the Year Award [683]

Democracy *see* Freedom

Demography

Prix Paul Leroy-Beaulieu [2282]

Dental research

Colyer Prize [9086]
Medical and Dental Postgraduate Research Scholarships [893]
Young Investigator's Award [4706]
Zsolnay Prize [4707]

Dentistry *see also* Dental research; Orthodontistry

Academic Prize [954]
Abdul Qassim Al-Zahrawi Prize [1360]
Jens Andreasen Award [6356]
Frank Ashley Undergraduate Prize [7260]
Bright Smiles, Bright Futures Award [6357]
Rod Cawson Prize Lecture [8699]
F. G. Christensen Memorial Prize [955]
Clinical Fellowship Awards [7261]
Davies Foundation Travelling Fellowship [8700]
Drummond-Jackson Essay Prize [9210]
Sir Wilfred Fish Research Prize [7262]
Goldene Nadel Award [2940]
Dr. Sam Harris Travel Bursaries [6358]
Honorary Fellowship [956]
Bengt Magnusson Memorial Prize [6359]
Meritorious Service Award [957]
Morita Prize [6360]
New Zealand Dental Therapist Student Award [4962]
Odontology Section President's Prize [9103]
Elida Ponds Prize [4421]
Winifred E. Preedy Postgraduate Bursary [343]
Presidential Commendation [958]
Research Grants [7263]
Student and Nurse Essay Prizes [9211]
Kenneth J. G. Sutherland Prize [959]

T. C. White Grant [8701]
Kay F. Thompson Award for Clinical Excellence in Dentistry [4113]
T. C. White Prize Lecture [8702]
Young Lecturer Award [960]

Dermatology

Best Free Communication [4027]
Best Poster of the Year [4028]
Book Prize [5936]
British Association of Dermatologists Fellowships [6960]
ESDR Travel Grants [6288]
Dr. Antonio Gonzalez Ochoa Award [4589]
Honorary Membership
    Dermatological Society of Malaysia [4538]
    European Society for Dermatological Research [6289]
Intercalated Degree Grant [6961]
Mor Kaposi Medal [3386]
Postgraduate Awards [6962]
V.S. Rajan Gold Medal [5937]
V.S. Rajan Memorial Fund [5938]
Research Grant [4539]
Undergraduate Award [6963]
Undergraduate Dermatology Elective/Project Grants [6964]
Undergraduate Essay Prize [6965]
Hugh Wallace's Registrars' Prize [9110]

Design *see also* Art; Architecture; Book and newspaper design; Costume design; Fiber science; Fashion; Graphic arts; Industrial design; Interior design; Jewelry design; Lighting design; Set design; Textile design

BeST Design Awards [4884]
BIDA Charitable Trust Bursary Award [7087]
BIDA Foundation BA Award [7088]
Braun Prize [2739]
Brick Awards [6915]
British Academy Television Awards [6932]
British Design Awards [7512]
Design Ambassador Awards [4885]
Design Award of the Federal Republic of Germany [2942]
Design Effectiveness Awards [7510]
Design Partnership Award [8389]
Dutch Design Awards [4646]
Emerging Talent Award [7102]
Estlander Prize [2068]
European Design Awards [3283]
Excellent Swedish Design Prize [6243]
Fennia Prize [2069]
FleurEx - Chrysal Competition [7060]
FleurEx - Smithers-Oasis Competition [7061]
FleurEx - Student Competition [7062]
Florist of the Year Competition [7063]
Founders Award [8037]
Kaj Franck Design Prize [2070]
Gerald Frewer Memorial Trophy [8038]
Dr. V. M. Ghatage Award [3441]
Glass Designer of the Year [2081]
Graduate Designer Awards [3850]
Graphic Designer of the Year [2082]
Hong Kong Awards for Industries - Consumer Product Design [5244]
Honorary Fellow [7418]
Honorary Membership [7064]
IDI Design Awards [3851]
International Designer Awards [4717]
International Student Design Competition [7449]
Logo Awards [5223]
Minerva Medal [7419]
Minerva Service Award [7420]
National Prize for the Most Beautiful Book [1245]
Newspaper of the Year Award [923]
Orange British Academy Film Awards [6933]
Ornamo Globe [2084]
Prince Philip Prize [7421]
Prince Philip Prize for the Designer of the Year [7513]
Dr. Biren Roy Trust Award [3447]
Royal Designer for Industry Award [8959]
Student Medals [7422]
Young Designer of the Year Prize [2071]
Piet Zwart Prize [4647]

Dietetics *see* Nutrition

Diplomacy *see* International relations

Diving safety *see* Water safety

Divorce *see* Family relations

Documentary films

AACTA Awards [349]
Amanda Award for Cinematographic Merit [5143]
British Academy Television Awards [6932]
Dance Screen Awards [1293]
The Documentary Award [5149]
Festival dei Popoli [4080]
FOXTEL Australian Documentary Prize [1080]
International Adventure Film Festival [2463]
International Filmfestival Mannheim/Heidelberg [3070]
International Visual Communications Association Awards [8250]
Sondrio International Documentary Film Festival on Parks [4153]
Tampere International Short Film Festival [2128]
Thessaloniki Film Festival [3313]
Uppsala International Short Film Festival [6245]
Visions du Reel International Documentary Film Festival [6532]

Dogs *see* Animal care and training

Drama *see also* Drama criticism; Theater

Arts Council of Northern Ireland Funding and Awards [6749]
Book Awards [5953]
Miles Franklin Literary Award [1084]
Fringe First Awards [7530]
Golden Chest International Television Festival [1789]
Grand Prix [2634]
Eric Gregory Awards [9249]
Hertzog Prize for Literature [5630]
Henri Jeanson Prize [2635]
Live Awards [9393]
Long Service Awards [8396]
Bruce Mason Playwrighting Award [5034]
Memorial Awards for Literature [5350]
New South Wales Premier's Literary Awards [906]
Norwegian Ibsen Award [5130]
Thomas Pringle Award [5542]
Prix Ex Aequo - International Children's and Youth Radio Drama Festival [6277]
Prix Nouveau Talent [2636]
Prize for Mountain Literature [6889]
Olive Schreiner Prize [5543]
Split Summer Festival [1867]
Teaterpriset [6217]
Village Roadshow Prize for Screen Writing [1068]
Brian Way Award [9387]
Peter Wolff Theatre Trust Award [6747]

Drama criticism

Thomas Pringle Award [5542]

Drawing *see also* Cartoons; Graphic arts; Illustration

Governor-General Art Award [4949]
Prix de Rome - Visual Arts [4811]
St. Cuthbert's Mill Award for Works on Paper [8970]
Prix de Dessin Pierre David Weill [2149]

Drug addiction

European Drug Prevention Prize [2350]
Medical Student Essay Prize in Addictions Psychiatry [8725]
National Drug and Alcohol Awards [331]
Poster Prize for Trainees in Addictions Psychiatry [8737]
Prime Minister's Award for Excellence and Outstanding Contribution in Drug and Alcohol Endeavours [332]
SSA Bursaries [9220]
SSA Traveling Scholarship [9221]

Education, elementary see Elementary education

Education, engineering see Engineering education

Education, geographic see Geographic education

Education, health see Health education

Education, higher see Higher education

Education, journalism see Journalism education

Education, legal see Legal education

Education, medical see Medical education

Education, music see Music education

Education, physical see Physical education

Education, science see Science education

Education, secondary see Secondary education

Education, special see Special education

Educational films

Australian Teachers of Media Awards [596]
Learning on Screen Awards [7291]
Andre Leroy Prize [2547]

Educational research

Bilbao Prize for the Promotion of a Culture of Human Rights [2648]
Bruce H. Choppin Memorial Award [4720]
National Assessment Awards [1096]
Dick Wolf Memorial Award [4721]

Electrical engineering see also Electronics

Achievement Medals [8019]
Blumlein-Brown-Willans Premium [8020]
CESA/Glenrand M.I.B. Engineering Excellence Awards [5535]
College of Electrical Engineers Student Prizes [775]
James Alfred Ewing Medal [7982]
Faraday Medal [8021]
Herbert-Kind-Preis [2788]
J. A. Lodge Award for Medical Engineering [8026]
John Madsen Medal [791]
Evan Parry Award [4915]
A. H. Reeves Premium [8030]
Sir Henry Royce Award [8031]
M. A. Sargent Medal [804]
J. Langham Thompson Premium [8033]
VDE/ETG Award [2789]
P.N. Yablochkov Prize [5877]

Electrical industry

Apprentice Awards [887]
Apprentice of the Year [9171]
Cecil Memorial Trust Competition [7521]
ELCINA/Dun & Bradstreet Awards for Excellence in Electronics Hardware [3478]
Electrotechnology School Student Awards [888]
Excellence Awards [889]
Student Lighting Design Awards [8311]

Electronics

Prof. S.V.C. Aiya Memorial Award [3752]
Apprentice Awards [887]
Audio and Home Theater Awards [5427]
Best Electrical Vehicle [1428]
Bimal Bose Award [3753]
Cave Radio and Electronics Group Award [6996]
Flt. Lt. Tanmaya Singh Dandass Memorial Award [3754]
Distinguished Member [2512]
E-Journal Prize [4240]
Electrotechnology School Student Awards [888]

Excellence Awards [889]
Honorary Member [2513]
Lord Kelvin Award [6374]
Alexander Kuznetsov Prize for Theoretical Electrochemistry [6443]
Prof. S.N. Mitra Memorial Award [3755]
Mobile Devices Awards [5428]
Mountbatten Medal [8028]
Paper Awards [3275]
Athanasios Papoulis Award [3276]
Quantum Electronics Prize [2397]
Prof. K. Sreenivasan Memorial Award [3756]
Technical Committee Award [2514]
J. Langham Thompson Premium [8033]
J. J. Thomson Medal [8034]
Hari Ramji Toshniwal Gold Medal [3757]
UIE Electroheat Prize for Young Engineers [2580]
Lal C. Verman Award [3758]
Ram Lal Wadhwa Gold Medal [3759]

Elementary education

Prix Joseph De Keyn [1602]
Luka Ritz Award [1883]

Emergency medicine

Ommaya Qurabi Al-Tajer Prize [1359]
Ambulance Service Medal [295]

Emergency services

112 Awards [1475]
Emergency Services Medal [312]

Employment practices see also Labor; Occupational health; Occupational safety; Personnel management; Training and development

Top Employer Award [1815]

Endocrinology

Bryan Hudson Clinical Endocrinology Award [702]
Roger Melick Young Investigator Award [207]
Novartis Junior Scientist Award [703]
Sol Posen Research Award [209]
Servier Young Investigator Award [704]
Von-Recklinghausen-Preis [2978]

Energy

Advancing Solar Energy Policy Award [3099]
Australian Institute of Energy Medal [390]
Karl W. Boer Solar Energy Medal of Merit [3100]
Farrington Daniels Award [3101]
Dow Energy Prize [4820]
Energy Efficiency Award [1410]
European Solar Prizes [2873]
Prix Gaz de France [2204]
Gold Medals [5192]
The Green Awards [4401]
Habitat Solaire, Habitat d'aujourd'hui [2594]
Heinrich Hertz Preis [3216]
James Prescott Joule Medal [7995]
Melchett Medal [7549]
Prix Ivan Peyches [2229]
Wal Read Memorial Student Prize [226]
Thring Award [7550]
Christopher A. Weeks Achievement through Action Award [3102]

Energy, atomic see Atomic energy

Energy conservation

Ashden Awards for Sustainable Energy [6753]
Dow Energy Prize [4820]
The Green Awards [4401]

Engineering see also Communications technology; Electronics; Energy; Engineering education; Materials science; Mining and metallurgy; Photogrammetry; Standards; Surveying; Testing; Water resources

ACE Engineering Excellence Awards [6762]
Achievement Award [4225]
Nikolai Alumae Medal [2038]
Andritz Oy Award [2093]
Asia Pacific Industrial Technologies Awards [5975]

The Associateship of the City and Guilds of London Institute [7430]
Australian Engineering Excellence Awards [767]
Automatica Prize Paper Award [1276]
Award for Achievement in Engineering Enterprise [769]
Award for Contribution to the Land Based Sector [7951]
Award of Merit [7952]
Awards for Excellence [664]
Awards of Excellence [4860]
Barker Silver Medal [7388]
Baroness Platt of Writtle Award [7552]
Beilby Medal and Prize [8978]
Best Emerging Young Woman Scientist Award [5685]
Best Paper Award [4226]
Shanti Swarup Bhatnagar Medal [3626]
Birmingham Medal [8040]
Scott Blair Biorheology Scholarship [7265]
O. F. Blakey Memorial Prize [770]
Douglas Bomford Paper Award [7953]
Dr. A. K. Bose Medal [3591]
British Foundry Medal and Prize [7828]
British Society of Rheology Annual Award [7266]
Bronze Medal [8041]
Frederick Brough Memorial Prize [772]
Bruce-Preller Prize Lectureship [9063]
Karen Burt Memorial Award [9458]
Fridrihs Canders Prize [4435]
Carter Bronze Medal [7389]
Richard Carter Prize [7396]
CESA/Glenrand M.I.B. Engineering Excellence Awards [5535]
Ceylon Development Engineering Award [6124]
Civil Engineering Students Papers Competition [7978]
Hans Cloos Medal [6037]
Collacott Prize [8017]
Conference Awards [8423]
Cooling Prize [7066]
E. R. Cooper Memorial Medal and Prize [5072]
J.M.C. Corlette Medal [777]
CPEA Educational Award [1899]
John Cranko Award [4906]
E. H. Davis Memorial Lecture [778]
Dell Award [8055]
Distinguished Achievement and Contributions Award [4227]
Distinguished International Fellow Award [821]
Distinguished Service Award [6584]
Distinguished Woman Scientist Award [5687]
Dufton Silver Medal [7390]
Duke of Edinburgh's Award [7891]
Russell Dumas Medal [779]
Michael Dwyer Memorial Prize [7954]
L.R. East Medal [780]
Education Award [4277]
Emblem of Appreciation [6177]
Engineer of the Year [5719]
Engineering Achievement Award [9577]
Engineering Excellence Awards [4523]
Engineering Heritage Award [7553]
Ergonomics Development Award [6585]
Excellence in Engineering Journalism Award [782]
Excellent Product Award [4278]
Finnish Engineering Award [2086]
Lady Finniston Award [9459]
Fourth-Year Student Award [4861]
Rosalind Franklin Award [8934]
Fulton-Downer Gold Medal [4908]
Gardner Award [9334]
Leon Gaster Memorial Award [7391]
Prix Gaz de France [2204]
Mary George Memorial Prize for Apprentices [8022]
Gold Medal
   British Society of Rheology [7267]
   Institution of Gas Engineers and Managers [8042]
   Royal Swedish Academy of Engineering Sciences [6178]
Gold Medals [5192]
Graduates and Students Papers Competition [7985]
Faldt Guthrie Medal [783]
P. H. Haviland Award [9578]
Fiona and Nicholas Hawley Award [7554]
Hector Memorial Medal and Prize [5075]

Dr. A.H. Heineken Prize for Environmental Sciences [4824]
Ian Henderson Award [784]
High Impact Paper Award [1277]
Dennis Hill Award [8023]
Holcim Green Built Bangladesh Contest [1374]
Honorary Fellows of CIBSE [7392]
Honorary Fellowship [7955]
Honorary Fellowship [5183]
Honorary Member's Emblem [6180]
Hume Prize [4910]
ICME Diploma [7831]
Industrial Achievement Award [1278]
Inose Award [4228]
International Medal [8580]
Arthur Thomas Ippen Award [6042]
K. Johinke Medal [785]
Johnson New Holland Trophy Award [7956]
James Prescott Joule Medal [7995]
Junior Inventor of the Year [6125]
Keith Jurgs Award [100]
Allen Knight Medal [787]
Jan Korevaar Outstanding Paper Award [822]
Krill Prizes for Excellence in Scientific Research [4000]
Lampen Medal [2096]
Ian Langlands Medal [788]
Digby Leach Medal [789]
Prix Charles Lemaire [1637]
Liberty Mutual Prize in Occupational Safety and Ergonomics [6586]
Local Government Engineering Medal [790]
MacLean Citation [4911]
MacRobert Award [8581]
Magsaysay Future Engineers/Technologists Award [5359]
Prasanta Chandra Mahalanobis Medal [3642]
MakDougall-Brisbane Prize [9069]
Arthur Mead Environmental Award [4912]
Medal for Distinguished Engineers [4279]
Medal for New Technology [4280]
Medal of Excellence in Engineering Education [2665]
Sir Eric Mensforth International Manufacturing Gold Medal [8027]
Mercia Prize [7555]
Meritorious Services Medal [7832]
John Monash Medal [793]
Mullard Award [8942]
G. T. Murray Memorial Award [4914]
Kevin Nash Gold Medal [8194]
NCE/ACE Young Consultant of the Year Award [6763]
Nathaniel B. Nichols Medal [1279]
General Pierre Nicolau Award [2475]
W.H.R. Nimmo Medal [794]
Thomas R. Odhiambo Prize in Basic and Applied Sciences [4372]
Orden al Merito Julio Garavito [1841]
Outstanding Book and/or Monograph Awards [5361]
Outstanding Educators Award [6587]
Outstanding Export Performance [3480]
Outstanding Scientific Paper Award [5362]
Outstanding Young Scientist Award [5363]
De Paepe-Willems Award [1545]
Sir Arvi Parbo Medal [795]
R. W. Parsons Memorial Prize [796]
Prix Blaise Pascal du GAMNI-SMAI [2226]
Paterson Prize [8002]
Professor E. O. E. Pereira Award [6126]
Plaquette of Merit [2098]
Louis Prangey Award [6378]
Premio Nacional [1830]
President's Award
   Association of Consulting Engineers of New Zealand [4862]
   International Ergonomics Association [6588]
President's Medal [8582]
President's Prize [797]
President's Shield [101]
R.A. Priddle Medal [798]
Prince Philip Medal [8583]
Prix de la SRBE [1664]
Professional Engineer of the Year [799]
Giorgio Quazza Medal [1280]
Rabone Award [4916]
Railway Engineering Award [801]

James Ransom Memorial Medals [8044]
Research Medal [1017]
Rooke Medal for the Public Promotion of Engineering [8584]
Dr. Biren Roy Memorial Lecture [3660]
Royal Medal [9071]
Peter Nicol Russell Memorial Medal [802]
Hassib Sabbagh Award for Engineering Construction Excellence [2666]
Mike Sargeant Career Achievement Award [8032]
Bernhard Schmidt Prize [2046]
Scott Trust Technology Bursaries [9460]
Scottish Engineering Award [9164]
Scottish Engineering/Hammermen Award [9165]
Service Awards [7556]
Kenneth Severn Award [8059]
Napier Shaw Bronze Medal [7393]
Silver Medal
   Institution of Gas Engineers and Managers [8045]
   Royal Academy of Engineering [8585]
Robert Sinave Prix [1665]
Major General Harkirat Singh Memorial Award [3467]
SKF Award [9579]
Cadzow Smith Award [7557]
K.U. Smith Student Paper Award [6589]
Stenback Plaquette [2099]
K. G. Stevens Award [9580]
Peter Stone Award [6804]
Sugg Heritage Award [8046]
Sustained Achievement Award [8586]
F. W. Taylor Medal [2476]
TDI Awards [8344]
Technician of the Year Award [4918]
Templin Scroll Competition [4919]
Transpower Neighborhood Engineers Award [4920]
Turner Award for Professional Commitment [4921]
UNESCO Science Prize [2659]
Carl von Linde Young Researcher Award [2538]
Walsh - Weston Memorial Award [7394]
Water Engineering Award [7559]
Sir Frank Whittle Medal [8587]
M. Selim Yalin Lifetime Achievement Award [6046]
Young Engineers Award [4282]
Young Professional Engineer of the Year [811]
Young Researchers' Award [4229]
Young Woman Engineer of the Year [8035]
Syed Husain Zaheer Medal [3673]

Engineering, aeronautical see Aeronautical engineering

Engineering, agricultural see Agricultural engineering

Engineering, automotive see Automotive engineering

Engineering, biomedical see Biomedical engineering

Engineering, ceramic see Ceramic engineering

Engineering, chemical see Chemical engineering

Engineering, civil see Civil engineering

Engineering, corrosion see Corrosion engineering

Engineering education

Brennan Medal [7958]
Fourth-Year Student Award [4861]
Dr. Eddah Gachukia Science Prize [4412]
IGIP Award [1302]
Innovation in Education Prize [8579]
Gustav Lorentzen Medal [2536]
Nathaniel B. Nichols Medal [1279]
Norman Selfe Medal [805]

Engineering, electrical see Electrical engineering

Engineering, human see Human engineering

Engineering, industrial see Industrial engineering

Engineering, marine see Naval engineering

Engineering, mechanical see Mechanical engineering

Engineering, military see Military engineering

Engineering, naval see Naval engineering

Engineering, nuclear see Nuclear engineering

Engineering, petroleum see Petroleum engineering

Engineering, sanitary see Sanitary engineering

English history

David Berry Prize [8802]
Templer Medal [9243]
Whitfield Book Prize [8808]

English literature

Benson Medal [9075]
Book Awards [2073]
David Cohen British Literature Prize [6745]
Rose Mary Crawshay Prize for English Literature [6924]
Gladstone History Book Prize [8805]
Sir Israel Gollancz Prize [6925]
Graduation Prize [4801]
Enid McLeod Literary Prize [7709]
NSES Award [4802]

Entertainment see also Animated films; Humor

Amused Moose Laugh Off Awards [7527]
Awards for Excellence - Accommodation Division [363]
Awards for Excellence - General Division [364]
Best of Bermuda Awards [1701]
British Comedy Awards [6871]
Digital Animation - Feature Film Award [5255]
Digital Animation - Short Film Award [5256]
Digital Entertainment Software Award [5257]
Funny Women Awards [7532]
Helpmann Awards [848]
Outstanding Achievement in Patron Transport Safety [366]
Rose d'Or Festival [6479]
Student Award [5258]
Young Hospitality Manager of the Year [3884]

Entomology see Zoology

Entrepreneurship see Business

Environmental conservation

ACCA Singapore Awards for Sustainability Reporting [5934]
ACCA U.K. Awards for Sustainability Reporting [6806]
ACHEMA Television Prize [3160]
Advanced Diploma [7855]
Advancing Solar Energy Policy Award [3099]
Asia Responsible Entrepreneurship Awards [4542]
Associate Member Diploma [7856]
Australian Medal for Landscape Architecture [396]
Award for Best Ecological Project [5563]
Christopher E. Barthel, Jr. Award [8245]
Be Sustainable Award [1420]
Best Environmental Management Program Award [4183]
Best Technical and/or Administrative Services Award [5904]
Bios Prizes [3270]
Blue Planet Prize [4206]
Karl W. Boer Solar Energy Medal of Merit [3100]
Britain in Bloom Awards [8813]
Certificate in Energy Efficiency For Domestic Central Heating [7857]

Clean City Awards [7436]
Community Wildlife Conservation Award [1188]
Conservation Follow-up Awards [7476]
Conservation Leadership Award [7477]
Distinguished Applied Research Manager [5905]
Distinguished Applied Research Team [5906]
Distinguished Applied Researcher [5907]
Dow Energy Prize [4820]
Eco Award Namibia [4621]
Eco Media Awards Namibia [4622]
ENERGY GLOBE Awards [1228]
Environment Award [6407]
Environmental Award [6398]
Environmental Awards [628]
Environmental Packaging Awards [5029]
Environmental Prize [4431]
Environmental Reporter Award [9574]
European Business Awards for the Environment [1460]
European Lifetime Achievement Award in Environmental Economics [4059]
European Practitioner Achievement Award in Applying Environmental Economic [4060]
Charles Fleming Award for Environmental Achievement [5073]
Ned Franklin Medal [7962]
Future Conservationist Awards [7478]
Global 500 [5318]
Global Compact Sri Lanka Network/CIMA Sustainability Awards [6119]
Green Apple Awards [7747]
The Green Awards [4401]
Green Gown Awards [7567]
The Green Star Awards [4402]
Greening the Future Awards [5572]
Hugh Greenwood Environmental Science Award [5358]
Elizabeth Haub Prize for Environmental Diplomacy [3059]
Elizabeth Haub Prize for Environmental Law [3060]
Honorary Member [5951]
Honorary Membership [8252]
Imhoff - Koch Award for Outstanding Contribution to Water Management and Science [8253]
IUCN - Reuters - COMplus Media Awards [6535]
Samuel H. Jenkins Outstanding Service Award [8254]
Erik Kempe Award in Environmental and Resource Economics [4061]
Les Diablerets Film Festival [6504]
Lillehammer Award [1424]
Prix de l'Institut Francais du Petrole [2216]
LivCom Awards [8090]
Macao Green Hotel Award [4503]
Kenton R. Miller Award for Innovation in Protected Areas Management [6536]
Natural and Organic Products Awards [9349]
Nature and Environment Prize [1980]
Nature Conservation Award [4634]
Oman Green Awards [5168]
Onassis Award for the Environment [3298]
Organization of Islamic Capitals and Cities Awards [5909]
Ozone Awards [4403]
Prix Pictet [7331]
Publishing Award [8255]
Sultan Qaboos Prize for Environmental Preservation [2655]
Qatar Today Green Awards [5436]
Reporter of the Year [9575]
Rolex Awards for Enterprise [6477]
Charles Rothschild and Miriam Rothschild Medal [9125]
Fritz Schumacher Prize [3207]
SEED Awards [4404]
SEED Awards for Entrepreneurship in Sustainable Development [4392]
SEED Gold Awards [4393]
Serventy Conservation Medal [1189]
Sorby Medal [4731]
Kate Stokes Award [7479]
Sture Centerwalls Pris [6187]
Sustainable City Awards [7438]
Technician Diploma [7858]
Umweltpreis der Landeshauptstadt Stuttgart [3194]
Josef Vavrousek Prize [1909]

Christopher A. Weeks Achievement through Action Award [3102]
Whitley Award [9447]
World Clean Air Congress Award [8246]
World Environment Day Awards [1094]
World Press Photo Contest [4849]
Young Conservationist Award [6541]

Environmental health

ACCA Hong Kong Awards for Sustainability Reporting [5221]
ACCA Ireland Sustainability Reporting Awards [3830]
ACCA Malaysia Sustainability Reporting Awards [4527]
ACCA Sri Lanka Awards for Sustainability Reporting [6115]
ACCA-WWF Pakistan Environmental Reporting Awards [5181]
Australia and New Zealand Awards for Sustainability Reporting [103]
Biodiversity Reporting Award [1724]
Frederick H. Buttel International Award for Distinguished Scholarship in Environmental Sociology [6078]
Champions of the Earth [4400]
Environment Award [4628]
European Business Awards for the Environment [1460]
European Responsible Care Awards [1455]
Fellow of the Australian Institute of Agricultural Science and Technology FAIAST [378]
Go-Green Journalism Award [4629]
Green Chemistry Challenge Awards [975]
Holcim Green Built Bangladesh Contest [1374]
National Award for Environmental Management [9518]
Sergey Soloviev Medal [2379]
Solvents Stewardship Awards [1457]
Tanzania Award for Scientific and Technological Achievements [9521]
Volvo Environment Prize [6247]
Zayed International Prize for the Environment [6673]

Epilepsy

Ambassador for Epilepsy Award [3855]
Award for Social Accomplishment [3856]

Equestrian see Horsemanship

Essays

Alexander Prize [8801]
Amerbach Prize [6519]
Award for Best Student Essay/Report [4374]
Barker Silver Medal [7388]
David Berry Prize [8802]
Blumlein-Brown-Willans Premium [8020]
Robert Alfred Carr Prize [7976]
Carter Bronze Medal [7389]
Civil Engineering Students Papers Competition [7978]
Coopers Hill War Memorial Prize [7979]
Crampton Prize [7980]
Curl Essay Prize [8640]
Bill Curtin Medal [7981]
J. B. Donne Essay Prize on the Anthropology of Art [8641]
Dufton Silver Medal [7390]
Aquileo J. Echeverria Prize [1857]
Dr. Wijnaendts Francken-prijs [4839]
Trench Gascoigne Prize [9139]
Leon Gaster Memorial Award [7391]
Graduates and Students Papers Competition [7985]
Halcrow Prize [7986]
History Today Prize [8807]
T. K. Hsieh Award [7991]
Renee Redfern Hunt Memorial Prize [7992]
IERE Benefactors Premium [8024]
James Prescott Joule Prize [7995]
John F. Kennedy Student Paper Competition [6043]
Lindapter Award [7997]
Memorial Awards for Literature [5350]
Johann Heinrich Merck Preis [2899]
New Scholar's Prize [8114]
Overseas Prize [7999]
Frederick Palmer Prize [8000]

Parkman Medal [8001]
Premio Nacional de Literatura [1827]
Reed and Mallik Medal [8005]
A. H. Reeves Premium [8030]
Safety in Construction Medal [8008]
Napier Shaw Bronze Medal [7393]
Gyorgy Striker Junior Paper Award [3405]
Telford Medal [8009]
J. Langham Thompson Premium [8033]
Trevithick Prize [8010]
Graham Turnbull Essay Competition [8295]
Walsh - Weston Memorial Award [7394]
James Watt Medal [8013]
Webb Prize [8014]
Wooden Horse Award [719]

Ethics

Church of Iceland Film Award [3419]

Ethnic affairs see also Culture

CRC Multicultural Award [1078]
Nancy Keesing Fellowship [1062]
Prix Henri Lavachery [1612]
Media Save Art Award [4089]
Nuremberg Award for Company Culture without Discrimination [2752]
Phonix UDA [2642]

European culture see also East European culture

Hamburg Max Brauer Prize [3200]
Henry Duncan Prize Lectureship [9067]
European Diploma [2348]
Flag of Honour [2351]
Dr. Wijnaendts Francken-prijs [4839]
Goethe Medaille [3031]
Gorsedd of Bards Membership [8391]
Herder Prizes [3202]
John Lotz Commemorative Medal [3390]
Somerset Maugham Awards [9253]
Plaque of Honour [2354]
Scottish Research Book Award [9155]
Sonning Prize [1995]
Henrik Steffens Prize [3209]
Endre Szirmai Prize [3391]

European history

Fraenkel Prize in Contemporary History [9449]
Dr. Wijnaendts Francken-prijs [4839]
Dr. A.H. Heineken Prize for History [4825]
Eoin O'Mahony Bursary [3930]
President of the Republic Genocide Prize [55]
Endre Szirmai Prize [3391]

European integration

Europe Prize [2347]
Herder Prizes [3202]
International Charlemagne Prize of Aachen [3185]
North-South Prize [2353]

European literature see also Dutch literature; English literature; French literature; Italian literature; Spanish literature

Aniara Prize [6235]
Literature Prize [1978]
John Lotz Commemorative Medal [3390]
Shakespeare Prize [3208]

Exhibiting

Awards for Excellence [708]
ICT Award [2644]
International Exhibition Logistics Associates Awards [8112]
Marketing Award [2645]
Operations Award [2646]

Exploration see also Geography

Australian Antarctic Medal [297]
Desiderius Erasmus Award [4678]
Livingstone Medal [8919]
Mungo Park Medal [8920]
Albert Renold Prize Lecture [2802]
Rolex Awards for Enterprise [6477]

Sagarmatha Award **[4643]**

Export *see International trade*

Family relations *see also Child welfare*

Individual Volunteer Award for Contributions to Sexual and Reproductive Health and Rights **[8161]**
International Award for Contributions to Sexual and Reproductive Health and Rights **[8162]**
Prix Malouet **[2287]**
Member Association Award for Contributions to Sexual and Reproductive Health and Rights **[8163]**
Mother of the Year Award **[1782]**
Staff Award for Contributions to Sexual and Reproductive Health and Rights **[8164]**
Youth Award for Contributions to Sexual and Reproductive Health and Rights **[8165]**

Fashion *see also Beauty contests; Cosmetology; Design; Hairstyling*

Best of Bermuda Awards **[1701]**
British Fashion Awards **[7052]**
Good Business Awards **[8966]**
International Designer Awards **[4717]**
Student Award **[4718]**
UK Fashion Export Awards **[9403]**

Feminism *see Women*

Fiber science *see also Textile design; Textile industry*

AFROSAI Prize **[4472]**
Jubilee Award **[9380]**
S. G. Smith Memorial Medal **[9383]**

Fiction *see also Science fiction; Short stories*

Afonso Arinos Prize **[1749]**
The Australian/Vogel Literary Award **[72]**
Award for Original Hebrew Novel **[3985]**
Azorin Prize **[6022]**
Bagutta Prize **[4036]**
Benson Medal **[9075]**
James Tait Black Memorial Prizes **[9426]**
Book Awards **[5953]**
Brian Burland Prize for Fiction **[1686]**
Hubert Church Best First Book Award for Fiction **[5010]**
Commonwealth Writers' Prize **[7465]**
Costa Book Awards **[6899]**
Aquileo J. Echeverria Prize **[1857]**
Festival Awards for Literature **[1044]**
Finlandia Prize for Literature **[2089]**
Soren Gyldendal Prisen **[1971]**
Joan Hessayon New Writers' Award **[8549]**
Independent Foreign Fiction Prize **[6906]**
Love Story of the Year **[8550]**
Somerset Maugham Awards **[9253]**
Memorial Awards for Literature **[5350]**
New South Wales Premier's Literary Awards **[906]**
Ondaatje Prize **[9076]**
Premi de les Lletres Catalanes Ramon Llull **[6023]**
Premier's Award **[1045]**
Premio de Novela Fernando Lara **[6024]**
Premio Nacional de Literatura **[1827]**
Premio Planeta de Novela **[6025]**
Prize for Mountain Literature **[6889]**
Prize for Young Adult Fiction **[1066]**
Prix Theophraste Renaudot **[2596]**
Romantic Novel of the Year (RoNA) Awards **[8551]**
Lilian Ida Smith Award **[5015]**
Strega Prize **[4155]**
Betty Trask Prize and Awards **[9259]**
Wales Book of the Year Awards **[6676]**

Field hockey *see Hockey*

Film competitions *see Film festivals*

Film criticism

FIPRESCI Prize **[3068]**

Film festivals

Air Tanzania Award for the Best East African Film **[9527]**

Amiens International Film Festival **[2309]**
Amnesty International Film Prize **[2716]**
Aruba International Film Festival **[60]**
Audience Award **[1887]**
Audience Prizes **[3247]**
Bahamas International Film Festival **[1343]**
Barbados International Film Festival **[1382]**
Alfred Bauer Prize **[2717]**
Belize International Film Festival **[1677]**
Berlin International Film Festival **[2718]**
Berlin Today Award **[2719]**
Berlinale Camera **[2720]**
Bermuda Children's Film Festival **[1696]**
Bermuda International Film Festival **[1697]**
Best Actor **[5417]**
Best Actress **[5418]**
Best Children's Film Prize **[3248]**
Best Direction **[5419]**
Best Fantasy Short **[5420]**
Best Film Award **[5421]**
Best Screenplay **[5422]**
Best Short/Animation Film **[9528]**
Best Short Film Prize **[3249]**
Best Special Effects **[5423]**
Bhutan National Film Festival **[1714]**
Biennial of Animation Bratislava **[5995]**
Brussels International Festival of Fantastic Film **[1417]**
Caligari Film Prize **[2721]**
Celtic Media Festival **[7335]**
Chairman's Award **[9529]**
Clermont-Ferrand International Short Film Festival **[2602]**
Clermont-Ferrand National Short Film Festival **[2603]**
CRC Multicultural Award **[1078]**
Crystal Bear Awards **[2722]**
DAAD Scholarship **[2723]**
Dendy Awards for Australian Short Films **[1079]**
Dominican Short Film Competition **[2005]**
East Africa Award **[9530]**
East African Talent Award **[9531]**
Ebensee Bear **[1247]**
Edinburgh International Film Festival **[7545]**
Emirates Film Competition **[6657]**
Femina Film Prize **[2724]**
Festival du Film Court de Villeurbanne **[2415]**
Fipresci Jury Prize **[9532]**
FIPRESCI Prize **[3068]**
Golden Apricot (Yerevan) International Film Festival **[53]**
Golden Bear Awards **[2725]**
Golden Horse Awards **[6593]**
Golden Impala Eastern Africa Short Film Award **[6650]**
Golden Zagreb Prize **[1888]**
Grand Prize **[1889]**
Hong Kong Independent Short Film and Video Awards **[5253]**
Honorary Golden Bear **[2726]**
Impact of Music on Film Competition **[1516]**
International Adventure Film Festival **[2463]**
International Children's Film Festival of India **[3459]**
International Competition for Film and Video **[1248]**
International Festival of the New Latin American Cinema **[1893]**
International Filmfestival Mannheim/Heidelberg **[3070]**
International Free Flight Film Festival **[2420]**
International Mystery Festival **[4048]**
Jakarta International Film Festival **[3822]**
Jordan Short Film Festival **[4355]**
Kaleva Award **[2121]**
Les Diablerets Film Festival **[6504]**
Little Bear Award **[2122]**
Monaco Charity Film Festival **[4607]**
Munich International Festival of Film Schools **[3106]**
NETPAC Prize **[2727]**
Norwegian International Film Festival **[5144]**
Norwegian Short Film Festival Prize **[5156]**
Odense Film Festival **[1987]**
Oporto International Film Festival - Fantasporto **[5424]**
Sembene Ousmane Prize **[9533]**
Panorama Audience Award **[2728]**
Peace Film Prize **[2729]**
St. Kilda Film Festival **[1036]**

Manfred Salzgeber Prize **[2730]**
San Sebastian International Film Festival Awards **[6094]**
Sao Paulo International Film Festival **[1768]**
Sarajevo Film Festival **[1728]**
Score Competition **[2731]**
Shorts Awards **[873]**
Signis Jury Award **[9534]**
Silver Bear Awards **[2732]**
Special Prize of the Jury **[5425]**
Stuttgart International Festival of Animated Film **[3196]**
Tampere International Short Film Festival **[2128]**
Tbilisi International Film Festival **[2688]**
Teddy Awards **[2733]**
TFL Kula Film Awards **[2060]**
Thessaloniki Film Festival **[3313]**
Tirana International Film Festival **[2]**
Tokyo International Film Festival **[4335]**
Turin International Film Festival **[4042]**
UNICEF Award **[9535]**
Unnim Mountain Film Festival **[6108]**
Uppsala International Short Film Festival **[6245]**
Verona Jury Award **[9536]**
Visions du Reel International Documentary Film Festival **[6532]**
West Australia Screen Awards **[723]**

Films *see also Animated films; Audiovisuals; Documentary films; Educational films; Entertainment; Film criticism; Film festivals; Television; Video*

AACTA Awards **[349]**
Age d'Or Prize **[1655]**
Amanda Award for Cinematographic Merit **[5143]**
Amnesty International Film Prize **[2716]**
Asia Pacific Screen Awards **[89]**
Audience Award
    The Norwegian Short Film Festival **[5148]**
    Swedish Film Institute **[6231]**
Alfred Bauer Prize **[2717]**
Berlin Today Award **[2719]**
Berlinale Camera **[2720]**
British Film Institute Fellowships **[7057]**
Caligari Film Prize **[2721]**
Channel 4 Archaeological Film Awards **[7290]**
Church of Iceland Film Award **[3419]**
Crystal Bear Awards **[2722]**
DAAD Scholarship **[2723]**
Dance Screen Awards **[1293]**
David Film Awards **[4052]**
Ecumenical Prize **[1661]**
Edda Awards for Icelandic Film and Television **[3425]**
European Film Awards **[2831]**
Femina Film Prize **[2724]**
Film Critics Award **[5150]**
Film Prize **[1977]**
Filmpolitiets Short Film Award **[5151]**
Golden Bear Awards **[2725]**
Golden Bug Award **[6232]**
The Golden Chair **[5152]**
Grand Prix **[2634]**
Grand Prix Grimstad **[5153]**
Gullspira Award **[6233]**
Hall of Fame **[255]**
Hong Kong Film Awards **[5260]**
Honorary Golden Bear **[2726]**
Hour Glass **[5154]**
Huesca International Short Film Contest **[6035]**
International Award for Cinematography **[256]**
International Visual Communications Association Awards **[8250]**
Henri Jeanson Prize **[2635]**
Cherry Kearton Medal and Award **[8794]**
Byron Kennedy Award **[350]**
LiteraVision Preis **[3137]**
Raymond Longford Award **[351]**
Milli Award **[257]**
National Awards for Cinematography **[258]**
NETPAC Prize **[2727]**
Norwegian Film Workers Association Technical Award **[5155]**
Opera Awards **[525]**
Orange British Academy Film Awards **[6933]**
Panorama Audience Award **[2728]**
Peace Film Prize **[2729]**

Praemium Imperiale [4262]
President of the Republic Youth Prize [57]
Prix Nouveau Talent [2636]
Prix UIP Grimstad [5157]
Prizes for the Distribution of Quality Films in Belgium [1656]
Promotional Prizes [3138]
Roquette Pinto Prize [1747]
Rosa Camuna [4038]
Manfred Salzgeber Prize [2730]
Score Competition [2731]
Screen Music Awards [141]
Silver Bear Awards [2732]
Sutherland Trophy [7058]
Teddy Awards [2733]
Terje Vigen Award [5158]
Ross Wood Memorial Award [259]

Finance *see also* *Accounting; Banking; Business; Economics; Financial planning; Insurance; Public finance*

Best Public Sector CFO of the Year [4900]
Covenant Assessment Provider of the Year [8462]
Excellence Awards [879]
Financial Reporting Awards [5488]
Bernhard Harms Prize [3111]
Innovation and Excellence Awards [933]
International Order of Educational Credit [1849]
Layborn Prize [7410]
Marjolin Prize [1239]
Medal of Honor of the Great Promoters of Education [1850]
National Institute of Insurance International Prizes [4024]
Onassis International Prize in Finance [3299]
Onassis Prize in Shipping, Trade and Finance [3304]
Pension Scheme Accountant of the Year [8464]
Solidarity of Educational Credit Order [1851]
Stockman Award [5162]

Financial journalism *see* *Business journalism*

Financial law *see* *Law*

Financial planning

Taxpayers Award [3198]

Fine arts *see* *Art; Arts and humanities; Music*

Fire fighting

Australian Fire Service Medal [301]
Merit Award [8383]
Queen's Fire Service Medal [7348]

Fire prevention

EPSC Award [7629]
Fire Excellence Awards [7693]
Fire Safety Award [6802]
Outstanding Service Award [6803]

Firearms

Queen's Prize [8408]

Fishing industry

Chandrakala Hora Memorial Medal [3638]
Icelandic Fisheries Awards [9484]

Fitness *see* *Health and fitness*

Flying

Aero Engine Services Trophy [5046]
Airways Corporation Trophy [5047]
D.M. Allan Memorial Cup [5049]
Sir Donald Anderson Trophy [609]
Australian Ballooning Hall of Fame [244]
Aviation Award (W.A. Branch) [610]
Jean Batten Memorial Trophy [5050]
Faith Bennet Navigation Trophy [7302]
Bledisloe Aviation Trophy [5051]
Mrs. Harry (Lores) Bonny Award [611]
Brabazon Cup [7303]
Jack Brackenbury Photography Trophy [7304]
Chairwoman's Challenge [7305]

Charts and Documents Award [612]
Naomy Christy Award [7306]
Leonardo da Vinci Parachuting Diploma [6302]
William Dean Award [245]
Santos Dumont Gold Airship Medal [6305]
Gedge Trophy [246]
Gliding Award [613]
Gold Parachuting Medal [6311]
Gold Rotorcraft Medal [6312]
Hang Gliding Cross Country Championship Trophy [8263]
Hang Gliding Cross Country Trophy [8264]
Hang Gliding Diploma [6314]
Hilda Hewlet Trophy [7307]
International Free Flight Film Festival [2420]
O.P. Jones Cup [7308]
Jean Lennox Bird Pendant [7309]
Life Members [247]
Life Membership of the GFA [743]
Lilienthal Gliding Medal [6318]
Pepe Lopes Hang Gliding Medal [6320]
Pelagia Majewska Gliding Medal [6321]
Jackie Moggridge Trophy [7310]
Montgolfier Ballooning Diploma [6322]
W. A. Morrison Trophy [5055]
Newman Cup [5057]
Shane O'Reilly Memorial Hang Gliding Competitions Trophy [8265]
Paragliding Cross Country Competitions Trophy [8266]
Paragliding Cross Country League Millennium Falcon Trophy [8267]
Robinson Silver Wings Award [614]
Rotorua Trophy [5059]
SA Branch Memorial Incentive Award [615]
Muriel Sells Trophy [7311]
Silver Medal [6328]
Sir Francis Boys Cup [5060]
G. M. Spence Trophy [5061]
Freda Thompson and Claire Embling Aviation Award [616]
Paul Tissandier Diploma [6329]
Waitemata Aero Club Cup [5062]
Nancy-Bird Walton Memorial Trophy [617]
Wanganui Trophy [5063]
Ivon Warmington Trophy [5064]
Ann Welch Diploma [6333]
Nancy Wells Award [618]
Wigram Cup [5065]
Wigram Cup (Sub-Competition) - Instrument Flying [5066]
Wigram Cup (Sub-Competition) - Junior Landing [5067]
Wigram Cup (Sub-Competition) - Non-instrument Circuits [5068]
Wigram Cup (Sub-Competition) - Senior Landing [5069]
Trevor Wilde Award [8268]

Folklore

Katharine Briggs Folklore Award [7697]
Fricis Brivzemnieks Prize [4434]
Coote Lake Medal for Folklore Research [7698]
A.N. Veselovskii Prize [5873]

Food *see also* *Dairy industry; Food processing; Nutrition; Restaurants; Wine*

Academic Achievement Award [5650]
Agritechnology, Life Sciences and Biotechnology Exporter of the Year [5023]
Best of Bermuda Awards [1701]
Best Product Award [5979]
Clarence Birdseye Young Researcher Award [2529]
A. H. Boerma Award [3371]
Charter Chef Competition [20]
Crystal Taste Award [1560]
Culinary Olympics [3181]
Culinary World Cup [4501]
Dreosti Award [5651]
FAB Awards, the International Food and Beverage Creative Excellence Awards [7664]
FHA Culinary Challenge [5973]
Food and Farming Awards [6981]
Ginsburg Award [5652]
Gold Medal [8415]
Good Business Awards [8966]

Great Taste Awards [7761]
Guild of Food Writers Award [7764]
Healthier Choice Award [5980]
Hidden Treasure Award [9352]
Innovation Awards [5981]
Koeppen Memorial Scholarship [5653]
Joseph Konig Gedenkmunze [2931]
Lifetime Achievement Award [9353]
LMA Award [846]
Meat to Go Awards [9167]
Aubrey Parsons Study Grant [5654]
Passionate Communicator Award [9354]
Dr. V. N. Patwardhan Prize [3556]
Prize for Meat and Technology [2553]
Benjamin Ward Richardson Gold Medal [8954]
Salon Culinaire International de Londres [7034]
Edouard Saouma Award [3372]
B. R. Sen Award [3373]
Silver Medal [8417]
Andre Simon Medal [8257]
SOFHT Awards [9311]
SOFHT Fellowship [9312]
Student Challenge Cook and Serve Competition [7035]
Superior Taste Award [1561]
Taste of Belize Culinary Competition [1680]
Toppers in Food Technology [3778]
Turks and Caicos Conch Festival [6643]
World Cheese Awards [7762]
Young Chef of the Year Award [7036]
Young Entrepreneur Award [9355]

Food processing

Clyde H. Bailey Medal [1250]
Lipids Group International Lecture [9288]
Manuel Mejia Award [1847]
Harald Perten Prize [1251]
Friedrich Schweitzer Medal [1252]
Richard Seligman Lecture [9295]
Supplier of the Year Awards [1191]

Food service *see also* *Restaurants*

Catering Manager of the Year [3882]
Food and Farming Awards [6981]
Student Challenge Cook and Serve Competition [7035]
Top Tea Places of the Year [9366]
Young Chef of the Year Award [7036]

Food technology *see* *Food processing*

Foreign policy

Prix Lucien de Reinach [2255]

Forestry *see also* *Paper industry; Wood and wood products*

Advisory Council Award [1307]
Barama Company Award [3344]
Best Poster Award [1308]
Certificate of Appreciation [1309]
Distinguished Service Award [1310]
Dwarka (Agriculture) Award [3345]
Tom Gill Memorial Award [7458]
Honorary Membership
  International Union of Forest Research Organizations [1311]
  Royal Geographical Society with the Institute of British Geographers [8793]
Outstanding Doctoral Research Award [1312]
Wilhelm Leopold Pfeil Prize [3205]
Queen's Award for Forestry [7459]
Randle Travel Fund [8782]
Dr. Y.S. Rao Forestry Research Award [4517]
RDS-Forest Service Irish Forestry Awards [3923]
Regional Awards [7460]
Research Medal [1017]
Schweighofer Prize [1317]
Scientific Achievement Award [1313]
Student Award for Excellence in Forest Sciences [1314]
Marcus Wallenberg Prize [6249]
World Congress Host Scientific Award [1315]
Yorkshire Bursary [8783]
Young Forester Award [7461]
Young Scientist Publication Award [7462]

Freedom

Anti-Slavery Award [6723]
Democracy Award [3961]
Free Market Award [5550]
Freedom to Create Prize [5943]
Gold Medal [7375]
Golden Pen of Freedom Award [2663]
International Democracy Award [3053]
International Simon Bolivar Prize [2653]
Dusko Kondor Civil Courage Award [1726]
Anton Lembede Award [5492]
Z.K. Matthews Award [5493]
Charlotte Maxeke Award [5494]
Sol Plaatje Award [5495]
Prize for Freedom [8304]
Albert Schweitzer Award [8067]
Prix Henri Texier I [2300]
United Nations Prize in the Field of Human
    Rights [6515]

French culture

Phenix UDA [2642]
V. S. Pustovoit Award [2571]

French history

Prix de la Fons-Melicocq [2159]
Prix Emile Le Senne [2163]
Prix Gabriel Monod [2290]
Prix Toutain-Blanchet [2171]

French literature

Prix Ernest Discailles [1606]
Prix Estrade-Delcros [2158]
Scott Moncrieff Prize [9256]
Prix du Jeune Ecrivain [2671]
Prix du Jeune Ecrivain Francophone [2672]

Friendship see Brotherhood

Furniture see also Interior design; Industrial design

Graduate Product Award [7090]

Games see also Recreation

International Mobile Gaming Awards [2592]
Swedish Video Game Awards [6135]

Gardening see Horticulture

Gastronomy see Food; Restaurants

Genealogy

Award for Meritorious Service to Family History [135]
Best Website Award [7674]
Julian Bickersteth Memorial Medal [7874]
Certificates, Diplomas, and Licentiates in Genealogy
    and Heraldry [7875]
Genealogist of the Year [5552]
GSI Medallion [3838]
Alexander Henderson Award [392]
Manuscript Award [393]
Eoin O'Mahony Bursary [3930]
President's Award [394]
Elizabeth Simpson Award [7675]

Genetics

Academy Medal for Contributions to Science and
    Technology [171]
Award for Excellent Oral Presentation [3981]
Award for Excellent Poster Presentation [3982]
Best Consumer Mobile Data Application
    Award [8368]
Dame Margaret Blackwood Prize [1105]
Carter Medal [7442]
D.G. Catcheside Prize [731]
Distinguished Scientist Award [8097]
Dwight Prize in Genetics [1114]
Alan Emery Prize [9091]
Gabor Medal [8935]
Ruth Stephens Gani Medal in Human Genetics [175]
Anton Hales Medal in Earth Sciences [177]
ISTT Prize [6068]
N.K. Kol'tsov Prize [5813]

Lifetime Achievement Award [8218]
Medal of Honor [3015]
Theodore Reich Young Investigator Award [8219]
Prix Joseph Schepkens [1642]
Spencer Smith-White Travel Prize [732]
Student Bursaries [5753]
Young Investigator Award [6069]
Young Investigator Awards [3894]
Young Scientist Award [8098]

Geochemistry

Award for the Environment [9270]
A.Y. Fersman Prize [5797]
Paul W. Gast Lecture Series [2360]
Houtermans Medal [2361]
Pieter Schenck Award [2807]
Science Innovation Award [2362]
Urey Medal [2363]
Verdeyen Prize for Soil Mechanics [1659]
A.P. Vinogradov Prize [5874]

Geographic education

AGTA Awards [355]

Geography see also Cartography; Exploration; Geographic education

African Urban Quarterly Prize [4407]
AGTA Awards [355]
Back Award [8785]
John Bartholomew Essay Competition [8915]
Premio Dr. Carlos A. Biedma [44]
Prix Binoux, Henri de Parville, Jean-Jaques Berger,
    Remlinger [2183]
W. S. Bruce Medal [9062]
Busk Medal [8787]
Monica Cole Research Grant [8788]
Coppock Research Medal [8917]
Distinguished Geographer Medal [4967]
Fellowship of the Institute of Australian Geogra-
    phers [753]
Galathea Medal [1991]
Geographical Award [8789]
Gill Memorial Award [8791]
Gold Medals [8792]
A.A. Grigorev Prize [5803]
Honorary Fellowship [8918]
Livingstone Medal [8919]
Premio Francisco P. Moreno Award [45]
Mungo Park Medal [8920]
Murchison Award [8795]
National Award for Middle School Teacher [5250]
National Award of Science and Technology for
    Young Geographer [5251]
Ness Award [8796]
Newbigin Prize [8921]
Cuthbert Peek Award [8797]
Postgraduate Award [754]
Premio Consagracion a la Geografia [46]
President's Medal [8922]
Prix du Duc de Loubat [2168]
Professional Associateship [8923]
Research Medal [1017]
Prix Saintour [2296]
F.P. Savarenskii Prize [5852]
Scottish Geographical Medal [8924]
O.Y. Shmidt Prize [5858]
Griffith Taylor Medal [755]
Joy Tivy Education Medal [8925]
University Medal [8926]
Victoria Medal [8799]
Darashaw Nosherwanji Wadia Medal [3672]

Geology and paleontology see also Geochemistry; Geophysics; Photogrammetry; Seismology

Aberconway Medal [7718]
Major John Sacheverell A'Deane Coke Medal [7719]
Friedrich von Alberti Prize [3146]
Mary Anning Award [8444]
Nigel Anstey Award [4674]
A.D. Arkhangelskii Prize [5784]
Prix Louis Armand [2177]
Prix Paul Bertrand, G. Deflandre, M. Deflandre-
    Rigaud, and Jean Cuvillier [2181]
Prix Leon Bertrand [2454]

Best Paper Award [1932]
Best Student Oral and Poster Presentation
    Award [1933]
Prix Paul Betrand, Georges Deflandre et Marthe
    Deflandre-Rigaud, Jean Cuvillier [2182]
Bigsby Medal [7720]
Bill Bishop Award [8524]
Guido Bonarelli Award [4675]
W.R. Browne Medal [734]
W. S. Bruce Medal [9062]
Bruce-Preller Prize Lectureship [9063]
Prix Henri Buttgenbach [1621]
Louis Cagniard Award [4676]
S.W. Carey Medal [735]
CERESIS Award [5320]
Dick Chorley Award for Postgraduate Re-
    search [7224]
Clarke Memorial Lectureship [1002]
Clarke Memorial Medal [1003]
Hans Cloos Medal [6037]
Clough Medal [7542]
Clough Memorial Award [7543]
Corstorphine Medal [5554]
Craford Prize [6183]
Herman Credner Preis [2944]
Danish Geology Prize [1968]
Des Pretorius Memorial Award [5555]
Distinguished Service Award [7721]
Draper Memorial Medal [5556]
Early Achievement Award [570]
Tilly Edinger Prize [3147]
Lorand Eotvos Award [4677]
Desiderius Erasmus Award [4678]
Exhibition Prize in Second-Year Geology [1119]
Exhibition Prize in Third-Year Geology [1121]
Norman Falcon Award [4679]
Major Edward D'Ewes Fitzgerald Coke Medal [7722]
Prix Fontannes [2455]
Prix Paul Fourmarier [1631]
Professor Raphael Freund Award [3963]
Sue Tyler Friedman Medal [7723]
Prix Raymond et Madeleine Furon [2456]
Gold Medal [571]
Gold Medals [5192]
Prix Gosselet [2457]
Dr. Peretz Grader Award [3964]
Greenland Prospector and Developer of the
    Year [3325]
David I. Groves Award [736]
I.M. Gubkin Prize [5804]
Assar Haddings pris [6171]
John Handley Award [5557]
Joe Harms Medal [737]
J.H. Harvey Prize [1125]
Haughton Award [5558]
Hector Memorial Medal and Prize [5075]
Hodson Award [8445]
Arthur Holmes Medal and Honorary Member-
    ship [2373]
Honorary Fellowships [7724]
Honorary Member [5559]
Honorary Membership [572]
Honours Award [5560]
Hutton Memorial Medal and Prize [5076]
IGS Medal [3965]
International Association of Sedimentologists
    Grants [4730]
Jubilee Medal [5561]
Keith Medal [9068]
Lapworth Medal [8446]
Life Membership Award [4680]
Prix Leon Lutaud [2218]
Lyell Medal [7725]
Mansel-Pleydell Trust Essay Competition [7522]
Mawson Medal and Lecture [184]
Prix et medaille Georges Millot [2220]
Ludger Mintrop Award [4681]
Mueller Medal [202]
Murchison Medal [7726]
Kevin Nash Gold Medal [8194]
New Research Workers' Awards [8525]
V.A. Obruchev Prize [5839]
Premio Giorgio Dal Piaz [4130]
Postgraduate QRA Meetings Award [8526]
President's Awards [7727]
President's Medal [8447]

Liley Medal for Health Research [4893]
MacDiarmid Young Scientist of the Year [4894]
Ian Macmillan Prize [8953]
Member Association Award for Contributions to
  Sexual and Reproductive Health and Rights [8163]
Quality Improvement Awards [289]
Sasakawa Health Prize [6554]
Staff Award for Contributions to Sexual and
  Reproductive Health and Rights [8164]
Student Science Award [1442]
George Sykes Memorial Award [8471]
Vice Presidents Emiriti Award [8955]
Wales Cares Awards [7333]
Young Investigator Award [7593]
Youth Award for Contributions to Sexual and
  Reproductive Health and Rights [8165]

Health care administration

Baxter Award for Healthcare Management in Eu-
  rope [1479]
Barnett Christie Lectureship [7084]
Honorary Fellows Award [8952]
Karolinska Medical Management Centre/EHMA
  Research Award [1480]
Vice Presidents Emiriti Award [8955]

Health education

Abu Abdulla Moh'd Al-Edreesi Prize [1354]
T. P. Gunton Grant [7120]
InBev-Baillet Latour Health Prize [1521]
Vice Presidents Emiriti Award [8955]

Hearing see Speech and hearing

Helicopters

Alan Marsh Medal [8613]

Heroism

Cacique's Crown of Valour [3336]
Citation of Merit [1538]
Cross of Valour [5212]
Diploma for Outstanding Airmanship [6304]
Distinguished Service Order [7340]
Prix Dulac [2262]
Gallantry Decorations [313]
George Cross [7341]
George Medal [7342]
Golden Arrow of Courage [3338]
Grand Prix d'Honneur [6424]
Hummingbird Medal [6616]
Dusko Kondor Civil Courage Award [1726]
Life Saving Cross [4486]
Lifeguard Awards [6984]
Lifesaving Hall of Fame [1539]
Medal for Bravery
  Office of the President of the Slovak Repub-
    lic [6003]
  Office of the Prime Minister of Malta [4572]
Medal for Courage [5172]
Medal of Honour [4512]
Medal of Honour of the Order of Saint Lucia [5893]
Medallion of the Republic of Iceland [3437]
Military Courage Medal [2679]
Military William Order [4649]
National Hero Award [2681]
Florence Nightingale Medal [6369]
Order of Lifesaving [1540]
Order of the Cross of Vytis (the Knight) [4491]
Fred M. Packard Award [6537]
Param Vir Chakra [3500]
Prince Philip Helicopter Rescue Award [7757]
Polaris Award [8116]
Police Public Bravery Awards [6810]
President's Award [1541]
Queen's Gallantry Medal [7349]
Rescue Medal [1542]
Rescue Medal of Valour [1543]
Prix Eugene Salvan [2297]
Shaurya Chakra [3502]
Victoria Cross [7353]
Vir Chakra [3503]

Higher education see also Alumni activities

African Development and Economic Consultants
  Prize [4406]

African Urban Quarterly Prize [4407]
Asian Commercial Community Academic
  Awards [4408]
Thenie Baddams Bursary [337]
Cathy Candler Bursary [338]
College Medal [261]
Barbara Crase Bursary [339]
Yusuf Dawood Award [4409]
Rahima Dawood Prize [4410]
Dr. A.C.L. De'Souza Memorial Prize [4411]
Diamond Jubilee Bursary [340]
Distinguished Former Student Award [5208]
Examination Prizes [1730]
Fellowship of the Australian College of Educa-
  tors [262]
Dr. Eddah Gachukia Science Prize [4412]
Kaplan and Stratton Prize [4413]
Kenya National Chamber of Commerce and
  Industry Prize [4414]
Lecturer Award [6044]
N.H.O. Mahondo Award [4415]
Doreen McCarthy Bursary [341]
Mutiso Menezes International Prize [4416]
Gandhi Smarak Nidhi Trustee Fund Gold
  Prize [4417]
Norbrook Award [4418]
Dr. Marjorie Oludhe Award [4419]
Daramola Oluyemisi Memorial Prize [4420]
Padnendadlu Undergraduate Bursary [342]
Elida Ponds Prize [4421]
Professor Arthur T. Porters Prize [4422]
PR, Marketing and Communications Awards [6816]
President's Award for Academic Excellence [1718]
Principal's Medal [1719]
Promising Former Student Award [5209]
Recognition Award [6387]
Sakarben Sheth Prize [4423]
Society for Research into Higher Education
  Awards [9206]
Student of the Year Award [1731]
Georgina Sweet Fellowship [344]
Paul Musili Wambua Award [4424]
Jigme Dorji Wangchuck Gold Medal [1720]
Professor L.R. Whittaker's Annual Prize [4425]

Highway safety

Achievement Award [4237]
MORR Trophy [8961]
Workforce Involvement in Safety and Health Tro-
  phy [8963]

Hiking see Recreation

Historic preservation see also Monument
  restoration

Awards of Excellence in Landscape Architec-
  ture [397]
Barbados National Trust Member [1384]
Concours Annuel de Sauvegarde [2661]
Conservation Grants [3876]
Christopher Dearnley Award [919]
Dorothea Award for Conservation [6768]
Engineering Heritage Award [7553]
European Union Prize for Cultural Heritage/Europa
  Nostra Awards [4672]
Fieldwork and Recording Awards [6769]
Gazzola Prize [2516]
Governor's Award for Preservation of CNMI His-
  tory [5112]
Honorary Membership [2517]
ICCROM Award [4088]
International Maritime Heritage Award [9492]
Charles Ivor Matthews Memorial Scholarship [920]
Onassis Award for Culture (Letters, Arts and Humani-
  ties) [3296]
Publications Award [6771]
Rural Wales Award [7328]
Prix Henri Texier II [2301]

History see also Antiquity; Biography; Culture;
  Genealogy; Historic preservation; History of science; Monument restoration; Social science
  research

Alexander Prize [8801]
Prix Gustave Chaix d'Est Ange [2242]

Article Award [4784]
The Australian/Vogel Literary Award [72]
Awards in History [4896]
Awards in Oral History [4897]
Bergson Award [4003]
Best Archaeological Book Award [7481]
Birger Scholdstroms pris [6197]
BP Prize Lectureship in the Humanities [9061]
Brandt Award [4004]
Buchman Award [4005]
Prix Hercule Catenacci [2471]
Prix Charles Clermont-Ganneau [2152]
Prix Victor Cousin [2251]
C. H. Currey Memorial Fellowship [1061]
Prix Baron de Saint-Genois [1605]
Christopher Dearnley Award [919]
Prix Demolombe [2257]
Prix Ernest Discailles [1606]
Prix Le Dissez de Penanrun [2258]
Distinguished Achievement Award [563]
Prix Drouyn de Lhuys [2260]
Prix Joseph du Teil [2261]
Prix Jules Duculot [1607]
Aquileo J. Echeverria Prize [1857]
Premio a Egresado [35]
Prix Estrade-Delcros [2158]
Fellowship of the Australian Society of Archi-
  vists [564]
Fellowships [996]
Festival dei Popoli [4080]
Prix Marcel Flach [2269]
Founders' Medal [9215]
Fraenkel Prize in Contemporary History [9449]
Frampton and Beazley Prizes [8803]
German History Society Essay Prize [8804]
Prix Roman et Tania Ghirshman [2161]
Gladstone History Book Prize [8805]
Axel Hirschs pris [6204]
History Scotland Prize [8806]
History Today Prize [8807]
Hodgson Prize [8609]
Professor Theodor Homen Prize [2104]
Honorary Member [565]
Honorary Membership [9216]
Honourary Life Membership [997]
Mander Jones Awards [567]
Journal of Olympic History Award [4785]
N.I. Kareev Prize [5808]
Kellgrenpriset [6206]
John Douglas Kerr Medal of Distinction for His-
  tory [998]
Prix Koenigswarter [2277]
Prix Eugene Lameere [1611]
Prix Jacques Lavalleye-Coppens [1593]
Prix Leon Leclere [1613]
Lee-Steere Western Australian History Prize [1021]
Lifetime Contribution Award [4786]
Prix Limantour [2284]
Prix Charles Lyon-Caen [2285]
MacGregor Medal [999]
Mansel-Pleydell Trust Essay Competition [7522]
Manufacturers' Award [7930]
Prix Gaston Maspero [2164]
Charles Ivor Matthews Memorial Scholarship [920]
Somerset Maugham Awards [9253]
Prix Georges Mauguin [2289]
Medal of Honour for the Promotion of History [5636]
Norton Medlicott Medal [7794]
Prix Gabriel Monod [2290]
Monograph Award [4787]
Keith Muckelroy Award [7484]
Najmann Award [4006]
Nordiska Priset [6209]
NSW Premier's Translation Prize [907]
Premio Enrique Pena [36]
Prix Paul-Michel Perret [2293]
Premier's History Awards [908]
Premio Academia Nacional de la Historia [37]
Premio Nacional de Historia [1826]
Prix du Duc de Loubat [2168]
Prix Gabriel-Auguste Prost [2169]
Prix Saintour [2296]
Prix Gustave Schlumberger [2170]
Schuckska priset [6212]
Scottish History Book of the Year Award [9154]
J. M. Sherrard Award [4873]

Prix Baron de Stassart [1616]
Prix de Stassart [1617]
Suntory Prize for Social Sciences and Humanities [4333]
Arveds Svabe Prize [4443]
Y.V. Tarle Prize [5865]
Prix Suzanne Tassier [1618]
John Thackray Medal [9217]
Prix Maurice Travers [2303]
Uveeler Award [4007]
Alwyne Wheeler Bursary [9218]
A. E. Williams History Prize [1022]
Wolfson History Prizes [9451]
Zibetska priset [6219]

History, American see American history

History, art see Art history

History, business see Business history

History, English see English history

History, European see European history

History, French see French history

History, Italian see Italian history

History, Jewish see Jewish history

History, military see Military history

History of art see Art history

History of science

Prix Binoux, Henri de Parville, Jean-Jaques Berger, Remlinger [2183]
Prix Franz Cumont [1600]
Partington Prize [9213]
Georg Uschmann Award for the History of Science [3127]

Hobbies and clubs see also Animal care and training; Automobiles; Book collecting; Crafts; Genealogy; Horticulture; Numismatics; Philately; Photography; Recreation

Sidney French Medal [7155]

Hockey

Diploma of Merit [6392]
International Ice Hockey Federation Championships [6400]
Pablo Negre Trophy [6393]
Order of Merit [6394]
Player of the Year Awards [6395]
President's Award [6396]

Home economics

Jessie Kinder Prize [5085]

Horse racing

Racehorse of the Year Award [8532]

Horsemanship

Best Athlete Award [6376]
British Show Pony Society Rosettes [7204]
Cubitt Award [8498]
Dublin Horse Show [3918]
Show Hunter Ponies Awards [7205]
Show Ponies Awards [7206]
Working Hunter Ponies Awards [7207]

Horticulture

Allotment Awards [3915]
Arboricultural Association Award [6728]
Associateship of Honour [8810]
Award for Production, Promotion, and Marketing of Biofertilizer [3482]
Banksian Medal [3927]
Peter Barr Memorial Cup [8811]
Bowles Cup [8812]
Christmas Tree Competition [7001]

Reginald Cory Memorial Cup [8814]
Rolf Dahlgrens Pris [6169]
Delphinium Society Awards [7508]
Devonshire Trophy [8815]
Dublin Horse Show [3918]
E. H. Trophy [8816]
Engleheart Cup [8817]
Farrer Trophy [8818]
Ron Fletcher Award [8414]
Franco-British Landscape Gardening Award [7708]
Garden Awards [1179]
Gold Medal [4713]
Gordon-Lennox Trophy [8819]
Roy Hay Memorial Award [7714]
Holford Medal [8820]
Honorary Fellowship [8821]
Honorary Membership [1182]
Horticulture Student of the Year Award [3920]
IMPHOS-FAI Award on the Role of Phosphorus on Yield and Quality of Crops [3483]
Industry Award [4714]
Lawrence Medal [8822]
Loder Rhododendron Cup [8823]
London's Green Corners Awards [7473]
George Moore Medal [8824]
National Landscape Architecture Awards [398]
Quality Award [4715]
Richardson Trophy [8825]
Mrs. F. E. Rivis Prize [8826]
Martin Robinson Award [8416]
Rothschild Challenge Cup [8827]
Veitch Memorial Medal [8828]
Victoria Medal of Honour in Horticulture [8829]
A. J. Waley Medal [8830]
Weed Book Prize [1183]
Westonbirt Orchid Medal [8831]
Wigan Cup [8832]
Williams Memorial Medal [8833]
Guy Wilson Memorial Vase [8834]

Hospital administration

Fred J. Boyd Award [1040]

Hotels see Travel

Housing see also Real estate

Building Excellence Awards [857]
Excellence in Building and Construction Awards [871]
Excellence in Building Awards [853]
Excellence in Housing and Construction Awards [859]
Excellence in Housing Awards
Master Builders Association - New South Wales [851]
Master Builders Association - Victoria [862]
Habitat Business Award [4395]
Housing and Construction Awards [942]
Housing Design Awards [8853]
Housing Excellence Awards [865]
Lecture Award [4396]
National Excellence in Building and Construction Awards [867]
National Export Awards [868]
National Lifestyle Housing for Seniors Award [869]
Scroll of Honour Award [4397]
Shaikh Khalifa Bin Salman Al Khalifa Habitat Award [4398]

Human engineering

Ulf Aberg Post Graduate Award [7860]
Sir Frederic Bartlett Medal [7861]
Paul Branton Meritorious Service Award [7862]
Otto Edholm Award [7863]
David Ferguson Award [748]
William Floyd Award [7864]
Richard Clive Holman Memorial Prize [7865]
John Lane Award [749]
Hywel Murrell Award [7866]
President's Medal [7867]
PRO LABORE SECURO Statuette [5381]
Society Medal [750]
Alan Welford Award [751]

Human relations

Prix Paul Vigne d'Octon [2259]
International Simon Bolivar Prize [2653]

Literature preis der Stadt Dortmund - Nelly-Sachs-Preis [2783]
Olof Palme Memorial Fund Scholarships [6161]
Olof Palme Prize [6162]
President of the Republic Genocide Prize [55]

Human resource management see Personnel management

Human rights see also Civil rights and liberties

Bilbao Prize for the Promotion of a Culture of Human Rights [2648]
Fellowship Award [6418]
Founders' Award [1091]
Front Line Award for Human Rights Defenders at Risk [3835]
Global Compact Sri Lanka Network/CIMA Sustainability Awards [6119]
Emil Grunzweig Human Rights Award [3938]
Human Rights Award
International Bar Association [8092]
International Service for Human Rights - Switzerland [6426]
Individual Volunteer Award for Contributions to Sexual and Reproductive Health and Rights [8161]
Integrity Awards [1799]
International Award for Contributions to Sexual and Reproductive Health and Rights [8162]
International Award for the Promotion of Human Understanding [6419]
The International Jose Marti Prize [2652]
Jurist of the Year Award [4390]
Dusko Kondor Civil Courage Award [1726]
Dr. Frantisek Kriegel Prize [1906]
Ludovic-Trarieux International Human Rights Prize [2465]
Member Association Award for Contributions to Sexual and Reproductive Health and Rights [8163]
Lorenzo Natali Journalism Prize [1463]
Nonviolence Award [6229]
Nuremberg International Human Rights Award [2753]
Onassis International Prize in Law [3300]
Outstanding Contribution to the Anti-Corruption Movement in Armenia [51]
Prince of Asturias Award for Communications and Humanities [6085]
Right Livelihood Award [6166]
Small Grants Program [3836]
Staff Award for Contributions to Sexual and Reproductive Health and Rights [8164]
United Nations Prize in the Field of Human Rights [6515]
Sir Ron Wilson Human Rights Award [275]
Youth Award for Contributions to Sexual and Reproductive Health and Rights [8165]

Humanitarianism

Australian Bravery Decorations [298]
Bronze Medal [8836]
Certificate of Commendation [8837]
Civilian Service Medal 1939-1945 [307]
Prix Felix de Beaujour [2254]
Elite Research Prize [1973]
Antonio Feltrinelli Prizes [4022]
Prix Jean Finot [2268]
Hansischer Goethe Prize [3201]
Humanitarian Overseas Service Medal [314]
In Memoriam Testimonial [8838]
Integrity Awards [1799]
International Humanitarian Medal [6402]
Malawi Award for Scientific and Technological Achievement [4515]
Medal of Icelandic Red Cross [3436]
Merit Prize for Development [6405]
Montaigne Prize [3204]
Outstanding Contribution to the Anti-Corruption Movement in Armenia [51]
Phenix UDA [2642]
Prince of Asturias Award for Concord [6086]
Resuscitation Certificate [8839]
Paul Reuter Prize [6370]
Royal Norwegian Order of St. Olav [5135]
SEED Awards for Entrepreneurship in Sustainable Development [4392]
SEED Gold Awards [4393]
Silver Medal [8840]

Stanhope Medal [8841]
Henrik Steffens Prize [3209]
Testimonial on Parchment [8842]
Testimonial on Vellum [8843]
World Mystical Poetry Prize [6092]

Humanities *see Arts and humanities*

Humanities research

British Academy Fellow [6920]
Elite Research Prize [1973]
Governor's Award for Research and Publication in the Humanities [5114]
Reuchlinpreis der Stadt Pforzheim [3183]

Humor *see also Cartoons; Entertainment*

Amused Moose Laugh Off Awards [7527]
British Comedy Awards [6871]
Roald Dahl Funny Prize [6904]
Funny Women Awards [7532]
Grand Prix de l'Humour [2630]
Henri Jeanson Prize [2635]
Live Awards [9393]

Hunting

Nature Conservation Officer of the Year [5595]
Coenraad Vermaak Award [5596]
Wildlife Utilisation Award [5597]

Hypnosis

Benjamin Franklin Gold Medal [4109]
Jay Haley Early Career Award for Innovative Contributions [4110]
Ernest R. Hilgard Award for Scientific Excellence [4111]
Pierre Janet Award for Clinical Excellence [4112]
Kay F. Thompson Award for Clinical Excellence in Dentistry [4113]

Ice hockey *see Hockey*

Illustration

Hans Christian Andersen Awards [6362]
Elsa Beskow Plaque [6236]
The Best of Finnish Graphic Design and Advertising Competition [2111]
Book of the Year Award: Early Childhood [645]
Book of the Year Award: Picture Books [647]
Book Prizes [3272]
Prix Catenacci [2139]
Prix Hercule Catenacci [2471]
CBCI Award [3824]
Russell Clark Award [4931]
Crichton Award for New Illustrators [649]
Early Years Awards [6905]
Kate Greenaway Medal [7378]
Honour List [6364]
Rudolf Koivu Prize [2114]
Elizabeth Mrazik-Cleaver Canadian Picture Book Award [6366]
National Calendar Awards [7176]
Red House Children's Book Award [7670]
White Ravens [3104]

Individual rights *see Civil rights and liberties*

Industrial arts

Prix Joseph De Keyn [1602]

Industrial chemistry

Canada International Award [9273]
Castner Medal and Lecture [9275]
Grand Prix de Chimie Industrielle [2437]
LeSueur Memorial Award [9283]
Leverhulme Lecture [9284]
Ivan Levinstein Memorial Lecture [9285]
Prix Frederic Swarts [1644]

Industrial design

British Design Awards [7512]
Design in Business Awards [4886]
Gold Compass Prize [4034]
Good Design Award [4268]

Prince Philip Prize for the Designer of the Year [7513]
Royal Designer for Industry Award [8959]
Student Lighting Design Awards [8311]
Heinrich Tessenow Gold Medal [3210]

Industrial engineering

Julian A. Banzon Medal for Applied Research [5357]
Ray Meyer Medal for Excellence in Student Design [4913]

Industries and trades *see also Business; Craftsmanship; specific industries and trades, e.g. Dairy industry*

Sven Berggrens pris [6168]
Caernarfon Award [7935]
Carothers Medal [9372]
Clinical Biomechanics Award [4075]
Prix Corbay [2250]
Benjamin Franklin Medal [8958]
Golden Ram Award [5578]
Graduateship of the City and Guilds of London Institute [7432]
Honorary Member [8065]
Industrialist of the Year [5245]
Innovation Awards [1473]
LeSueur Memorial Award [9283]
Medals for Excellence [7433]
Membership of the City and Guilds of London Institute [7434]
Merit Prize for Development [6405]
Prix Osiris [2473]
Papers Award [8243]
S. M. Perren Research Award [4076]
Prix Petit d'Ormoy, Carriere, Thebault [2228]
Purvis Memorial Award [9293]
Student Award [4078]
Vishwakarma Medal [3671]
Ian Wark Medal and Lecture [188]

Information management

APM Group IT Trainer of the Year [7003]
Isaac L. Auerbach Award [1268]
Award for Teachers [2953]
Kristian Beckman Award [1269]
BT Flagship Award for Innovation [7004]
Business Analyst of Year [7005]
Business-to-Business Project Award [7006]
Commercial Organisation of the Year [7007]
Consumer Goods and Services Organisation of the Year [7008]
Dissertation Prize [2954]
Entertainment and Media Project Award [7009]
Jason Farradane Award [9414]
Financial Sector Organisation of the Year [7010]
GCS Women in IT Award [7011]
Green Organisation of the Year [7012]
Innovation Prize [2955]
Intel IT Leader of the Year [7013]
IT Consultancy of the Year [7014]
Tony Kent Strix Award [9415]
Fritz Kutter-Preis [6499]
Lovelace Lecture and Medal [7015]
Mobile Technology Project Award [7016]
Namur Award [1270]
Roger Needham Award and Lecture [7017]
Manfred Paul Award [1272]
Project Manager of the Year [7018]
Public Sector Organisation of the Year [7019]
Research Award [9416]
Ricoh Information Security and Data Management Project Award [7020]
Service Manager of the Year [7021]
Brian Shackel Award [1273]
SME Supplier Organisation of the Year [7022]
Social Contribution Project Award [7023]
Student Bursary [9417]
Student Prize [8309]
Systems Developer of the Year [7024]
Web-based Technology Project Award [7025]
Young IT Practitioner of the Year [7027]

Innovation *see Inventions*

Instructional films *see Audiovisuals; Educational films*

Insurance

AIRMIC Prize [7404]
Book Prize [7098]
Stanley Brown Prize [7405]
Caribbean Education Award [1390]
The Chubb Insurance Company of Europe Prize [7406]
Finlaison Medal [7823]
Gold Medal [7824]
H. J. Greening Prize [7407]
Healthcare Award: Advanced Level [7408]
Insurance Company of the Year [1904]
International Underwriting Association Marine Prize [7409]
Prix Jules Lefort [2280]
Lifetime Achievement Award [1692]
London Business Interruption Association Prize [7411]
Ernst Meyer Prize [6354]
Boleslaw Monic Prize [7412]
National Institute of Insurance International Prizes [4024]
Morgan Owen Medal [7413]
John Poel Prize [7414]
Re(insurance) Person of the Year [1693]
Burton Rowe Prize [7415]
Rutter Gold Medal and Prize [7416]
Young Re(insurance) Person of the Year [1694]

Intellectual freedom

African Regional Intellectual Property Organisation Prize [4466]
Liberty Awards [8306]
Open Source Awards [8442]

Intellectual property *see Inventions*

Intelligence *see National security*

Interior design

Design Excellence Awards [5948]
Design for All Award [5949]
Emergent Designer Award [7089]
Graduate Product Award [7090]
Interior Design Awards [1702]
Interior Designer of the Year [2083]

International law

F.F. Martens Prize [5833]
James Brown Scott Prizes [6340]

International relations *see also European integration; World peace*

Andrew Mouravieff-Apostol Medal [6380]
King Baudouin International Development Prize [1569]
Canada Medal [9274]
J. G. Crawford Award [475]
Euro-Med Award for Dialogue between Cultures [2007]
Gold Star and Citation [4204]
Calouste Gulbenkian Foundation Grants [7315]
International Trophy [6404]
Japan Society Small Grants [8270]
F.F. Martens Prize [5833]
Jawaharlal Nehru Award for International Understanding [3518]
Onassis International Prize in Law [3300]
Hafiz Pashayev Award for the Promotion of U.S.-Azerbaijan Relations [1339]
President's Award [8175]
St. Olav Medal [5136]
Y.V. Tarle Prize [5865]
E.S. Varga Prize [5871]
Sir Ron Wilson Human Rights Award [275]
Writing for CEE Award [1201]

International trade

AmCham Annual Awards [3329]
APCAC Award [5919]
Award for Excellence in Exporting Legal Services [8284]
Champion Exporter Award [4185]
Champion Manufacturer [4176]

Bernhard Harms Prize [3111]
International Promotion Prize [6403]
Moroccan-American Trade and Investment Award [4618]
National Export Awards [868]
Onassis International Prize in Trade [3303]
Onassis Prize in Shipping, Trade and Finance [3304]
Prime Minister's Exporter of the Year Award [2064]
Private Sector Hall of Fame [4200]
Quality Prize of the Government of the Republic of Belarus [1394]
Rising Star Award [6598]
Seatrade Asia Awards [9175]
Seatrade Awards [9176]
Seatrade China Awards [9177]
Seatrade Middle East and Indian Subcontinent Awards [9179]

International understanding see also
Brotherhood; Human relations; Humanitarianism

Australian Alumni Awards [3815]
Rodrigo Gomez Prize [4579]
International Simon Bolivar Prize [2653]
Arthur Thomas Ippen Award [6042]
John F. Kennedy Student Paper Competition [6043]
Ramon Magsaysay Award [5337]
Mitsubishi Asian Children's Enikki Festa [4301]
Onassis Award for International Understanding and Social Achievement [3297]
Prince of Asturias Award for International Cooperation [6087]
Student Award for International Understanding [7608]
UNESCO Japan Fair Play Award [4302]
Philipp Franz von Siebold Award for Japanese Research [3233]
Youth Awards for International Understanding Activities [4303]

Inventions see also Technology

Best Student Paper Award [8187]
Arpad Bogsch Memory Medal [3398]
Genius Prize [3365]
Knut Holt Award [8188]
Innovators Mauritius Award [4577]
International Order of Merit of the Inventors [3399]
ISPIM-Wiley Innovation Management Dissertation Award [8189]
Junior Inventor of the Year [6125]
MacRobert Award [8581]
Paterson Medal and Prize [7918]
President's Medal [8582]
Prime Minister's Awards for Innovation and Invention [6618]
Prince Philip Medal [8583]
Rolex Awards for Enterprise [6477]
Scientific Panel Award [8190]
Silver Medal [8585]
Small and Medium Enterprise Innovation Research Award [6599]
SPUR: Support for Products Under Research [9412]
Vishwakarma Medal [3671]
Young Inventors' Award [5989]

Investment see Finance

Iron and steel industry

Asada Medal [4250]
Hattori Prize [4251]
Honorary Member [4252]
Meritorious Prize for Scientific Achievement [4253]
Mishima Medal [4254]
Nishiyama Medal [4255]
Satomi Prize [4256]
Tawara Gold Medal [4257]
G. Watanabe Medal [4258]

Irrigation

Best Paper Award [3761]
Best Performing National Committee Award [3762]
Best Performing Workbody Award [3763]
WatSave Awards [3764]
Jack Wright Memorial Travel Grants [9405]

Islamic culture

Aga Khan Award for Architecture [6251]

Prizes for Leadership in Islamic Thought and Applied Sciences [4012]
Abdus Salam Prize for Leadership in Islamic Thought and the Physical Sciences [4014]
Youth and Community Awards [7677]
Ahmed Zewail Prize for Leadership in Islamic Thought and Biological Science [4015]
Ahmed Zewail Prize for Leadership in Islamic Thought and Chemical Science [4016]

Israeli culture

Nathan Gottesdiener Prize [3992]
Emil Grunzweig Human Rights Award [3938]
Abdul Majeed Shoman International Award for Jerusalem [4368]

Italian culture

International Guido Dorso Prize [4032]
Grollo Ruzzene Foundation Prize for Writing about Italians in Australia [1067]
Serena Medal for Italian Studies [6929]

Italian history

I Tatti Fellowships [4169]

Italian literature

Bagutta Prize [4036]
Campiello Prize [4040]
Certamen Capitolinum [4115]
John Florio Prize [9248]
Italian PEN Prize [4139]

Japanese culture see also Asian studies

Daiwa Foundation Awards [7491]
Daiwa Scholarships [7493]
Suntory Prize for Community Cultural Activities [4332]
Suntory Prize for Social Sciences and Humanities [4333]
Philipp Franz von Siebold Award for Japanese Research [3233]

Jewelry design

German Award for Jewelry and Precious Stones [2875]
National Crafts Competition [3922]

Jewelry industry

Costume and Fashion Jewelry Award [3487]
Cut and Polished Colored Gemstones Award [3488]
Cut and Polished Diamonds Award [3489]
Cut and Polished Synthetic Stones Award [3490]
German Award for Jewelry and Precious Stones [2875]
Outstanding Achievement Award - Hong Kong Jewelry Industry [5264]
Pearls Award [3491]
Plain Gold Jewelry Award [3492]
Plain Precious Metal Jewelry Award [3493]
Sales to Foreign Tourists Award [3494]
Silver Jewelry Award [3495]
Studded Gold Jewelry Award [3496]
Studded Precious Metal Jewelry Award [3497]

Jewish culture

Award for Literary Criticism [3984]
Award for Original Hebrew Novel [3985]
Award for Original Hebrew Poetry [3986]
First Novel Award [3987]
First Poetry Book Award [3988]
Hebrew Play Award [3989]
Otto Hirsch Medaille [3192]
Solomon Prize [3953]

Jewish history

Fraenkel Prize in Contemporary History [9449]
Solomon Prize [3953]

Journalism see also Literature; Cartoons; Editing; Editorial writing; Journalism education; Media; Publications; Radio; School publications; Television; Travel literature; specific types of journalism, e.g. Broadcast journalism

ACCA Singapore Awards for Sustainability Reporting [5934]

Agricultural Journalism Awards [3840]
Asiavision Annual Awards [4521]
Awards for Editorial and Publishing Excellence [7256]
Ida Backmans Stipendium [6194]
Bagutta Prize [4036]
Bank of New Zealand Farm Business Writing Award [4972]
Bank of New Zealand Rongo Award [4973]
Best Journalist of the Year [3144]
Biodiversity Reporting Award [1724]
A. H. Boerma Award [3371]
Cavling Prize [1960]
Mark Chavhunduka Award [6857]
CNN MultiChoice African Journalist Awards [7444]
E-Journal Prize [4240]
Eco Media Awards Namibia [4622]
Editors of the Year Awards [7257]
Gun och Olof Engqvists stipendium [6200]
European Journalism Prize [1400]
Financial Journalism Awards [5611]
Financial Reporting Awards [5488]
Joaquin Garcia Monge Prize [1858]
Karin Gierows pris [6202]
Go-Green Journalism Award [4629]
Gold Medal [7375]
Grand Journalism Prize [5146]
IFAJ-Alltech Young Leaders in Agricultural Journalism Award [4737]
IUCN - Reuters - COMplus Media Awards [6535]
Journalist of the Year [8352]
Journalist Prize [3017]
Kellgrenpriset [6206]
Ramon Magsaysay Award [5337]
J.L. Manning Award [9359]
John Manyarara Investigative Journalism Awards [4625]
Bill McGowran Award [9360]
Medienpreis fur Sprachkultur [2961]
Lorenzo Natali Journalism Prize [1463]
Netherthorpe Communicator of the Year [7751]
Carsten Nielsen Prize [1961]
Nordiska Priset [6209]
Elizabeth O'Neill Journalism Award [3816]
Penguin Manuscript Prize [1098]
Premio Nacional de Periodismo [1828]
Premio Nacional de Periodismo Pio Viquez [1860]
Press Freedom Award [4626]
Thomas Pringle Award [5542]
SEAMEO-Australia Press Award [6606]
Sports Feature Writer Award [9361]
Sports Personalities of the Year (Men, Women, Team) [9362]
Sports Writer of the Year [9364]
Stanford Fellowship [9390]
Star Prize for Agricultural Photography [4738]
Star Prize for Print [4739]
Student Journalism Award [1048]
Student Journalist of the Year [8354]
Television Journalism Awards [9131]
Tenzing-Hillary Award [4644]
UNESCO Bangladesh Journalism Award [1376]
Markus Viljoen Medal for Journalism [5647]
The Walkley Awards [1176]
Van Walree Prize [4836]
Writing for CEE Award [1201]

Journalism education

Oxford University Fellowship [9389]

Judo see Martial arts

Justice see Civil rights and liberties

Juvenile literature see Children's literature

Karate see Martial arts

Kayak see Boating

Labor see also Occupational health; Occupational safety

Global Compact Sri Lanka Network/CIMA Sustainability Awards [6119]
Rene Kuczynski Prize [1261]

International Sports Event Management Awards [6338]
JRD Tata Corporate Leadership Award [3450]
Lambert Memorial Award [3886]
Lifetime Achievement Award for Management [3451]
Maple Leaf Award [1283]
Sir Eric Mensforth International Manufacturing Gold Medal [8027]
NTPC Book Award [3475]
Organization of Islamic Capitals and Cities Awards [5909]
Hans Ovelgonne - Purchasing Research Award [1284]
Wilfred Owen Awards [7883]
Parkman Medal [8001]
Pensions Management Institute Associateship [8465]
Petrie Memorial Award [7888]
President's Award for Excellence [5739]
Programme of the Year [6778]
Project Management Achievement Awards [421]
Project Management Excellence Award [5599]
Project Manager of the Year [6779]
Project of the Year [6780]
Public Service Excellence Award [3452]
Quality Award [5271]
Risk Manager of the Year [949]
Shiram Award [3476]
Lewis E. Spangler - Purchasing Professional Award [1285]
Dioscoro L. Umali Medal for Outstanding Science Administrator [5369]
Brian Willis Award [6781]

Manufacturing   *see also Industries and trades*

Albert Medal [8957]
Authors Club Certificate [1223]
Best Environmental Management Program Award [4183]
Best Paper Awards [1224]
Best Photo Award [1225]
Breakthrough Product of the Year [4184]
Champion Exporter Award [4185]
Excellence Awards [3580]
Excellence in Holography Awards [8143]
Dr. V. M. Ghatage Award [3441]
Ray Hadeed Award for Best Small and Medium-Sized Enterprise [4186]
Manufacturer of the Year [4187]
Medal of DAAAM International [1226]
Sir Eric Mensforth International Manufacturing Gold Medal [8027]
Ministry of Industry, Investment and Commerce Award for Competitiveness [4188]
G.P. Nair Awards [3578]
New Manufacturer of the Year [4189]
Viscount Nuffield Medal [8029]
Product Group Award [4190]
Dr. Biren Roy Trust Award [3447]
SEA Awards [3791]
Skills and Productivity Award [4191]
TDI Awards [8344]

Marine biology

Challenger Medal [7356]
Darwin Medal [8192]
Honorary Membership [4107]
Ron Kenny Prizes [458]
Ray Lankester Investigatorship [8346]
NM Tirmizi Gold Medal [5201]
Silver Jubilee Award [459]

Marine engineering   *see Naval engineering*

Marketing   *see also Advertising; Public relations; Merchandising*

Air Pacific Tabua Marketing Awards [2058]
B & T Awards [626]
Best of Europe - International Direct Marketing Awards [1512]
Brand Award Azerbaijan [1337]
Care Awards [1437]
DMA Awards [7517]
Euro Effie Awards [1438]
European Diploma [2348]
European Sponsorship Awards [7650]

Excellence Award for Best Paper [4668]
Flag of Honour [2351]
Seldon Gill Scholarship [86]
Golden Egg Award [8110]
Hall of Fame [87]
Lifetime Award [2910]
Marketing Awards [1532]
McKinsey Marketing Dissertation Award [1484]
Mercurio Award [42]
Newspaper of the Year Award [923]
Plaque of Honour [2354]
PR, Marketing and Communications Awards [6816]
Research Personality of the Year [2911]
Study of the Year Award [2912]
Tool of the Year Award [2913]
Young Researcher of the Year Award [4670]

Martial arts

Judo Hall of Fame [3402]

Materials science   *see also Ceramic engineering; Mining and metallurgy; Plastics and rubber*

Armourers and Brasiers' Company Award [8928]
Prix Professeur Louis Baes [1650]
Beilby Medal and Prize [8978]
G. D. Birla Memorial Gold Medal [3590]
Prix Gaz de France [2204]
J.H. Harvey Prize [1125]
Italian Association for Metallurgy Awards [4122]
Prix Charles Lemaire [1637]
Prize for Materials Science [3654]

Mathematics   *see also Statistics; Surveying*

Abel Prize [5138]
J.K. Aggarwal Prize [4231]
Aitken Prize [4977]
Alexander Prize [7452]
Prix Ampere d'Electricite de France [2176]
ANZIAM Medal [211]
Prix Louis Armand [2177]
Australian Mathematical Society Medal [464]
Cor Baayen Award [2404]
Balzan Prizes [4086]
Premio Giuseppe Bartolozzi [4135]
Maurice H. Belz Prizes in Statistics [1104]
Berwick Prize [8328]
Senior Berwick Prize [8329]
N.N. Bogoliubov Gold Medal [5791]
Guy Bomford Prize [3049]
Premio Renato Caccioppoli [4136]
Fridrihs Canders Prize [4435]
Georg Cantor Award [6073]
Prix Elie Cartan [2186]
CASTME Awards [7453]
Prix Eugene Catalan [1622]
Certificate of Appreciation [4232]
T. M. Cherry Prize [212]
Crafoord Prize [6183]
Prix Theophile de Donder [1624]
De Morgan Medal [8330]
Prix Ernest Dechelle [2194]
Prix Francois Deruyts [1626]
Prix Jacques Deruyts [1627]
Dirac Medal [4009]
Distinguished Service Award [3404]
Dwight Prize in Mathematical Statistics [1115]
Edgeworth-Pareto Award [6074]
Professor Magnus Ehrnrooth Prize [2103]
Fellow of ISIR [3407]
Antonio Feltrinelli Prizes [4022]
Prix Fonde par l'Etat [2201]
Francqui Prize [1527]
Hans Freudenthal Award [5430]
Carl Friedrich Gauss Prize [2967]
Gold Medal [6075]
Prix Grammaticakis-Neuman [2206]
Hector Memorial Medal and Prize [5075]
ICTP Prize [4011]
Keith Medal [9068]
Felix Klein Award [5431]
A.N. Kolmogorov Prize [5812]
S.V. Kovalevskaya Prize [5818]
A.N. Krylov Prize [5821]
Prix Charles Lagrange [1634]
M.A. Lavrent'ev Prize [5823]

Prix Leconte [2215]
N.I. Lobachevskii Prize [5826]
E. R. Love Prize [1135]
A.M. Lyapunov Prize [5828]
Thomas Ranken Lyle Medal [183]
Mahler Lectureship [465]
A.I. Maltsev Prize [5830]
A.A. Markov Prize [5832]
Norma McArthur Prize [1137]
Medal of the Society [2105]
J.H. Michell Medal [213]
Moran Medal [185]
MUPHAS Prize for Academic Excellence in Mathematics [1140]
Professor Nanson Prize [1141]
National Institute of Insurance International Prizes [4024]
Naylor Prize and Lectureship [8331]
Bernhard H. Neumann Prize [466]
NZMS Research Award [4978]
Outstanding Achievement Award [4233]
Outstanding Book and/or Monograph Awards [5361]
Outstanding Scientific Paper Award [5362]
Outstanding Young Scientist Award [5363]
Prix Blaise Pascal du GAMNI-SMAI [2226]
Prof. Amnon Pazy Memorial Award [3998]
I.G. Petrovskii Prize [5845]
Philippine Mathematical Olympiad [5364]
Pollock Memorial Lecture [1009]
Polya Prize [8332]
Prince of Asturias for Technical and Scientific Research [6090]
Eduardo A. Quisumbing Medal for Basic Research [5367]
Srinivasa Ramanujan Medal [3658]
Ramanujan Prize for Young Mathematicians from Developing Countries [4013]
Research Grant [9120]
Research Medal [1017]
Rolf Schock Prizes [6185]
Scientific Research Prizes [4591]
Section Grant [9121]
Prix Servant [2236]
Service Award [3408]
Dr. M. Raziuddin Siddiqi Prize for Scientists Under 40 [5194]
Sylvester Medal [8948]
George Szekeres Medal [467]
Prof. Luigi Tartufari Prizes [4025]
Premio Franco Tricerri [4137]
Prix Gabrielle Sand et Marie Guido Triossi [2237]
TWAS Prize for Young Scientist in the Philippines [5368]
TWAS Prize for Young Scientists in the South [5195]
Upper Secondary School Teachers Prizes [2107]
Gunning Victoria Jubilee Prize Lectureship [9073]
I.M. Vinogradov Prize [5875]
Whitehead Prize [8333]
Senior Whitehead Prize [8334]
Professor Wilson Prize [1158]
The Wolf Prizes [4001]
Young Scientist Award [4234]
P. Zamperoni Award [4235]

Mechanical engineering

A.A. Andronov Prize [5782]
Angus Award [4905]
Prix Louis Armand [2177]
Australian Geomechanics Award - John Jaeger Memorial Award [768]
N.N. Bogoliubov Gold Medal [5791]
CESA/Glenrand M.I.B. Engineering Excellence Awards [5535]
Prix du Commissariat a l'Energie Atomique [2190]
Contact Mechanics Award [944]
Contribution to Special Needs Award [8048]
James Alfred Ewing Medal [7982]
Georg A. Fischer Prize [6495]
Sir George Julius Medal [786]
A.N. Krylov Prize [5821]
M.A. Lavrent'ev Prize [5823]
A.M. Lyapunov Prize [5828]
Medal for Outstanding Paper [4281]
A. G. M. Michell Medal [792]
Prix Henri de Parville, Artur du Fay, Alexandre Givry [2225]

Prix Petit d'Ormoy, Carriere, Thebault [2228]
B.N. Petrov Prize [5844]
Premio Internazionale Panetti-Ferrari [4019]
Stephenson Award [7558]
Student Awards [8049]
James Watt Medal [8013]
Weir Minerals Design and Build Competition [810]

Media see also Communications; Journalism; Radio; Television

AIMIA Annual Awards [427]
B & T Awards [626]
BIMA Awards [7100]
CEVMA Awards [2750]
MEDEA Awards [1573]
Media Awards [1712]
Media Peace Awards [1093]

Medical education

Academic Prize [954]
AGC/GVS Fellowship [8689]
Prix Jean Dagnan-Bouveret [2192]
Rahima Dawood Prize [4410]
Eden Travelling Fellowship in Obstetrics and Gynaecology [8692]
Faculty of Medicine Prize [6524]
Sandoz Garcia Prize [3858]
Hamdan Award for the Best Medical College/Institute or Centre in the Arab World [6670]
Brigadier Haywood Prize [9095]
IFSC Travel Grants [3859]
Harold Johns Medal [8157]
MBC/IFSC Scholarship [3860]
Medical Student Elective Prize [9119]
William Pickles Lectureship [8684]
Undergraduate Project Prize [9122]

Medical journalism see also Science journalism

Garrod Prize [7239]
Ron Halmshaw Award [7093]
John Horder Award [8679]
Michael Mason Prize [7241]
Medical Book Awards [9255]
Minkowski Prize [2800]

Medical research see also Scientific research

Aaxis Pacific New Investigator Award [620]
Abbott Award [3085]
ACTM Medal for Outstanding Contributions to Tropical Medicine [131]
ACTM Medal for Students [133]
Professor B. K. Aikat Oration Award [3538]
Allied Health Fellowship [680]
Amgen-ANZBMS Outstanding Abstract Award [204]
Anaesthesia Essay Prize - Students [9079]
Dr. Nitya Anand Endowment Lecture [3619]
Anitschkow Prize [6137]
John Arderne Medal [9081]
Asthma Research Hall of Fame [108]
Asthma Research Postgraduate Scholarships [109]
Asthma Research Sustainability Grants [110]
AstraZeneca Award [8206]
Aujeszky Medal [3375]
AWMA Conference Awards [621]
BackCare Medal [6864]
Bernhard Baron Travelling Scholarship [8690]
Best Abstract Presentation Award [7631]
Best Practice Award [6785]
BGRC Silver Jubilee Oration Award [3540]
Jean-Paul Binet Prize [2422]
Robert Bing Prize [6481]
Biotest Best Oral Presentation Award [7633]
Boehringer Ingelheim Developing World Award [8207]
Boehringer Ingelheim Grant [6510]
Brahm's Young Investigators Award [2861]
Bristol-Myers Squibb AG Grant [6511]
Bruce-Preller Prize Lectureship [9063]
Alexander Ninian Bruce Prize [9064]
Kaye Merlin Brutton Prize [1107]
Donal Burke Memorial Lecture [3907]
Cardiology Section President's Medal [9085]
Career Award [1450]
Chalmers Memorial Medal [9114]

Basanti Devi Amir Chand Prize [3541]
Shakuntala Amir Chand Prizes [3542]
Jean-Martin Charcot Award [8371]
Dr. Dharamvir Datta Memorial Oration Award [3543]
Prix Marguerite Delahautemaison [4448]
Shri Dhanwantari Prize [3633]
Smt. Swaran Kanta Dingley Oration Award [3545]
Distinguished Member Award [8208]
Vera Down Grant [7118]
Down Syndrome Research Prize in the Eastern Mediterranean Prize [6550]
Austin Doyle Award [8209]
Henry Dryerre Prize Lectureship [9066]
Jacqueline du Pre Fellowship [8372]
ECCR Scholarships [7605]
Eckert and Ziegler Abstract Award [1233]
EGA Generic Medicines Award [1477]
Prix Leon-Alexandre Etancelin [2200]
Prix Fonde par l'Etat [2201]
Edgar Gentilli Prize [8693]
Genzyme Prize [2862]
Prix Jean-Marie Le Goff, Lemonon, Houry, Laveran [2205]
Maurice Goldblatt Cytology Award [3040]
Grand Prize [2423]
Graves Lecture [3909]
Green-Armytage and Spackman Travelling Scholarship [8694]
Daniel and Florence Guggenheim Memorial Lecture Award [6151]
R. T. Hall Prize [637]
Hamdan Award for Medical Research Excellence [6668]
Hamdan Award for Original Research Paper Published in SHAMS [6669]
Hamdan Award for the Best Medical College/Institute or Centre in the Arab World [6670]
Harington-De Visscher Prize [2863]
Nathaniel Bishop Harman Award [7121]
Charles Oliver Hawthorne Award [7122]
Adrienne and Frederick Herbert Prize [2424]
Doris Hillier Grant [7123]
Casey Holter Memorial Prize [9208]
Honorary Member Award [8210]
Honorary Membership [2853]
Bryan Hudson Clinical Endocrinology Award [702]
Humanitarian Award [8062]
Kaye Ibbertson Award for Metabolic Bone Disease [205]
Insole and Clegg Grant [7124]
Dr. M. O. T. Iyengar Memorial Award [3547]
Dr. C. G. S. Iyer Oration Award [3548]
H. C. Jacobaeus Lectures [1982]
Chaturvedi Kalawati Jaghmohan Das Memorial Award [3549]
T. V. James Fellowship [7125]
Prix Alexandre Joannides [2210]
Dr. Lee Jong-Wook Memorial Prize for Public Health [6551]
Prix Centre d'etudes Princesse Josephine-Charlotte [1523]
Journal of Infection Young Investigator's Prize [7085]
Stevo Julius Award [8211]
Smt. Suraj Kali Jain Award [3733]
Lala Ram Chand Kandhari Award [3551]
Prix de Biologie Alfred Kastler [2443]
Max Pierre Koenig/Organon/Nourypharma Poster Prize [2864]
Marie and August Krogh Prize [1983]
Prof. P.A. Kurup Endowment Award [3785]
Rose Lamarca Prize [2425]
Niels Lassen Award [6430]
John Lawson Prize [8695]
Prix Leconte [2215]
Lifetime Achievement Award [6431]
Eli Lilly/EASD Research Fellowship in Diabetes and Metabolism [2799]
Lissitzky Career Award [2865]
Louis-Jeantet Prize for Medicine [6336]
George Macdonald Medal [9116]
Donald Mackay Medal [9117]
C. J. Martin Overseas Biomedical Fellowship [892]
Christine and T. Jack Martin Research Travel Grant [206]
Medical and Dental Postgraduate Research Scholarships [893]

Dr. Janak H. Mehta Award [3512]
Roger Melick Young Investigator Award [207]
Merck-Serono Award [2866]
Merck-Serono Prize [2867]
Prof. Surindar Mohan Marwah Award [3554]
NAST-LELEDFI Award for Outstanding Research in Tropical Medicine [5360]
National Back Pain Association Medal [6865]
Christopher and Margie Nordin Young Investigator Poster Award [208]
Forbes Norris Award [8063]
Novartis Award for Hypertension Research [4294]
Novartis Junior Scientist Award [703]
Novo Nordisk Foundation Lecture [1984]
Masaaki Ohkoshi Award [8199]
Theodore Ott Prize [6482]
Overseas Surgical Fellowship [6850]
Paediatric Anaesthesia Research Fund Grant [6836]
Ana and John Paneboeuf Prize [2426]
Didier Patte Prize [2410]
Pfizer Award [8212]
Jacques Piraud Prize [2427]
Sol Posen Research Award [209]
Post Graduate PhD Studentship Grant [681]
Drs. Kunti and Om Prakash Oration Award [3557]
Prof. B.G. Prasad Award [3734]
Dr. D. N. Prasad Memorial Oration Award [3558]
President's Poster Prize [9229]
Prize for Biomedical Research Conducted in Underdeveloped Areas [3559]
Prize for Biomedical Research for Scientists Belonging to Underprivileged Communities [3560]
Prizes for Young Scientists in Atherosclerosis Research [6138]
Raine Award [8545]
Dr. T. Ramachandra Rao Award [3562]
Line Renaud Prize [2428]
Albert Renold Travel Fellowship [2803]
Research Award [7082]
Research Awards [540]
Research Visit Grant [7232]
H. C. Roscoe Research Grant [7126]
Prix Raymond Rosen [4449]
Prix Gustave Roussy [2234]
Smt. Kamal Satbir Award [3566]
Georg Schmorl Preis [3179]
Servier Young Investigator Award [704]
Society Medal [8230]
Maj. Gen. Saheb Singh Sokhey Award [3569]
Sports Award [7784]
Student Award [3003]
Student Researcher Award [6786]
Student Travel Award [7233]
Student Travel Bursaries [6145]
Lucien Tartois Prize [2429]
Robert Tigerstedt Award [8213]
Dr. T.S. Tirumurti Memorial Lecture [3670]
Travel Grants [6837]
Prijs Albert Van Dyck [1577]
Van Leeuwenhoek Distinctive Travel Award [2855]
Pauline van Wachem Award [4662]
Franz Volhard Award and Lectureship [8214]
Dr. Prem Nath Wahi Award [3572]
Van Walree Prize [4836]
Edith Walsh Grant [7128]
Wassermann Prize [6098]
Weissenberg Award [6027]
Elizabeth Wherry Award [7129]
Young Achiever Award [6787]
Young Cancer Researcher Award [7581]
Young Investigator [6099]
Young Investigator Award [1766]
Young Investigator Awards [6146]
Young Investigators Award [4295]
Young Scientist Award [836]
Young Scientists for Rainforests [7474]

Medical technology see also Biomedical engineering; Biotechnology

Abbott Award for Innovative Research and Development in Virology [5613]
Bactlab Systems Gold Award for the Best Paper [5614]
Bactlab Systems Premier Award for Best Paper [5615]

Bayer Diagnostics Academic Achievement Award [5616]
Bayer/Sakura Histology Achievement Award [5617]
Dade Behring Award [5618]
His Excellency Dr. Ali Fakhro Prize [1362]
International Cytotechnologist of the Year Award [3041]
Joseph Award [5619]
Labotec-Shandon Award for Achievement in the Field of Cytology [5620]
Merck Award [5621]
Oral Presentation Awards [1556]
Poster Awards [1557]
Roche Award [5622]
Technologist of the Year [5623]
Thistle Student Award [5624]

Medicine *see also* *Biomedical engineering; Biotechnology; Health care; Occupational health; Rehabilitation and therapy; Toxicology; specific fields of medicine, e.g. Anesthesiology*

AACR-Pezcoller International Award for Cancer Research [4149]
Aaxis Pacific New Investigator Award [620]
Abbott Award [3085]
Abbott Diagnostic Award [2406]
ACTM Medal for Outstanding Contributions to Tropical Medicine [131]
ACTM Medal for Outstanding Service to the College [132]
ACTM Medal for Students [133]
Adolescent Health Care Award in memory of Dr. Kathy Phipps [8672]
Dr. B. R. Ambedkar Centenary Award for Excellence in Biomedical Research [3539]
Amgen-ANZBMS Outstanding Abstract Award [204]
AMWA Awards [137]
Anaesthesia Essay Prize - Students [9079]
Asthma Research Postgraduate Scholarships [109]
Asthma Research Sustainability Grants [110]
Awards in Recognition of Women Obstetricians/ Gynecologists [8123]
AWMA Conference Awards [621]
Ayuda a la Investigacion [6101]
Albert Baikie Award [745]
Balzan Prizes [4086]
Dame Josephine Barnes Award [9082]
BASHH Undergraduate Prize [6956]
Prix Louis-Daniel Beauperthuy [2178]
Leon Bernard Foundation Prize [6547]
Claude Bernard Lecture [2798]
Jean Bernard Lifetime Achievement Award [4701]
Best Abstract Presentation Award [7631]
Best Consumer Mobile Data Application Award [8368]
Best Poster Award
    Australasian Society for Ultrasound in Medicine [158]
    European Society for Organ Transplantation [7632]
Best Research Presentation Award [159]
Best Sonographer Research Presentation Award [160]
Biotest Best Oral Presentation Award [7633]
Bird Healthcare Young Investigator Award [221]
Black and Minority Health Section Essay Prize [9083]
William Blair-Bell Memorial Lectureship in Obstetrics and Gynaecology [8691]
Boehringer Ingelheim Grant [6510]
Bristol-Myers Squibb AG Grant [6511]
Buchanan Medal [8929]
Henry Burger Prize [8148]
Caledonian Research Foundation Prize Lectureship in Biomedical Sciences and Arts and Letters [9065]
Cardiology Section President's Medal [9085]
Thelma Cardwell Foundation Award for Education and Research [1193]
Career Achievement Award [3078]
Jose Carreras Award [4702]
Britton Chance Award [3095]
Princess Chichibu Memorial TB Global Award [2573]
Sir Rickard Christophers Medal [9115]
Thomas Clarkson Prize [8149]
Comfeel Literary Awards [622]
Prix du Commisariat a l'Energie Atomique [2190]
Compumedics Poster Prize [222]
Marie Curie Training Grant [1232]

Darling Foundation Prize [6548]
Davies Foundation Travelling Fellowship [8700]
Frans Debruyne Lifetime Achievement Award [4690]
Elsdon Dew Medal [5590]
Disability Care Award [8673]
Distinguished Service Awards [264]
Ihsan Dogramaci Family Health Foundation Prize [6549]
Ian Donald Gold Medal [8223]
Maureen Downey Memorial Grant [3878]
GT du Toit Registrar Prize [5705]
Weary Dunlop Award [469]
Alan Edwards Prize [9089]
EGA Generic Medicines Award [1477]
Ellison-Cliffe Medal and Lecture [9090]
Ernst-von-Bergmann-Plakette [2964]
EULAR Stene Prize [6279]
Euroliver Foundation Award [7634]
European Postgraduate Grants [2857]
European Student Dietitian of the Year [2829]
Neil Hamilton Fairley Fellowships [891]
Antonio Feltrinelli Prizes [4022]
Juraj Ferin Award [3079]
FIGO/Ernst Schering Research Foundation Fellowship [1742]
John Flynn Placement Program Awards [265]
Foundation Council Award [8674]
Francqui Prize [1527]
Hans Frankel Scholarship [8229]
Paul Freeling Award [8675]
John Fry Award [8676]
Gagna A. and Ch. Van Heck Prize [1519]
Gardner Lectureship [2407]
Lars-Erik Gelin Conference Travel Award [2852]
Geriatrics and Gerontology Section Trainees' Prize [9093]
Chaturvedi Ghanshyam Das Jaigopal Memorial Award [3546]
GlaxoSmithKline Prize and Lecture [8936]
Gold Medal for Distinguished Merit [7119]
Gold Medal of Honor [6543]
Gottschalk Medal [176]
Marie Goubran Award [4735]
GP Registrar Awards [8677]
Willy Gregoir Medal [4691]
T.M. Gregory Memorial Scholarship Fund [5273]
Daniel and Florence Guggenheim Memorial Lecture Award [6151]
Garegin Harutyunyan Scholarship [48]
Reuben Harvey Memorial Prize [3913]
Brigadier Haywood Prize [9095]
Heine-Medin Award [2408]
Dr. A.H. Heineken Prize for Medicine [4826]
Gordon Holmes Prize [9096]
Hong Kong Nephrology Research Grants [5279]
Honorary Award [49]
Honorary Fellowship
    Australian College of Rural and Remote Medicine [266]
    International Society of Ultrasound in Obstetrics and Gynecology [8224]
Honorary Fellowship [8678]
Honorary Life Member [3879]
Honorary Member [2574]
Honorary Membership [267]
John Horder Award [8679]
Bryan Hudson Clinical Endocrinology Award [702]
Humane Education Award [8259]
Humanitarian Award [8062]
John Hunt Lectureship [8680]
Hunterian Medal [7804]
Kaye Ibbertson Award for Metabolic Bone Disease [205]
Ibrahim Memorial Award [4357]
ICCHK Scholarships [5280]
InBev-Baillet Latour Health Prize [1521]
Innovation Awards [2407]
International Women in Transfusion Award [4775]
ISBT Award [4776]
H.S. Jacobs President's Lecture [7054]
JALMA Trust Fund Oration Award [3550]
Janseen-Cilag Award for Excellence in Nephrology [3741]
Pierre Jaques Rural Doctor of the Year Award [5609]
Jephcott Lecture [9097]

E. Mead Johnson Award for Research in Pediatrics [6601]
Jean Julliard Prize [4777]
KFAS Awards in Islamic Medical Sciences [4427]
Melvin H. Knisely Award [3096]
Krill Prizes for Excellence in Scientific Research [4000]
Kshanika Oration Award [3552]
Life Fellowship [268]
Life Membership [223]
Lister Memorial Lecture [9289]
Prix Richard Lounsbery [2217]
Dietrich W. Lubbers Award [3097]
Lung Cancer Journalism Awards [7743]
MacDonald Award [7949]
Macfarlane Award [7782]
Ian MacKay Essay Prize [9099]
James Mackenzie Lectureship [8681]
John Macleod Memorial Award [8366]
Malcolm Black Travel Fellowship [8696]
Harold Malkin Prize [8697]
Mandy Award [1087]
Manson Medal [9118]
Hans Marberger Award [4692]
David Marsden Award [7610]
Marshall Scholarships [6815]
Christine and T. Jack Martin Research Travel Grant [206]
Crystal Matula Award [4693]
Kevin McCaul Prize [559]
Media Award [156]
Media Awards [163]
Medical Prize [6265]
Medical Rural Bonded Scholarship [269]
Medical Student Elective Grant [8302]
Medical Student Prize [4244]
MedicarePlus Procedural Training Grants [270]
Roger Melick Young Investigator Award [207]
Member Travel Fellowship [3805]
Amrut Mody Unichem Prize [3553]
MOTESZ Award [3369]
National GP of the Year Award [8682]
W.O. Neitz Junior Medal/Senior Medal [5591]
New Investigator Scholarship [746]
Niche Medical Best Oral Presentation [224]
Christopher and Margie Nordin Young Investigator Poster Award [208]
Forbes Norris Award [8063]
Novartis Award for Hypertension Research [4294]
Novartis Junior Scientist Award [703]
Novo Nordisk Prize [1985]
NSI Research Award [5160]
Nuffield Lecture [9102]
Lorenz Oken Medaille [3029]
Oral Presentation Awards [1556]
ORBEL Award [1415]
Osteoporosis Award [7242]
Bill O'Sullivan Fundraiser Award [3880]
Outstanding Book and/or Monograph Awards [5361]
Outstanding Scientific Paper Award [5362]
Outstanding Young Scientist Award [5363]
Overseas Surgical Fellowship [6850]
Palliative Care Section MSc/MA Research Prize [9104]
Paracelsus Medaille [2965]
Jacques Parisot Foundation Fellowship [6552]
Patient Participation Award [8683]
Patron's Prize [470]
Didier Patte Prize [2410]
Dr. V. N. Patwardhan Prize [3556]
Castelli Pedroli Prize [2801]
Prix Petit d'Ormoy, Carriere, Thebault [2228]
Dr. G.M. Phadke Oration [3806]
Late G.M. Phadke Travelling Award [3807]
William Pickles Lectureship [8684]
Platform Presentation Award [8203]
PMS Grants [8503]
Politzer Prize [8496]
Sol Posen Research Award [209]
Practitioner's Award for Excellence [1378]
President of the Republic Prize [56]
Presidential Award [4778]
Presidential Symposium Award [218]
President's Gold Medal [3808]
President's Medal
    Royal College of General Practitioners [8685]

South African Orthopaedic Association [5706]
Prince of Asturias for Technical and Scientific Research [6090]
Prix Madame Gay [2441]
Prize for Achievement [3087]
Raine Award [8545]
Dr. P. N. Raju Oration Award [3561]
Tilak Venkoba Rao Award [3563]
Herbert Reiss Trainees Prize [9107]
Line Renaud Prize [2428]
Research Grant [5199]
Research Grant [5707]
Research Prizes [6286]
RGCP/SAPC Elective Prize [8686]
Rose Prize [8687]
Prix Gaston Rousseau [2233]
Royal Colleges Medal [8907]
Karl Asmund Rudolphi Medal [2760]
Ronald Salinger Award [817]
Peter Schiff Award [219]
Hermann Schneider Prize [8151]
Norah Schuster Essay Prize [9108]
Scientific Prize [2575]
Scottish Science Award [9156]
Scoville Award [6544]
Robert E. Scully Young Investigator Award [8204]
M. N. Sen Oration Award [3567]
Servier Young Investigator Award [704]
Dr. A. T. Shousha Foundation Prize [6555]
Silver Medal [3911]
Dr. R. Sitharman Memorial Essay Competition [3809]
Marie Sklodowska-Curie Award [8158]
Smith/ASA Young Investigator Awards [560]
Society Medal [8230]
Spinal Cord Prize [8231]
Dr. J. B. Srivastav Oration Award [3570]
Andrija Stampar Medal [2324]
Patrick Steptoe Memorial Lecture [7055]
Stop TB Partnership/Kochon Prize [2576]
Pauls Stradins Prize [4441]
Student Research Award [3080]
Karel Styblo Public Health Prize [2577]
Lucien Tartois Prize [2429]
Teacher Travel Fellowship Award [3810]
Al-Sahabi Zaid Bin Thabit Prize [1366]
Thieme Award for Medicine [3126]
Travel Grant [5708]
Travel Grants/Scholarships [7652]
Anthony Tynan Award for Best Clinical Presentation [161]
The Union Medal [2578]
Premio Miguel Aleman Valdes [4585]
Prijs Franz Van Goidsenhoven [1578]
Pauline van Wachem Award [4662]
Oswald Vander Veken Prize [1525]
Weissenberg Award [6027]
Wellcome Medal for Anthropology as Applied to Medical Problems [8643]
Wing Award for Safety [8056]
Ian Wolboumers Award [2411]
The Wolf Prizes [4001]
WONCA Foundation Award [5993]
Young Investigator Award
  British Society for Rheumatology [7243]
  European Society for Organ Transplantation [7635]
  European Society of Intensive Care Medicine [1506]
  International Society for Aerosols in Medicine [3081]
  International Society for Pediatric and Adolescent Diabetes [3088]
  Latin American Thyroid Society [1766]
Young Investigators Award
  European Federation of Societies for Ultrasound in Medicine and Biology [7612]
  Japanese Society of Hypertension [4295]
Young Neurosurgeons Award [6545]
Young Scientist Award in Medical Physics [8159]

Medicine, emergency *see Emergency medicine*

Medicine, preventive *see Preventive medicine*

Medicine, sports *see Sports medicine*

Medicine, veterinary *see Veterinary medicine*

Meetings *see Conventions*

Mental health *see also Psychiatry*

Achievement Award [935]
Book of the Year Award [8350]
Champion of the Year [8351]
De Leo Fund Award [2483]
Early Career Award [3187]
European Bristol-Myers Squibb Prevention Award in Psychiatry [2401]
Farberow Award [2484]
John Hamilton Traveling Fellowship [8719]
Journalist of the Year [8352]
Ferdinande Johanna Kanjilal Traveling Fellowship [8722]
Life Esidimeni Award [5587]
Lifetime Career Award [3188]
Mental Health Matters Awards [875]
Mental Health Media Awards [8353]
Recognition Award [936]
Ringel Service Award [2485]
Dr. Vidya Sagar Award [3565]
Barbro Sandin Award [3292]
Alec Shapiro Prize [8742]
Stengel Research Award [2486]
Student Award [937]
Student Development Award [3189]
Zaccari Fellowship [925]

Mentally disabled

Philip Davis Prize [8713]
Distinguished Achievement Award - Research [8069]
Distinguished Achievement Award - Scientific Literature [8070]
Distinguished Achievement Award - Service [8071]
Distinguished Service Citation [8072]
Brian Oliver Prize [8732]
Roland Wagner Award [1205]
Zaccari Fellowship [925]

Merchandising

Best of Bermuda Awards [1701]
Distributor of the Year [128]
Peter Jowett Industry Award [129]
Fernanda Monti Award [4845]
New Zealand Post Book Awards [4870]

Metallurgy *see Mining and metallurgy*

Meteorology

Buys Ballot Medal [4816]
Vilhelm Bjerknes Medal [2370]
Broadcast Meteorologist Award [2837]
W. S. Bruce Medal [9062]
Forderpreis [2763]
Norbert Gerbier-Mumm International Award [6559]
Honorary Membership [2764]
International Meteorological Organization Prize [6560]
Edward Kidson Medal [4947]
Gordon Manley Weather Prize [8871]
Mason Gold Medal [8872]
Outreach and Communication Award [2838]
Kalpathi Ramakrishna Ramanathan Medal [3657]
Research Award for Young Scientists [6561]
Research Medal [1017]
Silver Medal [2839]
Symons Memorial Medal [8873]
TV Weather Forecast Trophy Award [2840]
Prof. Dr. Vilho Vaisala Award [6562]
Alfred Wegener Medaille [2765]
Young Scientist Award [2841]

Microbiology

Abbott Award for Innovative Research and Development in Virology [5613]
Arima Award for Applied Microbiology [4791]
Award for Advances in Clinical Microbiology [6291]
Award for Excellence in Clinical Microbiology and Infectious Diseases [6292]
Award for Outstanding Contributions to the Society [827]
Award of Excellence [828]
Bactlab Systems Premier Award for Best Paper [5615]

BD ASM Student Travel Award [542]
M. W. Beijerinck Virology Prize [4817]
Communications Award [9188]
Conference Poster Awards [829]
Conference Travel Grants [4866]
Distinguished Service Award [543]
Gertrude Elion Memorial Lecture Award [830]
Encouragement Award [6513]
Frank Fenner Award [544]
Carlos J. Finlay Prize [2649]
Garrod Medal [7219]
Dr. H.P. Heineken Prize for Biochemistry and Biophysics [4822]
Honorary Life Membership [545]
Lab Travel Grants [4867]
Leeuwenhoek Medal [4831]
Lifetime Achievement Award [3083]
Merck Award [5621]
Stuart Mudd Award for Studies in Basic Microbiology [4792]
Professor Shambu Nath De Memorial Lecture [3648]
Pfizer Animal Health Prize [1168]
W. H. Pierce Memorial Prize [9189]
William Prusoff Young Investigator Lecture Award [831]
Dr. Y. S. Narayana Rao Oration Award [3564]
Roy and Iris Simmons Award [1148]
Summer Conference Student Prizes [9190]
Teachers' Travel Award [546]
Technologist of the Year [5623]
Van Niel International Prize for Studies in Bacterial Systematics [4793]
S.N. Vinogradskii Prize [5876]
David White Excellence in Teaching Award [547]
Don Whitley Travel Scholarship [9191]
Young Investigator Awards for Research in Clinical Microbiology and Infectious Diseases [6293]

Microfilms *see Information management*

Military engineering

Arthur Corbett Medal [776]

Military history

Duke of Westminster Medal for Military Literature [9138]
Templer Medal [9243]

Military service

Afghanistan Medal [294]
Air Force Cross [7337]
Anniversary of National Service 1951-1972 Medal [296]
Australian Cadet Forces Service Medal [299]
Australian Service Medal [303]
Prix Lazare Carnot [2185]
Champion Shots Medal [306]
Chesney Gold Medal [9137]
Conspicuous Service Decorations [308]
Croix de Guerre [2431]
Defence Long Service Medal [310]
Distinguished Flying Cross [7339]
Distinguished Service Decorations [311]
Prix Edmond Freville [2270]
Gallantry Decorations [313]
Trench Gascoigne Prize [9139]
General Service Medal [5701]
International Force East Timor Medal [315]
Iraq Medal
  Australian Department of the Prime Minister and Cabinet - Awards and Culture Branch [316]
  Ministry of Defence - MOD Medal Office [8364]
Medaille Militaire [2432]
Medal for Military Service to Ukraine [6655]
Medal of Merit [6617]
Medal of the Founding Volunteers of the Lithuanian Army [4489]
Medalla Militar Francisco Jose de Caldas [1832]
Medalla Militar Soldado Juan Bautista Solarte Obando [1833]
Medalla Servicios Distinguidos a la Aviacion Naval [1834]
Medalla Servicios Distinguidos la Fuerza de Superficie [1835]
Military Courage Medal [2679]

Military Cross [7343]
Military Honor Medal [2680]
Military Merit Medal [5702]
Nursing Service Cross [318]
Orden del Merito Militar Antonio Narino [1836]
Orden del Merito Naval Almirante Padilla [1837]
Orden del Merito Sanitario Jose Fernandez
    Madrid [1838]
Order of Australia [319]
Order of Merit [7345]
Order of the British Empire [7347]
Param Vir Chakra [3500]
Param Vishisht Seva Medal [3501]
St. George's Victory Order [2683]
Service Medal [3896]
Servicios Distinguidos a la Fuerza Submarina [1839]
Shaurya Chakra [3502]
Unit Citations [322]
Unitas Medal [5703]
Vakhtang Gorgasal's Order [2684]
Vietnam Logistic and Support Medal [323]
Vir Chakra [3503]
Vishisht Seva Medal [3504]
War Service Decoration [4513]

Mineralogy

Georg Agricola Medaille [2767]
AIPEA Medals [1761]
Bradley Award [1762]
Prix Henri Buttgenbach [1621]
Collins Medal [8356]
Essar Gold Medal [3593]
A.Y. Fersman Prize [5797]
Viktor Moritz Goldschmidt Preis [2768]
Max Hey Medal [8357]
D.S. Korzhinskii Prize [5817]
Muller Award [5433]
Paul Ramdohr Prize [2769]
Manuel Rocha Medal [5434]
Schlumberger Medal [8358]
Abraham Gottlob Werner Medaille [2770]

Mining and metallurgy see also Materials
science

Prix Alcan [2175]
P.P. Anosov Prize [5783]
Atlas Copco Award [760]
Australian Geomechanics Award - John Jaeger
    Memorial Award [768]
Bablik Medal [7618]
I.P. Bardin Prize [5788]
Vidya Bharathi Prize [3588]
Binani Gold Medal [3589]
G. D. Birla Memorial Gold Medal [3590]
Dr. A. K. Bose Medal [3591]
Bralco Gold Medal [3592]
Brinell Medal [6176]
Ruston Bucyrus Award [7934]
Citation Award [7936]
Aldo Dacco Award [4119]
Felice de Carli Award [4120]
Essar Gold Medal [3593]
A.Y. Fersman Prize [5797]
Sir Padamji Ginwala Gold Medal [3594]
Gold Medal
    Brazilian Metallurgy and Materials Associa-
        tion [1756]
    Italian Association for Metallurgy [4121]
Gratitude Medal [3005]
Dr. Paul Grunfeld Commemorative Award [3006]
Hindustan Zinc Gold Medal [3595]
Historical Metallurgy Society Grants [7796]
Honorary Fellowship [7937]
Honorary Member [3596]
Robert Horne Memorial Lecture [9280]
Italian Association for Metallurgy Awards [4122]
O. P. Jindal Gold Medal [3597]
D.S. Korzhinskii Prize [5817]
Lessing Medal [8360]
Lifetime Achievement Award [3598]
Eugenio Lubatti Award [4123]
Marston Award [7938]
McPherson Memorial Lecture [7939]
MECON Award [3599]
N.V. Mel'nikov Prize [5835]
Metallurgist of the Year Award [3600]

Prix et medaille Georges Millot [2220]
Mining Analyst of the Year [6832]
J.B. Nakarmi Metalwork Award [4633]
National Metallurgist of the Year [3601]
Papers and Publications Committee Prizes [8361]
Ron Parrott Award [762]
Platinum Medal [3602]
Quality Awards [3603]
Reden Badge [3007]
Rolling Trophy [3604]
Sail Gold Medal [3605]
N.B. Sen Medal and Prize [3606]
Service Award [763]
Silver Medal [1757]
S.S. Smirnov Prize [5860]
SMS-DEMAG Excellence Award [3607]
Steel Eighties Award [3608]
Oliver Stubbs Medal [7833]
Tata Gold Medal [3609]
Travel Award [8362]
Young Metallurgist of the Year Award [3610]

Minority groups see Ethnic affairs

Monument restoration

Conservation Grants [3876]
Gazzola Prize [2516]
Fritz Schumacher Prize [3207]

Motion pictures see Films

Motorcycle racing

Best Paper Award [3761]
Best Performing National Committee Award [3762]
Best Performing Workbody Award [3763]
Fair Play Trophy [6408]
Gold Medal [6409]
Motorcycling Merit Diploma [6410]
WatSave Awards [3764]
World Motorcycle Championships [6411]

Museums

Colin Ford Award [8899]
Multimedia and Publication Design Awards [881]
Museum Prize [2352]

Music see also Conducting; Music competitions;
Music composition; Music education; Musical
instruments; Musicology; Opera; Performing
arts; Recording industry; specific types of
music, e.g. Choral music

Emily Anderson Prize for Violin [8884]
Arts Council of Northern Ireland Funding and
    Awards [6749]
Australian Country Music Industry Achiever
    Awards [675]
Award for Keyboard [8553]
Award for Strings [8554]
Balvenie Medal [7446]
Barbados Music Awards [1392]
Sir John Barbirolli Memorial Scholarship [8885]
Friedrich Baur Prize [2704]
Emil Berlanda Preis [1195]
Leslie Boosey Award [8886]
BRIT Awards [7171]
Irene Brown Memorial Prize [8555]
E.T. Bryant Memorial Prize [8084]
Callaway Doctoral Award [549]
Prix Hercule Catenacci [2471]
Classical Music Awards [472]
Country Music Awards of Australia [676]
Phillip Cranshaw Memorial Prize [8556]
Dublin Prize [1111]
Aquileo J. Echeverria Prize [1857]
Edison Classical Music Award [4664]
Edison Jazz/World Music Awards [4665]
Edison Popular Music Awards [4666]
Emma Awards [2118]
Excellence Award for Music Libraries [8085]
Pamela Faulkner Award for Singers [8557]
Fellowship of the Australian Society for Music Educa-
    tion [550]
Festival dei Popoli [4080]
Gen Foundation Awards [7716]
Ghana Music Awards [3251]

Glenfiddich Trophy [7447]
Gold Medal
    Guildhall School of Music and Drama [7779]
    Royal Philharmonic Society [8887]
Gold Medal and First Prize [8558]
Golden Harp [4658]
Golden Sail Most Performed Works Award [5240]
Golden Sail Music Awards [5241]
Grand Prix [2634]
Grand Prix de la Musique Symphonique [2628]
Grand Prix de l'Edition Musicale [2629]
Grand Prix du Disque Frederic Chopin [5387]
Sir Charles Grove Prizes [8339]
Hall of Fame Award [5242]
Honorary Member [8888]
Icelandic Music Awards [3421]
Impact of Music on Film Competition [1516]
International Music Award [2555]
Julius Isserlis Scholarship [8889]
Japan Gold Disk Awards [4318]
Junior Carnival Awards [6623]
Junior Eurovision Song Contest [6276]
Len Lickorish Memorial Prize [8559]
Mary Lindgren Award [5008]
Literarischer Marz [3239]
Local Education Authority Music Awards [8394]
Paul Lowin Prizes [473]
Marlin Awards [1349]
McCallum Prize [8560]
Merit Awards [2116]
MIDEM Classical Awards [1295]
Mitchell Award [8561]
MPG Awards [8378]
Music Awards
    Australasian Performing Rights Association [139]
    Music Industries Association - England [8376]
    Royal Philharmonic Society [8890]
Music Grants [2109]
Muuvi Awards [2119]
New Zealand Society Prize [8562]
NSW Premier's Translation Prize [907]
C. B. Oldman Prize [8086]
Olympiart [6413]
PCAM Music Award [8505]
Polar Music Prize [6164]
Pop Award [4659]
Postgraduate Performance Awards [8381]
Praemium Imperiale [4262]
Premio Nacional de Artes Musicales [1823]
Premio Tenco [4044]
President of the Republic Youth Prize in Classical
    Music [58]
Prince of Asturias Award for the Arts [6089]
Prix Nouveau Talent [2636]
Producers Guild Fellowship Award [8379]
Professional Development Awards [140]
Promotional Prizes [3138]
Reggae Academy Awards [4202]
St. Lucia Music Awards [5899]
Rolf Schock Prizes [6185]
Scholarships of the City of Munich [3139]
Screen Music Awards [141]
Senior Carnival Awards [6624]
Song of the Year [142]
Leonie Sonning Music Prize [1993]
Jakob Stainer Preis [1196]
Audrey Strange Memorial Prize [8563]
Sussex Prize [8564]
Lionel Tertis International Viola Festival and Competi-
    tion [7571]
Tiroler Landespreis fur Kunst [1197]
Donald Tovey Memorial Prize [9428]
TRIC Awards [9368]
Lorna Viol Memorial Prize [8565]
Ernst von Siemens Music Prize [3235]
W.S. Gwynn Williams Award [9440]
The Wolf Prizes [4001]
Young Composer of Dyfed [9504]

Music competitions see also Opera; Piano
competitions; Violin competitions; Vocal music

The Ammies, African Music Awards [6721]
Emily Anderson Prize for Violin [8884]
Award for Keyboard [8553]
Award for Strings [8554]
British Music Society Awards [7137]

Irene Brown Memorial Prize [8555]
Maria Callas Grand Prix for Opera [3267]
Concertino Prague International Radio Competition
   for Young Musicians [1930]
Coupe Mondiale International Competition for Ac-
   cordionists [4951]
Phillip Cranshaw Memorial Prize [8556]
Pamela Faulkner Award for Singers [8557]
Gibraltar Festival for Young Musicians [3259]
Gold Medal and First Prize [8558]
Philip and Dorothy Green Award for Young Concert
   Artists [8338]
Improvisation Competition [8153]
International Accordion Competition [4952]
International Carillon Competition - Queen Fa-
   biola [1652]
International Chopin Piano Competition, Darms-
   tadt [2748]
International Harp Contest in Israel [3955]
International Hilde Zadek Vocal Competition [1324]
International Joseph Haydn Chamber Music Compe-
   tition [1325]
International Karl Scheit Guitar Competition [1326]
International Robert Schumann Choral Competi-
   tion [3157]
International Villa-Lobos Guitar Competition [1770]
Interpretation Competition [8154]
Lily Laskine Harp Competition [2508]
Robert Levins Festspillfond [5120]
Maldives Breakout Festival [4555]
Mathy Awards [524]
Douglas May Award [8155]
McCallum Prize [8560]
Mitchell Award [8561]
New Zealand Society Prize [8562]
Carl Nielsen International Music Competitions [1975]
Carl Nielsen International Organ Competition [1989]
Sigbjorn Bernhoft Osas Festspillfond [5122]
Michele Pittaluga International Classical Guitar
   Competition - City of Alessandria Award [4151]
Prague Spring International Music Competi-
   tion [1928]
Premio Paolo Borciani - International String Quartet
   Competition [4157]
Queen Elisabeth International Music Competition of
   Belgium [1575]
Franz Schubert and Modern Music International
   Competition [1321]
Seoul International Music Festival Awards [5473]
Student Competition for Overseas Music Study
   Award [5474]
Lionel Tertis International Viola Festival and Competi-
   tion [7571]
Tokyo International Music Competition [4297]
Lorna Viol Memorial Prize [8565]
World Music Contest, Kerkrade [4843]
Young Concert Artists Trust Award [9506]
Young Performers Awards [1082]

Music composition

Tadeusz Baird Memorial Competition for Young Com-
   posers [5401]
Don Banks Music Award [167]
Sir John Barbirolli Memorial Scholarship [8885]
Besancon International Competition of Music Compo-
   sition [2418]
Gerda and Gunter Bialas Award [2705]
Prix Georges Bizet [2138]
Leslie Boosey Award [8467]
British Academy Television Awards [6932]
Prix Arthur DeGreef [1588]
Eurovision Song Contest [6274]
Prix Irene Fuerison [1590]
Grand Prix de la Chanson Francaise [2627]
Grand Prix du Jazz [2632]
International Carillon Composition Contest [1653]
International Composition Prize [4499]
International Mozart Competition [1319]
Korean Composition Awards [5472]
Prix Hector Lefuel [2144]
Witold Lutoslawski International Composers Compe-
   tition [5415]
Music Awards [8890]
Music Grants [2109]
Music Prize [1979]
Operasangerinnen Fanny Elstas Fond [5121]

Orange British Academy Film Awards [6933]
PCU Award [5402]
Prix Ars Electronica - International Competition for
   Cyberarts [1203]
Queen Elisabeth International Music Competition of
   Belgium [1575]
Harold Smart Competition [8911]
Leonie Sonning Music Prize [1993]
Swiss Music Edition [6506]
Young Composer Award [4769]
Young Composer of Dyfed [9504]
Maurice Yvain Prize [2637]

Music education

Callaway Doctoral Award [549]
Fellowship of the Australian Society for Music Educa-
   tion [550]
Leo Kestenberg Medal [3026]
Philip Morris Art Award [7783]
VDS-Media Award [3027]

Musical instruments

Award for Strings [8554]
Sir John Barbirolli Memorial Scholarship [8885]
Golden Viola Clef [4925]
Honorary Membership [4926]
Len Lickorish Memorial Prize [8559]
National Crafts Competition [3922]
Silver Viola Clef [4927]
Sussex Prize [8564]

Musicology

Derek Allen Prize [6919]
Dent Medal [8875]
Music Grants [2109]
PCU Award [5402]

Mycology

Applied Plant Pathology Award [5741]
Best Research Paper [3691]
Prof. S.N. Dasgupta Memorial Lecture [3692]
E.M. Doidge Memorial Lecture [5742]
Fellow of Indian Phytopathological Society [3693]
Inqaba Molecular Biology Prize [5745]
Jeersannidhi Award Lecture [3694]
K.C. Mehta and Manoranjan Mitra Award [3695]
K.P.V. Menon Best Poster Paper Award [3696]
John and Petakin Mildenhall Award [5746]
A.P. Misra Lifetime Achievement Award [3697]
Mundkur Memorial Lecture Award [3698]
Prof. M.J. Narasimhan Academic Merit Award Con-
   test [3699]
Pannar Seed Floating Trophy [5747]
Prof. M.K. Patel Memorial Young Scientist
   Award [3700]
Prof. M.S. Pavgi Award Lecture [3701]
Publicity Award [5749]
Travel Sponsorships for Young Scientists [3702]
J.E. Vanderplank Award [5750]
J.E. Vanderplank Lecture [5751]

Mystery writing

Ned Kelly Awards for Crime Writing [678]

Mythology

Prix Le Fevre-Deumier de Ports [2267]

National security

Prix Lamb [2214]
Prix Science et Defense [2433]

Natural history see Science

Natural science see Science

Nature

Award for Conservation Merit [6569]
Professor Blodwen Lloyd Binns Prize [7741]
Duke of Edinburgh Conservation Medal [6570]
Marsh Award for Conservation Biology [9510]

Nature photography

British Wildlife Photography Awards [7300]
Underwater Photo Competition [6646]

Naval architecture see Naval engineering

Naval engineering

Samuel Baxter Prize [8863]
Calder Prize [8864]
Challenger Medal [7356]
Denny Medal [7890]
William Froude Medal [8865]
Froude Research Scholarship in Naval Architec-
   ture [8866]
Stanley Gray Award - Branch Certificate [7892]
Stanley Gray Silver Medal [7893]
Donald Maxwell Award [7894]
Prix Plumey [2230]
Small Craft Group Medal [8867]
Kevin Stark Memorial Award [806]
Wakenham Prize [8868]
Sir William White Scholarship [8869]

Navigation

Asia Awards [8319]
Prix Binoux, Henri de Parville, Jean-Jaques Berger,
   Remlinger [2183]
Eagle Awards [6346]
Global Awards [8320]
Greek Shipping Awards [8321]
Honorary Fellow [8857]
Italian Shipping Awards [8322]
Middle East and Indian Subcontinent Awards [8323]
Navigation Distinction [2011]
De Paepe-Willems Award [1545]
Royal Institute of Navigation Fellowship [8858]
Turkish Shipping Awards [8324]

Neurology

Lucien Appel Prize [1508]
BNS Travel Grants [1412]
Boehringer Ingelheim FENS Research Award [2882]
A.W. Campbell Award [477]
Eckert and Ziegler Abstract Award [1233]
EJN Award [2883]
EJN Young Investigator Award [2884]
Gray Matter Medal [7222]
Gordon Holmes Prize [9096]
International Eppendorf and *Science* Prize for Neu-
   robiology [2792]
Kavli Prize in Neuroscience [5141]
Nina Kondelos Prize [478]
Otto Loewi Award [1208]
Membership Awards [6433]
Amrut Mody Unichem Prize [3553]
Franz Nissl Young Investigator Award [8216]
Paxinos-Watson Prize [479]
Research Fellowship for Young Investigators [1413]
Schilling Research Award [2969]
Sir Grafton Elliot Smith Award [480]
Spiegel-Wycis Award [4353]
Istvan Tork Prize [481]
Young Scientist Award
   International Society for Neurochemistry [836]
   International Society for Neuroimaging in Psychia-
      try [6434]

Newspapers see Journalism

Non-destructive testing see Testing

Nonfiction

Book Awards [5953]
Book Prize [7230]
Festival Awards for Literature [1044]
Louis Hiemstra Prize for Non-fiction [5631]
Calvin and Rose G. Hoffman Prize for Distinguished
   Publication on Christopher Marlowe [8274]
Inside Write Awards [8479]
BBC Samuel Johnson Prize for Non-Fiction [6900]
Magarey Medal [96]
E.H. McCormick Best First Book Award for Non-Fic-
   tion [5012]
New South Wales Premier's Literary Awards [906]
Eve Pownall Award for Information Books [651]
Prize for Mountain Literature [6889]
Prize for Non-Fiction [1690]
Prize for Science Writing [1065]

Royal Society Winton Prizes for Science
Books [8946]
Lilian Ida Smith Award [5015]
Strega Prize [4155]
Wales Book of the Year Awards [6676]
Whitfield Book Prize [8808]

Nuclear disarmament see World peace

Nuclear engineering see also Atomic energy

AINSE Awards [400]
Australian Nuclear Association Annual Award [483]
Gold Medal [401]
International Conference Award [8424]
Karl-Winnacker-Preis [2916]
Post Graduate Research Awards [402]
Rutherford Medal and Prize [7922]

Numismatics

Blunt Prize [7144]
Bronze Medal [485]
Prix Edmond Drouin [2155]
Prix Duchalais [2156]
Prix Roman et Tania Ghirshman [2161]
Gold Medal and Fellowship of the Society [486]
North Book Prize [7145]
Jeffrey North Medal for Service [7146]
John Sanford Saltus Gold Medal [7147]
Silver Medal and Associate Fellowship of the Society [487]
Prix Victor Tourneur [1619]

Nursing

His Excellency Mr. Jawad S. Al-Arrayed Prize [1351]
Rafida Bint Saad Al-Aslamiya Prize [1352]
Ibn Al-Nafees Prize [1357]
Ommaya Qurabi Al-Tajer Prize [1359]
Fatima Al-Zayani Prize [1361]
DermaTech Educational Award [326]
Ego Nurses Fellowship [327]
Galderma Research/Literature Award [328]
Consuelo Gomez Arabit Award for Excellence in
Perioperative Nursing [5348]
Her Highness Shaikha Hessa Prize [1363]
J and J Award [7814]
National Research Grants and Scholarships [989]
Florence Nightingale Medal [6369]
NISO Safety Representative of the Year
Award [3900]
Nursing Service Cross [318]
Occupational Health Practitioner of the Year [5722]
Ishaq bin Omran Prize [1364]
Christiane Reimann Prize [6372]
Royal Red Cross [7351]
Patricia Slater Award [990]
Stiefel Clinical Practice Award [329]

Nutrition

Danone International Prize for Nutrition [2358]
B. C. Guha Memorial Lecture [3714]
Journalist Prize [3017]
Hans Adolf Krebs Prize [3018]
Prix du Docteur et de Madame Henri Labbe [2212]
Julius Lewkowitsch Memorial Lecture [9287]
Premio Nacional de Ciencia y Tecnologia de Alimentos [4583]
Max Rubner Prize [3019]
Dr. Juan Salcedo Jr. Memorial Lecture [5346]

Occupational health

Bedford Award [7149]
Thomas Bedford Memorial Prize [7150]
Ned Franklin Medal [7962]
Malcolm Harrington Prize [9094]
David Hickish Award [7151]
Working for a Healthier Workplace - The Peter
Isaac Award [7152]
Ted King Award [7153]
Sector Awards [8962]

Occupational safety

Excellence Awards [7175]
Ned Franklin Medal [7962]
Lifetime Achievement Award [8051]

Sector Awards [8962]

Occupational therapy see Rehabilitation and therapy

Oceanography

Allen International Student Travel Award [456]
Cath Allen Prize [7355]
W. S. Bruce Medal [9062]
Albert Defant Medaille [2762]
A.A. Grigorev Prize [5803]
Norman Heaps Prize [7357]
Peter Holloway Oceanography Prize [457]
S.O. Makarov Prize [5829]
Prix des Sciences de la Mer de l'Ifremer [2219]
Prix et medaille Georges Millot [2220]
Fridtjof Nansen Medal [2375]
Prix de la Belgica [1641]
Research Medal [1017]
F.P. Savarenskii Prize [5852]

Oil painting see Painting

Oncology see Cancer

Opera see also Vocal music

Maria Callas Grand Prix for Opera [3267]
Boris Christoff International Competition for Young
Opera Singers [1793]
Bernhard Harms Prize [3111]
Long Service Awards [8396]
Mathy Awards [524]
Music Awards [8890]
Neue Stimmen International Singing Competition [2735]
Laurence Olivier Awards [9324]
Split Summer Festival [1867]

Operations research

Distinguished Principal Founding Member [1289]
Distinguished Service Medal [1402]
Doctoral Dissertation Award [1403]
EURO Doctoral Dissertation Award [1408]
Excellence in Practice Award [1404]
Gold Medal [1405]
Hodgson Prize [8609]
Honorary Scholar [1290]
Management Science Strategic Innovation
Prize [1406]
Peccei Scholarship [1291]

Ophthalmology

AMD Award [2971]
Mohamed el Aswad Prize [2020]
Adham Ayoub Prize [2021]
College Medal [962]
Dalov's Award [1791]
Distinguished Service Award [963]
Salwa Eid Prize [2022]
Yehia El-Gammal Prize [2023]
Amin El-Maghrabi Prize [2024]
Ahmed Abdel-Reheim Fahmy Prize [2025]
Glaucoma Research Award [2972]
Junior Award [2859]
Kamel Sabri Kamel Prize [2026]
Sabri Kamel Prize [2027]
Leonard Klein Award [2973]
M. Abdel Moneim Labib Prize [2028]
Meritorious Service Award [964]
Ibrahim Ahmed Mohamed Prize [2029]
Ophthalmological Gold Medal [2030]
Research Award for Innovative Work in Anterior-
Segment Surgery [2974]
Research Promotion for Innovative Work in Treating
Glaucoma With Medication [2975]
Retinitis Pigmentosa Research Award for Prevention
of Blindness [2976]
Wedad Saeed Prize [2031]
Mohamed Sobhi Prize [2032]

Optics

ICO/ICTP Gallieno Denardo Award [6054]
Satgur Prasad-Prag Parmeshwari Devi Memorial
Award [3774]

EOS Prize [2845]
Galileo Galilei Award [6055]
ICO-ICTP Gallieno Denardo Award [4010]
International Commission for Optics Prize [6056]
IUPAP Young Scientist Prize in Optics [6057]
Optical Society of India Award [3775]
D.S. Rozhdestvenskii Prize [5850]
Harbans Singh Memorial Award [3776]
Vision Scientist Memorial Fund [6725]
Thomas Young Medal and Prize [7926]

Optometry

Da Vinci Award [7029]
Dallos Award [7030]
EFCLIN Award [7614]
Laureate Award [7615]
SCO Prizes [6678]
Technology Award [7616]

Orchestral conducting see Conducting

Organizational service

Harry M. Ballantyne Award [6574]
Corporate Citizenship Award [4617]
Corporate Social Responsibility Awards [4605]
National Customer Service Awards [9410]

Oriental culture see Asian studies; Japanese culture

Ornithology

Conservation Follow-up Awards [7476]
Conservation Leadership Award [7477]
Foerderpreis der Werner-Sunkel-Stiftung [2980]
Future Conservationist Awards [7478]
Godman-Salvin Medal [7157]
Ibis Award [7158]
Jubilee Medal [7287]
Allen Keast Research Award [1551]
Stuart Leslie Bird Research Award [630]
Alfred Newton Lecture [7159]
Ornithologen-Preis [2981]
Preis der Horst Wiehe-Stiftung [2982]
Kate Stokes Award [7479]
Erwin-Stresemann-Foerderung [2983]
Bernard Tucker Medal [7288]
Union Medal [7160]

Orthodontistry

Beautiful E-line Award [4264]
Maurice Berman Prize [7162]
Chapman Prize Essay [7163]
Distinguished Teacher Award [7620]
Ernest Sheldon Friel Memorial Lecture [7621]
Grants to Eastern Europeans [7622]
W. J. B. Houston Research Awards [7623]
Houston Research Scholarship [7164]
Journal of Orthodontics Scientific Paper of the
Year [7165]
Northcroft Lectureship [7166]
Poster Award [7625]
Research and Audit Poster Prizes [7167]
Research Grants [7626]
Gunter Russell Prize [7168]
Beni Solow Award [7627]
Laurence Usiskin Student Elective Prize [7169]

Orthopedics

Oral Presentation Awards [1556]
Poster Awards [1557]

Packaging

Design Award [6474]
Environmental Packaging Awards [5029]
National Training Awards [7177]
Packaging Gravure Awards [2850]
Pro Carton/ECMA Awards [6475]
Tubes of the Year [2869]
UK Company of the Year [7178]

Painting see also Watercolor painting

Prix Jos Albert [1581]
Alufoil Trophy [2796]

Paleontology

Archibald Prize [78]
Prix Paul Artot [1582]
Prix Claude Berthault [2137]
BP Portrait Award [8402]
BP Young Artist Award [8403]
Prix Jeanne Burdy [2470]
Prix Gustave Camus [1584]
Prix Charles Caty [1586]
Prix Emma du Cayla-Martin [1587]
Prix Alphonse Cellier [2140]
De Laszlo Medal [8969]
Prix Louise Dehem [1589]
Portia Geach Memorial Award [1085]
Governor-General Art Award [4949]
Prix Rene Janssens [1592]
Jerwood Drawing Prize [8454]
Prix Hector Lefuel [2144]
Prix Constant Montald [1595]
Praemium Imperiale [4262]
Prix de Rome - Visual Arts [4811]
Prix Emile Sacre [1598]
St. Cuthbert's Mill Award for Works on Paper [8970]
Sir John Sulman Prize [79]
Summer Exhibition Awards [8570]
The Wolf Prizes [4001]
Charles Wollaston Award [8571]
The Wynne Prize [80]

Paleontology *see Geology and paleontology*

Paper industry *see also Forestry; Wood and wood products*

L. R. Benjamin Medal [74]
Johan Gullichsen Prize [2094]
C.J. Jansson Prize [2095]
Georg Jayme Denkmunze [2702]
Metso Paper Mechanical Pulping Award [2097]

Parachuting *see Flying*

Parenting *see Family relations*

Park planning *see also City planning*

Ian Galloway Memorial Cup [4996]

Parks *see Recreation*

Patents *see Inventions*

Pathology

Otto Appel Medal [2985]
Jean Bernard Lifetime Achievement Award [4701]
Jose Carreras Award [4702]
Gold-Headed Cane [4350]
Gold Medal [2624]
P.H. Gregory Prize [7235]
I.I. Mechnikov Prize [5834]
Pathology Section President's Prize [9105]
Research Grant [2625]
Gordon Signy Foreign Fellowship [4351]

Patriotism *see Citizenship and patriotism*

Peace *see World peace*

Pediatrics

Adolescent Health Care Award in memory of Dr. Kathy Phipps [8672]
Henning Andersen Prizes [7637]
Adalbert Czerny Preis [3021]
Tim David Prize [9088]
Dr. H. B. Dingley Memorial Award [3544]
Gold Medal [7644]
Otto Heubner Preis [3022]
Hormone Research Prize [7638]
Jacques Lefebvre Award [7645]
Outstanding Clinician Award [7639]
Poster Award [7646]
Andrea Prader Prize [7640]
President Award [7647]
Research Award [7641]
Schweisguth Prize [6448]
SIOP Awards [6449]
Young Investigator Award [7642]

Young Researcher Award [7648]

Performing arts *see also Ballet; Choreography; Costume design; Dance; Drama; Entertainment; Music; Puppetry; Theater*

Arts Council of Northern Ireland Funding and Awards [6749]
Friedrich Baur Prize [2704]
British Academy Television Awards [6932]
Circus Maniacs Awards [7427]
Hamilton Deane Award [7525]
Export Award [4657]
Gawad Alab ng Haraya (Alab ng Haraya Awards)- [5340]
International Robert Schumann and Piano and Song Competition [3156]
Live Awards [9393]
Music Prize [1979]
NSW Premier's Translation Prize [907]
Orange British Academy Film Awards [6933]
PCU Award [5402]
Silver Harp [4660]
Unicycling Awards [7428]

Perfumes *see Cosmetology*

Personal achievement *see Professional and personal achievement*

Personal finance *see Financial planning*

Personnel management *see also Employment practices; Training and development*

AHRI/The CEO Institute Business Leadership Awards [372]
Best HR Projects in Estonia [2049]
Best Potential in HR Management [2050]
Erehwon Award for Innovative HR Initiatives [3474]
HR Leadership Awards [373]
HR Student of the Year [374]
Organisational Awards [375]
Personnel Today Awards [8469]

Pest control *see Public health*

Petroleum engineering

Nigel Anstey Award [4674]
Guido Bonarelli Award [4675]
Louis Cagniard Award [4676]
Environment Award [494]
Lorand Eotvos Award [4677]
Desiderius Erasmus Award [4678]
Norman Falcon Award [4679]
Life Membership Award [4680]
Ludger Mintrop Award [4681]
JN Pierce Award for Media Excellence [495]
Safety Awards [496]
Reg Sprigg Medal [497]
Lewis G. Weeks Gold Medal [498]
Alfred Wegener Award [4684]

Petroleum industry

BTEC Advanced Certificate in Expedition Management [9193]
BTEC Advanced Certificate in Tropical Habitat Conservation [9194]
Dewhurst Lecture and Award [9489]
Environment Award [494]
Excellence Awards [9490]
Greenland Prospector and Developer of the Year [3325]
I.M. Gubkin Prize [5804]
H. E. Jones London Medal [8043]
Prof. M.L. Khorana Memorial Award [3677]
Organic Petrology Award [6059]
JN Pierce Award for Media Excellence [495]
Safety Awards [496]
Prof. M.L. Schroff Award [3679]
Reg Sprigg Medal [497]
Sugg Heritage Award [8046]
Thiessen Medal [6060]
Lewis G. Weeks Gold Medal [498]

Pets *see Animal care and training*

Pharmacology

Akabori Memorial Award [4287]
Abu Rayhan Al-Bayronni Prize [1353]
Dr. Nitya Anand Endowment Lecture [3619]
Award for Divisional Scientific Contributions [4309]
Award for Divisional Scientific Promotions [4310]
Award for Drug Discovery [9199]
Award for Drug Research and Development [4311]
Award for Young Investigator [4288]
Award for Young Scientists [4312]
Andre Bedat Award [4754]
Best Paper Award [6140]
Best Paper Awards [3675]
Professor K.P. Bhargava Memorial Medal [3625]
Bionorica Phytoneering Award [3174]
Fred J. Boyd Award [1040]
Chung-Wae Award [5468]
Distinguished Practice Award [4756]
Distinguished Science Award [4757]
Julije Domac Medal [1869]
Ehrennadel der Deutschen Apotheker [2879]
Eminent Pharmacist Award [3676]
Farmindustria Awards for Pharmacological Research [4141]
FARMOVS Prize for Pharmacology and Medicine Development [5628]
Fellowship of the Pharmacy Society of South Africa [5593]
FIP Fellowships [4759]
Prix Leon et Henri Fredericq [1632]
Honorary Member [4760]
Host-Madsen Medal [4761]
Albert Howells Award [7471]
JPS Award [4289]
Prix de Biologie Alfred Kastler [2443]
Lifetime Achievement Award
  Indian Pharmaceutical Association [3678]
  Pharmaceutical Society of Australia [927]
Lifetime Achievement in the Pharmaceutical Practice Award [4762]
Lifetime Achievement in the Pharmaceutical Science Award [4763]
Lister Memorial Lecture [9289]
Prix Charles Mentzer [2621]
Hans Meyer Medaille [2880]
Oswald Morton Essay Prize [9101]
New Safe Medicines Faster Award [6141]
Daramola Oluyemisi Memorial Prize [4420]
Pharmacist of the Year [928]
Pharmacy Award [6852]
Dr. D. N. Prasad Memorial Oration Award [3558]
Prix d'Encouragement a la Recherche en Chimie Therapeutique [2622]
PSJ Award [4313]
Redi Award [844]
Scheele Prize [6221]
Dr. Willmar Schwabe Award [3175]
Giorgio Segre Prize [6142]
Egon Stahl Award [3176]
Egon Stahl Award in Gold [3177]
Irma Tschudi Steiner Award [6530]
Third-Year Science Prize in Pharmacology [1153]
Young Investigator's Award [6143]
Young Pharmacist of the Year [929]
Young Scientist Award [5710]

Philanthropy

Science Prizes [1843]
Young Scientists for Rainforests [7474]

Philatelic journalism

Hunziker Medal [1259]

Philately

Award of Merit [6796]
Congress Medal [6797]
Crawford Medal [8880]
Medal for Research [6421]
Medal for Service [6422]
The Roll of Distinguished Philatelist [6798]
Tapling Medal [8881]
Tilleard Medal [8882]

Philology *see Linguistics*

Philosophy

Balzan Prizes [4086]
BP Prize Lectureship in the Humanities [9061]
Church of Iceland Film Award [3419]
Prix Victor Cousin [2251]
Prix Crouzet [2252]
Prix Polydore De Paepe [1604]
Prix Victor Delbos [2256]
Prix Demolombe [2257]
Prix Le Dissez de Penanrun [2258]
Prix Jules Duculot [1607]
Prix Estrade-Delcros [2158]
Prix Le Fevre-Deumier de Ports [2267]
Prix Gegner [2272]
Graham Medal [8892]
Kelvin Medal [8893]
Prix Charles Lambert [2278]
Prix Louis Liard [2283]
Prix Charles Lyon-Caen [2285]
Somerset Maugham Awards [9253]
G.V. Plekhanov Prize [5846]
Prix Joseph Saillet [2295]
Prix Saintour [2296]
Rolf Schock Prizes [6185]
Prix Stassart [2298]
Tom Stoppard Prize [1908]

Philosophy of science

Prix Binoux, Henri de Parville, Jean-Jaques Berger, Remlinger [2183]
Prix Grammaticakis-Neuman [2206]
James Scott Prize Lectureship [9072]

Photogrammetry

Brock Gold Medal Award [5294]
Gino Cassinis Award [5295]
The CATCON Prizes [5296]
Len Curtis Award [8538]
Eduard Dolezal Award [5297]
Samuel Gamble Award [5298]
U.V. Helava Award [5299]
Poster Paper Prize [8539]
President's Honorary Citation [5302]
Prizes for Best Papers by Young Authors [5303]
Remote Sensing and Photogrammetry Society Award [8540]
Willem Schermerhorn Award [5304]
Schwidefsky Medal [5305]
Student Awards [8541]
Taylor and Francis Best Letter Award [8542]
E. H. Thompson Award [8543]
Otto von Gruber Award [5306]
Wang Zhizhuo Award [5308]

Photography *see also* Nature photography; Photogrammetry; Photojournalism; Slide photography

AIPS Awards [6455]
Assistants Awards [6839]
Chrisi Bailey Award [6744]
Black and White Spider Awards [6885]
British Academy Television Awards [6932]
Centenary Medal [8895]
Commercial Photographer of the Year [413]
Communicators in Business Awards [7878]
Contemporary Book Award [2598]
Davies Medal [8896]
Prix de Boelpaepe [1623]
Discovery Award [2599]
Terence Donovan Award [8897]
Falklands Conservation Wildlife Photo Competition [7668]
Falklands Exposed! [2056]
Fenton Medal [8898]
Colin Ford Award [8899]
Governor-General Art Award [4949]
Highest Scoring Print of the Year Award [414]
Historical Book Award [2600]
Honorary Fellowship [8900]
Hood Medal [8901]
International Visual Communications Association Awards [8250]
J. Dudley Johnston Award [8902]
Cherry Kearton Medal and Award [8794]
Kodak Media Photography Award [4984]

Landscape Photographer of the Year [415]
Lumiere Award [8903]
Member's Award [8904]
National Calendar Awards [7176]
National Photographic Competition [2066]
Vic Odden Award [8905]
Open Category Award [416]
Orange British Academy Film Awards [6933]
Photographer of the Year Award [7077]
Photographers Awards [6840]
Photographic Competition [8399]
PIC Award [8473]
Portrait Photographer of the Year [417]
Prix de Rome - Visual Arts [4811]
Prix Pictet [7331]
Professional Photographer of the Year [418]
Progress Medal [8906]
Royal Colleges Medal [8907]
Saxby Award [8908]
Scottish Salon of Photography [9173]
Selwyn Award [8909]
Sports Photographer of the Year [9363]
Student Photographer of the Year [419]
Students Awards [6841]
Taylor Wessing Photographic Portrait Prize [8404]
Travel Photo of the Year Competition [9437]
World Cup [2413]
Young Photographer Awards [8967]

Photojournalism

Austrian Prize for Press Photography [1200]
The Walkley Awards [1176]
World Press Photo Contest [4849]

Physical education

Philip Noel Baker Research Award [3062]
Sport Science Award of the IOC President [3063]
Undergraduate Dissertation of the Year Award [6973]
UNESCO Award for Distinguished Services to Physical Education and Sport [2656]

Physical fitness *see* Health and fitness

Physical medicine *see* Rehabilitation and therapy

Physical science

Anil Kumar Bose Memorial Award [3630]
Bruce-Preller Prize Lectureship [9063]
Caledonian Research Foundation Prize Lectureship in Biomedical Sciences and Arts and Letters [9065]
Antonio Feltrinelli Prizes [4022]
Honorary Membership [4729]
R.J.W. Le Fevre Memorial Prize [182]
M.V. Lomonosov Great Gold Medal [5827]
MakDougall-Brisbane Prize [9069]
Outstanding Book and/or Monograph Awards [5361]
Outstanding Scientific Paper Award [5362]
Outstanding Young Scientist Award [5363]
Eduardo A. Quisumbing Medal for Basic Research [5367]
Science Communicator Award [4956]
Scottish Science Award [9156]
S. N. Seshadri Memorial Instrumentation Award [3689]
Sorby Medal [4731]

Physical therapy *see* Rehabilitation and therapy

Physics

Academician H. Abdullayev Award [1335]
Prix Anatole et Suzanne Abragam [2174]
Accelerator Prize [2387]
Hannes Alfven Prize [2388]
Gregori Aminoff Prize [6182]
Prix Ampere d'Electricite de France [2176]
Appleton Prize [1563]
Prix Louis Armand [2177]
L.A. Artsimovich Prize [5785]
Prof. Rango Krishna Asundi Memorial Lecture [3621]
Award for Best Thesis Presentation in Solid State Physics [3681]
Award for Outstanding Service to Physics in Australia [407]

Award for Promotion of Physics [5404]
Award for the Teaching of Physics [6103]
Award in Environmental Physics [2017]
Award in Nuclear and Particle Physics [2018]
Prof. C.V.K. Baba Award for Best Thesis Presentation in Nuclear Physics [3682]
A.A. Belopol'skii [5789]
Berthold Leibinger Innovation Prize [2737]
Best Poster Paper Awards [5293]
Homi Jehangir Bhabha Medal [3624]
Grzegorz Bialkowski Prize [5405]
R. D. Birla Award [3684]
Walter Boas Medal [408]
N.N. Bogoliubov Gold Medal [5791]
Max Born Medal and Prize [7900]
Max Born Prize [2772]
Satyendranath Bose Medal [3629]
Bragg Gold Medal for Excellence in Physics [409]
Bragg Medal and Prize [7901]
Prix Edmond Brun [2184]
Business and Innovation Medal [7902]
Buti Foundation Award [3685]
Fridrihs Canders Prize [4435]
Sadi Carnot Young Researcher Award [2530]
Willis H. Carrier Young Researcher Award [2532]
Prix L. La Caze, A. Policart-Lacassagne [2187]
Chadwick Medal and Prize [7903]
P.A. Cherenkov Prize [5795]
Murli M. Chugani Memorial Award for Excellence in Applied Physics [3686]
CISRA Prize in Physics [1109]
Prix du Commisariat a l'Energie Atomique [2190]
E. R. Cooper Memorial Medal and Prize [5072]
Marie Curie Medal [1494]
Prix Theophile de Donder [1624]
Prix Ernest Dechelle [2194]
Prix Deslandres [2195]
Dirac Medal
 Abdus Salam International Centre for Theoretical Physics [4009]
 Institute of Physics [7904]
Dwight Prize in Physics [1116]
Early Achievement Award [570]
Europhysics Prize [2389]
Experimental Physics Control Systems Prize [2390]
Faraday Medal [7905]
Fellowship Awards [6631]
V.A. Fok Prize [5799]
Prix Fonde par l'Etat [2201]
Founders' Prize [7928]
Jack Fowler Award [1495]
Francqui Prize [1527]
Franklin Medal and Prize [7906]
A.M. Fridman Prize [5800]
Gabor Medal and Prize [7907]
Prix Gaz de France [2204]
GEC-ESTRO Iridium Award [1496]
Pierre Gilles de Gennes Prize [2468]
Glazebrook Medal [7908]
Gold Medal [571]
Gribov Medal [2391]
Otto-Hahn-Preis fur Chemie und Physik [2773]
Vernon Harrison Annual Doctoral Prize [7268]
Hartle Awards [8226]
Hartnett-Irvine Award [6632]
Gustav Hertz Prize [2774]
Viktor Hess Preis [1210]
High Energy and Particle Physics Prize [2392]
High School Physics Prize [4975]
Gilles Holst Medal [4829]
Holweck Medal and Prize [7909]
Honorary Member [5300]
Honorary Membership
 Australian Society of Exploration Geophysicists [572]
 Polish Physical Society [5406]
Honorary Physicist Award [1497]
Hoyle Medal and Prize [7910]
Hughes Medal [8938]
Christiaan Huygens Science Award [4830]
ICTP Prize [4011]
A.F. Ioffe Prize [5805]
IPEM/AAPM Travel Award [7929]
Prix Jecker, Cahours, Paul Marguerite de la Charlonie, Houzeau, and J. B. Dumas [2209]
Harold Johns Medal [8157]

Physiology

Piano competitions

Placement *see Employment practices*

Planning *see also City planning; Park planning*

Plastics and rubber

Plays *see Drama; Theater*

Playwriting *see Drama*

Poetry

Police *see Law enforcement*

Polish culture

Political science *see also European integration; Foreign policy; Human relations; International relations; Legislative improvement; National security; Social science research; World peace*

Pollution control see Environmental conservation; Water conservation

Population see Demography

Poultry science

Poverty see Humanitarianism

Preventive medicine

Printed materials see Publications

Printing industry

Prints see Graphic arts

Professional and personal achievement
see also Academic achievement; Leadership

Psychiatry see also Mental health

Psychology

Zaccari Fellowship [925]

Public administration see also City
management; Government service; Historic
preservation; Planning; Public finance; Public
works

Alexis de Tocqueville Prize [4704]
Award for Best Student Essay/Report [4374]
Award for Excellence in the Teaching of Public
Administration in Africa [4375]
Award for Outstanding Contribution to Knowledge in
Public Administration and Management [4377]
Prix Odilon Barrot [2243]
Prix Edmond Freville [2270]
Giblin Lecture [200]
Gold Medal Award [4378]

Public affairs see also Community affairs;
Housing; Leadership; Legislative improvement;
Military service

Hans R. Bolliger Memorial Lecture [9272]
Richard Seligman Lecture [9295]

Public finance

Peggy and Richard Musgrave Prize [3073]
Young Economists Award [3074]

Public health

Ali Bin Al-Farabi Prize [1355]
Award for Divisional Scientific Promotions [4310]
Best Abstract Award [4709]
Buchanan Medal [8929]
Ihsan Dogramaci Family Health Foundation
Prize [6549]
Donald Mackay Medal [9117]
Premio Fundacion Alfredo Manzullo [26]
Jacques Parisot Foundation Fellowship [6552]
Population Science and Public Health Award [8076]
Dr. Comlan A. A. Quenum Prize for Public
Health [6553]
Dr. P. N. Raju Oration Award [3561]
Dr. M. K. Seshadri Prize [3568]
Dr. A. T. Shousha Foundation Prize [6555]
Prof. B. C. Srivastava Foundation Award [3571]
State of Kuwait Prize for Research in Health Promo-
tion [6556]
United Arab Emirates Health Foundation Prize [6557]
Premio Miguel Aleman Valdes [4585]

Public relations see also Advertising; Publicity

Arts and Business Awards [6734]
Gold Medal [5601]
Golden World Awards for Excellence [8174]
International Visual Communications Association
Awards [8250]
Long Service Award [5602]
National Golden Target Awards [939]
PR, Marketing and Communications Awards [6816]
PRCA Awards [8517]
President's Award [5603]
Prism Awards [5604]
Prix Herman Schoolmeesters [1615]
State Awards for Excellence [940]

Public sanitation see Sanitary engineering

Public service see also Community service;
Government service

Benemerenti Medal [9546]
Prix Bordin [2247]
British Empire Medal [7338]
Prix Rene Cassin [2249]
Croix de Guerre [2431]
EBU Award [6271]
Graduateship of the City and Guilds of London Insti-
tute [7432]
Prix de Joest [2276]
Medal for Service to the Republic [4573]
Medals for Excellence [7433]
Membership of the City and Guilds of London Insti-
tute [7434]
Most Honourable Order of the Bath [7344]
National Order of Merit [4574]
National Service Cross of the Order of Saint Lu-
cia [5895]

National Service Medal of the Order of Saint Lu-
cia [5896]
Onassis Award for the Environment [3298]
Orden al Merito Julio Garavito [1841]
Order of Australia [319]
Order of Pius [9547]
Order of St. Gregory the Great [9548]
Order of St. Michael and St. George [7346]
Order of the British Empire [7347]
Order of the Sacred Treasure [4272]
Padma Vibhushan [3499]
Prix du Baron de Joest [2167]
Public Officer of the Year [1683]
Public Service Medal [321]
Right Livelihood Award [6166]
Royal Norwegian Order of Merit [5134]
Royal Norwegian Order of St. Olav [5135]
Royal Victorian Order [7352]
Threadneedle/Spectator Parliamentarian of the Year
Awards [9357]
Prix Gabrielle Sand et Marie Guido Triossi [2237]
Twenty-Five Years Long Service Award [1684]
Hendrik Van Eck Medal [5681]

Public speaking

Lecturer Award [6044]
Ivor Spencer Best After Dinner Speaker of the
Year [7766]
T. C. White Prize Lecture [8702]

Public works

Australian Engineering Excellence Awards [767]
PTx2 Awards [1529]

Publications see also Company publications;
School publications; Travel literature

Award for Best New Journal [6829]
Awards for Editorial and Publishing Excel-
lence [7256]
Book Award [7181]
Editors of the Year Awards [7257]
Free Media Pioneer Award [1300]
Anne Keymer Prize [7047]
Malta Journalism Awards [4566]
Media Awards [7700]
Stafleu Medal [1256]

Publicity see also Advertising; Public relations

FE Cook Cup and Keliher [8519]
Zebra Awards [7540]

Publishing see also Bibliography; Book and
newspaper design; Book collecting; Editing; Illustration; Printing industry; Publications;
Typography

Advertising Sales Team of the Year [7496]
Award for Best New Journal [6829]
Award for Expanding the Retail Market [6891]
Award for Publishing Innovation [6830]
Awards for Editorial and Publishing Excel-
lence [7256]
Awards for Editorial Excellence [1954]
Best Book Awards [9516]
Best Magazine of the Year [1917]
Best Marketing of the Year [7497]
BHCA Awards [7080]
Book Design Awards [518]
Bookseller Industry Awards [6892]
British Book Design and Production Awards [7174]
Bronze Lion Award [1786]
Children's Bookseller of the Year [6893]
Children's Independent of the Year [6894]
Contemporary Book Award [2598]
Directory of the Year - Business [7498]
Directory of the Year - Consumer [7499]
International Guido Dorso Prize [4032]
European Awards for Quality and Excellence in
Directory Publishing [1440]
Golden Book Certificate [3940]
Green Initiative Award [6895]
Guild of Food Writers Award [7764]
Hegarty Prize [922]
Icelandic Literature Prize [3427]
Independent Bookseller of the Year [6896]

International Newspaper Color Quality Club
Awards [3035]
Jomo Kenyatta Prize for Literature [4388]
Knight of the Book Award [1787]
Fiona Macpherson New Editor of the Year
Award [7258]
Manager of the Year [6897]
Maori Language Award [4869]
Marcus Morris Award [8515]
The Most Beautiful and the Best Children's Books in
Slovakia [5996]
National Prize for the Most Beautiful Book [1245]
New Product of the Year [7500]
New Venture Award [9455]
New Zealand Post Book Awards [4870]
Nielsen BookData Booksellers' Choice Award [249]
Nihon Shinbun Kyokai Awards [4270]
Online Directory of the Year - Business [7501]
Online Directory of the Year - Consumer [7502]
Online Publishing Awards [9401]
Pandora Award [9456]
Platinum Book Certificate [3941]
PPC Annual Awards [8521]
PPC Quarterly Awards [8522]
Printer of the Year [7503]
Publisher of the Year [7504]
Scientific Book Award [1891]
Subscription Sales Team of the Year [7505]
Supplier of the Year [7506]
Walter Tiemann Award [2690]
Tieto-Finlandia Prize for Non-Fiction [2091]
Kim Scott Walwyn Prize [6911]
Raymond Williams Community Publishing
Prize [6746]
Young Authors' Award [3051]
Zlaty Stocek Golden Printing Block [1918]

Puppetry

Fritz Wortelmann Preis of the City of Bochum for
Amateur Puppetry [2781]

Quality control see Standards

Race relations see Ethnic affairs

Radio see also Broadcasting; Media; Television

ABU Prizes for Radio and Television Pro-
grams [4519]
Alexander the Great Award [3306]
All Malta Award [4568]
Ancient Greek Cities Award [3307]
Athenian Award [3308]
Athens Summer Olympic Games Award [3309]
Copenhagen Award [1943]
Countries Awards [9462]
Cross Country award [1944]
Danish Island Award [1945]
Danish Lighthouse Award [1946]
Danish Underground Radio Award [1947]
Diploma Mediterranean Award [4569]
Field Day Award [1948]
Graded Awards [9463]
Grand Prix [2634]
Greek Islands Award [3310]
Greenland Award [1949]
Heavenly Pilot Award [9464]
The Iceland Award [3429]
Iceland on Six Meters Award [3430]
Icelandic JOTA Award [3431]
Icelandic Radio Amateurs Award [3432]
Imison Award [9251]
IRA Zone 40 Award [3433]
Journalist Prize [3017]
The Lakes of Finland Award [2075]
Medal of Honour for Afrikaans Radio Feature Pro-
gramme [5635]
Medienpreis fur Sprachkultur [2961]
OH Awards [2076]
The OH County Award [2077]
The OHA Plaques [2078]
OHA-VHF Award [2079]
OZ Locator Award [1950]
OZ Prefix Award [1951]
Prix Ex Aequo - International Children's and Youth
Radio Drama Festival [6277]
Prix Nouveau Talent [2636]

Prize for Drama [1689]
RAAG Award [3311]
SIGNIS Award [1662]
Special Event Station Awards [9465]
TRIC Awards [9368]
Venezuelan Islands Award [9557]
The Walkley Awards [1176]
Worked All Nordic Countries Award [3434]
Worked Oscar Delta Award [4455]
ZB2 Award [7733]
ZB2BU Award [7734]

Radiology

Accuray Award [1492]
David Anderson-Berry Medal [9060]
George and Vera Ansell Poster Prize [8754]
Ellis Barnett Prize [8755]
Breur Lecture and Gold Medal Award [1493]
Marie Curie Medal [1494]
Frank Doyle Medal [8756]
Editor's Medal
  Cardiovascular and Interventional Radiological
    Society of Europe [1216]
  Royal College of Radiologists - United King-
    dom [8757]
Education Grants [1217]
Finzi Prize [9092]
Jack Fowler Award [1495]
GEC-ESTRO Iridium Award [1496]
Gold Medal
  Cardiovascular and Interventional Radiological
    Society of Europe [1218]
  European Society of Paediatric Radiology [7644]
Andreas Gruentzig Lecture [1219]
Robert and Elma Kemp Harper Prize [8758]
Honorary Physicist Award [1497]
Jacques Lefebvre Award [7645]
Nucletron Brachytherapy Award [1498]
Poster Award [7646]
Ella Preiskel Prize [8759]
President Award [7647]
Boris Rajewsky Medal [1241]
Regaud Lecture Award [1499]
Research Grant [1220]
Josef Roesch Lecture [1221]
Rolf M. Sievert Award [2559]
Sigmund's Prize [1920]
Ibn Sina Prize [1365]
Emmanuel van der Schueren Award [1500]
VARIAN-Juliana Denekamp Award [1501]
VARIAN Research Award [1502]
Professor L.R. Whittaker's Annual Prize [4425]
Young Researcher Award [7648]

Radiotherapy see Cancer

Railway transportation

Community Rail Awards [6818]
Industry Award [945]
Railway Engineering Award [001]
Student Thesis Award [946]
Webb Prize [8014]
Young Railway Engineers Award [947]

Real estate see also Construction; Housing

Ghana Property Awards [3255]
Prix d'Excellence [2561]
South East Asia Property Awards [6603]
Thailand Property Awards [6604]

Recording industry

AWIT Awards [5353]
BRIT Awards [7171]
Burkitt Medal for Biblical Studies [6921]
Certified Awards [7172]
Export Award [4657]
Gold Disc Award [5290]
Grand Prix du Disque Frederic Chopin [5387]
Platinum Disc Award [5291]
Jean Thevenot Medal [6382]

Recreation see also Hobbies and clubs

Campsite of the Year [6860]
Kite Flying Competition [6645]

Kruth Award [6239]
Sondrio International Documentary Film Festival on
  Parks [4153]
Waterford Crystal European Athlete of the Year
  Award [6269]
Young Amenity Horticulturist of the Year [5003]
Young Leisure Scholar Award [6083]

Recreation industry

Ian Galloway Memorial Cup [4996]
International Gaming Awards [8132]
Mark Mitchell Memorial Trophy [4997]
Outstanding Awards [4999]
Outstanding Contribution Award [5000]
Outstanding Research, Planning, and Policy
  Award [5001]
Paul Stuart Memorial Award [5002]

Refugees see Humanitarianism

Rehabilitation and therapy

Barbara Ansell Prize [9080]
Eric Bywaters Prize [9084]
Vona and Marie du Toit Foundation Student
  Prize [5585]
Vona du Toit Memorial Award and Lecture [5586]
Mildred Elson Award [9472]
Humanitarian Service Award [9473]
International Service Award [9474]
Leadership in Rehabilitation Award [9475]
Media Awards [590]
Recognition of Service Award [9476]
Albie Sachs Award [5588]

Religion see also Catholic literature; Christianity;
  Theology

Berakah Award [4143]
Church of Iceland Film Award [3419]
Prix Crouzet [2252]
Elmer Crowe Memorial Award [6575]
Prix Franz Cumont [1600]
Prix Eugene Goblet d'Alviella Prize [1601]
Prix Emile de Laveleye [1603]
Prix Victor Delbos [2256]
Ecumenical Prize [1661]
Prix Le Fevre-Deumier de Ports [2267]
Prix Roman et Tania Ghirshman [2161]
Gold Service Award [741]
International Paul VI Prize [4117]
International Sternberg Award [3057]
Malacological Society of London Annual
  Award [8341]
Albert Schweitzer Award [8067]
Sir Charles Maurice Yonge Award [8342]

Research see also Dental research; Educational
  research; Humanities research; Medical
  research; Research administration; Scientific
  research; Social science research

Yoshiaki Arata Award [2543]
ASSO Student Award [215]
Australian Engineering Excellence Awards [767]
Cor Baayen Award [2404]
Beale Medal [8432]
Berlyne Award [4857]
Cave Science and Technology Research Initiative
  Awards CSTRI [6997]
Copernicus Award [2991]
CRC for Polymers Prize [673]
DesCartes Prize for Collaborative, Transnational Re-
  search [1459]
Distinguished Applied Research Team [5906]
Distinguished Applied Researcher [5907]
Dufton Silver Medal [7390]
Early Career Award
  European Life Scientist Organization [2835]
  Leopoldina, the German Academy of Sci-
    ences [3121]
James Alfred Ewing Medal [7982]
Fiorini-Haardt Prize [1265]
Emilie Louise Frey Award for the Promotion of
  Talented Female Scholars [6528]
Leon Gaster Memorial Award [7391]
Geotechnical Research Medal [7983]
Goodeve Medal [8433]

John and Mary Goodyear Award [4669]
Graduate Student Award [2383]
Stanley Gray Silver Medal [7893]
Hannan Medal [178]
Honorary Fellowship [9486]
IUSSP Laureates [2582]
Junior Research Award in Gerontology [5780]
Karolinska Medical Management Centre/EHMA
  Research Award [1480]
Lawrence Memorial Grant [5772]
Gottfried Wilhelm Leibniz Prize [2992]
Lifetime Achievement Award [5574]
Lifetime Award [2910]
Heinz Maier-Leibnitz Prize [2993]
David Marsden Award [7610]
Albert Maucher Prize in Geoscience [2994]
Mellon Research Fellowship [4170]
Mid-Career Award [7661]
Moran Medal [185]
NZMS Research Award [4978]
Okuma Academic Commemorative Prize [4344]
Okuma Academic Encouragement Prize [4345]
Bill O'Sullivan Fundraiser Award [3880]
Outstanding Doctoral Research Award [1312]
Outstanding Researcher Award [5963]
Hans Ovelgonne - Purchasing Research
  Award [1284]
Sardar Patel Outstanding ICAR Institution
  Award [3530]
President's Awards [5575]
President's Medal [8434]
Prix Prestwich [2458]
Research Event Awards [588]
Research Personality of the Year [2911]
Scottish Research Book Award [9155]
Eugen and Ilse Seibold Prize [2995]
Napier Shaw Bronze Medal [7393]
Silver Jubilee Award [459]
Craig Hugh Smyth Visiting Fellowship [4171]
Stratis V. Sotirchos Memorial Lectureship [3287]
Study of the Year Award [2912]
Tool of the Year Award [2913]
Transforming the Science Cohort Award [5576]
Tsungming Tu Award [6591]
Norbert Wiener Memorial Gold Medal [9487]
Young Investigator Award [216]
Young Investigator Awards for Research in Clinical
  Microbiology and Infectious Diseases [6293]
Young Researcher Award [5964]
Young Scientist Award [8098]

Research administration

Research Award [9523]
Dioscoro L. Umali Medal for Outstanding Science
  Administrator [5369]

Restaurants

Annual Restaurant Merit Award [4594]
Continuing Education Grant [5036]
Eating and Drinking Awards [9392]
Innovator Award [5038]
Merit Scholarships for Hospitality Students [5039]
Merit Scholarships for Secondary School Stu-
  dents [5040]
Qatar Today Restaurant Awards [5437]
Tutor Work Study Grant [5041]

Retailing see Merchandising

Rhetoric see Public speaking

Riflery see Firearms; Hunting; Shooting

Rubber see Plastics and rubber

Rugby

International Coach of the Year [1026]
International Player of the Year [1027]
International Referee of the Year [1028]
Newcomer of the Year [1033]
Rookie of the Year [1029]
Rugby Medal for Excellence [1034]
Spirit of Rugby League Award [1030]
Team of the Year [1031]

Rural economics

Global Sanitation Award **[3798]**
Nestle Prize in Creating Shared Value **[6470]**
Prof. Bal Dattatraya Tilak Lecture **[3669]**

Safety *see also* *Crime prevention; Environmental health; Fire fighting; Fire prevention; Sanitary engineering; Security; specific types of safety, e.g. Aviation safety*

Hans R. Bolliger Memorial Lecture **[9272]**
Film Festival Award **[8138]**
International Rolleston Award **[8139]**
International Visual Communications Association Awards **[8250]**
Carol and Travis Jenkins Award **[8140]**
Gustave Magnel Prize **[1658]**
National Rolleston Award **[8141]**
Practical Project Award **[8052]**
Safety in Construction Medal **[8008]**
Technician Safety Practitioner Scholarship **[8053]**
Verdeyen Prize for Soil Mechanics **[1659]**

Salesmanship *see* *Marketing; Merchandising*

Sanitary engineering *see also* *Public works*

Communication Award **[1304]**
Habitat Business Award **[4395]**
Willy Hager Medal **[3166]**
Willy Hager Prize **[3167]**
Publication Award **[1305]**

Scholarly works

Best Poster Prizes **[7044]**
Cornforth Medal **[973]**
Emeritus Professor **[5956]**
Kenyon Medal for Classical Studies **[6926]**
Anne Keymer Prize **[7047]**
A.A. Phillips Prize **[97]**
C. S. Piper Prize **[981]**

School publications

PR, Marketing and Communications Awards **[6816]**

Science *see also* *History of science; Research administration; Science education; Scientific research; Technology; specific fields of science, e.g. Astronomy*

21st Anniversary Research Grants **[4888]**
Academic Prize **[4322]**
Academy Medal **[4815]**
Academy Prize **[5470]**
Achievement Awards
   National Research Council of the Philippines **[5344]**
   Worshipful Company of Scientific Instrument Makers **[9499]**
Daiwa Adrian Prizes **[7490]**
AILU Award **[6825]**
Iwan Akerman Award **[1518]**
Juan Alberto Olivares' Foundation Award **[9554]**
Joyce Allen Lecture **[198]**
AMOS Prize **[1102]**
H.G. Andrewartha Medal **[1012]**
Annual Award for Junior Researchers **[1875]**
Ansorge Bequest **[6697]**
ANZAAS Medal **[199]**
Henry E. Armstrong Memorial Lecture **[9267]**
Aryabhata Medal **[3620]**
ASA Travel Awards **[531]**
ASSO Student Award **[215]**
Australian Natural History Medallion **[721]**
Australian Skeptics Prize for Critical Thinking **[527]**
Award for the Environment **[9270]**
Awards in Science and Technology **[6626]**
Baekeland Lecture **[9271]**
Balzan Prizes **[4086]**
Julian A. Banzon Medal for Applied Research **[5357]**
Professor Sadhan Basu Memorial Lecture **[3623]**
Bavarian Academy of Science Prize **[2710]**
BDS Prize **[7038]**
Bene merenti Medals **[2711]**
Bent Spoon Award
   Australian Skeptics - NSW Branch **[528]**
   New Zealand Committee for the Scientific
    Investigation of Claims of the Paranormal **[4959]**
Prof. E. D. Bergmann Memorial Award **[3996]**
Berkeley Award **[7139]**
Prix Claude Berthault **[2244]**
Prix de Madame Claude Berthault **[2179]**
Best Emerging Young Woman Scientist Award **[5685]**
Best Paper Award for Young Scientists **[3048]**
Best Paper Awards **[8238]**
Best Scientific Work **[1396]**
Best Scientific Work of a Young Scientist **[1397]**
Best Student Scientific Work **[1398]**
Shanti Swarup Bhatnagar Award **[3509]**
BICI-UNESCO (ROSTE) **[4166]**
Professor Krishna Sahai Bilgrami Memorial Medal **[3627]**
Scott Blair Biorheology Scholarship **[7265]**
LeCoq de Boisbaudran Award **[6283]**
Boyle Medal for Scientific Excellence **[3916]**
Bradford Award **[6698]**
Braunschweig Research Prize **[2741]**
Bravo Awards **[4960]**
British Association Medal **[5734]**
British Society of Rheology Annual Award **[7266]**
Bronze Medal **[5735]**
MacFarlane Burnet Medal and Lecture **[172]**
Clare Butcher Awards **[4889]**
Career Award **[1450]**
Carus Medal **[3119]**
Castner Medal and Lecture **[9275]**
Certificate of Merit **[5736]**
Chairman's Medal **[655]**
G. P. Chatterjee Memorial Award **[3708]**
Dr. Guru Prajad Chatterjee Memorial Lecture **[3631]**
Murli M. Chugani Memorial Award for Excellence in Applied Physics **[3686]**
Fernand Collin Prize for Law **[1669]**
Comprehensive Research Grant **[4207]**
Prix Adrien Constantin de Magny **[2191]**
James Cook Medal **[1004]**
Prix Corbay **[2250]**
Cothenius Medal **[3120]**
Cribb Award **[6699]**
CSIR Case Award **[3471]**
Daiwa Foundation Small Project Grants **[7492]**
Dan David Prize **[3943]**
C.N. Davies Award **[6680]**
Duncan Davies Medal **[8547]**
Dr. B. C. Deb Memorial Award for Popularisation of Science **[3709]**
Debiopharm Life Sciences Award, Switzerland **[6260]**
Prix Ernest Dechelle **[2194]**
John Howard Dellinger Gold Medal **[1565]**
DesCartes Prize for Collaborative, Transnational Research **[1459]**
Gerhard Dierkes Prize **[3218]**
Distinguished Scientist Award for Contribution to the Improvement of the Quality of Life of Women **[5686]**
Distinguished Scientist of the Year **[5190]**
Distinguished Woman Scientist Award **[5687]**
Prix Paul Doistau - Emile Blutet de l'Information Scientifique **[2198]**
Doniach Lectureship and Award **[8459]**
International Guido Dorso Prize **[4032]**
Dublin Prize **[1111]**
Duke of Edinburgh's Award **[7891]**
Raj Kristo Dutt Memorial Award **[3711]**
Early Career Award
   European Life Scientist Organization **[2835]**
   Leopoldina, the German Academy of Sciences **[3121]**
ECCAI Travel Awards **[2818]**
Edwards Vacuum Ltd. Israel Research Excellence Prize **[3974]**
Howard Eggins Award **[7140]**
Egon - Elod Award **[3219]**
Professor Magnus Ehrnrooth Prize **[2103]**
Albert Einstein World Award of Science **[4602]**
Electrochimica Acta Travel Award for Young Electrochemists **[6440]**
Elite Research Prize **[1973]**
EMS Award **[2385]**
Environmental Award **[6128]**
European Lipid Awards **[2820]**
EUROTHERM Young Scientist Prizes and Awards **[4068]**

Excellence in Science and Technology **[3712]**
Michael Faraday Prize **[8933]**
Fellowship Competition **[6386]**
Fellowship of the City and Guilds of London Institute **[7431]**
Antonio Feltrinelli Prizes **[4022]**
Fine Craftsmanship Award for Young Foundrymen **[5227]**
Fissan-Pui-TSI International Collaboration Award **[2696]**
Matthew Flinders Medal and Lecture **[174]**
E.J. Fox Medal **[7829]**
K.J. Fox Memorial Awards **[4890]**
Francqui Prize **[1527]**
Frenkel Prize **[5915]**
Frisby-Green Dissertation Prize **[6794]**
Fuchs Memorial Award **[2697]**
Arnoldo Gabaldon Award **[9555]**
Dr. Gouri Ganguly Memorial Award for Young Scientists in Animal Science **[3713]**
Joaquin Garcia Monge Prize **[1858]**
Gardiner Award **[6700]**
Gauss Medal **[2743]**
Prix Gegner **[2272]**
Hugo Geiger Prize **[2892]**
General Research Committee Award **[6129]**
Geomechanics Award **[4969]**
John and Allan Gilmour Research Award **[1123]**
Bruce Given Awards **[4891]**
Gold Medal
   British Society of Rheology **[7267]**
   Pakistan Academy of Sciences **[5191]**
   Royal Irish Academy **[3929]**
Gold Medals **[5192]**
Goldsmid Award **[8239]**
L. J. Goodman Award for Insect Biology **[8770]**
Goudie Lectureship and Medal **[8460]**
Grand Medal **[4437]**
Grande Medaille
   French Academy of Sciences **[2435]**
   French Society for Metallurgy and Materials **[2451]**
Guest Lecturer Award **[4964]**
Soren Gyldendal Prisen **[1971]**
M.M. Hallett Award **[7830]**
Hamilton Memorial Prize **[5074]**
Hammond Award **[6701]**
Hannan Medal **[178]**
Carl Hanson Medal **[9277]**
Roland Harper Lecture **[9278]**
Havenga Prize **[5629]**
Hegel-Preis der Landeshauptstadt Stuttgart **[3191]**
Dr. A.H. Heineken Prize for Cognitive Science **[4823]**
Dr. A.H. Heineken Prize for Environmental Sciences **[4824]**
Heineken Young Scientists Awards **[4827]**
John F. W. Herschel Medal **[5606]**
Viktor Hess Preis **[1210]**
Hilditch Memorial Lecture **[9279]**
Dorothy Hill Award **[179]**
Professor Theodor Homen Prize **[2104]**
Honorary Fellow **[4386]**
Honorary Sign **[1801]**
Robert Horne Memorial Lecture **[9280]**
Human and Social Sciences Research Grant **[4208]**
Hurter Memorial Lecture **[9281]**
Javed Husain Prize for Young Scientists **[2651]**
ICPE Medal **[3766]**
Ernesto Illy Trieste Science Prize **[4159]**
Infosys Foundation - ISCA Travel Award **[3715]**
International Aerosol Fellow Award **[2698]**
IPS Prize **[3967]**
Otto Jaag-Gewasserschutz-Preis **[6498]**
Jaeger Medal **[180]**
Klaas Jan Beek Award **[4748]**
Japan Prize **[4320]**
Prix Jules et Louis Jeanbernat et Barthelemy de Ferrari Doria **[2472]**
Prix Jules et Louis Jeanbernat et Bathelemy de Ferrari Doria **[2275]**
Journal Prize **[5712]**
Journalism Award **[529]**
JSPS Prize **[4275]**
Junge Memorial Award **[2699]**
Junior Award **[6284]**
Kalinga Prize for the Popularization of Science **[2654]**
Alexander Petrowitsch Karpinskij Prize **[3203]**

Subject Index   Science

Subject Index

Prof. S. S. Katiyar Commemoration Lecture [3716]
Kavli Prize in Astrophysics [5139]
Cherry Kearton Medal and Award [8794]
Max Kehren Medal [3220]
Kharazmi International Award [3828]
King Charles II Medal [8939]
Haddon Forrester King Medal [181]
Issac Koga Gold Medal [1566]
Kohn Award [8940]
Daulat Singh Kothari Memorial Lecture Award [3639]
Krafft Medal [6049]
Krill Prizes for Excellence in Scientific Research [4000]
Kariamanikkam Srinivasa Krishnan Memorial Lecture [3640]
Kuczynski Prize [5916]
Kultureller Ehrenpreis [3136]
Kulturpreis der Stadt Villach [1328]
Laboratory Visit Grant [7133]
Landsforeningen mod Huntingtons Choreas Forskningsfond [1955]
Knud Lind Larsen Prize [1939]
LASA Award [8276]
Latsis-Preis [6500]
Lawrence Memorial Grant [5772]
Prix Leconte [2215]
Lenhosseks Prize [3378]
LeSueur Memorial Award [9283]
Letter of Appreciation [2041]
Levallois Medal [3050]
Life Membership Award [105]
Life Sciences Bursaries [6881]
Lifetime Achievement Award for Science [1880]
David Linton Award [7225]
Lister Memorial Lecture [9289]
Liversidge Lecture [201]
M.V. Lomonosov Great Gold Medal [5827]
John Lovering Prize [1136]
The Mackerras Medal [335]
Magsaysay Future Engineers/Technologists Award [5359]
Frank J. Malina Astronautics Medal [2500]
Malpighi Medal [2854]
Manamperi (Engineering) Award [6130]
Mansel-Pleydell Trust Essay Competition [7522]
Sir Ernest Marsden Medal for Outstanding Service to Science [4954]
Marsh Award for Insect Conservation [8773]
Martin Medal [7425]
Malcolm McIntosh Prize for Physical Scientist of the Year [357]
McWilliams Young Science Writers' Competition [3921]
Medal for Business Excellence [656]
Medal for Lifetime Achievement [657]
Medal for Young Scientists [3644]
Medal Lecturers [4160]
Medal of Honor [3221]
Medal of Merit
 Leopoldina, the German Academy of Sciences [3122]
 South African Society for Enology and Viticulture [5713]
Medal of Merit of the Order of Saint Lucia [5894]
Medal of the Estonian Academy of Sciences [2042]
Medal of the Royal Society of Western Australia [1019]
Medical and Veterinary Entomology Journal Award [8774]
Prof. R. C. Mehrotra Commemorative Lecture [3717]
Johann-Heinrich-Merck Ehrung [3240]
Merit Prize for Development [6405]
Microcirculation Conference Grant [7134]
Microscopy Award [7141]
Mining Analyst of the Year [6832]
Sisir Kumar Mitra Memorial Lecture [3645]
Asutosh Mookerjee Memorial Award [3718]
Moran Medal [185]
Prof. Sushil Kumar Mukherjee Commemorative Lecture [3719]
Mullard Award [8942]
Murdoch Award [8300]
Musgrave Medals [4173]
Professor K. Naha Memorial Medal [3646]
Professor Vishnu Vasudeva Narlikar Memorial Lecture [3647]

National Academy of Sciences Award [5476]
National Award for Environmental Management [9518]
National Award for Research in Science and Technology [9519]
National Awards for Science Technicians [9142]
Natural Science Grants [4209]
S. Meiring Naude Medal [5607]
Jawaharlal Nehru Birth Centenary Award [3720]
Jawaharlal Nehru Birth Centenary Lectures [3650]
Jawaharlal Nehru Birth Centenary Medal [3651]
Neill Medal [9070]
New Researcher Award [585]
New Zealand Science and Technology Medals [5077]
New Zealand Science, Mathematics and Technology Teacher Fellowship [5078]
Nigeria Prize for Science [5098]
Katsumi Niki Prize for Bioelectrochemistry [6444]
Alex Northover Award [761]
Prix Victor Noury, Thorlet, Henri Becquerel, Jules and Augusta Lazare [2224]
E. J. Nystrom Prize [2106]
Odem Technical Excellence Award [3975]
Thomas R. Odhiambo Prize in Basic and Applied Sciences [4372]
Lorenz Oken Medaille [3029]
Order of Merit [7345]
Order of the Netherlands Lion [4652]
Prix Osiris [2473]
Osmond-Russell Scholarship [106]
Outstanding Achievement Award [8240]
Outstanding Book and/or Monograph Awards [5361]
Outstanding Contributions Award [5228]
Outstanding Scientific Paper Award [5362]
Outstanding Young Scientist Award [5363]
Overseas Research Grant [4210]
Overseas Surgical Fellowship [6850]
Paper and Poster Prizes [5714]
Paracelsusring der Stadt Villach [1329]
Peace Prize of the German Book Trade [2989]
Peccei Scholarship [1291]
Prix Petit d'Ormoy, Carriere, Thebault [2228]
PhD of the Year [586]
PhD Study Award [587]
Physical Science Award [6131]
Physiological Entomology Journal Award [8775]
Postgraduate Student Prize [1013]
Postgraduate Travel Award [154]
Professor Brahm Prakash Memorial Medal [3652]
Drs. Kunti and Om Prakash Oration Award [3557]
Premio Nacional de Ciencias Aplicadas [1824]
Premio Nacional de Ciencias Naturales [1825]
President of the Republic Prize [56]
President's Award [7895]
President's Medal [582]
Derek John de Solla Price Memorial Medal [1553]
Prime Minister's Prize for Science [358]
Prince of Asturias for Technical and Scientific Research [6090]
Prix Debiopharm/Valais pour les Sciences de la Vie [6261]
Prix Science et Defense [2433]
Prize for Junior Scientists [3124]
Prize for Popularisation of Estonian Science [2044]
Prize for Science and Technology [5901]
Prize for Science Communication [1461]
Prize for Science Writing [1065]
Prizes for Leadership in Islamic Thought and Applied Sciences [4012]
Pro Scientia Transformatrix Award [5366]
Publication Medal [1014]
Alexander Sergeovich Pushkin Prize [5881]
Eduardo A. Quisumbing Medal for Basic Research [5367]
C. V. Raman Birth Centenary Award [3721]
Chandrasekhara Venkata Raman Medal [3656]
Srinivasa Ramanujan Birth Centenary Award [3722]
C.N.R. Rao Prize for Scientific Research [4161]
Research Award [4749]
Research Event Awards [588]
Research Grant [3423]
Rhodia European Colloid and Interface Prize [1795]
Sir Eric Rideal Lecture [9294]
Medaille Jean Rist [2452]
Rolex Awards for Enterprise [6477]

Rod Rookwood Award for Agriculture/Engineering Design [583]
Royal Medal [9071]
Royal Society and Academie des sciences Microsoft Award [8944]
The Royal Society-Daiwa Anglo-Japanese Foundation Joint Project Grants [7494]
Royal Society Pfizer Award [8945]
S & T Promotion Award [4635]
Anthony N. Sabga Caribbean Awards for Excellence [6613]
Meghnad Saha Medal [3661]
Prof R. C. Saha Memorial Lecture [3723]
Birbal Sahni Birth Centenary Award [3724]
Abdus Salam Medal for Science and Technology [4162]
Abdus Salam Prize for Leadership in Islamic Thought and the Physical Sciences [4014]
Samsonov Prize [5917]
SASEV Award [5715]
N. S. Satyamurthy Award for Young Scientists [3688]
Karl Schlossmann Medal [2045]
Bernhard Schmidt Prize [2046]
School Science Award [9520]
Schwizerhuesli Young Researchers Award [6529]
Science and Technology Award [4636]
Science and Technology Medal [2537]
Science Communicator Award [4956]
Science Minister's Prize for Life Scientist of the Year [360]
Scientific Achievement Competition [1802]
Scientific Award [2906]
Scientific Outreach Grants [6883]
Scientific Service Award [6637]
Selby Fellowship [187]
Richard Seligman Lecture [9295]
Prof. Anima Sen Memorial Lecture [3725]
Separation Science Lecture [9296]
Shorland Medal [4957]
Silver Medal of Special Merit [2712]
SMI-UNESCO (ROSTE) [4167]
Smoluchowski Award [2700]
Society's Medal [1010]
Arnold Sommerfeld Prize [2713]
South Africa Medal [5737]
Prix Baron de Stassart [1616]
M. T. Steyn Prize for Natural Science and Technical Achievement [5643]
Student Assistance Scheme [7135]
Student Award
 International Association of Logopedics and Phoniatrics [4727]
 New Zealand Geotechnical Society [4970]
 Royal Entomological Society [8776]
Student Awards [4442]
Student Prize
 Institute of Ergonomics and Human Factors [7868]
 South African Society for Enology and Viticulture [5716]
Student Research Prize [2047]
Dr. Yellapragada SubbaRow Memorial Lecture [3666]
Subsistence Award [7573]
Professor S. Swaminathan 60th Birthday Commemoration Lecture [3667]
Systematic Entomology Journal Award [8777]
Table Grape Award [5717]
Tanzania Award for Scientific and Technological Achievements [9521]
Technology Adoption Award [3472]
Thomson Medal [5080]
Prof. Bal Dattatraya Tilak Lecture [3669]
Tiroler Landespreis fur Wissenschaft [1198]
Travel Award
 Estuarine and Coastal Sciences Association [7574]
 New Zealand Freshwater Sciences Society [4965]
Prix Gabrielle Sand et Marie Guido Triossi [2237]
Tubitak-TWAS Science Award [6639]
TWAS Prizes [4164]
Dioscoro L. Umali Medal for Outstanding Science Administrator [5369]
Umicore Scientific Award [1524]
Undergraduate Student Bursaries [7142]
UNESCO Science Prize [2659]
Upper Secondary School Teachers Prizes [2107]
USB Certificate [1803]
Balthasar Van der Pol Gold Medal [1567]

Verco Medal [1015]
Prix Alfred Verdaguer [2239]
Pran Vohra Award [3728]
Joseph von Fraunhofer Prize [2894]
Carl Friedrich von Weizsacker Prize [3128]
Wahlbergska Minnesmedaljen I guld [6188]
George Walker Awards [6052]
Alfred Russel Wallace Award [8778]
Ian Wark Medal and Lecture [188]
Gordon Warwick Award [7227]
Weiss Medal [6783]
Weizmann Prizes [4592]
Werner-Risau Prize [3134]
Wilhelm Westrups Prize [6174]
Rowden White Foundation Prize [1156]
Whytlaw-Gray Studentship [6681]
Christo Wiese Medal for an Emerging Entrepreneur [5648]
Otto N. Witt Medal [3222]
Young Authors' Award [3051]
Young Investigator Award [8241]
Young Scientist Award
    International Radiation Commission [5446]
    Nepal Academy of Science and Technology [4637]
Young Scientist of the Year [2366]
Young Scientists' Awards [3729]
Ahmed Zewail Prize for Leadership in Islamic Thought and Chemical Science [4016]

Science education

Alexander Prize [7452]
Australian Museum Eureka Prizes [521]
Award for Chemistry Education [4217]
Award of Merit for Chemistry Education [4222]
Balmer Prize [6486]
BHP Billiton Science Awards [522]
Bragg Medal and Prize [7901]
Branches of the Year [5102]
CASTME Awards [7453]
Dr. A.C.L. De'Souza Memorial Prize [4411]
Distinguished and Sustained Service to Science Education Award [5103]
Distinguished Service Award [4923]
Excellence in Aerospace Education Award [3440]
Excellence in Psychology Education Award [7185]
Faculty of Science Prize [6526]
Jan Harabaszewski Medal [5392]
McWilliams Young Science Writers' Competition [3921]
New Zealand Science, Mathematics and Technology Teacher Fellowship [5078]
President's Award [5104]
Prime Ministers Prizes for Excellence in Science Teaching [359]
Royal Society Winton Prizes for Science Books [8946]
Abdul Hameed Shoman Award for Teachers of Science [4365]
Worlddidac Award [6567]
Young Scientists of the Year Awards [883]

Science fiction

Aurealis Awards [126]
Brussels International Festival of Fantastic Film [1417]
BSFA Awards [7199]
Arthur C. Clarke Award [9159]

Science journalism see also Medical journalism

Annual Award for Popularization and Promotion of Science [1876]
Best Paper Award [3574]
Excellence in Engineering Journalism Award [782]
Forderpreis der ITG [3037]
Sigmund Freud Preis [2897]
Indira Gandhi Prize for Popularization of Science [3634]
Medaille fur Naturwissenschaftliche Publizistik [2776]
Newbigin Prize [8921]
Preis der Gesellschaft Deutcher Chemiker fur Schriftsteller [2934]
Research Medal [4955]
Spearman Medal [7196]
VDE/ETG Award [2789]
Warner Memorial Medal [9384]

Scientific research

Prix Anatole et Suzanne Abragam [2174]
Prix Alcan [2175]
Prix Ampere d'Electricite de France [2176]
Annual Science Award [1877]
Appleton Medal and Prize [7899]
Award for Scientific Research [4429]
Prof. I.S. Bhatia Award [3781]
Boyle Medal for Scientific Excellence [3916]
Bronze Medal [2447]
Walter Burfitt Prize [1001]
Castner Medal and Lecture [9275]
Copley Medal [8930]
CORESTA Prize [2344]
Prix Dandrimont-Benicourt [2193]
Edgeworth David Medal [1005]
Prix de la Fondation Jean-Marie Delwart [1625]
Anthony Dipple Carcinogenesis Award [7578]
Dow Energy Dissertation Prizes [4819]
Neil Hamilton Fairley Fellowships [891]
Faustus Poster Awards [7579]
Carlos J. Finlay Prize [2649]
Gauss Medal [2743]
Gilchrist Fieldwork Award [8790]
Gold Medal
    French National Center for Scientific Research [2448]
    International Radiation Commission [5445]
Henry Granjon Prize [2545]
Great Gold Medal [6179]
Otto-Hahn-Preis fur Chemie und Physik [2773]
Heineken Young Scientists Awards [4827]
Hilti-Preis [6497]
Dorothy Hodgkin Fellowship [8937]
Honorary Member [6041]
Robert Horne Memorial Lecture [9280]
W. J. B. Houston Research Awards [7623]
W. J. B. Houston Scholarship Award [7624]
Humboldt Research Fellowships [3228]
Hurter Memorial Lecture [9281]
Javed Husain Prize for Young Scientists [2651]
Christiaan Huygens Science Award [4830]
William Inman Prize [7188]
International Hydrology Prize [2494]
Arthur Thomas Ippen Award [6042]
JNC Editors' Award [835]
Prix Alexandre Joannides [2210]
JSPS Research Fellowship for Postdoctoral Researchers [3229]
Jubilee Award [9380]
Junior Science Award [6635]
Prix de Biologie Alfred Kastler [2443]
John F. Kennedy Student Paper Competition [6043]
Prof. P.A. Kurup Endowment Award [3785]
Life Esidimeni Award [5587]
Lifetime Achievement Award - Academics and Researchers [7189]
Prix de l'Institut Francais du Petrole [2216]
Feodor Lynen Research Fellowships [3230]
C. J. Martin Overseas Biomedical Fellowship [892]
Michael Mason Prize [7241]
McWilliams Young Science Writers' Competition [3921]
Moseley Medal and Prize [7914]
Archibald D. Olle Prize [1007]
Prix Blaise Pascal du GAMNI-SMAI [2226]
Prix Paul Pascal [2227]
Max Planck Research Award [3231]
Presidents' Award [7194]
Prix des Jeunes [2314]
Frank Rampersad Scientific and Technological Award [6627]
Arne Richter Award for Outstanding Young Scientists [2377]
Andres Manuel del Rio National Prize in Chemistry [4581]
Prix Gaston Rousseau [2233]
Royal Medals [8943]
Prix Charles-Louis de Saulses de Freycinet [2235]
Science Award [6636]
Scientific Book Award [1891]
Abdul Hameed Shoman Award for Young Arab Researchers [4367]
T. K. Sidey Medal and Prize [5079]
Silver Medal [2449]
Thorarinsson Medal [6050]

Tison Award [2495]
Travel Fellowships [7580]
Van Leeuwenhoek Distinctive Travel Award [2855]
Alexander von Humboldt Award for Scientific Cooperation [3232]
Philipp Franz von Siebold Award for Japanese Research [3233]
Wager Medal [6051]
Wahlbergska Minnesmedaljen I guld [6188]
Van Walree Prize [4836]
Don Whitley Travel Scholarship [9191]
Young Cancer Researcher Award Lecture [7582]
Young Scientist of the Year [2366]

Sculpture

Annual Exhibition [8913]
Prix Claude Berthault [2137]
De Laszlo Medal [8969]
Jack Goldhill Award for Sculpture [8569]
Governor-General Art Award [4949]
Jerwood Sculpture Prize [8455]
Prix Hector Lefuel [2144]
Praemium Imperiale [4262]
Prix de Rome - Visual Arts [4811]
Prix Egide Rombaux [1597]
Summer Exhibition Awards [8570]
The Wolf Prizes [4001]
Charles Wollaston Award [8571]

Secondary education

Prix Joseph De Keyn [1602]
Luka Ritz Award [1883]

Security see also National security

Kristian Beckman Award [1269]
BSIA/IFSEC Security Industry Awards [7201]
ISIA Awards [3892]
Security Officer Awards [7202]

Seismology

Otto Glogau Award [5005]
Honorary Membership [6048]
Keith Medal [9068]
Ivan Skinner Award [5006]

Service

Australian of the Year Awards [885]
BASICS Award [6953]
Best of Vietnam Awards [9561]
Blue Service Award [740]
Centenary Medal [305]
Certificate of Merit [346]
College Medal [962]
Council of Women Award [1781]
Distinguished Service Award
    International Pharmaceutical Federation [4758]
    Royal Australian and New Zealand College of Ophthalmologists [963]
Emeritus Professor [5956]
Gold Service Award [741]
Golden Lion [9571]
Hall of Fame [1047]
Honorary Fellow Award [697]
Life Membership [1051]
Lifetime Achievement Award [153]
Meritorious Service Award [964]
National Medal [317]
Outstanding Service Award [5957]
Past Presidents Diploma [6325]
Rookie of the Year [1053]
Service Certificate [575]
Service Medal [576]
Silver Eagle [9572]
Society Medal [750]
Special Commendation [5958]
Vietnam Quality Award [9559]
WAGGGS Medal [9469]

Set design

Laurence Olivier Awards [9324]

Shooting

Champion Shots Medal [306]
Distinguished Service Award [8410]

Subject Index

Referee of the Year [7322]
Oscar Schwiglhofer Trophy [6792]
Singapore Sports Awards [5983]
Special Jury Prize [4614]
Sport Australia Hall of Fame [1057]
Sport Science Award of the IOC President [3063]
Sports Awards
  Botswana National Sports Council [1738]
  Samoa Association of Sport and National Olympic
    Committee [9563]
Sports Event for Peace of the Year [4615]
State Awards for Top-Level Sporting Achieve-
    ments [1884]
Statistician of the Year [6821]
Student Research Award [1059]
Under 14 Player of the Year [7323]
Under 17 Player of the Year [7324]
Under 21 Player of the Year [7325]
Undergraduate Dissertation of the Year Award [6973]
UNESCO Award for Distinguished Services to
    Physical Education and Sport [2656]
Volunteer of the Year [7326]
World Curling Freytag Award [9481]
The World Games [4795]
Young Researcher's Awards [5383]

Sports broadcasting

Media Awards [590]
Television Sports Awards [9132]

Sports journalism

Kodak Media Photography Award [4984]
Media Awards [590]

Sports medicine

Abo Yousif Yaqoub Al-Kindi Prize [1356]
Bronze Medal [4103]
Citation of Honor [4104]
Distinguished Contribution to the Field of Sport and
    Exercise Psychology Award [7183]
Geoffrey Dyson Lecture [3862]
Fellow Award [3863]
Gold Medal [4105]
Hans Gros New Investigator Award [3864]
Life Membership Award [3865]
H.T.A. Whiting Undergraduate Dissertation
    Prize [7197]

Sportsmanship

Jean Borotra World Fair Play Trophy [3393]
Pierre de Coubertin World Fair Play Trophy [3394]
Willi Daume World Fair Play Trophy [3395]
Fair Play Prizes [3396]
WJCC Sportsmanship Award [9480]
WWhCC Sportsmanship Award [9482]

Stamp collecting see Philately

Standards

Best Practice Award [1426]
Bhutan Seal of Excellence [1709]
Bhutan Seal of Quality [1710]
Deming Prizes [4337]
Georges Garel Award [6384]
Honeywell Prize [7897]
Japan Quality Medal [4338]
Nikkei QC Literature Prize [4339]
Quality Prize of the Government of the Republic of
    Belarus [1394]

Statistics

J.K. Aggarwal Prize [4231]
Maurice H. Belz Prizes in Statistics [1104]
Campbell Award [5020]
Certificate of Appreciation [4232]
Cochran-Hansen Prize [2497]
Prix Charles Dupin [2263]
Dwight Prize in Mathematical Statistics [1115]
Norma McArthur Prize [1137]
Moran Medal [185]
National Institute of Insurance International
    Prizes [4024]
Outstanding Achievement Award [4233]
Herbert Sichel Medal [5724]

Jan Tinbergen Awards for Young Statisticians from
    Developing Countries [4789]
Visiting Lecturer [5021]
Young Scientist Award [4234]
P. Zamperoni Award [4235]

Steel industry see Iron and steel industry

Stroke

New Investigators Awards [1070]

Surfing

European Surfing Championships - Open Cham-
    pion [7654]

Surgery

Hans Anderl Award [4686]
Best Paper Award [5108]
Best Poster Award [7632]
Robert Danis Prize [6451]
Davies Foundation Travelling Fellowship [8700]
Rahima Dawood Prize [4410]
Educational Grants [7588]
Euroliver Foundation Award [7634]
Consuelo Gomez-Arabit Award for Excellence in
    Perioperative Nursing [5348]
Honorary Fellowship [956]
Joseph Prize [2794]
Junior Award [2859]
Leibinger Prize [7589]
Rene Leriche Prize [6452]
Lester Lowe Awards [1555]
Hans Marberger Award [4692]
Meritorious Service Award [957]
MIA Prize [9100]
Mondeal Prize [7590]
Moynihan Prize [6849]
Hugo Obwegeser Travelling Scholarship [7591]
Oral Presentation Awards [1556]
Overseas Surgical Fellowship [6850]
Patey Prize [9228]
Poster Awards [1557]
Presidential Commendation [958]
President's Poster Prize [9229]
Prize of the Societe Internationale de Chirur-
    gie [6453]
Research Grant [5199]
Royal Colleges Medal [8907]
Hans von Seemen Preis [3024]
SICOT/SIROT Award [1558]
Adrian Tanner Prize [9109]
Undergraduate Essay Prize [6969]
Young Investigator Award [7635]

Surveying

ACES Award for Excellence in Property Manage-
    ment [6808]
Arthur Butcher Award [6995]
Richard Carter Prize [7396]
Early-Career Researcher Award [6031]
Faculty of Architecture and Surveying Innovation
    Award [7366]
Gold Medal of Honour [5508]
National President's Award [423]
Alex Pitcher Award [6998]
Service Award [4553]

Swedish culture

Sven Berggrens pris [6168]
Gun och Olof Engqvists stipendium [6200]
Grand Prize [6203]
Kellgrenpriset [6206]
Kungliga priset [6208]
Nordiska Priset [6209]

Swimming see also Surfing

Hans Belay Trophy [7106]
Henry Benjamin National Memorial Trophy [6703]
Mary Black Award [6704]
Breaststroke Trophy [7107]
James Brennan Memorial Trophy [7108]
Elise Brook Trophy [7109]
Tom Butcher Trophy [7110]
Citation of Merit [1538]

G. Melville Clark National Memorial Trophy [6705]
Dawdon Trophy [6706]
Harold Fern Award [6707]
Harold Fern National Trophy [6708]
George Hearn Trophy [6709]
Alan Hime Memorial Trophies [6710]
Holland Trophy [6711]
Alan Lawrence Trophy [6712]
Lifesaving Hall of Fame [1539]
Avril and Allan Mitchell Trophy [7111]
Harry Moffat Memorial Trophy [7112]
National Pool Lifeguard Award [4998]
Order of Lifesaving [1540]
President's Award [1541]
Rescue Medal [1542]
Rescue Medal of Valour [1543]
Shacklock Trophy [6713]
Fred Slater Trophy [7113]
Norma Thomas National Memorial Trophy [6714]
Triathlon Awards [3327]
Alfred H. Turner Award [6715]
Belle White National Memorial Trophy [6716]
Gemma Yates Trophy [6717]
T.M. Yeaden Memorial Trophy [6718]
T. M. Yeadon Memorial Trophy [6719]

Systems management see Information
management; Operations research

Tapestry see Textile design

Tattooing see Cosmetology

Teaching see also Education

Annual Teaching Excellence Award [5960]
Australian Museum Eureka Prizes [521]
Award for Excellent Chemistry Teachers [5453]
Award for Teachers [2953]
Award for the Teaching of Physics [6103]
BHP Billiton Science Awards [522]
Garth Boomer Award [291]
Bragg Medal and Prize [7901]
Centenary of Federation Teaching Awards in Chem-
    istry [971]
Certificate of Merit [346]
Credit Suisse Award for Best Teaching [6520]
Prix de Chenier [2153]
Degree Program Distinguished Teacher Award [4505]
Education Award [4277]
Excellence in Aerospace Education Award [3440]
Ivan Filipovic Award [1879]
Golden Torch Award [4193]
Governor's Award for Outstanding Humanities
    Teacher [5111]
Ben Hawthorne Award [4194]
John Holgate Memorial Award [9336]
Innovative Curriculum Award [292]
Edith-Dalton James Award [4195]
Long and Distinguished Service Medal [1733]
Prix Malouet [2287]
Medal for Outstanding Service to Language Teach-
    ing [347]
Meritorious Service Medal [1734]
Mid-Career Medal [1735]
Music Grants [2109]
Outstanding Educator Award [5961]
Paragon Lesotho Award [4462]
Robert Wichard Pohl Prize [2778]
Prime Ministers Prizes for Excellence in Science
    Teaching [359]
Thomas Pringle Award [5542]
Roll of Honour Award [4196]
SAALED Bursary [5656]
Silver Jubilee Medal [1736]
Elizabeth C. Steijn Medal [5642]
Svensklararpris [6216]
R.C. Tavares Award [4197]
Teaching English Excellence Award [9542]
Teaching Excellence Award [4507]
David White Excellence in Teaching Award [547]
Vasilis Xanthopoulos Award [3288]
Young Scientists of the Year Awards [883]

Technology see also Biotechnology; Computer
science; Engineering; Industrial arts; Inventions;
Science; Standards; Testing

Academician H. Abdullayev Award [1335]

Technology, color see Color technology

Technology, medical see Medical technology

Telecommunications see Communications

Television see also Broadcasting; Media; Radio; Video

Tennis

Testing

Textile design

Textile industry see also Fiber science

Theater

Theology

Therapy see Rehabilitation and therapy

Third world see Economic development

Tourism see Travel

Town planning see City planning

Toxicology

LRI Innovative Science Award [1456]
Redi Award [844]

Toys

Toy Design Competition [5316]
Toy Industry Awards [7279]
Toy Star Award [5230]

Track and field

Triathlon Awards [3327]

Trade see *Business; Finance; International trade*

Trade shows see *Conventions*

Trade unions see *Labor*

Trades see *Industries and trades*

Training and development

Asia-Pacific Cancer Society Training Grants (APCA-SOT) [6458]
International Visual Communications Association Awards [8250]
National Training Awards [3888]
Lewis F. Spangler - Purchasing Professional Award [1285]

Translations

Astellas and Novartis Research Fellowships [7281]
Best Translated Book of the Year [4480]
BTS/Morris Travelling Fellowship [7282]
Roy Calne Award [7283]
CBCI Award [3824]
Companion Prize [4481]
Dansk Oversaetterforbunds Aerespris [1963]
John Florio Prize [9248]
H.A.I. Goonetileke Prize for Translation [6121]
Calouste Gulbenkian Prize [9250]
Honour List [6364]
Premio Valle Inclan [9252]
Independent Foreign Fiction Prize [6906]
Johan Kruger Prize [5728]
Scott Moncrieff Prize [9256]
Oversattarpris [6210]
Sol Plaatje Award for Translation [5541]
Corneliu M. Popescu Prize for European Poetry Translation [8490]
Prize to Outstanding Student of Translation [3972]
Prizes for Outstanding Translation [5729]
Sahitya Akademi Translation Prize [3748]
St. Jerome Award [4482]
St. John Ambulance Air Wing Travelling Fellowship [7284]
Bernard Shaw Prize [9257]
Abdul Hameed Shoman Award for Translation [4366]
Stiftelsen Natur och Kulturs oversattarpris [6214]
Dominykas Urbas Prize [4483]
Vondel Translation Prize [9261]
Johann-Heinrich-Voss-Preis fur Uebersetzung [2900]
Wyeth Fellowship [7285]

Transportation see also *Aeronautics and aviation; Automobiles; Automotive engineering; Aviation safety; Helicopters; Highway safety; Navigation; Railway transportation; Trucking*

Achiever of the Year [642]
Asia Awards [8319]
Award for Most Meritorious Presentation [4942]
Award for Supply Chain Innovation [4943]
Contact Mechanics Award [944]
Eagle Awards [6346]
European Award for Logistics Excellence [1482]
European Parking Award [2847]
European Standard Parking Award [2848]
Excellence in Information Management Award [7380]
Excellence in Materials Handling Equipment and Technology Award [7381]
Excellence in Passenger Transport Award [7382]
Excellence in Transport Policy and Planning Award [7383]
Global Awards [8320]
Grand Prix d'Honneur [6424]
Greek Shipping Awards [8321]

James Harrison Young Researcher Award [2533]
Italian Shipping Awards [8322]
Sir Robert Lawrence Award [7384]
Local Transportation Company of the Year [4181]
Logistics Best Practice Award [7385]
Logistics Dissertation of the Year [7386]
Middle East and Indian Subcontinent Awards [8323]
Ministry of Transport Award for Best Student Research [4944]
MORR Trophy [8961]
Onassis International Prize in Shipping [3301]
PTx2 Awards [1529]
Norman Spencer Memorial Award [4945]
STUVA Prize [3214]
Turkish Shipping Awards [8324]
Workforce Involvement in Safety and Health Trophy [8963]
Young Achiever of the Year [643]

Travel

Achievement Award [6014]
Anguilla Tourism Awards [18]
Authentic Albania Quality Mark Award Program [9]
Award of Excellence [4620]
B & B Awards [6859]
Bahamas Hotel Awards/Cacique Awards [1341]
Benger-Sullivan Award [6065]
Best Overseas Tourism Project Award [7071]
Best Practices [365]
Best U.K. Tourism Project Award [7072]
Sir Richard Burton Medal [8649]
Campsite of the Year [6860]
Catering Manager of the Year [3882]
Cook Islands Tourism Awards [1855]
Crystal Pineapple Awards [4853]
Eco Award Namibia [4621]
Environmental Award [6398]
Excellence Awards [1706]
Globe Award [7073]
Gold Training Award [6800]
Anne Gregg/Ed Lacy Memorial Award for Travel Broadcasting [7074]
Hospitality Awards [6861]
Hotel Industry Awards for Excellence [369]
Hotel Manager of the Year [4073]
Hotel Worker of the Year [4178]
Hotelier of the Year [4179]
Housekeeper of the Year [6862]
Imvelo Awards for Responsible Tourism [5545]
Indonesia Travel and Tourism Awards [3820]
Abe Issa Award for Excellence [4180]
Lifetime Achievement Award
    British Guild of Travel Writers [7075]
    Caribbean Tourism Organization [1386]
    Visitor Industry Partnership [1707]
Macao Green Hotel Award [4503]
Paul Morrison Guide Awards [9436]
National Awards for Excellence [370]
National Tourism Awards [1679]
New Zealand Tourism Awards [5082]
Outstanding Community Service and Achievement Award [367]
Personality of the Year [4623]
Photographer of the Year Award [7077]
Safari Awards [7745]
Seatrade Insider Cruise Awards [9178]
SPIRIT Award [6066]
Stingray Tourism Awards [1817]
Sustainable Development in Tourism Awards [6096]
Tanzania Tourism Awards [9525]
Tourism Award [4641]
Tourism Business Leadership Award [5755]
Tourism Distinction Award [4359]
Tourism Recognition Awards [1997]
Tourism Society Award [9395]
Travel Photo of the Year Competition [9437]
Tom Tyrell Trophy and Award [4382]
Vanuatu Tourism Awards [9544]
Wanderlust Travel Awards [9438]
World Airline Awards - Passenger's Choice Awards [9183]
World Airport Awards [9184]
World Luxury Hotel Awards [5768]
World Travel Awards [9494]
Young Hospitality Manager of the Year [3884]

Travel literature

Somerset Maugham Awards [9253]
Members' Writing Awards [7076]
Silver Otter Award [7078]

Trucking

Fleet Awards [353]
Fleet News Awards [7695]

Typography

Gutenberg Award [3033]

Uniforms see *Fashion*

Unions see *Labor*

Urban development see *City planning*

Veterans see *Military service*

Veterinary medicine

Alison Alston Canine Award [8761]
Amoroso Award [7209]
Aujeszky Medal [3375]
Australian Veterinary Association (Australia) Prize [1162]
Australian Veterinary Association (Victoria) Prize [1163]
Berlin Poster Prize [4063]
Trevor Blackburn Award [7293]
Jan Blackburn Prize [1164]
Blaine Award [7210]
Boswell Award [5731]
Bourgelat Award [7211]
Alexander Ninian Bruce Prize [9064]
Cheiron Medal [1331]
Chiron Award [7294]
Csontos Medal [3376]
Dalrymple-Champneys Cup and Medal [7295]
Robert Daubney Research Fellowship in Virology and Helminthology [8762]
Prix Rene Dujarric de la Riviere [2199]
Dunkin Award [7212]
Premio Osvaldo Eckell [25]
Educational Trust Awards [6854]
Gamgee Gold Medal [1671]
Gilruth Prize [598]
GlaxoSmithKline Prize and Lecture [8936]
Gold Medal
    South African Veterinary Association [5732]
    World Organisation for Animal Health [2668]
Hills Prize in Small Animal Medicine [1165]
Honorary Life Membership [5025]
William Hunting Award [7296]
Intervet Prize in Animal Reproduction [1166]
Prix de Biologie Alfred Kastler [2443]
Kendall Oration and Medal [599]
Don Kerr Veterinary Student Award [600]
Kesteven Medal [601]
Langley Award [6855]
Lyppard/Provet Victoria Colin Basset Prize [1167]
Melton Award [7213]
Meritorious Medal [2669]
Meritorious Service Award [602]
Norbrook Award [4418]
NZVA Clinical Studies Award [5026]
Outstanding Service Award [5027]
Overseas Travel Grants [7297]
Petsavers Award [7214]
Pfizer Animal Health Prize [1168]
Dr. Antonio Pires Prize [27]
Prof. M. R. N. Prasad Memorial Lecture [3653]
Premio Bayer en Ciencias Veterinarias [31]
President's Prize [6789]
Bart Rispens Award [3243]
Science Award [5413]
Scottish Science Award [9156]
Dorothy Sidley Memorial Award [7802]
Simic-Grau Award [4064]
Simon Award [7215]
Harry Steele-Bodger Memorial Travel Scholarship [7298]
Undergraduate and Postgraduate Bursaries [6790]
Sir A.E. Rowden White Prize [1169]

J.A. Wight Memorial Award [7216]
Woodrow Award [7217]

Video

Australian Teachers of Media Awards [596]
Mike Baldock Award [7773]
BRIT Awards [7171]
British Academy Television Awards [6932]
Channel 4 Archaeological Film Awards [7290]
Communicators in Business Awards [7878]
Dance Screen Awards [1293]
Ecumenical Prize [1661]
Fellowship of the Guild of Television Camera-
men [7774]
Honorary Membership [7775]
International Competition for Film and Video [1248]
International Visual Communications Association
Awards [8250]
Learning on Screen Awards [7291]
Les Diablerets Film Festival [6504]
Muuvi Awards [2119]
Student Television Awards [9130]
Jean Thevenot Medal [6382]
Unnim Mountain Film Festival [6108]
The Walkley Awards [1176]
West Australia Screen Awards [723]

Visual Arts

Friedrich Baur Prize [2704]
CEVMA Awards [2750]
Contemporary Art Award [76]
Rolf Schock Prizes [6185]

Visually impaired see Blindness

Violin competitions

Emily Anderson Prize for Violin [8884]
Concertino Prague International Radio Competition
for Young Musicians [1930]
Hanover International Violin Competition [2888]
International Jean Sibelius Violin Competition [2126]
International Mozart Competition [1319]
International Violin Competition - Rodolfo Lipizer
Prize [4050]
International Fritz Kreisler Competition Prizes [1287]
Carl Nielsen International Music Competitions [1975]
Prague Spring International Music Competi-
tion [1928]
Queen Elisabeth International Music Competition of
Belgium [1575]

Vocal music see also Choral music; Opera

Maria Callas Grand Prix for Opera [3267]
Cardiff Singer of the World Competition [6980]
Eurovision Song Contest [6274]
Gibraltar Song Festival [3261]
Philip and Dorothy Green Award for Young Concert
Artists [8338]
Bernhard Harms Prize [3111]
International Hilde Zadek Vocal Competition [1324]
International Mozart Competition [1319]
International Robert Schumann Choral Competi-
tion [3157]
Mathy Awards [524]
McDonald's Operatic Aria [1076]
Music Awards [8890]
Operasangerinnen Fanny Elstas Fond [5121]
President of the Republic Youth Prize in Classical
Music [58]
Queen Elisabeth International Music Competition of
Belgium [1575]
Reggae Academy Awards [4202]
W. Towyn Roberts Vocal Scholarship [8392]
Leonie Sonning Music Prize [1993]
Tokyo International Music Competition [4297]
Francisco Vinas International Singing Contest [6113]
Young Concert Artists Trust Award [9506]
Young Performers Awards [1082]

Volunteerism

Business Volunteer of the Year Award [6736]
Council of Women Award [1781]

Walking see Track and field

Water conservation

Award for Excellence in European Aquacul-
ture [1510]
Best First Paper Prize [8125]
Best Paper Prize [8126]
Certificate and Diploma in Environmental Manage-
ment [7398]
William Dunbar Medal [2871]
Educational Fund Bursaries [8127]
Exhibitors Awards [5087]
Great Prizes [6159]
P. H. Haviland Award [9578]
Ronald Hicks Memorial Award [5088]
Hynds Paper of the Year Award [5089]
Innovative Coastal Research Grants [2639]
Living Wetlands Award [7399]
Orica Chemnet Operations Award [5090]
Poster of the Year Award [5091]
President's Award [7400]
Travel Grants [2640]
World of Difference Award [7401]
Young Members' Award [7402]

Water pollution control

Ernst-Kuntze Prize [2908]

Water resources see also Sanitary engineer-
ing

G.N. Alexander Medal [766]
Award for Excellence in European Aquacul-
ture [1510]
Best Technical and/or Administrative Services
Award [5904]
Dr. G. G. Cillie Floating Trophy [5761]
Distinguished Applied Research Manager [5905]
Gold Medals [5192]
P. H. Haviland Award [9578]
Peter Hughes Award [604]
International Award [4246]
Arthur Thomas Ippen Award [6042]
Paper Award [4247]
Reviewer Award [4248]
Stockholm Junior Water Prize [605]
Stockholm Water Prize [6190]
Swedish Baltic Sea Water Award [6191]
Umgeni Award [5764]
Undergraduate Water Prize [606]
Water Environment Merit Award [607]
Wilson Award [5766]
M. Selim Yalin Lifetime Achievement Award [6046]

Water safety

Aqua Vita Est Award [5759]
Burke Award [5760]
Foundation for Water Research (UK) Award [5762]
Port of the Year [8105]
Potable Water Award [5763]
Seafarer Centre of the Year [8106]
Shipping Company of the Year [8107]
Piet Vosloo Award [5765]
Welfare Personality of the Year [8108]

Water sports see also Boating; Surfing; Swim-
ming

Athlete of the Year [6464]
Hall of Fame [6465]
Order of Merit [6466]

Watercolor painting see also Painting

Sunday Times Watercolour Competition [8457]

Waterfowl management see Wildlife conser-
vation

Weather see Meteorology

Weightlifting

Award of Merit [3410]
Weightlifting Hall of Fame [3411]

Welding

Yoshiaki Arata Award [2543]
Edstrom Medal [2544]

Henry Granjon Prize [2545]
Guerrera Prize [2546]
Andre Leroy Prize [2547]
Evgenij Paton Prize [2548]
Arthur Smith Award [2549]
Sossenheimer Software Innovation Award [2550]
Thomas Medal [2551]

Welfare see Child welfare; Social service

Wildlife conservation see also
Environmental conservation

Ralph Brown Expedition Award [8786]
Community Wildlife Conservation Award [1188]
Gold Panda Award [6571]
Insect Conservation and Diversity Journal
Award [8771]
Marsh Award for Conservation Biology [9510]
Order of the Golden Ark [4651]
Roll of Honour [6572]
Serventy Conservation Medal [1189]
Neville Shulman Challenge Award [8798]
Sture Centerwalls Pris [6187]

Wine

Andre Simon Medal [8257]
Veritas Awards [5757]

Women

Alice Award [1042]
Thenie Baddams Bursary [337]
Dame Nita Barrow Award [9538]
Best Emerging Young Woman Scientist Award [5685]
Bourse Marcelle Blum [2246]
Nabila Breir Award [9539]
Henry Burger Prize [8148]
Karen Burt Memorial Award [9458]
Thomas Clarkson Prize [8149]
Rose Mary Crawshay Prize for English Litera-
ture [6924]
Distinguished Scientist Award for Contribution to the
Improvement of the Quality of Life of
Women [5686]
Essay Competition on Women in Society [6080]
European Sportsman and Sportswoman of the
Year [5385]
Excellence in Research on Improving Policing For
Women Award [279]
Fellowship Competition [6386]
Fellowship International Award [5668]
Harold Fern National Trophy [6708]
Lady Finniston Award [9459]
Rosalind Franklin Award [8934]
Emilie Louise Frey Award for the Promotion of
Talented Female Scholars [6528]
Mary George Memorial Prize for Apprentices [8022]
Hellweg Bravery Award [281]
HRH Princess Michael of Kent Award [9344]
International Recognition and Scholarship
Award [8088]
International Women in Transfusion Award [4775]
Nita B. Kibble Literary Award [1063]
Kshanika Oration Award [3552]
Ladies' British Open Amateur Championship [8278]
Pelagia Majewska Gliding Medal [6321]
Most Outstanding Female Administrator Award [283]
Most Outstanding Female Investigator Award [284]
Most Outstanding Female Leader Award [285]
Newman Cup [5057]
NSW Premier's Translation Prize [907]
Orange Award for New Writers [6907]
Orange Prize for Fiction [6908]
Padnendadlu Undergraduate Bursary [342]
Pandora Award [9456]
Mary Agard Pocock Award [5669]
Hansi Pollak Scholarship [5670]
Winifred E. Preedy Postgraduate Bursary [343]
President & Vice President's Choice Award [9345]
Prix des Dames [2615]
Recognition Award [6387]
Ricoh Women's British Open Championship [8279]
Hermann Schneider Prize [8151]
Rosemary Seymour Award [5093]
Isie Smuts Award [5671]
Bertha Stoneman Award [5672]

Georgina Sweet Fellowship [344]
Prix Tanesse [2299]
Prix Suzanne Tassier [1618]
Barbara Tate Award [9346]
Kim Scott Walwyn Prize [6911]
Winsor & Newton Choice Award [9347]
Women in Politics Prize [150]
Women in the City Achievement Awards [8419]

Women's rights

New Venture Award [9455]
Scott Trust Technology Bursaries [9460]

Wood and wood products see also
Forestry; Paper industry

Ron Cockcroft Award [6153]
IRG Travel Award [6154]
Schweighofer Prize [1317]

Work safety see Occupational safety

World peace

Best Corporate Social Responsibility Initiative of the
    Year [4609]
Best Project for Peace from an International Sports
    Federation [4610]
Champion for Peace of the Year [4611]
Founders' Award [1091]
Felix Houphouet-Boigny Peace Prize [2650]
The International Jose Marti Prize [2652]
International Peace Award [1092]
Luminosa Award for Unity [4082]
Media Peace Awards [1093]
Merit Awards [6256]
Niwano Peace Prize [4305]
Non-Governmental Organization for Peace of the
    Year [4612]
Olof Palme Memorial Fund Scholarships [6161]
Olof Palme Prize [6162]
Peace and Sport Image of the Year [4613]
Peace Prize of the German Book Trade [2989]
President's Award [8175]
Special Jury Prize [4614]
Sports Event for Peace of the Year [4615]
UNESCO Prize for Peace Education [2658]

Writing

Mona Brand Award Short Story Competition [715]
EduBlog Awards [700]
FOXTEL Fellowship for Excellence in Television Writ-
    ing [624]
Golden PEN Award [7562]
Arthur and Marjorie Goodchild Prize for Excellent
    English [8530]
Henries Awards [7749]

Hessell-Tiltman Prize [7563]
Louis Hiemstra Prize for Non-fiction [5631]
Hilarie Lindway Young Writers Short Story Competi-
    tion for School Children [716]
Maori Language Award [4869]
Mid-Career Writers Award [5013]
NZSA/Pindar Publishing Prize [5014]
Penguin Manuscript Prize [1098]
Prix Europa [2355]
Jerome Roche Prize [8876]
Grollo Ruzzene Foundation Prize for Writing about
    Italians in Australia [1067]
Tirlittan Prize [2130]
Union's Award for Merit [2131]
ZeBBie Awards [3890]

Yachting see Boating

Youth achievement

Chrisi Bailey Award [6744]
Celebrating Young Rwandan Achievers Award
    CYRWA [5887]
Creative Young Entrepreneur Luxembourg
    Award [4497]
Founders' Award [5945]
Global Youth Excellence Awards, an International
    Award Scheme [5946]
Governor General's Youth Award [1347]
Head of State Awards - Ghana [3257]
International Letter-Writing Competition for Young
    People [6517]
McWilliams Young Science Writers' Competi-
    tion [3921]
Luka Ritz Award [1883]
Rural Youth Europe Awards [2124]
Scouts of the World Award [6565]
Te Kura Pounamu Award [4938]
Young Achievers Awards [6652]
Young Active Citizens Award [2356]
Young Inventors' Award [5989]

Youth work

Bronze Wolf [6564]
Convoy For Kids Grant [666]
Culture and Literature Award [3802]
Distinguished Award of Honour for Service to
    Children's Charities [667]
Irish Youth Foundation Award [3898]
Life Governor [668]
Most Outstanding Volunteer [669]
President's Choice Award [670]
The President's International Award [2674]
Social Service Award [3803]
Youth Ambassador [671]
Youth and Community Awards [7677]

Zoology see also Ornithology

Agricultural and Forest Entomology Journal
    Award [8768]
Award to the Most Outstanding Third Year Student
    in Zoology [5770]
H. H. Bloomer Award [8314]
Pierre Bonnet Award [3090]
Paulo Marcello Brignoli Award [3091]
W. S. Bruce Medal [9062]
Phil Carne Prize [334]
Clarke Memorial Medal [1003]
F.H. Drummond Prize [1110]
Ecological Entomology Journal Award [8769]
Prix Foulon [2202]
Frink Medal for British Zoologists [9508]
Gold Medal [5771]
Hector Memorial Medal and Prize [5075]
Honorary Member [3092]
Sunder Lal Hora Medal [3637]
Hutton Memorial Medal and Prize [5076]
Thomas Henry Huxley Award [9509]
Insect Conservation and Diversity Journal
    Award [8771]
Insect Molecular Biology Journal Award [8772]
International Federation of Beekeepers' Associa-
    tions Medals [4095]
Prix Lamarck [1635]
Rudolph Leuckart Medal [2758]
Lifetime Achievement Award [3083]
Linnean Medal [8315]
Jasper Loftus-Hills Award [1134]
Mueller Medal [202]
Outstanding Researcher [4380]
E.N. Pavlovskii Prize [5843]
Gerhard Piekarski Prize [2759]
Frank A. Pitelka Award for Excellence in Re-
    search [833]
Fondation Max Poll [1640]
Prince Philip Award [9511]
Stamford Raffles Award [9512]
Research Medal [1017]
Scientific Medal [9513]
Junior Captain Scott Commemorative Medal [5640]
Silver Medal [9514]
Eugene Simon Award [3093]
Society Fellowship Award [4291]
Baldwin Spencer Prize [1149]
Stevenson - Hamilton Award [5773]
Student Prize [5774]
Professor Har Swarup Memorial Lecture [3668]
J.O. Westwood Medal for Excellence in Insect Tax-
    onomy [8779]
Whitley Awards [1024]
Wigglesworth Lecture and Medal Award [8780]
Young Scientist Award [4292]

The alphabetical Organization Index provides access to all sponsoring and administering organizations listed in both volumes, as well as to organization acronyms and alternate-language and former names. In the case of a sponsoring organization, the citation is to the specific award it sponsors. Each organization name is followed by the volume in which it appears. The numbers following the volume references are book entry numbers, not page numbers.

3D Society; International [Vol 1: 9479]
3M Health Care [Vol 1: 18097]
The 92nd Street Y [Vol 1: 1]
AACC International [Vol 1: 3]
AACE International [Vol 1: 13]
AAFRNC Trust for Philanthropy [Vol 1: 8651]
AAHPERD Research Consortium [Vol 1: 21]
Aaxis Pacific [Vol 2: 620]
Abbott Laboratories Ltd. [Vol 1: 6202]
ABC Canada [Vol 1: 6679]
Abdus Salam International Centre for Theoretical Physics [Vol 2: 4008, 6054]
ABET [Vol 1: 26]
Aboriginal Affairs and Northern Development Canada [Vol 1: 30]
Abraham Lincoln Association [Vol 1: 32]
Abu Dhabi Authority for Culture and Heritage [Vol 2: 6656]
ACA International [Vol 1: 35]
Acadamh Rioga na hEireann [Vol 2: 3928]
Academi - Welsh National Literature Promotion Agency and Society for Authors [Vol 2: 6674]
Academia Argentina de Letras [Vol 2: 38]
Academia Brasileira de Letras [Vol 2: 1748]
Academia de Ciencias Fisicas, Matematicas y Naturales [Vol 2: 9553]
Academia de la Investigacion Cientifica [Vol 2: 4590]
Academia Mexicana de Ciencias [Vol 2: 4590]
Academia Mexicana de Dermatologia [Vol 2: 4588]
Academia Nacional de Agronomia y Veterinaria [Vol 2: 23]
Academia Nacional de la Historia de la Republica Argentina [Vol 2: 34]
Academic Pediatric Association [Vol 1: 45]
Academie Canadienne de Parodontologie [Vol 1: 6162]
Academie des Beaux-Arts [Vol 2: 2134]
Academie des Inscriptions et Belles-Lettres [Vol 2: 2150]
Academie des Sciences [Vol 2: 2173]
Academie des Sciences - Institut de France [Vol 2: 2434]
Academie des Sciences Morales et Politiques [Vol 2: 2241]
L'Academie Internationale De Cytologie [Vol 2: 3039]
Academie Royale de Medecine de Belgique [Vol 2: 1576]
Academie Royale des Sciences, des Lettres et des Beaux-Arts de Belgique [Vol 2: 1579]
Academy of American Poets [Vol 1: 53]
Academy of Applied Osteopathy [Vol 1: 639]
Academy of Country Music [Vol 1: 60]
Academy of Country Music Entertainment [Vol 1: 6433]
Academy of Criminal Justice Sciences [Vol 1: 62]
Academy of Dentistry International [Vol 1: 69]
Academy of International Business [Vol 1: 76]
Academy of Marketing Science [Vol 1: 79]
Academy of Motion Picture Arts and Sciences [Vol 1: 83]
Academy of Natural Sciences [Vol 1: 90]
Academy of Operative Dentistry [Vol 1: 95]
Academy of Parish Clergy [Vol 1: 99]

Academy of Physical, Mathematical and Natural Sciences [Vol 2: 9553]
Academy of Psychosomatic Medicine [Vol 1: 103]
Academy of Science Fiction, Fantasy, and Horror Films [Vol 1: 110]
Academy of Sciences for the Developing World [Vol 2: 4372]
Academy of Sciences of Cuba [Vol 2: 1890]
Academy of Scientific Research [Vol 2: 4590]
Academy of Visual Arts - Leipzig College of Graphic Arts and Book Design [Vol 2: 2689]
Accademia delle Scienze di Torino [Vol 2: 4017]
Accademia Nazionale dei Lincei [Vol 2: 4020]
Accordeonistes; Confederation Internationale des [Vol 2: 2115]
Accordionists Confederation; International [Vol 2: 2115]
Accountants; Association of Government [Vol 1: 5353]
Accountants of Scotland; Institute of Chartered [Vol 2: 7834]
Accounting and Finance Association of Australia and New Zealand [Vol 2: 63]
Achilles Media Ltd. [Vol 1: 112]
ACM SIGGRAPH [Vol 1: 115]
Acoustical Society of America [Vol 1: 120]
Action for Nature Inc. [Vol 1: 130]
Action for Nuclear Disarmament [Vol 1: 17957]
Active Aging; International Council on [Vol 1: 9840]
Acton Institute for the Study of Religion and Liberty [Vol 1: 132]
Actors' Equity Association [Vol 1: 135]
Actuarial Society of South Africa [Vol 2: 5477]
Acuity [Vol 2: 6677]
Adapted Physical Activity; International Federation of [Vol 2: 2518]
ADARA: Professionals Networking for Excellence in Service Delivery with Individuals who are Deaf or Hard of Hearing [Vol 1: 140]
Addams Peace Association; Jane [Vol 1: 146]
Addiction Professionals; NAADAC: The Association for [Vol 1: 11341]
Adelaide Philosophical Society [Vol 2: 1011]
Ademe [Vol 2: 2594]
Adhesion Society [Vol 1: 148]
Adidas [Vol 1: 12844]
The Adirondack Council [Vol 1: 151]
Administration of the President of the Republic of Georgia [Vol 2: 2675]
Admiral of the Ocean Sea [Vol 1: 16652]
Adolescent Health and Medicine; Society for [Vol 1: 15010]
Adolescent Psychiatry; American Academy of Child and [Vol 1: 500]
Adolescent Psychiatry; American Society for [Vol 1: 3750]
Adult Education of the U.S.A. [Vol 1: 855]
Advanced Manufacturing Australia [Vol 2: 67]
Advancing Canadian Entrepreneurship [Vol 1: 153]
Advertising; American Academy of [Vol 1: 489]
Advertising and Design Club of Canada [Vol 1: 159]
Advertising Club of New York [Vol 1: 161]
Advertising Council [Vol 1: 163]

Advertising Media Credit Executives Association [Vol 1: 165]
Advertising Research Foundation [Vol 1: 167]
Advertising Women of New York [Vol 1: 172]
Aero Club of America [Vol 1: 11462]
Aero Club of South Africa [Vol 2: 5481]
Aeronautical Society of India [Vol 2: 3439]
Aeronautical Society - United Kingdom; Royal [Vol 2: 8602]
Aeronautics and Astronautics; American Institute of [Vol 1: 2498]
Aeronautics and Space Administration; National - Office of Human Capital Management [Vol 1: 11469]
Aerosol Society [Vol 2: 6679]
Aerospace Medical Association [Vol 1: 177]
AFL-CIO [Vol 1: 193]
AFL-CIO | International Labor Communications Association [Vol 1: 195]
Africa Investor [Vol 2: 5487]
Africagrowth Institute [Vol 2: 5489]
African Academy of Sciences [Vol 2: 4163, 4369]
African Association for Public Administration and Management [Vol 2: 4373]
African National Congress [Vol 2: 5491]
African Organization of Supreme Audit Institutions [Vol 2: 4471]
African Studies Association [Vol 1: 198]
African Studies Association of Australasia and the Pacific [Vol 2: 69]
African Studies Association of the United Kingdom [Vol 2: 6682]
Africare [Vol 1: 204]
AFS Intercultural Programs [Vol 1: 206]
Aga Khan Trust for Culture [Vol 2: 6250]
AGC Education and Research Foundation [Vol 1: 208]
Agence Nationale de Recherche sur le SIDA [Vol 2: 6343]
Agence Nationale de Recherches sur le SIDA [Vol 2: 6342]
AGFA Medical Systems [Vol 1: 6280]
Aging, Inc.; Center for the Study of [Vol 1: 7149]
Agricultural and Biological Engineers; American Society of [Vol 1: 4072]
Agricultural Economics Association of South Africa [Vol 2: 5496]
Agricultural Economics Society [Vol 2: 6685]
Agricultural Engineers; Institution of [Vol 2: 7950]
Agricultural History Society [Vol 1: 212]
Agricultural Institute of Canada [Vol 1: 219]
Agricultural Research; Indian Council of [Vol 2: 3519]
Agricultural Sciences; International Society for Southeast Asian [Vol 2: 5332]
Agricultural Society of England; Royal [Vol 2: 8626]
Agudat Hametargmim Beyisrael [Vol 2: 3971]
AHRA: The Association for Medical Imaging Management [Vol 1: 226]
AIIM - The Enterprise Content Management Association [Vol 1: 229]
Air and Waste Management Association [Vol 1: 233]
Air Force Association [Vol 1: 243]
Air Force Historical Foundation [Vol 1: 282]
Air League [Vol 2: 6688]

Air Shows; International Council of **[Vol 1: 9828]**
Air Traffic Control Association **[Vol 1: 291]**
Aircraft Owners and Pilots Association **[Vol 1: 306]**
Airline Passenger Experience Association **[Vol 1: 309]**
Airports Council International North America **[Vol 1: 313]**
Airts Cooncil o Norlin Airlann **[Vol 2: 6748]**
Akademiet for de Tekniske Videnskaber **[Vol 2: 1938]**
Alabama Sea Grant Consortium; Mississippi- **[Vol 1: 11216]**
Alarm and Security Association; Canadian **[Vol 1: 6866]**
Alaska-Siberia Research Center **[Vol 1: 318]**
Albania Art Institute **[Vol 2: 1]**
Albania; Bank of **[Vol 2: 6]**
Albanian Political Science Association **[Vol 2: 3]**
Alberta Amateur Boxing Association **[Vol 1: 320]**
Alberta Angus Association **[Vol 1: 326]**
Alberta Construction Safety Association **[Vol 1: 329]**
Alberta Irrigation Projects Association **[Vol 1: 334]**
Alberta Media Production Industries Association **[Vol 1: 336]**
Alberta Motion Picture Industries Association **[Vol 1: 336]**
Alberta Occupational Health Nurses Association **[Vol 1: 338]**
Alberta Publishers Association **[Vol 1: 5913]**
Alcoholism and Drug Dependence; National Council on **[Vol 1: 12244]**
Alcuin Society **[Vol 1: 342]**
Alexander Graham Bell Association for the Deaf and Hard of Hearing **[Vol 1: 344]**
Alger Association of Distinguished Americans; Horatio **[Vol 1: 347]**
Alger Society; Horatio **[Vol 1: 351]**
All-America Rose Selections **[Vol 1: 353]**
All India Management Association **[Vol 2: 3448]**
All Russia Association of the Blind **[Vol 2: 5775]**
Allen & Unwin Pty. Ltd. **[Vol 2: 71]**
Allergy/Asthma Information Association **[Vol 1: 357]**
Alliance Europeenne pour l'Ethique en Publicite **[Vol 2: 1425]**
Alliance for Children and Families **[Vol 1: 360]**
Alliance for Children and Television **[Vol 1: 18205]**
The Alliance for Coffee Excellence Inc. **[Vol 1: 364]**
Alliance for Community Media **[Vol 1: 366]**
Alliance for Continuing Medical Education **[Vol 1: 368]**
Alliance for Student Activities **[Vol 1: 372]**
L'Alliance Medias Jeunesse **[Vol 1: 18205]**
Alliance of Hazardous Materials Professionals **[Vol 1: 374]**
Alliance of the American Dental Association **[Vol 1: 386]**
Allied Artists of America **[Vol 1: 394]**
Alltech Canada Inc. **[Vol 1: 6927]**
Allyn & Bacon Publishers **[Vol 1: 14287]**
Alpert Foundation; Herb **[Vol 1: 10469]**
Alpha Chi Sigma **[Vol 1: 396]**
Alpha Chi Sigma Educational Foundation **[Vol 1: 399]**
Alpha Omega Alpha Honor Medical Society **[Vol 1: 402]**
Alpha Omega Dental Fraternity **[Vol 1: 405]**
Alpha Omega International Dental Fraternity **[Vol 1: 405]**
Alpha Tau Delta **[Vol 1: 407]**
Alpha Zeta Omega **[Vol 1: 412]**
Alpine Club of Canada **[Vol 1: 419]**
Altrusa International **[Vol 1: 426]**
Alumni Association of Princeton University **[Vol 1: 431]**
Alzheimer Society of Canada **[Vol 1: 434]**
Amakula Kampala Cultural Foundation **[Vol 2: 6649]**
Amateur Astronomers Association **[Vol 1: 439]**
Amateur Athletic Foundation of Los Angeles **[Vol 1: 10713]**
Amateur Athletic Union **[Vol 1: 441]**
Amateur Boxing Federation; United States of America **[Vol 1: 16697]**
Amateur Entomologists' Society **[Vol 2: 6696]**
Amateur Hockey Association of the United States **[Vol 1: 17418]**
Amateur Softball Association of America **[Vol 1: 480]**
Amateur Swimming Association **[Vol 2: 6702]**

Amaury Sport Organisation **[Vol 2: 2306]**
Ambulatory Pediatric Association **[Vol 1: 45]**
America-Israel Cultural Foundation **[Vol 1: 485]**
American Academy in Rome **[Vol 1: 487, 17507]**
American Academy of Advertising **[Vol 1: 489]**
American Academy of Arts and Sciences **[Vol 1: 492]**
American Academy of Child and Adolescent Psychiatry **[Vol 1: 500]**
American Academy of Child Psychiatry **[Vol 1: 500]**
American Academy of Clinical Psychiatrists **[Vol 1: 506]**
American Academy of Clinical Toxicology **[Vol 1: 508]**
American Academy of Dermatology **[Vol 1: 511]**
American Academy of Environmental Engineers **[Vol 1: 518]**
American Academy of Equine Art **[Vol 1: 523]**
American Academy of Facial Plastic and Reconstructive Surgery **[Vol 1: 533]**
American Academy of Family Physicians **[Vol 1: 544]**
American Academy of Forensic Psychology **[Vol 1: 568]**
American Academy of Kinesiology and Physical Education **[Vol 1: 11405]**
American Academy of Medical Administrators **[Vol 1: 570]**
American Academy of Neurology **[Vol 1: 579, 12612]**
American Academy of Nursing **[Vol 1: 599]**
American Academy of Occupational Medicine **[Vol 1: 1784]**
American Academy of Ophthalmology **[Vol 1: 603]**
American Academy of Ophthalmology and Otolaryngology **[Vol 1: 603]**
American Academy of Optometry **[Vol 1: 615]**
American Academy of Oral and Maxillofacial Radiology **[Vol 1: 627]**
American Academy of Oral Medicine **[Vol 1: 632]**
American Academy of Orthopaedic Surgeons **[Vol 1: 637]**
American Academy of Osteopathy **[Vol 1: 639]**
American Academy of Otolaryngology - Head and Neck Surgery **[Vol 1: 641]**
American Academy of Pediatric Dentistry **[Vol 1: 645]**
American Academy of Pediatrics **[Vol 1: 651]**
American Academy of Periodontology **[Vol 1: 717]**
American Academy of Physical Medicine and Rehabilitation **[Vol 1: 728]**
American Academy of Physician Assistants **[Vol 1: 734]**
American Academy of Political and Social Science **[Vol 1: 744]**
American Academy of Psychiatry and the Law **[Vol 1: 748, 3350]**
American Academy of Religion **[Vol 1: 750]**
American Academy of Sanitarians **[Vol 1: 758]**
American Academy of Sleep Medicine **[Vol 1: 761]**
American Academy of the History of Dentistry **[Vol 1: 764]**
American Academy of Veterinary Pharmacology and Therapeutics **[Vol 1: 767]**
American Accordionists' Association **[Vol 1: 772]**
American Advertising Federation **[Vol 1: 774]**
American Aging Association **[Vol 1: 782]**
American Agri-Women **[Vol 1: 786]**
American Agricultural Editors' Association **[Vol 1: 789]**
American Alliance for Health, Physical Education, Recreation and Dance **[Vol 1: 795]**
American Alliance for Theatre and Education **[Vol 1: 802]**
American Animal Hospital Association **[Vol 1: 818]**
American Anthropological Association **[Vol 1: 821]**
American Antiquarian Society **[Vol 1: 831]**
American Arbitration Association **[Vol 1: 835]**
American Art Therapy Association **[Vol 1: 837]**
American Artists Professional League **[Vol 1: 845]**
American Assembly for Men in Nursing **[Vol 1: 850]**
American Association for Active Lifestyles and Fitness - American Association for Leisure and Recreation **[Vol 1: 970]**
American Association for Adult and Continuing Education **[Vol 1: 855]**
American Association for Aerosol Research **[Vol 1: 861]**
American Association for Affirmative Action **[Vol 1: 866]**

American Association for Agricultural Education **[Vol 1: 870]**
American Association for Applied Linguistics **[Vol 1: 874]**
American Association for Artificial Intelligence **[Vol 1: 5109]**
American Association for Automotive Medicine **[Vol 1: 5115]**
American Association for Cancer Research **[Vol 1: 877]**
American Association for Clinical Chemistry **[Vol 1: 883]**
American Association for Collegiate Independent Study **[Vol 1: 930]**
American Association for Counseling and Development **[Vol 1: 1929]**
American Association for Employment in Education **[Vol 1: 938]**
American Association for Girls and Women in Sports **[Vol 1: 940]**
American Association for Hand Surgery **[Vol 1: 947]**
American Association for Health Education **[Vol 1: 949]**
American Association for History and Computing **[Vol 1: 955]**
American Association for Laboratory Animal Science **[Vol 1: 957]**
American Association for Marriage and Family Therapy **[Vol 1: 964]**
American Association for Physical Activity and Recreation **[Vol 1: 970]**
American Association for Public Opinion Research **[Vol 1: 972]**
American Association for State and Local History **[Vol 1: 978]**
American Association for the Advancement of Artificial Intelligence **[Vol 1: 4960]**
American Association for the Advancement of Science **[Vol 1: 982]**
American Association for the Advancement of Slavic Studies **[Vol 1: 5093]**
American Association for the History of Medicine **[Vol 1: 997]**
American Association for the History of Nursing **[Vol 1: 1004]**
American Association for Theatre in Secondary Education **[Vol 1: 802]**
American Association for Women in Community Colleges **[Vol 1: 1008]**
American Association for Women Radiologists **[Vol 1: 1011]**
American Association of Advertising Agencies **[Vol 1: 1015]**
American Association of Agricultural College Editors **[Vol 1: 4944]**
American Association of Anatomists **[Vol 1: 1019]**
American Association of Avian Pathologists **[Vol 1: 1040]**
American Association of Bioanalysts **[Vol 1: 1050]**
American Association of Blacks in Energy **[Vol 1: 1052]**
American Association of Blood Banks **[Vol 1: 1055]**
American Association of Bovine Practitioners **[Vol 1: 1069]**
American Association of Cereal Chemists **[Vol 1: 3]**
American Association of Certified Orthoptists **[Vol 1: 1079]**
American Association of Children's Residential Centers **[Vol 1: 1082]**
American Association of Christian Schools **[Vol 1: 1084]**
American Association of College Baseball Coaches **[Vol 1: 1474]**
American Association of Colleges for Teacher Education **[Vol 1: 1086]**
American Association of Collegiate Registrars and Admissions Officers **[Vol 1: 1096]**
American Association of Community Colleges **[Vol 1: 12148, 12149]**
American Association of Community Theatre **[Vol 1: 1105]**
American Association of Cost Engineers **[Vol 1: 13]**
American Association of Critical-Care Nurses **[Vol 1: 1116]**
American Association of Diabetes Educators **[Vol 1: 1126]**

American Association of Directors of Psychiatric
Residency Training [Vol 1: 1133]
American Association of Electromyography and Elec-
trodiagnosis [Vol 1: 1223]
American Association of Endodontists [Vol 1: 1138]
American Association of Engineering Societies [Vol
1: 1145]
American Association of Family and Consumer Sci-
ences [Vol 1: 1153]
American Association of Genito-Urinary Sur-
geons [Vol 1: 1159]
American Association of Gynecologic Laparosco-
pists [Vol 1: 1162]
American Association of Handwriting Analysts [Vol
1: 1166]
American Association of Healthcare Administrative
Management [Vol 1: 1168]
American Association of Homes and Services for
the Aging [Vol 1: 10768]
American Association of Hospital Dental Chiefs [Vol
1: 16073]
American Association of Housing Educators [Vol 1:
1173]
American Association of Immunologists [Vol 1: 1180]
American Association of Industrial Physicians and
Surgeons [Vol 1: 1784]
American Association of Law Libraries [Vol 1: 1186]
American Association of Meat Processors [Vol 1:
1199]
American Association of Motor Vehicle Administra-
tors [Vol 1: 1210]
American Association of Museums [Vol 1: 1214]
American Association of Neurological Surgeons [Vol
1: 1221]
American Association of Neuromuscular and Elec-
trodiagnostic Medicine [Vol 1: 1223]
American Association of Neuropathologists [Vol 1:
1228]
American Association of Neuroscience Nurses [Vol
1: 1232]
American Association of Nurse Anesthetists [Vol 1:
1238]
American Association of Nurse Attorneys [Vol 1:
1244]
American Association of Occupational Health
Nurses [Vol 1: 1247]
American Association of Oral and Maxillofacial Sur-
geons [Vol 1: 1252]
American Association of Orthodontists [Vol 1: 1259]
American Association of Osteopathic Specialists [Vol
1: 1299]
American Association of Pathologists and Bacteriolo-
gists [Vol 1: 3955]
American Association of Petroleum Geologists [Vol
1: 1265]
American Association of Physical Anthropolo-
gists [Vol 1: 1292]
American Association of Physician Specialists [Vol
1: 1299]
American Association of Physicists in Medicine [Vol
1: 1302]
American Association of Physicists in Medicine [Vol
2: 7929]
American Association of Physics Teachers [Vol 1:
1305]
American Association of Plastic Surgeons [Vol 1:
1314]
American Association of Poison Control Centers [Vol
1: 1319]
American Association of Political Consultants [Vol 1:
1321]
American Association of Public Health Dentistry [Vol
1: 1323]
American Association of Public Health Physi-
cians [Vol 1: 1330]
American Association of School Administrators [Vol
1: 1332]
American Association of School Librarians [Vol 1:
1337]
American Association of School Personnel Adminis-
trators [Vol 1: 1348]
American Association of State Colleges and Universi-
ties [Vol 1: 1350]
American Association of State Highway and
Transportation Officials [Vol 1: 1352]
American Association of Suicidology [Vol 1: 1357]

American Association of Teacher Educators in Agri-
culture [Vol 1: 870]
American Association of Teachers of German [Vol 1:
1360]
American Association of Teachers of Italian [Vol 1:
1365]
American Association of Teachers of Slavic and
East European Languages [Vol 1: 1367]
American Association of Teachers of Spanish and
Portuguese [Vol 1: 1372]
American Association of Textile Chemists and Color-
ists [Vol 1: 1378]
American Association of University Administra-
tors [Vol 1: 1383]
American Association of University Professors [Vol
1: 1387]
American Association of University Women [Vol 1:
1392]
American Association of University Women
Educational Foundation [Vol 1: 1395]
American Association of University Women Legal
Advocacy Fund [Vol 1: 1399]
American Association of Variable Star Observ-
ers [Vol 1: 1401]
American Association of Veterinary Laboratory Diag-
nosticians [Vol 1: 1406]
American Association of Wardens and Superinten-
dents [Vol 1: 13279]
American Association of Webmasters [Vol 1: 1408]
American Association of Women Dentists [Vol 1:
1413]
American Association of Zoo Keepers [Vol 1: 1415]
American Association of Zoological Parks and
Aquariums [Vol 1: 5559]
American Association on Intellectual and
Developmental Disabilities [Vol 1: 1421]
American Association on Mental Deficiency [Vol 1:
1421]
American Association on Mental Retardation [Vol 1:
1421]
American Astronautical Society [Vol 1: 1431]
American Astronomical Society [Vol 1: 1442]
American Auto Racing Writers and Broadcasters As-
sociation [Vol 1: 1456]
American Automatic Control Council [Vol 1: 2607]
American Award Manufacturers Association [Vol 1:
5747]
American Badminton Association [Vol 1: 17403]
American Bandmasters Association [Vol 1: 1460]
American Bar Association [Vol 1: 1463]
American Bar Association [Vol 1: 12585]
American Bar Association Criminal Justice Sec-
tion [Vol 1: 1469]
American Baseball Coaches Association [Vol 1:
1474]
American Bashkir Curly Registry [Vol 1: 1484]
American Basketball Association [Vol 1: 11973]
American Begonia Society [Vol 1: 1487]
American Bible Society [Vol 1: 1491]
American Birding Association [Vol 1: 1494]
American Board for Occupational Health Nurses [Vol
1: 1500]
American Board of Medical Laboratory Immunol-
ogy [Vol 1: 3991]
American Board of Medical Microbiology [Vol 1:
3991]
American Board of Orthodontics [Vol 1: 1506]
American Booksellers Association [Vol 1: 1511]
American Bottled Water Association [Vol 1: 9735]
American Bridge Teachers' Association [Vol 1: 1513]
American Bureau of Shipping [Vol 1: 15710]
American Burn Association [Vol 1: 1517]
American Business Council of Dubai and the
Northern Emirates [Vol 2: 6659]
American Business Women's Association [Vol 1:
1521]
American Camp Association [Vol 1: 1523]
American Cancer Society [Vol 1: 1529]
American Carbon Committee [Vol 1: 1537]
American Carbon Society [Vol 1: 1537]
American Catholic Historical Association [Vol 1:
1541]
American Catholic Philosophical Association [Vol 1:
1546]
American Ceramic Society [Vol 1: 1550]

American Chamber of Commerce Executives [Vol 1:
1581]
American Chamber of Commerce in Germany
(Frankfurt, Germany) [Vol 2: 2691]
American Chamber of Commerce in Lithuania [Vol
2: 4477]
American Chamber of Commerce in Moldova [Vol 2:
4604]
American Chamber of Commerce in Morocco [Vol 2:
4616]
American Chamber of Commerce in South Africa [Vol
2: 5501]
American Chamber of Commerce of Brazil (Rio de
Janeiro, Brazil) [Vol 2: 1741]
American Chamber of Commerce of Brazil (Sao
Paulo, Brazil) [Vol 2: 1743]
American Chamber of Commerce of Guatemala [Vol
2: 3328]
American Chemical Society [Vol 1: 397]
American Chemical Society [Vol 1: 1588]
American Chinese Medical Society [Vol 1: 7251]
American Chiropractic Association [Vol 1: 1680]
American Citizens Abroad [Vol 2: 6252]
American Civil Liberties Union [Vol 1: 1682]
American Classical League [Vol 1: 1684]
American Cleaning Institute [Vol 1: 13137]
American Cleft Palate Education Foundation [Vol 1:
7320]
American Coatings Association [Vol 1: 1689]
American College Health Association [Vol 1: 1693]
American College of Allergy, Asthma and Immunol-
ogy [Vol 1: 1700]
American College of Apothecaries [Vol 1: 1702]
American College of Cardiology [Vol 1: 1705]
American College of Cardiovascular Administra-
tors [Vol 1: 571]
American College of Clinical Pharmacology [Vol 1:
1716]
American College of Dentists [Vol 1: 1731]
American College of Emergency Physicians [Vol 1:
1743]
American College of Health Plan Management [Vol
1: 1748]
American College of Healthcare Executives [Vol 1:
1753]
American College of Hospital Administrators [Vol 1:
1753]
American College of Legal Medicine [Vol 1: 1763]
American College of Managed Care Administra-
tors [Vol 1: 1748]
American College of Medical Practice Execu-
tives [Vol 1: 1767]
American College of Musicians [Vol 1: 1774]
American College of Neuropsychopharmacology [Vol
1: 1776]
American College of Nurse-Midwives [Vol 1: 1782]
American College of Occupational and
Environmental Medicine [Vol 1: 1784]
American College of Oral and Maxillofacial Sur-
geons [Vol 1: 1789]
American College of Physicians [Vol 1: 1792]
American College of Preventive Medicine [Vol 1:
1806]
American College of Psychiatrists [Vol 1: 1811]
American College of Radiology [Vol 1: 1818]
American College of Surgeons [Vol 1: 1821]
American Community Theatre Association [Vol 1:
1105]
American Comparative Literature Association [Vol 1:
1825]
American Composers Alliance [Vol 1: 1833]
American Concrete Institute [Vol 1: 1835]
American Conference of Governmental Industrial
Hygienists [Vol 1: 1857]
American Congress of Rehabilitation Medicine [Vol
1: 1860]
American Congress on Surveying and Mapping [Vol
1: 1868, 12894]
American Consular Association [Vol 1: 2177]
American Contact Dermatitis Society [Vol 1: 1874]
American Coon Hunters Association [Vol 1: 1878]
American Correctional Association [Vol 1: 1880]
American Council for Better Broadcasts [Vol 1:
12975]
American Council for Polish Culture [Vol 1: 1887]

American Council of Engineering Companies [Vol 1: 1895]

American Council of Independent Laboratories [Vol 1: 1899]

American Council of Learned Societies [Vol 1: 1904]

American Council of the Blind [Vol 1: 1906]

American Council on Consumer Interests [Vol 1: 1912]

American Council on Education [Vol 1: 1919]

American Council on Industrial Arts Teacher Education [Vol 1: 10440]

American Council on the Teaching of Foreign Languages [Vol 1: 1921]

American Counseling Association [Vol 1: 1929]

American Craft Council [Vol 1: 1945]

American Crossword Puzzle Tournament [Vol 1: 1949]

American Crystallographic Association [Vol 1: 1951]

American Culinary Federation [Vol 1: 1963]

American Dairy Science Association [Vol 1: 1965]

American Dance Festival [Vol 1: 1988]

American Dance Guild [Vol 1: 1991]

American Darts Organization [Vol 1: 1994]

American Defense Institute [Vol 1: 1997]

American Dental Association [Vol 1: 1999]

American Dental Hygienists' Association [Vol 1: 2007]

American Design Awards [Vol 1: 2011]

American Diabetes Association [Vol 1: 2015]

American Dietetic Association Foundation [Vol 1: 2028]

American Documentation Institute [Vol 1: 3937]

American Donkey and Mule Society [Vol 1: 2046]

American Economic Association [Vol 1: 2049]

American Educational Research Association [Vol 1: 2054]

American Endurance Ride Conference [Vol 1: 2061]

American Enterprise Association [Vol 1: 2082]

American Enterprise Institute for Public Policy Research [Vol 1: 2082]

American Epilepsy Society [Vol 1: 2084]

American Ethical Union [Vol 1: 2086]

American Evaluation Association [Vol 1: 2088]

American Express Co. [Vol 1: 2462]

American Family Therapy Academy [Vol 1: 2094]

American Family Therapy Association [Vol 1: 2094]

American Farm Bureau Federation [Vol 1: 2097]

American Farrier's Association [Vol 1: 2099]

American Federation for Aging Research [Vol 1: 2106]

American Federation for Medical Research [Vol 1: 2109]

American Federation of Aviculture [Vol 1: 2113]

American Federation of Mineralogical Societies [Vol 1: 2115]

American Federation of Motorcyclists [Vol 1: 2120]

American Federation of Teachers [Vol 1: 2124]

American Feed Industry Association [Vol 1: 2126]

American Film Institute [Vol 1: 2136]

American Finance Association [Vol 1: 2139]

American Fisheries Society [Vol 1: 2143]

American Folklore Society [Vol 1: 2157]

American Football Coaches Association [Vol 1: 2166]

American Forage and Grassland Council [Vol 1: 2171]

American Foreign Service Association [Vol 1: 2177]

American Forensic Association [Vol 1: 2184]

American Forest and Paper Association [Vol 1: 2186]

American Foundation for the Blind [Vol 1: 2188]

American Friends of Magen David Adom [Vol 1: 2193]

American Fuchsia Society [Vol 1: 2195]

American Galvanizers Association [Vol 1: 2198]

American Gastroenterological Association [Vol 1: 2200]

American Gastroenterological Association Foundation [Vol 1: 8441]

American Gem Society [Vol 1: 2205]

American Gem Trade Association [Vol 1: 2207]

American Geographical Society [Vol 1: 2210]

American Geological Institute [Vol 1: 2221]

American Geophysical Union [Vol 1: 2225]

American Geriatrics Society [Vol 1: 2250]

American Goat Society [Vol 1: 2257]

American Guernsey Association [Vol 1: 2260]

American Guild of Organists [Vol 1: 2264]

American Gynecological and Obstetrical Society [Vol 1: 2268]

American Gynecological Society [Vol 1: 2268]

American Handwriting Analysis Foundation [Vol 1: 2271]

American Harp Society [Vol 1: 2274]

American Head and Neck Society [Vol 1: 2280]

American Headache Society [Vol 1: 2284]

American Health Assistance Foundation [Vol 1: 2288]

American Health Care Association [Vol 1: 2294]

American Healthcare Radiology Administrators [Vol 1: 226]

American Heart Association [Vol 1: 2298]

American Helicopter Society [Vol 1: 2317]

American Hemerocallis Society [Vol 1: 2333]

American Herbal Products Association [Vol 1: 2344]

American Hiking Society [Vol 1: 2348]

American Historical Association [Vol 1: 2356]

American Hockey Coaches Association [Vol 1: 2393]

American Hockey League [Vol 1: 2403]

American Home Economics Association Foundation [Vol 1: 1153]

American Horticultural Society [Vol 1: 2423]

American Horticultural Therapy Association [Vol 1: 2439]

American Hospital Association [Vol 1: 2445]

American Hospital Radiology Administrators [Vol 1: 226]

American Hosta Society [Vol 1: 2453]

American Hotel and Lodging Association [Vol 1: 2459]

American Hotel and Lodging Educational Foundation [Vol 1: 2461]

American Hotel & Motel Association [Vol 1: 2459]

American Humanist Association [Vol 1: 2466]

American Hungarian Foundation [Vol 1: 2471]

American Immigration Council [Vol 1: 2473]

American Immigration Law Foundation [Vol 1: 2473]

American Indian Ethnohistoric Conference [Vol 1: 3906]

American Indian Horse Registry [Vol 1: 2478]

American Industrial Arts Student Association [Vol 1: 16399]

American Industrial Hygiene Association [Vol 1: 2483]

American Institute for Decision Sciences [Vol 1: 7829]

American Institute for Public Service [Vol 1: 2496]

American Institute of Aeronautics and Astronautics [Vol 1: 2498]

American Institute of Architects [Vol 1: 2564]

American Institute of Architects, New York Chapter [Vol 1: 2580]

American Institute of Architects - *Sunset Magazine* [Vol 1: 16324]

American Institute of Biological Sciences [Vol 1: 2590]

American Institute of Building Design [Vol 1: 2593]

American Institute of Certified Public Accountants [Vol 1: 2595]

American Institute of Chemical Engineers [Vol 1: 398, 2603]

American Institute of Chemists [Vol 1: 2645]

American Institute of Fishery Research Biologists [Vol 1: 2649]

American Institute of Floral Designers [Vol 1: 2653]

American Institute of Graphic Arts [Vol 1: 2658]

American Institute of Indian Studies [Vol 1: 2662]

American Institute of Industrial Engineers [Vol 1: 9346]

American Institute of Iranian Studies [Vol 1: 2667]

American Institute of Mechanical Engineers [Vol 1: 4412]

American Institute of Mining, Metallurgical, and Petroleum Engineers [Vol 1: 2672]

American Institute of Mining, Metallurgical and Petroleum Engineers; Iron and Steel Society of the [Vol 1: 5028]

American Institute of Mining, Metallurgical and Petroleum Engineers; Society of Petroleum Engineers of the [Vol 1: 15748]

American Institute of Musical Studies [Vol 1: 12630]

American Institute of Physics [Vol 1: 2682]

American Institute of Planners [Vol 1: 3282]

American Institute of Professional Geologists [Vol 1: 2697]

American Institute of Steel Construction [Vol 1: 2702]

American Institute of Stress [Vol 1: 2706]

American Institute of Ultrasound in Medicine [Vol 1: 2708]

American Intellectual Property Law Association [Vol 1: 2713]

American Interior Designers [Vol 1: 4347]

American Intraocular Implant Society [Vol 1: 4135]

American Iron and Steel Institute [Vol 1: 2717]

American Jewish Committee [Vol 1: 2720]

American Jewish Congress [Vol 1: 2726]

American Jewish Historical Society [Vol 1: 2728]

American Jewish Press Association [Vol 1: 2734]

American Judicature Society [Vol 1: 2736]

American Kennel Club [Vol 1: 2742]

American Kidney Fund [Vol 1: 2746]

American Laryngological Association [Vol 1: 2749]

American Lawyers Auxiliary [Vol 1: 2755]

American Leather Chemists Association [Vol 1: 2759]

American Legislative Exchange Council [Vol 1: 2763]

American Library Association - Children's Services Division [Vol 1: 5054]

American Library Association - Ethnic and Multicultural Information Exchange Round Table [Vol 1: 2766]

American Library Association - Ethnic and Peoplecultural Information Exchange Roundtable [Vol 1: 2769]

American Library Association - Governance Office [Vol 1: 2771]

American Library Association - Office for Research and Statistics [Vol 1: 2791]

American Library Association - Reference and Adult Services Division [Vol 1: 14459]

American Library Association - Resources and Technical Services Division [Vol 1: 5046]

American Library Association - Social Responsibilities Round Table [Vol 1: 2793]

American Literary Translators Association [Vol 1: 2795]

American Liver Foundation [Vol 1: 2797]

American Lung Association [Vol 1: 2800]

American Marketing Association [Vol 1: 2802]

American Marketing Association Foundation [Vol 1: 2809]

American Mathematical Society [Vol 1: 2822]

American Meat Institute [Vol 1: 2844]

American Meat Science Association [Vol 1: 2848]

American Medical Association Foundation [Vol 1: 2859]

American Medical Technologists [Vol 1: 2863]

American Medical Women's Association [Vol 1: 2872]

American Medical Writers Association [Vol 1: 2875]

American Mensa [Vol 1: 2883]

American Mental Health Counselors Association [Vol 1: 2890]

American Meteor Society [Vol 1: 2894]

American Meteorological Society [Vol 1: 2898]

American Military Institute [Vol 1: 15196]

American Military Retirees Association [Vol 1: 2922]

American Mining Congress [Vol 1: 12608]

American Morgan Horse Association [Vol 1: 2924]

American Mosquito Control Association [Vol 1: 2936]

American Mothers Committee [Vol 1: 2942]

American Mothers, Inc. [Vol 1: 2942]

American Motorcyclist Association [Vol 1: 2945]

American Mule Association [Vol 1: 2947]

American Museum of Natural History [Vol 1: 2950]

American Musical Instrument Society [Vol 1: 2956]

American Musicological Society [Vol 1: 2960]

American National Standards Institute [Vol 1: 2967]

American Nephrology Nurses' Association [Vol 1: 2977]

American Newspaper Publishers Association Foundation [Vol 1: 13242]

American Numismatic Association [Vol 1: 2981]

American Numismatic Society [Vol 1: 3012]

American Nurses Association [Vol 1: 3017]

American Occupational Medical Association [Vol 1: 1784]

American Occupational Therapy Association [Vol 1: 3027]

American Occupational Therapy Foundation **[Vol 1: 3039]**

American Oil Chemists' Society **[Vol 1: 3044]**

American Ophthalmological Society **[Vol 1: 3050]**

American Optometric Association **[Vol 1: 3052]**

American Optometric Foundation **[Vol 1: 3057]**

American Orchid Society **[Vol 1: 3061]**

American Orff-Schulwerk Association **[Vol 1: 3086]**

American Ornithologists' Union **[Vol 1: 3091]**

American ORT and Women's American ORT **[Vol 1: 13702]**

American Orthopaedic Society for Sports Medicine **[Vol 1: 3097]**

American Orthopsychiatric Association **[Vol 1: 3101]**

American Osteopathic Foundation **[Vol 1: 3105]**

American Otological Society **[Vol 1: 3110]**

American Pain Society **[Vol 1: 3112]**

American Park and Recreation Society **[Vol 1: 3118]**

American Parkinson Disease Association **[Vol 1: 3121]**

American Patent Law Association **[Vol 1: 2713]**

American Peanut Council **[Vol 1: 3123]**

American Pediatric Society **[Vol 1: 3125]**

American Pet Products Association **[Vol 1: 3127]**

American Pet Products Manufacturers Association **[Vol 1: 3127]**

American Petroleum Institute **[Vol 1: 3129]**

American Pharmacists Association **[Vol 1: 3131]**

American Pharmacists Association - Academy of Pharmaceutical Research and Science **[Vol 1: 3140]**

American Pharmacists Association - Academy of Pharmacy Practice and Management **[Vol 1: 3148]**

American Pharmacists Association - Academy of Student Pharmacists **[Vol 1: 3157]**

American Philatelic Association **[Vol 1: 3163]**

American Philatelic Society **[Vol 1: 3163]**

American Philological Association **[Vol 1: 3167]**

American Philosophical Association **[Vol 1: 3170]**

American Philosophical Society **[Vol 1: 3182]**

American Physical Society **[Vol 1: 3192]**

American Physical Therapy Association **[Vol 1: 3228]**

American Physical Therapy Association, Private Practice Section **[Vol 1: 3245]**

American Physiological Society **[Vol 1: 3247]**

American Phytopathological Society **[Vol 1: 3272]**

American Planning Association **[Vol 1: 3282]**

American Planning Association - American Institute of Certified Planners **[Vol 1: 3293]**

American Plant Life Society **[Vol 1: 9741]**

American Podiatric Medical Association **[Vol 1: 3296]**

American Podiatry Association **[Vol 1: 3296]**

American Political Science Association **[Vol 1: 3299]**

American Polygraph Association **[Vol 1: 3312]**

American Pomological Society **[Vol 1: 3318]**

American Power Boat Association **[Vol 1: 3322]**

American Printing History Association **[Vol 1: 3328]**

American Probation and Parole Association **[Vol 1: 3331]**

American Protestant Health Association; College of Chaplains of the **[Vol 1: 5479]**

American Psychiatric Association **[Vol 1: 3341]**

American Psychological Association **[Vol 1: 14290, 14295]**

American Psychological Association - Adult Development and Aging Division (Division 20) **[Vol 1: 3370]**

American Psychological Association - American Society for the Advancement of Pharmacotherapy (Division 55) **[Vol 1: 3378]**

American Psychological Association - Committee on International Relations **[Vol 1: 3382]**

American Psychological Association - Committee on Women in Psychology **[Vol 1: 3384]**

American Psychological Association - Division of Applied Experimental and Engineering Psychology (Division 21) **[Vol 1: 3387]**

American Psychological Association - Division of Behavioral Analysis (Division 25) **[Vol 1: 3391]**

American Psychological Association - Division of Behavioral Neuroscience and Comparative Psychology (Division 6) **[Vol 1: 3397]**

American Psychological Association - Division of Developmental Psychology (Division 7) **[Vol 1: 3403]**

American Psychological Association - Division of Educational Psychology (Division 15) **[Vol 1: 3411]**

American Psychological Association - Division of Evaluation, Measurement and Statistics (Division 5) **[Vol 1: 3415]**

American Psychological Association - Division of Exercise and Sport Psychology (Division 47) **[Vol 1: 3420]**

American Psychological Association - Division of Family Psychology **[Vol 1: 3422]**

American Psychological Association - Division of Independent Practice **[Vol 1: 3430]**

American Psychological Association - Division of Intellectual and Developmental Disabilities (Division 33) **[Vol 1: 3434]**

American Psychological Association - Division of International Psychology (Division 52) **[Vol 1: 3436]**

American Psychological Association - Division of Media Psychology (Division 46) **[Vol 1: 3440]**

American Psychological Association - Division of Psychoanalysis (Division 39) **[Vol 1: 3444]**

American Psychological Association - Division of Psychotherapy **[Vol 1: 3448]**

American Psychological Association - Division of Rehabilitation Psychology (Division 22) **[Vol 1: 3456]**

American Psychological Association - Division of Trauma Psychology (Division 56) **[Vol 1: 3465]**

American Psychological Association - Health Psychology Division (Division 38) **[Vol 1: 3470]**

American Psychological Association - Psychologists in Public Service Division (Division 18) **[Vol 1: 3475]**

American Psychological Association - Psychology of Religion Division **[Vol 1: 3481]**

American Psychological Association - Psychopharmacology and Substance Abuse (Division 28) **[Vol 1: 3487]**

American Psychological Association - School Psychology Division (Division 16) **[Vol 1: 3490]**

American Psychological Association - Science Directorate **[Vol 1: 3497]**

American Psychological Association - Society for Child and Family Policy and Practice (Division 37)- **[Vol 1: 3502]**

American Psychological Association - Society for Community Research and Action - Division of Community Psychology (Division 27) **[Vol 1: 3507]**

American Psychological Association - Society for Consumer Psychology (Division 23) **[Vol 1: 3515]**

American Psychological Association - Society for General Psychology (Division 1) **[Vol 1: 3517]**

American Psychological Association - Society for Humanistic Psychology (Division 32) **[Vol 1: 3523]**

American Psychological Association - Society for Military Psychology (Division 19) **[Vol 1: 3526]**

American Psychological Association - Society for the Psychological Study of Lesbian, Gay, Bisexual and Transgender Issues (Division 44) **[Vol 1: 3531]**

American Psychological Association - Society for the Psychological Study of Men and Masculinity (Division 51) **[Vol 1: 3542]**

American Psychological Association - Society for the Psychology of Aesthetics, Creativity and the Arts (Division 10) **[Vol 2: 4854]**

American Psychological Association - Society for the Psychology of Women (Division 35) **[Vol 1: 3546]**

American Psychological Association - Society for the Teaching of Psychology (Division 2) **[Vol 1: 3553]**

American Psychological Association - Society for Theoretical and Philosophical Psychology (Division 24) **[Vol 1: 3559]**

American Psychological Association - Society of Addiction Psychology (Division 50) **[Vol 1: 3565]**

American Psychological Association - Society of Clinical Child and Adolescent Psychology (Division 53) **[Vol 1: 3571]**

American Psychological Association - Society of Clinical Psychology (Division 12) **[Vol 1: 3575]**

American Psychological Association - Society of Counseling Psychology (Division 17) **[Vol 1: 3587]**

American Psychological Association - Society of Group Psychology and Group Psychotherapy (Division 40) **[Vol 1: 3596]**

American Psychological Association - Society of Pediatric Psychology (Division 54) **[Vol 1: 3599]**

American Psychological Association - Society of Psychological Hypnosis (Division 30) **[Vol 1: 3605]**

American Psychological Association - State, Provincial, and Territorial Psychological Association Affairs (Division 31) **[Vol 1: 3614]**

American Psychological Foundation **[Vol 1: 3472]**

American Psychology-Law Society **[Vol 1: 3619]**

American Psychopathological Association **[Vol 1: 3628]**

American Public Gardens Association **[Vol 1: 3630]**

American Public Gas Association **[Vol 1: 3638]**

American Public Health Association **[Vol 1: 3641]**

American Public Power Association **[Vol 1: 3645]**

American Public Works Association **[Vol 1: 3659]**

American Radium Society **[Vol 1: 3666]**

American Real Estate and Urban Economics Association **[Vol 1: 3670]**

American Red Cross National Headquarters **[Vol 1: 3675]**

American Rental Association **[Vol 1: 3684]**

American Research Institute in Turkey **[Vol 1: 3691]**

American Rhinologic Society **[Vol 1: 3694]**

American Rhododendron Society **[Vol 1: 3697]**

American Risk and Insurance Association **[Vol 1: 3700]**

American Road and Transportation Builders Association **[Vol 1: 3705]**

American Road Builders Association **[Vol 1: 3705]**

American Rock Art Research Association **[Vol 1: 3712]**

American Romanian Academy of Arts and Sciences **[Vol 1: 3718]**

American Rottweiler Club **[Vol 1: 3721]**

American Rural Health Association **[Vol 1: 12789]**

American Samoa Chamber of Commerce **[Vol 2: 10]**

American School and Community Safety Association **[Vol 1: 970]**

American School Health Association **[Vol 1: 3725]**

American Scientific Glassblowers Society **[Vol 1: 3727]**

American Screenwriters Association **[Vol 1: 3730]**

American Sheep Industry Association **[Vol 1: 3735]**

American Shore and Beach Preservation Association **[Vol 1: 3741]**

American-Slovenian Polka Foundation **[Vol 1: 3746]**

American Society for Adolescent Psychiatry **[Vol 1: 3750]**

American Society for Aesthetic Plastic Surgery **[Vol 1: 3752]**

American Society for Bariatric Surgery **[Vol 1: 3966]**

American Society for Biochemistry and Molecular Biology **[Vol 1: 3754]**

American Society for Bioethics and Humanities **[Vol 1: 3762]**

American Society for Bone and Mineral Research **[Vol 1: 3766]**

American Society for Cell Biology **[Vol 1: 3777]**

American Society for Clinical Laboratory Science **[Vol 1: 3789]**

American Society for Clinical Pathology **[Vol 1: 3793]**

American Society for Clinical Pharmacology and Therapeutics **[Vol 1: 3798]**

American Society for Colposcopy and Cervical Pathology **[Vol 1: 3805]**

American Society for Competitiveness **[Vol 1: 3808]**

American Society for Composites **[Vol 1: 3810]**

American Society for Cybernetics **[Vol 1: 3815]**

American Society for Dermatologic Surgery **[Vol 1: 3819]**

American Society for Eighteenth-Century Studies **[Vol 1: 3821]**

American Society for Engineering Education **[Vol 1: 3834]**

American Society for Engineering Management **[Vol 1: 3887]**

American Society for Enology and Viticulture **[Vol 1: 3898]**

American Society for Environmental History **[Vol 1: 3901]**

American Society for Ethnohistory **[Vol 1: 3906]**

American Society for Experimental Pathology **[Vol 1: 3955]**

American Society for Gastrointestinal Endoscopy [Vol 1: 3908]

American Society for Gravitational and Space Biology [Vol 1: 3914]

American Society for Horticultural Science [Vol 1: 3919]

American Society for Information Science and Technology [Vol 1: 3937]

American Society for Investigative Pathology [Vol 1: 3955]

American Society for Investigative Pathology - International Society for Biological and Environmental Repositories [Vol 1: 3961]

American Society for Mass Spectrometry [Vol 1: 3964]

American Society for Metabolic and Bariatric Surgery [Vol 1: 3966]

American Society for Metals [Vol 1: 4829]

American Society for Microbiology [Vol 1: 3968]

American Society for Neurochemistry [Vol 1: 3994]

American Society for Nondestructive Testing [Vol 1: 3998]

American Society for Nutrition [Vol 1: 4009]

American Society for Nutritional Sciences [Vol 1: 4009]

American Society for Pain Management Nursing [Vol 1: 4022]

American Society for Parenteral and Enteral Nutrition [Vol 1: 4026]

American Society for Personnel Administration [Vol 1: 15100]

American Society for Pharmacology and Experimental Therapeutics [Vol 1: 4030]

American Society for Photobiology [Vol 1: 4038]

American Society for Public Administration [Vol 1: 4043, 11874]

American Society for Public Administration (ASPA)- [Vol 1: 11415]

American Society for Stereotactic and Functional Neurosurgery [Vol 1: 4053]

American Society for the Prevention of Cruelty to Animals [Vol 1: 4055]

American Society for Theatre Research [Vol 1: 4061]

American Society for Training and Development [Vol 1: 4067]

American Society of Agricultural and Biological Engineers [Vol 1: 4072]

American Society of Agricultural Engineers [Vol 1: 8400]

American Society of Agronomy [Vol 1: 4097, 15933]

American Society of Animal Science [Vol 1: 4109]

American Society of Association Executives [Vol 1: 4125]

American Society of Biological Chemists [Vol 1: 3754]

American Society of Business Press Editors [Vol 1: 4132]

American Society of Business Publication Editors [Vol 1: 4132]

American Society of Cataract and Refractive Surgery [Vol 1: 4135]

American Society of Certified Engineering Technicians [Vol 1: 4138]

American Society of Church History [Vol 1: 4144]

American Society of Cinematographers [Vol 1: 4150]

American Society of Civil Engineering [Vol 1: 4155]

American Society of Civil Engineers [Vol 1: 4155]

American Society of Clinical Hypnosis [Vol 1: 4251]

American Society of Clinical Pathologists [Vol 1: 3793]

American Society of Colon and Rectal Surgeons [Vol 1: 4256]

American Society of Composers, Authors and Publishers [Vol 1: 4258]

American Society of Consultant Pharmacists [Vol 1: 4266]

American Society of Criminology [Vol 1: 4270]

American Society of Cytopathology [Vol 1: 4275]

American Society of Echocardiography [Vol 1: 4285]

American Society of Electroencephalographic Technologists [Vol 1: 4294]

American Society of Electroneurodiagnostic Technologists [Vol 1: 4294]

American Society of Enologists [Vol 1: 3898]

American Society of Farm Managers and Rural Appraisers [Vol 1: 4296]

American Society of Furniture Designers [Vol 1: 4300]

American Society of Genealogists [Vol 1: 4302]

American Society of Health System Pharmacists [Vol 1: 4304]

American Society of Heating, Refrigerating and Air-Conditioning Engineers [Vol 1: 4309]

American Society of Hematology [Vol 1: 4334]

American Society of Human Genetics [Vol 1: 4339]

American Society of Ichthyologists and Herpetologists [Vol 1: 4341]

American Society of Interior Designers [Vol 1: 4347]

American Society of International Law [Vol 1: 4350]

American Society of Journalism School Administrators [Vol 1: 5507]

American Society of Journalists and Authors [Vol 1: 4355]

American Society of Landscape Architects [Vol 1: 4358]

American Society of Limnology and Oceanography [Vol 1: 5139]

American Society of Magazine Editors [Vol 1: 4371]

American Society of Magazine Editors [Vol 1: 10910]

American Society of Mammalogists [Vol 1: 4373]

American Society of Mechanical Engineers [Vol 1: 4379]

American Society of Mining and Reclamation [Vol 1: 4433]

American Society of Naturalists [Vol 1: 4437]

American Society of Naval Engineers [Vol 1: 4441]

American Society of Nephrology [Vol 1: 4448]

American Society of Neuroimaging [Vol 1: 4453]

American Society of Neuroradiology [Vol 1: 4456]

American Society of Neurorehabilitation [Vol 1: 4458]

American Society of News Editors [Vol 1: 4461]

American Society of Newspaper Editors [Vol 1: 4461]

American Society of Ophthalmic Administrators [Vol 1: 4469]

American Society of Ophthalmic Registered Nurses [Vol 1: 4471]

American Society of Oral Surgeons [Vol 1: 1252]

American Society of Orthopedic Professionals [Vol 1: 4478]

American Society of Pension Professionals and Actuaries [Vol 1: 4480]

American Society of Pharmacognosy [Vol 1: 4485]

American Society of Photogrammetry [Vol 1: 4860]

American Society of Planning Officials [Vol 1: 3282]

American Society of Plant Biologists [Vol 1: 4487]

American Society of Plant Taxonomists [Vol 1: 4494]

American Society of Primatologists [Vol 1: 4499]

American Society of Safety Engineers [Vol 1: 4506]

American Society of Sanitary Engineering [Vol 1: 4511]

American Society of Swedish Engineers [Vol 1: 4515]

American Society of Travel Agents [Vol 1: 4517]

American Society of Tropical Medicine and Hygiene [Vol 1: 4522]

American Society of Ultrasound Technical Specialists [Vol 1: 15613]

American Society of Zoologists [Vol 1: 15155]

American Society on Aging [Vol 1: 4526]

American Sociological Association [Vol 1: 4534]

American Speech and Hearing Association [Vol 1: 4542]

American Speech Language Hearing Association [Vol 1: 4542]

American Spinal Injury Association [Vol 1: 4547]

American Sports Medicine Institute [Vol 1: 4549]

American Sportscasters Association [Vol 1: 4551]

American Staffing Association [Vol 1: 4554]

American Statistical Association [Vol 1: 4558]

American Statistical Association [Vol 1: 7440]

American Steamship and Tourist Agents Association [Vol 1: 4517]

American String Teachers Association [Vol 1: 4567]

American Studies Association [Vol 1: 4570]

American Swimming Coaches Association [Vol 1: 4577]

American Symphony Orchestra League [Vol 1: 10777]

American Technical Education Association [Vol 1: 4582]

American Theatre Organ Society [Vol 1: 4587]

American Therapeutic Recreation Association [Vol 1: 4591]

American Thyroid Association [Vol 1: 4593]

American Topical Association [Vol 1: 4596]

American Trakehner Association [Vol 1: 4599]

American Translators Association [Vol 1: 4602]

American Truck Historical Society [Vol 1: 4607]

American Trucking Associations - Safety Management Council [Vol 1: 4610]

American TV Commercials Festival [Vol 1: 7330]

American Urological Association [Vol 1: 4617]

American Urological Association Foundation [Vol 1: 4628]

American Veterinary Medical Association [Vol 1: 4633]

American Water Resources Association [Vol 1: 4645]

American Watercolor Society [Vol 1: 4654]

American Welding Society [Vol 1: 4670]

American Whippet Club [Vol 1: 4696]

American Wine Society [Vol 1: 4699]

American Woman's Society of Certified Public Accountants [Vol 1: 4706]

Americans for the Arts [Vol 1: 4711]

Ames Research Center - NASA Astrobiology Institute [Vol 1: 4718]

Amgen Australia [Vol 2: 1101]

Amiene International Film Festival [Vol 2: 2300]

AMIT [Vol 1: 4721]

Amman Filmmakers Cooperative [Vol 2: 4354]

The Ammies, the African Music Awards [Vol 2: 6720]

Amputee Golf Association; National [Vol 1: 11513]

Amt der Tiroler Landesregierung, Kulturabteilung [Vol 2: 1194]

AMVETS [Vol 1: 4725]

Anaesthesiologists; Indian Association of Cardiovascular Thoracic [Vol 2: 3510]

Anaesthetists; Australian Society of [Vol 2: 554]

Analog-Digital Integrated Circuits; Center for Design of [Vol 1: 7132]

Anesthesia Educational Programs; Council on Accreditation of Nurse [Vol 1: 7685]

Anesthetists; American Association of Nurse [Vol 1: 1238]

Anguilla Hotel and Tourism Association [Vol 2: 17]

Anhinga Press [Vol 1: 4729]

ANIMAFEST Zagreb; Zagreb World Festival of Animated Films - [Vol 2: 1886]

Animal Aid; Wetnose [Vol 2: 9444]

Animal Behavior Society [Vol 1: 4732]

Animal Feed Manufacturers Association [Vol 2: 5504]

Animal Welfare Institute [Vol 1: 4737]

Anna Lindh Foundation [Vol 2: 2006]

Anna-Monika Foundation [Vol 2: 2693]

Anna-Monika-Stiftung [Vol 2: 2693]

ANSA McAL Foundation [Vol 2: 6612]

Anti-Defamation League [Vol 1: 4740]

Anti-Slavery International [Vol 2: 6722]

Antigua Charter Yacht Show [Vol 2: 19]

Antiquarian Field Club [Vol 2: 7520]

Antiviral Research; International Society for [Vol 2: 826]

Anvil Press [Vol 1: 4743]

Anxiety Disorders Association of America [Vol 1: 4745]

Aontas Teilgin Agus Amais na h'Eireann [Vol 2: 3901]

APA Committee on Women in Psychology [Vol 1: 3386]

APMI International [Vol 1: 11112]

Apothecaries; American College of [Vol 1: 1702]

Appalachian Studies Association [Vol 1: 4749]

Apparel Federation; International [Vol 2: 4716]

Appita - Technical Association for the Australian and New Zealand Pulp and Paper Industry [Vol 2: 73]

Applied Phycology; International Society for [Vol 2: 4106]

Applied Vision Association [Vol 2: 6724]

Aquariums; Association of Zoos and [Vol 1: 5559]

Arab American Institute [Vol 1: 4752]

Arab American National Museum [Vol 1: 4754]

Arab Fertilizer Association [Vol 2: 2008]

Arab Institute of Navigation [Vol 2: 2010]

Arab Web Awards Academy; Pan [Vol 2: 4450]

Arabian Business Magazine - ITP Publishing Group Ltd. [Vol 2: 6661]

Arbor Day Foundation [Vol 1: 4756]

Arboricultural Association [Vol 2: 6727]

Association des Comites Nationaux Olympiques **[Vol 2: 6255]**

L'Association des counseillers en orientation de l'Ontario **[Vol 1: 13594]**

Association des Ecoles de Sante Publique de la Regional Europeenne **[Vol 2: 2323]**

Association des Facultes de Pharmacie du Canada **[Vol 1: 5332]**

Association des Infirmieres et Infirmiers du Canada **[Vol 1: 6751]**

Association des Ingenieurs-Conseils du Canada **[Vol 1: 5293]**

Association des Journalistes Automobile du Canada **[Vol 1: 5707]**

L'Association des Malentendants Canadiens **[Vol 1: 6537]**

Association des Musees Canadiens **[Vol 1: 6720]**

Association des Pharmaciens du Canada **[Vol 1: 6784]**

Association des Psychiatres du Canada **[Vol 1: 6808]**

Association des Traducteurs et Traductrices Literariness du Canada **[Vol 1: 10865]**

Association des universites et colleges du Canada **[Vol 1: 5545]**

Association d'information sur l'allergie et l'asthme **[Vol 1: 357]**

L'Association du Barreau Canadien **[Vol 1: 6328]**

Association Espanola de Esclerosis Lateral Amiotrofica **[Vol 2: 6100]**

Association Europeene des Galvanisateurs **[Vol 2: 7617]**

Association Europeenne d'Athletisme **[Vol 2: 6268]**

L'Association Europeenne de Psychiatrie **[Vol 2: 2400]**

Association Europeenne des Editeurs d'Annuaires et Bases de Donrees **[Vol 1: 1439]**

Association Europeenne des Vehicules Electriques Routiers **[Vol 2: 1427]**

Association Europeenne Thyroide **[Vol 2: 2860]**

Association for Academic Surgery **[Vol 1: 4899]**

Association for Addiction Professionals; NAADAC: The **[Vol 1: 11341]**

Association for Aerosol Research **[Vol 2: 2695]**

Association for Applied and Therapeutic Humor **[Vol 1: 4903]**

Association for Applied Sport Psychology **[Vol 1: 4908]**

Association for Asian Studies **[Vol 1: 4912]**

Association for Behavioral and Cognitive Therapies **[Vol 1: 4918]**

Association for Business Communication **[Vol 1: 4924]**

Association for Canadian Studies in the United States **[Vol 1: 4928]**

Association for Career and Technical Education **[Vol 1: 4932]**

Association for Childhood Education International **[Vol 1: 4938]**

Association for Civil Rights in Israel **[Vol 2: 3937]**

Association for Clinical Biochemistry **[Vol 2: 6754]**

Association for Communication Excellence in Agriculture, Natural Resources, and Life and Human Sciences **[Vol 1: 4944]**

Association for Computer Educators **[Vol 1: 9522]**

Association for Computers and Taxation **[Vol 1: 4950]**

Association for Computing Machinery **[Vol 1: 4952]**

Association for Computing Machinery - Special Interest Group on Algorithms and Computation Theory **[Vol 1: 4965]**

Association for Computing Machinery - Special Interest Group on Computer Science Education **[Vol 1: 4969]**

Association for Computing Machinery - Special Interest Group on Knowledge Discovery and Data Mining **[Vol 1: 4972]**

Association for Consultancy and Engineering **[Vol 2: 6761]**

Association for Corporate Growth **[Vol 1: 4975]**

Association for Counselor Education and Supervision **[Vol 1: 4978]**

Association for Education and Rehabilitation of the Blind and Visually Impaired **[Vol 1: 4986]**

Association for Education in Journalism **[Vol 1: 4993]**

Association for Education in Journalism and Mass Communication **[Vol 1: 4993]**

Association for Educational Communications and Technology **[Vol 1: 5001]**

Association for Evolutionary Economics **[Vol 1: 5012]**

Association for Film and Television in the Celtic Countries **[Vol 2: 7334]**

Association for Financial Counseling and Planning Education **[Vol 1: 5014]**

Association for Fire Ecology **[Vol 1: 5017]**

Association for Gay, Lesbian and Bisexual Issues in Counseling **[Vol 1: 5039]**

Association for Gerontology in Higher Education **[Vol 1: 5020]**

Association for Gravestone Studies **[Vol 1: 5023]**

Association for Healthcare Philanthropy **[Vol 1: 5026]**

Association for Heritage Interpretation **[Vol 2: 6764]**

Association for Industrial Archaeology **[Vol 2: 6766]**

Association for Investment Management and Research **[Vol 1: 7165]**

Association for Iron and Steel Technology **[Vol 1: 5028]**

Association for Lesbian, Gay, Bisexual and Transgender Issues in Counseling **[Vol 1: 5039]**

Association for Library and Information Science Education **[Vol 1: 5042]**

Association for Library Collections and Technical Services **[Vol 1: 5046]**

Association for Library Service to Children **[Vol 1: 5054]**

Association for Library Trustees and Advocates **[Vol 1: 5394]**

Association for Literary and Linguistic Computing **[Vol 2: 6773]**

Association for Preservation Technology International **[Vol 1: 5072]**

Association for Professionals in Infection Control and Epidemiology **[Vol 1: 5075]**

Association for Project Management **[Vol 2: 6776]**

Association for Promotion of Skiing **[Vol 2: 5116]**

Association for Radiation Research **[Vol 2: 6782]**

Association for Research in Ophthalmology **[Vol 1: 5081]**

Association for Research in Otolaryngology, Inc. **[Vol 1: 5078]**

Association for Research in Vision and Ophthalmology **[Vol 1: 5081]**

Association for Science Teacher Education **[Vol 1: 5088]**

Association for Slavic, East European and Eurasian Studies **[Vol 1: 5093]**

Association for Social Economics **[Vol 1: 5105]**

Association for the Advancement of Applied Sport Psychology **[Vol 1: 4908]**

Association for the Advancement of Artificial Intelligence **[Vol 1: 5109]**

Association for the Advancement of Automotive Medicine **[Vol 1: 5115]**

Association for the Advancement of Baltic Studies **[Vol 1: 5117]**

Association for the Advancement of Behavior Therapy **[Vol 1: 4918]**

Association for the Advancement of Health Education **[Vol 1: 949]**

Association for the Advancement of Industrial Crops **[Vol 1: 5119]**

Association for the Advancement of International Education **[Vol 1: 5125]**

Association for the Advancement of Medical Instrumentation **[Vol 1: 5127]**

Association for the Advancement of Sustainability in Higher Education **[Vol 1: 5133]**

Association for the Education of Teachers in Science **[Vol 1: 5088]**

Association for the History of Chiropractic **[Vol 1: 5137]**

Association for the Sciences of Limnology and Oceanography **[Vol 1: 5139]**

Association for the Study of Afro-American Life and History **[Vol 1: 12302]**

Association for the Study of Australian Literature **[Vol 2: 92]**

Association for the Study of Obesity **[Vol 2: 6784]**

Association for Theatre in Higher Education **[Vol 1: 5142]**

Association for Theatre in Higher Education **[Vol 1: 10662]**

Association for Veterinary Teaching and Research Work **[Vol 2: 6788]**

Association for Women Geoscientists **[Vol 1: 5150]**

Association for Women in Aviation Maintenance **[Vol 1: 5152]**

Association for Women in Communications **[Vol 1: 5156]**

Association for Women in Computing **[Vol 1: 5168]**

Association for Women in Mathematics **[Vol 1: 5170]**

Association for Women in Science **[Vol 1: 5173]**

Association for Women in Sports Media **[Vol 1: 5176]**

Association for Women Veterinarians Foundation **[Vol 1: 5182]**

Association Forestiere Canadienne **[Vol 1: 6511]**

Association Francaise des Diabetiques **[Vol 2: 2440]**

Association Francois-Xavier Bagnoud **[Vol 1: 8678]**

Association Francophone pour le Savoir **[Vol 1: 5185]**

Association in Scotland to Research into Astronautics **[Vol 2: 6791]**

Association International pour l'Etude de l'Economie de l'Assurance **[Vol 2: 6353]**

Association Internationale de Geodesie **[Vol 2: 3047]**

Association Internationale de Geologie de l'Ingenieur **[Vol 2: 6036]**

Association Internationale de la Couleur **[Vol 2: 818]**

Association Internationale de la Presse Sportive **[Vol 2: 6454]**

Association Internationale de Navigation **[Vol 2: 1544]**

Association Internationale de Science Politique **[Vol 1: 10050]**

Association Internationale de Sedimentologistes **[Vol 2: 4728]**

Association Internationale de Sociologie **[Vol 2: 6076]**

Association Internationale de Volcanologie et de Chimie de l'Interieur de la Terre **[Vol 2: 6047]**

Association Internationale des Ecoles de Travail Social **[Vol 2: 5287]**

Association Internationale des Etudes Hongroises **[Vol 2: 3389]**

Association Internationale des Experts en Philatelie **[Vol 2: 1258]**

Association Internationale des Instituts de Navigation **[Vol 2: 8856]**

Association Internationale des Sciences Hydrologiques **[Vol 2: 2493]**

Association Internationale des Statisticiens d'Enquetes **[Vol 2: 2496]**

Association Internationale des Technologistes de Laboratoire Medical **[Vol 1: 9902]**

Association Internationale du Barreau **[Vol 2: 8091]**

Association Internationale du Droit Nucleaire **[Vol 2: 1549]**

Association Internationale du Film d'Animation **[Vol 2: 1870]**

Association Internationale du Theatre pour l'Enfance et la Jeunesse **[Vol 2: 1872]**

Association Internationale pour la Taxonomie Vegetale **[Vol 2: 1253]**

Association Internationale pour les Voiles Minces en Beton **[Vol 2: 6038]**

Association Internationale pour l'Etude des Argiles **[Vol 2: 1760]**

Association Internationale pour l'Evaluation du Rendement Scolaire **[Vol 2: 4719]**

Association Internationale Presse Professionelle Coiffure **[Vol 2: 2556]**

Association Media and Publishing **[Vol 1: 5190]**

Association mineralogique du Canada **[Vol 1: 11163]**

Association Mondiale des Journaux **[Vol 2: 2662]**

Association Mondiale des Radio-Amateurs et des Radioclubs Chretiens **[Vol 2: 9461]**

L'Association Motocycliste Canadienne **[Vol 1: 6716]**

Association of Accredited Advertising Agents Singapore **[Vol 2: 5930]**

Association of AE Business Leaders **[Vol 1: 5192]**

Association of Air Medical Services **[Vol 1: 5194]**

Association of American Colleges and Universities **[Vol 1: 5196]**

Association of American Editorial Cartoonists **[Vol 1: 5198]**

Association of American Geographers **[Vol 1: 5200]**

Association of American Library Schools **[Vol 1: 5042]**

Association Quebecoise des Critiques de Cinema **[Vol 1: 5573]**

Associazione Culturale Antonio Pedrotti **[Vol 2: 4029]**

Associazione Culturale "Rodolfo Lipizer" **[Vol 2: 4049]**

Associazione Internazionale Guido Dorso **[Vol 2: 4031]**

Associazione Italiana di Metallurgia **[Vol 2: 4118]**

Associazione per il Disegno Industriale **[Vol 2: 4033]**

Astellas Pharma US Inc. **[Vol 1: 4631]**

Asthma and Immunology; American College of Allergy, **[Vol 1: 1700]**

Asthma Foundation of New South Wales **[Vol 2: 107]**

ASTM International **[Vol 1: 5575]**

ASTM International **[Vol 1: 16250]**

AstraZeneca AB **[Vol 2: 8206]**

AstraZeneca Ltd. **[Vol 1: 15844]**

Astronautics; American Institute of Aeronautics and **[Vol 1: 2498]**

Astronomical League **[Vol 1: 5648]**

Astronomical Society of Australia **[Vol 2: 111]**

Astronomical Society of Canada; Royal **[Vol 1: 14617]**

Astronomical Society of New South Wales **[Vol 2: 117]**

Astronomical Society of Southern Africa **[Vol 2: 5509]**

Astronomical Society of the Pacific **[Vol 1: 5653]**

Astronomical Society; Royal **[Vol 2: 8654]**

Athenaeum International Cultural Center **[Vol 2: 3266]**

Athenaeum of Philadelphia **[Vol 1: 5661]**

Athletes; U.S. Association for Blind **[Vol 1: 16717]**

Athletic Association; National Christian College **[Vol 1: 12060]**

Athletic Directors; National Council of Secondary School **[Vol 1: 12193]**

The Athletics Congress of the USA **[Vol 1: 17453]**

Atlanta Tipoff Club **[Vol 1: 5666]**

Atlantic AME Association **[Vol 1: 5671]**

Atlantic Journalism Awards **[Vol 1: 5674]**

Atlantic Seaboard Wine Association **[Vol 1: 5679]**

Atlantis Films **[Vol 1: 6685]**

Atlas Economic Research Foundation **[Vol 1: 5681]**

Attorneys; American Association of Nurse **[Vol 1: 1244]**

Audio Engineering Society **[Vol 1: 5688]**

Audiovisual Libraries International; Federation of Commercial **[Vol 2: 7671]**

Augusta National Golf Club **[Vol 1: 5694]**

Aurealis Awards **[Vol 2: 125]**

Aurora Awards **[Vol 1: 5696]**

Australasian Association of Convenience Stores **[Vol 2: 127]**

Australasian Business Travel Association **[Vol 2: 903]**

Australasian College of Tropical Medicine **[Vol 2: 130]**

Australasian Federation of Family History Organisations **[Vol 2: 134]**

Australasian Medical Writers Association **[Vol 2: 136]**

Australasian Performing Rights Association **[Vol 2: 138]**

Australasian Pig Science Association **[Vol 2: 143]**

Australasian Political Studies Association **[Vol 2: 148]**

Australasian Quaternary Association **[Vol 2: 151]**

Australasian Society for Biomaterials **[Vol 2: 4865]**

Australasian Society for Biomaterials and Tissue Engineering **[Vol 2: 4865]**

Australasian Society for the Study of Obesity **[Vol 2: 214]**

Australasian Society for Traumatic Stress Studies **[Vol 2: 155]**

Australasian Society for Ultrasound in Medicine **[Vol 2: 157]**

Australasian Society of Clinical Immunology and Allergy **[Vol 2: 162]**

Australia Arts Victoria **[Vol 2: 1064]**

Australia Council - Literature Board **[Vol 2: 164]**

Australia Council for the Arts **[Vol 2: 166]**

Australia Council for the Arts - Visual Arts/Craft Board **[Vol 2: 168]**

Australian Academy of Science **[Vol 2: 170]**

Australian Academy of the Humanities **[Vol 2: 190]**

Australian Acoustical Society **[Vol 2: 192]**

Australian-American Fulbright Commission **[Vol 2: 194]**

Australian and New Zealand Association for the Advancement of Science **[Vol 2: 197]**

Australian and New Zealand Bone and Mineral Society **[Vol 2: 203]**

Australian and New Zealand College of Anaesthetists **[Vol 2: 558]**

Australian and New Zealand Industrial and Applied Mathematics ANZIAM **[Vol 2: 210]**

Australian and New Zealand Obesity Society **[Vol 2: 214]**

Australian and New Zealand Society of Blood Transfusion **[Vol 2: 217]**

Australian and New Zealand Society of Respiratory Science **[Vol 2: 220]**

Australian and New Zealand Solar Energy Society **[Vol 2: 225]**

Australian Archaeological Association **[Vol 2: 227]**

Australian Association for Cognitive and Behaviour Therapy **[Vol 2: 232]**

Australian Association of Consulting Archaeologists **[Vol 2: 235]**

Australian Association of the Deaf **[Vol 2: 682]**

Australian Athletes with a Disability **[Vol 2: 237]**

Australian Automotive Aftermarket Association **[Vol 2: 240]**

Australian Ballooning Federation **[Vol 2: 243]**

Australian Booksellers Association **[Vol 2: 248]**

Australian Business Awards **[Vol 2: 250]**

Australian Ceramic Society **[Vol 2: 252]**

Australian Cinematographers Society **[Vol 2: 254]**

Australian College of Educators **[Vol 2: 260]**

Australian College of Rural and Remote Medicine **[Vol 2: 263]**

Australian Council for Educational Leaders **[Vol 2: 271]**

Australian Council for International Development **[Vol 2: 274]**

Australian Council of Women and Policing **[Vol 2: 276]**

Australian Council on Healthcare Standards **[Vol 2: 287]**

Australian Curriculum Studies Association **[Vol 2: 290]**

Australian Department of the Prime Minister and Cabinet - Awards and Culture Branch **[Vol 2: 293]**

Australian Dermatology Nurses Association **[Vol 2: 325]**

Australian Drug Foundation **[Vol 2: 330]**

Australian Embassy in Indonesia **[Vol 2: 3814]**

Australian Entomological Society **[Vol 2: 333]**

Australian Federation of Graduate Women **[Vol 2: 336]**

Australian Federation of Modern Language Teachers Associations **[Vol 2: 345]**

Australian Federation of University Women - South Australia **[Vol 2: 336]**

Australian Film Institute **[Vol 2: 348]**

Australian Fleet Managers Association **[Vol 2: 352]**

Australian Geography Teachers Association **[Vol 2: 354]**

Australian Government Department of Innovation, Industry, Science and Research - Science Group **[Vol 2: 356]**

Australian Guild of Screen Composers **[Vol 2: 141]**

Australian Historical Association **[Vol 2: 96]**

Australian Hotels Association NSW **[Vol 2: 361]**

Australian Hotels Association South Australian Branch **[Vol 2: 368]**

Australian Human Resource Institute **[Vol 2: 371]**

Australian Institute of Agricultural Science and Technology **[Vol 2: 376]**

Australian Institute of Architects **[Vol 2: 380]**

Australian Institute of Energy **[Vol 2: 389]**

Australian Institute of Genealogical Studies **[Vol 2: 391]**

Australian Institute of Landscape Architects **[Vol 2: 395]**

Australian Institute of Nuclear Science and Engineering **[Vol 2: 399]**

Australian Institute of Packaging **[Vol 2: 403]**

Australian Institute of Physics **[Vol 2: 406]**

Australian Institute of Physics (NSW Branch) **[Vol 2: 1171]**

Australian Institute of Professional Photography **[Vol 2: 412]**

Australian Institute of Project Management • **[Vol 2: 420]**

Australian Institute of Quantity Surveyors **[Vol 2: 422]**

Australian Insurance Law Association **[Vol 2: 424]**

Australian Interactive Media Industry Association **[Vol 2: 426]**

Australian Library and Information Association **[Vol 2: 428]**

Australian Literature Society **[Vol 2: 92]**

Australian Mammal Society **[Vol 2: 451]**

Australian Marine Sciences Association **[Vol 2: 455]**

Australian Market and Social Research Society **[Vol 2: 460]**

Australian Mathematical Society **[Vol 2: 463]**

Australian Meteorological and Oceanographic Society **[Vol 2: 1102]**

Australian Military Medicine Association **[Vol 2: 468]**

Australian Music Centre **[Vol 2: 471]**

Australian National University - Crawford School of Economics and Government I Australian-Japan Research Centre **[Vol 2: 474]**

Australian Neuroscience Society **[Vol 2: 476]**

Australian Nuclear Association **[Vol 2: 482]**

Australian Numismatic Society **[Vol 2: 484]**

Australian Office of the Privacy Commissioner **[Vol 2: 488]**

Australian Packaging and Processing Machinery Association **[Vol 2: 491]**

Australian Packaging Machinery Association **[Vol 2: 491]**

Australian Petroleum Production and Exploration Association **[Vol 2: 493]**

Australian Physiological Society **[Vol 2: 499]**

Australian Psychological Society **[Vol 2: 504]**

Australian Publishers' Association **[Vol 2: 515]**

Australian Science Teachers Association **[Vol 2: 520]**

Australian Sesquicentennial Gift Trust for Awards in Oral History **[Vol 2: 4897]**

Australian Singing Competition **[Vol 2: 523]**

Australian Skeptics - NSW Branch **[Vol 2: 526]**

Australian Society for Antimicrobials **[Vol 2: 530]**

Australian Society for Biophysics **[Vol 2: 532]**

Australian Society for Fish Biology **[Vol 2: 536]**

Australian Society for Medical Research **[Vol 2: 539]**

Australian Society for Microbiology **[Vol 2: 541]**

Australian Society for Music Education **[Vol 2: 548]**

Australian Society for Parasitology **[Vol 2: 551]**

Australian Society of Anaesthetists **[Vol 2: 554]**

Australian Society of Archivists **[Vol 2: 562]**

Australian Society of Exploration Geophysicists **[Vol 2: 569]**

Australian Society of Plant Scientists **[Vol 2: 577]**

Australian Society of Sugar Cane Technologists **[Vol 2: 581]**

Australian Speech Science and Technology Association **[Vol 2: 584]**

Australian Sports Commission **[Vol 2: 589]**

Australian Steel Institute **[Vol 2: 591]**

Australian Subscription Television and Radio Association **[Vol 2: 593]**

Australian Teachers of Media **[Vol 2: 595]**

Australian Veterinary Association **[Vol 2: 597]**

Australian Veterinary Association (Australia) **[Vol 2: 1162]**

Australian Water Association **[Vol 2: 603]**

Australian Women Pilots' Association **[Vol 2: 608]**

Australian Wound Management Association **[Vol 2: 619]**

Australian Writers' Guild **[Vol 2: 623]**

Austria Ministry of Economics and Labour **[Vol 2: 1242]**

Austria Press Agency **[Vol 2: 1199]**

Austrian Broadcasting Corporation **[Vol 2: 1202]**

Austrian Computer Society **[Vol 2: 1204]**

Austrian Neuroscience Association **[Vol 2: 1207]**

Austrian Physical Society **[Vol 2: 1209]**

Austrian Society for Geriatrics and Gerontology **[Vol 2: 1213]**

Authority for Info-Communications Technology Industry of Brunei Darussalam **[Vol 2: 1772]**

Autism Research; International Society for **[Vol 1: 10143]**

Autism Society **[Vol 1: 5698]**

Autism Society of America **[Vol 1: 5698]**

Autodesk Canada **[Vol 1: 6212]**

Automated Imaging Association [Vol 1: 5705]
Automated Vision Association [Vol 1: 5705]
Automatic Control; International Federation of [Vol 2: 1275]
Automobile Association Ltd. - Hotel Services Section [Vol 2: 6858]
Automobile Club de l'Ouest [Vol 2: 2325]
Automobile Journalists Association of Canada [Vol 1: 5707]
Automotive Engineers; Society of [Vol 1: 15484]
Automotive Hall of Fame [Vol 1: 5712]
Automotive Industries Association of Canada [Vol 1: 5718]
Automotive Organization Team [Vol 1: 5712]
Avanti Polar Lipids Inc. [Vol 1: 3757]
Avenza [Vol 2: 6986]
Avian Pathologists; American Association of [Vol 1: 1040]
Aviation Association; Marine Corps [Vol 1: 10943]
Aviation Distributors and Manufacturers Association [Vol 1: 5721]
Aviation Hall of Fame [Vol 1: 11952]
Aviation Technician Education Council [Vol 1: 5723]
Aviation Week & Space Technology [Vol 1: 8374]
Avicultural Advancement Council of Canada [Vol 1: 5726]
AVS Science and Technology Society [Vol 1: 5728]
Awana Clubs International [Vol 1: 5743]
Awards and Recognition Association [Vol 1: 5747]
Ayn Rand Institute [Vol 1: 5752]
Azerbaijan Cartoonists Union [Vol 2: 1332]
Azerbaijan National Science Foundation [Vol 2: 1334]
B & T Magazine [Vol 2: 625]
Babson College - Blank Center for Entrepreneurship; The Arthur M. [Vol 1: 5754]
BackCare, The Charity for Healthier Backs [Vol 2: 6863]
Badminton England [Vol 2: 6866]
Badminton World Federation [Vol 2: 4528]
Bagutta Restaurant [Vol 2: 4035]
Bahamas Hotel Association [Vol 2: 1340]
Bahamas International Film Festival [Vol 2: 1342]
Bahamas Web Awards [Vol 2: 1344]
Baker Street Irregulars [Vol 1: 5762]
Balloon Federation of America [Vol 1: 5765]
The Banff Centre [Vol 1: 5773]
Banff School of Fine Arts [Vol 1: 5773]
Bangladesh Chemical Society [Vol 2: 1367]
Bangladesh University of Engineering and Technology - Department of Architecture [Vol 2: 1369]
Bank Insurance and Securities Association [Vol 1: 5778]
Bank of Albania [Vol 2: 6]
Bank Sarasin and Cie. [Vol 2: 6523]
Banksia Environmental Foundation [Vol 2: 627]
Bantrel [Vol 1: 6967]
Baptist Communicators Association [Vol 1: 5784]
Barbados Association of Medical Practitioners [Vol 2: 1377]
Barbados Employers' Confederation [Vol 2: 1379]
Barbados International Film Festival [Vol 2: 1381]
Barbados National Trust [Vol 2: 1383]
Barcelona Graduate School of Economics [Vol 2: 6019]
Barrick Gold Corp. [Vol 2: 1934]
Baseball Canada [Vol 1: 5789]
Baseball Hall of Fame and Museum; National [Vol 1: 11969]
Baseball Leagues; National Association of Professional [Vol 1: 11839]
Baseball; U.S.A. [Vol 1: 17407]
Baseball Writers Association of America [Vol 1: 5792, 11971, 11972]
BASF Catalysts LLC [Vol 1: 10059]
Basketball Association; National [Vol 1: 11973]
Basketball Association; National Wheelchair [Vol 1: 13036]
Bavarian Academy of Fine Arts [Vol 2: 2703]
Bavarian Academy of Sciences and Humanities [Vol 2: 2709]
Baxter International Foundation [Vol 1: 14897]
Bayerische Akademie der Schonen Kunste [Vol 2: 2703]
Bayerische Akademie der Wissenschaften [Vol 2: 2709]

Baylor College of Medicine - Huffington Center on Aging; Roy M. and Phyllis Gough [Vol 1: 5796]
Baywood Publishing Company [Vol 1: 8630]
BC Innovation Council [Vol 1: 5798]
BCA Productions [Vol 2: 6870]
Beatson Institute for Cancer Research [Vol 2: 6872]
Beckton Dickinson Co. [Vol 1: 5128]
Before Columbus Foundation [Vol 1: 5800]
Behavioral Ecology; International Society for [Vol 2: 832]
Belgian Luxembourg Chamber of Commerce in Great Britain [Vol 2: 6874]
Belgian Neurological Society [Vol 2: 1411]
Belgian Operations Research Society [Vol 2: 1414]
Belgische Vereniging voor Neurologie [Vol 2: 1411]
Belize Audubon Society [Vol 2: 1672]
Belize Chamber of Commerce and Industry [Vol 2: 1674]
Belize International Film Festival [Vol 2: 1676]
Belize Tourism Board [Vol 2: 1678]
Bell Association for the Deaf and Hard of Hearing; Parents' Section of the Alexander Graham [Vol 1: 13860]
Benin National Congress [Vol 2: 5094]
Bennett Neuropsychiatric Research Foundation; A. E. [Vol 1: 15560]
Bentley College - Center for Business Ethics [Vol 1: 5803]
Bergamo Film Meeting [Vol 2: 4037]
Bergen International Festival [Vol 2: 5119]
Berlin International Film Festival [Vol 2: 2715]
Bermuda Department of Community and Cultural Affairs [Vol 2: 1685]
The Bermuda Insurance Institute [Vol 2: 1691]
Bermuda International Film Festival [Vol 2: 1695]
Bermuda Public Services Union [Vol 2: 1698]
The Bermudian Publishing Co., Ltd. [Vol 2: 1700]
Beroepsorganisatie Nederlandse Ontwerpers [Vol 2: 4645]
Bertelsmann Stiftung [Vol 2: 2734]
Berthold Leibinger Stiftung GmbH [Vol 2: 2736]
Bertrand Russell Society [Vol 1: 5805]
Berufsverband Deutscher Markt- und Sozialforscher [Vol 2: 2909]
Beta Beta Beta [Vol 1: 5810]
Bethesda Lutheran Homes and Services [Vol 1: 5817]
Better Business Bureau of British Columbia [Vol 1: 5820]
Better Government Association [Vol 1: 5822]
Beverly Hills Theatre Guild [Vol 1: 5825]
Bharatiya Jnanpith [Vol 2: 3453]
Bhutan Department of Trade - Ministry of Economic Affairs [Vol 2: 1708]
Bhutan Ministry of Information and Communications [Vol 2: 1711]
Bibiana, International House of Art for Children [Vol 2: 5994]
Bibliographical Society of America [Vol 1: 5828]
Bibliographical Society - United Kingdom [Vol 2: 6876]
Bienal Internacional del Cartel Bolivia [Vol 2: 1721]
Bienek Stiftung; Horst [Vol 2: 2706]
Big Brothers Big Sisters of America [Vol 1: 5830]
Big Brothers of America [Vol 1: 5830]
Big East Conference [Vol 1: 5833]
Big Muddy Film Festival [Vol 1: 5836]
Big Sisters International [Vol 1: 5830]
Billboard - Prometheus Global Media [Vol 1: 5838]
Bioanalysts; American Association of [Vol 1: 1050]
Biochemical Societies; Federation of European [Vol 2: 3944]
Biochemical Society - England [Vol 2: 6878]
Bioelectrochemical Society [Vol 2: 2327]
Bioethics and Humanities; American Society for [Vol 1: 3762]
Biogeochemistry; International Society for Environmental [Vol 1: 10154]
BioIron Society; International [Vol 1: 9726]
Biological Chemists, India; Society of [Vol 2: 3779]
Biological Engineers; American Society of Agricultural and [Vol 1: 4072]
Biological Laboratory; Mount Desert Island [Vol 1: 11288]
Biologists; Society of Systematic [Vol 1: 15833]

Biology; American Society for Biochemistry and Molecular [Vol 1: 3754]
Biology; American Society for Cell [Vol 1: 3777]
Biology; Society for Integrative and Comparative [Vol 1: 15155]
Biology; Society for Leukocyte [Vol 1: 15167]
Biology Society; IEEE Engineering in Medicine and [Vol 1: 9085]
Biology Teachers; National Association of [Vol 1: 11645]
Biomedical Engineering Society [Vol 1: 5841]
Biometeorology; International Society of [Vol 1: 10291]
Biometric Society [Vol 1: 7440]
Biometric Society; International [Vol 1: 9728]
Biophysical Society [Vol 1: 5845]
Biopolitics International Organization [Vol 2: 3269]
Biosafety Associations; International Federation of [Vol 1: 9908]
Biosciences Federation [Vol 2: 9262]
Biotechnology Industry Organization [Vol 1: 5853]
Biotechnology, Japan; Society for [Vol 2: 4323]
Biotechnology; Society for Chemical Engineering and [Vol 2: 3158]
Bird Studies Canada [Vol 1: 5856]
Birds Australia [Vol 2: 629]
The Black and White Spider Awards [Vol 2: 6884]
Black Caucus of the American Library Association [Vol 1: 5858]
Black Culinarian Alliance [Vol 1: 5866]
Black Entertainment and Sports Lawyers Association [Vol 1: 5871]
Black Girls Rock! Inc. [Vol 1: 5873]
Blackwell Scientific Publications [Vol 2: 503]
Blazer Horse Association [Vol 1: 5875]
Blind; American Foundation for the [Vol 1: 2188]
Blind and Dyslexic; Recording for the [Vol 1: 10785]
Blind and Visually Impaired; Association for Education and Rehabilitation of the [Vol 1: 4986]
Blind Athletes; U.S. Association for [Vol 1: 16717]
Blind; National Federation of the [Vol 1: 12381]
Blinded Veterans Association [Vol 1: 5886]
Blue Ridge Literacy Council [Vol 1: 5891]
Bluegrass Music Association; International [Vol 1: 9731]
The Blues Foundation [Vol 1: 5895]
BMJ Group [Vol 2: 6886]
B'nai Brith Canada [Vol 1: 5899]
B'nai B'rith Hillel Foundations [Vol 1: 8919]
Boardgame Players Association [Vol 1: 5902]
Boardman Tasker Charitable Trust [Vol 2: 6888]
Boating Council; National Safe [Vol 1: 12795]
Boating Industry [Vol 1: 12598]
Boehringer Ingelheim (Canada) Ltd [Vol 1: 6889]
Boehringer Ingelheim GmbH [Vol 2: 8207]
Boeing Co. [Vol 1: 15641]
Boersenverein des Deutschen Buchhandels e.V. [Vol 2: 2988]
Boghossian Foundation [Vol 2: 56, 57, 58]
Bollywood Awards Inc. [Vol 1: 5907]
Bombay Natural History Society [Vol 2: 3456]
Bone and Mineral Research; American Society for [Vol 1: 3766]
Bonsai Clubs International [Vol 1: 5909]
Book Publishers Association of Alberta [Vol 1: 5913]
Book Publishers' Association of Israel - Bernstein Fund; Mordechai [Vol 2: 3939]
Books Abroad [Vol 1: 18054]
Bookseller Information Group [Vol 2: 6890]
Booksellers Association; American [Vol 1: 1511]
Booksellers Association of the United Kingdom and Ireland [Vol 2: 6898]
Booksellers New Zealand [Vol 2: 4868]
Booktrust [Vol 2: 6901]
Boone and Crockett Club [Vol 1: 5338]
Boston Athletic Association [Vol 1: 5924]
Boston College - Center for Corporate Citizenship [Vol 1: 5926]
Boston Municipal Research Bureau, Inc. [Vol 1: 5928]
Botanical Society of America [Vol 1: 5930]
Botanical Society of South Africa [Vol 2: 5516]
Botaniese Vereniging van Suid-Afrika [Vol 2: 5516]
Botswana Institute of Bankers [Vol 2: 1729]
Botswana Ministry of Education - Teaching Service Management Unit [Vol 2: 1732]

Botswana National Sports Council [Vol 2: 1737]

Bowling Proprietors' Association of America [Vol 1: 5945]

Bowling Writers Association of America [Vol 1: 5949]

Box Office Management International [Vol 1: 10455]

Boy Scouts Association of Zimbabwe [Vol 2: 9570]

Boy Scouts of America [Vol 1: 5958]

Boys and Girls Clubs of America [Vol 1: 5989]

Boys Clubs of America [Vol 1: 5989]

BP plc [Vol 2: 6735]

Brain Injury Association of New Jersey [Vol 1: 5994]

Brandeis University [Vol 1: 14600]

Brandeis University Alumni Association [Vol 1: 5998]

Brandon Society; Carl [Vol 1: 6002]

Braun GmbH [Vol 2: 2738]

Braunschweig City Cultural Office [Vol 2: 2740]

Brazil Office of the President [Vol 2: 1745]

Brazilian Academy of Letters [Vol 2: 1748]

Brazilian Book Chamber [Vol 2: 1751]

Brazilian Chamber of Commerce in Great Britain [Vol 2: 6912]

Brazilian Chemical Society [Vol 2: 1753]

Brazilian Metallurgy and Materials Association [Vol 2: 1755]

Brazilian Society of Biochemistry and Molecular Biology [Vol 2: 1758]

Breakout Festival; Maldives [Vol 2: 4554]

Brick Development Association [Vol 2: 6914]

Bridge School Foundation [Vol 1: 10140]

Bridgestone Bandag Tire Solutions [Vol 1: 12713]

Bridport Arts Centre [Vol 2: 6916]

Brigham Young University [Vol 1: 6102]

Brigham Young University - Redd Center for Western Studies; Charles [Vol 1: 6005]

Brisbane Warana Festival Ltd. [Vol 2: 631]

Brisbane Writers Festival [Vol 2: 631]

Bristol-Myers Squibb Canada Co. [Vol 1: 6013]

Bristol Myers Squibb Canada Co. [Vol 1: 6887]

Bristol-Myers Squibb Pharmaceutical Group [Vol 1: 6990]

British Academy [Vol 2: 6918]

British Academy of Film and Television Arts [Vol 2: 6931]

British Air Line Pilots Association [Vol 2: 6934]

British and Irish Association of Law Librarians [Vol 2: 6936]

British Animation Awards Ltd. [Vol 2: 6939]

British Association for Applied Linguistics [Vol 2: 6941]

British Association for Biological Anthropology and Osteoarchaeology [Vol 2: 6944]

British Association for Cancer Research [Vol 2: 6947]

British Association for Immediate Care [Vol 2: 6952]

British Association for Sexual Health and HIV [Vol 2: 6955]

British Association of Aviation Consultants [Vol 2: 6957]

British Association of Communicators in Business [Vol 2: 7876]

British Association of Dermatologists [Vol 2: 6959]

British Association of Industrial Editors [Vol 2: 7876]

British Association of Landscape Industries [Vol 2: 6966]

British Association of Otorhinolaryngologists - Head and Neck Surgeons [Vol 2: 6968]

British Association of Rheumatology and Rehabilitation [Vol 2: 7238]

British Association of Sport and Exercise Sciences [Vol 2: 6970]

British Astronomical Association [Vol 2: 6974]

British Broadcasting Corp. [Vol 2: 6902, 6979]

British Canoe Union [Vol 2: 6983]

British Cartographic Society [Vol 2: 6985]

British Cave Research Association [Vol 2: 6994]

British Christmas Tree Growers Association [Vol 2: 7000]

British Columbia Art Teachers' Association [Vol 1: 6015]

British Columbia Historical Federation [Vol 1: 6017]

British Columbia Psychological Association [Vol 1: 6025]

British Computer Society [Vol 2: 7002]

British Computer Society - Sri Lanka Section [Vol 2: 6116]

British Contact Lens Association [Vol 2: 7028]

British Council [Vol 2: 6737]

British Council for Offices [Vol 2: 7031]

British Culinary Federation [Vol 2: 7033]

British Dam Society [Vol 2: 7037]

British Deaf Association [Vol 2: 7039]

British Design and Art Direction [Vol 2: 7041]

British Direct Marketing Association [Vol 2: 7516]

British Ecological Society [Vol 2: 7043]

British Fashion Council [Vol 2: 7051]

British Fertility Society [Vol 2: 7053]

British Film Institute [Vol 2: 7056]

British Florist Association [Vol 2: 7059]

British Geotechnical Association [Vol 2: 7065]

British Grassland Society [Vol 2: 7068]

British Guild of Travel Writers [Vol 2: 7070]

British Health Care Association [Vol 2: 7079]

British HIV Association [Vol 2: 7081]

British Infection Society [Vol 2: 7083]

British Institute Interior Design [Vol 2: 7086]

British Institute of Architectural Technicians [Vol 2: 7358]

British Institute of Non-Destructive Testing [Vol 2: 7091]

British Insurance Law Association [Vol 2: 7097]

British Interactive Media Association [Vol 2: 7099]

British Interior Design Association [Vol 2: 7086]

British Interior Textiles Association [Vol 2: 7101]

British Italian Society [Vol 2: 9248]

British Lichen Society [Vol 2: 7103]

British Long Distance Swimming Association [Vol 2: 7105]

British Machine Vision Association and Society for Pattern Recognition [Vol 2: 7114]

British Medical Association [Vol 2: 7117]

British Mexican Society [Vol 2: 7130]

British Microcirculation Society [Vol 2: 7132]

British Music Society [Vol 2: 7136]

British Mycological Society [Vol 2: 7138]

British Numismatic Society [Vol 2: 7143]

British Occupational Hygiene Society [Vol 2: 7148]

British Origami Society [Vol 2: 7154]

British Ornithologists' Union [Vol 2: 7156]

British Orthodontic Society [Vol 2: 7161]

British Phonographic Industry [Vol 2: 7170]

British Printing Industries Federation [Vol 2: 7173]

British Psychological Society [Vol 2: 7179]

British Science Fiction Association [Vol 2: 7198]

British Security Industry Association [Vol 2: 7200]

British Show Pony Society [Vol 2: 7203]

British Small Animal Veterinary Association [Vol 2: 7208]

British Society for Antimicrobial Chemotherapy [Vol 2: 7218]

British Society for Clinical Neurophysiology [Vol 2: 7221]

British Society for Geomorphology [Vol 2: 7223]

British Society for Middle Eastern Studies [Vol 2: 7229]

British Society for Neuroendocrinology [Vol 2: 7231]

British Society for Plant Pathology [Vol 2: 7234]

British Society for Research on Ageing [Vol 2: 7236]

British Society for Rheumatology [Vol 2: 7238]

British Society of Animal Production [Vol 2: 7244]

British Society of Animal Science [Vol 2: 7244]

British Society of Hearing Aid Audiologists [Vol 2: 7253]

British Society of Magazine Editors [Vol 2: 7255]

British Society of Periodontology [Vol 2: 7259]

British Society of Rheology [Vol 2: 7264]

British Society of Scientific Glassblowers [Vol 2: 7269]

British Thematic Association [Vol 2: 7276]

British Toy and Hobby Association [Vol 2: 7278]

British Transplantation Society [Vol 2: 7280]

British Trust for Ornithology [Vol 2: 7286]

British Universities Film and Video Council [Vol 2: 7289]

British Universities Film and Video Council [Vol 2: 7289]

British Veterinary Association [Vol 2: 7292]

British Wildlife Photography Awards [Vol 2: 7299]

British Women Pilots' Association [Vol 2: 7301]

Broadcast Education Association [Vol 1: 11671]

Broadcast Educators Association of Canada [Vol 1: 6028]

Broadcast Technology Society; IEEE [Vol 2: 9046]

Broadway League [Vol 1: 6033]

Brown; James [Vol 1: 13250]

Brunei Darussalam Computer Society [Vol 2: 1774]

Brunei Ministry of Communications [Vol 2: 1776]

Brunei Ministry of Industry and Primary Resources [Vol 2: 1778]

Brussels International Festival of Fantastic Film [Vol 2: 1416]

BTC, the Belgian Development Agency - Trade for Development Centre [Vol 2: 1418]

Buchhandlung Ziemann & Ziemann, Buxtehude [Vol 2: 2745]

Buck International; Pearl S. [Vol 1: 6036]

Buckeye Children's Book Award Council [Vol 1: 6038]

Builder [Vol 1: 6041]

Building Designers Association of Australia [Vol 2: 633]

Building Owners and Managers Association International [Vol 1: 6043]

Building Performance Simulation Association; International [Vol 1: 9739]

Building Stone Institute [Vol 1: 6051]

Bula Fiji Tourism Exchange [Vol 2: 2057]

Bulgarian Academy of Sciences - Rostislaw Kaischew Institute of Physical Chemistry [Vol 2: 1783]

Bulgarian Book Association [Vol 2: 1785]

Bulgarian National Television [Vol 2: 1788]

Bulgarian Society of Ophthalmology [Vol 2: 1790]

Bulgarian Television and Radio [Vol 2: 1788]

Bulgarska Natcionalna Televiziya [Vol 2: 1788]

Bund der Steuerzahler Europa [Vol 2: 3197]

Bund Deutscher Innenarchitekten [Vol 2: 2957]

Bundesarztekammer [Vol 2: 2963]

Bundesarchitektenkammer [Vol 2: 2876]

Bundesverband der Edelstein- und Diamantindustrie [Vol 2: 2874]

Bundesverband Finanzdienstleistungen [Vol 2: 3143]

Bundesvereinigung Deutscher Apothekerverbande [Vol 2: 2878]

BundeszahnArztekammer-BZAK [Vol 2: 2939]

Bureau Canadien de l'Education Internationale [Vol 1: 6369]

Bureau of Security Control of Construction [Vol 2: 1657]

Burkina Faso Ministry of Culture, Tourism and Communication [Vol 2: 1806]

Burnett Fund; Carol [Vol 1: 17246]

The Burton Awards for Legal Achievement [Vol 1: 6053]

Business Administration; U.S. Small [Vol 1: 17103]

Business and Entrepreneurship; United States Association for Small [Vol 1: 16720]

Business and Industry Council; United States [Vol 1: 16746]

Business Archives Council [Vol 2: 7312]

Business Committee for the Arts [Vol 1: 6055]

Business Council of America; Small [Vol 1: 14937]

Business Forms Management Association [Vol 1: 6059]

Business History Conference [Vol 1: 6063]

Business Marketing Association [Vol 1: 6065]

Business News Publishing Co. [Vol 1: 12894]

Business Owners; National Association of Women [Vol 1: 11937]

Business Press Editors; American Society of [Vol 1: 4132]

Business/Professional Advertising Association [Vol 1: 6065]

Business Roundtable [Vol 1: 8208]

Business Technology Association [Vol 1: 6068]

Buxtehude; City of [Vol 2: 2745]

Byron Society; International [Vol 2: 8099]

Cable and Wireless (Jamaica) Ltd. [Vol 2: 4199]

Cable Telecommunications Engineers; Society of [Vol 1: 15576]

Cabletelevision Advertising Bureau [Vol 1: 6072]

CAD Society [Vol 1: 6076]

Cadillac-LaSalle Club [Vol 1: 6080]

Cafe des Deux Magots [Vol 2: 2330]

Cajal Club [Vol 1: 6086]

California Association for the Education of Young Children [Vol 1: 6089]

California Notary Association [Vol 1: 12619]

California Society of Anesthesiologists [Vol 1: 6093]

CaliforniaVolunteers [Vol 1: 6098]

Calorimetry Conference [Vol 1: 6101]

Calouste Gulbenkian Foundation [Vol 2: 7314]
Camanachd Association [Vol 2: 7316]
Camara Americana de Comercio de Sao Paulo [Vol 2: 1743]
Camara Brasileira do Livro [Vol 2: 1751]
Camara de Comercio Guatemalteco-Americana [Vol 2: 3328]
Camara Nacional de la Industria de Restaurantes y Alimentos Condimentados [Vol 2: 4593]
Cambodian Ministry of Foreign Affairs and International Cooperation [Vol 2: 1808]
Cambodian National Volleyball League (Disabled)- [Vol 2: 1810]
Cambridge Center for Behavioral Studies [Vol 1: 6106]
Cameroon Professional Society [Vol 1: 6108]
Camif Group [Vol 2: 2594]
Camille and Henry Dreyfus Foundation [Vol 1: 6114]
Camp Fire [Vol 1: 6118]
Camp Fire USA [Vol 1: 6118]
Campaign for the Protection of Rural Wales [Vol 2: 7327]
Campiello Foundation [Vol 2: 4039]
Canada Chacellery of Honors [Vol 1: 8746]
Canada Council for the Arts [Vol 1: 6121]
Canada Safety Council [Vol 1: 6146]
Canada's Aviation Hall of Fame [Vol 1: 6148]
Canada's National Ballet School [Vol 1: 6150]
Canada's National History Society [Vol 1: 6154]
Canada's Sports Hall of Fame [Vol 1: 6157]
Canada's Venture Capital and Private Equity Association [Vol 1: 6159]
Canadian Academy of Periodontology [Vol 1: 6162]
Canadian Academy of Psychiatric Epidemiology [Vol 1: 6815]
Canadian Academy of Recording Arts and Sciences [Vol 1: 6164]
Canadian Acoustical Association [Vol 1: 6166]
Canadian Actors' Equity Association [Vol 1: 6173]
Canadian Adult Recreational Hockey Association [Vol 1: 6176]
Canadian Advanced Technology Alliance [Vol 1: 6183]
Canadian Aeronautics and Space Institute [Vol 1: 6192]
Canadian Alarm and Security Association [Vol 1: 6866]
Canadian Anesthesiologists' Society [Vol 1: 6200]
Canadian Animal Health Institute [Vol 1: 6208]
Canadian Architect [Vol 1: 6210]
Canadian Association for Health, Physical Education, Recreation and Dance [Vol 1: 13996]
Canadian Association for Music Therapy [Vol 1: 6213]
Canadian Association for School Libraries [Vol 1: 6215]
Canadian Association for Theatre Research [Vol 1: 6218]
Canadian Association of Aquarium Clubs [Vol 1: 6224]
Canadian Association of Broadcasters [Vol 1: 6231]
Canadian Association of Career Educators and Employers [Vol 1: 6238]
Canadian Association of Critical Care Nurses [Vol 1: 6244]
Canadian Association of Emergency Physicians [Vol 1: 6247]
Canadian Association of Family Enterprise [Vol 1: 6252]
Canadian Association of Gastroenterology [Vol 1: 6254]
Canadian Association of Geographers [Vol 1: 6258]
Canadian Association of Gerontology [Vol 1: 6264]
Canadian Association of Gift Planners [Vol 1: 6270]
Canadian Association of Home and Property Inspectors [Vol 1: 6272]
Canadian Association of Home Inspectors [Vol 1: 6272]
Canadian Association of Journalists [Vol 1: 6275]
Canadian Association of Medical Radiation Technologists [Vol 1: 6278]
Canadian Association of Occupational Therapists [Vol 1: 6286]
Canadian Association of Oilwell Drilling Contractors [Vol 1: 6289]
Canadian Association of Pathologists [Vol 1: 6291]

Canadian Association of Physical Medicine and Rehabilitation [Vol 1: 6293]
Canadian Association of Physicists [Vol 1: 6298]
Canadian Association of Special Libraries and Information Services [Vol 1: 6305]
Canadian Association of Speech-Language Pathologists and Audiologists [Vol 1: 6307]
Canadian Association of University Teachers [Vol 1: 6309]
Canadian Astronomical Society [Vol 1: 6313, 14622]
Canadian Athletic Therapists Association [Vol 1: 6316]
Canadian Authors Association [Vol 1: 6322]
Canadian Bar Association [Vol 1: 6328]
Canadian Booksellers Association [Vol 1: 6346]
Canadian Botanical Association [Vol 1: 6359]
Canadian Brewing Awards [Vol 1: 6361]
Canadian Broadcasting Corp. [Vol 1: 6363]
Canadian Brown Swiss and Braunvieh Association [Vol 1: 6366]
Canadian Bureau for International Education [Vol 1: 6369]
Canadian Business Aviation Association [Vol 1: 6376]
Canadian Business Press [Vol 1: 6380]
Canadian Cable Telecommunications Association [Vol 1: 6382]
Canadian Camping Association [Vol 1: 6384]
Canadian Cancer Society Research Institute [Vol 1: 6389]
Canadian Cardiovascular Society [Vol 1: 6391]
Canadian Celiac Association [Vol 1: 6399]
Canadian Centre for Diversity [Vol 1: 6402]
Canadian Centre for Ecumenism [Vol 1: 6404]
Canadian Co-Operative Wool Growers [Vol 1: 6406]
Canadian College of Medical Geneticists [Vol 1: 6409]
Canadian Colleges Athletic Association [Vol 1: 6411]
Canadian Condominium Institute [Vol 1: 6421]
Canadian Conference of the Arts [Vol 1: 6424]
Canadian Council of Cardiovascular Nurses [Vol 1: 6427]
Canadian Council of Christians and Jews [Vol 1: 6402]
Canadian Council of Land Surveyors [Vol 1: 14254]
Canadian Council of Professional Engineers [Vol 1: 8123]
Canadian Council of Technicians and Technologists [Vol 1: 6429]
Canadian Country Music Association [Vol 1: 6433]
Canadian Courier and Logistics Association [Vol 1: 6435]
Canadian Culture of Peace Program [Vol 1: 6437]
Canadian Cystic Fibrosis Foundation [Vol 1: 6439]
Canadian Daily Newspaper Publishers Association [Vol 1: 6741]
Canadian Dam Association [Vol 1: 6442]
Canadian Dermatology Association [Vol 1: 6445]
Canadian Diabetes Association - Diabetes Educator Section [Vol 1: 6452]
Canadian Disc Jockey Association [Vol 1: 6455]
Canadian Economics Association [Vol 1: 6457]
Canadian Education Association [Vol 1: 6459]
Canadian Environmental Network [Vol 1: 6461]
Canadian Farm Writers' Federation [Vol 1: 6463]
Canadian Federation for Sexual Health [Vol 1: 6465]
Canadian Federation for the Humanities and Social Sciences [Vol 1: 6467]
Canadian Federation of Amateur Baseball [Vol 1: 6469]
Canadian Federation of Biological Societies [Vol 1: 6472]
Canadian Federation of Independent Business [Vol 1: 6475]
Canadian Federation of Independent Grocers [Vol 1: 6477]
Canadian Federation of Mental Health Nurses [Vol 1: 6479]
Canadian Federation of University Women [Vol 1: 6481]
Canadian Fertility and Andrology Society [Vol 1: 6490]
Canadian Film and Television Association [Vol 1: 6684]
Canadian Film and Television Production Association [Vol 1: 6684]

Canadian Fire Safety Association [Vol 1: 6495]
Canadian Football Council [Vol 1: 6501]
Canadian Football League [Vol 1: 6501]
Canadian Forestry Association [Vol 1: 6511]
Canadian Foundation for AIDS Research [Vol 1: 6513]
Canadian Foundation for Dietetic Research [Vol 1: 6515]
Canadian Foundation for Ileitis and Colitis [Vol 1: 7757]
Canadian Foundation for the Study of Infant Deaths [Vol 1: 6517]
Canadian Geomorphological Research Group [Vol 1: 6519]
Canadian Geophysical Union [Vol 1: 6522]
Canadian Geotechnical Society [Vol 1: 6525]
Canadian Gift and Tableware Association [Vol 1: 6527]
Canadian Golf Superintendents Association [Vol 1: 6530]
Canadian Hard of Hearing Association [Vol 1: 6537]
Canadian Health Information Management Association [Vol 1: 6543]
Canadian Health Libraries Association [Vol 1: 6545]
Canadian Healthcare Engineering Society [Vol 1: 6551]
Canadian Hemophilia Society [Vol 1: 6553]
Canadian HIV/AIDS Legal Network [Vol 1: 6555]
Canadian Hydrographic Association [Vol 1: 6557]
Canadian Image Processing and Pattern Recognition Society [Vol 1: 6559]
Canadian Independent Adjusters' Association [Vol 1: 6561]
Canadian Industrial Transportation Association [Vol 1: 6564]
Canadian Information Processing Society [Vol 1: 6566]
Canadian Institute for the Administration of Justice - University of Montreal [Vol 1: 6571]
Canadian Institute of Actuaries [Vol 1: 6573]
Canadian Institute of Child Health [Vol 1: 6575]
Canadian Institute of Food Science and Technology [Vol 1: 6578]
Canadian Institute of Forestry [Vol 1: 6586]
Canadian Institute of Marketing [Vol 1: 6597]
Canadian Institute of Mining, Metallurgy, and Petroleum [Vol 1: 6599]
Canadian Institute of Quantity Surveyors [Vol 1: 6621]
Canadian Institute of Traffic and Transportation [Vol 1: 6624]
Canadian International Amateur Film Festival [Vol 1: 6631]
Canadian International Annual Film/Video Festival [Vol 1: 6631]
Canadian Interuniversity Sport [Vol 1: 6633]
Canadian Intravenous Nurses Association [Vol 1: 7024]
Canadian Investment Awards Inc. [Vol 1: 6667]
Canadian Journalists for Free Expression [Vol 1: 6669]
Canadian Library Association [Vol 1: 6672]
Canadian Library Trustees Association [Vol 1: 6678]
Canadian Manufacturers and Exporters [Vol 1: 6681]
Canadian Media Production Association [Vol 1: 6684]
Canadian Mental Health Association [Vol 1: 6687]
Canadian Mental Health Association - Alberta Division [Vol 1: 6694]
Canadian Mental Health Association - British Columbia Division [Vol 1: 6701]
Canadian Mental Health Association - Central Alberta Region [Vol 1: 6703]
Canadian Mental Health Association - Ontario Division [Vol 1: 6705]
Canadian Meteorological and Oceanographic Society [Vol 1: 6707]
Canadian Motorcyle Association [Vol 1: 6716]
Canadian Museums Association [Vol 1: 6720]
Canadian Music Competition [Vol 1: 6724]
Canadian National Institute for the Blind [Vol 1: 6726]
Canadian Nautical Research Society [Vol 1: 6734]
Canadian Neurosurgical Society [Vol 1: 6739]
Canadian Newspaper Association [Vol 1: 6741]
Canadian Nuclear Society [Vol 1: 6743]
Canadian Nurses Association [Vol 1: 6751]

Canadian Nutrition Society **[Vol 1: 6754]**

Canadian Occupational Therapy Foundation **[Vol 1: 6756]**

Canadian Operational Research Society **[Vol 1: 6762]**

Canadian Organization of Medical Physicists **[Vol 1: 6300]**

Canadian Ornamental Plant Foundation **[Vol 1: 6765]**

Canadian Paediatric Society **[Vol 1: 6767]**

Canadian Parks and Recreation Association **[Vol 1: 6770]**

Canadian Parks and Wilderness Society **[Vol 1: 6777]**

Canadian Payroll Association **[Vol 1: 6779]**

Canadian Pharmacists Association **[Vol 1: 6784]**

Canadian Phytopathological Society **[Vol 1: 6793]**

Canadian Political Science Association **[Vol 1: 6798]**

Canadian Professional Sales Association **[Vol 1: 6804]**

Canadian Prostate Cancer Network **[Vol 1: 6806]**

Canadian Psychiatric Association **[Vol 1: 6808]**

Canadian Psychological Association **[Vol 1: 6820]**

Canadian Public Health Association **[Vol 1: 6829]**

Canadian Public Relations Society **[Vol 1: 6836]**

Canadian Quaternary Association **[Vol 1: 6847]**

Canadian Railroad Historical Association **[Vol 1: 6849]**

Canadian Recording Industry Association **[Vol 1: 6854]**

Canadian Remote Sensing Society **[Vol 1: 6856]**

Canadian Research Institute for the Advancement of Women **[Vol 1: 6859]**

Canadian Science Writers' Association **[Vol 1: 6862]**

Canadian Security Association **[Vol 1: 6866]**

Canadian Ski Council **[Vol 1: 6868]**

Canadian Society for Bioengineering **[Vol 1: 6871]**

Canadian Society for Brain, Behaviour and Cognitive Science **[Vol 1: 6879]**

Canadian Society for Chemical Engineering **[Vol 1: 6918]**

Canadian Society for Chemical Technology **[Vol 1: 6882]**

Canadian Society for Chemistry **[Vol 1: 6884]**

Canadian Society for Civil Engineering **[Vol 1: 6897]**

Canadian Society for Clinical Nutrition **[Vol 1: 6754]**

Canadian Society for Clinical Pharmacology - Pharmacological Society of Canada **[Vol 1: 6983]**

Canadian Society for International Health **[Vol 1: 6909]**

Canadian Society for Mechanical Engineering **[Vol 1: 6911]**

Canadian Society for Nutritional Sciences **[Vol 1: 6754]**

Canadian Society for Training and Development **[Vol 1: 6921]**

Canadian Society of Animal Science **[Vol 1: 6924]**

Canadian Society of Association Executives **[Vol 1: 6931]**

Canadian Society of Biochemistry, Molecular and Cellular Biology **[Vol 1: 6935]**

Canadian Society of Club Managers **[Vol 1: 6940]**

Canadian Society of Diagnostic Medical Sonographers **[Vol 1: 6945]**

Canadian Society of Hospital Pharmacists **[Vol 1: 6948]**

Canadian Society of Internal Medicine **[Vol 1: 6960]**

Canadian Society of Landscape Architects **[Vol 1: 6965]**

Canadian Society of Microbiologists **[Vol 1: 6975]**

Canadian Society of Petroleum Geologists **[Vol 1: 6978]**

Canadian Society of Pharmacology and Therapeutics **[Vol 1: 6983]**

Canadian Society of Zoologists **[Vol 1: 6992]**

Canadian Sociology and Anthropology Association **[Vol 1: 7001]**

Canadian Sociology Association **[Vol 1: 7001]**

Canadian Sport Council **[Vol 1: 16166]**

Canadian Sport Massage Therapists Association **[Vol 1: 7004]**

Canadian Sport Parachuting Association **[Vol 1: 7006]**

Canadian Sporting Goods Association **[Vol 1: 7008]**

Canadian Standards Association **[Vol 1: 16251]**

Canadian Toy Testing Council **[Vol 1: 7010]**

Canadian Trakehner Horse Society **[Vol 1: 7014]**

Canadian Urban Transit Association **[Vol 1: 7021]**

Canadian Vascular Access Association **[Vol 1: 7024]**

Canadian Veterinary Medical Association **[Vol 1: 7028]**

Canadian Water and Wastewater Association **[Vol 1: 7035]**

Canadian Water Resources Association **[Vol 1: 7038]**

Canadian Wildlife Federation **[Vol 1: 7040]**

Canadian Wood Council **[Vol 1: 7047]**

Cancer Hope Network **[Vol 1: 7049]**

Cancer; International Union Against **[Vol 2: 6456]**

Cancer Organization; European **[Vol 2: 1443]**

Cancer Registrars Association; National **[Vol 1: 12031]**

Cancer Research; American Association for **[Vol 1: 877]**

Cancer Research; British Association for **[Vol 2: 6947]**

Cancer Research; European Association for **[Vol 2: 7577]**

Cancer Research Foundation **[Vol 1: 7051]**

Cancer Research Institute, Inc. **[Vol 1: 7054]**

Cancer Society; American **[Vol 1: 1529]**

Candlestar **[Vol 2: 7329]**

Canon Information Systems Research Australia Pty. Ltd. **[Vol 2: 1109]**

Canon USA Inc. **[Vol 1: 14174]**

Canterbury Historical Association **[Vol 2: 4872]**

Cantors Assembly **[Vol 1: 7059]**

Cape Town Regional Chamber of Commerce and Industry **[Vol 2: 5527]**

Capital Corporation Image Institution **[Vol 2: 5222]**

Cardiac Society of Australia and New Zealand **[Vol 2: 635]**

Cardiovascular and Interventional Radiological Society of Europe **[Vol 2: 1215]**

Cardiovascular Society; Canadian **[Vol 1: 6391]**

Cardiovascular Thoracic Anaesthesiologists; Indian Association of **[Vol 2: 3510]**

Care Forum Wales **[Vol 2: 7332]**

Cargill Inc. **[Vol 1: 9550]**

Caribbean Conservation Corporation **[Vol 1: 14806]**

Caribbean Conservation Corporation and Sea Turtle Survival League **[Vol 1: 14806]**

Caribbean Studies Association **[Vol 1: 7066]**

Caribbean Tourism Organization **[Vol 2: 1385]**

Carnegie Hero Fund Commission **[Vol 1: 7068]**

Carnegie Mellon University - Hunt Institute for Botanical Documentation **[Vol 1: 7070]**

Carnegie Mellon University - Software Engineering Institute **[Vol 1: 7072]**

Carnegie Museum of Art **[Vol 1: 7077]**

Carolina Biological Supply Company **[Vol 1: 5090, 5092]**

Carreras Foundation; Jose **[Vol 2: 4702]**

Carton Manufacturers; Pro Carton, the Association of European Cartonboard and **[Vol 2: 6473]**

Cartonboard and Carton Manufacturers; Pro Carton, the Association of European **[Vol 2: 6473]**

Cartoonists Society; National **[Vol 1: 12033]**

Caspian Business Alliance LLC **[Vol 2: 1336]**

Casualty Actuarial Society **[Vol 1: 7079]**

Catalog and Multichannel Marketing Council **[Vol 1: 7084]**

Catalysis Society; North American **[Vol 1: 13285]**

Cataract and Refractive Surgery; American Society of **[Vol 1: 4135]**

Catboat Association **[Vol 1: 7088]**

Catching the Dream **[Vol 1: 7092]**

Catholic Academy for Communication Arts Professionals **[Vol 1: 7097]**

Catholic Broadcasting Association **[Vol 1: 7097]**

Catholic Campaign for Human Development **[Vol 1: 7099]**

Catholic Campus Ministry Association **[Vol 1: 7102]**

Catholic Church Extension Society of the U.S.A. **[Vol 1: 7104]**

Catholic Historical Association; American **[Vol 1: 1541]**

Catholic Library Association **[Vol 1: 7106]**

Catholic Philosophical Association; American **[Vol 1: 1546]**

Catholic Press Association **[Vol 1: 7108]**

Catholic Theological Society of America **[Vol 1: 7111]**

Caucus for a New Political Science **[Vol 1: 7114]**

Caucus for Television Producers, Writers, and Directors **[Vol 1: 7119]**

Caucus for Women in Statistics **[Vol 1: 7438]**

Cave Canem Foundation, Inc. **[Vol 1: 7123]**

Cayman Islands Society of Human Resource Professionals **[Vol 2: 1814]**

Cayman Islands Tourism Association **[Vol 2: 1816]**

Cayman National Cultural Foundation **[Vol 2: 1818]**

Cell Biology; American Society for **[Vol 1: 3777]**

Celtic Media Festival **[Vol 2: 7334]**

Center for Architecture Foundation **[Vol 1: 2581, 2586]**

Center for Chinese Studies **[Vol 2: 6581]**

Center for Communication **[Vol 1: 7125]**

Center for Creative Leadership **[Vol 1: 7127]**

Center for Critical Thinking **[Vol 1: 7130]**

Center for Democratic Policy **[Vol 1: 7144]**

Center for Design of Analog-Digital Integrated Circuits **[Vol 1: 7132]**

Center for Immigration Studies **[Vol 1: 7134]**

Center for Lesbian and Gay Studies **[Vol 1: 7136]**

Center for National Policy **[Vol 1: 7144]**

Center for Nonprofit Advancement **[Vol 1: 7146]**

Center for Public Resources - CPR Legal Program **[Vol 1: 7731]**

Center for Public Safety **[Vol 1: 9640]**

Center for Regional Development/Transparency International - Armenia **[Vol 2: 50]**

Center for the Study of Aging, Inc. **[Vol 1: 7149]**

Center for the Study of Canada **[Vol 1: 7151]**

Center for the Study of Sport in Society **[Vol 1: 13402]**

Center for the Study of the Presidency **[Vol 1: 7153]**

Centers for Disease Control and Prevention **[Vol 1: 11740]**

Central Association of Obstetricians and Gynecologists **[Vol 1: 7156]**

Central Chancery of the Orders of Knighthood - Honours and Appointments **[Vol 2: 7336]**

Central City Productions Inc. **[Vol 1: 7158]**

Central Institute for Labor Protection - National Research Institute **[Vol 2: 5380]**

Central Pennsylvania Festival of the Arts **[Vol 1: 7160]**

Centre canadien d'oecumenisme **[Vol 1: 6404]**

Centre de Cooperation pour les Recherches Scientifiques Relatives au Tabac **[Vol 2: 2343]**

Centre de recherche et d'enseignement sur les droits de la personne **[Vol 1: 17319]**

Centre de Recherches Mathematiques **[Vol 1: 6304]**

Centre de recherches mathematiques, Universite de Montreal **[Vol 1: 17304]**

Centre du Cinema Grec **[Vol 2: 3312]**

Centre for Asia Pacific Aviation **[Vol 2: 639]**

Centre for Latin American Monetary Studies **[Vol 2: 4578]**

Centre International de Recherche sur le Cancer **[Vol 2: 2479]**

Centre international d'etudes pour la conservation et la restauration des biens culturels **[Vol 2: 4087]**

Centre national de la recherche scientifique **[Vol 2: 2446]**

Centro de Estudios Monetarios Latinoamericanos **[Vol 2: 4578]**

Centro Gerontologico Latino **[Vol 1: 10753]**

Centro Regional de Sismologia para America del Sur **[Vol 2: 5319]**

Centro Studi Nuovo Mezzogiorno **[Vol 2: 4031]**

Centrum Foundation **[Vol 1: 6755]**

Cerebral Blood Flow and Metabolism; International Society for **[Vol 2: 6429]**

Ceres **[Vol 1: 5244]**

Certamen Internacional de Films Cortos, Ciudad de Huesca **[Vol 2: 6034]**

Cervical Cancer Coalition; National **[Vol 1: 12056]**

Ceska Radiologicka Spolecnost **[Vol 2: 1919]**

Ceska Spolecnost Chemicka **[Vol 2: 1910]**

Cesky Rozhlas, Praga **[Vol 2: 1929]**

Cetacean Society International **[Vol 1: 7163]**

Ceylon Development Engineering Company, Ltd. **[Vol 2: 6124]**

CFA Institute **[Vol 1: 7165]**

Challenger Society **[Vol 2: 7354]**

Challenger Society for Marine Science **[Vol 2: 7354]**

Chamber Music America **[Vol 1: 4259, 7175]**

Chamber of Commerce and Economy of Serbia [Vol 2: 5910]

Chamber of Commerce Executives; American [Vol 1: 1581]

Chamber of Commerce; Italy-America [Vol 1: 10537]

Chamber of Shipping of America [Vol 1: 7180]

Chancery of Netherlands Orders [Vol 2: 4648]

Charcot-Marie-Tooth Association [Vol 1: 7184]

Charity Film Festival Association; Monaco [Vol 2: 4606]

Charles A. and Anne Morrow Lindbergh Foundation [Vol 1: 7186]

Charlotte Touchdown Club [Vol 1: 8409]

Charta 77 Foundation [Vol 2: 1905]

Chartered Institute of Architectural Technologists [Vol 2: 7358]

Chartered Institute of Building [Vol 2: 7363]

Chartered Institute of Journalists [Vol 2: 7374]

Chartered Institute of Library and Information Professionals [Vol 2: 7376]

Chartered Institute of Logistics and Transport [Vol 2: 7379]

Chartered Institute of Logistics and Transport in Australia [Vol 2: 641]

Chartered Institute of Logistics and Transport in North America [Vol 1: 7192]

Chartered Institute of Management Accountants - Hong Kong Division [Vol 2: 5224]

Chartered Institute of Management Accountants - Sri Lanka [Vol 2: 6118]

Chartered Institute of Marketing [Vol 2: 5267]

Chartered Institution of Building Services Engineers - England [Vol 2: 7387]

Chartered Institution of Civil Engineering Surveyors [Vol 2: 7395]

Chartered Institution of Water and Environmental Management [Vol 2: 7397]

Chartered Insurance Institute [Vol 2: 7403]

Chartered Society of Designers [Vol 2: 7417]

Chelsea [Vol 1: 7194]

Chemical Development and Marketing Association [Vol 1: 7436]

Chemical Engineering and Biotechnology; Society for [Vol 2: 3158]

Chemical Engineers; American Institute of [Vol 1: 2603]

Chemical Engineers; Institution of [Vol 2: 7957]

Chemical Heritage Foundation [Vol 1: 7197]

Chemical Industry; Society of [Vol 2: 9266]

Chemical Institute of Canada [Vol 1: 7202]

Chemical Institute; Royal Australian [Vol 1: 965]

Chemical Institute; South African [Vol 2: 5673]

Chemical Marketing Research Association [Vol 1: 7433]

Chemical Organization of Mexico [Vol 2: 4580]

Chemical Society [Vol 2: 8971]

Chemical Society; American [Vol 1: 1588]

Chemical Society; Czech [Vol 2: 1910]

Chemical Society; French [Vol 2: 2436]

Chemical Society; German [Vol 2: 2922]

Chemical Society; Hungarian [Vol 2: 3379]

Chemical Society; Israel [Vol 2: 3956]

Chemical Society; Korean [Vol 2: 5447]

Chemical Society of Japan [Vol 1: 1659]

Chemical Society; Polish [Vol 2: 5391]

Chemical Society; Swiss [Vol 2: 6485]

Chemical Specialties Manufacturers Association [Vol 1: 7580]

Chemistry; American Association for Clinical [Vol 1: 883]

Chemistry and Laboratory Medicine; International Federation of Clinical [Vol 2: 4096]

Chemistry; Canadian Society for [Vol 1: 6884]

Chemistry; German Bunsen Society for Physical [Vol 2: 2917]

Chemistry of the Earth's Interior; International Association of Volcanology and [Vol 2: 6047]

Chemistry; Royal Society of [Vol 2: 8971]

Chemistry; Society of Environmental Toxicology and [Vol 1: 15622]

Chemists and Colorists; American Association of Textile [Vol 1: 1378]

Chemists' Club [Vol 1: 14993]

Chemists, India; Society of Biological [Vol 2: 3779]

Chemists of the Textile Industry; Association of [Vol 2: 2315]

Chemotherapy; International Society of [Vol 2: 8197]

Chess Journalists of America [Vol 1: 7209]

CHEST Foundation [Vol 1: 7211]

Chevron Corp. [Vol 1: 11703]

Chi Psi [Vol 1: 7214]

Chicago Film Critics Association [Vol 1: 7222]

Chicago International Festival of Children's Films [Vol 1: 8224]

Chicago Public Library Foundation [Vol 1: 7224]

Chicago Tribune [Vol 1: 7226]

Child and Adolescent Psychiatry; American Academy of [Vol 1: 500]

Child Health; Canadian Institute of [Vol 1: 6575]

Childhood Cancer Foundation - Candlelighters Canada [Vol 1: 7228]

Children as Teachers of Peace [Vol 1: 7230]

Children as the Peacemakers [Vol 1: 7230]

Children's Book Committee [Vol 1: 7232]

Children's Book Council of Australia [Vol 2: 644]

Children's Book Council of Iran [Vol 2: 3823]

Children's Books Ireland [Vol 2: 3831]

Children's Film Society, India [Vol 2: 3458]

Children's Hospice International [Vol 1: 7236]

Children's Literature Association [Vol 1: 7244]

Children's Literature Council of Southern California [Vol 1: 7249]

Chile Ministry of Education Library [Vol 2: 1822]

China Foundry Association [Vol 2: 5226]

China Toy Association [Vol 2: 5229]

Chinese American Librarians Association [Vol 2: 5231]

Chinese American Medical Society [Vol 1: 7251]

Chinese Anti-Cancer Association [Vol 2: 5233]

Chinese Chemical Society [Vol 2: 5236]

Chinese Studies; European Association for [Vol 2: 7583]

Chlotrudis Society for Independent Film [Vol 1: 7254]

Chopin Foundation of the United States [Vol 1: 7256]

Chopin-Gesellschaft in der Bundesrepublik Deutschland [Vol 2: 2747]

Chopin Society in the Federal Republic of Germany [Vol 2: 2747]

Chorus America [Vol 1: 7258]

Christian Booksellers Association of New Zealand [Vol 2: 4874]

Christian College Athletic Association; National [Vol 1: 12060]

Christian European Visual Media Association [Vol 2: 2749]

Christian Management Association [Vol 1: 7265]

Christian Ministries Management Association [Vol 1: 7265]

Christliche Europaische Arbeitsgemeinschaft fur Visuelle Medien [Vol 2: 2749]

Christoff International Competition for Young Opera Singers Foundation; Boris [Vol 2: 1792]

The Christophers [Vol 1: 7268]

The Christy Award LLC [Vol 1: 7270]

Chromatographic Society [Vol 1: 7423]

Church and Synagogue Library Association [Vol 1: 7272]

Churchill Centre [Vol 1: 7278]

Churchill Downs Inc. [Vol 1: 7282]

Churchill Foundation of the United States; Winston [Vol 1: 7285]

Churchill Study Unit [Vol 1: 7278]

CIBA Specialty Chemicals Education Foundation [Vol 1: 12820, 12821]

Cinema/Chicago [Vol 1: 7287]

Cinema Giovani - Torino Film Festival [Vol 2: 4041]

Cinema Novo Fantasporto [Vol 2: 5416]

Cinematheque Royale [Vol 2: 1654]

Circle of the Greek Children's Book [Vol 2: 3271]

Circuits; Center for Design of Analog-Digital Integrated [Vol 1: 7132]

Circus Maniacs [Vol 2: 7426]

Citizens Committee for New York City [Vol 1: 7289]

City and Guilds of London Institute [Vol 2: 7429]

City and Regional Magazine Association [Vol 1: 7291]

City and Regional Planners; International Society of [Vol 2: 4779]

City Council of Pforzheim [Vol 2: 3183]

City of London Corp. [Vol 2: 7435]

City of Nuremberg - Office of Human Rights [Vol 2: 2751]

City of Ottawa [Vol 1: 7293]

City of Sydney Eisteddfod [Vol 2: 1073]

City of Toronto [Vol 1: 7295, 16516]

Civil Engineering Forum for Innovation [Vol 1: 4205, 4216]

Civitan International [Vol 1: 7300]

Cladan Cultural Exchange Institute of Australia [Vol 2: 652]

Clan Hunter Association [Vol 2: 7439]

Clara Haskil Association [Vol 2: 6257]

Clarinet International [Vol 1: 9771]

Classic Car Club of America [Vol 1: 7312]

Classification Societies; International Federation of [Vol 2: 2521]

Clay Minerals Society [Vol 1: 7315]

Cleft Palate Foundation [Vol 1: 7320]

Clemson University [Vol 1: 15045]

Cleveland Institute of Music [Vol 1: 7323]

Cleveland State University Poetry Center [Vol 1: 7325]

CLFMA of India [Vol 2: 3460]

Clinical Genetics Society [Vol 2: 7441]

Clinton Global Initiative [Vol 1: 7328]

Clio Awards Inc. [Vol 1: 7330]

Clothing Manufacturers Association of India [Vol 2: 3462]

Clowns of America International [Vol 1: 7332]

Club Tenco [Vol 2: 4043]

CNN MultiChoice African Journalist Awards [Vol 2: 7443]

COACH: Canada's Health Informatics Association [Vol 1: 7336]

Coach Federation; International [Vol 1: 9774]

Coach Federation of New England; International [Vol 1: 9779]

Coaches Association; American Swimming [Vol 1: 4577]

Coal Preparation Society [Vol 2: 8359]

Coalition of Black Trade Unionists [Vol 1: 7339]

CODE [Vol 1: 7343]

Coffee Excellence Inc.; The Alliance for [Vol 1: 364]

COGEDIM [Vol 2: 2332]

Coiffure; Association Internationale Presse Professionelle [Vol 2: 2556]

Colegio de Ingenieros de Chile A.G [Vol 2: 1829]

Colgate-Palmolive Company [Vol 1: 15846, 15847]

Colitis Foundation of America; Crohn's and [Vol 1: 7753]

Collective Promotion for the Dutch Book [Vol 2: 4653]

College and University Professional Association for Human Resources [Vol 1: 7345]

College Art Association [Vol 1: 7351]

College Canadien de Geneticiens Medicaux [Vol 1: 6409]

College des Medecins de Famille du Canada [Vol 1: 7373]

College Gymnastics Association [Vol 1: 7361]

College International pour la Recherche en Productique [Vol 2: 2474]

College Media Advisers [Vol 1: 7366]

College of Chaplains of the American Protestant Health Association [Vol 1: 5479]

College of Family Physicians of Canada - Ontario Chapter [Vol 1: 7373]

College of Health Sciences [Vol 2: 1350]

College of Healthcare Information Management Executives [Vol 1: 8869]

College of Piping [Vol 2: 7445]

College of Psychologists of British Columbia [Vol 1: 6025]

College Ouest Africain des Chirurgiens [Vol 2: 5105]

College Reading and Learning Association [Vol 1: 7375]

College Sports Information Directors of America [Vol 1: 7378]

College Teaching and Learning; International Conference of [Vol 1: 9810]

Collymore Hall; Frank [Vol 2: 1387]

Colombia Ministry of National Defence [Vol 2: 1831]

Colombia Ministry of Transportation [Vol 2: 1840]

Colon and Rectal Surgeons; American Society of [Vol 1: 4256]

Colorado Association of Libraries [Vol 1: 7382]

Colorado Business Committee for the Arts [Vol 1: 7400]

Colorado Ranger Horse Association **[Vol 1: 7405]**

Colposcopy and Cervical Pathology; American Society for **[Vol 1: 3805]**

Columbia Basin Trust **[Vol 1: 7407]**

Columbia Scholastic Press Association **[Vol 1: 7409]**

Columbia University - Graduate School of Journalism **[Vol 1: 4372]**

Columbia University - Lamont-Doherty Earth Observatory **[Vol 1: 7412]**

Columbia University - Medical Center **[Vol 1: 7414]**

Columbia University - The Pulitzer Prizes **[Vol 1: 7416]**

Columbia University - Southern Asian Institute **[Vol 1: 7419]**

Columbus Fellowship Foundation; Christopher **[Vol 1: 7421]**

Columbus Foundation **[Vol 1: 10470]**

Columbus Foundation; Before **[Vol 1: 5800]**

Columbus International Film and Video Festival **[Vol 1: 7426]**

Combustion Institute **[Vol 1: 7428]**

Comite Europeen de Droit Rural **[Vol 2: 1467]**

Comite International de la Croix-Rouge **[Vol 2: 6368]**

Comite International des Sports des Sourds **[Vol 1: 9796]**

Comite International Olympique **[Vol 2: 6412]**

Comite International pour lo Controle des Performances en Elevage **[Vol 2: 4090]**

Comite pour la Recherche Spatiale **[Vol 2: 2334]**

Commerce; United States Department of - National Institute of Standards and Technology **[Vol 1: 16786]**

Commercial Audiovisual Libraries International; Federation of **[Vol 2: 7671]**

Commercial Development and Marketing Association **[Vol 1: 7433]**

Commission Electrotechnique Internationale **[Vol 2: 6373]**

Commission Internationale de Juristes - Section Canadienne **[Vol 1: 9789]**

Commission Internationale des Irrigations et du Drainage **[Vol 2: 3760]**

Commission Internationale des Oeufs **[Vol 2: 8109]**

Commission Internationale d'Optique **[Vol 2: 6053]**

Commission Internationale du Genie Rural **[Vol 2: 4238]**

Commission Oceanographique Intergouvernementale **[Vol 2: 2638]**

Commission on Presidential Scholars **[Vol 1: 16802]**

Committee of Presidents of Statistical Societies **[Vol 1: 7437, 9381]**

Committee on Space Research **[Vol 2: 2334]**

Committee to Protect Journalists **[Vol 1: 7443]**

Commonwealth Association for Public Administration and Management **[Vol 1: 7446]**

Commonwealth Association of Architects **[Vol 2: 7448]**

Commonwealth Association of Science and Mathematics Educators **[Vol 2: 7451]**

Commonwealth Association of Science, Technology and Mathematics Educators **[Vol 2: 7451]**

Commonwealth Bank of Australia **[Vol 2: 149]**

Commonwealth Broadcasting Association **[Vol 2: 7454]**

Commonwealth Forestry Association **[Vol 2: 7457]**

Commonwealth Foundation **[Vol 2: 7463]**

The Commonwealth Fund **[Vol 1: 7448]**

Commonwealth Games Federation **[Vol 2: 7466]**

Commonwealth Partnership for Technology Management **[Vol 2: 7468]**

Commonwealth Pharmaceutical Association **[Vol 2: 7470]**

Commonwealth Pharmacists Association **[Vol 2: 7470]**

Commonwealth Scientific and Industrial Research Organisation **[Vol 2: 654]**

Communal Studies Association **[Vol 1: 7450]**

Communication Agencies Association of New Zealand **[Vol 2: 4879]**

Communications Alliance **[Vol 2: 658]**

Communications and Technology; Association for Educational **[Vol 1: 5001]**

Community Counselling Service **[Vol 1: 5349]**

Community Development Society **[Vol 1: 7455]**

Community Media; Alliance for **[Vol 1: 366]**

Comparative Zoology; Museum of **[Vol 1: 11314]**

Compass Publications Inc. **[Vol 1: 10977, 12623]**

Competitive Eating; International Federation of **[Vol 1: 9914]**

COMplus **[Vol 2: 6535]**

Composers and Authors Society of Hong Kong **[Vol 2: 5239]**

Computer Graphics; European Association for **[Vol 2: 6262]**

Computer Measurement Group **[Vol 1: 7462]**

Computer Society; British **[Vol 2: 7002]**

Computer Society - Hungary; John Von Neumann **[Vol 2: 3412]**

Computer Society of Malta **[Vol 2: 4556]**

Computing Research Association **[Vol 1: 7465]**

Comune di Sondrio Mostra Internazionale dei Documentari sui Parchi **[Vol 2: 4152]**

Conamus **[Vol 2: 4656]**

Conamus; Stichting **[Vol 2: 4656]**

Conch Festival; Turks & Caicos **[Vol 2: 6642]**

Concorso Pianistico Internazionale Alessandro Casagrande **[Vol 2: 4045]**

Concours de musique du Canada **[Vol 1: 6724]**

Concours International de Ballet, Varna **[Vol 2: 1804]**

Concours International de Harpe en Israel **[Vol 2: 3954]**

Concours Internationaux de la Ville de Paris **[Vol 2: 2507]**

Concours Musical International Reine Elisabeth de Belgique **[Vol 2: 1574]**

Concrete Foundations Association **[Vol 1: 7469]**

Concrete Institute; American **[Vol 1: 1835]**

Concrete Institute of Australia **[Vol 2: 660]**

Concrete Reinforcing Steel Institute **[Vol 1: 7472]**

Concrete Society of Southern Africa **[Vol 2: 5530]**

Concurs Internacional de Cant Francesc Vinas **[Vol 2: 6112]**

Concurs Internacional de Piano **[Vol 2: 12]**

Conductors Guild **[Vol 1: 7474]**

Confederate Memorial Literary Society **[Vol 1: 7477]**

Confederate Stamp Alliance **[Vol 1: 7479]**

Confederation Europeenne de Baseball **[Vol 2: 2754]**

Confederation Internationale des Accordeonistes **[Vol 2: 2115]**

Confederation Internationale des Sages-Femmes **[Vol 2: 4734]**

Confederation Mondiale pour la Therapie Physique **[Vol 2: 9471]**

Confederation of European Baseball **[Vol 2: 2754]**

Confederation of Indian Textile Industry **[Vol 2: 3464]**

Conference Canadienne des arts **[Vol 1: 6424]**

Conference of California Historical Societies **[Vol 1: 7487]**

Conference of Consulting Actuaries **[Vol 1: 7496]**

Conference of Minority Public Administrators **[Vol 1: 7501]**

Conference on British Studies **[Vol 1: 13296]**

Conference on College Composition and Communication **[Vol 1: 7506]**

Conference on Latin American History **[Vol 1: 7511]**

Confrerie de la Chaine des Rotisseurs, Bailliage des U.S.A. **[Vol 1: 7518]**

Congregational Christian Historical Society **[Vol 1: 7525]**

Congres Mondiaux du Petrole **[Vol 2: 9488]**

Congress for the New Urbanism **[Vol 1: 7528]**

Congress of Neurological Surgeons **[Vol 1: 7531]**

Congressional Award Foundation **[Vol 1: 7536]**

Congressional Hispanic Caucus Institute **[Vol 1: 7538]**

Congressional Medal of Honor Society **[Vol 1: 7540]**

Conjunto Universitario Candido Mendes of Brazil **[Vol 2: 2564]**

Conrad Society of America; Joseph **[Vol 1: 7542]**

Conseil canadien de la securite **[Vol 1: 6146]**

Conseil Canadien des Infirmieres en Nursing Cardiovasculaire **[Vol 1: 6427]**

Conseil Canadien des Normes **[Vol 1: 16237]**

Conseil Canadien des Techniciens et Technologues **[Vol 1: 6429]**

Conseil Canadien du Ski **[Vol 1: 6868]**

Conseil Consultatif Canadiene de la Radio **[Vol 1: 14390]**

Conseil de l'Europe **[Vol 2: 2345]**

Conseil de recherches en sciences naturelles et en genie du Canada **[Vol 1: 13102]**

Conseil des Arts de Ile-du-Prince-Edouard **[Vol 1: 14143]**

Conseil Des Arts De L'Ontatio **[Vol 1: 13561]**

Conseil Europeen des Urbanistes **[Vol 2: 1470]**

Conseil International de la Musique **[Vol 2: 2554]**

Conseil International de l'Enseignement a Distance **[Vol 2: 5131]**

Conseil International d'Education des Adultes **[Vol 2: 9537]**

Conseil International des Associations Graphiques **[Vol 1: 9834]**

Conseil International des Grands Reseaux Electriques **[Vol 2: 2511]**

Conseil International des Infirmieres **[Vol 2: 6371]**

Conseil International des Monuments et des Sites **[Vol 2: 2515]**

Conseil International des Sciences Sociales **[Vol 2: 2562]**

Conseil International d'Etudes Canadiennes **[Vol 1: 9814]**

Conseil International du Droit de l'Environnement **[Vol 2: 3058]**

Conseil International pour l'Education Physique et la Science du Sport **[Vol 2: 3061]**

Conseil national de recherches Canada **[Vol 1: 12768]**

Consejo Cultural Mundial **[Vol 2: 4600]**

Consejo Mundial de Boxeo **[Vol 2: 4597]**

Consejo Nacional de Ciencia y Tecnologia **[Vol 2: 4582]**

Conservation and Research Foundation **[Vol 1: 5941]**

Conservation Foundation **[Vol 2: 7472]**

Conservation International - Bolivia **[Vol 2: 1723]**

Conservation Leadership Programme **[Vol 2: 7475]**

Conservation Society; Soil and Water **[Vol 1: 15920]**

Conservation Union; World **[Vol 2: 6533]**

Construction Innovation Forum **[Vol 1: 7547]**

Construction Specifications Canada **[Vol 1: 7549]**

Construction Specifications Institute **[Vol 1: 7552]**

Construction Writers Association **[Vol 1: 7565]**

Consuls; World Federation of **[Vol 2: 4203]**

Consult Australia **[Vol 2: 663]**

Consultant Dietitians in Health Care Facilities **[Vol 1: 7858]**

Consulting Engineers Association of India **[Vol 2: 3466]**

Consulting Engineers South Africa **[Vol 2: 5534]**

Consulting Psychologists Press Inc. **[Vol 1: 3589]**

Consumer Credit Industry Association **[Vol 1: 7572]**

Consumer Electronics Association **[Vol 1: 7574]**

Consumer Federation of America **[Vol 1: 7577]**

Consumer Specialty Products Association **[Vol 1: 7580]**

Consumers for World Trade **[Vol 1: 7582]**

Contact Lens Manufacturers Association **[Vol 1: 7584]**

Contemporary Music; International Society for **[Vol 2: 4768]**

Continental Basketball Association **[Vol 1: 7589]**

Convention Europeenne de la Construction Metallique **[Vol 2: 1464]**

Conveyancing Liability Solutions Ltd. **[Vol 2: 8289]**

Convoy For Kids **[Vol 2: 665]**

Cook Islands Tourism Awards **[Vol 2: 1854]**

Coop Schweiz **[Vol 2: 6521]**

Cooper Ecological Monitoring Inc. **[Vol 1: 7591]**

Cooper Ohioana Library Association; Martha Kinney **[Vol 1: 13488]**

Cooper Ornithological Society **[Vol 1: 7593]**

Cooperation Centre for Scientific Research Relative to Tobacco **[Vol 2: 2343]**

Cooperative Research Centre for Polymers **[Vol 2: 672]**

Coordinating Council for Women in History **[Vol 1: 7601]**

Cornea Society **[Vol 1: 7605]**

Cornell Lab of Ornithology **[Vol 1: 7609]**

Cornish American Heritage Society **[Vol 1: 7611]**

Corporation for Public Broadcasting **[Vol 1: 7616]**

Corporation Professionnelle des Psychologues du Quebec **[Vol 1: 13659]**

Corrosion Society; NACE International: The **[Vol 1: 11346]**

Corvette Restorers Society; National **[Vol 1: 12142]**

Deutsche Ophthalmologische Gesellschaft [Vol 2: 2970]

Deutsche Physikalische Gesellschaft [Vol 2: 2771]

Deutsche Phytomedizinische Gesellschaft e.V. [Vol 2: 2984]

Deutschen Gesellschaft fur Geowissenshaften [Vol 2: 2943]

Deutschen Gesellschaft fur Zerstorungsfreie Prufung [Vol 2: 3008]

Deutscher Verband fur Physiotherapie [Vol 2: 2905]

Deutscher Volkshochschul-Verband [Vol 2: 2901]

Deutscher Zentralausschuss fur Chemie [Vol 2: 2773]

Deutsches Atomforum [Vol 2: 2915]

Deutsches Forum fur Figurentheater und Puppenspielkunst e.V. [Vol 2: 2780]

Devis de Construction Canada [Vol 1: 7549]

Dewan Perniagaan dan Perindustrian Kebangsaan Malaysia [Vol 2: 4550]

DHL Worldwide Express, Bangladesh National Office [Vol 2: 1371]

Diabetes Association; American [Vol 1: 2015]

Diabetes; European Association for the Study of [Vol 2: 2797]

Dialogic Agency [Vol 2: 1421]

Dibner Fund [Vol 1: 15351]

Dickinson College [Vol 1: 7855]

Dickinson Press [Vol 1: 8196]

Die Misstofvereniging van Suid-Afrika [Vol 2: 5546]

Die Suid-Afrikaanse Akademie vir Wetenskap en Kuns [Vol 2: 5625]

Dierkundige Vereniging van Suidelike Afrika [Vol 2: 5769]

Dietetics in Health Care Communities [Vol 1: 7858]

Differentiation; International Society of [Vol 1: 10312]

Digestive Health and Nutrition; Foundation for [Vol 1: 8441]

Digital and Screen Printing Association [Vol 2: 7514]

Digital Integrated Circuits; Center for Design of Analog- [Vol 1: 7132]

Direct Mail/Marketing Educational Foundation [Vol 1: 7869]

Direct Marketing Association [Vol 2: 7516]

Direct Marketing Educational Foundation [Vol 1: 7869]

Direct Selling Association [Vol 1: 7872]

Direct Selling Association - United Kingdom [Vol 2: 7518]

Directors Guild of America [Vol 1: 7879]

Dirksen Congressional Leadership Research Center; Everett McKinley [Vol 1: 7889]

Disabled American Veterans [Vol 1: 7892]

Discover Dominica Authority [Vol 2: 1996]

Discover Worlds [Vol 1: 7895]

Dixie Council of Authors and Journalists [Vol 1: 8591]

Doctors of the World [Vol 1: 8678]

Document Management Industries Association [Vol 1: 14160]

Dominica Authority; Discover [Vol 2: 1996]

Dominican University [Vol 1: 7897]

DONA International [Vol 1: 7900]

Door and Hardware Institute [Vol 1: 7905]

Dorper Sheep Breeders' Society of South Africa [Vol 2: 5536]

Dorpers Skaaptelersgenootskap van Suid-Afrika [Vol 2: 5536]

Dorset Natural History [Vol 2: 7520]

Dorset Natural History and Archaeological Society [Vol 2: 7520]

Dortmund; City of [Vol 2: 2782]

Dow Chemical Co. [Vol 2: 4819, 4820]

Dow Jones Newspaper Fund [Vol 1: 7911]

Downeast Association of Physician Assistants [Vol 1: 7913]

Dracula Society [Vol 2: 7523]

Drama League [Vol 1: 7919]

Driving School Association of the Americas [Vol 1: 7923]

Dromkeen Collection Art Gallery [Vol 2: 686]

Drug Strategies [Vol 1: 7928]

Du Pont KEVLAR [Vol 1: 9644]

Dudley Observatory [Vol 1: 7930]

Duke University - Center for Documentary Studies [Vol 1: 7935]

Dutch Society for Biomaterials and Tissue Engineering [Vol 2: 4661]

D'Youville College Alumni Association [Vol 1: 7939]

Dyslexic; Recording for the Blind and [Vol 1: 10785]

Dystrophic Epidermolysis Bullosa Research Association of America [Vol 1: 7944]

Dystrophie Musculaire Canada [Vol 1: 11307]

E-Commerce Yemen Co., Ltd. [Vol 2: 9564]

EA Engineering [Vol 1: 15623]

Eaglehawk Dahlia and Arts Festival [Vol 2: 689]

Early Music America [Vol 1: 7946]

Earth Island Institute [Vol 1: 7950]

Earthwatch Institute [Vol 1: 7952]

East Coast Music Association [Vol 1: 7955]

East European Research; National Council for Eurasian and [Vol 1: 12150]

East Texas Historical Association [Vol 1: 7964]

Easter Seals [Vol 1: 7966]

Eastern Apicultural Society of North America [Vol 1: 7970]

Eastern Association of Mosquito Control Workers [Vol 1: 2936]

Eastern College Athletic Conference [Vol 1: 7973]

Eating; International Federation of Competitive [Vol 1: 9914]

Echocardiography; American Society of [Vol 1: 4285]

Eckhardt-Gramatte National Music Competition [Vol 1: 7978]

Ecolab Inc. [Vol 1: 2463, 9552]

Ecological Society; British [Vol 2: 7043]

Ecological Society of America [Vol 1: 7980]

Ecological Society of Australia [Vol 2: 691]

Ecological Society of Germany, Austria, and Switzerland [Vol 2: 2784]

Ecology; International Society for Behavioral [Vol 2: 832]

Econometric Society [Vol 1: 7990]

Economic History Association [Vol 1: 7992]

Economic Society of Australia [Vol 2: 695]

Economics Society; History of [Vol 1: 8945]

ECS Publishing [Vol 1: 2265]

Edinburgh Festival Fringe [Vol 2: 7526]

Edinburgh Geological Society [Vol 2: 7541]

Edinburgh International Film Festival [Vol 2: 7544]

Edison Electric Institute [Vol 1: 7999]

Edison Foundation [Vol 2: 4663]

Edison Fund; Charles [Vol 1: 15351]

Edison Stichting [Vol 2: 4663]

Editorial Planeta SA [Vol 2: 6021]

Editors; American Society of Business Press [Vol 1: 4132]

Editors Association [Vol 2: 5146]

Editors' Association of Canada [Vol 1: 8007]

Edmonton Epilepsy Association [Vol 1: 8009]

EduArt Inc. [Vol 2: 1812]

Edublog Awards [Vol 2: 699]

Education; Alliance for Continuing Medical [Vol 1: 368]

Education; American Council on [Vol 1: 1919]

Education; American Society for Engineering [Vol 1: 3834]

Education and Sports; Republic of Croatia Ministry of Science, [Vol 2: 1874]

Education Association; National [Vol 1: 12292]

Education Association; National Art [Vol 1: 11532]

Education Association; National Community [Vol 1: 12118]

Education; Botswana Ministry of - Teaching Service Management Unit [Vol 2: 1732]

Education Commission of the States [Vol 1: 8012]

Education Foundation; SME [Vol 1: 14941]

Education; International Council for Adult [Vol 2: 9537]

Education Library; Chile Ministry of [Vol 2: 1822]

Education; North American Association for Environmental [Vol 1: 13264]

Education physique et sante Canada [Vol 1: 13996]

Education Teachers; National Association of Special [Vol 1: 11897]

Education Writers Association [Vol 1: 8017]

Educational Audiology Association [Vol 1: 8019]

Educational Book and Media Association [Vol 1: 8022]

Educational Leaders; Australian Council for [Vol 2: 271]

Educational Paperback Association [Vol 1: 8022]

Educational, Scientific and Cultural Organization; United Nations [Vol 2: 2647]

Educational Testing Service [Vol 1: 8024]

Educational Theatre Association [Vol 1: 8028]

Educators Association; International Technology and Engineering [Vol 1: 10425]

Educators Serving the Community [Vol 1: 8033]

Eesti Ehitusmaterjalide Tootjate Liit [Vol 2: 2033]

Eesti Haridustootajate Liit [Vol 2: 2051]

Eesti Personalitoo Arendamise Uhing [Vol 2: 2048]

Eesti Psuhholoogide Liit [Vol 2: 2053]

Eesti Ringhaalingute Liit [Vol 2: 2035]

Eesti Teaduste Akadeemia [Vol 2: 2037]

Egypt Web Academy [Vol 2: 2012]

Egyptian Computer Society [Vol 2: 2014]

Egyptian Nuclear Physics Association [Vol 2: 2016]

Egyptian Ophthalmological Society [Vol 2: 2019]

Eidgenossische Technische Hochschule Zurich [Vol 2: 6494]

EIFS Industry Members Association [Vol 1: 8040]

Eisenhower Fellowships [Vol 1: 8042]

Eisteddfod Genedlaethol Frenhinol Cymr [Vol 2: 8390]

Elanco [Vol 1: 6926]

ELCINA Electronic Industries Association of India [Vol 2: 3477]

Electric Power Society - Association of German Electrical Engineers [Vol 2: 2787]

Electrical and Electronics Engineers; Institute of [Vol 1: 9284]

Electrical Apparatus Service Association [Vol 1: 8044]

Electrical Generating Systems Association [Vol 1: 8046]

Electricite de France [Vol 2: 2594]

Electro-Federation Canada [Vol 1: 8051]

Electroacoustic Music Studies Network [Vol 1: 10799]

Electrochemical Society [Vol 1: 8053]

Electrodiagnostic Medicine; American Association of Neuromuscular and [Vol 1: 1223]

Electromagnetic Compatibility Society; IEEE [Vol 1: 9077]

Electroneurodiagnostic Technologists; American Society of [Vol 1: 4294]

Electronic Document Systems Foundation [Vol 1: 8066]

Electronic Frontier Foundation [Vol 1: 8069]

Electronic Security Association [Vol 1: 8071]

Electronics and Telecommunication Engineers; Institution of [Vol 2: 3751]

Electronics Engineers; Institute of Electrical and [Vol 1: 9284]

Electronics Technicians Association International [Vol 1: 8074]

Eli Lilly [Vol 1: 6886]

Eli Lilly & Co. [Vol 1: 502]

Eli Lilly and Company [Vol 1: 8279]

Elsevier Science [Vol 1: 15563]

Elsevier Science Publishers [Vol 1: 9912, 9913]

Emap Ltd. [Vol 2: 7546]

Embassy of the United States in Azerbaijan [Vol 2: 1338]

Emergency Department Nurses Association [Vol 1: 8086]

Emergency Medicine Residents' Association [Vol 1: 8076]

Emergency Nurses Association [Vol 1: 8086]

Emirates Environmental Group [Vol 2: 6663]

Employee Involvement Association [Vol 1: 9021]

Endocrine Society [Vol 1: 8106]

Endocrine Society of Australia [Vol 2: 701]

Endocrinology; European Society for Paediatric [Vol 2: 7636]

endocrinology; International Society of Psychoneuro [Vol 1: 10353]

Endocrinology Nursing Society; Pediatric [Vol 1: 13884]

Endodontists; American Association of [Vol 1: 1138]

ENERGY GLOBE Portal [Vol 2: 1227]

Energy Institute [Vol 2: 7548]

Energy Medicine; International Society for the Study of Subtle Energies and [Vol 1: 10247]

Engineering; American Society of Sanitary [Vol 1: 4511]

Engineering and Biotechnology; Society for Chemical [Vol 2: 3158]

Engineering and Research; International Association of Hydraulic [Vol 2: 6040]

Engineering and Technology; Institution of [Vol 2: 8018]

Engineering; Australian Institute of Nuclear Science and [Vol 2: 399]

Engineering; Canadian Society for Civil [Vol 1: 6897]

Engineering; Canadian Society for Mechanical [Vol 1: 6911]

Engineering Companies; American Council of [Vol 1: 1895]

Engineering Education; American Society for [Vol 1: 3834]

Engineering Education Societies; International Federation of [Vol 1: 9918]

Engineering Educators Association; International Technology and [Vol 1: 10425]

Engineering Export Promotion Council [Vol 2: 3479]

Engineering in Medicine and Biology Society; IEEE [Vol 1: 9085]

Engineering Institute of Canada [Vol 1: 6901, 6903, 8115]

Engineering Management; American Society for [Vol 1: 3887]

Engineering ProActive Network; Women in [Vol 1: 17926]

Engineering; Royal Academy of [Vol 2: 8578]

Engineering Sciences; Royal Swedish Academy of [Vol 2: 6175]

Engineering Society of North America; Illuminating [Vol 1: 9152]

Engineering Society; Standards [Vol 1: 16246]

Engineers; American Academy of Environmental [Vol 1: 518]

Engineers; American Institute of Chemical [Vol 1: 2603]

Engineers; American Institute of Mining, Metallurgical, and Petroleum [Vol 1: 2672]

Engineers; American Society of Civil [Vol 1: 4155]

Engineers; American Society of Mechanical [Vol 1: 4379]

Engineers; American Society of Naval [Vol 1: 4441]

Engineers Association; Cyprus Professional [Vol 2: 1898]

Engineers' Association of Chile [Vol 2: 1829]

Engineers Australia - Society for Engineering in Agriculture [Vol 2: 705]

Engineers Australia/Engineers Australia; Institution of [Vol 2: 764]

Engineers Canada [Vol 1: 8123]

Engineers' Company [Vol 2: 7551]

Engineers' Council for Professional Development [Vol 1: 26]

Engineers; European Association of Geoscientists and [Vol 2: 4673]

Engineers; Institute of Domestic Heating and Environmental [Vol 2: 7854]

Engineers; Institute of Electrical and Electronics [Vol 1: 9284]

Engineers; Institute of Industrial [Vol 1: 9346]

Engineers; Institute of Transportation [Vol 1: 9412]

Engineers; Institution of Agricultural [Vol 2: 7950]

Engineers; Institution of Chemical [Vol 2: 7957]

Engineers; Institution of Civil [Vol 2: 7970]

Engineers; Institution of Electronics and Telecommunication [Vol 2: 3751]

Engineers; Institution of Structural [Vol 2: 8057]

Engineers; Japan Society of Mechanical [Vol 2: 4276]

Engineers; National Society of Professional [Vol 1: 12872]

Engineers New Zealand; Institution of Professional [Vol 2: 4904]

Engineers of New Zealand; Association of Consulting [Vol 2: 4859]

Engineers; Society of American Military [Vol 1: 15445]

Engineers; Society of Automotive [Vol 1: 15484]

Engineers; Society of Manufacturing [Vol 1: 15684]

Engineers; Society of Naval Architects and Marine [Vol 1: 15709]

Engineers; Society of Petroleum [Vol 1: 15748]

Engineers; Society of Plastics [Vol 1: 15782]

Engineers; Society of Women [Vol 1: 15894]

Engineers - Sri Lanka; Institution of [Vol 2: 6123]

Engineers; Zimbabwe Institute of [Vol 2: 9576]

English Academy of Southern Africa [Vol 2: 5538]

English Centre of International PEN [Vol 2: 7560]

English; National Council of Teachers of [Vol 1: 12201]

Enology and Viticulture; South African Society for [Vol 2: 5711]

Ensign Media (Bangkok) Co., Ltd. [Vol 2: 6602]

Ente David di Donatello [Vol 2: 4051]

Enterprise Asia [Vol 2: 4540]

Enterprise Foundation [Vol 1: 8458]

Entertainment and Leisure Software Publishers Association [Vol 2: 7564]

Entertainment Industries Council Inc. [Vol 1: 8132]

Entertainment Services and Technology Association [Vol 1: 8134]

Entomological Foundation [Vol 1: 8136]

Entomological Society of America [Vol 1: 8142]

Entomological Society of Canada [Vol 1: 8152]

Entomological Society of New Zealand [Vol 2: 4887]

Entomological Society; Royal [Vol 2: 8767]

Environment Africa [Vol 2: 9573]

Environment Council of Macao [Vol 2: 4502]

Environment Programme; United Nations - Division of Communication and Public Information [Vol 2: 4399]

Environmental and Resource Economists; European Association of [Vol 2: 4058]

Environmental Association for Universities and Colleges [Vol 2: 7566]

Environmental Biogeochemistry; International Society for [Vol 1: 10154]

Environmental Design Research Association [Vol 1: 8155]

Environmental Education; North American Association for [Vol 1: 13264]

Environmental Engineers; American Academy of [Vol 1: 518]

Environmental Engineers; Institute of Domestic Heating and [Vol 2: 7854]

Environmental Epidemiology; International Society for [Vol 1: 10156]

Environmental Ethics; International Society for [Vol 1: 10158]

Environmental History; American Society for [Vol 1: 3901]

Environmental Law Institute [Vol 1: 8159]

Environmental Law; International Council of [Vol 2: 3058]

Environmental Management; Chartered Institution of Water and [Vol 2: 7397]

Environmental Mutagen Society [Vol 1: 8161]

Environmental Protection Agency; United States [Vol 1: 16881]

Environmental Protection Associations; International Union of Air Pollution Prevention and [Vol 2: 8244]

Environmental Sciences and Technology; Institute of [Vol 1: 9315]

Environmental Technology; German Society for Mining, Metallurgy, Resource and [Vol 2: 3004]

Environmental Toxicology and Chemistry; Society of [Vol 1: 15622]

Environmental Transport Association [Vol 2: 7568]

Epidermolysis Bullosa Research Association of America; Dystrophic [Vol 1: 7944]

Epilepsy Foundation [Vol 1: 8165]

Epilepsy Newfoundland and Labrador [Vol 1: 8167]

Episcopal Communicators [Vol 1: 8171]

Eppendorf AG [Vol 2: 2790]

EPR (ESR) Society; International [Vol 1: 9887]

Epsilon Pi Tau [Vol 1: 8174]

Epsilon Sigma Phi [Vol 1: 8177]

Equator Initiative [Vol 1: 8184]

Equestre Internationale; Federation [Vol 2: 6375]

Equestrian Federation; International [Vol 2: 6375]

Equine Research Centre [Vol 1: 8186]

Ergonomics Society - England [Vol 2: 7859]

Ergonomics Society; Human Factors and [Vol 1: 8987]

Erin Arts Centre [Vol 2: 7570]

Ernst Von Siemens-Musikstiftung [Vol 2: 3234]

Escobar Foundation; Alejandro Angel [Vol 2: 1842]

ESOMAR: World Association of Opinion and Marketing Research Professionals [Vol 2: 4667]

ESPN Inc. [Vol 1: 8188]

Estonian Academy of Sciences [Vol 2: 2037]

Estonian Association for Personnel Development [Vol 2: 2048]

Estonian Education Personnel Union [Vol 2: 2051]

Estuarine and Coastal Sciences Association [Vol 2: 7572]

Eta Kappa Nu [Vol 1: 8190]

Ethics; International Society for Environmental [Vol 1: 10158]

Etudes d'Oiseaux Canada [Vol 1: 5856]

Eurasian and East European Research; National Council for [Vol 1: 12150]

EUREKA [Vol 2: 1423]

Eureka Secretariat [Vol 2: 1423]

Eurisys Measures [Vol 2: 2394]

Eurobest Advertising Festival [Vol 2: 7575]

Europa Nostra Pan European Federation for Heritage [Vol 2: 4671]

Europaische Foderation fur Chemie-Ingenieur-Wesen [Vol 2: 2821]

Europaische Kernenergie-Gesellschaft [Vol 2: 1485]

Europaischer Verband der Veranstaltungs-Centren [Vol 2: 2804]

European Academy of Facial Plastic Surgery [Vol 2: 2793]

European Advertising Standards Alliance [Vol 2: 1425]

European Aluminum Foil Association [Vol 2: 2795]

European Association for Animal Production [Vol 2: 4053]

European Association for Battery, Hybrid and Fuel Cell Electric Vehicles [Vol 2: 1427]

European Association for Cancer Research [Vol 2: 7577]

European Association for Chemical and Molecular Sciences [Vol 2: 1430]

European Association for Chinese Studies [Vol 2: 7583]

European Association for Computer Assisted Language Learning [Vol 2: 7585]

European Association for Computer Graphics [Vol 2: 6262]

European Association for Computer Science Logic [Vol 2: 5123]

European Association for Cranio-Maxillofacial Surgery [Vol 2: 7587]

European Association for Geochemistry [Vol 2: 2359]

European Association for Lexicography [Vol 2: 1965]

European Association for Palliative Care [Vol 2: 7592]

European Association for Programming Languages and Systems [Vol 2: 1229]

European Association for Research in Industrial Economics [Vol 2: 1433]

European Association for Signal and Image Processing [Vol 2: 3274]

European Association for Signal Processing [Vol 2: 3274]

European Association for Sociology of Sport [Vol 2: 5382]

European Association for the Study of Diabetes [Vol 2: 2797]

European Association for the Study of Obesity [Vol 2: 7594]

European Association for Theoretical Computer Science [Vol 2: 3277]

European Association of Archaeologists [Vol 2: 1921]

European Association of Communications Agencies [Vol 2: 1436]

European Association of Developmental Psychology [Vol 2: 3279]

European Association of Directory and Database Publishers [Vol 2: 1439]

European Association of Environmental and Resource Economists [Vol 2: 4058]

European Association of Event Centers [Vol 2: 2804]

European Association of Geoscientists and Engineers [Vol 2: 4673]

European Association of Hospital Pharmacists [Vol 2: 1441]

European Association of Nuclear Medicine [Vol 2: 1231]

European Association of Organic Geochemists [Vol 2: 2806]

European Association of Personality Psychology [Vol 2: 2808]

European Association of Plastic Surgeons [Vol 2: 4685]

European Association of Programmes in Health Services Studies [Vol 2: 1478]

European Association of Psychological Assessment [Vol 2: 2810]

European Association of Radiology [Vol 2: 1240]

European Association of Social Psychology [Vol 2: 2812]

European Association of Tax Law Professors [Vol 2: 4687]

European Association of Urology [Vol 2: 4689]

European Association of Veterinary Anatomists [Vol 2: 4062]

European Atherosclerosis Society [Vol 2: 6136]

European Athletic Association [Vol 2: 6268]

European Bar Human Rights Institute [Vol 2: 2465]

European Biophysical Societies' Association [Vol 2: 4694]

European Bridge League [Vol 2: 4065]

European Broadcasting Union [Vol 2: 6270]

European Cancer Organization [Vol 2: 1443]

European Cell Death Organization [Vol 2: 1449]

European Centre for Global Interdependence and Solidarity [Vol 2: 2353]

European Ceramic Society [Vol 2: 1451]

European Chemical Industry Council [Vol 2: 1454]

European Colloid and Interface Society [Vol 2: 1794]

European Commission [Vol 2: 1458, 2346]

European Commission - DG Development [Vol 2: 1462]

European Committee for the Advancement of Thermal Sciences and Heat Transfer [Vol 2: 4067]

European Consortium for Political Research [Vol 2: 7597]

European Convention for Constructional Steelwork [Vol 2: 1464]

European Coordinating Committee for Artificial Intelligence [Vol 2: 2816]

European Council for Agricultural Law [Vol 2: 1467]

European Council for Cardiovascular Research [Vol 2: 7604]

European Council of International Schools [Vol 2: 7606]

European Council of Spatial Planners [Vol 2: 1470]

European Design Awards [Vol 2: 3282]

European Disposables and Nonwovens Association [Vol 2: 1472]

European Dystonia Federation [Vol 2: 7609]

European Economic Association [Vol 2: 4069]

European Emergency Number Association [Vol 2: 1474]

European Environmental Mutagen Society [Vol 2: 2364]

European Federation for Medicinal Chemistry [Vol 2: 1234]

European Federation for Pharmaceutical Sciences [Vol 2: 6139]

European Federation for the Science and Technology of Lipids [Vol 2: 2819]

European Federation of Chemical Engineering [Vol 2: 2821]

European Federation of Corrosion [Vol 2: 2823]

European Federation of Food Science and Technology [Vol 2: 4696]

European Federation of Societies for Ultrasound in Medicine and Biology [Vol 2: 7611]

European Federation of the Associations of Dietitians [Vol 2: 2828]

European Federation of the Contact Lens Industry [Vol 2: 7613]

European Film Academy [Vol 2: 2830]

European Foundation for the Study of Diabetes [Vol 2: 2799, 2803]

European General Galvanizers Association [Vol 2: 7617]

European Generic Medicines Association [Vol 2: 1476]

European Geosciences Union [Vol 2: 2367]

European Health Management Association [Vol 2: 1478]

European Hematology Association [Vol 2: 4700]

European Histamine Research Society [Vol 2: 6144]

European Hotel Managers Association [Vol 2: 4072]

European Imaging and Sound Association [Vol 2: 5426]

European Institute of Public Administration [Vol 2: 4703]

European Landscape Contractors Association [Vol 2: 2832]

European League Against Rheumatism [Vol 2: 6278]

European Life Scientist Organization [Vol 2: 2834]

European Logistics Association [Vol 2: 1481]

European Marketing Academy [Vol 2: 1483]

European Materials Research Society [Vol 2: 2382]

European Membrane Society [Vol 2: 2384]

European Meteorological Society [Vol 2: 2836]

European Molecular Biology Organization [Vol 2: 2842]

European Money and Finance Forum [Vol 2: 1238]

European Nuclear Society [Vol 2: 1485]

European Optical Society [Vol 2: 2844]

European Organization for Caries Research [Vol 2: 4705]

European Organization for Testing New Flower Seeds [Vol 2: 4712]

European Orthodontic Society [Vol 2: 7619]

European Parking Association [Vol 2: 2846]

European Pharmaceutical Student Association [Vol 2: 1442]

European Photochemistry Association [Vol 2: 6280]

European Physical Society [Vol 2: 2386]

European Process Safety Centre [Vol 2: 7628]

European Psychiatric Association [Vol 2: 2400]

European Public Health Association [Vol 2: 4708]

European Rare-Earth Actinide Society [Vol 2: 6282]

European Research Consortium for Informatics and Mathematics [Vol 2: 2403]

European Research; National Council for Eurasian and East [Vol 1: 12150]

European Rhinologic Society [Vol 2: 6285]

European Rotogravure Association [Vol 2: 2849]

European Society for Clinical Virology [Vol 2: 2405]

European Society for Cognitive Psychology [Vol 2: 1487]

European Society for Dermatological Research [Vol 2: 6287]

European Society for Engineering Education [Vol 2: 1489]

European Society for Hyperthermic Oncology [Vol 2: 4710]

European Society for Microcirculation [Vol 2: 2851]

European Society for Organ Transplantation [Vol 2: 7630]

European Society for Paediatric Endocrinology [Vol 2: 7636]

European Society for Radiotherapy and Oncology [Vol 2: 1491]

European Society for Surgery of Shoulder and Elbow [Vol 2: 2409]

European Society for the Study of English [Vol 2: 2072]

European Society for Therapeutic Radiology and Oncology [Vol 2: 1491]

European Society of Anaesthesiology [Vol 2: 1503]

European Society of Biomechanics [Vol 2: 4074]

European Society of Clinical Microbiology and Infectious Diseases [Vol 2: 6290]

European Society of Gastrointestinal Endoscopy [Vol 2: 2856]

European Society of Intensive Care Medicine [Vol 2: 1505]

European Society of Neuroradiology [Vol 2: 1507]

European Society of Ophthalmic Plastic and Reconstructive Surgery [Vol 2: 2858]

European Society of Paediatric Radiology [Vol 2: 7643]

European Society of Radiology [Vol 2: 1240]

European Society of Rheology [Vol 2: 6026]

European Software Institute [Vol 2: 6028]

European Sponsorship Association [Vol 2: 7649]

European Sports Press Union [Vol 2: 5384]

European Study Group on Lysosomal Diseases [Vol 2: 7651]

European Surfing Federation [Vol 2: 7653]

European Survey Research Association [Vol 2: 6030]

European Thyroid Association [Vol 2: 2860]

European Tube Manufacturers Association [Vol 2: 2868]

European Water Association [Vol 2: 2870]

EUROSOLAR - The European Association for Renewable Energy [Vol 2: 2872]

Evaluation Network [Vol 1: 2088]

Evaluation Research Society [Vol 1: 2088]

Evangelical Christian Publishers Association [Vol 1: 8195]

Evangelical Lutheran Church of Iceland [Vol 2: 3418]

Evidence Photographers International Council [Vol 1: 8201]

Evolution Society; Human Behavior and [Vol 1: 8983]

Evonik Degussa Corp. [Vol 1: 14111]

Executive Office of the President [Vol 1: 8203]

Exhibit Designers and Producers Association [Vol 1: 8210]

Exhibition and Event Association of Australasia [Vol 2: 707]

Expediting Management Association [Vol 1: 8215]

Experimental Psychology Society [Vol 2: 7655]

Explorers Club [Vol 1: 8218]

Extremophiles; International Society for [Vol 2: 3082]

Eye Bank Association of America [Vol 1: 8221]

Eye Research; International Society for [Vol 1: 10160]

FAB Awards [Vol 2: 7663]

Fabless Semiconductor Association [Vol 1: 8679]

Facets Multi-Media Inc. [Vol 1: 8224]

Facial Plastic and Reconstructive Surgery; American Academy of [Vol 1: 533]

Faculty of Astrological Studies [Vol 2: 7665]

Fair Play Committee; International [Vol 2: 3392]

Falkland Islands Tourist Board [Vol 2: 2055]

Falklands Conservation [Vol 2: 7667]

Family, Career and Community Leaders of America [Vol 1: 8226]

Family Firm Institute [Vol 1: 8228]

Family Service Association of America [Vol 1: 360]

Farm Animal Reform Movement [Vol 1: 8235]

Farm Animal Rights Movement [Vol 1: 8235]

Farm Radio International [Vol 2: 8238]

Farm Writers' Federation; Canadian [Vol 1: 6463]

Farrer Memorial Trust [Vol 2: 709]

Father's Day/Mother's Day Council [Vol 1: 8240]

Fauchard Academy; Pierre [Vol 1: 8243]

Federacion Empresarial de la Industria Quimica Espanola [Vol 2: 6032]

Federacion Internacional de Asociaciones de Profesores de Ciencias [Vol 2: 4922]

Federacion Nacional de Cafeteros de Columbia [Vol 2: 1846]

Federal Association of the Gem, Stone and Diamond Industry [Vol 2: 2874]

Federal Bar Association [Vol 1: 8251]

Federal Chamber of Architects, Germany [Vol 2: 2876]

Federal Government Distance Learning Association [Vol 1: 8257]

Federal Government Distributed Learning Association [Vol 1: 8263]

Federal Ministry of Economy, Family and Youth [Vol 2: 1242]

Federal Union of German Associations of Pharmacists [Vol 2: 2878]

Federally Employed Women [Vol 1: 8268]

Federated Hospitality Association of Southern Africa [Vol 2: 5544]

Federation Aeronautique Internationale [Vol 2: 6294]

Federation Canadienne de la Faune [Vol 1: 7040]

Federation Canadienne de l'Entreprise Independante [Vol 1: 6475]

Federation Canadienne des Archers [Vol 1: 8283]

Federation Canadienne des Epiciers Independants [Vol 1: 6477]

Federation Canadienne des Femmes Diplomees des Universites [Vol 1: 6481]

Federation Canadienne des Festivals de Musique [Vol 1: 8291]

Federation Canadienne des Infirmieres et Infirmiers en Sante Mentale [Vol 1: 6479]

Federation Canadienne des Science Humanies et Sociales [Vol 1: 6467]

Federation canadienne des societes de biologie [Vol 1: 6472]

Federation Canadienne pour la sante sexuelle [Vol 1: 6465]

Federation des Associations de proprietaires de cinemas du Canada [Vol 1: 11282]

Federation des Jeux du Commonwealth [Vol 2: 7466]

Football Association; Liechtenstein [Vol 2: 4473]
Football Foundation and College Hall of Fame; National [Vol 1: 12401]
Football Hall of Fame; Pro [Vol 1: 14173]
Football League; National [Vol 1: 12410]
Football Writers Association of America [Vol 1: 8407]
Foraminiferal Research; Cushman Foundation for [Vol 1: 7785]
Foras Oiliuna agus Forbartha Eireann [Vol 2: 3887]
An Foras um Cheannacht agus Bainistocht Abhar [Vol 2: 3885]
Forbes [Vol 1: 6056, 6058]
Ford Motor Co. [Vol 1: 12186]
Fordham University - Donald McGannon Communication Research Center [Vol 1: 8413]
Foreign Affairs and International Trade Canada [Vol 1: 8415]
Foreign Correspondents' Association [Vol 2: 5611]
Foreign Languages; American Council on the Teaching of [Vol 1: 1921]
Foreign Languages; Northeast Conference on the Teaching of [Vol 1: 13393]
Foreign Press Association in London [Vol 2: 7699]
Forensic Association; American [Vol 1: 2184]
Forensic Association; National [Vol 1: 12412]
Forensic League; National [Vol 1: 12414]
Forensic Nurses; International Association of [Vol 1: 9665]
Forensic Science Society [Vol 2: 7701]
Forensic Sciences Foundation [Vol 1: 8419]
Forensic Toxicologists; The International Association of [Vol 2: 5441]
Forest History Society [Vol 1: 8425]
Forest Laboratories [Vol 1: 15563]
Forest Products Society [Vol 1: 8430]
Forest Resources Association [Vol 1: 8434]
Forest Roberts Theatre [Vol 1: 8437]
Forestry; Canadian Institute of [Vol 1: 6586]
Fork Lift Truck Association [Vol 2: 7705]
Forum for African Investigate Reporters [Vol 2: 4625]
FotoWeek DC Inc. [Vol 1: 8439]
Foundation for Australian Literary Studies [Vol 2: 727]
Foundation for Digestive Health and Nutrition [Vol 1: 8441]
Foundation for Independent Higher Education [Vol 1: 8450]
Foundation for Legal Research [Vol 1: 6336]
Foundation for Medical Research [Vol 2: 2421]
Foundation for Polish Science [Vol 2: 2991]
Foundation for Research and Technology - Hellas [Vol 2: 3286]
Foundation for the Promotion of Finnish Music [Vol 2: 2108]
Foundation of Lower Saxony [Vol 2: 2887]
Four Freedoms Foundation [Vol 1: 14596]
FOXTEL [Vol 2: 624]
Fragrance Foundation [Vol 1: 8454]
Fragrance Foundation and Fragrance Research Fund [Vol 1: 8454]
France Ministry of Defense [Vol 2: 2430]
Franchising and Licensing Association Singapore [Vol 2: 5939]
Franco-British Society [Vol 2: 7707]
Francqui Foundation [Vol 2: 1526]
Franklin and Eleanor Roosevelt Institute [Vol 1: 14596]
Franz Moll Foundation [Vol 2: 2889]
Fraunhofer-Gesellschaft zur Forderung der Angewandten Forschung [Vol 2: 2891]
Frederick Chopin Society [Vol 2: 5386]
Free Market Foundation [Vol 2: 5549]
Freedom Forum [Vol 1: 8457]
Freedom From Religion Foundation [Vol 1: 8461]
Freedom to Create Prize [Vol 2: 5942]
Freedoms Foundation at Valley Forge [Vol 1: 8465]
French Academy of Sciences [Vol 2: 2434]
French Aerospace Medical Association [Vol 1: 187]
French-Canadian Genealogical Society [Vol 1: 8467]
French Chemical Society [Vol 2: 2436]
French Diabetes Association [Vol 2: 2440]
French League for Animal Rights Foundation [Vol 2: 2442]
French Ministry of Culture and Communication [Vol 2: 2444]
French Ministry of Environment [Vol 2: 2594]

French National Center for Scientific Research [Vol 2: 2446]
French Society for Metallurgy and Materials [Vol 2: 2450]
Freshwater Biological Association [Vol 2: 7711]
Friends of Algonquin Park [Vol 1: 8470]
Friends of Libraries U.S.A. [Vol 1: 5394]
Friends of Libraries U.S.A. [Vol 1: 8472]
Friends of the Antigua Public Library [Vol 2: 21]
Friends of the Princeton University Library [Vol 1: 8475]
Friends Research Institute [Vol 1: 3489]
Front Line [Vol 2: 3834]
Fulfillment Management Association [Vol 1: 8477]
Functional Plan Biology [Vol 2: 578]
Fund for American Studies [Vol 1: 8481]
Fund for Modern Courts [Vol 1: 8491]
Fundacion Alejandro Angel Escobar [Vol 2: 1842]
Fundacion Miguel Aleman [Vol 2: 4584]
Fundacion Principe de Asturias [Vol 2: 6084]
Fusion Power Associates [Vol 1: 8496]
Future Problem Solving Program International [Vol 1: 8500]
Gadjah Mada University - Center for Population and Policy Studies [Vol 2: 3817]
Gairdner Foundation [Vol 1: 8505]
Gallaudet University Alumni Association [Vol 1: 8508]
Games; Federation of Gay [Vol 1: 8312]
Garden Club of America [Vol 1: 8511]
Garden Writers Association [Vol 1: 8513]
The Gardeners of America [Vol 1: 8517]
GARDENEX: Federation of Garden and Leisure Manufacturers [Vol 2: 7713]
Gardens of the Righteous Worldwide (GARIWO) - Sarajevo [Vol 2: 1725]
Gas Processors Association [Vol 1: 8523]
Gay Games; Federation of [Vol 1: 8312]
Gazette International Networking Institute [Vol 1: 14097]
GE Healthcare [Vol 1: 5129]
Gelber Music Foundation; Sylva [Vol 1: 8528]
Gem and Jewelry Export Promotion Council [Vol 2: 3486]
Gen Foundation [Vol 2: 7715]
Gen-Probe [Vol 1: 3976]
Genealogical Societies; Federation of [Vol 1: 8317]
Genealogical Society of Ireland [Vol 2: 3837]
Genealogical Society of South Africa [Vol 2: 5551]
General Aviation Manufacturers Association [Vol 1: 8530]
General Commission on Archives and History of the United Methodist Church [Vol 1: 8533]
General Federation of Women's Clubs [Vol 1: 8536]
General Mills Inc. [Vol 1: 8542]
General Monitors Inc. [Vol 1: 14909]
Genetic Alliance [Vol 1: 8544]
Genetics Society of America [Vol 1: 8547]
Genetics Society of Australasia [Vol 2: 730]
Geochemical Society [Vol 1: 8553]
Geographers; Royal Geographical Society with the Institute of British [Vol 2: 8784]
Geographical Society of China [Vol 2: 5249]
Geographical Society of Philadelphia [Vol 1: 8558]
Geographical Society; Royal Scottish [Vol 2: 8914]
Geographical Society with the Institute of British Geographers; Royal [Vol 2: 8784]
Geological Society of America [Vol 1: 5325, 8562]
Geological Society of Australia [Vol 2: 733]
Geological Society of Denmark [Vol 2: 1967]
Geological Society of France [Vol 2: 2453]
Geological Society of London [Vol 2: 7717]
Geological Society of South Africa [Vol 2: 5553]
Geologists; American Association of Petroleum [Vol 1: 1265]
Geology; Society for Sedimentary [Vol 1: 15306]
Geometres professionnels du Canada [Vol 1: 14254]
Geophysics Geology Division [Vol 1: 8568]
George Washington University - Center for Innovative Teaching and Learning [Vol 1: 8570]
George Washington University Law School [Vol 1: 8573]
Georgetown University - Institute for the Study of Diplomacy [Vol 1: 8587]
Georgia Public Policy Foundation [Vol 1: 8589]
Georgia Writers Association [Vol 1: 8591]
Geoscience Information Society [Vol 1: 8593]

Geoscientists and Engineers; European Association of [Vol 2: 4673]
Geothermal Resources Council [Vol 1: 8599]
Geriatrics; International Association of Gerontology and [Vol 2: 2489]
German Academic Exchange Service [Vol 1: 8603]
German Academy of Language and Poetry [Vol 2: 2895]
German Adult Education Association [Vol 2: 2901]
German Agricultural Society [Vol 2: 2903]
German Association for Physiotherapy [Vol 2: 2905]
German Association for Water, Wastewater and Waste [Vol 2: 2907]
German Association of Market and Social Researchers [Vol 2: 2909]
German Atomic Forum [Vol 2: 2915]
German Booksellers Association [Vol 2: 2988]
German Bunsen Society for Physical Chemistry [Vol 2: 2917]
German Chemical Society [Vol 2: 2922]
German Dental Association [Vol 2: 2939]
German Design Council [Vol 2: 2941]
German Geological Society [Vol 2: 2943]
German Geophysical Society [Vol 2: 2946]
German Informatics Society [Vol 2: 2952]
German Interior Architects Association [Vol 2: 2957]
German Language Society [Vol 2: 2960]
German Medical Association [Vol 2: 2963]
German Ministry for Economics and Technology [Vol 2: 2942]
German National Mathematical Society [Vol 2: 2966]
German Neuroscience Society [Vol 2: 2968]
German Nutrition Foundation [Vol 2: 3019]
German Ophthalmological Society [Vol 2: 2970]
German Organization of Endocrinology [Vol 2: 2977]
German Ornithologists' Society [Vol 2: 2979]
German Phytomedical Society [Vol 2: 2984]
German Publishers and Booksellers Association [Vol 2: 2988]
German Research Foundation [Vol 2: 2990]
German Society for Biochemistry and Molecular Biology [Vol 2: 2996]
German Society for Fat Science [Vol 2: 2998]
German Society for Medicinal Plant Research [Vol 2: 3173]
German Society for Mining, Metallurgy, Resource and Environmental Technology [Vol 2: 3004]
German Society for Non-Destructive Testing [Vol 2: 3008]
German Society of Glass Technology [Vol 2: 3011]
German Society of Human Genetics [Vol 2: 3014]
German Society of Metallurgical and Mining Engineers [Vol 2: 3004]
German Society of Nutrition [Vol 2: 3016]
German Society of Pediatrics and Adolescent Medicine [Vol 2: 3020]
German Society of Plastic and Reconstructive Surgery [Vol 2: 3023]
German Society of School Music Educators [Vol 2: 3025]
Gerontological Society of America [Vol 1: 8616]
Gerontological Society of the Russian Academy of Sciences [Vol 2: 5779]
Gerontology and Geriatrics; International Association of [Vol 2: 2489]
Geselleschaft fur deutsche Sprache [Vol 2: 2960]
Gesellschaft Deutscher Chemiker [Vol 2: 2918, 2919, 2922]
Gesellschaft Deutscher Naturforscher und Arzte [Vol 2: 3028]
Gesellschaft fuer Informatik [Vol 2: 2952]
Gesellschaft fur Aerosolforschung e.V. [Vol 2: 2695]
Gesellschaft fur Arzneipflanzenforschung [Vol 2: 3173]
Gesellschaft fur Bergbau, Metallurgie, Rohstoff-und Umwelttechnik e.V. [Vol 2: 3004]
Gesellschaft fur Biochemie und Molekularbiologie e.V. [Vol 2: 2996]
Gesellschaft fur Chemische Technik und Biotechnologie [Vol 2: 3158]
Gesellschaft fur Oekologie [Vol 2: 2784]
Gesellschaft fur Wirbelsaulenforschung [Vol 2: 3178]
Gesneriad Society [Vol 1: 8641]
Getty Grant Program [Vol 1: 8644]
Ghana Association of Software and IT Services Companies [Vol 2: 3253]

Ghana Base Music [Vol 2: 3250]
Ghana Internet Service Providers Association [Vol 2: 3253]
Ghana Ministry of Communications [Vol 2: 3252]
Ghana Property Awards [Vol 2: 3254]
Gibraltar Amateur Radio Society [Vol 2: 7732]
Gibraltar Festival for Young Musicians [Vol 2: 3258]
Gibraltar Song Festival [Vol 2: 3260]
Gibraltar Tourist Board [Vol 2: 7735]
Gibtelecom [Vol 2: 3263]
Gibtelecom International Chess Festival [Vol 2: 3262]
Girl Scout Committee of the Synagogue Council of America; National Jewish [Vol 1: 12569]
Girl Scouting; National Jewish Committee on [Vol 1: 12569]
Girls' Brigade Australia [Vol 2: 739]
Girls' Brigade International Council [Vol 2: 7737]
Giving U.S.A. Foundation [Vol 1: 8651]
Glasgow Natural History Society [Vol 2: 7740]
Glass Art Society [Vol 1: 8653]
The Glaucoma Foundation [Vol 1: 8656]
GlaxoSmithKline plc [Vol 1: 3977]
Gleitsman Foundation [Vol 1: 8660]
Gliding Federation of Australia [Vol 2: 742]
Global Awards for Excellence in BPM and Workflow [Vol 1: 8663]
Global Compact Sri Lanka Network [Vol 2: 6119]
Global Equity Organization [Vol 1: 8665]
Global Foundation for Democracy and Development [Vol 2: 2004]
Global Green U.S.A. [Vol 1: 8671]
Global Health Council [Vol 1: 8674]
Global Lung Cancer Coalition [Vol 2: 7742]
Global Scholars and Leaders Council [Vol 2: 5944]
Global Semiconductor Alliance [Vol 1: 8679]
Global Speakers Federation [Vol 1: 8685]
Global Warming International Center [Vol 1: 8687]
Godzilla Society of North America [Vol 1: 8689]
Goethe Institut [Vol 2: 3030]
Goethe Institute [Vol 2: 3030]
Golden Apricot (Yerevan) International Film Festival [Vol 2: 52]
Golden Key International Honour Society [Vol 1: 8691]
Golden Key National Honor Society [Vol 1: 8691]
Goldman Environmental Prize [Vol 1: 8712]
Golf Association; National Amputee [Vol 1: 11513]
Golf Course Superintendents Association of America [Vol 1: 8714]
Golf Writers Association of America [Vol 1: 8719]
Good Safari Guide - Miranda Travel Group [Vol 2: 7744]
Goodwill Industries International [Vol 1: 8721]
Google Inc. [Vol 1: 4957, 4964]
Gorsedd Board [Vol 2: 8391]
Gospel Music Association [Vol 1: 8731]
Gospel Music Association Canada [Vol 1: 8734]
Government Employees Insurance Company GEICO [Vol 1: 8736]
Government Finance Officers Association of United States and Canada [Vol 1: 8741]
Government of Belize - Ministry of the Public Service, Governance Improvement, Elections and Boundaries and Sports [Vol 2: 1681]
Government of India [Vol 2: 3518]
Government of St. Lucia [Vol 2: 5890]
Government of the Commonwealth of Dominica - Information and Communication Technology Unit [Vol 2: 1998]
Government of the Republic of Trinidad and Tobago - Office of the Prime Minister [Vol 2: 6614]
Governmental Industrial Hygienists; American Conference of [Vol 1: 1857]
Governmental Research Association [Vol 1: 8744]
Governor General of Canada [Vol 1: 8746]
Governor General's Youth Award [Vol 2: 1346]
Governor's Office for Women's Initiatives and Outreach [Vol 1: 8762]
Gowan Co. [Vol 1: 8144]
Grace and Company; W. R. [Vol 1: 13287, 13288]
GRAFIA - Association of Professional Graphic Designers in Finland [Vol 2: 2110]
Grand Aerie, Fraternal Order of Eagles [Vol 1: 8765]
Graphic Arts Technical Foundation [Vol 1: 14164]

Graphics; European Association for Computer [Vol 2: 6262]
Grassland Society of Southern Africa [Vol 2: 5562]
The Gratiaen Trust [Vol 2: 6120]
Gravestone Studies; Association for [Vol 1: 5023]
Gravure Association of America [Vol 1: 8772]
Gravure Education Foundation [Vol 1: 8774]
Great Lakes Commission [Vol 1: 8779]
Greater Lynn Photographic Association [Vol 1: 8781]
Greek Alzheimer's Association [Vol 2: 3289]
Greek America Foundation [Vol 1: 8783]
Green Organisation [Vol 2: 7746]
Greenland Bureau of Minerals and Petroleum [Vol 2: 3324]
Greeting Card Association [Vol 2: 7748]
Grenada Triathlon Association [Vol 2: 3326]
Griffin Trust for Excellence in Poetry [Vol 1: 8785]
Groundwater Foundation [Vol 1: 8788]
Groupe Consultatif International de Recherche sur le Colza [Vol 2: 2509]
Groupe International de Recherches sur la Preservation du Bois [Vol 2: 6152]
Groupe OCP [Vol 2: 4618]
Grune & Statton [Vol 1: 4337]
GSM Association - Mobile Innovation Section [Vol 1: 8792]
Guadalupe Cultural Arts Center [Vol 1: 8795]
Guide Dogs of America [Vol 1: 8797]
Guild of Agricultural Journalists [Vol 2: 7750]
Guild of Agricultural Journalists of Ireland [Vol 2: 3839]
Guild of Air Pilots and Air Navigators [Vol 2: 7752]
Guild of Air Traffic Control Officers [Vol 2: 7758]
Guild of Fine Food Retailers [Vol 2: 7760]
Guild of Food Writers [Vol 2: 7763]
Guild of International Professional Toastmasters [Vol 2: 7765]
Guild of Motoring Writers [Vol 2: 7767]
Guild of Television Cameramen [Vol 2: 7771]
Guild of Yachting Writers [Vol 2: 9500]
Guilde Europeenne du Raid [Vol 2: 2462]
Guildhall School of Music and Drama [Vol 2: 7778]
Gutenberg-Gesellschaft: Internationale Vereinigung fuer Geschichte und Gegenwart der Druckkunst [Vol 2: 3032]
Gutenberg Society [Vol 2: 3033]
Gutenberg Society: International Association for Past and Present History of the Art of Printing [Vol 2: 3032]
Guyana Awards Council [Vol 1: 8799]
Guyana Business Coalition on HIV/AIDS [Vol 2: 3330]
Guyana Central Arya Samaj [Vol 2: 3332]
Gyldendal [Vol 2: 1970]
Gynaecologists - United Kingdom; Royal College of Obstetricians and [Vol 2: 8688]
Gynecologic Laparoscopists; American Association of [Vol 1: 1162]
Gynecological and Obstetrical Society; American [Vol 1: 2268]
Gynecological Pathologists; International Society of [Vol 2: 8202]
Gynecology and Obstetrics; International Federation of [Vol 2: 8122]
Gyro International [Vol 1: 8801]
Ha-Merkar Le-Heker Yehudey Polin [Vol 2: 3952]
Haagudah Lezechuyot Haezrach Beyisrael [Vol 2: 3937]
Hachevrah Hayisraelit Lechimia [Vol 2: 3956]
Hacker Instruments [Vol 1: 12859]
Hackmatack Children's Choice Book Awards [Vol 1: 8806]
Haematology Society of Australia and New Zealand [Vol 2: 744]
Haemophilia Society [Vol 2: 7780]
Haiku Society of America [Vol 1: 8808]
Hairdressers Journal International [Vol 2: 7785]
Hairdressing Magazines Association; International Professional [Vol 2: 2556]
Handweavers Guild of America [Vol 1: 8815]
Handwriting Analysts; American Association of [Vol 1: 1166]
Hang 'Em High Productions [Vol 1: 8817]
Harbor-UCLA Medical Center - General Clinic Research Center [Vol 1: 8819]
Harness Tracks of America [Vol 1: 8823]

Harvard Business School [Vol 1: 8827, 8829]
Harvard University - Joan Shorenstein Center on the Press, Politics and Public Policy [Vol 1: 8833]
Harvard University Center for Italian Renaissance Studies [Vol 2: 4168]
Hastings Center [Vol 1: 8836]
Hasty Pudding Theatricals [Vol 1: 8838]
Hawaii Martial Arts International Society [Vol 1: 8841]
Hayastan All-Armenian Fund [Vol 2: 54]
Head and Neck Society; American [Vol 1: 2280]
Head Heritage Trust; Bessie [Vol 2: 1739]
The Head of State Award Scheme - Ghana [Vol 2: 3256]
Health and Human Services, Public Health Service; United States Department of - Centers for Disease Control and Prevention [Vol 1: 16816]
Health and Human Services; United States Department of - National Institutes of Health [Vol 1: 16814]
Health and Medical Research Council; National [Vol 2: 890]
Health and Medicine; Society for Adolescent [Vol 1: 15010]
Health Care Exhibitors Association [Vol 1: 8857]
Health Centers; National Association of Community [Vol 1: 11710]
Health Improvement Institute [Vol 1: 8843]
Health Industry Distributors Association [Vol 1: 8847]
Health; National Institutes of - National Institute of Nursing Research [Vol 1: 12555]
Health Physics Society [Vol 1: 8849]
Health Promotion Group Gibraltar [Vol 2: 3264]
Health Research Council of New Zealand [Vol 2: 4892]
Health Science Communications Association [Vol 1: 8853]
Health Sciences; College of [Vol 2: 1350]
Healthcare Convention and Exhibitors Association [Vol 1: 8857]
Healthcare Distribution Management Association [Vol 1: 8859]
Healthcare Financial Management Association [Vol 1: 8864]
Healthcare Information and Management Systems Society [Vol 1: 8867]
Healthcare People Management Association [Vol 2: 7787]
Hearst Corporation [Vol 1: 8208]
Heart Association; American [Vol 1: 2298]
Heart Rhythm Society [Vol 1: 8871]
Heating and Environmental Engineers; Institute of Domestic [Vol 2: 7854]
Heavy Specialized Carriers Conference [Vol 1: 16116]
Heberden Society [Vol 2: 7238]
Hebrew Union College - Jewish Institute of Religion [Vol 1: 8877]
Hebrew University of Jerusalem - Center for Research on the History and Culture of Polish Jews [Vol 2: 3952]
Heineken Fondsen Foundation; Alfred [Vol 2: 4823]
Heineken Foundation; Dr. H.P. [Vol 2: 4823]
Heinz Family Philanthropies [Vol 1: 8880]
Helen Keller Worldwide [Vol 1: 10648]
Helicopter Association International [Vol 1: 8886]
Helicopter Association of America [Vol 1: 8886]
Help Desk Institute [Vol 1: 8898]
Hematology Association; European [Vol 2: 4700]
Henkel [Vol 1: 150]
Herb Society of America [Vol 1: 8903]
Herff Jones Inc. [Vol 1: 11886]
Heritage Canada Foundation [Vol 1: 8909]
Heritage Center of Red Cloud Indian School [Vol 1: 8913]
Heritage Toronto [Vol 1: 8915]
Herpetologists' League [Vol 1: 8917]
Hiking Society; American [Vol 1: 2348]
Hill plc; William [Vol 2: 7789]
Hillel: The Foundation for Jewish Campus Life [Vol 1: 8919]
Hill's Pet Nutrition, Inc. [Vol 1: 4638]
Hillsdale College - Center for Constructive Alternatives/National Leadership Institute [Vol 1: 8922]
Hilton Foundation; Conrad N. [Vol 1: 8924]
Hip Society [Vol 1: 8926]

International Committee for Coal and Organic Petrology [Vol 2: 6058]

InterNational Committee for Information Technology Standards [Vol 1: 9793]

International Committee of Sports for the Deaf [Vol 1: 9796]

International Committee of Systematic Bacteriology [Vol 2: 4793]

International Committee of the Red Cross - Switzerland [Vol 2: 6368]

International Committee on Seafarers' Welfare [Vol 2: 8104]

International Communication Association [Vol 1: 9798]

International Community Corrections Association [Vol 1: 9803]

International Community of Women Living with HIV/AIDS [Vol 2: 6344]

International Competition of the City of Paris [Vol 2: 2507]

International Computer Music Association [Vol 1: 9805]

International Confederation for Thermal Analysis [Vol 2: 1763]

International Confederation for Thermal Analysis and Calorimetry [Vol 2: 1763]

International Confederation of Midwives [Vol 2: 4734]

International Conference of College Teaching and Learning [Vol 1: 9810]

International Conference of Labour and Social History [Vol 2: 1260]

International Consultative Research Group on Rapeseed [Vol 2: 2509]

International Copper Association [Vol 1: 15630]

International Coronelli Society for the Study of Globes [Vol 2: 1264]

International Corrosion Council [Vol 2: 6061]

International Cost Engineering Council [Vol 2: 820]

International Council for Adult Education [Vol 2: 9537]

International Council for Canadian Studies [Vol 1: 9814]

International Council for Health, Physical Education, Recreation, Sport, and Dance [Vol 1: 9817]

International Council for Machinery Lubrication [Vol 1: 9825]

International Council for Open and Distance Education [Vol 2: 5131]

International Council for the Control of Iodine Deficiency Disorders [Vol 2: 5569]

International Council for the Improvement of Reading [Vol 1: 10086]

International Council of Air Shows [Vol 1: 9828]

International Council of Associations for Science Education [Vol 2: 4922]

International Council of Christians and Jews [Vol 2: 3056]

International Council of Environmental Law [Vol 2: 3058]

International Council of Fine Arts Deans [Vol 1: 9832]

International Council of Graphic Design Associations [Vol 1: 9834]

International Council of Museums [Vol 1: 1218]

International Council of Nurses [Vol 2: 6371]

International Council of Shopping Centers [Vol 1: 9837]

International Council of Sport and Physical Education [Vol 2: 3061]

International Council of Sport Science and Physical Education [Vol 2: 3061]

International Council of the Aeronautical Sciences [Vol 2: 6150]

International Council on Active Aging [Vol 1: 9840]

International Council on Hotel, Restaurant, and Institutional Education [Vol 1: 9844]

International Council on Large Electric Systems [Vol 2: 2511]

International Council on Monuments and Sites [Vol 2: 2515]

International Country Music Conference [Vol 1: 9852]

International Cryogenic Materials Conference [Vol 1: 9855]

International Customer Service Association [Vol 1: 9859]

International Cytokine Society [Vol 1: 9861]

International Dairy Federation [Vol 2: 1530]

International Dairy Federation - Canadian National Committee [Vol 1: 9863]

International Dairy Foods Association [Vol 1: 9865]

International Design Awards [Vol 1: 9871]

International District Energy Association [Vol 1: 9873]

International Documentary Association [Vol 1: 9878]

International Dyslexia Association [Vol 1: 9885]

International Ecology Institute [Vol 2: 3064]

International Egg Commission [Vol 2: 8109]

International Electrotechnical Commission [Vol 2: 6373]

International EPR (ESR) Society [Vol 1: 9887]

International Equestrian Federation [Vol 2: 6375]

International Ergonomics Association [Vol 2: 6583]

International Erosion Control Association [Vol 1: 9889]

International Executive Service Corps [Vol 1: 9894]

International Exhibition Logistics Associates [Vol 2: 8111]

International Exhibitors Association [Vol 1: 16525]

International Facility Management Association [Vol 1: 9896]

International Fair Play Committee [Vol 2: 3392]

International Federation for Information Processing [Vol 2: 1267]

International Federation for Theatre Research [Vol 2: 8113]

International Federation of Adapted Physical Activity [Vol 2: 2518]

International Federation of Agricultural Journalists [Vol 2: 4736]

International Federation of Air Line Pilots Associations [Vol 2: 8115]

International Federation of Airworthiness [Vol 2: 8119]

International Federation of Asian and Western Pacific Contractors' Associations [Vol 2: 5329]

International Federation of Automatic Control [Vol 2: 1275]

International Federation of Beekeepers' Associations [Vol 2: 4094]

International Federation of Biomedical Laboratory Science [Vol 1: 9902]

International Federation of Biosafety Associations [Vol 1: 9908]

International Federation of Classification Societies [Vol 2: 2521]

International Federation of Clinical Chemistry and Laboratory Medicine [Vol 2: 4096]

International Federation of Clinical Neurophysiology [Vol 1: 9911]

International Federation of Competitive Eating [Vol 1: 9914]

International Federation of Consulting Engineers [Vol 2: 6377]

International Federation of Engineering Education Societies [Vol 1: 9918]

International Federation of Festival Organizations [Vol 1: 9920]

International Federation of Film Critics [Vol 2: 3067]

International Federation of Gynecology and Obstetrics [Vol 2: 8122]

International Federation of Hydrographic Societies [Vol 2: 8124]

International Federation of Interior Architects/Designers [Vol 2: 5947]

International Federation of Inventors' Associations [Vol 2: 3397]

International Federation of Landscape Architects [Vol 2: 1534]

International Federation of Library Associations and Institutions [Vol 2: 4740]

International Federation of Manufacturers and Converters of Pressure-Sensitive and Heatseals on Paper and Other Base Materials [Vol 2: 4850]

International Federation of Operational Research Societies [Vol 1: 9923]

International Federation of Operational Research Societies - Airline Group [Vol 1: 9926]

International Federation of Ophthalmological Societies [Vol 1: 9928]

International Federation of Pigment Cell Societies [Vol 2: 3767]

International Federation of Purchasing and Supply Management [Vol 2: 1281]

International Federation of Social Workers [Vol 2: 6379]

International Federation of Societies for Electroencephalography and Clinical Neurophysiology [Vol 1: 9911]

International Federation of Societies for Histochemistry and Cytochemistry [Vol 1: 9932]

International Federation of Societies of Cosmetic Chemists [Vol 2: 8128]

International Federation of Sound Hunters [Vol 2: 6381]

International Federation of Sports Medicine [Vol 2: 4102]

International Federation of Standards Users [Vol 2: 6383]

International Federation of Surgical Colleges [Vol 2: 3857]

International Federation of the Phonographic Industry - Finland [Vol 2: 2117]

International Federation of the Phonographic Industry - Hong Kong [Vol 2: 5289]

International Federation of Translators [Vol 1: 9936]

International Federation of University Women - Switzerland [Vol 2: 6385]

International Federation of Women's Travel Organizations [Vol 2: 6064]

International Fertilizer Industry Association [Vol 2: 2523]

International Festival of Films for TV [Vol 1: 112]

International Festival of Films on Art [Vol 1: 9941]

International Film Festival Mannheim-Heidelberg [Vol 2: 3069]

International Finn Association [Vol 2: 2526]

International Flanders Film Festival - Ghent [Vol 2: 1515]

International Flight Services Association [Vol 1: 9943]

International Formalwear Association [Vol 1: 9945]

International Franchise Association [Vol 1: 9947]

International Fritz Kreisler Competition [Vol 2: 1286]

International Furnishings and Design Association [Vol 1: 9951]

International Gaming Awards [Vol 2: 8131]

International Gay and Lesbian Human Rights Commission [Vol 1: 9955]

International Glaciological Society [Vol 2: 8133]

International Golf Federation [Vol 1: 9957]

International Guild of Candle Artisans [Vol 1: 9960]

International Handball Federation [Vol 2: 6388]

International Harm Reduction Association [Vol 2: 8137]

International Harp Contest in Israel [Vol 2: 3954]

International Hockey Federation [Vol 2: 6391]

International Hologram Manufacturers Association [Vol 2: 8142]

International Hospitality Awards Inc. [Vol 1: 9965]

International Hotel and Restaurant Association [Vol 2: 6397]

International House - World Trade Center [Vol 1: 18082]

International Ice Hockey Federation [Vol 2: 6399]

International Institute for Applied Systems Analysis [Vol 2: 1288]

International Institute for Geo-Information Science and Earth Observation [Vol 2: 4747]

International Institute for Promotion and Prestige [Vol 2: 6401]

International Institute for the Science of Sintering [Vol 2: 5914]

International Institute of Fisheries Economics and Trade [Vol 1: 9967]

International Institute of Municipal Clerks [Vol 1: 9970]

International Institute of Public Finance [Vol 2: 3071]

International Institute of Refrigeration [Vol 2: 2528]

International Institute of Space Law [Vol 2: 2539]

International Institute of Welding [Vol 2: 2542]

International Institution for Production Engineering Research [Vol 2: 2474]

International Internet Marketing Association [Vol 1: 9974]

International Isotope Society [Vol 1: 9976]

International Joseph A. Schumpeter Society [Vol 2: 3075]

International Judo Federation [Vol 2: 3400]

International Korfball Federation [Vol 2: 4750]

International Society of Air Safety Investigators [Vol 1: 10270]

International Society of Appraisers [Vol 1: 10272]

International Society of Arachnology [Vol 2: 3089]

International Society of Arboriculture [Vol 1: 10274]

International Society of Automation [Vol 1: 10277]

International Society of Bioethics [Vol 2: 6070]

International Society of Biomechanics [Vol 2: 837]

International Society of Biomechanics in Sports [Vol 2: 3861]

International Society of Biometeorology [Vol 1: 10291]

International Society of Blood Transfusion [Vol 2: 4774]

International Society of Certified Electronics Technicians [Vol 1: 10293]

International Society of Chemical Ecology [Vol 1: 10295]

International Society of Chemotherapy [Vol 2: 8197]

International Society of City and Regional Planners [Vol 2: 4779]

International Society of Coating Science and Technology [Vol 1: 10299]

International Society of Crime Prevention Practitioners [Vol 1: 10302]

International Society of Dermatology [Vol 1: 10310]

International Society of Developmental Biologists [Vol 2: 4242]

International Society of Differentiation [Vol 1: 10312]

International Society of Electrochemistry [Vol 2: 6435]

International Society of Explosives Engineers [Vol 1: 10314]

International Society of Exposure Analysis [Vol 1: 10317]

International Society of Exposure Science [Vol 1: 10317]

International Society of Gynecological Pathologists [Vol 2: 8202]

International Society of Heterocyclic Chemistry [Vol 2: 5309]

International Society of Hospitality Consultants [Vol 1: 10322]

International Society of Hypertension - United Kingdom [Vol 2: 8205]

International Society of Hypnosis [Vol 2: 4108]

International Society of Neuropathology [Vol 2: 8215]

International Society of Nurses in Cancer Care [Vol 1: 10326]

International Society of Offshore and Polar Engineers [Vol 1: 10330]

International Society of Olympic Historians [Vol 2: 4783]

International Society of Oncology Pharmacy Practitioners [Vol 1: 10336]

International Society of Orthopaedic Surgery and Traumatology [Vol 2: 1554]

International Society of Paddy and Water Environment Engineering [Vol 2: 4245]

International Society of Paediatric Oncology [Vol 2: 6447]

International Society of Political Psychology [Vol 1: 10341]

International Society of Protistologists [Vol 1: 10346]

International Society of Psychiatric Genetics [Vol 2: 8217]

International Society of Psychiatric-Mental Health Nurses [Vol 1: 10351]

International Society of Psychoneuroendocrinology [Vol 1: 10353]

International Society of Reliabilty Engineers [Vol 1: 15818]

International Society of Surgery [Vol 2: 6450]

International Society of Travel and Tourism Educators [Vol 1: 10358]

International Society of Tropical Dermatology [Vol 1: 10310]

International Society of Typographic Designers [Vol 2: 8220]

International Society of Ultrasound in Obstetrics and Gynecology [Vol 2: 8222]

International Society of Weekly Newspaper Editors [Vol 1: 10360]

International Society on General Relativity and Gravitation [Vol 2: 8225]

International Society on Multiple Criteria Decision Making [Vol 2: 6072]

International Society on Oxygen Transport to Tissue [Vol 2: 3094]

International Society on Thrombosis and Haemostasis [Vol 1: 10363]

International Society on Toxinology [Vol 2: 843]

International Sociological Association [Vol 2: 6076]

International Solar Energy Society [Vol 2: 3098]

International Solid Surface Fabricators Association [Vol 1: 10399]

International Solid Waste Association [Vol 2: 1303]

International Speech Communication Association [Vol 2: 2565]

International Spinal Cord Society [Vol 2: 8228]

International Sport Press Association [Vol 2: 6454]

International Statistical Institute [Vol 2: 4788]

International Studies Association [Vol 1: 10373]

International Sunflower Association [Vol 2: 2570]

International Superyacht Society [Vol 1: 10395]

International Surface Fabricators Association [Vol 1: 10399]

International Surfing Association [Vol 1: 10406]

International Swimming Hall of Fame [Vol 1: 10408]

International System Safety Society [Vol 1: 10416]

International Taste and Quality Institute [Vol 1: 1559]

International Technology and Engineering Educators Association [Vol 1: 10425]

International Technology Education Association - Council on Technology Teacher Education [Vol 1: 10440]

International Television Association [Vol 2: 8249]

International Television Festival of Monte Carlo [Vol 2: 1662]

International Tennis Federation [Vol 2: 8232]

International Tennis Hall of Fame [Vol 1: 10442]

International Thermoelectric Society [Vol 2: 8237]

International Thomas Merton Society [Vol 1: 10447]

International Thriller Writers [Vol 1: 10451]

International Ticketing Association [Vol 1: 10455]

International Trade Mart [Vol 1: 18082]

International Transactional Analysis Association [Vol 1: 10460]

International Triathlon Union [Vol 1: 10465]

International Trumpet Guild [Vol 1: 10468]

International Tube Association [Vol 2: 8242]

International Union Against Cancer [Vol 2: 6456]

International Union Against Tuberculosis and Lung Disease [Vol 2: 2572]

International Union for Electricity Applications [Vol 2: 2579]

International Union for the Scientific Study of Population [Vol 2: 2581]

International Union of Air Pollution Prevention and Environmental Protection Associations [Vol 2: 8244]

International Union of Architects [Vol 2: 2583]

International Union of Biochemistry and Molecular Biology [Vol 1: 10471]

International Union of Crystallography [Vol 2: 8247]

International Union of Forest Research Organizations [Vol 2: 1306]

International Union of Laboratories and Experts in Construction Materials, Systems and Structures [Vol 2: 2589]

International Union of Microbiological Societies [Vol 2: 4790]

International Union of Physical and Engineering Science in Medicine [Vol 1: 10474]

International Union of Pure and Applied Chemistry [Vol 1: 10476]

International Union of Pure and Applied Physics [Vol 2: 6057]

International Union of Radio Science [Vol 2: 1562]

International Viola Society [Vol 2: 4924]

International Visual Communications Association [Vol 2: 8249]

International Water Association [Vol 2: 8251]

International Water Association, Singapore National Committee [Vol 2: 5950]

International Waterski and Wakeboard Federation [Vol 2: 6463]

International Weightlifting Federation [Vol 2: 3409]

International Wild Waterfowl Association [Vol 1: 10478]

International Wine and Food Society (London, United Kingdom) [Vol 2: 8256]

International Women's Media Foundation [Vol 1: 10484]

International World Games Association [Vol 2: 4794]

International Youth Library [Vol 2: 3103]

Internationale Carl Nielsen Musik Konkurrencer [Vol 2: 1974]

Internationale Coronelli-Gesellschaft fuer Globenkunde [Vol 2: 1264]

Internationale Filmfestspiele Berlin [Vol 2: 2715]

Internationale Filmwoche Mannheim [Vol 2: 3069]

Internationale Gesellschaft fur Ingenieurpadagogik [Vol 2: 1301]

Internationale Jugendbibliothek [Vol 2: 3103]

Internationale Liberale [Vol 2: 8303]

Internationale Messtechnische Konfoderation [Vol 2: 3403]

Internationale Muenchner Filmwochen GmbH [Vol 2: 3105]

Internationale Tagung der Historikerinnen der Arbeiter-und anderer sozialer Bewegungen [Vol 2: 1260]

Internationale Vereinigung fur Bruckenbau und Hochbau [Vol 2: 6347]

Internationale Vereinigung Sport- und Freizeiteinrichtungen [Vol 2: 3045]

Internationalen Rat der Christen und Juden [Vol 2: 3056]

Internationaler Verband Forstlicher Forschungsanstalten [Vol 2: 1306]

Internationales Filmwochenende Wurzburg [Vol 2: 3246]

Internationales Musik Medienzentrum [Vol 2: 1292]

Internationales Trickfilm Festival Stuttgart [Vol 2: 3195]

Internews [Vol 1: 10487]

InterNICHE [Vol 2: 8258]

Interstate Mining Compact Commission [Vol 1: 10489]

Intervet [Vol 2: 1166]

Intervet Schering-Plough Animal Health [Vol 1: 7031]

Inuit Art Foundation [Vol 1: 10492]

Inventors; Association of Hungarian [Vol 2: 3364]

Inventors' Associations; International Federation of [Vol 2: 3397]

Inventory Research; International Society for [Vol 2: 3406]

Investigative Pathology; American Society for - International Society for Biological and Environmental Repositories [Vol 1: 3961]

Investigative Reporters and Editors [Vol 1: 10494]

Investor Relations Society [Vol 2: 8260]

Iodine Deficiency Disorders; International Council for the Control of [Vol 2: 5569]

Iota Sigma Pi [Vol 1: 10497]

Iowa Horse Council [Vol 1: 10505]

Iowa Horse Industry Council [Vol 1: 10505]

Iqbal Academy Pakistan [Vol 2: 5184]

Iranian Research Organization for Science and Technology [Vol 2: 3827]

IREM Foundation [Vol 1: 9408]

Irish American Cultural Institute [Vol 1: 10511]

Irish Astronomical Association [Vol 2: 3866]

Irish Exporters Association [Vol 2: 3868]

Irish Franchise Association [Vol 2: 3870]

Irish Georgian Society [Vol 2: 3875]

Irish Haemophilia Society [Vol 2: 3877]

Irish Hang Gliding and Paragliding Association [Vol 2: 8262]

Irish Hospitality Institute [Vol 2: 3881]

Irish Institute of Purchasing and Materials Management [Vol 2: 3885]

Irish Institute of Training and Development [Vol 2: 3887]

Irish Playwrights and Screenwriters Guild [Vol 2: 3889]

Irish Security Industry Association [Vol 2: 3891]

Irish Society of Human Genetics [Vol 2: 3893]

Irish Terrier Club of America [Vol 1: 10519]

Irish Times [Vol 2: 3916]

Irish United Nations Veterans Association [Vol 2: 3895]

Irish Youth Foundation [Vol 2: 3897]

Iron and Steel Institute of Japan [Vol 2: 4249]

Iron and Steel Society of the American Institute of Mining, Metallurgical and Petroleum Engineers [Vol 1: 5028]

Irrigation Association [Vol 1: 10525]

Islamic Academy of Sciences [Vol 2: 4356]

Islamic Capitals Organization [Vol 2: 5908]

Islamic Development Bank [Vol 2: 5900]

Islamic Organization for Medical Sciences [Vol 2: 4426]

Island Resources Foundation [Vol 1: 10531]

Islenskir Radioamatorar [Vol 2: 3428]

Israel Chemical Society [Vol 2: 3956]

Israel Democracy Institute [Vol 2: 3960]

Israel Geological Society [Vol 2: 3962]

Israel Physical Society [Vol 2: 3966]

Israel Society for Biochemistry and Molecular Biology [Vol 2: 3968]

Israel Translators Association [Vol 2: 3971]

Israel Vacuum Society [Vol 2: 3973]

Israeli Association of Grid Technologies [Vol 2: 3976]

Israeli Society for Bioinformatics and Computational Biology [Vol 2: 3978]

Israeli Society of Gene and Cell Therapy [Vol 2: 3980]

The Issue Exchange [Vol 1: 10533]

Issue Management Council [Vol 1: 10533]

Istituto Italiano Imballaggio [Vol 2: 4131]

Istituto Nazionale di Studi Romani [Vol 2: 4114]

Istituto Paolo VI: Centro Internazionale di Studi e Documentazione [Vol 2: 4116]

Istituto Paolo VI: International Centre for Study and Documentation [Vol 2: 4116]

Italian Association for Metallurgy [Vol 2: 4118]

Italian Chemical Society [Vol 2: 4124]

Italian Geological Society [Vol 2: 4129]

Italian Institute of Culture for the United Kingdom [Vol 2: 9248]

Italian Institute of Packaging [Vol 2: 4131]

Italian Mathematical Union [Vol 2: 4134]

Italian PEN Club [Vol 2: 4138]

Italian Pharmacological Society [Vol 2: 4140]

Italian Society of Pharmacology [Vol 2: 4140]

Italic Institute of America [Vol 1: 10535]

Italic Studies Institute [Vol 1: 10535]

Italy-America Chamber of Commerce [Vol 1: 10537]

Ivey Awards [Vol 1: 10539]

IZEA Inc. [Vol 1: 10541]

Jaguar Clubs of North America [Vol 1: 10543]

Jamaica Exporters Association [Vol 2: 4174]

Jamaica Hotel and Tourist Association [Vol 2: 4177]

Jamaica Manufacturers' Association [Vol 2: 4182]

Jamaica Teachers' Association [Vol 2: 4192]

Janssen-Ortho Inc. [Vol 1: 6466]

Japan Advertising Agencies Association [Vol 1: 4259]

Japan Art Association [Vol 2: 4261]

Japan Association of Adult Orthodontics [Vol 2: 4263]

Japan Construction Mechanization Association [Vol 2: 4265]

Japan Industrial Design Promotion Organization [Vol 2: 4267]

Japan Newspaper Publishers and Editors Association [Vol 2: 4269]

Japan Office of the Prime Minister [Vol 2: 4271]

Japan Prize Preparatory Foundation [Vol 2: 4319]

Japan Society for the Promotion of Science [Vol 2: 3229]

Japan Society for the Promotion of Science [Vol 2: 4273]

Japan Society of Mechanical Engineers [Vol 2: 4276]

Japan Society - United Kingdom [Vol 2: 8269]

Japanese American Citizens League [Vol 1: 10546]

Japanese Biochemical Society [Vol 2: 4283]

Japanese Peptide Society [Vol 2: 4286]

Japanese Society of Applied Entomology and Zoology [Vol 2: 4290]

Japanese Society of Hypertension [Vol 2: 4293]

Jef Denyn; Royal Carillon School [Vol 2: 1651]

Jenemann Foundation; Hans R. [Vol 2: 2918]

Jenkins Group Inc. [Vol 1: 10548]

Jerome Foundation [Vol 1: 14046]

Jeune Chambre Economique du Grand-Duche de Luxembourg - Federation Mondiale de Jeunes Leaders et Entrepreneurs [Vol 2: 4496]

Jewelry Export Promotion Council; Gem and [Vol 2: 3486]

Jewish Book Council [Vol 1: 10553]

Jewish Book Council/JWB (Jewish Welfare Board)- [Vol 1: 10553]

Jewish Campus Life; Hillel: The Foundation for [Vol 1: 8919]

Jewish Community Centers Association of North America [Vol 1: 10566]

Jewish Educators Assembly [Vol 1: 10569]

Jewish Foundation for Christian Resevers/ADL [Vol 1: 4741]

Jewish Foundation for the Righteous [Vol 1: 10571]

Jewish Institute for National Security Affairs [Vol 1: 10573]

Jewish National Fund [Vol 1: 10576]

Jewish Research; YIVO Institute for [Vol 1: 18176]

Jobs for America's Graduates [Vol 1: 10579]

Jockey Club of Canada [Vol 1: 10581]

John Deere [Vol 1: 13082]

John Von Neumann Computer Society - Hungary [Vol 2: 3412]

Johnson & Johnson Medical Inc. [Vol 1: 5077]

Johnson Foundation; Robert Wood [Vol 1: 5212, 9386, 9387]

Join Hands Day [Vol 1: 10583]

Joint Baltic American National Committee [Vol 1: 10585]

Jordan Hotel Association [Vol 2: 4358]

Jose Manuel Lara Foundation [Vol 2: 6024]

Joseph Foundation [Vol 1: 8879]

Journalism Education Association [Vol 1: 10587]

Journalistes Canadiens pour la Liberte d'Expression [Vol 1: 6669]

Jowett Car Club [Vol 2: 8271]

Joy in Singing [Vol 1: 10592]

Judge Advocate Foundation [Vol 1: 10598]

Judge Advocates Association [Vol 1: 10594]

Junior Achievement [Vol 1: 10599]

Junior Chamber International [Vol 1: 10601]

Junior Wireless Club [Vol 1: 14393]

Juvenile Products Manufacturers Association [Vol 1: 10622]

Kansas City Barbeque Society [Vol 1: 10624]

Kansas Crop Improvement Association [Vol 1: 10627]

Kansas Native Plant Society [Vol 1: 10629]

Kansas State University - Johnson Center for Basic Cancer Research [Vol 1: 10634]

Kanselarij der Nederlandse Orden [Vol 2: 4648]

Kappa Alpha Theta Foundation [Vol 1: 12259]

Kappa Delta Pi [Vol 1: 10637]

Karolinska MMC [Vol 2: 1480]

Keats-Shelley Association of America [Vol 1: 10641]

Keep America Beautiful [Vol 1: 10644]

Keller International; Helen [Vol 1: 10648]

Keller Worldwide; Helen [Vol 1: 10648]

Kennedy Center for Justice and Human Rights; Robert F. [Vol 1: 10653]

Kennedy Center for the Performing Arts; John F. [Vol 1: 10657]

Kennedy Center for the Performing Arts; John F. - Kennedy Center American College Theater Festival [Vol 1: 10659]

Kennedy Library Foundation; John F. [Vol 1: 10670]

Kent State University Alumni Association [Vol 1: 10673]

Kentucky Arts Council [Vol 1: 10675]

Kenya Association of Hotelkeepers and Caterers [Vol 2: 4381]

Kenya Institute of Management [Vol 2: 4383]

Kenya National Academy of Sciences - Ministry of Research, Science and Technology [Vol 2: 4385]

Kenyan Publishers Association [Vol 2: 4387]

Kenyan Section of the International Commission of Jurists [Vol 2: 4389]

Keren Wolf [Vol 2: 3999]

Keuka College Alumni Association [Vol 1: 10677]

Kidde-Grininer [Vol 2: 8624]

Kidney Fund; American [Vol 1: 2746]

Kiel Institute for the World Economy [Vol 2: 3107]

Kilby International Awards Foundation [Vol 1: 10683]

Kin Canada [Vol 1: 10685]

Kinesiology and Physical Education; American Academy of [Vol 1: 11405]

King Baudouin Foundation [Vol 2: 1568]

King County Bar Association [Vol 1: 10687]

King Fahd University of Petroleum and Minerals - Center for Environment and Water [Vol 2: 5903]

King's School [Vol 2: 8273]

Kiwanis International [Vol 1: 10692]

Kobenhavns Universitet [Vol 2: 1994]

Kochon Foundation [Vol 2: 2576]

Kodak Canada [Vol 1: 6686]

Kokusai Kotsu Anzen Gakkai [Vol 2: 4236]

Komen Breast Cancer Foundation; Susan G. [Vol 1: 10694]

Komen for the Cure; Susan G. [Vol 1: 10694]

Kongelige Danske Geografiske Selskab [Vol 2: 1990]

Koninklijk Nederlands Aardrijkskundig Genootschap [Vol 2: 4812]

Koninklijke Beiaardschool Jef Denyn [Vol 2: 1651]

Koninklijke Belgische Vereniging der Elektrotechnici [Vol 2: 1663]

Koninklijke Nederlandse Akademie van Wetenschappen [Vol 2: 4814]

Konrad Adenauer Foundation - Germany [Vol 2: 3112]

Konrad Adenauer Stiftung [Vol 2: 3112]

Korea Veterans Association of Canada [Vol 1: 10699]

Korean Chemical Society [Vol 2: 5447]

Korean Society for Biochemistry and Molecular Biology [Vol 2: 5464]

Korean Society of Pharmacology [Vol 2: 5467]

Korean Society of Soil Science and Fertilizer [Vol 2: 5469]

Kosciuszko Foundation [Vol 1: 10701]

Kristna Fredsrorelsen [Vol 2: 6228]

Kulturradet [Vol 2: 6222]

Kungl. Vetenskapsakademien [Vol 2: 6181]

Kungliga Fysiografiska Sallskapet [Vol 2: 6167]

Kurt J. Lesker Co. [Vol 1: 5732]

La Foundation Yves-Saint-Germain [Vol 1: 9249]

La Leche League International [Vol 1: 10705]

La Ligue des Families [Vol 2: 1570]

La Salle College [Vol 1: 10711]

La Salle University [Vol 1: 10711]

La Societe Canadienne de Genie Agroalimentaire et de Bioingenierie [Vol 1: 6871]

La Societe Canadienne de Pharmacologie et de Therapeutique [Vol 1: 6983]

La Societe Canadienne de Sante Internationale [Vol 1: 6909]

La Societe Canadienne de Sociologie [Vol 1: 7001]

La Societe Canadienne Pour la Recherche Nautique [Vol 1: 6734]

La Societe d'histoire nationale du Canada [Vol 1: 6154]

La Societe Geographique Royale du Canada [Vol 1: 14624]

La Societe pour l'etude de l'architecture au Canada [Vol 1: 15372]

LA84 Foundation [Vol 1: 10713]

Labor and Working Class History Association [Vol 1: 10715]

Labor Education and Research Project [Vol 1: 10719]

Labor Research Association [Vol 1: 10721]

Laboratory Animal Science Association [Vol 2: 8275]

Laboratory Diagnosticians; American Association of Veterinary [Vol 1: 1406]

Ladies' Golf Union [Vol 2: 8277]

Ladies Professional Golf Association [Vol 1: 10724]

Laerdal Medical Corp. [Vol 1: 11764]

Lake Placid Education Foundation [Vol 1: 13216]

Lamaze International [Vol 1: 10736]

Lambda Kappa Sigma [Vol 1: 10743]

Land Improvement Contractors of America [Vol 1: 10746]

Landeshauptstadt Stuttgart [Vol 2: 3190]

Landesstudio Oberosterreich [Vol 2: 1202]

Landscape Architects; American Society of [Vol 1: 4358]

Landscape Architects; International Federation of [Vol 2: 1534]

Landscape Association of Westfalen-Lippe [Vol 2: 3115]

Landscape Research Group [Vol 2: 8280]

Landschaftsverband Westfalen-Lippe [Vol 2: 3115]

Language Association of America; Modern [Vol 1: 11230]

Languages; American Council on the Teaching of Foreign [Vol 1: 1921]

Lanka Electricity Company [Vol 2: 6125]

Organization Index

National Association of Industrial and Office Properties [Vol 1: 11801]

National Association of Intercollegiate Athletics [Vol 1: 11804]

National Association of Journalism Directors [Vol 1: 10587]

National Association of Legal Investigators [Vol 1: 11814]

National Association of Licensed Paralegals [Vol 2: 8384]

National Association of Negro Business and Professional Women's Clubs [Vol 1: 11816]

National Association of Neonatal Nurses [Vol 1: 11819]

National Association of Parish Catechetical Directors [Vol 1: 12049, 12050]

National Association of Pediatric Nurse Practitioners [Vol 1: 11822]

National Association of Peoplecultural Rehabilitation Concerns [Vol 1: 11825]

National Association of Personal Financial Advisors [Vol 1: 11830]

National Association of Printing Ink Manufacturers [Vol 1: 11834]

National Association of Produce Market Managers [Vol 1: 11837]

National Association of Professional Baseball Leagues [Vol 1: 11839]

National Association of Professional Baseball Leagues [Vol 1: 11839]

National Association of Professional Gardeners [Vol 1: 14226]

National Association of Professional Insurance Agents [Vol 1: 11843]

National Association of Professional Organizers [Vol 1: 11847]

National Association of Purchasing Management [Vol 1: 9273]

National Association of Railroad Passengers [Vol 1: 11850]

National Association of Real Estate Editors [Vol 1: 11853]

National Association of Realtors [Vol 1: 11855]

National Association of Recording Merchandisers [Vol 1: 11857]

National Association of Regional Councils [Vol 1: 11861]

National Association of RV Parks and Campgrounds [Vol 1: 11865]

National Association of Sanitarians [Vol 1: 12320]

National Association of Scholars [Vol 1: 11869]

National Association of Schools of Public Affairs and Administration [Vol 1: 11873]

National Association of Science Writers [Vol 1: 11880]

National Association of Scientific Materials Managers [Vol 1: 11883]

National Association of Secondary School Principals [Vol 1: 11885]

National Association of Secretaries of State [Vol 1: 11889]

National Association of Shopfitters [Vol 2: 8388]

National Association of Social Workers [Vol 1: 11893]

National Association of Special Education Teachers [Vol 1: 11897]

National Association of State Chief Information Officers [Vol 1: 11904]

National Association of State Information Resource Executives [Vol 1: 11904]

National Association of State Park Directors [Vol 1: 11906]

National Association of State Procurement Officials [Vol 1: 11910]

National Association of State Purchasing Officials [Vol 1: 11910]

National Association of State Workforce Agencies [Vol 1: 11913]

National Association of Student Financial Aid Administrators [Vol 1: 11918]

National Association of Swedish Architects [Vol 2: 6155]

National Association of Television Program Executives [Vol 1: 11921]

National Association of Temporary Staffing Services [Vol 1: 4554]

National Association of Testing Authorities, Australia [Vol 2: 882]

National Association of the Bureau of Animal Industry Veterinarians [Vol 1: 11770]

National Association of the Remodeling Industry [Vol 1: 11923]

National Association of Theatre Owners [Vol 1: 11933]

National Association of Underwater Instructors [Vol 1: 11935]

National Association of Women Business Owners [Vol 1: 11937]

National Athletic Trainers' Association [Vol 1: 11942]

National Auctioneers Association [Vol 1: 11945]

National Audio-Visual Association [Vol 1: 9231]

National Audubon Society [Vol 1: 11949]

National Australia Day Council [Vol 2: 884]

National Aviation Hall of Fame [Vol 1: 11952]

National Back Pain Association [Vol 2: 6863]

National Ballet of Canada [Vol 1: 11955]

National Band Association [Vol 1: 11957]

National Bar Association [Vol 1: 11967]

National Baseball Hall of Fame and Museum [Vol 1: 11969]

National Basketball Association [Vol 1: 11973]

National Biplane Association [Vol 1: 11981]

National Black Police Association [Vol 1: 11986]

National Book Critics Circle [Vol 1: 11991]

National Book Development Council of Singapore [Vol 2: 5952]

National Book Foundation [Vol 1: 11993]

National Book League (England) [Vol 2: 6901]

National Bowling Writer's Association [Vol 1: 5949]

National Broadcasting Society - Alpha Epsilon Rho [Vol 1: 11995]

National Broiler Council [Vol 1: 14112]

National Burglar and Fire Alarm Association [Vol 1: 8071]

National Business Aircraft Association [Vol 1: 12015]

National Business and Disability Council [Vol 1: 12008]

National Business Aviation Association [Vol 1: 12015]

National Business Education Association [Vol 1: 12017]

National Business Incubation Association [Vol 1: 12023]

National Cable and Telecommunications Association [Vol 1: 12028]

National Cancer Institute [Vol 1: 4632]

National Cancer Institute of Canada [Vol 1: 6389]

National Cancer Registrars Association [Vol 1: 12031]

National Carnival Bands Association of Trinidad and Tobago [Vol 2: 6622]

National Cartoonists Society [Vol 1: 12033]

National Catholic Band Association [Vol 1: 12036]

National Catholic Bandmasters' Association [Vol 1: 12036]

National Catholic Committee on Scouting [Vol 1: 12039]

National Catholic Educational Association [Vol 1: 12041]

National Center for State Courts [Vol 1: 12052]

National Cervical Cancer Coalition [Vol 1: 12056]

National Chamber of Commerce and Industry of Malaysia [Vol 2: 4550]

National Chamber of the Restaurant and Seasoned Food Industry [Vol 2: 4593]

National Chicken Council [Vol 1: 14112]

National Child Labor Committee [Vol 1: 12058]

National Christian College Athletic Association [Vol 1: 12060]

National Civic League [Vol 1: 12071]

National Collegiate Athletic Association [Vol 1: 12073]

National Collegiate Athletic Association - Division 1 Track Coaches Association [Vol 1: 12075]

National Collegiate Baseball Writers Association [Vol 1: 12082]

National Collegiate EMS Foundation [Vol 1: 12087]

National Commercial Bank of Jamaica Ltd. [Vol 2: 4199]

National Commission for Culture and the Arts [Vol 2: 5338]

National Commission on Correctional Health Care [Vol 1: 12093]

National Committee for Employer Support of the Guard and Reserve [Vol 1: 12096]

National Committee for the Furtherance of Jewish Education [Vol 1: 12101]

National Committee on American Foreign Policy [Vol 1: 12105]

National Committee on Engineering Design [Vol 2: 810]

National Communication Association [Vol 1: 12109]

National Community Education Association [Vol 1: 12118]

National Conference of Bar Examiners [Vol 1: 12128]

National Congress of Parents and Teachers [Vol 1: 12724]

National Consumers League [Vol 1: 12130]

National Contract Management Association [Vol 1: 12133]

National Coordinating Council on Emergency Management [Vol 1: 9510]

National Correctional Industries Association [Vol 1: 12137]

National Corvette Restorers Society [Vol 1: 12142]

National Council for Community Behavioral Healthcare [Vol 1: 12145]

National Council for Community Relations [Vol 1: 12159]

National Council for Continuing Education and Training [Vol 1: 12147]

National Council for Eurasian and East European Research [Vol 1: 12150]

National Council for GeoCosmic Research [Vol 1: 12152]

National Council for Geographic Education [Vol 1: 12154]

National Council for Interior Design Qualification [Vol 1: 12157]

National Council for Marketing and Public Relations [Vol 1: 12159]

National Council for the Social Studies [Vol 1: 12164]

National Council of College Publications Advisers [Vol 1: 7366]

National Council of Commercial Plant Breeders [Vol 1: 7769]

National Council of Commercial Plant Breeders [Vol 1: 12178]

National Council of Engineering Examiners [Vol 1: 12182]

National Council of Examiners for Engineering and Surveying [Vol 1: 12182]

National Council of La Raza [Vol 1: 12185]

National Council of Less Commonly Taught Languages [Vol 1: 12191]

National Council of Secondary School Athletic Directors [Vol 1: 12193]

National Council of Social Security Management Associations [Vol 1: 12195]

National Council of Supervisors of Mathematics [Vol 1: 12199]

National Council of Teachers of English [Vol 1: 7508, 12201]

National Council of Teachers of English [Vol 1: 17947]

National Council of Teachers of Mathematics [Vol 1: 12222]

National Council on Aging [Vol 1: 12229]

National Council on Alcoholism and Drug Dependence [Vol 1: 12244]

National Council on Community Services and Continuing Education [Vol 1: 12147]

National Council on Community Services for Community and Junior Colleges [Vol 1: 12147]

National Council on Family Relations [Vol 1: 12247]

National Council on Public History [Vol 1: 12249]

National Council on U.S.-Arab Relations [Vol 1: 12254]

National Court Appointed Special Advocate Association [Vol 1: 12256]

National Court Reporters Association [Vol 1: 12260]

National Court Reporters Foundation [Vol 1: 12264]

National Cowboy and Western Heritage Museum [Vol 1: 12267]

National Cowboy and Western Heritage Museum [Vol 1: 14579, 14580]

National Cowboy Hall of Fame and Western Heritage Center **[Vol 1: 12267]**
National Dairy Shrine **[Vol 1: 12270]**
National Dance Association **[Vol 1: 12275]**
National Defense Transportation Association **[Vol 1: 12281]**
National Democratic Institute for International Affairs **[Vol 1: 12286]**
National Derby Rallies **[Vol 1: 12288]**
National Economic Association **[Vol 1: 12290]**
National Education Association **[Vol 1: 12292, 13132]**
National Eisteddfod of Wales **[Vol 2: 8390]**
National Electrical and Communications Association **[Vol 2: 886]**
National Electrical Manufacturers Representatives Association **[Vol 1: 12303]**
National Electronics Sales and Service Dealers Association **[Vol 1: 12305]**
National Electronics Service Dealers Association **[Vol 1: 12305]**
National Endowment for Democracy **[Vol 1: 12307]**
National Endowment for the Arts **[Vol 1: 12309]**
National Endowment for the Humanities **[Vol 1: 12317]**
National Environmental Health Association **[Vol 1: 759]**
National Environmental Health Association **[Vol 1: 12320, 13453]**
National Environmental, Safety and Health Training Association **[Vol 1: 12323]**
National Ethnic Coalition of Organizations **[Vol 1: 12328]**
National Farm-City Council **[Vol 1: 12330]**
National Federation of Abstracting and Information Services **[Vol 1: 12332]**
National Federation of Coffee Growers of Colombia **[Vol 2: 1846]**
National Federation of Music Clubs **[Vol 1: 7475, 12334]**
National Federation of Music Societies **[Vol 2: 8337]**
National Federation of Plastering Contractors **[Vol 2: 7678]**
National Federation of Press Women **[Vol 1: 12336]**
National Federation of State High School Associations **[Vol 1: 12338]**
National Federation of State High School Athletic Associations **[Vol 1: 12338]**
National Federation of State Poetry Societies **[Vol 1: 12341]**
National Federation of the Blind **[Vol 1: 12381]**
National Federation of UNESCO Associations in Japan **[Vol 2: 4300]**
National Fertilisers Ltd. **[Vol 2: 3482]**
National FFA Organization **[Vol 1: 12383]**
National Field Hockey Coaches Association **[Vol 1: 12389]**
National Fishing Lure Collectors Club **[Vol 1: 12394]**
National Flexible Packaging Association **[Vol 1: 8370]**
National Flute Association **[Vol 1: 12396]**
National Football Foundation and College Hall of Fame **[Vol 1: 12401]**
National Football Foundation and College Hall of Fame, Valley of the Sun Chapter **[Vol 1: 12406]**
National Football Foundation and Hall of Fame **[Vol 1: 12401]**
National Football League **[Vol 1: 12410]**
National Forensic Association **[Vol 1: 12412]**
National Forensic League **[Vol 1: 12414]**
National Forum for Black Public Administrators **[Vol 1: 12418]**
National Forum of Greek Orthodox Church Musicians **[Vol 1: 12422]**
National Foundation for Advancement in the Arts **[Vol 1: 12428]**
National Foundation for Infectious Diseases **[Vol 1: 12430]**
National Foundation for Peroneal Muscular Atrophy **[Vol 1: 7184]**
National Foundation for Unemployment Compensation and Workers Compensation **[Vol 1: 12432]**
National Frozen and Refrigerated Foods Association **[Vol 1: 12437]**
National Frozen Food Association **[Vol 1: 12437]**
National Funeral Directors Association **[Vol 1: 12439]**
National Gay and Lesbian Task Force **[Vol 1: 3538]**

National Genealogical Society **[Vol 1: 12441]**
National Geographic Society **[Vol 1: 8208]**
National Glass Association **[Vol 1: 12455]**
National Ground Water Association **[Vol 1: 12458]**
National Guard Association of the United States **[Vol 1: 12471]**
National Guild for Community Arts Education **[Vol 1: 12492]**
National Guild of Community Schools of the Arts **[Vol 1: 12492]**
National Guild of Hypnotists **[Vol 1: 12494]**
National Headache Foundation **[Vol 1: 12496]**
National Health and Medical Research Council **[Vol 2: 890]**
National Hearing Conservation Association **[Vol 1: 12499]**
National Hemophilia Foundation **[Vol 1: 12504]**
National High School Athletic Coaches Association **[Vol 1: 12506]**
National High School Rodeo Association **[Vol 1: 12508]**
National Highway Traffic Safety Administration **[Vol 1: 9640]**
National History Day **[Vol 1: 12510]**
National Hockey League Players' Association **[Vol 1: 12516]**
National Home Fashions League **[Vol 1: 9951]**
National Home Furnishings Association **[Vol 1: 12518]**
National Home Improvement Council **[Vol 1: 11923]**
National Horseshoe Pitchers Association of America **[Vol 1: 12520]**
National Hospice and Palliative Care Organization **[Vol 1: 12526]**
National Housing Conference **[Vol 1: 12530]**
National Independent Automobile Dealers Association **[Vol 1: 12532]**
National Indian Education Association **[Vol 1: 12537]**
National Institute for Farm Safety **[Vol 1: 10134]**
National Institute for Higher Education, Research, Science and Technology **[Vol 2: 6625]**
National Institute of Building Sciences **[Vol 1: 12543]**
National Institute of Ceramic Engineers **[Vol 1: 1558, 1562]**
National Institute of Diabetes and Digestive and Kidney Diseases **[Vol 1: 4632]**
National Institute of Governmental Purchasing **[Vol 1: 12549]**
National Institute of Real Estate Brokers **[Vol 1: 7670]**
National Institutes of Health - National Institute of Nursing Research **[Vol 1: 12555]**
National Intercollegiate Soccer Officials Association **[Vol 1: 12559]**
National InterScholastic Swimming Coaches Association of America **[Vol 1: 12565]**
National Irish Safety Organisation **[Vol 2: 3899]**
National Jewish Committee on Girl Scouting **[Vol 1: 12569]**
National Jewish Committee on Scouting **[Vol 1: 12571]**
National Jewish Girl Scout Committee of the Synagogue Council of America **[Vol 1: 12569]**
National Junior Classical League **[Vol 1: 12832]**
National Junior College Athletic Association **[Vol 1: 12577]**
National Lawyers Wives **[Vol 1: 2755]**
National League of Cities **[Vol 1: 12580]**
National Legal Aid and Defender Association **[Vol 1: 12583]**
National Library of Australia **[Vol 2: 894]**
National Library of Medicine **[Vol 1: 11069]**
National Library of Scotland **[Vol 2: 9155]**
National LP-Gas Association **[Vol 1: 12717]**
National Magazine Awards Foundation **[Vol 1: 12589]**
National Male Nurses Association **[Vol 1: 850]**
National Marine Educators Association **[Vol 1: 12591]**
National Marine Representatives Association **[Vol 1: 12597]**
National Medical Fellowships **[Vol 1: 12599]**
National Microfilm Association **[Vol 1: 229]**
National Middle School Association **[Vol 1: 12602]**
National Migraine Foundation **[Vol 1: 12496]**

National Military Intelligence Association **[Vol 1: 12606]**
National Mining Association **[Vol 1: 12608]**
National Multiple Sclerosis Society **[Vol 1: 12610]**
National Municipal League **[Vol 1: 12071]**
National Music Council of The United Kingdom **[Vol 2: 8393]**
National Newspaper Association **[Vol 1: 12617]**
National Notary Association **[Vol 1: 12619]**
National Ocean Industries Association **[Vol 1: 12622]**
National Office Paper Recycling Project **[Vol 1: 12624]**
National Opera Association **[Vol 1: 12626]**
National Operatic and Dramatic Association **[Vol 2: 8395]**
National Organization for Human Services **[Vol 1: 12631]**
National Organization for Victim Assistance **[Vol 1: 12637]**
National Organization of Human Service Educators **[Vol 1: 12631]**
National Organization on Disability **[Vol 1: 12645]**
National Orientation Directors Association **[Vol 1: 12647]**
National Orphan Train Complex **[Vol 1: 12650]**
National Paint and Coatings Association **[Vol 1: 1689]**
National Park Academy of the Arts **[Vol 1: 12653]**
National Park Service **[Vol 1: 12664]**
National Parks Association **[Vol 1: 12660]**
National Parks Conservation Association **[Vol 1: 12660]**
National Peace Corps Association **[Vol 1: 12665]**
National Peach Council **[Vol 1: 12671]**
National Peanut Council **[Vol 1: 3123]**
National Piers Society **[Vol 2: 8397]**
National Pigeon Association **[Vol 1: 12674]**
National Portrait Gallery **[Vol 2: 8401]**
National Postdoctoral Association **[Vol 1: 12676]**
National Press Club **[Vol 1: 12679]**
National Press Foundation **[Vol 1: 12690]**
National Press Foundation **[Vol 1: 12691]**
National Press Photographers Association **[Vol 1: 12696]**
National Private Truck Council **[Vol 1: 12711]**
National Productivity and Competitiveness Council **[Vol 2: 4576]**
National Propane Gas Association **[Vol 1: 12717]**
National Property Management Association **[Vol 1: 12722]**
National PTA **[Vol 1: 12724]**
National Quality Institute **[Vol 1: 12727]**
National Railroad Construction and Maintenance Association **[Vol 1: 12729]**
National Reading Conference **[Vol 1: 10860]**
National Ready Mixed Concrete Association **[Vol 1: 12731]**
National Recreation and Park Association **[Vol 1: 12737]**
National Recycling Coalition **[Vol 1: 12748]**
National Register of Warranted Builders **[Vol 2: 8405]**
National Rehabilitation Association **[Vol 1: 12750]**
National Rehabilitation Association - Vocational Evaluation and Work Adjustment Association **[Vol 1: 12757]**
National Rehabilitation Counseling Association **[Vol 1: 12760]**
National Remodeling Association **[Vol 1: 11923]**
National Research Council **[Vol 1: 12766]**
National Research Council of Canada **[Vol 1: 12768, 13102]**
National Research Council of Malawi **[Vol 2: 4514]**
National Research Council of the Philippines **[Vol 2: 5343]**
National Research Foundation **[Vol 2: 5573]**
National Restaurant Association **[Vol 1: 12771]**
National Restaurant Association Educational Foundation **[Vol 1: 12773]**
National Restaurant Association Foundation **[Vol 1: 12773]**
National Retail Federation **[Vol 1: 12776]**
National Retail Merchants Association **[Vol 1: 12776]**
National Rifle Association of America **[Vol 1: 12784]**
National Rifle Association of the United Kingdom **[Vol 2: 8407]**
National Rowing Foundation **[Vol 1: 12787]**

National Rural Health Association [Vol 1: 12789]
National Rural Health Care Association [Vol 1: 12789]
National Safe Boating Council [Vol 1: 12795]
National Safety Council [Vol 1: 12798]
National Scholastic Press Association [Vol 1: 12800]
National Scholastic Press Association [Vol 1: 16305]
National School Public Relations Association [Vol 1: 12803]
National School Transportation Association [Vol 1: 12807]
National Science Council of Taiwan [Vol 2: 6590]
National Science Foundation [Vol 1: 12811]
National Science Foundation - National Science Board [Vol 1: 12815]
National Science Teachers Association [Vol 1: 12818]
National Sculpture Society [Vol 1: 12829]
National Sea Grant Office [Vol 1: 8780]
National Senior Classical League [Vol 1: 12831]
National Sheriffs' Association [Vol 1: 12834]
National Small-Bore Rifle Association [Vol 2: 8409]
National Soccer Coaches Association of America [Vol 1: 12843]
National Society, Daughters of the American Revolution [Vol 1: 12846]
National Society for Experiential Education [Vol 1: 12849]
National Society for Histotechnology [Vol 1: 12856]
National Society for Performance and Instruction [Vol 1: 10191]
National Society of Arts and Letters [Vol 1: 12862]
National Society of Fingerprint Officers [Vol 2: 7688]
National Society of Insurance Premium Auditors [Vol 1: 12868]
National Society of Interior Design [Vol 1: 4347]
National Society of Newspaper Columnists [Vol 1: 12870]
National Society of Professional Engineers [Vol 1: 12872]
National Society of Professional Insurance Investigators [Vol 1: 12886]
National Society of Professional Surveyors [Vol 1: 12891]
National Society of Tole and Decorative Painters [Vol 1: 15610]
National Society, Sons of the American Revolution [Vol 1: 12895]
National Sojourners [Vol 1: 12916]
National Space Society [Vol 1: 12918]
National Space Society of Australia [Vol 2: 896]
National Speakers Association [Vol 1: 12925]
National Speleological Society [Vol 1: 12928]
National Sporting Club [Vol 2: 8411]
National Sportscasters and Sportswriters Association [Vol 1: 12930]
National Staff Development Council [Vol 1: 12933]
National Student Campaign Against Hunger and Homelessness [Vol 1: 12939]
National Student Employment Association [Vol 1: 12943]
National Swimming Pool Institute [Vol 1: 5473]
National Symphony Orchestra [Vol 1: 12950]
National Tattoo Association [Vol 1: 12952]
National Tattoo Club of the World [Vol 1: 12952]
National Tax Association [Vol 1: 12967]
National Tax Association [Vol 1: 12967]
National Taxpayers Union [Vol 1: 12971]
National Technical Honor Society [Vol 1: 4586]
National Telecommunications Cooperative Association [Vol 1: 12973]
National TeleMedia Council [Vol 1: 12975]
National Telephone Cooperative Association [Vol 1: 12973]
National Therapeutic Recreation Society [Vol 1: 12977]
National Thespian Society [Vol 1: 8028]
National Threshers Association [Vol 1: 12984]
National Tractor Pullers Association [Vol 1: 12986]
National Traditional Country Music Association [Vol 1: 12998]
National Trust for Historic Preservation [Vol 1: 13001]
National Turf Writers Association [Vol 1: 13005]
National Union of Public and General Employees [Vol 1: 13009]

National University Extension Association [Vol 1: 17379]
National University of Lesotho - Faculty of Education [Vol 2: 4460]
National University of Lesotho - Faculty of Law [Vol 2: 4465]
National University of Singapore [Vol 2: 5955]
National University of Singapore - Centre for Development of Teaching and Learning [Vol 2: 5959]
National University of Singapore - Division of Research and Technology [Vol 2: 5962]
National Urban League [Vol 1: 13014]
National Utility Contractors Association [Vol 1: 13017]
National Vegetable Society [Vol 2: 8413]
National Water Research Institute [Vol 1: 13021]
National Water Safety Congress [Vol 1: 13024]
National Weather Association [Vol 1: 13028]
National Wheelchair Basketball Association [Vol 1: 13036]
National Wild Turkey Federation [Vol 1: 13040]
National Wildlife Federation [Vol 1: 13043]
National Wildlife Rehabilitators Association [Vol 1: 13046]
National Woman's Party [Vol 1: 13050]
National Women's Political Caucus [Vol 1: 13052]
National Women's Studies Association [Vol 1: 13054]
National Wood Flooring Association [Vol 1: 13060]
National Wool Growers' Association of South Africa [Vol 2: 5577]
National Wrestling Coaches Association [Vol 1: 13065]
National Wrestling Hall of Fame & Museum [Vol 1: 13068]
National Writers Association [Vol 1: 13074]
National Writers Union [Vol 1: 13079]
National Writer's United Service Organization [Vol 1: 13080]
National Young Farmer Educational Association [Vol 1: 13081]
Nation's Restaurant News [Vol 1: 13085]
Natural Products Association [Vol 1: 13087]
Natural Resources Council of America [Vol 1: 13095]
Natural Resources Defense Council [Vol 1: 13099]
Natural Sciences and Engineering Research Council of Canada [Vol 1: 13102]
Nature Canada [Vol 1: 13106]
Nature Saskatchewan [Vol 1: 13110]
Nature's Window Art Gallery [Vol 1: 7043]
Nautilus Awards [Vol 1: 13116]
Naval Helicopter Association [Vol 1: 13118]
Naval Ships Association; Historic [Vol 1: 8932]
Naval Submarine League [Vol 1: 13123]
NBTA Asia Pacific [Vol 2: 903]
NCC Partners [Vol 2: 2591]
NCMS - Society of Industrial Security Professionals [Vol 1: 13129]
NEA Foundation [Vol 1: 13131]
NEA Foundation for the Improvement of Education [Vol 1: 13131]
NEA Health Information Network [Vol 1: 13136]
Near East South Asia Council of Overseas Schools [Vol 2: 3293]
Nebraska Library Association [Vol 1: 13138]
Nebraska Partnership for All-Bird Conservation [Vol 1: 13143]
Nederlandse Natuurkundige Vereniging [Vol 2: 4796]
Nederlandse Vereiniging voor Psychiatrie [Vol 2: 4798]
Nederlandse vereniging voor Biomaterialen en Tissue Engineering [Vol 2: 4661]
Nematological Society of Southern Africa [Vol 2: 5579]
Nematologiese Vereniging van Suidelike Afrika [Vol 2: 5579]
Nepal Academy of Science and Technology [Vol 2: 4630]
Nepal Vista [Vol 2: 4638]
Nestle SA - Creating Shared Value Section [Vol 2: 6469]
Netherlands Institute of Southern Africa [Vol 2: 4625]
Netherlands Physical Society [Vol 2: 4796]
Netherlands Psychiatric Association [Vol 2: 4798]
Netherlands Society for English Studies [Vol 2: 4800]
Networking Culture Ltd. [Vol 2: 8418]

Networking Institute; Gazette International [Vol 1: 14097]
Neumann Janos Szamitogep-tudomanyi Tarsasag [Vol 2: 3412]
Neurochemistry; American Society for [Vol 1: 3994]
neuroendocrinology; International Society of Psycho [Vol 1: 10353]
Neuroethology; International Society for [Vol 1: 10184]
Neurofeedback and Research; International Society for [Vol 1: 10186]
Neuroimaging; American Society of [Vol 1: 4453]
Neuroimaging in Psychiatry; International Society for [Vol 2: 6432]
Neurological Surgeons; American Association of [Vol 1: 1221]
Neuromuscular and Electrodiagnostic Medicine; American Association of [Vol 1: 1223]
Neuropathologists; American Association of [Vol 1: 1228]
Neuropsychopharmacology; American College of [Vol 1: 1776]
Neuroradiology; American Society of [Vol 1: 4456]
Neuroscience Society; Australian [Vol 2: 476]
Neurowissenschaftliche Gesellschaft e.V. [Vol 2: 2968]
Neutron Scattering Society of America [Vol 1: 13147]
New Brunswick Institute of Agrologists [Vol 1: 13152]
New England Theatre Conference [Vol 1: 13157]
New England Water Works Association [Vol 1: 13162]
New England Wild Flower Society [Vol 1: 13171]
New England Wildflower Preservation Society [Vol 1: 13171]
New Hampshire Audubon [Vol 1: 13178]
New Hampshire Developmental Disabilities Council [Vol 1: 13182]
New Jersey Library Association [Vol 1: 13186]
New Letters [Vol 1: 13190]
New Mexico Library Association [Vol 1: 13192]
New Mexico Music Awards [Vol 1: 13202]
New Orleans Time-Picayune [Vol 1: 17805]
New Peace History Society [Vol 1: 13875]
New South Wales Ministry for the Arts [Vol 2: 905]
New Statesman [Vol 2: 8420]
New York Academy of Sciences [Vol 1: 13204]
New York Botanical Garden - Institute of Systematic Botany [Vol 1: 13207]
New York City Section of the Illuminating Engineering Society [Vol 1: 9157]
New York Financial Writers' Association [Vol 1: 13209]
New York International Ballet Competition [Vol 1: 13211]
New York Library Association [Vol 1: 13213]
New York Press Club [Vol 1: 13220]
New York Racing Association [Vol 1: 13230]
New York Road Runners Club [Vol 1: 13232]
New York State Department of Health - Wadsworth Center [Vol 1: 13235]
The New York Times [Vol 1: 13238]
New Zealand Academy of Fine Arts [Vol 2: 4948]
New Zealand Accordion Association [Vol 2: 4950]
New Zealand Association of Scientists [Vol 2: 4953]
New Zealand Committee for the Scientific Investigation of Claims of the Paranormal [Vol 2: 4958]
New Zealand Dental Therapists' Association [Vol 2: 4961]
New Zealand Freshwater Sciences Society [Vol 2: 4963]
New Zealand Geographical Society [Vol 2: 4966]
New Zealand Geotechnical Society [Vol 2: 4968]
New Zealand Guild of Agricultural Journalists and Communicators [Vol 2: 4971]
New Zealand History Research Trust Fund [Vol 2: 4896]
New Zealand Institute of Physics [Vol 2: 4974]
New Zealand Library Association [Vol 2: 4928]
New Zealand Mathematical Society [Vol 2: 4976]
New Zealand Olympic Committee [Vol 2: 4979]
New Zealand Psychological Society [Vol 2: 4987]
New Zealand Recreation Association [Vol 2: 4995]
New Zealand Society for Earthquake Engineering [Vol 2: 5004]
New Zealand Society for Music Therapy [Vol 2: 5007]

New Zealand Society of Authors [Vol 2: 5009]
New Zealand Society of Designers [Vol 2: 4883]
New Zealand Society of Plant Biologists [Vol 2: 5016]
New Zealand Society of Plant Physiologists [Vol 2: 5016]
New Zealand Statistical Association [Vol 2: 5019]
New Zealand Trade and Enterprise [Vol 2: 5022]
New Zealand Veterinary Association [Vol 2: 5024]
New Zealand Water and Wastes Association [Vol 2: 5086]
Newcomer Supply [Vol 1: 12860]
Newhouse Newspapers [Vol 1: 17805]
Newmont Mining Corp. [Vol 2: 1935]
Newsletter and Electronic Publishers Foundation [Vol 1: 16127]
Newspaper Association of America [Vol 1: 13240]
Newspaper Association of America Foundation [Vol 1: 13242]
Newspaper Fund [Vol 1: 7911]
Newspaper Fund; Dow Jones [Vol 1: 7911]
The Newspaper Guild [Vol 1: 13245]
Next Generation Indie Book Awards [Vol 1: 13247]
NFL Players Association [Vol 1: 13249]
NHL Broadcasters' Association [Vol 1: 8961]
Niagara University [Vol 1: 13253]
Nielsen International Music Competitions; Carl [Vol 2: 1974]
Nigeria LNG Ltd. [Vol 2: 5096]
Nigerian Library Association [Vol 2: 5099]
Nihon Gakujutsu Shinko-kai [Vol 2: 4273]
Nihon Kensetsu Kikai-ka Kyokai [Vol 2: 4265]
Nihon Kikai Gakkai [Vol 2: 4276]
Nihon Shinbun Kyokai [Vol 2: 4269]
Nihon UNESCO Kyokai Renmei [Vol 2: 4300]
Nimrod: International Journal of Prose and Poetry [Vol 1: 13259]
The Ninety-Nines, Inc. [Vol 1: 11468]
Ninety-Nines, International Organization of Women Pilots [Vol 1: 13262]
Nippon Yakugakkai [Vol 2: 4308]
Niwano Heiwa Zaidan [Vol 2: 4304]
Niwano Peace Foundation [Vol 2: 4304]
Noir International Festival [Vol 2: 4047]
Nordic Association for Hydrology [Vol 2: 6158]
Nordic Council [Vol 2: 1976]
Nordisk Film [Vol 2: 5153]
Nordisk Hydrologisk Forening [Vol 2: 6158]
Nordiska Radet [Vol 2: 1976]
Norsk Presseforbund [Vol 2: 5145]
Norsk Selskap for Immunologi [Vol 2: 5159]
Norske Filmfestivalen [Vol 2: 5142]
Norske Finansanalytikeres Forening [Vol 2: 5161]
North American Academy of Liturgy [Vol 2: 4142]
North American Association for Environmental Education [Vol 1: 13264]
North American Association of Christians in Social Work [Vol 1: 13272]
North American Association of Food Equipment Manufacturers [Vol 1: 13275]
North American Association of Wardens and Superintendents [Vol 1: 13279]
North American Benthological Society [Vol 1: 15075]
North American Bluebird Society [Vol 1: 13281]
North American Broadcasters Association [Vol 1: 13283]
North American Catalysis Society [Vol 1: 13285]
North American Colleges and Teachers of Agriculture [Vol 1: 13290]
North American Conference on British Studies [Vol 1: 13296]
North American Council on Adoptable Children [Vol 1: 13302]
North American Gladiolus Council [Vol 1: 13306]
North American Hair Research Society [Vol 1: 13308]
North American Lily Society [Vol 1: 13311]
North American Membrane Society [Vol 1: 13314]
North American Mycological Association [Vol 1: 13319]
North American Patristics Society [Vol 1: 13322]
North American Peruvian Horse Association [Vol 1: 13324]
North American Police Work Dog Association [Vol 1: 13330]
North American Snowsports Journalists Association [Vol 1: 13334]

North American Society for Oceanic History [Vol 1: 13341]
North American Society for the Psychology of Sport and Physical Activity [Vol 1: 13343]
North American Society for the Sociology of Sport [Vol 1: 13347]
North American Society of Pacing and Electrophysiology [Vol 1: 8871]
North American Trail Ride Conference [Vol 1: 13350]
North American Vexillological Association [Vol 1: 13361]
North Carolina Health and Wellness Trust Fund [Vol 1: 13364]
North Carolina Library Association [Vol 1: 13366]
North Carolina Literary and Historical Association [Vol 1: 13370]
North Carolina Utility Contractors Association [Vol 1: 13377]
North Country Trail Association [Vol 1: 13381]
North-South Centre [Vol 2: 2353]
Northeast Asia Council [Vol 1: 4916]
Northeast Conference on the Teaching of Foreign Languages [Vol 1: 13393]
Northeastern Bird-Banding Association [Vol 1: 5335]
Northeastern Loggers Association [Vol 1: 13400]
Northeastern University - Center for the Study of Sport in Society [Vol 1: 13402]
Northern Mariana Islands Council for the Humanities [Vol 2: 5109]
Northern Michigan University Alumni Association [Vol 1: 13405]
Northern Territory Library [Vol 2: 909]
Northport/B.J. Spoke Gallery [Vol 1: 16159]
Northrop Grumman Corp. [Vol 1: 15901]
Northwest Film Center [Vol 1: 13409]
Northwest Film Study Center [Vol 1: 13409]
Northwest Public Power Association [Vol 1: 13413]
Northwestern University - Office of the Provost [Vol 1: 13417]
Northwestern University - Roberta Buffett Center for International and Comparative Studies [Vol 1: 13420]
Northwood University, Florida Campus [Vol 1: 13423]
Northwood University, Michigan Campus [Vol 1: 13426]
Norway Ministry of Foreign Affairs [Vol 2: 5133]
Norwegian Academy of Science and Letters [Vol 2: 5137]
Norwegian Broadcasting Corporation [Vol 2: 5146]
Norwegian Broadcasting Corp. [Vol 2: 5149, 5151]
Norwegian Elkhound Association of America [Vol 1: 13432]
Norwegian Film Critics Association [Vol 2: 5150]
Norwegian International Film Festival [Vol 2: 5142]
Norwegian Newspaper Publishers Association [Vol 2: 5146]
Norwegian Playwrights' Association [Vol 2: 5154]
Norwegian Press Association [Vol 2: 5145]
The Norwegian Short Film Festival [Vol 2: 5147]
Norwegian Society for Immunology [Vol 2: 5159]
Norwegian Society of Financial Analysts [Vol 2: 5161]
Norwegian Union of Journalists [Vol 2: 5146]
Norwich and Norfolk Terrier Club [Vol 1: 13437]
NOVA Chemicals Corp. [Vol 1: 7207]
Nova Scotia Library Association [Vol 1: 13446]
Novartis AG [Vol 2: 703]
Novo Nordisk Foundation [Vol 2: 1981]
NSF International [Vol 1: 13452]
Nuclear Age Peace Foundation [Vol 1: 13454]
Nuclear Energy Institute [Vol 1: 13459]
Nuclear Institute [Vol 2: 8422]
Nuclear Science and Engineering; Australian Institute of [Vol 2: 399]
Nurse Attorneys; American Association of [Vol 1: 1244]
Nursery and Garden Industry Australia [Vol 2: 911]
Nurses Association; American [Vol 1: 3017]
Nurses' Association; American Nephrology [Vol 1: 2977]
Nurses Association; Australian Dermatology [Vol 2: 325]
Nurses Association; Emergency [Vol 1: 8086]
Nurses; Association of PeriOperative Registered [Vol 1: 5464]

Nurses; International Association of Forensic [Vol 1: 9665]
Nurses; Society of Pediatric [Vol 1: 15740]
Nursing; American Assembly for Men in [Vol 1: 850]
Nursing; American Association for the History of [Vol 1: 1004]
Nursing Society; Oncology [Vol 1: 13527]
Nursing Society; Pediatric Endocrinology [Vol 1: 13884]
Nutrition Association; School [Vol 1: 14777]
Nutrition; Foundation for Digestive Health and [Vol 1: 8441]
Nutrition Foundation of the Philippines [Vol 2: 5345]
Obec Architektu [Vol 2: 1936]
Oberhasli Breeders of America [Vol 1: 13461]
Obesity; European Association for the Study of [Vol 2: 7594]
Obesity; International Association for the Study of [Vol 2: 8073]
Observatoire des Energies Renouvelables [Vol 2: 2593]
Observ'ER [Vol 2: 2593]
Obstetricians and Gynaecologists - United Kingdom; Royal College of [Vol 2: 8688]
Occupational and Environmental Medical Association of Canada [Vol 1: 13465]
Occupational Health Nurses; American Association of [Vol 1: 1247]
Occupational Health Nurses; American Board for [Vol 1: 1500]
Occupational Therapy Association of South Africa [Vol 2: 5584]
Occupational Therapy Foundation; American [Vol 1: 3039]
Ocean Conservancy [Vol 1: 13467]
Oceanography; American Society of Limnology and [Vol 1: 5139]
OCIC, for Cinema and Audiovisual [Vol 2: 1660]
Odense International Film Festival [Vol 2: 1986]
Odense International Organ Competition and Festival [Vol 2: 1988]
Oesterreichische Psysikalische Gesellschaft [Vol 2: 1209]
The Office of His Excellency the Governor of the Cayman Islands [Vol 2: 1820]
Office of the President of Iceland [Vol 2: 3435]
Office of the President of the Cooperative Republic of Guyana [Vol 2: 3334]
Office of the President of the Republic of Macedonia [Vol 2: 4508]
Office of the President of the Slovak Republic [Vol 2: 6002]
Office of the President of Ukraine [Vol 2: 6653]
Office of the Prime Minister of Malta [Vol 2: 4570]
Office of the Prime Minister of Papua New Guinea [Vol 2: 5210]
Ohio Academy of History [Vol 1: 13469]
Ohio Speech-Language-Hearing Association [Vol 1: 13475]
Ohio State University [Vol 1: 7427]
Ohio State University - Mershon Center for International Security Studies [Vol 1: 13480]
Ohio State University Press [Vol 1: 13486]
Ohioana Library Association [Vol 1: 13488]
Oil and Colour Chemists' Association [Vol 2: 8425]
Oil Firing Technical Association for the Petroleum Industry [Vol 2: 8429]
Oita Sports Association for the Disabled [Vol 2: 4306]
Oklahoma Archaeological Survey [Vol 1: 13498]
Oklahoma Association of School and Library Media Specialists [Vol 1: 13500]
Oklahoma Library Association - Oklahoma School Librarians Division [Vol 1: 13500]
Olympiques Speciaux Canada [Vol 1: 16113]
Oman Economic Review [Vol 2: 5167]
Omani Economic Association [Vol 2: 5169]
Omega Psi Phi Fraternity [Vol 1: 13504]
Omicron Chi Epsilon [Vol 1: 13509]
Omicron Delta Epsilon [Vol 1: 13509]
Omicron Delta Gamma [Vol 1: 13509]
Omicron Delta Kappa Society [Vol 1: 13512]
Omicron Kappa Upsilon [Vol 1: 13519]
Omospondia Ergodoton ke Biomichanon Kyprou [Vol 2: 1896]
Onassis Public Benefit Foundation; Alexander S. [Vol 2: 3295]

Oncology; European Society for Radiotherapy and [Vol 2: 1491]

Oncology Nursing Certification Corporation [Vol 1: 13522]

Oncology Nursing Society [Vol 1: 13527]

Oncology Social Work; Association of [Vol 1: 5445]

Online News Association [Vol 1: 13559]

Ontario Arts Council [Vol 1: 13561]

Ontario College of Art and Design [Vol 1: 13574]

Ontario Media Development Corp. [Vol 1: 13576]

Ontario Ministry of Citizenship and Immigration - Ontario Honours and Awards Secretariat [Vol 1: 13578]

Ontario Nature [Vol 1: 13583]

Ontario Psychological Association [Vol 1: 13592]

Ontario School Counsellor's Association [Vol 1: 13594]

Operating Room Nurses Association of the Philippines [Vol 2: 5347]

Operational Research Societies; International Federation of [Vol 1: 9923]

Operational Research Societies; International Federation of - Airline Group [Vol 1: 9926]

Operational Research Society of the United Kingdom [Vol 2: 8431]

Operations Research Society of America [Vol 1: 9253]

Operative Dentistry; Academy of [Vol 1: 95]

Operative Registered Nurses; Association of Peri [Vol 1: 5464]

Ophthalmic Administrators; American Society of [Vol 1: 4469]

Ophthalmic Registered Nurses; American Society of [Vol 1: 4471]

Ophthalmological Society; Egyptian [Vol 2: 2019]

Ophthalmological Society; German [Vol 2: 2970]

Ophthalmology; American Academy of [Vol 1: 603]

Ophthalmology; Association for Research in Vision and [Vol 1: 5081]

Oppenheim-John Downes Memorial Trust [Vol 2: 8435]

Optical Research Associates [Vol 1: 16148]

Optical Society of America [Vol 1: 13601]

Optical Society of India [Vol 2: 3773]

Optometry; American Academy of [Vol 1: 615]

Oral and Maxillofacial Radiology; American Academy of [Vol 1: 627]

Oral and Maxillofacial Surgery Foundation [Vol 1: 13623]

Oral History Association [Vol 1: 13628]

Oral Medicine; American Academy of [Vol 1: 632]

Orchestras Canada [Vol 1: 13635]

Orchestre Symphonique de Montreal [Vol 1: 11255]

Orchestres Canada [Vol 1: 13635]

Order of Daedalians [Vol 1: 13637]

Order of the Founders and Patriots of America [Vol 1: 13655]

Order Sons of Italy in America [Vol 1: 13657]

Ordre des Psychologues du Quebec [Vol 1: 13659]

Oregon Health and Science University - Neurological Sciences Institute [Vol 1: 13663]

Organ Historical Trust of Australia [Vol 2: 918]

Organisation de l'Aviation Civile Internationale [Vol 1: 9769]

Organisation des Capitales et des Villes Islamiques [Vol 2: 5908]

Organisation des Nations Unies pour l'Education, la Science et la Culture [Vol 2: 2647]

Organisation Internationale des Institutions Superieures de Control des Finances Publiques [Vol 2: 1296]

Organisation Internationale pour l'Elimination de Toutes les Formes de Discrimination Raciale [Vol 2: 6417]

Organisation Meteorologique Mondiale [Vol 2: 6558]

Organisation Mondiale de la Sante [Vol 2: 6546]

Organisation Mondiale de la Sante Animale [Vol 2: 2667]

Organisation Mondiale de Labourage [Vol 2: 4846]

Organisation Mondiale pour la Systemique et la Cybernetique [Vol 2: 9485]

Organisation pour l'Etude Phyto-Taxonomique de la Region Mediterraneenne [Vol 2: 4145]

Organisation Universitaire Interamericaine [Vol 1: 9438]

Organisme Europeen de Recherche sur la Carie [Vol 2: 4705]

Organizacion de Entidades Fiscalizadoras Superiors de Africa [Vol 2: 4471]

Organizacion de la Naciones Unidas para La Agricultura y la Alimentacion [Vol 2: 3370]

Organization de Paises Arabes Exportadores de Petroleo [Vol 2: 4428]

Organization Development Institute [Vol 1: 10189]

Organization for Entrepreneurial Development [Vol 1: 13666]

Organization for the Phyto-Taxonomic Investigation of the Mediterranean Area [Vol 2: 4145]

Organization for the Study of Sex Differences [Vol 1: 13669]

Organization of American Historians [Vol 1: 13671, 15083]

Organization of American States [Vol 1: 13691]

Organization of Arab Petroleum Exporting Countries [Vol 2: 4428]

Organization of Islamic Capitals and Cities [Vol 2: 5908]

Organizational Behavior Teaching Society [Vol 1: 13696]

Organizers; National Association of Professional [Vol 1: 11847]

Ornithological Society of the Middle East, the Caucasus and Central Asia [Vol 2: 8437]

Orphan Train Heritage Society of America [Vol 1: 12650]

ORT America [Vol 1: 13702]

Ortho Biotech [Vol 1: 6950]

Orthodontic Society; British [Vol 2: 7161]

Orthodontics; American Board of [Vol 1: 1506]

Orthodontists; American Association of [Vol 1: 1259]

Orthodox Society of America [Vol 1: 13711]

Orthopaedic Research Society [Vol 1: 13715]

Orthopaedic Society for Sports Medicine; American [Vol 1: 3097]

Orthopsychiatric Association; American [Vol 1: 3101]

Orthoptists; American Association of Certified [Vol 1: 1079]

Oryx Advertising Co. WLL [Vol 2: 5435]

Osterreichische Computer Gesellschaft [Vol 2: 1204]

Osterreichische Gesellschaft fuer Neurowissenschaften [Vol 2: 1207]

Osterreichische Gesellschaft fur Geriatrie und Gerontologie [Vol 2: 1213]

Otolaryngology - Head and Neck Surgery; American Academy of [Vol 1: 641]

Otological Society; American [Vol 1: 3110]

Ottawa Field-Naturalists' Club [Vol 1: 13721]

Ottawa International Animation Festival [Vol 1: 13729]

Oulu International Children's and Youth Film Festival [Vol 2: 2120]

Outdoor Advertising Association of America [Vol 1: 13738]

Outdoor Industries Women's Coalition [Vol 1: 13742]

Outdoor Writers of Canada [Vol 1: 13745]

Outer Critics Circle [Vol 1: 13747]

Outward Bound [Vol 1: 13749]

Overseas Press Club of America [Vol 1: 13751]

Oxford Preservation Trust [Vol 2: 8439]

Oxford University Press [Vol 1: 822]

Oxygen Transport to Tissue; International Society on [Vol 2: 3094]

Pace University [Vol 2: 3059]

Pacific Area Newspaper Publishers' Association [Vol 2: 921]

Pacific Association of Quantity Surveyors [Vol 2: 4552]

Pacific Science Association [Vol 1: 13771]

Pacific Sociological Association [Vol 1: 13774]

Packaging Council of New Zealand [Vol 2: 5028]

Packard Automobile Classics [Vol 1: 13779]

Packt Publishing Ltd. [Vol 2: 8441]

Paddy and Water Environment Engineering; International Society of [Vol 2: 4245]

Paediatric Endocrinology; European Society for [Vol 2: 7636]

PAGE International Screenwriting Awards [Vol 1: 13790]

Paine National Historical Association; Thomas [Vol 1: 13792]

Painting and Decorating Contractors of America [Vol 1: 13794]

Pakistan Academy of Sciences [Vol 2: 5187]

Pakistan Advertising Association [Vol 2: 5196]

Pakistan Society of Cardiovascular and Thoracic Surgeons [Vol 2: 5198]

Palaeontological Association [Vol 2: 8443]

Palanca Foundation; Carlos [Vol 2: 5349]

Paleontological Research Institution [Vol 1: 13798]

Paleontological Society [Vol 1: 13803]

Paleontological Society - Germany [Vol 2: 3145]

Palliative Care; European Association for [Vol 2: 7592]

Palliative Care Organization; National Hospice and [Vol 1: 12526]

Palme Memorial Fund for International Understanding and Common Security; Olof [Vol 2: 6160]

Palomino Horse Breeders of America [Vol 1: 13807]

Pambansang Komisyon para sa Kultura at mga Sining [Vol 2: 5338]

Pambansang Sanggunian sa Pananaliksik ng Pilipinas [Vol 2: 5343]

Pan-American Association of Educational Credit Institutions [Vol 1: 1848]

Pan-American Association of Ophthalmology [Vol 1: 13812]

Pan American Health and Education Foundation [Vol 1: 13814]

Pan Arab Web Awards Academy [Vol 2: 4450]

Panamerican Cultural Circle [Vol 1: 13819]

Pantheist Society; Universal [Vol 1: 17171]

Pantheon de l'Aviation de Canada [Vol 1: 6148]

Pantheon des Sports Canadiens [Vol 1: 6157]

Papanicolaou Society of Cytopathology [Vol 1: 13822]

Paper Industry Management Association [Vol 1: 13826]

Paper Industry Technical Association [Vol 2: 8448]

Parachute Industry Association [Vol 1: 13833]

PARADE [Vol 1: 9642]

Paralyzed Veterans of America [Vol 1: 13839]

Parapsychological Association [Vol 1: 13845]

Parapsychology Foundation [Vol 1: 13850]

Parasitological Society of Southern Africa [Vol 2: 5589]

Parasitologiese Vereniging van Suidelike Afrika [Vol 2: 5589]

Parent Cooperative Preschools International [Vol 1: 13853]

Parenthood Federation; International Planned [Vol 2: 8160]

Parenthood Federation of America; Planned [Vol 1: 14027]

Parents' Choice Foundation [Vol 1: 13858]

Parents' Section of the Alexander Graham Bell Association for the Deaf and Hard of Hearing [Vol 1: 13860]

Parents Without Partners [Vol 1: 13866]

The Paris Review [Vol 1: 13868]

Park Centre for Mental Health Treatment, Research and Education - Queensland Centre for Mental Health Research [Vol 2: 924]

Parker Harris Partnership [Vol 2: 8450]

Parkinson Disease Association; American [Vol 1: 3121]

Partitioning and Interiors Association [Vol 2: 6826]

Partitioning Industry Association [Vol 2: 6826]

Pascher + Heinz GmbH [Vol 2: 3149]

Pathological Society of Great Britain and Ireland [Vol 2: 8458]

Pathologists; American Association of Avian [Vol 1: 1040]

Pathology; American Society for Investigative - International Society for Biological and Environmental Repositories [Vol 1: 3961]

Pathology; United States and Canadian Academy of [Vol 1: 16701]

Patinage de Vitesse Canada [Vol 1: 16138]

PC World Communications Inc. [Vol 1: 13872]

Peace and Sport [Vol 2: 4608]

Peace History Society [Vol 1: 13875]

Peace Science Society International [Vol 1: 13877]

Pediatric AIDS Foundation [Vol 1: 13881]

Pediatric Dermatology; Society for [Vol 1: 15239]

Pediatric Endocrinology Nursing Society [Vol 1: 13884]

Pediatric Nurse Practitioners; National Association of [Vol 1: 11822]
Pediatric Nurses; Society of [Vol 1: 15740]
Pediatric Pathology; Society for [Vol 1: 15243]
Pediatric Radiology; Society for [Vol 1: 15250]
Pediatrics; American Academy of [Vol 1: 651]
Pediatrics and Adolescent Medicine; German Society of [Vol 2: 3020]
PEN American Center [Vol 1: 13890]
PEN Center USA [Vol 1: 13904]
PEN Club Italiano [Vol 2: 4138]
PEN/Faulkner Foundation [Vol 1: 13906]
PEN New England [Vol 1: 13908]
PEN New Zealand, Inc. [Vol 2: 5009]
Pennsylvania Science Teachers Association [Vol 1: 13911]
Pennsylvania State Education Association [Vol 1: 13915]
Pennsylvania State Nurses Association [Vol 1: 13924]
Pennsylvania State University - College of Communications [Vol 1: 13929]
Pennsylvania State University - Institute for the Study of Business Markets [Vol 1: 13931]
Pennsylvania State University - Kienle Center for Humanistic Medicine; Doctors [Vol 1: 13933]
Pensions Management Institute [Vol 2: 8461]
Penton Media, Inc. - *Restaurant Hospitality* [Vol 1: 13937]
People for the Ethical Treatment of Animals [Vol 1: 13939]
People to People International [Vol 1: 13941]
Pera [Vol 2: 7370]
Performance Warehouse Association [Vol 1: 13943]
Performing Right Society [Vol 2: 8466]
Periodical Publishers Association [Vol 2: 8514]
Permanent Court of Arbitration [Vol 2: 4803]
Persatuan Dermatologi Malaysia [Vol 2: 4537]
Persatuan Komputer Brunei Darussalam [Vol 2: 1774]
Personality Psychology; European Association of [Vol 2: 2808]
Personnel Today [Vol 2: 8468]
Peruvian Association for Conservation of Nature [Vol 2: 5317]
Peruvian Paso Horse Registry of North America [Vol 1: 13324]
The Pesticide Stewardship Alliance [Vol 1: 13947]
Petroleum and Minerals; King Fahd University of - Center for Environment and Water [Vol 2: 5903]
Petroleum; Canadian Institute of Mining, Metallurgy, and [Vol 1: 6599]
Petroleum Engineers; American Institute of Mining, Metallurgical, and [Vol 1: 2672]
Petroleum Engineers; Society of [Vol 1: 15748]
Petroleum Geologists; American Association of [Vol 1: 1265]
Petroleum Geologists; Canadian Society of [Vol 1: 6978]
Petroleum Production and Exploration Association; Australian [Vol 2: 493]
Petroleum Retailers and Allied Trades; Service Station Dealers of America/National Coalition of [Vol 1: 14842]
Pezcoller Foundation [Vol 2: 4148]
Pfizer Animal Health [Vol 2: 1168]
Pfizer Canada Inc. [Vol 1: 6930]
Pfizer Inc. [Vol 1: 6928, 8954, 9229]
Pharmaceutical and Healthcare Sciences Society [Vol 2: 8470]
Pharmaceutical Federation; International [Vol 2: 4753]
Pharmaceutical Manufacturers Association [Vol 1: 13950]
Pharmaceutical Research and Manufacturers of America [Vol 1: 13950]
Pharmaceutical Sciences; European Federation for [Vol 2: 6139]
Pharmaceutical Society of Australia [Vol 2: 926]
Pharmaceutical Society of Japan [Vol 2: 4308]
Pharmaceutical Society of South Africa [Vol 2: 5592]
Pharmacists; Canadian Society of Hospital [Vol 1: 6948]
Pharmacists; European Association of Hospital [Vol 2: 1441]

Pharmacology; American College of Clinical [Vol 1: 1716]
Phi Alpha Theta [Vol 1: 13952]
Phi Beta Kappa [Vol 1: 13961]
Phi Chi Pharmacy Fraternity [Vol 1: 13968]
Phi Delta Chi [Vol 1: 13968]
Phi Delta Phi International Legal Fraternity [Vol 1: 13970]
Phi Kappa Phi [Vol 1: 13975]
Phi Lambda Upsilon [Vol 1: 13978]
Phi Tau Sigma [Vol 1: 9335]
Phi Theta Kappa, International Honor Society [Vol 1: 13981]
Phi Upsilon Omicron [Vol 1: 13983]
Philanthropic Service for Institutions [Vol 1: 13988]
Philippine Association of the Record Industry [Vol 2: 5352]
Philippine Society of Anesthesiologists [Vol 2: 5354]
Philippines Department of Science and Technology - National Academy of Science and Technology [Vol 2: 5356]
Philological Association; American [Vol 1: 3167]
Philosophical Society; American [Vol 1: 3182]
Phoenix House [Vol 1: 13990]
Phoenix House Foundation [Vol 1: 13990]
Photo Imaging Council [Vol 2: 8472]
Photobiology; American Society for [Vol 1: 4038]
Photogrammetry and Remote Sensing; International Society for [Vol 2: 5292]
Photographers Association; National Press [Vol 1: 12696]
Photographic Society of Great Britain; Royal [Vol 2: 8894]
Phycological Society of America [Vol 1: 13992]
Phycology; International Society for Applied [Vol 2: 4106]
Physical and Health Education Canada [Vol 1: 13996]
Physical Society of Berlin [Vol 2: 3151]
Physical Therapy Association; American [Vol 1: 3228]
Physician Specialists; American Association of [Vol 1: 1299]
Physicians; American Academy of Family [Vol 1: 544]
Physicians and Surgeons of Canada; Royal College of [Vol 1: 14627]
Physicians and Surgeons of Glasgow; Royal College of [Vol 2: 8698]
Physics; Abdus Salam International Centre for Theoretical [Vol 2: 4008]
Physics; American Institute of [Vol 1: 2682]
Physics Association; Indian [Vol 2: 3680]
Physics; Australian Institute of [Vol 2: 406]
Physics; Institute of [Vol 2: 7898]
Physiological Society; Australian [Vol 2: 499]
Physiological Society of New Zealand [Vol 2: 5030]
Phytochemical Society of Europe [Vol 2: 8474]
Phytopathological Society of Japan [Vol 2: 4314]
Pi Kappa Phi [Vol 1: 13998]
Pi Lambda Theta [Vol 1: 14002]
Piano Technicians Guild [Vol 1: 14008]
Pickerington Area Chamber of Commerce [Vol 1: 14012]
Pierce-Arrow Society [Vol 1: 14016]
Pigment Cell Societies; International Federation of [Vol 2: 3767]
Pilots and Air Navigators; Guild of Air [Vol 2: 7752]
Pilots' Association; British Women [Vol 2: 7301]
Pilots; Society of Experimental Test [Vol 1: 15640]
Pilsner Urquell International Photography Awards [Vol 1: 14019]
Pitch and Putt Union of Ireland [Vol 2: 3901]
Pittaluga Premio Citta' di Alessandria; Concorso Internazionale di Chitarra Classica Michele [Vol 2: 4150]
Pittsburgh Conference on Analytical Chemistry and Applied Spectroscopy [Vol 1: 7200]
Pittsburgh New Music Ensemble [Vol 1: 14021]
Pixel Awards [Vol 1: 14023]
Plain English Campaign [Vol 2: 8476]
Planck Society; Max [Vol 2: 3231]
Planetary Society [Vol 1: 14025]
Planned Parenthood Federation; International [Vol 2: 8160]

Planned Parenthood Federation of America [Vol 1: 14027]
Planners; International Society of City and Regional [Vol 2: 4779]
Plant Engineering and Maintenance Association of Canada [Vol 1: 14030]
Plant Growth Regulation Society of America [Vol 1: 14032]
Plastic and Reconstructive Surgery; American Academy of Facial [Vol 1: 533]
Plastic Surgeons; American Association of [Vol 1: 1314]
Plastic Surgeons; European Association of [Vol 2: 4685]
Plastic Surgery Educational Foundation [Vol 1: 14035]
Plastic Surgery Foundation [Vol 1: 14035]
Plastics Academy [Vol 1: 14039]
Plastics Engineers; Society of [Vol 1: 15782]
Play Therapy International [Vol 2: 8484]
Playboy [Vol 1: 14041]
Playboy Foundation [Vol 1: 14043]
Players Inc. [Vol 1: 13250]
Playmarket [Vol 2: 5033]
Playwrights' Center [Vol 1: 14045]
Playwrights' Studio, Scotland [Vol 2: 8486]
PMNETwork [Vol 1: 14259]
Poetry [Vol 1: 14048]
The Poetry Center [Vol 1: 14055]
The Poetry Center & American Poetry Archives [Vol 1: 14055]
Poetry Foundation [Vol 1: 14052, 14053]
Poetry International Foundation [Vol 2: 4805]
Poetry Societies; National Federation of State [Vol 1: 12341]
Poetry Society [Vol 2: 8488]
Poetry Society of America [Vol 1: 14057]
Point-of-Purchase Advertising International [Vol 1: 14070]
Points of Light Foundation [Vol 1: 14072]
Points of Light Volunteer Organization [Vol 1: 14072]
Poison Control Centers; American Association of [Vol 1: 1319]
Polar Music Prize Committee [Vol 2: 6163]
Police Federation of England and Wales [Vol 2: 8491]
Polish American Historical Association [Vol 1: 14077]
Polish Chemical Society [Vol 2: 5391]
Polish Composers Union [Vol 2: 5400]
Polish Genealogical Society of America [Vol 1: 14080]
Polish Institute of Arts and Sciences of America [Vol 1: 14083]
Polish Physical Society [Vol 2: 5403]
Polish Society of Veterinary Science [Vol 2: 5412]
Polisher Research Institute [Vol 1: 8633]
Political Studies Association [Vol 2: 8493]
Politzer Society - International Society for Otological Surgery [Vol 2: 8495]
Polskie Towarzystwo Chemiczne [Vol 2: 5391]
Polskie Towarzystwo Fizyczne [Vol 2: 5403]
Polskie Towarzystwo Nauk Weterynaryjnych [Vol 2: 5412]
Polymers; Cooperative Research Centre for [Vol 2: 672]
Pompidou Group [Vol 2: 2350]
Pony Club [Vol 2: 8497]
Population Association of America [Vol 1: 14087]
Population Institute [Vol 1: 14091]
Portland Opera [Vol 1: 14093]
Portland State University - Institute on Aging [Vol 1: 14095]
Post Card and Souvenir Distributors Association [Vol 1: 16059]
Post-Polio Health International [Vol 1: 14097]
Postal History Society [Vol 1: 14099]
Postal History Society of Canada [Vol 1: 14103]
Postpartum Support International [Vol 1: 14106]
Poultry Science Association [Vol 1: 2128]
Poultry Science Association [Vol 1: 14108]
Pound-American Trial Lawyers Foundation; Roscoe [Vol 1: 14118]
Pound Civil Justice Institute [Vol 1: 14118]
Pound Foundation; Roscoe [Vol 1: 14118]
Powerhouse Museum [Vol 2: 930]
Practical Builder [Vol 1: 14190]

Royal Society of South Australia [Vol 2: 1011]
Royal Society of Tropical Medicine and Hygiene [Vol 2: 9113]
Royal Society of Victoria [Vol 2: 1016]
Royal Society of Western Australia [Vol 2: 1018]
Royal Society of Wildlife Trusts [Vol 2: 9123]
Royal Swedish Academy of Engineering Sciences [Vol 2: 6175]
Royal Swedish Academy of Music [Vol 2: 6185]
Royal Swedish Academy of Sciences [Vol 2: 6181]
Royal Television Society [Vol 2: 9126]
Royal Town Planning Institute [Vol 2: 9133]
Royal United Services Institute for Defence and Security Studies [Vol 2: 9136]
Royal University of Bhutan - Sherubtse College [Vol 2: 1717]
Royal Western Australian Historical Society [Vol 2: 1020]
Royal Zoological Society of New South Wales [Vol 2: 1023]
Royce Society; Josiah [Vol 1: 14650]
RTCA [Vol 1: 14653]
Rudder Memorial Fund; William [Vol 2: 6458]
Rugby League International Federation [Vol 2: 1025]
Rugby Union Players' Association [Vol 2: 1032]
Rumi Forum [Vol 1: 14655]
Runyon - Walter Winchell Cancer Fund; Damon [Vol 1: 7805]
Rural Doctors Association of Southern Africa [Vol 2: 5608]
Rural Sociological Society [Vol 1: 14657]
Rural Youth Europe [Vol 2: 2123]
Russian Academy of Sciences [Vol 2: 5781]
Russian Academy of Sciences - Section of Social Science [Vol 2: 5880]
Russian Council of Shopping Centers [Vol 2: 5882]
Russian PEN Club [Vol 2: 3206]
Rutgers University - National Center for Public Productivity [Vol 1: 14663]
Rwanda Development Board [Vol 2: 5888]
Sailing Federation; International [Vol 2: 8176]
Saint Bernard Club of America [Vol 1: 14665]
St. Bonaventure University - Russell J. Jandoli School of Journalism and Mass Communication [Vol 1: 14668]
St. Cecilia Society [Vol 1: 14673]
St. Kilda Film Festival [Vol 2: 1035]
Saint Louis University [Vol 1: 14675]
St. Lucia Music Awards [Vol 2: 5898]
St. Maarten Hospitality and Trade Association [Vol 2: 4852]
Sakura Finetek USA, Inc. [Vol 1: 12857]
Sakura Finetek U.S.A. Inc. [Vol 1: 12860]
Sales and Marketing Executives International [Vol 1: 14680]
Sales Professionals USA [Vol 1: 14690]
Sallie Mae Fund [Vol 1: 14692]
Salon du Livre de l'Estrie [Vol 1: 14697]
Salters' Institute [Vol 2: 9140]
Saltire Society [Vol 2: 9147]
Samoa Association of Sport and National Olympic Committee [Vol 2: 9562]
San Angelo Symphony [Vol 1: 14699]
San Antonio International Piano Competition [Vol 1: 14701]
San Diego County Fair - Exhibits Department [Vol 1: 14705]
San Francisco Film Society [Vol 1: 14707]
The San Francisco Foundation [Vol 1: 14709]
San Jose State University - Department of English and Comparative Literature [Vol 1: 14714]
San Remo Municipality [Vol 2: 4044]
San Sebastian International Film Festival [Vol 2: 6093]
Sanlam Life Insurance Ltd. [Vol 2: 5610]
sanofi-aventis [Vol 1: 3986]
Sao Paulo International Film Festival [Vol 2: 1767]
Sarajevo Film Festival [Vol 2: 1727]
SAS Institute Inc. [Vol 1: 14716]
Saskatchewan Library Association [Vol 1: 14718]
Saskatchewan Music Festival Association [Vol 1: 14721]
Saskatchewan Natural History Society [Vol 1: 13110]
Sauve Qui Peut le Court Metrage [Vol 2: 2601]
Save the Children Fiji [Vol 2: 2065]
Save the Frogs! [Vol 1: 14763]

Scandinavian Collectors Club [Vol 1: 14766]
Scandinavian Society for the Study of Diabetes [Vol 2: 1984]
Scarab Club [Vol 1: 14771]
Schenectady Museum Association [Vol 1: 14773]
Schering-Plough Animal Health [Vol 1: 7030]
Schizophrenias and Other Psychoses; International Society for the Psychological Treatments of the [Vol 2: 3291]
School Library Media Specialists of Southeastern New York [Vol 1: 14775]
School Nutrition Association [Vol 1: 14777]
Schumann Society Zwickau e.V.; Robert [Vol 2: 3155]
Schwartz Foundation; Ruth [Vol 1: 13571]
Schweighofer Privatstiftung Beteiligungsverwaltung GmbH [Vol 2: 1316]
Schweizer Musikedition [Vol 2: 6505]
Schweizerische Akademie der Medizinischen Wissenschaften [Vol 2: 6480]
Schweizerische Chemische Gesellschaft [Vol 2: 6485]
Schweizerische Gesellschaft fur Infektiologie [Vol 2: 6509]
Schweizerische Gesellschaft fur Theaterkultur [Vol 2: 6483]
Schweizerischer Elektrotechnischer Verein [Vol 2: 6492]
Science Academy; Indian National [Vol 2: 3618]
Science; American Association for the Advancement of [Vol 1: 982]
Science and Technology Foundation of Japan [Vol 2: 4319]
Science Association; American Dairy [Vol 1: 1965]
Science Congress Association; Indian [Vol 2: 3706]
Science Council of Japan [Vol 1: 13773]
Science, Education and Sports; Republic of Croatia Ministry of [Vol 2: 1874]
Science Fiction and Fantasy Writers of America [Vol 1: 14783]
Science Fiction Foundation [Vol 2: 9158]
Science Fiction Research Association [Vol 1: 14787]
Science Fiction Writers of America [Vol 1: 14783]
Science Foundation; National [Vol 1: 12811]
Science Service [Vol 1: 15303]
Science Teachers Association; National [Vol 1: 12818]
Science Teachers Association of Nigeria [Vol 2: 5101]
Sciences; American Academy of Arts and [Vol 1: 492]
Sciences; National Academy of - Institute of Medicine [Vol 1: 11419]
Scientific and Technical Research Council of Turkey [Vol 2: 6634]
Scientific Research Society of America [Vol 1: 14904]
Scientometrics and Informetrics; International Society for [Vol 2: 1552]
Scleroderma Foundation [Vol 1: 14790]
Scottish Arts Council [Vol 2: 7486]
Scottish Committee of Optometrists [Vol 2: 6677]
Scottish Ecological Design Association [Vol 2: 9160]
Scottish Engineering [Vol 2: 9163]
Scottish Federation of Meat Traders Association [Vol 2: 9166]
Scottish International Piano Competition [Vol 2: 9168]
Scottish Joint Industry Board for the Electrical Contracting Industry [Vol 2: 9170]
Scottish Motor Neurone Disease Association [Vol 2: 8365]
Scottish Photographic Federation [Vol 2: 9172]
Scottish Screen [Vol 2: 7486]
Scottish Studies Program/Scottish Studies Foundation [Vol 1: 14794]
Scouting Ireland CSI [Vol 2: 3931]
Screen Actors Guild [Vol 1: 14797]
Scribes, the American Society of Legal Writers [Vol 1: 14800]
SDR Clinical Technology [Vol 2: 503]
SDX Foundation [Vol 1: 15808]
Sea Grant Association [Vol 1: 14804]
Sea Grant College Program; Michigan [Vol 1: 11120]
Sea Grant Consortium; Mississippi-Alabama [Vol 1: 11216]

Sea Turtle Conservancy [Vol 1: 14806]
Seafarers' Welfare; International Committee on [Vol 2: 8104]
Search for Common Ground [Vol 1: 14809]
Seatrade Communications Ltd. [Vol 2: 9174]
Seattle Art Museum [Vol 1: 14812]
Seattle International Film Festival [Vol 1: 14814]
SECO: Technical Control Bureau for Construction [Vol 2: 1657]
Secondary School Admission Test Board [Vol 1: 14818]
Section for Women in Public Administration [Vol 1: 14820]
Securities and Insurance Licensing Association [Vol 1: 14824]
Securities Investors Association - Singapore [Vol 2: 5965]
Security Equipment Industry Association [Vol 1: 14831]
Security Industry Association [Vol 1: 14831]
SEED Initiative [Vol 2: 4391]
Seismological Society of America [Vol 1: 14833]
Seismological Society of Japan [Vol 2: 4321]
Semaine du commerce equitable [Vol 2: 1418]
SEMI International [Vol 1: 14838]
Semiconductor Equipment and Materials Institute [Vol 1: 14838]
Semiconductor Equipment and Materials International [Vol 1: 14838]
Seminar on the Acquisition of Latin American Library Materials [Vol 1: 14840]
Service Station Dealers of America/National Coalition of Petroleum Retailers and Allied Trades [Vol 1: 14842]
Servier Laboratories Australia [Vol 2: 704]
Seventh Day Baptist Historical Society [Vol 1: 14846]
Sheikh Hamdan Bin Rashid Award for Medical Sciences [Vol 2: 6665]
Shell Canada, Ltd. [Vol 1: 6969]
Shell Oil Co. [Vol 1: 12827]
Shiras Institute [Vol 1: 8438]
Shirika la Utafiti na Maendeleo va Viwanda, Tanzania [Vol 2: 9522]
Shoman Foundation; Abdul Hameed [Vol 2: 4363]
Shoqata Shqiptare e Shkencave Politike [Vol 2: 3]
Shoraye Ketabe Koodak [Vol 2: 3823]
Shreveport Civic Opera [Vol 1: 14850]
Shreveport Opera Company [Vol 1: 14850]
Shwachman-Diamond Syndrome Canada [Vol 1: 14852]
Sibelius Academy [Vol 2: 2125]
Sibelius Society of Finland [Vol 2: 2126]
Sidewise Awards for Alternate History [Vol 1: 14854]
Siemens AG [Vol 2: 2779]
Siemens Healthcare Diagnostics [Vol 2: 6758]
Siemens Medical Solutions Diagnostics Ltd. [Vol 2: 6759]
Sierra Club [Vol 1: 14856]
Sigma Alpha Iota Foundation [Vol 1: 14883]
Sigma Alpha Iota International Music Fraternity [Vol 1: 14883]
Sigma Delta Chi [Vol 1: 15812]
Sigma Delta Epsilon, Graduate Women in Science [Vol 1: 14885]
Sigma Diagnostics Inc. [Vol 1: 12860]
Sigma Gamma Tau [Vol 1: 14889]
Sigma Iota Epsilon [Vol 1: 14891]
Sigma Theta Tau International [Vol 1: 14893]
Sigma Xi [Vol 1: 14904]
Sigma Xi, The Scientific Research Society [Vol 1: 14904]
SIGNIS, World Catholic Association for Communication [Vol 2: 1660]
Sikorsky Aircraft [Vol 1: 8896]
Simon Fraser University - Office of Vice President, Research [Vol 1: 14908]
Simulation International; Society for Modeling and [Vol 1: 15230]
Singapore Association of Administrative Professionals [Vol 2: 5970]
Singapore Exhibition Services Pte. Ltd. [Vol 2: 5972]
Singapore Industrial Automation Association [Vol 2: 5974]
Singapore Infocomm Technology Federation [Vol 2: 5976]

Singapore Institute of Food Science and Technology **[Vol 2: 5978]**

Singapore National Olympic Council **[Vol 2: 5982]**

Singapore Psychological Society **[Vol 2: 5984]**

Singapore Retailers Association **[Vol 2: 5986]**

Single Service Institute **[Vol 1: 8401]**

Sir Henry Royce Memorial Foundation **[Vol 2: 9180]**

Sister Cities International **[Vol 1: 14910]**

Sister Kenny Rehabilitation Institute **[Vol 1: 14912]**

Site Global **[Vol 1: 14914]**

Sixteenth Century Society and Conference **[Vol 1: 14916]**

SJS Group (Oman) **[Vol 2: 5176]**

Skal, the International Association of Travel and Tourism Professionals **[Vol 2: 6095]**

Ski and Snowboard Association; United States **[Vol 1: 17067]**

SkillsUSA **[Vol 1: 14923]**

Skytrax Research **[Vol 2: 9182]**

Sloan Consortium **[Vol 1: 14926]**

Slobodna Dalmacija **[Vol 2: 1867]**

Slocum Society International; Joshua **[Vol 1: 14930]**

Slovenia Ministry of Higher Education, Science and Technology - Metrology Institute of the Republic of Slovenia **[Vol 2: 6010]**

Small Business Council of America **[Vol 1: 14937]**

SME Education Foundation **[Vol 1: 14941]**

Smith Breeden Associates Inc. **[Vol 1: 2142]**

Smith Memorial Fund; Merriman **[Vol 1: 17806]**

Smithsonian American Art Museum **[Vol 1: 14963]**

Smithsonian Institution - Smithsonian Women's Committee **[Vol 1: 14965]**

Snow Inc.; John **[Vol 1: 8678]**

Snowboard Association; United States Ski and **[Vol 1: 17067]**

Soaring Society of America **[Vol 1: 14967]**

SOCAN Foundation **[Vol 1: 14980]**

Social Issues Resources Series Inc. **[Vol 1: 10886, 13368]**

Social Research Association **[Vol 2: 9185]**

Social Science Research Council **[Vol 1: 14987]**

Social Studies; International Society for the **[Vol 1: 10245]**

Social Workers; International Federation of **[Vol 2: 6379]**

Sociedad Anatomica Espanola **[Vol 2: 6105]**

Sociedad Argentina de Estudios Geograficos **[Vol 2: 43]**

Sociedad Espanola de Quimica Industrial **[Vol 2: 2826]**

Sociedad Espanola para el Estudio de la Obesidad **[Vol 2: 6097]**

Sociedad Interamericana de Cardiologia **[Vol 2: 4586]**

Sociedad Interamericana de Prensa **[Vol 1: 9440]**

Sociedad Internacional de Bioetica **[Vol 2: 6070]**

Sociedad Quimica de Mexico **[Vol 2: 4580]**

Sociedade Brasileira de Bioquimica e Biologia Molecular **[Vol 2: 1758]**

Societa Chimica Italiana **[Vol 2: 4124]**

Societa Geologica Italiana **[Vol 2: 4129]**

Societa Italiana di Farmacologia **[Vol 2: 4140]**

Societas Europaea Anatomorum Veterinariorum **[Vol 2: 4062]**

Societas Internationalis Aerosolibus in Medicina **[Vol 2: 3077]**

Societas Scientiarum Fennica **[Vol 2: 2102]**

Societe Alzheimer du Canada **[Vol 1: 434]**

Societe Astronomique de France **[Vol 2: 2604]**

Societe Canadienne d'Astronomie **[Vol 1: 6313]**

Societe Canadienne de Cardiologie **[Vol 1: 6391]**

Societe canadienne de chimie **[Vol 1: 6884]**

Societe Canadienne de Fertilite et d'Andrologie **[Vol 1: 6490]**

Societe Canadienne de Genie Civil **[Vol 1: 6897]**

Societe Canadienne de Genie Mecanique **[Vol 1: 6911]**

Societe Canadienne de Geotechnique **[Vol 1: 6525]**

Societe Canadienne de la Sclerose en Plaques **[Vol 1: 11295]**

Societe Canadienne de l'Hemophilie **[Vol 1: 6553]**

Societe canadienne de medecine interne **[Vol 1: 6960]**

Societe Canadienne de Meteorologie et d'Oceanographique **[Vol 1: 6707]**

Societe Canadienne de Neurochirurgie **[Vol 1: 6739]**

Societe Canadienne de Nutrition **[Vol 1: 6754]**

Societe Canadienne de Pediatrie **[Vol 1: 6767]**

Societe Canadienne de Phytopathologie **[Vol 1: 6793]**

Societe Canadienne de Psychologie **[Vol 1: 6820]**

Societe Canadienne de Recherche Operationnelle **[Vol 1: 6762]**

Societe Canadienne de Science animale **[Vol 1: 6924]**

Societe canadienne de technologie chimique **[Vol 1: 6882]**

Societe Canadienne de Teledetection **[Vol 1: 6856]**

Societe Canadienne de Zoologie **[Vol 1: 6992]**

Societe Canadienne des Anesthesiologistes **[Vol 1: 6200]**

Societe canadienne des auteurs, compositeurs, et editeurs de musique **[Vol 1: 14980]**

Societe Canadienne des Directeurs d'Association **[Vol 1: 6931]**

Societe Canadienne des Directeurs de Clubs **[Vol 1: 6940]**

Societe Canadienne des Microbiologistes **[Vol 1: 6975]**

Societe Canadienne des pharmaciens d'Hopitaux **[Vol 1: 6948]**

Societe Canadienne des Relations Publiques **[Vol 1: 6836]**

Societe Canadienne des Sciences du Cerveau, du Comportement et de la Cognition **[Vol 1: 6879]**

Societe Canadienne d'Ingenierie des Services de Sante **[Vol 1: 6551]**

Societe Canadienne pour la Formation et le Perfectionnement **[Vol 1: 6921]**

Societe Chimique de Belgique **[Vol 2: 1666]**

Societe de Biologie Experimentale **[Vol 2: 9195]**

Societe de Chimie Industrielle **[Vol 2: 2437]**

Societe de Chimie Industrielle, American Section **[Vol 1: 14989]**

Societe de Chimie Therapeutique **[Vol 2: 2619]**

Societe de Geologie Appliquee aux Gites Mineraux **[Vol 2: 1931]**

Societe de la medecine rurale du Canada **[Vol 1: 15827]**

Societe de Pathologie Exotique **[Vol 2: 2623]**

Societe d'Entomologie du Canada **[Vol 1: 8152]**

Societe des Auteurs, Compositeurs et Editeurs de Musique **[Vol 2: 2626]**

Societe des Auteurs et Compositeurs Dramatiques **[Vol 2: 2633]**

Societe des Indexateurs **[Vol 2: 9318]**

Societe des Ornithologistes du Canada **[Vol 1: 15579]**

Societe Europeenne pour la Chirurgie de L'Epaule et du Coude **[Vol 2: 2409]**

Societe Europeenne pour la Formation des Ingenieurs **[Vol 2: 1489]**

Societe Francaise de Chimie **[Vol 2: 2436]**

Societe Francaise de Metallurgie et de Materiaux **[Vol 2: 2450]**

Societe Genealogique Canadienne-Francaise **[Vol 1: 8467]**

Societe Geologique de France **[Vol 2: 2453]**

Societe Internationale de Chimiotherapie **[Vol 2: 8197]**

Societe Internationale de Chirurgie **[Vol 2: 6450]**

Societe Internationale de Chirurgie Orthopedique et de Traumatologie **[Vol 2: 1554]**

Societe Internationale de Mecanique des Roches **[Vol 2: 5432]**

Societe Internationale de Mecanique des Sols et de la Geotechnique **[Vol 2: 8193]**

Societe Internationale de Neurochimie **[Vol 2: 834]**

Societe Internationale de Neuropathologie **[Vol 2: 8215]**

Societe Internationale de Transfusion Sanguine **[Vol 2: 4774]**

Societe Internationale d'Oncologie Pediatrique **[Vol 2: 6447]**

Societe Nucleaire Canadienne **[Vol 1: 6743]**

Societe pour la nature et les parcs du Canada **[Vol 1: 6777]**

Societe Royale Belge des Electriciens **[Vol 2: 1663]**

Societe Royale de Chimie **[Vol 2: 1666]**

Societe Royale Du Canada **[Vol 1: 14634]**

Societe Saint-Jean-Baptiste de Montreal **[Vol 1: 14994]**

Societe statistique du Canada **[Vol 1: 16285]**

Societe Suisse de Radiodiffusion et Television et la Ville de Montreux **[Vol 2: 6478]**

Societe Universitaire Europeenne de Recherches Financieres **[Vol 2: 1238]**

Society; Center for the Study of Sport in **[Vol 1: 13402]**

Society for Academic Emergency Medicine **[Vol 1: 15004]**

Society for Adolescent Health and Medicine **[Vol 1: 15010]**

Society for Adolescent Medicine **[Vol 1: 15010]**

Society for American Archaeology **[Vol 1: 15017]**

Society for American Baseball Research **[Vol 1: 15024]**

Society for Applied Anthropology **[Vol 1: 15032]**

Society for Applied Microbiology **[Vol 2: 9187]**

Society for Applied Spectroscopy **[Vol 1: 15034]**

Society for Back Pain Research **[Vol 2: 6864]**

Society For Biomaterials **[Vol 1: 15044]**

Society for Biotechnology, Japan **[Vol 2: 4323]**

Society for Chemical Engineering and Biotechnology **[Vol 2: 3158]**

Society for Cinema and Media Studies **[Vol 1: 15048]**

Society for Developmental Biology **[Vol 1: 15051]**

Society for Drug Research **[Vol 2: 9198]**

Society for East Asian Anthropology **[Vol 1: 15055]**

Society for Ecological Restoration International **[Vol 1: 15059]**

Society for Economic Botany **[Vol 1: 15063]**

Society for Environmental Exploration **[Vol 2: 9192]**

Society for Epidemiologic Research **[Vol 1: 15067]**

Society for Ethnomusicology **[Vol 1: 15069]**

Society for Experimental Biology **[Vol 2: 9195]**

Society for Film Art in Tampere **[Vol 2: 2127]**

Society for French Historical Studies **[Vol 1: 15073]**

Society for Freshwater Science **[Vol 1: 15075]**

Society for Geology Applied to Mineral Deposits **[Vol 2: 1931]**

Society for Historians of American Foreign Relations **[Vol 1: 15080]**

Society for Historians of the Early American Republic **[Vol 1: 15085]**

Society for Historical Archaeology **[Vol 1: 15089]**

Society for History in the Federal Government **[Vol 1: 15094]**

Society for Human Resource Management **[Vol 1: 15100]**

Society for In Vitro Biology **[Vol 1: 15106]**

Society for Industrial and Applied Mathematics **[Vol 1: 15114]**

Society for Industrial and Organizational Psychology **[Vol 1: 15132]**

Society for Industrial Microbiology **[Vol 1: 15143]**

Society for Information Display **[Vol 1: 15148]**

Society for Integrative and Comparative Biology **[Vol 1: 15155]**

Society for International Hockey Research **[Vol 1: 15157]**

Society for Investigative Dermatology **[Vol 1: 15159]**

Society for Italian Historical Studies **[Vol 1: 15161]**

Society for Judgment and Decision Making **[Vol 1: 15164]**

Society for Leukocyte Biology **[Vol 1: 15167]**

Society for Marine Mammalogy **[Vol 1: 15170]**

Society for Marketing Professional Services **[Vol 1: 15178]**

Society for Maternal-Fetal Medicine **[Vol 1: 15181]**

Society for Medical Anthropology **[Vol 1: 15186]**

Society for Medical Decision Making **[Vol 1: 15191]**

Society for Medicinal Plant Research **[Vol 2: 3173]**

Society for Medicines Research **[Vol 2: 9198]**

Society for Medieval Archaeology **[Vol 2: 9200]**

Society for Military History **[Vol 1: 15196]**

Society for Mining, Metallurgy, and Exploration **[Vol 1: 15202]**

Society for Modeling and Simulation International **[Vol 1: 15230]**

Society for Neuroscience **[Vol 1: 15233]**

Society for Nondestructive Testing **[Vol 1: 3998]**

Society for Pediatric Dermatology **[Vol 1: 15239]**

Society for Pediatric Pathology **[Vol 1: 15243]**

Society for Pediatric Radiology **[Vol 1: 15250]**

Society for Pediatric Research **[Vol 1: 15254]**

Society for Personality and Social Psychology **[Vol 1: 15262]**

Society for Prevention Research [Vol 1: 15269]

Society for Psychological Anthropology [Vol 1: 15280]

Society for Public Health Education [Vol 1: 15285]

Society for Range Management [Vol 1: 15290]

Society for Research in Child Development [Vol 1: 15296]

Society for Research into Higher Education [Vol 2: 9205]

Society for Research into Hydrocephalus and Spina Bifida [Vol 2: 9207]

Society for Science and the Public [Vol 1: 15303]

Society for Screen-Based Learning [Vol 2: 7289]

Society for Sedimentary Geology [Vol 1: 15306]

Society for Sedimentary Geology - Great Lakes Section [Vol 1: 15317]

Society for Sex Therapy and Research [Vol 1: 15326]

Society for Social Studies of Science [Vol 1: 15328]

Society for Social Work and Research [Vol 1: 15333]

Society for Spinal Research [Vol 2: 3178]

Society for Technical Communication [Vol 1: 15340]

Society for the Advancement of American Philosophy [Vol 1: 15344]

Society for the Advancement of Anaesthesia in Dentistry [Vol 2: 9209]

Society for the History of Alchemy and Chemistry [Vol 2: 9212]

Society for the History of Natural History [Vol 2: 9214]

Society for the History of Technology [Vol 1: 15349]

Society for the Psychological Study of Social Issues [Vol 1: 15357]

Society for the Scientific Study of Reading [Vol 1: 15367]

Society for the Scientific Study of Sexuality [Vol 1: 15370]

Society for the Study of Addiction to Alcohol and Other Drugs [Vol 2: 9219]

Society for the Study of Architecture in Canada [Vol 1: 15372]

Society for the Study of Evolution [Vol 1: 15374]

Society for the Study of Human Biology [Vol 2: 9222]

Society for the Study of Midwestern Literature [Vol 1: 15376]

Society for the Study of Postpartum (Postnatal) Depression [Vol 1: 15380]

Society for the Study of Reproduction [Vol 1: 15383]

Society for the Study of Social Problems [Vol 1: 15390]

Society for the Study of Southern Literature [Vol 1: 15395]

Society for the Study of Symbolic Interaction [Vol 1: 15397]

Society for Theatre Research [Vol 2: 9224]

Society for Utopian Studies [Vol 1: 15401]

Society for Vascular Ultrasound [Vol 1: 15404]

Society of Academic and Research Surgery [Vol 2: 9227]

Society of Actuaries [Vol 1: 15409]

Society of Allied Weight Engineers [Vol 1: 15411]

Society of American Archivists [Vol 1: 15416]

Society of American Business Editors and Writers [Vol 1: 15429]

Society of American Florists [Vol 1: 15431]

Society of American Foresters [Vol 1: 15434]

Society of American Military Engineers [Vol 1: 15445]

Society of American Travel Writers Foundation [Vol 1: 15464]

Society of Animal Artists [Vol 1: 15466]

Society of Antiquaries of Scotland [Vol 2: 9230]

Society of Architectural Historians [Vol 1: 15473]

Society of Architectural Historians of Great Britain [Vol 2: 9237]

Society of Army Historical Research [Vol 2: 9242]

Society of Arts and Crafts [Vol 1: 15481]

Society of Authors - England [Vol 2: 9244]

Society of Automotive Engineers [Vol 1: 15484]

Society of Automotive Engineers - Australasia [Vol 2: 1037]

Society of Automotive Historians [Vol 1: 15547]

Society of Behavioral Medicine [Vol 1: 15554]

Society of Biological Chemists, India [Vol 2: 3779]

Society of Biological Psychiatry [Vol 1: 15559]

Society of Biology [Vol 2: 9262]

Society of Border Leicester Sheep Breeders [Vol 2: 9264]

Society of Broadcast Engineers [Vol 1: 15565]

Society of Building Science Educators [Vol 1: 15571]

Society of Cable Telecommunications Engineers [Vol 1: 15576]

Society of Cable Television Engineers [Vol 1: 15576]

Society of Canadian Ornithologists [Vol 1: 15579]

Society of Cardiovascular Anesthesiologists [Vol 1: 15582]

Society of Chemical Industry [Vol 2: 9266]

Society of Children's Book Writers [Vol 1: 15584]

Society of Children's Book Writers and Illustrators [Vol 1: 15584]

Society of Competitive Intelligence Professionals [Vol 1: 16296]

Society of Consulting Psychology [Vol 1: 15589]

Society of Cosmetic Chemists [Vol 1: 15595]

Society of Cosmetic Scientists [Vol 2: 9298]

Society of Critical Care Medicine [Vol 1: 15601]

Society of Czech Architects [Vol 2: 1936]

Society of Decorative Painters [Vol 1: 15610]

Society of Diagnostic Medical Sonography [Vol 1: 15613]

Society of Dramatic Authors and Composers [Vol 2: 2633]

Society of Dyers and Colourists - England [Vol 2: 9300]

Society of Economic Geologists [Vol 1: 15616]

Society of Environmental Toxicology and Chemistry [Vol 1: 15622]

Society of Experimental Social Psychology [Vol 1: 15635]

Society of Experimental Test Pilots [Vol 1: 15640]

Society of Exploration Geophysicists [Vol 1: 15644]

Society of Film and Television Arts [Vol 2: 6931]

Society of Fire Protection Engineers [Vol 1: 15652]

Society of Flight Test Engineers [Vol 1: 15656]

Society of Floristry [Vol 2: 9307]

Society of Food Hygiene and Technology [Vol 2: 9310]

Society of Forensic Toxicologists [Vol 1: 15659]

Society of Gastroenterology Nurses and Associates [Vol 1: 15661]

Society of General Internal Medicine [Vol 1: 15666]

Society of German Cooks [Vol 2: 3180]

Society of Glass and Ceramic Decorated Products [Vol 1: 15676]

Society of Glass Technology [Vol 2: 9313]

Society of Hospital Medicine [Vol 1: 15679]

Society of Hospital Pharmacists of Australia [Vol 2: 1039]

Society of Indexers [Vol 2: 9318]

Society of Indonesian Films [Vol 2: 3821]

Society of Leather Technologists and Chemists [Vol 2: 9321]

Society of London Theatre [Vol 2: 9323]

Society of Magazine Writers [Vol 1: 4355]

Society of Manufacturing Engineers [Vol 1: 15684]

Society of Medical Laboratory Technologists of South Africa [Vol 2: 5612]

Society of Mexican American Engineers and Scientists [Vol 1: 15695]

Society of Motion Picture and Television Engineers [Vol 1: 15697]

Society of Municipal Arborists [Vol 1: 15707]

Society of National Association Publications [Vol 1: 5190]

Society of Naval Architects and Marine Engineers [Vol 1: 15709]

Society of Nematologists [Vol 1: 15721]

Society of Netherlands Literature [Vol 2: 4837]

Society of Nuclear Medicine [Vol 1: 15727]

Society of Ornamental Turners [Vol 2: 9325]

Society of Packaging and Handling Engineers [Vol 1: 15398]

Society of Paper Money Collectors [Vol 1: 15733]

Society of Pediatric Nurses [Vol 1: 15740]

Society of Petroleum Engineers [Vol 1: 15748]

Society of Petroleum Engineers of the American Institute of Mining, Metallurgical and Petroleum Engineers [Vol 1: 15748]

Society of Petrophysicists and Well Log Analysts [Vol 1: 15767]

Society of Physics Students [Vol 1: 15772]

Society of Plastics Engineers [Vol 1: 15782]

Society of Procurement Officers in Local Government [Vol 2: 9331]

Society of Professional Engineers [Vol 2: 9333]

Society of Professional Journalists [Vol 1: 15792]

Society of Publication Designers [Vol 1: 15816]

Society of Reliability Engineers [Vol 1: 15818]

Society of Research Administrators [Vol 1: 15820]

Society of Rheology [Vol 1: 15825]

Society of Rural Physicians of Canada [Vol 1: 15827]

Society of Southwest Archivists [Vol 1: 15423]

Society of Surgical Oncology [Vol 1: 15830]

Society of Systematic Biologists [Vol 1: 15833]

Society of Systematic Zoology [Vol 1: 15833]

Society of Teachers of Speech and Drama [Vol 2: 9335]

Society of Technical Analysts [Vol 2: 9337]

Society of Technical Writers and Publishers [Vol 1: 15340]

Society of the Plastics Industry - Alliance of Plastics Processors [Vol 1: 15835]

Society of the Plastics Industry - Thermoforming Institute [Vol 1: 15838]

Society of the Silurians [Vol 1: 15840]

Society of Toxicology [Vol 1: 15842]

Society of Trauma Nurses [Vol 1: 15855]

Society of Tribologists and Lubrication Engineers [Vol 1: 15857]

Society of United States Air Force Flight Surgeons [Vol 1: 15865]

Society of U.S. Naval Flight Surgeons [Vol 1: 15868]

Society of University Surgeons [Vol 1: 15873]

Society of Vertebrate Paleontology [Vol 1: 15875]

Society of West End Theatre [Vol 2: 9323]

Society of Wetland Scientists [Vol 1: 15881]

Society of Wildlife Artists [Vol 2: 9340]

Society of Woman Geographers [Vol 1: 15891]

Society of Women Artists [Vol 2: 9343]

Society of Women Engineers [Vol 1: 15894]

Society of Women Writers - Victoria [Vol 2: 1041]

Society of Wood Science and Technology [Vol 1: 15902]

Sociologists' AIDS Network [Vol 1: 15907]

Sociologists for Women in Society [Vol 1: 15911]

Sociology of Sport; North American Society for the [Vol 1: 13347]

Software and Information Industry Association [Vol 1: 15918]

Soil and Water Conservation Society [Vol 1: 15920]

Soil Association [Vol 2: 9348]

Soil Conservation Society of America [Vol 1: 15920]

Soil Science Society of America [Vol 1: 15927]

Solar Energy Society of Canada [Vol 1: 15937]

SOLE - The International Society of Logistics [Vol 1: 15939]

Solid Waste Association of North America [Vol 1: 15946]

Solvent Extractors' Association of India [Vol 2: 3790]

Sonangol [Vol 2: 14]

Sondrio Festival, the International Festival of Documentary Films on Parks [Vol 2: 4152]

Sonnings Music Foundation; Leonie [Vol 2: 1992]

Sonnings Musikfond; Leonie [Vol 2: 1992]

Sons of the Republic of Texas [Vol 1: 15953]

Sony Ericsson WTA Tour [Vol 1: 15956]

Soroptimist International of the Americas [Vol 1: 15962]

Sousa Foundation; John Philip [Vol 1: 15965]

South African Academy for Science and Arts [Vol 2: 5625]

South African Association for Food Science and Technology [Vol 2: 5649]

South African Association for Learning and Educational Difficulties [Vol 2: 5655]

South African Association of Botanists [Vol 2: 5657]

South African Association of Competitive Intelligence Professionals [Vol 2: 5664]

South African Association of Consulting Engineers [Vol 2: 5534]

South African Association of Women Graduates [Vol 2: 5667]

South African Chemical Institute [Vol 2: 5673]

South African Council of Shopping Centres [Vol 2: 5682]

South African Department of Science and Technology [Vol 2: 5684]

South African Geophysical Association [Vol 2: 5688]

Organization Index

United States Department of Labor - Bureau of Labor Statistics [Vol 1: 16833]

United States Department of Labor - Office of Job Corps [Vol 1: 16835]

United States Department of Navy - U.S. Naval Observatory [Vol 1: 16839]

United States Department of State [Vol 1: 16842]

U.S. Department of the Interior [Vol 1: 16857]

United States Department of Transportation [Vol 1: 16862]

United States Department of Transportation - Federal Highway Administration [Vol 1: 16864]

United States Department of Veterans Affairs - Office of Research and Development [Vol 1: 16866]

United States Dressage Federation [Vol 1: 16870]

U.S. Energy Association [Vol 1: 16879]

United States Environmental Protection Agency [Vol 1: 16881]

U.S. Environmental Protection Agency - Office of Research and Development [Vol 1: 16903]

United States Fencing Coaches Association [Vol 1: 16905]

United States Figure Skating Association [Vol 1: 16908]

United States Fish and Wildlife Service - Federal Duck Stamp Program [Vol 1: 16911]

United States Forest Service - Fire and Aviation Management [Vol 1: 16913]

U.S. Forest Service - Northern Research Station [Vol 1: 16919]

U.S. Fund for UNICEF [Vol 1: 16921]

United States General Services Administration [Vol 1: 16925]

U.S. Geological Survey - Land Remote Sensing Program [Vol 1: 16929]

United States Golf Association [Vol 1: 16931]

United States Hang Gliding and Paragliding Association [Vol 1: 16941]

United States Harness Writers' Association [Vol 1: 16947]

United States House of Representatives - Committee on Financial Services [Vol 1: 16956]

United States Institute for Theatre Technology [Vol 1: 16958]

United States Institute of Peace [Vol 1: 16971]

United States Intercollegiate Lacrosse Association [Vol 1: 16975]

U.S. International Film and Video Festival [Vol 1: 16984]

U.S.-Israel Binational Science Foundation [Vol 2: 3995]

United States Jaycees [Vol 1: 16986]

U.S. Junior Chamber of Commerce [Vol 1: 16986]

United States Lacrosse Association, Women's Division [Vol 1: 16989]

United States Lawn Tennis Association [Vol 1: 17126]

U.S. Marine Corps Combat Correspondents Association [Vol 1: 16993]

United States Masters Swimming [Vol 1: 16996]

U.S. Metric Association [Vol 1: 17000]

U.S.-Mexico Border Health Association [Vol 1: 17002]

United States Mexico Chamber of Commerce [Vol 1: 17004]

United States Naval Institute [Vol 1: 17006]

United States of America Amateur Boxing Federation [Vol 1: 16697]

United States Office of Personnel Management [Vol 1: 17010]

United States Olympic Committee [Vol 1: 17013]

United States Orienteering Federation [Vol 1: 17018]

U.S. Pan Asian American Chamber of Commerce [Vol 1: 17020]

U.S. Particle Accelerator School [Vol 1: 17022]

United States Patent and Trademark Office [Vol 1: 17024]

United States Police Canine Association [Vol 1: 17026]

United States Professional Tennis Association [Vol 1: 17030]

U.S. Psychotronics Association [Vol 1: 17035]

United States Racquetball Association [Vol 1: 17039]

United States Rowing Association [Vol 1: 17043]

United States Sailing Association [Vol 1: 17048]

United States Ski and Snowboard Association [Vol 1: 17067]

United States Ski Association [Vol 1: 17067]

United States Ski Writers Association [Vol 1: 13334]

U.S. Small Business Administration [Vol 1: 17103]

United States Space Foundation [Vol 1: 17110]

United States Stamp Society [Vol 1: 17114]

United States Synchronized Swimming [Vol 1: 17119]

United States Tennis Association [Vol 1: 17126]

U.S. Travel Association [Vol 1: 17144]

United States Trotting Association [Vol 1: 17147]

United States Women's Curling Association [Vol 1: 17151]

U.S. Yacht Racing Union [Vol 1: 17048]

United States Youth Soccer Association [Vol 1: 17153]

United Synagogue of Conservative Judaism [Vol 1: 17164]

United Way of America [Vol 1: 17166]

Unity-and-Diversity World Council [Vol 1: 17169]

Universal Pantheist Society [Vol 1: 17171]

Universal Postal Union [Vol 2: 6516]

Universal Ship Cancellation Society [Vol 1: 17173]

Universidad del Valle [Vol 2: 1852]

Universitat Basel [Vol 2: 6518]

Universitat Karlsruhe (Technische Hochschule) [Vol 2: 3215]

Universite de Montreal; Centre de recherches mathematiques, [Vol 1: 17304]

Universite Libre de Bruxelles [Vol 2: 3060]

Universities Council on Water Resources [Vol 1: 17177]

Universities Federation for Animal Welfare [Vol 2: 9422]

University Aviation Association [Vol 1: 17180]

University Continuing Education Association [Vol 1: 17379]

University Council for Educational Administration [Vol 1: 17184]

The University Foundation [Vol 2: 1668]

University Mozarteum, Salzburg [Vol 2: 1318]

The University Museum [Vol 1: 17322]

University of Alabama at Birmingham - Department of Theatre [Vol 1: 17188]

University of Alberta - Perinatal Research Centre [Vol 1: 17190]

University of Alberta, Department of Chemical and Materials Engineering [Vol 1: 6969]

University of Arizona - Department of Journalism [Vol 1: 17192]

University of Arizona - Udall Center for Studies in Public Policy [Vol 1: 17194]

University of Basel [Vol 2: 6518]

University of California at Berkeley - Hastings Natural History Reservation [Vol 1: 17196]

University of California, Los Angeles - Anderson School of Management [Vol 1: 17198]

University of California, San Diego - California Sea Grant College Program [Vol 1: 17200]

University of Chicago - Cancer Research Center [Vol 1: 17203]

University of Chicago - Medical and Biological Sciences Alumni Association [Vol 1: 17205]

University of Chicago Alumni Association [Vol 1: 17208]

University of Chicago Medical Alumni Association [Vol 1: 17205]

University of Chicago Press [Vol 1: 17215]

University of Colorado - School of Journalism and Mass Communication [Vol 1: 17217]

University of Colorado at Boulder - Center of the American West [Vol 1: 17219]

University of Copenhagen [Vol 2: 1994]

University of Dayton - Office of Provost [Vol 1: 17227]

University of Edinburgh - Department of English Literature [Vol 2: 9425]

University of Florida - Brechner Center for Freedom of Information [Vol 1: 17229]

University of Florida - Florida Freedom of Information Clearinghouse [Vol 1: 17229]

University of Georgia - Artificial Intelligence Center [Vol 1: 17231]

University of Georgia - Department of Language and Literary Education [Vol 1: 17233]

University of Georgia - Grady College of Journalism and Mass Communication [Vol 1: 17236]

University of Georgia - Institute for African American Studies [Vol 1: 17239]

University of Georgia Press [Vol 1: 17241]

University of Guyana - Faculty of Agriculture and Forestry [Vol 2: 3342]

University of Hawaii [Vol 1: 4995]

University of Hawaii at Manoa - Center for Korean Studies [Vol 1: 17243]

University of Hawaii at Manoa - School of Communications [Vol 1: 17245]

University of Illinois at Urbana-Champaign - Agricultural Bioprocess Laboratory [Vol 1: 17247]

University of Illinois at Urbana-Champaign - College of Fine & Applied Arts [Vol 1: 17250]

University of Illinois at Urbana-Champaign - Graduate School of Library and Information Science [Vol 1: 17252]

University of Iowa - Obermann Center for Advanced Studies [Vol 1: 17254]

University of Karachi - Marine Reference Collection and Resource Center [Vol 2: 5200]

University of Kentucky - Appalachian Center [Vol 1: 17258]

University of Kentucky - Markey Cancer Center [Vol 1: 17260]

University of Liechtenstein - Graduate School [Vol 2: 4475]

University of Louisville - College of Education and Human Development [Vol 1: 17262]

University of Louisville - Labor-Management Center [Vol 1: 17265]

University of Louisville - Louisville Presbyterian Theological Seminary [Vol 1: 17267]

University of Louisville - School of Music [Vol 1: 17269]

University of Manitoba [Vol 1: 14612]

University of Manitoba - Manitoba Centre for Nursing and Health Research [Vol 1: 17271]

University of Maryland [Vol 1: 8638]

University of Maryland - College of Information Studies [Vol 1: 17273]

University of Maryland - Maryland Technology Enterprise Institute [Vol 1: 17275]

University of Massachusetts Press [Vol 1: 17278]

University of Melbourne - Assessment Research Centre [Vol 2: 1095]

University of Melbourne - Faculty of Arts [Vol 2: 1097]

University of Melbourne - Faculty of Science [Vol 2: 1100]

University of Melbourne - Faculty of Veterinary Science [Vol 2: 1161]

University of Michigan [Vol 1: 17280]

University of Michigan - Center for Afroamerican and African Studies [Vol 1: 17282]

University of Michigan Press [Vol 1: 17286]

University of Minnesota - Children's Literature Research Collections [Vol 1: 17288]

University of Minnesota - Office of the Senior Vice President for Academic Affairs and Provost [Vol 1: 17291]

University of Missouri-Columbia - School of Journalism [Vol 1: 17293]

University of Missouri—Kansas City - Midwest Center for Nonprofit Leadership [Vol 1: 17297]

University of Missouri - St. Louis - Center for International Studies [Vol 1: 17299]

University of Missouri—St. Louis - Center for Trauma Recovery [Vol 1: 17301]

University of Montreal [Vol 1: 14613]

University of Montreal - Mathematics Research Center [Vol 1: 17304]

University of Music and Dramatic Arts in Graz [Vol 2: 1320]

University of Nairobi [Vol 2: 4405]

University of New Mexico - Alliance for Transportation Research Institute [Vol 1: 17308]

University of New South Wales [Vol 2: 1170]

University of North Carolina at Chapel Hill - Institute for the Study of the Americas [Vol 1: 17312]

University of Notre Dame - News and Information [Vol 1: 17316]

University of Otago [Vol 2: 5083]

University of Ottawa - Human Rights Research and Education Centre **[Vol 1: 17319]**

University of Oxford - Faculty of Music **[Vol 2: 9427]**

University of Pennsylvania Museum of Archaeology and Anthropology **[Vol 1: 17322]**

University of Pittsburgh - Pymatuning Laboratory of Ecology **[Vol 1: 17325]**

University of Pittsburgh Press **[Vol 1: 17329]**

University of Rhode Island - Rhode Island Transportation Research Center **[Vol 1: 17332]**

University of Rochester - Philosophy Dept. **[Vol 1: 17334]**

University of Rochester - Susan B. Anthony Institute for Gender and Women's Studies **[Vol 1: 17336]**

University of Southern California - Annenberg School for Communication **[Vol 1: 17338]**

University of Southern California - College of Letters, Arts and Sciences **[Vol 1: 17340]**

University of Southern Mississippi - School of Library and Information Science **[Vol 1: 17342]**

University of Tasmania **[Vol 2: 787]**

University of Tennessee, Knoxville - Center of Excellence in Livestock Diseases and Human Health **[Vol 1: 17344]**

University of the Philippines Alumni Association **[Vol 2: 5371]**

University of Toronto - Institute for Life Course and Aging **[Vol 1: 17346]**

University of Toronto - Ontario Tobacco Research Unit **[Vol 1: 17351]**

University of Toronto - Pulp and Paper Centre **[Vol 1: 17353]**

University of Toronto - University College **[Vol 1: 17357]**

University of Virginia - Center for Russian and East European Studies **[Vol 1: 17359]**

University of Virginia - Center for South Asian Studies **[Vol 1: 17361]**

University of Wisconsin - Eau Claire Alumni Association **[Vol 1: 17363]**

University of Wisconsin - Platteville Alumni Association **[Vol 1: 17365]**

University of Wisconsin—Madison - Center for South Asia **[Vol 1: 17369]**

University of Wisconsin - Madison - Cooperative Children's Book Center **[Vol 1: 17371]**

University of Wisconsin—Madison - Institute on Aging **[Vol 1: 17373]**

University of Wisconsin - Milwaukee - Center for Latin American and Caribbean Studies **[Vol 1: 17375]**

University of Wisconsin Press **[Vol 1: 17377]**

University Professional & Continuing Education Association **[Vol 1: 17379]**

Uppsala International Short Film Festival **[Vol 2: 6244]**

Urban Affairs Association **[Vol 1: 17398]**

Urban Land Institute **[Vol 1: 17401]**

Urban League; National **[Vol 1: 13014]**

Urological Society of India **[Vol 2: 3804]**

Urology; European Association of **[Vol 2: 4689]**

Ursa Astronomical Association **[Vol 2: 2132]**

U.S.A. Badminton **[Vol 1: 17403]**

U.S.A. Baseball **[Vol 1: 17407]**

USA Cycling **[Vol 1: 17411]**

U.S.A. Deaf Sports Federation **[Vol 1: 17413]**

USA Diving **[Vol 1: 17416]**

USA Hockey **[Vol 1: 17418]**

USA International Ballet Competition **[Vol 1: 17432]**

USA International Harp Competition **[Vol 1: 17434]**

U.S.A. Swimming **[Vol 1: 17436]**

USA Today Sports Weekly **[Vol 1: 15030]**

U.S.A. Track and Field **[Vol 1: 17453]**

U.S.A. Triathlon **[Vol 1: 17481]**

U.S.A. Ultimate **[Vol 1: 17483]**

U.S.A. Wrestling **[Vol 1: 17486]**

Utah Association for Gifted Children **[Vol 1: 17494]**

Utah State University - Jon M. Huntsman School of Business **[Vol 1: 17499]**

Utility Communicators International **[Vol 1: 17502]**

Uzbekistan Teachers of English Association **[Vol 2: 9541]**

Valent BiosSiences **[Vol 1: 14034]**

Valley Players **[Vol 1: 17504]**

Van Alen Institute: Projects in Public Architecture **[Vol 1: 17506]**

Vancouver International Film Festival **[Vol 1: 17508]**

Vanderbilt University - Autonomic Dysfunction Center **[Vol 1: 17510]**

Vanuatu Tourism Office **[Vol 2: 9543]**

Varian Associates **[Vol 1: 5739]**

VARIAN Medical Systems **[Vol 2: 1501, 1502]**

Varna International Ballet Competition **[Vol 2: 1804]**

Vatel-Club Luxembourg **[Vol 2: 4500]**

The Vatican **[Vol 2: 9545]**

Veeco Instruments, Inc. **[Vol 1: 5737]**

Vegetation Science; International Association for **[Vol 2: 4722]**

Ventana Medical Systems Inc. **[Vol 1: 12861]**

Venture Clubs **[Vol 1: 17512]**

Verband der Koche Deutschlands **[Vol 2: 3180]**

Verband Deutscher Schulmusiker **[Vol 2: 3025]**

Verein der Zellstoff-und Papier-Chemiker und-Ingenieure **[Vol 2: 2701]**

Verein Deutscher Textilveredlungsfachleute e.V **[Vol 2: 3217]**

Verein Fur Socialpolitik **[Vol 2: 3223]**

Verein Ungarischer Chemiker **[Vol 2: 3379]**

Vereniging van Geneeskundige Laboratorium Tegnoloe van Suid-Afrika **[Vol 2: 5612]**

Vernacular Architecture Forum **[Vol 1: 17514]**

Vertebrate Paleontology; Society of **[Vol 1: 15875]**

Vesalius Trust **[Vol 1: 17519]**

Vesterheim Norwegian-American Museum **[Vol 1: 17524]**

Veteran Motor Car Club of America **[Vol 1: 17528]**

Veteran Wireless Operators Association **[Vol 1: 17532]**

Veterans Association; Blinded **[Vol 1: 5886]**

Veterans of Foreign Wars of the United States **[Vol 1: 17536]**

Veterans of Foreign Wars of the United States I Ladies Auxiliary **[Vol 1: 17549]**

Veterinary Association; British Small Animal **[Vol 2: 7208]**

Veterinary Laboratory Diagnosticians; American Association of **[Vol 1: 1406]**

Veterinary Medical Association; American **[Vol 1: 4633]**

Via Christi Research, Inc. **[Vol 1: 17551]**

Viacom International Inc. - Nickelodeon **[Vol 1: 17553]**

Victorian Artists Society **[Vol 2: 1172]**

Victorian Society in America **[Vol 1: 17555]**

Vieilles Maisons Francaises **[Vol 2: 2660]**

Vienna University of Music and Performing Arts **[Vol 2: 1322]**

Vietnam Standards Center **[Vol 2: 9558]**

VietNamNet **[Vol 2: 9560]**

Viking Society for Northern Research **[Vol 2: 9429]**

Villa I Tatti - Harvard University Center for Italian Renaissance Studies **[Vol 2: 4168]**

Villa-Lobos Museum **[Vol 2: 1769]**

Villach; City of **[Vol 2: 1327]**

Village Voice LLC - *The Village Voice* **[Vol 1: 17559]**

Vinas International Singing Competition; Francisco **[Vol 2: 6112]**

Vinifera Wine Growers Association **[Vol 1: 5679]**

VinPro **[Vol 2: 5756]**

Virgin Islands Humanities Council **[Vol 1: 17561]**

Virginia Association of Chiefs of Police **[Vol 1: 17563]**

Virginia Department of Social Services - Office on Volunteerism and Community Service **[Vol 1: 17570]**

Virginia Film Office **[Vol 1: 17572]**

Virginia Interscholastic Athletic Administrators Association **[Vol 1: 17574]**

Virginia Police Chiefs Foundation **[Vol 1: 17564, 17566]**

Virginia Quarterly Review **[Vol 1: 17590]**

Virginia Recreation and Park Society **[Vol 1: 17592]**

Visions du Reel International Documentary Film Festival **[Vol 2: 6531]**

Visitor Industry Partnership **[Vol 2: 1705]**

Visual Arts Center of New Jersey **[Vol 1: 17607]**

Visual Effects Society **[Vol 1: 17609]**

Viticulture; South African Society for Enology and **[Vol 2: 5711]**

VMI Research Laboratories **[Vol 1: 17611]**

VM+SD **[Vol 1: 14533]**

Voice of the Listener and Viewer **[Vol 2: 9431]**

Volcanology and Chemistry of the Earth's Interior; International Association of **[Vol 2: 6047]**

Voluntary Protection Programs Participants' Association **[Vol 1: 17613]**

Volvo Environment Prize Foundation **[Vol 2: 6246]**

von Humboldt Foundation; Alexander **[Vol 1: 14635]**

von Humboldt-Stiftung Foundation; Alexander **[Vol 2: 3227]**

von Siemens Music Foundation; Ernst **[Vol 2: 3234]**

VSA Arts **[Vol 1: 17620]**

VSA - The International Organization on Arts and Disability **[Vol 1: 17620]**

Vserossiiskoe Obschestvo Slepykn **[Vol 2: 5775]**

Wakeboard Federation; International Waterski and **[Vol 2: 6463]**

Wales Craft Council **[Vol 2: 9433]**

Walking Horse Trainers Association **[Vol 1: 17623]**

Walkley Foundation **[Vol 2: 1175]**

Wallenberg Committee of the United States; Raoul **[Vol 1: 17627]**

Wallenberg Foundation; Marcus **[Vol 2: 6248]**

Walton League of America; Izaak **[Vol 1: 17630]**

WAMSO, Minnesota Orchestra Volunteer Association **[Vol 1: 17636]**

Wanderlust Magazine **[Vol 2: 9435]**

Waring International Piano Competition; Virginia **[Vol 1: 17641]**

Warringah Council **[Vol 2: 1177]**

Warsaw Philharmonic **[Vol 2: 5414]**

Waseda Daigaku **[Vol 2: 4340]**

Waseda University **[Vol 2: 4340]**

Washburn Alumni Association **[Vol 1: 17643]**

Washington Academy of Sciences **[Vol 1: 17646]**

Washington-Baltimore Newspaper Guild **[Vol 1: 17648]**

Washington College - Department of English **[Vol 1: 17650]**

Washington Crossing Foundation **[Vol 1: 17652]**

The Washington Monthly **[Vol 1: 17673]**

The Washington Post Company Educational Foundation **[Vol 1: 17675]**

Washington Theatre Awards Society **[Vol 1: 16485]**

Washington University in St. Louis - Diabetes Research and Training Center **[Vol 1: 17677]**

Washington University in St. Louis - Law School **[Vol 1: 17679]**

Washington Writers' Publishing House **[Vol 1: 17684]**

Washingtonian Magazine **[Vol 1: 17687]**

Waste Equipment Technology Association **[Vol 1: 17689]**

Water and Environmental Management; Chartered Institution of **[Vol 2: 7397]**

Water Association; Australian **[Vol 2: 603]**

Water Association; International **[Vol 2: 8251]**

Water Association; National Ground **[Vol 1: 12458]**

Water Conservation Society; Soil and **[Vol 1: 15920]**

Water Environment Federation **[Vol 1: 17694]**

Water Environment Research Foundation **[Vol 1: 17721]**

Water Institute of Southern Africa **[Vol 2: 5758]**

Water Institute; Stockholm International **[Vol 2: 6189]**

Water New Zealand **[Vol 2: 5086]**

Water Safety Congress; National **[Vol 1: 13024]**

Water Works Association; New England **[Vol 1: 13162]**

The Waterbird Society **[Vol 1: 17723]**

Waterski and Wakeboard Federation; International **[Vol 2: 6463]**

Weather Association; National **[Vol 1: 13028]**

Web Academy; Egypt **[Vol 2: 2012]**

Web Awards Academy; Pan Arab **[Vol 2: 4450]**

Web Awards; Syria **[Vol 2: 4456]**

Web Awards; UAE **[Vol 2: 4458]**

The Webby Awards **[Vol 1: 17729]**

Wedding and Portrait Photographers International **[Vol 1: 17734]**

Wedding Photographers International **[Vol 1: 17734]**

Wedding Photographers of America **[Vol 1: 17734]**

Weed Society of Victoria **[Vol 2: 1181]**

Weighing and Measurement; International Society for **[Vol 1: 10267]**

The Welch Foundation **[Vol 1: 17736]**

Welch Foundation; Robert A. **[Vol 1: 17736]**

Welding Technology Institute of Australia **[Vol 2: 1184]**

Welsh Amateur Music Federation **[Vol 2: 9439]**

Welsh Books Council **[Vol 2: 6676, 9441]**
Welsh National Centre for Children's Literature **[Vol 2: 9441]**
Welsh Society of Philadelphia **[Vol 1: 17738]**
Welt-Tierarztgesellschaft **[Vol 2: 1670]**
West African College of Surgeons **[Vol 2: 5105]**
West Coast Book Prize Society **[Vol 1: 17740]**
West Point Association of Graduates **[Vol 1: 17748]**
Westchester Library Association **[Vol 1: 17753]**
Western Economic Association International **[Vol 1: 17756]**
Western History Association **[Vol 1: 17758]**
Western Interpretation Association **[Vol 1: 11586]**
Western Michigan University - Medieval Institute **[Vol 1: 17764]**
Western North Carolina Historical Association - Smith-McDowell House Museum **[Vol 1: 17766]**
Western Political Science Association **[Vol 1: 17769]**
Western Thoracic Surgical Association **[Vol 1: 17771]**
Western Women Premier Bowlers **[Vol 1: 17775]**
Western Women Professional Bowlers **[Vol 1: 17775]**
Western Writers of America **[Vol 1: 17778]**
Westerners International **[Vol 1: 17781]**
Westerners International Association **[Vol 1: 13958]**
Westminster Kennel Club **[Vol 1: 17786]**
Wetnose Animal Aid **[Vol 2: 9444]**
Wexner Center for the Arts **[Vol 1: 17791]**
Wexner Foundation **[Vol 1: 17793]**
Wheelchair Basketball Association; National **[Vol 1: 13036]**
Whirly-Girls - International Women Helicopter Pilots **[Vol 1: 17795]**
White House Correspondents' Association **[Vol 1: 17803]**
White House News Photographers Association **[Vol 1: 17807]**
White House Office of Science and Technology Policy **[Vol 1: 12812]**
White Library; William Allen **[Vol 1: 17809]**
Whiting Foundation; Mrs. Giles **[Vol 1: 17811]**
Whitley Fund for Nature **[Vol 2: 9446]**
Whitney Awards Committee **[Vol 1: 17813]**
Why Hunger **[Vol 1: 17815]**
Wichita State University - Center for Entrepreneurship **[Vol 1: 17818]**
Wiener Library Institute of Contemporary History **[Vol 2: 9448]**
Wiesel Foundation for Humanity; Elie **[Vol 1: 17833]**
Wiesenthal Center; Simon **[Vol 1: 17836]**
Wilderness Medical Society **[Vol 1: 17839]**
The Wilderness Society **[Vol 1: 17841]**
Wildlife Management Institute **[Vol 1: 17845]**
Wildlife Preservation Society of Australia **[Vol 2: 1187]**
The Wildlife Society **[Vol 1: 17847]**
Wiley & Sons; John **[Vol 1: 9849, 9850]**
Wiley-Blackwell **[Vol 1: 9521]**
Wiley-Liss **[Vol 1: 1028]**
William Saroyan Foundation **[Vol 1: 16262]**
Wilson Company; H. W. **[Vol 1: 16105]**
Wilson National Fellowship Foundation; Woodrow **[Vol 1: 17999]**
Wilson Ornithological Society **[Vol 1: 17859]**
Wilson Sporting Goods Company **[Vol 1: 9471]**
Winchell Cancer Fund; Damon Runyon - Walter **[Vol 1: 7805]**
Wine Country Film Festival; Napa Sonoma **[Vol 1: 11363]**
Wine Industry Suppliers Australia **[Vol 2: 1190]**
Wine Spectator **[Vol 1: 17864]**
Wingfoot Lighter than Air Society **[Vol 1: 10845]**
Wire Association International **[Vol 1: 17867]**
Wireless Communications Association International **[Vol 1: 17870]**
Wisconsin Arts Board **[Vol 1: 17872]**
Wisconsin Educational Media and Technology Association **[Vol 1: 17878]**
Wisconsin Educational Media Association **[Vol 1: 17878]**
Wisconsin Health Information Management Association **[Vol 1: 17886]**
Wisconsin Historical Society **[Vol 1: 17893]**
Wisconsin Library Association **[Vol 1: 17895]**
Wissenschaftsstadt Darmstadt **[Vol 2: 3236]**
WMC Foundation **[Vol 2: 4842]**

Wofford College National Alumni Association **[Vol 1: 17899]**
Wolf Foundation **[Vol 2: 3999]**
Wolf Project **[Vol 1: 17903]**
Wolfe Society; Thomas **[Vol 1: 17905]**
Wolfson Foundation **[Vol 2: 9450]**
Women and Policing; Australian Council of **[Vol 2: 276]**
Women; Australian Federation of Graduate **[Vol 2: 336]**
Women Band Directors International **[Vol 1: 17909]**
Women Business Owners; National Association of **[Vol 1: 11937]**
Women; Canadian Federation of University **[Vol 1: 6481]**
Women Engineers; Society of **[Vol 1: 15894]**
Women for Faith and Family **[Vol 1: 17914]**
Women Graduates; South African Association of **[Vol 2: 5667]**
Women in Aerospace **[Vol 1: 17916]**
Women in Banking and Finance **[Vol 2: 9452]**
Women in Cable Telecommunications **[Vol 1: 17922]**
Women in Direct Marketing International **[Vol 1: 17924]**
Women in Engineering ProActive Network **[Vol 1: 17926]**
Women in Federal Law Enforcement **[Vol 1: 17931]**
Women in Film **[Vol 1: 17937]**
Women in Film and Video New England Chapter **[Vol 1: 17940]**
Women in Insurance and Financial Services **[Vol 1: 17942]**
Women in Literacy and Life Assembly **[Vol 1: 17946]**
Women in Livestock Development **[Vol 1: 17948]**
Women in Management **[Vol 1: 17950]**
Women in Publishing **[Vol 2: 9454]**
Women in Technology International **[Vol 1: 17952]**
Women in the Wind **[Vol 1: 17955]**
Women of Negara Brunei Darussalam; Council of **[Vol 2: 1780]**
Women Pilots' Association; Australian **[Vol 2: 608]**
Women Pilots' Association; British **[Vol 2: 7301]**
Women Radiologists; American Association for **[Vol 1: 1011]**
Women Surgeons; Association of **[Vol 1: 5550]**
Women's Action for New Directions **[Vol 1: 17957]**
Women's All-Star Association **[Vol 1: 17959]**
Women's Basketball Coaches Association **[Vol 1: 11362, 17966]**
Women's Business Enterprise National Council **[Vol 1: 17973]**
Women's Caucus for Art **[Vol 1: 17975]**
Women's Clubs; National Association of Negro Business and Professional **[Vol 1: 11816]**
Women's Engineering Society **[Vol 2: 9457]**
Women's Health and Economic Development Association **[Vol 2: 5107]**
Women's International League for Peace and Freedom U.S. Section **[Vol 1: 17977]**
Women's International Network of Utility Professionals **[Vol 1: 17979]**
Women's International Shipping and Trading Association Norway **[Vol 2: 5163]**
Women's National Book Association **[Vol 1: 17985]**
Women's Sports Foundation **[Vol 1: 17988]**
Women's Studies Association **[Vol 2: 5092]**
Women's Transportation Seminar **[Vol 1: 17993]**
Women's Veterinary Medical Association **[Vol 1: 5182]**
Wood Design and Building Magazine - Dovetail Communications **[Vol 1: 17997]**
Wood Science and Technology; Society of **[Vol 1: 15902]**
Woodrow Wilson National Fellowship Foundation **[Vol 1: 17999]**
Woodson Art Museum; Leigh Yawkey **[Vol 1: 18002]**
The Word Works **[Vol 1: 18004]**
Words+ Inc. **[Vol 1: 10142]**
Workforce Management - Crain Communications Inc. **[Vol 1: 18006]**
The Works Festival **[Vol 1: 6212]**
World Affairs Councils of America **[Vol 1: 18008]**
World Airline Entertainment Association **[Vol 1: 309]**
World Amateur Golf Council **[Vol 1: 9957]**
World Association for Public Opinion Research **[Vol 1: 18013]**

World Association for Small and Medium Enterprises **[Vol 2: 3811]**
World Association for the Advancement of Veterinary Parasitology **[Vol 1: 18016]**
World Association for the History of Veterinary Medicine **[Vol 2: 1330]**
World Association of Christian Radio Amateurs and Listeners **[Vol 2: 9461]**
World Association of Detectives **[Vol 2: 5202]**
World Association of Girl Guides and Girl Scouts **[Vol 2: 9466]**
World Association of Newspapers **[Vol 2: 2662]**
World Association of Non-Governmental Organizations **[Vol 1: 18020]**
World Association of Research Professionals **[Vol 2: 4844]**
World Association of Societies of Pathology and Laboratory Medicine **[Vol 2: 4349]**
World Bowling Writers **[Vol 1: 18029]**
World Boxing Council **[Vol 2: 4597]**
World Chess Federation **[Vol 2: 3314]**
World Confederation for Physical Therapy **[Vol 2: 9471]**
World Conservation Union **[Vol 2: 6533]**
World Council of Credit Unions **[Vol 1: 18034]**
World Council of Optometry **[Vol 1: 18036]**
World Cultural Council **[Vol 2: 4600]**
World Curling Federation **[Vol 2: 9477]**
World Environment Center **[Vol 1: 18038]**
World Fantasy Convention **[Vol 1: 18040]**
World Fashion Organization **[Vol 1: 18042]**
World Federation of Consuls **[Vol 2: 4203]**
World Federation of Engineering Organisations **[Vol 2: 2664]**
World Federation of Neurosurgical Societies **[Vol 2: 6542]**
World Federation of Occupational Therapists **[Vol 2: 1192]**
World Fishing Magazine - Mercator Media Ltd. **[Vol 2: 9483]**
World Folk Music Association **[Vol 1: 18044]**
The World Food Prize Foundation **[Vol 1: 18046]**
World Golf Hall of Fame **[Vol 1: 18048]**
World Health Organization **[Vol 2: 6546]**
World Hunger Year **[Vol 1: 17815]**
World Investigators Network **[Vol 1: 18050]**
World Literature Today **[Vol 1: 18054]**
World Luxury Hotel Awards **[Vol 2: 5767]**
World Meteorological Organization **[Vol 2: 6558]**
World Ocean and Cruise Liner Society **[Vol 1: 18057]**
World Organisation for Animal Health **[Vol 2: 2667]**
World Organisation of Systems and Cybernetics **[Vol 2: 9485]**
World Organization of Family Doctors **[Vol 2: 5992]**
World Organization of the Scout Movement **[Vol 2: 6563]**
World Petroleum Council **[Vol 2: 9488]**
World Phosphate Institute **[Vol 2: 3483]**
World Ploughing Organization **[Vol 2: 4846]**
World Press Photo **[Vol 2: 4848]**
World Research Foundation **[Vol 1: 18059]**
World Safety Organization **[Vol 1: 18061]**
World Science Fiction Society **[Vol 1: 18073]**
World Ship Trust - United Kingdom **[Vol 2: 9491]**
World Small Animal Veterinary Association **[Vol 1: 18075]**
World Society for Stereotactic and Functional Neurosurgery - Canada **[Vol 2: 4352]**
World Teleport Association **[Vol 1: 18080]**
World Trade Center Moscow **[Vol 2: 5884]**
World Trade Center of New Orleans **[Vol 1: 18082]**
World Trade Centre Vancouver **[Vol 1: 18085]**
World Travel Awards **[Vol 2: 9493]**
World Veterinary Association **[Vol 2: 1670]**
World Veterinary Poultry Association **[Vol 2: 3241]**
World Wildlife Fund **[Vol 2: 6568]**
Worlddidac Foundation **[Vol 2: 6566]**
WorldFest - Houston International Film and Video Festival **[Vol 1: 18092]**
WorldRadio **[Vol 1: 18094]**
World's Poultry Science Association **[Vol 2: 9495]**
Worldwide Association of Self-Adhesive Labels and Related Products **[Vol 2: 4850]**
Worshipful Company of Scientific Instrument Makers **[Vol 2: 9498]**
Worshipful Company Of Weavers' **[Vol 2: 9385]**

3 Apples Book Award **[Vol. 1: 13214]**
3M Award for Innovation in Libraries **[Vol. 2: 4929]**
3M ESPE Preventative Pediatric Dentistry Postdoctoral Research Fellowship **[Vol. 1: 646]**
3M Fellowship Award **[Vol. 1: 18097]**
3M Sustainable Packaging Award **[Vol. 1: 9399]**
5 Band WAZ Award **[Vol. 1: 7736]**
21st Anniversary Research Grants **[Vol. 2: 4888]**
50 Books/50 Covers Competition **[Vol. 1: 2659]**
"54" Founders Award **[Vol. 1: 17631]**
112 Awards **[Vol. 2: 1475]**
$500,000 Lemelson-MIT Prize **[Vol. 1: 10998]**
A-Level Chemistry Prizes **[Vol. 2: 9143]**
A-Prize **[Vol. 1: 10841]**
AAA/Oxford University Press Award for Excellence in Undergraduate Teaching of Anthropology **[Vol. 1: 822]**
AAA Scholarship for PELS **[Vol. 1: 17566]**
AAAI Fellows **[Vol. 1: 5110]**
AAAS Mass Media Science and Engineering Fellowship **[Vol. 1: 3248]**
AAAS Westinghouse Award for Public Understanding of Science and Technology **[Vol. 1: 986]**
AAAS Westinghouse Science Journalism Awards **[Vol. 1: 994]**
AABB-Baxter SBB Scholarship Awards **[Vol. 1: 1056]**
AABB-Baxter Transfusion Medicine Scholarships **[Vol. 1: 1057]**
AABB-Fenwal Specialist in Blood Bank Scholarships **[Vol. 1: 1056]**
AABB-Fenwal Transfusion Medicine Scholarships **[Vol. 1: 1057]**
AAC International Scholarship Endowment Fund **[Vol. 1: 10]**
AACC/NACB Award for Outstanding Contributions to Clinical Chemistry in a Selected Area of Research **[Vol. 1: 884]**
AACD Distinguished Professional Service Award **[Vol. 1: 1937]**
AACR-Pezcoller International Award for Cancer Research **[Vol. 2: 4149]**
AACT Fellow **[Vol. 1: 1106]**
AACTA Awards **[Vol. 2: 349]**
AAHA Award **[Vol. 1: 819]**
AAI-BD Biosciences Investigator Award **[Vol. 1: 1181]**
AAI-Dana Foundation Award in Human Immunology Research **[Vol. 1: 1183]**
AAI-Invitrogen Meritorious Career Award **[Vol. 1: 1182]**
AAI-Life Technologies Meritorious Career Award **[Vol. 1: 1182]**
AAIC Student of the Year Award **[Vol. 1: 5120]**
AALL/LexisNexis Call for Papers Awards **[Vol. 1: 1187]**
AALL Spectrum Article of the Year Award **[Vol. 1: 1188]**
AAMI/BD Professional Achievement Award **[Vol. 1: 5128]**
AAMI/GE Healthcare BMET of the Year Award **[Vol. 1: 5129]**
AAN Fellows **[Vol. 1: 600]**
AAP Honors **[Vol. 1: 5214]**
AAPOR Award **[Vol. 1: 973]**

AAS Prize in Agricultural Biosciences **[Vol. 2: 4370]**
AASL President's Award **[Vol. 1: 1342]**
AASL Research Grants **[Vol. 1: 1338]**
AASL/SIRS Intellectual Freedom Award **[Vol. 1: 1345]**
AAUP Design Show **[Vol. 1: 5219]**
Aaxis Pacific New Investigator Award **[Vol. 2: 620]**
Abafazi-Africana Women's Studies Essay Award **[Vol. 1: 13055]**
Abbot Nutrition Award **[Vol. 1: 2029]**
Abbot Nutrition Award in Women's Health **[Vol. 1: 2030]**
Abbott Award **[Vol. 2: 3085]**
Abbott Award for Innovative Research and Development in Virology **[Vol. 2: 5613]**
Abbott Award for Significant Contributions to Molecular Diagnostics **[Vol. 2: 4097]**
Abbott Diagnostic Award **[Vol. 2: 2406]**
Abbott Distinguished Research Award **[Vol. 1: 3268]**
Abbott Laboratories Award in Clinical and Diagnostic Immunology **[Vol. 1: 3969]**
Abbott Prize **[Vol. 2: 9255]**
ABC Champion Performance Horse **[Vol. 1: 1485]**
ABC-CLIO Leadership Grant **[Vol. 1: 1339]**
ABC Concerts and Vocal Competition **[Vol. 2: 1082]**
ABC Young Performers' Competition **[Vol. 2: 1082]**
ABCNews VideoSource Award **[Vol. 1: 9879]**
Abdullayev Award; Academician H. **[Vol. 2: 1335]**
Abel Award; Paul **[Vol. 1: 14445]**
Abel Cultural Arts, Literature, and Music Awards; Alice **[Vol. 1: 2943]**
Abel Prize **[Vol. 2: 5138]**
Abella; Prix Charles **[Vol. 2: 2135]**
Abelson Award for Visionary Leadership **[Vol. 1: 15485]**
Abelson Prize; Philip Hauge **[Vol. 1: 983]**
Aberconway Medal **[Vol. 2: 7718]**
Abercrombie Prize; Sir Patrick **[Vol. 2: 2584]**
Aberdeen Memorial Trophy; Stuart W. **[Vol. 1: 6634]**
Aberg Post Graduate Award; Ulf **[Vol. 2: 7860]**
Abiola Lecture; Bashorun MKO **[Vol. 1: 199]**
ABOA Foundation - National Scholastic Press Association Pacemaker Awards **[Vol. 1: 13244]**
ABOHN Research Grant **[Vol. 1: 1501]**
Aboriginal Canadians Scholarship **[Vol. 1: 13010]**
Above and Beyond Award **[Vol. 1: 12097]**
Abragam; Prix Anatole et Suzanne **[Vol. 2: 2174]**
Abrams Award; Eugene **[Vol. 2: 6253]**
Abrams Award in Geriatric Clinical Pharmacology; William B. **[Vol. 1: 3799]**
Abrams Award; Talbert **[Vol. 1: 4861]**
Abrams Medal; General Creighton W. **[Vol. 1: 5535]**
Abrams Prize; Mark **[Vol. 2: 9186]**
Abreu Award; Maria Isabel **[Vol. 1: 1373]**
Abromowicz Emerging Scholar Fellowship; Dina **[Vol. 1: 18177]**
Abstract Award for Outstanding Research in Molecular Pathology or Pharmacogenomics **[Vol. 1: 885]**
ABU Prizes for Radio and Television Programs **[Vol. 2: 4519]**
Abyss Award **[Vol. 1: 11260]**

Academic Achievement Award
    Data Management Association International **[Vol. 1: 7813]**
    South African Association for Food Science and Technology **[Vol 2: 5650]**
Academic All-American **[Vol. 1: 16766]**
Academic All-American Awards **[Vol. 1: 11805]**
Academic All-Canadian Awards **[Vol. 1: 6412]**
Academic Athletes of the Year (All Academic Team)- **[Vol. 1: 12076]**
Academic Award **[Vol. I: 7530]**
Academic Awards
    Big East Conference **[Vol. 1: 5834]**
    Faculty of Astrological Studies **[Vol 2: 7666]**
Academic Career Achievement Award **[Vol. 1: 9086]**
Academic Education Scholarship **[Vol. 1: 13885]**
Academic Excellence Award **[Vol. 1: 8077]**
Academic Excellence Prize **[Vol. 2: 5448]**
Academic Freedom Award **[Vol. 1: 11139]**
Academic Librarians' Distinguished Service Award **[Vol. 1: 6310]**
Academic Prize
    Royal Australasian College of Dental Surgeons **[Vol. 2: 954]**
    Seismological Society of Japan **[Vol 2: 4322]**
Academic/Research Librarian of the Year Award **[Vol. 1: 5256]**
Academy Awards **[Vol. 1: 84]**
Academy Fellow Award **[Vol. 1: 63]**
Academy Fellowship **[Vol. 1: 104]**
Academy Gold Medal **[Vol. 2: 5539]**
Academy Medal **[Vol. 2: 4815]**
Academy Medal for Contributions to Science and Technology **[Vol. 2: 171]**
Academy of Achievement - Sales and Marketing Hall of Fame **[Vol. 1: 14681]**
Academy of Authors **[Vol. 1: 9405]**
Academy of Country Music Awards **[Vol. 1: 61]**
Academy of Distinguished Entrepreneurs **[Vol. 1: 5755]**
Academy of Fellows **[Vol. 1: 11700]**
Academy of Fellows **[Vol. 1: 10426]**
Academy of Leaders Award **[Vol. 1: 4126]**
Academy of Pharmaceutical Research and Science Fellow **[Vol. 1: 3141]**
Academy of Wind and Percussion Arts Award **[Vol. 1: 11958]**
Academy Prize **[Vol. 2: 5470]**
Academy Research Grants **[Vol. 1: 984]**
ACCA Hong Kong Awards for Sustainability Reporting **[Vol. 2: 5221]**
ACCA Ireland Sustainability Reporting Awards **[Vol. 2: 3830]**
ACCA Malaysia Environmental and Social Reporting Awards **[Vol. 2: 4527]**
ACCA Malaysia Sustainability Reporting Awards **[Vol. 2: 4527]**
ACCA Singapore Awards for Sustainability Reporting **[Vol. 2: 5934]**
ACCA Sri Lanka Awards for Sustainability Reporting **[Vol. 2: 6115]**
ACCA U.K. Awards for Sustainability Reporting **[Vol. 2: 6806]**

ACCA-WWF Pakistan Environmental Reporting Awards [Vol. 2: 5181]
Accelerator Prize [Vol. 2: 2387]
Access Award for Disability Issues [Vol. 1: 7296]
Access Awards [Vol. 1: 2189]
Accessible America Award [Vol. 1: 12646]
Accomplishment Award [Vol. 1: 1200]
Accuray Award [Vol. 2: 1492]
ACD-AADE Prize for Dental Journalism [Vol. 1: 1732]
ACE Award [Vol. 1: 12034]
ACE Education Program Award [Vol. 1: 5298]
ACE Engineering Excellence Awards [Vol. 2: 6762]
ACES Award; Diamond [Vol. 1: 15957]
ACES Award for Excellence in Property Management [Vol. 2: 6808]
ACES Research Grants [Vol. 1: 4979]
ACHA Article Award [Vol. 1: 1754]
Acha Award for Veterinary Public Health; Pedro N. [Vol. 1: 13815]
ACHA World Championship [Vol. 1: 1879]
ACHEMA-Plakette in Titan [Vol. 2: 3159]
ACHEMA Plaque in Titanium [Vol. 2: 3159]
ACHEMA Television Prize [Vol. 2: 3160]
Acheson Award; Edward Goodrich [Vol. 1: 8054]
Achievement Award
    American Academy of Ophthalmology [Vol. 1: 604]
    American Association of Meat Processors [Vol 1: 1201]
    American Fuchsia Society [Vol 1: 2196]
    American Meat Science Association [Vol 1: 2849]
    American Scientific Glassblowers Society [Vol 1: 3729]
    Canadian Cardiovascular Society [Vol 1: 6392]
    IEEE - Ultrasonics, Ferroelectrics, and Frequency Control Society [Vol 1: 9040]
    Industrial Research Institute [Vol 1: 9223]
    Institute of Electronics, Information and Communication Engineers [Vol 2: 4225]
    The International Association of Forensic Toxicologists [Vol 2: 5442]
    International Association of Traffic and Safety Sciences [Vol 2: 4237]
    International Society of Oncology Pharmacy Practitioners [Vol 1: 10337]
    Lighter-Than-Air Society [Vol 1: 10846]
    National Association of County Agricultural Agents [Vol 1: 11738]
    National Black Police Association [Vol 1: 11987]
    National Peach Council [Vol 1: 12672]
    Ontario Nature [Vol 1: 13584]
    Psychotherapists and Counsellors Association of Western Australia [Vol 2: 935]
    Society for Maternal-Fetal Medicine [Vol 1: 15182]
    Society of Toxicology [Vol 1: 15843]
    Society of Women Engineers [Vol 1: 15895]
    Tourism and Hospitality Chamber of Slovenia [Vol 2: 6014]
    U.S.A. Baseball [Vol 1: 17408]
    Women in Aerospace [Vol 1: 17917]
Achievement Award for Real Property Innovation [Vol. 1: 16926]
Achievement Awards
    Canadian Mental Health Association - Ontario Division [Vol. 1: 6706]
    National Association of Regional Councils [Vol 1: 11862]
    National Horseshoe Pitchers Association of America [Vol 1: 12521]
    National Research Council of the Philippines [Vol 2: 5344]
    Rough and Smooth Collie Training Association [Vol 2: 8567]
    Technology Student Association [Vol 1: 16400]
    Worshipful Company of Scientific Instrument Makers [Vol 2: 9499]
Achievement Awards in Writing [Vol. 1: 12202]
Achievement in Applied Retirement Research Award [Vol. 1: 14536]
Achievement in Communication [Vol. 1: 9626]
Achievement in Consumer Education Awards [Vol. 1: 11727]
Achievement Medal [Vol. 1: 413]

Achievement Medal: Air Force [Vol. 1: 16654]
Achievement Medal: Coast Guard [Vol. 1: 16655]
Achievement Medal: Joint Service [Vol. 1: 16656]
Achievement Medal: Navy/Marine Corps [Vol. 1: 16657]
Achievement Medals [Vol. 2: 8019]
Achievement of Excellence [Vol. 1: 6385]
Achievement of Social Studies Education General Grant [Vol. 1: 12167]
Achievement of the Year Award [Vol. 1: 5354]
Achiever of the Year [Vol. 2: 642]
Achievers of the Year [Vol. 1: 8722]
Achieving Chapter Excellence Award [Vol. 1: 10638]
Achieving Excellence Awards [Vol. 1: 9866]
Achwal Gold Medal; Madhav [Vol. 2: 3582]
ACI Fellow [Vol. 1: 1836]
ACI Young Member Award for Professional Achievement [Vol. 1: 1837]
ACIL Scholarship [Vol. 1: 1900]
A.C.I.T. Award [Vol. 2: 2316]
Acker; Prix Ernest [Vol. 2: 1580]
Ackerley Prize for Autobiography; J. R. [Vol. 2: 7561]
Ackermann Award [Vol. 2: 5124]
Ackermann Medal for Excellence in Water Management; William C. [Vol. 1: 4646]
ACM Fellow [Vol. 1: 4953]
ACM SIGCOMM Award for Lifetime Achievement [Vol. 1: 16078]
ACM SIGCOMM Student Award [Vol. 1: 16079]
Acme Oyster Eating World Championship [Vol. 1: 9915]
ACMS Scientific Achievement Award [Vol. 1: 7253]
ACOMM Awards, the Communications Alliance and Communications Day Awards [Vol. 2: 659]
Acorn Grant [Vol. 1: 8420]
Acorn Poetry Award; Milton [Vol. 1: 14144]
ACRL/DLS Haworth Press Distance Learning Librarian Conference Sponsorship [Vol. 1: 5269]
ACS Award for Computers in Chemical and Pharmaceutical Research [Vol. 1: 1589]
ACS Award for Creative Advances in Environmental Science and Technology [Vol. 1: 1590]
ACS Award for Creative Invention [Vol. 1: 1591]
ACS Award for Creative Work in Synthetic Organic Chemistry [Vol. 1: 1592]
ACS Award for Distinguished Service in the Advancement of Inorganic Chemistry [Vol. 1: 1593]
ACS Award for Encouraging Disadvantaged Students into Careers in the Chemical Sciences [Vol. 1: 1594]
ACS Award for Encouraging Women into Careers in the Chemical Sciences [Vol. 1: 1595]
ACS Award for Nuclear Applications in Chemistry [Vol. 1: 1670]
ACS Award for Nuclear Chemistry [Vol. 1: 1670]
ACS Award for Outstanding Performance by Local Sections [Vol. 1: 1596]
ACS Award for Research at an Undergraduate Institution [Vol. 1: 1597]
ACS Award for Team Innovation [Vol. 1: 1598]
ACS Award in Analytical Chemistry [Vol. 1: 1599]
ACS Award in Applied Polymer Science [Vol. 1: 1600]
ACS Award in Chemical Education [Vol. 1: 1666]
ACS Award in Chromatography [Vol. 1: 1601]
ACS Award in Colloid and Surface Chemistry [Vol. 1: 1602]
ACS Award in Industrial Chemistry [Vol. 1: 1603]
ACS Award in Inorganic Chemistry [Vol. 1: 1604]
ACS Award in Organometallic Chemistry [Vol. 1: 1605]
ACS Award in Petroleum Chemistry [Vol. 1: 1662]
ACS Award in Polymer Chemistry [Vol. 1: 1606]
ACS Award in Pure Chemistry [Vol. 1: 1607]
ACS Award in Separations Science and Technology [Vol. 1: 1608]
ACS Award in the Chemistry of Materials [Vol. 1: 1609]
ACS Award in Theoretical Chemistry [Vol. 1: 1610]
ACS Chemical Biology Lectureship [Vol. 1: 1611]
ACS/NREF-AANS Faculty Career Development Awards [Vol. 1: 1222]
ACSM-CaGIS Map Design Competition Awards [Vol. 1: 1869]
ACT-NUCEA Innovations in Continuing Education Awards [Vol. 1: 17392]

Active Fellowships [Vol. 1: 2876]
Active State Member of the Year [Vol. 1: 9975]
ACTM Medal for Outstanding Contributions to Tropical Medicine [Vol. 2: 131]
ACTM Medal for Outstanding Service to the College [Vol. 2: 132]
ACTM Medal for Students [Vol. 2: 133]
Actor of the Year Award [Vol. 2: 7525]
ACUHO-I Award [Vol. 1: 5272]
Acura Someone to Watch Award [Vol. 1: 8354]
AD of the Year [Vol. 1: 17575]
ADA-ASP Young Investigator Innovation Award in Geriatric Endocrinology [Vol. 1: 2016]
ADA Foundation Scholarships [Vol. 1: 2031]
Adams Article Prize; Percy G. [Vol. 1: 15994]
Adams Award; Dorothy Garrigus [Vol. 1: 14898]
Adams Award for Conservation Photography; Ansel [Vol. 1: 14857]
Adams Award in Organic Chemistry; Roger [Vol. 1: 1612]
Adams Award; James Luther [Vol. 1: 16626]
Adams Chapter Heritage Award; Mildred [Vol. 1: 14894]
Adams Conservation Award; Ansel [Vol. 1: 17842]
Adams Founder's Award; Frank [Vol. 1: 12944]
Adams Lecture Award; Comfort A. [Vol. 1: 4671]
Adams Memorial Membership Award [Vol. 1: 4672]
Adams Prize; Henry [Vol. 1: 15095]
Adams Prize; Herbert Baxter [Vol. 1: 2357]
Adams Prize; Willi Paul [Vol. 1: 13672]
Adams Trophy; Mrs. Charles Francis [Vol. 1: 17049]
Adamson Award for Distinguished Service in the Advancement of Surface Chemistry; Arthur W. [Vol. 1: 1613]
Adapted Committee Award [Vol. 1: 17442]
Adaptive Re-Use Award [Vol. 1: 14382]
ADARN of the Year [Vol. 1: 144]
Adaskin Memorial Award; Canadian Music Centre John [Vol. 1: 13562]
Adcock Award; C.J. [Vol. 2: 4988]
Addams Award; Homer [Vol. 1: 4310]
Addams Children's Book Award; Jane
    Jane Addams Peace Association [Vol. 1: 147]
    Women's International League for Peace and Freedom U.S. Section [Vol 1: 17978]
Addams Medal; Jane [Vol. 1: 14571]
Addis Service to NACAC Award; Margaret E. [Vol. 1: 11563]
A'Deane Coke Medal; Major John Sacheverell [Vol. 2: 7719]
Adenauer Research Award; Konrad [Vol. 1: 14635]
Adequan/USDF All-Breed Awards [Vol. 1: 16871]
Adequan/USDF All-Breeds Dressage Sport Horse Breeding Awards [Vol. 1: 16872]
Adhesives Award [Vol. 1: 5576]
Adirondack Council Annual Awards [Vol. 1: 152]
Adivar Scholarship; Halide Edip [Vol. 1: 16580]
Adkins Memorial Instructor Membership Award; Howard E. [Vol. 1: 4673]
Adler Award [Vol. 1: 13916]
Adler Lectureship Award in the Field of Materials Physics; David [Vol. 1: 3193]
Adler Undergraduate Book Collecting Prize; Elmer [Vol. 1: 8476]
Administration Award [Vol. 1: 2100]
Administration-Management Award [Vol. 1: 13925]
Administrative Committee Prize [Vol. 1: 2729]
Administrative Grant [Vol. 2: 7487]
Administrative Professionals Award [Vol. 2: 5971]
Administrative Psychiatry Award [Vol. 1: 3342]
Administrator of the Year
    Trinidad and Tobago Football Federation [Vol. 2: 6629]
    Wisconsin Educational Media and Technology Association [Vol. 1: 17879]
Administrator of the Year Award [Vol. 1: 17967]
Administrator's Award [Vol. 1: 8029]
Admiral of the Ocean Sea [Vol. 1: 16651]
Adolescent Health Award [Vol. 1: 684]
Adolescent Health Care Award in memory of Dr. Kathy Phipps [Vol. 2: 8672]
Adolf-Dietzel-Industriepreis der DGG [Vol. 2: 3012]
Adolf-von-Baeyer-Denkmunze [Vol. 2: 2923]
Adopt-Action Service Award [Vol. 1: 13303]
Adoption Activist Awards [Vol. 1: 13303]

ADPD/SCDA Student Awards and Recognition Program **[Vol. 1: 16074]**

Adrian Awards **[Vol. 1: 8980]**

Adrian Prizes; Daiwa **[Vol. 2: 7490]**

ADSA Foundation Scholar Award **[Vol. 1: 1966]**

Adsit Excellence in Veterinary Medical Media Award; Milton E. **[Vol. 1: 8855]**

Adult Advisor of the Year Award **[Vol. 1: 2982]**

Adult Award for Promotion of International Education **[Vol. 2: 7607]**

Adult Volunteer of the Year **[Vol. 1: 2295]**

Advanced Ceramic Award **[Vol. 1: 5577]**

Advanced Diploma **[Vol. 2: 7855]**

Advanced Educational or Training Scholarships **[Vol. 1: 4472]**

Advanced Mountain Flight Training Scholarship **[Vol. 1: 17796]**

Advanced Oncology Certified Nurse of the Year Award **[Vol. 1: 13528]**

Advancing International Trade Awards **[Vol. 1: 11377]**

Advancing Solar Energy Policy Award **[Vol. 2: 3099]**

Advancing the Industry Award **[Vol. 1: 5305]**

Adventurer of the Year **[Vol. 2: 2463]**

Adventurous Programming Chamber Music Awards **[Vol. 1: 4259]**

Advertising and Promotions Contest Awards **[Vol. 1: 16311]**

Advertising Director of the Year **[Vol. 1: 16311]**

Advertising Effectiveness Awards **[Vol. 2: 3844]**

Advertising Hall of Achievement **[Vol. 1: 775]**

Advertising Hall of Fame **[Vol. 1: 776]**

Advertising Photographer of the Year **[Vol. 1: 14020]**

Advertising Sales Team of the Year **[Vol. 2: 7496]**

Advertising Woman of the Year **[Vol. 1: 173]**

Advisor of the Year **[Vol. 1: 11996]**

Advisor of the Year Award (Regional and International) **[Vol. 1: 8692]**

Advisor Professional Development Grant **[Vol. 1: 8693]**

Advisory Council Award **[Vol. 2: 1307]**

Advocacy Award **[Vol. 1: 10087]**

Advocacy Excellence Award **[Vol. 1: 8000]**

Advocacy-Legislative Award **[Vol. 1: 13926]**

Advocate Award **[Vol. 1: 9022]**

Advocate of the Year
    National Alliance for Medication Assisted Recovery **[Vol. 1: 11503]**
    National Space Society of Australia **[Vol 2: 897]**

ADwards **[Vol. 2: 4446]**

AE50 Awards **[Vol. 1: 4073]**

Aebersold Award; Paul C. **[Vol. 1: 15728]**

AECI Medal **[Vol. 2: 5677]**

AECT/SIRS Intellectual Freedom Award **[Vol. 1: 5002]**

Aelod o Orsedd Beirdd Ynys Prydain **[Vol. 2: 8391]**

AERA - American College Testing Program Award **[Vol. 1: 2057]**

AERA - PDK Award for Distinguished Contributions Relating Research to Practice **[Vol. 1: 2055]**

Aerial Achievement Medal **[Vol. 1: 16658]**

Aerial Photographer of the Year **[Vol. 1: 14181]**

Aero Club of America Trophy **[Vol. 1: 11464]**

Aero Engine Services Trophy **[Vol. 2: 5046]**

Aeroacoustics Award **[Vol. 1: 2499]**

Aerodynamic Measurement Technology Award **[Vol. 1: 2500]**

Aerodynamics Award **[Vol. 1: 2501]**

Aeromodelling Gold Medal **[Vol. 2: 6295]**

Aerospace Awareness Award **[Vol. 1: 17918]**

Aerospace Chair Award **[Vol. 1: 15486]**

Aerospace Communications Award **[Vol. 1: 2502]**

Aerospace Design Engineering Award **[Vol. 1: 2503]**

Aerospace Division/AIAA Educational Achievement Award **[Vol. 1: 3835]**

Aerospace Educator Award **[Vol. 1: 17919]**

Aerospace Engineering Leadership Award **[Vol. 1: 15487]**

Aerospace Medicine Technician of the Year **[Vol. 1: 15869]**

Aerospace Power Systems Award **[Vol. 1: 2504]**

Aerospace Software Engineering Award **[Vol. 1: 2505]**

AES Award **[Vol. 1: 5690]**

AES Student Prize **[Vol. 2: 334]**

Aesculapius Award of Excellence in Health Communications **[Vol. 1: 8844]**

AFA Annual Award **[Vol. 2: 2009]**

AFA Newsletter Award **[Vol. 1: 5344]**

AFAANZ Fellowship **[Vol. 2: 64]**

AFAEP Awards **[Vol. 2: 6840]**

AFAEP/Kodak Student Competition **[Vol. 2: 6841]**

AFAR Award of Distinction **[Vol. 1: 2108]**

AFC Annual Awards **[Vol. 2: 4525]**

Affiliate Award **[Vol. 1: 13107]**

Affiliate Clinical Development Award **[Vol. 2: 636]**

Affiliate Member Award **[Vol. 1: 11372]**

Affiliate of the Year Award
    International Society for Pharmaceutical Engineering **[Vol. 1: 10201]**
    National Council of La Raza **[Vol 1: 12186]**

Afghanistan Medal **[Vol. 2: 294]**

AFI Awards **[Vol. 2: 349]**

AFIA and American Society of Animal Science Nutrition Research Awards **[Vol. 1: 2127]**

AFIA and Poultry Science Association Award **[Vol. 1: 2128]**

AFMC Executive Management Award **[Vol. 1: 244]**

AFMC Junior Management Award **[Vol. 1: 245]**

AFMC Middle Management Award **[Vol. 1: 246]**

Africa Prize for Leadership for the Sustainable End of Hunger **[Vol. 1: 9013]**

AfricaCom Awards **[Vol. 2: 7816]**

African-American Culture and Philosophy Award **[Vol. 1: 14355]**

African Banker Awards **[Vol. 2: 7808]**

African Business Awards **[Vol. 2: 7809]**

African Development and Economic Consultants Prize **[Vol. 2: 4406]**

African Initiative Fellowship Program **[Vol. 1: 17283]**

African Most Popular Song of the Year **[Vol. 2: 6721]**

African Music Awards; The Ammies, **[Vol. 2: 6721]**

African Regional Intellectual Property Organisation Prize **[Vol. 2: 4466]**

African Union SMME of the Year **[Vol. 2: 5490]**

African Urban Quarterly Prize **[Vol. 2: 4407]**

AFROSAI Prize **[Vol. 2: 4472]**

Ag Communication Award **[Vol. 1: 13082]**

AGA Student Summer Research Fellowships **[Vol. 1: 8449]**

Agan Award; Tessie **[Vol. 1: 1174]**

Agassiz Medal; Alexander **[Vol. 1: 11420]**

Agatha Awards **[Vol. 1: 10927]**

AGC/GVS Fellowship **[Vol. 2: 8689]**

AGC/IAATI Award **[Vol. 1: 9505]**

AGCO National Student Design Competition **[Vol. 1: 4074]**

Age d'Or Prize **[Vol. 2: 1655]**

Agell Award for Excellence in Research; Gladys **[Vol. 1: 838]**

Agency Award for Excellence **[Vol. 1: 10075]**

Agency of the Year Award **[Vol. 1: 11728]**

Aggarwal Prize; J.K. **[Vol. 2: 4231]**

AGHE Award **[Vol. 1: 5022]**

Agility Dog of the Year **[Vol. 1: 16231]**

Agmashenebeli Order; David **[Vol. 2: 2676]**

Agnew Award for Outstanding AWIM Volunteers; Bill **[Vol. 1: 15488]**

AGO/ECS Publishing Award in Choral Composition **[Vol. 1: 2265]**

Agricola Medaille; Georg **[Vol. 2: 2767]**

Agricultural and Forest Entomology Journal Award **[Vol. 2: 8768]**

Agricultural Bioprocess Laboratory Awards **[Vol. 1: 17248]**

Agricultural Engineering Award **[Vol. 2: 765]**

Agricultural Engineering Award and Life Membership **[Vol. 2: 706]**

Agricultural Environmental Stewardship Award **[Vol. 1: 13153]**

Agricultural Initiative Award **[Vol. 1: 13154]**

Agricultural Journalism Awards **[Vol. 2: 3840]**

Agricultural Leadership Award **[Vol. 1: 13155]**

Agrinaut Award **[Vol. 1: 11487]**

Agritechnology, Life Sciences and Biotechnology Exporter of the Year **[Vol. 2: 5023]**

Agronomic Extension Education Award **[Vol. 1: 4098]**

Agronomic Industry Award **[Vol. 1: 4099]**

Agronomic Resident Education Award **[Vol. 1: 4100]**

Agronomic Service Award **[Vol. 1: 4101]**

AGS Award for Outstanding Contributions to Gravestone Studies **[Vol. 1: 5024]**

AGTA Awards **[Vol. 2: 355]**

AgustaWestland Community Service Award **[Vol. 1: 8887]**

Agway Inc. Young Scientist Award **[Vol. 1: 1970]**

Ahmad Shield; Naseer **[Vol. 2: 3343]**

Ahmed Award for Tribal Areas; Fakhruddin Ali **[Vol. 2: 3520]**

Ahn Award; Dr. Suzanne **[Vol. 1: 4823]**

AHNS-ACS Career Development Awards
    American Head and Neck Society **[Vol. 1: 2281]**
    Phi Kappa Phi **[Vol 1: 13976]**

AHNS Young Investigator Awards **[Vol. 1: 2282]**

AHRI/The CEO Institute Business Leadership Awards **[Vol. 2: 372]**

AHS/Merck US Human Health Migraine and Women's Health Research Award **[Vol. 1: 2285]**

AIA/ACSA Award for Architectural Education **[Vol. 1: 2565]**

AIA/ACSA Topaz Medallion for Excellence in Architectural Education **[Vol. 1: 2565]**

AIA/ALA Library Buildings Award **[Vol. 1: 2566]**

AIA Fellowship **[Vol. 1: 2567]**

AIASA Recognition Awards **[Vol. 1: 16401]**

AIC Fellowship **[Vol. 1: 220]**

AICP National Planning Pioneer Award **[Vol. 1: 3283]**

AICP Outstanding Student Awards **[Vol. 1: 3294]**

AICPA/AAA Notable Contributions to Accounting Literature Award **[Vol. 1: 2596]**

Aid to Advertising Education Award **[Vol. 1: 779]**

Aidlin Award; Joseph **[Vol. 1: 8600]**

AIGA Design Leadership Award **[Vol. 1: 2661]**

AIGA Medal **[Vol. 1: 2660]**

AIIE Award for Excellence in Productivity Improvement **[Vol. 1: 9347]**

Aikat Oration Award; Professor B. K. **[Vol. 2: 3538]**

Aikenhead Memorial Choral Scholarship; Roy **[Vol. 1: 14722]**

AILF Torchlight Awards **[Vol. 1: 2474]**

AILU Award **[Vol. 2: 6825]**

AIMIA Annual Awards **[Vol. 2: 427]**

AINSE Awards **[Vol. 2: 400]**

AIPEA Medals **[Vol. 2: 1761]**

AIPS Awards **[Vol. 2: 6455]**

Air Bag Safety Campaign **[Vol. 1: 9638]**

Air Breathing Propulsion Award **[Vol. 1: 2506]**

Air Force Academy Award **[Vol. 1: 283]**

Air Force Association AFLC Logistics Executive Management Award **[Vol. 1: 244]**

Air Force Association AFLC Logistics Junior Management Awards **[Vol. 1: 245]**

Air Force Association AFLC Logistics Middle Management Award **[Vol. 1: 246]**

Air Force Association AFSC Distinguished Award for Management **[Vol. 1: 244]**

Air Force Association AFSC Junior Management Award **[Vol. 1: 245]**

Air Force Association AFSC Management Awards **[Vol. 1: 246]**

Air Force Cross **[Vol. 2: 7337]**

Air Force ROTC Scholarship **[Vol. 1: 284]**

Air Force Test and Evaluation Team of the Year Award **[Vol. 1: 257]**

Air National Guard Outstanding Unit Award **[Vol. 1: 247]**

Air Pacific Tabua Marketing Awards **[Vol. 2: 2058]**

Air Reserve Forces Meritorious Service Medal **[Vol. 1: 16659]**

Air Sport Medal **[Vol. 2: 6296]**

Air Tanzania Award for the Best East African Film **[Vol. 2: 9527]**

Air Traffic Control Specialist of the Year Award **[Vol. 1: 292]**

Air War College Research and Writing Award **[Vol. 1: 285]**

Aircraft Design Award **[Vol. 1: 2507]**

Aircraft Maintenance Engineers Turnbuckle Award **[Vol. 2: 8603]**

Aircraft Technology Engineering and Maintenance Awards **[Vol. 2: 9399]**

Airline of the Year **[Vol. 2: 9183]**

AIRMIC Prize **[Vol. 2: 7404]**

Airport of the Year **[Vol. 2: 9184]**

Airway Facilities Technician of the Year **[Vol. 1: 293]**

Airway Transportation Systems Specialist of the Year **[Vol. 1: 293]**

Airways Corporation Trophy **[Vol. 2: 5047]**

Airwork Cup **[Vol. 2: 5048]**

Award Index

Aisenstadt Prize; Andre [Vol. 1: 17305]
Aitchison Memorial Trophy; Robert Swan [Vol. 2: 4980]
Aitken Prize [Vol. 2: 4977]
Aiya Memorial Award; Prof. S.V.C. [Vol. 2: 3752]
Aizstrauts Award; Arnie [Vol. 1: 442]
AJL Scholarship for Library School Students [Vol. 1: 5384]
Akabori Memorial Award [Vol. 2: 4287]
Akerman Award; Iwan [Vol. 2: 1518]
Akermarks Stipendium; Carl [Vol. 2: 6193]
Al-Arrayed Prize; His Excellency Mr. Jawad S. [Vol. 2: 1351]
Al-Aslamiya Prize; Rafida Bint Saad [Vol. 2: 1352]
Al-Bayronni Prize; Abu Rayhan [Vol. 2: 1353]
Al-Edreesi Prize; Abu Abdulla Moh'd [Vol. 2: 1354]
Al-Farabi Prize; Ali Bin [Vol. 2: 1355]
Al-Kindi Prize; Abo Yousif Yaqoub [Vol. 2: 1356]
Al-Nafees Prize; Ibn [Vol. 2: 1357]
Al Razi Prize; Muhammad Bin Zakariya [Vol. 2: 1358]
Al-Tajer Prize; Ommaya Qurabi [Vol. 2: 1359]
Al-Zahrawi Prize; Abdul Qassim [Vol. 2: 1360]
Al-Zayani Prize; Fatima [Vol. 2: 1361]
ALA/Information Today Inc. Library of the Future Award [Vol. 1: 2772]
ALA/Mecklermedia Library of the Future Award [Vol. 1: 2772]
Alab ng Haraya (Alab ng Haraya Awards); Gawad [Vol. 2: 5340]
Alabama Sportswriters Hall of Fame [Vol. 1: 10024]
Alabama State Poetry Society Award [Vol. 1: 12342]
Alaska Cup Award [Vol. 1: 17068]
Alaska-Siberia Lend-Lease Award [Vol. 1: 319]
Albers Award; Gerd [Vol. 2: 4780]
Albers Industry Relations Award; William H. [Vol. 1: 8396]
Albert Award for Outstanding Services to Australian Music; Ted [Vol. 2: 139]
Albert Award; Heather Leigh [Vol. 1: 16990]
Albert Award; Henry J. [Vol. 1: 10059]
Albert Medal [Vol. 2: 8957]
Albert O. Hirshchman Prize [Vol. 1: 14988]
Albert; Prix Jos [Vol. 2: 1581]
Alberta Book Awards
   Book Publishers Association of Alberta [Vol. 1: 5914]
   Book Publishers Association of Alberta [Vol 1: 5915]
   Book Publishers Association of Alberta [Vol 1: 5916]
   Book Publishers Association of Alberta [Vol 1: 5917]
   Book Publishers Association of Alberta [Vol 1: 5918]
   Book Publishers Association of Alberta [Vol 1: 5919]
   Book Publishers Association of Alberta [Vol 1: 5920]
   Book Publishers Association of Alberta [Vol 1: 5922]
   Book Publishers Association of Alberta [Vol 1: 5923]
   Writers Guild of Alberta [Vol 1: 18109]
Alberta Book Design Awards [Vol. 1: 5914]
Alberta Book Publishing Achievement Award [Vol. 1: 5915]
Alberta Book Publishing Awards [Vol. 1: 5921]
Alberta Emerging Publisher [Vol. 1: 5916]
Alberta Film and Television Awards [Vol. 1: 337]
Alberta Irrigation Projects Association Awards [Vol. 1: 335]
Alberta Literary Awards [Vol. 1: 18109]
Alberta Publisher of the Year Award [Vol. 1: 5917]
Alberti Prize; Friedrich von [Vol. 2: 3146]
Alberto Olivares' Foundation Award; Juan [Vol. 2: 9554]
Alberts Award for Excellence in Science Education; Bruce [Vol. 1: 3778]
Albion Book Prize [Vol. 1: 13297]
Albright Award; Fuller [Vol. 1: 3767]
Albritton, Jr. Award; Claude C. [Vol. 1: 9279]
Album Award; Manuel M. [Vol. 1: 647]
Album of the Year [Vol. 1: 9732]
Alcan Lecture Award [Vol. 1: 6895]
Alcan; Prix [Vol. 2: 2175]
Aldrich Award; C. Anderson [Vol. 1: 652]

Aldridge Prize; A. Owen [Vol. 1: 1826]
Aleph Emblem [Vol. 1: 12572]
Alex Awards [Vol. 1: 18215]
Alexander Award; J. Allen [Vol. 1: 3728]
Alexander Early Career Award; Michele [Vol. 1: 15358]
Alexander Medal; G.N. [Vol. 2: 766]
Alexander Media Awards; John [Vol. 1: 11296]
Alexander Prize
   Commonwealth Association of Science, Technology and Mathematics Educators [Vol. 2: 7452]
   Royal Historical Society - United Kingdom [Vol 2: 8801]
Alexander the Great Award [Vol. 2: 3306]
Alexis de Tocqueville Prize [Vol. 2: 4704]
Alfa Laval Agri Dairy Extension Award [Vol. 1: 1973]
Alfven Prize; Hannes [Vol. 2: 2388]
Alger Award; Horatio [Vol. 1: 348]
Alger Award; International Horatio [Vol. 1: 349]
Alger Prize; Chadwick F. [Vol. 1: 10374]
Algood Tuition Scholarships; Emma and Meloid [Vol. 1: 11660]
Algren Awards for Short Fiction; Nelson [Vol. 1: 7227]
Ali International Award; Salim [Vol. 2: 3457]
Aliant Creative Writing Award for Young People [Vol. 1: 14145]
The Aliant Creative Writing Awards for Young People [Vol. 1: 14146]
Alice Award
   National Woman's Party [Vol. 1: 13051]
   Society of Women Writers - Victoria [Vol 2: 1042]
Alice Paul Award [Vol. 1: 13051]
Alison Award; John R. [Vol. 1: 248]
All-America City Awards [Vol. 1: 12072]
All-America Honors (Men) [Vol. 1: 16906]
All-America Honors (Women) [Vol. 1: 16907]
All-America Racing Team [Vol. 1: 1457]
All-America Rose Selections Annual Winners [Vol. 1: 354]
All-America Rose Selections Certificate of Merit [Vol. 1: 355]
All-America Team
   Football Writers Association of America [Vol. 1: 8408]
   InterCollegiate Tennis Association [Vol 1: 9459]
All-America Teams [Vol. 1: 2167]
All-American [Vol. 1: 16767]
All American Association Award [Vol. 1: 443]
All-American Award [Vol. 1: 481]
All American Awards [Vol. 1: 13462]
All American Awards [Vol. 1: 12077]
All-American Awards [Vol. 1: 11806]
All American Club Award [Vol. 1: 2116]
All-American District Awards [Vol. 1: 443]
All-American Hall of Fame [Vol. 1: 12801]
All-American Scholar-Athlete Awards [Vol. 1: 11805]
All-Around Amateur Golden Horse [Vol. 1: 13808]
All-Around Cowboy [Vol. 1: 14250]
All Around Man/Woman Award [Vol. 1: 5876]
All Breed Master Judge [Vol. 1: 12675]
All-Canadian Awards [Vol. 1: 6413]
All-Island Overall Business Achiever [Vol. 2: 3934]
All Malta Award [Vol. 2: 4568]
All-NBA Team [Vol. 1: 11974]
All Sport Insurance Marketing Ltd. Volunteer of the Year Award [Vol. 1: 16169]
All Star Award [Vol. 1: 8899]
All-Tournament Teams/Outstanding Athlete Award [Vol. 1: 11807]
Allain Intellectual Freedom Award; Alex P. [Vol. 1: 10886]
Allan Award; William [Vol. 1: 4340]
Allan Memorial Cup; D.M. [Vol. 2: 5049]
Allderdice Award; Charles E. [Vol. 1: 7581]
Allee Award; Warder Clyde [Vol. 1: 4733]
Allen Award; Alfred [Vol. 1: 4987]
Allen Award; Alfred W. [Vol. 1: 1551]
Allen Award; Arthur A. [Vol. 1: 7610]
Allen Award; Beth [Vol. 1: 16991]
Allen Award for Scholarship and Service; Virginia French [Vol. 1: 16390]
Allen Award; P.W. [Vol. 2: 7702]
Allen Award; Ruth [Vol. 1: 3273]
Allen International Student Travel Award [Vol. 2: 456]

Allen Lecture; Joyce [Vol. 2: 198]
Allen Most Valuable Member Award; Clifford B. [Vol. 1: 9605]
Allen Prize; Cath [Vol. 2: 7355]
Allen Prize; David [Vol. 2: 112]
Allen Prize; Derek [Vol. 2: 6919]
Allen Scholarship; Dr. J. Frances [Vol. 1: 2144]
Allen Service Award; Mel [Vol. 1: 4552]
Allen Special Award; Lee [Vol. 1: 15025]
Allen Women's Player of the Year; Bob [Vol. 1: 17419]
Allendoerfer Awards; Carl B. [Vol. 1: 11010]
Allhands Essay Competition; James L. [Vol. 1: 209]
Alliance Award [Vol. 1: 814]
Alliance President's Awards [Vol. 1: 369]
Allied Arts Medal [Vol. 1: 14611]
Allied Health Fellowship [Vol. 2: 680]
Allied Health Professional Award [Vol. 1: 5421]
Allied Industry Individual Award [Vol. 1: 11488]
Allied Member Award [Vol. 1: 4518]
AlliedSignal Outstanding Student Branch Award [Vol. 1: 15513]
Allis Prize for Study of Ionized Gases; Will [Vol. 1: 3194]
Allison City of Sydney Piano Scholarship; John [Vol. 2: 1074]
Allison/Henderson Sydney Eisteddfod Piano Scholarship [Vol. 2: 1074]
Allotment Awards [Vol. 2: 3915]
Allport Prize; Gordon [Vol. 1: 15359]
Allstate James Cleveland Lifetime Achievement Award [Vol. 1: 7159]
Alltech Inc. Graduate Student Paper Publication Award [Vol. 1: 1967]
Alluisi Award for Early Career Achievement; Earl A. [Vol. 1: 3388]
Allwork Scholarship; Eleanor [Vol. 1: 2581]
Allyn and Bacon Psychology Awards [Vol. 1: 14287]
ALMA Awards [Vol. 1: 12187]
ALMA Humanitarian Award [Vol. 1: 12187]
Alouette Award [Vol. 1: 6193]
Alpaiwala Award [Vol. 2: 3772]
Alpha-1 Foundation/CHEST Foundation Clinical Research Award in Alpha-1 Antitrypsin (AAT) Deficiency [Vol. 1: 7212]
Alpha Chi Sigma Award in Pure Chemistry [Vol. 1: 397]
Alpha Kappa Psi Award [Vol. 1: 2808]
Alpha Omega Alpha Distinguished Teacher Awards [Vol. 1: 403]
Alpha Omega Alpha Student Essay Award [Vol. 1: 404]
Alpharma Award of Excellence [Vol. 1: 1070]
Alpine Domestic Coach of the Year [Vol. 1: 17069]
Alpine Skiing World Cup Champions [Vol. 2: 6428]
Alsberg-French-Schoch Memorial Lectureship Award [Vol. 1: 4]
ALSI/BWI Reading Program Grant [Vol. 1: 5055]
Alsobrook Industrial Minerals and Aggregates Distinguished Service Award; A. Frank [Vol. 1: 15203]
Alsop Award [Vol. 1: 2760]
Alston Canine Award; Alison [Vol. 2: 8761]
ALTA/Gale Outstanding Trustee Conference Grant [Vol. 1: 5395]
ALTA Outstanding Translations of the Year [Vol. 1: 2796]
ALTAFF/Gale Outstanding Trustee Conference Grant [Vol. 1: 5395]
Alter Cup; Hobie [Vol. 1: 17050]
Altieri Outstanding Coach Award [Vol. 1: 12407]
Altria Scholarship for the Institute for Leadership in Changing Times [Vol. 1: 17564]
Alufoil Trophy [Vol. 2: 2796]
Alumae Medal; Nikolai [Vol. 2: 2038]
Alumni Achievement Award
   Brandeis University Alumni Association [Vol. 1: 5999]
   Fund for American Studies [Vol 1: 8482]
   ORT America [Vol 1: 13703]
Alumni Achievement Awards [Vol. 1: 8828]
Alumni Awards [Vol. 1: 8482]
Alumni Medal [Vol. 1: 17209]
Alumni PRN Grant [Vol. 1: 408]
Alumni/Professional Coordinator of the Year [Vol. 1: 11997]

Alumni Recognition Award [Vol. 1: 7215]
Alumni Service Award
    D'Youville College Alumni Association [Vol. 1: 7940]
    Northern Michigan University Alumni Association [Vol 1: 13406]
Alumni Service Citations [Vol. 1: 17210]
Alumni Service Medal [Vol. 1: 17211]
Alumnus/Alumna of the Year Award [Vol. 1: 154]
Alumnus of the Year Award
    St. Bonaventure University - Russell J. Jandoli School of Journalism and Mass Communication [Vol. 1: 14669]
    University of Maryland - College of Information Studies [Vol 1: 17274]
Alvarez Memorial Award; Walter C. [Vol. 1: 2877]
Alzheimer's Disease Research Fellowship Award [Vol. 1: 2289]
Alzheimer's Disease Research Pilot Award [Vol. 1: 2290]
Alzheimer's Disease Research Standard Grant [Vol. 1: 2291]
AMA/Irwin/McGraw-Hill Distinguished Marketing Educator Award [Vol. 1: 2803]
Amakula Kampala International Film Festival [Vol. 2: 6650]
Amanda Award for Cinematographic Merit [Vol. 2: 5143]
Amanda Film - OG Fjernsynspris [Vol. 2: 5143]
Amateur Achievement Award [Vol. 1: 5654]
Amateur Astronomers Medal [Vol. 1: 440]
Amateur Athletic Fund Grants [Vol. 1: 16351]
Amateur Bowler of the Year [Vol. 1: 5950]
Amateur Cartoonist Extraordinary Award [Vol. 1: 12034]
Amateur Division Golden Horse [Vol. 1: 13808]
Amateur Photo Challenge [Vol. 1: 14174]
Amateur Wine Competition Awards [Vol. 1: 4700]
Ambassador Award
    American Council of the Blind [Vol. 1: 1911]
    Exhibit Designers and Producers Association [Vol 1: 8211]
    Federation of Fly Fishers [Vol 1: 8294]
    Global Speakers Federation [Vol 1: 8686]
Ambassador Award of Hospitality [Vol. 1: 12775]
Ambassador for Epilepsy Award [Vol. 2: 3855]
Ambassador of Free Enterprise [Vol. 1: 14681]
Ambassador's Trophy [Vol. 1: 7612]
Ambedkar Centenary Award for Excellence in Biomedical Research; Dr. B. R. [Vol. 2: 3539]
Ambulance Service Medal [Vol. 2: 295]
AmCham Annual Awards [Vol. 2: 3329]
AmCham Transatlantic Partnership Award [Vol. 2: 2692]
AMD Award [Vol. 2: 2971]
Amerbach Prize [Vol. 2: 6519]
America and the Sea Award [Vol. 1: 11333]
American Academy of Periodontology Student Award [Vol. 1: 727]
American Academy of Sanitarians/National Environmental Health Association Scholarship Award [Vol. 1: 759]
American and National League Managers of the Year [Vol. 1: 16171]
American Association of Individual Investors/ AREUEA Research Prize [Vol. 1: 3671]
American Association of University Women Award in Juvenile Literature [Vol. 1: 13371]
American Bar Association/Young Lawyers Division Outstanding Young Military Lawyer Award [Vol. 1: 10595]
American Bible Society Award [Vol. 1: 1492]
American Bible Society Scholarship [Vol. 1: 1493]
American Book Awards [Vol. 1: 5801]
American Bureau of Shipping - Captain Joseph H. Linnard Prize [Vol. 1: 15710]
American Business Award [Vol. 2: 6660]
American Cancer Society Eleanor Roosevelt International Cancer Fellowships [Vol. 2: 6457]
American Cancer Society International Fellowships for Beginning Investigators [Vol. 2: 6457]
American Chiropractic Foundation Scholarships [Vol. 1: 1681]
American College of Critical Care Medicine Distinguished Investigator Award [Vol. 1: 15602]
American College of Physicians Award [Vol. 1: 1793]

American Council of Learned Societies Fellowships [Vol. 1: 1905]
American Craft Council Fellows [Vol. 1: 1946]
American Craft Council Honorary Fellow [Vol. 1: 1946]
American Crossword Puzzle Champion [Vol. 1: 1950]
American Culinary Classic [Vol. 1: 1964]
American Cured Meat Championship Awards [Vol. 1: 1202]
American Dance Guild Annual Award [Vol. 1: 1992]
American Education Award [Vol. 1: 1333]
American Egg Board Research Award [Vol. 1: 14109]
American Eurocopter Flight Training Scholarship [Vol. 1: 17797]
American Express Building Leadership Award [Vol. 1: 9187]
American Express Scholarship [Vol. 1: 2462]
American Feed Industry Association Award [Vol. 1: 1968]
American Feed Industry Association Award in Ruminant Nutrition Research [Vol. 1: 4110]
American Feed Manufacturers Association Award [Vol. 1: 1968]
American Heritage Award [Vol. 1: 2475]
American Hiking Society Award [Vol. 1: 2349]
American Independent Award [Vol. 1: 14815]
American Indian Festival of Words Author Award [Vol. 1: 16576]
American Iron and Steel Institute Medal [Vol. 1: 2718]
American Jazz Masters Fellowship Awards [Vol. 1: 12312]
American Kennel Club Career Achievement Award in Canine Research [Vol. 1: 4634]
American Kennel Club Excellence in Research Awards [Vol. 1: 4635]
American League Most Valuable Player [Vol. 1: 5794]
American Liberties Medallion [Vol. 1: 2721]
American Liver Foundation Liver Scholar Awards [Vol. 1: 2798]
American Liver Foundation Special Research Initiatives [Vol. 1: 2799]
American Meteor Society Award [Vol. 1: 2895]
American Mineralogist Undergraduate Award [Vol. 1: 11177]
American Pharmacists Association Fellow [Vol. 1: 3149]
American Poultry Historical Society Award [Vol. 1: 14110]
American Society of Cytology Award for Meritorious Achievement in Cytology [Vol. 1: 4281]
American Society of Mammalogists Fellowship [Vol. 1: 4374]
American Society of Safety Engineers Fellow [Vol. 1: 4507]
American Spirit Award [Vol. 1: 12777]
American Stars Awards [Vol. 1: 16358]
American Therapeutic Recreation Association Awards [Vol. 1: 4592]
American Values Award [Vol. 1: 16747]
American Veterinary Medical Association Explorer Award [Vol. 1: 5959]
Americanism Award [Vol. 1: 17537]
Americanism Awards [Vol. 1: 4727]
Americas Award for Children's and Young Adult Literature [Vol. 1: 17376]
America's Marketplace Recycles! Awards Program [Vol. 1: 16882]
America's Old-Time Country Music Hall of Fame [Vol. 1: 12999]
America's Old-Time Fiddler's Hall of Fame [Vol. 1: 13000]
America's Ten Outstanding Young Men [Vol. 1: 16988]
AmeriStar Package Awards [Vol. 1: 9399]
Ames Histology Award [Vol. 2: 5617]
Amgen-ANZBMS Outstanding Abstract Award [Vol. 2: 204]
Amgen Australia Prize in Biotechnology [Vol. 2: 1101]
Amgen Award [Vol. 1: 3755]
Amgen Outstanding Investigator Award [Vol. 1: 3958]
Amiens International Film Festival [Vol. 2: 2309]
Amigo Del Libro [Vol. 2: 1752]

Amin Photographic Award; Mohamed [Vol. 2: 7444]
Aminoff Prize; Gregori [Vol. 2: 6182]
Amirikian Memorial Welding Award; Arsham [Vol. 1: 4674]
Amirikian Welding Scholarship; Arsham [Vol. 1: 4674]
Ammann Research Fellowship in Structural Engineering; O. H. [Vol. 1: 16302]
The Ammies, African Music Awards [Vol. 2: 6721]
Amnesty International Film Prize [Vol. 2: 2716]
Amoroso Award [Vol. 2: 7209]
Amory Prize [Vol. 1: 493]
AMOS Prize [Vol. 2: 1102]
Ampere d'Electricite de France; Prix [Vol. 2: 2176]
Amphibian Conservation Awards [Vol. 1: 14764]
AMS 50 Fellowships [Vol. 1: 2964]
Amsterdam Prize for Art [Vol. 2: 4821]
Amsterdam Prize for History [Vol. 2: 4825]
Amsterdam Prize for Medicine [Vol. 2: 4826]
Amsterdam Prize for the Environment [Vol. 2: 4824]
Amstutz-Williams Award [Vol. 1: 1071]
AMT's Outstanding Medical Assistant Students [Vol. 1: 2867]
Amused Moose Laugh Off Awards [Vol. 2: 7527]
AMWA Awards [Vol. 2: 137]
Anaesthesia and Intensive Care Best Paper Award [Vol. 2: 555]
Anaesthesia Essay Prize - Students [Vol. 2: 9079]
Analyst of the Year Award [Vol. 1: 8900]
Analytical Chemistry Division Award for Excellent Research [Vol. 2: 5449]
Anand Endowment Lecture; Dr. Nitya [Vol. 2: 3619]
Anastasi Early Career Award; Anne [Vol. 1: 3416]
Ancient Greek Cities Award [Vol. 2: 3307]
Anderl Award; Hans [Vol. 2: 4686]
Anders-Bording Prisen [Vol. 2: 1941]
Andersen Award; Hans Christian [Vol. 2: 6362]
Andersen Medal for Illustration; Hans Christian [Vol. 2: 6362]
Andersen Medal for Writing; Hans Christian [Vol. 2: 6362]
Andersen Memorial Award; William C. [Vol. 1: 14434]
Andersen Prizes; Henning [Vol. 2: 7637]
Anderson Award; Arthur R. [Vol. 1: 1838]
Anderson Award; Charles E. [Vol. 1: 2899]
Anderson Award; Elda E. [Vol. 1: 8850]
Anderson Award; Erin [Vol. 1: 2810]
Anderson Award; F. Paul [Vol. 1: 4311]
Anderson Award; H. C. L. [Vol. 2: 429]
Anderson Award; Harlan J. [Vol. 1: 5578]
Anderson Award; Mayer [Vol. 1: 14700]
Anderson Award of Merit; Inge [Vol. 1: 6443]
Anderson Award; William G. [Vol. 1: 796]
Anderson-Berry Medal; David [Vol. 2: 9060]
Anderson-Everett Award [Vol. 1: 9554]
Anderson Medal of Honor in Applied Geography; James [Vol. 1: 5201]
Anderson Memorial Intermediate Woodwind Scholarship; Mary [Vol. 1: 14723]
Anderson Memorial Senior Woodwind Scholarship; Mary [Vol. 1: 14724]
Anderson Prize for Violin; Emily [Vol. 2: 8884]
Anderson Prize; J.S. [Vol. 2: 1103]
Anderson Prize; Troyer Steele [Vol. 1: 2358]
Anderson Silver Medal; Sir Rowand [Vol. 2: 8845]
Anderson Trophy; Sir Donald [Vol. 2: 609]
Andes National Award; Ammon S. [Vol. 1: 14890]
Andreas Award [Vol. 2: 5144]
Andreasen Award; Jens [Vol. 2: 6356]
Andrew Mentor Award; Maureen [Vol. 1: 15255]
Andrew Mouravieff-Apostol Medal [Vol. 2: 6380]
Andrewartha Medal; H.G. [Vol. 2: 1012]
Andrews Award for Excellence in Baseball Sports Medicine; James R. [Vol. 1: 4550]
Andrews Bibliographical Award; Joseph L. [Vol. 1: 1189]
Andrews/Committee D-02 Scroll of Achievement; Sydney D. [Vol. 1: 5579]
Andritz Oy Award [Vol. 2: 2093]
Andronov Prize; A.A. [Vol. 2: 5782]
Andry Award; Nicolas [Vol. 1: 5231]
ANDY Awards [Vol. 1: 162]
Anfinsen Award; Christian B. [Vol. 1: 14280]
Ange; Prix Gustave Chaix d'Est [Vol. 2: 2242]
Angel Award [Vol. 1: 11261]
Angell Humanitarian Award; David [Vol. 1: 3731]

Angell Medal [Vol. 1: 17323]

Anguilla Tourism Awards [Vol. 2: 18]

Angus Award [Vol. 2: 4905]

Angus Medal; Robert W. [Vol. 1: 6912]

Anhinga Prize for Poetry [Vol. 1: 4730]

Aniara Priset [Vol. 2: 6235]

Aniara Prize [Vol. 2: 6235]

Aniello Award for Outstanding Emerging Theatre Company; John [Vol. 1: 16486]

Animal Behavior Society Best Student Paper Award [Vol. 1: 4733]

Animal Control Employee of the Year [Vol. 1: 11517]

Animal Growth and Development Award [Vol. 1: 4111]

Animal Industry Service Award [Vol. 1: 4112]

Animal Management Award [Vol. 1: 4113]

Animal Physiology and Endocrinology Award [Vol. 1: 4114]

Animal Technician Award [Vol. 1: 959]

Animal Welfare Award [Vol. 1: 4636]

The Animals and Society Course Awards [Vol. 1: 8998]

Anitschkow Prize [Vol. 2: 6137]

Anna-Monika Foundation Prize Competition [Vol. 2: 2694]

Annett Award for Children's Literature; R. Ross [Vol. 1: 18109]

Annin Award; Douglas H. [Vol. 1: 10278]

Anning Award; Mary [Vol. 2: 8444]

Anniversary of National Service 1951-1972 Medal [Vol. 2: 296]

Anniversary Prizes of the Society for Biochemistry and Molecular Biology [Vol. 2: 3945]

Anno Award of Excellence in Communication; B. Jaye [Vol. 1: 12094]

Annual Achievement Award [Vol. 1: 5003]

Annual Achievement Awards [Vol. 1: 3747]

Annual Art Competition [Vol. 1: 4889]

Annual Award for Junior Researchers [Vol. 2: 1875]

Annual Award for Popularization and Promotion of Science [Vol. 2: 1876]

Annual Awards Exhibitions [Vol. 1: 4803]

Annual Awards Program [Vol. 1: 18060]

Annual Central Prize [Vol. 1: 7157]

Annual Dissertation Award [Vol. 1: 7646]

Annual Exhibition
    Allied Artists of America [Vol. 1: 395]
    Royal Scottish Academy [Vol. 2: 8913]

Annual Gold Leaf Awards [Vol. 1: 6165]

Annual Prize for Hearing Research [Vol. 1: 10897]

Annual Prize for Psychological Research on Women and Gender by Students [Vol. 1: 3547]

Annual Report Awards [Vol. 2: 4899]

Annual Report Contest Award of Excellence [Vol. 1: 3646]

Annual Research Grant [Vol. 1: 948]

Annual Restaurant Merit Award [Vol. 2: 4594]

Annual School and College Publications Contest [Vol. 1: 12806]

Annual Science Award [Vol. 2: 1877]

Annual Teaching Excellence Award [Vol. 2: 5960]

Annual Tour Scholarship [Vol. 1: 15479]

Annual Wildlife Communications Award [Vol. 1: 16342]

Anosov Prize; P.P. [Vol. 2: 5783]

ANPA Foundation - Associated Collegiate Press Pacemakers Awards [Vol. 1: 13243]

ANRS/IAS Prize [Vol. 2: 6342]

Ansari Best Geosciences Reference Work Award; Mary B. [Vol. 1: 8594]

Ansari Distinguished Service Award; Mary B. [Vol. 1: 8595]

Ansari X Prize [Vol. 1: 18138]

Ansell Distinguished Service Award; John [Vol. 1: 6029]

Ansell Poster Prize; George and Vera [Vol. 2: 8754]

Ansell Prize; Barbara [Vol. 2: 9080]

Anson Award; Jack L. [Vol. 1: 5342]

Ansorge Bequest [Vol. 2: 6697]

Anstey Award; Nigel [Vol. 2: 4674]

Antarctic Medal; Australian [Vol. 2: 297]

Antarctica Service Medal [Vol. 1: 16660]

Anthem Essay Contest [Vol. 1: 5753]

Anthony Award; Susan B. [Vol. 1: 10065]

Anthony Memorial Award; Dennis [Vol. 2: 4520]

Anthropology in Media Award [Vol. 1: 823]

Anti-Slavery Award [Vol. 2: 6723]

Antigua & Barbuda Literary Festival [Vol. 2: 22]

Antigua Literary Award [Vol. 2: 22]

Antonov Aeromodelling Diploma [Vol. 2: 6297]

ANZ Private Bank and Australia Contemporary Award [Vol. 2: 76]

ANZAAS Medal [Vol. 2: 199]

Anzaldua Book Prize; Gloria [Vol. 1: 13056]

ANZIAM Medal [Vol. 2: 211]

AOTA COTA/OTR Partnership Award [Vol. 1: 3030]

AOTOS Mariner's Plaque [Vol. 1: 16652]

APA/NIMH Vestermark Psychiatry Teaching Award [Vol. 1: 3343]

APA/PDC Prize for Excellence and Innovation in Philosophy Programs [Vol. 1: 3171]

APCAC Award [Vol. 2: 5919]

APEX Award for Student Success [Vol. 1: 1097]

APEX Awards [Vol. 2: 3463]

APF/Division 29 Early Career Award [Vol. 1: 3449]

Apgar Award; Virginia [Vol. 1: 653]

APhA/APPM Merit Award [Vol. 1: 3150]

APIRE/Lilly Psychiatric Research Fellowship [Vol. 1: 3344]

Apker Award; LeRoy [Vol. 1: 3195]

APL Awards [Vol. 2: 6843]

Aplan Award [Vol. 1: 8914]

Aplan Award; Frank F. [Vol. 1: 2673]

APM Group IT Trainer of the Year [Vol. 2: 7003]

APO Award [Vol. 2: 4215]

APO National Awards [Vol. 2: 4214]

APO Regional Awards [Vol. 2: 4215]

APO Special National Award [Vol. 2: 4214]

Apollo Award [Vol. 1: 3053]

Apollo Prize [Vol. 2: 690]

Apotex Award [Vol. 1: 6949]

Apotex Fellowship in Clinical Pharmacology [Vol. 1: 6986]

Appel Medal; Otto [Vol. 2: 2985]

Appel Prize; Lucien [Vol. 1: 1508]

Appert Award; Nicholas [Vol. 1: 9331]

Applause Award [Vol. 1: 17974]

Applebaum Composers Award; Louis [Vol. 1: 13563]

Applebaum Memorial Scholarship; William [Vol. 1: 8394]

Applegate-Dorros Peace and International Understanding Award [Vol. 1: 12293]

Appleseed Award; Johnny [Vol. 1: 8518]

Appleton Medal and Prize [Vol. 2: 7899]

Appleton Prize [Vol. 2: 1563]

Application Award [Vol. 1: 10002]

Application to Practice Award [Vol. 1: 11179]

Applied Catalysis Award [Vol. 2: 8972]

Applied Consumer Economics Award [Vol. 1: 1913]

Applied Inorganic Chemistry Award [Vol. 2: 8973]

Applied Plant Pathology Award [Vol. 2: 5741]

Applied Research Medal [Vol. 2: 966]

Applied Social Issues Internship [Vol. 1: 15360]

Appraiser of the Year Award [Vol. 1: 11800]

Appreciation Award [Vol. 1: 10817]

Apprentice Awards [Vol. 2: 887]

Apprentice of the Year [Vol. 2: 9171]

APS College Awards of Distinction [Vol. 2: 505]

APS College of Forensic Psychologists (NSW Section) Annual Awards [Vol. 2: 506]

APS Fellow [Vol. 1: 3274]

APS Prize [Vol. 2: 507]

APSA Fellow [Vol. 2: 144]

APSA Medal [Vol. 2: 145]

Apsey Playwriting Award; Ruby Lloyd [Vol. 1: 17189]

Apt Lectureship; Leonard [Vol. 1: 654]

Apuraha tai Palkinto [Vol. 2: 2109]

Aqua Vita Est Award [Vol. 2: 5759]

Aquatic Horticulturist Award [Vol. 1: 6225]

Aquinas Medal [Vol. 1: 1547]

ARA Annual Award [Vol. 1: 3719]

Arab American Book Award [Vol. 1: 4755]

Arabia Corporate Social Responsibility Awards [Vol. 2: 6664]

Arabian Business Achievement Awards [Vol. 2: 6662]

Arata Award; Yoshiaki [Vol. 2: 2543]

Arbor Day Awards [Vol. 1: 4757]

Arboricultural Association Award [Vol. 2: 6728]

Arbuse Gold Medal; Gussie and Samuel [Vol. 1: 13212]

Arbuthnot Award [Vol. 1: 10088]

Arbuthnot Honor Lecture Award; May Hill [Vol. 1: 5056]

ARCA Championship Hall of Fame [Vol. 1: 10024]

Arch of Fame Lifetime Achievement Award [Vol. 1: 4933]

Archambault Award; George F. [Vol. 1: 4267]

Archambault Prize in Physical Sciences and Mathematics; Urgel [Vol. 1: 5186]

Archbishop Iakovos Distinguished Service Award [Vol. 1: 12423]

Archbishop's Years of Service Award [Vol. 1: 12424]

Archer Award; W. Harry [Vol. 1: 1790]

The Arches Brick Award [Vol. 2: 7528]

Archibald Prize [Vol. 2: 78]

Architectural Awards [Vol. 2: 2686]

Architectural Critics and Writers Award [Vol. 2: 5692]

Architectural Engineering Award [Vol. 1: 4156]

Architectural Photographer of the Year [Vol. 1: 14020]

Architecture Award [Vol. 2: 6577]

Architecture Awards [Vol. 1: 16959]

Architecture Firm Award [Vol. 1: 2568]

Archon X Prize for Genomics [Vol. 1: 18138]

Arcti Award; Stella [Vol. 2: 2133]

Arctowski Medal [Vol. 1: 11421]

Arcus Outstanding Family Life Educator Award; Margaret E. [Vol. 1: 12248]

Arderne Medal; John [Vol. 2: 9081]

Arenth Excellence in Cancer Nursing Management Award; Linda [Vol. 1: 13529]

Arete Best of Show Award
    Central Pennsylvania Festival of the Arts [Vol. 1: 7161]
    Central Pennsylvania Festival of the Arts [Vol 1: 7162]

Arid Lands Hydraulic Engineering Award [Vol. 1: 4157]

Arima Award for Applied Microbiology [Vol. 2: 4791]

Arinos Prize; Afonso [Vol. 2: 1749]

Ariste Medal; Paul [Vol. 2: 2039]

ARIT/Mellon Fellowships [Vol. 1: 3692]

ARIT/NEH Fellowships [Vol. 1: 3693]

Arizona State Poetry Society Award [Vol. 1: 12343]

Arizona Young Reader's Award [Vol. 1: 4783]

Arkhangelskii Prize; A.D. [Vol. 2: 5784]

ARL-Blackwells Practicum Prize [Vol. 2: 430]

ARL-DA Books Prize [Vol. 2: 431]

Arlt Award in the Humanities; Gustave O. [Vol. 1: 7667]

Armand; Prix Louis [Vol. 2: 2177]

Armed Forces Award [Vol. 1: 17538]

Armed Forces Expeditionary Medal [Vol. 1: 16661]

Armed Forces Reserve Medal [Vol. 1: 16662]

Armed Services Attorney Awards [Vol. 1: 10596]

Armourers and Brasiers' Company Award [Vol. 2: 8928]

Armstrong Medal [Vol. 1: 14394]

Armstrong Memorial Lecture; Henry E. [Vol. 2: 9267]

Army of Occupation Medal [Vol. 1: 16663]

Army Reserve Components Achievement Medal [Vol. 1: 16664]

Arnheim Award [Vol. 2: 4855]

Arnheim Award; Rudolf [Vol. 1: 839]

Arnold Award for Excellence in Aeronautical Program Management; Hap [Vol. 1: 2508]

Arnold Award; H. H. [Vol. 1: 249]

Arnow Award; Philip [Vol. 1: 16830]

Arpino Award [Vol. 1: 13212]

Arrington Award; Leonard J. [Vol. 1: 11277]

Arrington-Prucha Award [Vol. 1: 17759]

Arsenault Senior Arts Award; Father Adrien [Vol. 1: 14147]

Art Award [Vol. 1: 13221]

Art Directors Club of Toronto Awards and Show Presentation [Vol. 1: 160]

Art of Listening Award [Vol. 1: 8545]

Art of Reporting Award [Vol. 1: 8546]

Art Show and Auction [Vol. 1: 8824]

Art Spirit Foundation Gold Medal Award for Excellence in Pastel [Vol. 1: 846]

Art Therapy Clinician Award [Vol. 1: 840]

ARTBA Awards [Vol. 1: 3706]

Arthroscopy Research Grants [Vol. 1: 4813]

Arthur A. Hitchcock Award for Distinguished Service [Vol. 1: 1937]

Arthur, M.D. Award; Capt. Ransom J. [Vol. 1: 16997]

Article Award
    Canadian Railroad Historical Association [Vol. 1: 6850]
    Children's Literature Association [Vol 1: 7245]
    International Association for Relationship Research [Vol 1: 9579]
    International Society of Olympic Historians [Vol 2: 4784]
    Religious Communication Association [Vol 1: 14501]
Article Prize
    American Philosophical Association [Vol. 1: 3172]
    Law and Society Association [Vol 1: 10756]
Artificial Intelligence Dissertation Award [Vol. 2: 2817]
Artist Award for a Distinguished Body of Work [Vol. 1: 7352]
Artist Awards [Vol. 1: 15482]
Artist Humanitarian Award [Vol. 1: 7725]
Artist of the Year [Vol. 2: 1173]
Artist Program Support I APS1 [Vol. 1: 17873]
Artist-Teacher Award [Vol. 1: 4568]
Artistic Program Support II APS2 [Vol. 1: 17874]
Artists for Nature Foundation Award [Vol. 2: 9341]
Artists-in-Residence Program
    Studio Museum in Harlem [Vol. 1: 16307]
    Ucross Foundation [Vol 1: 16595]
The Artist's Magazine/Watercolor Magic Magazine Award [Vol. 1: 4655]
Artot; Prix Paul [Vol. 1: 1582]
Arts and Business Awards [Vol. 2: 6734]
Arts and Crafts in Architecture Award [Vol. 2: 9148]
Arts and Culture Award [Vol. 1: 11730]
Arts and Science Program Awards [Vol. 1: 13861]
Arts Challenge Initiative [Vol. 1: 17875]
Arts Council of Northern Ireland Funding and Awards [Vol. 2: 6749]
Arts Education Award [Vol. 1: 4712]
Arts Recognition and Talent Search [Vol. 1: 12429]
Artsimovich Prize; L.A. [Vol. 2: 5785]
Aruba International Film Festival [Vol. 2: 60]
Arya Samaj Award; National [Vol. 2: 3333]
Aryabhata Medal [Vol. 2: 3620]
The ASA Award [Vol. 1: 4527]
ASA Travel Awards [Vol. 2: 531]
ASABE Fellows [Vol. 1: 4075]
Asada Medal [Vol. 2: 4250]
ASAE Fellow [Vol. 1: 4127]
ASBC - Merck Award [Vol. 1: 3756]
ASBMB-Merck Award [Vol. 1: 3756]
ASC/DEStech Award in Composites [Vol. 1: 3811]
ASCA Awards of Excellence [Vol. 1: 4578]
ASCAP Foundation College Musical Theatre Award [Vol. 1: 10665]
ASEM Fellows [Vol. 1: 3888]
ASHA Scholarships [Vol. 1: 3726]
Ashden Awards for Sustainable Energy [Vol. 2: 6753]
Ashe Award for Leadership and Sportsmanship; Arthur [Vol. 1: 9460]
Asher Distinguished Teaching Award; Eugene [Vol. 1: 2359]
Asher-Hess Prize [Vol. 2: 6508]
Ashford Medal; Bailey K. [Vol. 1: 4523]
Ashley Award; Larry [Vol. 1: 6317]
Ashley Undergraduate Prize; Frank [Vol. 2: 7260]
Ashman Achievement Award; William D. [Vol. 1: 10008]
ASHRAE ASHAE - Homer Addams Award [Vol. 1: 4310]
ASHRAE Energy Awards [Vol. 1: 4333]
ASHRAE Fellow [Vol. 1: 4312]
ASHRAE Journal Paper Award [Vol. 1: 4313]
Ashram Trust Award; Hari Om [Vol. 2: 3521]
ASHS Scholars Awards [Vol. 1: 3920]
Ashy Award; Edna [Vol. 1: 4473]
Asia Awards [Vol. 2: 8319]
Asia Awards; Seatrade [Vol. 2: 9175]
Asia Mobile Awards [Vol. 1: 8793]
Asia-Pacific Cancer Society Training Grants (APCA-SOT) [Vol. 2: 6458]
Asia-Pacific Distance Education Award [Vol. 1: 8694]
Asia-Pacific Entrepreneurs Award [Vol. 1: 8695]
Asia Pacific Entrepreneurship Awards [Vol. 2: 4541]
Asia Pacific ICT Alliance Awards [Vol. 2: 1773]

Asia Pacific Industrial Technologies Awards [Vol. 2: 5975]
Asia-Pacific Outstanding Academic Achievement Award [Vol. 1: 8696]
Asia-Pacific Postgraduate Student Award [Vol. 1: 8697]
Asia Pacific Screen Awards [Vol. 2: 89]
Asia-Pacific Study Abroad Awards [Vol. 1: 8698]
Asia Responsible Entrepreneurship Awards [Vol. 2: 4542]
Asian American Literary Awards [Vol. 1: 4828]
Asian/Asian-American Award [Vol. 1: 3364]
Asian Commercial Community Academic Awards [Vol. 2: 4408]
Asian Television Awards [Vol. 2: 5991]
Asiavision Annual Awards [Vol. 2: 4521]
Asiavision Award for Contributions to ASEAN Television News [Vol. 2: 4522]
ASID Human Environment Award [Vol. 1: 4348]
ASJA Outstanding Author Award [Vol. 1: 4357]
ASJSA Citation of Merit Award [Vol. 1: 5508]
ASLA Council of Fellows [Vol. 1: 4359]
ASLA Medal [Vol. 1: 4360]
ASM Award in Applied and Environmental and Microbiology [Vol. 1: 3981]
ASM Fellow [Vol. 1: 4830]
ASM International and The Metallurgical Society Distinguished Lectureship in Materials and Society [Vol. 1: 4832]
ASME Medal [Vol. 1: 4380]
ASNT Fellow Award [Vol. 1: 3999]
ASNT Fellowship Awards [Vol. 1: 4000]
ASNT Gold Medal [Vol. 1: 4004]
ASOCIO IT Award [Vol. 2: 4212]
ASORN Honor Award [Vol. 1: 4474]
ASORN Local Chapter Honor Award [Vol. 1: 4475]
ASPA/NASPAA Distinguished Research Award [Vol. 1: 11874]
Aspen Filmfest [Vol. 1: 4848]
ASPEN Research Scholar Award [Vol. 1: 4027]
Aspen Shortsfest [Vol. 1: 4849]
ASPS-FPB Best Paper Award [Vol. 2: 578]
Asselin; Prix Olivar [Vol. 1: 14995]
Assistant Coach of the Year [Vol. 1: 12844]
Assistant Coach of the Year Award [Vol. 1: 9461]
Assistant Trainer of the Year [Vol. 1: 17624]
Assistants Award [Vol. 2: 6839]
ASSO Student Award [Vol. 2: 215]
Associate and Technicians Award [Vol. 2: 7971]
Associate Member Diploma [Vol. 2: 7856]
Associate Member of the Year
    North Carolina Utility Contractors Association [Vol. 1: 13378]
    Print Services and Distribution Association [Vol 1: 14161]
Associate of the Royal Academy of Dance [Vol. 2: 8573]
Associate of the Year [Vol. 1: 10400]
Associated Collegiate Press Pacemaker Awards [Vol. 1: 13243]
Associateship of Honour [Vol. 2: 8810]
The Associateship of the City and Guilds of London Institute [Vol. 2: 7430]
Association Award for Economic Research [Vol. 2: 5170]
Association Fellow [Vol. 1: 234]
Association of Subspecialty Professors Young Investigator Award in Geriatrics [Vol. 1: 12431]
Association Youth Sport Membership Award [Vol. 1: 444]
Association Youth Sport Programming Award [Vol. 1: 445]
Associations Advance America Award of Excellence [Vol. 1: 4128]
Associations Make A Better World Award [Vol. 1: 4129]
Associations-of-the-Year Award [Vol. 1: 17454]
Astar Award [Vol. 1: 14531]
Astellas and Novartis Research Fellowships [Vol. 2: 7281]
Asthma Research Hall of Fame [Vol. 2: 108]
Asthma Research Postgraduate Scholarships [Vol. 2: 109]
Asthma Research Sustainability Grants [Vol. 2: 110]
Astin Measurement Science Award; Allen V. [Vol. 1: 16787]

Astin-Polk International Standards Medal [Vol. 1: 2968]
ASTM Robert J. Painter Memorial Award; SES/ [Vol. 1: 16250]
Astor Memorial Leadership Essay Contest; Vincent [Vol. 1: 17007]
ASTRA Awards [Vol. 2: 594]
AstraZeneca Award [Vol. 2: 8206]
AstraZeneca Fellowship/Faculty Transition [Vol. 1: 2201]
AstraZeneca Trainee Presentation Award [Vol. 1: 6984]
AstraZeneca Traveling Lectureship Award [Vol. 1: 15844]
AstraZeneca Young Scientist Frank Rose Award [Vol. 2: 6948]
Astrobiology Award [Vol. 1: 4719]
Astronautics Literature Award [Vol. 1: 1434]
Astronomical League Award [Vol. 1: 5649]
Asturias Award for Communications and Humanities; Prince of [Vol. 2: 6085]
Asturias Award for Concord; Prince of [Vol. 2: 6086]
Asturias Award for International Cooperation; Prince of [Vol. 2: 6087]
Asturias Award for Sports; Prince of [Vol. 2: 6088]
Asturias Award for the Arts; Prince of [Vol. 2: 6089]
Asturias for Technical and Scientific Research; Prince of [Vol. 2: 6090]
Astwood Lecture Award; Edwin B. [Vol. 1: 8107]
Asundi Memorial Lecture; Prof. Rango Krishna [Vol. 2: 3621]
Aswad Prize; Mohamed el [Vol. 2: 2020]
A.T. Still Medallion of Honor [Vol. 1: 640]
ATA National Truck Rodeo [Vol. 1: 4613]
AT&T Foundation Awards [Vol. 1: 3881]
AT&T Nonfiction Award [Vol. 2: 6900]
ATCA Small Business Award [Vol. 1: 304]
Athena Cup [Vol. 1: 17160]
Athena Medals [Vol. 1: 7529]
Athenaeum Literary Award [Vol. 1: 5662]
Athenian Award [Vol. 2: 3308]
Athens Summer Olympic Games Award [Vol. 2: 3309]
Athlete of the Month [Vol. 1: 6414]
Athlete of the Year
    International Waterski and Wakeboard Federation [Vol. 2: 6464]
    Special Olympics Canada [Vol 1: 16114]
    United States Synchronized Swimming [Vol 1: 17120]
    U.S.A. Deaf Sports Federation [Vol 1: 17414]
Athletes Appreciation Award [Vol. 1: 17437]
Athletic Director of the Year
    Canadian Colleges Athletic Association [Vol. 1: 6415]
    National High School Athletic Coaches Association [Vol 1: 12507]
Athletic Director of the Year Award [Vol. 1: 12194]
Athletic Hall of Fame [Vol. 1: 17366]
Atkins Communications Award; George [Vol. 1: 8239]
Atkins Research Award; Bobbie [Vol. 1: 11826]
Atkinson Award; Joan [Vol. 1: 16544]
Atkinson Memorial Award; Hugh C. [Vol. 1: 5257]
Atlantic Journalism Awards [Vol. 1: 5675]
Atlantic Lottery Corporation Achievement Award [Vol. 1: 5676]
Atlantic Seaboard Wine Competition [Vol. 1: 5680]
Atlantis Award [Vol. 1: 11262]
Atlas Awards [Vol. 1: 5544]
Atlas Copco Award [Vol. 2: 760]
Atlas Travel Marketing Executive Award [Vol. 1: 5544]
Atrium Award [Vol. 1: 17237]
Atterberry Research Grant; Gwenyth [Vol. 1: 15381]
Attneave Diversity Award; Carolyn [Vol. 1: 3423]
Atwood Award; J. Leland [Vol. 1: 2509]
Atwood Award; John Leland [Vol. 1: 3835]
Aubin Aerospace Customer Support Award for Excellence; Bruce R. [Vol. 1: 15489]
Aubry Award; Claude [Vol. 2: 6363]
Auction of the Year [Vol. 1: 11948]
Audience Award
    Norwegian International Film Festival [Vol. 2: 5144]
    The Norwegian Short Film Festival [Vol 2: 5148]

Swedish Film Institute **[Vol 2: 6231]**

Zagreb World Festival of Animated Films - ANI-MAFEST Zagreb **[Vol 2: 1887]**

Audience Awards **[Vol. 1: 8380]**

Audience Favorite - Documentary **[Vol. 1: 4850]**

Audience Prize **[Vol 2: 6258]**

Audience Prizes **[Vol. 2: 3247]**

Audio and Home Theater Awards **[Vol. 2: 5427]**

Audubon Medal **[Vol. 1: 11950]**

Auerbach Award; Isaac L. **[Vol. 2: 1268]**

Auerbach Trophy; Red **[Vol. 1: 11975]**

Aufranc Award; Otto **[Vol. 1: 8927]**

August-Wilhelm-von-Hofmann-Denkmunze **[Vol. 2: 2924]**

Augustine Award for Outstanding Achievement in Engineering Communications; Norm **[Vol. 1: 1146]**

Aujeszky Medal **[Vol. 2: 3375]**

Ault Award **[Vol. 1: 11835]**

Aurbach Lecture Award; Gerald D. **[Vol. 1: 8108]**

Aurealis Awards **[Vol. 2: 126]**

Aurelio Award for Altruism; Santo J. **[Vol. 1: 12265]**

Aurora Awards **[Vol. 1: 5697]**

Aurora Borealis Prize for Outstanding Translation of Fiction Literature **[Vol. 1: 9937]**

Aurora Borealis Prize for Outstanding Translation of Non-Fiction Literature **[Vol. 1: 9938]**

Aurora Scholarship **[Vol. 2: 432]**

Austern Memorial Writing Competition; H. Thomas **[Vol. 1: 8392]**

Austin Award; Mike **[Vol. 2: 7945]**

Austin Public Library Friends Foundation Award for Best Children's/Young Adult Books **[Vol. 1: 16451]**

Australasian Ceramic Society/Ceramic Society of Japan Joint Ceramic Award **[Vol. 2: 253]**

Australia and New Zealand Awards for Sustainability Reporting **[Vol. 2: 103]**

Australia Day Awards **[Vol. 2: 1178]**

Australian Active Service Medal **[Vol. 2: 303]**

Australian Active Service Medal 1945-1975 **[Vol. 2: 303]**

Australian Alumni Awards **[Vol. 2: 3815]**

Australian Antarctic Medal **[Vol. 2: 297]**

Australian Awards for Excellence in Educational Publishing **[Vol. 2: 516]**

Australian Ballooning Hall of Fame **[Vol. 2: 244]**

Australian Biography of the Year **[Vol. 2: 517]**

Australian Book Industry Awards **[Vol. 2: 517]**

Australian Book of the Year **[Vol. 2: 517]**

Australian Bravery Decorations **[Vol. 2: 298]**

Australian Business Awards **[Vol. 2: 251]**

Australian Cadet Forces Service Medal **[Vol. 2: 299]**

Australian College of Education Medal **[Vol. 2: 261]**

Australian Country Music Industry Achiever Awards **[Vol. 2: 675]**

Australian Defence Medal **[Vol. 2: 300]**

Australian Ecology Research Award **[Vol. 2: 692]**

Australian Engineering Excellence Awards **[Vol. 2: 767]**

Australian Fire Service Medal **[Vol. 2: 301]**

Australian Geomechanics Award - John Jaeger Memorial Award **[Vol. 2: 768]**

Australian Illustrated Book of the Year **[Vol. 2: 517]**

Australian Institute of Energy Medal **[Vol. 2: 390]**

Australian Institute of Packaging Fellow **[Vol. 2: 404]**

Australian Library and Information Association Fellow **[Vol. 2: 433]**

Australian Literature Society Gold Medal **[Vol. 2: 93]**

Australian Mathematical Society Medal **[Vol. 2: 464]**

Australian Medal for Landscape Architecture **[Vol. 2: 396]**

Australian Medal of Agricultural Science **[Vol. 2: 377]**

Australian Museum Eureka Prizes **[Vol. 2: 521]**

Australian Natural History Medallion **[Vol. 2: 721]**

Australian Newcomer of the Year **[Vol. 2: 517]**

Australian Nuclear Association Annual Award **[Vol. 2: 483]**

Australian of the Year **[Vol. 2: 885]**

Australian of the Year Awards **[Vol. 2: 885]**

Australian Police Medal **[Vol. 2: 302]**

Australian Privacy Awards **[Vol. 2: 489]**

Australian Privacy Medal **[Vol. 2: 490]**

Australian Service Medal **[Vol. 2: 303]**

Australian Skeptics Prize for Critical Thinking **[Vol. 2: 527]**

Australian Sports Medal **[Vol. 2: 304]**

Australian Teachers of Media Awards **[Vol. 2: 596]**

Australian Universities Grant **[Vol. 2: 6386]**

Australian Veterinary Association (Australia) Prize **[Vol. 2: 1162]**

Australian Veterinary Association (Victoria) Prize **[Vol. 2: 1163]**

The Australian/Vogel Literary Award **[Vol. 2: 72]**

Australia's Local Hero **[Vol. 2: 885]**

Austrian Prize for Press Photography **[Vol. 2: 1200]**

Authentic Albania Quality Mark Award Program **[Vol. 2: 9]**

Author Emeritus Award **[Vol. 1: 14784]**

Author of the Year Award

American Society of Journalists and Authors **[Vol. 1: 4357]**

Canadian Booksellers Association **[Vol 1: 6347]**

Author's Awards **[Vol. 1: 5355]**

Authors Club Certificate **[Vol. 2: 1223]**

Autism Professional of the Year **[Vol. 1: 5699]**

Automated Imaging Achievement Award **[Vol. 1: 5706]**

Automatica Prize Paper Award **[Vol. 2: 1276]**

Automotive Achievement Award **[Vol. 1: 11107]**

Automotive Aftermarket Education Award **[Vol. 1: 13427]**

Automotive Dealer Education Award **[Vol. 1: 13428]**

Automotive Engineering Excellence Awards **[Vol. 2: 1038]**

Automotive Hall of Fame **[Vol. 1: 5713]**

Automotive Industry Leader of the Year **[Vol. 1: 5714]**

Automotive Innovation Award **[Vol. 1: 11108]**

Automotive Replacement Management Award **[Vol. 1: 13427]**

Autopsy Award for Pathologists-in-Training **[Vol. 1: 16702]**

Auxiliary Excellence Award **[Vol. 1: 2756]**

Ava Awards **[Vol. 1: 5402]**

Avanti Award in Lipids **[Vol. 1: 3757]**

Avenatti Award for Excellence in Pre-Trial and Trial Advocacy; Michael J. **[Vol. 1: 8574]**

Avenir Award **[Vol. 2: 2317]**

Avenza Award for Electronic Mapping **[Vol. 2: 6986]**

Avery Award; Oswald **[Vol. 1: 9227]**

Aviation and Space Award **[Vol. 1: 17539]**

Aviation Award (W.A. Branch) **[Vol. 2: 610]**

Aviation Awards for Excellence **[Vol. 2: 640]**

Aviation Hall of Fame Award **[Vol. 1: 11954]**

Aviation Journalism Award **[Vol. 1: 11497]**

Aviation Week and Space Technology Distinguished Service Award **[Vol. 1: 8374]**

AVID Excellence in Editing Award **[Vol. 1: 9880]**

Avioli Founders Award; Louis V. **[Vol. 1: 3768]**

Avion Awards **[Vol. 1: 310]**

AVMA Award **[Vol. 1: 4637]**

AVY Awards **[Vol. 1: 2114]**

Award for Achievement in Engineering Enterprise **[Vol. 2: 769]**

Award for Achievement in Environmental Law, Policy and Management **[Vol. 1: 8160]**

Award for Achievement in Scientific Research and Development **[Vol. 1: 18062]**

Award for Advancement of Industry **[Vol. 2: 5450]**

Award for Advancement of Science **[Vol. 2: 5451]**

Award for Advances in Clinical Microbiology **[Vol. 2: 6291]**

Award for Advancing Diversity and Social Change in Honor of Paul Davidoff **[Vol. 1: 3284]**

Award for Advocacy **[Vol. 1: 17515]**

Award for Affordable Green Chemistry **[Vol. 1: 1614]**

Award for an Exceptional Specific Prediction **[Vol. 1: 2900]**

Award for an Exemplary Program or Achievement in a Mathematics Department **[Vol. 1: 2823]**

Award for Behavioral Research Relevant to the Prevention of Nuclear War **[Vol. 1: 11422]**

Award for Best Canadian Feature Film **[Vol. 1: 16516]**

Award for Best Canadian First Feature Film **[Vol. 1: 16517]**

Award for Best Canadian Short Film **[Vol. 1: 16518]**

Award for Best Ecological Project **[Vol. 2: 5563]**

Award for Best Final Year Student in Agricultural Economics **[Vol. 2: 5497]**

Award for Best Financially Managed Semiconductor Company **[Vol. 1: 8680]**

Award for Best New Journal **[Vol. 2: 6829]**

Award for Best Student Essay/Report **[Vol. 2: 4374]**

Award for Best Thesis Presentation in Solid State Physics **[Vol. 2: 3681]**

Award for Best Undergraduate Paper in Psychology and Law **[Vol. 1: 3620]**

Award for Broadcast Meteorology **[Vol. 1: 2901]**

Award for Career Development in Honor of L.P. Cookingham **[Vol. 1: 9762]**

Award for Chemical Education **[Vol. 2: 5452]**

Award for Chemical Education **[Vol. 1: 7203]**

Award for Chemistry Education **[Vol. 2: 4217]**

Award for Chemistry in Service to Society **[Vol. 1: 11423]**

Award for Clinical Excellence **[Vol. 1: 15680]**

Award for Communication Excellence **[Vol. 1: 1582]**

Award for Community Service **[Vol. 1: 12456]**

Award for Conservation Merit **[Vol. 2: 6569]**

Award For Contribution to Gerontology **[Vol. 1: 6265]**

Award for Contribution to the Land Based Sector **[Vol. 2: 7951]**

Award for Contributions to Amateur Mycology **[Vol. 1: 13320]**

Award for Contributions to Correctional Psychology **[Vol. 1: 3621]**

Award for Creative Work in Fluorine Chemistry **[Vol. 1: 1615]**

Award for Creativity in Psychiatric Education **[Vol. 1: 1812]**

Award for Distinguished Career Contributions to Education and Training **[Vol. 1: 3566]**

Award for Distinguished Contribution to Education and Training **[Vol. 1: 3532]**

Award for Distinguished Contribution to Ethnic Minority Issues **[Vol. 1: 3533]**

Award for Distinguished Contribution to Practice in Community Psychology **[Vol. 1: 3508]**

Award for Distinguished Contribution to Psychology and Law **[Vol. 1: 3622]**

Award for Distinguished Contribution to the Advancement of Pharmacotherapy at the National Level **[Vol. 1: 3379]**

Award for Distinguished Contribution to the Advancement of Pharmacotherapy at the State Level **[Vol. 1: 3380]**

Award for Distinguished Contribution to Theory and Research in Community Psychology **[Vol. 1: 3509]**

Award for Distinguished Contributions in Education **[Vol. 2: 4098]**

Award for Distinguished Contributions to Asian Studies **[Vol. 1: 4913]**

Award for Distinguished Contributions to Education and Training in Psychology **[Vol. 1: 6821]**

Award for Distinguished Contributions to Education in Child Development **[Vol. 1: 15297]**

Award for Distinguished Contributions to Professional Psychology **[Vol. 2: 7180]**

Award for Distinguished Contributions to Psychology as a Profession **[Vol. 1: 6822]**

Award for Distinguished Contributions to Public or Community Service **[Vol. 1: 6823]**

Award for Distinguished Contributions to Public Policy for Children **[Vol. 1: 15298]**

Award for Distinguished Contributions to Research in Education **[Vol. 1: 2055]**

Award for Distinguished Contributions to the International Advancement of Psychology **[Vol. 1: 6824]**

Award for Distinguished Contributions to the Lives of Children **[Vol. 1: 15299]**

Award for Distinguished Contributions to the Society **[Vol. 1: 15300]**

Award for Distinguished Lifetime Contributions to Media Psychology **[Vol. 1: 3441]**

Award for Distinguished Professional Contribution **[Vol. 1: 3534]**

Award for Distinguished Public Service

American Mathematical Society **[Vol. 1: 2824]**

American Society of Heating, Refrigerating and Air-Conditioning Engineers **[Vol 1: 4314]**

United States Conference of Mayors **[Vol 1: 16771]**

Award for Distinguished Research in the Biomedical Sciences **[Vol. 1: 5209]**

Award for Distinguished Scientific Contribution **[Vol. 1: 3535]**

Award for Distinguished Scientific Contributions **[Vol. 1: 3567]**

Award for Distinguished Scientific Contributions to Child Development [Vol. 1: 15301]

Award for Distinguished Scientific Contributions to Clinical Psychology [Vol. 1: 3576]

Award for Distinguished Scientific Contributions to Media Psychology [Vol. 1: 3442]

Award for Distinguished Scientific Contributions to Public Interest [Vol. 1: 3568]

Award for Distinguished Scientific Contributions to the Application of Psychology [Vol. 1: 3569]

Award for Distinguished Scientific Early Career Contributions [Vol. 1: 3570]

Award for Distinguished Scientific or Professional Contributions to Psychological Assessment [Vol. 2: 2811]

Award for Distinguished Service [Vol. 1: 11015]

Award for Distinguished Service on Behalf of Social-Personality Psychology [Vol. 1: 15263]

Award for Distinguished Service to Building Simulation [Vol. 1: 9740]

Award for Distinguished Service to Children [Vol. 1: 11754]

Award for Distinguished Service to Museums [Vol. 1: 1215]

Award for Distinguished Service to N4A [Vol. 1: 11613]

Award for Distinguished Service to New Brunswick Agriculture [Vol. 1: 13156]

Award for Distinguished Service to the Cause of Unitarian Universalism [Vol. 1: 16622]

Award for Distinguished Service to the Profession of Wood Science and Technology [Vol. 1: 15903]

Award for Distinguished Service to the Society [Vol. 1: 15264]

Award for Distinguished Services to Art [Vol. 2: 4341]

Award for Distinguished Services to Sports [Vol. 2: 4342]

Award for Distinguished Student Contribution [Vol. 1: 3536]

Award for Distinguished Theoretical and Philosophical Contributions to Psychology [Vol. 1: 3560]

Award for Divisional Scientific Contributions [Vol. 2: 4309]

Award for Divisional Scientific Promotions [Vol. 2: 4310]

Award for Drug Discovery [Vol. 2: 9199]

Award for Drug Research and Development [Vol. 2: 4311]

Award for Early Career Contributions to Hypnosis [Vol. 1: 3606]

Award for Engaging Individuals with Disabilities [Vol. 1: 5458]

Award for Engaging Underserved Communities [Vol. 1: 5459]

Award for Environmentally Sustainable Use of Concrete [Vol. 2: 661]

Award for Excellence
 AHRA: The Association for Medical Imaging Management [Vol. 1: 227]
 American Public Health Association [Vol 1: 3642]
 National Catholic Committee on Scouting [Vol 1: 12040]
 South African Institute of Architects [Vol 2: 5693]

Award for Excellence and Innovation in Arts Access [Vol. 1: 5458]

Award for Excellence and Innovation in Glaucoma [Vol. 1: 8657]

Award for Excellence: Genealogical Methods and Sources [Vol. 1: 12442]

Award for Excellence: Genealogy and Family History Book [Vol. 1: 12443]

Award for Excellence in Adhesion Science [Vol. 1: 149]

Award for Excellence in Book Publication [Vol. 1: 754]

Award for Excellence in Clinical Microbiology and Infectious Diseases [Vol. 2: 6292]

Award for Excellence in Clinical Teaching [Vol. 1: 3232]

Award for Excellence in Community Crime Prevention [Vol. 1: 3332]

Award for Excellence in Economic Reporting [Vol. 1: 8483]

Award for Excellence in Editing [Vol. 1: 5143]

Award for Excellence in Encouraging Equity [Vol. 1: 11646]

Award for Excellence in Equality and Diversity [Vol. 2: 8283]

Award for Excellence in European Aquaculture [Vol. 2: 1510]

Award for Excellence in Exporting Legal Services [Vol. 2: 8284]

Award for Excellence in Human Research Protection [Vol. 1: 8845]

Award for Excellence in Integrated Pest Management [Vol. 1: 8137]

Award for Excellence in International Education [Vol. 1: 1098]

Award for Excellence in Marketing and Business Development [Vol. 2: 8285]

Award for Excellence in Nonfiction for Young Adults [Vol. 1: 18216]

Award for Excellence in Nutrition and Meat Sciences [Vol. 1: 6925]

Award for Excellence in Pain Research and Management [Vol. 1: 9596]

Award for Excellence in Perioperative Nursing [Vol. 1: 5465]

Award for Excellence in Pioneering Legal Services [Vol. 2: 8286]

Award for Excellence in Plasma Physics Research [Vol. 1: 3201]

Award for Excellence in Poetry for Children [Vol. 1: 12203]

Award for Excellence in Pre-College Physics Teaching [Vol. 1: 1306]

Award for Excellence in Productivity Improvement [Vol. 1: 9347]

Award for Excellence in Professional Writing [Vol. 1: 1093]

Award for Excellence in Pulmonary Hypertension Care [Vol. 1: 14343]

Award for Excellence in Science Broadcasting by a Broadcast Meteorologist [Vol. 1: 2902]

Award for Excellence in Social Responsibility [Vol. 2: 8287]

Award for Excellence in Teaching
 Society of Hospital Medicine [Vol. 1: 15681]
 Teachers of English to Speakers of Other Languages [Vol 1: 16391]

Award for Excellence in Teaching Geography [Vol. 1: 6259]

Award for Excellence in Teaching in Pediatrics [Vol. 1: 4286]

Award for Excellence in the Teaching of Natural Resources in the Earth Sciences K-12 [Vol. 1: 1266]

Award for Excellence in the Teaching of Public Administration in Africa [Vol. 2: 4375]

Award for Excellence in Training and Development [Vol. 2: 5266]

Award for Excellence in Undergraduate Physics Teaching [Vol. 1: 1307]

Award for Excellence in Workplace Volunteer Programs [Vol. 1: 14073]

Award for Excellent Chemistry Teachers [Vol. 2: 5453]

Award for Excellent Oral Presentation [Vol. 2: 3981]

Award For Excellent PhD Thesis in Psychology [Vol. 2: 508]

Award for Excellent Poster Presentation [Vol. 2: 3982]

Award for Excellent Research Paper [Vol. 2: 5454]

Award for Exceptional International Leadership [Vol. 1: 9794]

Award for Executive Excellence [Vol. 1: 7434]

Award for Exemplary Library Services to Diverse Populations [Vol. 1: 7383]

Award for Expanding the Retail Market [Vol. 2: 6891]

Award for Geography in the Service of Government or Business [Vol. 1: 6260]

Award for Heaviest Structure Moved On Dollies Under $30,000 [Vol. 1: 9703]

Award for Heaviest Structure Moved On Rubber Tires [Vol. 1: 9704]

Award for Heaviest Structure Moved Under $30,000 [Vol. 1: 9705]

Award for Human Immunology Research [Vol. 1: 1183]

Award for Humanistic Studies [Vol. 1: 494]

Award for Increasing Arts Access in Underserved Communities [Vol. 1: 5459]

Award for Industry's Most Respected Public Fabless Company [Vol. 1: 8681]

Award for Initiatives in Research [Vol. 1: 11424]

Award For Innovation [Vol. 1: 6416]

Award for Innovative Excellence in Teaching, Learning, and Technology [Vol. 1: 9811]

Award for Innovative Management [Vol. 2: 4376]

Award for International Scientific Cooperation [Vol. 1: 985]

Award for Keyboard [Vol. 2: 8553]

Award for Lifetime Service to the Computer Science Education Community [Vol. 1: 4970]

Award for Literary Criticism [Vol. 2: 3984]

Award for Local Sales Achievement [Vol. 1: 6073]

Award for Longest Structure Moved Under $30,000 [Vol. 1: 9706]

Award for Longest, Widest, Tallest Structure Moved [Vol. 1: 9707]

Award for Marketing Excellence [Vol. 2: 5267]

Award for Meritorious Service to Family History [Vol. 2: 135]

Award for Most Meritorious Presentation [Vol. 2: 4942]

Award for Most Unusual Move [Vol. 1: 9708]

Award for National Leadership in Government Service [Vol. 1: 545]

Award for Original Hebrew Novel [Vol. 2: 3985]

Award for Original Hebrew Poetry [Vol. 2: 3986]

Award for Outstanding Achievement in Biobanking [Vol. 1: 3962]

Award for Outstanding Achievement in International Business [Vol. 1: 18083]

Award for Outstanding Article in a Journal [Vol. 1: 5144]

Award for Outstanding Article in the History of the Neurosciences [Vol. 1: 10239]

Award for Outstanding Book in the History of the Neurosciences [Vol. 1: 10240]

Award for Outstanding Contribution in Research [Vol. 1: 1744]

Award for Outstanding Contribution to Computer Science Education [Vol. 1: 4971]

Award for Outstanding Contribution to Diversity in Alternative Dispute Resolution [Vol. 1: 7732]

Award for Outstanding Contribution to Knowledge in Public Administration and Management [Vol. 2: 4377]

Award for Outstanding Contribution to Psychology in Singapore [Vol. 2: 5985]

Award for Outstanding Contribution to Public Understanding of the Geosciences [Vol. 1: 2222]

Award for Outstanding Contribution to the Development of the IBS [Vol. 1: 9729]

Award for Outstanding Contributions in Education [Vol. 1: 886]

Award for Outstanding Contributions through Service to the Profession of Clinical Chemistry [Vol. 1: 887]

Award for Outstanding Contributions to Animal Clinical Chemistry [Vol. 1: 888]

Award for Outstanding Contributions to Health Psychology [Vol. 1: 3471]

Award for Outstanding Contributions to Pediatric and Maternal-Fetal Clinical Chemistry [Vol. 1: 889]

Award for Outstanding Contributions to Practice in Trauma Psychology [Vol. 1: 3466]

Award for Outstanding Contributions to the Science of Trauma Psychology [Vol. 1: 3467]

Award for Outstanding Contributions to the Society [Vol. 2: 827]

Award for Outstanding Dissertation in the Field of Trauma Psychology [Vol. 1: 3468]

Award for Outstanding Editorial or Publishing Contributions [Vol. 1: 5317]

Award for Outstanding Elected Official Leadership [Vol. 1: 5411]

Award for Outstanding Government Official [Vol. 2: 6459]

Award for Outstanding Individual Leadership [Vol. 1: 5412]

Award for Outstanding Leadership and Service to NHCA [Vol. 1: 12503]

Award for Outstanding Multidisciplinary Team Research in Agriculture and Allied Sciences [Vol. 2: 3522]

Construction Specifications Canada [Vol 1: 7550]

Door and Hardware Institute [Vol 1: 7906]

Eastern College Athletic Conference [Vol 1: 7974]

Federation of Genealogical Societies [Vol 2: 8318]

Institution of Agricultural Engineers [Vol 2: 7952]

International Association Auto Theft Investigators [Vol 1: 9506]

International Police Work Dog Association [Vol 1: 10046]

International Regional Magazine Association [Vol 1: 10112]

International Weightlifting Federation [Vol 2: 3410]

National Commission on Correctional Health Care [Vol 1: 12095]

National Genealogical Society [Vol 1: 12445]

National Water Safety Congress [Vol 1: 13025]

New England Water Works Association [Vol 1: 13163]

North American Association of Food Equipment Manufacturers [Vol 1: 13278]

Ontario Psychological Association [Vol 1: 13593]

Society for Historical Archaeology [Vol 1: 15090]

Society of Manufacturing Engineers [Vol 1: 15685]

South African Institute of Architects [Vol 2: 5694]

Swedish Council of America [Vol 1: 16346]

Tree Care Industry Association [Vol 1: 16547]

Western History Association [Vol 1: 17760]

Award of Merit - Commercial [Vol. 1: 7488]

Award of Merit for Chemistry Education [Vol. 2: 4222]

Award of Merit - Governmental [Vol. 1: 7489]

Award of Merit in Broadcasting [Vol. 1: 14493]

Award of Merit in Journalism [Vol. 1: 14493]

Award of Merit - Individual [Vol. 1: 7490]

Award of Merit - Industry [Vol. 1: 2656]

Award of Merit - Preservation [Vol. 1: 7491]

Award of Merit - Scholastic/Authorship [Vol. 1: 7492]

Award of Quality [Vol. 1: 3064]

Award of Recognition
AACE International [Vol. 1: 20]
La Leche League International [Vol 1: 10709]

Award of Recognition: AACRAO Internships [Vol. 1: 1097]

Award of Safety Excellence [Vol. 1: 14347]

Award of Special Merit [Vol. 1: 12245]

Award of Special Recognition [Vol. 1: 105]

Award of the Serbian Chamber of Commerce [Vol. 2: 5911]

Award of Valor
International Police Work Dog Association [Vol. 1: 10047]
North American Police Work Dog Association [Vol 1: 13331]

Award to the Most Outstanding Third Year Student in Zoology [Vol. 2: 5770]

Awards Competition [Vol. 1: 11769]

Awards for Achievement [Vol. 2: 9453]

Awards for Action on HIV/AIDS and Human Rights [Vol. 1: 6556]

Awards for Adult Literature [Vol. 1: 6323]

Awards for Best Posters [Vol. 1: 6810]

Awards for Business Excellence [Vol. 2: 3331]

Awards for Canine Excellence [Vol. 1: 2743]

Awards for Editorial and Publishing Excellence [Vol. 2: 7256]

Awards for Editorial Excellence [Vol. 2: 1954]

Awards for Excellence
Asphalt Recycling and Reclaiming Association [Vol. 1: 4858]
Australian Hotels Association NSW [Vol 2: 362]
Consult Australia [Vol 2: 664]
Exhibition and Event Association of Australasia [Vol 2: 708]
Fork Lift Truck Association [Vol 2: 7706]
Guild of Television Cameramen [Vol 2: 7772]
Institute of Leadership and Management [Vol 2: 7880]
International Society of City and Regional Planners [Vol 2: 4781]
Oil Firing Technical Association for the Petroleum Industry [Vol 2: 8430]
Rural Sociological Society [Vol 1: 14658]

Urban Land Institute [Vol 1: 17402]

Awards for Excellence - Accommodation Division [Vol. 2: 363]

Awards for Excellence, Automotive Service [Vol. 1: 4935]

Awards for Excellence - General Division [Vol. 2: 364]

Awards for Excellence in Alternative Dispute Resolution [Vol. 1: 7733]

Awards for Excellence in Book Design in Canada [Vol. 1: 343]

Awards for Excellence in Broadcasting [Vol. 2: 9432]

Awards for Excellence in Distance Learning [Vol. 1: 9426]

Awards for Excellence in eLearning [Vol. 1: 9426]

Awards for Excellence in Government Finance [Vol. 1: 8742]

Awards for Excellence in Research [Vol. 1: 2884]

Awards for Excellence in Research and Training/Service [Vol. 1: 18017]

Awards for Excellence in Teaching of the Classics [Vol. 1: 3168]

Awards for Excellence in the Study of Religion [Vol. 1: 751]

Awards for Innovation in Teaching Science Teachers [Vol. 1: 5089]

Awards for Investigative Journalism [Vol. 1: 6276]

Awards for Outstanding Achievement [Vol. 1: 6722]

Awards for Outstanding Achievement in Procurement [Vol. 2: 9332]

Awards for Outstanding Consultancy Practice [Vol. 2: 8517]

Awards for Outstanding Teaching and Mentoring [Vol. 1: 15361]

Awards for Science and Ethics in Transportation Research [Vol. 1: 17309]

Awards for Science Promotion [Vol. 1: 13103]

Awards for Scientific Achievement [Vol. 1: 17647]

Awards for Software Excellence [Vol. 2: 6029]

Awards for Young Composers [Vol. 1: 14986]

Awards in History [Vol. 2: 4896]

Awards in Oral History [Vol. 2: 4897]

Awards in Recognition of Women Obstetricians/Gynecologists [Vol. 2: 8123]

Awards in Science and Technology [Vol. 2: 6626]

Awards in Tropical Botany [Vol. 1: 8512]

Awards of Appreciation [Vol. 1: 8642]

Awards of Distinction [Vol. 1: 15836]

Awards of Excellence
Association for Communication Excellence in Agriculture, Natural Resources, and Life and Human Sciences [Vol. 1: 4945]
Association of Consulting Engineering Companies - Canada [Vol 1: 5294]
Association of Consulting Engineers of New Zealand [Vol 2: 4860]
Australian Packaging and Processing Machinery Association [Vol 2: 492]
Canadian Architect [Vol 1: 6211]
Canadian Public Relations Society [Vol 1: 6838]
Canadian Society of Landscape Architects [Vol 1: 6966]
Illinois Theatre Association [Vol 1: 9151]
International Magnesium Association [Vol 1: 10004]
International Parking Institute [Vol 1: 10044]
National Association of Community Health Centers [Vol 1: 11711]
National Council for Community Behavioral Healthcare [Vol 1: 12146]
Wedding and Portrait Photographers International [Vol 1: 17735]

Awards of Excellence in Housing and Community Development [Vol. 1: 11794]

Awards of Excellence in Landscape Architecture [Vol. 2: 397]

Awards of Merit
American Association of Blood Banks [Vol. 1: 1058]
American Society of Clinical Hypnosis [Vol. 1: 4252]
Historical Society of Michigan [Vol 1: 8942]

Awards of Merit in Housing and Community Development [Vol. 1: 11795]

Awards to Industry [Vol. 2: 241]

Awards to Young European Scientists [Vol. 2: 3285]

AWIT Awards [Vol. 2: 5353]

AWMA Conference Awards [Vol. 2: 621]

AWP Award Series
Association of Writers and Writing Programs [Vol. 1: 5555]
Association of Writers and Writing Programs [Vol 1: 5556]
Association of Writers and Writing Programs [Vol 1: 5557]
Association of Writers and Writing Programs [Vol 1: 5558]

AWP Prize for Creative Nonfiction [Vol. 1: 5555]

AWP Prize for the Novel [Vol. 1: 5556]

Axelby Outstanding Paper; George S. [Vol. 1: 9069]

Axelrod Award; Julius [Vol. 1: 4031]

Axelrod Mentorship Award; Julius [Vol. 1: 1777]

Axford Award for Elementary Guidance; Marion [Vol. 1: 13595]

Axiom Business Book Awards [Vol. 1: 10549]

AXIS Awards [Vol. 2: 4880]

Axium Producers Award [Vol. 1: 8355]

Axium Truer Than Fiction Award [Vol. 1: 8357]

Axton Award; Mae Boren [Vol. 1: 61]

Ayoub Prize; Adham [Vol. 2: 2021]

Ayres Award; A. Jean [Vol. 1: 3040]

Ayuda a la Investigacion [Vol. 2: 6101]

Azam Prize; Dr. M.N. [Vol. 2: 5188]

Azbee Awards of Excellence [Vol. 1: 4133]

AzLA/SIRS Intellectual Freedom Award [Vol. 1: 4780]

Azorin Prize [Vol. 2: 6022]

B & B Awards [Vol. 2: 6859]

B & T Awards [Vol. 2: 626]

Baayen Award; Cor [Vol. 2: 2404]

Baba Award for Best Thesis Presentation in Nuclear Physics; Prof. C.V.K. [Vol. 2: 3682]

Babbitt National Service Award; General George T. [Vol. 1: 10879]

Babcock-Hart Award [Vol. 1: 9332]

Baber Research Grant; Carol Preston [Vol. 1: 2792]

Bablik Medal [Vol. 2: 7618]

BACB National House Journal Competition [Vol. 2: 7878]

Bach Award [Vol. 1: 16309]

Bacharach Service Award; Jere L. [Vol. 1: 11140]

Bache Trophy; David [Vol. 2: 7036]

Bachus Gold Medal; Walter O. [Vol. 1: 15446]

Bacigalupi Program of Distinction Award; Tadini [Vol. 1: 12638]

Back Award [Vol. 2: 8785]

Back Pain Association Medal [Vol. 2: 6865]

BackCare Medal [Vol. 2: 6864]

Backmans Stipendium; Ida [Vol. 2: 6194]

Backus Award [Vol. 1: 11328]

Bacon Award; Paul [Vol. 1: 17070]

BACR Travel/Exchange Fellowships [Vol. 2: 6949]

Bactlab Systems Gold Award for the Best Paper [Vol. 2: 5614]

Bactlab Systems Premier Award for Best Paper [Vol. 2: 5615]

Baddams Bursary; Thenie [Vol. 2: 337]

Bader Award [Vol. 2: 8975]

Bader Award in Bioinorganic or Bioorganic Chemistry; Alfred [Vol. 1: 1619]

Bader Award in Organic Chemistry; Alfred [Vol. 1: 6885]

Bader Prize; Alfred [Vol. 2: 1911]

Badge of Honour [Vol. 2: 4751]

Badminton Hall of Fame [Vol. 1: 17406]

Baekeland Lecture [Vol. 2: 9271]

Baer Heart Fund Grants; Max [Vol. 1: 8766]

Baer Medal; Karl Ernst von [Vol. 2: 2040]

Baes; Prix Professeur Louis [Vol. 2: 1650]

Baethke - Eleanor J. Carlin Award for Excellence in Academic Teaching; Dorothy E. [Vol. 1: 3229]

Baethke - Eleanor J. Carlin Award for Teaching Excellence; Dorothy E. [Vol. 1: 3229]

Bagnoud Award; Francois Xavier [Vol. 1: 2318]

Baguley Award; R. M. [Vol. 2: 8500]

Bagutta Prize [Vol. 2: 4036]

Bahamas Hotel Awards/Cacique Awards [Vol. 2: 1341]

Bahamas International Film Festival [Vol. 2: 1343]

Bahamas Web Awards [Vol. 2: 1345]

Bahrain Web Awards [Vol. 2: 4451]

BAIE Editing for Industry Awards
  Institute of Internal Communication [Vol. 2: 7878]
  Institute of Internal Communication [Vol 2: 7878]
Baier Technical Achievement Award; Edward J. [Vol. 1: 2484]
Baikie Award; Albert [Vol. 2: 745]
Bailey Award; Alton E. [Vol. 1: 3046]
Bailey Award; Chrisi [Vol. 2: 6744]
Bailey Award; E.G. [Vol. 1: 10279]
Bailey Distinguished Member Award; Marilyn and Sturges W. [Vol. 1: 7316]
Bailey Medal; Clyde H. [Vol. 2: 1250]
Bailey Medal; Liberty Hyde [Vol. 1: 2424]
Baillie Award; Andrew D. [Vol. 1: 6979]
Baillie Student Award for Field Research [Vol. 1: 5857]
Bailly; Prix Antoine-Nicolas [Vol. 2: 2136]
Bainbridge Award [Vol. 1: 5536]
Bainton Book Prize; Roland H. [Vol. 1: 14917]
Bair Endowment Award; Clifford E. [Vol. 1: 12630]
Bairam Memorial Prize; Professor Erkin [Vol. 2: 5084]
Baird Audience Development Gold Ribbon Awards; Audrey [Vol. 1: 10778]
Baird Award; Tadeusz [Vol. 2: 5401]
Baird Excellence in Clinical Writing Award; Susan [Vol. 1: 13530]
Baird Memorial Competition for Young Composers; Tadeusz [Vol. 2: 5401]
Baker and Taylor Award [Vol. 1: 8473]
Baker and Taylor Entertainment Audio Music/Video Product Award [Vol. 1: 14318]
Baker and Taylor/YALSA Conference Grants [Vol. 1: 18217]
Baker Award for Highway Safety; J. Stannard
  International Association of Chiefs of Police [Vol. 1: 9640]
  National Sheriffs' Association [Vol 1: 12835]
Baker Award for Lifetime Achievement in Neurologic Education; A.B. [Vol. 1: 580]
Baker Best Conference Paper Award; Merl [Vol. 1: 3889]
Baker Bursary Award; Mike [Vol. 2: 5721]
Baker Distinguished Research Award; Dr. David F. [Vol. 1: 9349]
Baker Endowed Scholarships; Donna Jabara [Vol. 1: 17819]
Baker Fellowships; E. A. [Vol. 1: 6727]
Baker Medal [Vol. 2: 7972]
Baker Research Award; Philip Noel [Vol. 2: 3062]
Baker-Wilkins Award for Outstanding Deputy Chief of Mission [Vol. 1: 16843]
Bakewell Prize; Thomas [Vol. 2: 8704]
Bakh Prize; A.N. [Vol. 2: 5786]
Bakjian Award; Andy [Vol. 1: 17455]
Balakian Citation for Excellence in Reviewing Award; Nona [Vol. 1: 11992]
Balandin Prize; A.A. [Vol. 2: 5787]
Balasaraswati/Joy Ann Dewey Beinecke Endowed Chair for Distinguished Teaching [Vol. 1: 1989]
Balazs Prize; Endre A. [Vol. 1: 10161]
Balch Prizes; Emily Clark [Vol. 1: 17591]
Baldock Award; Mike [Vol. 2: 7773]
Baldwin Award; F. W. (Casey) [Vol. 1: 6194]
Baldwin Medal of Liberty Award; Roger N. [Vol. 1: 1683]
Balfour Professional of the Year Award; Frank C. [Vol. 1: 10122]
Balfour Scholarship [Vol. 1: 13971]
Balfour Silver and Golden Anniversary Award [Vol. 1: 11642]
Ballantyne Award; Harry M. [Vol. 2: 6574]
Ballard Breaux Visiting Fellowship [Vol. 1: 8361]
Ballew Directing Award; Leighton M. [Vol. 1: 16002]
Ballot Medal; Buys [Vol. 2: 4816]
Balmer Prize [Vol. 2: 6486]
Balodis Prize; Karlis [Vol. 2: 4433]
BALPA Award [Vol. 2: 6935]
Baltes Distinguished Research Achievement Award [Vol. 1: 3371]
Baltes Foundation Award; Margret M. and Paul B. [Vol. 1: 8617]
Baltic Democracy Award [Vol. 1: 10586]
Baltic Freedom Award [Vol. 1: 10586]
Balvenie Medal [Vol. 2: 7446]
Balzan Prizes [Vol. 2: 4086]

Banbury Award; Fernley H. [Vol. 1: 1620]
Bancroft Award [Vol. 1: 14636]
Bancroft - Mackerras Medal for Excellence [Vol. 2: 552]
Bancroft Memorial Scholarship; Mary A. [Vol. 1: 10630]
Band Booster Award [Vol. 1: 11959]
Bandura Graduate Research Award; Albert [Vol. 1: 14288]
Banff Centre Award for Creative Excellence [Vol. 1: 5776]
Banff Concours International de Quatuor A Cordes [Vol. 1: 5774]
Banff International String Quartet Competition [Vol. 1: 5774]
Banff Mountain Book Festival [Vol. 1: 5775]
Banff Mountain Film Festival [Vol. 1: 5776]
Banff Mountain Photography Competition [Vol. 1: 5777]
Banff World Television Festival
  Achilles Media Ltd. [Vol. 1: 113]
  Achilles Media Ltd. [Vol. 1: 114]
Bangladesh Business Awards [Vol. 2: 1372]
Bank of New Zealand Farm Business Writing Award [Vol. 2: 4972]
Bank of New Zealand Rongo Award [Vol. 2: 4973]
Banking Award Liechtenstein [Vol. 2: 4476]
Banks Composer Fellowship; Don [Vol. 2: 167]
Banks Music Award; Don [Vol. 2: 167]
Banksian Medal [Vol. 2: 3927]
Banner Society Awards [Vol. 1: 16627]
Banta Awards [Vol. 1: 17898]
Bantrel Award in Design and Industrial Practice [Vol. 1: 6967]
Banzon Medal for Applied Research; Julian A. [Vol. 2: 5357]
Bappu Memorial Award; Vainu [Vol. 2: 3622]
Barama Company Award [Vol. 2: 3344]
Barany Award for Young Investigators; Michael and Kate [Vol. 1: 5846]
Barany Prize; Ernst H. [Vol. 1: 10162]
Barash Media Award of Merit [Vol. 1: 7162]
Barbados Employers' Confederation Scholarship [Vol. 2: 1380]
Barbados International Film Festival [Vol. 2: 1382]
Barbados Music Awards [Vol. 2: 1392]
Barbados National Trust Member [Vol. 2: 1384]
Barbato Award; Lewis [Vol. 1: 1694]
Barbecue Products Award [Vol. 1: 9119]
Barbirolli Memorial Scholarship; Sir John [Vol. 2: 8885]
Barbizon Awards for Theatrical Design Excellence in Science, Costume, and Lighting Design [Vol. 1: 10660]
Barbosa Earth Fund Award; Joseph [Vol. 1: 14858]
Barbour Air Safety Award; Laura Taber [Vol. 1: 8375]
Barchi Prize; Richard H. [Vol. 1: 11153]
Bard Allied Professional Award; Morton [Vol. 1: 12639]
Bardeen Award; John [Vol. 1: 11180]
Bardin Prize; I.P. [Vol. 2: 5788]
Bardon Distinguished Service Award; Jack [Vol. 1: 3491]
Barkan Article Prize; Omer Lutfi [Vol. 1: 16581]
Barkan Memorial Award; Manuel [Vol. 1: 11533]
Barker Distinguished Research Contribution Award; Roger G. [Vol. 1: 3457]
Barker Silver Medal [Vol. 2: 7388]
Barlow Memorial Medal [Vol. 1: 6600]
Barnard Award; Bernard L. [Vol. 1: 9606]
Barnard Prize; Henry [Vol. 1: 8948]
Barnard Short Story Award; Marjorie [Vol. 2: 714]
Barnato Trophy; Woolf [Vol. 1: 16193]
Barneby Award; Rupert [Vol. 1: 13208]
Barner Teacher of the Year Award; John C. [Vol. 1: 803]
Barnes Award; Charles H. [Vol. 1: 6805]
Barnes Award; CMSAF Thomas N. [Vol. 1: 250]
Barnes Award; Dame Josephine [Vol. 2: 9082]
Barnes Award for Excellence for Community History Projects; Mary Faye [Vol. 1: 16464]
Barnes Award for Leadership in Chemical Research Management; Earle B. [Vol. 1: 1621]
Barnes Award; Rudolph John [Vol. 1: 14199]
Barnes Life Membership Award; Charles Reid [Vol. 1: 4488]

Barnes Student Paper Awards; K.K. [Vol. 1: 4077]
Barnett Award; Henry L. [Vol. 1: 656]
Barnett Prize; Ellis [Vol. 2: 8755]
Barnhart Memorial Lecture; Marion I. [Vol. 1: 10364]
Barnhisel Reclamation Researcher of the Year; Richard and Lela [Vol. 1: 4434]
Barnouw Award; Erik [Vol. 1: 13673]
Barnum Industry Award; Harold [Vol. 1: 9546]
Barnwell Award; John Blair [Vol. 1: 16867]
Baron Award in Fluid-Particle Systems; Thomas [Vol. 1: 2606]
Baron Travelling Scholarship; Bernhard [Vol. 2: 8690]
Barone Award; Joan Shorenstein [Vol. 1: 14411]
Baroness Platt of Writtle Award [Vol. 2: 7552]
Barr Award; Andy [Vol. 1: 5356]
Barr Award; Mel [Vol. 1: 12598]
Barr Award; Stephen [Vol. 1: 4133]
Barr, Jr. Award; Alfred H. [Vol. 1: 7353]
Barr Memorial Cup; Peter [Vol. 2: 8811]
Barraza Leadership Award; Maclovio [Vol. 1: 12188]
Barrer Award [Vol. 2: 8976]
Barringer Medal [Vol. 1: 1160]
Barringer Memorial Trophy; Lewin B. [Vol. 1: 14968]
Barrister of the Year Award [Vol. 2: 8288]
Barron Award; Frank X. [Vol. 2: 4856]
Barrot; Prix Odilon [Vol. 2: 2243]
Barrow Award; Dame Nita [Vol. 2: 9538]
Barry Award for Editorial Excellence; James P. [Vol. 1: 13489]
Barry Award; Redmond [Vol. 2: 434]
Bart Feminist Activist Award; Pauline [Vol. 1: 15912]
Bartels Medal; Julius [Vol. 2: 2368]
Bartelsmeyer Award; Ralph R. [Vol. 1: 3707]
Barthel, Jr. Award; Christopher E. [Vol. 2: 8245]
Bartholome Award for Ethical Excellence; William G. [Vol. 1: 657]
Bartholomew Award; Elizabeth Ann [Vol. 1: 16010]
Bartholomew Award; Harland [Vol. 1: 4159]
Bartholomew Award; John C. [Vol. 2: 6987]
Bartholomew Essay Competition; John [Vol. 2: 8915]
Bartholomew Globe [Vol. 2: 8916]
Bartlett Award; Charlie [Vol. 1: 8720]
Bartlett Award; George S. [Vol. 1: 16532]
Bartlett Durham Award [Vol. 1: 14137]
Bartlett Lecture; Sir Frederic [Vol. 2: 7656]
Bartlett Medal; Sir Frederic [Vol. 2: 7861]
Bartlett Membership Award; Ford [Vol. 1: 4862]
Bartley Award; Mel W. [Vol. 1: 6601]
Bartolozzi; Premio Giuseppe [Vol. 2: 4135]
Barton Gold Medal; Sir Derek [Vol. 2: 8977]
Barton Scholarship in Entrepreneurship; W. Frank [Vol. 1: 17820]
Barton Trophy; Karl-Heinz [Vol. 1: 4600]
Bartow Memorial Award; Buzz [Vol. 1: 11094]
Bartram Memorial Education Award; Walt [Vol. 1: 14942]
Bartter Award; Frederic C. [Vol. 1: 3770]
Baruch Essay Contest; Bernard M. [Vol. 1: 1861]
Baruch University Award; Mrs. Simon [Vol. 1: 16631]
Baseball Outstanding Volunteer Award [Vol. 1: 452]
Baseball Writers Most Valuable Player Award [Vol. 1: 5794]
BASES Annual Conference Awards [Vol. 2: 6971]
BASHH Undergraduate Prize [Vol. 2: 6956]
Bashinski Criminalistics Graduate Thesis Assistance Grant; Jan [Vol. 1: 8421]
Basic Behavior Analysis Dissertation Award [Vol. 1: 3392]
Basic Research in Biological Mineralization Award [Vol. 1: 9525]
Basic Research in Periodontal Disease Award [Vol. 1: 9526]
Basic Science Lecture Award [Vol. 1: 4276]
BASICS Award [Vol. 2: 6953]
Basker Memorial Prize; Eileen [Vol. 1: 15187]
Basmajian Award [Vol. 1: 1020]
Basnyat Technology Award; M.D. [Vol. 2: 4631]
Bass Award for Creativity in Independent Publishing; Miriam [Vol. 1: 5215]
Bass Service Award; Mamie L. [Vol. 1: 427]
Bassford Student Award; Forrest [Vol. 1: 10871]
Bassow Award; Whitman [Vol. 1: 13752]
Bastien Memorial Award; Vincent R.
  WAMSO, Minnesota Orchestra Volunteer Association [Vol. 1: 17637]

WAMSO, Minnesota Orchestra Volunteer Association **[Vol 1: 17640]**

Bastien Memorial Trophy; Aldege Baz **[Vol. 1: 2404]**

Basu Early Career Award in Sun-Earth Systems Science; Sunanda and Santimay **[Vol. 1: 2226]**

Basu Memorial Lecture; Professor Sadhan **[Vol. 2: 3623]**

Batchelder Award; Mildred L. **[Vol. 1: 5057]**

Batcher Memorial Award; Ralph **[Vol. 1: 14395]**

Bates Medal; Sir David Robert **[Vol. 2: 2369]**

Bates Memorial Award; P. H. **[Vol. 1: 5581]**

Bath and Body Line of the Year **[Vol. 1: 8455]**

Battan Author's Award; Louis J. **[Vol. 1: 2903]**

Batten Medal **[Vol. 1: 4462]**

Batten Memorial Trophy; Jean **[Vol. 2: 5050]**

Batterham Award **[Vol. 2: 146]**

Battisti Award; Eugenio **[Vol. 1: 15402]**

Battle Award for Excellence in Machinery Lubrication; John R. **[Vol. 1: 9826]**

Battle Award; Helen I. **[Vol. 1: 6993]**

Baudouin International Development Prize; King **[Vol. 2: 1569]**

Bauer Award; Dorothy **[Vol. 1: 12230]**

Bauer Founders Award; Louis H. **[Vol. 1: 178]**

Bauer Memorial Exhibit Award; Burton Saxton/George **[Vol. 1: 3006]**

Bauer Prize; Alfred **[Vol. 2: 2717]**

Bauman Award; Mary K. **[Vol. 1: 4988]**

Baumann Trophy; Hans **[Vol. 2: 6389]**

Baumgardt Memorial Fellowship; David **[Vol. 1: 3173]**

Baumgarten Award; Alexander Gottlieb **[Vol. 2: 4697]**

Baur Prize; Friedrich **[Vol. 2: 2704]**

Bavarian Academy of Science Prize **[Vol. 2: 2710]**

Baxter Allegiance Prize for Health Services Research **[Vol. 1: 5549]**

Baxter American Foundation Prize **[Vol. 1: 5549]**

Baxter Award for Healthcare Management in Europe **[Vol. 2: 1479]**

Baxter Corporation Canadian Research Awards in Anesthesia **[Vol. 1: 6201]**

Baxter Diagnostics MicroScan Young Investigator Award **[Vol. 1: 3989]**

Baxter Prize; Samuel **[Vol. 2: 8863]**

Bay Award; Christian **[Vol. 1: 7115]**

Bayer Award **[Vol. 2: 6759]**

Bayer Awards for Outstanding Contributions to Research and Teaching **[Vol. 1: 18018]**

Bayer Diagnostics Academic Achievement Award **[Vol. 2: 5616]**

Bayer-Mills Histology Award **[Vol. 2: 5617]**

Bayer/Sakura Histology Achievement Award **[Vol. 2: 5617]**

Bayer-Snoeyenbos New Investigator Award **[Vol. 1: 1041]**

Bayfield Award; St. Clair **[Vol. 1: 136]**

BBC National Short Story Award **[Vol. 2: 6902]**

BC Decker Research Paper Prize **[Vol. 1: 6549]**

BC Division Provincial Awards **[Vol. 1: 6702]**

BC Prize for Poetry **[Vol. 1: 17746]**

The BCA Ten: Best Companies Supporting the Arts in America **[Vol. 1: 6056]**

BCALA Literary Awards **[Vol. 1: 5859]**

BCIC Awards **[Vol. 1: 5799]**

BCO Awards **[Vol. 2: 7032]**

BD AFCB Distinguished Service Award **[Vol. 2: 5921]**

BD ASM Student Travel Award **[Vol. 2: 542]**

BD Award for Research in Clinical Microbiology **[Vol. 1: 3970]**

BDMA/Post Office Direct Marketing Awards **[Vol. 2: 7517]**

BDS Prize **[Vol. 2: 7038]**

Be Fair Award **[Vol. 2: 1419]**

Be Sustainable Award **[Vol. 2: 1420]**

Beach Comparative Psychology Award; Frank A. **[Vol. 1: 3398]**

Beacon Awards **[Vol. 1: 5320]**

Beadle Award; George W. **[Vol. 1: 8548]**

Beale Medal **[Vol. 2: 8432]**

Beale Memorial Award; John A. **[Vol. 1: 15436]**

Bealer Award; Alex W. **[Vol. 1: 4817]**

Beals Award; Carlyle S. **[Vol. 1: 6314]**

Beam Club Member of the Year **[Vol. 1: 4879]**

Beamish Award; Fred **[Vol. 1: 6886]**

Beamish Award; Jim **[Vol. 1: 6872]**

Bean Award; Edward H. **[Vol. 1: 5560]**

Bean Award; White Stag/Dan **[Vol. 1: 17099]**

Bean Memorial Trophy; Gladys **[Vol. 1: 6635]**

Bear Trap Award **[Vol. 1: 11907]**

Beaubien Award **[Vol. 1: 5295]**

Beaudet Award in Orchestra Conducting; Jean-Marie **[Vol. 1: 6122]**

Beauperthuy; Prix Louis-Daniel **[Vol. 2: 2178]**

Beauregard Judge of the Year Award; Sylvio **[Vol. 1: 8284]**

Beautification Award **[Vol. 1: 8519]**

Beautiful E-line Award **[Vol. 2: 4264]**

Bechtel Fellowship; Louise Seaman **[Vol. 1: 5058]**

Bechtel, Jr. Energy Award; Stephen D. **[Vol. 1: 4160]**

Bechtel Pipeline Engineering Award; Stephen D. **[Vol. 1: 4161]**

Beck Graduate Student Paper Award; Carl **[Vol. 1: 10375]**

Beck International Award **[Vol. 1: 17071]**

Beck Memorial Achievement Award; Don **[Vol. 1: 13834]**

Beckenbach Book Prize **[Vol. 1: 11011]**

Becker Award; Father **[Vol. 1: 12433]**

Becker Award; Joseph **[Vol. 1: 5029]**

Becker Distinguished Service Award; Samuel L. **[Vol. 1: 12110]**

Beckhard Practice Award; Richard **[Vol. 1: 8229]**

Beckman Award; Kristian **[Vol. 2: 1269]**

Beckman Founder Award; Arnold O. **[Vol. 1: 10280]**

Beckman Memorial Award; Aldo **[Vol. 1: 17804]**

The Becky Award **[Vol. 1: 2864]**

Becton Dickinson Career Achievement Award **[Vol. 1: 5128]**

Becton Innovation Award; Henry **[Vol. 1: 2017]**

Bedat Award; Andre **[Vol. 2: 4754]**

Bedell Award; Arthur Sidney **[Vol. 1: 17695]**

Bedford Award **[Vol. 2: 7149]**

Bedford Memorial Prize; Thomas **[Vol. 2: 7150]**

Beecher Award; Henry Knowles **[Vol. 1: 8837]**

Beer and E. Russell Johnston Jr. Outstanding New Mechanics Educator Award; Ferdinand P. **[Vol. 1: 3836]**

Beer of the Year **[Vol. 1: 6362]**

Beer Prize; George Louis **[Vol. 1: 2361]**

Beers Award; Clifford W. **[Vol. 1: 11099]**

Beeson Career Development Awards in Aging Research; Paul B. **[Vol. 1: 2107]**

Beeson Physician Faculty Scholar in Aging Research Award; Paul **[Vol. 1: 2107]**

Beethoven Piano Competition Vienna; International **[Vol. 2: 1323]**

Begay Award; Tony **[Vol. 1: 8914]**

Begley Award; Robert B. **[Vol. 1: 11678]**

Behavioral, Epidemiologic and Health Services Research Award **[Vol. 1: 9527]**

Behind the Scenes Award **[Vol. 1: 8087]**

Behnke Award; Albert R. **[Vol. 1: 16604]**

Behring National History Day Contest; Kenneth E. **[Vol. 1: 12511]**

Beigel Research Award; Hugo G. **[Vol. 1: 15371]**

Beijerinck Virology Prize; M. W. **[Vol. 2: 1817]**

Beilby Medal and Prize **[Vol. 2: 8978]**

Beilstein Denkmunze; Gmelin **[Vol. 2: 2925]**

Beinecke Endowed Chair for Distinguished Teaching; Balasaraswati/Joy Ann Dewey **[Vol. 1: 1989]**

Beinecke Fellowship in Western Americana; Frederick W. **[Vol. 1: 18145]**

Belair Memorial Award; Denis **[Vol. 1: 321]**

Belanger; Prix Leonidas- **[Vol. 1: 14370]**

Belarus; Quality Prize of the Government of the Republic of **[Vol. 2: 1394]**

Belay Trophy; Hans **[Vol. 2: 7106]**

Belcher Award; Ronald **[Vol. 2: 8979]**

Belcher Memorial Lectureship; Ronald **[Vol. 2: 8979]**

Belford Award; Elizabeth Russell **[Vol. 1: 14898]**

Belize Culinary Competition; Taste of **[Vol. 2: 1680]**

Belize International Film Festival **[Vol. 2: 1677]**

Belize Public Service Awards

Government of Belize - Ministry of the Public Service, Governance Improvement, Elections and Boundaries and Sports **[Vol. 2: 1682]**

Government of Belize - Ministry of the Public Service, Governance Improvement, Elections and Boundaries and Sports **[Vol 2: 1683]**

Government of Belize - Ministry of the Public Service, Governance Improvement, Elections and Boundaries and Sports **[Vol 2: 1684]**

Belkin Memorial Award; John N. **[Vol. 1: 2937]**

Bell Award; Alexander Graham **[Vol. 1: 345]**

Bell Award; Elliott V. **[Vol. 1: 13210]**

Bell Award; Grover E. **[Vol. 1: 2319]**

Bell Award in Video Art **[Vol. 1: 6123]**

Bell Award; Lindberg **[Vol. 1: 9560]**

Bell Award of Distinction; Alexander Graham **[Vol. 1: 13862]**

Bell Award; Robert E. **[Vol. 1: 13499]**

Bell DHHS Youth Achievement Award, Deaf and Hard of Hearing Section; Alexander Graham **[Vol. 1: 346]**

Bell Grant for Food Writers; Harry A. **[Vol. 1: 7781]**

Bell Helicopter Flight Training Scholarship **[Vol. 1: 17798]**

Bell, Jr. Travel Grants; Alfred D. **[Vol. 1: 8426]**

Bell Lifetime Achievement Award; Campton **[Vol. 1: 804]**

Bell Memorial Award; Lawrence D. **[Vol. 1: 8888]**

Bell Prize for Choral Conducting; Leslie **[Vol. 1: 13564]**

Bell Prize; Gordon **[Vol. 1: 4954]**

Bell Student Prize in Speech Communication and Behavioral Acoustics; Alexander Graham **[Vol. 1: 6167]**

Belleau Award; Bernard **[Vol. 1: 6887]**

Beller Medal; Esther Hoffman **[Vol. 1: 13602]**

Bellflasher Award **[Vol. 1: 141]**

Bellman Control Heritage Award; Richard E. **[Vol. 1: 2607]**

Bellmanpriset **[Vol. 2: 6195]**

Bello Award; Andres **[Vol. 1: 13692]**

Bellwether Prize for Fiction in Support of a Literature of Social Change **[Vol. 1: 13080]**

Belmont Book Award **[Vol. 1: 9853]**

Belmont Stakes **[Vol. 1: 13231]**

Belopol'skii; A.A. **[Vol. 2: 5789]**

Belozerskii Prize; A.N. **[Vol. 2: 5790]**

Belpre Award; Pura **[Vol. 1: 5059]**

Belt of Orion Award for Excellence **[Vol. 1: 6149]**

Belz Prizes in Statistics; Maurice H. **[Vol. 2: 1104]**

Bemis Trophy; F. Gregg **[Vol. 1: 17065]**

Benda Prize; Harry J. **[Vol. 1: 4914]**

Bendall; Medaille des Soixantenaire et Fondation Manley- **[Vol. 2: 2605]**

Bender Award **[Vol. 1: 8571]**

Bendix Automotive Electronics Engineering Award; Vincent **[Vol. 1: 15491]**

Bendix Award; Vincent **[Vol. 1: 3852]**

Bendix Minorities in Education Award; Vincent **[Vol. 1: 3852]**

Bene merenti Medals **[Vol. 2: 2711]**

Benemerenti Medal **[Vol. 2: 9546]**

Benger-Sullivan Award **[Vol. 2: 6065]**

Benham Award; Rhoda **[Vol. 1: 11079]**

Benin National Merit Award **[Vol. 2: 5095]**

Benitez Award for Clinical Excellence in Immigration Law; Manuel and Ana Maria **[Vol. 1: 8575]**

Benjamin Award for Creative Publishing; Curtis G. **[Vol. 1: 5216]**

Benjamin Award for Outstanding Article in the Field of Media Ecology; Walter **[Vol. 1: 11029]**

Benjamin Award; Robert Spiers **[Vol. 1: 13753]**

Benjamin Medal; L. R. **[Vol. 2: 74]**

Benjamin Memorial Award; Burton **[Vol. 1: 7444]**

Benjamin National Memorial Trophy; Henry **[Vol. 2: 6703]**

Bennet Navigation Trophy; Faith **[Vol. 2: 7302]**

Bennett Award; A. Leroy **[Vol. 1: 10376]**

Bennett Award; Hugh Hammond **[Vol. 1: 15921]**

Bennett Award; John **[Vol. 1: 17456]**

Bennett Memorial Award; William L. and Robbie S. **[Vol. 1: 3313]**

Bennett Prize; Douglas **[Vol. 2: 8705]**

Bennett Public Service Award; Walter J. **[Vol. 1: 13029]**

Bennett Research Awards; A. E. **[Vol. 1: 15560]**

Benoit Mid-Career Award; Anthony H. **[Vol. 1: 10887]**

Bensley Award in Cell Biology; R. R. **[Vol. 1: 1021]**

Benson and Hedges Awards **[Vol. 2: 1079]**

Benson Award; Clara **[Vol. 1: 6888]**

Benson Medal **[Vol. 2: 9075]**

Bent Spoon Award

Australian Skeptics - NSW Branch **[Vol. 2: 528]**

New Zealand Committee for the Scientific

Investigation of Claims of the Paranormal [Vol. 2: 4959]
Bentall Literary Award [Vol. 1: 14441]
Bentele Award for Engine Technology Innovation; Max [Vol. 1: 15492]
Benz Award; Carl [Vol. 1: 15548]
Berakah Award [Vol. 2: 4143]
Berber Memorial Award; Naomi [Vol. 1: 14165]
Berdie Memorial Research Award; Ralph F. [Vol. 1: 1930]
Berdon Award; Walter [Vol. 1: 15251]
Berens Award; Betty [Vol. 1: 14252]
Berg Award; Patty [Vol. 1: 10725]
Berg Awards; Fred [Vol. 1: 8020]
Bergan Career Development Award; Judge Francis [Vol. 1: 7931]
Bergan Memorial Award; Tom [Vol. 2: 8198]
Berger Award; Frederick J. [Vol. 1: 3837]
Berger Awards for Students of Architecture [Vol. 2: 1370]
Berger Memorial Prize; Fred [Vol. 1: 3174]
Berger, Remlinger; Prix Binoux, Henri de Parville, Jean-Jaques [Vol. 2: 2183]
Bergera Award for Best Biography; Ella Larsen Turner/Ella Ruth Turner [Vol. 1: 11281]
Berggrens pris; Sven [Vol. 2: 6168]
Bergh Medal of Honor; Henry [Vol. 1: 4056]
Bergmann Memorial Award; Prof. E. D. [Vol. 2: 3996]
Bergson Award [Vol. 2: 4003]
Bergstrom Award; Jonas [Vol. 1: 10198]
Bergstrom Memorial Research Award; E. Alexander [Vol. 1: 5336]
Berkeley Award [Vol. 2: 7139]
Berkeley Memorial Award; Maureen [Vol. 1: 4295]
Berkner Award; Lloyd V. [Vol. 1: 1432]
Berlanda Preis; Emil [Vol. 2: 1195]
Berlin International Film Festival [Vol. 2: 2718]
Berlin Memorial Outstanding Dissertation Award; James [Vol. 1: 7507]
Berlin Poster Prize [Vol. 2: 4063]
Berlin Today Award [Vol. 2: 2719]
Berlinale Camera [Vol. 2: 2720]
Berliner Award; Benjamin C. [Vol. 1: 3065]
Berliner Award; Emile [Vol. 1: 5693]
Berlyne Award [Vol. 2: 4857]
Berman Prize; Maurice [Vol. 2: 7162]
Berman Service Award; Richard S. [Vol. 1: 4268]
Bermuda Children's Film Festival [Vol. 2: 1696]
Bermuda International Film Festival [Vol. 2: 1697]
Bernabei Honor Award; Dr. Raymond [Vol. 1: 12560]
Bernal Prize; John Desmond [Vol. 1: 15329]
Bernard Award; Jessie [Vol. 1: 4536]
Bernard Foundation Prize; Leon [Vol. 2: 6547]
Bernard Lecture; Claude [Vol. 2: 2798]
Bernard Lifetime Achievement Award; Jean [Vol. 2: 4701]
Bernardin New Leadership Award; Cardinal [Vol. 1: 7100]
Bernath Book Prize; Stuart L. [Vol. 1: 15081]
Bernath Lecture Prize; Stuart L. [Vol. 1: 15082]
Bernath Scholarly Article Prize; Stuart L. [Vol. 1: 15083]
Berne Memorial Award; Eric [Vol. 1: 10461]
Bernfield Memorial Award; Merton [Vol. 1: 3779]
Bernhardt Distinguished Service Award; Homer I. [Vol. 1: 3838]
Bernheimer, Jr. Award; Leo G. Bill [Vol. 1: 10919]
Bernheimer Prize; Charles [Vol. 1: 1827]
Bernick New Leadership Award; Paul [Vol. 1: 13704]
Bernier Award; Roch [Vol. 1: 6014]
Bernstein Grant; Leslie F. [Vol. 1: 534]
Berntsen International Scholarship in Surveying [Vol. 1: 1870]
Berry/AMA Book Prize for Best Book in Marketing [Vol. 1: 2811]
Berry Award; Dave [Vol. 1: 658]
Berry Medal; Albert E. [Vol. 1: 6898]
Berry Medal; Leonard G. [Vol. 1: 11164]
Berry Prize; David [Vol. 2: 8802]
Berry Scholar Award; Chester A. [Vol. 1: 5277]
Berryman Award for Editorial Cartoons; Clifford K. and James T. [Vol. 1: 12692]
Bersheid-Hatfield Award for Distinguished Mid-Career Achievement [Vol. 1: 9580]
Berson-Yalow Award [Vol. 1: 15729]
Bertelson Award; Paul [Vol. 2: 1488]

Berthault; Prix Claude
    Academie des Beaux-Arts [Vol. 2: 2137]
    Academie des Sciences Morales et Politiques [Vol 2: 2244]
Berthault; Prix de Madame Claude [Vol. 2: 2179]
Berthelot; Medaille [Vol. 2: 2180]
Berthold Leibinger Innovation Prize [Vol. 2: 2737]
Berthold-Preis [Vol. 2: 3009]
Bertholf Award for Chapter Efficiency; Lloyd M. [Vol. 1: 5811]
Bertholf Award for Chapter Excellence; Lloyd M. [Vol. 1: 5811]
Berton Award; Pierre [Vol. 1: 6155]
Bertrand, G. Deflandre, M. Deflandre-Rigaud, and Jean Cuvillier; Prix Paul [Vol. 2: 2181]
Bertrand; Prix Leon [Vol. 2: 2454]
Berwick Prize [Vol. 2: 8328]
Berwick Prize; Senior [Vol. 2: 8329]
Besancon International Competition for Young Conductors [Vol. 2: 2417]
Besancon International Competition of Music Composition [Vol. 2: 2418]
Beskow Plaketten; Elsa [Vol. 2: 6236]
Beskow Plaque; Elsa [Vol. 2: 6236]
Beskowska resestipendiet [Vol. 2: 6196]
Bessaraboff Prize; Nicolas [Vol. 1: 2957]
Bessey Teaching Award; Charles Edwin [Vol. 1: 5931]
Best Abstract Award [Vol. 2: 4709]
Best Abstract in Breastfeeding Research Award [Vol. 1: 659]
Best Abstract of Interest to the Industry Division [Vol. 1: 891]
Best Abstract Presentation Award [Vol. 2: 7631]
Best Abstracts Physicians-in-Training Awards [Vol. 1: 660]
Best Actor [Vol. 2: 5417]
Best Actress [Vol. 2: 5418]
Best Annual Reports Awards [Vol. 2: 5268]
Best Annual SIR Paper Award [Vol. 1: 10228]
Best Applied Paper Award [Vol. 1: 3607]
Best Archaeological Book Award [Vol. 2: 7481]
Best Archaeological Project Award [Vol. 2: 7482]
Best Article Award [Vol. 1: 8949]
Best Article by an Active Duty Author [Vol. 1: 13124]
Best Article of the Year Award [Vol. 1: 5308]
Best Athlete [Vol. 2: 1901]
Best Athlete Award [Vol. 2: 6376]
Best Bet Awards [Vol. 1: 7012]
Best Black/White Design Sheet [Vol. 1: 12953]
Best Book Award
    International Studies Association [Vol. 1: 10377]
    Mormon History Association [Vol 1: 11278]
Best Book Awards [Vol. 2: 9516]
Best Book on East Texas History [Vol. 1: 7965]
Best Booth Award [Vol. 1: 1203]
Best Business Plan [Vol. 2: 4478]
Best Casual Game [Vol. 2: 2592]
Best Center Award [Vol. 2: 2805]
Best Children's Film Prize [Vol. 2: 3248]
Best Civil Engineering Student Award [Vol. 2: 7973]
Best Club in a Region [Vol. 1: 9717]
Best Conference Macro Paper Award [Vol. 1: 9515]
Best Conference Micro Paper Award [Vol. 1: 9516]
Best Conference Paper Award [Vol. 1: 9092]
Best Congress Paper Prize [Vol. 2: 2320]
Best Consumer Mobile Data Application Award [Vol. 2: 8368]
Best Contributed Paper Award [Vol. 2: 5498]
Best Contributed Poster Presentation Award [Vol. 1: 10206]
Best Corporate Mobile Data Application Award [Vol. 2: 8369]
Best Corporate Social Responsibility Initiative of the Year [Vol. 2: 4609]
Best Cover-Up Tattoo [Vol. 1: 12954]
BeST Design Awards [Vol. 2: 4884]
Best Direction [Vol. 2: 5419]
Best Dissertation Award
    Hong Kong Political Science Association [Vol. 2: 5275]
    International Society for Quality-of-Life Studies [Vol 1: 10229]
Best Doctoral Dissertation [Vol. 1: 8230]
Best Doctoral Dissertation Award [Vol. 1: 80]
Best Egglayer Award [Vol. 1: 6227]

Best Elected Recycling Leader [Vol. 1: 12749]
Best Electrical Vehicle [Vol. 2: 1428]
Best Emerging Franchise Award [Vol. 2: 3871]
Best Emerging Young Woman Scientist Award [Vol. 2: 5685]
Best Environment Development Program Award [Vol. 1: 10602]
Best Environmental Management Program Award [Vol. 2: 4183]
Best Evaluation of Staff Development Award [Vol. 1: 12934]
Best Fantasy Short [Vol. 2: 5420]
Best Feature-Length Mountain Film [Vol. 1: 5776]
Best Film Award [Vol. 2: 5421]
Best Film on Climbing [Vol. 1: 5776]
Best Film on Exploration and Adventure [Vol. 1: 5776]
Best Film on Mountain Culture [Vol. 1: 5776]
Best Film on Mountain Environment [Vol. 1: 5776]
Best Film on Mountain Sports [Vol. 1: 5776]
Best Financial Institution of the Year [Vol. 2: 1372]
Best Financial Journalist of the Year [Vol. 2: 5966]
Best First Article Award [Vol. 1: 13323]
Best First Book in the History of Religions Award [Vol. 1: 752]
Best First Feature Award [Vol. 1: 11364]
Best First Novel [Vol. 1: 10452]
Best First Paper Prize [Vol. 2: 8125]
Best Free Communication [Vol. 2: 4027]
Best Fund Raising Program Award [Vol. 1: 10603]
Best Gesneriad in Show [Vol. 1: 8643]
Best Graduate Animation [Vol. 1: 13730]
Best Guidebook Award [Vol. 1: 8596]
Best Hard Cover Novel [Vol. 1: 10453]
Best Hosta in a Tour Garden Award [Vol. 1: 2454]
Best Hosta Seedling or Sport in a Tour Garden Award [Vol. 1: 2455]
Best HR Projects in Estonia [Vol. 2: 2049]
Best Illustrated Children's Books of the Year [Vol. 1: 13239]
Best in American Living Awards [Vol. 1: 11792]
Best in Breed Award [Vol. 2: 9265]
Best in Business Awards [Vol. 1: 17821]
Best in Business Contest [Vol. 1: 15430]
Best In-Depth Reporting on Religion Awards [Vol. 1: 753]
Best in Financial Education [Vol. 1: 8666]
Best in Show [Vol. 1: 17787]
Best in Show Trophy [Vol. 1: 3066]
Best in Topical Awards [Vol. 1: 4597]
Best Information Science Book Award [Vol. 1: 3940]
Best Interactive Animation [Vol. 1: 13731]
Best International Development Program Award by a Local Organization [Vol. 1: 10604]
Best International Symposium Abstract Award [Vol. 1: 892]
Best JASIST Paper Award [Vol. 1: 3947]
Best JOHS Paper Award [Vol. 1: 10230]
Best Joint Venture Enterprise of the Year [Vol. 2: 1372]
Best Journalist of the Year [Vol. 2: 3144]
Best Kids' Menu in America Competition [Vol. 1: 13938]
Best Livebearer Award [Vol. 1: 6227]
Best Local Community Development Program Award [Vol. 1: 10605]
Best Local Individual Development Program Award [Vol. 1: 10606]
Best Local Public Relations Program Award [Vol. 1: 10607]
Best Magazine of the Year [Vol. 2: 1917]
Best Marketing of the Year [Vol. 2: 7497]
Best Master's Thesis Award [Vol. 2: 5499]
Best MBA Paper in Corporate Citizenship Competition [Vol. 1: 5927]
Best Membership Recruitment Program Award [Vol. 1: 10608]
Best Memorial Award; Elmer S. [Vol. 1: 8244]
Best Memorial Award; Robin [Vol. 1: 15171]
Best Music Video [Vol. 1: 13732]
Best New Advertising of the Year [Vol. 1: 8455]
Best New Design Award [Vol. 1: 5708]
Best New Facility Award [Vol. 1: 17593]
Best New Magazine Writer [Vol. 1: 12590]
Best New Program Award [Vol. 1: 17594]
Best New Renovation/Addition Award [Vol. 1: 17595]

Best New Special Event Award [Vol. 1: 17596]
Best New Technology Award [Vol. 1: 5709]
Best Newsletter Article [Vol. 1: 893]
Best Nursing School/College for Men in Nursing [Vol. 1: 851]
"Best of" Awards [Vol. 1: 11705]
Best of Beef Award [Vol. 1: 9120]
Best of Bermuda Awards [Vol. 2: 1701]
Best of Booth Award [Vol. 1: 9121]
Best of Breed/Best of Variety of Breed [Vol. 1: 17788]
Best of Europe - International Direct Marketing Awards [Vol. 2: 1512]
Best of Festival [Vol. 1: 16985]
The Best of Finnish Graphic Design and Advertising Competition [Vol. 2: 2111]
Best of *LRTS* Award [Vol. 1: 5047]
Best of Opposite Obedience [Vol. 1: 16232]
Best of Pork Award [Vol. 1: 9122]
Best of Show Award [Vol. 1: 6227]
Best of Show Awards
    Library Leadership and Management Association [Vol. 1: 10831]
    Specialty Sleep Association [Vol 1: 16130]
Best of the Bahamas Award [Vol. 2: 1345]
Best of the Press Award [Vol. 1: 7333]
Best of Vietnam Awards [Vol. 2: 9561]
Best One-Year Safety Record Award [Vol. 1: 14348]
Best Overseas Tourism Project Award [Vol. 2: 7071]
Best Packaging of the Year [Vol. 1: 8455]
Best Paper Award
    American Society for Composites [Vol. 1: 3812]
    European Federation for Pharmaceutical Sciences [Vol 2: 6140]
    Geoscience Information Society [Vol 1: 8597]
    Indian Dairy Association [Vol 2: 3574]
    Institute of Electronics, Information and Communication Engineers [Vol 2: 4226]
    International Commission on Irrigation and Drainage [Vol 2: 3761]
    International Cryogenic Materials Conference [Vol 1: 9856]
    International Institute of Public Finance [Vol 2: 3072]
    International Society of Offshore and Polar Engineers [Vol 1: 10331]
    Society for Geology Applied to Mineral Deposits [Vol 2: 1932]
    South African Geophysical Association [Vol 2: 5689]
    Women's Health and Economic Development Association [Vol 2: 5108]
Best Paper Award for the *IEEE Industrial Electronics Magazine* [Vol. 1: 9093]
Best Paper Award for the *IEEE Transactions on Industrial Electronics* [Vol. 1: 9094]
Best Paper Award for the *IEEE Transactions on Industrial Informatics* [Vol. 1: 9095]
Best Paper Award for Young Scientists [Vol. 2: 3048]
Best Paper Awards
    Canadian Fertility and Andrology Society [Vol. 1: 6492]
    DAAAM International Vienna [Vol 2: 1224]
    IEEE - Components, Packaging, and Manufacturing Technology Society [Vol 1: 9031]
    Indian Pharmaceutical Association [Vol 2: 3675]
    International Association for Mathematical Geosciences [Vol 1: 9573]
    International Thermoelectric Society [Vol 2: 8238]
    Special Interest Group on Mobility of Systems Users, Data, and Computing [Vol 1: 16088]
Best Paper in *Geophysics* Award [Vol. 1: 15645]
Best Paper of the Year Award [Vol. 1: 7435]
Best Paper Presented at the Annual Meeting Award [Vol. 1: 15646]
Best Paper Prize [Vol. 2: 8126]
Best Paper Published in the Speech Communication Journal [Vol. 2: 2566]
Best Paper Student Presentation [Vol. 1: 15318]
Best Paperback Original Novel [Vol. 1: 10454]
Best Performance of a Classical Work [Vol. 1: 14702]
Best Performance of a Romantic Work [Vol. 1: 14703]
Best Performing National Committee Award [Vol. 2: 3762]

Best Performing Workbody Award [Vol. 2: 3763]
Best PhD Dissertation Award [Vol. 2: 1230]
Best Photo Award [Vol. 2: 1225]
Best Plan Communications [Vol. 1: 8667]
Best Portrait Tattoo [Vol. 1: 12955]
Best Poster Award
    Australasian Society for Ultrasound in Medicine [Vol. 2: 158]
    European Society for Organ Transplantation [Vol 2: 7632]
    International Union of Forest Research Organizations [Vol 2: 1308]
Best Poster of the Year [Vol. 2: 4028]
Best Poster Paper Awards [Vol. 2: 5293]
Best Poster Presentation Prize [Vol. 2: 556]
Best Poster Prizes [Vol. 2: 7044]
Best Potential in HR Management [Vol. 2: 2050]
Best Practice Award
    Association for the Study of Obesity [Vol. 2: 6785]
    Association of Credit Union Internal Auditors [Vol 1: 5309]
    Dietetics in Health Care Communities [Vol 1: 7859]
    European Advertising Standards Alliance [Vol 2: 1426]
Best Practice Award for Professional Ethics and Moral Dispositions in Teacher Education [Vol. 1: 1087]
Best Practice Award for the Innovative Use of Technology [Vol. 1: 1088]
Best Practice Award in Support of Diversity [Vol. 1: 1089]
Best Practices [Vol. 2: 365]
Best Practices Award
    American Counseling Association [Vol. 1: 1931]
    National Association of Black Journalists [Vol 1: 11658]
    National Council on Aging [Vol 1: 12231]
Best Practices in Global Health Award [Vol. 1: 8675]
Best Presentation Award [Vol. 1: 9806]
Best Product Award [Vol. 2: 5979]
Best Program Administration [Vol. 1: 9023]
Best Project for Peace from an International Sports Federation [Vol. 2: 4610]
Best Promotional Effort Award - Basic Promotional Piece [Vol. 1: 17597]
Best Promotional Effort Award - Circular/Flyer/Poster [Vol. 1: 17598]
Best Promotional Effort Award - Electronic Media [Vol. 1: 17599]
Best Promotional Effort Award - Specialty or Apparel Piece [Vol. 1: 17600]
Best Public Sector CFO of the Year [Vol. 2: 4900]
Best Published Paper Prize [Vol. 2: 2321]
Best Real World Game [Vol. 2: 2592]
Best Research Award [Vol. 1: 12935]
Best Research Paper [Vol. 2: 3691]
Best Research Paper Award [Vol, 1: 3608]
Best Research Presentation Award [Vol. 2: 159]
Best Resident Paper Awards [Vol. 1: 661]
Best Retail Bank by Country Awards [Vol. 2: 5923]
Best Retail Bank in Asia Pacific [Vol. 2: 5924]
Best Retail Bank in Central Asia [Vol. 2: 5925]
Best Retail Bank in the Gulf States [Vol. 2: 5926]
Best Scientific Work [Vol. 2: 1396]
Best Scientific Work of a Young Scientist [Vol. 2: 1397]
Best Screenplay [Vol. 2: 5422]
Best Short/Animation Film [Vol. 2: 9528]
Best Short Animation Made for Children [Vol. 1: 13733]
Best Short Film Prize [Vol. 2: 3249]
Best Short Mountain Film [Vol. 1: 5776]
Best Sleeve [Vol. 1: 12956]
Best Sonographer Research Presentation Award [Vol. 2: 160]
Best Space Operations Crew Award [Vol. 1: 251]
Best Special Effects [Vol. 2: 5423]
Best Sports Game [Vol. 2: 2592]
Best Stand Award [Vol. 2: 9434]
Best State Public Library Services Award [Vol. 2: 5100]
Best Student Conference Paper Prizes [Vol. 2: 4989]
Best Student Magazine Writer [Vol. 1: 12590]

Best Student Oral and Poster Presentation Award [Vol. 2: 1933]
Best Student Paper and Poster Award [Vol. 1: 17724]
Best Student Paper and Poster Awards [Vol. 1: 15882]
Best Student Paper Award
    American Association of Petroleum Geologists [Vol. 1: 1267]
    American Society for Information Science and Technology [Vol 1: 3948]
    International Association for Chinese Management Research [Vol 1: 9517]
    International Institute of Fisheries Economics and Trade [Vol 1: 9968]
    International Society for Professional Innovation Management [Vol 2: 8187]
    International Speech Communication Association [Vol 2: 2567]
    Society of Nematologists [Vol 1: 15722]
Best Student Paper in Sociological Theory Award [Vol. 2: 6077]
Best Student Poster Award
    American Association of Petroleum Geologists [Vol. 1: 1268]
    Society for Judgment and Decision Making [Vol 1: 15165]
Best Student Scientific Work [Vol. 2: 1398]
Best Tattooed Female [Vol. 1: 12957]
Best Tattooed Male [Vol. 1: 12958]
Best Tattooist [Vol. 1: 12959]
Best Team [Vol. 2: 1902]
Best Technical and/or Administrative Services Award [Vol. 2: 5904]
Best Television Animation for Adults [Vol. 1: 13734]
Best Theoretical Paper Award [Vol. 1: 3609]
Best Time Saving Device Award [Vol. 1: 9711]
Best Traditional Tattoo [Vol. 1: 12960]
Best Translated Book of the Year [Vol. 2: 4480]
Best Transportation Dissertation/Thesis [Vol. 1: 17333]
Best U.K. Tourism Project Award [Vol. 2: 7072]
Best Unique Tattoo [Vol. 1: 12961]
Best Unpublished Research Paper [Vol. 1: 8231]
Best Unrestored Award [Vol. 1: 13780]
Best Use of Technology [Vol. 1: 8668]
Best Variegated Hosta in a Tour Garden Award [Vol. 1: 2456]
Best Website Award
    Federation of Family History Societies [Vol. 2: 7674]
    Geoscience Information Society [Vol 1: 8598]
Best Workplace for Men in Nursing [Vol. 1: 852]
Bestor Prize; Theodore C. [Vol. 1: 15056]
Beta Eta Teaching Assistant Scholarship Award [Vol. 1: 400]
Beta Phi Mu Award [Vol. 1: 2773]
Betrand, Georges Deflandre et Marthe Deflandre-Rigaud, Jean Cuvillier; Prix Paul [Vol. 2: 2182]
BETT Awards [Vol. 2: 7547]
Betta Award [Vol. 1: 6227]
Better Communications Contest [Vol. 1: 17503]
Better Newspaper Advertising Contest [Vol. 1: 12618]
Better Newspaper Contest [Vol. 1: 12618]
Bettineski Child Advocate of the Year Award; G. F. [Vol. 1: 12257]
Betton Youth Exhibit Award; James L. [Vol. 1: 2983]
Beveridge Award; Albert J. [Vol. 1: 2362]
Beveridge Family Teaching Award [Vol. 1: 2363]
Beverly Hills Theatre Guild Playwright Award [Vol. 1: 5826]
Beville, Jr. Award; Hugh Malcolm [Vol. 1: 11671]
Beydoun Memorial Award; Ziad [Vol. 1: 1269]
Beyond All Odds Award [Vol. 1: 5153]
Beyond Margins Awards [Vol. 1: 13897]
Beyonder [Vol. 1: 8501]
BGRC Silver Jubilee Oration Award [Vol. 2: 3540]
Bhabha Medal; Homi Jehangir [Vol. 2: 3624]
Bhaduri Memorial Lecture Award; A.N. [Vol. 2: 3780]
Bharathi Prize; Vidya [Vol. 2: 3588]
Bhargava Memorial Medal; Professor K.P. [Vol. 2: 3625]
Bhasha Samman Awards [Vol. 2: 3745]
Bhat Memorial Award for Indian Astronomy Olympiad; C.L. [Vol. 2: 3683]
Bhatia Award; Prof. I.S. [Vol. 2: 3781]

Bhatnagar Award; Shanti Swarup [Vol. 2: 3509]

Bhatnagar Medal; Shanti Swarup [Vol. 2: 3626]

Bhatt Memorial Oration; Late Brig PN [Vol. 2: 3511]

Bhatt Young Investigator Award; Pravin N. [Vol. 1: 958]

BHCA Awards [Vol. 2: 7080]

BHP Billiton Science Awards [Vol. 2: 522]

Bhubaneswor Low Cost Technology Award [Vol. 2: 4632]

Bhutan National Film Festival [Vol. 2: 1714]

Bhutan Seal of Excellence [Vol. 2: 1709]

Bhutan Seal of Quality [Vol. 2: 1710]

Bialas Award; Gerda and Gunter [Vol. 2: 2705]

Bialkowski Prize; Grzegorz [Vol. 2: 5405]

Bianchi Cup [Vol. 1: 12785]

Biancotto Aerobatics Diploma; Leon [Vol. 2: 6298]

Bicentenary Medal [Vol. 2: 8313]

BICI-UNESCO (ROSTE) [Vol. 2: 4166]

Bickel Award; John O. [Vol. 1: 4162]

Bickersteth Memorial Medal; Julian [Vol. 2: 7874]

Bicknell Essay Prize; Professor Joan [Vol. 2: 8706]

BIDA Charitable Trust Bursary Award [Vol. 2: 7087]

BIDA Foundation BA Award [Vol. 2: 7088]

Bidault de l'Isle; Prix Georges [Vol. 2: 2606]

Biedenbach Distinguished Service Award; Joseph M. [Vol. 1: 3839]

Biedma; Premio Dr. Carlos A. [Vol. 2: 44]

Bienek Preis fur Lyrik; Horst [Vol. 2: 2706]

Biennale Internationale de Gravure [Vol. 2: 6009]

Biennial Award [Vol. 1: 125]

Biennial Awards for Contributions to Hemostasis [Vol. 1: 10365]

Biennial of Animation Bratislava [Vol. 2: 5995]

Bier Award; William C. [Vol. 1: 3482]

Bietila Award; Paul [Vol. 1: 17072]

Big Brother of the Year [Vol. 1: 5831]

Big Muddy Film Festival Awards [Vol. 1: 5837]

Big Sister of the Year [Vol. 1: 5832]

Bigelow Trophy [Vol. 1: 7313]

Bigot de Morogues; Prix [Vol. 2: 2245]

Bigsby Medal [Vol. 2: 7720]

Bikila Award; Abebe [Vol. 1: 13233]

Bilbao Prize for the Promotion of a Culture of Human Rights [Vol. 2: 2648]

Bilezikian ISCD Global Leadership Award; Dr. John P. [Vol. 1: 10146]

Bilger Citation for Service; Thomas A. [Vol. 1: 1099]

Bilgrami Memorial Medal; Professor Krishna Sahai [Vol. 2: 3627]

Bilim Odulu [Vol. 2: 6636]

Bill Award; Raymond [Vol. 1: 14682]

Billard Award; Admiral Frederick C. [Vol. 1: 12607]

Billboard Music Awards [Vol. 1: 5839]

Billboard Radio Awards [Vol. 1: 5840]

Billings Good Sportsman Award; Bruce [Vol. 1: 3722]

Billington Award; Ray Allen [Vol. 1: 17761]

Billington Book Award; Ray A. [Vol. 1: 17782]

Billington Prize; Ray Allen [Vol. 1: 13674]

BIMA Awards [Vol. 2: 7100]

Binani Gold Medal [Vol. 2: 3589]

Bindrup Award; Jewel [Vol. 1: 17495]

Binet Prize; Jean-Paul [Vol. 2: 2422]

Bing Award; Elisabeth [Vol. 1: 10737]

Bing Prize; Robert [Vol. 2: 6481]

Bingham Fellowships for Writers; Robert [Vol. 1: 13892]

Bingham Medal [Vol. 1: 15826]

Bingo Operator Award [Vol. 2: 8132]

Binkhorst Medal and Lecture [Vol. 1: 4136]

Binkley Award; Thomas [Vol. 1: 7947]

Binkley-Stephenson Award [Vol. 1: 13675]

Binns Award; Professor Blodwen Lloyd [Vol. 2: 7741]

Binoux, Henri de Parville, Jean-Jaques Berger, Remlinger; Prix [Vol. 2: 2183]

Bio-Mega/Boehringer Ingelheim Award for Organic or Bioorganic Chemistry [Vol. 1: 6889]

Bio-Serv Award [Vol. 1: 4010]

Bio-Tech Award [Vol. 2: 4755]

Biobanking; Award for Outstanding Achievement in [Vol. 1: 3962]

Biodiversity Reporting Award [Vol. 2: 1724]

Bioinorganic Chemistry Award [Vol. 2: 8980]

Biological Physics Prize [Vol. 1: 3202]

Biology Student Award [Vol. 1: 7422]

Biomedical Engineering Outstanding Educator Award [Vol. 1: 3874]

Biomedical Instrumentation and Technology Outstanding Paper Awards [Vol. 1: 5130]

bioMerieux Sonnenwirth Award for Leadership in Clinical Microbiology [Vol. 1: 3971]

Bionorica Phytoneering Award [Vol. 3: 3174]

Bioorganic Chemistry Award [Vol. 2: 8981]

Bios Prizes [Vol. 2: 3270]

Biosafety Heroes Award [Vol. 1: 9909]

Biot Medal; Maurice A. [Vol. 1: 4163]

Biota Award for Medicinal Chemistry [Vol. 2: 967]

Biotechnology Heritage Award [Vol. 1: 7198]

Biotest Best Oral Presentation Award [Vol. 2: 7633]

Birch Award; Carroll L. [Vol. 1: 2873]

Birch Medal; A.J. [Vol. 2: 968]

Bird Healthcare Young Investigator Award [Vol. 2: 221]

Bird's Trophy; Peter [Vol. 2: 2463]

Birdsall Prize; Paul [Vol. 1: 2364]

Birdseye Young Researcher Award; Clarence [Vol. 2: 2529]

Birge Award; Stanley [Vol. 1: 7216]

Birger Scholdstroms pris [Vol. 2: 6197]

Birkhoff Prize in Applied Mathematics; George David [Vol. 1: 2825]

Birkmaier Award for Doctoral Dissertation Research in Foreign Language Education; Emma Marie [Vol. 1: 1922]

Birks Award [Vol. 1: 11128]

Birla Award; R. D. [Vol. 2: 3684]

Birla Awards [Vol. 2: 3465]

Birla Memorial Gold Medal; G. D. [Vol. 2: 3590]

Birmingham Medal [Vol. 2: 8040]

BIS Bibliographic Instruction Publication of the Year Award [Vol. 1: 5268]

Bischoff Award; Ernst [Vol. 1: 915]

Bishop Award; Bill [Vol. 2: 8524]

Bishop Award; Joan Fiss [Vol. 1: 14821]

Bisson Award; Edmond E. [Vol. 1: 15858]

Bisto Book of the Year Award [Vol. 2: 3832]

Bittner Extension Award in Horticulture; Carl S. [Vol. 1: 3927]

Bittner Service Citation; Walton S. [Vol. 1: 17380]

Bizet; Prix Georges [Vol. 2: 2138]

Bjerknes Medal; Vilhelm [Vol. 2: 2370]

Black and Minority Health Section Essay Prize [Vol. 2: 9083]

Black and White Spider Awards [Vol. 2: 6885]

Black Award; Charles A. [Vol. 1: 7633]

Black Award for Outstanding Achievement in the Practice of Counseling Psychology; John D. [Vol. 1: 3588]

Black Award for Outstanding Research in Counseling Health Psychology; Dorothy Booz [Vol. 1: 3589]

Black Award; Joseph [Vol. 2: 8982]

Black Award; Mary [Vol. 2: 6704]

Black Award; Murray [Vol. 2: 7245]

Black Award; SETAC/EA Engineering Jeff [Vol. 1: 15623]

Black Girls Rock! Awards [Vol. 1: 5874]

Black Memorial Prizes; James Tait [Vol. 2: 9426]

Black Prize; Duncan [Vol. 1: 14313]

Black Prize; Fischer [Vol. 2: 2140]

Black Tie Award [Vol. 1: 9946]

Blackall Machine Tool and Gage Award [Vol. 1: 4381]

Blackburn Award; Trevor [Vol. 2: 7293]

Blackburn New Professional Award; Richard D. [Vol. 1: 5278]

Blackburn Prize; Jan [Vol. 2: 1164]

Blackwell Medal; Elizabeth [Vol. 2: 2874]

Blackwell's Scholarship Award [Vol. 1: 5051]

Blackwood Prize; Dame Margaret [Vol. 2: 1105]

Blaine Award [Vol. 2: 7210]

Blair-Bell Memorial Lectureship in Obstetrics and Gynaecology; William [Vol. 2: 8691]

Blair Biorheology Scholarship; Scott [Vol. 2: 7265]

Blair Eminent Naturalist Award; W. Frank [Vol. 1: 16055]

Blair Service Award; Lucy [Vol. 1: 3230]

Blake Award for Distinguished Graduate Teaching; M. A. [Vol. 1: 3929]

Blakemore Prize; Harold [Vol. 2: 6847]

Blakeslee University Fellowships; Rennie Taylor/Alton [Vol. 1: 7655]

Blakey Memorial Prize; O. F. [Vol. 2: 770]

Blakney/Aviall Award; Earl [Vol. 1: 5672]

Blanc Prize; Armand [Vol. 2: 4239]

Blasters Leadership Award [Vol. 1: 10315]

Blau Early Career Award; Theodore H. [Vol. 1: 3577]

Blau Prize; Joseph J. [Vol. 1: 15345]

Blavatnik Awards for Young Scientists [Vol. 1: 13205]

Blaxter Scholarship; Sir Kenneth [Vol. 2: 7246]

Blaylock Medal; Selwyn G. [Vol. 1: 6602]

Blazer Hall of Fame [Vol. 1: 5877]

Bledisloe Aviation Trophy [Vol. 2: 5051]

Bledisloe Gold Medal for Landowners [Vol. 2: 8627]

Bledsoe Award; C. Warren [Vol. 1: 4989]

Blegen Award; Theodore C. [Vol. 1: 8427]

Blegen Diamond Award; Julius [Vol. 1: 17073]

Blenheim Award [Vol. 1: 7279]

Bleriot Medal; Louis [Vol. 2: 6299]

Blessing Certified Flight Instructor of the Year; W. A. (Dub) [Vol. 1: 8889]

BLG Awards [Vol. 1: 6636]

Blicq Award; Ronald S. [Vol. 1: 9113]

Bliss Award for Excellence in Investigative Journalism; George [Vol. 1: 5823]

Bliss Medal [Vol. 1: 15447]

Bliss Memorial Award; Gordon M. [Vol. 1: 4068]

Bloch Award; Herbert [Vol. 1: 4271]

Bloch Post-Doctoral Fellow Award; Austin [Vol. 1: 8618]

Block Award; Jack [Vol. 1: 15265]

Block Community Lecture; I. E. [Vol. 1: 15115]

Block Prize; Jochen [Vol. 2: 3161]

Blodger Diversity Award; John D. [Vol. 1: 11042]

Bloem Distinguished Service Award; Delmar L. [Vol. 1: 1839]

Blogger's Choice Awards [Vol. 1: 10542]

Blomska stipendiet [Vol. 2: 6198]

Blondel PhD Prize; Jean [Vol. 2: 7598]

Bloom Award; George [Vol. 1: 3672]

Bloom Memorial Award; A.A. [Vol. 1: 16586]

Bloomer Award; H. H. [Vol. 2: 8314]

Bloomfield Award; John J. [Vol. 1: 2485]

Blow Award for Fashion Creator; Isabella [Vol. 2: 7052]

Blue Pencil Awards [Vol. 1: 11777]

Blue Peter Book Awards [Vol. 2: 6903]

Blue Planet Prize [Vol. 2: 4206]

Blue Ribbon Industrial Research and Development Poster Presentation Award [Vol. 1: 18098]

Blue Ribbon Program Award [Vol. 1: 9191]

Blue Scholarships in Entrepreneurship; V. Jerry [Vol. 1: 17822]

Blue Service Award [Vol. 2: 740]

Bluebird Research Award [Vol. 1: 13282]

Bluegrass Event of the Year [Vol. 1: 9732]

Blues Hall of Fame [Vol. 1: 5896]

Blues Music Awards [Vol. 1: 5897]

Blum; Bourse Marcelle [Vol. 2: 2246]

Blum Distinguished Service to Research Award; Eleanor [Vol. 1: 4994]

Blum Research Grant; Stella [Vol. 1: 7620]

Blumer Graduate Student Paper Award; Herbert [Vol. 1: 15398]

Blumlein-Brown-Willans Premium [Vol. 2: 8020]

Blundell Grants; K. [Vol. 2: 9245]

Blunk Memorial Award; Jim [Vol. 1: 16729]

Blunt Prize [Vol. 2: 7144]

Bly Cub Reporter Award; Nellie [Vol. 1: 13222]

BMA Hall of Fame [Vol. 1: 6066]

BMJ Awards [Vol. 2: 6887]

BNS Travel Grants [Vol. 2: 1412]

Board Certification Educator Award [Vol. 1: 1139]

Board Citation [Vol. 1: 10804]

Board Leaders Award [Vol. 1: 8723]

Board of Directors Award
    Canadian Payroll Association [Vol. 1: 6780]
    Medical Fitness Association [Vol 1: 11053]

Board of Director's Award of Honor [Vol. 1: 4305]

Board of Directors Distinguished Service Award for Senior ACS Administrators [Vol. 1: 1622]

Board of Directors Student Paper Awards [Vol. 1: 7594]

Board of Governors Award [Vol. 1: 4151]

Board of Governors Award [Vol. 1: 5689]

Board of Publications Award for the Best Paper in *Toxicological Sciences* [Vol. 1: 15845]

Board of Trustees Award [Vol. 1: 2447]

Boas Award for Exemplary Service to Anthropology; Franz [Vol. 1: 824]

Boas Medal; Walter [Vol. 2: 408]
Boase Award; Arthur J. [Vol. 1: 1840]
Boating Safety Hall of Fame [Vol. 1: 12796]
Boating Safety Youth Award [Vol. 1: 12797]
Bocher Memorial Prize [Vol. 1: 2826]
Bock Award for Extraordinary Achievement; Frank and A.J. [Vol. 1: 3713]
Bock Prize; Frederick [Vol. 1: 14049]
Bock Prize; Gunter [Vol. 2: 2947]
Bocking Award; Douglas J. [Vol. 1: 6014]
Bocking Memorial Award; James H. [Vol. 1: 6329]
Bode - Norman Holmes Pearson Prize; Carl [Vol. 1: 4571]
Body Chapter of the Year Award; Lloyd [Vol. 1: 7551]
Boedecker Jr. Distinguished Service Award; Kenneth J. [Vol. 1: 5582]
Boehringer Ingelheim Developing World Award [Vol. 2: 8207]
Boehringer Ingelheim FENS Research Award [Vol. 2: 2882]
Boehringer Ingelheim Grant [Vol. 2: 6510]
Boehringer Mannheim S.A. Award [Vol. 2: 5622]
Boeing Award for Best Paper in Image Analysis and Interpretation [Vol. 1: 4863]
Boer Solar Energy Medal of Merit; Karl W. [Vol. 2: 3100]
Boerma Award; A. H. [Vol. 2: 3371]
Boger Award; Robert F. [Vol. 1: 7566]
Boggs Award; Larry [Vol. 1: 12029]
Boggs Award; Lindy [Vol. 1: 3029]
Boggs Award; Phil [Vol. 1: 17417]
Boggs Service Award; Andrew T. [Vol. 1: 4315]
Bogie Prize; David [Vol. 2: 7835]
Bogin Memorial Award; George [Vol. 1: 14058]
Bogoliubov Gold Medal; N.N. [Vol. 2: 5791]
Bogomolny National Service Award; Richard J. [Vol. 1: 7176]
Bogsch Memory Medal; Arpad [Vol. 2: 3398]
Bohlen Award; Avis [Vol. 1: 2178]
Boisbaudran Award; LeCoq de [Vol. 2: 6283]
Boisen Professional Service Award; Anton [Vol. 1: 5480]
Boivin Prize; Jean-Marc [Vol. 2: 2463]
Bok Award; Priscilla and Bart [Vol. 1: 1443]
The Bok Prize [Vol. 2: 113]
Bold Award; Harold C. [Vol. 1: 13993]
Boldrewood Award; Rolf [Vol. 2: 690]
Boldy Memorial Award; Julian [Vol. 1: 6603]
Bolivar Award; Simon [Vol. 1: 3346]
Bolivar Prize; International Simon [Vol. 2: 2653]
Bolivia - Bienal Internacional del Cartel Bolivia; International Poster Show of [Vol. 2: 1722]
Bolliger Award; Adolph [Vol. 2: 452]
Bolliger Memorial Lecture; Hans R. [Vol. 2: 9272]
Bollingen Prize in Poetry [Vol. 1: 18146]
Bollywood Movie Awards [Vol. 1: 5908]
Bolt Award for Drama; Carol [Vol. 1: 6324]
Bolton Award for Outstanding Bar Leadership [Vol. 1: 11634]
Bolton Award for Professional Excellence [Vol. 1: 11634]
Bolton-Cutter Award [Vol. 1: 17762]
Bolton-Johnson Prize [Vol. 1: 7512]
Bolus Medal [Vol. 2: 5517]
Bombard Prize; Alain [Vol. 2: 2463]
Bomford Paper Award; Douglas [Vol. 2: 7953]
Bomford Prize; Guy [Vol. 2: 3049]
Bonarelli Award; Guido [Vol. 2: 4675]
Bonazinga Award; Marie T. [Vol. 1: 15168]
Bond Awards; Polly [Vol. 1: 8172]
Bonder Scholarship for Applied Operations Research in Health Services; Seth [Vol. 1: 9254]
Bonder Scholarship for Applied Operations Research in Military Applications; Seth [Vol. 1: 9255]
Bonduelle; Prix Paul [Vol. 2: 1583]
Boneau Award; C. Alan [Vol. 1: 3518]
Bonica Public Service Award; John and Emma [Vol. 1: 3113]
Bonica Trainee Fellowship; John J. [Vol. 1: 9597]
Bonin Award; Wilbrod [Vol. 1: 6014]
Bonk Scholarship; Steve [Vol. 1: 7036]
Bonner Medal of Commendation; John A. [Vol. 1: 87]
Bonner Prize in Nuclear Physics; Tom W. [Vol. 1: 3196]

Bonnet Award; Pierre [Vol. 2: 3090]
Bonny Award; Mrs. Harry (Lores) [Vol. 2: 611]
Bono Engineering Communications Award; Jack [Vol. 1: 15653]
Book Award
    American Association for History and Computing [Vol. 1: 956]
    American Association for Public Opinion Research [Vol 1: 974]
    American Psychology-Law Society [Vol 1: 3624]
    Association for Applied and Therapeutic Humor [Vol 1: 4904]
    Association of Latina and Latino Anthropologists [Vol 1: 5391]
    Bertrand Russell Society [Vol 1: 5806]
    British Psychological Society [Vol 2: 7181]
    Canadian Academy of Periodontology [Vol 1: 6163]
    Canadian Railroad Historical Association [Vol 1: 6851]
    Children's Literature Association [Vol 1: 7246]
    International Association for Relationship Research [Vol 1: 9581]
    National Council on Public History [Vol 1: 12250]
    Oral History Association [Vol 1: 13629]
    The Poetry Center & American Poetry Archives [Vol 1: 14056]
    Religious Communication Association [Vol 1: 14501]
    Rhetoric Society of America [Vol 1: 14542]
    Scribes, the American Society of Legal Writers [Vol 1: 14801]
    Society for American Archaeology [Vol 1: 15018]
    University of Michigan Press [Vol 1: 17287]
Book Awards
    Catholic Press Association [Vol. 1: 7109]
    Children's Literature Council of Southern California [Vol 1: 7250]
    European Society for the Study of English [Vol 2: 2073]
    National Book Development Council of Singapore [Vol 2: 5953]
    Victorian Society in America [Vol 1: 17556]
Book Cover Award [Vol. 1: 8196]
Book Cover Design of the Year [Vol. 1: 5914]
Book Design Awards
    Australian Publishers' Association [Vol. 2: 518]
    Publishers Association of the West [Vol 1: 14338]
Book Design of the Year [Vol. 1: 5914]
Book Illustration of the Year [Vol. 1: 5914]
Book, Jacket and Journal Design Show [Vol. 1: 5219]
Book of the Decade Award [Vol. 1: 10378]
Book-of-the-Month Club Translation Prize [Vol. 1: 13902]
Book of the Season Award [Vol. 1: 13214]
Book of the Year [Vol. 2: 3388]
Book of the Year Award
    Academy of Parish Clergy [Vol. 1: 100]
    Healthcare Information and Management Systems Society [Vol 1: 8868]
    Mind - National Association for Mental Health [Vol 2: 8350]
Book of the Year Award: Early Childhood [Vol. 2: 645]
Book of the Year Award: Older Readers [Vol. 2: 646]
Book of the Year Award: Picture Books [Vol. 2: 647]
Book of the Year Award: Younger Readers [Vol. 2: 648]
Book Prize
    American Philosophical Association [Vol. 1: 3175]
    British Association for Applied Linguistics [Vol 2: 6942]
    British Insurance Law Association [Vol 2: 7098]
    British Society for Middle Eastern Studies [Vol 2: 7230]
    Dermatological Society of Singapore [Vol 2: 5936]
    Law and Society Association [Vol 1: 10758]
    Society for Historians of the Early American Republic [Vol 1: 15086]
Book Prizes [Vol. 2: 3272]
Book Publishers of Texas Children's/Young People's Award [Vol. 1: 16451]
Booker Gold Medal [Vol. 2: 1564]

Booker Sr. Health Promotion Award; Dr. Walter M. [Vol. 1: 5224]
Books Abroad/Neustadt International Prize [Vol. 1: 18055]
Books Across America Library Books Awards [Vol. 1: 13132]
Books for Children [Vol. 2: 813]
Bookseller Industry Awards [Vol. 2: 6892]
Bookseller of the Year Award [Vol. 1: 6348]
Boom Award; Roger W. [Vol. 1: 7778]
Boomer Award; Garth [Vol. 2: 291]
Boone and Crockett Award [Vol. 1: 5338]
Boosey Award; Leslie
    Performing Right Society [Vol. 2: 8467]
    Royal Philharmonic Society [Vol 2: 8886]
Booth Education Award; Taylor L. [Vol. 1: 9052]
Boothby Award; Walter M. [Vol. 1: 179]
Boothby-Edwards Award [Vol. 1: 179]
Boothe Endowed Memorial Scholarship; Byron W. [Vol. 1: 17823]
Boothman Bursary; Harry [Vol. 1: 6773]
Boots Romantic Novel of the Year [Vol. 2: 8551]
Borden Award
    American Dairy Science Association [Vol. 1: 1979]
    Association of American Medical Colleges [Vol 1: 5209]
Borden Award in Nutrition [Vol. 1: 6755]
Bordin; Prix [Vol. 2: 2247]
Borgia Prize; Dr. Joseph [Vol. 2: 4021]
Borgman Award for Surface Design; Lynn Goodwin [Vol. 1: 7802]
Borman Award; Alvah K. [Vol. 1: 3840]
Born Award; Max [Vol. 1: 13603]
Born Medal and Prize; Max [Vol. 2: 7900]
Born Prize; Max [Vol. 2: 2772]
Borotra World Fair Play Trophy; Jean [Vol. 2: 3393]
Bos Innovative Projects Grants; Candace C. [Vol. 1: 7647]
Bose Award; Bimal [Vol. 2: 3753]
Bose Medal; Dr. A. K. [Vol. 2: 3591]
Bose Medal; Jagadis Chandra [Vol. 2: 3628]
Bose Medal; Satyendranath [Vol. 2: 3629]
Bose Memorial Award; Anil Kumar [Vol. 2: 3630]
Bose prize; Aziz ul Haque and Hem Chandra [Vol. 2: 7689]
Bosley Award; John [Vol. 1: 11863]
Boss of the Year Award [Vol. 2: 4544]
Bossons Award; Fred H. [Vol. 1: 14557]
Boston Marathon [Vol. 1: 5925]
Bostrom Young Scholar Award; Robert [Vol. 1: 16041]
Boswell Award [Vol. 2: 5731]
Botany Prize [Vol. 2: 1106]
Botkin Prize; Benjamin A. [Vol. 1: 2158]
Botswana Teachers Day
    Botswana Ministry of Education - Teaching Service Management Unit [Vol. 2: 1733]
    Botswana Ministry of Education - Teaching Service Management Unit [Vol 2: 1734]
    Botswana Ministry of Education - Teaching Service Management Unit [Vol 2: 1735]
    Botswana Ministry of Education - Teaching Service Management Unit [Vol 2: 1736]
Bott Creative Excellence Award; Patricia Allen [Vol. 1: 15468]
Bottled Water Hall of Fame [Vol. 1: 9736]
Botto Award for Innovative Action and Entrepreneurial Zeal; Louis [Vol. 1: 7259]
Boucher-OCLC Distinguished Interlibrary Loan Librarian Award; Virginia [Vol. 1: 14460]
Bouchet Award; Edward A. [Vol. 1: 3197]
Bouffault International Animal Agriculture Award [Vol. 1: 4115]
Bouillon Award; Lincoln [Vol. 1: 4316]
Bound to Stay Bound Books Scholarships [Vol. 1: 5060]
Bourdon Service Award; Cathleen [Vol. 1: 5510]
Bourgelat Award [Vol. 2: 7211]
Bourke Award [Vol. 2: 8983]
Bourke Lectureship [Vol. 2: 8983]
Bourse Bancroft [Vol. 1: 14636]
Bourse de la SPE [Vol. 2: 2625]
Bourse Harry Boothman [Vol. 1: 6773]
Bourse Michener-Deacon [Vol. 1: 11119]

Bourses Commemoratives E. W. R. Steacie [Vol. 1: 13105]

Boutin Division Service Award; Delano L. [Vol. 1: 13827]

Bouwhuis Memorial Scholarship Program; Rev. Andrew L. [Vol. 1: 7107]

Bovee Award; Theodore L. Jahn and Eugene C. [Vol. 1: 10349]

Bovine Practitioner of the Year Award [Vol. 1: 1072]

Bovine Veterinary Student Recognition Award [Vol. 1: 1073]

Bowden International Fellowship; Ruth [Vol. 2: 6386]

Bowditch Award Lecture [Vol. 1: 3249]

Bowen Award; N.L. [Vol. 1: 2227]

Bowen Medal; R. W. [Vol. 2: 5699]

Bowen Memorial Award Competition; Betty [Vol. 1: 14813]

Bowie Medal; William [Vol. 1: 2228]

Bowie Young Investigator Award; Lemuel J. [Vol. 1: 894]

Bowie Young Investigator; Lemuel J. [Vol. 1: 895]

Bowis Award [Vol. 1: 1815]

Bowker/Ulrich's Serials Librarianship Award [Vol. 1: 5053]

Bowler of the Year
    Bowling Writers Association of America [Vol. 1: 5951]
    Western Women Premier Bowlers [Vol 1: 17776]

Bowler Prize; J.M. [Vol. 2: 152]

Bowlers of the Year [Vol. 1: 18030]

Bowles Cup [Vol. 2: 8812]

Bowling Reclamation Awards; Kenes C. [Vol. 1: 10490]

Bowman Memorial Award for Painting; Jean [Vol. 1: 524]

Boyce Bursary Awards; Margery [Vol. 1: 6266]

Boyce Prize; Professor Mary [Vol. 2: 8648]

Boyd Award; Donald R. [Vol. 1: 5416]

Boyd Award for Residential Architecture - Houses; Robin [Vol. 2: 381]

Boyd Award; Fred J. [Vol. 2: 1040]

Boyd Hall of Fame Award; John A. [Vol. 1: 7367]

Boyd Humanitarian Award; Benjamin F. [Vol. 1: 13813]

Boyd Literary Award for Excellence in Military Fiction; W.Y. [Vol. 1: 2774]

Boyer International Award for Excellence in Teaching, Learning, and Technology; Ernest L. [Vol. 1: 9812]

Boyer Lecture on Public Policy; Frances [Vol. 1: 2083]

Boyer Prize for Contributions to Psychoanalytic Anthropology [Vol. 1: 15281]

Boyle Award for Distinguished Public Service; Joseph F. [Vol. 1: 1794]

Boyle Award; Hal [Vol. 1: 13754]

Boyle Gold Award; Sister [Vol. 1: 14725]

Boyle Medal for Scientific Excellence [Vol. 2: 3916]

Boyle Medal; Robert [Vol. 2: 8984]

Boyle Memorial Senior French Music Scholarship; Sister Geraldine [Vol. 1: 14726]

Boyle Memorial Senior Hayden and Mozart Scholarship; Sister Geraldine [Vol. 1: 14727]

Boyle Prize for Analytical Science; Robert [Vol. 2: 8984]

Boynton Award; Melbourne W. [Vol. 1: 1433]

Boynton Award; Ruth E. [Vol. 1: 1695]

Boys - A Rahman Award; S. F. [Vol. 2: 8985]

Boys - A Rahman Lectureship; S. F. [Vol. 2: 8985]

Boys and Girls Club Medallion [Vol. 1: 5990]

Boys' Basketball Vision Award [Vol. 1: 465]

Boy's Medal and Prize [Vol. 2: 7914]

BP/A & B Sustained Partnership Award [Vol. 2: 6735]

BP Portrait Award [Vol. 2: 8402]

BP Prize Lectureship in the Humanities [Vol. 2: 9061]

BP Young Artist Award [Vol. 2: 8403]

BPAA Special Award [Vol. 1: 5948]

Brabazon Cup [Vol. 2: 7303]

Brabender Award; Carl Wilhelm [Vol. 1: 5]

Brace Award; Charles Loring [Vol. 1: 12651]

Brackenbury Photography Trophy; Jack [Vol. 2: 7304]

Brackett Memorial Award; Dexter [Vol. 1: 13164]

Braddock Award; CCCC Richard [Vol. 1: 12204]

Braddock Award; Richard [Vol. 1: 7508]

Braddom FRFDS Scholarship; Diana V. [Vol. 1: 10832]

Bradford Award [Vol. 2: 6698]

Bradford Distinguished Educator Award; David L. [Vol. 1: 13697]

Bradlee Editor of the Year Award; Benjamin [Vol. 1: 12693]

Bradley Award [Vol. 2: 1762]

Bradley Awards; Carol June [Vol. 1: 11317]

Bradley Distinguished Service Award; James J. [Vol. 1: 15549]

Brady Memorial Award for Excellence in Volunteer Leadership; Rod [Vol. 1: 2978]

Brady Memorial Awards; Gerald [Vol. 1: 8809]

Brady/Schuster Award [Vol. 1: 3488]

Bragg Gold Medal for Excellence in Physics [Vol. 2: 409]

Bragg Medal and Prize [Vol. 2: 7901]

Brahm's Young Investigators Award [Vol. 2: 2861]

Brahney Scholarship; James M. [Vol. 1: 10079]

Brakensiek "Caught Our Eye" Award [Vol. 1: 7802]

Bralco Gold Medal [Vol. 2: 3592]

Branches of the Year [Vol. 2: 5102]

Brand Award Azerbaijan [Vol. 2: 1337]

Brand Award Short Story Competition; Mona [Vol. 2: 715]

Branden Award; Carl [Vol. 1: 14281]

BrandNew Competition [Vol. 2: 3150]

Brandon Kindred Award; Carl [Vol. 1: 6003]

Brandon Parallax Award; Carl [Vol. 1: 6004]

Brandt Award [Vol. 2: 4004]

Brandt Volunteer Service Award; Sandy [Vol. 1: 11100]

Brannon Award; R. A. [Vol. 1: 11347]

Branscomb Award; Anne Wells [Vol. 1: 8576]

Branton Meritorious Service Award; Paul [Vol. 2: 7862]

BRASS Gale Cengage Learning Student Travel Award [Vol. 1: 14461]

BRASS Primark Student Travel Award [Vol. 1: 14461]

BRASS/Standard & Poor's Award for Outstanding Service to Minority Business Communities [Vol. 1: 14462]

Brasted Memorial Lecture [Vol. 1: 1623]

Braswell/Anderson Publishing Outstanding Student Paper Award; Michael C. [Vol. 1: 64]

Brattle Prizes in Corporate Finance [Vol. 1: 2141]

Brauer Prize; Hamburg Max [Vol. 2: 3200]

Braun Award; E. Lucy [Vol. 1: 7981]

Braun Prize [Vol. 2: 2739]

Braun Prize; Karl Ferdinand [Vol. 1: 15149]

Braunschweig Research Prize [Vol. 2: 2741]

Braunstein Memorial Award; Jules [Vol. 1: 1270]

Braunwald Award; Nina Starr [Vol. 1: 5551]

Braunwald Career Development Award; Nina Starr [Vol. 1: 16491]

Brautigam Award; Frank C. [Vol. 1: 5583]

Bravery Medal [Vol. 2: 298]

Bravo Award [Vol. 1: 7898]

Bravo Awards [Vol. 2: 4960]

Bray Award; Robert S. [Vol. 1: 1907]

Brazier Young Investigator Award; M. A. B. [Vol. 1: 9912]

Breakthrough Award [Vol. 1: 17927]

Breakthrough Director Award [Vol. 1: 9176]

Breakthrough Product of the Year [Vol. 2: 4184]

Breasted Prize; James Henry [Vol. 1: 2365]

Breaststroke Trophy [Vol. 2: 7107]

Breath of Life Award [Vol. 1: 6440]

Brechner Freedom of Information Award; Joseph L. [Vol. 1: 17230]

Bredikhin Prize; F.A. [Vol. 2: 5792]

Breed Award for Women Leaders; J. Cordell [Vol. 1: 15493]

Breeder of the Year [Vol. 1: 10017]

Breeder of the Year Award [Vol. 1: 2744]

Breeders' Award [Vol. 1: 6226]

Breeders Awards [Vol. 1: 8273]

Breem Memorial Award; Wallace [Vol. 2: 6937]

Bregger Essay Award [Vol. 1: 3319]

Breguet Trophy [Vol. 2: 8589]

Breir Award; Nabila [Vol. 2: 9539]

Breithaupt Award; Chef Herman [Vol. 1: 9845]

Breitkreutz Leadership Award; Emil [Vol. 1: 446]

Bremer Award for Best Graduate Student Paper; Stuart A. [Vol. 1: 13878]

Bremner Awards; M. D. K. [Vol. 1: 765]

Brennan Award; Thomas J. [Vol. 1: 5655]

Brennan Medal [Vol. 2: 7958]

Brennan Memorial Trophy; James [Vol. 2: 7108]

Brennan Scholarship; Joseph and Regina [Vol. 1: 17653]

Breslauer Prize for Bibliography [Vol. 1: 9986]

Bretnall Award; William B. [Vol. 1: 14819]

Brett Award; Philip [Vol. 1: 2961]

Brett Century of Service Award; George W. [Vol. 1: 17115]

Breunig Humanitarian Award; H. Latham [Vol. 1: 16404]

Breur Lecture and Gold Medal Award [Vol. 2: 1493]

Brewer Prize; Frank S. and Elizabeth D. [Vol. 1: 4145]

Brewer Research Travel Grant Award; Earl J. [Vol. 1: 662]

Brewer Trophy; Frank G. [Vol. 1: 11463]

Brewery of the Year [Vol. 1: 6362]

Brewster Memorial Award; William [Vol. 1: 3092]

Breyer Medal; Bruno [Vol. 2: 969]

Brick Awards [Vol. 2: 6915]

Bridge Awards [Vol. 1: 4629]

Bridge Book of the Year [Vol. 1: 1514]

Bridge School International Scholarship [Vol. 1: 10140]

Bridge Software of the Year [Vol. 1: 1515]

Bridges Memorial Award; Polly [Vol. 1: 13351]

Bridges Practitioner Award; T.K. [Vol. 1: 11827]

Bridport Prize [Vol. 2: 6917]

Brief-Writing Award [Vol. 1: 14802]

Briggs Award; Charles W. [Vol. 1: 5030]

Briggs Dissertation Award; George E. [Vol. 1: 3389]

Briggs Folklore Award; Katharine [Vol. 2: 7697]

Briggs Memorial Scientific Inquiry Award; Dorothy [Vol. 1: 3231]

Brigham Award; Reuben [Vol. 1: 4946]

Brigham Award; Richard and Grace [Vol. 1: 15550]

Bright Futures Award [Vol. 1: 10060]

Bright Idea Awards [Vol. 1: 16442]

Bright Memorial Award; Norman and Marion [Vol. 1: 6883]

Bright Smiles, Bright Futures Award [Vol. 2: 6357]

Brignoli Award; Paulo Marcello [Vol. 2: 3091]

Brijlal Open Chess Championship [Vol. 2: 2062]

Brill Award; Faye [Vol. 1: 16297]

Brimer Book Award; Ann Connor [Vol. 1: 13447]

Brindley Lecture; George W. [Vol. 1: 7317]

Brinell Medal [Vol. 2: 6176]

Briner Distinguished Achievement Award in Nuclear Pharmacy Practice; William H. [Vol. 1: 3151]

Brininger Award; F. Lee [Vol. 1: 12887]

Brink Award for Distinguished Service; Victor Z. [Vol. 1: 9367]

Brinker Award for Scientific Distinction [Vol. 1: 10695]

Brinker Award; Maureen Connolly [Vol. 1: 17127]

Brinker International Award for Breast Cancer Research [Vol. 1: 10696]

Brinker Outstanding Junior Girl Award; Maureen Connolly [Vol. 1: 17127]

Brinkhous Memorial Lecture; Kenneth M. [Vol. 1: 10366]

Brinkhous Young Investigator Prize in Thrombosis; Kenneth M. [Vol. 1: 2299]

Bristol Award [Vol. 1: 9228]

Bristol-Myers Squibb AG Grant [Vol. 2: 6511]

Bristol-Myers Squibb Mentorship Award [Vol. 1: 1717]

BRIT Awards [Vol. 2: 7171]

Britain in Bloom Awards [Vol. 2: 8813]

Britannia Trophy [Vol. 2: 8590]

British Academy Fellow [Vol. 2: 6920]

British Academy Television Awards [Vol. 2: 6932]

British Animation Awards [Vol. 2: 6940]

British Archaeological Awards [Vol. 2: 6767]

British Association Medal [Vol. 2: 5734]

British Association of Dermatologists Fellowships [Vol. 2: 6960]

British Book Design and Production Awards [Vol. 2: 7174]

British Cartographic Society Award [Vol. 2: 6988]

British Comedy Awards [Vol. 2: 6871]

British Council/AandB International Award [Vol. 2: 6737]

British Council Book Prize [Vol. 1: 13297]

British Design Awards [Vol. 2: 7512]

British Empire Medal [Vol. 2: 7338]

British Fashion Awards [Vol. 2: 7052]

British Federation Crosby Hall Fellowship [Vol. 2: 6386]

British Film Institute Fellowships [Vol. 2: 7057]

British Foundry Medal and Prize [Vol. 2: 7828]

British Grassland Society Award [Vol. 2: 7069]

British Hairdresser of the Year [Vol. 2: 7786]

British Hairdressing Awards [Vol. 2: 7786]

British Lichen Society Awards [Vol. 2: 7104]

British Music Society Awards [Vol. 2: 7137]

British Show Pony Society Rosettes [Vol. 2: 7204]

British Society of Rheology Annual Award [Vol. 2: 7266]

British Sport Books Awards [Vol. 2: 8412]

British Wildlife Photography Awards [Vol. 2: 7300]

Britt Literary Award [Vol. 1: 4796]

Brittell OTA/OT Partnership Award; Terry [Vol. 1: 3030]

Britten Prize; John [Vol. 2: 8604]

Brittingham Prize in Poetry [Vol. 1: 17378]

Britton Award; CEE James N. [Vol. 1: 12205]

Brivzemnieks Prize; Fricis [Vol. 2: 4434]

Broad Axe Award [Vol. 1: 7089]

Broadcast Engineer of the Year [Vol. 1: 15566]

Broadcast Journalism Awards [Vol. 1: 11306]

Broadcast Meteorologist Award [Vol. 2: 2837]

Broadcast of the Year [Vol. 1: 7956]

Broadcast Technology Society Special Service [Vol. 1: 9047]

Broadcaster of the Year
    Broadcast Educators Association of Canada [Vol. 1: 6030]
    International Bluegrass Music Association [Vol 1: 9732]
    National Weather Association [Vol 1: 13030]

Broadcasting Scholarship/Internship [Vol. 1: 5177]

Broadway Awards; Touring [Vol. 1: 6035]

Broch Fellowship in Modern German Literature; Hermann [Vol. 1: 18147]

Brock Gold Medal Award [Vol. 2: 5294]

Brodie Award; Frances [Vol. 2: 9478]

Brodie Award in Drug Metabolism; Bernard B. [Vol. 1: 4032]

Brodie Medal; John A. [Vol. 2: 771]

Brodman Award for the Academic Medical Librarian of the Year; Estelle [Vol. 1: 11061]

Brodsky Center Residency Award [Vol. 1: 9015]

Brody Lifetime Achievement Award; I. Lee [Vol. 1: 16405]

Brody Young Investigator Award; Michael J. [Vol. 1: 3250]

Broida Prize; Herbert P. [Vol. 1: 3198]

Brokaw Memorial Trophy; Irving [Vol. 1: 16909]

Bronfenbrenner Award for Lifetime Contribution to Developmental Psychology in the Service of Science and Society; Urie [Vol. 1: 3404]

Bronfman Award; Saidye [Vol. 1: 6124]

Bronze Anvil Awards [Vol. 1: 14327]

Bronze Award
    American Association of Webmasters [Vol. 1: 1409]
    Veteran Motor Car Club of America [Vol 1: 17529]

Bronze Good Citizenship Medal [Vol. 1: 12896]

Bronze Irrigation Award [Vol. 1: 335]

Bronze Lion Award [Vol. 2: 1786]

Bronze Medal
    Australian Numismatic Society [Vol. 2: 485]
    Federation Aeronautique Internationale [Vol 2: 6300]
    French National Center for Scientific Research [Vol 2: 2447]
    Institution of Gas Engineers and Managers [Vol 2: 8041]
    International Federation of Sports Medicine [Vol 2: 4103]
    National Association of Licensed Paralegals [Vol 2: 8385]
    Royal Humane Society [Vol 2: 8836]
    Southern Africa Association for the Advancement of Science [Vol 2: 5735]

Tau Sigma Delta [Vol 1: 16382]

Bronze Medal Award [Vol. 1: 5690]

Bronze Medal Award of Excellence [Vol. 1: 12940]

Bronze Medal of Honor [Vol. 1: 4656]

Bronze Plaque
    Columbus International Film and Video Festival [Vol. 1: 7427]
    International Regional Magazine Association [Vol 1: 10113]

Bronze Service Citation [Vol. 1: 8245]

Bronze Star of Excellence [Vol. 1: 7519]

Bronze TASTA Award [Vol. 2: 9521]

Bronze Wolf [Vol. 2: 6564]

Brood Bitch of the Year [Vol. 1: 16233]

Brood Mare Award [Vol. 1: 5878]

Brood Stallion Award [Vol. 1: 5879]

Brook Trophy; Elise [Vol. 2: 7109]

Brooker Collegiate Scholarship for Minorities; George M. [Vol. 1: 9406]

Brookes Award for Excellence in Journalism; Warren [Vol. 1: 2764]

Brooks Award for Best Graduate Paper; Juanita [Vol. 1: 11279]

Brooks Award for Best Undergraduate Paper; Juanita [Vol. 1: 11280]

Brooks Award for Excellence in Student Research; Frank G. [Vol. 1: 5812]

Brooks Award for Excellence in the Teaching of Culture; Nelson [Vol. 1: 1923]

Brooks Award for Outstanding Leadership in the Profession; Nelson H. [Vol. 1: 13394]

Brooks Award for Outstanding Service to the Society; Charles Franklin [Vol. 1: 2904]

Brooks Distinguished Mentor Award; David K. [Vol. 1: 1932]

Brooks Leader Award; Eric [Vol. 1: 420]

Brooks Memorial Life Award; Charles E. [Vol. 1: 8295]

Brooks, RN, Past President's Award; Ruth Anne [Vol. 1: 9671]

Brooks Undergraduate Essay Competition; F. G. [Vol. 1: 5812]

Brophy Distinguished Service Award; James E. [Vol. 1: 1260]

Brosseau Award for the Advancement of CSI; Robert P. [Vol. 1: 7553]

Brough Memorial Prize; Frederick [Vol. 2: 772]

Broun Award; Heywood [Vol. 1: 13246]

Broussard Best First Book Prize; James [Vol. 1: 15087]

Brouwer Award; Dirk [Vol. 1: 1444]

Brower Environmental Journalism Award; David R. [Vol. 1: 14859]

Brower Youth Awards [Vol. 1: 7951]

Brown & Associates Award of Merit [Vol. 1: 7162]

Brown Award for Meritorious Service; Lydia [Vol. 2: 6975]

Brown Award; Howard Mayer [Vol. 1: 7948]

Brown Award in Biomedical Research; Malcolm [Vol. 1: 6473]

Brown Award; James Barrett [Vol. 1: 1315]

Brown Award; Ronald H. [Vol. 1: 12059]

Brown Boettner Award for Outstanding Public Education; Beth [Vol. 1: 12749]

Brown Expedition Award; Ralph [Vol. 2: 8786]

Brown Grant; Amber [Vol. 1: 15588]

Brown-Hazen Lectureship for Research in Excellence in Life Science [Vol. 1: 13236]

Brown Literacy Award; Letha H. [Vol. 1: 428]

Brown Medical C.I.T. Abstract Ward; Dr. Jay [Vol. 1: 5225]

Brown Memorial Grant; Leslie [Vol. 1: 14435]

Brown Memorial Prize; Irene
    ROSL Arts [Vol. 2: 8555]
    ROSL Arts [Vol 2: 8555]

Brown Memorial Scholarship; Ronald H. [Vol. 1: 7502]

Brown Memorial Sportsmanship Award; Cecil J. [Vol. 1: 2925]

Brown Outstanding Student Paper Award; Barbara [Vol. 1: 13348]

Brown Practice/Research Recognition Award; Mary Louise [Vol. 1: 1248]

Brown Prize; John Nicholas [Vol. 1: 11089]

Brown Prize; Stanley [Vol. 2: 7405]

Brown Publication Award; James W. [Vol. 1: 5004]

Brown Trade Leadership Award; Doreen T. [Vol. 1: 7583]

Brown Trophy; Jack [Vol. 1: 17051]

Brown Volunteer/Community Service Award; H. Barksdale [Vol. 1: 361]

Browne Medal; W.R. [Vol. 2: 734]

Browne Memorial Bowl; George H. [Vol. 1: 16909]

Brownell Media Award; Emery A. [Vol. 1: 12584]

Brownell Press Award; Emery A. [Vol. 1: 12584]

Brownlow Award; Louis [Vol. 1: 4044]

Brownlow Book Award; Louis [Vol. 1: 11414]

Brownlow Publication Award; Cecil A. [Vol. 1: 8376]

Bruce Medal; Catherine Wolfe [Vol. 1: 5656]

Bruce Medal; W. S. [Vol. 2: 9062]

Bruce Memorial Award; James D. [Vol. 1: 1795]

Bruce-Preller Prize Lectureship [Vol. 2: 9063]

Bruce Prize; Alexander Ninian [Vol. 2: 9064]

Bruel Gold Medal for Noise Control and Acoustics; Per [Vol. 1: 4382]

Bruemmer Award; Mary A. [Vol. 1: 14676]

Bruhn Prize; Erik [Vol. 1: 11956]

Brun; Prix Edmond [Vol. 2: 2184]

Brunauer Award; S. [Vol. 1: 1552]

Brunauer Best Paper Award [Vol. 1: 1552]

Brunei Info-Communications Technology Awards [Vol. 2: 1773]

Brunei Information-Communication Technology Awards BICTA [Vol. 2: 1777]

Brunel Medal [Vol. 2: 7974]

Brunet Memorial Trophy; Jean-Pierre [Vol. 1: 16909]

Brunet; Prix Michel [Vol. 1: 9247]

Brunetti Award; Cledo [Vol. 1: 9285]

Brunner Grant; Arnold W. [Vol. 1: 2582]

Brunnstrom Award for Excellence in Clinical Teaching; Signe [Vol. 1: 3232]

Brunovsky Honorary Medal; Albin [Vol. 2: 5995]

Brussels International Festival of Fantastic Film [Vol. 2: 1417]

Brussels International Festival of Fantasy, Thriller, and Science-Fiction Films [Vol. 2: 1417]

Bruton Award; Ogden [Vol. 1: 663]

Brutton Prize; Kaye Merlin [Vol. 2: 1107]

Bryan Memorial Award for Traditional Landscape in Oil; Alden [Vol. 1: 847]

Bryant Award; Rachel [Vol. 1: 941]

Bryant Gold Medal; Henry Grier [Vol. 1: 8559]

Bryant Memorial Prize; E.T. [Vol. 2: 8084]

Bryant Outstanding Service Award; David C. [Vol. 1: 1107]

Bryson Memorial Senior Speech Arts Scholarship; L.I. [Vol. 1: 14728]

BSAS/Biosciences KTN Vacation Scholarships [Vol. 2: 7247]

BSFA Awards [Vol. 2: 7199]

BSIA/IFSEC Security Industry Awards [Vol. 2: 7201]

BSS Student Research Award [Vol. 1: 8619]

BSSC Exceptional Service Award [Vol. 1: 12544]

BSSC Honor Award [Vol. 1: 12545]

BT Flagship Award for Innovation [Vol. 2: 7004]

BTA Trophy [Vol. 2: 7277]

BTEC Advanced Certificate in Expedition Management [Vol. 2: 9193]

BTEC Advanced Certificate in Tropical Habitat Conservation [Vol. 2: 9194]

BTS/Morris Travelling Fellowship [Vol. 2: 7282]

BUBBA Award [Vol. 1: 16221]

Bucar National Sports Award; Franjo [Vol. 2: 1878]

Buchanan Award; Paul E. [Vol. 1: 17516]

Buchanan Medal [Vol. 2: 8929]

Bucher Lecture and Medal; Theodor [Vol. 2: 3946]

Bucher Medal; Walter H. [Vol. 1: 2229]

Buchman Award [Vol. 2: 4005]

Buchner Forschungsstiftung; DECHEMA Preis der Max [Vol. 2: 3162]

Buchner Preis; Georg [Vol. 2: 2896]

Buchner Research Foundation; DECHEMA Award of the Max [Vol. 2: 3162]

Buckendale Lecture; L. Ray [Vol. 1: 15494]

Buckeye Children's Book Awards [Vol. 1: 6039]

Buckley Condensed Matter Prize; Oliver E. [Vol. 1: 3199]

Buckwell Memorial Scholarship; Arthur [Vol. 1: 14612]

Bucyrus Award; Ruston [Vol. 2: 7934]

Buddingh' Prize; C. [Vol. 2: 4806]

Buell Award; Murray F. [Vol. 1: 7982]

Buerger Award; Martin J. [Vol. 1: 1952]

Buerki Golden Hammer Scenic Technology Award; Frederick A. [Vol. 1: 16960]

Bugnet Award for Novel; Georges [Vol. 1: 18109]

Build-to-Fit Award [Vol. 1: 14382]

Builder of the Year [Vol. 1: 14191]

Builders Award [Vol. 1: 17420]

Builders' Awards [Vol. 2: 5330]

Builder's Choice Awards for Excellence in Design and Planning [Vol. 1: 6042]

Builder's Choice Design and Planning Awards [Vol. 1: 6042]

Building Excellence Awards
    Master Builders Association - South Australia [Vol. 2: 857]
    Microanalysis Society [Vol 1: 11126]

Building Manager of the Year Awards [Vol. 2: 7364]

Building on Quality Awards [Vol. 2: 7853]

Bulletin Editors' Hall of Fame [Vol. 1: 2117]

Bullivant Student Prize; Mary [Vol. 2: 5031]

Bulpitt Woman of the Year Award; Mildred [Vol. 1: 1009]

Bulwer-Lytton Fiction Contest [Vol. 1: 14715]

Bunche Award; Ralph J. [Vol. 1: 3300]

Bundespreis Gute Form [Vol. 2: 2942]

Bunge Prize; Paul [Vol. 2: 2918]

Bunn Award; John [Vol. 1: 11360]

Buonocore Memorial Lecturer [Vol. 1: 97]

Bur Achievement in Membership Award; Louis [Vol. 1: 15495]

Burbank Award; Luther [Vol. 1: 2425]

Burbidge Award; Dean George A. [Vol. 1: 6785]

Burch Memorial Safety Award; Dr. Gary [Vol. 1: 11851]

Burchfield Award; Laverne [Vol. 1: 4045]

Burckett-Dodge Award [Vol. 1: 17074]

Burden Research Prize [Vol. 2: 8707]

Burdett, Jr. Army Aviation Flight Safety Award; Lt. Gen. Allen M. [Vol. 1: 13638]

Burdgick Award; Gary [Vol. 1: 12289]

Burdick Award for Distinguished Service to Clinical Pathology; Ward [Vol. 1: 3794]

Burdick-Thorne Gold Medal [Vol. 1: 16309]

Burdy; Prix Jeanne [Vol. 2: 2470]

Burfitt Prize; Walter [Vol. 2: 1001]

Burge Award; Cornelia [Vol. 1: 8388]

Burger Award in Medicinal Chemistry; Alfred [Vol. 1: 1624]

Burger Award; Warren E. [Vol. 1: 12053]

Burger Prize; Henry [Vol. 2: 8148]

Burgers Award; Hans [Vol. 1: 6552]

Burgess Forensic Nursing Research Award; Ann [Vol. 1: 9666]

Burggraf Award; Fred [Vol. 1: 16533]

Burka Award [Vol. 1: 9389]

Burkan Memorial Competition; Nathan [Vol. 1: 4260]

Burke Award [Vol. 2: 5760]

Burke Award; Edmund [Vol. 1: 10066]

Burke Essay Contest; Arleigh [Vol. 1: 17009]

Burke, Jr. Award; George W. [Vol. 1: 17696]

Burke Memorial Award; John "Sonny" [Vol. 1: 17027]

Burke Memorial Lecture; Donal [Vol. 2: 3907]

Burke Perpetual Challenge Machinery Trophy; Sir Roland [Vol. 2: 8628]

Burke Perpetual Challenge Trophy [Vol. 2: 8628]

Burket Alumni Service Award; Kevin [Vol. 1: 8482]

Burkhalter Award; Frank [Vol. 1: 5785]

Burkitt Medal for Biblical Studies [Vol. 2: 6921]

Burland Prize for Fiction; Brian [Vol. 2: 1686]

Burleigh Prize; J. C. [Vol. 2: 7836]

Burley Prize; Joseph Fraunhofer Award/Robert M. [Vol. 1: 13606]

Burlingame Humanitarian Service Award; Alice [Vol. 1: 2440]

Burma Memorial Lecture Award in Biological Sciences; D.P. [Vol. 2: 3782]

Burn Prevention Award [Vol. 1: 1518]

Burnet Medal and Lecture; MacFarlane [Vol. 2: 172]

Burnet Memorial Award; Sir John [Vol. 2: 8846]

Burnett Fund for Responsible Journalism; Carol [Vol. 1: 17246]

Burnett Prize in Journalism Ethics; UH Journalism Carol [Vol. 1: 17246]

Burnett/University of Hawaii/AEJMC Prize for Excellence in Ethics; Carol [Vol. 1: 4995]

Burnham Award for a Comprehensive Plan; Daniel [Vol. 1: 3285]

Burnham Manufacturing Management Award; Donald C. [Vol. 1: 15686]

Burns Award; Bernard J. [Vol. 1: 9179]

Burns Award; Jacob [Vol. 1: 8577]

Burr/Worzalla Award; Elizabeth [Vol. 1: 17896]

Burrill Award; Meredith F. [Vol. 1: 5202]

Burrin Award; Esther V. [Vol. 1: 9192]

Burrows Award [Vol. 2: 970]

Bursary Awards
    Brunei Darussalam Computer Society [Vol. 2: 1775]
    Royal British Society of Sculptors [Vol 2: 8670]

Bursary Competition [Vol. 1: 11552]

Burt Award for African Literature [Vol. 1: 7344]

Burt Award; Karen [Vol. 2: 7975]

Burt Memorial Award; Karen [Vol. 2: 9458]

Burton Award; Gale Cotton [Vol. 1: 17075]

Burton Awards for Legal Achievement [Vol. 1: 6054]

Burton Medal [Vol. 1: 11135]

Burton Medal; Sir Richard [Vol. 2: 8649]

Burwell Lectureship in Catalysis; Robert [Vol. 1: 13286]

Busa Award; Roberto [Vol. 2: 6774]

Busch Award; Paul L. [Vol. 1: 17722]

Bush Award; Vannevar [Vol. 1: 12816]

Bushkin Friend of the Foundation Award; Ellyn [Vol. 1: 13531]

Busignies Memorial Award; Henri [Vol. 1: 14396]

Business Achievement Awards [Vol. 1: 8699]

Business Achievers Awards [Vol. 2: 3934]

Business Analyst of Year [Vol. 2: 7005]

Business and Aging Awards [Vol. 1: 4528]

Business and Culture Award [Vol. 1: 10538]

Business and Industry Award [Vol. 1: 17310]

Business and Industry Hall of Fame [Vol. 1: 2597]

Business and Innovation Medal [Vol. 2: 7902]

Business and the Arts Awards [Vol. 1: 18086]

Business Aviation Meritorious Service Award [Vol. 1: 8377]

Business Award [Vol. 1: 7635]

Business Awards [Vol. 2: 11]

Business Enterprise Awards [Vol. 2: 8080]

Business Excellence Awards [Vol. 2: 5889]

Business Hall of Fame [Vol. 1: 18087]

Business in the Arts Awards [Vol. 1: 6056]

Business Leader Awards [Vol. 2: 757]

Business Leader of the Year [Vol. 2: 6468]

Business Leader of the Year Award [Vol. 1: 16067]

Business Management Award [Vol. 1: 15783]

Business Marketing Doctoral Award Support Competition [Vol. 1: 13932]

Business of the Quarter/Business of the Year [Vol. 1: 14013]

Business of the Year [Vol. 1: 13667]

Business of the Year Award [Vol. 1: 10303]

Business Partner Award [Vol. 1: 2349]

Business Partnership Award [Vol. 1: 17881]

Business Person of the Year [Vol. 1: 13668]

Business Person of the Year [Vol. 2: 1372]

Business Recognition Award [Vol. 1: 1249]

Business Start-Up Award [Vol. 2: 6595]

Business-to-Business Project Award [Vol. 2: 7006]

Business Valuation Hall of Fame Award [Vol. 1: 2598]

Business Volunteer of the Year Award [Vol. 2: 6736]

Businessman of the Year [Vol. 2: 6662]

Busk Medal [Vol. 2: 8787]

Busse Research Awards; Ewald W. [Vol. 2: 2490]

Bustad Companion Animal Veterinarian of the Year Award [Vol. 1: 4638]

Bustillo; Premio Jose Maria [Vol. 2: 24]

Buszek Memorial Award; Buz [Vol. 1: 8296]

Butcher Award; Arthur [Vol. 2: 6995]

Butcher Awards; Clare [Vol. 2: 4889]

Butcher Medal; Goler T. [Vol. 1: 4351]

Butcher Trophy; Tom [Vol. 2: 7110]

Buti Foundation Award [Vol. 2: 3685]

Butler Award; Wendell E. [Vol. 1: 8383]

Butler Faculty Research Awards; John Topham and Susan Redd [Vol. 1: 6012]

Butler Literary Award [Vol. 1: 10512]

Butler Literary Awards [Vol. 1: 10515]

Butlerov Prize; A.M. [Vol. 2: 5793]

Buttel International Award for Distinguished Scholarship in Environmental Sociology; Frederick H. [Vol. 2: 6078]

Butterfield Trophy; Jack A. [Vol. 1: 2405]

Butters Award; Nelson [Vol. 1: 11408]

Butterworth Prize [Vol. 1: 3067]

Butterworth Young Scientist Award; George [Vol. 2: 3280]

Buttgenbach; Prix Henri [Vol. 2: 1621]

Butts-Whiting Award [Vol. 1: 5279]

Buxtehuder Bulle [Vol. 2: 2746]

Buyer of the Year Award [Vol. 1: 12550]

Buzzell Best Paper Award; Robert D. [Vol. 1: 10983]

BVA Achievement Award [Vol. 1: 5890]

BWI/YALSA Collection Development Grant [Vol. 1: 18218]

Byrd Young Artist Competition; William C. [Vol. 1: 14674]

Byrne Memorial Literary Award; Ray [Vol. 1: 2984]

Bywaters Prize; Eric [Vol. 2: 9084]

C SADF Commendation Medal [Vol. 2: 5702]

CAA/Heritage Preservation Award for Distinction in Scholarship and Conservation [Vol. 1: 7354]

CAA National Awards [Vol. 2: 7450]

Caballo de Trabajo Award; El [Vol. 1: 16070]

Cabaud Memorial Award [Vol. 1: 3098]

CACA Award to Qualified Current Published Papers [Vol. 2: 5234]

Caccioppoli; Premio Renato [Vol. 2: 4136]

CACCN Research Grant [Vol. 1: 6245]

Cacique's Crown of Honour [Vol. 2: 3335]

Cacique's Crown of Valour [Vol. 2: 3336]

Cadbury Medal; Christopher [Vol. 2: 9124]

Cade Award; Tom [Vol. 1: 14436]

Cadmus Memorial Award; Bradford [Vol. 1: 9368]

CAEP Resident Research Award [Vol. 1: 6248]

Caernarfon Award [Vol. 2: 7935]

Caesar Award [Vol. 1: 5903]

Caffey Award for Excellence for Pre-Collegiate Teaching; W. Stewart [Vol. 1: 16465]

Cagniard Award; Louis [Vol. 2: 4676]

Cahn Lifetime Achievement Award; Sammy [Vol. 1: 11412]

Caille; Medaille Commemorative Pierre-Francois [Vol. 1: 9939]

Caille Memorial Medal; Pierre-Francois [Vol. 1: 9939]

Cajal Medal [Vol. 1: 6087]

Caldecott Medal; Randolph [Vol. 1: 5061]

Calder Cup [Vol. 1: 2406]

Calder Prize [Vol. 2: 8864]

Caldicott Leadership Award; Helen [Vol. 1: 17958]

Caldwell-Colbert Award for Distinguished Educator in Clinical Psychology; Toy [Vol. 1: 3578]

Caldwell Lifetime Achievement Award [Vol. 1: 7788]

Caledonian Research Foundation Prize Lectureship in Biomedical Sciences and Arts and Letters [Vol. 2: 9065]

Calgary/W.O. Mitchell Book Prize; City of [Vol. 1: 18110]

Calhoun International Relations Award; Dr. Nina Fay [Vol. 1: 429]

California History Day Award [Vol. 1: 7493]

California Sea Grant State Fellowship [Vol. 1: 17201]

Caligari Film Prize [Vol. 2: 2721]

Calihan Academic Fellowship [Vol. 1: 133]

Calihan Fellowships [Vol. 1: 133]

Calihan Lecture [Vol. 1: 134]

Calihan Travel Grants [Vol. 1: 133]

Call Centre Manager of the Year [Vol. 1: 8168]

Callahan Award; William F. (Bill) [Vol. 1: 11342]

Callas Grand Prix for Opera; Maria [Vol. 2: 3267]

Callas Grand Prix for Piano; Maria [Vol. 2: 3268]

Callas International Opera, Oratorio-Lied Competition; Maria [Vol. 2: 3267]

Callaway Award; Joe A. [Vol. 1: 137]

Callaway Doctoral Award [Vol. 2: 549]

Callimaci Memorial Supporters Award; Fulvio [Vol. 1: 6717]

Callison Award; Charles H. [Vol. 1: 11951]

Calne Award; Roy [Vol. 2: 7283]

Calnek Applied Poultry Research Achievement Award; Bruce W. [Vol. 1: 1042]

Calvin Award; Melvin [Vol. 1: 9977]

Calvo-Armengol International Prize [Vol. 2: 6020]

Calypso Award [Vol. 1: 11263]

Camakaris Best Paper by a Young Researcher Award; George [Vol. 2: 461]

Cambodian National Disability Awards [Vol. 2: 1811]

Camden Freeholders Award [Vol. 1: 9457]

Cameron Outstanding PhD Thesis Award; T. W. M. [Vol. 1: 6994]

Cameron Young Investigator Award; John R. [Vol. 1: 1303]

Cameroonian of the Year [Vol. 1: 6109]

Camp Applied Research Medal; Thomas R. [Vol. 1: 17697]

Camp Memorial Trophy; Mary C. [Vol. 1: 12786]

Campbell Award [Vol. 2: 5020]

Campbell Award; A. B. [Vol. 1: 11348]

Campbell Award; A.W. [Vol. 2: 477]

Campbell Award; Donald T. [Vol. 1: 15266]

Campbell Award; Estelle [Vol. 1: 12863]

Campbell Award; Francis Joseph [Vol. 1: 5511]

Campbell Award; Frank W. [Vol. 1: 14104]

Campbell Award of Merit; E. K. [Vol. 1: 4317]

Campbell Award; Roald [Vol. 1: 17185]

Campbell Fund; The Mona [Vol. 1: 6151]

Campbell; Medal in Memory of Ian [Vol. 1: 2223]

Campbell Memorial Award; Collie [Vol. 2: 9479]

Campbell Memorial Lecture; Edward DeMille [Vol. 1: 4831]

Campbell Memorial Prize; Malcolm [Vol. 2: 8986]

Campbell Pilot Award; Dr. Walter H. [Vol. 1: 10854]

Campbell Research Award; J.A. [Vol. 1: 6400]

Campbell Rookie of the Year Award; Jim [Vol. 1: 12945]

Campbell Space Simulation Award; John D. [Vol. 1: 9316]

Campbell Young Investigators Award; J.A. [Vol. 1: 6401]

Campiello Prize [Vol. 2: 4040]

Camping World Trucks [Vol. 1: 11608]

Campionato Europeo Baseball [Vol. 2: 2755]

Campos Memorial Award for Best International Student Paper; Carlos Walter M. [Vol. 1: 1271]

Campsite of the Year [Vol. 2: 6860]

Camptender Award [Vol. 1: 3736]

Campus Bookseller of the Year Award [Vol. 1: 6349]

Campus EMS Provider of the Year [Vol. 1: 12088]

Campus Sustainability Leadership Awards [Vol. 1: 5135]

Camus; Prix Gustave [Vol. 2: 1584]

Can-Am Civil Engineering Amity Award [Vol. 1: 4164]

Canada Awards for Business Excellence [Vol. 1: 12728]

Canada Awards for Excellence
  Canadian Federation of Independent Business [Vol. 1: 6476]
  National Quality Institute [Vol 1: 12728]

Canada Export Award [Vol. 1: 8416]

Canada International Award [Vol. 2: 9273]

Canada - Japan Literary Awards [Vol. 1: 6125]

Canada Medal [Vol. 2: 9274]

Canada Memorial Foundation Scholarships [Vol. 2: 6012]

Canada Packers' Medal [Vol. 1: 6925]

Canada Prize [Vol. 2: 2478]

Canada's Sports Hall of Fame [Vol. 1: 6158]

Canadian Agricultural Engineering of the Year Award. [Vol. 1: 6878]

Canadian Architect Art of CAD Competition [Vol. 1: 6212]

Canadian Architect Yearbook [Vol. 1: 6211]

Canadian Authors Association Award for Fiction [Vol. 1: 6326]

Canadian Award for Financial Reporting [Vol. 1: 8743]

Canadian Awards for International Cooperation [Vol. 1: 6682]

Canadian Basketball Hall of Fame [Vol. 1: 11358]

Canadian Brewing Awards [Vol. 1: 6362]

Canadian Business and Community Partnership Awards [Vol. 1: 9166]

Canadian Car of the Year [Vol. 1: 5710]

Canadian Coast Guard Exemplary Service Medal [Vol. 1: 8747]

Canadian Commission Prize [Vol. 1: 5774]

Canadian Conservation Achievement Awards [Vol. 1: 7041]

Canadian Country Music Association Awards [Vol. 1: 6434]

Canadian Farm Writers' and Broadcasters' Awards [Vol. 1: 6464]

Canadian Football Hall of Fame and Museum [Vol. 1: 6502]

Canadian Forest Management Group Achievement Award [Vol. 1: 6587]

Canadian Forestry Achievement Award [Vol. 1: 6588]

Canadian Forestry Scientific Achievement Award [Vol. 1: 6589]

Canadian Geotechnical Colloquium [Vol. 1: 6526]

Canadian Hospital Librarian of the Year Award [Vol. 1: 6546]

Canadian Information Productivity Awards [Vol. 1: 9242]

Canadian Innovation Awards [Vol. 1: 6683]

Canadian Institute of Chartered Accountants Prize [Vol. 2: 7837]

Canadian Insurance Claims Education Benevolent Foundation Award [Vol. 1: 6562]

Canadian International Amateur Film Festival [Vol. 1: 6632]

Canadian International Annual Film/Video Festival [Vol. 1: 6632]

Canadian International Medal Lecture [Vol. 2: 9273]

Canadian Investment Awards [Vol. 1: 6668]

Canadian Journal of Statistics Award [Vol. 1: 16286]

Canadian Master Merchandiser Awards [Vol. 1: 6478]

Canadian Music Competition [Vol. 1: 6725]

Canadian Outdoorsman of the Year Award [Vol. 1: 7043]

Canadian Pacific Railway Medal [Vol. 1: 8116]

Canadian Peace Awards [Vol. 1: 6438]

Canadian Pediatric Society Research Award [Vol. 1: 6768]

Canadian Pharmacist of the Year [Vol. 1: 6786]

Canadian Phytopathological Society Fellow [Vol. 1: 6795]

Canadian Region Member Recognition Award [Vol. 1: 4891]

Canadian School Library Association Merit Award [Vol. 1: 6217]

Canadian Software Systems Award [Vol. 1: 6567]

Canadian Student Film Festival [Vol. 1: 11258]

Canadian Truck of the Year [Vol. 1: 5711]

Canal+ Award
  Sauve Qui Peut le Court Metrage [Vol. 2: 2602]
  Sauve Qui Peut le Court Metrage [Vol 2: 2603]

Cancer Research Training Fellowship [Vol. 2: 2480]

Canders Prize; Fridrihs [Vol. 2: 4435]

Candle Artisan of the Year [Vol. 1: 9961]

Candler Bursary; Cathy [Vol. 2: 338]

Canham Graduate Studies Scholarship [Vol. 1: 17698]

Caniff Spirit of Flight Award; Milton [Vol. 1: 11953]

Cann Plaque; R. C. [Vol. 1: 11512]

Canning Trophy; Richard F. [Vol. 1: 2407]

Cannizzaro; Medaglia Stanislao [Vol. 2: 4125]

Cannon Award in Astronomy; Annie J. [Vol. 1: 1445]

Cannon Award Lecture; Physiology in Perspective: Walter B. [Vol. 1: 3262]

CANS Award [Vol. 2: 4881]

Canter Education and Training Paper Award; Mathilda B. [Vol. 1: 3450]

Cantor Award; Georg [Vol. 2: 6073]

Capa Award; Cornell [Vol. 1: 9750]

Capa Gold Medal Award; Robert [Vol. 1: 13755]

Caparne-Welch Medal [Vol. 1: 11044]

Capers Humanitarian Award; Hedges [Vol. 1: 10462]

Cappon Prize for Essay; Dorothy Churchill [Vol. 1: 13191]

Cappon Prize for Fiction; Alexander Patterson [Vol. 1: 13191]

Capps Green Zomaya Award [Vol. 2: 8987]

Capra Achievement Award; Frank [Vol. 1: 7880]

Capranica Prize [Vol. 1: 10185]

Captain Joseph H. Linnard Prize [Vol. 1: 15710]

Capute Award; Arnold J. [Vol. 1: 664]

Car of the Year Awards
  Automobile Journalists Association of Canada [Vol. 1: 5708]
  Automobile Journalists Association of Canada [Vol. 1: 5709]

Carbone Award; Paul P. [Vol. 2: 1547]

Card Award; George [Vol. 1: 1908]

Cardiff Singer of the World Competition [Vol. 2: 6980]

Cardinal Health Annual Representative to the Board Award [Vol. 1: 9672]

Cardiology Section President's Medal [Vol. 2: 9085]

Cardiovascular Nursing Clinical Excellence Award [Vol. 1: 6428]

Cardiovascular Sonographer Distinguished Teacher Award [Vol. 1: 4287]

Cardwell Foundation Award for Education and Research; Thelma [Vol. 2: 1193]

Care and Life Award [Vol. 1: 6493]

Care Awards [Vol. 2: 1437]

Care Practitioner Award [Vol. 2: 7333]

Career Achievement Award
  Colorado Association of Libraries [Vol. 1: 7384]
  Country Radio Broadcasters [Vol 1: 7726]
  International Documentary Association [Vol 1: 9881]
  International Society for Aerosols in Medicine [Vol 2: 3078]
  Professional Fraternity Association [Vol 1: 14214]
  Society for Medical Anthropology [Vol 1: 15188]

Career Achievement Award - Professional Theatre [Vol. 1: 5145]

Career Achievement Award - Theatre in Higher Education [Vol. 1: 5146]

Career Advancement for Women Award [Vol. 1: 7747]

Career Award
  Environmental Design Research Association [Vol. 1: 8156]
  European Cell Death Organization [Vol 2: 1450]
  Parapsychological Association [Vol 1: 13846]

Career Awards Program [Vol..1: 10848]

Career Contribution to the Sociology of HIV/AIDS Award [Vol. 1: 15908]

Career Development Award
  American Diabetes Association [Vol. 1: 2018]
  American Society of Echocardiography [Vol 1: 4288]
  National Institutes of Health - National Institute of Nursing Research [Vol 1: 12556]

Career Development Award in Adolescent Health [Vol. 1: 15011]

Career Development Award in Skin Research [Vol. 1: 7850]

Career Development Awards
  American Association for Cancer Research [Vol. 1: 878]
  Dermatology Foundation [Vol 1: 7850]

Career Development Grants [Vol. 1: 1396]

Career Development Travel Award [Vol. 1: 4746]

Career Education Citation [Vol. 1: 13596]

Career Enhancement Award [Vol. 1: 2510]

Career/Lifeskills Resources Award For Excellence in Career Education [Vol. 1: 13597]

Career/Lifetime Achievement Award [Vol. 1: 4919]

Career Scientist Award [Vol. 1: 6202]

Career Trajectory Award [Vol. 1: 15636]

Carey Award [Vol. 2: 9319]

Carey Award for Outstanding Journalism; James W. [Vol. 1: 11030]

Carey, Jr. Distinguished Service Award; W. N. [Vol. 1: 16534]

Carey Medal; S.W. [Vol. 2: 735]

Cargill Animal Nutrition Young Scientist Award [Vol. 1: 1970]

Carhartt National Team Award [Vol. 1: 12509]

Caribbean Education Award [Vol. 2: 1390]

Caritas Medal [Vol. 1: 13254]

Carlesson Memorial Award; Bert [Vol. 1: 7704]

Carleton Award; Robert H. [Vol. 1: 12819]

Carlier; Prix [Vol. 2: 2248]

Carlin Service Award; John J. [Vol. 1: 17044]

Carlisle Award; J. F. [Vol. 1: 5246]

Carll Award; John Franklin [Vol. 1: 15749]

Carlsburg Light People's Choice Award [Vol. 1: 16520]

Carlson Award for Innovation in Engineering Education; Chester F. [Vol. 1: 3841]

Carlson Awards; Karl [Vol. 1: 2275]

Carlton Brewery Chess Championship [Vol. 2: 2062]

Carnahan Prize; Charles Wendell [Vol. 1: 17680]

Carne Prize; Phil [Vol. 2: 334]

Carnegie International Exhibition [Vol. 1: 7078]

Carnegie Medal
  Carnegie Hero Fund Commission **[Vol. 1: 7069]**
  Chartered Institute of Library and Information
    Professionals **[Vol 2: 7377]**
Carnegie Medal for Excellence in Children's Video;
  Andrew **[Vol. 1: 5062]**
Carnegie Prize **[Vol. 1: 7078]**
Carnell Travelling Scholarship; Edith Jessie **[Vol. 2: 4930]**
Carney Endowed Scholarship; Frank and Zenda **[Vol. 1: 17824]**
Carney Endowed Scholarship in Entrepreneurship;
  Beverly and Daniel **[Vol. 1: 17825]**
Carnot; Prix Lazare **[Vol. 2: 2185]**
Carnot Young Researcher Award; Sadi **[Vol. 2: 2530]**
Carothers Medal **[Vol. 2: 9372]**
Carpenter Award; Joseph E. **[Vol. 1: 12732]**
Carpenter Award; Leroy H. **[Vol. 1: 8047]**
Carpenter Award; William W. **[Vol. 1: 13276]**
Carr Lifetime Achievement Award; Archie **[Vol. 1: 14807]**
Carr Outstanding Committee Chair Award;
  Davis **[Vol. 1: 7835]**
Carr Prize; Robert Alfred **[Vol. 2: 7976]**
Carrel Young Researcher Award; Alexis **[Vol. 2: 2531]**
Carreras Award; Jose **[Vol. 2: 4702]**
Carrier Award; Willis H. **[Vol. 1: 4318]**
Carrier Young Researcher Award; Willis H. **[Vol. 2: 2532]**
Carriere Award; Jean P. **[Vol. 1: 16239]**
Carringer Mental Health Journalism Award;
  Helen **[Vol. 1: 11102]**
Carroll Literary Award; John M. **[Vol. 1: 10868]**
Carron Award; I. Louis **[Vol. 1: 16488]**
Carron Keeper **[Vol. 1: 16488]**
Carski Foundation Distinguished Undergraduate
  Teaching Award **[Vol. 1: 3972]**
Carsoel; Prix Pierre **[Vol. 2: 1585]**
Carson Award; Rachel
  Society for Social Studies of Science **[Vol. 1: 15330]**
  Society of Environmental Toxicology and Chem-
    istry **[Vol 1: 15624]**
Carson Environmental Award; Rachel **[Vol. 1: 13088]**
Carson Prize; Rachel **[Vol. 1: 3902]**
Carstensen Memorial Award; Vernon **[Vol. 1: 213]**
Cartan; Prix Elie **[Vol. 2: 2186]**
Carter Bronze Medal **[Vol. 2: 7389]**
Carter Logistics Readiness Award; Maj. Gen. War-
  ren R. **[Vol. 1: 13639]**
Carter Medal **[Vol. 2: 7442]**
Carter Prize; Richard **[Vol. 2: 7396]**
Cartier Prize in Natural History; Jacques **[Vol. 1: 6735]**
Cartoons Award **[Vol. 1: 9441]**
Cartwright Student Award; L. J. **[Vol. 1: 6279]**
Carty Award for the Advancement of Science; John
  J. **[Vol. 1: 11431]**
Carus Lectures **[Vol. 1: 3176]**
Carus Medal **[Vol. 2: 3119]**
Caruso International Jazz Trumpet Solo Competi-
  tion; Carmine **[Vol. 1: 10469]**
Caruthers Memorial Award; Jimmy **[Vol. 1: 16730]**
Caruthers Memorial Championship Rookie Driver of
  the Year Award; Jimmy **[Vol. 1: 16730]**
CAS/GE Healthcare Canada Inc. Research Award in
  Perioperative Imaging **[Vol. 1: 6203]**
Casadesus International Piano Competition; Rob-
  ert **[Vol. 1: 7324]**
Casagrande International Piano Competition;
  Alessandro **[Vol. 2: 4046]**
Casagrande Professional Development Award;
  Arthur **[Vol. 1: 4165]**
CASE Award of Excellence **[Vol. 1: 12261]**
Case Gold Medal; Cyrus Hall McCormick - Jerome
  Increase **[Vol. 1: 4088]**
CASEY Award **[Vol. 1: 16158]**
Cash Awards **[Vol. 1: 16844]**
Cash-In-A-Flash Award Program **[Vol. 1: 16797]**
Casida Award; L. E. **[Vol. 1: 4116]**
Casimir Funk Natural Science Award **[Vol. 1: 14084]**
Casino Interior Design Award **[Vol. 2: 8132]**
Casino of the Year **[Vol. 1: 61]**
CASME Award **[Vol. 2: 7453]**

Cass Correctional Achievement Award; E. R. **[Vol. 1: 1881]**
Cassavetes Award; John **[Vol. 1: 7846]**
Casselberry Award **[Vol. 1: 2750]**
Casselberry Fund Award **[Vol. 1: 2750]**
Cassels Religion Reporter of the Year - Small-Sized
  Newspapers **[Vol. 1: 14495]**
Cassin; Prix Rene **[Vol. 2: 2249]**
Cassini Medal and Honorary Membership; Jean Do-
  minique **[Vol. 2: 2371]**
Cassinis Award; Gino **[Vol. 2: 5295]**
Castaing Award **[Vol. 1: 11129]**
Castellani - Reiss Medal and Award **[Vol. 1: 10311]**
Castle Trophy **[Vol. 1: 12785]**
Castleman Award; Benjamin **[Vol. 1: 16703]**
Castleton Award **[Vol. 1: 3714]**
CASTME Awards **[Vol. 2: 7453]**
Castner Medal and Lecture **[Vol. 2: 9275]**
Castroviejo Medal **[Vol. 1: 7606]**
Caswell Screenwriting Award; Mick **[Vol. 1: 3732]**
Cat of the Year **[Vol. 1: 4057]**
Cat of the Year Awards **[Vol. 2: 712]**
Catalan; Prix Eugene **[Vol. 2: 1622]**
Catalysis in Organic Chemistry Award **[Vol. 2: 8988]**
Catalyst Award **[Vol. 1: 16298]**
Catalyst Grants **[Vol. 1: 14429]**
Catcheside Prize; D.G. **[Vol. 2: 731]**
The CATCON Prizes **[Vol. 2: 5296]**
Catenacci; Prix **[Vol. 2: 2139]**
Catenacci; Prix Hercule **[Vol. 2: 2471]**
Catering Manager of the Year **[Vol. 2: 3882]**
Caterpillar Scholars Award **[Vol. 1: 14943]**
Cathey Award; H. Marc **[Vol. 1: 2426]**
Catholic Secondary Education Awards **[Vol. 1: 12042]**
Cattarulla Short Story Award; Kay **[Vol. 1: 16452]**
Cattell Cup **[Vol. 2: 9326]**
Cattell Memorial Award; McKeen **[Vol. 1: 1718]**
Cattleya Alliance Award; Masatoshi Miyamoto **[Vol. 1: 3068]**
Caty; Prix Charles **[Vol. 2: 1586]**
Cauble Short Play Award; John **[Vol. 1: 10661]**
Caucus Achievement Award **[Vol. 1: 6462]**
Caul Award; David **[Vol. 1: 10250]**
Caulfield, Jr. Medal for Exemplary Contributions to
  National Water Policy; Henry P. **[Vol. 1: 4647]**
Causey Award; Oscar **[Vol. 1: 10861]**
Cavallaro Medal **[Vol. 2: 2824]**
Cavanagh Medal; Kevin **[Vol. 2: 662]**
Cavanagh Award; Catherine A. M. **[Vol. 1: 12864]**
Cavanaugh Award for Excellence in Training and
  Education in Aging; Gloria **[Vol. 1: 4529]**
Cavanaugh Memorial Award; W. T. **[Vol. 1: 5584]**
Cave Canem Poetry Prize **[Vol. 1: 7124]**
Cave Radio and Electronics Group Award **[Vol. 2: 6996]**
Cave Science and Technology Research Initiative
  Awards CSTRI **[Vol. 2: 6997]**
Cavendish Excellence in Library Programming
  Award; Marshall **[Vol. 1: 2775]**
Caves Award; Philip K. **[Vol. 1: 10165]**
Cavett Award **[Vol. 1: 12926]**
Cavling Prize **[Vol. 2: 1960]**
Cavusgil Award; S. Tamar **[Vol. 1: 2812]**
Cawson Prize Lecture; Rod **[Vol. 2: 8699]**
Cayla-Martin; Prix Emma du **[Vol. 2: 1587]**
Caze, A. Policart-Lacassagne; Prix L. La **[Vol. 2: 2187]**
CBC Literary Awards **[Vol. 1: 6126]**
CBC Radio National Competition for Young Perform-
  ers **[Vol. 1: 6364]**
CBC Radio Talent Competition **[Vol. 1: 6364]**
CBC Young Composers Competition **[Vol. 1: 6127]**
CBCI Award **[Vol. 2: 3824]**
CBTU Grasshopper Awards **[Vol. 1: 7340]**
CCCC Outstanding Dissertation Award **[Vol. 1: 7507]**
CCFA Career Development Awards **[Vol. 1: 7754]**
CCFA Research Fellowship Awards **[Vol. 1: 7755]**
CCPE Faculty Teaching Award **[Vol. 1: 8127]**
CCWH/Berkshire Conference of Women Historians
  Graduate Student Fellowship **[Vol. 1: 7602]**
CDADIC Awards **[Vol. 1: 7133]**
CDC Best Student-Paper **[Vol. 1: 9070]**
CDC Medal of Excellence **[Vol. 1: 16818]**
CEC Outstanding Contributor Award **[Vol. 1: 7640]**

Cecil Award in Environmental Chemical Engineer-
  ing; Lawrence K. **[Vol. 1: 2608]**
Cecil Memorial Trust Competition **[Vol. 2: 7521]**
CEDR Medals **[Vol. 2: 1468]**
CEE Cultural Diversity Grant **[Vol. 1: 12206]**
Celebrate America Creative Writing Contest **[Vol. 1: 2476]**
Celebrating Young Rwandan Achievers Award
  CYRWA **[Vol. 2: 5887]**
Celebration Award
  Arbor Day Foundation **[Vol. 1: 4757]**
  Arbor Day Foundation **[Vol 1: 4757]**
Cellier; Prix Alphonse **[Vol. 2: 2140]**
Cellular Toxicology Award **[Vol. 1: 15107]**
Celtic Media Festival **[Vol. 2: 7335]**
Cements Award **[Vol. 1: 1554]**
Cena Frantisek Kriegel **[Vol. 2: 1906]**
Cena Jaroslava Seiferta **[Vol. 2: 1907]**
Cena Obce Architektu za Realizaci Roku **[Vol. 2: 1937]**
Centenarian Award **[Vol. 1: 14397]**
Centenary Award **[Vol. 2: 6879]**
Centenary Award for Outstanding Services to
  Shinty; Marine Harvest **[Vol. 2: 7320]**
Centenary Lectureships **[Vol. 2: 8989]**
Centenary Medal
  Aboriginal Affairs and Northern Development
    Canada **[Vol. 1: 31]**
  Australian Department of the Prime Minister and
    Cabinet - Awards and Culture Branch **[Vol 2: 305]**
  Royal Photographic Society of Great Britain **[Vol 2: 8895]**
  Royal Scottish Geographical Society **[Vol 2: 8917]**
  Society of Dyers and Colourists - England **[Vol 2: 9301]**
Centenary of Federation Teaching Awards in Chem-
  istry **[Vol. 2: 971]**
Centenary Prizes **[Vol. 2: 8989]**
Centennial Award
  Canadian Association of Aquarium Clubs **[Vol. 1: 6227]**
  Canadian Pharmacists Association **[Vol 1: 6787]**
Centennial Award for Excellence in Undergraduate
  Teaching **[Vol. 1: 10498]**
Centorino Award; James **[Vol. 1: 12592]**
Central Pennsylvania Festival of the Arts **[Vol. 1: 7161]**
Centrum Center for Nutrition Science Award **[Vol. 1: 4011]**
Century Award **[Vol. 1: 3647]**
Century Club Award **[Vol. 1: 1475]**
Century Scholarship **[Vol. 1: 5512]**
CEO Recognition Award **[Vol. 1: 17953]**
Ceres-ACCA North American Awards for Sustain-
  ability Reporting **[Vol. 1: 5244]**
CERESIS Award **[Vol. 2: 5320]**
Cermak Medal; Jack E. **[Vol. 1: 4166]**
Certamen Capitolinum **[Vol. 2: 4115]**
Certamen International de Films Cortos, Ciudad de
  Huesca **[Vol. 2: 6035]**
Certificate and Diploma in Environmental Manage-
  ment **[Vol. 2: 7398]**
Certificate for International Volunteer Service **[Vol. 1: 2000]**
Certificate for Young Botanists **[Vol. 2: 5658]**
Certificate in Energy Efficiency For Domestic
  Central Heating **[Vol. 2: 7857]**
Certificate of Achievement **[Vol. 1: 8904]**
Certificate of Achievement for Excellence in
  Financial Reporting **[Vol. 1: 8743]**
Certificate of Achievement in Leadership **[Vol. 1: 12581]**
Certificate of Achievement of Focused Studies **[Vol. 1: 101]**
Certificate of Appreciation
  American Occupational Therapy Associa-
    tion **[Vol. 1: 3031]**
  American Occupational Therapy Foundation **[Vol 1: 3041]**
  American Psychological Association - Division
    of Family Psychology **[Vol 1: 3424]**
  American Psychological Association - Society
    for the Psychological Study of Lesbian, Gay,

Chapman Medal; R. W. [Vol. 2: 773]
Chapman Memorial Award for Outstanding Contributions in Technical Services Law Librarianship; Renee D. [Vol. 1: 1190]
Chapman Memorial Award; Frank [Vol. 1: 16314]
Chapman Memorial Grant; Frank M. [Vol. 1: 2951]
Chapman Prize Essay [Vol. 2: 7163]
Chapter 17 - St. Louis Scholarship [Vol. 1: 14945]
Chapter Achievement [Vol. 1: 3158]
Chapter Achievement Award [Vol. 1: 17943]
Chapter Activities Award [Vol. 1: 1841]
Chapter Activity Award [Vol. 1: 9096]
Chapter Activity Awards [Vol. 1: 8252]
Chapter and Student Chapter of the Year Awards [Vol. 1: 17848]
Chapter Award [Vol. 1: 4023]
Chapter Award for Excellence in Membership Marketing [Vol. 1: 9897]
Chapter Award for Excellence in Newsletter Publishing [Vol. 1: 9898]
Chapter Awards
    American Association of Occupational Health Nurses [Vol. 1: 1250]
    Society of Cosmetic Chemists [Vol 1: 15596]
    Tau Beta Pi Association [Vol. 1: 16374]
Chapter Best Speaker Award [Vol. 1: 15596]
Chapter Communication Program of the Year Award [Vol. 1: 376]
Chapter Community Project Award [Vol. 1: 11924]
Chapter Competition [Vol. 1: 9378]
Chapter Corporate Partner of the Year [Vol. 1: 11938]
Chapter Distinguished Services Award [Vol. 1: 10880]
Chapter Event of the Year Award [Vol. 1: 3941]
Chapter Excellence Award
    American Association of Healthcare Administrative Management [Vol. 1: 1169]
    National Association of the Remodeling Industry [Vol 1: 11925]
    Oncology Nursing Society [Vol 1: 13532]
Chapter Excellence Awards
    Association for Professionals in Infection Control and Epidemiology [Vol. 1: 5076]
    International Society for Pharmaceutical Engineering [Vol 1: 10202]
    National Space Society [Vol 1: 12919]
Chapter History Award [Vol. 1: 5813]
Chapter Hope Chest Award [Vol. 1: 12611]
Chapter Innovation Award [Vol. 1: 15286]
Chapter Key Awards [Vol. 1: 14895]
Chapter Member of the Year Award [Vol. 1: 3942]
Chapter Membership Awards [Vol. 1: 547]
Chapter Merit Award [Vol. 1: 15596]
Chapter Merit Awards [Vol. 1: 4555]
Chapter Merit Awards for Students [Vol. 1: 15101]
Chapter/National Office of the Year Award [Vol. 1: 18063]
Chapter Newsletter of the Year Award [Vol. 1: 4797]
Chapter of Excellence Award [Vol. 1: 10192]
Chapter of the Year
    Alliance of Hazardous Materials Professionals [Vol. 1: 377]
    Autism Society [Vol 1: 5700]
    Information Systems Security Association [Vol 1: 9234]
Chapter of the Year
    ARMA International - The Association of Information Management Professionals [Vol. 1: 4798]
    International System Safety Society [Vol 1: 10417]
    National Broadcasting Society - Alpha Epsilon Rho [Vol 1: 11998]
    National Council on Alcoholism and Drug Dependence [Vol 1: 12246]
    National Space Society [Vol 1: 12919]
    National Space Society of Australia [Vol 2: 898]
    ORT America [Vol 1: 13705]
    United States Hang Gliding and Paragliding Association [Vol 1: 16942]
Chapter of the Year Award
    Logistics Officer Association [Vol. 1: 10881]
    Muscular Dystrophy Canada [Vol 1: 11308]
Chapter of the Year Award
    American Society for Information Science and Technology [Vol. 1: 3943]

American Society of Certified Engineering Technicians [Vol 1: 4139]
    Fund for American Studies [Vol 1: 8482]
    International Facility Management Association [Vol 1: 9899]
    Mail Systems Management Association [Vol 1: 10915]
    National Institute of Governmental Purchasing [Vol 1: 12551]
    TRI-M Music Honor Society [Vol 1: 16555]
Chapter-of-the-Year Award [Vol. 1: 9079]
Chapter One - Detroit Founding Chapter Scholarship [Vol. 1: 14946]
Chapter President of the Year Award [Vol. 1: 15179]
Chapter Publication of the Year Award [Vol. 1: 3944]
Chapter Research Advancement Award [Vol. 1: 14896]
Chapter Service Award [Vol. 1: 11661]
Chapter Service Award [Vol. 1: 5357]
Chapter Service Awards [Vol. 1: 8700]
Chapter Special Merit Awards [Vol. 1: 12920]
Chapters of the Year [Vol. 1: 11093]
Charcot Award; J. B. [Vol. 1: 14931]
Charcot Award; Jean-Martin [Vol. 2: 8371]
Charlie Award [Vol. 1: 7334]
Charlton Award of Outstanding Achievement; Margaret Ridley [Vol. 1: 6547]
Charlton Lifetime Achievement Award; Thomas L. [Vol. 1: 16466]
Charman Prize Competition [Vol. 2: 1704]
Charney Award; Jule G. [Vol. 1: 2905]
Charnley Award; John [Vol. 1: 8928]
Charter Awards [Vol. 1: 7530]
Charter Chef Competition [Vol. 2: 20]
Chartered Accountant of the Year; Hays [Vol. 2: 4901]
Charts and Documents Award [Vol. 2: 612]
Chase Award for Excellence in Issue Management; W. Howard [Vol. 1: 10534]
Chase Award; Joe M. [Vol. 1: 8378]
Chase Forest Bioproducts Division Award in Chemical Engineering; Andrew [Vol. 1: 2609]
Chasko Award; Lawrence J. [Vol. 1: 16075]
Chassis Inspectors Award [Vol. 1: 9375]
Chatt Award; Joseph [Vol. 2: 8990]
Chatt Lectureship; Joseph [Vol. 2: 8990]
Chattanooga Research Award [Vol. 1: 3233]
Chatterjee Memorial Award; G. P. [Vol. 2: 3708]
Chatterjee Memorial Lecture; Dr. Guru Prajad [Vol. 2: 3631]
Chaudesaigues; Prix [Vol. 2: 2141]
Chauncey Award for Distinguished Service to Assessment and Education Science; Henry [Vol. 1: 8025]
Chauveau Medal; Pierre [Vol. 1: 14637]
Chauvenet Prize [Vol. 1: 11013]
Chavee; Prix Honore [Vol. 2: 2151]
Chavez Accion y Compromiso Human and Civil Rights Award; Cesar [Vol. 1: 12294]
Chavez Award; Cesar Estrada [Vol. 1: 867]
Chavez Young Investigator Award; Professor Ignacio [Vol. 2: 4587]
Chavhunduka Award; Mark [Vol. 2: 6857]
Chavrid Award; Vladimir [Vol. 1: 11914]
Chayanov Prize; A.V. [Vol. 2: 5794]
Chayefsky Laurel Award for Television; Paddy [Vol. 1: 18118]
Chayes Prize for Excellence in Research in Mathematical Petrology; Felix [Vol. 1: 9574]
Cheek Exemplary Service Award; Willard D. [Vol. 1: 3843]
Chef Competition; Charter [Vol. 2: 20]
Chef Ireland
    American Culinary Federation [Vol. 1: 1964]
    Society of German Cooks [Vol 2: 3181]
Cheiron Medal [Vol. 2: 1331]
Chelsea Award for Poetry [Vol. 1: 7195]
Chelsea Award for Short Fiction [Vol. 1: 7196]
Chemeca Medal [Vol. 2: 774]
Chemical Dynamics Award [Vol. 2: 8991]
Chemical Education Medal [Vol. 2: 5674]
Chemical Institute of Canada Medal [Vol. 1: 7204]
Chemical Pioneer Awards [Vol. 1: 2646]
Chemical Society of Japan Award [Vol. 2: 4223]
Chemistry Award for Young Physical Chemists [Vol. 2: 5455]

Chemistry of Transition Metals Award [Vol. 2: 8992]
Chemistry Research Excellence Award [Vol. 2: 1108]
Chemistry Student Award [Vol. 1: 7424]
Chemistry World Entrepreneur of the Year [Vol. 2: 8993]
ChemLiminary Awards [Vol. 1: 1596]
Cheney Award; Frances Neel [Vol. 1: 16425]
Chennault Award; Lt. General Claire Lee [Vol. 1: 252]
Cherenkov Prize; P.A. [Vol. 2: 5795]
Chermside Award for Distinguished Contribution to Research Administration; Herbert B. [Vol. 1: 15821]
Cherry Prize; T. M. [Vol. 2: 212]
Cherry Tree Marathon [Vol. 1: 13234]
Chesed Award; Josef Hirsch [Vol. 1: 12102]
Chesney Gold Medal [Vol. 2: 9137]
Chess Journalism Awards [Vol. 1: 7210]
Chess Journalist of the Year [Vol. 1: 7210]
Chess World Champions [Vol. 2: 3315]
Chetwynd Award for Entrepreneurial Excellence [Vol. 1: 6685]
Chevalier; Prix Auguste [Vol. 2: 2188]
Chevy Entertainer of the Year [Vol. 1: 12187]
Chicago Award [Vol. 1: 7288]
Chicago Film Critics Awards [Vol. 1: 7223]
Chicago Folklore Prize [Vol. 1: 2159]
Chicago International Children's Film Festival [Vol. 1: 8225]
Chicago International Festival of Children's Films [Vol. 1: 8225]
Chicago International Film Festival [Vol. 1: 7288]
Chichibu Memorial TB Global Award; Princess [Vol. 2: 2573]
Chick Trophy; John [Vol. 1: 2408]
Chief Executive Officer Award [Vol. 1: 5289]
Chief of Engineers Design and Environmental Awards Program [Vol. 1: 16716]
Chief of the South African Defense Force Commendation Medal [Vol. 2: 5702]
Chief's Special Recognition Award [Vol. 1: 15319]
Chilcote Young Investigator Award; Max E. [Vol. 1: 895]
Child Advocate of the Year [Vol. 1: 13304]
Child and Adolescent Faculty Poster Prize for SHOs/ STs [Vol. 2: 8708]
Child and Adolescent Faculty Specialist Registrar Poster Prize [Vol. 2: 8709]
Child Award; Frank S. [Vol. 1: 15677]
Child Award; Julia [Vol. 1: 9656]
Child Cookbook Award; Julia [Vol. 1: 9656]
Child Health Foundation Prize [Vol. 2: 6549]
Child Research Seed Grants [Vol. 1: 17255]
Childers Award for Distinguished Graduate Teaching; Norman F. [Vol. 1: 3929]
Childhood Cancer Foundation Scholarships [Vol. 1: 7229]
Children of the Night Award [Vol. 2: 7524]
Children/Young Adult Book of the Year [Vol. 1: 5918]
Children's Africana Book Awards [Vol. 1: 200]
Children's and Young Adult's Book Awards [Vol. 1: 10092]
Children's Author/Illustrator Award [Vol. 1: 4782]
Children's Book Award
    Association of Jewish Libraries [Vol. 1: 5388]
    Children's Book Committee [Vol 1: 7233]
Children's Book Prize [Vol. 1: 17742]
Children's Bookseller of the Year [Vol. 2: 6893]
Children's Choice Award [Vol. 1: 7013]
Children's Independent of the Year [Vol. 2: 6894]
Children's Peace Literature Award [Vol. 2: 509]
Childs Award; Gayle B. [Vol. 1: 17381]
Chilton Prize; Ken [Vol. 1: 14619]
China Awards; Seatrade [Vol. 2: 9177]
China Service Medal - Navy, Marine Corps, Coast Guard [Vol. 1: 16665]
Chinard Prize; Gilbert [Vol. 1: 15074]
Chinese Martial Arts Outstanding Leadership Award [Vol. 1: 447]
Chinese Martial Arts Outstanding Service Award [Vol. 1: 448]
Chipp Memorial Award; Rodney D. [Vol. 1: 15896]
Chiron Award [Vol. 2: 7294]
Chiron Therapeutics Chapter Excellence Award [Vol. 1: 13532]

Chiron Therapeutics Susan Baird Excellence in Writing Awards in Clinical Practice and Nursing Research [Vol. 1: 13530]
Chiropractor of the Year [Vol. 1: 9754]
Chisholm Award for Lifetime Achievement; Jack [Vol. 1: 6686]
Chlotrudis Awards [Vol. 1: 7255]
Choate Scholarship; Ray [Vol. 2: 435]
Cholmondeley Award for Poets [Vol. 2: 9246]
Choong Most Promising Player of the Year Award; Eddy [Vol. 2: 4530]
Chope R and D Award; Rudolf [Vol. 1: 9097]
Chopin Piano Competition [Vol. 1: 10702]
Chopin Piano Competition; International Frederic [Vol. 2: 5388]
Choppin Memorial Award; Bruce H. [Vol. 2: 4720]
Chopra Lecture; Bashambar Nath [Vol. 2: 3632]
CHORAL: CBC Radio/Radio Canada National Competition for Amateur Choirs [Vol. 1: 6365]
Chorbachi Prizes; Walid [Vol. 2: 7838]
Chorley Award for Postgraduate Research; Dick [Vol. 2: 7224]
Chorpenning Playwright Award; Charlotte B. [Vol. 1: 805]
Chorus America/ASCAP Alice Parker Award [Vol. 1: 7260]
Chorus America/ASCAP Awards for Adventurous Programming [Vol. 1: 7261]
Choseed Memorial Fellowship; Prof. Bernard [Vol. 1: 18178]
Choucroun Prize; Nine [Vol. 2: 2467]
Chow Award; Ven Te [Vol. 1: 4167]
Chree Medal and Prize; Charles [Vol. 2: 7899]
Chris Awards [Vol. 1: 7427]
Chris Statuette [Vol. 1: 7427]
Christen Distinguished Undergraduate Student Award; Genevieve [Vol. 1: 1971]
Christensen Award for Innovations in Calorimetry; James J. [Vol. 1: 6102]
Christensen Award for Outstanding Contributions in Analytical Methods; Edith A. [Vol. 1: 6]
Christensen/John Jay Pittman Sr. Memorial Exhibit Award; Henry [Vol. 1: 2985]
Christensen Memorial Prize; F. G. [Vol. 2: 955]
Christian Album of the Year [Vol. 2: 4875]
Christian Awards; Henry [Vol. 1: 2110]
Christian Book Awards [Vol. 1: 8197]
Christian Book of the Year [Vol. 2: 4876]
Christian Management Award [Vol. 1: 7266]
Christian Stewardship Award [Vol. 1: 9747]
Christie Lectureship; Barnett [Vol. 2: 7084]
Christman Award; Luther [Vol. 1: 853]
Christmas Tree Competition [Vol. 2: 7001]
Christoff International Competition for Young Opera Singers; Boris [Vol. 2: 1793]
Christopher Awards [Vol. 1: 7269]
Christopher Leadership Award [Vol. 1: 7269]
Christopher Life Achievement Award [Vol. 1: 7269]
Christophers Medal; Sir Rickard [Vol. 2: 9115]
Christopherson Lectureship Award; E. H. [Vol. 1: 666]
Christus Magister Award [Vol. 1: 10907]
Christy Award; Naomy [Vol. 2: 7306]
Christy Award; Teresa E. [Vol. 1: 1005]
Christy Awards [Vol. 1: 7271]
Chrysal Competition; FleurEx - [Vol. 2: 7060]
The Chubb Insurance Company of Europe Prize [Vol. 2: 7406]
Chugaev Prize; L.A. [Vol. 2: 5796]
Chugani Memorial Award for Excellence in Applied Physics; Murli M. [Vol. 2: 3686]
Chung-Wae Award [Vol. 2: 5468]
Church Best First Book Award for Fiction; Hubert [Vol. 2: 5010]
Church Medal; Edwin F. [Vol. 1: 4383]
Church of Iceland Film Award [Vol. 2: 3419]
Churchill Award; H. V. [Vol. 1: 5585]
Churchill Award; Winston
    Winston Churchill Foundation of the United States [Vol. 1: 7286]
    International Public Debate Association [Vol 1: 10067]
Churchill Bowl [Vol. 1: 6661]
CIAA Prize [Vol. 1: 6563]
Ciapetta Lectureship in Catalysis; F. G. [Vol. 1: 13287]

Ciaudelli Award; Joseph P. [Vol. 1: 15597]
CIBA-GEIGY Exemplary Middle Level and High School Science Teaching Award [Vol. 1: 12820]
CIBA Specialty Chemicals Exemplary Middle Level and High School Principal Awards [Vol. 1: 12820]
CIBA Specialty Chemicals Exemplary Middle Level and High School Science Teaching Awards [Vol. 1: 12821]
CIC Fellowship [Vol. 1: 7205]
CICH Corporate Awards [Vol. 1: 6576]
Cichan Award; Michael [Vol. 1: 5932]
Cihon Memorial Exhibit Award; William C. Henderson/Fred [Vol. 1: 2992]
Cillie Floating Trophy; Dr. G. G. [Vol. 2: 5761]
CIM Fellowship [Vol. 1: 6604]
CIM Marketer of the Year Award [Vol. 2: 5267]
Cimino Award; Frank [Vol. 1: 5252]
CINDY Awards [Vol. 1: 9621]
CineFestival in San Antonio [Vol. 1: 8796]
Cinema Pioneer Award [Vol. 1: 11264]
Cinema Under the Stars [Vol. 1: 11258]
Cinematography; National Awards for [Vol. 2: 258]
Circle Award [Vol. 1: 7861]
Circle of Excellence Awards [Vol. 1: 15793]
Circus Maniacs Awards [Vol. 2: 7427]
CISRA Prize in Physics [Vol. 2: 1109]
Citation Award
    Awana Clubs International [Vol. 1: 5744]
    Canadian Society of Club Managers [Vol 1: 6941]
    Institute of Quarrying - England [Vol 2: 7936]
Citation Certificate [Vol. 1: 14232]
Citation for Career Achievement [Vol. 1: 15162]
Citation for Excellence in Community Architecture [Vol. 1: 2573]
Citation for Service [Vol. 1: 8524]
Citation of Excellence [Vol. 1: 11961]
Citation of Excellence in Advertising [Vol. 1: 17699]
Citation of Excellence in the Art of Puppetry [Vol. 1: 16619]
Citation of Honor
    Air Force Association [Vol. 1: 253]
    Associated Church Press [Vol 1: 4886]
    International Federation of Sports Medicine [Vol 2: 4104]
Citation of Merit
    International Life Saving Federation [Vol. 2: 1538]
    Women Band Directors International [Vol 1: 17910]
Citation of Outstanding Achievement [Vol. 1: 6774]
Citation of Outstanding Service to the Society [Vol. 1: 15698]
Citations for Contributions to Chemistry and the Chemical Profession [Vol. 2: 972]
Citations pour Service Eminent [Vol. 1: 6774]
Citizen Activist Award [Vol. 1: 8661]
Citizen Engineer Award [Vol. 1: 4168]
Citizen Leadership Award [Vol. 1: 12119]
Citizen of the Year [Vol. 1: 13505]
Citizen's Award [Vol. 1: 9193]
City and Guilds Prizes [Vol. 2: 9141]
City Livability Awards Program [Vol. 1: 16772]
City of Calgary/W.O. Mitchell Book Prize [Vol. 1: 18110]
City of Edmonton Book Prize [Vol. 1: 18111]
City of Sydney Piano Scholarship [Vol. 2: 1074]
Civic Achievement Award [Vol. 1: 5824]
Civic Courage Award [Vol. 1: 17628]
Civic Engagement in an Older America Project Awards [Vol. 1: 8620]
Civil Air Patrol Aerospace Education Cadet of the Year [Vol. 1: 254]
Civil Air Patrol Cadet of the Year [Vol. 1: 254]
Civil Aviation Authority (CAA) Trophy [Vol. 2: 5052]
Civil Engineering Awards [Vol. 2: 9149]
Civil Engineering Best Paper Award [Vol. 1: 3844]
Civil Engineering History and Heritage Award [Vol. 1: 4169]
Civil Engineering Manager of the Year Award [Vol. 2: 7977]
Civil Engineering Students Papers Competition [Vol. 2: 7978]
Civil Government Award [Vol. 1: 4170]
Civilian Service Medal 1939-1945 [Vol. 2: 307]

CJCLS EBESCO Community College Learning Resources and Library Achievement Awards [Vol. 1: 5258]
CLA Echo Program [Vol. 1: 6673]
Clagett Memorial Trophy; Nancy Leiter [Vol. 1: 17052]
CLAGS Fellowship [Vol. 1: 7137]
Clair Jr. Award; John J. [Vol. 1: 17076]
Claret Jug [Vol. 2: 8638]
Clarion Awards [Vol. 1: 5157]
Clarity Award [Vol. 1: 3538]
Clark Award; John [Vol. 1: 6873]
Clark Award; Justice Tom C. [Vol. 1: 8253]
Clark Award; Mary Higgins [Vol. 1: 11330]
Clark Award; Russell [Vol. 2: 4931]
Clark Distinguished Professional Award; David E. [Vol. 1: 3119]
Clark Distinguished Service Contribution Award; Beth [Vol. 1: 569]
Clark, Jr. National Sportsmanship Trophy; W. Van Alan [Vol. 1: 17053]
Clark Medal; Grahame [Vol. 2: 6922]
Clark Medal; John Bates [Vol. 1: 2050]
Clark Memorial Educational Scholarship; Robert A. [Vol. 1: 12857]
Clark Memorial Fund; Tony [Vol. 2: 8645]
Clark National Memorial Trophy; G. Melville [Vol. 2: 6705]
Clark/Seth Payne Award; Evert [Vol. 1: 11881]
Clark Student Research Award; Kenneth E. [Vol. 1: 7128]
Clarke Award; Arthur C. [Vol. 2: 9159]
Clarke Award for Excellence in Children's Care; Peter [Vol. 2: 7333]
Clarke Award; F.W. [Vol. 1: 8554]
Clarke Award; Polly [Vol. 1: 13501]
Clarke Memorial Award; Doug
    Canadian Wildlife Federation [Vol. 1: 7041]
    Canadian Wildlife Federation [Vol 1: 7042]
Clarke Memorial Lectureship [Vol. 2: 1002]
Clarke Memorial Medal [Vol. 1: 1003]
Clarke Outstanding Educator Award; Robert B. [Vol. 1: 7870]
Clarke Prize; Athalie Richardson Irvine [Vol. 1: 13023]
Clarke Trophy; Robert W. [Vol. 1: 2409]
Clarkson Prize; Thomas [Vol. 2: 8149]
Class Champions [Vol. 1: 2121]
Classic FM/A & B International Award [Vol. 2: 6737]
Classic Paper Award [Vol. 1: 5111]
Classical Commissioning Program [Vol. 1: 7177]
Classical Music Awards [Vol. 2: 472]
Classified Manager of the Year [Vol. 1: 16311]
Clavel-Lespiau; Prix [Vol. 2: 2189]
Clay Award; Garland W. [Vol. 1: 616]
Claypoole, Sr. Memorial Award; Ralph O. [Vol. 1: 1796]
Clayton Doctoral Dissertation Proposal Award; Alden G. [Vol. 1: 10984]
Clean Air Excellence Awards [Vol. 1: 16883]
C.L.E.A.N. Award [Vol. 1: 13137]
Clean City Awards [Vol. 2: 7436]
Cleanrun Trophy [Vol. 1: 13438]
Clear-Com Intercom Systems Sound Achievement Award [Vol. 1: 16961]
Cleary Award; Edward J. [Vol. 1: 519]
Cleaver Club Award [Vol. 1: 1205]
Cleghorn Award for Excellence and Leadership in Clinical Research; J.M. [Vol. 1: 6811]
Clemson Awards [Vol. 1: 15045]
Clermont-Ferrand International Short Film Festival [Vol. 2: 2602]
Clermont-Ferrand National Short Film Festival [Vol. 2: 2603]
Clermont-Ganneau; Prix Charles [Vol. 2: 2152]
Cleveland International Piano Competition [Vol. 1: 7324]
Cleveland Lifetime Achievement Award; Allstate James [Vol. 1: 7159]
Cleveland Prize; Newcomb [Vol. 1: 987]
Cleveland Quartet Award [Vol. 1: 7178]
CLFMA Award [Vol. 2: 3461]
Client of the Year Award [Vol. 2: 8852]
Clifford Prize; James L. [Vol. 1: 3822]
Climate Change Adaptation Award [Vol. 1: 10488]
Climate Change and Energy Award [Vol. 1: 10488]

Climate Change and Forests Award [Vol. 1: 10488]
Climate Change and Nature Award [Vol. 1: 10488]
Climate Change Negotiations Award [Vol. 1: 10488]
Climate Protection Awards [Vol. 1: 16884]
Climatics Award [Vol. 1: 9317]
Clinchard Award; Al and Dorothea [Vol. 1: 3314]
Cline Memorial Prize; Howard Francis [Vol. 1: 7513]
Clinedinst Memorial Medal; Benjamin West [Vol. 1: 4820]
Clinical Associate Physician Grant [Vol. 1: 8820]
Clinical Audit Prize, West Midlands Division [Vol. 2: 8710]
Clinical Biomechanics Award [Vol. 2: 4075]
Clinical Biomechanics Award [Vol. 2: 838]
Clinical/Biomedical Engineering Achievement Award [Vol. 1: 5131]
Clinical Excellence Award [Vol. 1: 8078]
Clinical Fellowship Awards [Vol. 2: 7261]
Clinical Instructor of the Year Award [Vol. 1: 1239]
Clinical Investigator Lecture Award [Vol. 1: 8109]
Clinical Lectureship [Vol. 1: 13533]
Clinical Medicine Person-in-Training Award [Vol. 1: 8621]
Clinical Medicine Research Award [Vol. 1: 8629]
Clinical Practice Award
    American College of Clinical Pharmacology [Vol. 1: 1719]
    International Society of Psychiatric-Mental Health Nurses [Vol. 1: 10352]
Clinical Research Award
    American Academy of Clinical Psychiatrists [Vol. 1: 507]
    European Cancer Organization [Vol 2: 1444]
Clinical Research Award in Periodontology [Vol. 1: 718]
Clinical Research Scholar Grant [Vol. 1: 8821]
Clinical Scholar Research Award [Vol. 1: 9501]
Clinical Scholars Award [Vol. 1: 2019]
Clinical Science Young Investigator Award [Vol. 1: 3251]
Clinical Scientist in Nephrology Fellowship [Vol. 1: 2747]
Clinical Scientist Training Award [Vol. 1: 2020]
Clinical Student Research Award [Vol. 1: 2251]
Clinical Surgery Fellowship [Vol. 1: 13624]
Clinical/Translational Award [Vol. 1: 2021]
Clinician Award [Vol. 1: 13089]
Clinician of the Year [Vol. 1: 1316]
Clinician of the Year Award
    American Geriatrics Society [Vol. 1: 2252]
    International Society for Clinical Densitometry [Vol 1: 10147]
Clinician's Professional Enrichment [Vol. 1: 6255]
Clinton Global Citizen Awards [Vol. 1: 7329]
Clio Awards [Vol. 1: 7331]
Clogg Award; Clifford C. [Vol. 1: 14088]
Cloos Medal; Hans [Vol. 2: 6037]
Clore International Award; Gerald R. [Vol. 1: 8724]
Clough Medal [Vol. 2: 7542]
Clough Memorial Award [Vol. 2: 7543]
Cloward and Frances Fox Piven Award; Richard [Vol. 1: 7116]
Clowes, Jr. MD, Memorial Research Career Development Award; George H. A. [Vol. 1: 1822]
Clowes Memorial Award; G. H. A. [Vol. 1: 879]
Clown of the Year [Vol. 1: 7335]
CLS Award for Excellence in Client Service [Vol. 2: 8289]
Club Achievement Awards [Vol. 1: 777]
Club Bulletin Contest [Vol. 1: 10855]
Club Development Award [Vol. 2: 3902]
Club of the Year [Vol. 2: 7317]
Clubmaker of the Year [Vol. 1: 14194]
Clubmakers Hall of Fame [Vol. 1: 14195]
Clubok Award; Miriam [Vol. 1: 12632]
Clurman Award; Richard M. [Vol. 1: 17281]
CMA/ASCAP Awards for Adventurous Programming [Vol. 1: 7179]
CNN MultiChoice African Journalist Awards [Vol. 2: 7444]
CNN MultiChoice African Journalist of the Year [Vol. 2: 7444]
Co-Founders Best Book Award [Vol. 1: 17782]
Co-op Feeds Young Scientist's Award [Vol. 1: 6930]
Coach of the Year
    Baseball Canada [Vol. 1: 5790]

Camanachd Association [Vol 2: 7318]
Canadian Colleges Athletic Association [Vol 1: 6417]
Ladies Professional Golf Association [Vol 1: 10726]
National Association of Basketball Coaches [Vol 1: 11637]
National Basketball Association [Vol 1: 11975]
National Christian College Athletic Association [Vol 1: 12061]
National High School Athletic Coaches Association [Vol 1: 12507]
Special Olympics Canada [Vol 1: 16115]
Speed Skating Canada [Vol 1: 16139]
Trinidad and Tobago Football Federation [Vol 2: 6629]
United States Synchronized Swimming [Vol 1: 17121]
Coach of the Year Award
    American Baseball Coaches Association [Vol. 1: 1476]
    American Swimming Coaches Association [Vol 1: 4579]
    Football Writers Association of America [Vol 1: 8412]
    National Association of Intercollegiate Athletics [Vol 1: 11808]
    National Soccer Coaches Association of America [Vol 1: 12844]
Coach of the Year Awards
    American Football Coaches Association [Vol. 1: 2168]
    National Wrestling Coaches Association [Vol. 1: 13066]
    United States Youth Soccer Association [Vol 1: 17154]
Coaches Hall of Fame [Vol. 1: 4580]
Coal and Energy Division Distinguished Service Award [Vol. 1: 15204]
Coal Award [Vol. 1: 6605]
Coast Guard Arctic Service Medal [Vol. 1: 16666]
Coast Guard Reserve Good Conduct Medal [Vol. 1: 16667]
Coastal Project Award [Vol. 1: 3742]
Cobb, Jr. Award for Initiative and Success in Trade Development; Charles E. [Vol. 1: 16845]
Cobb Young Investigator Award; W. A. [Vol. 1: 9913]
Cobbing Travelling Fellowship; Natalie [Vol. 2: 8711]
Coble Award for Young Scholars; Robert L. [Vol. 1: 1553]
Cochran-Hansen Prize [Vol. 2: 2497]
Cochrane Award; Vice Admiral E. L. [Vol. 1: 15711]
Cockayne Memorial Lecture; Leonard [Vol. 2: 5071]
Cockcroft Award; Ron [Vol. 2: 6153]
Cocker Award; Wesley [Vol. 2: 9276]
Codd Innovations Award; Edgar F. [Vol. 1: 16085]
Code of Silence Award [Vol. 1: 6277]
Codes and Standards Medal [Vol. 1: 4391]
CODiE Awards [Vol. 1: 15919]
Coe Award; Maynard [Vol. 1: 10135]
Coffee Conservation Award [Vol. 1: 7592]
Cogan Award [Vol. 1: 5082]
COGEL Award [Vol. 1: 7701]
Cohen Award for a Distinguished Edition of Letters; Morton N. [Vol. 1: 11231]
Cohen Award for Distinguished Contributions to Teaching and Mentoring; Jacob [Vol. 1: 3417]
Cohen Award; Lee [Vol. 1: 854]
Cohen Award; Riva [Vol. 1: 358]
Cohen Award; Seymour R. [Vol. 1: 2751]
Cohen British Literature Prize; David [Vol. 2: 6745]
Cohen/EMIERT Award; David [Vol. 1: 2767]
Cohen Gold Medal; Lord [Vol. 2: 8950]
Cohen Medal; Lord [Vol. 2: 7237]
Cohen National Playwriting Award; David Mark [Vol. 1: 10662]
Cohen Outstanding Service to KNPS; Sheldon H. [Vol. 1: 10631]
Cohen Sound Achievement Award; Robert E. [Vol. 1: 16961]
Cohn Hope Award; Norman [Vol. 1: 12611]
Coker Award; C. F. W. [Vol. 1: 15417]
Colaianni Award for Excellence and Achievement in Hospital Librarianship; Lois Ann [Vol. 1: 11062]

Colburn Award for Excellence in Publications by a Young Member of the Institute; Allan P. [Vol. 1: 2610]
Colburn Memorial Award; Wayne A. [Vol. 1: 1720]
Colby Award; William E. [Vol. 1: 14860]
Cole Award; Art [Vol. 1: 1108]
Cole Award for Automotive Engineering Innovation; Edward N. [Vol. 1: 15496]
Cole Distinguished Younger Member Award; Edward N. [Vol. 1: 15497]
Cole Grants in Aid; Arthur H. [Vol. 1: 7993]
Cole Nurse Practitioner Award; Frank L. [Vol. 1: 8088]
Cole Prize; Arthur H. [Vol. 1: 7994]
Cole Prize in Algebra; Frank Nelson [Vol. 1: 2827]
Cole Prize in Number Theory; Frank Nelson [Vol. 1: 2828]
Cole Research Grant; Monica [Vol. 2: 8788]
Cole Scholar; Alan [Vol. 1: 17520]
Cole Sportsmanship Award; Mark [Vol. 1: 12289]
Colen Memorial Grant; Kimberly [Vol. 1: 15588]
Coler - Maxwell Medal [Vol. 1: 10799]
Coles Medal for Landscape Archaeology; John [Vol. 2: 6923]
Coley Award; William B. [Vol. 1: 7055]
Colgate-Palmolive Awards for Student Research Training in Alternative Methods [Vol. 1: 15846]
Colgate-Palmolive Post-Doctoral Fellowship Award in In-Vitro Toxicology [Vol. 1: 15847]
Colgate-Palmolive Research Scholarship Award [Vol. 1: 1414]
Colgate Research Scholarship [Vol. 1: 1414]
Colibri Diploma [Vol. 2: 6301]
Collaboration Award [Vol. 1: 9194]
Collaborative Research Grant [Vol. 1: 9598]
Collaborative Research Grants [Vol. 1: 8645]
Collaborative School Library Award [Vol. 1: 1340]
Collacott Prize [Vol. 2: 8017]
Collection System Award [Vol. 1: 17700]
College and University Health and Safety Award [Vol. 1: 1625]
College Art Association/National Institute for Conservation Award [Vol. 1: 7354]
College Basketball Coach of the Year [Vol. 1: 16172]
College Basketball Player of the Year [Vol. 1: 16173]
College-Bound Award [Vol. 1: 10849]
College Community Service Awards [Vol. 1: 7408]
College Fiction Contest [Vol. 1: 14042]
College Football Coach of the Year [Vol. 1: 16174]
College Football Defensive Player of the Year Trophy [Vol. 1: 8409]
College Football Player of the Year [Vol. 1: 16175]
College Journalism Competition [Vol. 1: 14582]
College Medal
    Australian College of Educators [Vol. 2: 261]
    Royal Australian and New Zealand College of Ophthalmologists [Vol 2: 962]
College of Diplomates Award [Vol. 1: 12774]
College of Electrical Engineers Student Prizes [Vol. 2: 775]
College Player of the Year [Vol. 1: 17421]
College Press Freedom Award [Vol. 1: 16304]
College Scholar All-America Award [Vol. 1: 12845]
College Scholarship [Vol. 1: 13193]
College Scholarship Awards [Vol. 1: 13863]
College Scholarships [Vol. 1: 5715]
College Student Leadership Award [Vol. 1: 10428]
College/University Distinguished Teaching Achievement Award [Vol. 1: 12156]
Collegiate Athlete of the Year [Vol. 1: 17122]
Collegiate Bowlers of the Year [Vol. 1: 5952]
Collegiate or University Teacher of the Year [Vol. 1: 12018]
Collier Award for Forest History Journalism; John M. [Vol. 1: 8428]
Collier Trophy; Robert J. [Vol. 1: 11464]
Collin Prize for Law; Fernand [Vol. 2: 1669]
Colling Literary Achievement Medal; Russell L. [Vol. 1: 9561]
Collingwood Prize [Vol. 1: 4171]
Collins Award; Carr P. [Vol. 1: 16453]
Collins Award; George R. [Vol. 1: 959]
Collins Award; Joseph P. [Vol. 1: 12196]
Collins Award; Samuel C. [Vol. 1: 7775]
Collins Award; W. Leighton [Vol. 1: 3845]
Collins Diversity Award; Marva [Vol. 1: 7648]

Collins, Jr. Research Promotion Award; William J. **[Vol. 1: 4319]**

Collins Medal **[Vol. 2: 8356]**

Collins Memorial Award; Charles J. **[Vol. 1: 5253]**

Collins Memorial Award; Norman **[Vol. 2: 7270]**

Collison Prize; Jeanne **[Vol. 2: 557]**

Collymore Literary Awards; Frank **[Vol. 2: 1388]**

Colombe Unda **[Vol. 2: 1662]**

Colorado Blue Spruce Young Adult Book Award **[Vol. 1: 7385]**

Colorado Librarian of the Year **[Vol. 1: 7386]**

Colorado Library of the Year **[Vol. 1: 7387]**

Colorado Ocean Award **[Vol. 1: 11265]**

Colposcopy Recognition Award **[Vol. 1: 3806]**

Columbine Award **[Vol. 1: 11266]**

Columbine Poets of Colorado Award **[Vol. 1: 12344]**

Columbus Literary Awards **[Vol. 1: 16496]**

Column Contest **[Vol. 1: 12871]**

Colvin and Frank C. Laubach Award for Student Excellence; Ruth J. **[Vol. 1: 14263]**

Colwell Cooperative Engineering Medal; Arch T. **[Vol. 1: 15498]**

Colwell Merit Award; Arch T. **[Vol. 1: 15499]**

Colyer Prize **[Vol. 2: 9086]**

Comas Prize; Juan **[Vol. 1: 1293]**

Combat Readiness Medal **[Vol. 1: 16668]**

Combs Memorial Scholarship; Anne and Charles **[Vol. 1: 17655]**

Comfeel Literary Awards **[Vol. 2: 622]**

Comfort Prize; A. C. **[Vol. 2: 9087]**

Commandant's Aviation Trophy **[Vol. 1: 10944]**

Commandant's Distinguished Career Service Medal **[Vol. 1: 16753]**

Commandant's Superior Achievement Award (Bronze Medal) **[Vol. 1: 16754]**

Commander in Chief's Annual Award for Installation Excellence **[Vol. 1: 16801]**

Commander's Award for Civilian Service **[Vol. 1: 16755]**

Commander's Award for Sustained Excellence in the Federal Service **[Vol. 1: 16756]**

Commemorative Lecture Series **[Vol. 1: 1842]**

Commendation Award
   International Narcotic Enforcement Officers Association **[Vol. 1: 10026]**
     Soil and Water Conservation Society **[Vol 1: 15922]**

Commendation for Brave Conduct **[Vol. 2: 298]**

Commendation for Distinguished Service **[Vol. 2: 311]**

Commendation for Gallantry **[Vol. 2: 313]**

Commendation Medal: Navy/Marine Corps **[Vol. 1: 16669]**

Commentary/Column Writing **[Vol. 1: 4464]**

Commercial Award **[Vol. 1: 2427]**

Commercial Bacon Award **[Vol. 1: 9123]**

Commercial Breeder of the Year **[Vol. 1: 327]**

Commercial Horticulture Distinguished Achievement Award **[Vol. 1: 3921]**

Commercial Organisation of the Year **[Vol. 2: 7007]**

Commercial Photographer of the Year **[Vol. 2: 413]**

Commercial Style Ham - Bone In Award **[Vol. 1: 9124]**

Commercial Wine Competition Awards **[Vol. 1: 4702]**

Commisariat a l'Energie Atomique; Prix du **[Vol. 2: 2190]**

Commissioner's Award **[Vol. 1: 10727]**

Commissioner's Cup **[Vol. 1: 16014]**

Commissioner's Trophy Awards **[Vol. 1: 5835]**

Commitment to Interfaith Service Award **[Vol. 1: 14656]**

Committee D-12 Award **[Vol. 1: 5586]**

Committee D-20 Award of Excellence **[Vol. 1: 5587]**

Committee E-8 Best Student Paper Award **[Vol. 1: 5588]**

Committee of the Year **[Vol. 1: 11919]**

Committee Person of the Year **[Vol. 1: 1253]**

Common Award for Canadian History; Lela
   Canadian Authors Association **[Vol. 1: 6323]**
   Canadian Authors Association **[Vol 1: 6325]**

Common Ground Award for Journalism in the Middle East **[Vol. 1: 14811]**

Common Ground Awards **[Vol. 1: 14810]**

Commonwealth Fund Fellowships **[Vol. 1: 7449]**

Commonwealth Games **[Vol. 2: 7467]**

Commonwealth Scholarship and Fellowship Plan **[Vol. 2: 6813]**

Commonwealth Shared Scholarship Scheme **[Vol. 2: 6814]**

Commonwealth Short Story Competition **[Vol. 2: 7464]**

Commonwealth Writers' Prize **[Vol. 2: 7465]**

Communication Award
   International Solid Waste Association **[Vol. 2: 1304]**
   Sierra Club **[Vol 1: 14861]**

Communication Awards
   Alliance of the American Dental Association **[Vol. 1: 387]**
   Pennsylvania State Education Association **[Vol 1: 13917]**

Communication Excellence in Action Award **[Vol. 1: 9024]**

Communication Program of the Year **[Vol. 1: 9235]**

Communications Award
   American Institute of Aeronautics and Astronautics **[Vol. 1: 2512]**
   American Mathematical Society **[Vol 1: 2829]**
   American Staffing Association **[Vol 1: 4557]**
   Society for Applied Microbiology **[Vol 2: 9188]**
   Society for Ecological Restoration International **[Vol 1: 15060]**

Communications Center Director of the Year **[Vol. 1: 5492]**

Communications Contest **[Vol. 1: 12337]**

Communicator of the Year
   Institute of Internal Communication **[Vol. 2: 7877]**
   National Association of Government Communicators **[Vol 1: 11778]**

Communicator of the Year Award
   International Association of Business Communicators **[Vol. 1: 9626]**
   National Council for Marketing and Public Relations **[Vol 1: 12160]**
   North Country Trail Association **[Vol 1: 13382]**
   Utility Communicators International **[Vol 1: 17503]**

Communicators in Business Awards **[Vol. 2: 7878]**

Community Achievement Award **[Vol. 1: 13194]**

Community and Young People Award **[Vol. 2: 6738]**

Community Animal Welfare Footprints Achiever Awards **[Vol. 2: 8965]**

Community Award **[Vol. 1: 7814]**

Community Award **[Vol. 2: 912]**

Community Awareness Through Media Award **[Vol. 1: 3333]**

Community Conservation Enterprises **[Vol. 1: 14429]**

Community Contribution Award **[Vol. 2: 1050]**

Community Contribution Awards **[Vol. 1: 17496]**

Community Counselling Service Award for Outstanding Fundraising Professional **[Vol. 1: 5349]**

Community Crime Prevention Program Award **[Vol. 1: 10304]**

Community, Culture, and Prevention Science Award **[Vol. 1: 15270]**

Community Dentistry Award **[Vol. 1: 2001]**

Community Development Achievement Award **[Vol. 1: 7456]**

Community Development Projects (CDP) **[Vol. 1: 17876]**

Community Education Grants **[Vol. 1: 13183]**

Community Engagement Award of Excellence **[Vol. 1: 11706]**

Community Health and Safety Awards **[Vol. 1: 9759]**

Community Improvement Contest **[Vol. 1: 8537]**

Community Leadership Award **[Vol. 1: 430]**

Community Leadership Award **[Vol. 1: 9244]**

Community Leadership Awards **[Vol. 1: 14710]**

Community Legal Clinics Volunteer Service Award **[Vol. 1: 8578]**

Community Partnership Awards **[Vol. 1: 9760]**

Community Person of the Year **[Vol. 2: 3892]**

Community Preventive Dentistry Award **[Vol. 1: 2001]**

Community Project Grants **[Vol. 1: 13184]**

Community Rail Awards **[Vol. 2: 6818]**

Community Service Award
   Canadian Colleges Athletic Association **[Vol. 1: 6418]**
   National Indian Education Association **[Vol 1: 12538]**

Community Service Award
   American Academy of Facial Plastic and Reconstructive Surgery **[Vol. 1: 535]**
   American Association of Critical-Care Nurses **[Vol 1: 1117]**
   American Correctional Association **[Vol 1: 1882]**
   American Council of Engineering Companies **[Vol 1: 1897]**
   American Public Power Association **[Vol 1: 3648]**
   American Society of Landscape Architects **[Vol 1: 4361]**
   Canadian Society of Landscape Architects **[Vol 1: 6968]**
   Chinese American Medical Society **[Vol 1: 7252]**
   Inland Press Association **[Vol 1: 9244]**
   Keuka College Alumni Association **[Vol 1: 10678]**
   LeadingAge **[Vol 1: 10771]**
   National Council of Social Security Management Associations **[Vol 1: 12197]**
   Pickerington Area Chamber of Commerce **[Vol 1: 14014]**
   Sierra Club **[Vol 1: 14862]**
   UCLA Alumni Association **[Vol 1: 16589]**
   University of the Philippines Alumni Association **[Vol 2: 5372]**

Community Service Award for Fellows and Members **[Vol. 1: 1254]**

Community Service Photojournalism Award **[Vol. 1: 4463]**

Community Service Team Award **[Vol. 1: 16503]**

Community Sustainability Awards **[Vol. 1: 9761]**

Community Welfare Award **[Vol. 2: 3612]**

Community Wildlife Conservation Award **[Vol. 2: 1188]**

Compadre Award **[Vol. 1: 16070]**

Companion Membership **[Vol. 2: 9373]**

Companion of the RAeC **[Vol. 2: 8593]**

Companion of the Star of Melanesia **[Vol. 2: 5211]**

Companion Prize **[Vol. 2: 4481]**

Companions Awards **[Vol. 2: 7469]**

Company Award of Excellence **[Vol. 1: 11844]**

Company of Fellows
   AIIM - The Enterprise Content Management Association **[Vol. 1: 231]**
   ARMA International - The Association of Information Management Professionals **[Vol 1: 4799]**

Company of the Year Award **[Vol. 1: 10203]**

Company of the Year Awards **[Vol. 2: 4384]**

Compass Distinguished Achievement Award **[Vol. 1: 10977]**

Compass Industrial Award **[Vol. 1: 10978]**

Compass International Award **[Vol. 1: 10979]**

Competitie de Impact van Muziek op Film **[Vol. 2: 1516]**

Competition and Festival for Accordionists **[Vol. 1: 773]**

Competition Awards **[Vol. 1: 6227]**

Competition for Young Statisticians from Developing Countries **[Vol. 2: 4789]**

Competitions and Tournaments **[Vol. 2: 6148]**

Competitive Research and Equipment Grants **[Vol. 1: 17345]**

Competitive Workforce Award **[Vol. 1: 15103]**

Comprehensive Research Grant **[Vol. 2: 4207]**

Compton Medal for Leadership in Physics **[Vol. 1: 2683]**

Compton Medal for Leadership in Physics; Karl Taylor **[Vol. 1: 2684]**

Compumedics Poster Prize **[Vol. 2: 222]**

Computer Educator of the Year **[Vol. 2: 9523]**

Computer Entrepreneur Award **[Vol. 1: 9053]**

Computer Graphics Achievement Award **[Vol. 1: 116]**

Computer Pioneer Award **[Vol. 1: 9054]**

Computer Science and Engineering Undergraduate Teaching Award **[Vol. 1: 9055]**

Computer Sciences Man of the Year **[Vol. 1: 5376]**

Computing in Chemical Engineering Award **[Vol. 1: 2611]**

Computing in Civil Engineering Award **[Vol. 1: 4172]**

Computing Practice Award **[Vol. 1: 2612]**

Comstech Prize in Computer Sciences/Information Technology **[Vol. 2: 5189]**

Comstock Prize in Physics **[Vol. 1: 11432]**

Conable Award; Gordon M. **[Vol. 1: 14319]**

Conamus Export Prize **[Vol. 2: 4657]**

Conant Award in High School Chemistry Teaching; James Bryant [Vol. 1: 1626]

Conant Award; James Bryant [Vol. 1: 8014]

Conant Prize; Levi L. [Vol. 1: 2830]

Concerned Broadcaster of the Year [Vol. 1: 12002]

Concerned Citizen Award [Vol. 1: 18064]

Concerned Company/Corporation Award [Vol. 1: 18065]

Concerned Company/Corporation Honorable Mention Certificate [Vol. 1: 18066]

Concerned Organization Award [Vol. 1: 18067]

Concerned Professional Award [Vol. 1: 18068]

Concertino Prague International Radio Competition for Young Musicians [Vol. 2: 1930]

Conch Festival; Turks and Caicos [Vol. 2: 6643]

Concorso Internacional de Violao Villa-Lobos [Vol. 2: 1770]

Concorso Internazionale di Chitarra Classica Michele Pittaluga Premio Citta' di Alessandria [Vol. 2: 4151]

Concorso Internazionale di Violino - Premio Rodolfo Lipizer [Vol. 2: 4050]

Concorso Internazionale per Quartetto d'Archi [Vol. 2: 4157]

Concorso Pianistico Internazionale Alessandro Casagrande [Vol. 2: 4046]

Concours Annuel de Sauvegarde [Vol. 2: 2661]

Concours Canadien de Journalisme [Vol. 1: 6742]

Concours Clara Haskil [Vol. 2: 6258]

Concours de Musique du Canada [Vol. 1: 6725]

Concours et Seminaire International d'alto [Vol. 2: 7571]

Concours International de Ballet, Varna [Vol. 2: 1805]

Concours International de Campagnes de Marketing Direct [Vol. 2: 1512]

Concours International de Composition Musicale [Vol. 2: 2418]

Concours International de Harpe en Israel [Vol. 2: 3955]

Concours International de Jeunes Chanteurs d'Opera [Vol. 2: 1793]

Concours International de Jeunes Chefs d'Orchestre Besancon [Vol. 2: 2417]

Concours OSM [Vol. 1: 11256]

Concrete Achiever of the Year [Vol. 2: 5532]

Concurs Internacional de Cant Francesc Vinas [Vol. 2: 6113]

Concurso Internacional de Piano Villa-Lobos [Vol. 2: 1771]

Condon Prize for Best Student Essay in Psychological Anthropology [Vol. 1: 15282]

Confederate Philatelist Writers Award [Vol. 1: 7480]

Conference Award [Vol. 2: 3290]

Conference Awards
   Nuclear Institute [Vol. 2: 8423]
   Space Coast Writers' Guild [Vol. 1: 16065]

Conference Best Paper Award [Vol. 1: 17399]

Conference Bursaries [Vol. 2: 9238]

Conference Funding [Vol. 1: 8604]

Conference Grants [Vol. 2: 8764]

Conference on Latin American History Prize [Vol. 1: 7514]

Conference Poster Awards [Vol. 2: 829]

Conference Travel Grants [Vol. 2: 4866]

Congress Awards [Vol. 2: 8129]

Congress Medal [Vol. 2: 6797]

Congressional Award [Vol. 1: 17540]

The Congressional Award [Vol. 1: 7537]

Congressional Dialogue Service Award [Vol. 1: 14656]

Congressional Gold Medal [Vol. 1: 16957]

Congressional Medal of Honor [Vol. 1: 7541]

Congressional Research Awards [Vol. 1: 7890]

Congressional Scholarship Awards [Vol. 1: 8484]

Congressional Science Fellowship Program [Vol. 1: 2685]

Congressional Service Award
   American Society for Gastrointestinal Endoscopy [Vol. 1: 3909]
   Rumi Forum [Vol 1: 14656]

Congressional Space Medal of Honor [Vol. 1: 11470]

Conklin Award; Edwin Grant [Vol. 1: 15052]

Conklin Crusader for Lionism Award; Millard [Vol. 1: 10856]

Conkling Memorial Award; Robert J. [Vol. 1: 4675]

Conley Award; Dean [Vol. 1: 1754]

Conley Award; Fred O. [Vol. 1: 15784]

Connare Award for Distinguished Service; Bishop William G. [Vol. 1: 9748]

Connecticut Poetry Society Award [Vol. 1: 12345]

Connections Award of Merit [Vol. 1: 7162]

Connell Award; W. F. [Vol. 1: 6014]

Connelly Medal of Heroism; Robert P. [Vol. 1: 10693]

Conners Prize for Poetry; Bernard F. [Vol. 1: 13869]

Connor Award; Robert D. W. [Vol. 1: 13372]

Connor Environmental Award; John [Vol. 1: 15500]

ConocoPhillips Performance Award (Meet) [Vol. 1: 17438]

ConocoPhillips Performance Award (Year) [Vol. 1: 17439]

Conrad Award/Lecture; Miles [Vol. 1: 12333]

Conrady Award; A. E. [Vol. 1: 16148]

Conservation and Heritage Management Award [Vol. 1: 4759]

Conservation and Preservation Award [Vol. 1: 3715]

Conservation Award
   American Society of Primatologists [Vol. 1: 4500]
   Federation of Fly Fishers [Vol 1: 8297]
   International Wild Waterfowl Association [Vol 1: 10479]
   Nature Saskatchewan [Vol 1: 13111]
   New England Wild Flower Society [Vol 1: 13173]
   Ottawa Field-Naturalists' Club [Vol 1: 13722]
   Izaak Walton League of America [Vol 1: 17632]

Conservation Education Award [Vol. 1: 17849]

Conservation Follow-up Awards [Vol. 2: 7476]

Conservation Grants [Vol. 2: 3876]

Conservation Guest Scholars [Vol. 1: 8646]

Conservation Leadership Award [Vol. 2: 7477]

Conservation Medal [Vol. 1: 13173]

Conservation Research Grants [Vol. 2: 8438]

Conservationist of the Year [Vol. 1: 13044]

Considine Award; Bob [Vol. 1: 14670]

Consoli Film Award; Jim [Vol. 1: 841]

Conspicuous Service Cross [Vol. 2: 308]

Conspicuous Service Decorations [Vol. 2: 308]

Conspicuous Service Medal [Vol. 2: 308]

Constantin de Magny; Prix Adrien [Vol. 2: 2191]

Constantinides Memorial Translation Prize; Elizabeth [Vol. 1: 11227]

Construction Award [Vol. 1: 1843]

Construction Management Award [Vol. 1: 4173]

Construction Manager of the Year Awards [Vol. 2: 7365]

Consular Service Award [Vol. 1: 16856]

Consulting Psychology Journal Outstanding Article/Special Issue Award [Vol. 1: 15590]

Consumer Goods and Services Organisation of the Year [Vol. 2: 7008]

Consumer Horticulture Distinguished Achievement Award [Vol. 1: 3922]

Consumer Involvement Award [Vol. 1: 6688]

Consumer Journalism Award [Vol. 1: 12680]

Consumer Participation Award [Vol. 1: 6688]

Consumer Protection Award [Vol. 1: 7713]

Contact Mechanics Award [Vol. 2: 944]

Container Inspectors Award [Vol. 1: 9376]

Contemporary Art Award [Vol. 1: 76]

Contemporary Book Award [Vol. 2: 2598]

Continental Casualty Award [Vol. 1: 16737]

Continental Grain Company Poultry Products Research Award [Vol. 1: 14114]

Continuare Protessus Articulatus Excellare [Vol. 1: 12927]

Continuation of Service Grants [Vol. 1: 12666]

Continuing Education Awards
   Medical Library Association [Vol. 1: 11063]
   National Association for Pupil Transportation [Vol 1: 11591]

Continuing Education Grant [Vol. 2: 5036]

Continuing Education Grants [Vol. 1: 13195]

Continuing Publication Commendation [Vol. 1: 7554]

Contractor of the Year [Vol. 1: 7681]

Contractor of the Year [Vol. 1: 10747]

Contractor of the Year Award [Vol. 1: 7470]

Contractors' Awards [Vol. 2: 6827]

Contribution by Business Community Award [Vol. 2: 3613]

Contribution to Special Needs Award [Vol. 2: 8048]

Contributions Award [Vol. 1: 16086]

Contributions to Public Awareness of the Importance of Animals in Toxicology Research Award [Vol. 1: 15848]

Control System Technology Award [Vol. 1: 9071]

Control Systems Award [Vol. 1: 9286]

Convention Reimbursement Award [Vol. 1: 13886]

Converter of the Year [Vol. 1: 16353]

Convoy For Kids Grant [Vol. 2: 666]

Conway Prize for Physical Electrochemistry; Brian [Vol. 2: 6436]

Conway Review Lecture [Vol. 2: 3908]

Cook Award; Col. Donald G. [Vol. 1: 12607]

Cook-Douglas Medal [Vol. 1: 11044]

Cook Founders Award; Pete [Vol. 1: 378]

Cook Islands Tourism Awards [Vol. 2: 1855]

Cook Medal; James [Vol. 2: 1004]

Cook Memorial Scholarship; Jeffrey [Vol. 1: 15572]

Cook Peer Helping Award; Daryl L. [Vol. 1: 13598]

Cook Student Travel Award to PLEA; Jeffrey [Vol. 1: 15573]

Cookbook Awards [Vol. 1: 9656]

Cooke Personal Service Award; Harry M. [Vol. 1: 3639]

Cooke Visionary Program Award; Gregg [Vol. 1: 16883]

Cookingham; Award for Career Development in Memory of L.P. [Vol. 1: 9762]

Cookson Award; Isabel [Vol. 1: 5933]

Cooley Award for Recent Book or Article; Charles Horton [Vol. 1: 15399]

Cooley Award; George R. [Vol. 1: 4495]

Cooley Leadership Award; Denton A. [Vol. 1: 16449]

Cooley Memorial Award and Lectureship; Emily [Vol. 1: 1060]

Cooley Memorial Award; Michael Dillon [Vol. 1: 8579]

Cooley Memorial Lectureship; Emily [Vol. 1: 1060]

Coolidge Award; Edgar D. [Vol. 1: 1140]

Cooling Prize [Vol. 2: 7066]

Coomaraswamy Book Prize; Ananda Kentish [Vol. 1: 4915]

Cooney Award; Joe [Vol. 1: 11731]

Coonmel Medal; Howard [Vol. 1: 2970]

Coons Award; Steven A. [Vol. 1: 117]

Cooper and Dale Meyers Medal; Mario [Vol. 1: 4657]

Cooper Architecture Award; Shirley [Vol. 1: 1334]

Cooper Award [Vol. 1: 896]

Cooper Award; Billy H. [Vol. 1: 11080]

Cooper Award; W. S. [Vol. 1: 7983]

Cooper Lifetime Achievement Award; Jack [Vol. 1: 7009]

Cooper Memorial Medal and Prize; E. R. [Vol. 2: 5072]

Cooper Memorial Scholarship Award; Albert H. [Vol. 1: 401]

Cooperative Conservation Awards [Vol. 1: 16858]

Cooperative Research Award in Polymer Science and Engineering [Vol. 1: 1627]

Coopers Hill War Memorial Prize [Vol. 2: 7979]

Cope Award; Arthur C. [Vol. 1: 1628]

Cope Scholar Awards; Arthur C. [Vol. 1: 1629]

Cope Travel Grant; Arthur C. [Vol. 1: 1629]

Copeland Award; Edith Moore [Vol. 1: 14898]

Copeland Award; L. E. [Vol. 1: 1554]

Copeland Scholarship; Arthur E. [Vol. 1: 16718]

Copeland Scholarship; Helen [Vol. 1: 16719]

Copenhagen Award [Vol. 2: 1943]

Copernicus Award [Vol. 2: 2991]

Copley Medal [Vol. 2: 8930]

Copova Diploma [Vol. 2: 6016]

Copp Award; Nan [Vol. 1: 6637]

Copper Club Award [Vol. 1: 5589]

Coppock Research Medal [Vol. 2: 8917]

Copy Editing Scholarship/Internship [Vol. 1: 5178]

Corbay; Prix [Vol. 2: 2250]

Corbett Medal; Arthur [Vol. 2: 776]

Corbetta Concrete Constructor Award; Roger H. [Vol. 1: 1844]

Corbin Companion Animal Biology Award [Vol. 1: 4117]

Corbitt Memorial Award for Ultra Male Runner-of-the-Year; Ted [Vol. 1: 17457]

Corcoran Award; William H. [Vol. 1: 3846]

Corcoran Craft Awards; William and Mary [Vol. 1: 13565]

Corday-Morgan Prize [Vol. 2: 8994]

Core Student Award; Earl [Vol. 1: 16011]

CORESTA Prize [Vol. 2: 2344]
Corey Award; Albert B. [Vol. 1: 981]
Corey Award for Outstanding Contribution in
    Organic Synthesis by a Young Investigator; Elias
    J. [Vol. 1: 1630]
Corey Prize in Canadian-American Relations; Albert
    B. [Vol. 1: 2366]
Corlette Medal; J.M.C. [Vol. 2: 777]
Corliss Systematics Award; John O. [Vol. 1: 10347]
Cornell Religion Reporter of the Year - Mid-Sized
    Newspapers [Vol. 1: 14497]
Cornforth Award; Rita and John [Vol. 2: 8995]
Cornforth Medal [Vol. 2: 973]
Cornish Heritage Certificate [Vol. 1: 7613]
Corporate Award
    American Association of Community The-
        atre [Vol. 1: 1109]
    American Dietetic Association Foundation [Vol
        1: 2032]
    Ecological Society of America [Vol 1: 7984]
    Education Commission of the States [Vol 1:
        8015]
    Ontario Nature [Vol 1: 13585]
    Surface Mount Technology Association [Vol 1:
        16334]
Corporate Award for Balance [Vol. 1: 7187]
Corporate Citizenship Award
    American Chamber of Commerce in Mo-
        rocco [Vol. 2: 4617]
    Imagine Canada [Vol 1: 9167]
Corporate Commitment Award [Vol. 1: 16240]
Corporate Diversity Award [Vol. 1: 11655]
Corporate Engagement Award of Excellence [Vol. 1:
    14073]
Corporate Environmental Achievement Award [Vol.
    1: 1555]
Corporate Health Achievement Award [Vol. 1: 1785]
Corporate Innovation Recognition [Vol. 1: 9287]
Corporate Leadership Award
    American Institute of Graphic Arts [Vol. 1: 2661]
    Aspen Institute [Vol 1: 4852]
    CPR International Institute for Conflict Preven-
        tion and Resolution [Vol 1: 7734]
Corporate Leadership Scholarships [Vol. 1: 8775]
Corporate Organization of the Year [Vol. 2: 1679]
Corporate Patriot Award [Vol. 1: 13840]
Corporate Recognition Award [Vol. 1: 10009]
Corporate Service Award [Vol. 1: 9785]
Corporate Social Responsibility Award [Vol. 1: 5306]
Corporate Social Responsibility Awards [Vol. 2:
    4605]
Corporate Technical Achievement Award [Vol. 1:
    1556]
Corporation of the Year Award [Vol. 1: 5701]
Corr Award for Literature; Charles A. [Vol. 1: 7237]
Corrosion Science Award [Vol. 2: 8996]
Corstorphine Medal [Vol. 2: 5554]
Cory Award of Merit; Winnifred·C. [Vol. 1: 6538]
Cory Cup [Vol. 2: 8814]
Cory Memorial Cup; Reginald [Vol. 2: 8814]
Cory-Wright Cup [Vol. 2: 5053]
COSCDA Sterling Achievement Awards [Vol. 1:
    7679]
COSPAR Space Science Award [Vol. 2: 2335]
Cosslett Award [Vol. 1: 11130]
Costa Award; Joseph [Vol. 1: 12697]
Costa Book Awards [Vol. 2: 6899]
Costa Rica International Film Festival [Vol. 1: 8352]
Costello Fellowships; Jeanne Timmins [Vol. 1:
    11022]
Costello Prize; Harry Todd [Vol. 1: 14651]
Costume and Fashion Jewelry Award [Vol. 2: 3487]
Cothenius Medal [Vol. 2: 3120]
Cotran Young Investigator Award; Ramzi [Vol. 1:
    16704]
Cotter Award in Historical Archaeology; John L. [Vol.
    1: 15091]
Cottle Clinical Research Award [Vol. 1: 3695]
Cottle Honor Award; Dr. Maurice H. [Vol. 1: 3695]
Cotton Award; Marjorie [Vol. 2: 436]
Cottrell Free Animal Reporting Award; Ann [Vol. 1:
    12681]
Coubertin World Fair Play Trophy; Pierre de [Vol. 2:
    3394]
Coues Award; Elliott [Vol. 1: 3093]

Coulter Memorial Lecturer; John Stanley [Vol. 1:
    1862]
Council Appreciation Award [Vol. 1: 10506]
Council Award of Excellence [Vol. 1: 8298]
Council Medal [Vol. 2: 7959]
Council Meritorious Service Award [Vol. 1: 1745]
Council of Peers Award for Excellence/Speaker Hall
    of Fame [Vol. 1: 12927]
Council of the Year Award [Vol. 1: 9900]
Council of Women Award [Vol. 2: 1781]
Counseling Vision and Innovation Award [Vol. 1:
    4980]
Counselor Educator Advocacy Award [Vol. 1: 1933]
Counselor Educator of the Year [Vol. 1: 2891]
Counselor of the Year Award [Vol. 1: 12761]
Counsilman Coach of the Year Award [Vol. 1: 17440]
Counting Coup Award [Vol. 2: 2479]
Countries Awards [Vol. 2: 9462]
Country Music Association Awards [Vol. 1: 7719]
Country Music Awards of Australia [Vol. 2: 676]
Country Music DJ Hall of Fame [Vol. 1: 7727]
Country Music Hall of Fame [Vol. 1: 7720]
Country Radio Hall of Fame [Vol. 1: 7728]
County Courthouse Award [Vol. 1: 11732]
County Engineer of the Year Awards [Vol. 1: 11742]
County Leadership in Conservation Award [Vol. 1:
    11733]
County Leadership in the Arts Award [Vol. 1: 11734]
Coupe Mondiale International Competition for Ac-
    cordionists [Vol. 2: 4951]
Coupe Olympique [Vol. 2: 6414]
Courage Award [Vol. 1: 1530]
Courage in Journalism Awards [Vol. 1: 10485]
Courage in Student Journalism Awards [Vol. 1:
    16305]
Courage to Care Award [Vol. 1: 4741]
Courier Executive of the Year [Vol. 1: 6436]
Cournand and Comroe Young Investigator
    Award [Vol. 1: 2300]
Cousin; Prix Victor [Vol. 2: 2251]
Cousins National Chapter Award; Ruth Hubbard [Vol.
    1: 14289]
Coutts and Co. Award for Keyboard [Vol. 2: 8553]
Coutts Nijhoff International West European Special-
    ist Study Grant [Vol. 1: 5259]
Covenant Assessment Provider of the Year [Vol. 2:
    8462]
Covenant Awards [Vol. 1: 8735]
Covey Girls' Voice Scholarship [Vol. 1: 14729]
Covington Award for Research on Bar Admissions
    Testing; Joe E. [Vol. 1: 12129]
Covington, Jr. Award; Don K. [Vol. 1: 14684]
Cowan Promising Young Investigator Award;
    Marie [Vol. 1: 2301]
Coward Award in Gerontology; Helene and
    George [Vol. 1: 17347]
Cowart Plaque [Vol. 1: 15448]
Cowburn and Kay - Old and Bold Trophy [Vol. 2:
    8594]
Cowen Award for Public Architecture; Sir Zel-
    man [Vol. 2: 382]
Cowen Dissertation Award for the Promotion of
    Wellness; Emory L. [Vol. 1: 3511]
Cowie Prize; James M. [Vol. 2: 7839]
Cox Award; Morgan [Vol. 1: 18119]
Cox Award; Robert and Jessie [Vol. 1: 10379]
Cox-Johnson-Frazier Award [Vol. 1: 4537]
Cox Memorial Award; Revis A. [Vol. 1: 5280]
Cox Trophy; Whitcombe [Vol. 2: 8507]
CPA Partner Award [Vol. 1: 6782]
CPEA Educational Award [Vol. 2: 1899]
CPMT Electronics Manufacturing Technology
    Award [Vol. 1: 9032]
CPRS Lectern [Vol. 1: 6839]
CR/PACS Technology Award [Vol. 1: 6280]
The Crabtree Award [Vol. 1: 15019]
Crabtree Foundation Award; Harold [Vol. 1: 11552]
Crafoord Prize [Vol. 2: 6183]
Craft and Design Awards [Vol. 2: 9127]
Craft Award; Medal for Excellence in [Vol. 1: 15483]
Crafts National Exhibit [Vol. 1: 7161]
Craftsman Degree [Vol. 1: 13061]
Crago Award [Vol. 2: 118]
Crain Jr. Award; G. D. [Vol. 1: 6066]
Crampton Prize [Vol. 2: 7980]

Crane and Rigging Job of the Year Awards [Vol. 1:
    16117]
Crane and Rigging Safety/Safety Improvement
    Awards [Vol. 1: 16118]
Crane and Rigging Zero Accidents Award [Vol. 1:
    16119]
Crane Award; Julia [Vol. 1: 17313]
Crane Distinguished Service Award; Fred C. [Vol. 1:
    9350]
Craniofacial Biology Group Distinguished Scientist
    Award [Vol. 1: 9528]
Craniofacial Biology Research Award [Vol. 1: 9528]
Cranko Award; John [Vol. 2: 4906]
Cranshaw Memorial Prize; Phillip [Vol. 2: 8556]
Crase Bursary; Barbara [Vol. 2: 339]
Crater Software Award for Best Graduate Film [Vol.
    1: 13730]
Craven Award; Avery O. [Vol. 1: 13676]
Cravens Membership Award; James E. [Vol. 1:
    12134]
Crawford Award for Youth and Schools; Donella [Vol.
    2: 7319]
Crawford Award; J. G. [Vol. 2: 475]
Crawford Fantasy Award; William L. [Vol. 1: 9593]
Crawford Medal
    Australian Academy of the Humanities [Vol. 2:
        191]
    Royal Philatelic Society [Vol 2: 8880]
Crawford Young Professional Award; Robert W. [Vol.
    1: 12738]
Crawshay Prize for English Literature; Rose
    Mary [Vol. 2: 6924]
Cray Computer Engineering Award; Seymour [Vol.
    1: 9056]
Cray Computer Science and Engineering Award;
    Seymour [Vol. 1: 9056]
CRC for Polymers Prize [Vol. 2: 673]
CRC Multicultural Award [Vol. 2: 1078]
Creative Arts Awards [Vol. 1: 9480]
Creative Best of Show Award [Vol. 1: 14071]
Creative Circle Awards [Vol. 2: 5931]
Creative Commercial Production Awards [Vol. 1:
    6074]
Creative Communities Grants [Vol. 1: 17876]
Creative Drama Award [Vol. 1: 806]
Creative Writing Competition [Vol. 2: 6917]
Creative Young Entrepreneur Award [Vol. 1: 10609]
Creative Young Entrepreneur Luxembourg
    Award [Vol. 2: 4497]
Creativity and Innovation Award for Small Enter-
    prises [Vol. 2: 3449]
Creativity in Industry Prize [Vol. 2: 8997]
Credit Suisse Award for Best Teaching [Vol. 2: 6520]
Credner Preis; Herman [Vol. 2: 2944]
Creighton Lifetime Achievement Award; Dr.
    Helen [Vol. 1: 7957]
Crescendo Piano Competition [Vol. 2: 62]
Cressey Memorial Award; Donald R. [Vol. 1: 5241]
Cressman ACE Award Recognizing Commitment to
    Staff Development; Reginald J. [Vol. 1: 5299]
Cresta International Advertising Awards [Vol. 1:
    7739]
Cretsos Leadership Award; James M. [Vol. 1: 3945]
Crew Chief of the Year Award [Vol. 1: 250]
Cribb Award [Vol. 2: 6699]
Crichlow Trust Prize; Walter J. and Angeline H. [Vol.
    1: 2513]
Crichton Award for New Illustrators [Vol. 2: 649]
Crighton Trophy; Hec [Vol. 1: 6638]
Crisp Medal [Vol. 2: 149]
Crisp Television News Photographer of the Year;
    Ernie [Vol. 1: 12698]
The Cristy Award [Vol. 1: 14558]
Criswell Award; Jack [Vol. 1: 14685]
Critical Impact Awards [Vol. 1: 7694]
Crittenden Award; Eugene Casson [Vol. 1: 16788]
Crittenden Memorial Award; Christopher [Vol. 1:
    13373]
Crittenden Memorial Award; John and Jessie [Vol. 1:
    5749]
CRM-Fields-PIMS Prize [Vol. 1: 17306]
CRM-SSC Prize in Statistics [Vol. 1: 16287]
Croce Trophy; Beppe [Vol. 2: 8177]
Croes Medal; J. James R. [Vol. 1: 4174]
Croix de Guerre [Vol. 2: 2431]

Croke Memorial Traditional Music Award; Bernard [Vol. 1: 10513]

Croke Traditional Music Award; Bernard [Vol. 1: 10515]

Croly Award for Excellence in Journalism; Jane Cunningham [Vol. 1: 8538]

Crombie Lockwood Chartered Accountant of the Year [Vol. 2: 4901]

Cronin Awards for Procurement Excellence; George [Vol. 1: 11911]

Cronin Club Award [Vol. 1: 11911]

Crop Science Extension Education Award [Vol. 1: 7761]

Crop Science Teaching Award [Vol. 1: 7762]

Crosby Medallion; Philip [Vol. 1: 3809]

Crosman Memorial Award [Vol. 1: 9136]

Cross Award; Julie Y. [Vol. 1: 17932]

Cross Community Service Award; Ray H. [Vol. 1: 13828]

Cross Country award [Vol. 2: 1944]

Cross Country Coach of the Year [Vol. 1: 17077]

Cross Memorial Cup; Sir Lance [Vol. 2: 4981]

Cross of Valour
    Australian Department of the Prime Minister and Cabinet - Awards and Culture Branch [Vol. 2: 298]
    Australian Department of the Prime Minister and Cabinet - Awards and Culture Branch [Vol 2: 309]
    Governor General of Canada [Vol 1: 8748]
    Office of the Prime Minister of Papua New Guinea [Vol 2: 5212]

Crouch Medal; Herbert [Vol. 2: 93]

Crouzet; Prix [Vol. 2: 2252]

Crow Jr. Award; Horace [Vol. 1: 17458]

Crowbar Awards [Vol. 2: 5932]

Crowe Memorial Award; Elmer [Vol. 2: 6575]

Crowe Memorial Exhibit Award; Dr. Charles W. [Vol. 1: 2986]

Crowe Meritorious Service Award; Alberta [Vol. 1: 5953]

Crowley Scholarship; Francis X.
    New England Water Works Association [Vol. 1: 13165]
    New England Water Works Association [Vol. 1: 13169]

Crown Awards [Vol. 1: 7410]

Crown Leadership Award; Henry [Vol. 1: 4853]

Crowninshield Award; Louise du Pont [Vol. 1: 13002]

Cruce Trophy; 1-26 Marion C. [Vol. 1: 14969]

Cruess Award; William V. [Vol. 1: 9334]

Cruickshank Alumni Leadership Award [Vol. 1: 5756]

Cruickshank Education Award; Helen G. and Allan D. [Vol. 1: 8385]

Cruickshank Research Award; Helen G. and Allan D. [Vol. 1: 8386]

Cruise Awards; Seatrade Insider [Vol. 2: 9178]

Crum Distinguished Service Award; Roy W. [Vol. 1: 16535]

Crumbine Consumer Protection Award; Samuel J.
    Foodservice and Packaging Institute [Vol. 1: 8402]
    International Association for Food Protection [Vol 1: 9547]

Crymes Fellowship for Graduate Study; Ryan [Vol. 1: 16392]

Crymes TESOL Fellowship for Graduate Study; Ruth [Vol. 1: 16392]

Cryosphere Young Investigator Award [Vol. 1: 2230]

Crystal Apple Award [Vol. 1: 14847]

Crystal Award
    American Staffing Association [Vol. 1: 4557]
    Sugar Industry Technologists [Vol 1: 16315]

Crystal Awards
    Site Global [Vol. 1: 14915]
    Women in Film [Vol 1: 17938]

Crystal Bear Awards [Vol. 2: 2722]

Crystal Eagle Award [Vol. 1: 12533]

Crystal Pineapple Awards [Vol. 2: 4853]

Crystal Prism Award [Vol. 1: 174]

Crystal Scales of Justice Prize [Vol. 2: 2346]

Crystal Taste Award [Vol. 2: 1560]

Crystallographic Research Grant [Vol. 1: 11172]

CSA-Abbott Laboratories Resident Research Awards [Vol. 1: 6094]

CSA Trophy [Vol. 1: 7481]

CSAE/CSSBI Award [Vol. 1: 6877]

CSAE Fellow [Vol. 1: 6874]

Csallany Institutional Award for Exemplary Contributions to Water Resources Management; Sandor C. [Vol. 1: 4648]

CSAS Fellowship Award [Vol. 1: 6927]

CSCE Fellow [Vol. 1: 6899]

CSI Fellowship [Vol. 1: 7555]

CSIR Case Award [Vol. 2: 3471]

CSL Gold Medal [Vol. 1: 7193]

CSM/Roche Diagnostics Award [Vol. 1: 6976]

Csontos Medal [Vol. 2: 3376]

CSRT Essay Award [Vol. 1: 6279]

CTP Scholarship [Vol. 1: 12712]

Cub Scout Den Leader Award [Vol. 1: 5960]

Cub Scouter Award [Vol. 1: 5961]

Cubitt Award [Vol. 2: 8498]

Cubmaster Award [Vol. 1: 5962]

Cudecki International Business Award; Edwin [Vol. 1: 1924]

Cuff Medal; Leonard A. [Vol. 2: 4982]

Cugnot Award [Vol. 1: 15548]

Cugnot Award; Nicholas-Joseph [Vol. 1: 15551]

Culbertson Award; Jack A. [Vol. 1: 17186]

Culbertson Outstanding Volunteer Service Award; Charles V. [Vol. 1: 4508]

Culinary Arts Salon
    American Culinary Federation [Vol. 1: 1964]
    Society of German Cooks [Vol 2: 3181]

Culinary Masters
    American Culinary Federation [Vol. 1: 1964]
    Society of German Cooks [Vol 2: 3181]

Culinary Olympics [Vol. 2: 3181]

Culinary World Cup
    American Culinary Federation [Vol. 1: 1964]
    Society of German Cooks [Vol 2: 3181]
    Vatel-Club Luxembourg [Vol 2: 4501]

Culkin Award for Outstanding Praxis in the Field of Media Ecology; John [Vol. 1: 11031]

Cullis Grant; Winifred [Vol. 2: 6386]

Cullum Geographical Medal [Vol. 1: 2211]

Cultural Achievement Award [Vol. 1: 1888]

Cultural and Creative Arts Awards [Vol. 1: 2943]

Cultural and Economic Diversity Award [Vol. 1: 2096]

Cultural Award of the Year [Vol. 2: 1679]

Cultural Diversity Grant [Vol. 1: 10834]

Cultural Diversity Grant; CEE [Vol. 1: 12206]

Cultural Pluralism Award [Vol. 1: 5503]

Culture and Literature Award [Vol. 2: 3802]

Culver Distinguished Service Award; Essae M. [Vol. 1: 10888]

Cumberbatch Trophy [Vol. 2: 7753]

Cumming Award for Outstanding Service; Laurence G. [Vol. 1: 9080]

Cummings Award; Abbott Lowell [Vol. 1: 17517]

Cummings Memorial Award; Donald E. [Vol. 1: 2486]

Cummiskey Pro Bono Award; John W. [Vol. 1: 16265]

Cumont; Prix Franz [Vol. 2: 1600]

Cumulative Contribution to Marriage and Family Therapy Research Award [Vol. 1: 965]

Cumulative Mileage Awards [Vol. 1: 13352]

Cunningham Aviator of the Year Award; Alfred A. [Vol. 1: 10945]

Cunningham Award; Ed [Vol. 1: 13756]

Cunningham Award; Glenn [Vol. 1: 17459]

Cunningham Award; Thomas F. [Vol. 1: 18084]

Cunningham-Beatie Award [Vol. 2: 7254]

Cunningham Inter-American Award; Thomas F. [Vol. 1: 18084]

Cunningham Memorial International Fellowship [Vol. 1: 11064]

CUNY Student Paper Awards [Vol. 1: 7138]

Cup for Historic Grand Touring Cars [Vol. 2: 2504]

Cup for Thoroughbred Grand Prix Cars [Vol. 2: 2504]

Cup of Excellence Award [Vol. 1: 365]

Curatorial Research Fellowships [Vol. 1: 8647]

Curatorship Award [Vol. 1: 4770]

Cured Meats Hall of Fame [Vol. 1: 1204]

Curie Medal; Marie [Vol. 2: 1494]

Curie Training Grant; Marie [Vol. 1: 1232]

Curl Essay Award [Vol. 2: 8640]

Curnow Competition; Steven R. [Vol. 1: 7614]

Currey Book-Length Publications Award; Cecil B. [Vol. 1: 5540]

Currey Memorial Fellowship; C. H. [Vol. 2: 1061]

Curry Award; Alan [Vol. 2: 5443]

Curry-Lindahl Award; Kai [Vol. 1: 17725]

Curry Scholarship; Paul T. and Mary Jane [Vol. 1: 17826]

CURT Construction Industry Safety Excellence Awards [Vol. 1: 4880]

Curti Award; Merle [Vol. 1: 13677]

Curtin Medal; Bill [Vol. 2: 7981]

Curtin Plaque [Vol. 1: 15449]

Curtis Award; Len [Vol. 2: 8538]

Curtis Cup [Vol. 1: 16932]

Curtis Lecture Award; John A. [Vol. 1: 3847]

Cushman Award for Excellence in Foraminiferal Research; Joseph A. [Vol. 1: 7786]

Cushman Murphy Prize; Robert [Vol. 1: 17726]

Customer Service Excellence Award [Vol. 1: 1211]

Cut and Polished Colored Gemstones Award [Vol. 2: 3488]

Cut and Polished Diamonds Award [Vol. 2: 3489]

Cut and Polished Synthetic Stones Award [Vol. 2: 3490]

Cuthbertson Award; Kenneth M. [Vol. 1: 16256]

Cutler Award; Lady [Vol. 2: 650]

Cutler Memorial Award for Residential Lighting Design; Aileen Page [Vol. 1: 9153]

Cutting Edge Gemstone Competition [Vol. 1: 2208]

Cutts Scholarships; Donna [Vol. 1: 15418]

CVMA Award [Vol. 1: 7029]

CWI of the Year Award [Vol. 1: 4677]

Cymbidium and Paphiopedilum Awards [Vol. 1: 7791]

Cyprus Innovation Awards [Vol. 2: 1897]

Cytotechnologist Award of the American Society of Cytology [Vol. 1: 4277]

Cytotechnologist of the Year Award [Vol. 1: 4278]

Cytotechnologist Scientific Presentation Award [Vol. 1: 4277]

Cytotechnologists' Award for Outstanding Achievement [Vol. 1: 4278]

Czerny Preis; Adalbert [Vol. 2: 3021]

Da Vinci Award [Vol. 2: 7029]

da Vinci Award; Leonardo [Vol. 1: 7585]

da Vinci Medal; Leonardo
    European Society for Engineering Education [Vol. 2: 1490]
    Society for the History of Technology [Vol 1: 15350]

da Vinci Parachuting Diploma; Leonardo [Vol. 2: 6302]

da Vinci World Award of Arts; Leonardo [Vol. 2: 4601]

DAAD Scholarship [Vol. 2: 2723]

DACC Certificate of Recognition [Vol. 1: 897]

DACC Travel Award [Vol. 1: 898]

Dacco Award; Aldo [Vol. 2: 4119]

Dach Award for InVEST Agent of the Year [Vol. 1: 9180]

Dade Behring Award
    Association for Clinical Biochemistry [Vol. 2: 6758]
    Society of Medical Laboratory Technologists of South Africa [Vol 2: 5618]

Dade Behring MicroScan Young Investigator Award [Vol. 1: 3989]

Daedalian Civilian Air Safety Award [Vol. 1: 13646]

Daedalian Distinguished Achievement Award [Vol. 1: 13640]

Daedalian Scholarships [Vol. 1: 13641]

Daedalian Supply Effectiveness Award [Vol. 1: 13639]

Daedalian Weapons Systems Award [Vol. 1: 13642]

Dafoe Scholarship [Vol. 1: 6674]

Dagenais Award; Camille A. [Vol. 1: 6900]

Daggs Award; Ray G. [Vol. 1: 3252]

Daggy Youth/Student Scholarships [Vol. 1: 10448]

Dagnan-Bouveret; Prix [Vol. 2: 2253]

Dagnan-Bouveret; Prix Jean [Vol. 2: 2192]

Dahl Award of Merit; Marilyn [Vol. 1: 6539]

Dahl Funny Prize; Roald [Vol. 2: 6904]

Dahlgrens Pris; Rolf [Vol. 2: 6169]

Dahlquist Prize; Germund [Vol. 1: 15116]

Dahlquist Special Recognition Award; Gail H. [Vol. 1: 5121]

Dairy Education Awards [Vol. 1: 9864]

Dairy Industry Safety Recognition Awards [Vol. 1: 9867]

Daisey Outstanding Young Scientist Award; Joan M. **[Vol. 1: 10318]**

Daiwa Foundation Art Prize **[Vol. 2: 8451]**

Daiwa Foundation Awards **[Vol. 2: 7491]**

Daiwa Foundation Small Project Grants **[Vol. 2: 7492]**

Daiwa Scholarships **[Vol. 2: 7493]**

Dakin Distinguished Technical Contributions Award; Thomas W. **[Vol. 1: 9075]**

Daland Prize for Outstanding Achievement in Clinical Investigation; Judson **[Vol. 1: 3183]**

Dale Medical Products/AACN Excellent Clinical Nurse Specialist Award **[Vol. 1: 1118]**

Dale Prize; Henry **[Vol. 2: 8860]**

Dallas 100 Awards **[Vol. 1: 16031]**

Dallos Award **[Vol. 2: 7030]**

Dallos Award; Dr. Joseph **[Vol. 1: 7586]**

Dalov's Award **[Vol. 2: 1791]**

Dalrymple-Champneys Cup and Medal **[Vol. 2: 7295]**

Dalton Young Researchers Award **[Vol. 2: 8998]**

d'Alviella Prize; Prix Eugene Goblet **[Vol. 2: 1601]**

Daly Award; Sergeant Major Dan **[Vol. 1: 10971]**

Daly Medal; Charles P. **[Vol. 1: 2212]**

Dames of America Scholarship; Colonial **[Vol. 1: 15418]**

Dameshek Award; Dr. William **[Vol. 1: 10807]**

Dameshek Prize; William **[Vol. 1: 4335]**

Damien-Dutton Award **[Vol. 1: 7804]**

D'Amour Award; O'Neil **[Vol. 1: 12043]**

Dana Award; John Cotton **[Vol. 1: 16099]**

Dana Award; Margaret **[Vol. 1: 5590]**

Dana Library Public Relations Awards; John Cotton **[Vol. 1: 10835]**

Dana Publicity Award; John Cotton **[Vol. 1: 10835]**

Dance: Choreography Fellowship **[Vol. 1: 14154]**

Dance: Performance Scholarships **[Vol. 1: 14155]**

Dance Screen Awards **[Vol. 2: 1293]**

Dandass Memorial Award; Flt. Lt. Tanmaya Singh **[Vol. 2: 3754]**

Dandrimont-Benicourt; Prix **[Vol. 2: 2193]**

Dandurand Trophy; Leo **[Vol. 1: 6503]**

Dangal ng Haraya (Achievement Award) **[Vol. 2: 5339]**

Dangerfield Award; Elma **[Vol. 2: 8100]**

Daniel Award; Dr. William H. **[Vol. 1: 16215]**

Daniel Teaching Excellence Award; Robert S. **[Vol. 1: 3554]**

Danieli Young Professional Award; Chaim **[Vol. 1: 10261]**

Danieli Young Professional Award; Chaim and Bela **[Vol. 1: 10261]**

Daniels Award; Farrington **[Vol. 2: 3101]**

Danielson Award; Philip A. **[Vol. 1: 17783]**

Danis Prize; Robert **[Vol. 2: 6451]**

Danisco International Dairy Science Award **[Vol. 1: 1972]**

Danish Geology Prize **[Vol. 2: 1968]**

Danish Island Award **[Vol. 2: 1945]**

Danish Lighthouse Award **[Vol. 2: 1946]**

Danish Underground Radio Award **[Vol. 2: 1947]**

Dankworth Management Scholarship; Margaret A. **[Vol. 1: 5561]**

Danone International Prize for Nutrition **[Vol. 2: 2358]**

Dansk Oversaetterforbunds Aerespris **[Vol. 2: 1963]**

Danstrom Awards; Charlotte **[Vol. 1: 17951]**

Dantzig Dissertation Award; George B. **[Vol. 1: 9256]**

Dantzig Prize; George B. **[Vol. 1: 15117]**

Darbaker Prize **[Vol. 1: 5934]**

Darbaker Prize in Botany; Leasure K. **[Vol. 1: 17326]**

Darby Award for Inspirational Leadership and Excellence of Command; Jack N. **[Vol. 1: 13125]**

Darling Foundation Prize **[Vol. 2: 6548]**

Darling Medal for Distinguished Achievement in Collection Development in the Health Sciences; Louise **[Vol. 1: 11065]**

Dartmouth Medal **[Vol. 1: 14463]**

Darwin Lecture; George **[Vol. 2: 8657]**

Darwin Lifetime Achievement Award; Charles R. **[Vol. 1: 1294]**

Darwin Medal
   International Society for Reef Studies **[Vol. 2: 8192]**
   Royal Society **[Vol 2: 8931]**

Dasgupta Memorial Lecture; Prof. S.N. **[Vol. 2: 3692]**

Dasher Best Paper Award; Benjamin J. **[Vol. 1: 3848]**

Datascope Excellence in Collaboration Award - Multidisciplinary Teams **[Vol. 1: 1119]**

Datascope Excellence in Collaboration Award - Nurse to Family **[Vol. 1: 1120]**

Datta Lectureship and Medal **[Vol. 2: 3947]**

Datta Memorial Oration Award; Dr. Dharamvir **[Vol. 2: 3543]**

Daubney Research Fellowship in Virology and Helminthology; Robert **[Vol. 2: 8762]**

Daughters of Liberty Medal **[Vol. 1: 12899]**

Daughtrey Award; John **[Vol. 1: 8503]**

Daume World Fair Play Trophy; Willi **[Vol. 2: 3395]**

Davenport Memorial Exhibit Award; John S. **[Vol. 1: 2987]**

Davenport Prize; Margaret **[Vol. 2: 8712]**

Davenport Publication Award; Millia **[Vol. 1: 7621]**

David Award; Florence Nightingale **[Vol. 1: 7438]**

David Film Awards **[Vol. 2: 4052]**

David Medal; Edgeworth **[Vol. 2: 1005]**

David Prize; Dan **[Vol. 2: 3943]**

David Prize; Tim **[Vol. 2: 9088]**

Davidoff; Award for Advancing Diversity and Social Change in Honor of Paul **[Vol. 1: 3284]**

Davidoff Book Award; Paul **[Vol. 1: 5284]**

Davidoff National Award for Social Change and Diversity; Paul **[Vol. 1: 3284]**

Davids Award; Bob **[Vol. 1: 15026]**

Davidson Award; May **[Vol. 2: 7182]**

Davidson Award; Murray **[Vol. 1: 667]**

Davidson Medal **[Vol. 1: 15712]**

Davidson Medal; George **[Vol. 1: 2213]**

Davidson Memorial Trophy; Sam **[Vol. 1: 6639]**

Davidson Practice of the Profession Award; Park O. **[Vol. 1: 6026]**

Davidson President's Award for Practical Papers; John I. **[Vol. 1: 4864]**

Davies Award; C.N. **[Vol. 2: 6680]**

Davies Award; Valentine **[Vol. 1: 18120]**

Davies Foundation Travelling Fellowship **[Vol. 2: 8700]**

Davies Medal **[Vol. 2: 8896]**

Davies Medal; Duncan **[Vol. 2: 8547]**

Davies Memorial Scholar Award for Scholarly Activities in Humanities and History of Medicine; Nicholas E. **[Vol. 1: 1797]**

Davis and Helen Miles Davis Prize; Watson **[Vol. 1: 8952]**

Davis Award; Donald E. **[Vol. 1: 10946]**

Davis Award; Henry B. **[Vol. 1: 4512]**

Davis Award; John P. **[Vol. 1: 4384]**

Davis Award; Lloyd E. **[Vol. 1: 768]**

Davis Award; Miles **[Vol. 1: 8344]**

Davis Award; National Georgina MacDougall **[Vol. 1: 5158]**

Davis Award; W. Allison and Elizabeth Stubbs **[Vol. 1: 11299]**

Davis Award; Watson **[Vol. 1: 3946]**

Davis Center Book Prize **[Vol. 1: 5094]**

Davis Cup Award **[Vol. 1: 9137]**

Davis Cup Award of Excellence **[Vol. 2: 8234]**

Davis Graduate Scholarship; Dr. Keith **[Vol. 1: 14892]**

Davis International Award in Medicine; Dr. Nathan **[Vol. 1: 2860]**

Davis Lecture Series; Raymond E. **[Vol. 1: 1842]**

Davis Medal; George E. **[Vol. 2: 7960]**

Davis Memorial Award; Suzanne M. **[Vol. 1: 16003]**

Davis Memorial Award; William J. **[Vol. 1: 17187]**

Davis Memorial Lecture; E. H. **[Vol. 2: 778]**

Davis Prize; Philip **[Vol. 2: 8713]**

Davis Silver Medal Award; A. F. **[Vol. 1: 4676]**

Davis Special Recognition Award; Ronald **[Vol. 1: 1807]**

Davisson-Germer Prize in Atomic or Surface Physics **[Vol. 1: 3200]**

Davy Medal **[Vol. 2: 8932]**

Dawdon Trophy **[Vol. 2: 6706]**

Dawood Award; Yusuf **[Vol. 2: 4409]**

Dawood Prize; Rahima **[Vol. 2: 4410]**

Dawson Award for Excellence in Plasma Physics Research; John **[Vol. 1: 3201]**

Dawson Award for Programmatic Excellence; William **[Vol. 1: 5461]**

Dawson Medal; Sir John William **[Vol. 1: 14638]**

Day Award; Peter **[Vol. 2: 8999]**

Day Memorial Medal; Richard Hopper **[Vol. 1: 91]**

Day Prize and Lectureship; Arthur L. **[Vol. 1: 11433]**

Dayhoff Award; Margaret Oakley **[Vol. 1: 5847]**

Daytime Entertainment Emmy Awards **[Vol. 1: 11451]**

Daytona 200 **[Vol. 1: 2946]**

Daytona 500 **[Vol. 1: 7818]**

de Bary Medal; Anton **[Vol. 2: 2986]**

de Beaufort-prijs; Henriette **[Vol. 2: 4838]**

de Beaujour; Prix Felix **[Vol. 2: 2254]**

de Boelpaepe; Prix **[Vol. 2: 1623]**

de Carli Award; Felice **[Vol. 2: 4120]**

de Chenier; Prix **[Vol. 2: 2153]**

de Conway Little Medal of Honor; Helen **[Vol. 1: 8906]**

de Donder; Prix Theophile **[Vol. 2: 1624]**

De Florez Award for Flight Simulation **[Vol. 1: 2514]**

De Florez Award for Modeling and Simulation **[Vol. 1: 2514]**

de Gennes Prize **[Vol. 2: 9000]**

de Hevesy Nuclear Pioneer Award; Georg Charles **[Vol. 1: 15730]**

de Hueck and Norman Walford Career Achievement Awards; Paul **[Vol. 1: 13566]**

De Internationale Carl Nielsen Musik Konkurrencer **[Vol. 2: 1975]**

De Keyn; Prix Joseph **[Vol. 2: 1602]**

De la Court Prize **[Vol. 2: 4818]**

De La Vaulx Medal **[Vol. 2: 6303]**

de la Vega Prize; Josseph **[Vol. 2: 1514]**

De Laszlo Medal **[Vol. 2: 8969]**

de Laveleye; Prix Emile **[Vol. 2: 1603]**

De Leo Fund Award **[Vol. 2: 2483]**

De Morgan Medal **[Vol. 2: 8330]**

de Navarre Medal Award; Maison G. **[Vol. 1: 15598]**

de Nora Award; Vittorio **[Vol. 1: 8055]**

De Nora Foundation Prize of ISE on Electrochemical Technology and Engineering; Oronzio and Niccolo **[Vol. 2: 6437]**

De Nora Foundation Young Author Prize; Oronzio and Niccolo **[Vol. 2: 6438]**

De Paepe; Prix Polydore **[Vol. 2: 1604]**

de Reinach; Prix Lucien **[Vol. 2: 2255]**

de Saint-Genois; Prix Baron **[Vol. 2: 1605]**

de Sola Pool Award; Ithiel **[Vol. 1: 3301]**

De Vitoria Prize for Ethics and Values; Francisco **[Vol. 1: 5682]**

Deak Award; Francis **[Vol. 1: 9984]**

Deak Prize; Francis O. **[Vol. 1: 4353]**

Deal of the Year Award **[Vol. 1: 6160]**

Dealer Awards **[Vol. 1: 5751]**

Dealer Education Award **[Vol. 1: 13428]**

Dean Award for Creative Excellence; John **[Vol. 1: 18093]**

Dean Award for Research in Schizophrenia; Stanley **[Vol. 1: 1816]**

Dean Award; William **[Vol. 2: 245]**

Dean Memorial Award; H. Trendley **[Vol. 1: 9529]**

Deane Award; Hamilton **[Vol. 2: 7525]**

DeAngelo Memorial Teaching Award; Paul **[Vol. 1: 9432]**

Dean's Book Award **[Vol. 1: 17681]**

Dearnley Award; Christopher **[Vol. 2: 919]**

Deaver Award; Sally **[Vol. 1: 17078]**

Deb Memorial Award for Popularisation of Science; Dr. B. C. **[Vol. 2: 3709]**

Deb Memorial Award for Soil/Physical Chemistry; Dr. B. C. **[Vol. 2: 3710]**

DeBakey Award; Michael E. **[Vol. 1: 7823]**

Deballion Medal; Mary Swords **[Vol. 1: 11044]**

DeBellis Award; Anthony **[Vol. 1: 5591]**

DeBenedetti Prize in Peace History; Charles **[Vol. 1: 13876]**

Debiopharm Life Sciences Award, Switzerland **[Vol. 2: 6260]**

DebRA Research Grants **[Vol. 1: 7945]**

Debruyne Lifetime Achievement Award; Frans **[Vol. 2: 4690]**

Debs Award; Eugene V. **[Vol. 1: 7825]**

Debye Award in Physical Chemistry; Peter **[Vol. 1: 1631]**

DeCelle, Jr., Award; Robert E. **[Vol. 1: 17460]**

Dechelle; Prix Ernest **[Vol. 2: 2194]**

DECHEMA Ehrenmitgliedschaft **[Vol. 2: 3163]**

DECHEMA Honorary Membership **[Vol. 2: 3163]**

DECHEMA-Medaille **[Vol. 2: 3164]**

DECHEMA Medal **[Vol. 2: 3164]**

Decoration for Service to the Country **[Vol. 2: 4509]**

Decoration of the Republic of Macedonia **[Vol. 2: 4510]**
Dedicated Service Award
American Society of Mechanical Engineers **[Vol. 1: 4385]**
Society of Decorative Painters **[Vol 1: 15611]**
Dedication Award **[Vol. 1: 8079]**
Dedrick, Jr. Award; Dewey R. **[Vol. 1: 4513]**
Deen Distinguished Lectureship; Thomas B. **[Vol. 1: 16536]**
Deeper Perspective Photographer of the Year **[Vol. 1: 14020]**
Deere Awards; John **[Vol. 1: 13291]**
Deerr Gold Medal; Noel **[Vol. 2: 3795]**
Defant Medaille; Albert **[Vol. 2: 2762]**
Defence Long Service Medal **[Vol. 2: 310]**
Defender of the National Interest **[Vol. 1: 16748]**
Defense Distinguished Service Medal **[Vol. 1: 16670]**
Defense Meritorious Service Medal **[Vol. 1: 16671]**
Defense of Academic Freedom Award **[Vol. 1: 12165]**
Defense Superior Service Medal **[Vol. 1: 16672]**
Defensive Player of the Year
Continental Basketball Association **[Vol. 1: 7590]**
National Association of Basketball Coaches **[Vol 1: 11638]**
DeFiore Parental Choice Advocate Award; Leonard F. **[Vol. 1: 12044]**
DeForest Audion Award **[Vol. 1: 17533]**
DeForest Audion Gold Medal Award **[Vol. 1: 17533]**
DeForest Award; Lee **[Vol. 1: 14398]**
Defries Award; R. D. **[Vol. 1: 6831]**
DeGolyer Distinguished Service Medal **[Vol. 1: 15750]**
Degree Program Distinguished Teacher Award **[Vol. 2: 4505]**
DeGreef; Prix Arthur **[Vol. 2: 1588]**
Degussa Award for Achievement in Poultry Science; Evonik **[Vol. 1: 14111]**
Dehem; Prix Louise **[Vol. 2: 1589]**
deKieffer International Fellowship Award; Robert **[Vol. 1: 5005]**
Del Gaudio Service Award; Matthew W. **[Vol. 1: 2583]**
Delahautemaison; Prix Marguerite **[Vol. 2: 4448]**
Delalande-Guerineau; Prix **[Vol. 2: 2154]**
DeLaval Dairy Extension Award
American Dairy Science Association **[Vol. 1: 1973]**
American Dairy Science Association **[Vol. 1: 1973]**
Delavan Award **[Vol. 1: 2179]**
Delbos; Prix Victor **[Vol. 2: 2256]**
Delbruck Prize in Biological Physics; Max **[Vol. 1: 3202]**
Delco Electronics Intelligent Transportation Systems Award **[Vol. 1: 15501]**
Delegate Award **[Vol. 1: 8320]**
DeLeon Prize; Patrick H. **[Vol. 1: 3381]**
Delerue Prize for Best Music; George **[Vol. 1: 1516]**
Dell Award **[Vol. 2: 8055]**
Dellinger Gold Medal; John Howard **[Vol. 2: 1565]**
DELOS Distinguished Service Award **[Vol. 1: 3849]**
Delphinium Society Awards **[Vol. 2: 7508]**
Delta Air Lines "Puffer" Award **[Vol. 1: 11489]**
Delta Award; Penelope **[Vol. 2: 3273]**
Delta Pi Epsilon Research Awards **[Vol. 1: 7841]**
Delwart; Prix de la Fondation Jean-Marie **[Vol. 2: 1625]**
DeMaio Award for Trade Union Activism; Ernest **[Vol. 1: 10722]**
DeMarco-Becket Memorial Trophy **[Vol. 1: 6504]**
DEMCO/ALA Black Caucus Award for Excellence in Librarianship **[Vol. 1: 5861]**
DEMCO New Leaders Travel Grants **[Vol. 1: 14320]**
Dement Academic Achievement Award; William C. **[Vol. 1: 762]**
DeMille Award; Cecil B. **[Vol. 1: 8968]**
Deming Prizes **[Vol. 2: 4337]**
Demingu Sho **[Vol. 2: 4337]**
Demmond Award; Jack W. **[Vol. 1: 10947]**
Democracy Award
Israel Democracy Institute **[Vol. 2: 3961]**
National Endowment for Democracy **[Vol 1: 12308]**
Demolombe; Prix **[Vol. 2: 2257]**
Demonet Scholarships; Inez **[Vol. 1: 17521]**

Den Store Journalistprisen **[Vol. 2: 5146]**
Denardo Award; ICO/ICTP Gallieno **[Vol. 2: 6054]**
Dendy Awards for Australian Short Films **[Vol. 2: 1079]**
Dengo Memorial Award for Best International Paper; Gabriel **[Vol. 1: 1273]**
Denig Distinguished Performance Award; Robert L. **[Vol. 1: 16994]**
Denmark National Faculty Advisor Award; Florence L. **[Vol. 1: 14290]**
Dennis Award; Bill **[Vol. 1: 14275]**
Denny Medal **[Vol. 2: 7890]**
Densmore Prize; Frances **[Vol. 1: 2958]**
Dent Medal **[Vol. 2: 8875]**
Dental Health Education Award **[Vol. 1: 388]**
Dental Hygiene Student Merit Award for Outstanding Achievement in Community Dentistry **[Vol. 1: 1324]**
Dental Trade and Industry Award of Recognition **[Vol. 1: 8247]**
Dentist Award **[Vol. 1: 5422]**
Department of Defense Distinguished Service Award **[Vol. 1: 12282]**
Department of Education Young Writer's Award **[Vol. 1: 14148]**
Department of the Interior Environmental Achievement Awards **[Vol. 1: 16859]**
Department of Transportation Award for Heroism **[Vol. 1: 16863]**
Department of Veteran's Affairs Employee of the Year Award **[Vol. 1: 255]**
Derflinger Cup; Mavis **[Vol. 1: 17155]**
DermaTech Educational Award **[Vol. 2: 326]**
Dermatology Foundation Fellowships **[Vol. 1: 7851]**
deRoaldes Fund Award **[Vol. 1: 2752]**
DeRose-Hinkhouse Memorial Awards **[Vol. 1: 14492]**
Deruyts; Prix Francois **[Vol. 2: 1626]**
Deruyts; Prix Jacques **[Vol. 2: 1627]**
Derwent Award; Clarence **[Vol. 1: 138]**
Des Pretorius Memorial Award **[Vol. 2: 5555]**
Desai Prize Award; Dr. D.K. **[Vol. 2: 3738]**
DesCartes Prize for Collaborative, Transnational Research **[Vol. 2: 1459]**
Desforges Distinguished Teacher Award; Jane F. **[Vol. 1: 1798]**
Deshmukh Woman Agricultural Scientist Award; Punjab Rao **[Vol. 2: 3523]**
Design Ambassador Awards **[Vol. 2: 4885]**
Design and Application Award
International Magnesium Association **[Vol. 1: 10002]**
International Magnesium Association **[Vol 1: 10003]**
Design and Art Direction Awards **[Vol. 2: 7042]**
Design Award
American Concrete Institute **[Vol. 1: 1845]**
International Magnesium Association **[Vol. 1: 10003]**
Pro Carton, the Association of European Cartonboard and Carton Manufacturers **[Vol 2: 6474]**
Design Award Competition **[Vol. 1: 11105]**
Design Award of the Federal Republic of Germany **[Vol. 2: 2942]**
Design Awards
American Agricultural Editors' Association **[Vol. 1: 790]**
Concrete Reinforcing Steel Institute **[Vol 1: 7473]**
Hong Kong Institute of Landscape Architects **[Vol 2: 5262]**
International Superyacht Society **[Vol 1: 10396]**
Design Competition
American Institute of Building Design **[Vol. 1: 2594]**
Scottish Ecological Design Association **[Vol 2: 9161]**
Design Council Awards **[Vol. 2: 7512]**
Design Effectiveness Awards **[Vol. 2: 7510]**
Design Excellence Awards **[Vol. 2: 5948]**
Design for All Award **[Vol. 2: 5949]**
Design for Humanity Award **[Vol. 1: 4348]**
Design in Business Awards **[Vol. 2: 4886]**
Design Medal **[Vol. 1: 4362]**
Design Partnership Award **[Vol. 2: 8389]**
Designated Research Scholar Award in Geriatric Gastroenterology **[Vol. 1: 8442]**
Designer Awards; International **[Vol. 2: 4717]**

Designer of the Year Award **[Vol. 1: 8212]**
Designing with Roses Competition **[Vol. 1: 356]**
Designpreis der Bundesrepublik Deutschland **[Vol. 2: 2942]**
Desjardins CEO Award for Outstanding Service and Support; Carolyn **[Vol. 1: 1010]**
Desjardins President of the Year Award; Carolyn **[Vol. 1: 1010]**
Deslandres; Prix **[Vol. 2: 2195]**
Desnuelle; Prix Pierre **[Vol. 2: 2196]**
De'Souza Memorial Prize; Dr. A.C.L. **[Vol. 2: 4411]**
Detector Case of the Year **[Vol. 1: 17028]**
Deutsch Award; Karl
International Political Science Association **[Vol. 1: 10051]**
International Studies Association **[Vol 1: 10380]**
Deutsch Memorial Award; Wilbur **[Vol. 1: 15859]**
Deutsche Meteorologische Gesellschaft e.V. Jugendpreis **[Vol. 2: 2763]**
Deutscher Innenarchitektur Preis **[Vol. 2: 2958]**
Deutschmann Award for Excellence in Research; Paul J. **[Vol. 1: 4996]**
Deutz-Allis National Student Design Competition **[Vol. 1: 4074]**
Deux Magots Literary Prize **[Vol. 2: 2331]**
Developer of the Year **[Vol. 1: 11802]**
Developing Countries Project Grant **[Vol. 1: 9599]**
Developing Leaders Award **[Vol. 1: 11803]**
Development Award **[Vol. 2: 9374]**
Developmental Awards **[Vol. 1: 10844]**
Developmental Biology - Lifetime Achievement Award **[Vol. 1: 15053]**
Developmental Coach of the Year **[Vol. 1: 17441]**
Developmental Disabilities Awareness Awards for High School Seniors **[Vol. 1: 5818]**
Developmental Disabilities Awareness Awards for Lutheran Elementary Classes **[Vol. 1: 5819]**
Devi Memorial Award; Satgur Prasad-Prag Parmeshwari **[Vol. 2: 3774]**
DeVito Sr. Distinguished Service Award; Vincent J. **[Vol. 1: 9395]**
Devitt Distinguished Service to Justice Award; Edward J. **[Vol. 1: 2737]**
Devlin Award; Jones F. **[Vol. 1: 7181]**
Devlin Scholarship; Gertrude W. **[Vol. 1: 17827]**
Devonshire Trophy **[Vol. 2: 8815]**
Dew Medal; Elsdon **[Vol. 2: 5590]**
D'Ewe Medal; Dudley **[Vol. 2: 5519]**
Dewey Fellowship Award **[Vol. 1: 13215]**
Dewey Medal; Melvil **[Vol. 1: 2776]**
Dewey Scholarship **[Vol. 1: 13216]**
Dewhurst Lecture and Award **[Vol. 2: 9489]**
Dews Award for Research in Behavioral Pharmacology; P.B. **[Vol. 1: 4033]**
Dexter Prize **[Vol. 1: 15352]**
Dey Award; Joseph **[Vol. 1: 16933]**
Dhanwantari Prize; Shri **[Vol. 2: 3633]**
Dhere; Prix Charles **[Vol. 2: 2197]**
Di Carlo Distinguished Service Award; Frederick J. **[Vol. 1: 10257]**
Di Castagnola Award; Alice Fay **[Vol. 1: 14059]**
Diabetes Camp Educator Award **[Vol. 1: 1127]**
Diabetes Educator of the Year **[Vol. 1: 6453]**
Diabetes Educator of the Year Award **[Vol. 1: 1128]**
Dialogue Among Civilizations Award **[Vol. 1: 14656]**
Diamond ACES Award **[Vol. 1: 15957]**
Diamond Anniversary Book Award **[Vol. 1: 12112]**
Diamond Award; Julius Blegen **[Vol. 1: 17073]**
Diamond Clinical Fellowship in Headache Education; Seymour **[Vol. 1: 12497]**
Diamond Jubilee Bursary **[Vol. 2: 340]**
DIANA Award **[Vol. 1: 8860]**
Diana Award **[Vol. 1: 16082]**
Diaz-Alejandro Prize; Carlos **[Vol. 2: 1845]**
DiBello/Melvin and Leona Kohl Memorial Exhibit Award; Gaston **[Vol. 1: 2988]**
Dibner Award for Excellence in Museum Exhibits **[Vol. 1: 15351]**
Dick Medal of Merit; Charles **[Vol. 1: 12473]**
Dickason Award; Donald E. **[Vol. 1: 7346]**
Dickerman Award Lecture; Herbert W. **[Vol. 1: 13237]**
Dickerson Award; Ben F. **[Vol. 1: 15205]**
Dickinson Award for Teaching Excellence; Gary **[Vol. 1: 15502]**
Dickinson Award; *The Writer* Magazine/Emily **[Vol. 1: 14067]**

Distinguished Book Award
 American Alliance for Theatre and Education [Vol. 1: 807]
 American Psychological Association - Society for the Psychological Study of Lesbian, Gay, Bisexual and Transgender Issues (Division 44) [Vol 1: 3539]
 Society for Military History [Vol 1: 15197]
Distinguished Career Award
 Academic Pediatric Association [Vol. 1: 46]
 American Academy of Pediatrics [Vol 1: 668]
 American Psychological Association - Psychologists in Public Service Division (Division 18)- [Vol 1: 3476]
 Australian Association for Cognitive and Behaviour Therapy [Vol 2: 233]
 European Association for Computer Graphics [Vol 2: 6263]
 Fusion Power Associates [Vol 1: 8497]
 International Association for Relationship Research [Vol 1: 9583]
 International Society for Prevention of Child Abuse and Neglect [Vol 1: 10217]
 International Society on Thrombosis and Haemostasis [Vol 1: 10365]
 Southeastern Theatre Conference [Vol 1: 16004]
Distinguished Career Award for the Practice of Sociology [Vol. 1: 4539]
Distinguished Career Contribution to Gerontology Award [Vol. 1: 8622]
Distinguished Career Service Awards [Vol 1: 16831]
Distinguished Certificate Award [Vol. 2: 4091]
Distinguished Citizen Award
 National Consumers League [Vol. 1: 12132]
 Wofford College National Alumni Association [Vol 1: 17900]
Distinguished Clinical Chemist Award [Vol. 2: 4100]
Distinguished Clinician Award [Vol. 1: 729]
Distinguished Clinician Scholar Award [Vol. 1: 5499]
Distinguished Contribution Award
 American Urological Association [Vol. 1: 4619]
 International Association for Chinese Management Research [Vol 1: 9518]
 Project Management Institute [Vol 1: 14257]
Distinguished Contribution to Applied Behavior Analysis Award [Vol. 1: 3393]
Distinguished Contribution to Child Advocacy Award [Vol. 1: 3503]
Distinguished Contribution to Family Psychology Award [Vol. 1: 3425]
Distinguished Contribution to Family Systems Research Award [Vol. 1: 2095]
Distinguished Contribution to Science Education Through Research Award [Vol. 1: 11594]
Distinguished Contribution to Social Justice Award [Vol. 1: 2096]
Distinguished Contribution to Sociological Theory Award [Vol. 2: 6079]
Distinguished Contribution to the Field of Sport and Exercise Psychology Award [Vol. 2: 7183]
Distinguished Contribution to Workplace Learning and Performance Award [Vol. 1: 4070]
Distinguished Contributions to Clinical Hypnosis [Vol. 1: 3611]
Distinguished Contributions to Scientific Hypnosis Award [Vol. 1: 3610]
Distinguished Contributions to Slavic Studies Award [Vol. 1: 5095]
Distinguished Contributions to Sociological Practice Award [Vol. 1: 13775]
Distinguished Contributions to Teaching Award [Vol. 1: 4540]
Distinguished Contributions to the International Advancement of Psychology [Vol. 1: 3383]
Distinguished Convention Service Manager of the Year Award [Vol. 1: 14201]
Distinguished Crew Award [Vol. 1: 10397]
Distinguished Dairy Cattle Breeder Award [Vol. 1: 12271]
Distinguished Dissertation Award
 American Alliance for Theatre and Education [Vol. 1: 808]
 American Psychological Association - Division of Evaluation, Measurement and Statistics (Division 5) [Vol 1: 3418]

 Association for Canadian Studies in the United States [Vol 1: 4929]
Distinguished Dissertation in Teacher Education Award [Vol. 1: 5530]
Distinguished Donor Awards Program [Vol. 1: 8451]
Distinguished Eagle Scout Award [Vol. 1: 5963]
Distinguished Early Career Award [Vol. 1: 16710]
Distinguished Early Career Contributions Award [Vol. 1: 15133]
Distinguished Economic Botanist Award [Vol. 1: 15064]
Distinguished Educator and Service Award [Vol. 1: 3850]
Distinguished Educator Award
 American Association of Petroleum Geologists [Vol. 1: 1282]
 American Society for Gastrointestinal Endoscopy [Vol. 1: 3910]
 Association of Collegiate Schools of Planning [Vol 1: 5285]
 National Middle School Association [Vol 1: 12603]
 National Rural Health Association [Vol 1: 12790]
 North American Colleges and Teachers of Agriculture [Vol 1: 13292]
Distinguished Engineering Educator Award [Vol. 1: 15897]
Distinguished Executive Award [Vol. 1: 9519]
Distinguished Extension-Industry Service Award [Vol. 1: 2850]
Distinguished Fellow
 American Economic Association [Vol. 1: 2051]
 American Park and Recreation Society [Vol 1: 3119]
 Association for Financial Counseling and Planning Education [Vol 1: 5015]
Distinguished Fellow Award
 American Council on Consumer Interests [Vol. 1: 1914]
 British Machine Vision Association and Society for Pattern Recognition [Vol 2: 7115]
 Economic Society of Australia [Vol 2: 696]
 History of Economics Society [Vol 1: 8946]
 International Association of Forensic Nurses [Vol 1: 9667]
 Society for Public Health Education [Vol 1: 15287]
Distinguished Fellowship [Vol. 1: 71]
Distinguished Fellowship Award
 American College of Cardiology [Vol. 1: 1706]
 Royal Australian Chemical Institute [Vol 2: 974]
Distinguished Fifty-Year Member Award [Vol. 1: 4320]
Distinguished Flying Cross [Vol. 2: 7339]
Distinguished Flying Unit Plaques [Vol. 1: 12474]
Distinguished Former Student Award [Vol. 2: 5208]
Distinguished Friend to Behavior Therapy [Vol. 1: 4920]
Distinguished Geographer Medal [Vol. 2: 4967]
Distinguished Graduate Award [Vol. 1: 17749]
Distinguished Grantmaker Award [Vol. 1: 7695]
Distinguished Grasslander Award [Vol. 1: 2172]
Distinguished Group Psychologist Award [Vol. 1: 3598]
Distinguished Individual Service Award [Vol. 1: 11662]
Distinguished Informal Science Education Award [Vol. 1: 12822]
Distinguished Information Sciences Award [Vol. 1: 5376]
Distinguished International Colleague Award [Vol. 1: 8989]
Distinguished International Fellow Award [Vol. 2: 821]
Distinguished International Journalist Award [Vol. 1: 18009]
Distinguished International Scholar [Vol. 1: 4910]
Distinguished International Service Award [Vol. 1: 8178]
Distinguished Investigator Award
 American College of Clinical Pharmacology [Vol. 1: 1721]
 NARSAD: The Brain and Behavior Research Fund [Vol 1: 11368]
Distinguished Leadership and Service Award [Vol. 1: 3963]

Distinguished Leadership Award
 American Association for Marriage and Family Therapy [Vol. 1: 966]
 American College of Dentists [Vol 1: 1734]
 American Society of Health System Pharmacists [Vol 1: 4306]
 International Landslide Research Group [Vol 1: 9980]
 Parachute Industry Association [Vol 1: 13835]
Distinguished Lecturer [Vol. 1: 825]
Distinguished Lecturer Award
 IEEE - Ultrasonics, Ferroelectrics, and Frequency Control Society [Vol. 1: 9041]
 IEEE Photonics Society [Vol 1: 9103]
 International Society of Exposure Science [Vol 1: 10319]
Distinguished Lecturers [Vol. 1: 6606]
Distinguished Lectureship [Vol. 1: 16536]
Distinguished Lectureship in Materials and Society Award [Vol. 1: 4832]
Distinguished Lectureships [Vol. 1: 15617]
Distinguished Life Member
 American Ceramic Society [Vol. 1: 1557]
 ASM International [Vol 1: 4833]
Distinguished Life-time Achievement Award [Vol. 1: 16711]
Distinguished Lifetime Contribution to Neuropsychology Award [Vol. 1: 11409]
Distinguished Local Government Leadership Award [Vol. 1: 5358]
Distinguished Manager Award [Vol. 2: 5314]
Distinguished Marketing Leadership Award [Vol. 2: 5267]
Distinguished Meeting Professional of the Year Award [Vol. 1: 14202]
Distinguished Member
 American Society of Civil Engineers [Vol. 1: 4175]
 International Council on Large Electric Systems [Vol 2: 2512]
 National Wrestling Hall of Fame & Museum [Vol 1: 13069]
Distinguished Member and Fellow Award [Vol. 1: 5031]
Distinguished Member Award
 American Academy of Physical Medicine and Rehabilitation [Vol. 1: 730]
 American Congress of Rehabilitation Medicine [Vol 1: 1863]
 Association of Women Surgeons [Vol 1: 5552]
 Canadian Association of Gerontology [Vol 1: 6267]
 Dietetics in Health Care Communities [Vol 1: 7862]
 International Society of Hypertension - United Kingdom [Vol 2: 8208]
 National Cancer Registrars Association [Vol 1: 12032]
 Society for Mining, Metallurgy, and Exploration [Vol 1: 15206]
 Society of Petroleum Engineers [Vol 1: 15752]
 Wisconsin Health Information Management Association [Vol 1: 17887]
Distinguished Member of the Year Award [Vol. 1: 14203]
Distinguished Membership Award [Vol. 1: 3018]
Distinguished Mentor Award
 Association for Counselor Education and Supervision [Vol. 1: 4981]
 National Council for Geographic Education [Vol 1: 12155]
Distinguished Mentor Awards [Vol. 1: 15555]
Distinguished Mentorship in Gerontology Award [Vol. 1: 8623]
Distinguished Merit Award
 American Association of Community Theatre [Vol. 1: 1110]
 International Society of Nurses in Cancer Care [Vol 1: 10327]
Distinguished Mission Support Plaques [Vol. 1: 12475]
Distinguished New Engineer Award [Vol. 1: 15898]
Distinguished New Faculty Award [Vol. 1: 9813]
Distinguished Nurse Award [Vol. 1: 13927]
Distinguished Organization Award [Vol. 1: 11349]
Distinguished Pathologist Award [Vol. 1: 16705]

Distinguished Patriot Award [Vol. 1: 12900]

Distinguished Peace Leadership Award [Vol. 1: 13455]

Distinguished Performance Award [Vol. 1: 7921]

Distinguished Performance Awards Program [Vol. 1: 8452]

Distinguished Person Award [Vol. 2: 5325]

Distinguished Personality Psychologist Award [Vol. 2: 2809]

Distinguished Physician Award [Vol. 1: 1224]

Distinguished Pi Lambda Thetan Award [Vol. 1: 14003]

Distinguished Play Awards [Vol. 1: 809]

Distinguished Practice Award [Vol. 2: 4756]

Distinguished Primatologist Award [Vol. 1: 4501]

Distinguished Principal Founding Member [Vol. 2: 1289]

Distinguished Private Sector Service Award [Vol. 1: 17601]

Distinguished Professional Contributions Award [Vol. 1: 15134]

Distinguished Professional Practice Award [Vol. 1: 4911]

Distinguished Professional Service Award [Vol. 1: 4982]

Distinguished Programs in Teacher Education Award [Vol. 1: 5531]

Distinguished Psychologist Award for Contributions to Psychology and Psychotherapy [Vol. 1: 3451]

Distinguished Psychologist of the Year [Vol. 1: 3431]

Distinguished Public Involvement Award [Vol. 1: 13166]

Distinguished Public Leadership Award [Vol. 1: 3973]

Distinguished Public Service Award [Vol. 1: 731]

Distinguished Public Service Award
   American Psychological Association - Division of Independent Practice [Vol. 1: 3432]
   Center for National Policy [Vol 1: 7145]
   United States Department of Health and Human Services [Vol 1: 16813]

Distinguished Public Service Medal
   Mineralogical Society of America [Vol. 1: 11173]
   National Aeronautics and Space Administration - Office of Human Capital Management [Vol 1: 11471]

Distinguished Publication on Business Communication [Vol. 1: 4925]

Distinguished Quality of Life Researcher Award [Vol. 1: 10231]

Distinguished Recent Alumnus Award [Vol. 1: 5757]

Distinguished Research and Development Award [Vol. 1: 9608]

Distinguished Research Award
   American Meat Science Association [Vol. 1: 2851]
   National Council of Teachers of English [Vol 1: 12219]

Distinguished Research in Teacher Education Award [Vol. 1: 5532]

Distinguished Researcher Award
   American Association of Neuromuscular and Electrodiagnostic Medicine [Vol. 1: 1225]
   Association of Pediatric Hematology/Oncology Nurses [Vol 1: 5449]
   Oncology Nursing Society [Vol 1: 13534]

Distinguished Researcher's Award [Vol. 1: 10475]

Distinguished Rural Sociologist Award [Vol. 1: 14660]

Distinguished Sales and Marketing Award [Vol. 1: 14686]

Distinguished Salesperson Award [Vol. 2: 5269]

Distinguished Scholar Award
   Communal Studies Association [Vol. 1: 7451]
   International Association of Human-Animal Interaction Organizations [Vol 1: 9677]
   Keats-Shelley Association of America [Vol 1: 10642]
   Microbeam Analysis Society [Vol 1: 11131]
   North American Society for the Psychology of Sport and Physical Activity [Vol 1: 13344]

Distinguished Scholar Award in Health Education [Vol. 1: 9818]

Distinguished Scholar Award in Leisure and Recreation [Vol. 1: 9819]

Distinguished Scholar Award in Physical Education [Vol. 1: 9820]

Distinguished Scholar Award in Research [Vol. 1: 9821]

Distinguished Scholar in Sport and Olympic Movement [Vol. 1: 9822]

Distinguished Scholarship and Service Award [Vol. 1: 875]

Distinguished Scholarship Award [Vol. 1: 13776]

Distinguished School Administrators Award [Vol. 1: 1341]

Distinguished Science Award [Vol. 2: 4757]

Distinguished Scientific Achievement Award [Vol. 1: 8851]

Distinguished Scientific Award for the Applications of Psychology [Vol. 1: 3499]

Distinguished Scientific Contribution Award [Vol. 2: 511]

Distinguished Scientific Contribution Award
   American Psychological Association - Science Directorate [Vol. 1: 3500]
   American Psychological Association - Society for Consumer Psychology (Division 23) [Vol 1: 3516]

Distinguished Scientific Contributions Award [Vol. 1: 15368]

Distinguished Scientific Contributions Award [Vol. 1: 15135]

Distinguished Scientist Award
   American Association for Clinical Chemistry [Vol. 1: 900]
   American College of Cardiology [Vol 1: 1707]
   American Institute of Biological Sciences [Vol 1: 2591]
   Heart Rhythm Society [Vol 1: 8872]
   International Behavioural and Neural Genetics Society [Vol 2: 8097]
   Microscopy Society of America [Vol 1: 11136]
   Society of Behavioral Medicine [Vol 1: 15556]
   Society of Experimental Social Psychology [Vol 1: 15638]

Distinguished Scientist Award for Contribution to the Improvement of the Quality of Life of Women [Vol. 2: 5686]

Distinguished Scientist of the Year [Vol. 2: 5190]

Distinguished Section Member Award Honoring Noble R. Patterson [Vol. 1: 15503]

Distinguished Service/Achievement Awards [Vol. 1: 14863]

Distinguished Service and Achievement Award [Vol. 1: 5504]

Distinguished Service and Education Award [Vol. 1: 6985]

Distinguished Service Award
   Academy of Psychosomatic Medicine [Vol. 1: 106]
   American Agricultural Editors' Association [Vol 1: 791]
   American Association of Teachers of Slavic and East European Languages [Vol 1: 1368]
   American College of Health Plan Management [Vol 1: 1750]
   American Council for Polish Culture [Vol 1: 1889]
   American Guernsey Association [Vol 1: 2261]
   American Pain Society [Vol 1: 3114]
   American Rental Association [Vol 1: 3685]
   American Society for Pain Management Nursing [Vol 1: 4024]
   American Society of Primatologists [Vol 1: 4502]
   Association for the Advancement of Artificial Intelligence [Vol 1: 5112]
   Association of Medical Microbiology and Infectious Disease Canada [Vol 1: 5406]
   Biophysical Society [Vol 1: 5848]
   Canadian Bureau for International Education [Vol 1: 6370]
   Canadian Condominium Institute [Vol 1: 6422]
   College and University Professional Association for Human Resources [Vol 1: 7347]
   IEEE - Ultrasonics, Ferroelectrics, and Frequency Control Society [Vol 1: 9042]
   International Collegiate Licensing Association [Vol 1: 9786]
   International Ergonomics Association [Vol 2: 6584]
   International Police Work Dog Association [Vol 1: 10048]

International Society for Pharmacoepidemiology [Vol 1: 10212]

International Society for Quality-of-Life Studies [Vol 1: 10232]

International Union of Biochemistry and Molecular Biology [Vol 1: 10472]

Israeli Society for Bioinformatics and Computational Biology [Vol 2: 3979]

National Association of College and University Attorneys [Vol 1: 11686]

National Association of Student Financial Aid Administrators [Vol 1: 11920]

National Community Education Association [Vol 1: 12120]

North Country Trail Association [Vol 1: 13383]

Seismological Society of America [Vol 1: 14834]

Society for Freshwater Science [Vol 1: 15077]

Society for the Study of Reproduction [Vol 1: 15384]

Society for Vascular Ultrasound [Vol 1: 15405]

Society of Gastroenterology Nurses and Associates [Vol 1: 15662]

Special Interest Group on Mobility of Systems Users, Data, and Computing [Vol 1: 16089]

Special Interest Group on Programming Languages [Vol 1: 16093]

State Debt Management Network [Vol 1: 16273]

Statistical Society of Canada [Vol 1: 16288]

United States Aquaculture Society [Vol 1: 16712]

Washburn Alumni Association [Vol 1: 17644]

Waste Equipment Technology Association [Vol 1: 17690]

Wofford College National Alumni Association [Vol 1: 17901]

Women in Engineering ProActive Network [Vol 1: 17928]

Wound Healing Society [Vol 1: 18099]

Distinguished Service Award
   AAHPERD Research Consortium [Vol. 1: 22]
   AIIM - The Enterprise Content Management Association [Vol 1: 232]
   Alpine Club of Canada [Vol 1: 421]
   American Academy of Advertising [Vol 1: 490]
   American Academy of Family Physicians [Vol 1: 548]
   American Academy of Medical Administrators [Vol 1: 573]
   American Academy of Ophthalmology [Vol 1: 605]
   American Academy of Pediatrics [Vol 1: 669]
   American Art Therapy Association [Vol 1: 842]
   American Association for Agricultural Education [Vol 1: 871]
   American Association for Physical Activity and Recreation [Vol 1: 971]
   American Association of Collegiate Registrars and Admissions Officers [Vol 1: 1100]
   American Association of Housing Educators [Vol 1: 1175]
   American Association of Oral and Maxillofacial Surgeons [Vol 1: 1255]
   American Association of Petroleum Geologists [Vol 1: 1274]
   American Association of Public Health Dentistry [Vol 1: 1325]
   American Association of Public Health Physicians [Vol 1: 1331]
   American Association of School Administrators [Vol 1: 1335]
   American Association of School Librarians [Vol 1: 1342]
   American Association of Teachers of Italian [Vol 1: 1366]
   American Association of University Administrators [Vol 1: 1385]
   American Camp Association [Vol 1: 1525]
   American Cancer Society [Vol 1: 1531]
   American Chemical Society [Vol 1: 1632]
   American College of Cardiology [Vol 1: 1708]
   American College of Dentists [Vol 1: 1738]
   American College of Preventive Medicine [Vol 1: 1808]
   American Dairy Science Association [Vol 1: 1974]
   American Farm Bureau Federation [Vol 1: 2098]

American Feed Industry Association [Vol 1: 2129]

American Fisheries Society [Vol 1: 2146]

American Forensic Association [Vol 1: 2185]

American Hospital Association [Vol 1: 2448]

American Industrial Hygiene Association [Vol 1: 2487]

American Institute of Aeronautics and Astronautics [Vol 1: 2515]

American Institute of Biological Sciences [Vol 1: 2591]

American Institute of Chemical Engineers [Vol 1: 2613]

American Institute of Mining, Metallurgical, and Petroleum Engineers [Vol 1: 2674]

American Optometric Association [Vol 1: 3054]

American Phytopathological Society [Vol 1: 3276]

American Psychological Association - Division of Family Psychology [Vol 1: 3426]

American Psychological Association - Division of Rehabilitation Psychology (Division 22) [Vol 1: 3459]

American Psychological Association - Psychologists in Public Service Division (Division 18)- [Vol 1: 3477]

American Psychological Association - Psychology of Religion Division [Vol 1: 3483]

American Psychological Association - Society for the Psychological Study of Lesbian, Gay, Bisexual and Transgender Issues (Division 44) [Vol 1: 3540]

American Psychological Association - Society for Theoretical and Philosophical Psychology (Division 24) [Vol 1: 3561]

American Public Gas Association [Vol 1: 3640]

American Public Power Association [Vol 1: 3655]

American Society for Bioethics and Humanities [Vol 1: 3763]

American Society for Gastrointestinal Endoscopy [Vol 1: 3911]

American Society of Heating, Refrigerating and Air-Conditioning Engineers [Vol 1: 4321]

American Speech Language Hearing Association [Vol 1: 4543]

American Urological Association [Vol 1: 4620]

Association for Asian Studies [Vol 1: 4913]

Association for Computing Machinery [Vol 1: 4955]

Association for Educational Communications and Technology [Vol 1: 5006]

Association for Library Service to Children [Vol 1: 5063]

Association for Women Veterinarians Foundation [Vol 1: 5183]

Association of Professional Chaplains [Vol 1: 5481]

Association of Schools of Allied Health Professions [Vol 1: 5504]

Australian Society for Microbiology [Vol 2: 543]

Badminton World Federation [Vol 2: 4531]

Black Caucus of the American Library Association [Vol 1: 5862]

California Society of Anesthesiologists [Vol 1: 6095]

Canadian Society of Hospital Pharmacists [Vol 1: 6950]

Caucus for Television Producers, Writers, and Directors [Vol 1: 7120]

Chinese American Librarians Association [Vol 2: 5232]

Christian Management Association [Vol 1: 7267]

Colorado Association of Libraries [Vol 1: 7388]

Computing Research Association [Vol 1: 7466]

Conference on Latin American History [Vol 1: 7515]

Congress of Neurological Surgeons [Vol 1: 7532]

Congressional Hispanic Caucus Institute [Vol 1: 7539]

Construction Specifications Institute [Vol 1: 7556]

Council of Chief State School Officers [Vol 1: 7662]

Council of Supply Chain Management Professionals [Vol 1: 7683]

Deep Foundations Institute [Vol 1: 7832]

Direct Selling Association [Vol 1: 7873]

Easter Seals [Vol 1: 7967]

European Association for Animal Production [Vol 2: 4054]

Family, Career and Community Leaders of America [Vol 1: 8227]

Federally Employed Women [Vol 1: 8269]

Federation of Genealogical Societies [Vol 1: 8322]

Financial Planning Association [Vol 1: 8365]

Geological Society of America [Vol 1: 8563]

Geological Society of London [Vol 2: 7721]

Health Science Communications Association [Vol 1: 8854]

Healthcare Convention and Exhibitors Association [Vol 1: 8858]

Heart Rhythm Society [Vol 1: 8873]

IEEE Photonics Society [Vol 1: 9104]

Illuminating Engineering Society of North America [Vol 1: 9154]

International Association of Cancer Victors and Friends [Vol 1: 9632]

International Committee for Animal Recording [Vol 2: 4092]

International Council of Associations for Science Education [Vol 2: 4923]

International Institute of Fisheries Economics and Trade [Vol 1: 9969]

International Measurement Confederation [Vol 2: 3404]

International Pharmaceutical Federation [Vol 2: 4758]

International Society for Prevention of Child Abuse and Neglect [Vol 1: 10218]

International Union of Forest Research Organizations [Vol 2: 1310]

Lamaze International [Vol 1: 10737]

LeadingAge [Vol 1: 10772]

Lewis and Clark Trail Heritage Foundation [Vol 1: 10818]

Mail Systems Management Association [Vol 1: 10916]

Medical Fitness Association [Vol 1: 11055]

Minerals, Metals, and Materials Society [Vol 1: 11195]

NACE International: The Corrosion Society [Vol 1: 11350]

National Academy of Neuropsychology [Vol 1: 11410]

National Air Transportation Association [Vol 1: 11498]

National Alliance on Mental Illness [Vol 1: 11509]

National Association for Pupil Transportation [Vol 1: 11592]

National Association of Academies of Science [Vol 1: 11618]

National Association of Animal Breeders [Vol 1: 11620]

National Association of Biology Teachers [Vol 1: 11647]

National Association of Conservation Districts [Vol 1: 11722]

National Association of Realtors [Vol 1: 11856]

National Association of State Park Directors [Vol 1: 11908]

National Business Education Association [Vol 1: 12019]

National Council of Teachers of English [Vol 1: 12207]

National Court Reporters Association [Vol 1: 12262]

National Defense Transportation Association [Vol 1: 12283]

National Genealogical Society [Vol 1: 12447]

National Propane Gas Association [Vol 1: 12718]

National Retail Federation [Vol 1: 12778]

National School Transportation Association [Vol 1: 12808]

National Small-Bore Rifle Association [Vol 2: 8410]

National Society of Professional Engineers [Vol 1: 12873]

National Therapeutic Recreation Society [Vol 1: 12978]

Ohio Academy of History [Vol 1: 13471]

Oncology Nursing Society [Vol 1: 13535]

Optical Society of America [Vol 1: 13604]

Professional Geologists of Indiana [Vol 1: 14217]

Prospectors and Developers Association of Canada [Vol 1: 14276]

Radiation Research Society [Vol 1: 14384]

Royal Australian and New Zealand College of Ophthalmologists [Vol 2: 963]

Royal Society of Chemistry [Vol 2: 9001]

Society for Applied Spectroscopy [Vol 1: 15035]

Society for Range Management [Vol 1: 15293]

Society for Sedimentary Geology [Vol 1: 15307]

Society of American Archivists [Vol 1: 15419]

Society of Naval Architects and Marine Engineers [Vol 1: 15713]

Society of Petroleum Engineers [Vol 1: 15753]

Society of Petrophysicists and Well Log Analysts [Vol 1: 15768]

Society of Research Administrators [Vol 1: 15823]

South Dakota Library Association [Vol 1: 15976]

Standards Council of Canada [Vol 1: 16241]

Tax Foundation [Vol 1: 16388]

United States Association of Former Members of Congress [Vol 1: 16726]

Virginia Interscholastic Athletic Administrators Association [Vol 1: 17576]

Virginia Recreation and Park Society [Vol 1: 17602]

The Waterbird Society [Vol 1: 17727]

The Wildlife Society [Vol 1: 17854]

Wine Spectator [Vol 1: 17865]

Wisconsin Health Information Management Association [Vol 1: 17888]

World Council of Credit Unions [Vol 1: 18035]

Distinguished Service Award for an Administrator or Supervisor [Vol. 1: 12020]

Distinguished Service Award in Special Education [Vol. 1: 11899]

Distinguished Service Award (Outside the Profession) [Vol. 1: 11534]

Distinguished Service Award (Within the Profession)- [Vol. 1: 11535]

Distinguished Service Awards [Vol. 2: 264]

Distinguished Service Awards

American Psychiatric Association [Vol. 1: 3347]

Canadian Image Processing and Pattern Recognition Society [Vol 1: 6560]

National Association of Elementary School Principals [Vol 1: 11754]

National Center for State Courts [Vol 1: 12054]

National Institute of Governmental Purchasing [Vol 1: 12552]

University of Chicago - Medical and Biological Sciences Alumni Association [Vol 1: 17206]

Distinguished Service Citation

American Association of Physics Teachers [Vol. 1: 1308]

American Podiatric Medical Association [Vol 1: 3298]

American Society for Engineering Education [Vol 1: 3851]

Automotive Hall of Fame [Vol 1: 5716]

Ecological Society of America [Vol 1: 7985]

Pierre Fauchard Academy [Vol 1: 8248]

International Association for the Scientific Study of Intellectual Disabilities [Vol 2: 8072]

Lambda Kappa Sigma [Vol 1: 10744]

National FFA Organization [Vol 1: 12384]

Distinguished Service Citations [Vol. 1: 121]

Distinguished Service Contributions Award [Vol. 1: 15136]

Distinguished Service Cross [Vol. 2: 311]

Distinguished Service Decorations [Vol. 2: 311]

Distinguished Service in Psychiatry Award [Vol. 1: 1817]

Distinguished Service in Social Welfare Award [Vol. 1: 13274]

Distinguished Service Key and Certificate for Retiring Continuing Educators [Vol. 1: 17383]

Distinguished Service Medal

Association of European Operational Research Societies [Vol. 2: 1402]

Australian Department of the Prime Minister and Cabinet - Awards and Culture Branch [Vol 2: 311]

Canadian Institute of Mining, Metallurgy, and Petroleum [Vol 1: 6607]

Committee on Space Research [Vol 2: 2336]

National Aeronautics and Space Administration - Office of Human Capital Management [Vol 1: 11472]

National Guard Association of the United States [Vol 1: 12476]

Distinguished Service Order [Vol. 2: 7340]

Distinguished Service Prize [Vol. 1: 4966]

Distinguished Service Star [Vol. 1: 10700]

Distinguished Service to Children Award

National Association of Elementary School Principals [Vol 1: 11754]

Parents Without Partners [Vol 1: 13867]

Distinguished Service to College Award [Vol. 1: 5760]

Distinguished Service to Education Award [Vol. 1: 11754]

Distinguished Service to Health Education Award [Vol. 1: 950]

Distinguished Service to Powder Metallurgy Award [Vol. 1: 11109]

Distinguished Service to Public Works Award [Vol. 1: 3660]

Distinguished Service to Rural Life Award [Vol. 1: 14661]

Distinguished Service to Safety Education [Vol. 1: 971]

Distinguished Service to Science Education Award [Vol. 1: 12823]

Distinguished Service to the Cause of Liberal Religion [Vol. 1: 16622]

Distinguished Service to the RV Industry Award [Vol. 1: 14445]

Distinguished Services Award [Vol. 2: 4767]

Distinguished Society Award [Vol. 1: 17750]

Distinguished Society Service Award [Vol. 1: 10281]

Distinguished Student Paper Awards [Vol. 1: 13777]

Distinguished Student Practice Award in Clinical Psychology [Vol. 1: 3579]

Distinguished Student Research Award in Clinical Psychology [Vol. 1: 3580]

Distinguished Student Scholar Award [Vol. 1: 14004]

Distinguished Student Service Award in Clinical Psychology [Vol. 1: 3581]

Distinguished Teacher Award

American College of Physicians [Vol. 1: 1798]

American Mensa [Vol 1: 2885]

American Society of Animal Science [Vol 1: 4118]

Canadian Cardiovascular Society [Vol 1: 6393]

European Orthodontic Society [Vol 2: 7620]

Heart Rhythm Society [Vol 1: 8874]

Distinguished Teaching Achievement Awards [Vol. 1: 12156]

Distinguished Teaching Award

American Meat Science Association [Vol. 1: 2852]

College Reading and Learning Association [Vol 1: 7376]

National Science Teachers Association [Vol 1: 12824]

Ohio Academy of History [Vol 1: 13472]

Rider University Student Government Association [Vol 1: 14551]

Distinguished Teaching Awards [Vol. 1: 10674]

Distinguished Teaching Contributions Award [Vol. 1: 15137]

Distinguished Teaching in Journalism Award [Vol. 1: 15794]

Distinguished Teaching of Art Award [Vol. 1: 7356]

Distinguished Teaching of Art History Award [Vol. 1: 7357]

Distinguished Technical Achievement Award [Vol. 1: 15769]

Distinguished Technology Educator Award [Vol. 1: 10429]

Distinguished Topical Philatelist Award [Vol. 1: 4598]

Distinguished Trainer Award [Vol. 2: 5266]

Distinguished Vanguard Awards for Leadership [Vol. 1: 12029]

Distinguished Volunteer Service Award

Allergy/Asthma Information Association [Vol. 1: 359]

Virginia Recreation and Park Society [Vol 1: 17603]

Distinguished Woman Scientist Award [Vol. 2: 5687]

Distinguished Women's Awards [Vol. 1: 13424]

Distinguished Writing Award in Commentary/Column Writing [Vol. 1: 4464]

Distinguished Writing Award in Editorial Writing [Vol. 1: 4465]

Distinguished Writing Award in Local Accountability Reporting [Vol. 1: 4466]

Distinguished Writing Award in Local Watchdog Reporting [Vol. 1: 4466]

Distinguished Writing Award in Non-Deadline Writing [Vol. 1: 4467]

Distinguished Young Breeder Award [Vol. 1: 11200]

Distribution Executive of the Year [Vol. 1: 6565]

Distribution Management Award [Vol. 1: 8861]

Distributor of the Year

Australasian Association of Convenience Stores [Vol. 2: 128]

Souvenir Wholesale Distributors Association [Vol 1: 16060]

Distributor of the Year Award

Canadian Booksellers Association [Vol. 1: 6350]

Multi-Level Marketing International Association [Vol 1: 11293]

National Association of the Remodeling Industry [Vol 1: 11926]

Distributor Web Awards [Vol. 1: 14269]

District and Section Newsletter Award [Vol. 1: 9413]

District Award [Vol. 1: 13854]

District Award of Merit [Vol. 1: 5964]

District Coach of the Year [Vol. 1: 12078]

District Distinguished Service Awards [Vol. 1: 6608]

District Excellence Awards [Vol. 1: 11723]

Dita/NFHCA High School Coach of the Year [Vol. 1: 12390]

Ditchdigger of the Year Award [Vol. 1: 13018]

Dittus Award; Ray [Vol. 1: 13307]

DiValerio Technician of the Year Award; Lou [Vol. 1: 4001]

Diversity Award

American Psychological Association - Division of Psychotherapy [Vol. 1: 3452]

Federation of American Societies for Experimental Biology [Vol 1: 8278]

The Wildlife Society [Vol 1: 17850]

Diversity Award; Equity and [Vol. 1: 4997]

Diversity in Psychology and Law Research Award [Vol. 1: 3626]

Diversity Outreach Scholarship [Vol. 1: 9406]

Divine Award; Thomas F. [Vol. 1: 5106]

Division I Player of the Year [Vol. 1: 11639]

Division II Player of the Year [Vol. 1: 11640]

Division III Player of the Year [Vol. 1: 11641]

Division Leadership and Service Award [Vol. 1: 16364]

Division of Medicinal Chemistry Award [Vol. 1: 1633]

Division of the Year [Vol. 1: 17031]

Division Technical Awards [Vol. 1: 16365]

Divisional Road Rally Achievement Award [Vol. 1: 16194]

Divisions Council Awards [Vol. 1: 3286]

Dix Leadership Award; Marion Quin [Vol. 1: 11536]

Dixon Award; Russell A. [Vol. 1: 1915]

Dixon Medal; John W. [Vol. 1: 5537]

DMA Annual Award [Vol. 1: 7810]

DMA Awards [Vol. 2: 7517]

DMA/Royal Mail Direct Marketing Awards [Vol. 2: 7517]

DMFE Corporate Leadership [Vol. 1: 7085]

DMFE Educational Leadership [Vol. 1: 7086]

DMFE Vision [Vol. 1: 7087]

Doane Award; D. Howard [Vol. 1: 4297]

Doberaller Stipendium; Walter [Vol. 2: 1214]

Dobie-Paisano Writing Fellowships [Vol. 1: 16458]

Doblougska priset [Vol. 2: 6199]

Dobzhansky Prize; Theodosius [Vol. 1: 15375]

Dock Award; Lavinia L. [Vol. 1: 1006]

d'Octon; Prix Paul Vigne [Vol. 2: 2259]

Doctor Best Education Poster Awards; John [Vol. 1: 15054]

Dr. May K. Simon Memorial Scholarship [Vol. 1: 5384]

Doctoral Dissertation Award

Association for Computing Machinery [Vol. 1: 4956]

Association of European Operational Research Societies [Vol 2: 1403]

Council of Supply Chain Management Professionals [Vol 1: 7684]

Special Interest Group on Programming Languages [Vol 1: 16094]

Doctoral Dissertation Award for Arthritis Health Professionals [Vol. 1: 4808]

Doctoral Dissertation Fellowship [Vol. 1: 5260]

Doctoral Dissertation Grant Competition [Vol. 1: 491]

Doctoral Fellows Award [Vol. 1: 15335]

Doctoral Research Awards [Vol. 1: 435]

Doctoral Research Grant [Vol. 1: 8605]

Doctoral Scholarship [Vol. 1: 13953]

Doctoral Training Award [Vol. 1: 14853]

Doctorate of Bananistry Medal [Vol. 1: 9724]

Doctorate of Food Service Medallion [Vol. 1: 13277]

Documentaries of the World [Vol. 1: 11258]

The Documentary Award [Vol. 2: 5149]

Documentary Awards

International Documentary Association [Vol. 1: 9879]

International Documentary Association [Vol 1: 9883]

Dodd Memorial Award; M.E. [Vol. 1: 5786]

Dodge Award [Vol. 1: 18190]

Dodge Award; Harold F. [Vol. 1: 5592]

Dodge Foreign Language Advocate Award; James W. [Vol. 1: 13395]

Dodson Scholarship; Claudia [Vol. 1: 17577]

Doe Lectureship; Janet [Vol. 1: 11066]

Doerfer Engineering Concept of the Year Award

American Society of Agricultural and Biological Engineers [Vol. 1: 4092]

American Society of Agricultural and Biological Engineers [Vol 1: 4093]

Dog of the Year [Vol. 1: 4058]

Dog Show; Festival of the Wagging Tails [Vol. 2: 6648]

Dogan Foundation Prize in European Political Sociology; Mattei [Vol. 2: 7599]

Dogan Prize; Mattei [Vol. 2: 2563]

Dogan; Prize of the Foundation Mattei [Vol. 1: 10052]

Dogramaci Family Health Foundation Prize; Ihsan [Vol. 2: 6549]

Dohlman Award [Vol. 1: 7607]

Doidge Memorial Lecture; E.M. [Vol. 2: 5742]

Doistau - Emile Blutet de l'Information Scientifique; Prix Paul [Vol. 2: 2198]

Dolezal Award; Eduard [Vol. 2: 5297]

Doll Award; Edgar A. [Vol. 1: 3435]

Dolphin Award

Catboat Association [Vol. 1: 7090]

Moondance International Film Festival [Vol 1: 11268]

Dolphin Medal [Vol. 1: 4658]

Domac Medal; Julije [Vol. 2: 1869]

Domb Jewish Education Award; Sara [Vol. 1: 12103]

Dominica Award for Innovative Program Development; Sister Francis [Vol. 1: 7238]

Dominica Award of Honour [Vol. 2: 1999]

Dominican Short Film Competition [Vol. 2: 2005]

Donabedian Outcomes Research Lifetime Achievement Award; Avedis [Vol. 1: 10207]

Donald Gold Medal; Ian [Vol. 2: 8223]

Donald Medal [Vol. 2: 7961]

Donaldson Award of Merit; Mary [Vol. 1: 14719]

Donaldson Early Career Prize; Margaret [Vol. 2: 7184]

Donaldson Gold Medal [Vol. 2: 8951]

Donath Medal [Vol. 1: 8569]

Donehoo Essay Award [Vol. 1: 9609]

Dongchun Lecture [Vol. 2: 5465]

Doniach Lectureship and Award [Vol. 2: 8459]

Donlon Memorial Exhibit Award; Sidney W. Smith/William [Vol. 1: 3008]

Donne Essay Prize on the Anthropology of Art; J. B. [Vol. 2: 8641]

Donner Medal in Canadian Studies [Vol. 1: 4930]

Donnet Emerging Filmmaker Award; Jacqueline [Vol. 1: 9882]

Donohue Award; Mark [Vol. 1: 16195]

Donor of the Year - College Division [Vol. 1: 11624]

Donor of the Year - University Division **[Vol. 1: 11625]**
Donostia Award **[Vol. 2: 6094]**
Donovan Award; Terence **[Vol. 2: 8897]**
Donovan Individual Achievement Award; James D. **[Vol. 1: 3649]**
Doob Prize; Joseph L. **[Vol. 1: 2831]**
Doolan Best Building in Scotland Award; Andrew **[Vol. 2: 8847]**
Doolitte Award; Arthur K. **[Vol. 1: 1634]**
Doolittle Award; James H. **[Vol. 1: 15641]**
Dorfman Journal Paper Awards **[Vol. 1: 107]**
Dorn Distinguished Contributions to Teaching Award; Dean S. **[Vol. 1: 13778]**
Dornheim Award; Michael A. **[Vol. 1: 12682]**
Dorot Foundation Award in Memory of Joy Ungerleider Mayerson **[Vol. 1: 10562]**
Dorothea Award for Conservation **[Vol. 2: 6768]**
Dorroh Memorial Scholarship; Marion **[Vol. 1: 13196]**
Dorsey Most Notable Achievement Award; Thomas A. **[Vol. 1: 7159]**
Dorso Prize; International Guido **[Vol. 2: 4032]**
D'Orta Award; Augustine **[Vol. 1: 8080]**
Dorweiler Prize **[Vol. 1: 7080]**
Dott, Sr., Memorial Award; Robert H. **[Vol. 1: 1275]**
Doty Award; Donald B. **[Vol. 1: 17772]**
Doty Research Grant **[Vol. 1: 16501]**
Doubles Team of the Year **[Vol. 1: 15958]**
Doublespeak Award **[Vol. 1: 12208]**
Dougherty Award; John L. **[Vol. 1: 4895]**
Douglas Award; Marjory Stoneman **[Vol. 1: 12661]**
Douglas Award; William O. **[Vol. 1: 14864]**
Douglas Gold Medal; James **[Vol. 1: 2675]**
Douglas International Fellowship; CFUW A. Vibert **[Vol. 2: 6386]**
Douglas Scholarships; Tommy **[Vol. 1: 13011]**
Douglass Foundation Graduate Business Plan Competition **[Vol. 1: 5758]**
Douglass Prize; Jane Dempsey **[Vol. 1: 4146]**
Douthit Public Service Award; Richard **[Vol. 1: 2350]**
Dove Awards **[Vol. 1: 8732]**
Dove Medal Award; Allan B. **[Vol. 1: 17869]**
Dow Award; Robert S. **[Vol. 1: 13664]**
Dow Creative Minds in Residence Program; Alden B. **[Vol. 1: 13429]**
Dow Creativity Center Summer Residency Fellowships; Alden B. **[Vol. 1: 13429]**
Dow Energy Dissertation Prizes **[Vol. 2: 4819]**
Dow Energy Prize **[Vol. 2: 4820]**
Down Grant; Vera **[Vol. 2: 7118]**
Down Syndrome Research Prize in the Eastern Mediterranean Prize **[Vol. 2: 6550]**
Downes Jr. Memorial Award; William E. **[Vol. 1: 314]**
Downes Resident Research Award; John J. **[Vol. 1: 670]**
Downey Citation; Rob **[Vol. 1: 14413]**
Downey Memorial Grant; Maureen **[Vol. 2: 3878]**
Downing Award; Antoinette Forrester **[Vol. 1: 15474]**
Downing Award; C. N. **[Vol. 1: 6914]**
Downing Award; Glenn **[Vol. 1: 6875]**
Downs Intellectual Freedom Award; Robert B. **[Vol. 1: 17253]**
Doyle Award; Austin **[Vol. 2: 8209]**
Doyle Award; William H. **[Vol. 1: 2614]**
Doyle Medal; Frank **[Vol. 2: 8756]**
Drama League's Delia Austrian Medal for Distinguished Performance **[Vol. 1: 7921]**
Draper Health Promotion Award; Ron **[Vol. 1: 6832]**
Draper Medal; Henry **[Vol. 1: 11434]**
Draper Memorial Medal **[Vol. 2: 5556]**
Dream Garden Awards **[Vol. 1: 16325]**
Drechsel Award; Helmet E. **[Vol. 1: 3729]**
Dreher Memorial Award; Raymond H. **[Vol. 1: 9507]**
Drench Memorial Fellowship; Rose and Isidore **[Vol. 1: 18179]**
Dreosti Award **[Vol. 2: 5651]**
Drewes Scholarship; Tom and Roberta **[Vol. 1: 2777]**
Drexel Medal; Lucy Wharton **[Vol. 1: 17324]**
Dreyer Award in Applied Economic Geology; Robert M. **[Vol. 1: 15207]**
Dreyfus Teacher-Scholar Awards; Camille **[Vol. 1: 6115]**
Dried Beef Award **[Vol. 1: 9125]**
Drilling and Completions Award **[Vol. 1: 15754]**
Drilling Engineering Award **[Vol. 1: 15754]**
Drimmelen Medal; Dominee Pieter **[Vol. 2: 5626]**
Driver Award; Captain William **[Vol. 1: 13362]**

Driver Hall of Fame **[Vol. 1: 12713]**
Driver Memorial Lectureship Award; Muriel **[Vol. 1: 6287]**
Driver of the Year **[Vol. 1: 16222]**
Driver of the Year Award
 Guild of Motoring Writers **[Vol. 2: 7768]**
 National Ready Mixed Concrete Association **[Vol 1: 12733]**
Dromkeen Librarian's Award **[Vol. 1: 687]**
Dromkeen Medal **[Vol. 2: 688]**
Drotman Memorial Award; Jay S. **[Vol. 1: 3643]**
Drouin; Prix Edmond **[Vol. 2: 2155]**
Drouyn de Lhuys; Prix **[Vol. 2: 2260]**
Drum Memorial Scholarship Award; Douglas R. **[Vol. 1: 2923]**
Drummond-Jackson Essay Prize **[Vol. 2: 9210]**
Drummond Prize; F.H. **[Vol. 2: 1110]**
Dryburgh Memorial Trophy; Dave **[Vol. 1: 6505]**
Dryden Lectureship in Research **[Vol. 1: 2516]**
Dryerre Prize Lectureship; Henry **[Vol. 2: 9066]**
DSEF Circle of Honor Award **[Vol. 1: 7874]**
DSPA Awards for Printing **[Vol. 2: 7515]**
Du Bois-Mandela-Rodney Fellowship **[Vol. 1: 17284]**
Du Chatelet Award for Independent Scholarship; Emilie **[Vol. 1: 3823]**
du Pont Memorial Trophy; Richard C. **[Vol. 1: 14970]**
du Pre Fellowship; Jacqueline **[Vol. 2: 8372]**
du Teil; Prix Joseph **[Vol. 2: 2261]**
du Toit Foundation Student Prize; Vona and Marie **[Vol. 2: 5585]**
du Toit Medal for Business Leadership; Frans **[Vol. 2: 5627]**
du Toit Memorial Award and Lecture; Vona **[Vol. 2: 5586]**
du Toit Registrar Prize; GT **[Vol. 2: 5705]**
Duberman Fellowships; Martin **[Vol. 1: 7139]**
Dubin Award for Outstanding Contributions to the Profession and the Academy; Professor Alvin **[Vol. 1: 901]**
Dubin Outstanding Pro Member Award; Howard S. **[Vol. 1: 15795]**
Dublin Award; Louis I. **[Vol. 1: 1358]**
Dublin Horse Show **[Vol. 2: 3918]**
Dublin Prize **[Vol. 2: 1111]**
Dubner Research Prize; Ronald **[Vol. 1: 9600]**
Duboff Award; Samuel J. **[Vol. 1: 8492]**
DuBois Career of Distinguished Scholarship Award; W.E.B. **[Vol. 1: 4541]**
Dubois - Debauque; Prix **[Vol. 2: 1628]**
DuBois Fabric of Unionism Art Competition; Jenifer J. **[Vol. 1: 13918]**
Dubois-Johnson-Frazier Award **[Vol. 1: 4537]**
Duchalais; Prix **[Vol. 2: 2156]**
Duck New Scholars Award; Steve **[Vol. 1: 9584]**
Duckworth Award; Muriel **[Vol. 1: 6860]**
Duculot; Prix Jules **[Vol. 2: 1607]**
Duddell Medal and Prize **[Vol. 2: 7907]**
Duden Preis; Konrad **[Vol. 2: 3130]**
Dudley Award for Bibliographic Instruction; Miriam **[Vol. 1: 5261]**
Dudley Educational Awards and Grants **[Vol. 1: 7932]**
Dudley Instruction Librarian Award; Miriam **[Vol. 1: 5261]**
Dudley Medal; Charles B. **[Vol. 1: 5593]**
Dudrick Research Scholar Award; Stanley J. **[Vol. 1: 4027]**
Duer Scholarship Award; A. O. **[Vol. 1: 11809]**
Dufresne Award; A.O. **[Vol. 1: 6609]**
Dufton Silver Medal **[Vol. 2: 7390]**
Dugan Distinguished Service Award; David J. **[Vol. 1: 17773]**
Duggan Medal; G. H. **[Vol. 1: 6915]**
Dugger Odontoglossum Award; Robert B. **[Vol. 1: 3073]**
Duisberg Gedachtnispreis; Carl **[Vol. 2: 2926]**
Duisberg Plakette; Carl **[Vol. 2: 2927]**
Dujarric de la Riviere; Prix Rene **[Vol. 2: 2199]**
Duke and Duchess of York Prize in Photography **[Vol. 1: 6128]**
Duke Lifeline Earthquake Engineering Award; Charles Martin **[Vol. 1: 4176]**
Duke of Edinburgh Award
 Governor General's Youth Award **[Vol. 2: 1347]**
 The Head of State Award Scheme - Ghana **[Vol 2: 3257]**

Duke of Edinburgh Conservation Medal **[Vol. 2: 6570]**
Duke of Edinburgh's Award **[Vol. 2: 7891]**
Duke of Edinburgh's Designer's Prize **[Vol. 2: 7513]**
Duke of Westminster Medal for Military Literature **[Vol. 2: 9138]**
Dulac; Prix **[Vol. 2: 2262]**
Dulux Australia Prize **[Vol. 2: 1112]**
Dumas Medal; Russell **[Vol. 2: 779]**
Dumfries Octocentenary Trophy **[Vol. 2: 9173]**
DuMont Citation; Allen B. **[Vol. 1: 14399]**
Dumont Gold Airship Medal; Santos **[Vol. 2: 6305]**
Dun & Bradstreet Award for Outstanding Service to Minority Business Communities **[Vol. 1: 14462]**
Dun & Bradstreet Public Librarian Support Award **[Vol. 1: 14469]**
Dunbar Medal; William **[Vol. 2: 2871]**
Dunbar Memorial Award; Walter **[Vol. 1: 3334]**
Duncan Legacy Award; Todd **[Vol. 1: 12630]**
Duncan Media Award; Cameron **[Vol. 1: 14528]**
Duncan Prize Lectureship; Henry **[Vol. 2: 9067]**
Duncan Scholarship; Ernest **[Vol. 1: 12223]**
Dunkelblau Scholarships; Ed **[Vol. 1: 4905]**
Dunkin Award **[Vol. 2: 7212]**
Dunlap Kidney Fund Grants; D.D. **[Vol. 1: 8767]**
Dunlap Lecture Award **[Vol. 1: 7207]**
Dunleavy Award **[Vol. 1: 13255]**
Dunlop Award; Weary **[Vol. 2: 469]**
Dunn Award for Excellence; James Clement **[Vol. 1: 16847]**
Dunn Award; John T. **[Vol. 2: 5570]**
Dunning Award; H. A. B. **[Vol. 1: 3132]**
Dunning Prize; John H. **[Vol. 1: 2367]**
Dunton Memorial Award; Loren **[Vol. 1: 9694]**
Duntov Mark of Excellence Award **[Vol. 1: 12143]**
Dupin; Prix Charles **[Vol. 2: 2263]**
Dupont; Fondation Octave **[Vol. 2: 1629]**
DuPont Minorities in Engineering Award **[Vol. 1: 3852]**
Dupont; Prix Lucien **[Vol. 2: 2264]**
Durand Lectureship **[Vol. 1: 2517]**
Durante Children's Fund Grants; Jimmy **[Vol. 1: 8768]**
Durnbaugh Starting Scholar Award; Donald **[Vol. 1: 7452]**
Durward Volunteer of the Year Award; Greg **[Vol. 1: 8285]**
Duseigneur; Prix Raoul **[Vol. 2: 2157]**
Dusmet World Championship Cup; Edith Oliver **[Vol. 1: 9990]**
Dussich Founder's Award; John J. P. **[Vol. 1: 12640]**
Dutch Design Awards **[Vol. 2: 4646]**
Dutens; Prix Joseph **[Vol. 2: 2265]**
Duthie Booksellers' Choice Award; Bill **[Vol. 1: 17741]**
Dutt Memorial Award; Raj Kristo **[Vol. 2: 3711]**
Duvall Shock Compression Science Award; George E. **[Vol. 1: 3205]**
Duvernay; Prix Ludger- **[Vol. 1: 14996]**
D.W. Griffith Award **[Vol. 1: 7882]**
Dwarka (Agriculture) Award **[Vol. 2: 3345]**
Dwight Prize in Chemistry **[Vol. 2: 1113]**
Dwight Prize in Genetics **[Vol. 2: 1114]**
Dwight Prize in Mathematical Statistics **[Vol. 2: 1115]**
Dwight Prize in Physics **[Vol. 2: 1116]**
Dwyer Memorial Award; Johnny **[Vol. 2: 3846]**
Dwyer Memorial Prize; Michael **[Vol. 2: 7954]**
Dwyer Scholarships; Peter **[Vol. 1: 6129]**
DYBWAD Humanitarian Award **[Vol. 1: 1422]**
Dyckman Award for Service; Herbert P. **[Vol. 1: 1488]**
Dyer Aviation Education Award; Janice Marie **[Vol. 1: 5722]**
Dyer Award; Edward C. **[Vol. 1: 10948]**
Dyke Memorial Award; Cornelius G. **[Vol. 1: 4457]**
Dykes Memorial Medal **[Vol. 1: 11044]**
Dymond Public Service Award; J. R. **[Vol. 1: 13586]**
d'Youville Honor Award; Marguerite **[Vol. 1: 7941]**
Dyrbye Mental Health Award; Marita **[Vol. 1: 6757]**
Dyson Award; Anne **[Vol. 1: 671]**
Dyson Lecture; Geoffrey **[Vol. 2: 3862]**
Dystel Prize for Multiple Sclerosis Research; John **[Vol. 1: 581]**
Dystel Prize; John **[Vol. 1: 12612]**
e-Business Solution Award **[Vol. 2: 4557]**
E-Gre **[Vol. 1: 7979]**
E. H. Trophy **[Vol. 2: 8816]**

Employer Recognition Award
American Board for Occupational Health Nurses **[Vol. 1: 1502]**
Canadian Nurses Association **[Vol 1: 6752]**
Oncology Nursing Certification Corporation **[Vol 1: 13524]**
EMS Award
Environmental Mutagen Society **[Vol. 1: 8162]**
European Membrane Society **[Vol 2: 2385]**
EMT of the Year Award **[Vol. 1: 11756]**
EMT-Paramedic Emergency Medical Service of the Year Award **[Vol. 1: 11759]**
EMT-Paramedic of the Year Award **[Vol. 1: 11764]**
Encore Award **[Vol. 2: 9247]**
Encouragement Award **[Vol. 2: 6513]**
Endeavor Student Writing Award **[Vol. 1: 10824]**
Endurance Rider Award **[Vol. 1: 5880]**
Endzelins Prize; Janis **[Vol. 2: 4436]**
Energy Efficiency Award **[Vol. 2: 1410]**
ENERGY GLOBE Awards **[Vol. 2: 1228]**
Energy Innovator Award **[Vol. 1: 3650]**
Energy Star Awards **[Vol. 1: 16885]**
Energy Star Combined Heat and Power Awards **[Vol. 1: 16886]**
Energy Systems Award **[Vol. 1: 2518]**
Engel Award; Marian **[Vol. 1: 18130]**
Engel/Findley Award **[Vol. 1: 18130]**
Engel Teacher Innovation Grant; Rose C. **[Vol. 1: 6090]**
Engelberger Awards; Joseph F. **[Vol. 1: 14567]**
Engelberger Robotics Awards; Joseph F. **[Vol. 1: 14567]**
Engelbrecht International Achievement Award; Richard S. **[Vol. 1: 17703]**
Engell Prize; Hans-Jurgen **[Vol. 2: 6441]**
Engineer of the Year
International System Safety Society **[Vol. 1: 10419]**
South African Society for Professional Engineers **[Vol 2: 5719]**
Engineer of the Year Award **[Vol. 1: 2519]**
Engineering Achievement Award
American Institute of Mining, Metallurgical, and Petroleum Engineers **[Vol. 1: 2677]**
IEEE Photonics Society **[Vol 1: 9105]**
Zimbabwe Institute of Engineers **[Vol 2: 9577]**
Engineering Achievement Awards **[Vol. 1: 11672]**
Engineering Achievement in Radio **[Vol. 1: 11672]**
Engineering Achievement in Television **[Vol. 1: 11672]**
Engineering Ambassador Award **[Vol. 2: 6762]**
Engineering Award **[Vol. 1: 11672]**
Engineering Award for Connecting Professional Practice and Education **[Vol. 1: 12183]**
Engineering Dissertation Fellowships **[Vol. 1: 1393]**
Engineering Education Excellence Award **[Vol. 1: 12874]**
Engineering Excellence Awards
American Council of Engineering Companies **[Vol. 1: 1898]**
Asia-Pacific Broadcasting Union **[Vol 2: 4523]**
Engineering/Geology Scholarship **[Vol. 1: 14573]**
Engineering Heritage Award **[Vol. 2: 7553]**
Engineering Journalism Award **[Vol. 1: 1148]**
Engineering Manager of the Year Award **[Vol. 1: 3890]**
Engineering Materials Achievement Award **[Vol. 1: 4835]**
Engineering Medal **[Vol. 1: 14208]**
Engineering Meetings Board Outstanding Oral Presentation Award **[Vol. 1: 15504]**
Engineering/Technology Achievement Awards **[Vol. 1: 8702]**
Engineers Canada Awards
Engineers Canada **[Vol. 1: 8124]**
Engineers Canada **[Vol. 1: 8126]**
Engineers Canada **[Vol. 1: 8127]**
Engineers Canada **[Vol. 1: 8128]**
Engineers Canada **[Vol. 1: 8129]**
Engineers Canada **[Vol. 1: 8130]**
England Memorial Intermediate Haydn and Mozart Scholarship; Frances **[Vol. 1: 14730]**
Engleheart Cup **[Vol. 2: 8817]**
Engleman Award; Finis **[Vol. 2: 3294]**
Engler Gold Medal **[Vol. 2: 1254]**
Engler Silver Medal **[Vol. 2: 1255]**

English Award; Charles R. **[Vol. 1: 1470]**
English Badminton Award **[Vol. 2: 6867]**
English-Speaking Competition **[Vol. 2: 4506]**
Engqvists stipendium; Gun och Olof **[Vol. 2: 6200]**
Engstrom Award; Victor **[Vol. 1: 14769]**
Enhancement of Animal Welfare Award **[Vol. 1: 15850]**
Enlisted Essay Contest **[Vol. 1: 17008]**
Enners Outstanding Player Awards; Lt. Raymond J. **[Vol. 1: 16976]**
Ennes Scholarships; Harold E. **[Vol. 1: 15568]**
Ennis Award; Peter **[Vol. 1: 6640]**
Ennor Manufacturing Technology Award; William T. **[Vol. 1: 4386]**
Enright TESOL Interest Section Service Award; D. Scott **[Vol. 1: 16393]**
Enterostomal Therapist Recognition Award **[Vol. 1: 16645]**
Enterprise of the Year **[Vol. 2: 1372]**
Enterprises Award of Merit **[Vol. 1: 36]**
Entertainer of the Year **[Vol. 1: 9732]**
Entertainment and Media Project Award **[Vol. 2: 7009]**
Enthusiast of the Year **[Vol. 1: 12962]**
Entomology Journal Award; Agricultural and Forest **[Vol. 2: 8768]**
Entomology Journal Award; Ecological **[Vol. 2: 8769]**
Entrepreneur of the Year **[Vol. 2: 8326]**
Entrepreneur of the Year **[Vol. 1: 9948]**
Entrepreneur of the Year Award **[Vol. 1: 6161]**
Entrepreneurial Spirit Award **[Vol. 1: 7749]**
Entrepreneurial Success Award **[Vol. 1: 17104]**
Entrepreneurship Education Awards **[Vol. 1: 16721]**
Entrepreneurship Educator of the Year Award **[Vol. 1: 16722]**
Entrepreneurship Fellow Award **[Vol. 1: 5799]**
Entry Films Competition **[Vol. 1: 5837]**
Environment, Agriculture, and Rural Development Award **[Vol. 2: 3614]**
Environment and Energy Achievement Awards **[Vol. 1: 2187]**
Environment Award
Australian Petroleum Production and Exploration Association **[Vol. 2: 494]**
International Motorcycling Federation **[Vol 2: 6407]**
Namibia Nature Foundation **[Vol 2: 4628]**
World Association of Non-Governmental Organizations **[Vol 1: 18022]**
Environment, Health and Safety Award **[Vol. 1: 15757]**
Environment Medal **[Vol. 2: 9270]**
Environment Prize **[Vol. 2: 9003]**
Environment, Sustainability and Energy Forum Early Career Award **[Vol. 2: 9004]**
Environmental Achievement Award
Canadian Golf Superintendents Association **[Vol. 1: 6532]**
International Erosion Control Association **[Vol 1: 9891]**
Environmental Achievement Awards **[Vol. 1: 315]**
Environmental Alliance Award **[Vol. 1: 14866]**
Environmental and Social Responsibility Award **[Vol. 1: 14277]**
Environmental Award
International Hotel and Restaurant Association **[Vol. 2: 6398]**
Nursery and Garden Industry Australia **[Vol 2: 913]**
Sri Lanka Association for the Advancement of Science **[Vol 2: 6128]**
Environmental Awards
Banksia Environmental Foundation **[Vol. 2: 628]**
Oxford Preservation Trust **[Vol 2: 8440]**
Environmental Champion Award **[Vol. 1: 9874]**
Environmental Conservation Distinguished Service Award **[Vol. 1: 2676]**
Environmental Education Award **[Vol. 1: 15625]**
Environmental Education Award **[Vol. 1: 12324]**
Environmental Excellence Award **[Vol. 1: 12734]**
Environmental Excellence in Transportation Award E2T **[Vol. 1: 15505]**
Environmental Improvement Awards Program **[Vol. 1: 14238]**
Environmental Industry Associations' Hall of Fame Award **[Vol. 1: 17692]**

Environmental Legislator of the Year **[Vol. 1: 14512]**
Environmental Organization of the Year **[Vol. 2: 1679]**
Environmental Packaging Awards **[Vol. 2: 5029]**
Environmental Prize **[Vol. 2: 4431]**
Environmental Quality Research Award **[Vol. 1: 4102]**
Environmental Reporter Award **[Vol. 2: 9574]**
Environmental Science Award **[Vol. 1: 183]**
Environmental Stewardship Award
American Sheep Industry Association **[Vol. 1: 3737]**
Society for Freshwater Science **[Vol 1: 15078]**
Envision Award **[Vol. 1: 10401]**
EOS Prize **[Vol. 2: 2845]**
Eotvos Award; Lorand **[Vol. 2: 4677]**
Eotvos Medal; Lorand **[Vol. 2: 3361]**
EPIE Award **[Vol. 1: 7093]**
Epilepsy Foundation Awards **[Vol. 1: 8166]**
Epilepsy Research Award for Outstanding Contributions to the Pharmacology of Antiepileptic Drugs **[Vol. 1: 4034]**
Epilepsy Research Awards **[Vol. 1: 2085]**
Episteme Award **[Vol. 1: 14897]**
Eppendorf and Science Prize for Neurobiology **[Vol. 1: 988]**
Eppendorf Award for Young European Investigators **[Vol. 2: 2791]**
EPSC Award **[Vol. 2: 7629]**
Epson Aerial Photographer of the Year **[Vol. 1: 14181]**
Epstein Award **[Vol. 1: 3734]**
Epstein Award; Dena **[Vol. 1: 11318]**
Epstein Award for Technical Programming; Herb **[Vol. 1: 2615]**
Epstein Foundation Awards in Creative Writing; Norma **[Vol. 1: 17358]**
Equal Employment Opportunity Award **[Vol. 1: 16848]**
Equal Employment Opportunity Awards **[Vol. 1: 16832]**
Equal Employment Opportunity/Diversity Award **[Vol. 1: 16789]**
Equal Employment Opportunity Medal **[Vol. 1: 11473]**
Equal Opportunity/Affirmative Action Exemplary Practice Award **[Vol. 1: 4047]**
Equal Opportunity Award **[Vol. 1: 10797]**
Equal Opportunity Day Award **[Vol. 1: 13015]**
Equality Award **[Vol. 1: 2779]**
Equator Prize **[Vol. 1: 8185]**
Equine Mileage Program **[Vol. 1: 2062]**
Equine Research Centre Award **[Vol. 1: 8187]**
Equipment Design Award **[Vol. 1: 12459]**
Equity and Diversity Award **[Vol. 1: 4997]**
"Eqvalan Duo" Equine Thesis of the Year Award **[Vol. 2: 8629]**
Erasmus Award; Desiderius **[Vol. 2: 4678]**
ERDAS Award for Best Scientific Paper in Remote Sensing **[Vol. 1: 4865]**
ERDAS Internship **[Vol. 1: 4866]**
Erehwon Award for Innovative HR Initiatives **[Vol. 2: 3474]**
Ergonomics Development Award **[Vol. 2: 6585]**
Erickson Award; Bonnie **[Vol. 1: 8914]**
Erickson Continuous Service Award; James K. **[Vol. 1: 37]**
Ericson Award; Dick **[Vol. 1: 16216]**
Ericsson Medal; John **[Vol. 1: 4516]**
Erikson Early Career Award; Erik H. **[Vol. 1: 10342]**
Erikssons stipendium; Lydia och Herman **[Vol. 2: 6201]**
Erlbaum Awards in Cognitive Science **[Vol. 1: 14291]**
Ernst-Kuntze Prize **[Vol. 2: 2908]**
Ernst-von-Bergmann-Plakette **[Vol. 2: 2964]**
Errera; Prix Leo **[Vol. 2: 1630]**
Erskine Award; Ralph **[Vol. 2: 6156]**
Ertegun Award; Ahmet **[Vol. 1: 14569]**
Esau Award; Katherine **[Vol. 1: 5936]**
ESB Research Award **[Vol. 2: 4076]**
Eschenbach Best EMJ Journal Paper Award; Ted **[Vol. 1: 3891]**
ESDR Travel Grants **[Vol. 2: 6288]**
Eshelman Outstanding Campus Adviser Award; David L. **[Vol. 1: 15796]**
ESHO-BSD Award **[Vol. 2: 4711]**
Esidimeni Award; Life **[Vol. 2: 5587]**

Espenschade Memorial Scholarship; Park W. **[Vol. 1: 9318]**

Espirito Santo Trophy **[Vol. 1: 9959]**

Esposito Backbone Award; Bill **[Vol. 1: 7379]**

ESPY Awards **[Vol. 1: 8189]**

ESRI Award for Best Scientific Paper in Geographic Information Systems **[Vol. 1: 4867]**

Essar Gold Medal **[Vol. 2: 3593]**

Essay Competition on Women in Society **[Vol. 2: 6080]**

Essay Contest for Professionals in Rehabilitation **[Vol. 1: 1864]**

Essay Medal **[Vol. 2: 9239]**

Essay Prize in Informal Logic/Critical Thinking/ Argumentation Theory **[Vol. 1: 7131]**

Essey Award; Shelia **[Vol. 1: 582]**

Essig Award; Otto **[Vol. 1: 17462]**

ESSO Award **[Vol. 2: 781]**

Established Investigator Award **[Vol. 1: 11368]**

Established Investigator Grant **[Vol. 1: 14791]**

Estes Prize; J. Worth **[Vol. 1: 998]**

Estlander Prize **[Vol. 2: 2068]**

Estonian Concrete Construction of the Year **[Vol. 2: 2034]**

Estrade-Delcros; Prix **[Vol. 2: 2158]**

Estridge, Jr. Award; Capt. W. W. **[Vol. 1: 17181]**

Estrin Award; David **[Vol. 1: 6330]**

Etancelin; Prix Leon-Alexandre **[Vol. 2: 2200]**

ET&C Best Student Paper Award **[Vol. 1: 15626]**

ETG Innovation Award **[Vol. 2: 6493]**

Ethics and Professionalism Awards **[Vol. 1: 1735]**

Ethics in Journalism Awards **[Vol. 1: 15797]**

Ethics Prize **[Vol. 2: 513]**

Ethnic Minority Mentorship Award **[Vol. 1: 3512]**

ETR&D Young Scholar Award **[Vol. 1: 5007]**

ETS Award for Distinguished Service to Measurement **[Vol. 1: 8025]**

Etter Early Career Award; Margaret C. **[Vol. 1: 1953]**

Etter Student Lecturer Award; Margaret C. **[Vol. 1: 1954]**

Ettlingen International Competition for Young Pianists **[Vol. 2: 3142]**

Etz Chaim (Tree of Life) Award **[Vol. 1: 12573]**

Eu Achievement Award; March Fong **[Vol. 1: 12620]**

Eubank Services Award; Maj. Gen. Eugene L. **[Vol. 1: 13643]**

Eubanks Award; Jackie **[Vol. 1: 2794]**

EuCheMS Lecture **[Vol. 2: 1431]**

EULAR Stene Prize **[Vol. 2: 6279]**

Eure Ambassador of Hospitality Award; Thad and Alice **[Vol. 1: 12775]**

EURO Doctoral Dissertation Award **[Vol. 2: 1408]**

Euro Effie Awards **[Vol. 2: 1438]**

Euro-Med Award for Dialogue between Cultures **[Vol. 2: 2007]**

EuroBest Awards **[Vol. 2: 7576]**

EUROCALL Research Award **[Vol. 2: 7586]**

Eurocopter Golden Hour Award **[Vol. 1: 8890]**

Euroliver Foundation Award **[Vol. 2: 7634]**

Europa Nostra Awards; European Union Prize for Cultural Heritage/ **[Vol. 2: 4672]**

Europe Impresa Award **[Vol. 2: 3750]**

Europe Prize **[Vol. 2: 2347]**

European 1600 Cup for Autocross **[Vol. 2: 2504]**

European Academic Tax Thesis Award **[Vol. 2: 4688]**

European Archaeological Heritage Prize **[Vol. 2: 1922]**

European Award for Logistics Excellence **[Vol. 2: 1482]**

European Awards for Quality and Excellence in Directory Publishing **[Vol. 2: 1440]**

European Banker of the Year **[Vol. 2: 3055]**

European Baseball Championships **[Vol. 2: 2755]**

European Baseball Cup **[Vol. 2: 2756]**

European Bridge Champion **[Vol. 2: 4066]**

European Bristol-Myers Squibb Prevention Award in Psychiatry **[Vol. 2: 2401]**

European Bursaries for TV Film Writing **[Vol. 2: 6275]**

European Business Awards for the Environment **[Vol. 2: 1460]**

European Corrosion Medal **[Vol. 2: 2825]**

European Design Awards **[Vol. 2: 3283]**

European Diploma **[Vol. 2: 2348]**

European Diploma of Protected Areas **[Vol. 2: 2349]**

European Disposables and Nonwovens Association Awards **[Vol. 2: 1473]**

European Drag Racing Championship **[Vol. 2: 2504]**

European Drug Prevention Prize **[Vol. 2: 2350]**

European Film Academy Short Film Award **[Vol. 2: 5157]**

European Film Awards **[Vol. 2: 2831]**

European Football Supporters Award **[Vol. 2: 1422]**

European Grand Prize for TV Scenarios **[Vol. 2: 6275]**

European Historic Rally Trophy **[Vol. 2: 2504]**

European Journalism Prize **[Vol. 2: 1400]**

European Lifetime Achievement Award in Environmental Economics **[Vol. 2: 4059]**

European Lipid Awards **[Vol. 2: 2820]**

European Parking Award **[Vol. 2: 2847]**

European Postgraduate Grants **[Vol. 2: 2857]**

European Practitioner Achievement Award in Applying Environmental Economic **[Vol. 2: 4060]**

European Responsible Care Awards **[Vol. 2: 1455]**

European Shopping Centre Awards **[Vol. 1: 9838]**

European Solar Prizes **[Vol. 2: 2873]**

European Sponsorship Awards **[Vol. 2: 7650]**

European Sportsman and Sportswoman of the Year **[Vol. 2: 5385]**

European Standard Parking Award **[Vol. 2: 2848]**

European Steel Design Awards **[Vol. 2: 1465]**

European Student Dietitian of the Year **[Vol. 2: 2829]**

European Surfing Championships - Open Champion **[Vol. 2: 7654]**

European Sustainable Chemistry Award **[Vol. 2: 1432]**

European Trophy for Historic Sports Car **[Vol. 2: 2504]**

European Truck Racing Cup **[Vol. 2: 2504]**

European Union Prize for Cultural Heritage/Europa Nostra Awards **[Vol. 2: 4672]**

European Urban and Regional Planning Awards **[Vol. 2: 1471]**

Europhysics Prize **[Vol. 2: 2389]**

Eurosense Award **[Vol. 2: 8538]**

EUROTHERM Young Scientist Prizes and Awards **[Vol. 2: 4068]**

Eurovision Dance Contest **[Vol. 2: 6272]**

Eurovision for Young Dancers **[Vol. 2: 6273]**

Eurovision Song Contest **[Vol. 2: 6274]**

Euverard Innovation Award **[Vol. 1: 5595]**

Eva Award; William J. **[Vol. 1: 6580]**

Evans Award in Chemical Engineering Practice; Lawrence B. **[Vol. 2: 2616]**

Evans Award; Jefferson **[Vol. 1: 5867]**

Evans Award; John F. **[Vol. 1: 8580]**

Evans Award; John K. **[Vol. 1: 9541]**

Evans Award; Roche Diagnostics Alice C. **[Vol. 1: 3984]**

Evans Non-Fiction Prize; Hubert **[Vol. 1: 17743]**

Evans Trophy; Edward S. **[Vol. 1: 14970]**

Evening News Awards **[Vol. 2: 7529]**

Events of the Year **[Vol. 1: 17482]**

Everett Award; Woody **[Vol. 1: 3854]**

Everett Distinguished Life Service Award; Robinson O. **[Vol. 1: 10597]**

Ewald Prize **[Vol. 2: 8248]**

Ewing Layman Award; James **[Vol. 1: 15831]**

Ewing Lecturer; James **[Vol. 1: 15832]**

Ewing Medal; James Alfred **[Vol. 2: 7982]**

Ewing Medal; Maurice **[Vol. 1: 2232]**

Ex Libris Student Writing Award **[Vol. 1: 10824]**

Examination Prizes

    American Guild of Organists **[Vol. 1: 2266]**

    Botswana Institute of Bankers **[Vol 2: 1730]**

EXCEL Awards **[Vol. 1: 5191]**

Excel Awards for Professional Chapters **[Vol. 1: 15102]**

Excellence 200 Awards **[Vol. 1: 17021]**

Excellence Award

    Australian Library and Information Association **[Vol. 2: 437]**

    Black Entertainment and Sports Lawyers Association **[Vol. 1: 5872]**

    Direct Selling Association - United Kingdom **[Vol 2: 7519]**

    International Council of Graphic Design Associations **[Vol 1: 9835]**

    Society of Research Administrators **[Vol 1: 15822]**

Excellence Award for Best Accounting Graduate **[Vol. 2: 4547]**

Excellence Award for Best Paper **[Vol. 2: 4668]**

Excellence Award for Most Outstanding CPA Student **[Vol. 2: 4548]**

Excellence Award for Music Libraries **[Vol. 2: 8085]**

Excellence Award in Global Economic Affairs **[Vol. 2: 3108]**

Excellence Awards

    Association of Canadian Community Colleges **[Vol. 1: 5239]**

    Association of Event Organisers **[Vol 2: 6823]**

    British Printing Industries Federation **[Vol 2: 7175]**

    Indian Footwear Components Manufacturers Association **[Vol 2: 3580]**

    Information and Communications Technology Society of Trinidad and Tobago **[Vol 2: 6621]**

    Join Hands Day **[Vol 1: 10584]**

    Mortgage and Finance Association of Australia **[Vol 2: 879]**

    National Electrical and Communications Association **[Vol 2: 889]**

    Pakistan Advertising Association **[Vol 2: 5197]**

    Solid Waste Association of North America **[Vol 1: 15947]**

    Visitor Industry Partnership **[Vol 2: 1706]**

    World Petroleum Council **[Vol 2: 9490]**

Excellence in Academic Libraries Award **[Vol. 1: 5263]**

Excellence in Advanced Practice Award **[Vol. 1: 15742]**

Excellence in Advanced Practice Nursing Award **[Vol. 1: 1233]**

Excellence in Aerospace Education Award **[Vol. 2: 3440]**

Excellence in Alcohol and Drug Media Reporting **[Vol. 2: 331]**

Excellence in Art Education Award **[Vol. 1: 6016]**

Excellence in Aviation Education Award **[Vol. 1: 8531]**

Excellence in Blood and Marrow Transplantation Award **[Vol. 1: 13536]**

Excellence in Botany Award **[Vol. 1: 10632]**

Excellence in Building and Construction Awards **[Vol. 2: 871]**

Excellence in Building Awards

    Master Builders Association - Newcastle **[Vol. 2: 853]**

    Master Builders Association of the ACT **[Vol 2: 855]**

Excellence in Cancer Nursing Research Award **[Vol. 1: 13537]**

Excellence in Cancer Prevention and Early Detection Award **[Vol. 1: 13538]**

Excellence in Care of the Older Adult with Cancer Award **[Vol. 1: 13539]**

Excellence in Caring Practices Award **[Vol. 1: 1122]**

Excellence in Catering Award **[Vol. 2: 7333]**

Excellence in Clinical Practice **[Vol. 1: 1234]**

Excellence in Clinical Practice Award **[Vol. 1: 15743]**

Excellence in Clinical Research **[Vol. 1: 8822]**

Excellence in Communication Award **[Vol. 1: 14537]**

Excellence in Communication Leadership (EXCEL) Award **[Vol. 1: 9626]**

Excellence in Communications Award **[Vol. 1: 8891]**

Excellence in Communications Awards **[Vol. 1: 11724]**

Excellence in Construction Awards

    Associated Builders and Contractors **[Vol. 1: 4881]**

    Master Builders Association - New South Wales **[Vol 2: 850]**

    Master Builders Association - Victoria **[Vol 2: 861]**

    Master Builders Association - Western Australia **[Vol 2: 864]**

Excellence in Creating Healthy Sporting Communities **[Vol. 2: 331]**

Excellence in Dementia Care Award **[Vol. 2: 7333]**

Excellence in Design **[Vol. 2: 2592]**

Excellence in Education Award

    National Association for College Admission Counseling **[Vol. 1: 11564]**

    Society of Pediatric Nurses **[Vol 1: 15744]**

Excellence in Education Award

    American Society of Cytopathology **[Vol. 1: 4279]**

Minerals, Metals, and Materials Society **[Vol 1: 11185]**

National Association for Interpretation **[Vol 1: 11587]**

Precast/Prestressed Concrete Institute **[Vol 1: 14130]**

Project Management Institute **[Vol 1: 14258]**

Society of Wetland Scientists **[Vol 1: 15883]**

Society of Wood Science and Technology **[Vol 1: 15904]**

Soil and Water Conservation Society **[Vol 1: 15923]**

Standards Engineering Society **[Vol 1: 16247]**

Fellow Designation

American Association for Agricultural Education **[Vol. 1: 872]**

Illuminating Engineering Society of North America **[Vol 1: 9155]**

Fellow Grade Membership **[Vol. 1: 3855]**

Fellow Grade of Membership

Society of Automotive Engineers **[Vol 1: 15508]**

Society of Women Engineers **[Vol 1: 15899]**

Fellow Honor **[Vol. 1: 11351]**

Fellow Member Award **[Vol. 1: 4649]**

Fellow of ABET Award **[Vol. 1: 28]**

Fellow of Division 7 of APA **[Vol. 1: 3406]**

Fellow of ESA **[Vol. 1: 8146]**

Fellow of Indian Phytopathological Society **[Vol. 2: 3693]**

Fellow of ISIR **[Vol. 2: 3407]**

Fellow of the Academy of Professional Reporters **[Vol. 1: 12263]**

Fellow of the American Association of Anatomists **[Vol. 1: 1022]**

Fellow of the American Meteorological Society **[Vol. 1: 2906]**

Fellow of the American Society of Agronomy **[Vol. 1: 4103]**

Fellow of the Association **[Vol. 1: 13478]**

Fellow of The Athenaeum **[Vol. 1: 5663]**

Fellow of the Australian Institute of Agricultural Science and Technology FAIAST **[Vol. 2: 378]**

Fellow of the CPA **[Vol. 1: 6812]**

Fellow of the Crop Science Society of America **[Vol. 1: 7763]**

Fellow of the CSME **[Vol. 1: 6916]**

Fellow of the Institute **[Vol. 1: 6581]**

Fellow of the Metallurgical Society **[Vol. 1: 11185]**

Fellow of the National Genealogical Society **[Vol. 1: 12449]**

Fellow of the Phytopathological Society of Japan **[Vol. 2: 4315]**

Fellow of the Royal Academy of Dance **[Vol. 2: 8574]**

Fellow of the Society

Electrochemical Society **[Vol. 1: 8056]**

International Society for Magnetic Resonance in Medicine **[Vol 1: 10181]**

Society of Plastics Engineers **[Vol 1: 15785]**

Southern African Society for Plant Pathology **[Vol 2: 5743]**

Fellow of the Society

AVS Science and Technology Society **[Vol. 1: 5729]**

Society of Nematologists **[Vol 1: 15723]**

Fellow of the Society Award **[Vol. 1: 10010]**

Fellow of the Special Libraries Association **[Vol. 1: 16100]**

Fellow Recognition Award **[Vol. 1: 9952]**

Fellows and Honorary Members **[Vol. 1: 11067]**

Fellows Award

Nature Saskatchewan **[Vol. 1: 13112]**

Strategic and Competitive Intelligence Professionals **[Vol 1: 16299]**

Virginia Recreation and Park Society **[Vol 1: 17604]**

Fellow's Basic Research Award **[Vol. 1: 15256]**

Fellow's Clinical Research Award **[Vol. 1: 15257]**

Fellows of the American Statistical Association **[Vol. 1: 4559]**

Fellows of the Association **[Vol. 1: 11687]**

Fellows of the Association **[Vol. 1: 4544]**

Fellows of the Biophysical Society **[Vol. 1: 5849]**

Fellows of the Canadian Nuclear Society **[Vol. 1: 6744]**

Fellows of the Metallurgical Society of AIME **[Vol. 1: 11185]**

Fellows of the SID **[Vol. 1: 15150]**

Fellows of the Society **[Vol. 1: 15798]**

Fellows Program

American Council on Education **[Vol. 1: 1920]**

Arctic Institute of North America **[Vol 1: 4775]**

Fellows Program Award **[Vol. 1: 5505]**

Fellowship Award **[Vol. 2: 6418]**

Fellowship Award

American Academy of Periodontology **[Vol. 1: 719]**

American Society of Sanitary Engineering **[Vol 1: 4514]**

Fellowship Awards **[Vol. 2: 6631]**

Fellowship Competition **[Vol. 2: 6386]**

Fellowship in Aerospace History **[Vol. 1: 2371]**

Fellowship in Division 16 **[Vol. 1: 3492]**

Fellowship International Award **[Vol. 2: 5668]**

Fellowship of the Australian College of Educators **[Vol. 2: 262]**

Fellowship of the Australian Society for Music Education **[Vol. 2: 550]**

Fellowship of the Australian Society of Archivists **[Vol. 2: 564]**

Fellowship of the City and Guilds of London Institute **[Vol. 2: 7431]**

Fellowship of the Guild of Television Cameramen **[Vol. 2: 7774]**

Fellowship of the Institute of Australian Geographers **[Vol. 2: 753]**

Fellowship of the Pharmacy Society of South Africa **[Vol. 2: 5593]**

Fellowship Program **[Vol. 1: 1397]**

Fellowship to Faculty Transition Award **[Vol. 1: 2201]**

Fellowships **[Vol. 2: 996]**

Fellowships for Creative and Performing Artists and Writers **[Vol. 1: 832]**

Fellowships in Clinical Pharmacology **[Vol. 1: 6986]**

Feltrinelli Prizes; Antonio **[Vol. 2: 4022]**

Female Athlete of the Year **[Vol. 1: 16167]**

Female Vocalist of the Year **[Vol. 1: 9732]**

Femina Film Prize **[Vol. 2: 2724]**

Feminist Activist Award **[Vol. 1: 15912]**

Feminist Lecturer Award **[Vol. 1: 15913]**

Feminist Theory and Gender Studies Graduate Student Paper Award **[Vol. 1: 10381]**

Fenderbosch Leadership Award; Henry **[Vol. 1: 11927]**

Fenn Award **[Vol. 1: 10671]**

Fenner Award; Frank **[Vol. 2: 544]**

Fenner Medal **[Vol. 2: 173]**

Fennia Prize **[Vol. 2: 2069]**

Fenno Award; Richard **[Vol. 1: 3302]**

Fenton Medal **[Vol. 2: 8898]**

Fentress Memorial Award for Editorial Excellence; H. M. **[Vol. 1: 16443]**

Fenyo Student Paper Award; Jane K. **[Vol. 1: 81]**

Ferguson Award; David **[Vol. 2: 748]**

Ferguson Award; Diana **[Vol. 1: 6783]**

Ferguson Award; Virginia **[Vol. 1: 14868]**

Ferguson Lecture Series; Phil M. **[Vol. 1: 1842]**

Ferguson Memorial Award; Elmer **[Vol. 1: 8960]**

Ferguson; Premio Massey **[Vol. 2: 30]**

Ferguson Young Technical Author Medal; Cedric K. **[Vol. 1: 15755]**

Fergusson Excellence in Pediatric Hematology/Oncology Nursing Education Award; Jean **[Vol. 1: 5451]**

Fergusson Excellence in Pediatric Hematology/Oncology Nursing Practice Award; Jean **[Vol. 1: 5452]**

Ferin Award; Juraj **[Vol. 2: 3079]**

Fermi Award; Enrico **[Vol. 1: 16809]**

Fern Award; Harold **[Vol. 2: 6707]**

Fern National Trophy; Harold **[Vol. 2: 6708]**

Fernandez Award; Andy **[Vol. 1: 17174]**

Fernandez Trophy; Anthony **[Vol. 1: 17174]**

Fernbach Memorial Award; Sidney **[Vol. 1: 9058]**

Ferroelectrics Recognition Award **[Vol. 1: 9043]**

Fersman Prize; A.Y. **[Vol. 2: 5797]**

Ferst Award; Monie A. **[Vol. 1: 14905]**

Feser Award; Leo **[Vol. 1: 8715]**

Fessenden Award; Reginald **[Vol. 1: 15648]**

Fessenden Student Prize in Underwater Acoustics **[Vol. 1: 6170]**

Festival Awards **[Vol. 1: 1111]**

Festival Awards for Literature **[Vol. 2: 1044]**

Festival dei Popoli **[Vol. 2: 4080]**

Festival du Film Court de Villeurbanne **[Vol. 2: 2415]**

Festival du Nouveau Cinema de Montreal **[Vol. 1: 11254]**

Festival Internacional de Cinema do Porto - Fantasporto **[Vol. 2: 5424]**

Festival International du Court Metrage de Clermont-Ferrand **[Vol. 2: 2602]**

Festival International du Film d'Amiens **[Vol. 2: 2309]**

Festival International du Film d'Aventure de la Plagne **[Vol. 2: 2463]**

Festival International du Film de Vol Libre **[Vol. 2: 2420]**

Festival International du Film Fantastique, de Science-Fiction, et Thriller de Bruxelles **[Vol. 2: 1417]**

Festival International du Film sur l'Art Montreal **[Vol. 1: 9942]**

Festival Internazionale Cinema Giovani **[Vol. 2: 4042]**

Festival National du Court Metrage de Clermont-Ferrand **[Vol. 2: 2603]**

Festival of American Community Theatre **[Vol. 1: 1111]**

Festival of Asian Children's Art **[Vol. 2: 4301]**

Festival of the Americas **[Vol. 1: 18093]**

Festival of the Wagging Tails Dog Show **[Vol. 2: 6648]**

Fetch Award; Tom **[Vol. 1: 13781]**

Fevre-Deumier de Ports; Prix Le **[Vol. 2: 2267]**

FHA Culinary Challenge **[Vol. 2: 5973]**

FHA International Salon Culinaire **[Vol. 2: 5973]**

FIA Intercontinental Formula 3 Cup **[Vol. 2: 2504]**

FIA Marathon Trophy **[Vol. 2: 2504]**

FIA World Cup for Cross Country Rallies **[Vol. 2: 2504]**

Fiala Cultural Heritage Award; Stephen **[Vol. 1: 7798]**

FIAP Medals **[Vol. 1: 8782]**

Fiction Book Award **[Vol. 1: 17685]**

Fiction Book of the Year Award **[Vol. 1: 6352]**

Fiction Contest **[Vol. 1: 18123]**

FIDE Master **[Vol. 2: 3316]**

FIDOF Diploma **[Vol. 1: 9922]**

Field and Joe L. Franklin Award for Outstanding Achievement in Mass Spectrometry; Frank H. **[Vol. 1: 1638]**

Field Award; Crosby **[Vol. 1: 4322]**

Field Awards **[Vol. 1: 15941]**

Field Day Award **[Vol. 2: 1948]**

Field Maintenance Award **[Vol. 1: 1477]**

Field of the Year Awards **[Vol. 1: 16217]**

Fieldgate Trophy; Norm **[Vol. 1: 6506]**

Fieldwork and Recording Awards **[Vol. 2: 6769]**

Fieldwork Award **[Vol. 2: 6769]**

Fife Memorial Award; Mary Peery **[Vol. 1: 12865]**

FiFi Awards **[Vol. 1: 8455]**

Fifteen Year Service Award **[Vol. 1: 17578]**

Fifty Books of the Year **[Vol. 1: 2659]**

Fifty-Year Award **[Vol. 1: 8339]**

Fifty Year Club **[Vol. 1: 6611]**

Fighting Congressional Frosh **[Vol. 1: 16749]**

FIGO/Ernst Schering Research Foundation Fellowship **[Vol. 2: 1742]**

Fiji Chess Championships **[Vol. 2: 2062]**

Fiji Day Open Chess Championship **[Vol. 2: 2062]**

Filene Student Travel Award; Adele **[Vol. 1: 7622]**

Filipovic Award; Ivan **[Vol. 2: 1879]**

Filley Memorial Awards for Excellence in Respiratory Physiology and Medicine; Giles F. **[Vol. 1: 3253]**

Film Award for the Best Commercial Film **[Vol. 1: 4734]**

Film Critics Award

Norwegian International Film Festival **[Vol. 2: 5144]**

The Norwegian Short Film Festival **[Vol 2: 5150]**

Film Festival Award **[Vol. 2: 8138]**

Film Festival Awards **[Vol. 1: 4734]**

Film Finishing Fund Grants **[Vol. 1: 17939]**

Film of the Year Award **[Vol. 1: 7953]**

Film Prize **[Vol. 1: 1977]**

Film Scholarships **[Vol. 1: 14156]**

Filmmaker Award **[Vol. 1: 7936]**

Filmpolitiets Short Film Award **[Vol. 2: 5151]**

Filson Fellowships **[Vol. 1: 8362]**

Focus on Affordability Awards [Vol. 1: 6042]

Focus on World Cinema [Vol. 1: 11258]

Foerderpreis der Werner-Sunkel-Stiftung [Vol. 2: 2980]

Foerster Memorial Lecture; Theodor [Vol. 2: 2919]

Fofonoff Award; Nicholas P. [Vol. 1: 2907]

FOI Award [Vol. 1: 10495]

Fok Prize; V.A. [Vol. 2: 5799]

Folch-Pi Award; Jordi [Vol. 1: 3995]

Foley Injury Prevention Leadership Award; Barbara A. [Vol. 1: 8090]

Follett International Teacher-Librarian of the Year Award [Vol. 1: 6216]

Follett School Librarian of the Year Award [Vol. 1: 4781]

Follo Upper Peninsula History Award; Charles [Vol. 1: 8940]

Foltz Award; Clara Shortridge [Vol. 1: 12585]

Folz Memorial Award [Vol. 1: 12144]

FON Achievement Certificates [Vol. 1: 13590]

FON Conservation Award [Vol. 1: 13588]

FON Conservation Trophy [Vol. 1: 13587]

FON Distinguished Service Award [Vol. 1: 13586]

Fonda Young Playwrights Project; Henry [Vol. 1: 17622]

Fonde par l'Etat; Prix [Vol. 2: 2201]

Fones Award; Alfred C. [Vol. 1: 2009]

Fons-Melicocq; Prix de la [Vol. 2: 2159]

Fontannes; Prix [Vol. 2: 2455]

Food and Farming Awards [Vol. 2: 6981]

Food & Hotel Asia Competition
American Culinary Federation [Vol. 1: 1964]
Society of German Cooks [Vol 2: 3181]

Food Engineering Award [Vol. 1: 8400]

The Food Industry CEO of the Year Award [Vol. 1: 6582]

Food, Pharmaceutical and Bioengineering Division Award in Chemical Engineering [Vol. 1: 2618]

Food Technology Industrial Achievement Award [Vol. 1: 9336]

Foot in Mouth Award [Vol. 2: 8477]

Football Awards [Vol. 2: 6629]

Football Supporters Award; European [Vol. 2: 1422]

Footballer of the Year [Vol. 2: 6629]

Foote Award; Lucy B. [Vol. 1: 10889]

Footprint Marketing Awards [Vol. 2: 5683]

Forbes Award; Harriette Merrifield [Vol. 1: 5024]

Forbes Award; Malcolm [Vol. 1: 13760]

Force Health Protection Team Award [Vol. 1: 5424]

Forces for Nature Award [Vol. 1: 13100]

Ford Award; Colin [Vol. 2: 8899]

Ford Award; Lester R. [Vol. 1: 11014]

Ford Distinguished Fellow Award; Loretta C. [Vol. 1: 11823]

Ford Doctoral Dissertation Research Fellowships [Vol. 1: 17314]

Ford Graduate Student Research Award [Vol. 1: 1640]

Ford II Distinguished Award for Excellence in Automotive Engineering; Henry [Vol. 1: 15509]

Ford Memorial Award; Steven D. [Vol. 1: 12419]

Forderpreis
Deutsche Meteorologische Gesellschaft [Vol. 2: 2763]
German Interior Architects Association [Vol 2: 2959]

Forderpreis der ITG [Vol. 2: 3037]

Fordyce Clinical Investigator Award; Wilbert E. [Vol. 1: 3115]

Foreign Honorary Member [Vol. 1: 2053]

Foreign Language and Area Studies Fellowships
Columbia University - Southern Asian Institute [Vol. 1: 7420]
University of Wisconsin—Madison - Center for South Asia [Vol 1: 17370]

Foreman Award for Outstanding Community Service; Spencer [Vol. 1: 5211]

Forensic Faculty Poster Prizes for SpRs and STs 1 - 3 [Vol. 2: 8715]

Forensic Faculty Senior House Officer Poster Prize [Vol. 2: 8716]

Forensic Nursing Research Award; Ann Burgess [Vol. 1: 9666]

Forensic Nursing; Virginia A. Lynch Pioneer Award in [Vol. 1: 9668]

Forensic Sciences Award [Vol. 1: 5597]

Forest Capital of Canada Award [Vol. 1: 6512]

Forest Products Division Award in Chemical Engineering [Vol. 1: 2609]

Forest Service Award; Don [Vol. 1: 422]

Foresters' Ring [Vol. 1: 6595]

Forestry Program Accreditation [Vol. 1: 15708]

Forkosch Prize; Morris D. [Vol. 1: 2372]

Forman Engineering Excellence Awards; Paul F. [Vol. 1: 13605]

Formation Evaluation Award [Vol. 1: 15756]

Formula One World Champion [Vol. 2: 2505]

Forrestal III Leadership Award for Professional Ethics and Standards of Investment Practice; Daniel J. [Vol. 1: 7167]

Forsdale Award for Outstanding Educator in the Field of Media Ecology; Louis [Vol. 1: 11033]

Forster Distinguished Service Award; Eric O. [Vol. 1: 9076]

Fort Dodge Animal Health - Bovine Practitioner of the Year Award [Vol. 1: 1072]

Foss Award; Hal [Vol. 1: 11598]

Foster Outstanding Explorer Award; Norman H. [Vol. 1: 1276]

Foster Practicing Medical Anthropology Award; George [Vol. 1: 15189]

Foster Scholarship; Roger L. [Vol. 1: 17567]

FosterGrant Reading Glasses Romantic Novel of the Year [Vol. 2: 8551]

FotoWeek DC Awards [Vol. 1: 8440]

Fould; Prix Louis [Vol. 2: 2160]

Foulois Memorial Award; Maj. Gen. Benjamin D. [Vol. 1: 13645]

Foulon; Prix [Vol. 2: 2202]

Foundation Award
Association for Clinical Biochemistry [Vol. 2: 6755]
International Radio and Television Society Foundation [Vol 1: 10084]

Foundation Award for Outstanding Achievement [Vol. 1: 12590]

Foundation Council Award [Vol. 2: 8674]

Foundation for Water Research (UK) Award [Vol. 2: 5762]

Foundation Prize Awards [Vol. 1: 2269]

Founder Award [Vol. 1: 4608]

Founder's Award
Academy of Criminal Justice Sciences [Vol. 1: 65]
American Academy of Neurology [Vol 1: 584]
American Academy of Optometry [Vol 1: 619]
American Alliance for Theatre and Education [Vol 1: 815]
American Society for Gravitational and Space Biology [Vol 1: 3915]
Awards and Recognition Association [Vol 1: 5749]
La Leche League International [Vol 1: 10710]
Military Audiology Association [Vol 1: 11150]
National Hospice and Palliative Care Organization [Vol 1: 12528]
Republicans for Environmental Protection [Vol 1: 14513]
Surface Mount Technology Association [Vol 1: 16335]

Founders Award
American Academy of Arts and Sciences [Vol. 1: 496]
American Academy of Pediatrics [Vol 1: 675]
American Hockey Coaches Association [Vol 1: 2396]
American Statistical Association [Vol 1: 4560]
Biophysical Society [Vol 1: 5850]
Business Committee for the Arts [Vol 1: 6057]
Canadian College of Medical Geneticists [Vol 1: 6410]
Confederate Memorial Literary Society [Vol 1: 7478]
Door and Hardware Institute [Vol 1: 7907]
Health Physics Society [Vol 1: 8852]
Institution of Engineering Designers [Vol 2: 8037]
National Federation of State Poetry Societies [Vol 1: 12347]
Niagara University [Vol 1: 13256]
Omega Psi Phi Fraternity [Vol 1: 13506]
Packard Automobile Classics [Vol 1: 13782]
Society For Biomaterials [Vol 1: 15046]

Society of Environmental Toxicology and Chemistry [Vol 1: 15627]

Society of Paper Money Collectors [Vol 1: 15734]

Founders' Award
Educational Theatre Association [Vol. 1: 8030]
Global Scholars and Leaders Council [Vol 2: 5945]
National Association for Campus Activities [Vol 1: 11557]
National Association of Professional Organizers [Vol 1: 11848]
United Nations Association of Australia, Victorian Division [Vol 2: 1091]

Founders Award for Academic Excellence for Leadership of Engineering and Technical Management for Undergraduate Programs [Vol. 1: 3892]

Founders Award for Best Student Chapter [Vol. 1: 3893]

Founder's Award for Humane Excellence [Vol. 1: 4060]

Founders Award for Leadership [Vol. 1: 1102]

Founders Award for Outstanding Contributions to the Field of Chemical Engineering [Vol. 1: 2619]

Founders Award for Painting [Vol. 1: 525]

Founders Award for Sculpture [Vol. 1: 526]

Founders Awards [Vol. 1: 14898]

Founders Distinguished Service Award [Vol. 1: 3975]

Founder's Favorite Winner Award [Vol. 1: 12654]

Founder's JSAH Article Award [Vol. 1: 15475]

Founders Medal
Institute of Electrical and Electronics Engineers [Vol. 1: 9291]
SOLE - The International Society of Logistics [Vol 1: 15942]

Founders' Medal
Air League [Vol. 2: 6690]
Peace Science Society International [Vol 1: 13879]
Society for the History of Natural History [Vol 2: 9215]

Founders' Memorial Award [Vol. 1: 8147]

Founders of Adolescent Health Award [Vol. 1: 676]

Founders of SIGNA Medal [Vol. 1: 11044]

Founders' Prize
British Ecological Society [Vol. 2: 7046]
Institute of Physics and Engineering in Medicine [Vol 2: 7928]

Founders Trophy [Vol. 1: 7218]

Four Seasons Critics Awards [Vol. 1: 16519]

Four Wheel Drive Puller of the Year [Vol. 1: 12987]

Four-Year College Biology Research in Teaching Award [Vol. 1: 11648]

Four-Year University and College Achievement Award [Vol. 1: 10359]

Fourmarier; Prix Paul [Vol. 2: 1631]

Fournier; Prix Rodolphe- [Vol. 1: 14371]

Fourth Year Cardiology Subspecialty Fellowship Award [Vol. 1: 5226]

Fourth-Year Student Award [Vol. 2: 4861]

Fowler Award; Jack [Vol. 2: 1495]

Fowler Award; Raymond D. [Vol. 1: 3385]

Fowler Prizes [Vol. 2: 8659]

Fox Founder's Award; A. Roger [Vol. 1: 11758]

Fox, M.D. Lectureship; Everett C. [Vol. 1: 512]

Fox Medal; E.J. [Vol. 2: 7829]

Fox Memorial Awards; K.J. [Vol. 2: 4890]

Fox Memorial Scholarship; Terry [Vol. 1: 13012]

FOXTEL Australian Documentary Prize [Vol. 2: 1080]

FOXTEL Fellowship for Excellence in Television Writing [Vol. 2: 624]

Foy; Prix Percy W. [Vol. 1: 8468]

FPSA-FPEI Food Engineering Award [Vol. 1: 4080]

FQE Prizes [Vol. 2: 1429]

Fracture Mechanics Medal [Vol. 1: 5598]

Fraenkel Prize in Contemporary History [Vol. 2: 9449]

Fragrance Foundation Recognition Awards [Vol. 1: 8455]

Fragrance Hall of Fame [Vol. 1: 8455]

Frakes Continuing Education Award [Vol. 1: 2033]

Framed Scrolls [Vol. 2: 6691]

Frampton and Beazley Prizes [Vol. 2: 8803]

Frampton Award; Keith [Vol. 1: 8504]

France Telecom; Prix [Vol. 2: 2203]

Franchise of the Year [Vol. 2: 3872]

Franchise Person of the Year [Vol. 2: 3873]
Franchisee of the Year [Vol. 2: 3874]
Franchisor of the Year [Vol. 2: 5940]
Franck Award; Michael [Vol. 1: 16266]
Franck Design Prize; Kaj [Vol. 2: 2070]
Francke Leadership Mentor Award; Gloria Niemeyer [Vol. 1: 3133]
Francke Medal; Donald E. [Vol. 1: 4307]
Francken-prijs; Dr. Wijnaendts [Vol. 2: 4839]
Franco-British Landscape Gardening Award [Vol. 2: 7708]
Francois Golden Medal; Jules [Vol. 1: 9929]
Francou Legacy; Andre [Vol. 1: 14613]
Francqui Prize [Vol. 2: 1527]
Frank Award; Josette [Vol. 1: 7233]
Frank Award; Mimi S. [Vol. 1: 10564]
Frank Award; Morton [Vol. 1: 13761]
Frank Memorial Award and Lectureship; Sally [Vol. 1: 1063]
Frankel Prize; Charles [Vol. 1: 12319]
Frankel Scholarship; Hans [Vol. 2: 8229]
Frankl Student Research Award; Loren [Vol. 1: 3543]
Frankland Award [Vol. 2: 9007]
Frankland Fellowship; Sir Edward [Vol. 2: 9008]
Frankland Prize Lectureship; Sir Edward [Vol. 2: 9007]
Franklin Award; Ben [Vol. 1: 7427]
Franklin Award for Management of Federal Excess Personal Property [Vol. 1: 16915]
Franklin Award for Outstanding Achievement in Mass Spectrometry; Frank H. Field and Joe L. [Vol. 1: 1638]
Franklin Award for State Fire Assistance [Vol. 1: 16916]
Franklin Award for Volunteer Fire Assistance [Vol. 1: 16917]
Franklin Award; Rosalind [Vol. 2: 8934]
Franklin Awards; Benjamin [Vol. 1: 9174]
Franklin Fire Service Award for Valor; Benjamin [Vol. 1: 9664]
Franklin Gold Medal; Benjamin [Vol. 2: 4109]
Franklin Literary Award; Miles [Vol. 2: 1084]
Franklin Medal and Prize [Vol. 2: 7906]
Franklin Medal; Benjamin [Vol. 2: 8958]
Franklin Medal for Distinguished Achievement in the Sciences; Benjamin [Vol. 1: 3184]
Franklin Medal for Distinguished Public Service; Benjamin [Vol. 1: 3185]
Franklin Medal; Ned [Vol. 2: 7962]
Franklin Publication Prize; John Hope [Vol. 1: 4572]
Franklin Service Award; Jack [Vol. 1: 17045]
Franques Medal; Marti I. [Vol. 2: 2826]
Fraser Award for Best Translation of a Book; Soeurette Diehl [Vol. 1: 16454]
Fraser Sculpture Award; James Earle [Vol. 1: 12268]
Fraternalist of the Year Award [Vol. 1: 14633]
Fraunhofer Award/Robert M. Burley Prize; Joseph [Vol. 1: 13606]
Frederic Ives Medal [Vol. 1: 13610]
Fredericq; Prix Leon et Henri [Vol. 2: 1632]
Free Lectureship Award; Alfred H. [Vol. 1: 902]
Free Market Award [Vol. 2: 5550]
Free Media Pioneer Award [Vol. 2: 1300]
Free Press Africa Award [Vol. 2: 7444]
Free Spirit Award [Vol. 1: 8460]
Freedheim Student Development Paper Award; Donald K. [Vol. 1: 3453]
Freedley Memorial Award; George [Vol. 1: 16483]
Freedom Award
    International Rescue Committee USA [Vol. 1: 10120]
    National Association of Secretaries of State [Vol 1: 11890]
Freedom in Film Award [Vol. 1: 8459]
Freedom of Information Award [Vol. 1: 16426]
Freedom to Create Prize [Vol. 2: 5943]
Freeling Award; Paul [Vol. 2: 8675]
Freeman Award; Joseph T. [Vol. 1: 8626]
Freeman Award; Stephen A. [Vol. 1: 13397]
Freeman Fellowship [Vol. 1: 4179]
Freeman Lectureship in Geriatrics [Vol. 1: 8626]
Freeman Memorial Grant-in-Aid; Don [Vol. 1: 15588]
Freeman Philanthropic Services Award for Outstanding Corporation [Vol. 1: 5350]
Freeman Psychotherapy Award; Dr. Thomas [Vol. 2: 8717]

Freeman Scholar Award [Vol. 1: 4388]
Freeman Travel Grants; Kevin [Vol. 1: 11319]
Freeman Writing Award; Ned E. [Vol. 1: 1909]
Freese Environmental Engineering Award and Lecture; Simon W. [Vol. 1: 4180]
Freethinker of the Year Award [Vol. 1: 8463]
Freethought Heroine Award [Vol. 1: 8464]
Fregault; Prix Guy et Lilianne [Vol. 1: 9248]
French Fellowship; Edith and Richard [Vol. 1: 18150]
French Medal; Sidney [Vol. 2: 7155]
Frenkel Prize [Vol. 2: 5915]
Frenz Prize; Horst [Vol. 1: 1828]
Fresenius-Preis [Vol. 2: 2929]
Freshley Outstanding New Teacher Award; Dwight L. [Vol. 1: 16042]
Freud Preis; Sigmund [Vol. 2: 2897]
Freudenthal Award; Hans [Vol. 1: 5430]
Freudenthal Medal; Alfred M. [Vol. 1: 4181]
Freund Award; Clement J. [Vol. 1: 3856]
Freund Award; Professor Raphael [Vol. 2: 3963]
Freville; Prix Edmond [Vol. 2: 2270]
Frew National Leadership Award; Stephen A. [Vol. 1: 11761]
Frewer Memorial Trophy; Gerald [Vol. 2: 8038]
Frey Award for the Promotion of Talented Female Scholars; Emilie Louise [Vol. 2: 6528]
Freyssinet Award [Vol. 2: 4907]
Frick Award; Ford C. [Vol. 1: 11970]
Fridman Prize; A.M. [Vol. 2: 5800]
Friedberg Award [Vol. 1: 14241]
Friedberg Memorial Lecture; Arthur L. [Vol. 1: 1558]
Friedenberg Online Journalism Award; Joan M. [Vol. 1: 12683]
Friedenpreis des Deutschen Buchhandels [Vol. 2: 2989]
Friedenwald Memorial Award [Vol. 1: 5083]
Friedenwald Memorial Award; Jonas S. [Vol. 1: 5083]
Friedlander Award; Sheldon K. [Vol. 1: 862]
Friedman Award Medal; Lee Max [Vol. 1: 2731]
Friedman Medal; Sue Tyler [Vol. 1: 7723]
Friedman Professional Recognition Award; Edmund [Vol. 1: 4182]
Friedman Young Engineer Award for Professional Achievement; Edmund [Vol. 1: 4183]
Friedmann Award for Outstanding APA Contributions; Elly D. [Vol. 2: 2519]
Friedrich-Gerstaecker-Preis [Vol. 2: 2742]
Friedrichs Memorial Award; Gerda [Vol. 1: 4601]
Friel Memorial Lecture; Ernest Sheldon [Vol. 2: 7621]
Friend of Automotive History Award [Vol. 1: 15552]
Friend of Children Award [Vol. 1: 13305]
Friend of Conservation Award [Vol. 1: 11725]
Friend of ECPN Award [Vol. 1: 15272]
Friend of Education Award [Vol. 1: 12295]
Friend of History Award [Vol. 1: 13678]
Friend of Scholastic Journalism [Vol. 1: 10588]
Friend of the Alliance Award [Vol. 1: 379]
Friend of the Book [Vol. 2: 1752]
Friend of the Florida Trail Award [Vol. 1: 8390]
Friend of the Industry [Vol. 1: 14843]
Friend of the Industry Award [Vol. 1: 337]
Friend of the Legal Profession Award [Vol. 1: 10688]
Friend of the Library [Vol. 1: 15977]
Friend of the Rottweiler Award [Vol. 1: 3723]
Friend to Kids Award; Great [Vol. 1: 5248]
Friends of CAGP [Vol. 1: 6271]
Friends of Children Award [Vol. 1: 4939]
Friends of Libraries U.S.A. Award [Vol. 1: 8473]
Friends of the Dallas Public Library Award [Vol. 1: 16455]
Friends of the NAC Orchestra Association Award [Vol. 1: 11552]
Friendship Trophy [Vol. 2: 4847]
Friman Best of Show Award; Elmer [Vol. 1: 8855]
Fringe First Awards [Vol. 2: 7530]
Fringe Review Outstanding Theatre Awards [Vol. 2: 7531]
Frink Medal for British Zoologists [Vol. 2: 9508]
Fris Marine Air Command and Control Squadron of the Year Award; Edward S. [Vol. 1: 10949]
Frisby-Green Dissertation Prize [Vol. 2: 6794]
Frisch Medal Award [Vol. 1: 7991]
Fritz Medal; John [Vol. 1: 1149]
Fromm-Reichmann Fellowship Award [Vol. 1: 1134]
Front Line Award for Human Rights Defenders at Risk [Vol. 2: 3835]

Front Page Awards [Vol. 1: 17649]
Front Prize; Theodore [Vol. 1: 9499]
Frontiers in Anesthesia Research Award [Vol. 1: 9502]
Frontiers of Science and Society, the Rustum Roy Lecture [Vol. 1: 1559]
Frontline Person of the Year [Vol. 2: 1679]
Frost & Conn Inc. Booth of Distinction Award [Vol. 1: 7162]
Frost Literary Award; Dr. Lawrence A. [Vol. 1: 10869]
The Frost Medal [Vol. 1: 14061]
Froude Medal; William [Vol. 2: 8865]
Froude Research Scholarship in Naval Architecture [Vol. 2: 8866]
Frumkin Memorial Medal [Vol. 2: 6442]
Fry Award; John [Vol. 2: 8676]
Fry Book Award; Edward B. [Vol. 1: 10862]
Fry Lecture Award; Glenn A. [Vol. 1: 620]
Fry Medal; F.E.J. [Vol. 1: 6995]
Fry Memorial Lecture; William J. [Vol. 1: 2709]
Fry Victim Service Practitioner Award; Margery [Vol. 1: 12641]
Fryxell Award for Interdisciplinary Research [Vol. 1: 15020]
FSF-NUTEK Award [Vol. 2: 6225]
Fuchs Memorial Award [Vol. 2: 2697]
Fuchs Student Award; Henry O. [Vol. 1: 15510]
Fuels and Petrochemicals Division Award [Vol. 1: 2620]
Fuerison; Prix Irene [Vol. 2: 1590]
Fuertes Award; Louis Agassiz [Vol. 1: 17860]
Fuji/Association of Photographers Assistants' Awards [Vol. 2: 6839]
Fujita Research Achievement Award; T. Theodore [Vol. 1: 13031]
Fukumura Vandaceous Award; Roy T. [Vol. 1: 3075]
Fulbright Australian National University Distinguished Chair in American Political Science [Vol. 2: 195]
Fulbright Awards - American Program [Vol. 2: 195]
Fulbright Awards - Australian Program [Vol. 2: 196]
Fulbright New Century Scholar Program [Vol. 2: 196]
Fulbright Postdoctoral Scholarships [Vol. 2: 196]
Fulbright Postgraduate Scholarships
    Australian-American Fulbright Commission [Vol. 2: 195]
    Australian-American Fulbright Commission [Vol 2: 196]
Fulbright Professional Scholarships [Vol. 2: 196]
Fulbright Scholar in Residence [Vol. 2: 196]
Fulbright Senior Scholarships
    Australian-American Fulbright Commission [Vol. 2: 195]
    Australian-American Fulbright Commission [Vol 2: 196]
Fulfillment Hall of Fame [Vol. 1: 8478]
Fulfillment Manager of the Year Award [Vol. 1: 8479]
Fulkerson Prize; Delbert Ray [Vol. 1: 2833]
Full Community Inclusion Award [Vol. 1: 1423]
Full Frame Documentary Film Festival [Vol. 1: 7936]
Fuller Award; Josephine "Scout" Wollman [Vol. 1: 14309]
Fuller Award; Oliver Torry [Vol. 1: 5073]
Fuller Award; Solomon Carter [Vol. 1: 3349]
Fullerton Award; Jim [Vol. 1: 2394]
Fulling Award; Edmund H. [Vol. 1: 15065]
Fullum Award; Ernest F. [Vol. 1: 7933]
Fulrath Award; Richard M. [Vol. 1: 1560]
Fulton Award [Vol. 2: 5533]
Fulton-Downer Gold Medal [Vol. 2: 4908]
Fund for Educational Research and Development [Vol. 1: 10570]
Fund for the Advancement of Social Studies Education Grant [Vol. 1: 12167]
Funderberg Research Scholar Award [Vol. 1: 2202]
Fundraiser of the Year - College Division [Vol. 1: 11626]
Fundraiser of the Year - University Division [Vol. 1: 11627]
Funny Women Awards [Vol. 2: 7532]
Furkert Award [Vol. 2: 4909]
Furlong Grant; Miriam Fay [Vol. 1: 409]
Furness Consumer Media Service Award; Betty [Vol. 1: 7578]
Furniss Book Award; Edgar S. [Vol. 1: 13482]
Furon; Prix Raymond et Madeleine [Vol. 2: 2456]

Furuseth Award; Andrew [Vol. 1: 16652]

Fussell Distinguished Service Award; Sue Kraft [Vol. 1: 5343]

Futas Catalyst for Change Award; Elizabeth [Vol. 1: 2780]

Futrell Award; Mary Hatwood [Vol. 1: 12296]

Future Conservationist Awards [Vol. 2: 7478]

Future Leader Award [Vol. 1: 7742]

Future Leader Awards [Vol. 1: 9988]

Future Leader in Radiocommunications Scholarships [Vol. 1: 14391]

Future Leaders Initial NCTM Annual Meeting Attendance Awards [Vol. 1: 12224]

Fyan Public Library Research Grant; Loleta D. [Vol. 1: 2781]

Gabaldon Award; Arnoldo [Vol. 2: 9555]

Gabbay Award in Biotechnology and Medicine; Jacob Heskel [Vol. 1: 14599]

Gabby Awards [Vol. 1: 8784]

Gabor Award [Vol. 1: 10030]

Gabor Award; Dennis [Vol. 1: 16150]

Gabor Medal [Vol. 2: 8935]

Gabor Medal and Prize [Vol. 2: 7907]

Gabriel Award [Vol. 1: 7098]

Gabriel Dissertation Prize; Ralph Henry [Vol. 1: 4573]

Gachukia Science Prize; Dr. Eddah [Vol. 2: 4412]

Gad-el-Mawla Award; Nazli [Vol. 2: 1548]

Gaede-Langmuir Award [Vol. 1: 5730]

Gagarin Gold Medal; Yuri A. [Vol. 2: 6307]

Gagna A. and Ch. Van Heck Prize [Vol. 2: 1519]

Gagne Award for Graduate Student Research in Instructional Design; Robert M. [Vol. 1: 5008]

Gagne Family Award [Vol. 1: 16140]

Gaia Award [Vol. 1: 11269]

Gaige Fund Award [Vol. 1: 4342]

Gairdner International Awards [Vol. 1: 8506]

GALA Award [Vol. 1: 6568]

Galantiere Award; Lewis [Vol. 1: 4603]

Galathea Medaillen [Vol. 2: 1991]

Galathea Medal [Vol. 2: 1991]

Galatti Award for Outstanding Volunteer Service [Vol. 1: 207]

Galaxy Awards [Vol. 1: 6383]

Galbraith Award [Vol. 1: 7533]

Galderma Research/Literature Award [Vol. 2: 328]

Gale Cengage Learning Award for Excellence in Business Librarianship [Vol. 1: 14464]

Gale Cengage Learning Award for Excellence in Reference and Adult Library Services [Vol. 1: 14465]

Gale Cengage Learning Financial Development Award [Vol. 1: 2782]

Gale Group Financial Development Award [Vol. 1: 2782]

Galey, Sr. Memorial Public Service Award; John T. [Vol. 1: 2698]

Galilei Award; Galileo [Vol. 2: 6055]

Galkin Award; Harry [Vol. 1: 9610]

Gall Jr. CIO of the Year Award; John E. [Vol. 1: 8869]

Gallagher Award; F. Ann [Vol. 1: 2034]

Gallagher Award; Mike [Vol. 1: 17080]

Gallagher Distinguished Service Award; Marian Gould [Vol. 1: 1192]

Gallant Prize for Non-Fiction; Mavis [Vol. 1: 14374]

Gallantry Decorations [Vol. 2: 313]

Gallet; Prix [Vol. 2: 2271]

Gallimore Award; J.G. [Vol. 1: 17036]

Galloway Memorial Cup; Ian [Vol. 2: 4996]

Gallup Fellowship in American Literature; Donald C. [Vol. 1: 18151]

Galton Award; Sir Francis [Vol. 2: 4699]

Galvan Outstanding Graduate in Journalism Award; Julie [Vol. 1: 15800]

Galvani Prize; Luigi [Vol. 2: 2328]

GAMA Learn to Fly Award for Excellence in Aviation Education [Vol. 1: 8531]

Gamble Award; Samuel [Vol. 2: 5298]

Gamgee Gold Medal [Vol. 2: 1671]

Gamzu Prize; Dr. Haim [Vol. 2: 3991]

Gandhi Award; Mahatma [Vol. 1: 10068]

Gandhi Prize for Popularization of Science; Indira [Vol. 2: 3634]

Ganguly Memorial Award for Young Scientists in Animal Science; Dr. Gouri [Vol. 2: 3713]

Gani Medal in Human Genetics; Ruth Stephens [Vol. 2: 175]

Gannett Foundation Award for Technical Innovation in the Service of Digital Journalism [Vol. 1: 13560]

Gans Distinguished Overseas Lectureship; Stephen L. [Vol. 1: 677]

Gantrelle; Prix Joseph [Vol. 2: 1608]

Gantt Medal; Henry Laurence [Vol. 1: 4389]

Garant Awards; Serge [Vol. 1: 14981]

Garber Pioneer Award; Mary [Vol. 1: 5179]

Garber Scholarship/Internship (Sportswriting); Mary [Vol. 1: 5180]

Garcia Monge Prize; Joaquin [Vol. 2: 1858]

Garcia Prize; Sandoz [Vol. 2: 3858]

Garcia-Tunon Memorial Award in Human Dignity; Miguel [Vol. 1: 1696]

Gard Superior Citizen Volunteer Award; Robert E. [Vol. 1: 1112]

Gard Superior Volunteer Award; Robert E. [Vol. 1: 1112]

Garde Nationale Trophy [Vol. 1: 12477]

Garden Awards [Vol. 2: 1179]

Garden Centre Awards [Vol. 2: 914]

Garden State Children's Book Awards [Vol. 1: 13187]

Garden State Teen Book Awards [Vol. 1: 13188]

Gardeners of America/Men's Garden Clubs of America Scholarship [Vol. 1: 8520]

Gardening From the Heart Award [Vol. 1: 8521]

Gardiner Award [Vol. 2: 6700]

Gardiner Jr. Trophy; John H. [Vol. 1: 17060]

Gardner Award [Vol. 2: 9334]

Gardner Leadership Award; John W. [Vol. 1: 9188]

Gardner Lectureship [Vol. 2: 2407]

Gardner Subcommittee Chairman of the Year Award; Henry A. [Vol. 1: 5599]

Garel Award; Georges [Vol. 2: 6384]

Garland Commemorative Refrigeration Award for Project Excellence; Milton W. [Vol. 1: 4323]

Garland Educator Award; Robin F. [Vol. 1: 12699]

Garner-Themoin Medal [Vol. 2: 1282]

Garrett Award [Vol. 2: 6739]

Garrett Memorial Award; Dudley (Red) [Vol. 1: 2411]

Garrett Scholarships; Eileen J. [Vol. 1: 13851]

Garrett Turbomachinery and Applications Engineering Award; Cliff [Vol. 1: 15511]

Garrod Medal [Vol. 2: 7219]

Garrod Prize [Vol. 2: 7239]

Garry/Labbe Award for Contributions to Laboratory Assessment of Nutritional Status [Vol. 1: 903]

Garvan-John M. Olin Medal; Francis P. [Vol. 1: 1641]

Garvey Award; Joseph J. [Vol. 1: 960]

Gary Memorial Medal [Vol. 1: 2719]

Gas Balloon Championships [Vol. 1: 5768]

Gas Turbine Award [Vol. 1: 4390]

Gascoigne Medal for Wastewater Treatment Plant Operational Improvement [Vol. 1: 17705]

Gascoigne Prize; Trench [Vol. 2: 9139]

Gaskell Medal and Prize [Vol. 2: 8718]

Gassner Memorial Playwriting Award; John [Vol. 1: 13158]

Gassner Playwriting Award; John [Vol. 1: 13748]

Gast Lecture Series; Paul W. [Vol. 2: 2360]

Gaster Memorial Award; Leon [Vol. 2: 7391]

Gatchell Award; Willard Waddington [Vol. 1: 8581]

Gately Memorial Trophy; Michael [Vol. 1: 10520]

Gates Award for Global Health [Vol. 1: 8677]

Gatorade Predoctoral Investigator Award [Vol. 1: 3254]

Gatorade Rookie of the Year [Vol. 1: 10733]

Gatorade Young Investigator Award [Vol. 1: 3254]

Gatzke Outstanding Dissertation Award; Dr. Donald A. [Vol. 1: 1384]

Gaudin Award; Antoine M. [Vol. 1: 15209]

Gaudreau Memorial Prize; Jacques [Vol. 1: 17320]

Gaul Composition Competition; Harvey [Vol. 1: 14022]

Gaus Award; John [Vol. 1: 3303]

Gauss Award; Christian [Vol. 1: 13964]

Gauss Medal [Vol. 2: 2743]

Gauss Prize; Carl Friedrich [Vol. 2: 2967]

Gavel Award [Vol. 1: 836]

Gaver Scholarship; Mary V. [Vol. 1: 2783]

Gawad Alab ng Haraya (Alab ng Haraya Awards)- [Vol. 2: 5340]

Gawad Manlilikha Ng Bayan (GAMABA) [Vol. 2: 5341]

Gaynor Award; Richard D. [Vol. 1: 12736]

Gaz de France; Prix [Vol. 2: 2204]

Gazzola Prize [Vol. 2: 2516]

GCS Women in IT Award [Vol. 2: 7011]

GE Healthcare New Investigator Award [Vol. 1: 6937]

Geach Memorial Award; Portia [Vol. 2: 1085]

Gebhard Medal; Albert [Vol. 2: 2112]

GEC-ESTRO Iridium Award [Vol. 2: 1496]

Geddes Memorial Award; William F. [Vol. 1: 8]

Geddes Memorial Prize; Murray [Vol. 2: 5043]

Gedge Trophy [Vol. 2: 246]

Gediminas; Medal of the Order of the Lithuanian Grand Duke [Vol. 2: 4490]

Gediminas; Order of the Lithuanian Grand Duke [Vol. 2: 4492]

Gegner; Prix [Vol. 2: 2272]

Gehriger Diploma; Pirat [Vol. 2: 6308]

GEICO Life Scholarship [Vol. 1: 8703]

Geiger Award; General Roy S. [Vol. 1: 10972]

Geiger Prize; Hugo [Vol. 2: 2892]

Geijyutsu Korosha [Vol. 2: 4341]

Geilfuss Award for Wisconsin History; John C. [Vol. 1: 17894]

Geis Memorial Award [Vol. 1: 3548]

Geisel Medal; Theodor Seuss [Vol. 1: 5064]

Geisness Outstanding Lawyer or Non-Lawyer Award; Helen M. [Vol. 1: 10689]

Gelber Music Foundation Award; Sylva [Vol. 1: 8529]

Gelin Conference Travel Award; Lars-Erik [Vol. 2: 2852]

Gellar Award; Mort [Vol. 1: 449]

GEM Awards [Vol. 1: 15210]

Gemant Award; Andrew [Vol. 1: 2686]

Gemson Resident Award; Don [Vol. 1: 1809]

Gen Foundation Awards [Vol. 2: 7716]

Gen-Probe Joseph Public Health Award [Vol. 1: 3976]

Genealogical Publishing Company Award [Vol. 1: 14466]

Genealogist of the Year [Vol. 2: 5552]

General Aviation Award [Vol. 2: 2539]

General Aviation Service Technician Award [Vol. 1: 11500]

General Educator Fellowships [Vol. 1: 7954]

General Excellence in Online Journalism Award [Vol. 1: 13762]

General Motors Grand Jazz Award
    Festival International de Jazz de Montreal [Vol. 1: 8346]
    Festival International de Jazz de Montreal [Vol 1: 8346]

General Observer's Certificate [Vol. 2: 5511]

General Prize Essay Contest [Vol. 1: 17009]

General Research Committee Award [Vol. 2: 6129]

General Scholarly Incentive Awards [Vol. 1: 13852]

General Service Medal [Vol. 2: 5701]

Genesis Award [Vol. 1: 4735]

Genesis Awards [Vol. 1: 8999]

Genesis-Faraday/BSAS Vacation Scholarships [Vol. 2: 7247]

Genetics Society of America Medal [Vol. 1: 8549]

Geneva-Europe Prizes [Vol. 2: 6275]

Genius Prize [Vol. 2: 3365]

Gent Distinguished Student Paper Award; Alan [Vol. 1: 150]

Gentilli Prize; Edgar [Vol. 2: 8693]

Genzyme Prize [Vol. 2: 2862]

Genzyme Student Research Awards [Vol. 1: 904]

GEO Stars [Vol. 1: 8669]

Geochemistry Award [Vol. 2: 9009]

GeoEye Foundation Award [Vol. 1: 4869]

Geographical Award [Vol. 2: 8789]

Geomechanics Award [Vol. 2: 4969]

George Award; Alexander [Vol. 1: 10383]

George Civilian Airmanship Award; Lt. Gen. Harold L. [Vol. 1: 13646]

George Cross [Vol. 2: 7341]

George Medal [Vol. 2: 7342]

George Memorial Prize for Apprentices; Mary [Vol. 2: 8022]

George Public Service Award; John M. [Vol. 1: 13414]

Georgescu-Roegen Prize in Economics [Vol. 1: 16021]

Georgia Author of the Year Awards [Vol. 1: 8592]

Georgia Children's Book Award [Vol. 1: 17234]

Georgia Children's Picture Book Award [Vol. 1: 17235]

Georgia No Excuses Awards [Vol. 1: 8590]

Georgia Poetry Society Award [Vol. 1: 12348]

Geosciences in the Media Award [Vol. 1: 1277]

Geotechnical Research Medal [Vol. 2: 7983]

Geothermal Pioneer Award [Vol. 1: 8601]

Geothermal Special Achievement Award [Vol. 1: 8602]

Geppert Award; Leo J. [Vol. 1: 678]

Gerbier-Mumm International Award; Norbert [Vol. 2: 6559]

Gerboth Award; Walter [Vol. 1: 11320]

Gerdes Distinguished Service Award; Betty [Vol. 1: 12869]

Gerhold Award; Clarence (Larry) G. [Vol. 1: 2621]

Geriatric Oral Health Care Award [Vol. 1: 2002]

Geriatrics and Gerontology Section Trainees' Prize [Vol. 2: 9093]

German Award for Jewelry and Precious Stones [Vol. 2: 2875]

German History Society Essay Prize [Vol. 2: 8804]

German Studies Research Grants [Vol. 1: 8608]

German Summer-Study Scholarship [Vol. 1: 1362]

Germann Cup [Vol. 1: 16015]

Gerner Innovative Teaching Award; Deborah [Vol. 1: 10384]

Geron Corporation - Samuel Goldstein Distinguished Publication Award [Vol. 1: 8627]

Geroski Best Article of the Year Prize; Paul [Vol. 2: 1434]

Gerrity Award; Thomas P. [Vol. 1: 256]

Gerry Fellowships; Eloise [Vol. 1: 14886]

Gerschenkron Prize; Alexander [Vol. 1: 7995]

Gershoy Award; Leo [Vol. 1: 2373]

Gersoni Military Psychology Award; Charles S. [Vol. 1: 3528]

Gervais Award; Arthur J. [Vol. 1: 16197]

Geschwin Prize in Behavioral Neurology; Norman [Vol. 1: 585]

Getchell Award; Charles M. [Vol. 1: 16005]

Getty Award for Conservation Leadership; J. Paul [Vol. 1: 18091]

Getty Scholar Grants [Vol. 1: 8648]

Getty Wildlife Conservation Prize; J. Paul [Vol. 1: 18091]

Ghana ICT Awards [Vol. 2: 3253]

Ghana Music Awards [Vol. 2: 3251]

Ghana Property Awards [Vol. 2: 3255]

Ghandi Peace Award [Vol. 1: 14265]

Ghanshyam Das Jaigopal Memorial Award; Chaturvedi [Vol. 2: 3546]

Ghatage Award; Dr. V. M. [Vol. 2: 3441]

Ghirshman; Prix Roman et Tania [Vol. 2: 2161]

Ghoah Memorial Award; Professor B.N. [Vol. 2: 3514]

Giamatti Fellowship; A. Bartlett [Vol. 1: 18152]

Gianque Travel Award; William F. [Vol. 1: 6103]

Gibbs Brothers Medal [Vol. 1: 11436]

Gibbs, Jr. Memorial Award; Robert H. [Vol. 1: 4343]

Giblin Lecture [Vol. 2: 200]

Gibraltar Festival for Young Musicians [Vol. 2: 3259]

Gibraltar Song Festival [Vol. 2: 3261]

Gibran Spirit of Humanity Award; Kahlil [Vol. 1: 4753]

Gibson Award; Arrell M. [Vol. 1: 17763]

Gibson Award; Charlie [Vol. 1: 16223]

Gibson Distinguished Service Award; Duane L. [Vol. 1: 7457]

Gibson-Fawcett Award [Vol. 2: 9010]

Gibson Marine Command and Control Officer of the Year Award; Robert F. [Vol. 1: 10950]

Gibtelecom International Chess Festival [Vol. 2: 3263]

Giddings Award for Excellence in Education; J. Calvin [Vol. 1: 1642]

Gideon Prize; Miriam [Vol. 1: 9499]

Giegengack Award; Robert [Vol. 1: 17463]

Gierows pris; Karin [Vol. 2: 6202]

Gies Award; William J. [Vol. 1: 720]

Gies Award; William John [Vol. 1: 1736]

Gies Foundation Award in Oral and Maxillofacial Surgery; William J. [Vol. 1: 1256]

Giese Structures and Environment Award; Henry [Vol. 1: 4081]

Gift of Sight Award
    Eye Bank Association of America [Vol. 1: 8222]

Guide Dogs of America [Vol 1: 8798]

Gifted Educator Award [Vol. 1: 1709]

Giguere Award; John P. [Vol. 1: 10951]

Gil Award; Federico [Vol. 1: 17315]

Gilbert Aviation Ordnance Marine of the Year Award; Gaines G. [Vol. 1: 10952]

Gilbert Award; William
    American Geophysical Union [Vol. 1: 2237]
    American Historical Association [Vol. 1: 2374]

Gilbert Memorial Award; Glen A. [Vol. 1: 294]

Gilbert Memorial Trustee Award; Gloria F. "Mike" [Vol. 1: 3790]

Gilbert National Leadership Award; Glenn [Vol. 1: 12200]

Gilbert Prize; Geoffery [Vol. 1: 12398]

Gilbreth Industrial Engineering Award; Frank and Lillian [Vol. 1: 9352]

Gilchrist Fieldwork Award [Vol. 2: 8790]

Giles Clinical Vignettes; Ted [Vol. 1: 6961]

Gill Award for Oil Analysis Excellence; Augustus H. [Vol. 1: 9827]

Gill Medal [Vol. 2: 5512]

Gill Memorial Award [Vol. 2: 8791]

Gill Memorial Award; Harry C. [Vol. 1: 16218]

Gill Memorial Award; Tom [Vol. 2: 7458]

Gill Prize; Brendan [Vol. 1: 11300]

Gill Scholarship; Seldon [Vol. 2: 86]

Gilles de Gennes Prize; Pierre [Vol. 2: 2468]

Gillies Award; Sir Harold Delf [Vol. 1: 537]

Gillihan Award [Vol. 1: 8914]

Gilliland Trophy; James [Vol. 2: 5482]

Gillingham Award; Kent K. [Vol. 1: 180]

Gilliss Award for Outstanding Service; Captain James M. [Vol. 1: 16840]

Gilmore Award; Mary [Vol. 2: 94]

Gilmore - Woman Behind the Scenes Award; Diana Fell [Vol. 1: 16732]

Gilmour Research Award; John and Allan [Vol. 2: 1123]

Gilruth Prize [Vol. 2: 598]

Gilson Memorial Award; Hugh Cary [Vol. 2: 7712]

Giltner Memorial Trophy; Joe [Vol. 1: 14974]

Gilula Award; Norton B. [Vol. 1: 3781]

Gingras Humor Award; Angele [Vol. 1: 12684]

Gingrich Memorial Life Award; Arnold [Vol. 1: 8300]

Ginsberg Fellowship; George [Vol. 1: 1135]

Ginsburg Award [Vol. 1: 5652]

Ginwala Gold Medal; Sir Padamji [Vol. 2: 3594]

GIO Australia Ballet Scholarship [Vol. 2: 1075]

Girard; Prix Edmond [Vol. 2: 2609]

Girardeau; Prix Emile [Vol. 2: 2273]

Girenas; Medal of Darius and [Vol. 2: 4487]

Girls' 18 National Championships Sportsmanship Award [Vol. 1: 17128]

Girls' Basketball National Volunteer of the Year [Vol. 1: 471]

Gitelson Essay Awards; Moses Leo [Vol. 1: 7154]

Gitlin Literary Prize; Zelda [Vol. 1: 17906]

Gitlin Literary Prize; Zelda and Paul [Vol. 1: 17906]

Given Awards; Bruce [Vol. 1: 4891]

Gladstone History Book Prize [Vol. 2: 8805]

Glas-Greenwalt Memorial Lecture; Pia [Vol. 1: 10367]

Glaser Award; Robert J. [Vol. 1: 15668]

Glaser Distinguished Service Award; Jerome [Vol. 1: 679]

Glaser Distinguished Teacher Awards; Robert J. [Vol. 1: 403]

Glaser Scientist Award; Elizabeth [Vol. 1: 13882]

Glaser Student Essay Award; Helen H. [Vol. 1: 404]

Glasgow-Rubin Student Achievement Certificate [Vol. 1: 2874]

Glass Dealer of the Year [Vol. 1: 12457]

Glass Designer of the Year [Vol. 2: 2081]

Glass Globe [Vol. 2: 4813]

Glass Professional of the Year [Vol. 1: 12457]

Glassco Translation Prize; John [Vol. 1: 10866]

Glassie Award; Henry [Vol. 1: 17518]

Glaucoma Research Award [Vol. 2: 2972]

Glaus Credit Executive of the Year; O. D. [Vol. 1: 11744]

Glaxo Prize for Medical Writing [Vol. 2: 9255]

GlaxoSmithKline International Member of the Year Award [Vol. 1: 3977]

GlaxoSmithKline Prize and Lecture [Vol. 2: 8936]

Glazebrook Medal [Vol. 2: 7908]

Glazen Globe [Vol. 2: 4813]

Gleason Award; Henry Allan [Vol. 1: 5937]

Gleed Literary Award; Danuta [Vol. 1: 18132]

Glen Award; Esther [Vol. 2: 4934]

Glen Cause Marketing Award; Peter [Vol. 1: 14531]

Glenfiddich Trophy [Vol. 2: 7447]

Glenn Award; R. A. [Vol. 1: 5600]

Glick Lectureship; David [Vol. 1: 9933]

Gliding Award [Vol. 2: 613]

Global 500 [Vol. 2: 5318]

Global Award for Entrepreneurship Research [Vol. 2: 6225]

Global Award for Excellence in Engineering Education [Vol. 1: 9919]

Global Awards [Vol. 2: 8320]

Global Awards Competition [Vol. 1: 9511]

Global Citizen Award [Vol. 1: 17300]

Global Compact Sri Lanka Network/CIMA Sustainability Awards [Vol. 2: 6119]

Global Economy Prize [Vol. 2: 3109]

Global Environmental Award [Vol. 1: 9570]

Global Excellence in BPM and Workflow Awards [Vol. 1: 8664]

Global Media Awards
    National Academy of Television Arts and Sciences [Vol. 1: 11452]
    Population Institute [Vol 1: 14092]

Global Media Awards for College Sports [Vol. 1: 11453]

Global Mobile Awards [Vol. 1: 8794]

Global Outcomes Leadership Award [Vol. 1: 10208]

Global Prevention Prize [Vol. 1: 11457]

Global Sanitation Award [Vol. 2: 3798]

Global Student Entrepreneur Award [Vol. 2: 6226]

Global Television Writers' Apprentice Award [Vol. 1: 114]

Global War on Terrorism Expeditionary Medal [Vol. 1: 8204]

Global War on Terrorism Medals [Vol. 1: 8205]

Global War on Terrorism Service Medal [Vol. 1: 8205]

Global War on Terrorisms Medals [Vol. 1: 8204]

Global Young Advocate Award [Vol. 1: 16639]

Global Youth Excellence Awards, an International Award Scheme [Vol. 2: 5946]

Globe Award [Vol. 2: 7073]

Glogau Award; Otto [Vol. 2: 5005]

Gloucester Challenge Trophy [Vol. 2: 5054]

Glover Distinguished Member Award; Claire [Vol. 1: 11579]

Gluck ISCD Humanitarian Award; Dr. Oscar S. [Vol. 1: 10148]

Gluge; Prix Theophile [Vol. 2: 1633]

Glushien Award; Anne Williams [Vol. 1: 4659]

GM Liberal Arts Excellence Awards Program [Vol. 1: 8453]

GM of the Year [Vol. 1: 5904]

Go-Green Journalism Award [Vol. 2: 4629]

Godbout; Prix Archange- [Vol. 1: 8469]

Goddard Astronautics Award [Vol. 1: 2522]

Goddard Award [Vol. 1: 2522]

Goddard Award; George W. [Vol. 1: 16151]

Goddard Early Career Award; G.V. [Vol. 2: 4990]

Goddard/Libraries Ltd. Author Awards; Judy [Vol. 1: 4782]

Goddard Medal [Vol. 1: 15450]

Gode Medal; Alexander [Vol. 1: 4604]

Godel Prize
    Association for Computing Machinery - Special Interest Group on Algorithms and Computation Theory [Vol. 1: 4967]
    European Association for Theoretical Computer Science [Vol 2: 3278]

Godfrey Award; Kneeland "Ned" [Vol. 1: 7567]

Godin Award; Jean-Cleo [Vol. 1: 6219]

Godlove Award [Vol. 1: 9451]

Godman-Salvin Medal [Vol. 2: 7157]

Goethals Medal; George W. [Vol. 1: 15451]

Goethe Medaille [Vol. 2: 3031]

Goethe Prize; Hansischer [Vol. 2: 3201]

Goetze 21st Century Award; Mandy [Vol. 1: 9495]

Goff, Lemonon, Houry, Laveran; Prix Jean-Marie Le [Vol. 2: 2205]

Goffman Award for Outstanding Scholarship in the Ecology of Social Interaction; Erving [Vol. 1: 11034]

Gokcen Medal; Sabiha [Vol. 2: 6309]

Gold Air Medal **[Vol. 2: 6310]**
Gold and Platinum Awards **[Vol. 1: 6855]**
Gold Anvil Award **[Vol. 1: 14328]**
GOLD Award **[Vol. 1: 17645]**
Gold Award
   AHRA: The Association for Medical Imaging
     Management **[Vol. 1: 228]**
   American Association of Webmasters **[Vol 1:
     1410]**
   Chartered Institute of Architectural Technolo-
     gists **[Vol 2: 7359]**
   National Association of Emergency Medical
     Technicians **[Vol 1: 11759]**
   Veteran Motor Car Club of America **[Vol 1:
     17530]**
   Walkley Foundation **[Vol 2: 1176]**
Gold Award for Volunteer Services **[Vol. 1: 11760]**
Gold Awards for Exceptional Utility Performance **[Vol.
   1: 5417]**
Gold Baton Award **[Vol. 1: 10779]**
Gold Book Awards **[Vol. 1: 5315]**
Gold Camera Award **[Vol. 1: 16985]**
Gold Cane Award **[Vol. 1: 4621]**
Gold Chaine Star of Excellence **[Vol. 1: 7520]**
Gold Circle Awards
   American Society of Association Executives **[Vol.
     1: 4130]**
   Columbia Scholastic Press Association **[Vol 1:
     7411]**
Gold Compass Prize **[Vol. 2: 4034]**
Gold Crown Awards **[Vol. 1: 7410]**
Gold Cup **[Vol. 1: 3323]**
Gold Cystoscope Award **[Vol. 1: 4622]**
Gold Diploma of Honor **[Vol. 2: 3317]**
Gold Disc Award **[Vol. 2: 5290]**
Gold Edelweiss **[Vol. 2: 6108]**
Gold Good Citizenship Medal **[Vol. 1: 12902]**
Gold-Headed Cane
   Seventh Day Baptist Historical Society **[Vol. 1:
     14848]**
   World Association of Societies of Pathology and
     Laboratory Medicine **[Vol 2: 4350]**
Gold-Headed Cane Award **[Vol. 1: 3957]**
Gold Heart Award **[Vol. 1: 2312]**
Gold Key Award **[Vol. 1: 1865]**
Gold Key Awards
   Society of Professional Journalists **[Vol. 1:
     15812]**
   University of Chicago - Medical and Biological
     Sciences Alumni Association **[Vol 1: 17207]**
Gold Keyboard Award **[Vol. 1: 13226]**
Gold Leaf Award **[Vol. 1: 10275]**
Gold Lifesaving Medal **[Vol. 1: 16673]**
Gold Medal
   Academy of Natural Sciences **[Vol. 1: 92]**
   Acoustical Society of America **[Vol 1: 122]**
   Air League **[Vol 2: 6692]**
   American College of Radiology **[Vol 1: 1819]**
   American Craft Council **[Vol 1: 1947]**
   American Institute of Architects **[Vol 1: 2569]**
   American Institute of Chemists **[Vol 1: 2647]**
   American Rhododendron Society **[Vol 1: 3698]**
   ASM International **[Vol 1: 4836]**
   Association of European Operational Research
     Societies **[Vol 2: 1405]**
   Australian Council for Educational Leaders **[Vol
     2: 272]**
   Australian Council on Healthcare Standards **[Vol
     2: 288]**
   Australian Institute of Nuclear Science and Engi-
     neering **[Vol 2: 401]**
   Australian Society of Exploration Geophysi-
     cists **[Vol 2: 571]**
   Bangladesh Chemical Society **[Vol 2: 1368]**
   Brazilian Metallurgy and Materials Associa-
     tion **[Vol 2: 1756]**
   British Society of Rheology **[Vol 2: 7267]**
   Canadian Institute of Forestry **[Vol 1: 6590]**
   Canadian Remote Sensing Society **[Vol 1: 6857]**
   Cardiovascular and Interventional Radiological
     Society of Europe **[Vol 2: 1218]**
   Chartered Institute of Journalists **[Vol 2: 7375]**
   Ecological Society of Australia **[Vol 2: 693]**
   Entomological Society of Canada **[Vol 1: 8153]**
   European Society of Paediatric Radiology **[Vol
     2: 7644]**

Federation of International Bandy **[Vol 2: 6149]**
Filtration Society **[Vol 2: 7686]**
FLEUROSELECT **[Vol 2: 4713]**
French National Center for Scientific Re-
   search **[Vol 2: 2448]**
Guildhall School of Music and Drama **[Vol 2:
   7779]**
Institute of Actuaries - United Kingdom **[Vol 2:
   7824]**
Institute of Chartered Accountants of Scot-
   land **[Vol 2: 7840]**
Institute of Management **[Vol 2: 7887]**
Institution of Civil Engineers **[Vol 2: 7984]**
Institution of Gas Engineers and Managers **[Vol
   2: 8042]**
Institution of Structural Engineers **[Vol 2: 8058]**
International Federation of Sports Medicine **[Vol
   2: 4105]**
International Motorcycling Federation **[Vol 2:
   6409]**
International Radiation Commission **[Vol 2:
   5445]**
International Society for Magnetic Resonance in
   Medicine **[Vol 1: 10182]**
International Society on Multiple Criteria Deci-
   sion Making **[Vol 2: 6075]**
Italian Association for Metallurgy **[Vol 2: 4121]**
National Association of Licensed Paralegals **[Vol
   2: 8386]**
National Vegetable Society **[Vol 2: 8415]**
Pakistan Academy of Sciences **[Vol 2: 5191]**
Professional Grounds Management Society **[Vol
   1: 14227]**
Professional Institute of the Public Service of
   Canada **[Vol 1: 14233]**
Public Relations Institute of Southern Africa **[Vol
   2: 5601]**
Royal Architectural Institute of Canada **[Vol 1:
   14614]**
Royal Astronomical Society **[Vol 2: 8660]**
Royal Canadian Geographical Society **[Vol 1:
   14625]**
Royal Irish Academy **[Vol 2: 3929]**
Royal Philharmonic Society **[Vol 2: 8887]**
Royal Scottish Geographical Society **[Vol 2:
   8924]**
Royal Swedish Academy of Engineering Sci-
   ences **[Vol 2: 6178]**
Societe de Pathologie Exotique **[Vol 2: 2624]**
Society of Manufacturing Engineers **[Vol 1:
   15688]**
Society of Woman Geographers **[Vol 1: 15892]**
South African Chemical Institute **[Vol 2: 5675]**
South African Sugar Technologists' Associa-
   tion **[Vol 2: 5726]**
South African Veterinary Association **[Vol 2:
   5732]**
SPIE **[Vol 1: 16152]**
Statistical Society of Canada **[Vol 1: 16289]**
Tau Sigma Delta **[Vol 1: 16383]**
World Organisation for Animal Health **[Vol 2:
   2668]**
Zoological Society of Southern Africa **[Vol 2:
   5771]**
Gold Medal and Fellowship of the Society **[Vol. 2:
   486]**
Gold Medal and First Prize **[Vol. 2: 8558]**
Gold Medal Award
   African Association for Public Administration and
     Management **[Vol. 2: 4378]**
   American Academy of Periodontology **[Vol 1:
     721]**
   American College of Healthcare Executives **[Vol
     1: 1755]**
   American Society of Naval Engineers **[Vol 1:
     4442]**
   Association of Canadian Advertisers **[Vol 1:
     5233]**
   Audio Engineering Society **[Vol 1: 5691]**
   Engineers Canada **[Vol 1: 8125]**
   Fertilizer Society of South Africa **[Vol 2: 5547]**
   International Radio and Television Society Foun-
     dation **[Vol 1: 10085]**
   National Retail Federation **[Vol 1: 12779]**
   Society of Biological Psychiatry **[Vol 1: 15561]**

Gold Medal Award for Distinguished Archaeological
   Achievement **[Vol. 1: 4761]**
Gold Medal Award for Distinguished Lifetime
   Contributions to Canadian Psychology **[Vol. 1:
   6825]**
Gold Medal Award for Excellence in Dental Re-
   search **[Vol. 1: 2003]**
Gold Medal Award for Industry **[Vol. 2: 3919]**
Gold Medal Award for Technical Achievement **[Vol.
   1: 15770]**
Gold Medal Award of Excellence **[Vol. 1: 12941]**
Gold Medal for Architecture **[Vol. 2: 5695]**
Gold Medal for Botany **[Vol. 2: 5660]**
Gold Medal for Distinguished Achievement **[Vol. 1:
   3130]**
Gold Medal for Distinguished Merit **[Vol. 2: 7119]**
Gold Medal for Distinguished Service **[Vol. 1: 15446]**
Gold Medal for Excellence - Police Officers **[Vol. 1:
   8996]**
Gold Medal for International Corporate Achievement
   in Sustainable Development **[Vol. 1: 18039]**
Gold Medal for Outstanding Architectural Achieve-
   ment **[Vol. 2: 2585]**
Gold Medal of Honor
   American Watercolor Society **[Vol. 1: 4660]**
   World Federation of Neurosurgical Societies **[Vol
     2: 6543]**
Gold Medal of Honour **[Vol. 2: 5508]**
Gold Medal Student Award **[Vol. 1: 8126]**
Gold Medallion **[Vol. 1: 5991]**
Gold Medallion Award
   International Swimming Hall of Fame **[Vol. 1:
     10409]**
   National School Public Relations Associa-
     tion **[Vol 1: 12804]**
Gold Medallion Book Awards **[Vol. 1: 8197]**
Gold Medals
   Malaysian Institute of Certified Public Accoun-
     tants **[Vol. 2: 4549]**
   Pakistan Academy of Sciences **[Vol 2: 5192]**
   Royal Geographical Society with the Institute of
     British Geographers **[Vol 2: 8792]**
Gold Member **[Vol. 1: 9482]**
Gold Memorial Bowl **[Vol. 2: 9112]**
Gold Memorial Lifetime Achievement Award;
   Nathan **[Vol. 1: 15735]**
Gold Mondial Medal **[Vol. 1: 7521]**
Gold Nibs Award **[Vol. 1: 2273]**
Gold Panda Award **[Vol. 2: 6571]**
Gold Parachuting Medal **[Vol. 2: 6311]**
Gold Plaque **[Vol. 1: 10114]**
Gold/Platinum/Diamond Book Awards **[Vol. 1: 8198]**
Gold Quill Award **[Vol. 1: 4298]**
Gold Ribbon Award for Broadcast Excellence **[Vol.
   1: 6232]**
Gold Ribbon for Community Service (Radio) **[Vol. 1:
   6233]**
Gold Ribbon for Community Service (Specialty/Pay/
   PPV) **[Vol. 1: 6234]**
Gold Ribbon for Community Service (Television)-
   [Vol. 1: 6235]
Gold Ribbon for Distinguished Service **[Vol. 1: 6232]**
Gold Ribbon for Outstanding Community Service by
   an Individual Broadcaster **[Vol. 1: 6236]**
Gold Ribbon for Promotion of Musical Canadian Tal-
   ent (Radio) **[Vol. 1: 6237]**
Gold Rotorcraft Medal **[Vol. 2: 6312]**
Gold Screen Awards **[Vol. 1: 11779]**
Gold Service Award **[Vol. 2: 741]**
Gold, Silver, and Bronze Medals **[Vol. 2: 8595]**
Gold Space Medal **[Vol. 2: 6313]**
Gold Star and Citation **[Vol. 2: 4204]**
Gold Star Awards **[Vol. 1: 9787]**
Gold T-Square **[Vol. 1: 12035]**
Gold TASTA Award **[Vol. 2: 9521]**
Gold Training Award **[Vol. 2: 6800]**
Gold Triangle Awards **[Vol. 1: 513]**
Gold Wing Award **[Vol. 1: 12016]**
Gold Wings **[Vol. 2: 5483]**
Goldacre Award; Peter **[Vol. 2: 579]**
Goldberg Young Investigator Award; Leon I. **[Vol. 1:
   3801]**
Goldblatt Cytology Award; Maurice **[Vol. 2: 3040]**
Golde Award **[Vol. 1: 10538]**

Gospel Recorded Performance of the Year [**Vol. 1: 9732**]

Gosselet; Prix [**Vol. 2: 2457**]

Gossen Award [**Vol. 2: 3224**]

Gotham Independent Film Awards [**Vol. 1: 9177**]

Gotlieb Contribution Award; C. C. [**Vol. 1: 6569**]

Gottardi Prize [**Vol. 2: 5998**]

Gottesdiener Prize; Nathan [**Vol. 2: 3992**]

Gottesfeld Award; Kenneth R. [**Vol. 1: 15614**]

Gottlieb Prize; Murray [**Vol. 1: 11068**]

Gottlieb Trophy; Eddie [**Vol. 1: 11980**]

Gottschalk Medal [**Vol. 2: 176**]

Gottschalk Memorial Award; Fred W. [**Vol. 1: 8431**]

Gottschalk Prize; Louis [**Vol. 1: 3824**]

Goubran Award; Marie [**Vol. 2: 4735**]

Goudie Lectureship and Medal [**Vol. 2: 8460**]

Goueram-Toekenning [**Vol. 2: 5578**]

Gould Memorial Literary Award [**Vol. 1: 2991**]

Gould Young Composer Awards; Morton [**Vol. 1: 4261**]

Goulden Memorial Award; Loran L. [**Vol. 1: 8271**]

Goulding Social Justice Award; Robert and Mary [**Vol. 1: 10463**]

Governing Board's Award for the Best Paper [**Vol. 1: 17399**]

Government Achievement Award [**Vol. 1: 7815**]

Government Affairs Award [**Vol. 1: 11928**]

Government Affairs Award of Recognition [**Vol. 1: 6045**]

Government Attorney Award [**Vol. 1: 10789**]

Government Civil Engineer of the Year Award [**Vol. 1: 4184**]

Government Service Award [**Vol. 1: 15628**]

Governor and First Lady's Medals for Service [**Vol. 1: 6099**]

Governor and First Lady's Service Award [**Vol. 1: 6100**]

Governor-General Art Award [**Vol. 2: 4949**]

Governor General's Award [**Vol. 1: 6156**]

Governor General's Awards in Commemoration of the Persons Case [**Vol. 1: 16293**]

Governor General's Awards in Visual and Media Arts [**Vol. 1: 6131**]

Governor General's International Award for Canadian Studies [**Vol. 1: 9816**]

Governor General's Literary Awards [**Vol. 1: 6132**]

Governor General's Literary Awards for Children's Literature [**Vol. 1: 6132**]

Governor General's Literary Awards for Translation [**Vol. 1: 6132**]

Governor General's Youth Award [**Vol. 2: 1347**]

Governor of the Year [**Vol. 1: 12613**]

Governor of the Year Award [**Vol. 1: 5854**]

Governor's Achievement Award [**Vol. 1: 10858**]

Governor's Award [**Vol. 2: 7**]

Governor's Award for Design and Construction Excellence in the Cayman Islands [**Vol. 2: 1821**]

Governor's Award for Lifetime Achievement in the Humanities [**Vol. 2: 5110**]

Governor's Award for Outstanding Humanities Teacher [**Vol. 2: 5111**]

Governor's Award for Preservation of CNMI History [**Vol. 2: 5112**]

Governor's Award for Preservation of Traditional Cultural Practices [**Vol. 2: 5113**]

Governor's Award for Research and Publication in the Humanities [**Vol. 2: 5114**]

Governor's National Leadership Award [**Vol. 1: 11761**]

Governor's Screenwriting Competition [**Vol. 1: 17573**]

Governor's Volunteerism Awards [**Vol. 1: 17571**]

Gowdy Media Awards; Curt [**Vol. 1: 11361**]

GP of the Year Award; National [**Vol. 2: 8682**]

GP Registrar Awards [**Vol. 2: 8677**]

Graber Award of Special Merit; Thomas M. [**Vol. 1: 1261**]

Grace Award; Oliver R. [**Vol. 1: 7056**]

Grace Memorial Award; Dorman John [**Vol. 1: 12349**]

Graded Awards [**Vol. 2: 9463**]

Grader Award; Dr. Peretz [**Vol. 2: 3964**]

Gradiva Awards [**Vol. 1: 11610**]

Graduate and Undergraduate Scholarships [**Vol. 1: 10639**]

Graduate Assistantships [**Vol. 1: 17232**]

Graduate Award [**Vol. 1: 10850**]

Graduate Designer Awards [**Vol. 2: 3850**]

Graduate Education Award [**Vol. 2: 5237**]

Graduate Excellence in Materials Science Award GEMS [**Vol. 1: 1561**]

Graduate Fellows [**Vol. 1: 745**]

Graduate Fellowship [**Vol. 1: 7463**]

Graduate Fellowships [**Vol. 1: 13977**]

Graduate Fellowships in Mycology [**Vol. 1: 11328**]

Graduate Microbiology Teaching Award [**Vol. 1: 3978**]

Graduate of the Year [**Vol. 1: 8727**]

Graduate Prize [**Vol. 2: 3922**]

Graduate Product Award [**Vol. 2: 7090**]

Graduate Research Award [**Vol. 1: 16600**]

Graduate Research Award

    Herpetologists' League [**Vol. 1: 8918**]

    Institute of Industrial Engineers [**Vol 1: 9353**]

Graduate Research Awards

    AVS Science and Technology Society [**Vol. 1: 5731**]

    Northwestern University - Roberta Buffett Center for International and Comparative Studies [**Vol 1: 13421**]

Graduate Scholarship Award [**Vol. 1: 13057**]

Graduate Student Award

    Canadian Society of Microbiologists [**Vol. 1: 6977**]

    Chinese Chemical Society [**Vol 2: 5238**]

    European Materials Research Society [**Vol 2: 2383**]

    Society for Applied Spectroscopy [**Vol 1: 15036**]

Graduate Student Awards

    Biomedical Engineering Society [**Vol. 1: 5842**]

    International Association for the Fantastic in the Arts [**Vol 1: 9594**]

    Materials Research Society [**Vol 1: 11004**]

Graduate Student Essay Prize [**Vol. 1: 5096**]

Graduate Student Fellowship [**Vol. 1: 9106**]

Graduate Student Fellowship/Novartis Award [**Vol. 1: 15851**]

Graduate Student Mentor Award [**Vol. 1: 15190**]

Graduate Student Paper Competition Awards [**Vol. 1: 6928**]

Graduate Student Paper Contest [**Vol. 1: 4837**]

Graduate Student Paper Prize

    African Studies Association [**Vol. 1: 202**]

    Middle East Studies Association of North America [**Vol 1: 11141**]

Graduate Student Plant Breeding Award [**Vol. 1: 12179**]

Graduate Student Poster Presentation Award [**Vol. 1: 1023**]

Graduate Student Research Award [**Vol. 1: 967**]

Graduate Student Research Award

    AAHPERD Research Consortium [**Vol. 1: 23**]

    American Society on Aging [**Vol 1: 4530**]

Graduate Student Research Grants [**Vol. 1: 4496**]

Graduate Student Research Paper Award [**Vol. 1: 3825**]

Graduate Student Scholar Award [**Vol. 1: 14006**]

Graduate Student Scholarship Award [**Vol. 1: 13954**]

Graduate Student Teaching Award [**Vol. 1: 13293**]

Graduate Student Travel Award [**Vol. 1: 3454**]

Graduate Student Travel Grants

    American Association for Applied Linguistics [**Vol. 1: 876**]

    Labor and Working Class History Association [**Vol 1: 10716**]

Graduate Thesis/Dissertation Award [**Vol. 1: 9995**]

Graduates and Students Papers Competition [**Vol. 2: 7985**]

Graduateship of the City and Guilds of London Institute [**Vol. 2: 7432**]

Graduation Award [**Vol. 1: 7637**]

Graduation Prize [**Vol. 2: 4801**]

Grady Award for Interpreting Chemistry for the Public; James T. [**Vol. 1: 1644**]

Grady - James H. Stack Award for Interpreting Chemistry for the Public; James T. [**Vol. 1: 1644**]

Graff Excellence in Occupational Health Nursing Award; Marguerite Ahern [**Vol. 1: 1503**]

Graff Young Investigator Award; Ken [**Vol. 1: 680**]

Graffin Lectureship Award; George D. [**Vol. 1: 1538**]

Graham and Dodd Award [**Vol. 1: 7168**]

Graham Award; Duncan [**Vol. 1: 14628**]

Graham Award for Innovation in Improving Community Health; Fred [**Vol. 1: 1768**]

Graham Award of Merit; James H. [**Vol. 1: 14629**]

Graham Chance Award; Dr. [**Vol. 1: 6577**]

Graham Family Physician Executive Award; Robert [**Vol. 1: 554**]

Graham Medal [**Vol. 2: 8892**]

Graham Perpetual Trophy; Victor W. [**Vol. 2: 3842**]

Graham Prize for Health Services Research; William B. [**Vol. 1: 5549**]

Graham Scholarship in Entrepreneurship; Gerald [**Vol. 1: 17828**]

Gramatky Memorial Award; Hardie [**Vol. 1: 4661**]

Grambs Distinguished Career Research in Social Studies Award; Jean Dresden [**Vol. 1: 12168**]

Grammaticakis-Neuman; Prix [**Vol. 2: 2206**]

Grammaticakis-Neumann Prize [**Vol. 2: 6487**]

Gran Cruz de la Universidad del Valle [**Vol. 2: 1853**]

Grand Canyon Readers Awards [**Vol. 1: 4783**]

Grand Champion [**Vol. 1: 11983**]

Grand Companion of Logohu [**Vol. 2: 5213**]

Grand Concours Litteraire [**Vol. 1: 14698**]

Grand Cross of the Order of Saint Lucia [**Vol. 2: 5891**]

Grand Hamdan International Award [**Vol. 2: 6666**]

Grand Jazz Award [**Vol. 1: 8346**]

Grand Journalism Prize [**Vol. 2: 5146**]

Grand Jury Awards [**Vol. 1: 8381**]

Grand Master Award [**Vol. 1: 14785**]

Grand Medal [**Vol. 2: 4437**]

Grand National Exhibition Awards [**Vol. 1: 848**]

Grand National Pulling Circuit Rookie of the Year [**Vol. 1: 12988**]

Grand Prix

    Association Aeronautique et Astronautique de France [**Vol. 2: 2311**]

    Fiji Chess Federation [**Vol 2: 2062**]

    Society of Dramatic Authors and Composers [**Vol 2: 2634**]

Grand Prix d'Architecture [**Vol. 2: 2142**]

Grand Prix de Chimie Industrielle [**Vol. 2: 2437**]

Grand Prix de Jazz General Motors [**Vol. 1: 8346**]

Grand Prix de la Chanson Francaise [**Vol. 2: 2627**]

Grand Prix de la Musique Symphonique [**Vol. 2: 2628**]

Grand Prix de la Poesie [**Vol. 2: 2631**]

Grand Prix de la Societe de Chimie [**Vol. 2: 2437**]

Grand Prix de l'Edition Musicale [**Vol. 2: 2629**]

Grand Prix de l'Humour [**Vol. 2: 2630**]

Grand Prix des Poetes [**Vol. 2: 2631**]

Grand Prix d'Honneur [**Vol. 2: 6424**]

Grand Prix du Disque Frederic Chopin [**Vol. 2: 5387**]

Grand Prix du Jazz [**Vol. 2: 2632**]

Grand Prix Grimstad [**Vol. 2: 5153**]

Grand Prix in Architecture [**Vol. 2: 1937**]

Grand Prix of the Americas [**Vol. 1: 11258**]

Grand Prize

    Foundation for Medical Research [**Vol. 2: 2423**]

    Swedish Academy [**Vol 2: 6203**]

    Zagreb World Festival of Animated Films - ANIMAFEST Zagreb [**Vol 2: 1889**]

Grand Prize Cantabile [**Vol. 1: 6365**]

Grand Prize for Best Commissioned Animation [**Vol. 1: 13735**]

Grand Prize of the Flemish Community for Best Film [**Vol. 2: 1516**]

Grand Prize Winner Award [**Vol. 1: 12655**]

Grand Slams of Tennis [**Vol. 2: 8235**]

Grand Trophy Award [**Vol. 2: 2557**]

Grande Medaille

    French Academy of Sciences [**Vol. 2: 2435**]

    French Society for Metallurgy and Materials [**Vol 2: 2451**]

Grandjany Prize [**Vol. 1: 2276**]

Grandmaster [**Vol. 2: 3318**]

Granjon Prize; Henry [**Vol. 2: 2545**]

Grannis Award for Excellence in Research and Scientific Publication; George [**Vol. 1: 905**]

Grant Award; Eugene L. [**Vol. 1: 3857**]

Grant Competition [**Vol. 1: 16972**]

Grant Essay Prize; Julius [**Vol. 2: 8449**]

Grant for Student Research in Mineralogy and Petrology [**Vol. 1: 11174**]

Grant for the Enhancement of Geographic Literacy [**Vol. 1: 12169**]

Grant Medal; Robert P. [**Vol. 1: 10368**]

Grant Memorial Musical Theatre Scholarship; Regan [Vol. 1: 14739]

Grants for Arts Projects [Vol. 1: 12311]

Grants for Literacy Projects in Countries with Developing Economics [Vol. 1: 10094]

Grants for Postgraduate and Postdoctoral Workshops [Vol. 2: 7658]

Grants for Publication [Vol. 2: 7483]

Grants for Study Visits [Vol. 2: 7659]

Grants-in-Aid of Research [Vol. 1: 14906]

Grants-in-Aid Program [Vol. 1: 15362]

Grants to Eastern Europeans [Vol. 2: 7622]

Graphic Designer of the Year
    East Coast Music Association [Vol. 1: 7959]
    Finnish Association of Designers Ornamo [Vol 2: 2082]

Grass Foundation Lecture; Albert and Ellen [Vol. 1: 15234]

Grasso Literary Award; Ella [Vol. 1: 16611]

GrassRoots Action Network for Dairy Pioneer Award GRAND [Vol. 1: 9868]

Grateful Nation Award [Vol. 1: 10574]

The Gratiaen Prize [Vol. 2: 6122]

Gratitude Medal [Vol. 2: 3005]

Grau Turfgrass Science Award; Fred V. [Vol. 1: 7764]

Graves Lecture [Vol. 2: 3909]

Graves Nutrition Education Award; Lulu G. [Vol. 1: 2035]

Gravure Persons of the Year Awards [Vol. 1: 8776]

Grawemeyer Award for Ideas Improving World Order [Vol. 1: 17263]

Grawemeyer Award for Music Composition [Vol. 1: 17270]

Grawemeyer Award in Education [Vol. 1: 17264]

Grawemeyer Award in Religion [Vol. 1: 17268]

Gray Article Prize; Ralph D. [Vol. 1: 15088]

Gray Award; Asa [Vol. 1: 4497]

Gray Award - Branch Certificate; Stanley [Vol. 2: 7892]

Gray Award; Emily M. [Vol. 1: 5851]

Gray Award; Eva Kenworthy [Vol. 1: 1489]

Gray Citation of Merit; William S. [Vol. 1: 10095]

Gray/Elsevier Distinguished Educator Award; Henry [Vol. 1: 1024]

Gray/Lippincott Williams and Wilkins Scientific Achievement Award; Henry [Vol. 1: 1025]

Gray Matter Medal [Vol. 2: 7222]

Gray Medal [Vol. 1: 9792]

Gray Silver Medal; Stanley [Vol. 2: 7893]

Graybiel Award; Ashton [Vol. 1: 15870]

Greanoff Inspirational Leadership Award; COMO Charles S. [Vol. 1: 16759]

Great American Main Street Award [Vol. 1: 13003]

Great Friend to Kids Award [Vol. 1: 5248]

Great Gold Medal [Vol. 2: 6179]

Great Lakes Commission - Sea Grant Fellowship [Vol. 1: 11121]

Great Lakes Skakel Award [Vol. 1: 1540]

Great Mind Awards
    Advertising Research Foundation [Vol. 1: 168]
    Advertising Research Foundation [Vol 1: 169]
    Advertising Research Foundation [Vol 1: 171]

Great Prizes [Vol. 2: 6159]

Great Swedish Heritage Award [Vol. 1: 16347]

Great Taste Awards [Vol. 2: 7761]

Greater Lynn International Color Exhibition [Vol. 1: 8782]

Greater Union Awards [Vol. 2: 1079]

Greathouse Distinguished Leadership Award; Frank [Vol. 1: 5361]

Greathouse Medal; Walser S. [Vol. 1: 4662]

Greaves-Walker Award; Arthur Frederick [Vol. 1: 1562]

Grebe Award; Alfred H. [Vol. 1: 14401]

Grebenschikov Prize; L.V. [Vol. 2: 5802]

Greco Award; Richard E. [Vol. 1: 14484]

Greco Community Award; Joe [Vol. 1: 6077]

Greco-Roman Coach of the Year [Vol. 1: 17487]

Greco-Roman Wrestler of the Year [Vol. 1: 17488]

Greek Islands Award [Vol. 2: 3310]

Greek Shipping Awards [Vol. 2: 8321]

Greeley Award; Samuel Arnold [Vol. 1: 4185]

Green and Charles W. Ramsdell Award; Fletcher M. [Vol. 1: 16023]

Green Apple Awards
    Environmental Transport Association [Vol. 2: 7569]
    Green Organisation [Vol 2: 7747]

Green-Armytage and Spackman Travelling Scholarship [Vol. 2: 8694]

Green Award
    Foodservice Consultants Society International [Vol. 1: 8404]
    International Council on Active Aging [Vol 1: 9841]

Green Award; Alyce and Elmer [Vol. 1: 10248]

Green Award; Daniel H. [Vol. 1: 5601]

Green Award; David [Vol. 1: 11311]

Green Award; Fletcher M. [Vol. 1: 16023]

Green Award for Excellence in Journalism; Mark A. [Vol. 1: 10124]

Green Award for Young Concert Artists; Philip and Dorothy [Vol. 2: 8338]

Green Award; Paul E. [Vol. 1: 2813]

Green Award; Rick [Vol. 1: 9629]

The Green Awards [Vol. 2: 4401]

Green Built Bangladesh Contest; Holcim [Vol. 2: 1374]

Green Car Awards [Vol. 2: 7569]

Green Chemistry Award [Vol. 2: 9012]

Green Chemistry Challenge Awards [Vol. 2: 975]

Green Codes and Standards Medal; Melvin R. [Vol. 1: 4391]

Green Corners Awards; London's [Vol. 2: 7473]

Green Elephant Award for Citizen Achievement [Vol. 1: 14514]

Green Energy and Green Livelihoods Achievement Award [Vol. 1: 14869]

Green Globe Award for Environmental Achievement [Vol. 1: 8371]

Green Gown Awards [Vol. 2: 7567]

Green Idea of the Year Award [Vol. 1: 9026]

Green Initiative Award [Vol. 2: 6895]

Green Leaf Award [Vol. 1: 4301]

Green Organisation of the Year [Vol. 2: 7012]

Green Outstanding Young Scientist Award; Gordon J. [Vol. 1: 6796]

Green Power Leadership Awards
    United States Environmental Protection Agency [Vol. 1: 16887]
    United States Environmental Protection Agency [Vol 1: 16895]

Green Power Leadership Club [Vol. 1: 16888]

Green Power Partner of the Year [Vol. 1: 16889]

Green Power Purchase Award [Vol. 1: 16890]

Green Round Hill Trophy; Colonel [Vol. 1: 3324]

Green School Educator Award; Elizabeth A.H. [Vol. 1: 4569]

Green Section Award [Vol. 1: 16934]

Green Star Awards [Vol. 1: 14228]

The Green Star Awards [Vol. 2: 4402]

Greenaway Medal; Kate [Vol. 2: 7378]

Greenberg Award; Noah [Vol. 1: 2963]

Greenberg Media Award; Mel [Vol. 1: 17969]

Greenblatt Prizes; Robert B. [Vol. 2: 8150]

Greene, Jr., Award; General Wallace M. [Vol. 1: 10973]

Greene Leadership Award; Dr. Patricia [Vol. 1: 5453]

Greene Medal; Arnold [Vol. 2: 7963]

Greene Medical Student Award; Dr. Alexandra [Vol. 1: 8802]

Greene Memorial United States Numismatics - YN Exhibit Award; Gordon Z. [Vol. 1: 2989]

Greene Quality of Life Lectureship; Trish [Vol. 1: 13550]

Greenfield Award; Sylvia Sorkin [Vol. 1: 1304]

Greenford Award; Stephen [Vol. 1: 6273]

Greenhalgh Student Essay Competition; William [Vol. 1: 1471]

Greening Prize; H. J. [Vol. 2: 7407]

Greening the Future Awards [Vol. 2: 5572]

Greenland Award [Vol. 2: 1949]

Greenland Prospector and Developer of the Year [Vol. 2: 3325]

Greenlee Prize; Douglas [Vol. 1: 15346]

Greenwalt Memorial Award and Lectureship; Tibor [Vol. 1: 1064]

Greenwood Environmental Science Award; Hugh [Vol. 2: 5358]

Greer Achievement Award; Al [Vol. 1: 9433]

Greer Architectural Conservation and Craftsmanship Award; William [Vol. 1: 8916]

Greer Award; Clay M. [Vol. 1: 17511]

Greer Cup; Don [Vol. 1: 17156]

Gregg Award; Dr. Randy [Vol. 1: 6642]

Gregg/Ed Lacy Memorial Award for Travel Broadcasting; Anne [Vol. 2: 7074]

Gregoir Medal; Willy [Vol. 2: 4691]

Gregory Award; Joseph T. [Vol. 1: 15876]

Gregory Awards; Eric [Vol. 2: 9249]

Gregory Medal; Herbert E. [Vol. 1: 13772]

Gregory Memorial Scholarship Fund; T.M. [Vol. 2: 5273]

Gregory Prize; P.H. [Vol. 2: 7235]

Greim Award; Willard N. [Vol. 1: 450]

Grenadier Award; Judge Albert H. [Vol. 1: 8582]

Grenvik Memorial Award; Christer [Vol. 1: 15603]

Grenzebach Awards for Outstanding Research in Philanthropy for Educational Advancement; John [Vol. 1: 8652]

Gretzky Scholarship Foundation; Wayne and Walter [Vol. 1: 6729]

Greve Memorial Award; Belle [Vol. 1: 12752]

Grey Cup [Vol. 1: 6507]

Gribov Medal [Vol. 2: 2391]

Grierson Documentary Film Award [Vol. 2: 9150]

Grierson International Gold Medal Award; John [Vol. 1: 15699]

Griesbach Excellence in Airport Concessions Contest; Richard A. [Vol. 1: 316]

Griffin Award; Charles A. [Vol. 1: 961]

Griffin Award for Urban Design; Walter Burley [Vol. 2: 383]

Griffin Long and Outstanding Service Award; Robert [Vol. 1: 7377]

Griffin Poetry Prize [Vol. 1: 8786]

Griffin Rolex Award; Ellen [Vol. 1: 10728]

Griffin Service Award; John R. [Vol. 1: 12946]

Griffith Award; H. Winter [Vol. 1: 555]

Griffiths Obedience Trophy; Suzanne N. [Vol. 1: 10521]

Griffiths Property Person of the Year; Jack [Vol. 1: 12723]

Griffiths Teaching Award; John Cedric [Vol. 1: 9575]

Grigorev Prize; A.A. [Vol. 2: 5803]

Grigson Award; Jane [Vol. 1: 9656]

Grimes Award for Excellence in Chemical Engineering; William W. [Vol. 1: 2622]

Grimley Award; Horace [Vol. 2: 8272]

Grimm Leadership and Service Award; James C. [Vol. 1: 5273]

Grimm Prize; Harold J. [Vol. 1: 14918]

Grimme Preis; Adolf [Vol. 2: 2902]

Grimwade Medal; John [Vol. 2: 7092]

Grimwade Prize [Vol. 2: 1124]

Grindley Grants for Conference Attendance [Vol. 2: 7660]

Grindley Medal [Vol. 1: 221]

Griner Award; John [Vol. 1: 6932]

Grinter Distinguished Service Award; Linton E. [Vol. 1: 29]

Griscom Award; Ludlow [Vol. 1: 1495]

Griswold Outstanding Air Pollution Control Official Award; S. Smith [Vol. 1: 236]

Gritz Award for Excellence in Public Finance; Tanya [Vol. 1: 16274]

Grober Literaturpreis Wilhelm-Hausentein-Ehrung [Vol. 2: 2708]

Grolier Foundation Award [Vol. 1: 2789]

Grollman Award for Bereavement; Earl A. [Vol. 1: 7239]

Gros New Investigator Award; Hans [Vol. 2: 3864]

Gross Memorial Award; Barry R. [Vol. 1: 11870]

Grosser Literaturpreis der Bayerischen Akademie der Schonen Kunste [Vol. 2: 2707]

Grossman Award; Louis I. [Vol. 1: 1141]

Grossmann Young Author Award; Marcus A. [Vol. 1: 4838]

Groulx - Foundation Yves-Saint-Germain; Prix Lionel [Vol. 2: 9249]

Ground Testing Award [Vol. 1: 2523]

Ground Water Protection Award [Vol. 1: 12460]

Ground Water Remediation Award [Vol. 1: 12461]

Ground Water Supply Award [Vol. 1: 12462]

Grounds Management Awards [Vol. 1: 14228]

Group Achievement Award
  Library Leadership and Management Association [**Vol. 1:** 10836]
  National Aeronautics and Space Administration - Office of Human Capital Management [**Vol 1:** 11482]
  Royal Astronomical Society [**Vol 2:** 8661]
  The Wildlife Society [**Vol 1:** 17851]
Group Bravery Citation [**Vol. 2:** 298]
Group of the Year Award [**Vol. 1:** 2886]
Group Safety Improvement Award [**Vol. 1:** 16126]
Group Study Visit [**Vol. 1:** 8609]
Group Trophies [**Vol. 1:** 17789]
Group Volunteer of the Year [**Vol. 1:** 2296]
Grove Prizes; Sir Charles [**Vol. 2:** 8339]
Groves Award; David I. [**Vol. 2:** 736]
Groves Fund Awards; Donald [**Vol. 1:** 3013]
Grow Award; Malcolm C. [**Vol. 1:** 15866]
Grow Your Own at Your Library Institutional Scholarship [**Vol. 1:** 14322]
Growing Green Awards [**Vol. 1:** 13101]
Growth and Promotion Award [**Vol. 1:** 16489]
Gruber Fund Award; Lila [**Vol. 1:** 516]
Gruber International Research Award in Neuroscience; Peter and Patricia [**Vol. 1:** 15235]
Gruber Memorial Cancer Research Award and Lectureship; Lila [**Vol. 1:** 514]
Gruentzig Lecture; Andreas [**Vol. 2:** 1219]
Grulee Award; Clifford G. [**Vol. 1:** 681]
Grundler Prize; Otto [**Vol. 1:** 17765]
Grundy Memorial Scholarship; Joseph R. [**Vol. 1:** 17657]
Grunfeld Commemorative Award; Dr. Paul [**Vol. 2:** 3006]
Grunzweig Human Rights Award; Emil [**Vol. 2:** 3938]
Gruppo Augusta International Helicopter Fellowship Award [**Vol. 1:** 2321]
GSI Medallion [**Vol. 2:** 3838]
Guardia Memorial Trophy; Ed [**Vol. 1:** 16945]
Guardian Award [**Vol. 1:** 10842]
Guardians of the Children Award [**Vol. 1:** 4722]
Gubkin Prize; I.M. [**Vol. 2:** 5804]
Gude, Jr. Award; Adolph E. [**Vol. 1:** 4489]
Guenther Award in the Chemistry of Essential Oils and Related Products; Ernest [**Vol. 1:** 1645]
Guenther Award in the Chemistry of Natural Products; Ernest [**Vol. 1:** 1645]
Guerin; Prix Andre- [**Vol. 1:** 14997]
Guerrera Prize [**Vol. 2:** 2546]
Guest Lecturer Award [**Vol. 2:** 4964]
Guest of Honor [**Vol. 1:** 606]
Guest of Honor Award [**Vol. 1:** 12272]
Guetzkow Prize; Harold [**Vol. 1:** 13422]
Guggenheim Medal; Daniel [**Vol. 1:** 15512]
Guggenheim Memorial Lecture Award; Daniel and Florence [**Vol. 2:** 6151]
Guha Memorial Lecture; B. C. [**Vol. 2:** 3714]
Guiding Woman in Sport [**Vol. 1:** 942]
Guild Award; Elizabeth [**Vol. 1:** 11151]
Guild Award of Honour [**Vol. 2:** 7755]
Guild of Food Writers Award [**Vol. 2:** 7764]
Guild of Professional Toastmasters Best After Dinner Speaker of the Year [**Vol. 2:** 7766]
Guilday Prize; Peter [**Vol. 1:** 1543]
Guilford Undergraduate Research Awards; J. P. [**Vol. 1:** 14292]
Guise Medal; Arthur B. [**Vol. 1:** 15654]
Guiteras Award; Ramon [**Vol. 1:** 4623]
Gulbenkian Foundation Grants; Calouste [**Vol. 2:** 7315]
Gulbenkian Prize; Calouste [**Vol. 2:** 9250]
Guldbagge Award [**Vol. 2:** 6232]
Gulf Coast 4-Star National Best Condition Award [**Vol. 1:** 2063]
Gulick Medal; Luther Halsey [**Vol. 1:** 797]
Gullichsen Prize; Johan [**Vol. 2:** 2094]
Gullspira Award [**Vol. 2:** 6233]
Gundolf-Preis fur die Vermittlung deutscher Kultur im Ausland; Friedrich- [**Vol. 2:** 2898]
Gung and Dr. Charles Y. Hu Award for Distinguished Service to Mathematics; Yueh-Gin [**Vol. 1:** 11015]
Gunlogson Countryside Engineering Award; G. B. [**Vol. 1:** 4082]
Gunlogson Medal; G. B. [**Vol. 1:** 2428]
Gunn Award for Outstanding Professional Advocacy; Ira P. [**Vol. 1:** 7687]

Gunn Conservation Award; W. W. H. [**Vol. 1:** 13587]
Gunnells Intellectual Freedom Award; Danny [**Vol. 1:** 9197]
Gunning Jubilee Gift [**Vol. 2:** 9232]
Gunter Scholarships; Connie and Robert T. [**Vol. 1:** 14948]
Gunther Award; Frank A. [**Vol. 1:** 14402]
Gunton Grant; T. P. [**Vol. 2:** 7120]
Guptill Award; Nathanael M. [**Vol. 1:** 7527]
Gustin Memorial Intermediate Chopin Scholarship; Lyell [**Vol. 1:** 14743]
Gustin Memorial Senior Chopin Scholarship; The Lyell [**Vol. 1:** 14757]
Gutenberg Award [**Vol. 2:** 3033]
Gutenberg Medal; Beno [**Vol. 2:** 2372]
Gutenberg-Preis [**Vol. 2:** 3033]
Guth Award for Interior Lighting Design; Edwin F. [**Vol. 1:** 9156]
Guthrie Medal and Prize [**Vol. 2:** 7905]
Guthrie Medal; Faldt [**Vol. 2:** 783]
Guthrie Prize [**Vol. 2:** 7841]
Guttentag Promising New Evaluator Award; Marcia [**Vol. 1:** 2089]
Guttmacher Award; Manfred S. [**Vol. 1:** 3350]
Guttman Award; Sir Ludwig [**Vol. 2:** 238]
Guy Memorial Award; Sergio [**Vol. 1:** 14031]
Guyana Awards [**Vol. 1:** 8800]
Guyana National Cooperative Bank Award [**Vol. 2:** 3347]
Guyana Sugar Corporation Award for Soil Science [**Vol. 2:** 3348]
Guye; Prix Philippe A. [**Vol. 2:** 2207]
Guynn Family Foundation Book Scholarships [**Vol. 1:** 11663]
Guyton Awards for Excellence in Integrative Physiology; Arthur C. [**Vol. 1:** 3255]
GWA Fellow [**Vol. 1:** 8514]
Gwiazda Award [**Vol. 1:** 14081]
GWIC Award [**Vol. 1:** 8688]
Gwobrau Tir na n-Og [**Vol. 2:** 9443]
Gyldendal Prisen; Soren [**Vol. 2:** 1971]
Gyllenbergs pris; Fabian [**Vol. 2:** 6170]
Gymnastics National Volunteer of the Year [**Vol. 1:** 451]
Gyro Award of Merit [**Vol. 1:** 8802]
Gyro Honor Key [**Vol. 1:** 8803]
Gyro of the Year Award [**Vol. 1:** 8804]
Gysel Prize for Biomedical Research in Europe; Van [**Vol. 2:** 1520]
Gzowski Medal [**Vol. 1:** 6901]
Haber Award; Bernard [**Vol. 1:** 3996]
Haber Award; William
    Hillel: The Foundation for Jewish Campus Life [**Vol. 1:** 8920]
    ORT America [**Vol 1:** 13706]
Habermann Award; A. Nico [**Vol. 1:** 7467]
Habitat Business Award [**Vol. 2:** 4395]
Habitat Solaire, Habitat d'aujourd'hui [**Vol. 2:** 2594]
Hachemeister Prize; Charles A. [**Vol. 1:** 7081]
Hackerman Young Author Awards; Norman [**Vol. 1:** 8057]
Hackett Award; Thomas P. [**Vol. 1:** 108]
Hackett Memorial Award; Eleanor and Thomas P. [**Vol. 1:** 108]
Hackmatack Children's Choice Book Award [**Vol. 1:** 8807]
Hackney Award; L. R. Mike [**Vol. 1:** 15412]
Haddings pris; Assar [**Vol. 2:** 6171]
Hadeed Award for Best Small and Medium-Sized Enterprise; Ray [**Vol. 2:** 4186]
Hadford Professional Achievement Award; Gary [**Vol. 1:** 6570]
Hadley Memorial Achievement Award; Ross [**Vol. 1:** 16733]
Haemophilia Award [**Vol. 2:** 7781]
Hafner VTOL Prize [**Vol. 2:** 8606]
Hager Cup; Ben R. [**Vol. 1:** 11044]
Hager Medal; Willy [**Vol. 2:** 3166]
Hager Phalaenopsis Award; Herbert [**Vol. 1:** 3076]
Hager Prize; Willy [**Vol. 2:** 3167]
Haglund Prize for Excellence in Consultancy; Laila [**Vol. 2:** 236]
Hague Award; John L. [**Vol. 1:** 5602]
Hahn-Preis fur Chemie und Physik; Otto- [**Vol. 2:** 2773]

Haig-Brown Award; Roderick
    Canadian Wildlife Federation [**Vol. 1:** 7041]
    Federation of Fly Fishers [**Vol 1:** 8301]
Haight Award; Walter [**Vol. 1:** 13007]
Haiman Award; Mieczyslaw [**Vol. 1:** 14078]
Haimo Award for Distinguished College or University Teaching of Mathematics; Deborah and Franklin Tepper [**Vol. 1:** 11016]
Haines Award for Innovation and Leadership in Sustainability; Sharon G. [**Vol. 1:** 16339]
Hains Award; Robert A. [**Vol. 1:** 6626]
Hakanson Award; R. C. [**Vol. 1:** 8202]
Hake Translational Research Award; International Don [**Vol. 1:** 3394]
Hakluyt Award [**Vol. 1:** 14933]
Halbouty Memorial Human Needs Award; Michel T. [**Vol. 1:** 1278]
Halbouty Outstanding Leadership Award; Michel T. [**Vol. 1:** 1278]
Halcrow Prize [**Vol. 2:** 7986]
Hale Award; Sarah Josepha [**Vol. 1:** 14548]
Hale Prize; George Ellery [**Vol. 1:** 1446]
Halecki Award; Oscar [**Vol. 1:** 14079]
Hales Medal in Earth Sciences; Anton [**Vol. 2:** 177]
Hales Prize; Stephen [**Vol. 1:** 4490]
Haley Early Career Award for Innovative Contributions; Jay [**Vol. 2:** 4110]
Haley Memorial Award for Clinical Excellence; Sarah [**Vol. 1:** 10262]
Hall Award for Distinguished Contribution to Developmental Psychology; G. Stanley [**Vol. 1:** 3407]
Hall Book Prize; John Whitney [**Vol. 1:** 4916]
Hall Gold Medal; J and E [**Vol. 2:** 7941]
Hall/Harold F. Mayfield Award; George A. [**Vol. 1:** 17861]
Hall Juvenile Justice Award; Livingston [**Vol. 1:** 1472]
Hall Medal; Warren A. [**Vol. 1:** 17178]
Hall Memorial Award; Albert H. [**Vol. 1:** 12553]
Hall Memorial Trophy; Martha [**Vol. 1:** 10522]
Hall of Champions [**Vol. 1:** 3325]
Hall of Distinguished Americans [**Vol. 1:** 13070]
Hall of Fame
    American Baseball Coaches Association [**Vol. 1:** 1479]
    American Endurance Ride Conference [**Vol 1:** 2064]
    American Mensa [**Vol 1:** 2887]
    American Morgan Horse Association [**Vol 1:** 2927]
    American Society of Heating, Refrigerating and Air-Conditioning Engineers [**Vol 1:** 4324]
    American Theatre Organ Society [**Vol 1:** 4588]
    Art Directors Club [**Vol 1:** 4804]
    Asia-Pacific Professional Services Marketing Association [**Vol 2:** 87]
    Association for the Advancement of International Education [**Vol 1:** 5126]
    Association for Women in Communications [**Vol 1:** 5159]
    Association of Independent Corrugated Converters [**Vol 1:** 5369]
    Australian Cinematographers Society [**Vol 2:** 255]
    Awards and Recognition Association [**Vol 1:** 5750]
    Badminton World Federation [**Vol 2:** 4532]
    Business Committee for the Arts [**Vol 1:** 6057]
    Country Music Showcase International [**Vol 1:** 7722]
    Credit Union Executives Society [**Vol 1:** 7743]
    Garden Writers Association [**Vol 1:** 8515]
    Information Systems Security Association [**Vol 1:** 9236]
    International Bluegrass Music Association [**Vol 1:** 9732]
    International Coach Federation of New England [**Vol 1:** 9780]
    International Federation of Competitive Eating [**Vol 1:** 9916]
    International Federation of Operational Research Societies [**Vol 1:** 9924]
    International Waterski and Wakeboard Federation [**Vol 2:** 6465]
    Modular Building Institute [**Vol 1:** 11251]

National Academy of Television Arts and Sciences **[Vol 1: 11454]**

National Association for Sport and Physical Education **[Vol 1: 11604]**

National Association of Collegiate Marketing Administrators **[Vol 1: 11707]**

National Association of Hispanic Journalists **[Vol 1: 11784]**

National Baseball Hall of Fame and Museum **[Vol 1: 11971]**

National Christian College Athletic Association **[Vol 1: 12062]**

National Field Hockey Coaches Association **[Vol 1: 12391]**

National Forensic League **[Vol 1: 12415]**

National Sportscasters and Sportswriters Association **[Vol 1: 12931]**

National Wheelchair Basketball Association **[Vol 1: 13037]**

Palomino Horse Breeders of America **[Vol 1: 13809]**

Pi Kappa Phi **[Vol 1: 13999]**

Piano Technicians Guild **[Vol 1: 14010]**

Professional Bowlers Association of America **[Vol 1: 14186]**

Retail Advertising and Marketing Association **[Vol 1: 14530]**

Service Station Dealers of America/National Coalition of Petroleum Retailers and Allied Trades **[Vol 1: 14845]**

Special Libraries Association **[Vol 1: 16101]**

Special Olympics Australia **[Vol 2: 1047]**

Speed Skating Canada **[Vol 1: 16141]**

United States Curling Association **[Vol 1: 16776]**

U.S.A. Deaf Sports Federation **[Vol 1: 17415]**

Women in Technology International **[Vol 1: 17954]**

Women's All-Star Association **[Vol 1: 17960]**

World Bowling Writers **[Vol 1: 18031]**

World Boxing Council **[Vol 2: 4598]**

Hall of Fame Award

American Society for Horticultural Science **[Vol. 1: 3926]**

American Society on Aging **[Vol 1: 4531]**

American Sportscasters Association **[Vol 1: 4553]**

Asphalt Emulsion Manufacturers Association **[Vol 1: 4855]**

Composers and Authors Society of Hong Kong **[Vol 2: 5242]**

Direct Selling Association **[Vol 1: 7875]**

Federal Government Distance Learning Association **[Vol 1: 8260]**

Federal Government Distributed Learning Association **[Vol 1: 8265]**

International Franchise Association **[Vol 1: 9949]**

International Surface Fabricators Association **[Vol 1: 10403]**

Livestock Publications Council **[Vol 1: 10872]**

National Academy of Recording Arts and Sciences **[Vol 1: 11418]**

National Association for Campus Activities **[Vol 1: 11558]**

National Auctioneers Association **[Vol 1: 11946]**

National Aviation Hall of Fame **[Vol 1: 11954]**

National Forum for Black Public Administrators **[Vol 1: 12420]**

National Intercollegiate Soccer Officials Association **[Vol 1: 12561]**

National InterScholastic Swimming Coaches Association of America **[Vol 1: 12566]**

National School Transportation Association **[Vol 1: 12810]**

Restaurant Association of New Zealand **[Vol 2: 5037]**

Veterans of Foreign Wars of the United States **[Vol 1: 17544]**

Izaak Walton League of America **[Vol 1: 17633]**

Hall of Fame Awards

Consumer Electronics Association **[Vol. 1: 7575]**

Specialty Sleep Association **[Vol 1: 16131]**

Hall of Fame Horseman and Horsewoman of the Year **[Vol. 1: 10507]**

Hall of Fame in Philanthropy **[Vol 1: 16636]**

Hall of Fame Museum **[Vol 1: 9215]**

Hall of Fame of Distinguished Band Conductors **[Vol. 1: 11962]**

Hall of Fame Program **[Vol. 1: 11810]**

Hall of Flame **[Vol. 1: 10625]**

Hall of Great Names **[Vol. 2: 2491]**

Hall of Great Western Performers **[Vol. 1: 12269]**

Hall of Leaders **[Vol. 1: 17145]**

Hall of Outstanding Americans **[Vol. 1: 13070]**

Hall PhD Early Career Psychologist Award; Judy E. **[Vol. 1: 7657]**

Hall Prize for Poetry; Donald **[Vol. 1: 5557]**

Hall Prize; R. T. **[Vol. 2: 637]**

Haller Award for Excellence in Teaching; Jack O. **[Vol. 1: 15252]**

Haller Memorial Award for Sculpture; Evelyn and Peter **[Vol. 1: 15470]**

Hallett Award; M.M. **[Vol. 2: 7830]**

Hallinan Award; Archbishop Paul **[Vol. 1: 7103]**

Hallmark Award **[Vol. 1: 13982]**

Halmshaw Award; Ron **[Vol. 2: 7093]**

Halmstad Prize **[Vol. 1: 15410]**

Halonen Teaching Excellence Award; Jane S. **[Vol. 1: 3555]**

Halperin Electric Transmission and Distribution Award; Herman **[Vol. 1: 9292]**

Halpern Award for Distinguished Professional Contributions; Florence **[Vol. 1: 3582]**

Halsell Prize; Willie D. **[Vol. 1: 11219]**

Halstead Young Investigator's Award; Thora W. **[Vol. 1: 3916]**

Halverson Fair Play Award; John **[Vol. 1: 17040]**

Halverson Young Investigator Award; John **[Vol. 1: 3967]**

Hambleton Award; J. I. **[Vol. 1: 7971]**

Hambly Medal; Edmund **[Vol. 2: 7987]**

Hamdan Award for an Outstanding Clinical Department in the Public Sector in the UAE **[Vol. 2: 6667]**

Hamdan Award for Medical Research Excellence **[Vol. 2: 6668]**

Hamdan Award for Original Research Paper Published in SHAMS **[Vol. 2: 6669]**

Hamdan Award for the Best Medical College/Institute or Centre in the Arab World **[Vol. 2: 6670]**

Hamdan Award for Volunteers in Humanitarian Medical Services **[Vol. 2: 6671]**

Hamel; Prix Joseph **[Vol. 2: 2274]**

Hamer and Elizabeth Hamer Kegan Award; Philip M. **[Vol. 1: 15420]**

Hamilton Award; Alice **[Vol. 1: 2488]**

Hamilton Award; James A. **[Vol. 1: 1756]**

Hamilton Award; Jimmie **[Vol. 1: 4443]**

Hamilton Award; Mary Ellen **[Vol. 1: 12586]**

Hamilton Award on the Status of Women; Constance E. **[Vol. 1: 7297]**

Hamilton Award; Scott **[Vol. 1: 17464]**

Hamilton-Fairley Young Investigator Award **[Vol. 2: 6950]**

Hamilton Hospital Administrators' Book Award; James A. **[Vol. 1: 1756]**

Hamilton Memorial National CWI of the Year Award; Dalton E. **[Vol. 1: 4677]**

Hamilton Memorial Prize **[Vol. 2: 5074]**

Hamilton Prize; Alice **[Vol. 1: 3903]**

Hamilton Traveling Fellowship; John **[Vol. 2: 8719]**

Hammarksjold Award; Dag **[Vol. 1: 9684]**

Hammerman Spirit of Education Award; Harold **[Vol. 1: 11929]**

Hammett Award; Dashiell **[Vol. 1: 9654]**

Hamming Medal; Richard W. **[Vol. 1: 9293]**

Hammond Award **[Vol. 2: 6701]**

Hammond Memorial Prize; Sir John **[Vol. 2: 7248]**

Hammond Prize; Dr. George P. **[Vol. 1: 13956]**

Hampton Award for Excellence in Film and Digital Media; Henry **[Vol. 1: 7696]**

Han Prize for Student Landscape Architecture **[Vol. 2: 1536]**

Hancock Brick and Tile Soil and Water Engineering Award **[Vol. 1: 4083]**

Hancock Memorial Award in Piano **[Vol. 1: 14740]**

Hancock Memorial Award; Kenneth G. **[Vol. 1: 1646]**

Hancor Soil and Water Engineering Award **[Vol. 1: 4083]**

Handball Player of the Year **[Vol. 2: 6390]**

Handley Award; John **[Vol. 2: 5557]**

Handy Awards; W.C. **[Vol. 1: 5897]**

Hanes Natural History Award; Anne **[Vol. 1: 13723]**

Hanford Sr. Distinguished Faculty Award; Lloyd D. **[Vol. 1: 9407]**

Hang Gliding Cross Country Championship Trophy **[Vol. 2: 8263]**

Hang Gliding Cross Country Trophy **[Vol. 2: 8264]**

Hang Gliding Diploma **[Vol. 2: 6314]**

Hank IBA Defensive Player of the Year **[Vol. 1: 11638]**

Hanks, Jr., Scholarship in Meteorology; Howard H. **[Vol. 1: 2908]**

Hanks Memorial Award for Professional Excellence; Nancy **[Vol. 1: 1217]**

Hanlon Award **[Vol. 1: 8525]**

Hann Award; Elmer L. **[Vol. 1: 15714]**

Hanna, Jr. Fellowship in American History; Archibald **[Vol. 1: 18153]**

Hannah Medal; Jason A. **[Vol. 1: 14640]**

Hannan Medal **[Vol. 2: 178]**

Hanover International Violin Competition **[Vol. 2: 2888]**

Hanover Shoe Farms Caretaker of the Year Award **[Vol. 1: 8825]**

Hanover Shoe Farms Groom of the Year Award **[Vol. 1: 8825]**

Hansberger Leadership in Global Investing Award; Thomas L. **[Vol. 1: 7169]**

Hansberry Playwriting Award; Lorraine **[Vol. 1: 10663]**

Hansell Publication Award; Dorothy E. **[Vol. 1: 3633]**

Hansen Award; Ann **[Vol. 1: 17081]**

Hansen Diabetes Fund Grants; Robert W. **[Vol. 1: 8771]**

Hansen Publication Award; Kathryn G. **[Vol. 1: 7349]**

Hansens Bibliotekspris; R. Lysholt **[Vol. 2: 1957]**

Hanson Award; Abel **[Vol. 1: 5351]**

Hanson Fighter/Attack Squadron of the Year Award; Robert M. **[Vol. 1: 10953]**

Hanson Medal **[Vol. 2: 7964]**

Hanson Medal; Carl **[Vol. 2: 9277]**

Hanson Memorial Prize; John **[Vol. 1: 7497]**

Hanus Medal **[Vol. 2: 1912]**

Hanyo Award; George T. **[Vol. 1: 5732]**

Haque and Hem Chandra Bose prize; Aziz ul **[Vol. 2: 7689]**

Harabaszewski Medal; Jan **[Vol. 2: 5392]**

Harari Early Career Award; Carmi **[Vol. 1: 3524]**

Hardee Dissertation of the Year Award; Melvene D. **[Vol. 1: 11385]**

Hardesty Award; Shortridge **[Vol. 1: 4186]**

Hardin Memorial Award; David K. **[Vol. 1: 2814]**

Hardinge Award; Hal Williams **[Vol. 1: 15211]**

Hardingham Presidential Sword; Sir Robert **[Vol. 2: 8607]**

Hardison Award; J. Brown **[Vol. 1: 14443]**

Hardware Company of the Year **[Vol. 2: 3253]**

Hardy Award; Samuel **[Vol. 1: 10443]**

Hardy Medal Award; Robert Lansing **[Vol. 1: 11186]**

Harger Memorial Life Award; Don **[Vol. 1: 8302]**

Hargrove Award; Bill **[Vol. 1: 17465]**

Haring Prize; Clarence H. **[Vol. 1: 2375]**

Harington-De Visscher Prize **[Vol. 2: 2863]**

Harkin Conservation Award; J. B. **[Vol. 1: 6778]**

Harkin Medal; J. B. **[Vol. 1: 6778]**

Harkness Fellowships **[Vol. 1: 7449]**

Harkness Young Conrad Scholar Award; Bruce **[Vol. 1: 7543]**

Harley Award; Herbert **[Vol. 1: 2738]**

Harley Diplomate of the Year Award; Richard A. **[Vol. 1: 574]**

Harman Award; Nathaniel Bishop **[Vol. 2: 7121]**

Harman Research Award; Denham **[Vol. 1: 784]**

Harmon Award; Lt. Gens. Millard F. and Hubert R. **[Vol. 1: 13647]**

Harmon Cup; Larry **[Vol. 1: 17157]**

Harms Medal; Bernhard **[Vol. 2: 3110]**

Harms Medal; Joe **[Vol. 2: 737]**

Harms Prize; Bernhard **[Vol. 2: 3111]**

Harness Horse of the Year **[Vol. 1: 17148]**

Harper Lecture; Roland **[Vol. 2: 9278]**

Harper Prize; Robert and Elma Kemp **[Vol. 2: 8758]**

Harpers Ferry Memorial Scholarship **[Vol. 1: 16836]**

Harreveld Memorial Award; Van **[Vol. 1: 3256]**

Harriman Award for Distinguished Volunteer Service **[Vol. 1: 3679]**

Harriman Award; W. Averell **[Vol. 1: 2180]**

Harriman Democracy Award; W. Averell **[Vol. 1: 12287]**

Harrington Award in Historical Archaeology; J. C. **[Vol. 1: 15092]**

Harrington Book Award; Michael **[Vol. 1: 7117]**

Harrington-Lux Creative Design Award; Holly **[Vol. 1: 8855]**

Harrington Prize; Malcolm **[Vol. 2: 9094]**

Harris Award; Albert J. **[Vol. 1: 10096]**

Harris Award; Gilbert **[Vol. 1: 13799]**

Harris Award; John **[Vol. 2: 4935]**

Harris Equal Opportunity Award; William J. **[Vol. 1: 11916]**

Harris Fellow Award; Lewis E. **[Vol. 1: 1901]**

Harris Illustrated Children's Literature Prize; Christie **[Vol. 1: 17744]**

Harris, MD, Award; William H. **[Vol. 1: 13716]**

Harris Playwright Award Competition; Julie **[Vol. 1: 5826]**

Harris State Leadership Award; Jeffrey S. **[Vol. 1: 11762]**

Harris Travel Bursaries; Dr. Sam **[Vol. 2: 6358]**

Harrison Annual Doctoral Prize; Vernon **[Vol. 2: 7268]**

Harrison Award; Anne **[Vol. 2: 438]**

Harrison Award of Merit; Bernard P. **[Vol. 1: 12095]**

Harrison-Meldola Memorial Prize **[Vol. 2: 9013]**

Harrison Prize; Ross G. **[Vol. 2: 4243]**

Harrison Sr. Memorial Scholarship; Joe **[Vol. 1: 16316]**

Harrison Young Researcher Award; James **[Vol. 2: 2533]**

Hart Award of Merit for Lifetime Achievement; Kitty Carlisle **[Vol. 1: 8658]**

Hart Cup Award **[Vol. 1: 17082]**

Hart Graduate Scholarship; Dave **[Vol. 1: 16016]**

Hart Memorial Award; Moss **[Vol. 1: 13159]**

Hart Public Service Award; Philip **[Vol. 1: 7579]**

Hart Service Award; Ray L. **[Vol. 1: 755]**

Hart Trophy; Nelson C. **[Vol. 1: 6643]**

Hartford-Nicholsen Award **[Vol. 1: 15823]**

Hartle Awards **[Vol. 2. 8226]**

Hartman Award; Carl G. **[Vol. 1: 15385]**

Hartman Excellence in Sportswriting Award; Fred **[Vol. 1: 16444]**

Hartman Scholarships; R.T. **[Vol. 1: 17327]**

Hartmann Award; Frederick **[Vol. 1: 10385]**

Hartnett-Irvine Award **[Vol. 2: 6632]**

Hartranft Award; Joseph B. **[Vol. 1: 307]**

Hartshorne Trophies **[Vol. 1: 16909]**

Harutyunyan Scholarship; Garegin **[Vol. 2: 48]**

Harvard-Newcomen Postdoctoral Fellowship in Business History **[Vol. 1: 8829]**

Harvey Memorial Prize; Reuben **[Vol. 2: 3913]**

Harvey Prize; J.H. **[Vol. 2: 1125]**

Harvey Prize; Stanley **[Vol. 2: 1126]**

Harvey Short Story Award; S. D. **[Vol. 2: 678]**

Harwick Lifetime Achievement Award; Harry J. **[Vol. 1: 1769]**

Hasek Student Awards; Dr. Joseph **[Vol. 1: 7799]**

Haseltine Award; Florence P. **[Vol. 1: 13670]**

Haseltine Memorial Fellowship in Science Writing; Nate **[Vol. 1: 7655]**

Haskell Award for Student Journalism; Douglas **[Vol. 1: 2586]**

Haskil Competition; Clara **[Vol. 2: 6258]**

Haskins Medal **[Vol. 1: 11091]**

Hasler Award; Maurice F. **[Vol. 1: 16137]**

Hasse Prize; Merten M. **[Vol. 1: 11017]**

Hastings Student Award; Dr. John **[Vol. 1: 6833]**

Hatai Medal; Shinkishi **[Vol. 1: 13773]**

Hatch Award; James E. **[Vol. 1: 10954]**

Hatfield Award; W. Wilbur **[Vol. 1: 12207]**

Hatfield Award; William D. **[Vol. 1: 17706]**

Hatt-Bucher Prize; Heinrich **[Vol. 2: 6496]**

Hattaway Marine Aviation Ground Officer of the Year Award; Earle **[Vol. 1: 10955]**

Hatton Awards Competition for Junior Investigators; Edward H. **[Vol. 1: 9538]**

Hatton Awards Competition; Johnson and Johnson **[Vol. 1: 9538]**

Hatton Competition and Awards; Unilever **[Vol. 1: 9538]**

Hatton Memorial Grade B Male Voice Scholarship; Thomas and Don **[Vol. 1: 14741]**

Hatton Second Eleven Player of the Season; Les **[Vol. 2: 6820]**

Hattori Prize **[Vol. 2: 4251]**

Haub Prize for Environmental Diplomacy; Elizabeth **[Vol. 2: 3059]**

Haub Prize for Environmental Law; Elizabeth **[Vol. 2: 3060]**

Haueter Award; Paul E. **[Vol. 1: 2322]**

Haughton Award **[Vol. 2: 5558]**

Haughton Good Guy Award; William R. **[Vol. 1: 16948]**

Hauling Job of the Year Award **[Vol. 1: 16121]**

Havenga Prize **[Vol. 2: 5629]**

Havens Support and Classified Staff Development Award; Shirley **[Vol. 1: 12936]**

Haverland Citation Award; Harry **[Vol. 1: 9548]**

Haverstick Groundwater Hero Award; Vern **[Vol. 1: 8789]**

Haviland Award; P. H. **[Vol. 2: 9578]**

Hawkins Outstanding Volunteer Award; Richard **[Vol. 1: 452]**

Hawley Award; Fiona and Nicholas **[Vol. 2: 7554]**

Hawley Prize; Ellis W. **[Vol. 1: 13679]**

Haworth Memorial Lectureship **[Vol. 2: 9014]**

Hawryliuk Memorial Fund; Donald **[Vol. 1: 6550]**

Hawthorne Award; Ben **[Vol. 2: 4194]**

Hawthorne Award; Charles Oliver **[Vol. 2: 7122]**

Hay Award; Louise **[Vol. 1: 5171]**

Hay Medal; Logan **[Vol. 1: 33]**

Hay Memorial Award; Roy **[Vol. 2: 7714]**

Hayashi Awards; Chikio **[Vol. 2: 2522]**

Haycock Award for Promoting Librarianship; Ken **[Vol. 1: 2784]**

Hayden Emerging Researcher Award; Alice H. **[Vol. 1: 16371]**

Hayden Fellowship; Alice H. **[Vol. 1: 16371]**

Hayden - Harris Award **[Vol. 1: 766]**

Hayden Memorial Geological Award; F.V. **[Vol. 1: 93]**

Haydn Chamber Music Competition; International Joseph **[Vol. 2: 1325]**

Hayes Author/Illustrator Visit Award; Maureen **[Vol. 1: 5065]**

Hayes Award; Sheldon G. **[Vol. 1: 11554]**

Hayes Awards; Helen **[Vol. 1: 16486]**

Hayhow Award; Edgar C. **[Vol. 1: 1757]**

Hayman Award; Elise M. **[Vol. 2: 8169]**

Hayman Award; Max **[Vol. 1: 3102]**

Hayman Distinguished Staff Award; Harry **[Vol. 1: 9060]**

Hayman Prize for Published Work Pertaining to Traumatized Children and Adults **[Vol. 2: 8170]**

Haynes Prize for Best Paper **[Vol. 1: 78]**

Hays Award **[Vol. 1: 9390]**

Hays Award; Hazel **[Vol. 1: 8214]**

Hays Chartered Accountant of the Year **[Vol. 2: 4901]**

Haythornthwaite Cup **[Vol. 2: 9327]**

Haywood Prize; Brigadier **[Vol. 2: 9095]**

Hazardous Materials Professional of the Year **[Vol. 1: 380]**

Hazardous Waste Management Award **[Vol. 1: 17707]**

Hazen Education Prize; Joseph H. **[Vol. 1: 8953]**

H.D. Fellowship in English or American Literature **[Vol. 1: 18154]**

Head Arthur Ashe Sportsmanship Award **[Vol. 1: 9460]**

Head Book Award; Florence Roberts **[Vol. 1: 13490]**

Head Literature Awards; Bessie **[Vol. 2: 1740]**

Head of State Awards - Ghana **[Vol. 2: 3257]**

Headliner Award

Association for Women in Communications **[Vol. 1: 5160]**

Livestock Publications Council **[Vol 1: 10873]**

Heads Up Awards **[Vol. 1: 17784]**

Health Achievement in Occupational Medicine Award **[Vol. 1: 1785]**

Health Advocate Award **[Vol. 1: 3032]**

Health and Safety Achievement Award **[Vol. 1: 9217]**

Health Care Delivery Award **[Vol. 1: 47]**

Health Education Mentor Award **[Vol. 1: 15288]**

Health Education Professional of the Year Awards **[Vol. 1: 951]**

Health Improvement Institute Quality Award **[Vol. 1: 8846]**

Health Management Research Award **[Vol. 1: 1758]**

Health Professions Education and Training Award **[Vol. 1: 11712]**

Health, Safety, and Environment Award **[Vol. 1: 15757]**

Health, Safety, Security, Environment, and Social Responsibility Award **[Vol. 1: 15757]**

Health Science Award **[Vol. 1: 4624]**

Health Sciences Person-in-Training Award **[Vol. 1: 8628]**

Health Sciences Research Award **[Vol. 1: 8629]**

Healthcare Award: Advanced Level **[Vol. 2: 7408]**

Healthcare Executive of the Year **[Vol. 1: 1751]**

Healthcare Executive of the Year Award **[Vol. 1: 575]**

Healthier Choice Award **[Vol. 2: 5980]**

Healthy Workplace Initiative Award **[Vol. 1: 14304]**

Healy Award; T.W. **[Vol. 2: 1127]**

Heaps Prize; Norman **[Vol. 2: 7357]**

Hearing and Balance Science Research Grant **[Vol. 1: 7820]**

Hearn Trophy; George **[Vol. 2: 6709]**

Hearst Family-School Partnership Awards; Phoebe Apperson **[Vol. 1: 12725]**

Heart of Hospice **[Vol. 1: 12529]**

Heart of Humanity Award **[Vol. 1: 17170]**

Heart of Sarajevo Award **[Vol. 2: 1728]**

Heart of the Program Award **[Vol. 1: 14778]**

Heartland Award **[Vol. 1: 7802]**

Heartwell Jr. Award; William L. **[Vol. 1: 11917]**

Heat Transfer Memorial Award **[Vol. 1: 4392]**

Heath Achievement in Literacy Award; Stan **[Vol. 1: 6679]**

Heath Award **[Vol. 1: 17562]**

Heatley Award; Norman **[Vol. 2: 9015]**

Heavenly Pilot Award **[Vol. 2: 9464]**

Heaviest Structure Moved Award **[Vol. 1: 9712]**

Hebb Award **[Vol. 1: 10031]**

Hebb Award for Distinguished Contributions to Psychology as a Science; Donald O. **[Vol. 1: 6826]**

Hebb Distinguished Contribution Award; Donald O. **[Vol. 1: 6880]**

Hebb Distinguished Scientific Contribution Award; D. O. **[Vol. 1: 3399]**

Hebrew Play Award **[Vol. 2: 3989]**

Hecht Award; Max **[Vol. 1: 5603]**

Hecht Memorial Award; Jacob J. **[Vol. 1: 12104]**

Heck Award; Mathilda **[Vol. 1: 17640]**

Heck Prize; Gagna A. and Ch. Van **[Vol. 2: 1519]**

Heckel Award; George Baugh **[Vol. 1: 1690]**

Hector Memorial Medal and Prize **[Vol. 2: 5075]**

Hedberg Award in Energy; Hollis D. **[Vol. 1: 9280]**

Hedges Award; Phil **[Vol. 1: 13599]**

Hedrick Awards; U. P. **[Vol. 1: 3319]**

Hedrick Lectureship **[Vol. 1: 11018]**

Heeney Memorial Award; Robert C. **[Vol. 1: 11748]**

Heesom Medal; Denys **[Vol. 2: 5521]**

Hefley Educator of the Year Award; Sue **[Vol. 1: 10890]**

Hefner First Amendment Award; Hugh M. **[Vol. 1: 14044]**

Hefter Migraine Research Award; Thomas E. **[Vol. 1: 2286]**

Hegarty Prize **[Vol. 2: 922]**

Hegel-Preis der Landeshauptstadt Stuttgart **[Vol. 2: 3191]**

Heidseick Award; RPS Charles **[Vol. 2: 8890]**

Heifetz Memorial Fellowship; Vladimir and Pearl **[Vol. 1: 18180]**

Heilprin Literary Medal; Angelo **[Vol. 1: 8560]**

Heiman Impact Award for Excellence in Educational Support; John C. **[Vol. 1: 2623]**

Heine-Medin Award **[Vol. 2: 2408]**

Heineken Prize for Art; Dr. A.H. **[Vol. 2: 4821]**

Heineken Prize for Biochemistry and Biophysics; Dr. H.P. **[Vol. 2: 4822]**

Heineken Prize for Cognitive Science; Dr. A.H. **[Vol. 2: 4823]**

Heineken Prize for Environmental Sciences; Dr. A.H. **[Vol. 2: 4824]**

Heineken Prize for History; Dr. A.H. **[Vol. 2: 4825]**

Heineken Prize for Medicine; Dr. A.H. **[Vol. 2: 4826]**

Heineken Young Scientists Awards **[Vol. 2: 4827]**

Heineman Prize for Astrophysics; Dannie N. **[Vol. 1: 2687]**

Heineman Prize for Mathematical Physics; Dannie N. **[Vol. 1: 2688]**

Heineman Trophy **[Vol. 1: 14531]**

Heinl, Jr., Award; Colonel Robert Debs [Vol. 1: 10974]

Heinlein Memorial Award; Robert A. [Vol. 1: 12921]

Heinrich Award; K.F.J. [Vol. 1: 11132]

Heinz Award in Public Policy [Vol. 1: 8881]

Heinz Award in Technology, the Economy, and Employment [Vol. 1: 8882]

Heinz Award in the Arts and Humanities [Vol. 1: 8883]

Heinz Award in the Environment [Vol. 1: 8884]

Heinz Award in the Human Condition [Vol. 1: 8885]

Heinz Friend of Nursing Award; John [Vol. 1: 13928]

Heinz III Federal Public Service Award; H. John [Vol. 1: 12642]

Heinz Literature Prize; Drue [Vol. 1: 17330]

Heiskell Community Service Awards; Andrew [Vol. 1: 16503]

Heisler Graduate Student Paper Competition; Martin O. [Vol. 1: 10386]

Heisler Prize; Charlene [Vol. 2: 115]

Heizer Article Award; Robert F. [Vol. 1: 3907]

Helava Award; U.V. [Vol. 2: 5299]

Helfer Award; Ray E.
    Academic Pediatric Association [Vol. 1: 48]
    American Academy of Pediatrics [Vol 1: 682]

Heller Award; Florence G. [Vol. 1: 10567]

Heller Prize; Dr. Bernard [Vol. 1: 8878]

Hellinger Award; Mark [Vol. 1: 14672]

Hellings Award; Susan R. [Vol. 1: 12063]

Hellman Research Essay Award; Milo [Vol. 1: 1262]

Hellrung Award; Robert T. [Vol. 1: 11049]

Hellweg Bravery Award [Vol. 2: 281]

Helmerich Distinguished Author Award; Peggy V. [Vol. 1: 16577]

Helmholtz Award [Vol. 1: 10032]

Helms Award for Staff and Graduate Staff; Edgar J. [Vol. 1: 8728]

Help Desk Hero Award [Vol. 1: 8901]

Helpmann Awards [Vol. 2: 848]

Helt Memorial; Scott [Vol. 1: 9048]

Helton Manufacturing Scholarships; Clinton J. [Vol. 1: 14949]

Helyar Memorial Award; Frank [Vol. 1: 6622]

Hemingway Foundation Award; Ernest [Vol. 1: 13909]

Hemingway Foundation/PEN Award [Vol. 1: 13909]

Hemley Memorial Award; Cecil [Vol. 1: 14062]

Hemming Award; Val G. [Vol. 1: 683]

Hemphill-Jordan Leadership Award [Vol. 1: 1065]

Hemphill Memorial Award; Bernice [Vol. 1: 1065]

Hemschemeyer Award; Hattie [Vol. 1: 1783]

Henderson Award; Alexander [Vol. 2: 392]

Henderson Award; Ian [Vol. 2: 784]

Henderson Award; R.A. [Vol. 1: 6867]

Henderson/Fred Cihon Memorial Exhibit Award; William C. [Vol. 1: 2992]

Henderson Human Rights Scholarship; Gordon F. [Vol. 1: 17321]

Henderson MD Memorial Award; Peter [Vol. 1: 1136]

Henderson Memorial Award; Harold G. [Vol. 1: 8811]

Henderson Service to the Section Award; Julia [Vol. 1: 14822]

Henderson Student Award; Edward [Vol. 1: 2253]

Hendrick Award; Thomas "Mic" [Vol. 1: 10268]

Hendy Memorial Award; James C. [Vol. 1: 2412]

Henebry Professional of the Year Award; The Jack [Vol. 1: 18051]

Henebry Roll of Honor Award; Agnes [Vol. 1: 16108]

Henkin Student Travel Award; Paul [Vol. 1: 3493]

Henley Award; Butch [Vol. 1: 2351]

Henley Media Award; Vernon [Vol. 1: 1910]

Henne Award; Frances [Vol. 1: 1343]

Henne Research Grant; Frances [Vol. 1: 18220]

Henne/YALSA/VOYA Research Grant; Frances [Vol. 1: 18220]

Hennessy Awards [Vol. 1: 12772]

Hennessy Travelers Association Award of Excellence [Vol. 1: 12772]

Hennessy Trophy; John L. [Vol. 1: 12772]

Henning Prize [Vol. 2: 2862]

Henries Awards [Vol. 2: 7749]

Henry Award; Charles D. [Vol. 1: 798]

Henry Award for Magazine Journalism; O. [Vol. 1: 16456]

Henry Award; Patrick [Vol. 1: 12478]

Henry Best Paper Award; Edward C. [Vol. 1: 1563]

Henry Medal [Vol. 2: 7690]

Hensel Award; Cathy [Vol. 1: 7924]

Hensel Leadership Award; George [Vol. 1: 7925]

Henshall Warm Water Fisheries Award; Dr. James A. [Vol. 1: 8303]

Henshel Award; Colonel Harry D. [Vol. 1: 453]

Hensler Award; Bill and Sue [Vol. 1: 8914]

Hepburn Award for Contributions to the Health and Welfare of Children; Audrey [Vol. 1: 14899]

Heptathlon Award [Vol. 1: 17466]

Herb Society of America Research Grant [Vol. 1: 8907]

Herbal Hero Award [Vol. 1: 2345]

Herbal Industry Leader Award [Vol. 1: 2346]

Herbal Insight Award [Vol. 1: 2347]

Herbert-Kind-Preis [Vol. 2: 2788]

Herbert Medal [Vol. 1: 9742]

Herbert Prize; Adrienne and Frederick [Vol. 2: 2424]

Herder Prizes [Vol. 2: 3202]

Hereford Airport Communication Excellence Award; Peggy [Vol. 1: 317]

Hereford Award for Excellence in Communications; Peggy G. [Vol. 1: 317]

Hering Medal; Rudolph [Vol. 1: 4187]

Heritage Award
    American Psychological Association - Society for the Psychology of Women (Division 35)- [Vol. 1: 3549]
    Black Culinarian Alliance [Vol 1: 5868]
    Irish American Cultural Institute [Vol 1: 10514]
    Irish American Cultural Institute [Vol 1: 10515]
    National Dance Association [Vol 1: 12276]
    Swedish Council of America [Vol 1: 16347]

Heritage Award; Doris [Vol. 1: 17467]

Heritage Awards [Vol. 2: 8608]

Heritage Cross [Vol. 2: 1819]

Heritage Toronto Awards [Vol. 1: 8916]

Herlitzka; Premio [Vol. 2: 4018]

Herman Memorial Award; M. Justin [Vol. 1: 11796]

Herman Memorial Award; Robert H. [Vol. 1: 4013]

Herman Service Award; Susan [Vol. 1: 13698]

Hermann Memorial Award; Fred [Vol. 1: 9319]

Hermelin/Minkoff Award [Vol. 1: 13707]

Hermes Creative Awards [Vol. 1: 5403]

L'Hermite Medal; Robert [Vol. 2: 2590]

Herndon National Legislative Award; Maurice G. [Vol. 1: 9181]

Hero in Medicine Award [Vol. 1: 9685]

Hero of Baseball Award [Vol. 1: 15027]

Heroes of the 50 States: The State Government Hall of Fame [Vol. 1: 15801]

Heroism Award [Vol. 1: 5970]

Heroism Medal [Vol. 1: 12903]

Heron Prize; Alastair [Vol. 2: 514]

Heroy, Jr. Award for Distinguished Service to AGI; William B. [Vol. 1: 2224]

Herpetologists' League Award for Graduate Research [Vol. 1: 8918]

Herpetologists' League Student Prize [Vol. 1: 8918]

Herr Research Award for Disability Services; Twila Ann Janssen [Vol. 2: 439]

Herreshoff Trophy; Nathanael G. [Vol. 1: 17054]

Herrick Award in Neuroanatomy; C. J. [Vol. 1: 1026]

Herrick Award; James B. [Vol. 1: 2302]

Herrmann Outstanding Dissertation Award; Robert O. [Vol. 1: 1916]

Herschel Medal [Vol. 2: 8662]

Herschel Medal; John F. W. [Vol. 2: 5606]

Herschfus Memorial Award [Vol. 1: 633]

Hersey Award; Mayo D. [Vol. 1: 4393]

Hershberg Award for Important Discoveries in Medicinally Active Substances; E. B. [Vol. 1: 1647]

Hersholt Humanitarian Award; Jean [Vol. 1: 85]

Herskovits Award [Vol. 1: 203]

Herter Award; Christian A. [Vol. 1: 2181]

Hertert Memorial Award; Lucien Dean [Vol. 1: 1051]

Herty, Jr., Award; Charles W. [Vol. 1: 5033]

Hertz Memorial Fellowship; Aleksander and Alicja [Vol. 1: 18181]

Hertz Preis; Heinrich [Vol. 2: 3216]

Hertz Prize; Gustav [Vol. 2: 2774]

Hertzog Prize for Literature [Vol. 2: 5630]

Herzberg Gold Medal for Science and Engineering; Gerhard [Vol. 1: 13104]

Herzberg Medal [Vol. 1: 6299]

Hess Award; Barbara A. [Vol. 1: 5195]

Hess Award for Recognition of an Innovative Food or Culinary Effort; Mary Abbot [Vol. 1: 2036]

Hess Award; Henry [Vol. 1: 4394]

Hess Medal; Harry H. [Vol. 1: 2238]

Hess Memorial Scholarship; Beth B. [Vol. 1: 15914]

Hess Preis; Viktor [Vol. 2: 1210]

Hessa Prize; Her Highness Shaikha [Vol. 2: 1363]

Hessayon New Writers' Award; Joan [Vol. 2: 8549]

Hessell-Tiltman Prize [Vol. 2: 7563]

Heston Award for Outstanding Scholarship in Interpretation and Performance Studies; Lilla A. [Vol. 1: 12113]

Hestrin Prize [Vol. 2: 3969]

Hetherington Award [Vol. 1: 11406]

Heubner Preis; Otto [Vol. 2: 3022]

Heuer Award for Judging Excellence; Robert L. [Vol. 1: 9490]

Hewes Memorial Award for Distinguished Volunteer Service; Bettie [Vol. 1: 6695]

Hewett Book Prize; Ed A. [Vol. 1: 5097]

Hewitt and Maybelle Ellen Ball Hewitt Award; William Boright [Vol. 1: 3279]

Hewitt Award; Barnard [Vol. 1: 4063]

Hewitt Award; C. Gordon [Vol. 1: 8154]

Hewitt Memorial Award; Foster [Vol. 1: 8961]

Hewitt Team Achievement Award; John S. [Vol. 1: 6745]

Hewlet Trophy; Hilda [Vol. 2: 7307]

Hewlett Award; Lan [Vol. 1: 11614]

Hey Medal; Max [Vol. 2: 8357]

Heyrovsky-Ilkovic-Nernst Lecture [Vol. 2: 1913]

HGA Award [Vol. 1: 8816]

Hickish Award; David [Vol. 2: 7151]

Hickman Memorial Research Award; Susan [Vol. 1: 14107]

Hicks Award for Outstanding Contributions to Academic Law Librarianship; Frederick Charles [Vol. 1: 1193]

Hicks Graduate Scholarship; Dorothy [Vol. 1: 16017]

Hicks Memorial Award; Ronald [Vol. 2: 5088]

Hidden Treasure Award [Vol. 2: 9352]

Hideo Memorial Award; Yoshida [Vol. 2: 4260]

Hiemstra Prize for Non-fiction; Louis [Vol. 2: 5631]

Hieronymus - Posthumos [Vol. 1: 17037]

Higdon Distinguished Educator Award; Archie [Vol. 1: 3858]

Higgins Award; Lee Conroy [Vol. 1: 7942]

Higgins-Caditz Design Award [Vol. 1: 14135]

Higgins Gold Medal and Lecture Award; Boyle [Vol. 2: 3847]

Higgins Lectureship Award; T. R. [Vol. 1: 2703]

Higgins Redesign Award [Vol. 1: 14135]

High Energy and Particle Physics Prize [Vol. 2: 2392]

High Impact Paper Award [Vol. 2: 1277]

High Point Awards [Vol. 1: 13325]

High Point Horsemanship Award [Vol. 1: 13353]

High Point Performance Horse Awards [Vol. 1: 13326]

High Rising Trophy (Norwich Bitch) [Vol. 1: 13439]

High School All-American Awards [Vol. 1: 17404]

High School Awards Program [Vol. 1: 10714]

High School Flute Choir Competition [Vol. 1: 12397]

High School Physics Prize [Vol. 2: 4975]

High School Scholar All-America Award [Vol. 1: 12845]

High School Solo Competition [Vol. 1: 9772]

High School Soloist Competition [Vol. 1: 12398]

High Winds Medal [Vol. 1: 4663]

Higher Diploma in Floristry [Vol. 2: 9308]

Higher Education Student Achievement Award [Vol. 1: 11537]

Higher Education Teaching Award [Vol. 2: 9016]

Higher Education Writers Award [Vol. 1: 1390]

Highest Scoring Print of the Year Award [Vol. 2: 414]

Highly Commended Certificate [Vol. 1: 3077]

Highman Travel Grant Award [Vol. 1: 9169]

Highsmith Library Innovation Award [Vol. 1: 14323]

Highsmith Library Innovative Award [Vol. 1: 9138]

Highsmith Research Grants [Vol. 1: 1338]

Highway Research Board Distinguished Service Award [Vol. 1: 16535]

Higuchi Research Prize; Takeru [Vol. 1: 3143]

Hildebrand Award in the Theoretical and Experimental Chemistry of Liquids; Joel Henry [Vol. 1: 1648]

Hilditch Memorial Lecture [Vol. 2: 9279]

Hildreth Award; Harold M. [**Vol. 1: 3479**]
Hilgard Award for Distinguished Contributions to General Psychology; Ernest R. [**Vol. 1: 3519**]
Hilgard Award for Scientific Excellence; Ernest R. [**Vol. 2: 4111**]
Hilgard Best Graduate Level Academic Thesis Award; E. R. [**Vol. 1: 3612**]
Hilgard Hydraulic Prize; Karl Emil [**Vol. 1: 4188**]
Hilgard Lifetime Achievement Award; Ernest R. [**Vol. 1: 3519**]
Hill Award; Bill [**Vol. 1: 12719**]
Hill Award; Dennis [**Vol. 2: 8023**]
Hill Award; Dorothy [**Vol. 2: 179**]
Hill Award; Errol [**Vol. 1: 4064**]
Hill Award for Professional Achievement; Patty Smith [**Vol. 1: 4940**]
Hill Award; Jimmie D. [**Vol. 1: 12607**]
Hill Jr. Award; J. Eldred [**Vol. 1: 12434**]
Hill New Investigator Award; Martha N. [**Vol. 1: 2303**]
Hill Prize; James [**Vol. 2: 7988**]
Hill Sports Book of the Year; William [**Vol. 2: 7790**]
Hillenbrand Award [**Vol. 1: 72**]
Hillerman Award; Fred [**Vol. 1: 3078**]
Hillier Grant; Doris [**Vol. 2: 7123**]
Hillis Award for Choral Excellence; Margaret [**Vol. 1: 7262**]
Hill's Excellence in Veterinary Healthcare Award [**Vol. 1: 18076**]
Hills Fellowship; Debra [**Vol. 1: 14179**]
Hill's Pet Mobility Award [**Vol. 1: 18077**]
Hills Prize in Small Animal Medicine [**Vol. 2: 1165**]
Hilti-Preis [**Vol. 2: 6497**]
Hilton Humanitarian Prize [**Vol. 1: 8925**]
Hime Memorial Trophies; Alan [**Vol. 2: 6710**]
Himmelblau Award for Innovation in Computer-Based Chemical Engineering Education; David [**Vol. 1: 2624**]
Hinchley Medal; John William [**Vol. 2: 7965**]
Hincks Award; C. M. [**Vol. 1: 6689**]
Hinderstein Award; Jeanette Robinson [**Vol. 1: 10919**]
Hinds Award; Julian [**Vol. 1: 4189**]
Hindustan Zinc Gold Medal [**Vol. 2: 3595**]
Hine Awards; Lewis [**Vol. 1: 12059**]
Hines Memorial Award; Janice [**Vol. 1: 6758**]
Hinman Jr. Research Award; Wilbur S. [**Vol. 1: 17612**]
Hinman Research Awards; Maury and [**Vol. 1: 17612**]
Hinman Trophy; George R. [**Vol. 1: 17055**]
Hinton Research Training Award; William A. [**Vol. 1: 3979**]
Hippocratic Oath Award [**Vol. 1: 9633**]
Hire Awards of Excellence [**Vol. 2: 7792**]
Hirsch Award for Column Writing; Harold S. [**Vol. 1: 13335**]
Hirsch Award for Excellence in Broadcasting; Harold S. [**Vol. 1: 13336**]
Hirsch Award for Excellence in Ski Photography; Harold S. [**Vol. 1: 13337**]
Hirsch Award for Excellence in Snow Sports Photography; Harold S. [**Vol. 1: 13337**]
Hirsch Award for Most Promising Manitoba Writer; John [**Vol. 1: 10929**]
Hirsch Director's Award; John [**Vol. 1: 13567**]
Hirsch Medaille; Otto [**Vol. 2: 3192**]
Hirsch Prize; John [**Vol. 1: 6133**]
Hirschfeld Award; Tomas A. [**Vol. 1: 8281**]
Hirschmann Award in Peptide Chemistry; Ralph F. [**Vol. 1: 1649**]
Hirschs pris; Axel [**Vol. 2: 6204**]
Hirsh Award [**Vol. 1: 1764**]
Hiser Exemplary Publication Award; Paul T. [**Vol. 1: 8175**]
Hislop Award; David [**Vol. 2: 7989**]
Hislop Award for Outstanding Contributions to Professional Literature; Helen J. [**Vol. 1: 3234**]
Historic Naval Ship Maintenance/Preservation/Exhibition Award [**Vol. 1: 8935**]
Historic Sites in Journalism [**Vol. 1: 15802**]
Historical Achievement Award
    Ohio Academy of History [**Vol. 1: 13471**]
    Ohio Academy of History [**Vol. 1: 13473**]
Historical Book Award [**Vol. 2: 2600**]
Historical Category Award of Merit [**Vol. 1: 12656**]
Historical Landmarks Designation [**Vol. 1: 4839**]
Historical Metallurgy Society Grants [**Vol. 2: 7796**]

History Manuscript Award [**Vol. 1: 2524**]
History of Military Medicine Essay Award [**Vol. 1: 5425**]
History Scotland Prize [**Vol. 2: 8806**]
History Teacher of the Year [**Vol. 1: 15985**]
History Today Prize [**Vol. 2: 8807**]
Hitchcock Award; Edward [**Vol. 1: 1697**]
Hitchcock Book Award; Alice Davis [**Vol. 1: 15476**]
Hitchcock Distinguished Professional Service Award; Arthur A. [**Vol. 1: 1937**]
Hitchcock Medallion; Alice Davis [**Vol. 2: 9240**]
Hlushko Award to Young Cooperative Educators; William [**Vol. 1: 5300**]
Hnatyshyn Award for Law; Ramon John [**Vol. 1: 6331**]
Hoagland Award; Dennis Robert [**Vol. 1: 4491**]
Hoar Award [**Vol. 1: 6996**]
Hoard's Dairyman Youth Development Award [**Vol. 1: 1976**]
Hobart Memorial Award; W. H. [**Vol. 1: 4678**]
Hobart Seven Hats Award; Larry [**Vol. 1: 3651**]
Hobbs Award; Nicholas [**Vol. 1: 3504**]
Hobby Service Award [**Vol. 1: 5905**]
Hobbyist of the Year [**Vol. 1: 6228**]
Hoch Distinguished Service Award; Paul [**Vol. 1: 1780**]
Hochhausen Access Technology Research Award; E. (Ben) and Mary [**Vol. 1: 6730**]
Hochschullehrer-Nachwuchs Prize [**Vol. 2: 3168**]
Hochschulsommerkurse [**Vol. 1: 8614**]
Hockey Hall of Fame Award [**Vol. 1: 8962**]
Hockey Hall of Fame - Builder Category [**Vol. 1: 6177**]
Hockey Hall of Fame - International Friends Category [**Vol. 1: 6178**]
Hockey Hall of Fame - John Sergnese (Friends of CARHA) Category [**Vol. 1: 6179**]
Hockey Hall of Fame - Media Category [**Vol. 1: 6180**]
Hockey Hall of Fame - Player Category [**Vol. 1: 6181**]
Hockey Hall of Fame - Team Category [**Vol. 1: 6182**]
Hockley Award; Horace [**Vol. 2: 7946**]
Hodges International Piano Competition; Joanna [**Vol. 1: 17642**]
Hodgins Award for Outstanding Accomplishment; Agatha [**Vol. 1: 7688**]
Hodgkin Award; The Dorothy Crowfoot [**Vol. 1: 14282**]
Hodgkin Fellowship; Dorothy [**Vol. 2: 8937**]
Hodgkinson Research Prize; Virginia A. [**Vol. 1: 9189**]
Hodgkiss Canadian Outdoorsperson of the Year Award; Stan
    Canadian Wildlife Federation [**Vol. 1: 7041**]
    Canadian Wildlife Federation [**Vol. 1: 7043**]
Hodgson Distinguished Service Award; Kenneth O. [**Vol. 1: 13167**]
Hodgson Prize [**Vol. 2: 8609**]
Hodson Award [**Vol. 2: 8445**]
Hodson Award; Walter D. [**Vol. 1: 15860**]
Hoepfner Awards; Theodore Christian [**Vol. 1: 16029**]
Hoffman Award; Anna Louise [**Vol. 1: 10501**]
Hoffman Award; Dorothy M. and Earl S. [**Vol. 1: 5733**]
Hoffman Award for the Best Postgraduate Paper; Jerome J. [**Vol. 1: 1165**]
Hoffman Award; Paul R. [**Vol. 1: 12758**]
Hoffman Award; Phillip R. [**Vol. 1: 4190**]
Hoffman LaRoche Award of Excellence [**Vol. 1: 1070**]
Hoffman-LaRoche Ltd. Award [**Vol. 1: 6887**]
Hoffman Memorial Award; Cecile Pollack [**Vol. 1: 9634**]
Hoffman Memorial/Charles W. Shilling Award; Craig [**Vol. 1: 16605**]
Hoffman Prize for Distinguished Publication on Christopher Marlowe; Calvin and Rose G. [**Vol. 2: 8274**]
Hoffman Scholarship; Dorothy M. and Earl S. [**Vol. 1: 5734**]
Hofheimer Prize Award [**Vol. 1: 3345**]
Hofman Award; Jozef [**Vol. 1: 1890**]
Hofmann Award; Adele Dellenbaugh [**Vol. 1: 684**]
Hofmann Visiting Professor in Adolescent Medicine and Health Award [**Vol. 1: 15012**]
Hogan Distinguished Service Award; John F. [**Vol. 1: 14416**]

Hogan Environmental Law Essay Contest; Roscoe [**Vol. 1: 14315**]
Hogan/Smoger Access to Justice Essay Contest [**Vol. 1: 14315**]
Hogentogler Award; C. A. [**Vol. 1: 5604**]
Hogg Young Artist Competition; Ima [**Vol. 1: 8982**]
Hogle Distinguished Service Award; Cheryl M. [**Vol. 1: 13513**]
Hohl Service Award; Shirley [**Vol. 1: 3771**]
Hoidale Endowed Scholarship in Entrepreneurship; Peter B. [**Vol. 1: 17829**]
Hoke, Sr. Award; Henry [**Vol. 1: 10920**]
Hokin Prize; Bess [**Vol. 1: 14050**]
Holberg International Memorial Prize [**Vol. 2: 5126**]
Holberg Medal [**Vol. 2: 1964**]
Holbrook Alumni Award; Frances Morton [**Vol. 1: 13985**]
Holcim Green Built Bangladesh Contest [**Vol. 2: 1374**]
Holden Medal [**Vol. 2: 9375**]
Holden Street Theatre Award [**Vol. 2: 7533**]
Holdredge Award; Claire P. [**Vol. 1: 5324**]
Hole Medal; Dean [**Vol. 2: 8878**]
Holford Medal [**Vol. 2: 8820**]
Holgate Memorial Award; John [**Vol. 2: 9336**]
Holgersson Plaketten; Nils [**Vol. 2: 6237**]
Holgersson Plaque; Nils [**Vol. 2: 6237**]
Holladay Distinguished Fellow Award; Louise and Bill [**Vol. 1: 4325**]
Hollaender Award; Alexander [**Vol. 1: 8163**]
Holland Award for Outstanding Achievement in Career or Personality Research; John [**Vol. 1: 3590**]
Holland Award; Maurice [**Vol. 1: 9224**]
Holland Medal; Daniel M. [**Vol. 1: 12968**]
Holland Trophy [**Vol. 2: 6711**]
Hollander Award; Barbara [**Vol. 1: 8232**]
Holleman Prize, Dutch Foundation for Chemistry [**Vol. 2: 4828**]
Hollenback Prize [**Vol. 1: 98**]
Holley Award; Major General I. B. [**Vol. 1: 286**]
Holley Medal [**Vol. 1: 4395**]
Holliday Award; Polly [**Vol. 1: 16006**]
Hollist Service Award; Ladd [**Vol. 1: 10387**]
Hollister EMS Award; Jean [**Vol. 1: 8083**]
Holloway Award; Leonard [**Vol. 1: 5787**]
Holloway Award; Lisabeth M. [**Vol. 1: 4771**]
Holloway Medal; Tienie [**Vol. 2: 5632**]
Holloway Oceanography Prize; Peter [**Vol. 2: 457**]
Holly Memorial Award for Humanitarian Achievement; T. Kenyon [**Vol. 1: 16587**]
Holman Award; C. Hugh [**Vol. 1: 15396**]
Holman Memorial Prize; Richard Clive [**Vol. 2: 7865**]
Holmenkoll Medal [**Vol. 2: 5117**]
Holmenkollen Ski Festival [**Vol. 2: 5118**]
Holmenkollmedaljen [**Vol. 2: 5117**]
Holmes Awards for Post-Doctoral Studies; H.L. [**Vol. 1: 12769**]
Holmes Medal and Honorary Membership; Arthur [**Vol. 2: 2373**]
Holmes Memorial Award; Harry (Hap) [**Vol. 1: 2413**]
Holmes Pioneer Award; Joseph H. [**Vol. 1: 2710**]
Holmes Prize; Gordon [**Vol. 2: 9096**]
Holmes Travel Award; Oliver Wendell [**Vol. 1: 15421**]
Holonyak Jr. Award; Nick [**Vol. 1: 13608**]
Holroyd-Sherry Award [**Vol. 1: 685**]
Holst Medal; Gilles [**Vol. 2: 4829**]
Holt Award; Knut [**Vol. 2: 8188**]
Holt Fund; Charlotte S. [**Vol. 1: 17520**]
Holtby Memorial Prize; Winifred [**Vol. 2: 9076**]
Holter Memorial Prize; Casey [**Vol. 2: 9208**]
Holton Junior Scientist Award; James R. [**Vol. 1: 2239**]
Holweck Medal and Prize [**Vol. 2: 7909**]
Holzman Distinguished Educator Award; Albert G. [**Vol. 1: 9354**]
The Home Depot Humanitarian Award [**Vol. 1: 61**]
Homen Prize; Professor Theodor [**Vol. 2: 2104**]
Hometown Video Awards [**Vol. 1: 367**]
Homogeneous Catalysis Award [**Vol. 2: 9017**]
Honda Medal; Soichiro [**Vol. 1: 4396**]
Honens International Piano Competition; Esther [**Vol. 1: 8970**]
Honeywell Outstanding Collegiate Branch Award [**Vol. 1: 15513**]
Honeywell Prize [**Vol. 2: 7897**]

International Pharmaceutical Federation **[Vol 2: 4760]**

International Society for Photogrammetry and Remote Sensing **[Vol 2: 5300]**

International Society of Arachnology **[Vol 2: 3092]**

International Society of Automation **[Vol 1: 10285]**

International Union Against Tuberculosis and Lung Disease **[Vol 2: 2574]**

International Water Association, Singapore National Committee **[Vol 2: 5951]**

Iron and Steel Institute of Japan **[Vol 2: 4252]**

Medical Women's International Association **[Vol 1: 11086]**

National Marine Educators Association **[Vol 1: 12593]**

Ottawa Field-Naturalists' Club **[Vol 1: 13724]**

Phi Lambda Upsilon **[Vol 1: 13979]**

Royal Philharmonic Society **[Vol 2: 8888]**

Sigma Delta Epsilon, Graduate Women in Science **[Vol 1: 14887]**

Society of Motion Picture and Television Engineers **[Vol 1: 15700]**

Society of Nematologists **[Vol 1: 15724]**

South African Association of Botanists **[Vol 2: 5661]**

Southern African Society for Plant Pathology **[Vol 2: 5744]**

Special Libraries Association **[Vol 1: 16102]**

Ulster Teachers' Union **[Vol 2: 9407]**

Honorary Member Award
American Association of Petroleum Geologists **[Vol 1: 1279]**

American Water Resources Association **[Vol 1: 4650]**

Association of Women Surgeons **[Vol 1: 5553]**

Ecological Society of America **[Vol 1: 7987]**

Institute of Industrial Engineers **[Vol 1: 9355]**

International City/County Management Association **[Vol 1: 9763]**

International Society of Hypertension - United Kingdom **[Vol 2: 8210]**

Honorary Member (Individual) **[Vol. 1: 12450]**

Honorary Member (Institutional) **[Vol. 1: 12451]**

Honorary Member of the Year Award **[Vol. 1: 16477]**

Honorary Member of VOS **[Vol. 2: 5778]**

Honorary Members
Canadian Psychiatric Association **[Vol. 1: 6813]**

International Music and Media Centre **[Vol 2: 1294]**

Honorary Member's Emblem **[Vol. 2: 6180]**

Honorary Membership
Association of Canadian Archivists **[Vol. 1: 5235]**

Australian College of Rural and Remote Medicine **[Vol 2: 267]**

International Triathlon Union **[Vol 1: 10466]**

National Association of College and University Attorneys **[Vol 1: 11688]**

Society for Maternal-Fetal Medicine **[Vol 1: 15184]**

Society for the History of Natural History **[Vol 2: 9216]**

Honorary Membership
ACA International **[Vol. 1: 38]**

Agricultural Institute of Canada **[Vol 1: 222]**

Alpine Club of Canada **[Vol 1: 423]**

American Academy of Physician Assistants **[Vol 1: 736]**

American Association of Anatomists **[Vol 1: 1027]**

American Association of Collegiate Registrars and Admissions Officers **[Vol 1: 1103]**

American Association of Handwriting Analysts **[Vol 1: 1167]**

American Ceramic Society **[Vol 1: 1564]**

American Fisheries Society **[Vol 1: 2148]**

American Pharmacists Association **[Vol 1: 3135]**

American Romanian Academy of Arts and Sciences **[Vol 1: 3720]**

Association of College Unions International **[Vol 1: 5282]**

Association of Hungarian Geophysicists **[Vol 2: 3362]**

Association of State Dam Safety Officials **[Vol 1: 5523]**

Australian Society of Exploration Geophysicists **[Vol 2: 572]**

British Florist Association **[Vol 2: 7064]**

Canadian Actors' Equity Association **[Vol 1: 6174]**

Construction Specifications Institute **[Vol 1: 7558]**

Dermatological Society of Malaysia **[Vol 2: 4538]**

Deutsche Meteorologische Gesellschaft **[Vol 2: 2764]**

Electrochemical Society **[Vol 1: 8058]**

Entomological Society of America **[Vol 1: 8148]**

European Society for Dermatological Research **[Vol 2: 6289]**

European Society for Microcirculation **[Vol 2: 2853]**

German Society for Fat Science **[Vol 2: 2999]**

Guild of Television Cameramen **[Vol 2: 7775]**

International Association for Bridge and Structural Engineering **[Vol 2: 6348]**

International Association of Sedimentologists **[Vol 2: 4729]**

International Association of Volcanology and Chemistry of the Earth's Interior **[Vol 2: 6048]**

International Council on Monuments and Sites **[Vol 2: 2517]**

International Glaciological Society **[Vol 2: 8134]**

International Society for Applied Phycology **[Vol 2: 4107]**

International Union of Forest Research Organizations **[Vol 2: 1311]**

International Viola Society **[Vol 2: 4926]**

International Water Association **[Vol 2: 8252]**

D.H. Lawrence Society of North America **[Vol 1: 10761]**

National Association of Biology Teachers **[Vol 1: 11649]**

Oncology Nursing Society **[Vol 1: 13551]**

Polish Chemical Society **[Vol 2: 5393]**

Polish Physical Society **[Vol 2: 5406]**

Professional Institute of the Public Service of Canada **[Vol 1: 14234]**

Royal Geographical Society with the Institute of British Geographers **[Vol 2: 8793]**

Society for Sedimentary Geology **[Vol 1: 15309]**

Society of American Foresters **[Vol 1: 15437]**

Society of Exploration Geophysicists **[Vol 1: 15649]**

Society of Manufacturing Engineers **[Vol 1: 15689]**

Society of Petroleum Engineers **[Vol 1: 15758]**

Water Environment Federation **[Vol 1: 17708]**

Weed Society of Victoria **[Vol 2: 1182]**

The Wildlife Society **[Vol 1: 17852]**

World Conservation Union **[Vol 2: 6534]**

Honorary Membership Award
Solid Waste Association of North America **[Vol. 1: 15949]**

Statistical Society of Canada **[Vol 1: 16290]**

Honorary Membership Award
American Academy of Family Physicians **[Vol. 1: 556]**

American Nurses Association **[Vol 1: 3018]**

American Welding Society **[Vol 1: 4679]**

Association of Zoos and Aquariums **[Vol 1: 5566]**

International Society for Prevention of Child Abuse and Neglect **[Vol 1: 10219]**

National Athletic Trainers' Association **[Vol 1: 11943]**

National Fishing Lure Collectors Club **[Vol 1: 12395]**

Society for Applied Spectroscopy **[Vol 1: 15037]**

Southeastern Library Association **[Vol 1: 15996]**

Honorary Membership (Outstanding Contributors)- **[Vol. 1: 12079]**

Honorary Methadone Patient **[Vol 1: 11505]**

Honorary Nurse Practitioner Award **[Vol 1: 3020]**

Honorary Nursing Practice Award **[Vol 1: 3020]**

Honorary Physicist Award **[Vol 2: 1497]**

Honorary President
American Pharmacists Association **[Vol. 1: 3136]**

International Federation of Library Associations and Institutions **[Vol 2: 4742]**

Honorary President Award **[Vol. 2: 1873]**

Honorary Recognition Award
American Nurses Association **[Vol. 1: 3021]**

Contact Lens Manufacturers Association **[Vol 1: 7587]**

International Furnishings and Design Association **[Vol 1: 9953]**

Honorary Research Lecture **[Vol. 1: 3899]**

Honorary Scholar **[Vol. 2: 1290]**

Honorary Services to Writers Award **[Vol. 2: 3890]**

Honorary Sign **[Vol. 2: 1801]**

Honorary Vanguard Degree **[Vol. 1: 13062]**

Honorary Vice President **[Vol. 2: 9408]**

Honored Service Member Award **[Vol. 1: 15786]**

Honored Student Award **[Vol. 1: 3048]**

Honors of the Association
American Speech Language Hearing Association **[Vol. 1: 4545]**

Ohio Speech-Language-Hearing Association **[Vol. 1: 13479]**

Honour List **[Vol. 2: 6364]**

Honour Roll
Australian Drug Foundation **[Vol. 2: 331]**

National University of Singapore - Centre for Development of Teaching and Learning **[Vol 2: 5960]**

Honourary Life Membership **[Vol. 2: 997]**

Honourary Member **[Vol. 1: 14620]**

Honours Award **[Vol. 2: 5560]**

Honours Awards **[Vol. 2: 3832]**

Hood Award; E. I. **[Vol. 1: 6281]**

Hood Award for Diplomatic Correspondence; Edwin M. **[Vol. 1: 12685]**

Hood Medal **[Vol. 2: 8901]**

Hood Social Action Award; Thomas C. **[Vol. 1: 15391]**

Hook Memorial Award; Sidney
National Association of Scholars **[Vol. 1: 11871]**

Phi Beta Kappa **[Vol. 1: 13965]**

Hooke Distinguished Service Award; Casey **[Vol. 1: 5454]**

Hooker of the Year **[Vol. 1: 12989]**

Hoosier Intellectual Freedom Award **[Vol. 1: 9198]**

Hooten Plaque; George W. **[Vol. 1: 11512]**

Hoover Award; J. Edgar **[Vol. 1: 17545]**

Hoover Medal **[Vol. 1: 4398]**

Hoover Uncommon Student Awards; Herbert **[Vol. 1: 8972]**

HOPE Award **[Vol. 1: 7302]**

Hope Prize; A.D. **[Vol. 2: 95]**

Hopkins Promising Poet Award; Lee Bennett **[Vol. 1: 10098]**

Hopkinson Trophy; Walter W. **[Vol. 1: 17116]**

Hopper Award; Grace Murray **[Vol. 1: 4957]**

Hopps Award; Hope E. **[Vol. 1: 15110]**

Hora Medal; Sunder Lal **[Vol. 2: 3637]**

Hora Memorial Medal; Chandrakala **[Vol. 2: 3638]**

Horder Award; John **[Vol. 2: 8679]**

Horizon Award **[Vol. 1: 952]**

Horizon Interactive Awards **[Vol. 1: 8976]**

Horizon Pharma Fellow Abstract Prizes **[Vol. 1: 8445]**

Horizon Pharma Student Abstract Prizes **[Vol. 1: 8446]**

Hormone Research Prize **[Vol. 2: 7638]**

Hornaday Bronze and Silver Medals; William T. **[Vol. 1: 5966]**

Hornaday Gold Certificate; William T. **[Vol. 1: 5967]**

Hornaday Gold Medal; William T. **[Vol. 1: 5968]**

Hornaday Unit Award; William T. **[Vol. 1: 5969]**

Horne Memorial Award; John Robert **[Vol. 1: 11490]**

Horne Memorial Lecture; Robert **[Vol. 2: 9280]**

Horner Award; Wesley W. **[Vol. 1: 4192]**

Horner Sportsmanship Award; Frederic S. **[Vol. 1: 10544]**

Hornfeck Service Award; Anthony J. **[Vol. 1: 9099]**

Hornickel Award **[Vol. 1: 8914]**

Horning Memorial Award; Harry L. **[Vol. 1: 15514]**

Hornstein Medal in Operational Meteorology; Rube **[Vol. 1: 6708]**

Horonjeff Award of the Air Transport Division; Robert **[Vol. 1: 4193]**

Horowitz Jr. Memorial Graduate Award; Saul **[Vol. 1: 210]**

Horrocks Award for Library Leadership; Norman **[Vol. 1: 13448]**

Horror/Ghost Contest **[Vol. 1: 18124]**

Hors Concours **[Vol. 1: 11258]**

Horse Awards **[Vol. 1: 11716]**

Horse of the Year Award **[Vol. 1: 17625]**

Horse of the Year Awards [Vol. 1: 16873]
Horseback Hours Award [Vol. 1: 2480]
Horseback Miles Award [Vol. 1: 2481]
Horsemastership Awards [Vol. 1: 2928]
Horseshoe Hall of Fame [Vol. 1: 12522]
Horst-Wiehe Award [Vol. 2: 2785]
Hort Fellowship; Vivian Lefsky [Vol. 1: 18182]
Horta; Prix Baron [Vol. 2: 1591]
Horticultural Communication Award [Vol. 1: 2432]
Horticultural Therapy Award [Vol. 1: 2429]
Horticulture Awards [Vol. 1: 8274]
Horticulture Magazine Award for Garden Excellence [Vol. 1: 3635]
Horticulture Student of the Year Award [Vol. 2: 3920]
Horticuluture Writing Award [Vol. 1: 2432]
Hortie Memorial Award; Paul V. [Vol. 1: 322]
Horton Award; Robert E. [Vol. 1: 2240]
Horton Dining Awards; Loyal E. [Vol. 1: 11691]
Horvath Memorial; Alex [Vol. 1: 323]
Horwitz Award for Leadership in Inter-American Health; Abraham [Vol. 1: 13816]
Horwitz Prize; Louisa Gross [Vol. 1: 7415]
Hoskin Scientific Award [Vol. 1: 7039]
Hospital Awards for Volunteer Excellence [Vol. 1: 2451]
Hospital Pharmacy Student Award [Vol. 1: 6951]
Hospitality Awards [Vol. 2: 6861]
Host Communications Marketer of the Year [Vol. 1: 11708]
Host-Madsen Medal [Vol. 2: 4761]
Hosto Distinguished Service Award; Lester E. [Vol. 1: 11669]
Hot Bird TV Awards [Vol. 2: 4084]
Hotel Industry Awards for Excellence [Vol. 2: 369]
Hotel Manager of the Year
    European Hotel Managers Association [Vol. 2: 4073]
    Irish Hospitality Institute [Vol 2: 3883]
Hotel of the Year [Vol. 2: 1679]
Hotel Worker of the Year [Vol. 2: 4178]
Hotelier of the Year [Vol. 2: 4179]
Hotelympia
    American Culinary Federation [Vol. 1: 1964]
    Society of German Cooks [Vol. 2: 3181]
Hotelympia Competition [Vol. 2: 7034]
Houdry Award in Applied Catalysis; Eugene J. [Vol. 1: 13289]
Houghton Award; Henry G. [Vol. 1: 2909]
Houghton Lecture Award [Vol. 2: 3242]
Houle Award for Outstanding Literature in Adult Education; Cyril O. [Vol. 1: 856]
Houphouet-Boigny Peace Prize; Felix [Vol. 2: 2650]
Hour Glass [Vol. 2: 5154]
Hourani Book Award; Albert [Vol. 1: 11142]
House of Delegates Outstanding Service Award [Vol. 1: 737]
Housekeeper of the Year [Vol. 2: 6862]
Housing and Construction Awards [Vol. 2: 942]
Housing Design Awards
    Royal Institute of British Architects [Vol. 2: 8853]
    Saltire Society [Vol 2: 9151]
Housing Excellence Awards [Vol. 2: 865]
Housing Impact Award [Vol. 1: 1179]
Housing Person of the Year Award [Vol. 1: 12531]
Houssay Award; Bernardo A. [Vol. 1: 13693]
Houston Research Award; Charles S. [Vol. 1: 17840]
Houston Research Awards; W. J. B. [Vol. 2: 7623]
Houston Research Scholarship [Vol. 2: 7164]
Houston Scholarship Award; W. J. B. [Vol. 2: 7624]
Houston State University Award; Sam [Vol. 1: 3335]
Houtermans Medal [Vol. 2: 2361]
Houziaux; Prix Joseph [Vol. 1: 1609]
Hovey Trophy; Chandler [Vol. 1: 17056]
Howard/AMA Doctoral Dissertation Award; John A. [Vol. 1: 2815]
Howard Award; Ernest E. [Vol. 1: 4194]
Howard Award for Courage; Paul [Vol. 1: 2785]
Howard Award for Excellence in Horticulture; Nancy Putnam [Vol. 1: 8908]
Howard Citation of Musical Excellence for Military Concert Bands; Colonel George S. [Vol. 1: 15966]
Howard Medal [Vol. 2: 7990]
Howard Plaque; Mary B. [Vol. 1: 11512]
Howe Award [Vol. 1: 8914]
Howe Award; C. D. [Vol. 1: 6195]
Howe Cup [Vol. 2: 9328]

Howe Medal; Henry Marion [Vol. 1: 4841]
Howe Medal; Lucien [Vol. 1: 3051]
Howe Memorial Foundation Engineering Awards; C.D. [Vol. 1: 5546]
Howe Memorial Lecture [Vol. 1: 5034]
Howe Memorial Trophy; Henry Wainwright [Vol. 1: 16909]
Howell Award; A. Brazier [Vol. 1: 7595]
Howells Award; Albert [Vol. 2: 7471]
Howland Award; John [Vol. 1: 3126]
Howland Scholarships; Goldwin [Vol. 1: 6759]
Howley, Sr. Prize for Research in Arthritis; Lee C. [Vol. 1: 4809]
Howser Trophy; Dick [Vol. 1: 12083]
Hoyle Medal and Prize [Vol. 2: 7910]
Hoyt Award; National Milk Producers Federation Richard M. [Vol. 1: 1983]
HQF Career Development Grants [Vol. 1: 11581]
HQF New Quality Professional Grant [Vol. 1: 11582]
HR Leadership Awards [Vol. 2: 373]
HR Student of the Year [Vol. 2: 374]
HRD Award [Vol. 2: 6611]
Hrdlicka Prize; Ales [Vol. 1: 1295]
HRH Princess Michael of Kent Award [Vol. 2: 9344]
HRLSD Exceptional Service Award [Vol. 1: 5513]
Hromadka Excellence in Animal Care Award; Jean M. [Vol. 1: 1418]
Hromadka Excellence in Zoo Keeping Award; Jean M. [Vol. 1: 1418]
Hrycak Award; John and Judy [Vol. 1: 14742]
Hsieh Award; T. K. [Vol. 2: 7991]
HSMA Advertising Awards [Vol. 1: 8980]
Hsu Book Prize; Francis L.K. [Vol. 1: 15057]
Hu Award for Distinguished Service to Mathematics; Yueh-Gin Gung and Dr. Charles Y. [Vol. 1: 11015]
Hu Award; Shiu-ying [Vol. 1: 8964]
Hubbard Award for Race Relations; William P. [Vol. 1: 7298]
Hubbard Award; Prevost [Vol. 1: 5605]
Hubbard Memorial Prize; John [Vol. 2: 5032]
Hubbert Award; M. King [Vol. 1: 12463]
Hubbs Award; Carl L. [Vol. 1: 7853]
Hubele National Graduate Student Award; Glen E. [Vol. 1: 1938]
Huber Civil Engineering Research Prizes; Walter L. [Vol. 1: 4195]
Huber Learning Through Listening Awards; Marion [Vol. 1: 10786]
Huch-Preis; Ricarda- [Vol. 2: 3237]
HUD Secretary's Opportunity and Empowerment Award [Vol. 1: 3288]
Huddleson Memorial Award; Mary P. [Vol. 1: 2037]
Hudgens Memorial Award for Young Healthcare Executive of the Year; Robert S. [Vol. 1: 1760]
Hudgens Memorial Award - Young Hospital Administrator of the Year; Robert S. [Vol. 1: 1760]
Hudlicky Prize; Milos [Vol. 2: 1914]
Hudson Award in Carbohydrate Chemistry; Claude S. [Vol. 1: 1650]
Hudson Award; Roberts P. [Vol. 1: 16267]
Hudson Clinical Endocrinology Award; Bryan [Vol. 2: 702]
Hudson Medal; Manley O. [Vol. 1: 4354]
Hudson Service Award; Floyd G. [Vol. 1: 7651]
Huesca International Short Film Contest [Vol. 2: 6035]
Huff Award for Media Resources; Elmer [Vol. 1: 13600]
Huffington Leadership Award; Dale [Vol. 1: 931]
Huffman Memorial Award; Hugh M. [Vol. 1: 6104]
Hug Teacher of the Year Award; Clarissa [Vol. 1: 7638]
Huggins-Quarles Dissertation Award [Vol. 1: 13680]
Hughes Award; Howard [Vol. 1: 2324]
Hughes Award; John T. [Vol. 1: 12607]
Hughes Award; Lt. General Patrick M. [Vol. 1: 12607]
Hughes Award; Peter [Vol. 2: 604]
Hughes Jr. Memorial Award; Daniel C. [Vol. 1: 10011]
Hughes Medal [Vol. 2: 8938]
Hughes Memorial Graduate Student Prize; Tertia M.C. [Vol. 1: 6709]
Hugo Awards [Vol. 1: 18074]
Hull Award; T. J. [Vol. 1: 11352]
Hulse Memorial Award; William F. [Vol. 1: 5606]
Hulshoff Preis; Annette von Droste [Vol. 2: 3116]
Human and Civil Rights Awards [Vol. 1: 13919]

Human and Social Sciences Research Grant [Vol. 2: 4208]
Human Capital Business Leader of the Year Award [Vol. 1: 15103]
Human Capital Leadership Awards [Vol. 1: 15103]
Human Kinetics Writing Awards [Vol. 1: 6319]
Human Needs Award [Vol. 1: 1278]
Human Relations Award [Vol. 1: 11565]
Human Rights Award
    American Psychiatric Association [Vol. 1: 3351]
    International Bar Association [Vol 2: 8092]
    International Service for Human Rights - Switzerland [Vol 2: 6426]
    World Association of Non-Governmental Organizations [Vol 1: 18024]
Human Rights Prize [Vol. 2: 6515]
Human Values Award [Vol. 2: 3313]
Human Voices Award [Vol. 1: 10488]
Humane Award
    American Veterinary Medical Association [Vol. 1: 4639]
    Canadian Veterinary Medical Association [Vol 1: 7030]
Humane Awards [Vol. 1: 9000]
Humane Education Award [Vol. 2: 8259]
Humane Slaughter Association Award [Vol. 2: 7800]
Humane Teen of the Year Award [Vol. 1: 9004]
Humanist Distinguished Service Award [Vol. 1: 2467]
Humanist Fellow Award [Vol. 1: 2467]
Humanist Heroine Award [Vol. 1: 2468]
Humanist of the Year Award [Vol. 1: 2469]
Humanist Pioneer Award [Vol. 1: 2470]
Humanitarian Assistance Award [Vol. 1: 5426]
Humanitarian Award
    Academy of Dentistry International [Vol. 1: 74]
    American Academy of Family Physicians [Vol 1: 557]
    American Cancer Society [Vol 1: 1532]
    American Dental Association [Vol 1: 2004]
    B'nai Brith Canada [Vol 1: 5901]
    Canadian Psychological Association [Vol 1: 6827]
    Herbert Hoover Presidential Library Association [Vol 1: 8973]
    International Alliance of ALS/MND Associations [Vol 2: 8062]
    International Association of Cancer Victors and Friends [Vol 1: 9635]
    National Association of Recording Merchandisers [Vol 1: 11858]
    National Press Photographers Association [Vol 1: 12701]
    Painting and Decorating Contractors of America [Vol 1: 13795]
    People for the Ethical Treatment of Animals [Vol 1: 13940]
    Elie Wiesel Foundation for Humanity [Vol 1: 17834]
    Simon Wiesenthal Center [Vol 1: 17837]
    World Association of Non-Governmental Organizations [Vol 1: 18025]
Humanitarian of the Year [Vol. 1: 14938]
Humanitarian Overseas Service Medal [Vol. 2: 314]
Humanitarian PA of the Year [Vol. 1: 738]
Humanitarian Physician Assistant of the Year [Vol. 1: 738]
Humanitarian Service Award [Vol. 2: 9473]
Humanitarian Service Medal [Vol. 1: 16675]
Humanitas Prize [Vol. 1: 9009]
Humanities Symposium Grants [Vol. 1: 17256]
Humanities Texas Awards [Vol. 1: 9011]
Humble Newsletter Editor of the Year Award; Joe [Vol. 1: 4818]
Humboldt Research Fellowships [Vol. 2: 3228]
Hume Memorial Award for Excellence in Political Journalism; Sandy [Vol. 1: 12686]
Hume Prize [Vol. 2: 4910]
Hume-Rothery Award; William [Vol. 1: 11187]
Hummer Award; Glen S. [Vol. 1: 17443]
Hummingbird Medal [Vol. 2: 6616]
Humorous Poetry Award [Vol. 1: 12350]
Humphrey Award; Hubert H. [Vol. 1: 3137]
Humphrey Civil Rights Award; Hubert H. [Vol. 1: 10767]
Humphrey First Amendment Freedoms Prize; Hubert H. [Vol. 1: 4742]

Humphrey Freedom Award; John **[Vol. 1: 9752]**

Humphrey Software Process Achievement Award; Watts S. **[Vol. 1: 9061]**

Hunger Cleanup Rookie of the Year **[Vol. 1: 12942]**

Hunsaker Award in Aeronautical Engineering; J. C. **[Vol. 1: 11437]**

Hunt Award for Administrative Excellence; Leamon R. **[Vol. 1: 16849]**

Hunt Award for Management Excellence; Leamon R. **[Vol. 1: 16849]**

Hunt-Kelly Outstanding Paper Award **[Vol. 1: 5035]**

Hunt Lectureship; John **[Vol. 2: 8680]**

Hunt Memorial Award; Captain Alfred E. **[Vol. 1: 15861]**

Hunt Memorial Award; Fred T. **[Vol. 1: 2414]**

Hunt Memorial; Clyde M. **[Vol. 1: 9049]**

Hunt Memorial Prize; Renee Redfern **[Vol. 2: 7992]**

Hunt Trophy **[Vol. 2: 7759]**

Hunt Young Historian Award; Rockwell D. **[Vol. 1: 7494]**

Hunter Artists Awards; K. M. **[Vol. 1: 13568]**

Hunter Award **[Vol. 2: 4991]**

Hunter Award for Construction Document Education; J. Norman **[Vol. 1: 7559]**

Hunter, Jr. Thesis Prize; Charles A. **[Vol. 1: 2269]**

Hunter Leadership Award; Merle C. **[Vol. 1: 648]**

Hunter Memorial Award in Therapeutics; Oscar B. **[Vol. 1: 3802]**

Hunterdon Museum of Art Purchase Awards **[Vol. 1: 9015]**

Hunterian Medal **[Vol. 2: 7804]**

Hunting Award; William **[Vol. 2: 7296]**

Hunting Retriever Champion **[Vol. 1: 16633]**

Huntington Award; Merritt W. **[Vol. 1: 3079]**

Huntington Medal Award; Archer M. **[Vol. 1: 3014]**

Huntsman Australia for Research Excellence **[Vol. 2: 1128]**

Huntsman Australia Prize in Chemistry **[Vol. 2: 1129]**

Hunziker Medal **[Vol. 2: 1259]**

Hurd Award; James A. **[Vol. 1: 5274]**

Hurdis Award; John **[Vol. 1: 16142]**

Hurley Memorial Award for Aviation Traffic Management; David J. **[Vol. 1: 295]**

Hurst Award; John **[Vol. 2: 9201]**

Hurst Prize; J. Willard **[Vol. 1: 10757]**

Hurston Award; Zora Neale **[Vol. 1: 14467]**

Hurston Prize; Zora Neale **[Vol. 1: 2161]**

Hurter Memorial Lecture **[Vol. 2: 9281]**

Husain Prize for Young Scientists; Javed **[Vol. 2: 2651]**

Hutchins Award; Lee M. **[Vol. 1: 3280]**

Hutchins Educational Grant; Charles **[Vol. 1: 16336]**

Hutchinson Award; G. Evelyn **[Vol. 1: 5140]**

Hutchison Medal **[Vol. 2: 7966]**

Hutner Prize; Seymour H. **[Vol. 1: 10348]**

Hutton Memorial Award; Brig. Gen. Carl I. **[Vol. 1: 13648]**

Hutton Memorial Medal and Prize **[Vol. 2: 5076]**

Hutton Memorial Scholarship; Ann Hawkes **[Vol. 1: 17658]**

Hutton Memorial Scholarship; Edward **[Vol. 1: 17659]**

Hutton Memorial Scholarship; L. John **[Vol. 1: 17660]**

Hutton Memorial Scholarship; Rema **[Vol. 1: 17661]**

Huxley Award; Thomas Henry **[Vol. 2: 9509]**

Huygens Science Award; Christiaan **[Vol. 2: 4830]**

H.W. Wilson Library Staff Development Grant **[Vol. 1: 2786]**

Hyatt Benefit to Society Award; John W. **[Vol. 1: 15787]**

Hydar Memorial Award; Eleonora **[Vol. 1: 7015]**

Hyde Graduate Student Research Grant **[Vol. 1: 3550]**

Hydraulic Structures Medal **[Vol. 1: 4196]**

Hydrology Sciences Award **[Vol. 1: 2240]**

Hyman Ethics Award; Joseph **[Vol. 1: 2648]**

Hynds Paper of the Year Award **[Vol. 2: 5089]**

Hynes Award for New Investigators **[Vol. 1: 15079]**

I Tatti Fellowships **[Vol. 2: 4169]**

IAA Gold Medal **[Vol. 2: 1797]**

IABC Fellow **[Vol. 1: 9627]**

IABSE Prize **[Vol. 2: 6349]**

IADC Award **[Vol. 2: 4725]**

IAFIS-FPEI Food Engineering Award **[Vol. 1: 4080]**

IAGLR/Hydrolab Best Student Paper and Poster Competition **[Vol. 1: 9557]**

IAGLR Scholarship **[Vol. 1: 9558]**

IAHCSMM Cost Savers Award **[Vol. 1: 9674]**

IAHCSMM - Purdue University Scholarship Awards **[Vol. 1: 9675]**

Iakovos Distinguished Service Award; Archbishop **[Vol. 1: 12423]**

IAS/ANRS Young Investigator Award **[Vol. 2: 6343]**

IASL/Softlink Excellence Award **[Vol. 2: 814]**

Iatrides Best Dissertation Prize; John O. **[Vol. 1: 11228]**

Ibbertson Award for Metabolic Bone Disease; Kaye **[Vol. 2: 205]**

IBBY-Asahi Reading Promotion Award **[Vol. 2: 6365]**

Iben Award; Icko **[Vol. 1: 4651]**

Ibis Award **[Vol. 2: 7158]**

Ibrahim Memorial Award **[Vol. 2: 4357]**

Ibrahim Prize for Achievement in African Leadership; Mo **[Vol. 2: 7806]**

Ibsen Award; International **[Vol. 2: 5129]**

Ibsen Award; Norwegian **[Vol. 2: 5130]**

Ibuka Consumer Electronics Award; Masaru **[Vol. 1: 9294]**

ICA/UN Foundation Award **[Vol. 1: 9801]**

ICAAC Young Investigator Awards **[Vol. 1: 3980]**

ICCHK Scholarships **[Vol. 2: 5280]**

ICCROM Award **[Vol. 2: 4088]**

The Iceland Award **[Vol. 2: 3429]**

Iceland on Six Meters Award **[Vol. 2: 3430]**

Icelandic Fisheries Awards **[Vol. 2: 9484]**

Icelandic JOTA Award **[Vol. 2: 3431]**

Icelandic Literature Prize **[Vol. 2: 3427]**

Icelandic Music Awards **[Vol. 2: 3421]**

Icelandic Radio Amateurs Award **[Vol. 2: 3432]**

ICHCA Australia Award **[Vol. 2: 7811]**

ICHCA Finland Award **[Vol. 2: 7812]**

ICI Annual Award for Chemistry **[Vol. 2: 3848]**

ICI Award **[Vol. 2: 7482]**

ICIA Excellence in the Communications Industry Achievement Awards **[Vol. 1: 9232]**

Ickevaldspris **[Vol. 2: 6229]**

ICME Diploma **[Vol. 2: 7831]**

ICO-ICTP Gallieno Denardo Award **[Vol. 2: 4010]**

ICO-ICTP Prize **[Vol. 2: 4010]**

ICOM-US International Service Citation **[Vol. 1: 1218]**

ICPE Medal **[Vol. 2: 3766]**

ICT Award **[Vol. 2: 2644]**

ICTP Prize **[Vol. 2: 4011]**

ICU Design Citation **[Vol. 1: 15604]**

Ida and Henry Schuman Prize **[Vol. 1: 8956]**

IDA Documentary Awards

    International Documentary Association **[Vol. 1: 9880]**

    International Documentary Association **[Vol 1: 9881]**

    International Documentary Association **[Vol 1: 9882]**

    International Documentary Association **[Vol 1: 9884]**

IDF Award **[Vol. 2: 1531]**

IDI Design Awards **[Vol. 2: 3851]**

Iditarod Trail International Sled Dog Race **[Vol. 1: 9029]**

IEEE Education Medal **[Vol. 1: 9299]**

IEEE Life Members' Prize in Electrical History **[Vol. 1: 15354]**

IEEE Photonics Award **[Vol. 1: 9107]**

IERE Benefactors Premium **[Vol. 2: 8024]**

IEST Fellow **[Vol. 1: 9321]**

IFAJ-Alltech Young Leaders in Agricultural Journalism Award **[Vol. 2: 4737]**

IFAWPCA-CHOI Construction Fieldman Award **[Vol. 2: 5331]**

IFLA Medal **[Vol. 2: 4743]**

IFSC Travel Grants **[Vol. 2: 3859]**

IGIP Award **[Vol. 2: 1302]**

IGIP-Preis **[Vol. 2: 1302]**

IGS Medal **[Vol. 2: 3965]**

IGT Award **[Vol. 2: 3977]**

IHC Scholarship **[Vol. 1: 10508]**

IIE Distinguished Educator Award **[Vol. 1: 9354]**

IIE Doctoral Dissertation Award **[Vol. 1: 9361]**

IIE/Joint Publishers Book-of-the-Year Award **[Vol. 1: 9356]**

IIE Transactions Award **[Vol. 1: 9357]**

IIE Transactions Development and Applications Paper Award **[Vol. 1: 9359]**

IIS Award **[Vol. 1: 9978]**

ILDA Awards **[Vol. 1: 9982]**

Illingworth Award; Lady **[Vol. 2: 9370]**

Illinois Academic Librarian of the Year Award **[Vol. 1: 9139]**

Illumination Awards **[Vol. 1: 9153]**

Illy Trieste Science Prize; Ernesto **[Vol. 2: 4159]**

Image Award; EduSerc **[Vol. 1: 8036]**

Image Awards

    NAACP **[Vol. 1: 11339]**

    Women in Film and Video New England Chapter **[Vol 1: 17941]**

Imbrie Humanitarian; Frank **[Vol. 1: 16132]**

Imhoff - Koch Award for Outstanding Contribution to Water Management and Science **[Vol. 2: 8253]**

Imig Award for Distinguished Achievement in Teacher Education; David G. **[Vol. 1: 1090]**

Imison Award **[Vol. 2: 9251]**

Imison Memorial Award; Richard **[Vol. 2: 9251]**

Immerman and Abraham Nathan and Bertha Daskal Weinstein Memorial Fellowship; Abram and Fannie Gottlieb **[Vol. 1: 18183]**

Immigrant Achievement Awards **[Vol. 1: 2477]**

Impact Award **[Vol. 1: 7401]**

Impact Awards

    CREW Network **[Vol. 1: 7748]**

    CREW Network **[Vol 1: 7750]**

Impact of Music on Film Competition **[Vol. 2: 1516]**

IMPC Award for Excellence in Parking Design **[Vol. 1: 10044]**

IMPC Award for Excellence in Parking Design and Program Innovation **[Vol. 1: 10044]**

Imperial Tobacco Portrait Award **[Vol. 2: 8402]**

IMPHOS-FAI Award on the Role of Phosphorus on Yield and Quality of Crops **[Vol. 2: 3483]**

Implementing NCTM Standards in Your Own Classroom **[Vol. 1: 12225]**

Implications for Research and Innovations in Teaching **[Vol. 1: 5090]**

Implications for Research for Educational Practice Award **[Vol. 1: 5090]**

Imprisoned Artist Prize **[Vol. 2: 5943]**

Improvisation Competition **[Vol. 2: 8153]**

Imvelo Awards for Responsible Tourism **[Vol. 2: 5545]**

In-Depth Reporting Award **[Vol. 1: 9444]**

In-House Promotional Excellence Award **[Vol. 1: 10080]**

In Memoriam Testimonial **[Vol. 2: 8838]**

In-Print Award **[Vol. 1: 10081]**

In-Training Award **[Vol. 1: 15605]**

InBev-Baillet Latour Health Prize **[Vol. 2: 1521]**

Inclan; Premio Valle **[Vol. 2: 9252]**

Incubator Innovation Award **[Vol. 1: 12024]**

Incubator of the Year **[Vol. 1: 12025]**

Incubic/Milton Chang Student Travel Grants **[Vol. 1: 13609]**

Independence Foundation Scholarship **[Vol. 1: 17662]**

Independence Medal **[Vol. 2: 4485]**

Independent Bookseller of the Year **[Vol. 2: 6896]**

Independent Foreign Fiction Prize **[Vol. 2: 6906]**

Independent Investigator Award **[Vol. 1: 11369]**

Independent Publisher Book Awards **[Vol. 1: 10550]**

Independent Research and Creative Work Awards **[Vol. 1: 6007]**

Independent Research Award **[Vol. 1: 7842]**

Index of Investor-Owned Electric Utilities Award **[Vol. 1: 8003]**

Indian Country Officer of the Year Award **[Vol. 1: 9641]**

Indian Horse Hall of Fame Award **[Vol. 1: 2482]**

Indian Subcontinent Awards; Seatrade Middle East and **[Vol. 2: 9179]**

Indiana State Federation of Poetry Clubs Award **[Vol. 1: 12351]**

Indianapolis Motor Speedway Hall of Fame **[Vol. 1: 9215]**

Indies Choice Book Award **[Vol. 1: 1512]**

Indigenisation of Aeronautical Equipment Award **[Vol. 2: 3442]**

Individual Achievement Certificate **[Vol. 1: 10509]**

Individual Award

    American Printing History Association **[Vol. 1: 3329]**

South Dakota State Historical Society [**Vol 1:** 15986]

Individual Awards of Merit [**Vol. 1:** 10790]

Individual Citation [**Vol. 1:** 12979]

Individual Safety Advocate Award [**Vol. 1:** 12464]

Individual Volunteer Award for Contributions to Sexual and Reproductive Health and Rights [**Vol. 2:** 8161]

Indonesia Travel and Tourism Awards [**Vol. 2:** 3820]

Indonesian Feature Film Competition [**Vol. 2:** 3822]

Industrial Achievement Award [**Vol. 2:** 1278]

Industrial Appreciation Award [**Vol. 1:** 16]

Industrial Arts Teacher Educator of the Year [**Vol. 1:** 10441]

Industrial Award [**Vol. 1:** 296]

Industrial Chemistry Medal [**Vol. 2:** 5676]

Industrial Design Excellence Awards [**Vol. 1:** 9221]

Industrial Leadership Award [**Vol. 1:** 1436]

Industrial Minerals and Aggregates Young Scientist Award [**Vol. 1:** 15212]

Industrial Research and Development Award [**Vol. 1:** 2625]

Industrial Research Institute Medal [**Vol. 1:** 9225]

Industrial Safety Contest [**Vol. 1:** 4611]

Industrial Scientist Award [**Vol. 1:** 9337]

Industrial Water Quality Achievement Award [**Vol. 1:** 17709]

Industrialist of the Year [**Vol. 2:** 5245]

Industriepreis fur technisch-wissenschaftliche Arbeiten [**Vol. 2:** 3012]

Industry Achievement Award [**Vol. 1:** 14392]

Industry Achievement Award
    American Coatings Association [**Vol. 1:** 1691]
    Irrigation Association [**Vol 1:** 10526]

Industry Advancement Award [**Vol. 1:** 2845]

Industry and Technology Award [**Vol. 2:** 3615]

Industry Appreciation Award [**Vol. 1:** 11695]

Industry Award [**Vol. 2:** 945]

Industry Award [**Vol. 2:** 4714]

Industry Award of Distinction [**Vol. 1:** 8848]

Industry Awards
    Academy of Country Music [**Vol. 1:** 61]
    Florida Nursery, Growers and Landscape Association [**Vol 1:** 8383]

Industry Builder Award [**Vol. 1:** 7960]

Industry Champion Award [**Vol. 1:** 13090]

Industry Division Service Award [**Vol. 1:** 906]

Industry Excellence Awards [**Vol. 1:** 18173]

Industry/Government Graduate Fellowships [**Vol. 1:** 2910]

Industry Hall of Fame [**Vol. 1:** 14271]

Industry Innovation Award [**Vol. 1:** 14520]

Industry Leadership Award [**Vol. 1:** 6209]

Industry Merit Award [**Vol. 1:** 9473]

Industry Professional of the Year [**Vol. 1:** 7961]

Industry Recognition Award
    Electro-Federation Canada [**Vol. 1:** 8052]
    International Council on Hotel, Restaurant, and Institutional Education [**Vol. 1:** 9847]

Industry Research Scholar Awards [**Vol. 1:** 8447]

Industry Specific Group of the Year Award [**Vol. 1:** 4800]

Industry Star Award [**Vol. 1:** 10875]

Industry Statesman Awards [**Vol. 1:** 1692]

Industry Undergraduate Scholarships [**Vol. 1:** 2911]

Infinity Awards [**Vol. 1:** 9750]

Infocomm Singapore Awards [**Vol. 2:** 5977]

Infographics Award [**Vol. 1:** 9445]

Information Processing Public Service Award [**Vol. 1:** 5377]

Information Society Award [**Vol. 2:** 4558]

Information Systems Award [**Vol. 1:** 2525]

Information Technology Award [**Vol. 1:** 5427]

Information Technology Pathfinder Award [**Vol. 1:** 1344]

Information Technology Scholarship [**Vol. 1:** 16837]

INFORMS Fellow Award [**Vol. 1:** 9259]

INFORMS Prize [**Vol. 1:** 9260]

Infosys Foundation - ISCA Travel Award [**Vol. 2:** 3715]

Infrastructure, Utilities, and Transport [**Vol. 2:** 4905]

ING New York City Marathon [**Vol. 1:** 13234]

Ingall Memorial Award; Lindsay [**Vol. 2:** 573]

Ingbar Distinguished Lectureship Award; Sidney H. [**Vol. 1:** 4594]

Ingbar Distinguished Service Award; Sidney H. [**Vol. 1:** 8110]

Ingberg Award; S. H. [**Vol. 1:** 5607]

Ingelheim Award; Boehringer [**Vol. 1:** 6889]

Ingersoll Award; E. P. [**Vol. 1:** 15553]

Ingle Service Award; Robert [**Vol. 1:** 2090]

Inglehart First Amendment Award; Louis E. [**Vol. 1:** 7370]

Inglis Award; Rewey Belle [**Vol. 1:** 17947]

Ingraham Pediatric Optometry Residency Award; Terrance [**Vol. 1:** 622]

Initiative for Peace Award [**Vol. 1:** 12106]

Injury Prevention Institute Award [**Vol. 1:** 8091]

Inklings [**Vol. 1:** 11337]

INLA Prize [**Vol. 2:** 1550]

INMA Awards [**Vol. 1:** 10035]

Inman Prize; William [**Vol. 2:** 7188]

Inn of the Year [**Vol. 1:** 13972]

Inner City Physician Assistant of the Year [**Vol. 1:** 740]

Innes Achievement Award; Jack [**Vol. 1:** 6332]

Innis Aviation Command and Control Marine of the Year Award; Kenneth A. [**Vol. 1:** 10956]

Innis Award for Outstanding Thesis or Dissertation in the Field of Media Ecology; Harold A. [**Vol. 1:** 11035]

Innis-Gerin Medal [**Vol. 1:** 14641]

Innis Prize; Harold Adams [**Vol. 1:** 6468]

Innovation and Excellence Awards [**Vol. 2:** 933]

Innovation Award
    Federal Government Distributed Learning Association [**Vol. 1:** 8266]
    Supply Chain and Logistics Association Canada [**Vol 1:** 16329]
    Voluntary Protection Programs Participants' Association [**Vol 1:** 17614]

Innovation Award
    Advertising Research Foundation [**Vol. 1:** 168]
    American Diabetes Association [**Vol 1:** 2022]
    Association for Computing Machinery - Special Interest Group on Knowledge Discovery and Data Mining [**Vol 1:** 4973]
    Colorado Business Committee for the Arts [**Vol 1:** 7401]
    Federal Government Distance Learning Association [**Vol 1:** 8261]
    Professional Aerial Photographers Association [**Vol 1:** 14182]

Innovation Awards [**Vol. 2:** 5981]

Innovation Awards
    British Society for Rheumatology [**Vol. 2:** 7240]
    European Disposables and Nonwovens Association [**Vol 2:** 1473]
    Juvenile Products Manufacturers Association [**Vol 1:** 10623]

Innovation Competition [**Vol. 2:** 7367]

Innovation Excellence Awards [**Vol. 1:** 11701]

Innovation for Success Award [**Vol. 1:** 8861]

Innovation in Civil Engineering Award [**Vol. 1:** 4197]

Innovation in Education Prize [**Vol. 2:** 8579]

Innovation in Higher Education Award [**Vol. 1:** 8068]

Innovation in International Education Award [**Vol. 1:** 6371]

Innovation of the Year Awards [**Vol. 1:** 10773]

Innovation Prize [**Vol. 2:** 2955]

Innovations Design and Engineering Awards [**Vol. 1:** 7576]

Innovations in Occupational Health Award [**Vol. 1:** 1251]

Innovative Achievement Award [**Vol. 1:** 6746]

Innovative Applications of Artificial Intelligence Awards [**Vol. 1:** 5113]

Innovative Approaches Award [**Vol. 1:** 9649]

Innovative Business Solution Award [**Vol. 1:** 15103]

Innovative Coastal Research Grants [**Vol. 2:** 2639]

Innovative Course Design Competition [**Vol. 1:** 3826]

Innovative Curriculum Award [**Vol. 2:** 292]

Innovative Dairy Farmer of the Year [**Vol. 1:** 9869]

Innovative Engineering Award [**Vol. 1:** 12876]

Innovative Intermodal Solutions for Urban Transportation Paper Award [**Vol. 1:** 9415]

Innovative Management Award [**Vol. 1:** 9401]

Innovative Owl Award [**Vol. 1:** 2889]

Innovative Program Award [**Vol. 1:** 7458]

Innovative Research in Primary Care Award [**Vol. 1:** 11713]

Innovative Solutions Award [**Vol. 1:** 9842]

Innovative Teaching Grants [**Vol. 1:** 13920]

Innovative Technology Awards [**Vol. 1:** 17710]

Innovator Award
    American Society of Cataract and Refractive Surgery [**Vol. 1:** 4137]
    International Surface Fabricators Association [**Vol 1:** 10404]
    Restaurant Association of New Zealand [**Vol 2:** 5038]

Innovator of the Year [**Vol. 1:** 6186]

Innovator of the Year Award [**Vol. 1:** 18140]

Innovators Award [**Vol. 1:** 9843]

Innovators Mauritius Award [**Vol. 2:** 4577]

Inorganic Chemistry Division Award for Excellent Research [**Vol. 2:** 5457]

Inorganic Mechanisms Award [**Vol. 2:** 9018]

Inose Award [**Vol. 2:** 4228]

Inqaba Molecular Biology Prize [**Vol. 2:** 5745]

Insect Conservation and Diversity Journal Award [**Vol. 2:** 8771]

Insect Molecular Biology Journal Award [**Vol. 2:** 8772]

Inside Write Awards [**Vol. 2:** 8479]

Insole and Clegg Grant [**Vol. 2:** 7124]

Inspiration and Industry Awards [**Vol. 2:** 9019]

Institute Award [**Vol. 1:** 6583]

Institute Award for Excellence in Industrial Gases Technology [**Vol. 1:** 2626]

Institute Directors Award of Excellence [**Vol. 1:** 9971]

Institute Fellowship Award [**Vol. 2:** 6578]

Institute Honor Award for Architecture [**Vol. 1:** 2571]

Institute Honor Award for Interior Architecture [**Vol. 1:** 2572]

Institute Honor Award for Regional and Urban Design [**Vol. 1:** 2573]

Institute Honors for Collaborative Achievement [**Vol. 1:** 2574]

Institute Medal [**Vol. 2:** 9378]

Institute Medal for Design [**Vol. 2:** 9379]

Institute of Administrative Accountants Awards [**Vol. 2:** 7870]

Institute of Financial Accountants Awards [**Vol. 2:** 7870]

Institute of Metals Division Award [**Vol. 1:** 11194]

Institute of Metals Lecturer and Robert Franklin Mehl Award [**Vol. 1:** 11188]

Institute Recognition Award [**Vol. 1:** 223]

Institute Service Awards [**Vol. 1:** 14235]

Institution Medal and Premium (Local Association) Competition [**Vol. 2:** 7985]

Institution Medal and Premium (London Universities) Competition [**Vol. 2:** 7978]

Institution Medal and Premium (Universities) Competition [**Vol. 2:** 7978]

Institution or Organization Citation [**Vol. 1:** 12980]

Institutional Achievement Award [**Vol. 1:** 10359]

Institutional Award [**Vol. 1:** 3330]

Institutional Research Training Grant [**Vol. 1:** 15005]

Institutional Service Award [**Vol. 1:** 7628]

Instruction Section Innovation Award [**Vol. 1:** 5264]

Instructional Innovation Award [**Vol. 1:** 7830]

Instrumental Album of the Year [**Vol. 1:** 9732]

Instrumental and Vocal Competition [**Vol. 2:** 1082]

Instrumental Group of the Year [**Vol. 1:** 9732]

Instrumental Performers of the Year [**Vol. 1:** 9732]

Insurance Company of the Year [**Vol. 2:** 1904]

Insurance Media Awards [**Vol. 1:** 9430]

Insurance Prize [**Vol. 2:** 425]

Integrated Young Playwrights Project [**Vol. 1:** 17622]

Integrity Awards [**Vol. 2:** 1799]

Intel International Science and Engineering Fair [**Vol. 1:** 2714]

Intel International Science and Engineering Fair [**Vol. 1:** 15304]

Intel IT Leader of the Year [**Vol. 2:** 7013]

Intel Science Talent Search [**Vol. 1:** 15305]

Intellectual Freedom Award
    American Association of School Librarians [**Vol. 1:** 1345]
    Illinois Library Association [**Vol 1:** 9140]
    Louisiana Library Association [**Vol 1:** 10886]
    South Dakota Library Association [**Vol 1:** 15978]

Intellectual Property Organisation Prize; African Regional [**Vol. 2:** 4466]

Intensive Language Grant [**Vol. 1:** 8610]

Isker Award; Colonel Rohland A. **[Vol. 1: 14517]**

Isocrates Award **[Vol. 1: 10069]**

ISOPE Award **[Vol. 1: 10332]**

ISOPE EUROMS Award **[Vol. 1: 10333]**

ISOPE OMS Award **[Vol. 1: 10334]**

ISOPE PACOMS Award **[Vol. 1: 10335]**

ISP of the Year **[Vol. 2: 3253]**

ISPE Engineer of The Year **[Vol. 1: 10204]**

ISPIM-Wiley Innovation Management Dissertation Award **[Vol. 2: 8189]**

ispo BrandNew Awards **[Vol. 2: 3150]**

Israel Chemical Society Medal **[Vol. 2: 3957]**

Issa Award for Excellence; Abe **[Vol. 2: 4180]**

Isserlis Scholarship; Julius **[Vol. 2: 8889]**

ISSFA Champions **[Vol. 1: 10405]**

ISTT Prize **[Vol. 2: 6068]**

ISTTE Awards **[Vol. 1: 10359]**

IT Company Award **[Vol. 2: 4559]**

IT Consultancy of the Year **[Vol. 2: 7014]**

IT Education Award **[Vol. 2: 4560]**

IT Product Award **[Vol. 2: 4561]**

IT Project Award **[Vol. 2: 4562]**

Italian Association for Metallurgy Awards **[Vol. 2: 4122]**

Italian PEN Prize **[Vol. 2: 4139]**

Italian Shipping Awards **[Vol. 2: 8322]**

Itat'ev Prize; V.N. **[Vol. 2: 5806]**

Itschner Plaque **[Vol. 1: 15453]**

Ittleson Award for Research in Child and Adolescent Psychiatry; Blanche F. **[Vol. 1: 3352]**

IUCN - Reuters - COMplus Media Awards **[Vol. 2: 6535]**

IUPAP Young Scientist Prize in Optics **[Vol. 2: 6057]**

IUSSP Laureates **[Vol. 2: 2582]**

Ivers Award; William H. **[Vol. 1: 16278]**

Ives Medal/Quinn Prize; Frederic **[Vol. 1: 13610]**

Ivey Awards **[Vol. 1: 10540]**

Iyengar Memorial Award; Dr. M. O. T. **[Vol. 2: 3547]**

Iyer Oration Award; Dr. C. G. S. **[Vol. 2: 3548]**

J and J Award **[Vol. 2: 7814]**

Jaag-Gewasserschutz-Preis; Otto **[Vol. 2: 6498]**

Jabara Endowed Scholarship; Professor Fran **[Vol. 1: 17830]**

Jack Award; Colin E. **[Vol. 1: 6574]**

Jackling Award; Daniel C. **[Vol. 1: 15213]**

Jackson Award; Anna M. **[Vol. 1: 4375]**

Jackson Award; Dr. Nell C. **[Vol. 1: 944]**

Jackson Award; Hartley H. T. **[Vol. 1: 4376]**

Jackson Award; Sara E. **[Vol. 1: 8072]**

Jackson Award; William E. **[Vol. 1: 14654]**

Jackson Awards; C. C. **[Vol. 1: 17468]**

Jackson Brothers Fellowship **[Vol. 1: 18155]**

Jackson Cultural Diversity Award; Hobart **[Vol. 1: 10774]**

Jackson Distinguished Service Award; Henry M. "Scoop" **[Vol. 1: 10575]**

Jackson Fellowship; Beverley **[Vol. 1: 6484]**

Jackson Fellowship; John D. and Rose H. **[Vol. 1: 18156]**

Jackson-Gwilt Medal **[Vol. 2: 8663]**

Jackson Literary Award; Joseph Henry **[Vol. 1: 14711]**

Jackson Memorial Award; Bruce **[Vol. 1: 15871]**

Jackson Memorial Award; Dr. Glenn **[Vol. 1: 15736]**

Jackson Memorial Intermediate Piano Scholarship **[Vol. 1: 14744]**

Jackson Memorial Clay Scientist Award; Marion L. and Chrystie M. **[Vol. 1: 7318]**

Jackson Prize; John Brinckerhoff **[Vol. 1: 5204]**

Jackson Social Responsibility Award; Hobart **[Vol. 1: 10774]**

Jacob Book Prize; Herbert **[Vol. 1: 10758]**

Jacob K. Javits Public Service Award **[Vol. 1: 3353]**

Jacob Memorial Award; Max **[Vol. 1: 4401]**

Jacobaeus Lectures; H. C. **[Vol. 2: 1982]**

Jacobi Memorial Award; Abraham **[Vol. 1: 686]**

Jacobs Award; Alvin **[Vol. 1: 687]**

Jacobs Memorial Diversity Award; Raymond **[Vol. 1: 11568]**

Jacobs President's Lecture; H.S. **[Vol. 2: 7054]**

Jacobsen Award; Earl Grant **[Vol. 1: 14767]**

Jacobson Award for Women Working in Health Care Law; Elaine Osborne **[Vol. 1: 14119]**

Jacobus Award; Donald Lines **[Vol. 1: 4303]**

Jacquemetton; Prix Marius **[Vol. 2: 2610]**

Jaeger Medal **[Vol. 2: 180]**

Jaeger Memorial Award; Australian Geomechanics Award - John **[Vol. 2: 768]**

Jaeger Prize; Thomas A. **[Vol. 1: 9591]**

Jaffe Volunteer Award; Kathie **[Vol. 1: 9491]**

Jaghmohan Das Memorial Award; Chaturvedi Kalawati **[Vol. 2: 3549]**

Jahn and Eugene C. Bovee Award; Theodore L. **[Vol. 1: 10349]**

Jahnigen Memorial Award; Dennis W. **[Vol. 1: 2254]**

Jahns Distinguished Lecturer in Engineering Geology Award; Richard H. **[Vol. 1: 5325]**

Jahnsson Award; Yrjo **[Vol. 2: 4070]**

Jakarta International Film Festival **[Vol. 2: 3822]**

JALMA Trust Fund Oration Award **[Vol. 2: 3550]**

James Award; Edith-Dalton **[Vol. 2: 4195]**

James Award; William

    American Psychological Association - Psychology of Religion Division **[Vol. 1: 3485]**

    Institution of Engineering and Technology **[Vol 2: 8025]**

James Book Award; William **[Vol. 1: 3520]**

James Fellowship; T. V. **[Vol. 2: 7125]**

James International Award; John F. **[Vol. 1: 4327]**

James Living Principles Award; Muriel **[Vol. 1: 10464]**

James Shield and Trophy; Oscar Sydney **[Vol. 2: 3349]**

James Traveling Fellowship; Olivia **[Vol. 1: 4762]**

Jameson Archival Advocacy Award; J. Franklin **[Vol. 1: 15422]**

Jameson Prize; J. Franklin **[Vol. 1: 2377]**

Jamieson Award **[Vol. 2: 4992]**

Jamieson Fellowship; Donald **[Vol. 1: 6902]**

Jan Beek Award; Klaas **[Vol. 2: 4748]**

Janata Award; Rudolf A. **[Vol. 1: 7836]**

Jane Memorial Award; R.S. **[Vol. 1: 6970]**

Janet Award for Clinical Excellence; Pierre **[Vol. 2: 4112]**

Janet Writing Award; Pierre **[Vol. 1: 10251]**

Janeway Medal **[Vol. 1: 3667]**

Jankelow Trophy; Dennis **[Vol. 2: 5484]**

Janseen-Cilag Award for Excellence in Nephrology **[Vol. 2: 3741]**

Janssen; Prix Jules **[Vol. 2: 2611]**

Janssens; Prix Rene **[Vol. 2: 1592]**

Jansson Prize; C.J. **[Vol. 2: 2095]**

Japan Gold Disk Awards **[Vol. 2: 4318]**

Japan Prize **[Vol. 2: 4320]**

Japan Quality Medal **[Vol. 2: 4338]**

Japan Society Small Grants **[Vol. 2: 8270]**

Jaques Rural Doctor of the Year Award; Pierre **[Vol. 2: 5609]**

Jarabak Award; Louise Ada **[Vol. 1: 1263]**

Jarrett Award for Young Leaders; James A. **[Vol. 1: 1075]**

Jarrett Award of Marketing Excellence; James H. **[Vol. 1: 6598]**

Jarvis Award for Inspirational Leadership; Capt. David H. **[Vol. 1: 16760]**

Jaspers Awards; Jos **[Vol. 2: 2813]**

Javits Neuroscience Investigator Award; NINDS **[Vol. 1: 16815]**

Jaw Award; Jeoujang **[Vol. 2: 2338]**

Jayanti Award; Swarna **[Vol. 2: 3443]**

Jayezeye Shoraye Ketabe Koudak **[Vol. 2: 3824]**

Jayle; Prix Max-Fernand **[Vol. 2: 2208]**

Jayme Denkmunze; Georg **[Vol. 2: 2702]**

Jayne Excellence in Education Award; Hal **[Vol. 1: 15006]**

Jazz Lifetime Achievement Award **[Vol. 2: 4665]**

Jazz Masters Fellowships **[Vol. 1: 12312]**

Jazz/World Music Awards; Edison **[Vol. 2: 4665]**

JB Award **[Vol. 2: 4284]**

JB Awards **[Vol. 1: 13250]**

JC Penney - University of Missouri Awards in Lifestyle Journalism **[Vol. 1: 17295]**

JC Penney - University of Missouri Newspaper Awards **[Vol. 1: 17295]**

JCI Takamatsu Trophy **[Vol. 1: 10612]**

Jeanbernat et Barthelemy de Ferrari Doria; Prix Jules et Louis **[Vol. 2: 2472]**

Jeanbernat et Bathelemy de Ferrari Doria; Prix Jules et Louis **[Vol. 2: 2275]**

Jeanson Prize; Henri **[Vol. 2: 2635]**

Jecker, Cahours, Paul Marguerite de la Charlonie, Houzeau, and J. B. Dumas; Prix **[Vol. 2: 2209]**

Jeersannidhi Award Lecture **[Vol. 2: 3694]**

Jefferson Award; Thomas

    American Citizens Abroad **[Vol. 2: 6254]**

    Association of Private Enterprise Education **[Vol 1: 5476]**

    Society for Applied Spectroscopy **[Vol 1: 15038]**

Jefferson Awards **[Vol. 1: 2497]**

Jefferson Awards for Public Architecture; Thomas **[Vol. 1: 2575]**

Jefferson Freedom Award; Thomas **[Vol. 1: 2765]**

Jefferson Medal for Distinguished Achievement in the Arts, Humanities, and Social Sciences; Thomas **[Vol. 1: 3186]**

Jefferson Prize; Thomas **[Vol. 1: 15096]**

Jeffrey Memorial Award; Timothy B. **[Vol. 1: 3472]**

Jeffreys Award; Rees **[Vol. 2: 7994]**

Jeffreys Lecture; Harold **[Vol. 2: 8664]**

Jeffries Aerospace Medicine and Life Sciences Research Award **[Vol. 1: 2527]**

Jeffries Award; John **[Vol. 1: 2527]**

Jelavich Book Prize; Barbara **[Vol. 1: 5098]**

Jellicoe Award; Sir Geoffrey **[Vol. 1: 1535]**

Jenkins Award; Carol and Travis **[Vol. 2: 8140]**

Jenkins Award for Excellence in Teaching; Don **[Vol. 1: 16423]**

Jenkins Biography Prize; Annibel **[Vol. 1: 3827]**

Jenkins Outstanding Service Award; Samuel H. **[Vol. 2: 8254]**

Jenkinson Service Award; Marion **[Vol. 1: 3094]**

Jennings Award; Margaret **[Vol. 2: 566]**

Jennings Memorial Award; Charles H. **[Vol. 1: 4681]**

Jensen Award; Harry T. **[Vol. 1: 2325]**

Jensen Award; Paul **[Vol. 1: 14769]**

Jensen Memorial Trophy; Rudolf **[Vol. 1: 10523]**

Jenson Educational Stipend; Gaynold **[Vol. 1: 7863]**

Jephcott Lecture **[Vol. 2: 9097]**

Jeppson Medal; John **[Vol. 1: 1565]**

Jeremiah Division III Coach of the Year; Edward **[Vol. 1: 2395]**

Jerky Award **[Vol. 1: 9126]**

Jernigan Scholarship; Kenneth **[Vol. 1: 12382]**

Jerome Fellowships **[Vol. 1: 14046]**

Jerwood Drawing Prize **[Vol. 2: 8454]**

Jerwood Sculpture Prize **[Vol. 2: 8455]**

Jeske Award; Walter E. **[Vol. 1: 13265]**

Jesup Botanical Trophy; Ann and Phil **[Vol. 1: 3080]**

Jeter Award; Frank **[Vol. 1: 4947]**

Jewett Memorial Life Award; Lew **[Vol. 1: 8304]**

Jewish Caucus Scholarship **[Vol. 1: 13058]**

Jewish Programming Award **[Vol. 1: 5379]**

Jeyes Award; John **[Vol. 2: 9021]**

Jeyes Lectureship; John **[Vol. 2: 9021]**

Jindal Gold Medal; O. P. **[Vol. 2: 3597]**

Jnanpith Award **[Vol. 2: 3454]**

JNC Editors' Award **[Vol. 2: 835]**

JNMA Awards for Medical Journalism **[Vol. 1: 12601]**

Joachim Distinguished Service Award; Herman L. **[Vol. 1: 16366]**

Joannides; Prix Alexandre **[Vol. 2: 2210]**

Job Corps Hall of Fame **[Vol. 1: 16838]**

Job Creation Awards **[Vol. 2: 4199]**

Jobim Award; Antonio Carlos **[Vol. 1: 8347]**

Jobst Foundation Prize; Conrad **[Vol. 1: 1866]**

Joenk, Jr. Award; Rudolph J. **[Vol. 1: 9115]**

Joest; Prix de **[Vol. 2: 2276]**

Joest; Prix du Baron de **[Vol. 2: 2167]**

JOFA All-American Ice Hockey Teams (College Division) **[Vol. 1: 2400]**

JOFA All-American Ice Hockey Teams (University Division) **[Vol. 1: 2401]**

Jofa-Titan/USA Hockey Distinguished Achievement Award **[Vol. 1: 17423]**

Johinke Medal; K. **[Vol. 2: 785]**

John Deere Gold Medal **[Vol. 1: 4084]**

John Wiley and Sons Best *JASIST* Paper Award **[Vol. 1: 3947]**

Johns Award; Harold E. **[Vol. 1: 6390]**

Johns Award; Henry **[Vol. 2: 6989]**

Johns Medal; Harold **[Vol. 2: 8157]**

Johns Outstanding Teacher Educator in Reading Award; Jerry **[Vol. 1: 10099]**

Johnson Achievement Award; Alfred E. **[Vol. 1: 1353]**

Johnson Aerospace Vehicle Design and Development Award; Clarence L. (Kelly) **[Vol. 1: 15517]**

Johnson AMS 50 Dissertation Fellowships; Alvin H. **[Vol. 1: 2964]**

Johnson and Johnson Award for Excellence in Dental Hygiene [Vol. 1: 2010]

Johnson Award; Bob [Vol. 1: 17425]

Johnson Award; Charles A. [Vol. 1: 5610]

Johnson Award; Eleanor M. [Vol. 1: 10100]

Johnson Award for Career Contributions to Family Medicine Education; Thomas W. [Vol. 1: 558]

Johnson Award for Research in Pediatrics; E. Mead [Vol. 2: 6601]

Johnson Award for Young Professionals; A. Ivan [Vol. 1: 4652]

Johnson Award; G. Wesley [Vol. 1: 12251]

Johnson Award; John C. [Vol. 1: 5814]

Johnson Award; Kelly [Vol. 1: 15658]

Johnson Award; Mildred Biehn [Vol. 1: 2277]

Johnson Award; Mrs. Lyndon B. [Vol. 1: 10646]

Johnson-Award; Pyke [Vol. 1: 16537]

Johnson-Edwin Paget Distinguished Service Award; T. Earle [Vol. 1: 16043]

Johnson Exhibition Catalogue Award; Philip [Vol. 1: 15477]

Johnson Health Policy Fellowships; Robert Wood [Vol. 1: 9386]

Johnson Honorary Member Award; Philip D. [Vol. 1: 4002]

Johnson Image Award; Peter H. [Vol. 1: 11930]

Johnson Jr. Award; Howard J. [Vol. 1: 688]

Johnson, Jr., Award; J. E. [Vol. 1: 5036]

Johnson, Jr. Scholarship Program; Lloyd M. [Vol. 1: 11205]

Johnson Lifetime Achievement Award; Gordon [Vol. 1: 8048]

Johnson Matthew Student Award [Vol. 1: 10060]

Johnson Memorial Award; Palmer O. [Vol. 1: 2056]

Johnson Memorial Lecture; Shirley [Vol. 1: 10369]

Johnson Memorial Trophy; Joe [Vol. 1: 6644]

Johnson Meritorious Service Award; Edway R. [Vol. 1: 9396]

Johnson New Holland Trophy Award [Vol. 2: 7956]

Johnson Outstanding Achievement Award; A. Ivan [Vol. 1: 5611]

Johnson Pioneer Citation; Edgar F. [Vol. 1: 14403]

Johnson President's Trophy; John H. [Vol. 1: 11840]

Johnson Prize for Non-Fiction; BBC Samuel [Vol. 2: 6900]

Johnson Prize; Harry G. [Vol. 1: 6458]

Johnson SCJ Article Award; Rose B. [Vol. 1: 16044]

Johnson Special Award; Larry R. [Vol. 1: 13032]

Johnson Student Travel Award; Krystyna [Vol. 2: 9162]

Johnson Writing Award; Orinne [Vol. 1: 13986]

Johnson Young Investigator Award; Ned K. [Vol. 1: 3095]

Johnston Award; J. Dudley [Vol. 2: 8902]

Johnston Distinguished Lecture Award [Vol. 1: 10142]

Johnston Medal; W. A. [Vol. 1: 6848]

Johnston Service Award; Floyd T. [Vol. 1: 5326]

Johnstone Award; Cecilia I. [Vol. 1: 6333]

Joint Award for Excellence in Labor Diplomacy [Vol. 1: 16850]

Joint Service Commendation Medal [Vol. 1: 16676]

Jolliff Award for Lifetime Achievement in Clinical or Diagnostic Immunology; Carl R. [Vol. 1: 908]

Jonasson Distinguished Member Award; Olga [Vol. 1: 5552]

Jonckheere; Prix Tobie [Vol. 2: 1610]

Jones Award; Bob [Vol. 1: 16935]

Jones Award; Col. James L. [Vol. 1: 12607]

Jones Award; Dexter [Vol. 1: 12830]

Jones Award for Excellence in Education; Elizabeth W. [Vol. 1: 8550]

Jones Award for Fiction; Jesse [Vol. 1: 16457]

Jones Award; Mary Vaughan [Vol. 2: 9442]

Jones Awards for Best Papers; R.O. [Vol. 1: 6814]

Jones Awards; Mander [Vol. 2: 567]

Jones Community Service Award; Edward C. [Vol. 1: 2846]

Jones Cup; O.P. [Vol. 2: 7308]

Jones Distinguished Service Award; Reginald H. [Vol. 1: 11461]

Jones Fleet Engineer Award; Claud A. [Vol. 1: 4444]

Jones Leadership in Philanthropy Award; David R. [Vol. 1: 8485]

Jones Legend Award; Ambassador Bobby [Vol. 1: 7159]

Jones Lifetime Service Award; David R. [Vol. 1: 8486]

Jones London Medal; H. E. [Vol. 2: 8043]

Jones Male Athlete of the Year Award; Frank [Vol. 1: 8286]

Jones Medal; Rhys [Vol. 2: 228]

Jones Memorial Lecture; Hugh R. [Vol. 1: 8493]

Jones Outstanding Hybridizer Award; Bennett C. [Vol. 1: 11044]

Jones Principal's Leadership Award; Herff [Vol. 1: 11886]

Jones Prize; Alice Hanson [Vol. 1: 7996]

Jones Resident Humanitarian Award; Mary Louise Witmer [Vol. 1: 13934]

Jones Scholarship; Edward [Vol. 1: 17302]

Jones Stallion Award; Jim [Vol. 1: 2065]

Jones Trophy (Norwich Dog); John Paul [Vol. 1: 13440]

Jones Writing Fellowship; Jesse J. [Vol. 1: 16458]

Jong-Wook Memorial Prize for Public Health; Dr. Lee [Vol. 2: 6551]

Jonssons pris; Bengt [Vol. 2: 6172]

Jope Award; Martyn [Vol. 2: 9202]

Jordan Advertising Awards [Vol. 2: 4361]

Jordan Award [Vol. 2: 8427]

Jordan Short Film Festival [Vol. 2: 4355]

Jordan Web Awards [Vol. 2: 4362]

Jordon Lifetime Achievement Award [Vol. 1: 8199]

Jorgenson Award; Wally [Vol. 1: 11674]

Joseph Award [Vol. 2: 5619]

Joseph Award; Thomas L. [Vol. 1: 5037]

Joseph Prize [Vol. 2: 2794]

Joseph Prize; Roger E. [Vol. 1: 8879]

Joseph W. Rosenbluth Memorial Award [Vol. 1: 4519]

Josephine-Charlotte; Prix Centre d'etudes Princesse [Vol. 2: 1523]

Josey Scholarships; E.J. [Vol. 1: 5863]

Jost Memorial Lecture; Wilhelm [Vol. 2: 2920]

Jostens-Berenson Lifetime Achievement Award [Vol. 1: 17970]

Joukowsky Distinguished Service Award; Martha and Artemis [Vol. 1: 4763]

Joule Medal and Prize [Vol. 2: 7911]

Joule Medal; James Prescott [Vol. 2: 7995]

Joule Young Researcher Award; James [Vol. 2: 2534]

Jourard Student Award; Sidney M. [Vol. 1: 3525]

Journal Award
    American Association of Healthcare Administrative Management [Vol. 1: 1170]
    National Council on Public History [Vol 1: 12251]
    Society of Motion Picture and Television Engineers [Vol 1: 15701]

The Journal Award in Poetry [Vol. 1: 13487]

Journal Certificate of Merit [Vol. 1: 15701]

Journal Contributor Awards [Vol. 1: 4704]

Journal of Allied Health Award [Vol. 1: 5506]

Journal of Infection Young Investigator's Prize [Vol. 2: 7085]

Journal of Olympic History Award [Vol. 2: 4785]

Journal of Orthodontics Scientific Paper of the Year [Vol. 2: 7165]

Journal of Public Affairs Education Outstanding Article Award [Vol. 1: 11876]

Journal of Research in Science Teaching Award [Vol. 1: 11595]

Journal of Sedimentary Research Best Paper Award [Vol. 1: 15310]

Journal Prize [Vol. 2: 5712]

Journalism Achievement Awards [Vol. 1: 3753]

Journalism Award
    American Association of Petroleum Geologists [Vol. 1: 1277]
    American Farrier's Association [Vol 1: 2101]
    Australian Skeptics - NSW Branch [Vol 2: 529]
    International Association for Energy Economics [Vol 1: 9541]
    International Association of Assessing Officers [Vol 1: 9612]

Journalism Awards
    American Planning Association [Vol. 1: 3289]
    Specialized Information Publishers Association [Vol 1: 16128]

Journalist of the Year
    Mind - National Association for Mental Health [Vol. 2: 8352]
    National Association of Black Journalists [Vol 1: 11658]
    Suburban Newspapers of America [Vol 1: 16312]
    United Kingdom Warehousing Association [Vol 2: 9419]

Journalist Prize [Vol. 2: 3017]

Journalistenpreis of the DGE [Vol. 2: 3017]

Journalistic Leadership Award [Vol. 2: 1176]

Journalists in Distress Fund Awards [Vol. 1: 6671]

Jowett Industry Award; Peter [Vol. 2: 129]

Joy Award; Henry B. [Vol. 1: 13783]

Joy in Singing Award Competition [Vol. 1: 10593]

Joy of Effort Award [Vol. 1: 11605]

JPS Award [Vol. 2: 4289]

JRD Tata Corporate Leadership Award [Vol. 2: 3450]

JSID Outstanding Student Paper of the Year Award [Vol. 1: 15151]

JSPS Prize [Vol. 2: 4275]

JSPS Research Fellowship for Postdoctoral Researchers [Vol. 2: 3229]

Jubilee Award [Vol. 2: 9380]

Jubilee Medal
    British Trust for Ornithology [Vol. 2: 7287]
    Chromatographic Society [Vol 2: 7424]
    Geological Society of South Africa [Vol 2: 5561]

Judaica Reference Award [Vol. 1: 5386]

Judd Award [Vol. 2: 819]

Judd Freedom Award; Walter [Vol. 1: 8487]

Judeen Award; Erik [Vol. 1: 17083]

Judge Heart of New York Awards; Rev. Mychal [Vol. 1: 13227]

Judge Learned Hand Award [Vol. 1: 2722]

Judge of the Year Award [Vol. 1: 12258]

Judged Show Person Award [Vol. 1: 5881]

Judge's Award of Merit [Vol. 1: 12657]

Judge's Choice Award [Vol. 1: 9656]

Judges Choice Award [Vol. 1: 9962]

Judges' Commendation [Vol. 1: 3081]

Judkins Young Clinical Investigator Award; Melvin [Vol. 1: 2304]

Judo Hall of Fame [Vol. 2: 3402]

Julien; Prix Stanislas [Vol. 2: 2162]

Julin Trophy; Bengt [Vol. 1: 17063]

Julius Award; Stevo [Vol. 2: 8211]

Julius Medal; Sir George [Vol. 2: 786]

Julliard Prize; Jean [Vol. 2: 4777]

Jung-heun Young Scholar Award; Park [Vol. 2: 5322]

Junge Memorial Award [Vol. 2: 2699]

Jungfleisch; Prix Emile [Vol. 2: 2211]

Junior Award
    American Society of Mechanical Engineers [Vol. 1: 4394]
    European Rare-Earth Actinide Society [Vol 2: 6284]
    European Society of Ophthalmic Plastic and Reconstructive Surgery [Vol 2: 2859]

Junior Carnival Awards [Vol. 2: 6623]

Junior Champion of Champions Award [Vol. 1: 6227]

Junior Division Award [Vol. 1: 2066]

Junior Eurovision Song Contest [Vol. 2: 6276]

Junior Faculty Award [Vol. 1: 2023]

Junior Faculty Mentoring Award [Vol. 1: 3572]

Junior Faculty Research Grants [Vol. 1: 4747]

Junior Faculty Scholar Award [Vol. 1: 4336]

Junior Fellows [Vol. 1: 746]

Junior Fellowship Awards [Vol. 2: 8765]

Junior Female Athlete of the Year [Vol. 1: 16168]

Junior Grand Champion [Vol. 1: 13354]

Junior Handler of the Year [Vol. 1: 16234]

Junior High Average Horsemanship [Vol. 1: 13355]

Junior Hobbyist of the Year [Vol. 1: 6229]

Junior Hockey Award [Vol. 1: 12392]

Junior Inventor of the Year [Vol. 2: 6125]

Junior Investigator Award for Women [Vol. 1: 2305]

Junior Lawyer of the Year Award [Vol. 2: 8290]

Junior Lawyers Division Pro Bono Awards
    Law Society [Vol. 2: 8291]
    Law Society [Vol 2: 8296]

Junior Medal for Botany [Vol. 2: 5662]

Junior National Championship [Vol. 1: 13356]

Junior Paper Award [Vol. 1: 15718]

Junior Performance Competition [Vol. 1: 11323]

Junior Physician-Investigator Awards [Vol. 1: 2111]

Junior Player of the Year [**Vol. 1: 17426**]

Junior Research Award in Gerontology [**Vol. 2: 5780**]

Junior Research Fellowships [**Vol. 1: 2663**]

Junior Science Award [**Vol. 2: 6635**]

Junior/Young Rider Awards [**Vol. 1: 16874**]

Juniper Prizes [**Vol. 1: 17279**]

Juno Awards [**Vol. 1: 6165**]

Jurdant Prize in Environmental Science; Michel [**Vol. 1: 5187**]

Jurgs Award; Keith [**Vol. 2: 100**]

Juried Crafts Exhibition [**Vol. 1: 7161**]

Juried Design Competition Award [**Vol. 1: 9474**]

Jurist of the Year Award [**Vol. 2: 4390**]

Just Award; Elmore A. [**Vol. 1: 14196**]

Just Lecture Award; E.E. [**Vol. 1: 3782**]

Justice Award

    American Judicature Society [**Vol. 1: 2739**]

    Canadian Institute for the Administration of Justice - University of Montreal [**Vol 1: 6572**]

Justicia Award [**Vol. 1: 6334**]

Juta Prize [**Vol. 2: 4467**]

K-12 Dance Educator of the Year [**Vol. 1: 12277**]

K-12 Distinguished Teaching Achievement Award [**Vol. 1: 12156**]

K-12 Educator of the Year Award [**Vol. 1: 13266**]

Kabi Memorial Prize; Mokhele [**Vol. 2: 4468**]

Kable Electrification Award; George W. [**Vol. 1: 4094**]

Kafka Prize; Janet Heidiner [**Vol. 1: 17337**]

Kagin Family Paper Money Youth Exhibit Award [**Vol. 1: 2993**]

Kagy Education Award of Excellence; Frederick D. [**Vol. 1: 14168**]

Kahan Scholar's Prize; Gerald [**Vol. 1: 4065**]

Kahn Award; Noah A. [**Vol. 1: 5612**]

Kahuna Award [**Vol. 1: 10407**]

Kain Scholarship Fund; Karen [**Vol. 1: 6152**]

Kaischew Award; Professor Rostislaw [**Vol. 2: 1784**]

Kaiser Award; Emil Thomas [**Vol. 1: 14283**]

Kaiser Educational Award; L. U. "Luke" [**Vol. 1: 10921**]

Kaiser Family Foundation Award; Henry J. [**Vol. 2: 7444**]

Kaitz Award; Idell [**Vol. 1: 12029**]

Kal Kan Award [**Vol. 1: 820**]

Kalan Fund Award; Pavle [**Vol. 2: 6017**]

Kaletta Award; Father Paul [**Vol. 1: 9747**]

Kaleva Award [**Vol. 2: 2121**]

Kali Jain Award; Smt. Suraj [**Vol. 2: 3733**]

Kalinga Prize for the Popularization of Science [**Vol. 2: 2654**]

Kalish Innovative Publication Award; Richard [**Vol. 1: 8630**]

Kallebergerstipendiet [**Vol. 2: 6205**]

Kallman Executive Fellow Program; Ernest A. [**Vol. 1: 5804**]

Kallman Scientific Award; Burton [**Vol. 1: 13091**]

Kalmar Prize [**Vol. 2: 3413**]

Kalmus Gold Medal Award; Technicolor/Herbert T. [**Vol. 1: 15705**]

Kalven, Jr., Prize; Harry J. [**Vol. 1: 10759**]

Kamani Gold Medal [**Vol. 2: 3605**]

Kamel Prize; Kamel Sabri [**Vol. 2: 2026**]

Kamel Prize; Sabri [**Vol. 2: 2027**]

Kammer Merit in Authorship Award; Adolph G. [**Vol. 1: 1786**]

Kammerer Award; Gladys M. [**Vol. 1: 3305**]

Kanai Award; Tsutomu [**Vol. 1: 9062**]

Kandhari Award; Lala Ram Chand [**Vol. 2: 3551**]

Kandutsch Preis; Jorg [**Vol. 2: 1297**]

Kane Medal; Elisha Kent [**Vol. 1: 8561**]

Kane Rising Star Award; William [**Vol. 1: 1810**]

Kanellakis Theory and Practice Award; Paris [**Vol. 1: 4958**]

Kanin Playwriting Award Program; Michael [**Vol. 1: 10668**]

Kanjilal Traveling Fellowship; Ferdinande Johanna [**Vol. 2: 8722**]

Kansas Premier Seed Grower [**Vol. 1: 10628**]

Kanterman Memorial Merit Book Awards; Mildred [**Vol. 1: 8812**]

Kantorovich Prize; L.V. [**Vol. 2: 5807**]

Kapitan Award; Josef S. [**Vol. 1: 5038**]

Kapitza Young Researcher Award; Peter [**Vol. 2: 2535**]

Kaplan and Stratton Prize [**Vol. 2: 4413**]

Kaplan Award; David [**Vol. 1: 13763**]

Kaplan Award; Gordin [**Vol. 1: 6474**]

Kaplan Award; Sol [**Vol. 1: 14242**]

Kaplan Safe Driver of the Year Award; Joseph M. [**Vol. 1: 12799**]

Kaplan Sportsmanship Award; Bobby [**Vol. 1: 17129**]

Kaplun Foundation Award; Morris J. and Betty [**Vol. 1: 10560**]

Kapp Foundation Engineering Award; Martin S. [**Vol. 1: 4199**]

Kappa Alpha Theta Program Director of the Year Award [**Vol. 1: 12259**]

Kappa Delta Pi National Student Teacher/Intern of the Year Award [**Vol. 1: 5533**]

Kappe Award; Stanley E. [**Vol. 1: 522**]

Kareev Prize; N.I. [**Vol. 2: 5808**]

Kargin Prize; V.A. [**Vol. 2: 5809**]

Karl-Winnacker-Preis [**Vol. 2: 2916**]

Karlin Campus Organizing Award; Dr. Elizabeth [**Vol. 1: 11082**]

Karlin Grant; Barbara [**Vol. 1: 15588**]

Karling Graduate Student Research Award; J. S. [**Vol. 1: 5938**]

Karlsson Award for Leadership and Achievement through Collaboration; Hans [**Vol. 1: 9063**]

Karlsson Standards Award; Hans [**Vol. 1: 9063**]

Karlstrom Outstanding Educator Award; Karl V. [**Vol. 1: 4959**]

Karman Prize; Theodore von [**Vol. 1: 15119**]

Karmel Award; Marjorie [**Vol. 1: 10739**]

Karolinska Medical Management Centre/EHMA Research Award [**Vol. 2: 1480**]

Karpinskij Prize; Alexander Petrowitsch [**Vol. 2: 3203**]

Kaslow Distinguished Contributions to International Family Psychology Award; Florence W. [**Vol. 1: 3428**]

Kassirer Award; Eve [**Vol. 1: 6308**]

Kast Prize for Free Market Solutions to Poverty; Miguel [**Vol. 1: 5684**]

Kastler; Prix de Biologie Alfred [**Vol. 2: 2443**]

Kastler Prize; Gentner [**Vol. 2: 2775**]

Katiyar Commemoration Lecture; Prof. S. S. [**Vol. 2: 3716**]

Katritzky Junior Award in Heterocyclic Chemistry [**Vol. 2: 5310**]

Katz Award; Donald L. [**Vol. 1: 8526**]

Katz Award for Excellence in the Coverage of Immigration; Eugene [**Vol. 1: 7135**]

Katz Basic Research Prize; Louis N. and Arnold M. [**Vol. 1: 2306**]

Katz Basic Science Research Prize; Louis N. and Arnold M. [**Vol. 1: 2307**]

Katzell Award in I-O Psychology; Raymond A. [**Vol. 1: 15139**]

Kauffman Award [**Vol. 1: 11702**]

Kauffman Foundation Emerging Postdoctoral Entrepreneur Award [**Vol. 1: 12677**]

Kauffman Foundation Outstanding Postdoctoral Entrepreneur Award [**Vol. 1: 12678**]

Kauffman Gold Medal; Virgil [**Vol. 1: 15650**]

Kaufman Unselfish Cooperation in Research Award; Yoram J. [**Vol. 1: 2242**]

Kaufman Women's Scholarships; Lucile B. [**Vol. 1: 14950**]

Kaufmann Award; Richard Harold [**Vol. 1: 9295**]

Kaufmann Memorial Lecture [**Vol. 2: 3000**]

Kaufmann Prize; H. P. [**Vol. 2: 3001**]

Kautz Merit Award; Sena [**Vol. 1: 9199**]

Kavadas Memorial Award; Don and Pat [**Vol. 1: 454**]

Kavanagh Memorial Youth Baseball Research Award; Jack [**Vol. 1: 15028**]

Kavli Prize in Astrophysics [**Vol. 2: 5139**]

Kavli Prize in Nanoscience [**Vol. 2: 5140**]

Kavli Prize in Neuroscience [**Vol. 2: 5141**]

Kavod Award [**Vol. 1: 7060**]

Kay Award; Won Chuel [**Vol. 1: 181**]

Kay Co-op Scholarships; E. Wayne [**Vol. 1: 14951**]

Kay Community College Scholarships; E. Wayne [**Vol. 1: 14952**]

Kay Graduate Scholarship; E. Wayne [**Vol. 1: 14953**]

Kay High School Scholarships; E. Wayne [**Vol. 1: 14954**]

Kay Scholarship; E. Wayne [**Vol. 1: 14955**]

KCACTF Latino Playwriting Award [**Vol. 1: 10664**]

KCACTF Musical Theater Award [**Vol. 1: 10665**]

Kean Medal; Ben [**Vol. 1: 4524**]

Keane; Award for Career Excellence in Honor of Mark E. [**Vol. 1: 9764**]

Keane Award for Excellence; Mark E. [**Vol. 1: 9764**]

Keane Distinguished Service Award; Charles V. [**Vol. 1: 18**]

Kearns Credit Executive of the Year; Alfred W. [**Vol. 1: 166**]

Kearton Medal and Award; Cherry [**Vol. 2: 8794**]

Keast Research Award; Allen [**Vol. 2: 1551**]

Keats/Kerlan Memorial Fellowship; Ezra Jack [**Vol. 1: 17289**]

Keats Memorial Fellowship; Ezra Jack [**Vol. 1: 17289**]

Keats-Shelley Journal Essay Prize [**Vol. 1: 10643**]

Keefer Medal [**Vol. 1: 6903**]

Keeler Award; Leonarde [**Vol. 1: 3315**]

Keeley Book Prize; Edmund [**Vol. 1: 11229**]

Keeling Dissertation Award; William B. [**Vol. 1: 16542**]

Keener Meritorious Service Award; Joyce [**Vol. 1: 11828**]

Keep America Beautiful National Awards [**Vol. 1: 10647**]

Keepers Preservation Education Fund Fellowship [**Vol. 1: 15478**]

Keeping the Blues Alive Awards [**Vol. 1: 5898**]

Keesing Fellowship; Nancy [**Vol. 2: 1062**]

Keetman Assistance Fund; Gunild [**Vol. 1: 3087**]

Keeton Adult and Experiential Learning Award; Morris T. [**Vol. 1: 7629**]

Kegan Award; Philip M. Hamer and Elizabeth Hamer [**Vol. 1: 15420**]

Kegans Award for Victims Services in Probation and Parole; Joe [**Vol. 1: 3336**]

Kegel Bowler of the Month [**Vol. 1: 5954**]

Kehoe Award of Merit; Robert A. [**Vol. 1: 1787**]

Kehoe Memorial Award; Fr. George [**Vol. 1: 6645**]

Kehren Medal; Max [**Vol. 2: 3220**]

Kehrlein Award; Oliver [**Vol. 1: 14871**]

Keith Award [**Vol. 1: 15828**]

Keith Medal [**Vol. 2: 9068**]

Keithley Award for Advances in Measurement Science; Joseph F. [**Vol. 1: 3208**]

Kelleher Award; Judith C. [**Vol. 1: 8092**]

Kellendonk-prijs; Frans [**Vol. 2: 4840**]

Keller Achievement Awards; Helen [**Vol. 1: 2190**]

Keller Award; James [**Vol. 1: 7269**]

Keller Award; Spirit of Helen [**Vol. 1: 10649**]

Keller Behavioral Education Award; Fred S. [**Vol. 1: 3395**]

Keller High Average Award; Jean Fish-Pearl [**Vol. 1: 17961**]

Keller Humanitarian Award; Helen [**Vol. 1: 10650**]

Keller Innovations in Technology Award; J.J. [**Vol. 1: 16103**]

Keller Legacy Award; Helen [**Vol. 1: 10651**]

Keller Visionary Award; Helen [**Vol. 1: 10652**]

Kelley Consumer Leadership Award; Florence [**Vol. 1: 12131**]

Kelley Distinguished Public Service Award; Frank J. [**Vol. 1: 16268**]

Kellgrenpriset [**Vol. 2: 6206**]

Kelly Award for Cultural Leadership; Keith [**Vol. 1: 6426**]

Kelly Award; Jack [**Vol. 1: 17046**]

Kelly Award; Joe W. [**Vol. 1: 1847**]

Kelly Award; Stephen E. [**Vol. 1: 10909**]

Kelly Awards [**Vol. 1: 10909**]

Kelly Awards for Crime Writing; Ned [**Vol. 2: 678**]

Kelly Awards; Rita Mae [**Vol. 1: 14823**]

Kelly Cup; Francis J. "Frank" [**Vol. 1: 17158**]

Kelly Fair Play Award; Jack [**Vol. 1: 17014**]

Kelly Founders Award; John "Snooks" [**Vol. 1: 2396**]

Kelly Memorial Award; Robert [**Vol. 1: 12252**]

Kelly Memorial Prize in Women's History; Joan [**Vol. 1: 2378**]

Kelly Peace Poetry Awards; Barbara Mandigo [**Vol. 1: 13456**]

Kelly Trophy for Outstanding Goalie; Ensign C. Markland [**Vol. 1: 16977**]

Kelman Innovator's Lecture; Charles D. [**Vol. 1: 4137**]

Kelsey Award; Guy [**Vol. 1: 3708**]

Kelvin Award; Lord [**Vol. 2: 6374**]

Kelvin Medal [**Vol. 2: 8893**]

Kemeny Prize; John [**Vol. 2: 3414**]

Kempe Award in Environmental and Resource Economics; Erik [Vol. 2: 4061]

Kempe Lecturer Award; C. Henry [Vol. 1: 10220]

Kemper Award; Edward C. [Vol. 1: 2576]

Kempf Fund Award for Research Development in Psychobiological Psychiatry [Vol. 1: 3354]

Kempton Award; Rob [Vol. 1: 9730]

Kemula Medal; Wiktor [Vol. 2: 5394]

Kenaga SETAC Membership Award; Eugene [Vol. 1: 15629]

Kendall Award; Katherine [Vol. 2: 5288]

Kendall Oration and Medal [Vol. 2: 599]

Kendall Practice Award; Henry O. and Florence P. [Vol. 1: 3236]

Kendig, Jr. Award; Edwin L. [Vol. 1: 689]

Kennan Award for Distinguished Public Service; George F. [Vol. 1: 12107]

Kennard Award; Gavin B. [Vol. 2: 3350]

Kennedy Appreciation Award; Robert C. [Vol. 1: 14825]

Kennedy Astronautics Award; John F. [Vol. 1: 1437]

Kennedy Award; Annie [Vol. 1: 7901]

Kennedy Award; Byron [Vol. 2: 350]

Kennedy Award; Henry L. [Vol. 1: 1848]

Kennedy Award; William M. [Vol. 1: 15715]

Kennedy Book Awards; Robert F. [Vol. 1: 10654]

Kennedy Center Honors [Vol. 1: 10658]

Kennedy Equity Award; Charles [Vol. 1: 5290]

Kennedy Human Rights Award; Robert F. [Vol. 1: 10655]

Kennedy Journalism Awards; Robert F. [Vol. 1: 10656]

Kennedy Medal; Sir John [Vol. 1: 8119]

Kennedy Memorial Prize; Byron [Vol. 2: 350]

Kennedy New Frontier Awards; John F. [Vol. 1: 10671]

Kennedy Profile in Courage Award; John F. [Vol. 1: 10672]

Kennedy Student Essay Prize; Richard S. [Vol. 1: 17907]

Kennedy Student Paper Competition; John F. [Vol. 2: 6043]

Kennel and Marshall Klaus Award; John [Vol. 1: 7902]

Kenny Award; Dr. John J. [Vol. 1: 10808]

Kenny Prizes; Ron [Vol. 2: 458]

Kenshur Book Prize; Oscar [Vol. 1: 3828]

Kent Award; Donald P. [Vol. 1: 8631]

Kent Strix Award; Tony [Vol. 2: 9415]

Kentucky Derby [Vol. 1: 7283]

Kentucky Oaks [Vol. 1: 7284]

Kenya National Chamber of Commerce and Industry Prize [Vol. 2: 4414]

Kenyatta Prize for Literature; Jomo [Vol. 2: 4388]

Kenyon Medal for Classical Studies [Vol. 2: 6926]

Kerlan Award [Vol. 1: 17290]

Kern Award; Donald Q. [Vol. 1: 2628]

Kern Award; Jim [Vol. 1: 2352]

Kernot Scholarship in Chemistry; Professor [Vol. 2: 1126]

Kernot Scholarship in Earth Sciences; Professor [Vol. 2: 1125]

Kerr Basic Science Research Award; Frederick W.L. [Vol. 1: 3116]

Kerr Dissertation Awards; Malcolm H. [Vol. 1: 11143]

Kerr Medal of Distinction for History; John Douglas [Vol. 2: 998]

Kerr Prize; Sophie [Vol. 1: 17651]

Kerr Veterinary Student Award; Don [Vol. 2: 600]

Kertz Medal; Walter [Vol. 2: 2948]

Kerwin, Jr., Readiness Award; Walter T. [Vol. 1: 12479]

Kesler Memorial Achievement Award; John C. [Vol. 1: 10359]

Kestenberg Medal; Leo [Vol. 2: 3026]

Kesteven Medal [Vol. 2: 601]

Ketcham Memorial Award; Albert H. [Vol. 1: 1507]

Kettering Award; Charles F. [Vol. 1: 4492]

Key Awards [Vol. 1: 4131]

Keyes Award; Marjorie Hiscott [Vol. 1: 6690]

Keyes Medal [Vol. 1: 1161]

Keymer Prize; Anne [Vol. 2: 7047]

Keys Roundtable Award; Ted [Vol. 1: 9369]

KFAS Awards in Islamic Medical Sciences [Vol. 2: 4427]

Khan Award for Architecture; Aga [Vol. 2: 6251]

Khan Prize for Fiction; Aga [Vol. 1: 13870]

Kharazmi International Award [Vol. 2: 3828]

Khlopin Prize; V.G. [Vol. 2: 5810]

Khorana Memorial Award; Prof. M.L. [Vol. 2: 3677]

Khorana Prize [Vol. 2: 9022]

Kibble Literary Award; Nita B. [Vol. 2: 1063]

Kidd Award; J. Roby [Vol. 2: 9540]

Kidder Award for Eminence in the Field of American Archaeology; Alfred Vincent [Vol. 1: 826]

Kidder Early Career Award; Louise [Vol. 1: 15363]

Kideney Gold Medal Award; James William [Vol. 1: 2587]

Kids and Kindness Achievement Award [Vol. 1: 9005]

Kids Best Luncheon Meat Award [Vol. 1: 9127]

Kidson Medal; Edward [Vol. 2: 4947]

Kidwai Award; Rafi Ahmed [Vol. 2: 3524]

Kiefer Safety Commendation Award; Adolph [Vol. 1: 17444]

Kiene Fellowship in Electrical Energy; Julia [Vol. 1: 17984]

Kiene Fellowships in Electrical Energy; Julia [Vol. 1: 17980]

Kies Memorial Award; Marian [Vol. 1: 3997]

Kilbourne Award; Judith [Vol. 1: 6869]

Kilby International Awards [Vol. 1: 10684]

Kilgour Award for Research in Library and Information Technology; Frederick G. [Vol. 1: 10825]

Killam Memorial Prizes; Izaak Walton [Vol. 2: 6134]

Killam Memorial Scholarship; Elson T.
    New England Water Works Association [Vol. 1: 13168]
    New England Water Works Association [Vol 1: 13169]

Kilmer Prize [Vol. 1: 3144]

Kilpatrick Trophy; Macgregor [Vol. 1: 2415]

Kilrea Trophy; Wally [Vol. 1: 2422]

Kimball Award for Public and Applied Anthropology; Solon T. [Vol. 1: 827]

Kimball Innovators Award; Justin Ford [Vol. 1: 2452]

Kimball Medal; George E. [Vol. 1: 9261]

Kimball Medallion; Miles [Vol. 1: 10922]

Kimberly Cup [Vol. 1: 16198]

Kincheloe Award; Iven C. [Vol. 1: 15642]

KIND Children's Book Award [Vol. 1: 9007]

Kinder Prize; Jessie [Vol. 2: 5085]

King Award; Martin Luther [Vol. 1: 10070]

King Award; Ted [Vol. 2: 7153]

King Book Award; Coretta Scott [Vol. 1: 2770]

King Charles II Medal [Vol. 8: 8939]

King Contribution Award; Billie Jean [Vol. 1: 17990]

King, Jr. Award; Martin Luther [Vol. 1: 8341]

King Jr. Memorial Award; Martin Luther [Vol. 1: 12297]

King, Jr. Scholarship Award; Martin Luther [Vol. 1: 1883]

King Management Award; Kenneth K. [Vol. 1: 8729]

King Medal; Haddon Forrester [Vol. 2: 181]

King Medal; John Henry Garrood [Vol. 2: 7996]

King Memorial Award; Donald [Vol. 1: 16169]

King Memorial Award; Robert W. [Vol. 1: 5363]

King Memorial Certificate; Milton W. [Vol. 1: 12951]

King Prize; Alan [Vol. 2: 7360]

King Solomon Award [Vol. 1: 486]

Kingdon-Tomlinson Grants [Vol. 2: 5044]

Kingery Award; W. David [Vol. 1: 1566]

King's Prize [Vol. 2: 8408]

Kingslake Medal and Prize; Rudolf [Vol. 1: 16153]

Kingston Award; Albert J. [Vol. 1: 10863]

Kinias Service Award; George A. [Vol. 1: 12325]

Kinkeldey Award; Otto [Vol. 1: 2965]

Kinley Memorial Fellowship; Kate Neal [Vol. 1: 17251]

Kinnear/Journal of Public Policy and Marketing Award; Thomas C. [Vol. 1: 2816]

Kintner Award for Distinguished Service; Earl [Vol. 1: 8255]

Kiphuth Award; Robert J.H. [Vol. 1: 17445]

Kiplinger Distinguished Contributions to Journalism Award [Vol. 1: 12694]

Kipping Award in Silicon Chemistry; Frederic Stanley [Vol. 1: 1652]

Kirby Memorial Medal for Outstanding Service to Canadian Physics; Peter [Vol. 1: 6300]

Kirk Award for Outstanding Graduate Student Research; Barbara A. [Vol. 1: 3591]

Kirke Award; Sara [Vol. 1: 6187]

Kirschner Instructor Achievement Award; Fred [Vol. 1: 41]

Kisan Puruskar; Jagjivan Ram [Vol. 2: 3525]

Kishida International Award; Asabe [Vol. 1: 4085]

Kite Flying Competition [Vol. 2: 6645]

Kitz Award; James M. [Vol. 1: 6592]

Kiwanis Foundation Scholarship [Vol. 1: 17663]

Kiwanis of Wascana Senior Cello/Viola/Double Bass Scholarship [Vol. 1: 14745]

Kjellberg Award; Francesco [Vol. 1: 10053]

Klaus Award; John Kennel and Marshall [Vol. 1: 7902]

Klaus Award; Phyllis [Vol. 1: 7903]

Klausmeyer Distinguished Service Award; Otto [Vol. 1: 14018]

Kleberg Award for Excellence in Applied Wildlife Research; Caesar [Vol. 1: 17853]

Kleemeier Award; Robert W. [Vol. 1: 8632]

Klein Award; Felix [Vol. 2: 5431]

Klein Award; Lawrence R. [Vol. 1: 16834]

Klein Award; Leonard [Vol. 2: 2973]

Klein Prize for Poetry; A. M. [Vol. 1: 14374]

Klein Prize in Experimental Physics [Vol. 2: 1130]

Kleiner Memorial Award; Joseph J. [Vol. 1: 3791]

Kleinhans Fellowships [Vol. 1: 14430]

Kleinpeter Award; Hugh [Vol. 1: 16224]

Kleitman Distinguished Service Award; Nathaniel [Vol. 1: 763]

Klemin Award; Dr. Alexander [Vol. 1: 2326]

Klemm Postgraduate Research Award; Megan [Vol. 2: 1131]

Klemm Preis; Wilhelm [Vol. 2: 2930]

Klibansky Prize; Raymond [Vol. 1: 6468]

Klim Prize; Nils [Vol. 2: 5127]

Klineberg Award; Otto [Vol. 1: 15364]

Klingensmith EMS Administrator of the Year Award; William [Vol. 1: 11763]

Klinger Research Award; William A. [Vol. 1: 211]

Klinker Award; Mary T. [Vol. 1: 182]

Klopsteg Memorial Lecture [Vol. 1: 1309]

Klumpke - Isaac Roberts; Prix Dorothea [Vol. 2: 2612]

Klumpke-Roberts Award [Vol. 1: 5657]

Klyuchevskii Prize; V.O. [Vol. 2: 5811]

KM Fabrics Inc. Technical Production Award [Vol. 1: 16963]

Knacke Aerodynamic Decelerator Systems Award; Theodor W. [Vol. 1: 2528]

Knauss Marine Policy Fellowships [Vol. 1: 11122]

Knebel Best of Show Memorial Award; Clarence [Vol. 1: 1206]

Knee/Whitman Lifetime Achievement Award [Vol. 1: 11894]

Kneupper Award; Charles [Vol. 1: 14544]

Knight Award; Casper J. [Vol. 1: 8936]

Knight Award for Public Service [Vol. 1: 13560]

Knight Graduate Scholarship; David [Vol. 1: 16018]

Knight Medal; Allen [Vol. 2: 787]

Knight Memorial Grand Master Award; Damon
    Science Fiction and Fantasy Writers of America [Vol. 1: 14785]
    Science Fiction and Fantasy Writers of America [Vol 1: 14786]

Knight of the Book Award [Vol. 2: 1787]

Knight Research Grants; Elva [Vol. 1: 10101]

Knighton Service Award; Harry and Elsie [Vol. 1: 13321]

Knisely Award; Melvin H. [Vol. 2: 3096]

Knouff Line Officer of the Year Award; Scotia [Vol. 1: 3337]

Knowles Award for Outstanding Adult Education Program Leadership; Malcolm [Vol. 1: 857]

Knowles Award; Jeremy [Vol. 2: 9023]

Knowlton Medal [Vol. 1: 11044]

Knowlton Operator's Scholarship [Vol. 1: 13169]

Knox Honours Prize; Bruce [Vol. 2: 1132]

Knudsen Award; William S. [Vol. 1: 1788]

Knudsvig Memorial Scholarships; Glenn [Vol. 1: 1685]

Knuth Prize; Donald E. [Vol. 1: 4968]

Knutson Award; Jeanne N. [Vol. 1: 10343]

Kobayashi Computers and Communications Award; Koji [Vol. 1: 9296]

Koch Award for Early Career Contributions to Psychology; Sigmund [Vol. 1: 3562]

Koch Award for Outstanding Contribution to Water Management and Science; Imhoff - [Vol. 2: 8253]

Koch Award; Fred Conrad [Vol. 1: 8111]

Koch Memorial Medal Award; Carel C. [Vol. 1: 623]

Koch Scholarship in Entrepreneurship; Fred C. [Vol. 1: 17831]

Kodak Coach of the Year [Vol. 1: 11637]

Kodak Film Raw Stock Award [Vol. 1: 18093]

Kodak Media Photography Award [Vol. 2: 4984]

Kodama Award; Benjamin [Vol. 1: 3082]

Koenig/Organon/Nourypharma Poster Prize; Max Pierre [Vol. 2: 2864]

Koenigswarter; Prix [Vol. 2: 2277]

Koeppen Memorial Scholarship [Vol. 2: 5653]

Koerner Outstanding Electrical and Computer Engineering Student Award; Alton B. Zerby and Carl T. [Vol. 1: 8194]

Koga Gold Medal; Issac [Vol. 2: 1566]

Kohl Memorial Exhibit Award; Gaston DiBello/Melvin and Leona [Vol. 1: 2988]

Kohn Award [Vol. 2: 8940]

Kohrtz' stipendium; Ilona [Vol. 2: 6207]

Koivu Prize; Rudolf [Vol. 2: 2114]

Kokusai Seibutsugaku-sho [Vol. 2: 4274]

Kolb Prize; Eugene [Vol. 2: 3993]

Kolk Air Transportation Progress Award; Franklin W. [Vol. 1: 15518]

Kolmogorov Prize; A.N. [Vol. 2: 5812]

Kol'tsov Prize; N.K. [Vol. 2: 5813]

Komarov Diploma; V. M. [Vol. 2: 6316]

Komarov Prize; V.L. [Vol. 2: 5814]

Kondelos Prize; Nina [Vol. 2: 478]

Kondor Civil Courage Award; Dusko [Vol. 2: 1726]

Kondrat'ev Prize; N.D. [Vol. 2: 5815]

Konheim Award; Beatrice G. [Vol. 1: 1388]

Koni Prize; A.F. [Vol. 2: 5816]

Konig Gedenkmunze; Joseph [Vol. 2: 2931]

Konkurs Mlodych Kompozytorow im. Tadeusza Bairda [Vol. 2: 5401]

Konrad-Zuse-Medaille [Vol. 2: 2956]

Koob Merit Award; C. Albert [Vol. 1: 12046]

Kook Endowment Fund; Edward F. [Vol. 1: 16964]

Koplin Travel Award; James R. [Vol. 1: 14437]

Koprulu Book Prize; M. Fuat [Vol. 1: 16583]

Korea Foundation Fellowship for Field Research [Vol. 1: 17244]

Korean Composition Awards [Vol. 2: 5472]

Korean Service Medal [Vol. 1: 16677]

Korevaar Outstanding Paper Award; Jan [Vol. 2: 822]

Korn Award; Martin P. [Vol. 1: 14131]

Korn Founder's Award for Development of the Professional Choral Art; Michael [Vol. 1: 7263]

Korn Founders Award for Philanthropic Contribution to the Arts; Michael [Vol. 1: 7264]

Korolev Diploma [Vol. 2: 6317]

Korzhinskii Prize; D.S. [Vol. 2: 5817]

Kosar Award; William F. [Vol. 1: 8965]

Kosoff Founders Award; Abe [Vol. 1: 14243]

Kosoff Memorial Literary Award; Abe [Vol. 1: 2994]

Kossler, USCG Award; Captain William J. [Vol. 1: 2327]

Kostanecki Medal; Stanislaw [Vol. 2: 5395]

Kothari Memorial Lecture Award; Daulat Singh [Vol. 2: 3639]

Kotyk Award; Eugene [Vol. 1: 16597]

Kovacs Prize; Katherine Singer [Vol. 1: 11232]

Kovalenko Medal; Jessie Stevenson [Vol. 1: 11438]

Kovalevskaya Prize; S.V. [Vol. 2: 5818]

Kovalevskii Prize; A.O. [Vol. 2: 5819]

Kovalevskii Prize; M.M. [Vol. 2: 5820]

Krafft Medal [Vol. 2: 6049]

Kraft Community Service Award; Eve [Vol. 1: 17130]

Kraft Innovator Award; Jack A. [Vol. 1: 8992]

Kraft Teacher Training Scholarships; Maureen V. O'Donnell/Eunice E. [Vol. 1: 1687]

Krahman Medal [Vol. 2: 5690]

Kralik Distinguished Service Award; Gary M. [Vol. 1: 5613]

Kramer Award of Excellence; William S. [Vol. 1: 13520]

Kramer - John Preston Personal Service Award; Harold [Vol. 1: 3653]

Krasner Memorial Award; Jack D. [Vol. 1: 3449]

Kraus Fellowship in Early Books and Manuscripts; H.P. [Vol. 1: 18157]

Kraus Medal; Karl [Vol. 2: 5301]

Kraus Research Grant; Michael [Vol. 1: 2379]

Krebs Lecture and Medal; Sir Hans [Vol. 2: 3951]

Krebs Prize; Hans Adolf [Vol. 2: 3018]

Kreisler Competition Prizes; International Fritz [Vol. 2: 1287]

Krenek Solo Competition; Ernst [Vol. 1: 17642]

Kressel Award; Aron [Vol. 1: 9108]

Kretchmer Memorial Award in Nutrition and Development; Norman [Vol. 1: 4014]

Krieg Cortical Discoverer Prize [Vol. 1: 6087]

Krieg Cortical Kudos [Vol. 1: 6088]

Kriegel Prize; Dr. Frantisek [Vol. 2: 1906]

Krieghbaum Under 40 Award [Vol. 1: 4998]

Krill Prizes for Excellence in Scientific Research [Vol. 2: 4000]

Krishnamurthy Award; A. [Vol. 2: 3783]

Krishnamurti Lecture Award; C.R. [Vol. 2: 3784]

Krishnan Memorial Lecture; Kariamanikkam Srinivasa [Vol. 2: 3640]

Kriske Memorial Award; George W. [Vol. 1: 297]

Kristol Award and Lecture; Irving [Vol. 1: 2083]

Krochock Award; Richard H. [Vol. 1: 7837]

Krogh Prize; August [Vol. 2: 1983]

Krogh Prize; Marie and August [Vol. 2: 1983]

Krooss Prize for Best Dissertation in Business History; Herman E. [Vol. 1: 6064]

Krout Memorial Poetry Award; Helen and Laura [Vol. 1: 13491]

Krout Ohioana Poetry Award; Helen and Laura [Vol. 1: 13491]

Krueger Paper Money - YN Exhibit Award; Kurt [Vol. 1: 2993]

Kruger Prize; Johan [Vol. 2: 5728]

Krumbein Medal; William Christian [Vol. 1: 9576]

Krupsaw Award for Non-Traditional Teaching [Vol. 1: 17647]

Krusen Lifetime Achievement Award; Frank H. [Vol. 1: 732]

Kruth Award [Vol. 2: 6239]

Kruyskamp-prijs [Vol. 2: 4841]

Krylov Prize; A.N. [Vol. 2: 5821]

Krzhizhanovskii Prize; G.M. [Vol. 2: 5822]

Kshanika Oration Award [Vol. 2: 3552]

Ktytor Award of Merit; Moe [Vol. 1: 6239]

Ku Meritorious Award; P. M. [Vol. 1: 15863]

Kubal Prize; Viktor [Vol. 2: 5995]

Kubasik Lectureship Award; Norman P. [Vol. 1: 909]

Kubler-Ross Award for Outstanding Contribution; Elisabeth [Vol. 1: 7240]

Kucharski Young Investigator Award; David [Vol. 1: 10153]

Kuczynski Prize [Vol. 2: 5916]

Kuczynski Prize; Rene [Vol. 1: 1261]

Kuder Early Career Scientist/Practitioner Award; Fritz and Linn [Vol. 1: 3592]

Kuehl Prize for Documentary Editing; Arthur S. Link/Warren F. [Vol. 1: 15084]

Kuh Outstanding Contribution to Literature and/or Research Award; George D. [Vol. 1: 11386]

Kuhn Prize; Julius [Vol. 2: 2987]

Kuhring Award; Mike [Vol. 2: 4733]

Kuiper Prize; Gerard P. [Vol. 1: 1447]

Kukuljeviceva povelja [Vol. 2: 1864]

Kukuljevic's Charter [Vol. 2: 1864]

Kulp Memorial Award; Clarence Arthur [Vol. 1: 3701]

Kulp-Wright Book Award [Vol. 1: 3701]

Kultureller Ehrenpreis [Vol. 2: 3136]

Kulturpreis der Stadt Villach [Vol. 2: 1328]

Kumar Memorial Award; Prof. L. S. S. [Vol. 2: 3641]

Kundan Singh Open Chess Championship [Vol. 2: 2062]

Kungliga priset [Vol. 2: 6208]

Kunst Prize; Jaap [Vol. 1: 15070]

Kunstpreis der Stadt Darmstadt [Vol. 2: 3238]

Kupfer Award [Vol. 1: 5084]

Kupfmuller-Preis; Karl- [Vol. 2: 3038]

Kupfmuller Prize; Karl [Vol. 2: 3038]

Kurien Award; Dr. [Vol. 2: 3575]

Kurup Endowment Award; Prof. P.A. [Vol. 2: 3785]

Kusnetz Award [Vol. 1: 2489]

Kutter-Preis; Fritz [Vol. 2: 3641]

Kuwait Web Awards [Vol. 2: 5177]

Kuznetsov Prize for Theoretical Electrochemistry; Alexander [Vol. 2: 6443]

Kwapil Memorial Award; Joseph F. [Vol. 1: 16109]

Kwit Memorial Distinguished Service Award; Nathaniel T. [Vol. 1: 1725]

Kwolek Award; Stephanie L. [Vol. 2: 9024]

La Parada Award [Vol. 1: 16070]

La Semaine Nationale de la Culture [Vol. 2: 1807]

Lab of the Year Awards [Vol. 1: 14382]

Lab Travel Grants [Vol. 2: 4867]

Labatt Classic Film Award; John [Vol. 1: 16520]

Labatt's Award for the Most Popular Film [Vol. 1: 16520]

Labbe; Prix du Docteur et de Madame Henri [Vol. 2: 2212]

Laber International Freedom to Publish Award; Jeri [Vol. 1: 5217]

Labib Prize; M. Abdel Moneim [Vol. 2: 2028]

Labor Award [Vol. 1: 10723]

Labor-Management Center Award [Vol. 1: 17266]

Labor Media Awards [Vol. 1: 196]

Labor Media Contest Awards [Vol. 1: 197]

Labor Press Journalistic Awards Contest [Vol. 1: 196]

Laboratory Analyst Award [Vol. 1: 17711]

Laboratory Visit Grant [Vol. 2: 7133]

Labotec-Shandon Award for Achievement in the Field of Cytology [Vol. 2: 5620]

Lace Award; International [Vol. 2: 931]

Lachs Trophy; Manfred [Vol. 2: 2541]

Lackman Jr. Award; William F. [Vol. 1: 12607]

LaCugna Award for New Scholars; Catherine Mowry [Vol. 1: 7112]

Lacy Award; Ed [Vol. 2: 7736]

Lacy Memorial Award for Travel Broadcasting; Anne Gregg/Ed [Vol. 2: 7074]

Lada-Mocarski Award; Laura K. and Valerian [Vol. 1: 18158]

Ladd Medal; William E. [Vol. 1: 690]

Ladies' British Open Amateur Championship [Vol. 2: 8278]

Ladman Exemplary Service Award; AAA/Wiley A.J. [Vol. 1: 1028]

Lady Members Group Prize [Vol. 2: 7846]

Laerdal Award; Asmund S. [Vol. 2: 6954]

Laerdal Award for Excellence; Asmund S. [Vol. 1: 11764]

Laetare Medal [Vol. 1: 17317]

LaFage Graduate Student Research Award; Jeffery P. [Vol. 1: 8138]

Laferle Memorial Award; Charles [Vol. 1: 6627]

LaGasse Medal; Alfred B. [Vol. 1: 4364]

Lagerstrom Memorial Award; Elaine Louise [Vol. 1: 17640]

Lagrange; Prix Charles [Vol. 2: 1634]

Lahm Memorial Award for Flight Safety; Brig. Gen. Frank P. [Vol. 1: 13649]

Laidler Award; Keith [Vol. 1: 6890]

Laing Prize; Gordon J. [Vol. 1: 17216]

Lake Medal for Folklore Research; Coote [Vol. 2: 7698]

Lake Poster Award; John [Vol. 2: 537]

The Lakes of Finland Award [Vol. 2: 2075]

Lal Outstanding All-India Coordinated Research Project Award; Choudhary Devi [Vol. 2: 3526]

Lallemand; Prix Andre [Vol. 2: 2213]

Lally Distinguished Alumni Merit Award; Jack and Julie [Vol. 1: 14677]

Lamarca Prize; Rose [Vol. 2: 2425]

Lamarck; Prix [Vol. 2: 1635]

Lamaze Childbirth Educator Program Scholarship [Vol. 1: 10740]

Lamb Awards for Excellence in Country Music Journalism; Charlie [Vol. 1: 9854]

Lamb Outstanding Educator Award; Helen [Vol. 1: 1241]

Lamb; Prix [Vol. 2: 2214]

Lamb Prize; W. Kaye [Vol. 1: 5236]

Lambert Memorial Award [Vol. 2: 3886]

Lambert; Prix Charles [Vol. 2: 2278]

Lamberton Award for Teaching of Science in High School [Vol. 1: 17647]

Lameere; Prix Eugene [Vol. 2: 1611]

LaMer Award; Victor K. [Vol. 1: 1653]

Lamme Award; Benjamin Garver [Vol. 1: 3860]

Lamp of Service [Vol. 1: 6840]

Lampe-Kunkle Memorial Award [Vol. 1: 509]

Lampen Medal [Vol. 2: 2096]

Lampert Emerging Journalist Award; Herb [Vol. 1: 6863]

Lampert Memorial Award; Gerald [Vol. 1: 10783]

Lampitt Medal [Vol. 2: 9282]

Lancaster Award [Vol. 1: 1080]

Lanchester Prize; Frederick W. [Vol. 1: 9262]

Land Award; Gene L. [Vol. 1: 10125]

Land Medal; Edwin H. [Vol. 1: 13611]

Land Medal; Vice Admiral "Jerry" [Vol. 1: 15716]

Land of Enchantment Book Awards [Vol. 1: 13198]

Land O'Lakes, Inc. Award [Vol. 1: 1979]

Land O'Lakes/Purina Teaching Award in Dairy Production [Vol. 1: 1980]

Landis Medal; James N. [Vol. 1: 4402]

Landmark Award [Vol. 1: 4365]

Landon Translation Award; Harold Morton [Vol. 1: 54]

Landsberg Award; Helmut E. [Vol. 1: 2912]

Landscape Architecture Firm Award [Vol. 1: 4366]

Landscape Design Award [Vol. 1: 2430]

Landscape Photographer of the Year [Vol. 2: 415]

Landsforeningen mod Huntingtons Choreas Forskningsfond [Vol. 2: 1955]

Landsteiner Memorial Award and Lectureship; Karl [Vol. 1: 1066]

Lane Award; John [Vol. 2: 749]

Lane Award; Margaret T. [Vol. 1: 10891]

Lane Memorial Award; Diane [Vol. 1: 11518]

Lane Memorial Award; Sister M. Claude [Vol. 1: 15423]

Lang Prize Paper Award; Warren R.
    American Society of Cytopathology [Vol. 1: 4280]
    American Society of Cytopathology [Vol 1: 4280]

Lang Resident Physician Award; Warren R. [Vol. 1: 4280]

Lang-Rosen Award [Vol. 1: 15039]

Lang Trophy; Lewis [Vol. 2: 5485]

Lange/CQ Press Award; Marta [Vol. 1: 5265]

Lange International Award; John D. [Vol. 1: 11797]

Lange - Paul Taylor Prize; Dorothea [Vol. 1: 7938]

Langelier Award for Young Professionals; Claude [Vol. 1: 6776]

Langenhoven Prize; C. J. [Vol. 2: 5633]

Langer Award for Outstanding Scholarship in the Ecology of Symbolic Form; Susanne K. [Vol. 1: 11036]

Langer Award; Marion F. [Vol. 1: 3103]

Langer Nuclear Codes and Standards Award; Bernard F. [Vol. 1: 4403]

Langholz International Nutrition Award; Edna and Robert [Vol. 1: 2038]

Langlands Medal; Ian [Vol. 2: 788]

Langley Award [Vol. 2: 6855]

Langman Graduate Student Platform Presentation Award [Vol. 1: 1029]

Langmuir Award; Gaede- [Vol. 1: 5730]

Langmuir Award in Chemical Physics; Irving [Vol. 1: 1654]

Langmuir Prize in Chemical Physics; Irving [Vol. 1: 3209]

Lankester Investigatorship; Ray [Vol. 2: 8346]

Lansdown Prize for Interactive Digital Art; John [Vol. 2: 6264]

Lapham Award; Robert J. [Vol. 1: 14089]

Lapham Outstanding Service Award; Robert J. [Vol. 1: 7914]

Lapworth Medal [Vol. 2: 8446]

LaQue Memorial Award; Francis L. [Vol. 1: 5614]

Larew Memorial Scholarships; Christian [Vol. 1: 10826]

Larsen-Miller Community Service Award [Vol. 1: 11491]

Larsen Prize; Knud Lind [Vol. 2: 1939]

Larsen Prize; Libby [Vol. 1: 9499]

Larson Graduate Student Paper Award; Olaf [Vol. 1: 14662]

Larson Humanitarian Award; Barbara A. [Vol. 1: 15746]

Larson Memorial Award; Gustus L. [Vol. 1: 4404]

Las Cumbres Amateur Outreach Award [Vol. 1: 5658]

LASA Award [Vol. 2: 8276]

LaSalle Discovery Award [Vol. 1: 6081]

Lascoff Memorial Award; J. Leon [Vol. 1: 1703]

Lasher-Bottorff Award [Vol. 1: 1043]

Lashley Award; Karl Spencer [Vol. 1: 3187]

Lasker Award; Albert D. [Vol. 1: 2314]

Laskin Award for an Outstanding Predoctoral Educator in OMS; Daniel M. [Vol. 1: 1257]

Laskine Harp Competition; Lily [Vol. 2: 2508]

LASL Educator's Award [Vol. 1: 10890]

Lassen Award; Niels [Vol. 2: 6430]

Lasswell Award; Harold D. [Vol. 1: 10344]

Laszlo Award of Technical Excellence; Charles [Vol. 1: 6540]

Latham Sportsman Wild Turkey Service Award; Roger M. [Vol. 1: 13041]

Latsis-Preis [Vol. 2: 6500]

Laubach Award for Student Excellence; Ruth J. Colvin and Frank C. [Vol. 1: 14263]

Lauer Safety Award; A. R. [Vol. 1: 8993]

Laufer Award for Outstanding Scientific Achievement; Robert S. [Vol. 1: 10263]

Laufer; Prix Docteur Rene-Joseph [Vol. 2: 2279]

Laufman-Greatbatch Prize; AAMI Foundation [Vol. 1: 5132]

Laughlin Marketing Award; Sara [Vol. 1: 9200]

Laughlin Prize [Vol. 2: 8723]

Laureate Award [Vol. 2: 7615]

Laureate Recognition Award [Vol. 1: 609]

Laureateship of the Australian Society of Archivists [Vol. 2: 563]

Laurel Award for Screen [Vol. 1: 18121]

Laurel Crowned Circle Award [Vol. 1: 13514]

Laurel Leaf Award [Vol. 1: 1834]

Laurent; Prix Emile [Vol. 2: 1636]

Laurie Prize; James [Vol. 1: 4200]

Laursen Award; Capt. V. L. [Vol. 1: 17182]

Lautsch Award of Excellence; Joseph M. [Vol. 1: 7161]

Lautsch Family Award of Excellence [Vol. 1: 7162]

Lavachery; Prix Henri [Vol. 2: 1612]

Lavallee; Prix Calixa- [Vol. 1: 14998]

Lavalleye-Coppens; Prix Jacques [Vol. 2: 1593]

Lavarack Prize for Developmental Biology [Vol. 2: 1133]

Laventhol Prize for Deadline News Reporting; Jesse [Vol. 1: 4468]

Laver Award; Keith [Vol. 1: 6766]

Lavrent'ev Prize; M.A. [Vol. 2: 5823]

Law Award; Frank G. [Vol. 1: 4445]

Law Enforcement Award [Vol. 1: 11988]

Law Enforcement Commendation Medal [Vol. 1: 12905]

Law Enforcement Explorer Post Advisor of the Year [Vol. 1: 12836]

Law Firm Award of Excellence [Vol. 1: 10791]

Law Firm Award of Merit [Vol. 1: 10792]

Law Library Journal Article of the Year Award [Vol. 1: 1194]

Law Library Publications Award [Vol. 1: 1195]

Law-Related Education Teacher of the Year Award [Vol. 1: 2757]

Law-Review Award [Vol. 1: 14803]

LAWCHA Minority Graduate Student Conference Travel Award [Vol. 1: 10717]

Lawler Prize; Sylvia [Vol. 2: 9098]

Lawn Tennis Association National Awards [Vol. 2: 8298]

Lawrence Award for Children's Literature; Melinda [Vol. 1: 7241]

Lawrence Award; Sir Robert [Vol. 2: 7384]

Lawrence Distinguished Service Award; Robert L. [Vol. 1: 15950]

Lawrence Foundation Award [Vol. 1: 14122]

Lawrence Medal [Vol. 2: 8822]

Lawrence Memorial Award [Vol. 1: 7071]

Lawrence Memorial Grant [Vol. 2: 5772]

Lawrence Prize; Robert G. [Vol. 1: 6220]

Lawrence Trophy; Alan [Vol. 2: 6712]

Laws Award; Glenda [Vol. 1: 5205]

Laws of Life Essay Contest [Vol. 1: 16420]

Lawson Medals [Vol. 1: 6315]

Lawson Memorial Award; Bev [Vol. 2: 282]

Lawson Prize; John [Vol. 2: 8695]

Lawton Award; M. Powell [Vol. 1: 8633]

Lawton Distinguished Contribution Award for Applied Gerontology; M. Powell [Vol. 1: 3372]

Laxdal Memorial Grade B Female Voice Scholarship; Heather [Vol. 1: 14746]

Laxdal Memorial Vocal Award/Golan E. Hoole Memorial Shield; Heather [Vol. 1: 14747]

Lay Memorial Award; Herman W. [Vol. 1: 5477]

Layborn Prize [Vol. 2: 7410]

Lazarsfeld Evaluation Theory Award; Paul F. [Vol. 1: 2091]

Lazarus Memorial Award [Vol. 1: 2336]

Le Bel; Prix [Vol. 2: 2438]

Le Caine Awards; Hugh [Vol. 1: 14982]

Le Fevre Memorial Prize; R.J.W. [Vol. 2: 182]

Le Mans 24-hour Grand Prix d'Endurance [Vol. 2: 2326]

Le Prix d'Excellence Aliant en Journalisme Etudiant [Vol. 1: 5678]

Le Senne; Prix Emile [Vol. 2: 2163]

Le Sueur Young Persons Award; Herbert [Vol. 2: 8612]

Leab and Daniel J. Leab American Book Prices Current Exhibition Catalogue Awards; Katharine Kyes [Vol. 1: 5266]

Leach Medal; Digby [Vol. 2: 789]

Leacock Memorial Medal for Humour; Stephen [Vol. 1: 10764]

Leader Award [Vol. 1: 7402]

Leader of the Year Award [Vol. 1: 13515]

Leaderle Award in Human Nutrition [Vol. 1: 4011]

Leaders Award [Vol. 1: 1155]

Leaders Recognition Society Award [Vol. 1: 17944]

Leadership Achievement Award and Professional Achievement Award [Vol. 1: 5514]

Leadership and Professional Achievement Award [Vol. 1: 5514]

Leadership and Service Awards [Vol. 1: 5273]

Leadership Award
    American Psychological Association - Committee on Women in Psychology [Vol. 1: 3386]
    American Psychological Association - Division of Psychoanalysis (Division 39) [Vol 1: 3445]
    American Society on Aging [Vol. 1: 4532]
    Business Committee for the Arts [Vol 1: 6058]
    CAD Society [Vol 1: 6078]
    Cleft Palate Foundation [Vol 1: 7321]
    Emergency Medicine Residents' Association [Vol 1: 8084]
    International Association of Cancer Victors and Friends [Vol 1: 9636]
    Minerals, Metals, and Materials Society [Vol 1: 11189]
    National Apostolate for Inclusion Ministry [Vol 1: 11524]
    National Association for Equal Opportunity in Higher Education [Vol 1: 11574]
    National Association of Neonatal Nurses [Vol 1: 11820]
    Natural Resources Council of America [Vol 1: 13097]
    North Country Trail Association [Vol 1: 13384]
    Optical Society of America [Vol 1: 13612]
    Society for Academic Emergency Medicine [Vol 1: 15007]
    Society for Vascular Ultrasound [Vol 1: 15406]
    Standards Council of Canada [Vol 1: 16242]
    TRI-M Music Honor Society [Vol 1: 16556]
    University of Toronto - Pulp and Paper Centre [Vol 1: 17355]
    Women in Aerospace [Vol 1: 17921]

Leadership Awards
    Brain Injury Association of New Jersey [Vol. 1: 5996]
    Fusion Power Associates [Vol 1: 8499]

Leadership Circle Award [Vol. 1: 8059]

Leadership Citation [Vol. 1: 7675]

Leadership Hall of Fame Award [Vol. 1: 4556]

Leadership in Conservation Research Award [Vol. 1: 16340]

Leadership in Education Award [Vol. 1: 4269]

Leadership in Government Awards [Vol. 2: 758]

Leadership in Library Acquisitions Award [Vol. 1: 5049]

Leadership in Oncology Social Work Award [Vol. 1: 5446]

Leadership in Promoting Intergroup Relations Awards [Vol. 1: 13921]

Leadership in Public Service Award [Vol. 1: 12781]

Leadership in Rehabilitation Award [Vol. 2: 9475]

Leadership in Science Education Prize for High School Teachers [Vol. 1: 989]

Leadership in the Americas Award [Vol. 1: 9411]

Library Technician of the Year [Vol. 2: 440]
Libris Awards [Vol. 1: 6347]
Licensing/Registration Administrator of the Year [Vol. 1: 14826]
Lichten Award; Robert L. [Vol. 1: 2328]
Lichtenfelt Award; Richard [Vol. 1: 11692]
Lichvarik Award; George G. [Vol. 1: 13712]
Lickorish Memorial Prize; Len [Vol. 2: 8559]
Lidstone Female Athlete of the Year Award; Dorothy [Vol. 1: 8287]
Lieber Awards; Eleanor [Vol. 1: 14094]
Lieber Awards for Young Singers; Eleanor [Vol. 1: 14094]
Lieberman Student Poetry Award; Elias [Vol. 1: 14063]
Liebeskind Early Career Scholar Award; John C. [Vol. 1: 3117]
Liebig-Denkmunze [Vol. 2: 2932]
Liebman New Writer Excellence Award; Marcia C. [Vol. 1: 13553]
Liechtenstein Football Cup [Vol. 2: 4474]
Lienhard Award; Gustav O. [Vol. 1: 9387]
Lieutenant Governor's Award for Literary Excellence [Vol. 1: 17745]
Lieutenant Governor's Medal [Vol. 1: 8911]
Lieutenant-Governor's Medal for Historical Writing [Vol. 1: 6021]
Life Achievement Award
    National PTA [Vol. 1: 12726]
    Screen Actors Guild [Vol 1: 14798]
Life Cycle Management Award [Vol. 1: 298]
Life Esidimeni Award [Vol. 2: 5587]
Life Fellowship [Vol. 2: 268]
Life Governor [Vol. 2: 668]
Life Member Award
    American Chamber of Commerce Executives [Vol. 1: 1585]
    National Ground Water Association [Vol 1: 12465]
    Solid Waste Association of North America [Vol 1: 15951]
Life Members [Vol. 2: 247]
Life Membership
    Australian and New Zealand Society of Respiratory Science [Vol. 2: 223]
    Australian Archaeological Association [Vol 2: 229]
    National Association of College and University Attorneys [Vol 1: 11689]
Life Membership
    Astronomical Society of New South Wales [Vol. 2: 121]
    Canadian Actors' Equity Association [Vol 1: 6175]
    Professional Institute of the Public Service of Canada [Vol 1: 14236]
    Society of Exploration Geophysicists [Vol 1: 15651]
    Speech Pathology Australia [Vol 2: 1051]
Life Membership Award [Vol. 2: 105]
Life Membership Award
    Canadian Association of Career Educators and Employers [Vol. 1: 6240]
    European Association of Geoscientists and Engineers [Vol 2: 4680]
    International Society of Biomechanics in Sports [Vol 2: 3865]
    Northwest Public Power Association [Vol 1: 13415]
    Virginia Recreation and Park Society [Vol 1: 17605]
Life Membership of the GFA [Vol. 2: 743]
Life Saving Cross [Vol. 2: 4486]
Life Sciences Bursaries [Vol. 2: 6881]
Life Sciences Educator Award [Vol. 1: 7425]
Life-Time Membership Award [Vol. 1: 7723]
Life Time Special Members [Vol. 1: 10473]
Lifeguard Awards [Vol. 2: 6984]
Lifesaving Award [Vol. 1: 17568]
Lifesaving Hall of Fame [Vol. 2: 1539]
Lifetime Achievement [Vol. 1: 11506]
LifeTime Achievement Award [Vol. 1: 16985]
Lifetime Achievement Award
    Airline Passenger Experience Association [Vol. 1: 311]

American Agricultural Editors' Association [Vol 1: 792]
American Association of Colleges for Teacher Education [Vol 1: 1091]
American Association of Zoo Keepers [Vol 1: 1419]
American College of Cardiology [Vol 1: 1712]
American College of Dentists [Vol 1: 1738]
American Mensa [Vol 1: 2888]
American Numismatic Association [Vol 1: 2995]
American Psychological Association - Division of Rehabilitation Psychology (Division 22) [Vol 1: 3460]
American-Slovenian Polka Foundation [Vol 1: 3748]
American Society for Bioethics and Humanities [Vol 1: 3764]
American Society for Clinical Pathology [Vol 1: 3796]
American Society for Photobiology [Vol 1: 4039]
American Society of Business Publication Editors [Vol 1: 4133]
American Society of Cinematographers [Vol 1: 4153]
American Spinal Injury Association [Vol 1: 4548]
AMIT [Vol 1: 4723]
Asia-Pacific Satellite Communications Council [Vol 2: 5439]
Asian American Journalists Association [Vol 1: 4824]
Association for Women in Communications [Vol 1: 5162]
Association of Latina and Latino Anthropologists [Vol 1: 5392]
Association of Medical Microbiology and Infectious Disease Canada [Vol 1: 5408]
Association of Military Surgeons of the U.S. [Vol 1: 5428]
Australasian Quaternary Association [Vol 2: 153]
Badminton World Federation [Vol 2: 4533]
Before Columbus Foundation [Vol 1: 5802]
Belize Tourism Board [Vol 2: 1679]
The Bermuda Insurance Institute [Vol 2: 1692]
British Guild of Travel Writers [Vol 2: 7075]
Canadian Advanced Technology Alliance [Vol 1: 6188]
Canadian Booksellers Association [Vol 1: 6353]
Canadian Railroad Historical Association [Vol 1: 6852]
Canadian Society for International Health [Vol 1: 6910]
Caribbean Tourism Organization [Vol 2: 1386]
Conference of Consulting Actuaries [Vol 1: 7498]
Directors Guild of America [Vol 1: 7882]
European Consortium for Political Research [Vol 2: 7600]
Glass Art Society [Vol 1: 8655]
Gyro International [Vol 1: 8805]
Indian Institute of Metals [Vol 2: 3598]
Indian Pharmaceutical Association [Vol 2: 3678]
Indiana Library Federation [Vol 1: 9202]
Institute for the International Education of Students [Vol 1: 9276]
Institution of Occupational Safety and Health [Vol 2: 8051]
International Association of Diecutting and Diemaking [Vol 1: 9658]
International Center of Photography [Vol 1: 9750]
International Cryogenic Materials Conference [Vol 1: 9857]
International Microelectronic and Packaging Society [Vol 1: 10012]
International Society for Autism Research [Vol 1: 10144]
International Society for Cerebral Blood Flow and Metabolism [Vol 2: 6431]
International Society for Extremophiles [Vol 2: 3083]
International Society for Intelligence Research [Vol 1: 10170]
International Society for Iranian Studies [Vol 1: 10177]
International Society for Traumatic Stress Studies [Vol 1: 10264]

International Society of Psychiatric Genetics [Vol 2: 8218]
International Society of Psychoneuroendocrinology [Vol 1: 10354]
International Women's Media Foundation [Vol 1: 10486]
Journalism Education Association [Vol 1: 10589]
Leukemia and Lymphoma Society [Vol 1: 10809]
Logistics Officer Association [Vol 1: 10882]
Medical Dental Hospital Business Associates [Vol 1: 11050]
National Association of Social Workers [Vol 1: 11894]
National Cowboy and Western Heritage Museum [Vol 1: 12268]
National Research Foundation [Vol 2: 5574]
National Wildlife Rehabilitators Association [Vol 1: 13047]
North American Snowsports Journalists Association [Vol 1: 13338]
North Country Trail Association [Vol 1: 13385]
Oncology Nursing Society [Vol 1: 13554]
Pharmaceutical Society of Australia [Vol 2: 927]
Professional Aerial Photographers Association [Vol 1: 14183]
Professional Geologists of Indiana [Vol 1: 14218]
Professional Numismatists Guild [Vol 1: 14244]
Society for American Archaeology [Vol 1: 15021]
Society for Psychological Anthropology [Vol 1: 15283]
Society for Sedimentary Geology - Great Lakes Section [Vol 1: 15321]
Society of Wetland Scientists [Vol 1: 15886]
Specialty Coffee Association of Europe [Vol 2: 9353]
Visitor Industry Partnership [Vol 2: 1707]
Women's Caucus for Art [Vol 1: 17976]
World Affairs Councils of America [Vol 1: 18010]
Wound Healing Society [Vol 1: 18100]
Lifetime Achievement Award - Academics and Researchers [Vol. 2: 7189]
Lifetime Achievement Award for Management [Vol. 2: 3451]
Lifetime Achievement Award for Science [Vol. 2: 1880]
Lifetime Achievement Award in News Direction [Vol. 1: 7883]
Lifetime Achievement Award in Sports Direction [Vol. 1: 7884]
Lifetime Achievement Award in the History of Medicine [Vol. 1: 999]
Lifetime Achievement Award - Professional Psychology [Vol. 2: 7190]
Lifetime Achievement Awards
    American Chamber of Commerce Executives [Vol. 1: 1586]
    American Kennel Club [Vol 1: 2745]
    Magazine Publishers of America [Vol 1: 10910]
    National Council of Teachers of Mathematics [Vol 1: 12226]
Lifetime Achievement Awards in Fire Ecology and Management [Vol. 1: 5018]
Lifetime Achievement/Hall of Fame Award [Vol. 1: 8094]
Lifetime Achievement in Contemporary Sculpture Award [Vol. 1: 10129]
Lifetime Achievement in the Pharmaceutical Practice Award [Vol. 2: 4762]
Lifetime Achievement in the Pharmaceutical Science Award [Vol. 2: 4763]
Lifetime Advocacy Award [Vol. 1: 3505]
Lifetime Ambassador Award [Vol. 1: 5870]
Lifetime Award
    CAD Society [Vol. 1: 6079]
    German Association of Market and Social Researchers [Vol 2: 2910]
Lifetime Career Award
    International Society for Self and Identity [Vol. 1: 10235]
    Stress and Anxiety Research Society [Vol 2: 3188]
Lifetime Career Award for Distinguished Scientific Contribution [Vol. 1: 8985]
Lifetime Contribution Award [Vol. 2: 4786]
Lifetime Contribution to the History of the Neurosciences [Vol. 1: 10242]

Long Service Award
Astronomical Society of Southern Africa [**Vol. 2:** 5513]
Public Relations Institute of Southern Africa [**Vol 2:** 5602]
Royal Agricultural Society of England [**Vol 2:** 8632]
Long Service Awards [**Vol. 2:** 8396]
Long Service Medal
Government of the Commonwealth of Dominica - Information and Communication Technology Unit [**Vol. 2:** 2000]
International Sailing Federation [**Vol 2:** 8178]
Longacre Award; Raymond F. [**Vol. 1:** 185]
Longchamps; Prix Edmond de Selys [**Vol. 2:** 1638]
Longenecker Fellows; Justin G. [**Vol. 1:** 16723]
Longevity Awards
American Fuchsia Society [**Vol. 1:** 2197]
Specialized Carriers and Rigging Association [**Vol 1:** 16122]
Longford Award; Raymond [**Vol. 2:** 351]
Longstaff Medal [**Vol. 2:** 9026]
Longstaff Prize [**Vol. 2:** 9026]
Longtime Meritorious Service Award [**Vol. 1:** 11201]
Lonsdale Cup [**Vol. 2:** 4985]
Lopes Hang Gliding Medal; Pepe [**Vol. 2:** 6320]
Lord Lewis Prize [**Vol. 2:** 9027]
Lord Mayor's Dragon Awards [**Vol. 2:** 7437]
The Lord's Taverners Award [**Vol. 2:** 239]
Lorentz Award; Pare [**Vol. 2:** 9883]
Lorentz Medal [**Vol. 2:** 4832]
Lorentzen Medal; Gustav [**Vol. 2:** 2536]
Lorenzo Natali Prize for Journalists [**Vol. 2:** 1463]
Lorimer Memorial Award; Sir Robert [**Vol. 2:** 8848]
Los Angeles Times Book Prizes [**Vol. 1:** 10884]
Los Premios Nacionales Aquileo J. Echeverria [**Vol. 2:** 1857]
Los Premios Nacionales Interpretacion en Musica, Teatro, Danza [**Vol. 2:** 1859]
Losey Atmospheric Science Award [**Vol. 1:** 2530]
Losey Award; Robert M. [**Vol. 1:** 2530]
Losey Human Resource Research Award; Michael R. [**Vol. 1:** 15104]
Lotz Commemorative Medal; John [**Vol. 2:** 3390]
Lotz Janos Emlekerem [**Vol. 2:** 3390]
Loubat; Prix du Duc de [**Vol. 2:** 2168]
Loucks-Horsley Award; Susan [**Vol. 1:** 12937]
Lougheed Memorial Award; Robert [**Vol. 1:** 12268]
Louis/Emily F. Bourne Student Poetry Award; Louise [**Vol. 1:** 14063]
Louis-Jeantet Prize for Medicine [**Vol. 2:** 6336]
Louis Shores/Greenwood Publishing Group Award [**Vol. 1:** 14474]
Louisiana Literary Award [**Vol. 1:** 10892]
Louisiana State Poetry Society Award [**Vol. 1:** 12356]
Lounsbery Award; Richard [**Vol. 1:** 11439]
Lounsbery; Prix Richard [**Vol. 2:** 2217]
Lounsbury Award; John H. [**Vol. 1:** 12604]
Loup de Bronze [**Vol. 2:** 6564]
Louvain Award; Michel [**Vol. 1:** 11312]
Love Prize; E. R. [**Vol. 2:** 1135]
Love Prize in History; Walter D. [**Vol. 1:** 13299]
Love Story of the Year [**Vol. 2:** 8550]
Love Token Society Exhibit Award [**Vol. 1:** 2997]
Lovelace Award; Augusta Ada [**Vol. 1:** 5169]
Lovelace II Award; William Randolph [**Vol. 1:** 1438]
Lovelace Lecture and Medal [**Vol. 2:** 7015]
Loveland Memorial Award; Edward R. [**Vol. 1:** 1800]
Loveless Chapter of the Year Award; Bill H. [**Vol. 1:** 10932]
Lovell Award; Harry [**Vol. 2:** 405]
Lovering Prize; John [**Vol. 2:** 1136]
Lovett Award; E. Dean [**Vol. 1:** 1698]
Lovo Award for Outstanding Archery Contribution; D.M. [**Vol. 1:** 8288]
Low Award; George M. [**Vol. 1:** 11483]
Low Space Transportation Award; George M. [**Vol. 1:** 2531]
Lowe Awards; Lester [**Vol. 2:** 1555]
Lowell Award; Ralph [**Vol. 1:** 7617]
Lowell Mallett Award [**Vol. 1:** 13930]
Lowell President's Award; Richard E. [**Vol. 1:** 4859]
Lowell Prize; James Russell [**Vol. 1:** 11233]
Lowenfeld Award [**Vol. 1:** 11538]
Lowenheim Memorial Award; Frederick A. [**Vol. 1:** 5616]

Lowin Prizes; Paul [**Vol. 2:** 473]
Lowman Award; Edward W. [**Vol. 1:** 1867]
Lown Heart Hero Award; Louise [**Vol. 1:** 10901]
Lowry Extra Mile Award; Hugh [**Vol. 1:** 5892]
Lowther Memorial Award; Pat [**Vol. 1:** 10784]
LPGA Hall of Fame [**Vol. 1:** 10729]
LRI Innovative Science Award [**Vol. 2:** 1456]
LSDC Licentiateship [**Vol. 2:** 9302]
Lubalin Award; Herb [**Vol. 1:** 15817]
Lubar Award; Joel F. [**Vol. 1:** 10187]
Lubatti Award; Eugenio [**Vol. 2:** 4123]
Lubbers Award; Dietrich W. [**Vol. 2:** 3097]
Luby Jr. Distinguished Service Award; Mort [**Vol. 1:** 18032]
Luby Sr. Hall of Fame Award; Mort [**Vol. 1:** 5955]
Lucas Award for Sheriff of the Year; Ferris E. [**Vol. 1:** 12837]
Lucas Grant [**Vol. 1:** 8423]
Lucas Memorial Award; Tad [**Vol. 1:** 14579]
Lucas Public Landscape Award; Homer [**Vol. 1:** 13175]
Lucas Technical Leadership Gold Medal; Anthony F. [**Vol. 1:** 15759]
Lucia Trade Award [**Vol. 1:** 16344]
Lucie Award [**Vol. 1:** 14020]
Lucie Awards [**Vol. 1:** 10903]
Luck Award; James Murray [**Vol. 1:** 11425]
Ludington Memorial Award; Jeremiah [**Vol. 1:** 8023]
Ludovic-Trarieux International Human Rights Prize [**Vol. 2:** 2465]
Ludwig-Seidel Award [**Vol. 1:** 49]
Luehrs Memorial Award; Richard E. [**Vol. 1:** 15872]
Luer Pleurothallid Award; Carlyle A. [**Vol. 1:** 3083]
Luff Award [**Vol. 1:** 3165]
Lufkin Award; James M. [**Vol. 1:** 9116]
Luh International Award; Bor S. [**Vol. 1:** 9339]
Luikov Medal [**Vol. 2:** 6633]
Luke Award; Hugh J. [**Vol. 1:** 14124]
Lum Award; Anne [**Vol. 1:** 7943]
Lum Award; Louise L. and Y. T. [**Vol. 1:** 9408]
Lumen Awards [**Vol. 1:** 9157]
Lumen Christi Award [**Vol. 1:** 7105]
Lumiere Award [**Vol. 2:** 8903]
Luminosa Award for Unity [**Vol. 2:** 4082]
Luna Foreign Travel Scholarship; Lee G. [**Vol. 1:** 12858]
Luncheon Meats Award [**Vol. 1:** 9128]
Lund Public Service Award; Paul M. [**Vol. 1:** 14329]
Lundell-Bright Memorial Award [**Vol. 1:** 5617]
Lundvall Award; Bruce [**Vol. 1:** 8348]
Lung Cancer Journalism Awards [**Vol. 2:** 7743]
Lurani Trophy for Formula Junior Class [**Vol. 2:** 2504]
Lush Award in Animal Breeding; J. L. [**Vol. 1:** 1981]
Lusted Student Prizes; Lee B. [**Vol. 1:** 15193]
Lutaud; Prix Leon [**Vol. 2:** 2218]
Lutheran Educator of the Year [**Vol. 1:** 10907]
Luthi Award; Dr. Max [**Vol. 2:** 6488]
Lutoslawski International Composers Competition; Witold [**Vol. 2:** 5415]
Lutyens Award [**Vol. 2:** 6803]
Lyapunov Prize; A.M. [**Vol. 2:** 5828]
Lyell Medal [**Vol. 2:** 7725]
Lyle Medal; Thomas Ranken [**Vol. 2:** 183]
Lyman Award; Robert J. [**Vol. 1:** 14132]
Lyman Book Awards; John [**Vol. 1:** 13342]
Lynah Distinguished Achievement Award; James [**Vol. 1:** 7976]
Lynch Award; Twink [**Vol. 1:** 1113]
Lynch Pioneer Award in Forensic Nursing; Virginia A. [**Vol. 1:** 9668]
Lynch-Staunton Awards; Victor Martyn [**Vol. 1:** 6137]
Lyne Award; A.G. [**Vol. 1:** 453]
Lynen Research Fellowships; Feodor [**Vol. 2:** 3230]
Lyon-Caen; Prix Charles [**Vol. 2:** 2285]
Lyon Memorial Award; James P. [**Vol. 1:** 7977]
Lyons Award; Sir William [**Vol. 2:** 7769]
Lyppard/Provet Victoria Colin Basset Prize [**Vol. 2:** 1167]
Lyric Poetry Award [**Vol. 1:** 14064]
Lyster Award; Theodore C. [**Vol. 1:** 186]
Maas Achievement Award; Major General Melvin J. [**Vol. 1:** 5890]
Mabel Yaste Tricolor Award [**Vol. 1:** 2343]
MAC Foundation Scholarship [**Vol. 1:** 11165]
MAC Poster Award [**Vol. 1:** 3783]
Macao Green Hotel Award [**Vol. 2:** 4503]

MacArthur Award for Outstanding New Play or Musical; Charles [**Vol. 1:** 16486]
MacArthur Award for Outstanding Supporting Actor; James [**Vol. 1:** 16486]
MacArthur Award; Robert H. [**Vol. 1:** 7988]
MacArthur Bowl [**Vol. 1:** 12402]
Macaulay Prize Competition; Catharine [**Vol. 1:** 3829]
Macauley Award; Alvan [**Vol. 1:** 13784]
Macbeth Award [**Vol. 1:** 9452]
Maccabee Emblem [**Vol. 1:** 12574]
Maccoby Book Award in Developmental Psychology; Eleanor [**Vol. 1:** 3408]
MacColl Award; Hugh [**Vol. 2:** 7094]
MacDiarmid Young Scientist of the Year [**Vol. 2:** 4894]
MacDonald Award [**Vol. 2:** 7949]
Macdonald Medal; George [**Vol. 2:** 9116]
MacDonald Memorial Award; Thomas H. [**Vol. 1:** 1354]
MacDonald Outstanding Teacher Award; C. Holmes [**Vol. 1:** 8191]
Macdougall Medal [**Vol. 2:** 9497]
MacEachern Chief Executive Officer Award [**Vol. 1:** 14330]
Macelwane Medal; James B. [**Vol. 1:** 2244]
MacFarland Award; Douglas C. [**Vol. 1:** 4990]
Macfarlane Award [**Vol. 2:** 7782]
MacFarlane Award; Brian [**Vol. 1:** 15158]
MacGregor Medal [**Vol. 2:** 999]
Machado de Assis Prize [**Vol. 2:** 1750]
Machine Design Award [**Vol. 1:** 4406]
MacInnes Award; John [**Vol. 1:** 2397]
MacJannet Prize for Global Citizenship [**Vol. 1:** 16362]
Mack Junior Athlete of the Year Award; Tom [**Vol. 1:** 8289]
Mackay Award; J. Ross [**Vol. 1:** 6520]
MacKay Award; Roland P. [**Vol. 1:** 587]
Mackay Best First Book Award for Poetry; Jessie [**Vol. 2:** 5011]
MacKay Essay Prize; Ian [**Vol. 2:** 9099]
Mackay Medal; Donald [**Vol. 2:** 9117]
Mackay Trophy [**Vol. 1:** 11465]
MacKeller Distinguished Service Award; Lillian [**Vol. 1:** 17123]
MacKenzie Award; Agnes Mure [**Vol. 2:** 9154]
MacKenzie Book Prize; W. J. M. [**Vol. 2:** 8494]
Mackenzie Lectureship; James [**Vol. 2:** 8681]
MacKenzie Memorial Award; James T. [**Vol. 1:** 6628]
The Mackerras Medal [**Vol. 2:** 335]
Mackie Awards; Howard [**Vol. 1:** 6636]
MacKinnon Family Fellowship in Western Americana [**Vol. 1:** 18159]
MacLean Citation [**Vol. 2:** 4911]
Maclean Fellowship; Ida Smedley [**Vol. 2:** 6386]
MacLennan Prize for Fiction; Hugh [**Vol. 1:** 14374]
Macleod Memorial Award; John [**Vol. 2:** 8366]
MacMillan Awards; Sir Ernest [**Vol. 1:** 14983]
MacMillan Developer's Award; Viola R. [**Vol. 1:** 14278]
Macmillan Prize; Ian [**Vol. 2:** 8953]
Macmillan Writer's Prize for Africa [**Vol. 2:** 8336]
MacNab Medal [**Vol. 2:** 7967]
MacPhail Promotional Trophy; Larry [**Vol. 1:** 11842]
Macpherson New Editor of the Year Award; Fiona [**Vol. 2:** 7258]
Macpherson Prize; C.B. [**Vol. 1:** 6800]
Macquarie Award for Heritage; Lachlan [**Vol. 2:** 384]
MacRae Award in Creative Leadership; A. E. [**Vol. 1:** 14376]
Macres Award [**Vol. 1:** 11133]
MacRobert Award [**Vol. 2:** 8581]
Macromolecular Chemistry Division Award for Advancement of Science [**Vol. 2:** 5459]
Macromolecular Science and Engineering Award [**Vol. 1:** 7207]
Macular Degeneration Research Grant [**Vol. 1:** 2292]
Madison Award; James [**Vol. 1:** 3307]
Madison Medal; James [**Vol. 1:** 432]
Madison Prize; James [**Vol. 1:** 15097]
Madsen Medal; John [**Vol. 2:** 791]
MAE Award for Best Literature Program for Teens [**Vol. 1:** 18221]
Magarey Medal [**Vol. 2:** 96]
Magaw Outstanding Clinician Practitioner Award; Alice [**Vol. 1:** 7689]

Magazine Merit Awards [Vol. 1: 15587]
Magazine of the Year
    International Regional Magazine Association [Vol. 1: 10115]
    National Magazine Awards Foundation [Vol 1: 12590]
Magazine of the Year Awards [Vol. 1: 4134]
Magellanic Premium [Vol. 1: 3189]
Maggie Awards [Vol. 1: 14028]
Maggio Award; Charles [Vol. 1: 14851]
Magic of Persia Contemporary Art Prize [Vol. 2: 7330]
Magid Award; Nora [Vol. 1: 13893]
Magill Distinguished Service Award; Arthur Napier [Vol. 1: 6731]
Magnabosco Outstanding Local Section Member Award; Paul W. [Vol. 1: 16367]
Magnel Prize; Gustave [Vol. 2: 1658]
Magnussen Award; Ann [Vol. 1: 3680]
Magnusson Memorial Prize; Bengt [Vol. 2: 6359]
Magruder III Award; Colonel John H. [Vol. 1: 10975]
Magsaysay Award; Ramon [Vol. 2: 5337]
Magsaysay Future Engineers/Technologists Award [Vol. 2: 5359]
MaGuire Exceptional Achievement Award; James [Vol. 1: 10957]
A Magyar Konyvtarosok Egyesuleteert Emlekerem [Vol. 2: 3367]
Mahajan Award; Vijay [Vol. 1: 2817]
Mahalanobis Medal; Prasanta Chandra [Vol. 2: 3642]
Maher Award; John [Vol. 1: 10199]
Maheshwari Memorial Lecture; Prof. Panchanan [Vol. 2: 3643]
Mahler Lectureship [Vol. 2: 465]
Mahon Trainee Presentation Award; William [Vol. 1: 6987]
Mahondo Award; N.H.O. [Vol. 2: 4415]
Mahoney Award; Mary [Vol. 1: 3022]
Mai Service Award; Ludwig [Vol. 1: 5107]
Maibach Travel Award; Howard [Vol. 1: 1876]
Maier-Leibnitz Prize; Heinz [Vol. 2: 2993]
Mail Awards; World [Vol. 2: 9397]
Mail System Management Hall of Fame [Vol. 1: 10916]
Mailing Industry Ingenuity Award [Vol. 1: 10923]
Mailloux Award; Noel [Vol. 1: 13660]
Mailly; Prix Edouard [Vol. 2: 1639]
Main Excellence in Clinical Practice Award; Robyn [Vol. 1: 11821]
Main Group Chemistry Award [Vol. 2: 9028]
Main Student Section Award; Charles T. [Vol. 1: 4407]
Maio Award for Excellence in Adult Literacy; Jean [Vol. 1: 7393]
Maisondieu; Prix [Vol. 2: 2286]
Maisonneuve; Prix Chomedey-de- [Vol. 1: 14999]
Maisons solaire, maisons, d'aujourd'hui [Vol. 2: 2594]
Maitland Memorial Lecture Award; Frances M. [Vol. 1: 371]
Majewska Gliding Medal; Pelagia [Vol. 2: 6321]
Major Benefactor Citation [Vol. 1: 5397]
Major League Baseball Player of the Year [Vol. 1: 16176]
Major Prize; J. Russell [Vol. 1: 2383]
Majors/MLA Chapter Project of the Year Award [Vol. 1: 11070]
Makarov Prize; S.O. [Vol. 2: 5829]
MakDougall-Brisbane Prize [Vol. 2: 9069]
Make a Difference Day Awards [Vol. 1: 14074]
Make It With Meat Awards [Vol. 2: 9167]
Makeup Design Award [Vol. 1: 16966]
Maksymczuk Award; Julian G. [Vol. 1: 16598]
Malacological Society of London Annual Award [Vol. 2: 8341]
Malawi Award for Scientific and Technological Achievement [Vol. 2: 4515]
Malcolm Black Travel Fellowship [Vol. 2: 8696]
Maldives Breakout Festival [Vol. 2: 4555]
Male Thrower of the Year [Vol. 1: 17469]
Male Vocalist of the Year [Vol. 1: 9732]
Maleng Minister of Justice Award; Norm [Vol. 1: 1473]
Maley Spirit of Excellence Outstanding Graduate Student Citation; Donald [Vol. 1: 10432]
Malina Astronautics Medal; Frank J. [Vol. 2: 2500]

Malina Leonardo Award for Lifetime Achievement; Frank J. [Vol. 1: 10800]
Malinowski Social Science Award; Bronislaw [Vol. 1: 14085]
Malkin Prize; Harold [Vol. 2: 8697]
Mallett Student Award; Dr. Marshall [Vol. 1: 6282]
Mallory Cup; Clifford D. [Vol. 1: 17057]
Malloy Leadership Award; B. Charles [Vol. 1: 5618]
Malo Medal Award; Urbain J.H. [Vol. 1: 17869]
Malone Fellowship in Arab and Islamic Studies; Joseph J. [Vol. 1: 12255]
Malone Post-Doctoral Fellows Program; Joseph J. [Vol. 1: 12255]
Malone Prize; Tom [Vol. 2: 82]
Malouet; Prix [Vol. 2: 2287]
Maloy Graduate Student Research Award; Bernard Patrick [Vol. 1: 16163]
Malpighi Medal [Vol. 2: 2854]
Malta Journalism Awards [Vol. 2: 4566]
Malta Self-Government Re-introduction Seventy-Fifth Anniversary Medal [Vol. 2: 4571]
Maltsev Prize; A.I. [Vol. 2: 5830]
Mamer Fellowship; Louisan [Vol. 1: 17981]
Mamer Fellowship; Lyle [Vol. 1: 17984]
Mamer Fellowships; Lyle [Vol. 1: 17982]
Man and Woman of the Year Awards [Vol. 1: 2929]
Man of the Year
    Federation of Fly Fishers [Vol. 1: 8299]
    Hasty Pudding Theatricals [Vol 1: 8839]
    International Road Federation [Vol 1: 10127]
Management Accounting Award [Vol. 2: 5225]
Management Achievement Awards [Vol. 1: 5193]
Management and Administration Award [Vol. 1: 5429]
Management and Information Award [Vol. 1: 15760]
Management Award [Vol. 2: 6609]
Management Award [Vol. 1: 10082]
Management Division Award [Vol. 1: 2630]
Management Innovation Award [Vol. 1: 9759]
Management Science Strategic Innovation Prize [Vol. 2: 1406]
Manager Excellence Award [Vol. 1: 9697]
Manager of the Year
    Bookseller Information Group [Vol. 2: 6897]
    International System Safety Society [Vol 1: 10421]
    National Business and Disability Council [Vol 1: 12011]
Manager of the Year Award
    Baseball Writers Association of America [Vol. 1: 5793]
    Mail Systems Management Association [Vol 1: 10917]
    National Institute of Governmental Purchasing [Vol 1: 12554]
Manamperi (Engineering) Award [Vol. 2: 6130]
Manby Prize [Vol. 2: 7998]
Mance Award; Jeanne [Vol. 1: 6753]
Mance Memorial Trophy [Vol. 2: 7399]
Mandel Young Investigator Award; Lazaro J. [Vol. 1: 3257]
Mandel'shtam Prize; L.I. [Vol. 2: 5831]
Mandile Award; Julie [Vol. 2: 685]
Mandy Award [Vol. 2: 1087]
Mangled Skyscraper Award [Vol. 1: 8690]
Mangold Award; Walter S. [Vol. 1: 12322]
Manheim Medal for Translation; Ralph [Vol. 1: 13894]
Manitoba Nursing Research Institute Research Grants [Vol. 1: 17272]
Manjunatheswara Award; Dharmasthala [Vol. 2: 3583]
Manley Weather Prize; Gordon [Vol. 2: 8871]
Manly Memorial Medal; Charles M. [Vol. 1: 15520]
Mann Award for Global Health and Human Rights; Jonathan [Vol. 1: 8678]
Mann Citation; Margaret [Vol. 1: 5050]
Mann Plaque; Emerson O. [Vol. 1: 11512]
Mann Prize; John [Vol. 2: 7842]
Mann Prize; Thomas [Vol. 2: 2708]
Mannerfelt Gold Medal; Carl [Vol. 2: 8103]
Mannheim International Filmweek [Vol. 2: 3070]
Manning Award; J.L. [Vol. 2: 9359]
Mansel-Pleydell Trust Essay Competition [Vol. 2: 7522]
Manson Medal [Vol. 2: 9118]

Manton Award; Irene [Vol. 2: 9196]
Manton Prize; Irene [Vol. 2: 8316]
Manual Chapter Author Grant [Vol. 1: 13887]
Manufacturer Member of the Year [Vol. 1: 14161]
Manufacturer of the Year
    FeRFA Resin Flooring Association [Vol. 2: 7682]
    Performance Warehouse Association [Vol 1: 13944]
    Specialty Sleep Association [Vol 1: 16133]
Manufacturer of the Year [Vol. 2: 4187]
Manufacturer/Supplier Award [Vol. 1: 6070]
Manufacturers Award [Vol. 1: 12466]
Manufacturers' Award [Vol. 2: 7930]
Manuscript Award
    American Society of Ophthalmic Registered Nurses [Vol. 1: 4476]
    Australian Institute of Genealogical Studies [Vol 2: 393]
Manyarara Investigative Journalism Awards; John [Vol. 2: 4625]
Manyarara Investigative Journalist of the Year; John [Vol. 2: 4625]
Manyarara Upcoming Investigative Journalist of the Year; John [Vol. 2: 4625]
Manzullo; Premio Fundacion Alfredo [Vol. 2: 26]
Maori Language Award [Vol. 2: 4869]
Map Course Developer Award; Ed [Vol. 1: 932]
Maple Leaf Award
    Canadian Society for Bioengineering [Vol. 1: 6876]
    International Federation of Purchasing and Supply Management [Vol 2: 1283]
    United Ostomy Association of Canada [Vol 1: 16646]
Maple/Longman Memorial Travel Grant; Robert [Vol. 1: 16396]
Maplehurst Trophy [Vol. 1: 13441]
Marais Prize; Eugene [Vol. 2: 5634]
Maravich Memorial Award; Pete [Vol. 1: 12064]
Marberger Award; Hans [Vol. 2: 4692]
March Award; Francis Andrew [Vol. 1: 5313]
March of Dimes Prize in Developmental Biology [Vol. 1: 10942]
Marchal; Prix Joseph-Edmond [Vol. 2: 1594]
Marckwardt Travel Grants; Albert H. [Vol. 1: 16395]
MarCom Awards [Vol. 1: 5404]
Marconi Award; Guglielmo [Vol. 1: 13658]
Marconi Memorial Gold Medal of Service [Vol. 1: 17534]
Marconi Memorial Scroll of Honor [Vol. 1: 17535]
Marconi Radio Awards [Vol. 1: 11675]
Marconi Science Award [Vol. 1: 16612]
Marcus Family Endowed Scholarship in Entrepreneurship [Vol. 1: 17832]
Marcus Young Investigator Award in Basic Cardiovascular Sciences; Melvin L. [Vol. 1: 2310]
Mardigian Biotechnology Teaching Award; Ron [Vol. 1: 11650]
Marglieth Award; Andrew M. [Vol. 1: 691]
Marian Library Medal [Vol. 1: 17228]
Marimo; Prix Zerilli [Vol. 2: 2288]
Marine Corps Expeditionary Medal [Vol. 1: 16679]
Marine Education Award [Vol. 1: 12594]
Marine Harvest Centenary Award for Outstanding Services to Shinty [Vol. 2: 7320]
Marinelli Coccia Awards; Gladys [Vol. 1: 18209]
Marion; Prix Seraphin- [Vol. 1: 15000]
Mariucci Award; John [Vol. 1: 2398]
Marjolin Prize [Vol. 2: 1239]
Mark Division of Polymer Chemistry Award; Herman F. [Vol. 1: 1655]
Mark Memorial Award; Peter [Vol. 1: 5736]
Mark of Excellence Awards [Vol. 1: 15804]
Market Manager of the Year [Vol. 1: 11838]
Market Mover Award [Vol. 1: 10933]
Market Transformation Award [Vol. 1: 14521]
Marketing Achievement Award [Vol. 1: 15180]
Marketing and Publications Awards [Vol. 1: 17387]
Marketing and Sales Person of the Year Award [Vol. 1: 12138]
Marketing Award [Vol. 2: 2645]
Marketing Awards
    International Dairy Federation [Vol. 2: 1532]
    National Association of Recording Merchandisers [Vol 1: 11859]
Marketing Communications Award [Vol. 1: 7568]

Marketing Competition [**Vol. 1: 11948**]
Marketing Excellence Awards [**Vol. 1: 14687**]
Marketing Practitioner Award [**Vol. 1: 82**]
Markov Prize; A.A. [**Vol. 2: 5832**]
Markowe Public Education Prize; Morris [**Vol. 2: 8724**]
Marks Award; Louis B. [**Vol. 1: 9158**]
Marks of Excellence Award [**Vol. 1: 12421**]
Markwardt Award; L. J. [**Vol. 1: 5619**]
Markwardt Wood Engineering Award; L.J. [**Vol. 1: 8432**]
Marleau Official of the Year Award; Rene [**Vol. 1: 16143**]
Marlin Awards [**Vol. 2: 1349**]
Marloth Medal [**Vol. 2: 5524**]
Marlow Award [**Vol. 2: 9029**]
Marlow Medal and Prize [**Vol. 2: 9029**]
Marlowe Award; Donald E. [**Vol. 1: 3861**]
Marotta; Medaglia d'oro Domenico [**Vol. 2: 4126**]
The Marquette Excellence Award [**Vol. 1: 12940**]
Marquis Award for Excellence in School Programs; Carlo [**Vol. 1: 18011**]
Marquis *Behavioral Neuroscience* Award; D.G. [**Vol. 1: 3400**]
Marquis Memorial Award; John E. [**Vol. 1: 1567**]
Marra Award; George [**Vol. 1: 15905**]
Marraro Prize; Helen and Howard R. [**Vol. 1: 15163**]
Marraro Prize; Howard R. [**Vol. 1: 1544**]
Marraro Prize in Italian History; Helen and Howard R. [**Vol. 1: 2384**]
Marraro Prize in Italian History; Howard R. [**Vol. 1: 2384**]
Marroquin Prize for Student Outreach; Francisco [**Vol. 1: 5685**]
Marschall - Rhone - Poulenc International Dairy Science Award [**Vol. 1: 1972**]
Marsden Award; David [**Vol. 2: 7610**]
Marsden Award; Ralph W. [**Vol. 1: 15619**]
Marsden Medal for Outstanding Service to Science; Sir Ernest [**Vol. 2: 4954**]
Marsella Prize; Anthony J. [**Vol. 1: 14310**]
Marsh and Henning Awards [**Vol. 1: 17552**]
Marsh Award for Conservation Biology [**Vol. 2: 9510**]
Marsh Award for Ecology [**Vol. 2: 7048**]
Marsh Award for Insect Conservation [**Vol. 2: 8773**]
Marsh Distinguished Service Award; Burton W. [**Vol. 1: 9416**]
Marsh Fellowship for Graduate Study in Traffic and Transportation Engineering; Burton W. [**Vol. 1: 9417**]
Marsh Medal; Alan [**Vol. 2: 8613**]
Marsh Medal for Exemplary Contributions to the Protection and Wise Use of the Nation's Water Resources; Mary H. [**Vol. 1: 4653**]
Marsh Memorial Prize; James R. and Anne Steele [**Vol. 1: 9015**]
Marsh Prize; George Perkins [**Vol. 1: 3905**]
Marsh Safety Award; William O. [**Vol. 1: 11492**]
Marshall Award; Robert [**Vol. 1: 17843**]
Marshall Civil Liberties Award; Justice Thurgood [**Vol. 1: 8583**]
Marshall Education Award; Richard [**Vol. 1: 910**]
Marshall Graduate Student Awards; Thomas F. [**Vol. 1: 4066**]
Marshall Lifetime Achievement Award; Chief Justice [**Vol. 1: 10598**]
Marshall Medal; Dorothy [**Vol. 2: 9233**]
Marshall Medal; George Catlett [**Vol. 1: 5538**]
Marshall of Cambridge Medal [**Vol. 2: 6693**]
Marshall Poetry Prize; Lenore [**Vol. 1: 55**]
Marshall Scholarships [**Vol. 1: 6815**]
Marsters Promotion Award; James C. [**Vol. 1: 16406**]
Marston Award [**Vol. 2: 7938**]
Marten Prize for Social Entrepreneurship; Alberto [**Vol. 1: 5686**]
Martens Prize; F.F. [**Vol. 2: 5833**]
Marth Educator Award; Elmer [**Vol. 1: 9551**]
Marti Prize; The International Jose [**Vol. 2: 2652**]
Martin Award; Allie Beth [**Vol. 1: 14324**]
Martin Award; E. O. [**Vol. 1: 1300**]
Martin Award; Eric W. [**Vol. 1: 2879**]
Martin Award for Excellence in the Exhibition of Costume; Richard [**Vol. 1: 7624**]
Martin Award; G. Harold [**Vol. 1: 10412**]
Martin Award; Joseph J. [**Vol. 1: 3862**]
Martin Award; Sir James [**Vol. 2: 7756**]

Martin Fellowships; C. J. [**Vol. 2: 892**]
Martin Humanitarian Award; Edward [**Vol. 1: 2102**]
Martin Medal [**Vol. 2: 7425**]
Martin Memorial Award; Stan [**Vol. 1: 11866**]
Martin Memorial Scholarship; George [**Vol. 2: 5580**]
Martin Outstanding Younger Member Award; John [**Vol. 1: 9322**]
Martin Overseas Biomedical Fellowship; C. J. [**Vol. 2: 892**]
Martin Research Travel Grant; Christine and T. Jack [**Vol. 2: 206**]
Martinez-Marquez Award; Guillermo [**Vol. 1: 11785**]
Martino Outstanding Contributions to Bowling Award; John O. [**Vol. 1: 5953**]
Marty Public Understanding of Religion Award; Martin E. [**Vol. 1: 756**]
Marvel Creative Polymer Chemistry Award; Carl S. [**Vol. 1: 1656**]
Marvin Grant; Walter Rumsey [**Vol. 1: 13492**]
Marvin Hall of Fame for Design Excellence; William S. [**Vol. 1: 6042**]
Marvingt Award; Marie [**Vol. 1: 187**]
Mary Louise Brown Research Award [**Vol. 1: 1248**]
Maryland Quality Awards [**Vol. 1: 17276**]
Marzocco d'Ora [**Vol. 2: 4080**]
Masefield Gold Medal; Sir Peter [**Vol. 2: 6958**]
Mashman Safety Award; Joe [**Vol. 1: 8892**]
Mason Award for Excellence in Jewelry Design; John C. [**Vol. 1: 7162**]
Mason Award; Peter [**Vol. 2: 8398**]
Mason Gold Medal [**Vol. 2: 8872**]
Mason Playwrighting Award; Bruce [**Vol. 2: 5034**]
Mason Prize; Michael [**Vol. 2: 7241**]
Mason Project Award; Elizabeth B. [**Vol. 1: 13630**]
Mason Reference Award; Harold [**Vol. 1: 5386**]
Mason Scholarship; Val [**Vol. 1: 6942**]
Masonry Skills Challenge; International [**Vol. 1: 10994**]
Masotto Cup; Patricia L. [**Vol. 1: 17155**]
Maspero; Prix Gaston [**Vol. 2: 2164**]
Mass Communications Hall of Fame [**Vol. 1: 16470**]
Mass Communications Outstanding Alumni Awards [**Vol. 1: 16471**]
Massachusetts State Poetry Society Award [**Vol. 1: 12357**]
Masschelein Prize; Willy [**Vol. 1: 10042**]
Massey Award [**Vol. 2: 2339**]
Massey-Ferguson Educational Gold Medal [**Vol. 1: 4086**]
Massey Medal [**Vol. 1: 14626**]
Massey Medal and Prize; Harrie [**Vol. 2: 410**]
Massey Medal; Harrie [**Vol. 2: 7912**]
Masson Memorial Scholarship Prize [**Vol. 2: 977**]
Massonnet Award; Charles [**Vol. 2: 1466**]
Master Breeder Award [**Vol. 1: 2263**]
Master Builder of the Year Awards [**Vol. 2: 8406**]
Master Clinician Award [**Vol. 1: 722**]
Master Craftsman Degree [**Vol. 1: 13063**]
Master Diploma in Professional Floristry [**Vol. 2: 9309**]
Master Endoscopist Award [**Vol. 1: 3912**]
Master Judge Award [**Vol. 1: 12675**]
Master Mentor Award [**Vol. 1: 3373**]
Master Musician Award [**Vol. 1: 16557**]
Master of Bananistry Medal [**Vol. 1: 9725**]
Master of the Game Award [**Vol. 1: 10986**]
Master Teacher Award [**Vol. 1: 9682**]
Master Thesis Award [**Vol. 2: 6579**]
Master Toolmaker Award [**Vol. 2: 68**]
Master Trophy [**Vol. 1: 10582**]
Master Wildlife Artist [**Vol. 1: 18003**]
Masterclass Performers Competition [**Vol. 1: 12399**]
Mastermind Award [**Vol. 2: 6982**]
Masters Administrator of the Year [**Vol. 1: 17470**]
Masters Age Division Runners of the Year [**Vol. 1: 17471**]
Master's and First Professional Awards [**Vol. 1: 1394**]
Masters and Johnson Award [**Vol. 1: 15327**]
Masters Award [**Vol. 1: 17124**]
Masters Dissertation Award [**Vol. 2: 7369**]
Masters Golf Tournament [**Vol. 1: 5695**]
Masters Race Walker of the Year Award [**Vol. 1: 17472**]
Masters Series Award [**Vol. 1: 7707**]
Master's Thesis Fellowship [**Vol. 1: 8363**]
Masters Thesis Research Award [**Vol. 1: 14305**]

Masters Transportation Engineering Award; Frank M. [**Vol. 1: 4203**]
Masterships [**Vol. 1: 1801**]
Masubuchi Award; Professor Koichi [**Vol. 1: 4683**]
Masubuchi Lifetime Achievement Award; Kazumasa [**Vol. 2: 3042**]
Masur Fellowship in Civil Liberties; Robert [**Vol. 1: 11392**]
Masursky Award for Meritorious Service to Planetary Science; Harold [**Vol. 1: 1448**]
Material Chemistry Division Award for Excellent Research [**Vol. 2: 5460**]
Material for Industry - Derek Birchall Award [**Vol. 2: 9030**]
Mathematical Contest in Modeling [**Vol. 1: 15120**]
Mather Award; Frank Jewett [**Vol. 1: 7358**]
Mather Award; Katharine and Bryant [**Vol. 1: 5620**]
Mather Award; Stephen Tyng [**Vol. 1: 12662**]
Mathers Trophy; Frank [**Vol. 1: 2416**]
Mathewson Award; Champion H. [**Vol. 1: 11194**]
Mathias Grant; Mildred [**Vol. 1: 17197**]
Mathias Medal; Simao [**Vol. 2: 1754**]
Mathiasen Award; Geneva [**Vol. 1: 12233**]
Mathy Awards [**Vol. 2: 524**]
Matkin Awards; Noel D. [**Vol. 1: 8021**]
Matson Memorial Award; George C. [**Vol. 1: 1281**]
Matson Memorial Award; Theodore M. [**Vol. 1: 9418**]
Matsuda Award [**Vol. 2: 5333**]
Mattersdorf Memorial Fund Award; Jeanne S. [**Vol. 1: 12969**]
Matthew Award; Robert [**Vol. 2: 7450**]
Matthew Prize; Sir Robert [**Vol. 2: 2586**]
Matthews Award; Austin [**Vol. 1: 6646**]
Matthews Award; Z.K. [**Vol. 2: 5493**]
Matthews Awards; Keith [**Vol. 1: 6736**]
Matthews Graduate Student Poster Award; Whit [**Vol. 1: 5333**]
Matthews Memorial Scholarship; Charles Ivor [**Vol. 2: 920**]
Matthews Outstanding Chapter Award; R. C. [**Vol. 1: 16374**]
Matula Award; Crystal [**Vol. 2: 4693**]
Maucher Prize in Geoscience; Albert [**Vol. 2: 2994**]
Maugham Awards; Somerset [**Vol. 2: 9253**]
Mauguin; Prix Georges [**Vol. 2: 2289**]
Maurice Rookie of the Year; Lisa [**Vol. 1: 17963**]
Maury and Hinman Research Awards [**Vol. 1: 17612**]
Maury Research Award; Matthew Fontaine [**Vol. 1: 17612**]
Mavromatis Scholarship; Ann Lane [**Vol. 1: 2441**]
Mawson Medal and Lecture [**Vol. 2: 184**]
Max-Eyth-Gedenkmunze [**Vol. 2: 3132**]
Max Steinbock Award [**Vol. 1: 196**]
Maxeke Award; Charlotte [**Vol. 2: 5494**]
Maxwell Award; Donald [**Vol. 2: 7894**]
Maxwell Medal and Prize [**Vol. 2: 7913**]
Maxwell Prize for Plasma Physics; James Clerk [**Vol. 1: 3210**]
May Award; Douglas [**Vol. 2: 8155**]
Mayadas Leadership Award in Online Education; A. Frank [**Vol. 1: 14928**]
Maybee Award; Gordon Royal [**Vol. 1: 6584**]
Mayborn Award for Community Leadership; Frank [**Vol. 1: 16445**]
Mayer Award for Educational Leadership; Edward N. [**Vol. 1: 7871**]
Mayer Award for Young Investigators; Andre [**Vol. 2: 8074**]
Mayfield Award [**Vol. 1: 7534**]
Mayfield Cotton Engineering Award [**Vol. 1: 4087**]
Maynard Award; Harold H. [**Vol. 1: 2805**]
Maynard Book-of-the-Year Award; H. B. [**Vol. 1: 9356**]
Mayne Pharma Award (Oncology) [**Vol. 1: 6952**]
Mayor's Lifetime Achievement Award [**Vol. 1: 7847**]
Mayr Award in Systematic Biology; Ernst [**Vol. 1: 15834**]
Mayr Grants; Ernst [**Vol. 1: 11315**]
Mazzetti Scholarship; Giuliano [**Vol. 1: 14956**]
Mazzone Distinguished Service Award; Guilio [**Vol. 1: 11912**]
Mazzotti Awards Promote Women's Leadership [**Vol. 1: 14553**]
MBC/IFSC Scholarship [**Vol. 2: 3860**]
MBoC Paper of the Year Award [**Vol. 1: 3784**]
MCA Annual Merit Awards Program [**Vol. 1: 11105**]

McAdams Short-Term Study Stipend; A. James [**Vol. 1: 15244**]

McAlister Award; D.S. [**Vol. 1: 16019**]

McArthur Prize; Norma [**Vol. 2: 1137**]

McArthur Prize; Robert [**Vol. 2: 7843**]

McAulay Award; John H. [**Vol. 1: 4991**]

McAulay-Hope Prize for Original Biophysics [**Vol. 2: 533**]

McAuliffe Reach for the Stars Award; Christa [**Vol. 1: 12170**]

McBryde Medal; W. A. E. [**Vol. 1: 6892**]

McCall Life Pattern Fund (Training Award) [**Vol. 1: 15964**]

McCallum Prize [**Vol. 2: 8560**]

McCallum Scholarship; Heather [**Vol. 1: 6221**]

McCandless Award; Boyd [**Vol. 1: 3409**]

McCandliss Professional Service Award; Rhea [**Vol. 1: 2442**]

McCann Memorial Award; Gerry [**Vol. 1: 12306**]

McCanse Award; Jessie [**Vol. 1: 12976**]

McCarren Award [**Vol. 1: 9613**]

McCarthy Award of Merit; John and Sharon [**Vol. 1: 7162**]

McCarthy Bursary; Doreen [**Vol. 2: 341**]

McCarthy Good Guy Award; Clem [**Vol. 1: 16948**]

McCarthy Memorial Award [**Vol. 1: 7802**]

McCaughan, DO, Education Scholarships; Russell C. [**Vol. 1: 3106**]

McCaul Prize; Kevin [**Vol. 2: 559**]

McClarren Legislative Development Award; Robert R. [**Vol. 1: 9143**]

McCloskey Award; Michael [**Vol. 1: 14872**]

McCloy Memorial Award; John J. [**Vol. 1: 8494**]

McClung Award [**Vol. 1: 5815**]

McClure Award for Outstanding Environmental and Community Leadership; Tim [**Vol. 1: 12749**]

McClure Award for the Best Master's Student Paper; Edward [**Vol. 1: 5286**]

McClure Silver Ram Award [**Vol. 1: 3738**]

McCluskey Award of Excellence; Roger [**Vol. 1: 16734**]

McClusky Research Award; Dean and Sybil [**Vol. 1: 5010**]

McColl Family Fellowship [**Vol. 1: 2215**]

McCollum Award; E. V. [**Vol. 1: 4015**]

McCollum International Lectureship in Nutrition; E. V. [**Vol. 1: 4016**]

McConnell Award; Robert Earll [**Vol. 1: 2677**]

McConnell Distinguished Service Award; Douglas Rand [**Vol. 1: 2673**]

McConnell, MD, Award for Excellence in Volunteerism; Jack B. [**Vol. 1: 2861**]

McCord National Education Award; L. P. [**Vol. 1: 9182**]

McCormack Award [**Vol. 1: 5520**]

McCormick Award for Distinguished Early Career Contributions; Earnest J. [**Vol. 1: 15133**]

McCormick Best First Book Award for Non-Fiction; E.H. [**Vol. 2: 5012**]

McCormick - Jerome Increase Case Gold Medal; Cyrus Hall [**Vol. 1: 4088**]

McCormick Medal; Cyrus Hall [**Vol. 1: 4088**]

McCoy Distinguished Career Award; Charles A. [**Vol. 1: 7118**]

McCoy Service Award; Lois Clark [**Vol. 1: 11599**]

McCredie Award; Dr. Kenneth B. [**Vol. 1: 10810**]

McCree, Jr. Awards for the Advancement of Justice; Wade H. [**Vol. 1: 16270**]

McCulloch Award; Warren [**Vol. 1: 3816**]

McCulloch Prizes for Public Speaking; Andrina [**Vol. 1: 14377**]

McCullough Award; Constance M. [**Vol. 1: 10103**]

McCurdy Award [**Vol. 1: 6196**]

McCutcheon Marine Heavy Helicopter Squadron of the Year Award; Keith B. [**Vol. 1: 10958**]

McDaniel Ambassador Award; Durward K. [**Vol. 1: 1911**]

McDonald Award; Ralph E. [**Vol. 1: 649**]

McDonald Elder Statesman of Aviation Award; Wesley L. [**Vol. 1: 11466**]

McDonald House Charities Grants Program; Ronald [**Vol. 1: 14593**]

McDonald's Ballet Scholarship [**Vol. 2: 1075**]

McDonald's Operatic Aria [**Vol. 2: 1076**]

McDonough Award; Jim [**Vol. 1: 17855**]

McDowell Award; Fletcher H. [**Vol. 1: 4459**]

McDowell Award; W. Wallace [**Vol. 1: 9064**]

McEachern Internal Auditor of the Year Award; Terry [**Vol. 1: 5311**]

McEwan Memorial Award (Masters Athlete of the Year); Mae [**Vol. 1: 17124**]

McFarland Award; Forest R. [**Vol. 1: 15521**]

McFarland-SABR Baseball Research Award [**Vol. 1: 15029**]

McFarlane Environmental Leadership Award; Euan P. [**Vol. 1: 10532**]

McGannon Award for Social and Ethical Relevance in Communications Policy Research; Donald [**Vol. 1: 8414**]

McGavin Award for Prevention; Agnes Purcell [**Vol. 1: 3356**]

McGee Service Award; George [**Vol. 1: 13725**]

McGee Trophy; Francis J. [**Vol. 1: 12786**]

McGee Trophy; W. P. [**Vol. 1: 6647**]

McGibbon Award; Pauline [**Vol. 1: 13569**]

McGill Award; John [**Vol. 1: 16199**]

McGillivray Award for Investigative Journalism; Don [**Vol. 1: 6276**]

McGinnis Memorial Award; John H. [**Vol. 1: 16052**]

McGinnis-Ritchie Award [**Vol. 1: 16052**]

McGovern Award; John P. [**Vol. 1: 2880**]

McGovern Award Lectureship; John P. [**Vol. 1: 11071**]

McGovern Lecture in the Behavioral Sciences; John P. [**Vol. 1: 991**]

McGovern Umpires' Award; John T. [**Vol. 1: 17131**]

McGowan Memorial Award; Joe [**Vol. 1: 324**]

McGowran Award; Bill [**Vol. 2: 9360**]

McGraw Award; James H. [**Vol. 1: 3863**]

McGraw-Hill Biology Award [**Vol. 2: 1138**]

McGraw, Jr. Prize in Education; Harold W. [**Vol. 1: 11025**]

McGraw Research Award; Curtis W. [**Vol. 1: 3864**]

McGregor Award of Exceptional Achievement; Alice M.H. [**Vol. 1: 11745**]

McGroddy Prize for New Materials; James C. [**Vol. 1: 3211**]

McGruder Diversity Leadership Awards; Robert C. [**Vol. 1: 4898**]

McGuire Cup; James P. [**Vol. 1: 17159**]

McGuire Memorial Intermediate Piano Scholarship; Maude [**Vol. 1: 14748**]

McHenry Award; Lawrence C. [**Vol. 1: 588**]

McIlwaine Science Teaching Award [**Vol. 1: 13913**]

McIntosh Prize for Physical Scientist of the Year; Malcolm [**Vol. 2: 357**]

McIntyre Award [**Vol. 2: 5514**]

McIntyre Prize; A.K. [**Vol. 2: 500**]

McIver Public Health Nurse Award; Pearl [**Vol. 1: 3023**]

McKay - Helm Award [**Vol. 1: 4684**]

McKeachie Teaching Excellence Award; Wilbert J. [**Vol. 1: 3556**]

McKee Award; Harley J. [**Vol. 1: 5074**]

McKee Medal for Groundwater Protection, Restoration, and Sustainable Use; Jack Edward [**Vol. 1: 17712**]

McKee Trophy [**Vol. 1: 6197**]

McKenzie Award; Dorothy C. [**Vol. 1: 7250**]

McKenzie Award; Ken [**Vol. 1: 2417**]

McKenzie Award; R. Tait [**Vol. 1: 801**]

McKenzie Cup [**Vol. 1: 8306**]

McKenzie Memorial Prize; K.G. [**Vol. 1: 6740**]

McKenzie Plaque [**Vol. 1: 8306**]

McKinlay Scholarships; Arthur Patch [**Vol. 1: 1686**]

McKinley and Darbaker Resource Fellowships [**Vol. 1: 17328**]

McKinley Professional Leadership Award; Anne H. [**Vol. 1: 12234**]

McKinnell Award; Beverly Kerr [**Vol. 1: 10313**]

McKinney Award; William M. [**Vol. 1: 4454**]

McKinnon Award; Helen [**Vol. 1: 10338**]

McKinsey Marketing Dissertation Award [**Vol. 2: 1484**]

McKitterick Prize [**Vol. 2: 9254**]

McKnight Advancement Grants [**Vol. 1: 14047**]

McKnight Artist Fellowships for Writers [**Vol. 1: 10877**]

McLauchlan Prize; Juliet [**Vol. 1: 7544**]

McLaughlin Award [**Vol. 1: 12139**]

McLaughlin Award of Merit; Kenneth P. [**Vol. 1: 12703**]

McLaughlin, Jr. Award for Outstanding Midfielder; Lt. Donald [**Vol. 1: 16979**]

McLaughlin Medal [**Vol. 1: 14642**]

McLaughry Award; Tuss [**Vol. 1: 2169**]

McLemore Prize [**Vol. 1: 11220**]

McLennan Award; Ethel [**Vol. 2: 1139**]

McLeod Founder's Award for Distinguished Service to the Profession [**Vol. 1: 15231**]

McLeod Literary Prize; Enid [**Vol. 2: 7709**]

McLintock Prize; Sir William [**Vol. 2: 7844**]

McLuhan Award for Outstanding Book in the Field of Media Ecology; Marshall [**Vol. 1: 11038**]

McMahon Award for Excellence in Pre-Collegiate Independent Study; Monty [**Vol. 1: 933**]

McMahon Dedicated Service Award [**Vol. 1: 16243**]

McMaster Gold Medal; Robert C. [**Vol. 1: 4004**]

McMenemy Prize; John [**Vol. 1: 6801**]

McMillan Lecture Award; Mary [**Vol. 1: 3237**]

McMullen Weapon System Maintenance Award; Maj. Gen. Clements [**Vol. 1: 13651**]

McNamara Convenors' Award for Excellence; Peter [**Vol. 2: 126**]

McNamee CSJ Award; Catherine T. [**Vol. 1: 12047**]

McNaughton Exemplary Communication Award; Shirley [**Vol. 1: 10141**]

McNeer Award; Lenore [**Vol. 1: 12633**]

McNeil Medal for the Public Awareness of Science [**Vol. 1: 14643**]

McNichol Prize; J. N. [**Vol. 2: 951**]

McNiven Medal [**Vol. 2: 122**]

McNutt Award for Excellence in Automotive Policy Analysis; Barry D. [**Vol. 1: 15522**]

McParland Memorial Award; Donald J. [**Vol. 1: 6612**]

McPherson Memorial Lecture [**Vol. 2: 7939**]

McQuade Memorial Award; Gerard [**Vol. 1: 10481**]

McRae Award; Ian [**Vol. 1: 6748**]

McShan Inspirational Leadership Award; MCPO Angela M. [**Vol. 1: 16761**]

McTague Memorial Award; Thomas J. [**Vol. 1: 6629**]

McWilliams Award; Carey [**Vol. 1: 3308**]

McWilliams Pre-Doctoral Fellowship; Dr. Margaret [**Vol. 1: 6486**]

McWilliams Young Science Writers' Competition [**Vol. 2: 3921**]

Meacham Award; Monte [**Vol. 1: 811**]

Mead Award for Lifetime Achievement; George Herbert [**Vol. 1: 15400**]

Mead Award; Margaret
   American Anthropological Association [**Vol. 1: 828**]
   International Community Corrections Association [**Vol 1: 9804**]

Mead Environmental Award; Arthur [**Vol. 2: 4912**]

Mead Johnson Award [**Vol. 1: 4017**]

Mead Johnson Research Award in Endocrinology and Metabolism [**Vol. 1: 3258**]

Mead Jr. Distinguished Leadership Award; Robert G. [**Vol. 1: 1375**]

Mead Prize; Sidney E. [**Vol. 1: 4147**]

Mead Prizes; Daniel W. [**Vol. 1: 4204**]

Meade Award; CEE Richard A. [**Vol. 1: 12211**]

Meade Award; George and Eleanore [**Vol. 1: 16317**]

Meadows Award for Excellence in the Arts; Algur H. [**Vol. 1: 16033**]

Meadows Prize [**Vol. 1: 16033**]

Meany-Lane Kirkland Human Rights Award; George [**Vol. 1: 194**]

Mears Good Guy Award; Rick [**Vol. 1: 1459**]

Meat Processing Award [**Vol. 1: 2855**]

Meat to Go Awards [**Vol. 2: 9167**]

Meats Research Award [**Vol. 1: 4121**]

Mechanic of the Year Award [**Vol. 1: 16735**]

Mechanical Engineering Prize [**Vol. 2: 786**]

Mechanics and Control of Flight Award [**Vol. 1: 2532**]

Mechnikov Prize; I.I. [**Vol. 2: 5834**]

MECON Award [**Vol. 2: 3599**]

Medaglia d'Oro [**Vol. 2: 4121**]

Medaille de l'ACP pour Contribution Exceptionnelle a la Physique [**Vol. 1: 6302**]

Medaille des Anciens Presidents [**Vol. 2: 2613**]

Medaille d'Or [**Vol. 2: 2624**]

Medaille du Lieutenant-Gouverneur [**Vol. 1: 8911**]

Medaille Flavelle [**Vol. 1: 14639**]

Medaille fur Naturwissenschaftliche Publizistik [**Vol. 2: 2776**]

Medaille Gabrielle Leger [**Vol. 1: 8910**]

Medaille Henry Marshall [Vol. 1: 14648]

Medaille Innis - Gerin [Vol. 1: 14641]

Medaille Jason A. Hannah [Vol. 1: 14640]

Medaille Jean Thevenot [Vol. 2: 6382]

Medaille Lorne Pierce [Vol. 1: 14645]

Medaille McLaughlin [Vol. 1: 14642]

Medaille Militaire [Vol. 2: 2432]

Medaille Pierre Chauveau [Vol. 1: 14637]

Medaille Willet G. Miller [Vol. 1: 14644]

Medailles et Diplomes Olympique [Vol. 2: 6415]

Medal Award

    Illuminating Engineering Society of North America [Vol. 1: 9159]

    Society of Exploration Geophysicists [Vol 1: 15648]

Medal Class Awards [Vol. 1: 2930]

Medal Federacion Espanola de Montanismo [Vol. 2: 6108]

Medal for Bravery

    Canadian Institute of Mining, Metallurgy, and Petroleum [Vol. 1: 6613]

    Office of the President of the Slovak Republic [Vol 2: 6003]

    Office of the Prime Minister of Malta [Vol 2: 4572]

Medal for Business Excellence [Vol. 2: 656]

Medal for Courage [Vol. 2: 5172]

Medal for Distinction in Engineering Education [Vol. 1: 8127]

Medal for Distinguished Engineers [Vol. 2: 4279]

Medal for Distinguished Philanthropy [Vol. 1: 1219]

Medal for Efficiency [Vol. 2: 5173]

Medal for Excellence in Craft Award [Vol. 1: 15483]

Medal for Excellence in Teaching Undergraduate Physics [Vol. 1: 6301]

Medal for Excellent Service [Vol. 2: 5175]

Medal for Gallantry [Vol. 2: 313]

Medal for Irreproachable Service [Vol. 2: 6654]

Medal for Lifetime Achievement [Vol. 2: 657]

Medal for Lifetime Achievement in Physics [Vol. 1: 6302]

Medal for Long Service and Good Conduct [Vol. 2: 5174]

Medal for Military Service to Ukraine [Vol. 2: 6655]

Medal for New Technology [Vol. 2: 4280]

Medal for Outstanding Achievement in Industrial and Applied Physics [Vol. 1: 6303]

Medal for Outstanding Paper [Vol. 2: 4281]

Medal for Outstanding Service to Language Teaching [Vol. 2: 347]

Medal for Public Understanding of Physics [Vol. 2: 2393]

Medal for Research [Vol. 2: 6421]

Medal for Scientific Achievement [Vol. 2: 2568]

Medal for Service [Vol. 2: 6422]

Medal for Service to the Country [Vol. 2: 4511]

Medal for Service to the Republic [Vol. 2: 4573]

Medal for Services to Bibliography [Vol. 2: 6877]

Medal for the Advancement of Research [Vol. 1: 4842]

Medal for Young Scientists [Vol. 2: 3644]

Medal in Medicine [Vol. 1: 14630]

Medal in Surgery [Vol. 1: 14631]

Medal Lecturers [Vol. 2: 4160]

Medal Mariana Smoluchowskiego [Vol. 2: 5409]

Medal of Appreciation [Vol. 1: 12907]

Medal of Bravery [Vol. 1: 8750]

Medal of Courage [Vol. 1: 13071]

Medal of DAAAM International [Vol. 2: 1226]

Medal of Darius and Girenas [Vol. 2: 4487]

Medal of Distinction [Vol. 2: 5696]

Medal of Excellence [Vol. 1: 4367]

Medal of Excellence in Engineering Education [Vol. 2: 2665]

Medal of Honor

    American Cancer Society [Vol. 1: 1533]

    American Mosquito Control Association [Vol 1: 2938]

    Fragrance Foundation [Vol 1: 8456]

    German Society of Human Genetics [Vol 2: 3015]

    Herb Society of America [Vol 1: 8906]

    Institute of Electrical and Electronics Engineers [Vol 1: 9298]

    Niagara University [Vol 1: 13257]

    Society of Automotive Engineers [Vol 1: 15523]

    Verein Deutscher Textilveredlungsfachleute e.V [Vol 2: 3221]

Medal of Honor for Career Service [Vol. 1: 15771]

Medal of Honor of the Great Promoters of Education [Vol. 2: 1850]

Medal of Honour

    British Deaf Association [Vol. 2: 7040]

    International Triathlon Union [Vol 1: 10467]

    Office of the President of the Republic of Macedonia [Vol 2: 4512]

Medal of Honour for Afrikaans Radio Feature Programme [Vol. 2: 5635]

Medal of Honour for the Promotion of History [Vol. 2: 5636]

Medal of Honour of the Order of Saint Lucia [Vol. 2: 5893]

Medal of Icelandic Red Cross [Vol. 2: 3436]

Medal of January 13 [Vol. 2: 4488]

Medal of Liberty [Vol. 1: 1683]

Medal of Merit

    American Numismatic Association [Vol. 1: 2998]

    Boy Scouts of America [Vol 1: 5970]

    Government of the Republic of Trinidad and Tobago - Office of the Prime Minister [Vol 2: 6617]

    Journalism Education Association [Vol 1: 10590]

    Leopoldina, the German Academy of Sciences [Vol 2: 3122]

    National Sheriffs' Association [Vol 1: 12838]

    South African Society for Enology and Viticulture [Vol 2: 5713]

Medal of Merit of the Order of Saint Lucia [Vol. 2: 5894]

Medal of Military Valour [Vol. 1: 8751]

Medal of Service [Vol. 2: 3339]

Medal of the Endocrine Society [Vol. 1: 8111]

Medal of the Estonian Academy of Sciences [Vol. 2: 2042]

Medal of the Founding Volunteers of the Lithuanian Army [Vol. 2: 4489]

Medal of the Order of the Lithuanian Grand Duke Gediminas [Vol. 2: 4490]

Medal of the Royal Society of Western Australia [Vol. 2: 1019]

Medal of the Society [Vol. 2: 2105]

Medal of the Society of Dyers and Colourists [Vol. 2: 9303]

Medal of Valor

    International Narcotic Enforcement Officers Association [Vol. 1: 10027]

    National Sheriffs' Association [Vol 1: 12839]

Medal of Valor Award

    American Correctional Association [Vol. 1: 1885]

    International Association for Healthcare Security and Safety [Vol 1: 9562]

Medalja Julije Domac [Vol. 1: 1869]

Medalla de Oro [Vol. 1: 15696]

Medalla Militar Francisco Jose de Caldas [Vol. 2: 1832]

Medalla Militar Soldado Juan Bautista Solarte Obando [Vol. 2: 1833]

Medalla Servicios Distinguidos a la Aviacion Naval [Vol. 2: 1834]

Medalla Servicios Distinguidos la Fuerza de Superficie [Vol. 2: 1835]

Medallion Award

    American Forage and Grassland Council [Vol. 1: 2173]

    Council of Residential Specialists [Vol 1: 7672]

    National Association of Secretaries of State [Vol 1: 11891]

Medallion de Oro [Vol. 1: 13327]

Medallion de Plata [Vol. 1: 13328]

Medallion of Excellence for Leadership and Community Service [Vol. 1: 7539]

Medallion of Merit [Vol. 1: 2865]

Medallion of the Republic of Iceland [Vol. 2: 3437]

Medals for Excellence [Vol. 2: 7433]

Medals of the Orders [Vol. 2: 5214]

Medawar Prize [Vol. 1: 16530]

MEDEA Awards [Vol. 2: 1573]

Media Award

    American Association of Critical-Care Nurses [Vol. 1: 1124]

    American Association on Intellectual and Developmental Disabilities [Vol. 1: 1425]

    American College of Neuropsychopharmacology [Vol 1: 1781]

    Arbor Day Foundation [Vol 1: 4757]

    Australasian Society for Traumatic Stress Studies [Vol 2: 156]

    Canadian Mental Health Association [Vol 1: 6691]

    Canadian Mental Health Association - Alberta Division [Vol 1: 6696]

    Colorado Association of Libraries [Vol 1: 7394]

    Emergency Nurses Association [Vol 1: 8095]

    International Society for the Study of Trauma and Dissociation [Vol 1: 10252]

    International Society of Appraisers [Vol 1: 10273]

    National Hearing Conservation Association [Vol 1: 12500]

    Veterans of Foreign Wars of the United States [Vol 1: 17546]

Media Awards

    American Academy of Nursing [Vol. 1: 602]

    American Institute of Biological Sciences [Vol 1: 2592]

    Australasian Society of Clinical Immunology and Allergy [Vol 2: 163]

    Australian Sports Commission [Vol 2: 590]

    Bhutan Ministry of Information and Communications [Vol 2: 1712]

    Catholic Press Association [Vol 1: 7110]

    Communication Agencies Association of New Zealand [Vol 2: 4882]

    Foreign Press Association in London [Vol 2: 7700]

    International Association Emergency Managers [Vol 1: 9511]

    Latin American Studies Association [Vol 1: 10749]

    Plain English Campaign [Vol 2: 8480]

    Sigma Theta Tau International [Vol 1: 14900]

Media Awards Competition [Vol. 1: 16745]

Media Awards for Journalists [Vol. 1: 4546]

Media Citation [Vol. 1: 10588]

Media Eclipse Awards [Vol. 1: 16494]

Media Excellence Award [Vol. 1: 14656]

Media Festival Awards [Vol. 1: 8855]

Media-Field Award [Vol. 1: 4945]

MedIA-MICCAI Prizes [Vol. 1: 11058]

Media of the Year Award [Vol. 1: 10305]

Media Orthopaedic Reporting Excellence Awards MORE [Vol. 1: 638]

Media Peace Awards [Vol. 2: 1093]

Media Person of the Year Award [Vol. 1: 455]

Media Save Art Award [Vol. 2: 4089]

Median Iris Awards [Vol. 1: 11044]

Medical and Dental Postgraduate Research Scholarships [Vol. 2: 893]

Medical and Veterinary Entomology Journal Award [Vol. 2: 8774]

Medical Book Awards

    American Medical Writers Association [Vol. 1: 2881]

    Society of Authors - England [Vol 2: 9255]

Medical Book Prizes [Vol. 2: 9255]

Medical Executive Award [Vol. 1: 1772]

Medical Logistics Award [Vol. 1: 5430]

Medical Practice Executive of the Year Award [Vol. 1: 1771]

Medical Prize [Vol. 2: 6265]

Medical Rural Bonded Scholarship [Vol. 2: 269]

Medical Scholars Award [Vol. 1: 2019]

Medical Student Elective Grant [Vol. 2: 8302]

Medical Student Elective Prize [Vol. 2: 9119]

Medical Student Essay Award [Vol. 1: 6294]

Medical Student Essay Prize in Addictions Psychiatry [Vol. 2: 8725]

Medical Student Essay Prize in Child and Adolescent Mental Health [Vol. 2: 8726]

Medical Student Essay Prize in Forensic Psychiatry [Vol. 2: 8727]

Medical Student Essay Prize in General and Community Psychiatry [Vol. 2: 8728]

Medical Student Essay Prize in Liaison Psychiatry [Vol. 2: 8729]

Medical Student Excellence in Emergency Medicine Award [Vol. 1: 15008]

Medical Student Humanitarian Award [Vol. 1: 13935]

Medical Student Prize [Vol. 2: 4244]

Medical Technologist of the Year [Vol. 1: 3796]

MedicarePlus Procedural Training Grants [Vol. 2: 270]

Medienpreis fur Sprachkultur [Vol. 2: 2961]

Medieval Archaeology Research Grant [Vol. 2: 9203]

Medina Award; Jose Toribio [Vol. 1: 14841]

Medlicott Medal; Norton [Vol. 2: 7794]

Medola Medal and Prize [Vol. 2: 9013]

Medwick Memorial Award; Lucille [Vol. 1: 14065]

Meek Award; Howard B. [Vol. 1: 9848]

Meeker Award [Vol. 1: 17085]

Meeks Award for Deputy Sheriff of the Year; Charles "Bud" [Vol. 1: 12840]

Mees Medal; C. E .K. [Vol. 1: 13616]

Megariotis Award; Nicholas J. [Vol. 1: 17664]

Meggers Award; William F. [Vol. 1: 13617]

Meggers Project Award; William F. and Edith R. [Vol. 1: 2689]

Mehlman Award; Constance L. [Vol. 1: 10320]

Mehr Award; Robert I. [Vol. 1: 3702]

Mehrotra Commemorative Lecture; Prof. R. C. [Vol. 2: 3717]

Mehta and Manoranjan Mitra Award; K.C. [Vol. 2: 3695]

Mehta Award; Dr. Janak H. [Vol. 2: 3512]

Meiklejohn Award for Academic Freedom; Alexander [Vol. 1: 1389]

Meinzer Award; O. E. [Vol. 1: 8565]

Meiselman Memorial Award for Painting; Leonard J. [Vol. 1: 527]

Meiselman Memorial Award for Realistic Painting; Leonard J. [Vol. 1: 15471]

Meiselman Memorial Award for Realistic Sculpture; Leonard J. [Vol. 1: 15472]

Meiselman Memorial Award for Sculpture; Leonard J. [Vol. 1: 528]

Meitner Prize; Lise [Vol. 2: 2394]

Mejia Award; Manuel [Vol. 2: 1847]

Melbourne Award for Excellence in the Advancement of Automotive Sheet Steel; SAE/AISI Sydney H. [Vol. 1: 15524]

Melcher Scholarships; Frederic G. [Vol. 1: 5066]

Melchers Memorial Medal; Gari [Vol. 1: 4821]

Melchett Medal [Vol. 2: 7549]

Melezin Fellowship; Abraham and Rachela [Vol. 1: 18184]

Melick Young Investigator Award; Roger [Vol. 2: 207]

Melies Award; Georges [Vol. 1: 17610]

Mellon Environmental Stewardship Award; Richard Beatty [Vol. 1: 238]

Mellon Fellowships; [Vol. 1: 7709]

Mellon Post-Dissertation Fellowship [Vol. 1: 833]

Mellon Research Fellowship [Vol. 2: 4170]

Mellor Award; Samuel [Vol. 1: 12704]

Mellow Prize; Ila and John [Vol. 1: 15347]

Mel'nikov Prize; N.V. [Vol. 2: 5835]

Meltas Award for Enhancing Our Knowledge of the History of Clinical Chemistry; Sam [Vol. 1: 911]

Melton Award [Vol. 2: 7213]

Melton Early Achievement Award; Arthur W. [Vol. 1: 3529]

Melville Medal [Vol. 1: 4408]

Member Association Award for Contributions to Sexual and Reproductive Health and Rights [Vol. 2: 8163]

Member Association Director Award [Vol. 1: 11621]

Member Association Safety Program Awards [Vol. 1: 17713]

Member Award [Vol. 1: 12547]

Member of Honour [Vol. 1: 11087]

Member of Logohu [Vol. 2: 5215]

Member of Note [Vol. 1: 14011]

Member of Technical Distinction Award [Vol. 1: 16337]

Member of the Year

   American Feed Industry Association [Vol. 1: 2133]

   Caucus for Television Producers, Writers, and Directors [Vol 1: 7122]

   National Association of Women Business Owners [Vol 1: 11939]

   National Therapeutic Recreation Society [Vol 1: 12981]

   Ottawa Field-Naturalists' Club [Vol 1: 13726]

   Parachute Industry Association [Vol 1: 13837]

Print Services and Distribution Association [Vol 1: 14162]

   Society of Cable Telecommunications Engineers [Vol 1: 15578]

   Waste Equipment Technology Association [Vol 1: 17693]

   Women's Transportation Seminar [Vol 1: 17994]

Member of the Year Award

   ACA International [Vol. 1: 43]

   American Probation and Parole Association [Vol 1: 3338]

   American Shore and Beach Preservation Association [Vol 1: 3743]

   American Society of Certified Engineering Technicians [Vol 1: 4142]

   Dance Masters of America [Vol 1: 7811]

   International Association of Assessing Officers [Vol 1: 9614]

   Malaysian Association of Professional Secretaries and Administrators [Vol 2: 4545]

   National Weather Association [Vol 1: 13033]

   Theatre Historical Society of America [Vol 1: 16478]

Member of the Year - Regional [Vol. 1: 6061]

Member Organization of the Year [Vol. 1: 17132]

Member Recognition Award [Vol. 1: 169]

Member Scholarship [Vol. 1: 17983]

Member-to-Member Business Award [Vol. 1: 7750]

Member Travel Fellowship [Vol. 2: 3805]

Member's Award [Vol. 2: 8904]

Members Award [Vol. 1: 6614]

Members Choice Award [Vol. 1: 9963]

Members' Writing Awards [Vol. 2: 7076]

Membership Achievement Awards [Vol. 1: 1587]

Membership Award

   Alliance of the American Dental Association [Vol. 1: 390]

   American Institute of Aeronautics and Astronautics [Vol 1: 2533]

Membership Award [Vol. 2: 6433]

Membership Bell [Vol. 1: 14688]

Membership in Omicron Kappa Upsilon [Vol. 1: 13521]

Membership of the City and Guilds of London Institute [Vol. 2: 7434]

Membership Recognition [Vol. 1: 5237]

Membres Honoraires a Vie [Vol. 1: 6775]

Memorial Awards for Deceased Continuing Higher Education Professionals [Vol. 1: 17388]

Memorial Awards for Literature [Vol. 2: 5350]

Memorial Fellowship Award [Vol. 1: 6487]

Memorial Hall of Fame Award [Vol. 1: 2712]

Memorial Lecturer Award and Honoree [Vol. 1: 2939]

Memorial NAMA Fellowship [Vol. 1: 11328]

Memorial Scholarship [Vol. 1: 17801]

Mendel Medal [Vol. 2: 3123]

Mendel Memorial Award in Strings and Trophy; Fred S. [Vol. 1: 14749]

Mendel Memorial Senior Violin Scholarship and Trophy; Mrs. Clare K. [Vol. 1: 14750]

Mendel; Prix Gustave [Vol. 2: 2165]

Mendelson Memorial Awards; Robin H. [Vol. 1: 3792]

Mendes Award; Chico [Vol. 1: 14873]

Menefee Honorary Life Membership Award; Jim [Vol. 1: 13357]

Menezes International Prize; Mutiso [Vol. 2: 4416]

Menger Memorial Awards; Karl [Vol. 1: 2834]

Menninger Memorial Award; William C. [Vol. 1: 1802]

Menon Best Poster Paper Award; K.P.V. [Vol. 2: 3696]

Men's Garden Clubs of America Scholarship; Gardeners of America/ [Vol. 1: 8520]

Mensa International Competitions [Vol. 2: 8348]

Mensforth International Manufacturing Gold Medal; Sir Eric [Vol. 2: 8027]

Mental Health Counselor of the Year [Vol. 1: 2892]

Mental Health in the Workplace Award [Vol. 1: 6692]

Mental Health Matters Awards [Vol. 2: 875]

Mental Health Media Awards

   Mental Health America [Vol. 1: 11102]

   Mind - National Association for Mental Health [Vol 2: 8353]

Mention in Dispatches [Vol. 1: 8752]

Mentkowski Sports Law Alumnus of the Year Award; Charles W. [Vol. 1: 10987]

Mentor Award

   American Association for the Advancement of Science [Vol. 1: 992]

   American Psychological Association - Adult Development and Aging Division (Division 20)- [Vol 1: 3373]

Mentor Award in Developmental Psychology [Vol. 1: 3410]

Mentor-Based Minority Postdoctoral Fellowship [Vol. 1: 2025]

Mentor-Based Postdoctoral Fellowships [Vol. 1: 2026]

Mentor of the Year Award [Vol. 1: 12877]

Mentoring Award

   American Association of Critical-Care Nurses [Vol. 1: 1125]

   American Contact Dermatitis Society [Vol 1: 1877]

   International Association for Relationship Research [Vol 1: 9585]

   Middle East Studies Association of North America [Vol 1: 11144]

   Sociologists for Women in Society [Vol 1: 15915]

Mentorship Awards in Aging [Vol. 1: 3373]

Mentorship Grants [Vol. 1: 13309]

Mentzer; Prix Charles [Vol. 2: 2621]

Menzel Award; Margaret [Vol. 1: 5939]

Menzies Bursary Award; Donald [Vol. 1: 6269]

Mer de l'Ifremer; Prix des Sciences de la [Vol. 2: 2219]

Mercer Award; George [Vol. 1: 7989]

Mercer Award; Johnny [Vol. 1: 11412]

Mercer Footage Researcher of the Year; Jane [Vol. 2: 7672]

Mercer Joint Prize; Thomas T. [Vol. 1: 863]

Merchant Manufacturing Medal of ASME/SME; M. Eugene [Vol. 1: 4409]

Mercia Prize [Vol. 2: 7555]

Merck Award

   Royal Society of Chemistry [Vol. 2: 9031]

   Society of Medical Laboratory Technologists of South Africa [Vol 2: 5621]

Merck Award for Achievement in Poultry Science [Vol. 1: 14111]

Merck Ehrung; Johann-Heinrich- [Vol. 2: 3240]

Merck Frosst Canada Inc. Postgraduate Pharmacy Fellowship Award [Vol. 1: 5334]

Merck Frosst Centre for Therapeutic Research Lecture Award [Vol. 1: 6893]

Merck Frosst Fellowship in Clinical Pharmacology [Vol. 1: 6986]

Merck Frosst Prize [Vol. 1: 6937]

Merck KGaA Prize [Vol. 2: 2867]

Merck Medal [Vol. 2: 5677]

Merck Preis; Johann Heinrich [Vol. 2: 2899]

Merck-Serono Award [Vol. 2: 2866]

Merck-Serono Prize [Vol. 2: 2867]

Merck Sharp & Dohme Lecture Award [Vol. 1: 6893]

Merck US Human Health Migraine and Women's Health Research Award; AHS/ [Vol. 1: 2285]

Mercure Awards; Pierre [Vol. 1: 14984]

Mercurio Award [Vol. 2: 42]

Mercury Awards [Vol. 1: 17146]

Merial Excellence in Preventive Medicine in Beef Award [Vol. 1: 1076]

Merial Excellence in Preventive Medicine in Dairy Award [Vol. 1: 1077]

Meriam/Wiley Distinguished Author Award [Vol. 1: 3865]

Merit Award

   American Forage and Grassland Council [Vol. 1: 2174]

   American Society for Enology and Viticulture [Vol 1: 3900]

   Canadian Athletic Therapists Association [Vol 1: 6320]

   Canadian Nautical Research Society [Vol 1: 6737]

   Decalogue Society of Lawyers [Vol 1: 7828]

   Indiana Library Federation [Vol 1: 9199]

   Institute for Landscape Architecture in South Africa [Vol 2: 5565]

   Interior Design Educators Council [Vol 1: 9475]

   International Commission of Agricultural Engineering [Vol 2: 4241]

   Korean Chemical Society [Vol 2: 5461]

National Association of Hospital Fire Officers [Vol 2: 8383]

Society of Cosmetic Chemists [Vol 1: 15600]

Society of Toxicology [Vol 1: 15853]

Society of Wetland Scientists [Vol 1: 15887]

Soil and Water Conservation Society [Vol 1: 15925]

Merit Award for Distinguished Service as a Public Library Trustee [Vol. 1: 6680]

Merit Awards

Association of National Olympic Committees [Vol. 2: 6256]

Botanical Society of America [Vol 1: 5940]

International Accordionists Confederation [Vol 2: 2116]

Portland State University - Institute on Aging [Vol 1: 14096]

Merit Awards for Travel [Vol. 1: 15386]

Merit of Breeding Award [Vol. 1: 2047]

Merit Prize for Development [Vol. 2: 6405]

Merit Scholarships for Hospitality Students [Vol. 2: 5039]

Merit Scholarships for Secondary School Students [Vol. 2: 5040]

Meritorious Accountant of the Americas [Vol. 1: 9455]

Meritorious Achievement Award

American Conference of Governmental Industrial Hygienists [Vol. 1: 1858]

American Industrial Hygiene Association [Vol 1: 2490]

Lewis and Clark Trail Heritage Foundation [Vol 1: 10819]

Meritorious Award

Alpha Zeta Omega [Vol. 1: 414]

Awana Clubs International [Vol 1: 5745]

South African Association of Competitive Intelligence Professionals [Vol 2: 5665]

Strategic and Competitive Intelligence Professionals [Vol 1: 16300]

Meritorious Medal [Vol. 2: 2669]

Meritorious Prize for Scientific Achievement [Vol. 2: 4253]

Meritorious Service Award

American Rental Association [Vol. 1: 3686]

American Society of Echocardiography [Vol 1: 4289]

International Morab Registry [Vol 1: 10018]

Meritorious Service Award

Alpha Omega International Dental Fraternity [Vol. 1: 406]

American Baseball Coaches Association [Vol 1: 1481]

American Fisheries Society [Vol 1: 2149]

American Horticultural Society [Vol 1: 2431]

American Mosquito Control Association [Vol 1: 2940]

American National Standards Institute [Vol 1: 2973]

American Occupational Therapy Foundation [Vol 1: 3043]

Australian Veterinary Association [Vol 2: 602]

Badminton World Federation [Vol 2: 4534]

Government of the Commonwealth of Dominica - Information and Communication Technology Unit [Vol 2: 2001]

Illuminating Engineering Society of North America [Vol 1: 9160]

Iowa Horse Council [Vol 1: 10510]

LeadingAge [Vol 1: 10775]

National Association for Interpretation [Vol 1: 11588]

National Christian College Athletic Association [Vol 1: 12065]

National Council of Examiners for Engineering and Surveying [Vol 1: 12184]

National Guard Association of the United States [Vol 1: 12480]

National Therapeutic Recreation Society [Vol 1: 12982]

Nebraska Library Association [Vol 1: 13140]

Occupational and Environmental Medical Association of Canada [Vol 1: 13466]

Royal Australasian College of Dental Surgeons [Vol 2: 957]

Royal Australian and New Zealand College of Ophthalmologists [Vol 2: 964]

Society of Nematologists [Vol 1: 15725]

Meritorious Service Award for Community Service [Vol. 1: 8128]

Meritorious Service Award for Professional Service [Vol. 1: 8129]

Meritorious Service Awards [Vol. 1: 3120]

Meritorious Service Certificate [Vol. 1: 12481]

Meritorious Service Cross - Civil Division [Vol. 1: 8753]

Meritorious Service Cross - Military Division [Vol. 1: 8754]

Meritorious Service in Communication Award [Vol. 1: 4299]

Meritorious Service Medal

Botswana Ministry of Education - Teaching Service Management Unit [Vol. 2: 1734]

National Society, Sons of the American Revolution [Vol 1: 12908]

United States Air Force - Defense Logistics Agency [Vol 1: 16680]

Meritorious Service Medal - Civil Division [Vol. 1: 8755]

Meritorious Service Medal - Military Division [Vol. 1: 8756]

Meritorious Services Medal [Vol. 2: 7832]

Meritorious Unit Citation [Vol. 2: 322]

Merlin Medal [Vol. 2: 6977]

Merriam Award; C. Hart [Vol. 1: 4377]

Merriam Award; Charles [Vol. 1: 3309]

Merrill Nordic Award; Al [Vol. 1: 17086]

Merriman Award; Wayne [Vol. 1: 13785]

Merritt Service Award; Emma [Vol. 1: 14586]

Merryfield Design Award; Fred [Vol. 1: 3866]

Mertz Trophy; Allegra Knapp [Vol. 1: 17058]

Mervyn Stutter's Spirit of the Fringe Awards [Vol. 2: 7534]

Merwin Distinguished Service Award; Richard E. [Vol. 1: 9065]

MESBEC Scholarships [Vol. 1: 7094]

Messick Award for Distinguished Scientific Contributions; Samuel J. [Vol. 1: 3419]

Metal Mining Division Award [Vol. 1: 6615]

Metal Mining Society Award [Vol. 1: 6615]

Metallurgist of the Year Award [Vol. 2: 3600]

Metalor Technologies Graduate Student Award [Vol. 1: 10060]

Metcalf Exemplary Dissertation Award; Larry [Vol. 1: 12171]

Metchnikoff Prize; Elie [Vol. 2: 1533]

Metras Trophy; J. P. [Vol. 1: 6648]

Metro Awards [Vol. 1: 17821]

Metro New York Chapter Student Award [Vol. 1: 10060]

Metropolitan Award [Vol. 1: 11643]

Metso Paper Mechanical Pulping Award [Vol. 2: 2097]

Mettler Award for Leadership in Health Promotion; Molly [Vol. 1: 12235]

Mewaldt-King Student Research Award [Vol. 1: 7596]

Meyer Lectureship; Adolf [Vol. 1: 3357]

Meyer Medaille; Hans [Vol. 2: 2880]

Meyer Medal for Excellence in Student Design; Ray [Vol. 1: 4913]

Meyer Medal for Plant Genetic Resources; Frank N. [Vol. 1: 7766]

Meyer Outstanding Teacher Awards; Agnes [Vol. 1: 17676]

Meyer Prize; Carl S. [Vol. 1: 14919]

Meyer Prize; Ernst [Vol. 2: 6354]

Meyer-Schutzmeister Award; Luise [Vol. 1: 5174]

Meyer-Whitworth Award [Vol. 2: 8487]

Meyers Award; John F. [Vol. 1: 12048]

Mezinarodni hudebni soutez Prazske jaro [Vol. 2: 1928]

Mezinarodni Rozhlasova Soutez Mladych Hudebniku Concertino Praha [Vol. 2: 1930]

Mhatre Gold Medal; Baburao [Vol. 2: 3584]

MIA Prize [Vol. 2: 9100]

Michaels Memorial Film Award; John [Vol. 1: 5837]

Michel Award for Industry Advancement of Research; Henry L. [Vol. 1: 4205]

Michel Special Project Grants; Robert H. [Vol. 1: 7891]

Michelbacher Prize [Vol. 1: 7082]

Michell Medal; A. G. M. [Vol. 2: 792]

Michell Medal; J.H. [Vol. 2: 213]

Michels New Investigator Award; Eugene [Vol. 1: 3238]

Michelson Award; A.A. [Vol. 1: 7464]

Michener Award [Vol. 1: 11118]

Michener Conservation Award; Roland

Canadian Wildlife Federation [Vol. 1: 7041]

Canadian Wildlife Federation [Vol 1: 7044]

Michener-Deacon Fellowship [Vol. 1: 11119]

Michigan Industrial Hygiene Society Award [Vol. 1: 2491]

Mickle Award; D. Grant [Vol. 1: 16538]

Micro-Enterprise Award [Vol. 2: 4563]

Microcirculation Conference Grant [Vol. 2: 7134]

Microcomputer in the Media Center Award [Vol. 1: 1344]

Microscopy Award [Vol. 2: 7141]

Mid-Career Award

American Council on Consumer Interests [Vol. 1: 1918]

Experimental Psychology Society [Vol 2: 7661]

Mid-Career Medal [Vol. 2: 1735]

Mid-Career Research and Mentorship Award [Vol. 1: 15670]

Mid-Career Writers Award [Vol. 2: 5013]

Midalja ghall-Qadi tar-Repubblika [Vol. 2: 4573]

Midalja ghall-Qlubija [Vol. 2: 4572]

MidAmerica Award [Vol. 1: 15377]

Midda Fellowship; Marsh [Vol. 2: 7261]

Middle Atlantic Section Distinguished Teaching Award [Vol. 1: 3867]

Middle East and Indian Subcontinent Awards [Vol. 2: 8323]

Middle East and Indian Subcontinent Awards; Seatrade [Vol. 2: 9179]

Middlebrooks Award; Thomas A. [Vol. 1: 4206]

Middleton Award; William S. [Vol. 1: 16868]

MIDEM Classical Awards [Vol. 2: 1295]

Midwestern Studies Book Award [Vol. 1: 15378]

Miedzynarodowy Konkurs Kompozytorski im-Witolda Lutoslawskiego [Vol. 2: 5415]

Migel Medal [Vol. 1: 2191]

Migliore Award for Lifetime Achievement [Vol. 1: 10937]

Mignault Award; Jean de [Vol. 1: 6014]

Miklukho-Maklai Prize; N.N. [Vol. 2: 5836]

Milankovic Medal; Milutin [Vol. 2: 2374]

Milazzo Prize; Giulio [Vol. 2: 2329]

Milch Award for Palliative Pain and Symptoms Management; Robert A. [Vol. 1: 7242]

Mildenberger Outstanding NESDA Officer Award; Richard [Vol. 1: 12306]

Mildenberger Prize; Kenneth W. [Vol. 1: 11234]

Mildenhall Award; John and Petakin [Vol. 2: 5746]

Mildon Award; James R. [Vol. 1: 9323]

Mileage Awards [Vol. 1: 10019]

Miles Distinguished Service Award; Margaret S. [Vol. 1: 15747]

Miles - Marschall International Award [Vol. 1: 1972]

Milestone Awards [Vol. 1: 8941]

Military Astronautics Award [Vol. 1: 1439]

Military Courage Medal [Vol. 2: 2679]

Military Cross [Vol. 2: 7343]

Military Honor Medal [Vol. 2: 2680]

Military Merit Medal [Vol. 2: 5702]

Military Photographer of the Year [Vol. 1: 12705]

Military William Order [Vol. 2: 4649]

Milk Industry Foundation and Kraft Foods Teaching Award in Dairy Science [Vol. 1: 1982]

Milk Production Awards [Vol. 1: 2259]

Mill Manager of the Year [Vol. 1: 13830]

Millar Award for Innovative Approaches to Adolescent Health Care [Vol. 1: 15014]

Millar Award; Preston S. [Vol. 1: 1902]

Millennium Awards [Vol. 1: 8672]

Miller Award; Carroll R. [Vol. 1: 12673]

Miller Award; Douglas [Vol. 1: 6335]

Miller Award; Elizabeth McWilliams [Vol. 1: 14898]

Miller Award for Early Career Achievement; Gerald R. [Vol. 1: 9586]

Miller Award for Innovation in Protected Areas Management; Kenton R. [Vol. 2: 6536]

Miller Award for Young Adult Literature; Peggy [Vol. 1: 7250]

Miller Award; George A. [Vol. 1: 3522]

Miller Award in Geography; E. Willard and Ruby S. [Vol. 1: 5206]

Miller Award in Safety/Loss Prevention; Norton H. Walton/Russell L. [Vol. 1: 2642]

Miller Award; Merl K. [Vol. 1: 3868]

Miller Award; Russell R. [Vol. 1: 1726]

Miller Award; Samuel Charles [Vol. 1: 635]

Miller Awards; Cheryl Allyn [Vol. 1: 15916]

Miller Awards; Saul

AFL-CIO l International Labor Communications Association [Vol. 1: 196]

AFL-CIO l International Labor Communications Association [Vol 1: 197]

Miller Chapter Service Awards; Susan E. [Vol. 1: 14874]

Miller International Award; S. Ray [Vol. 1: 9659]

Miller ISCD Service Award; Dr. Paul D. [Vol. 1: 10149]

Miller Lite Women's Sports Journalism Awards [Vol. 1: 17992]

Miller Medal; Osborn Maitland [Vol. 1: 2216]

Miller Medal; Willet G. [Vol. 1: 14644]

Miller Memorial Award; Barse [Vol. 1: 4664]

Miller Memorial Medal Award; Samuel Wylie [Vol. 1: 4685]

Miller Prize; Zvi [Vol. 2: 1536]

Miller Research Award; Loye and Alden [Vol. 1: 7597]

Miller Ruppe Award for Outstanding Community Service; Loret [Vol. 1: 12668]

Miller Young Writers Award; Isabel [Vol. 1: 18112]

Milli Award [Vol. 2: 257]

Milligan Award for Effective Committee Management; Gene [Vol. 1: 9795]

Milligan Trophy and Prize; Spike [Vol. 2: 8730]

Millikan Medal; Robert A. [Vol. 1: 1310]

Million Dollar Hall of Fame [Vol. 1: 13015]

Million Miler Safety Award [Vol. 1: 16123]

Million Miler Safety Awards [Vol. 1: 16126]

Millot; Prix et medaille Georges [Vol. 2: 2220]

Mills Award; C. Wright [Vol. 1: 15393]

Mills Award for Meritorious Service [Vol. 1: 1746]

Mills Award; Harlan D. [Vol. 1: 9066]

Mills Outstanding Contribution to Emergency Medicine Award; James D. [Vol. 1: 1746]

Millson Award for Invention; Henry E. [Vol. 1: 1381]

Milne Memorial Award; Jack [Vol. 1: 454]

Milner Award; Brenda A. [Vol. 1: 3401]

Milstein Award; Seymour and Vivian [Vol. 1: 10173]

Milstein Travel Awards; Seymour and Vivian [Vol. 1: 10174]

Milstein Young Investigator Awards; Seymour and Vivian [Vol. 1: 10175]

Minah Distinguished Service Award; Theodore W. [Vol. 1: 11693]

Minasian Award; George T. [Vol. 1: 239]

Mindlin Award; Raymond D. [Vol. 1: 4207]

Mine Safety Awards [Vol. 1: 14574]

Miner Award; Neil A. [Vol. 1: 11773]

Mineral Economics Award [Vol. 1: 2678]

Mineral Education Awards [Vol. 1: 10491]

Mineral Industry Education Award [Vol. 1: 2679]

Mineralogical Society of America Award [Vol. 1: 11175]

Minerva Medal [Vol. 2: 7419]

Minerva Service Award [Vol. 2: 7420]

Mini-Grants for Special Projects [Vol. 1: 4941]

Mining Analyst of the Year [Vol. 2: 6832]

Mining and Exploration Division Distinguished Service Award [Vol. 1: 15214]

Mining and Exploration Outstanding Young Professional Award [Vol. 1: 15215]

Ministere des Affaires etrangeres et du Commerce International [Vol. 1: 8416]

Minister's Award [Vol. 2: 1679]

Minister's Award for Consular Excellence [Vol. 1: 8417]

Minister's Award for Foreign Policy Excellence [Vol. 1: 8418]

Minister's Certificate of Merit [Vol. 2: 1881]

Ministry/Department of the Year [Vol. 2: 1682]

Ministry of Agriculture Award [Vol. 2: 3351]

Ministry of Agriculture Award for Soil Science [Vol. 2: 3352]

Ministry of Industry, Investment and Commerce Award for Competitiveness [Vol. 2: 4188]

Ministry of Transport Award for Best Student Research [Vol. 2: 4944]

Minkowski Prize [Vol. 2: 2800]

Minks Award; Nancy [Vol. 1: 2454]

Minority Fellowships [Vol. 1: 968]

Minority Initiatives Award [Vol. 1: 3239]

Minority Recruitment and Retention Award [Vol. 1: 16045]

Minority Scholarships Program for Residents and Medical Students [Vol. 1: 559]

Minority Travel Fellowship Awards [Vol. 1: 3259]

Minshall Award; Lewis [Vol. 2: 7691]

Minter Award; Jerry B. [Vol. 1: 14405]

Mintrop Award; Ludger [Vol. 2: 4681]

Minute Award [Vol. 1: 12358]

Minuteman Award [Vol. 1: 12909]

Minville; Prix Edras- [Vol. 1: 15001]

Mirbeau et Valentine Allorge; Prix Octave [Vol. 2: 2221]

Mishima Medal [Vol. 2: 4254]

Misra Lifetime Achievement Award; A.P. [Vol. 2: 3697]

Miss America [Vol. 1: 11210]

Miss America Women of Achievement Award [Vol. 1: 11211]

Miss Bhutan [Vol. 2: 1716]

Miss Tall International [Vol. 1: 16360]

Miss Teen USA [Vol. 1: 11213]

Miss Universe [Vol. 1: 11214]

Miss USA [Vol. 1: 11215]

Missile Systems Awards [Vol. 1: 2534]

Mission Accomplished Creative Commercial Production Awards [Vol. 1: 6074]

Mission Support Trophy [Vol. 1: 12482]

Mississippi-Alabama Sea Grant Consortium Grants [Vol. 1: 11217]

Mississippi Poetry Society Award [Vol. 1: 12359]

Missouri Honor Medal [Vol. 1: 17294]

Missouri Lifestyle Journalism Award [Vol. 1: 17295]

Missouri State Poetry Society Award [Vol. 1: 12360]

Mistral Award; Gabriela [Vol. 1: 13694]

Misumi Award [Vol. 2: 5323]

Mita Society for Library and Information Science Prize [Vol. 2: 4299]

Mita Toshokan Joho Gakkai-Sho [Vol. 2: 4299]

Mitchell Award [Vol. 2: 8561]

Mitchell Award; Charles L. [Vol. 1: 2913]

Mitchell Award for C4 Excellence; General Billy [Vol. 1: 259]

Mitchell Award; Gen. Billy [Vol. 1: 259]

Mitchell Award; H. L. [Vol. 1: 16024]

Mitchell Award; S. Weir [Vol. 1: 589]

Mitchell Book Prize; City of Calgary/W.O. [Vol. 1: 18110]

Mitchell Bowl MVP Award [Vol. 1: 6649]

Mitchell Medal; Sydney B. [Vol. 1: 11044]

Mitchell Memorial Intermediate Cello/Viola/Double Bass Scholarship; Johanna [Vol. 1: 14751]

Mitchell Memorial Intermediate Violin Scholarship and Trophy; Robert C. [Vol. 1: 14752]

Mitchell Memorial Trophy; Mark [Vol. 2: 4997]

Mitchell Prize for Research in Early British Serials; William L. [Vol. 1: 5829]

Mitchell Trophy; Avril and Allan [Vol. 2: 7111]

Mitchell Trophy; Doug [Vol. 1: 6636]

Mitchell Young Extension Worker Award; Nolan [Vol. 1: 4089]

Mitofsky Innovators Award; Warren J. [Vol. 1: 975]

Mitra Memorial Award; Prof. S.N. [Vol. 2: 3755]

Mitra Memorial Lecture; Sisir Kumar [Vol. 2: 3645]

Mitsubishi Asian Children's Enikki Festa [Vol. 2: 4301]

Mittasch Medal; Alwin [Vol. 2: 3169]

Mittelstadt Ski Jumping Officials Award [Vol. 1: 17087]

Mittlemann Achievement Award; Dr. Ing. Eugene [Vol. 1: 9100]

Mixon First Prize [Vol. 1: 7324]

Mizel Memorial Exhibit Award; Menachem Chaim and Simcha Tova [Vol. 1: 2999]

MLA Scholarship [Vol. 1: 11072]

MLM Company of the Year [Vol. 1: 11294]

MobiCom Best Student Paper Award [Vol. 1: 16090]

Mobile Ambassador Award [Vol. 1: 10875]

Mobile Awards [Vol. 1: 17731]

Mobile Devices Awards [Vol. 2: 5428]

Mobile Excellence Awards [Vol. 1: 10875]

Mobile Innovation Grand Prix [Vol. 1: 8794]

Mobile Technology Project Award [Vol. 2: 7016]

Moch Lifetime Achievement Award; Frank J. [Vol. 1: 12306]

Model Chapter Awards [Vol. 1: 14293]

Model Shareholder of the Year Award [Vol. 2: 5967]

Modeling and Simulation Hall of Fame [Vol. 1: 15232]

Modisette Award; James O. [Vol. 1: 10893]

Mody Unichem Prize; Amrut [Vol. 2: 3553]

Moe Prize in the Humanities; Henry Allen [Vol. 1: 3190]

Moffat - Frank E. Nichol Harbor and Coastal Engineering Award; John G. [Vol. 1: 4208]

Moffat Memorial Trophy; Harry [Vol. 2: 7112]

Moffatt Award; Gordon [Vol. 2: 1174]

Moffett Award; CEE James [Vol. 1: 12212]

Moffett Memorial Teaching Excellence Award; Mary Margaret [Vol. 1: 3557]

Moffitt Human Rights Awards; Letelier - [Vol. 1: 9269]

Moggridge Trophy; Jackie [Vol. 2: 7310]

Mohamed Prize; Ibrahim Ahmed [Vol. 2: 2029]

Mohan Marwah Award; Prof. Surindar [Vol. 2: 3554]

Mohawk-Hudson Region Art Exhibition Award [Vol. 1: 14774]

Mohr Medal; William

Aril Society International [Vol. 1: 4777]

Median Iris Society [Vol 1: 11044]

Moir Medal; James [Vol. 2: 5678]

Moisseiff Award [Vol. 1: 4209]

Moldovan Mentoring Award; Steve [Vol. 1: 2337]

Moletsane and Sets'abi Award [Vol. 2: 4461]

Molfenter-Preis der Landeshauptstadt Stuttgart/Galerie; Hans- [Vol. 2: 3193]

Molinari Memorial Scholarship; Antoinette [Vol. 1: 3058]

Moll Quality Management Award; Dale C. [Vol. 1: 7560]

Mollenhoff Award for Excellence in Investigative Reporting; Clark [Vol. 1: 8488]

Moller/AGO Award in Choral Competition [Vol. 1: 2265]

Molodovsky Award; Nicholas [Vol. 1: 7170]

Molotsky Award for Excellence in Coverage of Higher Education; Iris [Vol. 1: 1390]

Mols Award; Herbert Joseph [Vol. 1: 456]

Molson Prizes [Vol. 1: 6138]

Monaco Charity Film Festival [Vol. 2: 4607]

Monash Medal; John [Vol. 2: 793]

Moncado Prizes for Best Article [Vol. 1: 15198]

Moncrieff Prize; Scott [Vol. 2: 9256]

Mond Award; Ludwig [Vol. 2: 9032]

Mond Health and Safety Award [Vol. 2: 9290]

Mond Lectureship; Ludwig [Vol. 2: 9032]

Mondeal Prize [Vol. 2: 7590]

Mondial Bronze Medal [Vol. 1: 7522]

Mondial Silver Medal [Vol. 1: 7523]

Monette-Roger Horwitz Dissertation Prize; Paul [Vol. 1: 7140]

Monic Prize; Boleslaw [Vol. 2: 7412]

Monod; Prix Gabriel [Vol. 2: 2290]

Monograph Award [Vol. 2: 4787]

Monpetit; Prix Michel [Vol. 2: 2222]

Monroe Library Adult Services Award; Margaret E. [Vol. 1: 14468]

Monsanto Crop Science Distinguished Career Award [Vol. 1: 7767]

Monsen Award; Elaine [Vol. 1: 2040]

Montague Distinguished Resident Award in Radiation Oncology; Eleanor [Vol. 1: 1012]

Montaigne Prize [Vol. 2: 3204]

Montald; Prix Constant [Vol. 2: 1595]

Montana New Zealand Book Awards [Vol. 2: 4870]

Montgolfier Ballooning Diploma [Vol. 2: 6322]

Montgomery Distinguished Service Award; Reid H. [Vol. 1: 7371]

Montgomery Medal [Vol. 1: 12483]

Montgomery/PEI Literature for Children Award; Lucy Maud [Vol. 1: 14150]

Monthly Design Contest [Vol. 1: 2012]

Monti Award; Fernanda [Vol. 2: 4845]

Montreal International Festival of New Cinema and Video [Vol. 1: 11254]

Montreal Medal [Vol. 1: 7208]

Montreal World Film Festival [Vol. 1: 11258]

Monty Distinguished Service Award; Michael [Vol. 1: 6031]

Montyon de Physiologie; Prix [Vol. 2: 2223]

Mookerjee Memorial Award; Asutosh [Vol. 2: 3718]

Moonbeam Children's Book Awards [Vol. 1: 10552]

Mooney Distinguished Technology Award; Melvin [Vol. 1: 1657]

Moore Award [Vol. 1: 1229]

Moore Award for Outstanding New Academic Faculty Member; Margaret L. [Vol. 1: 3240]

Moore Award for Voluntary Service; Clarence H. [Vol. 1: 13817]

Moore Award; Gordon E. [Vol. 1: 15304]

Moore Award; Harry T. [Vol. 1: 10762]

Moore Award; Ray [Vol. 1: 13367]

Moore Award; Royal N. [Vol. 1: 10959]

Moore Jr. Award; Walter P. [Vol. 1: 4210]

Moore Jr. Faculty Achievement Award; Walter P. [Vol. 1: 1849]

Moore "Making a Difference" Awards; Pearl [Vol. 1: 13555]

Moore Medal for Paleontology; Raymond C. [Vol. 1: 15311]

Moore Medal; George [Vol. 2: 8824]

Moore Medal; Gordon E.
   Electrochemical Society [Vol. 1: 8061]
   Society of Chemical Industry [Vol 2: 9291]

Moore Medal; Leo B. [Vol. 1: 16249]

Moore Memorial Award in Biological Science; Barrington [Vol. 1: 15438]

Moore Memorial Award; Robert P. [Vol. 1: 11984]

Moore Prize; Glover [Vol. 1: 11221]

Moore Prize; Jane [Vol. 2: 6945]

Moore Prize; Virginia P. [Vol. 1: 6139]

Moore Research Article Prize; E.H. [Vol. 1: 2835]

Moore Superintendent of the Year; Brookshire [Vol. 1: 13831]

Moore Young Anatomist's Publication Award; Keith and Marion [Vol. 1: 1031]

Moortidevi Award [Vol. 2: 3455]

Moosa Lecture [Vol. 2: 5466]

Mor Kaposi Medal [Vol. 2: 3386]

Mora Award; Estela and Raul [Vol. 1: 14477]

Morab Award Programs [Vol. 1: 14360]

Morab Horse of the Year [Vol. 1: 10020]

Morab Horseman of the Year Award [Vol. 1: 14361]

Morales Latin American Bonsai Design Award; Pedro J. [Vol. 1: 5911]

Moran Medal [Vol. 2: 185]

Moran National Portrait Prize; Doug [Vol. 2: 877]

Moran Portraiture Prize; Douglas J. [Vol. 2: 877]

Morando Lifetime Achievement Award; Rocco V. [Vol. 1: 11765]

Mordecai Ben David Award [Vol. 1: 18175]

Mordica Memorial Award [Vol. 1: 17868]

Moreno Award; Premio Francisco P. [Vol. 2: 45]

Moreno; Premio Enrique Martinez [Vol. 2: 6106]

Morey Award; George W. [Vol. 1: 1568]

Morey Book Award; Charles Rufus [Vol. 1: 7359]

Morgan Award for Distinguished Service; Clifford T. [Vol. 1: 3402]

Morgan Award; Joseph F. [Vol. 1: 15111]

Morgan Award; Kathy Lee [Vol. 1: 12867]

Morgan Global Humanitarian Award; James C. [Vol. 1: 16398]

Morgan Individual Achievement Award; Frederick C. [Vol. 1: 8865]

Morgan Medal; Thomas Hunt [Vol. 1: 8551]

Morgan Memorial Scholarship; Thomas S. [Vol. 1: 13954]

Morgan Operational Solutions Medal; Philip F. [Vol. 1: 17714]

Morgan Prize for Outstanding Research in Mathematics by an Undergraduate Student; Frank and Brennie
   American Mathematical Society [Vol. 1: 2836]
   Society for Industrial and Applied Mathematics [Vol 1: 15121]

Morgan Research Award; Agnes Fay [Vol. 1: 10502]

Morgan-Wood Medal [Vol. 1: 11044]

Morgenthau Award; Hans J. [Vol. 1: 12108]

Morgenthau Memorial Award; Hans J. [Vol. 1: 12108]

Morgotch Award for Photography; Larry [Vol. 1: 13113]

Moricoli; Research Award in Honor of John C. [Vol. 1: 15789]

Morin; Prix Victor- [Vol. 1: 15002]

Morison Prize; Samuel Eliot [Vol. 1: 15199]

Morita Prize [Vol. 2: 6360]

Moritsugu Memorial Award; Donna Jones [Vol. 1: 3107]

Morlan Faculty Secretary Award; Robert L. [Vol. 1: 13516]

Morley Distinguished Service Award; Alfred C. [Vol. 1: 7171]

Morley Distinguished Service Award; Col. John [Vol. 1: 8716]

Morley-Montgomery Award [Vol. 1: 5764]

Morley Outstanding Programmer Award; Patsy [Vol. 1: 11560]

Morningstar Public Librarian Support Award [Vol. 1: 14469]

Moroccan-American Trade and Investment Award [Vol. 2: 4618]

Morphological Sciences Award [Vol. 1: 1032]

MORR Trophy [Vol. 2: 8961]

Morrell Memorial Award; David [Vol. 1: 16200]

Morrill Award for Outstanding Volunteer; Lisa [Vol. 1: 5893]

Morrill Award; Justin [Vol. 1: 15041]

Morris Art Award; Philip [Vol. 2: 7783]

Morris Award; Arthur J. [Vol. 1: 7573]

Morris Award; Charles [Vol. 1: 628]

Morris Award; Marcus [Vol. 2: 8515]

Morris Award; Old Tom [Vol. 1: 8717]

Morris Award; Robert [Vol. 1: 17739]

Morris Memorial Trophy; Ted [Vol. 1: 6650]

Morris Sustaining Member Award; J. W. [Vol. 1: 15454]

Morris YA Debut Award; William C. [Vol. 1: 18222]

Morrison & Foerster Regulatory Innovation Award [Vol. 1: 6054]

Morrison Award [Vol. 1: 4122]

Morrison Award; Frances [Vol. 1: 14720]

Morrison Communication Award; B.Y. [Vol. 1: 2432]

Morrison Communicator Award; Thomas [Vol. 1: 16851]

Morrison Guide Awards; Paul [Vol. 2: 9436]

Morrison Information Management Award; Thomas [Vol. 1: 16851]

Morrison Jr. Award; Major Gen. John E. [Vol. 1: 12607]

Morrison Trophy; W. A. [Vol. 2: 5055]

Morrow Award; Elizabeth Cutter [Vol. 1: 18212]

Morrow Public Outreach Award; Douglas S. [Vol. 1: 17111]

MORS Prize [Vol. 1: 11154]

Morse Lectureship Award; Philip McCord [Vol. 1: 9263]

Morse Medal; Samuel Finley Breese [Vol. 1: 2217]

Morse Outstanding Teaching/Extension Service/Regulatory Award; Roger A. [Vol. 1: 7972]

Morse Writer's Award; Robert T. [Vol. 1: 3358]

Morsey Award; David [Vol. 1: 9756]

Mortimer Memorial Sterling Silver Trophy; James [Vol. 1: 17790]

Morton Essay Prize; Oswald [Vol. 2: 9101]

MOSAID Technologies Award for Fiction [Vol. 1: 6326]

MOSAID Technologies Inc. Award for Fiction [Vol. 1: 6323]

Mosby Award; Henry S. [Vol. 1: 13042]

Moscicki Medal; Ignacy [Vol. 2: 5396]

Moseley Award; Harry G. [Vol. 1: 188]

Moseley Medal and Prize [Vol. 2: 7914]

Moser Memorial Trophy; Mike [Vol. 1: 6651]

Mosher and Frederick C. Mosher Award; William E. [Vol. 1: 4048]

Mosisili Memorial Award; Maile [Vol. 2: 4470]

Mosse Prize; George L. [Vol. 1: 2385]

Mossman Developmental Biologist Award; H. W. [Vol. 1: 1033]

Most Active Woman Award [Vol. 1: 11493]

Most Admired Bank [Vol. 2: 5927]

The Most Beautiful and the Best Children's Books in Slovakia [Vol. 2: 5996]

Most Beautiful Books of Austria (Staatspreis fur die Schonsten Bucher Osterreichs) [Vol. 2: 1245]

Most Distinguished Technical Paper Award [Vol. 1: 9892]

Most Honourable Order of the Bath [Vol. 2: 7344]

Most Improved Award
   Advancing Canadian Entrepreneurship [Vol. 1: 155]
   Pulp and Paper Safety Association [Vol 1: 14349]

Most Improved Awards [Vol. 1: 8037]

Most Improved Chapter Award [Vol. 1: 9081]

Most Improved Chapter of the Year [Vol. 1: 12000]

Most Improved Driver [Vol. 1: 16225]

Most Improved Driver Award [Vol. 1: 16736]

Most Improved Golfer Award [Vol. 1: 11514]

Most Improved Player Award
   National Basketball Association [Vol. 1: 11976]
   Sony Ericsson WTA Tour [Vol. 1: 15959]

Most Influential PLDI Paper Award [Vol. 1: 16095]

Most Influential POPL Paper Award [Vol. 1: 16096]

Most Innovative and Creative Plan Design [Vol. 1: 8670]

Most Innovative Game [Vol. 2: 2592]

Most Innovative Move Award [Vol. 1: 9713]

Most Outstanding Abstract Award [Vol. 1: 3772]

Most Outstanding Chapter President Award [Vol. 1: 10611]

Most Outstanding Female Administrator Award [Vol. 2: 283]

Most Outstanding Female Investigator Award [Vol. 2: 284]

Most Outstanding Female Leader Award [Vol. 2: 285]

Most Outstanding Female Practitioner Award [Vol. 2: 286]

Most Outstanding LOM Project Award [Vol. 1: 10612]

Most Outstanding Member Award [Vol. 1: 10613]

Most Outstanding NOM President [Vol. 1: 10614]

Most Outstanding Senator Award [Vol. 1: 10615]

Most Outstanding Trainer Award [Vol. 1: 10616]

Most Outstanding Volunteer [Vol. 2: 669]

Most Outstanding Wrestler [Vol. 1: 13067]

Most Realistic Tattoo [Vol. 1: 12964]

Most Supportive Business Advisory Board Member of the Year Award [Vol. 1: 156]

Most Supportive Dean or Department Chair of the Year Award [Vol. 1: 157]

Most Transparent Company Award [Vol. 2: 5968]

Most Valuable Player [Vol. 2: 6629]

Most Valuable Player Award
   Baseball Writers Association of America [Vol. 1: 5794]
   National Basketball Association [Vol 1: 11977]
   National Wheelchair Basketball Association [Vol 1: 13038]

Most Valuable Player in the Rose Bowl [Vol. 1: 16522]

Most Valuable Volunteer Award [Vol. 1: 7499]

Most Versatile Horse Award [Vol. 1: 7406]

Mostofi Distinguished Service Award; F. K. [Vol. 1: 16706]

Mostra Internazionale die Documentari Sui Parchi [Vol. 2: 4153]

Moten Award; Ollie B. [Vol. 1: 1699]

MOTESZ Award [Vol. 2: 3369]

Mother/Father of the Year Award [Vol. 1: 12614]

Mother of the Year [Vol. 1: 2944]

Mother of the Year Award [Vol. 2: 1782]

Motivator Award [Vol. 1: 17890]

Motley EMT of the Year Award; Robert E. [Vol. 1: 11756]

Motorcycle Safety Foundation Awards [Vol. 1: 11287]

Motorcycling Merit Diploma [Vol. 2: 6410]

Motsinger New Horizon Award; David L. [Vol. 1: 3316]

Mott Jr. Park Leadership Award; William Penn [Vol. 1: 12663]

Mott/Kappa Tau Alpha Research Award; Frank Luther [Vol. 1: 17296]

Mott Medal and Prize [Vol. 2: 7915]

Mott Scholarship; Gerald O. [Vol. 1: 7768]

Moulton Award; Bette [Vol. 1: 6541]

Moulton Medal [Vol. 2: 7968]

Moulton Medal; Junior [Vol. 2: 7969]

Mountbatten Medal [Vol. 2: 8028]

Mouravieff-Apostol Medal; Andrew [Vol. 2: 6380]

Movement Disorders Research Award [Vol. 1: 590]

Movies of the Year [Vol. 2: 2137]

Moye; Prix Marcel [Vol. 2: 2614]

Moynihan Award; Senator Daniel Patrick [Vol. 1: 5411]

Moynihan Cup; Laura [Vol. 1: 17162]

Moynihan Prize [Vol. 2: 6849]

MPD Outstanding Young Engineer Award [Vol. 1: 15216]

MPG Awards [Vol. 2: 8378]

Mrazik-Cleaver Canadian Picture Book Award; Elizabeth [Vol. 2: 6366]

MRS Medal [Vol. 1: 11005]

MSFC Faculty Mentor Award [Vol. 1: 11083]

MSFC Hats Off Fundraising Award [Vol. 1: 11084]

MSI Annual Doctoral Dissertation Proposal Award [Vol. 1: 10984]

The MTM:UK Musical Theatre Matters Awards [Vol. 2: 7535]

MTNA National Student Composition Contest [Vol. 1: 11326]

MTV Positive Change Award [Vol. 1: 10488]

Muckelroy Award; Keith [Vol. 2: 7484]

Mudd Award for Studies in Basic Microbiology; Stuart [Vol. 2: 4792]

Mudge Award; Isadore Gilbert [Vol. 1: 14470]

Mudge Citation; Isadore Gilbert [Vol. 1: 14470]

Mueller Award and Lecture; James I. [Vol. 1: 1569]

Mueller Medal [Vol. 2: 202]

Muhlmann Prize; Maria and Eric [Vol. 1: 5659]

Muir Award; John [Vol. 1: 14875]

Mukherjee Commemorative Lecture; Prof. Sushil Kumar [Vol. 2: 3719]

Mullard Award [Vol. 2: 8942]

Mullen National Arts and Humanities Award; Dorothy [Vol. 1: 12739]

Muller Award [Vol. 2: 5433]

Muller Jr. Undergraduate Business Plan Competition; John H. [Vol. 1: 5759]

Muller Prize for Behavioural and Social Sciences; Dr. Hendrik [Vol. 2: 4833]

Mulligan Jr. Education Medal; James H. [Vol. 1: 9299]

Mullins Award; Nicholas C. [Vol. 1: 15332]

Mullins Memorial Trophy; Thomas H. [Vol. 1: 10524]

Multi-Event Outstanding Women Award [Vol. 1: 17466]

Multicultural Excellence Awards [Vol. 1: 5444]

Multicultural Leadership and Involvement Award [Vol. 1: 12121]

Multidisciplinary Design Optimization Award [Vol. 1: 2535]

Multidisciplinary Team Award [Vol. 1: 10221]

Multimedia and Publication Design Awards [Vol. 2: 881]

Multinational Force and Observers Medal [Vol. 1: 16681]

Mulvaney Book Award; John [Vol. 2: 230]

Mumford Award for Outstanding Scholarship in the Ecology of Technics; Lewis [Vol. 1: 11039]

Munday Award; Don and Phyllis [Vol. 1: 5775]

Mundi Cantant - International Choir Festival [Vol. 2: 1925]

Mundkur Memorial Lecture Award [Vol. 2: 3698]

Mundt Congress Trophy; Senator Karl E. [Vol. 1: 12416]

Mungo Park Medal [Vol. 2: 8920]

Munich International Festival of Film Schools [Vol. 2: 3106]

Munro Award for Inspirational Leadership; Douglas A. [Vol. 1: 16762]

MUPHAS Prize for Academic Excellence in Mathematics [Vol. 2: 1140]

Murchison Award [Vol. 2: 8795]

Murchison Medal [Vol. 2: 7726]

Murdoch Award [Vol. 2: 8300]

Murdoch Award; Connie [Vol. 1: 14939]

Murie Award; Olaus and Margaret [Vol. 1: 17844]

Murphree Award in Industrial and Engineering Chemistry; E. V. [Vol. 1: 1658]

Murphy Award for Excellence in Copy Editing; John [Vol. 1: 16446]

Murphy Award; Glenn [Vol. 1: 3869]

Murphy Award; John Killam [Vol. 1: 7091]

Murphy Excellence in Teaching Award; Mother Evelyn [Vol. 1: 7899]

Murphy Prize; Forbes [Vol. 2: 7845]

Murphy Scholarship; Joseph [Vol. 1: 13169]

Murray Award; Henry A. [Vol. 1: 15267]

Murray Award; John Courtney [Vol. 1: 7113]

Murray Award; Robert J. [Vol. 1: 14851]

Murray Distinguished Educator Award; Grover E. [Vol. 1: 1282]

Murray Distinguished Mentor Award; Sylvester [Vol. 1: 7503]

Murray - Green Award [Vol. 1: 194]

Murray-Green-Meany-Kirkland Award for Community Service [Vol. 1: 194]

Murray Medal [Vol. 2: 5478]

Murray Memorial Award; G. T. [Vol. 2: 4914]

Murrell Award; Hywel [Vol. 2: 7866]

Murrow Award; Edward R.

Corporation for Public Broadcasting [Vol. 1: 7618]

Overseas Press Club of America [Vol 1: 13764]

Murrow Awards; Edward R. [Vol. 1: 14417]

Museum Director's Award [Vol. 1: 529]

Museum of Haiku Literature Awards [Vol. 1: 8813]

Museum Prize [Vol. 2: 2352]

Museum Publications Design Competition [Vol. 1: 1220]

Musgrave Medals [Vol. 2: 4173]

Musgrave Prize; Peggy and Richard [Vol. 2: 3073]

Music Awards

Australasian Performing Rights Association [Vol. 2: 139]

Music Industries Association - England [Vol 2: 8376]

Royal Philharmonic Society [Vol 2: 8890]

Music Camper Citation [Vol. 1: 11963]

Music Grants [Vol. 2: 2109]

Music Prize [Vol. 2: 1979]

Musica Religiosa - International Choir Festival of Sacred and Clerical Music [Vol. 2: 1926]

Musical Freestyle Rider Awards [Vol. 1: 16875]

Musical Theatre Matters Awards; The MTM:UK [Vol. 2: 7535]

Musician/Bandleader/Instrumentalist Awards [Vol. 1: 61]

Musicians Achievement Award [Vol. 1: 7962]

Musikpris [Vol. 2: 1979]

Muskett Award; Nevva [Vol. 2: 8549]

Muskie Distinguished Public Service Award; Edmund S. [Vol. 1: 7145]

Musson Prize for Poetry; Cecile N. [Vol. 2: 1687]

Mustard Seed Awards [Vol. 1: 12049]

Muteau; Prix Fondation du General [Vol. 2: 2291]

Mutharika International Law Awarded; Christophine G. [Vol. 1: 17682]

Muuvi Awards [Vol. 2: 2119]

Muybridge Award [Vol. 2: 839]

MVSA Goue Medalje [Vol. 2: 5547]

MVSA Silwer Medalje vir Navorsing [Vol. 2: 5548]

Myer Award; Haydn [Vol. 1: 7484]

Myers Award for Applied Research in the Workplace; M. Scott [Vol. 1: 15140]

Myers Award for Outstanding Student Paper [Vol. 1: 15525]

Myers Award; Paul W. [Vol. 1: 260]

Myers Man of the Year Award; Howdy [Vol. 1: 16980]

Myers Writers Award; Cordelia [Vol. 1: 3033]

Myrdal Evaluation Practice Award; Alva and Gunnar [Vol. 1: 2092]

Myrdal Government Evaluation Award; Alva and Gunnar [Vol. 1: 2093]

Myrdal Human Service Delivery Award; Gunnar [Vol. 1: 2092]

Mythopoeic Fantasy Awards [Vol. 1: 11337]

NABA International Achievement Award [Vol. 1: 13284]

Nabokov Award [Vol. 1: 13895]

NACBS-Huntington Library Fellowship [Vol. 1: 13300]

NACD Deutz/Allis Chalmers Conservation District Awards [Vol. 1: 11723]

NACE/Chevron Award [Vol. 1: 11703]

Nachtsheim Award; John [Vol. 1: 5621]

Nadai Medal [Vol. 1: 4410]

Nadal Entrance Awards; Irwin Allen [Vol. 1: 18197]

Nadal Entrance Awards; Miles Spencer [Vol. 1: 18198]

Nadine International Inc. Awards [Vol. 1: 6498]

NAE/Spencer Postdoctoral Fellowship Program [Vol. 1: 11402]

NAEA Art Educator of the Year [Vol. 1: 11539]

NAEA State/Province Newsletter Editor Award [Vol. 1: 11549]

Nafziger-White-Salwen Dissertation Award [Vol. 1: 4999]

Nagel Most Improved Chapter Award; R. H. [Vol. 1: 16374]

Nagroda Zwiazku Kompozytorow Polskich [Vol. 2: 5402]

Naguib Memorial Prize; Mohsen [Vol. 2: 8731]

Nagurski Award; Bronko [Vol. 1: 8409]

Naha Memorial Medal; Professor K. [Vol. 2: 3646]

NAHWW/Stanley Awards [Vol. 1: 11790]

Naik Award; Vasantrao [Vol. 2: 3527]

NAIOP Man of the Year Award [Vol. 1: 11802]

Nair Awards; G.P. [Vol. 2: 3578]

Naismith Award; Frances Pomeroy [Vol. 1: 11362]

Naismith College Coach of the Year [Vol. 1: 5667]

Naismith College Players of the Year [Vol. 1: 5668]

Naismith High School Player of the Year Awards [Vol. 1: 5669]

Naismith Outstanding Contribution to Basketball Award [Vol. 1: 5670]

Naismith Trophy [Vol. 1: 5668]

Najmann Award [Vol. 2: 4006]

Nakane Prize; Paul [Vol. 1: 9934]

Nakanishi Prize [Vol. 1: 1659]

Nakarmi Metalwork Award; J.B. [Vol. 2: 4633]

Nakkula Award for Police Reporting; Al [Vol. 1: 17218]

NAMIC Engineering Safety Award [Vol. 1: 4090]

NAMS Annual Meeting Student Travel Awards [Vol. 1: 13316]

Namur Award [Vol. 2: 1270]

Nansen Award for Young Scientists; Peter [Vol. 1: 18019]

Nansen Medal [Vol. 2: 4596]

Nansen Medal; Fridtjof [Vol. 2: 2375]

Nansen Refugee Award [Vol. 2: 4596]

Nanson Prize; Professor [Vol. 2: 1141]

Napolitano Award; Luigi G. [Vol. 2: 2501]

Narasimhan Academic Merit Award Contest; Prof. M.J. [Vol. 2: 3699]

Narlikar Memorial Lecture; Professor Vishnu Vasudeva [Vol. 2: 3647]

NASAR Service Award [Vol. 1: 11599]

NASCAR Championships [Vol. 1: 11608]

Nash Gold Medal; Kevin [Vol. 2: 8194]

Nash History Journal Prize [Vol. 1: 13955]

Nash Layman Junior Award; Paul [Vol. 1: 17088]

Nashville Film Festival [Vol. 1: 11382]

NASPAA/ASPA Distinguished Research Award [Vol. 1: 4049]

NASPAA Public Courage Award [Vol. 1: 11879]

Nast Award; Thomas [Vol. 1: 13765]

NAST-LELEDFI Award for Outstanding Research in Tropical Medicine [Vol. 2: 5360]

Natali Journalism Prize; Lorenzo [Vol. 2: 1463]

Natelson Research Award; Samuel R. [Vol. 1: 912]

Nath De Memorial Lecture; Professor Shambu [Vol. 2: 3648]

Nath Memorial Lecture; Professor Vishwa [Vol. 2: 3649]

Nathan Award; Etta [Vol. 1: 5797]

Nathan Award in Hematology/Oncology; David G. [Vol. 1: 15258]

Nathan's Famous Fourth of July International Hot Dog Eating Contest [Vol. 1: 9917]

Nathanson Award for Conducting; Moshe [Vol. 1: 7061]

National 100 Mile Award [Vol. 1: 2069]

National Academic Squad and Team Award [Vol. 1: 12393]

National Academics and Fine Arts Competition [Vol. 1: 1085]

National Academy of Sciences Award [Vol. 2: 5476]

National Academy of Sciences Award in Microbiology [Vol. 1: 11446]

National Academy of Western Art Exhibition [Vol. 1: 12268]

National Achievement Award

Canadian Council of Technicians and Technologists [Vol. 1: 6431]

Heritage Canada Foundation [Vol 1: 8912]

National Advisor of the Year Award [Vol. 1: 410]

National Aeronautical Prize [Vol. 2: 3444]

National Agricultural Award [Vol. 2: 8633]

National Amputee Invitational Champion [Vol. 1: 11515]

National Art Educator Award [Vol. 1: 11539]

National Arts and Culture Awards [Vol. 2: 1819]

National Arya Samaj Award [Vol. 2: 3333]

National Assessment Awards [Vol. 2: 1096]

National Association of Realtors Research Award [Vol. 1: 3674]

National Athletic Director of the Year [Vol. 1: 12194]

National Award
   American Cancer Society [Vol. 1: 1533]
   John F. Kennedy Center for the Performing Arts - Kennedy Center American College Theater Festival [Vol 1: 10666]
   National Water Safety Congress [Vol 1: 13026]

National Award for an Engineering Project or Achievement [Vol. 1: 8130]

National Award for Career Achievements in Medical Education [Vol. 1: 15671]

National Award for Demonstrated Leadership [Vol. 1: 13857]

National Award for Environmental Management [Vol. 2: 9518]

National Award for Media Excellence [Vol. 1: 12740]

National Award for Middle School Teacher [Vol. 2: 5250]

National Award for Research in Science and Technology [Vol. 2: 9519]

National Award for Smart Growth Achievement [Vol. 1: 16891]

National Award for Technical Culture Faust Vrancic [Vol. 2: 1882]

National Award of Merit [Vol. 1: 5524]

National Award of Science and Technology for Young Geographer [Vol. 2: 5251]

National Awards [Vol. 2: 9432]

National Awards [Vol. 1: 13119]

National Awards Contest [Vol. 1: 5157]

National Awards for Cinematography [Vol. 2: 258]

National Awards for Education Reporting [Vol. 1: 8018]

National Awards for Excellence [Vol. 2: 370]

National Awards for Scholarship in Medical Education [Vol. 1: 15672]

National Awards for Science Technicians [Vol. 2: 9142]

National Awards for SMEs [Vol. 2: 1779]

National Awards Program
   AMVETS [Vol. 1: 4727]
   Freedoms Foundation at Valley Forge [Vol 1: 8466]
   National Telecommunications Cooperative Association [Vol 1: 12974]

National Back Pain Association Medal [Vol. 2: 6865]

National Bank of Industry and Commerce Award [Vol. 2: 3353]

National Best Quality Software Awards [Vol. 2: 6117]

National Book Awards [Vol. 1: 11994]

National Book Critics Circle Awards [Vol. 1: 11992]

National Business Calendar Awards [Vol. 2: 7176]

National Calendar Awards [Vol. 2: 7176]

National Career Award Competition
   National Society of Arts and Letters [Vol. 1: 12863]
   National Society of Arts and Letters [Vol 1: 12864]
   National Society of Arts and Letters [Vol 1: 12865]
   National Society of Arts and Letters [Vol 1: 12866]
   National Society of Arts and Letters [Vol 1: 12867]

National Certificate of Merit [Vol. 1: 5970]

National Champions [Vol. 1: 1995]

National Championship
   American Baseball Coaches Association [Vol. 1: 1482]
   American Motorcyclist Association [Vol 1: 2946]

National Championship Regatta [Vol. 1: 9457]

National Championship Trophy [Vol. 1: 16768]

National Championships
   American Endurance Ride Conference [Vol. 1: 2070]
   Canadian Sport Parachuting Association [Vol 1: 7007]
   National Rifle Association of America [Vol 1: 12785]
   United States Curling Association [Vol 1: 16777]

   U.S.A. Badminton [Vol 1: 17405]
   USA Cycling [Vol 1: 17412]

National Chapter of the Year [Vol. 1: 16558]

National Chicken Council Broiler Research Award [Vol. 1: 14112]

National Chopin Piano Competition [Vol. 1: 7257]

National Citation Awards [Vol. 1: 12762]

National City and Regional Magazine Awards [Vol. 1: 7292]

National Coach of the Year [Vol. 1: 12080]

National Collegiate and Scholastic Swimming Trophy [Vol. 1: 12567]

National Community Service Award [Vol. 1: 11817]

National Company Representative of the Year [Vol. 1: 11845]

National Congressional Award [Vol. 1: 12741]

National Conservation Achievement Awards [Vol. 1: 13044]

National Conservation Award [Vol. 2: 6834]

National Convention Research Awards [Vol. 1: 14294]

National Corporate Humanitarian Award [Vol. 1: 12742]

National Council Auditions [Vol. 1: 11116]

National Courage Award [Vol. 2: 3892]

National Court of Honor Lifesaving and Meritorious Action Awards [Vol. 1: 5970]

National Crafts Competition [Vol. 2: 3922]

National Credit Executive of the Year [Vol. 1: 11744]

National Crew Person Award [Vol. 1: 5769]

National Culture Week of Burkina Faso [Vol. 2: 1807]

National Customer Service Awards [Vol. 2: 9410]

National Defense Service Medal [Vol. 1: 16682]

National Design Awards [Vol. 2: 634]

National Diploma of the Society of Floristry [Vol. 2: 9309]

National Distinguished Friends of Extension Award [Vol. 1: 8179]

National Distinguished Professional Award [Vol. 1: 12743]

National Distinguished Service Award
   Canadian Mental Health Association [Vol. 1: 6693]
   National Rehabilitation Counseling Association [Vol 1: 12763]

National Distinguished Service Ruby Award [Vol. 1: 8180]

National Division Art Educator Award [Vol. 1: 11540]

National Division Art Educator of the Year [Vol. 1: 11540]

National Driver of the Year Award [Vol. 1: 4612]

National Drug and Alcohol Awards [Vol. 2: 331]

National Editor's Award [Vol. 1: 1171]

National Education Service Award [Vol. 1: 14446]

National Endowment for the Arts Programs [Vol. 1: 12311]

National Endowment for the Humanities Grant Programs [Vol. 1: 12318]

National Engineering Award [Vol. 1: 1150]

National Environment Quality Award [Vol. 1: 13098]

National Environmental Achievement Awards [Vol. 1: 11683]

National Environmental Leadership Awards in Asthma Management [Vol. 1: 16892]

National Equal Employment/Affirmative Action Exemplary Practices Award [Vol. 1: 4047]

National Established Investigator Award [Vol. 1: 2311]

National Excellence in Building and Construction Awards [Vol. 2: 867]

National Exhibition of Folk-Art in the Norwegian Tradition - Rosemaling Award [Vol. 1: 17525]

National Exhibition of Folk-Art in the Norwegian Tradition - Weaving Award [Vol. 1: 17526]

National Exhibition of Folk-Art in the Norwegian Tradition - Woodworking Award [Vol. 1: 17527]

National Export Awards [Vol. 2: 868]

National Family and Consumer Sciences Home Economics Teacher of the Year Award [Vol. 1: 1156]

National Federation of Music Clubs Awards and Scholarships [Vol. 1: 12335]

National Federation of the Blind Scholarship Program [Vol. 1: 12382]

National Film Board Award for Best Short Film [Vol. 1: 16518]

National Film Board of Canada Public Prize [Vol. 1: 13736]

National Food and Energy Council Electric Technology Award [Vol. 1: 4094]

National Forensic Association Awards [Vol. 1: 12413]

National Fresenius Award [Vol. 1: 13980]

National Genealogy Hall of Fame [Vol. 1: 12452]

National Geographic Society New Mapmaker Award [Vol. 2: 6990]

National Glaucoma Research Grant [Vol. 1: 2293]

National Gold Pin Awards [Vol. 1: 457]

National Golden Target Awards
   Public Relations Institute of Australia [Vol. 2: 939]
   Public Relations Institute of Australia [Vol 2: 940]

National Goodwill Worker of the Year [Vol. 1: 8722]

National GP of the Year Award [Vol. 2: 8682]

National Health Leadership Award [Vol. 1: 7690]

National Heritage Fellowships [Vol. 1: 12315]

National Hero Award [Vol. 2: 2681]

National High Point Awards [Vol. 1: 11717]

National High School Essay Contest [Vol. 1: 15805]

National High School Finals Rodeo [Vol. 1: 12509]

National High School Flute Choir [Vol. 1: 12397]

National High School Journalism Teacher of the Year [Vol. 1: 7912]

National High School Sports Hall of Fame Awards [Vol. 1: 12339]

National History Day History of Agriculture and Rural Life Award [Vol. 1: 216]

National Honor Award [Vol. 1: 1527]

National Honor Society Scholarship Program [Vol. 1: 11887]

National Honorary Member Award [Vol. 1: 10503]

National Housing Quality Award [Vol. 1: 14192]

National Human Relations Award [Vol. 1: 2724]

National Humanitarian Award [Vol. 1: 12744]

National Humanities Medal [Vol. 1: 12319]

National Institute of Insurance International Prizes [Vol. 2: 4024]

National Inventor of the Year [Vol. 1: 9437]

National Inventor's Hall of Fame [Vol. 1: 17025]

National Iqbal Award [Vol. 2: 5186]

National Jewish Book Award - Biography/ Autobiography/Memoir [Vol. 1: 10554]

National Jewish Book Award - Children's and Young Adult Literature [Vol. 1: 10555]

National Jewish Book Award - Contemporary Jewish Life and Practice [Vol. 1: 10556]

National Jewish Book Award - Fiction [Vol. 1: 10557]

National Jewish Book Award - Holocaust [Vol. 1: 10558]

National Jewish Book Award - Illustrated Children's Book [Vol. 1: 10559]

National Jewish Book Award - Israel [Vol. 1: 10560]

National Jewish Book Award - Jewish History [Vol. 1: 10561]

National Jewish Book Award - Modern Jewish Thought and Experience [Vol. 1: 10562]

National Jewish Book Award - Scholarship [Vol. 1: 10563]

National Jewish Book Award - Sephardic Culture [Vol. 1: 10564]

National Jewish Book Award - Visual Arts [Vol. 1: 10565]

National Journalism Awards [Vol. 1: 4825]

National Junior Team MVP [Vol. 1: 5791]

National Junior Tennis League Chapter of the Year Award [Vol. 1: 17133]

National Juried Print Exhibition Awards [Vol. 1: 9015]

National Key Accounts Outstanding Customer Service Awards [Vol. 1: 8004]

National KIND Teacher Award [Vol. 1: 9006]

National Krishi Vigyan Kendra Award [Vol. 2: 3528]

National Landscape Architecture Awards [Vol. 2: 398]

National Landscape Awards [Vol. 2: 6967]

National Leadership Award
   National Council for Continuing Education and Training [Vol. 1: 12148]
   Simon Wiesenthal Center [Vol 1: 17838]

National Leadership Awards [Vol. 1: 10580]

National League Most Valuable Player [Vol 1: 5794]

National League Rookie of the Year [Vol. 1: 16177]

National Legislative Award [Vol. 1: 14447]

National Lifestyle Housing for Seniors Award [Vol. 2: 869]

National Lifetime Achievement Award [Vol. 2: 1878]

National Limited Distance Mileage Champion [Vol. 1: 2071]

National Living Treasures Awards [Vol. 2: 5341]

National Logohu Medal [Vol. 2: 5216]

National Looking Glass Poetry Competition for a Single Poem [Vol. 1: 14340]

National Magazine Awards
 American Society of Magazine Editors [Vol. 1: 4372]
  National Magazine Awards Foundation [Vol 1: 12590]

National Mass Media Award [Vol. 1: 2725]

National Materials Advancement Award [Vol. 1: 8336]

National Medal [Vol. 2: 317]

National Medal of Arts [Vol. 1: 12316]

National Media Awards
 American College of Allergy, Asthma and Immunology [Vol. 1: 1701]
 American Society of Colon and Rectal Surgeons [Vol 1: 4257]

National Member of the Year Award [Vol. 1: 411]

National Meritorious Award [Vol. 1: 4686]

National Metallurgist of the Year [Vol. 2: 3601]

National Methadone Conference [Vol. 1: 11507]

National Mileage Championship [Vol. 1: 2072]

National Military Intelligence Association Annual Awards [Vol. 1: 12607]

National Milk Producers Federation Richard M. Hoyt Award [Vol. 1: 1983]

National Music Festival [Vol. 1: 8292]

National Newspaper Awards [Vol. 1: 6742]

National Officials Outstanding Service Award [Vol. 1: 17455]

National Order of Merit [Vol. 2: 4574]

National Outstanding Advisor Award [Vol. 1: 16376]

National Outstanding Logger Award [Vol. 1: 8435]

National Outstanding Small and Medium Enterprise Award [Vol. 2: 6597]

National Peace Essay Contest [Vol. 1: 16973]

National Person of the Year Award [Vol. 1: 12148]

National Photographic Competition [Vol. 2: 2066]

National Planning Excellence Awards [Vol. 1: 3295]

National Planning Leadership Award for a Distinguished Contribution [Vol. 1: 3290]

National Planning Leadership Award for a Student Planner [Vol. 1: 3291]

National Poetry Competition [Vol. 2: 8489]

National Police Award for Traffic Safety [Vol. 1: 6147]

National Police Shooting Championships [Vol. 1: 12786]

National Pool Lifeguard Award [Vol. 2: 4998]

National Preservation Honor Awards [Vol. 1: 13004]

National President's Award [Vol. 1: 6456]

National President's Award
 American Association of Healthcare Administrative Management [Vol. 1: 1172]
 Australian Institute of Quantity Surveyors [Vol 2: 423]

National President's Awards [Vol. 1: 5364]

National Prize for Advertising [Vol. 2: 1243]

National Prize for Consulting [Vol. 2: 1244]

National Prize for the Most Beautiful Book [Vol. 2: 1245]

National Prizes of Arts and Literature [Vol. 2: 1807]

National Psychologist Trainee Register Credentialing Scholarships [Vol. 1: 7658]

National Public Service Awards [Vol. 1: 11415]

National Quality Award [Vol. 2: 6011]

National Quality Dealer Award [Vol. 1: 12535]

National Recreational Fisheries Awards [Vol. 1: 8369]

National Recycling Coalition Annual Awards [Vol. 1: 12749]

National Register Early Career Psychologist Credentialing Scholarships [Vol. 1: 7659]

National Research Competition [Vol. 1: 12151]

National Research Grants and Scholarships [Vol. 2: 989]

National Research Service Awards [Vol. 1: 12557]

National Responsible Business Award [Vol. 2: 4495]

National Rifle and Pistol Championship Trophy Match [Vol. 1: 16782]

National Rolleston Award [Vol. 2: 8141]

National Safety Awards [Vol. 1: 6379]

National Safety Excellence Awards [Vol. 1: 4882]

National Scholar-Athlete Awards [Vol. 1: 12403]

National Scholarships [Vol. 1: 4708]

National Scholastic Award [Vol. 1: 14448]

National Scholastic Press Association Pacemaker Awards [Vol. 1: 13244]

National School Library Media Program of the Year Award [Vol. 1: 1346]

National Service Award
 Chamber Music America [Vol. 1: 7176]
  Recreation Vehicle Industry Association [Vol 1: 14449]

National Service Cross of the Order of Saint Lucia [Vol. 2: 5895]

National Service Medal of the Order of Saint Lucia [Vol. 2: 5896]

National Short Story Award; BBC [Vol. 2: 6902]

National Ski Safety Award [Vol. 1: 6870]

National Small Business Person of the Year [Vol. 1: 17105]

National Small Works Exhibition [Vol. 1: 16553]

National Smokey Bear Awards [Vol. 1: 16918]

National Softball Hall of Fame [Vol. 1: 483]

National Sportscaster and Sportswriter of Year [Vol. 1: 12932]

National Staff Award and NCIA Honor Roll [Vol. 1: 12140]

National Student Advertising Competition [Vol. 1: 780]

National Student Award [Vol. 2: 7362]

National Student Awards Program [Vol. 1: 6032]

National Student Paper Award [Vol. 1: 16332]

National Student Playwriting Award [Vol. 1: 10666]

National Student Production Awards Competition [Vol. 1: 12007]

National Student Teacher/Intern of the Year [Vol. 1: 10640]

National Superintendent of the Year Award [Vol. 1: 1336]

National Sweepstakes Champion [Vol. 1: 13358]

National Target Championships [Vol. 1: 11529]

National Teacher of the Year [Vol. 1: 7663]

National Teacher of the Year Award [Vol. 1: 1156]

National Technical Writing Award [Vol. 1: 8436]

National Torchbearer Award [Vol. 1: 2748]

National Tourism Awards [Vol. 2: 1679]

National Track and Field Hall of Fame [Vol. 1: 17473]

National Training Awards [Vol. 2: 3888]

National Training Awards [Vol. 2: 7177]

National Transit Corporate Recognition Awards [Vol. 1: 7022]

National Transit Employee Recognition Awards [Vol. 1: 7023]

National Translation Award [Vol. 1: 2796]

National Transportation Award [Vol. 1: 12284]

National Treasure Award [Vol. 1: 18193]

National Truck Driving Championships [Vol. 1: 4613]

National Truck Safety Contest [Vol. 1: 4614]

National Turkey Federation Research Award [Vol. 1: 14113]

National Voluntary Service Award [Vol. 1: 12745]

National Volunteer Award [Vol. 1: 6432]

National Wastewater Management Excellence Awards [Vol. 1: 16893]

National Water and Energy Conservation Award [Vol. 1: 10527]

National Wildlife Photo Contest [Vol. 1: 13045]

National Wildlife Week Awards [Vol. 1: 7045]

National Wohelo Order Award [Vol. 1: 6120]

National Young Artists Competition in Organ Performance [Vol. 1: 2267]

National Young Astronomer Award [Vol. 1: 5650]

National Youth Award [Vol. 1: 11818]

The Nations Cup [Vol. 2: 6428]

Nationwide Series [Vol. 1: 11608]

Native American Child Health Advocacy Award [Vol. 1: 692]

Native Educator Scholarships [Vol. 1: 7095]

NATO Awards [Vol. 1: 11934]

Natta; Medaglia d'oro Giulio [Vol. 2: 4127]

Natural and Organic Products Awards [Vol. 2: 9349]

Natural Science Grants [Vol. 2: 4209]

Nature and Ecology Student Paper Award [Vol. 1: 8157]

Nature and Environment Prize [Vol. 2: 1980]

Nature Conservancy Applied Conservation Award [Vol. 2: 694]

Nature Conservation Award [Vol. 2: 4634]

Nature Conservation Officer of the Year [Vol. 2: 5595]

Nature Photographer of the Year [Vol. 1: 14020]

Naude Medal; S. Meiring [Vol. 2: 5607]

Naukowa Scientific Prize; Nagroda [Vol. 2: 5407]

Nauta Award on Pharmacochemistry [Vol. 2: 1235]

Nautica/U.S. SAILING Youth Championship [Vol. 1: 17066]

Nautilus Book Awards [Vol. 1: 13117]

Nauts Service Award; Helen Coley [Vol. 1: 7058]

Naval Reserve Medal [Vol. 1: 16683]

Naval Submarine Literary Awards
 Naval Submarine League [Vol. 1: 13124]
  Naval Submarine League [Vol 1: 13126]

Navigation Distinction [Vol. 2: 2011]

Navy Expeditionary Medal [Vol. 1: 16684]

Navy Occupation Service Medal [Vol. 1: 16685]

NAWBO/Wells Fargo Trailblazer Award [Vol. 1: 11940]

Nax Trophy [Vol. 1: 3080]

Naylor Prize and Lectureship [Vol. 2: 8331]

Naylor Working Writer Fellowship; Phyllis [Vol. 1: 13896]

NBA All-Star Team [Vol. 1: 16178]

NBA Coach of the Year [Vol. 1: 16179]

NBA MVP [Vol. 1: 16180]

NBA Player of the Year [Vol. 1: 16180]

NBA Rookie of the Year [Vol. 1: 16181]

NBC-LEO City Cultural Diversity Awards [Vol. 1: 12582]

NCCPB Genetics and Plant Breeding Award for Industry [Vol. 1: 7769]

NCE/ACE Young Consultant of the Year Award [Vol. 2: 6763]

NCEA Merit Award [Vol. 1: 12046]

NCLA/SIRS Intellectual Freedom Award [Vol. 1: 13368]

NCUCA Scholarship [Vol. 1: 13379]

NEA/TCG Career Development Program for Designers [Vol. 1: 16473]

NEA/TCG Career Development Program for Theatre Directors [Vol. 1: 16474]

Near Presidential Award; Elwood G. [Vol. 1: 9563]

Neaverson Awards; Peter [Vol. 2: 6770]

Nebraska Land Stewardship Award [Vol. 1: 13145]

Nebraska State Poetry Society Award [Vol. 1: 12361]

Nebula Awards [Vol. 1: 14786]

NECCC Medal [Vol. 1: 8782]

NECTFL Service [Vol. 1: 13398]

Needham Award and Lecture; Roger [Vol. 2: 7017]

Neel Medal; Louis [Vol. 2: 2376]

Neff Distinguished Service Award; Thelma J. [Vol. 1: 391]

Negre Trophy; Pablo [Vol. 2: 6393]

Nehru Award for International Understanding; Jawaharlal [Vol. 2: 3518]

Nehru Award; Jawaharlal [Vol. 2: 3529]

Nehru Birth Centenary Award; Jawaharlal [Vol. 2: 3720]

Nehru Birth Centenary Lectures; Jawaharlal [Vol. 2: 3650]

Nehru Birth Centenary Medal; Jawaharlal [Vol. 2: 3651]

Nehru Literacy Award [Vol. 2: 3506]

Neighborhood Conservation Award [Vol. 1: 14765]

Neil Prize for Innovation in Drug Development; Gary [Vol. 1: 3803]

Neill Medal [Vol. 2: 9070]

Neilson Award; John B. [Vol. 1: 4892]

Neitz Junior Medal/Senior Medal; W.O. [Vol. 2: 5591]

Nelson Award for Diagnosis of Yield-Limiting Factors; Werner L. [Vol. 1: 4106]

Nelson Fellowship; Morley [Vol. 1: 14438]

Nelson Fly Tying Teaching Award; Dick [Vol. 1: 8307]

Nelson Government Service Award; E. Benjamin [Vol. 1: 8790]

Nelson Prize; Elizabeth H. [Vol. 1: 18015]

Nelson Prize; William [Vol. 1: 14504]

Nelson Service Award; Harold E. [Vol. 1: 15655]

Nelvana Grand Prize for Independent Short Animation [Vol. 1: 13737]

Nemchinov Prize; V.S. [Vol. 2: 5837]

Nemet Award [Vol. 2: 7095]

Nemmers Prize in Economics; Erwin Plein [Vol. 1: 13418]

Nemmers Prize in Mathematics; Frederic Esser [Vol. 1: 13419]

NEMRA Manufacturer of the Year [Vol. 1: 12304]

Neonatal Education Award [Vol. 1: 693]

Neonatal Landmark Award [Vol. 1: 694]

Neptune Award [Vol. 1: 11271]

Ner Tamid (Eternal Light) Emblem [Vol. 1: 12575]

Nerken Award; Albert [Vol. 1: 5737]

Nernst-Haber-Bodenstein-Preis [Vol. 2: 2921]

Neruda Prize for Poetry; Pablo [Vol. 1: 13260]

Nesburn Playwright Award; Dr. Henry and Lilian [Vol. 1: 5826]

NESDA Awards [Vol. 1: 12306]

Nesmeyanov Prize; A.N. [Vol. 2: 5838]

Ness Award [Vol. 2: 8796]

Ness Book Award; Frederic W. [Vol. 1: 5197]

Ness Memorial Award; John Harrison [Vol. 1: 8535]

Nestle Prize in Creating Shared Value [Vol. 2: 6470]

NETA Special Service Award [Vol. 1: 12325]

Netherthorpe Communicator of the Year [Vol. 2: 7751]

NETPAC Prize [Vol. 2: 2727]

Netter Award; Frank [Vol. 1: 17522]

Network/Syndicated Personality of the Year [Vol. 1: 11675]

Neue Stimmen International Singing Competition [Vol. 2: 2735]

Neue Stimmen Internationaler Gesangswettbewerb [Vol. 2: 2735]

Neufeld Memorial Award; Prof. Henry [Vol. 2: 3997]

Neuharth Free Spirit Awards; Al [Vol. 1: 8460]

Neuharth Free Spirit Journalism Award; Al [Vol. 1: 8460]

Neuman Award; William F. [Vol. 1: 3773]

Neumann Award; Harold E. [Vol. 1: 9492]

Neumann Medal [Vol. 2: 3415]

Neumann Memorial Award; Selma [Vol. 1: 8982]

Neumann Plaquette and Certificate [Vol. 2: 3416]

Neumann Prize; Bernhard H. [Vol. 2: 466]

Neumueller Award in Optics; Julius F. [Vol. 1: 624]

Neurath Award; Hans [Vol. 1: 14284]

Neuroscience Research Prize [Vol. 1: 591]

Neustadt International Prize for Literature [Vol. 1: 18055]

Neustadt Prize for Children's Literature; NSK [Vol. 1: 18056]

Neustein Memorial Award; Harry B. [Vol. 1: 15245]

Nevada Poetry Society Award [Vol. 1: 12362]

Neversink Trophy [Vol. 1: 13442]

Nevins Physiology and Human Environment Award; Ralph G. [Vol. 1: 4328]

Nevins Prize; Allan [Vol. 1: 7997]

New Achievers Award [Vol. 1: 1157]

New America Award [Vol. 1: 15806]

New Barwis-Holliday Award [Vol. 2: 8650]

New Directors Competition [Vol. 1: 14817]

New Educator Award [Vol. 1: 13700]

New Entrants Prize [Vol. 2: 3922]

New Focus Student Travel Grants [Vol. 1: 13609]

New Frontiers in Animal Nutrition Award [Vol. 1: 2134]

New Genre Prize [Vol. 1: 9499]

New Holland Young Researcher Award [Vol. 1: 4091]

New Horizons Award for Innovation [Vol. 1: 10801]

New Hospital Pharmacy Practitioner Award [Vol. 1: 6953]

New Investigator Award
    American Society for Photobiology [Vol. 1: 4040]
    Canadian Society of Internal Medicine [Vol 1: 6962]
    International Association for the Study of Obesity [Vol 2: 8075]
    Society for the Study of Reproduction [Vol 1: 15387]

New Investigator Awards
    American Geriatrics Society [Vol. 1: 2255]
    Mount Desert Island Biological Laboratory [Vol 1: 11289]
    University of Wisconsin—Madison - Institute on Aging [Vol 1: 17374]

New Investigator Grant [Vol. 1: 14793]

New Investigator Recognition Awards [Vol. 1: 13717]

New Investigator Research Award [Vol. 1: 5077]

New Investigator Scholarship [Vol. 2: 746]

New Investigators Awards [Vol. 2: 1070]

New Jersey Poetry Society Award [Vol. 1: 12363]

New Lawyer Award of Excellence [Vol. 1: 10793]

New Leaders Travel Grant [Vol. 1: 14320]

New Leadership Award [Vol. 1: 4724]

New Letters Literary Awards [Vol. 1: 13191]

New Librarian of the Year [Vol. 1: 15980]

New Manufacturer of the Year [Vol. 2: 4189]

New Member Abstract Award [Vol. 1: 1727]

New Member Recognition Award [Vol. 1: 6241]

New Mexico Library Amigo Award [Vol. 1: 13200]

New Mexico Library Leadership Award [Vol. 1: 13201]

New Mexico Music Awards [Vol. 1: 13203]

New Nepali Website Award [Vol. 2: 4639]

New Play Project [Vol. 1: 16005]

New Practitioner Award [Vol. 1: 6789]

New Product Award
    American Association of Law Libraries [Vol. 1: 1196]
    National Society of Professional Engineers [Vol 1: 12878]

New Product of the Year [Vol. 2: 7500]

New Product Showcase Awards [Vol. 1: 3128]

New Professional Award [Vol. 1: 14485]

New Professional Reporter Grant [Vol. 1: 12266]

New Research Workers' Awards [Vol. 2: 8525]

New Researcher Award [Vol. 2: 585]

New Safe Medicines Faster Award [Vol. 2: 6141]

New Scholar's Prize [Vol. 2: 8114]

New Scientist Award for Outstanding Research [Vol. 1: 6755]

New South Wales Premier's Literary Awards [Vol. 2: 906]

New Spirit of Community Partnership Awards [Vol. 1: 9166]

New Student Prize; Peter K. [Vol. 1: 15033]

New Venture Award [Vol. 2: 9455]

New Vision Award [Vol. 2: 1343]

New Voices Award [Vol. 1: 14366]

New Web Site Award [Vol. 1: 6227]

New York International Ballet Competition [Vol. 1: 13212]

New York Poetry Forum Award [Vol. 1: 12364]

New Yorkers for Better Neighborhood Grants [Vol. 1: 7290]

New Zealand Christian Book of the Year [Vol. 2: 4877]

New Zealand Dental Therapist Student Award [Vol. 2: 4962]

New Zealand Herald Challenge Trophy [Vol. 2: 5056]

New Zealand Olympic Order [Vol. 2: 4986]

New Zealand Post Book Awards
    Booksellers New Zealand [Vol. 2: 4869]
    Booksellers New Zealand [Vol 2: 4870]

New Zealand Post Children's Book Awards [Vol. 2: 4871]

New Zealand Science and Technology Medals [Vol. 2: 5077]

New Zealand Science, Mathematics and Technology Teacher Fellowship [Vol. 2: 5078]

New Zealand Society Prize [Vol. 2: 8562]

New Zealand Tourism Awards [Vol. 2: 5082]

Newbery Medal; John [Vol. 1: 5067]

Newbigin Prize [Vol. 2: 8921]

Newbold V/STOL Award; F. E. [Vol. 1: 2536]

Newcomb Award for Research Achievement; Simon [Vol. 1: 16841]

Newcomb Award; Simon [Vol. 1: 14621]

Newcomb Fund Award; James E. [Vol. 1: 2753]

Newcombe Doctoral Dissertation Fellowship; Charlotte W. [Vol. 1: 18000]

Newcomen Book Award [Vol. 1: 8830]

Newcomen-Harvard Article Award [Vol. 1: 8831]

Newcomen-Harvard Special Award [Vol. 1: 8832]

Newcomer Healthcare Executive of the Year Award; William [Vol. 1: 575]

Newcomer of the Year
    Rugby Union Players' Association [Vol. 2: 1033]
    Sony Ericsson WTA Tour [Vol. 1: 15960]

Newcomer Supply Student Scholarship [Vol. 1: 12860]

Newcomer to Care Award [Vol. 2: 7333]

Newell Award; Allen [Vol. 1: 4960]

Newell Prize; W. W. [Vol. 1: 2163]

Newfoundland Government Air Services Memorial Award [Vol. 1: 5673]

Newington Award [Vol. 1: 849]

Newkirk Award; Burt L. [Vol. 1: 4411]

Newman Award for State Innovation; Frank [Vol. 1: 8016]

Newman Cup [Vol. 2: 5057]

Newman Graduate Research Award; Edwin B. [Vol. 1: 14295]

Newman Graduate Research Award; Psi Chi/APA Edwin B. [Vol. 1: 3501]

Newman Leadership Awards; Frank [Vol. 1: 6204]

Newmark Medal; Nathan M. [Vol. 1: 4211]

News and Documentary Emmy Awards [Vol. 1: 11455]

News Coverage Award [Vol. 1: 9446]

News Picture Contest [Vol. 1: 9245]

Newsfilm Cameramen of the Year [Vol. 1: 12698]

Newsletter Association Journalism Awards [Vol. 1: 16128]

Newsletter Award [Vol. 1: 6022]

Newsletter Awards
    American Hemerocallis Society [Vol. 1: 2338]
    Association of Government Accountants [Vol 1: 5365]

Newsletter Competition [Vol. 1: 12453]

Newsletter Excellence Award [Vol. 1: 6083]

Newsletter Journalism Award [Vol. 1: 12687]

Newsletter of the Year
    United States Hang Gliding and Paragliding Association [Vol. 1: 16944]
    United States Professional Tennis Association [Vol. 1: 17033]

Newsletter of the Year Award [Vol. 1: 12859]

Newsletter of the Year Merit Award [Vol. 1: 12859]

Newspaper Award [Vol. 1: 416]

Newspaper in Education Award [Vol. 1: 9447]

Newspaper of the Year Award [Vol. 2: 923]

Newton Award; Michael [Vol. 1: 4714]

Newton Lecture; Alfred [Vol. 2: 7159]

Newton Medal; Isaac [Vol. 2: 7916]

NEWWA Scholarships [Vol. 1: 13169]

Newydd Short Story Competition; Lingo [Vol. 2: 6675]

Next Generation Achievement Award [Vol. 1: 5466]

Next Generation Award [Vol. 1: 2974]

Next Generation Indie Book Awards [Vol. 1: 13248]

Nexus Award for Lifetime Achievement [Vol. 1: 8862]

Nexus Sport Aviation Journalist of the Year Trophy [Vol. 2: 8596]

Neyman Lecture [Vol. 1: 9382]

NFHS Citations [Vol. 1: 12340]

NFID - Burroughs Welcome Fund Young Investigator Awards [Vol. 1: 12431]

NFL All-Star Team [Vol. 1: 16182]

NFL Coach of the Year [Vol. 1: 16183]

NFL Player of the Year [Vol. 1: 16184]

NFL Rookie of the Year [Vol. 1: 16185]

Nganakarrawa Award [Vol. 2: 273]

Ngoma Awards [Vol. 2: 9569]

NHL All-Star Team [Vol. 1: 16186]

NHL Coach of the Year [Vol. 1: 16187]

NHL Player of the Year [Vol. 1: 16188]

NHL Rookie of the Year [Vol. 1: 16189]

Nia Award for Lifetime Achievement [Vol. 1: 11664]

Nicest Studio Award [Vol. 1: 12965]

Niche Medical Best Oral Presentation [Vol. 2: 224]

Nichol Harbor and Coastal Engineering Award; John G. Moffat - Frank E. [Vol. 1: 4208]

Nicholls Award; Percy W.
    American Society of Mechanical Engineers [Vol. 1: 4412]
    Society for Mining, Metallurgy, and Exploration [Vol 1: 15217]

Nichols Award for Environmental Excellence; Charles Walter [Vol. 1: 3661]

Nichols Medal; Nathaniel B. [Vol. 2: 1279]

Nicholson Award for International Caregiver; Evelyn [Vol. 2: 8373]

Nicholson Award; Lt. Col. Arthur D. [Vol. 1: 12607]

Nicholson Gold Medal; Gunnar [Vol. 1: 16368]

Nicholson Noncommissioned Officer Leadership Award; James E. [Vol. 1: 10960]

Nicholson Student Paper Competition; George [Vol. 1: 9264]

Nickelodeon Kid's Choice Awards [Vol. 1: 17554]

Nickens Award; Herbert W. [**Vol. 1:** 15673]
Nickerson Service Award [**Vol. 1:** 9453]
Nickins Epidemiology Award; Dr. Herbert [**Vol. 1:** 5227]
Nicolai Award; Walter R. [**Vol. 1:** 785]
Nicolau Award; General Pierre [**Vol. 2:** 2475]
Nidhi Trustee Fund Gold Prize; Gandhi Smarak [**Vol. 2:** 4417]
NIDRR Scholars Program [**Vol. 1:** 16805]
Niederman Award; Allan and Joyce [**Vol. 1:** 8914]
Nielsen BookData Booksellers' Choice Award [**Vol. 2:** 249]
Nielsen International Music Competitions; Carl [**Vol. 2:** 1975]
Nielsen International Organ Competition; Carl [**Vol. 2:** 1989]
Nielsen Prize; Carsten [**Vol. 2:** 1961]
Nies Medal; Eric [**Vol. 1:** 11044]
Nigeria Prize for Literature [**Vol. 2:** 5097]
Nigeria Prize for Science [**Vol. 2:** 5098]
Nightclub of the Year [**Vol. 1:** 61]
Nightingale; Medaille Florence [**Vol. 2:** 6369]
Nightingale Medal; Florence [**Vol. 2:** 6369]
NIGP Fellow Award [**Vol. 1:** 12553]
Nihon Shinbun Kyokai Awards [**Vol. 2:** 4270]
Nihon Yakugakkai Gakujutsukokensho [**Vol. 2:** 4309]
Nihon Yakugakkai Gijutsusho [**Vol. 2:** 4311]
Nihon Yakugakkai sho [**Vol. 2:** 4313]
Nihon Yakugakkai Shoreisho [**Vol. 2:** 4312]
Niki Prize for Bioelectrochemistry; Katsumi [**Vol. 2:** 6444]
Nikkei QC Literature Prize [**Vol. 2:** 4339]
Nikolsky Honorary Lectureship; Alexander A. [**Vol. 1:** 2329]
Nikon-Walkley Press Photographer Prizes [**Vol. 2:** 1176]
Nile Gold Medal [**Vol. 2:** 6323]
Nimmo Medal; W.H.R. [**Vol. 2:** 794]
NINDS Javits Neuroscience Investigator Award [**Vol. 1:** 16815]
The Ninety-Nines Awards [**Vol. 1:** 13263]
Nininger Award; Alexander R. [**Vol. 1:** 17751]
Niotis Cup; D. J. [**Vol. 1:** 17157]
NISC Founders Award [**Vol. 1:** 12236]
NISC Research Award [**Vol. 1:** 12237]
Nishiyama Medal [**Vol. 2:** 4255]
NISO Safety Representative of the Year Award [**Vol. 2:** 3900]
Nissan - Fitzgerald [**Vol. 1:** 16196]
Nissen Award [**Vol. 1:** 7364]
Nissen-Emery Award [**Vol. 1:** 7364]
Nissim Prize; Rudolf [**Vol. 1:** 4262]
Nissl Young Investigator Award; Franz [**Vol. 2:** 8216]
Niwano Peace Prize [**Vol. 2:** 4305]
NJTL Chapter of the Year Award [**Vol. 1:** 17133]
NM Tirmizi Gold Medal [**Vol. 2:** 5201]
NMRT Mid-Career Award [**Vol. 1:** 10887]
Nobel Laureate Signature Award for a Graduate Student in Chemistry [**Vol. 1:** 1660]
Nobel Laureate Signature Award for Graduate Education in Chemistry [**Vol. 1:** 1660]
Nobel Prizes [**Vol. 2:** 6184]
Noble Educational Scholarship; Leonard [**Vol. 1:** 12857]
Noble Prize; Alfred [**Vol. 1:** 4212]
NODA Scholarship [**Vol. 1:** 12649]
Noether Awards; Gottfried E. [**Vol. 1:** 4561]
Nofflet Williams Up-and-Coming Leadership Award [**Vol. 1:** 17389]
NOGI Awards [**Vol. 1:** 16608]
Nolte Award for Extraordinary Leadership; Julius M. [**Vol. 1:** 17390]
Non-Broadcast Productions Telly Award [**Vol. 1:** 16414]
Non-Deadline Writing [**Vol. 1:** 4467]
Non-Fiction Book of the Year Award [**Vol. 1:** 6354]
Non-Governmental Organization for Peace of the Year [**Vol. 2:** 4612]
Nonfiction Contest [**Vol. 1:** 13075]
Nonnenmacher Industry Service Award; Tom [**Vol. 1:** 9623]
Nonprofit Marketer of the Year [**Vol. 1:** 2818]
Nonviolence Award [**Vol. 2:** 6229]
Noranda Lecture Award [**Vol. 1:** 6890]
Norbrook Award [**Vol. 2:** 4418]
Nordberg Medal; William [**Vol. 2:** 2340]

Nordberg Shield [**Vol. 2:** 5568]
Nordic Award [**Vol. 1:** 9903]
Nordic Combined World Cup Leaders [**Vol. 2:** 6428]
Nordic World Cup Leaders [**Vol. 2:** 6428]
Nordin Young Investigator Poster Award; Christopher and Margie [**Vol. 2:** 208]
Nordiska Priset [**Vol. 2:** 6209]
Nordlinger Child Welfare Leadership Award; Samuel Gerson [**Vol. 1:** 362]
Noriega Morales Award; Manuel [**Vol. 1:** 13695]
Norman Medal [**Vol. 1:** 4213]
Normann Medal; Wilhelm [**Vol. 2:** 3002]
Norris Award; Forbes [**Vol. 2:** 8063]
Norris Award in Physical Organic Chemistry; James Flack [**Vol. 1:** 1661]
Norris Career Achievement Award; Kenneth S. [**Vol. 1:** 15175]
North American Championship Trophy [**Vol. 1:** 9991]
North American Conservation Award [**Vol. 1:** 5568]
North American Mixing Forum Award [**Vol. 1:** 2631]
North Book Prize [**Vol. 2:** 7145]
North Medal for Service; Jeffrey [**Vol. 2:** 7146]
North Memorial Trophy; Rexford L. [**Vol. 1:** 12495]
North Shore Trophy [**Vol. 2:** 5058]
North-South Prize [**Vol. 2:** 2353]
Northcroft Lectureship [**Vol. 2:** 7166]
Northcutt Award; Susan [**Vol. 1:** 10390]
Northeastern Loggers' Association Awards [**Vol. 1:** 13401]
Northern Light Award [**Vol. 1:** 14934]
Northern New England Playwrights Award [**Vol. 1:** 17505]
Northern Print Biennale [**Vol. 2:** 8453]
Northern Science Award [**Vol. 1:** 31]
Northern Territory Literary Awards [**Vol. 2:** 910]
Northover Award; Alex [**Vol. 2:** 761]
Northrop Distinguished Service Award; Cynthia [**Vol. 1:** 1245]
Northrop Grumman Lunar Lander Challenge [**Vol. 1:** 18137]
Northwater Capital Management Award in Aging [**Vol. 1:** 17348]
Northwest Film and Video Festival [**Vol. 1:** 13410]
Northwest Filmmakers' Festival [**Vol. 1:** 13410]
Northwestern Mutual Best Master's Thesis Award [**Vol. 1:** 9271]
Norton Award; Andre [**Vol. 1:** 14786]
Norton Award; Joseph [**Vol. 1:** 5040]
Norton Award; Margaret Cross [**Vol. 1:** 11147]
Norton Distinguished Ceramist Award; F. H. [**Vol. 1:** 1570]
Norton-Griffiths Challenge Trophy [**Vol. 2:** 8597]
Norton Memorial Scholarship Award for Women; Mary R. [**Vol. 1:** 5622]
Norwegian Film Workers Association Technical Award [**Vol. 2:** 5155]
Norwegian Ibsen Award [**Vol. 2:** 5130]
Norwegian International Film Festival [**Vol. 2:** 5144]
Norwegian Short Film Festival Prize [**Vol. 2:** 5156]
Notable Trade Books for Young People [**Vol. 1:** 12172]
Notable Wisconsin Authors [**Vol. 1:** 17897]
Notary of the Year Award [**Vol. 1:** 12621]
Notre Dame Award [**Vol. 1:** 17318]
Noury, Thorlet, Henri Becquerel, Jules and Augusta Lazare; Prix Victor [**Vol. 2:** 2224]
NOVA Award [**Vol. 1:** 7548]
Nova Award [**Vol. 1:** 1403]
Nova Awards [**Vol. 1:** 8826]
NOVA Program of Distinction Awards [**Vol. 1:** 12638]
Novak Award [**Vol. 1:** 134]
Novak Collegiate Journalism Award; Robert [**Vol. 1:** 8489]
Novartis Award for Hypertension Research [**Vol. 2:** 4294]
Novartis Award; Graduate Student Fellowship/ [**Vol. 1:** 15851]
Novartis Award (Pharmoeconomics) [**Vol. 1:** 6954]
Novartis Junior Scientist Award [**Vol. 2:** 703]
Novartis Nematology Award [**Vol. 1:** 15726]
Novartis Oration Award for Research in the Field of Cancer [**Vol. 2:** 3555]
Novel Disease Model Awards [**Vol. 1:** 3260]
Novel Manuscript Award [**Vol. 1:** 13076]
Novella Contest [**Vol. 1:** 14368]
Novice Award [**Vol. 1:** 17175]

Novikoff Memorial Award; Philip A. [**Vol. 1:** 6842]
Novitski Prize; Edward [**Vol. 1:** 8552]
Novo Nordisk Canada-CAS Research Awards [**Vol. 1:** 6205]
Novo Nordisk Foundation Lecture [**Vol. 2:** 1984]
Novo Nordisk Prize [**Vol. 2:** 1985]
NovoPharm Award [**Vol. 1:** 6955]
Nowotny Excellence in Cancer Nursing Education Award; Mary [**Vol. 1:** 13556]
Noyes Award; Marcia C. [**Vol. 1:** 11073]
NRCA Fellow Award [**Vol. 1:** 12764]
NSES Award [**Vol. 2:** 4802]
NSI Research Award [**Vol. 2:** 5160]
NSK Neustadt Prize for Children's Literature [**Vol. 1:** 18056]
NSPE Award [**Vol. 1:** 12879]
NSPS Scholarships [**Vol. 1:** 12893]
NSW Premier's Translation Prize [**Vol. 2:** 907]
NTPC Book Award [**Vol. 2:** 3475]
Nuclear-Free Future Award [**Vol. 2:** 2890]
Nucletron Brachytherapy Award [**Vol. 2:** 1498]
Nuffield Lecture [**Vol. 2:** 9102]
Nuffield Medal; Viscount [**Vol. 2:** 8029]
Numismatic Art Award for Excellence in Medallic Sculpture [**Vol. 1:** 3000]
Numismatic Error Collectors Exhibit Award [**Vol. 1:** 3001]
Nunn Media and Conservation Award; Carl [**Vol. 1:** 13588]
Nuremberg Award for Company Culture without Discrimination [**Vol. 2:** 2752]
Nuremberg International Human Rights Award [**Vol. 2:** 2753]
Nurse Exemplar Award [**Vol. 1:** 4025]
Nurse Manager Award [**Vol. 1:** 8096]
Nurse of the Year Award
    Care Forum Wales [**Vol. 2:** 7333]
    National Hemophilia Foundation [**Vol 1:** 12505]
Nursery Extension Award for Distinguished Service to the Nursery Industry [**Vol. 1:** 3927]
Nurse's Humanitarian Award in Honor of Lawrence F. Kienle, MD [**Vol. 1:** 13936]
Nursing Award [**Vol. 1:** 5431]
Nursing Competence in Aging Award [**Vol. 1:** 8097]
Nursing Education Award [**Vol. 1:** 8098]
Nursing Excellence Award [**Vol. 1:** 6480]
Nursing Practice Award [**Vol. 1:** 8099]
Nursing Professionalism Award [**Vol. 1:** 8100]
Nursing Research Award [**Vol. 1:** 8101]
Nursing Research Award; Ann Burgess Forensic [**Vol. 1:** 9666]
Nursing Service Cross [**Vol. 2:** 318]
Nursing; Virginia A. Lynch Pioneer Award in Forensic [**Vol. 1:** 9668]
Nutrition Award [**Vol. 1:** 695]
Nutrition Education Award [**Vol. 1:** 1129]
Nutrition Professionals, Inc. Applied Dairy Nutrition Award [**Vol. 1:** 1984]
Nutting Award for Exemplary Historical Research and Writing; Mary Adelaide [**Vol. 1:** 1007]
NWC Nonfiction Contest [**Vol. 1:** 13075]
NWC Novel Manuscript Award [**Vol. 1:** 13076]
NWC Poetry Award [**Vol. 1:** 13077]
NWC Short Story Award [**Vol. 1:** 13078]
NWRA Grants [**Vol. 1:** 13048]
Nycomed Prize [**Vol. 2:** 6449]
Nyholm Lectureship; Sir Ronald [**Vol. 2:** 9033]
Nyholm Prize for Education [**Vol. 2:** 9033]
Nystrom Award; J. Warren [**Vol. 1:** 5207]
Nystrom Prize; E. J. [**Vol. 2:** 2106]
Nystroms Prize; Professor E. J. [**Vol. 2:** 2106]
NZMS Research Award [**Vol. 2:** 4978]
NZSA/Pindar Publishing Prize [**Vol. 2:** 5014]
NZVA Clinical Studies Award [**Vol. 2:** 5026]
Oakley Certificate of Merit [**Vol. 1:** 5025]
Obasanjo Prize in Technological Innovation; Olusegun [**Vol. 2:** 4371]
Oberle Award [**Vol. 1:** 8217]
Oberle Award for Outstanding Teaching in Grades K-12; Marcella E. [**Vol. 1:** 12114]
Oberly Award for Bibliography in the Agricultural or Natural Sciences [**Vol. 1:** 5267]
Oberly Memorial Award; Eunice Rockwell [**Vol. 1:** 5267]
Oberman and Rich Award [**Vol. 1:** 9144]
Obermann Fellowships [**Vol. 1:** 17257]

Oberst Award; Byron B. [Vol. 1: 696]
OBIE Awards [Vol. 1: 13739]
Obie Awards [Vol. 1: 17560]
O'Brien Award; Jane [Vol. 1: 9145]
O'Brien Award; Morrough P. [Vol. 1: 3744]
O'Brien Award; Robert F. [Vol. 1: 12037]
O'Brien Championship Trophy; Larry [Vol. 1: 11978]
O'Brien New Investigator Award; Bernie J. [Vol. 1: 10209]
Obruchev Prize; V.A. [Vol. 2: 5839]
Observer Awards [Vol. 1: 1404]
Obstetricians/Gynecologists; Awards in Recognition of Women [Vol. 2: 8123]
Obwegeser Travelling Scholarship; Hugo [Vol. 2: 7591]
O'Byrne Award; Father Patrick [Vol. 1: 17465]
Occhialini Medal and Prize [Vol. 2: 7917]
Occupational Health Practitioner of the Year [Vol. 2: 5722]
Ocean Sciences Award [Vol. 1: 2245]
Oceaneering International Award [Vol. 1: 16606]
Oceania Zonal Chess Championship [Vol. 2: 2062]
Ochal Award for Distinguished Service to the Profession; Bethany J. [Vol. 1: 1197]
Ockerman State and Regional Professional Activity Award; Elbert W. [Vol. 1: 1104]
O'Connor Award for Short Fiction; Flannery [Vol. 1: 17242]
O'Connor Award; Neil [Vol. 2: 7191]
O'Connor Essay Award; Richard [Vol. 1: 4814]
O'Connor Film Award; John E. [Vol. 1: 2386]
ODAS Youth Achievement Award [Vol. 1: 346]
O'Day Trophy; George D. [Vol. 1: 17059]
Odden Award; Vic [Vol. 2: 8905]
O'Dell Award; William [Vol. 1: 2806]
Odem Technical Excellence Award [Vol. 2: 3975]
Odems Memorial Award; Lingiam [Vol. 1: 299]
Odense Film Festival [Vol. 2: 1987]
Odense International Organ Competition [Vol. 2: 1989]
Odhiambo Prize in Basic and Applied Sciences; Thomas R. [Vol. 2: 4372]
O'Donnell/Eunice E. Kraft Teacher Training Scholarships; Maureen V. [Vol. 1: 1687]
O'Donoghue Sports Injury Research Award [Vol. 1: 3100]
Odontology Section President's Prize [Vol. 2: 9103]
Odyssey Award for Excellence in Audiobook Production [Vol. 1: 5068]
Odyssey Diploma [Vol. 2: 6324]
Oelke Memorial Award for Painting; Kimbel E. [Vol. 1: 530]
Oenslager Scholastic Achievement Awards; Mary P. [Vol. 1: 10787]
Oersted Medal [Vol. 1: 1311]
Oertel Interventional Cytopathologist Award; Yolanda [Vol. 1: 13824]
Office Directors' Award/Cross Category Award [Vol. 1: 16894]
Officer of Logohu [Vol. 2: 5217]
Official of the Year [Vol. 1: 17489]
O'Flaherty Service Award; Fred [Vol. 1: 2761]
Ofsthun Award; Stan [Vol. 1: 15819]
Ogden Award; H. R. "Russ" [Vol. 1: 5623]
Ogden Memorial Prize; Bill [Vol. 2: 8536]
Ogilvy Award; Grand [Vol. 1: 170]
Ogilvy Awards; David [Vol. 1: 170]
OH Awards [Vol. 2: 2076]
The OH County Award [Vol. 2: 2077]
The OHA Plaques [Vol. 2: 2078]
OHA-VHF Award [Vol. 2: 2079]
O'Hagan Award for Short Fiction; Howard [Vol. 1: 18109]
O'Harris Award; Pixie [Vol. 2: 519]
Ohio Award [Vol. 1: 12365]
Ohio Women's Hall of Fame [Vol. 1: 8763]
Ohioana Award for Editorial Excellence [Vol. 1: 13489]
Ohioana Book Awards [Vol. 1: 13493]
Ohioana Career Award [Vol. 1: 13494]
Ohioana Citations [Vol. 1: 13495]
Ohioana Pegasus Award [Vol. 1: 13496]
Ohkoshi Award; Masaaki [Vol. 2: 8199]
Oil and Fats Group International Lecture [Vol. 2: 9288]

Oita International Wheelchair Marathon [Vol. 2: 4307]
Oke Trophy; F. G. (Teddy) [Vol. 1: 2418]
Oken Medaille; Lorenz [Vol. 2: 3029]
Okes Award; Imogene [Vol. 1: 858]
Oklahoma Centennial Award [Vol. 1: 12268]
Oklahoma School Administrator Award [Vol. 1: 13502]
Okuma Academic Commemorative Prize [Vol. 2: 4344]
Okuma Academic Encouragement Prize [Vol. 2: 4345]
Okuma Gakujutsu Kinensho [Vol. 2: 4344]
Okuma Gakujutsu Shoreisho [Vol. 2: 4345]
Olah Award in Hydrocarbon or Petroleum Chemistry; George A. [Vol. 1: 1662]
Olander In-Service Training Grants; Clarence [Vol. 1: 12227]
Olave Award [Vol. 2: 9468]
Old Guard Prizes [Vol. 1: 4413]
Old Walrus Award [Vol. 1: 8937]
Ol'denburg Prize; S.F. [Vol. 2: 5840]
Oldenburger Medal; Rufus [Vol. 1: 4414]
Oldendorf Award; William H. [Vol. 1: 4455]
Oldfield Award [Vol. 2: 9314]
Oldfield Cup; Lucy [Vol. 2: 7272]
Oldfield Distinguished Service Award; Barney [Vol. 1: 14418]
Oldman Prize; C. B. [Vol. 2: 8086]
O'Leary Award; Bart [Vol. 1: 11750]
Olivarez La Raza Award; Graciela [Vol. 1: 12189]
Oliver Award; Ross L. [Vol. 1: 12467]
Oliver Prize; Brian [Vol. 2: 8732]
Oliver Rock Art Photography Award [Vol. 1: 3716]
Oliveros Prize; Pauline [Vol. 1: 9499]
Olivier Award; C.P. [Vol. 1: 2896]
Olivier Awards; Laurence [Vol. 2: 9324]
Olle Prize; Archibald D. [Vol. 2: 1007]
Olman Publishers Award; Abe [Vol. 1: 11412]
Olmsted Award; Sterling [Vol. 1: 3870]
Olmsted Medal; Frederick Law [Vol. 1: 4368]
Olney Medal for Achievement in Textile Chemistry [Vol. 1: 1382]
Olsen Engineering Executive of the Year Award; Sid [Vol. 1: 15526]
Olsson Award; Axel [Vol. 1: 13800]
Oludhe Award; Dr. Marjorie [Vol. 2: 4419]
Oluyemisi Memorial Prize; Daramola [Vol. 2: 4420]
Olympiad Awards; Physics [Vol. 2: 3687]
Olympiart [Vol. 2: 6413]
Olympic Cup [Vol. 2: 6414]
Olympic Medals and Diplomas [Vol. 2: 6415]
Olympic Order [Vol. 2: 6416]
Olympic Order; New Zealand [Vol. 2: 4986]
Olympic Spirit Award [Vol. 1: 17015]
O'Mahony Bursary; Eoin [Vol. 2: 3930]
O'Malley Art Award
    Irish American Cultural Institute [Vol. 1: 10515]
    Irish American Cultural Institute [Vol 1: 10517]
O'Malley Award; General Jerome F. [Vol. 1: 261]
Oman Green Awards [Vol. 2: 5168]
Oman Web Awards [Vol. 2: 5178]
Omega Man of the Year Award [Vol. 1: 13507]
Omega Protein Innovative Research Award [Vol. 1: 4123]
Omicron Delta Kappa Scholarships [Vol. 1: 13517]
Omni Intermedia Awards [Vol. 1: 11027]
OMNII Pediatric Dentistry Postdoctoral Fellowship [Vol. 1: 646]
Omran Prize; Ishaq bin [Vol. 1: 1364]
On Behalf of Youth Award [Vol. 1: 6119]
On-site Generation Award [Vol. 1: 16895]
On-the-Spot Awards [Vol. 1: 16799]
Onassis Award for Culture (Letters, Arts and Humanities) [Vol. 2: 3296]
Onassis Award for International Understanding and Social Achievement [Vol. 2: 3297]
Onassis Award for the Environment [Vol. 2: 3298]
Onassis International Prize in Finance [Vol. 2: 3299]
Onassis International Prize in Law [Vol. 2: 3300]
Onassis International Prize in Shipping [Vol. 2: 3301]
Onassis International Prize in the Humanities [Vol. 2: 3302]
Onassis International Prize in Trade [Vol. 2: 3303]
Onassis Medal; Jacqueline Kennedy [Vol. 1: 11301]

Onassis Prize for Man and Culture - Olympia [Vol. 2: 3296]
Onassis Prize for Man and His Environment - Delphi [Vol. 2: 3298]
Onassis Prize in Shipping, Trade and Finance [Vol. 2: 3304]
Oncology Certified Nurse (OCN) of the Year [Vol. 1: 13525]
Oncology Social Worker of the Year [Vol. 1: 5447]
Ondaatje Ballet Fund; Christopher [Vol. 1: 6153]
Ondaatje Prize [Vol. 2: 9076]
One-Club Award [Vol. 1: 14876]
One-Design Awards [Vol. 1: 17060]
O'Neal Safety Award; Jack [Vol. 1: 16737]
O'Neill Award; Joseph E. [Vol. 1: 10988]
O'Neill Journalism Award; Elizabeth [Vol. 2: 3816]
O'Neill Memorial Award; Gerard K. [Vol. 1: 12922]
Ong Memorial Award; William A. "Bill" [Vol. 1: 11501]
Online Directory of the Year - Business [Vol. 2: 7501]
Online Directory of the Year - Consumer [Vol. 2: 7502]
Online Film and Video Awards [Vol. 1: 17732]
Online Journalism Awards [Vol. 1: 13560]
Online Publishing Awards [Vol. 2: 9401]
Ono Memorial Awards for Academic Studies; Azusa [Vol. 2: 4346]
Ono Memorial Awards for Art; Azusa [Vol. 2: 4347]
Ono Memorial Awards for Sports; Azusa [Vol. 2: 4348]
Onsager Prize; Lars [Vol. 1: 3212]
Ontario College of Art & Design Scholarships [Vol. 1: 13575]
Ontario Medal for Firefighter Bravery [Vol. 1: 13579]
Ontario Medal for Good Citizenship [Vol. 1: 13580]
Ontario Medal for Police Bravery [Vol. 1: 13581]
Ontario Waste Minimization Awards [Vol. 1: 14456]
Ontario's Family Physicians of the Year [Vol. 1: 7374]
Open Award for Technical Excellence in Architectural Technology [Vol. 2: 7361]
Open Book Award [Vol. 1: 13897]
Open Category Award [Vol. 2: 416]
Open Championship [Vol. 2: 8638]
Open Competition Awards [Vol. 1: 2931]
Open Palm Award [Vol. 1: 9176]
Open Source Awards [Vol. 2: 8442]
Open Water Swimmer of the Year [Vol. 1: 17446]
Opera Awards [Vol. 2: 525]
Operasangerinnen Fanny Elstas Fond [Vol. 2: 5121]
Operation Safe Shop Competition [Vol. 1: 5370]
Operational Achievement Award (Individual and Group) [Vol. 1: 13034]
Operational Medicine Award [Vol. 1: 5432]
Operations Award [Vol. 2: 2646]
Operator of the Year [Vol. 1: 13086]
Ophthalmological Gold Medal [Vol. 2: 2030]
Opie Prize; Peter and Iona [Vol. 1: 2164]
Opinion Award [Vol. 1: 9448]
Oporto International Film Festival - Fantasporto [Vol. 2: 5424]
Oppenheim-John Downes Memorial Trust Awards [Vol. 2: 8436]
Oppenheimer Award [Vol. 1: 3871]
Oppenheimer Award; Ernst [Vol. 1: 8112]
Opperman Award for Judicial Excellence; Dwight D. [Vol. 1: 2740]
Oppermann Memorial Award for Lifetime Achievement; Martin [Vol. 1: 10359]
Optical Society of India Award [Vol. 2: 3775]
OPTIMA Gold Medal [Vol. 2: 4146]
OPTIMA Silver Medal [Vol. 2: 4147]
Optimas Awards [Vol. 1: 18007]
Optometrist of the Year Award [Vol. 1: 3055]
Ora Award [Vol. 1: 12570]
Oral and Poster Presentation Prize [Vol. 2: 8733]
Oral and Poster Prize in the Psychiatry of Learning Disability [Vol. 2: 8734]
Oral Presentation Awards [Vol. 2: 1556]
Oral Science Research Award [Vol. 1: 9539]
Orange Award for New Writers [Vol. 2: 6907]
Orange British Academy Film Awards [Vol. 2: 6933]
Orange Prize for Fiction [Vol. 2: 6908]
Orban Memorial Prize; Balint [Vol. 1: 723]
ORBEL Award [Vol. 2: 1415]
Orbeli Prize; L.A. [Vol. 2: 5841]
Orbis Books Prize for Polish Studies [Vol. 1: 5100]

Orbis Pictus Award for Outstanding Nonfiction for Children [Vol. 1: 12213]
Orchard Medal; William J. [Vol. 1: 17715]
Orchestral Audition and Masterclass Competition [Vol. 1: 12400]
Orde van Oranje-Nassau [Vol. 2: 4650]
Orden al Merito Julio Garavito [Vol. 2: 1841]
Orden del Merito Militar Antonio Narino [Vol. 2: 1836]
Orden del Merito Naval Almirante Padilla [Vol. 2: 1837]
Orden del Merito Sanitario Jose Fernandez Madrid [Vol. 2: 1838]
Orden ng Gawad Pambansang Alagad ng Sining [Vol. 2: 5342]
Order of Australia [Vol. 2: 319]
Order of Canada [Vol. 1: 8757]
Order of Excellence of Guyana [Vol. 2: 3340]
Order of Honor [Vol. 2: 2682]
Order of Honour Service Awards [Vol. 1: 14209]
Order of Hospitality [Vol. 2: 5885]
Order of Lifesaving [Vol. 2: 1540]
Order of Mariposa [Vol. 1: 10765]
Order of Merit
    Central Chancery of the Orders of Knighthood - Honours and Appointments [Vol. 2: 7345]
    International Hockey Federation [Vol 2: 6394]
    International Waterski and Wakeboard Federation [Vol 2: 6466]
    National Wrestling Hall of Fame & Museum [Vol 1: 13072]
Order of National Artists of the Philippines [Vol. 2: 5342]
Order of Ontario [Vol. 1: 13582]
Order of Orange-Nassau [Vol. 2: 4650]
Order of Pius [Vol. 2: 9547]
Order of Red Triangle [Vol. 1: 18191]
Order of Rio Branco [Vol. 2: 1746]
Order of Roraima of Guyana [Vol. 2: 3341]
Order of St. Gregory the Great [Vol. 2: 9548]
Order of St. Michael and St. George [Vol. 2: 7346]
Order of St. Sylvester [Vol. 2: 9549]
Order of Sancta Barbara [Vol. 1: 6616]
Order of the Academic Palms [Vol. 2: 2445]
Order of the Bell [Vol. 1: 14689]
Order of the Bird [Vol. 1: 9689]
Order of the British Empire [Vol. 2: 7347]
Order of the Cross of Vytis (the Knight) [Vol. 2: 4491]
Order of the Egg [Vol. 1: 9690]
Order of the Falcon [Vol. 2: 3438]
Order of the Golden Ark [Vol. 2: 4651]
Order of the Golden Microscope [Vol. 1: 2866]
Order of the Golden Spur (Golden Militia) [Vol. 2: 9550]
Order of the Lapis Lazuli [Vol. 1: 8308]
Order of the Lithuanian Grand Duke Gediminas [Vol. 2: 4492]
Order of the Netherlands Lion [Vol. 2: 4652]
Order of the Royal Huntsman [Vol. 2: 7440]
Order of the Sacred Treasure [Vol. 2: 4272]
Order of the White Double Cross [Vol. 2: 6004]
Order of Vytautas the Great [Vol. 2: 4493]
Ordinary Fellow [Vol. 2: 6920]
Ordnance Survey MasterMap Award [Vol. 2: 6991]
O'Reilly Memorial Hang Gliding Competitions Trophy; Shane [Vol. 2: 8265]
Orenstein Memorial Convention Travel Fund; Doris [Vol. 1: 5387]
Orford String Quartet Scholarship [Vol. 1: 13570]
Organ Honorary Member Award; Claude [Vol. 1: 5553]
Organic Chemistry Division Award for Excellent Research [Vol. 2: 5462]
Organic Food Awards [Vol. 2: 9350]
Organic Industry Chemistry Award [Vol. 2: 9034]
Organic Lectureship [Vol. 2: 978]
Organic Petrology Award [Vol. 2: 6059]
Organic Stereochemistry Award [Vol. 2: 9035]
Organisational Awards [Vol. 2: 375]
Organist of the Year [Vol. 1: 4590]
Organization of Islamic Capitals and Cities Awards [Vol. 2: 5909]
Organization of the Year Award [Vol. 1: 14827]
Organizational Achievement Award [Vol. 1: 11343]
Organizational Award
    National Rehabilitation Association [Vol. 1: 12753]

South Dakota State Historical Society [Vol 1: 15987]
Organizational Certificate of Appreciation [Vol. 1: 7561]
Organizational Contribution Award [Vol. 1: 969]
Organizational Leader in Experiential Education Award: Community-Based Organization [Vol. 1: 12851]
Organizational Leader in Experiential Education Award: Corporate/Foundation [Vol. 1: 12852]
Organizational Leader in Experiential Education Award: Higher Education [Vol. 1: 12853]
Organizational Leader in Experiential Education Award: K-12 [Vol. 1: 12854]
Organizing Excellence Award [Vol. 1: 11849]
Organometallic Chemistry Award
    Royal Australian Chemical Institute [Vol. 2: 979]
    Royal Society of Chemistry [Vol 2: 9036]
Orica Chemnet Operations Award [Vol. 2: 5090]
Orion Award for Excellence in Experimental Education [Vol. 1: 11335]
Orme Prize; Margaret [Vol. 2: 9430]
Ormond Medal; Francis [Vol. 2: 952]
Ornamo Globe [Vol. 2: 2084]
Ornish Award; Natalie [Vol. 1: 16459]
Ornithologen-Preis [Vol. 2: 2981]
Orr Air Force Spouse of the Year Award; Joan [Vol. 1: 262]
Orr Award; Verne [Vol. 1: 263]
ORSA Prize [Vol. 1: 9260]
Orthopedic Allied Professional of the Year [Vol. 1: 4479]
Orton Award; Samuel T. [Vol. 1: 9886]
Orton, Jr., Memorial Lecture; Edward [Vol. 1: 1571]
Orwell Award for Distinguished Contribution to Honesty and Clarity in Public Language; George [Vol. 1: 12214]
Orzalli Memorial Award; Margene [Vol. 1: 12947]
OSA Leadership Award - New Focus/Bookham Prize [Vol. 1: 13612]
Osas Festspillfond; Sigbjorn Bernhoft [Vol. 2: 5122]
Osborn Post-Doctoral Research Fellowship in British Studies; James M. [Vol. 1: 18160]
Osborn Teacher-Scholar Award; Michael M. [Vol. 1: 16046]
Osborne and Mendel Award [Vol. 1: 4018]
Osborne Medal; Thomas Burr [Vol. 1: 9]
Osborne Memorial Award [Vol. 2: 8481]
Oscar dell'imballaggio Award [Vol. 2: 4132]
Oscars [Vol. 1: 84]
Oser Food Ingredient Safety Award; Bernard L. [Vol. 1: 9340]
Osetek Educator Award; Edward M. [Vol. 1: 1142]
Osiris; Prix [Vol. 2: 2473]
Osler Award [Vol. 1: 6014]
The Osler Award [Vol. 1: 6963]
Osler Medal; William [Vol. 1: 1000]
OSM Standard Life Competition [Vol. 1: 11256]
Osmond-Russell Scholarship [Vol. 1: 106]
Ossofsky Award; Jack [Vol. 1: 12238]
Osteoporosis Award [Vol. 2: 7242]
Oster Gold Heart Award; Richard M. [Vol. 1: 2312]
Osterweil Award for Poetry; Joyce [Vol. 1: 13898]
Ostwald Medal; Wilhelm [Vol. 2: 2043]
Ostwald Original Band Composition Award [Vol. 1: 1462]
OSU Photography and Cinema Alumni Society Award [Vol. 1: 7427]
O'Sullivan Award for Professional Development; Tim [Vol. 1: 5569]
O'Sullivan Fundraiser Award; Bill [Vol. 2: 3880]
Osuna Sportsmanship Award [Vol. 1: 9464]
Osuna Sportsmanship Award; Rafael [Vol. 1: 9464]
OTA Award of Excellence [Vol. 1: 3034]
Othmer Gold Medal [Vol. 1: 14991]
Othmer Sophomore Academic Excellence Award; Donald F. [Vol. 1: 2636]
Otis Lifetime Achievement Award; John [Vol. 1: 11379]
Otological Research Fellowship for Medical Students [Vol. 1: 7821]
O'Toole Agency Awards [Vol. 1: 1016]
O'Toole Multicultural Advertising Award [Vol. 1: 1017]
O'Toole Public Service Award [Vol. 1: 1018]
Otremba Memorial Award; Elke [Vol. 1: 7016]

Ott Award for Outstanding Contribution to Children's Literature; Helen Keating [Vol. 1: 7273]
Ott; Prix Theodore [Vol. 2: 6482]
Ott Prize; Theodore [Vol. 2: 6482]
Ottawa Architectural Conservation Awards [Vol. 1: 7294]
Ottawa University School of Medicine Award [Vol. 1: 6014]
Ottum Award; Selina Roberts [Vol. 1: 4715]
Our American Indian Heritage Award [Vol. 1: 12366]
Our Native American Heritage Award [Vol. 1: 12366]
Ousmane Prize; Sembene [Vol. 2: 9533]
Outdoor Communications Awards [Vol. 1: 13746]
Outdoor/Environmental Commercial Telly Award [Vol. 1: 16415]
Outdoor Writing Awards [Vol. 1: 13746]
Outer Critics Circle Awards [Vol. 1: 13748]
Outland Trophy [Vol. 1: 8410]
Outler Prize in Ecumenical Church History; Albert C. [Vol. 1: 4148]
Outreach and Communication Award [Vol. 2: 2838]
Outreach Award
    North Country Trail Association [Vol. 1: 13386]
    Southern States Communication Association [Vol 1: 16047]
    Voluntary Protection Programs Participants' Association [Vol 1: 17615]
Outreach Prize [Vol. 2: 2395]
Outreach Services Award [Vol. 1: 4786]
Outstanding Academic Librarian Award [Vol. 1: 10894]
Outstanding Achievement Award
    Canadian Association of Career Educators and Employers [Vol. 1: 6242]
    Canadian Public Relations Society [Vol 1: 6843]
    International Association for Pattern Recognition [Vol 2: 4233]
    International Thermoelectric Society [Vol 2: 8240]
    Modular Building Institute [Vol 1: 11252]
    National Society of Professional Insurance Investigators [Vol 1: 12888]
    Parapsychological Association [Vol 1: 13847]
    Renewable Natural Resources Foundation [Vol 1: 14506]
    Society of Woman Geographers [Vol 1: 15893]
    Western North Carolina Historical Association - Smith-McDowell House Museum [Vol 1: 17767]
    Youth Media Alliance [Vol 1: 18207]
Outstanding Achievement Award - Group [Vol. 1: 2650]
Outstanding Achievement Award - Hong Kong Jewelry Industry [Vol. 2: 5264]
Outstanding Achievement Award - Individual [Vol. 1: 2651]
Outstanding Achievement Awards
    American Association of Blood Banks [Vol. 1: 1067]
    Public Risk Management Association [Vol. 1: 14335]
Outstanding Achievement in Adolescent Medicine Award [Vol. 1: 15015]
Outstanding Achievement in Management Award [Vol. 1: 9358]
Outstanding Achievement in Mentorship Award [Vol. 1: 5467]
Outstanding Achievement in Patron Transport Safety [Vol. 2: 366]
Outstanding Achievement in Perioperative Clinical Nursing Education Award [Vol. 1: 5468]
Outstanding Achievement in Perioperative Clinical Nursing Practice Award [Vol. 1: 5469]
Outstanding Achievement in Perioperative Nursing Management Award [Vol. 1: 5470]
Outstanding Achievement in Perioperative Nursing Research Award [Vol. 1: 5471]
Outstanding Achievement in Perioperative Patient Education [Vol. 1: 5472]
Outstanding Administration Award [Vol. 1: 9823]
Outstanding Administrator Award [Vol. 1: 16144]
Outstanding Advertising Campaign [Vol. 1: 12012]
Outstanding Advising Awards [Vol. 1: 11396]
Outstanding Advising Program Awards [Vol. 1: 11397]
Outstanding Advisor Award [Vol. 1: 5163]

Outstanding Section and Collegiate Chapter Partnership Award [Vol. 1: 15527]

Outstanding Section Awards
AACE International [Vol. 1: 19]
American Institute of Aeronautics and Astronautics [Vol 1: 2537]

Outstanding Section Member Award [Vol. 1: 15528]

Outstanding Service Award
ACM SIGGRAPH [Vol. 1: 118]
NARTS - The Association of Resale Professionals [Vol 1: 11374]
States Organization for Boating Access [Vol 1: 16280]

Outstanding Service Award
American Academy of Family Physicians [Vol. 1: 560]
American Academy of Psychiatry and the Law [Vol 1: 749]
American Association of Meat Processors [Vol 1: 1207]
American Association of Teachers of Spanish and Portuguese [Vol 1: 1376]
American College of Dentists [Vol 1: 1739]
American Physical Therapy Association, Private Practice Section [Vol 1: 3246]
ASPRS - The Imaging and Geospatial Information Society [Vol 1: 4873]
Association of Building Engineers [Vol 2: 6803]
Care Forum Wales [Vol 2: 7333]
Council on Governmental Ethics Laws [Vol 1: 7702]
Fellows of the American Bar Foundation [Vol 1: 8339]
International Federation for Information Processing [Vol 2: 1271]
International Wild Waterfowl Association [Vol 1: 10482]
National Association of Underwater Instructors [Vol 1: 11936]
National Space Society of Australia [Vol 2: 899]
National University of Singapore [Vol 2: 5957]
New Zealand Veterinary Association [Vol 2: 5027]
Soil and Water Conservation Society [Vol 1: 15926]
TRI-M Music Honor Society [Vol 1: 16559]
Virginia Interscholastic Athletic Administrators Association [Vol 1: 17580]

Outstanding Service Award for Military Pediatrics [Vol. 1: 698]

Outstanding Service Awards
National Agricultural Aviation Association [Vol. 1: 11494]
National InterScholastic Swimming Coaches Association of America [Vol 1: 12568]

Outstanding Service Medallion [Vol. 1: 859]

Outstanding Service to a Chapter Award [Vol. 1: 14205]

Outstanding Service to Environmental Education Award [Vol. 1: 13268]

Outstanding Service to Environmental Education by an Individual Award [Vol. 1: 13269]

Outstanding Service to Environmental Education by an Organization Award [Vol. 1: 13270]

Outstanding Service to Karate Award [Vol. 1: 458]

Outstanding Service to Libraries Award [Vol. 1: 13218]

Outstanding Service to Music Award [Vol. 1: 16379]

Outstanding Service to People with Disabilities [Vol. 1: 7308]

Outstanding Service to the Forest Industry [Vol. 1: 13401]

Outstanding Service to the Profession Award [Vol. 2: 4902]

Outstanding Show Poster Award [Vol. 1: 8330]

Outstanding Small Chapter Award [Vol. 1: 9311]

Outstanding Social Work Doctoral Dissertation Award [Vol. 1: 15337]

Outstanding Southeastern Author Award [Vol. 1: 15997]

Outstanding Southeastern Library Program Award [Vol. 1: 15998]

Outstanding Special Education Teacher Award [Vol. 1: 11903]

Outstanding SPS Chapter Advisor Award [Vol. 1: 2690]

Outstanding State Association Award [Vol. 1: 11521]

Outstanding State Leader Award [Vol. 1: 5482]

Outstanding State, Provincial or Territorial Psychological Association Award [Vol. 1: 3618]

Outstanding State Representative Award [Vol. 1: 7838]

Outstanding Statistical Application Awards [Vol. 1: 4562]

Outstanding Structure Award [Vol. 2: 6352]

Outstanding Student Achievement in Contemporary Sculpture Award [Vol. 1: 10131]

Outstanding Student Award [Vol. 1: 2867]

Outstanding Student Award for Undergraduate Research [Vol. 1: 15778]

Outstanding Student Chapter Contest Award [Vol. 1: 15218]

Outstanding Student Leader Award [Vol. 1: 1740]

Outstanding Student Poster Award [Vol. 1: 3473]

Outstanding Student Recognition Awards [Vol. 1: 12278]

Outstanding Student Research Award [Vol. 1: 10196]

Outstanding Support Staff Award [Vol. 1: 9208]

Outstanding Teacher Award
International Society for the Social Studies [Vol. 1: 10246]
National Marine Educators Association [Vol 1: 12595]

Outstanding Teacher Educator in Reading Award [Vol. 1: 10099]

Outstanding Teacher of American History Contest [Vol. 1: 12848]

Outstanding Teacher of the Year Awards [Vol. 1: 1377]

Outstanding Teacher of Theatre in Higher Education Award [Vol. 1: 5149]

Outstanding Technical Contributions Award [Vol. 2: 6266]

Outstanding Technical Program Award [Vol. 1: 4583]

Outstanding Technical Student Award [Vol. 1: 4584]

Outstanding Technical Teacher Award [Vol. 1: 4585]

Outstanding Technologist Award [Vol. 1: 15731]

Outstanding Tennis Facility Awards [Vol. 1: 17134]

Outstanding Ticketing Professional Award [Vol. 1: 10457]

Outstanding Torch Club [Vol. 1: 9719]

Outstanding Total Community Service [Vol. 1: 7309]

Outstanding Training Program Award [Vol. 1: 3574]

Outstanding Trustee Award [Vol. 1: 9209]

Outstanding Ultrasonic Application [Vol. 1: 16602]

Outstanding Undergraduate Award [Vol. 1: 7468]

Outstanding Undergraduate Educator Award [Vol. 1: 3933]

Outstanding Undergraduate Horticulture Student Award [Vol. 1: 3934]

Outstanding Undergraduate Student Member of the Year Award [Vol. 1: 7642]

Outstanding Use of Oral History in a Nonprint Format [Vol. 1: 13633]

Outstanding Use of Wood [Vol. 1: 13401]

Outstanding Volunteer [Vol. 1: 10912]

Outstanding Volunteer Awards [Vol. 1: 12615]

Outstanding Website or Newsletter Award [Vol. 1: 459]

Outstanding Woman in Business [Vol. 2: 1372]

Outstanding Woman Veterinarian of the Year [Vol. 1: 5184]

Outstanding Women in Music Award [Vol. 1: 16379]

Outstanding Wrestling Official of the Year [Vol. 1: 449]

Outstanding Young Agents Committee Award [Vol. 1: 9183]

Outstanding Young Agrologist Award [Vol. 1: 225]

Outstanding Young Alumni Award [Vol. 1: 13408]

Outstanding Young Alumnus Award [Vol. 1: 8509]

Outstanding Young Citizen [Vol. 1: 13713]

Outstanding Young Electrical and Computer Engineer Award [Vol. 1: 8193]

Outstanding Young Farmer Awards [Vol. 1: 16987]

Outstanding Young Industrial Engineer Award [Vol. 1: 9360]

Outstanding Young Investigator Award [Vol. 1: 11006]

Outstanding Young Manufacturing Engineer Award [Vol. 1: 15690]

Outstanding Young Member Award [Vol. 1: 873]

Outstanding Young Numismatist of the Year [Vol. 1: 3004]

Outstanding Young Range Professional Award [Vol. 1: 15294]

Outstanding Young Researcher Award [Vol. 2: 6686]

Outstanding Young Scientist Award
European Geosciences Union [Vol. 2: 2377]
Philippines Department of Science and Technology - National Academy of Science and Technology [Vol 2: 5363]

Outstanding Young Scientist Prize [Vol. 2: 3958]

Outstanding Younger Member Award [Vol. 1: 15529]

Outstanding Youth Project [Vol. 1: 7310]

Outstanding Youth Services Librarian Award [Vol. 1: 4790]

Outstanding Zone Campus Activity Coordinator Award [Vol. 1: 3886]

Outward Bound Wilderness Leadership Awards for Youth [Vol. 1: 13750]

Ovchinnikov Prize; Y.A. [Vol. 2: 5842]

Ovelgonne - Purchasing Research Award; Hans [Vol. 2: 1284]

Overly Memorial Graduate Scholarship; Helene M. [Vol. 1: 17995]

Oversattarpris [Vol. 2: 6210]

Overseas Prize [Vol. 2: 7999]

Overseas Research Grant [Vol. 2: 4210]

Overseas Surgical Fellowship [Vol. 2: 6850]

Overseas Travel Grants [Vol. 2: 7297]

Owen Award of Recognition for Innovative Nutrition Education; Anita [Vol. 1: 2041]

Owen Awards; Wilfred [Vol. 2: 7883]

Owen Book Prize; Walter [Vol. 1: 6336]

Owen Medal; Morgan [Vol. 2: 7413]

Owen Memorial Scholarship; Charles and Melva T. [Vol. 1: 12382]

Owen Memorial Trophy [Vol. 1: 16909]

Owen Poetry Prize; Guy [Vol. 1: 16035]

Owens Award; Jesse [Vol. 1: 17474]

Owens Scholarly Achievement Award; William A. [Vol. 1: 15141]

Owsley Award; Frank L. and Harriet C. [Vol. 1: 16025]

Oxford Preservation Trust Awards [Vol. 2: 8440]

Oxford University Fellowship [Vol. 2: 9389]

OZ Locator Award [Vol. 2: 1950]

OZ Prefix Award [Vol. 2: 1951]

Ozone Awards [Vol. 2: 4403]

PA Service to the Underserved Award [Vol. 1: 740]

PACE Award [Vol. 1: 460]

Pace Award; Frank [Vol. 1: 9895]

PACE Awards [Vol. 1: 1213]

Pacemaker Awards [Vol. 1: 12802]

Pacemaker Awards; Associated Collegiate Press [Vol. 1: 13243]

Pacemaker Awards; National Scholastic Press Association [Vol. 1: 13244]

Pacesetter Award
Alberta Construction Safety Association [Vol. 1: 330]
National Academic Advising Association [Vol 1: 11398]

Pacesetter of the Year Award [Vol. 1: 12161]

Pacific Biometrics Research Foundation Award [Vol. 1: 916]

Pacific Southwest Section Outstanding Community College Educator Award [Vol. 1: 3873]

Pacing Triple Crown [Vol. 1: 17149]

Pack Trainer Award [Vol. 1: 5971]

Packaging Design Competition [Vol. 1: 5371]

Packaging Gravure Awards [Vol. 2: 2850]

Packard Award; Fred M. [Vol. 2: 6537]

Packard Memorial Scholarship; Arthur J. [Vol. 1: 2464]

Packard Outstanding Educator Award; Robert L. [Vol. 1: 16056]

Packer Engineering Safety Award [Vol. 1: 4090]

Padgett Early Career Achievement Award; Deborah K. [Vol. 1: 15338]

Padma Vibhushan [Vol. 2: 3499]

Padnendadlu Undergraduate Bursary [Vol. 2: 342]

Paediatric Anaesthesia Research Fund Grant [Vol. 2: 6836]

Paepe-Willems Award; De [Vol. 2: 1545]

PAGE International Screenwriting Awards [Vol. 1: 13791]

Page Medal [Vol. 2: 116]

Page Outstanding Service Award; John A. [Vol. 1: 8870]

Page Prize; Gillian [Vol. 2: 8735]

Page Young Investigator Research Award; Irvine H. [Vol. 1: 2313]

Pagels Human Rights of Scientists Award; Heinz R. [Vol. 1: 13206]

Pahlsons pris; Margit [Vol. 2: 6211]

Paine Journalism Award; Thomas [Vol. 1: 13793]

Paine Memorial Award; Thomas O. [Vol. 1: 14026]

Painter Memorial Award; SES/ASTM Robert J. [Vol. 1: 16250]

Painter-Stainers Prize; Lynn [Vol. 2: 8456]

Painton Award; Harry R. [Vol. 1: 7598]

Pais Prize for History of Physics; Abraham [Vol. 1: 2691]

Pake Prize; George E. [Vol. 1: 3215]

Palaios Outstanding Paper Award [Vol. 1: 15312]

Palanca Hall of Fame [Vol. 2: 5351]

Paleontological Society Medal [Vol. 1: 13804]

Paley Prize for Short Fiction; Grace [Vol. 1: 5558]

Palladio Awards [Vol. 1: 16528]

Palladium Award; Olin [Vol. 1: 8062]

Palliative Care Section MSc/MA Research Prize [Vol. 2: 9104]

Palme Memorial Fund Scholarships; Olof [Vol. 2: 6161]

Palme Prize; Olof [Vol. 2: 6162]

Palmer Award; Joe [Vol. 1: 13008]

Palmer Award; Katherine [Vol. 1: 13801]

Palmer Prize; Frederick [Vol. 2: 8000]

Palmes Academiques [Vol. 2: 2445]

Pan Arab Web Awards [Vol. 2: 4453]

Pancyprian Ballet Competition [Vol. 2: 1895]

Pandora Award [Vol. 2: 9456]

Paneboeuf Prize; Ana and John [Vol. 2: 2426]

Panetti International Prize with Gold Medal; Professor Modesto [Vol. 2: 4019]

Pankow Award for Innovation; Charles [Vol. 1: 4216]

Pannar Seed Floating Trophy [Vol. 2: 5747]

Pannell Award; Lucile Micheels [Vol. 1: 17986]

Panofsky Prize in Experimental Particle Physics; W. K. H. [Vol. 1: 3216]

Panorama Audience Award [Vol. 2: 2728]

Panowski Playwriting Award; Mildred and Albert [Vol. 1: 8438]

Panting Award for New Scholars; Gerry [Vol. 1: 6738]

Papalia Award for Excellence in Teacher Education; Anthony [Vol. 1: 1925]

Papanicolaou Award [Vol. 1: 4281]

Paper and Poster Prizes [Vol. 2: 5714]

Paper Award [Vol. 2: 4247]

Paper Awards
    American Society of Agricultural and Biological Engineers [Vol. 1: 4092]
    European Association for Signal and Image Processing [Vol 2: 3275]

Papers and Publications Committee Prizes [Vol. 2: 8361]

Papers Award [Vol. 2: 8243]

Papi - Gaston Leduc; Prix Ugo [Vol. 2: 2292]

Papoulis Award; Athanasios [Vol. 2: 3276]

Pappas Award; Doug [Vol. 1: 15030]

Paracelsus Medaille [Vol. 2: 2965]

Paracelsus Prize [Vol. 2: 6489]

Paracelsusring der Stadt Villach [Vol. 1: 1329]

Parada Award; La [Vol. 1: 16070]

Parade - IACP Police Service Award [Vol. 1: 9642]

Paragliding Cross Country Competitions Trophy [Vol. 2: 8266]

Paragliding Cross Country League Millennium Falcon Trophy [Vol. 2: 8267]

PAragon
    American Academy of Physician Assistants [Vol. 1: 735]
    American Academy of Physician Assistants [Vol 1: 742]

Paragon Awards [Vol. 1: 12162]

Paragon Lesotho Award [Vol. 2: 4462]

PAragon Publishing Award [Vol. 1: 741]

Param Vir Chakra [Vol. 2: 3500]

Param Vishisht Seva Medal [Vol. 2: 3501]

Paraprofessional of the Year Award [Vol. 1: 4792]

Parapsychological Association Research Endowment [Vol. 1: 13848]

Parbo Medal; Sir Arvi [Vol. 2: 795]

Parcel - Leif J. Sverdrup Civil Engineering Management Award; John I. [Vol. 1: 4217]

Pard'ners Award [Vol. 1: 2073]

Pardoe Space Award; Geoffrey [Vol. 2: 8614]

Paredes Prize; Americo [Vol. 1: 2165]

Parent-Infant Preschool Services [Vol. 1: 13864]

Parent of the Year [Vol. 1: 12541]

Parent-Patient Leadership Award [Vol. 1: 7321]

Parenteau Memorial Award; William A. [Vol. 1: 300]

Parents' Choice Awards [Vol. 1: 13859]

Parents' Choice Classic Award [Vol. 1: 13859]

Parents' Choice FunStuff Award [Vol. 1: 13859]

Parents of the Year [Vol. 1: 5703]

Parish Pastor of the Year [Vol. 1: 102]

Parisot Foundation Fellowship; Jacques [Vol. 2: 6552]

Park of the Year [Vol. 1: 11867]

Parker Award; Chorus America/ASCAP Alice [Vol. 1: 7260]

Parker Education Gold Ribbon Awards; Sally [Vol. 1: 10780]

Parker Medal for Distinguished Service to the Profession of Pharmacy; Paul F. [Vol. 1: 1728]

Parker Memorial Award; Jim [Vol. 1: 11740]

Parker Memorial Award; R. Hunt [Vol. 1: 13374]

Parker Memorial Medal; Ben H. [Vol. 1: 2700]

Parker Prize; Virginia [Vol. 1: 6139]

Parker Prize; William Riley [Vol. 1: 11235]

Parkman Medal [Vol. 2: 8001]

Parks Award; Rosa [Vol. 1: 868]

Parks Memorial Award; Rosa [Vol. 1: 12298]

Parlin Award; Charles Coolidge [Vol. 1: 2807]

Parmeshwar Memorial Open; Rajnesh [Vol. 2: 2062]

Parmley Young Author Achievement Award; William P. [Vol. 1: 1713]

Parrish Scholarship; William E. [Vol. 1: 13954]

Parrott Award; Ron [Vol. 2: 762]

Parry Award; Evan [Vol. 2: 4915]

Parsons Award; Charles Lathrop [Vol. 1: 1663]

Parsons Memorial Prize; R. W. [Vol. 2: 796]

Parsons Prize; Talcott [Vol. 1: 497]

Parsons Study Grant; Aubrey [Vol. 2: 5654]

Partee Trophy [Vol. 1: 13443]

Partington Prize [Vol. 2: 9213]

Partner of the Year [Vol. 1: 10528]

Partners Against Leukemia and Lymphoma Award [Vol. 1: 10811]

Partner's Award [Vol. 1: 9567]

Partners Award [Vol. 1: 331]

Partnership Award
    American Chamber of Commerce in Moldova [Vol. 2: 4605]
    Direct Selling Association [Vol 1: 7876]
    Indiana Library Federation [Vol 1: 9210]

Parville, Artur du Fay, Alexandre Givry; Prix Henri de [Vol. 2: 2225]

Parville, Jean-Jaques Berger, Remlinger; Prix Binoux, Henri de [Vol. 2: 2183]

Pascal du GAMNI-SMAI; Prix Blaise [Vol. 2: 2226]

Pascal; Prix Paul [Vol. 2: 2227]

Pashayev Award for the Promotion of U.S.-Azerbaijan Relations; Hafiz [Vol. 2: 1339]

Pashkoff Prize; Daniil [Vol. 2: 3245]

Passenger's Choice Awards; World Airline Awards - [Vol. 2: 9183]

Passionate Communicator Award [Vol. 2: 9354]

Past President's Award
    American Association for Clinical Chemistry [Vol. 1: 917]
    International Federation of Biomedical Laboratory Science [Vol 1: 9904]
    International Society of Nurses in Cancer Care [Vol 1: 10328]
    Union of Estonian Psychologists [Vol 2: 2054]

Past Presidents' Award for Merit in Transportation [Vol. 1: 9419]

Past Presidents' Canadian Legislator Award [Vol. 1: 7046]

Past Presidents Diploma [Vol. 2: 6325]

Past President's Intermediate Brass Scholarship [Vol. 1: 14753]

Past-Presidents' Medal [Vol. 1: 11166]

Past Presidents' Memorial Medal [Vol. 1: 6617]

Paster Award; Vera S. [Vol. 1: 3104]

Pasteur Medal for Excellence in Health Research Journalism; Aventis [Vol. 1: 7037]

Pasteur Medal for Excellence in Health Research Journalism; Sanofi [Vol. 1: 7037]

PAT Paper Prize Awards [Vol. 1: 13956]

PAT/Western Front Association Undergraduate Essay Prize [Vol. 1: 13957]

PAT/Westerners International Award [Vol. 1: 13958]

PAT/World History Association Paper Prizes [Vol. 1: 13959]

Patch Awards; Dan [Vol. 1: 16950]

Pate Leadership for Children Award; Maurice [Vol. 1: 16923]

Pate Memorial Award; Tom [Vol. 1: 6509]

Patel Memorial Young Scientist Award; Prof. M.K. [Vol. 2: 3700]

Patel Outstanding ICAR Institution Award; Sardar [Vol. 2: 3530]

Paterno; Medaglia Emanuele [Vol. 2: 4128]

Paterson Medal and Prize [Vol. 2: 7918]

Paterson Media Award; John G. [Vol. 1: 14306]

Paterson Prize [Vol. 2: 8002]

Patey Prize [Vol. 2: 9228]

Pathfinder Award
    American Association for Girls and Women in Sports [Vol 1: 945]
    Institute for Public Relations [Vol 1: 9272]

Pathology Section President's Prize [Vol. 2: 9105]

Patient Care Achievement Award for Health Promotion [Vol. 1: 6790]

Patient Care Achievement Award for Innovation [Vol. 1: 6791]

Patient Care Achievement Award for Specialty Practice [Vol. 1: 6792]

Patient Participation Award [Vol. 2: 8683]

Paton Award; R. Townley [Vol. 1: 8223]

Paton Prize; Evgenij [Vol. 2: 2548]

Patriarch Athenagoras Medal [Vol. 1: 12425]

Patriot Award [Vol. 1: 12098]

Patriot Medal [Vol. 1: 12911]

Patriquin International Fellowship for Education; Heidi [Vol. 1: 15253]

Patrol Case of the Year [Vol. 1: 17029]

Patron/Matrons Award [Vol. 2: 5106]

Patron of Architecture Award [Vol. 2: 5697]

Patron of the American Community Theatre Association [Vol. 1: 1106]

Patrons and Fellows [Vol. 2: 3576]

Patron's Prize [Vol. 2: 470]

Patsaama Award; Saki [Vol. 1: 18077]

PatsyLu Prize [Vol. 1: 9499]

Patt Visiting Professorship; Workmen's Circle/Dr. Emanuel [Vol. 1: 18188]

Patte Prize; Didier [Vol. 2: 2410]

Patterson Award; A. L. [Vol. 1: 1956]

Patterson Award; Clair C. [Vol. 1: 8556]

Patterson Innovation in Education Leadership Award; Paul [Vol. 1: 6816]

Patterson Memorial Grant; Bryan [Vol. 1: 15877]

Patwardhan Prize; Dr. V. N. [Vol. 2: 3556]

Paul Award [Vol. 2: 9315]

Paul Award; Manfred [Vol. 2: 1272]

Paul Career Award; John [Vol. 2: 6873]

Paul Prize; Barbara [Vol. 1: 14378]

Paul VI Prize; International [Vol. 2: 4117]

Paulin Automotive Aftermarket Scholarship Awards; Arthur [Vol. 1: 5719]

Pauling Poster Prize [Vol. 1: 1957]

Pavement Awards [Vol. 1: 11554]

Pavgi Award Lecture; Prof. M.S. [Vol. 2: 3701]

Pavlovskii Prize; E.N. [Vol. 2: 5843]

Pawsey Medal [Vol. 2: 186]

Paxinos-Watson Prize [Vol. 2: 479]

Payen Award; Anselme [Vol. 1: 1664]

Payne Award; Ed [Vol. 1: 15414]

Payne-Gaposchkin Medal and Prize [Vol. 2: 7919]

Payne Medal; J.A. [Vol. 1: 11044]

Pazy Memorial Award; Prof. Amnon [Vol. 2: 3998]

PCAM Music Award [Vol. 2: 8505]

PCU Award [Vol. 2: 5402]

Peabody Awards Collection [Vol. 1: 17238]

Peabody Awards; George Foster [Vol. 1: 17238]

Peace and Security Award [Vol. 1: 18027]

Peace and Sport Image of the Year [Vol. 2: 4613]

Peace Film Prize [Vol. 2: 2729]

Peace from an International Sports Federation; Best Project for **[Vol. 2: 4610]**

Peace of the Year; Champion for **[Vol. 2: 4611]**

Peace of the Year; Non-Governmental Organization for **[Vol. 2: 4612]**

Peace of the Year; Sports Event for **[Vol. 2: 4615]**

Peace Prize of the German Book Trade **[Vol. 2: 2989]**

Peace Scholars **[Vol. 1: 16974]**

Peacock Medal **[Vol. 1: 11166]**

Peak Performance Awards **[Vol. 1: 11684]**

Peale Award; Norman Vincent **[Vol. 1: 350]**

Peanut Research and Education Award **[Vol. 1: 3124]**

Pearce Award; William T. **[Vol. 1: 5624]**

Pearl Awards **[Vol. 1: 7789]**

Pearls Award **[Vol. 2: 3491]**

Pearson Award; Clarence Ike **[Vol. 1: 11812]**

Pearson Award; L. B. "Mike" **[Vol. 1: 6652]**

Pearson Award; Lester B. **[Vol. 1: 12517]**

Pease Award; Theodore Calvin **[Vol. 1: 15425]**

Peaslee Memorial Brazing Award; Robert L. **[Vol. 1: 4687]**

Peccei Scholarship **[Vol. 2: 1291]**

Peck Award; A. Wells and Catherine **[Vol. 1: 13433]**

Peck Award; Ralph B. **[Vol. 1: 4218]**

Peck Award; Walter D. **[Vol. 1: 14444]**

Pecora Award; William T. **[Vol. 1: 16930]**

Pedersens Biblioteksfonds Forfatterpris; Edvard **[Vol. 2: 1958]**

Pederson Award in Solid-State Circuits; Donald O. **[Vol. 1: 9300]**

Pederson, CTC Award; Melva C. **[Vol. 1: 4521]**

Pediatric Dentist of the Year Award **[Vol. 1: 650]**

Pediatric Dermatology Award for Dermatologists in Developing Countries **[Vol. 1: 15240]**

Pediatric Dermatology Fellows/Residents Research Award **[Vol. 1: 15241]**

Pediatric Dermatology Research Grants **[Vol. 1: 15242]**

Pediatric Founders Award **[Vol. 1: 4290]**

Pedler Award **[Vol. 2: 9037]**

Pedler Lectureship **[Vol. 2: 9037]**

Pedroli Prize; Castelli **[Vol. 2: 2801]**

Pedrotti; Concurso Internazionale per Direttori d'Orchestra Antonio **[Vol. 2: 4030]**

Pedrotti International Competition for Orchestra Conductors; Antonio **[Vol. 2: 4030]**

Peek Award; Cuthbert **[Vol. 2: 8797]**

Peele Memorial Award; Robert **[Vol. 1: 15219]**

Peer Excellence Award **[Vol. 1: 11635]**

Peikoff Service to Others Award; Pauline **[Vol. 1: 8510]**

Pelander Award; Carl E. **[Vol. 1: 14768]**

Pelican Island Award for Habitat Conservation **[Vol. 1: 14515]**

Pellas-Graham Ryder Award; Paul **[Vol. 1: 11114]**

Pels Foundation Awards for Drama; Laura **[Vol. 1: 13899]**

Peltier Award; Leslie C. **[Vol. 1: 5651]**

Peltier Plaque **[Vol. 1: 15455]**

Pelton Award; Jeanette Siron **[Vol. 1: 5941]**

Pelzer Memorial Award; Louis **[Vol. 1: 13685]**

Pemberton Trophy **[Vol. 2: 7770]**

PEN/Faulkner Award for Fiction **[Vol. 1: 13907]**

PEN/O. Henry Awards **[Vol. 1: 14432]**

Pena; Premio Enrique **[Vol. 2: 36]**

Penaud Aeromodelling Diploma; Alphonse **[Vol. 2: 6326]**

Pendray Aerospace Literature Award **[Vol. 1: 2538]**

Pendray Award; G. Edward **[Vol. 1: 2538]**

Penguin Manuscript Prize **[Vol. 2: 1098]**

Penguin Young Readers Group Award **[Vol. 1: 5069]**

Penner Prize; Donald W. **[Vol. 1: 6292]**

Penrose Division I Coach of the Year; Spencer **[Vol. 1: 2399]**

Penrose Gold Medal; R.A.F. **[Vol. 1: 15620]**

Penrose Medal Award **[Vol. 1: 8566]**

Pension Scheme Accountant of the Year **[Vol. 2: 8464]**

Pensions Management Institute Associateship **[Vol. 2: 8465]**

Penston Astronomy Prize; Michael **[Vol. 2: 8665]**

People Initiative Awards **[Vol. 2: 375]**

People Management Awards **[Vol. 2: 372]**

People Photographer of the Year **[Vol. 1: 14020]**

People's Choice Award

    Bahamas Web Awards **[Vol. 2: 1345]**

    Toronto International Film Festival Group **[Vol 1: 16520]**

People's Choice Awards **[Vol. 1: 11046]**

Peplau Award; Hildegard **[Vol. 1: 3024]**

Pepler International Award; George **[Vol. 2: 9134]**

PEPP Chair Award **[Vol. 1: 12880]**

PEPP Merit Award **[Vol. 1: 12881]**

PEPP Professional Development Awards **[Vol. 1: 12882]**

PEPP QBS Award **[Vol. 1: 12883]**

Pepper Award for Excellence in Community-Based Long-Term Care; Claude **[Vol. 1: 12239]**

Pera Prize **[Vol. 2: 7370]**

Perdue Live Poultry Food Safety Award; Frank **[Vol. 1: 14114]**

Pereira Award; Professor E. O. E. **[Vol. 2: 6126]**

Perfect Ten (Equine Only) Award **[Vol. 1: 2074]**

Performance Gelding Award **[Vol. 1: 5882]**

Performance Mare Award **[Vol. 1: 5883]**

Performance Stallion Award **[Vol. 1: 5884]**

Performance Test Codes Medal **[Vol. 1: 4415]**

Performing Arts/Program Achievement Award **[Vol. 1: 11561]**

Perkin Family Physician of the Year; Reg L. **[Vol. 1: 7374]**

Perkin Medal

    Societe de Chimie Industrielle, American Section **[Vol. 1: 14992]**

    Society of Dyers and Colourists - England **[Vol 2: 9304]**

Perkin Prize for Organic Chemistry **[Vol. 2: 9038]**

Perkins Award for Professional Excellence; R. Marlin **[Vol. 1: 5570]**

Perkins Award; Marlin **[Vol. 1: 1418]**

Perkins Government Relations Award; Carl D. **[Vol. 1: 1940]**

Perkins, Jr. Memorial Award for International Physiologists; John F. **[Vol. 1: 3261]**

Perkins Outstanding Service Award; Carl **[Vol. 1: 4936]**

Perlemuter Piano Scholarship; Vlado **[Vol. 2: 7710]**

Perlman Award; Itzhak **[Vol. 1: 17621]**

Perreault Memorial Award; Robert **[Vol. 1: 7844]**

Perren Research Award; S. M. **[Vol. 2: 4076]**

Perret; Prix Paul-Michel **[Vol. 2: 2293]**

Perret Prize; Auguste **[Vol. 2: 2587]**

Perry Award; Ted **[Vol. 2: 7942]**

Perry Career Service Award; Nathan **[Vol. 1: 3474]**

Perry Distinguished Authors Award; J. Warren **[Vol. 1: 5506]**

Pershing Plaque **[Vol. 1: 12484]**

Persian Language Study in Tehran Scholarships **[Vol. 2: 2668]**

Person of the Year

    Minnesota Holstein Association **[Vol. 1: 11202]**

    Performance Warehouse Association **[Vol 1: 13945]**

Person of the Year Award **[Vol. 1: 10529]**

Personal Education and Leadership Development Grants **[Vol. 1: 13185]**

Personal Trainer of the Year **[Vol. 2: 9019]**

Personality of the Year

    Hospitality Association of Namibia **[Vol. 2: 4623]**

    International Road Federation **[Vol 1: 10127]**

Personality of the Year Awards **[Vol. 2: 6913]**

Personality Psychologist Award; Distinguished **[Vol. 2: 2809]**

Personnel Today Awards **[Vol. 2: 8469]**

Persons Awards **[Vol. 1: 16293]**

Persoon Medal; Christiaan Hendrik **[Vol. 2: 5748]**

Perspectives Award **[Vol. 1: 5344]**

Perten Prize; Harald **[Vol. 2: 1251]**

Pertzoff Prize; Vladimir A. **[Vol. 1: 17360]**

Peryam Award; David R. **[Vol. 1: 5625]**

Pessin Stroke Leadership Prize; Michael S. **[Vol. 1: 592]**

Peters Award; John P. **[Vol. 1: 4449]**

Peterson Agricultural Scholarship Award; John W. **[Vol. 1: 16779]**

Peterson Award; Oscar **[Vol. 1: 8349]**

Peterson Award; Roger Tory **[Vol. 1: 1496]**

Peterson Consumer Service Award; Esther **[Vol. 1: 8397]**

Peterson Excellence in Diversity Award; Angela **[Vol. 1: 5571]**

Peterson Fellows; Charles E. **[Vol. 1: 5664]**

Peterson Goalie of the Year; Dave **[Vol. 1: 17427]**

Peterson Research Fellowships and Internships; Charles E. **[Vol. 1: 5664]**

Peterson's Award for Promoting an Inclusive Graduate Community **[Vol. 1: 7669]**

Petit d'Ormoy, Carriere, Thebault; Prix **[Vol. 2: 2228]**

Petrie Memorial Award **[Vol. 2: 7888]**

Petrie Memorial Award; Dr. **[Vol. 1: 6283]**

Petrizzo Award for Career Achievement; D. Richard **[Vol. 1: 12163]**

Petro-Canada Award in New Media **[Vol. 1: 6140]**

Petrochemical Heritage Award **[Vol. 1: 7199]**

Petrov Prize; B.N. **[Vol. 2: 5844]**

Petrovskii Prize; I.G. **[Vol. 2: 5845]**

Pets in Cities Award **[Vol. 1: 9678]**

Petsavers Award **[Vol. 2: 7214]**

Pettifor Memorial Award; Dick **[Vol. 1: 14307]**

Pettigrew Award for Officials; Kenneth J. **[Vol. 1: 17447]**

Pettijohn Medal; Francis J. **[Vol. 1: 15313]**

Pettinos Award; Charles E. **[Vol. 1: 1539]**

Peurifoy Construction Research Award **[Vol. 1: 4219]**

Peyches; Prix Ivan **[Vol. 2: 2229]**

Peyton Award for Cold Regions Engineering; Harold R. **[Vol. 1: 4220]**

Pezcoller Foundation-ECCO Recognition for Contributions to Oncology **[Vol. 1: 1448]**

Pezzano Scholarships; Chuck **[Vol. 1: 5956]**

Pfeffer Peace Prize; International **[Vol. 1: 8342]**

Pfeifer Award; Ignac **[Vol. 2: 3381]**

Pfeil Prize; Wilhelm Leopold **[Vol. 2: 3205]**

Pfister Award; Oskar **[Vol. 1: 3359]**

Pfizer Animal Health Distinguished Service Award **[Vol. 1: 1078]**

Pfizer Animal Health Physiology Award **[Vol. 1: 1985]**

Pfizer Animal Health Prize **[Vol. 2: 1168]**

Pfizer Award

    History of Science Society **[Vol. 1: 8954]**

    International Society of Hypertension - United Kingdom **[Vol 2: 8212]**

Pfizer Award in Enzyme Chemistry **[Vol. 1: 1665]**

Pfizer Award (Long Term Health Care) **[Vol. 1: 6956]**

Pfizer Extension Award **[Vol. 1: 14115]**

Pfizer Fellowship in Clinical Pharmacology **[Vol. 1: 6986]**

Pfizer Outstanding Investigator Award **[Vol. 1: 3958]**

Pfizer Predoctoral Excellence in Renal Research Award **[Vol. 1: 3265]**

Pfizer Senior Scientist Award **[Vol. 1: 6988]**

Pfizer Young Investigator Award in Vaccine Development **[Vol. 1: 9229]**

PGA Assistants' Championship **[Vol. 2: 8508]**

PGA Championship **[Vol. 1: 14220]**

PGA Professional Championship **[Vol. 2: 8509]**

PGA Seniors Championship **[Vol. 2: 8510]**

Phadke Oration; Dr. G.M. **[Vol. 2: 3806]**

Phadke Travelling Award; Late G.M. **[Vol. 2: 3807]**

Pharmacia-ASPET Award for Experimental Therapeutics **[Vol. 1: 4036]**

Pharmacist of the Year **[Vol. 2: 928]**

Pharmacy Award **[Vol. 2: 6852]**

Pharmingen Investigator Award **[Vol. 1: 1181]**

PHBA National Youth Congress Horse Show High Point Youth **[Vol. 1: 13811]**

PhD Dissertation Award **[Vol. 1: 17179]**

PhD of the Year **[Vol. 2: 586]**

PhD Publication Prize **[Vol. 2: 501]**

PhD Research Scholarship Award **[Vol. 1: 3814]**

PhD Study Award **[Vol. 2: 587]**

Phelan Art Awards; James Duval **[Vol. 1: 14712]**

Phelan Literary Award; James Duval **[Vol. 1: 14713]**

Phelan Memorial Award; Paul F. **[Vol. 1: 3709]**

Phenix UDA **[Vol. 2: 2642]**

Pherigo Tutorial Citation; George L. **[Vol. 1: 4006]**

Phibro Animal Health Excellence in Poultry Research Award **[Vol. 1: 1045]**

Philanthropy Award

    American Chamber of Commerce in Moldova **[Vol. 2: 4605]**

    Colorado Business Committee for the Arts **[Vol 1: 7403]**

Philatelic Hall of Fame **[Vol. 1: 3166]**

Philbin Award **[Vol. 1: 11751]**

Philbro Extension Award [Vol. 1: 14115]

Philip Award; Margaret Dale [Vol. 1: 6488]

Philip Helicopter Rescue Award; Prince [Vol. 2: 7757]

Philip Morris International Prize [Vol. 2: 2344]

Philip Morris USA Scholarship for the Institute for Leadership in Changing Times [Vol. 1: 17564]

Philippine Mathematical Olympiad [Vol. 2: 5364]

Philippine Physics Olympiad [Vol. 2: 5365]

Philips Award for Prevention; Irving [Vol. 1: 501]

Philips Award; Frederik [Vol. 1: 9301]

Philips Prize; Henry M. [Vol. 1: 3191]

Phillips Award; A.T. [Vol. 1: 9509]

Phillips Award; Dr. Jackson R. E. [Vol. 1: 5496]

Phillips Award; Melba Newell [Vol. 1: 1312]

Phillips Award; Roy A. [Vol. 1: 16244]

Phillips Award; Winston J. [Vol. 2: 3354]

Phillips Collegiate Journalism Award; Thomas L. [Vol. 1: 8489]

Phillips Leadership Award; Sarah Thorniley [Vol. 1: 13987]

Phillips Memorial Award; John [Vol. 1: 1803]

Phillips Memorial Medal; John C. [Vol. 2: 6538]

Phillips Prize; A.A. [Vol. 2: 97]

Phillips Top Awards; Susan D. [Vol. 1: 13434]

Phinney Commemorative Scholarships; Ed [Vol. 1: 1688]

Phipps; Adolescent Health Care Award in memory of Dr. Kathy [Vol. 2: 8672]

Phoenix Award [Vol. 1: 7248]

Phoenix Award for Outstanding Contributions to Disaster Recovery [Vol. 1: 17106]

Phoenix Award for Small Business Disaster Recovery [Vol. 1: 17107]

Phoenix Group Diploma [Vol. 2: 6327]

Phoenix House Award for Public Service [Vol. 1: 13991]

Phoenix Trophy; Lloyd [Vol. 1: 17061]

Photo Award Program [Vol. 1: 8275]

Photogrammetric (Fairchild) Award [Vol. 1: 4874]

Photographer of the Year Award [Vol. 2: 7077]

Photographers Awards [Vol. 2: 6840]

Photographic Competition [Vol. 2: 8399]

Photography Award [Vol. 1: 9449]

Photography Awards [Vol. 1: 793]

Photography Book of the Year [Vol. 1: 14020]

Photography Contests [Vol. 1: 8539]

Photon Award [Vol. 1: 4041]

Physica Prize [Vol. 2: 4797]

Physical Chemistry Division Medal [Vol. 2: 980]

Physical Organic Chemistry Award [Vol. 2: 9039]

Physical Rehabilitation Award [Vol. 1: 8738]

Physical Science Award [Vol. 2: 6131]

Physician Award [Vol. 1: 5433]

Physician Executive of the Year Award [Vol. 1: 1772]

Physician of the Year

    American Association of Physician Specialists [Vol. 1: 1301]

    United States Amateur Boxing, Inc. [Vol 1: 16698]

Physician of the Year Award [Vol. 1: 7917]

Physician-PA Partnership Award [Vol. 1: 742]

Physician-Scientist Training Award [Vol. 1: 2020]

Physics Olympiad Awards [Vol. 2: 3687]

Physik-Preis [Vol. 2: 1211]

Physiological Entomology Journal Award [Vol. 2: 8775]

Physiological Section Li-COR Award [Vol. 1: 5942]

Physiology in Perspective: Walter B. Cannon Award Lecture [Vol. 1: 3262]

Phytochemical Society of Europe Medal [Vol. 2: 8475]

Pi Kapp Scholar's Award [Vol. 1: 14000]

Pi Tau Sigma Gold Medal [Vol. 1: 4416]

Piafsky Trainee Presentation Award; K.M. [Vol. 1: 6989]

Piafsky Young Investigator Award; K.M. [Vol. 1: 6990]

Piafsky Young Investigator Award of the Canadian Society for Clinical Pharmacology; K. M. [Vol. 1: 6990]

Piaget Producers Award [Vol. 1: 8355]

Piaz; Premio Giorgio Dal [Vol. 2: 4130]

PIC Award [Vol. 2: 8473]

Piccolo Prix [Vol. 1: 11552]

Pickell Award; Mark [Vol. 1: 10269]

Pickles Lectureship; William [Vol. 2: 8684]

Pictet; Prix [Vol. 2: 7331]

Picture Book Hall of Fame [Vol. 1: 1512]

"Picture It Painted Professionally" Awards [Vol. 1: 13796]

Pied Piper Award [Vol. 1: 4263]

Piekara Prize; Arkadiiusz [Vol. 2: 5408]

Piekarski Prize; Gerhard [Vol. 2: 2759]

Pier of the Year Award [Vol. 2: 8400]

Pierce Award for Media Excellence; JN [Vol. 2: 495]

Pierce Award; Janette [Vol. 1: 8173]

Pierce Medal; Lorne [Vol. 1: 14645]

Pierce Memorial Prize; W. H. [Vol. 2: 9189]

Pierce Prize in Astronomy; Newton Lacy [Vol. 1: 1449]

Piercy Award; Esther J. [Vol. 1: 5052]

Pieri Memorial Award; Louis A. R. [Vol. 1: 2419]

Pilgrim Award [Vol. 1: 14788]

Pilkington Outstanding Educator Award; Theo C. [Vol. 1: 3874]

Pillar Award

    Federal Government Distance Learning Association [Vol. 1: 8262]

    Federal Government Distributed Learning Association [Vol 1: 8267]

The Pillar Award [Vol. 1: 2868]

Pillsbury Bake-Off (R) Contest [Vol. 1: 8543]

Pilot and Feasibility Awards

    Cystic Fibrosis Foundation [Vol. 1: 7794]

    Washington University in St. Louis - Diabetes Research and Training Center [Vol 1: 17678]

Pilot of the Year Award [Vol. 1: 8893]

Pilot Project Award [Vol. 1: 15242]

Pilot Project Research Awards [Vol. 1: 17261]

Pilot Research Award for Junior Faculty and Child Psychiatry Fellows [Vol. 1: 502]

Pilot Safety Award [Vol. 1: 8894]

Pimentel Award in Chemical Education; George C. [Vol. 1: 1666]

Pimlott Award; Douglas H. [Vol. 1: 13108]

Pimsleur Award for Research in Foreign Language Education; Paul [Vol. 1: 1926]

Pinch Medal [Vol. 1: 11167]

Pinchot Medal; Gifford [Vol. 1: 15440]

Pinckney Award; Robert L. [Vol. 1: 2330]

Pine Memorial Award; John [Vol. 1: 13953]

Pinehurst Bronze Medal [Vol. 1: 16309]

Pinkard Leader in Federal Equity Award; Mary D. [Vol. 1: 16757]

Pinkett Minority Student Award; Harold T. [Vol. 1: 15426]

Pinnacle Award

    Canadian Society of Association Executives [Vol. 1: 6933]

    Evangelical Christian Publishers Association [Vol 1: 8200]

    Medical Dental Hospital Business Associates [Vol 1: 11051]

    Sales and Marketing Executives International [Vol 1: 14681]

    Specialized Carriers and Rigging Association [Vol 1: 16124]

Pinnacle Awards

    Association Media and Publishing [Vol. 1: 5191]

    Canadian Health Information Management Association [Vol 1: 6544]

    Marble Institute of America [Vol 1: 10938]

    Society for Human Resource Management [Vol 1: 15105]

Pinnacle Design Achievement Awards [Vol. 1: 4301]

Pintrich Dissertation Award; Paul R. [Vol. 1: 3412]

Pioneer Award

    American Association of Petroleum Geologists [Vol. 1: 1283]

    American Endurance Ride Conference [Vol 1: 2075]

    American Institute of Ultrasound in Medicine [Vol 1: 2710]

    Association for Communication Excellence in Agriculture, Natural Resources, and Life and Human Sciences [Vol 1: 4947]

    International Society for Traumatic Stress Studies [Vol 1: 10264]

    International Society of Hospitality Consultants [Vol 1: 10323]

    National Dairy Shrine [Vol 1: 12273]

Performance Warehouse Association [Vol 1: 13946]

    Science Fiction Research Association [Vol 1: 14789]

    Society for Vascular Ultrasound [Vol 1: 15407]

Pioneer Awards

    Anguilla Hotel and Tourism Association [Vol. 2: 18]

    Electronic Frontier Foundation [Vol 1: 8070]

Pioneer Citation [Vol. 1: 14403]

Pioneer Hi-Bred Forage Award [Vol. 1: 1986]

Pioneer in Cardiac Pacing and Electrophysiology Award [Vol. 1: 8875]

Pioneer in Clay Science Lecture [Vol. 1: 7319]

Pioneering Woman Award [Vol. 1: 13744]

Pioneers of Underwater Acoustics Medal [Vol. 1: 126]

Piore Award; Emanuel R. [Vol. 1: 9302]

Piper General Aviation Award [Vol. 1: 2539]

Piper Prize; C. S. [Vol. 2: 981]

Piraud Prize; Jacques [Vol. 2: 2427]

Pires Prize; Dr. Antonio [Vol. 2: 27]

Pirx de Traduction Fondation Cole [Vol. 1: 14374]

Pisk Award; Paul A. [Vol. 1: 2966]

Pistilli Silver Veterans' Medal; Philip [Vol. 1: 16563]

Pitcher Award; Alex [Vol. 2: 6998]

Piteau Outstanding Young Member Award; Douglas R. [Vol. 1: 5328]

Pitelka Award for Excellence in Research; Frank A. [Vol. 2: 833]

Pitsenbarger Award [Vol. 1: 266]

Pittaluga International Classical Guitar Competition - City of Alessandria Award; Michele [Vol. 2: 4151]

Pittcon Heritage Award [Vol. 1: 7200]

Pittman Sr. Memorial Exhibit Award; Henry Christensen/John Jay [Vol. 1: 2985]

Pittman Wildlife Art Award; Major General and Mrs. Don D. [Vol. 1: 12268]

Pittsburgh Dietetic Association Leadership Development Award [Vol. 1: 2042]

Pitzer Distinguished Service Award; Donald E. [Vol. 1: 7454]

Piven Award; Richard Cloward and Frances Fox [Vol. 1: 7116]

Pixel Awards [Vol. 1: 14024]

Pizzy Award for Leadership in Product Stewardship [Vol. 1: 13949]

Plaatje Award for Translation; Sol [Vol. 2: 5541]

Plaatje Award; Sol [Vol. 2: 5495]

Plain English Awards [Vol. 2: 8482]

Plain Gold Jewelry Award [Vol. 2: 3492]

Plain Precious Metal Jewelry Award [Vol. 2: 3493]

Plaisterers' Trophy [Vol. 2: 7679]

Planck Medaille; Max [Vol. 2: 2777]

Planck Research Award; Max [Vol. 2: 3231]

Planje - St. Louis Refractories Award; Theodore J. [Vol. 1: 1573]

Plant Award; Richard [Vol. 1: 6222]

Plants Award for Special Events; Helen I. [Vol. 1: 3875]

Plaque of Honour [Vol. 2: 2354]

Plaquette of Merit [Vol. 2: 2098]

Plarski Award; Lea [Vol. 1: 12578]

Plaskett Medal [Vol. 1: 14622]

Plasmadynamics and Lasers Award [Vol. 1: 2540]

Plass Award; William T. [Vol. 1: 4435]

Plastics Hall of Fame [Vol. 1: 14040]

Platform Presentation Award [Vol. 2: 8203]

Plath Media Award; David [Vol. 1: 15058]

Platinum Awards for Utility Excellence [Vol. 1: 5418]

Platinum Book Certificate [Vol. 2: 3941]

Platinum Disc Award [Vol. 2: 5291]

Platinum Jubilee Award [Vol. 2: 3616]

Platinum Medal [Vol. 2: 3602]

Plaut Community Leadership Award; Johanna Cooke [Vol. 1: 7969]

Play Competition for Youth Theatre [Vol. 1: 5827]

Play Therapy International Award [Vol. 2: 8485]

Player of the Week [Vol. 1: 16769]

Player of the Year

    Camanachd Association [Vol. 2: 7321]

    Canadian Colleges Athletic Association [Vol 1: 6419]

    InterCollegiate Tennis Association [Vol 1: 9465]

    Sony Ericsson WTA Tour [Vol 1: 15961]

Trinidad and Tobago Football Federation [Vol 2: 6629]
United States Professional Tennis Association [Vol 1: 17034]
Player of the Year Awards
Badminton World Federation [Vol. 2: 4535]
International Hockey Federation [Vol 2: 6395]
Player Portrait Award; John [Vol. 2: 8402]
Player to Watch [Vol. 1: 9466]
Playwright Award Competition [Vol. 1: 5826]
Playwright Discovery Award [Vol. 1: 17622]
Playwriting Fellowship [Vol. 1: 14157]
Pleissner Memorial Award; Ogden [Vol. 1: 4665]
Pleissner Memorial Award; Ogden and Mary [Vol. 1: 4665]
Plekhanov Prize; G.V. [Vol. 2: 5846]
Pless International Graduate of the Year; J. Will [Vol. 1: 13973]
Pletscher Award; Elisabeth [Vol. 1: 9905]
Plimpton Prize [Vol. 1: 13871]
Pludonis Prize; Vilis [Vol. 2: 4439]
Plumey; Prix [Vol. 2: 2230]
Plummer Memorial Educational Lecture Award [Vol. 1: 4688]
Plyler Prize for Molecular Spectroscopy and Dynamics; Earle K. [Vol. 1: 3217]
PMRS Awards [Vol. 2: 9338]
PMS Grants [Vol. 2: 8503]
Pocock Award; Mary Agard [Vol. 2: 5669]
Podesta Prize Spirit of Washington [Vol. 1: 8440]
Podgorecki Prize; Adam [Vol. 2: 6081]
Poe Award; Edgar A. [Vol. 1: 17805]
Poe Awards; Edgar Allan [Vol. 1: 11330]
Poe II Award; General Bryce [Vol. 1: 287]
Poehlman Award; William J. [Vol. 1: 15042]
Poel Memorial Festival; William [Vol. 2: 9225]
Poel Prize; John [Vol. 2: 7414]
Poetker Award; Frances Jones [Vol. 1: 2433]
Poetry Award
Canadian Authors Association [Vol. 1: 6323]
National Writers Association [Vol 1: 13077]
Poetry Books Award [Vol. 1: 17686]
Poetry Center Prizes [Vol. 1: 7326]
Poetry Contest [Vol. 1: 18125]
Poetry Day Prizes [Vol. 2: 4807]
Poetry International Festival [Vol. 2: 4808]
Poetry Society of Michigan Award [Vol. 1: 12367]
Poetry Society of Oklahoma Award [Vol. 1: 12368]
Poetry Society of Tennessee Award [Vol. 1: 12369]
Poetry Society of Texas Award [Vol. 1: 12370]
Poet's Award [Vol. 1: 61]
Poets Greatest Hits National Archive [Vol. 1: 14341]
Poets' Roundtable of Arkansas Award [Vol. 1: 12371]
Poggendorff Lecture [Vol. 2: 1008]
Pohl Prize; Robert Wichard [Vol. 2: 2778]
Point of Care Coordinator of the Year Award [Vol. 1: 918]
Points and Awards Program [Vol. 1: 16070]
Points Champions [Vol. 1: 1996]
Polak Charitable Foundation Award; Vasek and Anna Maria [Vol. 1: 8490]
Polanyi Award; John C. [Vol. 1: 6894]
Polar Music Prize [Vol. 2: 6164]
Polaris Award [Vol. 2: 8116]
Police Bravery Award [Vol. 2: 8492]
Police Exemplary Service Medal [Vol. 1: 8758]
Police Officer of the Year Award [Vol. 1: 9642]
Police Overseas Service Medal [Vol. 2: 320]
Police Public Bravery Awards [Vol. 2: 6810]
Policy Impact Award [Vol. 1: 976]
Policymaker of The Year Award [Vol. 1: 4937]
Polish Chemical Society Medal [Vol. 2: 5397]
Political Journalism Award [Vol. 1: 12686]
Politiek Award; Romert [Vol. 2: 4056]
Politzer Prize [Vol. 2: 8496]
Polka Music Awards [Vol. 1: 10057]
Poll; Fondation Max [Vol. 2: 1640]
Pollack Award for Productive Aging; Maxwell A. [Vol. 1: 8634]
Pollak Scholarship; Hansi [Vol. 2: 5670]
Pollie Awards [Vol. 1: 1322]
Pollitzer Student Travel Prize; William [Vol. 1: 1296]
Pollock Award; Herbert C. [Vol. 1: 7934]
Pollock Award; R. C. [Vol. 1: 2856]
Pollock Memorial Lecture [Vol. 2: 1009]

Pollock Supreme Undergraduate Award; Jay L. [Vol. 1: 415]
Pollock Trophy; Sam [Vol. 1: 2420]
Polya Award; George [Vol. 1: 11019]
Polya Lectureship; George [Vol. 1: 11019]
Polya Prize [Vol. 2: 8332]
Polya Prize; George [Vol. 1: 15122]
Polymer Physics Prize [Vol. 1: 3218]
Polytechnic Award [Vol. 2: 3170]
Pomer Award; Vic [Vol. 1: 11552]
Pomerance Award for Scientific Contributions to Archaeology [Vol. 1: 4765]
Pomerance Fellowship; Harriet and Leon [Vol. 1: 4766]
Pomeroy Award for Outstanding Contributions to Teacher Education; Edward C. [Vol. 1: 1095]
Pon Memorial Award; Ernest M. [Vol. 1: 11577]
PONCHO Special Recognition Award [Vol. 1: 14813]
Ponds Prize; Elida [Vol. 2: 4421]
Pop Award [Vol. 2: 4659]
Pope Award; E. P. [Vol. 1: 1407]
Popescu Prize for European Poetry Translation; Corneliu M. [Vol. 2: 8490]
Popp Excellence in Teaching Award; Richard [Vol. 1: 4291]
Poppele Broadcast Award; Jack [Vol. 1: 14406]
Pops Medal Award; Horace [Vol. 1: 17869]
Popular Annual Financial Reporting Award Program [Vol. 1: 8743]
Popular Choice Award [Vol. 1: 531]
Popularisation of Estonian Science; Prize for [Vol. 2: 2044]
Population Science and Public Health Award [Vol. 2: 8076]
Population Specific Research Project Award [Vol. 1: 10697]
Porraz International Coastal Engineering Award; Mauricio [Vol. 1: 4198]
Port of the Year [Vol. 2: 8105]
Porter Award; Charles [Vol. 1: 15144]
Porter Award; USFCC/J. Roger [Vol. 1: 3992]
Porter Emerging Hospitality Leader of the Year; Stevan [Vol. 1: 2460]
Porter Lecture Award; William C. [Vol. 1: 5434]
Porter Memorial Book Prize; John [Vol. 1: 7003]
Porter Physiology Fellowships for Minorities [Vol. 1: 3263]
Porter Prize; Arthur Kingsley [Vol. 1: 7360]
Porter Prize for Fiction; Katherine Anne [Vol. 1: 13261]
Porter Tradition of Excellence Book Award; John [Vol. 1: 7003]
Porterfield Award; Robert [Vol. 1: 16007]
Porters Prize; Professor Arthur T. [Vol. 2: 4422]
Portland International Film Festival [Vol. 1: 13411]
Portland Opera Lieber Awards [Vol. 1: 14094]
Portrait Photographer of the Year [Vol. 2: 417]
Ports Employees of the Year [Vol. 2: 18]
Posen Research Award; Sol [Vol. 2: 209]
Positive Image Award [Vol. 1: 16372]
Positive Images in the Media Award [Vol. 1: 16372]
Posner Award; Fellows' Ernst [Vol. 1: 15427]
Posner Memorial Award; Louis [Vol. 1: 10559]
Post-Doctoral Fellowship [Vol. 1: 13483]
Post-Doctoral Fellowships
Ames Research Center - NASA Astrobiology Institute [Vol. 1: 4720]
Louisiana State University - Kresge Hearing Research Laboratory [Vol 1: 10898]
Post Doctoral Research Awards [Vol. 1: 436]
Post Graduate PhD Studentship Grant [Vol. 2: 681]
Post Graduate Research Awards [Vol. 2: 402]
Post-graduate Research Prize [Vol. 2: 2101]
Post Prize; Felix [Vol. 2: 8736]
Postal History Journal Awards [Vol. 1: 14101]
Postal History Society Medal [Vol. 1: 14102]
Postcard Awards [Vol. 1: 16061]
Postcard Story Competition [Vol. 1: 18133]
PostDoc Publication Prize [Vol. 2: 502]
Postdoctoral Fellowship in Physiological Genomics [Vol. 1: 3264]
Postdoctoral Fellowship Program [Vol. 1: 2953]
Postdoctoral Fellowships [Vol. 1: 8650]
Postdoctoral Platform Presentation Award [Vol. 1: 1034]

Postdoctoral Poster Presentation Award [Vol. 1: 1035]
Poster Award
Australasian Pig Science Association [Vol. 2: 147]
European Orthodontic Society [Vol 2: 7625]
European Society of Biomechanics [Vol 2: 4077]
European Society of Paediatric Radiology [Vol 2: 7646]
International Federation of Societies of Cosmetic Chemists [Vol 2: 8130]
Poster Awards
International Society for Magnetic Resonance in Medicine [Vol. 1: 10183]
International Society of Orthopaedic Surgery and Traumatology [Vol 2: 1557]
Poster of the Year Award [Vol. 2: 5091]
Poster Paper Prize [Vol. 2: 8539]
Poster Presentation Grant [Vol. 1: 13888]
Poster Prize [Vol. 2: 7355]
Poster Prize for Trainees in Addictions Psychiatry [Vol. 2: 8737]
Poster Session Awards [Vol. 1: 2492]
Postgraduate Award [Vol. 2: 754]
Postgraduate Awards [Vol. 2: 6962]
Postgraduate Best Paper Award [Vol. 1: 3145]
Postgraduate Essay Prize [Vol. 2: 70]
Postgraduate Performance Awards [Vol. 2: 8381]
Postgraduate Prize [Vol. 2: 7131]
Postgraduate QRA Meetings Award [Vol. 2: 8526]
Postgraduate Scholarship [Vol. 1: 11709]
Postgraduate Scholarship
British Association for Applied Linguistics [Vol. 2: 6943]
Canadian Meteorological and Oceanographic Society [Vol 1: 6710]
National Association of Athletic Development Directors [Vol 1: 11628]
Postgraduate Student Prize [Vol. 2: 1013]
Postgraduate Student Travel Prize [Vol. 2: 9223]
Postgraduate Travel Award [Vol. 2: 154]
PostPartum Depression Best Research Thesis Award [Vol. 1: 15382]
Postsecondary Teacher of the Year [Vol. 1: 12021]
Potable Water Award [Vol. 2: 5763]
Potamkin Prize for Research in Pick's, Alzheimer's, and Related Diseases [Vol. 1: 593]
Pott Memorial Award; Anthony [Vol. 2: 6730]
Potter Award of Special Recognition; Helen [Vol. 1: 5108]
Potter Award; Stuart G. [Vol. 1: 5722]
Potter Gold Medal; James Harry [Vol. 1: 4417]
Potter Lifetime Professional Service Award; Louis B. [Vol. 1: 7839]
Pottle Fellowship in 18th-Century British Studies; Frederick A. and Marion S. [Vol. 1: 18161]
Pottorff Professional Designee of the Year Award; Verne W. [Vol. 1: 9616]
Potts Memorial Award; John H. [Vol. 1: 5691]
Potts Memorial Fellowship Award; Ralph H. [Vol. 1: 3049]
Pouliot Prize in Scientific Cooperation; Adrien [Vol. 1: 5188]
Poultry Catching Award [Vol. 2: 7801]
Poultry Products Award [Vol. 1: 9129]
Poultry Products Research Award [Vol. 1: 14114]
Poultry Science Association Fellows [Vol. 1: 14116]
Poultry Welfare Research Award [Vol. 1: 14117]
Pourbaix Award for Promotion of International Cooperation; Marcel [Vol. 2: 6062]
Powder Metallurgy Design Excellence Competition [Vol. 1: 11110]
Powder Metallurgy Pioneer Award [Vol. 1: 11111]
Powell Award; Cedric [Vol. 1: 5626]
Powell Award; Elizabeth [Vol. 1: 17394]
Powell Award; William and Mousie [Vol. 1: 10730]
Powell Memorial Medal; Cecil F. [Vol. 2: 2396]
Powell Prize; John Wesley [Vol. 1: 15098]
Power Award; General Thomas S. [Vol. 1: 267]
Power of Prevention Awards [Vol. 1: 13365]
Power Strategic Combat Missile Crew Award; General Thomas S. [Vol. 1: 267]
Powers Fellowship for Sea Turtle Research and Conservation; Joshua B. [Vol. 1: 14808]
Powers Memorial Award; Sidney [Vol. 1: 1284]

Pownall Award for Information Books; Eve **[Vol. 2: 651]**

Pozzetta Dissertation Research Award; George E. **[Vol. 1: 9170]**

PPC Annual Awards **[Vol. 2: 8521]**

PPC Quarterly Awards **[Vol. 2: 8522]**

PPFA Hall of Fame **[Vol. 1: 14246]**

PR, Marketing and Communications Awards **[Vol. 2: 6816]**

PR Professional of the Year **[Vol. 1: 14332]**

Pracejus Preis; Horst **[Vol. 2: 2933]**

Practical Project Award **[Vol. 2: 8052]**

Practice Excellence Award **[Vol. 1: 3156]**

Practitioner of the Year **[Vol. 2: 12160]**

Practitioner of the Year Award **[Vol. 2: 7193]**

Practitioner Research Award **[Vol. 1: 4641]**

Practitioner's Award for Excellence **[Vol. 2: 1378]**

Prader Prize; Andrea **[Vol. 2: 7640]**

Praemium Imperiale **[Vol. 2: 4262]**

Prague Spring International Music Competition **[Vol. 2: 1928]**

Prairie Pasque Children's Book Award **[Vol. 1: 15981]**

Prakash Memorial Medal; Professor Brahm **[Vol. 2: 3652]**

Prakash Oration Award; Drs. Kunti and Om **[Vol. 2: 3557]**

Prakken Professional Cooperation Award **[Vol. 1: 10433]**

Prangey Award; Louis **[Vol. 2: 6378]**

Pras Hestrin **[Vol. 2: 3969]**

Pras l'Bikoret Sifrutit **[Vol. 2: 3984]**

Pras l'Roman Ivri Mekori **[Vol. 2: 3985]**

Pras l'Sefer Shira Ivri Mekori **[Vol. 2: 3986]**

Prasad Award; Prof. B.G. **[Vol. 2: 3734]**

Prasad Memorial Lecture; Prof. M. R. N. **[Vol. 2: 3653]**

Prasad Memorial Oration Award; Dr. D. N. **[Vol. 2: 3558]**

Prasad Puruskar; Dr. Rajendra **[Vol. 2: 3531]**

Prather Award; Victor A. **[Vol. 1: 1440]**

Pratley Award; P. L. **[Vol. 1: 6905]**

Pratley Awards; Gerald **[Vol. 1: 8359]**

Pratt Award; Haraden **[Vol. 1: 9303]**

Pratt Award; Harold W. **[Vol. 1: 11680]**

Pratt Memorial Award; Wallace E. **[Vol. 1: 1285]**

Pratt-Severn Best Student Research Paper Award **[Vol. 1: 3948]**

PRCA Awards **[Vol. 2: 8517]**

Pre-College Award **[Vol. 1: 1306]**

Preakness Stakes **[Vol. 1: 10990]**

Prechter Award for Automotive Excellence; Heinz C. **[Vol. 1: 15530]**

Predoctoral Dental Student Merit Award for Outstanding Achievement in Community Dentistry **[Vol. 1: 1327]**

Predoctoral Excellence in Renal Research Award **[Vol. 1: 3265]**

Preedy Postgraduate Bursary; Winifred E. **[Vol. 2: 343]**

Prego Prize; Antonio J. **[Vol. 2: 28]**

Preis der Deutschen Physikalische Gesellschaft **[Vol. 2: 2774]**

Preis der Gesellschaft Deutcher Chemiker fur Schriftsteller **[Vol. 2: 2934]**

Preis der Gesellschaft Deutscher Chemiker fur Journalistin und Schrif tsteller **[Vol. 2: 2934]**

Preis der Horst Wiehe-Stiftung **[Vol. 2: 2982]**

Preis Prize; Karel **[Vol. 2: 1915]**

Preisich Award; Miklos **[Vol. 2: 3382]**

Preiskel Prize; Ella **[Vol. 2: 8759]**

Prelinger Award; Catherine **[Vol. 1: 7603]**

Preller Prize; Gustav **[Vol. 2: 5637]**

Premi David di Donatello per la Cinematografia Internazionale **[Vol. 2: 4052]**

Premi de les Lletres Catalanes Ramon Llull **[Vol. 2: 6023]**

Premi Principat d'Andorra International Piano Competition **[Vol. 2: 13]**

Premi SIF Farmindustria **[Vol. 2: 4141]**

Premier Award

    British Universities Film and Video Council **[Vol. 2: 7291]**

    Irish Security Industry Association **[Vol 2: 3892]**

Premier Technology Shandon Award **[Vol. 2: 5620]**

Premier Youth **[Vol. 1: 13463]**

Premier's Award **[Vol. 2: 1045]**

Premier's History Awards **[Vol. 2: 908]**

Premies voor de verspreiding van de betere film in Belgie **[Vol. 2: 1656]**

Premio a Investigadores Noveles **[Vol. 2: 6104]**

Premio Academia Argentina de Letras **[Vol. 2: 39]**

Premio Academia Argentina de Letras e Egresados de la carrera de Letras de universidades estatales o privadas **[Vol. 2: 40]**

Premio Academia Nacional de Agronomia y Veterinaria **[Vol. 2: 29]**

Premio Academia Nacional de la Historia **[Vol. 2: 37]**

Premio al Desarrollo Agropecuario **[Vol. 2: 30]**

Premio Balzan **[Vol. 2: 4086]**

Premio Bayer en Ciencias Veterinarias **[Vol. 2: 31]**

Premio Bolsa de Cereales de Buenos Aires **[Vol. 2: 32]**

Premio Camara Arbitral de la Bolsa de Cereales de Buenos Aires **[Vol. 2: 33]**

Premio Campiello **[Vol. 2: 4040]**

Premio Ceresis **[Vol. 2: 5320]**

Premio Comillas de Biografia, Autobiografia y Memorias **[Vol. 2: 6110]**

Premio Compasso d'oro **[Vol. 2: 4034]**

Premio Consagracion a la Geografia **[Vol. 2: 46]**

Premio de Novela Fernando Lara **[Vol. 2: 6024]**

Premio del Rey **[Vol. 1: 2387]**

Premio Iberoamericano Book Award **[Vol. 1: 10750]**

Premio Internazionale Panetti-Ferrari **[Vol. 2: 4019]**

Premio Internazionali dell' Instituto Nazionale delle Assicurazioni **[Vol. 2: 4024]**

Premio Joven Investigador Profesor Ignacio Chavez **[Vol. 2: 4587]**

Premio La Sonrisa Vertical **[Vol. 2: 6111]**

Premio Mercurio **[Vol. 2: 42]**

Premio Mesquite Audience Award **[Vol. 1: 8796]**

Premio Nacional **[Vol. 2: 1830]**

Premio Nacional de Artes Musicales **[Vol. 2: 1823]**

Premio Nacional de Ciencia y Tecnologia de Alimentos **[Vol. 2: 4583]**

Premio Nacional de Ciencias Aplicadas **[Vol. 2: 1824]**

Premio Nacional de Ciencias Naturales **[Vol. 2: 1825]**

Premio Nacional de Historia **[Vol. 2: 1826]**

Premio Nacional de Literatura **[Vol. 2: 1827]**

Premio Nacional de Periodismo **[Vol. 2: 1828]**

Premio Nacional de Periodismo Pio Viquez **[Vol. 2: 1860]**

Premio Paolo Borciani - International String Quartet Competition **[Vol. 2: 4157]**

Premio Planeta de Novela **[Vol. 2: 6025]**

Premio Tenco **[Vol. 2: 4044]**

Premios de Investigacion Cientifica **[Vol. 2: 4591]**

Premios Principe de Asturias **[Vol. 2: 6085]**

Premios Weizmann de la Academia Mexicana de Ciencias **[Vol. 2: 4592]**

Prentice Medal; Charles F. **[Vol. 1: 625]**

Prescott Award; Gerald W. **[Vol. 1: 13994]**

Prescott Award; Samuel Cate **[Vol. 1: 9341]**

Preservation and Scholarship Award **[Vol. 1: 9884]**

Preservation Award **[Vol. 1: 6853]**

Preservation Awards **[Vol. 1: 17557]**

Preservation Publication Award **[Vol. 1: 15428]**

President & Vice President's Choice Award **[Vol. 2: 9345]**

President Award

    European Society of Paediatric Radiology **[Vol. 2: 7647]**

    International Committee for Animal Recording **[Vol 2: 4093]**

President Citations **[Vol. 1: 15631]**

President of the Republic Genocide Prize **[Vol. 2: 55]**

President of the Republic Prize **[Vol. 2: 56]**

President of the Republic Youth Prize **[Vol. 2: 57]**

President of the Republic Youth Prize in Classical Music **[Vol. 2: 58]**

Presidential Academic Fitness Awards **[Vol. 1: 16807]**

Presidential Award

    American Academy of Periodontology **[Vol. 1: 724]**

    American Association for Girls and Women in Sports **[Vol 1: 946]**

American Association of Blood Banks **[Vol 1: 1067]**

American Society for Engineering Management **[Vol 1: 3894]**

American Society of Naturalists **[Vol 1: 4438]**

American Society of Neurorehabilitation **[Vol 1: 4460]**

Canadian Institute of Forestry **[Vol 1: 6593]**

Interior Design Educators Council **[Vol 1: 9476]**

International Association of Diecutting and Diemaking **[Vol 1: 9660]**

International Association of Gerontology and Geriatrics **[Vol 2: 2492]**

International Society of Blood Transfusion **[Vol 2: 4778]**

National Association of Black Social Workers **[Vol 1: 11665]**

National Horseshoe Pitchers Association of America **[Vol 1: 12523]**

Rehabilitation International **[Vol 1: 14489]**

Society for Prevention Research **[Vol 1: 15274]**

Presidential Award for Outstanding Contributions to the Promotion of Scholarship in the Third World **[Vol. 1: 5541]**

Presidential Award for Reading and Technology **[Vol. 1: 10089]**

Presidential Award for Sustained Executive Achievement **[Vol. 1: 11860]**

Presidential Award of Merit **[Vol. 1: 10188]**

Presidential Award of the RES - Annie R. Beasley Memorial Award **[Vol. 1: 15169]**

Presidential Awards

    American Society of Clinical Hypnosis **[Vol. 1: 4253]**

    Society for Leukocyte Biology **[Vol 1: 15169]**

Presidential Awards for Excellence in Mathematics and Science Teaching **[Vol. 1: 12812]**

Presidential Citation

    American Academy of Otolaryngology - Head and Neck Surgery **[Vol 1: 644]**

    American College of Cardiology **[Vol 1: 1714]**

    American Mosquito Control Association **[Vol 1: 2941]**

    American Psychological Association - Society for the Psychological Study of Lesbian, Gay, Bisexual and Transgender Issues (Division 44) **[Vol 1: 3541]**

    International Association Emergency Managers **[Vol 1: 9513]**

    Rotary International **[Vol 1: 14605]**

    United States Hang Gliding and Paragliding Association **[Vol 1: 16945]**

    YWCA of the U.S.A. **[Vol 1: 18223]**

Presidential Citation Award

    American Forage and Grassland Council **[Vol. 1: 2175]**

    National Art Education Association **[Vol 1: 11543]**

Presidential Citations

    American Congress on Surveying and Mapping **[Vol. 1: 1872]**

    American Urological Association **[Vol 1: 4625]**

    Czechoslovak Society of Arts and Sciences **[Vol 1: 7800]**

Presidential Citations and Awards **[Vol. 1: 12983]**

Presidential Citations for Meritorious Service **[Vol. 1: 4875]**

Presidential Citizens Medal **[Vol. 1: 8206]**

Presidential Commendation

    Executive Office of the President **[Vol. 1: 8209]**

    Royal Australasian College of Dental Surgeons **[Vol 2: 958]**

Presidential Design Awards **[Vol. 1: 16928]**

Presidential Distinguished Service Award **[Vol. 1: 15732]**

Presidential Early Career Award for Scientist and Engineers PECASE **[Vol. 1: 16869]**

Presidential Green Chemistry Challenge Awards

    American Chemical Society **[Vol. 1: 1667]**

    United States Environmental Protection Agency **[Vol 1: 16896]**

Presidential Honor Award **[Vol. 1: 10413]**

Presidential Leadership Award **[Vol. 1: 11766]**

Presidential Master's Prize **[Vol. 1: 1830]**

Presidential Medal of Freedom **[Vol. 1: 8207]**

Presidential Proclamation **[Vol. 1: 15702]**

Presidential Public Safety Communication
Award [Vol. 1: 8209]
Presidential Recognition Award
Society for American Archaeology [Vol. 1: 15022]
Water Environment Federation [Vol 1: 17715]
Presidential Scholars in the Arts [Vol. 1: 12429]
Presidential Scholarship [Vol. 1: 4483]
Presidential Student Awards [Vol. 1: 11137]
Presidential Symposium Award [Vol. 2: 218]
Presidential Undergraduate Prize [Vol. 1: 1831]
President's Achievement Award [Vol. 1: 10422]
President's Award
Actuarial Society of South Africa [Vol. 2: 5479]
Advertising Women of New York [Vol 1: 175]
Alberta Amateur Boxing Association [Vol 1: 325]
American Academy of Family Physicians [Vol 1: 561]
American Association for Affirmative Action [Vol 1: 869]
American Association of Petroleum Geologists [Vol 1: 1275]
American Association of Petroleum Geologists [Vol 1: 1285]
American Forage and Grassland Council [Vol 1: 2176]
American Handwriting Analysis Foundation [Vol 1: 2273]
American Probation and Parole Association [Vol 1: 3339]
American Society for Bone and Mineral Research [Vol 1: 3774]
American Society for Gravitational and Space Biology [Vol 1: 3917]
American Society of Cinematographers [Vol 1: 4154]
American Society of Cytopathology [Vol 1: 4282]
Association of Consulting Engineers of New Zealand [Vol 2: 4862]
Association of Metropolitan Water Agencies [Vol 1: 5419]
Association of Rheumatology Health Professionals [Vol 1: 5500]
Astronomical Society of New South Wales [Vol 2: 123]
Australian Institute of Genealogical Studies [Vol 2: 394]
Balloon Federation of America [Vol 1: 5770]
Canadian Association of Home and Property Inspectors [Vol 1: 6274]
Canadian Bar Association [Vol 1: 6337]
Canadian Institute of Food Science and Technology [Vol 1: 6585]
Canadian Mental Health Association - Alberta Division [Vol 1: 6697]
Canadian Nuclear Society [Vol 1: 6750]
Canadian Prostate Cancer Network [Vol 1: 6807]
Canadian Society for Training and Development [Vol 1: 6922]
Canadian Society of Club Managers [Vol 1: 6943]
Canadian Veterinary Medical Association [Vol 1: 7032]
Chartered Institution of Water and Environmental Management [Vol 2: 7400]
COACH: Canada's Health Informatics Association [Vol 1: 7338]
Country Radio Broadcasters [Vol 1: 7729]
Educational Theatre Association [Vol 1: 8032]
The Glaucoma Foundation [Vol 1: 8659]
Industrial Accident Prevention Association [Vol 1: 9218]
Institute for Operations Research and the Management Sciences [Vol 1: 9265]
Institute of Environmental Sciences and Technology [Vol 1: 9324]
Institute of Marine Engineering, Science and Technology [Vol 2: 7895]
Institution of Professional Engineers New Zealand [Vol 2: 4908]
Insurance Regulatory Examiners Society [Vol 1: 9434]
International Association of Business Communicators [Vol 1: 9625]
International Association of Business Communicators Ottawa [Vol 1: 9630]

International Association of Correctional Training Personnel [Vol 1: 9650]
International Association of Registered Financial Consultants [Vol 1: 9695]
International Coach Federation [Vol 1: 9778]
International Commission on Glass [Vol 2: 5999]
International Ergonomics Association [Vol 2: 6588]
International Flight Services Association [Vol 1: 9944]
International Hockey Federation [Vol 2: 6396]
International Life Saving Federation [Vol 2: 1541]
International Public Relations Association [Vol 2: 8175]
International Society for Agricultural Safety and Health [Vol 1: 10136]
International Society for Quality of Life Research [Vol 1: 10224]
International Society of Explosives Engineers [Vol 1: 10316]
Lamaze International [Vol 1: 10741]
Library Leadership and Management Association [Vol 1: 10838]
Medical Library Association [Vol 1: 11074]
National Association of State Park Directors [Vol 1: 11909]
National Defense Transportation Association [Vol 1: 12285]
National Institute of Building Sciences [Vol 1: 12548]
National Marine Educators Association [Vol 1: 12596]
National Organization for Human Services [Vol 1: 12636]
National Press Photographers Association [Vol 1: 12707]
National Society of Professional Insurance Investigators [Vol 1: 12889]
National Student Employment Association [Vol 1: 12948]
Natural Products Association [Vol 1: 13092]
North American Association for Environmental Education [Vol 1: 13271]
North American Association of Food Equipment Manufacturers [Vol 1: 13278]
North American Society for the Psychology of Sport and Physical Activity [Vol 1: 13346]
Print Services and Distribution Association [Vol 1: 14163]
Professional Grounds Management Society [Vol 1: 14229]
Public Relations Institute of Southern Africa [Vol 2: 5603]
Puppeteers of America [Vol 1: 14351]
Radio Club of America [Vol 1: 14407]
Royal Academy of Dance [Vol 2: 8576]
Royal Aeronautical Society - United Kingdom [Vol 2: 8615]
Science Teachers Association of Nigeria [Vol 2: 5104]
Society of Cable Telecommunications Engineers [Vol 1: 15577]
Society of Naval Architects and Marine Engineers [Vol 1: 15711]
Southeastern Library Association [Vol 1: 15999]
Theatre Historical Society of America [Vol 1: 16480]
United Ostomy Association of Canada [Vol 1: 16647]
University of Wisconsin - Eau Claire Alumni Association [Vol 1: 17364]
U.S.A. Track and Field [Vol 1: 17475]
Victorian Society in America [Vol 1: 17558]
Women's Basketball Coaches Association [Vol 1: 17971]
Women's Caucus for Art [Vol 1: 17976]
Presidents' Award
American Association of Petroleum Geologists [Vol. 1: 1286]
American Society of Civil Engineers [Vol 1: 4221]
Association of State Dam Safety Officials [Vol 1: 5525]
British Psychological Society [Vol 2: 7194]
Committee of Presidents of Statistical Societies [Vol 1: 7440]

Driving School Association of the Americas [Vol 1: 7926]
Midwest Archives Conference [Vol 1: 11148]
President's Award Certificate [Vol. 2: 5515]
President's Award for Academic Excellence [Vol. 2: 1718]
President's Award for Air Force Reserve Command [Vol. 1: 268]
President's Award for Best Conference Presentation [Vol. 1: 12326]
President's Award for Distinguished Federal Civilian Service [Vol. 1: 17012]
President's Award for Environmental Stewardship [Vol. 1: 8718]
President's Award for Excellence [Vol. 2: 5739]
President's Award for Exceptional and Innovative Leadership in Adult and Continuing Education [Vol. 1: 860]
President's Award for Innovation [Vol. 1: 7680]
President's Award for Journalism [Vol. 1: 2975]
President's Award for Merit [Vol. 1: 15943]
Presidents' Award for Public Service [Vol. 1: 9239]
President's Award of Distinction [Vol. 1: 10253]
President's Award of Excellence [Vol. 1: 14780]
President's Award of Excellence, Honor and Merit [Vol. 1: 4370]
President's Award of Merit [Vol. 1: 9972]
President's Awards
Geological Society of London [Vol. 2: 7727]
Metal Construction Association [Vol 1: 11105]
National Research Foundation [Vol 2: 5575]
President's Awards for Council Excellence [Vol. 1: 18012]
President's Certificate [Vol. 1: 562]
President's Challenge Award [Vol. 1: 11944]
President's Challenge Physical Activity and Fitness Awards Program [Vol. 1: 14142]
President's Choice Award [Vol. 2: 670]
President's Circle Award [Vol. 2: 19]
President's Citation
Federation of Genealogical Societies [Vol. 1: 8323]
LeadingAge [Vol 1: 10770]
Society for Mining, Metallurgy, and Exploration [Vol 1: 15220]
President's Commendation [Vol. 1: 6817]
President's Community Volunteer Award [Vol. 1: 14075]
President's Continuing Education Grant [Vol. 1: 1519]
President's Corporate Council Award [Vol. 1: 3935]
President's Cup
Canadian Dermatology Association [Vol. 1: 6448]
International Public Debate Association [Vol 1: 10071]
Society of Ornamental Turners [Vol 2: 9329]
Society of Plastics Engineers [Vol 1: 15790]
Sports Car Club of America [Vol 1: 16202]
Presidents Cup [Vol. 1: 13358]
President's "E" Award for U.S. Exporters [Vol. 1: 16784]
President's "E Star" Award [Vol. 1: 16785]
President's Education Award Program [Vol. 1: 16807]
President's Environment and Conservation Challenge Awards [Vol. 1: 8208]
President's Environmental Merit Awards Program [Vol. 1: 16897]
President's Environmental Youth Awards [Vol. 1: 16897]
President's Fishery Conservation Award [Vol. 1: 2150]
President's Gold Medal [Vol. 2: 3808]
President's Honorary Citation [Vol. 2: 5302]
The President's International Award [Vol. 2: 2674]
The President's Maori Scholarship [Vol. 2: 4993]
President's Medal
American Society of Landscape Architects [Vol. 1: 4369]
Australian Society of Sugar Cane Technologists [Vol 2: 582]
Bowling Proprietors' Association of America [Vol 1: 5947]
British Academy [Vol 2: 6927]
British Ecological Society [Vol 2: 7049]

Prize for Distinguished Service to the Profession [Vol. 1: 15123]

Prize for Drama [Vol. 2: 1689]

Prize for Encouragement of Globe Studies [Vol. 2: 1266]

Prize for Excellence [Vol. 2: 3959]

Prize for Freedom [Vol. 2: 8304]

Prize for Independent Scholars [Vol. 1: 11239]

Prize for Industrial Applications of Physics [Vol. 1: 2692]

Prize for Innovative Applied Physics of the Division of Industrial and Applied Physics [Vol. 1: 6303]

Prize for Junior Scientists [Vol. 2: 3124]

Prize for Materials Science [Vol. 2: 3654]

Prize for Meat and Technology [Vol. 2: 2553]

Prize for Mountain Literature [Vol. 2: 6889]

Prize for Non-Fiction [Vol. 2: 1690]

Prize for Outstanding Student Research [Vol. 1: 13148]

Prize for PhD Thesis in Photochemistry [Vol. 2: 6281]

Prize for Popularisation of Estonian Science [Vol. 2: 2044]

Prize for Science and Technology [Vol. 2: 5901]

Prize for Science Communication [Vol. 2: 1461]

Prize for Science Writing [Vol. 1: 1065]

Prize for the Teaching of OR/MS Practice [Vol. 1: 9266]

Prize for Young Adult Fiction [Vol. 2: 1066]

Prize for Young Life Scientists [Vol. 1: 993]

Prize in Applied Oceanography [Vol. 1: 6712]

Prize in Life Sciences for a Young Scientist [Vol. 2: 1759]

Prize in OR in Development [Vol. 1: 9925]

Prize in Theoretical and Mathematical Physics
  Canadian Association of Physicists [Vol. 1: 6304]
  University of Montreal - Mathematics Research Center [Vol 1: 17307]

Prize of Excellence [Vol. 2: 5132]

Prize of the Societe Internationale de Chirurgie [Vol. 2: 6453]

Prize to Outstanding Student of Translation [Vol. 2: 3972]

Prizes for Best Papers by Young Authors [Vol. 2: 5303]

Prizes for Leadership in Islamic Thought and Applied Sciences [Vol. 2: 4012]

Prizes for Outstanding Translation [Vol. 2: 5729]

Prizes for the Distribution of Quality Films in Belgium [Vol. 2: 1656]

Prizes for Young Chemists [Vol. 1: 10477]

Prizes for Young Scientists in Atherosclerosis Research [Vol. 2: 6138]

Prizes in Islamic Economics and Islamic Banking [Vol. 2: 5902]

Pro Bono Publico Award [Vol. 1: 1466]

Pro Carton/ECMA Awards [Vol. 2: 6475]

Pro-Comm Awards Competition [Vol. 1: 6067]

Pro Ecclesia et Pontifice Medal [Vol. 2: 9551]

Pro Football Hall of Fame [Vol. 1: 14175]

PRO LABORE SECURO Statuette [Vol. 2: 5381]

Pro-Line Athletic National Players of the Week [Vol. 1: 12084]

Pro Patria Award [Vol. 1: 12099]

Pro Rodeo Hall of Fame [Vol. 1: 14249]

Pro Scientia Transformatrix Award [Vol. 2: 5366]

Pro Stock Puller of the Year [Vol. 1: 12990]

Process Award [Vol. 1: 10004]

Process Safety Management Award [Vol. 1: 6971]

Process Technology Award [Vol. 2: 9040]

Procirep's Award for Best Producer [Vol. 2: 2603]

Procter and Gamble Award in Applied and Environmental Microbiology [Vol. 1: 3981]

Procter and Gamble Complex PE Scholars Grant [Vol. 1: 3108]

Procter Memorial Prize [Vol. 2: 9322]

Procter Prize for Scientific Achievement; William [Vol. 1: 14907]

Proctor Medal [Vol. 1: 5085]

Proctor Research Medal Award; Francis I. [Vol. 1: 5085]

Procurement Executive Award [Vol. 1: 16810]

Producers Guild Fellowship Award [Vol. 2: 8379]

Product Group Award [Vol. 2: 4190]

Product of the Year [Vol. 1: 12013]

Production and Operations Award [Vol. 1: 15761]

Production Award [Vol. 1: 6367]

Production Engineering Award [Vol. 1: 15761]

Production Nursery Awards [Vol. 2: 915]

Production Technology Award [Vol. 2: 3445]

Products and Processes Awards [Vol. 2: 5928]

Professional Achievement Award
  Data Management Association International [Vol. 1: 7816]
  Keuka College Alumni Association [Vol 1: 10680]
  Solid Waste Association of North America [Vol 1: 15952]
  Special Libraries Association - Transportation Division [Vol 1: 16112]

Professional Achievement Awards [Vol. 1: 16591]

Professional Achievement Citations [Vol. 1: 17212]

Professional Agent of the Year [Vol. 1: 11846]

Professional Associateship [Vol. 2: 8923]

Professional Award
  American Horticultural Society [Vol. 1: 2434]
  Association for Communication Excellence in Agriculture, Natural Resources, and Life and Human Sciences [Vol 1: 4948]
  Association of Jewish Aging Services [Vol 1: 5380]
  Ordre des Psychologues du Quebec [Vol 1: 13662]
  Special Libraries Association [Vol 1: 16104]

Professional Awards
  American Society of Landscape Architects [Vol. 1: 4365]
  American Society of Landscape Architects [Vol 1: 4370]

Professional Board Staff Member Award [Vol. 1: 5291]

Professional Care Award [Vol. 1: 6698]

Professional Chapter Awards [Vol. 1: 5165]

Professional Citation [Vol. 1: 3636]

Professional Communications Awards [Vol. 1: 16550]

Professional Contribution by an ACE Member [Vol. 1: 5303]

Professional Development Award
  American Counseling Association [Vol. 1: 1941]
  Institute for the International Education of Students [Vol 1: 9277]
  International System Safety Society [Vol 1: 10423]

Professional Development Awards
  Australasian Performing Rights Association [Vol. 2: 140]
  School Nutrition Association [Vol 1: 14781]

Professional Development Program Awards [Vol. 1: 14924]

Professional Development Scholarships [Vol. 1: 17984]

Professional Engineer of the Year [Vol. 2: 799]

Professional Engineers Citizenship Award [Vol. 1: 14210]

Professional Engineers Gold Medal [Vol. 1: 14211]

Professional Leadership Award [Vol. 1: 4985]

Professional Member of the Year [Vol. 1: 12002]

Professional of the Year
  Ladies Professional Golf Association [Vol. 1: 10731]
  Wisconsin Educational Media and Technology Association [Vol 1: 17884]

Professional Photographer of the Year [Vol. 2: 418]

Professional Practice Ethics and Leadership Award [Vol. 1: 4223]

Professional Progress Award for Outstanding Progress in Chemical Engineering [Vol. 1: 2632]

Professional Promise Award [Vol. 1: 11615]

Professional Safety Paper Awards [Vol. 1: 4509]

Professional Secretary Award [Vol. 2: 5971]

Professional Service Award
  National Community Education Association [Vol. 1: 12124]
  States Organization for Boating Access [Vol 1: 16281]

Professional Service to Health Education Award [Vol. 1: 953]

Professionalism Award [Vol. 1: 11931]

Professors' Prize [Vol. 2: 6757]

Progistix National Student Logistics Paper Award [Vol. 1: 16332]

Program Award [Vol. 1: 11525]

Program Director of the Year [Vol. 1: 9020]

Program Director of the Year Award [Vol. 1: 1242]

Program Excellence Award [Vol. 1: 10434]

Program Excellence Awards
  International City/County Management Association [Vol. 1: 9766]
  NASBITE International [Vol 1: 11380]

Program Leadership Award [Vol. 1: 14522]

Program of the Year: Community-Based Institutions [Vol. 1: 5780]

Program of the Year: Large National and Regional Institutions [Vol. 1: 5781]

Program of the Year: Regional Institutions [Vol. 1: 5782]

Program Participation Award [Vol. 1: 1143]

Program to Recognize Excellence in Student Literary Magazines [Vol. 1: 12215]

Programme Awards [Vol. 2: 9129]

Programme of the Year [Vol. 2: 6778]

Programming Award [Vol. 1: 9211]

Programming Languages Achievement Award [Vol. 1: 16097]

Programming Systems and Languages Paper Award [Vol. 1: 4963]

Progress Award [Vol. 1: 461]

Progress in Equity Award [Vol. 1: 1400]

Progress Medal [Vol. 2: 8906]

Progress Medal Award [Vol. 1: 15703]

Progressive Automotive X Prize [Vol. 1: 18138]

Progressive Dairy Producer Awards [Vol. 1: 12274]

Progressive School Library Media Award [Vol. 1: 9212]

Project Award [Vol. 1: 4757]

Project Management Achievement Awards [Vol. 2: 421]

Project Management Excellence Award [Vol. 2: 5599]

Project Manager of the Year [Vol. 2: 6779]

Project Manager of the Year [Vol. 2: 7018]

Project of the Year [Vol. 2: 6780]

Project of the Year
  Builder [Vol. 1: 6042]
  FeRFA Resin Flooring Association [Vol 2: 7683]
  National Space Society of Australia [Vol 2: 900]

Project of the Year Award [Vol. 1: 14259]

Projects, Facilities and Construction Award [Vol. 1: 15762]

Prolific Owl Award [Vol. 2: 2889]

Promega Biotechnology Research Award [Vol. 1: 3982]

Prometheus Award [Vol. 1: 10821]

Prometheus Hall of Fame [Vol. 1: 10822]

Promise to Earth Award [Vol. 1: 4757]

Promising Former Student Award [Vol. 2: 5209]

Promising Franchisor of the Year [Vol. 2: 5941]

Promising Performer Award [Vol. 1: 339]

Promising Practice Award [Vol. 1: 5249]

Promising Researcher Award [Vol. 1: 12216]

Promising Young Scientist Award [Vol. 2: 840]

Promising Young Writers Program [Vol. 1: 12217]

Promoter of the Year
  Academy of Country Music [Vol. 1: 61]
  United States Auto Club [Vol 1: 16738]

Promoting Fulfilled Lives Award [Vol. 2: 7333]

Promotion and Education Awards [Vol. 1: 11304]

Promotion of Savings, Consumer Protection, and Export Performance Award [Vol. 2: 3617]

Promotional Prizes [Vol. 2: 3138]

Promotions Award [Vol. 1: 462]

Propellants and Combustion Award [Vol. 1: 2541]

Property Awards; Ghana [Vol. 2: 3255]

Property Tax Achievement Award [Vol. 1: 9617]

ProQuest Intellectual Freedom Award [Vol. 1: 13219]

Prosky Award for Outstanding Lead Actor; Robert [Vol. 1: 16486]

Prost; Prix Gabriel-Auguste [Vol. 2: 2169]

Protagoras Cup [Vol. 1: 10072]

Prous Institute-Overton and Meyer Award on New Technologies in Drug Discovery [Vol. 2: 1236]

Prouty and Elsie S. Prouty Memorial Award; Morton D. [Vol. 1: 12372]

Prouty Award; Bob [Vol. 1: 16226]

Provasoli Award; Luigi [Vol. 1: 13995]

Provincial Police Award [Vol. 2: 6810]

Provisional Horse Award [Vol. 1: 5885]

Provost; Prix Honorius- [Vol. 1: 14372]

Proximity Achievement Award [Vol. 1: 16951]

Prudential/A & B People Development Award [Vol. 2: 6741]

Prudential Spirit of Community Award [Vol. 1: 11888]

Prusoff Young Investigator Lecture Award; William [Vol. 2: 831]

Pruvost; Prix Fondation Pierre [Vol. 2: 2459]

Pruzansky Memorial Fund for Maternal and Child Health Nursing; Donna [Vol. 1: 7322]

Pryanishnikov Prize; D.N. [Vol. 2: 5847]

PSA Contemporary Medal [Vol. 1: 8782]

PSA Medal [Vol. 1: 8782]

PSA Yankee Medal [Vol. 1: 8782]

PSJ Award [Vol. 2: 4313]

Psychiatry Section Mental Health Foundation Research Prize [Vol. 2: 9106]

Psychoanalytic Training Today Award [Vol. 2: 8171]

Psychotherapy Prize [Vol. 2: 8738]

PTx2 Awards [Vol. 2: 1529]

Public Access to Government Information Award [Vol. 1: 1198]

Public Affairs Competition [Vol. 1: 1213]

Public and Community Service Emmy Awards [Vol. 1: 11457]

Public Art Network Award [Vol. 1: 4716]

Public Awareness Award [Vol. 1: 6998]

Public Citizen of the Year [Vol. 1: 11895]

Public Communications Award
   American Society for Microbiology [Vol. 1: 3983]
   Society of Toxicology [Vol 1: 15854]

Public Education Award
   Canadian Society of Zoologists [Vol. 1: 6999]
   National Weather Association [Vol 1: 13035]

Public Education Awards
   Canadian Dermatology Association [Vol. 1: 6449]
   Water Environment Federation [Vol 1: 17716]

Public Health Award [Vol. 1: 563]

Public History Award [Vol. 1: 13474]

Public Information Program Award [Vol. 1: 9618]

Public Interest Award [Vol. 2: 4994]

Public Officer of the Year [Vol. 2: 1683]

Public Plant Breeding Award [Vol. 1: 12181]

Public Policy and Advocacy Award [Vol. 1: 50]

Public Policy Award
   American Institute of Aeronautics and Astronautics [Vol. 1: 2542]
   American Mathematical Society [Vol 1: 2837]

Public-Private Partnership Award [Vol. 1: 12240]

Public Programming Awards [Vol. 1: 6008]

Public Relations Award [Vol. 1: 463]

Public Relations Film/Video Competition [Vol. 1: 14327]

Public Relations Recognition Award [Vol. 1: 1243]

Public Relations Scholarship/Internships [Vol. 1: 5181]

Public Risk Manager of the Year Award [Vol. 1: 14336]

Public Safety/Injury Prevention Award [Vol. 1: 8102]

Public Safety Officer Medal of Valor [Vol. 1: 16826]

Public Sector Leadership [Vol. 1: 6191]

Public Sector Leadership Awards [Vol. 1: 9402]

Public Sector Organisation of the Year [Vol. 2: 7019]

Public Service Award
   American Woman's Society of Certified Public Accountants [Vol. 1: 4709]
   Conference of Minority Public Administrators [Vol 1: 7504]
   National Society of Professional Insurance Investigators [Vol 1: 12890]
   Society for Prevention Research [Vol 1: 15276]
   Wildlife Management Institute [Vol 1: 17846]

Public Service Award
   Advertising Council [Vol. 1: 164]
   American Association of Immunologists [Vol 1: 1185]
   American Association of Public Health Dentistry [Vol 1: 1328]
   American Crystallographic Association [Vol 1: 1958]
   American Institute of Aeronautics and Astronautics [Vol 1: 2543]
   American Institute of Certified Public Accountants [Vol 1: 2601]
   American Institute of Professional Geologists [Vol 1: 2698]
   American Public Power Association [Vol 1: 3654]

American Society for Cell Biology [Vol 1: 3785]
   American Veterinary Medical Association [Vol 1: 4642]
   Associated Press Managing Editors - Managing Editors Association [Vol 1: 4896]
   Friends of Libraries U.S.A. [Vol 1: 8474]
   National Rehabilitation Association [Vol 1: 12755]
   National Science Foundation - National Science Board [Vol 1: 12817]
   Society of Petroleum Engineers [Vol 1: 15763]
   UCLA Alumni Association [Vol 1: 16592]

Public Service Awards [Vol. 1: 1287]

Public Service Awards of Excellence [Vol. 1: 16545]

Public Service Citations [Vol. 1: 17213]

Public Service Excellence Award [Vol. 2: 3452]

Public Service Medal [Vol. 2: 321]

Public Transport Times Two Awards [Vol. 2: 1529]

Public Understanding of Technology Award [Vol. 1: 10435]

Public Welfare Medal [Vol. 1: 11440]

Publication Award
   Archivists and Librarians in the History of the Health Sciences [Vol. 1: 4772]
   Association of Environmental and Engineering Geologists [Vol 1: 5329]
   Canadian Society of Pharmacology and Therapeutics [Vol 1: 6991]
   International Solid Waste Association [Vol 2: 1305]

Publication Awards [Vol. 1: 8276]

Publication Grants [Vol. 1: 6009]

Publication Medal [Vol. 2: 1014]

Publications and Electronic Media Awards [Vol. 1: 12806]

Publications Award
   AACE International [Vol. 1: 19]
   Association for Industrial Archaeology [Vol 2: 6771]
   Audio Engineering Society [Vol 1: 5692]
   Flight Safety Foundation [Vol 1: 8376]

Publications Prize [Vol. 2: 9299]

Publicity Award [Vol. 2: 5749]

Publicity Book Contest [Vol. 1: 8540]

Publisher Award [Vol. 1: 13901]

Publisher of the Year [Vol. 2: 7504]

Publisher of the Year Award [Vol. 1: 6355]

Publishing Award [Vol. 2: 8255]

Publius Award [Vol. 1: 7155]

Pueble, Jr. Alumnus of the Year Award; Robert C. [Vol. 1: 7220]

Pufahl Spirit Award; Kathy [Vol. 1: 17485]

Puffin/Nation Prize for Creative Citizenship [Vol. 1: 11393]

Pugi Award; Kalev [Vol. 2: 9292]

Pulaski Scholarship [Vol. 1: 1891]

Pulitzer Fellowships [Vol. 1: 7417]

Pulitzer Prizes [Vol. 1: 7418]

Pull of the Year [Vol. 1: 12991]

Puller of the Year [Vol. 1: 12997]

Pulliam Fellowship for Editorial Writing; Eugene C. [Vol. 1: 15808]

Pulliam First Amendment Award; Eugene S. [Vol. 1: 15809]

Pulliam/Kilgore First Amendment Internships [Vol. 1: 15810]

Pulliam/Kilgore Freedom of Information Internships [Vol. 1: 15810]

Pulling Family of the Year [Vol. 1: 12992]

Pulling Hall of Fame [Vol. 1: 12993]

Pulp Biology and Regeneration Group Award [Vol. 1: 9530]

Pulp Press International Three-Day Novel Competition [Vol. 1: 4744]

Pundik Prize; Mendel and Eva [Vol. 2: 3994]

Puppeteers of America Award [Vol. 1: 14352]

Purchasing Manager of the Year Award [Vol. 1: 12554]

Purdy Award; Ken W. [Vol. 1: 10022]

Purdy Award; Ross Coffin [Vol. 1: 1574]

Purdy Award to End Discrimination; Rona and Ken [Vol. 1: 11510]

Purdy Distinguished Achievement Award; Richard B. [Vol. 1: 10204]

Purebred Breeder of the Year [Vol. 1: 328]

Purina Mills, Inc. Teaching Award [Vol. 1: 1980]

Purple Heart [Vol. 1: 12841]

Purse Doctoral Fellowship; Ross C. [Vol. 1: 6732]

Pursuit of Excellence Award [Vol. 1: 12440]

Purves Grant; Daphne [Vol. 2: 6386]

Purvis Memorial Award [Vol. 2: 9293]

Puschkin Prize; Alexander Sergejewitsch [Vol. 2: 3206]

Pushcart Prize: Best of the Small Presses [Vol. 1: 14364]

Pushkin Prize; Alexander Sergeovich [Vol. 2: 5881]

Pustovoit Award; V. S. [Vol. 2: 2571]

- Putnam & Grosset Group Award [Vol. 1: 5069]

Putnam Inspirational Leadership Award; George R. [Vol. 1: 16763]

Putnam Publishing Group Award [Vol. 1: 5069]

Putnam Service Award; Allan Ray [Vol. 1: 4843]

PVA Donor Recognition Award [Vol. 1: 13840]

Pyeatt Award; Madelyn [Vol. 1: 14877]

Pyne Awards [Vol. 1: 14138]

Pyramid Award [Vol. 1: 4652]

Qaboos Police Medal; Sultan [Vol. 2: 5175]

Qaboos Prize for Environmental Preservation; Sultan [Vol. 2: 2655]

Qantas/ABTA Excellence Awards [Vol. 2: 904]

Qatar Today Green Awards [Vol. 2: 5436]

Qatar Today Restaurant Awards [Vol. 2: 5437]

Qatar Web Awards [Vol. 2: 5179]

QSPELL Awards [Vol. 1: 14374]

Qualey Memorial Article Award; Carlton C. [Vol. 1: 9171]

Quality Award
   FLEUROSELECT [Vol. 2: 4715]
   Hong Kong Management Association [Vol 2: 5271]

Quality Awards [Vol. 2: 3603]

Quality Care Award [Vol. 1: 699]

Quality Improvement Awards [Vol. 2: 289]

Quality in Construction Award [Vol. 1: 11554]

Quality of Life Award [Vol. 1: 13557]

Quality Prize of the Government of the Republic of Belarus [Vol. 2: 1394]

Quantum Electronics Award [Vol. 1: 9109]

Quantum Electronics Prize [Vol. 2: 2397]

Quarter Midgets of America Hall of Fame [Vol. 1: 10024]

Quaternary Conference Fund Awards [Vol. 2: 8527]

Quaternary Research Fund Awards [Vol. 2: 8528]

Quazza Medal; Giorgio [Vol. 2: 1280]

Queaneau Palladium Medal; Joan Hodges [Vol. 1: 1151]

Queen Elisabeth International Music Competition of Belgium [Vol. 2: 1575]

Queen Elizabeth II Coronation Award [Vol. 2: 8577]

Queen Elizabeth II Silver Jubilee Endowment Fund for Study in a Second Official Language Award Program [Vol. 1: 5547]

Queen's Award [Vol. 2: 7739]

Queen's Award for Forestry [Vol. 2: 7459]

Queen's Fire Service Medal [Vol. 2: 7348]

Queen's Gallantry Medal [Vol. 2: 7349]

Queen's Medal for Champion Shot [Vol. 1: 8759]

Queen's Police Medal for Distinguished Service [Vol. 2: 7350]

Queen's Prize [Vol. 2: 8408]

Queensland Division Chemical Branch Award [Vol. 2: 800]

Queensland Library Achiever of the Year Award [Vol. 2: 441]

Queensland Library Technician of the Year (Recent Graduate) Award [Vol. 2: 442]

Queeny Safety Professional of the Year Award; Edgar Monsanto [Vol. 1: 4510]

Quenum Prize for Public Health; Dr. Comlan A. A. [Vol. 2: 6553]

Quern Quality Award; Arthur [Vol. 1: 14559]

Quesada Award; General E. R. [Vol. 1: 301]

Quesada Memorial Award; General E. R. [Vol. 1: 301]

Quest Award [Vol. 1: 5972]

QUEST Travel Award [Vol. 2: 8003]

QUEST Undergraduate Scholarship [Vol. 2: 8004]

Quilici Outstanding Member Award; Al [Vol. 1: 13797]

Quill Award [Vol. 1: 9973]

Quill Medal; Jeffrey [Vol. 2: 6694]

Quilt National Awards [Vol. 1: 7802]

Quilts Japan Prize [Vol. 1: 7802]

Quinn Award; Robert G. **[Vol. 1: 3876]**

Quisumbing Medal for Basic Research; Eduardo A. **[Vol. 2: 5367]**

QWF Literary Awards **[Vol. 1: 14374]**

R & D Award **[Vol. 2: 4564]**

R38 Memorial Prize **[Vol. 2: 8616]**

RAAG Award **[Vol. 2: 3311]**

Rabb Award; Sidney R. **[Vol. 1: 8398]**

Rabbitt History of Geology Award; Mary C. **[Vol. 1: 8567]**

Rabi Prize in Atomic, Molecular and Optical Physics; I. I. **[Vol. 1: 3220]**

Rabin Award; Yitzah **[Vol. 1: 13709]**

Rabinow Applied Research Award; Jacob **[Vol. 1: 16790]**

Rabone Award **[Vol. 2: 4916]**

Race Organizer of the Year **[Vol. 1: 16738]**

Racehorse of the Year Award **[Vol. 2: 8532]**

Racial/Ethnic Minority Graduate Scholarship **[Vol. 1: 15394]**

RACie Awards
    Retail Advertising and Marketing Association **[Vol. 1: 14530]**
    Retail Advertising and Marketing Association **[Vol 1: 14531]**

Racolin Memorial Fellowship; Natalie and Mendel **[Vol. 1: 18185]**

Racquetball Hall of Fame **[Vol. 1: 17041]**

Radcliffe Travelling Fellowship in Reliability and Quality Assurance; Frank **[Vol. 2: 8617]**

Raddall Atlantic Fiction Award; Thomas Head **[Vol. 1: 18106]**

Radde Educator of the Year Award; Leon R. **[Vol. 1: 9371]**

Radharc Awards **[Vol. 2: 3853]**

Radin Distinguished Service Award; Alex **[Vol. 1: 3655]**

Radio Awards **[Vol. 1: 61]**

Radio Humanitarian Award **[Vol. 1: 7730]**

Radio Mercury Awards **[Vol. 1: 14389]**

Radio Technical Commission for Aeronautics **[Vol. 1: 14654]**

Radish Marine Enlisted Aircrew of the Year Award; Danny **[Vol. 1: 10961]**

Radix Pin; Harry E. **[Vol. 1: 16909]**

Radix Trophy **[Vol. 1: 16909]**

Radix Trophy; Henry E. **[Vol. 1: 14225]**

Radovic Prize; Dusko **[Vol. 2: 5913]**

RAeS Bronze Medal **[Vol. 2: 8618]**

RAeS Gold Medal **[Vol. 2: 8619]**

RAeS Silver Medal **[Vol. 2: 8620]**

Raeymaekers; Prix Jules **[Vol. 2: 1596]**

Rafael Research Excellence Award **[Vol. 2: 3974]**

Rafaty Memorial Award; F. Mark **[Vol. 1: 538]**

Raffles Award; Stamford **[Vol. 2: 9512]**

Ragazzini Award; John R. **[Vol. 1: 2633]**

Rahman Prize for Computational Physics; Aneesur **[Vol. 1: 3221]**

Rahman Prize in Chemistry; Dr. Atta Ur **[Vol. 2: 5193]**

Rahn Education Award; Ivan B. **[Vol. 1: 15221]**

RAI Research Grants **[Vol. 2: 8646]**

Raiken-Sender Lifetime Achievement Award **[Vol. 1: 5783]**

Raikes Medal **[Vol. 2: 5679]**

Railway Engineering Award **[Vol. 2: 801]**

Rain Bird Engineering Concept of the Year Award **[Vol. 1: 4093]**

Rainbowmaker Award **[Vol. 1: 11206]**

Raine Award **[Vol. 2: 8545]**

Raise Your Sites Award **[Vol. 1: 8887]**

Raiziss/de Palchi Translation Awards **[Vol. 1: 56]**

Rajan Gold Medal; V.S. **[Vol. 2: 5937]**

Rajan Memorial Fund; V.S. **[Vol. 2: 5938]**

Rajchman Prize; Jan **[Vol. 1: 15152]**

Rajewsky Medal; Boris **[Vol. 2: 1241]**

Raju Oration Award; Dr. P. N. **[Vol. 2: 3561]**

Raleigh Award for Fiction; Sir Walter **[Vol. 1: 13375]**

Ralph W. Westcott Award **[Vol. 1: 17143]**

Ralston Purina Company Teaching Award in Dairy Science **[Vol. 1: 1980]**

The Ram Award **[Vol. 1: 5400]**

Rama Scholarships for the American Dream **[Vol. 1: 2465]**

Ramachandran 60th Birthday Commemoration Medal; Prof. G. N. **[Vol. 2: 3655]**

Ramaermedaille **[Vol. 2: 4799]**

Raman Birth Centenary Award; C. V. **[Vol. 2: 3721]**

Raman Medal; Chandrasekhara Venkata **[Vol. 2: 3656]**

Ramanathan Medal; Kalpathi Ramakrishna **[Vol. 2: 3657]**

Ramanujan Birth Centenary Award; Srinivasa **[Vol. 2: 3722]**

Ramanujan Medal; Srinivasa **[Vol. 2: 3658]**

Ramanujan Prize for Young Mathematicians from Developing Countries **[Vol. 2: 4013]**

Ramdohr Prize; Paul **[Vol. 2: 2769]**

Ramm Prize in Experimental Physics **[Vol. 2: 1142]**

Ramo Medal; Simon **[Vol. 1: 9304]**

Ramos Award; Elsie **[Vol. 1: 4922]**

Ramos Memorial Student Poster Award; Elise **[Vol. 1: 4922]**

Rampersad Scientific and Technological Award; Frank **[Vol. 2: 6627]**

Ramsay Medal; Erskine **[Vol. 1: 15222]**

Ramsay Memorial Fellowships for Postdoctoral Chemical Research **[Vol. 2: 8534]**

Ramsdell Award; Charles **[Vol. 1: 16023]**

Ramsdell Award; Fletcher M. Green and Charles W. **[Vol. 1: 16023]**

Ramsey Award; Alice H. **[Vol. 1: 13786]**

Rand Division of Animal Clinical Chemistry Past-Chair's Award; Royden N. **[Vol. 1: 919]**

Rand Memorial Gold Medal; Charles F. **[Vol. 1: 2680]**

Randall Award; Ollie A. **[Vol. 1: 12241]**

Randle Lecture; Sir Philip **[Vol. 2: 6882]**

Randle Travel Fund **[Vol. 2: 8782]**

Randolph-Perry Medal **[Vol. 1: 11044]**

Randolph Senior Fellowship Program; Jennings **[Vol. 1: 16974]**

Raney Fund Award **[Vol. 1: 4344]**

Ranga Farmer Award For Diversified Agriculture; N. G. **[Vol. 2: 3532]**

Ranki Prize; Gyorgi **[Vol. 1: 7998]**

Rankine Lecture **[Vol. 2: 7067]**

Ransom Memorial Medals; James **[Vol. 2: 8044]**

Rao Award; Dr. T. Ramachandra **[Vol. 2: 3562]**

Rao Award; Tilak Venkoba **[Vol. 2: 3563]**

Rao Forestry Research Award; Dr. Y.S. **[Vol. 2: 4517]**

Rao Memorial Award; P.B. Rama **[Vol. 2: 3786]**

Rao Memorial Lecture; Prof. K. Rangadhama **[Vol. 2: 3659]**

Rao Oration Award; Dr. Y. S. Narayana **[Vol. 2: 3564]**

Rao Prize for Scientific Research; C.N.R. **[Vol. 2: 4161]**

Raper Award; Howard **[Vol. 1: 629]**

Raphel Memorial Award; Arnold L. **[Vol. 1: 16852]**

Rapkin Award for Best Paper in *JPER*; Chester **[Vol. 1: 5287]**

Rardon Aviation Maintenance Technician Student of the Year Award; James **[Vol. 1: 5725]**

RAS-Blackwell Prize **[Vol. 2: 8667]**

Rasmussen Award; Wayne D. **[Vol. 1: 217]**

Rasmussen Emerging Artist Memorial Award; Cathy **[Vol. 1: 7802]**

Raspletin Prize; A.A. **[Vol. 2: 5848]**

Rather Convention Award; Hal **[Vol. 1: 12832]**

Ratner Pediatric Allergy and Immunology Research Award; Bret **[Vol. 1: 700]**

Rattlesnake Award; Jimmy **[Vol. 1: 6470]**

Raven Award **[Vol. 1: 11331]**

Raven Award; Peter **[Vol. 1: 4498]**

Raver Community Service Award; Paul J. **[Vol. 1: 13416]**

Rawley Prize; James A. **[Vol. 1: 13686]**

Rawley Silver Awards for Excellence **[Vol. 1: 844]**

Rawlings Award for Energy Conservation (Manager and Technician); General Edwin W. **[Vol. 1: 269]**

Rawlings Awards for Environmental Achievement; General Edwin W. **[Vol. 1: 269]**

Rawls-Palmer Progress in Medicine Award **[Vol. 1: 3804]**

Ray Award **[Vol. 1: 11864]**

Ray Award in Memory of Margaret Sutermeister; Isaac **[Vol. 1: 3360]**

Ray Memorial Award; Professor Priyadaranjan **[Vol. 2: 3515]**

Ray of Sunshine Award **[Vol. 2: 5144]**

Rayleigh Award **[Vol. 1: 9045]**

Rayleigh Medal **[Vol. 2: 7818]**

Rayleigh Medal and Prize **[Vol. 2: 7921]**

Raymond Memorial Award; Rossiter W. **[Vol. 1: 2681]**

RBK Hockey All-American Teams (College Division)- **[Vol. 1: 2400]**

RBK Hockey All-American Teams (University Division) **[Vol. 1: 2401]**

RBMS Exhibition Catalogue Awards **[Vol. 1: 5266]**

RCA Awards **[Vol. 1: 14501]**

RDS-Forest Service Irish Forestry Awards **[Vol. 2: 3923]**

Read Memorial Student Prize; Wal **[Vol. 2: 226]**

Reading Award Program Grants **[Vol. 1: 7096]**

Ready for Work Design Award **[Vol. 1: 16008]**

Reagan Humanitarian Award; Dodi **[Vol. 2: 12716]**

Reagan Lecture Award; James W. **[Vol. 2: 3043]**

Real Estate Journalism Competition **[Vol. 1: 11854]**

Reason Memorial Award; George **[Vol. 1: 6284]**

Rebbot Award; Olivier **[Vol. 1: 13766]**

Rebinder Prize; P.A. **[Vol. 2: 5849]**

Recent Graduate Award **[Vol. 1: 10681]**

Receptive Service of the Year **[Vol. 1: 1679]**

Rechel Award; Amy Lutz **[Vol. 1: 5174]**

Reckord Trophy; Major General Milton A. **[Vol. 1: 12485]**

Reclamation Researcher of the Year **[Vol. 1: 4434]**

Reclamationist of the Year **[Vol. 1: 4436]**

Recognition Award
    American Federation of Mineralogical Societies **[Vol. 1: 2118]**
    American Society for Cybernetics **[Vol 1: 3817]**
    Association for Science Teacher Education **[Vol 1: 5091]**
    Council on Licensure, Enforcement and Regulation **[Vol 1: 7715]**
    Gas Processors Association **[Vol 1: 8527]**
    International Federation of University Women - Switzerland **[Vol 2: 6387]**
    National Association of Diaconate Directors **[Vol 1: 11752]**
    National Intercollegiate Soccer Officials Association **[Vol 1: 12563]**
    Psychotherapists and Counsellors Association of Western Australia **[Vol 2: 936]**

Recognition Award in Entomology **[Vol. 1: 8149]**

Recognition Award in Insect Physiology, Biochemistry and Toxicology **[Vol. 1: 8150]**

Recognition Award Program **[Vol. 1: 13997]**

Recognition Awards **[Vol. 1: 1320]**

Recognition Awards for Outstanding Achievement in the Field of Information Technology **[Vol. 1: 11905]**

Recognition of Achievement Award **[Vol. 1: 4856]**

Recognition of Goodness Award **[Vol. 1: 10572]**

Recognition of Merit **[Vol. 1: 4773]**

Recognition of Outstanding Service and Involvement **[Vol. 1: 7909]**

Recognition of Professional Service Award **[Vol. 1: 5480]**

Recognition of Service Award **[Vol. 2: 1052]**

Recognition of Service Award **[Vol. 2: 9476]**

Recorded Event of the Year **[Vol. 1: 9732]**

Recording and Fieldwork Awards **[Vol. 2: 6772]**

Recruiting Recognition Award **[Vol. 1: 5254]**

Recycler of the Year **[Vol. 1: 12749]**

Recycler of the Year Award **[Vol. 1: 12625]**

Red Award; Chief Master Sergeant Dick **[Vol. 1: 270]**

Red Cloud Indian Art Show **[Vol. 1: 8914]**

Red House Children's Book Award **[Vol. 2: 7670]**

Red Ochre Award **[Vol. 2: 169]**

Redd Student Award in Women's History; Annaley Naegle **[Vol. 1: 6010]**

Reddick Memorial Scholarship Award; Dr. Lawrence Dunbar **[Vol. 1: 5542]**

Reden Badge **[Vol. 2: 3007]**

Redhouse Student Prize; James W. **[Vol. 1: 16584]**

Redi Award **[Vol. 2: 844]**

Redmond Award; Juanita **[Vol. 1: 271]**

Redwood Award; Theophilus **[Vol. 2: 9041]**

Redwood Lectureship; Theophilus **[Vol. 2: 9041]**

Ree Academic Award; Taikyue **[Vol. 2: 5463]**

Reebok Human Rights Award **[Vol. 1: 14458]**

Reed Aeronautics Award **[Vol. 1: 2544]**

Reed and Mallik Medal **[Vol. 2: 8005]**

Reed Award; Sylvanus Albert **[Vol. 1: 2544]**

Reed Medal; Walter **[Vol. 1: 4525]**

Reed Technology Medal; Robert F. **[Vol. 1: 14169]**

Rees Award; Charles **[Vol. 2: 9042]**

Reese Fellowship in American Bibliography and the History of the Book in the Americas **[Vol. 1: 18162]**

Reese Research Prize; Raymond C. [Vol. 1: 4224]

Reese Structural Research Award; Raymond C. [Vol. 1: 1850]

Reeve Memorial Award; John Peter [Vol. 1: 17356]

Reeves International Award; Jim [Vol. 1: 61]

Reeves Member Contribution Award; James [Vol. 1: 7681]

Reeves Premium; A. H. [Vol. 2: 8030]

Referee of the Year
  Camanachd Association [Vol. 2: 7322]
  Trinidad and Tobago Football Federation [Vol 2: 6629]

Reference Service Press Award [Vol. 1: 14472]

Reference Services Award [Vol. 1: 9146]

Refinement Awards [Vol. 1: 4738]

REFORMA Scholarship [Vol. 1: 14478]

Regaud Lecture Award [Vol. 2: 1499]

Reger Memorial Award; Harley B. [Vol. 1: 12765]

Reggae Academy Awards [Vol. 2: 4202]

Reggae Icon Award [Vol. 2: 4202]

Reggae Legend Award [Vol. 2: 4202]

Reggae Trailblazer Award [Vol. 2: 4202]

Reggie Awards [Vol. 1: 14267]

Region Merit Awards [Vol. 2: 8006]

Region Newsletter of the Year Award [Vol. 1: 4876]

Region of the Year [Vol. 1: 12003]

Region of the Year Award [Vol. 1: 4877]

Regional Assistant Coach of the Year [Vol. 1: 12844]

Regional Awards
  Commonwealth Forestry Association [Vol. 2: 7460]
  NASPA - Student Affairs Administrators in Higher Education [Vol 1: 11388]
  National Park Academy of the Arts [Vol 1: 12658]
  National Water Safety Congress [Vol 1: 13027]
  Naval Helicopter Association [Vol 1: 13120]
  New England Theatre Conference [Vol 1: 13160]

Regional Awards of Merit [Vol. 1: 5526]

Regional Best Condition Award [Vol. 1: 2076]

Regional Chairs' Award [Vol. 1: 9477]

Regional Chapter Awards [Vol. 1: 14296]

Regional Chapter Research Advancement Award [Vol. 1: 14896]

Regional Director of the Year
  National Broadcasting Society - Alpha Epsilon Rho [Vol. 1: 12004]
  Society of Professional Journalists [Vol 1: 15811]

Regional Distinguished Mid-Career Award [Vol. 1: 8181]

Regional Distinguished Service Award [Vol. 1: 8182]

Regional Distinguished Team Award [Vol. 1: 8183]

Regional Diver of the Year Award [Vol. 1: 16609]

Regional Division Art Educator Award [Vol. 1: 11544]

Regional Division Art Educator of the Year [Vol. 1: 11544]

Regional Faculty Advisor Awards [Vol. 1: 14297]

Regional Horse Awards [Vol. 1: 13359]

Regional Leadership Award [Vol. 1: 12149]

Regional Medallions [Vol. 1: 13329]

Regional Person of the Year Award [Vol. 1: 3688]

Regional Person of the Year Award [Vol. 1: 12149]

Regional Presidents' Award [Vol. 1: 11694]

Regional Recognition Award [Vol. 1: 6243]

Regional Research Awards [Vol. 1: 14298]

Regional Road Rally Achievement Award [Vol. 1: 16203]

Regional Scientific Achievement Awards [Vol. 1: 10258]

Regional Service Award [Vol. 1: 9161]

Regional Society Member of the Year Award [Vol. 1: 15664]

Regional Technical Award [Vol. 1: 9162]

Regional Television and Multi-Market Cable Commercial Telly Award [Vol. 1: 16416]

Register of Merit [Vol. 1: 4697]

Registered Manager Award [Vol. 2: 7333]

Registrar of Merit Excellent [Vol. 1: 4698]

Regnone Service Award; Debbie [Vol. 1: 14526]

Regular Research Grants [Vol. 1: 6516]

Regulatory Excellence Award [Vol. 1: 7716]

Rehabilitation Award [Vol. 1: 5436]

Rehabilitation Project of the Year Award [Vol. 1: 5527]

Rehnquist Award for Judicial Excellence; William H. [Vol. 1: 12055]

Reich Young Investigator Award; Theodore [Vol. 2: 8219]

Reichart Award; Stuart R. [Vol. 1: 272]

Reichelderfer Award; Francis W. [Vol. 1: 2914]

Reid Award for Animal Science; Ptolemy A. [Vol. 2: 3355]

Reid Award for Crop Science; Ptolemy A. [Vol. 2: 3356]

Reid Award; John E. [Vol. 1: 3317]

Reid Medal; Harry Fielding [Vol. 1: 14836]

Reid Memorial Award; Crawford [Vol. 1: 10530]

Reid Memorial Fellowship; J.H. Stewart [Vol. 1: 6311]

Reid Prize in Mathematics; W. T. and Idalia [Vol. 1: 15124]

Reimann Prize; Christiane [Vol. 2: 6372]

Reiner Award; Miriam [Vol. 1: 920]

Reiner Diamond Pin Award; Abraham [Vol. 1: 636]

Reingold Prize; Nathan [Vol. 1: 8956]

Reinhart and Henry Butch Kuhlmann Award; Frank W. [Vol. 1: 5627]

Reinhart Award; Frank W. [Vol. 1: 5628]

Reinhart Ring; Hans [Vol. 2: 6484]

Reinhold Award for Innovation in Teaching; Van Nostrand [Vol. 1: 9849]

Re(insurance) Person of the Year [Vol. 2: 1693]

Reiss Trainees Prize; Herbert [Vol. 2: 9107]

Related Industry Award [Vol. 1: 11495]

Relating Research to Practice Award [Vol. 1: 2059]

Reliability Test and Evaluation Award [Vol. 1: 9325]

Religion and the Arts Award [Vol. 1: 757]

Religious Educational Excellence Award [Vol. 1: 12050]

Romi Awards [Vol. 1: 18093]

Remington Honor Medal [Vol. 1: 3138]

Remington Painting Award; Frederic [Vol. 1: 12268]

Remlinger; Prix Binoux, Henri de Parville, Jean-Jaques Berger, [Vol. 2: 2183]

Remmers Award; H.H. [Vol. 1: 14357]

Remote Sensing and Photogrammetry Society Award [Vol. 2: 8540]

Remote Sensing Prize [Vol. 1: 2915]

Remote Sensing Society Medal [Vol. 2: 8540]

Remote Sensing Society President's Prize [Vol. 2: 8543]

Renaissance Great Comebacks Award [Vol. 1: 16648]

Renaud Prize; Line [Vol. 2: 2428]

Renaudot; Prix Theophraste [Vol. 2: 2596]

Rencken Emerging Professional Leader Award; Robert [Vol. 1: 1942]

Renee River Award [Vol. 1: 11375]

Renie; Prix [Vol. 1: 2278]

Renner Award for Outstanding Crime Reporting; Thomas [Vol. 1: 10496]

Renner Medal; Janos [Vol. 2: 3363]

Rennie Medal; James [Vol. 2: 8007]

Rennie Memorial Award for Excellence in Government Public Relations; Don [Vol. 1: 6844]

Rennie Memorial Medal [Vol. 2: 982]

Renold Prize Lecture; Albert [Vol. 2: 2802]

Renold Travel Fellowship; Albert [Vol. 2: 2803]

Renovated Laboratory of the Year [Vol. 1: 14382]

Renqvist Prize; Alvar [Vol. 2: 2090]

Rental Hall of Fame [Vol. 1: 3689]

Repligen Corporation Award in Chemistry of Biological Processes [Vol. 1: 1669]

Replogle Award for Management Improvement; Luther I. [Vol. 1: 16853]

Reporter Awards [Vol. 1: 15779]

Reporter of the Year [Vol. 2: 9575]

Representative Excellence Award [Vol. 1: 9698]

Reproductive Health and Rights; Individual Volunteer Award for Contributions to Sexual and [Vol. 2: 8161]

Reproductive Health and Rights; International Award for Contributions to Sexual and [Vol. 2: 8162]

Reproductive Health and Rights; Member Association Award for Contributions to Sexual and [Vol. 2: 8163]

Reproductive Health and Rights; Staff Award for Contributions to Sexual and [Vol. 2: 8164]

Reproductive Health and Rights; Youth Award for Contributions to Sexual and [Vol. 2: 8165]

Reptile Humanitarian of the Year [Vol. 1: 14509]

Reptile Researcher of the Year [Vol. 1: 14510]

Rescue Medal [Vol. 2: 1542]

Rescue Medal of Valour [Vol. 2: 1543]

Research Achievement Award
  American Heart Association [Vol. 1: 2314]
  Canadian Cardiovascular Society [Vol 1: 6394]

Research Achievement Award in the Pharmaceutical Sciences [Vol. 1: 3146]

Research Achievement Awards [Vol. 1: 170]

Research and Audit Poster Prizes [Vol. 2: 7167]

Research and Development Award
  American Diabetes Association [Vol. 1: 2018]
  Association of Military Surgeons of the U.S. [Vol 1: 5437]
  Institute of Food Technologists [Vol 1: 9342]

Research and Special Libraries Award [Vol. 1: 5386]

Research Appointments [Vol. 1: 17303]

Research Article Award [Vol. 1: 8331]

Research Associateship Programs [Vol. 1: 12767]

Research Award
  Academy of Psychosomatic Medicine [Vol. 1: 109]
  American Academy of Veterinary Pharmacology and Therapeutics [Vol 1: 769]
  American Society for Photobiology [Vol 1: 4042]
  European Society for Paediatric Endocrinology [Vol 2: 7641]
  National Association for Drama Therapy [Vol 1: 11569]
  Society for the Study of Reproduction [Vol 1: 15388]
  Tanzania Industrial Research and Development Organization [Vol 2: 9523]
  United Kingdom eInformation Group [Vol 2: 9416]

Research Award
  Academic Pediatric Association [Vol. 1: 51]
  American Academy of Clinical Toxicology [Vol 1: 510]
  American Alliance for Theatre and Education [Vol 1: 808]
  American Association on Intellectual and Developmental Disabilities [Vol 1: 1426]
  American Counseling Association [Vol 1: 1943]
  American Diabetes Association [Vol 1: 2027]
  American Institute of Aeronautics and Astronautics [Vol 1: 2516]
  British HIV Association [Vol 2: 7082]
  Charcot-Marie-Tooth Association [Vol 1: 7185]
  Fellows of the American Bar Foundation [Vol 1: 8338]
  International Institute for Geo-Information Science and Earth Observation [Vol 2: 4749]
  Lamaze International [Vol 1: 10742]
  National Association of Animal Breeders [Vol 1: 11622]
  Radiation Research Society [Vol 1: 14387]

Research Award Competition [Vol. 1: 1916]

Research Award for Innovative Work in Anterior-Segment Surgery [Vol. 2: 2974]

Research Award for Young Scientists [Vol. 2: 6561]

Research Award in Geriatric Neurology [Vol. 1: 595]

Research Award in Teacher Education [Vol. 1: 5532]

Research Award of Merit [Vol. 1: 13241]

Research Awards
  International Society for Agricultural Safety and Health [Vol. 1: 10138]
  Papanicolaou Society of Cytopathology [Vol. 1: 13825]

Research Awards
  American Rhinologic Society [Vol. 1: 3696]
  American Society for Mass Spectrometry [Vol 1: 3965]
  Arthritis Foundation [Vol 1: 4810]
  Australian Society for Medical Research [Vol 2: 540]
  Governmental Research Association [Vol 1: 8745]
  National Institutes of Health - National Institute of Nursing Research [Vol 1: 12558]
  Oral and Maxillofacial Surgery Foundation [Vol 1: 13626]
  Post-Polio Health International [Vol 1: 14098]
  Society for Theatre Research [Vol 2: 9226]

Research, Development and Demonstration Project Grants [Vol. 1: 11075]

Research Dissemination Award [Vol. 1: 14901]

Ringwood Award for Drama; Gwen Pharis [Vol. 1: 18109]

Rio National Prize in Chemistry; Andres Manuel del [Vol. 2: 4581]

Rio; Premio Nacional de Quimica Andres Manuel del [Vol. 2: 4581]

Rio Tinto Alcan Award [Vol. 1: 6895]

Riopelle Award; James and Marie [Vol. 1: 3084]

Ripperton Environmental Educator Award; Lyman A. [Vol. 1: 240]

Ripples of Hope Award in Biotechnology & Entrepreneurship [Vol. 1: 5799]

Riseborough Prize; Ronald [Vol. 2: 1144]

Rising Moon Outstanding Youth Services Librarian Award [Vol. 1: 4790]

Rising Star Award
  Advertising Research Foundation [Vol. 1: 171]
  Association for Women in Communications [Vol 1: 5166]
  Association of Military Surgeons of the U.S. [Vol 1: 5438]
  Emergency Nurses Association [Vol 1: 8103]
  International Society of Hospitality Consultants [Vol 1: 10324]
  Medical Fitness Association [Vol 1: 11056]
  North Country Trail Association [Vol 1: 13387]
  Taiwan Ministry of Economic Affairs - Small and Medium Enterprise Administration [Vol 2: 6598]
  United States Harness Writers' Association [Vol 1: 16952]
  Wisconsin Health Information Management Association [Vol 1: 17891]

Rising Star in Clinical Practice Award [Vol. 1: 1237]

Rising Star in Urology Awards [Vol. 1: 4631]

Rising Stars Secondary Recognition Award [Vol. 1: 11546]

Risk Manager of the Year [Vol. 2: 949]

Rispens Award; Bart [Vol. 2: 3243]

Rist; Medaille Jean [Vol. 2: 2452]

Rist Prize; David [Vol. 1: 11154]

RITA Award [Vol. 1: 14587]

Rittenhouse Award [Vol. 1: 11076]

Ritter Award, R. Max [Vol. 1: 16714]

Rittle, Sr. Scholarship; Paul H. [Vol. 1: 9409]

Ritz Award; Luka [Vol. 2: 1883]

Rivenes Award; David G. [Vol. 1: 464]

River Bend Trophy [Vol. 1: 13444]

River Prize; Charles [Vol. 1: 4643]

Rivera Award in Transgender Studies; Sylvia [Vol. 1: 7141]

Rivera Children's Book Award; Tomas [Vol. 1: 16468]

Rivers Innovation Award; Lee W. [Vol. 1: 7436]

Rivis Prize; Mrs. F. E. [Vol. 2: 8826]

Rivkin Award; William R. [Vol. 1: 2182]

Rivot; Prix L. E. [Vol. 2: 2232]

Rizzuto Award; Antonio R. [Vol. 1: 16613]

RMA of the Year [Vol. 1: 2869]

Roadrunners of the Year Award [Vol. 1: 14562]

Roanoke-Chowan Award for Poetry [Vol. 1: 13376]

Roark Jr. Meritorious Service Award; Eldridge W. [Vol. 1: 13518]

Roback Scholarship; Herbert [Vol. 1: 11416]

Robb Fellowship; Preston [Vol. 1: 11023]

Robbins Award; Chandler [Vol. 1: 1498]

Robbins Outstanding Competitor Award; Paul [Vol. 1: 13339]

Robbins Prize; David R. [Vol. 1: 2838]

Robe of Achievement [Vol. 1: 14849]

Robel Award [Vol. 2: 5390]

Robert J. Jaeger Student Award for Graduate Research [Vol. 1: 8918]

Roberts Award for Clinical Leadership; C.A. [Vol. 1: 6818]

Roberts Award; Frances F. [Vol. 1: 7599]

Roberts Award; Harold R. [Vol. 1: 10370]

Roberts Award; Summerfield G. [Vol. 1: 15955]

Roberts Lifetime Achievement Award; Nora [Vol. 1: 14588]

Roberts Memorial Scholarships; Marion [Vol. 1: 5720]

Roberts Playwriting Award; Forest A. [Vol. 1: 8438]

Roberts Public Library Distinguished Service Award; William H. [Vol. 1: 13369]

Roberts Vocal Scholarship; W. Towyn [Vol. 2: 8392]

Robertson Award; Bob [Vol. 2: 534]

Robertson Continuing Professional Educator Award; Adelle F. [Vol. 1: 17395]

Robertson Fund; Alan [Vol. 2: 7250]

Robertson Memorial Award; J. Stuart [Vol. 1: 6630]

Robertson Memorial Lecture [Vol. 1: 11441]

Robertson Memorial Prize; James Alexander [Vol. 1: 7516]

Robertson Memorial Trophy; Heaton R. [Vol. 1: 16909]

Robichaux Award; Joseph [Vol. 1: 17476]

Robie Award for Achievement in Industry [Vol. 1: 14564]

Robie Humanitarianism Award [Vol. 1: 14565]

Robillard Award; Pierre [Vol. 1: 16291]

Robinson Award; Charlie [Vol. 1: 14325]

Robinson Award; J. Franklin [Vol. 1: 504]

Robinson Award; Martin [Vol. 2: 8416]

Robinson Award; Renault [Vol. 1: 11989]

Robinson Award; Robert [Vol. 2: 9043]

Robinson Awards; Robert L. [Vol. 1: 3361]

Robinson Coach of the Year; Eddie [Vol. 1: 8412]

Robinson-Cunningham Award [Vol. 1: 504]

Robinson Distinguished Service Award; Stanley C. [Vol. 1: 17396]

Robinson Grants; Helen M. [Vol. 1: 10105]

Robinson Helicopter R22/R44 Safety Course Scholarship [Vol. 1: 17800]

Robinson Lectureship; Robert [Vol. 2: 9043]

Robinson Marine Naval Flight Officer of the Year Award; Robert Guy [Vol. 1: 10962]

Robinson Memorial Award [Vol. 1: 15988]

Robinson Memorial Medal for Begonia Hybrid; Alfred D. [Vol. 1: 1490]

Robinson Periodontal Regeneration Award; R. Earl [Vol. 1: 725]

Robinson Prize for Historical Analysis; Michael C. [Vol. 1: 12253]

Robinson Prize; James Harvey [Vol. 1: 2388]

Robinson Prize; Joan Cahalin [Vol. 1: 15355]

Robinson Scholarship Award; Thelma A. [Vol. 1: 7475]

Robinson Silver Wings Award [Vol. 2: 614]

Robinson Vision Award; Julius [Vol. 1: 465]

Rocha Medal; Manuel [Vol. 2: 5434]

Roche Award [Vol. 2: 5622]

Roche Diagnostics Alice C. Evans Award [Vol. 1: 3984]

Roche Diagnostics Award [Vol. 1: 6938]

Roche Prize; Jerome [Vol. 2: 8876]

Rochester International Film Festival [Vol. 1: 11291]

Rock and Roll Hall of Fame [Vol. 1: 14569]

Rock Mechanics Award [Vol. 1: 15224]

Rockefeller Prentice Memorial Award in Animal Breeding and Genetics [Vol. 1: 4124]

Rockefeller Prize [Vol. 1: 3177]

Rockman Instruction Publication of the Year Award; Ilene F. [Vol. 1: 5268]

Rockower Awards for Excellence in Jewish Journalism; Simon [Vol. 1: 2735]

Rockwell Award; Martha [Vol. 1: 17089]

The Rocky Advertising Awards [Vol. 1: 10940]

Rodan Excellence in Mentorship Award; Gideon A. [Vol. 1: 3775]

Rodeo Hall of Fame [Vol. 1: 14580]

Roderick Lectures; Colin [Vol. 2: 728]

Roderick Prizes for Australian Literature; Colin [Vol. 2: 729]

Rodermund Service Award; Matthew [Vol. 1: 7083]

Rodgers Award; Richard [Vol. 1: 4264]

Rodli Award [Vol. 1: 12141]

Roe Award; John Orlando [Vol. 1: 540]

Roe Award; Joseph H. [Vol. 1: 921]

Roe Award; Kenneth Andrew [Vol. 1: 1152]

Roe Award; Ralph Coats [Vol. 1: 3877]

Roe Medal; Ralph Coats [Vol. 1: 4420]

Roe Memorial Alcoholism and Drug Abuse Counselor of the Year; Lora [Vol. 1: 11344]

Roebling Award [Vol. 1: 4227]

Roebling Medal [Vol. 1: 11176]

Roelen Medal; Otto [Vol. 2: 3171]

Roelker Mentorship Award; Nancy Lyman [Vol. 1: 2389]

Roelker Prize; Nancy Lyman [Vol. 1: 14920]

Roentgen Resident/Fellow Research Award [Vol. 1: 14427]

Roesch Lecture; Josef [Vol. 2: 1221]

Roeske Certificate of Recognition for Excellence in Medical Student Education; Nancy C. A. [Vol. 1: 3362]

Roethlisberger Award; Fritz [Vol. 1: 13701]

Rogers Award; David E. [Vol. 1: 5212]

Rogers Bursaries; Hal [Vol. 1: 10686]

Rogers Information Advancement Award; Thomson Reuters/Frank Bradway [Vol. 1: 11077]

Rogers Memorial Exhibit Award; Lelan G. [Vol. 1: 3005]

Rogosa Award; Morrison [Vol. 1: 3985]

Rokkan Prize in Comparative Social Science Research; Stein
  European Consortium for Political Research [Vol. 2: 7601]
  International Social Science Council [Vol 2: 2564]

Role Model/Mentor Awards [Vol. 1: 8039]

Rolex Awards for Enterprise [Vol. 2: 6477]

Rolex International Women's Keelboat Championship [Vol. 1: 17063]

Rolex Player of the Year Award [Vol. 1: 10732]

Rolex Player to Watch [Vol. 1: 9466]

Rolex World Sailor of the Year Award [Vol. 2: 8179]

The Roll of Distinguished Philatelist [Vol. 2: 6798]

Roll of Honor
  Military Vehicle Preservation Association [Vol. 1: 11161]
  Parachute Industry Association [Vol. 1: 13838]

Roll of Honour [Vol. 2: 6572]

Roll of Honour Award [Vol. 2: 4196]

Rolling Trophy [Vol. 2: 3604]

Rollins Grant; William [Vol. 1: 631]

Rolls-Royce Award for Exceptional News Feature [Vol. 2: 7456]

Rolls-Royce Excellence in Helicopter Maintenance Award [Vol. 1: 8895]

Romance Contest [Vol. 1: 18126]

Romanell Lecture on Philosophical Naturalism; Patrick [Vol. 1: 3178]

Romanell - Phi Beta Kappa Professorship in Philosophy [Vol. 1: 13966]

Romanowski Medal; Miroslaw [Vol. 1: 14646]

Romantic Novel of the Year [Vol. 2: 8551]

Romantic Novel of the Year (RoNA) Awards [Vol. 2: 8551]

Rombaux; Prix Egide [Vol. 2: 1597]

Romberg Award for Residential Architecture - Multiple Housing; Frederick [Vol. 2: 385]

Rome Memorial Newspaper Award; Sidney R. [Vol. 1: 416]

Rome Prize [Vol. 1: 488]

Romeo Talent Buyer of the Year; Don [Vol. 1: 61]

Romer - G. G. Simpson Medal; A. S. [Vol. 1: 15878]

Romer Prize; Alfred Sherwood [Vol. 1: 15879]

Romero Award; Oscar [Vol. 1: 14609]

Romero First Book Publication Prize; Lora [Vol. 1: 4574]

Rominger Plaque; William E. [Vol. 1: 11512]

Romney Volunteer Center of the Year Award; George W. [Vol. 1: 14076]

Ron Kenny Student Poster Prize [Vol. 2: 458]

Ron Kenny Student Presentation Prize [Vol. 2: 458]

Rooke Medal for the Public Promotion of Engineering [Vol. 2: 8584]

Rookie Chapter of the Year [Vol. 1: 12005]

Rookie Member of the Year [Vol. 1: 12006]

Rookie of the Meet Award [Vol. 1: 17448]

Rookie of the Year
  Rugby League International Federation [Vol. 2: 1029]
  Speech Pathology Australia [Vol 2: 1053]
  Sportscar Vintage Racing Association [Vol 1: 16227]
  Western Women Premier Bowlers [Vol 1: 17777]

Rookie of the Year Award (National Sprint Care Div.) [Vol. 1: 16739]

Rookie of the Year Award (Silver Crown Div.) [Vol. 1: 16740]

Rookie Player of the Year [Vol. 1: 9467]

Rookwood Award for Agriculture/Engineering Design; Rod [Vol. 2: 583]

Roosevelt American History Awards; Theodore [Vol. 2: 4834]

Roosevelt Award for Excellence in Recreation and Park Research; Theodore and Franklin [Vol. 1: 12746]

Roosevelt Award; Franklin Delano [Vol. 1: 15099]

Roosevelt Award; Theodore [Vol. 1: 12074]

Roosevelt Distinguished Service Medal; Theodore [Vol. 1: 14595]

Roosevelt Four Freedoms Medals; Franklin D. [Vol. 1: 14597]

Roosevelt Fund Award; Eleanor [Vol. 1: 1398]

Roosevelt Leadership Award for Company Grade Officers; Theodore [Vol. 1: 12486]

Roosevelt Memorial Grant; Theodore [Vol. 1: 2954]

Roosevelt/Woodrow Wilson Award; Theodore [Vol. 1: 2390]

Root Award; H. Paul [Vol. 1: 2808]

Root Award; Lt. Charles S. [Vol. 1: 12607]

Roozeboom Medal; Bakhuys [Vol. 2: 4835]

Roquemore Memorial Award; A.D. [Vol. 1: 2339]

Roquette Pinto Prize [Vol. 2: 1747]

Rosa Award; Edward Bennett [Vol. 1: 16791]

Rosa Camuna [Vol. 2: 4038]

Roscoe Research Grant; H. C. [Vol. 2: 7126]

Rose Award; AstraZeneca Young Scientist Frank [Vol. 2: 6948]

Rose Award; Rod [Vol. 1: 15824]

Rose Award; William C. [Vol. 1: 3759]

Rose Bowl Player of the Game [Vol. 1: 16522]

Rose Brand Award for Scene Design [Vol. 1: 16967]

Rose d'Or Festival [Vol. 2: 6479]

Rose-Hulman Award [Vol. 1: 9571]

Rose Jr.; Pinnacle Award for Volunteerism in Memory of William E. [Vol. 1: 4470]

Rose Prize [Vol. 2: 8687]

Rose Teaching Award; Martha [Vol. 1: 13634]

Rosen Lectureship; Aaron [Vol. 1: 15339]

Rosen; Prix Raymond [Vol. 2: 4449]

Rosenbaum Memorial Award; Colonel Samuel [Vol. 1: 12493]

Rosenbaum Memorial Award; Samuel [Vol. 1: 7062]

Rosenberg Academic Achievement Award; Martin [Vol. 1: 4484]

Rosenberg Award; Bill [Vol. 1: 8236]

Rosenblum Cancer Dissertation Award; Barbara [Vol. 1: 15917]

Rosenbluth Memorial Travel Agent of the Year Award; Joseph W. [Vol. 1: 4519]

Rosenstiel Award for Distinguished Work in Basic Medical Research; Lewis S. [Vol. 1: 14600]

Rosenthal Awards; Richard and Hinda [Vol. 1: 1804]

Rosenthal Early Career Research Award [Vol. 1: 3461]

Rosenwald Student Poster Award; A.S. [Vol. 1: 1047]

Rosenzweig Distinguished Service Award [Vol. 1: 4791]

Rosenzweig Distinguished Service Award; Roy [Vol. 1: 13687]

Rosica, Jr. Memorial Award; Albert E. [Vol. 1: 1704]

Rosie Awards [Vol. 1: 337]

Roslyn Faculty Research Award [Vol. 1: 4901]

Ross Aviation Safety Award; Pete [Vol. 1: 10963]

Ross Award; Alan [Vol. 1: 6769]

Ross Award for Excellence in Clinical Research; Norton M. [Vol. 1: 2005]

Ross Award; Madeline Dane [Vol. 1: 13767]

Ross Award; Thomas [Vol. 2: 8849]

Ross Dissertation Award; Jacqueline A. [Vol. 1: 8026]

Ross Leadership Award [Vol. 2: 7864]

Ross Long Distance Running Merit Award; H. Browning [Vol. 1: 17477]

Ross Medal; Will [Vol. 1: 2801]

Ross Prize; John Munn [Vol. 2: 7847]

Ross Student Paper Award; Carl A. [Vol. 1: 4750]

Rossby Research Medal; Carl-Gustaf [Vol. 1: 2916]

Rossi; Prix [Vol. 2: 2294]

Rossi Prize; Bruno [Vol. 1: 1450]

Rossiter History of Women in Science Prize; Margaret W. [Vol. 1: 8957]

Roster of Fellows [Vol. 1: 3035]

Roster of Honor [Vol. 1: 3036]

Rostkowski Award; Nicolaus [Vol. 1: 8914]

Roswell Student Dissertation Award; Virginia A. [Vol. 1: 4923]

ROTC Award [Vol. 1: 4727]

ROTC Awards [Vol. 1: 12917]

ROTC Medals [Vol. 1: 12912]

Roth Award for a Translation of a Literary Work; Lois [Vol. 1: 11240]

Roth Manufacturing Engineering Scholarships; Edward S. [Vol. 1: 14957]

Roth Persian Translation Prize; Lois [Vol. 1: 2670]

Rothman Memorial Award; Stephen [Vol. 1: 15160]

Rothmans Foundation Ballet Scholarship [Vol. 2: 1075]

Rothrock Award [Vol. 1: 16000]

Rothschild and Miriam Rothschild Medal; Charles [Vol. 2: 9125]

Rothschild Challenge Cup [Vol. 2: 8827]

Rothstein Golden Pen Award for Scientific Writing; Jules M. [Vol. 1: 3241]

Rotorua Trophy [Vol. 2: 5059]

Roulston/COTF Innovation Award [Vol. 1: 6761]

Rous-Whipple Award [Vol. 1: 3959]

Rouse Hydraulic Engineering Lecture; Hunter [Vol. 1: 4228]

Rousseau; Prix Gaston [Vol. 2: 2233]

Roussy; Prix Gustave [Vol. 2: 2234]

Routh Student Research Grants; Marion and Donald [Vol. 1: 3601]

Routledge Distance Learning Librarian Conference Sponsorship [Vol. 1: 5269]

Routman Teacher Recognition Grant; Regie [Vol. 1: 10106]

Rouyer; Prix [Vol. 2: 2146]

Rovelstad Scholarship in International Librarianship [Vol. 1: 7710]

Rowan-Legg Award; Edward K. [Vol. 1: 6338]

Rowan Marine Botany Prize; Kingsley [Vol. 2: 1145]

Rowe Award in Perinatal Cardiology; Richard D. [Vol. 1: 15260]

Rowe Award; N.E. [Vol. 2: 8621]

Rowe Prize; Burton [Vol. 2: 7415]

Rowing Hall of Fame [Vol. 1: 12788]

Rowland Prevention Award; Lela [Vol. 1: 11103]

Rowland Prize; Thomas Fitch [Vol. 1: 4229]

Rowlands Male Student-Athlete of the Year; David [Vol. 1: 12579]

Rowse Award for Press Criticism; Arthur [Vol. 1: 12688]

Roxane Laboratories Linda Arenth Excellence in Cancer Nursing Management Award [Vol. 1: 13529]

Roy Lecture; Frontiers of Science and Society, the Rustum [Vol. 1: 1559]

Roy Memorial Lecture; Dr. Biren [Vol. 2: 3660]

Roy Space Science and/or Design Award; Dr. Biren [Vol. 2: 3446]

Roy Trust Award; Dr. Biren [Vol. 2: 3447]

Royal Aero Club Diploma [Vol. 1: 8600]

Royal Asiatic Society Award [Vol. 2: 8651]

Royal Canadian Mounted Police Long Service Medal [Vol. 1: 8760]

Royal Canin Award [Vol. 1: 4644]

Royal Canin Veterinary Diet Award [Vol. 1: 820]

Royal Colleges Medal [Vol. 2: 8907]

Royal Designer for Industry Award [Vol. 2: 8959]

Royal Economic Society Prize [Vol. 2: 8766]

Royal Gold Medal [Vol. 2: 8854]

Royal Institute of British Architects Awards [Vol. 2: 8855]

Royal Institute of Navigation Fellowship [Vol. 2: 8858]

Royal Medal [Vol. 2: 9071]

Royal Medals [Vol. 2: 8943]

Royal Norwegian Order of Merit [Vol. 2: 5134]

Royal Norwegian Order of St. Olav [Vol. 2: 5135]

Royal Order of Sahametrei [Vol. 2: 1809]

Royal Red Cross [Vol. 2: 7351]

Royal Society and Academie des sciences Microsoft Award [Vol. 2: 8944]

The Royal Society-Daiwa Anglo-Japanese Foundation Joint Project Grants [Vol. 2: 7494]

Royal Society Pfizer Award [Vol. 2: 8945]

Royal Society Prizes for Science Books [Vol. 2: 8946]

Royal Society Winton Prizes for Science Books [Vol. 2: 8946]

Royal Victorian Order [Vol. 2: 7352]

Royce Award; Sir Henry [Vol. 2: 8031]

Royce Foundation Trophy; Sir Henry [Vol. 2: 9181]

Royce Lectures in the Philosophy of the Mind [Vol. 1: 3179]

Royce Prize in American Idealist Thought; Josiah [Vol. 1: 14652]

Rozhdestvenskii Prize; D.S. [Vol. 2: 5850]

RR Donnelley Awards [Vol. 1: 17898]

Rs of Excellence Awards [Vol. 1: 14454]

RSA Fellow [Vol. 1: 14545]

RSPB Fine Art Award [Vol. 2: 9342]

RSPCA Award for Innovative Developments in Animal Welfare [Vol. 2: 7251]

RTNDA National Awards [Vol. 1: 14423]

RTNDA/UNITY Awards [Vol. 1: 14419]

Rubens-Alcais Award [Vol. 1: 9797]

Rubin Award; Leonard R. [Vol. 1: 1318]

Rubincam Youth Award [Vol. 1: 12454]

Rubinshtein Prize; S.L. [Vol. 2: 5851]

Rubinstein Award [Vol. 1: 1230]

Rubinstein International Piano Master Competition; Arthur [Vol. 2: 3936]

Rubner Prize; Max [Vol. 2: 3019]

Ruby Award; National Distinguished Service [Vol. 1: 8180]

Rudd Award; Steele [Vol. 2: 632]

Rudolfs Medal for Industrial Waste Management; Willem [Vol. 1: 17717]

Rudolph Student Athlete Achievement Award; Wilma [Vol. 1: 11616]

Rudolphi-Medaille; Carl-Asmund- [Vol. 2: 2760]

Rudolphi Medal; Karl Asmund [Vol. 2: 2760]

Rugby League Award; Spirit of [Vol. 2: 1030]

Rugby Medal for Excellence [Vol. 2: 1034]

Ruger World Team Trophy; William B. [Vol. 1: 12786]

Ruggles Travel Grant Awards; Richard and Nancy [Vol. 1: 9589]

Ruhe Meritorious Achievement Award for Professional of the Year; Lutz [Vol. 1: 1420]

Ruhlmann; Prix [Vol. 2: 2147]

Ruhr Coach of the Year; Lionel [Vol. 1: 6471]

Ruiz Award; Enrique Labrador [Vol. 1: 13821]

Rule Award; Wilma [Vol. 1: 10054]

Rule of Law Award [Vol. 2: 8093]

Rumbaugh Outstanding Student Leader Award [Vol. 1: 15532]

Rumford Medal [Vol. 2: 8947]

Rumford Prize [Vol. 1: 498]

Rumi Peace and Dialogue Awards [Vol. 1: 14656]

Rumsey Buyers' Choice Award; Nona Jean Hulsey [Vol. 1: 12268]

Rumsey Student Award for Advancement of Avian Medicine; Reed [Vol. 1: 1048]

Runcorn-Florensky Medal [Vol. 2: 2378]

Runcorn Prize; Keith [Vol. 2: 8667]

Runcorn Travel Award; Keith [Vol. 2: 2378]

Runermark Award; Jan [Vol. 2: 1486]

Runyon Clinical Investigator Awards; Damon [Vol. 1: 7806]

Runyon Fellowship Award; Damon [Vol. 1: 7807]

Runyon-Rachleff Innovation Awards; Damon [Vol. 1: 7808]

Runyon - Walter Winchell Cancer Fund Fellowships; Damon [Vol. 1: 7807]

Ruppe Distinguished Service Award; Carol V. [Vol. 1: 15093]

Ruptash-Mandryk Nurse of the Year Award [Vol. 1: 340]

Rural and Remote Opportunities Grant [Vol. 1: 6550]

Rural County Engineer of the Year Award [Vol. 1: 11742]

Rural Electricity Resource Council Electric Technology Award [Vol. 1: 4094]

Rural Health Practitioner of the Year [Vol. 1: 12794]

Rural Service Award [Vol. 1: 15829]

Rural Wales Award [Vol. 2: 7328]

Rural Youth Europe Awards [Vol. 2: 2124]

Rush and Frances Hubbs Miller Award; Robert [Vol. 1: 7854]

Rush Award; Benjamin [Vol. 1: 3363]

Rush Award; Gertrude E. [Vol. 1: 11968]

Rushing Early Career Research Award; Janice Hocker [Vol. 1: 16048]

Russell and Burch Award [Vol. 1: 9001]

Russell Award; Diane H. [Vol. 1: 5174]

Russell Award for Distinguished Research in the Teaching of English; David H. [Vol. 1: 12219]

Russell Award; Frances E. [Vol. 2: 6367]

Russell Award; Walter McRae [Vol. 2: 98]

Russell, Jr., Award; Louis B. [Vol. 1: 2315]

Russell Lectureship; Henry Norris [**Vol. 1: 1451**]

Russell Memorial Medal; Peter Nicol [**Vol. 2: 802**]

Russell Naval Aviation Flight Safety Award; Adm. James S. [**Vol. 1: 13652**]

Russell Prize; Gunter [**Vol. 2: 7168**]

Russell Scholarships; Norman K. [**Vol. 1: 12649**]

Russell Society Award; Bertrand [**Vol. 1: 5808**]

Russo Food Writers Grant; Linda D. [**Vol. 1: 7783**]

Rustgi International Travel Awards; Moti L. and Kamla [**Vol. 1: 8448**]

Rustin Human Rights Award; Bayard [**Vol. 1: 2125**]

Ruth Digital Avionics Award; Dr. John C. [**Vol. 1: 2545**]

Rutherford Medal and Prize [**Vol. 2: 7922**]

Rutherford Memorial Lecture [**Vol. 2: 7922**]

Rutter Gold Medal and Prize [**Vol. 2: 7416**]

Ruzicka-Preis [**Vol. 2: 6501**]

Ruzicka Prize [**Vol. 2: 6501**]

Ruzzene Foundation Prize for Writing about Italians in Australia; Grollo [**Vol. 2: 1067**]

RV Automotive Achievement Award [**Vol. 1: 14450**]

Ryan Award; Cornelius [**Vol. 1: 13768**]

Ryan Editorial Award; Robert G. [**Vol. 1: 7910**]

Ryan Prize for Anatomy; T.F. [**Vol. 2: 1146**]

Ryan Trophies; John T. [**Vol. 1: 6618**]

Ryan Winners Circle Acting Awards; Irene [**Vol. 1: 10667**]

Ryan Winners Circle Evening of Scenes; Irene [**Vol. 1: 10667**]

Ryder Cup [**Vol. 1: 14221**]

Ryle Award for Excellence in Writing on the Problems of Geriatrics; Joseph D. [**Vol. 1: 12689**]

Ryle Memorial Medal [**Vol. 2: 8511**]

Ryser SGI [**Vol. 2: 6989**]

S & T Promotion Award [**Vol. 2: 4635**]

S. Lewis Elmer Award [**Vol. 1: 2266**]

SA Branch Memorial Incentive Award [**Vol. 2: 615**]

SA Eagle Trophy [**Vol. 2: 5486**]

SAALED Bursary [**Vol. 2: 5656**]

SABAM Prize for the Best Scenario [**Vol. 2: 1516**]

Sabbagh Award for Engineering Construction Excellence; Hassib [**Vol. 2: 2666**]

Sabga Caribbean Awards for Excellence; Anthony N. [**Vol. 2: 6613**]

Sabin Metal Student Award [**Vol. 1: 10060**]

Sabina Fund Grants [**Vol. 1: 8237**]

Sabine Medal; Wallace Clement [**Vol. 1: 127**]

Saccamanno, M.D. New Frontiers in Cytology Award; Geno [**Vol. 1: 4283**]

Sacerdoti Award; Cesare [**Vol. 2: 8172**]

Sacher Student Award; George [**Vol. 1: 8635**]

Sachs Award; Albie [**Vol. 2: 5588**]

Sachs Award; Curt [**Vol. 1: 2959**]

Sack Award; Ernest [**Vol. 2: 2318**]

Sackett Senior Investigator Award; Dr. David [**Vol. 1: 6964**]

Sacre; Prix Emile [**Vol. 2: 1598**]

Saddle Sore Award [**Vol. 1: 2949**]

Saddlemyer Award; Ann [**Vol. 1: 6223**]

SAE/AEM Outstanding Young Engineer Award [**Vol. 1: 15533**]

SAE Foundation Young Industry Leadership Award [**Vol. 1: 15534**]

SAE Foundation Young Manufacturing Leadership Award [**Vol. 1: 15534**]

SAE/InterRegs Standards and Regulations Award for Young Engineers [**Vol. 1: 15535**]

Saeed Prize; Wedad [**Vol. 2: 2031**]

Saenger Award for Distinguished Service; Eugene L. [**Vol. 1: 15195**]

Safari Awards [**Vol. 2: 7745**]

Safe Contractor of the Year Awards [**Vol. 1: 12730**]

Safe Drinking Water Studentship Award [**Vol. 1: 5409**]

Safe Driver Award Program [**Vol. 1: 12799**]

Safe Driving Award [**Vol. 1: 16854**]

Safe Mileage Award [**Vol. 1: 17956**]

Safety Achievement Award
    Chamber of Shipping of America [**Vol. 1: 7182**]
    Edison Electric Institute [**Vol 1: 8005**]

Safety and Health Achievement Award [**Vol. 1: 17616**]

Safety and Health Award [**Vol. 1: 4689**]

Safety and Health Outreach Award [**Vol. 1: 17617**]

Safety Award
    Industrial Accident Prevention Association [**Vol. 1: 9219**]
    International Association of Diecutting and Diemaking [**Vol 1: 9661**]
    National Propane Gas Association [**Vol 1: 12720**]
    Pickerington Area Chamber of Commerce [**Vol 1: 14015**]

Safety Award for Superior Accomplishment [**Vol. 1: 16792**]

Safety Awards
    Australian Petroleum Production and Exploration Association [**Vol. 2: 496**]
    Canadian Association of Oilwell Drilling Contractors [**Vol 1: 6290**]
    North Carolina Utility Contractors Association [**Vol 1: 13380**]
    Tree Care Industry Association [**Vol 1: 16551**]

Safety Codes and Standards Medal [**Vol. 1: 4421**]

Safety Contest Awards [**Vol. 1: 3656**]

Safety Director of the Year Award [**Vol. 1: 4616**]

Safety Engineer of the Year [**Vol. 1: 10419**]

Safety, Health, Environment Award [**Vol. 2: 2525**]

Safety in Construction Medal [**Vol. 2: 8008**]

Safety in Seas Award [**Vol. 1: 12623**]

Safety Manager of the Year [**Vol. 1: 10421**]

Safety Recognition Awards [**Vol. 1: 14239**]

SAGA-FUGRO Best Paper Award [**Vol. 2: 5689**]

Sagan Award for Public Understanding of Science [**Vol. 1: 7676**]

Sagar Award; Dr. Vidya [**Vol. 2: 3565**]

Sagarmatha Award [**Vol. 2: 4643**]

Sage Best Transactions Paper Award; Andrew P. [**Vol. 1: 9036**]

Sagebrush Award for a Young Adult Reading or Literature Program [**Vol. 1: 18221**]

Sager Awards; Thomas L. [**Vol. 1: 11207**]

Saget; Prix Julien [**Vol. 2: 2617**]

Saha Medal; Meghnad [**Vol. 2: 3661**]

Saha Memorial Lecture; Prof R. C. [**Vol. 2: 3723**]

Sahametrei; Royal Order of [**Vol. 2: 1809**]

Sahitya Akademi Awards [**Vol. 2: 3746**]

Sahitya Akademi Fellowship [**Vol. 2: 3747**]

Sahitya Akademi Translation Prize [**Vol. 2: 3748**]

SAHM/Mead Johnson Nutritionals New Investigator Award [**Vol. 1: 15016**]

Sahni Birth Centenary Award; Birbal [**Vol. 2: 3724**]

Saidi-Sirjani Memorial Book Prize [**Vol. 1: 10178**]

Sail Gold Medal [**Vol. 2: 3605**]

Sailing Hall of Fame [**Vol. 2: 8180**]

Saillet; Prix Joseph [**Vol. 2: 2295**]

Sainsbury's Baby Book Award [**Vol. 2: 6905**]

St. Catherine of Sienna Distinguished Service Award [**Vol. 1: 1548**]

St. Cuthbert's Mill Award for Works on Paper [**Vol. 2: 8970**]

St. George National Award [**Vol. 1: 1534**]

St. George's Victory Order [**Vol. 2: 2683**]

St. Jerome Award [**Vol. 2: 4482**]

St. John Ambulance Air Wing Travelling Fellowship [**Vol. 1: 7284**]

St. Kilda Film Festival [**Vol. 2: 1036**]

St. Lawrence Section Outstanding Educator Award [**Vol. 1: 3878**]

St. Louis Refractories Award [**Vol. 1: 1573**]

St. Lucia Cross [**Vol. 2: 5897**]

St. Lucia Music Awards [**Vol. 2: 5899**]

Saint Luke's Lecture [**Vol. 2: 3910**]

St. Olav Medal [**Vol. 2: 5136**]

St. Petersburg Yacht Club Trophy [**Vol. 1: 17064**]

St. Romanos the Melodist Medallion [**Vol. 2: 12426**]

Saintour; Prix [**Vol. 2: 2296**]

Saito Award [**Vol. 2: 4326**]

Sakakibara Prize; Yasuo [**Vol. 1: 4575**]

Saks Engineering Award; Andrew [**Vol. 1: 16407**]

Saksena Memorial Medal; Professor Shyam Bahadur [**Vol. 2: 3662**]

Sakura Finetek Student Scholarship [**Vol. 1: 12860**]

Sakurai Prize for Theoretical Particle Physics; J. J. [**Vol. 1: 3222**]

Salam Medal for Science and Technology; Abdus [**Vol. 2: 4162**]

Salam Prize for Leadership in Islamic Thought and the Physical Sciences; Abdus [**Vol. 2: 4014**]

Salazar Award for Communications; Ruben [**Vol. 1: 12190**]

Salcedo Jr. Memorial Lecture; Dr. Juan [**Vol. 2: 5346**]

Saleh Award; Ismail [**Vol. 1: 5912**]

Salem Conference Grant; Dr. Shawky [**Vol. 2: 4744**]

Sales Achievement Awards [**Vol. 1: 6075**]

Sales and Marketing Hall of Fame; Academy of Achievement - [**Vol. 1: 14681**]

Sales Professionals USA Annual Awards [**Vol. 1: 14691**]

Sales Representative Excellence Award [**Vol. 1: 10436**]

Sales Representative of the Year Award [**Vol. 1: 6356**]

Sales to Foreign Tourists Award [**Vol. 2: 3494**]

Salierno Memorial Scholarship; Vincent [**Vol. 1: 3059**]

Salin Prize; Kasper [**Vol. 2: 6157**]

Salinger Award; Ronald [**Vol. 2: 817**]

Salinpriset; Kasper [**Vol. 2: 6157**]

Salivary Research Award [**Vol. 1: 9534**]

Salk Distinguished Service Award; Lee [**Vol. 1: 3602**]

The Sallie Mae 911 Education Fund [**Vol. 1: 14693**]

The Sallie Mae Fund American Dream [**Vol. 1: 14694**]

The Sallie Mae Fund First in My Family [**Vol. 1: 14695**]

The Sallie Mae Fund Unmet Need [**Vol. 1: 14696**]

Sallie Mae MembersFirst Source for Education Scholarship [**Vol. 1: 8707**]

Salmon Award; Dr. Daniel E. [**Vol. 1: 11771**]

Salon Culinaire International de Londres [**Vol. 2: 7034**]

Salon Culinaire Mondial
    American Culinary Federation [**Vol. 1: 1964**]
    Society of German Cooks [**Vol 2: 3181**]

Saloutos Memorial Award; Theodore [**Vol. 1: 218**]

Saloutos Memorial Book Award in Immigration History; Theodore [**Vol. 1: 9172**]

Salter Award; Janet & Maxwell [**Vol. 1: 5826**]

Salters Advanced Chemistry Prize [**Vol. 2: 9143**]

Salters' Graduate Prizes [**Vol. 2: 9144**]

Salters Horners Advanced Physics Prize [**Vol. 2: 9145**]

Salters-Nuffield Advanced Biology Awards [**Vol. 2: 9146**]

Saltire Society and The Royal Bank of Scotland - Scottish Science Award [**Vol. 2: 9156**]

Saltire Society Scottish Literary Awards [**Vol. 2: 9153**]

Saltus Gold Medal; John Sanford [**Vol. 2: 7147**]

Saltus Medal Award; J. Sanford [**Vol. 1: 3015**]

Salute to Excellence Awards
    Center for Nonprofit Advancement [**Vol. 1: 7147**]
    National Association of Black Journalists [**Vol 1: 11657**]
    National Restaurant Association Educational Foundation [**Vol 1: 12774**]

Salvan; Prix Eugene [**Vol. 2: 2297**]

Salvatori Prize; Henry [**Vol. 1: 8923**]

Salzberg Mentorship Award; Arnold M. [**Vol. 1: 703**]

Salzgeber Prize; Manfred [**Vol. 2: 2730**]

Salzman Award for Excellence in International Economic Performance; Herbert [**Vol. 1: 16855**]

SAM/Organon Visiting Professor in Adolescent Research Award [**Vol. 1: 15013**]

Sample Student Excellence Award; W. Frederick [**Vol. 1: 15615**]

Sampson Excellence in Teaching Award; Donald K. [**Vol. 1: 6027**]

Samson Resident Prize; Paul C. [**Vol. 1: 17774**]

Samsonov Prize [**Vol. 2: 5917**]

San Antonio International Piano Competition [**Vol. 1: 14704**]

San Francisco International Film Festival [**Vol. 1: 14708**]

San Sebastian International Film Festival Awards [**Vol. 2: 6094**]

Sanchez Awards; Dr. Priscilla C. [**Vol. 2: 5334**]

Sanchez Memorial Award; George I. [**Vol. 1: 14478**]

Sandak Young Investigator Award; Rebecca L. [**Vol. 1: 15369**]

Sandburg Literary Award; Carl [**Vol. 1: 7225**]

Sandcastle Award [**Vol. 1: 11272**]

Sanderow Outstanding Technical Paper Award; Howard I [**Vol. 1: 11112**]

Sanderson Attack Squadron of the Year Award; Lawson H. M. [**Vol. 1: 10964**]

Sanderson Award; A. B. [**Vol. 1: 6906**]

Sandin Award; Barbro [**Vol. 2: 3292**]
The Sandlot Kid [**Vol. 1: 16176**]
Sandmeyer Prize [**Vol. 2: 6490**]
Sandoz Award; Mari [**Vol. 1: 13141**]
Sandoz Oration Award for Research in Cancer [**Vol. 2: 3555**]
Sandrof Lifetime Achievement Award; Ivan [**Vol. 1: 11992**]
Sands Award; Grahame [**Vol. 2: 574**]
Sanford Award; Nevitt [**Vol. 1: 10345**]
Sanger Award; Margaret [**Vol. 1: 14029**]
Sangster Memorial Award; Allan [**Vol. 1: 6327**]
Sanitarian's Award [**Vol. 1: 9552**]
Sanofi-Aventis Award (Specialty Practice in Cardiology) [**Vol. 1: 6957**]
sanofi-aventis ICAAC Award [**Vol. 1: 3986**]
Sansum Medal; W.E. [**Vol. 2: 803**]
Santarelli Award for Public Policy; Donald E. [**Vol. 1: 12643**]
Sao Paulo International Film Festival [**Vol. 2: 1768**]
Saouma Award; Edouard [**Vol. 2: 3372**]
Sarabhai Medal; Vikram [**Vol. 2: 2341**]
Sarajevo Film Festival [**Vol. 2: 1728**]
Sarason Award for Community Research and Action; Seymour B. [**Vol. 1: 3514**]
Saraswati Extension Scientist/Worker Award; Swamy Sahajanand [**Vol. 2: 3533**]
Sarber Award; Raymond W. [**Vol. 1: 3987**]
Sarbin Award; Theodore [**Vol. 1: 3563**]
Sarchet Award; Bernard R. [**Vol. 1: 3895**]
Sargeant Career Achievement Award; Mike [**Vol. 2: 8032**]
Sargent, Jr. Award; Lowrie B. [**Vol. 1: 5630**]
Sargent Medal [**Vol. 1: 15457**]
Sargent Medal; M. A. [**Vol. 2: 804**]
Sargent Progress Award; Albert M. [**Vol. 1: 15691**]
Sargeson Inorganic Lectureship Award; Alan [**Vol. 2: 983**]
Sarhan's Award [**Vol. 2: 2015**]
Sarma Memorial Award; P.S. [**Vol. 2: 3787**]
Sarnat Award; Bernard G. [**Vol. 1: 9535**]
Sarnoff Award; David [**Vol. 1: 9306**]
Sarnoff Citation [**Vol. 1: 14408**]
Sarnoff Medal Award; David [**Vol. 1: 15704**]
Saroyan International Prize for Writing; William [**Vol. 1: 16262**]
Sarton Medal; George [**Vol. 1: 8958**]
Sasakawa Health Prize [**Vol. 2: 6554**]
SASEV Award [**Vol. 2: 5715**]
Saskatchewan Choral Federation Choral Scholarship [**Vol. 1: 14754**]
Sasol Golden Key Excellence Awards [**Vol. 1: 8708**]
Sasol Post-Graduate Medal [**Vol. 2: 5680**]
Sass Award for Distinguished Service to Journalism and Mass Communication; Gerald M. [**Vol. 1: 5508**]
Sass Medal; Hans and Jacob [**Vol. 1: 11044**]
Satbir Award; Smt. Kamal [**Vol. 2: 3566**]
Satellite Executive of the Year [**Vol. 2: 5440**]
Satomi Prize [**Vol. 2: 4256**]
Satter Award; Ruth [**Vol. 1: 5174**]
Satter Prize in Mathematics; Ruth Lyttle [**Vol. 1: 2839**]
Saturn Awards [**Vol. 1: 111**]
Satyamurthy Award for Young Scientists; N. S. [**Vol. 2: 3688**]
Saulses de Freycinet; Prix Charles-Louis de [**Vol. 2: 2235**]
Saunders Award; Harold E. [**Vol. 1: 4446**]
Saunders Gold Medal; William Lawrence [**Vol. 1: 15225**]
Saunders Natural History Award; W. E. [**Vol. 1: 13590**]
Saunders Sr. Award; Harris [**Vol. 1: 4609**]
Sauveur Achievement Award; Albert [**Vol. 1: 4844**]
Savage Memorial Award; Warren F. [**Vol. 1: 4690**]
Savage Memorial Scientific Award; Dr. Daniel D. [**Vol. 1: 5228**]
Savago New Voice Award; Joe [**Vol. 1: 14366**]
Savarenskii Prize; F.P. [**Vol. 2: 5852**]
Save Our Earth Award [**Vol. 1: 12373**]
Save Our Streams Award [**Vol. 1: 17634**]
Savory Shield Award [**Vol. 1: 2455**]
SAWE Fellow [**Vol. 1: 15415**]
Sawyer Award; Gordon E. [**Vol. 1: 87**]
Sawyer Award; R. Tom [**Vol. 1: 4422**]

Sawyer Award; Robert D. [**Vol. 1: 7471**]
Sax Memorial Hunger Relief Grant; Richard [**Vol. 1: 7784**]
Saxby Award [**Vol. 2: 8908**]
Saxton/George Bauer Memorial Exhibit Award; Burton [**Vol. 1: 3006**]
Sayen Award; Clarence N. [**Vol. 2: 8117**]
SBE Fellow [**Vol. 1: 15569**]
SBET/Replacement Parts Industries BMET of the Year Award [**Vol. 1: 5129**]
SCA Distinguished Service Award [**Vol. 1: 12110**]
SCA Golden Anniversary Fund Awards [**Vol. 1: 12112**]
Scaglione Prize for a Translation of a Literary Work; Aldo and Jeanne [**Vol. 1: 11241**]
Scaglione Prize for a Translation of a Scholarly Study of Literature; Aldo and Jeanne [**Vol. 1: 11242**]
Scaglione Prize for Comparative Literary Studies; Aldo and Jeanne [**Vol. 1: 11243**]
Scaglione Prize for French and Francophone Studies; Aldo and Jeanne [**Vol. 1: 11244**]
Scaglione Prize for Italian Studies; Aldo and Jeanne [**Vol. 1: 11245**]
Scaglione Prize for Studies in Germanic Languages and Literatures; Aldo and Jeanne [**Vol. 1: 11246**]
Scaglione Prize for Studies in Slavic Languages and Literatures; Aldo and Jeanne [**Vol. 1: 11247**]
Scales Memorial Award; Trooper Christopher [**Vol. 1: 5997**]
Scanlan Medal; Robert H. [**Vol. 1: 4230**]
Scattergood System Achievement Award; E. F. [**Vol. 1: 3657**]
SCC Award Medals [**Vol. 1: 14769**]
Scene Design Award [**Vol. 1: 16968**]
Schaar Playwright Award; Ruby Yoshino [**Vol. 1: 10547**]
Schachern Award for Online Religion Section of the Year [**Vol. 1: 14498**]
Schaefer Award; Hugo H. [**Vol. 1: 3139**]
Schaeffer Environmental Award; William D. [**Vol. 1: 14170**]
Schaeffler Award; Willy [**Vol. 1: 17090**]
Schafer Award; George E. [**Vol. 1: 15867**]
Schafer Prize; Alice T. [**Vol. 1: 5172**]
Schaff Prize; Philip [**Vol. 1: 4149**]
Schaffer Young Investigator Award; Rita [**Vol. 1: 5844**]
Schaffner Achievement Award; Franklin J. [**Vol. 1: 7888**]
Schapler Memorial Book Award; Mark [**Vol. 1: 12833**]
Schatz Award; Jack [**Vol. 1: 466**]
Schawlow Prize in Laser Science; Arthur L. [**Vol. 1: 3223**]
Schechter Award; Solomon [**Vol. 1: 17165**]
Scheckter Memorial Scholarship; I. Jerome and Harriet R. [**Vol. 1: 17665**]
Scheel Prize; Karl [**Vol. 2: 3152**]
Scheele Medal; Herbert [**Vol. 2: 6868**]
Scheele Prize; Herbert [**Vol. 2: 6221**]
Scheele Trophy; Herbert [**Vol. 2: 4536**]
Scheepers Prize for Youth Literature [**Vol. 2: 5638**]
Scheit Guitar Competition; International Karl [**Vol. 2: 1326**]
Schell Award; Herbert S. [**Vol. 1: 15989**]
Schell Memorial Intermediate Piano Scholarship; Minnie [**Vol. 1: 14755**]
Schelpe Award [**Vol. 2: 5525**]
Schenck Award; Carl Alwin [**Vol. 1: 15441**]
Schenck Award; Pieter [**Vol. 2: 2807**]
Schenkel Player of the Year; Chris [**Vol. 1: 14187**]
Schenley Award - Most Outstanding Player [**Vol. 1: 6508**]
Schepkens; Prix Joseph [**Vol. 2: 1642**]
Scherago-Rubin Award [**Vol. 1: 3988**]
Schering-Plough Research Institute Award [**Vol. 1: 3761**]
Schering Veterinary Award [**Vol. 1: 7031**]
Schermerhorn Award; Willem [**Vol. 2: 5304**]
Schiebold-Gedenkmunze [**Vol. 2: 3010**]
Schiff Award; Peter [**Vol. 2: 219**]
Schilling Award; David C. [**Vol. 1: 274**]
Schilling Research Award [**Vol. 2: 2969**]
Schindler Award; Rudolf V. [**Vol. 1: 3913**]
Schindler Clinical Excellence Award; Gabriele [**Vol. 1: 15665**]

Schleiden Medal [**Vol. 2: 3125**]
Schlenk Preis; Arfvedson [**Vol. 2: 2935**]
Schlenz Public Education Medal; Harry E. [**Vol. 1: 17718**]
Schlesinger Award for Distinguished Service; Emily K. [**Vol. 1: 9117**]
Schlesinger Outstanding Service Award; Ed [**Vol. 1: 13435**]
Schlich Memorial Award; Sir William [**Vol. 1: 15442**]
Schlossmann Medal; Karl [**Vol. 2: 2045**]
Schlueter Stroke Awards [**Vol. 1: 4581**]
Schlumberger Award; Conrad [**Vol. 2: 4682**]
Schlumberger Medal [**Vol. 2: 8358**]
Schlumberger; Prix Gustave [**Vol. 2: 2170**]
Schlumpf Award; Mildred [**Vol. 1: 2340**]
Schmeidler Award for Outstanding Student; Gertrude [**Vol. 1: 13849**]
Schmeisser Award for Outstanding Defensive Player; William [**Vol. 1: 16981**]
Schmeisser Memorial Trophy; William [**Vol. 1: 16981**]
Schmidt Prize; Bernhard [**Vol. 2: 2046**]
Schmitt Award for Outstanding Corporate Leadership; Fred [**Vol. 1: 12749**]
Schmitt Award; Harrison [**Vol. 1: 1288**]
Schmitt Grants; Bernadotte [**Vol. 1: 2391**]
Schmitz Award for Outstanding Contributions to the Frontiers in Education Conference; Ronald J. [**Vol. 1: 3879**]
Schmocker Memorial Breeders' Award; Hanna [**Vol. 1: 7017**]
Schmorl Preis; Georg [**Vol. 2: 3179**]
Schnabel Jr. Award for Career Excellence in Earth Retaining Structures; Harry [**Vol. 1: 4231**]
Schneider Award; David M. [**Vol. 1: 829**]
Schneider Award; Herbert [**Vol. 1: 15348**]
Schneider Director Award; Alan [**Vol. 1: 16475**]
Schneider Family Book Award [**Vol. 1: 2788**]
Schneider Prize; Hermann [**Vol. 2: 8151**]
Schneider Prize in Linear Algebra; Hans [**Vol. 1: 9993**]
Schnurr Award; Eleanore [**Vol. 1: 16641**]
Schock Prizes; Rolf [**Vol. 2: 6185**]
Schoemaker Award; Harold Jan [**Vol. 2: 6045**]
Schoenberg International Award in Neuroepidemiology; Bruce S. [**Vol. 1: 596**]
Schoenfield Media Award; Al [**Vol. 1: 10414**]
Scholander Award [**Vol. 1: 3267**]
Scholar All-America Awards [**Vol. 1: 12845**]
Scholar/Artist Award [**Vol. 1: 12279**]
Scholar Athlete Award [**Vol. 1: 6420**]
Scholar-Athlete Award [**Vol. 1: 9468**]
Scholar-Athlete Awards [**Vol. 1: 12409**]
Scholar Award [**Vol. 1: 954**]
Scholar Awards [**Vol. 1: 16573**]
Scholar-Patriot Award [**Vol. 1: 499**]
Scholarly Activity Award [**Vol. 1: 15910**]
Scholarly and Academic Book of the Year [**Vol. 1: 5920**]
Scholarly Book Prizes [**Vol. 1: 6468**]
Scholarly Paper Competition [**Vol. 1: 12629**]
Scholar's Scholarship [**Vol. 1: 17666**]
Scholarship Award [**Vol. 1: 3446**]
Scholarship Foundation Award [**Vol. 1: 2119**]
Scholarships of the City of Munich [**Vol. 2: 3139**]
Scholastic Achievement Awards [**Vol. 1: 10787**]
Scholastic Library Publishing Award [**Vol. 1: 2789**]
Scholastic Press Freedom Award [**Vol. 1: 16304**]
Scholl Preis; Geschwister [**Vol. 2: 3140**]
Scholl Showmanship Award; Art [**Vol. 1: 9829**]
Schonfeld Award; William A. [**Vol. 1: 3751**]
Schonstedt Scholarship in Surveying [**Vol. 1: 1873**]
School Administrators Distinguished Library Service Award [**Vol. 1: 1341**]
School Age Financial Aid [**Vol. 1: 13865**]
School Art Program Standards Award [**Vol. 1: 11547**]
School Librarian's Workshop Scholarship [**Vol. 1: 1347**]
School Library Media Specialist Award [**Vol. 1: 10895**]
School Library Technology Innovation Award [**Vol. 2: 815**]
School of Advanced Air and Space Studies Award [**Vol. 1: 288**]
School of Information Management Graduate Award [**Vol. 1: 13450**]

SGA-Newmont Gold Medal [Vol. 2: 1935]

Sgambati Award; Fred [Vol. 1: 6654]

SGL Carbon Award [Vol. 1: 1540]

SGT Fellowship [Vol. 2: 9316]

SGT Travel Grant [Vol. 2: 9317]

Shaara Outstanding Writer Award; Michael [Vol. 1: 16065]

Shackel Award; Brian [Vol. 2: 1273]

Shacklock Trophy [Vol. 2: 6713]

Shadakshara Swamy Endowment Lecture Award; Prof. M. [Vol. 2: 3788]

Shadle Fellowship; Albert R. and Alma [Vol. 1: 4378]

Shaffer Award for Academic Excellence as a Graduate Faculty Member; Robert H. [Vol. 1: 11389]

Shaffer Award; Robert H. [Vol. 1: 5345]

Shaffer Award; Thomas E. [Vol. 1: 709]

Shah Award; Saleem [Vol. 1: 3627]

Shah Memorial Lecture; Professor R. C. [Vol. 2: 3726]

Shaikh Khalifa Bin Salman Al Khalifa Habitat Award [Vol. 2: 4398]

Shakespeare Prize [Vol. 2: 3208]

Shakhmatov Prize; A.A. [Vol. 2: 5854]

Shakow Early Career Award; David [Vol. 1: 3583]

Shaler Company's Rislone Most Improved Championship Driver Award [Vol. 1: 16736]

Shalom Peace Award [Vol. 1: 10577]

Shands, Jr., MD, Award; Alfred R. [Vol. 1: 13718]

Shankar Memorial Lecture; Dr. Jagdish [Vol. 2: 3664]

Shannon Fellowships [Vol. 1: 10449]

Shantz Award; Stan [Vol. 1: 14105]

Shapiro Award; M.B. [Vol. 2: 7195]

Shapiro Prize; Alec [Vol. 2: 8742]

Sharman Award [Vol. 2: 568]

Sharp Award; A.J. [Vol. 1: 5943]

Sharp Memorial Prize; Frank Chapman [Vol. 1: 3181]

Sharpe Award; Norma [Vol. 1: 6214]

Sharpe Prize; Roy [Vol. 2: 7096]

Sharpest Knife in North America Award [Vol. 1: 1208]

Sharples Perpetual Award; Laurence P. [Vol. 1: 308]

Sharr Medal; F. A. [Vol. 2: 443]

Shastri Young Scientist Award; Lal Bahadur [Vol. 2: 3534]

Shatskii Prize; N.S. [Vol. 2: 5855]

Shattner Award; Gertrude [Vol. 1: 11570]

Shattuck Public Service Awards; Henry L. [Vol. 1: 5929]

Shaughnessy Prize; Mina P. [Vol. 1: 11248]

Shaurya Chakra [Vol. 2: 3502]

Shaw Award; Cliff [Vol. 1: 13114]

Shaw Award; Donna Mary [Vol. 1: 6934]

Shaw Bronze Medal; Napier [Vol. 2: 7393]

Shaw Deaf Australian of the Year Award; Dorothy [Vol. 2: 683]

Shaw Golden Age Award; Bob [Vol. 1: 12966]

Shaw International Fellowship; Marjorie [Vol. 2: 6386]

Shaw Memorial Award; Peter [Vol. 1: 11872]

Shaw Memorial Award; Val [Vol. 1: 6858]

Shaw Postdoctoral Prize in Acoustics; Edgar and Millicent [Vol. 1: 6171]

Shaw Prize; Bernard [Vol. 2: 9257]

Shaw-Worth Memorial Scholarship [Vol. 1: 9002]

Shea Award; James H. [Vol. 1: 11775]

Shea Prize; John Gilmary [Vol. 1: 1545]

Sheahan Award; John Drury [Vol. 1: 7683]

Shedd Aquarium Award; John G. [Vol. 1: 15176]

Sheehan Memorial Educational Scholarship; Dezna C. [Vol. 1: 12857]

Sheeline Award for Excellence in Public Relations; Randall D. [Vol. 1: 2634]

Sheep Heritage Foundation Memorial Scholarship [Vol. 1: 3739]

Sheerin, Sr. Service Award; Thomas F. [Vol. 1: 13832]

Shelburne Memorial Award; Tilton E. [Vol. 1: 5633]

Shelkan Award for Mentoring; Gregor [Vol. 1: 7063]

Shell Science Teaching Award [Vol. 1: 12827]

Shelley Award for Outstanding Fictional Work; Mary [Vol. 1: 11040]

Shelley Memorial Award [Vol. 1: 14066]

Shelton Award for Sustained Chapter Excellence; Robert M. [Vol. 1: 8866]

Shelton Search and Discovery Award; John W. [Vol. 1: 1289]

Shemyakin Prize; M.M. [Vol. 2: 5856]

Shenk Award [Vol. 1: 11530]

Shepard Award [Vol. 1: 3320]

Shepard Award; Glenn [Vol. 1: 12985]

Shepard Distinguished Service Award; Earl E. and Wilma S. [Vol. 1: 1508]

Shepard Medal for Excellence in Marine Geology; Francis P. [Vol. 1: 15314]

Shepard Medal for Marine Geology; Francis P. [Vol. 1: 15314]

Shepard Science Award; Charles C. [Vol. 1: 16817]

Shepheard Award; Halert C. [Vol. 1: 7183]

Shepherd Distinguished Composer of the Year Award [Vol. 1: 11325]

Shepherd's Award for Media [Vol. 1: 3740]

Sheppard Award; C. Stewart [Vol. 1: 7172]

Sheps Award; Mindel C. [Vol. 1: 14090]

Sheridan Canadian Research Awards; David S. [Vol. 1: 6206]

Sherif Award; Carolyn Wood [Vol. 1: 3551]

Sherlock Meritorious Service Award; Charles N. [Vol. 1: 4007]

Sherrard Award; J. M. [Vol. 2: 4873]

Sherry Memorial Lecture; Sol [Vol. 1: 10371]

Sherwin International Award; Raymond J. [Vol. 1: 14878]

Sheth Foundation/Journal of Marketing Award [Vol. 1: 2819]

Sheth Prize; Sakarben [Vol. 2: 4423]

Shiebler Award; George L. [Vol. 1: 7977]

Shield of Public Service [Vol. 1: 6845]

Shields-Gillespie Scholarships [Vol. 1: 3089]

Shields Medal [Vol. 1: 15458]

Shields-Trauger Award [Vol. 1: 5771]

Shigo Award for Excellence in Arboricultural Education; Alex L. [Vol. 1: 10276]

Shils Award; Edward B. [Vol. 1: 2006]

Shinbum Kyokai Sho [Vol. 2: 4270]

Shingo Prize for Operational Excellence [Vol. 1: 17500]

Shingo Research and Publication Award [Vol. 1: 17501]

Ship of the Year [Vol. 1: 18058]

Shipley Award; Robert M. [Vol. 1: 2206]

Shipman Gold Medal Award; J. [Vol. 1: 9274]

Shipping Company of the Year [Vol. 2: 8107]

Shiram Award [Vol. 2: 3476]

Shiras Institute/Mildred & Albert Panowski Playwriting Award [Vol. 1: 8438]

Shirley Award; Franklin [Vol. 1: 16049]

Shirley Fellowship in American Children's Literature; Betsy Beinecke [Vol. 1: 18163]

Shmal'gauzen Prize; I.I. [Vol. 2: 5857]

Shmidt Prize; O.Y. [Vol. 2: 5858]

Shneidman Award; Edwin [Vol. 1: 1359]

Shock Compression Science Award [Vol. 1: 3205]

Shock New Investigator Award; Nathan [Vol. 1: 8637]

Shockley Memorial Award; Woodland G. [Vol. 1: 5634]

Shoemaker Award; Norma J. [Vol. 1: 15606]

Shoemaker Award of Merit; Ralph J. [Vol. 1: 16110]

Shoemaker Grant for Critical Care Nursing Research; Norma J. [Vol. 1: 15607]

Shofar Award (Ram's Horn) [Vol. 1: 12576]

Shoman Award for Children's Literature; Abdul Hameed [Vol. 2: 4364]

Shoman Award for Teachers of Science; Abdul Hameed [Vol. 2: 4365]

Shoman Award for Translation; Abdul Hameed [Vol. 2: 4366]

Shoman Award for Young Arab Researchers; Abdul Hameed [Vol. 2: 4367]

Shoman International Award for Jerusalem; Abdul Majeed [Vol. 2: 4368]

Shooting Sports Outstanding Achievement Award [Vol. 1: 5974]

Shopping Center Awards [Vol. 2: 5883]

Shore Award; Eddie [Vol. 1: 2421]

Shore Award of Honor; Dr. Herbert [Vol. 1: 5381]

Shores Award; Louis [Vol. 1: 14474]

Shorland Medal [Vol. 2: 4957]

Short Film Award [Vol. 1: 11365]

Short-Form Award [Vol. 1: 14855]

Short Play Awards Program [Vol. 1: 10661]

Short Prose Competition for Developing Writers [Vol. 1: 18134]

Short Short Story Competition [Vol. 1: 18103]

Short Story and Poetry Contest [Vol. 1: 8541]

Short Story Award [Vol. 1: 13078]

Short Story Contest [Vol. 1: 18128]

Short-Term Fellowship for Visiting Scholars [Vol. 1: 18164]

Short Term Lectureship [Vol. 1: 8613]

Short-term Senior Fellowships in Iranian Studies [Vol. 1: 2671]

Shorten Award; Sarah [Vol. 1: 6312]

Shorts Awards [Vol. 2: 873]

Shotwell Memorial Award; Ambrose M. [Vol. 1: 4992]

Shousha Foundation Prize; Dr. A. T. [Vol. 2: 6555]

Show Awards [Vol. 1: 6368]

Show Hunter Ponies Awards [Vol. 2: 7205]

Show Ponies Awards [Vol. 2: 7206]

ShowCanada Showmanship Awards [Vol. 1: 11283]

Shriver Award for Humanitarian Service; Sargent [Vol. 1: 12670]

Shropshire Outstanding Club Award; Dr. Courtney [Vol. 1: 7311]

Shryock Medal; Richard H. [Vol. 1: 1002]

Shubin-Weil Award for Excellence in Bedside Teaching [Vol. 1: 15608]

Shubitz Award; Simon M. [Vol. 1: 17204]

Shull Award; Charles Albert [Vol. 1: 4493]

Shull Prize in Neutron Science; Clifford G. [Vol. 1: 13150]

Shulman Book Prize; Marshall [Vol. 1: 5101]

Shulman Challenge Award; Neville [Vol. 2: 8798]

Shumway Award; F. Ritter [Vol. 1: 14253]

Shuster Memorial Award; Ben [Vol. 1: 541]

Shy Award; G. Milton [Vol. 1: 597]

Sia Community Pediatrics Medical Home Leadership and Advocacy Award; Calvin C.J. [Vol. 1: 710]

SIA Service Award [Vol. 1: 14832]

SIAD Medal [Vol. 2: 7419]

SIAG/Linear Algebra Prize [Vol. 1: 15125]

SIAG/Optimization Prize [Vol. 1: 15126]

SIAM/ACM Prize in Computational Science and Engineering [Vol. 1: 4962]

SIAM Prize in Numerical Analysis and Scientific Computing [Vol. 1: 15131]

Sibelius Violin Competition; International Jean [Vol. 2: 2126]

Sibert Informational Book Medal; Robert F. [Vol. 1: 5070]

SIBI Prize [Vol. 2: 6071]

Sibley Fellowships; Mary Isabel [Vol. 1: 13967]

Sichel Medal; Herbert [Vol. 2: 5724]

Sicher First Research Essay Award; Harry [Vol. 1: 1264]

SICOT/SIROT Award [Vol. 2: 1558]

Siday Musical Creativity Award; Eric [Vol. 1: 9808]

Siddiqi Prize for Scientists Under 40; Dr. M. Raziuddin [Vol. 2: 5194]

Sidewalk Sale and Exhibition [Vol. 1: 7162]

Sidewise Awards for Alternate History [Vol. 1: 14855]

Sidey Medal and Prize; T. K. [Vol. 2: 5079]

Sidley Memorial Award; Dorothy [Vol. 2: 7802]

Siegel International Transportation Safety Award; Arnold W. [Vol. 1: 15537]

Siegel Memorial Award; Joseph A. [Vol. 1: 15692]

Siegel Service Award; Joseph A. [Vol. 1: 15692]

Siemens Award Lecture [Vol. 2: 6758]

Siemens Healthcare Diagnostics Young Investigator Award [Vol. 1: 3989]

Siemens Medal [Vol. 2: 6759]

Siesel Award for Community Service; E. Hank [Vol. 1: 12456]

Siess Award for Excellence in Structural Research; Chester Paul [Vol. 1: 1850]

Sievers Trophy; Art [Vol. 1: 12785]

Sievert Award; Rolf M. [Vol. 2: 2559]

SIG Excellence Award [Vol. 1: 13558]

SIG Excellence in Advanced Practice Award [Vol. 1: 11820]

SIG Member of the Year Award [Vol. 1: 3949]

SIG of the Year Award [Vol. 1: 3950]

SIG Publication of the Year Award [Vol. 1: 3951]

Sigal Memorial Award; Merck Irving S. [Vol. 1: 3990]

Sigal Young Investigator Award; Irving [Vol. 1: 14285]

Sigma Delta Chi Awards [Vol. 1: 15812]

Sigma Diagnostics Student Scholarship [Vol. 1: 12860]

Sigma Iota Epsilon Scholarships [Vol. 1: 14892]

Sigma Pi Sigma Undergraduate Research Award [Vol. 1: 15780]
SIGMOD Innovations Award [Vol. 1: 16085]
Sigmund's Prize [Vol. 2: 1920]
Signal Service Award [Vol. 1: 2857]
Signe Ekblad-Eldhs pris [Vol. 2: 6213]
Significant Achievement Award
　　National Wildlife Rehabilitators Association [Vol. 1: 13049]
　　Rotary International [Vol 1: 14607]
Significant New Researcher Award [Vol. 1: 119]
SIGNIS Award [Vol. 2: 1662]
Signis Jury Award [Vol. 2: 9534]
Signum Fidei Medal [Vol. 1: 10712]
Signy Foreign Fellowship; Gordon [Vol. 2: 4351]
SIGP Prize for Best Published Paper on Psychopharmacology [Vol. 2: 8743]
Sikes Slide Sequence Award; Sarah [Vol. 1: 2341]
Sikorsky Award for Humanitarian Service; Igor [Vol. 1: 8896]
Sikorsky International Trophy; Igor I. [Vol. 1: 2331]
Silva Service Award [Vol. 1: 17019]
Silver Antelope Award [Vol. 1: 5975]
Silver Anvil Awards [Vol. 1: 14333]
Silver Award
　　American Association of Webmasters [Vol. 1: 1411]
　　Veteran Motor Car Club of America [Vol 1: 17531]
Silver Baton [Vol. 1: 17913]
Silver Bear Awards [Vol. 2: 2732]
Silver Beaver Award [Vol. 1: 5976]
Silver Bowl Award [Vol. 1: 10190]
Silver Buffalo Award [Vol. 1: 5977]
Silver Certificate Award [Vol. 1: 17869]
Silver Chris [Vol. 1: 7427]
Silver Combustion Medal [Vol. 1: 7431]
Silver Core Award [Vol. 2: 1274]
Silver Crown Awards [Vol. 1: 7410]
Silver Dirac Medal [Vol. 2: 1171]
Silver Eagle [Vol. 2: 9572]
Silver Edelweiss [Vol. 2: 6108]
Silver Elephant Award [Vol. 2: 3459]
Silver Gavel Awards for Media and the Arts [Vol. 1: 1467]
Silver-gilt Medal for Bibliography [Vol. 2: 6877]
Silver Good Citizenship Medal [Vol. 1: 12913]
Silver Hard Hat Award [Vol. 1: 7569]
Silver Harp [Vol. 2: 4660]
Silver Hawk Award [Vol. 1: 10965]
Silver Helmet Awards [Vol. 1: 4728]
Silver Jewelry Award [Vol. 1: 3495]
Silver Jubilee Award [Vol. 2: 459]
Silver Jubilee Commemoration Medal [Vol. 2: 3665]
Silver Jubilee Medal [Vol. 2: 1736]
Silver King Award [Vol. 1: 8310]
Silver Lifesaving Medal [Vol. 1: 16688]
Silver Medal
　　American Advertising Federation [Vol. 1: 781]
　　American Rhododendron Society [Vol 1: 3699]
　　Brazilian Metallurgy and Materials Association [Vol 2: 1757]
　　European Meteorological Society [Vol 2: 2839]
　　Federation Aeronautique Internationale [Vol 2: 6328]
　　French National Center for Scientific Research [Vol 2: 2449]
　　The Gardeners of America [Vol 1: 8522]
　　Institute of Actuaries - United Kingdom [Vol 2: 7823]
　　Institution of Gas Engineers and Managers [Vol 2: 8045]
　　International Society of Chemical Ecology [Vol 1: 10296]
　　National Association of Licensed Paralegals [Vol 2: 8387]
　　National Vegetable Society [Vol 2: 8417]
　　Royal Academy of Engineering [Vol 2: 8585]
　　Royal Academy of Medicine in Ireland [Vol 2: 3911]
　　Royal Humane Society [Vol 2: 8840]
　　Society of Economic Geologists [Vol 1: 15621]
　　Tau Sigma Delta [Vol 1: 16384]
　　Zoological Society of London [Vol 2: 9514]
Silver Medal and Associate Fellowship of the Society [Vol. 2: 487]

Silver Medal Award
　　Advertising Women of New York [Vol. 1: 176]
　　Audio Engineering Society [Vol 1: 5693]
　　Fertilizer Society of South Africa [Vol 2: 5548]
Silver Medal Award of Excellence [Vol. 1: 12942]
Silver Medal of Honor [Vol. 1: 4667]
Silver Medal of Special Merit [Vol. 2: 2712]
Silver Medallion [Vol. 1: 5993]
Silver Medallion Award [Vol. 1: 10536]
Silver Medals [Vol. 1: 9888]
Silver Member [Vol. 1: 9483]
Silver Memorial Award; Henry K. [Vol. 1: 11824]
Silver Otter Award [Vol. 2: 7078]
Silver Page Award [Vol. 1: 4298]
Silver Palette Award [Vol. 1: 15612]
Silver Pin Awards [Vol. 1: 467]
Silver Plaque [Vol. 1: 10116]
Silver Plaque Award [Vol. 1: 12782]
Silver Quill Editorial Achievement Award [Vol. 1: 4691]
Silver Ring [Vol. 1: 6595]
Silver Rope Award for Leadership [Vol. 1: 424]
Silver Rose Bowl [Vol. 2: 4847]
Silver Screen Award [Vol. 1: 16985]
The Silver Service Award [Vol. 1: 2870]
Silver Shovel Award [Vol. 1: 10036]
Silver Slugger Awards [Vol. 1: 16190]
Silver Star: Navy [Vol. 1: 16689]
Silver Star of Excellence [Vol. 1: 7524]
Silver Star of Excellence Award [Vol. 1: 4586]
Silver T-Square [Vol. 1: 12035]
Silver TASTA Award [Vol. 2: 9521]
Silver Torch Award [Vol. 1: 11698]
Silver Viola Clef [Vol. 2: 4927]
Silver World Award [Vol. 1: 5978]
Silvered Turnbuckle Award [Vol. 2: 8603]
Silverstein-Simeone Award Lecture [Vol. 1: 10297]
Silvert Award; Kalman [Vol. 1: 10751]
SIM Fellowship [Vol. 1: 15145]
Simic-Grau Award [Vol. 2: 4064]
Simkin Award; Penny [Vol. 1: 7904]
Simkins Award; Francis B. [Vol. 1: 16026]
Simko Award for Excellence at a Clinical Poster Session; Margaret Dullea [Vol. 1: 2043]
Simmons Award; Edwin H. [Vol. 1: 15200]
Simmons Award; Roy and Iris [Vol. 2: 1148]
Simon/Anderson Publishing Outstanding Paper Award; William L. [Vol. 1: 67]
Simon Award [Vol. 2: 7215]
Simon Award; Eugene [Vol. 2: 3093]
Simon Award; Marcel [Vol. 1: 9727]
Simon Award; Norma P. [Vol. 1: 5517]
Simon Medal; Andre [Vol. 2: 8257]
Simon Memorial Prize [Vol. 2: 7923]
Simons Memorial Award; Bernard [Vol. 2: 8094]
Simons Prize; Harden [Vol. 1: 3882]
Simpson Automotive Transmission and Driveline Innovation Award; SAE/Timken-Howard [Vol. 1: 15538]
Simpson Award; Elizabeth [Vol. 2: 7675]
Simpson Medal; A. S. Romer - G. G. [Vol. 1: 15878]
Simpson Technical Editors Award; Maurice [Vol. 1: 9327]
Sims Encouragement Fund Award for Work in the Comedic Arts; Tim [Vol. 1: 13572]
Simulation and Ground Testing Award [Vol. 1: 2523]
Sina Prize; Ibn [Vol. 2: 1365]
Sinave Prix; Robert [Vol. 2: 1665]
Sinclair Award; David [Vol. 1: 864]
Sinclaire Award; Matilda W. [Vol. 1: 2183]
Sinclaire Language Award [Vol. 1: 2183]
Singapore Corporate Governance Award [Vol. 2: 5969]
Singapore Environmental and Social Reporting Awards [Vol. 2: 5934]
Singapore Literature Prize [Vol. 2: 5954]
Singapore Sports Awards [Vol. 2: 5983]
Singarimbun Research Awards; Masri [Vol. 2: 3818]
Singer Award; Colonel Merton [Vol. 1: 14518]
Singer Award for Management Excellence; Eugene [Vol. 1: 16354]
Singer Friedlander/Sunday Times Watercolour Competition [Vol. 2: 8457]
Singer of the Year Competition [Vol. 1: 14851]
Singh Award for Excellence in Journalism in Agricultural Research and Development;

Chaudhary Charan [Vol. 2: 3535]
Singh Memorial Award; Harbans [Vol. 2: 3776]
Singh Memorial Award; Major General Harkirat [Vol. 2: 3467]
Single Action Awards [Vol. 1: 13121]
Sinha Memorial Award; Professor Umakant [Vol. 2: 3727]
Sinking Creek Film Celebration [Vol. 1: 11382]
Sinor Medal; Denis [Vol. 2: 8652]
SIOP Awards [Vol. 2: 6449]
Sir Francis Boys Cup [Vol. 2: 5060]
Sisco Excellence in Teaching Award; John I. [Vol. 1: 16050]
Sise Outstanding Alpine Masters Award; Al [Vol. 1: 17091]
Sisserou Award of Honour [Vol. 2: 2003]
Sister Cities Expressions of Peace Youth Art Contest [Vol. 1: 14911]
Sister Irene Award [Vol. 1: 12652]
Sister Mary Arthur "Sharing the Light" Award [Vol. 1: 6285]
Sisyphus Award [Vol. 1: 12153]
Site Management Awards [Vol. 2: 7371]
Site of the Month [Vol. 2: 4640]
Site of the Year [Vol. 2: 4640]
Site of the Year Award [Vol. 1: 1412]
Sitharman Memorial Essay Competition; Dr. R. [Vol. 2: 3809]
Siukola Memorial; Matti M. [Vol. 1: 9050]
Sixteenth Century Journal Literature Prize [Vol. 1: 14921]
Sixteenth Century Society and Conference Medal [Vol. 1: 14922]
Sixth Man Award [Vol. 1: 11979]
Skalny Scholarship for Polish Studies [Vol. 1: 1893]
Skater of the Year [Vol. 1: 16145]
Skellerup Award [Vol. 2: 4917]
SKF Award [Vol. 2: 9579]
Ski Magazine Cup Award [Vol. 1: 17092]
Skier of the Year [Vol. 2: 6428]
Skiing Magazine Development Cup [Vol. 1: 17093]
Skills and Productivity Award [Vol. 2: 4191]
SkillsUSA Championships [Vol. 1: 14925]
Skinner Award; Bradley [Vol. 1: 13787]
Skinner Award; Clarence R. [Vol. 1: 16623]
Skinner Award; Constance Lindsay [Vol. 1: 17987]
Skinner Award; Ivan [Vol. 2: 5006]
Skinner Award; Morris F. [Vol. 1: 15880]
Skinner Memorial Fund Award; John E. [Vol. 1: 2152]
Skinner New Researcher Award; B. F. [Vol. 1: 3396]
Skinner Sermon Award [Vol. 1: 16623]
Skinner Special Recognition Award; Kayla [Vol. 1: 14813]
Sklodowska-Curie Award; Marie
　　American Association for Women Radiologists [Vol. 1: 1013]
　　International Organization for Medical Physics [Vol 2: 8158]
Sklodowska-Curie Medal; Maria [Vol. 2: 5397]
Skolnik Award; Herman [Vol. 1: 1671]
Skryabin Prize; K.I. [Vol. 2: 5859]
Skrzypek Award; Alexander J. [Vol. 1: 9147]
Skuja Prize; Heinrichs [Vol. 2: 4440]
Slack Award in Plant Biology; Roger [Vol. 2: 5017]
Slagle Lectureship; Eleanor Clarke [Vol. 1: 3038]
Slate - MacDaniels Award [Vol. 1: 13312]
Slater Award; Patricia [Vol. 2: 990]
Slater Trophy; Fred [Vol. 2: 7113]
Slaughter Association Award; Humane [Vol. 2: 7800]
Slaymaker Award; Olav [Vol. 1: 6521]
Sled of the Year [Vol. 1: 12994]
Sleep Science Award [Vol. 1: 598]
Sleeter Bull Award [Vol. 1: 9130]
Sless Award; Ephraim G. [Vol. 1: 417]
Sless Award; Simon I. [Vol. 1: 418]
Slichter Award; William P. [Vol. 1: 16793]
Sliffe Awards for Distinguished Junior High and High School Mathematics Teaching; Edyth May [Vol. 1: 11020]
Slipper Gold Medal; Stanley [Vol. 1: 6981]
Sloan-C Awards for Excellence in Online Teaching and Learning [Vol. 1: 14929]
Sloan Memorial Award; Norman J. [Vol. 2: 5206]
Slocum Award [Vol. 1: 14935]
Slot Manager Award [Vol. 2: 8132]
Slote Award; Bernice [Vol. 1: 14125]

Slovenian Business Excellence Prize [Vol. 2: 6012]
Smail Memorial Award; Mary Winston
WAMSO, Minnesota Orchestra Volunteer Association [Vol. 1: 17638]
WAMSO, Minnesota Orchestra Volunteer Association [Vol. 1: 17640]
Smales Award; Paul [Vol. 1: 7615]
Small and Disadvantaged Business Award [Vol. 1: 302]
Small and Medium Enterprise Innovation Research Award [Vol. 2: 6599]
Small Animal Practitioner Award [Vol. 1: 7033]
Small Award for Specifications Writing; Ben John [Vol. 1: 7563]
Small Business Advocates of the Year [Vol. 1: 17108]
Small Business Award [Vol. 2: 4199]
Small Business Exporter of the Year [Vol. 1: 17109]
Small Business Innovation Research Program SBIR [Vol. 1: 16898]
Small Business Person of the Year [Vol. 1: 14940]
Small Craft Group Medal [Vol. 2: 8867]
Small Ecological Project Grants [Vol. 2: 7050]
Small Grants Program [Vol. 2: 3836]
Small Hotel of the Year [Vol. 2: 1679]
Small Museums Collection Care Grant [Vol. 1: 7625]
Small Press Publisher of the Year Award [Vol. 1: 6357]
Small Project and Travel Awards [Vol. 2: 9423]
Small Project Grants for Canadian Researchers [Vol. 1: 17352]
Small Research Project Grants [Vol. 2: 6946]
Small Vendor of the Year [Vol. 2: 1679]
SMART [Vol. 2: 9412]
Smart Competition; Harold [Vol. 2: 8911]
SME Award [Vol. 2: 4605]
SME Education Foundation Family Scholarship [Vol. 1: 14958]
SME Progress Award [Vol. 1: 15691]
SME Research Medal [Vol. 1: 15693]
SME Supplier Organisation of the Year [Vol. 2: 7022]
Smedley Memorial Award; Glenn [Vol. 1: 3007]
SMFA Brass Award [Vol. 1: 14753]
The SMFA Senior Speech Arts Scholarship [Vol. 1: 14728]
The SMFA Senior Woodwind Scholarship [Vol. 1: 14724]
SMFM/AAOGF Scholarship [Vol. 1: 15185]
SMI-UNESCO (ROSTE) [Vol. 2: 4167]
Smiley Prize; Donald [Vol. 1: 6802]
Smirnov Prize; S.S. [Vol. 2: 5860]
Smith American Democracy Award; Margaret Chase [Vol. 1: 11892]
Smith/ASA Young Investigator Awards [Vol. 2: 560]
Smith Award; Adam [Vol. 1: 5478]
Smith Award; Arthur [Vol. 2: 2549]
Smith Award; Cadzow [Vol. 2: 7557]
Smith Award; Daniel B. [Vol. 1: 3156]
Smith Award for Distinguished Pathology Educator; H. P. [Vol. 1: 3797]
Smith Award for Excellence in Nonprofit Leadership; Edward A. [Vol. 1: 17298]
Smith Award for Freestyle Wrestler of the Year; John [Vol. 1: 17490]
Smith Award for Submarine Support Achievement; Levering [Vol. 1: 13127]
Smith Award; Georgina M. [Vol. 1: 1391]
Smith Award; Homer H. [Vol. 1: 4451]
Smith Award; Horton [Vol. 1: 14222]
Smith Award; Howard DeWitt [Vol. 1: 5635]
Smith Award; I. W. [Vol. 1: 6917]
Smith Award; Job Lewis [Vol. 1: 711]
Smith Award; Lilian Ida [Vol. 2: 5015]
Smith Award; Merriam [Vol. 1: 17806]
Smith Award; Nila Banton [Vol. 1: 10107]
Smith Award; Reginald Heber [Vol. 1: 12587]
Smith Award; Robert M. [Vol. 1: 712]
Smith Award; Roger C. [Vol. 1: 5518]
Smith Award; Sir Grafton Elliot [Vol. 2: 480]
Smith Award; Wilbur S. [Vol. 1: 4233]
Smith Awards for Science Promotion; Michael [Vol. 1: 13103]
Smith Book Awards; Lillian [Vol. 1: 16037]
Smith Breeden Prizes [Vol. 1: 2142]
Smith Distinguished Transportation Educator Award; Wilbur S. [Vol. 1: 9421]
Smith Fellowships; Al [Vol. 1: 10676]

Smith Hydraulic Fellowship; J. Waldo [Vol. 1: 4234]
Smith Individual Artist Fellowship; Al [Vol. 1: 10676]
Smith International Trumpet Solo Competition; Ellsworth [Vol. 1: 10470]
Smith Jr. Outstanding Young Lawyer of the Year Award; William Reece [Vol. 2: 8095]
Smith Jr. Student Paper Award; W. David [Vol. 1: 2636]
Smith Medal; Blakely [Vol. 1: 15717]
Smith Medal; Gilbert Morgan [Vol. 1: 11442]
Smith Medal; H. G. [Vol. 2: 984]
Smith Medal; J. Lawrence [Vol. 1: 11443]
Smith Medal; Julian C. [Vol. 1: 8121]
Smith Medal; Waldo E. [Vol. 1: 2247]
Smith Medal; William [Vol. 2: 7729]
Smith Memorial Award; Dale A. [Vol. 1: 1068]
Smith Memorial Award; H. G. [Vol. 2: 984]
Smith Memorial Medal; S. G. [Vol. 1: 9383]
Smith Memorial Mentoring Award; Jamie [Vol. 1: 15580]
Smith National Award; Sidney O. [Vol. 1: 9184]
Smith Playwriting Award; Jean Kennedy [Vol. 1: 10668]
Smith Practice Excellence Award; Daniel B. [Vol. 1: 3156]
Smith Prize; Rufus Z. [Vol. 1: 4931]
Smith Research Award; Bob [Vol. 2: 8501]
Smith Sr. Award; Bruce [Vol. 1: 68]
Smith Singer of the Year Competition; Mary Jacob [Vol. 1: 14851]
Smith Student Paper Award; K.U. [Vol. 2: 6589]
Smith-White Travel Prize; Spencer [Vol. 2: 732]
Smith/William Donlon Memorial Exhibit Award; Sidney W. [Vol. 1: 3008]
Smithers-Oasis Competition; FleurEx - [Vol. 2: 7061]
Smithers-Oasis Trophy [Vol. 2: 7061]
Smiths Educational Award [Vol. 1: 6246]
Smithsonian Craft Show [Vol. 1: 14966]
SMME Awards [Vol. 2: 5490]
Smoked Whole Turkey Award [Vol. 1: 9131]
Smoluchowski Award [Vol. 2: 2700]
Smoluchowski Medal; Marian [Vol. 2: 5409]
Smoluchowski-Warburg Prize [Vol. 2: 5410]
Smoot Organizational Meritorious Award; Willie [Vol. 1: 11990]
SMS-DEMAG Excellence Award [Vol. 2: 3607]
Smuts Award; Isie [Vol. 2: 5671]
Smyth Nuclear Statesman Award; Henry DeWolf [Vol. 1: 13460]
Smyth-Ravenel Prize for Excellence in Publication Design; Frances [Vol. 1: 1220]
Smyth Visiting Fellowship; Craig Hugh [Vol. 2: 4171]
Smythe Trophy; D. Verner [Vol. 1: 17065]
Smythies Award; Jill [Vol. 2: 8317]
Snack Sticks Award [Vol. 1: 9132]
Snedecor Award; George W. [Vol. 1: 7442]
Sniadecki Medal; Jedrzej [Vol. 2: 5398]
Snively Memorial Award; Dr. George G. [Vol. 1: 16205]
Snodgrass Award; Bill [Vol. 1: 13788]
Snodgrass Memorial Research Award [Vol. 1: 8141]
Snow Award for Early Contributions; Richard E. [Vol. 1: 3413]
Snow Award; Leigh Anne [Vol. 2: 685]
Snow Award; Roland B. [Vol. 1: 1576]
Snow Foundation Prize; John Ben [Vol. 1: 13301]
Snowcem Award [Vol. 2: 3585]
Snyder Award; Walter F. [Vol. 1: 13453]
Snyder Distinguished Service to College Award; Richard J. [Vol. 1: 5760]
Snyder Memorial Landscape Award; Rachel [Vol. 1: 10633]
Snypp Award; Wilbur [Vol. 1: 12085]
Soaring Eagle Award [Vol. 1: 9870]
Soaring Hall of Fame [Vol. 1: 14976]
Sobek Outstanding Contribution Award; Joe [Vol. 1: 17042]
Sobels Award; Frits [Vol. 2: 2365]
Sober Lectureship; Herbert A. [Vol. 1: 3760]
Sobhi Prize; Mohamed [Vol. 2: 2032]
Soccer Coach of the Year [Vol. 1: 6655]
Social Action Leadership Award [Vol. 1: 16628]
Social Contribution Project Award [Vol. 2: 7023]
Social Gerontology Award [Vol. 1: 8638]
Social Issues Dissertation Award [Vol. 1: 15366]
Social Justice Award [Vol. 1: 3594]

Social Research, Policy and Practice Student Research Award [Vol. 1: 8639]
Social Science Prize of the American Academy [Vol. 1: 497]
Social Service Award [Vol. 2: 3803]
Social Studies Programs of Excellence [Vol. 1: 12176]
Social Worker of the Year [Vol. 1: 11896]
Socially Responsible Retailer Award [Vol. 1: 13093]
Society Award
International Thomas Merton Society [Vol. 1: 10450]
Society for Biotechnology, Japan [Vol 2: 4327]
Society Award [Vol. 2: 9297]
Society Citation [Vol. 1: 9230]
Society Fellow [Vol. 1: 4019]
Society Fellows [Vol. 1: 1577]
Society Fellowship Award [Vol. 2: 4291]
Society for Analytical Chemistry Silver Medal [Vol. 2: 9045]
Society for Research into Higher Education Awards [Vol. 2: 9206]
Society Medal
British Cartographic Society [Vol. 2: 6992]
International Spinal Cord Society [Vol 2: 8230]
Society Medal [Vol. 2: 750]
Society of Children's Book Writers and Illustrators Grants [Vol. 1: 15588]
Society of Consulting Psychology Service Award [Vol. 1: 15594]
Society of Early Americanists Essay Competition [Vol. 1: 3830]
Society of Petroleum Engineers of AIME Distinguished Service Award [Vol. 1: 15753]
Society of West End Theatre [Vol. 2: 9324]
Society Research Awards [Vol. 1: 6207]
Society's Medal [Vol. 2: 1010]
Sodersten Award for Interior Architecture; Emil [Vol. 2: 387]
Soderstromska medaljen i guld [Vol. 2: 6186]
SOFHT Awards [Vol. 2: 9311]
SOFHT Fellowship [Vol. 2: 9312]
Soft Matter and Biophysical Chemistry Award [Vol. 2: 9046]
Software Process Achievement Award [Vol. 1: 7076]
Software System Award [Vol. 1: 4963]
Soil Science Applied Research Award [Vol. 1: 15929]
Soil Science Distinguished Service Award [Vol. 1: 15930]
Soil Science Education Award [Vol. 1: 15931]
Soil Science Industry and Professional Leadership Award [Vol. 1: 15932]
Soil Science Professional Service Award [Vol. 1: 15932]
Soil Science Research Award [Vol. 1: 15933]
Sokhey Award; Maj. Gen. Saheb Singh [Vol. 2: 3569]
Solandt Award; Omond [Vol. 1: 6764]
Solar Energy Policy Award; Advancing [Vol. 2: 3099]
Solar Observer Awards [Vol. 1: 1405]
Solberg Award [Vol. 1: 4447]
Solberg Award; Myron [Vol. 1: 9343]
Solicitor of the Year Award [Vol. 2: 8294]
Solid-State Circuits Award [Vol. 1: 9300]
Solidarity of Educational Credit Order [Vol. 2: 1851]
Sollenberger Trophy; John B. [Vol. 1: 2422]
Sollmann Award in Pharmacology; Torald [Vol. 1: 4037]
Solo Cup [Vol. 1: 16206]
Solo Divisional of the Year Award [Vol. 1: 16207]
Solo Driver of Eminence Award [Vol. 1: 16208]
Solo Driver of the Year [Vol. 1: 16209]
Solo Rookie of the Year [Vol. 1: 16210]
Solomon Prize [Vol. 2: 3953]
Soloviev Medal; Sergey [Vol. 2: 2379]
Solow Award; Beni [Vol. 2: 7627]
Solvents Stewardship Awards [Vol. 2: 1457]
Sommer Award; Ralph F. [Vol. 1: 1144]
Sommerfeld Prize; Arnold [Vol. 2: 2713]
Sommerville Prize; Helen [Vol. 2: 7848]
Somogyi-Sendroy Award [Vol. 1: 923]
Somorjai Award for Creative Research in Catalysis; Gabor A. [Vol. 1: 1672]
Sonangol Literature Prize - Grand Prize [Vol. 2: 15]
Sonangol Literature Prize - Revelation Prize [Vol. 2: 16]

Sonatina, Sonata, Early and Advanced Bach Programs [Vol. 1: 1775]

Sondrio International Documentary Film Festival on Parks [Vol. 2: 4153]

Song Award; John S. [Vol. 1: 15112]

Song Foundation Award for Plant Tissue Culture; John S. [Vol. 1: 15112]

Song of the Year
    Australasian Performing Rights Association [Vol. 2: 142]
    International Bluegrass Music Association [Vol 1: 9732]

Songwriter of the Year [Vol. 2: 1392]

Songwriters Hall of Fame [Vol. 1: 11412]

Sonnenwirth Memorial Award [Vol. 1: 3971]

Sonning Music Prize; Leonie [Vol. 2: 1993]

Sonning Prize [Vol. 2: 1995]

Sonnings Musikpris; Leonie [Vol. 2: 1993]

Sonntag Award; Al [Vol. 1: 15864]

Sons of Martha Medal [Vol. 1: 14209]

Sons of Norway Jumping Award [Vol. 1: 17094]

Soo Award; Kun-Po [Vol. 1: 3364]

Soper Award for Excellence in Health Literature; Fred L. [Vol. 1: 13818]

Sorantin Award for Young Artists; Hemphill-Wells [Vol. 1: 14700]

Sorantin Young Artist Competition [Vol. 1: 14700]

Sorby Medal [Vol. 2: 4731]

Sorum Assembly Member-in-Training Award; William [Vol. 1: 3365]

Sosman Award; Dr. J. Leland [Vol. 1: 17095]

Sosman Memorial Award and Lecture; Robert B. [Vol. 1: 1578]

Sosnovsky Award in Cancer Therapy; George and Christine [Vol. 2: 9047]

Sossenheimer Software Innovation Award [Vol. 2: 2550]

Sotirchos Memorial Lectureship; Stratis V. [Vol. 2: 3287]

Souder Award; Wilmer [Vol. 1: 9537]

South Africa Medal [Vol. 2: 5737]

South African High Commission Award [Vol. 2: 4464]

South African Initiatives Office Research Grant [Vol. 1: 17285]

South Asia Foreign Language and Area Studies Fellowships [Vol. 1: 17362]

South Australian Library Achiever of the Year Award [Vol. 2: 444]

South East Asia Property Awards [Vol. 2: 6603]

South West Division Innovation Prize [Vol. 2: 8744]

South West Division Poster Prize [Vol. 2: 8745]

South West Division Trainees Prize [Vol. 2: 8746]

Southcomb Award; Kenneth W. [Vol. 1: 10966]

Southeast Review Poetry Contest [Vol. 1: 15991]

Southern Cross Award [Vol. 2: 124]

Southern Entertainment Awards [Vol. 1: 8818]

Southgate Memorial Trophy; Hugh M. [Vol. 1: 17117]

Southwest Asia Service Medal [Vol. 1: 16690]

Southwick Memorial Award; Justin A. [Vol. 1: 10483]

Souvenir Awards [Vol. 1: 16063]

Souza Award; Felipa de [Vol. 1: 9956]

Sovereign Awards [Vol. 1: 10582]

Sowards Award; Dale [Vol. 1: 11736]

Spaatz Award; General Carl "Tooey" [Vol. 1: 289]

Spaatz Trophy [Vol. 1: 12487]

Space Achievement Award [Vol. 1: 17112]

Space Flight Award [Vol. 1: 1441]

Space Flight Medal [Vol. 1: 11485]

Space Operations and Support Award [Vol. 1: 2546]

Space Pioneer Award [Vol. 2: 901]

Space Pioneer Awards [Vol. 1: 12923]

Space Processing Award [Vol. 1: 2547]

Space Science Award [Vol. 1: 2548]

Space Systems Award [Vol. 1: 2549]

Space Technology Hall of Fame [Vol. 1: 17113]

Spacecraft Design Award [Vol. 1: 2549]

SPAIG Award [Vol. 1: 4563]

Spalding Player of the Year [Vol. 1: 11640]

Spangler Award; Kenneth C. [Vol. 1: 2917]

Spangler - Purchasing Professional Award; Lewis E. [Vol. 2: 1285]

Spanos Best Graduate Student Paper Award; Nicholas P. [Vol. 1: 3613]

Spark Design and Architecture Awards [Vol. 1: 16072]

Sparks Medal; Ben C. [Vol. 1: 4423]

Sparks-Thomas Award [Vol. 1: 1673]

Sparks Tutoring Award; G'Anne [Vol. 1: 5894]

Spaulding Award; William B. [Vol. 1: 4893]

Speaker Hall of Fame; Council of Peers Award for Excellence/ [Vol. 1: 12927]

Spearman Medal [Vol. 2: 7196]

Speas Airport Award; Jay Hollingsworth [Vol. 1: 2550]

Special Achievement Award
    Academy of Motion Picture Arts and Sciences [Vol. 1: 88]
    DHL Worldwide Express, Bangladesh National Office [Vol 2: 1372]
    Health Science Communications Association [Vol 1: 8856]
    National Association of Personal Financial Advisors [Vol 1: 11831]
    National Council of Social Security Management Associations [Vol 1: 12198]
    Register of Professional Archaeologists [Vol 1: 14482]
    Securities and Insurance Licensing Association [Vol 1: 14829]
    Standards Council of Canada [Vol 1: 16245]

Special Achievements for the ACHMM [Vol. 1: 382]

Special Ad Hoc Awards [Vol. 1: 10899]

Special Award
    American Association of Petroleum Geologists [Vol. 1: 1288]
    American Association on Intellectual and Developmental Disabilities [Vol. 1: 1428]
    American Society for Information Science and Technology [Vol 1: 3952]
    International Animated Film Association [Vol 2: 1871]
    National Association for Interpretation [Vol 1: 11589]
    National Legal Aid and Defender Association [Vol 1: 12586]
    Psychological Society of Ireland [Vol 2: 3904]
    Recreation Vehicle Industry Association [Vol 1: 14451]

Special Award for Dedicated Service [Vol. 1: 11399]

Special Award for Public Health Promotion through Pharmacoepidemiology [Vol. 1: 10215]

Special Award of Honor [Vol. 1: 10028]

Special Award of Recognition [Vol. 1: 2657]

Special Awards
    Association of Environmental and Engineering Geologists [Vol. 1: 5330]
    New England Theatre Conference [Vol 1: 13161]

Special Awards Established by the President [Vol. 1: 8209]

Special Banking Awards [Vol. 2: 5929]

Special Breed Master Judge [Vol. 1: 12675]

Special Certificate of Appreciation [Vol. 1: 4626]

Special Citation Award [Vol. 1: 2705]

Special Citations
    American Academy of Periodontology [Vol. 1: 726]
    National Press Photographers Association [Vol 1: 12708]

Special Commendation
    Children's Book Council of Iran [Vol. 2: 3826]
    National University of Singapore [Vol 2: 5958]

Special Commendation and Award [Vol. 1: 10981]

Special Distinguished & Outstanding Service Awards [Vol. 1: 3918]

Special Education Research Award [Vol. 1: 7643]

Special Educational Merit Award for Women [Vol. 1: 10446]

Special Event Station Awards [Vol. 2: 9465]

Special Focus Awards [Vol. 1: 6042]

Special Grand Prix of the Jury [Vol. 1: 11258]

Special Grant in Chemical Sciences [Vol. 1: 6117]

Special Honors [Vol. 1: 11658]

Special Honour Award [Vol. 2: 3813]

Special Jury Prize [Vol. 2: 4614]

Special Membership Award [Vol. 1: 11832]

Special Merit Award
    American Association of Public Health Dentistry [Vol. 1: 1329]
    Canadian Association of Emergency Physicians [Vol. 1: 6250]

Special Merit Citation [Vol. 1: 2741]

Special Olympics Award [Vol. 1: 4727]

Special President's Award of Merit [Vol. 1: 1356]

Special Prize [Vol. 2: 5411]

Special Prize of the Jury [Vol. 2: 5425]

Special Prizes [Vol. 1: 12514]

Special Project Award [Vol. 1: 9478]

Special Project Grants [Vol. 1: 14158]

Special Recognition [Vol. 1: 16135]

Special Recognition Award
    Alberta Construction Safety Association [Vol. 1: 332]
    American Academy of Ophthalmology [Vol 1: 613]
    American Association of Community Theatre [Vol 1: 1114]
    American Board of Orthodontics [Vol 1: 1509]
    American Camp Association [Vol 1: 1528]
    American Institute of Certified Public Accountants [Vol 1: 2602]
    American Meat Science Association [Vol 1: 2858]
    Asian American Journalists Association [Vol 1: 4826]
    Association for Research in Vision and Ophthalmology [Vol 1: 5086]
    Canadian Athletic Therapists Association [Vol 1: 6321]
    Canadian Psychiatric Association [Vol 1: 6819]
    International Listening Association [Vol 1: 9999]
    International Technology and Engineering Educators Association [Vol 1: 10437]
    Manufacturers' Agents for the Foodservice Industry [Vol 1: 10934]
    Regulatory Affairs Professionals Society [Vol 1: 14486]
    States Organization for Boating Access [Vol 1: 16282]
    University of the Philippines Alumni Association [Vol 2: 5379]

Special Recognition Awards
    American Association of School Personnel Administrators [Vol. 1: 1349]
    Asphalt Recycling and Reclaiming Association [Vol 1: 4858]
    Society for Information Display [Vol 1: 15153]
    United States Auto Club [Vol 1: 16741]

Special Recognition Plaques [Vol. 1: 5864]

Special Recognition Service Award [Vol. 1: 17856]

Special Service/Achievement Awards [Vol. 1: 14879]

Special Service Award
    American Rental Association [Vol. 1: 3690]
    Canadian Mental Health Association - Alberta Division [Vol 1: 6699]
    Canadian Mental Health Association - Central Alberta Region [Vol 1: 6704]

Special Service Award
    American Association of Avian Pathologists [Vol. 1: 1049]
    Association for Educational Communications and Technology [Vol 1: 5011]
    CFA Institute [Vol 1: 7173]
    College Gymnastics Association [Vol 1: 7365]
    Indiana Library Federation [Vol 1: 9213]
    Institute of Nuclear Materials Management [Vol 1: 9397]

Special Service Citation [Vol. 1: 2551]

Special Service Medal [Vol. 2: 2569]

Special Service Recognition Award [Vol. 1: 17885]

Special Services Award [Vol. 1: 14409]

Special Student Awards [Vol. 1: 1429]

Special VIAAA Award [Vol. 1: 17582]

Specialists in Blood Banking Scholarship Awards [Vol. 1: 1056]

Specialized Topic Award [Vol. 1: 9651]

Specialties in Pharmacy Practice Award [Vol. 1: 6958]

Specialty Books Excellence in Research Award [Vol. 1: 934]

Specialty Bookseller of the Year Award [Vol. 1: 6358]

Spector Memorial Award for Excellence in Senior Housing Service; Sid [Vol. 1: 12242]

Spectrum Awards Design Competition [Vol. 1: 2209]

Speed and Figure Skating National Championships [Vol. 1: 16700]

Speedo/USMS Coach of the Year Award [Vol. 1: 16998]

Speedy Award [Vol. 1: 13842]

Starz Denver International Film Festival **[Vol. 1: 7846]**

Starz People's Choice Award **[Vol. 1: 7848]**

Stassart; Prix **[Vol. 2: 2298]**

Stassart; Prix Baron de **[Vol. 2: 1616]**

Stassart; Prix de **[Vol. 2: 1617]**

State Achievement Awards **[Vol. 1: 11905]**

State Association Leadership Award **[Vol. 1: 12125]**

State Awards **[Vol. 1: 13176]**

State Awards and National Awards **[Vol. 1: 11720]**

State Awards for Excellence **[Vol. 2: 940]**

State Awards for Top-Level Sporting Achievements **[Vol. 2: 1884]**

State Boating Access Program Excellence Award **[Vol. 1: 16283]**

State/Canadian Province Award **[Vol. 1: 11600]**

State Chairperson of the Year **[Vol. 1: 17491]**

State Clean Vessel Act Program Excellence Award **[Vol. 1: 16284]**

State Council/Chapter Government Affairs Award **[Vol. 1: 8104]**

State Department Science Fellowship Program **[Vol. 1: 2694]**

State Director of the Year Award **[Vol. 1: 12721]**

State Executive of the Year **[Vol. 1: 11868]**

State History Awards **[Vol. 1: 8942]**

State Legislation Award **[Vol. 1: 12126]**

State of Kuwait Prize for Research in Health Promotion **[Vol. 2: 6556]**

State of the Art Award **[Vol. 1: 14133]**

State-of-the-Art of Civil Engineering Award **[Vol. 1: 4236]**

State/Province Art Educator Award **[Vol. 1: 11548]**

State/Province Art Educator of the Year **[Vol. 1: 11548]**

State/Province Association/Issues Group Newsletter Award **[Vol. 1: 11549]**

State/Province Programs or Associations Award **[Vol. 1: 10306]**

States Student Award; John D. **[Vol. 1: 5116]**

Statesman Award **[Vol. 1: 16727]**

Statesman/Stateswoman Award **[Vol. 1: 13094]**

Statistician of the Year **[Vol. 2: 6821]**

Statistics in Chemistry Award **[Vol. 1: 4564]**

Statton Lecture; Henry M **[Vol. 1: 4337]**

Statue of Freedom Medal **[Vol. 1: 17118]**

Staubs Precollege Outreach Award; Harry **[Vol. 1: 2553]**

Staudinger Preis; Hermann **[Vol. 2: 2936]**

Stauffer Award; Leonard **[Vol. 1: 14487]**

Stauffer Meritorious Service Award; Isabel E. **[Vol. 1: 6959]**

Stauffer Prizes; Joseph S. **[Vol. 1: 6142]**

Staunton Prize; Sir George **[Vol. 2: 8653]**

Steacie Memorial Fellowships; E. W. R. **[Vol. 1: 13105]**

Steacie Prize **[Vol. 1: 16295]**

Stead Award of Achievement **[Vol. 1: 743]**

Steavenson Memorial Award **[Vol. 2: 6978]**

Stebbins Medal **[Vol. 1: 1257]**

Steck - Vaughn Award **[Vol. 1: 16451]**

Steel Awards **[Vol. 2: 592]**

Steel Distinguished Service Award; John B. **[Vol. 1: 6533]**

Steel Eighties Award **[Vol. 2: 3608]**

Steele-Bodger Memorial Travel Scholarship; Harry **[Vol. 2: 7298]**

Steele Memorial Senior Romantic Music Scholarship; Maude **[Vol. 1: 14759]**

Steele Prize for Lifetime Achievement; Leroy P. **[Vol. 1: 2840]**

Steele Prize for Mathematical Exposition; Leroy P. **[Vol. 1: 2841]**

Steele Prize for Seminal Contributions to Research; Leroy P. **[Vol. 1: 2842]**

Stefanik Cross; M.R. **[Vol. 2: 6006]**

Stefanko Best Paper Award **[Vol. 1: 15226]**

Steffens Prize; Henrik **[Vol. 2: 3209]**

Stegman Award for Distinguished Service; Samuel J. **[Vol. 1: 3820]**

Stegner Award; Wallace **[Vol. 1: 17220]**

Steiger Memorial Award; William
American Conference of Governmental Industrial Hygienists **[Vol. 1: 1859]**
American Industrial Hygiene Association **[Vol 1: 2493]**

Steijn Medal; Elizabeth C. **[Vol. 2: 5642]**

Stein International Award; Sidney J. **[Vol. 1: 10014]**

Steinberg Award; S. S. **[Vol. 1: 3710]**

Steinbock Award; Max **[Vol. 1: 197]**

Steindler, MD, Award; Arthur **[Vol. 1: 13719]**

Steiner Award; Ben **[Vol. 2: 6845]**

Steiner Award for Leadership in Foreign Language Education, K-12; Florence **[Vol. 1: 1927]**

Steiner Award for Leadership in Foreign Language Education, Postsecondary; Florence **[Vol. 1: 1928]**

Steiner Award; Irma Tschudi **[Vol. 2: 6530]**

Steiner Prize; Herbert **[Vol. 2: 1263]**

Steinmetz Award; Charles Proteus **[Vol. 1: 9307]**

Stellar Gospel Music Awards **[Vol. 1: 7159]**

Stenback Plaquette **[Vol. 2: 2099]**

Stengel Memorial Award; Alfred **[Vol. 1: 1805]**

Stengel Research Award **[Vol. 2: 2486]**

Stennis Student Congress Awards; John C. **[Vol. 1: 12417]**

Steno Medal **[Vol. 2: 1969]**

STEP Platinum **[Vol. 1: 4883]**

Stepanek Champion Award; Mattie **[Vol. 1: 7243]**

Stephansson Award for Poetry; Stephan G. **[Vol. 1: 18109]**

Stephens Industry Award; Vivian **[Vol. 1: 14589]**

Stephens Lecture **[Vol. 2: 7819]**

Stephenson Award **[Vol. 2: 7558]**

Stepinsnki Fund Award **[Vol. 2: 6018]**

Steptoe Memorial Lecture; Patrick **[Vol. 2: 7055]**

Stern Award **[Vol. 2: 8428]**

Stern Award; Louis W. **[Vol. 1: 2820]**

Stern Humanitarian Award; Rabbi Malcolm H. **[Vol. 1: 8324]**

Stevens Article of the Year Award; Edward B. **[Vol. 1: 1773]**

Stevens Award; J. C. **[Vol. 1: 4237]**

Stevens Award; K. G. **[Vol. 2: 9580]**

Stevens Award; Wallace **[Vol. 1: 57]**

Stevens Groundwater Educator Award; Edith **[Vol. 1: 8791]**

Stevens Memorial Award; Barbara **[Vol. 1: 12375]**

Stevenson Award; RBK **[Vol. 2: 9235]**

Stevenson - Hamilton Award **[Vol. 2: 5773]**

Stevenson Trophy **[Vol. 1: 9379]**

Stewardson Keefe LeBrun Travel Grants **[Vol. 1: 2588]**

Stewart Award; Chet **[Vol. 1: 17428]**

Stewart Award; James E. **[Vol. 1: 1054]**

Stewart Award; Larry **[Vol. 1: 3462]**

Stewart Awards; Paul A. **[Vol. 1: 17862]**

Stewart Cup; Ross **[Vol. 1: 17160]**

Stewart Engineering-Humanities Award; Robert E. **[Vol. 1: 4095]**

Stewart Excellence in Occupational Health Case Management Award; Ada Mayo **[Vol. 1: 1504]**

Steyn Prize for Natural Science and Technical Achievement; M. T. **[Vol. 2: 5643]**

Stiefel Clinical Practice Award **[Vol. 2: 329]**

Stier Award; Elizabeth Fleming **[Vol. 1: 9344]**

Stiftelsen Kortfilmfestivalen **[Vol. 2: 5156]**

Stiftelsen Natur och Kulturs oversattarpris **[Vol. 2: 6214]**

Stiles Memorial Award for Outstanding Defensive Player; William C. **[Vol. 1: 16982]**

Stillwell Award; F.L. **[Vol. 2: 738]**

Stimulation of Research Award **[Vol. 1: 3147]**

Stinchcomb Memorial Lecture and Award; Wayne W. **[Vol. 1: 5636]**

Stine Award in Materials Engineering and Science; Charles M. A. **[Vol. 1: 2635]**

Stingray Tourism Awards **[Vol. 1: 1817]**

Stirling Medal; John B. **[Vol. 1: 8122]**

Stirling Memorial Award; Nadin **[Vol. 1: 6700]**

Stirling Prize for Best Published Work in Psychological Anthropology **[Vol. 1: 15284]**

STLE National Award **[Vol. 1: 15862]**

Stock Gedachtnispreis; Alfred **[Vol. 2: 2937]**

Stockberger Achievement Award; Warner W. **[Vol. 1: 10077]**

Stockholm Junior Water Prize **[Vol. 2: 605]**

Stockholm Water Prize **[Vol. 2: 6190]**

Stockman Award **[Vol. 2: 5162]**

Stoddart Award for Outstanding Performance; Richard R. **[Vol. 1: 9083]**

Stoker Awards; Bram **[Vol. 1: 8978]**

Stokes Award; Kate **[Vol. 2: 7479]**

Stokes Award; Sir George **[Vol. 2: 9049]**

Stokes Medal; R.H. **[Vol. 2: 985]**

Stokes Memorial Award **[Vol. 1: 12524]**

Stokes Memorial Award for Innovation in Administrative Dietetics; Judy Ford **[Vol. 1: 2044]**

Stokinger Award; Herbert E. **[Vol. 1: 2494]**

Stokstad Award; E.L.R. **[Vol. 1: 4020]**

Stoletov Prize; A.G. **[Vol. 2: 5862]**

Stolper Award; Gustav **[Vol. 2: 3226]**

Stommel Research Award; Henry **[Vol. 1: 2918]**

Stompin' Tom Award **[Vol. 1: 7963]**

Stone Award; Donald C. **[Vol. 1: 4050]**

Stone Award for Excellence in Education; Donald C. **[Vol. 1: 3662]**

Stone Award for Poetry; Jean **[Vol. 2: 717]**

Stone Award; Peter **[Vol. 2: 6804]**

Stone Cup; Andy **[Vol. 1: 17161]**

Stone Distinguished Service Award; Judge J. C. (Jake) **[Vol. 1: 10794]**

Stone Graduate Fellowship in Cave and Karst Studies; Ralph W. **[Vol. 1: 12929]**

Stone Memorial Award; Walter **[Vol. 2: 718]**

Stone Pioneer Award; Cliffie **[Vol. 1: 61]**

Stoneman Award; Bertha **[Vol. 2: 5672]**

Stoneridge Freestyle Award **[Vol. 1: 7018]**

Stookey Lecture of Discovery **[Vol. 1: 1580]**

Stop TB Partnership/Kochon Prize **[Vol. 2: 2576]**

Stoppard Prize; Tom **[Vol. 2: 1908]**

Stopper of the Year **[Vol. 1: 12086]**

Stora priset **[Vol. 2: 6203]**

Storch Award in Fuel Chemistry; Henry H. **[Vol. 1: 1674]**

Storer Award **[Vol. 1: 4345]**

Stork Fellow; Charles Wharton **[Vol. 1: 5665]**

Stouffer Award **[Vol. 1: 4541]**

Stoughton Award for Young Teachers; Bradley **[Vol. 1: 4845]**

Stoughton Award for Young Teachers of Metallurgy; Bradley **[Vol. 1: 4845]**

Stover Memorial Award; Elizabeth Matchett **[Vol. 1: 16053]**

Stowe Award; Allen B. **[Vol. 1: 17138]**

Stowe Sportsmanship Award; Dr. Allen B. **[Vol. 1: 17138]**

Stowell-Orbison Awards **[Vol. 1: 16707]**

Stoye Awards **[Vol. 1: 4346]**

STP Most Improved Championship Driver Award **[Vol. 1: 16736]**

Straatsma Award for Excellence in Resident Education **[Vol. 1: 614]**

Strader Memorial Award; Noel Ross **[Vol. 1: 7372]**

Stradins Prize; Pauls **[Vol. 2: 4441]**

Strandness, MD, Scientific Award for Excellence in Research; D.E. **[Vol. 1: 15408]**

Strange Award; Susan **[Vol. 1: 10392]**

Strange Memorial Prize; Audrey **[Vol. 2: 8563]**

Stranks Awards; Don **[Vol. 2: 986]**

Strategic HR Leadership Award **[Vol. 1: 15103]**

Strategic Leadership and Governance Awards **[Vol. 1: 9766]**

Stratton Award; Samuel Wesley **[Vol. 1: 16794]**

Stratton Medal; Henry M. **[Vol. 1: 4337]**

Straus Award; Flora Stieglitz **[Vol. 1: 7235]**

Straus Award; Ralph I. **[Vol. 1: 12616]**

Strausbaugh Club Relations Award; Bill **[Vol. 1: 14223]**

Strauss Prize; Lotte **[Vol. 1: 15247]**

Strega Prize **[Vol. 2: 4155]**

Streifer Scientific Achievement Award; William **[Vol. 1: 9110]**

Strem Chemicals Award for Pure or Applied Inorganic Chemistry **[Vol. 1: 6896]**

Stresemann-Foerderung; Erwin- **[Vol. 2: 2983]**

Strickler Innovation in Instruction Award; Les B. **[Vol. 1: 3703]**

Striker Junior Paper Award; Gyorgy **[Vol. 2: 3405]**

Strimple Award; Harrell L. **[Vol. 1: 13806]**

String Teacher of the Year Award **[Vol. 1: 4569]**

Strive and Succeed Award **[Vol. 1: 352]**

Striving for Excellence Award **[Vol. 1: 12091]**

Strock Award; Lester W. **[Vol. 1: 15043]**

Stroobant; Prix Paul et Marie **[Vol. 2: 1643]**

Stroud Bursary; Dorothy **[Vol. 2: 9241]**

Stroud Memorial Award; Clara and Ida Wells **[Vol. 1: 4668]**

Stroukoff Memorial Trophy; Larissa **[Vol. 1: 14978]**

Strousse Award [**Vol. 1: 14127**]
Structural Awards [**Vol. 2: 8060**]
Structural Engineering Award [**Vol. 1: 1845**]
Structural Materials Division Distinguished Materials Scientist/Engineer Award [**Vol. 1: 11196**]
Structural Materials Division Distinguished Service Award [**Vol. 1: 11197**]
Structures, Structural Dynamics, and Materials Award [**Vol. 1: 2554**]
Stuart Education Award; Mary [**Vol. 1: 13728**]
Stuart Memorial Award; Paul [**Vol. 2: 5002**]
Stuart Prize; Ackroyd [**Vol. 2: 8622**]
Stubbs Medal; Oliver [**Vol. 2: 7833**]
Stuckenbruck Person of the Year Award; Linn [**Vol. 1: 14260**]
Stuckey Award; Bill [**Vol. 1: 2079**]
Stud Dog [**Vol. 1: 14667**]
Stud Dog of the Year [**Vol. 1: 16236**]
Studded Gold Jewelry Award [**Vol. 2: 3496**]
Studded Precious Metal Jewelry Award [**Vol. 2: 3497**]
Student Achievement Grants [**Vol. 1: 13135**]
Student Achievement/Research Award [**Vol. 1: 7461**]
Student Activity Award [**Vol. 1: 8151**]
Student Aid Award [**Vol. 1: 17513**]
Student and New Investigator Travel Awards [**Vol. 1: 8164**]
Student and Nurse Essay Prizes [**Vol. 2: 9211**]
Student and Postdoctoral Travel Award [**Vol. 1: 1036**]
Student Art Awards [**Vol. 2: 3924**]
Student Assistance Scheme [**Vol. 2: 7135**]
Student Association for Fire Ecology Graduate and Undergraduate Student Excellence Awards [**Vol. 1: 5019**]
Student-Athlete of the Week [**Vol. 1: 12067**]
Student Award
    American Association on Intellectual and Developmental Disabilities [**Vol. 1: 1430**]
    American Institute of Architects, New York Chapter [**Vol. 1: 2589**]
    American Society of Heating, Refrigerating and Air-Conditioning Engineers [**Vol 1: 4330**]
    Australian Library and Information Association [**Vol 1: 445**]
    Canadian Dam Association [**Vol 1: 6444**]
    Canadian Hydrographic Association [**Vol 1: 6558**]
    Canadian Society of Microbiologists [**Vol 1: 6977**]
    European Association of Archaeologists [**Vol 2: 1923**]
    European Society of Biomechanics [**Vol 2: 4078**]
    Federation of Analytical Chemistry and Spectroscopy Societies [**Vol 1: 8282**]
    German Society for Fat Science [**Vol 2: 3003**]
    Hong Kong Digital Entertainment Association [**Vol 2: 5258**]
    International Apparel Federation [**Vol 2: 4718**]
    International Association of Logopedics and Phoniatrics [**Vol 2: 4727**]
    National Federation of State Poetry Societies [**Vol 1: 12376**]
    New Zealand Geotechnical Society [**Vol 2: 4970**]
    Psychotherapists and Counsellors Association of Western Australia [**Vol 2: 937**]
    Royal Entomological Society [**Vol 2: 8776**]
Student Award for Achievement in Periodontology [**Vol. 1: 727**]
Student Award for Excellence [**Vol. 1: 9362**]
Student Award for Excellence in Forest Sciences [**Vol. 2: 1314**]
Student Award for International Understanding [**Vol. 2: 7608**]
Student Award for Scholarly Writing [**Vol. 1: 15050**]
Student Award for Technical Excellence [**Vol. 2: 7362**]
Student Award in Systematic Paleontology [**Vol. 1: 13802**]
Student Award of Excellence [**Vol. 1: 6846**]
Student Award - Postgraduate Division [**Vol. 2: 7860**]
Student Award - Undergraduate Division [**Vol. 2: 7866**]
Student Awards
    American Institute of Chemical Engineers [**Vol. 1: 2636**]
    Institution of Mechanical Engineers [**Vol 2: 8049**]

International Astronautical Federation [**Vol 2: 2502**]
    Latvian Academy of Sciences [**Vol 2: 4442**]
    Remote Sensing and Photogrammetry Society [**Vol 2: 8541**]
    Society for Chemical Engineering and Biotechnology [**Vol 2: 3172**]
    Speech Pathology Australia [**Vol 2: 1054**]
Student Awards for Outstanding Research [**Vol. 1: 15047**]
Student Awards for Precious Metals Research [**Vol. 1: 10060**]
Student Best Essay Award [**Vol. 2: 7798**]
Student Best Paper Award [**Vol. 1: 9101**]
Student Book Prize [**Vol. 1: 7759**]
Student Bursaries [**Vol. 2: 5753**]
Student Bursary [**Vol. 2: 9417**]
Student Business Initiative Award [**Vol. 1: 5761**]
Student Business of the Year Award [**Vol. 1: 5761**]
Student Challenge [**Vol. 2: 7372**]
Student Challenge Cook and Serve Competition [**Vol. 2: 7035**]
Student Chapter Advisor of the Year [**Vol. 1: 17857**]
Student Chapter Award [**Vol. 1: 9422**]
Student Chapter Awards [**Vol. 1: 1761**]
Student Chapter of the Year Award
    American Society for Information Science and Technology [**Vol. 1: 3953**]
    International Facility Management Association [**Vol 1: 9901**]
Student Chapter Sponsor Award of Excellence [**Vol. 1: 11550**]
Student Community Outreach Award [**Vol. 1: 565**]
Student Competition for Overseas Music Study Award [**Vol. 2: 5474**]
Student Composition Competition [**Vol. 1: 11326**]
Student Design Competition
    Association of Independent Corrugated Converters [**Vol. 1: 5372**]
    Environmental Design Research Association [**Vol 1: 8158**]
    International Federation of Landscape Architects [**Vol 2: 1536**]
    Retail Design Institute [**Vol 1: 14534**]
    Southeastern Theatre Conference [**Vol 1: 16008**]
Student Design Contest [**Vol 1: 2014**]
Student Design Project Competition [**Vol. 1: 4330**]
Student Development Award [**Vol. 2: 3189**]
Student Dissertation Award [**Vol. 1: 3506**]
Student/Dissertation Research Award [**Vol. 1: 3443**]
Student Diversity Paper Award [**Vol. 1: 3452**]
Student Educational Award [**Vol. 1: 3745**]
Student Employee of the Year [**Vol. 1: 12949**]
Student Essay Prize [**Vol. 1: 5809**]
Student Gold Medal Awards [**Vol. 1: 6919**]
Student Grants [**Vol. 1: 13484**]
Student International Research Awards [**Vol. 1: 3439**]
Student Journalism Award [**Vol. 2: 1048**]
Student Journalist of the Year [**Vol. 2: 8354**]
Student Leader Award (Regional and International)- [**Vol. 1: 8709**]
Student Leader of the Year Award [**Vol. 1: 158**]
Student Leadership Award [**Vol. 1: 4943**]
Student Leadership Awards [**Vol. 1: 3161**]
Student Leadership in Internationalization Award [**Vol. 1: 6375**]
Student Liaison Award [**Vol. 1: 7564**]
Student Lighting Design Awards [**Vol. 2: 8311**]
Student Literary Award [**Vol. 1: 12280**]
Student Medal [**Vol. 1: 14615**]
Student Medals [**Vol. 2: 7422**]
Student/Medical Technologist Abstract Award for Outstanding Research in Molecular Pathology or Pharmacogenomics [**Vol. 1: 924**]
Student Meritorious Paper Award [**Vol. 1: 9858**]
Student/New Investigators' Award [**Vol. 1: 10225**]
Student of the Year Award
    American Psychological Association - Society for the Psychological Study of Men and Masculinity (Division 51) [**Vol. 1: 3545**]
    Association for Women in Aviation Maintenance [**Vol 1: 5155**]
    Botswana Institute of Bankers [**Vol 2: 1731**]
Student Outstanding Research Award [**Vol. 1: 10864**]
Student Paper Award
    American Psychological Association - Society

for Theoretical and Philosophical Psychology (Division 24) [**Vol. 1: 3564**]
    American Society for Bioethics and Humanities [**Vol 1: 3765**]
Student Paper Awards
    Center for Lesbian and Gay Studies [**Vol. 1: 7142**]
    Society of Naval Architects and Marine Engineers [**Vol 1: 15718**]
Student Paper of the Year Award [**Vol. 1: 14261**]
Student Paper Prize
    Association of Latina and Latino Anthropologists [**Vol. 1: 5393**]
    Society for Industrial and Applied Mathematics [**Vol 1: 15127**]
Student Participation Award [**Vol. 1: 14151**]
Student Photographer of the Year [**Vol. 2: 419**]
Student/Postdoctoral Awards for Completed Research [**Vol. 1: 3376**]
Student/Postdoctoral Education Research Award [**Vol. 1: 1037**]
Student Poster Award [**Vol. 1: 15023**]
Student Poster Competition [**Vol. 1: 15906**]
Student Poster Session Awards [**Vol. 1: 8063**]
Student Presentation Award
    Canadian Acoustical Association [**Vol. 1: 6172**]
    Canadian Cardiovascular Society [**Vol. 1: 6396**]
Student Presentation Prizes [**Vol. 2: 503**]
Student Prize
    Association for Literary and Linguistic Computing [**Vol. 2: 6775**]
    Institute of Ergonomics and Human Factors [**Vol 2: 7868**]
    Library and Information Research Group [**Vol 2: 8309**]
    South African Society for Enology and Viticulture [**Vol 2: 5716**]
    Zoological Society of Southern Africa [**Vol 2: 5774**]
Student Prizes [**Vol. 2: 7704**]
Student Professional Paper Award [**Vol. 1: 5331**]
Student Project Awards [**Vol. 1: 3292**]
Student Publication Award [**Vol. 1: 3455**]
Student Research Award
    Association for Academic Surgery [**Vol. 1: 4902**]
    Sport Management Association of Australia and New Zealand [**Vol 2: 1059**]
Student Research Award
    American Psychological Association - Division of Family Psychology [**Vol. 1: 3429**]
    American Psychological Association - Division of Rehabilitation Psychology (Division 22) [**Vol 1: 3463**]
    Gerontological Society of America [**Vol 1: 8639**]
    International Society for Aerosols in Medicine [**Vol 2: 3080**]
    National Academic Advising Association [**Vol 1: 11400**]
Student Research Award Competition [**Vol. 1: 3603**]
Student Research Award for Clinical Child Psychology [**Vol. 1: 3584**]
Student Research Awards
    American Association for Clinical Chemistry [**Vol. 1: 904**]
    American Psychological Association - Adult Development and Aging Division (Division 20)- [**Vol 1: 3377**]
Student Research Fellowship Award [**Vol. 1: 2204**]
Student Research Fellowships [**Vol. 1: 8449**]
Student Research Prize [**Vol. 2: 2047**]
Student Research Scholarship [**Vol. 1: 17523**]
Student Researcher Award [**Vol. 2: 6786**]
Student/Resident Award [**Vol. 1: 1226**]
Student Retreat Scholarship [**Vol. 1: 15574**]
Student Scholars Award [**Vol. 1: 6534**]
Student Scholarships
    National Society for Histotechnology [**Vol. 1: 12860**]
    Society of Wetland Scientists [**Vol 1: 15890**]
Student Science Award [**Vol. 2: 1442**]
Student Section Advisor Award [**Vol. 1: 4425**]
Student Service Award [**Vol. 1: 11571**]
Student Services Award [**Vol. 1: 935**]
Student Spouse Award [**Vol. 1: 393**]
Student Sustainability Leadership Awards [**Vol. 1: 5136**]

Training and Education Award [Vol. 1: 5441]
Training Award
  Nursery and Garden Industry Australia [Vol. 2: 917]
  United Kingdom Warehousing Association [Vol 2: 9420]
Training System Award [Vol. 1: 9652]
Trampoline and Tumbling National Leadership Award [Vol. 1: 473]
Trans-Canada (McKee) Trophy [Vol. 1: 6197]
Transforming the Science Cohort Award [Vol. 2: 5576]
Translation Prize [Vol. 1: 13902]
Translational Research Award [Vol. 2: 6951]
Translators Association Unger Award [Vol. 1: 4606]
Transport and Energy Processes Division Award [Vol. 1: 2639]
Transportation Achievement Award [Vol. 1: 9423]
Transportation Administrator of the Year [Vol. 1: 11592]
Transportation Fleet Safety/Safety Improvement Awards [Vol. 1: 16125]
Transportation Research Board Distinguished Service Award [Vol. 1: 16534]
Transportation Safety Awards [Vol. 1: 16126]
Transpower Neighborhood Engineers Award [Vol. 2: 4920]
Trask Prize and Awards; Betty [Vol. 2: 9259]
Tratman Award; E.K. [Vol. 2: 6999]
Trauma Leadership Award [Vol. 1: 15856]
Trautman Award; George M. [Vol. 1: 16510]
Travel Agent of the Year Award [Vol. 1: 4519]
Travel Award
  Estuarine and Coastal Sciences Association [Vol. 2: 7574]
  Minerals Engineering Society [Vol 2: 8362]
  New Zealand Freshwater Sciences Society [Vol 2: 4965]
  North American Membrane Society [Vol 1: 13317]
Travel Awards
  Association for Research in Otolaryngology, Inc. [Vol. 1: 5080]
  Society of Physics Students [Vol 1: 15781]
  University of Alberta - Perinatal Research Centre [Vol 1: 17191]
Travel Fellowship Award [Vol. 1: 15563]
Travel Fellowships
  European Association for Cancer Research [Vol. 2: 7580]
  Kansas State University - Johnson Center for Basic Cancer Research [Vol 1: 10636]
Travel Grant
  Conference of Minority Public Administrators [Vol. 1: 7505]
  International Society of Oncology Pharmacy Practitioners [Vol 1: 10340]
  South African Orthopaedic Association [Vol 2: 5708]
Travel Grants
  Albanian Political Science Association [Vol. 2: 5]
  American Association for Cancer Research [Vol 1: 882]
  Association of Paediatric Anaesthetists of Great Britain and Ireland [Vol 2: 6837]
  Chemical Heritage Foundation [Vol 1: 7201]
  UNESCO - Intergovernmental Oceanographic Commission [Vol 2: 2640]
Travel Grants for Educators [Vol. 1: 10109]
Travel Grants/Scholarships [Vol. 2: 7652]
Travel Hall of Fame [Vol. 1: 4520]
Travel Industry Awards for Excellence [Vol. 1: 17146]
Travel Industry Hall of Leaders [Vol. 1: 17145]
Travel Journalist of the Year Award [Vol. 1: 4521]
Travel Photo of the Year Competition [Vol. 2: 9437]
Travel Research Grants [Vol. 1: 7626]
Travel Sponsorships for Young Scientists [Vol. 2: 3702]
Travel Writer of the Year Award [Vol. 2: 7076]
Traveling Fellowship [Vol. 1: 1520]
Traveling Fellowships to the European Society of Cardiology [Vol. 2: 638]
Travelling Jam Pot: Fund for Graduate Students [Vol. 1: 3831]
Travelling Scholarships [Vol. 2: 9260]
Travers; Prix Maurice [Vol. 2: 2303]

Tree of Learning Award [Vol. 2: 6540]
Tree of Life Award
  Canadian Institute of Forestry [Vol. 1: 6596]
  Jewish National Fund [Vol 1: 10578]
  Leukemia and Lymphoma Society [Vol 1: 10814]
Tregre Award; Louis S. [Vol. 1: 12158]
Treibs Award; Alfred [Vol. 1: 8557]
Trejo Librarian of the Year Award [Vol. 1: 14479]
TREK Diagnostic Professional Recognition Award [Vol. 1: 3991]
Trend Award [Vol. 2: 2833]
Trendsetter Award [Vol. 1: 8406]
Trenholm Memorial Award; H. Councill [Vol. 1: 12300]
Trent-Crede Medal [Vol. 1: 128]
Trent Division Research Presentation Prize [Vol. 2: 8750]
Tresley Research Award; Ira [Vol. 1: 542]
Trevethan Award; P. J. [Vol. 1: 8730]
Trevithick Prize [Vol. 2: 8010]
Trial Lawyer of the Year Award [Vol. 1: 14316]
Triandis Doctoral Thesis Award; Harry and Pola [Vol. 2: 5285]
Triangle Award [Vol. 1: 11285]
Triathlon Awards [Vol. 2: 3327]
Tribute to Women in Industry Award [Vol. 1: 18204]
Tribute to Women in International Industry [Vol. 1: 18204]
TRIC Awards [Vol. 2: 9368]
Tricerri; Premio Franco [Vol. 2: 4137]
Tricolor Medal [Vol. 1: 2343]
Trieschman Award; Albert E. [Vol. 1: 1083]
Trillium Book Award [Vol. 1: 13577]
Trillium Book Award for Poetry [Vol. 1: 13577]
Trimble Memorial Award; Robert E. [Vol. 1: 8897]
Trimmer Excellence in Teaching Award; John [Vol. 1: 4884]
Trinity Cross [Vol. 2: 6619]
Triossi; Prix Gabrielle Sand et Marie Guido [Vol. 2: 2237]
Triple Crown Champion [Vol. 1: 7283]
Triple Tiara [Vol. 1: 7284]
Trobman Memorial Award; Charles [Vol. 1: 17683]
Troland Research Awards [Vol. 1: 11445]
Troll Preis; Thaddaeus [Vol. 2: 2886]
Trollope Medal; D. H. [Vol. 2: 807]
Trombetta, MD Teaching Award; George C. [Vol. 1: 3807]
Tromp Scientific Award [Vol. 1: 10292]
Trooper of the Year Award [Vol. 1: 9645]
Trophee du Fairplay FIM [Vol. 2: 6408]
Trost Award; Jan [Vol. 1: 10133]
Trotter Prize; Mildred [Vol. 1: 1297]
Trotting Triple Crown [Vol. 1: 17150]
Troublemaker Awards [Vol. 1: 10720]
Troughton Memorial Award; Ellis [Vol. 2: 454]
Troup Prize; Gilbert [Vol. 2: 561]
Troutman Cornea Prize [Vol. 1: 7608]
Truck Fleet of the Year [Vol. 1: 2135]
Truck Puller of the Year [Vol. 1: 12987]
Trueblood Award; Kenneth N. [Vol. 1: 1960]
Truer Than Fiction Award [Vol. 1: 8357]
Truesdail Award for Outstanding Service; Roger [Vol. 1: 1903]
Truman Award; Harry S [Vol. 1: 12489]
Truman Book Award; Harry S. [Vol. 1: 16567]
Truman Good Neighbor Award; Harry S. [Vol. 1: 16564]
Truman Good Neighbor Scholarships; Harry S. [Vol. 1: 16565]
Trumpeter Award [Vol. 1: 12132]
Trumpler Award; Robert J. [Vol. 1: 5660]
Truog Soil Science Award; Emil [Vol. 1: 15936]
TRUST Award [Vol. 1: 5980]
Trustee Award [Vol. 1: 16429]
Trustee Awards [Vol. 1: 13714]
Trustee Citation [Vol. 1: 5398]
Trustee Citation Award [Vol. 1: 13142]
Trustee Leadership Award [Vol. 1: 5292]
Trustee of the Year [Vol. 1: 15983]
Trustee of the Year Award
  Association of Jewish Aging Services [Vol. 1: 5382]
  Illinois Library Association [Vol 1: 9149]
  LeadingAge [Vol 1: 10776]
Trustee's Award [Vol. 1: 14353]

Trustees Award [Vol. 1: 9750]
Trustees Honor Roll [Vol. 1: 3749]
Trustees Trophy [Vol. 1: 7486]
Truth Award for Excellence in American Literature; Sojourner [Vol. 1: 16861]
Tsander Prize; F.A. [Vol. 2: 5867]
Tsao Leonardo Award; Makepeace [Vol. 1: 10802]
Tschumi Prize; Jean [Vol. 2: 2588]
Tsiolkovskii Prize; K.E. [Vol. 2: 5868]
TSL Trophy [Vol. 2: 7274]
Tu Award; Tsungming [Vol. 2: 6591]
Tubes of the Year [Vol. 2: 2869]
Tubitak-TWAS Science Award [Vol. 2: 6639]
Tucker Architectural Awards Competition [Vol. 1: 6052]
Tucker Award; Richard [Vol. 1: 16569]
Tucker Career Grants; Richard [Vol. 1: 16570]
Tucker Fund Award; Gabriel F. [Vol. 1: 2754]
Tucker Medal; Bernard [Vol. 2: 7288]
Tucker/Stephen F. Cohen Dissertation Prize; Robert C. [Vol. 1: 5103]
Tucker Study Grants; Sarah [Vol. 1: 16571]
Tudor Medal [Vol. 1: 15462]
Tully Medal in Oceanography; J.P. [Vol. 1: 6714]
Tully Memorial Grant; Stephen R. [Vol. 1: 14439]
Tulsa Library Trust Award for Young Readers' Literature [Vol. 1: 16578]
tum Suden Professional Opportunity Awards; Caroline [Vol. 1: 3270]
Tunner Aircrew Award; Lt. General William H. [Vol. 1: 276]
Tunstall, Jr. Scholarship; Graydon A. [Vol. 1: 13960]
Tuntland Memorial Award; Paul E. [Vol. 1: 14979]
Tupolev Aeromodelling Diploma; Andrei [Vol. 2: 6330]
Tupolev Aeromodelling Medal; Andrei [Vol. 2: 6331]
Tupolev Prize; A.N. [Vol. 2: 5869]
Turbayne International Berkeley Essay Prize Competition; Colin and Ailsa [Vol. 1: 17335]
Turin International Film Festival [Vol. 2: 4042]
Turing Award; A. M. [Vol. 1: 4964]
Turkish Shipping Awards [Vol. 2: 8324]
Turks and Caicos Conch Festival [Vol. 2: 6643]
Turnbull Award for Outstanding Attackman; Lt. Col. J.L. [Vol. 1: 16983]
Turnbull Award; John [Vol. 1: 6877]
Turnbull Essay Competition; Graham [Vol. 2: 8295]
Turnbull Lecture; W. Rupert [Vol. 1: 6198]
Turnbull Lectureship; David [Vol. 1: 11007]
Turnbull Trophy; Jack [Vol. 1: 16983]
Turner Award [Vol. 2: 6000]
Turner Award; Alfred H. [Vol. 2: 6715]
Turner Award for Outstanding Service to NASPA; Fred [Vol. 1: 11390]
Turner Award for Professional Commitment [Vol. 2: 4921]
Turner Award; Frederick Jackson [Vol. 1: 13690]
Turner Award; Wava Banes [Vol. 1: 16380]
Turner Early Career Award for Distinguished Contributions to Diversity in Clinical Psychology; Samuel M. [Vol. 1: 3586]
Turner/Ella Ruth Turner Bergera Award for Best Biography; Ella Larsen [Vol. 1: 11281]
Turner Entrepreneur Award; Arthur E. [Vol. 1: 13431]
Turner Lecture; Francis C. [Vol. 1: 4244]
Turner Medal; Henry C. [Vol. 1: 1851]
Turner Prize; Dr. Lynn W. [Vol. 1: 13956]
Turner - Scholefield Award [Vol. 2: 9305]
Turner Sportsmanship Award; Bob [Vol. 1: 12289]
Turnquist Trophy [Vol. 1: 7314]
Tutor Work Study Grant [Vol. 2: 5041]
Tutt Award; William Thayer [Vol. 1: 17429]
Tuttle Award; Arnold D. [Vol. 1: 191]
TV Programs of the Year [Vol. 1: 2138]
TV Programs, Segments, and Promotional Pieces Telly Award [Vol. 1: 16418]
TV Weather Forecast Trophy Award [Vol. 2: 2840]
Twain Award; Mark [Vol. 1: 15379]
Twain Comedy Playwriting Award; Mark [Vol. 1: 10669]
TWAS-AAS-Microsoft Award for Young Scientists [Vol. 2: 4163]
TWAS Prize for Young Scientist in the Philippines [Vol. 2: 5368]
TWAS Prize for Young Scientists in the South [Vol. 2: 5195]

Urey Medal [Vol. 2: 2363]
Urey Prize; Harold C. [Vol. 1: 1453]
Uribe Award for Creative Leadership in Human Rights; Virginia [Vol. 1: 12301]
Urist, MD, Award; Marshall R. [Vol. 1: 13720]
Urology Medal [Vol. 1: 713]
Urology Research Prize [Vol. 1: 714]
Urquell International Photography Awards; Pilsner [Vol. 1: 14020]
US Air Force Personnel Manager Award [Vol. 1: 278]
US Youth Soccer Cup [Vol. 1: 17162]
USA/British Isles Visiting Fellowship [Vol. 2: 8689]
USA-CA Award [Vol. 1: 7737]
USA International Ballet Competition [Vol. 1: 17433]
USA International Harp Competition [Vol. 1: 17435]
USA Swimming Award [Vol. 1: 17451]
USA Today Sports Weekly Award [Vol. 1: 15030]
USAdult Ironman of the Year [Vol. 1: 17430]
USAF Personnel Manager of the Year [Vol. 1: 278]
USB Certificate [Vol. 2: 1803]
Uschmann Award for the History of Science; Georg [Vol. 2: 3127]
USDF/Dover Saddlery Adult Amateur Medal [Vol. 1: 16877]
User Feedback Award [Vol. 1: 14717]
USFCC/J. Roger Porter Award [Vol. 1: 3992]
Usher Prize; Abbott Payson [Vol. 1: 15356]
Usher Research Award in Dermatology; Barney [Vol. 1: 6450]
Ushkow Community Service Award; Martin C. [Vol. 1: 715]
USHWAn of the Year [Vol. 1: 16953]
USHWAn of the Year; Bob Zellner [Vol. 1: 16955]
Usiskin Student Elective Prize; Laurence [Vol. 2: 7169]
USPS Gold Mailbox Award [Vol. 1: 7868]
USRowing Medal [Vol. 1: 17047]
USSA Outstanding Alpine Masters Award [Vol. 1: 17091]
USTA Junior and Boys' Sportsmanship Award [Vol. 1: 17138]
USX Foundation Award in Molecular Biology [Vol. 1: 11429]
Utah State Poetry Society Award [Vol. 1: 12378]
Uteck Bowl [Vol. 1: 6661]
Uteck Bowl MVP Award [Vol. 1: 6662]
Utility Design Awards [Vol. 1: 3650]
Utilization Award [Vol. 1: 11585]
Utley Prize for Advancing Liberty; Freda [Vol. 1: 5687]
Utmarkt Svensk Form [Vol. 2: 6243]
Utzon Award for International Architecture; John [Vol. 2: 388]
Uveeler Award [Vol. 2: 4007]
Uyisenga Scholars Program [Vol. 1: 7896]
Vachon Award; Romeo [Vol. 1: 6199]
Vadnais, Jr. Award; Henry A. [Vol. 1: 8938]
Vahue Award of Merit; L. Ray [Vol. 1: 13741]
Vaisala Award; New Prof. Dr. Vilho [Vol. 2: 6562]
Vaisala Award; Prof. Dr. Vilho [Vol. 2: 6562]
Vakhtang Gorgasal's Order [Vol. 2: 2684]
Valdes; Premio Miguel Aleman [Vol. 2: 4585]
Vale Medal [Vol. 1: 6620]
Valent BiosSiences Best Paper Award [Vol. 1: 14034]
Valero Scholarships; Lucy [Vol. 1: 13923]
Valicek Medal; Anna [Vol. 1: 9927]
Valkanas State Arts Advocacy Award; Alene [Vol. 1: 4717]
Valley Forge Certificate [Vol. 1: 12490]
Valley Forge Cross for Heroism [Vol. 1: 12491]
Valley, Jr. Prize; George E. [Vol. 1: 3225]
Valor Award
    National Association for Search and Rescue [Vol. 1: 11601]
    World Conservation Union [Vol 2: 6537]
Valued Customer Award [Vol. 1: 12014]
van Ameringen Award in Psychiatric Rehabilitation; Arnold L. [Vol. 1: 3367]
Van Antwerpen Award for Service to the Institute; F. J. and Dorothy [Vol. 1: 2640]
Van Beneden; Prix Pierre-Joseph et Edouard [Vol. 2: 1646]
Van Biesbroeck Prize; George [Vol. 1: 1454]
van Buren Structural Engineering Award; Maurice P. [Vol. 1: 1845]
Van Cleef Memorial Medal [Vol. 1: 2218]

Van Couvering Memorial Award; Martin C. [Vol. 1: 2701]
van de Jonge Jury; Prijs [Vol. 2: 4654]
van de Nederlandse Kinderjury; Prijs [Vol. 2: 4655]
Van Den Heever Prize for Jurisprudence; Toon [Vol. 2: 5645]
Van Der Linde Award [Vol. 2: 5582]
Van Der Merwe Award; Marina [Vol. 1: 6663]
van der Merwe Prize; Koos [Vol. 2: 5505]
Van der Pol Gold Medal; Balthasar [Vol. 2: 1567]
van der Schueren Award; Emmanuel [Vol. 2: 1500]
van der Smissen Leadership Award; Betty [Vol. 1: 16165]
Van Dyck; Prijs Albert [Vol. 2: 1577]
Van Eck Medal; Hendrik [Vol. 2: 5681]
Van Ertborn; Prix Baron [Vol. 2: 1647]
Van Goidsenhoven; Prijs Franz [Vol. 2: 1578]
Van Grover Youth Exhibit Award; Melissa [Vol. 1: 3009]
Van Hook Industry Award; Daryl [Vol. 1: 11695]
Van Leeuwenhoek Distinctive Travel Award [Vol. 2: 2855]
van Niekerk/AFMA Technical Person of the Year; Barney [Vol. 2: 5506]
Van Niel International Prize for Studies in Bacterial Systematics [Vol. 2: 4793]
Van Nostrand Memorial Award; John [Vol. 1: 9470]
Van Nostrand Reinhold Research Award [Vol. 1: 9851]
Van Remortel Service Award; Harold [Vol. 1: 926]
Van Slyke Foundation Grants [Vol. 1: 927]
Van Son Distinguished Service Award; Allene [Vol. 1: 1131]
van Straelen; Prix [Vol. 2: 2460]
Van Vliet Trophy; Maury L. [Vol. 1: 6662]
van Vught Award; Jean [Vol. 1: 5250]
van Wachem Award; Pauline [Vol. 2: 4662]
van Weelden Award; Arie [Vol. 2: 4683]
van Wesemael Literary Prize; Guust [Vol. 2: 4745]
Van Winkle Award; Rip [Vol. 1: 14776]
van Wyk Louw Medal; N. P. [Vol. 2: 5646]
Van Zandt Citizenship Award; James E. [Vol. 1: 17547]
Vanags Prize; Gustavs [Vol. 2: 4444]
Vance Award; James A. [Vol. 1: 6907]
Vance Award; John C. [Vol. 1: 16539]
Vance Award; Robert W. [Vol. 1: 7779]
Vance Tribute; Cyrus R. [Vol. 1: 8495]
Vanchiere Award; Charles [Vol. 1: 716]
Vancouver International Film Festival [Vol. 1: 17509]
Vandenberg Award; Hoyt S. [Vol. 1: 279]
Vanderlinden; Prix Georges [Vol. 2: 1648]
Vanderlinden Public Official Award; Spence [Vol. 1: 3658]
Vanderplank Award; J.E. [Vol. 2: 5750]
Vanderplank Lecture; J.E. [Vol. 2: 5751]
Vanderveen Distinguished Service Award; Bart [Vol. 1: 11162]
Vandiver Award; Willard T. [Vol. 1: 474]
Vanguard Award
    American Academy of Medical Administrators [Vol. 1: 578]
    North Country Trail Association [Vol 1: 13392]
Vanguard Award for Cable Operations Management [Vol. 1: 12030]
Vanguard Degree [Vol. 1: 13064]
Vanguard Leadership Award [Vol. 1: 10745]
Vanier Cup Trophy [Vol. 1: 6664]
Vanier Medal [Vol. 1: 9403]
VanMeter Humanitarian Award for International Relations; Harriet [Vol. 1: 9734]
Vanuatu Tourism Awards [Vol. 2: 9544]
Vardon Trophy [Vol. 1: 14225]
Vardon Trophy; Harry [Vol. 2: 8513]
Vare Trophy [Vol. 1: 10735]
Varga Prize; E.S. [Vol. 2: 5871]
Varian Award; Russell and Sigurd [Vol. 1: 5739]
VARIAN-Juliana Denekamp Award [Vol. 2: 1501]
VARIAN Research Award [Vol. 2: 1502]
Varna International Ballet Competition [Vol. 2: 1805]
Varnell Memorial Award for Small Business; Charles E. [Vol. 1: 304]
Vars Award; Harry M. [Vol. 1: 4029]
Vasconcelos World Award of Education; Jose [Vol. 2: 4603]
Vastola Award; Dr. Anthony P. [Vol. 1: 16614]

Vaughan and Bushnell Awards (Golden Hammer Awards) [Vol. 1: 11790]
Vavrousek Prize; Josef [Vol. 2: 1909]
Vawter Pathologist-in-Training Award; Gordon L. [Vol. 1: 15248]
VDE/ETG Award [Vol. 2: 2789]
VDS-Media Award [Vol. 2: 3027]
Veblen - Commons Award [Vol. 1: 5013]
Vegetable Breeding Working Group Award of Excellence [Vol. 1: 3936]
Vehicle Theft Award of Merit [Vol. 1: 9647]
Veitch Award for Excellence in Indigenous Engagement; Bruce [Vol. 2: 231]
Veitch Memorial Medal [Vol. 2: 8828]
Veken Prize; Oswald Vander [Vol. 2: 1525]
Veksler Prize; V.I. [Vol. 2: 5872]
Velben Prize in Geometry; Oswald [Vol. 1: 2843]
Velluz; Prix Leon [Vol. 2: 2238]
Vendelfelts minnesfond; Stipendium ur Lena [Vol. 2: 6218]
Venezuelan Islands Award [Vol. 2: 9557]
Venison Summer Sausage Award [Vol. 1: 9133]
Ventana Medical Systems In Situ Hybridization Awards [Vol. 1: 12861]
Ventris Memorial Award; Michael [Vol. 2: 6731]
Venturing Advisor Award of Merit [Vol. 1: 5981]
Venturing Bronze Award [Vol. 1: 5982]
Venturing Gold Award [Vol. 1: 5983]
Venturing Leadership Award [Vol. 1: 5984]
Venturing Ranger Award [Vol. 1: 5985]
Venturing Silver Award [Vol. 1: 5986]
Venue of the Year [Vol. 1: 61]
Verbatim Award [Vol. 2: 1966]
Verco Medal [Vol. 2: 1015]
Verco Medal; Sir Joseph [Vol. 2: 1015]
Verdaguer; Prix Alfred [Vol. 2: 2239]
Verdeyen Prize for Soil Mechanics [Vol. 2: 1659]
Veritas Award
    American Agri-Women [Vol. 1: 788]
    Romance Writers of America [Vol 1: 14590]
Veritas Awards [Vol. 2: 5757]
Vermaak Award; Coenraad [Vol. 2: 5596]
Verman Award; Lal C. [Vol. 2: 3758]
Vermeulen Memorial Award; Buster [Vol. 1: 6623]
Vermont Playwrights Award [Vol. 1: 17505]
Verner Awards; Elizabeth O'Neill [Vol. 1: 15974]
Verona Award; Eva [Vol. 2: 1865]
Verona Jury Award [Vol. 2: 9536]
Versatility Award [Vol. 1: 13445]
Versatility Award of Merit [Vol. 1: 13436]
Versatility Hall of Fame [Vol. 1: 2048]
Versele; Prix Bernard [Vol. 2: 1571]
Vertical Smile La Sonrisa Vertical [Vol. 2: 6111]
Vertin Award; James R. [Vol. 1: 7174]
Very Special Arts Young Playwrights Program [Vol. 1: 17622]
VES Awards [Vol. 1: 17610]
Veselovskii Prize; A.N. [Vol. 2: 5873]
Vess Avionics Marine of the Year Award; Paul G. [Vol. 1: 10968]
Veteran's Administration Employee of the Year Award [Vol. 1: 255]
Veteran's Award [Vol. 1: 475]
Veteran's Bowl [Vol. 1: 475]
Veterans Memorial Scholarship [Vol. 1: 17669]
Vetlesen Prize [Vol. 1: 7413]
Vetter Award for Research; Betty [Vol. 1: 17929]
VFW Emergency Medical Technician Award [Vol. 1: 17542]
VGP Award [Vol. 1: 2227]
Vice Presidents Emiriti Award [Vol. 2: 8955]
Vick Outstanding Province President Award; A. Frank [Vol. 1: 13974]
Vickers Prize; Jill [Vol. 1: 6803]
Victoria Cross [Vol. 2: 7353]
Victoria Cross for Australia [Vol. 2: 313]
Victoria Jubilee Prize Lectureship; Gunning [Vol. 2: 9073]
Victoria Medal [Vol. 2: 8799]
Victoria Medal of Honour in Horticulture [Vol. 2: 8829]
Viener Book Prize; Saul [Vol. 1: 2732]
Viennet-Damien; Prix [Vol. 2: 2618]
Vietnam Campaign Medal [Vol. 1: 16693]
Vietnam Logistic and Support Medal [Vol. 2: 323]

Walker Bookseller of the Year Award; Steffie [Vol. 1: 14591]

Walker Community Service Award; John [Vol. 1: 2444]

Walker Cup [Vol. 1: 16940]

Walker Distinguished Humanitarian Award; Bishop John T. [Vol. 1: 205]

Walker Education Award; Sylvia [Vol. 1: 11829]

Walker, Jr. Award; John K. [Vol. 1: 11156]

Walker Memorial Award; Morris R. [Vol. 1: 5242]

Walker Scholarship; Myrtle and Earl [Vol. 1: 14960]

Walkley Awards; The [Vol. 2: 1176]

Wall, DMD, Award; Thomas P. [Vol. 1: 4255]

Wall Memorial Award; Richard [Vol. 1: 16484]

Wall Young Investigator Award; Patrick D. [Vol. 1: 9603]

Wallace Award; Alfred Russel [Vol. 2: 8778]

Wallace Dissertation Award; S. Rains [Vol. 1: 15142]

Wallace Memorial Award; Karl R. [Vol. 1: 12115]

Wallace's Registrars' Prize; Hugh [Vol. 2: 9110]

Wallenberg "A Hero for Our Time" Award; Raoul [Vol. 1: 17629]

Wallenberg Prize; Marcus [Vol. 2: 6249]

Wallenberg World of Heroes Award; Raoul [Vol. 1: 17629]

Wallin Education of Handicapped Children Award; J. E. Wallace [Vol. 1: 7644]

Wallin Special Education Lifetime Achievement Award; J. E. Wallace [Vol. 1: 7644]

Wallis Award; Helen [Vol. 2: 8146]

Wallis Memorial Intermediate Beethoven Scholarship; Gordon C. [Vol. 1: 14760]

Wallis Memorial Senior Beethoven Scholarship; Gordon C. [Vol. 1: 14761]

Wallis Memorial Silver Award [Vol. 1: 14762]

Walree Prize; Van [Vol. 2: 4836]

Walsh Award for Lifetime Contributions to Family Medicine; John G. [Vol. 1: 567]

Walsh Grant; Edith [Vol. 2: 7128]

Walsh Medal for Service to Industry; Alan [Vol. 2: 411]

Walsh Teaching the Psychology of Women Award; Mary Roth [Vol. 1: 3552]

Walsh - Weston Memorial Award [Vol. 2: 7394]

Walters Award; Lt. General Vernon A. [Vol. 1: 12607]

Walther Cup; Fred and Barbara [Vol. 1: 11044]

Walton Award; A. Ronald [Vol. 1: 12192]

Walton Memorial Trophy; Nancy-Bird [Vol. 2: 617]

Walton/Russell L. Miller Award in Safety/Loss Prevention; Norton H. [Vol. 1: 2642]

Walwyn Prize; Kim Scott [Vol. 2: 6911]

Wambua Award; Paul Musili [Vol. 1: 4424]

Wanderlust Travel Awards [Vol. 2: 9438]

Wang Young Investigator Award; Shih-Chun [Vol. 1: 3271]

Wanganui Trophy [Vol. 2: 5063]

Wangchuck Gold Medal; Jigme Dorji [Vol. 2: 1720]

Wanner Award; Vance R. [Vol. 1: 11157]

Wapensky Award; V. A. [Vol. 1: 5948]

War Service Decoration [Vol. 2: 4513]

War Service Medal [Vol. 1: 12914]

Warburg Medaille; Otto [Vol. 2: 2997]

Ward Award; Arch [Vol. 1: 7381]

Ward Exceptional Service Award; Herb [Vol. 1: 15634]

Ward Library Instruction Award; James E. [Vol. 1: 16431]

Ward Memorial Award; Earl F. [Vol. 1: 305]

Ward Memorial Award; Julian E. [Vol. 1: 192]

Ward Memorial Film Award; Jack [Vol. 1: 4734]

Ward Memorial Posthumous Award; R.D. "Bob" [Vol. 1: 11522]

Ward Memorial Prize; Lynd [Vol. 1: 9015]

Ward Outstanding New Children's Theatre Company Award; Winifred [Vol. 1: 813]

Ward Prize in Experimental Physics; E.M. and J.F. [Vol. 2: 1155]

Ward Scholar; Winifred [Vol. 1: 813]

Warden of the Year [Vol. 1: 13280]

Warder Award for Outstanding Achievement; Frederick B. [Vol. 1: 13128]

Wardle Award; Robert Arnold [Vol. 1: 7000]

Ware Award for Distinguished (Undergraduate) Teaching; L. M. [Vol. 1: 3933]

Warehouse Person of the Year [Vol. 2: 9421]

Waring International Piano Competition; Virginia [Vol. 1: 17642]

Wark Medal and Lecture; Ian [Vol. 2: 188]

Warkany Lecturer Award; Josef [Vol. 1: 16436]

Warman International Students Design Award Competition [Vol. 2: 810]

Warmington Trophy; Ivon [Vol. 2: 5064]

Warner Award; Edward [Vol. 1: 9770]

Warner Award; Jo [Vol. 1: 6062]

Warner Awards Program; William Everett [Vol. 1: 8176]

Warner Medal; Worcester Reed [Vol. 1: 4428]

Warner Memorial Medal [Vol. 2: 9384]

Warner Memorial Medal Award; Samuel L. [Vol. 1: 15706]

Warner Prize for Astronomy; Helen B. [Vol. 1: 1455]

Warren Diffraction Physics Award; Bertram E. [Vol. 1: 1961]

Warren Medal [Vol. 2: 8011]

Warren Medal; W. H. [Vol. 2: 809]

Warren Prize; G. K. [Vol. 1: 11448]

Wartenweiler Memorial Lecture [Vol. 2: 841]

Wartha Memorial Plaquettes; Vince [Vol. 2: 3384]

Warwick Award; Gordon [Vol. 2: 7227]

Wascana Senior Cello/Viola/Double Bass Scholarship; Kiwanis of [Vol. 1: 14745]

Washburn Award; Jennie Hassler [Vol. 1: 8584]

Washburn Prize; Sherwood L. [Vol. 1: 1298]

Washington Craft Show [Vol. 1: 14966]

Washington Crossing Foundation Scholarships [Vol. 1: 17670]

Washington Medal; Martha [Vol. 1: 12915]

The Washington Monthly Journalism Award [Vol. 1: 17674]

The Washington Post Award for Excellence in Nonprofit Management [Vol. 1: 7148]

Washington Prize [Vol. 1: 18005]

Washington Regional Reporting Award [Vol. 1: 12690]

Washington State Reserve Police Association Trophy [Vol. 1: 12786]

Washingtonians of the Year [Vol. 1: 17688]

Wason Medal for Materials Research [Vol. 1: 1852]

Wason Medal for Most Meritorious Paper [Vol. 1: 1853]

Wasserman Foundation Prizes; Leo [Vol. 1: 2733]

Wassermann Award for Lifetime Achievement; Friedrich [Vol. 2: 7595]

Wassermann Prize [Vol. 2: 6098]

Waste Management Award [Vol. 1: 242]

Watanabe Medal; G. [Vol. 2: 4258]

Water Drop Patch Project [Vol. 1: 16900]

Water Engineering Award [Vol. 2: 7559]

Water Environment Merit Award [Vol. 2: 607]

Water Quality Improvement Award [Vol. 1: 17720]

Water Works State Leadership Award [Vol. 1: 13170]

Waterbury Award for Outdoor Lighting Design; Paul [Vol. 1: 9164]

Watercolor U.S.A. [Vol. 1: 16229]

Waterfall Award; Wallace [Vol. 1: 5645]

Waterford Crystal European Athlete of the Year Award [Vol. 2: 6269]

Waterman Award; Alan T. [Vol. 1: 12814]

Watkins Award; J. B. C. [Vol. 1: 6144]

Watkins Best Paper Award; Campbell [Vol. 1: 9544]

WatSave Awards [Vol. 2: 3764]

Watson Award; Clarence W. [Vol. 1: 2156]

Watson Award for Consular Excellence; Barbara M. [Vol. 1: 16856]

Watson Award; Robert C. [Vol. 1: 2716]

Watson, Jr.; Assistant Excellence in Leadership Award in Memory of Buford M. [Vol. 1: 9768]

Watson, Jr. Medal of Excellence; William C. [Vol. 1: 16818]

Watson Medal; Garth [Vol. 2: 8012]

Watson Medal; James Craig [Vol. 1: 11449]

Watson Prize; Albert J. [Vol. 2: 7849]

Watson Prize; Frank [Vol. 1: 14796]

Watt Award; Virginia J. [Vol. 1: 10493]

Watt Gold Medal; Oswald [Vol. 1: 994]

Watt Medal; James [Vol. 2: 8013]

Watt Prize for Excellence in Conrad Scholarship; Ian P. [Vol. 1: 7545]

Watters Memorial Scholarship; George E. [Vol. 1: 13169]

Way Award; Brian [Vol. 2: 9387]

Wayburn Award; Edgar [Vol. 1: 14881]

Wayne Award; Peter [Vol. 2: 8082]

The WCA Award for Excellence in Non-Profit Management [Vol. 1: 7148]

WCO Emeritus [Vol. 1: 18037]

We Dig America Award [Vol. 1: 13020]

Weatherford Award; W. D. [Vol. 1: 17259]

Weaver Memorial Award; Thelma [Vol. 1: 8585]

Weaver's Company Medal and Prize [Vol. 2: 9385]

Web Award [Vol. 2: 8483]

Web Awards; Bahrain [Vol. 2: 4451]

Web Awards; Egypt [Vol. 2: 2013]

Web Awards; Jordan [Vol. 2: 4362]

Web Awards; Kuwait [Vol. 2: 5177]

Web Awards; Lebanon [Vol. 2: 4452]

Web Awards; Oman [Vol. 2: 5178]

Web Awards; Pan Arab [Vol. 2: 4453]

Web Awards; Qatar [Vol. 2: 5179]

Web Awards; Syria [Vol. 2: 4457]

Web Awards; UAE [Vol. 2: 4459]

Web Awards; Yemen [Vol. 2: 9565]

Web-based Technology Project Award [Vol. 2: 7025]

Web Site of the Year [Vol. 1: 12092]

Webb Award; Aileen Osborn [Vol. 1: 1948]

Webb Award; James E. [Vol. 1: 4052]

Webb Medal; William H. [Vol. 1: 15720]

Webb Prize [Vol. 2: 8014]

Webb Service Award; Aileen Osborn [Vol. 1: 1948]

Webb Studentship; Bernard [Vol. 2: 6732]

Webelos Den Leader Award [Vol. 1: 5987]

Weber Award; Max [Vol. 2: 2714]

Weber Engineering Leadership Recognition; Ernst [Vol. 1: 9309]

Website and Electronic Communications Awards [Vol. 1: 7570]

Website Award
 British Columbia Historical Federation [Vol. 1: 6023]
 Overseas Press Club of America [Vol 1: 13762]

Website Awards
 Psi Chi, the National Honor Society in Psychology [Vol. 1: 14299]
 The Webby Awards [Vol 1: 17733]

Webster Award; Betty [Vol. 1: 13636]

Webster Award; Daniel [Vol. 1: 10073]

WEC Gold Medal for International Corporate Environmental Achievement [Vol. 1: 18039]

Wedel Award; Cynthia [Vol. 1: 3682]

Wedemeyer Award; Charles A. [Vol. 1: 17397]

Weed Book Prize [Vol. 2: 1183]

Weeder Scholarship [Vol. 1: 17671]

Weeks Achievement through Action Award; Christopher A. [Vol. 2: 3102]

Weeks Gold Medal; Lewis G. [Vol. 2: 498]

Weems Award [Vol. 1: 9393]

Weetabix Women's British Open Championship [Vol. 2: 8279]

Wegener Award; Alfred [Vol. 2: 4684]

Wegener Medaille; Alfred [Vol. 2: 2765]

Wegener Medal and Honorary Membership; Alfred [Vol. 2: 2380]

Wegmann; Prix [Vol. 2: 2461]

Weickhardt Medal for Distinguished Contribution to Economic Advancement [Vol. 2: 987]

Weightlifting Hall of Fame [Vol. 2: 3411]

Weigley Graduate Student Travel Awards; Russell F. [Vol. 1: 15201]

Weil Award [Vol. 1: 1231]

Weil Awards; Frank L. [Vol. 1: 10568]

Weil Prize; Martin Eli [Vol. 1: 15373]

Weill; Prix de Dessin Pierre David [Vol. 2: 2149]

Weinberg Memorial Award for Geriatric Psychiatry; Jack [Vol. 1: 3368]

Weinberg Plaque; Al [Vol. 1: 11512]

Weinsier Award for Excellence in Medical/Dental Nutrition Education; Roland L. [Vol. 1: 4021]

Weinstein Memorial Fellowship; Abram and Fannie Gottlieb Immerman and Abraham Nathan and Bertha Daskal [Vol. 1: 18183]

Weinstock Person of the Year; Morris F. [Vol. 1: 8073]

Weintal Prize for Diplomatic Reporting; Edward [Vol. 1: 8588]

Weinzweig Grand Prize; John [Vol. 1: 14986]

Weir Minerals Design and Build Competition [Vol. 2: 810]

Weir Prize; C. J. **[Vol. 2: 7850]**

Weisel Scholarships; William E. **[Vol. 1: 14961]**

Weisenfeld Award for Excellence in Ophthalmology; Mildred **[Vol. 1: 5087]**

Weisfeld Costume Design and Technology Award; Zelma H. **[Vol. 1: 16970]**

Weisinger Award; Mort **[Vol. 1: 4356]**

Weiss Award; George L. **[Vol. 1: 13789]**

Weiss Award; Rosalee G. **[Vol. 1: 3433]**

Weiss Literary Award Competition; Jeffrey **[Vol. 1: 16481]**

Weiss Medal **[Vol. 2: 6783]**

Weiss Student Scholarship; Fannie **[Vol. 1: 1993]**

Weissenberg Award **[Vol. 2: 6027]**

Weitbrecht Telecommunication Access Award; Robert H. **[Vol. 1: 16408]**

Weiten Teaching Excellence Award; Wayne **[Vol. 1: 3558]**

Weitzman Award; Richard E. **[Vol. 1: 8113]**

Weizmann Prizes **[Vol. 2: 4592]**

Weizmann Prizes of the Academy of Scientific Research (Premios Weizmann de la Academia de la Investigacion Cientifica) **[Vol. 2: 4592]**

Welch Award in Chemistry **[Vol. 1: 17737]**

Welch Award; Medard W. **[Vol. 1: 5741]**

Welch Diploma; Ann **[Vol. 2: 6333]**

Welch Medal; William H. **[Vol. 1: 1003]**

Welch Memorial Award; Ann **[Vol. 2: 8601]**

Welfare Personality of the Year **[Vol. 2: 8108]**

Welford Award; Alan **[Vol. 2: 751]**

Wellcome Diagnostics Student Award **[Vol. 2: 5624]**

Wellcome Medal and Prize; Sir Henry **[Vol. 1: 5442]**

Wellcome Medal for Anthropology as Applied to Medical Problems **[Vol. 2: 8643]**

Wollcome Prize **[Vol. 2: 8936]**

Wellek Prize; Rene **[Vol. 1: 1832]**

Wellington Prize; Arthur M. **[Vol. 1: 4246]**

Wellmann Memorial Award; Klaus **[Vol. 1: 3717]**

Wellner Award; Alfred M. **[Vol. 1: 7660]**

Wells Appreciation Award; Cliff **[Vol. 1: 11644]**

Wells Award; Ida B. **[Vol. 1: 7604]**

Wells Award; Nancy **[Vol. 2: 618]**

Wells Graduate Student Fellowship; Ida B. **[Vol. 1: 7604]**

Wells Memorial Award; Elizabeth B. **[Vol. 1: 11798]**

Wells Memorial Key **[Vol. 1: 15815]**

Welsh Arts Council Prizes **[Vol. 2: 6676]**

Welsh Community Service Award; Paul **[Vol. 1: 4727]**

Welsh Society Medallion **[Vol. 1: 17739]**

Weltmeister im Pflugen **[Vol. 2: 4847]**

Welty Prize in Fiction; Eudora **[Vol. 1: 16039]**

Wenner Strong Inference Award; Adrien M. **[Vol. 1: 15156]**

Wereld Muziek Concours Kerkrade **[Vol. 2: 4843]**

Werner Award; Wallace "Buddy" **[Vol. 1: 17098]**

Werner Medaille; Abraham Gottlob **[Vol. 2: 2770]**

Werner Prize **[Vol. 2: 6491]**

Werner-Risau Prize **[Vol. 2: 3134]**

Wertheimer Award **[Vol. 2: 8077]**

Wesley-Logan Prize **[Vol. 1: 2392]**

Wesolowski Award; Jerome J. **[Vol. 1: 10321]**

Wesson Memorial Physician of the Year Award; Dr. Ray **[Vol. 1: 16698]**

West Agro Inc. Award **[Vol. 1: 1987]**

West Australia Screen Awards **[Vol. 2: 723]**

West Coast Scholarship **[Vol. 1: 17672]**

Westcott USTA Family of the Year Award; Ralph W. **[Vol. 1: 17143]**

Westerfield Award; Samuel Z. **[Vol. 1: 12291]**

Western Australia Film and Video Festival **[Vol. 2: 723]**

Western Australian Artist Award **[Vol. 2: 83]**

Western Australian Indigenous Art Award **[Vol. 2: 83]**

Western Australian Premier's Indigenous Art Awards **[Vol. 2: 83]**

Western Auto NASCAR Mechanics Hall of Fame **[Vol. 1: 10024]**

Western Cape Exporter of the Year **[Vol. 2: 5528]**

Western Conference Trophy **[Vol. 1: 6506]**

Western Electric Fund Award **[Vol. 1: 3881]**

Western Garden Design Wards **[Vol. 1: 16325]**

Western Heritage Awards **[Vol. 1: 12269]**

Western Home Awards **[Vol. 1: 16327]**

Western Political Science Association Awards **[Vol. 1: 17770]**

Westfaelischer Kurstpreis **[Vol. 2: 3117]**

Westfaelischer Literaturpreis **[Vol. 2: 3116]**

Westinghouse Medals; George **[Vol. 1: 4429]**

Westinghouse Science Talent Search **[Vol. 1: 15305]**

Weston Environmental Chemistry Award; Roy F. **[Vol. 1: 15633]**

Weston Grant; Martha **[Vol. 1: 15588]**

Weston Research Award; William **[Vol. 1: 15242]**

Westonbirt Orchid Medal **[Vol. 2: 8831]**

Westpac Outstanding New Member of the Year **[Vol. 2: 4903]**

Westrups Prize; Wilhelm **[Vol. 2: 6174]**

Westwood Medal for Excellence in Insect Taxonomy; J.O. **[Vol. 2: 8779]**

Wetland Program Development Grants **[Vol. 1: 16901]**

Wetnose Awards **[Vol. 2: 9445]**

Wetzel Travel Awards; Lawrence T. **[Vol. 1: 16437]**

Wetzsteon Award; Ross **[Vol. 1: 17560]**

Wexner Graduate Fellow **[Vol. 1: 17794]**

Wexner Prize **[Vol. 1: 17792]**

Weyand and the Business Pinnacle Award; Ruth **[Vol. 1: 5167]**

Weyant Lifetime Achievement Award; J. Thomas **[Vol. 1: 12783]**

Weyerhaeuser Award; Charles A. **[Vol. 1: 8429]**

Weyl International Glass Science Award; Woldemar A. **[Vol. 2: 6001]**

Weyman Young Investigator's Award; Arthur E. **[Vol. 1: 4293]**

WGSS Award for Career Achievement in Women's Studies Librarianship **[Vol. 1: 5270]**

Whaley Book Prize; Sara **[Vol. 1: 13059]**

Whaley Incubator of the Year; Randall M. **[Vol. 1: 12025]**

Wham Leadership Medal; George S. **[Vol. 1: 2976]**

Wheadon Education Award; Lynn **[Vol. 1: 6542]**

Wheatley Award; John **[Vol. 1: 3226]**

Wheatley Award; William A. **[Vol. 1: 17183]**

Wheatley Medal **[Vol. 2: 9320]**

Wheeler Best Conference Paper Award; Tony **[Vol. 2: 462]**

Wheeler Bursary; Alwyne **[Vol. 2: 9218]**

Wheeler Legacy Award; A. O. **[Vol. 1: 425]**

Wheeler Men's Cross Country Award **[Vol. 1: 12068]**

Wheeler Prize; Charles B. **[Vol. 1: 13487]**

Wheeler Track and Field Awards **[Vol. 1: 12069]**

Wherry Award; Edgar T. **[Vol. 1: 5944]**

Wherry Award; Elizabeth **[Vol. 1: 7129]**

Whetten Award; Nellie Yeoh **[Vol. 1: 5742]**

Whirly-Girls Helicopter Add-On Flight Training Scholarship **[Vol. 1: 17801]**

Whirly-Girls Memorial Flight Training Scholarship **[Vol. 1: 17802]**

Whitaker Distinguished Lectureship **[Vol. 1: 5843]**

Whitaker Graduate Student Awards **[Vol. 1: 5842]**

Whitaker Science Journalism Awards **[Vol. 1: 994]**

Whitaker Young Investigator Award **[Vol. 1: 5844]**

Whitby Award for Distinguished Teaching and Research; George Stafford **[Vol. 1: 1677]**

Whitby Award; Kenneth T. **[Vol. 1: 865]**

White Award; David C. **[Vol. 2: 4772]**

White Award; Marsh W. **[Vol. 1: 2696]**

White Award; Paul **[Vol. 1: 14420]**

White Awards **[Vol. 1: 7292]**

White Children's Book Awards; William Allen **[Vol. 1: 17810]**

White Distinguished Teacher Award; Albert Easton **[Vol. 1: 4846]**

White Excellence in Teaching Award; David **[Vol. 2: 547]**

White Fellowship; Harold **[Vol. 2: 895]**

White Foundation Prize; Rowden **[Vol. 2: 1156]**

White Golden Quill Award; Carson **[Vol. 1: 13340]**

White House Fellows **[Vol. 1: 14140]**

White Humanitarian Award; Byron "Whizzer" **[Vol. 1: 13252]**

White Medal; C. G. **[Vol. 1: 11044]**

White Medal; Clarence G. **[Vol. 1: 4778]**

White Memorial Award for Electronic Journalism; Paul **[Vol. 1: 14420]**

White Memorial Award; Philip R. **[Vol. 1: 15113]**

White Memorial Trophy **[Vol. 1: 6719]**

White National Championship; J.R. **[Vol. 2: 2062]**

White National Defense Award; Thomas D. **[Vol. 1: 16696]**

White National Memorial Trophy; Belle **[Vol. 2: 6716]**

White Prize; Frederick **[Vol. 2: 189]**

White Prize Lecture; T. C. **[Vol. 2: 8702]**

White Prize; Sir A.E. Rowden **[Vol. 2: 1169]**

White Ravens **[Vol. 2: 3104]**

White Research and Mentoring Award; D.C. **[Vol. 1: 3993]**

White Scholarship; Sir William **[Vol. 2: 8869]**

White Stag Award **[Vol. 1: 17099]**

White Stag/Dan Bean Award **[Vol. 1: 17099]**

Whitebread Literary Awards **[Vol. 2: 6899]**

Whitehead Award for Best Design of a Trade Book; Fred **[Vol. 1: 16462]**

Whitehead Awards for Excellence in Reporting on Drug and Alcohol Problems; Nancy Dickerson **[Vol. 1: 7929]**

Whitehead Prize **[Vol. 2: 8333]**

Whitehead Prize; Senior **[Vol. 2: 8334]**

Whitfield Award; Willis J. **[Vol. 1: 9329]**

Whitfield Book Prize **[Vol. 2: 8808]**

Whitfield Regional Newsletter Award; Earl **[Vol. 1: 14212]**

Whiting Award; John **[Vol. 2: 6747]**

Whiting Undergraduate Dissertation Prize; H.T.A. **[Vol. 2: 7197]**

Whitley Award **[Vol. 2: 9447]**

Whitley Awards **[Vol. 1: 1024]**

Whitley Memorial Student Award; Gilbert P. **[Vol. 2: 538]**

Whitley Travel Scholarship; Don **[Vol. 2: 9191]**

Whitlock Award; Marvin **[Vol. 1: 15544]**

Whitman Award; Walt **[Vol. 1: 59]**

Whitney Award **[Vol. 1: 13363]**

Whitney Award; Willis Rodney **[Vol. 1: 11356]**

Whitney Awards **[Vol. 1: 17814]**

Whitney Lecture Award; Harvey A.K. **[Vol. 1: 4308]**

Whitney Medal; Charles S. **[Vol. 1: 1854]**

Whitney Memorial Award; Eli **[Vol. 1: 15694]**

Whitney Productivity Award; Eli **[Vol. 1: 15694]**

Whitrow Lecture; Gerald **[Vol. 2: 8668]**

Whittaker's Annual Prize; Professor L.R. **[Vol. 2: 4425]**

Whitten Medal; Charles A. **[Vol. 1: 2249]**

Whitten Silver Medallion Award; E. B. **[Vol. 1: 12756]**

Whittington Excellence in Teaching Award; Leslie A. **[Vol. 1: 11878]**

Whittle Medal; Sir Frank **[Vol. 2: 8587]**

Whittle Safety Award **[Vol. 2: 8121]**

Whitworth Award for Educational Research **[Vol. 1: 6460]**

Whyte Award; Andrew **[Vol. 1: 10545]**

Whyte Memorial Essay Prize; Jon **[Vol. 1: 18113]**

Whytlaw-Gray Studentship **[Vol. 2: 6681]**

Wiant Distinguished Service and Leadership Award; Rik **[Vol. 1: 3287]**

Wichelns Memorial Award for Distinguished Scholarship in Rhetoric and Public Address; James A. Winans/Herbert A. **[Vol. 1: 12116]**

Wickersham Award **[Vol. 1: 2279]**

Wickham Award; Mary Ann **[Vol. 1: 11313]**

Wickham Prize; John **[Vol. 2: 1388]**

Wiebenson Graduate Student Prize; Dora **[Vol. 1: 3832]**

Wiechert Medal; Emil **[Vol. 2: 2950]**

Wied Lifetime Achievement Award; George L. **[Vol. 2: 3044]**

Wiegenstein Award for Meritorious Service **[Vol. 1: 1747]**

Wiegenstein Leadership Award; John G. **[Vol. 1: 1747]**

Wiener Award; Norbert **[Vol. 1: 9037]**

Wiener Medal; Norbert **[Vol. 1: 3818]**

Wiener Memorial Gold Medal; Norbert **[Vol. 2: 9487]**

Wiener Prize; Norbert **[Vol. 1: 15130]**

Wieners Award **[Vol. 1: 9134]**

Wiese Medal for an Emerging Entrepreneur; Christo **[Vol. 2: 5648]**

Wiesel Award for Jewish Arts and Culture; Elie **[Vol. 1: 8921]**

Wiesel Prize in Ethics; Elie **[Vol. 1: 17835]**

Wiesenthal Center National Leadership Award; Simon **[Vol. 1: 17838]**

WIFLE Scholarship **[Vol. 1: 17936]**

Wig & Pen Prize **[Vol. 2: 8296]**

Wigan Cup **[Vol. 2: 8832]**

Wigglesworth Lecture and Medal Award [Vol. 2: 8780]

Wight Memorial Award; J.A. [Vol. 2: 7216]

Wightman Award [Vol. 1: 8507]

Wigilia Medal [Vol. 1: 14082]

Wigor Award for Studies in Aging; Leon and Blossom [Vol. 1: 17350]

Wigram Cup [Vol. 2: 5065]

Wigram Cup (Sub-Competition) - Instrument Flying [Vol. 2: 5066]

Wigram Cup (Sub-Competition) - Junior Landing [Vol. 2: 5067]

Wigram Cup (Sub-Competition) - Non-instrument Circuits [Vol. 2: 5068]

Wigram Cup (Sub-Competition) - Senior Landing [Vol. 2: 5069]

Wijnstroom Fund; Margaret [Vol. 2: 4746]

Wilbur Award; Cornelia [Vol. 1: 10255]

Wilbur Awards [Vol. 1: 14493]

Wilby Memorial Scholarship; Ernest [Vol. 1: 14616]

Wilcher Award; Denny and Ida [Vol. 1: 14882]

Wilcox Award; Bill [Vol. 1: 2355]

Wild Animal Welfare Award [Vol. 2: 9424]

Wild Leitz Photogrammetric Fellowship Award [Vol. 1: 4866]

Wilde Award; Trevor [Vol. 2: 8268]

Wildenmann Prize [Vol. 2: 7603]

Wilder Award; Laura Ingalls [Vol. 1: 5071]

Wilder Award; Russell [Vol. 1: 17100]

Wilder Fellowship in Wilder Studies; Thornton [Vol. 1: 18165]

Wilder Medal [Vol. 1: 3321]

Wildfang Award; Henry [Vol. 1: 10969]

Wildland Fire Safety Award [Vol. 1: 9722]

Wildlife Category Award of Merit [Vol. 1: 12659]

Wildlife Leadership Awards [Vol. 1: 14577]

Wildlife Publication Awards [Vol. 1: 17858]

Wildlife Utilisation Award [Vol. 2: 5597]

Wilds Award for Distinguished Service; Claudia [Vol. 1: 1499]

Wiley and Sons Award for Innovation in Teaching; John [Vol. 1: 9849]

Wiley and Sons Lifetime Research Achievement Award; John [Vol. 1: 9850]

Wiley Award [Vol. 2: 7228]

Wiley Award for Excellence in Engineering Technology Education [Vol. 1: 3837]

Wiley-Berger Award for Volunteer Service [Vol. 1: 1158]

Wiley-Blackwell *Management and Organization Review* Young Scholar Award [Vol. 1: 9521]

Wiley Memorial Best Research Paper of the Year Award; W. Bradford [Vol. 1: 9851]

Wiley Memorial Novella Contest; Ruthanne [Vol. 1: 7327]

Wiley Prize in Psychology [Vol. 2: 6930]

Wilhelm Award in Chemical Reaction Engineering; R. H. [Vol. 1: 2643]

Wilhelmi-Haskell Stewardship Award [Vol. 1: 12070]

Wiliford Constitutional Law Award; Immogen [Vol. 1: 8586]

Wilke Memorial Award; Louis G. [Vol. 1: 477]

Wilkerson Early Career Award; Deborah L. [Vol. 1: 1855]

Wilkes Award [Vol. 2: 7026]

Wilkes Service to Keuka Award; Eleanor Judd [Vol. 1: 10682]

Wilkinson Meritorious Service Award [Vol. 1: 10439]

Wilkinson Outstanding Young Electrical Engineer Award; Roger I. [Vol. 1: 8193]

Wilkinson Prize in Numerical Analysis and Scientific Computing; James H. [Vol. 1: 15131]

Wilks Award [Vol. 1: 16058]

Wilks Memorial Awards; [Vol. 1: 4565]

Willan Grand Prize; Healey [Vol. 1: 6365]

Willan Prize; Healey [Vol. 1: 6145]

Willems Prize; Gustave [Vol. 2: 1545]

Willendorf Award [Vol. 2: 8078]

Willensky Fund; Elliot [Vol. 1: 11302]

Willey Distinguished Service Award; Calvert L. [Vol. 1: 9345]

Williams Applied Research Award; Phil [Vol. 1: 11]

Williams Assembly Speaker's Award; Warren [Vol. 1: 3369]

Williams Award; Boyce R. [Vol. 1: 145]

Williams Award; Burt [Vol. 1: 12710]

Williams Award; Cenie "Jomo" [Vol. 1: 11667]

Williams Award for Excellence in Collegiate Independent Study; Helen [Vol. 1: 936]

Williams Award for Research in Physical Therapy; Marian [Vol. 1: 3243]

Williams Award; George E. [Vol. 1: 8326]

Williams Award; James K. [Vol. 1: 18071]

Williams Award; Lee C. [Vol. 1: 8480]

Williams Award; William Carlos [Vol. 1: 14068]

Williams Award; W.S. Gwynn [Vol. 2: 9440]

Williams Community Publishing Prize; Raymond [Vol. 2: 6746]

Williams Distinguished Leadership Award; Robert H. [Vol. 1: 8114]

Williams Distinguished Scientific Achievement Award; R.T. [Vol. 1: 10259]

Williams History Prize; A. E. [Vol. 2: 1022]

Williams/James S. Brown Service Award; Cratis D. [Vol. 1: 4751]

Williams, Jr., Design Award; Alexander C. [Vol. 1: 8994]

Williams Jr. International Adaptive Aquatics Award; John K. [Vol. 1: 10415]

Williams Memorial Award; John David [Vol. 2: 8201]

Williams Memorial Medal

Royal Horticultural Society [Vol. 2: 8826]

Royal Horticultural Society [Vol 2: 8833]

Williams Scholarship; Dr. Richard Allen [Vol. 1: 5229]

Williams Space Logistics Medal; Jack L. [Vol. 1: 15944]

Williamson Award; J.C. [Vol. 2: 848]

Williamson Best Student Paper Award; Merrit [Vol. 1: 3896]

Williamson Memorial Trust Fund Bursaries; Peter [Vol. 1: 16146]

Williamson Prize; Ronald [Vol. 2: 7851]

Williamson-White Medal [Vol. 1: 11044]

Willis Award; Brian [Vol. 2: 6781]

Willis Award; George E. [Vol. 1: 4695]

Willis Award of Merit [Vol. 1: 12519]

Williston Medal; Arthur L. [Vol. 1: 4430]

Wills Alliance Award; Barbara Salisbury [Vol. 1: 814]

Willson Award; Cedric [Vol. 1: 1856]

Wilsmore Research Prize; Norman Thomas Mortimer [Vol. 2: 1157]

Wilson Award [Vol. 2: 5766]

Wilson Award; Dr. Alice E. [Vol. 1: 6489]

Wilson Award; E. H. [Vol. 1: 13313]

Wilson Award; Gill Robb [Vol. 1: 281]

Wilson Award in Spectroscopy; E. Bright [Vol. 1: 1678]

Wilson Award; James Lee [Vol. 1: 15316]

Wilson Award; Margo [Vol. 1: 8986]

Wilson Award; Ralph C. [Vol. 1: 12747]

Wilson Award; Robert E. [Vol. 1: 2644]

Wilson Award; Woodrow

Alumni Association of Princeton University [Vol. 1: 433]

American Red Cross National Headquarters [Vol 1: 3683]

Wilson Awards; Kenneth R. [Vol. 1: 6381]

Wilson Coach of the Year Award [Vol. 1: 9471]

Wilson Company Award; H. W. [Vol. 1: 16105]

Wilson Cypripedioideae Award; W. W. [Vol. 1: 3085]

Wilson Dissertation Fellowship in Women's Studies; Woodrow [Vol. 1: 18001]

Wilson Fiction Prize; Ethel [Vol. 1: 17747]

Wilson Foundation Award; Woodrow [Vol. 1: 3311]

Wilson History Award; Andrew H. [Vol. 1: 6920]

Wilson Human Rights Award; Sir Ron [Vol. 2: 275]

Wilson Leadership Award; Janie Menchaca [Vol. 1: 11788]

Wilson Leadership Award; Kay [Vol. 1: 14300]

Wilson Medal; E. B. [Vol. 1: 3786]

Wilson Medal; J. Tuzo [Vol. 1: 6523]

Wilson Memorial Award; Peter [Vol. 2: 4864]

Wilson Memorial Lecture Award; John Arthur [Vol. 1: 2762]

Wilson Memorial Vase; Guy [Vol. 2: 8834]

Wilson National High School Coaches - AD of the Year [Vol. 1: 12507]

Wilson Presentation Award [Vol. 1: 16438]

Wilson Prize; Alexander [Vol. 1: 17863]

Wilson Prize for Achievement in the Physics of Particle Accelerators; Robert R. [Vol. 1: 3227]

Wilson Prize; Professor [Vol. 2: 1158]

Wilson Publication Award; James G. [Vol. 1: 16439]

Wilson Scholarships; H.W. [Vol. 1: 6676]

Wilson Service to Education Award; Gayle C. [Vol. 1: 11566]

Wilson State/Regional Leadership Award; Norton [Vol. 1: 11714]

Wilson - Toekenning [Vol. 2: 5766]

Winans/Herbert A. Wichelns Memorial Award for Distinguished Scholarship in Rhetoric and Public Address; James A. [Vol. 1: 12116]

Windler Award; Richard and Minnie [Vol. 1: 16012]

Window Cleaner of the Month [Vol. 1: 11001]

Window Cleaner of the Year [Vol. 1: 11002]

Wing Award for Safety [Vol. 2: 8056]

Wingquist Award [Vol. 2: 9579]

Winner Award; Lewis and Beatrice [Vol. 1: 15154]

Winner Memorial Award; Robert H. [Vol. 1: 14069]

Winners' Circle Award [Vol. 1: 12379]

Winokur Research Award; George [Vol. 1: 507]

Winship Award; Laurence L. [Vol. 1: 13910]

Winship Secondary School Theatre Award; F. Loren [Vol. 1: 815]

Winsor and Newton Award [Vol. 1: 4669]

Winsor & Newton Choice Award [Vol. 2: 9347]

Winter Award; George [Vol. 1: 4247]

Winter-Klein; Prix Aniuta [Vol. 2: 2240]

Winthrop-Sears Award [Vol. 1: 14993]

Winzen Lifetime Achievement Award; Otto C. [Vol. 1: 2559]

Wirsam Scientific Award [Vol. 2: 5583]

Wischmeyer Memorial Scholarships; Albert E. [Vol. 1: 14962]

Wisconsin Artist Fellowships Awards [Vol. 1: 17877]

Wisconsin Arts Boards Fellowships [Vol. 1: 17877]

Wisdom Grant in Aid of Research; William B. [Vol. 1: 17908]

Wise Award for Best Director; De Robert [Vol. 2: 1516]

Wise Award; Stephen S. [Vol. 1: 2727]

Wise Award; Tony [Vol. 1: 17101]

Wise - Warren Susman Prize; Gene [Vol. 1: 4576]

Wisely American Civil Engineer Award; William H. [Vol. 1: 4248]

Wiseman Book Award; James R. [Vol. 1: 4767]

Wiseman Coach of the Year Award; Hank [Vol. 1: 8290]

Wishinsky Award for Distinguished International Service; Henry [Vol. 2: 4101]

Wiskirchen Jazz Award; Reverend George C. [Vol. 1: 12038]

Wismer Award; D.C. [Vol. 1: 15739]

WISTA Personality of the Year [Vol. 2: 5164]

Wister Award; Owen [Vol. 1: 17780]

Wister Medal; John C. [Vol. 1: 11044]

Witherspoon Inspirational Leadership Award; Capt. John G. [Vol. 1: 16764]

Withrow Distinguished Speaker Award; Lloyd L. [Vol. 1: 15545]

Witkin-Okonji Memorial Fund Award [Vol. 2: 5286]

Witmer Award; Lightner [Vol. 1: 3496]

Witt Award; Robert C. [Vol. 1: 3704]

Witt Medal; Otto N. [Vol. 2: 3222]

Witt Supplier of the Year Award; F. W. [Vol. 1: 1209]

Witteveen Award for Article of the Year; Gordon [Vol. 1: 6536]

Witty Short Story Award; Paul A. [Vol. 1: 10110]

WJCC Sportsmanship Award [Vol. 2: 9480]

Wofford Award; Harris [Vol. 1: 18210]

Wohelo Order [Vol. 1: 6120]

Wohl Outstanding Career Award; Joseph [Vol. 1: 9038]

Wohlberg Award for Composition; Max [Vol. 1: 7064]

Wohler Preis fur Ressourcenschonende Prozesse; Friedrich [Vol. 2: 2938]

Wolboumers Award; Ian [Vol. 2: 2411]

Wolf Award; C. R. [Vol. 1: 8966]

Wolf-Fenton Award [Vol. 1: 8966]

Wolf Memorial Award; Dick [Vol. 2: 4721]

Wolf Memorial Award; Kate [Vol. 1: 18045]

The Wolf Prizes [Vol. 2: 4001]

Wolf Project Award [Vol. 1: 17904]

Wolfe Literary Award; Thomas [Vol. 1: 17768]

Wolfe Society Literary Prize; Thomas [Vol. 1: 17907]

Wolfensohn Award; James D. [Vol. 2: 8374]

Wolff Lecture Award; Harold G. [Vol. 1: 2287]

Wolff Theatre Trust Award; Peter [Vol. 2: 6747]

Award Index

Wynn Kent Public Communications Award **[Vol. 1: 7500]**

Wynne Fellowship in British Literature; Marjorie G. **[Vol. 1: 18166]**

Wynne Gold Medal; Arthur **[Vol. 1: 6939]**

The Wynne Prize **[Vol. 2: 80]**

WYOpoets Award **[Vol. 1: 12380]**

X Prizes **[Vol. 1: 18138]**

Xanthopoulos Award; Vasilis **[Vol. 2: 3288]**

Xanthopoulos Prize **[Vol. 2: 8227]**

Xirka Gieh ir-Repubblika **[Vol. 2: 4575]**

Xplorer of the Year Award **[Vol. 1: 18141]**

Yablochkov Prize; P.N. **[Vol. 2: 5877]**

Yachtsman of the Year Award **[Vol. 2: 9501]**

Yaciuk Award; Walter **[Vol. 1: 17431]**

Yale Center for International and Area Studies Awards **[Vol. 1: 18168]**

Yale Series of Younger Poets Competition **[Vol. 1: 18143]**

Yalin Lifetime Achievement Award; M. Selim **[Vol. 2: 6046]**

Yamagiwa-Yoshida Memorial International Cancer Study Grants **[Vol. 2: 6462]**

Yandle Best Article Award; Anne and Philip **[Vol. 1: 6024]**

Yang Award; Chen Ning **[Vol. 2: 5219]**

Yant Award; William B. **[Vol. 1: 2495]**

Yara Prize for an African Green Revolution **[Vol. 2: 5166]**

Yarshater Award; Latifeh **[Vol. 1: 10179]**

YASD/*School Library Journal* Author Achievement Award **[Vol. 1: 18219]**

YASD/*School Library Journal* Young Adult Author Award **[Vol. 1: 18219]**

Yasme Award **[Vol. 1: 18170]**

Yasme Excellence Award **[Vol. 1: 18171]**

Yates Advocacy Award; Sidney R. **[Vol. 1: 5463]**

Yates Trophy; Gemma **[Vol. 2: 6717]**

YBP Award for Collection Services **[Vol. 2: 4940]**

YBP/Lindsay and Croft Research Award for Collection Services **[Vol. 2: 450]**

Yeaden Memorial Trophy; T.M. **[Vol. 2: 6718]**

Yeadon Memorial Trophy; T. M. **[Vol. 2: 6719]**

Year 12 Perspectives People's Choice Award **[Vol. 2: 84]**

Years of Dedicated Service Award **[Vol. 1: 341]**

Yemen Panther Award **[Vol. 2: 9567]**

Yemen Web Awards **[Vol. 2: 9565]**

Yerkes Award; Robert M. **[Vol. 1: 3530]**

Ylvisaker Award for Public Policy Engagement; Paul **[Vol. 1: 7699]**

Yokelson Medal Award; Marshall V. **[Vol. 1: 17869]**

Yonex National Badminton Awards **[Vol. 2: 6869]**

Yonge Award; Sir Charles Maurice **[Vol. 2: 8342]**

Yoos Distinguished Service Award; George **[Vol. 1: 14546]**

Yorkdale Memorial Award; Alan H. **[Vol. 1: 5647]**

Yorkshire Bursary **[Vol. 2: 8783]**

Yorzyk Memorial Award; David **[Vol. 1: 16999]**

Youden Award in Interlaboratory Testing; W. J. **[Vol. 1: 4566]**

Young Achiever Award **[Vol. 2: 6787]**

Young Achiever of the Year **[Vol. 2: 643]**

Young Achievers Awards **[Vol. 2: 6652]**

Young Active Citizens Award **[Vol. 2: 2356]**

Young Adult Author Award **[Vol. 1: 4782]**

Young Adult Volunteer of the Year Award **[Vol. 1: 2297]**

Young Alumni Award **[Vol. 1: 8482]**

Young Alumni Service Citations **[Vol. 1: 17214]**

Young Alumnus of the Year **[Vol. 1: 17902]**

Young Amenity Horticulturist of the Year **[Vol. 2: 5003]**

Young American Awards **[Vol. 1: 5988]**

Young American Creative Patriotic Art Awards **[Vol. 1: 17550]**

Young American Medal for Bravery **[Vol. 1: 16827]**

Young American Medal for Service **[Vol. 1: 16828]**

Young Archeologist of the Year Award **[Vol. 2: 7485]**

Young Architects Award **[Vol. 1: 2578]**

Young Artist Awards **[Vol. 1: 12335]**

Young Artist Competition **[Vol. 1: 17640]**

Young Artists Competition **[Vol. 1: 9773]**

Young Artists Contest **[Vol. 2: 6334]**

Young Artists Showcase **[Vol. 1: 14911]**

Young Asian Biotechnologist Prize **[Vol. 2: 4330]**

Young Australian of the Year **[Vol. 2: 885]**

Young Authors' Award **[Vol. 2: 3051]**

Young Award; Cy **[Vol. 1: 5795]**

Young Award; Hugh Hampton **[Vol. 1: 4627]**

Young Biophysicist Award **[Vol. 2: 535]**

Young Cancer Researcher Award **[Vol. 2: 7581]**

Young Cancer Researcher Award Lecture **[Vol. 2: 7582]**

Young Chapter of the Year Award; Lorne **[Vol. 1: 6423]**

Young Chef of the Year Award **[Vol. 2: 7036]**

Young Competitor Award **[Vol. 1: 7020]**

Young Composer Award **[Vol. 2: 4769]**

Young Composer of Dyfed **[Vol. 2: 9504]**

Young Concert Artists Trust Award **[Vol. 2: 9506]**

Young Conservationist Award **[Vol. 2: 6541]**

Young Consultants Award **[Vol. 1: 9424]**

Young Contributor's Award **[Vol. 1: 1359]**

Young Crop Scientist Award **[Vol. 1: 7771]**

Young Dermatologists' Volunteer Award **[Vol. 1: 6451]**

Young Designer of the Year Prize **[Vol. 2: 2071]**

Young Director Prize **[Vol. 2: 2463]**

Young Eco-Hero Awards **[Vol. 1: 131]**

Young Economist Award **[Vol. 2: 698]**

Young Economists Award **[Vol. 2: 3074]**

Young Economists' Essay Awards **[Vol. 2: 1435]**

Young Educator Award **[Vol. 1: 6257]**

Young Emerging Scholar Awards; Alma H. **[Vol. 1: 17400]**

Young Engineer Achievement Award **[Vol. 1: 8131]**

Young Engineer Award **[Vol. 1: 15229]**

Young Engineer of the Year Award

    Canadian Society for Bioengineering **[Vol. 1: 6878]**

    National Society of Professional Engineers **[Vol 1: 12885]**

Young Engineers Award **[Vol. 2: 4282]**

Young Enterprise Award **[Vol. 2: 5490]**

Young Entrepreneur Award **[Vol. 2: 9355]**

Young Faculty Travel Award **[Vol. 1: 1039]**

Young Fellows Bursaries **[Vol. 2: 9236]**

Young Filmmaker of the Year **[Vol. 2: 723]**

Young Filmmakers Festival **[Vol. 1: 13412]**

Young Forester Award **[Vol. 2: 7461]**

Young Forester Leadership Award **[Vol. 1: 15444]**

Young Government Civil Engineer of the Year Award **[Vol. 1: 4249]**

Young Guns Competition **[Vol. 1: 4806]**

Young Handler Award **[Vol. 2: 8183]**

Young Hazardous Materials Professional of the Year **[Vol. 1: 385]**

Young Histochemist Awards **[Vol. 1: 9935]**

Young Hospitality Manager of the Year **[Vol. 2: 3884]**

Young Industrialist Awards of Hong Kong **[Vol. 2: 5246]**

Young Industrialist of the Year Award **[Vol. 2: 9058]**

Young Inventors' Award **[Vol. 2: 5989]**

Young Investigator **[Vol. 2: 6099]**

Young Investigator Abstract Award for Outstanding Research in Molecular Pathology or Pharmacogenomics **[Vol. 1: 928]**

Young Investigator Award

    American College of Clinical Pharmacology **[Vol. 1: 1729]**

    American Society for Biochemistry and Molecular Biology **[Vol 1: 3761]**

    American Society for Bone and Mineral Research **[Vol 1: 3776]**

    American Society of Nephrology **[Vol 1: 4452]**

    Australian and New Zealand Obesity Society **[Vol 2: 216]**

    British Society for Rheumatology **[Vol 2: 7243]**

    Canadian Cardiovascular Society **[Vol 1: 6398]**

    Canadian Society of Pharmacology and Therapeutics **[Vol 1: 6990]**

    European Association for Palliative Care **[Vol 2: 7593]**

    European Society for Organ Transplantation **[Vol 2: 7635]**

    European Society for Paediatric Endocrinology **[Vol 2: 7642]**

    European Society of Intensive Care Medicine **[Vol 2: 1506]**

    International Association for Dental Research **[Vol 1: 9539]**

    International College of Angiology **[Vol 1: 9783]**

    International Society for Aerosols in Medicine **[Vol 2: 3081]**

    International Society for Microbial Ecology - Netherlands **[Vol 2: 4773]**

    International Society for Pediatric and Adolescent Diabetes **[Vol 2: 3088]**

    International Society for Transgenic Technologies **[Vol 2: 6069]**

    International Thermoelectric Society **[Vol 2: 8241]**

    Latin American Thyroid Society **[Vol 2: 1766]**

    NARSAD: The Brain and Behavior Research Fund **[Vol 1: 11370]**

    Society for Academic Emergency Medicine **[Vol 1: 15009]**

    Society for Neuroscience **[Vol 1: 15238]**

    Society for Pediatric Research **[Vol 1: 15261]**

    Society of Critical Care Medicine **[Vol 1: 15609]**

    Turkish Society of Cardiology **[Vol 2: 6641]**

    Wound Healing Society **[Vol 1: 18101]**

Young Investigator Awards

    Cancer Research Foundation **[Vol. 1: 7053]**

    CHEST Foundation **[Vol 1: 7213]**

    European Histamine Research Society **[Vol 2: 6146]**

    International Neural Network Society **[Vol 1: 10033]**

    International Society of Biomechanics **[Vol 2: 842]**

    Irish Society of Human Genetics **[Vol 2: 3894]**

    Japanese Biochemical Society **[Vol 2: 4285]**

    National Foundation for Infectious Diseases **[Vol 1: 12431]**

Young Investigator Awards for Research in Clinical Microbiology and Infectious Diseases **[Vol. 2: 6293]**

Young Investigator Research Award **[Vol. 1: 438]**

Young Investigator Research Grant **[Vol. 1: 15249]**

Young Investigator Travel Award **[Vol. 1: 10357]**

Young Investigator Travel Awards **[Vol. 1: 16440]**

Young Investigator's Award

    European Federation for Pharmaceutical Sciences **[Vol. 2: 6143]**

    European Organization for Caries Research **[Vol 2: 4706]**

    Society of Hospital Medicine **[Vol 1: 15683]**

Young Investigators Award

    American Academy of Dermatology **[Vol. 1: 517]**

    European Federation of Societies for Ultrasound in Medicine and Biology **[Vol 2: 7612]**

    International Association of Therapeutic Drug Monitoring and Clinical Toxicology **[Vol 1: 9715]**

    Japanese Society of Hypertension **[Vol 2: 4295]**

Young Investigators Awards **[Vol. 1: 8876]**

Young Investigators' Prizes **[Vol. 1: 4440]**

Young Investigators United Best Thesis Award **[Vol. 2: 7596]**

Young IT Practitioner of the Year **[Vol. 2: 7027]**

Young, Jr., Award; Whitney M. **[Vol. 1: 2579]**

Young Lawyers' Pro Bono Award **[Vol. 1: 6345]**

Young Leader Award **[Vol. 1: 10325]**

Young Leadership and Excellence Award **[Vol. 1: 5717]**

Young Leadership Award **[Vol. 1: 6001]**

Young Lecturer Award **[Vol. 2: 960]**

Young Leisure Scholar Award **[Vol. 2: 6083]**

Young Logistician Award **[Vol. 1: 15945]**

Young Medal and Prize; Thomas **[Vol. 2: 7926]**

Young Member Outstanding Service Award **[Vol. 1: 15766]**

Young Members' Award **[Vol. 2: 7402]**

Young Metallurgist of the Year Award **[Vol. 2: 3610]**

Young Naturalist Awards **[Vol. 1: 2955]**

Young NDT Professional Award **[Vol. 1: 4008]**

Young Nephrology Investigator Scholarship **[Vol. 2: 5281]**

Young Neurosurgeons Award **[Vol. 2: 6545]**

Young Nursery Professional of the Year **[Vol. 1: 8383]**

Young Oncologist Essay Awards **[Vol. 1: 3668]**

Young Oncologist Travel Grants **[Vol. 1: 3669]**

Young Optometrist of the Year **[Vol. 1: 3056]**

Young Oration; Thomas **[Vol. 2: 7926]**

Young Particle Physicist Prize **[Vol. 2: 2399]**

Award Index